The
New York
State
Directory

2007-2008

The New York State Directory

Grey House Publishing

MILLERTON, NY 12546

PUBLISHER:	Leslie Mackenzie
EDITOR:	Richard Gottlieb
EDITORIAL DIRECTOR:	Laura Mars-Proietti
EDITORIAL COORDINATOR:	Jael Powell
EDITORIAL RESEARCH:	Alysia Giglio, Sarah Miles, Erica Schneider
PRODUCTION MANAGER:	Karen Stevens
COMPOSITION:	David Garoogian
CONTRIBUTOR:	Allison Blake
MARKETING DIRECTOR:	Jessica Moody

Grey House Publishing, Inc.
185 Millerton Road
Millerton, NY 12546
518.789.8700
FAX 518.789.0545
www.greyhouse.com
e-mail: books @greyhouse.com

While every effort has been made to ensure the reliability of the information presented in this publication, Grey House Publishing neither guarantees the accuracy of the data contained herein nor assumes any responsibility for errors, omissions or discrepancies. Grey House accepts no payment for listing; inclusion in the publication of any organization, agency, institution, publication, service or individual does not imply endorsement of the editors or publisher.

Errors brought to the attention of the publisher and verified to the satisfaction of the publisher will be corrected in future editions.

Except by express prior written permission of the Copyright Proprietor no part of this work may be copied by any means of publication or communication now known or developed hereafter including, but not limited to, use in any directory or compilation or other print publication, in any information storage and retrieval system, in any other electronic device, or in any visual or audio-visual device or product.

This publication is an original and creative work, copyrighted by Grey House Publishing, Inc. and is fully protected by all applicable copyright laws, as well as by laws covering misappropriation, trade secrets and unfair competition.

Grey House has added value to the underlying factual material through one or more of the following efforts: unique and original selection; expression; arrangement; coordination; and classification.

Grey House Publishing, Inc. will defend its rights in this publication.

The New York State directory. -- [1st ed.] (1983)-

Annual
ISSN: 0737-1314

1. New York (State)--Officials and employees--Directories. 2. Government executives--New York (State)--Directories. 3. Legislators--New York (State)--Directories.

JK3430 .N52
353.9747002

ISBN: 978-1-59237-190-7

TABLE OF CONTENTS

Introduction
Organization
Acronyms

NEW YORK STATE BRANCHES OF GOVERNMENT

Executive Branch	3
Legislative Branch	19
Senate Membership & Committees	21
Assembly Membership & Committees	34
Judicial Branch	55

POLICY AREAS

Agriculture	79
Banking & Finance	90
Commerce, Industry & Economic Development	98
Corporations, Authorities & Commissions	113
Crime & Corrections	129
Education	143
Elections	157
Energy, Utility & Communication Services	168
Environment & Natural Resources	177
Government Operations	194
Health	211
Housing & Community Development	228
Human Rights	237
Insurance	245
Judicial & Legal Systems	252
Labor & Employment Practices	268
Mental Hygiene	278
Municipal & Local Governments	287
Public Employees	295
Real Property	301
Social Services	307
Taxation & Revenue	324
Tourism, Arts & Sports	332
Transportation	348
Veterans & Military	360

STATE & LOCAL PUBLIC INFORMATION

Public Information Offices	371
US Congress, Membership & Committees	381
County Government	396
Municipal Government	414

POLITICS

Political Parties	447
Lobbyists	454
Political Action Committees	533

BUSINESS
    Chambers of Commerce
    Economic & Industrial Development Organizations 569

NEWS MEDIA
    Newspapers, News Services, Magazines, Radio & Television 591

EDUCATION
    Colleges & Universities 611
    Public School Districts 638

FINANCIAL PLAN OVERVIEW 681

BIOGRAPHIES
    Executive Branch 685
    New York State Assembly 686
    New York State Senate 712
    US Senate: New York Delegation 723
    US House of Representatives: New York Delegation 724

INDEXES
    Name Index 733
    Organizations Index 809
    Geographic Index 877
    World Wide Web (URL) Index 931

DEMOGRAPHIC MAPS
    Congressional Districts 997
    Core Based Statistical Areas, Counties, and Independent Cities 998
    Population 999
    Percent White Alone 1000
    Percent Black Alone 1001
    Percent Asian Alone 1002
    Percent Hispanic 1003
    Average Household Size 1004
    Median Age 1005
    Median Household Income 1006
    Percent of Population Living in Poverty 1007
    Median Home Value 1008
    Percent of Population Who Own Their Own Homes 1009
    Percent High School Graduates 1010
    Percent College Graduates 1011
    Percent of Population Who Voted for George Bush in 2004 1012

INTRODUCTION

Welcome to the latest edition of *The New York State Directory*. Published for 20 years by Walker's Research in California, the *New York State Directory* has been published by Grey House Publishing in Millerton, New York since 2004.

The New York State Directory is a comprehensive and easy-to-use guide to accessing public officials and private sector organizations and individuals who influence public policy in the state of New York. In this new edition, you will find all listings updated with current data, as well as additional listings in several sections, including Political Action Committees and Lobbyists. The four-color Demographic Map section offers data on congressional districts, employment and education levels, income distribution, and ethnic and racial population density.

Section One of *The New York State Directory* begins with an introduction to various offices and officers that form the executive, legislative, and judicial branches of the New York state government. This section includes important information on all New York State legislators and congressional representatives, key committee assignments, and staff rosters.

Section Two comprises twenty-five chapters covering the most significant public policy issue areas from Agriculture to Veterans & Military. Each chapter identifies the state, local, and federal agencies and officials that formulate or implement policy. At the end of each chapter is a list of private sector experts and advocates who influence the policy process.

Section Three provides public information on state and local government, plus comprehensive sections on political party officials, lobbyists, political action committees, chambers of commerce, print and electronic media, colleges, universities, school districts and a financial plan overview that includes numbers from 2005 to 2011.

In addition, you'll find a comprehensive **Biographies** section that includes detailed biographical sketches of all 247 key state officials, including US Senators and House Representatives. Individual e-mail addresses make it easy to contact these influential individuals. Following the Biographies are four indexes and 4-color **Demographic Maps**.

Every reasonable effort has been made to ensure that information in *The New York State Directory* is as easily accessible and as comprehensive as possible. Organizational and personnel entries in the *Directory* were updated before publication; follow-up verifications and editorial changes were made as late as June 2007. Continuing assistance and cooperation from state, regional, county, municipal, and federal officials and staff have helped make *The New York State Directory* a unique and valuable resource. We are grateful to these individuals and the private sector sources listed for their generous contributions of time and insight.

In addition to *The New York State Directory*, Grey House offers a companion volume -- *Profiles of New York State*. This comprehensive volume provides demographic, economic, religious, geographic and historical detail on the more than 2,300 counties and place names that make up New York state. *Profiles of New York State* includes chapters on Education, Ancestry, Hispanic and Asian Populations, Weather and Maps, with comparative statistics and rankings.

— The Editors

ORGANIZATION of DATA

Section 1: New York State Branches of Government
Executive Branch. Outlines key staff in the Governor's and Lieutenant Governor's offices and senior officials in New York state executive departments and agencies. Biographies for the senior executive branch officials appear in the *Biographies* section at the back of the book.

Legislative Branch. Covers the state Senate and Assembly leadership, membership, administrative staff, and standing committees and subcommittees. Committee listings include the Chairperson, Ranking Minority Member, Majority and Minority committee members, committee staff, and key Senate or Assembly Majority and Minority staff assignments. Biographies with district office information for Senators and Assembly members appear in the *Biographies* section at the back of the book.

Judicial Branch. Identifies the state courts, judges who currently sit on these courts, and the clerk of each court. Includes the Court of Appeals, Appellate Division courts, Supreme Court, Court of Claims, New York City courts, county courts, district courts and city courts outside New York City. The county judge section identifies the specific court with which the judge is associated.

Section 2: Policy Areas
This section classifies New York state government activity into 25 major policy areas. Each policy area lists key individuals in the New York state government, federal government, and the private sector who have expertise in the area of government activity. All entries show organization name, individual name, title, address, telephone number, and fax number. Internet and e-mail addresses are included where available. Each policy area includes the following information:

<u>NEW YORK STATE</u>
Governor's Office. Identifies the Governor's legal and program staff assigned to the policy area.

Executive Department & Related Agencies. Provides a complete organizational description of the primary state departments and agencies responsible for the policy area. Also includes those state departments and agencies whose activities relate to the policy area.

Corporations, Authorities & Commissions. Covers independent public and quasi-private sector agencies in the state, as well as intrastate bodies to which New York sends a representative.

Legislative Standing Committees. Lists committees and subcommittees which oversee governmental activities in that policy area, their respective chairpersons, and ranking minority members.

<u>U.S. GOVERNMENT</u>
Executive Departments & Related Agencies. Identifies federal departments and agencies located in or assigned to the New York region.

U.S. Congress. Lists congressional committees which oversee federal activities in that policy area, their respective chairpersons, ranking minority members, and NY delegation members.

<u>PRIVATE SECTOR SOURCES</u>
Includes an alphabetized list of public interest groups, trade and professional associations, corporations, and academia, with the associated individuals who have expertise in the policy area.

Section 3: State & Local Government Public Information

Public Information Offices. Lists key contacts in state government public information offices and libraries.

U.S. Congress. Lists all New York State delegates to the Senate and the House of Representatives with their Washington, DC office, phone and fax numbers, and e-mail addresses. Biographies with district office information for each New York Senator and Representative appear in the *Biographies* section at the back of the book. Provides a comprehensive list of all Senate and House standing, select, and special committees and subcommittees. Each committee and subcommittee entry includes the chairperson, ranking minority member, and assigned members from the New York delegation.

County Government. Identifies senior government officials in all New York counties.

Municipal Government. Identifies senior public officials for cities, towns, and villages in New York with populations greater than 20,000. All New York City departments are included in the city listing.

Politics
Political Parties. Lists statewide party officials and county chairpersons for the Conservative, Democratic, Independence and Republican parties.

Lobbyists. Identifies registered lobbyists and clients.

Political Action Committees. Lists registered political action committees and their treasurers.

Business
Chambers of Commerce. Lists contact information for chambers of commerce, and economic and industrial development organizations and their primary officials.

Media
Identifies daily and weekly newspapers in New York, major news services with reporters assigned to cover state government, radio stations with a news format, and television stations with independent news staff. Newspapers are categorized by the primary city they serve. Staff listings include managing, news, and editorial page editors, and political reporters. News service entries include bureau chiefs and reporters. Radio and television entries include the news director.

Education
SUNY and Other Universities and Colleges. Includes the board of trustees, system administration, the four University Centers, and all colleges and community colleges in the SUNY system; the central administration and all colleges in the CUNY system; and independent colleges and universities. Each college includes the name of its top official, usually the president or dean, as well as address, telephone number and Internet address.

Public School Administrators. Lists school district administrators by county and school district. The New York City School's subsection includes officials in the Chancellor's office. Following are BOCES District Superintendents by supervisory district and the education administrators of schools operated by the state or other public agencies.

Financial Plan Overview
Provides information excerpted from the New York State 2007-2008 Enacted Budget Financial Plan, published April 19, 2007.

Biographies
Includes 247 political biographies of individuals representing New York state's Executive Branch, New York state Assembly members, New York state Senate members, US Senators from New York, and US Representatives from New York

Indexes

Name Index. Includes every official and executive name listed in *The New York State Directory*.

Organizations Index. Includes the names of the top three organization levels in all New York state executive departments and agencies, as well as public corporations, authorities, and commissions. In addition, this index includes all organizations listed in the Private Sector section of each policy chapter, as well as lobbyist organizations and political action committees, chambers of commerce, newspapers, news services, radio and television stations, SUNY and CUNY locations, and private colleges.

Geographic Index. Includes the organizations listed in the *Government and Private Sector Organizations Index* (see above) arranged by the city location.

World Wide Web (URL) Index. Provides Internet addresses for all organizations listed in the *Directory*.

Demographic Maps
    Congressional Districts
    Core Based Statistical Areas, Counties, and Independent City
    Population
    Percent White Alone
    Percent Black Alone
    Percent Asian Alone
    Percent Hispanic
    Average Household Size
    Median Age
    Median Household Income
    Percent of Population Living in Poverty
    Median Home Value
    Percent of Population Who Own Their Own Homes
    Percent High School Graduates
    Percent College Graduates
    Percent of Population Who Voted for George Bush in 2004

ACRONYMS IN *New York State Directory*

AAA	Automobile Association of America
AAAA	Army Aviation Association of America
AARP	American Association of Retired Persons
AFA	Air Force Association
AFL-CIO	American Federation of Labor/Congress of Industrial Organizations
AFSA	Air Force Sergeants Association
AFSCME	American Federation of State, County & Municipal Employees
AFWOA	Air Force Women Officers Association
AHRC	Association for the Help of Retarded Children
AIA	American Institute of Architects
AIVF	Association of Independent Video & Filmmakers
AMAC	Association for Metroarea Autistic Children
AMSUS	Association of Military Surgeons of the US
ASPCA	American Society for the Prevention of Cruelty to Animals
AUSA	Association of the US Army
BAC	Bricklayers & Allied Craftsmen
BIANYS	Brain Injury Association of NYS
BLS	Bureau of Labor Statistics
BOCES	Board of Cooperative Educational Services
CASES	Center for Alternative Sentencing & Employment Services
CBVH	Commission for the Blind & Visually Handicapped
CGR	Center for Governmental Research
CHIP	Community Housing Improvement Program
CIO	Chief Information Office
COA	Commissioned Officers Association
COMPA	Committee of Methadone Program Administrators
COPE	Committee on Political Education
CPB	Customs & Border Protection
CPR	Institute for Conflict Prevention and Resolution
CSD	Central School District
CUNY	City University of New York
DHS	Department of Homeland Security
FEGS	Federation Employment & Guidance Service
FEMA	Federal Emergency Management Agency
FRA	Fleet Reserve Association
FRIA	Friends & Relatives of Institutionalized Aged
HANNYS	Hunger Action Network of New York State
HFA	Housing Finance Agency

IBPAT	International Brotherhood of Painters & Allied Trades
IBT	International Brotherhood of Teamsters
ILGWU	International Ladies' Garment Workers' Union
IOLA	Interest on Lawyers Account
IUE	International Union of Electrical, Radio & Machine Workers
IUOE	International Union of Operating Engineers
MADD	Mothers Against Drunk Driving
MBBA	Municipal Bond Bank Agency
MCA	Military Chaplains Association
MCL	Marine Corps League
MOAA	Military Officers Association of America
MOPH	Military Order of the Purple Heart
MTA	Metropolitan Transportation Authority
NAIFA	North American Insurance & Finance Association
NERA	National Enlisted Reserve Association
NGAUS	National Guard Association of the US
NLN	National League for Nursing
NLUS	Navy League of the US
NMFA	National Military Family Association
NOFA	Northeast Organization Farming Association
NOW	National Organization for Women
NRA	National Reserve Association
NYC	New York City
NYANA	New York Association for New Americans
NYAPRS	New York Association of Psychiatric Rehabilitation Services
NYATEP	New York Association of Training & Employment Professionals
NYCCT	New York Community College Trustees
NYS	New York State
NYSARC	New York State Association for Retarded Citizens
NYSANA	New York State Association of Nurse Anesthetists
NYSHESC	New York State Higher Education Services Corp
NYSIR	New York State Insurance Reciprocal
NYSID	New York State Industries for the Disabled
NYSSMA	New York State School Music Association
NYSEG	New York State Electric & Gas Corporation
NYSTEC	New York State Technology Enterprise Corporation
NYSTEA	New York State Transportation Engineering Alliance
NYU	New York University
OOA	Office of Administration
PAC	Political Action Committee
PACE	Political Action for Candidates' Election
PAF	Political Action Fund

PAT	Political Action Team
PBA	Patrolmen's Benevolent Association
PCNY	Police Conference of New York
PEF	Political Education Fund – and – Public Employees Federation
PRLDEF	Puerto Rican Legal Defense and Education Fund
PSRC	Professional Standards Review Council
RCIL	Resource Center for Independent Living
RID	Rid Intoxicated Drivers
RIOC	Roosevelt Island Operating Corporation
ROA	Reserve Officers Association
SCAA	Schuyler Center for Analysis & Advocacy
SEMO	State Emergency Management Office
SENSES	Statewide Emergency Network for Social & Economic Security
SIFMA	Securities Industry and Financial Markets Association
SONYMA	State of New York Mortgage Agency
SUNY	State University of New York
UNYAN	United New York Ambulance Network
USWA	United Steel Workers of America
VESID	Vocational & Educational Services for Individuals with Disabilities Office
VFW	Veterans of Foreign Wars
VISN	Veterans Integrated Service Network
VWIN	Veterans Widows International Network
WHEDCO	Women's Housing & Economic Development Corporation

Section 1:
BRANCHES OF GOVERNMENT

EXECUTIVE BRANCH

This chapter provides a summary of officials in the Executive Branch. For a more detailed listing of specific executive and administrative departments and agencies, refer to the appropriate policy area in Section 2 or to the Organizations Index. Biographies for the senior Executive Branch officials appear in a separate section in the back of the book.

New York State

Governor (also see Governor's Office):
Eliot Spitzer 518-474-8390
Lieutenant Governor (also see Lieutenant Governor's Office):
David A Paterson . . . . 518-474-4623 or 212-681-4532
Chief Information Officer (also see Technology, Office of):
Melodie Mayberry-Stewart 518-408-2140
Comptroller (also see State Comptroller, Office of the):
Thomas P DiNapoli 518-474-4040
Attorney General (also see Law Department):
Andrew M Cuomo 518-474-7330
Secretary of State (also see State Department):
Lorraine A Cortes-Vazquez 518-474-0050

Governor's Office
Executive Chamber
State Capitol
Albany, NY 12224
518-474-8390 Fax: 518-474-1513
Web site: www.ny.gov/governor

Governor:
  Eliot Spitzer . . . . 518-474-8390 or 212-681-4580
Secretary to the Governor:
  Richard Baum 518-474-4246
Counsel to the Governor:
  David Nocenti 518-474-8343
Director, Communications:
  Darren Dopp 518-474-8418
Special Counsel:
  Richard Rifkin 518-486-9671
Director, Policy:
  Peter Pope 518-486-9671
Senior Advisor to the Governor:
  Lloyd Constantine 518-486-9671
Chief of Staff:
  Marlene Turner 518-474-8390

Office of the Secretary
Secretary to the Governor:
  Richard Baum 518-474-4246
First Deputy Secretary to the Governor:
  Sean Maloney 518-474-4246
Director, State Operations:
  Olivia Golden 518-486-9871
Deputy Secretary, Appointments:
  Francine James 518-474-0491
Deputy Secretary, Economic Development & Infrastructure:
  Timothy Gilchrist 518-408-2552
Deputy Secretary, Education:
  Manuel Rivera 518-408-2833

Deputy Secretary, Environment:
  Judith Enck 518-472-5442
Deputy Secretary, General Services, Technology & Labor Relations:
  Sylvia Hamer 518-408-2576
Deputy Secretary, Health & Human Services:
  Dennis Whalen 518-408-2500
Deputy Secretary, Intergovernmental Affairs:
  Martin Mack 518-408-3522
Deputy Secretary, Public Safety:
  Michael Balboni 518-474-3522
Chief of Staff to the First Lady:
  Uri Perrin 518-408-2588
Assistant Secretary, Energy:
  Steve Mitnick 518-473-5442
Assistant Deputy Secretary, Criminal Justice:
  Lai Sun Yee 518-474-3522
Assistant Deputy Secretary, Education:
  John Reid 518-408-2833
Assistant Deputy Secretary, Health & Human Services:
  Joseph Baker 518-486-4079
Assistant Secretary, Homeland Security:
  William Howard 518-408-2552
Assistant Secretary to the Governor:
  Drew Warshaw 518-474-4246
Assistant Deputy Secretary, Labor Relations:
  Arlene Smoller 518-408-2576
Special Advisor, Public Safety:
  James Sherry 518-474-3522
Assistant Director, Policy:
  Julieta Lozano 518-486-9671

Appointments
Deputy Secretary for Appointments:
  Francine James 518-474-0491
Assistant Secretary for Appointments:
  Jean Woodard 518-474-0491
Assistant Secretary for Appointments:
  Mary Bernet 518-474-0491
Counsel to the Deputy Secretary for Appointments:
  David Szuchman 518-474-0491

Communications
Director, Communications:
  Darren Dopp 518-474-8418
Press Secretary:
  Christine Anderson 518-474-8418
Deputy Press Secretary:
  Paul Larrabee 518-474-8418
Press Officer:
  Christine Pritchard 518-474-8418
Press Officer:
  Marc Violette 518-474-8418

Offices and agencies generally appear in alphabetical order, except when specific order is requested by listee.

EXECUTIVE BRANCH / New York State

Press Officer:
Brad Maione 518-474-8418

Counsel
Counsel to the Governor:
David Nocenti 518-474-8343
First Assistant Counsel to the Governor:
Terryl Brown-Clemons 518-474-8434
Asst Counsel to the Governor-Energy & Environment:
Vincent Esposito 518-474-1310
Asst Counsel to the Governor-Economic Development:
William Estes 518-474-8494
Asst Counsel to the Governor-Criminal Justice:
Robin Forshaw 518-474-1310
Asst Counsel to the Governor-Housing, Local Governments & Arts:
Amanda Hiller 518-474-8494
Asst Counsel to the Governor:
Steven Krantz 518-474-1310
Asst Counsel to the Governor-Transportation & Infrastructure:
Timothy B Lennon 518-474-1310
Asst Counsel to the Governor-General Government Operations & Human Services:
David Rose 518-474-2266
Asst Counsel to the Governor-Education, Elections & the Judiciary:
Mariya Treisman 518-474-8494
Asst Counsel to the Governor-Health & Mental Hygiene:
Lisa Ullman 518-474-2266
Asst Counsel to the Governor-Business & Financial Services:
Gaurav Vasisht 518-474-2266
Asst Counsel to Governor-Labor & Retirement:
David Weinstein 518-474-8434

Intergovernmental Affairs
Deputy Secretary, Intergovernmental Affairs:
Martin Mack 518-408-2555
Senior Advisor, Intergovernmental Affairs:
Michael Schell 518-408-2555
Director, Legislative Affairs:
James Clancy 518-486-9896

Operations/Administration
Director, Executive Chamber Operations:
Peter Drago 518-474-4727
Director, Administration:
Theresa Brennan 518-474-3036
Chief, Computer Services:
Thomas Irvin 518-473-5632

New York City Office
633 Third Ave, 38th Fl, New York, NY 10017
Director, NYC Intergovernmental Affairs:
Carl Andrews 212-681-4580
Director, Community Affairs:
Lila Kirton 212-681-4580
Press Secretary:
Christine Anderson 212-681-4580
Press Officer:
Jennifer Givner 212-681-4580
Office Manager:
Bette Bissram 212-681-4580
Director, Scheduling:
Maribel Torres 212-681-4580

Washington Office for the Governor
444 N Capitol St NW, Washington, DC 20001
Director:
Derek Douglas 202-434-7100

Lieutenant Governor's Office
Executive Chamber
State Capitol
Albany, NY 12224
518-474-4623 Fax: 518-486-4170

633 Third Ave
38th Fl
New York, NY 10017
212-681-4532
Fax: 212-681-4533

Lieutenant Governor:
David A Paterson . . . . 518-474-4623 or 212-681-4532
Chief of Staff:
Charles J O'Byrne 518-474-4623
Deputy Chief of Staff:
Sarah Lewis 518-474-4623
Press Secretary:
Mari Arce 518-474-4623
Counsel to Lt Governor:
Jeff Pearlman 518-474-4623
Director, Communications & Intergovernmental Affairs:
Richard Schwabacher 518-474-4623
Director, Policy:
Mark Leinung 518-474-4623

EXECUTIVE DEPARTMENTS AND RELATED AGENCIES

Aging, Office for the
2 Empire State Plaza
Albany, NY 12223
518-474-4425 or 800-342-9871 Fax: 518-474-0608
Web site: www.aging.state.ny.us

Director:
Michael Burgess 518-474-4425
Executive Deputy Director:
Laurie Pferr 518-474-7012
Deputy Director, Executive Division:
Greg Olsen 518-474-4552
Assistant Director:
Gail Koser 518-474-8422
Counsel:
Jennifer Seehase 518-474-7011
Public Information Officer:
Reza Mizbani 518-474-7181/fax: 518-473-6565
Deputy Director, Local Program Operations:
Marcus Harazin 518-473-5705
Deputy Director, Finance & Administration:
James Foy 518-473-4808

Agriculture & Markets Department
10B Airline Dr
Albany, NY 12235
518-457-3880 or 800-554-4501 Fax: 518-457-3087
e-mail: info@agmkt.state.ny.us
Web site: www.agmkt.state.ny.us

Offices and agencies generally appear in alphabetical order, except when specific order is requested by listee.

EXECUTIVE BRANCH / New York State

Commissioner:
  Patrick Hooker 518-457-8876
  e-mail: commissioner@agmkt.state.ny.us
First Deputy Commissioner:
  Thomas Lindberg 518-457-2771
Deputy Commissioner:
  Jeremiah Cosgrove 518-457-3136
  e-mail: cathy.durand@agmkt.state.ny.us
Deputy Commissioner:
  Catherine Durand 518-485-7728
Deputy Commissioner:
  Jacqueline Moody-Czub 518-457-0752
Counsel:
  Ruth Moore 518-457-1059
Executive Assistant:
  Richard Bennett 518-457-8876
Public Information Officer:
  Jessica Chittenden 518-457-3136/fax: 518-457-3087
  e-mail: jessica.chittenden@agmkt.state.ny.us

Alcoholic Beverage Control, Division of (State Liquor Authority)
317 Lenox Ave
New York, NY 10027
212-961-8385 Fax: 212-961-8299
Web site: www.abc.state.ny.us

80 S Swan St, Ste 900
Albany, NY 12210-8002
518-486-4767
Fax: 518-402-4015

Chair:
  Daniel B Boyle . . . . 212-961-8347 or 518-473-6559
  fax: 212-961-8283
Chief Executive Officer:
  Joshua B Troas 518-486-4767/fax: 518-402-4015
Commissioner:
  Lawrence J Gedda 212-961-8347
Senior Deputy Commissioner, Administration:
  J Mark Anderson 518-474-4139
Deputy Commissioner, Zone 1 (NYC) Licensing & Enforcement:
  Fred J Gioffre 212-961-8301
Deputy Commissioner, Government Affairs:
  Thomas O'Connor 518-486-4701
Counsel:
  Thomas J Donohue 518-402-4429
Director, Communications:
  William Crowley 518-486-4767

Alcoholism & Substance Abuse Services, Office of
1450 Western Ave
Albany, NY 12203
518-485-1660 Fax: 518-457-5474
e-mail: communications@oasas.state.ny.us
Web site: www.oasas.state.ny.us

501 Seventh Ave
8th Fl
New York, NY 10018
646-728-4533

Commissioner:
  Karen M Carpenter-Palumbo 518-457-1758
Associate Cmsr, Financial, Capital & Information Technology Mgmt:
  Michael Lawler 518-457-5312
Associate Commissioner, Prevention & Treatment Services:
  Frances M Harding 518-485-6022
Acting Associate Commissioner, Systems/Program Performance & Analysis:
  Timothy P Williams 518-485-2322
Associate Cmsr, Management Resources & Quality Assurance:
  Neil C Grogin 518-485-2257
Executive Deputy Commissioner:
  Kathleen Caggiano-Siino 518-485-2312
Director, Communications:
  Jennifer Farrell 518-485-1768/fax: 518-485-6014
  e-mail: jenniferfarrell@oasas.state.ny.us
Public Information Officer:
  Joseph Morrissey 518-485-1768
  e-mail: josephmorrissey@oasas.state.ny.us

Banking Department
One State Street
New York, NY 10004-1417
212-709-3500 or 877-226-5697
Web site: www.banking.state.ny.us

80 S Swan Street
Suite 1157
Albany, NY 12210-8003
518-473-6160
Fax: 518-473-7204

Superintendent of Banks & Chair:
  Richard H Neiman 212-709-3501/fax: 212-709-3520
  e-mail: richard.neiman@banking.state.ny.us
Secretary to the Board:
  Sam L Abram 212-709-1658
  e-mail: sam.abram@banking.state.ny.us
Acting General Counsel:
  Rosanne Notaro 212-709-1652
  e-mail: rosanne.notaro@banking.state.ny.us
Director, Criminal Investigations Bureau:
  John Dinin 212-709-3540
  e-mail: john.dinin@banking.state.ny.us
Chief Information Officer:
  William Rachmiel 212-709-5420
  e-mail: william.rachmiel@banking.state.ny.us
Deputy Superintendent, Consumer Services Division:
  Steven Kirchgraber 212-709-3591
  e-mail: steven.kirchgraber@banking.state.ny.us
Deputy Superintendent, Community & Regional Banks Division:
  Manuel Kursky 212-709-1610
  e-mail: manuel.kursky@banking.state.ny.us
Chief of Staff & Director, Communications:
  James Fuchs 212-709-1690
  e-mail: james.fuchs@banking.state.ny.us

Budget, Division of the
State Capitol
Albany, NY 12224
518-473-3885
e-mail: bdgord@budget.state.ny.us
Web site: www.budget.state.ny.us

Offices and agencies generally appear in alphabetical order, except when specific order is requested by listee.

EXECUTIVE BRANCH / New York State

Director:
   Paul E Francis 518-474-2300
First Deputy Director:
   Laura L Anglin 518-474-6323
Deputy Director:
   Ron Rock 518-474-6300
Deputy Director:
   Kim Fine 518-474-6300
Counsel:
   Kathy Bennett 518-474-2300
Director, Communications:
   Jeffrey Gordon 518-473-3885
Press Officer:
   Scott Reif 518-473-3885

CIO Office & Office for Technology
State Capitol
Empire State Plaza
PO Box 2062
Albany, NY 12220-0062

CIO Office
Web site: www.cio.state.ny.us
Chief Information Officer:
   Melodie Mayberry-Stewart, PhD 518-408-2140/fax: 518-402-2976
   e-mail: cio@cio.state.ny.us
Associate Chief Information Officer:
   Ram Shenoy 518-408-2140
Senior Advisor:
   Michael Mittleman 518-408-2140
Assistant to the CIO:
   Marie Potter 518-408-2140

Office for Technology
Web site: www.oft.state.ny.us
Acting Director:
   Melodie Mayberry-Stewart, PhD 518-473-9450/fax: 518-402-2976
Deputy Counsel:
   Darlene VanSickle 518-473-5115/fax: 518-402-2976
Deputy Director, Administration:
   Margaret Becker 518-473-7041/fax: 518-402-2976
Deputy Director, Applications:
   Ellen B Kattleman 518-402-2010/fax: 518-486-4344
Deputy Director, Networking Technologies:
   David A Runyon 518-486-9200/fax: 518-408-4693

Children & Family Services, Office of
52 Washington St
Rensselaer, NY 12144-2735
518-473-8437
Web site: www.ocfs.state.ny.us

Commissioner:
   Gladys Carrion, Esq 518-473-8437
Executive Deputy Commissioner:
   Larry G Brown 518-402-3108
Assistant Commissioner, Public Affairs:
   Sandra A Brown 518-402-3130
   e-mail: cfspio@dfa.state.ny.us
Deputy Commissioner, Legal Affairs & General Counsel:
   Vacant 518-473-8418
Deputy Commissioner, Administration:
   William T Gettman, Jr 518-486-7218
Deputy Commissioner, Development & Prevention Services:
   Jane G Lynch 518-474-3377

Acting Deputy Commissioner, Rehabilitative Services:
   Ines Nieves 518-476-6766
Acting Director, Youth Development:
   Matt Murell 518-402-3830
Deputy Commissioner, Information Technology:
   William E Travis, Jr 518-402-3194
Associate Commissioner, Blind & Visually Handicapped Commission:
   Brian Daniels 518-474-7299

Council on Children & Families . . . . fax: 518-473-2570
52 Washington Street, Room 256W, Rensselaer, NY 12144-2735
518-473-3652 Fax: 518-473-2570
e-mail: council@ccf.state.ny.us
Web site: www.ccf.state.ny.us
Acting Executive Director:
   Deborah Benson 518-473-3652/fax: 518-473-2570
   e-mail: debbie.benson@dfa.state.ny.us
Counsel:
   Vacant 518-473-4857
Director-Bureau of Policy, Planning & Research/Head Start Project Director:
   Robert Frawley 518-473-8081
Director-Bureau of Interagency Coordination & Case Resolution:
   Janet Sapio-Mayta 518-474-8443

Civil Service Department
Alfred E Smith State Ofc Bldg
Albany, NY 12239
518-457-2487 Fax: 518-457-7547
Web site: www.cs.state.ny.us

Commissioner:
   Nancy G Groenwegen 518-457-3701
Executive Deputy Commissioner:
   Patricia Hite 518-457-6212
Deputy Commissioner, Operations:
   Hector Millan 518-485-7515
Special Counsel:
   Thomas F Brennan 518-485-7278
Counsel:
   Judith Ratner 518-457-3177
Director, Workforce & Occupational Planning:
   Nancy B Kiyonaga 518-485-9274
Director, Employee Benefits:
   Robert Dubois 518-457-9391/fax: 518-485-8952
Director, Public Information:
   Erin Barlow 518-457-9375/fax: 518-457-6654
   e-mail: erin.barlow@cs.state.ny.us
Public Records Access Officer:
   Erin Barlow 518-457-6875/fax: 518-457-6654

Civil Service Commission
President:
   Nancy G Groenwegen . . . . 518-457-3701 or 518-457-2575
Commissioner:
   Daniel E Wall . . . . 518-457-3504 or 518-457-2575
Commissioner:
   Caroline W Ahl . . . . 518-457-5444 or 518-457-2575
Director, Commission Operations:
   Stella Chen Harding 518-457-2575

Consumer Protection Board
5 Empire State Plaza
Ste 2101
Albany, NY 12223-1556

Offices and agencies generally appear in alphabetical order, except when specific order is requested by listee.

EXECUTIVE BRANCH / New York State

518-474-3514 or 800-697-1220 Fax: 518-474-3514
Web site: www.nyconsumer.gov

1740 Broadway
15th Fl
New York, NY 10019
212-459-8850
Fax: 212-459-8855

Chairperson & Executive Director:
  Mindy A Bockstein............................. 518-486-4852
Executive Deputy Director & General Counsel:
  Lisa R Harris................................. 518-474-3514

Correctional Services Department
1220 Washington Ave
Bldg 2 State Campus
Albany, NY 12226-2050
518-457-8126 Fax: 518-457-7252
Web site: www.docs.state.ny.us

Commissioner:
  Brian Fischer................................. 518-457-8134
Assistant Commissioner & Executive Assistant:
  Edward J McSweeney............................ 518-457-1281
Special Assistant to Commissioner:
  Terri Pratt................................... 518-457-8134
Executive Deputy Commissioner:
  Vacant.. 518-457-1748
Deputy Commissioner & Counsel:
  Anthony Annucci.............. 518-485-9613 or 518-457-4951
Associate Commissioner & Inspector General:
  Richard D Roy................................. 518-457-7261
Deputy Commissioner, Administrative Services:
  Gayle Haponik................................. 518-457-8188
Deputy Commissioner, Correctional Facility Operations:
  Lucien LeClaire............................... 518-457-8138
Deputy Commissioner, Health Services Division/Chief Medical Officer:
  Lester Wright................ 518-457-7073 or 212-961-4027
Deputy Commissioner, Program Services:
  John Nuttall.................................. 518-457-5555
Public Information Officer:
  Vacant..................... 518-457-8182/fax: 518-457-7070
Asst Public Information Officer:
  Linda Foglia............... 518-457-8182/fax: 518-457-7070
  e-mail: lmfoglia@docs.state.ny.us

Council on the Arts
175 Varick St
3rd Fl
New York, NY 10014-4604
212-627-4455 or TDD: 800-895-9838 Fax: 212-620-5911
Web site: www.nysca.org

Chair:
  Richard J Schwartz............................ 212-627-4455
Vice Chair:
  Debra R Black................................. 212-627-4455
Director, Special Projcets/Assistant to Chair:
  Sasha Soreff.................................. 212-627-5656
  e-mail: ssoreff@nysca.org
Acting Executive Director:
  Richard J Schwartz............................ 212-627-4440
  e-mail: rschwartz@nysca.org

Deputy Director:
  Al Berr....................................... 212-627-8444
  e-mail: aberr@nysca.org
Deputy Director:
  Jack Lindahl.................................. 212-627-3338
  e-mail: glindahl@nysca.org
Deputy Director:
  Debby Silverfine.............................. 212-627-7778
  e-mail: dsilverfine@nysca.org
Director, Information Technology:
  Lenn Ditman................................... 212-627-5545
  e-mail: lditman@nysca.org

Crime Victims Board
55 Hanson Place
10th Fl
Brooklyn, NY 11217-1523
718-923-4325 Fax: 718-923-4332
e-mail: cvbinfo@cvb.state.ny.us
Web site: www.cvb.state.ny.us

1 Columbia Circle, Ste 200
Albany, NY 12203-6383
518-457-8727
Fax: 518-457-8658

65 Court Street
Buffalo, NY 14202
716-847-7992
Fax: 716-847-7995

Chairwoman:
  Joan A Cusack................................. 718-923-4331
Commissioner:
  Louis A Mosiello.............................. 718-923-4336
Commissioner:
  Alton R Waldron, Jr........................... 718-923-4331
Commissioner:
  Jacqueline C Mattina.......................... 716-847-7948
Commissioner:
  Benedict J Monachino.......................... 718-923-4400
General Counsel:
  John Watson................ 518-457-8066/fax: 518-457-8658
Executive Director:
  Virginia A Miller.......... 518-457-9320/fax: 518-485-9154
Director, MIS:
  David Loomis.................................. 518-485-2763
Contract Supervisor:
  Raymond Parafinczuk........................... 518-485-2763

Criminal Justice Services, Division of
Four Tower Place
Albany, NY 12203-3764
518-457-1260 Fax: 518-457-3089
e-mail: infodcjs@dcjs.state.ny.us
Web site: www.criminaljustice.state.ny.us

Commissioner:
  Denise E O'Donnell............................ 518-457-1260
Executive Deputy Commissioner:
  Sean Byrne.................................... 518-457-6091
Special Counsel to the Commissioner:
  Michael Barrett............................... 518-485-7913

Offices and agencies generally appear in alphabetical order, except when specific order is requested by listee.

EXECUTIVE BRANCH / New York State

Special Counsel & Host Agency Coordination/Support:
  Mary Kavaney 518-485-8495
Deputy Commissioner, Strategic Planning:
  Beth Ryan 518-485-7433
Deputy Commissioner, Administration:
  Don Capone 518-457-6110
Deputy Commissioner, Legal Services & Counsel:
  Gina Bianchi 518-457-4181
Deputy Commissioner, Public Safety Office:
  Cedric Alexander 518-457-6101
Deputy Commissioner, Criminal Justice Operations Office:
  Daniel Foro 518-485-2995
Director, Financial Administration:
  Kimberly J Szady 518-457-6105
Director, Bureau of Justice Research & Innovation:
  Donna Hall, PhD 518-457-7301
Executive Director, Justice Information Systems:
  James Shea 518-457-8724
Director, Identification Operations:
  William Sillery 518-457-6050
Public Information Officer:
  John Caher 518-457-8828/fax: 518-485-7715

Developmental Disabilities Planning Council
155 Washington Ave
2nd Fl
Albany, NY 12210
518-486-7505 or 800-395-3372 Fax: 518-402-3505
e-mail: ddpc@ddpc.state.ny.us
Web site: www.ddpc.state.ny.us

Chairperson:
  George E Fertal Sr 518-486-7505
Vice Chairperson:
  Rose Marie Toscano 518-486-7505
Executive Director:
  Sheila M Carey 518-486-7505
Deputy Executive Director:
  Anna Lobosco 518-486-7505
  e-mail: alobosco@ddpc.state.ny.us
Public Information Officer:
  Thomas F Lee 518-486-7505
  e-mail: tlee@ddpc.state.ny.us

Education Department
State Education Bldg
89 Washington Ave
Albany, NY 12234
518-474-5215 Fax: 518-486-5631
Web site: www.nysed.gov

Commissioner, University President:
  Richard P Mills 518-474-5844
  e-mail: rmills@mail.nysed.gov
Assistant to the Commissioner:
  Peggy Rivers 518-474-5845
  e-mail: privers@mail.nysed.gov
Counsel & Deputy Commissioner, Legal Affairs:
  Kathy A Ahearn 518-474-6400
  e-mail: kahearn@mail.nysed.gov
Chief of Staff & Deputy Commissioner, Innovation:
  David Miller 518-486-1713
  e-mail: dmiller@mail.nysed.gov

Deputy Commissioner, Cultural Education Office:
  Jeffrey Cannell 518-474-5976/fax: 518-486-4850
  e-mail: jcannell@mail.nysed.gov
Associate Commissioner, Higher Education:
  Joseph P Frey 518-486-3633
Associate Commissioner, Curriculum & Instructional Support:
  Jean Stevens 518-474-5915/fax: 518-486-2233
  e-mail: jstevens@mail.nysed.gov
Deputy Commissioner, Office of P-16 Education:
  Johanna Duncan-Poitier 518-474-3812
  e-mail: jpoitier@mail.nysed.gov
Deputy Commissioner, Vocational & Educational Services for Individuals with Disabilities Office (VESID):
  Rebecca Cort 518-474-2714
  e-mail: rcort@mail.nysed.gov
Deputy Commissioner, Management Fiscal Services:
  Theresa E Savo 518-474-2547/fax: 518-473-2827
Director, Communications:
  Alan Ray 518-474-1201/fax: 518-473-2977
  e-mail: aray@mail.nysed.gov

Elections, State Board of
40 Steuben St
Albany, NY 12207
518-474-6220 or TTY: 800-367-8683 Fax: 518-486-4068
e-mail: info@elections.state.ny.us
Web site: www.elections.state.ny.us

Co-Chair:
  Neil W Kelleher 518-474-8113
Co-Chair:
  Douglas A Kellner 518-474-8113
Commissioner:
  Evelyn J Aquila 518-474-8113
Commissioner:
  Helena M Donohue 518-474-8113
Co-Executive Director:
  Peter S Kosinski 518-474-6236
  e-mail: pkosinski@elections.state.ny.us
Co-Executive Director:
  Stanley L Zalen 518-474-8100
Special Counsel:
  Todd D Valentine 518-474-6367
Election Law Enforcement Counsel:
  Vacant 518-474-2063
Director, Election Operations:
  Anne E Svizzero 518-473-5086/fax: 518-486-4546
Director, Public Information:
  Lee Daghlian 518-474-1953/fax: 518-473-8315
  e-mail: ldaghlian@elections.state.ny.us
Coordinator, Registration Operations:
  Gregory Fiozzo 518-474-1953

Emergency Management Office, NYS (SEMO)
1220 Washington Ave
Bldg 22, Ste 101
Albany, NY 12226-2251
518-292-2275
Web site: www.semo.state.ny.us

Director:
  John R Gibb 518-292-2301
First Deputy Director:
  Andrew X Feeney 518-292-2275

Offices and agencies generally appear in alphabetical order, except when specific order is requested by listee.

EXECUTIVE BRANCH / New York State

Deputy Director, Operations:
  Thomas Fargione 518-292-2275
Deputy Director, Preparedness:
  Greg Brunelle 518-292-2275
Deputy Director, Administration:
  John A Agostino 518-292-2275
Program Assistant:
  Judy Williams 518-292-2301/fax: 518-322-4978

Administration
Chief Budget Analyst:
  Susan Mutch 518-292-2325
Manager, Recovery Section:
  Les Radford 518-292-2391

Community Affairs
Asst Director:
  Dennis J Michalski 518-292-2310
Public Information Officer:
  Donald L Maurer 518-292-2312/fax: 518-457-4923
  e-mail: donald.maurer@semo.state.ny.us

Preparedness
Chief, Training/Exercises:
  William Campbell 518-292-2350
Chief, Planning:
  Robert Olazagasti 518-292-2360

Support Services
Assistant Director, Technology:
  Kevin Ross 518-292-2260
Manager, Supply Services:
  John Zobel 518-292-2270

Empire State Development Corporation
633 Third Ave
New York, NY 10017
212-803-3100
Web site: www.empire.state.ny.us

30 South Pearl Street
Albany, NY 12245
518-292-5100

420 Main St, Ste 717
Buffalo, NY 14202
716-856-8111

Co-Chair Downstate:
  Patrick J Foye 212-803-3700
Co-Chair Upstate:
  Daniel C Gundersen . . . . 518-292-5100 or 716-856-8111
President & Chief Operating Officer:
  Avi Schick 212-803-3730
Chief Operating Officer (Upstate):
  Kenneth A Schoetz 716-856-8111
Director, Communications:
  A J Carter 212-803-3740
Senior VP, Legal & General Counsel:
  Anita W Laremont 212-803-3750
Chief Financial Officer:
  Frances A Walton 212-803-3510

Employee Relations, Governor's Office of
Two Empire State Plz
Bldg 2
Albany, NY 12223-1250
518-473-8766 Fax: 518-473-6795
e-mail: info@goer.state.ny.us
Web site: www.goer.state.ny.us

Director:
  Gary Johnson 518-474-6988/fax: 518-486-7304
Deputy Director, Contract Negotiations & Administration:
  John V Currier 518-474-4800
General Counsel:
  Walter J Pellegrini 518-474-4090
Director, Administration:
  Mary Hines 518-473-3467/fax: 518-473-6725
  e-mail: pshatsoff@goer.state.ny.us
Management/Confidential Affairs:
  Craig Dickinson 518-473-3130/fax: 518-473-6795
  e-mail: mgmcdonald@goer.state.ny.us

Environmental Conservation Department
625 Broadway
Albany, NY 12207
518-402-8545 Fax: 518-402-9016
Web site: www.dec.ny.gov

Commissioner:
  Alexander B (Pete) Grannis 518-402-8540/fax: 518-402-8541
Executive Deputy Commissioner:
  Stuart Gruskin 518-402-8560
Deputy Commissioner & General Counsel:
  Vacant 518-402-2794/fax: 518-402-9018
Deputy Commissioner, Air & Waste Management:
  Vacant 518-402-8549
Assistant Commissioner, Hearings & Mediation Services Office:
  Louis Alexander 518-402-8537
Deputy Commissioner, Natural Resources & Water Quality:
  Vacant 518-402-8543
Assistant Commissioner, Administration:
  Jack McKeon 518-402-9401
Assistant Commissioner, Public Protection:
  Henry Hamilton 518-402-8552/fax: 518-402-8830
Assistant Commissioner, Legislative Affairs:
  Maureen Coleman 518-402-8533
Asst Commissioner, Media Relations:
  Maureen Wren 518-402-8000/fax: 518-402-2209

Freshwater Wetlands Appeals Board
625 Broadway, Room 145
Albany, NY 12233-1070
518-402-0566 Fax: 518-402-0588
Web site: www.dec.state.ny.us/website/fwab/

Chairwoman:
  Rhonda K Amoroso 518-402-0566
Counsel:
  Michele M Stefanucci 518-402-0566
Co-Counsel:
  Pamela J Armstrong 518-402-0566
Docket Clerk & Board Secretary:
  Carol A Goldstein 518-402-0566

Offices and agencies generally appear in alphabetical order, except when specific order is requested by listee.

EXECUTIVE BRANCH / New York State

General Services, Office of
Corning Tower, 41st Fl
Empire State Plaza
Albany, NY 12242
518-474-3899 Fax: 518-474-1546
Web site: www.ogs.state.ny.us

633 Third Ave
New York, NY 10017
212-681-4580
Fax: 212-681-4558

Commissioner:
   John C Egan 518-474-5991/fax: 518-486-9179
   e-mail: john.egan@ogs.state.ny.us
First Deputy Commissioner:
   Robert J Fleury 518-473-6953/fax: 518-486-9179
   e-mail: robert.fleury@ogs.state.ny.us
Deputy Commissioner, Administration:
   Trina Mead 518-473-8550
Acting Deputy Commissioner, Design & Construction:
   James Davies 518-474-0337/fax: 518-486-9135
Deputy Commissioner, Information Technology & Procurement Services:
   Carla Chiaro 518-473-3933/fax: 518-486-9166
   e-mail: carla.chiaro@ogs.state.ny.us
Deputy Commissioner, Legal Services & Counsel:
   Howard Zwickel 518-474-5988/fax: 518-473-4973
Deputy Commissioner, Support Services:
   John J Spano 212-967-6090
Deputy Commissioner, Real Property Management & Development:
   William L Hill Jr 518-474-5390/fax: 518-474-1546
   e-mail: william.hill@ogs.state.ny.us
Assistant Commissioner, Public Affairs:
   Brad Maione 518-474-5987/fax: 518-474-3187
   e-mail: brad.maione@ogs.state.ny.us

Health Department
Corning Tower
Empire State Plaza
Albany, NY 12237
518-474-7354
Web site: www.nyhealth.gov

Commissioner:
   Richard F Daines, MD 518-474-2011
Chief of Staff:
   Wendy Saunders 518-473-0458
Deputy Commissioner, Administration:
   Robert W Reed 518-474-8565
Director, Human Resources & Operations:
   John R Conroy 518-473-3394/fax: 518-486-7374
Deputy Commissioner & State Medicaid Director:
   Deborah Bachrach 518-474-3018/fax: 518-486-6852
Director, Coverage & Enrollment:
   Judith A Arnold 518-474-0180
Director, Governmental Affairs:
   Wendy Saunders 518-473-1124/fax: 518-473-9674
General Counsel:
   Thomas Conway 518-474-7553
Chief Counsel, Professional Medical Conduct:
   Vacant 518-473-4282/fax: 518-473-2430
Assistant Director, Executive & Advisory Council Operations:
   Donna Peterson 518-474-8009

Director, AIDS Institute:
   Guthrie S Birkhead 518-473-7542/fax: 518-486-1315
Director, Center for Community Health:
   Guthrie S Birkhead 518-402-5382/fax: 518-486-1455
Director, Minority Health Office:
   Wilma E Waithe 518-474-2180/fax: 518-474-4695
Director, Health Facilities Management:
   Val S Gray 518-474-2772/fax: 518-474-0611
Director, The Wadsworth Center:
   Lawrence S Sturman 518-474-7592/fax: 518-474-3439
Director, Public Affairs:
   Claudia Hutton 518-474-7354

Housing & Community Renewal, Division of
Hampton Plaza
38-40 State St
Albany, NY 12207
866-275-3427 or 518-402-3728
e-mail: dhcrinfo@dhcr.state.ny.us
Web site: www.dhcr.state.ny.us

25 Beaver St
New York, NY 10004-2319
866-275-3427

Commissioner:
   Deborah VanAmerongen . . . . 518-473-8384 or 212-480-6705
   fax: 518-473-9462
First Deputy Commissioner:
   Brian Lawlor . . . . 518-473-0632 or 212-480-6718
Executive Assistant:
   Vacant 518-473-0632
Managing Attorney:
   Sheldon Melnitsky 212-480-6789/fax: 212-480-7416
Acting Deputy Commissioner, Administration:
   Catherine Johnson 518-486-3370/fax: 518-473-9462
Deputy Commissioner, Community Development:
   Gary Hallock 212-480-6446/fax: 212-480-7450
Deputy Commissioner, Housing Operations:
   David Cabrera 212-480-6440/fax: 212-480-7169
Deputy Commissioner, Policy & Intergovernmental Relations:
   Lorrie Pizzola 518-474-9553/fax: 518-473-9462
Deputy Commissioner, Rent Administration:
   Leslie Torres 718-262-4822/fax: 718-262-4008
Assistant Commissioner, Section Eight:
   Alan Smith 518-473-6183/fax: 518-474-5752
Director, Communications:
   James Plastiras . . . . 518-473-2526 or 212-480-6732
   fax: 518-474-5752

Hudson River Valley Greenway
Capitol Bldg, Rm 254
Capitol Station
Albany, NY 12224
518-473-3835 Fax: 518-473-4518
e-mail: hrvg@hudsongreenway.state.ny.us
Web site: www.hudsongreenway.state.ny.us

Greenway Conservancy for the Hudson River Valley
Board Chair:
   Kevin J Plunkett 518-473-3835
Executive Director:
   Mary Mangione 518-473-3835

Offices and agencies generally appear in alphabetical order, except when specific order is requested by listee.

Hudson River Valley Greenway Communities Council
Board Chair:
  Barnabas McHenry 518-473-3835/fax: 212-681-4552
Executive Director:
  Mary Mangione 518-473-3835

Human Rights, State Division of
1 Fordham Plaza, 4th Fl
Bronx, NY 10458
718-741-8400 Fax: 718-741-3214
e-mail: pubinfo@dhr.state.ny.us
Web site: www.dhr.state.ny.us

Commissioner:
  Kumiki Gibson 718-741-8326
Special Advisor to the Commissioner:
  Spencer B Freedman 718-741-8328
Special Advisor to the Commissioner:
  Alphonso B David 718-741-8415
Deputy Commissioner, Enforcement:
  Joshua Zinner 718-741-8330
Acting General Counsel:
  Caroline Downey 718-741-8398
Director, Administration:
  Stephen Lopez 718-741-8358
Director, Federal Programs:
  Edward A Watkins 718-741-8330
Deputy Commissioner, External Relations:
  Thomas D Shanahan 718-741-3223

Inspector General (NYS), Office of the
Executive Chamber
State Capitol
Albany, NY 12224
518-474-1010 Fax: 518-486-3745
Web site: www.ig.state.ny.us

61 Broadway
12th Floor
New York, NY 10006
212-635-3150
Fax: 212-809-6287

State Inspector General:
  Kristine Hamann . . . . 212-635-3150 or 518-474-1010
  e-mail: inspector.general@ig.state.ny.us
First Deputy Inspector General:
  Michael Boxer 212-635-3150
Deputy Chief of Investigator:
  Dennis Saville 518-474-1010
Deputy Director, Administration:
  Margaret Gaudet 518-474-1010
Director, Public Information:
  Stephen Del Giacco 518-474-1010
  e-mail: steve.delgiacco@ig.state.ny.us

Insurance Department
25 Beaver St
New York, NY 10004
212-480-6400 Fax: 212-480-7454
Web site: www.ins.state.ny.us

One Commerce Plaza
Albany, NY 12257
518-474-4567
Fax: 518-473-6814

Superintendent:
  Eric R Dinallo . . . . 518-474-4567 or 212-480-2289
  fax: 518-473-6814
First Deputy Superintendent:
  Kermitt Brooks . . . . 212-480-2292 or 518-474-4567
Deputy Superintendent & General Counsel:
  Robert H Easton 212-480-5259
  e-mail: counsel@ins.state.ny.us
Deputy Superintendent, Policy & Chief Ethics Officer:
  Susan Donnellan 212-480-5282
Deputy Superintendent, Frauds & Disaster Preparedness:
  Louis W Pietroluongo . . . . 212-480-6074 or 518-474-4567
Deputy Superintendent, Health:
  Troy Oechsner 212-480-5242
  e-mail: health@ins.state.ny.us
Director, Communications:
  David Neustadt 212-480-5262
  e-mail: public-affairs@ins.state.ny.us

Insurance Fund (NYS)
15 Computer Drive West
Albany, NY 12205
518-437-5220
Web site: www.nysif.com

199 Church St
New York, NY 10007
212-312-9000

Executive Director/CEO:
  David P Wehner 518-437-5220
First Deputy Executive Director:
  Christopher Barclay 518-437-5220
Deputy Executive Director & Marketing Director:
  Ann F Formel 518-437-1879
Deputy Executive Director, Project Management:
  Stephen D Nelson 518-437-6196
Chief Fiscal Officer:
  Susan D Sharp 518-437-6168
Public Information Officer:
  Robert Lawson 518-437-3504/fax: 518-437-1849
General Attorney:
  Gregory Allen 518-437-5220
Director, Administration:
  Joseph Mullen 518-437-5220

Insurance Fund Board of Commissioners
Chair:
  Robert H Hurlbut 518-437-5220
Vice Chair:
  Donald T DeCarlo 518-437-5220
Secretary to the Board:
  Christopher Barclay 518-437-5220

Labor Department
Building 12, Room 500
State Campus
Albany, NY 12240

Offices and agencies generally appear in alphabetical order, except when specific order is requested by listee.

EXECUTIVE BRANCH / New York State

518-457-2741 Fax: 518-457-6908
e-mail: nysdol@labor.state.ny.us
Web site: www.labor.state.ny.us

Commissioner:
   M Patricia Smith.................................518-457-2746
Executive Deputy Commissioner:
   Mario Musolino..................................518-457-4318
Counsel:
   Maria Colavito...................................518-457-7069
Inspector General:
   Vacant...518-457-7012
Deputy Commissioner, Administration & CFO:
   Vacant...518-457-3905
Deputy Commissioner, Federal Programs:
   Margaret M Moree...............................518-485-6410
   e-mail: margaret.moree@labor.state.ny.us
Deputy Commissioner, Worker Protection:
   Pico Ben-Amotz..................................518-457-4317
Associate Commissioner, Human Resources:
   Andrew Adams...................................518-457-9570
Director, Communications:
   Leo Rosales.....................518-457-5519/fax: 518-485-1126
Chief Information Officer:
   Robert Vitello.................518-457-7994/fax: 518-485-1126

Law Department
State Capitol
Albany, NY 12224-0341
518-474-7330 Fax: 518-402-2472
Web site: www.oag.state.ny.us

120 Broadway
New York, NY 10271-0332
212-416-8000
Fax: 212-416-8796

Attorney General:
   Andrew M Cuomo..............518-474-7330 or 212-416-8050
   fax: 518-402-2472
First Deputy Attorney General:
   Michele Hirshman................212-416-8040 or 518-474-7330
Assistant First Deputy Attorney General:
   Francine James....................212-416-8036 or 518-474-7330
Executive Director, Administration:
   Sylvia Hamer......................518-473-7900 or 212-416-6561
   fax: 212-416-6024
Counsel to Attorney General:
   David Nocenti.....................212-416-8095 or 518-474-7330
Deputy Attorney General, Operations:
   Kermitt J Brooks..................212-416-8492 or 518-473-7900
Deputy Attorney General, Criminal Division:
   Peter B Pope.......................212-416-8058 or 914-422-8782
   fax: 212-416-8026
Deputy Attorney General, Public Advocacy Division:
   Dietrich Snell.....................212-416-8041/fax: 212-416-8068
Assistant Deputy Attorney General, Regional Offices:
   Christopher T Walsh.............518-402-2184/fax: 518-473-8153
Deputy Attorney General, State Counsel Division:
   Richard Rifkin.....................518-473-7190 or 212-416-8525
   fax: 212-416-6001
Solicitor General, Appeals & Opinions:
   Caitlin J Halligan.................212-416-8016 or 518-474-8101
   fax: 212-416-8962

Director, Communications:
   Darren Dopp......................518-473-5525 or 212-416-8060
   fax: 518-402-2271
Director, Public Information & Correspondence:
   Peter A Drago......................518-474-7330/fax: 518-402-2472

Lottery, Division of
One Broadway Center
PO Box 7500
Schenectady, NY 12301-7500
518-388-3300 Fax: 518-388-3423
Web site: www.nylottery.org

Director:
   Robert J McLaughlin............................518-388-3400
Deputy Director:
   Susan E Miller..................................518-388-3404
Acting General Counsel:
   Julie B Silverstein Barker......................518-388-3408
Director, Communications:
   Vacant.............................518-388-3415/fax: 518-388-3423
Deputy Director, Finance & Administration:
   Gardner Gurney................................518-388-3406
Director, Operations:
   Joseph E Seeley................................518-388-3411
Director, Advertising:
   Fred Chick......................................518-388-3430
Director, Administration:
   Art DelSignore..................................518-388-3404

Mental Health, Office of
44 Holland Ave
Albany, NY 12229
518-474-4403 or 800-597-8481 Fax: 518-474-2149
Web site: www.omh.state.ny.us

Commissioner:
   Michael F Hogan, PhD.........................518-474-4403
Executive Deputy Commissioner:
   Vacant.............................518-474-7056/fax: 518-402-2361
Deputy Commissioner & Counsel:
   John Tauriello...................518-474-1331/fax: 518-473-7863
Deputy Commissioner, Public Affairs & Planning:
   Keith E Simons..................518-473-7612/fax: 518-473-4690
Medical Director:
   Lloyd I Sederer, MD............518-486-4302/fax: 518-474-8469
Senior Deputy Cmsr/Deputy Director, Info Tech & Eval Research:
   Chip Felton......................518-474-7359/fax: 518-473-2778
Deputy Commissioner, Investigation & Audit:
   Vacant.............................518-473-5940/fax: 518-473-3456
Acting Director, Public Affairs:
   Jill Daniels........................518-474-6540/fax: 518-473-3456

Mental Retardation & Developmental Disabilities, Office of
44 Holland Avenue
Albany, NY 12229
866-946-9733 or TTY: 866-933-4889 Fax: 518-474-1335
e-mail: public.affairs@omr.state.ny.us
Web site: www.omr.state.ny.us

Commissioner:
   Diana Jones Ritter...............................518-473-1997

Offices and agencies generally appear in alphabetical order, except when specific order is requested by listee.

EXECUTIVE BRANCH / New York State

Special Assistant to Commissioner:
   Tracy Durfee.....................................518-473-1997
Executive Deputy Commissioner:
   Max Chmura......................................518-474-8115
General Counsel:
   Patricia Martinelli, Esq............................518-474-7700
Deputy Commissioner, Administration & Revenue Support:
   James F Moran...................................518-473-2747
Associate Commissioner, NYC Regional Office:
   Kathleen M Broderick..............212-229-3231/fax: 212-229-3234
Associate Commissioner, Upstate Support:
   Michele Gatens...................................518-474-9897
Director, Public Affairs:
   Deborah Sturm Rausch.............................518-474-6601

Military & Naval Affairs, Division of
330 Old Niskayuna Rd
Latham, NY 12110-2224
518-786-4500 Fax: 518-786-4325
Web site: www.dmna.state.ny.us

Adjutant General:
   Maj Gen Joseph J Taluto...........................518-786-4502
Deputy Adjutant General:
   Maj Gen Robert A Knauff..........................518-786-4502
Inspector General, Federal:
   Col James D McDonough, Jr........518-786-4679/fax: 518-786-4694
Legal Counsel:
   Robert G Conway, Jr...............................518-786-4541
Joint Chief of Staff:
   Col Timothy G Vaughan............................518-786-4503
Director, Governmental Affairs:
   Michael Ostrander.................................518-786-4580
Deputy Director, Government & Community Affairs:
   Christian Bradley.................................518-786-4738
Director, Public Affairs:
   Scott Sandman...................518-786-4581/fax: 518-786-4649
   e-mail: scott.sandman1@us.army.mil
Director, Budget & Finance:
   Robert A Martin..................................518-786-4513

Motor Vehicles Department
Swan Street Building 6
Empire State Plaza
Albany, NY 12228
518-474-0841 or 800-225-5368
Web site: www.nysdmv.com

Commissioner:
   David J Swarts....................518-474-0841/fax: 518-474-0712
Executive Deputy Commissioner:
   Wayne Benjamin..................518-474-0846/fax: 518-474-0712
Deputy Commissioner, Administration:
   Gregory J Kline...................................518-474-6876
Deputy Commissioner, Legal Affairs:
   Jill A Dunn......................................518-474-1003
Deputy Commissioner, Operations & Customer Service:
   Jack Hope..518-402-2379
Deputy Commissioner, Safety, Consumer Protection & Clean Air:
   Terri Egan.......................................518-402-4860
Director, Information Technology:
   Adam Gigandet...................................518-474-0605
Project Manager, Real ID Project Team:
   Kelly Smith-Lawless..............................518-474-8328

Director, Motor Carrier & Driver Safety:
   Kevin P O'Brien..................................518-474-0855
Associate Commissioner, Communications:
   Gail Tyner-Taylor.................518-473-7000/fax: 518-473-1930

NYS Commission on Quality of Care & Advocacy for Persons with Disabilities
1 Empire State Plaza
Ste 1001
Albany, NY 12223-1150
800-624-4143 or 800-522-4369 Fax: 518-388-2800
Web site: www.cqcapd.state.ny.us

Chair:
   Gary O'Brien.....................................518-388-1281
Commissioner:
   Patricia Okoniewski..............................518-388-1281
Commissioner:
   Bruce G Blower...................................518-388-1281
Counsel, Fiscal Investigations & Policy Analysis:
   Robert Boehlert...................518-388-1270/fax: 518-388-1275
Director, Advocacy & Outreach:
   Rosemary Lamb....................518-474-2826/fax: 518-473-6005
Deputy Advocate, Counsel & Public Information Officer:
   Gary Masline.....................................518-388-1270

NYS Foundation for Science, Technology & Innovation
30 South Pearl St
11th Fl
Albany, NY 12207
518-292-5700 Fax: 518-292-5798
e-mail: contact@nystar.state.ny.us
Web site: www.nystar.state.ny.us

Executive Director:
   Michael J Relyea.................................518-292-5700
Director, Communications:
   Jannette Rondo....................518-292-5700/fax: 518-292-5798
   e-mail: contact@nystar.state.ny.us
Director, Programs:
   Kathleen J Wise..................................518-292-5700
Deputy Counsel:
   Paul Jesep.......................................518-292-5700
Director, Finance:
   Edward J Hamilton................................518-292-5700

Parks, Recreation & Historic Preservation, NYS Office of
Empire State Plaza
Bldg 1
Albany, NY 12238
518-474-0456 or TDD: 518-486-1899 Fax: 518-486-2924
Web site: www.nysparks.com

Commissioner:
   Carol Ash..518-474-0443
Executive Deputy Commissioner:
   Andy Beers........................518-473-5385/fax: 518-474-4492
Deputy Commissioner, Finanace & Administration:
   Pete Finn..518-474-0440

Offices and agencies generally appear in alphabetical order, except when specific order is requested by listee.

EXECUTIVE BRANCH / New York State

Deputy Commissioner, Operations:
  Daniel Kane 518-474-0414
Deputy Commissioner, Open Space:
  Erik Kulleseid 518-474-0402
Counsel:
  Glen Bruening 518-474-0447
Director, Communication:
  Eileen Larrabee 518-486-1868
Acting Director, Natural Heritage Trust:
  Elaine Bartley 518-474-2997
Director, Law Enforcement:
  James Warwick 518-474-4029

Parole, Division of
97 Central Ave
Albany, NY 12206
518-473-9400 Fax: 518-473-6037
e-mail: nysparole@parole.state.ny.us
Web site: www.parole.state.ny.us

Chief Executive Officer:
  George B Alexander 518-473-9548
Executive Director:
  Felix M Rosa 518-473-9672
Chief Counsel:
  Terrence X Tracy 518-473-5671/fax: 518-473-9760
Chair, Parole Board:
  George B Alexander 518-473-9548
Public Information Offficer:
  Mark Johnson 518-486-4631/fax: 518-473-6037
Director, Administrative Services:
  Jeffrey Nesich 518-473-9531/fax: 518-474-0852
Director, Operations:
  Angela Jiminez 518-473-5421/fax: 518-402-3653
Director, Support Operations:
  George W Hemstead 518-473-5790/fax: 518-486-4167

Prevention of Domestic Violence, Office for the
80 Wolf Rd
Ste 406
Albany, NY 12205
518-457-5800 Fax: 518-457-5810
Web site: www.opdv.state.ny.us

90 Church St, 13th Fl
New York, NY 10007
212-417-4477
Fax: 212-268-7921

Executive Director:
  Amy Barasch, Esq 518-457-5800
Director, NYC Program:
  Sujata Warrier 212-417-4477
Director, Prevention, Training & Planning:
  Gwen Wright 518-457-5916
Administrative Officer:
  Linda Cassidy 518-457-7995
Public Information Officer:
  Suzanne Cecala 518-457-5744
  e-mail: suzanne.cecala@opdv.state.ny.us

Probation & Correctional Alternatives, Division of
80 Wolf Rd
Ste 501
Albany, NY 12205
518-485-7692 Fax: 518-485-5140
Web site: www.dpca.state.ny.us

State Director:
  Robert Maccarone 518-485-7692
Secretary to the Director:
  Barbara J Flanigan 518-485-7692
Executive Deputy Director:
  Thomas Slater . . . . 518-485-7692 or 518-485-2394
General Counsel:
  Linda Valenti 518-485-2394
Administrative Officer:
  Howard Bancroft 518-485-5145/fax: 518-485-5140

Public Employment Relations Board
80 Wolf Rd
Albany, NY 12205
518-457-2854 Fax: 518-457-2664
e-mail: perbinfo@perb.state.ny.us
Web site: www.perb.state.ny.us

Chair:
  Jerome Lefkowitz 518-457-2578
Member:
  Robert S Hite 518-457-2578
Executive Director:
  James R Edgar 518-457-2676
Deputy Chair & Counsel (Acting):
  Deborah A Sabin 518-457-2614
Secretary to the Board:
  Sheila Talavera 518-457-2578
Director, Conciliation:
  Richard A Curreri 518-457-2690
Director, Employment Practices & Representation:
  Monte Klein 518-457-6410

Public Service Commission
NYS Dept of Public Service
3 Empire State Plaza
Albany, NY 12223-1350
518-474-7080 Fax: 518-473-2838
Web site: www.dps.state.ny.us

90 Church St
New York, NY 10007-2919
212-417-2378

295 Main St
Buffalo, NY 14203
716-847-3400

Chairwoman:
  Patricia L Acampora 518-474-2523/fax: 518-486-1947
Commissioner:
  Maureen F Harris . . . . 518-474-2503 or 212-417-3168
  fax: 518-473-2838

Offices and agencies generally appear in alphabetical order, except when specific order is requested by listee.

EXECUTIVE BRANCH / New York State

Commissioner:
  Robert E Curry Jr . . . . 518-474-2503 or 212-417-3168
  fax: 518-473-2838
Commissioner:
  Cheryl A Buley . . . . 518-474-2503 or 212-417-3168
  fax: 518-473-2838
Secretary to the Commission:
  Jaclyn A Brilling 518-474-6530/fax: 518-486-6081
  e-mail: secretary@dps.state.ny.us
Acting Executive Deputy:
  Judith Lee 518-473-4544/fax: 518-473-2838
Acting General Counsel:
  Peter McGowan 518-474-2510/fax: 518-486-5710
Director, Consumer Services Office:
  Sandra Sloane . . . . 518-474-3280 or 212-417-6161
  fax: 518-486-7868
  e-mail: csd@dps.state.ny.us
Director, Electricity & Environment Office:
  James Gallagher . . . . 518-473-7248 or 212-474-2199
  fax: 518-486-1672
Director, Gas & Water Office:
  Thomas Dvorsky . . . . 518-473-6080 or 212-417-2234
  fax: 518-473-4992
Director, Office of Administration:
  Debra Renner 518-474-2508/fax: 518-474-0413
Director, Telecommunications:
  Robert H Mayer . . . . 518-474-1668 or 212-417-2191
  fax: 518-474-5616
Director, Accounting, Finance & Economics Office:
  Charles Dickson 518-474-4508/fax: 518-486-7524
Director, Public Affairs:
  James Denn 518-474-7080/fax: 518-473-0421

Racing & Wagering Board
1 Broadway Center
Ste 600
Schenectady, NY 12305-2553
518-395-5400 Fax: 518-347-1250
e-mail: info@racing.state.ny.us
Web site: www.racing.state.ny.us

Chair:
  Daniel D Hogan 518-395-5400
Member:
  Michael J Hoblock, Jr. 518-395-5400
Member:
  John B Simoni 518-395-5400
Executive Director:
  John G Cansdale 518-395-5400
Counsel:
  Robert A Feuerstein 212-417-2103
Chief, Racing Operations:
  Joseph Lynch 518-395-5400
Secretary to the Board:
  Gail Pronti 518-395-5400
Public Information Officer:
  Dan Toomey 518-395-5400/fax: 518-453-8867
Director, Audits & Investigations:
  Tom Casaregola 518-395-5400/fax: 518-453-8867
Director, Administration:
  Kevin Dempsey 518-395-5400/fax: 518-453-8867
Manager, Licensing:
  Nicole Robilotto 518-395-5400/fax: 518-453-8867
Director, Gaming Regulation:
  Bruce Samboy 518-395-5400

Director, Racing Officials:
  Brian Barry 518-395-5400

Real Property Services, Office of
16 Sheridan Ave
Albany, NY 12210-2714
518-486-5446 Fax: 518-474-9276
e-mail: nysorps@orps.state.ny.us
Web site: www.orps.state.ny.us

Chair, State Board of Real Property Services:
  George E Herren 518-474-5711
Executive Director, Board Secretary:
  Donald C DeWitt 518-474-5711
Executive Deputy Director:
  Steve King 518-473-6914
Acting Counsel:
  James O'Keefe 518-474-6753
Research, Information & Policy Development:
  James F Dunne 518-473-4532
  e-mail: jim.dunne@orps.state.ny.us
Director, Public Information:
  Geoffrey T Gloak 518-486-5446
  e-mail: geoffrey.gloak@orps.state.ny.us

Regulatory Reform, Governor's Office of
Agency Bldg 1, 4th Fl
Empire State Plaza, PO Box 2107
Albany, NY 12220-0107
518-486-3292 Fax: 518-473-9342
e-mail: gorr@gorr.state.ny.us
Web site: www.gorr.state.ny.us

Director:
  Robert Hermann 518-473-8197
Counsel:
  Amelia Stern 518-473-0620/fax: 518-473-9342
Public Information Officer:
  Tim Beadnell 518-486-3292
  e-mail: tbeadnell@gorr.state.ny.us
Director, Administration:
  Sandra L Curry 518-408-2055

Small Cities, Office for
4 Empire State Plaza
Suite 600
Albany, NY 12223
518-474-2057 Fax: 518-474-5247
Web site: www.nysmallcities.com

Executive Director:
  Joseph J Rabito 518-474-2057
Associate Counsel:
  Brian McCartney 518-474-2057
Program Manager:
  Gail Hammond 518-474-2057
Finance Officer:
  Leslie Haggerty 518-474-2057
Director, Communications:
  Joseph Picchi 518-474-2057

Offices and agencies generally appear in alphabetical order, except when specific order is requested by listee.

EXECUTIVE BRANCH / New York State

State Comptroller, Office of the
110 State St
Albany, NY 12236-0001
518-474-4044 Fax: 518-473-3004
Web site: www.osc.state.ny.us

633 Third Ave, 31st Fl
New York, NY 10017-6754
212-681-4489
Fax: 212-681-4468

State Comptroller:
   Thomas P DiNapoli . . . . 518-474-4040 or 212-681-4489
Chief of Staff:
   Jack Chartier. . . . . 212-681-4498 or 518-402-2516
First Deputy Comptroller:
   Thomas Sanzillo. 518-474-2909 or 212-681-4469
Executive Deputy Comptroller:
   Diana J Ritter 518-474-3610
Deputy Chief of Staff:
   Roberta Rubin. . . . . 212-681-4495 or 518-474-4040
Director, Business Communication:
   Ellen J Evans . . . . 518-473-1323 or 212-681-4489
Deputy Comptroller, Office of Budget & Policy Analysis:
   Kim Fine. 518-473-4333
Deputy Comptroller, Investigations:
   Robert Brackman . . . . 212-681-4474 or 518-402-4926
Deputy Comptroller, Intergovernmental Affairs & Community Relations:
   Myrna Santiago 212-383-2662
State Deputy Comptroller for New York City:
   Kenneth Bleiwas. 212-383-3900
General Counsel:
   Alan Lebowitz . . . . 518-474-3444 or 212-681-6069
Deputy Comptroller, Administration:
   Harris Lirtzman 518-402-4884
Deputy Comptroller, Local Government Services & Economic Development:
   Mark P Pattison 518-474-4037
   e-mail: localgov@osc.state.ny.us
Assistant Comptroller, Payroll & Revenue Services:
   Daniel Berry 518-408-4149
Deputy Comptroller, Pension Investment & Cash Management:
   David Loglisci 518-474-4003
Deputy Comptroller, Retirement Services:
   Laura Anglin. 518-474-2600
Deputy Comptroller, State Services:
   Jerry Barber . . . . 518-474-5598 or 212-417-5200
Deputy Comptroller, Enterprise Initiatives:
   Margaret Sherman 518-473-7520
Director, Communications:
   Daniel Weiller . . . . 518-474-4015 or 212-681-4840
   fax: 518-473-8940
Chief Information Officer:
   Jeffrey S Grunfeld 518-408-2915/fax: 518-473-3004
Press Secretary:
   Jeffrey Gordon . . . . 518-474-4015 or 212-681-4825
   fax: 518-473-8940
   e-mail: jgordon@osc.state.ny.us

State Department
123 William St
New York, NY 10038-3804
212-417-5801 Fax: 212-417-5805
e-mail: info@dos.state.ny.us
Web site: www.dos.state.ny.us

41 State St
Albany, NY 12231-0001
518-474-0050
Fax: 518-474-4765

Secretary of State:
   Lorraine A Cortes-Vazquez 518-474-0050
First Deputy Secretary of State:
   Daniel Shapiro 518-474-4750
Counsel:
   Susan Watson 518-474-6740/fax: 518-473-9211
Deputy Secretary of State, Public Affairs:
   Eamon Moynihan. 212-417-5800
Deputy Secretary of State, Business & Licensing Services Division:
   Albert P Jurczynski 518-474-4429/fax: 518-473-6648
   e-mail: licensing@dos.state.ny.us
Deputy Secretary of State, Local Government & Community Services:
   Matthew Andrus 518-486-9888/fax: 518-474-6572
Assistant Secretary of State, Communications:
   Laurence Sombke 518-474-4752/fax: 518-474-4597
   e-mail: info@dos.state.ny.us

State Police, Division of
Bldg 22, State Campus
1220 Washington Ave
Albany, NY 12226-2252
518-457-2180
Web site: www.troopers.state.ny.us

Superintendent:
   Preston L Felton 518-457-6721
First Deputy Superintendent:
   James L Harney. 518-457-6711/fax: 518-485-7505
Counsel:
   Glenn P Valle 518-457-6137/fax: 518-485-1164
Deputy Superintendent, Administration:
   Steven F Cumoletti 518-457-6621/fax: 518-485-5051
Deputy Superintendent, Employee Relations:
   Francis P Christensen 518-457-3572/fax: 518-485-7505
Deputy Superintendent, Field Command:
   Bart R Johnson 518-457-5936/fax: 518-457-4779
Deputy Superintendent, Internal Affairs:
   Pedro J Perez 518-485-6018/fax: 518-485-1493
Technical Lieutenant, Public Information:
   Glenn R Miner. 518-457-2180/fax: 518-485-7818
   e-mail: piooffice@troopers.state.ny.us

Tax Appeals, Division of
Riverfront Professional Tower
500 Federal St, 4th Fl
Troy, NY 12180
518-266-3000 Fax: 518-271-0886
e-mail: nysdota@nysdta.org
Web site: www.nysdta.org

Tax Appeals Tribunal
President & Commissioner:
   Charles H Nesbitt 518-266-3050
Commissioner:
   Carroll R Jenkins 518-266-3050
Commissioner:
   Robert J McDermott. 518-266-3050
Counsel:
   Donna M Gardiner 518-266-3052

Offices and agencies generally appear in alphabetical order, except when specific order is requested by listee.

Secretary to the Tribunal:
 Jean A McDonnell 518-266-3036

Administrative Law Judges & Officers
Chief Administrative Law Judge:
 Andrew F Marchese 518-266-3000
Assistant Chief Administrative Law Judge:
 Daniel J Ranalli 518-266-3000
Director, Administration:
 George J Cannon 518-266-3041

Taxation & Finance Department
State Campus
Bldg 9, Rm 227
Albany, NY 12227
518-457-4242 Fax: 518-457-2486
Web site: www.tax.state.ny.us

Acting Commissioner:
 Barbara G Billet 518-457-2244
Executive Deputy Commissioner:
 Barbara G Billet 518-457-7358
Deputy Commissioner & Counsel:
 Daniel Smirlock................... 518-457-3746/fax: 518-457-8247
Deputy Commissioner & Treasurer:
 Aida M Brewer 518-474-4250/fax: 518-402-4118
Deputy Commissioner, Tax Enforcement:
 William Comisky............ 518-457-9692 or 800-225-5829
Deputy Commissioner, Tax Policy Analysis:
 Robert D Plattner 518-457-4357
Deputy Commissioner, Administration:
 Margaret Sherman 518-457-1000
Chief Financial Officer & Budget/Management Analysis:
 Patricia Mitchell 518-457-1000
Director, Public Information:
 Thomas Bergin 518-457-4242

Temporary & Disability Assistance, Office of
40 N Pearl St
Albany, NY 12243
518-474-9003 or 800-342-3004 Fax: 518-474-7870
e-mail: nyspio@otda.state.ny.us
Web site: www.otda.state.ny.us

Commissioner:
 David A Hansell 518-474-4152/fax: 518-486-6255
  e-mail: david.hansell@otda.state.ny.us
Deputy Commissioner, Child Support Enforcement:
 Scott E Cade 518-474-1078
Acting Deputy Commissioner, Disability Determinations:
 Gloria S Toal 518-473-0070
Director, Budget, Finance & Data Management:
 Michael Normile..................................... 518-474-0183
Deputy Commissioner, Program Support & Quality Improvement:
 John Paolucci 518-473-3912
Deputy Commissioner, Information Technology:
 Vacant 518-473-7858
Deputy Commissioner, Employment & Transitional Supports:
 Russell Sykes................... 518-474-9222/fax: 518-474-5281
General Counsel:
 John P Bailly Jr...................................... 518-474-9502
Director, External & Intergovernmental Affairs Office:
 Elizabeth Segal..................................... 518-474-7420

Director Public Information:
 Michael Hayes................... 518-474-9516/fax: 518-486-6935
  e-mail: nyspio@otda.state.ny.us

Transportation Department
50 Wolf Road
6th Fl
Albany, NY 12232
518-457-5100 or 518-457-6195 Fax: 518-457-5583
Web site: www.nysdot.gov

Commissioner:
 Astrid C Glynn 518-457-4422
Deputy Commissioner:
 Stanley Gee... 518-457-4422
Chief Operating Officer:
 Brian O Rowback.................................... 518-485-0887
CFO:
 Michael Novakowski 518-457-2320
Acting Chief Administrative Officer:
 Michael J McCarthy 518-457-6300
Director, Legal Affairs Office:
 Thomas Perreault 518-457-2412
Director, Transportation Policy & Performance Office:
 Robert Zerrillo 518-457-6700
Chief Counsel:
 Bruce Feldman 518-457-2412
Chief Engineer:
 Michael Shamma 518-457-4430
Director, Public Affairs:
 Jennifer Post 518-457-6400/fax: 518-457-6506
  e-mail: jpost@dot.state.ny.us

Veterans' Affairs, Division of
5 Empire State Plaza
Ste 2836
Albany, NY 12223-1551
518-474-6114 or 888-838-7697 Fax: 518-473-0379
e-mail: info@veterans.state.ny.us
Web site: www.veterans.state.ny.us

Director:
 George P Basher.................................... 518-474-6114
Executive Deputy Director:
 Vacant 518-474-6784
Deputy Director, Western Division:
 Joseph H Vogtli Jr 716-847-3414
Deputy Director, Eastern Division:
 Benjamin Weisbroth.................................. 212-807-3162
Counsel:
 William J Brennan 518-474-6114
Deputy Director, Program Development:
 Michelle LaRock 518-474-6114

Welfare Inspector General, Office of NYS
22 Cortland St
11th Fl
New York, NY 10007
212-417-5822 Fax: 212-417-5849

40 N Pearl St, Sect 10B
Albany, NY 12243

Offices and agencies generally appear in alphabetical order, except when specific order is requested by listee.

EXECUTIVE BRANCH / New York State

518-474-9636
Fax: 518-486-6148

Inspector General:
   Brian P Sanvidge 212-417-5840
Deputy Inspector General & Counsel:
   Andrew Weiss 212-417-2395
Chief Investigator:
   Joseph R Bucci 212-417-2026
Administrative Asst to Inspector General:
   Wanda Hernandez 212-417-5822

Workers' Compensation Board
20 Park Street
Albany, NY 12207
877-632-4996 Fax: 518-473-1415
Web site: www.wcb.state.ny.us

Executive Director:
   Glenn Warren 518-474-6670
Chair, Board of Commissioners:
   Donna Ferrara 518-474-6670/fax: 518-473-1415
Vice Chair:
   Fran Libous 518-474-6670/fax: 518-473-1415
Secretary to the Board:
   Sandra Olson 518-402-6071
Deputy Executive Director, Adminstration:
   Ann Kutter. 518-473-8900/fax: 518-486-6411
Deputy Executive Director, Operations:
   Vacant. 518-486-7143/fax: 518-474-9367
Deputy Executive Director, Systems Modernization:
   Thomas Schofield 518-486-7143/fax: 518-474-9367
General Counsel:
   Cheryl Wood 518-486-9564/fax: 518-473-2233
Director, Public Information:
   Vacant. 518-474-6670/fax: 518-473-1415
Advocate for Injured Workers:
   Edwin Ruff. . . . . 800-580-6665 or 518-474-8182
  fax: 518-486-7510
Fraud Inspector General:
   John H Burgher Jr. . . . . 888-363-6001 or 518-473-4839
  fax: 518-402-1059

Offices and agencies generally appear in alphabetical order, except when specific order is requested by listee.

LEGISLATIVE BRANCH SENATE

Members of the Senate welcome e-mail correspondence from the public. They may reply by e-mail, or by mail when more extensive follow-up is necessary. Please include both an e-mail and mailing address in all correspondence. Biographies of Legislative Branch Senate and Assembly Members appear in a separate section in the back of the book.

State Senate Leadership

State Capitol
Albany, NY 12247
Web site: www.senate.state.ny.us

Administration

Steven M Boggess................518-455-2051/fax: 518-455-3332
Title: Secretary of the Senate

Gail M Skelos....................518-455-2201/fax: 518-426-6978
Title: Director, Appointments Office

General Information............................800-342-9860
Title: Bill Status Hotline

Chris J Cook....................518-455-2318/fax: 518-426-6841
Title: Director, Document Room

Thomas A Testo..................518-455-2245/fax: 518-426-6842
Title: Journal Clerk

Paul Graffeo....................518-455-3216/fax: 518-426-6813
Title: Supervisor, Legislative Assistance & Services

Ellen Breslin....................518-455-2468/fax: 518-426-6901
Title: Legislative Librarian, Legislative Library

James Giliberto..................518-455-2468/fax: 518-426-6901
Title: Legislative Librarian, Legislative Library

Ed Stahr........................518-455-2558/fax: 518-426-6911
Title: Director, Constituent Relations

Rosemary Vogt...................518-455-2173/fax: 518-455-3552
Title: Director, Senate Research Services

William C Martin................518-455-2338/fax: 518-455-3332
Title: Sergeant-at-Arms

Krista Ketterer..................518-455-2611/fax: 518-432-5470
Title: Director, Student Programs Office

Tracy Starr......................518-455-3145/fax: 518-426-6831
Title: District Office Coordinator

Edward S Lurie..................518-455-2550/fax: 518-426-6835
Title: Director, Legislative Services (Senate Research)

Frank W Patience................518-455-3376/fax: 518-426-6927
Title: Personnel Officer

James Bell......................518-455-2313/fax: 518-455-7339
Title: Director, Technology Services

Majority Leadership

Joseph L Bruno (R)...............................518-455-3191
e-mail: bruno@senate.state.ny.us
Title: President Pro Tempore & Majority Leader

Owen H Johnson (R)..............................518-455-3411
e-mail: ojohnson@senate.state.ny.us
Title: Chair of Senate Finance Committee

Frank Padavan (R)...............................518-455-3381
e-mail: padavan@senate.state.ny.us
Title: Vice President Pro Tempore

Dean G Skelos (R)...............................518-455-3171
e-mail: skelos@senate.state.ny.us
Title: Deputy Majority Leader for Legislative Operations

Thomas W Libous (R)............................518-455-2677
e-mail: senator@senatorlibous.com
Title: Senior Asst Majority Leader/Liaison to the Executive Branch

Dale M Volker (R)...............................518-455-3471
e-mail: volker@senate.state.ny.us
Title: Assistant Majority Leader on Conference Operations

Caesar Trunzo (R)...............................518-455-2111
e-mail: trunzo@senate.state.ny.us
Title: Assistant Majority Leader for House Operations

Kenneth P LaValle (R)...........................518-455-3121
e-mail: lavalle@senate.state.ny.us
Title: Chair of Majority Conference

Hugh T Farley (R)...............................518-455-2181
e-mail: farley@senate.state.ny.us
Title: Chair of Majority Program Development Committee

Offices and agencies generally appear in alphabetical order, except when specific order is requested by listee.

LEGISLATIVE BRANCH SENATE / State Senate Leadership

James L Seward (R) 518-455-3131
e-mail: seward@senate.state.ny.us
Title: Majority Whip

Serphin R Maltese (R) 518-455-3281
e-mail: maltese@senate.state.ny.us
Title: Vice Chair of Majority Conference

William J Larkin Jr (R) 518-455-2770
e-mail: larkin@senate.state.ny.us
Title: Secretary of Majority Conference

Kemp Hannon (R) 518-455-2200
e-mail: hannon@senate.state.ny.us
Title: Deputy Majority Whip

Stephen M Saland (R) 518-455-2441
e-mail: saland@senate.state.ny.us
Title: Chair of Majority Steering Committee

Michael F Nozzolio (R) 518-455-2366
e-mail: nozzolio@senate.state.ny.us
Title: Assistant Majority Whip

John A DeFrancisco (R) 518-455-3511
e-mail: jdefranc@senate.state.ny.us
Title: Deputy Majority Leader for Intergovernmental Affairs

James W Wright (R) 518-455-2346
e-mail: wright@senate.state.ny.us
Title: Deputy Majority Leader for Policy

Mary Lou Rath (R) 518-455-3161
e-mail: rath@senate.state.ny.us
Title: Deputy Majority Leader for State/Federal Relations

Majority Staff

Michael Avella 518-455-2675/fax: 518-426-6830
Title: Counsel to the Majority

Francis J Gluchowski 518-455-2563/fax: 518-426-2265
Title: Legislative Counsel to the Majority

Richard Burdick 518-455-2381/fax: 518-426-6818
Title: Director, Majority District Operations

Robert J Hess 518-455-2591/fax: 518-426-6979
Title: Bill Clerk

Peter L Rupert 518-455-2578/fax: 518-426-6803
Title: Home Rule Counsel

Louise Guiliano 518-455-2595/fax: 518-426-6996
Title: Special Projects Coordinator

Janet L Reilly 518-455-2589/fax: 518-426-6815
Title: Majority Calendar Clerk

Jeffrey Lovell 518-455-3198/fax: 518-426-6958
Title: Secretary to the Finance Committee

Robert Mujica 518-455-2880/fax: 518-426-6836
Title: Deputy Secretary, Budget & Fiscal Analysis

Magaret Law 518-455-2567/fax: 518-426-6936
Title: Director, Majority Correspondence

John E McArdle 518-455-2264/fax: 518-455-2260
Title: Director, Majority Communications

Linda Marano 518-455-3541/fax: 518-426-6917
Title: Director, Majority Media Services

Edward S Lurie 518-455-2550/fax: 518-426-6835
Title: Director, Majority Legislative Services

Matthew Walter 518-455-2264/fax: 518-455-2448
Title: Assistant Majority Press Secretary

Minority Leadership

Malcolm A Smith (D) 518-455-2701
e-mail: masmith@senate.state.ny.us
Title: Minority Leader

Jeffrey D Klein (D) 518-455-3595
e-mail: jdklein@senate.state.ny.us
Title: Deputy Minority Leader

William T Stachowski (D) 518-455-2426
e-mail: stachows@senate.state.ny.us
Title: Ranking Minority Member of Senate Finance Committee

Diane J Savino (D) 518-455-2437
e-mail: savino@senate.state.ny.us
Title: Assistant Minority Leader for Conference Operations

Thomas K Duane (D) 518-455-2451
e-mail: duane@senate.state.ny.us
Title: Assistant Minority Leader for Policy & Administration

John L Sampson (D) 518-455-2788
e-mail: sampson@senate.state.ny.us
Title: Secretary, Minority Conference

Martin Malave Dilan (D) 518-455-2177
e-mail: dilan@senate.state.ny.us
Title: Chair of Minority Conference

George Onorato (D) 518-455-3486
e-mail: onorato@senate.state.ny.us
Title: Vice Chair of Minority Conference

Kevin S Parker (D) 518-455-2580
e-mail: parker@senate.state.ny.us
Title: Minority Whip

John D Sabini (D) 518-455-2529
e-mail: sabini@senate.state.ny.us
Title: Assistant Minority Leader, International Affairs

Offices and agencies generally appear in alphabetical order, except when specific order is requested by listee.

LEGISLATIVE BRANCH SENATE / State Senate Roster

Suzi Oppenheimer (D)..........................518-455-2031
e-mail: oppenhei@senate.state.ny.us
Title: Deputy Minority Whip

Toby Ann Stavisky (D)..........................518-455-3461
e-mail: stavisky@senate.state.ny.us
Title: Assistant Minority Whip

Velmanette Montgomery (D)....................518-455-3451
e-mail: montgome@senate.state.ny.us
Title: Assistant Minority Leader, Floor Operations

Jose M Serrano (D)............................518-455-2795
e-mail: serrano@senate.state.ny.us
Title: Chair, Minority Policy Committee

Liz Krueger (D)...............................518-455-2297
e-mail: lkrueger@senate.state.ny.us
Title: Chair, Minority Program Development

Minority Staff

Mortimer Lawrence.............................518-455-3401
Title: Chief of Staff to the Minority Leader

Douglas Forand................518-455-2701/fax: 518-455-2816
Title: Deputy Chief of Staff

Celeste Knight................518-455-3401/fax: 518-455-2816
Title: Secretary to the Minority Leader

Meredith Henderson............518-455-2701/fax: 518-455-2816
Title: Deputy Secretary

Shelley Mayer.................518-455-2711/fax: 518-426-6955
Title: Legislative Counsel

Mary K Berger.................518-455-2636/fax: 518-455-2816
Title: Director, Minority Operations

Michael Weber.................518-455-2217/fax: 518-426-6839
Title: Comptroller, Senate Minority

Indira Noel...................518-455-2966/fax: 518-426-6840
Title: Director, Minority Policy Development

Curtis Taylor.................518-455-2415/fax: 518-426-6933
Title: Director, Communications

Tracey Pierce-Smith...........518-455-2501/fax: 518-426-6930
Title: Director, Minority Conference Services

James Plastiras...............518-455-2415/fax: 518-426-6933
Title: Press Secretary to the Minority Leader

State Senate Roster

Multiple party abbreviations following the names of legislators indicate that those legislators ran as the Senate candidate for each identified party. Source: NYS Board of Elections. Party abbreviations: Conservative (C), Democrat (D), Green (G), Independent (I), Liberal (L), Republican (R), Working Families (WF)

Eric Adams (D).................518-455-2431/fax: 518-426-6856
District: 20 *Room:* 413 LOB *e-mail:* eadams@senate.state.ny.us
Committees: Aging; Civil Service & Pensions; Codes; Crime Victims, Crime & Correction (Ranking Minority Member); Veterans, Homeland Security & Military Affairs (Ranking Minority Member)
Senior Staff: Ingrid Lewis-Martin

James S Alesi (R-C-I)..........518-455-2015/fax: 518-426-6968
District: 55 *Room:* 905 LOB *e-mail:* alesi@senate.state.ny.us
Committees: Banks; Commerce, Economic Development & Small Business (Chair); Crime Victims, Crime and Correction; Energy & Telecommunications; Higher Education; Insurance; Labor; Tourism, Recreation and Sports Development
Senior Staff: Melissa Pugliese

John J Bonacic (R-I-C).........518-455-3181/fax: 518-426-6948
District: 42 *Room:* 815 LOB *e-mail:* bonacic@senate.state.ny.us
Committees: Banks; Codes; Commerce, Economic Development & Small Business; Housing, Construction & Community Development (Chair); Judiciary; Labor; Local Government; Tourism, recreation & Sports Development
Senior Staff: Langdon Chapman

Neil D Breslin (D-I)...........518-455-2225/fax: 518-426-6807
District: 46 *Room:* 414 CAP *e-mail:* breslin@senate.state.ny.us
Title: Ranking Minority Member, Finance Committee
Committees: Agriculture; Banks; Codes; Insurance (Ranking Minority Member); Judiciary; Labor
Senior Staff: Darcy L Green

Joseph L Bruno (R-I)...........518-455-3191/fax: 518-455-2448
District: 43 *Room:* 909 LOB *e-mail:* bruno@senate.state.ny.us
Title: President Pro Tempore & Majority Leader; ex officio member of all committees
Committees: Rules (Chair)
Senior Staff: Rick Burdick

Martin Connor (D-WF)...........518-455-2625/fax: 518-426-6956
District: 25 *Room:* 408 LOB *e-mail:* connor@senate.state.ny.us
Committees: Banking (Ranking Minority Member); Codes; Finance; Insurance; Judiciary; Labor; Rules
Senior Staff: Martin Algaze

Offices and agencies generally appear in alphabetical order, except when specific order is requested by listee.

LEGISLATIVE BRANCH SENATE / State Senate Roster

John A DeFrancisco (R-I-C-WF) . . 518-455-3511/fax: 518-426-6952
District: 50 *Room:* 307 LOB *e-mail:* jdefranc@senate.state.ny.us
Title: Deputy Majority Leader, Intergovernmental Affairs
Committees: Banks; Codes; Energy & Telecommunications; Health; Judiciary (Chair); Tourism, Recreation & Sports Development
Senior Staff: Carole Luther

Ruben Diaz, Sr (D) 518-455-2511/fax: 518-426-6945
District: 32 *Room:* 304 LOB *e-mail:* diaz@senate.state.ny.us
Committees: Aging (Ranking Minority Member); Higher Education; Mental Health & Developmental Disabilities (Ranking Minority Member); Social Services, Children & Families; Veterans, Homeland Security & Military Affairs
Senior Staff: Marcos A Crespo

Martin M Dilan (D-WF) 518-455-2177/fax: 518-426-6947
District: 17 *Room:* 606 LOB *e-mail:* dilan@senate.state.ny.us
Title: Chair, Minority Conference
Committees: Banks; Education; Elections (Ranking Minority Member); Finance; Judiciary; Transportation
Senior Staff: Lorenda Harris

Thomas K Duane (D-WF) 518-455-2451/fax: 518-426-6846
District: 29 *Room:* 808 LOB *e-mail:* duane@senate.state.ny.us
Title: Asst Minority Leader, Policy & Administration
Committees: Civil Service & Pensions; Codes; Finance; Health; Investigations & Government Operations (Ranking Minority Member); Judiciary; Rules
Senior Staff: Mark Furnish

Hugh T Farley (R-C-I) 518-455-2181/fax: 518-455-2271
District: 44 *Room:* 412 LOB *e-mail:* farley@senate.state.ny.us
Title: Chair, Majority Program Development Committee
Committees: Aging; Banks (Chair); Ethics; Finance; Health; Judiciary; Rules
Senior Staff: David Smingler

John J Flanagan (R-I-C) 518-455-2071/fax: 518-426-6904
District: 2 *Room:* 817 LOB *e-mail:* flanagan@senate.state.ny.us
Committees: Aging; Corporations, Authorities & Commissions (Chair); Transportation; Veterans, Homeland Security & Military Affairs
Senior Staff: Raymond Bennardo

Charles J Fuschillo, Jr (R-I-C) 518-455-3341/fax: 518-426-6823
District: 8 *Room:* 915 LOB *e-mail:* fuschill@senate.state.ny.us
Committees: Civil Service & Pensions; Commerce, Economic Development & Small Business; Consumer Protection (Chair); Education; Health; Labor; Transportation
Senior Staff: Michael James DeMartino

Martin J Golden (R-I-C) 518-455-2730/fax: 518-426-6910
District: 22 *Room:* 946 LOB *e-mail:* golden@senate.state.ny.us
Committees: Aging (Chair); Banks; Codes; Crime Victims, Crime & Correction; Education; Insurance; Investigations & Government Operations; Veterans, Homeland Security & Military Affairs
Senior Staff: Walter A Pacholczak

Efrain Gonzalez, Jr (D) 518-455-3395/fax: 518-426-6858
District: 33 *Room:* 420 CAP *e-mail:* gonzalez@senate.state.ny.us
Title: Chair, Minority Conference
Committees: Banks; Commerce, Economic Development & Small Business (Ranking Minority Member); Corporations, Authorities & Commissions; Energy & Telecommunications; Finance; Labor
Senior Staff: Amy Class

Joseph A Griffo (R-C) 518-455-3334/fax: 518-426-6921
District: 47 *Room:* 944 LOB *e-mail:* griffo@senate.state.ny.us
Committees: Aging; Banks; Consumer Protection; Elections (Chair); Energy & Telecommunications; Environmental Conservation; Higher Education; Racing, Gaming & Wagering
Senior Staff: Dwight Evans

Kemp Hannon (R-I-C) 518-455-2200/fax: 516-747-7430
District: 6 *Room:* 501 CAP *e-mail:* hannon@senate.state.ny.us
Title: Deputy Majority Whip
Committees: Codes; Corporations, Authorities & Commissions; Elections; Finance; Health (Chair); Judiciary; Rules
Senior Staff: Jane Preston

Ruth Hassell-Thompson (D-I-WF) 518-455-2061/fax: 518-426-6998
District: 36 *Room:* 613 LOB *e-mail:* hassellt@state.senate.ny.us
Title: Asst Minority Leader for Floor Operations
Committees: Commerce, Economic Development & Small Business; Consumer Protection; Crime Victims, Crime & Correction; Housing, Construction & Community Development; Judiciary (Ranking Minority Member); Rules
Senior Staff: Jerry W Williams

Shirley L Huntley (D) 518-455-3531/fax: 518-426-6859
District: 10 *Room:* 508 LOB *e-mail:* shuntley@senate.state.ny.us
Committees: Education; Higher Education; Mental Health & Developmental Disabilities; Transportation
Senior Staff: Ruben Wills

Craig M Johnson (D-WF) 518-455-2622
District: 7 *Room:* 604 LOB *e-mail:* johnson@senate.state.ny.us
Committees: Environmental Conservation (Ranking Minority Member); Ethics; Local Government
Senior Staff: Cari Abatemarco

Owen H Johnson (R-C) 518-455-3411/fax: 518-426-6973
District: 4 *Room:* 913 LOB *e-mail:* ojohnson@senate.state.ny.us
Title: Chair, Finance Committee
Committees: Banks; Consumer Protection; Environmental Conservation; Finance (Chair); Rules; Social Services, Children & Families; Transportation
Senior Staff: Rory P Whelan

Jeffrey Klein (D) 518-455-3595/fax: 518-426-6887
District: 34 *Room:* 313 LOB *e-mail:* jdklein@senate.state.ny.us
Title: Deputy Minority Leader
Committees: Agriculture; Codes; Consumer Protection (Ranking Minority Member); Finance; Health; Investigations & Government Operations; Judiciary; Labor
Senior Staff: Shelley Andrews

Liz Krueger (D-WF) 518-455-2297/fax: 518-426-6874
District: 26 *Room:* 302 LOB *e-mail:* lkrueger@senate.state.ny.us
Title: Chair, Minority Program Development
Committees: Banks; Consumer Protection; Finance; Higher Education; Housing, Construction & Community Development (Ranking Minority Member); Rules
Senior Staff: Brad Usher

Carl Kruger (D) 518-455-2460/fax: 518-426-6855
District: 27 *Room:* 608 LOB *e-mail:* kruger@senate.state.ny.us
Committees: Aging (Ranking Minority Member); Crime Victims, Crime & Correction; Energy & Telecommunications; Finance; Insurance; Social

Offices and agencies generally appear in alphabetical order, except when specific order is requested by listee.

LEGISLATIVE BRANCH SENATE / State Senate Roster

Services, Children & Families (Chair); Veterans, Homeland Security & Military Affairs
Senior Staff: Jason Koppel

Kenneth P LaValle (R-I-C) 518-455-3121/fax: 518-426-6826
District: 1 *Room:* 806 LOB *e-mail:* lavalle@senate.state.ny.us
Title: Chair of Majority Conference
Committees: Aging; Agriculture; Education; Finance; Higher Education (Chair); Insurance; Judiciary; Rules
Senior Staff: Ann Eisenhut

Andrew J Lanza (R-I) 518-455-3215/fax: 518-426-6852
District: 24 *Room:* 947 LOB *e-mail:* lanza@senate.state.ny.us
Committees: Cities; Codes; Education; Ethics (Chair); Judiciary; Tramsportation
Senior Staff: John Turoski

William J Larkin, Jr (R-C) 518-455-2770/fax: 518-426-6923
District: 39 *Room:* 612 LOB *e-mail:* larkin@senate.state.ny.us
Title: Secretary, Majority Conference
Committees: Agriculture; Commerce, Economic Development & Small Business; Elections; Finance; Health; Insurance; Racing, Gaming & Wagering (Chair); Rules; Transportation; Veterans, Homeland Security & Military Affairs
Senior Staff: Jennifer Downs

Vincent L Leibell, III (R-I-C) 518-455-3111/fax: 518-426-6977
District: 40 *Room:* 609 LOB *e-mail:* leibell@senate.state.ny.us
Committees: Aging; Civil Service & Pensions; Corporations, Authorities & Commissions (Chair); Elections; Environmental Conservation; Housing, Construction & Community Development; Insurance; Veterans, Homeland Security & Military Affairs (Chair)
Senior Staff: Lynne Klein

Thomas W Libous (R-C) 518-455-2677/fax: 518-455-2065
District: 52 *Room:* 512 LOB *e-mail:* senator@senatorlibous.com
Title: Senior Asst Majority Leader/Liaison to the Executive Branch
Committees: Finance; Health; Racing, Gaming & Wagering; Tourism, Recreation & Sports Development; Transportation (Chair); Rules
Senior Staff: Robert N Nielson Jr

Elizabeth O'Connor Little (R-I-C) 518-455-2811/fax: 518-426-6873
District: 45 *Room:* 903 LOB *e-mail:* little@senate.state.ny.us
Committees: Agriculture; Crime Victims, Crime & Correction; Education; Environmental Conservation; Health; Housing, Construction & Community Development; Local Government (Chair); Racing, Gaming & Wagering; Tourism, Recreation & Sports Development
Senior Staff: Rebecca Marino

Serphin R Maltese (R-I-C) 518-455-3281/fax: 518-426-6951
District: 15 *Room:* 413 CAP *e-mail:* maltese@senate.state.ny.us
Title: Vice Chair, Majority Conference
Committees: Cities (Chair); Civil Service & Pensions; Codes; Finance; Higher Education; Judiciary; Rules
Senior Staff: Victoria Vattimo

Carl L Marcellino (R-I-C) 518-455-2390/fax: 518-426-6975
District: 5 *Room:* 812 LOB *e-mail:* marcelli@senate.state.ny.us
Committees: Civil Service & Pensions; Consumer Protection; Education; Environmental Conservation (Chair); Labor; Mental Health & Developmental Disabilities; Social Services, Children & Families
Senior Staff: Vacant

George D Maziarz (R-I-C) 518-455-2024/fax: 518-426-6987
District: 62 *Room:* 811 LOB *e-mail:* maziarz@senate.state.ny.us
Committees: Aging; Corporations, Authorities & Commissions; Crime Victims, Crime & Correction; Energy & Telecommunications; Finance; Judiciary; Labor
Senior Staff: Renea Molineaux

Velmanette Montgomery (D-WF) 518-455-3451/fax: 518-426-6854
District: 18 *Room:* 306 LOB *e-mail:* montgome@senate.state.ny.us
Title: Assistant Minority Leader, Floor Operations
Committees: Crime Victims, Crime & Correction; Education; Finance; Health; Mental Health & Developmental Disabilities; Rules; Social Services, Children & Families (Ranking Minority Member)
Senior Staff: Nancy M Santiago

Thomas P Morahan (R-C-I-WF) .. 518-455-3261/fax: 518-455-2959
District: 38 *Room:* 848 LOB *e-mail:* morahan@senate.state.ny.us
Committees: Agriculture; Banks; Education; Elections; Labor; Local Government; Mental Health & Developmental Disabilities; Rules; Social Services; Children & Families (Ranking Minority Member)
Senior Staff: Patricia Ramondo

Michael F Nozzolio (R-I-C) 518-455-2366/fax: 518-426-6953
District: 54 *Room:* 409 LOB *e-mail:* nozzolio@senate.state.ny.us
Title: Assistant Majority Whip
Committees: Crime Victims, Crime & Correction (Chair); Finance; Investigations & Government Operations; Judiciary; Racing, Gaming & Wagering; Tourism; Recreation & Sports Development; Transportation
Senior Staff: Justin J McCarthy

George Onorato (D) 518-455-3486/fax: 518-426-6929
District: 12 *Room:* 315 LOB *e-mail:* onorato@senate.state.ny.us
Title: Vice Chair, Minority Conference
Committees: Banks; Energy & Telecommunications; Health, Insurance; Labor (Ranking Minority Member); Racing, Gaming & Wagering
Senior Staff: Candyce Propper

Suzi Oppenheimer (D-WF) 518-455-2031/fax: 518-426-6860
District: 37 *Room:* 515 LOB *e-mail:* oppenhei@senate.state.ny.us
Title: Deputy Minority Whip
Committees: Cities; Education (Ranking Minority Member); Environmental Conservation; Ethics; Finance; Higher Education; Transportation
Senior Staff: Steven Otis

Frank Padavan (R-I-C) 518-455-3381/fax: 518-455-2008
District: 11 *Room:* 416 CAP *e-mail:* padavan@senate.state.ny.us
Title: Vice President Pro Tempore
Committees: Cities; Energy & Telecommunication; Finance; Mental Health & Developmental Disabilities; Rules; Transportation; Veterans, Homeland Security & Military Affairs
Senior Staff: John C Googas, Jr

Kevin S Parker (D-WF) 518-455-2580/fax: 518-426-6843
District: 21 *Room:* 517 LOB *e-mail:* parker@senate.state.ny.us
Title: Minority Whip
Committees: Commerce, Economic Development & Small Business; Energy & Telecommunications (Ranking Minority Member); Environmental Conservation; Finance; Higher Education; Insurance; Veterans, Homeland Security & Military Affairs
Senior Staff: Glynda Carr

Offices and agencies generally appear in alphabetical order, except when specific order is requested by listee.

LEGISLATIVE BRANCH SENATE / State Senate Roster

Bill Perkins (D) 518-455-2441/fax: 518-426-2816
District: 30 *Room:* 617 LOB *e-mail:* perkins@senate.state.ny.us
Committees: Civil Service & Pensions; Codes; Corporations, Authorities & Commissions (Ranking Minority Member); Judiciary; Transportation
Senior Staff: Cordell Cleare

Mary Lou Rath (R-C-I) 518-455-3161/fax: 518-426-6963
District: 61 *Room:* 310 LOB *e-mail:* rath@senate.state.ny.us
Title: Deputy Majority Leader, State/Federal Relations
Committees: Elections; Finance; Health; Higher Education; Local Government; Racing, Gaming & Wagering; Tourim, Recreation & Sports Development (Chair)
Senior Staff: Sharon Rich

Joseph E Robach (R-I-C-WF) 518-455-2909/fax: 518-426-6938
District: 56 *Room:* 902 LOB *e-mail:* robach@senate.state.ny.us
Committees: Banks; Civil Service & Pensions (Chair); Commerce, Economic Development & Small Business; Consumer Protection; Higher Education; Labor; Tourism, Recreation & Sports Development; Transportation
Senior Staff: Tim Ragazzo

John D Sabini (D-WF) 518-455-2529/fax: 518-426-6906
District: 13 *Room:* 513 LOB *e-mail:* sabini@senate.state.ny.us
Title: Assistant Minority Leader, International Affairs
Committees: Consumer Protection; Education; Elections; Environmental Conservation; Rules; Racing, Gaming & Wagering (Ranking Minority Member); Transportation (Ranking Minority Member)
Senior Staff: Katharine Pichardo-Erskine

Stephen M Saland (R-C-I) 518-455-2411/fax: 518-426-6920
District: 41 *Room:* 708 LOB *e-mail:* saland@senate.state.ny.us
Title: Chair, Majority Steering Committee
Committees: Banks; Codes; Education (Chair); Ethics; Finance; Insurance; Judiciary; Rules
Senior Staff: Toni Dickinson

John L Sampson (D-WF) 518-455-2788/fax: 518-426-8806
District: 19 *Room:* 506 LOB *e-mail:* sampson@senate.state.ny.us
Title: Secretary, Minority Conference
Committees: Codes; Crime Victims, Crime & Correction; Health (Ranking Minority Member); Judiciary; Racing, Gaming & Wagering; Veterans, Homeland Security & Military Affairs
Senior Staff: Michelle Trotman

Diane J Savino (D-I-WF) 518-455-2437/fax: 518-426-6943
District: 23 *Room:* 406 LOB *e-mail:* savino@senate.state.ny.us
Title: Asst Minority Leader, Conference Operations
Committees: Civil Service & Pensions (Ranking Minority Member); Environmental Conservation; Housing, Construction & Community Development; Judiciary; Labor; Tourism, Recreation & Sports Development; Transportation
Senior Staff: Robert Cataldo

Eric T Schneiderman (D-WF) 518-455-2041/fax: 518-426-6847
District: 31 *Room:* 711B LOB *e-mail:* schneide@senate.state.ny.us
Title: Deputy Minority Leader
Committees: Codes; Education; Investigations & Government Operations; Judiciary; Mental Health & Developmental Disabilities; Rules
Senior Staff: Michael Clements

Jose M Serrano (D-WF) 518-455-2795/fax: 518-426-6886
District: 28 *Room:* 706 LOB *e-mail:* serrano@senate.state.ny.us
Title: Chair, Minority Policy Committee
Committees: Education; Environmental Conservation; Higher Education; Local Government; Rules; Transportation, Recreation & Sports Development
Senior Staff: George Torres

James L Seward (R-I-C) 518-455-3131/fax: 518-455-3123
District: 51 *Room:* 917 LOB *e-mail:* seward@senate.state.ny.us
Title: Majority Whip
Committees: Agricultural; Education; Finance; Higher Education; Insurance (Chair); Rules; Transportation
Senior Staff: Duncan Davie

Dean G Skelos (R-I-C) 518-455-3171/fax: 518-426-6950
District: 9 *Room:* 503 CAP *e-mail:* skelos@senate.state.ny.us
Title: Deputy Majority Leader for Legislative Operations
Committees: Civil Service & Pensions; Codes; Finance; Insurance; Investigations & Government Operations; Judiciary; Rules
Senior Staff: Tracy Lloyd

Malcolm A Smith (D-WF-C) 518-455-2701/fax: 518-426-2816
District: 14 *Room:* 508 LOB *e-mail:* masmith@senate.state.ny.us
Title: Minority Leader
Committees: Rules
Senior Staff: Mortimer Lawrence

William T Stachowski (D-C-WF) . . 518-455-2426/fax: 518-426-6851
District: 58 *Room:* 802 LOB *e-mail:* stachows@senate.state.ny.us
Title: Ranking Minority Member, Senate Finance Committee
Committees: Agriculture (Ranking Minority Member); Ethics (Ranking Minority Member); Finance; Insurance; Investigations & Government Operations (Ranking Minority Member); Labor; Local Government; Racing, Gaming & Wagering; Rules
Senior Staff: Kim Bosy

Toby Ann Stavisky (D-WF) 518-455-3461/fax: 518-426-6857
District: 16 *Room:* 504 LOB *e-mail:* stavisky@senate.state.ny.us
Title: Assistant Minority Whip
Committees: Aging; Civil Service & Pensions; Education; Finance; Higher Education (Ranking Minority Member); Tourism, Recreations & Sports Development; Transportation
Senior Staff: Marilyn Dyer

Andrea Stewart-Cousins (D) 518-455-2585/fax: 518-426-6811
District: 35 *Room:* 415 LOB *e-mail:* scousins@senate.state.ny.us
Committees: Commerce, Economic Development & Small Business; Finance; Judiciary; Local Govenment (Ranking Minority Member); Tourism, Recreation & Sports Development
Senior Staff: Jose Gustavo-Rivera

Antoine M Thompson (D-WF) 518-455-3371/fax: 518-426-6969
District: 60 *Room:* 615 LOB *e-mail:* athompso@senate.state.ny.us
Committees: Cities (Ranking Minority Member); Commerce, Economic Development & Small Business; Finance; Tourism, Recreation & Sports Development; Veterans, Homeland Security & Military Affairs
Senior Staff: Mark Boyd

Offices and agencies generally appear in alphabetical order, except when specific order is requested by listee.

LEGISLATIVE BRANCH SENATE / State Senate Standing Committees

Caesar Trunzo (R-I-C)............ 518-455-2111/fax: 518-455-2113
District: 3 *Room:* 711 LOB *e-mail:* trunzo@senate.state.ny.us
Title: Asst Majority Leader, House Operations
Committees: Civil Service & Pensions; Corporations, Authorities & Commissions; Environmental Conservation; Finance; Local Government; Rules; Transportation
Senior Staff: Christopher Molluso

David J Valesky (D-WF).......... 518-455-2838/fax: 518-426-6885
District: 49 *Room:* 707 LOB *e-mail:* valesky@senate.state.ny.us
Committees: Agriculture (Ranking Minority Member); Banks; Energy & Telecommunications; Health; Higher Education; Tourism, Recreation & Sports Development; Transportation
Senior Staff: Cort Ruddy

Dale M Volker (R-I-C)............ 518-455-3471/fax: 518-426-6949
District: 59 *Room:* 427 CAP *e-mail:* volker@senate.state.ny.us
Title: Assistant Majority Leader, Conference Operations
Committees: Codes (Chair); Corporations, Authorities & Commissions; Crime Victims, Crime & Correction; Ethics; Finance; Judiciary; Mental Health & Developmental Disabilities; Rules
Senior Staff: John R Drexielius

George H Winner Jr (R-C-I)...... 518-455-2091/fax: 518-426-6976
District: 53 *Room:* 814 LOB *e-mail:* winner@senate.state.ny.us
Committees: Crime Victims, Crime & Correction; Elections; Energy & Telecommunication; Health; Higher Education; Investigations & Government Operations (Chair); Judiciary
Senior Staff: Sperry J Navone

James W Wright (R-C-I).......... 518-455-2346/fax: 518-455-2365
District: 48 *Room:* 509 LOB *e-mail:* wright@senate.state.ny.us
Title: Deputy Majority Leader for Policy
Committees: Commerce, Economic Development & Small Business; Crime Victims, Crime & Correction; Energy & Telecommunications (Chair); Finance; Housing, Cmty Dev & Constr; Labor; Tourism, Recreation & Sports Develop; Veterans, Homeland Security & Military Affairs
Senior Staff: Graham Wise

Catharine M Young (R-C-I)...... 518-455-3563/fax: 518-426-6905
District: 57 *Room:* 805 LOB *e-mail:* cyoung@senate.state.ny.us
Committees: Agriculture (Chair); Health; Higher Education; Housing, Construction & Community Development; Insurance; Mental Health & Developmental Disabilities

State Senate Standing Committees

Aging
Chair:
  Martin J Golden (R)............................... 518-455-2730
Ranking Minority Member:
  Ruben Diaz, Sr (D)................................ 518-455-2511

Committee Staff
Executive Assistant & Committee Clerk:
  Patricia Donnelly 518-455-2730
Director, Legislation:
  Robert Herz 518-455-2730

Key Senate Staff Assignments
Senate Majority Counsel/Program Services/Program Associate:
  Michelle Di Bacco 518-455-2597
Senate Minority Policy Development & Counsel Staff:
  Francis McKearin.................................. 518-455-2975

Membership
Majority
  Hugh T Farley   John J Flanagan
  Kenneth LaValle   Andrew J Lanza
  Vincent L Leibell, III   George D Maziarz
Minority
  Eric Adams   Carl Kruger
  Jose E Serrano   Toby Ann Stavisky

Agriculture
Chair:
  Catharine M Young (R) 518-455-3563
Ranking Minority Member:
  David J Valesky (D)............................... 518-455-2838

Committee Staff
Clerk:
  Jessica Phelan.................................... 518-455-3563
Committee Director:
  Catherine Mural 518-455-3563

Key Senate Staff Assignments
Senate Majority Counsel/Program Services Assistant Counsel:
  Karen Moreau...................................... 518-455-3413
Senate Research Service Analyst:
  Todd Kusnierz 518-455-2153
Senate Minority Policy Development & Counsel Staff:
  Jim Watson.. 518-455-2977

Membership
Majority
  Kenneth P LaValle   William J Larkin
  Elizabeth O'Connor Little   Thomas P Morahan
  James L Seward
Minority
  Neil D Breslin   William T Stachowski

Banks
Chair:
  Hugh T Farley (R) 518-455-2181
Ranking Minority Member:
  Martin Connor (D)................................. 518-455-2625

Committee Staff
Director:
  Peter A Edman 518-455-2181
Clerk:
  Tracy Cullen...................................... 518-455-2181

Key Senate Staff Assignments
Senate Majority Counsel/Program Services Principal Program Assoc:
  Bernard McGarry................................... 518-455-2986
Senate Research Service Analyst:
  Art DiLello....................................... 518-455-2296
Senate Minority Policy Development & Counsel Staff:
  Francis McKearin.................................. 518-455-2975

Offices and agencies generally appear in alphabetical order, except when specific order is requested by listee.

LEGISLATIVE BRANCH SENATE / State Senate Standing Committees

Membership

Majority
- James S Alesi
- John A DeFrancisco
- Martin J Golden
- Thomas P Morahan
- Stephen M Saland
- John J Bonacic
- Owen H Johnson
- Carl L Marcellino
- Joseph E Robach
- Dale M Volker

Minority
- Neil D Breslin
- Martin M Dilan
- Liz Krueger
- David J Valesky
- Ruben Diaz, Sr
- Efrain Gonzalez, Jr
- George Onorato

Cities
Chair:
  Serphin R Maltese (R) 518-455-3281
Ranking Minority Member:
  Antoine Thompson (D) 518-455-3371

Committee Staff
Counsel:
  Kathryn Coward 518-455-1260
Clerk:
  Jason Lansley 518-455-3281

Key Senate Staff Assignments
Senate Majority Counsel/Program Home Rule Counsel:
  Peter Rupert 518-455-2578
Senate Research Service Analyst:
  Chris Anderson 518-455-3501
Senate Minority Policy Development & Counsel Staff:
  Edna Jackson 518-455-2981

Membership

Majority
- Dale M Volker
- Frank Padavan
- Andrew J Lanza

Minority
- Suzi Oppenheimer
- Ruth Hassell-Thompson

Civil Service & Pensions
Chair:
  Joseph E Robach (R) 518-455-2909
Ranking Minority Member:
  Diane J Savino (D) 518-455-2437

Committee Staff
Director, Operations & Legislation:
  Timothy Ragazzo 518-455-2909

Key Senate Staff Assignments
Senate Majority Counsel/Program Services Assistant Counsel:
  Edward Bartholomew 518-455-2424
Senate Research Service Analyst:
  Steven Koczak 518-455-2295

Membership

Majority
- Vincent L Leibell, III
- Carl L Marcellino
- Charles J Fuschillo, Jr
- Serphin R Maltese
- Dean G Skelos
- Caesar Trunzo

Minority
- Eric Adams
- Bill Perkins
- Thomas K Duane
- Diane J Savino

Toby Ann Stavisky

Codes
Chair:
  Dale M Volker (R) 518-455-3471
Ranking Minority Member:
  Eric Schneiderman (D) 518-455-2041

Committee Staff
Counsel:
  J R Drexelius 518-455-3471
Clerk:
  Colleen Purcell 518-455-3471

Key Senate Staff Assignments
Senate Majority Counsel/Program Services Assistant Counsel:
  Joseph Messina 518-455-2342
Senate Research Service Analyst:
  Kandi Corey-Terry 518-455-2134
Senate Minority Policy Development & Counsel Staff:
  Keith St John 518-455-2842

Membership

Majority
- John J Bonacic
- Martin J Golden
- Andrew J Lanza
- Stephen M Saland
- John A DeFrancisco
- Kemp Hannon
- Serphin R Maltese
- Dean G Skelos

Minority
- Eric Adams
- Martin Connor
- Bill Perkins
- Eric T Schneiderman
- Neil D Breslin
- Thomas K Duane
- John L Sampson

Commerce, Economic Development & Small Business
Chair:
  James S Alesi (R) 518-455-2015
Ranking Minority Member:
  Efrain Gonzalez, Jr (D) 518-455-3395

Committee Staff
Counsel:
  Melissa Pugliese 518-455-2015
Clerk:
  Michelle Laranjo 518-455-2015

Key Senate Staff Assignments
Senate Majority Counsel/Program Services Assistant Counsel:
  Heather Briccetti 518-455-3413
Senate Research Service Analyst:
  Jason Wheatley 518-455-2151
Senate Minority Policy Development & Counsel Staff:
  Graham Ennis 518-455-2879

Membership

Majority
- John J Bonacic
- Joseph A Griffo
- William J Larkin, Jr
- Charles J Fuschillo, Jr
- Joseph E Robach
- James W Wright

Minority
- Efrain Gonzalez
- Kevin S Parker
- Ruth Hassell-Thompson
- Andrea Stewart-Cousins

Offices and agencies generally appear in alphabetical order, except when specific order is requested by listee.

LEGISLATIVE BRANCH SENATE / State Senate Standing Committees

Consumer Protection
Chair:
  Charles J Fuschillo, Jr (R) 518-455-3341
Ranking Minority Member:
  Carl Kruger (D) 518-455-2460

Committee Staff
Counsel:
  Michael James DeMartino III. 518-455-3341
Clerk:
  Timothy Ellis 518-455-3341

Key Senate Staff Assignments
Senate Majority Counsel/Program Services Assistant Counsel:
  Marcus Ferguson 518-455-3413
Senate Research Service Analyst:
  Art DiLello. 518-455-2296
Senate Minority Policy Development & Counsel Staff:
  Francis McKearin. 518-455-2975

Membership

Majority
  Joseph E Robach   Owen H Johnson
  John J Flanagan   Carl L Marcellino
  Joseph A Griffo

Minority
  Ruth Hassell-Thompson   Liz Krueger
  John D Sabini

Corporations, Authorities & Commissions
Chair:
  John J Flanagan (R) 518-455-3341
Ranking Minority Member:
  Bill Perkins (D). 518-455-2441

Committee Staff
Director:
  John Conklin. 518-455-2071
Clerk:
  Susan Conte-Zimmer 518-455-2071

Key Senate Staff Assignments
Senate Majority Counsel/Program Services Assistant Counsel:
  Maston Sansom 518-455-3413
Senate Research Service Analyst:
  Tracey Tudor 518-455-2546
Senate Minority Policy Development & Counsel Staff:
  Keith St John 518-455-2842

Membership

Majority
  Kemp Hannon   George D Maziarz
  Caesar Trunzo

Minority
  Efrain Gonzalez Jr

Crime Victims, Crime & Correction
Chair:
  Michael F Nozzolio (R) 518-455-2366
Ranking Minority Member:
  Eric Adams (D). 518-455-2431

Committee Staff
Director:
  Justin McCarthy 518-455-2366

Clerk:
  Meagan Fitzgerald 518-455-2366

Key Senate Staff Assignments
Senate Majority Counsel/Program Assistant Counsel:
  Kenneth Connolly 518-455-2342
Senate Research Service Analyst:
  Kandi Corey-Terry. 518-455-2134
Senate Minority Policy Development & Counsel Staff:
  Christina Dickinson 518-455-2823

Membership

Majority
  James S Alesi   Martin J Golden
  Elizabeth O'Connor Little George D Maziarz
  George H Winner, Jr   Dale M Volker
  James W Wright

Minority
  Ruth Hassell-Thompson   Carl Kruger
  John L Sampson   Velmanette Montgomery

Education
Chair:
  Stephen M Saland (R) 518-455-2411
Ranking Minority Member:
  Suzi Oppenheimer (D) 518-455-2031

Committee Staff
Legislative Director:
  Caroline Chauvin 518-455-2411
Counsel:
  Megha Godambe 518-455-2631

Key Senate Staff Assignments
Senate Majority Counsel/Program Services Program Associate:
  Michael Fox 518-455-3413
Senate Research Service Analyst:
  Ken Kienzle 518-455-2525
Senate Minority Policy Development & Counsel Staff:
  Greg Roberts 518-455-2870

Membership

Majority
  Charles J Fuschillo, Jr   Martin J Golden
  Andrew J Lanza   Kenneth P LaValle
  Elizabeth O'Connor Little Carl L Marcellino
  Thomas P Morahan   James L Seward
  Joseph Robach

Minority
  Martin M Dilan   Suzi Oppenheimer
  Shirley Huntley   Velmanette Montgomery
  John D Sabini   Eric T Schneiderman
  Toby Ann Stavisky   Jose E Serrano

Elections
Chair:
  Joseph A Griffo (R) 518-455-3334
Ranking Minority Member:
  Martin M Dilan (D) 518-455-2177

Committee Staff
Legislative Director:
  John Conklin. 518-455-2071

Offices and agencies generally appear in alphabetical order, except when specific order is requested by listee.

LEGISLATIVE BRANCH SENATE / State Senate Standing Committees

Key Senate Staff Assignments
Senate Majority Counsel/Program Services Assistant Counsel:
  Michael Melkonian 518-455-7501
Senate Research Service Analyst:
  Tracey Tudor 518-455-2546
Senate Minority Policy Development & Counsel Staff:
  Christopher Higgins 518-455-3447

Membership

Majority
Kemp Hannon	George H Winner
Thomas P Morahan	Mary Lou Rath

Minority
John D Sabini

Energy & Telecommunications
Chair:
  James W Wright (R) 518-455-2346
Ranking Minority Member:
  Kevin S Parker (D) 518-455-2580

Committee Staff
Counsel:
  Frank Moroney 518-455-2346
Director:
  Kim Ireland 518-455-2346

Key Senate Staff Assignments
Senate Majority Counsel/Program Services Principal Program Assoc:
  Bernard McGarry 518-455-2986
Senate Research Service Analyst:
  Todd Kusnierz 518-455-2153
Senate Minority Policy Development & Counsel Staff:
  Marcy Palmer 518-455-2830

Membership

Majority
James S Alesi	John A DeFrancisco
George D Maziarz	Joseph A Griffo
Frank Padavan	George H Winner

Minority
Efrain Gonzalez Jr	Carl Kruger
George Onorato	David J Valesky

Environmental Conservation
Chair:
  Carl L Marcellino (R) 518-455-2390
Ranking Minority Member:
  Craig Johnson (D) 518-455-2622

Committee Staff
Director:
  Deborah Peck Kelleher 518-455-2390

Key Senate Staff Assignments
Senate Majority Counsel/Program Services Program Associate:
  Darren Suarez 518-455-2342
Senate Minority Policy Development & Counsel Staff:
  Marcy Palmer 518-455-2830

Membership

Majority
John J Bonacic	Owen H Johnson
Vincent L Leibell, III	Elizabeth O'Connor Little
Joseph A Griffo	Caesar Trunzo

Catharine M Young

Minority
Suzi Oppenheimer	Kevin S Parker
John D Sabini	Diane J Savino
Jose E Serrano	

Ethics
Chair:
  Andrew J Lanza (R) 518-455-3215
Ranking Minority Member:
  Jeffrey Klein (D) 518-455-3595

Key Senate Staff Assignments
Senate Majority Counsel/Program Services Legislative Counsel:
  Francis Gluchowski 518-455-2563
Senate Minority Policy Development & Counsel Staff:
  Keith St John 518-455-2842

Membership

Majority
Hugh T Farley	Stephen M Saland

Minority
Craig Johnson	Suzi Oppenheimer

Finance
Chair:
  Owen H Johnson (R) 518-455-3411
Ranking Minority Member:
  William Stachowski (D) 518-455-2426

Committee Staff
Secretary to the Committee:
  Jeffrey Lovell 518-455-3198
Assistant Secretary:
  David J Natoli 518-455-2417
Counsel:
  Jay Bove 518-455-3411
Communications Director:
  Kathleen O'Neill 518-455-3411
Clerk:
  Louis Sitrin 518-455-3232

Key Senate Staff Assignments
Senate Majority Finance Budget Studies Director:
  Robert Mujica 518-455-2880
Secretary to Minority Finance:
  Michael Weber 518-455-2217
Senate Minority Finance Budget Studies Director:
  Ahmed Diomande 518-455-2641
Senate Minority Finance Fiscal Studies Director:
  Michael J Laccetti 518-455-2641

Membership

Majority
Hugh T Farley	Kemp Hannon
John D DeFrancisco	Michael F Nozzolio
William J Larkin, Jr	Kenneth P LaValle
Thomas W Libous	Serphin R Maltese
Vincent L Leibell III	James W Wright
Frank Padavan	Stephen M Saland
James L Seward	Dean G Skelos
George D Maziarz	Caesar Trunzo
Mary Lou Rath	Dale M Volker

Minority
Thomas K Duane	Efrain Gonzalez, Jr

Offices and agencies generally appear in alphabetical order, except when specific order is requested by listee.

LEGISLATIVE BRANCH SENATE / State Senate Standing Committees

Martin Connor
Antoine Thompson
Suzi Oppenheimer
John L Sampson
Martin M Dilan
Toby Ann Stavisky
Carl Kruger
Velmanette Montgomery
Kevin S Parker
Andrea Stewart-Cousins
Liz Krueger

Health
Chair:
  Kemp Hannon (R) 518-455-2200
Ranking Minority Member:
  John L Sampson (D) 518-455-2788

Committee Staff
Executive Director:
  Jane Preston 518-455-2200
Clerk:
  Lori Gradwell 518-455-2200

Key Senate Staff Assignments
Senate Majority Counsel/Program Services Principal Program Assoc:
  Caron O'Brien Crummey 518-455-2597
Senate Minority Policy Development & Counsel Staff:
  Cathy Bern-Smith 518-455-2957

Membership

Majority
John A DeFrancisco
Charles J Fuschillo, Jr
Thomas W Libous
George H Winner, Jr
Catharine M Young
Hugh T Farley
William J Larkin, Jr
Elizabeth O'Connor Little
Mary Lou Rath

Minority
Thomas K Duane
Velmanette Montgomery
Eric Schneiderman
Efrain Gonzalez Jr
George Onorato
David J Valesky

Higher Education
Chair:
  Kenneth P LaValle (R) 518-455-3121
Ranking Minority Member:
  Toby Ann Stavisky (D) 518-455-3461

Committee Staff
Director:
  John D'Agati 518-455-3121
Assistant Director:
  Leslea Snyder 518-455-3121

Key Senate Staff Assignments
Senate Majority Counsel/Program Services Assistant Counsel:
  Nicole Burckard 518-455-7924
Senate Research Service Analyst:
  Darryl B Hayes 518-455-3322
Senate Minority Policy Development & Counsel Staff:
  Greg Roberts 518-455-2870

Membership

Majority
James S Alesi
Joseph A Griffo
George H Winner, Jr
Joseph E Robach
Catharine M Young
John J Flanagan
Serphin R Maltese
Mary Lou Rath
James L Seward

Minority
Shirley Huntley
Ruben Diaz, Sr

Liz Krueger
Kevin S Parker
David J Valesky
Suzi Oppenheimer
Jose E Serrano

Housing, Construction & Community Development
Chair:
  John J Bonacic (R) 518-455-3181
Ranking Minority Member:
  Liz Krueger (D) 518-455-2297

Committee Staff
Director/Counsel:
  Langdon Chapman 518-455-3181
Asst Director/Clerk:
  Darlene Leder 518-455-3181

Key Senate Staff Assignments
Senate Majority Counsel/Program Services Principal Program Assoc:
  Bernard McGarry 518-455-2986
Senate Research Service Analyst:
  Jason Wheatley 518-455-2151
Senate Minority Policy Development & Counsel Staff:
  Vacant 518-455-2966

Membership

Majority
Vincent L Leibell, III
Elizabeth O'Connor Little
James W Wright
Catharine M Young

Minority
Ruth Hassell-Thompson
Diane J Savino

Insurance
Chair:
  James L Seward (R) 518-455-3131
Ranking Minority Member:
  Neil D Breslin (D) 518-455-2225

Committee Staff
Counsel:
  Kristina Baldwin 518-455-3131
Clerk:
  Laurie Heimroth 518-455-3131

Key Senate Staff Assignments
Senate Majority Counsel/Program Services Assistant Counsel:
  Damon Stewart 518-455-2986
Senate Research Service Analyst:
  Art DiLello 518-455-2296
Senate Minority Policy Development & Counsel Staff:
  Francis McKearin 518-455-2975

Membership

Majority
James S Alesi
John J Flanagan
Kenneth P LaValle
Thomas W Libous
Dean G Skelos
Martin J Golden
William J Larkin, Jr
Vincent L Leibell, III
Stephen M Saland
Catharine M Young

Minority
Martin Connor
George Onorato
Carl Kruger
Neil D Breslin
William T Stachowski
Kevin S Parker

Offices and agencies generally appear in alphabetical order, except when specific order is requested by listee.

LEGISLATIVE BRANCH SENATE / State Senate Standing Committees

Investigations & Government Operations
Chair:
George H Winner Jr (R) 518-455-2091
Ranking Minority Member:
William T Stachowski (D) 518-455-3531

Committee Staff
Counsel:
Teresa Russi 518-455-2091

Key Senate Staff Assignments
Senate Majority Counsel/Program Services Assistant Counsel:
Mike Avella 518-455-3413
Senate Research Service Analyst:
Tracey Tudor 518-455-2546
Senate Minority Policy Development & Counsel Staff:
Christina Dickinson 518-455-2823

Membership

Majority
- Martin J Golden
- Michael F Nozzolio
- Thomas W Libous
- Dean G Skelos

Minority
- Thomas K Duane
- Eric T Schneiderman

Judiciary
Chair:
John A DeFrancisco (R) 518-455-3511
Ranking Minority Member:
Ruth Hassell-Thompson (D) 518-455-2061

Committee Staff
Senior Counsel:
Kevin Engel 518-455-3511
Clerk:
Carole Luther 518-455-3511

Key Senate Staff Assignments
Senate Majority Counsel/Program Services Assistant Counsel:
John Cahill 518-455-2342
Senate Research Service Analyst:
Tracey Tudor 518-455-2546
Senate Minority Policy Development & Counsel Staff:
Keith St John 518-455-2842

Membership

Majority
- John J Bonacic
- Kemp Hannon
- Serphin R Maltese
- Andrew J Lanza
- Stephen M Saland
- George H Winner, Jr
- Hugh T Farley
- Kenneth P LaValle
- Michael F Nozzolio
- George Maziarz
- Dean G Skelos
- Dale M Volker

Minority
- Neil D Breslin
- Martin M Dilan
- Bill Perkins
- Eric T Schneiderman
- Diane J Savino
- Martin Connor
- Thomas K Duane
- John L Sampson
- Andrea Stewart-Cousins

Labor
Chair:
George D Maziarz (R) 518-455-2024
Ranking Minority Member:
George Onorato (D) 518-455-3486

Committee Staff
Committee Director:
Joseph Erdman 518-455-2024

Key Senate Staff Assignments
Senate Majority Counsel/Program Services Assistant Counsel:
Edward Bartholomew 518-455-2424
Senate Research Service Analyst:
Steven Koczak 518-455-2295

Membership

Majority
- James S Alesi
- John J Bonacic
- Charles J Fuschillo, Jr
- Joseph E Robach
- Thomas P Morahan
- John J Flanagan
- Carl L Marcellino
- James W Wright

Minority
- Neil D Breslin
- Efrain Gonzalez, Jr
- Martin Connor
- Diane J Savino
- Bill Perkins
- William T Stachowski

Local Government
Chair:
Elizabeth O'Connor Little (R) 518-455-2811
Ranking Minority Member:
Andrea Stewart-Cousins (D) 518-455-2585

Committee Staff
Clerk:
Mary Pat McDonald 518-455-2811

Key Senate Staff Assignments
Senate Majority Counsel/Program Services Home Rule Counsel:
Peter Rupert 518-455-2578
Senate Research Service Analyst:
Chris Anderson 518-455-3501
Senate Minority Policy Development & Counsel Staff:
Jim Watson 518-455-2977

Membership

Majority
- John J Bonacic
- Mary Lou Rath
- Thomas P Morahan
- Caesar Trunzo

Minority
- Jose E Serrano
- Craig M Johnson

Mental Health & Developmental Disabilities
Chair:
Thomas P Morahan (R) 518-455-3261
Ranking Minority Member:
Ruben Diaz, Sr (D) 518-455-2511

Committee Staff
Legislative Counsel:
Kristin Gran Sinclair 518-455-3261

Key Senate Staff Assignments
Senate Majority Counsel/Program Services Program Associate:
Beth Colombo 518-455-2484
Senate Minority Policy Development & Counsel Staff:
Cathy Bern-Smith 518-455-2957

Membership

Majority
- Andrew J Lanza
- Frank Padavan
- Carl L Marcellino
- Dale M Volker

Offices and agencies generally appear in alphabetical order, except when specific order is requested by listee.

LEGISLATIVE BRANCH SENATE / State Senate Standing Committees

Catharine M Young

Minority
Shirley L Huntley
Eric T Schneiderman
Velmanette Montgomery

Racing, Gaming & Wagering
Chair:
William J Larkin, Jr (R) 518-455-2770
Ranking Minority Member:
John D Sabini (D) 518-455-2529

Committee Staff
Director:
Charlotte Johnson 518-455-2775
Counsel:
J Stephen Casscles 518-455-2770

Key Senate Staff Assignments
Senate Majority Counsel/Program Services Program Associate:
Jon McCloskey 518-455-3413
Senate Research Service Analyst:
Jason Wheatley 518-455-2151
Senate Minority Policy Development & Counsel Staff:
Christopher Higgins 518-455-3447

Membership
Majority
Thomas W Libous
Michael F Nozzolio
Joseph A Griffo
Elizabeth O'Connor Little
Mary Lou Rath

Minority
George Onorato
William T Stachowski
John L Sampson

Rules
Chair:
Joseph L Bruno (R) 518-455-3191
Ranking Minority Member:
Malcom A Smith (D) 518-455-2701

Membership
Majority
Hugh T Farley
Owen H Johnson
Stephen M Saland
Frank Padavan
Dean G Skelos
Caesar Trunzo
Dale M Volker
Kemp Hannon
Kenneth P LaValle
Thomas W Libous
James L Seward
William J Larkin Jr
Serphin R Maltese

Minority
Thomas K Duane
Liz Krueger
John D Sabini
Martin Connor
William T Stachowski
Ruth Hassell-Thompson
Velmanette Montgomery
Eric T Schneiderman
Jose M Serrano

Social Services, Children & Families
Chair:
Carl Kruger (R) 518-455-2460
Ranking Minority Member:
Velmanette Montgomery (D) 518-455-3451

Committee Staff
Legislative Director:
Emma Steckman 518-455-2430

Key Senate Staff Assignments
Senate Majority Counsel/Program Services Program Assoc:
Michelle DiBacco 518-455-2597
Senate Minority Policy Development & Counsel Staff:
Francis McKearin 518-455-2975

Membership
Majority
Owen H Johnson
Mary Lou Rath
Carl L Marcellino

Minority
Ruben Diaz, Sr

Tourism, Recreation & Sports Development
Chair:
Mary Lou Rath (R) 518-455-3161
Ranking Minority Member:
Jose E Serrano (D) 518-455-2795

Committee Staff
Director:
John Emery 518-455-3161
Clerk:
Deadra Morrissey 518-455-3161

Key Senate Staff Assignments
Senate Majority Counsel/Program Services Assistant Counsel:
Karen Moreau 518-455-3413
Senate Research Service Analyst:
Jason Wheatley 518-455-2151
Senate Minority Policy Development & Counsel Staff:
Marcy Palmer 518-455-2830

Membership
Majority
James S Alesi
Thomas W Libous
Michael F Nozzolio
James W Wright
John A DeFrancisco
Elizabeth O'Connor Little
Joseph E Robach

Minority
Antoine Thompson
Diane J Savino
David J Valesky
Andrea Stewart-Cousins
Toby Ann Stavisky

Transportation
Chair:
Thomas W Libous (R) 518-455-2677
Ranking Minority Member:
John D Sabini (D) 518-455-2529

Committee Staff
Legislative Director:
Aaron M Martin 518-455-2674
Deputy Director:
Matthew W Moyse 518-455-7973
Legislative Asst:
John T Knadler 518-455-7972

Key Senate Staff Assignments
Senate Majority Counsel/Program Services Assistant Counsel:
Michael Melkonian 518-455-7501

Offices and agencies generally appear in alphabetical order, except when specific order is requested by listee.

LEGISLATIVE BRANCH SENATE / Joint Legislative Commissions

Senate Research Service Analyst:
   Michael Cartenuto 518-455-2154
Senate Minority Policy Development & Counsel Staff:
   Graham Ennis 518-455-2879

Membership

Majority
- John J Flanagan
- Owen H Johnson
- Michael F Nozzolio
- Joseph E Robach
- Andrew J Lanza
- Charles J Fuschillo, Jr
- William J Larkin, Jr
- Frank Padavan
- James L Seward
- Caesar Trunzo

Minority
- Martin M Dilan
- Suzi Oppenheimer
- Toby Ann Stavisky
- David J Valesky
- Shirley L Huntley
- Bill Perkins
- Diane J Savino

Veterans, Homeland Security & Military Affairs
Chair:
   Vincent L Leibell III (R) 518-455-3111
Ranking Minority Member:
   Eric Adams (D) 518-455-2431

Committee Staff
Chief Counsel:
   Robert Farley 518-455-3111
Chief of Staff:
   Raymond Maguire 518-455-1650

Key Senate Staff Assignments
Senate Majority Counsel/Program Services Assistant Counsel:
   Richard Consentino 518-455-2424
Senate Majority Counsel/Program Assistant Counsel:
   Kenneth Connolly 518-455-2342
Senate Minority Policy Development & Counsel Staff:
   Francis McKearin 518-455-2975

Membership

Majority
- John J Flanagan
- William J Larkin, Jr
- Thomas P Morahan
- James W Wright
- Martin J Golden
- Joseph A Griffo
- Frank Padavan

Minority
- Antoine Thompson
- Kevin S Parker
- Carl Kruger
- Ruben Diaz, Sr
- John L Sampson

SENATE SELECT & SPECIAL COMMITTEES & SPECIAL TASK FORCES

Arts & Cultural Affairs, Special Committee on the
Chair:
   Serphin R Maltese (R) 518-455-3281
Chief of Staff:
   Victoria Vattimo 518-455-3281

Disabled, Select Committee on the
Chair:
   Thomas W Libous (R) 518-455-2677
Legislative Director:
   Aaron Martin 518-455-2674

Interstate Cooperation, Select Committee on
Chair:
   Hugh T Farley (R) 518-455-2181

Joint Legislative Commissions

Administrative Regulations Review, Legislative Commission on
Senate Co-Chair:
   Catharine M Young (R) 518-455-3563
Assembly Co-Chair:
   Michael N Gianaris (D) 518-455-5014
Senate Director:
   John Koury 518-455-2731/fax: 518-426-6820
Assembly Program Manager:
   Rich Murphy 518-455-5070/fax: 518-455-4175

Critical Transportation Choices, Legislative Commission on
Senate Chair:
   Thomas W Libous (R) 518-455-2677
Assembly Vice Chair:
   Vacant 518-455-0000
Program Manager:
   Heidi Kromphardt 518-455-4031/fax: 518-455-4859

Demographic Research & Reapportionment, Legislative Task Force on
Senate Co-Chair:
   Dean G Skelos (R) 518-455-3171
Assembly Co-Chair:
   Carl Heastie (D) 518-455-4800
Senate Co-Executive Dir:
   Debra A Levine 212-618-1100/fax: 212-618-1135
Assembly Co-Executive Director:
   Lewis M Hoppe 212-618-1100/fax: 212-618-1135

Ethics Committee, Legislative
Senate Co-Chair:
   Andrew J Lanza (R) 518-455-3215
Assembly Co-Chair:
   Kevin A Cahill (D) 518-455-4436
Director/Counsel:
   Melissa Ryan 518-455-2142/fax: 518-426-6850

Offices and agencies generally appear in alphabetical order, except when specific order is requested by listee.

LEGISLATIVE BRANCH SENATE / Joint Legislative Commissions

Government Administration, Legislative Commission on
Senate Vice-Chair:
  Owen H Johnson (R) 518-455-3411
Assembly Chair:
  Joan Millman (D) 518-455-5426
Senior Program Manager:
  Philip Johnson 518-455-3632/fax: 518-455-4574

Health Care Financing, Council on
Senate Chair:
  Joseph L Bruno (R) 518-455-3191
Assembly Vice Chair:
  Vacant 518-455-5282
Executive Director:
  Allan Filler. 518-455-2067/fax: 518-426-6925

Rural Resources, Legislative Commission on
Senate Chair:
  George H Winner Jr (R) 518-455-2091
Assembly Chair:
  David R Koon (D) 518-455-5784
Senate Executive Director:
  Ronald C Brach 518-455-2544/fax: 518-426-6960
Assembly Director:
  Susan Bartle. 518-455-3999/fax: 518-455-4175
Counsel:
  Donald A Walsh 518-455-2544

Science & Technology, Legislative Commission on
Assembly Chair:
  William B Magnarelli (D) 518-455-4826

Senate Vice Chair:
  Vacant 518-455-0000
Senior Program Manager:
  Philip Johnson 518-455-5081/fax: 518-455-4859

Solid Waste Management, Legislative Commission on
Assembly Chair:
  William Colton (D). 518-455-5828
Senate Vice Chair:
  Vacant 518-455-0000
Program Manager:
  Richard D Morse, Jr 518-455-3711/fax: 518-455-3837

Toxic Substances & Hazardous Waste, Legislative Commission on
Senate Chair:
  Vacant 518-455-0000
Assembly Vice Chair:
  David R Koon (D) 518-455-5784
Program Manager:
  Richard D Morse, Jr 518-455-3711/fax: 518-455-3837

Water Resources Needs of New York State & Long Island, Legislative Commission
Assembly Co-Chair:
  Vacant 518-455-0000
Program Manager:
  Richard D Morse, Jr 518-455-3711/fax: 518-455-3837

Offices and agencies generally appear in alphabetical order, except when specific order is requested by listee.

LEGISLATIVE BRANCH ASSEMBLY

State Assembly Leadership

Members of the Assembly welcome e-mail correspondence from the public. They may reply by e-mail, or by mail when more extensive follow-up is necessary. Please include both an e-mail and mailing address in all correspondence.

State Capitol
Albany, NY 12248
Web site: www.assembly.state.ny.us

Administration

June Egeland 518-455-4242/fax: 518-455-4935
Title: Clerk of the Assembly

Wayne P Jackson 518-455-3797/fax: 518-455-4445
Title: Sergeant-at-Arms, Chamber

John Longo 518-455-5767/fax: 518-455-4963
Title: Director, Communication & Information Services

John P Wellspeak 518-455-4411/fax: 518-455-4298
Title: Director, Administration

Vacant 518-455-4999/fax: 518-455-4989
Title: District Office Administrator

Kathleen McCarty 518-455-4704/fax: 518-455-4705
Title: Director, Internship Program

Mike Gaffney 518-455-5165/fax: 518-455-4741
Title: Superintendent, Document Room

Sharon Walsh 518-455-4218/fax: 518-455-5175
Title: Public Information Officer

Ellen Breslin 518-455-2468/fax: 518-426-6901
Title: Reference Librarian, Legislative Library

Joseph E O'Brien 518-455-5190/fax: 518-455-4517
Title: Director, Operations

Majority Leadership

Sheldon Silver (D) 518-455-3791
e-mail: speaker@assembly.state.ny.us
Title: Speaker

Ron Canestrari (D) 518-455-4474
e-mail: canestr@assembly.state.ny.us
Title: Majority Leader

Herman D Farrell, Jr (D) 518-455-5491
e-mail: farrelh@assembly.state.ny.us
Title: Chair, Ways & Means Committee

Ivan C Lafayette (D) 518-455-4545
e-mail: lafayei@assembly.state.ny.us
Title: Deputy Speaker

Aurelia Greene (D) 518-455-5671
e-mail: greenea@assembly.state.ny.us
Title: Speaker Pro Tempore

Harvey Weisenberg (D) 518-455-3028
e-mail: weisenh@assembly.state.ny.us
Title: Assistant Speaker Pro Tempore

Rhoda S Jacobs (D) 518-455-5385
e-mail: jacobsr@assembly.state.ny.us
Title: Assistant Speaker

William L Parment (D) 518-455-4511
e-mail: parmenw@assembly.state.ny.us
Title: Chair, Committee on Standing Committees

Earlene Hooper (D) 518-455-5861
e-mail: hoopere@assembly.state.ny.us
Title: Deputy Majority Leader

Vivian E Cook (D) 518-455-4203
e-mail: cookv@assembly.state.ny.us
Title: Assistant Majority Leader

N Nick Perry (D) 518-455-4166
e-mail: perryn@assembly.state.ny.us
Title: Majority Whip

Dov Hikind (D) 518-455-5721
e-mail: hikindd@assembly.state.ny.us
Title: Deputy Majority Whip

Barbara Clark (D) 518-455-4711
e-mail: clarkb@assembly.state.ny.us
Title: Assistant Majority Whip

William Colton (D) 518-455-5828
e-mail: coltonw@assembly.state.ny.us
Title: Chair, Majority Conference

Offices and agencies generally appear in alphabetical order, except when specific order is requested by listee.

LEGISLATIVE BRANCH ASSEMBLY / State Assembly Leadership

Steven Cymbrowitz (D)....................518-455-5214
e-mail: cymbrows@assembly.state.ny.us
Title: Vice Chair, Majority Conference

Francine DelMonte (D)....................518-455-5284
e-mail: delmonf@ssembly.state.ny.us
Title: Secretary, Majority Conference

John J McEneny (D).......................518-455-4178
e-mail: mcenenj@assembly.state.ny.us
Title: Chair, Majority Steering Committee

Patricia Eddington (D)...................518-455-4901
e-mail: eddingp@assembly.state.ny.us
Title: Vice Chair, Majority Steering Committee

Anthony S Seminerio (D)..................518-455-4621
e-mail: seminea@assembly.state.ny.us
Title: Chair, Majority Program Committee

Majority Staff

Judy R Rapfogel.............212-312-1400/fax: 212-312-1418
Title: Chief of Staff to the Speaker

Charles Carrier............518-455-3888/fax: 518-455-3858
Title: Press Secretary to the Speaker

Kevin C McGraw.............518-455-4303/fax: 518-455-4380
Title: First Deputy to the Speaker for Majority Program & Policy

Karen McCann...............518-455-4736/fax: 518-455-5428
Title: Director, Legislative Services

John Hudder................518-455-4386/fax: 518-455-5573
Title: Director, Program Development

Bill Collins...............518-455-4191/fax: 518-455-4103
Title: Counsel to the Majority

Dean Fuleihan..............518-455-3786/fax: 518-455-4445
Title: Secretary to the Majority Committee on Ways & Means

Minority Leadership

James N Tedisco (R).......................518-455-3751
e-mail: tediscj@assembly.state.ny.us
Title: Minority Leader

Brian M Kolb (R)..........................518-455-5772
e-mail: kolbb@assembly.state.ny.us
Title: Minority Leader Pro Tempore

James D Conte (R).........................518-455-5732
e-mail: contej@assembly.state.ny.us
Title: Assistant Minority Leader Pro Tempore

Nancy Calhoun (R).........................518-455-5441
e-mail: calhoun@assembly.state.ny.us
Title: Ranking Minority Member, Committee on Standing Committees

Robert C Oaks (R).........................518-455-5655
e-mail: oaksr@assembly.state.ny.us
Title: Deputy Minority Leader

Thomas W Alfano (R).......................518-455-4627
e-mail: alfanot@assembly.state.ny.us
Title: Assistant Minority Leader

William A Barclay (R).....................518-455-5841
e-mail: barclaw@assembly.state.ny.us
Title: Assistant Minority Leader

Diedre K Scozzafava (R)...................518-455-5797
e-mail: scozzad@assembly.state.ny.us
Title: Minority Whip

Gary D Finch (R)..........................518-455-5878
e-mail: finchg@assembly.state.ny.us
Title: Deputy Minority Whip

Clifford Crouch (R).......................518-455-5741
e-mail: crouchc@assembly.state.ny.us
Title: Assistant Minority Whip

James G Bacalles (R)......................518-455-5791
e-mail: bacallj@assembly.state.ny.us
Title: Chair, Minority Conference

Daniel J Burling (R)......................518-455-5314
e-mail: burlind@assembly.state.ny.us
Title: Vice Chair, Minority Conference

Teresa R Sayward (R)......................518-455-5565
e-mail: saywart@assembly.state.ny.us
Title: Secretary, Minority Conference

David R Townsend Jr (R)...................518-455-5334
e-mail: townsed@assembly.state.ny.us
Title: Chair, Minority Joint Conference Committee

Fred W Thiele, Jr (R).....................518-455-5997
e-mail: thielef@assembly.state.ny.us
Title: Vice Chair, Minority Joint Conference Committee

William Reilich (R).......................518-455-4664
e-mail: reilicw@assembly.state.ny.us
Title: Chair, Minority Steering Committee

Rob Walker (R)............................518-455-4684
e-mail: walkerr2@ssembly.state.ny.us
Title: Vice Chair, Minority Steering Committee

Roy McDonald (R)..........................518-455-5404
e-mail: mcdonar@assembly.state.ny.us
Title: Chair, Minority Program Committee

Thomas F O'Mara (R).......................518-455-4538
e-mail: omarat@assembly.state.ny.us
Title: Vice Chair, Minority Program Committee

Offices and agencies generally appear in alphabetical order, except when specific order is requested by listee.

LEGISLATIVE BRANCH ASSEMBLY / State Assembly Roster

James P Hayes (R) 518-455-4618
e-mail: hayesj@assembly.state.ny.us
Title: Ranking Minority Member, Ways & Means

Minority Staff

Bill Sherman..................... 518-455-3751/fax: 518-455-3750
Title: Chief of Staff

Phil Oliva........................ 518-455-3756/fax: 518-455-3750
Title: Director, Minority Communications

Howard Becker.................. 518-455-4689/fax: 518-455-3750
Title: Executive Director

Greg Amorosi................... 518-455-3741/fax: 518-455-4494
Title: Counsel to the Minority

Harry MacAvoy................. 518-455-5002/fax: 518-455-5829
Title: Director, Minority Research & Program Development

Rebecca D'Agati................ 518-455-5161/fax: 518-455-4550
Title: Director, Minority Ways & Means Staff

Judith A Skype.................. 518-455-4211/fax: 518-455-3758
Title: Director, Minority Administration & Personnel

State Assembly Roster

Multiple party abbreviations following the names of legislators indicate that those legislators ran as the Assembly candidate for each identified party. Source: NYS Board of Elections. Party abbreviations: Conservative (C), Democrat (D), Green (G), Independent (I), Liberal (L), Republican (R), Right to Life (RL), Veterans (VE), Working Families (WF)

Peter J Abbate, Jr (D) 518-455-3053/fax: 518-455-5524
District: 49 *Room:* 839 LOB *e-mail:* abbatep@assembly.state.ny.us
Committees: Aging; Banks; Consumer Affairs & Protection; Governmental Employees (Chair); Labor
Senior Staff: Barbara M O'Neill

Marc S Alessi (D) 518-455-5294/fax: 518-455-4740
District: 1 *Room:* 326 LOB *e-mail:* alessim@assembly.state.ny.us
Committees: Aging; Agriculture; Energy; Labor; Local Governments; Transportation; Veterans Affairs
Senior Staff: Vacant

Thomas W Alfano (R-I-C-WF).... 518-455-4627/fax: 518-455-4643
District: 21 *Room:* 404 LOB *e-mail:* alfanot@assembly.state.ny.us
Title: Assistant Minority Leader
Committees: Children & Families; Higher Education; Judiciary (Ranking Minority Member); Labor
Senior Staff: M Scott Cushing

Carmen E Arroyo (D)............ 518-455-5402/fax: 518-455-4681
District: 84 *Room:* 734 LOB *e-mail:* arroyoc@assembly.state.ny.us
Committees: Aging; Alcoholism and Drug Abuse; Children & Families; Education
Senior Staff: Richard Izquierdo

Darrel J Aubertine (D)........... 518-455-5545/fax: 518-455-5751
District: 118 *Room:* 602 LOB *e-mail:* aubertd@assembly.state.ny.us
Committees: Agriculture; Economic Development, Job Creation, Commerce & Industry; Energy; Higher Education; Transportation; Veterans Affairs
Senior Staff: Ed Gaffney

Jeffrion L Aubry (D-L) 518-455-4561/fax: 518-455-4565
District: 35 *Room:* 526 LOB *e-mail:* aubryj@assembly.state.ny.us
Committees: Correction (Chair); Economic Development, Job Creation, Commerce & Industry; Governmental Employees; Social Services; Ways & Means
Senior Staff: Mary C Nicholson

James G Bacalles (R-C)........... 518-455-5791/fax: 518-455-4644
District: 136 *Room:* 439 LOB *e-mail:* bacallj@assembly.state.ny.us
Title: Chair, Minority Conference
Committees: Cities; Corporations, Authorities & Commissions (Ranking Minority Member); Environmental Conservation; Health; Transportation
Senior Staff: Robin Lattimer

Greg Ball (R) 518-455-5783/fax: 518-455-5543
District: 99 *Room:* 543 LOB *e-mail:* ballg@assembly.state.ny.us
Committees: Election Law; Energy; Housing; Social Services; Veterans Affairs
Senior Staff: Rob DiFrancesco

William A Barclay (R-I-C)........ 518-455-5841/fax: 518-455-5362
District: 124 *Room:* 546 LOB *e-mail:* barclaw@assembly.state.ny.us
Title: Assistant Minority Leader
Committees: Corporations, Authorities & Commissions; Ethics & Guidance; Insurance (Ranking Minority Member); Judiciary; Ways & Means
Senior Staff: Jen Cook

Robert D Barra (R-C) 518-455-4656/fax: 518-455-4337
District: 14 *Room:* 723 LOB *e-mail:* barrar@assembly.state.ny.us
Committees: Aging; Local Governments; Mental Health; Racing & Wagering (Ranking Minority Member)
Senior Staff: Rosemary Pugliese

Michael R Benedetto (D).......... 518-455-5296/fax: 518-455-4641
District: 82 *Room:* 919 LOB *e-mail:* benedem@assembly.state.ny.us
Committees: Agriculture; Consumer Affairs & Protection; Education; Governmental Operations; Housing; Labor
Senior Staff: John Collazzi

Michael A Benjamin (D-WF) 518-455-5272/fax: 518-455-5925
District: 79 *Room:* 549 LOB *e-mail:* benjamm@assembly.state.ny.us
Committees: Banks; Children & Families; Correction; Election Law; Housing; Libraries & Education Technology
Senior Staff: Kennedy Benjamin

Offices and agencies generally appear in alphabetical order, except when specific order is requested by listee.

LEGISLATIVE BRANCH ASSEMBLY / State Assembly Roster

Jonathan L Bing (D) 518-455-4794/fax: 518-455-4629
District: 73 *Room:* 744 LOB *e-mail:* bingj@assembly.state.ny.us
Committees: Banks; Health; Housing; Judiciary; Social Services; Tourism, Arts & Sports Development
Senior Staff: Barry Klein

William F Boyland, Jr (D) 518-455-4466/fax: 518-455-3894
District: 55 *Room:* 540 LOB *e-mail:* boylanw@assembly.state.ny.us
Committees: Aging; Banks; Economic Development, Job Creation, Commerce & Industry; Housing; Local Goverments
Senior Staff: Vacant

Philip Boyle (R-I-C) 518-455-4611
District: 8 *Room:* 718 LOB *e-mail:* boylep@assembly.state.ny.us
Committees: Aging; Codes; Economic Development, Job Creation, Commerce & Industry; Libraries & Education Technology
Senior Staff: Amy Grega

Adam T Bradley (D) 518-455-5397/fax: 518-455-5041
District: 89 *Room:* 529 LOB *e-mail:* bradlea@assembly.state.ny.us
Committees: Children & Families; Election Law; Environmental Conservation; Insurance; Judiciary; Veterans' Affairs
Senior Staff: Justin Smith

James F Brennan (D) 518-455-5377/fax: 518-455-5592
District: 44 *Room:* 842 LOB *e-mail:* brennaj@assembly.state.ny.us
Committees: Cities (Chair); Codes; Corporations, Authorities & Commissions; Education; Real Property Taxation; Rules
Senior Staff: Lorrie Smith

Richard L Brodsky (D) 518-455-5753/fax: 518-455-5920
District: 92 *Room:* 422 LOB *e-mail:* brodskr@assembly.state.ny.us
Committees: Banks; Corporations, Authorities & Commissions (Chair); Tourism, Arts & Sports Development
Senior Staff: Kelly MacMillan

Alec Brook-Krasny (D) 518-455-4811/fax: 518-455-5654
District: 46 *Room:* 428 LOB *e-mail:* brookkrasny@assembly.state.ny.us
Committees: Aging; Cities; Election Law; Governmental Employees; Housing; Social Services

Daniel J Burling (R-I-C) 518-455-5314/fax: 518-455-5691
District: 147 *Room:* 635 LOB *e-mail:* burlind@assembly.state.ny.us
Title: Vice Chair, Minority Conference
Committees: Environmental Conservation; Rules; Veterans Affairs; Ways & Means
Senior Staff: Barbara Finke

Marc W Butler (R-I-C) 518-455-5393/fax: 518-455-5889
District: 117 *Room:* 318 LOB *e-mail:* butlerm@assembly.state.ny.us
Committees: Agriculture; Economic Development, Job Creation, Commerce & Industry (Ranking Minority Member); Higher Education; Insurance
Senior Staff: Laurel D Corby

Kevin A Cahill (D) 518-455-4436/fax: 518-455-5576
District: 101 *Room:* 557 LOB *e-mail:* cahillk@assembly.state.ny.us
Title: Vice Chair, Majority Steering Committee
Committees: Ethics & Guidance (Chair); Economic Development, Job Creation, Commerce & Industry; Health; Higher Education; Ways & Means
Senior Staff: Kathy Keyser

Nancy Calhoun (R-C) 518-455-5441/fax: 518-455-5884
District: 96 *Room:* 525 LOB *e-mail:* calhoun@assembly.state.ny.us
Title: Ranking Minority Member, Committee on Standing Committees
Committees: Insurance; Labor; Real Property Taxation; Ways & Means
Senior Staff: Marianne D Crary

Karim Camara (D) 518-455-5262/fax: 518-455-5768
District: 43 *Room:* 827 LOB *e-mail:* camarak@assembly.state.ny.us
Committees: Banks; Children & Families; Consumer Affairs & Protection; Education; Housing; Mental Health
Senior Staff: Hasoni Pratts

Ronald J Canestrari (D) 518-455-4474/fax: 518-455-4727
District: 106 *Room:* 926 LOB *e-mail:* canestr@assembly.state.ny.us
Title: Majority Leader
Committees: Banks
Senior Staff: Cathy Krasnopolski

Ann-Margaret E Carrozza (D) 518-455-5425/fax: 518-455-4648
District: 26 *Room:* 656 LOB *e-mail:* carroza@assembly.state.ny.us
Committees: Aging; Banks; Election Law; Governmental Employees; Insurance
Senior Staff: Evelyn R Lewis

Joan K Christensen (D) 518-455-5383/fax: 518-455-5417
District: 119 *Room:* 502 LOB *e-mail:* christj@assembly.state.ny.us
Title: Chair, Cmsn on Skills Development & Vocational Education
Committees: Housing; Insurance; Labor; Real Property Taxation; Small Business
Senior Staff: Sally Drake

Barbara M Clark (D) 518-455-4711/fax: 518-455-3740
District: 33 *Room:* 702 LOB *e-mail:* clarkb@assembly.state.ny.us
Title: Assistant Majority Whip
Committees: Children & Families; Education; Environmental Conservation; Labor; Libraries & Education Technology
Senior Staff: Rachael Fauss

Mike Cole (R-I-C) 518-455-4601
District: 142 *Room:* 545 LOB *e-mail:* colem@assembly.state.ny.us
Committees: Alcoholism & Drug Abuse; Cities; Consumer Affairs & Protection; Higher Education; Local Governments; Tourism, Arts & Sports Development
Senior Staff: Carol Volker

William Colton (D) 518-455-5828/fax: 518-455-5706
District: 47 *Room:* 733 LOB *e-mail:* coltonw@assembly.state.ny.us
Title: Chair, Majority Conference
Committees: Correction; Environmental Conservation; Governmental Employees; Labor; Ways & Means
Senior Staff: Stacy Bandhold

James D Conte (R-I-C) 518-455-5732/fax: 518-455-5553
District: 10 *Room:* 521 LOB *e-mail:* contej@assembly.state.ny.us
Committees: Health; Higher Education; Insurance; Labor
Senior Staff: Jenifer J Pratico

Vivian E Cook (D) 518-455-4203/fax: 518-455-3606
District: 32 *Room:* 331 LOB *e-mail:* cookv@assembly.state.ny.us
Title: Assistant Majority Leader
Committees: Codes; Corporations, Authorities & Commissions; Housing; Insurance; Rules; Ways & Means
Senior Staff: Joyce Corker

Offices and agencies generally appear in alphabetical order, except when specific order is requested by listee.

LEGISLATIVE BRANCH ASSEMBLY / State Assembly Roster

Clifford W Crouch (R)............518-455-5741/fax: 518-455-5864
District: 107 *Room:* 450 LOB *e-mail:* crouchc@assembly.state.ny.us
Title: Assistant Minority Whip
Committees: Agriculture (Ranking Minority Member); Economic Development, Job Creation, Commerce & Industry; Labor; Rules; Ways & Means
Senior Staff: Kathleen Moore

Michael J Cusick (D)..............518-455-5526/fax: 518-455-4760
District: 63 *Room:* 727 LOB *e-mail:* cusikm@assembly.state.ny.us
Committees: Governmental Employees; Higher Education; Mental Health; Transportation; Veterans Affairs
Senior Staff: Sharon L Grobe

Steven H Cymbrowitz (D).......518-455-5214/fax: (518) 455-5738
District: 45 *Room:* 538 LOB *e-mail:* cymbros@assembly.state.ny.us
Title: Vice Chair, Majority Conference
Committees: Codes; Environmental Conservation; Health; Housing; Insurance
Senior Staff: Sharon Messer

Francine DelMonte (D)...........518-455-5284/fax: 518-455-5694
District: 138 *Room:* 553 LOB *e-mail:* delmonf@assembly.state.ny.us
Title: Secretary, Majority Conference
Committees: Agriculture; Economic Development, Job Creation, Commerce & Industry; Energy; Racing & Wagering; Tourism, Arts & Sports Development; Transportation
Senior Staff: Seth Piccirillo

RoAnn M Destito (D-WF)........518-455-5454/fax: 518-455-5928
District: 116 *Room:* 621 LOB *e-mail:* destitr@assembly.state.ny.us
Committees: Aging; Agriculture; Economic Development, Job Creation, Commerce & Industry; Governmental Operations (Chair); Ways & Means
Senior Staff: Stephen M Longo

Luis M Diaz (D)...................518-455-5511/fax: 518-455-5449
District: 86 *Room:* 921 LOB *e-mail:* diazl@assembly.state.ny.us
Committees: Aging; Banks; Higher Education; Housing; Social Services
Senior Staff: Suzy A Lind

Ruben Diaz, Jr (D)................518-455-5514/fax: 518-455-5827
District: 85 *Room:* 419 LOB *e-mail:* diazr@assembly.state.ny.us
Title: Co-Chair, Cmsn on Administrative Regulations Review
Committees: Children & Families; Education; Environmental Conservation; State-Federal Relations; Transportation; Ways & Means
Senior Staff: Paul DelDuca

Jeffrey Dinowitz (D-L-WF)......518-455-5965/fax: 518-455-4437
District: 81 *Room:* 627 LOB *e-mail:* dinowij@assembly.state.ny.us
Committees: Alcoholism & Drug Abuse (Chair); Election Law; Environmental Conservation; Health; Judiciary
Senior Staff: Vacant

Janet L Duprey (R-I-C)...........518-455-5943/fax: 518-455-5761
District: 114 *Room:* 937 LOB *e-mail:* dupreyj@assembly.state.ny.us
Committees: Aging; Correction; House Operations; Mental Health; Real property taxation; Social Services
Senior Staff: Vikki Fisher

Patricia A Eddington (D-I-WF)...518-455-4901/fax: 518-455-5908
District: 3 *Room:* 639 LOB *e-mail:* eddingp@assembly.state.ny.us
Title: Vice Chair, Majority Steering Committee
Committees: Education; Governmental Operations; Health; Higher Education; Labor
Senior Staff: Donna Lent

Steven C Englebright (D).........518-455-4804/fax: 518-455-5795
District: 4 *Room:* 824 LOB *e-mail:* engles@assembly.state.ny.us
Committees: Aging (Chair); Education; Energy; Higher Education; Tourism, Arts & Sports Development
Senior Staff: Maria Weisenberg

Joseph A Errigo (R-C)............518-455-5662/fax: 518-455-5918
District: 130 *Room:* 427 LOB *e-mail:* errigoj@assembly.state.ny.us
Committees: Banks; Children & Families (Ranking Minority Member); Economic Development, Job Creation, Commerce & Industry; Transportation
Senior Staff: Bonnie Turner

Adriano Espaillat (D-WF)........518-455-5807/fax: 518-455-4908
District: 72 *Room:* 652 LOB *e-mail:* espaila@assembly.state.ny.us
Title: Vice-Chair, Majority Conference
Committees: Alcoholism & Drug Abuse; Corporations, Authorities & Commissions; Environmental Conservation; Insurance; Oversight, Analysis & Investigation; Ways & Means
Senior Staff: Rosemarie Longo

Herman D Farrell, Jr (D)........518-455-5491/fax: 518-455-5776
District: 71 *Room:* 923 LOB *e-mail:* farrelh@assembly.state.ny.us
Title: Chair, Ways & Means Committee
Committees: Rules; Ways & Means (Chair)
Senior Staff: Marcia Coleman

Ginny Fields (D-WF).............518-455-5937/fax: 518-455-4784
District: 5 *Room:* 432 LOB *e-mail:* fieldsg@assembly.state.ny.us
Committees: Aging; Consumer Affairs & Protection; Corporations, Authorities & Commissions; Oversight; Analysis & Investigation; Real Property Taxation; Tourism, Arts & Sports Development
Senior Staff: Vacant

Gary D Finch (R-C)...............518-455-5878/fax: 518-455-3895
District: 123 *Room:* 320 LOB *e-mail:* finchg@assembly.state.ny.us
Title: Deputy Minority Whip
Committees: Agriculture; Alcoholism & Drug Abuse; Economic Development, Job Creation, Commerce & Industry; Energy; Environmental Conservation
Senior Staff: Suzanne Redmond

Michael J Fitzpatrick (R-I-C).....518-455-5021/fax: 518-455-4394
District: 7 *Room:* 544 LOB *e-mail:* fitzpam@assembly.state.ny.us
Committees: Higher Education; Housing; Local Government; Small Business
Senior Staff: Margie Ranalli

Dennis H Gabryszak (D).........518-455-5921/fax: 518-455-3962
District: 143 *Room:* 920 LOB *e-mail:* gabryszakd@assembly.state.ny.us
Committees: Banks; Consumer Affairs & Protection; Energy; Local Government; Tourism, Arts & Sports Development; Transportation
Senior Staff: Whitney Kemp

Sandra R Galef (D-WF)..........518-455-5348/fax: 518-455-5728
District: 90 *Room:* 540 LOB *e-mail:* galefs@assembly.state.ny.us
Committees: Corporations Authorities & Commissions; Election Law; Governmental Operations; Health; Real Property Taxation (Chair)
Senior Staff: Rebecca Southard-Kreiger

Offices and agencies generally appear in alphabetical order, except when specific order is requested by listee.

LEGISLATIVE BRANCH ASSEMBLY / State Assembly Roster

David F Gantt (D) 518-455-5606/fax: 518-455-5419
District: 133 *Room:* 830 LOB *e-mail:* ganttd@assembly.state.ny.us
Committees: Economic Development, Job Creation, Commerce & Industry; Local Governments; Rules; Transportation (Chair); Ways & Means
Senior Staff: Robert Cook

Michael N Gianaris (D) 518-455-5014/fax: 518-455-4044
District: 36 *Room:* 742 LOB *e-mail:* gianrm@assembly.state.ny.us
Committees: Consumer Affairs & Protection; Election Law; Environmental Conservation; Judiciary; Tourism, Arts & Sports Development
Senior Staff: Michael Sais

Joe Giglio (R-I-C) 518-455-5241
District: 149 *Room:* 550 LOB *e-mail:* giglioj@assembly.state.ny.us
Committees: Aging; Correction (Chair); Labor; Trransportation
Senior Staff: Mike Brisky

Deborah J Glick (D) 518-455-4841/fax: 518-455-4649
District: 66 *Room:* 844 LOB *e-mail:* glickd@assembly.state.ny.us
Committees: Environmental Conservation; Higher Education (Chair); Rules; Ways & Means
Senior Staff: Theresa Swidorski

Diane M Gordon (D) 518-455-5912/fax: 518-455-3891
District: 40 *Room:* 441 LOB *e-mail:* gordond@assembly.state.ny.us
Committees: Alcoholism & Drug Abuse; Corporations, Authorities & Commissions; Correction; Health; Real Property Taxation; Social Services
Senior Staff: Marcia Chandler

Tim Gordon (I) 518-455-5777/fax: 518-455-5923
District: 108 *Room:* 529 LOB *e-mail:* gordont@assembly.state.ny.us
Committees: Aging; Agriculture; Banks; Energy; Racing & Wagering; Small Business
Senior Staff: Mark Jordan

Richard N Gottfried (D-WF) 518-455-4941/fax: 518-455-5939
District: 75 *Room:* 822 LOB *e-mail:* gottfrr@assembly.state.ny.us
Committees: Health (Chair); Higher Education; Rules
Senior Staff: Richard Conti

Aurelia Greene (D) 518-455-5671/fax: 518-455-5461
District: 77 *Room:* 646 LOB *e-mail:* greenea@assembly.state.ny.us
Title: Speaker Pro Tempore
Committees: Cities; Education; Rules; Social Services; Ways & Means
Senior Staff: Sarah Curry-Cobb

Aileen M Gunther (D-WF) 518-455-5355/fax: 518-455-5239
District: 98 *Room:* 428 LOB *e-mail:* gunthea@assemby.state.ny.us
Committees: Agriculture; Environmental Conservation; Health; Racing & Wagering; Real Property Taxation; Tourism, Arts & Sports Development
Senior Staff: Steven Wilkinson

Stephen Hawley (R-I-C) 518-455-5811
District: 139 *Room:* 433 LOB *e-mail:* hawles@assembly.state.ny.us
Committees: Aging; Agriculture; Corporations, Authorities & Commissions; Economic Development, Job Creation, Commerce & Industry; Health; Racing & Wagering
Senior Staff: Pamela LaGrou

James P Hayes (R-C-I) 518-455-4618/fax: 518-455-5258
District: 148 *Room:* 444 CAP *e-mail:* hayesj@assembly.state.ny.us
Title: Ranking Minority Member, Ways & Means
Committees: Rules; Ways & Means
Senior Staff: Mary Jo Tamburlin

Carl E Heastie (D) 518-455-4800/fax: 518-455-5103
District: 83 *Room:* 417 LOB *e-mail:* heastic@assembly.state.ny.us
Committees: Aging; Corporations, Authorities & Commissions; Housing; Labor; Small Business
Senior Staff: Vacant

Andrew Hevesi (D) 518-455-4926/fax: 518-455-5173
District: 28 *Room:* 833 LOB *e-mail:* hevesia@assembly.state.ny.us
Committees: Alcoholism & Drug Abuse; Cities; Consumer Affairs & Protection; Corporations, Authorities & Commissions; Energy; Labor
Senior Staff: Todd Ferrara

Dov Hikind (D) 518-455-5721/fax: 518-455-5948
District: 48 *Room:* 551 LOB *e-mail:* hikindd@assembly.state.ny.us
Title: Deputy Majority Whip
Committees:
Senior Staff: Marc B Kronenberg

Earlene Hooper (D-L) 518-455-5861/fax: 518-455-4329
District: 18 *Room:* 939 LOB *e-mail:* hoopere@assembly.state.ny.us
Title: Deputy Majority Leader
Committees: Economic Development, Job Creation, Commerce & Industry; Education; Labor; Rules
Senior Staff: Arndreia M Goodbee

William (Sam) Hoyt, III (D) 518-455-4886/fax: 518-455-4890
District: 144 *Room:* 454 LOB *e-mail:* hoyts@assembly.state.ny.us
Committees: Cities; Energy; Local Governments (Chair); Tourism, Arts & Sports Development; Transportation; Ways & Means
Senior Staff: Sarah Kolberg

Janele Hyer-Spencer (D) 518-455-5716/fax: 518-455-5970
District: 60 *Room:* 628 LOB *e-mail:* hyerspencerd@assembly.state.ny.us
Committees: Aging; Alcoholism & Drug Abuse; Children & Families; Judiciary; Transportation

Rhoda S Jacobs (D) 518-455-5385/fax: 518-455-3881
District: 42 *Room:* 736 LOB *e-mail:* jacobsr@assembly.state.ny.us
Title: Assistant Speaker
Committees: Health; Higher Education; Insurance; Rules
Senior Staff: Mary-Jo Ehrlich

Ellen Jaffee (D) 518-455-5118/fax: 518-455-5119
District: 95 *Room:* 637 LOB *e-mail:* jaffeee@assembly.state.ny.us
Committees: Children & Families; Consumer Affairs & Protection; Environmental Conservation; Local Government; Mental Health
Senior Staff: Kathleen Conroy

Hakeem Jeffries (D) 518-455-5325/fax: 518-455-3684
District: 57 *Room:* 523 LOB *e-mail:* jeffriesh@assembly.state.ny.us
Committees: Banks; Cities; Corporations, Authorities & Commissions; Housing; Judiciary
Senior Staff: Daisy James

Susan V John (D) 518-455-4527/fax: 518-455-5342
District: 131 *Room:* 522 LOB *e-mail:* johns@assembly.state.ny.us
Committees: Education; Energy; Judiciary; Labor (Chair); Libraries & Education Technology
Senior Staff: Patricia L Rzepka

Brian P Kavanagh (D) 518-455-5506/fax: 518-455-4801
District: 74 *Room:* 431 LOB *e-mail:* kavanaghb@assembly.state.ny.us
Committees: Cities; Corporations, Authorities & Commissions; Election Law; Environmental Conservation; Housing; Labor

Offices and agencies generally appear in alphabetical order, except when specific order is requested by listee.

LEGISLATIVE BRANCH ASSEMBLY / State Assembly Roster

Thomas J Kirwan (R-C) 518-455-5762/fax: 518-455-5593
District: 100   *Room:* 725 LOB   *e-mail:* kirwant@assembly.state.ny.us
Committees: Alcoholism & Drug Abuse; Cities (Ranking Minority Member); Codes; Education
Senior Staff: Thilde Rafferty

Brian M Kolb (R-I-C) 518-455-5772/fax: 518-455-4650
District: 129   *Room:* 458 LOB   *e-mail:* kolbb@assembly.state.ny.us
Title: Minority Leader Pro Tempore
Committees: Rules; Ways & Means
Senior Staff: Doug Finch

David R Koon (D-I) 518-455-5784/fax: 518-455-4639
District: 135   *Room:* 643 LOB   *e-mail:* koond@assembly.state.ny.us
Title: Chair, Commission on Rural Resources
Committees: Alcoholism & Drug Abuse; Economic Development, Job Creation, Commerce & Industry; Libraries & Education Technology; Local Government; Small Business
Senior Staff: John J Joyce

Ivan C Lafayette (D-WF) 518-455-4545/fax: 518-455-4547
District: 34   *Room:* 646 LOB   *e-mail:* lafayei@assembly.state.ny.us
Title: Deputy Speaker
Committees: Banks; Insurance; Rules; Transportation; Ways & Means
Senior Staff: Evan Schneider

Rory I Lancman (D) 518-455-5172/fax: 518-455-5479
District: 25   *Room:* 549 LOB   *e-mail:* lancmanr@assembly.state.ny.us
Committees: Banks; Cities; Governmental Operations; Housing; Judiciary; Labor
Senior Staff: Diane Barrett

George Latimer (D) 518-455-4897/fax: 518-455-4861
District: 91   *Room:* 820 LOB   *e-mail:* latimeg@assembly.state.ny.us
Committees: Environmental Conservation; Governmental Operations; Insurance; Labor; Local Governments; Transportation
Senior Staff: Deborah Sacks Chapin

Charles D Lavine (D) 518-455-5456/fax: 518-455-5467
District: 13   *Room:* 325 LOB   *e-mail:* lavinec@assembly.state.ny.us
Committees: Alcoholism & Drug Abuse; Codes; Judiciary; Local Governments; Social Services
Senior Staff: Carol Hammond

Joseph R Lentol (D) 518-455-4477/fax: 518-455-4599
District: 50   *Room:* 632 LOB   *e-mail:* lentolj@assembly.state.ny.us
Committees: Codes (Chair); Election Law; Ethics & Guidance; Rules; Ways & Means
Senior Staff: Catherine E Peake

Barbara S Lifton (D-WF) 518-455-5444/fax: 518-455-4640
District: 125   *Room:* 555 LOB   *e-mail:* liftonb@assembly.state.ny.us
Committees: Agriculture; Economic Development, Job Creation, Commerce & Industry; Election Law; Environmental Conservation; Higher Education; Mental Health
Senior Staff: Susan Pratt

Peter D Lopez (R-I-C) 518-455-5363
District: 127   *Room:* 429 LOB   *e-mail:* lopezd@assembly.state.ny.us
Committees: Agriculture; Consumer Affairs & Protection; Environmental Conservation; Social Services

Vito J Lopez (D) 518-455-5537/fax: 518-455-5789
District: 53   *Room:* 943 LOB   *e-mail:* lopezv@assembly.state.ny.us
Committees: Economic Development, Job Creation, Commerce & Industry; Housing (Chair); Rules; Social Services
Senior Staff: Jonathan Harkavy

Donna A Lupardo (D) 518-455-5431/fax: 518-455-5693
District: 126   *Room:* 834 LOB   *e-mail:* lupardd@assembly.state.ny.us
Committees: Election Law; Environmental Conservation; Higher Education; Mental Health; Transportation; Veterans Affairs
Senior Staff: Michael Kennerknecht

William Magee (D) 518-455-4807/fax: 518-455-5237
District: 111   *Room:* 828 LOB   *e-mail:* mageew@assembly.state.ny.us
Committees: Aging; Agriculture (Chair); Banks; Higher Education; Local Government
Senior Staff: Troy Waffner

William B Magnarelli (D-WF) 518-455-4826/fax: 518-455-5498
District: 120   *Room:* 519 LOB   *e-mail:* magnarw@assembly.state.ny.us
Title: Vice Chair, Majority Conference
Committees: Economic Development, Job Creation, Commerce & Industry; Education; Health; Oversight, Analysis & Investigation; Veterans Affairs
Senior Staff: Susan McSweeney

Alan Maisel (D) 518-455-5211
District: 59   *Room:* 528 LOB   *e-mail:* maisela@assembly.state.ny.us
Committees: Agriculture; Banks; Correction; Education; Social Services; Transportation
Senior Staff: Sharon Long

Margaret M Markey (D) 518-455-4755/fax: 518-455-5032
District: 30   *Room:* 654 LOB   *e-mail:* markeym@assembly.state.ny.us
Committees: Agriculture; Consumer Affairs & Protection; Governmental Operations; House Operations (Chair); Labor; Racing & Wagering; Tourism, Arts & Sports Development
Senior Staff: Eileen Boland

Nettie Mayersohn (D-C) 518-455-4404/fax: 518-455-5408
District: 27   *Room:* 746 LOB   *e-mail:* mayersn@assembly.state.ny.us
Committees: Health; Labor
Senior Staff: Mary A Schlotter

Roy J McDonald (R-I-C) 518-455-5404/fax: 518-455-3727
District: 112   *Room:* 426 LOB   *e-mail:* mcdonar@assembly.state.ny.us
Committees: Agriculture; Racing & Wagering; Veterans Affairs; Ways & Means
Senior Staff: Mark Luciano

David G McDonough (R-C-I) 518-455-4633/fax: 518-455-5559
District: 19   *Room:* 533 LOB   *e-mail:* mcdonod@assembly.state.ny.us
Committees: Banks; Consumer Affairs & Protection (Ranking Minority Member); Education; Health
Senior Staff: Lynette Liverani

John J McEneny (D) 518-455-4178/fax: 518-455-5737
District: 104   *Room:* 648 LOB   *e-mail:* mcenenj@assembly.state.ny.us
Title: Chair, Majority Steering Committee
Committees: Agriculture; Ethics & Guidance; Governmental Employees; Social Services; Tourism, Arts & Sports Development; Ways & Means
Senior Staff: Joe Galu

Offices and agencies generally appear in alphabetical order, except when specific order is requested by listee.

LEGISLATIVE BRANCH ASSEMBLY / State Assembly Roster

Tom McKevitt (R-C-I) 518-455-5341
District: 17 *Room:* 534 LOB *e-mail:* mckevit@assembly.state.ny.us
Committees: Judiciary; Mental Health; Small Business; Social Services
Senior Staff: Lynn Schaefering

Joel M Miller (R-I) 518-455-5725/fax: 518-455-5729
District: 102 *Room:* 722 LOB *e-mail:* millerj@assembly.state.ny.us
Committees: Education; Election Law; Health; Higher Education (Ranking Minority Member)
Senior Staff: Keri Peterson

Joan L Millman (D) 518-455-5426/fax: 518-455-4787
District: 52 *Room:* 510 CAP *e-mail:* millmaj@assembly.state.ny.us
Title: Chair, Cmsn on Government Administration
Committees: Aging; Corporations, Authorities & Commissions; Labor; Small Business; Transportation
Senior Staff: Sam Cooper

Marcus Molinaro (R-I-C) 518-455-5177
District: 103 *Room:* 532 LOB *e-mail:* molinarom@assembly.state.ny.us
Committees: Children & Families; Corporations, Authorities & Commissions; Economic Development, Job Creation, Commerce & Industry; Governmental Operations; Libraries & Education Technology; Local Governments
Senior Staff: Frank Harris

Joseph D Morelle (D) 518-455-5373/fax: 518-455-5647
District: 132 *Room:* 716 LOB *e-mail:* morellj@assembly.state.ny.us
Committees: Economic Development, Job Creation, Commerce & Industry; Higher Education; Rules; Ways & Means
Senior Staff: Kristin Anderson, COS

Catherine T Nolan (D) 518-455-4851/fax: 518-455-3847
District: 37 *Room:* 424 LOB *e-mail:* nolanc@assembly.state.ny.us
Committees: Corporations, Authorities & Commissions; Education (Chair); Rules; Veterans' Affairs; Ways & Means
Senior Staff: Geraldine A Reilly

Daniel J O'Donnell (D) 518-455-5603/fax: 518-455-3812
District: 69 *Room:* 819 LOB *e-mail:* odonned@assembly.state.ny.us
Committees: Codes; Environmental Conservation; Judiciary; Local Governments; Oversight, Analysis & Investigation; Tourism, Arts & Sports Development
Senior Staff: Robin Chappelle

Thomas F O'Mara (R) 518-455-4538/fax: 518-455-5922
District: 137 *Room:* 720 LOB *e-mail:* omarat@assembly.state.ny.us
Title: Vice Chair, Minority Program Committee
Committees: Banks; Energy; Ethics & Guidance; Judiciary; Tourism, Arts & Sports Development
Senior Staff: Michael Fuller

Robert C Oaks (R-C) 518-455-5655/fax: 518-455-5407
District: 128 *Room:* 437 LOB *e-mail:* oaksr@assembly.state.ny.us
Title: Deputy, Minority Leader
Committees: Aging; Ethics & Guidance (Ranking Minority Member); Housing; Insurance; Rules
Senior Staff: Laurie Levine

Felix W Ortiz (D) 518-455-3821/fax: 518-455-3828
District: 51 *Room:* 542 LOB *e-mail:* ortizf@assembly.state.ny.us
Committees: Banks; Correction; Economic Development, Job Creation, Commerce & Industry; Labor; Rules; Veterans Affairs (Chair)
Senior Staff: Linda A Buckley

William L Parment (D) 518-455-4511/fax: 518-455-4328
District: 150 *Room:* 547 LOB *e-mail:* parmenw@assembly.state.ny.us
Title: Chair, Committee on Standing Committees
Committees: Education; Environmental Conservation; Mental Health; Veterans' Affairs; Ways & Means
Senior Staff: Amy Abbati

Amy R Paulin (D) 518-455-5585/fax: 518-455-5409
District: 88 *Room:* 327 LOB *e-mail:* paulina@assembly.state.ny.us
Committees: Children & Families; Education; Health; Higher Education; Libraries & Education Technology
Senior Staff: Nancy Fisher

Crystal D Peoples (D) 518-455-5005/fax: 518-455-5471
District: 141 *Room:* 619 LOB *e-mail:* peoplec@assembly.state.ny.us
Committees: Alcoholism & Drug Abuse; Environmental Conservation; Governmental Operations; Health; Insurance; Social Services
Senior Staff: Shrita Sterlin

Jose R Peralta (D-WF) 518-455-4567/fax: 518-455-5375
District: 39 *Room:* 528 LOB *e-mail:* peraltj@assembly.state.ny.us
Committees: Banks; Consumer Affairs & Protection; Correction; Election Law; Higher Education; Labor
Senior Staff: Yonel Letellier

N Nick Perry (D) 518-455-4166/fax: 518-455-5478
District: 58 *Room:* 452 LOB *e-mail:* perryn@assembly.state.ny.us
Title: Majority Whip
Committees: Banks; Codes; Insurance; Labor; Transportation; Ways & Means
Senior Staff: Marjorie Forbes

Audrey I Pheffer (D) 518-455-4292/fax: 518-455-4723
District: 23 *Room:* 941 LOB *e-mail:* pheffea@assembly.state.ny.us
Committees: Aging; Consumer Affairs & Protection (Chair); Governmental Employees; Higher Education; Veterans' Affairs
Senior Staff: JoAnn Shapiro

Adam Clayton Powell, IV (D) 518-455-4781/fax: 518-455-3893
District: 68 *Room:* 527 LOB *e-mail:* powella@assembly.state.ny.us
Committees: Corporations, Authorities & Commissions; Housing; Insurance; Small Business
Senior Staff: France Blanco-Bardia

James Gary Pretlow (D) 518-455-5291/fax: 518-455-5447
District: 87 *Room:* 845 LOB *e-mail:* pretloj@assembly.state.ny.us
Committees: Cities; Codes; Insurance; Racing & Wagering (Chair); Rules; Ways & Means
Senior Staff: Janet E Edwards

Jack Quinn (R-C-I) 518-455-4462/fax: 518-455-5560
District: 146 *Room:* 721 LOB *e-mail:* quinnj@assembly.state.ny.us
Committees: Banks; Governmental Operations; Health; Housing; Judiciary
Senior Staff: Mary Lou Palmer

Annie Rabbitt (R-C-I) 518-455-5991/fax: 518-455-5929
District: 97 *Room:* 719 LOB *e-mail:* rabbita@assembly.state.ny.us
Committees: Environmental Conservation; Housing; Local Governments (Ranking Minority Member); Small Business; Tourism, Arts & Sports Development
Senior Staff: Betty Nolte

Offices and agencies generally appear in alphabetical order, except when specific order is requested by listee.

LEGISLATIVE BRANCH ASSEMBLY / State Assembly Roster

Andrew P Raia (R-C-I-WF)......518-455-5952/fax: 518-455-5804
District: 9 *Room:* 629 LOB *e-mail:* raiaa@assembly.state.ny.us
Committees: Banks; Corporations, Authorities & Commissions; Health; Housing; Social Services
Senior Staff: Judy VanAmburgh

Philip R Ramos (D-WF)..........518-455-5185/fax: 518-455-5236
District: 6 *Room:* 650 LOB *e-mail:* ramosp@assembly.state.ny.us
Committees: Aging; Economic Development, Job Creation, Commerce & Industry; Education; Housing; Local Governments
Senior Staff: Luis Montes

William Reilich (R-C-I)..........518-455-4664/fax: 518-455-3093
District: 134 *Room:* 322 LOB *e-mail:* reilicw@assembly.state.ny.us
Title: Chair, Minority Steering Committee
Committees: Aging; Banks; Education; Small Business; Transportation
Senior Staff: Michelle Marini

Robert Reilly (D-I-WF)..........518-455-5931/fax: 518-455-5840
District: 109 *Room:* 430 LOB *e-mail:* reillyr@assembly.state.ny.us
Committees: Agriculture; Corporations, Authorities & Commissions; Education; Governmental Operations; Racing & Wagering; Tourism, Arts & Sports Development
Senior Staff: Tim Nichols

Jose Rivera (D)................518-455-5414/fax: 518-455-5322
District: 78 *Room:* 536 LOB *e-mail:* riveraj@assembly.state.ny.us
Committees: Aging; Insurance; Small Business
Senior Staff: Diane Gamble

Naomi Rivera (D)..............518-455-5844/fax: 518-455-5596
District: 80 *Room:* 530 LOB *e-mail:* naomirivera2004@aol.com
Committees: Children & Families; Cities; Health; Real Property Taxation; Tourism, Arts & Sports Development
Senior Staff: Bertha A Saldana

Peter M Rivera (D).............518-455-5102/fax: 518-455-3693
District: 76 *Room:* 826 LOB *e-mail:* riverap@assembly.state.ny.us
Committees: Agriculture; Consumer Affairs & Protection; Judiciary; Mental Health (Chair); Rules
Senior Staff: Guillermo A Martinez

Annette M Robinson (D).........518-455-5474/fax: 518-455-5857
District: 56 *Room:* 729 LOB *e-mail:* robinsa@assembly.state.ny.us
Committees: Children & Families; Housing; Oversight, Analysis & Investigation; Real Property Taxation; Small Business
Senior Staff: Vacant

Linda B Rosenthal (D).........................518-455-5802
District: 67 *Room:* 821 LOB *e-mail:* rosentl@assembly.state.ny.us
Committees: Agriculture; Alcoholism & Drug Abuse; Corporations, Authorities & Commissions; Energy; Higher Education; Housing
Senior Staff: David Weinberg

Joseph S Saladino (R)..........518-455-5305/fax: 518-455-5024
District: 12 *Room:* 722 LOB *e-mail:* saladij@assembly.state.ny.us
Committees: Consumer Affairs & Protection; Education; Environmental Conservation; Governmental Employees (Ranking Minority Member); Governmental Operations
Senior Staff: Christine Giordano

Teresa R Sayward (R-I-C).......518-455-5565/fax: 518-455-5710
District: 113 *Room:* 940 LOB *e-mail:* saywart@assembly.state.ny.us
Title: Secretary, Minority Conference
Committees: Children & Families; Correction (Ranking Minority Member); Education; Environmental Conservation; Tourism, Arts & Sports Development
Senior Staff: Meg Wood

William D Scarborough (D-WF)..518-455-4451/fax: 518-455-5522
District: 29 *Room:* 622 LOB *e-mail:* scarbow@assembly.state.ny.us
Committees: Banks; Children & Families (Chair); Corporations, Authorities & Commissions; Correction; Energy
Senior Staff: Robyn L Montgomery

Michelle Schimel (D-I-WF)......................518-455-5192
District: 16 *Room:* 324 LOB *e-mail:*
Committees: Energy; Environmental Conservation; Local Governments; Transportation; Veterans Affairs

Robin L Schimminger (D-I-C)....518-455-4767/fax: 518-455-4724
District: 140 *Room:* 847 LOB *e-mail:* schimmr@assembly.state.ny.us
Committees: Codes; Economic Development, Job Creation, Commerce & Industry (Chair); Health; Ways & Means
Senior Staff: Kenneth L Berlinski

Mark J F Schroeder (D).........518-455-4691/fax: 518-455-5238
District: 145 *Room:* 323 LOB *e-mail:* schroem@assembly.state.ny.us
Committees: Insurance; Local Governments; Mental Health; Oversight, Analysis & Investigation; Small Business; Veterans Affairs
Senior Staff: Patrick Curry

Dierdre K Scozzafava (R).......518-455-5797/fax: 518-455-5289
District: 122 *Room:* 329 LOB *e-mail:* scozzad@assembly.state.ny.us
Committees: Banks; Codes (Ranking Minority Member); Ethics & Guidance; Rules; Ways & Means
Senior Staff: Dayle B Burgess

Anthony S Seminerio (D-C)......518-455-4621/fax: 518-455-5361
District: 38 *Room:* 818 LOB *e-mail:* seminea@assembly.state.ny.us
Title: Chair, Majority Program Committee
Committees: Banks; Cities; Governmental Employees; Racing & Wagering; Rules
Senior Staff: Jody Rickert

Sheldon Silver (D).............518-455-3791/fax: 518-455-5459
District: 64 *Room:* 932 LOB *e-mail:* speaker@assembly.state.ny.us
Title: Speaker
Committees: Rules (Chair); ex officio to all committees
Senior Staff: Judy R Rapfogel

Mike Spano (R-I-C).............518-455-3662/fax: 518-455-5499
District: 93 *Room:* 402 LOB *e-mail:* spanom@assembly.state.ny.us
Committees: Banks; Codes; Education; Labor; Oversight & Analysis; Rules
Senior Staff: Joyce Gould

Albert Stirpe (D)..............518-455-4505/fax: 518-455-5523
District: 121 *Room:* 430 LOB *e-mail:* stirpea@assembly.state.ny.us
Committees: Aging; Agriculture; Economic Development, Job Creation, Commerce & Industry; Higher Education; Small Business; Veterans Affairs

Offices and agencies generally appear in alphabetical order, except when specific order is requested by listee.

LEGISLATIVE BRANCH ASSEMBLY / State Assembly Standing Committees

Robert K Sweeney (D) 518-455-5787/fax: 518-455-3976
District: 11 *Room:* 837 LOB *e-mail:* sweeney@assembly.state.ny.us
Committees: Education; Environmental Conservation (Chair); Rules; Veterans Affairs
Senior Staff: Stephen Liss

James N Tedisco (R-I-C) 518-455-3751/fax: 518-455-3750
District: 110 *Room:* 933 LOB *e-mail:* tediscj@assembly.state.ny.us
Title: Minority Leader
Committees: Rules
Senior Staff: Howard Becker

Fred W Thiele, Jr (R-I-WF) 518-455-5997/fax: 518-455-5963
District: 2 *Room:* 443 LOB *e-mail:* thielef@assembly.state.ny.us
Title: Vice-Chair, Minority Joint Conference Committee
Committees: Education; Election Law; Environmental Conservation; Transportation; Ways & Means
Senior Staff: Rebecca McGrory

Matthew Titone (D) 518-455-4677
District: 611 *Room:* 938 LOB *e-mail:*
Committees: Banks; Environmental Conservation; Judiciary; Social Services; Tourism, Arts & Sports Development; Transportation

Michele R Titus (D) 518-455-5668/fax: 518-455-3892
District: 31 *Room:* 741 LOB *e-mail:* titusm@assembly.state.ny.us
Committees: Children & Families; Codes; Ethics & Guidance; Judiciary; Local Governments; Small Business
Senior Staff: Richard A McKoy

Louis Tobacco (R) 518-455-4495/fax: 518-455-3892
District: 62 *Room:* 433 LOB *e-mail:* tobaccol@assembly.state.ny.us
Committees: Aging; Cities; Governmental Employees; Higher Education; Social Services; Transportation

Paul D Tonko (D) 518-455-5197/fax: 518-455-5435
District: 105 *Room:* 713 LOB *e-mail:* tonkop@assembly.state.ny.us
Committees: Agriculture; Education; Energy (Chair); Racing & Wagering; Transportation
Senior Staff: Thomas J Lynch

Darryl C Towns (D) 518-455-5821/fax: 518-455-5591
District: 54 *Room:* 841 LOB *e-mail:* townsd@assembly.state.ny.us
Committees: Banks (Chair); Economic Development, Job Creation, Commerce & Industry; Health; Mental Health;
Senior Staff: Natashua Rice

David R Townsend, Jr (R-C-I-WF) 518-455-5334/fax: 518-455-5391
District: 115 *Room:* 458 LOB *e-mail:* townsed@assembly.state.ny.us
Title: Chair, Minority Joint Conference Committee
Committees: Codes; Corporations, Authorities & Commissions; Governmental Employees; Labor
Senior Staff: Claudia Tenney

Rob Walker (R-C-I) 518-455-4684/fax: 518-455-5477
District: 15 *Room:* 633 LOB *e-mail:* walkerr2@assembly.state.ny.us
Title: Vice Chair, Minority Steering Committee
Committees: Aging; Election Law; Energy; Tourism, Arts & Sports Development; Veterans Affairs

Helene E Weinstein (D) 518-455-5462/fax: 518-455-5752
District: 41 *Room:* 831 LOB *e-mail:* weinsth@assembly.state.ny.us
Committees: Aging; Codes; Judiciary (Chair); Rules; Ways & Means
Senior Staff: Sarah Beaver

Harvey Weisenberg (D) 518-455-3028/fax: 518-455-5769
District: 20 *Room:* 731 LOB *e-mail:* weisenh@assembly.state.ny.us
Title: Assistant Speaker Pro Tempore
Committees: Banks; Correction; Education; Environmental Conservation; Mental Health; Transportation
Senior Staff: Marie Curley

Mark Weprin (D) 518-455-5806/fax: 518-455-5977
District: 24 *Room:* 626 LOB *e-mail:* weprinm@assembly.state.ny.us
Committees: Aging; Codes; Insurance; Judiciary; Small Business (Chair)
Senior Staff: Ruth Wimpfheimer

Keith L T Wright (D) 518-455-4793/fax: 518-455-3890
District: 70 *Room:* 749 LOB *e-mail:* wrightk@assembly.state.ny.us
Committees: Codes; Corrections; Housing; Social Services (Chair)
Senior Staff: Vacant

Ellen Young (D) 518-455-5411/fax: 518-455-4995
District: 22 *Room:* 920 LOB *e-mail:* younge@assembly.state.ny.us
Committees: Aging; Alcoholism & drug Abuse; Corporations, Authorities & Commissions; Economic Development, Job Creation, Commerce & Industry; Housing; Libraries & Education Technology
Senior Staff: Dot Dugan

Kenneth Zebrowski (D) 518-455-5735/fax: 518-455-5561
District: 94 *Room:* 631 LOB *e-mail:* zebrowk@assembly.state.ny.us
Committees: Judiciary

State Assembly Standing Committees

Aging
Chair:
  Steven C Englebright (D) 518-455-4804
Ranking Minority Member:
  Philip Boyle (R) 518-455-4611

Committee Staff
Clerk:
  Shay Bergin 518-455-4804

Key Assembly Staff Assignments
Majority Program & Counsel Legislative Analyst:
  Jennifer Best 518-455-4371

Membership

Majority
Peter J Abbate, Jr	Marc S Alessi
Carmen E Arroyo	William F Boyland, Jr
Alec Brook-Krasny	Ann Margaret E Carrozza
RoAnn M Destito	Luis M Diaz

Offices and agencies generally appear in alphabetical order, except when specific order is requested by listee.

LEGISLATIVE BRANCH ASSEMBLY / State Assembly Standing Committees

Ginny Fields
Carl E Heastie
William Magee
Audrey I Pheffer
Jose Rivera
Mark Weprin
Ellen Young

Tim Gordon
Janele Hyer-Spencer
Joan L Millman
Philip R Ramos
Albert Stirpe
Helene E Weinstein

Minority
Robert Barra
Joe Giglio
William Reilich

Janet L Duprey
Robert C Oaks
Rob Walker

Agriculture
Chair:
William Magee (D)..................518-455-4807
Ranking Minority Member:
Clifford W Crouch (R)..................518-455-5741

Committee Staff
Clerk:
Christin Nowak..................518-455-4807

Key Assembly Staff Assignments
Majority Program & Counsel Legislative Analyst:
William Ketzer..................518-455-4355
Majority Program & Counsel Associate Counsel:
Elizabeth Hogan..................518-455-4355
Minority Associate Counsel:
Anne S Tarpinian..................518-455-4285
Minority Research & Program Development Legislative Analyst:
Charles Marshall..................518-455-5002

Membership
Majority
Marc S Alessi
Michael Benedetto
RoAnn M Destito
Barbara S Lifton
Margaret M Markey
Robert P Reilly
Linda B Rosenthal
Paul D Tonko

Darrel J Aubertine
Francine DelMonte
Aileen M Gunther
Alan Maisel
John J McEneny
Peter M Rivera
Albert Stirpe

Minority
Marc W Butler
Tim Gordon
Peter D Lopez

Gary D Finch
Stephen Hawley
Roy J McDonald

Alcoholism & Drug Abuse
Chair:
Jeffrey Dinowitz (D)..................518-455-5965
Ranking Minority Member:
Gary D Finch (R)..................518-455-5878

Committee Staff
Clerk:
Edward Woda..................518-455-5965

Key Assembly Staff Assignments
Majority Program & Counsel Legislative Analyst:
William Eggler..................518-455-4371
Majority Program & Counsel Associate Counsel:
Elana Marton..................518-455-4371
Minority Associate Counsel:
Nancylynn Ferrini..................518-455-4515
Minority Research & Program Development Legislative Analyst:
Kristin Zielinksi..................518-455-5002

Membership
Majority
Carmen E Arroyo
Sylvia Friedman
Andrew Hevesi
David R Koon
Crystal D Peoples
Ellen Young

Adriano Espaillat
Diane Gordon
Janele Hyer-Spencer
Charles D Lavine
Linda B Rosenthal

Minority
Mike Cole

Thomas J Kirwan

Banks
Chair:
Darryl C Towns (D)..................518-455-5821
Ranking Minority Member:
Andrew P Raia (R)..................518-455-5952

Committee Staff
Clerk:
Kent Sopris..................518-455-5821

Key Assembly Staff Assignments
Majority Program & Counsel Legislative Analyst:
Yolanda Bostic..................518-455-4928
Majority Program & Counsel Associate Counsel:
Teri Kleinmann..................518-455-4928
Minority Associate Counsel:
Jessica Reinhardt..................518-455-4260
Minority Research & Program Development Legislative Analyst:
Angelo Cafaro..................518-455-5002

Membership
Majority
Peter J Abbate, Jr
Jonathan L Bing
Richard L Brodsky
Ann-Margaret E Carrozza
Dennis Gabryszak
Ivan C Lafayette
William Magee
Felix W Ortiz
N Nick Perry
Anthony S Seminerio
Harvey Weisenberg

Michael Benjamin
William F Boyland, Jr
Karim Camara
Luis M Diaz
Hakeem Jeffries
Rory I Lancman
Alan Maisel
Jose R Peralta
William D Scarborough
Matthew Titone

Minority
Joseph A Errigo
David G McDonough
Jack Quinn
Deirdre K Scozzafava

Tim Gordon
Thomas F O'Mara
William Reilich
Mike Spano

Children & Families
Chair:
William Scarborough (D)..................518-455-4451
Ranking Minority Member:
Joseph A Errigo (R)..................518-455-5662

Committee Staff
Clerk:
Shawn Chin-Chance..................518-455-4764

Key Assembly Staff Assignments
Majority Program & Counsel Legislative Analyst:
Judi West..................518-455-4371
Majority Program & Counsel Associate Counsel:
Bacqueline Vacant..................518-455-4371

Offices and agencies generally appear in alphabetical order, except when specific order is requested by listee.

LEGISLATIVE BRANCH ASSEMBLY / State Assembly Standing Committees

Minority Associate Counsel:
Nancylynn Ferrini 518-455-4264
Minority Research & Program Development Legislative Analyst:
Laura Wood 518-455-5002

Membership

Majority

Carmen E Arroyo	Michael A Benjamin
Adam T Bradley	Karim Camara
Barbara M Clark	Ruben Diaz, Jr
Deborah J Glick	Carl E Heastie
Janele Hyer-Spencer	Ellen Jaffee
Amy Paulin	Naomi Rivera
Annette M Robinson	Michele R Titus

Minority

Thomas W Alfano	Marcus Molinaro
Teresa R Sayward	

Cities

Chair:
James F Brennan (D) 518-455-5377
Ranking Minority Member:
Thomas J Kirwan (R) 518-455-5762

Committee Staff

Clerk:
Lisa Forkas 518-455-5377

Key Assembly Staff Assignments
Majority Program & Counsel Legislative Analyst:
Deborah Stevens 518-455-4363
Counsel:
Julia Mallalieu 518-455-4363
Minority Associate Counsel:
Edmund V Wick 518-455-4262
Minority Research & Program Development Legislative Analyst:
Angelo Cafaro 518-455-5002

Membership

Majority

Alec Brook-Krasny	Aurelia Greene
Andrew D Hevesi	William (Sam) Hoyt, III
Hakeem Jeffries	Brian Kavanagh
Rory I Lancman	Jose R Peralta
James Gary Pretlow	Naomi Rivera
Anthony S Seminerio	

Minority

James Bacalles	Mike Cole
Louis Tobacco	

Codes

Chair:
Joseph R Lentol (D) 518-455-4477
Ranking Minority Member:
David R Townsend Jr (R) 518-455-5334

Committee Staff

Clerk:
Wilda Lang 518-455-4484

Key Assembly Staff Assignments
Senior Team Counsel:
Marty Rosenbaum 518-455-4313
Counsel:
Jonathan Bailey 518-455-4313

Majority Program & Associate Counsel:
Kathleen O'Keefe 518-455-4313
Minority Associate Counsel:
Nancylynn Ferrini 518-455-4265
Minority Research & Program Development Principal Legislative Analyst:
Kim Halayko 518-455-5002

Membership

Majority

James F Brennan	Vivian E Cook
Steven Cymbrowitz	Charles D Lavine
Daniel J O'Donnell	Nick N Perry
James Gary Pretlow	Robin L Schimminger
Dede Scozzafava	Michele R Titus
Mark Weprin	Keith L Wright

Minority

Philip Boyle	Thomas J Kirwan
Mike Spano	Helene E Weinstein

Consumer Affairs & Protection

Chair:
Audrey I Pheffer (D) 518-455-4292
Ranking Minority Member:
Peter D Lopez (R) 518-455-5363

Committee Staff

Clerk:
Kim Lease 518-455-4292

Key Assembly Staff Assignments
Majority Program & Counsel Legislative Analyst:
Jeff O'Donnell 518-455-4355
Minority Associate Counsel:
Edmund V Wick 518-455-4262
Minority Research & Program Development Legislative Analyst:
Marc G Lundberg 518-455-5002

Membership

Majority

Peter J Abbate, Jr	Michael Benedetto
Karim Camara	Ginny Fields
Dennis Gabryszak	Michael N Gianaris
Andrew Hevesi	Ellen Jaffee
Margaret M Markey	Peter M Rivera

Minority

David G McDonough	Joseph S Saladino

Corporations, Authorities & Commissions

Chair:
Richard L Brodsky (D) 518-455-5753
Ranking Minority Member:
Stephen Hawley (R) 518-455-5811

Committee Staff

Clerk:
Jim Malatras 518-455-5753

Key Assembly Staff Assignments
Majority Program & Counsel Legislative Analyst:
Caitlin Shaheen 518-455-4881
Majority Counsel:
William Thornton 518-455-4881
Minority Associate Counsel:
Jessica Reinhardt 518-455-4264
Minority Research & Program Development Legislative Analyst:
Angelo Cafaro 518-455-5002

Offices and agencies generally appear in alphabetical order, except when specific order is requested by listee.

LEGISLATIVE BRANCH ASSEMBLY / State Assembly Standing Committees

Membership

Majority

James F Brennan	Vivian E Cook
Adriano Espaillat	Ginny Fields
Sandra R Galef	Diane Gordon
Carl E Heastie	Andrew Hevesi
Hakeem Jeffries	Brian P Kavanagh
Joan L Millman	Catherine T Nolan
Adam Clayton Powell, IV	Robert P Reilly
Linda B Rosenthal	William D Scarborough
Ellen Young	

Minority

William A Barclay	Marcus Molinaro
Andrew P Raia	David R Townsend Jr

Correction

Chair:
Jeffrion L Aubry (D) 518-455-4561
Ranking Minority Member:
Joe Giglio (R) 518-455-5241

Committee Staff

Clerk:
Indira Noel 518-455-4548

Key Assembly Staff Assignments

Majority Program & Counsel Legislative Analyst:
  Richard McDonald 518-455-4313
Majority Program & Counsel Legislative Analyst:
  Dominique Tauzin 518-455-4313
Majority Program & Counsel Senior Team Counsel:
  Tracey Brooks 518-455-4313
Minority Associate Counsel:
  Nancylynn Ferrini 518-455-4265
Minority Research & Program Development Principal Legislative Analyst:
  Kim Halayko 518-455-5002

Membership

Majority

Michael A Benjamin	William Colton
Diane Gordon	Alan Maisel
Felix W Ortiz	Jose R Peralta
William D Scarborough	Harvey Weisenberg
Keith L T Wright	

Minority

Janet L Duprey	Teresa R Sayward

Economic Development, Job Creation, Commerce & Industry

Chair:
Robin L Schimminger (D) 518-455-4767
Ranking Minority Member:
Marc W Butler (R) 518-455-5393

Committee Staff

Clerk:
Judi Giuliano 518-455-4767

Key Assembly Staff Assignments

Majority Program & Counsel Legislative Analyst:
  Vacant 518-455-4928
Majority Program & Counsel Associate Counsel:
  Teri Kleinmann 518-455-4928
Minority Associate Counsel:
  Michelle Pellegri 518-455-4637

Minority Research & Program Development Legislative Analyst:
  Jessica Howard 518-455-5002

Membership

Majority

Darrel J Aubertine	Jeffrion L Aubry
William F Boyland, Jr	Philip Boyle
Kevin A Cahill	Francine DelMonte
RoAnn M Destito	David F Gantt
Earlene Hooper	David R Koon
Barbara S Lifton	Vito J Lopez
William B Magnarelli	Joseph D Morelle
Felix W Ortiz	Philip R Ramos
Albert Stirpe	Darryl C Towns
Ellen Young	

Minority

Clifford W Crouch	Joseph A Errigo
Gary D Finch	Stephen Hawley
Marcus Molinaro	

Education

Chair:
Catherine Nolan (D) 518-455-4851
Ranking Minority Member:
Fred W Thiele Jr (R) 518-455-5997

Committee Staff

Clerk:
Debra Triblet 518-455-4851
Counsel:
Geraldine Reilly 518-455-4851

Key Assembly Staff Assignments

Minority Associate Counsel:
  Laura Cail 518-455-4515
Minority Research & Program Development Legislative Analyst:
  Chelsey Tulis 518-455-5002

Membership

Majority

Carmen E Arroyo	Michael Benedetto
James F Brennan	Karim Camara
Barbara M Clark	Ruben Diaz, Jr
Patricia A Eddington	Steven C Englebright
Aurelia Greene	Earlene Hooper
Susan V John	John W Lavelle
William B Magnarelli	Alan Maisel
William L Parment	Amy R Paulin
Philip R Ramos	Robert P Reilly
Robert K Sweeney	Paul D Tonko
Harvey Weisenberg	

Minority

Thomas J Kirwan	David G McDonough
Joel M Miller	William Reilich
Joseph S Saladino	Teresa R Sayward
Mike Spano	

Election Law

Chair:
Ann Margaret Carrozza (D) 518-455-5425
Ranking Minority Member:
Joel M Miller (R) 518-455-5725

Offices and agencies generally appear in alphabetical order, except when specific order is requested by listee.

LEGISLATIVE BRANCH ASSEMBLY / State Assembly Standing Committees

Committee Staff
Clerk:
  Laurie Barone..................................518-455-5425

Key Assembly Staff Assignments
Majority Program & Counsel Legislative Analyst:
  Laurie Barone..................................518-455-4313
Majority Program & Counsel Associate Counsel:
  Kathleen O'Keefe...............................518-455-4313
Minority Associate Counsel:
  Douglas Goldman................................518-455-4637
Minority Research & Program Development Legislative Analyst:
  Dan Moser......................................518-455-5002

Membership

Majority
  Michael A Benjamin   Adam T Bradley
  Alec Brook-Krasny   Jeffrey Dinowitz
  Sandra R Galef   Michael N Gianaris
  Brian P Kavanagh   Joseph R Lentol
  Barbara Lifton   Donna Lupardo
  Jose R Peralta

Minority
  Greg Ball   Fred W Thiele Jr
  Rob Walker

Energy
Chair:
  Paul D Tonko (D).................................518-455-5197
Ranking Minority Member:
  Thomas O'Mara (R)................................518-455-4538

Committee Staff
Clerk:
  Matthew Beebe....................................518-455-4779

Key Assembly Staff Assignments
Majority Program & Counsel Associate Counsel:
  Julia Mallalieu..................................518-455-4363
Minority Associate Counsel:
  Anne S Tarpinian.................................518-455-4285
Minority Research & Program Development Legislative Analyst:
  Angelo Cafaro....................................518-455-5002

Membership

Majority
  Marc S Alessi   Darrel J Aubertine
  Francine DelMonte   Steven C Englebright
  Dennis Gabryzsak   Andrew Hevesi
  William (Sam) Hoyt, III   Susan V John
  Linda B Rosenthal   William D Scarborough
  Michelle Schimel

Minority
  Greg Ball   Gary D Finch
  Tim Gordon   Rob Walker

Environmental Conservation
Chair:
  Robert K Sweeney (D).............................518-455-5787
Ranking Minority Member:
  Teresa R Sayward (R).............................518-455-5565

Committee Staff
Clerk:
  Rebecca Rasmussen................................518-455-5787

Key Assembly Staff Assignments
Committee Counsel:
  Stephen Liss.....................................518-455-4363
Majority Program & Counsel Associate Counsel:
  Julia Mallalieu..................................518-455-4363
Minority Associate Counsel:
  Anne S Tarpinian.................................518-455-4285
Minority Research & Program Development Legislative Analyst:
  Charles Marshall.................................518-455-5002

Membership

Majority
  Adam T Bradley   Barbara M Clark
  William Colton   Steven Cymbrowitz
  Ruben Diaz, Jr   Jeffrey Dinowitz
  Adriano Espaillat   Michael N Gianaris
  Deborah J Glick   Aileen M Gunther
  Ellen Jaffee   Brian P Kavanagh
  George S Latimer   Barbara S Lifton
  Donna Lupardo   Daniel J O'Donnell
  William L Parment   Crystal D Peoples
  Michelle Schimel   Matthew Titone
  Harvey Weisenberg

Minority
  James Bacalles   Daniel J Burling
  Gary D Finch   Peter D Lopez
  Annie Rabbitt   Joseph S Saladino
  Fred W Thiele, Jr

Ethics & Guidance
Chair:
  Kevin A Cahill (D)...............................518-455-4436
Ranking Minority Member:
  Robert C Oaks (R)................................518-455-5655

Membership

Majority
  Joseph R Lentol   John J McEneny
  Michele R Titus

Minority
  William A Barclay   Thomas F O'Mara
  Dierdre K Scozzafava

Governmental Employees
Chair:
  Peter J Abbate, Jr (D)...........................518-455-3053
Ranking Minority Member:
  Joseph S Saladino (R)............................518-455-5305

Committee Staff
Clerk:
  Christine Epplemann..............................518-455-3053

Key Assembly Staff Assignments
Minority Associate Counsel:
  Douglas L Goldman................................518-455-4637
Minority Research & Program Development Legislative Analyst:
  William Backes...................................518-455-5002

Membership

Majority
  Jeffrion L Aubry   Alec Brook-Krasny
  Ann-Margaret E Carrozza   William Colton
  Michael J Cusick   John J McEneny
  Audrey I Pheffer   Anthony S Seminerio

Offices and agencies generally appear in alphabetical order, except when specific order is requested by listee.

LEGISLATIVE BRANCH ASSEMBLY / State Assembly Standing Committees

Minority
- Louis Tobacco
- David R Townsend Jr

Governmental Operations
Chair:
RoAnn M Destito (D)..................518-455-5454
Ranking Minority Member:
Vacant (R)..........................518-455-0000

Committee Staff
Clerk:
Alyssa McCoy.........................518-455-5436

Key Assembly Staff Assignments
Majority Program & Counsel Legislative Analyst:
Cheryl Couser.......................518-455-4355
Majority Program & Counsel Associate Counsel:
Elizabeth Hogan......................518-455-4355
Minority Associate Counsel:
Charles E Crandall..................518-455-4626
Minority Research & Program Development Principal Legislative Analyst:
Mark G Lundberg.....................518-455-5002

Membership

Majority
- Michael Benedetto
- Sandra R Galef
- George S Latimer
- Crystal D Peoples
- Patricia A Eddington
- Rory I Lancman
- Margaret M Markey
- Robert P Reilly

Minority
- Marcus Molinaro
- Joseph S Saladino
- Jack Quinn

Health
Chair:
Richard N Gottfried (D)...............518-455-4941
Ranking Minority Member:
James Bacalles (R)...................518-455-5791

Committee Staff
Executive Director:
Richard Conti.......................518-455-4941
Clerk:
Helen Dong..........................518-455-4941

Key Assembly Staff Assignments
Legislative Analyst & Counsel:
Esti Alonso.........................518-455-4371
Majority Program & Counsel Associate Counsel:
Jennifer Seehase....................518-455-4371
Minority Associate Counsel:
Campbell Wallace....................518-455-4258
Minority Research & Program Development Legislative Analyst:
Kristin Zielinski...................518-455-5002

Membership

Majority
- Jonathan L Bing
- Steven Cymbrowitz
- Patricia A Eddington
- Diane M Gordon
- Rhoda S Jacobs
- Nettie Mayersohn
- Crystal D Peoples
- Robin L Schimminger
- Kevin A Cahill
- Jeffrey Dinowitz
- Sandra R Galef
- Aileen M Gunther
- William B Magnarelli
- Amy R Paulin
- Naomi Rivera
- Darryl C Towns

Minority
- James D Conte
- David G McDonough
- Jack Quinn
- Stephen Hawley
- Joel M Miller
- Andrea P Raia

Higher Education
Chair:
Deborah J Glick (D)..................518-455-4841
Ranking Minority Member:
Joel M Miller (R)....................518-455-5725

Committee Staff
Clerk:
Susan Nowogodzki....................518-455-4841

Key Assembly Staff Assignments
Minority Associate Counsel:
Laura Cail..........................518-455-4515
Minority Research & Program Development Legislative Analyst:
Chelsey Tulis.......................518-455-5002

Membership

Majority
- Darrel J Aubertine
- Michael J Cusick
- Patricia A Eddington
- Richard N Gottfried
- Barbara S Lifton
- William Magee
- Jose R Peralta
- Audrey I Pheffer
- Albert Stirpe
- Kevin A Cahill
- Luis M Diaz
- Steven C Englebright
- Rhoda S Jacobs
- Donna Lupardo
- Joseph D Morelle
- Amy R Paulin
- Linda B Rosenthal

Minority
- Thomas W Alfano
- Mike Cole
- Michael J Fitzpatrick
- Marc W Butler
- James D Conte
- Louis Tobacco

Housing
Chair:
Vito J Lopez (D).....................518-455-5537
Ranking Minority Member:
Michael J Fitzpatrick (R)............518-455-5021

Committee Staff
Chief of Staff:
Jonathan Harkavy....................518-455-5537
Clerk:
Lindsay Florek......................518-455-5500

Key Assembly Staff Assignments
Majority Program & Counsel Legislative Analyst:
Linda Camoin........................518-455-4355
Majority Program & Counsel Associate Counsel:
Don Lebowitz........................518-455-4355
Minority Associate Counsel:
Edmund V Wick.......................518-455-4262
Minority Research & Program Development Legislative Analyst:
Mark G Lundberg.....................518-455-5002

Membership

Majority
- Michael Benedetto
- Jonathan L Bing
- Karim Camara
- Vivian E Cook
- Rory I Lancman
- Michael Benjamin
- William F Boyland, Jr
- Joan K Christensen
- Steven Cymbrowitz
- Brian P Kavanagh

Offices and agencies generally appear in alphabetical order, except when specific order is requested by listee.

LEGISLATIVE BRANCH ASSEMBLY / State Assembly Standing Committees

Hakeem Jeffries
Alec Brook-Krasny
Luis M Diaz
Adam Clayton Powell, IV
Annette M Robinson
Ellen Young
Linda B Rosenthal
Carl E Heastie
Philip R Ramos
Keith L T Wright

Minority
Greg Ball
Jack Quinn
David R Townsend Jr
Robert Oaks
Michael J Fitzpatrick
Annie Rabbitt
Andrew P Raia

Insurance
Chair:
Vacant 518-455-0000
Ranking Minority Member:
William A Barclay (R) 518-455-5841

Key Assembly Staff Assignments
Majority Program & Counsel Legislative Analyst:
LouAnn Ciccone 518-455-4928
Majority Program & Counsel Associate Counsel:
Teri Kleinmann 518-455-4928
Minority Associate Counsel:
Campbell Wallace 518-455-4258
Minority Research & Program Development Legislative Analyst:
Harry J MacAvoy 518-455-5002

Membership

Majority
Adam T Bradley
Joan K Christensen
Steven H Cymbrowitz
Rhoda S Jacobs
George S Latimer
N Nick Perry
James Gary Pretlow
Mark J Schroeder
Ann Margaret E Carrozza
Vivian E Cook
Adriano Espaillat
Ivan C Lafayette
Crystal D Peoples
Adam Clayton Powell, IV
Jose Rivera
Mark Weprin

Minority
Marc W Butler
James Conte
Robert C Oaks
Nancy Calhoun
Brian M Kolb
Thomas F O'Mara

Judiciary
Chair:
Helene E Weinstein (D) 518-455-5462
Ranking Minority Member:
Jack Quinn (R) 518-455-4462

Committee Staff
Advisory Counsel:
Ken Munnelly 518-455-5462
Clerk:
Sarah Beaver 518-455-5462

Key Assembly Staff Assignments
Majority Program & Counsel Legislative Analyst:
Clayton Rivet 518-455-4313
Majority Program & Counsel Legislative Analyst:
Lowell Siegel 518-455-4313
Majority Program & Counsel Legislative Analyst:
Lisa Seemann 518-455-4313
Majority Program & Counsel Senior Team Counsel:
Richard Ancowitz 518-455-4313
Minority Associate Counsel:
Michelle Pellegri 518-455-5230

Minority Research & Program Development Legislative Analyst:
Dan Moser 518-455-5002

Membership

Majority
Jonathan L Bing
Jeffrey Dinowitz
Janele Hyer-Spencer
Charles D Lavine
Peter M Rivera
Mark Weprin
Adam T Bradley
Michael N Gianaris
Susan V John
Daniel J O'Donnell
Michele R Titus

Minority
Thomas Alfano
Tom McKevitt
William A Barclay
Thomas O'Mara

Labor
Chair:
Susan V John (D) 518-455-4527
Ranking Minority Member:
Thomas Alfano (R) 518-455-4627

Committee Staff
Clerk:
Kate Mahon 518-455-4527

Key Assembly Staff Assignments
Majority Program Counsel:
Harry Bronson 518-455-4311
Minority Associate Counsel:
Douglas L Goldman 518-455-4637
Minority Research & Program Development Legislative Analyst:
Dan Moser 518-455-5002

Membership

Majority
Peter J Abbate, Jr
Michael Benedetto
Barbara M Clark
Patricia A Eddington
Andrew Hevesi
Brian P Kavanaugh
George S Latimer
Nettie Mayersohn
Felix W Ortiz
N Nick Perry
Marc S Alessi
Joan K Christensen
William Colton
Carl E Heastie
Earlene Hooper
Rory I Lancman
Margaret M Markey
Joan L Millman
Jose R Peralta

Minority
Nancy Calhoun
Joe Giglio
David R Townsend, Jr
Clifford W Crouch
Mike Spano

Libraries & Education Technology
Chair:
Amy Paulin (D) 518-455-5585
Ranking Minority Member:
Marcus Molinaro (R) 518-455-5177

Committee Staff
Clerk:
Cathy Corellis 518-455-4901

Key Assembly Staff Assignments
Majority Program & Counsel Legislative Analyst:
Vacant 518-455-4881
Majority Program & Counsel Associate Counsel:
William Thornton 518-455-4881

Offices and agencies generally appear in alphabetical order, except when specific order is requested by listee.

LEGISLATIVE BRANCH ASSEMBLY / State Assembly Standing Committees

Minority Associate Counsel:
 Laura Cail.......................................518-455-4515
Minority Research & Program Development Legislative Analyst:
 Chelsey Tulis....................................518-455-5002

Membership

Majority
- Michael A Benjamin
- Susan V John
- Ellen Young
- Barbara M Clark
- David R Koon

Minority
- Philip Boyle

Local Government
Chair:
 William (Sam) Hoyt III (D).......................518-455-4886
Ranking Minority Member:
 Ann G Rabbitt (R)................................518-455-5991

Committee Staff
Clerk:
 Barrett Wadsworth................................518-455-4886

Key Assembly Staff Assignments
Majority Program & Counsel Legislative Analyst:
 Michelle Milot...................................518-455-4363
Majority Program & Counsel Associate Counsel:
 Julia Mallalieu..................................518-455-4363
Minority Associate Counsel:
 Charles E Crandall...............................518-455-4626
Minority Research & Program Development Legislative Analyst:
 Dan Moser..518-455-5002

Membership

Majority
- Marc S Alessi
- Dennis Gabryszak
- Ellen Jaffee
- George S Latimer
- William Magee
- Philip R Ramos
- Mark J Schroeder
- William F Boyland, Jr
- David F Gantt
- David R Koon
- Charles D Lavine
- Daniel J O'Donnell
- Michelle Schimel
- Michele R Titus

Minority
- Robert Barra
- Michael J Fitzpatrick
- Mike Cole
- Marcus Molinaro

Mental Health
Chair:
 Peter M Rivera (D)...............................518-455-5102
Ranking Minority Member:
 Tom McKevitt (R).................................518-455-5341

Committee Staff
Clerk:
 Anton Konev......................................518-455-5102

Key Assembly Staff Assignments
Majority Program & Counsel Legislative Analyst:
 Amy Nickson......................................518-455-4371
Majority Program & Counsel Associate Counsel:
 Elana Marton.....................................518-455-4371
Minority Associate Counsel:
 Campbell Wallace.................................518-455-4258
Minority Research & Program Development Legislative Analyst:
 Kristin Zielinski................................518-455-5002

Membership

Majority
- Karim Camara
- Ellen Jaffee
- Barbara S Lifton
- William L Parment
- Darryl C Towns
- Michael J Cusick
- John W Lavelle
- Donna Lupardo
- Mark J Schroeder
- Harvey Weisenberg

Minority
- Robert D Barra
- Janet L Duprey

Oversight, Analysis & Investigation
Chair:
 Adriano Espaillat (D)............................518-455-5807
Ranking Minority Member:
 Mike Spano (R)...................................518-455-3662

Committee Staff
Majority Committee Counsel:
 Thomas J Fox.....................................518-455-3039
Minority Associate Counsel:
 Edmund V Wick....................................518-455-4262

Membership

Majority
- Ginny Fields
- Daniel J O'Donnell
- Mark J Schroeder
- William B Magnarelli
- Annette Robinson

Racing & Wagering
Chair:
 James Gary Pretlow (D)...........................518-455-5291
Ranking Minority Member:
 Robert D Barra (R)...............................518-455-4656

Committee Staff
Clerk:
 Gregory O Smiley.................................518-455-5291

Key Assembly Staff Assignments
Majority Program & Counsel Legislative Analyst:
 Stephen Bochnak..................................518-455-4311
Majority Program & Counsel Associate Counsel:
 Vacant...518-455-4311
Minority Associate Counsel:
 Edmund V Wick....................................518-455-4262
Minority Research & Program Development Legislative Analyst:
 Laura Wood.......................................518-455-5002

Membership

Majority
- Francine DelMonte
- Margaret M Markey
- Anthony S Seminerio
- Aileen Gunther
- Robert P Reilly
- Paul D Tonko

Minority
- Tim Gordon
- Roy McDonald
- Stephen Hawley

Real Property Taxation
Chair:
 Sandra R Galef (D)...............................518-455-5348
Ranking Minority Member:
 Nancy Calhoun (R)................................518-455-5441

Offices and agencies generally appear in alphabetical order, except when specific order is requested by listee.

LEGISLATIVE BRANCH ASSEMBLY / State Assembly Standing Committees

Committee Staff
Clerk:
Rebecca Southard-Krieger 518-455-5348

Key Assembly Staff Assignments
Majority Program & Counsel Legislative Analyst:
Karen Smeaton 518-455-4311
Majority Program & Counsel Associate Counsel:
Tony Cantore 518-455-4311
Minority Associate Counsel:
Michelle Pellegri 518-455-5230
Minority Research & Program Development Legislative Analyst:
Laura Wood 518-455-5002

Membership

Majority
- James F Brennan
- Ginny Fields
- Aileen M Gunther
- Annette M Robinson
- Joan K Christensen
- Diane M Gordon
- Naomi Rivera

Minority
- Janet L Duprey (R)

Rules
Chair:
Sheldon Silver (D) 518-455-3791
Ranking Minority Member:
James N Tedisco (R) 518-455-3751

Committee Staff
Clerk:
June Egeland 518-455-3791
Counsel to the Minority:
Michael Cuevas 518-455-3751

Membership

Majority
- James F Brennan
- Vivian E Cook
- David F Gantt
- Aurelia Greene
- Rhoda S Jacobs
- Joseph R Lentol
- Joseph D Morelle
- Felix W Ortiz
- Anthony S Seminario
- Peter M Rivera
- Helene E Weinstein
- Ronald J Canestrari
- Herman D Farrell, Jr
- Richard N Gottfried
- Earlene Hooper
- Ivan C Lafayette
- Vito J Lopez
- Catherine T Nolan
- James Gary Pretlow
- Robert K Sweeney
- Paul A Tokasz

Minority
- Daniel J Burling
- Jim Hayes
- Robert C Oaks
- Mike Spano
- Clifford W Crouch
- Brian M Kolb
- Dede Scozzafava

Small Business
Chair:
Mark S Weprin (D) 518-455-5806
Ranking Minority Member:
William Reilich (R) 518-455-4664

Committee Staff
Clerk:
Darlene Mullally 518-455-5806

Key Assembly Staff Assignments
Majority Program & Counsel Legislative Analyst:
Benita Leigh-Lewis 518-455-4928
Majority Program & Counsel Associate Counsel:
Teri Kleinmann 518-455-4928
Minority Associate Counsel:
Michelle Pellegri 518-455-4637
Minority Research & Program Development Legislative Analyst:
Mark G Lundberg 518-455-5002

Membership

Majority
- Joan K Christensen
- David R Koon
- Adam Clayton Powell, IV
- Annette M Robinson
- Albert Stirpe
- Carl E Heastie
- Joan L Millman
- Jose Rivera
- Mark J F Schroeder
- Michele R Titus

Minority
- Michael J Fitzpatrick
- Tom McKevitt
- Tim Gordon
- Annie Rabbitt

Social Services
Chair:
Keith L T Wright (D) 518-455-4793
Ranking Minority Member:
Louis Tobacco (R) 518-455-4495

Committee Staff
Acting Clerk:
Jeanine Johnson 518-455-4793

Key Assembly Staff Assignments
Majority Program & Counsel Legislative Analyst:
Jill Poklemba 518-455-4371
Majority Program Counsel:
Jeanine Johnson 518-455-4371
Minority Associate Counsel:
Nancylynn Ferrini 518-455-4264
Minority Research & Program Development Legislative Analyst:
Laura Wood 518-455-5002

Membership

Majority
- Jeffrion L Aubry
- Luis M Diaz
- Diane M Gordon
- Charles D Lavine
- Alan Maisel
- Crystal D Peoples
- Jonathan L Bing
- Alec Brook-Krasny
- Aurelia Greene
- Vito J Lopez
- John J McEneny
- Matthew Titone

Minority
- Greg Ball
- Peter D Lopez
- Janet L Duprey
- Tom McKevitt

Tourism, Arts & Sports Development
Chair:
Joseph D Morelle (D) 518-455-5373
Ranking Minority Member:
Rob Walker (R) 518-455-4684

Committee Staff
Clerk:
Dan Farfaglia 518-455-5373

Key Assembly Staff Assignments
Majority Program & Counsel Legislative Analyst:
Brendan Fitzgerald 518-455-4928

Offices and agencies generally appear in alphabetical order, except when specific order is requested by listee.

LEGISLATIVE BRANCH ASSEMBLY / State Assembly Standing Committees

Majority Program & Counsel Associate Counsel:
  Teri Kleinmann 518-455-4928
Minority Associate Counsel:
  Jessica Reinhardt 518-455-4265
Minority Research & Program Development Legislative Analyst:
  Jessica C Howard 518-455-5002

Membership

Majority

Jonathan L Bing	Richard L Brodsky
Francine DelMonte	Steven C Englebright
Ginny Fields	Dennis Gabryszak
Michael N Gianaris	Aileen M Gunther
William (Sam) Hoyt, III	Margaret M Markey
John J McEneny	Daniel J O'Donnell
Robert P Reilly	Naomi Rivera
Matthew Titone	

Minority

Mike Cole	Thomas F O'Mara
Annie Rabbitt	Teresa R Sayward

Transportation

Chair:
  David F Gantt (D). 518-455-5606
Ranking Minority Member:
  David G McDonough (R). 518-455-4633

Committee Staff

Clerk:
  Kathryn F Curren 518-455-5606

Key Assembly Staff Assignments

Majority Program & Counsel Legislative Analyst:
  Julie Barney 518-455-4881
Majority Program & Counsel Associate Counsel:
  William Thornton 518-455-4881
Minority Associate Counsel:
  Jessica Reinhardt 518-455-4264
Minority Research & Program Development Legislative Analyst:
  Jessica C Howard 518-455-5002

Membership

Majority

Marc A Alessi	Darrel J Aubertine
Michael J Cusick	Francine DelMonte
Ruben Diaz, Jr	William (Sam) Hoyt, III
Janelle Hyer-Spencer	Dennis Gabryszak
Ivan C Lafayette	George S Latimer
John W Lavelle	Donna Lupardo
Alan Maisel	Brian M McLaughlin
Joan L Millman	N Nick Perry
Michelle Schimel	Matthew Titone
Paul D Tonko	Harvey Weisenberg

Minority

James G Bacalles	Joe Giglio
Joseph A Errigo	William R Reilich
Matthew Mirones	Louis Tobacco
Fred W Thiele Jr	

Veterans' Affairs

Chair:
  Felix W Ortiz (D). 518-455-3821
Ranking Minority Member:
  Greg Ball (R) 518-455-5783

Committee Staff

Clerk:
  Ann M McGrath 518-455-3821

Key Assembly Staff Assignments

Majority Program & Counsel Legislative Analyst:
  Joanne Martin 518-455-4355
Majority Program & Counsel Legislative Counsel:
  Elizabeth Hogan 518-455-4355
Minority Associate Counsel:
  Charles E Crandall 518-455-4626
Minority Research & Program Development Legislative Analyst:
  Mark G Lundberg 518-455-5002

Membership

Majority

Marc S Alessi	Darrel J Aubertine
Adam T Bradley	Michael J Cusick
Donna Lupardo	William B Magnarelli
Catherine T Nolan	William L Parment
Audrey I Pheffer	Mark J Schroeder
Michelle Schimel	Albert Stirpe
Robert K Sweeney	

Minority

Daniel J Burling	Stephen Hawley
Roy J McDonald	Rob Walker

Ways & Means

Chair:
  Herman D Farrell, Jr (D) 518-455-5491
Ranking Minority Member:
  James P Hayes (R) 518-455-4618

Committee Staff

Executive Director:
  Marcia Coleman 518-455-5491
Secretary to the Committee:
  Dean Fuleihan 518-455-3786
Deputy Secretary to the Committee:
  Stephen M August 518-455-4049
Counsel to the Chair:
  Michael L Johnson 518-455-5491
Clerk:
  Emma Leigh 518-455-4026
Clerk:
  Deb Devine 518-455-4026

Key Assembly Staff Assignments

Majority Tax & Fiscal Studies Director:
  Steven Pleydle 518-455-4051
Director of Economic Research:
  Audra Nowosilski 518-455-4006
Chief Economist (Modeling/Forecasting & Economic Analysis):
  InBong Kang 518-455-4006
Majority Director of Budget Studies:
  Stephen M August 518-455-4054
Majority Deputy Budget Director (Education & General Government):
  Jocelyn Dax 518-455-4026
Majority Deputy Budget Director (Environment/Energy, General Govt & Social Svcs):
  Tom Andriola 518-455-4026
Majority Deputy Budget Director (Economic Development & Higher Education):
  Matthew Howard 518-455-4026
Majority Deputy Budget Director (Budget Services):
  Victor Franco 518-455-4026

Offices and agencies generally appear in alphabetical order, except when specific order is requested by listee.

LEGISLATIVE BRANCH ASSEMBLY / Joint Legislative Commissions

Majority Deputy Budget Director (Health, Mental Hygiene, Children & Families):
  Mary Ann Donnaruma 518-455-4026
Majority Deputy Budget Director (Infrastructure, Criminal Justice, Public Safety, Gen Govt & labor):
  Lou Tobias 518-455-4026
Majority Counsel (Taxation):
  Brien R Downes 518-455-3933
Majority Deputy Fiscal Director (Taxation):
  Scott Palladino 518-455-3933
Majority Deputy Fiscal Director (State & Local Finance):
  Phillip Fields 518-455-4051
Minority Ways & Means Director:
  Rebecca P D'Agati 518-455-5161
Minority Ways & Means First Deputy Director:
  Lauren O'Hare 518-455-5161
Minority Deputy Directory for Economic Development:
  David Young 518-455-5161
Minority Deputy Director of Budget Studies:
  Edward V Golden 518-455-5161

Membership

Majority
- Jeffrion L Aubry
- William Colton
- RoAnn M Destito
- Adriano Espaillat
- Deborah J Glick
- William (Sam) Hoyt, III
- Joseph R Lentol
- Joseph D Morelle
- William L Parment
- James Gary Pretlow
- Helene E Weinstein
- Kevin A Cahill
- Vivian E Cook
- Ruben Diaz, Jr
- David F Gantt
- Aurelia Greene
- Ivan C Lafayette
- John J McEneny
- Catherine T Nolan
- N Nick Perry
- Robin L Schimminger

Minority
- William A Barclay
- Nancy Calhoun
- Brian M Kolb
- Dierdre K Scozzafava
- Daniel J Burling
- Clifford W Crouch
- Roy J McDonald
- Fred W Thiele, Jr

ASSEMBLY TASK FORCES & CAUCUS

Food, Farm & Nutrition, Task Force on
Chair:
  Jose Rivera (D) 518-455-5414

Program Manager:
  Robert Stern 518-455-5203

People with Disabilities Task Force
Chair:
  Michele R Titus (D) 518-455-5668

Puerto Rican/Hispanic Task Force
Chair:
  Peter M Rivera (D) 518-455-5102
Co-Chair:
  Vito J Lopez (D) 518-455-5537

Skills Development & Career Education, Legislative Commission on
Assembly Chair:
  Joan K Christensen (D) 518-455-5383
Program Manager:
  Brenda Carter 518-455-4865/fax: 518-455-4175

State-Local Relations, Legislative Commission on
Assembly Chair:
  Darrel J Aubertine (D) 518-455-5545
Program Manager:
  William Kraus 518-455-5035/fax: 518-455-5396

University-Industry Cooperation, Task Force on
Chair:
  William B Magnarelli (D) 518-455-4826
Coordinator:
  Maureen Schoolman 518-455-4884/fax: 518-455-4175

Women's Issues, Task Force on
Chair:
  Barbara Lifton (D) 518-455-5444
Coordinator:
  Jean Emery 518-455-3632/fax: 518-455-4574

Joint Legislative Commissions

Administrative Regulations Review, Legislative Commission on
Assembly Co-Chair:
  Michael N Gianaris (D) 518-455-5014
Senate Co-Chair:
  Catharine M Young (R) 518-455-3563
Senate Director:
  John Koury 518-455-2731/fax: 518-426-6820
Assembly Program Manager:
  Rich Murphy 518-455-5070/fax: 518-455-4175

Critical Transportation Choices, Legislative Commission on
Senate Chair:
  Thomas W Libous (R) 518-455-2677
Assembly Vice Chair:
  Vacant 518-455-0000
Program Manager:
  Heidi Kromphardt 518-455-4031

Demographic Research & Reapportionment, Legislative Task Force on
Assembly Co-Chair:
  Carl Heastie (D) 518-455-4800

Offices and agencies generally appear in alphabetical order, except when specific order is requested by listee.

LEGISLATIVE BRANCH ASSEMBLY / Joint Legislative Commissions

Senate Co-Chair:
  Dean G Skelos (R) 518-455-3171
Assembly Co-Executive Director:
  Lewis M Hoppe 212-618-1100/fax: 212-618-1135
Senate Co-Executive Director:
  Debra A Levine 212-618-1100/fax: 212-618-1135

Ethics Committee, Legislative
Assembly Co-Chair:
  Kevin A Cahill (D) 518-455-4436
Senate Co-Chair:
  Andrew J Lanza (R) 518-455-3215
Director/Counsel:
  Melissa Ryan 518-455-2142/fax: 518-426-6850

Government Administration, Legislative Commission on
Assembly Chair:
  Joan Millman (D) 518-455-5426
Senate Vice Chair:
  Owen H Johnson (R) 518-455-3411
Senior Program Manager:
  Philip Johnson 518-455-3632/fax: 518-455-4574

Health Care Financing, Council on
Senate Chair:
  Joseph L Bruno (R) 518-455-3191
Assembly Vice-Chair:
  Vacant 518-455-0000
Executive Director:
  Allan Filler 518-455-2067/fax: 518-426-6925

Rural Resources, Legislative Commission on
Assembly Chair:
  David R Koon (D) 518-455-5784
Senate Chair:
  George H Winner Jr (R) 518-455-2091
Senate Executive Director:
  Ronald C Brach 518-455-2544/fax: 518-426-6960

Assembly Director:
  Susan Bartle 518-455-3999/fax: 518-455-4175
Counsel:
  Donald A Walsh 518-455-2544

Science & Technology, Legislative Commission on
Assembly Chair:
  William B Magnarelli (D) 518-455-4826
Senate V Chair:
  Vacant 518-455-0000
Senior Program Manager:
  Philip Johnson 518-455-5081/fax: 518-455-4859

Solid Waste Management, Legislative Commission on
Assembly Chair:
  William Colton (D) 518-455-5828
Senate Vice Chair:
  Vacant 518-455-0000
Program Manager:
  Richard D Morse, Jr 518-455-3711/fax: 518-455-3837

Toxic Substances & Hazardous Wastes, Legislative Commission on
Senate Chair:
  Vacant 518-455-0000
Assembly Vice Chair:
  David R Koon (D) 518-455-5784
Program Manager:
  Richard D Morse, Jr 518-455-3711/fax: 518-455-3837

Water Resource Needs of NYS & Long Island, Legislative Commission on
Assembly Co-Chair:
  Vacant 518-455-0000
Program Manager:
  Richard D Morse, Jr 518-455-3711/fax: 518-455-3837

Offices and agencies generally appear in alphabetical order, except when specific order is requested by listee.

JUDICIAL BRANCH

Court of Appeals

The Court of Appeals is the highest court in New York State, hearing both civil and criminal appeals. This court consists of the Chief Judge and six Associate Judges. Judges are appointed by the Governor for fourteen-year terms or until age seventy, whichever comes first. The Court of Appeals receives direct appeal on matters where the only question relates to the constitutionality of a State or Federal statute. The Court also establishes policy for administration of the New York State Unified Court System.

Court of Appeals
20 Eagle St
Albany, NY 12207-1095
518-455-7700

Clerk of the Court:
  Stuart M Cohen 518-455-7700/fax: 518-463-8782
  e-mail: coa@courts.state.ny.us

Public Information Officer:
  Gary Spencer 518-455-7711
Judith S Kaye: 2007   Chief Judge

Associate Judges
Carmen Beauchamp Ciparick: 2007
Theodore Jones: 2016
Susan Phillips Read
Victoria A Graffeo: 2010
Eugene F Pigott, Jr
Robert S Smith: 2014

Appellate Divisions

The Appellate Divisions of the Supreme Court exist for each of New York State's four Judicial Departments. Each Judicial Department is comprised of one or more of the State's twelve judicial districts and has Governor appointed Presiding and Associate Justices. The Presiding Justice serves the duration of his/her term as a Supreme Court Justice. Associate Justices serve for the shorter of a five-year term or the balance of their term. Supreme Court Justices are required to retire at age seventy, unless they become "Certificated" by the Administrative Board of the Courts. Justices may serve after age seventy under Certification for two-year terms, until age seventy-six. The Appellate Divisions review appeals from the Superior Court decisions in civil and criminal cases, and from Appellate Terms and County Courts in civil cases.

1st Department
Judicial Districts 1, 12
Courthouse
27 Madison Ave
New York, NY 10010
212-340-0400 Fax: 212-889-4412

Clerk of the Court:
  Catherine O'Hagan Wolfe 212-340-0418
John T Buckley   Presiding Justice

Associate Justices
Richard T Andrias: 2013
Betty W Ellerin (Cert): 2005
Luis A Gonzalez: 2010
Angela Mazzarelli: 2012
David B Saxe: 2018
John W Sweeny: 2013
Milton L Williams (Cert): 2006
James M Catterson: 2012
David Friedman: 2011
George Marlow: 2011
Eugene Nardelli (Cert): 2006
Joseph P Sullivan (Cert): 2005
Peter Tom: 2018

2nd Department
Judicial Districts 2, 9, 10, 11
45 Monroe Pl
Brooklyn, NY 11201

718-875-1300 Fax: 718-858-2446

Clerk of the Court:
  James E Pelzer 718-875-1300
A Gail Prudenti: 2014   Presiding Justice

Associate Justices
Daniel D Angiolillo: 2011
Edward D Carni: 2007
Stephen G Crane: 2017
Mark C Dillon: 2013
Anita R Florio
Gabriel Krausman (Cert): 2007
William F Mastro: 2007
Howard Miller: 2007
Reinaldo E Rivera
Robert W Schmidt
Robert A Spolzino: 2007
Ruth C Balkin
Joseph Covello: 2007
Thomas A Dickerson: 2013
Steven Fisher: 2007
Gloria Goldstein (Cert): 2007
Robert A Lifson: 2007
William E McCarthy
David S Ritter (Cert): 2007
Fred T Santucci (Cert): 2007
Peter B Skelos: 2007

3rd Department
Judicial Districts 3, 4, 6
Capitol Station
PO Box 7288
Albany, NY 12224-0288
518-474-3609

Offices and agencies generally appear in alphabetical order, except when specific order is requested by listee.

JUDICIAL BRANCH / Supreme Court

Clerk of the Court:
  Michael Novack 518-471-4777/fax: 518-471-4750
Anthony V Cardona: 2018   Presiding Justice

Associate Justices
Anthony J Carpinello: 2008
Anthony T Kane: 2009
Thomas E Mercure: 2009
Karen K Peters: 2009
Edward O Spain
D Bruce Crew III: 2007
John A Lahtinen: 2011
Carl J Mugglin: 2007
Robert S Rose: 2013

4th Department
Judicial Districts 5, 7, 8

50 East Ave
Rochester, NY 14604-2214
585-530-3100 Fax: 585-530-3247

Clerk of the Court:
  JoAnn M Wahl 585-530-3100
Presiding Justice:
  Henry J Scudder

Associate Justices
Jerome C Gorski: 2016
Robert G Hurlbutt: 2009
Elizabeth W Pine (Cert): 2006
Nancy E Smith
Samuel L Green
Salvatore R Martoche: 2010
Henry J Scudder: 2010

Supreme Court

The Supreme Court consists of twelve Judicial Districts, which are comprised of County Courts within NYS (See County Court information in related section). Justices are elected by their Judicial Districts for fourteen-year terms, unless they reach age seventy before term expiration. Justices may serve beyond age seventy if Certificated (see Apellate Divisions for definition). The Supreme Court generally hears cases outside the jurisdiction of other courts, such as: civil matters with monetary limits exceeding that of the lower courts; divorce, separation and annulment proceedings; equity suits; and criminal prosecutions of felonies.

1st Judicial District
New York County
Jacqueline W Silberman: 2004   Administrative Judge, Civil
Micki A Scherer: 2008   Administrative Judge, Criminal
Chief Clerk, Civil Branch:
  Norman Goodman 646-386-5955
Chief Clerk, Criminal Branch:
  Alan Murphy 646-386-3900
  e-mail: amurphy@courts.state.ny.us

Judges
Sheila Abdus-Salaam: 2007
Eileen Bransten: 2013
Herman Cahn (Cert): 2006
Leland G DeGrasse: 2016
Nicholas Figueroa (Cert): 2005
Emily Jane Goodman: 2018
Sherry Klein Heitler: 2014
Phyllis Gangel Jacob (Cert): 2004
Barbara Kapnick: 2015
Doris Ling-Cohan: 2016
Richard B Lowe: 2016
William P McCooe (Cert): 2005
Karla Moskowitz
Charles E Ramos: 2007
Alice Schlesinger: 2013
Stanley L Sklar (Cert): 2004
Lucindo Suarez: 2009
Edwin Torres (Cert): 2005
Troy K Webber: 2016
James A Yates: 2011

Rolando T Acosta: 2016
Richard F Braun: 2017
William J Davis (Cert): 2007
Carol R Edmead: 2016
Helen E Freedman: 2016
Budd G Goodman (Cert): 2005
Carol E Huff: 2016
Marcy L Kahn: 2007
Edward H Lehner
Joan Lobis: 2020
Joan Madden: 2011
Donna Marie Mills: 2013
Eduardo Padro: 2015
Rosalyn H Richter: 2016
Martin Schoenfeld: 2008
John EH Stackhouse: 2017
Milton A Tingling: 2014
Laura Visitacion-Lewis: 2011
Lottie E Wilkins
Louis B York: 2014

2nd Judicial District
Richmond & Kings Counties
Neil Jon Firetog: 2009   Administrative Judge, Criminal
Theodore T Jones: 2017   Administrative Judge, Civil
Chief Clerk, Criminal Division:
  James Imperatrice 347-396-1100

Chief Clerk, Civil Division:
  Edward J Volpe 347-296-1800

Judges
Thomas P Aliotta: 2015
Betsy Barros: 2011
Ariel Belen: 2008
Bert A Bunyan: 2010
Anthony J Cutrona: 2008
Carolyn E Demarest
Lewis L Douglass (Cert): 2006
Anne G Feldman (Cert): 2006
Robert Gigante: 2013
L Priscilla Hall: 2007
Gerald S Held (Cert): 2006
Allen Z Hurkin-Torres: 2015
Laura Lee Jacobson: 2016
Theodore T Jones: 2017
Herbert Kramer: 2007
Joseph S Levine (Cert): 2007
Plummer E Lott: 2008
Larry D Martin: 2007
Philip G Minardo: 2009
Michelle Weston Patterson: 2018
Eric I Prus: 2018
Francois A Rivera: 2010
Leon Ruchelsman: 2016
Wayne P Saitta: 2018
Martin Schneier (Cert): 2006
James G Starkey (Cert): 2007
James P Sullivan: 2016
David B Vaughan

Bruce M Balter: 2018
Bernadette Bayne: 2017
Michael J Brennan: 2011
Cheryl E Chambers: 2007
Gloria Dabiri: 2009
Patricia DiMango: 2015
Deborah A Dowling: 2010
Abraham G Gerges (Cert): 2008
Raymond Guzman: 2017
Ira B Harkavy (Cert): 2005
Sylvia O Hinds-Radix: 2018
M Randolph Jackson: 2016
Diana A Johnson: 2014
Lawrence S Knipel: 2011
John M Leventhal: 2007
Yvonne Lewis
Louis John Marrero
Christopher Mega (Cert): 2006
Mark I Partnow: 2016
Michael L Pesce: 2013
Gustin L Reichbach: 2012
Gerard H Rosenberg (Cert): 2005
Howard A Ruditzky: 2014
Arthur M Schack: 2007
Martin M Solomon: 2017
Marsha Steinhardt: 2008
Albert Tomei: 2007

3rd Judicial District
Albany, Columbia, Greene, Rensselaer, Schoharie, Sullivan & Ulster Counties
George B Ceresia Jr: 2007   Administrative Judge
District Executive:
  Felicia D LaReau 518-285-8300/fax: 518-426-1604

Offices and agencies generally appear in alphabetical order, except when specific order is requested by listee.

JUDICIAL BRANCH / Supreme Court

Judges
Vincent Bradley: 2009
John C Egan Jr: 2020
E Michael Kavanagh: 2012
William E McCarthy: 2018
Robert A Sackett: 2017
Joseph C Teresi: 2007
George B Ceresia Jr: 2007
Stephen A Ferradino: 2008
Michael C Lynch: 2020
Thomas J Spargo: 2013
Leslie E Stein: 2016

4th Judicial District
Counties: Clint, Essex, Frankln, Fultn, Hamiltn, Montg, St Lawr, Saratga, Schenectady, Warren & Wash
Vito C Caruso: 2008   Administrative Judge
Executive Assistant to Administrative Judge:
  Marilyn F Jordan 518-587-3019/fax: 518-587-3179

Judges
Richard T Aulisi: 2012
James P Dawson: 2008
Stephen A Ferradino: 2008
Thomas D Nolan: 2013
Joseph M Sise: 2012
Vito C Caruso: 2008
David R Demarest: 2007
David B Krogmann: 2017
Vincent J Reilly: 2014
Frank B Williams: 2007

5th Judicial District
Herkimer, Jefferson, Lewis, Oneida, Onondaga & Oswego Counties
James C Tormey: 2009   Administrative Judge
Executive Assistant to Administrative Judge:
  John R Voninski 315-671-2111/fax: 315-671-1175

Judges
John J Brunetti (Acting): 2010
John V Centra: 2013
Brian F DeJoseph: 2014
Hugh A Gilbert: 2017
Robert F Julian: 2014
Joseph D McGuire: 2014
Thomas J Murphy (Cert): 2007
Bernadette Romano: 2010
Anthony F Shaheen: 2011
Edward D Carni: 2015
Michael E Daley: 2015
John J Elliott (Acting)
Donald A Greenwood: 2018
Deborah H Karalunas: 2016
James P Murphy: 2018
Anthony J Paris: 2013
Norman W Seiter Jr: 2017

6th Judicial District
Broome, Chemung, Chenango, Cortland, Delaware, Madison, Otsego, Schuyler, Tioga & Tompkins Counties
Judith F O'Shea: 2013   Administrative Judge
Executive Assistant to Administrative Judge:
  G Russell Oechsle 607-721-8541/fax: 607-721-8634

Judges
Kevin M Dowd: 2012
Robert C Mulvey: 2014
Walter J Relihan Jr (Cert): 2006
Jeffrey A Tait: 2017
Ferris D Lebous: 2019
Judith F O'Shea: 2013
Philip R Rumsey: 2007

7th Judicial District
Cayuga, Livingston, Monroe, Ontario, Seneca, Steuben, Wayne & Yates Counties
Thomas M VanStrydonck: 2012   Administrative Judge
Executive Assistant to Administrative Judge:
  Harry Salis 585-454-4242/fax: 716-325-1396

Judges
Francis A Affronti: 2017
David M Barry: 2012
David D Egan: 2014
John J Ark: 2007
Raymond E Cornelius
Kenneth R Fisher: 2009
Evelyn Frazee
Robert J Lunn: 2008
Matthew A Rosenbaum: 2019
Ann Marie Taddeo: 2018
Thomas M Van Strydonck: 2012
Harold Galloway
William P Polito: 2008
Thomas A Stander: 2018
Joseph D Valentino: 2015

8th Judicial District
Allegany, Cattaraugus, Chautauqua, Erie, Genesee, Niagara, Orleans & Wyoming Counties
Sharon S Townsend: 2017   Administrative Judge
Executive Assistant to Administrative Judge:
  Andrew B Isenberg 716-845-2505/fax: 716-858-4828

Judges
Ralph A Boniello, III: 2014
John M Curran: 2018
Kevin M Dillon: 2010
Eugene M Fahey: 2010
Amy J Fricano: 2013
Deborah A Haendiges: 2019
Joseph G Makowski: 2012
John A Michalek: 2008
Patrick H NeMoyer: 2011
Erin M Peradotto: 2017
Rose H Sconiers: 2007
Donna M Siwek: 2014
Penny Wolfgang: 2013
Christopher J Burns: 2009
Diane Y Devlin: 2020
Vincent E Doyle (Cert): 2006
Paula L Feroleto: 2018
Joseph R Glownia: 2018
John P Lane (Cert): 2006
Frederick J Marshall: 2014
Joseph D Mintz
John F O'Donnell: 2009
Janice M Rosa: 2016
Frank A Sedita
Gerald Whalen: 2019

9th Judicial District
Dutchess, Orange, Putnam, Rockland & Westchester Counties
Francis A Nicolai: 2014   Administrative Judge
Executive Assistant to Administrative Judge:
  Tomme Berg 914-824-5100/fax: 914-995-4111

Judges
Lester B Adler: 2018
Daniel D Angiolillo: 2014
Orazio Bellantoni: 2009
Nicholas Colabella: 2016
Mark Dillon: 2013
Margaret Garvey: 2017
Lawrence I Horowitz: 2017
William Kelly: 2019
Richard Lebowitz: 2019
Lewis Lubell: 2018
Richard Molea
Aldo Nastasi (Cert): 2006
Joseph G Owen (Cert): 2005
Kenneth W Rudolph
Mary H Smith: 2016
Bruce E Tolbert: 2018
Joseph Alessandro: 2019
Louis A Barone (Cert): 2005
James V Brands: 2016
Thomas A Dickerson: 2016
W Denis Donovan (Cert): 2006
William J Giacomo: 2018
Linda S Jamieson: 2016
John R LaCava: 2012
Joan B Lefkowitz: 2018
John McGuirk: 2013
J Emmett Murphy: 2010
Andrew P O'Rourke
Peter P Rosato (Cert): 2006
William E Sherwood: 2007
Christine A Sproat: 2017
Alfred Weiner: 2018

10th Judicial District
Nassau & Suffolk Counties
Anthony F Marano: 2013   Administrative Judge, Nassau
H Patrick Leis III   Administrative Judge, Suffolk
Executive Assistant to Administrative Judge, Nassau:
  Susan Sharp 516-571-3542/fax: 516-571-3653
Executive Assistant to Administrative Judge, Suffolk:
  Thomas F Lorito 631-853-7742/fax: 631-853-7741

Judges
Bruce D Alpert
Paul J Baisley, Jr: 2011
Leonard B Austin: 2012
Ruth C Balkin

Offices and agencies generally appear in alphabetical order, except when specific order is requested by listee.

JUDICIAL BRANCH / Court of Claims

Howard Berler (Cert): 2006
Donald R Blydenburgh: 2010
Peter Fox Cohalan: 2008
Joseph Covello: 2013
Kenneth A Davis: 2008
Arthur M Diamond: 2018
John P Dunne (Cert): 2005
Anthony Falanga: 2013
Patrick Henry (Cert): 2005
Zelda Jonas (Cert): 2006
Burton S Joseph (Cert): 2005
Ute W Lally
Daniel J Loughlin (Cert): 2006
Anthony Marano: 2007
Edward W McCarty
Denise F Molia: 2012
Geoffrey J O'Connell: 2007
Anthony L Parga: 2007
Emily Pines: 2016
William B Rebolini: 2017
Robert A Ross: 2015
Sandra L Sgroi: 2014
Elaine J Stack (Cert): 2007
Ira B Warshawsky: 2011
Ira H Wexner (Cert): 2005
F Dana Winslow: 2010

John C Bivona: 2009
Stephen A Bucaria: 2009
Ralph F Costello: 2010
Robert B Cozzens: 2011
Joseph A DeMaro: 2007
Robert W Doyle
Elizabeth H Emerson: 2009
Thomas Feinman: 2017
Angela G Iannacci: 2007
John J J Jones, Jr: 2013
William J Kent: 2008
William R Lamarca (Cert): 2005
Roy S Mahon: 2011
Edward G McCabe (Cert): 2005
Marion T McNulty: 2018
Karen Murphy: 2019
Robert W Oliver (Cert): 2005
Thomas P Phelan: 2009
Arthur G Pitts: 2013
Robert Roberto Jr (Cert): 2006
Marvin E Segal (Cert): 2004
Joseph P Spinola: 2017
Melvyn Tanenbaum
Mary M Werner (Cert): 2005
Thomas F Whelan: 2014
Michele M Woodard: 2014

Robert J Hanophy (Cert): 2006
Ronald D Hollie: 2014
Peter Joseph Kelly: 2016
Robert C Kohm
Leslie G Leach: 2016
Daniel Lewis: 2009
James M McGuire: 2018
Thomas V Polizzi (Cert): 2005
Jaime Antonio Rios: 2008
Martin E Ritholtz: 2015
Roger N Rosengarten: 2007
Frederick D R Sampson: 2008
Martin J Schulman: 2008
Sidney F Strauss: 2008
Charles J Thomas (Cert): 2007
Allan B Weiss: 2011

Duane A Hart: 2015
Richard D Huttner: 2014
Orin R Kitzes: 2007
Gregory L Lasak: 2017
Alan Levine (Cert): 2005
Robert J McDonald: 2013
Peter O'Donoghue: 2015
Arnold N Price (Cert): 2005
Joseph J Risi (Cert): 2005
Sheri S Roman: 2008
Seymour Rotker (Cert): 2005
Patricia P Satterfield: 2012
Mark H Spires (Cert): 2006
Janice A Taylor: 2011
Jeremy S Weinstein: 2013

12th Judicial District
Bronx County
Barry Salman: 2018   Chief Administrative Judge, Civil
John P Collins: 2007   Administrative Judge, Criminal
Chief Clerk, Criminal Division:
   Steven B Clark 718-590-3985
Chief Clerk, Civil Division:
   Tracy Pardo . . . . 718-590-3985 or 212-791-6000

Judges
John A Barone: 2014
Janice L Bowman: 2010
Edward Davidowitz (Cert): 2006
Joseph Fisch (Cert): 2007
Yvonne Gonzalez: 2013
Bertram Katz (Cert): 2007
La Tia W Martin: 2016
Richard L Price: 2016
Nelson Roman: 2016
Robert A Sackett: 2017
George D Salerno (Cert): 2007
Howard R Silver (Cert): 2008
David Stadtmauer (Cert): 2007
Robert E Torres: 2018
Paul A Victor (Cert): 2007

Lawrence H Bernstein (Cert): 2006
Mary Brigantí-Hughes: 2018
Laura G Douglas: 2013
Mark Friedlander: 2015
Alexander W Hunter: 2008
Sallie Manzanet: 2015
Douglas E McKeon: 2017
Dianne T Renwick: 2015
Norma Ruiz: 2013
Alan J Saks (Cert): 2005
Barry Salman: 2018
Harold Silverman (Cert): 2005
Kenneth Thompson, Jr: 2009
Alison Y Tuitt: 2017

11th Judicial District
Queens County
Leslie G Leach: 2017   Administrative Judge
Chief Clerk:
   Anthony D'Angelis 718-298-1150

Judges
Augustus C Agate: 2018
Laura D Blackburne: 2007
Evelyn L Braun
Arthur J Cooperman (Cert): 2007
Joseph P Dorsa
David Elliot: 2017
William M Erlbaum: 2018
Phyllis Orlikoff Flug: 2017
Joseph G Golia: 2014

Michael B Aloise: 2017
Valerie Brathwaite Nelson: 2018
Richard Lance Buchter
James P Dollard (Cert): 2007
Roberta L Dunlop
Randall T Eng: 2018
Timothy J Flaherty (Cert): 2006
James J Golia: 2018
Marguerite A Grays: 2016

Court of Claims

*The Court of Claims is a special trial court that hears and determines only claims against the State of New York. Court of Claims judges are appointed by the Governor for nine-year terms. Certain judges of this court, as designated herein by an *, also serve as acting Supreme Court Justices for the assigned judicial district.*

Court of Claims
Justice Bldg
Capitol Station
PO Box 7344
Albany, NY 12224
518-432-3437 Fax: 518-432-3483

Clerk of the Court:
   Robert T DeCataldo 518-432-3411/fax: 518-432-3483
   e-mail: rdecatal@courts.state.ny.us
Presiding Judge:
   Richard E Sise 518-432-3435/fax: 518-432-3428

Judges
Michael R Ambrecht*: 2008
John J Brunetti*: 2010
Russell P Buscaglia*: 2015
Thomas J Carroll*: 2013
Margaret L Clancy*: 2013
Francis T Collins: 2015
Matthew J D'Emic*: 2013
William C Donnino*: 2007
Anthony Giacobbe*: 2007
Judith A Hard: 2009
Michael E Hudson: 2015

Antonio I Brandveen: 2007
Edward D Burke*: 2008
Gregory Carro*: 2013
Caesar Cirigliano*
Robert J Collini*: 2013
Michael A Corriero*: 2008
Vincent M Del Guidice*: 2013
Diane L Fitzpatrick: 2007
Philip M Grella*: 2010
Alan L Honorof*: 2013
John G Ingram*: 2013

Offices and agencies generally appear in alphabetical order, except when specific order is requested by listee.

JUDICIAL BRANCH / New York City Courts

Richard C Kloch: 2013
Ferris D Lebous
Joseph J Maltese*: 2007
Martin Marcus*: 2008
Daniel Martin*: 2013
Thomas J McNamara*: 2013
Stephen J Mignano: 2011
Richard Molea*
Michael F Mullen*: 2013

James J Lack: 2012
Albert Lorenzo*: 2009
Guy J Mangano, Jr*: 2010
Alan C Marin: 2015
Dominic R Massaro*: 2013
Nicholas V Midey Jr: 2010
Renee Forgensi Minarik: 2014
Jeremiah J Moriarity III: 2012
S Michael Nadel: 2009

Juanita B Newton: 2007
Philip J Patti: 2011
Mario J Rossetti*: 2009
Melvin Schweitzer: 2008
Norman I Siegel*
Lewis Bart Stone*: 2008
Ronald H Tills*: 2010
Alton R Waldon, Jr
Maxwell T Wiley*: 2009

Joseph C Pastoressa: 2009
Stephen J Rooney*: 2013
Terry J Ruderman: 2015
Thomas H Scuccimarra: 2015
Richard E Sise: 2013
Charles J Tejada*: 2008
Rena K Uviller*: 2007
William A Wetzel*: 2008
Ronald A Zweibel*: 2010

New York City Courts

*New York City has its own Civil, Criminal and Family courts, separate from the County Court system. The NYC Civil Court hears civil cases involving amounts up to $25,000, and its judges are elected for ten-year terms. The NYC Criminal Court conducts trials of misdemeanors and violations. Criminal Court judges act as magistrates for all criminal offenses and are appointed by the City's Mayor for ten-year terms. The NYC Family Court hears matters involving children and families, such as: child protection, delinquency, domestic violence, guardianship, parental rights and spousal and child support. Family Court judges are appointed by the City's Mayor for ten-year terms. Certain judges of the Civil Court, as designated herein by an *, are also assigned to serve in other courts.*

Civil Court, NYC
Administrative Judge:
  Fern A Fisher
Chief Clerk:
  Jack Baer 646-386-5409/fax: 212-374-5709

Bronx County
851 Grand Concourse, Bronx, NY 10451
Chief Clerk:
  Joseph Monastra 646-386-5700

Kings County
141 Livingston St, Brooklyn, NY 11201
Chief Clerk:
  Stewart Feigel 646-386-5700

New York County
111 Centre St, New York, NY 10013
Chief Clerk:
  Mary Lee Andronaco 646-386-5700

Queens County
89-17 Sutphin Blvd, Jamaica, NY 11435
Chief Clerk:
  Thomas Touhey 646-386-5700

Richmond County
927 Castleton Ave, Staten Island, NY 10310
Chief Clerk:
  Lorraine Stergious 646-386-5700

Judges
Sharon A Aarons: 2013
Harold Adler*: 2011
Loren Baily-Schiffman: 2008
Johnny Lee Baynes*: 2014
Lucy Billings*: 2007
Arlene P Bluth: 2014
Dorothy K Chin Brandt*: 2007
Denis J Butler: 2011
Raul Cruz: 2012
Mitchell Danzinger: 2009
Marylin G Diamond*: 2010
Timothy J Dufficy: 2012
Arthur F Engoron: 2012

Rachel Amy Adams*: 2009
Francis M Alessandro: 2009
Jack M Battaglia: 2010
Harold B Beeler*: 2007
Arthur Birnbaum*
John A K Bradley: 2004
Raymond L Bruce*: 2011
Matthew F Cooper: 2010
Anna Culley: 2013
Catherine M DiDomenico: 2017
Monica Drinane*
Gerald J Dunbar: 2014
Joseph J Esposito: 2014

Saralee Evans*: 2013
Anthony J Ferrara*: 2007
Kathryn E Freed: 2013
Robin S Garson: 2012
Ellen Frances Gesmer*: 2013
Ira R Globerman*
Ferne J Goldstein
Stephen S Gottlieb: 2013
Desmond A Green*: 2013
Wilma Guzman: 2008
Barbara Jaffe: 2011
Deborah A Kaplan*: 2011
Cynthia S Kern: 2009
Kathy J King: 2013
Shirley W Kornreich*: 2004
Evelyn J LaPorte*: 2014
Diane A Lebedeff: 2012
Nelida Maleve*: 2014
Milagros A Matos: 2014
Judith N McMahon*: 2012
Peter H Moulton: 2013
Ann E O'Shea*: 2013
Jose A Padilla: 2014
Kibbie F Payne*: 2012
Geraldine Pickett*: 2014
Eileen A Rakower*
Karen B Rothenberg: 2007
Laura Safer-Espinoza*: 2010
Saliann Scarpulla: 2011
Marilyn Shafer*: 2013
Martin Shulman: 2007
Debra Silber*: 2007
Joseph Silverman*: 2007
Anil C Singh: 2012
Ruth E Smith
Faviola Soto*: 2013
Michael D Stallman*: 2016
Peter Paul Sweeney: 2011
Delores J Thomas
Analisa Torres*: 2009
George R Villegas*: 2012
Edgar G Walker: 2010
Betty J Williams: 2010

Paul G Feinman*
Fern A Fisher: 2007
Marcy S Friedman*: 2013
Darrell L Gavrin*: 2013
Judith J Gische*: 2013
Lila P Gold: 2013
Lizbeth Gonzalez: 2014
Bernard J Graham: 2014
Stanley Green*: 2009
Shlomo S Hagler: 2013
Debra A James*: 2014
Joan M Kenney: 2010
Kevin Kerrigan: 2009
Stephen A Knopf
Sarah L Krauss*: 2014
Howard G Lane: 2013
Robert D Lippmann*: 2013
Ira H Margulis*: 2013
Lee A Mayersohn: 2014
Manuel J Mendez: 2013
Eileen N Nadelson*: 2008
Jeffrey K Oing: 2013
Barbara I Panepinto*
Steven W Paynter*
Diccia T Pineda-Kirwan: 2012
Julia I Rodriguez: 2013
Alice Fisher Rubin: 2008
Debrarose Samuels: 2012
Larry S Schachner: 2013
Howard E Sherman: 2009
Bernice Daun Siegal: 2011
George J Silver: 2014
ShawnDaya L Simpson*: 2013
Karen Smith*: 2016
Jane S Solomon*
Ellen M Spodek*: 2012
Philip S Straniere
Fernando Tapia: 2012
Walter Tolub*: 2009
Wavny Toussaint: 2012
Eric N Vitaliano*: 2011
Dolores L Waltrous: 2008
John H Wilson*: 2014

Offices and agencies generally appear in alphabetical order, except when specific order is requested by listee.

JUDICIAL BRANCH / New York City Courts

Geoffrey D Wright: 2007

Housing Court Judges
Paul L Alpert
Gilbert Badillo: 2007
Joseph E Capella: 2009
Oymin Chin: 2008
Mitchell Danzinger: 2015
Timmie E Elsner: 2007
Anthony J Fiorella Jr: 2008
James R Grayshaw: 2007
Sheldon J Halprin: 2008
Douglas E Hoffman: 2012
Pam B Jackman-Brown: 2008
Anne Katz: 2008
Bruce Marc Kramer: 2009
John S Lansden: 2008
Gerald Lebovits: 2007
Jaya Madhaven: 2009
Kevin C McClanahan: 2007
Maria Milin: 2008
Michael J Pinckney: 2009
Maria Ressos
Bruce E Scheckowitz: 2009
Michelle D Schreiber: 2009
Brenda S Spears
Elizabeth J Yalin Tao: 2009
Deighton S Waithe: 2009

Alex J Zigman*: 2016

Ava P Alterman
Ronni D Birnbaum
Ernest J Cavallo: 2007
David B Cohen: 2009
Marian C Doherty
Marc Finkelstein: 2009
Thomas M Fitzpatrick: 2009
Arlene H Hahn: 2009
George M Heymann
Inez Hoyos: 2008
Dawn M Jimenez: 2009
Jerald R Klein: 2007
Lydia C Lai: 2008
Laurie L Lau: 2008
Ulysses B Leverett: 2009
Gary F Marton: 2009
Margaret P McGowan
Inez Muniz-Hoyos: 2008
Eardell J Rashford
Jose Rodriguez
Jean T Schneider: 2007
Marcia Sikowitz: 2008
John Stanley: 2010
Pierre B Turner: 2011
Peter M Wendt: 2008

Criminal Court, NYC
Administrative Judge:
 Juanita Bing Newton
Chief Clerk:
 William H Etheridge 646-386-4600/fax: 212-374-4835

Bronx County
215 E 161st St., Bronx, NY 10451
 Clerk in Charge:
  William Kalish 718-590-2858

Kings County
120 Schermerhorn St, Brooklyn, NY 11201
 Borough Chief Clerk:
  John Hayes 718-643-4044

New York County
100 Centre St, New York, NY 10013
 Borough Chief Clerk:
  Serena Springle 646-386-4511

Queens County
125-01 Queens Blvd, Kew Gardens, NY 11415
 Borough Chief Clerk:
  Brian Wynne 718-520-3855

Richmond County
67 Targee St, Staten Island, NY 10304
 Borough Chief Clerk:
  Andrew Hassell 718-390-8742

Judges
Bruce Allen
Allen G Alpert: 2012
Jeffrey M Atlas: 2009
A Kirke Bartley: 2008
Carol Berkman: 2009
Joel L Blumenfeld: 2010
James M Burke: 2012
Alexander Calabrese: 2016

Richard N Allman: 2007
Efrain L Alvarado: 2010
Steven Lloyd Barrett: 2008
Peter J Benitez: 2011
Miriam Best: 2012
Denis J Boyle: 2011
John N Byrne
Fernando M Camacho: 2008

Richard D Carruthers: 2012
John Cataldo: 2008
Darcel D Clark: 2008
John P Collins: 2007
Joseph J Dawson: 2008
Ralph A Fabrizio: 2007
Joann Ferdinand: 2011
Daniel P Fitzgerald: 2011
William E Garnett: 2009
Lenora Gerald: 2011
Arlene D Goldberg: 2008
Ethan Greenberg: 2010
Michael A Gross: 2013
Josephe Gubbay: 2008
Gerald Harris: 2008
Charles J Heffernan: 2007
Douglas E Hoffman: 2012
Melissa C Jackson: 2007
Eileen Koretz: 2015
John B Latella
Judith A Levitt
Gene R Lopez: 2008
Seth L Marvin: 2011
William L McGuire Jr: 2013
Edward J McLaughlin: 2012
Alan J Meyer: 2012
Deborah S Modica: 2008
William I Mogulescu: 2009
John S Moore: 2010
Barbara F Newman: 2016
Patricia M Nunez: 2012
Michael J Obus
Sheryl L Parker: 2007
Ruth Pickholz: 2009
Leonard P Rienzi: 2011
Micki A Scherer: 2007
Robert G Seewald: 2013
Brenda S Soloff
Michael R Sonberg: 2007
Robert M Stolz: 2011
Joan C Sudolnik: 2009
John P Walsh: 2008
Richard M Weinberg: 2007
Patricia Anne Williams: 2009
Douglas S Wong: 2011
Joseph A Zayas: 2009

John W Carter: 2012
Danny K Chun: 2008
Ellen M Coin: 2013
Miriam Cyrulnik: 2015
Laura E Drager: 2011
Thomas A Farber: 2011
Neil Jon Firetog: 2009
Bernard J Fried: 2009
Michael A Gary: 2010
James D Gibbons: 2012
Joel M Goldberg: 2012
James P Griffin
Joseph A Grosso: 2012
William M Harrington: 2012
Roger S Hayes: 2011
Patricia E Henry: 2017
Nicholas Iacovetta
Diane R Kiesel: 2008
Barry Kron: 2016
Jeffrey Lebowitz: 2014
Judith S Lieb: 2011
Alan D Marrus: 2012
Robert C Mc Gann: 2007
Joseph K McKay: 2013
Suzanne J Melendez: 2010
William Miller: 2012
Salvatore J Modica: 2009
Suzanne M Mondo: 2008
Pauline Mullings: 2014
Juanita B Newton: 2013
Mary O'Donoghue: 2009
Eugene Oliver: 2007
Ann Pfau: 2008
Robert M Raciti: 2007
Neil E Ross: 2008
Matthew Sciarrino Jr: 2015
Arlene Silverman: 2008
Charles H Solomon: 2009
Larry R Stephen: 2007
Robert H Straus: 2000
Megan Tallmer: 2014
Laura A Ward: 2013
Renee A White: 2007
Bonnie G Wittner: 2010
Alvin M Yearwood: 2008

Family Court, NYC
Administrative Judge:
 Joseph M Lauria
Chief Clerk:
 James E Kenny . . . . 646-386-5170 or 646-386-5200
fax: 212-374-3257

Bronx County
900 Sheridan Ave, Bronx, NY 10451
 Clerk of Court:
  Paul Moriarity 718-590-3318/fax: 718-590-2681

Kings County
33 Jay St, Brooklyn, NY 11201
 Clerk of Court:
  Robert Ratanski 347-401-9600/fax: 347-401-9609

New York County
60 Lafayette St, New York, NY 10013
 Clerk of Court:
  Evelyn Hasanoeddin 646-386-5200/fax: 212-748-5272

Offices and agencies generally appear in alphabetical order, except when specific order is requested by listee.

JUDICIAL BRANCH / County Courts

Queens County
151-20 Jamaica Ave, Jamaica, NY 11432
Clerk of Court:
George Cafasso 718-298-0197/fax: 718-297-2826

Richmond County
100 Richmond Terrace, Staten Island, NY 10301
Clerk of Court:
William J Quirk. 718-390-5460/fax: 718-390-5247

Judges
Jody Adams: 2012
Mary E Bednar: 2015
Rhoda J Cohen: 2012
Tandra L Dawson: 2015
Lee Hand Elkins
Nora L Freeman: 2012
Michael A Ambrosio: 2012
Stephen J Bogacz: 2015
Susan S Danoff: 2011
Guy P DePhillips: 2012
Maryellen Fitzmaurice: 2010
Rhea G Friedman: 2008
Sidney Gribetz: 2009
Bryanne A Hamill: 2011
John M Hunt
Susan R Larabee: 2009
Arnold Lim: 2009
Harold J Lynch
Ruben A Martino: 2012
Martin P Murphy: 2016
Jane Pearl: 2009
Edwina G Richardson: 2014
Gayle P Roberts: 2016
Sara P Schechter: 2008
Gloria Sosa-Lintner: 2012
Carol Ann Stokinger: 2009
Jeffrey S Sunshine: 2013
Stewart H Weinstein: 2010
Paul H Grosvenor: 2010
Paula J Hepner: 2010
George L Jurow: 2008
Joseph M Lauria: 2008
Fran L Lubow: 2008
Myrna Martinez-Perez: 2012
Maureen A McLeod: 2011
Emily M Olshansky: 2007
Clark V Richardson: 2014
Marybeth S Richroath: 2011
Barbara Salinitro: 2013
Marian R Shelton: 2007
Betty E Staton: 2011
Helen C Sturm: 2009
Daniel Turbow: 2015

County Courts

NYS has three types of courts designated at a county level: County Court, Family Court and Surrogate's Court. The County Court is authorized to handle criminal prosecutions of offenses committed within the county and hears civil cases involving amounts up to $25,000. County Court judges are elected for ten-year terms. The Family Court hears matters involving children and families (for types of court matters see NYC Courts). Family Court judges are elected for ten-year terms. The Surrogate's Court hears cases involving the affairs of decedents, including the probate of wills, and administration of estates and adoptions. Surrogates are elected for ten-year terms. This section also includes Supreme Court clerks and their addresses. Additional information and a list of judges for the NYS Supreme Court is provided in the related Section.

Albany County

Judges
Thomas A Breslin: 2012   County
Cathryn M Doyle: 2010   Surrogate
W Dennis Duggan: 2013   Family
Stephen W Herrick: 2011   County
Gerard E Maney: 2011   Family
Margaret T Walsh: 2014   Family

County Court
Albany County Judicial Center, 6 Lodge Street, Albany, NY 12207

Family Court
30 Clinton Ave, Albany, NY 12207
Chief Clerk:
David B Cardona. 518-285-8600/fax: 518-462-4248

Supreme & Surrogate's Courts
Courthouse, Room 102, 16 Eagle St, Albany, NY 12207
Chief Clerk-Supreme/County:
Charles Diamond. 518-285-8989/fax: 518-487-5020
Chief Clerk-Surrogate:
Stacy L Pettit 518-285-8585

Allegany County

Judges
Thomas Paul Brown: 2009   Multi-Bench
James E Euken: 2007   Multi-Bench

Supreme, County, Family & Surrogate's Courts
7 Court St, Belmont, NY 14813-1084
Chief Clerk-County/Supreme:
Kathleen C Johnson 585-268-5813
e-mail: kcjohnso@courts.state.ny.us

Chief Clerk-Family/Surrogate:
Carolyn J Miller 585-268-5815
e-mail: cjmiller@courts.state.ny.us

Bronx County

Judges
Lee L Holzman: 2011   Surrogate

COUNTY & FAMILY COURTS: See New York City Courts

Supreme & Surrogate's Courts
851 Grand Concourse, Bronx, NY 10451
Chief Clerk-Criminal Division:
Steven B Clark 718-590-3985
Chief Clerk-Civil Division:
Tracy Pardo 718-590-3985
Chief Clerk-Surrogate:
Michael L Prisco 718-590-3618

Broome County

Judges
Peter P Charnetsky: 2014   Family
Rita Connerton: 2011   Family
Patrick H Mathews: 2007   County
Eugene E Peckham: 2010   Surrogate
Spero Pines: 2013   Family
Herbert B Ray: 2014   Family
Martin E Smith: 2010   County

County, Family & Surrogate's Courts
65 Hawley St, PO Box 1766, Binghamton, NY 13902

Offices and agencies generally appear in alphabetical order, except when specific order is requested by listee.

JUDICIAL BRANCH / County Courts

Chief Clerk-Family:
  Marcia DiRose 607-778-2156/fax: 907-778-2439
Chief Clerk-County/Supreme:
  Michael P Husar 607-778-2448/fax: 607-778-6426
Chief Clerk-Surrogate:
  Marilyn A Vescio 607-778-2111/fax: 607-7782308

Supreme Court
92 Court St, Binghamton, NY 13901

Cattaraugus County

Judges
Larry M Himelein: 2012   Multi-Bench
Michael L Nenno: 2011   Multi-Bench

Family Court
1 Leo Moss Dr, Olean, NY 14760
Chief Clerk:
  Ruth Dickerson 716-373-8035/fax: 716-373-0449
  e-mail: rdickers@courts.state.ny.us

Supreme, County & Surrogate's Courts
Courthouse, 303 Court St, Little Valley, NY 14755
Chief Clerk-Surrogate:
  Christine Wrona 716-938-9111 x2327
  e-mail: cwrona@courts.state.ny.us
Chief Clerk-County:
  Sandra A Wogick 716-938-9111 x2388
  e-mail: swogick@courts.state.ny.us

Cayuga County

Judges
Peter E Corning   County/Family
Mark H Fandrich: 2011   Surrogate

Family Court
Old Historic PO Bldg, 157 Genesee St, Auburn, NY 13021-3476
Chief Clerk:
  Nancy Delaney 315-255-4306
Chief Clerk-Surrogate:
  Barbara A Carmody 315-255-4320
Chief Clerk-County/Supreme:
  Kelly J Wejko 315-255-4320

Chautauqua County

Judges
Stephen W Cass: 2010   Surrogate
Judith S Claire: 2008   Family
John T Ward: 2012   County

Family Court
Gerace Bldg, Courthouse, PO Box 149, Mayville, NY 14757
Chief Clerk-Family:
  Frank Baggiano 716-753-4351/fax: 716-753-4350
  e-mail: fbaggian@courts.state.ny.us

Supreme & County Courts
Courthouse, PO Box 292, Mayville, NY 14757-0292
Chief Clerk:
  Kathleen Krauza 716-753-4266/fax: 716-753-4993
  e-mail: kkrauza@courts.state.ny.us

Surrogate Court
Gerace Bldg, Courthouse, PO Box C, Mayville, NY 14757

Chief Clerk:
  Lydia Romer 716-753-4339/fax: 716-753-4600
  e-mail: lromer@courts.state.ny.us

Chemung County

Judges
David M Brockway: 2007   Family
Peter C Buckley: 2007   County/Surrogate
James T Hayden: 2009   Surrogate

Family Court
203-209 William St, PO Box 588, Elmira, NY 14902-0558
Chief Clerk:
  Rebecca Kelley 607-737-2902/fax: 607-737-2898

Supreme & County Courts
Corthouse, 224 Lake St, PO Box 588, Elmira, NY 14902-0588
Chief Clerk-County/Supreme:
  John A Buturla 607-737-2084/fax: 607-732-8879

Surrogate Court
224 Lake St, PO Box 588, Elmira, NY 14902-0588
Chief Clerk-Surrogate:
  Patricia Kreitzer 607-737-2946/fax: 607-737-2874

Chenango County

Judges
W Howard Sullivan: 2009   Multi-Bench

Supreme, County, Family & Surrogate's Courts
5 Court St, Norwich, NY 13815
Chief Clerk-Surrogate:
  Linda Wiley 607-337-1827/fax: 607-337-1834
Chief Clerk-Family:
  Carole S Dunham 607-337-1824/fax: 607-337-1835
Chief Clerk-County/Supreme:
  Catherine A Schell 607-337-1457/fax: 607-337-1835
  e-mail: cschell@courts.state.ny.us

Clinton County

Judges
Timothy J Lawliss: 2008   Family
Patrick R McGill: 2009   County
Kevin K Ryan   County/Surrogate

Supreme, County, Family & Surrogate's Courts
Government Ctr, 137 Margaret St, Plattsburgh, NY 12901
Chief Clerk-Family:
  Cathy Williams 518-565-4658
Chief Clerk-County:
  Jan M Lavigne 518-565-4715
Chief Clerk-Surrogate:
  Patricia A LeClerc 518-565-4630

Columbia County

Judges
Paul Czajka: 2014   Multi-Bench
Jonathan D Nichols: 2013   Multi-Bench

Supreme, County, Family & Surrogate's Courts
Courthouse, 401 Union St, Hudson, NY 12534
Chief Clerk-Multi:
  Dorothy Prestigiacomo 518-828-7858/fax: 518-828-1603

Offices and agencies generally appear in alphabetical order, except when specific order is requested by listee.

JUDICIAL BRANCH / County Courts

Chief Clerk-Surrogate:
Lee Norton 518-828-0414

Cortland County

Judges
William F Ames: 2008 Multi-Bench
Julie A Campbell: 2013 Multi-Bench

Supreme, County, Family & Surrogate's Courts
Courthouse, 46 Greenbush St, Ste 301, Cortland, NY 13045-2725
Chief Clerk-Family:
Laurie L Case 607-753-5353/fax: 607-756-3409
e-mail: lcase@courts.state.ny.us
Chief Clerk-County/Supreme:
Christina DeMass 607-753-5013/fax: 607-756-3409
e-mail: cdemass@courts.state.ny.us
Chief Clerk-Surrogate:
Maxine Ripley 607-753-5355/fax: 607-756-3409
e-mail: mripley@courts.state.ny.us

Delaware County

Judges
Carl F Becker: 2012 Multi-Bench

Supreme, County, Family & Surrogate's Courts
Courthouse, 3 Court St, Delhi, NY 13753
Chief Clerk-County/Supreme:
Allison Barnes 607-746-2131
Chief Clerk-Surrogate:
Nancy A Smith 607-746-2126
Chief Clerk-Family:
Lori Metzko 607-746-2298

Dutchess County

Judges
Damian J Amodeo: 2008 Family
Thomas J Dolan: 2012 County
Peter M Forman: 2007 Family
Gerald V Hayes: 2010 County
James D Pagones: 2008 Surrogate
Valentino T Sammarco: 2013 Family

Family Court
50 Market St, Poughkeepsie, NY 12601
Chief Clerk-Family:
Peter A Palladino 845-486-2500/fax: 845-486-2510

Supreme, County & Surrogate's Courts
Courthouse, 10 Market St, Poughkeepsie, NY 12601
Chief Clerk-Surrogate:
John J Atherton 845-486-2235/fax: 845-486-2234
Chief Clerk-County:
Ronald Varricchio 845-486-2260/fax: 845-486-5403

Erie County

Judges
Rosalie Bailey: 2007 Family
Paul G Buchanan: 2013 Family
Kevin M Carter: 2012 Family
Michael L D'Amico County
James H Dillon: 2010 Family
Sheila DiTullio County
Timothy J Drury: 2007 County

Barbara Howe: 2013 Surrogate
Patricia A Maxwell: 2011 Family
Michael F Pietruszka: 2008 County
Margaret O Szczur: 2014 Family
Shirley Troutman: 2012 County

Family Court
One Niagara Plz, Buffalo, NY 14202
Chief Clerk:
Frank J Boccio 716-845-7444
e-mail: fboccio@courts.state.ny.us

Supreme & Surrogate's Court
Erie County Hall, 92 Franklin St, Buffalo, NY 14202
Chief Clerk-Surrogate:
Mary Dee Martoche 716-845-2568/fax: 716-853-3741
e-mail: mmartoch@courts.state.ny.us

County Court
25 Delaware Ave, Buffalo, NY 14202
Chief Clerk-County/Supreme:
Christine Nestor 716-845-9301/fax: 716-851-3293
e-mail: cnestor@courts.state.ny.us

Essex County

Judges
Richard D Meyer: 2015 Multi-Bench

Supreme, County, Family & Surrogate's Courts
Courthouse, 7559 Court St, PO Box 217, Elizabethtown, NY 12932
Chief Clerk-Surrogate:
Elaine Caldwell 518-873-3385
Chief Clerk-County/Family:
Darlene K Gough . . . . 518-873-3375 or 518-873-3320

Franklin County

Judges
Robert G Main, Jr: 2008 Multi-Bench

Supreme, County, Family & Surrogate's Courts
Courthouse, 355 W Main St, Malone, NY 12953
Acting Chief Clerk-Multi-Bench:
Martha A LaBarge 518-481-1748/fax: 518-481-5456
Chief Clerk-Family:
Janice F Mock 518-481-1742

Fulton County

Judges
Richard C Giardino County/Surrogate
Polly A Hoye: 2011 County/Surrogate
David F Jung: 2009 Family

Family Court
County Ofc Bldg, 11 N William St, Johnstown, NY 12095
Chief Clerk-Family:
Geraldine Bastolla 518-762-3840/fax: 518-762-9540

Supreme, County & Surrogate's Courts
County Ofc Bldg, 223 W Main St, Johnstown, NY 12095
Chief Clerk-County/Supreme:
Patricia Caravella 518-736-5539/fax: 518-762-5078
Chief Clerk-Surrogate:
Barbara Shattuck 518-736-5685

Offices and agencies generally appear in alphabetical order, except when specific order is requested by listee.

JUDICIAL BRANCH / County Courts

Genesee County

Judges
Eric R Adams: 2010   Family
Robert C Noonan: 2016   Multi-Bench

Supreme, County, Family & Surrogate's Courts
County Courts Facility, 1 W Main St, Batavia, NY 14020-2019
Chief Clerk-Family:
  Kathleen Blake 585-344-2550 x2231/fax: 585-344-8520
  e-mail: kblake@courts.state.ny.us
Chief Clerk-County:
  Nelson L Green 585-344-2550 x2239/fax: 585-344-8517
  e-mail: ngreen@courts.state.ny.us
Chief Clerk-Surrogate:
  Vacant

Greene County

Judges
Daniel K Lalor: 2010   Multi-Bench
George J Pulver, Jr   Multi-Bench

Supreme, County, Family & Surrogate's Courts
Courthouse, 320 Main St, Catskill, NY 12414
Chief Clerk-County/Supreme:
  Kathleen Barry Gorczyea 518-943-2230/fax: 518-943-0247
Chief Clerk-Surrogate:
  Eric Maurer 518-943-2484
Chief Clerk-Family:
  Brenda Vandermark 518-943-5711/fax: 518-943-1864

Hamilton County

Judges
S Peter Feldstein: 2009   Multi-Bench

Supreme, County, Family & Surrogate's Courts
County Ofc Bldg, 79 White Birch Ln, PO Box 780, Indian Lake, NY 12842
Chief Clerk:
  Catherine Linton 518-648-5411/fax: 518-648-6286

Herkimer County

Judges
Patrick L Kirk: 2011   County/Surrogate
Henry A LaRaia: 2014   Family

Family Court
County Office & Court Facility, 301 N Washington St, 4th Fl, Herkimer, NY 13350
Chief Clerk:
  Lynn M Kohl 315-867-1139/fax: 315-867-1369

Supreme, County & Surrogate's Courts
County Office & Court Facility, 301 N Washington St, Herkimer, NY 13350
Chief Clerk:
  Constance A Vertucci 315-867-1209/fax: 315-866-1802

Jefferson County

Judges
Richard V Hunt: 2014   Family
Kim H Martusewicz: 2009   County
Peter A Schwerzmann: 2010   Surrogate

County, Family & Surrogate's Courts
163 Arsenal St, Watertown, NY 13601
Chief Clerk-Family:
  Tanice A Gebo 315-785-3001/fax: 315-785-3198
Chief Clerk-Surrogate:
  Benjamin Cobb 315-785-3019/fax: 315-785-5194

Supreme Court
State Office Bldg, 317 Washington St, Watertown, NY 13601
Chief Clerk-County/Supreme:
  Bonnie Johnston 315-785-7906/fax: 315-785-7909

Kings County

Judges
Margarita Lopez Torres: 2019   Surrogate

COUNTY & FAMILY COURTS: See New York City Courts

Supreme Court
Civil: 360 Adams St, Criminal: 320 Jay St, Brooklyn, NY 11201
Chief Clerk-Criminal:
  James Imperatrice 347-396-1100
Chief Clerk-Civil:
  Edward J Volpe 347-296-1800

Surrogate's Court
2 Johnson St, Brooklyn, NY 11201
Chief Clerk-Surrogate:
  Stephen Chepiga . . . . 718-643-7098 or 347-404-9700

Lewis County

Judges
Charles C Merrell: 2012   Multi-Bench

Supreme, County, Family & Surrogate's Courts
Courthouse, 7660 N State St, Lowville, NY 13367
Chief Clerk-Family:
  Judy Meekins 315-376-5345/fax: 315-376-5189
Chief Clerk-Surrogate:
  Lori Pfendler 315-376-5344/fax: 315-376-4145
Chief Clerk-County/Supreme:
  Bart R Pleskach 315-376-5366/fax: 315-376-4145

Livingston County

Judges
Dennis S Cohen: 2015   County
Robert B Wiggins: 2015   County

Supreme, County, Family & Surrogate's Courts
Courthouse, 2 Court St, Geneseo, NY 14454-1030
Chief Clerk:
  Diane Murphy 585-243-7060/fax: 585-243-7067

Madison County

Judges
Biagio J DiStefano: 2007   Multi-Bench
Dennis K McDermott: 2011   Multi-Bench

Supreme, County, Family & Surrogate's Courts
Courthouse, N Court St, Wampsville, NY 13163-0545
Chief Clerk-Family:
  Cheryl Collins 315-366-2291/fax: 315-366-2828

Offices and agencies generally appear in alphabetical order, except when specific order is requested by listee.

JUDICIAL BRANCH / County Courts

Chief Clerk-County/Supreme:
  Marianne Kincaid 315-366-2267/fax: 315-366-2539
Chief Clerk-Surrogate:
  Andrea Slivinski 315-366-2392/fax: 315-366-2539

Monroe County

Judges
Elma A Bellini: 2010   County
Edmund A Calvaruso: 2009   Surrogate
John J Connell: 2014   County
Raymond E Cornelius: 2014   Family
Gail A Donofrio: 2008   Family
Frank P Geraci: 2008   County
Richard A Keenan: 2010   County
Joan S Kohout: 2008   Family
Patricia D Marks: 2014   County
Marilyn L O'Connor: 2007   Family
Alex R Renzi: 2012   County
John J Rivoli: 2010   Family
Dandrea L Ruhlmann: 2013   Family

Supreme, County, Family & Surrogate's Courts
Hall of Justice, 99 Exchange Blvd, 5th Fl, Rochester, NY 14614
Chief Clerk-Surrogate:
  William Brongo 585-428-1779
Chief Clerk-County:
  James Hendricks 585-428-2020/fax: 585-428-2331
  e-mail: monroe_superior@courts.state.ny.us
Chief Clerk-Family:
  Ronald W Pawelczak 585-428-5429

Montgomery County

Judges
Felix J Catena: 2009   County
Philip V Cortese: 2012   Family
Guy P Tomlinson   Surrogate

Supreme, County, Family & Surrogate's Courts
Courthouse, 58 Broadway, PO Box 1500, Fonda, NY 12068-1500
Chief Clerk-Surrogate:
  Ella Bowerman 518-853-8108/fax: 518-853-8230
Chief Clerk-Family:
  Donna Caravella 518-853-8134
Chief Clerk-County/Supreme:
  Timothy J Riley 518-853-4516/fax: 518-853-3596

Nassau County

Judges
David J Ayres: 2013   County
Meryl J Berkowitz: 2009   County
Jeffrey S Brown: 2009   County
Joseph Calabrese: 2013   County
Jerald S Carter: 2007   County
Julianne S Eisman: 2007   Family
Carnell Foskey: 2008   Family
John M Galasso: 2007   County
Steven M Jaeger: 2014   County
John L Kase: 2014   County
Richard Lapera: 2007   County
Richard S Lawrence: 2007   Family
John G Marks: 2012   Family
James P McCormack   County
Daniel Palmieri: 2015   County
George R Peck: 2012   County
John B Riordan: 2010   Surrogate
Tammy S Robbins: 2014   County
David P Sullivan: 2012   County
Hope Schwartz Zimmerman: 2014   Family

County & Surrogate's Courts
262 Old Country Rd, Mineola, NY 11501
Chief Clerk-County:
  Katharine A Cunningham 516-571-2800
Chief Clerk-Surrogate:
  Michael Ryan 516-571-2847

Family Court
1200 Old Country Rd, Westbury, NY 11590
Chief Clerk:
  Rosalie Fitzgerald 516-571-9033

Supreme Court
Supreme Court Bldg, 100 Supreme Court Dr, Mineola, NY 11501
Chief Clerk:
  Kathryn D Hopkins 516-571-2904

New York County

Judges
Kristin B Glenn: 2015   Surrogate
Renee R Roth: 2008   Surrogate

COUNTY & FAMILY COURTS: See New York City Courts

SUPREME COURT, Civil Term
60 Centre St, New York, NY 10007
Chief Clerk:
  Norman Goodman 646-386-5955

SUPREME COURT, Criminal Term
100 Centre St, New York, NY 10013
Chief Clerk:
  Alan Murphy 646-386-3900

Surrogate's Court
31 Chambers St, New York, NY 10007
Chief Clerk:
  Jane Passenant 212-374-8232

Niagara County

Judges
John F Batt: 2007   Family
Peter L Broderick: 2007   County/Surrogate
David E Seaman: 2012   Family
Sara S Sperrazza: 2010   County/Surrogate

County, Family & Surrogate's Courts
Courthouse, 175 Hawley St, Lockport, NY 14094
Chief Clerk-Family:
  William F McCarthy 716-439-7172/fax: 716-439-7170
  e-mail: wmccarth@courts.state.ny.us
Chief Clerk-Supreme:
  Mary Ellen Florian 716-278-1800/fax: 716-278-1809
  e-mail: mflorian@courts.state.ny.us
Chief Clerk-Surrogate:
  Ronald A Sutton 716-439-7130
  e-mail: rsutton@courts.state.ny.us

Supreme & Family Courts
Angelo A Delsignore Civic Bldg, 775 Third St, Niagara Falls, NY 14302

Offices and agencies generally appear in alphabetical order, except when specific order is requested by listee.

JUDICIAL BRANCH / County Courts

Oneida County

Judges
Randall B Caldwell: 2013   Family
Barry M Donalty: 2013   County
Michael L Dwyer: 2009   County
James R Griffith: 2008   Family
David A Murad: 2015   Surrogate

Supreme & County Courts
Courthouse, 200 Elizabeth St, Utica, NY 13501
Chief Clerk:
　Joseph Panella 315-798-5889/fax: 315-798-6047
Chief Clerk:
　Barbara L Tokarski 315-337-7492

Surrogate's Court
County Office Bldg, 800 Park Ave, 8th Fl, Utica, NY 13501
Chief Clerk:
　Martha R Hoffman 315-336-6860/fax: 315-797-9237

Onondaga County

Judges
Anthony F Aloi: 2009   County
Joseph E Fahey   County
Michael Hanuszczak: 2010   Family
Bryan R Hedges: 2014   Family
Martha Walsh Hood: 2010   Family
Family:
　Martha E Mulroy
Robert J Rossi: 2007   Family
William D Walsh: 2011   County
Peter N Wells: 2009   Surrogate

County Court
505 S State St, Syracuse, NY 13202-2104
Chief Clerk:
　Patricia J Knoll 315-671-1020/fax: 315-671-1191

Supreme, Family & Surrogate's Courts
Courthouse, 401 Montgomery St, Syracuse, NY 13202
Chief Clerk-Family:
　Sherree Jackson 315-671-2000/fax: 315-671-1163
Chief Clerk-Surrogate:
　Ava S Raphael 315-671-2100/fax: 315-671-1163

Ontario County

Judges
Craig Doran: 2009   County
James R Harvey: 2009   County
Frederick G Reed: 2011   Surrogate

Supreme, County, Family & Surrogate's Courts
Courthouse, 27 N Main St, Canandaigua, NY 14424-1459
Chief Clerk-Surrogate:
　Donna Crudele 585-396-4055
Chief Clerk-Family:
　Michael R Morrisey 585-396-4272
Chief Clerk-County:
　Kathleen D Sweeney 585-396-4239/fax: 585-396-4576

Orange County

Judges
Jeffrey G Berry: 2010   County
Andrew P Bivona: 2008   Family
Nicholas DeRosa: 2007   County
County:
　Robert H Freehill
Debra Kiedaisch   Family
Carol S Klein: 2010   Family
Stewart Rosenwasser: 2009   County
Elaine Slobod: 2014   Surrogate
Lori Currier Woods: 2015   Family

Supreme, County & Family Courts
285 Main St, Goshen, NY 10924
Chief Clerk-County/Supreme:
　Thomas Adams 845-291-3111/fax: 845-291-2595
Chief Clerk-Family:
　Elizabeth Holbrook 845-291-3031/fax: 845-291-3054

Surrogate's Court
Courthouse, 30 Park Pl, Goshen, NY 10924
Chief Clerk:
　Joy V Morse 845-291-2193

Orleans County

Judges
James P Punch: 2010   Multi-Bench

Supreme, County, Family & Surrogate's Courts
Courthouse Square, 3 S Main St, Albion, NY 14411-1497
Chief Clerk-Surrogate:
　Deborah Berry 585-589-4457
　e-mail: dberry@courts.state.ny.us
Chief Clerk-Family:
　Laurie A Bower 585-589-4457
　e-mail: lbower@courts.state.ny.us
Chief Clerk-County/Supreme:
　Barbara Hale 585-589-5458
　e-mail: bhale@courts.state.ny.us

Oswego County

Judges
John J Elliott: 2008   Surrogate
Walter W Hafner, Jr: 2008   County
James W McCarthy: 2012   County
David J Roman: 2007   Family

Family Court
Public Safety Ctr, 39 Churchill Rd, Oswego, NY 13126
Chief Clerk-Family:
　Sherryl Waldron 315-349-3350/fax: 315-349-3457

Supreme, County & Surrogate's Courts
Courthouse, 25 E Oneida St, Oswego, NY 13126
Chief Clerk-Surrogate:
　Judy Cooper 315-349-3295/fax: 315-349-8514
Chief Clerk-County/Supreme:
　Theresa M Stephens 315-349-3277/fax: 315-349-8513

Otsego County

Judges
Brian D Burns: 2010   Multi-Bench
Michael V Coccoma: 2014   Multi-Bench

Supreme, County, Family & Surrogate's Courts
197 Main St, Cooperstown, NY 13326

Offices and agencies generally appear in alphabetical order, except when specific order is requested by listee.

JUDICIAL BRANCH / County Courts

Chief Clerk-County/Supreme:
  Gloria Chandler.................607-547-4364/fax: 607-547-7567
  e-mail: gchandle@courts.state.ny.us
Chief Clerk-Family:
  Karen A Nichols.................607-547-4264/fax: 607-547-6412
Chief Clerk-Surrogate:
  Judy M McBrearty................607-547-4213/fax: 607-547-7566

Putnam County

Judges
James F Reitz: 2007   Multi-Bench
James T Rooney: 2010   Multi-Bench

Supreme, County, Family & Surrogate's Courts
44 Gleneida Ave, Carmel, NY 10512
Chief Clerk-Family:
  Karen O'Connor............845-225-3641 x286/fax: 845-225-4395
Chief Clerk-County/Supreme:
  Leonard A Pace............845-225-3641 x336/fax: 845-225-6784
Chief Clerk-Surrogate:
  Linda M Schwark...........845-225-3641 x293/fax: 845-225-4395

Queens County

Judges
Robert L Nahman: 2007   Surrogate

COUNTY & FAMILY COURTS: See New York City Courts

Supreme & Surrogate's Courts
88-11 Sutphin Blvd, Jamaica, NY 11435
Chief Clerk:
  Alicemarie E Rice................718-298-0400/fax: 718-298-0500

Rensselaer County

Judges
Catherine Cholakis: 2012   Family
Linda C Griffin: 2013   Family
Christian F Hummel: 2011   Surrogate
Robert M Jacon: 2015   County
Patrick J McGrath: 2013   County

Family Court
1504 5th Ave, Troy, NY 12180-4107
Chief Clerk:
  Patricia Beeler...................518-270-3761/fax: 518-270-6573

Supreme, County & Surrogate's Courts
Courthouse, 72 Second St, Troy, NY 12180
Chief Clerk-Surrogate:
  Paul Morgan Jr..................................518-270-3724
Chief Clerk-County/Supreme:
  Richard Reilly...................518-270-3709/fax: 518-270-3714

Richmond County

Judges
John A Fusco: 2007   Surrogate

COUNTY & FAMILY COURTS: See New York City Courts

Supreme & Surrogate's Courts
County Courthouse, 18 Richmond Terrace, Staten Island, NY 10301

Chief Clerk-Surrogate:
  Ronald M Cerrachio............................718-390-5403
Chief Clerk-Supreme:
  Joseph Como....................................718-390-8670

Rockland County

Judges
Robert M Berliner   Family/Surrogate
Linda Christopher: 2014   Family
William A Kelly: 2007   County
William K Nelson: 2007   County
Kenneth H Resnik: 2010   County
William P Warren: 2008   Family

Supreme, County, Family & Surrogate's Courts
Courthouse, 1 S Main St, New City, NY 10956
Chief Clerk-Family:
  Eileen Stanford...................845-638-5300/fax: 845-638-5619
Chief Clerk-County:
  John F Hussey.....................845-638-5393/fax: 845-638-5312
Chief Clerk-Surrogate:
  Virginia Athens...................845-638-5330/fax: 845-638-5632

Saratoga County

Judges
Gilbert L Abramson: 2010   Family
Courtenay W Hall: 2008   Family
Jerry J Scarano Jr: 2014   County
Harry W Seibert: 2012   Surrogate

Family Court
Municipal Ctr, Bldg 2, 35 W High St, Ballston Spa, NY 12020
Chief Clerk:
  Susan P Janczak................................518-884-9207

Supreme, County & Surrogate's Courts
30 McMaster St, Ballston Spa, NY 12020
Chief Clerk-Surrogate:
  Debra D Baker..................................518-884-4722
Chief Clerk-County/Supreme:
  Carolyn Hall....................................518-885-2224

Schenectady County

Judges
Jo Anne Assini (Acting): 2010   Family
Karen A Drago: 2014   County
Barry D Kramer: 2013   Surrogate
Mark L Powers: 2011   Family

Family Court
County Office Bldg, 620 State St, Schenectady, NY 12305
Chief Clerk:
  Melissa Mills....................................518-285-8435

Supreme, County & Surrogate's Courts
Courthouse, 612 State St, Schenectady, NY 12305
Chief Clerk-Surrogate:
  Paula Miller....................................518-285-8455
Chief Clerk-County/Supreme:
  Sharon Sheffer..................................518-285-8401

Schoharie County

Judges
George R Bartlett, III: 2015   Multi-Bench

Offices and agencies generally appear in alphabetical order, except when specific order is requested by listee.

JUDICIAL BRANCH / County Courts

Supreme, County, Family & Surrogate's Courts
Courthouse, 290 Main St, PO Box 669, Schoharie, NY 12157-0669
Chief Clerk:
  Christian F Spies 518-295-8342/fax: 518-295-7226

Schuyler County

Judges
J C Argetsinger: 2007   Multi-Bench

Supreme, County, Family & Surrogate's Courts
Courthouse, 105 9th St, Unit 35, Watkins Glen, NY 14891
Chief Clerk-Family:
  Lynda LoPresti 607-535-7143/fax: 607-535-4918
  e-mail: lloprest@courts.state.ny.us
Chief Clerk-County:
  Karen H Morgan 607-535-7760/fax: 607-535-4918
  e-mail: kmorgan@courts.state.ny.us
Chief Clerk-Surrogate:
  Frances Pierce 607-535-7144/fax: 607-535-4918
  e-mail: fpierce@courts.state.ny.us

Seneca County

Judges
Dennis F Bender: 2013   Multi-Bench

Supreme, County, Family & Surrogate's Courts
Courthouse, 48 W Williams St, Waterloo, NY 13165
Chief Clerk:
  Elizabeth C Young 315-539-7021/fax: 315-539-7929

St Lawrence County

Judges
Barbara R Potter: 2012   Family
Jerome J Richards: 2014   County
Kathleen Martin Rogers: 2008   Surrogate

Supreme, County, Family & Surrogate's Courts
Courthouse, 48 Court St, Canton, NY 13617-1194
Chief Clerk-County/Supreme:
  Mary B Curran 315-379-2219/fax: 315-379-2423
  e-mail: mcurran@courts.state.ny.us
Chief Clerk-Family:
  Christy Q Bass 315-379-2410/fax: 315-386-3197
  e-mail: cbass@courts.state.ny.us
Chief Clerk-Surrogate:
  Debra Dow 315-379-2217/fax: 315-379-2372

Steuben County

Judges
Peter C Bradstreet: 2012   Multi-Bench
Marianne Furfure: 2007   Surrogate
Joseph W Latham: 2008   Multi-Bench

Supreme, County, Family & Surrogate's Courts
Courthouse, 3 Pulteney Sq E, Bath, NY 14810
Chief Clerk:
  William Deninger 607-776-7879/fax: 607-776-5226

Suffolk County

Judges
Stephen L Braslow: 2010   County
Marlene Budd: 2010   Family
Andrew A Crecca: 2007   County
John M Czygier, Jr: 2011   Surrogate
James F X Doyle: 2012   County
Joseph Farnetti: 2008   County
David Freundlich: 2008   Family
Ralph T Gazzillo: 2016   County
Joan M Genchi: 2012   Family
C Randall Hinrichs: 2011   County
James C Hudson: 2010   County
Barbara Kahn: 2015   County
John Kelly: 2013   Family
Martin J Kerins: 2008   County
Martha L Luft: 2015   Family
Barbara Lynaugh: 2010   Family
Jeffrey Arlen Spinner: 2008   County
Patrick A Sweeney: 2011   Family
Gary J Weber: 2012   County

County Court
210 Center Dr, Riverhead, NY 11901
Chief Clerk:
  Victor Rossomano 631-852-2120

Family Court
Courthouse, 400 Carleton Ave, Central Islip, NY 11722
Chief Clerk:
  Patricia S Herlihy 631-853-4647

Supreme Court
235 Griffing Ave, Riverhead, NY 11901
Chief Clerk:
  Michael Scardino 631-852-2334

Surrogate's Court
320 Center Dr, Riverhead, NY 11901
Chief Clerk:
  Michael Cipollino 631-852-1746

Sullivan County

Judges
Frank J Labuda   County/Surrogate
Burton Ledina: 2007   County/Surrogate
Mark M Meddaugh: 2012   Family

Family & Surrogate's Courts
Government Ctr, 100 North St, Monticello, NY 12701
Chief Clerk-Family:
  Cathy Emerson 845-794-3000/fax: 845-794-0199
Chief Clerk-Surrogate:
  LuAnn Hering 845-794-3000/fax: 845-794-0310

Supreme & County Courts
Courthouse, 414 Broadway, Monticello, NY 12701
Chief Clerk:
  Earl L Lilley 845-794-4066/fax: 845-791-6170

Tioga County

Judges
Vincent Sgueglia: 2012   Multi-Bench

Family & Surrogate's Courts
Court Annex, 20 Court St, PO Box 10, Owego, NY 13827
Chief Clerk-Family:
  Denise Marsili 607-687-1730/fax: 607-687-3240
Chief Clerk-Surrogate:
  Deborah Stone 607-687-1303/fax: 607-687-3240

Offices and agencies generally appear in alphabetical order, except when specific order is requested by listee.

JUDICIAL BRANCH / County Courts

Supreme & County Courts
Courthouse Sq, 16 Court St, Owego, NY 13827
Chief Clerk:
   JoAnn Peet 607-687-0544/fax: 607-687-3240

Tompkins County

Judges
John C Rowley: 2010   Multi-Bench
M John Sherman: 2007   Multi-Bench

Supreme, County, Family & Surrogate's Courts
Courthouse, 320 N Tioga St, PO Box 70, Ithaca, NY 14851-0070
Chief Clerk-Surrogate:
   Constance L Delaney 607-277-0622/fax: 607-256-2572
Chief Clerk-County/Supreme:
   Nancy M Joch 607-272-0466/fax: 607-256-0301
Chief Clerk-Family:
   Cheryl Lidell Obenauer. 607-272-1517/fax: 607-272-5027
   e-mail: clidell@courts.state.ny.us

Ulster County

Judges
J Michael Bruhn: 2013   County
Marianne O Mizel: 2013   Family
Steven Nussbaum   County
Mary MacMaster Work: 2014   Surrogate
Anthony McGinty: 2015   Family

Family Court
16 Lucas Ave, Kingston, NY 12401-3708
Chief Clerk:
   Kathy Lasko 845-340-3600/fax: 845-340-3626

Supreme & County Courts
Courthouse, 285 Wall St, Kingston, NY 12401
Chief Clerk:
   Florence Brandt. 845-340-3377/fax: 845-340-3387

Surrogate's Court
240 Fair St, Kingston, NY 12401
Chief Clerk:
   Mary Ellen Sullivan 845-340-3348

Warren County

Judges
J Timothy Breen: 2009   Family
John S Hall Jr: 2013   County/Surrogate

Supreme, County, Family & Surrogate's Courts
Municipal Ctr, 1340 State Rte 9, Lake George, NY 12845
Chief Clerk-Family:
   Ann Marie Lavigne 518-761-6500/fax: 518-761-6230
Chief Clerk-Surrogate:
   Shirley Friday 518-761-6512/fax: 518-761-6511
Chief Clerk-County/Supreme:
   Joseph R Hughes, Jr 518-761-7965/fax: 518-761-7698

Washington County

Judges
Philip A Berke: 2012   Multi-Bench
Stanley L Pritzker: 2014   Multi-Bench

Supreme, County, Family & Surrogate's Courts
Courthouse, 383 Broadway, Fort Edward, NY 12828-1015

Chief Clerk-County/Supreme:
   Kathleen M LaBelle 518-746-2521/fax: 518-746-2519
Chief Clerk-Family:
   Patricia A Ross 518-746-2501/fax: 518-746-2503
Chief Clerk-Surrogate:
   Barbara Smith 518-746-2545/fax: 518-746-2547

Wayne County

Judges
Multi-Bench:
   Dennis M Kehoe
John B Nesbitt: 2010   Multi-Bench
Stephen R Sirkin: 2009   Multi-Bench

Supreme, County, Family & Surrogate's Courts
Hall of Justice, 54 Broad St, Rm 106, Lyons, NY 14489-1199
Chief Clerk:
   Ellis W Bozzolo 315-946-5459/fax: 315-946-5456

Westchester County

Judges
Rory J Bellantoni: 2013   County
Jeffrey Cohen: 2016   County
Susan Cacace: 2014   County
Kathie E Davidson: 2013   Family
Robert M Di Bella: 2013   County
Colleen Duffy: 2008   County
Sandra B Edlitz: 2016   Family
Nilda Morales Horowitz: 2010   Family
David Klein: 2010   Family
Gerald E Loehr: 2015   County
Anthony A Scarpino: 2007   County/Surrogate
Sam D Walker: 2012   County
Barbara G Zambelli: 2007   County

Supreme, County & Family Courts
111 Dr Martin Luther King Jr Blvd, White Plains, NY 10601
Chief Clerk-Family:
   James McAllister 914-824-5500
Chief Clerk-County/Supreme:
   Donna Minort 914-824-5300/fax: 914-995-3427

Surrogate's Court
140 Grand St, White Plains, NY 10601-4831
Chief Clerk:
   John W Kelly. 914-824-5656/fax: 914-995-3728

Wyoming County

Judges
Mark H Dadd: 2013   Multi-Bench
Michael F Griffith: 2011   Multi-Bench

Supreme, County, Family & Surrogate's Courts
Courthouse, 147 N Main St, Warsaw, NY 14569
Chief Clerk-Surrogate:
   William D Beyer. 585-786-3148/fax: 585-786-3800
   e-mail: wbeyer@courts.state.ny.us
Chief Clerk-Family:
   Jacqueline Domkowski 585-786-3148/fax: 585-786-3800
   e-mail: jdomkows@courts.state.ny.us
Chief Clerk-County:
   Rebecca Miller 585-786-3148/fax: 585-786-2818
   e-mail: rmmiller@courts.state.ny.us

Offices and agencies generally appear in alphabetical order, except when specific order is requested by listee.

JUDICIAL BRANCH / District Courts

Yates County

Judges
W Patrick Falvey: 2008   Multi-Bench

Supreme, County, Family & Surrogate's Courts
Courthouse, 415 Liberty St, Penn Yan, NY 14527-1191
Chief Clerk:
  Margaret D DiMartino 315-536-5129/fax: 315-536-5190

District Courts

District Courts exist in Nassau County and in five western towns of Suffolk County. District Courts have civil jurisdiction up to $15,000, and criminal jurisdiction for misdemeanors, violations and lesser offenses. Judges are elected for six-year terms by their judicial districts.

Nassau County

Chief Clerk:
  Eileen Bianchi 516-572-2157

1st, 2nd & 4th District Courts
99 Main St, Hempstead, NY 11550
Deputy Chief Clerk, 4th:
  Michael Beganskas 516-572-2355
Deputy Chief Clerk, 1st & 2nd:
  Kenneth Roll 516-572-2355

3rd District Court
435 Middle Neck Rd, Great Neck, NY 11023
Deputy Chief Clerk, 3rd:
  Christine Harasek 516-571-8402

Judges

Anna Anzalone: 2009	Joel K Asarch
Valerie Bullard	Bonnie P Chaikin: 2010
Vito M Destefano: 2009	Scott Fairgrieve
Kenneth L Gartner	Sharon MJ Gianelli: 2012
Dana M Jaffe: 2008	Norman Janowitz: 2012
Gary F Knobel: 2012	Randy Sue Marber: 2007
Edward A Maron	Martin J Massell: 2008
Howard S Miller: 2007	William J O'Brien
Anthony W Paradiso: 2012	Sondra K Pardes: 2009
Erica L Prager: 2007	Christopher G Quinn: 2010
Margaret C Reilly: 2010	Francis Ricigliano: 2008
Lea Ruskin: 2008	Denise L Sher: 2007
Norman St George: 2010	

Suffolk County

Chief Clerk:
  Roger Huguenin 631-853-4530

1ST DISTRICT COURT, Civil Term . . . . . . fax: 631-854-9681
  3105 Veterans Memorial Hwy, Ronkonkoma, NY 11779
  631-854-9676 Fax: 631-854-9681

1ST DISTRICT COURT, Criminal Term . . . fax: 631-853-4505
  Courthouse, 400 Carleton Ave, Central Islip, NY 11722
  631-853-7500 Fax: 631-853-4505

2nd District Court . . . . fax: 631-854-1956
  375 Commack Rd, Deer Park, NY 11729
  631-854-1950 Fax: 631-854-1956

3rd District Court . . . . fax: 631-854-4549
  1850 New York Ave, Huntington Station, NY 11746
  631-854-4545 Fax: 631-854-4549

4th District Court . . . . fax: 631-853-5951
  Veterans' Memorial Highway, North County Cplx Bldg C158, Hauppauge, NY 11787
  631-853-5408 Fax: 631-853-5951

5th District Court . . . . fax: 631-854-9683
  3105 Veterans Memorial Hwy, Ronkonkoma, NY 11779
  631-854-9673 Fax: 631-854-9683

6th District Court . . . . fax: 631-854-1444
  150 W Main St, Patchogue, NY 11772
  631-854-1440 Fax: 631-854-1444

Judges

Salvatore A Alamia: 2010	W Gerard Asher: 2010
Patrick J Barton: 2007	Toni A Bean: 2010
Stephen M Behar Sr: 2009	Howard M Bergson: 2008
William J Burke, III: 2007	Kevin J Crowley: 2007
Lawrence Donohue: 2010	Martin I Efman: 2010
Patricia M Filiberto: 2009	Madeleine A Fitzgibbon: 2009
James P Flanagan: 2009	C Stephen Hackeling: 2008
Paul M Hensley: 2008	John Iliou: 2012
Steven A Lotto: 2009	Gaetan B Lozito: 2007
Glenn A Murphy: 2009	Joseph A Santorelli: 2010
G Ann Spellman: 2011	John J Toomey, Jr: 2008
Hertha C Trotto: 2008	Georgia A Tschiember: 2008

City Courts Outside New York City

City Courts outside New York City have civil jurisdiction up to $15,000 and criminal jurisdiction over misdemeanors or lesser offenses. City Court judges are either elected or appointed for terms of ten years for full-time judges and six years for part-time judges.

Albany

Judges

William A Carter: 2012	John Egan, Jr: 2019	Helena Heath-Roland: 2011	Thomas K Keefe: 2012
		Gary F Stiglmeier: 2014	

Offices and agencies generally appear in alphabetical order, except when specific order is requested by listee.

JUDICIAL BRANCH / City Courts Outside New York City

Civil Court
Albany City Hall, Room 209, 24 Eagle Street, Albany, NY 12207
Chief Clerk:
Linda File 518-434-5115

Criminal Court
Public Safety Bldg, 1 Morton Ave, Albany, NY 12202
Chief Clerk:
Janice Cellucci 518-462-6714

Traffic Court
Albany City Hall, Basement, 24 Eagle St, Albany, NY 12207
Chief Clerk:
Vicki McManus 518-434-5095

Amsterdam

Judges
Howard M Aison: 2008   Paul L Wollman

Civil & Criminal Courts
Public Safety Bldg, Rm 208, 1 Guy Park Ave Ext, Amsterdam, NY 12010
Chief Clerk:
Melanie Hartman 518-842-9510

Auburn

Judges
Michael F McKeon: 2008   Thomas J Shamon: 2008

Civil & Criminal Courts
157 Genesee St, Auburn, NY 13021
Chief Clerk:
Deborah L Robillard 315-253-1570/fax: 315-253-1085

Batavia

Judges
Robert J Balbick: 2010   Michael A DelPlato: 2009

Civil & Criminal Courts . . . . fax: 585-344-8556
Facility Bldg, 1 W Main St, Batavia, NY 14020
585-344-255 x2417 Fax: 585-344-8556
Chief Clerk:
Linda M Giambrone 585-344-2550 x2426

Beacon

Judges
Rebecca S Mensch (Acting)   Timothy G Pagones

Civil & Criminal Courts
1 Municipal Plz, Ste 2, Beacon, NY 12508
Chief Clerk:
Debra Antonelli 845-838-5030/fax: 845-838-5041

Binghamton

Judges
Mary Anne Lehmann   Robert C Murphy: 2008
William C Pelella: 2014

Civil & Criminal Courts
City Hall, Governmental Plz, 38 Hawley St, 5th Fl, Binghamton, NY 13901

Chief Clerk:
Catherine R Maloney 607-772-7006/fax: 607-772-7041
e-mail: cmaloney@courts.state.ny.us

Buffalo

Judges
Thomas P Amodeo: 2014   Patrick M Carney: 2014
Joseph A Fiorella: 2011   Thomas P Franczyk: 2007
Debra L Givens: 2012   Craig D Hannah: 2007
Kevin J Keane: 2013   Sharon M LoVallo: 2007
David M Manz: 2011   James A McLeod: 2008
Henry J Nowak: 2012   E Jeanette Ogden: 2007
Robert T Russell: 2007

Civil & Criminal Courts . . . . fax: 716-847-8257
50 Delaware Ave, Buffalo, NY 14202
716-845-2600 Fax: 716-847-8257
Chief Clerk:
Sharon A Thomas 716-845-2689
e-mail: sthomas@courts.state.ny.us

Canandaigua

Judges
Stephen D Aronson: 2009   John A Schuppenhauer: 2007

Civil & Criminal Courts
2 N Main St, Canandaigua, NY 14424
Chief Clerk:
Lisa Schutz 585-396-5011/fax: 585-396-5012

Cohoes

Judges
Richard R Maguire: 2010   Stephen J Van Ullen: 2009

Civil, Criminal & Traffic Courts
City Hall, 97 Mohawk St, PO Box 678, Cohoes, NY 12047
Chief Clerk:
Janet LeBeau 518-233-2133

Corning

Judges
Robert H Cole, Jr: 2009   David B Kahl: 2008

Civil & Criminal Courts
12 Civic Ctr Plz, Corning, NY 14830
Chief Clerk:
Julie L Callahan 607-936-4111/fax: 607-936-0519

Cortland

Judges
Elizabeth Burns: 2007   Thomas A Meldrim: 2009

Civil & Criminal Courts
City Hall, 25 Court St, Cortland, NY 13045
Chief Clerk:
Kelley Preston 607-753-1811/fax: 607-753-9932

Dunkirk

Judges
Walter F Drag: 2007   John M Kuzdale (Acting): 2011

Offices and agencies generally appear in alphabetical order, except when specific order is requested by listee.

JUDICIAL BRANCH / City Courts Outside New York City

Civil & Criminal Courts
City Hall, 342 Central Ave, Dunkirk, NY 14048-2122
Chief Clerk:
Jean Dill 716-366-2055/fax: 716-366-3622
e-mail: jdill@courts.state.ny.us

Elmira

Judges
Steven W Forrest: 2009   Thomas E Ramich

Civil & Criminal Courts
317 E Church St, Elmira, NY 14901
Chief Clerk:
Teresa B Seeley. 607-737-5681/fax: 607-737-5820
e-mail: tseeley@courts.state.ny.us

Fulton

Judges
Spencer J Ludington: 2008   Jerome A Mirabito: 2007

Civil & Criminal Courts
Municipal Bldg, 141 S First St, Fulton, NY 13069
Chief Clerk:
Maureen Ball. 315-593-8400/fax: 315-592-3415
e-mail: mball@courts.state.ny.us

Geneva

Judges
Timothy J Buckley: 2009   Walter C Gage: 2007
Elisabeth A Toole: 2009

Civil & Criminal Courts
255 Exchange St, Geneva, NY 14456
Chief Clerk:
Josephine Guard 315-789-6560/fax: 315-781-2802

Glen Cove

Judges
Richard J McCord

Civil & Criminal Courts
13 Glen St, Glen Cove, NY 11542
Chief Clerk:
Heddy Amstel. 516-676-0109

Glens Falls

Judges
Gary C Hobbs (Part Time)   Richard P Tarantino: 2014

Civil & Criminal Courts
Glens Falls City Hall, 42 Ridge St, 3rd Fl, Glens Falls, NY 12801
Chief Clerk:
Philip Simms. 518-798-4714/fax: 518-798-0137

Gloversville

Judges
Vincent Desantis   Mario J Papa

Civil & Criminal Courts
City Hall, 3 Frontage Rd, Gloversville, NY 12078

Chief Clerk:
Jodi L Ferguson 518-773-4527

Hornell

Judges
Joseph E Damrath: 2007   David A Shults: 2009

Civil & Criminal Courts
PO Box 627, 82 Main St, Hornell, NY 14843
Chief Clerk:
Laura Beltz 607-324-7531/fax: 607-324-6325

Hudson

Judges
William F Cranna (Part Time): 2008   Barry Sack: 2008

Civil & Criminal Courts
427 Warren St, Hudson, NY 12534
Chief Clerk:
Rosemary Zukowski. 518-828-3100

Ithaca

Judges
Marjorie Z Olds: 2007   Judith A Rossiter: 2010

Civil & Criminal Courts
118 E Clinton St, Ithaca, NY 14850
Chief Clerk:
James R Jecen 607-273-2263/fax: 607-277-3702

Jamestown

Judges
John J LaMancuso: 2013   George Panebianco (Acting): 2010

Civil & Criminal Courts
Municipal Bldg, 200 E 3rd St, Jamestown, NY 14701
Chief Clerk:
Cheryl Dove 716-483-7561/fax: 716-483-7519
e-mail: cdove@courts.state.ny.us

Johnstown

Judges
Frederick R Stortecky   Thomas C Walsh: 2007

Civil & Criminal Courts
City Hall, 33-41 E Main St, Johnstown, NY 12095
Chief Clerk:
Stephen Russo 518-762-0007

Kingston

Judges
Edward T Feeney: 2009   James P Gilpatric: 2011

Civil & Criminal Courts
Kingston City Court, 1 Garraghan Dr, Kingston, NY 12401
Chief Clerk:
Janet Strauss. 845-338-2974

Offices and agencies generally appear in alphabetical order, except when specific order is requested by listee.

JUDICIAL BRANCH / City Courts Outside New York City

Lackawanna

Judges
Joseph V Deren: 2008
Frederic J Marrano: 2007

Civil & Criminal Courts
City Hall, 714 Ridge Rd, Lackawanna, NY 14218
Chief Clerk:
Vacant 716-827-6486

Little Falls

Judges
Bart M Carrig (Acting): 2007
Edward J Rose: 2007

Civil & Criminal Courts
City Hall, 659 E Main St, Little Falls, NY 13365
Chief Clerk:
Jane B Fortuna. 315-823-1690/fax: 315-823-1623

Lockport

Judges
William J Watson
Thomas M DiMillo: 2011

Civil & Criminal Courts
1 Locks Plz, Lockport, NY 14094
Chief Clerk:
Colleen Kelly 716-439-6672/fax: 716-439-6684
e-mail: ckelly@courts.state.ny.us

Long Beach

Judges
Stanley A Smolkin: 2009
Roy Tepper: 2013

Civil & Criminal Courts
1 W Chester St, Long Beach, NY 11561
Chief Clerk:
Robert Davis. 516-431-1000

Mechanicville

Judges
James F Hughes (Acting): 2008
Joseph W Sheehan: 2014

Civil & Criminal Courts
City Hall, 36 N Main St, Mechanicville, NY 12118
Chief Clerk:
Francine Baker 518-664-9876

Middletown

Judges
Steven Brockett: 2016
Michael Schwartz: 2010

Civil & Criminal Courts
2 James St, Middletown, NY 10940
Chief Clerk:
Linda Padden. 845-346-4050/fax: 845-343-5737

Mount Vernon

Judges
Brenda L Dowery-Rodriquez: 2009
Mark A Gross: 2016
William Edwards: 2013
Adam Seiden

Civil & Criminal Courts
Roosevelt Square, Mount Vernon, NY 10550
Chief Clerk:
Lawrence Darden 914-665-2400/fax: 914-665-1230

New Rochelle

Judges
John P Colangelo: 2012
Gail B Rice (Acting): 2008
Preston S Scher

Civil & Criminal Courts
475 North Ave, New Rochelle, NY 10801
Chief Clerk:
James Generoso. 914-654-2207/fax: 914-654-0344

Newburgh

Judges
Peter M Kulkin: 2014
B Harold Ramsey: 2013

Civil & Criminal Courts
57 Broadway, Newburgh, NY 12550
Chief Clerk:
Sharon Reed 845-565-3208/fax: 845-565-1244

Niagara Falls

Judges
Angelo J Morinello: 2012
Robert M Restaino: 2011
Mark A Violante

Civil & Criminal Courts
Public Safety Bldg, 520 Hyde Park Blvd, Niagara Falls, NY 14302
Chief Clerk:
Martha J Farbo-Lincoln. 716-278-9800/fax: 716-278-9809
e-mail: mfarbo@courts.state.ny.us

North Tonawanda

Judges
R Thomas Burgasser: 2011
William R Lewis: 2011

Civil & Criminal Courts
City Hall, 216 Payne Ave, North Tonawanda, NY 14120
Chief Clerk:
Sheila D McQuade 716-693-1010/fax: 716-743-1754
e-mail: smcquade@courts.state.ny.us

Norwich

Judges
Maureen A Byrne (Acting)
James Downey

Civil & Criminal Courts
1 Court Plz, Norwich, NY 13815
Chief Clerk:
Linda Roys-Jones 607-334-1224/fax: 607-334-8494

Ogdensburg

Judges
George Silver

Civil & Criminal Courts
330 Ford St, Ogdensburg, NY 13669

Offices and agencies generally appear in alphabetical order, except when specific order is requested by listee.

JUDICIAL BRANCH / City Courts Outside New York City

Chief Clerk:
Lisa Marie Meyer 315-393-3941/fax: 315-393-6839

Olean
Judges
William H Mountain III   Daniel R Palumbo (Acting): 2011

Civil & Criminal Courts
101 E State St, PO Box 631, Olean, NY 14760
Chief Clerk:
Stella Johnson 716-376-5620/fax: 716-376-5623
e-mail: ssjohnst@courts.state.ny.us

Oneida
Judges
Anthony P Eppolito: 2007   Michael J Misiaszek (Acting): 2008

Civil & Criminal Courts
Municipal Bldg, 109 N Main St, Oneida, NY 13421
Chief Clerk:
Lynne Mondrick 315-363-1310/fax: 315-363-3230

Oneonta
Judges
Lucy P Bernier: 2009   Walter L Terry, III: 2009

Civil & Criminal Courts
Public Safety Bldg, 81 Main St, Oneonta, NY 13820
Chief Clerk:
Patricia Pettit 607-432-4480/fax: 607-432-2328

Oswego
Judges
James M Metcalf: 2007   Thomas A Reynolds (Acting): 2007

Civil & Criminal Courts
Conway Municipal Ctr, 20 W Oneida St, Oswego, NY 13126
Chief Clerk:
Cassie Kinney 315-343-0415/fax: 315-343-0531

Peekskill
Judges
Thomas R Langan (Acting): 2010   William L Maher: 2013

Civil & Criminal Courts
2 Nelson Ave, Peekskill, NY 10566
Chief Clerk:
Janice Laughlin 518-563-7870/fax: 518-563-3124

Plattsburgh
Judges
Penelope D Clute: 2012   Mark J Rogers (Acting): 2007

Civil & Criminal Courts
24 US Oval, Plattsburgh, NY 12903
Chief Clerk:
Robin Germain 518-563-7870/fax: 518-563-3124

Port Jervis
Judges
Victoria B Campbell: 2008   Robert A Onofry: 2008

Civil & Criminal Courts
20 Hammond St, Port Jervis, NY 12771-2495
Chief Clerk:
Catherine Quinn 845-858-4034/fax: 845-856-2767

Poughkeepsie
Judges
John B Garrity: 2010   Ronald J McGaw

Civil & Criminal Courts
62 Civic Ctr Plz, PO Box 300, Poughkeepsie, NY 12601
Chief Clerk:
Jean Jicha 845-451-4091/fax: 845-451-4094

Rensselaer
Judges
Kathleen L Robichaud: 2007

Civil & Criminal Courts
City Hall, 505 Broadway, Rensselaer, NY 12144
Chief Clerk:
Patricia Wiesmaier 518-462-6751

Rochester
Judges
Melchor E Castro: 2011   Charles F Crimi: 2007
Mija Dixon   John E Elliott: 2014
Teresa D Johnson: 2010   Stephen T Miller: 2015
Thomas R Morse: 2007   John R Schwartz: 2013
Ellen Yacknin: 2012

Civil Court . . . . fax: 585-428-2588
6 Hall of Justice, Rochester, NY 14614
585-428-2444 Fax: 585-428-2588
Chief Clerk:
Sandra Petrella 585-428-3527

Criminal Court . . . . fax: 585-428-2732
123 Public Safety Bldg, Rochester, NY 14614
585-428-2447 Fax: 585-428-2732
Chief Clerk:
Sandra Petrella 585-428-3527

Rome
Judges
John C Gannon   Daniel C Wilson: 2013

Civil & Criminal Courts
100 W Court St, Rome, NY 13440
Chief Clerk:
Eleanor T Coniglio 315-337-6440/fax: 315-338-0343

Rye
Judges
John L Alfano: 2007   Peter Lane: 2009

Offices and agencies generally appear in alphabetical order, except when specific order is requested by listee.

JUDICIAL BRANCH / City Courts Outside New York City

Civil & Criminal Courts
21 McCullough Pl, Rye, NY 10580
Chief Clerk:
Antoinette Cipriano. 914-967-1599/fax: 914-967-3308

Salamanca

Judges
William J Gabler (Acting): 2010   Ronald D Ploetz

Civil & Criminal Courts
225 Wildwood Ave, Salamanca, NY 14779
Chief Clerk:
Stella Johnston 716-945-4153/fax: 716-945-2362
e-mail: ssjohnst@courts.state.ny.us

Saratoga Springs

Judges
James E Doern (Part Time): 2010   Douglas C Mills: 2008

Civil & Criminal Courts
City Hall, 474 Broadway, Ste 3, Saratoga Springs, NY 12866
Chief Clerk:
Elizabeth M Thornhill 518-581-1797

Schenectady

Judges
Christine Clark   Guido A Loyola: 2008
Vincent W Versaci: 2008

Civil Court
City Hall, 105 Jay St, Schenectady, NY 12305
Chief Clerk:
Patricia Jordan 518-382-5077

Criminal Court
531 Liberty St, Schenectady, NY 12305
Chief Clerk:
Patricia Jordan 518-382-5077

Sherrill

Judges
Neal P Rose: 2008

Civil & Criminal Courts
373 Sherrill Rd, Sherrill, NY 13461
Chief Clerk:
Carol A Shea 315-363-0996/fax: 315-363-1176

Syracuse

Judges
James H Cecile: 2007   Stephen J Dougherty: 2012
Thomas W Higgins: 2010   Langston C McKinney: 2007
Jeffrey R Merrill: 2014   Kate Rosenthal: 2010
Karen M Uplinger: 2011   Kevin G Young

Civil & Criminal Courts
505 S State St, Syracuse, NY 13202
Chief Clerk:
Lucia Sanders 315-671-2782/fax: 315-671-2741

Tonawanda

Judges
Joseph J Cassata: 2011   S Michael Rua (Acting): 2007

Civil & Criminal Courts. fax: 716-693-1612
200 Niagara St, Tonawanda, NY 14150
716-846-2160 Fax: 716-693-1612
Chief Clerk:
Mary Strobel. 716-845-2164
e-mail: mstrobel@courts.state.ny.us

Troy

Judges
Christopher T Maier: 2014   Matthew J Turner: 2010

Civil & Criminal Court
51 State St, 3rd Fl, Troy, NY 12180
Chief Clerk:
Karen DeBenedetto 518-271-1604

Utica

Judges
John S Balzano: 2008   Ralph J Eannace: 2013
Gerald J Popeo: 2010

Civil & Criminal Courts
411 Oriskany St W, Utica, NY 13502
Chief Clerk:
Steven V Pecheone 315-724-8157/fax: 315-792-8038

Watertown

Judges
Eugene R Renzi (Part Time): 2008

Civil & Criminal Courts
Municipal Bldg, 245 Washington St, Watertown, NY 13601
Chief Clerk:
Agnes Zaremba 315-785-7785/fax: 315-785-7917

Watervliet

Judges
Thomas Lamb: 2010   Susan B Reinfurt (Acting): 2010

Civil & Criminal Courts
2 - 15th St, Watervliet, NY 12189
Chief Clerk:
Robin Robillard 518-270-3803

White Plains

Judges
JoAnn Friia   Brian Hansbury: 2009
Barbara A Leak: 2007   Eric P Press: 2009

Civil & Criminal Courts
77 S Lexington Ave, White Plains, NY 10601
Chief Clerk:
Patricia Lupi 914-824-5675/fax: 914-422-6058

Offices and agencies generally appear in alphabetical order, except when specific order is requested by listee.

JUDICIAL BRANCH / City Courts Outside New York City

Yonkers

Judges
Robert C Cerrato: 2010
Arthur J Doran: 2012
Thomas R Daly: 2010
Arthur J Doran III: 2013
Michael A Martinelli: 2015

Civil & Criminal Courts
100 S Broadway, Yonkers, NY 10701
Chief Clerk:
    Marisa Garcia 914-377-6326/fax: 914-377-6395

Offices and agencies generally appear in alphabetical order, except when specific order is requested by listee.

Section 2:
POLICY AREAS

AGRICULTURE
New York State

GOVERNOR'S OFFICE

Governor's Office
Executive Chamber
State Capitol
Albany, NY 12224
518-474-8390 Fax: 518-474-1513
Web site: www.state.ny.us

Governor:
  Eliot Spitzer 518-474-8390
Secretary to the Governor:
  Richard Baum 518-474-4246
Counsel to the Governor:
  David Nocenti 518-474-8343
Senior Advisor to the Governor:
  Lloyd Constantine 518-486-9671
Director, Communications:
  Darren Dopp 518-474-8418
Deputy Secretary, Environment:
  Judith Enck 518-472-5442

EXECUTIVE DEPARTMENTS AND RELATED AGENCIES

Agriculture & Markets Department
10B Airline Dr
Albany, NY 12235
518-457-3880 Fax: 518-457-3087
e-mail: info@agmkt.state.ny.us
Web site: www.agmkt.state.ny.us

Commissioner:
  Patrick Hooker 518-457-8876
First Deputy Commissioner:
  Thomas Lindberg 518-457-2771
Deputy Commissioner:
  Jeremiah Cosgrove 518-457-3136
Deputy Commissioner:
  Catherine Durand 518-485-7728
Deputy Commissioner:
  Jacqueline Moody-Czub 518-457-0752
Special Assistant:
  Robert Haggerty 518-457-0752
Special Assistant:
  Chip Pratt 518-457-0752
Special Assistant:
  Rebecca Smith 518-457-3136
Special Assistant:
  Vacant 518-485-7728
Executive Assistant:
  Richard Bennett 518-457-8876
Public Information Officer:
  Jessica Chittenden 518-457-3136/fax: 518-457-3087
  e-mail: jessica.chittenden@agmkt.state.ny.us

Agricultural Protection & Development Services
Director:
  William Kimball 518-457-7076/fax: 518-457-2716
  Migrant Labor Programs
  Coordinator:
    Vacant 518-457-7076
  Agricultural Protection Unit
  Chief:
    Bob Somers 518-457-2713

Animal Industry .... fax: 518-485-7773
Director:
  John Huntley 518-457-3502
Assistant Director:
  Bruce Ackey 518-457-3502
Companion Animal & Dog Licensing:
  Roberta Brooks 518-485-7965
Milk Ring Tests:
  Erin Bond 518-457-7757
DAHP & Pullorum:
  Mary Beth Dobrucki 518-457-5558
NYSCHAP, Tuberculosis & Brucellosis:
  Sandy McKay 518-457-5365
Animal Exports & Imports:
  Pat Panepinto 518-457-3971
Veterinarian Accreditation:
  Pam Hull 518-485-9964

Counsel's Office .... fax: 518-457-8842
Counsel:
  Ruth Moore 518-457-1059
Supervising Attorney:
  Michael McCormick 518-457-2449
Penalty Litigation Unit:
  Nancy Bogaard 518-485-8741

Fiscal Management .... fax: 518-485-7750
Director:
  Lucy Roberson 518-457-2080

Food Laboratory .... fax: 518-485-8097
Director:
  Daniel Rice 518-457-4477
Assistant Director:
  Debra Oglesby 518-485-5012
Associate Food Chemist:
  Kurt Mangione 518-457-2453
Associate Food Chemist:
  Virginia Greene 518-485-8098

Food Safety & Inspection .... fax: 518-485-8986
Director:
  Joseph Corby 518-457-4492
Assistant Director:
  Curtis Vincent 518-457-5382
Director, Field Operations:
  Steve Stich 518-457-5380
Food Products Quality Manager:
  William Lyons 518-457-2090

Offices and agencies generally appear in alphabetical order, except when specific order is requested by listee.

AGRICULTURE / New York State

Supervisor, Compliance:
  Erin Sawyer 518-457-2840
Poultry, Fruit & Vegetable Inspector:
  Michael Jones 518-457-2090
  Field Operations
    Brooklyn . . . . fax: 718-722-2836
    55 Hanson Place, Rm 378, Brooklyn, NY 11217-1583
      Chief Inspector:
        Richard Olson 718-722-2838
    Buffalo . . . . fax: 716-847-3155
    Donovan St Ofc Bldg, 125 Main St, Buffalo, NY 14203
      Supervising Inspector:
        Dan Gump 716-847-3185
    Hauppauge . . . . fax: 631-952-3390
    Suffolk State Office Bldg, Veteran's Memorial Hwy, Hauppauge, NY 11787-5532
      Farm Prod Grading Inspector 3:
        Steve Macomber 631-952-3079
    Rochester . . . . fax: 585-424-1248
    900 Jefferson Rd, Rochester, NY 14623
      Supervising Food Inspector:
        Evelyn Miles 585-427-2273
      Chief Inspector:
        Vacant 716-427-0200
    Syracuse
    Art & Home Center, New York State Fairgrounds, Syracuse, NY 13209
      Supervising Food Regional Supervisor:
        John Luker 315-487-0852/fax: 315-487-1064

Human Resources . . . . fax: 518-457-8852
Director:
  Karen Stenard 518-457-3216

Information Systems . . . . fax: 518-457-7815
Director:
  Dolores C Dybas 518-457-7368

Internal Audit . . . . fax: 518-457-3087
Director:
  Vacant 518-457-4418

Milk Control & Dairy Services . . . . fax: 518-485-8730
Director:
  Will Francis 518-457-1772
Assistant Director:
  James Fitts 518-457-5731
Supervisor, Milk Licensing:
  Charles Huff 518-457-4142
Compliance Officer:
  Casey McCue 518-457-8870

New York City Office . . . . fax: 718-722-2836
55 Hanson Place, Brooklyn, NY 11217-1583
Chief, Food Safety & Inspection:
  Rich Olson 718-722-2876
Office Manager:
  Melba Delgado 718-722-2850
Director, Kosher Law Enforcement:
  Luzer Weiss 718-722-2852
Director, Kosher Food Marketing:
  Vacant 718-722-2834

Plant Industry . . . . fax: 518-457-1204
Director:
  Robert J Mungari 518-457-2087

Soil & Water Conservation Committee . . . . fax: 518-457-3412
10B Airline Dr, Albany, NY 12235

518-457-3738 Fax: 518-457-3412
Web site: www.nys-soilandwater.org
Chair:
  Dennis Hill 518-457-3738
Director:
  Ron Kaplewicz 518-457-3738
  e-mail: ron.kaplewicz@agmkt.state.ny.us
Assistant Director:
  Mike Latham 518-457-3738
  e-mail: michael.latham@agmkt.state.ny.us
Coordinator, Agricultural Environmental Management Program:
  Jeff Ten Eyck 518-457-3738
  e-mail: jeff.teneyck@agmkt.state.ny.us

State Fair . . . . fax: 315-487-9260
581 State Fair Blvd, Syracuse, NY 13209
315-487-7711 Fax: 315-487-9260
Web site: www.nysfair.org/fair
Director:
  Daniel O'Hara 315-487-7711 x1200
Deputy Director:
  Matthew Morgan 315-487-7711 x1221

Statistics . . . . fax: 518-453-6564
Fax: 518-453-6564
Web site: www.nass.usda.gov/ny
State Statistician:
  Stephen C Ropel 518-457-5570
Deputy State Statistician:
  Blair Smith 518-487-5870

Weights & Measures . . . . fax: 518-457-5693
Director:
  Ross Andersen 518-457-3146
Metrologist:
  William Fishman 518-485-8377
Metrologist:
  Edward Szesnat 518-457-4781

NEW YORK STATE LEGISLATURE

See Legislative Branch in Section 1 for additional Standing Committee and Subcommittee information.

Assembly Standing Committees

Agriculture
Chair:
  William Magee (D) 518-455-4807
Ranking Minority Member:
  Clifford W Crouch (R) 518-455-5741

Assembly Task Force

Food, Farm & Nutrition, Task Force on
Chair:
  Jose Rivera (D) 518-455-5414
Program Manager:
  Robert Stern 518-455-5203

Senate Standing Committees

Agriculture
Chair:
  Catharine M Young (R) 518-455-3563

Offices and agencies generally appear in alphabetical order, except when specific order is requested by listee.

AGRICULTURE / U.S. Government

Ranking Minority Member:
  David J Valesky (D)..............................518-455-2838

Senate/Assembly Legislative Commissions

Rural Resources, Legislative Commission on
Senate Chair:
  George H Winner Jr (R)..........................518-455-2091
Assembly Vice Chair:
  David R Koon (D)................................518-455-5784
Senate Executive Director:
  Ronald C Brach..................518-455-2544/fax: 518-426-6960
Assembly Director:
  Susan Bartle....................518-455-3999/fax: 518-455-4175
Counsel:
  Donald A Walsh..................................518-455-2544

Toxic Substances & Hazardous Wastes, Legislative Commission on
Senate Chair:
  Vacant..518-455-0000
Assembly Vice Chair:
  David R Koon (D)................................518-455-5784
Program Manager:
  Richard D Morse, Jr.............518-455-3711/fax: 518-455-3837

Water Resource Needs of NYS & Long Island, Legislative Commission on
Assembly Co-Chair:
  Vacant..518-455-0000
Senate Co-Chair:
  Vacant..518-455-0000
Program Manager:
  Richard D Morse, Jr.............518-455-3711/fax: 518-455-3837

U.S. Government

EXECUTIVE DEPARTMENTS AND RELATED AGENCIES

Commodity Futures Trading Commission
Web site: www.cftc.gov

Eastern Region
140 Broadway, New York, NY 10005
Regional Coordinator:
  Stephen J Obie...................646-746-9700/fax: 646-746-9766

US Commerce Department
Web site: www.doc.gov

National Oceanic & Atmospheric Administration

National Weather Service, Eastern Region
630 Johnson Ave, Ste 202, Bohemia, NY 11716
Web site: www.nws.noaa.gov
Director:
  Dean Gulezian...................631-244-0100/fax: 631-244-0109
  e-mail: dean.gulezian@noaa.gov
Deputy Director:
  Mickey J Brown..................................631-244-0102
Public Affairs Officer:
  Marcie Katcher..................631-244-0149/fax: 631-244-0167
Chief, Meteorological Services Division:
  John Guiney.....................................631-244-0121
Chief, Regional Hydrology Division:
  Peter Gabrielsen................................631-244-0111
Chief, Scientific Services Division:
  Kenneth Johnson.................................631-244-0136

US Department of Agriculture
Web site: www.usda.gov

Agricultural Marketing Service

Dairy Programs
Web site: www.ams.usda.gov
  Northeast Marketing Area....................fax: 518-464-6468
  1 Columbia Circle, Albany, NY 12203
  Assistant Market Administrator:
    John F Poole..................................518-452-4410

Fruit & Vegetable Division
  Fresh Products Branch - Bronx Field Office......fax: 718-589-5108
  465B NYC Terminal Market, Bronx, NY 10474
  Officer-in-Charge:
    Cathy Hance...................................718-991-7665
  Market News Branch—New York State..........fax: 718-378-0891
  NYC Terminal Market, Rm 4A, Bronx, NY 10474
  Officer-in-Charge:
    Edward Martello...............................718-542-2225

USDA-AMS Poultry Grading Branch
  Gastonia Region—New York Office.............fax: 518-459-5163
  21 Aviation Rd, Albany, NY 12205
  Federal-State Supervisor:
    Dennis McAuliffe..............................518-459-5487

Agricultural Research Service

North Atlantic Area
  Ithaca NY Research Units
  Plant Genetic Resources Unit....................fax: 315-787-2339
  USDA, 630 W North St, Geneva, NY 14456-0462
  Research Leader:
    Philip Forsline...............................315-787-2356

Animal Plant Health Inspection Service
Web site: www.aphis.usda.gov

Plant Protection Quarantine (PPQ) Programs-Eastern Region....fax: 919-855-7393
920 Main Campus Dr, Ste 200, Raleigh, NC 27606-5213
Eastern Regional Director:
  Victor Harabin..................................919-716-5576
  Avoca Work Unit.............................fax: 607-566-2081
  8237 Kanona Rd, Avoca, NY 14809-9729
  Director:
    Daniel J Kepich...............................607-566-2212
    e-mail: daniel.j.kepich@aphis.usda.gov
  Batavia Work Station........................fax: 585-343-5538
  29 Liberty St, Ste 1, Batavia, NY 14020
  PPQ Officer:
    Lewis Tandy...............................585-343-9167 x1033
    e-mail: lewis.tandy@aphis.usda.gov
  Big Flats Work Station......................fax: 607-562-3470
  USDA Plant Material Ctr, 3266-B State Rte 352, Corning, NY 14830

Offices and agencies generally appear in alphabetical order, except when specific order is requested by listee.

AGRICULTURE / U.S. Government

PPQ Officer:
Lawrence R Kershaw 607-562-3459
Canandaigua Work Station . . . . fax: 585-394-8367
3037 County Rd 10, Canandaigua, NY 14424
Senior PPQ Officer:
Cynthia A Estey 585-394-0525 x5
e-mail: cynthia.a.estey@aphis.usda.gov
JFK International Airport Inspection Station
230-59 Intl Airport Ctr Blvd, Jamaica, NY 11413
Supervising PPQ Officer:
Lubomira Rydl 718-553-1732/fax: 718-553-0060
New York State Office . . . . fax: 518-869-5136
500 New Karner Rd, Albany, NY 12205
State Plant Health Director:
Yvonne Demrino 518-869-5540
Oneida Work Station
248 Main St, 1st Fl, Oneida, NY 13421
Senior PPQ Officer:
Paul F Wrege 315-361-4281/fax: 315-363-3657
e-mail: paul.f.wrege@usda.gov
Westhampton Beach Work Station . . . . fax: 631-288-6021
4 Stewart Ave, Westhampton Beach, NY 11978-1103
PPQ Officer:
Willy Hsiang 631-288-4191

Veterinary Services
NY Animal Import Center
200 Drury Lane, Rock Tavern, NY 12575
Veterinarian-in-Charge:
Dr Kenneth Davis 845-564-2950/fax: 845-564-1075
New York Area Office
500 New Karner Rd, 2nd Fl, Albany, NY 12205
Veterinarian-in-Charge, New York Area:
Roxanne C Mullaney 518-869-9007/fax: 518-869-6135

Cornell Cooperative Extension Service
Roberts Hall, Rm 365, Cornell University, Ithaca, NY 14853-5905
State Director:
Helene Dillard 607-255-2237/fax: 607-255-0788

Farm Service Agency, New York State Office . . . . fax: 315-477-6323
441 S Salina St, Rm 536, Syracuse, NY 13202-2455
State Director:
Brymer Humphreys 315-477-6303

Food & Nutrition Service

Albany Field Office . . . . fax: 518-431-4271
O'Brien Federal Bldg, Rm 752, 1 Clinton Ave & N Pearl St, Albany, NY 12207
Officer-in-Charge:
Claudia Ortiz 518-431-4274
e-mail: claudia.ortiz@FNS.usda.gov

New York City Field Office . . . . fax: 212-620-6948
201 Varick St, Rm 609, New York, NY 10014
Assistant Director:
Denise Thomas 212-620-7360

Rochester Field Office
Federal Bldg, 100 State St, Rm 318, Rochester, NY 14614
Officer in Charge:
Claudia Ortiz 585-263-6748/fax: 585-263-5807

Food Safety & Inspection Service
Web site: www.fsis.usda.gov

Field Operations - Albany District Office . . . . fax: 518-452-3118
230 Washington Ave Ext, Albany, NY 12203-5388

District Manager:
Louis C Leny 518-452-6870

National Agricultural Statistics Service-NYS Office . . . . fax: 518-485-8719
10B Airline Dr, Albany, NY 12235
800-821-1276 Fax: 518-485-8719
Director:
Stephen C Ropel 518-457-5570

Office of the Inspector General, Northeast Region . . . . . . fax: 212-264-8416
26 Federal Plaza, Room 1409, New York, NY 10278
Special Agent-in-Charge, Investigation:
Brian L Haaser 212-264-8400
Assistant Special Agent-in-Charge, Investigation:
Bethanne Marik 212-264-8400
Assistant Special Agent-in-Charge, Investigation:
William G Squires 212-264-8400

Rural Development
Web site: www.rurdev.usda.gov/ny

New York State Office . . . . fax: 315-477-6438
The Galleries of Syracuse, 441 S Salina St, Ste 357, 5th Fl, Syracuse, NY 13202-2425
TTY: 315-477-6447 or 315-477-6400 Fax: 315-477-6438
Acting State Director:
Scott Collins 315-477-6400
Special Projects Representative:
Vacant 315-477-6433
Program Director, Rural Business-Cooperative Service:
Walter D Schermerhorn 315-477-6425
e-mail: walter.schermerhorn@ny.usda.gov
Program Director, Rural Utilities Service:
David Miller 315-477-6427
e-mail: david.miller@ny.usda.gov
Program Director, Rural Housing Service:
George Von Pless 315-477-6419
e-mail: george.vonpless@ny.usda.gov
Human Resources Manager:
Brenda Chewning-Kulick 315-477-6439

USDA/GIPSA, Packers & Stockyards Pgms-Atlantic Region . . . . fax: 404-562-5848
75 Spring St, Ste 230, Atlanta, GA 30303
Regional Supervisor:
Elkin Parker 404-562-5840

US Department of Homeland Security (DHS)
Web site: www.dhs.gov

Customs & Border Protection (CBP)
202-354-1000
Web site: www.cbp.gov

Agricultural Inspections (AI)
Brooklyn, Port of
6405 7th Ave, 3rd Fl, Brooklyn, NY 11220
Supervising Ag Specialist:
Willie J Martin 718-340-5225/fax: 718-340-5224
Buffalo, Port of
1 Peace Bridge Plaza, Room 316, Buffalo, NY 14213
Supervisor:
Brent Speicher 716-884-5701/fax: 716-884-5679
Champlain, Port of . . . . fax: 518-298-8395
237 West Service Rd, Suite 2, Champlain, NY 12919
518-298-8327 Fax: 518-298-8395

Offices and agencies generally appear in alphabetical order, except when specific order is requested by listee.

AGRICULTURE / Private Sector

Agriculture Specialist:
　Vacant....................................518-298-4332
JFK International Airport Area Office...........fax: 718-487-5191
　JFK Int'l Airport, Bldg #77, 2nd Fl, Jamaica, NY 11430
　718-487-5164 Fax: 718-487-5191
　Port Director:
　　Camille Polimeni..........................718-487-5164
　Canine Kennel:
　　James Armstrong...........................718-553-1659

Plum Island Animal Disease Center
PO Box 848, Greenport, NY 11944
Deputy Director of Operations:
　Gerald Jennings....................631-323-3202/fax: 631-323-3295

U.S. CONGRESS

See U.S. Congress Chapter for additional Standing Committee and Subcommittee information.

House of Representatives Standing Committees

Agriculture
Chair:
　Collin C Peterson (D-MN)..........................202-225-2165
Ranking Minority Member:
　Bob Goodlatte (R-VA).............................202-225-5431

Appropriations
Chair:
　David R Obey (D-WI)..............................202-225-3365
Ranking Minority Member:
　Jerry Lewis (R-CA)...............................202-225-5861
New York Delegate:
　Maurice D Hinchey (D)............................202-225-6335
New York Delegate:
　Nita M Lowey (D)................................202-225-6506
New York Delegate:
　Jose E Serrano (D)...............................202-225-4361
New York Delegate:
　John E Sweeney (R)...............................202-225-5614
New York Delegate:
　James T Walsh (R)................................202-225-3705

　Subcommittee
　Agriculture, Rural Development, FDA & Related Agencies
　Chair:
　　Rosa DeLauro (D-CT)..........................202-225-2638
　Ranking Minority Member:
　　Jack Kingston (R-GA).........................202-225-5831
　New York Delegate:
　　Maurice D Hinchey (D)........................202-225-6335

Senate Standing Committees

Agriculture, Nutrition & Forestry
Chair:
　Tom Harkin (D-IA)...............................202-224-3254
Ranking Republican Member:
　Saxby Chambliss (R-GA)..........................202-224-3521

Appropriations
Chair:
　Robert C Byrd (D-WV)............................202-224-3954
Ranking Minority Member:
　Thad Cochran (R-MS).............................202-224-5054

　Subcommittee
　Agriculture, Rural Development, FDA & Related Agencies
　Chair:
　　Herb Kohl (D-WI)............................202-224-5653
　Ranking Minority Member:
　　Robert Bennett (R-UT).......................202-224-5444

Private Sector

Agricultural Affiliates
638 Lake St, PO Box 10, Wilson, NY 14172-0010
716-751-9331 Fax: 716-751-6141
e-mail: agaffiliat@aol.com
Peter Russell, President
Advise & inform agriculture industry on labor issues & related public policy

American Farmland Trust, Northeast Regional Office
112 Spring Street, Suite 207, Saratoga Springs, NY 12866
518-581-0078 Fax: 518-581-0079
e-mail: neaft@farmland.org
Web site: www.farmland.org
David Haight, Northeast Regional Director
Advocacy & education to protect farmland & promote environmentally sound farming practices

American Society for the Prevention of Cruelty to Animals (ASPCA)
424 E 92nd St, New York, NY 10128-6804
212-876-7700 x4552 Fax: 212-360-6875
e-mail: government@aspca.org
Web site: www.aspca.org
Lisa Weisberg, Senior Vice President, Government Affairs & Public Policy, Senior Policy Advisor
Promoting humane treatment of animals, education & advocacy programs & conducting statewide anti-cruelty investigation & enforcement

Associated New York State State Food Processors Inc
16 Loretta Dr, Ste 100, Spencerport, NY 14559
585-352-7766 Fax: 585-349-2334
e-mail: jackie@nyfoodprocessors.org
Web site: www.nyfoodprocessors.org
Jacqueline J Arnold, Executive Secretary

Offices and agencies generally appear in alphabetical order, except when specific order is requested by listee.

AGRICULTURE / Private Sector

Birds Eye Foods Inc
90 Linden Oaks, PO Box 20670, Rochester, NY 14602-0670
585-383-1850
e-mail: media@birdseyefoods.com
Web site: www.birdseyefoods.com
Bea Slizewski, Vice President, Corporate Communications
Produces & markets processed food products

Christmas Tree Farmers Association of New York Inc
646 Finches Corners Rd, Red Creek, NY 13143
315-754-8132 Fax: 315-754-8499
e-mail: bnorris@usadatanet.net
Web site: www.christmastreesny.org
Robert D Norris, Executive Director
Fresh Christmas trees & evergreen wreaths

Consumers Union
101 Truman Ave, Yonkers, NY 10703-1057
914-378-2000 Fax: 914-378-2900
Web site: www.consumerreports.org; www.consumersunion.org
Jean Halloran, Director, Consumer Policy Institute
Food safety issues including genetically engineered food, microbial safety of food, toxic chemical issues, pesticides, integrated pest management, sustainable agriculture

Cornell Cooperative Extension
365 Roberts Hall, Cornell University, Ithaca, NY 14853-5905
607-255-2237 Fax: 607-255-0788
e-mail: cedir@cornell.edu
Web site: www.cce.cornell.edu
Helene Dillard, Director
Extension educational system & outreach

Community & Rural Development Institute
43 Warren Hall, Cornell University, Ithaca, NY 14853
607-255-9510 Fax: 607-255-2231
e-mail: cardi@cornell.edu
Web site: www.cardi.cornell.edu
Rod Howe, Executive Director
Provides research, education & policy analysis on critical community & rural development issues

Cornell Cooperative Extension, Pesticide Management Education Program
5123 Comstock Hall, Cornell University, Ithaca, NY 14853-0901
607-255-1866 Fax: 607-255-3075
e-mail: rdg5@cornell.edu
Web site: pmep.cce.cornell.edu
Ronald D Gardner, Senior Extension Associate

Cornell Cooperative Extension, Urban Agriculture & Markets Program
Cornell University, 16 East 34th St, New York, NY 10016
212-340-2946 Fax: 212-340-2908
e-mail: jma20@cornell.edu
Web site: www.cce.cornell.edu
John Ameroso, Extension Educator
Farmer recruitment & training for urban farmers' markets; community gardens advisory; food access/food security policy

Cornell Farmedic Training Program
Cornell University, 777 Warren Rd, Ithaca, NY 14850
800-437-6010 Fax: 607-253-3907
e-mail: farmedic@cornell.edu
Web site: www.farmedic.com
Eric Hallman, Director Ag. Health & Safety Program
Training programs for emergency providers & agricultural workers to reduce mortality, injury & property loss from agricultural emergencies

Cornell University, College of Agriculture & Life Sciences, Animal Science
149 Morrison Hall, Ithaca, NY 14853
607-255-2862 or 607-255-5497 Fax: 607-255-9829
e-mail: wrb2@cornell.edu; anscinfo@cornell.edu
Web site: www.ansci.cornell.edu
W R Butler, Department Chair
Nutritional physiology

Cornell University, Community, Food & Agriculture Program
Dept of Rural Sociology, 216 Warren Hall, Ithaca, NY 14853
607-255-0417 Fax: 607-254-2896
e-mail: hmm1@cornell.edu
Web site: www.cfap.org
Heidi Mouillesseaux-Kunzman, Program Coordinator
To support food & agriculture based community development in NY & the Northeast through integrated, multi-disciplinary & participating teaching, research & extension activities

Cornell University, Department of Applied Economics & Management
357 Warren Hall, Ithaca, NY 14853-7801
607-255-4534 Fax: 607-255-1589
e-mail: ell4@cornell.edu
Web site: www.aem.cornell.edu/profiles/ladue.htm
Eddy L LaDue, W I Myers Professor of Agricultural Finance
Agricultural finance

Cornell University, Development Sociology
Community Food & Agriculture Program, 216 Warren Hall, Ithaca, NY 14853
607-255-4413 Fax: 607-254-2896
e-mail: dlh3@cornell.edu
Web site: www.cfap.org
Duncan Hilchey, Agricultural Development Specialist
Ethnic markets, cooperatives, farmers' markets, agritourism, agricultural marketing, regional identity

Cornell University, FarmNet Program
Dept of Applied Economics & Management, 415 Warren Hall, Ithaca, NY 14853-7801
607-255-4121 or 800-547-3276 Fax: 607-254-7435
e-mail: nyfarmnet@cornell.edu
Web site: www.nyfarmnet.org
Ed Staehr, Program Director
Farm family resource library; financial & family consultations; workshops for agricultural services professionals & farmers

Offices and agencies generally appear in alphabetical order, except when specific order is requested by listee.

AGRICULTURE / Private Sector

Cornell University, Program on Dairy Markets & Policy
Agriculture & Life Sciences, 316 Warren Hall, Ithaca, NY 14853-7801
607-255-7602 Fax: 607-255-9984
e-mail: amn3@cornell.edu
Web site: www.cpdmp.cornell.edu
Andrew Novakovic, Director
Applied research and extension education program

Dairylea Cooperative Inc
PO Box 4844, Syracuse, NY 13221-4844
315-433-0100 or 800-654-8838 Fax: 315-433-2345
e-mail: clyde.rutherford@dairylea.com
Web site: www.dairylea.com
Clyde Rutherford, President
Maximizes net returns at the farm by preserving and enhancing milk markets and milk-marketing relationships, and by providing services and programs that create real economic value.

Empire State Honey Producers Association
273 Randall Rd, Lisbon, NY 13658
315-322-4208
e-mail: harmonydeb@starband.net
Web site: www.eshpa.org
Deborah Kalicin, Secretary/Treasurer
Promote & protect the interests of beekeepers in NYS

Empire State Potato Growers Inc
PO Box 566, Stanley, NY 14561-0566
585-526-5356 Fax: 585-526-6576
e-mail: mwickham@empirepotatogrowers.com
Web site: www.empirepotatogrowers.com
Melanie Wickham, Executive Secretary
To foster the potato industry in NYS

Farm Sanctuary
PO Box 150, Watkins Glen, NY 14891
607-583-2225 Fax: 607-583-2041
e-mail: info@farmsancturary.org
Web site: www.farmsanctuary.org
Gene Baur, President
Farm animal rescue; public information programs & advocacy for the humane treatment of animals

Farmers' Market Federation of NY
2100 Park St, Syracuse, NY 13208
315-475-1101 Fax: 315-362-5012
e-mail: diane.eggert@verizon.net
Web site: www.nyfarmersmarket.com
Diane Eggert, Director
Education & services to NY's farmers markets.

Food Industry Alliance of New York State Inc
130 Washington Ave, Albany, NY 12210
518-434-1900 Fax: 518-434-9962
e-mail: michael@fiany.com
Web site: www.fiany.com
Michael Rosen, Vice President for Government Relations & General Counsel
Assn of retail grocery, wholesale & supplier/manufacturer food companies

Fund for Animals (The)
200 W 57th St, New York, NY 10019
212-757-3425 Fax: 212-246-2633
Web site: www.fund.org
Marian Probst, Chair
Working to protect all animals through education, legislation, litigation & hands-on care

New York State Flower Industries Inc
Garden Gate Greenhouse
11649 W Perrysburg Rd, Perrysburg, NY 14129
716-532-6282
Gary Patterson, President
Greenhouse plant production

Global Gardens Program, New York Botanical Garden (The)
200th St & Kazimiroff Blvd, Bronx, NY 10458-5126
718-817-8700 Fax: 718-817-8178
e-mail: emccarthy@nybg.org
Web site: www.nybg.org
Toby Adams, Family Garden Manager
Promoting understanding of ethnic diversity & the interconnectedness of cultures through gardening

GreenThumb
49 Chambers Street, Room 1020, New York, NY 10007
212-788-8070 Fax: 212-788-8052
e-mail: edie@greenthumbnyc.org
Web site: www.greenthumbnyc.org
Edie Stone, Director
Development & preservation of community gardens; reclamation of urban land for green space

Greenmarket/Council on the Environment of NYC
51 Chambers Street, Room 228, New York, NY 10007
212-788-7900 Fax: 212-788-7913
e-mail: conyc@cenyc.org
Web site: www.cenyc.org
Robert Kafin, Director
Direct to consumer farmers' markets, sustainable agriculture

Hill & Gosdeck
99 Washington Ave, Ste 400, Albany, NY 12210-2823
518-463-5449 x3102 Fax: 518-463-0947
e-mail: tjgosdeck@aol.com
Thomas J Gosdeck, Partner
Workers compensation, group self insurance and food industry regulation

Humane Society of the United States, Mid Atlantic Regional Office
270 US Hwy 206, Flanders, NJ 07836
973-927-5611 Fax: 973-927-5617
e-mail: maro@hsus.org
Web site: www.hsus.org
Nina Austenberg, Regional Director

Policy Areas

Offices and agencies generally appear in alphabetical order, except when specific order is requested by listee.

AGRICULTURE / Private Sector

Long Island Farm Bureau
104 Edwards Ave, Suite 3, Calverton, NY 11923
631-727-3777 Fax: 631-727-3721
e-mail: askus@lifb.com
Web site: www.lifb.com
Joseph M Gergela, III, Executive Director
Provides strong, networked and allied Farm Bureau organizations at the local, state and national organization levels. Goal is to protect and strengthen the nation's agricultural industry.

Long Island Nursery & Landscape Association Inc
PO Box 1165, Farmingdale, NY 11735
516-249-0545 Fax: 516-249-0740
e-mail: linla@nysnla.com
Ruth Dougherty, Secretary
A professional association serving retail garden center, nursery and landscape businesses on Long Island. Fosters professionalism in the green industry while cultivating a high standard of business ethics.

National Potato Board
McCormick Farms Inc
4189 Route 78, Bliss, NY 14024
585-322-7274 Fax: 585-322-7495
James P McCormick, NYS Delegate

My-T Acres Inc
8127 Lewiston Rd, Batavia, NY 14020
585-343-1026 Fax: 585-343-2051
Peter Call, Co-Owner
Vegetable crops & grain

NOFA-NY Certified Organic LLC
840 Upper Front St, Binghamton, NY 13905-1542
607-724-9851 Fax: 607-724-9853
e-mail: certifiedorganic@nofany.org
Web site: www.nofany.org
Carol King, Program Representative
Organic farming certification

NY Farms!
125 Williams Rd, Candor, NY 13743
607-659-3710 or 888-NYFARMS Fax: 607-659-3710
e-mail: nyfarms@nyfarms.info
Web site: www.nyfarms.info
Gene Pierce, President
Campaign to promote farming & protect farmland in NYS

NYS Agricultural Society
493 Charlton Rd, Ballston Spa, NY 12020
518-384-1715
e-mail: penny@nysagsociety.org
Web site: www.nysagsociety.org
Penny Heritage, Executive Secretary
To improve the condition of agriculture through education, leadership development & recognition programs

NYS Arborists
PO Box 306, Pawling, NY 12564-0306
845-855-0225 Fax: 845-855-0387
e-mail: execsec@newyorkstatearborists.com
Web site: www.newyorkstatearborists.com
David Hayner, Executive Secretary
Professional arborists & educators; promote public interest, foster research & education in the care & benefits of trees, shrubs & their environment

NYS Association For Food Protection
Cornell University, Dept of Food Science, 172 Stocking Hall, Ithaca, NY 14853
607-255-2892 Fax: 607-255-7619
e-mail: jgg3@cornell.edu
Web site: www.foodscience.cornell.edu/nysfsanit/index.html
Janene Lucia, Executive Secretary

NYS Association of Veterinary Technicians Inc
119 Washington Ave, 2nd Floor, Albany, NY 12210
518-426-7920 Fax: 518-432-5902
e-mail: nysavt@aol.com
Web site: www.nysavt.org
Jan Dorman, Executive Director

NYS Berry Growers Association
14 State Street, Bloomfield, NY 14469
585-657-5328 Fax: 585-657-4642
e-mail: goodberries@frontiernet.net
Web site: www.nysbga.org
Jim Altemus, Executive Secretary

NYS Cheese Manufacturers Association, Department of Food Science
Cornell University, 413 Stocking Hall, Ithaca, NY 14853
607-255-3111 Fax: 607-254-4868
e-mail: kjb4@cornell.edu
Web site: www.newyorkcheese.org
Kathryn Boor, Secretary & Scientific Advisor
Cheese manufacturing education & product promotion

NYS Grange
100 Grange Place, Cortland, NY 13045
607-756-7553 Fax: 607-756-7757
e-mail: nysgrange@nysgrange.com
Web site: www.nysgrange.com
Bruce Croucher, President
Advocacy, education & services for farm, rural & suburban families

NYS Horticultural Society
PO Box 462, Hedrick Hall, Room 116, Geneva, NY 14462
315-787-2404 Fax: 315-787-2216
e-mail: wilsonk36@hotmail.com
Web site: www.nyshs.org
Paul Baker, Executive Director
Advocacy, education & member services for the fruit industry

AGRICULTURE / Private Sector

NYS Nursery/Landscape Association
24 Martin Road, Voorheesville, NY 12186
518-320-8760 or 877-210-4518 Fax: 518-694-4431
e-mail: nysnla@aol.com; suzannemm@nycap.rr.com
Web site: www.nylandscaper.com
Suzanne M Maloney, Executive Director
Trade Association

NYS Turfgrass Association
PO Box 612, Latham, NY 12110
518-783-1229 Fax: 518-783-1258
e-mail: nysta@nysta.org
Web site: www.nysta.org
Beth Seme, Executive Director
Grow & manage turf for golf courses, ball fields & landscape

NYS Vegetable Growers Association Inc
PO Box 70, Kirkville, NY 13082-0070
315-687-5734 Fax: 315-687-5734
e-mail: nysvga@twcny.rr.com
Jeff & Lindy Kubecka, Co-Contacts

NYS Weights & Measures Association
8292 State Rt 3, Harrisville, NY 13648
315-543-2820 Fax: 315-376-5874
e-mail: bcooper@lewiscountyny.org
Web site: lewiscountyny.net/wt-measures
Barbara J Cooper, Secretary
Promote uniformity in measure accuracy, enforcement standards & legal requirements

National Coffee Association
15 Maiden Ln, Ste 1405, New York, NY 10038
212-766-4007 Fax: 212-766-5815
e-mail: info@ncausa.org
Web site: www.ncausa.org
Robert F Nelson, President & Chief Executive Officer

National Grape Cooperative-Welch Foods Inc
575 Virginia Rd, 3 Concord Farms, Concord, MA 01742-9101
978-371-1000 Fax: 978-371-3707
Web site: www.welchs.com
Dave Lukiewski, President & Chief Executive Officer
Manufacturers of juices, jams and jellies.

New York Agriculture in the Classroom
Cornell University, Dept of Education, 106 Kennedy Hall, Ithaca, NY 14853
607-255-9252 or 607-255-9252 Fax: 607-255-7905
e-mail: nfw3@cornell.edu; nyaitc@cornell.edu
Web site: www.cerp.cornell.edu/aitc
Nancy Schaff, Director
An agricultural literacy program providing resources and professional development opportunities for teachers to facilitate the integration of food and fiber systems education into the curriculum

New York Apple Association Inc
7645 Main St, PO Box 350, Fishers, NY 14453-0350
585-924-2171 Fax: 585-924-1629
e-mail: jimallen@nyapplecountry.com
Web site: www.nyapplecountry.com
James Allen, President
Promote NYS apples & apple products

New York Beef Industry Council Inc
PO Box 250, Westmoreland, NY 13490
315-339-6922 Fax: 315-339-6931
e-mail: cgillis@nybeef.org
Web site: www.nybeef.org
Carol Gillis, Executive Director
Producer-directed & funded organization conducting beef promotion & information programs

New York Center for Agricultural Medicine & Health, Bassett Healthcare
1 Atwell Rd, Cooperstown, NY 13326
800-343-7527 or 607-547-6023 Fax: 607-547-6087
e-mail: info@nycamh.com
Web site: www.nycamh.com
John May, MD, Director
Occupational health & medicine in agriculture

New York Farm Bureau
159 Wolf Road, PO Box 5330, Albany, NY 12205-0330
518-436-8495 Fax: 800-342-4143
Web site: www.nyfb.org
Julie Suarez, Contact
Resources, education, advocacy, services & programs for the farming industry & community

New York Field Corn Growers Association
2269 DeWindt Rd, Newark, NY 14513
315-331-7791 Fax: 315-331-1294
e-mail: svanvoo338@aol.com
Web site: www.nycorn.org
Steven VanVoorhis, President

New York Holstein Association
957 Mitchell St, Ithaca, NY 14851
607-273-7591 or 800-834-4644 Fax: 607-273-7612
e-mail: pgifford@nyholsteins.com
Web site: www.nyholsteins.com
Patricia G Gifford, Executive Manager
Promoting the Holstein breed for the economic & social benefit of junior & senior members

New York Pork Producers Coop
12 North Pork Street, Seneca Falls, NY 13141
315-568-2750 Fax: 315-568-2752
Michael Hargrave, President
Education & promotion of pork industry in NY

Offices and agencies generally appear in alphabetical order, except when specific order is requested by listee.

AGRICULTURE / Private Sector

New York Seed Improvement Project, Cornell University, Plant Breeding Department
103C Leland Lab, Cornell University, Ithaca, NY 14853
607-255-9869 Fax: 607-255-9048
e-mail: aaw4@cornell.edu
Web site: SeedPotato.NewYork.cornell.edu
Alan Westra, Manager
Official seed certifying agency for the state of NY & foundation seedstocks agency

New York State Association of Agricultural Fairs Inc
67 Verbeck Ave, Schaghticoke, NY 12154
518-753-4956 Fax: 518-753-0208
e-mail: carousels4@aol.com
Web site: www.nyfairs.org
Norma W Hamilton, Executive Secretary

New York State Dairy Foods Inc
201 S Main St, Suite 302, North Syracuse, NY 13212
315-452-6455 Fax: 315-452-1643
Web site: www.nysdfi.org
Bruce W Krupke, Executive Vice President
Full service trade association representing dairy processing/distribution industry

New York State Maple Producers Association Inc
PO Box 210, Watkins Glens, NY 14891
607-535-9790 Fax: 607-535-9794
Web site: www.nysmaple.com
Mary Jeanne Packer, Secretary
Promoting quality maple products through education & research

New York State Veterinary Medical Society
9 Highland Ave, Albany, NY 12205-5417
518-437-0787 or 800-876-9867 Fax: 518-437-0957
e-mail: info@nysvms.org
Web site: www.nysvms.org
Julie Lawton, Executive Director

New York Thoroughbred Breeders Inc
Saratoga Spa State Park, 19 Roosevelt Drive, Saratoga Springs, NY 12866
518-580-0100 Fax: 518-580-0500
e-mail: nybreds@nybreds.com
Web site: www.nybreds.com
Martin G Kinsella, Executive Director

New York Wine & Grape Foundation
800 South Main Street, Suite 200, Canadaigua, NY 14424
585-394-3620 Fax: 585-394-3649
e-mail: info@newyorkwines.org
Web site: www.newyorkwines.org
James Trezise, President
Promotion of winery products & tours; research for wine & grape related products

NYS Bar Assn, Food, Drug & Cosmetic Law Section
North Shore-Long Island Jewish Health System
Office of Legal Affairs, 150 Community Dr, Great Neck, NY 11021
516-465-8379 Fax: 516-465-8105
e-mail: cmcgowan2@nshs.edu
Coreen McGowan, Esquire

Northeast Organic Farming Association of New York
PO Box 880, Cobleskill, NY 12043
607-652-6632
e-mail: office@nofany.org
Web site: www.nofany.org
Greg Swartz, Executive Director
Education for farmers, gardeners & consumers; organic certification program

Public Markets Partners / Baum Forum
5454 Palisade Ave, Bronx, NY 10471
718-884-5716
e-mail: hilarybaum@aol.com
Web site: www.baumforum.org
Hilary Baum, President
Partnerships with communities to develop & manage public markets to revitalize urban areas & promote regional agriculture; educational programs

Regional Farm & Food Project
PO Box 8628, Albany, NY 12208
518-271-0744
e-mail: billie@farmandfood.org
Web site: www.farmandfood.org
Billie Best, Executive Director
Building supply and demand for farm fresh local foods in the Hudson-Mohawk Valley foodshed.

Rural Opportunities Inc
400 East Ave, Rochester, NY 14607-1910
585-340-3366 Fax: 585-340-3309
e-mail: lbeaulac@ruralinc.org
Web site: www.ruralinc.org
Lee Beaulac, President
Housing & related assistance for farmworkers, seniors & the rural poor

Seneca Foods Corporation
3736 South Main St, Marion, NY 14505
315-926-8100 Fax: 315-926-8300
e-mail: webmaster@senecafoods.com
Web site: www.senecafoods.com
Kraig H Kayser, President & CEO
Vegetable food products

NYS Bar Association
Special Committee on Animals & the Law
1 Elk Street, Albany, NY 12207
518-463-3200 Fax: 518-463-4276
e-mail: hkpassantino@aol.com
Web site: www.nysba.org
Holly Kennedy Passantino, Chair

Offices and agencies generally appear in alphabetical order, except when specific order is requested by listee.

AGRICULTURE / Private Sector

Tea Association of the USA Inc
420 Lexington Ave, Suite 825, New York, NY 10170
212-986-9415 Fax: 212-697-8658
e-mail: info@teausa.com
Web site: www.teausa.com
Joe Simrany, President
Trade association for the tea industry

United Dairy Cooperative Services Inc
12 North Park St, Seneca Falls, NY 13148
315-568-2750 Fax: 315-568-2752
e-mail: unitedag@flare.net
James G Patsos, Chief Executive Officer
Management, accounting & payroll services to agriculture industry

Upstate Niagara Cooperative Inc
25 Anderson Rd, Buffalo, NY 14225
716-892-3156 Fax: 716-892-3157
Web site: www.upstateniagara.com
Bob Hall, General Manager & Chief Executive Officer

Venture Vineyards Inc
PO Box 185, Lodi, NY 14860
607-582-6774 Fax: 607-582-6342
e-mail: venturev@capital.net
Melvin P Nass, President
Produce wholesaler of grapes/juices

Offices and agencies generally appear in alphabetical order, except when specific order is requested by listee.

BANKING AND FINANCE

New York State

GOVERNOR'S OFFICE

Governor's Office
Executive Chamber
State Capitol
Albany, NY 12224
518-474-8390 Fax: 518-474-1513
Web site: www.state.ny.us

Governor:
  Eliot Spitzer 518-474-8390
Secretary to the Governor:
  Richard Baum. 518-474-4246
Counsel to the Governor:
  David Nocenti. 518-474-8343
Senior Advisor to the Governor:
  Lloyd Constantine 518-486-9671
Assistant Counsel to the Governor-Business & Financial Services:
  Gaurav Vasisht. 518-474-2266
Deputy Secretary, Economic Development & Infrastructure:
  Timothy Gilchrist. 518-408-2552
Director, Communications:
  Darren Dopp. 518-474-8418

EXECUTIVE DEPARTMENTS AND RELATED AGENCIES

Banking Department
One State St
New York, NY 10004-1417
212-709-3500 or 877-226-5697
Web site: www.banking.state.ny.us

80 S Swan Street
Suite 1157
Albany, NY 12210-8003
518-473-6160
Fax: 518-473-7204

Superintendent of Banks & Chair:
  Richard H Neiman. 212-709-3501/fax: 212-709-3520
  e-mail: richard.neiman@banking.state.ny.us
Chief Administrative Officer:
  Diana Rulon 518-473-6160
  e-mail: diana.rulon@banking.state.ny.us
Chief of Staff & Director, Communications:
  James Fuchs 212-709-1690
  e-mail: james.fuchs@banking.state.ny.us
Acting General Counsel:
  Rosanne Notaro 212-709-1652
  e-mail: rosanne.notaro@banking.state.ny.us
Director, Criminal Investigations Bureau:
  John Dinin 212-709-3540
  e-mail: john.dinin@banking.state.ny.us

Chief Information Officer:
  William Rachmiel. 212-709-5420
  e-mail: william.rachmiel@banking.state.ny.us
Information Security Officer:
  Walter Jones 212-709-1535
Information Security Officer:
  Jae Sohn 212-709-5401
  e-mail: jae.sohn@banking.state.ny.us
Secretary, NYS Banking Board:
  Sam L Abram 212-709-1658
  e-mail: sam.abram@banking.state.ny.us

Communication & Media Relations
Deputy Superintendent:
  Vacant 212-709-1698

Community and Regional Banks Division
Deputy Superintendent:
  Manuel Kursky. 212-709-1610
  e-mail: manuel.kursky@banking.state.ny.us

Consumer Services Division
Deputy Superintendent:
  Steven Kirchgraber. 212-709-3591
  e-mail: steven.kirchgraber@banking.state.ny.us

Criminal Investigations Bureau
Director:
  John Dinin 212-709-3540/fax: 212-709-3555
  e-mail: john.dinin@banking.state.ny.us

Foreign and Wholesale Banks Division
Deputy Superintendent:
  David Fredsall 212-709-1551
  e-mail: david.fredsall@banking.state.ny.us

Human Resources
Director:
  Vacant. 212-709-5444/fax: 212-709-5450

Information Technology Division
Director:
  William Rachmiel 212-709-5420/fax: 212-709-5427
  e-mail: william.rachmiel@banking.state.ny.us

Licensed Financial Services Division
Deputy Superintendent:
  Regina A Stone 212-709-5500/fax: 212-709-5513
  e-mail: regina.stone@banking.state.ny.us

Mortgage Banking Division
Deputy Superintendent:
  Rholda Ricketts 212-709-5540/fax: 212-709-5555
  e-mail: rholda.ricketts@banking.state.ny.us

Regional Offices

London Office
Sardinia House, 52 Lincoln's Inn Fields, London, UK WC2A 3LZ
011 44-20-7405-5474

Offices and agencies generally appear in alphabetical order, except when specific order is requested by listee.

BANKING AND FINANCE / New York State

Upstate Office . . . . fax: 315-428-4052
333 E Washington St, 5th Fl, Syracuse, NY 13202
315-428-4049 Fax: 315-428-4052

Research, Applications & Technical Assistance Division
Assistant Deputy Superintendent:
   Vacant 212-709-1613

Law Department
State Capitol
Albany, NY 12224-0341
518-474-7330 Fax: 518-402-2472
Web site: www.oag.state.ny.us

120 Broadway
New York, NY 10271-0332
212-416-8000
Fax: 212-416-8942

Attorney General:
   Andrew M Cuomo 518-474-7330
First Deputy Attorney General:
   Michele Hirshman 212-416-8050
Director, Public Information & Correspondence:
   Peter A Drago 518-474-7330/fax: 518-402-2472

Public Advocacy Division
Deputy Attorney General:
   Dietrich Snell 212-416-8041/fax: 212-416-8068
Special Counsel:
   Mary Ellen Burns 212-416-6155

Consumer Fraud & Protection Bureau
Bureau Chief:
   Thomas G Conway 518-474-2374/fax: 518-474-3618

Investment Protection Bureau
Bureau Chief:
   David Brown 212-416-8198/fax: 212-416-6377

CORPORATIONS, AUTHORITIES AND COMMISSIONS

Municipal Assistance Corporation for the City of New York
420 Lexington Avenue
Room 1756
New York, NY 10170
212-840-8255 Fax: 212-840-8570
e-mail: macnyc@earthlink.net

Chairman:
   Jonathan A Ballan 212-840-8255
Executive Director:
   Nancy H Henze 212-840-8255

New York State Housing Finance Agency (HFA)
641 Lexington Ave
4th Floor
New York, NY 10022
212-688-4000 Fax: 212-872-0789
Web site: www.nyhomes.org

Chair:
   Judd Levy 212-688-4000
President & CEO:
   Priscilla Almodovar 212-688-4000
Senior VP, COO & CFO:
   Ralph J Madalena 212-688-4000
Senior VP & Counsel:
   Justin Driscoll 212-688-4000
Senior VP & Special Assistant to President/CEO for Policy Development & Programs:
   James P Angley 212-688-4000
Senior VP, Debt Issuance:
   Bernard Abramowitz 212-688-4000 x530
Vice President, Director of Development:
   Maria LaSorsa 212-688-4000 x688
Vice President, Policy & Planning:
   Tracy A Oats 212-688-4000 x678
Vice President, Intergovernmental Relations:
   Michael Houseknecht 518-434-2118/fax: 518-432-7158

Affordable Housing Corporation
Senior VP & Special Assistant to Pres/CEO for Policy Development & Programs:
   James P Angley 212-688-4000

New York State Mortgage Loan Enforcement & Administration Corporation
633 Third Ave
37th Fl
New York, NY 10017-6754
212-803-3700 Fax: 212-803-3775
Web site: www.empire.state.ny.us

Senior Vice President:
   Anita W Laremont 212-803-3750
Senior Vice President & Chief Financial Officer:
   Frances A Walton 212-803-3510

New York State Project Finance Agency
641 Lexington Ave
New York, NY 10022
212-688-4000 Fax: 212-872-0678

Chair:
   Judd Levy 212-688-4000
President & CEO:
   Priscilla Almodovar 212-688-4000
Senior VP, COO & CFO:
   Ralph J Madalena 212-688-4000
Senior VP & General Counsel:
   Justin Driscoll 212-688-4000
Senior VP, Debt Issuance:
   Bernard Abramowitz 212-688-4000 x530
Vice President, Director of Development:
   Jonathan Cortrell 212-688-4000 x688
Vice President, Policy & Planning:
   Tracy A Oats 212-688-4000 x678

State of New York Mortgage Agency (SONYMA)
641 Lexington Ave
New York, NY 10022

Offices and agencies generally appear in alphabetical order, except when specific order is requested by listee.

BANKING AND FINANCE / U.S. Government

212-688-4000 Fax: 212-872-0678
Web site: www.nyhomes.org

Chair:
   Judd Levy 212-688-4000
President & CEO:
   Priscilla Almodovar 212-688-4000
Senior VP & Special Assistant to Pres/CEO for Policy Development & Programs:
   James P Angley 212-688-4000
Senior VP, COO & CFO:
   Ralph J Madalena 212-688-4000
Senior VP & General Counsel:
   Justin Driscoll 212-688-4000
Vice President/Director, SONYMA Mortgage Insurance Fund:
   Michael Friedman 212-688-4000 x714
Senior VP, Single Family Programs & Financing:
   Charles Rosenwald 212-688-4000 x531
Vice President, Policy & Planning:
   Tracy A Oats 212-688-4000 x678
Vice President, Intergovernmental Relations:
   Michael Houseknecht 518-434-2118/fax: 518-434-7158

State of New York Municipal Bond Bank Agency (MBBA)
641 Lexington Ave
New York, NY 10022
212-688-4000 Fax: 212-872-0678
Web site: www.nymbba.org

Chair:
   Judd Levy 212-688-4000
President & CEO:
   Priscilla Almodovar 212-688-4000

Senior VP, CFO, COO:
   Ralph J Madalena 212-688-4000
Senior VP & Counsel:
   Justin Driscoll 212-688-4000
Senior VP & Special Assistant to Pres & CEO for Policy Development & Programs:
   James P Angley 212-688-4000
Senior VP, Debt Issuance:
   Bernard Abramowitz 212-688-4000 x530
Vice President, Policy & Planning:
   Tracy A Oats 212-688-4000 x678

NEW YORK STATE LEGISLATURE

See Legislative Branch in Section 1 for additional Standing Committee and Subcommittee information.

Assembly Standing Committees

Banks
Chair:
   Darryl C Towns (D) 518-455-5821
Ranking Minority Member:
   Andrew P Raia (R) 518-455-5952

Senate Standing Committees

Banks
Chair:
   Hugh T Farley (R) 518-455-2181
Ranking Minority Member:
   Martin Connor (D) 518-455-2625

U.S. Government

EXECUTIVE DEPARTMENTS AND RELATED AGENCIES

Export Import Bank of the United States
Web site: www.exim.gov

Northeast Regional Office .... fax: 212-809-2687
33 Whitehall St, 22nd Fl Ste B, New York, NY 10004
212-809-2650 Fax: 212-809-2687
Regional Director:
   Thomas Cummings 212-809-2652/fax: 212-809-2646
   e-mail: thomas.cummings@exim.gov
Administrative Assistant:
   Jennifer Drakes 212-809-2649
   e-mail: jennifer.drakes@exim.gov

Federal Deposit Insurance Corporation
800-334-9593 or 917-320-2500
Web site: www.fdic.gov

Division of Supervision & Consumer Protection .... fax: 917-320-2919
   20 Exchange Place, 4th Fl, New York, NY 10005

Regional Director:
   James C Watkins 917-320-2570

Federal Reserve System

Federal Reserve Bank of New York
33 Liberty St, New York, NY 10045-0001
212-720-5000 or TTY: 212-720-5387
e-mail: general.info@ny.frb.org
Web site: www.newyorkfed.org
President:
   Timothy F Geithner 212-720-5000
Senior Vice President, Public Information:
   Calvin Mitchell, III 212-720-6136
   e-mail: peter.bakstansky@ny.frb.org
Assistant Vice President:
   Rae Rosen 212-720-1935/fax: 212-720-6628
   e-mail: rae.rosen@ny.frb.org

Buffalo Branch
40 Fountain Plaza, Ste 650, Buffalo, NY 14202
716-849-5000
Senior Vice President & Branch Manager:
   Kausar Hamdani 716-849-5000

Offices and agencies generally appear in alphabetical order, except when specific order is requested by listee.

BANKING AND FINANCE / Private Sector

National Credit Union Administration

Albany Region
9 Washington Sq, Washington Ave Ext, Albany, NY 12205
Acting Regional Director:
  Mark A Treichel 518-862-7400/fax: 518-862-7420

US Treasury Department
Web site: www.ustreas.gov

Comptroller of the Currency
Web site: www.occ.treas.gov

Northeastern District
341 Madison Avenue, 5th Floor, New York, NY 10017
Deputy Comptroller:
  Toney Bland 212-790-4001/fax: 212-790-4058
Assistant Deputy Comptroller:
  Beverly Cole. 212-790-4007
District Counsel:
  Jonathan Rushdoony 212-790-4010

Office of Thrift Supervision
Web site: www.ots.treas.gov

Northeast Region (serving NY)
Harborside Financial Center, Plaza 5, Suite 1600, Jersey City, NJ 07311
Regional Director:
  Robert C Albanese 201-413-1000/fax: 201-413-7543

US Mint . . . . fax: 845-446-6258
Rt 218, PO Box 37, West Point, NY 10996
Fax: 845-446-6258
Web site: www.usmint.gov
Superintendent:
  Ellen McCullom 845-446-6201
Administrative Officer:
  Vacant 845-446-6203
Chief, Mint Police:
  John Bennett. 845-446-6235

U.S. CONGRESS

See U.S. Congress Chapter for additional Standing Committee and Subcommittee information.

House of Representatives Standing Committees

Financial Services
Chair:
  Barney Frank (D-MA) 202-225-5931
Ranking Minority Member:
  Spencer Bachus (R-AL) 202-225-4921
New York Delegate:
  Gary L Ackerman (D) 202-225-2601
New York Delegate:
  Joseph Crowley (D) 202-225-3965
New York Delegate:
  Vito Fossella (R). 202-225-3371
New York Delegate:
  Steve Israel (D). 202-225-3335
New York Delegate:
  Sue W Kelly (R). 202-225-5441
New York Delegate:
  Carolyn B Maloney (D) 202-225-7944
New York Delegate:
  Carolyn McCarthy (D) 202-225-5516
New York Delegate:
  Gregory W Meeks (D) 202-225-3461
New York Delegate:
  Nydia M Velasquez (D) 202-225-2361

Senate Standing Committees

Banking, Housing & Urban Affairs
Chair:
  Christopher J Dodd (D-CT) 202-224-2823
Ranking Minority Member:
  Richard C Shelby (R-AL). 202-224-5744
New York Delegate:
  Charles E Schumer (D). 202-224-6542

Private Sector

Alliance Bank
Tower II, 120 Madison St 18th Floor, Syracuse, NY 13202
315-475-2100 or 800-310-6275 Fax: 315-475-4421
e-mail: abnaweb@alliancebankna.com
Web site: www.alliancebankna.com
Jack H Webb, President & Chief Executive Officer

American Express Company
200 Vesey St, 48th Fl, New York, NY 10285-4811
212-640-5028 Fax: 212-640-9602
Web site: www.americanexpress.com
Stephen Lemson, Vice President, State & Government Affairs
Consumer lending, travel services, proprietary database marketing, insurance underwriting & investment services

American International Group Inc
70 Pine St, 36th Fl, New York, NY 10270
212-770-6114 Fax: 212-785-4214
e-mail: ned.cloonan@aig.com
Web site: www.aig.com
Edward T Cloonan, Vice President International & Corporate Affairs
International business, government & financial services

Antalek & Moore Insurance Agency
340 Main St, Beacon, NY 12508
845-831-4300 or 866-894-1026 Fax: 845-831-5631
e-mail: fantalek@antalek-moore.com
Web site: www.antalek-moore.com
Frederick N Antalek, Sr, President
NYS Banking Board member

Offices and agencies generally appear in alphabetical order, except when specific order is requested by listee.

BANKING AND FINANCE / Private Sector

Apple Banking for Savings
122 East 42nd St, 9th Fl, New York, NY 10168
212-224-6410 Fax: 212-224-6580
Web site: www.applebank.com
Alan Shamoon, President & Chief Executive Officer
NYS Banking Board member

Community Bankers Assn of NY State, Banking Law & Regulations Cmte
Astoria Federal Savings & Loan
1 Astoria Federal Plaza, Lake Success, NY 11042-1085
516-327-3000 Fax: 516-327-7860
e-mail: banking@astoriafederal.com
Web site: www.astoriafederal.com
Alan P Eggleston, Member

Bank of Akron
46 Main St, Akron, NY 14001
716-542-5401 Fax: 716-542-5510
Web site: www.bankofakron.com
E Peter Forrestel, II, President & Chief Executive Officer
NYS Banking Board member/ Director - Independent Bankers Association of New York State (IBANYS)

Bear Stearns & Co Inc
383 Madison Ave, 11th Fl, New York, NY 10179
212-272-2000 Fax: 212-272-5188
e-mail: bforan@bear.com
Web site: www.bearstearns.com
James E Cayne, Chairman & Chief Executive Officer
Public finance

SIFMA
Bond Market Association (The)
360 Madison Ave, Ste 18, New York, NY 10017-7111
646-637-9200 or 212-808-1000 Fax: 646-637-9126
e-mail: namiel@bondmarkets.com
Web site: www.bondmarkets.com
Jon Teall, Vice President, Media Relations
Represent securities firms & banks that underwrite, trade & sell debt securities

Brown Brothers Harriman & Co, Bank Asset Management Group
140 Broadway, New York, NY 10005-1101
212-483-1818 Fax: 212-493-7657
e-mail: carl.terzer@bbh.com
Web site: www.bbh.com
Carl E Terzer, Senior Vice President & Marketing Director

Canandaigua National Bank & Trust Co
72 S Main St, Canandaigua, NY 14424
585-394-4260 or 800-724-2621 Fax: 585-396-1355
e-mail: ghamlin@cnbank.com
Web site: www.cnbank.com
George W Hamlin, President
Full service banking

Citigroup
399 Park Avenue, New York, NY 10043
212-559-5248 or 800-285-3000 Fax: 212-793-8011
e-mail: thomsonte@citi.com
Web site: www.citigroup.com
Terri Thomson, Director, State Civic Affairs

Citigroup Inc
399 Park Ave, 2nd Fl, New York, NY 10043
212-793-0141 Fax: 212-793-2008
e-mail: schleinm@citigroup.com
Web site: www.citigroup.com
Michael Schlein, Senior Vice President, Global Corporate Affairs, Human Resources & Business Practices
Commercial & retail banking

Cornell University, Economics Department
450 Uris Hall, Ithaca, NY 14853-7601
607-255-6283 Fax: 607-255-2818
e-mail: dae3@cornell.edu
Web site: www.arts.cornell.edu/econ
David Easley, Professor
Microeconomic theory, financial economics

Credit Advocate Counseling Corporation
237 First Ave, Ste 305, New York, NY 10003
212-260-2776 or 866-MYBILLS Fax: 646-218-4599
e-mail: info@creditadvocates.com
Web site: www.creditadvocates.com
Steve Burman, President
Advice & assistance in eliminating credit card debt by consolidating & handling bill payments while reducing interest rates

Deutsche Bank
60 Wall Street, New York, NY 10005
212-250-2500
e-mail: thomas.curtis@db.com
Web site: www.db.com
Thomas Curtis, Global Head of Business Development & Strategic Planning & Communications

Federal Home Loan Bank of New York
101 Park Ave, New York, NY 10178-0599
212-681-6000 Fax: 212-441-6890
Web site: www.fhlbny.com
Alfred A DelliBovi, President

Financial Services Forum
708 3rd Avenue, 17th Fl, New York, NY 10015
212-692-0828 Fax: 212-692-0830
Web site: www.estandardsforum.com
George J Vojta, Chairman, Estandardsforum Inc
NYS Banking Board member; organization of CEOs of twenty one of the largest & most diversified financial institutions

Offices and agencies generally appear in alphabetical order, except when specific order is requested by listee.

BANKING AND FINANCE / Private Sector

Goldman Sachs & Co
101 Constitution Avenue NW, Suite 1000 East, Washington, DC 20001
202-637-3700 Fax: 202-637-3773
Web site: www.gs.com
Ann S Costello, Managing Director & Head of Global Government Affairs

Community Bankers Assn of NY State, Accounting & Taxation Cmte
North Fork Bank
275 Broadhollow Road, Melville, NY 11747
631-844-1004 Fax: 631-531-2759
Web site: www.northforkbank.com
Carolyn Dresel, Co-Chair

HSBC Bank USA
452 Fifth Ave, New York, NY 10018
212-525-6533 Fax: 212-525-8447
e-mail: janet.l.burak@us.hsbc.com
Janet L Burak, General Counsel

HSBC USA Inc
452 Fifth Ave, New York, NY 10018
212-525-3800 Fax: 212-525-0109
e-mail: linda.s.recupero@us.hsbc.com
Web site: www.us.hsbc.com
Linda Recupero, Executive Vice President, Public Affairs-North America
Bank holding company

IRX Therapeutics Inc
140 West 57th, Ste 9-C, New York, NY 10019
212-582-1199 Fax: 212-582-3659
e-mail: jhwang@immunorx.com
Web site: www.irxtherapeutics.com
Jeffrey Hwang, Chief Financial Officer
NYS Banking Board member

Independent Bankers Association of NYS
125 State St, Albany, NY 12207
518-436-4646 Fax: 518-436-4648
e-mail: info@ibanys.net
Web site: ibanys.net
William Y Crowell, III, Executive Director
Representing New York's community banks

Kudlow & Company LLC
1375 Kings Highway E, Ste 260, Fairfield, CT 06824
203-228-5050 Fax: 203-228-5040
e-mail: svarga@kudlow.com
Web site: www.kudlow.com
Vacant, Managing Director
NYS Banking Board member

Lake Shore Savings
128 East Fourth St, Dunkirk, NY 14048
716-366-4070 Fax: 716-366-2965
e-mail: dave.mancuso@lakeshoresavings.com
Web site: www.lakeshoresavings.com
David C Mancuso, President & Chief Executive Officer
NYS Banking Board member

Law Offices of Wesley Chen
641 Lexington Ave, 20th Fl, New York, NY 10022
212-751-7100 Fax: 212-371-6632
e-mail: wchenlaw@aol.com
Wesley Chen, Attorney
NYS Banking Board member

M&T Bank Corporation
One M&T Plaza, Buffalo, NY 14203-2399
716-842-5425 Fax: 716-842-5220
e-mail: rwilmers@mandtbank.com
Web site: www.mandtbank.com
Robert G Wilmers, Chairman
Commercial, savings & mortgage banking services

MBIA Insurance Corporation
113 King St, Armonk, NY 10504
914-273-4545 Fax: 914-765-3555
e-mail: ethel.geisinger@mbia.com
Web site: www.mbia.com
Ethel Z Geisinger, Vice President, Government Relations
Insure municipal bonds & structured transactions

Mallory Factor Inc
555 Madison Ave, New York, NY 10022
212-350-0000 Fax: 212-350-0001
Mallory Factor, President
NYS Banking Board member

Merrill Lynch & Co Inc
222 Broadway, 16th Fl, New York, NY 10038-2510
212-670-0302 Fax: 212-670-4501
e-mail: andrew_kandel@ml.com
Web site: www.ml.com
Andrew Kandel, First Vice President & Assistant General Counsel, State Regulation, Legislation & Government Relations
Securities, capital markets & financial services

Morgan Stanley
1585 Broadway, New York, NY 10036
212-761-4000 Fax: 212-762-7994
Web site: www.morganstanley.com
John Mack, Chairman & Chief Executive Officer
Investment banking

Municipal Credit Union
22 Cortlandt St, New York, NY 10007-3107
212-238-3361 Fax: 212-416-7050
Web site: www.nymcu.org
Thomas G Siciliano, General Counsel
NYS Banking Board member

Offices and agencies generally appear in alphabetical order, except when specific order is requested by listee.

BANKING AND FINANCE / Private Sector

NBT Bancorp Inc.
PO Box 351, Norwich, NY 13815
607-337-2265 Fax: 607-336-6545
e-mail: customerservice@nbtbank.com
Web site: www.nbtbank.com
Martin A Dietrich, President & Chief Executive Officer
Commercial banking

NYS Credit Union League
19 British American Blvd, Latham, NY 12110
518-437-8100 Fax: 518-782-4212
e-mail: akramer@nyscul.org
Web site: www.nyscul.org
Amy Kramer, Vice President/Governmental Affairs
Serving & support credit unions

National Federation of Community Development Credit Unions
116 John St, 33rd Fl, New York, NY 10038
212-809-1850 Fax: 212-809-3274
e-mail: info@cdcu.coop
Web site: www.cdcu.coop
Cliff Rosenthal, Executive Director

New York Bankers Association
99 Park Ave, 4th Fl, New York, NY 10016-1502
212-297-1664 Fax: 212-297-1622
e-mail: bbosies@nyba.com
Web site: www.nyba.com
William J Bosies, Senior Vice President, Legislation & Regulation
Advocacy for commercial banking industry

Community Bankers Assn of NY State, Mortgages & Real Estate Cmte
New York Community Bank
615 Merrick Ave, Westbury, NY 11590
516-683-4100 Fax: 516-683-8344
Web site: www.mynycb.com
Joseph R Ficalora, President & Chief Executive Officer

New York State Credit Union League Inc
19 British American Blvd, Latham, NY 12110
800-342-9835 Fax: 518-782-8284
e-mail: mlanotte@nyscul.org
Web site: www.nyscul.org
Michael A Lanotte, Senior Vice President, Governmental & Regulatory Affairs
Trade association for over 600 not-for-profit, member owned credit unions in New York

New York Stock Exchange
Government Relations, 11 Wall St, 6th Fl, New York, NY 10005
212-656-3000 Fax: 212-656-5605
e-mail: pagurto@nyse.com
Web site: www.nyse.com
Richard G Ketchum, Chief Regulatory Officer

Norddeutsche Landesbank Girozentrale
1114 Ave of the Americas, 37th Fl, New York, NY 10036
212-398-7300 Fax: 212-812-6860
e-mail: thomas.buerkle@nordlb.com
Web site: www.nordlbnewyork.com
Thomas S Buerkle, Executive Vice President & General Manager

Community Bankers Assn of NY State, Bank Operations & Admin Cmte
North Country Savings Bank
127 Main St, Canton, NY 13617
315-386-4533 Fax: 315-386-3739
Web site: www.northcountrysavings.com
Michael A Noble, Chair

Community Bankers Assn of NY State, Government Relations Cmte
Pioneer Savings Bank
21 Second St, Troy, NY 12180
518-274-4800 Fax: 518-274-1060
e-mail: troybranch@pioneersb.com
Web site: www.pioneersb.com
Dawn Gendron, Sales Development Officer/Senior Branch Manager

Securities Industry Association (SIA)
120 Broadway, 35th Fl, New York, NY 10271-0800
212-608-1500 Fax: 212-968-0703
e-mail: info@sia.com
Web site: www.sia.com
Mark Lackritz, President

Sullivan & Cromwell
125 Broad St, New York, NY 10004
212-558-3534 Fax: 212-558-3588
Web site: www.sullcrom.com
H Rodgin Cohen, Partner & Chairman
Bank regulation & acquisition law

TD Banknorth
237 Glen St, PO Box 318, Glens Falls, NY 12801
518-792-1151 Fax: 518-792-4837
e-mail: jeffrey.rivenburgh@TDBanknorth.com
Web site: www.TDBanknorth.com
Jeffrey Rivenburgh, President & Chief Executive Officer
Commercial, retail & investment banking

The Clearing House Association, LLC
100 Broad St, New York, NY 10004
212-612-9205 Fax: 212-612-9253
e-mail: norm.nelson@theclearinghouse.org
Web site: www.theclearinghouse.org
Norman R Nelson, General Counsel
Electronic funds transfer

Offices and agencies generally appear in alphabetical order, except when specific order is requested by listee.

BANKING AND FINANCE / Private Sector

Tompkins Trustco Inc
110 N Tioga St, PO Box 460, Ithaca, NY 14851
607-273-3210 Fax: 607-273-0063
e-mail: sromaine@tompkinstrust.com
Web site: www.tompkinstrustco.com
Stephen S Romaine, President & CEO
$2.2 Billion financial services holding company headquartered in Ithaca, NY. Parent company to three community banks, Tompkins Trust Company, The Bank of Castile and Mahopac National Bank, as well as Tompkins Insurance Agencies

Ulster Savings Bank
180 Schwank Dr, Kingston, NY 12401
845-338-6322 or 800-762-0449 Fax: 845-339-9008
Web site: www.ulstersavings.com
Clifford Miller, President & Chief Executive Officer
NYS Banking Board member

Union State Bank
100 Dutch Hill Rd, Orangeburg, NY 10962
845-365-4605 or 800-616-3491 Fax: 845-365-2130
e-mail: customerservices@unionstate.com
Web site: www.unionstate.com
Thomas E Hales, Pres & Chief Executive Officer
NYS Banking Board member

Valley National Bank
925 Allwood Road, Clifton, NJ 07012
973-916-2250 Fax: 973-779-7563
e-mail: fcosentino@valleynationalbank.com
Web site: www.valleynationalbank.com
Frank T Cosentino, SVP-Corporate & Government Services
Full-service banking, cash management, municipal leasing & public finance

Washington Mutual
589 5th Avenue, New York, NY 10117-1923
212-353-6230 Fax: 212-673-5118
Web site: www.wamu.com
Donna Wilson, Senior Vice President, Regional President
National financial services company that provides a diversified line of products to consumers & small to mid-sized businesses

White & Case LLP
1155 Ave of the Americas, New York, NY 10036-2787
212-819-8200 Fax: 212-354-8113
e-mail: dwall@whitecase.com
Web site: www.whitecase.com
Duane D Wall, Partner
Advises domestic & foreign banks on the nature & structure of their operations & activities in the US & abroad

Wilber National Bank
245 Main St, PO Box 430, Oneonta, NY 13820
607-432-1700 Fax: 607-433-4161
e-mail: dgulotty@wilberbank.com
Web site: www.wilberbank.com
Douglas C Gulotty, President & Chief Executive Officer
Commercial & retail banking

Offices and agencies generally appear in alphabetical order, except when specific order is requested by listee.

COMMERCE, INDUSTRY & ECONOMIC DEVELOPMENT

New York State

GOVERNOR'S OFFICE

Governor's Office
Executive Chamber
State Capitol
Albany, NY 12224
518-474-8390 Fax: 518-474-1513
Web site: www.state.ny.us

Governor:
  Eliot Spitzer 518-474-8390
Secretary to the Governor:
  Richard Baum 518-474-4246
Counsel to the Governor:
  David Nocenti 518-474-8343
Senior Advisor to the Governor:
  Lloyd Constantine 518-486-9671
Deputy Secretary, Economic Development & Infrastructure:
  Timothy Gilchrist 518-408-2552
Assistant Counsel to the Governor-Economic Development:
  William Estes 518-474-8494
Director, Communications:
  Darren Dopp 518-474-8418

EXECUTIVE DEPARTMENTS AND RELATED AGENCIES

Alcoholic Beverage Control, Division of (State Liquor Authority)
80 S Swan St, Ste 900
Albany, NY 12210-8002
518-486-4767 Fax: 518-402-4015
Web site: www.abc.state.ny.us

317 Lenox Ave
New York, NY 10027
212-961-8385
Fax: 212-961-8299

Chair:
  Daniel B Boyle .... 212-961-8347 or 518-473-6559
  fax: 212-961-8283
Commissioner:
  Lawrence J Gedda 212-961-8347
Commissioner:
  Noreen Healey 212-961-8355
Chief Executive Officer:
  Joshua B Toas 518-486-4767
Deputy Commissioner, Government Affairs:
  Thomas O'Connor 518-486-4701

Counsel:
  Thomas J Donohue 518-402-4429

Administration
Senior Deputy Commissioner, Administration:
  J Mark Anderson 518-474-4139
Director, Financial Administration:
  Franklin A Hecht 518-474-4546
Director, Human Resources:
  Dan Cunningham 518-473-5995
Director, Communications:
  William Crowley 518-486-4767

Licensing & Enforcement

Albany (Zone II)
80 S Swan St, Ste 900, 2nd Fl, Albany, NY 12210-8002
Director, Licensing:
  Kerri O'Brien 518-474-7604
Associate Counsel:
  Leslie Trebby 518-474-6750
Assistant Director, ABC Compliance:
  Daniel Malay 518-474-0385/fax: 518-473-7527
Supervising Beverage Control Investigator:
  Robert Benedetto 518-474-0385

Buffalo (Zone III)
Iskalo Electric Tower, 535 Washington St, Ste 303, Buffalo, NY 14203
716-847-3035
Executive Officer:
  Brandon Noyes 716-847-3060
Senior Beverage Control Investigator:
  Gary Bartikofsky 716-847-3039

New York City (Zone I)
317 Lenox Avenue, New York, NY 10027
212-961-8385
Deputy Commissioner:
  Fred Gioffre 212-961-8301
Supervising Attorney:
  Stephen Kalinsky 212-961-8351

Budget, Division of the
State Capitol
Albany, NY 12224
518-473-3885
e-mail: bdgord@budget.state.ny.us
Web site: www.budget.state.ny.us

Director:
  Paul E Francis 518-474-2300
First Deputy Director:
  Laura L Anglin 518-474-6323
Deputy Director:
  Ron Rock 518-474-6300

Offices and agencies generally appear in alphabetical order, except when specific order is requested by listee.

COMMERCE, INDUSTRY & ECONOMIC DEVELOPMENT / New York State

Deputy Director:
 Kim Fine...518-474-6300
Counsel:
 Kathy Bennett......................................518-474-2300
Director, Communications:
 Jeffrey Gordon....................................518-473-3885
Press Officer:
 Scott Reif..518-473-3885

Consumer Protection Board
5 Empire State Plaza
Ste 2101
Albany, NY 12223-1556
518-474-3514 or 800-697-1220 Fax: 518-474-3514
Web site: www.nyconsumer.gov

1740 Broadway
15th Fl
New York, NY 10019
212-459-8850
Fax: 212-459-8855

Chairperson & Executive Director:
 Mindy A Bockstein................................518-486-4852
Executive Deputy Director & General Counsel:
 Lisa R Harris..518-474-3514

Empire State Development Corporation
633 Third Ave
New York, NY 10017
212-803-3100
Web site: www.empire.state.ny.us

30 South Pearl Street
Albany, NY 12245
518-292-5100

420 Main St, Ste 717
Buffalo, NY 14202
716-856-8111

Co-Chair Downstate:
 Patrick J Foye......................................212-803-3700
Co-Chair Upstate:
 Daniel C Gundersen...............518-292-5100 or 716-856-8111
President & Chief Operating Officer:
 Avi Schick...212-803-3730
Chief Operating Officer (Upstate):
 Kenneth A Schoetz.................................716-856-8111
Senior VP, Legal & General Counsel:
 Anita W Laremont.................................212-803-3750
Director, Communications:
 A J Carter..212-803-3740
Chief Financial Officer:
 Frances A Walton..................................212-803-3510

Law Department
120 Broadway
New York, NY 10271-0332
212-416-8000 Fax: 212-416-8796

State Capitol
Albany, NY 12224-0341
518-474-7330
Fax: 518-402-2472

Attorney General:
 Andrew M Cuomo..................................518-474-7330
First Deputy Attorney General:
 Michele Hirshman..................................212-416-8050
Executive Director, Administration:
 Sylvia Hamer..................212-416-6561 or 518-473-7900
Director, Public Information & Correspondence:
 Peter A Drago....................518-474-7330/fax: 518-402-2472
Director, Communications:
 Darren Dopp....................212-416-8060 or 518-473-5525
 fax: 212-416-6005

Public Advocacy Division
Deputy Attorney General:
 Dietrich Snell..................212-416-8041/fax: 212-416-8068
Special Counsel:
 Mary Ellen Burns..................................212-416-6155

 Antitrust Bureau
 Bureau Chief:
  Jay L Himes..................212-416-8282/fax: 212-416-6015

 Consumer Fraud & Protection Bureau
 Bureau Chief:
  Thomas G Conway..............518-472-2374/fax: 518-474-3618

 Internet Bureau
 Bureau Chief:
  Jane Azia......................212-416-8433/fax: 212-416-8369

 Investment Protection Bureau
 Bureau Chief:
  David Brown...................212-416-8198/fax: 212-416-6377

State Counsel Division
Deputy Attorney General:
 Richard Rifkin......................................518-473-7190
Assistant Deputy Attorney General:
 Patricia Martinelli...............518-473-0648/fax: 518-486-9777
Assistant Deputy Attorney General:
 Susan L Watson.................212-416-8579/fax: 212-416-6001

 Claims Bureau
 Bureau Chief:
  Susan Pogoda..................212-416-8516/fax: 212-416-8946

Regulatory Reform, Governor's Office of
Agency Bldg 1, 4th Fl, Empire State Plz
PO Box 2107
Albany, NY 12220-0107
518-486-3292 Fax: 518-473-9342
Web site: www.gorr.state.ny.us

Director:
 Robert Hermann...................................518-473-8197
Counsel:
 Amelia Stern....................518-473-0620/fax: 518-473-9342
Public Information Officer:
 Tim Beadnell..518-486-3292
 e-mail: tbeadnell@gorr.state.ny.us
Director, Administration:
 Sandra L Curry......................................518-408-2055

Offices and agencies generally appear in alphabetical order, except when specific order is requested by listee.

COMMERCE, INDUSTRY & ECONOMIC DEVELOPMENT / New York State

NYS Foundation for Science, Technology & Innovation
30 South Pearl St
11th Fl
Albany, NY 12207
518-292-5700 Fax: 518-292-5798
Web site: www.nystar.state.ny.us

Executive Director:
　Michael J Relyea 518-292-5700
Director, Communications:
　Jannette Rondo 518-292-5700/fax: 518-292-5798
Director, Programs:
　Kathleen J Wise 518-292-5700
Deputy Counsel:
　Paul Jesep 518-292-5700
Director, Finance:
　Edward J Hamilton 518-292-5700

Centers for Advanced Technology

Center for Advanced Ceramic Technology at Alfred University
352 McMahon Engineering Bldg, 2 Pine St, Alfred, NY 14802-1296
Director:
　Vasantha Amarakoon 607-871-2486/fax: 607-871-3469

Center for Advanced Materials Processing at Clarkson Univ
Box 5665, Potsdam, NY 13699-5665
Director:
　S V Babu 315-268-2336/fax: 315-268-7615

Center for Advanced Tech in Biomedical & Bioengineering
SUNY at Buffalo, 162K Farber Hall, 3435 Main St, Buffalo, NY 14214-3092
Deputy Director:
　Cathy M Buyea 716-829-2561/fax: 716-829-3945
　e-mail: buyea@buffalo.edu

Sensor CAT-Diagnostic Tools & Sensor Systems
SUNY Stony Brook, 214 Old Chemistry Bldg, 2nd Fl, Stony Brook, NY 11794-3717
Web site: www.sensorcat.sunysb.edu
Director:
　Serge Luryi 631-632-1368/fax: 631-632-8529

Center for Advanced Tech in Electronic Imaging Systems
Univ of Rochester, Taylor Hall, 260 Hutchinson Rd, Rochester, NY 14627-0194
Director:
　Eby Friedman 585-275-1022/fax: 585-276-0200

Center for Advanced Technology in Info Mgmt
Columbia University, 630 W 168th St, PH-15-1501, New York, NY 10032
Director:
　Edward H Shortliffe 212-305-2944/fax: 212-305-0196

Center for Advanced Technology in Life Science Enterprise
Cornell University, 130 Biotechnology Bldg, Ithaca, NY 14853-2703
Director:
　Stephen Kresovich 607-255-2300/fax: 607-255-6249

Center for Advanced Technology in Photonic Applications
Dept of Physics, City College of CUNY, 138th St & Convent Ave Rm J419, New York, NY 10031
Director:
　Robert R Alfano 212-650-5531/fax: 212-650-5530

Ctr for Advanced Tech in Telecommunications at Polytech Univ
5 MetroTech Center, Room LC 208, Brooklyn, NY 11201
Director:
　Shivendra S Panwar 718-260-3050/fax: 718-260-8687

Center for Automation Technologies at Rensselaer
CII Bldg, Rm 8015, Troy, NY 12180-3590
Director:
　Ray Puffer . . . . 518-276-8990 or 518-276-8087
　fax: 518-276-4897

Center for Advanced Tech-Medical Biotechnology
SUNY at Stony Brook, Psychology A, 3rd Fl, Stony Brook, NY 11794-2580
Director:
　Clinton T Rubin 631-632-8521/fax: 631-632-8577

Center for Computer Applications & Software Engineering
Syracuse University, 2-212 Ctr for Science & Tech, Syracuse, NY 13244
Director:
　Shui-Kai Chin 315-443-1060/fax: 315-443-4745

Center in Nanomaterials and Nanoelectronics
Albany Institue for Materials, CESTM Bldg, 251 Fuller Rd, Rm B110, Albany, NY 12203
President:
　Alain E Kaloyeros 518-437-8686/fax: 518-437-8687

Future Energy Systems CAT at Rensselaer Polytechnic Inst
Ctr for Integrated Electronics and, 9023 Low Ctr for Industrial Innovation, 110 8th St, Troy, NY 12180
Director:
　Omkaram Nalamasu 518-276-3290/fax: 518-276-2990

Integrated Electronics Engineering Center
Thomas J Watson School of Engineering, S, Vestal Pkwy East, PO Box 6000, Binghamton, NY 13902-6000
Director:
　Bahgat Sammakia 607-777-4332/fax: 607-777-4683

Regional Technology Development Centers

Alliance for Manufacturing & Technology
59 Court St, 6th Fl, State St Entrance, Binghamton, NY 13901
Executive Director:
　Edward Gaetano 607-774-0022 x304/fax: 607-774-0026

Center for Economic Growth
63 State St, Albany, NY 12207
President:
　Kelly Lovell 518-465-8975/fax: 518-465-6681

Central New York Technology Development Organization
1201 E Fayette St, Syracuse, NY 13210
President:
　Robert I Trachtenberg 315-425-5144/fax: 315-233-1259

Council for Interntl Trade, Tech, Education & Communication
Peyton Hall, Rm 101, Main St, Potsdam, NY 13676
Executive Director:
　Thomas Plastino 315-268-3778 x24/fax: 315-268-4432

High Technology of Rochester
Chamber of Commerce Bldg, 5 Bragdon Pl, Rochester, NY 14604
Executive Director:
　Paul Wettenhall 585-327-7920/fax: 585-327-7931

Hudson Valley Technology Development Center
300 Westage Business Ctr, Ste 130, Fishkill, NY 12524
Executive Director:
　Thomas J Phillips, Sr 845-896-6934 x3006/fax: 845-896-7006

Industrial & Technology Assistance Corp
253 Broadway, Rm 302, New York, NY 10007

Offices and agencies generally appear in alphabetical order, except when specific order is requested by listee.

COMMERCE, INDUSTRY & ECONOMIC DEVELOPMENT / New York State

President:
Sara Garretson.................212-442-2990/fax: 212-442-4567

Long Island Forum for Technology
111 West Main St, Bayshore, NY 11706
Executive Director:
Patricia Howley.................631-969-3700/fax: 631-969-4489

Mohawk Valley Applied Technology Corp
207 Genesee St, Ste 405, Utica, NY 13501
President:
Paul MacEnroe 315-793-8050/fax: 315-793-8057

INSYTE Consulting (Western NY Technology Development Ctr)
726 Exchange St, Ste 620, Buffalo, NY 14210
President:
Robert J Martin.................716-636-3626/fax: 716-845-6418

Small Cities, Office for
4 Empire State Plaza
Suite 600
Albany, NY 12223
518-474-2057 Fax: 518-474-5247
Web site: www.nysmallcities.com

Executive Director:
Joseph J Rabito......................................518-474-2057
Associate Counsel:
Brian McCartney 518-474-2057
Program Manager:
Gail Hammond.......................................518-474-2057
Director, Communications:
Joseph Picchi...518-474-2057
Executive Assistant:
Drue Paige 518-474-2057

State Department
41 State Street
Albany, NY 12231
518-474-4750 Fax: 518-474-4765
Web site: www.dos.state.ny.us

123 William St
New York, NY 10038
212-417-5801
Fax: 212-417-5805

Secretary of State:
Lorraine A Cortes-Vazquez........................518-474-0050
First Deputy Secretary of State:
Daniel Shapiro 518-474-4750
Deputy Secretary of State, Public Affairs:
Eamon Moynihan....................................212-417-5800
Assistant Secretary of State, Communications:
Laurence Sombke 518-474-4752/fax: 518-474-4597
e-mail: info@dos.state.ny.us
Counsel:
Susan Watson 518-474-6740/fax: 518-473-9211
Deputy Secretary of State, Local Government & Community Services:
Matthew Andrus 518-486-9888/fax: 518-474-6572

Business & Licensing Services Division
Deputy Secretary of State:
Al Jurczynski.....................518-473-2728/fax: 518-473-6648
e-mail: licensing@dos.state.ny.us

Administrative Rules Division
Manger, Publications:
Deborah Ritzko 518-474-6957/fax: 518-473-9055
e-mail: adminrules@dos.state.ny.us

Cemeteries Division
Director:
Richard D Fishman ....518-474-6226 or 212-417-5713
fax: 518-473-0876
e-mail: cemeteries@dos.state.ny.us

Corporations, State Records & UCC Division
Director:
Daniel E Shapiro.................518-473-2281/fax: 518-474-1418
e-mail: corporations@dos.state.ny.us

Taxation & Finance Department
State Campus
Bldg 9, Rm 227
Albany, NY 12227
518-457-4242 Fax: 518-457-2486
Web site: www.tax.state.ny.us

Acting Commissioner:
Barbara G Billet 518-457-2244
Executive Deputy Commissioner:
Barbara G Billet 518-457-7358
Deputy Commissioner & Counsel:
Daniel Smirlock..................518-457-3746/fax: 518-457-8247
Special Assistant to Commissioner for Business:
Holly Chamberlin....................................518-485-5080
Director, Conciliation & Mediation Services:
Barry M Bresler 518-485-8063
Director, Executive Correspondence Control Unit:
Elizabeth Amodeo 518-457-6118
Director, Legislative Affairs:
Maryann Tucker.....................................518-457-2398
Director, Public Information:
Thomas Bergin......................................518-457-4242

Information Office
Chief Information Officer:
Brian Digman..518-457-4362

Office of Administration (OOA)
Deputy Commissioner:
Margaret Sherman 518-457-1000

Human Resources Management
Director:
Kiaran Johnson-Lew 518-457-2786

Operations Support Bureau
Director:
Lisa Negus 518-485-7891

Office of Budget & Management Analysis
Chief Financial Officer:
Patricia Mitchell....................................518-457-1000

Budget & Accounting Services
Director:
Eric Mostert 518-485-6731

Planning & Management Analysis Bureau
Director:
Mary Ellen Nagengast 518-457-8660

Offices and agencies generally appear in alphabetical order, except when specific order is requested by listee.

COMMERCE, INDUSTRY & ECONOMIC DEVELOPMENT / New York State

Tax Enforcement, Office of
Deputy Commissioner:
  William Comisky 518-457-9692

Audit Division
Director, Tax Audits:
  Nonie Manion. 518-457-2750

Tax Compliance Division
Director:
  Joseph F Gecewicz. 518-457-1138

Tax Policy Analysis, Office of
Deputy Commissioner:
  Robert D Plattner 518-457-4357

Technical Services Division
Director:
  Marilyn M Kaltenborn 518-457-1153

Taxpayer Services & Revenue Division
Director:
  Jamie Woodward 518-457-2261

Treasury Division
Deputy Commissioner & Treasurer:
  Aida Brewer. 518-474-4250/fax: 518-402-4118

E-MPIRE
Director:
  Terry Atwater 518-457-7929

CORPORATIONS, AUTHORITIES AND COMMISSIONS

Central New York Regional Market Authority
2100 Park St
Syracuse, NY 13208
315-442-8647 Fax: 315-442-6897

Executive Director:
  Benjamin Vitale 315-422-8647
Counsel:
  Robert Scalione 315-422-1311

Development Authority of the North Country
Dulles State Office Bldg, Ste 414
317 Washington St
Watertown, NY 13601
315-785-2593 Fax: 315-785-2591
Web site: www.danc.org

Chair:
  Thomas Hefferon 315-785-2593
Executive Director:
  Robert S Juravich 315-785-2593
  e-mail: juravich@danc.org
Engineer:
  Carrie M Tuttle. 315-782-8661
  e-mail: ctuttle@danc.org
Deputy Executive Director:
  Thomas R Sauter 315-785-2593
  e-mail: tsauter@danc.org
Finance Director:
  Denise A Gray 315-785-2593

Solid Waste Management Facility General Manager:
  E William Seifried 315-232-3236
Director, Project Development:
  Kevin J Jordan 315-785-2593
  e-mail: kjordan@danc.org

Great Lakes Commission
2805 S Industrial Hwy
Ste 100
Ann Arbor, MI 48104-6791
734-971-9135 Fax: 734-971-9150
e-mail: teder@glc.org
Web site: www.glc.org

Chairman:
  John Cherry 517-373-6800
Vice Chair:
  Patrick Quinn 312-814-4866
New York State Commissioner:
  Alexander B Grannis. 518-402-8540/fax: 518-402-8541
Executive Director:
  Tim A Eder. 734-971-9135
  e-mail: teder@glc.org
Program Manager, Resource Management:
  Thomas R Crane. 734-971-9135
  e-mail: tcrane@glc.org
Program Manager, Transportation & Sustainable Development:
  Dave Knight 734-971-9135
  e-mail: dknight@glc.org
Program Manager, Communications & Internet Technology:
  Christine Manninen 734-971-9135
  e-mail: manninen@glc.org
Program Manager, Data & Information Management:
  Roger Gauthier 734-971-9135
  e-mail: gauthier@glc.org
Program Manager, Environmental Quality:
  Matthew Doss. 734-971-9135
  e-mail: mdoss@glc.org

New York State Liquor Authority
80 S Swan St, Ste 900
Albany, NY 12210
518-486-4767
Web site: www.abc.state.ny.us

Chairman:
  Daniel B Boyle. . . . . 518-486-4767 or 212-961-8347
Commissioner:
  Lawrence J Gedda . . . . 518-486-4767 or 212-961-8347
Commissioner:
  Noreen Healey . . . . 518-486-4767 or 212-961-8347
Chief Executive Officer:
  Joshua B Toas, Esq. 518-486-4767
Counsel:
  Thomas J Donohue. 518-486-4767
Deputy Commissioner, Licensing, NYC:
  Fred J Gioffre 212-961-8301
Senior Deputy Commissioner, Administration:
  J Mark Anderson 518-486-4767
Deputy Commissioner, Government Affairs:
  Thomas J O'Connor 518-486-4767
Public Information Officer, NYC:
  Kimberly Morella. 212-961-8331

Offices and agencies generally appear in alphabetical order, except when specific order is requested by listee.

COMMERCE, INDUSTRY & ECONOMIC DEVELOPMENT / New York State

Director, Communications:
William Crowley 518-486-4767
e-mail: pressoffice@abc.state.ny.us

United Nations Development Corporation
Two United Nations Plaza, 27th Fl
New York, NY 10017-4403
212-888-1618 Fax: 212-588-0758
e-mail: info@undc.org
Web site: www.undc.org

Chair, Board of Directors:
George Klein 212-888-1618
President & CEO:
Roy M Goodman 212-888-1618
Executive VP, Director of Development:
Jeffrey Feldman 212-888-1618
Senior VP, Controller:
Jorge Ortiz 212-888-1618
Senior VP, Operations:
Robert M Preissner 212-888-1618

NEW YORK STATE LEGISLATURE

See Legislative Branch in Section 1 for additional Standing Committee and Subcommitee information.

Assembly Standing Committees

Cities
Chair:
James F Brennan (D) 518-455-5377
Ranking Minority Member:
Thomas J Kirwan (R) 518-455-5762

Consumer Affairs & Protection
Chair:
Audrey I Pheffer (D) 518-455-4292
Ranking Minority Member:
Peter D Lopez (R) 518-455-5363

Corporations, Authorities & Commissions
Chair:
Richard L Brodsky (D) 518-455-5753
Ranking Minority Member:
Stephen Hawley (R) 518-455-5811

Economic Development, Job Creation, Commerce & Industry
Chair:
Robin L Schimminger (D) 518-455-4767
Ranking Minority Member:
Marc Butler (R) 518-455-5393

Small Business
Chair:
Mark Weprin (D) 518-455-5806

Ranking Minority Member:
William Reilich (R) 518-455-4664

Assembly Task Forces

University-Industry Cooperation, Task Force on
Chair:
William B Magnarelli (D) 518-455-4826
Coordinator:
Maureen Schoolman 518-455-4884/fax: 518-455-4175

Senate Standing Committees

Cities
Chair:
Serphin R Maltese (R) 518-455-3281
Ranking Minority Member:
Antoine Thompson (D) 518-455-3371

Commerce, Economic Development & Small Business
Chair:
James S Alesi (R) 518-455-2015
Ranking Minority Member:
Efrain Gonzalez, Jr (D) 518-455-3395

Consumer Protection
Chair:
Charles J Fuschillo, Jr (R) 518-455-3341
Ranking Minority Member:
Carl Kruger (D) 518-455-2460

Corporations, Authorities & Commissions
Chair:
John J Flanagan (R) 518-455-3341
Ranking Minority Member:
Bill Perkins (D) 518-455-2441

Senate/Assembly Legislative Commissions

Rural Resources, Legislative Commission on
Senate Chair:
George H Winner Jr (R) 518-455-2091
Assembly Vice Chair:
David R Koon (D) 518-455-5784
Assembly Program Manager:
Susan Bartle 518-455-3999/fax: 518-455-4175
Senate Program Manager:
Ronald C Brach 518-455-2544/fax: 518-426-6960
Counsel:
Donald A Walsh 518-455-2544

Science & Technology, Legislative Commission on
Assembly Chair:
William B Magnarelli (D) 518-455-4826
Senior Vice Chair:
Vacant 518-455-0000
Senior Program Manager:
Philip Johnson 518-455-5081

Offices and agencies generally appear in alphabetical order, except when specific order is requested by listee.

COMMERCE, INDUSTRY & ECONOMIC DEVELOPMENT / U.S. Government

U.S. Government

EXECUTIVE DEPARTMENTS AND RELATED AGENCIES

Commodity Futures Trading Commission
Web site: www.cftc.gov

Eastern Region
140 Broadway, New York, NY 10005
Regional Coordinator:
Stephen J Obie..................... 646-746-9700/fax: 646-746-9766

Consumer Product Safety Commission
609-927-1840 Fax: 609-927-4013
Web site: www.cpsc.gov

Eastern Regional Center .... fax: 212-620-5338
201 Varick St, Rm 903, New York, NY 10014
Acting Director:
Beverly Kohen 212-620-6180

Export Import Bank of the United States
Web site: www.exim.gov

Northeast Regional Office .... fax: 212-809-2687
33 Whitehall St, 22nd Fl Ste B, New York, NY 10004
212-809-2650 Fax: 212-809-2687
Regional Director:
Thomas Cummings 212-809-2652/fax: 212-809-2646
e-mail: thomas.cummings@exim.gov
Administrative Assistant:
Jennifer Drakes.................................... 212-809-2649
e-mail: jennifer.drakes@exim.gov

Federal Trade Commission
212-607-2828 Fax: 212-607-2822
Web site: www.ftc.gov

Northeast Regional Office .... fax: 212-607-2822
1 Bowling Green, Ste 318, New York, NY 10004
Regional Director:
Barbara Anthony 212-607-2829
Senior Assistant Regional Director:
Thomas Cohn 212-607-2829

Small Business Administration
Web site: www.sba.gov

Region II New York .... fax: 212-264-4963
26 Federal Plaza, Ste 3108, New York, NY 10278
212-264-4354 Fax: 212-264-4963
e-mail: michael.carbone@sba.gov
Regional Administrator:
William Mangler Jr................................. 212-264-1450
Regional Advocate:
Christine Glassnerg 212-264-7752

District Offices
Buffalo .... fax: 716-551-4418
Niagara Center, 130 S Elmwood Avenue, Suite 540, Buffalo, NY 14202
716-551-4301 Fax: 716-551-4418
District Director:
Franklin J Sciortino 716-551-4301/fax: 716-551-4418
New Jersey
2 Gateway Center, 15th Floor, Newark, NJ 07102
973-645-2434
District Director:
James A Kocsi............................. 973-645-2434
New York City................................ fax: 212-264-4963
26 Federal Plaza, Ste 3100, New York, NY 10278
212-264-4354 Fax: 212-264-4963
District Director:
Jose Sifontes................ 212-264-4354/fax: 212-264-4963
Syracuse .... fax: 315-471-9288
401 S Salina St, 5th Fl, Syracuse, NY 13202
315-471-9393 Fax: 315-471-9288
District Director:
Bernard J Paprocki 315-471-9393/fax: 315-471-9288

New York Business Information Center
1 Computer Dr South, Albany, NY 12205
Director:
Daniel O'Connell............ 518-446-1118 x231/fax: 518-446-1228
e-mail: daniel.oconnel@sba.gov

US Commerce Department
Web site: www.doc.gov

Census Bureau
Web site: www.census.gov

Boston Region (includes upstate New York)
4 Copley Pl, Ste 301, PO Box 9108, Boston, MA 02117-9108
Regional Director:
Kathleen Ludgate 617-424-4501/fax: 617-424-0547

New York Region
395 Hudson St, Ste 800, New York, NY 10014-7451
Regional Director:
Lester A Farthing 212-584-3400/fax: 212-478-4800

Economic Development Administration
Web site: www.doc.gov/eda/

Philadelphia Region (includes New York)
Curtis Ctr, Ste 140 South, Independence Sq West, Philadelphia, PA 19106
Representative, NYC & Long Island:
Edward Hummel 215-597-6767/fax: 215-597-6669

Upstate New York Office
620 Erie Blvd W, Ste 104, Syracuse, NY 13204-2442
Representative:
Harold J Marshall 315-448-0938/fax: 315-448-0939

Minority Business Development Agency
Web site: www.mbda.gov

New York Region
26 Federal Plaza, Rm 3720, New York, NY 10278
Regional Director:
Heyward B Davenport............. 212-264-3262/fax: 212-264-0725

Offices and agencies generally appear in alphabetical order, except when specific order is requested by listee.

COMMERCE, INDUSTRY & ECONOMIC DEVELOPMENT / U.S. Government

National Oceanic & Atmospheric Administration

National Weather Service, Eastern Region
630 Johnson Ave, Ste 202, Bohemia, NY 11716
Web site: www.nws.noaa.gov
Director:
    Dean Gulezian 631-244-0100/fax: 631-244-0109
    e-mail: dean.gulezian@noaa.gov
Deputy Director:
    Mickey J Brown 631-244-0102
Public Affairs Officer:
    Marcie Katcher 631-244-0149/fax: 631-244-0167
Chief, Meteorological Services Division:
    John Guiney 631-244-0121
Chief, Regional Hydrology Division:
    Peter Gabrielsen 631-244-0111
Chief, Scientific Services Division:
    Kenneth Johnson 631-244-0136

US Commercial Service - International Trade Administration

Web site: www.export.gov

Buffalo US Export Assistance Center
130 South Elmwood Ave, Suite 530, Buffalo, NY 14202
Director:
    James C Mariano 716-551-4191/fax: 716-551-5290
    e-mail: james.mariano@mail.doc.gov

Harlem US Export Assistance Center
163 West 125th St, Ste 901, New York, NY 10027
Director:
    K L Fredericks 212-860-6200/fax: 212-860-6203
    e-mail: kl.fredericks@mail.doc.gov

Long Island US Export Assistance Center
20 Exchange Place, 40th Floor, New York, NY 10005
Director:
    Kenneth Reidbord 212-809-2642/fax: 212-809-2687
    e-mail: kenneth.reidbord@mail.doc.gov

New York US Export Assistance Center
20 Exchange Pl, 40th Fl, New York, NY 10005
Director, NY-NJ Hub:
    William D Spitler 212-809-2642/fax: 212-809-2687
    e-mail: william.spitler@mail.doc.gov

Rochester US Export Assistance Center
400 Andrews St, Ste 710, Rochester, NY 14604
Web site: www.export.gov
Director:
    Erin Cole 585-263-6480/fax: 585-325-6505
    e-mail: erin.cole@mail.doc.gov

Westchester US Export Assistance Center
707 Westchester Ave, Ste 209, White Plains, NY 10604
Director:
    Joan Kanlian 914-682-6712/fax: 914-682-6698
    e-mail: joan.kanlian@mail.doc.gov

US Department of Agriculture

Rural Development

Web site: www.rurdev.usda.gov/ny

New York State Office . . . . fax: 315-477-6438
The Galleries of Syracuse, 441 S Salina St, Ste 357, 5th Fl, Syracuse, NY 13202-2425
TTY: 315-477-6447 or 315-477-6400 Fax: 315-477-6438
Acting State Director:
    Scott Collins 315-477-6400
Special Projects Representative:
    Vacant 315-477-6433
Program Director, Rural Business-Cooperative Service:
    Walter D Schermerhorn 315-477-6425
    e-mail: walter.schermerhorn@ny.usda.gov

US Justice Department

Web site: www.usdoj.gov

Antitrust Division-New York Field Office
26 Federal Plaza, Rm 3630, New York, NY 10278-0096
Chief:
    Ralph T Giordano 212-264-0391/fax: 212-264-7453
    e-mail: ralph.giordano@usdoj.gov
Assistant Chief:
    John McReynolds 212-264-0394/fax: 212-264-7453

Civil Division-Commercial Litigation Branch
26 Federal Plz, Rm 346, New York, NY 10278
Attorney-in-Charge:
    Barbara S Williams 212-264-9240/fax: 212-264-1916

Community Relations Service-Northeast & Carribean Region
26 Federal Plaza, Ste 36-118, New York, NY 10278
Regional Director:
    Reinaldo Rivera, Jr 212-264-0700/fax: 212-264-2143

US Securities & Exchange Commission

Web site: www.sec.gov

Northeast Region . . . . fax: 212-336-1322
3 World Financial Center, Ste 400, New York, NY 10281
212-336-1100 Fax: 212-336-1322
e-mail: newyork@sec.gov
Regional Director:
    Mark Schonfeld 212-336-1100

Broker-Dealer Inspection Program
Associate Regional Director:
    Robert A Sollazzo 212-336-1070

Enforcement Division
Associate Regional Director:
    Robert B Blackburn 212-336-1050

Investment Management
Associate Regional Director:
    Vacant 212-336-0199

U.S. CONGRESS

See U.S. Congress Chapter for additional Standing Committee and Subcommittee information.

House of Representatives Standing Committees

Energy & Commerce
Chair:
    John D Dingell (D-MI) 202-225-2927
Ranking Minority Member:
    Joe Barton (R-TX) 202-225-2002
New York Delegate:
    Eliot L Engel (D) 202-225-2464
New York Delegate:
    Vito Fossella (R) 202-225-3371

Offices and agencies generally appear in alphabetical order, except when specific order is requested by listee.

COMMERCE, INDUSTRY & ECONOMIC DEVELOPMENT / Private Sector

New York Delegate:
   Edolphus Towns (D).................................202-225-5936

Foreign Affairs
Chair:
   Tom Lantos (D-CA).................................202-225-3531
Ranking Minority Member:
   Ileana Ros Lehtinen (R-FL).......................202-225-3931
New York Delegate:
   Gary L Ackerman (D)..............................202-225-2601
New York Delegate:
   Joseph Crowley (D)................................202-225-3965
New York Delegate:
   Eliot L Engel (D)...................................202-225-2464
New York Delegate:
   Amory Houghton (R)..............................202-225-3161
New York Delegate:
   Peter T King (R)...................................202-225-7896
New York Delegate:
   Gregory W Meeks (D)............................202-225-3461

Small Business
Chair:
   Nydia Velazquez (D-NY).........................202-225-2361
Ranking Minority Member:
   Steve Chabot (R-OH).............................202-225-2216
New York Delegate:
   Sue W Kelly (R)....................................202-225-5441

Joint Senate & House Standing Committees

Economic Committee, Joint
Chair:
   Sen Charles E Schumer (D-NY)................202-224-6542

Vice Chair:
   Rep Carolyn B Maloney (D-NY)..............202-225-7944
Ranking Republican Member:
   Rep Jim Saxton (R-NJ)...........................202-225-4765
New York Delegate:
   Carolyn Maloney (D)..............................202-225-7944
New York Delegate:
   Maurice D Hinchey (D)...........................202-225-6335

Senate Standing Committees

Commerce, Science & Transportation
Chair:
   Daniel K Inouye (D-HI)............................202-224-3934
Ranking Minority Member:
   Ted Stevens (R-AK)................................202-224-3004

Finance
Chair:
   Max Baucus (D-MT)...............................202-224-2651
Ranking Minority Member:
   Chuck Grassley (R-IA)............................202-224-3744

Foreign Relations
Chair:
   Joseph R Biden, Jr (D-DE)........................202-224-5042
Ranking Minority Member:
   Richard G Lugar (R-IN)...........................202-228-0360

Small Business & Entrepreneurship
Chair:
   John F Kerry (D-MA)..............................202-224-2742
Ranking Minority Member:
   Oympia J Snowe (R-ME).......................202-224-5344

Private Sector

AeA New York Council
255 Fuller Rd, Albany Nanotechnology Complex, Albany, NY 12203
518-437-8820 Fax: 518-437-8821
e-mail: justin-wright@aeanet.org
Web site: www.aeanet.org
Justin Wright, Executive Director
Electronics, software & information technology industries; support of high tech industry goals

Altria Corporate Services
120 Park Ave, 16th Fl, New York, NY 10017
917-663-4000
Web site: www.altria.com
Louis C Camilleri, Chairman & Chief Executive Officer
Manufacturing & marketing of foods, tobacco, alcoholic beverages

American Chemistry/American Plastics Council
One Commerce Plaza, 99 Washington Ave, Ste 701, Albany, NY 12210
518-432-7835 Fax: 518-426-2276
e-mail: steve_rosario@americanchemistry.com
Web site: www.americanchemistry.com
Stephen Rosario, Director

American Council of Engineering Companies of NY (ACEC New York)
6 Airline Drive, Albany, NY 12205
518-452-8611 Fax: 518-452-1710
e-mail: jay@acecny.org
Web site: www.acecny.org
Jay J Simson, Executive Director
Business association for consulting engineering

American Institute of Architects (AIA) New York State Inc
52 S Pearl St, 3rd Fl, Albany, NY 12207
518-449-3334 Fax: 518-426-8176
e-mail: aianys@aianys.org
Web site: www.aianys.org
Edward C Farrell, Executive Director
Architectural regulations, state policy & smart growth

American Management Association International
1601 Broadway, New York, NY 10019
212-586-8100 or 800-262-9699 Fax: 212-903-8168
Web site: www.amanet.org
Edward T Reilly, President & Chief Executive Officer
Business education & management development programs for individuals & organizations

Offices and agencies generally appear in alphabetical order, except when specific order is requested by listee.

COMMERCE, INDUSTRY & ECONOMIC DEVELOPMENT / Private Sector

Associated Builders & Contractors, Empire State Chapter
6369 Collamer Dr, East Syracuse, NY 13057-1115
315-463-7539 or 800-477-7743 Fax: 315-463-7621
e-mail: empire@abcnys.org
Web site: www.abcnys.org
Rebecca Meinking, President
Merit shop construction trade association

Associated General Contractors of America, NYS Chapter
10 Airline Dr, Ste 203, Albany, NY 12205-1025
518-456-1134 Fax: 518-456-1198
e-mail: agcadmin@agcnys.org
Web site: www.agcnys.org
A J Castelbuono, President & Chief Executive Officer

Association Development Group Inc
119 Washington Ave, Ste 300, Albany, NY 12210
518-465-7085 Fax: 518-427-9495
e-mail: info@adgcommunications.com
Web site: www.adgcommunications.com
Kathleen A Van De Loo, President
Association management, communications, education & training, strategic planning, graphic design, web design, database design

Association for a Better New York
355 Lexington Ave, 11th Fl, New York, NY 10017
212-370-5800 Fax: 212-661-5877
e-mail: info@abny.org
Web site: www.abny.org
Michelle Adams, Executive Director
NYC public policy issues forums & committees

Association of Graphic Communications
330 Seventh Ave, 9th Fl, New York, NY 10001
212-279-2100 x108 Fax: 212-279-5381
e-mail: spindrvrk@agcomm.org
Web site: www.agcomm.org
Vicki R Keenan, VP, Public Affairs
Promote the economic well-being & public perception of printing & graphic communications within the NY/NJ/CT metro area

Better Business Bureau of Metropolitan New York
257 Park Ave South, 4th Fl, New York, NY 10010-7384
212-533-6200 Fax: 212-477-4912
e-mail: inquiry@newyork.bbb.org
Web site: www.newyork.bbb.org
Susan D McMillan, President
Membership organization promoting ethical business practices

NYS Bar Assn, Public Relations Cmte
Brown & Kelly, LLP
424 Main St, 1500 Liberty Bldg, Buffalo, NY 14202-3615
716-854-2620 Fax: 716-854-0082
e-mail: phassett@brownkelly.com
Paul Michael Hassett, Chair

Building Contractors Association
451 Park Ave South, 4th Fl, New York, NY 10016
212-683-8080 Fax: 212-683-0404
e-mail: nybca1@aol.com
Web site: www.ny-bca.com
Paul J O'Brien, Managing Director
Commercial contractors

Building Industry Association of NYC Inc
3225 Victory Blvd, Staten Island, NY 10314
718-720-3070 Fax: 718-720-3088
e-mail: lbrinker@webuildnyc.com
Web site: www.webuildnyc.com
Laurence H Brinker, Executive Vice President

Business Council for International Understanding
1212 Ave of the Americas, 10th Fl, New York, NY 10036
212-490-0460 Fax: 212-697-8526
Web site: www.bciu.org
Peter J Tichansky, President & Chief Executive Officer
Promoting dialogue & action between the business & government communities to expand international commerce

Business Council of New York State Inc
152 Washington Ave, Albany, NY 12210
518-465-7511 or 800-358-1202 Fax: 518-465-4389
e-mail: dan.walsh@bcnys.org
Web site: www.bcnys.org
Daniel B Walsh, President & Chief Executive Officer
Create an economic renaissance for NYS & its people

Center for Economic Growth Inc
63 State Street, Albany, NY 12207
518-465-8975 Fax: 518-465-6681
e-mail: ceg@ceg.org
Web site: www.ceg.org
F Michael Tucker, President/Chief Executive Officer
Business membership nonprofit promoting economic & business development in the Capital Region and Tech Valley

Columbia University, Science & Technology Ventures
80 Claremont Avenue, 4th Fl, New York, NY 10027
212-854-6777 Fax: 212-854-8463
e-mail: mc1378@columbia.edu
Web site: www.stv.columbia.edu
Michael Cleare, Executive Director
Identify & patent new inventions & copyright materials; interact with industry to setup collaborative research agreements

Conference Board (The)
845 Third Ave, New York, NY 10022
212-339-0300 Fax: 212-836-3805
e-mail: gail.fosler@conference-board.org
Web site: www.conference-board.org
Gail Fosler, Executive Vice President & Chief Economist
Research for business

Offices and agencies generally appear in alphabetical order, except when specific order is requested by listee.

COMMERCE, INDUSTRY & ECONOMIC DEVELOPMENT / Private Sector

Construction Contractors Association of the Hudson Valley Inc
330 Meadow Ave, Newburgh, NY 12550
845-562-4280 Fax: 845-562-1448
Web site: www.constructioncontractorsassociation.com
James Jay Bodrato, Executive Director

Consumers Union
101 Truman Ave, Yonkers, NY 10703-1057
914-378-2000 Fax: 914-378-2905
Web site: www.consumerreports.org; www.consumersunion.org
Jean Halloran, Director, Consumer Policy Institute
Publisher of Consumer Reports magazine; independent, nonprofit testing & information organization serving only consumers

Cornell University, Economics Department
450 Uris Hall, Ithaca, NY 14853-7601
607-255-6283 Fax: 607-255-2818
e-mail: dae3@cornell.edu
Web site: www.arts.cornell.edu/econ
David Easley, Professor
Microeconomic theory, financial economics

Dale Carnegie & Associates Inc
290 Motor Parkway, Hauppauge, NY 11788-5102
631-415-9300 or 800-231-5800 Fax: 631-415-9358
e-mail: peter_handal@dale-carnegie.com
Web site: www.dale-carnegie.com
Peter Handal, President & Chief Executive Officer
Executive leadership training

Davis Polk & Wardwell
450 Lexington Ave, New York, NY 10017
212-450-4000 Fax: 212-450-3800
e-mail: henry.king@dpw.com
Web site: www.dpw.com
Henry L King, Senior Counsel
Securities litigation & antitrust law

Decision Strategies Group
111 Washington Ave, Ste 409, Albany, NY 12210
518-436-0607 Fax: 518-432-4359
e-mail: lynnmueller@dsgny.com
Web site: www.decisionstrategiesgroup.com
I Lynn Mueller, President
Strategic planning & communications consulting

Development Counsellors International
215 Park Ave S, 10th Floor, New York, NY 10003
212-725-0707 Fax: 212-725-2254
e-mail: andy.levine@dc-intl.com
Web site: www.aboutdci.com
Andrew T Levine, President
Marketing services for economic development & tourism

EVCI Career Colleges Holding Corp
1 Van Der Donck St, Yonkers, NY 10701-7049
914-623-0700 Fax: 914-964-8222
e-mail: info@evcinc.com
Web site: www.evcinc.com
Dr John J McGrath, President/Chief Executive Officer
Own & operate accredited career & college centers in NY & PA emphasizing business, technology & allied health programs

Eastern Contractors Association Inc
6 Airline Dr, Albany, NY 12205-1095
518-869-0961 Fax: 518-869-2378
e-mail: info@ecainc.org
Web site: www.ecainc.org
Todd G Helrich, Managing Director
Commercial development & construction

Eastman Kodak Company
1250 H Street, Ste 800, Washington, DC 20005
202-857-3474 Fax: 202-857-3401
e-mail: stephen.ciccone@kodak.com
Web site: www.kodak.com
Stephen J Ciccone, Director & Vice President of Public Affairs
Manufactures & markets imaging systems & related services

Empire Center for New York State Policy
PO Box 7113, Albany, NY 12224
518-434-3100 Fax: 518-434-3130
e-mail: info@empirecenter.org
Web site: www.empirecenter.org
Edmund J McMahon, Director
An independent nonpartisan research organization dedicated to fostering greater economic growth, opportunity, and individual responsibility in the Empire State. The Empire Center is a project of the Manhattan Inst for Policy Research.

Empire State Restaurant & Tavern Association Inc
40 Sheridan Ave, Albany, NY 12210
518-436-8121 Fax: 518-436-7287
e-mail: esrta@verizon.net
Web site: www.esrta.org
Scott Wexler, Executive Director

Empire State Society of Association Executives Inc
991 Broadway, Suite 208, Albany, NY 12204
518-463-1755 Fax: 518-463-5257
e-mail: penny@essae.org
Web site: www.essae.org
Penny Murphy, President & Chief Executive Officer
Education, information, research & networking for professional staff of not-for-profit trade business & professional associations

Eric Mower & Associates
500 Plum St, Syracuse, NY 13204
315-466-1000 Fax: 315-466-2000
e-mail: csteenstra@mower.com
Web site: www.mower.com
Chris Steenstra, Senior Partner
Marketing communications & issues management

Offices and agencies generally appear in alphabetical order, except when specific order is requested by listee.

COMMERCE, INDUSTRY & ECONOMIC DEVELOPMENT / Private Sector

NYS Bar Assn, Antitrust Law Section
Federal Trade Commission
One Bowling Green, Ste 318, New York, NY 10004
212-607-2828
e-mail: banthony@ftc.gov
Barbara Anthony, Chair

Food Industry Alliance of New York State Inc
130 Washington Ave, Albany, NY 12210
518-434-8144 Fax: 518-434-9962
e-mail: michael@fiany.com
Web site: www.fiany.com
Michael Rosen, Vice President for Government Relations & General Counsel
Assn of retail grocery, wholesale & supplier/manufacturer food companies

General Building Contractors of NYS/AGC
6 Airline Dr, Albany, NY 12205
518-869-2207 Fax: 518-869-0846
e-mail: jeffz@gbcnys.agc.org
Web site: www.gbcnys.agc.org
Jeffrey J Zogg, Executive Director

General Contractors Association of NY
60 East 42nd St, Rm 3510, New York, NY 10165
212-687-3131 Fax: 212-808-5267
e-mail: felice@gca.gcany.net
Felice Farber, Director, Government Relations
Heavy construction, transportation

Geto & deMilly Inc
130 E 40th St, New York, NY 10016
212-686-4551 Fax: 212-213-6850
e-mail: pr@getodmilly.com
Ethan Geto, President
Public & government relations

Gilbert Tweed Associates Inc
415 Madison Ave, 20th Fl, New York, NY 10017
212-758-3000 Fax: 212-832-1040
e-mail: spinson@gilberttweed.com
Web site: www.gilberttweed.com
Stephanie L Pinson, President
Executive searches & recruitment in public transit, transportation, energy, utilities, communication & insurance

NYS Bar Assn, Intellectual Property Law Section
Hartman & Winnicki, PC
115 W Century Rd, Paramus, NJ 7654
201-967-8040 Fax: 201-967-0590
e-mail: rick@ravin.com
Richard L Ravin, Chair

IBM Corporation
80 State St, Albany, NY 12207
518-487-6733 Fax: 518-487-6679
Web site: www.ibm.com
Jim Costa, Director, Government Affairs

Intermagnetics General Corporation
450 Old Niskyuna Rd, PO Box 461, Latham, NY 12110-0461
518-782-1122 Fax: 518-786-8216
e-mail: corporate@igc.com
Web site: www.igc.com
Kathy Sheehan, Vice President & General Counsel

International Flavors & Fragrances Inc
521 West 57th Street, New York, NY 10019-2960
212-765-5500 Fax: 212-708-7132
Web site: www.iff.com
Dennis M Meany, Senior Vice President, General Counsel & Secretary
Create & manufacture flavors & fragrances for consumer products

Macy's East Inc
151 W 34th St, 18th Fl, New York, NY 10001
212-494-5568 Fax: 212-494-1857
e-mail: ed.goldberg@macys.com
Edward Jay Goldberg, Senior Vice President Government & Consumer Affairs
Retail department/specialty stores

Manhattan Institute for Policy Research
52 Vanderbilt Avenue, 2nd Floor, New York, NY 10017
212-599-7000 x315 Fax: 212-599-3494
e-mail: communications@manhattan-institute.org
Web site: www.manhattan-institute.org
Lindsay Y Craig, Executive Director, Communications
Think-tank promoting the development & dissemination of new ideas that foster greater economic choice & individual responsibility

Manufacturers Association of Central New York
One Webster's Landing, 5th Fl, Syracuse, NY 13202-1044
315-474-4201 Fax: 315-474-0524
e-mail: kburns@macny.org
Web site: www.macny.org
Karyn E Burns, Director, Communications & Government Relations
Training, education, compensation data & government relations services, HR services, consulting, purchasing consortiums

NYS Bar Assn, Business Law Section
Menaker & Herrmann LLP
10 East 40th Street, New York, NY 10016
212-545-1900 Fax: 212-545-1656
e-mail: sfa@mhjur.com
Web site: www.mhjur.com
Samuel F Abernethy, Chair
Advice and counsel in Commercial Litigation, Corporate Securities & Finance and Commodities and Derivitives land

Mid-Hudson Pattern for Progress
6 Albany Post Rd, Newburgh, NY 12550-1439
914-565-4900 Fax: 914-565-4918
e-mail: mditullo@pfprogress.org
Web site: www.pattern-for-progress.org
Jonathan Drapkin, President
Regional planning, research & policy development

Offices and agencies generally appear in alphabetical order, except when specific order is requested by listee.

COMMERCE, INDUSTRY & ECONOMIC DEVELOPMENT / Private Sector

NYS Bar Assn, Commercial & Federal Litigation Section
Montclare & Wachtler
67 Wall St, 22nd Fl, New York, NY 10005
212-509-3900 Fax: 212-509-7239
e-mail: ljwachtler@montclarewachtler.com
Web site: www.montclarewachtler.com
Lauren J Wachtler, Chair

NY Society of Association Executives Inc (NYSAE)
322 Eighth Avenue, Suite 501, New York, NY 10001-8001
212-206-8230 Fax: 212-645-1147
e-mail: jdolci@nysaenet.org
Web site: www.nysaenet.org
Joel A Dolci, President & Chief Executive Officer

NYS Association of Electrical Contractors
16 Wade Rd, Latham, NY 12110
518-785-3676 or 800-724-1904 Fax: 518-785-0912
Web site: www.nysaec.org
Jay Mangione, Managing Director

NYS Builders Association Inc
One Commerce Plaza, Ste 704, Albany, NY 12210
518-465-2492 Fax: 518-465-0635
e-mail: phill@nysba.com
Web site: www.nysba.com
Philip A LaRocque, Executive Vice President
Advocate for building and housing industry on all legislative & regulatory issues impacting builders and housing

NYS Building & Construction Trades Council
71 West 23 St, New York, NY 10010
212-647-0700 Fax: 212-647-0705
Edward J Malloy, President

NYS Clinical Laboratory Association Inc
62 William St, 2nd Fl, New York, NY 10005
212-664-7999 Fax: 212-248-3008
e-mail: info@nyscla.com
Web site: www.nyscla.com
Tom Rafalsky, President
Promote the common business and regulataory interests of clinical laboratories located or operated within the state

NYS Economic Development Council
19 Dove Street, Ste 101, Albany, NY 12210
518-426-4058 Fax: 518-426-4059
e-mail: mcmahon@nysedc.org
Web site: www.nysedc.org
Brian McMahon, Executive Director
Economic development professionals membership organization

NYS Society of Certified Public Accountants
3 Park Ave, 18th Fl, New York, NY 10016-5991
212-719-8300 or 800-633-6320 Fax: 212-719-3364
e-mail: lgrumet@nysscpa.org
Web site: www.nysscpa.org
Louis Grumet, Executive Director

NYS Trade Adjustment Assistance Center
81-85 State Street, 4th Floor, Binghamton, NY 13901
607-771-0875 Fax: 607-724-2404
e-mail: information@nystaac.org
Web site: www.nystaac.org
Louis G McKeage, Director
Advises US manufacturers on competing with foreign imports

National Association of Black Accountants, NY Chapter
PO Box 2791, Grand Central Station, New York, NY 10163
212-969-0560 Fax: 646-349-9620
e-mail: info@nabany.org
Web site: www.nabany.org
L Matthew Perry, President
Represents the interest of African Americans & other minorities in accounting, auditing, business, consulting, finance & information technology

National Federation of Independent Business
1 Commerce Plaza, Ste 1119, Albany, NY 12260-1000
518-434-1262 Fax: 518-221-7513
e-mail: mike.elmendorf@NFIB.org
Web site: www.nfib.org
Michael Elmendorf, State Director
Small business advocacy; supporting pro-small business candidates at the state & federal levels

New York Association of Convenience Stores
130 Washington Ave, Suite 300, Albany, NY 12210-2219
518-432-1400 Fax: 518-432-7400
e-mail: info@nyacs.org
Web site: www.nyacs.org
Jim Calvin, President
Retail & small business issues

New York Biotechnology Association (The)
25 Health Sciences Drive, Ste 203, Stony Brook, NY 11790
631-444-8895 Fax: 631-444-8896
e-mail: info@nyba.org
Web site: www.nyba.org
Karin A Duncker, Executive Director
Development & growth of NYS-based biotechnology-related industries & institutions; strengthen competitiveness of the state as a location for biotech/biomed research, education & industry

New York Building Congress
44 W 28th St, 12th Fl, New York, NY 10001-4212
212-481-9230 Fax: 212-447-6037
e-mail: rtanders55@aol.com
Web site: www.buildingcongress.com
Richard T Anderson, President
Coalition of design, construction & real estate organizations

New York Business Development Corporation
50 Beaver St, 6th Fl, Albany, NY 12207
518-463-2268 Fax: 518-463-0494
e-mail: rlazar@nybdc.com
Web site: www.nybdc.com
Robert W Lazar, President & Chief Executive Officer
Small business lending

Offices and agencies generally appear in alphabetical order, except when specific order is requested by listee.

COMMERCE, INDUSTRY & ECONOMIC DEVELOPMENT / Private Sector

New York Mercantile Exchange Inc
1 North End Ave, New York, NY 10282-1101
212-299-2000 Fax: 212-301-4568
Web site: www.nymex.com
Mitchell Steinhause, Chair
Commodity trading

New York State Auto Dealers Association
37 Elk St, Albany, NY 12207
518-463-1148 x204 Fax: 518-432-1309
e-mail: bob@nysada.com
Web site: www.nysada.com
Robert Vancavage, President

New York State Restaurant Association
409 New Karner Rd, Albany, NY 12205
518-452-4222 Fax: 518-452-4497
e-mail: ricks@nysra.org
Web site: www.nysra.org
Rick J Sampson, President & Chief Executive Officer

Berkley Center for Entrepreneurial Studies NYU, Stern School of Business
44 West Fourth Street, Suite 7-91, New York, NY 10012-1126
212-998-8943 Fax: 212-995-4211
e-mail: william.baumol@nyu.edu
Web site: http://pages.stern.nyu.edu/~wbaumol
William J Baumol, Professor of Economics & Academic Director of B.C.E.S.
Productivity growth, downsizing, scale economies; trade, anti-trust; economics of industry, the environment, the arts & entrpreneurship

Northeast Equipment Dealers Association Inc
128 Metropolitan Park Dr, Liverpool, NY 13088
315-457-0314 Fax: 315-451-3548
e-mail: rgaiss@ne-equip.com
Web site: www.ne-equip.com
Ralph F Gaiss, CEO
Agricultural, industrial & outdoor power equipment

Partnership for New York City
One Battery Park Plaza, 5th Fl, New York, NY 10004-1479
212-493-7403 or 212-493-7564 Fax: 212-493-7778
Web site: www.partnershipfornyc.org
MarySol Rodriguez, Vice President, Government Affairs
Government Affairs; Business organization working in partnership with government, labor & the nonprofit sector to enhance the NYC economy

Pepsi Co
700 Anderson Hill Rd, MD 3/1-311, Purchase, NY 10577
914-253-2609 Fax: 914-249-8203
e-mail: pwilcox@pepsi.com
Web site: www.pepsi.com
Peter G Wilcox, Director, Government Affairs
Manufacture, sell & distribute soft drinks, concentrates, syrups, snack foods & beverages

Perry Davis Associates
25 W 45th St, Suite 1405, New York, NY 10036
212-840-1166 Fax: 212-840-1514
e-mail: perry@perrydavis.com
Web site: www.perrydavis.com
Perry Davis, President
Economic development & fundraising & management consulting for nonprofit organizations

NYS Bar Assn, Multi-Jurisdictional Practice Cmte
Proskauer Rose LLP
1585 Broadway, New York, NY 10036-8299
212-969-3245 Fax: 212-969-2900
e-mail: keppler@proskauer.com
Web site: www.proskauer.com
Klaus Eppler, Chair

Public Policy Institute of NYS Inc
152 Washington Ave, Albany, NY 12210
518-465-7511 Fax: 518-432-4537
e-mail: david.shaffer@bcnys.org
Web site: www.ppinys.org
David Shaffer, President
Conduct & publish research on NYS economic development issues

Regional Plan Association
4 Irving Place, 7th Fl, New York, NY 10003
212-253-2727 Fax: 212-253-5666
e-mail: yaro@rpa.org
Web site: www.rpa.org
Robert D Yaro, President
Develops & implements land-use, community design, transportation, open-space preservation, economic development & social equity proposals

Retail Council of New York State
258 State St, PO Box 1992, Albany, NY 12201
518-465-3586 or 800-442-3589 Fax: 518-465-7960
e-mail: info@retailcouncilnys.com
Web site: www.retailcouncilnys.com
James R Sherin, President & Chief Executive Officer

Sawchuk Brown Associates
41 State St, Ste 500, Albany, NY 12207
518-462-0318 Fax: 518-462-0688
e-mail: info@sawchukbrown.com
Web site: www.sawchukbrown.com
Sean Casey, Senior Vice President, Public Affairs
Public affairs, public relations, marketing, association communication

Society of Professional Engineers Inc (NYS)
RPI Technology Park, 385 Jordan Rd, Troy, NY 12180-7620
518-283-7490 Fax: 518-283-7495
e-mail: knorris@nysspe.org
Web site: www.nysspe.org
Kelly K Norris, Executive Director
Promotes and defends the lawful and ethical practice of engineering

---

Offices and agencies generally appear in alphabetical order, except when specific order is requested by listee.

COMMERCE, INDUSTRY & ECONOMIC DEVELOPMENT / Private Sector

Software & Information Industry Association
1090 Vermont Ave, NW, 6th Fl, Washington, DC 20005-4095
202-289-7442 Fax: 202-289-7097
Web site: www.siia.net
Ken Wasch, President
Issues affecting the software & information industry, in particular electronic commerce & the digital marketplace

Support Services Alliance Inc
107 Prospect St, PO Box 130, Schoharie, NY 12157
800-322-3920 or 518-295-7966 Fax: 518-295-8556
e-mail: info@ssamembers.com
Web site: www.smallbizgrowth.com
Steven Cole, President
Provides representation & group purchasing for small businesses

UHY Advisors
66 State St, Albany, NY 12207
518-449-3166 Fax: 518-449-5832
e-mail: rkotlow@uhy-us.com
Web site: www.uhyadvisors-us.com
Richard Kotlow, Chief Executive Officer
Professional financial, tax, business & tax advisory services for mid-sized to larger companies

Wegmans Food Markets Inc
1500 Brooks Ave, PO Box 30844, Rochester, NY 14603-0844
585-464-4760 Fax: 585-464-4669
e-mail: comments@wegmans.com
Web site: www.wegmans.com
Mary Ellen Burris, Senior Vice President, Consumer Affairs

Women's Business Training Center of New York State
200 Genesee St, Utica, NY 13502
315-733-9848 or 877-844-9848 Fax: 315-733-0247
e-mail: nywbc@aol.com
Web site: www.nywbc.org
Donna L Rebisz, Project Director
Dedicated to helping women reach their entrepreneurial goals & aspirations through assistance and training

Women's Venture Fund Inc
545 5th Ave, 17th Fl, New York, NY 10018
212-563-0499 Fax: 212-868-9116
e-mail: info@wvf-ny.org
Web site: www.womensventurefund.org
Maria Otero, President & Founder
Multi-service micro-lender that targets women entrepreneurs in under-served urban communities

Zogby International
901 Broad St, Utica, NY 13501
315-624-0200 or 877-462-7655 Fax: 315-624-0210
e-mail: marketing@zogby.com
Web site: www.zogby.com
John Zogby, President/CEO
Political polling & analysis; social science research; business & consumer public opinion surveys & market research

Offices and agencies generally appear in alphabetical order, except when specific order is requested by listee.

CORPORATIONS, AUTHORITIES & COMMISSIONS

New York State

Adirondack Park Agency
1133 NYS Route 86
Ray Brook, NY 12977
518-891-4050 Fax: 518-891-3938
Web site: www.apa.state.ny.us

Chair:
   Vacant 518-891-4050
Executive Director:
   Vacant 518-891-4050
Counsel:
   John S Banta 518-891-4050
Associate Counsel:
   Barbara A Rottier 518-891-4050
Public Relations:
   Keith McKeever 518-891-4050

Agriculture & NYS Horse Breeding Development Fund
90 State St, Ste 809
Albany, NY 12207
518-436-8713 Fax: 518-426-1490
e-mail: agfund@nysirestakes.com
Web site: www.nysirestakes.com

Executive Director:
   Peter Goold 518-436-8713
Counsel:
   Steven Losquadro 518-436-8713

Albany County Airport Authority
Administration Bldg, 2nd Fl
Albany International Airport
Albany, NY 12211-1507
518-242-2222 x1 Fax: 518-242-2641
e-mail: info@albanyairport.com
Web site: www.albanyairport.com

Chief Executive Officer:
   John A O'Donnell PE 518-242-2222 x1
Chief Fiscal Officer:
   J Dwight Hadley 518-242-2222 x1
Director, Public Affairs:
   Doug Myers 518-242-2222 x1
Counsel:
   Peter F Stuto 518-242-2222 x1
Airport Planner:
   Stephen A Iachetta 518-242-2222 x1
Purchasing Agent:
   Mary Ann Mysliwiec 518-242-2222 x2
Administrative Services Manager:
   Ginger Olthoff CM, A.C.E. Ops 518-242-2222 x1

Albany Port District Commission
Administration Bldg
Port of Albany
Albany, NY 12202
518-463-8763 Fax: 518-463-8767
e-mail: portofalbany@portofalbany.com
Web site: www.portofalbany.com

Chair:
   Robert F Cross 518-463-8763
General Manager:
   Frank W Keane 518-463-8763
Counsel:
   Thomas Owens 518-694-0910

Atlantic States Marine Fisheries Commission
1444 Eye St NW
6th Fl
Washington, DC 20005
202-289-6400 Fax: 202-289-6051
e-mail: info@asmfc.org
Web site: www.asmfc.org

Chair, Maine:
   George D Lapointe 207-624-6553
Administrative Commissioner, New York:
   Gordon C Colvin 631-444-0433
Governor's Appointee, New York:
   Pat Augustine 631-928-1524
Legislative Commissioner, New York:
   Senator Owen H Johnson 631-669-9200
Executive Director:
   John V O'Shea 202-289-6400
   e-mail: voshea@asmfc.org
Public Affairs & Resource Specialist:
   Tina Berger 202-289-6400
   e-mail: tberger@asmfc.org

Battery Park City Authority (Hugh L Carey)
One World Financial Center, 24th Fl
New York, NY 10281
212-417-2000 Fax: 212-417-2001
e-mail: info@bpcauthor.org
Web site: www.batteryparkcity.org

Chairman:
   James F Gill 212-417-2000
Vice Chairman:
   Charles J Urstadt 212-417-2000
President & Chief Executive Officer:
   James E Cavanaugh 212-417-4205/fax: 212-417-4153

Offices and agencies generally appear in alphabetical order, except when specific order is requested by listee.

CORPORATIONS, AUTHORITIES & COMMISSIONS / New York State

Member:
   David B Cornstein 212-417-2000
Member:
   Andy K Shenoy 212-417-2000
Member:
   Evelyn K Rollins 212-417-2000
Member:
   Frank J Branchini 212-417-2000
Member:
   Robert J Mueller. 212-417-2000
Press Liaison:
   Leticia M Remauro 212-417-2276/fax: 212-417-2279
   e-mail: remaurol@bpcauthor.org

Brooklyn Navy Yard Development Corporation
63 Flushing Ave, Unit #300
Bldg 292, 3rd Fl
Brooklyn, NY 11205-1054
718-907-5900 Fax: 718-643-9296
Web site: www.brooklynnavyyard.com

Chair:
   Alan H Fishman 718-907-5900
President & Chief Executive Officer:
   Andrew H Kimball. 718-907-5900
Senior Vice President, External Affairs:
   Richard Drucker 718-907-5936
   e-mail: rdrucker@brooklynnavyyard.com

Buffalo & Fort Erie Public Bridge Authority (Peace Bridge Authority)
One Peace Bridge Plaza
Buffalo, NY 14213-2494
716-884-6744 Fax: 716-884-2089
Web site: www.peacebridge.com

Chair (Canadian):
   John A Lopinski 716-884-6744/fax: 716-883-7246
Vice Chair (US):
   Paul J Koessler 716-884-6744/fax: 716-883-7246
General Manager:
   Ron Rienas 716-884-6744

Capital Defender Office
2 Rector Street
13th Floor
New York, NY 10006
212-608-3352 Fax: 212-608-4558
Web site: www.nycdo.org

Capital Defender:
   Kevin Doyle. 212-608-3352 x208
First Deputy Capital Defender, New York City Office:
   Susan Salomon 212-608-3352 x206

Capital District Regional Off-Track Betting Corporation
510 Smith St
Schenectady, NY 12305
518-370-5151 or 800-292-2387 Fax: 518-370-5460
Web site: www.capitalotb.com

Chair:
   Marcel Webb 518-344-5225
President & Chief Executive Officer:
   Michael J Connery 518-344-5225
Vice President/CFO:
   John F Signor 518-344-5224
Executive Assistant to the President:
   Tod Grenci 518-344-5408
Board Secretary:
   Willis Vermilyea 518-482-5615
Comptroller:
   Nancy Priputen-Madrian 518-344-5233

Capital District Regional Planning Commission
One Park Place
Suite 102
Albany, NY 12205-1606
518-453-0850 Fax: 518-453-0856
e-mail: cdrpc@cdrpc.org
Web site: www.cdrpc.org

Executive Director:
   Rocco Ferraro 518-453-0850

Capital District Transportation Authority
110 Watervliet Ave
Albany, NY 12206
518-437-8300 Fax: 518-437-8318
Web site: www.cdta.org

Chair:
   David M Stackrow 518-437-8311
Vice Chair:
   Donald C MacElroy 518-437-8311
Executive Director:
   Ray Melleady 518-437-8300
General Counsel:
   David Winans. 518-437-8300
Chief Financial Officer:
   Milt Pratt. 518-437-8300
Deputy Executive Director, Business Development:
   Carm Basile 518-437-8300

Catskill Off-Track Betting Corporation
Park Place
Box 3000
Pomona, NY 10970
845-362-0400 Fax: 845-362-0419
e-mail: otb@interbets.com
Web site: www.interbets.com

President & Chief Executive Officer:
   Donald J Groth 845-362-0400

Central New York Regional Market Authority
2100 Park St
Syracuse, NY 13208
315-422-8647 Fax: 315-422-6897

Executive Director:
   Benjamin Vitale 315-422-8647

Offices and agencies generally appear in alphabetical order, except when specific order is requested by listee.

CORPORATIONS, AUTHORITIES & COMMISSIONS / New York State

Counsel:
  Robert Scalione 315-422-1311

Central New York Regional Transportation Authority
200 Cortland Ave
PO Box 820
Syracuse, NY 13205-0820
315-442-3300 Fax: 315-442-3337
Web site: www.centro.org

Chair, Board of Directors:
  Robert E Colucci 315-442-3300
Executive Director:
  Frank Kobliski 315-442-3360
  e-mail: fkobliski@centro.org
Senior VP, Finance & Administration:
  Steven M Share 315-442-3358
Senior VP, Corporate Operations:
  John Renock 315-442-3388

Central Pine Barrens Joint Planning & Policy Commission
PO Box 587
3525 Sunrise Hwy, 2nd Fl
Great River, NY 11739
631-224-2604 Fax: 631-224-7653
e-mail: info@pb.state.ny.us
Web site: www.pb.state.ny.us

Chair & Governor's Appointee & Region 1 Director DEC:
  Peter A Scully 631-224-2604
Executive Director:
  Ray Corwin 631-224-2604
Member & Suffolk County Executive:
  Steve Levy 631-224-2604
Member & Brookhaven Town Supervisor:
  Brian X Foley 631-224-2604
Member & Riverhead Town Supervisor:
  Philip J Cardinale 631-224-2604
Member & Southampton Town Supervisor:
  Patrick A Heaney 631-224-2604

City University Construction Fund
555 W 57th St, 11th Fl
New York, NY 10019
212-541-0171 Fax: 212-541-1014

Interim Chair:
  Philip Berry 212-541-0171
Executive Director:
  Iris Weinshall 212-541-5315
  e-mail: iris.weinshall@mail.cuny.edu
Counsel:
  Frederick Schaffer 212-794-5506
Accountant:
  Carlos Mena 212-541-0173
  e-mail: carlos.mena@mail.cuny.edu
Administrative Officer:
  Denise Phillips 212-541-0190
  e-mail: denise.phillips@mail.cuny.edu

Delaware River Basin Commission
25 State Police Drive
PO Box 7360
West Trenton, NJ 08628-0360
609-883-9500 Fax: 609-883-9522
Web site: www.drbc.net

New York Member:
  Eliot Spitzer 518-474-8390
Executive Director:
  Carol R Collier 609-883-9500 x200
  e-mail: carol.collier@drbc.state.nj.us
Deputy Executive Director:
  Robert Tudor 609-883-9500 x208
  e-mail: robert.tudor@drbc.state.nj.us
Commission Secretary & Assistant General Counsel:
  Pamela Bush 609-883-9500 x203
  e-mail: pamela.bush@drbc.state.nj.us
General Counsel:
  Kenneth J Warren 215-977-2276
  e-mail: kwarren@wolfblock.com
Communications Manager:
  Clarke Rupert 609-883-9500 x260
  e-mail: clarke.rupert@drbc.state.nj.us

Development Authority of the North Country
Dulles State Office Bldg, Ste 414
317 Washington St
Watertown, NY 13601
315-785-2593 Fax: 315-785-2591
Web site: www.danc.org

Chair:
  Thomas Hefferon 315-785-2593
Executive Director:
  Robert S Juravich 315-785-2593
  e-mail: juravich@danc.org
Engineer:
  Carrie M Tuttle 315-782-8661
  e-mail: ctuttle@danc.org
Deputy Executive Director:
  Thomas R Sauter 315-785-2593
  e-mail: tsauter@danc.org
Finance Director:
  Denise A Gray 315-785-2593
Solid Waste Management Facility General Manager:
  E William Seifried 315-232-3236
Director, Project Development:
  Kevin J Jordan 315-785-2593
  e-mail: kjordan@danc.org

Empire State Development Corporation
633 Third Ave
New York, NY 10017
212-803-3100
Web site: www.empire.state.ny.us

30 South Pearl Street
Albany, NY 12245
518-292-5100

Offices and agencies generally appear in alphabetical order, except when specific order is requested by listee.

CORPORATIONS, AUTHORITIES & COMMISSIONS / New York State

420 Main St, Ste 717
Buffalo, NY 14202
716-856-8111

Co-Chair Downstate:
   Patrick J Foye 212-803-3700
Co-Chair Upstate:
   Daniel C Gundersen .... 518-292-5100 or 716-856-8111
President & Chief Operating Officer:
   Avi Schick 212-803-3730
Chief Operating Officer (Upstate):
   Kenneth A Schoetz 716-856-8111
Director, Communications:
   A J Carter 212-803-3740
Senior Vice President, General Counsel:
   Anita W Laremont 212-803-3750
Chief Financial Officer:
   Frances A Walton 212-803-3510

Great Lakes Commission

2805 S Industrial Hwy
Ste 100
Ann Arbor, MI 48104-6791
734-971-9135 Fax: 734-971-9150
e-mail: teder@glc.org
Web site: www.glc.org

Chairman:
   John Cherry 517-373-6800
Vice Chair:
   Patrick Quinn 312-814-4866
New York State Commissioner:
   Alexander B Grannis 518-402-8540/fax: 518-402-8541
Executive Director:
   Tim A Eder 734-971-9135
   e-mail: teder@glc.org
Program Manager, Resource Management:
   Thomas R Crane 734-971-9135
   e-mail: tcrane@glc.org
Program Manager, Transportation & Sustainable Development:
   Dave Knight 734-971-9135
   e-mail: dknight@glc.org
Program Manager, Communications & Internet Technology:
   Christine Manninen 734-971-9135
   e-mail: manninen@glc.org
Program Manager, Data & Information Management:
   Roger Gauthier 734-971-9135
   e-mail: gauthier@glc.org
Program Manager, Environmental Quality:
   Matthew Doss 734-971-9135
   e-mail: mdoss@glc.org

Hudson River-Black River Regulating District

Hudson River Area Office
350 Northern Blvd
Albany, NY 12204
518-465-3491 Fax: 518-432-2485
e-mail: hrao@hrbrrd.com
Web site: www.hrbrrd.com

Chair:
   Anne B McDonald 518-465-3491
Executive Director:
   Glenn A LaFave 518-465-3491

Chief Engineer:
   Robert S Foltan 518-465-3491
Chief Fiscal Officer:
   Richard J Ferrara 518-465-3491
General Counsel:
   William L Busler 518-465-3491

Interest on Lawyer Account (IOLA) Fund of the State of NY

11 East 44th St
Ste 1406
New York, NY 10017
646-865-1541 or 800-222-4652 Fax: 646-865-1545
e-mail: iolaf@iola.org
Web site: www.iola.org

Chair:
   William R Nojay 646-865-1541
Executive Director:
   Lorna Blake 646-865-1541
   e-mail: lblake@iola.org
General Counsel:
   Stephen Brooks 646-865-1541
   e-mail: sgbrooks@iola.org
Assistant Director & Director of Administration:
   Odette M McNeil 646-865-1541
   e-mail: omcneil@iola.org

Interstate Environmental Commission

311 W 43rd St, Ste 201
New York, NY 10036
212-582-0380 Fax: 212-581-5719
e-mail: iecmail@iec-nynjct.org
Web site: www.iec-nynjct.org

Chair:
   John Atkin 212-582-0380
Executive Director & Chief Engineer:
   Howard Golub 212-582-0380
General Counsel:
   Eileen D Millett 212-582-0380

Interstate Oil & Gas Compact Commission

PO Box 53127
Oklahoma City, OK 73152-3127
405-525-3556 Fax: 405-525-3592
e-mail: iogcc@iogcc.state.ok.us
Web site: www.iogcc.state.ok.us

Chair:
   John Hoeven 405-525-3556
Vice Chair:
   Victor Carrillo 405-525-3556
Executive Director:
   Christine Hansen 405-525-3556
New York State Official Representative:
   Bradley J Field 518-402-8076
Communications Manager:
   Erica Carr 405-525-3556

Offices and agencies generally appear in alphabetical order, except when specific order is requested by listee.

CORPORATIONS, AUTHORITIES & COMMISSIONS / New York State

Lake George Park Commission
75 Fort George Rd
PO Box 749
Lake George, NY 12845-0749
518-668-9347 Fax: 518-668-5001
e-mail: info@lgpc.state.ny.us
Web site: www.lgpc.state.ny.us

Chair:
   Bruce E Young....................................518-668-9347
Vice Chair:
   Thomas K Conerty..............................518-668-9347
Executive Director:
   Michael P White.................................518-668-9347
Secretary/Treasurer:
   John A Pettica, Jr................................518-668-9347

Lawyers' Fund for Client Protection
119 Washington Ave
Albany, NY 12210
518-434-1935 or 800-442-FUND Fax: 518-434-5641
e-mail: info@nylawfund.org
Web site: www.nylawfund.org

Chair:
   Eleanor Breitel Alter............................518-434-1935
Vice Chair:
   Bernard F Ashe..................................518-434-1935
Executive Director & Counsel:
   Timothy O'Sullivan.............................518-434-1935
Deputy Counsel:
   Michael J Knight................................518-434-1935

Legislative Bill Drafting Commission
Capitol, Rm 308
Albany, NY 12224
518-455-7500 Fax: 518-455-7598

Commissioner:
   Michael H Melkonian..........................518-455-7501
   e-mail: melkonian@lbdc.state.ny.us
Commissioner:
   Randall G Bluth.................................518-455-7506
   e-mail: bluth@lbdc.state.ny.us
Counsel:
   Jamie-Lynne Elacqua.........................518-455-7538
   e-mail: elacqua@lbdc.state.ny.us

Legislative Retrieval System................fax: 518-455-7679
   55 Elk St, Albany, NY 12210
   800-356-6566 Fax: 518-455-7679
Director:
   Burleigh McCutcheon..........................518-455-7669
   e-mail: mccutcheon@lbdc.state.ny.us

Long Island Power Authority
333 Earle Ovington Blvd
Suite 403
Uniondale, NY 11553
516-222-7700 Fax: 516-222-9137
e-mail: info@lipower.org
Web site: www.lipower.org

Chairman:
   Kevin S Law......................................516-222-7700
CEO/President:
   Richard M Kessel..............................516-222-7700
Acting General Counsel:
   Lynda Nicolino.................................516-222-7700
Vice President, Communications:
   Bert Cunningham..............................516-719-9838
   e-mail: bcunningham@lipower.org
Executive Director, Government Relations:
   William Davidson..............................516-719-9852

MTA (Metropolitan Transportation Authority)
347 Madison Ave
New York, NY 10017
212-878-7000 Fax: 212-878-7030
Web site: www.mta.info

Chairman & CEO:
   Peter S Kalikow.................................212-878-7200
Executive Director/Chief Operating Officer:
   Elliot Sander....................................212-878-7274
Deputy Executive Director, Director of Security:
   William Morange..............................212-878-7155
Deputy Executive Director, Corporate & Community Affairs:
   Christopher P Boylan.........................212-878-7160
Deputy Executive Director, Policy/Special Advisor, Safety & Environmental Issues:
   Linda Kleinbaum..............................212-878-7206
Director, Labor Relations:
   Gary Dellaverson..............................212-878-7438
Director, Budgets & Financial Management:
   Gary Lanigan....................................212-878-7236
Director, Finance:
   Vacant...212-878-7278
Director, Human Resources:
   Margaret Connor..............................212-878-7017
Director, Government Affairs:
   Hilary Ring..............212-878-7313/fax: 212-878-7050
MTA Chief of Police:
   Kevin J McConville...........................212-878-1084
Press Secretary:
   Jeremy Soffin..................................212-878-7145

MTA Bridges & Tunnels
2 Broadway
22nd Floor
New York, NY 10004-2801
646-252-7000 Fax: 646-252-7408
Web site: www.mta.info/bandt

Chairman & CEO:
   Peter S Kalikow.................................212-878-7200
President:
   Susan Kupferman.............................212-360-3100
Vice President & Chief Engineer:
   Thomas Bach...................................212-360-3080
Vice President, Labor Relations:
   Sharon Gallo-Kotcher........................212-360-3015
Executive Vice President, Operations:
   Martha Walther................................212-360-3060
Vice President, Procurement & Materials:
   Roy Parks..646-252-7084
Vice President, Staff Services & Chief of Staff:
   Catherine T Sweeney.........................646-252-7421

Offices and agencies generally appear in alphabetical order, except when specific order is requested by listee.

CORPORATIONS, AUTHORITIES & COMMISSIONS / New York State

Chief Financial Officer:
  David Moretti..................................646-252-7100
Chief Technology Officer:
  Tariq Habib......................................646-252-7230
General Counsel:
  Robert O'Brien.................................646-252-7617
Director, Public Affairs:
  Frank Pascual..................................646-252-7416
Executive Director, MTA:
  Katherine N Lapp..............................646-252-7000

MTA Bus Company
341 Madison Avenue
New York, NY 10017
212-878-7174 Fax: 212-878-0205
Web site: www.mta.info/busco

Chairman & CEO:
  Peter S Kalikow.................................212-878-7200
President:
  Thomas J Savage...............................212-878-7174
Administrative Assistant:
  Marian Noel.....................................212-878-7174

MTA Capital Construction
2 Broadway
8th Floor
New York, NY 10002
646-252-4200
Web site: www.mta.info/capconstr

Chairman & CEO:
  Peter S Kalikow.................................212-878-7200
President:
  Mysore L Nagaraja............................646-252-4277
Chief Financial Officer:
  Anthony D'Amico..............................646-252-4200
Vice President & General Counsel:
  Veronique Hakim...............................646-252-4278
Vice President, Project Controls:
  Shawn Kildare..................................646-252-3723
Vice President, Program Executive & Chief Engineer:
  Joseph Trainor..................................646-252-3467
Program Executive, Fulton Street & Special Projects:
  Richard Miras...................................646-252-4556
Executive Assistant to the President:
  Vacant..646-252-4278
Deputy Vice President, Finance & Administration:
  Joseph Petrocelli...............................646-252-3813
Deputy Program Executive, Design Integrity:
  Mike Kyriacou...................................646-252-4500
Program Manager, Security Projects:
  Ron Pizak..646-252-4756
Program Manager, Security Projects:
  Joe Christen....................................646-252-3841
Program Manager, Manhattan East Side Access:
  Dilip Patel..212-967-0236
Program Manager, Fulton Street Transit Center:
  Uday Durg.......................................646-252-4932
Program Manager, 7 West Extension:
  Philip McGrade.................................646-252-4107
Program Manager, 2nd Avenue Subway:
  Anil Parikh......................................212-510-2154
Chief Budget Officer:
  Susan Jurman..................................646-252-4260

Senior Director, Policy & Implementation:
  Patricia Hoag...................................646-252-4656

MTA Long Island Bus
700 Commercial Ave
Garden City, NY 11530
516-542-0100 Fax: 516-542-1428
Web site: www.mta.info/libus

Chairman & CEO:
  Peter S Kalikow.................................212-878-7200
President:
  Neil S Yellin.............................516-542-0100 x4525
Senior Vice President, Operations:
  William Norwich.........................516-542-0100 x4334
Vice President, Finance:
  Joseph Pokorny..........................516-542-0100 x4439
General Counsel & VP, Legal/Human Resources:
  Cheryl Hartell............................516-542-0100 x4429

MTA Long Island Rail Road
Jamaica Station
Jamaica, NY 11435
718-558-7400 Fax: 718-558-8212
Web site: www.mta.info/lirr

Chairman & CEO:
  Peter S Kalikow.................................212-878-7200
Acting President:
  Raymond P Kenny..............................718-558-8252
Executive Vice President:
  Albert Cosenza..................................718-558-7993
  e-mail: accosen@lirr.org
Chief Information Officer:
  Frederick A Wedley.............................718-588-8166
  e-mail: fawedley@lirr.org
Vice President & Chief Fiscal Officer:
  Nicholas DiMola.................................718-558-7777
  e-mail: ndimola@lirr.org
Acting Vice President, General Counsel & Secretary:
  Frank Kronenberg..............................718-558-8264
Acting Vice President, Labor Relations:
  Steve Drayzen..................................718-558-7405
Acting Vice President, Market Development & Public Affairs:
  Susan McGowan................................718-558-7301
Vice President, Service, Planning, Technology & Capital Program Management:
  John Coulter....................................718-558-7363
  e-mail: jwcoult@lirr.org
Vice President, System Safety:
  Jose R Fernandez..............................718-558-7711
  e-mail: jrferna@lirr.org
Chief Fire Marshal:
  William Rice.....................................718-558-3094

MTA Metro-North Railroad
347 Madison Ave
New York, NY 10017
212-340-2677 Fax: 212-340-4995
Web site: www.mta.info/mnr

Chairman & CEO:
  Peter S Kalikow.................................212-878-7200

Offices and agencies generally appear in alphabetical order, except when specific order is requested by listee.

CORPORATIONS, AUTHORITIES & COMMISSIONS / New York State

President:
   Peter A Cannito 212-340-2677
Vice President & General Counsel:
   Richard Bernard 212-340-4933
VP, Finance & Informational Systems:
   Leonard DeSimone 212-340-2636
Director, Operating Capital Projects:
   George Walker 212-499-4300
Senior VP, Planning Procurement & Business Development:
   Howard Permut 212-340-2500
Chief of Staff & Director, Corporate Communications:
   Donna Evans 212-340-2766/fax: 212-340-3460
Chief Safety Officer:
   Mark Campbell 212-340-4913
Senior Director, Capital Programs:
   Ronald T Yutko 212-340-4913
Senior Director, Customer Service:
   Thomas Tendy 212-672-1251

MTA New York City Transit
370 Jay St
Brooklyn, NY 11201
718-330-3000 Fax: 718-596-2146
Web site: www.mta.info/nyct

Chairman & CEO:
   Peter S Kalikow 212-878-7200
President:
   Howard H Roberts Jr 646-252-5800
Executive Vice President:
   Barbara R Spencer 646-252-5888
Senior Vice President, Buses:
   Millard Seay 646-252-5872
Senior Vice President, Capital Program Management:
   Cosema Crawford 646-252-3034
Vice President, Corporate Communications:
   Paul Fleuranges 646-252-5873
Senior Vice President, Subways:
   Michael Lombardi 646-252-5860
Senior Vice President, System Safety:
   Cheryl Kennedy 646-252-5934
Vice President & General Counsel:
   Martin Schnabel 718-694-3900
Vice President, Labor Relations:
   Ralph Agritelley 646-252-5880
Chief Officer, Staten Island Railway:
   John McCabe 718-876-8239

MTA Office of the Inspector General
111 West 40th St
5th Fl
New York, NY 10018
212-878-0000 or 800-682-4448 Fax: 212-878-0003
e-mail: complaints@mtaig.org
Web site: www.mtaig.state.ny.us

Inspector General:
   Barry L Kluger 212-878-0007

Municipal Assistance Corporation for the City of New York
420 Lexington Avenue
Room 1756
New York, NY 10170
212-840-8255 Fax: 212-840-8570
e-mail: macnyc@earthlink.net

Chairman:
   Jonathan A Ballan 212-840-8255
Executive Director:
   Nancy H Henze 212-840-8255

NYS Commission on Quality of Care & Advocacy for Persons with Disabilities
1 Empire State Plaza
Ste 1001
Albany, NY 12223-1150
800-624-4143 or 800-522-4369 Fax: 518-388-2800
Web site: www.cqcapd.state.ny.us

Chair:
   Gary O'Brien 518-388-1281
Commissioner:
   Patricia Okoniewski 518-388-1281
Commissioner:
   Bruce G Blower 518-388-1281
Press Officer:
   Gary W Masline 518-388-1270/fax: 518-388-1275

Administrative Services Bureau
Director:
   Richard H Schaefer 518-388-2804

Advisory Council
Chair:
   Vacant 518-388-1270

Advocacy Services Bureau
Director:
   Marcel Chaine 518-388-2892

Counsel, Policy Analysis, Fiscal Investigations
Counsel/Director:
   Robert J Boehlert 518-388-1270

Medical Review Board
Executive Secretary:
   Thomas Harmon 518-388-1281

Quality Assurance
Director:
   Mark Keegan 518-388-2888

Surrogate Decision-Making Committees Program
Program Director:
   Thomas Fisher 518-388-2820

Nassau Regional Off-Track Betting Corporation
220 Fulton Ave
Hempstead, NY 11550
516-572-2800 Fax: 516-572-2840
e-mail: webmaster@nassauotb.com
Web site: www.nassauotb.com

Offices and agencies generally appear in alphabetical order, except when specific order is requested by listee.

CORPORATIONS, AUTHORITIES & COMMISSIONS / New York State

President:
  Dino G Amoroso 516-572-2800
Executive Director of Operations:
  Richard T Bennett, Jr. 516-572-2800 x155
Director, Public Affairs:
  Joseph Galante 516-572-2800 x152
Comptroller:
  Joah Sapphire 516-572-2800 x141

New England Interstate Water Pollution Control Commission
116 John St
Lowell, MA 01852-1124
978-323-7929 Fax: 978-323-7919
e-mail: mail@neiwpcc.org
Web site: www.neiwpcc.org

Chair:
  Harry Stewart 603-271-3308
Vice Chair:
  Alicia Good 401-222-4700
Commissioner, New York State:
  Denise M Sheehan 518-485-8940
Executive Director:
  Ronald F Poltak 978-323-7929
Deputy Director:
  Susan Sullivan 978-323-7929

New York City Housing Development Corporation
110 William St
10th Fl
New York, NY 10038
212-227-5500 Fax: 212-227-6865
e-mail: info@nychdc.com
Web site: www.nychdc.com

Chairperson:
  Shaun Donovan 212-863-6100
President:
  Emily Youssouf 212-227-3600
Executive Vice President & Chief of Staff:
  John Crotty 212-227-6846/fax: 212-227-9807
Senior Vice President & General Counsel:
  Richard Froehlich 212-227-7435
Senior Vice President, Portfolio Management:
  Teresa Gigliello 212-227-9133
Senior Vice President & Chief Fiscal Officer:
  Eileen O'Reilly 212-227-7494/fax: 212-227-6757
Chief Credit Officer:
  Urmas Naeris 212-227-9724
Vice President, Development:
  Rachel Grossman 212-227-9373
Director, Communications:
  Aaron Donovan 212-227-9496/fax: 212-227-8580
Board Member:
  Mathew Wambua 718-788-3098
Board Member:
  Harry E Gould 212-227-5500
Board Member:
  Michael W Kelly 212-227-5500
Board Member:
  Charles G Moerdler 212-227-5500

Board Member:
  Mark Page 212-788-5900
Board Member:
  Martha E Stark 212-669-4855

New York City Residential Mortgage Insurance Corporation

Chair:
  Shaun Donovan 212-863-6100
President:
  Emily Youssouf 212-227-3600

New York City Off-Track Betting Corporation
1501 Broadway
New York, NY 10036-5572
212-221-5200 Fax: 212-221-8025
Web site: www.nycotb.com

President:
  Raymond V Casey 212-704-5101
Executive Vice President & Chief Operating Officer:
  John Van Lindt 212-704-5108
Chief of Staff:
  Denise DePrima 212-704-5107
Executive Vice President & Chief Fiscal Officer:
  Vacant 212-221-5200 x5214
Executive Vice President & General Counsel:
  Ira H Block 212-221-5200 x5311
Executive Director, Legislative Affairs:
  Daniel Wray 212-221-5200 x5230
Acting Inspector General:
  Norma Papamichael-Walsh 212-221-5200
Senior Vice President, Marketing, Media & Communications:
  Ron Ceisler 212-704-5152
Senior Vice President, New Business, Real Estate, Facilities & Community Affairs:
  Robert E Unger 212-704-5642

New York City School Construction Authority
30-30 Thomson Ave
Long Island City, NY 11101-3045
718-472-8000 Fax: 718-472-8840
Web site: schools.nyc.gov/Offices/SCA

Chair/Chancellor:
  Joel I Klein 718-472-8000
President & Chief Executive Officer:
  Sharon Greenberger 718-472-8001
Vice President & General Counsel:
  Ross J Holden 718-472-8220
VP, Finance:
  Marianne Egri 718-472-8012
VP, Project Management & Operations:
  Chester Yee, PE 718-472-8015
VP, Architecture & Engineering:
  Bruce Barrett, RA 718-472-8710
Senior Director, Real Estate:
  Lorraine Grillo 718-472-8216

New York Convention Center Operating Corporation
655 W 34th St
New York, NY 10001-1188

Offices and agencies generally appear in alphabetical order, except when specific order is requested by listee.

CORPORATIONS, AUTHORITIES & COMMISSIONS / New York State

212-216-2000 Fax: 212-216-2588
e-mail: moreinfo@javitscenter.com
Web site: www.javitscenter.com

President & Chief Executive Officer:
  Gerald T McQueen 212-216-2130
General Manager:
  Anthony Bracco 212-216-2217
Chief Financial Officer:
  Edward B MacDonald 212-216-2369
General Counsel:
  Elizaeth Bradford 212-216-2125
Vice President, Sales & Marketing:
  Doreen Guerin 212-216-2103

New York Metropolitan Transportation Council
199 Water St, 22nd Fl
New York, NY 10038
212-383-7200 Fax: 212-383-2418
e-mail: nymtc-web@dot.state.ny.us
Web site: www.nymtc.org

Executive Director:
  Joel Ettinger 212-383-7236
Deputy Director, Administration Group:
  Alan Borenstein 212-383-7294
  e-mail: aborenstein@dot.state.ny.us
Assistant Director, Planning Group:
  Gerard J Bogacz 212-383-7260
  e-mail: gbogacz@dot.state.ny.us
Assistant Director, Technical Group:
  Kuo-Ann Chiao 212-383-7212
  e-mail: kchiao@dot.state.ny.us

New York Power Authority
123 Main St
White Plains, NY 10601-3170
914-681-6200 Fax: 914-390-8190
e-mail: info@nypa.gov
Web site: www.nypa.gov

30 South Pearl St
Albany, NY 12207
518-433-6700
Fax: 518-433-1406

Chairman:
  Frank S McCullough, Jr 914-287-3636
President & Chief Executive Officer:
  Timothy S Carey 914-287-3501
Senior Vice President, Public & Government Affairs:
  Brian Vattimo 518-433-6734
Executive Director, Public/Governmental Affairs:
  Paul Finnegan 518-433-6740
Director, Media Relations:
  Michael Saltzman 914-390-8181

New York State Assn of Fire Districts
PO Box 1419
Massapequa, NY 11758
516-799-8575 or 800-520-9594 Fax: 516-799-2516
Web site: www.firedistnys.com

President:
  Randall Rider .... 716-876-1214 or 716-875-0183
  fax: 716-876-9566
  e-mail: adrilleye@aol.com
First Vice President:
  Lawrence Pierce 585-624-4673/fax: 585-624-4047
  e-mail: lpierce@rochester.rr.com
Second Vice President:
  John LoScalzo 631-549-5729/fax: 631-549-2030
  e-mail: mcque@verizon.net
Secretary & Treasurer:
  Frank A Nocerino 516-799-8575/fax: 516-799-2516
  e-mail: fnoc@aol.com
Counsel:
  William N Young .... 800-349-2904 or 518-456-6767
  fax: 518-869-5142
  e-mail: byoung@wyfklaw.com

New York State Athletic Commission
123 William St
20th Fl
New York, NY 10038-3804
212-417-5700 Fax: 212-417-4987
e-mail: athletic@dos.state.ny.us
Web site: www.dos.state.ny.us/athletic.html

Chair:
  Ron Scott Stevens 212-417-5700

New York State Board of Law Examiners
Corporate Plaza Bldg 3
254 Washington Ave Ext
Albany, NY 12203
518-452-8700 Fax: 518-452-5729
Web site: www.nybarexam.org

Chair:
  Diane F Bosse 518-452-8700
Executive Director:
  John J McAlary 518-452-8700

New York State Bridge Authority
Mid-Hudson Bridge Plaza
PO Box 1010
Highland, NY 12528
845-691-7245 Fax: 845-691-3560
Web site: www.nysba.net

Chair:
  James P Sproat 845-691-7245
Vice Chair:
  Roderick O Dressel 845-691-7245
Executive Director:
  George C Sinnott 845-691-7245
Deputy Executive Director:
  James J Bresnan 845-691-7245
  e-mail: jbresnan@nysba.state.ny.us
General Counsel:
  Carl Whitbeck 518-828-4107
Public Information Officer, Director Planning & Public Relations:
  John R Bellucci 845-691-5953/fax: 845-691-3636
  e-mail: jbellucci@nysba.state.ny.us

Offices and agencies generally appear in alphabetical order, except when specific order is requested by listee.

CORPORATIONS, AUTHORITIES & COMMISSIONS / New York State

New York State Commission of Correction
80 Wolf Road
4th Fl
Albany, NY 12205
518-485-2346 Fax: 518-485-2467
e-mail: infoscoc@scoc.state.ny.us
Web site: www.scoc.state.ny.us

Chairman:
  Daniel L Stewart 518-485-2330
Assistant to Chair:
  Patricia Amati 518-485-2330
Counsel:
  Michael F Donegan 518-485-2346
Chair, Citizens' Policy & Complaint Review Council:
  Frances Sullivan 518-485-2346
Chair, Medical Review Board:
  Frederick C Lamy 518-485-2346
Director, Operations:
  James Lawrence 518-485-2346
Director, Human Resource Management:
  Alyce Ashe 518-457-6110
Press Secretary:
  John Caher 518-485-2346

New York State Commission on Judicial Nomination
c/o Patterson Belknap Webb & Tyler LLP
1133 Ave of the Americas, 20th Fl
New York, NY 10036-6710
212-841-0715 Fax: 212-262-5152

Chair:
  John F O'Mara 607-733-4635
Senior Counsel:
  Stuart A Summit 212-977-9700
  e-mail: ssummit@phillipsnizer.com
Counsel:
  Stephen P Younger 212-336-2000
  e-mail: spyounger@pbwt.com

New York State Commission on the Restoration of the Capitol
Corning Tower, 31st Fl
Empire State Plaza
Albany, NY 12242
518-473-0341 Fax: 518-486-5720

Executive Director:
  Andrea J Lazarski 518-473-0341
  e-mail: andrea.lazarski@ogs.state.ny.us

New York State Disaster Preparedness Commission
Building 22, Suite 101
1220 Washington Ave
Albany, NY 12226-2251
518-292-2301 or 518-292-2200 Fax: 518-322-4978
Web site: www.semo.state.ny.us/dpc/

Director:
  John R Gibb 518-292-2301

New York State Dormitory Authority
515 Broadway
Albany, NY 12207-2964
518-257-3000 Fax: 518-257-3100
e-mail: dabonds@dasny.org
Web site: www.dasny.org

One Penn Plaza
52nd Fl
New York, NY 10119-0098
212-273-5000
Fax: 212-273-5121

539 Franklin St
Buffalo, NY 14202-1109
716-884-9780
Fax: 716-884-9787

Chair:
  Gail H Gordon 518-257-3180/fax: 518-257-3183
Executive Director:
  David D Brown, IV 518-257-3180/fax: 518-257-3183
Deputy Executive Director:
  Michael T Corrigan 518-257-3192/fax: 518-257-3183
Chief Fiscal Officer:
  John G Pasicznyk 518-257-3630/fax: 518-257-3100
  e-mail: jpasiczn@dasny.org
General Counsel:
  Jeffrey M Pohl 518-257-3120/fax: 518-257-3101
  e-mail: jpohl@dasny.org
Associate General Counsel:
  Debbie Drescher 518-257-3120
Associate General Counsel:
  George Weissman 518-257-3120
Associate General Counsel:
  Deborah Paden 518-257-3120
Managing Director, Construction:
  James M Gray, RA 518-257-3200/fax: 518-257-3100
  e-mail: jgray@dasny.org
Managing Director, Portfolio Management:
  Lora K Lefebvre 518-257-3163/fax: 518-257-3387
  e-mail: llefebvr@dasny.org
Managing Director, Public Finance:
  Cheryl Ishmael 518-257-3362/fax: 518-257-3100
  e-mail: cishmael@dasny.org
Director, Communications & Marketing:
  Paul Burgdorf 518-257-3380/fax: 518-257-3387
  e-mail: pburgdor@dasny.org

New York State Energy Research & Development Authority
17 Columbia Circle
Albany, NY 12203-6399
518-862-1090 Fax: 518-862-1091
Web site: www.nyserda.org

Chairman:
  Vincent A DeIorio 518-862-1090

Offices and agencies generally appear in alphabetical order, except when specific order is requested by listee.

CORPORATIONS, AUTHORITIES & COMMISSIONS / New York State

President & CEO:
   Peter R Smith.................................518-862-1090 x3320
   e-mail: prs@nyserda.org
General Counsel (Acting):
   Hal Brodie......................................518-862-1090 x3280
   e-mail: hb1@nyserda.org
Vice President, Programs:
   Robert Callender.............................518-862-1090 x3233
   e-mail: rgc@nyserda.org
Treasurer:
   Jeffrey J Pitkin...............................518-862-1090 x3223
   e-mail: jjp@nyserda.org
Director, Communications (Acting):
   Colleen Q Ryan.............518-862-1090 x3359/fax: 518-464-8249
   e-mail: cqr@nyserda.org

New York State Environmental Facilities Corp
625 Broadway
Albany, NY 12207-2997
518-402-6924 or 800-882-9721 Fax: 518-486-9323
Web site: www.nysefc.org

Chair:
   Alexander B Grannis......................518-402-6924
President & CEO:
   David Sterman..............................518-402-6924
Executive Vice President:
   Matthew J Millea..........................518-402-6924
Senior VP & General Counsel:
   James R Levine............................518-402-6969
Chief Financial Officer:
   James T Gebhardt........................518-402-6985
Director, Engineering & Program Management:
   Robert E Davis............................518-402-7396
Director, Technical Advisory Services:
   Frederick D McCandless..............518-402-7461
Director, Corporate Communications:
   Susan Mayer...............................518-402-6957
Controller & Director, Corporate Operations:
   Michael Malinoski........................518-486-9267

New York State Ethics Commission
Alfred E Smith State Office Bldg
11th Fl, Ste 1147
Albany, NY 12210
518-474-8320 or 800-873-8442 Fax: 518-474-8322
e-mail: ethics@dos.state.ny.us
Web site: www.dos.state.ny.us/ethc/ethics.html

Chair:
   John D Feerick............................518-474-8320
Commissioner:
   Robert J Giuffra, Jr......................518-474-8320
Commissioner:
   Carl H Loewenson, Jr..................518-474-8320
Commissioner:
   Lynn Millane...............................518-474-8320
Commissioner:
   Susan E Shepard.........................518-474-8320
Acting Executive Director:
   Suzanne Dugan...........................518-474-8320
Counsel:
   Suzanne Dugan...........................518-474-4533

Public Information Officer:
   Walter C Ayres............................518-474-4418
   e-mail: wayres@dos.state.ny.us

New York State Financial Control Board
123 William St
23rd Fl
New York, NY 10038-3804
212-417-5046 Fax: 212-417-5055
e-mail: nysfcb@fcb.state.ny.us
Web site: www.fcb.state.ny.us

Acting Executive Director:
   Jeffrey Sommer............................212-417-5066
Deputy Director, Expenditure Analysis:
   Dennis DeLisle.............................212-417-5069
Deputy Director, Financial & Capital Analysis:
   Jewel A Douglas..........................212-417-5067
Acting Deputy Director, Economic & Revenue Analysis:
   Martin Fischman...........................212-417-5068
Associate Director:
   Mattie W Taylor...........................212-417-5053

New York State Higher Education Services Corp (NYSHESC)
99 Washington Ave
Albany, NY 12255
518-473-7087 or 888-697-4372 Fax: 518-474-2839
Web site: www.hesc.org

President & Chief Executive Officer:
   James Ross..................................518-474-5592
Executive Vice President:
   Corinne M Biviano........................518-474-5775
Senior Vice President, Corporate Finance & Chief Fiscal Officer:
   Warren Wallin.............................518-402-3584
Senior Vice President, Chief Operating Officer:
   Leonard Sippel............................518-473-2523
   e-mail: lsippel@hesc.org
Senior Vice President, Communications:
   Ronald Kermani...........................518-473-1264
   e-mail: rkermani@hesc.org
Senior Vice President, Information Technology:
   Victor Stucchi..............................518-474-7083
   e-mail: vstucchi@hesc.org
Assistant Vice President, Customer Relations:
   John Austin.................................518-473-0733
   e-mail: jaustin@hesc.org
Director, Human Resources Management:
   Linda Dillon.................................518-474-0510
   e-mail: ldillon@hesc.org

New York State Housing Finance Agency (HFA)
641 Lexington Ave
4th Floor
New York, NY 10022
212-688-4000 Fax: 212-872-0789
Web site: www.nyhomes.org

Chair:
   Judd Levy....................................212-688-4000
President & CEO:
   Priscilla Almodovar.......................212-688-4000

Offices and agencies generally appear in alphabetical order, except when specific order is requested by listee.

CORPORATIONS, AUTHORITIES & COMMISSIONS / New York State

Senior Vice President, Chief Operating Officer & Chief Fiscal Officer:
   Ralph J Madalena..212-688-4000
Senior Vice President & Counsel:
   Justin Driscoll..212-688-4000
Senior Vice President & Special Assistant to President/Chief Executive Officer for Policy Development & Programs:
   James P Angley...212-688-4000
Senior Vice President, Debt Issuance:
   Bernard Abramowitz...........................212-688-4000 x530
Vice President, Director of Development:
   Maria LaSorsa......................................212-688-4000 x688
Vice President, Policy & Planning:
   Tracy A Oats.......................................212-688-4000 x678
Vice President, Intergovernmental Affairs:
   Michael R Houseknecht 518-434-2118/fax: 518-432-7158

Affordable Housing Corporation
Senior Vice President & Special Assistant to President/Chief Executive Officer for Policy Development & Programs:
   James P Angley...212-688-4000

New York State Judicial Conduct Commission
61 Broadway
12th Floor
New York, NY 10006
212-809-0566 Fax: 212-809-3664
e-mail: scjc@scjc.state.ny.us
Web site: www.scjc.state.ny.us

Chair:
   Raoul Lionel Felder, Esq 212-809-0566
Vice Chair:
   Thomas A Klonick..................................212-809-0566
Administrator & Counsel:
   Robert H Tembeckjian.............................212-809-0566
Chief Attorney, Albany Office:
   Cathleen Cenci.......................................518-474-5617
Chief Attorney, Rochester Office:
   John J Postel..585-232-5756
Chief Attorney, New York Office:
   Alan W Friedberg...................................212-809-0566
Clerk:
   Jean M Savanyu, Esq 212-809-0566

New York State Law Reporting Bureau
One Commerce Plaza, Ste 1750
Albany, NY 12210
518-474-8211 Fax: 518-463-6869
Web site: www.courts.state.ny.us/reporter

State Reporter:
   Gary D Spivey.......................................518-474-8211
Deputy State Reporter:
   Charles A Ashe......................................518-474-8211
   e-mail: Reporter@courts.state.ny.us

New York State Law Revision Commission
80 New Scotland Ave
Albany, NY 12208
518-472-5858 Fax: 518-445-2303
Web site: www.lawrevision.state.ny.us

Chairman:
   Robert M Pitler......................................518-472-5858

Executive Director:
   Rose Mary Bailly...................................518-472-5858

New York State Liquor Authority
80 S Swan St, Ste 900
Albany, NY 12210
518-486-4767
Web site: www.abc.state.ny.us

Chairman:
   Daniel B Boyle...................518-486-4767 or 212-961-8347
Commissioner:
   Lawrence J Gedda ....518-486-4767 or 212-961-8347
Commissioner:
   Noreen Healey....................518-486-4767 or 212-961-8347
Chief Executive Officer:
   Joshua B Toas, Esq..................................518-486-4767
Counsel:
   Thomas J Donohue.................................518-486-4767
Deputy Commissioner, Licensing, NYC:
   Fred J Gioffre..212-961-8301
Senior Deputy Commissioner, Administration:
   J Mark Anderson 518-486-4767
Deputy Commissioner, Government Affairs:
   Thomas J O'Connor................................518-486-4767
Public Information Officer, NYC:
   Kimberly Morella...................................212-961-8331
Director, Communications:
   William Crowley 518-486-4767
   e-mail: pressoffice@abc.state.ny.us

New York State Mortgage Loan Enforcement & Administration Corporation
633 Third Ave, 37h Fl
New York, NY 10017-6754
212-803-3700 Fax: 212-803-3775
Web site: www.empire.state.ny.us

Senior Vice President:
   Anita W Laremont..................................212-803-3750
Senior Vice President & Chief Financial Officer:
   Frances A Walton...................................212-803-3510

New York State Olympic Regional Development Authority
Olympic Center
2634 Main Street
Lake Placid, NY 12946
518-523-1655 Fax: 518-523-9275
e-mail: info@orda.org
Web site: www.orda.org

Chair:
   Pat Barrett......................................518-523-1655 x201
President & CEO:
   Ted Blazer......................................518-523-1655 x201
   e-mail: blazer@orda.org
Senior Vice President:
   Jeffrey Byrne..................................518-523-1655 x203
   e-mail: byrne@orda.org
Olympic Center Manager:
   Denny Allen..................................518-523-1655 x222
   e-mail: allen@orda.org

Offices and agencies generally appear in alphabetical order, except when specific order is requested by listee.

CORPORATIONS, AUTHORITIES & COMMISSIONS / New York State

Marketing Director:
Fran Sayers..518-523-1655 x209
e-mail: sayers@orda.org
Director, Events:
Jim Goff...518-523-1655 x212
e-mail: jgoff@orda.org
Director, Finance:
Kathy Bushy..518-523-1655 x217
e-mail: bushy@orda.org
Director, Communications:
Sandy Caligiore..518-523-1655 x213
e-mail: sandyc@orda.org

New York State Teachers' Retirement System
10 Corporate Woods Dr
Albany, NY 12211-2395
518-447-2900 or 800-348-7298 Fax: 518-447-2695
e-mail: communit@nystrs.state.ny.us
Web site: www.nystrs.org

Executive Director:
George M Philip..518-447-2666
e-mail: execdir@nystrs.state.ny.us
General Counsel:
Wayne Schneider...518-447-2722
Actuary:
Richard Young..518-447-2692
Director, Administration:
William S O'Brien..518-447-2730
Director, Member Realtions:
Sheila Gardella...518-447-2684
Manager, Public Information:
John Cardillo...518-447-4743
Real Estate Investment Officer:
John Virtanen..518-447-2751
Securities Investment Officer:
Lawrence A Johansen......................................518-447-2611

New York State Temporary Commission of Investigation
59 Maiden Lane, 31st Fl
New York, NY 10038
212-344-6660 Fax: 212-344-6868
e-mail: commissioner@sic.state.ny.us
Web site: www.sic.state.ny.us

Chairman:
Alfred D Lerner..212-344-6660
Deputy Commissioner & Chief Counsel:
Anthony T Cartusciello....................................212-344-6670
Chief Investigator:
Anthony Hellmer...212-344-6660

New York State Temporary Commission on Lobbying
2 Empire State Plaza
18th Floor
Albany, NY 12223-1254
518-474-7126 Fax: 518-473-6492
e-mail: lobcom@nytscol.org
Web site: www.nylobby.state.ny.us

Chair:
Hon. James P King...518-474-7126
Vice Chair:
Andrew G Celli, Jr...518-474-7126
Commissioner:
Patrick J Bulgaro..518-474-7126
Commissioner:
Kenneth J Baer..518-474-7126
Commissioner:
Michael A Lenz..518-474-7126
Executive Director:
David M Grandeau...518-474-7126
Director, Program & Finance Administration:
Jeannine M Clemente......................................518-474-7126

New York State Thoroughbred Breeding & Development Fund Corporation
Saratoga Spa State Park
19 Roosevelt Dr, Ste 250
Saratoga Springs, NY 12866
518-580-0100 Fax: 518-580-0500
e-mail: nybreds@nybreds.com
Web site: www.nybreds.com

Executive Director:
Martin G Kinsella..518-580-0100

New York State Thruway Authority
200 Southern Blvd
Albany, NY 12209
518-436-2700 Fax: 518-436-2899
Web site: www.nysthruway.gov

Chair:
John L Buono..518-436-3000
Executive Director:
Michael R Fleischer.......................................518-436-2900
General Counsel:
Sharon O'Conor...518-436-2840
Deputy Counsel:
Katherine McCartney.....................................518-436-3188
Director, Government Relations:
Pamela Davis.....................518-436-2860/fax: 518-471-4340
Director, Public Information:
Vacant..............................518-436-2983/fax: 518-426-3995

New York State Canal Corporation
Web site: www.nyscanals.gov
Director:
Carmella Mantello...518-436-3055

New York State Tug Hill Commission
Dulles State Office Bldg
317 Washington St
Watertown, NY 13601
315-785-2380 Fax: 315-785-2574
e-mail: tughill@tughill.org
Web site: www.tughill.org

Chair:
Kenneth W Vigus..315-785-2380

Offices and agencies generally appear in alphabetical order, except when specific order is requested by listee.

CORPORATIONS, AUTHORITIES & COMMISSIONS / New York State

Executive Director:
　John K Bartow, Jr.....................................315-785-2380
　e-mail: john@tughill.org
Counsel:
　James P McClusky..................................315-232-4551

Niagara Falls Bridge Commission
PO Box 1031
Niagara Falls, NY 14302
716-285-6322　Fax: 716-282-3292
e-mail: general_inquiries@niagarafallsbridges.com
Web site: www.niagarafallsbridges.com

Chair:
　Janice A Thomson.................................716-285-6322
General Manager/Secretary/Treasurer:
　Thomas E Garlock..................................716-285-6322

Niagara Frontier Transportation Authority
181 Ellicott St
Buffalo, NY 14203
716-855-7300　Fax: 716-855-6655
e-mail: info@nfta.com
Web site: www.nfta.com

Chair:
　Gregory Stamm.......................................716-855-7232
Executive Director:
　Lawrence M Meckler...............................716-855-7369
　e-mail: lawrence_meckler@nfta.com
Chief Financial Officer:
　Deborah Leous..716-855-7250
General Counsel:
　David M Gregory....................................716-855-7230
Director, Aviation:
　William Vanecek.....................................716-630-6030
Director, Human Resources:
　Diane Ruszala...716-855-7373
Director, Surface Transportation:
　Walter D Zmuda......................................716-855-7252
Director, Engineering:
　Michael Bykowski...................................716-855-7412
Director, Public Affairs:
　C Douglas Hartmayer..............................716-855-7420

Northeastern Forest Fire Protection Commission
21 Parmenter Terrace
PO Box 6192
China Village, ME 04926-6192
207-968-3782　Fax: 207-968-3782
e-mail: info@nffpc.org
Web site: www.nffpc.org

Chair of Commissioners:
　Walter Fanning..902-758-7236
　e-mail: fanninwf@gov.ns.ca
Vice Chair of Commissioners:
　Philip A Bryce...603-271-2217
　e-mail: pbryce@dred.state.nh.us
Executive Director:
　Thomas G Parent....................................207-968-3782
　e-mail: necompact@fairpoint.net

Operations Committee, Chair:
　Andrew Jacob...518-402-8832
　e-mail: atjacob@gw.dec.state.ny.us
New York Fire Prevention:
　Adam Pickett..315-823-9252
　e-mail: ajpicket@gw.dec.state.ny.us

Northeastern Queens Nature & Historical Preserve Commission
Bldg 635, Bayside St, Box 5
Fort Totten, NY 11359-1012
718-229-8805　Fax: 718-229-6131
e-mail: sneq@aol.com
Web site: www.sneq.com

Chair:
　Bernard Haber..718-229-8805
Vice Chair:
　William Nieter..718-229-8805
Executive Director:
　Joan M Vogt..718-229-8805

Ogdensburg Bridge & Port Authority
One Bridge Plaza
Ogdensburg, NY 13669
315-393-4080　Fax: 315-393-7068
e-mail: obpa@ogdensport.com
Web site: www.ogdensport.com

Chair:
　Fredrick J Carter.....................................315-393-4080
Executive Director:
　Wade A Davis...315-393-4080
　e-mail: wadavis@ogdensport.com

Ohio River Valley Water Sanitation Commission
5735 Kellogg Ave
Cincinnati, OH 45228-1112
513-231-7719　Fax: 513-231-7761
e-mail: info@orsanco.org
Web site: www.orsanco.org

New York State Commissioner:
　Douglas E Conroe...................................513-231-7719
New York State Commissioner:
　T Lee Servatius.......................................513-231-7719
New York State Commissioner:
　Alexander B Grannis...............................513-231-7719
Executive Director:
　Alan H Vicory, Jr....................................513-231-7719
　e-mail: avicory@orsanco.org
Legal Counsel:
　Ross Wales...513-231-7719
Public Information Programs Manager:
　Jeanne Ison..513-231-7719
　e-mail: jison@orsanco.org

Offices and agencies generally appear in alphabetical order, except when specific order is requested by listee.

CORPORATIONS, AUTHORITIES & COMMISSIONS / New York State

Port Authority of New York & New Jersey
225 Park Ave South
18th Fl
New York, NY 10003
212-435-7000 Fax: 212-435-4032
Web site: www.panynj.gov

Chair, New Jersey:
  Anthony R Coscia...................................212-435-7000
Vice Chair, New York:
  Henry R Silverman................................212-435-7000
Executive Director:
  Anthony E Shorris..................................212-435-7271
First Deputy Executive Director:
  James P Fox..212-435-6667
Deputy Executive Director:
  William H Goldstein................................212-435-6668
Deputy Executive Director:
  Ernesto Butcher.....................................212-435-7887
Director, Government & Community Relations:
  Shawn K Laurenti..................................212-435-6903
General Counsel:
  Darrell Buchbinder.................................212-435-3515
Chief Financial Officer:
  A Paul Blanco.......................................212-435-7738
Chief Administrative Officer:
  Louis J LaCapra.....................................212-435-8140
Chief of Public & Government Affairs:
  Stephen Sigmund..................................212-435-8041
Chief Engineer:
  Francis J Lombardi................................212-435-7449
Director, Public Affairs:
  John J McCarthy..................................212-435-6502
Office of Secretary:
  Karen E Eastman..................................212-435-6528

Port of Oswego Authority
1 East Second St
Oswego, NY 13126
315-343-4503 Fax: 315-343-5498
e-mail: shipping@portoswego.com
Web site: www.portoswego.com

Chairman:
  Richard Tesoriero.................................315-343-8095
Acting Executive Director:
  James Cloonan....................................315-343-4503
Counsel:
  Timothy Fennell..................................315-343-6363

Rochester-Genesee Regional Transportation Authority
1372 E Main St
PO Box 90629
Rochester, NY 14609
585-654-0200 Fax: 585-654-0224
Web site: www.rgrta.com

Chair:
  John G Doyle, Jr...................................585-654-0200
Chief Executive Officer:
  Mark R Aesch.....................................585-654-0200
Chief Operating Officer:
  Stephen W Hendershott........................585-654-0200
Chief Financial Officer:
  Robert W Frye....................................585-654-0200
Director, Transit Operations:
  Bruce G Philpott..................................585-654-0200

Roosevelt Island Operating Corporation (RIOC)
591 Main St
Roosevelt Island, NY 10044
212-832-4540 Fax: 212-832-4582
e-mail: info@roosevelt-island.ny.us
Web site: www.rioc.com

President:
  Stephen H Shane................................212-832-4540
Vice President, Operations:
  Vacant..212-832-4540
Chairperson, Board of Directors (ex officio):
  Deborah VanAmerogen........................212-480-6705
General Counsel:
  Kenneth A Leitner.........................212-832-4540 x311
Chief Financial Officer:
  Carla Van de Walle..............................212-832-4540
Public Information Officer:
  Vacant..212-832-4540

State of New York Mortgage Agency (SONYMA)
641 Lexington Ave
New York, NY 10022
212-688-4000 Fax: 212-872-0678
Web site: www.nyhomes.org

Chair:
  Judd Levy...212-688-4000
President & CEO:
  Priscilla Almodovar...............................212-688-4000
Senior Vice President & Special Assistant to President/Chief Ececutive Officer for Policy Development & Programs:
  James P Angley..................................212-688-4000
Senior Vice President, Chief Operating Officer & Chief Fiscal Officer:
  Ralph J Madalena................................212-688-4000
Senior Vice President & General Counsel:
  Justin Driscoll.....................................212-688-4000
Vice President/Director, SONYMA Mortgage Insurance Fund:
  Michael Friedman..........................212-688-4000 x714
Senior Vice President, Single Family Programs & Financing:
  Charles Rosenwald........................212-688-4000 x531
Vice President, Policy & Planning:
  Tracy A Oats..................................212-688-4000 x678
Vice President, Intergovernmental Affairs:
  Michael R Houseknecht............518-434-2118/fax: 518-432-7158

State of New York Municipal Bond Bank Agency (MBBA)
641 Lexington Ave
New York, NY 10022
212-688-4000 Fax: 212-872-0678
Web site: www.nymbba.org

Chair:
  Judd Levy...212-688-4000

Offices and agencies generally appear in alphabetical order, except when specific order is requested by listee.

CORPORATIONS, AUTHORITIES & COMMISSIONS / New York State

President & CEO:
 Priscilla Almodovar 212-688-4000
Senior Vice President & Special Assistant to President & Chief Executive Officer for Policy Development & Programs:
 James P Angley 212-688-4000
Senior Vice President, Chief Fiscal Officer & Chief Operating Officer:
 Ralph J Madalena 212-688-4000
Senior Vice President & Counsel:
 Justin Driscoll 212-688-4000
Vice President, Policy & Planning:
 Tracy A Oats 212-688-4000 x678

State University Construction Fund
353 Broadway
Albany, NY 12246
518-689-2500 Fax: 518-689-2634
Web site: www.sucf.suny.edu

General Manager:
 Philip W Wood 518-689-2501
Acting General Counsel:
 William K Barczak 518-689-2514/fax: 518-689-2634

Suffolk Regional Off-Track Betting Corporation
5 Davids Dr
Hauppauge, NY 11788-2004
631-853-1000 Fax: 631-853-1086
e-mail: customerservice@suffolkotb.com
Web site: www.suffolkotb.com

President/Chief Executive Officer:
 Jeffrey A Casale 631-853-1000
Vice President:
 Marietta M Seaman 631-853-1000
Corporate Counsel/Executive Director, External Affairs:
 Neil H Tiger 631-853-1000
Comptroller:
 Celine M Gazes 631-853-1000

Thousand Islands Bridge Authority
PO Box 428, Collins Landing
43530 Interstate 81
Alexandria Bay, NY 13607
315-482-2501 or 315-658-2281 Fax: 315-482-5925
e-mail: info@tibridge.com
Web site: www.tibridge.com

Chair:
 Donald J Grant 315-482-2501
Executive Director:
 Robert G Horr, III 315-482-2501
 e-mail: roberthorr@tibridge.com
Legal Counsel:
 Anderson Wise 315-482-2501

Uniform State Laws Commission
c/o Coughlin & Gerhart LLP, 20 Hawley St
East Tower
Binghamton, NY 13902-2039
607-584-4193 Fax: 607-723-1530

Chair:
 Richard B Long 607-584-4193
 e-mail: rlong@cglawllp.com
Member:
 Sandra Stern 212-207-8150

United Nations Development Corporation
Two United Nations Plaza, 27th Fl
New York, NY 10017-4403
212-888-1618 Fax: 212-588-0758
e-mail: info@undc.org
Web site: www.undc.org

Chair, Board of Directors:
 George Klein 212-888-1618
President & CEO:
 Roy M Goodman 212-888-1618
Executive VP & Director of Development:
 Jeffrey Feldman 212-888-1618
Senior VP, Controller:
 Jorge Ortiz 212-888-1618
Senior VP, Operations:
 Robert M Preissner 212-888-1618

Waterfront Commission of New York Harbor
39 Broadway, 4th Fl
New York, NY 10006
212-742-9280 Fax: 212-480-0587
Web site: www.wcnyh.org

Commissioner, New York:
 Michael C Axelrod 212-742-9280
Commissioner, New Jersey:
 Michael J Madonna 212-742-9280
Executive Director:
 Thomas De Maria 212-905-9201

Western Regional Off-Track Betting Corp
8315 Park Road
Batavia, NY 14020-1272
585-343-1423 Fax: 585-344-6188
e-mail: info@westernotb.com
Web site: www.westernotb.com

Chair:
 Joseph Gallo 585-343-1423
President & Chief Executive Officer:
 Martin C Basinait 585-343-1423
Executive Vice President:
 Patrick T Murphy 585-343-1423
Vice President, Racing & Gaming:
 Michael Kane 585-343-1423
General Counsel:
 Timothy A McCarthy 585-343-1423
Comptroller:
 Jacquelyne A Leach 585-343-1423
Director Marketing:
 Martin Biniasz 585-343-1423
Mutuels/Communications:
 James M Haas 585-343-1423

Offices and agencies generally appear in alphabetical order, except when specific order is requested by listee.

CRIME & CORRECTIONS

New York State

GOVERNOR'S OFFICE

Governor's Office
Executive Chamber
State Capitol
Albany, NY 12224
518-474-8390 Fax: 518-474-1513
Web site: www.state.ny.us

Governor:
   Eliot Spitzer 518-474-8390
Secretary to the Governor:
   Richard Baum 518-474-4246
Counsel to the Governor:
   David Nocenti 518-474-8343
Deputy Secretary, Public Safety:
   Michael Balboni 518-474-3522
Assistant Deputy Secretary, Criminal Justice:
   Lai Sun Yee 518-474-3522
Assistant Counsel to the Governor-Criminal Justice:
   Robin Forshaw 518-474-1310
Assistant Counsel to the Governor-Criminal Justice:
   Steven Krantz 518-474-1310
Director, Communications:
   Darren Dopp 518-474-8418

EXECUTIVE DEPARTMENTS AND RELATED AGENCIES

Correctional Services Department
1220 Washington Ave
Bldg 2 State Campus
Albany, NY 12226-2050
518-457-8126 Fax: 518-457-7252
Web site: www.docs.state.ny.us

Commissioner:
   Brian Fischer 518-457-8134
Executive Deputy Commissioner:
   Vacant 518-457-1748
Deputy Commissioner & Counsel:
   Anthony Annucci 518-485-9613
Associate Commissioner & Inspector General:
   Richard D Roy 518-457-7261
Assistant Commissioner & Executive Assistant:
   Edward J McSweeney 518-457-1281
Special Assistant to Commissioner:
   Terri Pratt 518-457-8134
Public Information Officer:
   Vacant 518-457-8182/fax: 518-457-7070
Asst Public Information Officer:
   Linda Foglia 518-457-8182/fax: 518-457-7070

Administrative Services
Deputy Commissioner:
   Gayle Haponik 518-457-8188

Budget & Finance Division
Assistant Commissioner/Chief Fiscal Officer:
   Vacant 518-457-7135
Director, Budget & Finance:
   Bruce A Johnson 518-457-3808

Diversity Management
Director:
   Charlie R Harvey 518-435-9494
ADA Coordinator:
   Robert Raymond 518-485-5806

Human Resources Management Division
  Personnel Bureau
   Director:
     Daniel Martuscello 518-457-5393
  Support Operations Division
  550 Broadway, Menands, NY 12204
   Director:
     Stewart Kidder 518-436-7886

Inmate Grievance
Director:
   Vacant 518-457-1885

Internal Controls
Director:
   Deborah Coons 518-485-1394

Labor Relations Bureau
Director:
   Peter Brown 518-457-7383

Training Academy
1134 New Scotland Rd, Albany, NY 12208
Director:
   Bruce Olsen 518-489-9072

Workers' Compensation Investigation Unit
Director:
   Paul DiMura 518-457-3112

Correctional Facility Operations
Deputy Commissioner:
   Lucien LeClaire 518-457-8138
Assistant Commissioner:
   Diane Van Buren 518-457-5902
Assistant Commissioner:
   Donald Selsky 518-457-5902
Assistant Commissioner:
   Paul Kikendall 518-457-4118

Agri-Business
Eastern NY Correctional Facility, Box 333, Napanoch, NY 12458
Director:
   Vacant 914-647-7400

Correctional Industries Division . . . . fax: 518-436-6007
Corcraft Products, 550 Broadway, Albany, NY 12204

Offices and agencies generally appear in alphabetical order, except when specific order is requested by listee.

CRIME & CORRECTIONS / New York State

Fax: 518-436-6007
Web site: www.corcraft.org
Director:
   James Hoffman..................518-436-6321

Facilities
Adirondack Correctional Facility
Box 110, Ray Brook, NY 12977-0110
Superintendent:
   Leo Bisceglia 518-891-1343/fax: 518-891-3299
Albion Correctional Facility
3595 State School Rd, Albion, NY 14411
Superintendent:
   William Powers 585-589-5511/fax: 585-589-1247
Altona Correctional Facility
555 Devil's Den Rd, Box 125, Altona, NY 12910-0125
Acting Superintendent:
   Bruce Yelich 518-236-7841
Arthur Kill Correctional Facility
2911 Arthur Kill Rd, Staten Island, NY 10309-1197
Superintendent:
   Dennis Breslin.................718-356-7333
Attica Correctional Facility
Box 149, Attica, NY 14011-0149
Superintendent:
   James Conway.................585-591-2000
Auburn Correctional Facility
135 State St, Auburn, NY 13021
Superintendent:
   Harold Graham.................315-253-8401
Bare Hill Correctional Facility
Caller Box #20 181 Brand Rd, Malone, NY 12953
Superintendent:
   John Donelli.................518-483-8411
Bayview Correctional Facility
550 West 20th St, New York, NY 10011-2878
Superintendent:
   Catherine Cook.................212-255-7590
Beacon Correctional Facility
PO Box 780, Beacon, NY 12508-0780
Superintendent:
   Gail Thomas.................845-831-4200
Bedford Hills Correctional Facility
247 Harris Rd, Bedford Hills, NY 10507-2499
Superintendent:
   Ada Perez.................914-241-3100
Buffalo Correctional Facility
PO Box 300, Alden, NY 14004
Superintendent:
   Carol Woughter 716-937-3786/fax: 716-937-3789
Butler Correctional Facility
PO Box 388, Rt 370, Red Creek, NY 13143
Superintendent:
   James Morrissey.................315-754-6216
Camp Gabriels
Box 100, Gabriels, NY 12939-0100
Superintendent:
   Jeff Tedford.................518-327-3111
Camp Georgetown
RD #1, Box 48, Georgetown, NY 13072-9307
Superintendent:
   Vacant.................315-837-4446
Camp Pharsalia
486 Center Rd, South Plymouth, NY 13844-6777
Superintendent:
   Rickey Bartlett.................607-334-2264
Cape Vincent Correctional Facility
Route 12E, Box 599, Cape Vincent, NY 13618
Superintendent:
   Warren D Barkley............315-654-4100/fax: 315-654-4103

Cayuga Correctional Facility
PO Box 1150, Moravia, NY 13119-1150
Superintendent:
   Michael Corcoran............315-497-1110/fax: 315-497-3617
Chateaugay Correctional Facility
PO Box 320, Route 11, Chateaugay, NY 12920
Superintendent:
   Vacant 518-497-3300/fax: 497-3300 x2099
Clinton Correctional Facility
PO Box 2000, Dannemora, NY 12929
Superintendent:
   Dale Artus 518-492-2511 x2099/fax: 518-492-7892
Collins Correctional Facility
PO Box 490, Taylor Hollow Rd, Collins, NY 14034-0490
Superintendent:
   James Berbary.................716-532-4588
Coxsackie Correctional Facility
Box 200, West Coxsackie, NY 12051-0200
Superintendent:
   William Lape.................518-731-2781
Downstate Correctional Facility
PO Box 445, Fishkill, NY 12524-0445
Superintendent:
   Paul Annetts.................845-831-6600
Eastern NY Correctional Facility
Box 338, Napanoch, NY 12458-0338
Superintendent:
   William Brown.................845-647-7400
Edgecombe Correctional Facility
611 Edgecombe Ave, New York, NY 10032-4398
Superintendent:
   Cynthia Morton.................212-923-2575
Elmira Correctional Facility
Box 500, Elmira, NY 14902-0500
Superintendent:
   Vacant.................607-734-3901
Fishkill Correctional Facility
PO Box 307, Beacon, NY 12508
Superintendent:
   William Connolly.................845-831-4800
Five Points Correctional Facility
Caller Box 400, State Rte 96, Romulus, NY 14541
Superintendent:
   Thomas Poole.................607-869-5111
Franklin Correctional Facility
PO Box 10, Malone, NY 12953
Superintendent:
   Lawrence Sears.................518-483-6040
Fulton Correctional Facility
1511 Fulton Ave, Bronx, NY 10457-8398
Superintendent:
   Elnora Porter.................718-583-8000
Gouverneur Correctional Facility
PO Box 370, Gouverneur, NY 13642-0370
Superintendent:
   Justin Taylor.................315-287-7351
Gowanda Correctional Facility
PO Box 350, South Rd, Gowanda, NY 14070-0350
Superintendent:
   Richard Savage.................716-532-0177
Great Meadow Correctional Facility
Box 51, Comstock, NY 12821
Superintendent:
   Darwin Laclair.................518-639-5516
Green Haven Correctional Facility
Rte 216, Stormville, NY 12582
Acting Superintendent:
   Robert Ercole.................845-221-2711

Offices and agencies generally appear in alphabetical order, except when specific order is requested by listee.

CRIME & CORRECTIONS / New York State

Greene Correctional Facility
PO Box 8, Coxsackie, NY 12051-0008
Superintendent:
Peter Behrle 518-731-2741/fax: 518-731-9377

Groveland Correctional Facility
Route 36, Sonyea Rd, Sonyea, NY 14556-0001
Superintendent:
Carl Hunt. 585-658-2871

Hale Creek ASACTC
279 Maloney Rd, Johnstown, NY 12095
Superintendent:
Hazel Lewis 518-736-2094

Hudson Correctional Facility
Box 576, Hudson, NY 12534-0576
Superintendent:
Jeff McKoy. 518-828-4311/fax: 518-828-5559

Lakeview Shock Incarceration Correctional Facility
PO Box T, Brocton, NY 14716
Superintendent:
Ronald Moscicki 716-792-7100/fax: 792-7197 x3099

Lincoln Correctional Facility
31-33 West 110th St, New York, NY 10026-4398
Superintendent:
Joseph Williams. 212-860-9400

Livingston Correctional Facility
Route 36, Sonyea Rd, Sonyea, NY 14556-0049
Acting Superintendent:
Malcolm Cully. 585-658-3710

Lyon Mountain Correctional Facility
Box 276, Lyon Mountain, NY 12952-0276
Superintendent:
Mark Vann. 518-735-4546

Marcy Correctional Facility
PO Box 5000, Marcy, NY 13403
Superintendent:
James Mance 315-768-1400/fax: 315-768-1419

Mid-Orange Correctional Facility
900 Kings Hwy, Warwick, NY 10990-0900
Superintendent:
Vacant. 845-986-2291

Mid-State Correctional Facility
PO Box 216, Marcy, NY 13403-0216
Superintendent:
Kenneth Perlman. 315-768-8581

Mohawk Correctional Facility
6100 School Rd, PO Box 8450, Rome, NY 13440
Superintendent:
Leo E Payant 315-339-5232 x2000/fax: 339-5232 x2099

Monterey Shock Incarceration Correctional Facility
2150 Evergreen Hill Rd, RD #1, Beaver Dams, NY 14812-9718
Superintendent:
Vacant. 607-962-3184

Moriah Shock Incarceration Correctional Facility
PO Box 999, Mineville, NY 12956-0999
Superintendent:
John Lemke 518-942-7561 x2000/fax: 942-7561 x2099

Mt McGregor Correctional Facility
1000 Mt McGregor Rd, PO Box 2071, Wilton, NY 12831-5071
Superintendent:
Harold McKinney 518-587-3960

Ogdensburg Correctional Facility
One Correction Way, Ogdensburg, NY 13669-2288
Superintendent:
Vacant. 315-393-0281

Oneida Correctional Facility
6100 School Rd, Rome, NY 13440
Superintendent:
Susan Connell 315-339-6880

Orleans Correctional Facility
35-31 Gaines Basin Rd, Albion, NY 14411
Superintendent:
David Unger 585-589-6820

Otisville Correctional Facility
Box 8, Otisville, NY 10963-0008
Superintendent:
Vacant. 845-386-1490

Queensboro Correctional Facility
47-04 Van Dam St, Long Island City, NY 11101-3081
Superintendent:
Dennis Crowley. 718-361-8920

Riverview Correctional Facility
PO Box 158, Ogdensburg, NY 13669
Superintendent:
Calvin Rabsatt 315-393-8400/fax: 315-394-1189

Rochester Correctional Facility
470 Ford St, Rochester, NY 14608-2499
Superintendent:
Carol Woughter 585-454-2280/fax: 585-454-3412

Shawangunk Correctional Facility
PO Box 750, Wallkill, NY 12589-0750
Superintendent:
Joseph Smith 845-895-2081

Sing Sing Correctional Facility
354 Hunter St, Ossining, NY 10562-5442
Superintendent:
Luis Marshall. 914-941-0108

Southport Correctional Facility
236 Bob Masia Drive, PO Box 2000, Pine City, NY 14871
Superintendent:
David Napoli 607-737-0850

Sullivan Correctional Facility
PO Box 116, Riverside Dr, Fallsburg, NY 12733-0116
Superintendent:
James Walsh 845-434-2080

Summit Shock Incarceration Correctional Facility
RFD, Dibbles Rd, Summit, NY 12175-9608
Superintendent:
Theodore Inserra. 518-287-1721/fax: 518-287-1241

Taconic Correctional Facility
250 Harris Rd, Bedford Hills, NY 10507-2498
Superintendent:
Delores Thornton. 914-241-3010

Ulster Correctional Facility
Berme Rd, PO Box 800, Napanoch, NY 12458
Superintendent:
Scott C Carlsen 845-647-1670

Upstate Correctional Facility
PO Box 2000, 309 Bare Hill Rd, Malone, NY 12953
Superintendent:
Robert Uloops 518-483-6997

Wallkill Correctional Facility
Box G, Wallkill, NY 12589-0286
Superintendent:
Vacant. 845-895-2021

Washington Correctional Facility
Box 180, Comstock, NY 12821-0180
Superintendent:
James Plescia 518-639-4486/fax: 518-639-4073

Watertown Correctional Facility
23147 Swan Rd, Watertown, NY 13601-9340
Superintendent:
Ekpe Ekpe 315-782-7490

Wende Correctional Facility
3622 Wende Rd, PO Box 1187, Alden, NY 14004-1187
Superintendent:
Robert Kirkpatrick 716-937-4000/fax: 937-4000 x2099

Offices and agencies generally appear in alphabetical order, except when specific order is requested by listee.

CRIME & CORRECTIONS / New York State

Willard Drug Treatment Center
7116 County Route 132, PO Box 303, Willard, NY 14588
Superintendent:
Melvin L Williams 607-869-5500
Woodbourne Correctional Facility
Riverside Dr, Woodbourne, NY 12788
Superintendent:
Raymond Cunningham 845-434-7730
Wyoming Correctional Facility
Dunbar Rd, PO Box 501, Attica, NY 14011
Superintendent:
Michael Giambruno 585-591-1010

Facilities Planning & Development
One Watervliet Ave Extension, Albany, NY 12206
Director:
Vacant 518-485-5576

Security Staffing Unit
One Watervliet Ave Extension, Albany, NY 12206
Director:
Phil Battiste 518-485-5407

Special Operations
Director, Crisis Intervention Unit:
Mike Hogan 518-457-2006
Director, Corrections Emergency Response Team (Cert):
Edward Bly 518-457-2006
Director, Shock Incarceration Program:
Cheryl Clark 518-457-8144
Director, Special Housing/Inmate Disciplinary Program:
Vacant 518-457-2337

Health Services Division
Deputy Commissioner, Chief Medical Officer:
Lester Wright 518-457-7072
Assistant Commissioner:
John Sheridan 518-457-7072

Correctional Health Services
Director:
Teresa Wuerdeman 518-457-7072

Dental Services
Director:
Vacant 518-457-7072

Mental Health
Director:
John Culkin 518-457-5067

Nursing & Ancillary Services
Director:
Donna Constant 518-457-7072

Population Management
Associate Commissioner & Inspector General:
Richard D Roy 518-457-7261

Classification & Movement/Transportation
Director:
Terry Knapp-David 518-457-6022

Management Information Services
Director:
Thomas Herzog 518-457-2540

Program Planning, Research & Evaluation
Assistant Director:
Paul Korotkin 518-457-3007

Temporary Release
Director:
Debra Joy 518-457-2655

Program Services
Deputy Commissioner:
John Nuttall 518-457-5555

Education
Director:
Linda Hollmen 518-457-8142

Guidance & Counseling
Director:
Vacant 518-457-5652

Library Services
Supervising Librarian:
Jean Clancy-Botta 518-485-7109

Ministerial & Family Services
Director:
Mark Leonard 518-457-8106

Substance Abuse Treatment Services
Director:
Dwight Bradford 518-485-7903

Volunteer Services
Director:
Vacant 518-485-9204

Crime Victims Board
1 Columbia Circle, Ste 200
Albany, NY 12203-6383
518-457-8727 or 800-247-8035 Fax: 518-457-8658
e-mail: cvbinfo@cvb.state.ny.us
Web site: www.cvb.state.ny.us

55 Hanson Place
10th Fl
Brooklyn, NY 11217-1523
718-923-4325
Fax: 718-923-4332

65 Court St
Rm 308
Buffalo, NY 14202-3406
716-847-7992
Fax: 716-847-7995

Chairwoman:
Joan A Cusack 718-923-4331
Commissioner:
Benedict J Monachino 718-923-4400
Commissioner:
Louis A Mosiello 718-923-4336
Commissioner:
Alton R Waldron, Jr 718-923-4331
Commissioner:
Jacqueline C Mattina 716-847-7948
Executive Director:
Virginia A Miller 518-457-9320/fax: 518-485-9154
Contract Supervisor:
Raymond Parafinczuk 518-485-2763
General Counsel:
John Watson 518-457-8066/fax: 518-457-8658

Offices and agencies generally appear in alphabetical order, except when specific order is requested by listee.

CRIME & CORRECTIONS / New York State

Director, MIS:
David Loomis 518-485-2763

Criminal Justice Services, Division of
Four Tower Place
Albany, NY 12203-3764
518-457-1260 Fax: 518-457-3089
Web site: www.criminaljustice.state.ny.us

Commissioner:
Denise E O'Donnell 518-457-1260
Executive Deputy Commissioner:
Sean Byrne 518-457-6091
Special Counsel to the Commissioner:
Michael Barrett 518-485-7913
Special Counsel & Host Agency Coordination/Support:
Mary Kavaney 518-485-8495
Affirmative Action Officer:
Vacant 518-457-6110
Public Information Officer:
John Caher 518-457-8828/fax: 518-485-7715

Administration Office
Deputy Commissioner, Administration:
Don Capone 518-457-6110

Administrative Services
Director:
Phyllis M Foster 518-457-1696

Human Resources Management
Director:
Alyce Ashe 518-457-6110

State Finance & Budget
Director, Financial Administration:
Kimberly J Szady 518-457-6105
Director, Internal Audit & Compliance:
Bob Wright 518-485-5823

Advisory Groups

Juvenile Justice Advisory Group
Chair:
Anne Marie Strano 518-457-8462

NYS Motor Vehicle & Insurance Fraud Prevention Board
Chair:
Eileen Langer-Smith 518-485-7921

Legal Services
Deputy Commissioner & Counsel:
Gina Bianchi 518-457-4181

Missing & Exploited Children Clearinghouse
Director:
Kenneth R Buniak 518-485-7632

Commission on Forensic Science

Office of Forensic Services
Director:
John Hicks 518-457-7287

Office of Criminal Justice Operations
Deputy Commissioner:
Daniel Foro 518-485-2995

Office of Operations
Director:
William J Sillery 518-457-6050

Assistant Director:
Michael Tymeson 518-457-6050
Chief, Operations:
James Stanco 518-457-6051
Manager, Civil Identification:
Ann Sammons 518-485-5763

Office of Justice Information Services
Executive Director:
James Shea 518-457-8724
Deputy Commissioner/CIO:
Anne Roest 518-485-7176

Information Technology Development Group
Director:
Connie Snyder 518-485-7154

Information Technology Services Group
Assistant Director:
Alex Roberts 518-457-3743

Office of Sex Offender Management
Director:
Luke Martland 518-485-1897

Office of Justice Statistics & Performance
Director:
Terry Salo 518-457-0439
Chief, Crimestat Unit:
Paula K Lockhart 518-485-7122
Chief, Crime Reporting & Statistical Services Unit:
Susan Jacobsen 518-457-8381

Office of Public Safety

Law Enforcement Accreditation Council

Municipal Police Training Council

State Committee for Coordination of Police Services for Elderly (TRIAD)

Statewide Law Enforcement Telecommunications Committee
Deputy Commissioner:
Cedric Alexander 518-457-6101
Director:
Mark R Lindsay 518-457-2667
Assistant Director:
John R Digman 518-485-1414
Chief, Administrative Services:
David H Mahany 518-457-4135
Chief, Program Services:
Mark Fettinger 518-485-1410
Chief, Security Guard Advisory Council:
David H Mahany 518-457-6101

Office of Strategic Planning
Deputy Commissioner:
Beth Ryan 518-485-7433

Bureau of Justice Research & Innovation
Director:
Donna Hall, PhD 518-457-7301

Crime Reduction Strategies Unit
Chief:
Thomas Mitchell 518-457-7301

Justice Systems Analysis Unit
Chief:
David vanAlstyne 518-457-7301

Offices and agencies generally appear in alphabetical order, except when specific order is requested by listee.

CRIME & CORRECTIONS / New York State

Offender Management Analysis Unit
Chief:
   Bruce Frederick 518-457-3724

Funding & Program Assistance Office
Director:
   AnneMarie Strano 518-457-8462

Operation IMPACT Coordinator
Director:
   Julie Pasquini 518-485-7923
Director, Technical Assistance:
   John Bilich 518-457-7832

Inspector General (NYS), Office of the
Executive Chamber
State Capitol
Albany, NY 12224
518-474-1010 Fax: 518-486-3745
Web site: www.ig.state.ny.us

61 Broadway
12th Fl
New York, NY 10006
212-635-3150
Fax: 212-809-6287

State Inspector General:
   Kristine Hamann................. 212-635-3150 or 518-474-1010
   e-mail: inspector.general@ig.state.ny.us
First Deputy Inspector General:
   Michael Boxer 212-635-3150
Deputy Chief of Investigator:
   Dennis Saville.................................. 518-474-1010
Deputy Director, Administration:
   Margaret Gaudet 518-474-1010
Director, Public Information:
   Stephen Del Giacco 518-474-1010
   e-mail: steve.delgiacco@ig.state.ny.us

Law Department
120 Broadway
New York, NY 10271-0332
212-416-8000 Fax: 212-416-8796

State Capitol
Albany, NY 12224-0341
518-474-7330
Fax: 518-402-2472

Attorney General:
   Andrew M Cuomo 518-474-7330
First Deputy Attorney General:
   Michele Hirshman 212-416-8050
Director, Public Information & Correspondence:
   Peter A Drago 518-474-7330/fax: 518-402-2472

Appeals & Opinions Division
Solicitor General:
   Caitlin J Halligan................... 212-416-8016/fax: 212-416-8942
Deputy Solicitor General:
   Michael Belohlavek.............. 212-416-8028/fax: 212-416-8962
Deputy Solicitor General:
   Wayne L Benjamin 518-474-7138/fax: 518-473-8963
Deputy Solicitor General:
   Michelle Aronowitz............... 212-416-8027/fax: 212-416-8962
Deputy Solicitor General:
   Daniel Smirlock.................... 518-473-0903/fax: 518-486-3176
Legal Records:
   Cynthia Bogardus............................... 518-474-5241

Law Library
Chief, Library Services:
   Sarah Browne 518-474-3840/fax: 518-402-2271
Senior Librarian, New York City Office:
   Franette Sheinwald 212-416-8012/fax: 212-416-6130

Criminal Division
Deputy Attorney General:
   Peter B Pope 212-416-8058/fax: 212-416-8026
Assistant Deputy Attorney General:
   Julieta Lozano 212-416-8090/fax: 212-416-8026

Criminal Prosecutions Bureau
Chief:
   Janet Cohn.......................... 518-474-4096/fax: 518-474-3364
Deputy Bureau Chief, NYC:
   Laurie M Israel 212-416-8741/fax: 212-416-8026
Deputy Bureau Chief, Albany:
   Viola Abbitt........................ 518-474-4096/fax: 518-474-3364

Investigations Bureau
Chief Investigator:
   William M Casey.................. 212-416-6328 or 518-486-4540

Medicaid Fraud Control Unit
120 Broadway, 13th Fl, New York, NY 10271-0007
Deputy Attorney General-in-Charge:
   William J Comisky 212-417-5250/fax: 212-417-5274
First Deputy Attorney General:
   Peter M Bloch 212-417-5261/fax: 212-417-5274
Assistant Deputy Attorney General:
   George Quinlan 716-853-8584
Regional Director, Albany:
   Steven Krantz 518-474-3032/fax: 518-474-4519
Deputy Regional Director, Buffalo:
   Gary A Baldauf 716-853-8507/fax: 716-853-8525
Regional Director, Long Island:
   Alan Buonpastore 631-952-6400/fax: 631-952-6382
Regional Director, NYC:
   Richard Harrow.................... 212-417-5391/fax: 212-417-4725
Regional Director, Rochester:
   Jerry Solomon 716-262-2860/fax: 716-262-2866
Regional Director, Syracuse:
   Ralph Tortora, III 315-423-1104/fax: 315-423-1120
Deputy Regional Director, Westchester/Rockland:
   Anne S Jardine 845-732-7500/fax: 845-732-7555
Regional Director for Special Projects Unit:
   Patrick Lupinetti 845-732-7550/fax: 845-732-7557

Organized Crime Task Force
Deputy Attorney General-in-Charge:
   J Christopher Prather............. 518-474-1620/fax: 518-474-7258

Public Advocacy Division
Deputy Attorney General:
   Dietrich Snell...................... 212-416-8041/fax: 212-416-8068
Special Counsel:
   Mary Ellen Burns................................ 212-416-6155

Antitrust Bureau
Bureau Chief:
   Jay L Himes........................ 212-416-8282/fax: 212-416-6015

Offices and agencies generally appear in alphabetical order, except when specific order is requested by listee.

CRIME & CORRECTIONS / New York State

Charities Bureau
Bureau Chief:
Gerald Rosenberg 212-416-8490/fax: 212-416-8393

Civil Rights Bureau
Bureau Chief:
Dennis Parker 212-416-8250/fax: 212-416-8074

Consumer Frauds & Protection Bureau
Bureau Chief:
Thomas G Conway 518-474-2374/fax: 518-474-3618

Environmental Protection Bureau
Bureau Chief:
Peter Lehner 212-416-8450/fax: 212-416-6007

Healthcare Bureau
Bureau Chief:
Joseph R Baker, III 212-416-8521/fax: 212-416-8034

Internet Bureau
Bureau Chief:
Jane Azia 212-416-8433/fax: 212-416-8369

Investment Protection Bureau
Bureau Chief:
David Brown 212-416-8198/fax: 212-416-8816

Telecommunications & Energy Bureau
Bureau Chief:
Vacant 212-416-8333/fax: 212-416-8877

State Counsel Division
Deputy Attorney General:
Richard Rifkin 518-473-7190
Assistant Deputy Attorney General:
Patricia Martinelli 518-473-0648/fax: 518-486-9777
Assistant Deputy Attorney General:
Susan L Watson 212-416-8579/fax: 212-416-6001

Civil Recoveries Bureau
Bureau Chief:
Mary E House 518-474-7131/fax: 518-473-1635

Claims Bureau
Bureau Chief, NYC:
Susan Pogoda 212-416-8516/fax: 212-416-8946

Labor Bureau
Bureau Chief:
M Patricia Smith 212-416-8710

Litigation Bureau
Bureau Chief, Albany:
Bruce D Feldman 518-473-8328/fax: 518-473-1572
Bureau Chief, NYC:
James B Henley 212-416-8523/fax: 212-416-6075

Real Property Bureau
Bureau Chief:
Henry A DeCotis 518-474-7151/fax: 518-473-5106

Parole, Division of
97 Central Ave
Albany, NY 12206
518-473-9400 Fax: 518-473-6037
e-mail: nysparole@parole.state.ny.us
Web site: www.parole.state.ny.us

314 W 40th St
New York, NY 10018

212-239-6000
Fax: 212-239-6160

Executive Office . . . . fax: 518-486-5858
Chief Executive Officer:
George B Alexander 518-473-9548
Executive Director:
Felix M Rosa 518-473-9672
Public Information Officer:
Mark Johnson 518-486-4631

Administrative Services
Director:
Jeffrey Nesich 518-473-9531
Director, Finance:
J Dennis Casey 518-473-9419
Director, Human Resource Management:
Jose Burgos 518-473-6041
Labor Relations Representative:
Vacant 518-474-5612
Director, Support Operations:
George Hemstead 518-473-5790

Board of Parole
Chairman:
George B Alexander 518-473-9548/fax: 518-473-6037
Secretary to the Board:
Vacant 518-473-5424/fax: 518-402-3456

Clemency Unit
845 Central Ave, Albany, NY 12206
Director:
Frank Herman 518-485-8953

Information Services
Chief:
Lawrence Hammond 518-445-7558

Office of Counsel
Chief Counsel:
Terrence X Tracy 518-473-5671/fax: 518-473-9760
Associate Counsel:
Steven Philbrick 518-473-5673/fax: 518-473-9760

Parole Operations Unit
Director, Operations:
Angela Jiminez 518-473-5421
Deputy Director of Operations:
Timothy O'Brien 518-473-4064
Director, Bureau of Special Svcs/Senior Parole Officer:
James Shapiro 212-239-6158
Director, Parole Violations Unit:
Gerald McCord 212-239-5176
Director, Strategic Planning:
Mary Ellen Flynn 212-239-5766
Director, ACCESS:
Robert Smith 212-239-5735
Regional Dir-Region I:
Milton Brown 212-736-9880
Regional Dir-Region II:
James Dress 718-254-2007
Regional Dir-Region III:
Michael Burdi 914-654-8691
Regional Dir-Region IV:
Michael Hayden 518-459-7469
Regional Dir-Region V:
Eugenio Russi 585-232-6927

Offices and agencies generally appear in alphabetical order, except when specific order is requested by listee.

CRIME & CORRECTIONS / New York State

Policy Analysis
Director:
Michael R Buckman 518-445-6071

Victim Impact Unit .... fax: 518-493-9659
Parole Officer:
Barbara Tobin 518-486-4400
Parole Officer:
Christine Robinson 518-486-4400

Prevention of Domestic Violence, Office for the
80 Wolf Road
Ste 406
Albany, NY 12205
518-457-5800 Fax: 518-457-5810
Web site: www.opdv.state.ny.us

90 Church St, 13th Fl
New York, NY 10007
212-417-4477
Fax: 212-268-7921

Executive Director:
Amy Barasch, Esq 518-457-5800
Director, Prevention, Training & Planning:
Gwen Wright 518-457-5916
Administrative Officer:
Linda Cassidy 518-457-7995
Public Information Officer:
Suzanne Cecala 518-457-5744
e-mail: suzanne.cecala@opdv.state.ny.us

Probation & Correctional Alternatives, Division of
80 Wolf Rd
Ste 501
Albany, NY 12205
518-485-7692 Fax: 518-485-5140
Web site: www.dpca.state.ny.us

State Director:
Robert Maccarone 518-485-7692
Secretary to the Director:
Barbara J Flanigan 518-485-7692
Executive Deputy Director:
Thomas Slater 518-485-7692
General Counsel:
Linda Valenti 518-485-2394
Administrative Officer:
Howard Bancroft 518-485-5145/fax: 518-485-5140

Interstate/Intrastate Transfers Unit
Supervisor:
Sandra Layton 518-485-2399/fax: 518-485-7198

New York State Probation Commission
Chair/State Director:
Robert Maccarone 518-485-7692
Member/Chief Administrative Judge:
Jonathan Lippman .... 212-428-2812 or 518-473-6087
Member:
Wayne D'Arcy 518-274-9159
Member:
Harold Brilliant 845-897-4291

Member:
Robert Burns 716-428-5765
Member:
Rocco Pozzi 914-995-3500
Member:
Terri Theobald 607-746-2075

State Police, Division of
Building 22, State Campus
1220 Washington Ave
Albany, NY 12226-2252
518-457-2180
Web site: www.troopers.state.ny.us

Superintendent:
Preston L Felton 518-457-6721
First Deputy Superintendent:
James L Harney 518-457-6711/fax: 518-485-7505
Counsel:
Glenn P Valle 518-457-6137/fax: 518-485-1164

Administration
Deputy Superintendent:
Steven F Cumoletti 518-457-6621/fax: 518-485-5051

Forensic Investigation Center
Director, Staff Inspector:
Gerald M Zeosky 518-457-2466/fax: 518-457-2477

Public Information
Director, Technical Lieutenant:
Glenn R Miner 518-457-2180/fax: 518-485-7818
e-mail: piooffice@troopers.state.ny.us
Crime Prevention Coordinator:
Sgt Kern Swoboda 518-457-2180/fax: 518-485-7818

Employee Relations
Deputy Superintendent:
Francis P Christensen 518-457-3572/fax: 518-485-7505

Human Resources
Deputy Superintendent:
Deborah J Campbell 518-485-5044/fax: 518-485-2293

State Police Academy
Director:
Major Ellwood A Sloat, Jr 518-457-7254/fax: 518-485-1454

Field Command
Deputy Superintendent:
Bart R Johnson 518-457-5936/fax: 518-457-4779

Internal Affairs
Deputy Superintendent:
Pedro J Perez 518-485-6018/fax: 518-485-1493

CORPORATIONS, AUTHORITIES AND COMMISSIONS

Capital Defender Office
2 Rector Street
13th Floor
New York, NY 10006
212-608-3352 Fax: 212-608-4558
Web site: www.nycdo.org

Offices and agencies generally appear in alphabetical order, except when specific order is requested by listee.

CRIME & CORRECTIONS / U.S. Government

Capital Defender:
    Kevin Doyle...................................212-608-3352 x208
First Deputy Capital Defender, New York City Office:
    Susan Salomon 212-608-3352 x206

New York State Commission of Correction
80 Wolf Road
4th Fl
Albany, NY 12205
518-485-2346 Fax: 518-485-2467
e-mail: infoscoc@scoc.state.ny.us
Web site: www.scoc.state.ny.us

Chairman:
    Daniel L Stewart.................................518-485-2330
Assistant to Chair:
    Patricia Amati....................................518-485-2330
Counsel:
    Michael F Donegan 518-485-2346
Chair, Citizens' Policy & Complaint Review Council:
    Frances Sullivan..................................518-485-2346
Chair, Medical Review Board:
    Frederick C Lamy.................................518-485-2346
Director, Human Resource Management:
    Alyce Ashe..518-457-6110
Director, Operations:
    James Lawrence..................................518-485-2346
Press Secretary:
    John Caher.......................................518-485-2346

NEW YORK STATE LEGISLATURE

See Legislative Branch in Section 1 for additional Standing Committee and Subcommittee information.

Assembly Standing Committees

Alcoholism & Drug Abuse
Chair:
    Jeffrey Dinowitz (D)..............................518-455-5965
Ranking Minority Member:
    Gary D Finch (R) 518-455-5878

Codes
Chair:
    Joseph R Lentol (D) 518-455-4477
Ranking Minority Member:
    David R Townsend Jr (R).........................518-455-5334

Correction
Chair:
    Jeffrion L Aubry (D) 518-455-4561
Ranking Minority Member:
    Joe Giglio (R).....................................518-455-5241

Senate Standing Committees

Codes
Chair:
    Dale M Volker (R)................................518-455-3471
Ranking Minority Member:
    Eric Schneiderman (D)...........................518-455-2041

Crime Victims, Crime & Correction
Chair:
    Michael F Nozzolio (R)...........................518-455-2366
Ranking Minority Member:
    Eric Adams (D)...................................518-455-2431

U.S. Government

EXECUTIVE DEPARTMENTS AND RELATED AGENCIES

US Justice Department
Web site: www.usdoj.gov

Bureau of Alcohol, Tobacco, Firearms & Explosives
Web site: www.atf.gov

New York Field Division.......................fax: 718-650-4041
241 37th St, 3rd Floor, Brooklyn, NY 11232
718-650-4040 Fax: 718-650-4041
Special Agent-in-Charge:
    William McMahon 718-650-4040/fax: 718-650-4071
Public Information Officer:
    Joseph G Green 718-650-4040

Drug Enforcement Administration - New York Task Force...fax: 212-337-3978
99 Tenth Ave, New York, NY 10011
Fax: 212-337-3978
Web site: www.usdoj.gov/dea/deahome.html
Special Agent-in-Charge:
    John P Gilbride..................................212-337-2912

Associate Special Agent-in-Charge:
    Wilbert L Plummer...............................212-337-2901
Associate Special Agent-in-Charge:
    Jimmy S Fox.....................................212-620-4910
Associate Special Agent-in-Charge:
    Daniel S Anderson 212-337-2903

Federal Bureau of Investigation - New York Field Offices
Web site: www.fbi.gov

Albany ....fax: 518-431-7463
200 McCarty Ave, Albany, NY 12209
518-465-7551 Fax: 518-431-7463
Web site: www.albany.fbi.gov
Special Agent-in-Charge:
    William Chase...................................518-465-7551

Buffalo ....fax: 716-843-5288
One FBI Plaza, Buffalo, NY 14202-2698
716-856-7800 Fax: 716-843-5288
Web site: www.buffalo.fbi.gov
Special Agent-in-Charge:
    Lori Bennett.....................................716-856-7800

New York City................................fax: 212-384-2745
26 Federal Plaza, 23rd Fl, New York, NY 10278-0004
212-384-1000 Fax: 212-384-2745

Offices and agencies generally appear in alphabetical order, except when specific order is requested by listee.

CRIME & CORRECTIONS / U.S. Government

Assistant Director-in-Charge:
   Mark J Mershon 212-384-1000

Federal Bureau of Prisons
Web site: www.bop.gov

Brooklyn Metropolitan Detention Center . . . . fax: 718-840-5001
80 29th St, Brooklyn, NY 11232
718-840-4200 Fax: 718-840-5001
Warden:
   Pete Laird 718-840-4200/fax: 718-840-5005

Federal Correctional Institution at Otisville
Two Mile Drive, Sanitorium Road, PO Box 600, Otisville, NY 10963
Warden:
   Craig Apker 845-386-6700/fax: 845-386-6727

Metropolitan Correctional Center
150 Park Row, New York, NY 10007-1779
Warden:
   Marvin D Morrison 646-836-6423/fax: 646-836-7751

Ray Brook Federal Correctional Institution
PO Box 300, Ray Brook, NY 12977
Warden:
   T R Craig 518-897-4000/fax: 518-897-4216

Secret Service - New York Field Offices

Albany
39 N Pearl St, Ste 2, Albany, NY 12207-2785
Resident Agent-in-Charge:
   William Leege 518-436-9600/fax: 518-436-9635

Buffalo
610 Main St, Ste 300, Buffalo, NY 14202
Special Agent-in-Charge:
   Michael Bryant 716-551-4401/fax: 716-551-5075

JFK/LGA . . . . fax: 718-553-7626
230-59 Rockaway Blvd, Bldg 59, Suite 265, Springfield Gardens, NY 11413
718-553-0911 Fax: 718-553-7626
Resident Agent-in-Charge:
   Kenneth J Cronin 718-553-0911

Melville . . . . fax: 631-293-4389
145 Pinelawn Rd, Ste 200N, Melville, NY 11747
631-293-4028 Fax: 631-293-4389
Resident Agent-in-Charge:
   Kenneth Pleasant 631-293-4028

New York City . . . . fax: 718-840-1001
335 Adams St, Brooklyn, NY 11201
718-840-1000 Fax: 718-840-1001
Special Agent-in-Charge:
   A T Smith 718-840-1000

Rochester
1820 HSBC Plaza, 100 Chestnut St, Rochester, NY 14604
585-232-4160
Resident Agent:
   Michael de Stefano 585-232-4160/fax: 585-232-4662

Syracuse . . . . fax: 315-448-0302
100 S Clinton St, PO Box 7006, Syracuse, NY 13261
315-448-0304 Fax: 315-448-0302
Resident Agent-in-Charge:
   Timothy Kirk 315-448-0304

White Plains
140 Grand St, White Plains, NY 10601
914-682-6300

Resident Agent-in-Chg:
   Milton D Johnson 914-682-6300/fax: 914-682-6182

US Attorney's Office - New York

Eastern District . . . . fax: 718-254-6479
147 Pierrepont St, Brooklyn, NY 11201
718-254-7000 Fax: 718-254-6479
US Attorney:
   Roslynn R Mauskopf 718-254-7000/fax: 718-254-6319
Chief Assistant United States Attorney:
   Eric Covngold 718-254-7000/fax: 718-254-6300
Executive Assistant United States Attorney:
   William J Muller 718-254-7000/fax: 718-254-6329
Administrative Assistant United States Attorney:
   John Lenior 718-254-6255
Chief Assistantt United States Attorney, Criminal Division:
   Bridget Rohde 718-254-6238/fax: 718-254-6150
Chief Assistant United States Attorney, Civil Division:
   Susan Riley 718-254-6037/fax: 718-254-7483
Chief Assistant United States Attorney, Appeals Division:
   Peter Norling 718-254-6280
Administrative Officer:
   Peter Kurtin 718-254-6587/fax: 718-254-6550

Northern District . . . . fax: 518-431-0249
518-431-0247 Fax: 518-431-0249
   Albany
      James T Foley US Courthouse, #218, 455 Broadway, Albany, NY 12207
      Assistant United States Attorney, Chief Criminal Justice:
         Grant C Jaquith 518-431-0247/fax: 518-431-0249
   Binghamton . . . . fax: 607-773-2901
      US Courthouse, 304 Federal Bldg, 15 Henry St, Binghamton, NY 13901
      607-773-2887 Fax: 607-773-2901
      Supervising Assistant United States Attorney:
         Thomas P Walsh 607-773-2887/fax: 607-773-2901
   Syracuse . . . . fax: 315-448-0689
      J F Hanley Fed Bldg, 100 S Clinton St, Rm 900, Syracuse, NY 13261
      315-448-0672 Fax: 315-448-0689
      United States Attorney:
         Glenn Suddaby 315-448-0672
      First Assistant United States Attorney:
         Andrew T Baxter 315-448-0672
      Assistant United States Attorney, Chief Civil Division:
         William H Pease 315-448-0672
      Administrative Officer:
         Martha Stratton 315-448-0672/fax: 315-448-0689

Southern District . . . . fax: 212-637-2611
1 Saint Andrews Plaza, New York, NY 10007
212-637-2200 Fax: 212-637-2611
   New York City
      United States Attorney:
         Michael Garcia 212-637-1025
      Associate United States Attorney:
         John M McEnany 212-637-2571
      Chief United States Appellate Attorney:
         Celeste Koeleveld 212-637-1044
      Chief, Civil Division:
         James Cott 212-637-2695
      Chief, Criminal Division:
         Lev Dassin 212-637-2508
      Administrative Officer:
         Edward Tyrrell 212-637-2269/fax: 212-637-0084
   White Plains . . . . fax: 914-682-3392
      300 Quarropas St, 3rd Fl, White Plains, NY 10601
      914-993-1907 Fax: 914-682-3392

Offices and agencies generally appear in alphabetical order, except when specific order is requested by listee.

CRIME & CORRECTIONS / U.S. Government

Chief Assistant United States Attorney:
Margery Feinzig 914-993-1909

Western District
Buffalo . . . . fax: 716-551-3052
138 Delaware Ave, Buffalo, NY 14202
716-843-5700 Fax: 716-551-3052
United States Attorney:
Terrance P Flynn 716-843-5814
First Assistant United States Attorney:
Kathleen M Mehltretter 716-843-5817
Assistant United States Attorney, Civil Division Chief:
Mary Pat Fleming 716-843-5867
Assistant United States Attorney, Narcotics & Violent Crime Division Chief:
Joseph M Guerra, III 716-843-5824
Assistant United States Attorney, Strike Force Division Chief:
Anthony M Bruce 716-843-5886
Assistant United States Attorney, White Collar & General Crimes Division Chief:
Paul J Campana 716-843-5819
Administrative Officer:
Barbara A Sweitzer 716-843-5826/fax: 716-551-3170
Rochester . . . . fax: 585-263-6226
620 Federal Bldg, 100 State St, Rochester, NY 14614
585-263-6760 Fax: 585-263-6226
Assistant United States Attorney-in-Charge:
Bradley E Tyler 585-263-5717

US Marshals' Service - New York

Eastern District
Brooklyn
225 Cadman Plaza East, Suite G-20, Brooklyn, NY 11201
718-260-0440
United States Marshal:
Eugene J Corcoran 718-260-0401/fax: 718-260-0436
Central Islip
310 Federal Plaza, Central Islip, NY 11722
631-715-6160
United States Marshal:
Eugene J Corcoran 631-715-6201/fax: 631-715-4425

Northern District
Albany
US Courthouse, 2nd Fl, 445 Broadway, Albany, NY 12207
United States Marshal:
James J Parmley 518-431-0101/fax: 518-431-0100
Syracuse
Federal Bldg, 100 S Clinton St, 10th Fl, PO Box 7260, Syracuse, NY 13261
Unitede States Marshal:
James J Parmley 315-448-0341/fax: 315-448-0343

Southern District
500 Pearl St, Ste 400, New York, NY 10007

United States Marshal:
Joseph R Guccione 212-331-7100/fax: 212-637-6130

Western District
Buffalo
Courthouse Bldg, Rm 129, 68 Court St, Buffalo, NY 14202
United States Marshal:
Peter Lawrence 716-551-4851/fax: 716-551-5505
Rochester
US Courthouse, Rm 284, 100 State St, Rochester, NY 14614
United States Marshal:
Peter Lawrence 585-263-5787/fax: 585-263-6741

US Parole Commission
5550 Friendship Blvd, Ste 420, Chevy Chase, MD 20815
Chairman:
Edward F Reilly 301-492-5990/fax: 301-492-5543

U.S. CONGRESS

See U.S. Congress Chapter for additional Standing Committee and Subcommittee information.

House of Representatives Standing Committees

Judiciary
Chair:
John Conyers, Jr (D-MI) 202-225-5126
Ranking Minority Member:
Lamar Smith (R-TX) 202-225-4236
New York Delegate:
Jerrold Nadler (D) 202-225-5635
New York Delegate:
Anthony D Weiner (D) 202-225-6616

Subcommittee
Crime, Terrorism & Homeland Security
Chair:
Robert C Scott (D-VA) 202-225-8351
Ranking Minority Member:
J Randy Forbes (R-VA) 202-225-6365
New York Delegate:
Anthony D Weiner (D) 202-225-6616

Senate Standing Committees

Judiciary
Chair:
Patrick J Leahy (D-VT) 202-224-4242
Ranking Minority Member:
Arlen Specter (R-PA) 202-224-4254
New York Delegate:
Charles E Schumer (D) 202-224-6542

Offices and agencies generally appear in alphabetical order, except when specific order is requested by listee.

CRIME & CORRECTIONS / Private Sector

Private Sector

American Society for the Prevention of Cruelty to Animals (ASPCA)
424 E 92nd St, New York, NY 10128-6804
212-876-7700 x4552 Fax: 212-360-6875
e-mail: government@aspca.org
Web site: www.aspca.org
Lisa Weisberg, Sr VP, Government Affairs & Public Policy, Sr Policy Advisor
Promoting humane treatment of animals, education & advocacy programs & conducting statewide anti-cruelty investigation & enforcement

Associated Licensed Detectives of New York State
575 Madison Avenue, Suite 1006, New York, NY 10022
646-320-0143 Fax: 212-605-0222
e-mail: info@aldonys.org
Web site: www.aldonys.org
William C Vassell, President
Licensed NYS private investigators & watch, guard & patrol license holders

Berkshire Farm Center & Services for Youth
13640 Route 22, Canaan, NY 12029
518-781-4567 Fax: 518-781-4577
e-mail: jmessina@berkshirefarm.org
Web site: www.berkshirefarm.org
Harith Flagg, Chief Executive Officer
Multi-function agency for troubled youth & families

CUNY John Jay College of Criminal Justice
899 10th Ave, Room 625, New York, NY 10019
212-237-8600 or 212-237-8606 Fax: 212-237-8607
e-mail: jtravis@jjay.cuny.edu
Web site: www.jjay.cuny.edu
Jeremy Travis, President
Criminal justice, police & fire science, clinical psychology & forensic psychology, human dignity & human rights

Center for Alternative Sentencing & Employment Services (CASES)
346 Broadway, 3rd Fl, New York, NY 10013
212-732-0076 Fax: 212-571-0292
e-mail: jcopperman@cases.org
Web site: www.cases.org
Joel Copperman, President/Chief Executive Officer
Advocacy for the use of community sanctions that are fair, affordable & consistent with public safety

Center for Law & Justice
Pine West Plaza, Bldg 2, Washington Ave Ext, Albany, NY 12205
518-427-8361 Fax: 518-427-8362
e-mail: cflj@verizon.net
Web site: www.timesunion.com/communities/cflj
Alice P Green, Executive Director
Advocacy for fair treatment of poor people & communities of color by the legal & criminal justice systems; referral, workshops, community lawyering & education

Coalition Against Domestic Violence, NYS
350 New Scotland Ave, Albany, NY 12208
518-482-5465 Fax: 518-482-3807
e-mail: vasquez@nyscadv.org
Web site: www.nyscadv.org
Jessica Vasquez, Director, Public Policy

Coalition Against Sexual Assault (NYS)
28 Essex Street, Albany, NY 12206
518-482-4222 Fax: 518-482-4248
e-mail: lafo@nyscasa.org
Web site: www.nyscasa.org
Anne Liske, Executive Director
Advocacy, public education, technical assistance & training

Correctional Association of New York
135 E 15th St, New York, NY 10003
212-254-5700 Fax: 212-473-2807
e-mail: rgangi@correctionalassociation.org
Web site: www.correctionalassociation.org
Robert Gangi, Executive Director
Drug law reform/improved prison conditions

NYS Bar Assn, Public Trust & Confidence in the Legal System
Debevoise & Plimpton LLP
919 Third Ave, New York, NY 10022
212-909-6096 Fax: 212-909-6836
e-mail: elieberman@debevoise.com
Web site: www.debevoise.com
Ellen Lieberman,

Education & Assistance Corporation Inc
50 Clinton St, Ste 107, Hempstead, NY 11550
516-539-0150 Fax: 516-539-0160
e-mail: lelder@eacinc.org
Web site: www.eacinc.org
Lance W Elder, President & CEO
Rehabilitation for nonviolent offenders; advocacy, education & counseling programs for youth, elderly & families

Fortune Society (The)
53 W 23rd St, 8th Fl, New York, NY 10010
212-691-7554 x501 Fax: 212-255-4948
e-mail: jpfortune@aol.com
Web site: www.fortunesociety.org
JoAnne Page, Executive Director
Education & vocational training for ex-offenders, alternatives to incarceration, counseling, drug treatment & HIV/AIDS services & referrals & transitional housing facility

Hofstra University, School of Law
121 Hofstra University, Hempstead, NY 11549-1210
212-864-6092
e-mail: lawdny@hofstra.edu
Web site: www.hofstra.edu/law
David N Yellen, Emeritus Professor of Law
Antitrust, criminal law, evidence

Offices and agencies generally appear in alphabetical order, except when specific order is requested by listee.

CRIME & CORRECTIONS / Private Sector

Law Offices of Stanley N Lupkin
98 Cutter Mill Road, Suite 227N, Great Neck, NY 11021
516-482-1223 Fax: 516-466-2799
e-mail: slupkin@gnlaw.com
Stanley N Lupkin, White Collar Criminal Defense
Corporate, criminal & financial investigations

Legal Action Center of the City of NY Inc
153 Waverly Place, New York, NY 10014
212-243-1313 Fax: 212-675-0286
e-mail: lacinfo@lac.org
Web site: www.lac.org
Paul N Samuels, President & Director
Legal & policy issues, alcohol/drug abuse, AIDS & criminal justice

Legal Aid Society
199 Water Street, New York, NY 10013
212-557-3300 Fax: 212-509-8761
e-mail: jpreble@legal-aid.org
Web site: www.legal-aid.org
Judith Preble, Supervising Attorney, Criminal Defense Division
Criminal defense & appeals

NYS Bar Assn, Criminal Justice Section
Michael T Kelly, Esq
1217 Delaware Ave, Apt 1003, Buffalo, NY 14209
716-886-1922 Fax: 716-886-1922
e-mail: mkelly1005@aol.com
Michael T Kelly, Chair

Mothers Against Drunk Driving (MADD) of NYS
790 Watervliet-Shaker Road, Suite #6, Latham, NY 12110
518-785-6233 or 800-245-6233 Fax: 518-782-1806
e-mail: ny.state@madd.org
Web site: www.madd.org
Donna Kopec, Executive Director
Advocacy, public education & victim support

NYS Association of Chiefs of Police Inc
2697 Hamburg Street, Schenectady, NY 12303
518-355-3371 Fax: 518-356-5767
e-mail: nysacop@nycap.rr.com
Web site: www.nychiefs.org
John Grebert, Executive Director

NYS Correctional Officers & Police Benevolent Association Inc
102 Hackett Blvd, Albany, NY 12209
518-427-1551 or 888-484-7279 Fax: 518-426-1635
e-mail: nyscopba@nyscopba.org
Web site: www.nyscopba.org
Richard Harcrow, President

NYS Council of Probation Administrators
c/o Council of Community Svcs of NYS, Box 2, 272 Broadway, Albany, NY 12204-2941
518-434-9194 Fax: 518-434-0392
e-mail: president@nyscopa.org
Web site: www.nyscopa.org
Patricia Aikens, President
Provide supervision & investigation services to courts

NYS Defenders Association
194 Washington Ave, Ste 500, Albany, NY 12210-2314
518-465-3524 Fax: 518-465-3249
e-mail: info@nysda.org
Web site: www.nysda.org
Jonathan E Gradess, Executive Director
Criminal defense

NYS Deputies Association Inc
61 Laredo Dr, Rochester, NY 14624
585-247-9322 Fax: 585-247-6661
e-mail: tross1@rochester.rr.com
Web site: www.nysdeputy.org
Thomas H Ross, Executive Director

NYS Law Enforcement Officers Union, Council 82, AFSCME, AFL-CIO
Hollis V Chase Bldg, 63 Colvin Ave, Albany, NY 12206
518-489-8424 Fax: 518-435-1523
e-mail: c82@council82.org
Web site: www.council82.org
James Lyman, President

NYS Sheriffs' Association
27 Elk St, Albany, NY 12207-1002
518-434-9091 Fax: 518-434-9093
e-mail: pkehoe@nysheriffs.org
Web site: www.nysheriffs.org
Peter R Kehoe, Executive Director

New York State Law Enforcement Council
One Hogan Place, New York, NY 10013
212-335-8927 Fax: 212-335-3808
Web site: www.nyslec.org
Leroy Frazer, Jr, Coordinator
Founded in 1982 as a legislative advocate for NY's law enforcement community. The members represent leading law enforcement professionals throughout the state. An active voice and participant in improving the quality of justice and a safer NY.

Osborne Association
809 Westchester Avenue, Bronx, NY 10455
718-707-2600 or 718-842-0500 Fax: 718-707-3102
e-mail: info@osborneny.org
Web site: www.osborneny.org
Elizabeth A Gaynes, Director of Employment & Training
Career/educational counseling, job referrals & training for recently released prisoners, substance abuse treatment, case management, HIV/AIDS counseling & prevention, family services, parenting education, re-entry services, housing placement assistan

Pace University, School of Law, John Jay Legal Services Inc
80 N Broadway, White Plains, NY 10603-3711
914-422-4333 Fax: 914-422-4391
e-mail: vmerton@law.pace.edu
Web site: www.law.pace.edu
Vanessa Merton,
Health law, poverty law, domestic violence, immigration

Offices and agencies generally appear in alphabetical order, except when specific order is requested by listee.

CRIME & CORRECTIONS / Private Sector

Palladia Inc
2006 Madison Avenue, New York, NY 10035
212-979-8800 Fax: 212-979-0100
e-mail: info@palladiainc.org
Web site: www.palladiainc.org
Susan Ohanesian, Vice President, Residential Services
Outpatient treatment, substance abuse treatment & counseling, alternatives to incarceration & parole transitional services

Patrolmen's Benevolent Association
40 Fulton St, 17th Fl, New York, NY 10038
212-233-5531 Fax: 212-233-3952
e-mail: union@nycpba.org
Web site: www.nycpba.org
Patrick Lynch, President
NYC patrolmen's union

Police Conference of NY Inc (PCNY)
112 State St, Ste 1120, Albany, NY 12207
518-463-3283 Fax: 518-463-2488
Web site: www.pcny.org
Edward W Guzdek, President
Advocacy for law enforcement officers

Prisoners' Legal Services of New York
114 Prospect St, Ithaca, NY 14850-5616
607-273-2283 Fax: 607-272-9122
e-mail: sjohnson@plsny.org
Susan Johnson, Executive Director

Remove Intoxicated Drivers (RID-USA Inc)
1013 Nott St, PO Box 520, Schenectady, NY 12301
518-372-0034 or 518-393-4357 Fax: 518-370-4917
e-mail: daiken2@nycap.rr.com
Web site: www.rid-usa.org
Doris Aiken, President
Victims' rights, alcohol policy & public awareness

Pearls' Prison Families of NY
Rochester Interfaith Jail Ministry Inc
130 Plymouth Avenue South, Rochester, NY 14614
585-428-3802
e-mail: rochesterjail/ministry@yahoo.com
Harry Bronson, Executive Director
Support services for ex-offenders, the incarcerated & their families

SUNY at Stony Brook, NY State Drinking Driver Program
Social & Behavioral Sciences, Rm North 231, Stony Brook, NY 11794-4326
631-632-7060 Fax: 631-632-4224
e-mail: pbrennan@notes.cc.sunysb.edu
Patricia Brennan, Director
Drinking & driving education & prevention

Stillman, Friedman & Shechtman PC
425 Park Ave, New York, NY 10022
212-223-0200 Fax: 212-223-1942
e-mail: cstillman@stillmanfriedman.com
Web site: www.stillmanfriedman.com
Charles A Stillman, Partner
White collar criminal law

Trooper Foundation-State of New York Inc
3 Airport Park Blvd, Latham, NY 12110-1441
518-785-1002 Fax: 518-785-1003
e-mail: rmincher@nystf.org
Web site: www.nystrooperfoundation.org
Rachel L Mincher, Foundation Administrator
Supports programs & services of the NYS Police

Vera Institute of Justice
233 Broadway, 12th Fl, New York, NY 10279-1299
212-334-1300 Fax: 212-941-9407
e-mail: mgolden@vera.org
Web site: www.vera.org
Michael Jacobson, Director
Research, design & implementation of demonstration projects in criminal justice & social equity in partnership with governmental community organizations

Women's Prison Association & Home Inc
110 Second Ave, New York, NY 10003
646-336-6100 Fax: 212-677-1981
Web site: www.wpaonline.org
Ann Jacobs, Executive Director
Community corrections & family preservation programs

Offices and agencies generally appear in alphabetical order, except when specific order is requested by listee.

EDUCATION

New York State

GOVERNOR'S OFFICE

Governor's Office
Executive Chamber
State Capitol
Albany, NY 12224
518-474-8390 Fax: 518-474-1513
Web site: www.state.ny.us

Governor:
   Eliot Spitzer 518-474-8390
Secretary to the Governor:
   Richard Baum 518-474-4246
Counsel to the Governor:
   David Nocenti 518-474-8343
Senior Advisor to the Governor:
   Lloyd Constantine 518-486-9671
Deputy Secretary, Education:
   Manuel Rivera 518-408-2833
Assistant Deputy Secretary, Education:
   John Reid 518-408-2833
Director, Communications:
   Darren Dopp 518-474-8418

EXECUTIVE DEPARTMENTS AND RELATED AGENCIES

Board of Regents
89 Washington Ave
Rm 110
Albany, NY 12234
518-474-5889 Fax: 518-486-2405
Web site: www.regents.nysed.gov

Chancellor:
   Robert M Bennett (2010) 716-882-4300
Vice Chancellor:
   Merryl H Tisch (2011) 212-879-9414
Education Commissioner, USNY President:
   Richard P Mills 518-474-5844
   e-mail: rmills@mail.nysed.gov
Secretary to the Board:
   David Johnson 518-474-5889
   e-mail: djohnson@mail.nysed.gov
Member:
   Charles R Bendit (2012) 212-220-9945
Member:
   Karen Brooks Hopkins (2010) 718-636-4135
Member:
   Anthony S Bottar (2011) 315-422-3466
Member:
   Joseph E Bowman, Jr (2009) 518-442-4987
Member:
   Geraldine Chapey (2008) 718-634-8471
Member:
   Milton L Cofield (2012) 585-248-8494
Member:
   Saul B Cohen (2009) 914-633-7889
Member:
   James C Dawson (2010) 518-643-9289
Member:
   Arnold B Gardner (2009) 716-845-6000
Member:
   Natalie M Gomez-Velez (2008) 716-340-4523
Member:
   Harry Phillips, III (2010) 914-948-2228
Member:
   James R Tallon, Jr (2012) 212-494-0777
Member:
   Roger B Tilles (2010) 516-364-2533

Children & Family Services, Office of
52 Washington St
Rensselaer, NY 12144-2735
518-473-8437
Web site: www.ocfs.state.ny.us

Commissioner:
   Gladys Carrion, Esq 518-473-8437
Executive Assistant:
   Laura Velez 518-473-8437
Executive Deputy Commissioner:
   Larry G Brown 518-402-3108
Executive Assistant:
   Lee Lounsbury 518-402-8400
Assistant Commissioner, Public Affairs:
   Sandra A Brown 518-402-3130
   e-mail: cfspio@dfa.state.ny.us
Director, Strategic Planning & Policy Development:
   Nancy W Martinez 518-473-1776
Acting Deputy Director, Equal Employment & Diversity Development:
   Emy Murphy 518-474-3715
Director, Bureau of Early Childhood Services (BECS):
   Suzanne Sennett 518-474-9454
NYC Regional Office Regional Coordinator:
   Digna Sanchez 212-383-1823

Regional Operations
Director, Regional Operations & Practice Improvement (ROPI):
   Bill McLaughlin 518-474-9465
Acting Director, Youth Development:
   Matt Murell 518-402-3830

Education Department
State Education Bldg
89 Washington Ave
Albany, NY 12234
518-474-5215 Fax: 518-486-5631
Web site: www.nysed.gov

Offices and agencies generally appear in alphabetical order, except when specific order is requested by listee.

EDUCATION / New York State

Commissioner, University President:
  Richard P Mills...................518-474-5844
  e-mail: rmills@mail.nysed.gov
Assistant to the Commissioner:
  Peggy Rivers......................518-474-5845
  e-mail: privers@mail.nysed.gov
Counsel & Deputy Commissioner, Legal Affairs:
  Kathy A Ahearn....................518-474-6400
  e-mail: kahearn@mail.nysed.gov
Chief of Staff & Deputy Commissioner, Innovation:
  David Miller......................518-486-1713
  e-mail: dmiller@mail.nysed.gov

Cultural Education Office
10A 33 Cultural Education Center, Madison Avenue, Albany, NY 12230
Web site: www.oce.nysed.gov
Deputy Commissioner:
  Jeffrey Cannell............518-474-5976/fax: 518-486-4850
  e-mail: jcannell@mail.nysed.gov

Educational Television & Public Broadcasting
Director:
  Elizabeth Hood....................518-474-5862
Public Broadcasting Financial Aid:
  Mark Waldman......................518-474-4731
Educational Services:
  Jane Briggs.......................518-486-3843
Senior Administrative Analyst:
  Alexander Gyamfi..................518-473-2907

State Archives
Assistant Commissioner & State Archivist:
  Christine Ward....................518-474-6926
  e-mail: cward@mail.nysed.gov
Archives Operations:
  Kathleen Roe......................518-474-6926
Archival Services:
  Maria Holden......................518-474-6926
Reference & Research Services:
  James Folts.......................518-474-8955
State Records Center Services:
  John Welter.......................518-457-3171
Government Records Services:
  Geoff Huth........................518-402-5371
Grants Administration:
  Kathleen Roe......................518-474-6926
Administrative & Technical Services:
  Loraine Wilson....................518-474-6926
Public Programs & Outreach:
  Judy Hohmann......................518-474-6926

State Library
Empire State Plaza, Cultural Education Center, Albany, NY 12230
Web site: www.nysl.nysed.gov
Assistant Commissioner & State Librarian:
  Janet Welch.......................518-474-5930
  e-mail: jwelch2@mail.nysed.gov
NYS Library Director:
  Loretta Ebert.....................518-473-1189
Acting Library Administrative Officer:
  Mary Woodward.....................518-474-1195
Public Relations/Public Information:
  Valerie Chevrette.........518-474-5961/fax: 518-486-2152
Technical Services & Systems:
  Liza Duncan.......................518-474-5946
  Reference Services
  518-474-2274
Coordinator Statewide Library Services:
  Carol Desch.......................518-474-7196

Talking Book & Braille Library:
  Sharon Phillips...................518-474-7586

State Museum Office
Assistant Commissioner & Director:
  Clifford A Siegfried..............518-474-5812
  e-mail: csiegfri@mail.nysed.gov
Exhibits/Public Programs Director:
  Mark Schaming.....................518-402-5952
State Geologist:
  William Kelly.....................518-474-5816

Research and Collections
Director:
  John Hart.........................518-474-5816
Assistant Director:
  Robert Daniels....................518-474-5816
Assistant Director:
  Penelope Drooker..................518-474-5816
Operations & Museum Administration Center:
  Clifford Siegfried................518-474-5812
Chartering:
  David Palmquist...................518-473-3131
Museum Education Director:
  Jeanine Grinage...................518-486-2003
Registrar:
  Vacant............................518-474-4812

Innovation
Deputy Commissioner:
  David Miller......................518-486-1713
Director, Communications:
  Alan Ray..........................518-474-1201
Director, Governmental Relations:
  Diana Hinchcliff..................518-486-5644
Coordinator, Organizational Effectiveness:
  Rebecca Kennard...................518-486-5289
Secretary to the Board of Regents:
  David Johnson.....................518-474-5889

Office of Higher Education
89 Washington Ave, 2nd Fl Mezzanine, EB West, Albany, NY 12234
Web site: www.highered.nysed.gov
Associate Commissioner:
  Joseph P Frey.....................518-474-3633

Office of K-16 Initiatives & Access Programs
Executive Coordinator:
  Stanley S Hansen, Jr.......518-474-3719/fax: 518-474-7468
  e-mail: shansen2@mail.nysed.gov
  College & University Evaluation
  Coordinator:
    Barbara D Meinert...............518-474-1551
  Proprietary School Supervision
  Chief:
    Carole Yates....................518-474-3969
  Research & Information Systems
  Lead Contact:
    Glenwood Rowse..................518-474-5091
    e-mail: growse@mail.nysed.gov

Office of Teaching Initiatives
Teacher Certification, Teacher Policy & School Personnel Review
Executive Director:
  Robert Bentley................518-474-3817 x340
  e-mail: rbentley@mail.nysed.gov

Office of Operations & Management Services
Web site: www.oms.nysed.gov
Deputy Commissioner:
  Theresa E Savo.............518-474-2547/fax: 518-473-2827

Offices and agencies generally appear in alphabetical order, except when specific order is requested by listee.

EDUCATION / New York State

Administration
Diversity, Ethics & Access:
  Steven Earle 518-474-1265
Facilities & Business Services:
  George Webb 518-474-7770
Human Resources Management:
  Gayle Bowden 518-474-5883

Fiscal Services
Chief Financial Officer:
  Theresa E Savo 518-474-2547
  e-mail: tsavo@mail.nysed.gov
Budget Coordination:
  Lenton D Simms 518-474-6571
Education Finance Director:
  Burt Porter 518-474-8825
Fiscal Management:
  Michael DiVirgilio 518-474-7751
Child Nutrition Reimbursement:
  Theresa Cary 518-486-1766
Categorical Aid:
  Margaret Zollo 518-473-4815
Program Services Reimbursement:
  Thomas Hamel 518-486-2991
STAC (Systems to Track & Account for Children):
  Harold Matott 518-474-7116

Information Technology Services
Chief Information Officer:
  David Walsh 518-486-1702
Information Technology Services (ITS) Director:
  Richard Melita 518-474-4640

Planning & Policy Development
Audit Services:
  James Conway 518-473-3863

Office of P-16 Education
89 Washington Ave, EB West 2nd Fl Mezzanine, Albany, NY 12234
Senior Deputy Commissioner:
  Johanna Duncan-Poiter 518-474-3812/fax: 518-473-2056
  e-mail: jpoiter@mail.nysed.gov
Lead Contact, Management Operations:
  Leslie E Templeman 518-474-3862
Lead Contact, District Superintendent's Office:
  Raymond Kesper 518-474-8076/fax: 518-473-2860
  e-mail: rkesper@mail.nysed.gov
Lead Contact, Administrative Support Group:
  John Delaney 518-486-1544

Curriculum & Instructional Support
Associate Commissioner:
  Jean Stevens 518-474-5915
  e-mail: jstevens@mail.nysed.gov
Adult Education & Workforce Development
Lead Contact:
  Thomas Orsini 518-474-8940
Career & Technical Education
Lead Contact:
  Pat Hodgins 518-486-1547
Lead Contact:
  Vic Perun 518-486-1547
Curriculum, Instruction & Instructional Technology
Lead Contact:
  Anne Schiano 518-402-5544/fax: 518-486-1385
Summer Initiatives
Lead Contact:
  Mary Daley 518-474-8773

Bilingual Education
Lead Contact:
  Pedro Ruiz 518-474-8775

School Improvement & Community Services (NYC) fax: 718-722-4559
55 Hanson Place, Brooklyn, NY 11217
Associate Commissioner:
  Shelia Evans-Tranumn .... 718-722-2796 or 518-474-4715
  e-mail: sevans-tra@mail.nysed.gov
Coordinator, School Accountability Workgroup:
  Ira Schwartz 718-722-2796
  e-mail: ischwart@mail.nysed.gov
Early Education & Reading Initiatives
89 Washington Ave, EBA, Rm 381, Albany, NY 12234
Lead Contact:
  Cynthia Gallagher 518-474-5807/fax: 518-486-7290
NYC Intra/Interagency Group
Lead Contact:
  Sandra Herndon 718-722-2784
NYC School Improvement
Lead Contact:
  Sandra Norfleet 718-722-2636
Title I School & Community Services
Lead Contact:
  Roberto Reyes 518-473-0295

School Improvements & Community Services (Regional)
Executive Director:
  James Viola 518-474-4817
  e-mail: jviola@mail.nysed.gov
Native American Education
Lead Contact:
  Adrian Cooke 518-474-0537
Planning & Professional Development
Lead Contact:
  Laurie Rowe 518-473-7155
Public School Choice
Lead Contact:
  Darlene Mengel 518-474-1762
Student Support Services
Lead Contact:
  Robert Jaffarian 518-486-6090/fax: 518-474-8299

School Operations & Management Services
Coordinator:
  Charles Szuberla 518-474-2238
Child Nutrition Program Administration
Lead Contact:
  Frances O'Donnell 518-473-8781
Educational Management Services
Lead Contact:
  Deborah Cunningham 518-474-6541
Facilities & Management Services
Lead Contact:
  Carl Thurnau 518-474-3906
Grants Management
Lead Contact:
  Jeanette Canaday 518-474-6541
Nonpublic School Services
Lead Contact:
  Tom Hogan 518-474-3879

Standards, Assessment & Reporting
Assistant Commissioner:
  David Abrams 518-473-7880
  e-mail: dabrams@mail.nysed.gov
Information & Reporting Services
Lead Contact:
  Martha Musser 518-474-7965
  e-mail: mmusser@mail.nysed.gov

Offices and agencies generally appear in alphabetical order, except when specific order is requested by listee.

EDUCATION / New York State

State Assessment
Lead Contact, Administration & Development:
Steven Katz 518-474-5099

Office of the Professions . . . . fax: 518-473-3863
89 Washington Ave, EB, 2nd Fl, West Mezz, Albany, NY 12234
Fax: 518-473-3863
Web site: www.op.nysed.gov
Associate Commissioner:
Frank Munoz 518-474-3817 x440
e-mail: opopr@mail.nysed.gov
Executive Coordinator, Professional Practice:
Anthony Lofrumento 518-474-3817 x570
e-mail: op4info@mail.nysed.gov

Office of Professional Responsibility
Executive Director:
Vacant 518-474-3817 x440
e-mail: opexdir@mail.nysed.gov
Office of Special Projects & Legislation
Coordinator:
Sarah Benson 518-474-3817 x440
Professional Assistance Program
Executive Secretary:
Lawrence DeMers 518-474-3817 x480
Professional Discipline
475 Park Ave South, New York, NY 10016
Director:
Louis Catone 212-951-6400
Director, Investigations:
Daniel Kelleher 212-951-6400
Director, Legal Services:
Andrew Tolkoff 212-951-6550
Director, Prosecutions:
George Ding 212-951-6400
State Review
Chief:
Paul Kelly 518-485-9373

Professional Education Program Review
Supervisor:
Vacant 518-474-3817 x360
e-mail: opprogs@mail.nysed.gov

Professional Licensing Services
Director:
Anthony Lofrumento 518-474-3817 x340
e-mail: opdpls@mail.nysed.gov
Chief, Office of Comparative Education:
Leonard Lapinski 518-474-3817 x300

State Boards for the Professions
Architecture & Landscape Architecture
Executive Secretary:
Robert Lopez 518-474-3817 x110
Chiropractic
Executive Secretary:
Douglas Lentivech 518-474-3817 x190
Dentistry & Optometry
Executive Secretary:
Milton Lawney 518-474-3817 x550
Engineering & Land Surveying & Interior Design
Executive Secretary:
Jane Blair 518-474-3817 x140
Medicine, Diet-Nutrn, Athltc Trning, Medical Physics & Vet Med
Executive Secretary:
Vacant 518-474-3817 x560
Nursing & Respiratory Therapy
Executive Secretary:
Barbara Zittel 518-474-3817 x120

Pharmacy & Midwifery
Executive Secretary:
Lawrence H Mokhiber 518-474-3817 x130
Psychology & Massage Therapy
Executive Secretary:
Kathleen M Doyle 518-474-3817 x150
Public Accountancy & Certified Shorthand Reporting
Executive Secretary:
Daniel J Dustin 518-474-3817 x160
Social Work & Mental Health Practitioners
Executive Secretary:
David Hamilton 518-474-3817 x450
Speech Language Pathology & Audiology, Acupuncture & Occupational Therapy
Executive Secretary:
Lawrence DeMers 518-474-3817 x100

Vocational & Educational Services for Individuals With Disabilities Office (VESID) . . . . fax: 518-474-8802
One Commerce Plaza, Rm 1606, Albany, NY 12234
Fax: 518-474-8802
Web site: www.vesid.nysed.gov
Deputy Commissioner:
Rebecca Cort 518-474-2714
e-mail: rcort@mail.nysed.gov
Assistant Commissioner:
Edward Placke 518-473-4818

Fiscal & Administrative Services
Coordinator:
Rosemary Ellis Johnson 518-486-4038
Manager, Data Collection:
Inni Barone 518-486-4678
Manager, Contracts & Grants:
Jack LaFrank 518-486-6585
Manager, Support Services:
Michael Plotzker 518-473-4823
Manager, Budget & Finance:
William Keane 518-473-4824
Manager, Technology:
Lori Scalera 518-486-4037
Quality Assurance - Statewide Special Education
Statewide Coordinator:
James DeLorenzo 518-402-3353
Upstate Regional Coordinator:
Daniel Johnson 518-486-6221
State School for the Blind at Batavia
2A Richmond Ave, Batavia, NY 14020
Acting Superintendent:
James Knowles 585-343-5384
State School for the Deaf at Rome
401 Turin St, Rome, NY 13340
Superintendent:
Carriann Ray 315-337-8400

Program Develpmnt & Support Svcs/Special Ed Policy & Ptshps
Coordinator:
Vacant 518-486-7462
Manager, Deaf & Hard of Hearing Services:
Dorothy Steele 518-474-1711
Supervisor, Lifelong Services:
Daniel J Ryan 518-486-7462
Supervisor, Special Education Policy & Partnerships:
Vacant 518-473-2878

Special Education Quality Assurance Regional Offices
Central Regional Office
State Office Bldg, 333 E Washington St, Syracuse, NY 13202
Region Office Supervisor:
Jackie Bumbalo 315-428-3287/fax: 315-428-3286

Offices and agencies generally appear in alphabetical order, except when specific order is requested by listee.

EDUCATION / New York State

Eastern Regional Office
One Commerce Plaza, Rm 1623, Albany, NY 12234
Regional Office Supervisor:
Vacant 518-486-6366/fax: 518-486-7693
Hudson Valley Regional Office
1950 Edgewater St, Yorktown Heights, NY 10598
Regional Office Supervisor:
Christine Efner 518-473-1185/fax: 518-402-3582
Long Island Regional Office
The Kellum Education Center, 887 Kellum St, Lindenhurst, NY 11757
Regional Office Supervisor:
Stephen Berman 631-884-8530/fax: 631-884-8540
New York City Regional Office
55 Hanson Place, Rm 545, Brooklyn, NY 11217-1580
NYC Regional Coordinator:
Patricia Shubert 718-722-4544/fax: 718-722-2032
Western Regional Office
2A Richmond Ave, Batavia, NY 14020
Regional Office Supervisor:
Phyllis Powers 585-344-2002/fax: 585-344-2422

Vocational Rehabilitation Operations
Acting Director, District Office Administration:
Debora Brown-Grant 518-473-1626
e-mail: dbrowngr@mail.nysed.gov
Director, Operations-District Office Administration:
Ronald Strohl 518-486-4035
e-mail: rstrohl@mail.nysed.gov
Manager, Independent Living Centers:
Robert Gumson 518-474-2925
Albany District Office
80 Wolf Road, Albany, NY 12205
Regional Director:
David Segalla 518-473-8097
Bronx District Office
1215 Zerega Ave, Bronx, NY 10462
District Office Manager:
Mary Faulkner 718-931-3500
Brooklyn District Office
55 Hanson Pl, Brooklyn, NY 11217-1578
District Office Manager:
Frank Stechel 718-722-6700
Buffalo District Office
508 Main St, Buffalo, NY 14202
Regional Coordinator:
Susan Piper 716-848-8001
Hauppauge District Office
State Office Bldg, Veterans Memorial Hwy, Hauppauge, NY 11788-5127
District Office Manager:
Ingo Gloeckner 631-952-6357
Hempstead District Office
50 Clinton St, Rm 708, Hempstead, NY 11550
District Office Manager:
Aurora Farrington 518-483-6510
Malone District Office
209 W Main St, Malone, NY 12953
District Office Manager:
Steve Novacich 518-483-3530
Manhattan District Office
116 West 32nd St, 6th Fl, New York, NY 10001
Regional Coordinator:
William Ursillo 212-630-2300
Mid-Hudson District Office
Manchester Mill Ctr, 301 Manchester Rd, Ste 200, Poughkeepsie, NY 12603
District Office Manager:
Bruce Solomkin 845-452-5325

Queens District Office
One LeFrak City Plaza, 20th Fl, 59-17 Junction Blvd, Corona, NY 11368
Regional Coordinator:
John Nardozzi 718-271-9346
Rochester District Office
Wilson Bldg, 109 S Union St, 2nd Fl, Rochester, NY 14607
District Office Manager:
Nicolette Leathersich 585-238-2900
Southern Tier District Office
44 Hawley St, Binghamton, NY 13901
Regional Coordinator:
Richard Bohman 607-721-8400
Syracuse District Office
333 E Washington St, 2nd Fl, Rm 230, Syracuse, NY 13202-1428
Regional Coordinator:
Duane Watson 315-428-4179
Utica District Office
207 Genesee St, Rm 801, Utica, NY 13501-2812
District Office Manager:
John Tracy 315-793-2536
White Plains District Office
75 South Broadway, 1st Fl, White Plains, NY 10601
District Office Manager:
Mark Ridgeway 914-946-1313

NYS Foundation for Science, Technology & Innovation

30 South Pearl St
11th Fl
Albany, NY 12207
518-292-5700 Fax: 518-292-5798
e-mail: contact@nystar.state.ny.us
Web site: www.nystar.state.ny.us

Executive Director:
Michael J Relyea 518-292-5700
Director, Communications:
Jannette Rondo 518-292-5700/fax: 518-292-5798
Director, Programs:
Kathleen J Wise 518-292-5700
Deputy Counsel:
Paul Jesep 518-292-5700
Director, Finance:
Edward J Hamilton 518-292-5700

Centers for Advanced Technology

Center for Advanced Ceramic Technology at Alfred University
352 McMahon Engineering Bldg, 2 Pine St, Alfred, NY 14802-1296
Director:
Vasantha Amarakoon 607-871-2486/fax: 607-871-3469

Center for Advanced Materials Processing at Clarkson Univ
Box 5665, Potsdam, NY 13699-5665
Director:
S V Babu 315-268-2336/fax: 315-268-7615

Center for Advanced Tech in Biomedical & Bioengineering
SUNY at Buffalo, 162K Farber Hall, 3435 Main St, Buffalo, NY 14214-3092
Deputy Director:
Cathy M Buyea 716-829-2561/fax: 716-829-3945
e-mail: buyea@buffalo.edu

Sensor CAT-Diagnostic Tools & Sensor Systems
SUNY at Stony Brook, 214 Old Chemistry Bldg, 2nd Fl, Stony Brook, NY 11794-3717

Offices and agencies generally appear in alphabetical order, except when specific order is requested by listee.

EDUCATION / New York State

Web site: www.sensorcat.sunybsb.edu
Director:
    Serge Luryi 631-632-1368/fax: 631-632-8529

Center for Advanced Technology in Electronic Imaging Systems
Univ of Rochester, Taylor Hall, 260 Hutchison Rd, Rochester, NY 14627
Director:
    Eby Friedman 585-275-1022/fax: 585-276-0200

Center for Advanced Technology in Information Management
Columbia University, 630 W 168th St, PH-15-1501, New York, NY 10032
Director:
    Edward H Shortliffe 212-305-2944/fax: 212-305-0196

Center for Advanced Technology in Life Science Enterprise
Cornell University, 130 Biotechnology Bldg, Ithaca, NY 14853-2703
Director:
    Stephen Kresovich 607-255-2300/fax: 607-255-6249

Center for Advanced Technology in Photonic Applications
Dept of Physics, City College of CUNY, 138th St & Convent Ave Rm J419, New York, NY 10031
Director:
    Robert R Alfano 212-650-5531/fax: 212-650-5530

Center for Automation Tech at Rensselaer Polytechnic Inst
CII Bldg, Rm 8015, Troy, NY 12180-3590
Director:
    Ray Puffer . . . . 518-276-8990 or 518-276-8087
    fax: 518-276-4897

Center for Advanced Tech-Medical Biotechnology
SUNY at Stony Brook, Psychology A, 3rd Fl, Stony Brook, NY 11794-2580
Director:
    Clinton T Rubin 631-632-8521/fax: 631-632-8577

Center for Computer Applications & Software Engineering
Syracuse University, 2-212 Ctr for Science & Tech, Syracuse, NY 13244
Director:
    Shui-Kai Chin 315-443-1060/fax: 315-443-4745

Center in Nanomaterials and Nanoelectronics
Albany Institue for Materials, CESTM Bldg, 251 Fuller Rd, Rm B110, Albany, NY 12203
President:
    Alain E Kaloyeros 518-437-8686/fax: 518-437-8687

Ctr for Advanced Tech in Telecommunications at Polytech Univ
5 MetroTech Center, Rm LC 208, Brooklyn, NY 11201
Director:
    Shivendra S Panwar 718-260-3050/fax: 718-260-3074

Future Energy Systems CAT at Rensselaer Polytechnic Inst
Ctr for Integrated Electronics and, 9023 Low Ctr for Industrial Innovation, 110 8th St, Troy, NY 12180
Director:
    Omkaram Nalamasu 518-276-3290/fax: 518-276-2990

Integrated Electronics Engineering Center
Thomas J Watson School of Engineering, S, Vestal Pkwy East, PO Box 6000, Binghamton, NY 13902-6000
Director:
    Bahgat Sammakia 607-777-4332/fax: 607-777-4683

Regional Technology Development Centers

Alliance for Manufacturing & Technology
59 Court St, 6th Fl, State St Entrance, Binghamton, NY 13901
Executive Director:
    Edward Gaetano 607-774-0022 x304/fax: 607-774-0026

Center for Economic Growth
63 State St, Albany, NY 12207
President:
    Kelly Lovell 518-465-8975/fax: 518-465-6681

Central New York Technology Development Organization
1201 E Fayette St, Syracuse, NY 13210
President:
    Robert I Trachtenberg 315-425-5144/fax: 315-233-1259

Council for Interntl Trade, Tech, Education & Communication
Peyton Hall, Rm 101, Main St, Potsdam, NY 13676
Executive Director:
    Thomas Plastino 315-268-3778 x24/fax: 315-268-4432

High Technology of Rochester
Chamber of Commerce Bldg, 5 Bragdon Pl, Rochester, NY 14604
Executive Director:
    Paul Wettenhall 585-327-7920/fax: 585-327-7931

Hudson Valley Technology Development Center
300 Westage Business Ctr, Ste 130, Fishkill, NY 12524
Executive Director:
    Thomas J Phillips, Sr 845-896-6934 x3006/fax: 845-896-7006

Industrial & Technology Assistance Corp
253 Broadway, Rm 302, New York, NY 10007
President:
    Sara Garretson 212-442-2990/fax: 212-442-4567

Long Island Forum for Technology
111 West Main St, Bayshore, NY 11706
Executive Director:
    Patricia Howley 631-969-3700/fax: 631-969-4489

Mohawk Valley Applied Technology Corp
207 Genesee St, Ste 405, Utica, NY 13501
President:
    Paul MacEnroe 315-793-8050/fax: 315-793-8057

INSYTE Consulting (Western NY Technology Development Ctr)
726 Exchange St, Ste 620, Buffalo, NY 14210
President:
    Robert J Martin 716-636-3626/fax: 716-845-6418

CORPORATIONS, AUTHORITIES AND COMMISSIONS

City University Construction Fund
555 W 57th St
11th Fl
New York, NY 10019
212-541-0171 Fax: 212-541-1014

Interim Chair:
    Philip Berry 212-541-0171
Executive Director:
    Iris Weinshall 212-541-5315
    e-mail: iris.weinshall@mail.cuny.edu
Counsel:
    Frederick Schaffer 212-794-5506
Accountant:
    Carlos Mena 212-541-0173
    e-mail: carlos.mena@mail.cuny.edu
Administrative Officer:
    Denise Phillips 212-541-0190
    e-mail: denise.phillips@mail.cuny.edu

Offices and agencies generally appear in alphabetical order, except when specific order is requested by listee.

EDUCATION / New York State

New York City School Construction Authority
30-30 Thomson Ave
Long Island City, NY 11101-3045
718-472-8000 Fax: 718-472-8840
Web site: schools.nyc.gov/Offices/SCA

Chair/Chancellor:
  Joel I Klein 718-472-8000
President & Chief Executive Officer:
  Sharon Greenberger 718-472-8001
Vice President, General Counsel:
  Ross J Holden 718-472-8220
VP, Finance:
  Marianne Egri 718-472-8012
VP, Project Management & Operations:
  Chester Yee, PE 718-472-8015
VP, Architecture & Engineering:
  Bruce Barrett, RA 718-472-8710
Senior Director, Real Estate:
  Lorraine Grillo 718-472-8216

New York State Dormitory Authority
515 Broadway
Albany, NY 12207-2964
518-257-3000 Fax: 518-257-3100
e-mail: dabonds@dasny.org
Web site: www.dasny.org

One Penn Plaza
52nd Fl
New York, NY 10119-0098
212-273-5000
Fax: 212-273-5121

539 Franklin St
Buffalo, NY 14202-1109
716-884-9780
Fax: 716-884-9787

Chair:
  Gail H Gordon 518-257-3180/fax: 518-257-3183
Executive Director:
  David D Brown, IV 518-257-3180/fax: 518-257-3183
Deputy Executive Director:
  Michael T Corrigan 518-257-3192/fax: 518-257-3183
Chief Fiscal Officer:
  John G Pasicznyk 518-257-3630/fax: 518-257-3100
  e-mail: jpasiczn@dasny.org
General Counsel:
  Jeffrey M Pohl 518-257-3120/fax: 518-257-3101
  e-mail: jpohl@dasny.org
Managing Director, Construction:
  James M Gray, RA 518-257-3200/fax: 518-257-3100
  e-mail: jgray@dasny.org
Managing Director, Portfolio Management:
  Lora K Lefebvre 518-257-3163/fax: 518-257-3387
  e-mail: llefebvr@dasny.org
Managing Director, Public Finance:
  Cheryl Ishmael 518-257-3362/fax: 518-257-3100
  e-mail: cishmael@dasny.org
Director, Communications & Marketing:
  Paul Burgdorf 518-257-3380/fax: 518-257-3387
  e-mail: pburgdor@dasny.org

New York State Higher Education Services Corp (NYSHESC)
99 Washington Ave
Albany, NY 12255
518-473-7087 or 888-697-4372 Fax: 518-474-2839
Web site: www.hesc.org

President & Chief Executive Officer:
  James Ross 518-474-5592
Executive Vice President:
  Corinne M Biviano 518-474-5775
Senior Vice President, Corporate Finance & Chief Fiscal Officer:
  Warren Wallin 518-402-3584
Senior Vice President, Chief Operating Officer:
  Leonard Sippel 518-473-2523
  e-mail: lsippel@hesc.org
Senior Vice President, Communications:
  Ronald Kermani 518-473-1264
  e-mail: rkermani@hesc.org
Senior Vice President, Information Technology:
  Victor Stucchi 518-474-7083
  e-mail: vstucchi@hesc.org
Assistant Vice President, Customer Relations:
  John Austin 518-473-0733
  e-mail: jaustin@hesc.org
Director, Human Resources Management:
  Linda Dillon 518-474-0510
  e-mail: ldillon@hesc.org

New York State Teachers' Retirement System
10 Corporate Woods Dr
Albany, NY 12211-2395
518-447-2900 or 800-348-7298 Fax: 518-447-2695
e-mail: communit@nystrs.state.ny.us
Web site: www.nystrs.org

Executive Director:
  George M Philip 518-447-2666
  e-mail: execdir@nystrs.state.ny.us
General Counsel:
  Wayne Schneider 518-447-2722
Actuary:
  Richard Young 518-447-2692
Director, Administration:
  William S O'Brien 518-447-2730
Director, Member Relations:
  Sheila Gardella 518-447-2684
Manager, Public Information:
  John Cardillo 518-447-4743
Real Estate Investment Officer:
  John Virtanen 518-447-2751
Securities Investment Officer:
  Lawrence A Johansen 518-447-2611

State University Construction Fund
353 Broadway
Albany, NY 12246
518-689-2500 Fax: 518-689-2634
Web site: www.sucf.suny.edu

General Manager:
  Philip W Wood 518-689-2501

Offices and agencies generally appear in alphabetical order, except when specific order is requested by listee.

EDUCATION / U.S. Government

Acting General Counsel:
William K Barczak 518-689-2514/fax: 518-689-2634

NEW YORK STATE LEGISLATURE

See Legislative Branch in Section 1 for additional Standing Committee and Subcommittee information.

Assembly Standing Committees

Education
Chair:
Catherine Nolan (D) 518-455-4851
Ranking Minority Member:
Fred W Thiele Jr (R) 518-455-5997

Higher Education
Chair:
Deborah J Glick (D) 518-455-4841
Ranking Minority Member:
Joel M Miller (R) 518-455-5725

Libraries & Education Technology
Chair:
Patricia A Eddington (D) 518-455-4901
Ranking Minority Member:
Donna Ferrara (R) 518-455-4684

Assembly Task Forces

Skills Development & Career Education, Legislative Commission on
Assembly Chair:
Joan K Christensen (D) 518-455-5283

Program Manager:
Brenda Carter 518-455-4865/fax: 518-455-4175

University-Industry Cooperation, Legislative Task Force on
Chair:
William B Magnarelli (D) 518-455-4826
Coordinator:
Maureen Schoolman 518-455-4884/fax: 518-455-4175

Senate Standing Committees

Education
Chair:
Stephen M Saland (R) 518-455-2411
Ranking Minority Member:
Suzi Oppenheimer (D) 518-455-2031

Subcommittee
Libraries
Chair:
Hugh T Farley (R) 518-455-2181
Legislative Associate:
Marian Crounse 518-455-2181/fax: 518-455-2271

Higher Education
Chair:
Kenneth P LaValle (R) 518-455-3121
Ranking Minority Member:
Toby Ann Stavisky (D) 518-455-3461

U.S. Government

EXECUTIVE DEPARTMENTS AND RELATED AGENCIES

National Archives & Records Administration

Franklin D Roosevelt Presidential Library & Museum
4079 Albany Post Rd, Hyde Park, NY 12538
846-486-7770
Web site: www.fdrlibrary.marist.edu
Director:
Cynthia M Koch 845-486-7770/fax: 845-486-1147
e-mail: roosevelt.library@nara.gov

US Defense Department
e-mail: www.defenselink.mil

US Military Academy
West Point, NY 10996
845-938-4011
Web site: www.usma.edu
Superintendent:
Lt Gen Franklin L Hagenbeck 845-938-2610
Director, Public Affairs:
LTC Kent Cassella 845-938-3808/fax: 845-446-5820

US Education Department
Web site: www.ed.gov

Region 2 - NY, NJ, PR, VI .... fax: 646-428-3843
32 Old Slip, 25th Floor, New York, NY 10005
646-428-3900 or TDD: 877-521-2172 Fax: 646-428-3843
e-mail: OCR.NewYork@ed.gov
Secretary's Regional Representative:
Valarie Smith 646-428-3907
e-mail: valarie.smith@ed.gov
Deputy Secretary's Regional Representative:
Orysia Dmytrenko 646-428-3906

Civil Rights
Regional Director:
Randolph Wills 646-428-3839
e-mail: randolph.wills@ed.gov
Chief Civil Rights Attorney:
Timothy Blanchard 646-428-3805
e-mail: timothy.blanchard@ed.gov

Federal Student Aid
NY Team Area Case Director:
William Swift 646-428-3755
e-mail: william.swift@ed.gov

Offices and agencies generally appear in alphabetical order, except when specific order is requested by listee.

EDUCATION / Private Sector

Director, Loan Client Account Management Group Team Leader:
  David A Sola 617-565-5810/fax: 617-565-8636
  e-mail: david.sola@ed.gov

Financial Partner Services
Director, Eastern Regions:
  AnnMaria Fusco 646-428-3774
  e-mail: ann.maria.fusco@ed.gov

Office of Inspector General
Regional Inspector General, Audit:
  Daniel Schultz 646-428-3888
  e-mail: daniel.schultz@ed.gov
Regional Inspector General, Investigations:
  Gary Mathison 212-264-4104/fax: 212-637-0603
  e-mail: gary.mathison@ed.gov

Regional Grants Representative
Regional Grants Representative:
  Earl Williams 646-428-3935
  e-mail: earl.williams@ed.gov

US Transportation Department

US Merchant Marine Academy . . . . fax: 516-773-5774
  300 Steamboat Road, Kings Point, NY 11024-1699
  516-773-5000 Fax: 516-773-5774
  Web site: www.usmma.edu
Superintendent:
  VAdm Joseph D Stewart 516-773-5348/fax: 516-773-5347

U.S. CONGRESS

See U.S. Congress Chapter for additional Standing Committee and Subcommittee information.

House of Representatives Standing Committees

Education & Labor
Chair:
  George Miller (D-CA) 202-225-2095
Ranking Minority Member:
  Howard P (Buck) McKeon (R-CA) 202-225-1956
New York Delegate:
  Timothy H Bishop (D) 202-225-3826
New York Delegate:
  Carolyn McCarthy (D) 202-225-5516
New York Delegate:
  Major R Owens (D) 202-225-6231
New York Delegate:
  John R (Randy) Kuhl, Jr (R) 202-225-3161

Subcommittee
Education Reform
  Chair:
    Michael N Castle (R-DE) 202-225-4165
  Ranking Minority Member:
    Lynn Woolsey (D-CA) 202-225-5161
  New York Delegate:
    John R (Randy) Kuhl, Jr (R) 202-225-3161

Senate Standing Committees

Health, Education, Labor & Pensions
Chair:
  Edward M Kennedy (D-MA) 202-224-4543
Ranking Minority Member:
  Michael B Enzi (R-WY) 202-224-3424
New York Delegate:
  Hillary Rodham Clinton (D) 202-224-4451

Private Sector

ASPIRA of New York Inc
520 Eighth Ave, 22nd Fl, New York, NY 10018
212-564-6880 Fax: 212-564-7152
e-mail: hgesualdo@ny.aspira.org
Web site: www.nyaspira.org
Hector Gesualdo, Executive Director
Foster the social advancement of the PuertoRican/Latino community by supportig its youth through community & leadership development

Advocates for Children of New York Inc
151 West 30th St, 5th Fl, New York, NY 10001
212-947-9779 Fax: 212-947-9790
e-mail: info@advocatesforchildren.org
Web site: www.advocatesforchildren.org; www.insideschools.org
Matthew Lenaghan, Executive Director
Advocacy for public school students

Africa-America Institute (The)
420 Lexington Ave, Suite 1706, New York, NY 10170-0002
212-949-5666 Fax: 212-682-6174
e-mail: aainy@aaionline.org
Web site: www.aaionline.org
Mora McLean, President & Chief Executive Officer
Promoting enlightened engagement between Africa & America through education, training & dialogue

After-School Corporation (The)
925 Ninth Ave, New York, NY 10019
212-547-6950 Fax: 212-548-6983
e-mail: info@tascorp.org
Web site: www.tascorp.org
John P Albert, Vice President, External Relations
Non-profit organization dedicated to enhancing the quality, availability & sustainability of in-school, after-school programs in NYS

Offices and agencies generally appear in alphabetical order, except when specific order is requested by listee.

EDUCATION / Private Sector

Agudath Israel of America
42 Broadway, 14th Fl, New York, NY 10004
212-797-7385 Fax: 646-254-1650
e-mail: dzwiebel@agudathisrael.org
David Zwiebel, Executive Vice President, Government & Public Affairs
Religious school education; Orthodox Judaism

American Higher Education Development Corporation
Two Penn Plaza, Ste 1500, New York, NY 10121
212-292-5658 Fax: 212-292-4957
e-mail: jmdevaney@earthlink.net
James M Devaney, President
Acquisition of & investment in post-secondary education institutions

Association of Presidents of Public Community Colleges
c/o Onondaga Community College, 4585 W Seneca Tpk, Syracuse, NY 13215-4585
315-498-2211 Fax: 315-469-4475
Debbie L Sydow PhD, Executive Committee

Associated Medical Schools of New York
10 Rockefeller Plaza, Suite 1120, New York, NY 10020
212-218-4610 Fax: 212-218-5644
e-mail: jo.wiederhorn@amsny.org
Web site: www.amsny.org
Jo Wiederhorn, Executive Director
AMS is a consortium of the fourteen public and private medical schools in New York State. Our mission is to support quality health care in New York State.

Association of Proprietary Colleges
1259 Central Ave, Albany, NY 12205
518-437-1867 Fax: 518-437-1048
e-mail: lnhol@aol.com
Web site: www.apc-colleges.org
Ellen Hollander, President

Board of Jewish Education of Greater New York
520 - 8th Ave, New York, NY 10018
646-472-5300 Fax: 646-472-5421
e-mail: judyopp@bjeny.org
Web site: www.bjeny.org
Chaim Lauer, Executive Vice President

Campaign for Fiscal Equity, Inc
110 William St, Ste 2602, New York, NY 10038
212-867-8455 Fax: 212-867-8460
e-mail: cfeinfo@cfequity.org
Web site: www.cfequity.org
Michael Rebell, Executive Director & Counsel

Catholic School Administrators Association of NYS
406 Fulton St, Ste 512, Troy, NY 12180
518-273-1205 Fax: 518-273-1206
e-mail: nysadm@csdsl.net
Web site: www.csaanys.org
Carol Geddis, Executive Director

Center for Educational Innovation - Public Education Association
28 W 44th St, Ste 300, New York, NY 10036-6600
212-302-8800 Fax: 212-302-0088
e-mail: info@pea-online.org
Web site: www.cei-pea.org
Judy Roth Berkowitz, Chairman
Advocacy & public information for NYC public education

Cerebral Palsy Associations of New York State
330 W 34th St, New York, NY 10001
212-947-5770 x201 Fax: 212-356-0746
e-mail: sconstantino@cpofnys.org
Web site: www.cpofnys.org
Susan Constantino, President & CEO
Advocate & provide direct services with & for individuals with cerebral palsy & other significant disabilities, & their families

Coalition of New York State Career Schools (The)
437 Old Albany Post Rd, Garrison, NY 10524
845-788-5070 Fax: 845-788-5071
e-mail: tzaleski@sprynet.com
Web site: www.coalitionofnewyorkstatecareerschools.com
Terence M Zaleski, Special Counsel
Licensed post-secondary career schools

Commission on Independent Colleges & Universities
17 Elk St, PO Box 7289, Albany, NY 12224
518-436-4781 Fax: 518-436-0417
e-mail: abe@cicu.org
Web site: www.cicu.org
Abraham M Lackman, President
Represent public policy interests of member colleges & universities

Conference of Big 5 School Districts
One Steuben Place, 5th Fl Loft, Albany, NY 12207-2106
518-465-4274 Fax: 518-465-0638
e-mail: big5@nycap.rr.com
Georgia Asciutto, Executive Director

Cornell University
305 Day Hall, Ithaca, NY 14853
607-255-9029 Fax: 607-255-5572
e-mail: spj2@cornell.edu
Web site: www.govrelations.cornell.edu
Stephen Philip Johnson, Vice President for Government & Community Relations

Cornell University, Rural Schools Association of NYS
111 Kennedy Hall, Ithaca, NY 14853
607-255-8709 Fax: 607-255-7905
e-mail: lak35@cornell.edu
Web site: www.education.cornell.edu/rsp
Lawrence Kiley, Executive Director
Advocacy for small & rural schools throughout New York

Offices and agencies generally appear in alphabetical order, except when specific order is requested by listee.

EDUCATION / Private Sector

Cornell University, School of Industrial & Labor Relations
368 Ives Hall, Ithaca, NY 14853-3901
607-255-2742 or 607-257-1402 Fax: 607-255-1836
e-mail: jhb5@cornell.edu
Web site: www.ilr.cornell.edu
John Bishop, Professor
Education, workforce preparedness; student peer culture, employee training, recruitment & selection practices

Council of School Supervisors & Administrators
16 Court St, 4th Fl, Brooklyn, NY 11241
718-852-3000 Fax: 718-403-0278
e-mail: ernest@csa-nyc.org
Web site: www.csa-nyc.org
Ernest Logan, President

Council on the Environment of NYC, Environmental Education
51 Chambers St, Rm 228, New York, NY 10007
212-788-7900 or 212-788-7932 Fax: 212-788-7913
e-mail: cenyctso@hotmail.com
Web site: www.cenyc.org
Michael Zamm, Program Director
Environmental education & action training programs for students

Fordham University
Admin Bldg, 441 E Fordham Rd, Rm 220, Bronx, NY 10458
718-817-3023 Fax: 718-817-5722
e-mail: massiah@fordham.edu
Web site: www.fordham.edu
Lesley A Massiah, Assistant Vice President, Government Relations

Learning Leaders
80 Maiden Lane, 11th Fl, New York, NY 10038
212-213-3370 Fax: 212-213-0787
e-mail: mduitz@learningleaders.org
Web site: www.learningleaders.org
Mindy Duitz, President
Helps NYC public school students (K-12) succeed in school by training volunteers who provide tutoring and other school-based support, and by equipping parents to foster their own children's educational development

MDRC
16 East 34th St, 19th Floor, New York, NY 10016-4326
212-532-3200 Fax: 212-684-0832
e-mail: information@mdrc.org
Web site: www.mdrc.org
Gordon Berlin, President
Nonprofit research & field testing of education & employment programs for disadvantaged adults & youth

Museum Association of New York
265 River St, Troy, NY 12180
518-273-3400 Fax: 518-273-3416
e-mail: info@manyonline.org
Web site: www.manyonline.org
Anne Ackerson, Director

NYC Board of Education Employees, Local 372/AFSCME, AFL-CIO
125 Barclay Street, 6th Fl, New York, NY 10007
212-815-1372 Fax: 212-815-1347
Web site: www.local372.com
Veronica Montgomery-Costa, President, District Council 37/372

NYS Alliance for Arts Education
PO Box 2217, Albany, NY 12220-0217
800-ARTS-N-ED or 518-473-0823 Fax: 518-486-7329
e-mail: info@nysaae.org
Web site: www.nysaae.org
Amy Williams, Executive Director
State & local advocacy, professional development, technical assistance & information for educators, organizations, artists, parents & policymakers

NYS Association for Health, Physical Education, Recreation & Dance
77 North Ann St, Little Falls, NY 13365
315-823-1015 Fax: 315-823-1012
e-mail: ccorsi@nysahperd.org
Web site: www.nysahperd.org
Colleen Corsi, Executive Director
Promoting, educating & creating opportunites for physical education, health, recreation & dance professionals

NYS Association for the Education of Young Children
230 Washington Ave Ext, Albany, NY 12203-5390
518-867-3517 Fax: 518-867-3520
e-mail: nysaeyc@capital.net
Web site: www.nysaeyc.org
Patricia A Myers, Executive Director
Supporting the development of professionals to promote quality care & education for the well-being of all young children & their families

NYS Association of Library Boards
PO Box 11048, Albany, NY 12211
518-445-9505 Fax: 518-426-8240
Web site: www.nysalb.org
Margaret Malicki, Association Manager

NYS Association of School Business Officials
7 Elk St, #1, Albany, NY 12207-1002
518-434-2281 Fax: 518-434-1303
e-mail: steve@nysasbo.org
Web site: www.nysasbo.org
Steve Van Hoesen, Director of Governement Relations
Leadership in the practice of school business management

NYS Head Start Association
230 Washington Ave Ext, Albany, NY 12203
518-452-0897 Fax: 518-452-0898
e-mail: nyshsa@capital.net
Web site: www.nysheadstart.org
Steven Moskowitz, Executive Director
Educational program designed to meet the needs of low-income children & their families

Offices and agencies generally appear in alphabetical order, except when specific order is requested by listee.

EDUCATION / Private Sector

NYS Public High School Athletic Association
8 Airport Park Blvd, Latham, NY 12110
518-690-0771 Fax: 518-690-0775
e-mail: nvanerk@nysphsaa.org
Web site: www.nysphsaa.org
Nina Van Erk, Executive Director
Provide equitable & safe competition through interschool athletic activities at secondary schools

NYS Reading Association
PO Box 874, Albany, NY 12201-0874
518-434-4748 Fax: 518-434-4748
e-mail: information@capital.net
Web site: www.nysreading.org
Dolores Watford, President
Literacy education advocacy & professional development programs for educators

NYS Theatre Institute
37 First St, Troy, NY 12180
518-274-3200 Fax: 518-274-3815
e-mail: nysti@capital.net
Web site: www.nysti.org
Patricia Di Benedetto Snyder, Producing Artistic Director
Professional theater productions for family and school audiences; training & education, internships, community/school outreach & cultural exchange programs

Nelson A Rockefeller Inst of Govt, Higher Education Program
411 State St, Albany, NY 12203
518-443-5835 or 518-443-5843 Fax: 518-443-5788
e-mail: burkejo@rockinst.org
Web site: www.rockinst.org
Joseph C Burke, Director
Accountability & autonomy in public higher education; system governance; performance funding, budgeting, reporting & assessment

New York Community College Trustees (NYCCT)
State University Plaza, N-110, Albany, NY 12246-0001
518-443-5136 or 518-443-5133 Fax: 518-443-5100
Anton Kasanof, President
Trustee education, legislative advocacy & communication

New York Library Association (The)
252 Hudson Ave, Albany, NY 12210-1802
518-432-6952 Fax: 518-427-1697
e-mail: director@nyla.org
Web site: www.nyla.org
Michael J Borges, Executive Director
Advocacy on behalf of public, academic and school libraries on funding and legislation.

New York State Association of Independent Schools
12 Jay St, Schenectady, NY 12305-1913
518-346-5662 Fax: 518-346-7390
e-mail: hq@nysais.org
Web site: www.nysais.org
Elizabeth P Riegelman, Executive Director

New York State Catholic Conference
465 State St, Albany, NY 12203-1004
518-434-6195 Fax: 518-434-9796
e-mail: info@nyscatholic.org
Web site: www.nyscatholic.org
Richard E Barnes, Executive Director
Identify, formulate & implement public policy objectives of the NYS Bishops in health, education, welfare, human & civil rights

New York State Congress of Parents & Teachers Inc
One Wembley Court, Albany, NY 12205-3830
518-452-8808 Fax: 518-452-8105
e-mail: office@nyspta.org
Web site: www.nyspta.org
Maria L DeWald, President
Advocating education, health, welfare of children & parent involvement

New York State Council of School Superintendents
7 Elk St, 3rd Floor, Albany, NY 12207-1002
518-449-1063 Fax: 518-426-2229
Web site: www.nyscoss.org
Thomas L Rogers, Executive Director

New York State School Boards Association
24 Century Hill Drive, Ste 200, Latham, NY 12110-2125
518-783-0200 Fax: 518-783-0211
e-mail: info@nyssba.org
Web site: www.nyssba.org
Timothy G Kremer, Executive Director
Public school leadership advocates

New York State School Music Association (NYSSMA)
718 The Plain Rd, Westbury, NY 11590-5931
888-697-7621 Fax: 516-997-1700
e-mail: executive@nyssma.org
Web site: www.nyssma.org
Steven Schopp, Executive Administrator
Advocacy for a quality school music education for every student

New York State United Teachers/AFT, NEA, AFL-CIO
800 Troy-Schenectady Road, Latham, NY 12110-2455
518-213-6000 or 800-342-9810 Fax: 518-213-6428
Web site: www.nysut.org
Richard Iannuzzi, President
Representing employees & retirees of NY's public schools, colleges & healthcare facilities

New York University
25 West 4th St, 5th Fl - Rm 503, New York, NY 10012
212-998-6840 Fax: 212-995-4021
e-mail: john.beckman@nyu.edu
Web site: www.nyu.edu
John Beckman, Vice President
Office of Public Affairs

Offices and agencies generally appear in alphabetical order, except when specific order is requested by listee.

EDUCATION / Private Sector

Niagara University
Alumni Hall, Niagara University, NY 14109-2014
716-286-8360 Fax: 716-286-8349
e-mail: mpf@niagara.edu
Web site: www.niagara.edu
Dr Marilynn P Fleckenstein, Associate Vice President for Academic Affairs

ProLiteracy Worldwide
1320 Jamesville Ave, Syracuse, NY 13210-4224
315-422-9121 Fax: 315-422-6369
e-mail: info@proliteracy.org
Web site: www.proliteracy.org
Rochelle A Cassella, Director, Corporate Communications
Sponsors educational programs & services to empower adults & families through the acquisition of literacy skills & practices

Rensselaer Polytechnic Institute
110 8th St, Troy, NY 12180-3590
518-276-2840 Fax: 518-276-6091
e-mail: bourgt@rpi.edu
Web site: www.rpi.edu
Theresa Bourgeois, Director, Media Relations
Assistant to the President for Media & Public Relations

Research Foundation of SUNY
State University Plz, Albany, NY 12246
518-434-7066 Fax: 518-434-9108
e-mail: cathy.kaszluga@rfsuny.org
Web site: www.rfsuny.org
Cathy Kaszluga, Vice President, Corporate Communications
Facilitate research, education & public service at SUNY campuses

Rochester School for the Deaf
1545 St Paul St, Rochester, NY 14621
585-544-1240 Fax: 585-544-0383
e-mail: hmowl@rsdeaf.org
Web site: www.rsdeaf.org
Harold Mowl, Jr, Superintendent
Complete educational program for deaf children to age 21

SCAA - Schuyler Center for Analysis & Advocacy
150 State St, 4th Fl, Albany, NY 12207-1626
518-463-1896 x25 Fax: 518-463-3364
e-mail: kschimke@scaany.org
Web site: www.scaany.org
Karen Schimke, President & Chief Executive Officer
Advocacy, analysis & forums on education, child welfare, health, economic security, mental health, revenue & taxation issues

School Administrators Association of NYS
8 Airport Park Blvd, Latham, NY 12110
518-782-0600 Fax: 518-782-9552
e-mail: kcasey@saanys.org
Web site: www.saanys.org
Kevin S Casey, Executive Director

Sports & Arts in Schools Foundation
58-12 Queens Blvd, Suite 1 - 59th Entrance, Woodside, NY 11377
718-786-7110 Fax: 718-786-7635
e-mail: info@sasfny.org
Web site: www.sasfny.org
James R O'Neill, Executive Director
After-school, summer camps & clinics, winter-break festival

Syracuse University, Maxwell School of Citizenship & Public Affairs
200 Eggers Hall, Syracuse, NY 13244-1020
315-443-2252 Fax: 315-443-1081
e-mail: ctrpol@syr.edu
Web site: www.maxwell.syr.edu
Timothy Smeeding, Professor of Public Policy; Director
Education, healthcare, entrepreneurship policies, social welfare, income distribution & comparative social policies

Syracuse University, Office of Government & Community Relations
Room 2-212, Center for Science & Technology, Syracuse, NY 13244-4100
315-443-3919 Fax: 315-443-3676
e-mail: earougeu@syr.edu
Web site: govt-comm.syr.edu
Elizabeth A Rougeux, Executive Director, Government & Community Relations

Teachers College, Columbia University
525 W 120th St, Box 7, New York, NY 10027
212-678-3000 Fax: 212-678-3682
e-mail: ts171@columbia.edu
Web site: www.tc.columbia.edu
Thomas Sobol, Professor
Education policy

Teaching Matters Inc
475 Riverside Dr, Ste 1270, New York, NY 10115-0122
212-870-3505 Fax: 212-870-3516
e-mail: lguastaferro@teachingmaters.org
Web site: www.teachingmatters.org
Lynette Guastaferro, Executive Director
Technology planning & professional development for NYC public schools

United Federation of Teachers
52 Broadway, New York, NY 10004
212-777-7500 Fax: 212-260-6393
e-mail: rweigarte@aol.com
Web site: www.uft.org
Randi Weingarten, President

United University Professions
PO Box 15143, Albany, NY 12212-5143
518-640-6600 or 800-342-4206 Fax: 518-640-6698
e-mail: contact@uupmail.org
Web site: www.uupinfo.org
William E Scheuerman, President
SUNY labor union of academic & other professional faculty

Offices and agencies generally appear in alphabetical order, except when specific order is requested by listee.

EDUCATION / Private Sector

Western New York Library Resources Council
4455 Genesee St, PO Box 400, Buffalo, NY 14225-0400
716-633-0705 Fax: 716-633-1736
e-mail: sknab@wnylrc.org; www.wnyinfo.org
Web site: www.wnylrc.org;
www.wnylibraries.org;www.askus247.org
Sheryl Knab, Executive Director
Dedicated to enhancing access to information, encouraging resource sharing & promoting library interests

ELECTIONS

New York State

GOVERNOR'S OFFICE

Governor's Office
Executive Chamber
State Capitol
Albany, NY 12224
518-474-8390 Fax: 518-474-1513
Web site: www.state.ny.us

Governor:
   Eliot Spitzer 518-474-8390
Secretary to the Governor:
   Richard Baum 518-474-4246
Counsel to the Governor:
   David Nocenti 518-474-8343
Director, Communications:
   Darren Dopp 518-474-8418
Deputy Secretary, Intergovernmental Affairs:
   Martin Mack 518-408-2555
Assistant Counsel to the Governor-Education, Elections & the Judiciary:
   Mariya Treisman 518-474-8494
Assistant Counsel to the Governor-General Government Operations & Human Services:
   David Rose 518-474-2266
Assistant Counsel to the Governor-Housing, Local Governments & Arts:
   Amanda Hiller 518-474-8494

New York City Office
633 Third Ave, 38th Fl, New York, NY 10017
Director, NYC Intergovernmental Affairs:
   Carl Andrews 212-681-4580
Director, Community Affairs:
   Lila Kirton 212-681-4580
Press Secretary:
   Christine Anderson 212-681-4640
Press Officer:
   Jennifer Givner 212-681-4640

EXECUTIVE DEPARTMENTS AND RELATED AGENCIES

Elections, State Board of
40 Steuben St
Albany, NY 12207-2108
518-474-6220 or TTY: 800-367-8683 Fax: 518-486-4068
Web site: www.elections.state.ny.us

Co-Chair:
   Neil W Kelleher 518-474-8113
Co-Chair:
   Douglas A Kellner 518-474-8113
Commissioner:
   Evelyn Aquila 518-474-8113
Commissioner:
   Helena M Donohue 518-474-8113
Co-Executive Director:
   Peter S Kosinski 518-474-6236
Co-Executive Director:
   Stanley L Zalen 518-474-8100
Director, Public Information:
   Lee Daghlian 518-474-1953/fax: 518-473-8315
   e-mail: ldaghlian@elections.state.ny.us
Deputy, Public Information:
   Robert Brehm 518-474-1953

Administrative Services
Administrative Officer:
   Patricia Tracey 518-474-6336
Special Counsel:
   Todd D Valentine 518-474-6367
Deputy Counsel:
   Patricia L Murray 518-474-6367

Campaign Finance
Senior Accountant:
   Josephine Jackson 518-474-8200

Counsel/Enforcement
Counsel:
   Vacant 518-474-2063
Deputy Enforcement Counsel:
   William McCann 518-474-2063

County Boards of Elections

Albany . . . . fax: 518-487-5077
32 N Russell Rd, Albany, NY 12206
Commissioner:
   John A Graziano, Sr (R) 518-487-5060
Commissioner:
   Vacant (D) 518-487-5060
Deputy Commissioner:
   Ellen Graziano (R) 518-487-5060
Deputy Commissioner:
   Karen A Shea (D) 518-487-5060

Allegany . . . . fax: 585-268-9406
6 Schuyler Street, Belmont, NY 14813
Commissioner:
   James Gallman (R) 585-268-9294
Commissioner:
   John F Colligan (D) 585-268-9294
Deputy Commissioner:
   Elaine Herdman (R) 585-268-9294
   e-mail: herdmae@allegany.co.com
Deputy Commissioner:
   Catherine Lorow (D) 585-268-9294
   e-mail: lorowem@allegany.co.com

Broome . . . . fax: 607-778-2174
Gov't Plaza, 44 Hawley St, PO Box 1766, Binghamton, NY 13902
Commissioner:
   Eugene D Faughnan (R) 607-778-2172
Commissioner:
   John Perticone (D) 607-778-2172

Offices and agencies generally appear in alphabetical order, except when specific order is requested by listee.

ELECTIONS / New York State

Deputy Commissioner:
   John Sejan (R) 607-778-2172
Deputy Commissioner:
   Mary E Pines (D) 607-778-2172

Cattaraugus .... fax: 716-938-6347
302 Court Street, Little Valley, NY 14755
Fax: 716-938-6347
Web site: www.cattco.org
Commissioner:
   Sue A Fries (R) 716-938-9111 x2405
   e-mail: SAFries@cattco.org
Commissioner:
   Kevin Burleson (D) 716-938-9111 x2404
   e-mail: KCBurleson@cattco.org
Deputy Commissioner:
   Kristie L Virga (R) 716-938-9111 x2401
Deputy Commissioner:
   Karen L Byrne (D) 716-938-9111 x2403

Cayuga .... fax: 315-253-1289
10 Court St, Auburn, NY 13021
Fax: 315-253-1289
Web site: www.co.cayuga.ny.us/election
Commissioner:
   Cherl Heary (R) 315-253-1285
Commissioner:
   Dennis Sedor (D) 315-253-1285
Deputy Commissioner:
   Tom Prystal (R) 315-253-1285
Deputy Commissioner:
   Deborah Calarco (D) 315-253-1285

Chautauqua .... fax: 716-753-4111
7 North Erie St, Mayville, NY 14757
716-753-4580 Fax: 716-753-4111
e-mail: vote@co.chautauqua.ny.us
Web site: www.votechautauqua.com
Commissioner:
   Terry Niebel (R) 716-753-4226
Commissioner:
   Norman P Green (D) 716-753-4580

Chemung .... fax: 607-737-5499
378 S Main Street, PO Box 588, Elmira, NY 14902-0588
607-737-5475 Fax: 607-737-5499
Web site: www.chemungcounty.com
Commissioner:
   Marilyn O'Mara (R) 607-737-5475
   e-mail: momara@co.chemung.ny.us
Commissioner:
   Keith H Osborne (D) 607-737-5475
   e-mail: kosborne@co.chemung.ny.us
Deputy Commissioner:
   Linda A Forrest (R) 607-737-5475
   e-mail: lforrest@co.chemung.ny.us
Deputy Commissioner:
   Mary O'Dell (D) 607-737-5475
   e-mail: modell@co.chemung.ny.us

Chenango .... fax: 607-337-1766
5 Court Street, Norwich, NY 13815
607-337-1760 Fax: 607-337-1766
Web site: www.co.chenango.ny.us
Commissioner:
   Harriet L Jenkins (R) 607-337-1764
   e-mail: harrietj@co.chenango.ny.us
Commissioner:
   Carol A Franklin (D) 607-337-1765
   e-mail: carolf@co.chenango.ny.us

Clinton .... fax: 518-565-4508
County Gov't Center, 137 Margaret St, Ste 104, Plattsburgh, NY 12901
Fax: 518-565-4508
e-mail: boe@co.clinton.ny.us
Web site: www.clintoncountygov.com
Commissioner:
   Judith C Layhee (R) 518-565-4740
Commissioner:
   John W Brunell (D) 518-565-4740
Deputy Commissioner:
   Lois M McShane (R) 518-565-4740
Deputy Commissioner:
   Debra L Bruno (D) 518-565-4740

Columbia .... fax: 518-828-2624
401 State St, Hudson, NY 12534
Commissioner:
   Donald R Kline (R) 518-828-3115
Commissioner:
   Kenneth J Dow (D) 518-828-3115
Deputy Commissioner:
   Michael P Nabozny (R) 518-828-3115
Deputy Commissioner:
   Geeta Cheddie-Musall (D) 518-828-3115

Cortland .... fax: 607-758-5513
County Court House, 60 Central Ave, Ste 102, Cortland, NY 13045-2746
607-758-5032 Fax: 607-758-5513
Commissioner:
   Robert C Howe (R) 607-753-5032
Commissioner:
   William J Wood (D) 607-753-5032

Delaware .... fax: 607-746-6516
3 Gallant Ave, Delhi, NY 13753
Fax: 607-746-6516
e-mail: elec@co.delaware.ny.us
Web site: www.co.delaware.ny.us
Commissioner:
   William J Campbell (R) 607-746-2315
Commissioner:
   William J Buccheri (D) 607-746-2315
Deputy Commissioner:
   Robin L Alger (R) 607-746-2315
Deputy Commissioner:
   Janice G Burdick (D) 607-746-2315

Dutchess .... fax: 845-486-2483
47 Cannon St, Poughkeepsie, NY 12601
Fax: 845-486-2483
Web site: www.dutchesselections.com
Commissioner:
   David J Gamache (R) 845-486-2473
   e-mail: dgamache@co.dutchess.ny.us
Commissioner:
   Frances A Knapp (D) 845-486-2473
   e-mail: fknapp@co.dutchess.ny.us
Deputy Commissioner:
   John M Kennedy (R) 845-486-2473
   e-mail: jkennedy@co.dutchess.ny.uc
Deputy Commissioner:
   Daniel J French (D) 845-486-2473

Erie .... fax: 716-858-8282
134 West Eagle St, Buffalo, NY 14202
Commissioner:
   Ralph M Mohr (R) 716-858-8891
Commissioner:
   Dennis Ward (D) 716-858-8891

Offices and agencies generally appear in alphabetical order, except when specific order is requested by listee.

ELECTIONS / New York State

Deputy Commissioner:
  Dennis V Ryan (R)..........................716-858-8891
Deputy Commissioner:
  Alonzo W Thompson (D)....................716-858-8891

Essex..fax: 518-873-3479
7551 Court Street, PO Box 217, Elizabethtown, NY 12932
518-873-3474 Fax: 518-873-3479
Web site: www.co.essex.ny.us/elect.asp
Commissioner:
  Lewis W Sanders (R).........................518-873-3478
Commissioner:
  David Mace (D)..............................518-873-3475
  e-mail: dmace@co.essex.ny.us
Deputy Commissioner:
  Patti L Doyle (R)............................518-873-3476
  e-mail: pdoyle@co.essex.ny.us
Deputy Commissioner:
  Steven W Laundree (D)......................518-873-3477

Franklin..fax: 518-481-6018
335 West Main St, Ste 155, Malone, NY 12953-1823
518-481-1663 Fax: 518-481-6018
Web site: franklincony.org
Commissioner:
  Beverly C Mills (R)..........................518-481-1663
  e-mail: bmills@co.franklin.ny.us
Commissioner:
  Kathy M Fleury (D)..........................518-481-1663
  e-mail: kfleury@co.franklin.ny.us
Deputy Commissioner:
  Veronica B King (R).........................518-481-1663
  e-mail: vking@co.franklin.ny.us
Deputy Commissioner:
  Cheryl A Dumas (D).........................518-481-1663
  e-mail: cdumas@co.franklin.ny.us

Fulton..fax: 518-736-1612
2714 State Highway 29, Ste 1, Johnstown, NY 12095-9946
Commissioner:
  Dexter J Risedorph (R)......................518-736-5526
Commissioner:
  Marilyn J Cornell (D)........................518-736-5526
Deputy Commissioner:
  Linda M Madison (R)........................518-736-5526
Deputy Commissioner:
  Linda L Coons (D)...........................518-736-5526

Genesee..fax: 585-344-8562
County Bldg One, 15 Main St, PO Box 284, Batavia, NY 14021
Fax: 585-344-8562
Web site: www.co.genesee.ny.us
Commissioner:
  Richard Siebert (R)..........................585-344-2550
Commissioner:
  Dawn E Cassidy (D).........................585-344-2550
Deputy Commissioner:
  Sharon E White (R).........................585-344-2250
Deputy Commissioner:
  Karen S Gannon (D).........................585-344-2250

Greene...fax: 518-719-3784
411 Main St, 4th Fl, PO Box 307, Catskill, NY 12414
Commissioner:
  Frank DeBenedictus (R).....................518-719-3550
Commissioner:
  Thomas J Burke (D).........................518-719-3550
Deputy Commissioner:
  Gina Legari (R)..............................518-719-3550

Deputy Commissioner:
  Marie Metzler (D)...........................518-719-3550

Hamilton.......................................fax: 518-548-6345
Route 8, PO Box 175, Lake Pleasant, NY 12108
Commissioner:
  Judith L Peck (R)............................518-548-4684
Commissioner:
  Cathleen E Rogers (D)......................518-548-4684
Deputy Commissioner:
  Deborah A O'Rourke (R)....................518-548-4684
Deputy Commissioner:
  William Parslow (D).........................518-548-4684

Herkimer.......................................fax: 315-867-1106
109 Mary Street, Suite 1306, Herkimer, NY 13350
315-867-1102 Fax: 315-867-1106
Commissioner:
  Marty L Smith (R)...........................315-867-1104
  e-mail: msmith@herkimercounty.org
Commissioner:
  Toni M Scalise (D)..........................315-867-1103
  e-mail: tscalise@herkimercounty.org

Jefferson......................................fax: 315-785-5197
175 Arsenal St, Watertown, NY 13601
Fax: 315-785-5197
Web site: www.co.jefferson.ny.us
Commissioner:
  James E Fitzpatrick (R).....................315-785-3027
Commissioner:
  Keith F Crimmins (D).......................315-785-3027
Deputy Commissioner:
  Sandra Corey (R)............................315-785-3027
  e-mail: sandyc@co.jefferson.ny.us
Deputy Commissioner:
  Cindy Corbett (D)...........................315-785-3027
  e-mail: cindyc@co.jefferson.ny.us

Lewis..fax: 315-376-2860
7660 N State St, Lowville, NY 13367
Commissioner:
  Ann M Nortz (R)............................315-376-5329
Commissioner:
  Elaine M McLear (D)........................315-376-5330

Livingston.....................................fax: 585-243-7015
County Government Ctr, 6 Court St, Rm 104, Geneseo, NY 14454-1043
Commissioner:
  Gerald L Smith (R)..........................585-243-7090
  e-mail: gsmith@co.livingston.ny.us
Commissioner:
  Susan N Guenther (D).......................585-243-7090
  e-mail: sguenther@co.livingston.ny.us
Deputy Commissioner:
  Nancy L Leven (R)..........................585-243-7090
  e-mail: nleven@co.livingston.ny.us
Deputy Commissioner:
  Laura M Schoonover (D)....................585-243-7090
  e-mail: lschoonover@co.livingston.ny.us

Madison.......................................fax: 315-366-2532
North Court St, County Office Bldg, PO Box 666, Wampsville, NY 13163
Commissioner:
  Lynne M Jones (R)..........................315-366-2231
Commissioner:
  Laura P Costello (D).........................315-366-2231

Monroe
39 Main St West, Rochester, NY 14614

Offices and agencies generally appear in alphabetical order, except when specific order is requested by listee.

ELECTIONS / New York State

e-mail: mcboe@monroecounty.gov
Web site: www.monroe.county.gov
Commissioner:
   Peter M Quinn (R)................585-428-4550/fax: 585-753-1521
   e-mail: pQuinn@monroecounty.gov
Commissioner:
   Thomas F Ferrarese (D)...........585-428-4550/fax: 585-753-1531
   e-mail: tFerrarese@monroecounty.gov
Deputy Commissioner:
   Douglas E French (R).............................585-428-4550
Deputy Commissioner:
   Sheila Fleischauer (D)............................585-428-4550

Montgomery......................................fax: 518-853-8392
Old Court House, 9 Park St, PO Box 1500, Fonda, NY 12068-1500
518-853-8180 Fax: 518-853-8392
Commissioner:
   Lyn A May (R)....................................518-853-8182
Commissioner:
   Joan M Grainer (D)...............................518-853-8181
Deputy Commissioner:
   Debra J Shang (R)................................518-853-8185
Deputy Commissioner:
   Marcia M Baranowski (D)..........................518-853-8180

Nassau...fax: 516-571-2058
New Administration Bldg, 400 County Seat Dr, Mineola, NY 11501
Commissioner:
   John A DeGrace (R)...............................516-571-2411
Commissioner:
   William T Biamonte (D)...........................516-571-2411
Deputy Commissioner:
   Carol Demauro Busketta (R).......................516-571-2411
Deputy Commissioner:
   Eleanor Sciglibaglio (D).........................516-571-2411

New York City....................................fax: 212-487-5349
32 Broadway, 7th Fl, New York, NY 10004
Fax: 212-487-5349
Web site: www.vote.nyc.ny.us
Executive Director:
   John Ravitz (R)..................................212-487-5300
Deputy Executive Director:
   George Gonzalez (D)..............................212-487-5300
Administrative Manager:
   Pamela Green Perkins (D).........................212-487-5300
   Bronx
   1780 Grand Concourse, 5th Fl, Bronx, NY 10457
   Commissioner:
      Vacant (R)...................................718-299-9017
   Commissioner:
      Nero Graham, Jr (D)..........................718-299-9017
   Deputy Chief Clerk:
      Victor B Tosi (R)............................718-299-9017
   Deputy Chief Clerk:
      Anna Torres (D)..............................718-299-9017
   Kings..fax: 718-522-6227
   345 Adams St, 4th Fl, Brooklyn, NY 11201
   Commissioner:
      Nancy Mottola Schacher (R)...................718-797-8800
   Commissioner:
      Vacant (D)...................................718-797-8800
   Chief Clerk:
      Diane Haslett Rudiano (R)....................718-797-8800
   Chief Clerk:
      Maryrose Sattie (D)..........................718-797-8800
   New York
   200 Varick St, 10th Fl, New York, NY 10014
   Commissioner:
      Frederic M Umane (R)........................212-886-2100
   Commissioner:
      Gregory C Soumas (D)........................212-886-2100
   Chief Clerk:
      Troy Johnson (R)............................212-886-2100
   Deputy Chief Clerk:
      Timothy Gay (D).............................212-886-2100
   Queens
   126-06 Queens Blvd, Kew Gardens, NY 11415
   Commissioner:
      Anthony Como (R)............................718-730-6730
   Commissioner:
      Terrence C O'Connor (D).....................718-730-6730
   Deputy Chief Clerk:
      Kathrine A James (R)........................718-730-6730
   Chief Clerk:
      Barbara Conacchio (D).......................718-730-6730
   Richmond
   1 Edgewater Plaza, Staten Island, NY 10305
   Commissioner:
      Mary Ann Yennella (R).......................718-876-0079
   Commissioner:
      James Joseph Sampel (D).....................718-876-0079
   Deputy Chief Clerk:
      Anthony Andruili (R)........................718-876-0079
   Chief Clerk:
      Barbara Kett (D)............................718-876-0079

Niagara..fax: 716-438-4054
111 Main Street, Ste 100, Lockport, NY 14094
Fax: 716-438-4054
Web site: www.elections.niagara.ny.us
Commissioner:
   Scott P Kiedrowski (R)...........................716-438-4040
Commissioner:
   Nancy L Smith (D)................................716-438-4041
Deputy Commissioner:
   Mary Ann Casamento (R)...........................716-438-4040
Deputy Commissioner:
   Lora A Allen (D).................................716-438-4041

Oneida...fax: 315-798-6412
Union Station, 321 Main St, 3rd Fl, Utica, NY 13501
Fax: 315-798-6412
Web site: www.oneidacounty.org
Commissioner:
   Patricia Ann DiSpirito (R).......................315-798-5765
Commissioner:
   Angela Pedone Longo (D)..........................315-798-5765
Deputy Commissioner:
   Catherine A Dumka (R)............................315-798-5765
Deputy Commissioner:
   Carolann Cardone (D).............................315-798-5765

Onondaga...fax: 315-435-8451
Civic Center, 421 Montgomery St, 15th Fl, Syracuse, NY 13202
Fax: 315-435-8451
Web site: www.ongov.net
Commissioner:
   Helen M Kiggins (R)..............................315-435-3312
Commissioner:
   Edward J Szczesniak (D)..........................315-435-3312

Ontario..fax: 585-393-2941
20 Ontario St, Canandaigua, NY 14424
Fax: 585-393-2941
Web site: www.co.ontario.ny.us/elections
Commissioner:
   Michael J Northrup (R)...........................585-396-4005
Commissioner:
   Mary Q Salotti (D)...............................585-396-4005

Offices and agencies generally appear in alphabetical order, except when specific order is requested by listee.

ELECTIONS / New York State

Deputy Commissioner:
    Elaine Mallaber (R) 585-396-4005
Deputy Commissioner:
    Joan F Luther (D) 585-396-4005

Orange . . . . fax: 845-291-2437
25 Court Lane, PO Box 30, Goshen, NY 10924
Commissioner:
    David C Green (R) 845-291-2444
Commissioner:
    Susan Bahren (D) 845-291-2444
Deputy Commissioner:
    Courtney Canfield Greene (R) 845-291-2444
Deputy Commissioner:
    Ellouise S Raffo (D) 845-291-2444

Orleans . . . . fax: 585-589-2771
County Admin Bldg, 14016 State Rte 31, Albion, NY 14411
Commissioner:
    Dennis J Piedimonte (R) 585-589-3274
Commissioner:
    Helen L Zelazny (D) 585-589-3274
Deputy Commissioner:
    Clara L Martin (R) 585-589-3274
Deputy Commissioner:
    Janice E Grabowski (D) 585-589-3274

Oswego . . . . fax: 315-349-8357
185 E Seneca St, Box 9, Oswego, NY 13126
Commissioner:
    Donald M Wart (R) 315-349-8350
Commissioner:
    William W Scriber (D) 315-349-8350

Otsego . . . . fax: 607-547-4248
140 County Hwy 33W, Ste 2, Cooperstown, NY 13326
Commissioner:
    Charlotte Koniuto (R) 607-547-4247
    e-mail: ckoniuto@otsegocounty.com
Commissioner:
    Henry J Nicols (D) 607-547-4247
    e-mail: hjnicols@otsegocounty.com
Deputy Commissioner:
    Sheila M Ross (R) 607-547-4247
Deputy Commissioner:
    Lucinda A Jarvis (D) 607-547-4247

Putnam . . . . fax: 845-278-6798
One Geneva Rd, Brewster, NY 10509
Commissioner:
    Anthony G Scannapieco, Jr (R) 845-278-6970
Commissioner:
    Robert J Bennett (D) 845-278-6970
Deputy Commissioner:
    Nancy M Quis (R) 845-278-6970
Deputy Commissioner:
    Andrea Basli (D) 845-278-6970

Rensselaer . . . . fax: 518-270-2909
Ned Pattison Gov Ctr, 1600 Seventh Ave, Troy, NY 12180
Commissioner:
    Larry A Bugbee (R) 518-270-2990
Commissioner:
    Edward G McDonough (D) 518-270-2990

Rockland . . . . fax: 845-638-5196
11 New Hempstead Rd, New City, NY 10956
Fax: 845-638-5196
Web site: www.co.rockland.ny.us
Commissioner:
    Joan M Silvestri (R) 845-638-5172

Commissioner:
    Ann Marie Kelly (D) 845-638-5172
Deputy Commissioner:
    Ruth A Vezzetti (R) 845-638-5172
Deputy Commissioner:
    Kathleen Pietanza (D) 845-638-5172

Saint Lawrence . . . . fax: 315-386-2737
48 Court St, Canton, NY 13617
Fax: 315-386-2737
Web site: www.co.st-lawrence.ny.us
Commissioner:
    Deborah J Pahler (R) 315-379-2202
Commissioner:
    Robin M St Andrews (D) 315-379-2202
Deputy Commissioner:
    Cathy A Marich (R) 315-379-2202
Deputy Commissioner:
    Sandra Ragan (D) 315-379-2202

Saratoga . . . . fax: 518-884-4751
50 W High St, Ballston Spa, NY 12020
Fax: 518-884-4751
Web site: www.co.saratoga.ny.us
Commissioner:
    Diane Wade (R) 518-885-2249
Commissioner:
    William Fruci (D) 518-885-2249
Deputy Commissioner:
    Kathleen Anderson (R) 518-885-2249
Deputy Commissioner:
    Carol Turney (D) 518-885-2249

Schenectady . . . . fax: 518-377-2716
388 Broadway, Ste E, Schenectady, NY 12305-2520
Fax: 518-377-2716
Web site: www.schenectadyelections.com
Commissioner:
    Art Brassard (R) 518-377-2469
Commissioner:
    Brian Quail (D) 518-377-2469
Deputy Commissioner:
    Neil E Buhrmaster (R) 518-377-2469
Deputy Commissioner:
    Marie M Woodward (D) 518-377-2469

Schoharie . . . . fax: 518-295-8419
County Office Bldg, 284 Main St, PO Box 99, Schoharie, NY 12157
Commissioner:
    Lewis L Wilson (R) 518-295-8388
Commissioner:
    Clifford C Hay (D) 518-295-8388
Deputy Commissioner:
    Anne W Hendrix (R) 518-295-8388
Deputy Commissioner:
    Diane J Becker (D) 518-295-8388

Schuyler . . . . fax: 607-535-8364
County Ofc Bldg, 105 Ninth St, Unit 13, Watkins Glen, NY 14891-9972
Commissioner:
    Joseph Fazzary (R) 607-535-8195
Commissioner:
    John L Vona (D) 607-535-8195
Deputy Commissioner:
    Donna J Kelley (R) 607-535-8195
Deputy Commissioner:
    Carolyn Elkins (D) 607-535-8195

Seneca . . . . fax: 315-539-3710
1 DiPronio Dr, Waterloo, NY 13165

Offices and agencies generally appear in alphabetical order, except when specific order is requested by listee.

ELECTIONS / New York State

Fax: 315-539-3710
Web site: www.co.seneca.ny.us/boe
Commissioner:
    Elaine M Catanise (R) 315-539-1760
    e-mail: ecatanise@co.seneca.ny.us
Commissioner:
    Ruth V Same (D) 315-539-1760
    e-mail: rsame@co.seneca.ny.us
Deputy Commissioner:
    Joan P Mooney (R)................................... 315-539-1760
    e-mail: jmooney@co.seneca.ny.us
Deputy Commissioner:
    Barbara R McCann (D) 315-539-1760
    e-mail: bmccann@co.seneca.ny.us

Steuben.. fax: 607-664-1200
3 E Pulteney Square, Bath, NY 14810
607-664-2260 Fax: 607-664-1200
Web site: www.steubencony.org
Commissioner:
    Sharlene J Thompson (R)............................ 607-664-2261
    e-mail: Sharlenet@co.steubenco.ny.us
Commissioner:
    Allan C Johnson (D)................................. 607-664-2262
    e-mail: Allanj@co.steubenco.ny.us
Deputy Commissioner:
    Penny M Ruest (R).................................. 607-664-2260
Deputy Commissioner:
    Kelly J Austin (D) 607-664-2263

Suffolk .... fax: 631-852-4590
Yaphank Ave, PO Box 700, Yaphank, NY 11980
Commissioner:
    Cathy L Richter Geier (R) 631-852-4500
Commissioner:
    Anita S Katz (D).................................... 631-852-4500
Deputy Commissioner:
    Wayne Rogers (R) 631-852-4500
Deputy Commissioner:
    Jeanne O'Rourke (D) 631-852-4500

Sullivan... fax: 845-794-0183
Government Ctr, 100 North St, PO Box 5012, Monticello, NY 12701-5192
845-794-3000 x5024 Fax: 845-794-0183
Commissioner:
    Rodney Gaebel (R).................................. 845-794-3000
Commissioner:
    Timothy E Hill (D).................................. 845-794-3000
    e-mail: timothy.hill@co.sullivan.ny.us
Deputy Commissioner:
    Joanne Clements (R) 845-794-3000
    e-mail: joanne.clements@co.sullivan.ny.us
Deputy Commissioner:
    Faith Kaplan (D) 845-794-3000
    e-mail: faith.kaplan@co.sullivan.ny.us

Tioga... fax: 607-687-6348
County Office Bldg, 56 Main St, Owego, NY 13827
607-687-8261 Fax: 607-687-6348
Web site: www.tiogacountyny.com/boardofelections.asp
Commissioner:
    Bernadette M Toombs (R)........................... 607-687-8218
    e-mail: toombsb@co.tioga.ny.us
Commissioner:
    Cinda Lou Goodrich (D) 607-687-8219
    e-mail: goodrichc@co.tioga.ny.us
Deputy Commissioner:
    Arrah M Richards (R) 607-687-8220
Deputy Commissioner:
    Sandra Saddlemire (D)............................... 607-687-8217

Tompkins .... fax: 607-274-5533
Court House Annex, 128 E Buffalo St, Ithaca, NY 14850
Fax: 607-274-5533
Web site: www.tompkins-co.org/boe
Commissioner:
    Elizabeth W Cree (R)............................... 607-274-5522
    e-mail: ecree@tompkins-co.org
Commissioner:
    Stephen M DeWitt (D)............................... 607-274-5522
    e-mail: sdewitt@tompkins-co.org
Deputy Commissioner:
    Krystal Hastings (R)................................ 607-274-5522
Deputy Commissioner:
    Thomas M Paolangeli (D) 607-274-5522

Ulster .... fax: 845-334-5434
284 Wall Street, Kingston, NY 12401
Commissioner:
    Thomas F Turco (R)................................ 845-334-5470
Commissioner:
    John Parete (D).................................... 845-334-5470
Deputy Commissioner:
    Joan M Millham (R)................................ 845-334-5470
Deputy Commissioner:
    Stuart Fraser (D)................................... 845-334-5470

Warren.. fax: 518-761-6480
County Municipal Center, 1340 State Rte 9, Lake George, NY 12845
518-761-6456 Fax: 518-761-6480
Commissioner:
    Mary Beth Casey (R) 518-761-6458
    e-mail: caseym@co.warren.ny.us
Commissioner:
    William A Montfort (D)............................. 518-761-6459
    e-mail: montfortw@co.warren.ny.us
Deputy Commissioner:
    Constance L Service (R) 518-761-6457
    e-mail: servicec@co.warren.ny.us
Deputy Commissioner:
    M Suzanne O'Dea (D)............................... 518-761-6456
    e-mail: odeas@co.warren.ny.us

Washington .... fax: 518-746-2179
383 Broadway, Fort Edward, NY 12828
518-746-2180 Fax: 518-746-2179
Commissioner:
    Donna English (R).................................. 518-746-2180
    e-mail: denglish@co.washington.ny.us
Commissioner:
    Patricia A Haley (D)................................ 518-746-2180
    e-mail: phaley@co.washington.ny.us
Deputy Commissioner:
    Linda Falkouski (R)................................. 518-746-2180
Deputy Commissioner:
    Jeffrey J Curtis (D)................................. 518-746-2180

Wayne... fax: 315-946-7409
157 Montezuma St Ext, PO Box 636, Lyons, NY 14489
Fax: 315-946-7409
Web site: www.co.wayne.ny.us
Commissioner:
    Richard E Clark (R) 315-946-7400
Commissioner:
    Jack W Bailey (D) 315-946-7400
Deputy Commissioner:
    Kelley M Borrelli (R)................................ 315-946-7400
Deputy Commissioner:
    Joyce A Krebbeks (D) 315-946-7400
    e-mail: jkrebbeks@co.wayne.ny.us

Offices and agencies generally appear in alphabetical order, except when specific order is requested by listee.

ELECTIONS / New York State

Westchester .... fax: 914-995-3190
25 Quarropas Street, White Plains, NY 10601
Commissioner:
   Carolee C Sunderland (R) 914-995-5700
Commissioner:
   Reginald A LaFayette (D) 914-995-5700/fax: 914-995-7753
Deputy Commissioner:
   Melissa Nacerino (R) 914-995-5700
Deputy Commissioner:
   Jeannie L Palazola (D) 914-995-5700

Wyoming .... fax: 585-786-8843
76 N Main St, Warsaw, NY 14569-1329
Fax: 585-786-8843
Web site: www.wyoming.co.net
Commissioner:
   James E Schlick (R) 585-786-8931
Commissioner:
   Anna Mae Balmas (D) 585-786-8931
Deputy Commissioner:
   Wendy Simpson (R) 585-786-8931
   e-mail: wesimpson@frontiernet.net
Deputy Commissioner:
   Jeanne M Williams (D) 585-786-8931
   e-mail: jewilliams@frontiernet.net

Yates .... fax: 315-536-5523
417 Liberty St, Ste 1124, Penn Yan, NY 14527
Commissioner:
   Pamela A Welker (R) 315-536-5135
Commissioner:
   Vacant (D) 315-536-5135
Deputy Commissioner:
   Helen J Scarpechi (R) 315-536-5135
Deputy Commissioner:
   Patricia Selwood (D) 315-536-5135

Election Law Enforcement
Investigator:
   Javan Owens 518-474-2371

Election Operations
Director:
   Anna E Svizzero 518-473-5086
Deputy Director:
   Allison Carr 518-473-5086

General Information
Coordinator, Registration Operations:
   Gregory Fiozzo 518-474-1953

Information Technology Unit
Supervisor:
   George Stanton 518-473-4803

CORPORATIONS, AUTHORITIES AND COMMISSIONS

New York State Temporary Commission on Lobbying
2 Empire State Plaza
18th Floor
Albany, NY 12223-1254

518-474-7126 Fax: 518-473-6492
e-mail: lobcom@nytscol.org
Web site: www.nylobby.state.ny.us

Chair:
   Hon. James P King 518-474-7126
Vice Chair:
   Andrew G Celli, Jr 518-474-7126
Commissioner:
   Patrick J Bulgaro 518-474-7126
Commissioner:
   Kenneth J Baer 518-474-7126
Commissioner:
   Michael A Lenz 518-474-7126
Executive Director:
   David M Grandeau 518-474-7126
Director, Program & Finance Administration:
   Jeannine M Clemente 518-474-7126

NEW YORK STATE LEGISLATURE

See Legislative Branch in Section 1 for additional Standing Committee and Subcommittee information.

Assembly Standing Committees

Election Law
Chair:
   Ann Margaret Carrozza (D) 518-455-5425
Ranking Minority Member:
   Joel M Miller (R) 518-455-5725

Senate Standing Committees

Elections
Chair:
   Joseph A Griffo (R) 518-455-3334
Ranking Minority Member:
   Martin Malave Dilan (D) 518-455-2177

Senate/Assembly Legislative Commissions

Demographic Research & Reapportionment, Legislative Task Force on
Assembly Co-Chair:
   Carl Heastie (D) 518-455-4800
Senate Co-Chair:
   Dean G Skelos (R) 518-455-3171
Assembly Program Manager:
   Lewis M Hoppe 212-618-1100/fax: 212-618-1135
Senate Program Manager:
   Debra A Levine 212-618-1110/fax: 212-618-1135

Offices and agencies generally appear in alphabetical order, except when specific order is requested by listee.

ELECTIONS / U.S. Government

U.S. Government

EXECUTIVE DEPARTMENTS AND RELATED AGENCIES

Federal Election Commission
999 E St NW
Washington, DC 20463
202-694-1100 or 800-424-9530 Fax: 202-219-8504
Web site: www.fec.gov

Chairman:
   Robert D Lenhard 202-694-1000
   e-mail: commissionerlenhard@fec.gov
Vice Chair:
   David M Mason 202-694-1000
   e-mail: commissionermason@fec.gov
Acting General Counsel:
   Thomasenia P Duncan 202-694-1000
Inspector General:
   Lynne A McFarland 202-694-1015/fax: 202-501-8134
   e-mail: oig@fec.gov
Chief Communications Officer:
   Art Forster 202-694-1100
Director, Congressional, Legislative & Intergovernmental Affairs:
   Tina VanBrakle 202-694-1006
Press Officer:
   Robert Biersack 202-694-1220/fax: 202-501-3283

US Commission on Civil Rights
Web site: www.usccr.gov

EASTERN REGION (includes New York State)
624 9th St NW, Ste 500, Washington, DC 20425
Regional Director:
   Ivy Davis 202-376-7533/fax: 202-376-7548

U.S. CONGRESS

See U.S. Congress Chapter for additional Standing Committee and Subcommittee information.

House of Representatives Standing Committees

Government Reform
Chair:
   Henry A Waxman (D-CA) 202-225-3976
Ranking Minority Member:
   Thomas M Davis, III (R-VA) 202-225-1492
New York Delegate:
   Brian M Higgins (D) 202-225-3306
New York Delegate:
   Carolyn B Maloney (D) 202-225-7944
New York Delegate:
   John R McHugh (R) 202-225-4611
New York Delegate:
   Edolphus Towns (D) 202-225-5936

Subcommittee
Federal Workforce, Postal Service and the District of Columbia
   Chair:
      Danny K Davis (D-IL) 202-225-5006
   Ranking Minority Member:
      Kenny Marchant (R-TX) 202-225-6605
   New York Delegate:
      Major R Owens (D) 202-225-6231

Standards of Official Conduct
Chair:
   Stephanie Tubbs Jones (D-OH) 202-225-7032
Ranking Minority Member:
   Doc Hastings (R-WA) 202-225-5816

Senate Standing Committees

Ethics, Select Committee on
Chair:
   Barbara Boxer (D-CA) 202-224-3553
Vice Chair:
   John Cornyn (R-TX) 202-224-2934

Homeland Security & Governmental Affairs
Chair:
   Joseph I Liberman (D-CT) 202-224-4041
Vice Chair:
   Susan Collins (R-ME) 202-224-2523

Private Sector

Arthur J Finkelstein & Associates Inc
16 N Astor, Irvington, NY 10533
914-591-8142 Fax: 914-591-4013
Arthur J Finkelstein, President
Election polling & consulting

Branford Communications
611 Broadway, New York, NY 10012
212-260-9905 Fax: 212-260-9908
Ernest Lendler, Principal
Media consulting; print production & advertising

Bynum, Thompson, Ryer
44 Travis Corners, Garrison, NY 10524
845-424-4300 Fax: 845-424-3850
e-mail: bynum@btrsc.com
Web site: www.btrsc.com
Peter Bynum, President
Campaign communication, strategy & media production

Offices and agencies generally appear in alphabetical order, except when specific order is requested by listee.

ELECTIONS / Private Sector

CUNY Graduate School, Center for Urban Research
365 5th Ave, New York, NY 10016-4309
212-817-2046 Fax: 212-817-1575
e-mail: jmollenkopf@gc.cuny.edu
Web site: www.gc.cuny.edu
John Hull Mollenkopf, Director
Political participation, voting behavior, NYC politics & urban economic & demographic change

Century Foundation (The)
41 East 70th St, New York, NY 10021
212-535-4441 Fax: 212-879-9197
e-mail: info@tcf.org
Web site: www.tcf.org
Christy Hicks, Vice President, Public Affairs
Sponsor the Federal Election Reform Network; co-organizer of the National Commission on Federal Election Reform; provide policymakers with new ideas to address challenges facing the nation

Citizen Action of New York
94 Central Ave, Albany, NY 12206
518-465-4600 x113 Fax: 518-465-2890
e-mail: rkirsch@citizenactionny.org
Web site: www.citizenactionny.org
Richard Kirsch, Executive Director
Campaign finance reform; health care advocacy & consumer protection; education

Columbia Law School, Legislative Drafting Research Fund
435 W 116th St, New York, NY 10027-7297
212-854-2640 Fax: 212-854-7946
e-mail: rb34@columbia.edu
Web site: www.law.columbia.edu
Richard Briffault, Professor of Legislation
State & local government law, property law & election law

Common Cause/NY
155 Ave of the Americas, 4th Fl, New York, NY 10013
212-691-6506 Fax: 212-807-1809
e-mail: cocauseny@aol.com
Web site: www.commoncause.org/ny
Rachel Leon, Executive Director
Campaign finance reform, ballot access, political gift disclosure & public interest lobbying

Conservative Party of NYS
325 Parkview Dr, Schenectady, NY 12303
518-356-7882 Fax: 518-356-3773
e-mail: cpnys@nycap.rr.com
Web site: www.cpnys.org
Shaun Marie Levine, Executive Director
Campaign consulting services & funding for Conservative Party political candidates

Cookfair Media Inc
536 Buckingham Ave, Syracuse, NY 13210
315-478-3359 Fax: 315-478-5236
e-mail: cookfair@aol.com
John R Cookfair, III, President
Campaign media production, print production & advertising

Democratic Congressional Campaign Committee
430 South Capitol St, SE, Washington, DC 20003
202-863-1500 Fax: 202-485-3436
Web site: www.dccc.org
Rahm Emanuel, Chair
Funding for Democratic congressional candidates; campaign strategy

Election Computer Services Inc
197 County Route 7, Pine Plains, NY 12567-9664
518-398-8844 or 212-750-8844 Fax: 518-398-9370
e-mail: ecs@taconic.net
Margo Marabon, President
Computer services, voter lists & direct mail

EMILY's List
1120 Connecticut Ave NW, Ste 1100, Washington, DC 20036-3949
202-326-1400 Fax: 202-326-1415
Web site: www.emilyslist.org
Johnatha Parker, Political Director
Political network for pro-choice Democratic women political candidates

Garth Group Inc (The)
1 W 67th St, #206, New York, NY 10023-6200
212-838-8800 Fax: 212-873-5252
e-mail: garthgroup@aol.com
David Garth, Chairman
Political & media consulting

Harris Interactive Inc
60 Corporate Woods, Rochester, NY 14623-1457
585-272-8400 or 800-866-7655 Fax: 585-272-8763
e-mail: info@harrisinteractive.com
Web site: www.harrisinteractive.com
Greg Novak, President & Chief Executive Officer
Market research

League of Women Voters of New York State
62 Grand Street, Albany, NY 12207-2712
518-465-4162 Fax: 518-465-0812
e-mail: rob@lwvny.org
Web site: www.lwvny.org
Kristen Hansen, Executive Director
Public policy issues forum; good government advocacy

Marist Institute for Public Opinion
Marist College, 3399 North Road, Poughkeepsie, NY 12601
845-575-5050 Fax: 845-575-5111
e-mail: lee.miringoff@marist.edu
Web site: www.maristpoll.marist.edu
Lee M Miringoff, Director
Develops & conducts nonpartisan public opinion polls on elections & issues

Offices and agencies generally appear in alphabetical order, except when specific order is requested by listee.

ELECTIONS / Private Sector

NY League of Conservation Voters/NY Conservation Education Fund
30 Broad Street, 30th Floor, New York, NY 10004
212-361-6350 x208 Fax: 212-361-6363
e-mail: mbystryn@nylcv.org
Web site: www.nylcv.org
Marcia Bystryn, Executive Director
Endorsement of pro-environmental candidates; environmental advocacy & education statewide

NYC Campaign Finance Board
40 Rector St, 7th Fl, New York, NY 10006-1705
212-306-7100 Fax: 212-306-7143
e-mail: info@nyccfb.info
Web site: www.nyccfb.info
Amy M Loprest, Executive Director
Public funding of candidates for NYC elective offices

NYS Right to Life Committee
41 State St, Ste 100, Albany, NY 12207
518-434-1293 Fax: 518-426-1200
e-mail: admin@nysrighttolife.com
Web site: www.nysrighttolife.org
Lori Kehoe, Executive Director

National Organization for Women, NYS
1500 Central Avenue, Albany, NY 12205
518-452-3944 Fax: 518-452-3861
e-mail: newyorkstatenow@aol.com
Web site: www.nownys.com
Marcia Pappas, President
Campaign assistance & funding for political candidates who support feminist agenda; legislative lobbying on women's issues

New School University, Department of Political Science
65 5th Ave, New York, NY 10011
212-229-5784 Fax: 212-807-1669
e-mail: hattamv@newschool.edu
Web site: www.newschool.edu
Victoria Hattam, Associate Professor of Political Science
Business unionism in the US; political parties & elections

New York Republican State Committee
315 State St, Albany, NY 12210
518-462-2601 Fax: 518-449-7443
Web site: www.nygop.org
Joseph N Mondello, Executive Director

New York State Democratic Committee
60 Madison Ave, Ste 1201, New York, NY 10010
212-725-8825 Fax: 212-725-8867
e-mail: rodneyc@nysdems.org
Web site: www.nydems.org
Edna Ishayik, Executive Director

New York University, Departmentt of Politics
19 West 4th Street, New York, NY 10003-9580
212-998-8500 Fax: 212-995-4184
e-mail: russell.hardin@nyu.edu
Web site: www.nyu.edu/gsas/dept/politics
Russell Hardin, Professor of Politics
Ethics in public life; collective action & social movements; nationalism & ethnic conflict

New York University, Graduate School of Journalism
20 Cooper Square, 6th Floor, New York, NY 10003
212-998-7980 Fax: 212-995-4148
e-mail: jr3@nyu.edu
Web site: www.journalism.nyu.edu
Jay Rosen, Chair, Journalism Department
Political role of the press

New York Wired
One Commerce Plz, Ste 301, PO Box 3945, Albany, NY 12203
518-462-1780 x211
Web site: www.newyorkwired.com
Tom Owens, Consulting & Legal

Nostradamus Advertising
884 West End Ave, Ste 2, New York, NY 10025
212-581-1362
e-mail: nos@nostradamus.net
Web site: www.nostradamus.net
Barry N Sher, President
Print production, media consulting, direct mail development

Public Agenda
6 East 39th St, 9th Fl, New York, NY 10016
212-686-6610 Fax: 212-889-3461
e-mail: info@publicagenda.org
Web site: www.publicagenda.org
Claudia Feurey, Vice President, Communications & External Relations
Nonpartisan, nonprofit organization dedicated to conducting unbiased public opinion research & producing fair-minded citizen education materials

SUNY at Albany, Nelson A Rockefeller College
135 Western Ave, Albany, NY 12222
518-442-5378 Fax: 518-442-5298
e-mail: zimmer@albany.edu
Web site: www.albany.edu/rockefeller
Joseph F Zimmerman, Professor
Intergovernmental relations; NY state & local government; ethics in government; election systems & voting

SUNY at New Paltz, College of Liberal Arts & Sciences
614 Faculty Tower, New Paltz, NY 12561-2499
845-257-3520 Fax: 845-257-3520
e-mail: benjamig@newpaltz.edu
Web site: www.newpaltz.edu
Gerald Benjamin, Dean & Professor of Political Science
Local & state government process & structure; regionalism; politics & election law

Offices and agencies generally appear in alphabetical order, except when specific order is requested by listee.

ELECTIONS / Private Sector

Sheinkopf Communications
152 Madison Avenue, Suite 1603, New York, NY 10016
212-725-2378 Fax: 212-725-6896
e-mail: info@scheinkopf.com
Web site: www.sheikopf.com
Henry A Sheinkopf, President
Strategic message counseling for corporate & political clients

US Term Limits Foundation
240 Waukegan Road, Suite 200, Glenview, IL 60025
847-657-7429 or 800-733-6440 Fax: 847-657-7502
e-mail: howrch@cs.com
Web site: www.ustermlimits.org
Howard Rich, President
Publishers of

Women's Campaign Fund
734 15th St NW, Ste 500, Washington, DC 20005
202-393-8164 or 800-446-8170 Fax: 202-393-0649
e-mail: susanmedalie@wcfonline.org
Web site: www.wcfonline.org
Ilana Goldman, Executive Director
Training, education & funding for pro-choice women political candidates

Women's City Club of New York
307 Seventh Ave, Ste 1403, New York, NY 1001
212-353-8070 Fax: 212-228-4665
e-mail: info@wccny.org
Web site: www.wccny.org
Ruth Acker, President
Nonpartisan, nonprofit civic organization whose mission is to shape public policy through education, advocacy and citizen participation

Working Families Party
2-4 Nevins Street, 3rd Flr, Brooklyn, NY 11217
718-222-3796 Fax: 718-246-3718
e-mail: wfp@workingfamiliesparty.org
Web site: www.workingfamiliesparty.org
Dan Cantor, Executive Director

Zogby International
901 Broad St, Utica, NY 13501
315-624-0200 Fax: 315-624-0210
e-mail: mail@zogby.com
Web site: www.zogby.com
John Zogby, President
Political polling & analysis; social science research; business & consumer public opinion surveys & market research

Offices and agencies generally appear in alphabetical order, except when specific order is requested by listee.

ENERGY, UTILITY & COMMUNICATION SERVICES

New York State

GOVERNOR'S OFFICE

Governor's Office
Executive Chamber
State Capitol
Albany, NY 12224
518-474-8390 Fax: 518-474-1513
Web site: www.state.ny.us

Governor:
  Eliot Spitzer 518-474-8390
Secretary to the Governor:
  Richard Baum 518-474-4246
Counsel to the Governor:
  David Nocenti 518-474-8343
Senior Advisor to the Governor:
  Lloyd Constantine 518-486-9671
Assistant Secretary, Energy:
  Steve Mitnick 518-473-5442
Assistant Counsel to the Governor-Energy & Environment:
  Vincent Esposito 518-474-1310
Director, Communications:
  Darren Dopp 518-474-8418

EXECUTIVE DEPARTMENTS AND RELATED AGENCIES

CIO Office & Office for Technology
State Capitol, ESP
PO Box 2062
Albany, NY 12220-0062

CIO Office
  Web site: www.cio.state.ny.us
Chief Information Officer:
  Melodie Mayberry-Stewart, PhD 518-408-2140/fax: 518-402-2976
  e-mail: cio@cio.state.ny.us
Associate Chief Information Officer:
  Ram Shenoy 518-408-2140
Senior Advisor:
  Michael Mittleman 518-408-2140
Assistant to the CIO:
  Marie Potter 518-408-2140

Office for Technology
  Web site: www.oft.state.ny.us
Acting Director:
  Melodie Mayberry-Stewart, PhD 518-473-9450/fax: 518-402-2976

Administration
Deputy Director:
  Margaret Becker 518-473-7041
Administrative Support:
  Max Morehouse 518-437-0927
Budget & Fiscal Administration:
  Kevin Nephew 518-402-4874/fax: 518-402-4807
Human Resources:
  Elaine Ehlinger 518-473-1935/fax: 518-402-4924

Counsel
Deputy Counsel:
  Darlene VanSickle 518-473-5115/fax: 518-486-7923

Operations
Deputy Director, Customer Service:
  Daniel Healy 518-473-2658/fax: 518-474-1196
Customer Networking Solutions:
  John Benson 518-474-9254
Deputy Director, Applications:
  Ellen B Kattleman 518-402-2010/fax: 518-486-4344
Deputy Director, Networking Technologies:
  Dave A Runyon 518-486-9200/fax: 518-408-4693
Director, Telecommunications:
  Daniel Corcoran 518-474-3019/fax: 518-473-7145
Acting Deputy Director, Computing:
  Eileen Fitzsimmons 518-474-8345/fax: 518-473-7532
IT Services & Support:
  Jerry Foster 518-473-5071

Statewide Initiatives
HIPAA Coord:
  Anne Marie Rainville 518-473-2658/fax: 518-474-1196
NYS Technology Academy:
  Terri Daly 518-473-2658/fax: 518-474-1196

Statewide Wireless Network
Deputy Director:
  Hanford Thomas 518-474-9112/fax: 518-443-2787

Consumer Protection Board
5 Empire State Plaza
Ste 2101
Albany, NY 12223-1556
518-474-3514 or 800-697-1220 Fax: 518-474-3514
Web site: www.nyconsumer.gov

1740 Broadway
15th Fl
New York, NY 10019
212-459-8850
Fax: 212-459-8855

Chairperson & Executive Director:
  Mindy A Bockstein 518-486-4852
Executive Deputy Director & General Counsel:
  Lisa R Harris 518-474-3514

Offices and agencies generally appear in alphabetical order, except when specific order is requested by listee.

ENERGY, UTILITY & COMMUNICATION SERVICES / New York State

Law Department
120 Broadway
New York, NY 10271-0332
212-416-8000 Fax: 212-416-8796

State Capitol
Albany, NY 10271-0332
518-474-7330
Fax: 518-402-2472

Attorney General:
   Andrew M Cuomo 518-474-7330
First Deputy Attorney General:
   Michele Hirshman 212-416-8050
Director, Public Information & Correspondence:
   Peter A Drago 518-474-7330/fax: 518-402-2472

Public Advocacy Division
Deputy Attorney General:
   Dietrich Snell. 212-416-8041/fax: 212-416-8068
Special Counsel:
   Mary Ellen Burns 212-416-6155

   Internet Bureau
   Bureau Chief:
      Jane Azia. 212-416-8433/fax: 212-416-8369

   Telecommunications & Energy Bureau
   Bureau Chief:
      Vacant 212-416-8333/fax: 212-416-8877

Public Service Commission
NYS Dept of Public Service
3 Empire State Plaza
Albany, NY 12223-1350
518-474-7080 Fax: 518-473-2838
Web site: www.dps.state.ny.us

90 Church St
New York, NY 10007-2919
212-417-2378

295 Main St
Buffalo, NY 14203
716-847-3400

Chairwoman:
   Patricia L Acampora 518-474-2523/fax: 518-486-1947
Acting Executive Deputy:
   Judith Lee 518-473-4544/fax: 518-473-2838
Acting General Counsel:
   Peter McGowan. 518-474-2510/fax: 518-486-5710
Director, Public Affairs:
   James Denn 518-474-7080/fax: 518-473-2838

Accounting, Finance & Economics Office
Director:
   Charles M Dickson 518-474-4508/fax: 518-486-7524

Consumer Services Office
Director:
   Sandra Sloane 518-474-3280/fax: 518-486-7868
   e-mail: csd@dps.state.ny.us

Electricity & Environment Office
Director:
   James Gallagher. 518-473-7248/fax: 518-486-1672
Deputy Director:
   James Austin 518-474-8702/fax: 518-486-1672
Chief, Administration & Planning:
   Frederick Carr 518-486-2892/fax: 518-473-2420
Chief, Energy Resources & The Environment:
   Douglas K May 518-474-5368/fax: 518-474-5026
Chief, Rates & Tariffs:
   Doug Lutzy 518-473-3329/fax: 518-473-1498
Chief, Bulk Transmission Systems:
   Howard A Tarler 518-486-2483/fax: 518-473-2420

Gas & Water Office
Director:
   Thomas Dvorsky 518-473-6080/fax: 518-473-4992
Chief, Gas Rates:
   Michael Scott. 518-474-1372/fax: 518-473-4992
Chief, Safety Section:
   Gavin S Nicoletta 518-486-2496/fax: 518-473-5625
Chief, Policy Section:
   Sheila A Rappazzo 518-486-1645/fax: 518-473-4992
Chief, Water Rates:
   Arthur Gordon 518-474-8656/fax: 518-473-5625

Hearings & Alternative Dispute Resolution Office
Chief Administrative Law Judge:
   Judith Lee 518-474-4520/fax: 518-473-3263

Office of Administration
Director:
   Debra Renner. 518-474-2508/fax: 518-474-0413
Adminstrative Management:
   William Reilly 518-474-1990/fax: 518-474-0413
Finance & Budget:
   Sorelle Brauth 518-474-2516/fax: 518-473-9990
Human Resources:
   Barbara Herbert 518-486-2633/fax: 518-473-9990
Information Services Director:
   Jane Craig 518-486-4960/fax: 518-473-7815
Internal Audit:
   Steve Suriano. 518-473-2079/fax: 518-474-0413

Office of Telecommunications
Director:
   Robert H Mayer. 518-474-1668/fax: 518-474-5616
Deputy Director, Cable:
   Chad Hume 518-474-1939/fax: 518-486-5727

Public Service Commission
Chairwoman:
   Patricia L Acampora 518-474-2523/fax: 518-486-1947
Secretary to the Commission:
   Jaclyn A Brilling 518-474-6530/fax: 518-486-6081
   e-mail: secretary@dps.state.ny.us

Utility Security Office
Director:
   John J Sennett 518-473-0547/fax: 518-474-5026

CORPORATIONS, AUTHORITIES AND COMMISSIONS

Interstate Oil & Gas Compact Commission
PO Box 53127
Oklahoma City, OK 73152-3127

Offices and agencies generally appear in alphabetical order, except when specific order is requested by listee.

ENERGY, UTILITY & COMMUNICATION SERVICES / U.S. Government

405-525-3556 Fax: 405-525-3592
e-mail: iogcc@iogcc.state.ok.us
Web site: www.iogcc.state.ok.us

Chair:
  John Hoeven.....................................405-525-3556
Vice Chair:
  Victor Carrillo....................................405-525-3556
Executive Director:
  Christine Hansen.................................405-525-3556
New York State Official Representative:
  Bradley J Field...................................518-402-8076
Communications Manager:
  Erica Carr..405-525-3556

Long Island Power Authority
333 Earle Ovington Blvd
Suite 403
Uniondale, NY 11553
516-222-7700 Fax: 516-222-9137
e-mail: info@lipower.org
Web site: www.lipower.org

Chairman:
  Kevin S Law......................................516-222-7700
CEO/President:
  Richard M Kessel.................................516-222-7700
Acting General Counsel:
  Lynda Nicolino...................................516-222-7700
Vice President, Communications:
  Bert Cunningham.................................516-719-9838
  e-mail: bcunningham@lipower.org
Executive Director, Government Relations:
  William Davidson.................................516-719-9852

New York Power Authority
123 Main St
White Plains, NY 10601-3170
914-681-6200 Fax: 914-390-8190
e-mail: info@nypa.gov
Web site: www.nypa.gov

30 South Pearl St
Albany, NY 12207
518-433-6700
Fax: 518-433-1406

Chairman:
  Frank S McCullough, Jr...........................914-287-3636
President & Chief Executive Officer:
  Timothy S Carey..................................914-287-3501

Senior Vice President, Public & Government Affairs:
  Brian Vattimo....................................518-433-6734
Executive Director, Public/Governmental Affairs:
  Paul Finnegan....................................518-433-6740
Director, Media Relations:
  Michael Saltzman.................................914-390-8181

New York State Energy Research & Development Authority
17 Columbia Circle
Albany, NY 12203-6399
518-862-1090 Fax: 518-862-1091
Web site: www.nyserda.org

Chairman:
  Vincent A DeIorio................................518-862-1090
President & CEO:
  Peter R Smith..............................518-862-1090 x3320
  e-mail: prs@nyserda.org
General Counsel (Acting):
  Hal Brodie.................................518-862-1090 x3280
  e-mail: hb1@nyserda.org
Vice President, Programs:
  Robert Callender...........................518-862-1090 x3233
  e-mail: rgc@nyserda.org
Treasurer:
  Jeffrey J Pitkin............................518-862-1090 x3223
  e-mail: jjp@nyserda.org
Director, Communications (Acting):
  Colleen Q Ryan 518-862-1090 x3359/fax: 518-464-8249
  e-mail: cqr@nyserda.org

NEW YORK STATE LEGISLATURE

See Legislative Branch in Section 1 for additional Standing Committee and Subcommittee information.

Assembly Standing Committees

Energy
Chair:
  Paul D Tonko (D)..................................518-455-5197
Ranking Minority Member:
  Thomas O'Mara (R)................................518-455-4538

Senate Standing Committees

Energy & Telecommunications
Chair:
  James W Wright (R)...............................518-455-2346
Ranking Minority Member:
  Kevin S Parker (D)................................518-455-2580

U.S. Government

EXECUTIVE DEPARTMENTS AND RELATED AGENCIES

Federal Communications Commission
Web site: www.fcc.gov

Office of Media Relations
445 12th St SW, Rm CY-C314, Washington, DC 20554

Offices and agencies generally appear in alphabetical order, except when specific order is requested by listee.

ENERGY, UTILITY & COMMUNICATION SERVICES / U.S. Government

Director:
  David Fiske......................................202-418-0500

Nuclear Regulatory Commission
Web site: www.nrc.gov

REGION I (includes New York State)
475 Allendale Rd, King of Prussia, PA 19406-1415
Regional Administrator:
  Samuel J Collins...............610-337-5299/fax: 610-337-5241
Senior Public Affairs Officer:
  Diane P Screnci...................................610-337-5330
Public Affairs Officer:
  Neil A Sheehan....................................610-337-5331

US Department of Agriculture
Web site: www.usda.gov

Rural Development
Web site: www.rurdev.usda.gov/ny

New York State Office..........................fax: 315-477-6438
The Galleries of Syracuse, 441 S Salina St, Ste 357, 5th Fl, Syracuse, NY 13202-2425
TTY: 315-477-6447 or 315-477-6400 Fax: 315-477-6438
Acting State Director:
  Scott Collins.....................................315-477-6400
Special Projects Representative:
  Vacant...315-477-6433
Program Director, Rural Utilities Service:
  David Miller.....................................315-477-6427
  e-mail: david.miller@ny.usda.gov

US Department of Energy
Web site: www.doe.gov

Federal Energy Regulatory Commission

New York Regional Office
19 W 34th St, Ste 400, New York, NY 10001
Regional Engineer:
  Charles P Goggins...............212-273-5910/fax: 212-631-8124
Deputy Regional Engineer:
  Peter Valeri......................................212-273-5930

Office of External Affairs
888 First St NE, Washington, DC 20426
202-502-8004
Director:
  J Mclane Layton................202-502-8004/fax: 202-208-2106

Laboratories

Brookhaven National Laboratory
  Brookhaven Group
    53 Bell Ave, Bldg 464, Upton, NY 11973-5000
    Site Manager:
      Michael Holland............631-344-3424/fax: 631-344-3444
  Community Involvement/Public Affairs
    35 Brookhaven Ave, Upton, NY 11973
    Assistant Lab Director:
      Margaret Lynch.............631-344-4747/fax: 631-344-5004
    Media & Communications Manager:
      Mona Rowe..................631-344-5056/fax: 631-344-3368
  Office of the Director
    40 Brookhaven Ave, Bldg 460, Upton, NY 11973-5000
    Director:
      Sam Aronson................631-344-2772/fax: 631-344-5803

Knolls Atomic Power Laboratory- KAPL Inc
PO Box 1072, Schenectady, NY 12301-1072
General Manager:
  Michael F Quinn..................518-395-4200/fax: 518-395-6469

U.S. CONGRESS

See U.S. Congress Chapter for additional Standing Committee and Subcommittee information.

House of Representatives Standing Committees

Appropriations
Chair:
  David R Obey (D-WI)...............................202-225-3365
Ranking Minority Member:
  Jerry Lewis (R-CA)................................202-225-5861
New York Delegate:
  Maurice D Hinchey (D).............................202-225-6335
New York Delegate:
  Nita M Lowey (D)..................................202-225-6506
New York Delegate:
  Jose E Serrano (D)................................202-225-4361
New York Delegate:
  John E Sweeney (R)................................202-225-5614
New York Delegate:
  James T Walsh (R).................................202-225-3701

  Subcommittee
    Energy & Water Development
      Chair:
        Peter J Visclosky (D-IN)....................202-225-2461
      Ranking Minority Member:
        David L Hobson (R-OH)

Energy & Commerce
Chair:
  John D Dingell, Jr (D-MI).........................202-225-2927
Ranking Minority Member:
  Joe Barton (R-TX).................................202-225-2002
New York Delegate:
  Eliot L Engel (D).................................202-225-2464
New York Delegate:
  Vito Fossella (R).................................202-225-3371
New York Delegate:
  Edolphus Towns (D)................................202-225-5936

  Subcommittee
    Energy & Air Quality
      Chair:
        Rick Boucher (D-VA).........................202-225-3861
      Ranking Minority Member:
        J Dennis Hastert (R-IL).....................202-225-2976
      New York Delegate:
        Eliot L Engel (D)...........................202-225-2464
      New York Delegate:
        Vito Fossella (R)...........................202-225-3371

Natural Resources
Chair:
  Nick J Rahall, II (D-WV)..........................202-225-6065
Ranking Minority Member:
  Don Young (R-AK)...................................202-225-5765

Offices and agencies generally appear in alphabetical order, except when specific order is requested by listee.

ENERGY, UTILITY & COMMUNICATION SERVICES / Private Sector

Subcommittees
Energy & Mineral Resources
Chair:
  Jim Costa (D-CA) 202-225-9297
Ranking Minority Member:
  Stevan Pearce (R-NM) 202-225-2365
Water & Power
Chair:
  Grace F Napolitano (D-CA) 202-225-8331
Ranking Minority Member:
  Cathy McMorris Rodgers (WA) 202-225-2006

Science & Technology
Chair:
  Bart Gordon (D-TN) 202-225-4231
Ranking Minority Member:
  Ralph M Hall (R-TX) 202-225-6673

Subcommittee
Energy & Environment
Chair:
  Nick Lampson (D-TX) 202-225-5951
Ranking Minority Member:
  Bob Inglis (R-SC) 202-225-6030

Senate Standing Committees

Appropriations
Chair:
  Robert C Byrd (D-WV) 202-224-3954
Ranking Minority Member:
  Thad Cochran (R-MS) 202-224-5054

Subcommittee
Energy & Water Development
Chair:
  Byron Dorgan (D-ND) 202-224-2551
Ranking Minority Member:
  Pete V Domenici (R-NM) 202-224-6621

Commerce, Science & Transportation
Chair:
  Daniel K Inouye (D-HI) 202-224-3934
Ranking Minority Member:
  Ted Stevens (R-AK) 202-224-30045

Subcommittee
Aviation Operations, Safety & Security
Chair:
  John D Rockefeller, IV (D-WV) 202-224-6472
Ranking Minority Member:
  Trent Lott (R-MS) 202-224-6253
Space, Aeronautics and Related Sciences
Chair:
  Bill Nelson (D-FL) 202-224-5724
Ranking Minority Member:
  Kay Bailey Hutchison (R-TX) 202-224-5922

Energy & Natural Resources
Chair:
  Jeff Bingaman (D-NM) 202-224-5521
Ranking Minority Member:
  Pete V Domenici (R-NM) 202-224-6621

Private Sector

AT&T Corporation
One AT&T Way, Bedminster, NJ 7921
908-532-1835 Fax: 908-532-1702
e-mail: morrisse@lga.att.com
Web site: www.att.com
Michael Morrissey, Vice President, Law & Government Affairs
Telecommunications services & systems

AeA New York Council
255 Fuller Rd, Albany Nanotechnology Complex, Albany, NY 12203
518-437-1530 Fax: 732-340-1533
e-mail: justin-wright@aeanet.org
Web site: www.aeanet.org
Justin Wright, Executive Director
Electronics, software & information technology industries; support of high tech industry goals

Amerada Hess Corporation
1185 Ave of the Americas, New York, NY 10036
212-997-8500 Fax: 212-536-8390
Web site: www.hess.com
John B Hess, Chief Executive Officer
Manufacture & market petroleum products; operate gasoline outlets

Association of Public Broadcasting Stations of NY Inc
33 Elk St, Ste 200, Albany, NY 12207
518-462-1590 Fax: 518-462-1390
e-mail: apbs@wxxi.org
Peter Repas, Executive Director
Public television

Business Council of New York State Inc
152 Washington Ave, Albany, NY 12210
518-465-7511 x223 Fax: 518-465-4389
e-mail: anne.vanburen@bcnys.org
Web site: www.bcnys.org
Anne Van Buren, Director, Energy & Telecommunications
Telecommunications, small business, financial services, insurance

CBS Corporation
51 W 52nd St, New York, NY 10019
212-975-4321 Fax: 212-975-6035
Web site: www.cbs.com
Martin Franks, Executive Vice President, CBS Television & Senior Vice President, Viacom
TV & radio broadcasting, news, entertainment

Offices and agencies generally appear in alphabetical order, except when specific order is requested by listee.

ENERGY, UTILITY & COMMUNICATION SERVICES / Private Sector

Cable Telecommunications Association of New York Inc
80 State St, 10th Fl, Albany, NY 12207
518-463-6676 Fax: 518-463-0574
e-mail: rfa@nycap.rr.com
Web site: www.cabletvny.com
Richard F Alteri, President
Advocate & represent the interests of the cable television industry

Cablevision Systems Corporation
1111 Stewart Ave, Bethpage, NY 11714-3581
516-803-2580 Fax: 516-803-2585
e-mail: lrosenbl@cablevision.com
Web site: www.cablevision.com
Lisa Rosenblum, Senior Vice President, Government Relations
Own & operate cable television systems & programming networks, telecommunications, Madison Square Garden, Radio City Music Hall, pro sports teams

Central Hudson Gas & Electric Corporation
284 South Ave, Poughkeepsie, NY 12601
845-486-5218 Fax: 845-486-5544
e-mail: jglusko@cenhud.com
Web site: www.cenhud.com
John P Glusko, Director, Governmental Affairs & Economic Development
Governmental relations, corporate relocations & economic development

Consolidated Edison Energy
4 Irving Pl, Rm 1650S, New York, NY 10276-0138
212-460-2706 or 800-752-6633 Fax: 212-614-1821
e-mail: banksjo@coned.com
Web site: www.coned.com
John H Banks, Vice President, Government Relations

Constellation NewEnergy Inc
Metro-North Region, 810 7th Avenue, Suite 400, New York, NY 10019
212-885-6400 Fax: 212-883-5888
e-mail: cnesalesny@constellation.com
Web site: www.newenergy.com
Charles C Sutton, Vice President
Retail energy supply & energy services

Crane, Parente & Cherubin
90 State Street, Ste 1515A, Albany, NY 12207
518-432-8000 Fax: 518-432-0086
e-mail: jcrane@cpclaw.net
James B Crane, II, Managing Partner
Governmental relations, banking & financial services, corporate law, construction law, energy, utilities, communications, land use, environmental & wireless telecommunications law

Educational Broadcasting Corporation
450 West 33rd St, New York, NY 10001
212-560-1313 Fax: 212-560-1314
e-mail: rae@thirteen.org
Web site: www.thirteen.org
Kathleen Rae, Director Governmental Affairs

Empire State Petroleum Association Inc
80 Wolf Rd, St 308, Albany, NY 12205
518-449-0702 Fax: 518-449-0779
e-mail: tpeters@espa.net
Web site: www.espa.net
Thomas J Peters, Executive Vice President
Petroleum industry lobby & trade association

Energy Association of New York State
111 Washington Ave, Suite 601, Albany, NY 12210
518-449-3440 Fax: 518-449-3446
Patrick J Curran, Executive Director
Electric & gas utility companies

Entek Power Services
11 Satterly Rd, East Setauket, NY 11733
631-751-9800 Fax: 631-980-3759
e-mail: info@entekpower.com
Web site: www.entekpower.com
Harry Davitian, President
Energy consulting

Entergy Nuclear Northeast
440 Hamilton Ave, White Plains, NY 10601
914-272-3200 Fax: 914-272-3205
Web site: www.entergy.com
Michael R Kansler, President
Second largest operator of nuclear power plants in the US

Exxon Mobil Corporation
1400 Old Country Rd, Ste 203, Westbury, NY 11590
516-333-3177 Fax: 516-333-3428
e-mail: donald.l.clarke@exxonmobil.com
Web site: www.exxonmobil.com
Donald L Clarke, Manager, Public Affairs Northeast

Frontier, A Citizens Communications Co
19 John St, Middletown, NY 10940
845-344-9801 Fax: 845-343-3768
e-mail: claudia.maroney@frontiercorp.com
Web site: www.frontieronline.com
Claudia Maroney, Operations Director
Full service telecommunications provider

Fund for the City of New York, Center for Internet Innovation
121 Ave of the Americas, 6th Fl, New York, NY 10013
212-925-6675 Fax: 212-925-5675
e-mail: mmccormick@fcny.org
Web site: www.fcny.org
Mary McCormick, President
Developing technology systems & applications that help nonprofits & government streamline operations, expand services, improve performance

Offices and agencies generally appear in alphabetical order, except when specific order is requested by listee.

ENERGY, UTILITY & COMMUNICATION SERVICES / Private Sector

Getty Petroleum Marketing Inc
1500 Hempstead Turnpike, East Meadow, NY 11554
516-542-5055 Fax: 516-832-8443
e-mail: mlewis@getty.com
Web site: www.getty.com
Michael G Lewis, Vice President & General Counsel
Petroleum products sales & distribution

NYS Bar Assn, Electronic Communications Task Force
Heslin Rothenberg Farley & Mesiti PC
5 Columbia Cir, Albany, NY 12203
518-452-5600 Fax: 518-452-5579
e-mail: dpm@hrfmlaw.com
Web site: www.hrfmlaw.com
David P Miranda, Chair

NYS Bar Assn, Media Law Committee
Hogan & Hartson LLP
875 3rd Ave, 25th Fl, New York, NY 10022
212-918-3637 Fax: 212-918-3100
e-mail: srmetcalf@hhlaw.com
Slade R Metcalf, Chair

Independent Oil & Gas Association of New York
5743 Walden Drive, Lake View, NY 14085
716-627-4250 Fax: 716-627-4375
e-mail: brgill@iogany.org
Web site: www.iogany.org
Bradley Gill, Executive Director
Trade association representing oil & natural gas producers, drillers & affiliated service companies

Independent Power Producers of NY Inc
19 Dove Street, Ste 302, Albany, NY 12210
518-436-3749 Fax: 518-436-0369
e-mail: gavin@ippny.org
Web site: www.ippny.org
Gavin J Donohue, President & Chief Executive Officer
Companies developing alternative, environmentally friendly electric generating facilities

KeySpan Corporation
1377 Motor Parkway, Hauppauge, NY 11749
631-300-3700 Fax: 631-300-3702
e-mail: tdejesu@keyspanenergy.com
Thomas DeJesu, Director, Government Relations
Electric generation & gas utility

Komanoff Energy Associates
636 Broadway, Rm 602, New York, NY 10012-2623
212-260-5237
e-mail: kea@igc.org
Web site: www.carbontax.org
Charles Komanoff, Director
Energy, utilities & transportation consulting

Mechanical Technology Incorporated
431 New Karner Road, Albany, NY 12205
518-533-2200 Fax: 518-533-2201
Web site: www.mechtech.com
Cynthia A Scheuer, Chairman & Chief Executive Officer
New energy technologies, precision measurement & testing instruments

Municipal Electric Utilities Association
445 Electronics Pkwy, Ste 207, Liverpool, NY 13088-6001
315-453-7851 Fax: 315-453-7849
e-mail: info@meua.org
Web site: www.meua.org
Robert Mullane, Executive Director

NY Oil Heating Association
14 Penn Plaza, Ste 1102, New York, NY 10122
212-695-1380 Fax: 212-594-6583
e-mail: nyoilheating@nyoha.org
Web site: www.nyoha.org
John Maniscalco, Executive Vice President
Fuel dealers & auxiliary industries

NY Press Association
1681 Western Ave, Albany, NY 12203
518-464-6483 Fax: 518-464-6489
e-mail: mkrea@nynewspapers.com
Web site: www.nynewspapers.com
Michelle Rea, Executive Director
Weekly community & ethnic newspaper publishers

NY Propane Gas Association
PO Box 760, Clifton Park, NY 12065
518-383-3823 Fax: 518-383-3824
e-mail: nypga1@aol.com
Web site: www.nypropane.com
John Hamilton, President; Roland Penta, State/National Director
Provides services that communicate, promote and educate the propane industry in New York.

NYS Broadcasters Association
1805 Western Ave, Albany, NY 12203
518-456-8888 Fax: 518-456-8943
Web site: www.nysbroadcasters.org
Joseph Reilly, President
Trade association for NYS Broadcasters

NYS Technology Enterprise Corporation (NYSTEC)
100 State St, Ste 900, Albany, NY 12207
518-431-7020 Fax: 518-431-7037
e-mail: nystec@nystec.com
Web site: www.nystec.com
Geoff Plante, Director, Business Development
Technology acquisition, technology management & engineering services to government clients

Offices and agencies generally appear in alphabetical order, except when specific order is requested by listee.

ENERGY, UTILITY & COMMUNICATION SERVICES / Private Sector

National Economic Research Associates
308 N Cayuga St, Ithaca, NY 14850
607-277-3007 Fax: 607-277-1581
e-mail: alfred.kahn@nera.com
Web site: www.nera.com
Alfred E Kahn, Professor Emeritus & Special Consultant
Utility & transportation regulation, deregulation & antitrust

National Fuel Gas
800 North 3rd Street, Ste 410, Box 1145, Harrisburg, PA 17108
717-232-7236 Fax: 717-232-8238
e-mail: morrisong@nat.fuel.com
Web site: www.nationalfuel.com
Gary L Morrison, General Manager, Government Affairs

NYS Bar Assn, Public Utility Law Committee
National Fuel Gas Distribution
Legal Department, 6363 Main Street, Buffalo, NY 14221
716-857-7313
Michael W Reville, Chair

Nelson A Rockefeller Inst of Government, NY Forum for Info
411 State St, Albany, NY 12203-1003
518-443-5001 Fax: 518-443-5006
e-mail: gbenson@nysfirm.org
Web site: www.nysfirm.org
Gregory M Benson Jr, Executive Director
Information management; public access to government information; privacy & confidentiality; intellectual property; public/private partnerships

New York Independent System Operator - Not For Profit
10 Krey Blvd, Rensselaer, NY 12144
518-356-8728 Fax: 518-356-7524
e-mail: gbrown@nyiso.com
Web site: www.nyiso.com
Garry Brown, VP, External Affairs
Grid operator

New York Newspaper Publishers Association
291 Hudson Avenue, Suite A, Albany, NY 12210
518-449-1667 Fax: 518-449-5053
Web site: www.nynpa.com
Diane Kennedy, President

New York Press Photographers Association
225 E 36th St, Ste 1-P, New York, NY 10016
212-889-6633 Fax: 212-889-6634
e-mail: nyppa@aol.com
Web site: www.nyppa.org
Bernie Nunez, President

New York State Electric & Gas Corporation (NYSEG)
18 Link Drive, Box 5224, Binghamton, NY 13902-5224
607-762-7310 Fax: 607-762-8751
e-mail: ctchadwick@nyseg.com
Web site: www.nyseg.com
Cindy T Chadwick, Manager, Public Affairs

New York State Petroleum Council
150 State St, Albany, NY 12207
518-465-3563 Fax: 518-465-4022
e-mail: nyspc@nycap.rr.com
Web site: www.api.org
Michael R Doyle, Executive Director
Petroleum industry lobby

New York State Telecommunications Association Inc
100 State St, Ste 650, Albany, NY 12207
518-443-2700 Fax: 518-443-2810
e-mail: rpuckett@nysta.com
Web site: www.nysta.com
Robert R Puckett, President

Niagara Mohawk - A National Grid Company
300 Erie Blvd West, Syracuse, NY 13202
315-428-5430 Fax: 315-428-3406
e-mail: susan.crossett@us.ngrid.com
Susan Crossett, Vice President, Public Affairs

Northeast Gas Association
75 Second Ave, Ste 510, Needham, MA 02494-2824
781-455-6800 Fax: 781-455-6828
e-mail: tkiley@northeastgas.org
Web site: www.northeastgas.org
Thomas M Kiley, President & CEO
Gas Industry Trade Association

Oil Heat Institute of Long Island
200 Parkway Drive S, Ste 202, Hauppauge, NY 11788
631-360-0200 Fax: 631-360-0781
e-mail: info@ohili.org
Web site: www.ohili.org
Kevin M Rooney, Chief Executive Officer
Heating oil industry association

Orange & Rockland Utilities Inc
One Blue Hill Plz, Pearl River, NY 10965
845-352-6000 Fax: 845-577-6914
e-mail: struckr@oru.com
Web site: www.oru.com
John D McMahon, President & Chief Executive Officer
New business development

Plug Power Inc
968 Albany-Shaker Rd, Latham, NY 12110
518-782-7700 x1970 Fax: 518-782-9060
Web site: www.plugpower.com
Gerard L Conway, Jr, General Counsel
Fuel cell research & development for small stationary applications

Public Utility Law Project of New York Inc
194 Washington Ave, Ste 420, Albany, NY 12210-2314
518-449-3375 Fax: 518-449-1769
e-mail: info@pulp.tc
Web site: www.pulp.tc
Gerald A Norlander, Executive Director
Advocacy of universal service, affordability & customer protection for residential utility consumers

---

Offices and agencies generally appear in alphabetical order, except when specific order is requested by listee.

ENERGY, UTILITY & COMMUNICATION SERVICES / Private Sector

Rochester Gas & Electric Corporation
89 East Ave, Rochester, NY 14649
585-771-2230 Fax: 585-724-8799
e-mail: marion@rge.com
Web site: www.rge.com
Dick Marion, Manager, Corporate Communications

Sithe Energies Inc
335 Madison Ave, New York, NY 10017
212-351-0266 Fax: 212-351-0800
Web site: www.sithe.com
Frank Gomez, Office Manager
Independent electric power producer & generator

Spanish Broadcasting System Network Inc
26 W 56th St, New York, NY 10019
646-710-2629 Fax: 212-541-9295
Web site: www.lamusica.com
Luis A Miranda, Jr, Director, Public Affairs
Spanish language FM radio stations

Sunwize Technologies Inc
1155 Flatbush Rd, Kingston, NY 12401
845-336-0146 x124 Fax: 845-336-0457
e-mail: sunwize@sunwize.com
Web site: www.sunwize.com
Bruce Gould, Vice President, Sales
Solar electric energy development & product distribution

Verizon Communications
140 West Street, New York, NY 10007
518-396-1086 Fax: 518-436-0141
Web site: www.verizon.com
David Lamendola, Director, Government Affairs-State of NY
Telecommunications services for northeastern US

Viacom Inc
1515 Broadway, New York, NY 10036
212-258-6000
Web site: www.viacom.com
Sumner M Redstone, Chairman & Chief Executive Officer
International media, entertainment

Wall Street Journal (The)
200 Liberty St, New York, NY 10281
212-416-2000 Fax: 212-416-2720
e-mail: paul.steiger@dowjones.com
Web site: www.wsj.com
Paul E Steiger, Managing Editor

Offices and agencies generally appear in alphabetical order, except when specific order is requested by listee.

ENVIRONMENT & NATURAL RESOURCES

New York State

GOVERNOR'S OFFICE

Governor's Office
Executive Chamber
State Capitol
Albany, NY 12224
518-474-8390 Fax: 518-474-1513
Web site: www.state.ny.us

Governor:
   Eliot Spitzer 518-474-8390
Secretary to the Governor:
   Richard Baum. 518-474-4246
Counsel to the Governor:
   David Nocenti. 518-474-8343
Senior Advisor to the Governor:
   Lloyd Constantine 518-486-9671
Deputy Secretary, Environment:
   Judith Enck 518-472-5442
Assistant Counsel to the Governor-Energy & Environment:
   Vincent Esposito. 518-474-1310
Director, Communications:
   Darren Dopp 518-474-8418

EXECUTIVE DEPARTMENTS AND RELATED AGENCIES

Empire State Development Corporation
633 Third Ave
New York, NY 10017
212-803-3100
Web site: www.empire.state.ny.us

30 South Pearl Street
Albany, NY 12245
518-292-5100

420 Main St, Ste 717
Buffalo, NY 14202
716-856-8111

Co-Chair Downstate:
   Patrick J Foye 212-803-3700
Co-Chair Upstate:
   Daniel C Gundersen . . . . 518-292-5100 or 716-856-8111
President & Chief Operating Officer:
   Avi Schick 212-803-3730
Chief Operating Officer (Upstate):
   Kenneth A Schoetz. 716-856-8111
Director, Communications:
   A J Carter 212-803-3740

Environmental Conservation Department
625 Broadway
Albany, NY 12233
518-402-8545 Fax: 518-402-9016
Web site: www.dec.ny.gov

Commissioner:
   Alexander B (Pete) Grannis. 518-402-8540/fax: 518-402-8541
Executive Deputy Commissioner:
   Stuart Gruskin. 518-402-8560

Air & Waste Management Office
Deputy Commissioner:
   Vacant 518-402-8549

Air Resources Division
Director:
   David Shaw 518-402-8452/fax: 518-402-9035

Environmental Remediation Division
Director:
   Dale Desnoyers 518-402-9706/fax: 518-402-9020

Solid & Hazardous Materials Division
Director:
   Stephen Hammond 518-402-8651/fax: 518-402-9024

General Counsel's Office
Deputy Commissioner & General Counsel:
   Vacant. 518-402-2794/fax: 518-485-8484

Environmental Enforcement Division
Director:
   Charles Sullivan 518-402-9509/fax: 518-402-9019

Environmental Justice Division
Environmental Justice Coordinator:
   Monica L Kreshik 518-402-8556/fax: 518-402-9018

Legal Affairs Division
Acting Director:
   Bill Little 518-402-9184/fax: 518-402-9018

Hearings & Mediation Services Office
Asst Commissioner:
   Louis Alexander 518-402-8537
Chief Administrative Law Judge:
   James McClymonds. 518-402-9003/fax: 518-402-9037

Legislative Affairs Office
Asst Commissioner:
   Maureen Coleman 518-402-8533/fax: 518-402-9016

Natural Resources & Water Quality Office
Deputy Commissioner:
   Vacant 518-402-8543

Offices and agencies generally appear in alphabetical order, except when specific order is requested by listee.

ENVIRONMENT & NATURAL RESOURCES / New York State

Fish, Wildlife & Marine Resources Division
Director:
  Gerald Barnhart 518-402-8924/fax: 518-402-8925

Lands & Forests Division
Director:
  Robert Davies 518-402-9405/fax: 518-402-9028

Mineral Resources Division
Director:
  Bradley J Field 518-402-8076/fax: 518-402-8060

Water Division
Director:
  Sandra Allen 518-402-8233/fax: 518-402-8230

Office of Administration
Asst Commissioner:
  Jack McKeon 518-402-9401

Environmental Permits Division
Director:
  Jeffrey Sama 518-402-9182/fax: 518-402-9168

Information Services Division
Director:
  Eugene Pezdek 518-402-9860/fax: 518-402-9031

Management & Budget Services Division
Director:
  Nancy Lussier 518-402-9228/fax: 518-402-9230

Operations Division
Director:
  Michael Turley 518-402-9055/fax: 518-402-9053

Public Affairs & Education Division
Director:
  Laurel Remus 518-402-8049/fax: 518-402-8050

Office of Employee Relations
Director:
  Joe Lattanzio 518-402-9388/fax: 518-486-9957

Office of Media Affairs
Asst Commissioner, Media Relations:
  Maureen Wren 518-402-8000

Freedom of Information Law
Records Access Officer:
  Ruth Earl 518-402-8000

Public Protection Office
Asst Commissioner:
  Henry Hamilton 518-402-8552

Forest Protection & Fire Management Division
Director:
  Andrew T Jacob 518-402-8839/fax: 518-402-8840

Law Enforcement Division
Director:
  Vacant 518-402-8829/fax: 518-402-8830

Regional Offices

Region 1
SUNY - Bldg 40, Rm 121, Stony Brook, NY 11790-2356
Director:
  Peter A Scully 631-444-0345/fax: 631-444-0349

Region 2
One Hunters Pt Plaza, 47-40 21st St, Long Island City, NY 11101-5407
Acting Director:
  Louis Oliva 718-482-4949/fax: 718-482-4954

Region 3
21 S Putt Corners Rd, New Paltz, NY 12561-1696
Director:
  Marc Moran 845-256-3000/fax: 845-255-3042

Region 4
1150 N Westcott Rd, Schenectady, NY 12306-2014
Director:
  Steve Schassler 518-357-2068/fax: 518-357-2087

Region 5
Rte 86, PO Box 296, Ray Brook, NY 12977
Director:
  Stuart Buchanan 518-897-1220/fax: 518-897-1394

Region 6
317 Washington St, Watertown, NY 13601-3787
Director:
  Sandra L LeBarron 315-785-2239/fax: 315-785-2242

Region 7
615 Erie Blvd West, Syracuse, NY 13204-2400
Director:
  Kenneth Lynch 315-426-7403/fax: 315-426-7408

Region 8
6274 E Avon-Lima Rd, Avon, NY 14414-9519
Director:
  Sean Hanna 585-226-2466/fax: 585-226-9485

Region 9
270 Michigan Ave, Buffalo, NY 14203-2999
Director:
  Gerald Mikol 716-851-7000/fax: 716-851-7211

Special Programs

Great Lakes Program
Region 9 NYS DEC, 270 Michigan Ave, Buffalo, NY 14203
Coordinator:
  Donald Zelazny 716-851-7220/fax: 716-851-7226

Hudson River Estuary Program
Region 3 NYS DEC, 21 S Putt Corners Rd, New Paltz, NY 12561
Special Asst:
  Frances Dunwell 845-256-3016/fax: 845-255-3649
  e-mail: hrep@gw.dec.state.ny.us

New York Natural Heritage Program
625 Broadway, 5th Fl, Albany, NY 12233-4757
Director:
  David Van Leuven 518-402-8935/fax: 518-402-8925

Freshwater Wetlands Appeals Board
625 Broadway, Room 145
Albany, NY 12233-1070
518-402-0566 Fax: 518-402-0588
Web site: www.dec.state.ny.us/website/fwab/

Chairwoman:
  Rhonda K Amoroso 518-402-0566
Counsel:
  Michele M Stefanucci 518-402-0566
Co-Counsel:
  Pamela J Armstrong 518-402-0566
Docket Clerk & Board Secretary:
  Carol A Goldstein 518-402-0566

Offices and agencies generally appear in alphabetical order, except when specific order is requested by listee.

ENVIRONMENT & NATURAL RESOURCES / New York State

Health Department
Corning Tower
Empire State Plaza
Albany, NY 12237
518-474-7354
Web site: www.nyhealth.gov

Commissioner:
   Richard F Daines, MD 518-474-2011
Chief of Staff:
   Wendy Saunders.................................... 518-473-0458
Deputy Commissioner, Administration:
   Robert W Reed..................................... 518-474-8565
Director, Human Resources & Operations:
   John R Conroy................... 518-473-3394/fax: 518-486-7374

Public Affairs
Director:
   Claudia Hutton 518-474-7354

Center for Environmental Health .... fax: 518-402-7509
547 River St, Troy, NY 12180
Director:
   Ronald Tramontano 518-402-7500

Division of Environmental Health Investigation
Associate Director:
   G Anders Carlson................................... 518-402-7501

Environmental Health Assessment Division
Director:
   Nancy Kim 518-402-7511/fax: 518-402-7509
Associate Director:
   John Wilson 518-402-7511

Environmental Protection
Director:
   Richard Svenson.................................... 518-402-7510

Wadsworth Center
Director:
   Lawrence S Sturman 518-474-7592/fax: 518-474-3439
Deputy Director:
   Jill Taylor 518-474-3157
Director, Education:
   Kathy Zdeb 518-474-6713/fax: 518-474-5049
Associate Director, Operations & Administration:
   Barbara Ryan.................... 518-474-1151/fax: 518-474-3439
Director, Policy & Planning:
   Ann Willey 518-486-2523/fax: 518-474-3439
Director, Research:
   Robert Trimble 518-486-2565/fax: 518-402-5540

Environmental Disease Prevention
Director:
   Ken Aldous 518-474-7161/fax: 518-473-2895
Deputy Director:
   Patrick Parsons 518-474-7161/fax: 518-473-2895

Hudson River Valley Greenway
Capitol Building, Rm 254
Capitol Station
Albany, NY 12224
518-473-3835 Fax: 518-473-4518
e-mail: hrvg@hudsongreenway.state.ny.us
Web site: www.hudsongreenway.state.ny.us

Greenway Conservancy for the Hudson River Valley
Board Chair:
   Kevin J Plunkett................................... 518-473-3835
Executive Director:
   Mary Mangione 518-473-3835

Hudson River Valley Greenway Communities Council
Board Chair:
   Barnabas McHenry.................................. 518-473-3835
Executive Director:
   Mary Mangione 518-473-3835

Law Department
120 Broadway
New York, NY 10271-0332
212-416-8000 Fax: 212-416-8796

State Capitol
Albany, NY 12224-0341
518-474-7330
Fax: -18-402-2472

Attorney General:
   Andrew M Cuomo 518-474-7330
First Deputy Attorney General:
   Michele Hirshman 212-416-8050
Asst Deputy Attorney General, Program Development:
   Vacant 212-416-8167
Asst Attorney General, Legislative Bureau:
   Kathy Bennett..................................... 518-486-3000
Director, Public Information & Correspondence:
   Peter Drago 518-474-7330/fax: 518-402-2472

Public Advocacy Division
Deputy Attorney General:
   Dietrich Snell.................... 212-416-8041/fax: 212-416-8068
Special Counsel:
   Mary Ellen Burns 212-416-6155

Environmental Protection Bureau
Bureau Chief:
   Peter Lehner 212-416-8450/fax: 212-416-6007

Parks, Recreation & Historic Preservation, NYS Office of
Empire State Plaza
Bldg 1
Albany, NY 12238
518-486-0456 Fax: 518-486-2924
Web site: www.nysparks.com

Commissioner:
   Carol Ash 518-474-0443
Executive Deputy Commissioner:
   Andy Beers....................................... 518-473-5385
Deputy Commissioner, Finance & Administration:
   Pete Finn... 518-474-0440
Deputy Commissioner, Operations:
   Daniel Kane 518-474-0414
Deputy Commissioner, Open Space:
   Erik Kulleseid.................................... 518-474-0402
Counsel:
   Glen Bruening 518-474-0447
Director, Communication:
   Eileen Larrabee................................... 518-486-1868

Offices and agencies generally appear in alphabetical order, except when specific order is requested by listee.

ENVIRONMENT & NATURAL RESOURCES / New York State

Acting Director, Natural Heritage Trust:
    Elaine Bartley 518-474-2997
Director, Natural Resources:
    Ralph Odell 845-889-4100
Director, Law Enforcement:
    James Warwick 518-474-4029

Historic Preservation

Field Services
Peebles Island, Waterford, NY 12118
Director:
    Ruth Pierpont 518-237-8643

Historic Sites Bureau
Peebles Island, Waterford, NY 12118
Director:
    James P Gold 518-237-8643

Marine & Recreational Vehicles

Director:
    Brian Kempf 518-474-0445

Resource Management

Environmental Management
Director:
    Thomas Lyons 518-474-0409

Planning & Development
Director:
    Robert W Reinhardt 518-474-0415

Advisory Groups

State Board for Historic Preservation
Chairman:
    Robert MacKay 631-692-4664

State Council of Parks, Recreation & Historic Preservation
Agency Contact:
    Carol Ash 518-486-1868

State Comptroller, Office of the

110 State St, 15th Fl
Albany, NY 12236-0001
518-474-4040 Fax: 518-473-3004
Web site: www.osc.state.ny.us

633 Third Ave, 31st Fl
New York, NY 10017-0001
212-681-4491
Fax: 212-681-4468

State Comptroller:
    Thomas DiNapoli . . . . 518-474-4040 or 212-681-4491

Executive Office
Chief of Staff:
    Jack Chartier 212-681-4498
First Deputy Comptroller:
    Thomas Sanzillo 518-474-2909
Executive Deputy Comptroller:
    Diana J Ritter 518-474-3610
Deputy Chief of Staff:
    Roberta Rubin . . . . 212-681-4495 or 518-474-4040

Oil Spill Fund Office
Executive Director:
    Anne Hohenstein 518-474-6657/fax: 518-474-9979

State Department

123 William St
New York, NY 10038
212-417-5801 Fax: 212-417-5805
Web site: www.dos.state.ny.us

41 State St
Albany, NY 12231
518-474-0050
Fax: 518-474-4765

Secretary of State:
    Lorraine A Cortes-Vazquez 518-474-0050
First Deputy Secretary of State:
    Daniel Shapiro 518-474-4750
Assistant Secretary of State, Communications:
    Laurence Sombke 518-474-4752/fax: 518-474-4597
    e-mail: info@dos.state.ny.us
Deputy Secretary of State, Public Affairs:
    Eamon Moynihan 212-417-5800
Counsel:
    Susan Watson 518-474-6740/fax: 518-473-9211

Local Government & Community Services
Deputy Secretary of State:
    Matthew Andrus 518-486-9888/fax: 518-474-6572

Coastal Resources & Waterfront Revitalization Division
Director:
    George Stafford 518-474-6000/fax: 518-473-2464
    e-mail: coastal@dos.state.ny.us

Community Services Division
Director:
    Evelyn M Harris 518-474-5741/fax: 518-486-4663
    e-mail: commserv@dos.state.ny.us

Fire Prevention & Control Office
State Fire Administrator:
    James A Burns 518-474-6746/fax: 518-474-3240
    e-mail: fire@dos.state.ny.us
    New York State Academy of Fire Science
      600 College Ave, Montour Falls, NY 14865-9634
      Director:
        Richard Nagle 607-535-7136/fax: 607-535-4841

CORPORATIONS, AUTHORITIES AND COMMISSIONS

Adirondack Park Agency
1133 NYS Route 86
Ray Brook, NY 12977
518-891-4050 Fax: 518-891-3938
Web site: www.apa.state.ny.us

Chair:
    Vacant 518-891-4050
Executive Director:
    Vacant 518-891-4050
Counsel:
    John S Banta 518-891-4050
Associate Counsel:
    Barbara A Rottier 518-891-4050
Public Relations:
    Keith McKeever 518-891-4050

Offices and agencies generally appear in alphabetical order, except when specific order is requested by listee.

ENVIRONMENT & NATURAL RESOURCES / New York State

Atlantic States Marine Fisheries Commission
1444 Eye St NW
6th Fl
Washington, DC 20005
202-289-6400 Fax: 202-289-6051
e-mail: info@asmfc.org
Web site: www.asmfc.org

Chair, Maine:
   George D Lapointe.................................207-624-6553
Administrative Commissioner, New York:
   Gordon C Colvin....................................516-444-0433
Governor's Appointee, New York:
   Pat Augustine..631-928-1524
Legislative Commissioner, New York:
   Senator Owen H Johnson.........................516-669-9200
Executive Director:
   John V O'Shea......................................202-289-6400
   e-mail: voshea@asmfc.org
Public Affairs & Resource Specialist:
   Tina Berger..202-289-6400
   e-mail: tberger@asmfc.org

Central Pine Barrens Joint Planning & Policy Commission
PO Box 587
3525 Sunrise Hwy, 2nd Fl
Great River, NY 11739
631-224-2604 Fax: 631-224-7653
e-mail: info@pb.state.ny.us
Web site: www.pb.state.ny.us

Chair & Governor's Appointee & Region 1 Director DEC:
   Peter A Scully.......................................631-224-2604
Executive Director:
   Ray Corwin..631-224-2604
Member & Suffolk County Executive:
   Steve Levy...631-224-2604
Member & Brookhaven Town Supervisor:
   Brian X Foley.......................................631-224-2604
Member & Riverhead Town Supervisor:
   Philip J Cardinale..................................631-224-2604
Member & Southampton Town Supervisor:
   Patrick A Heaney..................................631-224-2604

Delaware River Basin Commission
25 State Police Dr
PO Box 7360
West Trenton, NJ 08628-0360
609-883-9500 Fax: 609-883-9522
Web site: www.drbc.net

New York Member:
   Eliot Spitzer...518-474-8390
Executive Director:
   Carol R Collier..............................609-883-9500 x200
   e-mail: carol.collier@drbc.state.nj.us
Deputy Executive Director:
   Robert Tudor.................................609-883-9500 x208
   e-mail: robert.tudor@drbc.state.nj.us
Commission Secretary & Assistant General Counsel:
   Pamela Bush.................................609-883-9500 x203
   e-mail: pamela.bush@drbc.state.nj.us

General Counsel:
   Kenneth J Warren.................................215-977-2276
   e-mail: kwarren@wolfblock.com
Communications Manager:
   Clarke Rupert................................609-883-9500 x260
   e-mail: clarke.rupert@drbc.state.nj.us

Great Lakes Commission
2805 S Industrial Hwy
Ste 100
Ann Arbor, MI 48104-6791
734-971-9135 Fax: 734-971-9150
e-mail: teder@glc.org
Web site: www.glc.org

Chairman:
   John Cherry...517-373-6800
Vice Chair:
   Patrick Quinn.......................................312-814-4866
New York State Commissioner:
   Alexander B Grannis................518-402-8540/fax: 518-402-8541
Executive Director:
   Tim A Eder..734-971-9135
   e-mail: teder@glc.org
Program Manager, Communications & Internet Technology:
   Christine Manninen................................734-971-9135
   e-mail: manninen@glc.org
Program Manager, Data & Information Management:
   Roger Gauthier.....................................734-971-9135
   e-mail: gauthier@glc.org
Program Manager, Environmental Quality:
   Matthew Doss......................................734-971-9135
   e-mail: mdoss@glc.org
Program Manager, Resource Management:
   Thomas R Crane...................................734-971-9135
   e-mail: tcrane@glc.org
Program Manager, Transportation & Sustainable Development:
   Dave Knight..734-971-9135
   e-mail: dknight@glc.org

Hudson River-Black River Regulating District
Hudson River Area Office
350 Northern Blvd
Albany, NY 12204
518-465-3491 Fax: 518-432-2485
e-mail: hrao@hrbrrd.com
Web site: www.hrbrrd.com

Chair:
   Anne B McDonald.................................518-465-3491
Executive Director:
   Glenn A LaFave....................................518-465-3491
Chief Engineer:
   Robert S Foltan....................................518-465-3491
Chief Fiscal Officer:
   Robert J Ferrara...................................518-465-3491
General Counsel:
   William L Busler..................................518-465-3491

Interstate Environmental Commission
311 W 43rd St
Ste 201
New York, NY 10036

Offices and agencies generally appear in alphabetical order, except when specific order is requested by listee.

ENVIRONMENT & NATURAL RESOURCES / New York State

212-582-0380 Fax: 212-581-5719
e-mail: iecmail@iec-nynjct.org
Web site: www.iec-nynjct.org

Chair:
  John Atkin 212-582-0380
Executive Director & Chief Engineer:
  Howard Golub 212-582-0380
General Counsel:
  Eileen D Millett 212-582-0380

Interstate Oil & Gas Compact Commission
PO Box 53127
Oklahoma City, OK 73152-3127
405-525-3556 Fax: 405-525-3592
e-mail: iogcc@iogcc.state.ok.us
Web site: www.iogcc.state.ok.us

Chair:
  John Hoeven 405-525-3556
Vice Chair:
  Victor Carrillo 405-525-3556
Executive Director:
  Christine Hansen 405-525-3556
New York State Official Representative:
  Bradley J Field 518-402-8076
Communications Manager:
  Erica Carr 405-525-3556

Lake George Park Commission
75 Fort George Rd
PO Box 749
Lake George, NY 12845-0749
518-668-9347 Fax: 518-668-5001
e-mail: info@lgpc.state.ny.us
Web site: www.lgpc.state.ny.us

Chair:
  Bruce E Young 518-668-9347
Vice Chair:
  Thomas K Conerty 518-668-9347
Executive Director:
  Michael P White 518-668-9347
Secretary/Treasurer:
  John A Pettica, Jr 518-668-9347

New England Interstate Water Pollution Control Commission
Boott Mills South
100 Foot of John St
Lowell, MA 01852-1124
978-323-7929 Fax: 978-323-7919
e-mail: mail@neiwpcc.org
Web site: www.neiwpcc.org

Chair:
  Harry Stewart 603-271-3380
Vice Chair:
  Alicia Good 401-222-4700
Commissioner, New York State:
  Denise M Sheehan 518-485-8940

Executive Director:
  Ronald F Poltak 978-323-7929
Deputy Director:
  Susan Sullivan 978-323-7929

New York State Energy Research & Development Authority
17 Columbia Circle
Albany, NY 12203-6399
518-862-1090 Fax: 518-862-1091
Web site: www.nyserda.org

Chairman:
  Vincent A DeIorio 518-862-1090
President & CEO:
  Peter R Smith 518-862-1090 x3320
  e-mail: prs@nyserda.org
General Counsel (Acting):
  Hal Brodie 518-862-1090 x3280
  e-mail: hb1@nyserda.org
Vice President, Programs:
  Robert Callender 518-862-1090 x3233
  e-mail: rgc@nyserda.org
Treasurer:
  Jeffrey J Pitkin 518-862-1090 x3223
  e-mail: jjp@nyserda.org
Director, Communications (Acting):
  Colleen Q Ryan 518-862-1090 x3359/fax: 518-464-8249
  e-mail: cqr@nyserda.org

New York State Environmental Facilities Corp
625 Broadway
Albany, NY 12207-2997
518-402-6924 or 800-882-9721 Fax: 518-486-9323
Web site: www.nysefc.org

Chair:
  Alexander B Grannis 518-402-6924
President & CEO:
  David Sterman 518-402-6924
Executive Vice President:
  Matthew Millea . . . . 518-402-6924 or J
Senior VP & General Counsel:
  James R Levine 518-402-6969
Chief Financial Officer:
  James T Gebhardt 518-402-6985
Director, Engineering & Program Management:
  Robert E Davis 518-402-7396
Director, Technical Advisory Services:
  Frederick D McCandless 518-402-7461
Director, Corporate Communications:
  Susan Mayer 518-402-6957
Controller & Director, Corporate Operations:
  Michael Malinoski 518-486-9267

New York State Tug Hill Commission
Dulles State Office Bldg
317 Washington St
Watertown, NY 13601
315-785-2380 Fax: 315-785-2574
e-mail: tughill@tughill.org
Web site: www.tughill.org

Offices and agencies generally appear in alphabetical order, except when specific order is requested by listee.

ENVIRONMENT & NATURAL RESOURCES / New York State

Chair:
   Kenneth W Vigus..................................315-785-2380
Executive Director:
   John K Bartow, Jr................................315-785-2380
   e-mail: john@tughill.org
Counsel:
   James P McClusky.................................315-232-4551

Northeastern Forest Fire Protection Commission
21 Parmenter Terrace
PO Box 6192
China Village, ME 04926-6192
207-968-3782 Fax: 207-968-3782
e-mail: info@nffpc.org
Web site: www.nffpc.org

Chair of Commissioners:
   Walter Fanning....................................902-758-7236
   e-mail: fanninwf@gov.ns.ca
Vice Chair of Commissioners:
   Philip A Bryce....................................603-271-2217
   e-mail: pbryce@dred.state.nh.us
Executive Director:
   Thomas G Parent...................................207-968-3782
   e-mail: necompact@fairpoint.net
Operations Committee, Chair:
   Andrew Jacob......................................518-402-8832
   e-mail: atjacob@gw.dec.state.ny.us
New York State Fire Prevention:
   Adam Pickett......................................315-823-9252
   e-mail: ajpicket@gw.dec.state.ny.us

Northeastern Queens Nature & Historical Preserve Commission
Bldg 635, Bayside St, Box 5
Fort Totten, NY 11359-1012
718-229-8805 Fax: 718-229-6131
e-mail: sneq@aol.com
Web site: www.sneq.com

Chair:
   Bernard Haber.....................................718-229-8805
Vice Chair:
   William Nieter....................................718-229-8805
Executive Director:
   Joan M Vogt.......................................718-229-8805

Ohio River Valley Water Sanitation Commission
5735 Kellogg Ave
Cincinnati, OH 45228-1112
513-231-7719 Fax: 513-231-7761
e-mail: info@orsanco.org
Web site: www.orsanco.org

New York State Commissioner:
   Douglas E Conroe..................................513-231-7719
New York State Commissioner:
   T Lee Servatius...................................513-231-7719
New York State Commissioner:
   Alexander B Grannis...............................518-457-3446

Executive Director:
   Alan H Vicory, Jr.................................513-231-7719
   e-mail: avicory@orsanco.org
Legal Counsel:
   Ross Wales..513-231-7719
Public Information Programs Manager:
   Jeanne Ison.......................................513-231-7719
   e-mail: jison@orsanco.org

NEW YORK STATE LEGISLATURE

See Legislative Branch in Section 1 for additional Standing Committee and Subcommittee information.

Assembly Standing Committees

Environmental Conservation
Chair:
   Robert K Sweeney (D).............................518-455-5787
Ranking Minority Member:
   Teresa Sayward (R)...............................518-455-5565

Senate Standing Committees

Environmental Conservation
Chair:
   Carl L Marcellino (R)............................518-455-2390
Ranking Minority Member:
   Craig Johnson (D)................................518-455-2622

Senate/Assembly Legislative Commissions

Rural Resources, Legislative Commission on
Senate Chair:
   George H Winner Jr (R)...........................518-455-2091
Assembly Vice Chair:
   David R Koon (D).................................518-455-5784
Senate Executive Director:
   Ronald C Brach............518-455-2544/fax: 518-426-6960
Assembly Director:
   Susan Bartle..............518-455-3999/fax: 518-455-4175
Counsel:
   Donald A Walsh...................................518-455-2544

Solid Waste Management, Legislative Commission on
Assembly Chair:
   William Colton (D)...............................518-455-5828
Senate Vice Chair:
   Vacant...518-455-0000
Program Manager:
   Richard D Morse, Jr.......518-455-3711/fax: 518-455-3837

Toxic Substances & Hazardous Wastes, Legislative Commission on
Senate Chair:
   Vacant...518-455-0000
Assembly Vice Chair:
   David R Koon (D).................................518-455-5784
Program Manager:
   Richard D Morse, Jr.......518-455-3711/fax: 518-455-3837

Water Resource Needs of NYS & Long Island, Legislative Commission on
Assembly Co-Chair:
   Vacant...518-455-0000

Offices and agencies generally appear in alphabetical order, except when specific order is requested by listee.

ENVIRONMENT & NATURAL RESOURCES / U.S. Government

Senate Co-Chair:
   Vacant 518-455-0000

Program Manager:
   Richard D Morse, Jr 518-455-3711/fax: 518-455-3837

U.S. Government

EXECUTIVE DEPARTMENTS AND RELATED AGENCIES

US Commerce Department
Web site: www.doc.gov

National Oceanic & Atmospheric Administration

National Marine Fisheries Svc, Northeast Region Headquarters . . fax: 978-281-9333
One Blackburn Dr, Gloucester, MA 01930
Fax: 978-281-9333
Web site: www.nero.noaa.gov/nero/
Regional Administrator:
   Patricia A Kurkul 978-281-9200

National Weather Service, Eastern Region
630 Johnson Ave, Ste 202, Bohemia, NY 11716
Web site: www.nws.noaa.gov
Director:
   Dean Gulezian 631-244-0100/fax: 631-244-0109
   e-mail: dean.gulezian@noaa.gov
Deputy Director:
   Mickey J Brown 631-244-0102
Public Affairs Specialist:
   Marcie Katcher 631-244-0149/fax: 631-244-0167
Chief, Meteorological Services Division:
   John Guiney 631-244-1021

US Defense Department
e-mail: www.defenselink.mil

Army Corps of Engineers
Web site: www.usace.army.mil

Great Lakes & Ohio River Division (Western NYS)
550 Main St, PO Box 1159, Cincinnati, OH 45201-1159
Commander:
   BG Bruce A Berwick 513-684-3002/fax: 513-684-2085
   Buffalo District Office . . . . fax: 716-879-4195
      1776 Niagara St, Buffalo, NY 14207-3199
      716-879-4200 Fax: 716-879-4195
      Deputy Commander:
         Maj R Brian Phillips 716-879-4200
      District Commander:
         LTC Timothy B Touchette 716-879-4201

North Atlantic Division
302 General Lee Ave, Ft Hamilton Military Cmty, Brooklyn, NY 11252
Commander:
   William T Grisoli 718-765-7000
Deputy Commander:
   Christopher Larsen 718-765-7001
Executive Officer:
   Steve Sattinger 718-765-7002
Emergency Mgmt Specialist:
   Carmine Leone 718-765-7074
Public Affairs Officer:
   David J Lipsky 718-765-7018/fax: 718-765-7173

Program Directorate
Director of Programs:
   Lloyd Caldwell 718-765-7129
Supervisory Civil Engineer, Civil Works Integration Div:
   Larry Petrosino 718-765-7060
Supervisory Civil Engineer, Military Integration Div:
   Bob Mawhinney 718-765-7120
Supervisory Civil Engineer, Program Support Div:
   Joseph Vietri 718-765-7080
Regional Business Directorate
Regional Business Director:
   Mohan Singh 718-765-7055
Director/Financial Manager:
   Irma Nanez 718-765-7033
Supervisory Program Manager, Business Mgmt Div:
   Larry Mazzola 718-765-7127
Supervisory Civil Engineer, Business Technical Div:
   John Bianco 718-765-7086

US Department of Agriculture

Forest Service-Northeastern Area State & Private Forestry
11 Campus Blvd, Ste 200, Newtown Square, PA 19073
Area Director:
   Kathryn P Maloney 610-557-4103/fax: 610-557-4177
Deputy Director:
   Larry Mastic 610-557-4103/fax: 610-557-4177
Asst Director, Forest Health & Economics:
   Jerry Boughton 610-557-4139/fax: 610-557-4136
Asst Director, Fire Management:
   Billy Terry 610-557-4152/fax: 610-557-4154
Asst Director, Forest Management:
   N Robin Morgan 610-557-4124/fax: 610-557-4136
Asst Director, Information Management & Analysis:
   Susan E Lacy 610-557-4114/fax: 610-557-4177

Forest Service-Northern Research Station
11 Campus Blvd, Ste 200, Newton Square, PA 19073
Director:
   Michael T Rains 610-557-4017
Deputy Director:
   Roy Patton 610-557-4107

Forest Service-Region 9
Web site: www.fs.fed.us

Green Mountain & Finger Lakes . . . . fax: 802-747-6766
231 N Main St, Rutland, VT 05701
802-747-6700 Fax: 802-747-6766
   Finger Lakes National Forest . . . . fax: 607-546-4474
   5218 State Route 414, Hector, NY 14841
   District Ranger:
      Mike Liu 607-546-4470

Natural Resources Conservation Service . . . . fax: 315-477-6550
441 S Salina St, Suite 354, Syracuse, NY 13202-2450
Fax: 315-477-6550
Web site: www.ny.nrcs.usda.gov
State Conservationist:
   Ron Alverado 315-477-6504

Offices and agencies generally appear in alphabetical order, except when specific order is requested by listee.

ENVIRONMENT & NATURAL RESOURCES / U.S. Government

US Department of Homeland Security (DHS)

Environmental Measurements Laboratory
201 Varick St, 5th Fl, New York, NY 10014-7447
Web site: www.eml.st.dhs.gov
Director:
  Mitchell D Erickson 212-620-3619/fax: 212-620-3651
  e-mail: mitchell.erickson@dhs.gov

Administration
Director:
  Richard Larsen 212-620-3524/fax: 212-620-3600
  e-mail: richard.larsen@dhs.gov

Systems Division
Director:
  Lawrence Ruth 212-620-3609/fax: 212-620-3600
  e-mail: lawrence.ruth@dhs.gov

Testbeds Division
Director:
  Adam Hutter 212-620-3619/fax: 212-620-3651
  e-mail: adam.hutter@dhs.gov

US Department of the Interior
e-mail: webteam@ios.doi.gov
Web site: www.doi.gov

Bureau of Land Management
e-mail: woinfo@blm.gov
Web site: www.blm.gov

Eastern States Office (includes New York State) . . . . fax: 703-440-1701
7450 Boston Blvd, Springfield, VA 22153
State Director:
  Michael D Nedd 703-440-1711

Fish & Wildlife Service . . . . fax: 413-253-8303
413-253-8200 Fax: 413-253-8303
e-mail: northeast@fws.gov
Web site: www.fws.gov

Northeast Region (includes New York State) . . . . fax: 413-253-8308
300 Westgate Center Dr, Hadley, MA 01035
Regional Director:
  Marvin E Moriarty 413-253-8200

Geological Survey
Web site: ny.usgs.gov

Water Resources Division - New York State District Office
425 Jordan Rd, Troy, NY 12180-8349
District Chief:
  Rafael W Rodriguez 518-285-5659/fax: 518-285-5601
  Coram Sub-District Office . . . . fax: 631-736-4283
  2045 Rte 112, Bldg 4, Coram, NY 11727
  Sub-District Chief:
    Vacant 631-736-0783 x102
  Ithaca Sub-District Office . . . . fax: 607-266-0521
  30 Brown Rd, Ithaca, NY 14850-1573
  Sub-District Chief:
    Edward Bugliosi 607-266-0217 x3005

National Park Service-Northeast Region
200 Chestnut St, US Custom House, Philadelphia, PA 19106
Web site: www.nps.gov
Northeast Regional Director:
  Mary A Bomar 215-597-7013/fax: 215-597-0815

Fire Island National Seashore . . . . fax: 631-289-4898
120 Laurel St, Patchogue, NY 11772

631-289-4810 Fax: 631-289-4898
Superintendent:
  Michael Reynolds 631-289-4810/fax: 631-289-4898

Office of the Secretary, Environmental Policy & Compliance

Northeast Region (includes New York State)
408 Atlantic Ave, Rm 142, Boston, MA 02210-3334
Regional Environmental Officer:
  Andrew L Raddant 617-223-8565/fax: 617-223-8569

Office of the Solicitor

Northeast Region (includes New York State) . . . . fax: 617-527-6848
One Gateway Center, Ste 612, Newton, MA 02458-2881
Regional Solicitor:
  Anthony R Conte 617-527-3400
Deputy Regional Solicitor:
  James E Epstein 617-527-3400
Attorney Advisor:
  Martha F Ansty 802-872-0629 x17
Attorney Advisor:
  Mark D Barash 617-527-3400
Attorney Advisor:
  Marcia F Gittes 617-527-3400
Attorney Advisor:
  J Robin Lepore 617-527-3400
Attorney Advisor:
  Katherine Buttolph 617-527-3400
Attorney Advisor:
  David Rothstein 617-527-3400
Attorney Advisor:
  Katharine M Costenbader 617-527-3400
Attorney Advisor:
  Andrew Tittler 617-527-3400

US Environmental Protection Agency
Web site: www.epa.gov

Region 2 - New York . . . . fax: 212-637-3526
290 Broadway, New York, NY 10007
212-637-3660 Fax: 212-637-3526
Regional Administrator:
  Alan Steinberg 212-637-5000
Acting Deputy Regional Administrator:
  Kathleen Callahan 212-637-5000

Caribbean Environmental Protection Division (CEPD)
Director:
  Carl-Axel P Soderberg 787-977-5814

Division of Enforcement & Compliance Assistance (DECA)
Director:
  Dore LaPosta 212-637-4031

Division of Environmental Planning & Protection (DEPP)
Director:
  Walter Mugdan 212-637-3725

Division of Environmental Science & Assessment (DESA)
2890 Woodbridge Ave, Edison, NJ 08837-3679
Director:
  Barbara A Finazzo 732-321-6754
  e-mail: finazzo.barbara@epa.gov

Emergency & Remedial Response Division (ERRD)
Director:
  George Pavlou 212-637-4391

Offices and agencies generally appear in alphabetical order, except when specific order is requested by listee.

ENVIRONMENT & NATURAL RESOURCES / U.S. Government

Inspector General, Office of (OIG)
Divisional Inspector General, Investigation:
    Paul Zammit 212-637-3042/fax: 212-637-3071
    e-mail: zammit.paul@epa.gov

OCEFT/Criminal Investigations Division
Special-Agent-In-Charge:
    William V Lometti 212-637-3610
    e-mail: lometti.william@epa.gov

Policy & Management, Office of
Asst Regional Administrator for Policy & Management:
    Donna Vizian 212-637-3581

Public Affairs Division (PAD)
Director:
    Bonnie Bellow 212-637-3660/fax: 212-637-5046
    e-mail: bellow.bonnie@epa.gov

Regional Counsel, Office of (ORC)
Deputy Regional Counsel:
    Eric Schaaf 212-637-3107
    e-mail: schaaf.eric@epa.gov

U.S. CONGRESS

See U.S. Congress Chapter for additional Standing Committee and Subcommittee information.

House of Representatives Standing Committees

Agriculture
Chair:
    Collin C Peterson (D-MN) 202-225-2165
Ranking Minority Member:
    Bob Goodlatte (R-VA) 202-225-5431
    Subcommittees
    Department Operations, Oversight, Nutrition & Forestry
    Chair:
        Joe Baca (D-CA) 202-225-6161
    Ranking Minority Member:
        Jo Bonner (R-AL) 202-225-4931
    General Farm Commodities & Risk Management
    Chair:
        Bob Etheridge (D-NC) 202-225-4531
    Ranking Minority Member:
        Jerry Moran (R-KS) 202-225-2715
    Horticulture and Organic Agriculture
    Chair:
        Dennis A Cardoza (D-CA) 202-225-6131
    Ranking Minority Member:
        Randy Neugebauer (R-TX) 202-225-4005
    Specialty Crops, Rural Development and Foreign Agriculture
    Chair:
        Mike McIntyre (D-NC) 202-225-2731
    Ranking Minority Member:
        Marilyn N Musgrave (R-CO) 202-225-4676

Energy & Commerce
Chair:
    John D Dingell (D-MI) 202-225-2927
Ranking Minority Member:
    Joe Barton (R-TX) 202-225-2002
New York Delegate:
    Eliot L Engel (D) 202-225-2464
New York Delegate:
    Vito Fossella (R) 202-225-3371
New York Delegate:
    Edolphus Towns (D) 202-225-5936
    Subcommittees
    Energy & Air Quality
    Chair:
        Rick Boucher (D-VA) 202-225-3861
    Ranking Minority Member:
        J Dennis Hastert (R-IL) 202-225-2976
    New York Delegate:
        Eliot L Engel (D) 202-225-3371
    New York Delegate:
        Vito Fossella (R) 202-225-3371
    Environment & Hazardous Materials
    Chair:
        Albert R Wynn (D-MD) 202-225-8699
    Ranking Minority Member:
        John Shimkus (R-IL) 202-225-5271
    New York Delegate:
        Vito Fossella (R) 202-225-3371

Natural Resources
Chair:
    Nick J Rahall, II (D-WV) 202-225-6065
Ranking Minority Member:
    Don Young (R-AK) 202-225-5765

Science & Technology
Chair:
    Bart Gordon (D-TN) 202-225-4231
Ranking Minority Member:
    Ralph M Hall (R-TX) 202-225-6673
    Subcommittee
    Energy & Environment
    Chair:
        Nick Lampson (D-TX) 202-225-5951
    Ranking Minority Member:
        Bob Inglis (R-SC) 202-225-6030

Transportation & Infrastructure
Chair:
    James L Oberstar (D-MN) 202-225-4472
Ranking Minority Member:
    John L Mica (FL) 202-225-4035
New York Delegate:
    Timothy Bishop (D) 202-225-3826
New York Delegate:
    Sherwood Boehlert (R) 202-225-3665
New York Delegate:
    Brian M Higgins (D) 202-225-3306
New York Delegate:
    Sue W Kelly (R) 202-225-5441
New York Delegate:
    John R (Randy) Kuhl (R) 202-225-3161
New York Delegate:
    Jerrold Nadler (D) 202-225-5635
New York Delegate:
    Anthony Weiner (D) 202-225-6616
    Subcommittee
    Water Resources & Environment
    Chair:
        Eddie Bernice Johnson (D-TX) 202-225-0060
    Ranking Minority Member:
        Richard H Baker (R-LA) 202-225-3901
    New York Delegate:
        Timothy Bishop (D) 202-225-3826
    New York Delegate:
        Sherwood L Boehlert (R) 202-225-3665

Offices and agencies generally appear in alphabetical order, except when specific order is requested by listee.

ENVIRONMENT & NATURAL RESOURCES / Private Sector

New York Delegate:
   Brian M Higgins (D) 202-225-3306
New York Delegate:
   Sue W Kelly (R) 202-225-5441

Senate Standing Committees

Agriculture, Nutrition & Forestry
Chair:
  Tom Harkin (D-IA) 202-224-3254
Ranking Republican Member:
  Saxby Chambliss (R-GA) 202-224-3521

Subcommittee
Rural Revitalization, Conservation, Forestry and Credit
  Chair:
    Debbie Stabenow (D-MI) 202-224-4822
  Ranking Minority Member:
    Mike Crapo (R-ID) 202-224-6142

Commerce, Science & Transportation
Chair:
  Daniel K Inouye (D-HI) 202-224-3934

Ranking Minority Member:
  Ted Stevens (R-AK) 202-224-3004

Subcommittee
Oceans, Atmosphere, Fisheries and Coast Guard
  Chair:
    Maria Cantwell (D-WA) 202-224-3441
  Ranking Minority Member:
    Olympia J Snowe (R-ME) 202-224-5344

Energy & Natural Resources
Chair:
  Jeff Bingaman (D-NM) 202-224-4971
Ranking Minority Member:
  Pete V Domenici (R-NM) 202-224-4971

Environment & Public Works
Chair:
  Barbara Boxer (D-CA) 202-224-8832
Ranking Minority Member:
  James M Inhofe (R-OK) 202-224-6176
New York Delegate:
  Hillary Rodham Clinton (D) 202-224-4451

Private Sector

Adirondack Council Inc (The)
103 Hand Ave, Ste 3, Box D-2, Elizabethtown, NY 12932
518-873-2240 Fax: 518-873-6675
e-mail: info@adirondackcouncil.org
Web site: www.adirondackcouncil.org
Brian L Houseal, Executive Director
The Council's mission is to ensure the ecological integrity and wild character of the Adirondack Park.

Adirondack Mountain Club Inc
301 Hamilton Street, Albany, NY 12210-1738
518-449-3870 Fax: 518-449-3875
e-mail: adk@nycap.rr.com; marisatedesco@nycap.rr.com
Web site: www.adk.org
Neil F Woodworth, Executive Director;, Marisa Tedesco, Conservation & Legislative Director; Ian Brown, Land Use Planner
Hiking, nonmotorized recreation, conservation & education

American Museum of Natural History
Central Park West at 79th St, New York, NY 10024-5192
212-769-5100 Fax: 212-769-5018
e-mail: info@amnh.org
Web site: www.amnh.org
Ellen V Futter, President
Education, exhibition & scientific research

Audubon New York
200 Trillium Lane, Albany, NY 12203
518-869-9731 Fax: 518-869-0737
e-mail: nasny@audubon.org
Web site: ny.audubon.org
David J Miller, Executive Director
Protecting birds, other wildlife & their habitats

Audubon Society of NYS Inc (The) / Audubon International
Hollyhock Hollow Sanctuary, 46 Rarick Rd, Selkirk, NY 12158
518-767-9051 x20 Fax: 518-767-0069
e-mail: hjack@auduboninternational.org
Web site: www.auduboninternational.org
Howard A Jack, Vice President & Chief Operating Officer
Wildlife & water conservation; environmental education; sustainable land management

Brooklyn Botanic Garden
1000 Washington Ave, Brooklyn, NY 11225-1099
718-623-7200 Fax: 718-857-2430
Web site: www.bbg.org
Scot Medbury, President & CEO
Comprehensive study of plant biodiversity in metropolitan New York; home gardener's resource center

Business Council of New York State Inc
152 Washington Ave, Albany, NY 12210
518-465-7511 x205 Fax: 518-465-4389
e-mail: ken.pokalsky@bcnys.org
Web site: www.bcnys.org
Kenneth J Pokalsky, Director, Environmental & Manufacturing Programs
Environment, manufacturing, economic development

CWM Chemical Services LLC
1550 Balmer Rd, PO Box 200, Model City, NY 14107
716-754-8231 Fax: 716-754-0211
e-mail: cwmmdc@wm.com
Web site: www.cwmlandfill.com
Michael Mahar, District Manager
Hazardous waste treatment, storage & disposal

Offices and agencies generally appear in alphabetical order, except when specific order is requested by listee.

ENVIRONMENT & NATURAL RESOURCES / Private Sector

Catskill Center for Conservation & Development
PO Box 504, Route 28, Arkville, NY 12406-0504
845-586-2611 Fax: 845-586-3044
e-mail: cccd@catskillcenter.org
Web site: www.catskillcenter.org
Tom Alworth, Executive Director
Advocacy for environmental & economic health of the Catskill Mountain region

Center for Environmental Information Inc
55 St Paul St, Rochester, NY 14604-1314
585-262-2870 Fax: 585-262-4156
e-mail: cei@frontiernet.net
Web site: www.ceinfo.org
Public information & education on environmental topics

Citizens' Environmental Coalition
119 Washington Ave, Albany, NY 12210
518-462-5527 Fax: 518-465-8349
e-mail: cectoxic@igc.org
Web site: www.cectoxic.org ; www.kodakstoxicolors.org
Michael Schade, Western NY Director
Organizing & assistance for communities concerned about toxic waste, air & water contamination & pollution prevention

Colgate University, Department of Geology
13 Oak Dr, Hamilton, NY 13346
315-228-7201 Fax: 315-228-7187
e-mail: bselleck@mail.colgate.edu
Web site: departments.colgate.edu/geology
Bruce Selleck, Chair of Geology
Marine geology; coastal geology

Columbia University, MPA in Environmental Science & Policy
420 W 118th St, Rm 1314, New York, NY 10027
212-854-4445 or 212-854-3142 Fax: 212-864-4847
e-mail: sc32@columbia.edu
Web site: www.columbia.edu/~sc32
Steven Cohen, Director
Urban & environmental policy; public management

Commodore Applied Technologies Inc
150 East 58th St, Ste 3238, New York, NY 10155-0001
212-308-5800 Fax: 212-753-0731
e-mail: jdeangelis@commodore.com
Web site: www.commodore.com
James DeAngelis, Senior Vice President/Chief Financial & Administration Officer
Develops technologies for destroying hazardous waste, PCBs, dioxins, mixed waste & chemical weapons

Cornell Cooperative Extension, Environment & Natural Resources Initiative
108 Fernow Hall, Cornell University, Ithaca, NY 14853
607-255-2115 Fax: 607-255-2815
e-mail: cce-nat-res@cornell.edu
Web site: www.dnr.cornell.edu/extension
Diana Bryant, Department Extension Leader
Working to improve the quality & sustainability of human environments & natural resources

Cornell Cooperative Extension, NY Sea Grant
Cornell University, 112 Rice Hall, Ithaca, NY 14853-5601
607-255-2832 Fax: 607-255-2812
e-mail: drb17@cornell.edu
Web site: www.nyseagrant.org
Dale Baker, Program Leader
Research, education & training related to ocean, coastal & Great Lakes resources

Cornell University Center for the Environment
200 Rice Hall, Ithaca, NY 14853-5601
607-255-7535 Fax: 215-701-1844
Web site: environment.cornell.edu
Mark B Bain, Director
Environmental research

Council on the Environment of NYC (The)
51 Chambers St, Rm 228, New York, NY 10007
212-788-7900 Fax: 212-788-7913
e-mail: conyc@cenyc.org
Web site: www.cenyc.org
Marcel Van Ooyen, Executive Director
Promotes environmental awareness & develops solutions to environmental problems

Dakota Software Corporation
95 Allens Creek Rd, #2-302, Rochester, NY 14618
585-244-3300 Fax: 585-244-3301
e-mail: info@dakotasoft.com
Web site: www.dakotasoft.com
Arlene Davidson, Marketing Director
Environmental health & safety regulatory software systems design

Dionondehowa Wildlife Sanctuary & School - Not For Profit
148 Stanton Rd, Shushan, NY 12873
518-854-7764 Fax: 518-854-3648
e-mail: dionondehowa@yahoo.com
Web site: www.dionondehowa.org
Bonnie Hoag, Co-Founder & Director
Conservation & land use issues, conscious living, nature studies & healing & expressive arts

ENSR
3495 Winton Place, Suite E295, Rochester, NY 14623
585-381-2210 Fax: 585-381-5392
e-mail: pnielsen@ensr.aecom.com; askensr@ensr.aecom.com
Web site: www.ensr.aecom.com
Peter Nielsen, Senior Program Manager
Environmental consulting, engineering, remediation & related services

Ecology & Environment Inc
368 Pleasant View Dr, Lancaster, NY 14086-1397
716-684-8060 Fax: 716-684-0844
e-mail: dcastle@ene.com
Web site: www.ene.com
Gerhard J Neumaier, President
Environmental scientific & engineering consulting

Offices and agencies generally appear in alphabetical order, except when specific order is requested by listee.

ENVIRONMENT & NATURAL RESOURCES / Private Sector

Empire State Forest Products Association
828 Washington Ave, Albany, NY 12203-1622
518-463-1297 x2 Fax: 518-426-9502
e-mail: kking@esfpa.org
Web site: www.esfpa.org
Kevin S King, Executive Vice President

Environmental Advocates of New York
353 Hamilton St, Albany, NY 12210
518-462-5526 x238 Fax: 518-427-0381
e-mail: info@eany.org
Web site: www.eany.org
Erica Ringewald, Assistant Director
The state's government watchdog, holding lawmakers and agencies accountable for enacting and enforcing laws that protect natural resources and safeguard public health.

Environmental Business Association of NYS Inc
126 State St, 3rd Fl, Albany, NY 12207-1637
518-432-6400 x227 Fax: 518-432-1383
e-mail: suzanne@eba-nys.org
Web site: www.eba-nys.org
Suzanne Maloney, Executive Director
Supports businesses that provide products & services to prevent, monitor, control or remediate pollution or generate, conserve and/or recycle energy & resources

Environmental Defense
257 Park Ave South, 17th Fl, New York, NY 10010
212-505-2100 Fax: 212-505-2375
e-mail: adarrell@environmentaldefense.org
Web site: www.environmentaldefense.org
Andrew Darrell, NY Regional Director

Ethan C Eldon Associates Inc
1350 Broadway, Ste 612, New York, NY 10018
212-967-5400 Fax: 212-967-2747
e-mail: info@ethanceldon.com
Web site: www.ethanceldon.com
Ethan C Eldon, President
Environmental, EIS, traffic, hazardous & solid waste consulting

NYS Bar Assn, Environmental Law Section
Farrell Fritz, PC
1320 Reckosn Plaza, Uniondale, NY 11556-1320
516-227-0700 Fax: 516-227-0777
e-mail: mvillani@farrellfritz.com
Web site: www.farrellfritz.com
Miriam Villani, Chair

Great Lakes United
Buffalo State College, Cassety Hall, 1300 Elmwood Ave, Buffalo, NY 14222
716-886-0142 Fax: 716-204-9521
e-mail: glu@glu.org
Web site: www.glu.org
Derrick Stack, Executive Director
Great Lakes & St Lawrence River issues

GreenThumb
49 Chambers Street, Room 1020, New York, NY 10007
212-788-8070 Fax: 212-788-8052
e-mail: edie@greenthumbnyc.org
Web site: www.greenthumbnyc.org
Edie Stone, Director
Development & preservation of community gardens; reclamation of urban land for green space

Greene County Soil & Water Conservation District
907 County Office Building, Cairo, NY 12413
518-622-3620 Fax: 518-622-0344
e-mail: rene@gcswcd.com
Web site: www.gcswcd.com
Rene Van Schaack, Executive Director
Natural resource conservation & water quality programs & public access to Hudson River, stormwater management, wetland mitigation

Hawk Creek Wildlife Center Inc
PO Box 662, East Aurora, NY 14052
716-652-8646 Fax: 716-652-8646
e-mail: info@hawkcreek.org
Web site: www.hawkcreek.org
Loretta C Jones, President
Hawk Creek's mission is to create understanding & knowledge of the natural world & its relationship to humankind through conservation, environmental education & research

Hofstra University, School of Law
121 Hofstra University, Hempstead, NY 11549
212-864-6092
Web site: www.hofstra.edu
William R Ginsberg, Emeritus Professor of Law
Land use & environmental law

Hudson River Environmental Society
6626 Stitt Road, Altamont, NY 12009-4523
518-861-8020 Fax: 518-861-8020
e-mail: hres@nycap.rr.com
Web site: www.hres.org
Stephen Wilson, Executive Director
Facilitates & coordinates research in the physical & biological sciences, environmental engineering & resource management in the Hudson River region

Hudson River Sloop Clearwater Inc
112 Little Market St, Poughkeepsie, NY 12601
845-454-7673 Fax: 845-454-7953
e-mail: office@clearwater.org
Web site: www.clearwater.org
Gregg Swanzey, Executive Director
Hudson River water quality, environmental education & advocacy

Offices and agencies generally appear in alphabetical order, except when specific order is requested by listee.

ENVIRONMENT & NATURAL RESOURCES / Private Sector

Hudson Valley Grass Roots Energy & Environmental Network
PO Box 208, Red Hook, NY 12571
845-486-7070
e-mail: hvgreentimes@hotmail.com
Web site: www.hvgreentimes.org
Brian Reid, Board Member
Public environmental education & journalism

INFORM Inc
5 Hanover Square, New York, NY 10004
212-361-2400 Fax: 212-361-2412
e-mail: inform@informinc.org
Web site: www.informinc.org
Katherine O'Dea, Interim Executive Director
Advocacy, research & education on practical methods to protect natural resources & public health

Institute of Ecosystem Studies
PO Box A B, Millbrook, NY 12545
845-677-5359 Fax: 845-677-6455
e-mail: quillenl@ecostudies.org
Web site: www.ecostudies.org
Lori Quillen, Director & President
Ecosystem research; curriculum development & on-site ecology education

Land Trust Alliance Northeast Program
112 Spring St, Suite 205, PO Box 792, Saratoga Springs, NY 12866
518-587-0774 Fax: 518-587-9586
e-mail: newyork@lta.org
Web site: www.lta.org
Lynn Schumann, Northeast Director
Promotes voluntary land conservation; provides leadership, information, skills & resources needed by land trusts

Messinger Woods Wildlife Care & Education Center Inc
PO Box 508, Orchard Park, NY 14127
716-648-8091
e-mail: mike@messingerwoods.org
Web site: www.messingerwoods.org
Michael Olek, President
Promoting community awareness, education, instruction, involvement, understanding, appreciation & acceptance of our wildlife in order to conserve it

Modutank Inc
41-04 35th Ave, Long Island City, NY 11101
718-392-1112 Fax: 718-786-1008
e-mail: info@modutank.com
Web site: www.modutank.com
Reed Margulis, President
Rent & sell modular storage tanks for potable water, wastewater & liquid chemicals

NY League of Conservation Voters/NY Conservation Education Fund
30 Broad Street, 30th Floor, New York, NY 10006-3201
212-361-6350 x208 Fax: 212-361-6363
e-mail: info@nylcv.org
Web site: www.nylcv.org
Marcia Bystryn, Executive Director
Endorsement of pro-environmental candidates; environmental advocacy & education statewide

NYC Neighborhood Open Space Coalition
232 E 11th St, New York, NY 10003
212-228-3126 Fax: 212-471-9987
e-mail: nosc@treebranch.com
Web site: www.treebranch.com; www.walkny.org
David Lutz, Executive Director
Works to preserve/expand NYC's parks, waterfront, community gardens & other public open space

NYS Association of Solid Waste Management
PO Box 13461, Albany, NY 12212
518-783-2827 Fax: 518-786-7331
e-mail: info@newyorkwaste.org
Web site: www.newyorkwaste.org
F Joseph Stockbridge, President
Waste management & recycling professionals providing advocacy & education for responsible integrated solid waste management

NYS Water Resources Institute of Cornell University
Cornell University, 207 Rice Hall, Ithaca, NY 14853-5601
607-255-5941
e-mail: nyswri@cornell.edu
Web site: wri.eas.cornell.edu
Keith S Porter, Director
Education, research, investigation & technical assistance to agencies & communities concerned with water resources

National Wildlife Federation
1400 16th Street NW, Suite 501, Washington, DC 20036
202-797-6800 Fax: 202-797-6646
e-mail: spencer@nwf.org
Web site: www.nwf.org
Rick Spencer, Regional Representative
Conservation education, litigation & advocacy for policies to restore habitat & return wildlife to natural environs

Natural Resources Defense Council
40 W 20th St, 11th Fl, New York, NY 10011
212-727-2700 Fax: 212-727-1773
e-mail: nrdcinfo@nrdc.org
Web site: www.nrdc.org
Frances Beinecke, President
Litigation, legislation advocacy & public education to preserve & protect the environment & public health

Offices and agencies generally appear in alphabetical order, except when specific order is requested by listee.

ENVIRONMENT & NATURAL RESOURCES / Private Sector

Nature Conservancy (The)
195 New Karner Rd, Ste 200, Albany, NY 12205
518-690-7850 Fax: 518-869-2332
e-mail: dsavage@tnc.org
Web site: www.nature.org
Henry Tepper, New York State Director
Preserve plants, animals & natural communities by protecting the land & water which they need to survive

New York Forest Owners Association Inc
PO Box 541, Lima, NY 14485
800-836-3566
e-mail: info@nyfoa.org
Web site: www.nyfoa.org
Mary Jeanne Packer, Executive Director
Promote & nurture private woodland owners stewardship

New York Public Interest Research Group
9 Murray St, 3rd Fl, New York, NY 10007
212-349-6460 Fax: 212-349-1366
e-mail: nypirg@nypirg.org
Web site: www.nypirg.org
Christopher Meyer, Executive Director
Environmental preservation, public health, consumer protection & government reform

New York State Conservation Council
8 E Main St, Ilion, NY 13357-1899
315-894-3302 Fax: 315-894-2893
e-mail: nyscc@nyscc.com
Web site: www.nyscc.com
Harold I Palmer, President
Promotes conservation & wise use & management of natural resources

New York State Woodsmen's Field Days Inc
PO Box 123, 118-120 Main St, Boonville, NY 13309
315-942-4593 Fax: 315-942-4452
e-mail: fielddays@aol.com
Web site: www.starinfo.com/woodsmen/
Phyllis W White, Executive Coordinator
Promoting the forest products industry

New York Water Environment Association Inc (NYWEA)
525 Plum Street, Suite 102, Syracuse, NY 13204
315-422-7811 Fax: 315-422-3851
e-mail: pcr@nywea.org
Web site: www.nywea.org
Patricia Cerro-Reehil, Executive Director
Water quality education, protection & enhancement of water environment.

Northeastern Loggers' Association
PO Box 69, Old Forge, NY 13420
315-369-3078 Fax: 315-369-3736
e-mail: nela@northernlogger.com
Web site: www.northernlogger.com
Joseph E Phaneuf, Executive Director & Treasurer

Open Space Institute
1350 Broadway, Ste 201, New York, NY 10018-7799
212-290-8200 Fax: 212-244-3441
Web site: www.osiny.org
Christopher J Elliman, Chief Executive Officer
Protects scenic, natural and historic landscapes to ensure public employment, conserve habitats and sustain community character. OSI achieves its goal through land acquisition, conservation, easements, special loan programs, fiscal sponsorships.

Pace University, School of Law Center for Environmental Legal Studies
78 N Broadway, White Plains, NY 10603
914-422-4244 Fax: 914-422-4261
e-mail: nrobinson@law.pace.edu
Web site: www.law.pace.edu
Nicholas Robinson, Co-Director
US & international environmental law

Proskauer Rose LLP
1585 Broadway, 23rd Fl, New York, NY 10036-1507
212-969-3000 Fax: 212-969-2900
e-mail: rkafin@proskauer.com
Web site: www.proskauer.com
Robert J Kafin, General Counsel
Environmental law

Radiac Environmental Services
261 Kent Ave, Brooklyn, NY 11211
718-963-2233 Fax: 718-388-5107
e-mail: jtekin@radiacenv.com
John V Tekin, Jr, Operations Manager
Radioactive & chemical waste disposal, decontamination & remediation

Radon Testing Corp of America Inc
2 Hayes St, Elmsford, NY 10523
914-345-3380 or 800-457-2366 Fax: 914-345-8546
e-mail: rtca97@att.net
Web site: www.rtca.com
Nancy Bredhoff, President
Radon detection services for health departments, municipalities, homeowners; manufacture canister detectors

Rensselaer Polytechnic Inst, Ecological Economics, Values & Policy Program
Dept of Science & Tech Studies, 110 Eighth St, Troy, NY 12180
518-276-8509 Fax: 518-276-2659
e-mail: hessd@rpi.edu
Web site: www.rpi.edu/dept/sts/eevp
David Hess, Professor & Director
Educating leaders for a sustainable future

Riverhead Foundation for Marine Research & Preservation (The)
467 E Main St, Riverhead, NY 11901
631-369-9840 Fax: 631-369-9826
Web site: www.riverheadfoundation.org
Kimberly Durham, Rescue Program Director/Biologist
Preservation & protection of the marine environment through education, rehabilitation & research

Offices and agencies generally appear in alphabetical order, except when specific order is requested by listee.

ENVIRONMENT & NATURAL RESOURCES / Private Sector

Riverkeeper Inc
828 South Broadway, Suite 101, Tarrytown, NY 10591
914-478-4501 Fax: 914-478-4527
e-mail: info@riverkeeper.org
Web site: www.riverkeeper.org
Alex Matthiessen, Hudson Riverkeeper & President
Nonprofit member supported environmental organization protecting the ecological integrity of the Hudson and its tributaries, also safeguards NYC drinking water supply watershed.

Rural Water Association
PO Box 487, Claverack, NY 12513-0487
518-828-3155 Fax: 518-828-0582
Patricia C Scalera, Executive Director

SCS Engineers PC
140 Rte 303, Valley Cottage, NY 10989-1923
845-353-5727 Fax: 845-353-5731
e-mail: pkuniholm@scsengineers.com
Web site: www.scsengineers.com
Peter Kuniholm, Vice President
Environmental consulting

SUNY at Cortland, Center for Environmental & Outdoor Education
PO Box 2000, Cortland, NY 13045
607-753-5488 Fax: 607-753-5985
e-mail: sheltmirej@cortland.edu
Web site: www.cortland.edu
Jack Sheltmire, Director

Scenic Hudson
1 Civic Center Plaza, #200, Poughkeepsie, NY 12601
845-473-4440 Fax: 845-473-2648
e-mail: info@scenichudson.org
Web site: www.scenichudson.org
Ned Sullivan, President
Environmental advocacy, air & water quality, riverfront protection, land/historic preservation, smart growth planning

Sierra Club, Atlantic Chapter
353 Hamilton St, Albany, NY 12210-1709
518-426-9144
e-mail: john.stouffer@sierraclub.org
Web site: www.sierraclub.org/chapters/ny/
John Stouffer, Legislative Director
Environmental protection advocacy & education; outdoor recreation

Spectra Environmental Group Inc
19 British American Blvd, Latham, NY 12110
518-782-0882 Fax: 518-782-0973
e-mail: gsovas@spectraenv.com
Web site: www.spectraenv.com
Gregory H Sovas, Vice President, Government Affairs
Environmental & infrastructure engineering, architecture, surveying, air quality, ground penetrating radar & power generation consulting & services

St John's University, School of Law
8000 Utopia Pkwy, Jamaica, NY 11439
718-990-6628 Fax: 718-990-6649
e-mail: weinberp@stjohns.edu
Philip Weinberg, Professor
Environmental law

Syracuse University Press
621 Skytop Rd, Syracuse, NY 13244-5290
315-443-5543 Fax: 315-443-5545
e-mail: msevans@syr.edu
Web site: www.syracuseuniversitypress.syr.edu
Mary Selden Evans, Executive Editor
Adirondack & regional NYS studies series

Syracuse University, Maxwell School of Citizenship & Public Affairs
200 Eggers Hall, Syracuse, NY 13244-1020
315-443-2252 Fax: 315-443-1075
e-mail: whlambri@maxwell.syr.edu
Web site: www.maxwell.syr.edu
W Henry Lambright, Director & Professor
Environmental policy; science, technology & public policy

Trees New York
51 Chambers St, Ste 1412A, New York, NY 10007
212-227-1887 Fax: 212-732-5325
e-mail: info@treesny.com
Web site: www.treesny.com
Susan Gooberman, Executive Director
Planting, preserving & protecting street trees; urban forestry resources & reference materials & programs in NYC

University of Rochester School of Medicine
Box EHSC, Rochester, NY 14642
585-275-3911 Fax: 585-256-2591
e-mail: tom_clarkson@urmc.rochester.edu
Web site: www2.envmed.rochester.edu
Thomas Clarkson, Professor, Department of Environmental Medicine
Mercury poisoning

Upstate Freshwater Institute
PO Box 506, Syracuse, NY 13214
315-431-4962 Fax: 315-431-4969
e-mail: sweffler@upstatefreshwater.org
Web site: www.upstatefreshwater.org
Steven Effler, Executive Director
Freshwater water quality research

Waterkeeper Alliance
50 South Buckhout Street, Suite 302, Irvington, NY 10533
914-674-0622 Fax: 914-674-4560
e-mail: info@waterkeeper.org
Web site: www.waterkeeper.org
Steve Fleischli, Executive Director
Protect & restore the quality of the world's waterways

Offices and agencies generally appear in alphabetical order, except when specific order is requested by listee.

ENVIRONMENT & NATURAL RESOURCES / Private Sector

Whiteman Osterman & Hanna LLP
One Commerce Plaza, Albany, NY 12260
518-487-7619 Fax: 518-487-7777
e-mail: druzow@woh.com
Web site: www.woh.com
Daniel A Ruzow, Senior Partner
Environmental & zoning law

Wildlife Conservation Society
2300 Southern Blvd, Bronx, NY 10460
718-220-5100 Fax: 718-220-6890
e-mail: jcalvelli@wcs.org
Web site: www.wcs.org
John Calvelli, Senior Vice President, Public Affairs

Offices and agencies generally appear in alphabetical order, except when specific order is requested by listee.

GOVERNMENT OPERATIONS

New York State

GOVERNOR'S OFFICE

Governor's Office
Executive Chamber
State Capitol
Albany, NY 12224
518-474-8390 Fax: 518-474-1513
Web site: www.state.ny.us

Governor:
   Eliot Spitzer 518-474-8390
Secretary to the Governor:
   Richard Baum 518-474-4246
Counsel to the Governor:
   David Nocenti 518-474-8343
Special Counsel:
   Richard Rivkin 518-486-9671
Director, Policy:
   Peter Pope 518-486-9671
Senior Advisor to the Governor:
   Lloyd Constantine 518-486-9671
Chief of Staff:
   Marlene Turner 518-474-8390
First Deputy Secretary:
   Sean Maloney 518-474-4246
Deputy Secretary, Appointments:
   Francine James 518-474-0491
Deputy Secretary, Intergovernmental Affairs:
   Martin Mack 518-408-2555
Deputy Secretary, General Services, Technology & Labor Relations:
   Sylvia Hamer 518-408-2576
Deputy Secretary, Public Safety:
   Michael Balboni 518-474-3522
Assistant Deputy Secretary, Education:
   John Reid 518-408-2833
Director, Communications:
   Darren Dopp 518-474-8418

New York City Office
633 Third Ave, 38th Fl, New York, NY 10017
Director, NYC Intergovernmental Affairs:
   Carl Andrews 212-681-4580
Director, Community Affairs:
   Lila Kirton 212-681-4580
Press Secretary:
   Christine Anderson 212-681-4640
Press Officer:
   Jennifer Givner 212-681-4640

Washington Office of the Governor
444 N Capitol St NW, Washington, DC 20001
Director:
   Derek Douglas 202-434-7100

Lieutenant Governor's Office
Executive Chamber
State Capitol
Albany, NY 12224
518-474-4623 Fax: 518-486-4170

633 Third Ave
38th Fl
New York, NY 10017
212-681-4532
Fax: 212-681-4533

Lieutenant Governor:
   David A Paterson . . . . 518-474-4623 or 212-681-4532
Chief of Staff:
   Charles J O'Byrne 518-474-4623
Deputy Chief of Staff:
   Sarah Lewis 518-474-4623
Press Secretary:
   Mari Arce 518-474-4623
Counsel to Lt Governor:
   Jeff Pearlman 518-474-4623
Director, Communications & Intergovernmental Affairs:
   Richard Schwabacher 518-474-4623
Director, Policy:
   Mark Leinung 518-474-4623

EXECUTIVE DEPARTMENTS AND RELATED AGENCIES

Budget, Division of the
State Capitol
Albany, NY 12224
518-473-3885
e-mail: bdgord@budget.state.ny.us
Web site: www.budget.state.ny.us

Director:
   Paul E Francis 518-474-2300
First Deputy Director:
   Laura L Anglin 518-474-6323
Deputy Director:
   Ron Rock 518-474-6300
Deputy Director:
   Kim Fine 518-474-6300
Counsel:
   Kathy Bennett 518-474-2300
Director, Communications:
   Jeffrey Gordon 518-473-3885
Press Officer:
   Scott Reif 518-473-3885

Offices and agencies generally appear in alphabetical order, except when specific order is requested by listee.

GOVERNMENT OPERATIONS / New York State

CIO Office & Office for Technology
State Capitol, ESP
PO Box 2062
Albany, NY 12220-0062

CIO Office
Web site: www.cio.state.ny.us
Chief Information Officer:
  Melodie Mayberry-Stewart, PhD 518-408-2140/fax: 518-402-2976
  e-mail: cio@cio.state.ny.us
Associate Chief Information Officer:
  Ram Shenoy 518-408-2140
Senior Advisor:
  Michael Mittleman 518-408-2140
Assistant to the CIO:
  Marie Potter 518-408-2140

Office for Technology
Web site: www.oft.state.ny.us
Acting Director:
  Melodie Mayberry-Stewart, PhD 518-473-9450/fax: 518-402-2976

Administration
Deputy Director, Administration:
  Margaret Becker 518-473-7041
Administrative Support:
  Max Morehouse 518-437-0927
Budget & Fiscal Admin:
  Kevin Nephew 518-402-4874/fax: 518-402-4807
Human Resources:
  Elaine Ehlinger 518-473-1935/fax: 518-402-4924

Counsel
Deputy Counsel:
  Darlene VanSickle 518-473-5115/fax: 518-486-7923

Operations
Deputy Director, Customer Service:
  Daniel Healy 518-473-2658/fax: 518-474-1196
Customer Networking Solutions:
  John Benson 518-474-9254
Deputy Director, Applications:
  Ellen Kattleman 518-402-2010/fax: 518-486-4344
Deputy Director, Networking Technologies:
  Dave Runyon 518-486-9200/fax: 518-408-4693
Director, Telecommunications:
  Daniel Corcoran 518-474-3019/fax: 518-473-7145
Acting Deputy Director, Computing:
  Eileen Fitzsimmons 518-474-8345/fax: 518-473-7532
IT Services & Support:
  Jerry Foster 518-473-5071

Statewide Initiatives
HIPAA Coord:
  Anne Marie Rainville 518-473-2658/fax: 518-474-1196
NYS Technology Academy:
  Terri Daly 518-473-2658/fax: 518-474-1196

Statewide Wireless Network
Deputy Director:
  Hanford Thomas 518-474-9112/fax: 518-443-2787

Emergency Management Office, NYS (SEMO)
1220 Washington Ave
Bldg 22, Ste 101
Albany, NY 12226-2251
518-292-2275
Web site: www.semo.state.ny.us

Director:
  John R Gibb 518-292-2301
First Deputy Director:
  Andrew X Feeney 518-292-2275
Deputy Director, Operations:
  Thomas Fargione 518-292-2275
Deputy Director, Preparedness:
  Greg Brunelle 518-292-2275
Deputy Director, Administration:
  John A Agostino 518-292-2275
Program Assistant:
  Judy Williams 518-292-2301/fax: 518-322-4978

Administration
Chief Budget Analyst:
  Susan Mutch 518-292-2325
Manager, Recovery Section:
  Les Radford 518-292-2391

Community Affairs
Asst Director:
  Dennis J Michalski 518-292-2310
Public Information Officer:
  Donald L Maurer 518-292-2312/fax: 518-457-4923
  e-mail: donald.maurer@semo.state.ny.us

Preparedness
Chief, Training/Exercises:
  William Campbell 518-292-2350
Chief, Planning:
  Robert Olazagasti 518-292-2360

Support Services
Assistant Director, Technology:
  Kevin Ross 518-292-2260
Manager, Supply Services:
  John Zobel 518-292-2270

General Services, Office of
Corning Tower, 41st Fl
Empire State Plaza
Albany, NY 12242
518-474-3899 Fax: 518-474-1546
Web site: www.ogs.state.ny.us

633 Third Ave
New York, NY 10017
212-681-4580
Fax: 212-681-4558

Commissioner:
  John C Egan 518-474-5991
  e-mail: john.egan@ogs.state.ny.us
First Deputy Commissioner:
  Robert J Fleury 518-473-6953
  e-mail: robert.fleury@ogs.state.ny.us
Deputy Commissioner, Legal Services:
  Howard Zwickel 518-474-5988/fax: 518-473-4973
Special Asst to Commissioner:
  Vacant 518-473-7345
Assistant Commissioner, Public Affairs:
  Brad Maione 518-474-5987/fax: 518-474-3187
  e-mail: brad.maione@ogs.state.ny.us

Administration
Deputy Commissioner:
  Trina Mead 518-473-8550

Offices and agencies generally appear in alphabetical order, except when specific order is requested by listee.

GOVERNMENT OPERATIONS / New York State

Director, Administration:
  Franklin A Hecht 518-474-4546/fax: 518-486-3651
Director, Financial Administration:
  Linda Decker 518-474-4546
Director, Food Services:
  Vincent Brewer 518-474-1606
Director, Human Resources Management:
  Dan Cunningham 518-474-5995/fax: 518-473-8610
Director, Personnel:
  Mary Beth Metzger 518-408-1497
Acting Director, Bureau of Risk & Insurance Management:
  Tomlynn Yacono 518-474-4725/fax: 518-474-7867

Empire State's Convention & Cultural Events Office
Director:
  Heather Flynn 518-474-3195
Manager, Convention Center:
  Dick Hallock 518-474-0558
Director, Marketing:
  Michael J Snyder 518-474-0538
Director, Curatorial & Tour Services:
  Dennis Anderson 518-473-7521
Curator, NYS Vietnam Memorial:
  Robert Allyn 518-473-5546/fax: 518-486-3948

Design & Construction
Acting Deputy Commissioner:
  James M Davies 518-474-0337
Director, Construction:
  Robert Palmer 518-474-0333/fax: 518-474-8201
Director, Contract Administration:
  John D Lewyckyj 518-474-0201/fax: 518-486-1650
Director, Design:
  James Dirolf 518-474-0222

Information Technology & Procurement Services
Deputy Commissioner:
  Carla Chiaro 518-473-3933
  e-mail: carla.chiaro@ogs.state.ny.us

Information Resource Management
Director:
  Vacant 518-473-4788
Asst Director, Technical Services:
  Kevin Baxter 518-473-4788
Asst Director, Applications Services/Web Unit:
  Barbara Draiss 518-473-4788/fax: 518-474-1997
Information Security Officer:
  Brett Lewis 518-474-5502/fax: 518-486-9166

Procurement Services Group
Acting Director:
  Jerry Gerard 518-474-6710/fax: 518-486-6099
Acting Deputy Director:
  Monica Wilkes 518-474-3695/fax: 518-486-6099
Asst Director, Customer Services & Admin:
  Dixon J Ross 518-474-3855/fax: 518-474-2437
Asst Director:
  Donald R Greene 518-474-3418
Asst Director:
  Bruce Hallenbeck 518-408-1705
Asst Director:
  James Mastromarchi 518-474-3416

Real Estate Planning & Development Group
Deputy Commissioner:
  William L Hill Jr 518-474-5390
  e-mail: william.hill@ogs.state.ny.us
Director, Real Estate Planning & Development:
  James Sproat 518-474-4944
Director, Real Estate Planning & Development:
  Daniel Kennedy 518-474-4944
Director, Real Estate Planning & Development:
  Vacant 518-474-4944
Bureau Chief, Land Management:
  Charles Sheifer 518-474-2195
Bureau Chief, Space Planning & Lease Construction & Compliance:
  Anne M Carr 518-473-9887
Bureau Chief, Space Planning & Lease Construction & Compliance:
  John T Culliton 518-473-9887
Bureau Chief, Real Estate Planning - Downstate:
  Joseph V Luvera 518-474-7963
Asst Director, Real Estate Planning - Upstate:
  Timothy J Leonard 518-486-1484
Bureau Chief, Special Projects:
  Vacant 518-473-9887
Asst Director, Real Estate Planning - Downstate:
  Robert Lazarou 518-474-4944

Real Property Management Group
Deputy Commissioner:
  William L Hill Jr 518-474-5390
  e-mail: william.hill@ogs.state.ny.us
Director:
  Martin J Gilroy 518-474-6057/fax: 518-474-1523
Manager, Capital Planning:
  Richard Stock 518-473-3927/fax: 518-474-1523
Director, Construction Management:
  Kevin O'Connor 518-473-2041/fax: 518-473-2189
Director, Downstate Regional Buildings:
  Richard Gallagher 718-923-4448/fax: 718-923-4451
Director, Empire State Plaza & Downtown Buildings:
  Thomas E Casey 518-474-8894/fax: 518-474-4182
Director, Upstate Harriman State Office Campus:
  Tom O'Connell 518-457-2290/fax: 518-457-8297
Director, Utilities Management:
  Robert Lobdell 518-474-3249/fax: 518-402-5682

Support Services
Deputy Commissioner:
  John J Spano 212-967-6090
  e-mail: john.spano@ogs.state.ny.us
Director, Support Services Operations:
  Brian Moody 518-402-5557
Director, Food Distribution & Warehousing:
  Tom Osterhout 518-474-5122
Director, Properties & Fleet Administration:
  Ronald Ottman 518-457-1744
Bureau Chief, Parking Management:
  Dennis Moffre 518-486-5437
Program Manager, Central Printing & Copy Center:
  Tony DeMagistris 518-457-6593
Director, Clean Fueled Vehicles Program:
  Eileen Redmond 518-408-1491
Distribution Ctr Mgr: Mail & Freight Security:
  James Cerone 518-402-5750

Inspector General (NYS), Office of the
Executive Chamber
State Capitol
Albany, NY 12224
518-474-1010 Fax: 518-486-3745
Web site: www.ig.state.ny.us

61 Broadway
12th Fl

Offices and agencies generally appear in alphabetical order, except when specific order is requested by listee.

GOVERNMENT OPERATIONS / New York State

New York, NY 10006
212-635-3150
Fax: 212-809-6287

State Inspector General:
  Kristine Hamann.....................212-635-3150 or 518-474-1010
  e-mail: inspector.general@ig.state.ny.us
First Deputy Inspector General:
  Michael Boxer.......................................212-635-3150
Deputy Chief of Investigator:
  Dennis Saville......................................518-474-1010
Deputy Director, Administration:
  Margaret Gaudet....................................518-474-1010
Director, Public Information:
  Stephen Del Giacco..................................518-474-1010
  e-mail: steve.delgiacco@ig.state.ny.us

Law Department
120 Broadway
New York, NY 10271-0332
212-416-8000 Fax: 212-416-8796

State Capitol
Albany, NY 10271-0332
518-474-7330
Fax: 518-402-2472

Attorney General:
  Andrew M Cuomo......................................518-474-7330
Asst Attorney General, Legislative Bureau:
  Kathy Bennett......................................518-486-3000

Administration
Agency Bldg 4, Empire State Plaza, Albany, NY 12224-0341
Executive Director, Administration:
  Sylvia Hamer......................518-473-7900/fax: 518-474-0680
Assistant Director:
  Jean M Woodard...................518-474-7969/fax: 518-474-0680

Intergovernmental Relations
Director:
  Lila Kirton......................212-416-6044/fax: 212-416-8539
First Deputy Director:
  Galen Kirkland.....................518-402-2185 or 212-416-6342
  fax: 212-416-8539

Regulatory Reform, Governor's Office of
Agency Bldg 1, 4th Fl, Empire State Plz
PO Box 2107
Albany, NY 12220-0107
518-486-3292 Fax: 518-473-9342
Web site: www.gorr.state.ny.us

Director:
  Robert Hermann.....................................518-473-8197
Counsel:
  Amelia Stern.....................518-473-0620/fax: 518-473-9342
Public Information Officer:
  Tim Beadnell......................................518-486-3292
  e-mail: tbeadnell@gorr.state.ny.us
Director, Administration:
  Sandra L Curry....................................518-408-2055

State Comptroller, Office of the
110 State St
15th Fl
Albany, NY 12236-0001
518-474-4040 Fax: 518-473-3004
Web site: www.osc.state.ny.us

633 Third Ave, 31st Fl
New York, NY 10017-6754
212-681-4491
Fax: 212-681-4468

State Comptroller:
  Thomas P DiNapoli..................518-474-4040 or 212-681-4491

Administration
Deputy Comptroller:
  Harris Lirtzman...................................518-402-4884

Financial Administration
Director:
  Larry Appel.......................................518-474-7574

Information Technology Services
Director:
  Richard Green.....................................518-474-7476

Management Services
Director:
  Paul Capobianco...................................518-473-0675

Oil Spill Fund Office
Executive Director:
  Anne Hohenstein..............518-474-6657/fax: 518-474-9979

Division of Intergovernmental Affairs & Community Relations
Deputy Comptroller:
  Myrna Santiago....................................212-383-2662
Director, Intergovernmental Affairs & Community Relations:
  Sam Nicolas.......................................518-473-2449
Director, Intergovernmental Affairs, Upstate & Long Island Rural Liais:
  Victor Mallison...................................518-473-2449
Director, Intergovernmental Affairs, NYC, Brooklyn & Staten Island:
  Samuel Nicolas....................................212-383-2672

Division of Investigations
Deputy Comptroller:
  Robert Brackman...................212-681-4474 or 518-402-4926
Asst Comptroller for Internal Audit & Division Operations:
  Stephen R Hillerman..........................518-286-2622 x105
Chief Investigative Counsel:
  Samantha Biletsky..................212-681-4475 or 518-486-3501
Director, Internal Audit:
  Robert Kosky.................................518-286-2622 x110

Division of Local Govt Services & Economic Development
Deputy Comptroller:
  Mark P Pattison..................518-474-4037/fax: 518-486-6479
Asst Comptroller:
  Steve Hancox......................................518-474-4037
Asst Comptroller:
  John Clarkson.....................................518-474-4037

Division of State Services
Deputy Comptroller:
  Jerry Barber......................................518-474-5598

Offices and agencies generally appear in alphabetical order, except when specific order is requested by listee.

GOVERNMENT OPERATIONS / New York State

State Audit Group
Asst Comptroller:
  Jerry Barber 518-474-5598
Director, Administration:
  Bob Blot 518-474-3271
Director, Audit:
  Steve Sossei 518-474-3271
Director, Audit:
  David R Hancox 518-474-3271

State Financial Services Group
Asst Comptroller:
  Joan Sullivan 518-402-4103
Director, Accounting Operations Bureau:
  Tom Mahoney 518-474-4017
Director, Accounting Systems Bureau:
  Bob Campano 518-474-8657

Executive Office
Chief of Staff:
  Jack Chartier 212-681-4498
First Deputy Comptroller:
  Thomas Sanzillo 518-474-2909
Executive Deputy Comptroller:
  Diana J Ritter 518-474-3610
Deputy Chief of Staff:
  Roberta Rubin . . . . 212-681-4495 or 518-474-4040
Director, Business Communication:
  Ellen J Evans . . . . 518-473-1323 or 212-681-4489
Chief Information Officer:
  Jeffrey S Grunfeld 518-408-2915/fax: 518-473-3004

Human Resources & Affirmative Action Office
Asst Comptroller:
  Jacquelyn J Hawkins 518-474-5512
Director, Affirmative Action:
  Celia Gonzalez 518-473-1368
Director, Personnel:
  Jay Canetto 518-474-7662
Director, Employee Relations & Training Services:
  Artis Reed 518-473-7317
Assistant Director, Personnel:
  Gregory Hurd 518-474-0010
EAP Coordinator:
  Joe Quinlan 518-473-8838

Legal Services
Counsel:
  Alan Lebowitz . . . . 518-474-3444 or 212-681-6069
Deputy Counsel:
  Helen Fanshawe 518-474-6036
Counsel, Division of Retirement Services:
  George King 518-474-3592
Associate Counsel, Finance:
  Maurice Peaslee 518-474-5426
Associate Counsel, Local:
  Mitchell Morris 518-474-5586
Associate Counsel, State:
  John K Dalton 518-474-6011
Associate Counsel, State Audit:
  Albert Brooks 518-474-5490
Associate Counsel, Legislative Policy & Research:
  William Murray 518-474-9024

Office of Budget & Policy Analysis
Deputy Comptroller:
  Kim Fine 518-473-4333
Chief Economist:
  Thomas Marks 518-402-2670

Deputy Comptroller:
  Christine Rutigliano 518-486-7982

Payroll & Revenue Services Div
Deputy Comptroller:
  Daniel Berry 518-408-4149
Director, Unclaimed Funds:
  Lawrence Schantz 518-473-6438
Director, State Payroll Services:
  Robin R Rabii 518-474-3400

Pension Investment & Public Finance
Deputy Comptroller:
  David Loglisci 518-474-4003
Asst Comptroller:
  Thad McTigue 518-408-3156
Asst Comptroller:
  William Barrett 518-473-6396
Real Estate Investment:
  Marjorie Tsang 212-383-1508
Director, Private Equity:
  Nick Smirensky 212-678-4019
Director, Corporate Governance:
  Julie Gresham 212-681-4480
Director, Domestic Equities & Fixed Income Investment:
  Robert J Limage 518-474-6035

Press Office
Director, Communications:
  Daniel Weiller 518-474-4015/fax: 518-473-8940
Press Secretary:
  Jeffrey Gordon 518-474-4015
  e-mail: jgordon@osc.state.ny.us

Retirement Services
Deputy Comptroller:
  Laura Anglin 518-474-2600
Asst Comptroller:
  Nancy Burton 518-474-4600

Accounting Bureau
Director:
  Daniel Burns 518-474-3670

Actuarial Bureau
Actuary:
  Teri Landin 518-474-4537

Administration Services & Quality Performance
Director:
  Melanie MacPherson 518-408-4193

Advisory Counsel Affairs
Director:
  George S King 518-474-3592

Benefit Calculations & Disbursements
Director:
  Veronica D'Alauro 518-473-0983

Benefit Information Services
Director:
  Keith Zeto 518-474-5728

Disability Processing/Hearing Administration
Director:
  Kathy Nowak 518-473-1347

Matrimonial & Hearing Review
Director:
  Carolyn D'Agostino 518-474-1253

Offices and agencies generally appear in alphabetical order, except when specific order is requested by listee.

GOVERNMENT OPERATIONS / New York State

Member & Employee Services
Director:
Ginger Dame 518-474-1101

Retirement Communications
Director:
Paul Kentoffio 518-474-7096

State Deputy Comptroller for New York City
59 Maiden Lane, 29th Fl, New York, NY 10038
Deputy Comptroller:
Kenneth Bleiwas. 212-383-3900

Agency Analysis Bureau
Director:
Mark Chernoff 212-383-3870

Bureau of Economic Development & Policy Analysis
Director:
Adam Freed 212-383-3930

Bureau of Tax & Economic Analysis
Director:
Vacant 212-383-3921

Infrastructure & Citywide Expenditure Analysis
Director:
Christopher Wieda 212-383-3936

State Department
41 State St
Albany, NY 12231
518-474-4750   Fax: 518-474-4765
Web site: www.dos.state.ny.us

123 William St
New York, NY 10038
212-417-5801
Fax: 212-417-5805

Secretary of State:
Lorraine A Cortes-Vazquez 518-474-0050
First Deputy Secretary of State:
Daniel Shapiro 518-474-4750
Deputy Secretary of State, Public Affairs:
Eamon Moynihan 212-417-5800
Counsel:
Susan Watson 518-474-6740/fax: 518-473-9211
Assistant Secretary of State, Communications:
Laurence Sombke 518-474-4752/fax: 518-474-4597
e-mail: info@dos.state.ny.us

Business & Licensing Services Division
Deputy Secretary of State:
Al Jurczynski 518-473-2728/fax: 518-473-6648
e-mail: licensing @dos.state.ny.us

Administrative Rules Division
Manager, Publications:
Deborah Ritzko 518-474-6957/fax: 518-473-9055
e-mail: adminrules@dos.state.ny.us

Cemeteries Division
Director:
Richard D Fishman . . . . 518-474-6226 or 212-417-5713
fax: 518-473-0876
e-mail: cemeteries@dos.state.ny.us

Corporations, State Records & UCC Division
Director:
Daniel E Shapiro 518-473-2281/fax: 518-474-5173
e-mail: corporations@dos.state.ny.us

Ethics Commission
Alfred E Smith State Offc Bldg, 11th Fl, Ste 1147, Albany, NY 12210
Acting Executive Director:
Suzanne Dugan 518-474-8320/fax: 518-474-8322
e-mail: ethics@dos.state.ny.us
Chair:
John D Feerick 518-474-8320

Local Government & Community Services
Deputy Secretary of State:
Matthew Andrus 518-486-9888/fax: 518-474-6572

Coastal Resources & Waterfront Revitalization Division
Director:
George Stafford 518-474-6000/fax: 518-473-2464
e-mail: coastal@dos.state.ny.us

Code Enforcement & Administration Division
Director:
Ronald E Piester 518-474-4073/fax: 518-486-4487
e-mail: codes@dos.state.ny.us

Community Services Division
Director:
Evelyn M Harris 518-474-5741/fax: 518-486-4663
e-mail: commserv@dos.state.ny.us

Fire Prevention & Control Office
State Fire Administrator:
James A Burns 518-474-6746/fax: 518-474-3240
e-mail: fire@dos.state.ny.us
New York State Academy of Fire Science
600 College Ave, Montour Falls, NY 14865-9634
Director:
Richard Nagle 607-535-7136/fax: 607-535-4841

Local Government Services Division
Director:
Barbara Murphy 518-473-3355/fax: 518-474-6572
e-mail: localgov@dos.state.ny.us

Open Government Committee
Executive Director:
Robert J Freeman 518-474-2518/fax: 518-474-1927
e-mail: opengov@dos.state.ny.us

Operations
Director, Administration & Management:
Judith E Kenny 518-474-4751/fax: 518-474-4765

Administrative Support Services
Director:
Rebecca Sabesta 518-473-8221/fax: 518-473-7182

Affirmative Action . . . . fax: 518-473-3294
Affirmative Action Officer:
Antonio Cortes 518-474-2752

Fiscal Management
Director:
Kym Landry 518-474-2754/fax: 518-474-4777

Human Resources Management
Director:
Debra L Frisch 518-474-2752/fax: 518-473-3294

Offices and agencies generally appear in alphabetical order, except when specific order is requested by listee.

GOVERNMENT OPERATIONS / New York State

Internal Audit
Director:
Ralph Bizarro 518-474-3772

Systems Management Bureau
Director:
Steven S Lovelett 518-474-8512/fax: 518-474-6239

Regional Affairs Division
Director:
John Haggerty 518-486-9896/fax: 518-473-0073

Regional Offices
Albany
Ofc of Local Gov't & Reg Affairs St C, Exec Chamber Rm 236, Albany, NY 12224
Regional Representative:
John Haggerty 518-486-9896/fax: 518-473-0073
Binghamton
State Office Bldg Annex, 44 Hawley St, 16th Fl, Rm 1605, Binghamton, NY 13901
Regional Representative:
Donald Leonard 607-721-8751/fax: 607-721-8755
Buffalo
65 Court St, Buffalo, NY 14202
Upstate Regional Director:
Jennifer McNamara 716-847-7110
Regional Representative:
Richard Solecky 716-847-7110/fax: 716-847-7969
Hicksville
303 Old Country Road, Hicksville, NY 11802
Regional Representative:
Heidi Callahan 516-934-8572/fax: 516-934-8001
Olean
Municipal Bldg, PO Box 624, 101 East State St, Olean, NY 14760
Regional Representative:
William Heaney 716-376-5706/fax: 716-376-5700
Peekskill
2 John Walsh Blvd, Ste 206, Peekskill, NY 10566
Regional Representative:
Cheryl Murray 914-734-1347/fax: 914-734-1763
Plattsburgh
22 US Oval, Bldg 426, Ste 1210, Plattsburgh, NY 12903
Regional Representative:
Candace Luck 518-562-3640/fax: 518-562-3645
Poughkeepsie
State Ofc Bldg, 4 Burnett Blvd, Poughkeepsie, NY 12603-2553
Regional Representative:
John Bellucci 845-437-5140/fax: 845-437-5142
Rochester
1530 Jefferson Rd, Rochester, NY 14623
Regional Representative:
Kelli O'Conner 585-424-9927/fax: 585-424-3658
Suffolk
State Office Bldg, 250 Veterans Memorial Hwy, Hauppauge, NY 11788
Regional Representative:
Steven Halsey 631-952-6583/fax: 631-952-7910
Syracuse
St Ofc Bldg, 333 E Washington St, Rm 514, Syracuse, NY 13202
Regional Representative:
Bebette Yunis 315-428-4337/fax: 315-428-4261
Utica
State Office Bldg, 207 Genesee St, Utica, NY 13501
Regional Representative:
Carole Kelly 315-793-2535/fax: 315-793-2635
Watertown
State Office Bldg, 317 Washington St, 4th Fl, Watertown, NY 13601
Regional Representative:
Joanne Dicob 315-785-2561/fax: 315-785-2563

State Athletic Commission
123 William St, 20th Fl, New York, NY 10038
Chair:
Ron Scott Stevens 212-417-5700/fax: 212-417-4987
e-mail: athletic@dos.state.ny.us

Welfare Inspector General, Office of NYS
22 Cortland St
11th Fl
New York, NY 10007
212-417-5822 Fax: 212-417-5849

40 N Pearl St, Sect 10B
Albany, NY 12243
518-474-9636
Fax: 518-486-6148

Inspector General:
Brian P Sanvidge 212-417-5840
Deputy Inspector General & Counsel:
Andrew J Weiss 212-417-2395
Chief Investigator:
Joseph R Bucci 212-417-2026
Administrative Asst to Inspector General:
Wanda Hernandez 212-417-5822

CORPORATIONS, AUTHORITIES AND COMMISSIONS

Legislative Bill Drafting Commission
Capitol, Rm 308
Albany, NY 12224
518-455-7500 Fax: 518-455-7598

Commissioner:
Michael H Melkonian 518-455-7501
e-mail: melkonian@lbdc.state.ny.us
Commissioner:
Randall G Bluth 518-455-7506
e-mail: bluth@lbdc.state.ny.us
Counsel:
Jamie-Lynne Elacqua 518-455-7538
e-mail: elacqua@lbdc.state.ny.us

Legislative Retrieval System . . . . fax: 518-455-7679
55 Elk St, Albany, NY 12210
800-356-6566 Fax: 518-455-7679
Director:
Burleigh McCutcheon 518-455-7669
e-mail: mccutcheon@lbdc.state.ny.us

New York State Athletic Commission
123 William St
20th Fl
New York, NY 10038-3804
212-417-5700 Fax: 212-417-4987
e-mail: athletic@dos.state.ny.us
Web site: www.dos.state.ny.us/athletic.html

Chair:
Ron Scott Stevens 212-417-5700

Offices and agencies generally appear in alphabetical order, except when specific order is requested by listee.

GOVERNMENT OPERATIONS / New York State

New York State Commission on the Restoration of the Capitol
Corning Tower, 31st Fl
Empire State Plaza
Albany, NY 12242
518-473-0341 Fax: 518-486-5720

Executive Director:
　Andrea J Lazarski 518-473-0341
　e-mail: andrea.lazarski@ogs.state.ny.us

New York State Disaster Preparedness Commission
Building 22, Suite 101
1220 Washington Ave
Albany, NY 12226-2251
518-292-2301 or 518-292-2200 Fax: 518-322-4978
Web site: www.semo.state.ny.us/dpc/

Chairman:
　John R Gibb 518-292-2301

New York State Dormitory Authority
515 Broadway
Albany, NY 12207-2964
518-257-3000 Fax: 518-257-3100
e-mail: dabonds@dasny.org
Web site: www.dasny.org

One Penn Plaza
52nd Fl
New York, NY 10119-0098
212-273-5000
Fax: 212-273-5121

539 Franklin St
Buffalo, NY 14202-1109
716-884-9780
Fax: 716-884-9787

Chair:
　Gail H Gordon 518-257-3180/fax: 518-257-3183
Executive Director:
　David D Brown, IV 518-257-3180/fax: 518-257-3183
Deputy Executive Director:
　Michael T Corrigan 518-257-3192/fax: 518-257-3183
Chief Fiscal Officer:
　John G Pasicznyk 518-257-3630/fax: 518-257-3100
　e-mail: jpasiczn@dasny.org
General Counsel:
　Jeffrey M Pohl 518-257-3120/fax: 518-257-3101
　e-mail: jpohl@dasny.org
Managing Director, Construction:
　James M Gray, RA 518-257-3200/fax: 518-257-3100
　e-mail: jgray@dasny.org
Managing Director, Portfolio Management:
　Lora K Lefebvre 518-257-3163/fax: 518-257-3387
　e-mail: llefebvr@dasny.org
Managing Director, Public Finance:
　Cheryl Ishmael 518-257-3362/fax: 518-257-3100
　e-mail: cishmael@dasny.org

Director, Communications & Marketing:
　Paul Burgdorf 518-257-3380/fax: 518-257-3387
　e-mail: pburgdor@dasny.org

New York State Ethics Commission
Alfred E Smith State Office Bldg
11th Fl, Ste 1147
Albany, NY 12210
518-474-8320 or 800-873-8442 Fax: 518-474-8322
e-mail: ethics@dos.state.ny.us
Web site: www.dos.state.ny.us/ethc/ethics.html

Chair:
　John D Feerick 518-474-8320
Commissioner:
　Robert J Giuffra, Jr 518-474-8320
Commissioner:
　Carl H Loewenson, Jr 518-474-8320
Commissioner:
　Lynn Millane 518-474-8320
Commissioner:
　Susan E Shepard 518-474-8320
Acting Executive Director:
　Suzanne Dugan 518-474-8320
Counsel:
　Suzanne Dugan 518-474-4533
Public Information Officer:
　Walter C Ayres 518-474-4418
　e-mail: wayres@dos.state.ny.us

New York State Financial Control Board
123 William St
23rd Fl
New York, NY 10038-3804
212-417-5046 Fax: 212-417-5055
e-mail: nysfcb@fcb.state.ny.us
Web site: www.fcb.state.ny.us

Acting Executive Director:
　Jeffrey Sommer 212-417-5066
Deputy Director, Expenditure Analysis:
　Dennis DeLisle 212-417-5069
Acting Deputy Director, Economic & Revenue Analysis:
　Martin Fischman 212-417-5068
Associate Director:
　Mattie W Taylor 212-417-5053

New York State Law Reporting Bureau
One Commerce Plaza, Ste 1750
Albany, NY 12210
518-474-8211 Fax: 518-463-6869
Web site: www.courts.state.ny.us/reporter

State Reporter:
　Gary D Spivey 518-474-8211
Deputy State Reporter:
　Charles A Ashe 518-474-8211
　e-mail: Reporter@courts.state.ny.us

Offices and agencies generally appear in alphabetical order, except when specific order is requested by listee.

GOVERNMENT OPERATIONS / New York State

New York State Temporary Commission of Investigation
59 Maiden Lane, 31st Fl
New York, NY 10038
212-344-6660 Fax: 212-344-6868
e-mail: commissioner@sic.state.ny.us
Web site: www.sic.state.ny.us

Chairman:
  Aldred D Lerner...................................212-344-6660
Deputy Commissioner & Chief Counsel:
  Anthony T Cartusciello.........................212-344-6670
Chief Investigator:
  Anthony Hellmer...................................212-344-6660

New York State Temporary Commission on Lobbying
2 Empire State Plaza
18th Floor
Albany, NY 12223-1254
518-474-7126 Fax: 518-473-6492
e-mail: lobcom@nytscol.org
Web site: www.nylobby.state.ny.us

Chair:
  Hon. James P King................................518-474-7126
Vice Chair:
  Andrew G Celli, Jr................................518-474-7126
Commissioner:
  Patrick J Bulgaro..................................518-474-7126
Commissioner:
  Kenneth J Baer....................................518-474-7126
Commissioner:
  Michael A Lenz....................................518-474-7126
Executive Director:
  David M Grandeau................................518-474-7126
Director, Program & Finance Administration:
  Jeannine M Clemente.............................518-474-7126

Uniform State Laws Commission
c/o Coughlin & Gerhart LLP, 20 Hawley St
East Tower
Binghamton, NY 13902-2039
607-584-4193 Fax: 607-723-1530

Chair:
  Richard B Long....................................607-584-4193
    e-mail: rlong@cglawllp.com
Member:
  Sandra Stern...212-207-8150
Member:
  Justin L Vigdor......................................585-232-5300
    e-mail: jvigdor@boylanbrown.com
Member:
  Norman L Greene..................................212-661-5030
    e-mail: normlg510@aol.com

United Nations Development Corporation
2 United Nations Plaza
27th Fl
New York, NY 10017-4403
212-888-1618 Fax: 212-588-0758
e-mail: info@undc.org
Web site: www.undc.org

Chair, Board of Directors:
  George Klein...212-888-1618
President & CEO:
  Roy M Goodman...................................212-888-1618
Executive VP & Director of Development:
  Jeffrey Feldman.....................................212-888-1618
Senior VP, Operations:
  Robert M Preissner.................................212-888-1618
Senior VP, Controller:
  Jorge Ortiz..212-888-1618

NEW YORK STATE LEGISLATURE

See Legislative Branch in Section 1 for additional Standing Committee and Subcommittee information.

Assembly Standing Committees

Consumer Affairs & Protection
Chair:
  Audrey I Pheffer (D)..............................518-455-4292
Ranking Minority Member:
  Peter D Lopez (R)..................................518-455-5363

Corporations, Authorities & Commissions
Chair:
  Richard L Brodsky (D)............................518-455-5753
Ranking Minority Member:
  Stephen Hawley (R)................................518-455-5811

Ethics & Guidance
Chair:
  Kevin A Cahill (D).................................518-455-4436
Ranking Minority Member:
  Robert Oaks (R)....................................518-455-5655

Governmental Operations
Chair:
  RoAnn M Destito (D).............................518-455-5454
Ranking Minority Member:
  Vacant (R)...518-455-0000

Oversight, Analysis & Investigation
Chair:
  Adriano Espaillat (D)..............................518-455-5807
Ranking Minority Member:
  Mike Spano (R).....................................518-455-3662

Rules
Chair:
  Sheldon Silver (D).................................518-455-3791
Ranking Minority Member:
  James N Tedisco (R)...............................518-455-3751

Ways & Means
Chair:
  Herman D Farrell, Jr (D).........................518-455-5491
Ranking Minority Member:
  James P Hayes (R).................................518-455-4618

Offices and agencies generally appear in alphabetical order, except when specific order is requested by listee.

GOVERNMENT OPERATIONS / U.S. Government

Assembly Task Forces & Caucus

State-Local Relations, Legislative Commission on
Assembly Chair:
  Darrel Aubertine................................518-455-5545
Program Manager:
  William Kraus....................518-455-5035/fax: 518-455-5396

Senate Select Committees

Interstate Cooperation, Select Committee on
Chair:
  Hugh T Farley (R)................................518-455-2181

Senate Standing Committees

Civil Service & Pensions
Chair:
  Joseph E Robach (R)..............................518-455-2909
Ranking Minority Member:
  Diane J Savino (D)...............................518-455-2437

Consumer Protection
Chair:
  Charles J Fuschillo, Jr (R)......................518-455-3341
Ranking Minority Member:
  Carl Kruger (D)..................................518-455-2460

Corporations, Authorities & Commissions
Chair:
  John J Flanagan (R)..............................518-455-3341
Ranking Minority Member:
  Bill Perkins (D).................................518-455-2441

Ethics
Chair:
  Andrew J Lanza (R)...............................518-455-3215

Ranking Minority Member:
  Jeffrey Klein (D)................................518-455-3595

Finance
Chair:
  Owen H Johnson (R)...............................518-455-3411
Ranking Minority Member:
  William Stachowski (D)...........................518-455-2426

Investigations & Government Operations
Chair:
  George H Winner, Jr (R)..........................518-455-2091
Ranking Minority Member:
  Shirley Huntley (D)..............................518-455-3531

Rules
Chair:
  Joseph L Bruno (R)...............................518-455-3191
Ranking Minority Member:
  Malcolm A Smith (D)..............................518-455-2701

Senate/Assembly Legislative Commissions

Ethics Committee, Legislative
Senate Co-Chair:
  Andrew J Lanza (R)...............................518-455-3215
Assembly Co-Chair:
  Kevin A Cahill (D)...............................518-455-4436
Director/Counsel:
  Melissa Ryan.....................518-455-2142/fax: 518-426-6850

Government Administration, Legislative Commission on
Assembly Chair:
  Joan Millman (D).................................518-455-5426
Senate Vice Chair:
  Owen H Johnson (R)...............................518-455-3411
Senior Program Manager:
  Philip Johnson...................518-455-3632/fax: 518-455-4574

U.S. Government

EXECUTIVE DEPARTMENTS AND RELATED AGENCIES

Peace Corps
Web site: www.peacecorps.gov

New York Regional Office...................fax: 212-352-5441
  201 Varick St, Ste 1025, New York, NY 10014
  212-352-5440 Fax: 212-352-5441
  e-mail: nyinfo@peacecorps.gov
Regional Manager:
  Vincent Wickes...................................212-352-5440
  e-mail: nyinfo@peacecorps.gov
Public Affairs Specialist:
  Molly Jennings...................................212-352-5446

US Department of Homeland Security (DHS)
Web site: www.dhs.gov

Bureau of Immigration & Customs Enforcement (ICE)
Web site: www.ice.gov

New York District Office
601 W 26th St, Ste 700, New York, NY 10001
Special Agent-in-Charge:
  Martin Ficke.....................................646-230-3200
  Albany Sub Office
  1086 Troy-Schenectady Rd, Latham, NY 12110
  Group Supervisor:
    LeRoy Tario....................................518-220-2100
  Resident Agent-in-Charge:
    Jack McQuade...................................518-220-2100

Customs & Border Protection (CBP)
202-354-1000
Web site: www.cbp.gov

Agriculture Inspections (AI)
  Brooklyn, Port of
  6405 7th Ave, 3rd Fl, Brooklyn, NY 11220
  Supervising Ag Specialist:
    Willie J Martin................................718-340-5225
  Buffalo, Port of
  1 Peace Bridge Plaza, Room 316, Buffalo, NY 14213
  Supervisor:
    Brent Speicher.............716-884-5701/fax: 716-884-5679
  Champlain, Port of..........................fax: 518-298-8395
  237 West Service Rd, Suite 2, Champlain, NY 12919

Offices and agencies generally appear in alphabetical order, except when specific order is requested by listee.

GOVERNMENT OPERATIONS / U.S. Government

      518-298-8327 Fax: 518-298-8395
    Ag Specialist:
      Vacant 518-298-4332/fax: 518-298-4486
    JFK International Airport Area Office . . . . fax: 718-487-5191
    JFK Int'l Airport, Bldg #77, 2nd Fl, Jamaica, NY 11430
    718-487-5164 Fax: 718-487-5191
    Port Director:
      Camille Polimeni 718-487-5164/fax: 718-487-5191

Buffalo Field Office
4455 Genesee St, Buffalo, NY 14225
716-626-0400
Director:
  James Engleman. 716-626-0400 x201/fax: 716-626-9281
  Albany, Port of
    445 Broadway, Room 216, Albany, NY 12207
    518-431-0200
    Port Director:
      Drew Wescott 518-431-0200/fax: 518-431-0203
  Buffalo, Port of
    Larkin at Exchange, 726 Exchange, Suite 400, Buffalo, NY 14210
    716-843-8300
    Port Director:
      Joseph Wilson 716-843-8300
  Champlain, Port of
    198 W Service Rd, Champlain, NY 12919
    Area Port Director:
      Christopher Perry 518-298-8347/fax: 518-298-8314
  Ogdensburg, Port of
    104 Bridge Approach Rd, Ogdensburg, NY 13669
    Port Director:
      William Mitchell 315-393-1390/fax: 315-393-7472

New York Field Office . . . . fax: 646-733-3245
1 Penn Plaza, 11th Fl, New York, NY 10119
646-733-3100 Fax: 646-733-3245
Director, Field Operations:
  Susan T Mitchell 646-733-3100
Press Officer:
  Janet Rapaport 212-514-8324/fax: 212-344-3755
  Field Counsel - New York
    Associate Chief Counsel:
      Judith Altman 646-733-3200
  Laboratory Division
    Director:
      Tom Governo. 973-368-1901

Environmental Measurements Laboratory
201 Varick St, 5th Fl, New York, NY 10014-7447
Web site: www.eml.st.dhs.gov
Director:
  Mitchell D Erickson 212-620-3619/fax: 212-620-3651
  e-mail: mitchell.erickson@dhs.gov

Administration
Director:
  Richard Larsen 212-620-3524/fax: 212-620-3600
  e-mail: richard.larsen@dhs.gov

Systems Division
Director:
  Lawrence Ruth 212-620-3609/fax: 212-620-3600
  e-mail: lawrence.roth@dhs.gov

Testbeds Division
Director:
  Adam Hutter 212-620-3619/fax: 212-620-3651
  e-mail: adam.hutter@dhs.gov

Federal Emergency Management Agency (FEMA)
TTY: 800-462-7585 or 800-621-3362
Web site: www.fema.gov

National Disaster Medical System . . . . fax: 212-680-3608
26 Federal Plz, Rm 3835, New York, NY 10278
Coordinator:
  Captain Bonita Pyler, USPHS 212-680-8542
  e-mail: pyler@dhs.gov

New York Regional Office . . . . fax: 212-680-3681
26 Federal Plz, Ste 1311, New York, NY 10278
Regional Director:
  Stephen Kempf, Jr 212-680-3612

Federal Protective Service (The)
26 Federal Plaza, Rm 17-130, New York, NY 10278
Director:
  John A Ulianko 212-264-4255/fax: 212-264-9803

Plum Island Animal Disease Center
PO Box 848, Greenport, NY 11944
Deputy Director of Operations:
  Gerald Jennings 631-323-3202/fax: 631-323-3295

Transportation Security Administration (TSA)
201 Varick St, Rm 603, New York, NY 10014
Regional Spokesperson:
  Mark Hatfield 212-337-2260/fax: 212-337-2261
  e-mail: mark.hatfield@dhs.gov

US Citizenship & Immigration Services (USCIS)
TTY: 800-767-1833 or 800-375-5283
Web site: www.uscis.gov

Buffalo District Office . . . . fax: 716-551-3131
Federal Center, 130 Delaware Ave, Buffalo, NY 14202
District Director:
  M Frances Holmes 716-551-4741 x6000
  Albany Sub Office
    1086 Troy-Schenectady Rd, Latham, NY 12110
    Officer-in-Charge:
      Gary Hale. 518-220-2100

CIS Asylum Offices
  New York Asylum Office . . . . fax: 718-723-1121
    One Cross Island Plaza, 3rd Fl, Rosedale, NY 11422
    Director:
      Patricia A Jackson 718-723-5954
    Deputy Director:
      Mick Dedvukaj 718-723-5954
  Newark Asylum Offc-Including NYS not served by New York City fax:
    201-531-1877
    1200 Wall St, West 4th Fl, Lyndhurst, NJ 07071
    Director:
      Susan Raufer 201-531-0555
    Deputy Director:
      Aster Zeleke. 201-531-0555

New York City District Office
26 Federal Plaza, New York, NY 10278
District Director:
  Mary Ann Gantner 212-264-3972
  Garden City Satellite Office
    711 Stewart Ave, Garden City, NY 11530
    Officer-in-Charge:
      Linda Pritchett . . . . 516-228-9242 or 516-288-9243

US General Services Administration
Web site: www.gsa.gov

Offices and agencies generally appear in alphabetical order, except when specific order is requested by listee.

GOVERNMENT OPERATIONS / U.S. Government

Region 2—New York
26 Federal Plaza, Rm 18-102, New York, NY 10278
212-264-9290
Regional Administrator:
 Emily R Baker 212-264-2600/fax: 212-264-3998
 e-mail: emily.baker@gsa.gov
Deputy Regional Administrator:
 Steve Ruggiero 212-264-2600/fax: 212-264-3998
 e-mail: steve.ruggiero@gsa.gov
Regional Counsel:
 Lionel Bately, Jr 212-264-8306/fax: 212-264-1987
Regional Counsel:
 Carol Latterman 212-264-8308/fax: 212-264-1987
 e-mail: carol.latterman@gsa.gov

Administration
Director, Program Support & Human Resources:
 Joseph J Giorgianni 212-264-0780/fax: 212-264-6798
 e-mail: joseph.giorgianni@gsa.gov

Federal Supply Service
Asst Regional Administrator:
 Charles B Weill 212-264-3590/fax: 212-264-9759

Federal Technology Service
Asst Regional Administrator (Acting):
 Steve Ruggiero 212-264-3590
 e-mail: steve.ruggiero@gsa.gov

Inspector General's Office
Asst Regional Inspector, Investigations:
 Daniel Walsh 212-264-7300/fax: 212-264-7154
Regional Director, Audit:
 Joseph Mastropietro 212-264-8620

Public Buildings Service
Asst Regional Administrator:
 John Scorcia 212-264-4282/fax: 212-264-2232
 e-mail: john.scorcia@gsa.gov
Deputy Asst Regional Administrator:
 Vacant 212-264-4285
Director, Property Management:
 David Segermeister 212-264-4273/fax: 212-264-2746
Director, Realty Services:
 Donald W Eigendorff 212-264-4210/fax: 212-264-9400

US Government Printing Office
e-mail: infonewyork@gpo.gov
Web site: www.gpo.gov

Region 2-I (New York)
Printing Procurement Office . . . . fax: 212-264-2413
26 Federal Plaza, Room 2930, New York, NY 10278
212-264-2252 Fax: 212-264-2413
Manager, NYC & Philadelphia Ofcs:
 Ira Fishkin 212-620-3321/fax: 212-620-3378

US Postal Service
Web site: www.usps.gov

NORTHEAST AREA (Includes part of New York State) . . . . fax: 860-285-1253
6 Griffin Rd North, Windsor, CT 06006-7010
Vice President, Area Operations:
 Megan Brennan 860-285-7040

New York Metro Area . . . . fax: 718-321-7150
142-02 20th Ave, Rm 318, Flushing, NY 11351-0001
Vice President, Area Operations:
 David L Solomon 718-321-5823

US State Department
Web site: www.state.gov

Bureau of Educational & Cultural Affairs-NY Pgm Branch . . . . fax: 212-399-5783
666 Fifth Ave, Ste 603, New York, NY 10103
212-399-5750 Fax: 212-399-5783
Web site: exchanges.state.gov
Director:
 Donna Shirreffs 212-399-5750

US Mission to the United Nations
140 East 45th St, New York, NY 10017
US Representative to the United Nations:
 Acting Ambassador Ann Patterson 212-415-4404
Deputy US Representative to the United Nations:
 Ambassador Ann Patterson 212-415-4410
US Representative for UN Management & Reform:
 Ambassador Patrick Kennedy 212-415-4032
US Representative to ECOSOC:
 Ambassador Sichan Siv 212-415-4278
Chief of Staff:
 Thomas A Schweich 212-415-4481
Counselor for Host Country:
 Russell F Graham 212-415-4131
Counselor for International Legal Affairs:
 Charles Nicholas Rostow 212-415-4220
Counselor for Political Affairs:
 William J Brencick 212-415-4363
Director, Communications, Spokesman:
 Richard Grenell 212-415-4058
Military Staff Committee:
 Col John B O'Dowd 212-415-4147

U.S. CONGRESS

See U.S. Congress Chapter for additional Standing Committee and Subcommittee information.

House of Representatives Standing Committees

Government Reform
Chair:
 Henry A Waxman (D-CA)
Ranking Minority Member:
 Henry A Waxman (D-CA) 202-225-3976
New York Delegate:
 Brian M Higgins (D) 202-225-3306
New York Delegate:
 Carolyn B Maloney (D) 202-225-7944
New York Delegate:
 John M McHugh (R) 202-225-4611
New York Delegate:
 Major R Owens (D) 202-225-6231
New York Delegate:
 Edolphus Towns (D) 202-225-5936

Homeland Security
Chair:
 Bennie G Thompson (D-MS) 202-225-5876

Offices and agencies generally appear in alphabetical order, except when specific order is requested by listee.

GOVERNMENT OPERATIONS / Private Sector

Ranking Minority Member:
  Peter T King (R-NY) 202-225-7896
New York Delegate:
  Nita M Lowey (D) 202-225-6506
  Subcommittees
    Emergency Communications, Preparedness and Response
      Chair:
        Henry Cuellar (D-TX) 202-225-1640
      Ranking Minority Member:
        Charlie Dent (R-PA) 202-225-6411
    Emerging Threats, Cybersecurity and Science & Technology
      Chair:
        James R Langevin (D-RI) 202-225-2736
      Ranking Minority Member:
        Michael McCaul (R-TX) 202-225-2401
    Intelligence Information Sharing & Terrorism Risk Assessment
      Chair:
        Robert R Simmons (R-CT) 202-225-2076
      Ranking Minority Member:
        Zoe Lofgren (D-CA) 202-225-3072
      New York Delegate:
        Nita M Lowey (D) 202-225-6506
    Management, Investigations and Oversight
      Chair:
        Christopher P Carney (D-PA) 202-225-3731
      Ranking Minority Member:
        Mike Rogers (R-AL) 202-225-3261
    Transportation Security and Infrastructure Protection
      Chair:
        Sheila Jackson Lee (D-TX) 202-225-3816
      Ranking Minority Member:
        Dan Lungren (R-CA) 202-225-5716

Intelligence, Permanent Select Committee on
Chair:
  Silvestre Reyes (D-TX) 202-225-4831
Ranking Minority Member:
  Peter Hoekstra (R-MI) 202-225-4401
New York Delegate:
  John McHugh (R) 202-225-4611
  Subcommittee
    Technical & Tactical Intelligence
      Chair:
        C A Dutch Ruppersberger (D-MD) ... 202-225-3061
      Ranking Minority Member:
        Heather Wilson (R-NM) 202-225-6316
      New York Delegate:
        John McHugh (R) 202-225-4611

Standards of Official Conduct
Chair:
  Stephanie Tubbs Jones (D-OH) 202-225-4472

Ranking Minority Member:
  Doc Hastings (R-WA) 202-225-5816

Senate Standing Committees

Ethics, Select Committee on
Chair:
  Barbara Boxer (D-CA) 202-224-3553
Vice Chair:
  John Cornyn (R-TX) 202-224-2934

Homeland Security & Governmental Affairs
Chair:
  Joseph I Lieberman (D-CT) 202-224-4041
Ranking Minority Member:
  Susan Collins (R-ME) 202-224-2523

Indian Affairs, Committee on
Chair:
  Byron L Dorgan (D-ND) 202-224-2251
Vice Chair:
  Craig Thomas (R-WY) 202-224-2251

Intelligence, Select Committee on
Chair:
  John D Rockefeller, IV (D-WV) 202-224-6472
Vice Chair:
  Christopher S Bond (R-MO) 202-224-5721

Judiciary
Chair:
  Patrick J Leahy (D-VT) 202-224-4242
Ranking Minority Member:
  Arlen Specter (R-PA) 202-227-4254
New York Delegate:
  Charles E Schumer (D) 202-224-6542
  Subcommittees
    Immigration, Refugees and Border Security
      Chair:
        Edward M Kennedy (D-MA) 202-224-4543
      Ranking Minority Member:
        John Cornyn (R-TX) 202-224-2394
      New York Delegate:
        Charles E Schumer (D) 202-224-6542
    Terrorism, Technology & Homeland Security
      Chair:
        Dianne Feinstein (D-CA) 202-224-3841
      Ranking Minority Member:
        Jon Kyl (R-AZ) 202-224-4521

Private Sector

Academy of Political Science
475 Riverside Drive, Ste 1274, New York, NY 10115-1274
212-870-2500 Fax: 212-870-2202
e-mail: aps@psqonline.org
Web site: www.psqonline.org
Demetrios James Caraley, President
Analysis of government, economic & social issues

Albany Law School, Government Law Center
80 New Scotland Ave, Albany, NY 12208
518-445-2311 Fax: 518-445-2303
e-mail: glc@albanylaw.edu
Web site: www.als.edu
Patricia Salkin, Associate Dean & Director, Governmental Law
Legal aspects of public policy reform

Offices and agencies generally appear in alphabetical order, except when specific order is requested by listee.

GOVERNMENT OPERATIONS / Private Sector

Association of Government Accountants, NY Capital Chapter
PO Box 1923, Albany, NY 12201
518-427-4765 or 212-872-5733
e-mail: lvacarro@kpmg.com
Web site: www.aganycap.org
Lori Vaccaro, Chapter President
Education for the government financial management community

Business Council of New York State Inc
152 Washington Ave, Albany, NY 12210
518-465-7511 x204 Fax: 518-465-4389
e-mail: elliott.shaw@bcnys.org
Web site: www.bcnys.org
Elliott A Shaw, Jr, Director, Government Affairs
Resources for business

Cayuga Nation
PO Box 11, Versailles, NY 14168
716-532-4847 Fax: 716-532-5417
e-mail: cayuga@sixnations.org
Web site: www.sixnations.org
Clint Halftown, Representative
Tribal government

Center for Governmental Research Inc (CGR)
1 South Washington St, Ste 400, Rochester, NY 14614-1125
585-325-6360 Fax: 585-325-2612
e-mail: kgardner@cgr.org
Web site: www.cgr.org
Kent Gardner, Executive Director
Nonprofit, nonpartisan institution devoted to analyzing public policies to ensure that they benefit the community at large

Center for Technology in Government, University at Albany, SUNY
187 Wolf Rd, Ste 301, Albany, NY 12205-1138
518-442-3892 Fax: 518-442-3886
e-mail: info@ctg.albany.edu
Web site: www.ctg.albany.edu
Alison Heaphy, Director
Works with government to develop well-informed information strategies that foster innovation and enhance the quality and coordination of public services through applied research and partnership projects

Citizens Union of the City of New York
299 Broadway, Rm 700, New York, NY 10007-1978
212-227-0342 Fax: 212-227-0345
e-mail: citizens@citizensunion.org
Web site: www.citizensunion.org
Dick Dadey, Executive Director
Government watchdog organization; city and state public policy issues; political and goverment reform.

Coalition of Fathers & Families NY, PAC
PO Box 782, Clifton Park, NY 12065
518-383-8202
e-mail: fafny@fafny.org
Web site: www.fafny.org/fafnypac.htm
James Hays, Treasurer
Political Action for fathers and families in New York

Columbia University, Exec Graduate Pgm in Public Policy & Administration
420 W 118th St, Rm 1314, New York, NY 10027
212-854-4445 Fax: 212-854-5765
e-mail: sc32@columbia.edu
Web site: www.columbia.edu/~sc32
Steven Cohen, Director
Urban & environmental policy; public management

Common Cause/NY
155 Ave of the Americas, 4th Fl, New York, NY 10013
212-691-6421 Fax: 212-807-1809
e-mail: cocauseny@aol.com
Web site: www.commoncause.org/ny
Rachel Leon, Executive Director
Campaign finance reform, ballot access, political gift disclosure & public interest lobbying

NYS Bar Assn, Task Force to Review Terrorism Legislation Cmte
Connors & Vilardo
1000 Liberty Bldg, 424 Main St, Buffalo, NY 14202-3510
716-852-5533 Fax: 716-852-5649
e-mail: ved@connors-vilardo.com
Web site: www.connors-vilardo.com
Vincent E Doyle, III, Chair

Council of State Governments, Eastern Conference
40 Broad St, Ste 2050, New York, NY 10004-2317
212-482-2320 Fax: 212-482-2344
e-mail: alan@csgeast.org
Web site: www.csgeast.org
Alan V Sokolow, Regional Director
Training, research & information sharing for state government officials

Crane, Parente & Cherubin
90 State Street, Ste 1515A, Albany, NY 12207
518-432-8000 Fax: 518-432-0086
e-mail: jcrane@cpclaw.net
James B Crane, II, Managing Partner
Governmental relations, banking & financial services, corporate law, construction law, energy, utilities, communications, land use, environmental & wireless telecommunications law

Offices and agencies generally appear in alphabetical order, except when specific order is requested by listee.

GOVERNMENT OPERATIONS / Private Sector

DeGraff, Foy, Kunz & Devine, LLP
90 State St, Albany, NY 12207
518-462-5300 Fax: 518-436-0210
e-mail: firm@degraff-foy.com
Web site: www.degraff-foy.com
David Kunz, Managing Partner
Government relations, administrative law & tax exempt/municipal financing, education, energy, transportation, public authorities & the environment

Fiscal Policy Institute
1 Lear Jet Lane, Latham, NY 12110
518-786-3156
e-mail: mauro@fiscalpolicy.org
Web site: www.fiscalpolicy.org
Frank Mauro, Executive Director
Nonpartisan research & education; tax, budget, economic & related public policy issues that affect quality of life & economic well-being

Fordham University, Department of Political Science
113 W 60th Street, New York, NY 10023
212-636-6334 Fax: 212-636-7153
e-mail: sbeck@fordham.edu
Web site: www.fordham.edu
Susan Beck, Associate Professor of Political Science
Women in public office; importance of gender in understanding modes of governance

Geto & deMilly Inc
130 E 40th St, New York, NY 10016
212-686-4551 Fax: 212-213-6850
e-mail: pr@getodmilly.com
Ethan Geto, President
Public & government relations

NYS Bar Assn, Legislative Policy Cmte
Greenberg Traurig, LLP
MetLife Building, 200 Park Avenue, New York, NY 10166
212-801-9200 Fax: 212-801-6400
e-mail: greenbergh@gtlaw.com
Web site: www.gtlaw.com
Henry M Greenberg, Chair

Institute of Public Administration/NYU Wagner
295 Lafayette St, 2nd Floor, New York, NY 10012-9604
212-998-7400
e-mail: wagner@nyu.edu
Web site: www.wagner.nyu.edu
David Mammen, President
Non-profit research, consulting & educational institute

KPMG LLP
515 Broadway, Albany, NY 12207-2974
518-427-4600 Fax: 518-689-4717
e-mail: rhannmann@kpmg.com
Web site: www.kpmg.com
John R Miller, Vice Chair, Health Care & Public Sector
State & local government audit & advisory service

League of Women Voters of New York State
62 Grand Street, Albany, NY 12207-2712
518-465-4162 Fax: 518-465-0812
e-mail: rob@lwvny.org
Web site: www.lwvny.org
Rob Marchiony, Executive Director
Public policy issues forum; good government advocacy

Manhattan Institute (The)
52 Vanderbilt Ave, 2nd Fl, New York, NY 10017
212-599-7000 Fax: 212-599-3494
Web site: www.manhattan-institute.org
Lawrence J Mone, President
Research on public policy issues including taxes, welfare, crime, the legal system, urban life, race & education

Manhattan Institute for Policy Research
52 Vanderbilt Avenue, 2nd Floor, New York, NY 10017
212-599-7000 x315 Fax: 212-599-3494
e-mail: communications@manhattan-institute.org
Web site: www.manhattan-institute.org
Lindsay M Young, Executive Director, Communications
Think tank promoting the development & dissemination of new ideas that foster greater economic choice & individual responsibility

NYS Bar Assn, Court Structure & Judicial Selection Cmte
McMahon & Grow
301 N Washington St, PO Box 4350, Rome, NY 13442-4350
315-336-4700 Fax: 315-336-5851
e-mail: mgglaw@dreamscape.com
Hon Richard D Simons, Chair
Retired Judge-NYS Court of Appeals

NYS Bar Assn, Federal Constitution & Legislation Cmte
Mulholland & Knapp, LLP
641 Lexington Avenue, New York, NY 10022-4503
212-702-9027 Fax: 212-702-9092
e-mail: robknapp@mklex.com
Web site: www.mklex.com
Robert Knapp, Chair

NY Coalition of 100 Black Women - Not For Profit
PO Box 2555, Grand Central Station, New York, NY 10163
212-517-5700 Fax: 212-772-8771
e-mail: ngriffith@cobwfounders.org
Natatia Griffith, President
Leadership by example; advocates & agents for changes-improving the quality of life by focusing resources in education, health & community services

NY StateWatch Inc
100 State St, Ste 440, Albany, NY 12207
518-449-7425 Fax: 518-449-7431
e-mail: rob@statewatch.com
Web site: www.statewatch.com
Robert Dusablon, Executive Director
Legislative news/bill tracking service

Offices and agencies generally appear in alphabetical order, except when specific order is requested by listee.

GOVERNMENT OPERATIONS / Private Sector

NYS Association of Counties
111 Pine Street, Albany, NY 12207
518-465-1473 Fax: 518-465-0506
e-mail: sacquario@nysac.org
Web site: www.nysac.org
Stephen J Acquario, Executive Director
Lobbying, research & training services

NYS Bar Assn, Mass Disaster Response Committee
NYS Grievance Committee
Renaissance Plz, 335 Adams St, Ste 2400, Brooklyn, NY 11201
718-923-6300 Fax: 718-624-2978
e-mail: rsaltzma@courts.state.ny.us
Robert J Saltzman, Chair

NYS Bar Assn, Law Youth & Citizenship Committee
NYS Supreme Court
92 Franklin Street, 2nd Floor, Buffalo, NY 14202
716-845-9327 Fax: 716-851-3229
e-mail: oyoung@courts.state.ny.us
Oliver C Young, Chair

Nelson A Rockefeller Institute of Government
411 State St, Albany, NY 12203-1003
518-443-5522 Fax: 518-443-5788
e-mail: nathanr@rockinst.org
Web site: www.rockinst.org
Richard P Nathan, Director
Management & finance of welfare, health & employment of state & local governments nationally & especially in NY

New York Public Interest Research Group
9 Murray St, 3rd Fl, New York, NY 10007
212-349-6460 Fax: 212-349-1366
e-mail: nypirg@nypirg.org
Web site: www.nypirg.org
Christopher Meyer, Executive Director
Environmental preservation, public health, consumer protection & government reform

New York State Directory
185 Millerton Road, PO Box 860, Millerton, NY 12546
518-789-8700 or 800-562-2139 Fax: 518-789-0556
e-mail: customerservice@greyhouse.com
Web site: www.greyhouse.com
Leslie Mackenzie, Publisher
State government public policy directory

Oneida Indian Nation
Turning Stone Resort & Casino, Executive Offices, Patrick Road, Vernon, NY 13478
315-361-7633 Fax: 315-361-7721
Web site: www.oneida-nation.org
Ray Halbritter, Nation Repesentative & Chief Eexecutive Officer, Nation Enterprises
Tribal government

Onondaga Nation
Box 319-B, RR #1, Nedrow, NY 13120
315-492-4210 Fax: 315-469-1725
Web site: www.onondaganation.org
Irving Powless, Jr, Chief
Tribal government

Community Bankers Assn of NY State, Government Relations Cmte
Pioneer Savings Bank
21 Second St, Troy, NY 12180
518-274-4800 Fax: 518-274-3560
Web site: www.pioneersb.com
John M Scarchilli, President & CEO

PricewaterhouseCoopers LLP
State St Ctr, 80 State St, Albany, NY 12207
518-462-2030 Fax: 518-427-4499
Web site: www.pwc.com
Rich Grant, Managing Partner

NYS Bar Assn, Civil Rights/Spec Cmte on Collateral Consequence of Criminal Proceedings
Proskauer Rose LLP
1585 Broadway, New York, NY 10036-8299
212-969-3261 Fax: 212-969-2900
e-mail: psherwin@proskauer.com
Web site: www.proskauer.com
Peter J W Sherwin, Chair

Public Agenda
6 East 39th St, 9th Fl, New York, NY 10016
212-686-6610 Fax: 212-889-3461
e-mail: info@publicagenda.org
Web site: www.publicagenda.org
Claudia Feurey, Vice President, Communications & External Relations
Nonpartisan, nonprofit organization dedicated to conducting unbiased public opinion research & producing fair-minded citizen education materials

SUNY at Albany, Center for Women in Government & Civil Society
135 Western Ave, Draper Hall, Rm 302, Albany, NY 12222
518-442-3900 Fax: 518-442-3877
e-mail: cwig@albany.edu
Web site: www.cwig.albany.edu
Judith R Saidel, Executive Director
Through research, teaching, leadership development, networking & public education, the center works to strengthen women's public policy leadership, broaden access to policy knowledge, skills & influence; advance equity, enhance nonprofit mgmnt

Offices and agencies generally appear in alphabetical order, except when specific order is requested by listee.

GOVERNMENT OPERATIONS / Private Sector

SUNY at Albany, Nelson A Rockefeller College of Public Affairs & Policy
135 Western Ave, Albany, NY 12222
518-442-5244 Fax: 518-442-5298
e-mail: thompson@albany.edu
Web site: www.albany.edu/rockefeller
Frank J Thompson, Dean
Health policy, policy implementation, public personnel policy, administrative politics

SUNY at Albany, Rockefeller College
135 Western Ave, Albany, NY 12222
518-442-5378 Fax: 518-442-5298
Joseph F Zimmerman, Professor
Intergovernmental relations; NY state & local government; ethics in government; election systems & voting

SUNY at New Paltz, College of Liberal Arts & Sciences
614 Faculty Tower, New Paltz, NY 12561-2499
845-257-2901
e-mail: benjamig@newpaltz.edu
Web site: www.newpaltz.edu
Gerald Benjamin, Dean & Professor of Political Science
Local & state government process & structure; regionalism; politics & election law

SUNY at New Paltz, Department of History
75 South Manheim Blvd, New Paltz, NY 12561
845-257-3523 Fax: 845-257-2735
Laurence Hauptman, Professor of History
American Indian policies

Seneca Nation of Indians
PO Box 231, Salamanca, NY 14779
716-945-1790 Fax: 716-945-1565
e-mail: sni@localnet.com
Web site: www.sni.org
Maurice A John, Sr, President
Tribal government

Shinnecock Indian Nation
PO Box 5006, Southampton, NY 11969-5006
631-283-6143 ext 1 or 631-287-3752 Fax: 631-283-0751
e-mail: sination@optionline.net
Web site: www.shinnecocknation.com
Randy King, Chairman, Tribal Trustees
Tribal government

St Regis Mohawk Tribe
412 State Route 37, Hogansburg, NY 13655
518-358-2272 Fax: 518-358-3203
Web site: www.stregismohawktribe.com
Barbara Lazori, Chief
Tribal government

Syracuse University, Maxwell School of Citizenship & Public Affairs
400 Eggers Hall, Syracuse, NY 13244-1020
315-443-2252 Fax: 315-443-1081
e-mail: ctrpol@syr.edu
Web site: www.maxwell.syr.edu
Timothy Smeeding, Professor of Public Policy; Director
Education, healthcare, entrpreneurship policies, social welfare, income distribution & comparative social policies

Unkechauq Nation
Poospatuck Reservation, Box 86, Mastic, NY 11950
631-281-6464 Fax: 631-281-2125
e-mail: hwal1@aol.com
Harry Wallace, Chief
Tribal government

Offices and agencies generally appear in alphabetical order, except when specific order is requested by listee.

HEALTH

New York State

GOVERNOR'S OFFICE

Governor's Office
Executive Chamber
State Capitol
Albany, NY 12224
518-474-8390 Fax: 518-474-1513
Web site: www.state.ny.us

Governor:
  Eliot Spitzer 518-474-8390
Secretary to the Governor:
  Richard Baum..................................... 518-474-4246
Counsel to the Governor:
  David Nocenti.................................... 518-474-8343
Senior Advisor to the Governor:
  Lloyd Constantine 518-486-9671
Deputy Secretary, Health & Human Services:
  Dennis Whalen.................................... 518-408-2500
Assistant Deputy Secretary, Health & Human Services:
  Joseph Baker..................................... 518-486-4079
Assistant Counsel to the Governor-Health & Mental Hygiene:
  Lisa Ullman 518-474-2266
Director, Communications:
  Darren Dopp...................................... 518-474-8418

EXECUTIVE DEPARTMENTS AND RELATED AGENCIES

Alcoholism & Substance Abuse Services, Office of
1450 Western Ave
Albany, NY 12203
518-485-1660 Fax: 518-457-5474
Web site: www.oasas.state.ny.us

501 7th Ave
8th Fl
New York, NY 10018
646-728-4533

Commissioner:
  Karen M Carpenter-Palumbo 518-457-1758
Executive Deputy Commissioner:
  Kathleen Caggiano-Siino 518-485-2312
Director, Communications:
  Jennifer Farrell................... 518-485-1768/fax: 518-485-6014
  e-mail: jenniferfarrell@oasas.state.ny.us
Director, Human Resources Management:
  Thomas M Torino 518-457-2963
Director, Internal Audit:
  Richard Kaplan................................... 518-485-2039
Affirmative Action Officer:
  Henry Gonzalez 518-457-2963

Public Information Officer:
  Joseph Morrissey 518-485-1768
  e-mail: josephmorrissey@oasas.state.ny.us

Financial, Capital & Information Tech Management Division
Associate Commissioner:
  Michael Lawler................................... 518-457-5312
  e-mail: michaellawler@oasas.state.ny.us

  Bureau of Budget Management
  Director:
    Jay Runkel..................................... 518-485-2193

  Bureau of Capital Management
  Director:
    Laurie Felter.................................. 518-457-2545

  Bureau of Financial & Emergency Management
  Director:
    Vito Manzella.................................. 518-457-4742

  Bureau of Health Care Financing & 3rd Party Reimbursement
  Director:
    Nicholas Colamaria 518-485-2207

  Bureau of Information Technology
  Director:
    David Gardam 518-485-2351

Legal Affairs Division
Associate Commsioner:
  Henry F Zwack.................................... 518-485-2312

  Bureau of Counsel
  Director:
    Dick Hogle..................................... 518-485-2317

  Bureau of Governmental & NYC Affairs
  Director:
    Jeff Cleary 518-485-2337

  Bureau of Certification
  Director:
    Virginia Martin................................ 518-485-2247

  Bureau of Enforcement
  Director:
    Charles Monson................................. 518-485-2312

Management Resources & Quality Assurance Division
Associate Commissioner:
  Neil Grogin...................................... 518-485-2257
Client Advocacy:
  Michael Yorio.................................... 800-553-5790

  Bureau of Quality Assurance
  Director:
    William Lachanski.............................. 518-485-2260
  Training/Technical Assistance:
    Steve Therriault............................... 518-485-2027
  Training/Technical Assistance:
    Joseph Chelales 646-728-4644

Offices and agencies generally appear in alphabetical order, except when specific order is requested by listee.

HEALTH / New York State

Bureau of Workforce Development
Director:
  Joseph Burke 518-485-2033

Prevention & Treatment Services Division
Associate Commissioner:
  Frances M Harding.............................. 518-485-6022

Bureau of Prevention
Director:
  John Ernst..................................... 518-485-2132

Bureau of ATCs
Director:
  Thomas Nightingale............................. 518-457-7077

Bureau of Treatment
Director:
  Rob Piculell 518-485-2123

Bureau of Systems Development & Public Education
Director:
  William Barnette 518-457-6206

Systems/Program Performance & Analysis Division
Acting Associate Commissioner:
  Timothy P Williams 518-485-2322

Bureau of Planning & Practice Improvement
Acting Associate Commissioner:
  Bob Gallati.................................... 518-457-5989

Bureau of Evaluation & Practice Improvement
Director:
  Alan Kott 518-485-7189

Bureau of Statewide Field Operations
Director:
  Edward Freeman 518-457-8240

Education Department
State Education Bldg
89 Washington Ave
Albany, NY 12234
518-474-5215 Fax: 518-486-5631
Web site: www.nysed.gov

Commissioner, University President:
  Richard P Mills................................ 518-474-5844
  e-mail: rmills@mail.nysed.gov
Assistant to the Commissioner:
  Peggy Rivers................................... 518-474-5845
  e-mail: privers@mail.nysed.gov
Counsel & Deputy Commissioner, Legal Affairs:
  Kathy A Ahearn 518-474-6400
  e-mail: kahearn@mail.nysed.gov
Chief of Staff & Deputy Commissioner, Innovation:
  David Miller................................... 518-486-1713
  e-mail: dmiller@mail.nysed.gov

Office of the Professions .... fax: 518-473-2056
  89 Washington Ave, EB, 2nd Fl, West Mezz, Albany, NY 12234
  Fax: 518-473-2056
  Web site: www.op.nysed.gov
Associate Commissioner:
  Frank Munoz.................................... 518-474-3817 x440
  e-mail: opopr@mail.nysed.gov
Executive Coordinator, Professional Practice:
  Anthony Lofrumento............................. 518-474-3817 x570
  e-mail: op4info@mail.nysed.gov

Office of Professional Responsibility
Executive Director:
  Vacant 518-474-3817 x440
  e-mail: opexdir@mail.nysed.gov

Professional Education Program Review
Supervisor:
  Vacant 518-474-3817 x360
  e-mail: opprogs@mail.nysed.gov

Professional Licensing Services
Director:
  Anthony Lofrumento............................. 518-474-3817 x340
  e-mail: opdpls@mail.nysed.gov

State Boards for the Professions
  Chiropractic
    Executive Secretary:
      Douglas Lentovich 518-474-3817 x190
  Dentistry & Optometry
    Executive Secretary:
      Milton Lawney 518-474-3817 x550
  Medicine, Diet-Nutrn, Athltc Trning, Medical Physics & Vet Med
    Executive Secretary:
      Vacant 518-474-3817 x560
  Nursing & Respiratory Therapy
    Executive Secretary:
      Barbara Zittel 518-474-3817 x120
  Pharmacy & Midwifery
    Executive Secretary:
      Lawrence H Mokhiber 518-474-3817 x130
  Psychology & Massage Therapy
    Executive Secretary:
      Kathleen M Doyle 518-474-3817 x150
  Social Work & Mental Health Practitioners
    Executive Secretary:
      David Hamilton 518-474-3817 x450
  Speech Language Pathology & Audiology, Acupuncture & Occupational Therapy
    Executive Secretary:
      Lawrence DeMers 518-474-3817 x100

Health Department
Corning Tower
Empire State Plaza
Albany, NY 12237
518-474-7354
Web site: www.nyhealth.gov

Commissioner:
  Richard F Daines, MD 518-474-2011
Chief of Staff:
  Wendy Saunders................................. 518-473-0458
Deputy Commissioner, Administration:
  Robert W Reed 518-474-8565
Ombudsman:
  David V Wollner 518-474-3920
Interim Records Access Officer:
  Robert LoCicero................................ 518-474-8734

AIDS Institute
Director:
  Guthrie S Birkhead 518-473-7542/fax: 518-486-1315
Co-Executive Deputy Director:
  Barbara DeVore 518-473-7542
Co-Executive Deputy Director:
  Humberto Cruz.................................. 212-417-5500

Offices and agencies generally appear in alphabetical order, except when specific order is requested by listee.

HEALTH / New York State

Associate Director:
Sue Klein 518-473-8778
Director, Systems Development:
Vida Chernoff. 518-402-6790
Director, Information Systems Office:
Bonita Scott 518-473-8459
Director, Special Projects:
Andrea Small 518-473-2903
Director, Program Evaluation & Research:
James Tesoriero 518-402-6814
Medical Director:
Bruce D Agins 212-417-4536

HIV Health Care & Community Services
Co-Director:
Mona Scully 518-474-5577
Co-Director:
Ira Feldman 518-486-1383

HIV Prevention
Director:
Daniel O'Connell 518-473-2300
Associate Director:
Alma Candela 212-417-4693

Center for Community Health
Director:
Guthrie S Birkhead 518-402-5382/fax: 518-486-1455
Executive Deputy Director:
Ellen Anderson 518-474-5073/fax: 518-473-8389
Deputy Director:
Phyllis Silver 518-473-0771/fax: 518-473-8389

Chronic Disease Prevention & Adult Health
Director:
Mark S Baptiste 518-474-0512/fax: 518-473-2853
Associate Director:
Thomas Blake 518-473-4438/fax: 518-473-2853

Epidemiology Division
Director:
Perry F Smith 518-474-1055/fax: 518-473-2301
Associate Director:
Karen Savicki 518-474-4394

Family Health Division
Director:
Barbara McTague 518-473-7922/fax: 518-473-2015
Associate Director:
Vacant 518-473-4441
Pediatric Director:
Christopher A Kus 518-473-9883
Office of the Medical Director:
Marilyn A Kacica 518-473-9883

Information Technology & Project Management
Director:
Robert B Fletcher 518-473-4261/fax: 518-473-0476
Assistant Director:
Catherine Sciara 518-473-4261/fax: 518-473-0476

Local Health Services
Director:
Sylvia Pirani 518-473-4223/fax: 518-473-8714
Assistant Director:
Marie Miller 518-473-4223/fax: 518-473-8714

Minority Health
Director:
Wilma Waithe 518-474-2180/fax: 518-474-4695

Nutrition Division
Director:
Patricia Hess 518-402-7090/fax: 518-402-7398
Associate Director:
Mary Warr Cowans 518-402-7090

Center for Environmental Health . . . . fax: 518-402-7509
547 River St, Troy, NY 12180
Director:
Ronald Tramontano 518-402-7500

Division of Environmental Health Investigation
Associate Director:
G Anders Carlson 518-402-7501

Environmental Health Assessment Division
Director:
Nancy Kim 518-402-7511/fax: 518-402-7509
Associate Director:
John Wilson 518-402-7511

Environmental Protection
Director:
Richard Svenson 518-402-7510

Executive Offices

Executive & Advisory Council Operations
Director:
Vacant 518-474-8009
Assistant Director:
Donna Peterson 518-474-8009

Office of Governmental Affairs
Director:
Wendy Saunders 518-473-1124/fax: 518-473-9674

Office of Health Insurance Programs
Deputy Commissioner & State Medicaid Director:
Deborah Bachrach 518-474-3018/fax: 518-486-6852
Medical Director:
Foster Gesten MD 518-486-6865
Medical Director:
James Figge MD 518-474-9138
Director, Coverage & Enrollment:
Judith Arnold 518-474-0180
Director, Program Operations & Systems:
Gabriel Deyo 518-408-0647
Director, Managed Care & Program Evaluation:
Kathleen Shure 518-474-1590
Director, Financial Planning & Policy:
Gregory Allen 518-473-0919
Director, Health Care Financing:
John Ulberg 518-474-6350
Director, Administration:
Katherine Napoli 518-486-6830

Office of Long Term Care
Deputy Commissioner:
Mark Kissinger 518-402-5673

School of Public Health, SUNY at Albany . . . . fax: 518-402-0283
One University Place, Rensselaer, NY 12144
518-402-0414 Fax: 518-402-0283
Interim Dean:
Mary Applegate MD 518-402-0281/fax: 518-402-0329
Assistant Dean, Administration:
Larry D Preston 518-402-0281

Task Force On Life & The Law
90 Church St, New York, NY 10007

Offices and agencies generally appear in alphabetical order, except when specific order is requested by listee.

HEALTH / New York State

Director:
    Tia Powell 212-417-5444
Counsel:
    Vacant 212-417-5444
Policy Analyst:
    Kelly Pike 212-417-5444

Health Facilities Management
Director:
    Val S Gray 518-474-2772/fax: 518-474-0611

Helen Hayes Hospital
Rte 9W, West Haverstraw, NY 10993-1195
845-786-4000
Web site: www.helenhayeshospital.org
Director & CEO:
    Magdalena Ramirez 845-786-4202/fax: 845-947-0036
Deputy Director:
    Edmund Zybert 845-786-4201

New York State Veterans' Home at Batavia
220 Richmond Ave, Batavia, NY 14020
585-345-2000
Administrator:
    Joanne I Hernick 585-345-2076/fax: 585-345-9030
Medical Director:
    Bruce Small MD 585-345-2042
Director, Nursing:
    Barbara Bates 585-345-2000 x2041

New York State Veterans' Home at Montrose . . . . . . fax: 914-788-6100
2090 Albany Post Rd, Montrose, NY 10548
Administrator:
    Nancy Baa-Danso 914-788-6003
Medical Director:
    Wellington Liu MD 914-788-6025

New York State Veterans' Home at Oxford
4211 State Highway 220, Oxford, NY 13830
607-843-3100
Administrator:
    Vathsala Venugopalan 607-843-3129/fax: 607-843-3199
Medical Director:
    Philip Dzwonczyk MD 607-843-3140

New York State Veterans' Home at St Albans
178-50 Linden Blvd, Jamaica, NY 11434-1467
718-990-0300
Administrator:
    Neville Goldson 718-990-0329
Medical Director:
    Thomas Bizarro MD 718-990-0328
Director, Nursing:
    Elaine Boy-Brown 718-990-0316

Health Research Inc
One University Place, Rensselaer, NY 12144
Web site: www.hrinet.org
Executive Director:
    Michael Nazarko 518-431-1204

Health Systems Management Office
Deputy Commissioner:
    James W Clyne Jr 518-474-7028

Acute & Primary Care Services Division
Director:
    Martin J Conroy 518-402-1003/fax: 518-402-1010

Continuing Care Offices
    Home & Community Based Care Division . . . . fax: 518-408-1145
    518-408-1132 Fax: 518-408-1145

    Quality & Surveillance for Nursing Homes & ICF/MRs . . . . fax:
    518-408-1271
    518-408-1267 Fax: 518-408-1271

Health Care Quality & Safety Office
Director:
    John N Morley MD 518-408-1828/fax: 518-474-2881

Health Care Standards & Surveillance Division
Director:
    Lisa M McMurdo 518-402-1040/fax: 518-402-1042

Health Facility Planning Division
Director:
    Neil Benjamin 518-402-0967/fax: 518-402-0971

Professional Medical Conduct
Director:
    Keith Servis 518-402-0855

Human Resources & Operations
Director:
    John R Conroy 518-473-3394/fax: 518-486-7374

Human Resources Management Group
Director:
    Vacant 518-473-3394

Operations Management Group
Director:
    M Colleen Driscoll 518-474-6936/fax: 518-474-8163

Information Systems & Health Statistics Group
Director:
    Brian Y Scott 518-474-8373/fax: 518-474-2288
Assistant Director:
    Robert Pennacchia 518-474-1301

    Administrative Operations - Tower/Administrative Operations
    800 N Pearl Street,
    Director:
        Robert Pennacchia 518-474-1301

    Bureau of Production Systems Management
    800 N Pearl Street,
    Director:
        Peter Carucci 518-474-5245

HEALTHCOM Services
Acting Director:
    Janet Carmack 518-473-2902

Legal Affairs
General Counsel:
    Thomas Conway 518-474-7553/fax: 518-473-2802
Deputy General Counsel:
    Janet S Cohn 518-474-7553/fax: 518-473-2802
Director, Bureau of Adjudication:
    Sean D O'Brien 518-402-0748/fax: 518-402-0751
Director, Bureau of Administrative Hearings:
    Edmund Russell Altone 518-473-1707/fax: 518-486-1858
Director, Bureau of House Counsel:
    Barbara Asheld 518-473-3233/fax: 518-473-2019
Director, Bureau of Litigation:
    Joseph Bierman 518-473-4631/fax: 518-473-2802
Director, Bureau of Health Insurance Programs:
    Gregor N Macmillan 518-408-1495/fax: 518-473-2802
Chief Counsel, Professional Medical Conduct Unit:
    Vacant 518-473-4282/fax: 518-473-2430

Offices and agencies generally appear in alphabetical order, except when specific order is requested by listee.

HEALTH / New York State

Public Affairs
Director:
  Claudia Hutton....................518-474-7354 x1

Regional/Area Offices

Capital District Regional Office
Frear Bldg, One Fulton St, Troy, NY 12180-3281
518-408-5300
Regional Director:
  Geraldine Bunn.....................518-408-5277
Assistant Regional Director:
  Robert Welch......................518-408-5277

Central New York Regional Office
217 S Salina St, Syracuse, NY 13202-1380
315-477-8100
Associate Director:
  Ronald Heerkens...................315-477-8484
Associate Director:
  Pauline Frazier...................315-477-8485

Metropolitan Area/Regional Office
90 Church St, New York, NY 10007
212-417-4100
Regional Director:
  Celeste M Johnson.................212-417-5550
Deputy Regional Director:
  Ellen Poliski.....................212-417-5550

Western Regional Office
584 Delaware Ave, Buffalo, NY 14202-1295
716-847-4500
Acting Regional Director:
  William Hoogland..................716-847-4302

Roswell Park Cancer Institute Corporation
Elm & Carlton Streets, Buffalo, NY 14263-0999
716-845-2300
Web site: www.roswellpark.org
President/CEO:
  Donald Trump...............716-845-5770/fax: 716-845-8261
Associate Director, Administration:
  Jeff Walker.......................716-845-3385
Medical Director:
  Judy Smith........................716-845-7724
Senior VP, Scientific Administration:
  Youcef Rustum.....................716-845-2389
Legal Counsel:
  Michael Sexton....................716-845-5770
Executive Director, Government Affairs:
  Lisa Damiani......................716-845-3079
  e-mail: lisa.damiani@roswellpark.org

Wadsworth Center
Director:
  Lawrence S Sturman..........518-474-7592/fax: 518-474-3439
Deputy Director:
  Jill Taylor.......................518-474-3157
Assistant Director:
  Vicky Derbyshire..................518-474-3157
Associate Director, Operations & Administration:
  Barbara Ryan.................518-474-1151/fax: 518-474-3439
Associate Director, Research & Technology:
  Carmen Manella...............518-474-0109/fax: 518-402-5381
Director, Education:
  Kathy Zdeb...................518-474-6713/fax: 518-474-5049
Director, Policy & Planning:
  Ann Willey...................518-486-2523/fax: 518-474-3439

Director, Research:
  Robert Trimble...............518-486-2565/fax: 518-402-5540

Environmental Disease Prevention
Director:
  Ken Aldous...................518-474-7161/fax: 518-473-2895
Deputy Director:
  Patrick Parsons...................518-474-7161

Genetic Disorders
Director:
  Marlene Belfort..............518-473-3345/fax: 518-474-3181
Deputy Director:
  Michele Caggana.............518-473-3854/fax: 518-486-2693

Herbert W Dickerman Library
Director:
  Thomas Flynn.................518-474-6172/fax: 518-474-3933

Infectious Disease
Director:
  Harry Taber..................518-474-8660/fax: 518-473-1326
Deputy Director:
  Ron Limberger................518-474-4177/fax: 518-486-7971

Laboratory Operations
Director:
  Barbara Ryan.................518-474-1151/fax: 518-474-3439
Deputy Director:
  Elizabeth Mahoney............518-474-6163/fax: 518-474-5719

Molecular Medicine
Director:
  Carmen Mannella..............518-474-0109/fax: 518-402-5381
Deputy Director:
  Erasmus Schneider.................518-474-2088

Insurance Department
25 Beaver St
New York, NY 10004
212-480-6400 Fax: 212-480-7454
Web site: www.ins.state.ny.us

One Commerce Plaza
Albany, NY 12257
518-474-4567
Fax: 518-473-6814

Superintendent:
  Eric R Dinallo...............518-474-4567/fax: 518-473-6814

Health Bureau
Co-Chief, NYC:
  Charles Rapacciulo...........212-480-5120/fax: 212-480-5216
Co-Chief, Albany:
  Tom Zyra.....................518-474-6272/fax: 518-473-4600
Chief, Accident & Health Rating:
  James M Gutterman.................518-474-5394

Life Bureau
Chief Examiner:
  Jeffrey Angelo....................212-480-5026

Public Affairs & Research Bureau
Director, Communications:
  David Neustadt...............212-480-5262/fax: 212-480-6077
  e-mail: public-affairs@ins.state.ny.us

Offices and agencies generally appear in alphabetical order, except when specific order is requested by listee.

HEALTH / New York State

Labor Department
Building 12
Room 500, State Campus
Albany, NY 12240
518-457-2741 Fax: 518-457-6908
e-mail: nysdol@labor.state.ny.us
Web site: www.labor.state.ny.us

Commissioner:
  M Patricia Smith................................518-457-2746
Director, Communications:
  Leo Rosales......................518-457-5519/fax: 518-485-1126

Worker Protection
Deputy Commissioner, Workforce Protection, Standards & Licensing:
  Pico Ben-Amotz..............................518-457-4317
Deputy Commissioner, Wage & Immigrant Services:
  Terri Gerstein..............................518-473-3905

Safety & Health Division
Director:
  Maureen Cox..................518-457-3518/fax: 518-457-1519

Asbestos Control Bureau
Program Manager:
  Robert Perez.................518-457-1255/fax: 518-485-8054

Industry Inspection Unit
Program Manager:
  Joe Gallagher...............518-457-1212/fax: 518-485-8054

On-Site Consultation Unit
Program Manager:
  James Rush..................518-457-2238/fax: 518-457-3454

Public Employees Safety & Health (PESH) Unit
Program Manager:
  Normand Labbe.............518-457-1263/fax: 518-457-5545

Law Department
State Capitol
Albany, NY 12224-0341
518-474-7330 Fax: 518-402-2472
Web site: www.oag.state.ny.us

120 Broadway
New York, NY 10271-0332
212-416-8000
Fax: 212-416-8942

Attorney General:
  Andrew M Cuomo................................518-474-7330
First Deputy Attorney General:
  Michele Hirshman..............................212-416-8050
Director, Public Information & Correspondence:
  Peter A Drago.....................518-474-7330/fax: 518-402-2472

Criminal Division
Deputy Attorney General:
  Peter B Pope....................212-416-8058/fax: 212-416-8026
Assistant Deputy Attorney General:
  Julieta Lozano..................212-416-8090/fax: 212-416-8026

Medicaid Fraud Control Unit
120 Broadway, 13th Fl, New York, NY 10271-0007
Deputy Attorney General-in-Charge:
  William J Comisky..........212-417-5250/fax: 212-417-5274
First Asst Dep Attny General:
  Peter M Bloch................212-417-5261/fax: 212-417-5274

Assistant Deputy Attorney General:
  George Quinlan................................716-853-8584
Regional Director, Albany:
  Steve Krantz....................518-474-3032/fax: 518-474-4519
Deputy Regional Director, Buffalo:
  Gary A Baldauf.................716-853-8507/fax: 716-853-8525
Regional Director, Long Island:
  Alan Buonpastore...............631-952-6400/fax: 631-952-6382
Regional Dir, NYC:
  Richard Harrow.................212-417-5391/fax: 212-417-4725
Regional Director, Rochester:
  Jerry Solomon..................716-262-2860/fax: 716-262-2866
Regional Director, Syracuse:
  Ralph Tortora, III.............315-423-1104/fax: 315-423-1120
Deputy Regional Director, Westchester/Rockland:
  Anne S Jardine.................845-732-7500/fax: 845-732-7555
Regional Director for Special Projects Unit:
  Patrick Lupinetti..............845-732-7550/fax: 845-732-7557

Public Advocacy Division
Deputy Attorney General:
  Dietrich Snell..................212-416-8041/fax: 212-416-8068
Special Counsel:
  Mary Ellen Burns...............................212-416-6155

Healthcare Bureau
Bureau Chief:
  Joseph R Baker, III............212-416-8521/fax: 212-416-8034

State Counsel Division
Deputy Attorney General:
  Richard Rifkin.................................518-473-7190

Claims Bureau
Bureau Chief:
  Susan Pogoda...................212-416-8516/fax: 212-416-8946

Litigation Bureau
Bureau Chief, Albany:
  Bruce D Feldman................518-473-8238/fax: 518-473-1572
Bureau Chief, NYC:
  James B Henley.................212-416-8523/fax: 212-416-6075

CORPORATIONS, AUTHORITIES AND COMMISSIONS

New York State Dormitory Authority
515 Broadway
Albany, NY 12207-2964
518-257-3000 Fax: 518-257-3100
e-mail: dabonds@dasny.org
Web site: www.dasny.org

One Penn Plaza
52nd Fl
New York, NY 10119-0098
212-273-5000
Fax: 212-273-5121

539 Franklin St
Buffalo, NY 14202-1109
716-884-9780
Fax: 716-884-9787

Offices and agencies generally appear in alphabetical order, except when specific order is requested by listee.

HEALTH / U.S. Government

Chair:
   Gail H Gordon 518-257-3180/fax: 518-257-3183
Executive Director:
   David D Brown, IV 518-257-3180/fax: 518-257-3183
Deputy Executive Director:
   Michael T Corrigan 518-257-3192/fax: 518-257-3183
Chief Fiscal Officer:
   John G Pasicznyk 518-257-3630/fax: 518-257-3100
   e-mail: jpasiczn@dasny.org
General Counsel:
   Jeffrey M Pohl 518-257-3120/fax: 518-257-3101
   e-mail: jpohl@dasny.org
Managing Director, Construction:
   James M Gray, RA 518-257-3200/fax: 518-257-3100
   e-mail: jgray@dasny.org
Managing Director, Portfolio Management:
   Lora K Lefebvre 518-257-3163/fax: 518-257-3387
   e-mail: llefebvr@dasny.org
Managing Director, Public Finance:
   Cheryl Ishmael 518-257-3362/fax: 518-257-3100
   e-mail: cishmael@dasny.org
Director, Communications & Marketing:
   Paul Burgdorf 518-257-3380/fax: 518-257-3387
   e-mail: pburgdor@dasny.org

NEW YORK STATE LEGISLATURE

See Legislative Branch in Section 1 for additional Standing Committee and Subcommittee information.

Assembly Standing Committees

Aging
Chair:
   Steven C Englebright (D) 518-455-4804
Ranking Minority Member:
   Philip Boyle (R) 518-455-4611

Alcoholism & Drug Abuse
Chair:
   Jeffrey Dinowitz (D) 518-455-5965
Ranking Minority Member:
   Gary D Finch (R) 518-455-5878

Children & Families
Chair:
   William Scarborough (D) 518-455-4451
Ranking Minority Member:
   Joseph A Errigo (R) 518-455-5662

Consumer Affairs & Protection
Chair:
   Audrey I Pheffer (D) 518-455-4292

Ranking Minority Member:
   Peter D Lopez (R) 518-455-5363

Health
Chair:
   Richard N Gottfried (D) 518-455-4941
Ranking Minority Member:
   James Bacalles (R) 518-455-5791

Senate Standing Committees

Aging
Chair:
   Martin J Golden (R) 518-455-2730
Ranking Minority Member:
   Ruben Diaz, Sr (D) 518-455-2511

Consumer Protection
Chair:
   Charles J Fuschillo, Jr (R) 518-455-3341
Ranking Minority Member:
   Carl Kruger (D) 518-455-2460

Health
Chair:
   Kemp Hannon (R) 518-455-2200
Ranking Minority Member:
   John L Sampson (D) 518-455-2788

Social Services, Children & Families
Chair:
   Carl Kruger (R) 518-455-2460
Ranking Minority Member:
   Velmanette Montgomery (D) 518-455-3451

Senate/Assembly Legislative Commissions

Health Care Financing, Council on
Senate Chair:
   Joseph L Bruno (R) 518-455-3191
Assembly Vice Chair:
   Vacant 518-455-0000
Executive Director:
   Al Cardillo 518-455-2067/fax: 518-426-6925

Toxic Substances & Hazardous Wastes, Legislative Commission on
Senate Chair:
   Vacant 518-455-0000
Assembly Vice Chair:
   David R Koon (D) 518-455-5784
Program Manager:
   Richard D Morse, Jr 518-455-3711/fax: 518-455-3837

U.S. Government

EXECUTIVE DEPARTMENTS AND RELATED AGENCIES

US Department of Agriculture
Web site: www.usda.gov

Food & Nutrition Service

Albany Field Office
O'Brien Federal Bldg, Rm 752, 1 Clinton Ave & N Pearl St, Albany, NY 12207

Offices and agencies generally appear in alphabetical order, except when specific order is requested by listee.

HEALTH / U.S. Government

Officer in Charge:
Claudia Ortiz 518-431-4274/fax: 518-431-4271
e-mail: claudia.ortiz@FNS.usda.gov

New York City Field Office . . . . fax: 212-620-6948
201 Varick St, Rm 609, New York, NY 10014
Assistant Director:
Denise Thomas 212-620-7360

Rochester Field Office
Federal Bldg, 100 State St, Rm 318, Rochester, NY 14614
Officer in Chg:
Claudia Ortiz 585-263-6748/fax: 585-263-5807
e-mail: claudia.ortiz@FNS.usda.gov

Food Safety & Inspection Service
Web site: www.fsis.usda.gov

Field Operations-Albany District Office . . . . fax: 518-452-3118
230 Washington Ave Ext, Albany, NY 12203-5388
District Manager:
Louis C Leny 518-452-6870

US Department of Health & Human Services
Web site: www.os.dhhs.gov; www.hhs.gov/region2/

Administration for Children & Families . . . . fax: 212-264-4881
26 Federal Plaza, Rm 4114, New York, NY 10278
Fax: 212-264-4881
Web site: www.acf.hhs.gov
Regional Administrator:
MaryAnn Higgins 212-264-2890 x103
e-mail: mhiggins@acf.hhs.gov

Administration on Aging . . . . fax: 212-264-0114
26 Federal Plaza, Rm 38-102, New York, NY 10278
Fax: 212-264-0114
Web site: www.aoa.gov
Regional Administrator:
Daniel A Quirk 212-264-2976
e-mail: dan.quirk@aoa.hhs.gov

Centers for Disease Control & Prevention
Web site: www.cdc.gov

Agency for Toxic Substances & Disease Registry-EPA Region 2
290 Broadway, 28th Fl, New York, NY 10007
Web site: www.atsdr.cdc.gov
Senior Regional Representative:
Arthur Block 212-637-4305/fax: 212-637-3253

New York Quarantine Station . . . . fax: 718-553-1524
Terminal 4E, Rm 219 016, JFK Airport, Jamaica, NY 11430-1081
718-553-1685   Fax: 718-553-1524
Officer-in-Charge:
Margaret A Becker 718-553-1685/fax: 718-553-1524

Centers for Medicare & Medicaid Services
26 Federal Plaza, Rm 3811, New York, NY 10278
Web site: www.cms.hhs.gov
Regional Administrator:
James T Kerr 212-616-2205/fax: 212-264-6189
e-mail: james.kerr@cms.hhs.gov
Deputy Regional Administrator:
Gilbert Kunken 212-616-2205/fax: 212-264-6189
e-mail: gilbert.kunken@cms.hhs.gov

Medicaid and Children's Health (DMCH)
Associate Regional Administrator:
Sue Kelly 212-616-2428/fax: 212-264-6814
e-mail: sue.kelly@cms.hhs.gov

Medicare Financial Management (DMFM)
Associate Regional Administrator:
Peter Reisman 212-616-2505/fax: 212-264-2790
e-mail: peter.reisman@cms.hhs.gov

Medicare Operations Division (DMO)
Associate Regional Administrator:
Jose Mirabal 212-616-2333/fax: 212-264-2665
e-mail: jose.mirabal@cms.hhs.gov

Food & Drug Administration
888-463-6332
Web site: www.fda.gov

Northeast Region
158-15 Liberty Ave, Jamaica, NY 11433
Regional Director:
Vacant 718-662-5416/fax: 718-662-5434

New York District Office
District Director:
Vacant 718-662-5447/fax: 718-662-5665

Northeast Regional Laboratory
158-15 Liberty Ave, Queens, NY 11433
Director:
Michael J Palmieri 718-662-5450/fax: 718-662-5439

Health Resources & Svcs Admin Office of Performance Review . . . . fax: 212-264-2673
26 Federal Bldg, Rm 3337, New York, NY 10278
Regional Division Director:
Ron Moss 212-264-2664
e-mail: robert.moss@hrsa.hhs.gov
Operations Director:
Margaret Lee 212-264-2571
e-mail: margaret.lee@hrsa.hhs.gov
Director, Office of Engineering Services:
Emilio Pucillo 212-264-3600
e-mail: emilio.pucillo@hrsa.hhs.gov

Indian Health Services-Area Office . . . . fax: 615-467-1501
711 Stewarts Ferry Pike, Nashville, TN 37214-2634
Director:
Richie Grinnell 615-467-1500

Office of Secretary's Regional Representative-Region 2-NY . . . . fax: 212-264-3620
26 Federal Plaza, Rm 3835, New York, NY 10278
Regional Director:
Deborah Konopko 212-264-4600
e-mail: deborah.konopko@hhs.gov
Senior Intergovernmental Affairs Specialist:
Joel S Truman 212-264-4600
e-mail: joel.truman@hhs.gov
Intergovernmental Affairs Specialist:
Katherine Williams 212-264-4600
e-mail: katherine.williams@hhs.gov

Office for Civil Rights . . . . fax: 212-264-3039
26 Federal Plaza, Rm 3312, New York, NY 10278
Fax: 212-264-3039
Web site: www.hhs.gov/ocr
Regional Manager:
Michael Carter 212-264-3313/fax: 212-264-3039
Deputy Regional Manager:
Linda Colon 212-264-3313

Office of General Counsel
26 Federal Plaza, Rm 3908, New York, NY 10278
Chief Counsel:
Joel Lerner 212-264-6373

Offices and agencies generally appear in alphabetical order, except when specific order is requested by listee.

HEALTH / U.S. Government

Office of Inspector General
Regional Inspector General, Audit:
   James P Edert....................................212-264-4620
Regional Inspector General & Regional Coordinator, Investigations:
   Gary Heuer.......................................212-264-1691
Regional Inspector General, Evaluations & Inspections:
   Jodi Nudelman...................................212-264-1998

Office of Public Health & Science
26 Federal Plaza, Rm 3835, New York, NY 10278
Regional Health Administrator:
   Robert Amler....................................212-264-2560
   e-mail: ramler@osophs.dhhs.gov
Deputy Regional Health Administrator:
   Robert L Davidson...............................212-264-2560
Regional Family Planning Consultant:
   Robin Lane......................................212-264-3935
   e-mail: rlane@osophs.hhs.gov
Regional Minority Health Consultant:
   Claude Colimon..................................212-264-2560
Regional Women's Health Coordinator:
   Sandra Estepa...................................212-264-2560

US Department of Homeland Security (DHS)
Web site: www.dhs.gov

Federal Emergency Management Agency (FEMA)
TTY: 800-462-7585 or 800-621-3362

National Disaster Medical System................fax: 212-680-3608
26 Federal Plz, Rm 3835, New York, NY 10278
Coordinator:
   Captain Bonita Pyler, USPHS.....................212-680-8542
   e-mail: pyler@dhs.gov

New York Regional Office......................fax: 212-680-3681
26 Federal Plz, Ste 1311, New York, NY 10278
Regional Director:
   Stephen Kempf, Jr...............................212-680-3612

US Labor Department
Web site: www.dol.gov

Occupational Safety & Health Adminstration (OSHA)
201 Varick St, Rm 670, New York, NY 10014
212-337-2378
Web site: www.osha.gov
Regional Administrator:
   Patricia K Clark..................212-337-0118/fax: 212-337-2371

Albany Area Office
401 New Karner Rd, Ste 300, Albany, NY 12205-3809
Area Director:
   Edward Jerome.................518-464-4338/fax: 518-464-4337

Buffalo Area Office
5360 Genesee St, Browmansville, NY 14026
Area Director:
   Art Dube......................716-551-3053/fax: 716-551-3126

Manhattan Area Office
201 Varick St, Rm 908, New York, NY 10014
Area Director:
   Richard Mendelson.............212-620-3200/fax: 212-620-4121

Queens Area Office
45-17 Marathon Parkway, Little Neck, NY 11362
Assistant Area Director:
   Kevin Brennan.................718-279-9060/fax: 718-279-9057

Syracuse Area Office
3300 Vickery Rd, North Syracuse, NY 13212
Area Director:
   Christopher Adams.............315-451-0808/fax: 315-451-1351

Tarrytown Area Office
660 White Plains Rd, Tarrytown, NY 10591
Area Director:
   Diana Cortez..................914-524-7510/fax: 914-524-7515

U.S. CONGRESS

See U.S. Congress Chapter for additional Standing Committee and Subcommittee information.

House of Representatives Standing Committees

Agriculture
Chair:
   Collin C Peterson (D-MN).........................202-225-2165
Ranking Minority Member:
   Bob Goodlatte (R-VA).............................202-225-5431

   Subcommittee
   Department Operations, Oversight, Nutrition & Forestry
   Chair:
     Joe Baca (D-CA)..............................202-225-6161
   Ranking Minority Member:
     Jo Bonner (R-AL).............................202-225-4931

Energy & Commerce
Chair:
   John D Dingell, Jr (D-MI)........................202-225-2927
Ranking Minority Member:
   Joe Barton (R-TX)................................202-225-2002
New York Delegate:
   Eliot L Engel (D)................................202-225-2464
New York Delegate:
   Vito Fossella (R)................................202-225-3371
New York Delegate:
   Edolphus Towns (D)...............................202-225-5936

   Subcommittee
   Health
   Chair:
     Frank J Pallone, Jr (D-NJ)...................202-225-4671
   Ranking Minority Member:
     Nathan Deal (R-GA)...........................202-225-5211
   New York Delegate:
     Eliot L Engel (D)............................202-225-2464

Ways & Means
Chair:
   Charles B Rangel (D-NY)..........................202-225-4365
Ranking Minority Member:
   Charles B Rangel (D-NY)..........................202-225-4365
New York Delegate:
   Michael R McNulty (D)............................202-225-5076
New York Delegate:
   Thomas M Reynolds (R)............................202-225-5265

   Subcommittee
   Health
   Chair:
     Fortney Pete Stark (D-CA)....................202-225-5065
   Ranking Minority Member:
     Dave Camp (R-MI).............................202-225-3561

Offices and agencies generally appear in alphabetical order, except when specific order is requested by listee.

HEALTH / Private Sector

Senate Standing Committees

Aging, Special Committee on
Chair:
  Herb Kohl (D-WI) 202-224-5653
Ranking Minority Member:
  Gordon Smith (R-OH) 202-224-3753

Agriculture, Nutrition & Forestry
Chair:
  Tom Harkin (D-IA) 202-224-3254
Ranking Minority Member:
  Saxby Chambliss (R-GA) 202-224-3521

Health, Education, Labor & Pensions
Chair:
  Edward M Kennedy (D-MA) 202-224-4543
Ranking Minority Member:
  Michael B Enzi (R-WY) 202-224-3424
New York Delegate:
  Hillary Rodham Clinton (D) 202-224-4451

Subcommittees
Retirement & Aging
Chair:
  Barbara Mikulski (D-MD) 202-224-4654
Ranking Minority Member:
  Richard Burr (R-NC) 202-224-3154
New York Delegate:
  Hillary Rodham Clinton (D) 202-224-4451

Private Sector

AIDS Council of Northeastern New York
927 Broadway, Albany, NY 12207-1306
518-434-4686 Fax: 518-427-8184
e-mail: info@aidscouncil.org
Web site: www.aidscouncil.org
Michele McClave, Executive Director
Provide HIV/AIDS education & outreach to at-risk individuals & the public; offer direct assistance & service coordination; serve as public advocates

Adelphi NY Statewide Breast Cancer Hotline & Support Program
Adelphi University, School of Social Work, 1 South Ave, PO Box 701, Garden City, NY 11530
800-877-8077 or 516-877-4320 Fax: 516-877-4336
e-mail: breastcancerhotline@adelphi.edu
Web site: www.adelphi.edu/nysbreastcancer
Hillary Rutter, Director
Breast cancer support, information & referral hotline for all of New York State; community education, support groups, counseling & advocacy

Alzheimer's Association, Northeastern NY
85 Watervliet Ave, Albany, NY 12206
518-438-2217 Fax: 518-438-2219
e-mail: marvin.leroy@alz.org
Web site: www.alzneny.org
Monika Boekmann, President & Chief Executive Officer

American Cancer Society-Eastern Division
19 Dove St, Ste 103, Albany, NY 12210
518-449-5438 Fax: 518-449-7283
e-mail: peter.slocum@cancer.org
Web site: www.cancer.org
Peter Slocum, Director, Advocacy for NY State

American College of Nurse-Midwives, NYC Chapter
450 Clarkson Ave, Box 1227, Brooklyn, NY 11203-2098
718-270-7759 Fax: 718-270-7634
e-mail: gholmes@downstate.edu
Web site: www.nysmidwives.org; www.nyc.org
Grace Holmes, Chair
Midwifery/women's health

American College of Obstetricians & Gynecologists/NYS
152 Washington Ave, Albany, NY 12210
518-436-3461 Fax: 518-426-4728
e-mail: info@ny.acog.org
Web site: www.acogny.org
Donna Montalto Williams, Executive Director
Women's health care & physician education

American College of Physicians, New York Chapter
100 State St, Ste 700, Albany, NY 12207
518-427-0366 Fax: 518-427-1991
Web site: www.acponline.org/chapters/ny
Linda Lambert, Executive Director
Develops & advocates policies on health issues

American Heart Association Northeast Affiliate
17 Technology Place, East Syracuse, NY 13057
315-234-4700 Fax: 315-234-4701
e-mail: csugrue@heart.org
Web site: www.americanheart.org
William J Sugrue, Jr, Executive Vice President
Research, education & community service to reduce disability & death from heart disease & stroke

American Fertility Association
305 Madison Ave, Ste 449, New York, NY 10165
888-917-3777
e-mail: info@americaninfertility.org
Web site: www.theafa.org
Pamela Madsen, Executive Director
Infertility, reproductive disorders, adoption; education, research, advocacy, support & referral

Offices and agencies generally appear in alphabetical order, except when specific order is requested by listee.

HEALTH / Private Sector

American Liver Foundation, Western NY Chapter
25 Canterbury Rd, Ste 316, Rochester, NY 14607
585-271-2859 Fax: 585-271-8642
e-mail: nkoris@liverfoundation.org
Web site: www.liverfoundation.org
Nancy Koris, Executive Director
Disease research, public education & patient support

American Lung Association of NYS Inc
155 Washington Ave, Ste 210, Albany, NY 12210
518-465-2013 Fax: 518-465-2926
e-mail: tnichols@alanys.org
Web site: www.alanys.org
Timothy Nichols, Director, Government Affairs
To prevent lung disease & promote lung health

Associated Medical Schools of New York
10 Rockefeller Plaza, Suite 1120, New York, NY 10020
212-218-4610 Fax: 212-218-5644
e-mail: jo.wiederhorn@amsny.org
Web site: www.amsny.org
Jo Wiederhorn, Executive Director
AMS is a consortium of the fourteen public and private medical schools in New York state. Our mission is to support quality health care in New York State.

Association of Military Surgeons of the US (AMSUS), NY Chapter
105 Franklin Ave, Malverne, NY 11565-1926
516-542-0025 Fax: 516-593-3114
e-mail: amsusny@aol.com
Col John J Hassett, USAR, President NY Chapter
Improve federal healthcare service; support & represent military & other health care professionals

Bausch & Lomb Inc
One Bausch & Lomb Place, Rochester, NY 14604-2701
585-338-6000 Fax: 585-338-6007
Web site: www.bausch.com
Meg Graham, Vice President, Corporate Communication
Development, manufacture & marketing of contact lenses & lens care products, opthalmic surgical & pharmaceutical products

Bellevue Hospital Center, Department of Emergency Medicine Training Division
1st Ave & 27th St, Rm A-345, New York, NY 10016
212-562-3346 Fax: 212-562-3001
e-mail: goldfl03@popmail.med.nyu.edu
Lewis Goldfrank, Director, Emergency Medicine
Emergency medicine; medical toxicology

Brain Injury Association of NYS (BIANYS)
10 Colvin Ave, Albany, NY 12206
518-459-7911 or 800-228-8201 Fax: 518-482-5285
e-mail: info@bianys.org
Web site: www.bianys.org
Judith I Avner, Esq, Executive Director
Public education & advocacy for brain injury persons & their families

Bristol-Myers Squibb Co
PO Box 4755, Syracuse, NY 13221-4755
315-432-2709 Fax: 315-432-2619
Web site: www.bms.com
Pamela M Brunet, Manager of Community Affairs
Develops & markets pharmaceuticals

Bronx-Lebanon Hospital Center
1276 Fulton Ave, Bronx, NY 10456
718-901-8595 Fax: 718-299-5447
Web site: www.bronxcare.org
Errol Schneer, Vice President-Planning, Marketing & Public Relations

Cerebral Palsy Associations of New York State
90 State St, Albany, NY 12207-1709
518-436-0178 Fax: 518-436-8619
e-mail: malvaro@cpofnys.org
Web site: www.cpofnys.org
Michael Alvaro, Executive Vice President
Advocate & provide direct services with & for individuals with cerebral palsy & other significant disabilities, & their families

Coalition of Fathers & Families NY
PO Box 782, Clifton Park, NY 12065
518-383-8202
e-mail: fafny@fafny.org
Web site: www.fafny.org/fafnypac.htm
James Hays, President
Working to keep fathers and families together

Columbia University, Mailman School of Public Health
Heilbrunn Dept of Population & Family He, 60 Haven Ave, B-2, New York, NY 10032
212-304-5281 Fax: 212-305-7024
e-mail: lpf1@columbia.edu
Web site: cpmcnet.columbia.edu/dept/sph/popfam
Lynn P Freedman, Associate Professor & Director
Theory, analysis & development of policy & programs supporting public health & human rights

Columbia University, Mailman School of Public Health, Center for Public Health
722 W 168th St, Ste 522, New York, NY 10032
212-342-1290 Fax: 212-543-8793
e-mail: eng9@columbia.edu
Web site: www.cpmcnet.columbia.edu/dept/sph
Eric N Gebbie, Project Coordinator

Commissioned Officers Assn of the US Public Health Svc Inc (COA)
8201 Corporate Dr, Ste 200, Landover, MD 20785
301-731-9080 Fax: 301-731-9084
e-mail: gfarrell@coausphs.org
Web site: www.coausphs.org
Jerry Farrell, Executive Director
Committed to improving the public health of the US; supports corps officers & advocates for their interests through leadership, education & communication

Offices and agencies generally appear in alphabetical order, except when specific order is requested by listee.

HEALTH / Private Sector

Committee of Methadone Program Administrators Inc of NYS (COMPA)
1 Columbia Place, 4th Fl, Albany, NY 12207
518-689-0457 Fax: 518-426-1046
e-mail: compahb@hotmail.com
Web site: www.compa-ny.org
Henry Bartlett, Executive Director
Methadone treatment & substance abuse coalition building; advocacy, community education, standards & regulatory review & policy development

Commonwealth Fund
One E 75th St, New York, NY 10021-2692
212-606-3800 Fax: 212-606-3500
e-mail: cmwf@cmwf.org
Web site: www.cmwf.org
Karen Davis, President
Supports independent research on health access, coverage & quality issues affecting minorities, women, elderly & low income

Community Health Care Association of NYS
254 West 31st Street, 9th Fl, New York, NY 10001
212-279-9686 Fax: 212-279-3851
e-mail: eswain@chcanys.org
Web site: www.chcanys.org
Elizabeth Swain, Chief Executive Officer
Advocacy, education & services for the medically underserved throughout NYS

Community Healthcare Network
79 Madison Avenue, Fl 6, New York, NY 10016-7802
212-366-4500 Fax: 212-463-8411
e-mail: cabate@chnnyc.org
Web site: www.chnnyc.org
Catherine Abate, President & Chief Executive Officer
Health & social services for low-income, ethnically diverse, medically underserved neighborhoods of NYC

Continuum Health Partners Inc
555 West 57th, 18th Fl, New York, NY 10019
212-523-7772 Fax: 212-523-7885
e-mail: jmandler@chpnet.org
Web site: wehealnewyork.org
Jim Mandler, Assistant Vice President, Public Affairs

Cornell Cooperative Extension, College of Human Ecology, Nutrition, Health
185 MVR Hall, Cornell University, Ithaca, NY 14853-4401
607-255-2247 Fax: 607-255-3794
e-mail: jas56@cornell.edu
Web site: www.cce.cornell.edu
Josephine Swanson, Associate Director, Assistant Dean
Promoting nutritional well-being; safe preparation & storage of food; reducing food insecurity; improving access to health services

County Nursing Facilities of New York Inc
c/o NYSAC, 111 Pine Street, Albany, NY 12207
518-465-1473 Fax: 518-465-0506
e-mail: rmaloney@nysac.org
Web site: www.nysac.org
Richard J Maloney, Executive Director

Dental Hygienists' Association of the State of New York Inc
23 Burton Lane, Massapequa, NY 11758
516-541-4540
e-mail: dhasny@aol.com
Web site: www.dhasny.org
Jean Hall, Administrative Manager
Professional association representing registered dental hygienists; working to improve the oral health of New Yorkers

Doctors Without Borders USA
333 7th Ave, Fl 2, New York, NY 10001-5004
212-679-6800 Fax: 212-679-7016
e-mail: doctors@newyork.msf.org
Web site: www.doctorswithoutborders.org
Nicolas de Torrente, Executive Director
International medical assistance for victims of natural or man-made disasters & armed conflict

Empire Blue Cross & Blue Shield
11 West 42nd St, 18th Fl, New York, NY 10036
212-476-1000 Fax: 212-476-1281
e-mail: deborah.bohren@empireblue.com
Web site: www.empireblue.com
Deborah Bohren, Senior Vice President, Communications
Health insurance

Empire State Association of Assisted Living
646 Plank Rd, Ste 207, Clifton Park, NY 12065
518-371-2573 Fax: 518-371-3774
e-mail: lnewcomb1@aol.com
Web site: www.esaal.org
Lisa Newcomb, Executive Director
Trade association representing NYS assisted living providers

Epilepsy Coalition of New York State Inc
111 Washington Ave, Albany, NY 12210
518-434-4360 Fax: 518-434-4542
e-mail: ecnys@epilepsyny.org
Web site: www.epilepsyny.org
Janice W Gay, President
Promotes awareness of epilepsy & its consequences

Excellus Health Plan Inc
165 Court Street, Rochester, NY 14647
585-327-7581 Fax: 585-327-7585
e-mail: stephen.sloan@excellus.com
Web site: www.excellus.com
Stephen R Sloan, Senior Vice President & General Counsel
Health insurance

Eye-Bank for Sight Restoration Inc (The)
120 Wall St, New York, NY 10005-3902
212-742-9000 Fax: 212-269-3139
e-mail: info@ebsr.org
Web site: www.eyedonation.org
Patricia Dahl, Executive Director/Chief Executive Officer
Cornea & scleral transplants

Offices and agencies generally appear in alphabetical order, except when specific order is requested by listee.

HEALTH / Private Sector

Family Planning Advocates of New York State
17 Elk St, Albany, NY 12207-1002
518-436-8408 Fax: 518-436-0004
e-mail: smitj@fpaofnys.org
Web site: www.fpaofnys.org
JoAnn M Smith, President/Chief Executive Officer
Reproductive rights

Friends & Relatives of Institutionalized Aged Inc (FRIA)
18 John St, Suite 905, New York, NY 10038
212-732-5667 or 212-732-4455 Fax: 212-732-6945
e-mail: fria@fria.org
Web site: www.fria.org
Amy Paul, Executive Director
Free telephone helpline for information, assistance and complaints related to nursing homes, assisted living and other long term care issues.

Generic Pharmaceutical Association
2300 Clarendon Blvd, Ste 400, Arlington, VA 22201-3367
703-647-2480 Fax: 703-647-2481
e-mail: info@gphaonline.org
Web site: www.gphaonline.org
Kathleen Jaeger, President & Chief Executive Officer
Education & consumer information on the quality & effectiveness of generic drugs; generic drug issues

Gertrude H Sergievsky Center (The)
630 West 168th St, New York, NY 10032
212-305-2391 Fax: 212-305-2518
e-mail: rpm2@columbia.edu
Richard Mayeux, Director
Neurological disease research correlating epidemiological techniques with genetic analysis & clinical investigation

Greater New York Hospital Association
555 W 57th St, New York, NY 10019
212-246-7100 Fax: 212-262-6350
e-mail: raske@gnyha.org
Web site: www.gnyha.org
Kenneth E Raske, President
Trade association representing more than 250 not-for-profit hospitals

Group Health Inc
441 9th Ave, New York, NY 10001
212-615-0891 Fax: 212-563-8561
e-mail: jgoodwin@ghi.com
Jeffrey Goodwin, Director, Governmental Relations
Affordable, quality health insurance for working individuals & families

Healthcare Association of New York State
1 Empire Dr, Rensselaer, NY 12144
518-431-7600 Fax: 518-431-7915
e-mail: skroll@hanys.org
Web site: www.hanys.org
Steven Kroll, Vice President, Governmental Affairs & External Relations
Representing New York's not-for-profit hospitals, health systems & continuing care providers

Home Care Association of New York State Inc
194 Washington Ave, Suite 400, Albany, NY 12210-2314
518-426-8764 x214 Fax: 518-426-8788
e-mail: mkissinger@hcanys.org
Web site: www.hcanys.org
Mark L Kissinger, President
Advocacy for home health care & related health services

Hospice & Palliative Care Association of NYS Inc
21 Aviation Rd, Ste 9, Albany, NY 12205
518-446-1483 Fax: 518-446-1484
e-mail: info@hpcanys.org
Web site: www.hpcanys.org
Kathy A McMahon, President & Chief Executive Officer
Hospice & palliative care information & referral service; educational programs; clinical, psychosocial & bereavement issues

INFORM Inc
5 Hanover Square, New York, NY 10004
212-361-2400 Fax: 212-361-2412
e-mail: inform@informinc.org
Web site: www.informinc.org
Katherin O'Dea, Interim Executive Director
Advocacy, research & education on practical methods to protect natural resources & public health

Institute for Family Health (The)
16 East 16th St, New York, NY 10003
212-633-0800 x255 Fax: 212-691-4610
e-mail: ncalman@institute2000.org
Web site: www.institute2000.org
Neil S Calman, President/Chief Executive Officer
Family practice healthcare for NYC's underserved; health professions training; research & advocacy

Iroquois Healthcare Alliance
17 Halfmoon Executive Park Dr, Clifton Park, NY 12065
518-383-5060 Fax: 518-383-2616
e-mail: gfitzgerald@iroquois.org
Web site: www.iroquois.org
Gary Fitzgerald, President
Represents healthcare providers in upstate New York

Jewish Home & Hospital (The)
120 West 106 St, New York, NY 10025
212-870-4600 Fax: 212-870-4895
e-mail: aweiner@jhha.org
Web site: www.jewishhome.org
Audrey Weiner, President & Chief Executive Officer
Long term care & rehabilitation

League for the Hard of Hearing
50 Broadway, Fl 5, New York, NY 10004-1607
917-305-7700 or TTY: 917-305-7999 Fax: 917-305-7888
e-mail: postmaster@lhh.org
Web site: www.lhh.org
Laurie Hanin, Co-Executive Director
Rehabilitation & other services for the deaf & hard of hearing

Offices and agencies generally appear in alphabetical order, except when specific order is requested by listee.

HEALTH / Private Sector

Lighthouse International
111 East 59th St, New York, NY 10022
212-821-9484 Fax: 212-821-9712
e-mail: cstuen@lighthouse.org
Web site: www.lighthouse.org
Cynthia Stuen, Senior Vice President, Policy & Professional Affairs
Vision rehabilitation, research, education & awareness

Marion S Whelan School of Practical Nursing
Geneva General Hospital, 196 North St, Geneva, NY 14456
315-787-4005 Fax: 315-787-4770
e-mail: VictoriaRecord@flhealth.org
Web site: www.flhealth.org - Services & Programs
Victoria Record MS, RN, Director
Health education/diabetes education

Medical Society of the State of NY, Governmental Affairs Division
One Commerce Plaza, Ste 408, Albany, NY 12210
518-465-8085 Fax: 518-465-0976
e-mail: gconway@mssny.org
Web site: www.mssny.org
Gerard L Conway, Senior VP/Chief Legislative Council
Healthcare legislation & advocacy

Memorial Sloan-Kettering Cancer Center
1275 York Ave, New York, NY 10021
212-639-3627 Fax: 212-639-3576
Web site: www.mskcc.org
Christine Hickey, Director, Communications
Nat'l Cancer Institute designated comprehensive cancer center

Mount Sinai Medical Center
One Gustave L Levy Plaza, New York, NY 10029-6514
212-241-6500 Fax: 212-410-6111
e-mail: brad.beckstrom@mssm.edu
Web site: www.mountsinaihospital.org
Brad Beckstrom, Director, Government Affairs

NY Health Information Management Association Inc
19 Aviation Rd, Albany, NY 12205
518-435-0422 Fax: 518-435-0362
e-mail: art.ambuhl@nyhima.org
Web site: www.nyhima.org
Arthur Ambuhl, Executive Director

NY Physical Therapy Association
5 Palisades Dr, Ste 330, Albany, NY 12205-1443
518-459-4499 Fax: 518-459-8953
e-mail: lesliew@nypta.org
Web site: www.nypta.org
Leslie Wood, Executive Director

NY State Society of Physician Assistants
251 New Karner Rd, Ste 10A, Albany, NY 12205
877-769-7722 Fax: 856-423-3420
e-mail: info@nysspa.org
Web site: www.nysspa.org
Kenneth Cleveland, Executive Director

NYS Academy of Family Physicians
260 Osborne Rd, Loudonville, NY 12211-1822
518-489-8945 or 800-822-0700 Fax: 518-489-8961
e-mail: fp@nysafp.org
Web site: www.nysafp.org
Vito Grasso, CAE, Executive Vice President

NYS Association of County Health Officials
One United Way, Pine West Plaza, Albany, NY 12205
518-456-7905 Fax: 518-452-5435
e-mail: jab@nysacho.org
Web site: www.nysacho.org
JoAnn Bennison, Executive Director

NYS Association of Health Care Providers
99 Troy Road, Ste 200, East Greenbush, NY 12061
518-463-1118 Fax: 518-463-1606
e-mail: johnston@nyshcp.org
Web site: www.nyshcp.org
Christy Johnston, Executive Vice President
Home health care; health care services for the aging

NYS Association of Nurse Anesthetists (NYSANA)
PO Box 8867, Albany, NY 12208-0867
518-861-8876 Fax: 518-861-8876
e-mail: webmaster@nysana.com
Web site: www.nysana.com
Kathy O'Donnell, Executive Director

NYS Dental Association
121 State St, Albany, NY 12207
518-465-0044 Fax: 518-427-0461
Web site: www.nysdental.org
Roy E Lasky, Executive Director

NYS Federation of Physicians & Dentists
521 5th Ave, Ste 1700, New York, NY 10175-0003
212-986-3859
Larry Nathan, Executive Director

NYS Optometric Association Inc
119 Washington Avenue, Albany, NY 12210
518-449-7300 Fax: 518-432-5902
e-mail: nysoa2020@aol.com
Web site: www.nysoa.org
Jan Dorman, Executive Director

NYS Public Health Association
150 State St, 4th Fl, Albany, NY 12207
518-427-5835 Fax: 518-427-5835
e-mail: info@nyspha.org
Web site: www.nyspha.org
Erin Sinisgalli, President
Reviewing & advocating for stronger legislation/regulation to protect public health in NYS

Offices and agencies generally appear in alphabetical order, except when specific order is requested by listee.

HEALTH / Private Sector

National Amputation Foundation Inc
40 Church St, Malverne, NY 11565
516-887-3600 Fax: 516-887-3667
e-mail: amps76@aol.com
Web site: www.nationalamputation.org
Paul Bernacchio, President
Programs & services geared to help the amputee; donated medical equipment give-away program. Items must be picked up at the office-for anyone in need.

National League for Nursing (NLN)
61 Broadway, New York, NY 10006
212-363-5555 Fax: 212-812-0392
e-mail: oceo@nln.org
Web site: www.nln.org
Dr Beverly Malone, Chief Executive Officer
Advances quality nursing education that prepares the nursing workforce to meet the needs of diverse populations in an ever-changing healthcare environment

National Marfan Foundation
22 Manhasset Ave, Port Washington, NY 11050
516-883-8712 Fax: 516-883-8040
e-mail: staff@marfan.org
Web site: www.marfan.org
Carolyn Levering, President & Chief Executive Officer
Marfan syndrome research, education & support

New School University, Milano Graduate School of Mgmt & Urban Policy
72 Fifth Ave, 6th Fl, New York, NY 10011
212-229-5311 x1516 Fax: 212-229-5335
Web site: www.newschool.edu
Peter Issinger, Director, Health Policy Research Center

New York AIDS Coalition
231 W 29th St, New York, NY 10001
212-629-3075 Fax: 212-629-8403
Web site: www.nyaidscoalition.org
James Darden, Office Manager
HIV/AIDS-related public policy & education

New York Association of Homes & Services for the Aging
150 State St, Ste 301, Albany, NY 12207-1698
518-449-2707 Fax: 518-455-8908
e-mail: cyoung@nyahsa.org
Web site: www.nyahsa.org
Carl Young, President
Long-term care

New York Business Group on Health Inc
61 Broadway, Suite 2705, New York, NY 10006
212-252-7440 x223 Fax: 212-252-7448
e-mail: laurel@nybgh.org
Web site: www.nybgh.org
Laurel Pickering, Executive Director
Business employers addressing healthcare cost & quality; Non-profit coalition of 150 businesses devoted to health benefits issues.

New York Counties Registered Nurses Association
70 W 36th St, Rm 601, New York, NY 10018-1262
212-673-7110 Fax: 212-673-7762
e-mail: nycrna@aol.com
Web site: www.nysna.org/districts/13.htm
Marlene S Gerber, Executive Director

New York Health Care Alliance
39 Broadway, Ste 1710, New York, NY 10006
212-425-5050 or 877-HI-NYHCA Fax: 212-968-7710
e-mail: njheyman@nyhca.com
Web site: www.nyhca.com
Neil Heyman, CEO
An affiliation of 48 skilled nursing facilities that provide sub-acute, rehabilitation and long term care services in the NY Metropolitan Area. A managed care contracting entity responsible for group contracts with all major health plans in NY Area.

New York Health Plan Association
90 State St, Ste 825, Albany, NY 12207-1717
518-462-2293 Fax: 518-462-2150
e-mail: lmarks@nyhpa.org
Web site: www.nyhpa.org
Lee Marks, Director, Government Affairs
Promotes the development of managed healthcare plans

New York Medical College
Basic Science Bldg, Valhalla, NY 10595
914-594-4110 Fax: 914-594-4944
e-mail: francis_belloni@nymc.edu
Web site: www.nymc.edu
Francis L Belloni, Dean, Graduate School of Basic Medical Sciences
Cardiovascular physiology, graduate education

New York Medical College, Department of Community & Preventive Medicine
Munger Pavilion, Valhalla, NY 10595
914-594-4254 Fax: 914-594-4576
e-mail: joseph_cimino@nymc.edu
Web site: www.nymc.edu
Joseph A Cimino, Professor & Chairman
Health policy & public health

New York Medical College, Department of Medicine
Munger Pavilion, Valhalla, NY 10595
914-594-4415
e-mail: lerner@nymc.edu
Web site: www.nymc.edu
Robert G Lerner, Professor, Vice Chair-Department of Medicine
Hematology, oncology, research of coagulation & clotting

New York Medical College, School of Public Health
School of Public Health, Valhalla, NY 10595
914-594-4531 Fax: 914-594-4292
e-mail: james_obrien@nymc.edu
Web site: www.nymc.edu
James J O'Brien, Dean & Acting Vice President
Graduate education for public health & the health sciences

Offices and agencies generally appear in alphabetical order, except when specific order is requested by listee.

HEALTH / Private Sector

New York Presbyterian Hospital
Public Affairs Ofc, 525 East 68th St, Box 144, New York, NY 10021
212-821-0560 Fax: 212-821-0576
e-mail: krobinso@med.cornell.edu
Web site: www.med.cornell.edu; www.nyp.org
Kathleen Robinson, Director, Media Relations

New York State Association of Ambulatory Surgery Centers
c/o Harrison Center Outpatient Surgery I, 550 Harrison St, Suite 230, Syracuse, NY 13202
315-472-7315 Fax: 315-475-8056
e-mail: palteri@harrisonsurgery.com
Web site: nysaasc.org
Margaret M Alteri, President & Executive Director
Ambulatory surgery

New York State Health Facilities Association Inc
33 Elk St, Ste 300, Albany, NY 12207-1010
518-462-4800 x10 Fax: 518-426-4051
e-mail: rherrick@nyshfa.org
Web site: www.nyshfa.org
Richard J Herrick, President & Chief Executive Officer
Nursing homes & continuing care services

New York State Nurses Association
11 Cornell Rd, Latham, NY 12110
518-782-9400 x279 Fax: 518-782-1706
e-mail: executive@nysna.org
Web site: www.nysna.org
Chief Executive Officer, Executive Director
Labor union & professional association for registered nurses

New York State Ophthalmological Society
10 Colvin Ave, Albany, NY 12206
518-438-2020 Fax: 518-438-3008
e-mail: nysos2020@aol.com
Web site: www.nysos.com
Robin M Pellegrino, Executive Director

New York State Osteopathic Medical Society
1855 Broadway, New York, NY 10023
212-261-1784 Fax: 212-261-1786
e-mail: info@nysoms.org
Web site: www.nysoms.org
Martin Diamond, Executive Director
Advance the art & science of the osteopathic medical philosophy & practice through continuing medical education programs

New York State Podiatric Medical Association
1255 Fifth Ave, New York, NY 10029
212-996-4400 Fax: 646-672-9344
e-mail: nyspma@nyspma.org
Web site: www.nyspma.org
Leonard Thaler, Executive Director
To promote and pursue manifest excellence in all aspects of the art and science and podiatric medicine; to promote appreciation for that excellence on the past of patients, policy makers, other health care professionals, and the public.

New York State Radiological Society Inc
9 E 40th St, New York, NY 10016
212-448-1866 Fax: 212-448-1863
e-mail: nysrad@aol.com
Richard Schiffer, Executive Director

New York University, Graduate School of Public Service
295 Lafayette St, 2nd Fl, New York, NY 10012
212-998-7455 or 212-998-7440 Fax: 212-995-4166
e-mail: john.billings@nyu.edu
Web site: www.nyu.edu/wagner
John Billings, Director, Center for Health & Public Service Research
Health care reform

New York University, Robert F Wagner Graduate School of Public Service
295 Lafayette, 2nd Floor, New York, NY 10012
212-998-7410 Fax: 212-995-4162
e-mail: jo.boufford@nyu.edu
Web site: www.nyu.edu/wagner
Jo Ivey Boufford, Professor of Public Administration
Health policy & management

Next Wave Inc
24 Madison Ave Ext, Albany, NY 12203
518-452-3351 Fax: 518-452-3358
e-mail: contact@nextwave.info
Web site: www.nextwave.info
John Shaw, President
Health services research, management consulting & evaluation

NYS Bar Assn, Food, Drug & Cosmetic Law Section
North Shore-Long Island Jewish Health System
Office of Legal Affairs, 150 Community Dr, Great Neck, NY 11021
516-465-8379 Fax: 516-465-8105
e-mail: cmcgowan2@nshs.edu
Coreen McGowan, Esquire

Nurse Practitioners Assn NYS (The)
12 Corporate Dr, Clifton Park, NY 12065
518-348-0719 Fax: 518-348-0720
e-mail: info@thenpa.org
Web site: www.thenpa.org
Seth Gordon, President/Chief Executive Officer
Representation, communication & advocacy

Pharmacists Society of the State of New York
210 Washington Ave Extenstion, Albany, NY 12203
518-869-6595 Fax: 518-464-0618
e-mail: craigb@pssny.org
Web site: www.pssny.org
Craig Burridge, Executive Director
Continuing education, public information, health advocacy

Procter & Gamble Pharmaceuticals
PO Box 191, Norwich, NY 13815
607-335-2111 Fax: 607-335-2700
Web site: www.pg.com
Pamela Traister, Manager, Public Affairs
Research & development of prescription pharmaceuticals

Offices and agencies generally appear in alphabetical order, except when specific order is requested by listee.

HEALTH / Private Sector

Professional Standards Review Council of America Inc (PSRC)
200 Madison Ave, Suite 2108, New York, NY 10016
646-419-4020 Fax: 212-779-9307
e-mail: cwielk@psrc-of-america.org
Web site: www.psrc-of-america.org
Carol A Wielk, Executive Director
Health care QA/UR management; credentialing

Radon Testing Corp of America Inc
2 Hayes St, Elmsford, NY 10523
914-345-3380 or 800-457-2366 Fax: 914-345-8546
e-mail: rtca97@att.net
Web site: www.rtca.com
Nancy Bredhoff, President
Radon detection services for health departments, municipalities, homeowners; manufacture canister detectors

Regeneron Pharmaceuticals Inc
777 Old Saw Mill River Rd, Tarrytown, NY 10591-6707
914-345-7400 Fax: 914-345-7688
e-mail: info@regeneron.com
Web site: www.regeneron.com
Stephen L Holst, Vice President, Quality Assurance & Regulatory Affairs
Discovers, develops & intends to commercialize therapeutic drugs for serious medical conditions, including rheumatoid arthritis, cancer, asthma & obesity

Robert P Borsody, PC
666 Fifth, 29th Fl, New York, NY 10103
212-841-0566 Fax: 212-262-5152
e-mail: rborsody@phillipsnizer.com
Web site: www.borsodyhealthlaw.com
Robert P Borsody, Attorney
Health care law

SUNY at Albany, School of Public Health, Center for Public Health Preparedness
One University Pl, Rensselaer, NY 12144-3456
518-486-7921 Fax: 518-402-4656
e-mail: mwatson@albany.edu
Web site: www.ualbanycphp.org
Margaret R Watson, Project Coordinator

The Bachmann-Strauss Dystonia & Parkinson Foundation
Mount Sinai Medical Center, One Gustave L Levy Place, Box 1490, New York, NY 10029
212-241-5614 Fax: 212-987-0662
e-mail: bachmann.strauss@mssm.edu
Web site: www.dystonia-parkinsons.org
Helen Miller, Executive Director
Funds research & creates public awareness of dystonia, Parkinson's disease

True & Walsh, LLP
950 Danby Road, Suite 310, Ithaca, NY 14850
607-273-2301 Fax: 607-272-1901
e-mail: stt@truewalshlaw.com
Web site: www.truewalshlaw.com
Sally T True, Partner
Health care, corporate law & estate planning/administration

United Hospital Fund of New York
Empire State Building, 350 Fifth Ave, 23rd Fl, New York, NY 10118-2399
212-494-0777 Fax: 212-494-0830
e-mail: jtallon@uhfnyc.org
Web site: www.uhfnyc.org
James R Tallon, Jr, President
Health services research & philanthropic organization

United New York Ambulance Network (UNYAN)
119 Washington Ave, Ste 300, Albany, NY 12210
518-694-4420 Fax: 518-427-9495
e-mail: info@unyan.net
Web site: unyan.net
Alan Lewis, Chairman
Ambulance trade association

We Move
204 W 84th St, New York, NY 10024
800-437-6682 Fax: 212-875-8389
e-mail: wemove@wemove.org
Web site: www.wemove.org
Susan B Bressman, President
Education & information about movement disorders for both healthcare providers & patients

NYS Bar Assn, Health Law Section
Wilson Elser Moskowitz Edelman & Dicker
677 Broadway, Albany, NY 12207
518-449-8893 Fax: 518-449-4292
e-mail: philip.rosenberg@wilsonelser.com
Phillip Rosenberg,

Winthrop University Hospital
286 Old Country Road, Mineola, NY 11501
516-663-2706 Fax: 516-663-2713
e-mail: jbroder@winthrop.org
Web site: www.winthrop.org
John P Broder, Vice President, External Affairs & Development

Yeshiva University, A Einstein Clg of Med, OB/GYN & Wmn's Health
1300 Morris Park Ave, Ste B-502, Bronx, NY 10461
718-430-4192 Fax: 718-430-8813
e-mail: chairobgyn@aol.com
Web site: www.yu.edu
Irwin R Merkatz, Chair

Offices and agencies generally appear in alphabetical order, except when specific order is requested by listee.

HOUSING & COMMUNITY DEVELOPMENT

New York State

GOVERNOR'S OFFICE

Governor's Office
Executive Chamber
State Capitol
Albany, NY 12224
518-474-8390 Fax: 518-474-1513
Web site: www.state.ny.us

Governor:
　Eliot Spitzer 518-474-8390
Secretary to the Governor:
　Richard Baum 518-474-4246
Counsel to the Governor:
　David Nocenti 518-474-8434
Senior Advisor to the Governor:
　Lloyd Constantine 518-486-9671
Director, Communications:
　Darren Dopp 518-474-8418
Assistant Counsel to Governor-Housing, Local Governments & Arts:
　Amanda Hiller 518-474-8494

EXECUTIVE DEPARTMENTS AND RELATED AGENCIES

Housing & Community Renewal, Division of
Hampton Plaza
38-40 State St
Albany, NY 12207
866-275-3427 or 518-402-3728
Web site: www.dhcr.state.ny.us

25 Beaver St
New York, NY 10004-2319
866-275-3427

Commissioner:
　Deborah VanAmerogen 518-473-8384/fax: 518-473-9462
First Deputy Commissioner:
　Brian Lawlor 518-473-0632
Executive Assistant:
　Vacant 518-473-0632
Director, Communications:
　James Plastiras 518-473-2526/fax: 518-474-5752

Administration
Acting Deputy Commissioner:
　Catherine Johnson 518-486-3370/fax: 518-473-9462

Housing Information Systems
Director:
　David Dietrich 518-473-5681/fax: 518-486-5056

Internal Audit

Office of Financial Administration
Acting Director:
　Mary Kozlowski 518-486-6399/fax: 518-473-3260

Office of Training & Professional Development
Director:
　Richard Washburn 518-486-5021/fax: 518-486-5027

Personnel
Director:
　Gerald Burke 518-473-6977/fax: 518-486-5007

Support Services/Processing Services Unit
Director:
　Theodore T Minissale 518-486-6166/fax: 518-486-3366

Community Development
Deputy Commissioner:
　Gary Hallock 212-480-6446/fax: 212-480-7450
Assistant Commissioner, Capital Development:
　Sean Fitzgerald 518-473-8536/fax: 518-474-7292
Asst Commissioner, Underwriting & Design Services:
　Ellen M Coyle 518-473-3890/fax: 518-473-7357
Asst Director, Community Development:
　Robert Shields 518-486-3305/fax: 518-486-3410

Community Service Bureau/Technical Assistance Unit
Director:
　Pat Doyle 518-473-3247/fax: 518-486-5186

Energy Services Bureau/Weatherization
Director:
　Thom Carey 518-474-5700/fax: 518-474-9907

Environmental Analysis Unit
Director:
　Barbara Wigzell 518-473-0457

Housing Trust Fund Program
Program Manager:
　Thomas Koenig 518-486-7682/fax: 518-486-3410

Regional Offices
　Buffalo
　　107 Delaware Ave, Ste 600, Buffalo, NY 14213
　　Reg Director:
　　　Thomas H VanNortwick 716-842-2244/fax: 716-842-2724
　Capital District
　　Hampton Plaza, 38-40 State St, 9th Fl, Albany, NY 12207
　　Regional Director:
　　　Deb Devine 518-486-5012/fax: 518-474-5752
　New York City
　　25 Beaver St, New York, NY 10004
　　Regional Director:
　　　Kim Swan 212-480-4543
　Syracuse
　　800 South Wilbur Ave, Syracuse, NY 13204

Offices and agencies generally appear in alphabetical order, except when specific order is requested by listee.

HOUSING & COMMUNITY DEVELOPMENT / New York State

Regional Director:
Daniel P Buyer 315-473-6930/fax: 315-473-6937

Fair Housing & Equal Opportunity
Director:
Cecil Brown. 518-474-6157/fax: 518-473-3173

Housing Operations
Deputy Commissioner:
David Cabrera 212-480-6440/fax: 212-480-7169
Asst Commissioner, Section 8:
Alan Smith. 518-473-6183/fax: 518-474-5752
Asst Commissioner, Housing Operations:
Richmond McCurnin. 212-480-6444/fax: 212-480-7169

Architecture & Engineering Bureau
Director:
Robert Damico 212-480-6266/fax: 212-480-6268

Housing Audits & Accounts Bureau
Director:
Vincent Giammarino. 212-480-7224/fax: 212-480-7042

Housing Management Bureau
Director:
Jane Berrie. 212-480-7252/fax: 212-480-7270
Mobile Home Unit
Director:
Dominic Cardillo. . . . . 800-432-4210 or 518-486-6267
fax: 518-486-3366
Subsidy Services
Director:
Linda Kedzierski 212-480-6482/fax: 212-480-6481

Legal Affairs

Albany Unit
Managing Attorney:
Brian P McCartney 518-486-6337/fax: 518-473-8206
Closing Coordinator:
Vacant 518-486-6337/fax: 518-473-8206

General Law
Managing Attorney:
Sheldon Melnitsky 212-480-6789/fax: 212-480-7416
Senior Supervising Attorney:
Cullen McVoy. 212-480-6787/fax: 212-480-7416

Policy & Intergovernmental Relations
Deputy Commissioner:
Lorrie Pizzola 518-474-9553/fax: 518-473-9462
Legislative Liaison:
Vacant. 518-473-2519/fax: 518-474-5752

Rent Administration
92-31 Union Hall St, Jamaica, NY 11433
Deputy Commissioner:
Leslie Torres 718-262-4822/fax: 718-262-4008

Luxury Decontrol/Overcharge
Bureau Chief:
Gerald Garfinkle 718-262-4725/fax: 718-262-7932

Owner Multiple Applications
Bureau Chief:
Paul Fuller. 718-262-4768/fax: 718-262-7938

Rent Control/ETPA
Bureau Chief/Deputy Counsel:
Michael Rosenblatt 718-262-4713/fax: 718-262-4008

Rent Information & Mediation
Bureau Chief:
Bruce Falbo. 718-262-4914/fax: 718-262-4008

Services Compliance Owner Restoration Enforcement/SCORE
Bureau Chief:
Patrick Siconolfi 718-262-4765/fax: 718-262-4008

Law Department
120 Broadway
New York, NY 10271-0332
212-416-8000 Fax: 212-416-8796

State Capitol
Albany, NY 12224-0341
518-474-7330
Fax: 518-402-2472

Attorney General:
Andrew M Cuomo 518-474-7330
First Deputy Attorney General:
Michele Hirshman 212-416-8050
Director, Public Information & Correspondence:
Peter A Drago 518-474-7330/fax: 518-402-2472

Public Advocacy Division
Deputy Attorney General:
Dietrich Snell. 212-416-8041/fax: 212-416-8068
Special Counsel:
Mary Ellen Burns 212-416-6155

Civil Rights Bureau
Bureau Chief:
Dennis Parker 212-416-8250/fax: 212-416-8074

Consumer Fraud & Protection Bureau
Bureau Chief:
Thomas G Conway 518-474-2374/fax: 518-474-3618

State Counsel Division
Deputy Attorney General:
Richard Rifkin 518-473-7190
Assistant Deputy Attorney General:
Patricia Martinelli 518-473-0648/fax: 518-486-9777
Assistant Deputy Attorney General:
Susan L Watson. 212-416-8579/fax: 212-416-6001

Litigation Bureau
Bureau Chief, Albany:
Bruce D Feldman 518-473-8328/fax: 518-473-1572
Bureau Chief, NYC:
James B Henley. 212-416-8523/fax: 212-416-6075

Real Property Bureau
Bureau Chief:
Henry A DeCotis. 518-474-7151/fax: 518-473-5106

Small Cities, Office for
4 Empire State Plaza
Suite 600
Albany, NY 12223
518-474-2057 Fax: 518-474-5247
Web site: www.nysmallcities.com

Executive Director:
Joseph J Rabito. 518-474-2057

Offices and agencies generally appear in alphabetical order, except when specific order is requested by listee.

HOUSING & COMMUNITY DEVELOPMENT / New York State

Associate Counsel:
 Brian McCartney 518-474-2057
Program Manager:
 Gail Hammond 518-474-2057
Executive Assistant:
 Drue Paige 518-474-2057
Director, Communications:
 Joseph Picchi 518-474-2057

CORPORATIONS, AUTHORITIES AND COMMISSIONS

Capital District Regional Planning Commission
One Park Place
Suite 102
Albany, NY 12205-1606
518-453-0850 Fax: 518-453-0856
e-mail: cdrpc@cdrpc.org
Web site: www.cdrpc.org

Executive Director:
 Rocco Ferraro 518-453-0850

Development Authority of the North Country
Dulles State Office Bldg, Ste 414
317 Washington St
Watertown, NY 13601
315-785-2593 Fax: 315-785-2591
Web site: www.danc.org

Chair:
 Thomas Hefferon 315-785-2593
Executive Director:
 Robert S Juravich 315-785-2593
 e-mail: juravich@danc.org
Engineer:
 Carrie M Tuttle 315-785-8661
 e-mail: ctuttle@danc.org
Deputy Exec Director:
 Thomas R Sauter 315-785-2593
 e-mail: tsauter@danc.org
Finance Director:
 Denise A Gray 315-785-2593
Solid Waste Management Facility General Manager:
 E William Seifried 315-232-3236
Director, Project Development:
 Kevin J Jordan 315-785-2593
 e-mail: kjordan@danc.org

Empire State Development Corporation
633 Third Ave
New York, NY 10017
212-803-3100
Web site: www.empire.state.ny.us

30 South Pearl Street
Albany, NY 12245
518-292-5100

420 Main St, Ste 717
Buffalo, NY 14202
716-856-8111

Co-Chair Downstate:
 Patrick J Foye 212-803-3700
Co-Chair Upstate:
 Daniel C Gundersen .... 518-292-5100 or 716-856-8111
President & Chief Operating Officer:
 Avi Schick 212-803-3730
Chief Operating Officer (Upstate):
 Kenneth A Schoetz 716-856-8111
Director, Communications:
 A J Carter 212-803-3740
Senior VP, General Counsel:
 Anita W Laremont 212-803-3750

New York City Housing Development Corporation
110 William St
10th Fl
New York, NY 10038
212-227-5500 Fax: 212-227-6865
e-mail: info@nychdc.com
Web site: www.nychdc.com

Chairman:
 Shaun Donovan 212-863-6100
President:
 Emily Youssouf 212-227-3600
Executive Vice President & Chief of Staff:
 John Crotty 212-227-6846/fax: 212-227-9807
Senior Vice President & General Counsel:
 Richard Froehlich 212-227-7435
Senior Vice President, Portfolio Mgt:
 Teresa Gigliello 212-227-9133
Senior Vice President & Chief Fiscal Officer:
 Eileen O'Reilly 212-227-7494/fax: 212-227-6757
Chief Credit Officer:
 Urmas Naeris 212-227-9724
Vice President, Development:
 Rachel Grossman 212-227-9373
Director, Communications:
 Aaron Donovan 212-227-9496/fax: 212-227-8580

New York City Residential Mortgage Insurance Corporation
Chair:
 Shaun Donovan 212-863-6100
President:
 Emily Youssouf 212-227-3600

New York State Housing Finance Agency (HFA)
641 Lexington Ave
4th Floor
New York, NY 10022
212-688-4000 Fax: 212-872-0789
Web site: www.nyhomes.org

Chair:
 Judd Levy 212-688-4000
President & CEO:
 Priscilla Almodovar 212-688-4000

Offices and agencies generally appear in alphabetical order, except when specific order is requested by listee.

HOUSING & COMMUNITY DEVELOPMENT / New York State

Senior VP & Special Asst to Pres/CEO for Policy Dev & Programs:
James P Angley 212-688-4000
Senior VP, COO & CFO:
Ralph J Madalena 212-688-4000
Senior VP & Counsel:
Justin Driscoll 212-688-4000
Senior VP, Debt Issuance:
Bernard Abramowitz 212-688-4000 x530
Vice President, Director of Development:
Maria LaSorsa 212-688-4000 x688
Vice President, Policy & Planning:
Tracy A Oats 212-688-4000 x678
Vice President, Intergovernmental Relations:
Michael Houseknecht 518-434-2118/fax: 518-434-7158

Affordable Housing Corporation
Senior VP & Special Asst to Pres/CEO for Policy Dev & Programs:
James P Angley 212-688-4000

New York State Mortgage Loan Enforcement & Administration Corporation
633 Third Ave
37th Fl
New York, NY 10017-6754
212-803-3700 Fax: 212-803-3775
Web site: www.empire.state.ny.us

Senior Vice President:
Anita W Laremont 212-803-3750
Senior Vice President & Chief Financial Officer:
Frances A Walton 212-803-3510

New York State Project Finance Agency
641 Lexington Ave
New York, NY 10022
212-688-4000 Fax: 212-872-0678

Chair:
Judd Levy 212-688-4000
President & CEO:
Priscilla Almodovar 212-688-4000
Senior VP, COO & CFO:
Ralph J Madalena 212-688-4000
Senior VP & Counsel:
Justin Driscoll 212-688-4000
Senior VP, Debt Issuance:
Bernard Abramowitz 212-688-4000 x530
Vice President, Director of Development:
Jonathan Cortrell 212-688-4000 x688
Vice President, Policy & Planning:
Tracy A Oats 212-688-4000 x678

Roosevelt Island Operating Corporation (RIOC)
591 Main St
Roosevelt Island, NY 10044
212-832-4540 Fax: 212-832-4582
e-mail: info@roosevelt-island.ny.us
Web site: www.rioc.com

President:
Stephen H Shane 212-832-4540
Vice President, Operations:
Vacant 212-832-4540

Chairperson, Board of Directors (ex officio):
Deborah VanAmerogen 212-480-6705
General Counsel:
Kenneth A Leitner 212-832-4540 x311
Chief Financial Officer:
Carla Van de Walle 212-832-4540
Public Information Officer:
Vacant 212-832-4540

State of New York Mortgage Agency (SONYMA)
641 Lexington Ave
New York, NY 10022
212-688-4000 Fax: 212-872-0678
Web site: www.nyhomes.org

Chair:
Judd Levy 212-688-4000
President & CEO:
Priscilla Almodovar 212-688-4000
Senior VP & Special Asst to Pres/CEO for Policy Dev & Programs:
James P Angley 212-688-4000
Senior VP, COO & CFO:
Ralph J Madalena 212-688-4000
Senior VP & General Counsel:
Justin Driscoll 212-688-4000
Senior VP, Single Family Programs & Financing:
Charles Rosenwald 212-688-4000 x531
Vice President, Director, SONYMA Mortgage Insurance Fund:
Michael Friedman 212-688-4000 x714
Vice President, Policy & Planning:
Tracy A Oats 212-688-4000 x678
Vice President, Intergovernmental Relations:
Michael Houseknecht 518-434-2118/fax: 518-434-7158

NEW YORK STATE LEGISLATURE

See Legislative Branch in Section 1 for additional Standing Committee and Subcommittee information.

Assembly Standing Committees

Housing
Chair:
Vito J Lopez (D) 518-455-5537
Ranking Minority Member:
Michael J Fitzpatrick (R) 518-455-5021

Local Government
Chair:
William (Sam) Hoyt III (D) 518-455-4886
Ranking Minority Member:
Annie G Rabbitt (R) 518-455-5991

Senate Standing Committees

Housing, Construction & Community Development
Chair:
John J Bonacic (R) 518-455-3181
Ranking Minority Member:
Liz Krueger (D) 518-455-2297

Offices and agencies generally appear in alphabetical order, except when specific order is requested by listee.

HOUSING & COMMUNITY DEVELOPMENT / U.S. Government

Local Government
Chair:
  Elizabeth O'Connor Little (R) 518-455-2811

Ranking Minority Member:
  Andrea Stewart-Cousins (D) 518-455-2585

U.S. Government

EXECUTIVE DEPARTMENTS AND RELATED AGENCIES

US Department of Agriculture

Rural Development
Web site: www.rurdev.usda.gov/ny

New York State Office . . . . fax: 315-477-6438
  The Galleries of Syracuse, 441 S Salina St, 5th Fl, Ste 357, Syracuse, NY 13202-2425
  TTY: 315-477-6447 or 315-477-6400 Fax: 315-477-6438
  Acting State Director:
    Scott Collins 315-477-6400
  Special Projects Representative:
    Vacant 315-477-6433
  Program Director, Rural Business-Cooperative Service:
    Walter D Schermerhorn 315-477-6425
    e-mail: walter.schermerhorn@ny.usda.gov
  Program Director, Rural Utilities Service:
    David Miller 315-477-6427
    e-mail: david.miller@ny.usda.gov
  Program Director, Rural Housing Service:
    George Von Pless 315-477-6419
    e-mail: george.vonpless@ny.usda.gov
  Human Resources Manager:
    Brenda Chewning-Kulick 315-477-6405

US Housing & Urban Development Department
Web site: www.hud.gov

New York State Office . . . . fax: 212-264-3068
  26 Federal Plaza, 35th Fl, Rm 3541, New York, NY 10278-0068
  212-264-8000 Fax: 212-264-3068
  Regional Director:
    Marisel Morales 212-264-1161/fax: 212-264-9377
  Deputy Regional Director:
    Carmen McCulloch 212-264-8000 x3173
  Public Affairs Officer:
    Adam Glantz 212-264-8000 x3158

  Administration (Admin Service Center 1)
  Deputy Director:
    Lisa Surplus 212-264-8000 x3331

  Community Planning & Development
  Director:
    Robert Cardillo 212-264-2885 x3401

  Fair Housing & Equal Opportunity Office
  Director:
    Stanley Seidenfeld 212-264-1290 x3501

  Field Offices
    Albany Area Office & Financial Operations Center fax: 518-464-4300
      52 Corporate Circle, Albany, NY 12203-5121
      Director Financial Operations Center:
        Lester J West 518-464-4200
      Field Office Director:
        Robert Scofield 518-464-4201/fax: 518-464-4300
    Buffalo Area Office . . . . fax: 716-551-5752
      465 Main St, Lafayette Court, 2nd Fl, Buffalo, NY 14203
      Field Office Director:
        Stephen T Banko, III 716-551-5755/fax: 716-551-5752
        e-mail: stephen_t._banko@hud.gov

  General Counsel
  Asst General Counsel:
    Henry Czauski 212-264-8000 x3201

  Housing
  Director:
    Deborah VanAmerongen 212-264-0777 x3701

  Inspector General
  Special Agent-in-Charge, Investigation:
    Ruth A Ritzema 212-264-8062
  District Inspector General, Audit:
    Alexander C Malloy 212-264-8000 x3976

  Public Housing
  Director:
    Mirza Negron Morales 212-264-0903 x3601

U.S. CONGRESS

See U.S. Congress Chapter for additional Standing Committee and Subcommittee information.

House of Representatives Standing Committees

Financial Services
Chair:
  Barney Frank (D-MA) 202-225-5931
Ranking Minority Member:
  Spencer Bachus (R-AL) 202-225-4921
New York Delegate:
  Gary L Ackerman (D) 202-225-2601
New York Delegate:
  Joseph Crowley (D) 202-225-3965
New York Delegate:
  Vito Fossella (R) 202-225-3371
New York Delegate:
  Steve Israel (D) 202-225-3335
New York Delegate:
  Sue W Kelly (R) 202-225-5441
New York Delegate:
  Peter T King (R) 202-225-7896
New York Delegate:
  Carolyn B Maloney (D) 202-225-7944
New York Delegate:
  Carolyn McCarthy (D) 202-225-5516
New York Delegate:
  Gregory W Meeks (D) 202-225-3461
New York Delegate:
  Nydia M Velazquez (D) 202-225-2361

Offices and agencies generally appear in alphabetical order, except when specific order is requested by listee.

HOUSING & COMMUNITY DEVELOPMENT / Private Sector

Subcommittee
Housing & Community Opportunity
Chair:
Maxine Waters (D-CA) 202-225-2201
Ranking Minority Member:
Judy Biggert (R-IL) 202-225-3515
New York Delegate:
Nydia M Velazquez (D) 202-225-2361

Transportation & Infrastructure
Chair:
James L Oberstar (D-MN) 202-225-4472
Ranking Republican Member:
John L Mica (R-FL) 202-225-4035
New York Delegate:
Timothy H Bishop (D) 202-225-3826
New York Delegate:
Sherwood L Boehlert (R) 202-225-3665
New York Delegate:
Brian M Higgins (D) 202-225-3306
New York Delegate:
Sue W Kelly (R) 202-225-5441
New York Delegate:
John R (Randy) Kuhl (R) 202-225-3161

New York Delegate:
Jerrold Nadler (D) 202-225-5635
New York Delegate:
Anthony Weiner (D) 202-225-6616
Subcommittee
Economic Development, Public Buildings & Emergency Management
Chair:
Eleanor Holmes Norton (D-DC) 202-225-9961
Ranking Minority Member:
Sam Graves (R-MO) 202-225-7041
New York Delegate:
John R (Randy) Kuhl, Jr (R) 202-225-3161

Senate Standing Committees
Banking, Housing & Urban Affairs
Chair:
Christopher J Dodd (D-CT) 202-224-2823
Ranking Minority Member:
Richard C Shelby (R-AL) 202-224-5744
New York Delegate:
Charles E Schumer (D) 202-224-6542

Private Sector

Albany County Rural Housing Alliance Inc
PO Box 407, 24 Martin Road, Voorheesville, NY 12186
518-765-2425 Fax: 518-765-9014
Web site: www.acrha.org
Judith A Eisgruber, Executive Director
Development & management of low income housing; home repair programs; housing counseling & education

American Institute of Architects (AIA) New York State Inc
52 S Pearl St, 3rd Fl, Albany, NY 12207
518-449-3334 Fax: 518-426-8176
e-mail: aianys@aianys.org
Web site: www.aianys.org
Edward C Farrell, Executive Director
Architectural regulations, state policy, smart growth & affordable housing

Association for Community Living
632 Plank Road, Suite 110, Clifton Park, NY 12065
518-688-1682 Fax: 518-688-1686
e-mail: info@aclnys.org
Web site: www.aclnys.org
Antonia Lasicki, Director
Membership organization for agencies that provide housing & rehab services to individuals diagnosed with serious mental illness

Association for Neighborhood & Housing Development
50 Broad St, Suite 1125, New York, NY 10004-2376
212-747-1117 Fax: 212-747-1114
e-mail: irene.b@anhd.org
Web site: www.anhd.org
Irene Baldwin, Executive Director
Umbrella organization providing assistance to NYC nonprofits advocating for affordable housing & neighborhood preservation

Association for a Better New York
355 Lexington Ave, 11th Fl, New York, NY 10017
212-370-5800 Fax: 212-661-5877
e-mail: info@abny.org
Web site: www.abny.org
Michelle Adams, Executive Director
Business recruitment & retention, NYC public policy issues forums & committees

Brooklyn Housing & Family Services Inc
415 Albemarle Rd, Brooklyn, NY 11218
718-435-7585 Fax: 718-435-7605
e-mail: ljayson@brooklynhousing.org; carol@brooklynhousing.org
Web site: www.brooklynhousing.org
Larry Jayson, Executive Director
Homelessness prevention, landlord/tenant dispute resolution & advocacy, immigration services

CUNY Hunter College, Urban Affairs & Planning Department
695 Park Ave, New York, NY 10021
212-772-5515 Fax: 212-772-5593
e-mail: smoses@hunter.cuny.edu
Web site: www.hunter.cuny.edu
Stanley Moses, Chair
History of planning, employment & education

Center for an Urban Future
120 Wall St, 20th Fl, New York, NY 10005
212-479-3319 Fax: 212-479-3338
e-mail: cuf@nycfuture.org
Web site: www.nycfuture.org
Johnathan Bowle, Director
Policy institute dedicated to aggressively pursuing solutions to critical problems facing cities

Offices and agencies generally appear in alphabetical order, except when specific order is requested by listee.

HOUSING & COMMUNITY DEVELOPMENT / Private Sector

Citizens Housing & Planning Council of New York
50 East 42nd St, Ste 407, New York, NY 10017
212-286-9211 Fax: 212-286-9214
e-mail: info@chpcny.org
Web site: www.chpcny.org
Marsha Nicholson, Executive Director

Community Housing Improvement Program (CHIP)
377 Broadway, 3rd Floor, New York, NY 10013
212-838-7442 Fax: 212-838-7456
e-mail: info@chipnyc.org
Web site: www.chipnyc.org
Patrick J Siconolfi, Executive Director
Representing NYC apartment building owners

Community Preservation Corporation (The)
28 East 28th Street, 9th Floor, New York, NY 10016-7943
212-869-5300 x511 Fax: 212-683-0694
e-mail: mlappin@communityp.com
Web site: www.communityp.com
Michael D Lappin, President & Chief Executive Officer
Multifamily housing rehabilitation financing for NYC & NJ neighborhoods

Community Service Society of New York
105 E 22nd St, New York, NY 10010
212-614-5492 Fax: 212-614-9441
e-mail: vbach@cssny.org
Web site: www.cssny.org
Victor Bach, Senior Housing Policy Analyst
Research & advocacy for public policies & programs that improve housing conditions & opportunities for low-income NYC residents & communities

Cornell Cooperative Extension, Community & Economic Vitality Program
43 Warren Hall, Cornell University, Ithaca, NY 14853
607-255-9510 Fax: 607-255-2231
e-mail: rlh13@cornell.edu
Web site: www.cce.cornell.edu
Rod Howe, Assistant Director
Work with community leaders, extension educators & elected officials to strengthen the vitality of New York's communities

Council on the Environment of NYC, Open Space Greening Program
51 Chambers St, Rm 228, New York, NY 10007
212-788-7900 or 212-788-7928 Fax: 212-788-7913
e-mail: conyc@cenyc.org
Web site: www.cenyc.org
Gerard Lordahl, Director
Material & technical assistance for housing groups to create & maintain open community gardens & other public open spaces in NYC

Federal Home Loan Bank of New York
101 Park Ave, New York, NY 10178-0599
212-681-6000 Fax: 212-441-6890
e-mail: info@fhlbny.com
Web site: www.fhlbny.com
Joseph Gallo, Vice President & Director, Community Investment

Hofstra University, School of Law
121 Hofstra University, Hempstead, NY 11549
212-864-6092
Web site: www.hofstra.edu
William R Ginsberg, Emeritus Professor of Law
Land use & environmental law

Homes for the Homeless/Institute for Children & Parties
36 Cooper Square, 6th Fl, New York, NY 10003
212-529-5252 Fax: 212-529-7698
e-mail: info@homesforthehomeless.com
Web site: www.homesforthehomeless.com
Christy Forshey, Media Contact
Private non-profit providing education, social services & transitional housing for homeless children & families in NYC

Housing Action Council Inc - Not For Profit
55 S Broadway, Tarrytown, NY 10591
914-332-4144 Fax: 914-332-4147
e-mail: rnoonan@affordablehomes.org
Rosemarie Noonan, Executive Director
Financial feasibility, land use & zoning & affordable housing

Housing Works Inc
57 Willoughby Street, Brooklyn, NY 11201
347-473-7400 Fax: 347-473-7464
Web site: www.housingworks.org
Michael Kink, Statewide Advocacy Coordinator & Legislative Counsel
Housing, health care, advocacy, job training & support services for homeless NY residents with HIV or AIDS

Local Initiative Support Corporation
501 7th Ave, Fl 7, New York, NY 10018
212-455-9800 Fax: 212-682-5929
Web site: www.liscnet.org
Norman R Bobins, President & Chief Executive Officer
Support the development of local leadership & the creation of affordable housing, commercial, industrial & community facilities, businesses & jobs

Mid-Hudson Pattern for Progress
6 Albany Post Rd, Newburgh, NY 12550-1439
845-565-4900 Fax: 845-565-4918
e-mail: jdrapkin@pfprogress.org
Web site: www.pattern-for-progress.org
Jonathan Drapkin, President & Chief Executive Officer
Regional planning, research & policy development

NY Housing Association Inc
35 Commerce Ave, Albany, NY 12206
518-435-9858 Fax: 518-435-9839
e-mail: info@nyhousing.org
Web site: www.nyhousing.org
Nancy Geer, Executive Director
Manufactured, factory built, modular & mobile housing

Offices and agencies generally appear in alphabetical order, except when specific order is requested by listee.

HOUSING & COMMUNITY DEVELOPMENT / Private Sector

NYS Tenants & Neighbors Coalition
236 West 27th St, 4th Fl, New York, NY 10001
212-608-4320 Fax: 212-619-7476
e-mail: info@tandn.org
Web site: www.tandn.org
Miriam Serrano, Executive Director
Advocacy for tenant protection legislation & affordable housing, tenant education and empowerment

National Trust for Historic Preservation
NE Office, 7 Faneuil Hall Marketplace, 4th Fl, Boston, MA 2109
617-523-0885 Fax: 617-523-1199
e-mail: wendy_nicholas@nthp.org
Web site: www.nthp.org
Wendy Nicholas, Director
Advocacy, education, technical assistance & funding for preservation & community revitalization

Neighborhood Preservation Coalition of NYS Inc
40 Colvin Ave, Ste 102, Albany, NY 12206-1104
518-432-6757 Fax: 518-432-6758
e-mail: agostine@npcnys.org
Web site: www.npcnys.org
Joseph A Agostine, Jr, Executive Director
Community organizations united to preserve & revitalize neighborhoods

Nelson A Rockefeller Inst of Govt, Urban & Metro Studies
411 State St, Albany, NY 12203-1003
518-443-5522 Fax: 518-443-5788
e-mail: wrightd@rockinst.org
Web site: www.rockinst.org
David J Wright, Director
Research on community capacity building, impacts of welfare reform on community development corporations, empowerment zone/enterprise communities & neighborhood preservation

New School University, Milano Graduate School of Mgmt & Urban Policy
72 Fifth Ave, New York, NY 10011
212-229-5400
Web site: www.newschool.edu
Edwin Melendez, Professor
Research, policy analysis & evaluation on community development & urban poverty

New York Building Congress
44 W 28th St, 12th Fl, New York, NY 10001-4212
212-481-9230 Fax: 212-447-6037
e-mail: rtanders55@aol.com
Web site: www.buildingcongress.com
Richard T Anderson, President
Coalition of design, construction & real estate organizations

New York Community Bank
One Jericho Plz, PO Box 9005, Jericho, NY 11753
516-942-6994 Fax: 516-942-6995
e-mail: d.coniglio@mynycb.com
Web site: www.mynycb.com
Donna Coniglio, Chair

New York Landmarks Conservancy
1 Whitehall St, 21 Fl, New York, NY 10004
212-995-5260 Fax: 212-995-5268
e-mail: nylandmarks@nylandmarks.org
Web site: www.nylandmarks.org
Peg Breen, President
Technical & financial assistance for preservation & reuse of landmark buildings

New York Lawyers for the Public Interest
151 W 30th Street, 11th Floor, New York, NY 10001
212-244-4664 Fax: 212-244-4570
e-mail: mar@nylpi.org
Web site: www.nylpi.org
Michael Rothenberg, Executive Director
Disability rights law; access to health care; pro bono clearingouse; environmental justice and community development

New York State Community Action Association
2 Charles Blvd, Guilderland, NY 12084
518-690-0491 Fax: 518-690-0498
e-mail: dan@nyscaaonline.org
Web site: www.nyscaaonline.org
Daniel Maskin, Chief Executive Officer
Dedicated to the growth & education of community action agencies in NYS to sustain their efforts in advocating & improving the lives of low-income New Yorkers

New York State Rural Advocates
PO Box 104, Blue Mountain Lake, NY 12812
518-352-7787
Nancy Berkowitz, Coordinator
Advocacy & education for affordable housing for rural New Yorkers

New York State Rural Development Council
c/o NYS Dept of State, 41 State St, Ste 900, Albany, NY 12231
518-473-7290 Fax: 518-474-6572
e-mail: localgov@dos.state.ny.us
Web site: www.dos.state.ny.us
Patricia M Walsh, Executive Director
Identifies, discusses & takes action on issues important to rural NY, especially economic development & availability of community services

New York State Rural Housing Coalition Inc
879 Madison Ave, 2nd Fl, Albany, NY 12208
518-458-8696 Fax: 518-458-8896
e-mail: rhc@ruralhousing.org
Web site: www.ruralhousing.org
Blair W Sebastian, Executive Director
Rural & small city housing; community & economic development

New York University, Wagner Graduate School
295 Lafayette Street, 2nd Floor, New York, NY 10012
212-998-7400 Fax: 212-995-4162
e-mail: mitchell.moss@nyu.edu
Web site: www.nyu.edu/wagner
Mitchell Moss, Professor of Urban Policy & Planning
Research on urban planning & development, with special emphasis on technology & the future of cities

---

Offices and agencies generally appear in alphabetical order, except when specific order is requested by listee.

HOUSING & COMMUNITY DEVELOPMENT / Private Sector

Park Resident Homeowners' Association Inc
PO Box 68, Ontario, NY 14519
315-524-6703 Fax: 315-524-6703
e-mail: info@prho.com
Web site: www.prho.com
George R Miles, President
Protecting the rights of homeowners living in mobile/manufactured park communities in NYS

Parodneck Foundation (The)
121 6th Ave, Suite 501, New York, NY 10013
212-431-9700 Fax: 212-431-9783
e-mail: info@parodneckfoundation.org
Harold DeRienzo, President
Resident-controlled housing; community development

Pratt Center for Community Development
379 Dekalb Ave, 2nd Fl, Brooklyn, NY 11205
718-636-3486 Fax: 718-636-3709
e-mail: mmcgrego@pratt.edu
Web site: www.prattcenter.edu
Brad Lander, Director
Training & technical assistance in community economic development & housing

Project for Public Spaces
700 Broadway, 4th Fl, New York, NY 10003
212-620-5660 Fax: 212-620-3821
e-mail: pps@pps.org
Web site: www.pps.org
Fred I Kent, President
Nonprofit organization providing community planning, design & development services

Regional Plan Association
4 Irving Place, 7th Fl, New York, NY 10003
212-253-2727 Fax: 212-253-5666
e-mail: yaro@rpa.org
Web site: www.rpa.org
Robert D Yaro, President
Develops & implements land-use, transportation, open space preservation, economic development & social equity proposals

Rent Stabilization Assn of NYC Inc
123 William St, New York, NY 10038
212-214-9200 x222 Fax: 212-732-0618
Web site: www.rsanyc.org
Joseph Strasburg, President
NYC landlord organization

Rural Housing Action Corporation
400 East Ave, Rochester, NY 14607-1910
585-340-3366 Fax: 585-340-3309
e-mail: lbeaulac@ruralinc.org
Web site: www.ruralinc.org
Lee Beaulac, President
Rental, first-time homebuyer, property management & home improvement programs for farmworkers, seniors & the rural poor

Settlement Housing Fund Inc
1780 Broadway, 6th Fl, New York, NY 10019
212-265-6530 Fax: 212-757-0571
Web site: www.settlementhousingfund.org
Carol Lamberg, Executive Director
Low & moderate income housing development, leasing, community development

Turner/Geneslaw Inc
2 Executive Blvd, Suite 401, Suffern, NY 10901
845-368-1472 Fax: 845-368-1572
e-mail: rgeneslaw@tgiplanning.com
Web site: www.tgiplanning.com
Robert Geneslaw, Consultant
Community planning & zoning

Urban Homesteading Assistance Board
120 Wall St, 20th Fl, New York, NY 10005
212-479-3300 Fax: 212-344-6457
e-mail: info@uhab.org
Web site: www.uhab.org
Andrew Reicher, Executive Director
Training, technical assistance & services for development & preservation of low income cooperative housing

Women's Housing & Economic Development Corporation (WHEDCO)
50 E 168th St, Bronx, NY 10452
718-839-1103 Fax: 718-839-1170
e-mail: nbiberman@whedco.org
Web site: www.whedco.org
Nancy Biberman, President
Non-profit organization dedicated to the economic advancement of low-income women & their families

Offices and agencies generally appear in alphabetical order, except when specific order is requested by listee.

HUMAN RIGHTS

New York State

GOVERNOR'S OFFICE

Governor's Office
Executive Chamber
State Capitol
Albany, NY 12224
518-474-8390 Fax: 518-474-1513
Web site: www.state.ny.us

Governor:
　Eliot Spitzer 518-474-8390
Secretary to the Governor:
　Richard Baum 518-474-4246
Counsel to the Governor:
　David Nocenti 518-474-8343
Senior Advisor to the Governor:
　Lloyd Constantine 518-486-9671
Deputy Secretary, Health & Human Services:
　Dennis Whalen 518-408-2500
Assistant Deputy Secretary, Health & Human Services:
　Joseph Baker 518-486-4079
Director, Communications:
　Darren Dopp 518-474-8418

EXECUTIVE DEPARTMENTS AND RELATED AGENCIES

Civil Service Department
Alfred E Smith State Ofc Bldg
Albany, NY 12239
518-457-2487 Fax: 518-457-7547
Web site: www.cs.state.ny.us

Commissioner:
　Nancy G Groenwegen 518-457-3701
Executive Deputy Commissioner:
　Patricia Hite 518-457-6212
Deputy Commissioner, Operations:
　Hector Millan 518-485-7515
Director, Public Information:
　Erin Barlow 518-457-9375/fax: 518-457-6654
　e-mail: erin.barlow@cs.state.ny.us
Public Records Access Officer:
　Erin Barlow 518-457-6875/fax: 518-457-6654

Classification & Compensation Division
Director:
　Nicholas J Vagianelis 518-457-6226/fax: 518-457-8081

Diversity, Planning & Management Division
Director:
　Frank E Abrams 518-457-4146/fax: 518-457-0399
Coordinator, Community Outreach:
　George Swiers 518-457-7661/fax: 518-457-0399

Developmental Disabilities Planning Council
155 Washington Ave
2nd Fl
Albany, NY 12210
518-486-7505 or 800-395-3372 Fax: 518-402-3505
Web site: www.ddpc.state.ny.us

Chairperson:
　George E Fertal Sr 518-486-7505
Vice Chairperson:
　Rose Marie Toscano 518-486-7505
Executive Director:
　Sheila M Carey 518-486-7505
Deputy Executive Director:
　Anna Lobosco 518-486-7505
　e-mail: alobosco@ddpc.state.ny.us
Public Information Officer:
　Thomas F Lee 518-486-7505
　e-mail: tlee@ddpc.state.ny.us

Human Rights, State Division of
1 Fordham Plaza, 4th Fl
Bronx, NY 10458-5871
718-741-8400 Fax: 718-741-3214
Web site: www.dhr.state.ny.us

Commissioner:
　Kumiki Gibson 718-741-8326
Special Advisor to the Commissioner:
　Spencer B Freedman 718-741-8328
Special Advisor to the Commissioner:
　Alphonso B David 718-741-8415
Deputy Commissioner, Enforcement:
　Joshua Zinner 718-741-8330
Director, Federal Programs:
　Edward A Watkins 718-741-8330
Director, Administration:
　Stephen Lopez 718-741-8358
Acting General Counsel:
　Caroline Downey 718-741-8398
Chief Information Officer:
　Stephen Lopez 718-741-8376
Administrator, Affirmative Action:
　Rockwell J Chin 718-741-8309

Regional Offices

Albany
Empire State Plaza, Corning Tower, 25th Fl, Albany, NY 12220
Regional Director:
　Rey F Torres 518-474-2705/fax: 518-473-3422

Binghamton
44 Hawley St, Rm 603, Binghamton, NY 13901
Regional Director:
　Rey Torres 607-721-8467/fax: 607-721-8470

Offices and agencies generally appear in alphabetical order, except when specific order is requested by listee.

HUMAN RIGHTS / New York State

Brooklyn
55 Hanson Place, Rm 304, Brooklyn, NY 11217
Regional Director:
  William Lamot 718-722-2856/fax: 718-722-2869

Buffalo
W J Mahoney State Ofc Bldg, 65 Court St, Ste 506, Buffalo, NY 14202
Regional Director:
  Tasha Moore 716-847-7632/fax: 716-847-7625

Manhattan (Lower)
20 Exchange Place, 2nd Fl, New York, NY 10005
Regional Director:
  Leon Dimaya 212-480-2522/fax: 212-480-0143

Manhattan (Upper)
State Ofc Bldg, 163 W 125th St, 4th Fl, New York, NY 10027
Regional Director:
  Wilson Ortiz 212-961-8650/fax: 212-961-4425

Nassau County
175 Fulton Ave, 4th Fl, Hempstead, NY 11550
Regional Director:
  Leah Jefferson 516-538-1360/fax: 516-483-6589

Peekskill
8 John Walsh Blvd, Ste 204, Peekskill, NY 10566
Regional Director:
  Margaret Gormley-King 914-788-8050/fax: 914-788-8059

Rochester
One Monroe Sq, 259 Monroe Ave, Ste 308, Rochester, NY 14607
Regional Director:
  Julia Day 585-238-8250/fax: 585-238-8259

Suffolk County
Perry B Duryea State Ofc Bldg, Rm 3A-15 Veterans Memorial Hwy, Hauppauge, NY 11788
Regional Director:
  Leah Jefferson 631-952-6434/fax: 631-952-6436

Syracuse
333 E Washington St, Rm 443, Syracuse, NY 13202
Regional Director:
  Julia Day 315-428-4633/fax: 315-428-4638

Law Department
120 Broadway
New York, NY 10271-0332
212-416-8000 Fax: 212-416-8796

State Capitol
Albany, NY 12224-0341
518-474-7330
Fax: 518-402-2472

Attorney General:
  Andrew M Cuomo 518-474-7330/fax: 518-402-2472
First Deputy Attorney General:
  Michele Hirshman 212-416-8050
Director, Public Information & Correspondence:
  Peter A Drago 518-474-7330/fax: 518-402-2472

Public Advocacy Division
Deputy Attorney General:
  Dietrich Snell 212-416-8041/fax: 212-416-8068
Special Counsel:
  Mary Ellen Burns 212-416-6155

Civil Rights Bureau
Bureau Chief:
  Dennis Parker 212-416-8250/fax: 212-416-8074

NYS Commission on Quality of Care & Advocacy for Persons with Disabilities
1 Empire State Plaza
Ste 1001
Albany, NY 12223-1150
800-624-4143 or 800-522-4369 Fax: 518-388-2800
Web site: www.cqcapd.state.ny.us

Chair:
  Gary O'Brien 518-388-1281
Deputy Advocate & Counsel, Public Info Officer:
  Gary Masline 518-388-1270
  e-mail: oapwdinfo@oapwd.org

Temporary & Disability Assistance, Office of
40 N Pearl St
Albany, NY 12243
518-474-9003 or 800-342-3004 Fax: 518-474-7870
e-mail: nyspio@otda.state.ny.us
Web site: www.otda.state.ny.us

Commissioner:
  David A Hansell 518-474-4152/fax: 518-486-6255
  e-mail: david.hansell@otda.state.ny.us
Director, External & Intergovernmental Affairs Office:
  Elizabeth Segal 518-474-7420
Director, Public Information:
  Michael Hayes 518-474-9516/fax: 518-486-6935
  e-mail: nyspio@otda.state.ny.us

Employment & Transitional Supports
Deputy Commissioner:
  Russell Sykes 518-474-9222/fax: 518-474-5281

Program Support & Quality Improvement
Deputy Commissioner:
  John Paolucci 518-473-3912

NEW YORK STATE LEGISLATURE

See Legislative Branch in Section 1 for additional Standing Committee and Subcommittee information.

Assembly Standing Committees

Aging
Chair:
  Steven C Englebright (D) 518-455-4804
Ranking Minority Member:
  Philip Boyle (R) 518-455-4611

Correction
Chair:
  Jeffrion L Aubry (D) 518-455-4561
Ranking Minority Member:
  Joe Giglio (R) 518-455-5241

Offices and agencies generally appear in alphabetical order, except when specific order is requested by listee.

HUMAN RIGHTS / U.S. Government

Labor
Chair:
　Susan V John (D) 518-455-4527
Ranking Minority Member:
　Thomas W Alfano (R) 518-455-4627

Mental Health
Chair:
　Peter M Rivera (D) 518-455-5102
Ranking Minority Member:
　Tom McKevitt (R) 518-455-5341

Assembly Task Forces

Puerto Rican/Hispanic Task Force
Chair:
　Peter M Rivera (D) 518-455-5102
Co-Chair:
　Vito J Lopez (D) 518-455-5537

Women's Issues, Task Force on
Chair:
　Barbara Lifton (D) 518-455-5444
Coordinator:
　Jean Emery 518-455-3632/fax: 518-455-4574

Senate Standing Committees

Aging
Chair:
　Martin J Golden (R) 518-455-2730
Ranking Minority Member:
　Ruben Diaz, Sr (D) 518-455-2511

Crime Victims, Crime & Correction
Chair:
　Michael F Nozzolio (R) 518-455-2366
Ranking Minority Member:
　Eric Adams (D) 518-455-2431

Labor
Chair:
　George D Maziarz (R) 518-455-2024
Ranking Minority Member:
　George Onorato (D) 518-455-3486

Mental Health & Developmental Disabilities
Chair:
　Thomas P Morahan (R) 518-455-3261
Ranking Minority Member:
　Ruben Diaz, Sr (D) 518-455-2511

U.S. Government

EXECUTIVE DEPARTMENTS AND RELATED AGENCIES

Equal Employment Opportunity Commission
Web site: www.eeoc.gov

New York District
33 Whitehall St, 5th Fl, New York, NY 10004
District Director:
　Spencer H Lewis, Jr .... 800-669-4000 or 800-669-6820 tty
fax: 212-336-3790

Buffalo Local
6 Fountain Plaza, Ste 350, Buffalo, NY 14202
Director:
　Elizabeth Cadle 800-669-4000/fax: 716-551-4387

US Commerce Department
Web site: www.doc.gov

Minority Business Development Agency
Web site: www.mbda.gov

New York Region
26 Federal Plaza, Rm 3720, New York, NY 10278
Regional Director:
　Heyward B Davenport 212-264-3262/fax: 212-264-0725

US Commission on Civil Rights
Web site: www.usccr.gov

EASTERN REGION (includes New York State)
624 9th St NW, Ste 500, Washington, DC 20425
Regional Director:
　Ivy Davis 202-376-7533/fax: 202-376-7548

US Department of Health & Human Services
Web site: www.os.dhhs.gov; www.hhs.gov/region2/

Office of Secretary's Regional Representative-Region 2-NY .... fax: 212-264-3620
26 Federal Plaza, Rm 3835, New York, NY 10278
Regional Director:
　Deborah Konopko 212-264-4600
　e-mail: deborah.konopko@hhs.gov
Senior Intergovernmental Affairs Specialist:
　Joel S Truman 212-264-4600
　e-mail: joel.truman@hhs.gov
Intergovernmental Affairs Specialist:
　Katherine Williams 212-264-4600
　e-mail: katherine.williams@hhs.gov

Office for Civil Rights .... fax: 212-264-3039
26 Federal Plaza, Rm 3312, New York, NY 10278
Fax: 212-264-3039
Web site: www.hhs.gov/ocr
Regional Manager:
　Michael Carter 212-264-3313/fax: 212-264-3039
Deputy Regional Manager:
　Linda Colon 212-264-3313

US Department of Homeland Security (DHS)
Web site: www.dhs.gov

US Citizenship & Immigration Services (USCIS)
TTY: 800-767-1833 or 800-375-5283
Web site: www.uscis.gov

Buffalo District Office .... fax: 716-551-3131
Federal Center, 130 Delaware Ave, Buffalo, NY 14202
District Director:
　M Frances Holmes 716-551-4741 x6000

Offices and agencies generally appear in alphabetical order, except when specific order is requested by listee.

HUMAN RIGHTS / Private Sector

Albany Sub Office
1086 Troy-Schenectady Rd, Latham, NY 12110
Officer-in-Charge:
Gary Hale 518-220-2100

CIS Asylum Offices
New York Asylum Office . . . . fax: 718-723-1121
One Cross Island Plaza, 3rd Fl, Rosedale, NY 11422
Director:
Patricia A Jackson 718-723-5954
Deputy Director:
Mick Dedvukaj 718-723-5954
Newark Asylum Offc-Including NYS not served by New York City fax: 201-531-1877
1200 Wall St, West 4th Fl, Lyndhurst, NJ 07071
Director:
Susan Raufer 201-531-0555
Deputy Director:
Aster Zeleke 201-531-0555

New York City District Office
26 Federal Plaza, New York, NY 10278
District Director:
Mary Ann Gantner 212-264-3972
Garden City Satellite Office
711 Stewart Ave, Garden City, NY 11530
Officer-in-Charge:
Linda Pritchett . . . . 516-228-9242 or 516-288-9243

U.S. CONGRESS

See U.S. Congress Chapter for additional Standing Committee and Subcommittee information.

House of Representatives Standing Committees

Education & Labor
Chair:
George Miller (D-CA) 202-225-2095
Ranking Minority Member:
Howard P (Buck) McKeon (R-CA) 202-225-1956
New York Delegate:
Timothy H Bishop (D) 202-225-3826
New York Delegate:
Carolyn McCarthy (D) 202-225-5516
New York Delegate:
Major R Owens (D) 202-225-6231
New York Delegate:
John R (Randy) Kuhl, Jr (R) 202-225-3161

Foreign Affairs
Chair:
Tom Lantos (D-CA) 202-225-3531
Ranking Minority Member:
Ileana Ros Lehtinen (R-FL) 202-225-3931
New York Delegate:
Gary L Ackerman (D) 202-225-2601
New York Delegate:
Joseph Crowley (D) 202-225-3965
New York Delegate:
Eliot L Engel (D) 202-225-2464
New York Delegate:
Amory Houghton (R) 202-225-3161
New York Delegate:
Peter T King (R) 202-225-7896
New York Delegate:
Gregory W Meeks (D) 202-225-3461

Subcommittee
Terrorism, Nonproliferation and Trade
Chair:
Brad Sherman (D-CA) 202-225-5911
Ranking Minority Member:
Edward R Royce (R-CA) 202-225-4111

Senate Standing Committees

Indian Affairs, Committee on
Chair:
Byron L Dorgan (D-ND) 202-224-2251
Vice Chair:
Craig Thomas (R-WY) 202-224-2251

Private Sector

American Jewish Committee
165 E 56th St, New York, NY 10022-2709
212-751-4000 Fax: 212-891-1450
e-mail: pr@ajc.org
Web site: www.ajc.org
David Harris, Executive Director
Promoting tolerance, mutual respect & understanding among diverse ethnic, racial & religious groups

Amnesty International USA
5 Penn Plaza, 14th Floor, New York, NY 10001
212-807-8400 Fax: 212-627-1451
e-mail: aimember@aiusa.org
Web site: www.amnestyusa.org
William F Schulz, Executive Director
Worldwide campaigning movement working to promote internationally recognized human rights

Anti-Defamation League
605 Third Ave, New York, NY 10158
212-885-7707 Fax: 212-697-0109
e-mail: afoxman@adl.org
Web site: www.adl.org
Abraham H Foxman, National Director
Fighting anti-Semitism worldwide

Asian American Legal Defense and Education Fund
99 Hudson St, 12th Fl, New York, NY 10013-2815
212-966-5932 or 800-966-5946 Fax: 212-966-4303
e-mail: info@aaldef.org
Web site: www.aaldef.org
Margaret Fung, Executive Director
Defend civil rights of Asian Americans through litigation, legal advocacy & community education

Offices and agencies generally appear in alphabetical order, except when specific order is requested by listee.

HUMAN RIGHTS / Private Sector

NYS Bar Assn, Gender Equity Task Force Cmte
Bond Schoeneck & King PLLC
One Lincoln Ctr, Syracuse, NY 13202-1355
315-218-8000 Fax: 315-218-8100
e-mail: crichardson@bsk.com
M Catherine Richardson, Co-Chair

CIDNY - Queens
137-02A Northern Blvd, Flushing, NY 11354
646-442-1520 or TTY 718-886-0427 Fax: 718-886-0428
Web site: www.cidny.org
Susan Dooha, Executive Director
Rights & advocacy for the disabled

Cardozo School of Law
55 Fifth Ave, New York, NY 10003
212-790-0200 Fax: 212-790-0205
e-mail: mrosnfld@ymail.yu.edu
Web site: www.cardozo.yu.edu
Michel Rosenfeld, Justice Sidney L Robins Professor of Human Rights
Law & theory of human rights

Center for Constitutional Rights
666 Broadway, 7th Fl, New York, NY 10012
212-614-6464 Fax: 212-614-6499
e-mail: info@ccr.ny.org
Web site: www.ccr-ny.org
Vincent Warren, Legal Director
Dedicated to advancing & protecting rights guaranteed by the US Constitution & the Universal Declaration of Human Rights

Center for Independence of the Disabled in NY (CIDNY)
841 Broadway, Ste 301, New York, NY 10003
212-674-2300 or TTY: 212-674-5619 Fax: 212-254-5953
Web site: www.cidny.org
Susan Dooha, Executive Director
Rights & advocacy for the disabled

Center for Migration Studies of New York Inc
27 Carmine Street, New York, NY 10014
718-351-8800 Fax: 718-667-4598
e-mail: cms@cmsny.org
Web site: www.cmsny.org
Rev Joseph Fugolo, Executive Director
Facilitate the study of sociodemographic, historical, economic, political, legislative & pastoral aspects of human migration & refugee movements

Children's Rights Inc
330 Seventh Avenue, 4th Floor, New York, NY 10001
212-683-2210 Fax: 212-683-4015
e-mail: info@childrensrights.org
Web site: www.childrensrights.org
Marcia Robinson Lowry, Executive Director
Advocacy & litigation on behalf of abused & neglected children

Citizens' Committee for Children of New York Inc
105 E 22nd St, 7th Fl, New York, NY 10010
212-673-1800 Fax: 212-979-5063
e-mail: info@cccnewyork.org
Web site: www.cccnewyork.org
Gail B Nayowith, Executive Director
Public policy advocacy for children's rights & services

Columbia University, Mailman School of Public Health
Heilbrunn Dept of Population & Family He, 60 Haven Ave, B-2, New York, NY 10032
212-304-5281 Fax: 212-305-7024
e-mail: lpf1@columbia.edu
Web site: cpmcnet.columbia.edu/dept/sph/popfam
Lynn P Freedman, Associate Professor & Director
Theory, analysis & development of policy & programs supporting public health & human rights

Cornell University, School of Industrial & Labor Relations
Ives Hall, Ithaca, NY 14853-3901
607-255-4381 Fax: 607-255-4496
e-mail: fdb4@cornell.edu
Web site: www.ilr.cornell.edu
Francine Blau, Professor
Inequality, discrimination & sexual harassment; occupational segregation

Drum Major Institute for Public Policy - Not For Profit
40 Exchange Place, Suite 2001, New York, NY 10005
212-909-9663 Fax: 212-909-9493
e-mail: dmi@drummajorinstitute.org
Web site: www.drummajorinstitute.org
Andrea Batista Schlesinger, Executive Director
Progressive think tank sponsoring frank dialogue on social problems & developing public policy to promote social & economic justice & equity

Family Planning Advocates of New York State
17 Elk St, Albany, NY 12207-1002
518-436-8408 Fax: 518-436-0004
e-mail: smitj@fpaofnys.org
Web site: www.fpaofnys.org
JoAnn M Smith, President/Chief Executive Officer
Reproductive rights

Filipino American Human Services Inc
185-14 Hillside Ave, Jamaica, NY 11432
718-883-1295 Fax: 718-523-9606
e-mail: fahsi@fahsi.org
Web site: www.fahsi.org
Venessa G Manzano, Executive Director
FAHSI is a community-based non-profit organization dedicated to serving the most vulnerable segments of the Filipino community of New York-particularly youth, women, recent immigrants, and the elderly.

Offices and agencies generally appear in alphabetical order, except when specific order is requested by listee.

HUMAN RIGHTS / Private Sector

Hispanic Outreach Services
40 North Main Ave, Albany, NY 12203
518-453-6655 Fax: 518-641-6830
e-mail: anne.tranelli@rcda.org
Web site: www.hispanicoutreachservices.org
Sister Anne Tranelli, CSJ, Executive Director
Social service, youth guidance, language translation & immigration assistance programs

Human Rights First
333 Seventh Ave, 13th Fl, New York, NY 10001
212-845-5200 Fax: 212-845-5299
e-mail: nyc@humanrightsfirst.org
Web site: www.humanrightsfirst.org
Michael Posner, President
Advocacy for the promotion & protection of fundamental human rights worldwide

Human Rights Watch
350 Fifth Ave, 34th Fl, New York, NY 10118-3299
212-290-4700 Fax: 212-736-1300
e-mail: hrwnyc@hrw.org
Web site: www.hrw.org
Kenneth Roth, Executive Director
Working with victims & activists to prevent discrimination, uphold political freedom, protect people from inhumane conduct in wartime & to bring offenders to justice

International Institute of Buffalo, NY, Inc
864 Delaware Ave, Buffalo, NY 14209
716-883-1900 Fax: 716-883-9529
e-mail: pkefi@iibuff.org
Web site: www.iibuff.org
Pamela Kefi, Executive Director
Assist newly arrived refugees & immigrants to find work, learn English; legal immigration service, translations & interpreting school advocacy

Jewish Community Relations Council of NY Inc
70 W 36th Street, Ste 700, New York, NY 10018
212-983-4800 Fax: 212-983-4084
e-mail: millerm@jcrcny.org
Web site: www.jcrcny.org
Michael Miller, Executive Vice President
JCRC is an umbrella organization for more than 60 Jewish organizations ranging from community based councils to local chapters of national educational, cvic and religious agencies.

Lambda Legal Defense & Education Fund Inc
120 Wall St, Ste 1500, New York, NY 10005-3904
212-809-8585 Fax: 212-809-0055
e-mail: lambda@lambdalegal.org
Web site: www.lambdalegal.org
Kevin M Cathcart, Executive Director
Gay rights & AIDS issues

Lesbian, Gay, Bisexual & Transgender Community Ctr - Not For Profit
208 West 13th Street, New York, NY 10011-7702
212-620-7310 Fax: 212-924-2657
e-mail: info@gaycenter.org
Web site: www.gaycenter.org
Miriam Yeung, Director, Public Policy
Mental health counseling, out-patient chemical dependency treatment center, after-school youth services, HIV/AIDS services, advocacy, cultural programs, affordable meeting and conference services, and community-building.

NYS Bar Assn, Issues Affecting People with Disabilities Cmte
NYS Education Department
Education Bldg, Rm 148, 89 Washington Ave, Albany, NY 12234
518-473-4921 Fax: 518-473-2925
e-mail: ksurgall@mail.nysed.gov
Melinda Saran, Chair

National Council of Jewish Women
53 W 23rd St, 6th Fl, New York, NY 10010
212-645-4048 Fax: 212-645-7466
e-mail: action@ncjw.org
Web site: www.ncjw.org
Phyllis Snyder, President
Human rights & social service advocacy & education

National Organization for Women, NYS
1500 Central Avenue, Albany, NY 12205
518-452-3944 Fax: 518-452-3861
e-mail: newyorkstatenow@aol.com
Web site: www.nownys.com
Marcia Pappas, President
Legislative lobbying on issues affecting women

New School University, Department of Political Science
65 Fifth Ave, New York, NY 10003
212-228-5747 X3088 Fax: 212-807-1669
e-mail: pollis@newschool.edu
Adamantia Pollis, Professor Emeritus, Political Science
Comparative politics, human rights, nationalism & ethnicity

New School University, Intl Center for Migration, Ethnicity & Citizenship
65 Fifth Ave, Room 227, New York, NY 10003
212-229-5399 Fax: 212-989-0504
e-mail: icmec@newschool.edu
Web site: www.newschool.edu/icmec
Aristide R Zolberg, Director
International migrations, refugees

New York Civil Liberties Union
125 Broad Street, 19th Floor, New York, NY 10004
212-607-3300 Fax: 212-607-3318
Web site: www.nyclu.org
Donna Lieberman, Executive Director
Civil rights & civil liberties

Offices and agencies generally appear in alphabetical order, except when specific order is requested by listee.

HUMAN RIGHTS / Private Sector

New York Civil Rights Coalition
3 W 35th Street, Penthouse, New York, NY 10001-2204
212-563-5636 Fax: 212-563-9757
e-mail: nycrc@aol.com
Web site: www.nycivilrights.org
Michael Meyers, Executive Director
Advocacy of racial equality & multiracial cooperation in advancing social progress through the protection & enforcement of civil rights & the unlearning of stereotypes

New York Immigration Coalition (The)
137 W 25th Street, 12th Floor, New York, NY 10001
212-627-2227 x221 Fax: 212-627-9314
e-mail: jwong@thenyic.org
Web site: www.thenyic.org
Chung-Wha Hong, Executive Director
Nonprofit umbrella advocacy organization for groups assisting immigrants

New York Lawyers for the Public Interest
151 W 30th Street, 11th Floor, New York, NY 10001
212-244-4664 Fax: 212-244-4570
e-mail: mar@nylpi.org
Web site: www.nylpi.org
Michael Rothenberg, Executive Director
Disability rights law; access to health care; pro bono clearinghouse; environmental justice and community development

New York State Council of Churches
18 Computer Dr West, Suite 107, Albany, NY 12205
518-436-9319 Fax: 518-427-6705
e-mail: nyscoc@aol.com
Web site: www.nyscoc.org
Mary Lu Bowen, Executive Director

NYS Bar Assn, Minorities in the Profession Cmte
Office of the Attorney General
120 Broadway, New York, NY 10271
212-416-6303 Fax: 212-416-8539
e-mail: lila.kirton@oag.state.ny.us
Lila E Kirton, Chair

Open Society Institute
400 West 59th St, New York, NY 10019
212-548-0600 Fax: 212-548-4600
Web site: www.soros.org
Stewart Paperin, Executive Vice President
Promotes open societies by shaping government policy & supporting education, media, public health, human & women's rights, as well as social, legal & economic reform

Puerto Rican Legal Defense & Education Fund Inc (PRLDEF)
99 Hudson St, 14th Fl, New York, NY 10013-2815
212-219-3360 or 800-328-2322 Fax: 212-431-4276
e-mail: info@prldef.org
Web site: www.prldef.org
Cesar Perales, President & General Counsel
Secure, promote & protect the civil & human rights of the Puerto Rican & wider Latino community through litigation, policy analysis & education

Resource Center for Independent Living (RCIL)
401-409 Columbia St, PO Box 210, Utica, NY 13503-0210
315-797-4642 or TTY 315-797-5837 Fax: 315-797-4747
e-mail: rcil@rcil.com
Web site: www.rcil.com
Burt Danovitz, Executive Director
Services & advocacy for the disabled; public information & community education & awareness

SUNY Buffalo Human Rights Center
SUNY Buffalo, School of Law, 523 O'Brian Hall, Buffalo, NY 14260-1100
716-645-6184 Fax: 716-645-2064
e-mail: bhrc@buffalo.edu
Web site: wings.buffalo.edu/law/bhrlc
Makau Mutua, Professor & Director
Fostering scholarship, coursework, research & internships in international & human rights law

Self Advocacy Association of NYS
500 Balltown Rd, Bldg #5, Schenectady, NY 12304
518-382-1454 Fax: 518-382-1594
e-mail: sholmes@earthlink.net
Web site: www.sanys.org
Steve Holmes, Administrative Coordinator
Advocacy for & by persons with developmental disabilities to ensure civil rights & opportunities

Simon Wiesenthal Center, NY Tolerance Center
50 E 42nd St, Ste 1600, New York, NY 10017-5405
212-370-0320 Fax: 212-883-0895
e-mail: swcny@swcny.org
Web site: www.wiesenthal.com
Rhonda Barad, Eastern Director
Preserve the memory of the Holocaust by fostering tolerance & understanding through community involvement, educational outreach & social action

Tanenbaum Center for Interreligious Understanding
350 Fifth Ave, Ste 3502, New York, NY 10118
212-967-7707 Fax: 212-967-9001
e-mail: info@tanenbaum.org
Web site: www.tanenbaum.org
Joyce S Dubensky, Executive Vice President
Puts interreligious understanding into practice; defuse the verbal & physical violence done in the name of religion

NYS Bar Assn, Gender Equity Task Force Cmte
The Legal Aid Society
One West Main Street, Suite 800, Rochester, NY 14614
585-232-4090 Fax: 585-232-2352
e-mail: cpalumbo@lasroc.org
Carla M Palumbo, Division Director

NYS Bar Assn, Issues Affecting Same Sex Couples
Whiteman Osterman & Hanna LLP
One Commerce Plz, Ste 1900, Albany, NY 12260-2015
518-487-7600 Fax: 518-487-7777
e-mail: mw@woh.com
Web site: www.woh.com
Michael Whiteman, Chair

Offices and agencies generally appear in alphabetical order, except when specific order is requested by listee.

HUMAN RIGHTS / Private Sector

Women's Commission for Refugee Women & Children
122 East 42nd St, New York, NY 10168-1289
212-551-3000 or 212-551-3111 Fax: 212-551-3180
e-mail: wcrwc@womenscommission.org
Web site: www.womenscommission.org
Carolyn Makinson, Executive Director
Advocacy on behalf of refugee women & children world-wide

Offices and agencies generally appear in alphabetical order, except when specific order is requested by listee.

INSURANCE

New York State

GOVERNOR'S OFFICE

Governor's Office
Executive Chamber
State Capitol
Albany, NY 12224
518-474-8390 Fax: 518-474-1513
Web site: www.state.ny.us

Governor:
  Eliot Spitzer 518-474-8390
Secretary to the Governor:
  Richard Baum. 518-474-4246
Counsel to the Governor:
  David Nocenti. 518-474-8343
Senior Advisor to the Governor:
  Lloyd Constantine 518-486-9671
Assistant Counsel to the Governor-General Government Operations & Human Services:
  David Rose. 518-474-2266
Director, Communications:
  Darren Dopp. 518-474-8418

EXECUTIVE DEPARTMENTS AND RELATED AGENCIES

Insurance Department
25 Beaver St
New York, NY 10004
212-480-6400 Fax: 212-480-7454
Web site: www.ins.state.ny.us

One Commerce Plaza
Albany, NY 12257
518-474-4567
Fax: 518-473-6814

Superintendent:
  Eric R Dinallo 518-474-4567/fax: 518-473-6814
First Deputy Superintendent:
  Kermitt Brooks. . . . . 212-480-2292 or 518-474-4567
Deputy Superintendent & General Counsel:
  Robert H Easton 212-480-5259
  e-mail: counsel@ins.state.ny.us
Deputy Superintendent, Policy & Chief Ethics Officer:
  Susan Donnellan. 212-480-5282
Deputy Superintendent, Frauds & Disaster Preparedness:
  Louis W Pietroluongo. . . . . 212-480-6074 or 518-474-4567
Deputy Superintendent, Health:
  Troy Oechsner 212-480-5242
Director, Communications:
  David Neustadt 212-480-5262/fax: 212-480-6077
  e-mail: public-affairs@ins.state.ny.us

Administration & Operations
Director:
  Christopher Rulon 518-474-6848/fax: 518-486-6600
  Licensing Services Unit
  Director:
    Salvatore Castiglione 518-474-7159/fax: 518-474-5048
  Taxes & Accounts Unit
  Director:
    Lori Fraser 518-474-8567

Consumer Services Bureau
Chief:
  Salvatore Castiglione 518-474-6600
  e-mail: scastigl@ins.state.ny.us
Assistant Chief:
  Mitchel Gennaovi 212-480-4697/fax: 212-480-4735

Health Bureau
Co-Chief, Albany:
  Tom Zyra. 518-474-6272/fax: 518-473-4600
Co-Chief, NYC:
  Charles Rapacciulo 212-480-5120/fax: 212-480-5216
Chief, Accident & Health Rating:
  James M Gutterman 518-474-5394

Information Systems & Technology Bureau
Chief:
  Geoff Morse 212-480-2332
  e-mail: systems@ins.state.ny.us

Insurance Frauds Bureau
Director:
  Charles Bardong. 212-480-6074

Life Bureau
Chief Examiner:
  Jeffrey Angelo 212-480-5026

Liquidation Bureau
123 William St, New York, NY 10038
Special Deputy Superintendent:
  Mark Peters. 212-341-6400

Property Bureau
Chief:
  Vacant 212-480-5565

Public Affairs & Research Bureau
Director, Communications:
  David Neustadt 212-480-5262/fax: 212-480-6077
  e-mail: public-affairs@ins.state.ny.us

Insurance Fund (NYS)
15 Computer Drive West
Albany, NY 12205
518-437-5220
Web site: www.nysif.com

Offices and agencies generally appear in alphabetical order, except when specific order is requested by listee.

INSURANCE / New York State

199 Church St
New York, NY 10007
212-312-9000

Executive Director/CEO:
  David P Wehner...................................518-437-5220
First Deputy Executive Director:
  Christopher Barclay.............................518-437-5220
Chief Fiscal Officer:
  Susan D Sharp....................................518-437-6168
General Attorney:
  Gregory Allen.....................................518-437-5220
Deputy Executive Director & Marketing Director:
  Ann F Formel.....................................518-437-1879
Deputy Executive Director, Project Management:
  Stephen D Nelson................................518-437-6196
Public Information Officer:
  Robert Lawson............518-437-3504/fax: 518-437-1849

Administration
Director:
  Joseph Mullen....................................518-437-5220

Claims & Medical Operations
Director:
  Edward Hiller....................................212-312-7880

Confidential Investigations
Director:
  Laurence LaPointe...............................631-756-4007

Field Services
Director:
  Armin Holdorf....................................212-587-5225

Information Technology Service
Chief Information Officer:
  Sean O'Brien.....................................518-437-4361
Director, ITS:
  Laurie Endries...................................518-437-3130

Insurance Fund Board of Commissioners
Chair:
  Robert H Hurlbut................................518-437-5220
Vice Chair:
  Donald T DeCarlo................................518-437-5220
Secretary to the Board:
  Christopher Barclay.............................518-437-5220
Asst Secretary to the Board:
  Albert K DiMeglio................................518-437-5220
Member (ex-officio)/Commissioner, NYS Dept of Labor:
  M Patricia Smith.................................518-437-5220
Member:
  John F Carpenter.................................518-437-5220
Member:
  C Scott Bowen....................................518-437-5220
Member:
  Donald T DeCarlo................................518-437-5220
Member:
  Jane A Halbritter................................518-437-5220
Member:
  Charles L Loiodice...............................518-437-5220
Member:
  William A O'Loughlin, Jr.......................518-437-5220

Investments
Director:
  Miriam Martinez.................................212-587-6550

NYSIF District Offices

Albany
One Watervliet Ave Ext, Albany, NY 12206
Business Manager:
  Edward Obertubbesing............518-437-6401/fax: 518-437-8021

Buffalo
225 Oak St, Buffalo, NY 14203
Business Manager:
  Ronald Reed......................716-851-2004/fax: 716-851-2131

Endicott
Glendale Technology Park, 2001 E Perimeter Rd, Endicott, NY 13760
Business Manager:
  James Fehrer....................607-741-6023/fax: 607-741-5029

Nassau County, Long Island
8 Corporate Center Dr, 2nd Fl, Melville, NY 11747
Business Manager:
  Cliff Meister.....................631-756-4003/fax: 631-756-4030

Rochester
100 Chestnut St, Ste 1000, Rochester, NY 14604
Business Manager:
  Lisa Ellsworth...................585-258-2100/fax: 585-258-2065

Suffolk County, Long Island
8 Corporate Center Dr, 3rd Fl, Melville, NY 11747
Business Manager:
  Eileen Wojnar....................631-756-4330/fax: 631-756-4260

Syracuse
1045 Seventh North St, Liverpool, NY 13088
Business Manager:
  Kathleen Campbell..............315-453-8300/fax: 315-453-8313

White Plains
105 Corporate Park Dr, Ste 200, White Plains, NY 10604
Business Manager:
  Carl Heitner....................914-701-6292/fax: 914-701-2181

Premium Audit
Director:
  Glenn Cunningham..............................212-587-7470

Underwriting
Director:
  John Massetti....................................212-312-7012

Labor Department
Building 12, Room 500
State Campus
Albany, NY 12240
518-457-2741 Fax: 518-457-6908
e-mail: nysdol@labor.state.ny.us
Web site: www.labor.state.ny.us

Commissioner:
  M Patricia Smith.................................518-457-2746
Executive Deputy Commissioner:
  Mario Musolino..................................518-457-4318
Director, Communications:
  Leo Rosales.....................518-457-5519/fax: 518-485-1126

Employment & Unemployment Insurance Advisory Council
Chair:
  Vacant..518-457-2878

Offices and agencies generally appear in alphabetical order, except when specific order is requested by listee.

INSURANCE / New York State

Employment Relations Board
Chair:
  Vacant 212-564-2441

Industrial Board of Appeals
Chair:
  Evelyn Heady 518-474-4789

Unemployment Insurance Appeal Board
Chair:
  Michael Greason 518-402-0205
Executive Director:
  Lisa Connors-Wright 518-402-0205

Unemployment Insurance Division
Director:
  Vacant 518-457-2878/fax: 518-485-8604

Law Department
120 Broadway
New York, NY 10271-0332
212-416-8000 Fax: 212-416-8796

State Capitol
Albany, NY 12224-0341
518-474-7330
Fax: 518-402-2472

Attorney General:
  Andrew M Cuomo 518-474-7330
First Deputy Attorney General:
  Michele Hirshman 212-416-8050
Director, Public Information & Correspondence:
  Peter A Drago 518-474-7330/fax: 518-402-2472

State Counsel Division
Deputy Attorney General:
  Richard Rifkin 518-473-7190
Asst Deputy Attorney General:
  Patricia Martinelli 518-473-0648/fax: 518-486-9777
Asst Deputy Attorney General:
  Susan L Watson 212-416-8579/fax: 212-416-6009

Civil Recoveries Bureau
Bureau Chief:
  Mary E House 518-474-7131/fax: 518-474-1635

Claims Bureau
Bureau Chief:
  Susan Pogoda 212-416-8516/fax: 212-416-8946

Labor Bureau
Bureau Chief:
  M Patricia Smith 212-416-8710

Litigation Bureau
Bureau Chief, NYC:
  James B Henley 212-416-8523/fax: 212-416-6075

Real Property Bureau
Bureau Chief:
  Henry A DeCotis 518-474-7151/fax: 518-473-5106

Workers' Compensation Board
20 Park Street
Albany, NY 12207
877-632-4996 Fax: 518-473-1415
Web site: www.wcb.state.ny.us

Executive Director:
  Glenn Warren 518-474-6670
Chair, Board of Commissioners:
  Donna Ferrara 518-474-6670/fax: 518-473-1415
Vice Chair:
  Fran Libous 518-474-6670/fax: 518-473-1415
General Counsel:
  Cheryl Wood 518-486-9564/fax: 518-473-2233
Director, Division of Appeals:
  Carl Copps 518-402-0160/fax: 518-473-2233
Director, Internal Audit:
  Albert Blackman 518-473-6447/fax: 518-473-4761
Director, Public Information:
  Vacant 518-474-6670/fax: 518-473-1415
Fraud Inspector General:
  John Burgher .... 888-363-6001 or 518-473-4839
  fax: 518-402-1059
Advocate for Business:
  Vacant 518-486-3331
Advocate for Injured Workers:
  Edwin Ruff .... 800-580-6665 or 518-471-8182
  fax: 518-486-7510

Administration
Deputy Executive Director:
  Ann Kutter 518-473-8900/fax: 518-486-6411
Administrative Services:
  Vacant 518-486-3334
Director, Security:
  Joseph V Smith 518-402-0172/fax: 518-402-1059
Director, Finance & Policy:
  Kathleen Griffin 518-486-9596
Director, Human Resources:
  Lisa Sunkes .... 718-802-6612 or 518-474-2685
  fax: 718-834-2123
Affirmative Action Officer:
  Jaime Benitez 518-486-5128/fax: 518-486-6364

Operations
Deputy Executive Director:
  Vacant 518-486-7143/fax: 518-474-9367
Director, Operations:
  David M Donohue 518-486-3345/fax: 518-486-6411
Director, Disability Benefits:
  Nicholas Dogias .... 718-802-6947 or 518-474-6680
  fax: 718-802-6971
Director, Bureau of Compliance:
  Brian Collins 518-474-9598/fax: 518-402-0701

District Offices
Albany
  100 Broadway-Menands, Albany, NY 12241
  District Administrator:
    Linda Spano 866-750-5157/fax: 518-473-9166
  District Manager:
    Pat Wright 518-474-2661
Binghamton
  State Office Bldg, 44 Hawley St, Binghamton, NY 13901
  District Administrator:
    Vacant 866-802-3604/fax: 607-721-8464
  District Manager:
    David Wiktorek 866-802-3604
Brooklyn
  111 Livingston St, Brooklyn, NY 11201
  District Administrator:
    Edward Joyce 800-877-1373/fax: 718-802-6642

Offices and agencies generally appear in alphabetical order, except when specific order is requested by listee.

INSURANCE / U.S. Government

District Manager:
  Tom Agostino 800-877-1373
Buffalo
Statler Towers, 3rd Fl, 107 Delaware Ave, Buffalo, NY 14202-2898
District Administrator:
  Jeffrey Quinn 866-211-0645/fax: 716-842-2171
District Manager:
  Barbara Townsend 866-211-0645/fax: 716-842-2171
Hauppauge
220 Rabro Drive, Ste 100, Hauppauge, NY 11788-4230
District Administrator:
  Vacant 866-681-5354/fax: 631-952-7966
District Manager:
  Robert F Williams 866-681-5354/fax: 631-952-7966
Hempstead
175 Fulton Ave, Hempstead, NY 11550
District Administrator:
  Alan Landman 866-805-3630/fax: 516-560-7807
District Manager:
  Alan Gotlinsky 866-805-3630/fax: 516-560-7807
Manhattan
215 W 125th St, New York, NY 10027
District Administrator:
  Frank Vernuccio, Jr 800-877-1373/fax: 212-932-1488
Peekskill
41 N Division St, Peekskill, NY 10566
District Administrator:
  Vacant 866-746-0552/fax: 914-788-5793
District Manager:
  Luis A Torres 866-746-0552/fax: 914-788-5793
Queens
168-46 91st Ave, Jamaica, NY 11432
District Administrator:
  Wayne Allen 800-877-1373/fax: 718-291-7248
District Manager:
  Vacant 800-877-1373
Rochester
130 Main St West, Rochester, NY 14614
District Admin:
  George A Park, Jr 866-211-0644/fax: 585-238-8351
District Manager:
  MaryBeth Goodsell 866-211-0644/fax: 585-238-8351
Syracuse
935 James Street, Syracuse, NY 13203
District Administrator:
  Janet Burman 866-802-3730/fax: 315-423-2938
District Manager:
  Marc Johnson 866-802-3730/fax: 315-423-2938

Systems Modernization
Deputy Executive Director:
  Thomas Schofield 518-486-7143/fax: 518-474-9367
Director, Management Information Systems:
  Thomas Wegener 518-486-5143/fax: 518-473-6379

Workers' Compensation Board of Commissioners
Commissioner:
  Fran Libous 518-474-6670

Commissioner:
  Mona Bargnesi 716-842-2149
Commissioner:
  Michael T Berns 718-802-6849
Commissioner:
  Donna Ferrara 518-474-6670
Commissioner:
  Candace K Finnegan 914-788-5890
Commissioner:
  Agatha Edel Groski 518-402-6135
Commissioner:
  Karl A Henry 716-842-2140
Commissioner:
  Ellen O Paprocki 315-423-1276
Commissioner:
  Robert Zinck 877-657-4994
Secretary to the Board:
  Susan M Olson 518-402-6071

NEW YORK STATE LEGISLATURE

See Legislative Branch in Section 1 for additional Standing Committee and Subcommittee information.

Assembly Standing Committees

Insurance
Chair:
  Vacant 518-455-0000
Ranking Minority Member:
  William Barclay (R) 518-455-5481

Labor
Chair:
  Susan V John (D) 518-455-4527
Ranking Minority Member:
  Thomas W Alfano (R) 518-455-4627

Senate Standing Committees

Insurance
Chair:
  James L Seward (R) 518-455-3131
Ranking Minority Member:
  Neil D Breslin (D) 518-455-2225

Labor
Chair:
  George D Maziarz (R) 518-455-2024
Ranking Minority Member:
  George Onorato (D) 518-455-3486

U.S. Government

U.S. CONGRESS

See U.S. Congress Chapter for additional Standing Committee and Subcommittee information.

House of Representatives Standing Committees

Financial Services
Chair:
  Barney Frank (D-MA) 202-225-5931

Offices and agencies generally appear in alphabetical order, except when specific order is requested by listee.

INSURANCE / Private Sector

Ranking Minority Member:
  Spencer Bachus (R-AL) 202-225-4921
New York Delegate:
  Gary L Ackerman (D) 202-225-2601
New York Delegate:
  Joseph Crowley (D) 202-225-3965
New York Delegate:
  Vito Fossella (R) 202-225-3371
New York Delegate:
  Steve Israel (D) 202-225-3335
New York Delegate:
  Sue W Kelly (R) 202-225-5441
New York Delegate:
  Carolyn B Maloney (D) 202-225-7944
New York Delegate:
  Carolyn McCarthy (D) 202-225-5516
New York Delegate:
  Gregory W Meeks (D) 202-225-3461
New York Delegate:
  Nydia M Velazquez (D) 202-225-2361

Subcommittee
Capital Markets, Insurance & Government Sponsored Enterprises
Chair:
  Paul E Kanjorski (D-PA) 202-225-6511
Ranking Minority Member:
  Deborah Pryce (R-OH) 202-225-2015
New York Delegate:
  Gary L Ackerman (D) 202-225-2601
New York Delegate:
  Joseph Crowley (D) 202-225-3965
New York Delegate:
  Vito Fossella (R) 202-225-3371

New York Delegate:
  Steve Israel (D) 202-225-3335
New York Delegate:
  Sue W Kelly (R) 202-225-5441
New York Delegate:
  Carolyn McCarthy (D) 202-225-5516
New York Delegate:
  Gregory W Meeks (D) 202-225-3461
New York Delegate:
  Nydia M Velazquez (D) 202-225-2361

Senate Standing Committees
Finance
Chair:
  Max Baucus (D-MT) 202-224-2651
Ranking Minority Member:
  Chuck Grassley (R-IA) 202-224-3744

Subcommittees
Healthcare
Chair:
  John D Rockefeller, IV (D-WV) 202-224-6472
Ranking Minority Member:
  Orrin G Hatch (R-UT) 202-224-5251
Social Security, Pensions and Family Policy
Chair:
  John F Kerry (D-MA) 202-224-2742
Ranking Minority Member:
  Jim Bunning (R-KY) 202-224-4343

Private Sector

American International Group Inc
70 Pine St, 36th Fl, New York, NY 10270
212-770-6114 Fax: 212-785-4214
e-mail: ned.cloonan@aig.com
Web site: www.aig.com
Edward T Cloonan, Vice President International & Corporate Affairs
International business, government & financial services

Aon Services Corporation
199 Water St, 35th Fl, New York, NY 10038
212-441-1150 Fax: 212-441-1929
e-mail: ellen_perle@aon.com
Web site: www.aon.com
Ellen Perle, Associate General Counsel
Insurance brokerage, risk management & financing

Associated Risk Managers of New York Inc
4 Airline Drive, Suite 205, Albany, NY 12205
518-690-2072 or 800-735-5441 Fax: 518-690-2074
e-mail: arm@armnortheast.com
Web site: www.armnortheast.com
John McLaughlin, Executive Director

NYS Bar Assn, Torts, Insurance & Compensation Law Section
Connors & Corcoran LLP
Times Square Bldg, 45 Exchange St, Ste 250, Rochester, NY 14614
585-232-5885 Fax: 585-546-3631
e-mail: ebaholtz@connorscorcoran.com
Web site: www.connorscorcoran.com
Eileen E Buholtz, Partner

DeGraff, Foy, Kunz & Devine, LLP
90 State Street, Albany, NY 12207
518-462-5300 Fax: 518-436-0210
e-mail: firm@degraff-foy.com
Web site: www.degraff-foy.com
David Kunz, Managing Partner
Tax law & procedure, administrative law

Dupee & Monroe, PC
30 Matthews St, Box 470, Goshen, NY 10924
845-294-8900 Fax: 845-294-3619
e-mail: law@dupeelaw.com
Web site: www.dupeelaw.com
James E Monroe, Managing Partner
Litigation, personal injury law, medical malpractice, product liability, civil rights, discrimination, sexual harassment

---

Offices and agencies generally appear in alphabetical order, except when specific order is requested by listee.

INSURANCE / Private Sector

Empire Blue Cross & Blue Shield
11 West 42nd St, 18th Fl, New York, NY 10036
212-476-1000 Fax: 212-476-1281
e-mail: deborah.bohren@empireblue.com
Web site: www.empireblue.com
Deborah Bohren, Senior Vice President, Communications
Health insurance

Equitable Life Assurance Society of the US
1290 Ave of the Americas, New York, NY 10104
212-314-3828 Fax: 212-707-1890
e-mail: wendy.cooper@axa.financial.com
Web site: www.axa-financial.com
Wendy E Cooper, Senior Vice President & Associate General
    Counsel, Government Relations
Life insurance regulation

Excellus Health Plan Inc
165 Court Street, Rochester, NY 14647
585-327-7581 Fax: 585-327-7585
e-mail: stephen.sloan@excellus.com
Web site: www.excellus.com
Stephen R Sloan, Senior Vice President & General Counsel
Health insurance

Excess Line Association of New York
One Exchange Plz, 55 Broadway, 29th Fl, New York, NY 10006
646-292-5555 Fax: 626-292-5505
e-mail: dmaher@elany.org
Web site: www.elany.org
Daniel F Maher, Executive Director
Industry advisory association; facilitate & encourage compliance with the excess line law

Group Health Inc
441 9th Ave, 8th Fl, New York, NY 10001
212-615-0891 Fax: 212-563-8561
e-mail: jgoodwin@ghi.com
Web site: www.ghi.com
Jeffrey Goodwin, Director, Governmental Relations
Affordable, quality health insurance for working individuals & families

Insurance Brokers' Association of the State of New York
555 Fifth Ave, 8th Fl, New York, NY 10017
212-867-0228 Fax: 212-867-2544
e-mail: info@ibany.org
Web site: www.ibany.org
Susan Phillips, Executive Director

Levene, Gouldin & Thompson LLP
PO Box F-1706, Binghamton, NY 13902
607-584-5706 Fax: 607-763-9212
e-mail: dgouldin@binghamtonlaw.com
Web site: www.binghamtonlaw.com
David M Gouldin, Partner
Professional liability insurance

Life Insurance Council of New York, Inc
551 Fifth Ave, 29th Floor, New York, NY 10176
212-986-6181 Fax: 212-986-6549
e-mail: tworkman@licony.org
Web site: www.licony.org
Thomas E Workman, President & Chief Executive Officer
Promote a legislative, regulatory & judicial environment that encourages members to conduct & grow their business

Marsh & McLennan Companies
1166 6th Ave, New York, NY 10036-2774
212-345-5000
e-mail: barbara.perlmutter@mmc.com
Web site: www.mmc.com
Barbara S Perlmutter, Senior Vice President, Public Affairs
Risk & insurance services; investment management; consulting

Medical Society of the State of New York, Div of Socio-Medical Economics
420 Lakeville Rd, PO Box 5404, Lake Success, NY 11042
516-488-6100 x332 Fax: 516-488-6136
e-mail: rmcnally@mssny.org
Web site: www.mssny.org
William Abrams, Executive Vice President
Workers compensations; health insurance programs

MetLife
27-01 Queens Plaza North, Long Island City, NY 11101
212-578-3968 Fax: 212-578-8869
e-mail: jfdonnellan@metlife.com
Web site: www.metlife.com
James F Donnellan, Vice President Government & Industry
    Relations

NY Life Insurance Co
51 Madison Ave, Suite 1111, New York, NY 10010
212-576-7000 Fax: 212-576-4473
e-mail: gayle_yeomans@newyorklife.com
Web site: www.newyorklife.com
Gayle A Yeomans, Vice President Government Affairs
Insurance products & financial services

NY Property Insurance Underwriting Association
100 William St, New York, NY 10038
212-208-9700 Fax: 212-344-9879
Web site: www.nypiua.com
Joseph Calvo, President

NYMAGIC Inc
919 3rd Ave, 10th Fl, New York, NY 10022-3919
212-551-0600 Fax: 212-551-0724
e-mail: info@mmo.com
Web site: www.nymagic.com
A George Kallop, President & CEO
Marine insurance & excess & surplus lines

Offices and agencies generally appear in alphabetical order, except when specific order is requested by listee.

INSURANCE / Private Sector

New York Insurance Association Inc
130 Washington Ave, Albany, NY 12210
518-432-4227 Fax: 518-432-4220
e-mail: bbourdeau@nyia.org
Web site: www.nyia.org
Bernard N Bourdeau, President
Property & casualty insurance

New York Long-Term Care Brokers Ltd
11 Halfmoon Executive Park, Clifton Park, NY 12065
518-371-5522 x116 Fax: 518-371-6131
e-mail: kjohnson@nyltcb.com
Web site: www.nyltcb.com
Kevin Johnson, President & CEO
Long-term care, life & disability insurance; consulting & sales to individual consumers & financial service industry professionals

New York Municipal Insurance Reciprocal (NYMIR)
24 Aviation Rd, Ste 204, Albany, NY 12205
518-437-1171 Fax: 518-437-1182
Web site: www.nymir.org
Gale M Hatch, President
Insurance services for municipalities

New York Schools Insurance Reciprocal (NYSIR)
333 Earle Ovington Blvd, Uniondale, NY 11553
516-227-3355 x1468 or 1-800-476-9747 Fax: 516-227-2352
e-mail: jgoncalves@wrightrisk.com
Web site: www.nysir.org
Joseph Goncalves, Executive Director
Insurance & risk management services for public school districts

NAIFA - New York State
38 Sheridan Ave, Albany, NY 12210
518-462-5567 Fax: 518-462-5569
e-mail: naifanewyork@aol.com
Web site: www.naifanys.org
Mark L Yavornitzki, Executive Vice President & Chief Administrative Officer
Association of individuals engaged in the sale of life, health & property/casualty insurance & related financial services

Professional Insurance Agents of New York State
25 Chamberlain St, PO Box 997, Glenmont, NY 12077-0997
800-424-4244 Fax: 888-225-6935
e-mail: kenb@piaonline.org
Web site: www.piany.org
Ken Bessette, President/Chief Executive Officer

SBLI USA Mutual Life Insurance Company Inc
460 W 34th St, Suite 800, New York, NY 10001-2320
212-356-0327 Fax: 212-624-0700
e-mail: dklugman@sbliusa.com
Web site: www.sbliusa.com
Vikki Pryor, President & Chief Executive Officer
Corporate insurance regulatory law & government affairs

St John's University-Peter J Tobin College of Business, School of Risk Mgmt
101 Murray St, New York, NY 10007
212-962-4111
Web site: www.stjohns.edu
Ellen Thrower, Executive Director

Stroock & Stroock & Lavan LLP
180 Maiden Lane, New York, NY 10038-4982
212-806-5541 Fax: 212-806-2541
e-mail: dgabay@stroock.com
Donald D Gabay, Attorney
Insurance, reinsurance, corporate & regulatory law

Support Services Alliance Inc
107 Prospect St, PO Box 130, Schoharie, NY 12157
800-322-3920 or 518-295-7966 Fax: 518-295-8556
e-mail: info@ssamembers.com
Web site: www.smallbizgrowth.com
Steven Cole, President
Small business support services & insurance

Unity Mutual Life Insurance Co
507 Plum St, PO Box 5000, Syracuse, NY 13250-5000
315-448-7000 Fax: 315-448-7100
e-mail: jwason@unity-life.com
Web site: www.unity-life.com
Jay Wason, Jr, General Counsel

Utica Mutual Insurance Co
PO Box 530, Utica, NY 13503-0530
1-800-274-1914 Fax: 315-734-2662
Web site: www.uticanational.com
Richard Creedon, Senior Vice President, Claims & General Counsel
Property, casualty insurance

Offices and agencies generally appear in alphabetical order, except when specific order is requested by listee.

JUDICIAL & LEGAL SYSTEMS

New York State

GOVERNOR'S OFFICE

Governor's Office
Executive Chamber
State Capitol
Albany, NY 12224
518-474-8390 Fax: 518-474-1513
Web site: www.state.ny.us

Governor:
  Eliot Spitzer 518-474-8390
Secretary to the Governor:
  Richard Baum 518-474-4246
Counsel to the Governor:
  David Nocenti 518-474-8343
Senior Advisor to the Governor:
  Lloyd Constantine 518-486-9671
Director, Communications:
  Darren Dopp 518-474-8418
Deputy Secretary, Intergovernmental Affairs:
  Martin Mack 518-408-2555
Deputy Secretary, Appointments:
  Francine James 518-474-0491
Assistant Counsel to the Governor-Education, Elections & the Judiciary:
  Mariya Treisman 518-474-8494
Director, Legislative Affairs:
  James Clancy 518-486-9896

EXECUTIVE DEPARTMENTS AND RELATED AGENCIES

Criminal Justice Services, Division of
Four Tower Place
Albany, NY 12203-3764
518-457-1260 Fax: 518-457-3089
Web site: www.criminaljustice.state.ny.us

Commissioner:
  Denise E O'Donnell 518-457-1260
Executive Deputy Commissioner:
  Sean Byrne 518-457-6091
Special Counsel to the Commissioner:
  Michael Barrett 518-485-7913
Special Counsel & Host Agency Coordination/Support:
  Mary Kavaney 518-485-8495
Affirmative Action Officer:
  Vacant 518-457-6110
Public Information Officer:
  John Caher 518-457-8828/fax: 518-485-7715

Administration Office
Deputy Commissioner, Administration:
  Don Capone 518-457-6110

Administrative Services
Director:
  Phyllis M Foster 518-457-1696

Human Resources Management
Director:
  Alyce Ashe 518-457-6110

State Finance & Budget
Director, Financial Administration:
  Kimberly J Szady 518-457-6105
Director, Internal Audit & Compliance:
  Bob Wright 518-485-5823

Advisory Groups

Juvenile Justice Advisory Group
15 Van Dyke Ave, Amsterdam, NY 12010
Chair:
  Anne Marie Strano 518-457-8462

NYS Motor Vehicle & Insurance Fraud Prevention Board
Chair/Commissioner:
  Eileen Langer-Smith 518-485-7921

Legal Services
Deputy Commissioner & Counsel:
  Gina Bianchi 518-457-4181

Missing & Exploited Children Clearinghouse
Director:
  Kenneth R Buniak 518-485-7632

Commission on Forensic Science

Office of Forensic Services
Director:
  John Hicks 518-457-7287

Office of Criminal Justice Operations
Deputy Commissioner:
  Daniel Foro 518-485-2995

Office of Operations
Director:
  William J Sillery 518-457-6050
Assistant Director:
  Michael Tymeson 518-457-6050
Chief, Operations:
  James Stanco 518-457-6051
Manager, Civil Identification:
  Ann Sammons 518-485-5763

Office of Justice Information Services
Executive Director:
  James Shea 518-457-8724
Deputy Commissioner/CIO:
  Anne Roest 518-485-7176

Information Technology Development Group
Director:
  Connie Snyder 518-485-7154

Offices and agencies generally appear in alphabetical order, except when specific order is requested by listee.

JUDICIAL & LEGAL SYSTEMS / New York State

Information Technology Services Group
Director:
Alex Roberts................................ 518-457-3743

Office of Sex Offender Management
Director:
Luke Martland............................. 518-485-1897

Office of Justice Statistics & Performance
Director:
Terry Salo.................................... 518-457-0439
Chief, Crimestat Unit:
Paula K Lockhart......................... 518-485-7122
Chief, Crime Reporting & Statistical Services Unit:
Susan Jacobsen........................... 518-457-8381

Office of Public Safety

Law Enforcement Accreditation Council

Municipal Police Training Council

State Committee for Coordination of Police Services for Elderly (TRIAD)

Statewide Law Enforcement Telecommunications Committee
Deputy Commissioner:
Cedric Alexander......................... 518-457-6101
Director:
Mark R Lindsay........................... 518-457-2667
Assistant Director:
John R Digman............................ 518-485-1414
Chief, Administrative Services:
David H Mahany.......................... 518-457-4135
Chief, Program Services:
Mark Fettinger............................. 518-485-1410
Chief, Security Guard Advisory Council:
David H Mahany.......................... 518-457-6101

Office of Strategic Planning
Deputy Commissioner:
Beth Ryan.................................... 518-485-7433

Bureau of Justice Research & Innovation
Director:
Donna Hall, PhD.......................... 518-457-7301

Crime Reduction Strategies Unit
Chief:
Thomas Mitchell......................... 518-457-7301

Justice Systems Analysis Unit
Chief:
David vanAlstyne........................ 518-457-7301

Offender Management Analysis Unit
Chief:
Bruce Frederick.......................... 518-457-3724

Funding & Program Assistance Office
Director:
AnneMarie Strano....................... 518-457-8462

Operation IMPACT Coordinator
Director:
Julie Pasquini.............................. 518-485-7923
Director, Technical Assistance:
John Bilich.................................. 518-457-7832

Law Department
120 Broadway
New York, NY 10271-0332
212-416-8000 Fax: 212-416-8796
Web site: www.oag.state.ny.us

State Capitol
Albany, NY 12224-0341
518-474-7330
Fax: 518-402-2472

Attorney General:
Andrew M Cuomo........................ 518-474-7330

Administration
Agency Bldg 4, Empire State Plaza, Albany, NY 12224-0341
Executive Director:
Sylvia Hamer.................. 518-473-7900 or 212-416-6561
fax: 518-474-0680
Assistant Director:
Jean M Woodard............ 518-474-7969/fax: 518-474-0680

Administrative Services
Director:
Catherine Mead............ 518-474-6765/fax: 518-473-8224

Budget & Fiscal Management
Director:
Cynthia Itzo................. 518-473-7699/fax: 518-474-0714

Human Resources
Director:
Eric Schwenzfeier........ 518-474-4848/fax: 518-474-3578

Legal Technology & Systems Management
Director:
Robert J Vitello........... 518-474-9048/fax: 518-473-7483

Training & Staff Development
Manager:
Michael Kopcza........... 518-486-2234/fax: 518-486-5936

Appeals & Opinions Division
Solicitor General:
Caitlin J Halligan........ 212-416-8016/fax: 212-416-8942
Deputy Solicitor General:
Wayne L Benjamin....... 518-474-7138/fax: 518-473-8963
Deputy Solicitor General:
Daniel Smirlock........... 518-473-0903/fax: 518-486-3176
Deputy Solicitor General:
Michael Belohlavek...... 212-416-8028/fax: 212-416-8962
Deputy Solicitor General:
Michelle Aronowitz...... 212-416-8027/fax: 212-416-8962
Legal Records:
Cynthia Bogardus....................... 518-474-5241

Law Library
Chief, Library Services:
Sarah Browne.............. 518-474-3840/fax: 518-402-2271
Senior Librarian, New York City Office:
Franette Sheinwald...... 212-416-8012/fax: 212-416-6130

Criminal Division
Deputy Attorney General:
Peter B Pope............... 212-416-8058/fax: 212-416-8026
Assistant Deputy Attorney General:
Julieta Lozano............. 212-416-8090/fax: 212-416-8026

Criminal Prosecutions Bureau
Chief:
Janet Cohn.................. 518-474-4096/fax: 518-474-3364
Deputy Bureau Chief, NYC:
Laurie M Israel........... 212-416-8741/fax: 212-416-8026

Offices and agencies generally appear in alphabetical order, except when specific order is requested by listee.

JUDICIAL & LEGAL SYSTEMS / New York State

Deputy Bureau Chief, Albany:
  Viola Abbitt............................518-474-4096/fax: 518-474-3364

Investigations Bureau
Chief Investigator:
  William M Casey...................212-416-6328 or 518-486-4540

Medicaid Fraud Control Unit
120 Broadway, 13th Fl, New York, NY 10271-0007
Deputy Attorney General in Charge:
  William J Comiskey..............212-417-5250/fax: 212-417-5274
First Asst Deputy Attorney General:
  Peter M Bloch.....................212-417-5261/fax: 212-417-5274
Asst Deputy Attorney General:
  George Quinlan...716-853-8584
Regional Director, Albany:
  Steve Krantz........................518-474-3032/fax: 518-474-4519
Deputy Regional Director, Buffalo:
  Gary A Baldauf....................716-853-8507/fax: 716-853-8525
Regional Director, Long Island:
  Alan Buonpastore................631-952-6400/fax: 631-952-6382
Regional Director, NYC:
  Richard Harrow....................212-417-5391/fax: 212-417-4725
Regional Director, Rochester:
  Jerry Solomon......................716-262-2860/fax: 716-262-2866
Regional Director, Syracuse:
  Ralph Tortora, III.................315-423-1104/fax: 315-423-1120
Deputy Regional Director, Westchester/Rockland:
  Anne S Jardine....................845-732-7500/fax: 845-732-7555
Regional Director for Special Projects Unit:
  Patrick Lupinetti...................845-732-7550/fax: 845-732-7557

Organized Crime Task Force
Deputy Attorney General-in-Charge:
  J Christopher Prather.............914-422-8714/fax: 914-422-8835

Intergovernmental Relations
Director:
  Lila Kirton...........................212-416-6044/fax: 212-416-8738
Deputy Director:
  Galen Kirkland....................212-416-6342/fax: 212-416-8738
Director, Policy Resources:
  Mindy Bockenstein...............212-416-8147/fax: 212-416-8738

Office of the Attorney General
First Deputy Attorney General:
  Michele Hirshman..212-416-8050
Asst First Deputy Attorney General:
  Francine James..212-416-8050
Executive Director, Administration:
  Sylvia Hamer.....................212-416-6561 or 518-473-7900
Counsel to Attorney General:
  David Nocenti..212-416-8050
Deputy Counsel to Attorney General:
  Avi Schick...212-416-8050
Deputy Attorney General, Operations:
  Kermitt J Brooks...212-416-8050
Deputy Attorney General:
  Debra L W Cohn...212-416-8054
Asst Deputy Attorney General, Program Development:
  Vacant..212-416-8167
Asst Attorney General, Legal Recruitment:
  Camille Chin-Kee-Fatt.....................................212-416-8080
Asst Attorney General, Legislative Bureau:
  Kathy Bennett..518-486-3000
Director, Public Information & Correspondence:
  Peter A Drago....................518-474-7330/fax: 518-402-2472
Scheduler:
  Marlene Turner...212-416-8050

Deputy Chief of Staff:
  Joseph Palozzola...212-416-8050
Press Office
Director, Communications:
  Darren Dopp.....................212-416-8060 or 518-473-5525
  fax: 212-416-6005
Press Secretary:
  Juanita Scarlett..212-416-8060
Senior Press Officer:
  Marc Violette...518-473-5525
Press Officer:
  Brad F Maione...212-416-8060

Public Advocacy Division
Deputy Attorney General:
  Dietrich Snell......................212-416-8041/fax: 212-416-8068
Special Counsel:
  Mary Ellen Burns...212-416-6155

Antitrust Bureau
Bureau Chief:
  Jay L Himes.......................212-416-8282/fax: 212-416-6015

Charities Bureau
Bureau Chief:
  Gerald Rosenberg..............212-416-8490/fax: 212-416-8393

Civil Rights Bureau
Bureau Chief:
  Dennis Parker....................212-416-8250/fax: 212-416-8074

Consumer Fraud & Protection Bureau
Bureau Chief:
  Thomas G Conway.............518-474-2374/fax: 518-474-3618

Environmental Protection Bureau
Bureau Chief:
  Peter Lehner......................212-416-8450/fax: 212-416-6007

Healthcare Bureau
Bureau Chief:
  Joseph R Baker, III.............212-416-8521/fax: 212-416-8034

Internet Bureau
Bureau Chief:
  Jane Azia...........................212-416-8433/fax: 212-416-8369

Investment Protection Bureau
Bureau Chief:
  David Brown......................212-416-8198/fax: 212-416-8816

Telecommunications & Energy Bureau
Bureau Chief:
  Vacant................................212-416-8333/fax: 212-416-8877

Regional Offices Division
Assistant Deputy Attorney General, Regional Offices:
  Christopher T Walsh............518-402-2184/fax: 518-473-8153

Binghamton
State Office Bldg, 44 Hawley St, 17th Fl, Binghamton, NY 13901-4433
Asst Attorney General in Charge:
  Dennis McCabe...................607-721-8771/fax: 607-721-8789

Brooklyn
55 Hanson Place, Brooklyn, NY 11217-1523
Asst Attorney General in Charge:
  Lois Booker Williams............718-722-3949/fax: 718-722-3951

Buffalo
Statler Towers, 107 Delaware Ave, 4th Fl, Buffalo, NY 14202-3473
Asst Attorney General in Charge:
  Kenneth Schoetz..................716-853-6271/fax: 716-853-8571

Offices and agencies generally appear in alphabetical order, except when specific order is requested by listee.

JUDICIAL & LEGAL SYSTEMS / New York State

Harlem
163 West 125th St, New York, NY 10027-8201
Asst Attorney General in Charge:
  Guy H Mitchell 212-961-4475/fax: 212-961-4003

Nassau
200 Old Country Rd, Ste 460, Mineola, NY 11501-4241
Asst Attorney General in Charge:
  Juan Merchan 516-248-3322/fax: 516-747-6432

Plattsburgh
70 Clinton St, Plattsburgh, NY 12901-2818
Asst Attorney General in Charge:
  Robert Glennon 518-562-3282/fax: 518-562-3294

Poughkeepsie
235 Main St, 3rd Fl, Poughkeepsie, NY 12601-3194
Asst Attorney General in Charge:
  Mary Kavaney 845-485-3900/fax: 845-452-3303

Rochester
144 Exchange Blvd, 2nd Fl, Rochester, NY 14614-2176
Asst Attorney General in Charge:
  Robert Colon 585-546-7430/fax: 585-546-7514

Suffolk
300 Motor Pkwy, Ste 205, Hauppauge, NY 11788-5127
Asst Attorney General in Charge:
  Denis McElligott 631-231-2424/fax: 631-435-4757

Syracuse
615 Erie Blvd West, Suite 102, Syracuse, NY 13210-2339
Asst Attorney General in Charge:
  Winthrop Thurlow 315-448-4800/fax: 315-448-4853

Utica
207 Genesee St, Room 504, Utica, NY 13501-2812
Asst Attorney General in Charge:
  Joel L Marmelstein 315-793-2225/fax: 315-793-2228

Watertown
Dulles St Ofc Bldg, 317 Washington St, Watertown, NY 13601-3744
Asst Attorney General in Charge:
  John Sullivan 315-785-2444/fax: 315-785-2294

Westchester
101 East Post Rd, White Plains, NY 10601-5008
Asst Attorney General in Charge:
  Gary Brown 914-422-8755/fax: 914-422-8706

State Counsel Division
Deputy Attorney General:
  Richard Rifkin 518-473-7190
Asst Deputy Attorney General:
  Patricia Martinelli 518-473-0648/fax: 518-486-9777
Asst Deputy Attorney General:
  Susan L Watson 212-416-8579/fax: 212-416-6001

Civil Recoveries Bureau
Bureau Chief:
  Mary E House 518-474-7131/fax: 518-473-1635

Claims Bureau
Bureau Chief:
  Susan Pogoda 212-416-8516/fax: 212-416-8946

Labor Bureau
Bureau Chief:
  M Patricia Smith 212-416-8710

Litigation Bureau
Bureau Chief, Albany:
  Bruce D Feldman 518-473-8328/fax: 518-473-1572

Bureau Chief, NYC:
  James B Henley 212-416-8523/fax: 212-416-6075

Real Property Bureau
Bureau Chief:
  Henry A DeCotis 518-474-7151/fax: 518-473-5106

JUDICIAL SYSTEM AND RELATED AGENCIES

Attorney Grievance Committee

1st Judicial Dept, Judicial Dist 1, 12
61 Broadway, 2nd Fl, New York, NY 10006
Chief Counsel:
  Thomas J Cahill 212-401-0800/fax: 212-401-0810

2nd Judicial Dept, Judicial Dist 2, 9, 10, 11

Judicial Dist 2, 11
Renaissance Plz, 335 Adams St, Ste 2400, Brooklyn, NY 11201-3745
Chief Counsel:
  Diana M Kearse 718-923-6300/fax: 718-624-2978

Judicial Dist 9
399 Knollwood Rd, Ste 200, White Plains, NY 10603
Chief Counsel:
  Gary L Casella 914-949-4540/fax: 914-949-0997

Judicial Dist 10
150 Motor Pkwy, Ste 102, Hauppauge, NY 11788
Chief Counsel:
  Faith Lorenzo 631-231-3775/fax: 516-364-7355

3rd Judicial Dept, Judicial Dist 3, 4, 6
40 Steuben St, Albany, NY 12207-2109
Web site: www.courts.state.ny.us/ad3
Chief Counsel:
  Mark S Ochs 518-474-8816/fax: 518-474-0389
  e-mail: AD3COPS@courts.state.ny.us

4th Judicial Dept, Dist 5, 7, 8
Web site: www.courts.state.ny.us/ad4

Judicial Dist 5 . . . . fax: 315-471-0123
224 Harrison St, Ste 408, Syracuse, NY 13202-3066
Chief Counsel:
  Gregory J Huether 315-471-1835
Principal Counsel:
  Anthony J Gigliotti 315-471-1835

Judicial Dist 7 . . . . fax: 585-530-3191
50 East Ave, Ste 404, Rochester, NY 14604-2206
Chief Counsel:
  Gregory J Huether 585-530-3180
Principal Counsel:
  Daniel A Drake 585-530-3180

Judicial Dist 8 . . . . fax: 716-856-2701
438 Main St, Ste 800, Buffalo, NY 14202
Chief Counsel:
  Gregory J Huether 716-845-3630
Deputy Chief Counsel:
  Vincent L Scarsella 716-845-3630

Law Guardian Program

1st Judicial Dept
41 Madison Ave, 39th Fl, New York, NY 10010

Offices and agencies generally appear in alphabetical order, except when specific order is requested by listee.

JUDICIAL & LEGAL SYSTEMS / New York State

Director:
  Jane Schreiber 212-340-0502/fax: 212-340-0550

2nd Judicial Dept
335 Adams St, Ste 2400, Brooklyn, NY 11201
Director:
  Harriet Weinberger 718-923-6350/fax: 718-624-5603
  e-mail: hweinber@courts.state.ny.us

3rd Judicial Dept . . . . fax: 518-471-4757
PO Box 7288, Capital Station, Albany, NY 12224-0288
Fax: 518-471-4757
Web site: www.courts.state.ny.us/ad3/lg
Director:
  John E Carter, Jr 518-471-4825
  e-mail: lgp3d@courts.state.ny.us
Assistant Director:
  Betsy R Ruslander 518-471-4826

4th Judicial Dept . . . . fax: 585-530-3175
50 East Ave, Ste 304, Rochester, NY 14604
Fax: 585-530-3175
Web site: www.courts.state.ny.us/ad4/
Director:
  Tracy M Hamilton . . . . 585-530-3170 or 585-530-3176
  e-mail: thamilto@courts.state.ny.us
Assistant Program Director:
  Christine Constantine 585-530-3178
  e-mail: cconstan@courts.state.ny.us

Mental Hygiene Legal Service

1st Judicial Dept . . . . fax: 212-779-1894
60 Madison Ave, 2nd Fl, New York, NY 10010
Director:
  Marvin Bernstein 212-779-1734

2nd Judicial Dept
170 Old Country Rd, Rm 500, Mineola, NY 11501
Director:
  Sidney Hirschfeld 516-746-4545/fax: 516-746-4372

3rd Judicial Dept
40 Steuben St, Ste 501, Albany, NY 12207-2109
Web site: www.courts.state.ny.us/ad3/mhls/
Acting Director:
  David M LeVine 518-474-4453/fax: 518-473-5849

4th Judicial Dept
50 East Ave, Ste 402, Rochester, NY 14604
Web site: www.courts.state.ny.us/ad4/mhls/
Director:
  Emmett J Creahan 585-530-3050
Deputy Director:
  Neil J Rowe 585-530-3050/fax: 585-530-3079

Unified Court System
25 Beaver St
New York, NY 10004
212-428-2700 Fax: 212-428-2508
Web site: www.nycourts.gov

Agency Bldg 4, 20th Fl
Empire State Plaza
Albany, NY 12223
518-473-6087
Fax: 518-473-5514

Administrative Board of the Courts
Appellate Division
  1st Judicial Department
    Courthouse, 27 Madison Ave, New York, NY 10010
    Presiding Justice:
      John T Buckley 212-340-0400
  2nd Judicial Department
    45 Monroe Place, Brooklyn, NY 11201
    Presiding Justice:
      A Gail Prudenti 718-875-1300
  3rd Judicial Department
    Justice Bldg, Rm 511, ESP, PO Box 7288, Albany, NY 12224
    Presiding Justice:
      Anthony V Cardona 518-471-4763
  4th Judicial Department
    50 East Ave, Rochester, NY 14604
    Presiding Justice:
      Henry Scudder 585-530-3100

Court of Appeals
230 Park Ave, Suite 826, New York, NY 10169
Chief Judge:
  Judith S Kaye 212-661-6787/fax: 212-682-2778

Court Administration
Chief Administrative Judge:
  Jonathan Lippman 212-428-2100
Administrative Director, Office of Court Admin:
  Lawrence K Marks 212-428-2884
First Deputy Chief Administrative Judge, Management Support:
  Ann T Pfau 212-428-2120/fax: 212-428-2190
Deputy Chief Administrative Judge, Courts in NYC:
  Joan B Carey 646-386-4200
Deputy Chief Administrative Judge, Courts outside NYC:
  Jan Plumadore 518-891-3816
Deputy Chief Admin Judge, Justice Initiatives/Admin Judge NYC Criminal:
  Juanita Bing Newton 646-386-4700
Deputy Chief Admin Judge, Court Operations & Planning:
  Judy Harris Kluger 212-428-2130
Administrative Judge, Matrimonial Matters:
  Jacqueline W Silbermann 212-428-2140/fax: 212-428-2197
Executive Assistant to Deputy Chief Admin Judge, Courts in NYC:
  Maria Logus 646-386-4201
Executive Assistant to Deputy Chief Admin Judge, Courts outside NYC:
  David Sullivan 518-474-3828
Chief of Staff:
  Paul Lewis 212-428-2120
Chief of Operations:
  Ron Younkins 212-428-2120

Administrative Judge to the Court of Claims (NYS). fax: 866-413-1069
Justice Bldg, Capitol Station, PO Box 7433, Albany, NY 12224
Presiding Judge:
  Richard E Sise 518-432-3435

Administrative Judges to the Courts in New York City
  1st Judicial District (Judicial Department 1)
    Administrative Judge, Civil Term:
      Jacqueline W Silbermann 646-386-3170
    Administrative Judge, Criminal Term:
      Micki A Scherer 646-386-3888
  2nd Judicial District (Judicial Department 2)
    320 Jay St, Brooklyn, NY 11201
    Administrative Judge:
      Neil Jon Firetog 347-296-1200
  Civil Court
    111 Centre St, New York, NY 10013
    Administrative Judge:
      Fern Fisher 646-386-5400/fax: 212-374-5709

Offices and agencies generally appear in alphabetical order, except when specific order is requested by listee.

JUDICIAL & LEGAL SYSTEMS / New York State

Criminal Court
    100 Centre St, Rm 549A, New York, NY 10013
    Administrative Judge:
        Juanita Bing Newton 646-386-4700/fax: 212-374-3004

Family Court
    60 Lafayette St, 11th Floor, New York, NY 10013
    Administrative Judge:
        Joseph M Lauria..............646-386-5190/fax: 212-374-2127

Administrative Judges to the Courts outside New York City

3rd Judicial District (Judicial Department 3)
    Courthouse, 80 Second St, Troy, NY 12180
    Administrative Judge:
        George Ceresia..............518-270-3739/fax: 518-270-3788

4th Judicial District (Judicial Department 3)
    612 State St, Schenectady, NY 12305
    Administrative Judge:
        Vito Caruso..................518-388-4327/fax: 518-587-3179

5th Judicial District (Judicial Department 4)
    Onondaga County Court House, 401 Montgomery St, Syracuse, NY 13202
    Administrative Judge:
        James C Tormey, III..........315-671-2111/fax: 315-671-1183

6th Judicial District (Judicial Department 3)
    203 Lake St, Hazlett Bldg, PO Box 588, Elmira, NY 14902-0588
    Administrative Judge:
        Judith F O'Shea..............607-737-3560/fax: 607-737-3562

7th Judicial District (Judicial Department 4)
    Hall of Justice, Civic Center Plz, 99 Exchange Blvd, Rochester, NY 14614
    Administrative Judge:
        Thomas M VanStrydonck......585-428-2885/fax: 585-428-2105

8th Judicial District (Judicial Department 4)
    Erie County Hall, 92 Franklin St, Buffalo, NY 14202
    Administrative Judge:
        Sharon Townsend............716-845-2500/fax: 716-855-1611

9th Judicial District (Judicial Department 2)
    County Court House, 111 Dr Martin Luther King Blvd, White Plains, NY 10601
    Administrative Judge:
        Francis A Nicolai............914-824-5100/fax: 914-285-4111

10th Judicial District (Judicial Department 2)
    Administrative Judge, Nassau County:
        Anthony F Marano..........516-571-2684/fax: 516-571-3713
    Administrative Judge, Suffolk County:
        H Patrick Leis, III............631-853-5368/fax: 631-853-7741

11th Judicial District (Judicial Department 2)
    88-11 Sutphin Blvd, Jamaica, NY 11432
    Administrative Judge:
        Jeremy Weinstein............718-298-1100/fax: 718-520-2499

12th Judicial District (Judicial Department 1)
    851 Grand Concourse, Bronx, NY 10451
    Administrative Judge (Civil):
        Barry Salman................................718-590-3795
    Administrative Judge (Criminal):
        John P Collins..............................718-590-3804

Counsel's Office
Counsel:
    Michael Colodner................212-428-2160/fax: 212-428-2155

Management Support
First Deputy Chief Administrative Judge:
    Ann T Pfau.....................212-428-2120/fax: 212-428-2190
Administrative Services Office
    Director:
        Laura Weigley Ross..........212-428-2860/fax: 212-428-2819
    Deputy Director:
        Vacant....................212-428-2812/fax: 212-428-2819

Court Operations
    Director:
        Nancy M Mangold..........212-428-2761/fax: 518-428-2768
    Coordinator, Alternative Dispute Resolution Program:
        Daniel M Weitz..............212-428-2863/fax: 212-428-2819
        e-mail: dweitz@courts.state.ny.us
    Director, Court Research & Technology:
        Chester Mount..............212-428-2990/fax: 212-428-2987
    Chief of Court Security Services:
        Howard Metzdorff..........212-428-2766/fax: 212-428-2768
    Director, Internal Controls Office:
        Dennis Donnelly............518-238-4303/fax: 518-238-2086
    Special Inspector General, Bias Complaints:
        Kay-Ann Porter..............646-386-3507 or 212-514-7158
        fax: 212-428-2190
    Chief Law Librarian, Legal Info & Records Mgmt:
        Ellen Robinson..............518-238-4373/fax: 518-238-2894
    Records Management Chief:
        Richard Hogan...............................212-428-2877

Financial Management & Audit Services
    Empire State Plaza, Bldg 4, Ste 2001, Albany, NY 12223-1450
    Director:
        Joseph M deChants..........518-474-8513/fax: 518-474-3218

Human Resources & Employee Relations
    Director:
        Lauren DeSole..............212-428-2515/fax: 212-428-2513
    Deputy Director, Career Services:
        Juanita Norman..............646-386-5630/fax: 212-406-4534
    Deputy Director, Equal Employment Opportunity Division:
        Alice Chapman-Minutello.....212-428-2540/fax: 212-428-2545
    Administrator, Judicial Benefits Division:
        William Gilchrist..............212-428-2550/fax: 212-428-2555
    Dean, Judicial Institute of Education & Training:
        Robert G M Keating..........914-824-5806/fax: 914-997-8964
    Deputy Director, Personnel Division:
        Michael S Miller..............212-428-2600/fax: 212-428-2606

Public Affairs Office
    Director:
        Gregory Murray..............212-428-2116/fax: 212-428-2117
    Director, Communications:
        David Bookstaver............212-428-2500/fax: 212-428-2507
    Communications Specialist:
        Arelene Hackel................................212-428-2116
    Public Information Officer:
        Tony Walters.................................212-428-2116

CORPORATIONS, AUTHORITIES AND COMMISSIONS

Capital Defender Office
2 Rector Street
13th Floor
New York, NY 10006
212-608-3352 Fax: 212-608-4558
Web site: www.nycdo.org

Capital Defender:
    Kevin Doyle.....................................212-608-3352 x208
First Deputy Capital Defender, New York City Office:
    Susan Salomon................................212-608-3352 x206

Offices and agencies generally appear in alphabetical order, except when specific order is requested by listee.

JUDICIAL & LEGAL SYSTEMS / New York State

Interest on Lawyer Account (IOLA) Fund of the State of NY
11 East 44th St
Ste 1406
New York, NY 10017
646-865-1541 or 800-222-4652 Fax: 646-865-1545
e-mail: iolaf@iola.org
Web site: www.iola.org

Chair:
   William R Nojay..................................646-865-1541
Executive Director:
   Lorna Blake......................................646-865-1541
   e-mail: lblake@iola.org
General Counsel:
   Stephen Brooks...................................646-865-1541
   e-mail: sgbrooks@iola.org
Assistant Director & Director of Administration:
   Odette M McNeil..................................646-865-1541
   e-mail: omcneil@iola.org

Lawyers' Fund for Client Protection
119 Washington Ave
Albany, NY 12210
518-434-1935 or 800-442-FUND Fax: 518-434-5641
e-mail: info@nylawfund.org
Web site: www.nylawfund.org

Chair:
   Eleanor Breitel Alter..............................518-434-1935
Vice Chair:
   Bernard F Ashe...................................518-434-1935
Executive Director & Counsel:
   Timothy O'Sullivan................................518-434-1935
Deputy Counsel:
   Michael J Knight..................................518-434-1935

New York State Board of Law Examiners
Corporate Plaza Bldg 3
254 Washington Ave Ext
Albany, NY 12203
518-452-8700 Fax: 518-452-5729
Web site: www.nybarexam.org

Chair:
   Diane F Bosse....................................518-452-8700
Executive Director:
   John J McAlary...................................518-452-8700

New York State Commission on Judicial Nomination
c/o Patterson Belknap Webb & Tyler LLP
1133 Ave of the Americas, 20th Fl
New York, NY 10036-6710
212-841-0715 Fax: 212-262-5152

Chair:
   John F O'Mara....................................607-733-4635
Senior Counsel:
   Stuart A Summit..................................212-977-9700
   e-mail: ssummit@phillipsnizer.com

Counsel:
   Stephen P Younger................................212-336-2000
   e-mail: spyounger@pbwt.com

New York State Judicial Conduct Commission
61 Broadway
12th Fl
New York, NY 10006
212-809-0566 Fax: 212-809-3664
e-mail: scjc@scjc.state.ny.us
Web site: www.scjc.state.ny.us

Chair:
   Raoul Lionel Felder, Esq..........................212-809-0566
Vice Chair:
   Thomas A Klonick.................................212-809-0566
Administrator & Counsel:
   Robert H Tembeckjian.............................212-809-0566
Chief Attorney, Albany Office:
   Cathleen Cenci...................................518-474-5617
Chief Attorney, Rochester Office:
   John J Postel....................................585-232-5756
Chief Attorney, New York Office:
   Alan W Friedberg.................................212-809-0566
Clerk:
   Jean M Savanyu, Esq..............................212-809-0566

New York State Law Reporting Bureau
One Commerce Plaza, Ste 1750
Albany, NY 12210
518-474-8211 Fax: 518-463-6869
Web site: www.courts.state.ny.us/reporter

State Reporter:
   Gary D Spivey....................................518-474-8211
Deputy State Reporter:
   Charles A Ashe...................................518-474-8211
   e-mail: Reporter@courts.state.ny.us

New York State Law Revision Commission
80 New Scotland Ave
Albany, NY 12208
518-472-5858 Fax: 518-445-2303
Web site: www.lawrevision.state.ny.us

Chairman:
   Robert M Pitler..................................518-472-5858
Executive Director:
   Rose Mary Bailly.................................518-472-5858

Uniform State Laws Commission
c/o Coughlin & Gerhart LLP
20 Hawley St, East Tower
Binghamton, NY 13902-2039
607-584-4193 Fax: 607-723-1530

Chair:
   Richard B Long...................................607-584-4193
   e-mail: rlong@cglawllp.com
Member:
   Norman L Greene..................................212-661-5030

Offices and agencies generally appear in alphabetical order, except when specific order is requested by listee.

JUDICIAL & LEGAL SYSTEMS / U.S. Government

Member:
  Sandra Stern 212-207-8150
Member:
  Justin L Vigdor 585-232-5300

NEW YORK STATE LEGISLATURE

See Legislative Branch in Section 1 for additional Standing Committee and Subcommittee information.

Assembly Standing Committees

Codes
Chair:
  Joseph R Lentol (D) 518-455-4477
Ranking Minority Member:
  David R Townsend Jr (R) 518-455-5334

Judiciary
Chair:
  Helene E Weinstein (D) 518-455-5462
Ranking Minority Member:
  Jack Quinn (R) 518-455-4462

Senate Standing Committees

Codes
Chair:
  Dale M Volker (R) 518-455-3471
Ranking Minority Member:
  Eric Schneiderman (D) 518-455-2041

Judiciary
Chair:
  John A DeFrancisco (R) 518-455-3511
Ranking Minority Member:
  Ruth Hassell-Thompson (D) 518-455-2061

U.S. Government

EXECUTIVE DEPARTMENTS AND FEDERAL COURTS

US Federal Courts

US Bankruptcy Court - New York

Eastern District
271 Cadman Plaza E, Ste 1595, Brooklyn, NY 11201
347-394-1700
Web site: www.nyeb.uscourts.gov
Chief Judge:
  Carla E Craig 347-394-1700
Clerk of the Court:
  Joseph P Hurley 347-394-1700

Northern District
Web site: www.nynb.uscourts.gov
Chief Bankruptcy Judge:
  Stephen D Gerling 315-266-1122
Court Unit Executive:
  Richard G Zeh, Sr 518-257-1661

Southern District
Alexander Hamilton Custom House, 1 Bowling Green, New York, NY 10004-1408
212-668-2870
Web site: www.nysb.uscourts.gov
Chief Judge:
  Stuart M Bernstein 212-668-2304
Clerk of the Court:
  Kathleen Farrell-Willoughby 212-668-2870

Western District
Web site: www.nywb.uscourts.gov
Chief Bankruptcy Judge:
  Carl L Bucki 585-613-4200
Clerk of the Court:
  Paul R Warren 585-613-4200
  e-mail: pwarren@nywb.uscourts.gov

US Court of Appeals for the Second Circuit
500 Pearl St, New York, NY 10007
212-857-8500
Web site: www.ca2.uscourts.gov
Circuit Executive:
  Karen Milton 212-857-8700/fax: 212-857-8680
Clerk of the Court:
  Roseann B MacKechnie 212-857-8500

US Court of International Trade . . . . fax: 212-264-1085
One Federal Plaza, New York, NY 10278
212-264-2800 Fax: 212-264-1085
Web site: www.cit.uscourts.gov
Chief Judge:
  Jane A Restani 212-264-2018
Acting Clerk:
  Louis Tumminia, Jr 212-264-2814

US DISTRICT COURT - NEW YORK (part of the Second Circuit)
225 Cadman Plaza E, Brooklyn, NY 11201
Web site: www.nyed.uscourts.gov

Eastern District
718-613-2600
Chief District Judge:
  Edward R Korman 718-613-2470
Chief Magistrate Judge:
  Michael L Orenstein 613-712-5700
District Executive:
  James E Ward 718-260-2260
Clerk of the Court:
  Robert C Heinemann 718-260-2600
Chief Probation Officer:
  Tony Garoppolo 347-534-3400/fax: 347-534-3509

Northern District
100 S Clinton St, PO Box 7367, Syracuse, NY 13261
315-234-8500
Web site: www.nynd.uscourts.gov
Chief District Judge:
  Norman A Mordue 315-234-8570
Chief Magistrate Judge:
  Gustave J DiBianco 315-234-8600
Clerk of the Court:
  Lawrence K Baerman 315-234-8500

Offices and agencies generally appear in alphabetical order, except when specific order is requested by listee.

JUDICIAL & LEGAL SYSTEMS / U.S. Government

Chief Probation Officer:
  Paul DeFelice 315-234-8700/fax: 315-234-8701
Southern District
US Courthouse, 40 Centre St, New York, NY 10007-1581
212-805-0136
Web site: www.nysd.uscourts.gov
Chief District Judge:
  Kimba M Wood 212-805-0258
Chief Magistrate Judge:
  Lisa Margaret Smith 212-805-0036
District Executive:
  Clifford P Kirsch 212-805-0500
Clerk of the Court:
  J Michael McMahon 212-805-0136
Chief Probation Officer:
  Chris J Stanton 212-805-0040/fax: 212-805-0045
Western District .... fax: 716-551-4850
304 US Courthouse, 68 Court St, Buffalo, NY 14202
716-551-4211 Fax: 716-551-4850
Web site: www.nywd.uscourts.gov
Chief District Judge:
  Richard J Arcara 716-332-7810/fax: 716-551-4850
Clerk of the Court:
  Rodney C Early 716-332-1700
Chief Probation Off:
  Joseph A Giacobbe 716-551-4241/fax: 716-551-4988

US Tax Court
Chief Judge:
  John O Colvin 202-521-0777
Clerk of the Court:
  Robert BiTrolio 202-521-4600

US Justice Department
Web site: www.usdoj.gov

Antitrust Division—New York Field Office
26 Federal Plaza, Rm 3630, New York, NY 10278-0096
Chief:
  Ralph T Giordano 212-264-0391/fax: 212-264-7453
  e-mail: ralph.giordano@usdoj.gov
Assistant Chief:
  John McReynolds 212-264-0394/fax: 212-264-7453

Civil Division - Commercial Litigation Branch
26 Federal Plz, Rm 346, New York, NY 10278
Attorney-in-Charge:
  Barbara S Williams 212-264-9240/fax: 212-264-1916

Community Relations Service - Northeast & Caribbean Region
26 Federal Plaza, Suite 36-118, New York, NY 10278
Regional Director:
  Reinaldo Rivera, Jr 212-264-0700/fax: 212-264-2143

OFFICE OF INSPECTOR GENERAL (including New York State)

Audit Division
701 Market St, Ste 201, Philadelphia, PA 19106
Regional Manager:
  Ferris B Polk 215-580-2111/fax: 215-597-1348

Investigations Division
JFK Airport, N Boundary Rd, Bldg 77, Penthouse 2, Jamaica, NY 11430
Spl-Agent-in-Chg:
  James E Tomlinson 718-553-7520/fax: 718-553-7533

US Attorney's Office - New York
Eastern District .... fax: 718-254-6479
147 Pierrepont St, Brooklyn, NY 11201
718-254-7000 Fax: 718-254-6479
US Attorney:
  Roslynn R Mauskopf 718-254-7000/fax: 718-254-6319
Chief Asst US Atty:
  Eric Covngold 718-254-7000/fax: 718-254-6300
Executive Asst US Attorney:
  William J Muller 718-254-7000/fax: 718-254-6329
Administrative Asst US Attorney:
  John Lenior 718-254-6255
Chief Asst US Attorney, Criminal Division:
  Bridget Rohde 718-254-6238/fax: 718-254-6150
Chief Asst US Attorney, Civil Division:
  Susan Riley 718-254-6037/fax: 718-254-7483
Chief Asst US Attorney, Appeals Division:
  Peter Norling 718-254-6280
Administrative Officer:
  Peter Kurtin 718-254-6587/fax: 718-254-6550
Northern District
  Albany .... fax: 518-431-0249
  James T Foley US Courthouse, #218, 445 Broadway, Albany, NY 12207
  518-431-0247 Fax: 518-431-0249
  Supervising Asst US Attorney:
    Grant C Jaquith 518-431-0247/fax: 518-431-0249
  Binghamton .... fax: 607-773-2901
  US Courthouse, 304 Federal Bldg, 15 Henry St, Binghamton, NY 13901
  607-773-2887 Fax: 607-773-2901
  Assistant United States Attorney, Chief Criminal Justice:
    Thomas P Walsh 607-773-2887/fax: 607-773-2901
  Syracuse .... fax: 315-448-0689
  J F Hanley Fed Bldg, 100 S Clinton St, Rm 900, Syracuse, NY 13261
  315-448-0672 Fax: 315-448-0689
  United States Attorney:
    Glenn Suddaby 315-448-0672
  First Assistant United States Attorney:
    Andrew T Baxter 315-448-0672
  Asst US Attorney, Chief Civil Division:
    William H Pease 315-448-0672
  Administrative Officer:
    Martha Stratton 315-448-0672/fax: 315-448-0689
Southern District .... fax: 212-637-2611
212-637-2200 Fax: 212-637-2611
  New York City
  1 Saint Andrews Plaza, New York, NY 10007
  212-637-2200
  US Attorney:
    Michael Garcia 212-637-1025
  Associate US Attorney:
    John M McEnany 212-637-2571
  Chief US Appellate Attorney:
    Celeste Koeleveld 212-637-1044
  Chief, Civil Division:
    James Cott 212-637-2695
  Chief, Criminal Division:
    Lev Dassin 212-637-2508
  Administrative Officer:
    Edward Tyrrell 212-637-2269/fax: 212-637-0084
  White Plains .... fax: 914-682-3392
  300 Quarropas St, 3rd Fl, White Plains, NY 10601
  914-993-1907 Fax: 914-682-3392
  Chief Asst US Attorney:
    Margery B Feinzig 914-993-1909

Offices and agencies generally appear in alphabetical order, except when specific order is requested by listee.

JUDICIAL & LEGAL SYSTEMS / Private Sector

Western District
Buffalo .... fax: 716-551-3052
    138 Delaware Ave, Buffalo, NY 14202
    716-843-5700 Fax: 716-551-3052
    US Attorney:
        Terrance P Flynn 716-843-5814
    First Asst US Attorney:
        Kathleen M Mehltretter 716-843-5817
    Asst US Attorney, Civil Division Chief:
        Mary Pat Fleming 716-843-5867
    Asst US Attorney, Narcotics & Violent Crime Division Chief:
        Joseph M Guerra, III 716-843-5824
    Asst US Attorney, Strike Force Division Chief:
        Anthony M Bruce 716-843-5886
    Asst US Attorney, White Collar & General Crimes Division Chief:
        Paul J Campana 716-843-5819
    Administrative Officer:
        Barbara A Sweitzer 716-843-5826/fax: 716-551-3170
Rochester .... fax: 585-263-6226
    620 Federal Bldg, 100 State St, Rochester, NY 14614
    585-263-6760 Fax: 585-263-6226
    Asst US Attorney-in-Charge:
        Bradley E Tyler 585-263-5717

US Marshals' Service - New York

Eastern District
Brooklyn
    225 Cadman Plaza East, Suite G-20, Brooklyn, NY 11201
    718-260-0440
    US Marshal:
        Eugene J Corcoran 718-260-0401/fax: 718-260-0436

Eastern District .... fax: 631-715-4425
310 Federal Plaza, Central Islip, NY 11722
631-715-6160 Fax: 631-715-4425
    US Marshal:
        Eugene J Corcoran 631-715-6201/fax: 631-715-4425

Northern District
Albany
    US Courthouse, 2nd Fl, Rm 206, 445 Broadway, Albany, NY 12207
    US Marshal:
        James J Parmley 518-431-0101/fax: 518-431-0100
Syracuse
    Federal Bldg, 100 S Clinton St, 10th Fl, PO Box 7260, Syracuse, NY 13261
    US Marshal:
        James J Parmley 315-448-0341/fax: 315-448-0343

Southern District
500 Pearl St, Ste 400, New York, NY 10007
    US Marshal:
        Joseph R Guccione 212-331-7100/fax: 212-637-6130

Western District
Buffalo
    Courthouse Bldg, Rm 129, 68 Court St, Buffalo, NY 14202
    US Marshal:
        Peter Lawrence 716-551-4851/fax: 716-551-5505
Rochester
    US Courthouse, Rm 284, 100 State St, Rochester, NY 14614
    US Marshal:
        Peter A Lawrence 585-263-5787/fax: 585-263-6741

US Trustee - Bankruptcy, Region 2
33 Whitehall St, 21st Fl, New York, NY 10004-2112
US Trustee:
    Deidre A Martini 212-510-0500/fax: 212-668-2255

U.S. CONGRESS

See U.S. Congress Chapter for additional Standing Committee and Subcommittee information.

House of Representatives Standing Committees

Judiciary
Chair:
    John Conyers, Jr (D-MI) 202-225-5126
Ranking Minority Member:
    Lamar S Smith (R-TX) 202-225-4236
New York Delegate:
    Jerrold Nadler (D) 202-225-5635
New York Delegate:
    Anthony D Weiner (D) 202-225-6616

Subcommittee
The Constitution
    Chair:
        Steve Chabot (R-OH) 202-225-2216
    Ranking Minority Member:
        Jerrold Nadler (D-NY) 202-225-5635

Senate Standing Committees

Judiciary
Chair:
    Patrick J Leahy (D-VT) 202-224-4242
Ranking Minority Member:
    Arlen Specter (R-PA) 202-224-4254
New York Delegate:
    Charles E Schumer (D) 202-224-6542

Private Sector

NYS Bar Assn, Judicial Independence Cmte
714 East 241st St, Bronx, NY 10470-1302
718-325-5000 Fax: 718-324-0333
e-mail: mspfeifer@aol.com
Maxwell S Pfeifer, Chair

NYS Bar Assn, International Law & Practice Section
Alston & Bird LLP
90 Park Ave, 15th Fl, New York, NY 10016-1387
212-210-9540 Fax: 212-210-9444
e-mail: pmfrank@alston.com
Paul M Frank, Chair

Offices and agencies generally appear in alphabetical order, except when specific order is requested by listee.

JUDICIAL & LEGAL SYSTEMS / Private Sector

NYS Bar Assn, Lawyer Referral Service Cmte
Amdursky Pelky Fennell & Wallen
26 E Oneida St, Oswego, NY 13126-2695
315-343-6363 Fax: 315-343-0134
e-mail: apfwlaw@twcny.rr.com
Web site: www.apfwlaw.com
Timothy J Fennell, Chair

Asian American Legal Defense and Education Fund
99 Hudson St, 12th Fl, New York, NY 10013-2815
212-966-5932 or 800-966-5946 Fax: 212-966-4303
e-mail: info@aaldef.org
Web site: www.aaldef.org
Margaret Fung, Executive Director
Defend civil rights of Asian Americans through litigation, legal advocacy & community education

Association of the Bar of the City of New York
42 W 44th St, New York, NY 10036-6689
212-382-6655 Fax: 212-768-8630
e-mail: jbigelsen@nycbar.org
Web site: www.nycbar.org
Jayne Bigelsen, Director, Communications/Legislative Affrs

NYS Bar Assn, Review the Code of Judicial Conduct Cmte
Securities Industry & Financial Markets Association (SIFMA)
360 Madison Ave, 18th Fl, New York, NY 10017-7111
646-637-9200 Fax: 646-637-9126
e-mail: mgross@bondmarkets.com
Web site: www.sifma.org
Herbert H McDade III, Chair

NYS Bar Assn, President's Cmte on Access to Justice
Boylan Brown
2400 Chase Sq, Rochester, NY 14604
585-232-5300 x256 Fax: 585-232-3528
e-mail: info@boylanbrown.com
Web site: www.boylanbrown.com
C Bruce Lawrence, Co-Chair

NYS Bar Assn, Tort System Cmte
Bracken & Margolin LLP
1 Suffolk Sq, Ste 300, Islandia, NY 11749
631-234-8585 Fax: 631-234-8702
e-mail: jbracken@bracken-margolin.com
Web site: www.bracken-margolin.com
John P Bracken, Co-Chair, Torts Comm

Brooklyn Law School
250 Joralemon St, Brooklyn, NY 11201
718-780-7900 Fax: 718-780-0393
e-mail: joan.wexler@brooklaw.edu
Web site: www.brooklaw.edu
Joan G Wexler, Dean
Legal clinics include immigration, criminal defense, bankruptcy, real estate, and securities arbitration

NYS Bar Assn, Cyberspace Law Cmte
Thelen Reid Brown Raysman & Steiner
875 Third Ave, New York, NY 10022
212-603-2196 Fax: 212-603-2001
e-mail: jneuburger@thelen.com
Web site: www.thelen.com
Jeffrey D Neuburger, Chair

CASA - Advocates for Children of NYS
32 Essex St, Albany, NY 12206
518-426-5354 Fax: 518-426-5348
e-mail: mail@casanys.org
Web site: www.casanys.org
Robin M Robinson, Executive Director
Volunteer advocates appointed by family court judges to represent abused & neglected children in court

CPR, The International Institute for Conflict Prevention & Resolution
575 Lexington Ave, 21st Fl, New York, NY 10022
212-949-6490 Fax: 212-949-8859
e-mail: info@cpradr.org
Web site: www.cpradr.org
Kathleen A Bryan, President & Chief Executive Officer
Alternative dispute resolution

Center for Court Innovation
520 8th Ave, New York, NY 10018
212-397-3050 Fax: 212-397-0985
e-mail: info@courtinnovation.org
Web site: www.courtinnovation.org
Greg Berman, Director
Foster innovation within NYS courts addressing quality-of-life crime, substance abuse, child neglect, domestic violence & landlord-tenant disputes

Center for Judicial Accountability Inc
PO Box 8220, White Plains, NY 10602
914-421-1200 Fax: 914-428-4994
e-mail: cja@judgewatch.org
Web site: www.judgewatch.org
Elena Roth Sassower, Director
Nonpartisan citizens' organization documenting politicization & corruption of the judicial selection & discipline processes

Center for Law & Justice
Pine West Plaza, Bldg 2, Washington Ave Ext, Albany, NY 12205
518-427-8361 Fax: 518-427-8362
e-mail: cflj@verizon.net
Web site: www.timesunion.com/communities/cflj
Alice P Green, Executive Director
Advocacy for fair treatment of poor people & communities of color by the justice system; referral, workshops, community lawyering & education

Offices and agencies generally appear in alphabetical order, except when specific order is requested by listee.

JUDICIAL & LEGAL SYSTEMS / Private Sector

Coalition of Fathers & Families NY, PAC
PO Box 782, Clifton Park, NY 12065
518-383-8202
e-mail: pac@fafny.org
Web site: www.fafny.org/fafnypac.htm
James Hays, Treasurer
Political Action for fathers and families in New York

NYS Bar Assn, Trial Lawyers Section
Connors & Connors, PC
766 Castleton Ave, Staten Island, NY 10310
718-442-1700 Fax: 718-442-1717
e-mail: jpc@connorslaw.com
Web site: www.connorslaw.com
John P Connors, Jr, Chair

NYS Bar Assn, Torts, Insurance & Compensation Law Section
Connors & Corcoran LLP
Times Square Bldg, 45 Exchange St, Ste 250, Rochester, NY 14614
585-232-5885 Fax: 585-546-3631
e-mail: law@connorscorcoran.com
Web site: www.connorscorcoran.com
Eileen E Buholtz, Chair

Cornell Law School, Legal Information Institute
Myron Taylor Hall, Ithaca, NY 14853
607-255-1221 Fax: 607-255-7193
e-mail: lii@lii.law.cornell.edu
Web site: www.law.cornell.edu
Thomas R Bruce, Director
Distributes legal documents via the web & electronic mail

NYS Bar Assn, Judicial Section
Court of Claims
140 Grand St, Ste 507, White Plains, NY 10601
914-289-2310 Fax: 914-289-2313
e-mail: truderma@courts.state.ny.us
Hon Terry Jane Ruderman, Chair

NYS Bar Assn, Federal Constitution & Legislation Cmte
Day Pitney LLP
7 Times Square, New York, NY 10036-7311
973-966-8180 Fax: 973-966-1015
e-mail: jmaloney@daypitney.com
Web site: www.daypitney.com
John C Maloney Jr,
PO Box 1945, Morristown, NJ 07962-1945

NYS Bar Assn, Trusts & Estates Law Section
Day Pitney LLP
7 Times Square, 41st & 42nd St, New York, NY 10036
212-297-5800 Fax: 212-916-2940
e-mail: gwwhitaker@dbh.com
Web site: www.daypitney.com
G Warren Whitaker,
Domestic and international trusts and estates.

NYS Bar Assn, Public Trust & Confidence in the Legal System
Debevoise & Plimpton LLP
919 Third Ave, New York, NY 10022
212-909-6000 Fax: 212-909-6836
e-mail: azgorgun@debevoise.com
Web site: www.debevoise.com
Ellen Lieberman,

NYS Bar Assn, Alternative Dispute Resolution Cmte
Elayne E Greenberg, MS, Esq
25 Potters Lane, Great Neck, NY 11024
516-829-5521 Fax: 516-466-8130
e-mail: elayneegreenberg@juno.com
Elayne E Greenberg, Chair

Empire Justice Center
119 Washington Ave, Albany, NY 12210
518-462-6831 Fax: 518-462-6687
e-mail: hbrown@empirejustice.org
Web site: www.empirejustice.org
Anne Erickson, President & CEO
Policy analysis and research in issues impacting civil legal matters for low-income residents

NYS Bar Assn, Review Judicial Nominations Cmte
Englert Coffey & McHugh
224 State St, PO Box 1092, Schenectady, NY 12305
518-370-4645 Fax: 518-370-4979
e-mail: mpardi@ecmlaw.com
Web site: www.englertcoffeymchugh.com
Peter V Coffey, Chair

NYS Bar Assn, Cmte on the Jury System
FitzGerald Morris et al
One Broad St Plz, PO Box 2017, Glens Falls, NY 12801-4360
518-745-1400 Fax: 518-745-1576
e-mail: pdf@fmbf-law.com
Peter D FitzGerald, Chair

Fund for Modern Courts (The)
351 W 54th St, New York, NY 10019
212-541-6741 Fax: 212-541-7301
e-mail: justice@moderncourts.org
Web site: www.moderncourts.org
Dennis R Hawkins, Executive Director
Improve the administration & quality of justice in NYS courts

NYS Bar Assn, Court Operations Cmte
Getnick, Livingston, Atkinson, Gigliotti & Priore LLP
258 Genesee St, Ste 401, Utica, NY 13502-4642
315-797-9261 Fax: 315-732-0755
e-mail: mgetnick@glagplawfirm.com
Michael E Getnick, Chair

NYS Bar Assn, Labor & Employment Law Section
Goodman & Zuchlewski LLP
500 5th Ave, Ste 5100, New York, NY 10110-5197
212-869-1940 Fax: 212-768-3020
e-mail: pz@goodznyc.com
Pearl Zuchlewski, Chair

Offices and agencies generally appear in alphabetical order, except when specific order is requested by listee.

JUDICIAL & LEGAL SYSTEMS / Private Sector

NYS Bar Assn, Review Attorney Fee Regulation Cmte
Harris Beach LLP
99 Garnsey Rd, Pittsford, NY 14534
585-419-8800 Fax: 585-419-8801
e-mail: vbuzard@harrisbeach.com
Web site: www.nysba.org
A Vincent Buzard, Co-Chair/Bar President Elect

NYS Bar Assn, Intellectual Property Law Section
Hartman & Winnicki, PC
115 W Century Rd, Paramus, NJ 7654
201-967-8040 Fax: 201-967-0590
e-mail: rick@ravin.com
Web site: www.hartmanwinnicki.com
Richard L Ravin, Chair
Internet and Computer Law, Intellectual Property Law, and Debtors & Creditors Rights.

NYS Bar Assn, Procedures for Judicial Discipline Cmte
Hollyer Brady et al
551 Fifth Ave, 27th Fl, New York, NY 10176-0001
212-818-1110 Fax: 212-818-0494
e-mail: arh-esq@worldnet.att.net
A Rene Hollyer, Chair

JAMS
280 Park Ave, 28th Fl, 28th Floor, New York, NY 10017
212-607-2763 Fax: 212-972-0027
e-mail: mshaw@jamsadr.com
Web site: www.jamsadr.com
Margaret L Shaw, Principal
Mediation of civil, commercial & employment disputes; training & systems design

NYS Bar Assn, Children & the Law Committee
Law Office of Anne Reynolds Copps
126 State St, 6th Fl, Albany, NY 12207
518-436-4170 Fax: 518-436-1456
e-mail: arcopps@nycap.rr.com
Web site: arcopps.net
Anne Reynolds Copps, Chair

NYS Bar Assn, General Practice Section
Law Offices of Frank G. D'Angelo & Associates
999 Franklin Ave, Ste 100, Garden City, NY 11530-2909
516-742-7601 Fax: 516-742-6070
e-mail: fgdangeloesq@aol.com
Frank G D'Angelo, Chair
Queens Village Office- 224-44 Braddock Ave, Queens Village, NY 11428 Phone; 718-776-7475

Legal Action Center Inc
225 Varick Street, 4th Floor, New York, NY 10014
212-243-1313 Fax: 212-675-0286
e-mail: lacinfo@lac.org
Web site: www.lac.org
Paul N Samuels, President & Director
Legal & policy issues, alcohol/drug abuse, AIDS & criminal justice

Legal Aid Society
199 Water Street, New York, NY 10038
212-577-3300 Fax: 212-509-8761
Web site: www.legal-aid.org
Theodore A Levine, President
Civil & criminal defense, appeals, juvenile rights, civil legal services

Legal Aid Society, Community Law Offices
199 Water Street, New York, NY 10038
212-577-3300 Fax: 212-509-8761
e-mail: dwweschler@legal-aid.org
Web site: www.legal-aid.org
David W Weschler, Attorney-in-Charge, Volunteer Director
Public interest law, housing & economic development, AIDS, elder law, domestic relations, landlord-tenant, low-income taxpayer clinic

NYS Bar Assn, Legal Aid Cmte/Funding for Civil Legal Svcs Cmte
Legal Services of the Hudson Valley
4 Cromwell Pl, White Plains, NY 10601-5006
914-949-1305 x136 Fax: 914-949-6213
e-mail: bfinkelstein@lshv.org
Web site: www.lshv.org
Barbara D Finkelstein, Executive Director
Established to provide free legal representation in civil matters to low-income people. Legal assistance is provided in the following areas; Westchester, Putnam, Dutchess, Orange, Sullivan and Ulster Counties.

NYS Bar Assn, Tort System Cmte
Levene, Gouldin & Thompson LLP
450 Plaza Dr, Binghamton, NY 13902-0106
607-763-9200 Fax: 607-763-9212
e-mail: dgouldin@binghamtonlaw.com
Web site: www.binghamtonlaw.com
David M Gouldin,

NYS Bar Assn, Elder Law Section
Littman Krooks LLP
399 Knollwood Rd, White Plains, NY 10603
914-684-2100 Fax: 914-684-9865
e-mail: hkrooks@lkllp.com
Web site: www.lkrlaw.com
Harold S Krooks, Chair

NYS Bar Assn, Unlawful Practice of Law Cmte
Schlather, Geldenhuys, Stumbar & Salk
200 E Buffalo St, PO Box 353, Ithaca, NY 14851
607-273-2202 Fax: 607-273-4436
e-mail: mjs@lsss-law.com
Web site: www.ithacalaw.com
Mark J Solomon, Chair

NYS Bar Assn, Court Structure & Judicial Selection Cmte
McMahon & Grow
301 N Washington St, PO Box 4350, Rome, NY 13442-4350
315-336-4700 Fax: 315-336-5851
e-mail: mgglaw@dreamscape.com
Web site: www.mgglaw.com
Hon Richard D Simons, Chair

Offices and agencies generally appear in alphabetical order, except when specific order is requested by listee.

JUDICIAL & LEGAL SYSTEMS / Private Sector

NYS Bar Assn, Resolutions Committee
Meyer Suozzi English & Klein, PC
990Stewart Ave, Garden City, NY 11530-9194
516-592-5704 Fax: 516-741-6706
e-mail: atlevin@nysbar.com
A Thomas Levin, Chair

NYS Bar Assn, Criminal Justice Section
Michael T Kelly, Esq
1217 Delaware Ave, Apt 1003, Buffalo, NY 14209
716-886-1922 Fax: 716-886-1922
e-mail: mkelly1005@aol.com
Michael T Kelly, Chair

NYS Bar Assn, Commercial & Federal Litigation Section
Montclare & Wachtler
67 Wall St, 22nd Fl, New York, NY 10005
212-509-3900 Fax: 212-509-7239
e-mail: ljwachtler@montclarewachtler.com
Lauren J Wachtler, Chair

NY County Lawyers' Association
14 Vessey St, New York, NY 10007
212-267-6646 Fax: 212-406-9252
e-mail: mflood@nycla.org
Web site: www.nycla.org
Catherine Ann Christian, President

NYS Association of Criminal Defense Lawyers
245 Fifth Ave, 19th Fl, New York, NY 10016
212-532-4434 Fax: 212-532-4668
e-mail: nysacdl@aol.com
Web site: www.nysacdl.org
Patricia Marcus, Executive Director
Criminal law

NYS Bar Assn, Cmte on Diversity & Leadership Development
1 Elk St, Albany, NY 12207
518-487-5555 or 212-351-4670 Fax: 212-878-8641
e-mail: kstandard@ebglaw.com
Kenneth G Standard, Co-Chair

NYS Council of Probation Administrators
Box 2 272 Broadway, Albany, NY 12204
518-434-9194 Fax: 518-434-0392
e-mail: president@nyscopa.org
Web site: www.nyscopa.org
Patricia Aikens, President
Provide supervision & investigation services to courts

NYS Court Clerks Association
170 Duane St, New York, NY 10013
212-941-5700 Fax: 212-941-5705
Kevin E Scanlon, Sr, President

NYS Defenders Association
194 Washington Ave, Ste 500, Albany, NY 12210-2314
518-465-3524 Fax: 518-465-3249
e-mail: info@nysda.org
Web site: www.nysda.org
Jonathan E Gradess, Executive Director
Criminal defense

NYS Dispute Resolution Association
255 River St, #4, Troy, NY 12180
518-687-2240 Fax: 518-687-2245
e-mail: nysdra@nysdra.org
Web site: www.nysdra.org
Lisa U Hicks, Executive Director
Dispute resolution-mediation, arbitration, facilitation

NYS Magistrates Association
267 Delaware Ave, Delmar, NY 12054-1124
518-439-1087 Fax: 518-439-1204
e-mail: nysma@juno.com
Web site: www.nysmagassoc.homestead.com
Thomas W Baldwin, Executive Director
Association of town & village justices

NYS Bar Assn, Civil Practice Law & Rules Committee
NYS Supreme Court
50 Delaware Ave, Buffalo, NY 14202
716-845-9478 Fax: 716-851-3265
e-mail: sgerstma@courts.state.ny.us
Sharon Stern Gerstman, Chair

National Academy of Forensic Engineers
174 Brady Ave, Hawthorne, NY 10532
914-741-0633 Fax: 914-747-2988
e-mail: nafe@nafe.org
Web site: www.nafe.org
Marvin M Specter, Executive Director
Engineering consultants to legal professionals & expert witnesses in court, arbitration & administrative adjudication proceedings

NYS Bar Assn, Public Utility Law Committee
National Fuel Gas Distribution
455 Main St, Buffalo, NY 14203
716-686-6123
Web site: www.natfuel.com
Michael W Reville, Chair

NYS Bar Assn, Municipal Law Section
New York State Court of Claims
500 Court Exchange Bldg, 144 Exchange Blvd, Rochester, NY 14614
585-987-4212 Fax: 585-262-3019
e-mail: rminarik@courts.state.ny.us
Web site: www.nyscourtofclaims.courts.state.ny.us/
Hon Renee Forgensi Minarik, Chair

Offices and agencies generally appear in alphabetical order, except when specific order is requested by listee.

JUDICIAL & LEGAL SYSTEMS / Private Sector

New York State Law Enforcement Council
One Hogan Place, New York, NY 10013
212-335-8927 Fax: 212-335-3808
Web site: www.nyslec.org
Leroy Frazer, Jr, Coordinator
Founded in 1982 as a legislative advocate for NY's law enforcement community. The members represent leading law enforcement professionals throughout the state. An active voice and participant in improving the quality of justice and a safer NY.

New York State Supreme Court Officers Association
299 Broadway, Suite 1100, New York, NY 10007-1921
212-406-4292 or 212-406-4276 Fax: 212-791-8420
e-mail: lbroderick@nysscoa.org
Web site: www.nysscoa.org
John P McKillop, President
Supreme Court officers union

New York State Trial Lawyers
132 Nassau St, 2nd Fl, New York, NY 10038-2486
212-349-5890 Fax: 212-608-2310
e-mail: info@nystla.org
Web site: www.nystla.org
Elizabeth Coleman, Executive Director

New York University School of Law
40 Washington Square South, Rm 413, New York, NY 10012-1099
212-998-6217 Fax: 212-995-4881
e-mail: chase@juris.law.nyu.edu
Web site: www.law.nyu.edu/institutes/judicial
Alison Kinney, Program Coordinator-Inst of Judicial Administration
Judicial education & research

New York University, Law School
40 Washington Square South, New York, NY 10012-1012
212-998-6264 Fax: 212-995-4658
e-mail: stephen.gillers@nyu.edu
Stephen Gillers, Professor of Law
Legal ethics

NYS Bar Assn, Media Law Committee
New Yorker
4 Times Square, 20th Fl, New York, NY 10036
212-286-5857 Fax: 212-286-5025
e-mail: lynn_oberlander@newyorker.com
Web site: www.newyorker.com
Lynn Oberlander, Chair

NYS Bar Assn, Courts of Appellate Jurisdiction Cmte
Norman A Olch, Esq
233 Broadway, New York, NY 10279
212-964-6171 Fax: 212-964-7634
e-mail: nao5@columbia.edu
Norman A Olch, Chair

NYS Bar Assn, Judicial Campaign Monitoring Cmte
Ostertag O'Leary & Barrett
17 Collegeview Ave, Poughkeepsie, NY 12603
845-486-4300 Fax: 845-486-4080
e-mail: r.ostertag@verizon.net
Robert L Ostertag, Chair

Pace University, School of Law, John Jay Legal Services Inc
80 N Broadway, White Plains, NY 10603-3711
914-422-4333 Fax: 914-422-4391
e-mail: vmerton@law.pace.edu
Web site: www.law.pace.edu
Vanessa Merton,
Health law, poverty law, domestic violence, immigration

Prisoners' Legal Services of New York
114 Prospect St, Ithaca, NY 14850-5616
607-273-2283 Fax: 607-272-9122
e-mail: sjohnson@plsny.org
Susan Johnson, Executive Director

Pro Bono Net
151 West 30th St, 10th Fl, New York, NY 10001
212-760-2554 Fax: 212-760-2557
e-mail: info@probono.net
Web site: www.probono.net; www.lawhelp.org
Mark O'Brien, Executive Director
Connects & organizes the public interest legal community in an online environment; a lawyer-to-lawyer network

NYS Bar Assn, Multi-jurisdictional Practice Cmte
Proskauer Rose LLP
1585 Broadway, New York, NY 10036-8299
212-969-3000 Fax: 212-969-2900
e-mail: keppler@proskauer.com
Web site: www.proskauer.com
Klaus Eppler, Partner
Business Law, Securities

NYS Bar Assn, Fiduciary Appointments Cmte
Pruzansky & Besunder LLP
One Suffolk Sq, Ste 315, Islandia, NY 11749
631-234-9240 Fax: 631-234-9278
e-mail: jmp@prubeslaw.com
Joshua M Pruzansky, Chair

Puerto Rican Legal Defense & Education Fund Inc (PRLDEF)
99 Hudson St, 14th Fl, New York, NY 10013-2815
212-219-3360 or 800-328-2322 Fax: 212-431-4276
e-mail: info@prldef.org
Web site: www.prldef.org
Cesar A Perales, President & General Counsel
Secure, promote & protect the civil & human rights of the Puerto Rican & wider Latino community through litigation, policy analysis & education

NYS Bar Assn, Judicial Campaign Conduct Cmte
Supreme Court
401 Montgomery St, Rm 401, Syracuse, NY 13202-2127
315-671-1100 Fax: 315-671-1183
e-mail: maklein@courts.state.ny.us
Michael A Klein, Chair

Offices and agencies generally appear in alphabetical order, except when specific order is requested by listee.

JUDICIAL & LEGAL SYSTEMS / Private Sector

Vera Institute of Justice
233 Broadway, 12th Fl, New York, NY 10279-1299
212-334-1300 Fax: 212-941-9407
e-mail: contactvera@vera.org
Web site: www.vera.org
Michael Jacobson, Director
Research, design & implementation of demonstration projects in criminal justice & social equity in partnership with government & nonprofit organizations

NYS Bar Assn, Family Law Section
Vincent F Stempel, Jr Esq
1205 Franklin Ave, Ste 280, Garden City, NY 11530
516-742-8620 Fax: 516-742-6859
e-mail: vstempel@yahoo.com
Vincent F Stempel, Jr, Chair

Volunteers of Legal Service, Inc
54 Greene St, New York, NY 10013
212-966-4400 Fax: 212-219-8943
e-mail: wdean@volsprobono.org
William J Dean, Executive Director
Providing pro bono civil legal services to poor people in New York City.

NYS Bar Assn, Diversity & Leadership Development Cmte
Whiteman Osterman & Hanna LLP
One Commerce Plz, Albany, NY 12260
518-487-7600 Fax: 518-487-7777
e-mail: lptharp@woh.com
Web site: www.woh.com
Lorraine Power Tharp, Chair

NYS Bar Assn, Health Law Section
Wilson Elser Moskowitz Edelman & Dicker
677 Broadway, Albany, NY 12207
518-449-8893 Fax: 518-449-4292
e-mail: philip.rosenberg@wilsonelser.com
Phillip Rosenberg,

Women's Bar Association of the State of New York
PO Box 936, Planetarium Station, New York, NY 10024-0546
212-362-4445 Fax: 212-721-1620
e-mail: info@wbasny.org
Web site: www.wbasny.org
Maria T Cortese, President

LABOR & EMPLOYMENT PRACTICES

New York State

GOVERNOR'S OFFICE

Governor's Office
Executive Chamber
State Capitol
Albany, NY 12224
518-474-8390 Fax: 518-474-1513
Web site: www.state.ny.us

Governor:
  Eliot Spitzer 518-474-8390
Secretary to the Governor:
  Richard Baum 518-474-4246
Counsel to the Governor:
  David Nocenti 518-474-8343
Senior Advisor to the Governor:
  Lloyd Constantine 518-486-9671
Assistant Deputy Secretary, Labor Relations:
  Arlene Smoller 518-408-2576
Assistant Counsel to the Governor-Labor & Retirement:
  David Weinstein 518-474-8434
Deputy Secretary, General Services, Technology & Labor Relations:
  Syliva Hamer 518-474-8434
Director, Communications:
  Darren Dopp 518-474-8418

EXECUTIVE DEPARTMENTS AND RELATED AGENCIES

Insurance Fund (NYS)
15 Computer Drive West
Albany, NY 12205
518-437-5220
Web site: www.nysif.com

199 Church St
New York, NY 10007
212-312-9000

Executive Director/CEO:
  David P Wehner 518-437-5220
First Deputy Executive Director:
  Christopher Barclay 518-437-5220
Chief Fiscal Officer:
  Susan D Sharp 518-437-6168
General Attorney:
  Gregory Allen 518-437-5220
Deputy Exec Director & Marketing Director:
  Ann F Formel 518-437-1879
Deputy Executive Director, Project Management:
  Stephen D Nelson 518-437-6196
Public Information Officer:
  Robert Lawson 518-437-3504/fax: 518-437-1849

Administration
Director:
  Joseph Mullen 518-437-5220

Claims & Medical Operations
Director:
  Edward Hiller 212-312-7880

Confidential Investigations
Director:
  Laurence LaPointe 631-756-4007

Field Services
Director:
  Armin Holdorf 212-587-5225

Information Technology Service
Chief Information Officer:
  Sean O'Brien 518-437-4361
Director, ITS:
  Laurie Endries 518-437-3130

Insurance Fund Board of Commissioners
Chair:
  Robert H Hurlbut 518-437-5220
Vice Chair:
  Donald T DeCarlo 518-437-5220
Secretary to the Board:
  Christopher Barclay 518-437-5220
Asst Secretary to the Board:
  Albert K DiMeglio 518-437-5220
Member(ex-offico)/Commissioner, NYS Dept of Labor:
  M Patricia Smith 518-437-5220
Member:
  John F Carpenter 518-437-5220
Member:
  C Scott Bowen 518-437-5220
Member:
  Donald T DeCarlo 518-437-5220
Member:
  Jane A Halbritter 518-437-5220
Member:
  Charles L Loiodice 518-437-5220
Member:
  William A O'Loughlin, Jr 518-437-5220

Investments
Director:
  Miriam Martinez 212-587-6550

NYSIF District Offices

Albany
15 Computer Drive West, Albany, NY 12205
Business Manager:
  Edward Obertubbesing 518-437-6401/fax: 518-437-8021

Buffalo
225 Oak St, Buffalo, NY 14203
Business Manager:
  Ronald Reed 716-851-2004/fax: 716-851-2131

Offices and agencies generally appear in alphabetical order, except when specific order is requested by listee.

LABOR & EMPLOYMENT PRACTICES / New York State

Endicott
Glendale Technology Park, 2001 E Perimeter Rd, Endicott, NY 13760
Business Manager:
James Fehrer 607-741-6023/fax: 607-741-5029

Nassau County, Long Island
8 Corporate Center Dr, 2nd Fl, Melville, NY 11747
Business Manager:
Cliff Meister 631-756-4003/fax: 631-756-4030

Rochester
100 Chestnut St, Ste 1000, Rochester, NY 14604
Business Manager:
Lisa Ellsworth 585-258-2100/fax: 585-258-2065

Suffolk County, Long Island
8 Corporate Center Dr, 3rd Fl, Melville, NY 11747
Business Manager:
Eileen Wojnar 631-756-4330/fax: 631-756-4260

Syracuse
1045 Seventh North St, Liverpool, NY 13088
Business Manager:
Kathleen Campbell 315-453-8300/fax: 315-453-8313

White Plains
105 Corporate Park Dr, Ste 200, White Plains, NY 10604
Business Manager:
Carl Heitner 914-701-6292/fax: 914-701-2181

Premium Audit
Director:
Glenn Cunningham 212-587-7470

Underwriting
Director:
John Massetti 212-312-7012

Labor Department
Building 12, Room 500
State Campus
Albany, NY 12240
518-457-2741 Fax: 518-457-6908
e-mail: nysdol@labor.state.ny.us
Web site: www.labor.state.ny.us

Commissioner:
M Patricia Smith 518-457-2746
Executive Deputy Commissioner:
Mario Musolino 518-457-4318

Employment & Unemployment Insurance Advisory Council
Chair:
Vacant 518-457-2878

Employment Relations Board
Chair:
Vacant 212-564-2441

Industrial Board of Appeals
Chair:
Evelyn Heady 518-474-4789

Unemployment Insurance Appeal Board
Chair:
Michael Graeson 518-402-0205
Executive Director:
Lisa Connors-Wright 518-402-0205

Administration & Public Affairs
Deputy Commissioner, Administration & CFO:
Vacant 518-457-3905
Associate Commissioner, Human Resources:
Andrew Adams 518-457-9570
Director, Administrative Finance Bureau:
Roger Bailie 518-457-2647
Director, Communications:
Leo Rosales 518-457-5519/fax: 518-485-1126
Director, Personnel:
Debora O'Brien-Jordan 518-457-6651
Director, Staff & Organization Development:
Michael Cunningham 518-457-1168
Affirmative Action Administrator:
Margaret Sheehan-Nolan 518-457-1984

Counsel's Office
Counsel:
Maria Colavito 518-457-7069
Deputy Counsel:
Joan Connell 518-457-7069
Legislative Counsel:
Kevin Kerwin 518-457-4380

Federal Programs
Deputy Commissioner, Federal Programs:
Margaret Moree 518-485-6410

Employment Services Division
Director:
Karen Papandrea 518-457-3584
Assistant Director:
Russell Oliver 518-457-3584

Unemployment Insurance Division
Director:
Vacant 518-457-2878/fax: 518-485-8604

Workforce Development & Training Division
Acting Director:
Yue Yee 518-457-0380/fax: 518-457-9526
Employability Development/Apprentice Training
Director:
Christine Timber 518-457-6820

Inspector General's Office
Inspector General:
Vacant 518-457-7012
Director, Internal Audit:
Karen Stackrow 518-457-9016

Labor Planning & Technology
Chief Information Officer:
Robert Vitello 518-457-7994

Research & Statistics Division
Deputy Director:
David J Trzaskos 518-457-6369
Chief of Labor Market Information:
Norman Steele 518-457-6638
Statewide Labor Market Analyst:
Kevin Jack 518-457-2919

Veterans Services
Deputy Commissioner, Veterans Affairs:
Ronald Tocci 518-457-1343
Program Coordinator:
Earl Wallace 518-457-1343

Offices and agencies generally appear in alphabetical order, except when specific order is requested by listee.

LABOR & EMPLOYMENT PRACTICES / New York State

Employer Services
Director:
  Timothy O'Keefe................518-457-6821
Rural Labor Services:
  Valerie Sewell.................518-485-8539

Regional Offices
Central/Mohawk Valley................fax: 315-793-2342
207 Genesee St, Ste 712, Utica, NY 13501
Regional Administrator:
  Kelli Owens....................315-793-2716
Finger Lakes Region..................fax: 585-258-8859
130 West Main St, Rochester, NY 14614
Regional Administrator:
  Peter Pecor....................585-258-8858
Greater Capital District..............fax: 518-462-2777
175 Central Ave, Albany, NY 12206-2902
Regional Administrator:
  David Wallingford..............518-462-7600
Hudson Valley........................fax: 914-287-2058
120 Bloomingdale Rd, White Plains, NY 10605
Acting Regional Administrator:
  Frank Surdey...................914-997-8711
Long Island Region...................fax: 516-934-8553
303 W Old County Rd, Hicksville, NY 11801
Regional Administrator:
  Diane Wicklund.................516-934-8547
New York City........................fax: 212-621-0730
247 West 54th St, New York, NY 10019
Regional Administrator:
  Sara Spatz.....................212-621-9346
Southern Tier........................fax: 607-741-4516
2001 Perimeter Rd East, Ste 3, Endicott, NY 13760
Regional Administrator:
  John Flynn.....................607-741-4519
Western Region.......................fax: 716-851-2792
290 Main St, Buffalo, NY 14202
Regional Administrator:
  Samuel J Drago.................716-851-2752

Worker Protection
Deputy Commissioner, Workforce Protection, Standards & Licensing:
  Pico Ben-Amotz.................518-457-4317
Deputy Commissioner, Wage & Immigrant Services:
  Terri Gerstein.................518-473-3905

Labor Standards Division
Acting Director:
  Carmine Ruberto................518-457-2460

Public Work Bureau
Director:
  Chris Alund....................518-457-5589

Safety & Health Division
Director:
  Maureen Cox...........518-457-3518/fax: 518-457-1519
Asbestos Control Bureau
Program Manager:
  Robert Perez.........518-457-1255/fax: 518-485-8054
Industry Inspection Unit
Program Manager:
  Joe Gallagher........518-457-1212/fax: 518-485-8054
On-site Consultation Unit
Program Manager:
  James Rush...........518-457-2238/fax: 518-457-3454
Public Employees Safety & Health (PESH) Unit
Program Manager:
  Normand Labbe........518-457-1263/fax: 518-457-5545

Law Department
State Capitol
Albany, NY 12224-0341
518-474-7330 Fax: 518-402-2472
Web site: www.oag.state.ny.us

120 Broadway
New York, NY 12224-0341
212-416-8000
Fax: 212-416-8942

Attorney General:
  Andrew M Cuomo.................518-474-7330
First Deputy Attorney General:
  Michele Hirshman...............212-416-8050
Director, Public Information & Correspondence:
  Peter A Drago.........518-474-7330/fax: 518-402-2472

Public Advocacy Division
Deputy Attorney General:
  Dietrich Snell........212-416-8041/fax: 212-416-8068
Special Counsel:
  Mary Ellen Burns...............212-416-6155

Civil Rights Bureau
Bureau Chief:
  Dennis Parker.........212-416-8250/fax: 212-416-8074

State Counsel Division
Deputy Attorney General:
  Richard Rifkin.................518-473-7190
Assistant Deputy Attorney General:
  Patricia Martinelli...518-473-0648/fax: 518-486-9777
Assistant Deputy Attorney General:
  Susan L Watson........212-416-8579/fax: 212-416-6001

Labor Bureau
Bureau Chief:
  M Patricia Smith...............212-416-8710

Workers' Compensation Board
20 Park Street
Albany, NY 12207
877-632-4996 Fax: 518-473-1415
Web site: www.wcb.state.ny.us

Executive Director:
  Glenn Warren...................518-474-6670
Chair, Board of Commissioners:
  Donna Ferrara.........518-474-6670/fax: 518-473-1415
Vice Chair:
  Fran Libous...........518-474-6670/fax: 518-473-1415
General Counsel:
  Cheryl Wood...........518-486-9564/fax: 518-473-2233
Director, Division of Appeals:
  Carl Copps............518-402-0160/fax: 518-473-2233
Director, Internal Audit:
  Albert Blackman.......518-473-6447/fax: 518-473-4761
Director, Public Information:
  Vacant................518-474-6670/fax: 518-473-1415
Fraud Inspector General:
  John Burgher..........888-363-6001/fax: 518-402-1059
Advocate for Business:
  Vacant.........................518-486-3331
Advocate for Injured Workers:
  Edwin Ruff............800-580-6665/fax: 518-486-7510

Offices and agencies generally appear in alphabetical order, except when specific order is requested by listee.

LABOR & EMPLOYMENT PRACTICES / New York State

Administration
Deputy Executive Director:
    Ann Kutter 518-473-8900/fax: 518-486-6411
Director, Administrative Services:
    Vacant 518-486-3334
Director, Security:
    Joseph V Smith 518-402-0172/fax: 518-402-1059
Director, Finance & Policy:
    Kathleen Griffin 518-486-9596
Director, Human Resources:
    Lisa Sunkes 718-802-6612/fax: 718-834-2123
Affirmative Action Officer:
    Jaime Benitez. 518-486-5128/fax: 518-486-6364

Operations
Deputy Executive Director:
    Vacant. 518-486-7143/fax: 518-474-9367
Director, Operations:
    David M Donohue 518-486-3345/fax: 518-486-6411
Director, Disability Benefits:
    Nicholas Dogias. 718-802-6947/fax: 718-802-6971
Director, Bureau of Compliance:
    Brian Collins 518-474-2686/fax: 518-402-0701

District Offices
Albany
100 Broadway-Menands, Albany, NY 12241
  District Administrator:
    Linda Spano 866-750-5157/fax: 518-473-9166
  District Manager:
    Pat Wright. 866-750-5157/fax: 518-473-9166

Binghamton
State Office Bldg, 44 Hawley St, Binghamton, NY 13901
  District Administrator:
    Vacant 866-802-3604/fax: 607-721-8464
  District Manager:
    David Wiktorek 866-802-3604/fax: 607-721-8464

Brooklyn
111 Livingston St, Brooklyn, NY 11201
  District Administrator:
    Edward Joyce 800-877-1373/fax: 718-802-6642
  District Manager:
    Tom Agostino. 800-877-1373/fax: 718-802-6642

Buffalo
Statler Towers, 3rd Fl, 107 Delaware Ave, Buffalo, NY 14202-2898
  District Administrator:
    Jeffrey Quinn 866-211-0645/fax: 716-842-2171
  District Manager:
    Barbara Townsend 866-211-0645/fax: 716-842-2171

Hauppauge
220 Rabro Drive, Ste 100, Hauppauge, NY 11788-4230
  District Administrator:
    Vacant 866-681-5354/fax: 631-952-7966
  District Manager:
    Robert F Williams 866-681-5354/fax: 631-952-7966

Hempstead
175 Fulton Ave, Hempstead, NY 11550
  District Administrator:
    Alan Landman 866-805-3630/fax: 516-560-7807
  District Manager:
    Alan Gotlinsky 866-805-3630/fax: 516-560-7807

Manhattan
215 W 125th St, New York, NY 10027
  District Administrator:
    Frank Vernuccio, Jr 800-877-1373/fax: 212-932-1488

Peekskill
41 N Division St, Peekskill, NY 10566
  District Administrator:
    Vacant 866-746-0552/fax: 914-788-5793

  District Manager:
    Luis A Torres 866-746-0552/fax: 914-788-5793

Queens
168-46 91st Ave, Jamaica, NY 11432
  District Administrator:
    Wayne Allen. 800-877-1373/fax: 718-291-7248
  District Administrator:
    Vacant 800-877-1373/fax: 718-291-7248

Rochester
130 Main St West, Rochester, NY 14614
  District Administrator:
    George A Park, Jr 866-211-0644/fax: 585-238-8351
  District Manager:
    MaryBeth Goodsell 866-211-0644/fax: 585-238-8351

Syracuse
935 James Street, Syracuse, NY 13203
  District Administrator:
    Janet Burman 866-802-3730/fax: 315-423-2938
  District Manager:
    Marc Johnson 866-802-3730/fax: 315-423-2938

Systems Modernization
Deputy Exec Director:
    Thomas Schofield 518-486-7143/fax: 518-474-9367
Director, Management Information Systems:
    Thomas Wegener. 518-486-5143/fax: 518-473-6379

Workers' Compensation Board of Commissioners
Commissioner:
    Fran Libous. 518-474-6670
Commissioner:
    Mona Bargnesi 716-842-2149
Commissioner:
    Michael T Berns 718-802-6849
Commissioner:
    Donna Ferrara 518-474-6670
Commissioner:
    Candace K Finnegan. 914-788-5890
Commissioner:
    Agatha Edel Groski 518-402-6135
Commissioner:
    Karl A Henry 716-842-2140
Commissioner:
    Ellen O Paprocki 315-423-1276
Commissioner:
    Robert Zinck 877-657-4994
Secretary to the Board:
    Susan M Olson 518-402-6071

CORPORATIONS, AUTHORITIES AND COMMISSIONS

Waterfront Commission of New York Harbor
39 Broadway
4th Fl
New York, NY 10006
212-742-9280 Fax: 212-480-0587
Web site: www.wcnyh.org

Commissioner, New York:
    Michael C Axelrod 212-742-9280
Commissioner, New Jersey:
    Michael J Madonna 212-742-9280
Executive Director:
    Thomas De Maria. 212-905-9201

Offices and agencies generally appear in alphabetical order, except when specific order is requested by listee.

LABOR & EMPLOYMENT PRACTICES / U.S. Government

NEW YORK STATE LEGISLATURE

See Legislative Branch in Section 1 for additional Standing Committee and Subcommittee information.

Assembly Standing Committees

Labor
Chair:
  Susan V John (D) 518-455-4527
Ranking Minority Member:
  Thomas W Alfano (R) 518-455-4627

Assembly Task Forces

Puerto Rican/Hispanic Task Force
Chair:
  Peter M Rivera (D) 518-455-5102
Co-Chair:
  Vito J Lopez (D) 518-455-5537

Skills Development & Career Education, Legislative Commission on
Assembly Chair:
  Joan K Christensen (D) 518-455-5283
Program Manager:
  Brenda Carter 518-455-4865

Women's Issues, Task Force on
Chair:
  Barbara Lifton (D) 518-455-5444
Coordinator:
  Jean Emery 518-455-3632/fax: 518-455-4574

Senate Standing Committees

Labor
Chair:
  George D Maziarz (R) 518-455-2024
Ranking Minority Member:
  George Onorato (D) 518-455-3486

U.S. Government

EXECUTIVE DEPARTMENTS AND RELATED AGENCIES

Equal Employment Opportunity Commission
Web site: www.eeoc.gov

New York District
33 Whitehall St, 5th Fl, New York, NY 10004
District Director:
  Spencer H Lewis, Jr .... 800-669-4000 or 800-669-6820 tty
  fax: 212-336-3790

  Buffalo Local
  6 Fountain Plaza, Ste 350, Buffalo, NY 14202
  Director:
    Elizabeth Cadle .... 800-669-4000 or 800-669-3820 tty
    fax: 716-551-4387

Federal Labor Relations Authority
Web site: www.flra.gov

Boston Regional Office .... fax: 617-565-6262
Thomas P O'Neill Jr Federal Building, 10 Causeway Street, Suite 472, Boston, MA 02222
617-565-5100 Fax: 617-565-6262
Regional Director:
  Richard D Zaiger 617-565-5100/fax: 617-565-6262

Federal Mediation & Conciliation Service
Web site: www.fmcs.gov

Northeastern Region .... fax: 732-726-2124
517 US Hwy 1 So, Ste 3020, Iselin, NJ 08830
732-726-3120 Fax: 732-726-2124
Regional Director:
  John F Buettner 732-726-3120

Director, Mediation Services:
  John E Sweeney 732-726-3120

National Labor Relations Board
Web site: www.nlrb.gov

Region 2 - New York City Metro Area ...... fax: 212-264-2450
26 Federal Plaza, Rm 3614, New York, NY 10278-0104
212-264-0300 Fax: 212-264-2450
Regional Director:
  Celeste J Mattina 212-264-0300/fax: 212-264-2450

Region 29 - Brooklyn Area .... fax: 718-330-7579
Two MetroTech Center, 100 Myrtle Ave, 5th Fl, Brooklyn, NY 11201-4201
718-330-7713 Fax: 718-330-7579
Regional Director:
  Alvin P Blyer..................... 718-330-7713/fax: 718-330-7579

Region 3 - New York Except Metro Area ... fax: 716-551-4972
Niagara Center Building, 130 South Elmowood Ave, Ste 630, Buffalo, NY 14202-2387
716-551-4931 Fax: 716-551-4972
Regional Dir:
  Helen Marsh 716-551-4931/fax: 716-551-4972

  Albany Resident Office .... fax: 518-431-4157
  Leo W O'Brien Fed Bldg, Rm 342, Clinton Ave and N Pearl St, Albany, NY 12207-2350
  518-431-4155 Fax: 518-431-4157
  Resident Officer:
    Jon Mackle 518-431-4155/fax: 518-431-4157

US Labor Department
Web site: www.dol.gov

Bureau of Labor Statistics (BLS)
201 Varick St, Rm 808, New York, NY 10014
Web site: www.bls.gov

Offices and agencies generally appear in alphabetical order, except when specific order is requested by listee.

LABOR & EMPLOYMENT PRACTICES / U.S. Government

Regional Commissioner (NY & Boston):
　Dennis McSweeney . . . . 212-337-2451 or 617-565-2331
Reg Comm (NY):
　Michael L Dolfman 212-337-2500/fax: 212-337-2411

Employee Benefits Security Administration (EBSA)
33 Whitehall St, Ste 1200, New York, NY 10004
Regional Director:
　Jonathan Kay 212-607-8600/fax: 212-607-8681

Employment & Training Administration (ETA)
JFK Federal Bldg, RmE/350, Boston, MA 2203
Regional Administrator:
　William Carlson 617-788-0170/fax: 617-788-0101

Employment Standards Administration

Federal Contract Compliance Programs Office (OFCCP)
201 Varick St, Rm 750, New York, NY 10014
Regional Director:
　Lorenzo Harrison 646-264-3170/fax: 646-264-3009

Labor-Management Standards Office (OLMS)
Web site: www.olms.dol.gov
　Buffalo District Office
　　111 W Huron St, Rm 1310, Buffalo, NY 14202
　　District Director:
　　　Joseph Wasik 716-842-2900/fax: 716-842-2901
　New York District Office
　　201 Varick St, Rm 878, New York, NY 10014
　　District Director:
　　　Ralph Gerchak 646-264-3190/fax: 646-264-3191

Wage-Hour Division (WHD)-Northeast Regional Office
170 So Independence Mall, Ste 850 West, Philadelphia, PA 19106
Regional Admin:
　Corlis L Sellers 215-861-5800/fax: 215-861-5840
　Albany District Office
　　Leo W O'Brien Fed Bldg, Rm 822, Albany, NY 12207
　　District Director:
　　　Christopher Martin 518-431-4278/fax: 518-431-4281
　Long Island District Office
　　1400 Old Country Rd, Ste 410, Westbury, NY 11590
　　District Director:
　　　Irv Miljoner 516-338-1890/fax: 516-338-8901
　New York City District Office
　　26 Federal Plz, Rm 3700, New York, NY 10278
　　District Director:
　　　Philip Jacobson 212-264-8185/fax: 212-264-9548

Workers' Compensation Programs (OWCP)
201 Varick St, Rm 740, New York, NY 10014
Regional Director:
　Jaye Weirman 646-264-3000/fax: 646-264-3006

Inspector General

Inspector General's Office for Audit (OIG-A)
201 Varick St, Rm 871, New York, NY 10014
Regional Inspector General, Audit:
　Mark Schwartz 646-264-3500/fax: 646-264-3501

Inspector General's Office for Investigations (OIG-I)
201 Varick St, Rm 849, New York, NY 10014
Special Agent-in-Charge:
　Marjorie Franzman 646-264-3550/fax: 646-264-3502

Occupational Safety & Health Administration (OSHA)
201 Varick St, Rm 670, New York, NY 10014
212-337-2378
Web site: www.osha.gov

Regional Administrator:
　Patricia K Clark 212-337-0118/fax: 212-337-2371
　Albany Area Office
　　401 New Karner Rd, Ste 300, Albany, NY 12205-3809
　　Area Director:
　　　Edward Jerome 518-464-4338/fax: 518-464-4337
　Buffalo Area Office
　　5360 Genesee St, Bowmansville, NY 14026
　　Area Director:
　　　Art Dube 716-551-3053/fax: 716-551-3126
　Manhattan Area Office
　　201 Varick St, Rm 908, New York, NY 10014
　　Area Director:
　　　Richard Mendelson 212-620-3200/fax: 212-620-4121
　Queens Area Office
　　45-17 Marathon Parkway, Little Neck, NY 11362
　　Assistant Area Director:
　　　Kevin Brennan 718-279-9060/fax: 718-279-9057
　Syracuse Area Office
　　3300 Vickery Rd, North Syracuse, NY 13212
　　Area Director:
　　　Christopher Adams 315-451-0808/fax: 315-451-1351
　Tarrytown Area Office
　　660 White Plains Rd, Tarrytown, NY 10591
　　Area Director:
　　　Diana Cortez 914-524-7510/fax: 914-524-7515

Office of Asst Secretary for Administration & Mgmt (OASAM)
201 Varick St, Rm 813, New York, NY 10014
Regional Administrator (NY & Boston):
　Debbra Williams . . . . 646-264-5050 or 617-788-2818
fax: 212-337-2631

Office of the Solicitor
201 Varick St, Rm 983, New York, NY 10014
Reg Solicitor:
　Patricia M Rodenhausen 212-337-2078/fax: 212-337-2112

Region 2 - New York Office of Secretary's Representative
201 Varick St, Rm 605-B, New York, NY 10014
Secretary's Regional Representative (SRR):
　Angelica O Tang 212-337-2317/fax: 212-337-2586
　Jobs Corps (JC)
　　JFK Fed Bldg, Room E350, Boston, NY 02203
　　Regional Director:
　　　Joseph A Semansky 617-788-0197/fax: 617-788-0184
　Office of Public Affairs (OPA) (serving New York State)
　　JFK Federal Bldg, Rm E120, Boston, MA 2203
　　Regional Director, Public Affairs:
　　　John Chavez 617-565-2072/fax: 617-565-2076

Region 2 New York - Women's Bureau (WB)
201 Varick St, Rm 602, New York, NY 10014
Regional Administrator:
　Jacqueline Cooke 212-337-2389/fax: 212-337-2394

US Merit Systems Protection Board
Web site: www.mspb.gov

New York Field Office
26 Federal Plaza, Ste 3137A, New York, NY 10278-0022

Offices and agencies generally appear in alphabetical order, except when specific order is requested by listee.

LABOR & EMPLOYMENT PRACTICES / Private Sector

Chief Administrative Judge:
Arthur Joseph....................212-264-9372/fax: 212-264-1417

US Office of Personnel Management
Web site: www.usajobs.opm.gov

PHILADELPHIA SERVICE CENTER (serving New York)
William J Green Fed Bldg, Rm 3400, 600 Arch St, Philadelphia, PA 19106
Director:
Joseph D Stix....................215-861-3031/fax: 215-861-3030
e-mail: philadelphia@opm.gov

US Railroad Retirement Board
Web site: www.rrb.gov

New York District Offices

Albany....................fax: 518-431-4000
O'Brien Fed Bldg, Rm 264, Clinton Ave & N Pearl St, Albany, NY 12201
518-431-4004 Fax: 518-431-4000
District Manager:
Daniel M Layton, Jr..............518-431-4004/fax: 518-431-4000
e-mail: albany@rrb.gov

Buffalo....................fax: 716-551-3802
186 Exchange Streeet, Suite 110, Buffalo, NY 14204-2026
716-551-4141 Fax: 716-551-3802
District Manager:
Philip C Dissek..................716-551-4141/fax: 716-551-3802
e-mail: buffalo@rrb.gov

New York....................fax: 212-264-1687
26 Federal Plaza, Rm 3404, New York, NY 10278
212-264-9820 Fax: 212-264-1687
District Manager:
Rose I Jonas....................212-264-9820/fax: 212-264-1687
e-mail: newyork@rrb.gov

Westbury....................fax: 516-334-4763
1400 Old Country Rd, Ste 202, Westbury, NY 11590
516-334-5940 or 716-835-7808 Fax: 516-334-4763
District Manager:
Marie Baran....................516-334-5940/fax: 516-334-4763

U.S. CONGRESS

See U.S. Congress Chapter for additional Standing Committee and Subcommittee information.

House of Representatives Standing Committees

Education & Labor
Chair:
George Miller (D-CA)..............................202-225-2095
Ranking Minority Member:
Howard P (Buck) McKeon (CA).......................202-225-1956
New York Delegate:
Timothy H Bishop (D)..............................202-225-3826
New York Delegate:
Carolyn McCarthy (D)..............................202-225-5516
New York Delegate:
Major R Owens (D).................................202-225-6231
New York Delegate:
John R (Randy) Kuhl, Jr (R).......................202-225-3161

Small Business
Chair:
Nydia Velazquez (D-NY)............................202-225-2361
Ranking Minority Member:
Steve Chabot (R-OH)...............................202-225-2216
New York Delegate:
Sue W Kelly (R)...................................202-225-5441

Subcommittees
Contracting and Technology
Chair:
Bruce Braley (D-IA)...........................202-225-2911
Ranking Minority Member:
David Davis (R-TN)............................202-225-6356
Investigations and Oversight
Chair:
Jason Altmire (D-PA)..........................202-225-2565
Ranking Minority Member:
Louie Gohmert (R-TX)..........................202-225-3035

Senate Standing Committees

Health, Education, Labor & Pensions
Chair:
Edward M Kennedy (D-MA)...........................202-224-4543
Ranking Minority Member:
Michael B Enzi (R-WY).............................202-224-3424
New York Delegate:
Hillary Rodham Clinton (D)........................202-224-4451

Small Business & Entrepreneurship
Chair:
John F Kerry (D-MA)...............................202-224-2742
Ranking Minority Member:
Olympia J Snowe (R-ME)............................202-224-5344

Private Sector

1199 SEIU United Healthcare Workers East
310 W 43rd St, New York, NY 10036
212-261-2222 Fax: 212-956-5140
Web site: www.1199seiuonline.org
Dennis Rivera, President
Representing New York State healthcare workers

Abilities Inc, National Center for Disability Services
201 IU Willets Rd, Albertson, NY 11507-1599
516-465-1400 or 516-747-5355 (TTY) Fax: 516-465-3757
e-mail: ftishman@abilitiesinc.org
Web site: www.abilitiesinc.org
Charles W Hunt, Executive Director
Provides comprehensive services to help individuals with disabilities reach their employment goals; provides support services & technical assistance to employers who hire persons with disabilities

Offices and agencies generally appear in alphabetical order, except when specific order is requested by listee.

LABOR & EMPLOYMENT PRACTICES / Private Sector

American Federation of Teachers
555 New Jersey Ave NW, Washington, DC 20001
800-238-1133 Fax: 202-393-7479
e-mail: emcelroy@aft.org
Web site: www.aft.org
Edward J McElroy, President

Associated Builders & Contractors, Construction Training Center of NYS
6369 Collamer Drive, East Syracuse, NY 13057-1115
315-463-7539 or 800-477-7743 Fax: 315-463-7621
e-mail: info@abc.org
Web site: www.abc.org/newyork
Thomas Schlueter, Vice President of Education Programs
Merit shop construction trades apprenticeship program

Blitman & King LLP
443 N Franklin St, Ste 300, Syracuse, NY 13204
315-422-7111 Fax: 315-471-2623
e-mail: btking@bklawyers.com
Web site: www.bklawyers.com
Bernard T King, Attorney/Senior Partner
Labor & employee benefits

Center for an Urban Future
120 Wall St, 20th Fl, New York, NY 10005
212-479-3319 Fax: 212-479-3338
e-mail: cuf@nycfuture.org
Web site: www.nycfuture.org
Johnathan Bowles, Director
Policy institute dedicated to aggressively pursuing solutions to critical problems facing cities

Civil Service Employees Union (CSEA), Local 1000, AFSCME, AFL-CIO
143 Washington Ave, Capitol Station Box 7125, Albany, NY 12210-0125
518-257-1000 or 800-342-4146 Fax: 518-462-3639
Web site: www.csealocal1000.org
Danny Donohue, President
Public/private employees union

Communications Workers of America, District 1
80 Pine St, 37th Floor, New York, NY 10005
212-344-2515 Fax: 212-425-2947
Web site: www.cwa-union.org
Christopher Shelton, Vice President

Cornell University, Institute on Conflict Resolution
621 Ives Hall, Ithaca, NY 14853-3901
607-255-5378 Fax: 607-255-6974
e-mail: dbl4@cornell.edu
Web site: www.ilr.cornell.edu
David Lipsky, Professor Collective Bargaining & Director
Collective bargaining; dispute resolution, negotiation

Cornell University, Sch of Industr & Labor Relations Institute for Workplace Studies
16 E 34th Street, 4th Fl, New York, NY 10016
212-340-2850 Fax: 212-340-2893
e-mail: sb22@cornell.edu
Web site: www.ilr.cornell.edu/iws
Samuel B Bacharach, McKelvey-Grant Professor & Director
Substance abuse in the workplace; power & bargaining in organizations

Cornell University, School of Industrial & Labor Relations
Ives Hall, Ithaca, NY 14853-3901
607-255-4375 or 607-255-2223 Fax: 607-255-1836
e-mail: vmb2@cornell.edu
Web site: www.ilr.cornell.edu
Vernon Briggs, Professor
Immigration policy; labor market trends & analysis

Cornell University, School of Industrial & Labor Relations
356 ILR Research Bldg, Ithaca, NY 14853-3901
607-255-7581 Fax: 607-255-0245
e-mail: klb23@cornell.edu
Web site: www.ilr.cornell.edu
Kate Bronfenbrenner, Director, Labor Education Research
Public sector organizations; leadership; temporary & contract workers; union organizing; & collective bargaining

Cornell University, School of Industrial & Labor Relations
340 ILR Research Bldg, Ithaca, NY 14853-3901
607-255-2765 Fax: 607-255-2513
e-mail: rwh8@cornell.edu
Web site: www.ilr.cornell.edu
Richard Hurd, Professor Industrial & Labor Relations
Trade union administration & strategy

Cullen & Dykman LLP
100 Quentin Roosevelt Blvd, Garden City Ctr, Garden City, NY 11530-4850
516-357-3703 Fax: 516-296-9155
e-mail: gfishberg@cullenanddykman.com
Web site: www.cullenanddykman.com
Gerard Fishberg, Partner
Municipal & labor law

Empire State Regional Council of Carpenters
1284 Central Avenue, Ste 1, Albany, NY 12205
518-459-7182 Fax: 518-459-7798
e-mail: kevinrhicks@usa.com
Kevin R Hicks, Political & Legislative Director & Region 3 Director

JAMS
45 Broadway, 28th Floor, New York, NY 10006
212-751-2700 Fax: 212-751-4099
Web site: www.jamsadr.com
Carol Wittenberg, Arbitrator/Mediator
Mediation of civil, commercial & employment disputes: training & systems design

Offices and agencies generally appear in alphabetical order, except when specific order is requested by listee.

LABOR & EMPLOYMENT PRACTICES / Private Sector

Kaye Scholer LLP
425 Park Ave, 8th Fl, New York, NY 10022
212-836-8558 Fax: 212-836-6458
e-mail: jwaks@kayescholer.com
Web site: www.kayescholer.com
Jay W Waks, Partner
Chair, Labor & Employment Law Group (representing employers)

NYS Bar Assn, Labor & Employment Law Section
Kraus & Zuchlewski LLP
500 Fifth Ave, Ste 5100, New York, NY 10110
212-869-4646 Fax: 212-869-4648
e-mail: pz@goodznyc.com
Pearl Zuchlewski, Chair

Lancer Insurance Co/Lancer Compliance Services
370 West Park Ave, Long Beach, NY 11561-3245
516-432-5000 Fax: 516-431-0926
e-mail: bcrescenzo@lancer-ins.com
Bob Crescenzo, Vice President
Substance abuse management & testing services for the transportation industry

MDRC
16 East 34th St, 19th Floor, New York, NY 10016-5936
212-532-3200 Fax: 212-684-0832
e-mail: information@mdrc.org
Web site: www.mdrc.org
Gordon Berlin, President
Nonprofit research & field testing of education & employment programs for disadvantaged adults & youth

Manhattan-Bronx Minority Business Enterprise Center
225 W 34th St, Ste 2007, New York, NY 10122
212-947-5351 or 212-947-4900 Fax: 212-947-1506
e-mail: mbmbdc@manhattanmbec.com
Web site: www.manhattanmbec.com
Lorraine Kelsey, Executive Director
Information & advocacy for local employment & business & contract opportunities

NY Association of Training & Employment Professionals (NYATEP)
175 Central Avenue, 3rd Floor, Albany, NY 12206
518-433-1200 Fax: 518-433-7424
e-mail: jtwomey@nyatep.org
Web site: www.nyatep.org
John Twomey, Executive Director
Represent local workforce development partnerships

NYS Building & Construction Trades Council
71 West 23 St, New York, NY 10010
212-647-0700 Fax: 212-647-0705
Edward J Malloy, President

NYS Industries for the Disabled (NYSID) Inc
155 Washington Ave, Ste 400, Albany, NY 12210-2329
518-463-9706 or 800-221-5994 Fax: 518-463-9708
e-mail: administrator@nysid.org
Web site: www.nysid.org
Lawrence L Barker, Jr, President & Chief Executive Officer
Business development through 'preferred source' purchasing to increase employment opportunities for people with disabilities

National Federation of Independent Business
1 Commerce Plaza, Ste 1119, Albany, NY 12260-1000
518-434-1262 Fax: 518-426-8799
e-mail: mike.elmendorf@nfib.org
Web site: www.nfib.org
Michael Elmendorf, State Director
Small business advocacy; supporting pro-small business candidates at the state & federal levels

National Writers Union
113 University Pl, 6th Fl, New York, NY 10003
212-254-0279 Fax: 212-254-0673
e-mail: nwu@nwu.org
Web site: www.nwu.org
Gerard Colby, President

New York Committee for Occupational Safety & Health
116 John St, Ste 604, New York, NY 10038
212-227-6440 Fax: 212-227-9854
e-mail: nycosh@nycosh.org
Web site: www.nycosh.org
Joel Shufro, Executive Director
Provide occupational safety & health training & technical assistance

New York State Nurses Association
11 Cornell Rd, Latham, NY 12110
518-782-9400 x279 Fax: 518-783-5207
e-mail: executive@nysna.org
Web site: www.nysna.org
Labor union & professional association for registered nurses

New York University, Graduate School of Journalism
20 Cooper Square, 6th Floor, New York, NY 10003
212-998-7980 Fax: 212-995-4148
Web site: www.nyu.edu/gsas/dept/journal
Bill Serrin, Director, Graduate Studies
Labor issues & reporting

Osborne Association
809 Westchester Avenue, Bronx, NY 10455
718-707-2600 or 718-842-0500 Fax: 718-707-3102
e-mail: info@osborneny.org
Web site: www.osborneny.org
Elizabeth A Gaynes, Director of Employment & Training
Career/educational counseling, job referrals & training for recently released prisoners, substance abuse treatment, case management, HIV/AIDS counseling & prevention, family services, parenting education, re-entry services, housing placement assistan

Offices and agencies generally appear in alphabetical order, except when specific order is requested by listee.

LABOR & EMPLOYMENT PRACTICES / Private Sector

Public/Private Ventures
The Chanin Building, 122 East 42nd St, 42nd Fl, New York, NY 10168
212-822-2400 Fax: 212-949-0439
e-mail: melliott@ppv.org
Web site: www.ppv.org
Mark Elliott, Executive Vice President
Action-based research, public policy & program development organization

Realty Advisory Board on Labor Relations
292 Madison Ave, New York, NY 10017
212-889-4100 Fax: 212-889-4105
e-mail: jberg@rabolr.com
Web site: www.rabolr.com
James Berg, President
Labor negotiations for realtors & realty firms

Transport Workers Union of America, AFL-CIO
1700 Broadway, 2nd Fl, New York, NY 10019
212-259-4900 Fax: 212-265-5704
Web site: www.twu.com
James C Little, International President
Bus, train, railroad & airline workers' union

UNITE HERE
275 7th Ave, Fl 11, New York, NY 10001-6708
212-265-7000 Fax: 212-765-7751
e-mail: brayor@unitehere.org
Web site: www.uniteunion.org
Bruce Raynor, General President

United Food & Commercial Workers Local 1
5911 Airport Road, Oriskany, NY 13424
315-797-9600 or 800-697-8329 Fax: 315-793-1182
e-mail: organize@ufcwone.org
Web site: www.ufcwone.org
Frank C DeRiso, President

Vedder Price Kaufman & Kammholz PC
1633 Broadway, New York, NY 10019
212-407-7750 or 917-214-6441 Fax: 212-407-7799
e-mail: akoral@vedderprice.com
Web site: www.vedderprice.com
Alan M Koral, Shareholder
Employment law

Vladeck, Waldman, Elias & Engelhard PC
1501 Broadway, Suite 800, New York, NY 10036
212-403-7300 Fax: 212-221-3172
e-mail: jvladeck@vladeck.com
Judith Vladeck, Senior Law Partner
Employment law, including discrimination cases

Offices and agencies generally appear in alphabetical order, except when specific order is requested by listee.

MENTAL HYGIENE

New York State

GOVERNOR'S OFFICE

Governor's Office
Executive Chamber
State Capitol
Albany, NY 12224
518-474-8390 Fax: 518-474-1513
Web site: www.state.ny.us

Governor:
  Eliot Spitzer 518-474-8390
Secretary to the Governor:
  Richard Baum 518-474-4246
Counsel to the Governor:
  David Nocenti 518-474-8343
Senior Advisor to the Governor:
  Lloyd Constantine 518-486-9671
Deputy Secretary, Health & Human Services:
  Dennis Whalen 518-408-2500
Assistant Counsel to the Governor-Health & Mental Hygiene:
  Lisa Ullman 518-474-2266
Director, Communications:
  Darren Dopp 518-474-8418

EXECUTIVE DEPARTMENTS AND RELATED AGENCIES

Alcoholism & Substance Abuse Services, Office of
1450 Western Ave
Albany, NY 12203
518-485-1660 Fax: 518-457-5474
Web site: www.oasas.state.ny.us

501 7th Ave
8th Fl
New York, NY 10018
646-728-4533

Commissioner:
  Karen M Carpenter-Palumbo 518-457-1758
Executive Deputy Commissioner:
  Kathleen Caggiano-Siino 518-485-2312
Director, Communications:
  Jennifer Farrell 518-485-1768/fax: 518-485-6014
  e-mail: jenniferfarrell@oasas.state.ny.us
Director, Human Resources Management:
  Thomas M Torino 518-457-2963
Director, Internal Audit:
  Richard Kaplan 518-485-2039
Affirmative Action Officer:
  Henry Gonzalez 518-457-2963

Public Information Officer:
  Joseph Morrissey 518-485-1768
  e-mail: josephmorrissey@oasas.state.ny.us

Financial, Capital & Information Tech Management Division
Associate Commissioner:
  Michael Lawler 518-457-5312
  e-mail: michaellawler@oasas.state.ny.us

Bureau of Budget Management
Director:
  Jay Runkel 518-485-2193

Bureau of Capital Management
Director:
  Laurie Felter 518-457-2545

Bureau of Financial & Emergency Management
Director:
  Vito Manzella 518-457-4742

Bureau of Health Care Financing & 3rd Party Reimbursement
Director:
  Nicholas Colamaria 518-485-2207

Bureau of Information Technology
Director:
  David Gardam 518-485-2351

Legal Affairs Division
Associate Commsioner:
  Henry F Zwack 518-485-2312

Bureau of Counsel
Director:
  Dick Hogle 518-485-2317

Bureau of Governmental & NYC Affairs
Director:
  Jeff Cleary 518-485-2337

Bureau of Certification
Director:
  Virginia Martin 518-485-2247

Bureau of Enforcement
Director:
  Charles Monson 518-485-2312

Management Resources & Quality Assurance Division
Associate Commissioner:
  Neil Grogin 518-485-2257
Client Advocacy:
  Michael Yorio 800-553-5790

Bureau of Quality Assurance
Director:
  William Lachanski 518-485-2260
Training/Technical Assistance:
  Steve Therriault 518-485-2027
Training/Technical Assistance:
  Joseph Chelales 646-728-4644

Offices and agencies generally appear in alphabetical order, except when specific order is requested by listee.

MENTAL HYGIENE / New York State

Bureau of Workforce Development
Director:
Joseph Burke 518-485-2033

Prevention & Treatment Services Division
Associate Commissioner:
Frances M Harding 518-485-6022

Bureau of Prevention
Director:
John Ernst 518-485-2132

Bureau of ATCs
Director:
Thomas Nightingale 518-457-7077

Bureau of Treatment
Director:
Rob Piculell 518-485-2123

Bureau of Systems Development & Public Education
Director:
William Barnette 518-457-6206

Systems/Program Performance & Analysis Division
Acting Associate Commissioner:
Timothy P Williams 518-485-2322

Bureau of Planning & Practice Improvement
Acting Associate Commissioner:
Bob Gallati 518-457-5989

Bureau of Evaluation & Practice Improvement
Director:
Alan Kott 518-485-7189

Bureau of Statewide Field Operations
Director:
Edward Freeman 518-457-8240

Developmental Disabilities Planning Council
155 Washington Ave
2nd Fl
Albany, NY 12210
518-486-7505 or 800-395-3372   Fax: 518-402-3505
Web site: www.ddpc.state.ny.us

Chairperson:
George E Fertal Sr 518-486-7505
Vice Chairperson:
Rose Marie Toscano 518-486-7505
Executive Director:
Sheila M Carey 518-486-7505
Deputy Executive Director:
Anna Lobosco 518-486-7505
  e-mail: alobosco@ddpc.state.ny.us
Public Information Officer:
Thomas F Lee 518-486-7505
  e-mail: tlee@ddpc.state.ny.us

Education Department
State Education Bldg
89 Washington Ave
Albany, NY 12234
518-474-5215   Fax: 518-486-5631
Web site: www.nysed.gov

Commissioner, University President:
Richard P Mills 518-474-5844
  e-mail: rmills@mail.nysed.gov
Assistant to the Commissioner:
Peggy Rivers 518-474-5845
  e-mail: privers@mail.nysed.gov
Counsel & Deputy Commissioner, Legal Affairs:
Kathy A Ahearn 518-474-6400
  e-mail: kahearn@mail.nysed.gov
Chief of Staff & Deputy Commissioner, Innovation:
David Miller 518-486-1713
  e-mail: dmiller@mail.nysed.gov

Office of the Professions . . . . fax: 518-474-3863
89 Washington Ave, EB, 2nd Fl, West Mezz, Albany, NY 12234
Fax: 518-474-3863
Web site: www.op.nysed.gov
Associate Commissioner:
Frank Munoz 518-474-3817 x440
  e-mail: opopr@mail.nysed.gov
Executive Coordinator, Professional Practice:
Anthony Lofrumento 518-474-3817 x570
  e-mail: op4info@mail.nysed.gov

Office of Professional Responsibility
Executive Director:
Vacant 518-474-3817 x440
  e-mail: opexdir@mail.nysed.gov

Professional Education Program Review
Supervisor:
Vacant 518-474-3817 x360
  e-mail: opprogs@mail.nysed.gov

Professional Licensing Services
Director:
Anthony Lofrumento 518-474-3817 x340
  e-mail: opdpls@mail.nysed.gov

Vocational & Educational Services for Individuals With Disabilities Office (VESID) . . . . fax: 518-474-8802
One Commerce Plz, Rm 1606, Albany, NY 12234
Fax: 518-474-8802
Web site: www.vesid.nysed.gov
Deputy Commissioner:
Rebecca Cort 518-474-2714
  e-mail: rcort@mail.nysed.gov
Asst Commissioner:
Edward Placke 518-473-4818

Fiscal & Administrative Services
Coordinator:
Rosemary Ellis Johnson 518-486-4038

Program Develpmnt & Support Svcs/Special Ed Policy & Ptshps
Coordinator:
Vacant 518-486-7462

Quality Assurance - Statewide Special Education
Statewide Coordinator:
James DeLorenzo 518-402-3353

State School for the Blind at Batavia
2A Richmond Ave, Batavia, NY 14020
Acting Superintendent:
James Knowles 585-343-5384

Vocational Rehabilitation Operations
Acting Director, District Office Administration:
Debora Brown-Grant 518-473-1626
  e-mail: dbrowngr@mail.nysed.gov

Offices and agencies generally appear in alphabetical order, except when specific order is requested by listee.

MENTAL HYGIENE / New York State

Asst Director, District Office Administration:
Richard Strohl 518-486-4035
e-mail: rstrohl@mail.nysed.gov

Mental Health, Office of
44 Holland Ave
Albany, NY 12229
518-474-4403 Fax: 518-474-2149
Web site: www.omh.state.ny.us

Commissioner:
Michael F Hogan, PhD 518-474-4403
Executive Deputy Commissioner:
Vacant 518-474-7056/fax: 518-402-2361
Medical Director:
Lloyd I Sederer, MD 518-486-4302/fax: 518-474-8469
Deputy Commissioner & Counsel:
John V Tauriello 518-474-1331/fax: 518-473-7863
Investigation & Audit:
Vacant 518-473-5940

Division of Adult Services
Senior Deputy Commissioner:
Robert Myers 518-474-5222/fax: 518-473-7926
Senior Associate Commissioner:
Al Holmes 518-474-4447

Division of Children and Family Services
Deputy Commissioner:
David Woodlock 518-473-6328/fax: 518-473-4690

Center for Human Resource Management
Director:
Deborah Wagoner 518-474-7952/fax: 518-402-4086

Center for Information Technology & Evaluation Research
Senior Deputy Commissioner/Division Director:
Chip J Felton 518-474-7359/fax: 518-473-2778

Division of Forensic Services
Associate Commissioner:
Richard Miraglia 518-474-7219/fax: 518-473-4098

Facilities

Bronx Children's Psychiatric Center
1000 Waters Place, Bronx, NY 10461-2799
Executive Director:
Mark Bienstock 718-239-3600/fax: 718-862-3669

Bronx Psychiatric Center
1500 Waters Place, Bronx, NY 10461-2796
Executive Director:
LeRoy Carmichael 718-862-3300/fax: 718-826-4858

Brooklyn Children's Center
1819 Bergen St, Brooklyn, NY 11233
Acting Executive Director:
Diane Aman 718-221-4500/fax: 718-221-4581

Buffalo Psychiatric Center
400 Forest Ave, Buffalo, NY 14213-1298
Executive Director:
Thomas Dodson 716-885-2261/fax: 716-885-4852

Capital District Psychiatric Center
75 New Scotland Ave, Albany, NY 12208-3474
Executive Director:
Lew Campbell 518-447-9611/fax: 518-434-0041

Central New York Psychiatric Center
PO Box 300, Marcy, NY 13404-0300
Executive Director:
Donald Sawyer 315-765-3600/fax: 315-765-3629

Creedmoor Psychiatric Center
80-45 Winchester Blvd, Queens Village, NY 11427-2199
Executive Director:
Kathleen Iverson 718-464-7500/fax: 718-264-3636

Elmira Psychiatric Center
100 Washington St, Elmira, NY 14902-1527
Executive Director:
William L Benedict 607-737-4711/fax: 607-737-9080

Greater Binghamton Health Center
425 Robinson St, Binghamton, NY 13904-1775
Executive Director:
Margaret Dugan 607-724-1391/fax: 607-773-4387

Hudson River Psychiatric Center
10 Ross Cir, Poughkeepsie, NY 12601-1197
Executive Director:
Jean L Wolfersteig 845-452-8000/fax: 845-452-8040

Hutchings Psychiatric Center
620 Madison St, Syracuse, NY 13210-2319
Executive Director:
Colleen Zackoski 315-426-3600/fax: 315-426-3603

Kingsboro Psychiatric Center
681 Clarkson Ave, Brooklyn, NY 11203-2199
Acting Executive Director:
Martin Darcy 718-221-7700/fax: 718-221-7206

Kirby Forensic Psychiatric Center
600 East 125th St, Wards Island, NY 10035
Acting Executive Director:
Stephen Rabinowitz 646-672-5800/fax: 646-672-6893

Manhattan Psychiatric Center
600 East 125th St, Wards Island, NY 10035-6098
Acting Executive Director:
Stephen Rabinowitz 646-672-6000/fax: 646-672-6446

Mid-Hudson Forensic Psychiatric Center
Box 158, Route 17-M, New Hampton, NY 10958
Executive Director:
Howard Holanchock 845-374-3171/fax: 845-374-3961

Mohawk Valley Psychiatric Center
1400 Noyes St, Utica, NY 13502-3082
Executive Director:
Maureen Ruben 315-738-3800/fax: 315-738-4412

Nathan S Kline Institute for Psychiatric Research
140 Old Orangeburg Rd, Orangeburg, NY 10952-1197
Executive Director:
Harold S Koplewicz, MD 845-398-5500/fax: 845-398-5510

New York Psychiatric Institute
1051 Riverside Dr, New York, NY 10032-2695
Director:
Jeffrey A Lieberman, MD 212-543-5000/fax: 212-543-6012

Pilgrim Psychiatric Center
998 Crooked Hill Rd, West Brentwood, NY 11717-1087
Executive Director:
Dean Weinstock 631-761-3500/fax: 631-761-2600

Queens Children's Psychiatric Center
74-03 Commonwealth Blvd, Bellerose, NY 11426-1890
Executive Director:
Keith Little 718-264-4500/fax: 718-740-0968

Offices and agencies generally appear in alphabetical order, except when specific order is requested by listee.

MENTAL HYGIENE / New York State

Rochester Psychiatric Center
1111 Elmwood Ave, Rochester, NY 14620-3972
Executive Director:
  Michael P Zuber 585-241-1200/fax: 585-241-1424

Rockland Children's Psychiatric Center
599 Convent Rd, Orangeburg, NY 10962-1199
Executive Director:
  Raul Silva, MD 845-680-4040/fax: 845-680-8905

Rockland Psychiatric Center
140 Old Orangeburg Rd, Orangeburg, NY 10962-1196
Executive Director:
  James Bopp 845-359-1000/fax: 845-359-1744

Sagamore Children's Psychiatric Center
197 Half Hollow Rd, Dix Hills, NY 11746
Executive Director:
  Dennis Dubey, PhD 631-370-1700/fax: 631-370-1714

South Beach Psychiatric Center
777 Seaview Ave, Staten Island, NY 10305-3499
Executive Director:
  William F Henri 718-667-2300/fax: 718-667-2344

St Lawrence Psychiatric Center
1 Chimney Point Dr, Ogdensburg, NY 13669-2291
Executive Director:
  Sam Bastien 315-541-2001/fax: 315-541-2041

Western New York Children's Psychiatric Center
1010 East & West Rd, West Seneca, NY 14224-3699
Acting Executive Director:
  Kathe Hayes 716-674-9730/fax: 716-675-6455

Office of Consumer Affairs
Director, Recipient Affairs:
  John Allen 518-473-6579
Coordinator, Cultural Competence:
  Cathy Cave 518-408-2026

Office of Financial Management
Deputy Commissioner:
  Martha J Schaefer Hayes 518-474-3631/fax: 518-473-4690

Office of Public Affairs and Planning
Deputy Commissioner:
  Keith E Simons 518-473-7612/fax: 518-473-4690
Acting Director, Public Affairs:
  Jill Daniels 518-474-6540/fax: 518-473-3456

Office of Quality Management
Division Director:
  Jayne Van Bramer 518-474-6587/fax: 518-474-8998

Mental Retardation & Developmental Disabilities, Office of
44 Holland Ave
Albany, NY 12229
866-946-9733 or TTY: 866-933-4889 Fax: 518-474-1335
e-mail: public.affairs@omr.state.ny.us
Web site: www.omr.state.ny.us

Commissioner:
  Diana Jones Ritter 518-473-1997
Special Asst to the Commissioner:
  Tracy Durfee 518-473-1997
Executive Deputy Commissioner:
  Max Chmura 518-474-8115
General Counsel:
  Patricia Martinelli, Esq 518-474-7700
Deputy Commissioner, Admin & Revenue Support:
  James F Moran 518-473-2747
Associate Commissioner, Upstate Support:
  Michael Gatens 518-474-9897
Director, Policy & Planning:
  Gary R Lind 518-473-9697
Director, Public Affairs:
  Deborah Sturm Rausch 518-474-6601
Director, Intergovernmental & Legislative Affairs:
  Carl Letson 518-473-8084
Affirmative Action Administrator:
  Dolores Lark 518-473-8084
Director, Internal Audit:
  James Nelligar 518-474-4376

New York City Regional Office
75 Morton St, New York, NY 10014
Associate Commissioner:
  Kathleen M Broderick 212-229-3231/fax: 212-229-3234

Information Support Services
Balltown & Consaul Roads, Schenectady, NY 12304
Director:
  Robert Vasko 518-381-2110

Developmental Disabilities Services Offices

Bernard Fineson Developmental Disabilities Services Office
Hillside Complex Bldg 12, 80-45 Winchester Blvd, Queens Vlg, NY 11427
Director:
  Frank Parisi 718-217-4242/fax: 718-217-4724

Brooklyn Developmental Disabilities Services Office
888 Fountain Ave, Brooklyn, NY 11208
Director:
  Peter Uschakow 718-642-6000/fax: 718-642-6282
Director:
  Patricia McDonnell 607-770-0211/fax: 607-770-8037

Capital District Developmental Disabilities Services Office
Balltown & Consaul Rds, Schenectady, NY 12304
Director:
  David Slingerland 518-370-7370/fax: 518-370-7401

Central New York Developmental Disabilities Services Office
101 W Liberty St, Box 550, Rome, NY 13442
Director:
  Stephen M Smits 315-336-2300/fax: 315-339-5456

Finger Lakes Developmental Disabilities Services Office
620 Westfall Rd, Rochester, NY 14620
Director:
  James Whitehead 585-461-8500/fax: 585-461-0618

Hudson Valley Developmental Disabilities Services Office
Admin Bldg, 2 Ridge Rd, PO Box 470, Thiells, NY 10984
Director:
  Janet Wheeler 845-947-6000/fax: 845-947-6004

Long Island Developmental Disabilities Services Office
45 Mall Dr, Ste 1, Commack, NY 11725
Interim Director:
  Irene McGinn 631-493-1700/fax: 631-493-1803

Metro New York Developmental Disabilities Services Office
75 Morton St, New York, NY 10014
Director:
  Hugh D Tarpley 212-229-3000/fax: 212-924-0580

Offices and agencies generally appear in alphabetical order, except when specific order is requested by listee.

MENTAL HYGIENE / New York State

Staten Island Developmental Disabilities Services Office
1150 Forest Hill Rd, Staten Island, NY 10314
Director:
David Booth 718-983-5200/fax: 718-983-9768

Sunmount Developmental Disabilities Services Office
2445 State Rte 30, Tupper Lake, NY 12986-2502
Director:
Joseph Colarusso 518-359-3311/fax: 518-359-2276

Taconic Developmental Disabilities Services Office
26 Center Circle, Wassaic, NY 12592
Director:
John Mizerak 845-877-6821/fax: 845-877-9177

Valley Ridge Developmental Disabilities Services Office
19 Eaton Ave, Norwich, NY 13815
Interim Director:
Charles Kearley 607-337-7000

Western New York Developmental Disabilities Services Office
1200 East & West Rd, West Seneca, NY 14224
Director:
Bruce Korotkin 716-674-6300/fax: 716-674-7488

Institute for Basic Research in Developmental Disabilities
1050 Forest Hill Rd, Staten Island, NY 10314
Director:
W Ted Brown 718-494-0600/fax: 718-698-3803

JUDICIAL SYSTEM AND RELATED AGENCIES

Mental Hygiene Legal Service

1st Judicial Dept . . . . fax: 212-779-1894
60 Madison Ave, 2nd Fl, New York, NY 10010
Director:
Marvin Bernstein 212-779-1734

2nd Judicial Dept
170 Old Country Rd, Rm 500, Mineola, NY 11501
Director:
Sidney Hirschfeld 516-746-4545/fax: 516-746-4372

3rd Judicial Dept
40 Steuben St, Ste 501, Albany, NY 12207-2109
Web site: www.courts.state.ny.us/ad3/mhls/
Acting Director:
David M LeVine 518-474-4453/fax: 518-473-5849

4th Judicial Dept
50 East Ave, Ste 402, Rochester, NY 14604
Web site: www.courts.state.ny.us/ad4/mhls/
Director:
Emmett J Creahan 585-530-3050
Deputy Director:
Neil J Rowe 585-530-3050/fax: 585-530-3079

CORPORATIONS, AUTHORITIES AND COMMISSIONS

NYS Commission on Quality of Care & Advocacy for Persons with Disabilities
1 Empire State Plaza
Ste 1001
Albany, NY 12223-1150
800-624-4143 or 800-522-4369 Fax: 518-388-2800
Web site: www.cqcapd.state.ny.us

Chair:
Gary O'Brien 518-388-1281
Commissioner:
Patricia Okoniewski 518-388-1281
Commissioner:
Bruce G Blower 518-388-1281
Executive Assistant:
Mindy Becker 518-388-1281
Press Officer:
Gary W Masline 518-388-1270/fax: 518-388-1275

Administrative Services Bureau
Director:
Richard H Schaefer 518-388-2804

Advisory Council
Chair:
Vacant 518-388-1270

Advocacy Services Bureau
Director:
Marcel Chaine 518-388-2892

Counsel/Policy Analysis/Fiscal Investigations
Counsel/Director:
Robert J Bochlert 518-388-2835

Medical Review Board
Executive Secretary:
Thomas Harmon 518-388-1281

Quality Assurance
Director:
Mark Keegan 518-388-2888

Surrogate Decision-Making Committees Program
Program Director:
Thomas Fisher 518-388-2820

NEW YORK STATE LEGISLATURE

See Legislative Branch in Section 1 for additional Standing Committee and Subcommittee information.

Assembly Standing Committees

Alcoholism & Drug Abuse
Chair:
Jeffrey Dinowitz (D) 518-455-5965
Ranking Minority Member:
Gary D Finch (R) 518-455-5878

Offices and agencies generally appear in alphabetical order, except when specific order is requested by listee.

MENTAL HYGIENE / Private Sector

Mental Health
Chair:
  Peter M Rivera (D) 518-455-5102
Ranking Minority Member:
  Tom McKevitt (R) 518-455-5341

Senate Standing Committees

Mental Health & Developmental Disabilities
Chair:
  Thomas P Morahan (R) 518-455-3261
Ranking Minority Member:
  Ruben Diaz, Sr (D) 518-455-2511

Senate/Assembly Legislative Commissions

Health Care Financing, Council on
Senate Chair:
  Joseph L Bruno (R) 518-455-3191
Assembly Vice Chair:
  Vacant 518-455-0000
Executive Director:
  Al Cardillo 518-455-2067/fax: 518-426-6925

Private Sector

AIM Services Inc
3257 Route 9, Saratoga Springs, NY 12866
518-587-3208 Fax: 518-587-7236
e-mail: aimservices@aimservicesinc.org
Web site: www.aimservicesinc.org
Charlene Endal, Executive Director
Residential & home-based services for individuals with developmental disabilities & traumatic brain injuries

AMAC, Association for Metroarea Autistic Children
25 W 17th St, New York, NY 10011
212-645-5005 Fax: 212-645-0170
e-mail: rica@amac.org
Web site: www.amac.org
Frederica Blausten, Executive Director
Providing lifelong services to austistic & special needs children & adults; specializing in applied behavior analysis (ABA) methodology; serving ages 2 years to adults, schools, camps, group homes

Association for Addiction Professionals of New York
PO Box 4053, Albany, NY 12204
877-862-2769 Fax: 585-394-1111
e-mail: info@appnycounselor.com
Web site: www.aapnycounselor.com
Ferd Haverly, President
Alcohol & chemical dependency counselor organization; addiction treatment & prevention

Association for Community Living
632 Plank Road, Suite 110, Clifton Park, NY 12065
518-688-1682 Fax: 518-688-1686
e-mail: info@aclnys.org
Web site: www.aclnys.org
Antonia Lasicki, Director
Membership organization for agencies that provide housing & rehab services to individuals diagnosed with serious mental illness

Association for Eating Disorders - Capital Region
PO Box 3123, Saratoga Springs, NY 12866
518-464-9043
e-mail: CRAEDOffice@GMail.com
Web site: www.craed.org
William Friske, Treasurer
Support & referral services, wellness programs & education for recovering individuals, parents & health professionals

Association for the Help of Retarded Children/AHRC
83 Maiden Lane, New York, NY 10038
212-780-2500 or 212-780-2692 Fax: 212-780-2353
e-mail: webmaster@ahrcnyc.org
Web site: www.ahrcnyc.org
Michael Goldfarb, Executive Director
Also known as the NYS Chapter of NYSARC, Inc. Social services, advocacy & public information on developmental disabilities

Brain Injury Association of NYS (BIANYS)
10 Colvin Ave, Albany, NY 12206
518-459-7911 Fax: 518-482-5285
e-mail: info@bianys.org
Web site: www.bianys.org
Judith I Avner, Executive Director
Public education & advocacy for persons with brain injury & their families

Cerebral Palsy Associations of New York State
330 W 34th Street, New York, NY 10001
212-947-5770 x201 Fax: 212-356-0746
e-mail: sconstantino@cpofnys.org
Web site: www.cpofnys.org
Susan Constantino, President & CEO
Advocate and provide direct services with and for individuals with cerebral palsy and other significant disabilities and their families

Children's Village (The)
Echo Hills, Dobbs Ferry, NY 10522
914-693-0600 x1201 Fax: 914-674-9208
e-mail: jkohomban@childrensvillage.org
Web site: www.childrensvillage.org
Jeremy Kohomban, PhD, President & Chief Executive Officer
Residential school, located 20 minutes outside of NYC. Treatment & prevention of behavioral problems for youth; residential &

Offices and agencies generally appear in alphabetical order, except when specific order is requested by listee.

MENTAL HYGIENE / Private Sector

community-based services; mental health, education, employment & runaway shelter services

Coalition of Behavioral Health Agencies, Inc (The)
90 Broad St, New York, NY 10004-2205
212-742-1600 x115 Fax: 212-742-2080
e-mail: mailbox@coalitionny.org
Web site: www.coalitionny.org
Phillip Saperia, Executive Director
Advocacy organization representing over 100 nonprofit, community-based mental health agencies in NYC

Committee of Methadone Program Administrators Inc of NYS (COMPA)
1 Columbus Place, 4th Fl, Albany, NY 12207
518-689-0457 Fax: 518-426-1046
e-mail: compahb@hotmail.com
Web site: www.compa-ny.org
Henry Bartlett, Executive Director
Methadone treatment & substance abuse coalition building; advocacy, community education, standards & regulatory review & policy development

Families Together in NYS Inc
737 Madison Avenue, Albany, NY 12208
518-432-0333 x20 or 888-326-8644 (referr Fax: 518-434-6478
e-mail: info@ftnys.org
Web site: www.ftnys.org
Paige Pierce, Executive Director
Advocacy for families with children having special social, emotional & behavioral needs; working to improve services & support for children & families

Federation Employment & Guidance Service (FEGS) Inc
315 Hudson St, 9th Fl, New York, NY 10013
212-366-8400 Fax: 212-366-8441
e-mail: info@fegs.org
Web site: www.fegs.org
Jonas Waizer, PhD, Chief Executive Officer
Diversified health & human services system to help individuals achieve their potential at work, at home, at school and in the community

Federation of Organizations Inc
One Farmingdale Road, Route 109, West Babylon, NY 11704-6207
631-669-5355 Fax: 631-669-1114
e-mail: bfaron@fedoforg.org
Web site: www.fedoforg.org
Barbara Faron, Executive Director
Social welfare agency with programs in mental health & aging

InterAgency Council of Mental Retardatn & Developmental Disabilities
150 W 30th Street, 15th Floor, New York, NY 10001
212-645-6360 Fax: 212-627-8847
e-mail: mames@iacny.org
Web site: www.iacny.org
Margery E Ames, Executive Director

Jewish Board of Family & Children's Services
120 W 57th St, New York, NY 10019
212-582-9100 or 888-523-2769 Fax: 212-956-5676
e-mail: asiskind@jbfcs.org
Web site: www.jbfcs.org
Alan B Siskind, PhD, Executive Vice President & Chief Executive Officer
Mental health services/human services

Lesbian, Gay, Bisexual & Transgender Community Ctr - Not For Profit
208 W 13th St, New York, NY 10011-7702
212-620-7310 Fax: 212-924-2657
e-mail: enealy@gaycenter.org
Web site: www.gaycenter.org
Miriam Yeung, Director, Public Policy
Mental health counseling, out-patient chemical dependency treatment center, after-school youth services, HIV/AIDS services, advocacy, culutral programs, affordable meeting and conference services, and community-building.

Lifespire
350 5th Ave, Ste 301, New York, NY 10118-0301
212-741-0100 Fax: 212-242-0696
e-mail: info@lifespire.org
Web site: www.lifespire.org
Mark Vanvoorst, Executive Director
Services for adults with developmental disabilites throughout the five boroughs of New York City

Mental Health Association of NYC Inc
666 Broadway, Ste 200, New York, NY 10012
212-254-0333 x307 Fax: 212-529-1959
e-mail: helpdesk@mhaofnyc.org
Web site: www.mhaofnyc.org
Giselle Stolper, Executive Director
Advocacy, public education, community-based services

Mental Health Association of NYS Inc
194 Washington Ave, Ste 415, Albany, NY 12210
518-434-0439 Fax: 518-427-8676
e-mail: info@mhanys.org
Web site: www.mhanys.org
Glen Liebman, Chief Executive Officer
Technical assistance, advocacy, training & resource clearinghouse

NAMI-NYS
260 Washington Ave, Albany, NY 12210
518-462-2000 Fax: 518-462-3811
e-mail: naminys@naminys.org
Web site: www.naminys.org
J David Seay, Executive Director
Family advocates for the mentally ill

Offices and agencies generally appear in alphabetical order, except when specific order is requested by listee.

MENTAL HYGIENE / Private Sector

NY Council on Problem Gambling
119 Washington Ave, Albany, NY 12210
518-427-1622 Fax: 518-427-6181
e-mail: jmaney@nyproblemgambling.org
Web site: www.nyproblemgambling.org
James Maney, Executive Director
Statewide helpline, public information, referral svcs, advocacy for treatment & support svcs, in-service training & workshops

NY Counseling Association Inc
PO Box 12636, Albany, NY 12212-2636
518-235-2026 Fax: 518-235-0910
e-mail: nycaoffice@nycounseling.org
Web site: www.nycounseling.org
Donald Newell, Executive Manager
Counseling professionals in education, mental health, career, employment, rehabilitation & adult development

NYS Association of Community & Residential Agencies
99 Pine St, Ste C-110, Albany, NY 12207
518-449-7551 Fax: 518-449-1509
e-mail: nysacra@nysacra.org
Web site: www.nysacra.org
Ann M Hardiman, Executive Director
Advocating for agencies that serve individuals with developmental disabilities

NYS Conference of Local Mental Hygiene Directors
99 Pine Street, Ste C100, Albany, NY 12207
518-462-9422 Fax: 518-465-2695
e-mail: ds@clmhd.org
Web site: www.clmhd.org
Duane Spilde, LCSWR, ACSW, Executive Director

NYS Council for Community Behavioral Healthcare
155 Washington Ave, 2nd Flr, Albany, NY 12210-2329
518-445-2642 Fax: 518-463-2543
e-mail: nyscouncil@nycap.rr.com
Web site: www.nccbh.org
Laurie Cole, Executive Director
Statewide membership organization representing community mental health centers

NYS Psychological Association
6 Executive Park Dr, Albany, NY 12203
800-732-3933 Fax: 518-437-0177
e-mail: nyspa@nyspa.org
Web site: www.nyspa.org
Gayle Everitt, Executive Director
Promote & advance profession of psychology; referral service

NYSARC Inc
393 Delaware Ave, Delmar, NY 12054
518-439-8311 Fax: 518-439-1893
e-mail: info@nysarc.org
Web site: www.nysarc.org
Marc N Brandt, Executive Director
Mental retardation & developmental disabilities programs, services & advocacy

New York Association of Psychiatric Rehabilitation Services (NYAPRS)
1 Columbia Place, 2nd Floor, Albany, NY 12207
518-436-0008 Fax: 518-436-0044
e-mail: HarveyR@nyaprs.org
Web site: www.nyaprs.org
Harvey Rosenthal, Executive Director
Promoting the recovery, rehabilitation & rights of New Yorkers with psychiatric disabilities

New York Presbyterian Hospital, Department of Psychiatry
180 Fort Washington Ave, Room 270, New York, NY 10032
212-305-9249 Fax: 212-305-4724
e-mail: hjs1@columbia.edu
Herbert J Schlesinger, PhD, Director, Division of Clinical Psychology
Psychotherapy & public policy

New York State Rehabilitation Association
155 Washington Ave, Suite 410, Albany, NY 12210
518-449-2976 Fax: 518-426-4329
e-mail: nysra@nyrehab.org
Web site: www.nyrehab.org
Jeff Wise, JD, Vice President
Political advocacy, education, communications, networking & referral services for people with disabilities

Postgrad Center for Mental Health, Child, Adolescent & Family-Couples
138 E 26th St, Fl 4, New York, NY 10010-1843
212-576-4190 Fax: 212-576-4129
Diana Daimwood, Director
Psychotherapy & assessment services for children, adolescents & families

Postgraduate Center for Mental Health
344 W 36th St, New York, NY 10018
212-560-6757 Fax: 212-244-2034
e-mail: mholman@pgcmh.org
Web site: www.pgcmh-institute.org
Marcia Holman, CSW/Vice President, Clinical Services
Community-based rehabilitation & employment services for adults with mental illness

Research Foundation for Mental Hygiene Inc
Riverview Center, 150 Broadway, Suite 301, Menands, NY 12204
518-474-5661 Fax: 518-474-6995
Robert E Burke, Managing Director
Not-for-profit responsible for administering grants & sponsored research contracts for the NYS Department of Mental Health & its agencies

Offices and agencies generally appear in alphabetical order, except when specific order is requested by listee.

MENTAL HYGIENE / Private Sector

SUNY at Albany, Professional Development Program, NE States Addiction
Rockefeller College, 1400 Washington Ave, Room 412A, Albany, NY 12222
518-956-7800 Fax: 518-956-7865
e-mail: lparsons@pdp.albany.edu
Web site: www.pdp.albany.edu
Eugene J Monaco, Director
Dissemination of current research & best clinical practice information; coursework & programs for professionals in the field of addictions

Samaritan Village Inc
138-02 Queens Blvd, Briarwood, NY 11435
718-206-2000 Fax: 718-657-6982
Web site: www.samaritanvillage.org
Ron Solarz, Executive Director
Substance abuse treatment; residential & outpatient therapeutic community

Schuyler Center for Analysis & Advocacy (SCAA)
150 State St, 4th Fl, Albany, NY 12207
518-463-1896 x29 Fax: 518-463-3364
e-mail: drobinson@scaany.org
Web site: www.scaany.org
Davin Robinson, Senior Policy Associate
Advocacy, analysis & forums on mental health issues

Self Advocacy Association of NYS
Capital District DSO, 500 Balltown Rd, Bldg #5, Schenectady, NY 12304
518-382-1454 Fax: 518-382-1594
e-mail: sholmes@earthlink.net
Web site: www.sanys.org
Steve Holmes, Executive Director
Advocacy for & by persons with developmental disabilities to ensure civil rights & opportunities

Springbrook
2705 State Hwy 28, Oneonta, NY 13820
607-286-7171 Fax: 607-286-7166
e-mail: kennedyp@springbrookny.org
Web site: www.springbrookny.org
Patricia E Kennedy, Executive Director
Education/mental hygiene

St Joseph's Rehabilitation Center Inc
PO Box 470, Saranac Lake, NY 12983
518-891-3950 or 518-891-3801 Fax: 518-891-3986
e-mail: stjoes@sjrcrehab.org
Web site: www.sjrcrehab.org
Janet Reichert, Interim CEO
Inpatient & outpatient alcohol & substance abuse treatment

Statewide Black & Puerto Rican/Latino Substance Abuse Task Force
2730 Atlantic Ave, Brooklyn, NY 11207-2820
718-647-8275 Fax: 718-647-7889
e-mail: info@nytaskforce.org; nystaskforce@ad.com
Web site: www.nytaskforce.org
Ralph Gonzalez, Executive Director
Substance abuse, HIV/AIDS & HepC prevention & treatment

University at Buffalo, Research Institute on Addictions
1021 Main St, Buffalo, NY 14203-1016
716-887-2566 Fax: 716-887-2252
e-mail: connors@ria.buffalo.edu
Web site: www.ria.buffalo.edu
Gerard Connors, Director
Alcohol & substance abuse prevention, treatment & policy research

YAI/National Institute for People with Disabilities
460 W 34th St, New York, NY 10001-2382
212-273-6110 or 866-2-YAI-LINK Fax: 212-947-7524
e-mail: jmlcares@yai.org
Web site: www.yai.org
Joel M Levy, Chief Executive Officer
Programs, services & advocacy for people with autism, mental retardation & other developmental disabilities as well as learning disabilities of all ages & their families; special education & early learning programs

Yeshiva University, A Einstein Clg of Med, Div of Subs Abuse
1500 Waters Place, Bronx, NY 10461
718-409-9450 x312 Fax: 718-892-7115
e-mail: imarion@dosa.aecom.yu.edu
Web site: www.aecom.yu.edu
Ira J Marion, Executive Director
Screening, assessment, diagnosis, treatment, support services, research & teaching & training related to chemical dependency & substance abuse

Offices and agencies generally appear in alphabetical order, except when specific order is requested by listee.

MUNICIPAL & LOCAL GOVERNMENTS

New York State

GOVERNOR'S OFFICE

Governor's Office
Executive Chamber
State Capitol
Albany, NY 12224
518-474-8390 Fax: 518-474-1513
Web site: www.state.ny.us

Governor:
   Eliot Spitzer 518-474-8390
Secretary to the Governor:
   Richard Baum 518-474-4246
Counsel to the Governor:
   David Nocenti 518-474-8343
Senior Advisor to the Governor:
   Lloyd Constantine 518-486-9671
Director, Communications:
   Darren Dopp 518-474-8418
Deputy Secretary, Appointments:
   Francine James 518-474-0491
Deputy Secretary, Intergovernmental Affairs:
   Martin Mack 518-408-2555
Senior Advisor, Intergovernmental Affairs:
   Michael Schell 518-408-2555
Assistant Counsel to the Governor-General Government Operations &
  Human Services:
   David Rose 518-474-2266
Director, Administration:
   Theresa Brennan 518-474-3036

New York City Office
633 Third Ave, 38th Fl, New York, NY 10017
Director, NYC Intergovernmental Affairs:
   Carl Andrews 212-681-4580
Director, Community Affairs:
   Lila Kirton 212-681-4580

EXECUTIVE DEPARTMENTS AND RELATED AGENCIES

Budget, Division of the
State Capitol
Albany, NY 12224
518-473-3885
e-mail: bdgord@budget.state.ny.us
Web site: www.budget.state.ny.us

Director:
   Paul E Francis 518-474-2300
First Deputy Director:
   Laura L Anglin 518-474-6323
Deputy Director:
   Ron Rock 518-474-6300

Deputy Director:
   Kim Fine 518-474-6300
Counsel:
   Kathy Bennett 518-474-2300
Director, Communications:
   Jeffrey Gordon 518-473-3885
Press Officer:
   Scott Reif 518-473-3885

Civil Service Department
Alfred E Smith State Ofc Bldg
Albany, NY 12239
518-457-2487 Fax: 518-457-7547
Web site: www.cs.state.ny.us

Commissioner:
   Nancy G Groenwegen 518-457-3701
Executive Deputy Commissioner:
   Patricia Hite 518-457-6212
Deputy Commissioner, Operations:
   Hector Millan 518-485-7515
Special Counsel:
   Thomas F Brennan 518-485-7278
Counsel:
   Judith Ratner 518-457-3177
Director, Workforce & Occupational Planning:
   Nancy B Kiyonaga 518-485-9274
Director, Internal Audit:
   Joseph Kulkus 518-457-7355
Director, Public Information:
   Erin Barlow 518-457-9375/fax: 518-457-6654
   e-mail: erin.barlow@cs.state.ny.us
Public Records Access Officer:
   Erin Barlow 518-457-6875/fax: 518-457-6654

Administration

Administrative Services Unit
Director, Financial Administration:
   Michael Bosanko 518-457-6490/fax: 518-457-5116

Classification & Compensation Division
Director:
   Nicholas J Vagianelis 518-457-6226/fax: 518-457-8081

Commission Operations
Director:
   Stella Chen Harding 518-457-2575

Diversity, Planning & Management Division
Director:
   Frank E Abrams 518-457-4146/fax: 518-457-0399
Coordinator, Community Outreach:
   George Swiers 518-457-7661/fax: 518-457-0399

Employee Benefits Division
Director:
   Robert DuBois 518-457-9391/fax: 518-485-8952
Director, Employee Insurance Programs:
   Mary B Frye 518-457-1771/fax: 518-457-1311

Offices and agencies generally appear in alphabetical order, except when specific order is requested by listee.

MUNICIPAL & LOCAL GOVERNMENTS / New York State

Asst Director, Financial Management & Accounting:
David Boland 518-457-5159/fax: 518-457-1311

Employee Health Services Division
Administrator, EHS:
Maria C Steinbach. 518-457-6142/fax: 518-485-1995
Director, Health Services Nursing:
Mary M McSweeney 518-457-2616

Information Resource Management
Director:
Frank Slade 518-457-1775/fax: 518-485-5752
e-mail: frank.slade@cs.state.ny.us

Municipal Services Division
Director:
Richard Ciprioni 518-457-9553/fax: 518-485-8244
Local Examinations:
Will Martin. 518-457-4487

Personnel
Director:
Susan China. 518-457-1077/fax: 518-457-6875

Planning Division
Director:
Frank R Santora 518-457-5507

Staffing Services Division
Director:
Terry Jordan 518-457-5781/fax: 518-457-4239
Asst Director:
Blaine Ryan-Lynch 518-457-5445
Attendance & Leave Unit:
Margaret Harrigan 518-457-2295

Testing Services Division
Director:
Paul Kaiser 518-457-9499/fax: 518-457-4239
Assistant Director:
Debbi Parrington 518-457-5465

Civil Service Commission
President:
Nancy G Groenwegen 518-457-3701
Commissioner:
Daniel E Wall 518-457-3504
Commissioner:
Caroline W Ahl. 518-457-5444

Criminal Justice Services, Division of
Four Tower Place
Albany, NY 12203-3764
518-457-1260 Fax: 518-457-3089
Web site: www.criminaljustice.state.ny.us

Commissioner:
Denise E O'Donnell 518-457-1260
Executive Deputy Commissioner:
Sean Byrne 518-457-6091
Special Counsel to the Commissioner:
Michael Barrett 518-485-7913
Special Counsel & Host Agency Coordination/Support:
Mary Kavaney 518-485-8495
Affirmative Action Officer:
Vacant 518-457-6110
Public Information Officer:
John Caher. 518-457-8828/fax: 518-485-7715

Administration Office
Deputy Commissioner, Administration:
Don Capone 518-457-6110

Administrative Services
Director:
Phyllis M Foster 518-457-1696

Human Resources Management
Director:
Alyce Ashe 518-457-6110

State Finance & Budget
Director, Financial Administration:
Kimberly J Szady 518-457-6105
Director, Internal Audit & Compliance:
Bob Wright. 518-485-5823

Legal Services
Deputy Commissioner & Counsel:
Gina Bianchi. 518-457-4181

Missing & Exploited Children Clearinghouse
Director:
Kenneth R Buniak 518-485-7632

Office of Forensic Services
Director:
John Hicks 518-457-7287

Office of Criminal Justice Operations
Deputy Commissioner:
Daniel Foro 518-485-2995

Office of Justice Information Services
Executive Director:
James Shea 518-457-8724
Deputy Commissioner/CIO:
Anne Roest 518-485-7176

Office of Public Safety

Law Enforcement Accreditation Council

Municipal Police Training Council

State Committee for Coordination of Police Services for Elderly (TRIAD)

Statewide Law Enforcement Telecommunications Committee

Security Guard Advisory Council

Deputy Commissioner:
Cedric Alexander 518-457-6101
Director:
Mark R Lindsay 518-457-2667

Office of Strategic Planning
Deputy Commissioner:
Beth Ryan 518-485-7433

Bureau of Justice Research & Innovation
Director:
Donna Hall, PhD 518-457-7301

Crime Reduction Strategies Unit
Chief:
Thomas Mitchell 518-457-7301

Justice Systems Analysis Unit
Chief:
David vanAlstyne 518-457-7301

Offices and agencies generally appear in alphabetical order, except when specific order is requested by listee.

MUNICIPAL & LOCAL GOVERNMENTS / New York State

Offender Management Analysis Unit
Chief:
　Bruce Frederick 518-457-3724

Funding & Program Assistance Office
Director:
　AnneMarie Strano 518-457-8462

Emergency Management Office, NYS (SEMO)
1220 Washington Ave
Bldg 22, Ste 101
Albany, NY 12226-2251
518-292-2275
Web site: www.semo.state.ny.us

Director:
　John R Gibb 518-292-2301
First Deputy Director:
　Andrew X Feeney 518-292-2275
Deputy Director, Operations:
　Thomas Fargione 518-292-2275
Deputy Director, Preparedness:
　Greg Brunelle 518-292-2275
Deputy Director, Administration:
　John A Agostino 518-292-2275
Program Assistant:
　Judy Williams 518-292-2301/fax: 518-322-4978

Administration
Chief Budget Analyst:
　Susan Mutch 518-292-2325
Manager, Recovery Section:
　Les Radford 518-292-2391

Community Affairs
Asst Director:
　Dennis J Michalski 518-292-2310
Public Information Officer:
　Donald L Maurer 518-292-2312/fax: 518-457-4923
　e-mail: donald.maurer@semo.state.ny.us

Preparedness
Chief, Training/Exercises:
　William Campbell 518-292-2350
Chief, Planning:
　Robert Olazagasti 518-292-2360

Support Services
Assistant Director, Technology:
　Kevin Ross 518-292-2260
Manager, Supply Services:
　John Zobel 518-292-2270

Real Property Services, Office of
16 Sheridan Ave
Albany, NY 12210-2714
518-486-5446 Fax: 518-474-9276
e-mail: nysorps@orps.state.ny.us
Web site: www.orps.state.ny.us

Executive Director:
　Donald C DeWitt 518-474-5711
Executive Deputy Director:
　Steve King 518-473-6914
Acting Counsel:
　James O'Keefe 518-474-6753

Director, Public Information:
　Geoffrey T Gloak 518-486-5446
　e-mail: geoffrey.gloak@orps.state.ny.us

Research, Information & Policy Development
Director:
　James Dunne 518-473-4532
　e-mail: jim.dunne@orps.state.ny.us

Regional Customer Service Delivery
Director:
　David Williams 518-473-7574
　e-mail: dave.williams@orps.state.ny.us

Albany (Northern Region) . . . . fax: 518-486-7752
16 Sheridan Ave, Albany, NY 12210
Regional Director:
　Jeffrey Green 518-486-4403
　e-mail: internet.northern@orps.state.ny.us

Batavia (Western Region)
Genesee County Bldg 2, 3837 W Main Rd, Batavia, NY 14020
Regional Director:
　Joseph Muscarella 585-343-6329/fax: 585-343-9740
　e-mail: internet.western@orps.state.ny.us

Long Island Satellite Office . . . . fax: 631-952-3729
250 Veterans Memorial Hgwy, Rm 2B-44, Hauppauge, NY 11788
Manager:
　Louis Cubello 631-952-3650
　e-mail: internet.metro@orps.state.ny.us

Newburgh (Southern Region) . . . . fax: 845-567-2690
263 Route 17K, Ste 2001, Newburgh, NY 12550-8310
Regional Director:
　John Wolham 845-567-2648
　e-mail: internet.southern@orps.state.ny.us

Saranac Lake Satellite Office . . . . fax: 518-891-2639
43 Broadway, Saranac Lake, NY 12983
Office Manager:
　Dan Lancor 518-891-1780
　e-mail: internet.saranac@orps.state.ny.us

Syracuse (Central Region) . . . . fax: 315-471-3634
401 South Salina St, Syracuse, NY 13202-2415
Regional Director:
　Teresa Frank 315-471-2347
　e-mail: internet.central@orps.state.ny.us

State Board of Real Property Services
Chair:
　George E Herren 518-474-5711
Executive Secretary:
　Donald C DeWitt 518-474-5711
Asst to the Board:
　Darlene A Maloney 518-474-3793/fax: 518-474-9276

Small Cities, Office for
4 Empire State Plaza
Suite 600
Albany, NY 12223
518-474-2057 Fax: 518-474-5247
Web site: www.nysmallcities.com

Executive Director:
　Joseph J Rabito 518-474-2057
Associate Counsel:
　Brian McCartney 518-474-2057

Offices and agencies generally appear in alphabetical order, except when specific order is requested by listee.

MUNICIPAL & LOCAL GOVERNMENTS / New York State

Program Manager:
　Gail Hammond 518-474-2057
Executive Assistant:
　Drue Paige 518-474-2057
Director, Communications:
　Joseph Picchi 518-474-2057

State Comptroller, Office of the
633 Third Ave
31st Fl
New York, NY 10017-6754
212-681-4491 Fax: 212-681-4468

110 State St
15th Fl
Albany, NY 12236-0001
518-474-4040
Fax: 518-473-3004

State Comptroller:
　Thomas P DiNapoli . . . . 518-474-4040 or 212-681-4491

Administration
Deputy Comptroller:
　Harris Lirtzman 518-402-4884

Financial Administration
Director:
　Larry Appel 518-474-7574

Information Technology Services
Director:
　Richard Green 518-474-7476

Management Services
Director:
　Paul Capobianco 518-473-0675

Oil Spill Fund Office
Executive Director:
　Anne Hohenstein 518-474-6657/fax: 518-474-9979

Division of Intergovernmental Affairs & Community Relations
Deputy Comptroller:
　Myrna Santiago 212-383-2662
Director, Intergovernmental Affairs & Community Relations:
　Sam Nicolas 518-473-2449
Director, Community Relations & Constituent Services:
　Nicholas Acquafredda 212-417-5487
Director, Intergovernmental Affairs, Upstate & Long Island Rural Liais:
　Victor Mallison 518-473-2449
Director, Intergovernmental Affairs, NYC, Brooklyn & Staten Island:
　Samuel Nicolas 212-383-2672

Division of Investigations
Deputy Comptroller:
　Robert Brackman . . . . 212-681-4474 or 518-402-4926
Asst Comptroller for Internal Audit & Division Operations:
　Stephen R Hillerman 518-286-2622 x105
Chief Investigative Counsel:
　Samantha Biletsky . . . . 212-681-4475 or 518-486-3501
Director, Internal Audit:
　Robert Kosky 518-286-2622 x110

Division of Local Govt Services & Economic Development
Deputy Comptroller:
　Mark P Pattison 518-474-4037/fax: 518-486-6479

Asst Comptroller:
　Steve Hancox 518-474-4037
Asst Comptroller:
　John Clarkson 518-474-4037

Division of State Services
Deputy Comptroller:
　Jerry Barber 518-474-5598

State Audit Group
Asst Comptroller:
　Jerry Barber 518-474-5598
Director, Administration:
　Bob Blot 518-474-3271
Director, Audit:
　Steve Sossei 518-474-3271
Director, Audit:
　David R Hancox 518-474-3271

State Financial Services Group
Asst Controller:
　Joan Sullivan 518-402-4103
Director, Accounting Operations Bureau:
　Tom Mahoney 518-474-4017
Director, Accounting Systems Bureau:
　Bob Campano 518-474-8657

Executive Office
Chief of Staff:
　Jack Chartier 212-681-4498
First Deputy Comptroller:
　Thomas Sanzillo 518-474-2909
Executive Deputy Comptroller:
　Diana J Ritter 518-474-3610
Deputy Chief of Staff:
　Roberta Rubin . . . . 212-681-4495 or 518-474-4040
Director, Business Communication:
　Ellen J Evans . . . . 518-473-1323 or 212-681-4489
Chief Information Officer:
　Jeffrey S Grunfeld 518-408-2915/fax: 518-473-3004

Office of Budget & Policy Analysis
Deputy Comptroller:
　Kim Fine 518-473-4333
Chief Economist:
　Thomas Marks 518-402-3117
Deputy Comptroller:
　Christine Rutigliano 518-474-4541

Press Office
Director, Communications:
　Daniel Weiller 518-474-4015/fax: 518-473-8940
Press Secretary:
　Jeffrey Gordon 518-474-4015
　e-mail: jgordon@osc.state.ny.us

State Department
41 State St
Albany, NY 12231
518-474-4750 Fax: 518-474-4765
Web site: www.dos.state.ny.us

123 William St
New York, NY 10038
212-417-5801
Fax: 212-417-5805

Offices and agencies generally appear in alphabetical order, except when specific order is requested by listee.

MUNICIPAL & LOCAL GOVERNMENTS / New York State

Secretary of State:
   Lorraine A Cortes-Vazquez 518-474-0050
First Deputy Secretary of State:
   Daniel Shapiro 518-474-4750
Deputy Secretary of State, Public Affairs:
   Eamon Moynihan 212-417-5800
Counsel:
   Susan Watson 518-474-6740/fax: 518-473-9211
Assistant Secretary of State, Communications:
   Laurence Sombke 518-474-4752/fax: 518-474-4597
   e-mail: info@dos.state.ny.us

Ethics Commission
Alfred E Smith State Offc Bldg, 11th Fl, Ste 1147, Albany, NY 12210
Acting Executive Director:
   Suzanne Dugan 518-474-8320/fax: 518-474-8322
   e-mail: ethics@dos.state.ny.us
Chair:
   John D Feerick 518-474-8320

Local Government & Community Services
Deputy Secretary of State:
   Matthew Andrus 518-486-9888/fax: 518-474-6572

Coastal Resources & Waterfront Revitalization Division
Director:
   George Stafford 518-474-6000/fax: 518-473-2464
   e-mail: coastal@dos.state.ny.us

Code Enforcement & Administration Division
Director:
   Ronald E Piester 518-474-4073/fax: 518-486-4487
   e-mail: codes@dos.state.ny.us

Community Services Division
Director:
   Evelyn M Harris 518-474-5741/fax: 518-486-4663
   e-mail: commserv@dos.state.ny.us

Fire Prevention & Control Office
State Fire Administrator:
   James A Burns 518-474-6746/fax: 518-474-3240
   e-mail: fire@dos.state.ny.us

Local Government Services Division
Director:
   Barbara Murphy 518-473-3355/fax: 518-474-6572
   e-mail: localgov@dos.state.ny.us

New York State Academy of Fire Science
600 College Ave, Montour Falls, NY 14865-9643
Director:
   Richard Nagle 607-535-7136/fax: 607-535-4841

Open Government Committee
Executive Director:
   Robert J Freeman 518-474-2518/fax: 518-474-1927
   e-mail: opengov@dos.state.ny.us

CORPORATIONS, AUTHORITIES AND COMMISSIONS

Municipal Assistance Corporation for the City of New York
420 Lexington Avenue
Room 1756
New York, NY 10170
212-840-8255 Fax: 212-840-8570
e-mail: macnyc@earthlink.net

Chairman:
   Jonathan A Ballan 212-840-8255
Executive Director:
   Nancy H Henze 212-840-8255

New York State Assn of Fire Districts
PO Box 1419
Massapequa, NY 11758
516-799-8575 or 800-520-9594 Fax: 516-799-2516
Web site: www.firedistnys.com

President:
   Randall J Rider .... 716-875-0183 or 716-876-1214
   fax: 716-876-9566
   e-mail: adrilleye@aol.com
First Vice President:
   Lawrence Pierce 585-624-4673/fax: 585-624-4047
   e-mail: lpierce@rochester.rr.com
Second Vice President:
   John LoScalzo 631-549-5729/fax: 631-549-2030
   e-mail: mcque@verizon.net
Secretary & Treasurer:
   Frank A Nocerino .... 516-799-8575 or 800-520-9594
   fax: 516-799-2516
   e-mail: fnoc@aol.com
Counsel:
   William N Young .... 800-349-2904 or 518-456-6767
   fax: 518-869-5142
   e-mail: byoung@wyfklaw.com

New York State Disaster Preparedness Commission
Building 22, Suite 101
1220 Washington Ave
Albany, NY 12226-2251
518-292-2301 or 518-292-2200 Fax: 518-322-4978
Web site: www.semo.state.ny.us/dpc/

Chairman:
   John R Gibb 518-292-2301

State of New York Municipal Bond Bank Agency (MBBA)
641 Lexington Ave
New York, NY 10022
212-688-4000 Fax: 212-872-0678
Web site: www.nymbba.org

Chair:
   Judd Levy 212-688-4000
President & CEO:
   Priscilla Almodovar 212-688-4000
Senior VP, CFO & COO:
   Ralph J Madalena 212-688-4000
Senior VP & Counsel:
   Robert M Drillings 212-688-4000
Senior VP, Debt Issuance:
   Bernard Abramowitz 212-688-4000 x530
Vice President, Policy & Planning:
   Tracy A Oats 212-688-4000 x678

Offices and agencies generally appear in alphabetical order, except when specific order is requested by listee.

MUNICIPAL & LOCAL GOVERNMENTS / Private Sector

NEW YORK STATE LEGISLATURE

See Legislative Branch in Section 1 for additional Standing Committee and Subcommittee information.

Assembly Legislative Commissions

State-Local Relations, Legislative Commission on
Assembly Chair:
  Darrel J Aubertine (D) 518-455-5545
Program Manager:
  William Kraus 518-455-5035/fax: 518-455-5396

Assembly Standing Committees

Cities
Chair:
  James F Brennan (D) 518-455-5377
Ranking Minority Member:
  Thomas J Kirwan (R) 518-455-5762

Economic Development, Job Creation, Commerce & Industry
Chair:
  Robin L Schimminger (D) 518-455-4767
Ranking Minority Member:
  Marc W Butler (R) 518-455-5393

Housing
Chair:
  Vito J Lopez (D) 518-455-5537
Ranking Minority Member:
  Michael J Fitzpatrick (R) 518-455-5021

Local Government
Chair:
  William (Sam) Hoyt III (D) 518-455-4886
Ranking Minority Member:
  Annie G Rabbitt (R) 518-455-5991

Transportation
Chair:
  David F Gantt (D) 518-455-5606
Ranking Minority Member:
  David G McDonough (R) 518-455-4633

Ways & Means
Chair:
  Herman D Farrell, Jr (D) 518-455-5491
Ranking Minority Member:
  James P Hayes (R) 518-455-4618

Senate Standing Committees

Cities
Chair:
  Serphin R Maltese (R) 518-455-3281
Ranking Minority Member:
  Antoine Thompson (D) 518-455-3371

Commerce, Economic Development & Small Business
Chair:
  James S Alesi (R) 518-455-2015
Ranking Minority Member:
  Efrain Gonzalez, Jr (D) 518-455-3395

Finance
Chair:
  Owen H Johnson (R) 518-455-3411
Ranking Minority Member:
  William Stachowski (D) 518-455-2426

Housing, Construction & Community Development
Chair:
  John J Bonacic (R) 518-455-3181
Ranking Minority Member:
  Liz Krueger (D) 518-455-2297

Local Government
Chair:
  Elizabeth O'Connor Little (R) 518-455-2811
Ranking Minority Member:
  Andrea Stewart-Cousins (D) 518-455-2585

Transportation
Chair:
  Thomas W Libous (R) 518-455-2677
Ranking Minority Member:
  John D Sabini (D) 518-455-2529

Private Sector

Association of Fire Districts of the State of NY Inc
948 North Bay Avenue, North Massapequa, NY 11758-2581
516-799-8575 or 800-520-9594 Fax: 516-799-2516
e-mail: FNOC@aol.com
Web site: www.firedistnys.com
Frank A Nocerino, Secretary-Treasurer
Obtain greater economy in the administration of fire district affairs

Association of Towns of the State of New York
150 State St, Albany, NY 12207
518-465-7933 Fax: 518-465-0724
e-mail: jhaber@nytowns.org
Web site: www.nytowns.org
G Jeffrey Haber, Executive Director
Advocacy, education for local government

Citizens Budget Commission
One Penn Plaza, Ste 640, New York, NY 10119
212-279-2605 Fax: 212-868-4745
e-mail: cmb2@ls2.nyu.edu
Web site: www.cbcny.org
Charles Brecher, Executive VP & Director, Research
Nonpartisan, nonprofit civic organization devoted to influencing constructive change in the finances and services of New York City and New York State government

Offices and agencies generally appear in alphabetical order, except when specific order is requested by listee.

MUNICIPAL & LOCAL GOVERNMENTS / Private Sector

Citizens Union of the City of New York
299 Broadway, Rm 700, New York, NY 10007-1978
212-227-0342 Fax: 212-227-0345
e-mail: citizens@citizensunion.org
Web site: www.citizensunion.org
Dick Dadey, Executive Director
Government watchdog organization; city & state public policy issues; political and government reform

Columbia Law School, Legislative Drafting Research Fund
435 W 116th St, New York, NY 10027-7297
212-854-2640 Fax: 212-854-7946
e-mail: rb34@columbia.edu
Web site: www.law.columbia.edu
Richard Briffault, Vice Dean & Executive Director
State & local government law, property law & election law

Council of State Governments, Eastern Conference
100 Wall St, 20th Fl, New York, NY 10005
212-482-2320 Fax: 212-482-2344
e-mail: alan@csgeast.org
Web site: www.csgeast.org
Alan V Sokolow, Regional Director
Training, research & information sharing for state government officials

Cullen & Dykman LLP
100 Quentin Roosevelt Blvd, Garden City Ctr, Garden City, NY 11530-4850
516-357-3703 Fax: 516-396-9155
e-mail: gfishberg@cullenanddykman.com
Web site: www.cullenanddykman.com
Gerard Fishberg, Partner
Municipal & labor law

Fordham University, Department of Political Science
441 E Fordham Road, Bronx, NY 10458
718-817-3960 Fax: 718-817-3972
e-mail: kantor@fordham.edu
Paul Kantor, Professor of Political Science
Urban politics, urban economic development and the social condition of American cities.

Fund for the City of New York
121 Ave of the Americas, 6th Fl, New York, NY 10013
212-925-6675 Fax: 212-925-5675
e-mail: mmccormick@fcny.org
Web site: www.fcny.org
Mary McCormick, President
Innovations in policy, programs, practice & technology to advance the functioning of government & nonprofit organizations in NYC & beyond

Genesee Transportation Council
50 West Main Street, Suite 8112, Rochester, NY 14614-1227
585-232-6240 Fax: 585-262-3106
e-mail: rperrin@gtcmpo.org
Web site: www.gtcmpo.org
Richard Perrin, Executive Director
Nine-county metropolitan planning organization

Hawkins Delafield & Wood LLP
One Chase Manhattan Plaza, 42nd Fl, New York, NY 10005
212-820-9300 Fax: 212-514-8425
e-mail: srkramer@hdw.com
Web site: www.hawkins.com
Howard Zucker, Partner
Transportation, municipal & local government law

Housing Action Council Inc - Not For Profit
55 S Broadway, Tarrytown, NY 10591
914-332-4144 Fax: 914-332-4147
e-mail: rnoonan@affordablehomes.org
Rosemarie Noonan, Executive Director
Financial feasibility, land use & zoning & affordable housing

Institute of Public Administration/NYU Wagner
295 Lafayette St, 2nd Floor, New York, NY 10012-9604
212-998-7400
e-mail: wagner@nyu.edu
Web site: www.wagner.nyu.edu
David Mammen, President
Non-profit research, consulting & educational institute

KPMG LLP
345 Park Ave, Rm 4095, New York, NY 10154
212-758-9700 Fax: 212-409-8340
e-mail: jrmiller@kpmg.com
Web site: www.kpmg.com
Michael D V Rake, Chairman, International & Senior Partner
Accounting

League of Women Voters of New York State
62 Grand St, Albany, NY 12207-2712
518-465-4162 Fax: 518-465-0812
e-mail: lwvny@lwvny.org
Web site: www.lwvny.org
Kristen Hansen, Executive Director
Public policy issues forum; good government advocacy

MBIA Insurance Corporation
113 King St, Armonk, NY 10504
914-273-4545 Fax: 914-765-3555
e-mail: ethel.geisinger@mbia.com
Web site: www.mbia.com
Ethel Z Geisinger, Vice President, Government Relations
Insure municipal bonds & structured transactions

Manhattan Institute, Center for Civic Innovation
52 Vanderbilt Ave, 2nd Fl, New York, NY 10017
212-599-7000 Fax: 212-599-3494
Web site: www.manhattan-institute.org
Lindsay Young, Executive Director, Communications
Urban policy, reinventing government, civil society

Moody's Investors Service, Public Finance Group
99 Church St, New York, NY 10007
212-553-7780 Fax: 212-298-7113
e-mail: dennis.farrell@moodys.com
Web site: www.moodys.com
Dennis M Farrell, Group Managing Director
Municipal debt ratings & analysis

Offices and agencies generally appear in alphabetical order, except when specific order is requested by listee.

MUNICIPAL & LOCAL GOVERNMENTS / Private Sector

NY Association of Local Government Records Officers
PO Box 208, Buffalo, NY 14201
315-785-5149 Fax: 315-785-5145
e-mail: benc@co.jefferson.ny.us
Web site: www.nyalgro.org
Benjamin Cobb, President
Education advisory network for the development of sound records & information management programs

NY State Association of Town Superintendents of Highways Inc
119 Washington Avenue, Suite 300, Albany, NY 12210
518-694-9313 Fax: 518-694-9314
e-mail: info@nystownhwys.org
Web site: www.nystownhwys.org
Michael K Thompson, Executive Secretary & Treasurer

NYS Association of Counties
111 Pine Street, Albany, NY 12207
518-465-1473 Fax: 518-465-0506
e-mail: info@NYSAC.org
Web site: www.nysac.org
Stephen J Acquario, Executive Director
Lobbying, research & training services

NYS Conference of Mayors & Municipal Officials
119 Washington Ave, Albany, NY 12210
518-463-1185 Fax: 518-463-1190
e-mail: info@nycom.org
Web site: www.nycom.org
Peter Baynes, President
Legislative advocacy for NYS cities & villages

NYS Magistrates Association
267 Delaware Ave, Delmar, NY 12054-1124
518-439-1087 Fax: 518-439-1204
e-mail: nysma@juno.com
Web site: www.nysmagassoc.homestead.com
Thomas W Baldwin, Executive Director
Association of town & village justices

New York Municipal Insurance Reciprocal (NYMIR)
24 Aviation Rd, Ste 204, Albany, NY 12205
518-437-1171 Fax: 518-437-1182
Web site: www.nymir.org
Gale M Hatch, President
Insurance services for municipalities

NYS Bar Assn, Municipal Law Section
New York State Court of Claims
500 Court Exchange Bldg, 144 Exchange Blvd, Rochester, NY 14614
585-262-2320 Fax: 585-262-3019
e-mail: rminarik@courts.state.ny.us
Hon Renee Forgensi Minarik, Chair

New York State Government Finance Officers Association Inc
126 State St, 5th Fl, Albany, NY 12207
518-465-1512 Fax: 518-434-4640
e-mail: info@nysgfoa.org
Web site: www.nysgfoa.org
Kevin Spacher, CPA, President
Membership organization dedicated to the professional management of governmental resources

New York State Society of Municipal Finance Officers
13 West Oneida Street, Oswego, NY 13126
315-342-8107 Fax: 315-342-8171
e-mail: dcoad@oswegony.org
Web site: www.nysmunicipalfinanceofficers.org
Deborah Coad, Secretary & Treasurer
Improve municipal financial & accounting operations & procedures in NYS

New York University, Wagner Graduate School
295 Lafayette Street, 2nd Floor, New York, NY 10012
212-998-7400 Fax: 212-995-4162
e-mail: mitchell.moss@nyu.edu
Web site: www.nyu.edu/wagner
Mitchell Moss, Professor of Urban Policy & Planning
Research on urban planning & development, with special emphasis on technology & the future of cities

Syracuse University, Maxwell School of Citizenship & Public Affairs
215 Eggers Hall, Syracuse, NY 13244-1090
315-443-4000 Fax: 315-443-9721
e-mail: sibretsc@maxwell.syr.edu
Stuart Bretschneider, Associate Dean & Chair, Professor of Public Administration
Capital financing & debt management; public employee pensions; financial management

Urbanomics
115 Fifth Ave, 3rd Fl, New York, NY 10003
212-353-7462 Fax: 212-353-7494
e-mail: d-sundell@peapc.com
Web site: www.urbanomics.org
David Sundell, Researcher
Economic development planning studies, market studies, tax policy analyses, program evaluations & economic & demographic forecasts

Whiteman Osterman & Hanna LLP
One Commerce Plaza, Albany, NY 12260
518-487-7600 Fax: 518-487-7777
e-mail: druzow@woh.com
Web site: www.woh.com
Daniel A Ruzow, Senior Partner
Environmental & zoning law

Offices and agencies generally appear in alphabetical order, except when specific order is requested by listee.

PUBLIC EMPLOYEES

New York State

GOVERNOR'S OFFICE

Governor's Office
Executive Chamber
State Capitol
Albany, NY 12224
518-474-8390 Fax: 518-474-1513
Web site: www.state.ny.us

Governor:
   Eliot Spitzer 518-474-8390
Secretary to the Governor:
   Richard Baum 518-474-4246
Counsel to the Governor:
   David Nocenti 518-474-8343
Senior Advisor to the Governor:
   Lloyd Constantine 518-486-9671
Director, Communications:
   Darren Dopp 518-474-8418
Deputy Secretary, Intergovernmental Affairs:
   Martin Mack 518-408-2555
Assistant Deputy Secretary, Labor Relations:
   Arlene Smoller 518-474-3522
Assistant Counsel to the Governor-Labor & Retirement:
   David Weinstein 518-474-8434

EXECUTIVE DEPARTMENTS AND RELATED AGENCIES

Civil Service Department
Alfred E Smith State Ofc Bldg
Albany, NY 12239
518-457-2487 Fax: 518-457-7547
Web site: www.cs.state.ny.us

Commissioner:
   Nancy G Groenwegen 518-457-3701
Executive Deputy Commissioner:
   Patricia Hite 518-457-6212
Deputy Commissioner, Operations:
   Hector Millan 518-485-7515
Special Counsel:
   Thomas F Brennan 518-485-7278
Counsel:
   Judith Ratner 518-457-3177
Director, Workforce & Occupational Planning:
   Nancy B Kiyonaga 518-485-9274
Director, Internal Audit:
   Joseph Kulkus 518-457-7355
Director, Public Information:
   Erin Barlow 518-457-9375/fax: 518-457-6654
   e-mail: erin.barlow@cs.state.ny.us
Public Records Access Officer:
   Erin Barlow 518-457-6875/fax: 518-457-6654

Administration

Administrative Services Unit
Director, Financial Administration:
   Michael Bosanko 518-457-6490/fax: 518-457-5116

Classification & Compensation Division
Director:
   Nicholas J Vagianelis 518-457-6226/fax: 518-457-8081

Commission Operations
Director:
   Stella Chen Harding 518-457-2575

Diversity, Planning & Management Division
Director:
   Frank E Abrams 518-457-4146/fax: 518-457-0399
Coordinator, Community Outreach:
   George Swiers 518-457-7661/fax: 518-457-0399

Employee Benefits Division
Director:
   Robert DuBois 518-457-9391/fax: 518-485-8952
Director, Employee Insurance Programs:
   Mary B Frye 518-457-1771/fax: 518-457-1311
Asst Director, Financial Management & Accounting:
   David Boland 518-457-5159/fax: 518-457-1311

Employee Health Services Division
Administrator, EHS:
   Maria C Steinbach 518-457-6142/fax: 518-485-1995
Director, Health Services Nursing:
   Mary M McSweeney 518-457-2616

Information Resource Management
Director:
   Frank Slade 518-457-1775/fax: 518-485-5752
   e-mail: frank.slade@cs.state.ny.us

Municipal Services Division
Director:
   Richard Ciprioni 518-457-9553/fax: 518-485-8244
Local Examinations:
   Will Martin 518-457-4487

Personnel
Director:
   Susan China 518-457-1077/fax: 518-457-6875

Planning & Training Division
Director:
   Frank R Santora 518-457-5507

Staffing Services Division
Director:
   Terry Jordan 518-457-5781/fax: 518-457-4239
Asst Director:
   Blaine Ryan-Lynch 518-457-5445
Attendance & Leave Unit:
   Margaret Harrigan 518-457-2295

Testing Services Division
Director:
   Paul Kaiser 518-457-9499/fax: 518-457-4239

Offices and agencies generally appear in alphabetical order, except when specific order is requested by listee.

PUBLIC EMPLOYEES / New York State

Assistant Director:
Debbi Parrington 518-457-5465

Civil Service Commission
President:
Nancy G Groenwegen 518-457-3701
Commissioner:
Daniel E Wall 518-457-3504
Commissioner:
Caroline W Ahl 518-457-5444

Employee Relations, Governor's Office of
Two Empire State Plz
Bldg 2
Albany, NY 12223-1250
518-473-8766 Fax: 518-473-6795
e-mail: info@goer.state.ny.us
Web site: www.goer.state.ny.us

Director:
Gary Johnson 518-474-6988/fax: 518-486-7304
Deputy Director, Contract Negotiations & Administration:
John V Currier 518-474-4800
General Counsel:
Walter J Pellegrini 518-474-4090
Director, Administration:
Mary Hines 518-473-3467/fax: 518-473-6725
Director, Employee Benefits Unit:
Priscilla Feinberg 518-473-6211/fax: 518-423-6294
Director, Information Management Unit:
Debi Orton 518-473-6202/fax: 518-473-6725
Director, Research Unit:
Peter Sennett 518-473-7233/fax: 518-486-5602
Assistant Director, Workforce Training & Development Unit:
Onnolee Smith 518-474-6613/fax: 518-474-8587
Management/Confidential Affairs:
Craig Dickinson 518-473-3130/fax: 518-473-6795

Labor/Management Committees

Family Benefits Committee
55 Elk St, Rm 301C, Albany, NY 12210-2331
Staff Director:
Deborah Long Miller 518-473-8091/fax: 518-473-3581

NYS/CSEA Discipline Unit .... fax: 518-486-9737
55 Elk St, Rm 301D, Albany, NY 12210-2333
Arbitration Panel Coordinator:
Linda Ronda 518-473-6070

NYS/CSEA Partnership for Education & Training .. fax: 518-473-9457
240 Washington Ave Extension, Ste 502, Albany, NY 12203
800-253-4332 or 518-486-7814 Fax: 518-473-9457
Co-Director:
Deb Berg 518-473-8991
Co-Director:
Ira Baumgarten 518-473-8991

NYS/SSU Joint Labor-Management Committee .... fax: 518-457-9445
55 Elk St, Rm 301-B, Albany, NY 12210
Employee Program Assistant:
Patricia Merola 518-457-9420

NYS/UUP Labor-Management Committee .... fax: 518-457-9445
55 Elk St, Rm 301-B, Albany, NY 12210
Executive Director:
Tina Kaplan 518-486-4666

Statewide Employee Assistance Programs .... fax: 518-486-9796
55 Elk St, Rm 301A, Albany, NY 12210-2316
800-822-0244 Fax: 518-486-9796
Asst Director:
Michael Brace 518-486-9769

Public Employment Relations Board
80 Wolf Rd
Albany, NY 12205
518-457-2854 Fax: 518-457-2664
e-mail: perbinfo@perb.state.ny.us
Web site: www.perb.state.ny.us

Chair:
Jerome Lefkowitz 518-457-2578
Member:
Robert S Hite 518-457-2578
Executive Director:
James R Edgar 518-457-2676
Deputy Chair & Counsel (Acting):
Deborah A Sabin 518-457-2614
Asst Counsel to the Board:
Vacant 518-457-2614
Secretary to the Board:
Sheila Talavera 518-457-2578

Administration Section
Administrative Officer:
Patricia Bredenko 518-457-2922

Conciliation Section
Director:
Richard A Curreri 518-457-2690
Asst Director:
Vacant 518-457-2690

District Offices
Buffalo .... fax: 716-847-3690
125 Main St, Buffalo, NY 14203
Regional Director:
Scott Marchant 716-847-3449

New York City .... fax: 718-722-4550
55 Hanson Pl, Ste 700, Brooklyn, NY 11217
Regional Director:
Philip Maier 718-722-4545

Employment Practices & Representation Section
Director:
Monte Klein 518-457-6410
Asst Director:
Susan Comenzo 518-457-6410

Legal Section
Associate Counsel (Acting):
Sandra Nathan 518-457-2678
Asst Counsel for Litigation:
Vacant 518-457-2678

State Comptroller, Office of the
110 State St, 15th Fl
Albany, NY 12236-0001
518-474-4040 Fax: 518-473-3004
Web site: www.osc.state.ny.us

Offices and agencies generally appear in alphabetical order, except when specific order is requested by listee.

PUBLIC EMPLOYEES / New York State

633 Third Ave, 31st Fl
New York, NY 10017-6754
212-681-4491
Fax: 212-681-4468

State Comptroller:
  Thomas P DiNapoli . . . . 518-474-4040 or 212-681-4491

Division of State Services
Deputy Comptroller:
  Jerry Barber 518-474-5598

Payroll & Revenue Services Division
Deputy Comptroller:
  Daniel Berry 518-408-4149
Director, Unclaimed Funds:
  Lawrence Schantz 518-473-6438
Director, State Payroll Services:
  Robin R Rabii 518-474-3400

Executive Office
Chief of Staff:
  Jack Chartier 212-681-4498
First Deputy Comptroller:
  Thomas Sanzillo 518-474-2909
Executive Deputy Comptroller:
  Diana J Ritter 518-474-3610
Deputy Chief of Staff:
  Roberta Rubin . . . . 212-681-4495 or 518-474-4040
Director, Business Communication:
  Ellen J Evans . . . . 518-473-1323 or 212-681-4489
Chief Information Officer:
  Jeffrey S Grunfeld 518-408-2915/fax: 518-473-3004
Internal Control Officer:
  Raymond H Harris 518-473-6017

Retirement Services
Deputy Comptroller:
  Laura Anglin 518-474-2600
Asst Comptroller:
  Nancy Burton 518-474-4600

Accounting Bureau
Director:
  Daniel Burns 518-474-3670

Actuarial Bureau
Actuary:
  Teri Landin 518-474-4537

Benefit Calculations & Disbursements
Director:
  Veronica D'Alauro 518-474-5556

Disability Processing/Hearing Administration
Director:
  Kathy Nowak 518-473-1347

Member & Employee Services
Director:
  Ginger Dame 518-474-1101

Retirement Communications
Director:
  Paul Kentoffio 518-474-7096

CORPORATIONS, AUTHORITIES AND COMMISSIONS

New York State Teachers' Retirement System
10 Corporate Woods Dr
Albany, NY 12211-2395
518-447-2900 or 800-348-7298 Fax: 518-447-2695
e-mail: communit@nystrs.state.ny.us
Web site: www.nystrs.org

Executive Director:
  George M Philip 518-447-2666
  e-mail: execdir@nystrs.state.ny.us
General Counsel:
  Wayne Schneider 518-447-2722
Actuary:
  Richard Young 518-447-2692
Director, Administration:
  William S O'Brien 518-447-2730
Director, Member Relations:
  Sheila Gardella 518-447-2684
Manager, Public Information:
  John Cardillo 518-447-4743
Real Estate Investment Officer:
  John Virtanen 518-447-2751
Securities Investment Officer:
  Lawrence A Johansen 518-447-2611

New York State Temporary Commission of Investigation
59 Maiden Lane, 31st Fl
New York, NY 10038
212-344-6660 Fax: 212-344-6868
e-mail: commissioner@sic.state.ny.us
Web site: www.sic.state.ny.us

Chairman:
  Alfred D Lerner 212-344-6660
Deputy Commissioner & Chief Counsel:
  Anthony T Cartusciello 212-344-6670
Chief Investigator:
  Anthony Hellmer 212-344-6660

NEW YORK STATE LEGISLATURE

See Legislative Branch in Section 1 for additional Standing Committee and Subcommittee information.

Assembly Standing Committees

Governmental Employees
Chair:
  Peter J Abbate, Jr (D) 518-455-3053
Ranking Minority Member:
  Joseph S Saladino (R) 518-455-5305

Labor
Chair:
  Susan V John (D) 518-455-4527
Ranking Minority Member:
  Thomas W Alfano (R) 518-455-4627

Offices and agencies generally appear in alphabetical order, except when specific order is requested by listee.

PUBLIC EMPLOYEES / U.S. Government

Senate Standing Committees

Civil Service & Pensions
Chair:
  Joseph E Robach (R) 518-455-2909
Ranking Minority Member:
  Diane J Savino (D) 518-455-2437

Labor
Chair:
  George D Maziarz (R) 518-455-2024
Ranking Minority Member:
  George Onorato (D) 518-455-3486

Senate/Assembly Legislative Commissions

Government Administration, Legislative Commission on
Assembly Chair:
  Joan Millman (D) 518-455-5426
Senate Vice Chair:
  Owen H Johnson (R) 518-455-3411
Senior Program Manager:
  Philip Johnson 518-455-3632/fax: 518-455-4574

U.S. Government

EXECUTIVE DEPARTMENTS AND RELATED AGENCIES

US Merit Systems Protection Board
Web site: www.mspb.gov

New York Field Office
26 Federal Plaza, Room 3137A, New York, NY 10278-0022
Chief Administrative Judge:
  Arthur Joseph 212-264-9372/fax: 212-264-1417

US Office of Personnel Management
Web site: www.usajobs.opm.gov

PHILADELPHIA SERVICE CENTER (serving New York)
William J Green Fed Bldg, Rm 3400, 600 Arch St, Philadelphia, PA 19106
Director:
  Joseph D Stix 215-861-3031/fax: 215-861-3030
  e-mail: philadelphia@opm.gov

U.S. CONGRESS

See U.S. Congress Chapter for additional Standing Committee and Subcommittee information.

House of Representatives Standing Committees
Chair:
  Henry A Waxman (D-CA) 202-225-3976
Ranking Minority Member:
  Thomas M Davis, III (R-VA) 202-225-1492
New York Delegate:
  Brian M Higgins (D) 202-225-3306
New York Delegate:
  Carolyn B Maloney (D) 202-225-7944
New York Delegate:
  John M McHugh (R) 202-225-4611
New York Delegate:
  Major R Owens (D) 202-225-6231
New York Delegate:
  Edolphus Towns (D) 202-225-5936

Subcommittee
Federal Workforce, Postal Service and the District of Columbia
Chair:
  Danny K Davis (D-IL) 202-225-5871
Ranking Minority Member:
  Kenny Marchant (R-TX) 202-225-6605
New York Delegate:
  Major R Owens (D) 202-225-6231

Senate Standing Committees

Homeland Security & Governmental Affairs
Chair:
  Joseph I Liberman (D-CT) 202-224-4041
Ranking Minority Member:
  Susan Collins (R-ME) 202-224-2523

Private Sector

AFSCME District Council 37
150 State St, Albany, NY 12207
518-436-0665 or 212-815-1550 Fax: 518-436-1066
Wanda Williams, Director
NYC employees union

AFSCME, New York
212 Great Oaks Blvd, Albany, NY 12203
518-869-2245 Fax: 518-869-8649
e-mail: bmcdonnell@organize.afscme.org
Web site: www.afscme.org
Brian McDonnell, Legislative Political Director
Union representing public service & healthcare workers; American Federation of State, County & Municipal Employees

Offices and agencies generally appear in alphabetical order, except when specific order is requested by listee.

PUBLIC EMPLOYEES / Private Sector

Civil Service Employees Assn of NY (CSEA), Local 1000, AFSCME, AFL-CIO
143 Washington Ave, Albany, NY 12210
518-257-1000 or 800-342-4146 Fax: 518-462-3639
Web site: www.csealocal1000.org
Danny Donohue, President
Public/private employees union

Cornell University, School of Industrial & Labor Relations
356 ILR Research Bldg, Ithaca, NY 14853-3901
607-255-7581 Fax: 607-255-0245
e-mail: klb23@cornell.edu
Web site: www.ilr.cornell.edu
Kate Bronfenbrenner, Director, Labor Education Research
Public sector organizations; leadership; temporary & contract workers; union organizing; & collective bargaining

District Council 37, AFSCME, AFL-CIO
125 Barclay St, New York, NY 10007
212-815-1000 Fax: 212-815-1402
e-mail: dsullivan@dc37.net
Web site: www.dc37.net
Dennis Sullivan, Director, Research & Negotiations
NYC employees union

NYC Board of Education Employees, Local 372/AFSCME, AFL-CIO
125 Barclay Street, 6th Floor, New York, NY 10007
212-815-1372 Fax: 212-815-1347
Web site: www.local372.com
Veronica Montgomery-Costa, President - District Council 37/372

NYS Association of Chiefs of Police Inc
2697 Hamburg Street, Schenectady, NY 12303-3783
518-355-3371 Fax: 518-356-5767
e-mail: nysacop@nycap.rr.com
Web site: www.nychiefs.org
Joseph S Dominelli, Executive Director

NYS Association of Fire Chiefs
1670 Columbia Turnpike, Box 328, East Schodack, NY 12063-0328
518-477-2631 Fax: 518-477-4430
e-mail: tlabelle@nysfirechiefs.com
Web site: www.nysfirechiefs.com
Thomas LaBelle, Executive Director

NYS Correctional Officers & Police Benevolent Association Inc
102 Hackett Blvd, Albany, NY 12209
518-427-1551 Fax: 518-426-1635
e-mail: nyscopba@nyscopba.org
Web site: www.nyscopba.org
Larry Flanagan, Jr, President

NYS Court Clerks Association
170 Duane St, New York, NY 10013
212-941-5700 Fax: 212-941-5705
Kevin E Scanlon, Sr, President

NYS Deputies Association Inc
61 Laredo Dr, Rochester, NY 14624
585-247-9322 Fax: 585-247-6661
e-mail: tross1@rochester.rr.com
Web site: www.nysdeputy.org
Thomas H Ross, Executive Director

NYS Bar Assn, Attorneys in Public Service Cmte
NYS Health Department
433 River St, 5th Fl, Ste 330, Troy, NY 12180-2299
518-402-0748 Fax: 518-402-0751
e-mail: jfh01@health.state.ny.us
Hon James F Horan, Chair
Advancing the interests of NY governmental & not-for-profit attorneys

NYS Law Enforcement Officers Union, Council 82, AFSCME, AFL-CIO
Hollis V Chase Bldg, 63 Colvin Ave, Albany, NY 12206
518-489-8424 Fax: 518-489-8430
e-mail: c82@council82.org
Web site: www.council82.org
Kathy B McCormack, Legislative Director

NYS Parole Officers Association
PO Box 5821, Albany, NY 12205-0821
518-393-6541 Fax: 518-393-6541
e-mail: hsj195@localnet.com
H Susan Jeffords, President
Professional association representing NYS parole affairs

NYS Sheriffs' Association
27 Elk St, Albany, NY 12207-1002
518-434-9091 Fax: 518-434-9093
e-mail: pkehoe@nysheriffs.org
Web site: www.nysheriffs.org
Peter R Kehoe, Executive Director

New York State Law Enforcement Council
One Hogan Place, New York, NY 10013
212-335-8927 Fax: 212-335-3808
Web site: www.nyslec.org
Leroy Frazer, Jr, Coordinator
Founded in 1982 as a legislative advocate for NY's law enforcement community. The members represent leading law enforcement professionals throughout the state. An active voice and participant in improving the quality of justice and a safer NY.

New York State Public Employees Federation (PEF)
1168-70 Troy-Schenectady Rd, PO Box 12414, Albany, NY 12212
518-785-1900 x211 Fax: 518-783-1117
e-mail: kbrynien@pef.org
Web site: www.nyspef.org
Kenneth D Brynien, President
Professional, scientific & technical employees union

Offices and agencies generally appear in alphabetical order, except when specific order is requested by listee.

PUBLIC EMPLOYEES / Private Sector

New York State Supreme Court Officers Association
299 Broadway, Suite 1100, New York, NY 10007-1921
212-406-4292 or 212-406-4276 Fax: 212-791-8420
e-mail: lbroderick@nysscoa.org
Web site: www.nysscoa.org
John P McKillop, President
Supreme Court Officers Union

New York State United Teachers/AFT, AFL-CIO
800 Troy-Schenectady Road, Latham, NY 12110-2455
518-213-6000 or 800-342-9810
Web site: www.nysut.org
Richard Iannuzzi, President

Organization of NYS Management Confidential Employees
3 Washington Square, Albany, NY 12205
518-456-5241 or 800-828-6623 Fax: 518-456-3838
e-mail: nysomce@gmail.com
Web site: www.nysomce.org
Barbara Zaron, President
Professional organization of state management & confidential employees

Patrolmen's Benevolent Association
40 Fulton St, 17th Fl, New York, NY 10038
212-233-5531 Fax: 212-233-3952
e-mail: union@nycpba.org
Web site: www.nycpba.org
Patrick Lynch, President
NYC patrolmen's union

Police Conference of NY Inc (PCNY)
112 State St, Ste 1120, Albany, NY 12207
518-463-3283 Fax: 518-463-2488
e-mail: pcnyinfo@pcny.org
Web site: www.pcny.org
Edward W Guzdek, President
Advocacy for law enforcement officers

Professional Fire Fighters Association Inc (NYS)
111 Washington Ave, Suite 207, Albany, NY 12210-6511
518-436-8827 Fax: 518-436-8830
e-mail: suite207@nyspffa.org
Web site: www.nyspffa.org
Charles Morello, President
Union representing city, village & town firefighters

Retired Public Employees Association
435 New Karner Road, Albany, NY 12205-3833
518-869-2542 ext 25 or 518-265-9284 Fax: 518-869-0631
e-mail: mail@rpea.org
Web site: www.rppa.org
Donald Hirshorn, Legislative Liaison & Counsel
Advocacy for retired public employees & their families

State Employees Federal Credit Union
1239 Washington Avenue, Albany, NY 12206-1067
518-452-8234 Fax: 518-464-5227
Web site: www.sefcu.com
John Gallagher, Director, Internal Audit

Syracuse University, Maxwell School of Citizenship & Public Affairs
215 Eggers Hall, Syracuse, NY 13244-1090
315-443-4000 Fax: 315-443-9721
e-mail: sibretsc@maxwell.syr.edu
Stuart Bretschneider, Associate Dean & Chair, Professor of Public Administration
Capital financing & debt management; public employee pensions; financial management

Trooper Foundation-State of New York Inc
3 Airport Park Blvd, Latham, NY 12110-1441
518-785-1002 Fax: 518-785-1003
e-mail: rmincher@nystf.org
Web site: www.nystrooperfoundation.org
Rachael L Mincher, Foundation Administrator
Supports programs & services of the NYS Police

Uniformed Fire Officers Association
225 Broadway, Suite 401, New York, NY 10007
212-293-9300 Fax: 212-292-1560
e-mail: administrator@ufoa.org
Web site: www.ufoa.org
Peter L Gorman, President
NYC fire officers' union

United Transportation Union
35 Fuller Rd, Suite 205, Albany, NY 12205
518-438-8403 Fax: 518-438-8404
e-mail: sjnasca@aol.com
Web site: www.utu.org
Samuel Nasca, Legislative Director
Federal government railroad, bus & airline employees; public employees

United University Professions
PO Box 15143, Albany, NY 12212-5143
518-640-6600 Fax: 518-640-6698
e-mail: feedback@uupmail.org
Web site: www.uupinfo.org
William E Scheuerman, President
SUNY labor union of academic & other professional faculty

Offices and agencies generally appear in alphabetical order, except when specific order is requested by listee.

REAL PROPERTY

New York State

GOVERNOR'S OFFICE

Governor's Office
Executive Chamber
State Capitol
Albany, NY 12224
518-474-8390 Fax: 518-474-1513
Web site: www.state.ny.us

Governor:
   Eliot Spitzer 518-474-8390
Secretary to the Governor:
   Richard Baum 518-474-4246
Counsel to the Governor:
   David Nocenti 518-474-8343
Senior Advisor to the Governor:
   Lloyd Constantine 518-486-9671
Director, Communications:
   Darren Dopp 518-474-8418
Assistant Counsel to the Governor-Housing, Local Governments & Arts:
   Amanda Hiller 518-474-8494
Senior Advisor, Intergovernmental Affairs:
   Michael Schell 518-408-2555

EXECUTIVE DEPARTMENTS AND RELATED AGENCIES

General Services, Office of
Corning Tower, 41st Fl
Empire State Plaza
Albany, NY 12242
518-474-3899 Fax: 518-474-1546
Web site: www.ogs.state.ny.us

633 Third Ave
New York, NY 10017
212-681-4580
Fax: 212-681-4558

Commissioner:
   John C Egan 518-474-5991
   e-mail: john.egan@ogs.state.ny.us
First Deputy Commissioner:
   Robert J Fleury 518-473-6953
   e-mail: robert.fleury@ogs.state.ny.us
Assistant Commissioner, Public Affairs:
   Brad Maione 518-474-5987/fax: 518-474-3187
   e-mail: brad.maione@ogs.state.ny.us

Real Estate Planning & Development Group
Deputy Commissioner:
   William L Hill Jr 518-474-5390
   e-mail: william.hill@ogs.state.ny.us
Director, Real Estate Planning & Development:
   James Sproat 518-474-4944
Director, Real Estate Planning & Development:
   Vacant 518-474-4944
Bureau Chief, Land Management:
   Charles Sheifer 518-474-2195
Bureau Chief, Space Planning & Lease Construction & Compliance:
   Anne M Carr 518-473-9887
Bureau Chief, Space Planning & Lease Construction & Compliance:
   John T Culliton 518-473-9887
Bureau Chief, Real Esatte Planning - Downstate:
   Joseph V Luvera 518-474-7963
Asst Director, Real Estate Planning - Upstate:
   Timothy J Leonard 518-473-9887
Asst Director, Real Estate Planning - Downstate:
   Robert W Lazarou 518-486-7963

Real Property Management Group
Deputy Commissioner:
   William L Hill Jr 518-474-5390/fax: 518-474-1523
   e-mail: william.hill@ogs.state.ny.us
Director:
   Martin J Gilroy 518-474-6057/fax: 518-474-1523
Manager, Capital Planning:
   Richard Stock 518-473-3927/fax: 518-473-2189
Director, Construction Management:
   Kevin O'Connor 518-473-2041/fax: 518-473-2189
Director, Downstate Regional Buildings:
   Richard Gallagher 718-923-4448/fax: 718-923-4451
Director, Empire State Plaza & Downtown Buildings:
   Thomas E Casey 518-474-8894/fax: 518-474-4182
Director, Upstate Harriman State Office Campus:
   Tom O'Connell 518-457-2290/fax: 518-457-8297
Director, Utilities Management:
   Robert Lobdell 518-474-3249/fax: 518-402-5682

Law Department
State Capitol
Albany, NY 12224-0341
518-474-7330 Fax: 518-402-2472
Web site: www.oag.state.ny.us

120 Broadway
New York, NY 10271-0332
212-416-8000
Fax: 212-416-8942

Attorney General:
   Andrew M Cuomo 518-474-7330

Public Advocacy Division
Deputy Attorney General:
   Dietrich Snell 212-416-8041/fax: 212-416-8068
Special Counsel:
   Mary Ellen Burns 212-416-6155

Offices and agencies generally appear in alphabetical order, except when specific order is requested by listee.

REAL PROPERTY / New York State

Civil Rights Bureau
Bureau Chief:
 Dennis Parker 212-416-8250/fax: 212-416-8074

Investment Protection Bureau
Bureau Chief:
 David Brown 212-416-8198/fax: 212-416-6377

State Counsel Division
Deputy Attorney General:
 Richard Rifkin 518-473-7190
Assistant Deputy Attorney General:
 Patricia Martinelli 518-473-0648/fax: 518-486-9777
Assistant Deputy Attorney General:
 Susan L Watson 212-416-8579/fax: 212-416-6001

Claims Bureau
Bureau Chief:
 Susan Pogoda 212-416-8516/fax: 212-416-8946

Real Property Bureau
Bureau Chief:
 Henry A DeCotis 518-474-7151/fax: 518-473-5106

Real Property Services, Office of
16 Sheridan Ave
Albany, NY 12210-2714
518-486-5446   Fax: 518-474-9276
e-mail: nysorps@orps.state.ny.us
Web site: www.orps.state.ny.us

Executive Director:
 Donald C DeWitt 518-474-5711
Executive Deputy Director:
 Steve King 518-473-6914
Acting Counsel:
 James O'Keefe 518-474-6753
Director, Public Information:
 Geoffrey T Gloak 518-486-5446
 e-mail: geoffrey.gloak@orps.state.ny.us

Research, Information & Policy Development
Director:
 James Dunne 518-473-4532
 e-mail: jim.dunne@orps.state.ny.us

Regional Customer Service Delivery
Director:
 David Williams 518-473-7574
 e-mail: dave.williams@orps.state.ny.us

Albany (Northern Region) .... fax: 518-486-7752
16 Sheridan Ave, Albany, NY 12210
Regional Director:
 Jeffrey Green 518-486-4403
 e-mail: internet.northern@orps.state.ny.us

Batavia (Western Region)
Genesee County Bldg 2, 3837 W Main Rd, Batavia, NY 14020
Regional Director:
 Joseph Muscarella 585-343-6329/fax: 585-343-9740
 e-mail: internet.western@orps.state.ny.us

Long Island Satellite Office .... fax: 631-952-3729
250 Veterans Memorial Hgwy, Rm 2B-44, Hauppauge, NY 11788
Manager:
 Louis Cubello 631-952-3650
 e-mail: internet.metro@orps.state.ny.us

Newburgh (Southern Region) .... fax: 845-567-2690
263 Route 17K, Ste 2001, Newburgh, NY 12550-8310
Regional Director:
 John Wolham 845-567-2648
 e-mail: internet.southern@orps.state.ny.us

Saranac Lake Satellite Office .... fax: 518-891-2639
43 Broadway, Saranac Lake, NY 12983
Office Manager:
 Dan Lancor 518-891-1780
 e-mail: internet.saranac@orps.state.ny.us

Syracuse (Central Region) .... fax: 315-471-3634
401 South Salina St, Syracuse, NY 13202
Regional Director:
 Teresa Frank 315-471-2347
 e-mail: internet.central@orps.state.ny.us

State Board of Real Property Services
Chair:
 George E Herren 518-474-5711
Executive Secretary:
 Donald C DeWitt 518-474-5711
Asst to the Board:
 Darlene A Maloney 518-474-3793/fax: 518-474-9276

Transportation Department
50 Wolf Rd, 6th Fl
Albany, NY 12232
518-457-5100 or 518-457-6195   Fax: 518-457-5583
Web site: www.nysdot.gov

Commissioner:
 Astrid C Glynn 518-457-4422
Chief Operating Officer:
 Brian O Rowback 518-457-4422
 e-mail: browback@dot.state.ny.us

Engineering Division
Chief Engineer:
 Michael Shamma 518-457-4430
Director, Environmental Analysis:
 Mary E Ivey 518-457-5672
Director, Design:
 Daniel D'Angelo 518-457-6452

NEW YORK STATE LEGISLATURE

See Legislative Branch in Section 1 for additional Standing Committee and Subcommittee information.

Assembly Standing Committees

Economic Development, Job Creation, Commerce & Industry
Chair:
 Robin L Schimminger (D) 518-455-4767
Ranking Minority Member:
 Marc Butler (R) 518-455-5393

Housing
Chair:
 Vito J Lopez (D) 518-455-5537
Ranking Minority Member:
 Michael J Fitzpatrick (R) 518-455-5021

Offices and agencies generally appear in alphabetical order, except when specific order is requested by listee.

REAL PROPERTY / U.S. Government

Real Property Taxation
Chair:
 Sandra R Galef (D) 518-455-5348
Ranking Minority Member:
 Nancy Calhoun (R) 518-455-5441

Senate Standing Committees

Commerce, Economic Development & Small Business
Chair:
 James S Alesi (R) 518-455-2015

Ranking Minority Member:
 Efrain Gonzalez, Jr (D) 518-455-3395

Housing Construction & Community Development
Chair:
 John J Bonacic (R) 518-455-3181
Ranking Minority Member:
 Liz Krueger (D) 518-455-2297

U.S. Government

EXECUTIVE DEPARTMENTS AND RELATED AGENCIES

US Department of Agriculture

Rural Development
Web site: www.rurdev.usda.gov/ny

New York State Office .... fax: 315-477-6438
The Galleries of Syracuse, 441 S Salina St, Ste 357, 5th Fl, Syracuse, NY 13202-2425
TTY: 315-477-6447 or 315-477-6400 Fax: 315-477-6438
Acting State Director:
 Scott Collins 315-477-6400
Special Projects Representative:
 Vacant 315-477-6433

US General Services Administration
Web site: www.gsa.gov

Region 2—New York
26 Federal Plaza, Rm 18-102, New York, NY 10278
212-264-9290
Regional Administrator:
 Emily R Baker 212-264-2600/fax: 212-264-3998
 e-mail: emily.baker@gsa.gov
Deputy Regional Administrator:
 Steve Ruggiero 212-264-2600/fax: 212-264-3998
 e-mail: steve.ruggiero@gsa.gov

Administration
Director, Program Support & Human Resources:
 Joseph J Giorgianni 212-264-0780/fax: 212-264-6798
 e-mail: joseph.giorgianni@gsa.gov

Federal Supply Service
Acting Asst Regional Administrator:
 Charles B Weill 212-264-3590/fax: 212-264-9759

Federal Technology Service
Asst Regional Administrator (Acting):
 Steve Ruggiero 212-264-3590
 e-mail: steve.ruggiero@gsa.gov

Inspector General's Office
Asst Regional Inspector, Investigations:
 Daniel Walsh 212-264-7300/fax: 212-264-7154
Regional Director, Audit:
 Joseph Mastropietro 212-264-8620

Public Buildings Service
Asst Regional Administrator:
 John Scorcia 212-264-4282/fax: 212-264-2232
 e-mail: john.scorcia@gsa.gov
Deputy Asst Regional Administrator:
 Vacant 212-264-4285
Director, Property Management:
 David Segermeister 212-264-4273/fax: 212-264-2746
Director, Realty Services:
 Donald W Eigendorff 212-264-4210/fax: 212-264-9400

Private Sector

Appraisal Education Network School & Merrell Institute
1461 Lakeland Ave, Bohemia, NY 11716
631-563-7720 Fax: 631-563-7719
e-mail: bcm@doctor.com
Web site: www.merrellinstitute.com
Bill C Merrell, Director
Real estate sales, broker, appraiser, mortgage & property management education courses, paralegal, continuing education, home inspection

Brookfield Properties Corporation
Three World Financial Center, 200 Vesey Street, 11th Floor, New York, NY 10281
212-417-7000 Fax: 212-417-7214
e-mail: kkane@brookfieldproperties.com
Web site: www.brookfieldproperties.com
Kathleen G Kane, General Counsel
Commercial real estate

Offices and agencies generally appear in alphabetical order, except when specific order is requested by listee.

REAL PROPERTY / Private Sector

Building & Realty Institute
80 Business Park Dr, Armonk, NY 10504
914-273-0730 Fax: 914-273-7051
e-mail: aaaa@buildersinstitute.org
Web site: www.buildersinstitute.org
Albert A Annunziata, Executive Director
Building, realty & construction industry membership organization

Colliers ABR Inc
40 E 52nd St, New York, NY 10022
212-758-0800 Fax: 212-758-6190
Web site: www.colliersabr.com
Mark P Boisi, Chairman
Commercial real estate & property management

NYS Bar Assn, Real Property Law Section
D H Ferguson, Attorney, PLLC
141 Sully's Trail, Suite 12, Pittsford, NY 14534
585-586-0459 or 585-586-0450 Fax: 585-586-2297
e-mail: dhferguson@frontiernet.net
Dorothy H Ferguson, Chair

Ernst & Young
5 Times Square, New York, NY 10036-6350
212-773-4500 Fax: 212-773-4986
e-mail: dale.reiss@ey.com
Web site: www.ey.com
Dale Anne Reiss, Global & Americas Director-Real Estate, Hospitality & Construction

Fisher Brothers
299 Park Ave, New York, NY 10171
212-752-5000 Fax: 212-940-6879
Arnold Fisher, Partner
Real estate investment & development

GVA Williams
380 Madison Ave, 3rd Floor, New York, NY 10017
212-716-3555 Fax: 212-716-3710
e-mail: mtcohen@gvawilliams.com
Web site: www.gvawilliams.com
Michael T Cohen, Chairman of the Executive Committee
Real estate brokerage, ownership, sales, leasing, management & consulting

Glenwood Management Corporation
1200 Union Turnpike, New Hyde Park, NY 11040
718-343-6400 Fax: 718-343-0009
Web site: www.glenwoodmanagement.com
Leonard Litwin, President
Property management

Greater Rochester Association of Realtors Inc
930 East Avenue, Rochester, NY 14607
585-292-5000 Fax: 585-292-5008
e-mail: karenw@grar.net
Web site: www.homesteadnet.com
Karen Wingender, Chief Executive Officer

Greater Syracuse Association of Realtors Inc
1020 Seventh North St, Ste 140, Liverpool, NY 13088
315-457-5979 Fax: 315-457-5884
e-mail: fetyko@cnyrealtor.com
Web site: www.cnyrealtor.com
Lynnore Fetyko, Chief Executive Officer

H J Kalikow & Co LLC
101 Park Ave, 25th Fl, New York, NY 10178
212-808-7000 Fax: 212-573-6380
Web site: www.hjkalikow.com
Peter S Kalikow, President
Real estate development

J J Higgins Properties Inc
20 North Main St, Pittsford, NY 14534
585-381-6030 Fax: 585-381-0571
e-mail: jjhigginsproperties@frontiernet.net
Web site: www.jjhigginsproperties.com
John J Higgins, President
Residential properties, relocation, commercial properties, home sales & listings, buyer agency

Landauer Realty Group Inc
1177 Avenue of the Americas, New York, NY 10036
212-759-9700 or 212-326-4752 Fax: 212-326-4802
e-mail: david.arena@grubb-ellis.com
Web site: www.landauer.com
David Arena, President
Commercial real estate appraisers, analysts & transaction consultants

MJ Peterson Corporation
501 Audubon Pkwy, Amherst, NY 14228
716-688-1234 Fax: 716-688-5463
e-mail: corporate@mjpeterson.com
Web site: www.mjpeterson.com
Victor L Peterson, Jr, President
Residential, commercial, property management, development and new homes

Mancuso Business Development Group
56 Harvester Ave, Batavia, NY 14020
585-343-2800 Fax: 585-343-7096
e-mail: tom@mancusogroup.com
Web site: www.mancusogroup.com
Tom Mancuso, President
Improve operating performances of multi tenant industrial and office and business incubator properties

Metro/Colvin Realty Inc
2211 Sheridan Dr, Kenmore, NY 14223
716-874-0110 Fax: 716-874-9015
e-mail: metrocolvin1@aol.com
John Riordan, President
Residential & commercial property

Offices and agencies generally appear in alphabetical order, except when specific order is requested by listee.

REAL PROPERTY / Private Sector

Metro/Horohoe-Leimbach
3199 Delaware Ave, Kenmore, NY 14217
716-873-5404 Fax: 716-873-8901
e-mail: whorohoe@aol.com
Web site: metrohorohoe.com
William Horohoe, Vice President
Residential real estate

NY Commercial Association of Realtors
130 Washington Ave, Albany, NY 12210
518-463-5315 Fax: 518-462-5474
e-mail: nyscar@att.net
Web site: www.nyscarxchange.com
David M Dworkin, President
Commercial real estate

NYS Association of Realtors
130 Washington Ave, Albany, NY 12210-2298
518-463-0300 Fax: 518-462-5474
e-mail: admin@nysar.com
Web site: www.nysar.com
Charles M Staro, Chief Executive Officer

NYS Land Title Association
2 Rector St, Ste 901, New York, NY 10006-1819
212-964-3701 Fax: 212-964-7185
e-mail: nyslta@nyslta.org
Web site: www.nyslta.org
Sharon Sabol, Executive Vice President
Trade association for title insurance industry

NYS Society of Real Estate Appraisers
130 Washington Ave, Albany, NY 12210-2298
518-463-0300 Fax: 518-462-5474
e-mail: nyssrea@nysar.com
Web site: www.nyrealestateappraisers.com
Carol DiSento, President
Real estate appraisal

Community Bankers Assn of NY State, Mortgages & Real Estate Cmte
New York Community Bank
615 Merrick Ave, Westbury, NY 11590
516-683-4100 Fax: 516-683-8344
Web site: www.mynycb.com
James O'Donovan, Chair

New York Landmarks Conservancy
1 Whitehall St, 21 Fl, New York, NY 10004
212-995-5260 Fax: 212-995-5268
e-mail: nylandmarks@nylandmarks.org
Web site: www.nylandmarks.org
Peg Breen, President
Technical & financial assistance for preservation & reuse of landmark buildings

New York State Assessors' Association
PO Box 888, Middletown, NY 10940
845-344-0292 Fax: 845-343-8238
e-mail: nysaa@nyassessor.com
Web site: www.nyassessor.com
Thomas Frey, Executive Secretary
Real property tax issues

Pomeroy Appraisal Associates Inc
Pomeroy Pl, 225 W Jefferson St, Syracuse, NY 13202
315-422-7106 Fax: 315-476-1011
e-mail: dfisher@pomeroyappraisal.com
Web site: pomeroyappraisal.com
Donald A Fisher, MAI, ARA
Real estate appraisal & consultation

R W Bronstein Corporation
3666 Main St, Buffalo, NY 14226
716-835-7400 or 800-642-2500 Fax: 716-835-7419
e-mail: value@bronstein.net
Web site: www.bronstein.net
Richard W Bronstein, President
Real estate, appraisals & auctions; valuation & marketing of all types of realty and chattels

Real Estate Board of New York Inc
570 Lexington Ave, New York, NY 10022
212-532-3120 Fax: 212-481-0122
e-mail: stevenspinola@rebny.com
Web site: www.rebny.com
Steven Spinola, President
Representing real estate professionals & firms in New York City

Realty Advisory Board on Labor Relations
292 Madison Ave, New York, NY 10017
212-889-4100 Fax: 212-889-4105
e-mail: jberg@rabolr.com
Web site: www.rabolr.com
James Berg, President
Labor negotiations for realtors & realty firms

Realty USA
6505 E Quaker Rd, Orchard Park, NY 14127
716-662-2000 Fax: 716-662-3385
e-mail: mwhitehead@realtyusa.com
Web site: www.realtyusa.com
Merle Whitehead, President & Chief Executive Officer
Residential real estate

Red Barn Properties
Six Schoen Pl, Pittsford, NY 14534
585-381-2222 x11 Fax: 585-381-1854
e-mail: estelle@redbarnproperties.com
Web site: www.redbarnproperties.com
Estelle O'Connell, Relocation Director
Specializing in local, national & global residential relocation

Offices and agencies generally appear in alphabetical order, except when specific order is requested by listee.

REAL PROPERTY / Private Sector

Related Companies LP
60 Columbus Circle, 19th Fl, New York, NY 10023
212-421-5333 Fax: 212-801-1036
e-mail: bbeal@related.com
Web site: www.related.com
Bruce A Beal, Jr, Executive Vice President, NY Development Group
Residential & commercial real estate

Robert Schalkenbach Foundation
149 Madison Ave, Ste 601, New York, NY 10016
212-683-6424 Fax: 212-683-6454
e-mail: msullivan@schalkenbach.org
Web site: www.schalkenbach.org
Mark A Sullivan, Administrative Director
Land value taxation, real property & economic publications

Roohan Realty
519 Broadway, Saratoga Springs, NY 12866-2208
518-587-4500 Fax: 518-587-4509
e-mail: troohan@roohanrealty.com
Web site: www.roohanrealty.com
J Thomas Roohan, President
Commercial & residential property

Silverstein Properties Inc
7 World Trade Center, 250 Greenwich Street, 38th Floor, New York, NY 10036
212-490-0666 Fax: 212-687-0067
Larry A Silverstein, President, Chief Executive Officer
NYC commercial real estate

Sonnenblick-Goldman Company
712 Fifth Ave, New York, NY 10019
212-841-9200 Fax: 212-262-4224
e-mail: asonnenblick@sonngold.com
Web site: www.sonngold.com
Arthur I Sonnenblick, Senior Managing Director
Real estate investment banking

Tishman Speyer Properties
Rockefeller Center, 45 Rockefeller Plaza, New York, NY 10111
212-715-0300 Fax: 212-319-1745
e-mail: jspeyer@tishmanspeyer.com
Web site: www.tishmanspeyer.com
Jerry I Speyer, President
Owners/builders

United Jewish Appeal-Federation of Jewish Philanthropies
130 E 59th St, New York, NY 10022
212-980-1000 Fax: 212-836-1653
e-mail: flynnc@ujafedny.org
Web site: www.ujafedny.org
John S Ruskay, Executive Vice President & Chief Executive Officer
Real property portfolio management

Offices and agencies generally appear in alphabetical order, except when specific order is requested by listee.

SOCIAL SERVICES

New York State

GOVERNOR'S OFFICE

Governor's Office
Executive Chamber
State Capitol
Albany, NY 12224
518-474-8390 Fax: 518-474-1513
Web site: www.state.ny.us

Governor:
   Eliot Spitzer 518-474-8390
Secretary to the Governor:
   Richard Baum 518-474-4246
Counsel to the Governor:
   David Nocenti 518-474-8343
Senior Advisor to the Governor:
   Lloyd Constantine 518-486-9671
Director, Communications:
   Darren Dopp 518-474-8418
Deputy Secretary, Health & Human Services:
   Dennis Whalen 518-408-2500
Assistant Deputy Secretary, Health & Human Services:
   Joseph Baker 518-486-4079
Assistant Counsel to the Governor-Labor & Retirement:
   David Weinstein 518-474-8434
Director, State Operations:
   Olivia Golden 518-486-9871

EXECUTIVE DEPARTMENTS AND RELATED AGENCIES

Aging, Office for the
2 Empire State Plaza
Albany, NY 12223
518-474-4425 or 800-342-9871 Fax: 518-474-0608
Web site: www.aging.state.ny.us

Director:
   Michael Burgess 518-474-4425
Executive Deputy Director:
   Laurie Pferr 518-474-7012
Deputy Director, Executive Division:
   Greg Olsen 518-474-4552
Assistant Director:
   Gail Koser 518-474-8422
Counsel:
   Jennifer Seehase 518-474-7011
Public Information Officer:
   Reza Mizbani 518-474-7181/fax: 518-473-6565

Advisory Groups

Aging Services Advisory Committee
Constituency Liaison:
   Gail Myers 518-474-4395/fax: 518-486-2225

Governor's Advisory Committee
Constituency Liaison:
   Gail Myersr 518-474-4395/fax: 518-486-2225

Federal Relations
Staff Liaison:
   Sandra Longworth 518-474-5041/fax: 518-474-1398

Finance & Administration Division
Deputy Director:
   James Foy 518-473-4808/fax: 518-474-0608
Asst Director:
   Jack Lynch 518-474-2631

Local Program Operations
Deputy Director:
   Marcus Harazin 518-473-5705

Targeting Services & Equal Opportunity Programs
Director:
   Carmen Cunningham 518-474-5041

Agriculture & Markets Department
10B Airline Dr
Albany, NY 12235
518-457-3880 Fax: 518-457-3087
e-mail: info@agmkt.state.ny.us
Web site: www.agmkt.state.ny.us

Commissioner:
   Patrick Hooker 518-457-8876
First Deputy Commissioner:
   Thomas Lindberg 518-457-2771
Public Information Officer:
   Jessica Chittenden 518-457-3136/fax: 518-457-3087
   e-mail: jessica.chittenden@agmkt.state.ny.us

Migrant Labor Programs
Coordinator:
   Vacant 518-457-7076

Alcoholism & Substance Abuse Services, Office of
1450 Western Ave
Albany, NY 12203
518-485-1660 Fax: 518-457-5474
Web site: www.oasas.state.ny.us

501 7th Ave
8th Fl
New York, NY 10018
646-728-4533

Commissioner:
   Karen M Carpenter-Palumbo 518-457-1758

Offices and agencies generally appear in alphabetical order, except when specific order is requested by listee.

SOCIAL SERVICES / New York State

Executive Deputy Commissioner:
   Kathleen Caggiano-Siino 518-485-2312
Director, Communications:
   Jennifer Farrell. 518-485-1768/fax: 518-485-6014
   e-mail: jenniferfarrell@oasas.state.ny.us
Director, Human Resources Management:
   Thomas M Torino 518-457-2963
Director, Internal Audit:
   Richard Kaplan 518-485-2039
Affirmative Action Officer:
   Henry Gonzalez 518-457-2963
Public Information Officer:
   Joseph Morrissey 518-485-1768
   e-mail: josephmorrissey@oasas.state.ny.us

Financial, Capital & Information Tech Management Division
Associate Commissioner:
   Michael Lawler 518-457-5312
   e-mail: michaellawler@oasas.state.ny.us

Bureau of Budget Management
Director:
   Jay Runkel 518-485-2193

Bureau of Capital Management
Director:
   Laurie Felter 518-457-2545

Bureau of Financial & Emergency Management
Director:
   Vito Manzella 518-457-4742

Bureau of Health Care Financing & 3rd Party Reimbursement
Director:
   Nicholas Colamaria 518-485-2207

Bureau of Information Technology
Director:
   David Gardam 518-485-2351

Legal Affairs Division
Associate Commsioner:
   Henry F Zwack 518-485-2312

Bureau of Counsel
Director:
   Dick Hogle 518-485-2317

Bureau of Governmental & NYC Affairs
Director:
   Jeff Cleary 518-485-2337

Bureau of Certification
Director:
   Virginia Martin 518-485-2247

Bureau of Enforcement
Director:
   Charles Monson 518-485-2312

Management Resources & Quality Assurance Division
Associate Commissioner:
   Neil Grogin 518-485-2257
Client Advocacy:
   Michael Yorio 800-553-5790

Bureau of Quality Assurance
Director:
   William Lachanski 518-485-2260
Training/Technical Assistance:
   Steve Therriault 518-485-2027

Training/Technical Assistance:
   Joseph Chelales 646-728-4644

Bureau of Workforce Development
Director:
   Joseph Burke 518-485-2033

Prevention & Treatment Services Division
Associate Commissioner:
   Frances M Harding 518-485-6022

Bureau of Prevention
Director:
   John Ernst 518-485-2132

Bureau of ATCs
Director:
   Thomas Nightingale 518-457-7077

Bureau of Treatment
Director:
   Rob Piculell 518-485-2123

Bureau of Systems Development & Public Education
Director:
   William Barnette 518-457-6206

Systems/Program Performance & Analysis Division
Acting Associate Commissioner:
   Timothy P Williams 518-485-2322

Bureau of Planning & Practice Improvement
Acting Associate Commissioner:
   Bob Gallati 518-457-5989

Bureau of Evaluation & Practice Improvement
Director:
   Alan Kott 518-485-7189

Bureau of Statewide Field Operations
Director:
   Edward Freeman 518-457-8240

Children & Family Services, Office of
52 Washington St
Rensselaer, NY 12144-2735
518-473-8437
Web site: www.ocfs.state.ny.us

Commissioner:
   Gladys Carrion, Esq 518-473-8437
Executive Assistant:
   Laura Velez 518-473-8437
Executive Secretary:
   Donna Quirk 518-473-8437
Ombudsman:
   Viola I Abbitt 518-486-7082
Executive Deputy Commissioner:
   Larry G Brown 518-402-3108
Executive Assistant:
   Lee Lounsbury 518-402-8400
Executive Secretary:
   Evelyn D'Ambro 518-402-3108

Executive Office, NYC
80 Maiden Lane, 24th Fl, New York, NY 10038
212-383-1823
Associate Commissioner:
   Digna Sanchez 212-383-1823

Offices and agencies generally appear in alphabetical order, except when specific order is requested by listee.

SOCIAL SERVICES / New York State

Regional Coordinator, NYC Office:
  Digna Sanchez 212-383-1823
Special Assistant:
  Yessenia Cardona 212-383-1823

Administration Division
Deputy Commissioner:
  William T Gettman, Jr 518-486-7218

Audit & Quality Control
Acting Director:
  Lynn Dobriko 518-402-3985
External, Contract & Fiscal Audits:
  Don Nicklas 518-486-1118
Internal Audits:
  Lynn Dobriko 518-402-3985

Contract Management
Director:
  Karen Lopiccolo 518-486-7224
Assistant Director:
  Harry Ritter 518-473-6001
Assistant Director:
  James Spoor 518-486-6380

Financial Management
Associate Commissioner:
  Edna Mae Reilly 518-486-1110
Director, Budget:
  Deborah J Hanor 518-474-1361
Director, Financial Operations:
  Susan A Costello 518-486-3848
Director, Grants Management:
  Dawn Rowan 518-473-1085
Director, Rate Setting:
  Daniel Zeidman 518-474-1384

Human Resources
Associate Commissioner:
  Mikki Ward-Harper 518-473-8453
Acting Deputy Director, Equal Employment & Diversity Development:
  Emy Murphy 518-474-3715
Director, Human Resources:
  John Monteiro 518-402-3211
Director, Labor Relations:
  Walter Greenberg 518-486-4240
Director, Personnel:
  Charles Breiner 518-474-5207
Director, Training:
  Peter Miraglia 518-474-9645

Management & Support
Director:
  Stephanie Donato 518-402-3208
Capital Services:
  Raymond Beaudoin 518-473-0487
Management Services:
  Pamela Relyea 518-402-3926
Security & Emergency Preparedness:
  Joseph Impicciatore 518-402-3984

Commission for the Blind & Visually Handicapped (CBVH)
Associate Commissioner:
  Brian Daniels 518-474-7299
Director:
  Peter Crowley 518-473-1801
Director, Bureau of Program Evaluation, Support & Business Svcs:
  Kenneth Galarneau 518-474-7812

Director, Bureau of Field Operations:
  Priscilla Wrobel 518-473-9685

Development & Prevention Services Division
Deputy Commissioner:
  Jane G Lynch 518-473-3377

Central Services
Associate Commissioner:
  Christine Heywood 518-402-3213
State Central Registry
Director:
  David R Peters 518-474-9607
Native American Services
Affairs Specialist:
  Kim Thomas 716-847-3123

Program Support
Assistant Commissioner:
  Renee Rider 518-474-9431
Adult Protective Services
Director:
  Vacant 518-402-6782
Adoption Services
Director:
  Brenda Rivers 518-473-1901

Bureau of Early Childhood Services (BECS)
Director:
  Suzanne Sennett 518-474-9454

Information Technology Division
40 N Pearl Street, Albany, NY 12243
Deputy Commissioner:
  William E Travis, Jr 518-402-3194
Director, Applications:
  Fred Krough 518-474-9362

Connections
Project Director:
  Carolyn Glisson 518-473-6976
Assistant Information Technology Director:
  Joel Schensul 518-486-6388
Director, Technical Support:
  Kevin Sternberg 518-486-6292

Legal Affairs Division
Deputy Commissioner & General Counsel:
  Vacant 518-473-8418
Deputy Counsel:
  John Ouimet 518-473-8418
Deputy Counsel:
  Anthony Pietrafesa 518-473-3226
Deputy Counsel:
  Lee Prochera 518-473-3226

Public Information Division
Assistant Commissioner:
  Sandra A Brown 518-402-3130
Records Access Officer:
  Sandra A Brown 518-402-3130
Public Information Officer:
  Brian Marchetti 518-473-7793

Regional Operations
Regional Operations & Practice Improvement (ROPI)
Director:
  Bill McLaughlin 518-474-9465

Offices and agencies generally appear in alphabetical order, except when specific order is requested by listee.

SOCIAL SERVICES / New York State

Youth Development
Acting Director:
  Matt Murell 518-402-3830

Rehabilitative Services Division
Acting Deputy Commissioner:
  Ines Nieves 518-476-6766

Facility Operations
Associate Commissioner:
  Anthony Hough 518-473-4411
Facility Coordinator:
  Edgardo Lopez 315-479-8356
Facility Coordinator:
  Ruth Noriega 212-961-4121
Facility Coordinator:
  Ruben Reyes. 845-561-5620
ACA Accreditation Coordinator:
  Kurt Pfisterer 518-408-3825
Supervisor, Facilities Fire Safety:
  Chris Ost. 518-473-4488
  Bureau of Management & Program Support
  Director:
    Merle Brandwene 518-473-5325

Program Services
Associate Commissioner:
  Ines Nieves. 518-486-6766
Director, Bureau of Behavioral Health Services:
  Lois Shapiro 518-402-7653
Acting Director, Bureau of Counseling Services:
  Jerome Hall 518-486-7098
Director, Bureau of Education & Employment Services:
  Timothy Bromirski. 518-402-6754
Director, Bureau of Health Services:
  Michael D Cohen MD 518-474-9560
Director, Bureau of Intervention Coordination & Enhancement:
  Mark French. 518-474-1709
Coordinator, Chaplaincy:
  Father Kofi Amissah 518-474-9400
Director, Classification & Movement:
  Robert Pollack 518-473-8985

Program Support & Community Partnerships
Associate Commissioner:
  Felipe Franco 518-473-4411
Upstate Community Services Coordinator:
  Daniel Maxwell 518-486-5513
Downstate Community Services Coordinator:
  Robert Ellis. 212-961-4116
Director, Detention Services Unit:
  Terry Portelli 518-474-1308
Director, EBCI:
  Terry Portelli 518-474-1308
Director, IT Automation:
  Jeff Evans. 518-486-4335
Director, Workforce Development:
  Tana Fileccia-Flagg 518-473-1813

Special Investigations Unit
Director:
  Kevin W Mahar 518-474-9478

Strategic Planning & Policy Development, Office of
Director:
  Nancy W Martinez. 518-473-1776
Assistant Director:
  Dianne Ewashko. 518-473-7373
Director, Evaluation & Research:
  Sue Mitchell-Herzfeld 518-474-9486

Director, Management Information:
  Lillian Denton. 518-474-6947
Director, Planning & Intervention Design:
  Larry Pasti 518-473-1274
Director, Policy Analysis:
  Jamie Greenberg. 518-473-1327
Director, Special Projects:
  Greg Owens 518-473-3990

Regional Offices

Albany Regional Office
155 Washington Ave, 3rd Fl, Albany, NY 12210-2329
Serving the counties of: Albany, Clinton, Columbia, Delaware, Essex, Franklin, Fulton, Greene, Hamilton, Montgomery, Otsego, Rensselaer, Saratoga, Schenectady, Schoharie, Warren, Washington
Director:
  Glenn Humphreys 518-486-7078/fax: 518-486-7625
  Youth Development . . . . fax: 518-473-6692
  52 Washington Ave, Room 309 S, Rensselaer, NY 12144
  518-473-4453 Fax: 518-473-6692
  Coordinator:
    Steve Conti
    Serving the counties of: Albany, Dutchess, Montgomery, Orange, Otsego, Sullivan, Ulster
  Coordinator:
    Matt Beck
    Serving the counties of: Columbia, Delaware, Fulton, Greene, Saratoga, Schenectady, Schoharie, Warren, Washington
  Coordinator:
    Larry Hayes
    Serving the counties of: Clinton, Essex, Franklin, Hamilton, Rensselaer

Buffalo Regional Office. . . . . fax: 716-847-3742
295 Main St, Ellicott Sq Bldg, Rm 545, 5th Fl, Buffalo, NY 14203
716-847-3145 Fax: 716-847-3742
Serving the counties of: Allegany, Cattaraugus, Chautauqua, Erie, Genesee, Niagara, Orleans, Wyoming
Director:
  Linda C Brown
  Youth Development . . . . fax: 716-847-3692
  716-847-3323 Fax: 716-847-3692
  Coordinator:
    Joseph Proietti
    Serving the counties of: Genesee, Orleans, Cattaraugus, Allegany, Wyoming
  Coordinator:
    Christine Garmon-Salaam
    Serving the counties of: Erie, Chautauqua, Niagara
  Upstate Area Manager:
    Andrew Johnson 716-847-3321
  Native American Services . . . . fax: 716-847-3812
  716-847-3123 Fax: 716-847-3812
  Affairs Specialist:
    Kim Thomas
    Serving the nine tribal communities across New York State

New York City Regional Office . . . . fax: 212-383-1709
80 Maiden Lane, 24th Fl, New York, NY 10038
212-383-4703 Fax: 212-383-1709
Director:
  Vacant
  Youth Development . . . . fax: 212-383-4707
  212-383-4703 Fax: 212-383-4707
  Coordinator: Sonia Tate
    Serving the counties of: Bronx, Manhattan, Richmond
  Coordinator: Gail Branch-Muhammad
    Serving the counties of: Kings, Queens

Offices and agencies generally appear in alphabetical order, except when specific order is requested by listee.

SOCIAL SERVICES / New York State

Downstate Area Manager/Liaison to NYC Office:
   Vacant

Rochester Regional Office . . . . fax: 585-238-8289
259 Monroe Avenue, Monroe Sq, 3rd Fl, Rochester, NY 14607
585-238-8201 Fax: 585-238-8289
Serving the counties of: Chemung, Livingston, Monroe, Ontario, Schuyler, Seneca, Steuben, Wayne, Yates
Director:
   Linda Kurtz
   Youth Development . . . . fax: 585-238-8213
      585-238-8281 Fax: 585-238-8213
      Coordinator:
         Lydia Dzus
         Serving the counties of: Chemung, Livingston, Monroe, Ontario, Seneca, Schuyler, Steuben, Wayne, Yates

Syracuse Regional Office . . . . fax: 315-423-1198
The Atrium Bldg, 3rd Fl, 100 S Salina St, Ste 350, Syracuse, NY 13202
315-423-1200 Fax: 315-423-1198
Serving the counties of: Broome, Cayuga, Chenango, Cortland, Herkimer, Jefferson, Lewis, Madison, Oneida, Onondaga, Oswego, St Lawrence, Tioga, Tompkins
Director:
   Jack Klump
   Youth Development . . . . fax: 315-423-5499
      315-423-5486 Fax: 315-423-5499
      Coordinator:
         Denise Dyer
         Serving the counties of: Broome, Chenango, Jefferson, Oneida, Oswego, Onondaga, Tompkins
      Coordinator:
         Thomas Mitchell
         Serving the counties of: Cayuga, Cortland, Madison, Herkimer, Lewis, St Lawrence, Tioga

Yonkers Regional Office . . . . fax: 914-377-2083
525 Nepperhan Ave, Room 205, Yonkers, NY 10703
914-377-2080 Fax: 914-377-2083
Serving the counties of: Dutchess, Nassau, Orange, Putnam, Rockland, Suffolk, Sullivan, Ulster, Westchester
Director:
   Patricia Sheehy
   Youth Development . . . . fax: 516-564-4453
      516-564-4430 Fax: 516-564-4453
      Coordinator:
         Princella Stover
         Serving the counties of: Westchester, Nassau, Suffolk, Putnam, Rockland

Council on Children & Families
52 Washington St, Room 256W, Rensselaer, NY 12144-2735
Web site: www.ccf.state.ny.us
Acting Executive Director:
   Deborah Benson 518-473-3652/fax: 518-473-2570
Counsel:
   Vacant 518-473-4857

Bureau of Policy, Research & Planning
Director & Head Start Project Director:
   Robert Frawley 518-473-8081

Bureau of Interagency Coordination & Case Resolution
Director:
   Janet Sapio-Mayta 518-474-8443

Crime Victims Board
1 Columbia Circle, Ste 200
Albany, NY 12203-6383
518-457-8727 or 800-247-8035 Fax: 518-457-8658
e-mail: cvbinfo@cvb.state.ny.us
Web site: www.cvb.state.ny.us

55 Hanson Place
10th Fl
Brooklyn, NY 11217
718-923-4325
Fax: 718-923-4332

65 Court St
Rm 308
Buffalo, NY 14202
716-847-7992
Fax: 716-847-7995

Chairwoman:
   Joan A Cusack 718-923-4331
Commissioner:
   Louis A Mosiello 718-923-4336
Commissioner:
   Alton R Waldron, Jr 718-923-4331
Commissioner:
   Jacqueline C Mattina 716-847-7948
Commissioner:
   Benedict J Monachino 718-923-4400
General Counsel:
   John Watson 518-457-8066/fax: 518-457-8658
Executive Director:
   Virginia A Miller 518-457-9320
Director, MIS:
   David Loomis 518-485-2763
Contract Supervisor:
   Raymond Parafinczuk 518-485-2763

Developmental Disabilities Planning Council
155 Washington Ave
2nd Fl
Albany, NY 12210
518-486-7505 or 800-395-3372 Fax: 518-402-3505
Web site: www.ddpc.state.ny.us

Chairperson:
   George E Fertal Sr 518-486-7505
Vice Chairperson:
   Rose Marie Toscano 518-486-7505
Executive Director:
   Sheila M Carey 518-486-7505
Deputy Executive Director:
   Anna Lobosco 518-486-7505
   e-mail: alobosco@ddpc.state.ny.us
Public Information Officer:
   Thomas F Lee 518-486-7505
   e-mail: tlee@ddpc.state.ny.us

Education Department
State Education Bldg
89 Washington Ave
Albany, NY 12234
518-474-5215 Fax: 518-486-5631
Web site: www.nysed.gov

Offices and agencies generally appear in alphabetical order, except when specific order is requested by listee.

SOCIAL SERVICES / New York State

Commissioner, University President:
Richard P Mills..................................518-474-5844
e-mail: rmills@mail.nysed.gov
Assistant to the Commissioner:
Peggy Rivers....................................518-474-5845
e-mail: privers@mail.nysed.gov
Counsel & Deputy Commissioner, Legal Affairs:
Kathy A Ahearn................................518-474-6400
e-mail: kahearn@mail.nysed.gov
Chief of Staff & Deputy Commissioner, Innovation:
David Miller....................................518-486-1713
e-mail: dmiller@mail.nysed.gov

Office of the Professions .... fax: 518-474-3863
89 Washington Ave, EB, 2nd Fl, West Mezz, Albany, NY 12234
Fax: 518-474-3863
Web site: www.op.nysed.gov
Associate Commissioner:
Frank Munoz...........................518-474-3817 x440
e-mail: opopr@mail.nysed.gov
Executive Coordinator, Professional Practice:
Anthony Lofrumento..................518-474-3817 x570
e-mail: op4info@mail.nysed.gov

Office of Professional Responsibility
Executive Director:
Vacant.................................518-474-3817 x440
e-mail: opexdir@mail.nysed.gov

Professional Education Program Review
Supervisor:
Vacant.................................518-474-3817 x360
e-mail: opprogs@mail.nysed.gov

Professional Licensing Services
Director:
Anthony Lofrumento..................518-474-3817 x340
e-mail: opdpls@mail.nysed.gov

Vocational & Educational Services for Individuals With Disabilities Office (VESID) .... fax: 518-474-8802
One Commerce Plaza, Rm 1606, Albany, NY 12234
Fax: 518-474-8802
Web site: www.vesid.nysed.gov
Deputy Commissioner:
Rebecca Cort....................................518-474-2714
e-mail: rcort@mail.nysed.gov
Asst Commissioner:
Edward Placke..................................518-473-4818

Fiscal & Administrative Services
Coordinator:
Rosemary Ellis Johnson....................518-486-4038

Program Develpmnt & Support Svcs/Special Ed Policy & Ptshps
Coordinator:
Vacant...518-486-7462
Deaf & Hard of Hearing Services
Manager:
Dorothy Steele............................518-474-1711
Lifelong Services
Supervisor:
Daniel J Ryan.............................518-486-7462
Special Education Policy & Partnerships
Supervisor:
Vacant..518-473-2878

Quality Assurance - Statewide Special Education
Statewide Coordinator:
James DeLorenzo.............................518-402-3353

State School for the Blind at Batavia
2A Richmond Ave, Batavia, NY 14020
Acting Superintendent:
James Knowles..................................585-343-5384

Vocational Rehabilitation Operations
Acting Director, District Ofc Administration:
Debora Brown-Grant.........................518-473-1626
e-mail: dbrowngr@mail.nysed.gov
Asst Director, District Office Administration:
Richard Strohl..................................518-486-4035
e-mail: rstrohl@mail.nysed.gov

Labor Department
Building 12, Room 500
State Campus
Albany, NY 12240
518-457-2741 Fax: 518-457-6908
e-mail: nysdol@labor.state.ny.us
Web site: www.labor.state.ny.us

Commissioner:
M Patricia Smith..............................518-457-2746
Executive Deputy Commissioner:
Mario Musolino...............................518-457-4318
Counsel:
Maria Colavito.................................518-457-7069
Inspector General:
Vacant...518-457-7012
Director, Communications:
Leo Rosales..................518-457-5519/fax: 518-485-1126

Federal Programs
Deputy Commissioner, Federal Programs:
Margaret Moree...............................518-485-6410

Unemployment Insurance Division
Director:
Vacant....................518-457-2878/fax: 518-485-8604

Workforce Development & Training Division
Acting Director:
Yue Yee.....................518-457-0380/fax: 518-457-9526

Workforce Protection, Standards & Licensing
Deputy Commissioner:
Pico Ben-Amotz................................518-457-4317

Labor Standards Division
Acting Director:
Carmine Ruberto..............................518-457-2460

Safety & Health Division
Director:
Maureen Cox..................518-457-3518/fax: 518-457-1519

Prevention of Domestic Violence, Office for the
80 Wolf Rd
Ste 406
Albany, NY 12205
518-457-5800 Fax: 518-457-5810
Web site: www.opdv.state.ny.us

Executive Director:
Amy Barasch, Esq.............................518-457-5800
Director, Prevention, Training & Planning:
Gwen Wright....................................518-457-5916

Offices and agencies generally appear in alphabetical order, except when specific order is requested by listee.

SOCIAL SERVICES / New York State

Director, NYC Program:
  Sujata Warrier..................................212-417-4477
Administrative Officer:
  Linda Cassidy....................................518-457-7995
Public Information Officer:
  Suzanne Cecala..................................518-457-5744
  e-mail: suzanne.cecala@opdv.state.ny.us

Temporary & Disability Assistance, Office of
40 N Pearl St
Albany, NY 12243
518-474-9003 or 800-342-3004 Fax: 518-474-7870
e-mail: nyspio@otda.state.ny.us
Web site: www.otda.state.ny.us

Commissioner:
  David A Hansell...............518-474-4152/fax: 518-486-6255
  e-mail: david.hansell@otda.state.ny.us
Director, External & Intergovernmental Affairs Office:
  Elizabeth Segal..................................518-474-7420

Budget, Finance & Data Management
Director:
  Michael Normile..................................518-474-0183

Child Support Enforcement Division
Deputy Commissioner & Director:
  Scott E Cade......................................518-474-1078

Disability Determinations Division
Acting Deputy Commissioner:
  Gloria S Toal.....................................518-473-0070

Employment & Transitional Supports
Deputy Commissioner:
  Russell Sykes..................518-474-9222/fax: 518-474-5281

Information Technology Services
Director:
  Vacant..518-473-7858

Legal Affairs Division
General Counsel:
  John P Bailly Jr..................................518-474-9502

Program Support & Quality Improvement
Deputy Commissioner:
  John Paolucci....................................518-473-3912

Public Information
Director:
  Michael Hayes..................518-474-9516/fax: 518-486-6935
  e-mail: nyspio@otda.state.ny.us

Welfare Inspector General, Office of NYS
22 Cortland St
11th Fl
New York, NY 10007
212-417-5822 Fax: 212-417-5849

40 N Pearl St, Sect 10B
Albany, NY 12243
518-474-9636
Fax: 518-486-6148

Inspector General:
  Brian P Sanvidge.................................212-417-5840
Deputy Inspector General & Counsel:
  Andrew J Weiss...................................212-417-2395
Chief Investigator:
  Joseph R Bucci...................................212-417-2026
Administrative Asst to Inspector General:
  Wanda Hernandez..................................212-417-5822

NEW YORK STATE LEGISLATURE

See Legislative Branch in Section 1 for additional Standing Committee and Subcommittee information.

Assembly Standing Committees

Aging
Chair:
  Steven C Englebright (D)..........................518-455-4804
Ranking Minority Member:
  Philip Boyle (R).................................518-455-4611

Alcoholism & Drug Abuse
Chair:
  Jeffrey Dinowitz (D).............................518-455-5965
Ranking Minority Member:
  Gary D Finch (R).................................518-455-5878

Children & Families
Chair:
  William Scarborough (D)..........................518-455-4451
Ranking Minority Member:
  Joseph A Errigo (R)..............................518-455-5662

Social Services
Chair:
  Deborah J Glick (D)..............................518-455-4841
Ranking Minority Member:
  Vincent Ignizio (R)..............................518-455-4495

Assembly Task Forces

Puerto Rican/Hispanic Task Force
Chair:
  Peter M Rivera (D)...............................518-455-5102
Co-Chair:
  Vito J Lopez.....................................518-455-5537

Women's Issues, Task Force on
Chair:
  Barbara Lifton (D)...............................518-455-5444
Coordinator:
  Jean Emery....................518-455-3632/fax: 518-455-4574

Senate Standing Committees

Aging
Chair:
  Martin J Golden (R)..............................518-455-2730
Ranking Minority Member:
  Ruben Diaz, Sr (D)...............................518-455-2511

Social Services, Children & Families
Chair:
  Carl Kruger (R)..................................518-455-2460

Offices and agencies generally appear in alphabetical order, except when specific order is requested by listee.

SOCIAL SERVICES / U.S. Government

Ranking Minority Member:
  Velmanette Montgomery (D) 518-455-3451

U.S. Government

EXECUTIVE DEPARTMENTS AND RELATED AGENCIES

Corporation for National & Community Service
Web site: www.cns.gov

New York Program Office
Federal Bldg, 1 Clinton Sq, Ste 900, Albany, NY 12207
State Director:
  Donna M Smith 518-431-4150/fax: 518-431-4154
  e-mail: ny@cns.gov

Social Security Administration
Web site: www.socialsecurity.gov

Region 2—New York .... fax: 212-264-1444
26 Federal Plz, Rm 40-120, New York, NY 10278
Regional Commissioner:
  Beatrice M Disman 212-264-3915
Deputy Regional Commissioner:
  Paul M Doersam 212-264-3915
Asst Regional Commissioner, Management & Operations Support:
  Julio Infiesta 212-264-2507
Asst Regional Commissioner, Processing Center Operations:
  Anne Jacobosky 718-557-5000

Office of Hearings & Appeals
Regional Chief Administrative Law Judge:
  G Stephen Wright 212-264-4036

Office of Quality Assurance
Director:
  Susan Pike 212-264-2827

Office of the General Counsel
Chief Counsel:
  Barbara Spivak 212-264-3650

Program Operations Center
Director:
  Dennis Moss 212-264-4004

Public Affairs
Regional Communications Director:
  John E Shallman 212-264-2500/fax: 212-264-1444

US Department of Health & Human Services
Web site: www.os.dhhs.gov; www.hhs.gov/region2/

Administration for Children & Families .... fax: 212-264-4881
26 Federal Plaza, Rm 4114, New York, NY 10278
Fax: 212-264-4881
Web site: www.acf.hhs.gov
Regional Administrator:
  MaryAnn Higgins 212-264-2890 x103
  e-mail: mhiggins@acf.hhs.gov

Administration on Aging .... fax: 212-264-0114
26 Federal Plaza, Rm 38-102, New York, NY 10278

212-264-2976 Fax: 212-264-0114
Web site: www.aoa.gov
Regional Administrator:
  Daniel A Quirk 212-264-2976
  e-mail: dan.quirk@aoa.hhs.gov

Centers for Disease Control & Prevention
Web site: www.cdc.gov

Agency for Toxic Substances & Disease Registry-EPA Region 2
290 Broadway, 28th Fl, New York, NY 10007
Web site: www.atsdr.cdc.gov
Senior Regional Representative:
  Arthur Block 212-637-4305/fax: 212-637-4942

New York Quarantine Station .... fax: 718-553-1524
Terminal 4E, Rm 219 016, JFK Airport, Jamaica, NY 11430-1081
718-553-1685 Fax: 718-553-1524
Officer-in-Charge:
  Margaret A Becker 718-553-1685/fax: 718-553-1524

Centers for Medicare & Medicaid Services
26 Federal Plaza, Rm 3811, New York, NY 10278
Web site: www.cms.hhs.gov
Regional Administrator:
  James T Kerr 212-616-2205/fax: 212-264-6189
  e-mail: james.kerr@cms.hhs.gov
Deputy Regional Administrator:
  Gilbert Kunken 212-616-2205/fax: 212-264-6189
  e-mail: gilbert.kunken@cms.hhs.gov

Medicaid and Children's Health (DMCH)
Associate Regional Administrator:
  Sue Kelly 212-616-2428/fax: 212-264-6814
  e-mail: sue.kelly@cms.hhs.gov

Medicare Financial Management (DMFM)
Associate Regional Administrator:
  Peter Reisman 212-616-2505/fax: 212-264-2790
  e-mail: peter.reisman@cms.hhs.gov

Medicare Operations Division (DMO)
Associate Regional Administrator:
  Jose Mirabal 212-616-2333/fax: 212-264-2665
  e-mail: jose.mirabal@cms.hhs.gov

Food & Drug Administration
888-463-6332
Web site: www.fda.gov

Northeast Region
158-15 Liberty Ave, Jamaica, NY 11433
Regional Director:
  Vacant 718-662-5416/fax: 718-662-5434
  New York District Office
  District Director:
    Vacant 718-662-5447/fax: 718-662-5665
  Northeast Regional Laboratory
  158-15 Liberty Ave, Queens, NY 11433
  Director:
    Michael J Palmieri 718-662-5450/fax: 718-662-5439

Offices and agencies generally appear in alphabetical order, except when specific order is requested by listee.

SOCIAL SERVICES / Private Sector

Health Resources & Svcs Admin Office of Performance Review .... fax: 212-264-2673
   26 Federal Plaza, Rm 3337, New York, NY 10278
   Regional Division Director:
     Ron Moss 212-264-2664
     e-mail: robert.moss@hrsa.hhs.gov
   Operations Director:
     Margaret Lee 212-264-2571
     e-mail: margaret.lee@hrsa.hhs.gov
   Director, Ofc of Engineering Services:
     Emilio Pucillo 212-264-3600
     e-mail: emilio.pucillo@hrsa.hhs.gov

Indian Health Services-Area Office .... fax: 615-467-1501
   711 Stewarts Ferry Pike, Nashville, TN 37214-2634
   Director:
     Richie Grinnell 615-467-1500

Office of Secretary's Regional Representative-Region 2-NY .... fax: 212-264-3620
   26 Federal Plaza, Rm 3835, New York, NY 10278
   Regional Director:
     Deborah Konopko 212-264-4600
     e-mail: deborah.konopko@hhs.gov
   Sr Intergovernmental Affairs Specialist:
     Dennis Gonzalez 212-264-4600
     e-mail: dennis.gonzalez@hhs.gov
   Intergovernmental Affairs Specialist:
     Katherine Williams 212-264-4600
     e-mail: katherine.williams@hhs.gov

   Office for Civil Rights .... fax: 212-264-3039
   26 Federal Plaza, Rm 3312, New York, NY 10278
   Fax: 212-264-3039
   Web site: www.hhs.gov/ocr
   Regional Manager:
     Michael Carter 212-264-3313/fax: 212-264-3039
   Deputy Regional Manager:
     Linda Colon 212-264-3313

   Office of General Counsel
   26 Federal Plaza, Rm 3908, New York, NY 10278
   Chief Counsel:
     Joel Lerner 212-264-6373

   Office of Inspector General
   Regional Inspector General, Audit:
     James P Edert 212-264-4620
   Regional Inspector General & Regional Coordinator, Investigations:
     Gary Heuer 212-264-1691
   Regional Inspector General, Evaluations & Inspections:
     Jodi Nudelman 212-264-1998

   Office of Public Health & Science
   26 Federal Plaza, Rm 3835, New York, NY 10278

   Acting Regional Health Administrator:
     Robert Davidson 212-264-2560
     e-mail: rdavidson@osophs.dhhs.gov
   Deputy Regional Health Administrator:
     Robert L Davidson 212-264-2560
     e-mail: rdavidson@osophs.dhhs.gov
   Regional Family Planning Consultant:
     Robin Lane 212-264-3935
     e-mail: rlane@osophs.hhs.gov
   Regional Minority Health Consultant:
     Claude Colimon 212-264-2560
   Regional Women's Health Coordinator:
     Sandra Estepa 212-264-2560

U.S. CONGRESS

See U.S. Congress Chapter for additional Standing Committee and Subcommittee information.

House of Representatives Standing Committees

Ways & Means
Chair:
   Charles B Rangel (D-NY) 202-225-4365
Ranking Minority Member:
   Charles B Rangel (D-NY) 202-225-4365
New York Delegate:
   Michael R McNulty (D) 202-225-5076
New York Delegate:
   Thomas M Reynolds (R) 202-225-5265

   Subcommittee
   Social Security
   Chair:
     Michael R McNulty (D-NY) 202-225-5076
   Ranking Minority Member:
     Sam Johnson (R-TX) 202-225-4201

Senate Standing Committees

Health, Education, Labor & Pensions
Chair:
   Edward M Kennedy (D-MA) 202-224-4543
Ranking Minority Member:
   Michael B Enzi (R-WY) 202-224-2523
New York Delegate:
   Hillary Rodham Clinton (D-NY) 202-224-4451

Aging, Special Committee on
Chair:
   Herb Kohl (D-WI) 202-224-5653
Ranking Minority Member:
   Gordon Smith (R-OR) 202-224-2753

Private Sector

AARP
780 3rd Ave, Fl 33, New York, NY 10017-2024
866-227-7442 Fax: 212-644-6390
Web site: www.aarp.org
Lois Aronstein, NY State Director
AARP

Offices and agencies generally appear in alphabetical order, except when specific order is requested by listee.

SOCIAL SERVICES / Private Sector

Abilities Inc, National Center for Disability Services
201 IU Willets Rd, Albertson, NY 11507-1599
516-465-1400 or 516-747-5355 (TTY) Fax: 516-465-3757
e-mail: ftishman@abilitiesinc.org
Web site: www.abilitiesinc.org
Charles W Harles, Executive Director
Provides comprehensive services to help individuals with disabilities reach their employment goals; provides support services & technical assistance to employers who hire persons with disabilities

Action for a Better Community Inc
550 E Main St, Rochester, NY 14604
585-325-5116 or 585-295-1726 Fax: 585-325-9108
e-mail: fcaldwell@abcinfo.org
Web site: www.abcinfo.org
Freddie Caldwell, Deputy Director
Advocacy for programs enabling the low-income to become self-sufficient; social services for the needy

Agenda for Children Tomorrow
c/o Administration for Children's Servic, 2 Washington St, 20th Fl,
New York, NY 10004
212-487-8284 or 212-487-8285 Fax: 212-487-8581
e-mail: actnet1@earthlink.net
Web site: www.actnyc.org
Eric B Brettschneider, Executive Director
Public, private & community collaboration to identify, plan for & deliver social & community services to families

American Red Cross in NYS
33 Everett Rd, Albany, NY 12205-1437
518-458-8111 x3021 Fax: 518-459-8262
e-mail: briand@redcrossneny.org
Elizabeth H Briand, Director, State Government Relations

Asian American Federation of New York
120 Wall St, 3rd Fl, New York, NY 10005
212-344-5878 Fax: 212-344-5636
e-mail: info@aafny.org
Web site: www.aafny.org
Cao K. O, Executive Director
Nonprofit leadership organization for member health & human services agencies serving the Asian American community

Asian Americans for Equality
108 Norfolk Street, New York, NY 10002
212-979-8381 Fax: 212-979-8386
e-mail: info@aafe.org
Web site: www.aafe.org
Christopher Kui, Executive Director
Equal opportunities for minorities; affordable housing development, homeownership counseling, immigration services, housing rights

Berkshire Farm Center & Services for Youth
13640 Route 22, Canaan, NY 12029
518-781-4567 Fax: 518-781-4577
e-mail: jmessina@berkshirefarm.org
Web site: www.berkshirefarm.org
Harith Flagg, Chief Executive Officer
Multi-function agency for troubled youth & families

Big Brothers Big Sisters of NYC
223 East 30th St, New York, NY 10016
212-686-2042 Fax: 212-779-1221
e-mail: help@bigsnyc.org
Web site: www.bigsnyc.org
Allan Luks, Executive Director
Providing disadvantaged youth with one-to-one, long-term relationships with a trained volunteer

CIDNY - Queens
137-02A Northern Blvd, Flushing, NY 11354
646-442-1520 or TTY 718-886-0427 Fax: 718-886-0428
Web site: www.cidny.org
Susan Dooha, Executive Director
Rights & advocacy for the disabled

CASA - Advocates for Children of NYS
32 Essex St, Albany, NY 12206
518-426-5354 Fax: 518-426-5348
e-mail: mail@casanys.org
Web site: www.casanys.org
Robin M Robinson, Executive Director
Volunteer advocates appointed by family court judges to represent abused & neglected children in court

Camp Venture Inc
25 Smith Street, Suite 510, Nanuet, NY 10954
845-624-3862 Fax: 845-624-7064
Web site: www.campventure.org
Daniel Lukens, Executive Director
Services for the developmentally disabled

Catholic Charities
1654 W Onondaga St, Syracuse, NY 13204
315-424-1812 Fax: 315-424-8274
Web site: www.ccoc.us
Eleanor Carr, Director, Elder Abuse Prevention Program

Center for Anti-Violence Education Inc
327 7th St, 2nf Fl, Brooklyn, NY 11215
718-788-1775 Fax: 718-499-2284
e-mail: cae@cae-bklyn.org
Web site: www.cae-bklyn.org
Tracy Hobson, Executive Director
Self-defense & violence prevention education for children, youth, women & LGBT people

Center for Family & Youth (The)
Administrative Ofc, 135 Ontario St, PO Box 6240, Albany, NY 12206
518-462-4745 or 518-462-4630 Fax: 518-427-1464
e-mail: dbosworth@ctrfamyouth.com
David A Bosworth, Executive Director
Child welfare services, Project STRIVE

Center for Independence of the Disabled in NY (CIDNY)
841 Broadway, Ste 301, New York, NY 10003
212-674-2300 or TTY: 212-674-5619 Fax: 212-254-5953
Web site: www.cidny.org
Susan Dooha, Executive Director
Rights & advocacy for the disabled

Offices and agencies generally appear in alphabetical order, except when specific order is requested by listee.

SOCIAL SERVICES / Private Sector

Center for Urban Community Services
120 Wall St, 25th Fl, New York, NY 10005
212-801-3300 Fax: 212-635-2191
e-mail: cucsinfo@cucs.org
Web site: www.cucs.org
Anthony Hannigan, Executive Director
Services to the homeless & low-income individuals, training & technical assistance to not-for-profit organizations

Center for Disability Services
314 S Manning Blvd, Albany, NY 12208
518-437-5700 Fax: 518-437-5705
Web site: www.cfdsny.org
Alan Krafchin, President & Chief Executive Officer
Medical & dental services; education, adult & residential services & service coordination

Cerebral Palsy Associations of New York State
90 State Street, Suite 929, Albany, NY 12207-1709
518-436-0178 Fax: 518-436-8619
e-mail: malvaro@cpofnys.org
Web site: www.cpofnys.org
Michael Alvaro, Executive Vice President
Advocate and provide direct services with and for individuals with cerebral palsy and other significant disabilities and their families

Children's Aid Society (The)
105 E 22nd St, New York, NY 10010
212-949-4921 Fax: 212-460-5941
e-mail: pmoses@childrensaidsociety.org
Web site: www.childrensaidsociety.org
C Warren Moses, Chief Executive Officer
Child welfare, health, foster care/adoption, preventive services, community centers & public schools, camps

Children's Rights Inc
330 Seventh Ave, 4th Floor, New York, NY 10001
212-683-2210 Fax: 212-683-4015
e-mail: info@childrensrights.org
Web site: www.childrensrights.org
Marcia Robinson Lowry, Executive Director
Advocacy & class action lawsuits on behalf of abused & neglected children

Children's Village (The)
Echo Hills, Dobbs Ferry, NY 10522
914-693-0600 x1201 Fax: 914-674-9208
e-mail: jkohomban@childrensvillage.org
Web site: www.childrensvillage.org
Jeremy Kohomban, PhD, President & Chief Executive Officer
Residential school, located 20 minutes outside of NYC. Treatment & prevention of behavioral problems for youth; residential & community-based services; mental health, education, employment & runaway shelter services

Citizens' Committee for Children of New York Inc
105 E 22nd St, 7th Fl, New York, NY 10010
212-673-1800 Fax: 212-979-5063
e-mail: info@cccnewyork.org
Web site: www.cccnewyork.org
Gail B Nayowith, Executive Director
Public policy advocacy for children's rights & services; promoting improved quality of life for NYC children & families in need

Coalition Against Domestic Violence, NYS
350 New Scotland Ave, Albany, NY 12208
518-482-5465 Fax: 518-482-3807
e-mail: vasquez@nyscadv.org
Web site: www.nyscadv.org
Jessica Vasquez, Director, Public Policy

Coalition for Asian American Children & Families
50 Broad St, Rm 1701, New York, NY 10004
212-809-4675 Fax: 212-785-4601
e-mail: cacf@cacf.org
Web site: www.cacf.org
Wayne H Ho, Executive Director
Advocacy for programs & policies supporting Asian American children & families; training & resources for service providers

Coalition for the Homeless
129 Fulton St, 1st Flr, New York, NY 10038
212-776-2000 Fax: 212-964-1303
e-mail: info@cfthomeless.org
Web site: www.coalitionforthehomeless.org
Mary Brosnahan Sullivan, Executive Director
Food, shelter, clothing assistance program, services for homeless New Yorkers

Coalition of Animal Care Societies (The)
437 Old Albany Post Rd, Garrison, NY 10524
845-788-5070 Fax: 845-788-5071
e-mail: tzaleski@sprynet.com
Terence M Zaleski, Special Counsel
Association of humane societies & animal welfare groups in NYS

Coalition of Fathers & Families NY
PO Box 782, Clifton Park, NY 12065
518-383-8202
e-mail: fafny@fafny.org
Web site: www.fafny.org/fafnypac.htm
James Hays, President
Working to keep fathers & families together

Commission on Economic Opportunity for the Greater Capital Region
2331 Fifth Ave, Troy, NY 12180
518-272-6012 Fax: 518-272-0658
e-mail: kgordon@ceo-cap.org
Web site: www.ceo-cap.org
Karen E Gordon, Executive Director
Preserve & advance the self-sufficiency, well-being & growth of individuals & families through education, guidance & resources

Offices and agencies generally appear in alphabetical order, except when specific order is requested by listee.

SOCIAL SERVICES / Private Sector

Community Healthcare Network
79 Madison Avenue, Fl 6, New York, NY 10016-7802
212-366-4500 Fax: 212-463-8411
e-mail: cabate@chnnyc.org
Web site: www.chnnyc.org
Catherine Abate, President & Chief Executive Officer
Health & social services for low-income, ethnically diverse, medically underserved neighborhoods of NYC

Cornell Cooperative Extension, College of Human Ecology, Nutrition, Health
186 Martha Van Rensselaer Hall, Cornell University, Ithaca, NY 14853-4401
607-255-2247 Fax: 607-254-4403
e-mail: jas56@cornell.edu
Web site: www.cce.cornell.edu
Josephine Swanson, Associate Director, Assistant Dean
Children, youth & family economic & social well-being

Council of Community Services of NYS Inc
272 Broadway, Albany, NY 12204
518-434-9194 x103 Fax: 518-434-0392
e-mail: info@ccsnys.org
Web site: www.ccsnys.org
Doug Sauer, Executive Director
Build healthy, caring communities & human care delivery systems through a strong charitable nonprofit sector & quality community-based planning

Council of Family & Child Caring Agencies
254 West 31st Street, 5th Floor, New York, NY 10001
212-929-2626 Fax: 212-929-0870
e-mail: cofcca@cofcca.org
Web site: www.cofcca.org
James F Purcell, Executive Director
Child welfare services membership organization

EPIC-Every Person Influences Children Inc
1000 Main St, Buffalo, NY 14202
716-332-4100 Fax: 716-332-4101
Web site: www.epicforchildren.org
Vito J Borrello, President
Uniting parents, teachers & community members to prevent child abuse & neglect, school dropout, juvenile crime, substance abuse & teenage pregnancy

Education & Assistance Corp Inc
50 Clinton St, Ste 107, Hempstead, NY 11550
516-539-0150 Fax: 516-539-0160
e-mail: lelder@eacinc.org
Web site: www.eacinc.org
Lance W Elder, President & Chief Executive Officer
Rehabilitation for nonviolent offenders; advocacy, education & counseling programs for youth, elderly & families

Empire Justice Center
119 Washington Ave, Albany, NY 12210
518-462-6831 Fax: 518-462-6687
e-mail: nkrupski@empirejustice.org
Web site: www.empirejustice.org
Anne Erickson, President & Chief Executive Officer
Empire Justice protects and strengthens the legal rights of people in New York State who are poor, disabled or disenfranchised.

Family Planning Advocates of New York State
17 Elk St, Albany, NY 12207
518-436-8408 Fax: 518-436-0004
e-mail: info@fpaofnys.org
Web site: www.fpaofnys.org
JoAnn M Smith, President/Chief Executive Officer
Reproductive rights

Federation Employment & Guidance Service (FEGS) Inc
315 Hudson St, 9th Fl, New York, NY 10013
212-366-8400 Fax: 212-366-8441
e-mail: info@fegs.org
Web site: www.fegs.org
Gail Magaliff, Chief Executive Officer
Diversified health & human services system to help individuals achieve their potential at work, at home, at school and in the community

Federation of Protestant Welfare Agencies Inc
281 Park Ave South, New York, NY 10010
212-777-4800 x322 Fax: 212-673-4085
e-mail: fgoldman@fpwa.org
Web site: www.fpwa.org
Fatima Goldman, Executive Director
Childcare & child welfare, HIV/AIDS, elderly, income security

Filipino American Human Services Inc
185-14 Hillside Ave, Jamaica, NY 11432
718-883-1295 Fax: 718-523-9606
e-mail: fahsi@fahsi.org
Web site: www.fahsi.org
Sherry Lynn Peralta, Executive Director
Youth program, family counseling referral, community education/advocacy & citizenship assistance services

Fordham University, Graduate School of Social Service
113 West 60th Street, Lincoln Center, New York, NY 10023
212-636-6616 Fax: 212-636-7876
e-mail: vaughan@fordham.edu
Web site: www.fordham.edu
Peter B Vaughan, Dean
Social work education, clinical social work, administration, client centered management

Offices and agencies generally appear in alphabetical order, except when specific order is requested by listee.

SOCIAL SERVICES / Private Sector

Friends & Relatives of Institutionalized Aged Inc (FRIA)
18 John St, Suite 905, New York, NY 10038
212-732-5667 or 212-732-4455 Fax: 212-732-6945
e-mail: fria@fria.org
Web site: www.fria.org
Amy Paul, Executive Director
Free telephone helpline for information assistance and complaints about nursing homes, assisted living and other long-term care issues.

Green Chimneys School-Green Chimneys Children's Services Inc
400 Doansburg Rd, Box 719, Brewster, NY 10509
845-279-2995 x119 Fax: 845-279-3077
Web site: www.greenchimneys.org
Joseph A Whalen, Executive Director
Residential treatment programs for emotionally troubled children & youths; therapeutic/educational Farm & Wildlife Conservation Center programs; therapeutic day school program

Guide Dog Foundation for the Blind Inc
371 East Jericho Turnpike, Smithtown, NY 11787-2976
631-930-9000 or 800-548-4337 Fax: 631-930-9009
e-mail: info@guidedog.org
Web site: www.guidedog.org
Wells B Jones, Chief Executive Officer
Provide guide dogs without charge to sight-impaired persons seeking enhanced mobility & independence

HeartShare Human Services of New York, Roman Catholic Diocese of Brooklyn
191 Joralemon St, Brooklyn, NY 11201
718-422-HEART Fax: 718-522-4506
e-mail: info@heartshare.org
Web site: www.heartshare.org
William R Guarinello, President & Chief Executive Officer
Service for the developmentally disabled children & family services & programs for people with HIV/AIDS

Helen Keller Services for the Blind
57 Willoughby Street, Brooklyn, NY 11201
718-522-2122 Fax: 718-935-9463
e-mail: info@helenkeller.org
Web site: www.helenkeller.org
John P Lynch, Executive Director
Preschool, rehabilitation, employment & senior services, low vision & braille library services

Hispanic Federation
55 Exchange Place, 5th Floor, New York, NY 10005
212-233-8955 Fax: 212-233-8996
Web site: www.hispanicfederation.org
Lillian Rodriguez Lopez, President
Technical assistance, capacity building, grantmaking & advocacy for Latino nonprofit service providers

Hispanic Outreach Services
40 North Main Ave, Albany, NY 12203
518-453-6655 Fax: 518-641-6830
e-mail: anne.tranelli@rcda.org
Web site: www.hispanicoutreachservices.org
Sister Anne Tranelli, Executive Director
Social service, youth guidance, language translation & immigration assistance programs

Homes for the Homeless/Institute for Children & Poverty
36 Cooper Square, 6th Fl, New York, NY 10003
212-529-5252 Fax: 212-529-7698
e-mail: info@homesforthehomeless.com
Web site: www.homesforthehomeless.com
Christy Forshey, Media Contact
Private non-profit providing education, social services & transitional housing for homeless children & families in NYC.

Hospice & Palliative Care Association of NYS Inc
21 Aviation Rd, Ste 9, Albany, NY 12205
518-446-1483 Fax: 518-446-1484
e-mail: info@hpcanys.org
Web site: www.hpcanys.org
Kathy A McMahon, President & Chief Executive Officer
Hospice & palliative care information & referral service; educational programs; clinical, psychosocial & bereavement issues

Housing Works Inc
57 Willoughby Street, Brooklyn, NY 11201
347-473-7400 Fax: 347-473-7464
Web site: www.housingworks.org
Michael Kink, Statewide Advocacy Coordinator & Legislative Counsel
Housing, health care, advocacy, job training & support services for homeless NY residents with HIV or AIDS

Humane Society of the United States, Mid Atlantic Regional Office
270 US Hwy 206, Flanders, NJ 07836
973-927-5611 Fax: 973-927-5617
e-mail: maro@hsus.org
Web site: www.hsus.org
Nina Austenberg, Regional Director

Hunger Action Network of NYS (HANNYS)
275 State St, Albany, NY 12210
518-434-7371 Fax: 518-434-7390
e-mail: bhpham@hungeractionnys.org
Web site: www.hungeractionnys.org
Bich Ha Pham, Executive Director
Developing unified efforts to address the root causes of hunger & promote social justice

Offices and agencies generally appear in alphabetical order, except when specific order is requested by listee.

SOCIAL SERVICES / Private Sector

Hunter College, Brookdale Center for Healthy Aging and Longevity
425 E 25th St, New York, NY 10010
212-481-5420 or 212-481-4595 Fax: 212-481-3791
e-mail: mfahs@huntercuny.edu
Web site: www.brookdale.org
Marianne Fahs, Executive Director
Policy research & development, training, publications & resources for institutions & community agencies

Institute for Socio-Economic Studies
10 New King St, White Plains, NY 10604
914-686-7112 Fax: 914-686-0581
e-mail: info@socioeconomic.org
Web site: www.socioeconomic.org
Leonard M Greene, President
Welfare reform, socioeconomic incentives, tax & healthcare reform

Japanese American Social Services Inc
100 Gold St, Lower Level, New York, NY 10038
212-442-1541 Fax: 212-442-8627
e-mail: info@jassi.org
Web site: www.jassi.org
Margaret Fung, Executive Director
Bilingual/bicultural programs; assistance with government benefits, housing, immigration & legal rights

Korean Community Services of Metropolitan NY
149 West 24th St, 6th Fl, New York, NY 10011
212-463-9685 Fax: 212-463-8347
e-mail: kcskcsny.org
Web site: www.kcsny.org
Shin Son, Executive Director
Develop & deliver social services to support & assist members of the Korean & neighboring communities

NYS Bar Assn, Children & the Law Committee
Law Office of Anne Reynolds Copps
126 State St, 6th Fl, Albany, NY 12207
518-436-4170 Fax: 518-436-1456
e-mail: arcopps@nycap.rr.com
Anne Reynolds Copps, Chair

Lesbian, Gay, Bisexual & Transgender Community Ctr - Not For Profit
208 W 13th Street, New York, NY 10011-7702
212-620-7310 Fax: 212-924-2657
e-mail: info@gaycenter.org
Web site: www.gaycenter.org
Miriam Yeung, Director, Public Policy
Mental health counseling, out-patient chemical dependency treatment center, after-school youth services, HIV/AIDS services, advocacy, cultural programs, affordable meeting and conference services, and community-building.

Little Flower Children & Family Services
186 Joralemon St, Brooklyn, NY 11201-4326
718-875-3500 ext3650 Fax: 718-260-8863
e-mail: stupph@lfchild.org
Web site: www.littleflowerny.org
Hon. Herbert W Stupp, Chief Executive Officer
Foster care, adoption, child welfare, residential treatment services and residences for the developmentally disabled & day care; union free school district

Littman Krooks LLP
655 Third Ave, New York, NY 10017
212-490-2020 Fax: 212-490-2990
e-mail: bkrooks@littmankrooks.com
Web site: www.littmankrooks.com
Bernard A Krooks, Partner
Elder law and special needs planning

March of Dimes Birth Defects Foundation
1275 Mamaroneck Ave, White Plains, NY 10605
914-997-4641 Fax: 914-997-4662
e-mail: dstaples@marchofdimes.com
Web site: www.marchofdimes.com
Douglas Staples, Senior Vice President Strategic Marketing and Communications

New York Association for New Americans, Inc (NYANA)
2 Washington St, 9th Fl, New York, NY 10004-1102
212-425-2900 Fax: 212-344-1621
e-mail: shenry@nyana.org
Web site: www.nyana.org
Sylvie Henry, Chief Financial Officer
Social service referrals for immigrants

NY Counseling Association Inc
PO Box 12636, Albany, NY 12212-2636
518-235-2026 Fax: 518-235-0910
e-mail: nycaoffice@nycounseling.org
Web site: www.nycounseling.org
Donald Newell, Executive Manager
Counseling professionals in education, mental health, career, employment, rehabilitation & adult development

NY Foundation for Senior Citizens Inc
11 Park Place, 14th Fl, New York, NY 10007-2801
212-962-7559 Fax: 212-227-2952
e-mail: nyfscinc@aol.com
Web site: www.nyfsc.org
Linda Hoffman, President
Social services for seniors in New York City

NYC Coalition Against Hunger
16 Beaver St, 3rd Fl, New York, NY 10004
212-825-0028 Fax: 212-825-0267
e-mail: jberg@nyccah.org
Web site: www.nyccah.org
Joel Berg, Executive Director

Offices and agencies generally appear in alphabetical order, except when specific order is requested by listee.

SOCIAL SERVICES / Private Sector

NYS Association of Area Agencies on Aging
272 Broadway, Albany, NY 12204-2717
518-449-7080 Fax: 518-449-7055
e-mail: nysaaaa@aol.com
Web site: www.nysaaaa.org
Laura A Cameron, Executive Director
Agencies working to enhance effectiveness of programs for older persons

NYS Child Care Coordinating Council
230 Washington Ave Ext, Albany, NY 12203-5390
518-690-4217 Fax: 518-690-2887
e-mail: csaginaw@nyscccc.org
Web site: www.nyscccc.org
Carol Saginaw, Executive Director
Advocacy & education for the development of accessible and affordable, quality child care services

NYS Corps Collaboration
24 Century Hill Drive, Ste 200, Latham, NY 12110
518-470-4995 Fax: 518-783-3577
e-mail: info@nyscc.net
Web site: www.nyscc.net
Linda J Cohen, Executive Director
Statewide youth service & conservation corps addressing society's unmet needs & buiding self-esteem, a sense of civic responsibility & leadership skills

NYS Industries for the Disabled (NYSID) Inc
155 Washington Ave, Ste 400, Albany, NY 12210
518-463-9706 or 800-221-5994 Fax: 518-463-9708
e-mail: administrator@nysid.org
Web site: www.nysid.org
Lawrence L Barker, Jr, President & Chief Executive Officer
Business development through 'preferred source' purchasing to increase employment opportunities for people with disabilities

National Association of Social Workers, NYS Chapter
188 Washington Ave, Albany, NY 12210-2304
518-463-4741 or 800-724-6279 Fax: 518-463-6446
e-mail: info@naswnys.org
Web site: www.naswnys.org
Thea Griffin, Assistant Executive Director
Professional development & specialized training for professional social workers; standards for social work practice; advocacy for policies, services & programs that promote social justice

National Council of Jewish Women
53 W 23rd St, 6th Fl, New York, NY 10010
212-645-4048 Fax: 212-645-7466
e-mail: action@ncjw.org
Web site: www.ncjw.org
Phyllis Snyder, President
Human rights & social service advocacy & education

National Urban League Inc (The)
120 Wall St, New York, NY 10005
212-558-5300 Fax: 212-344-5332
e-mail: info@nul.org
Web site: www.nul.org
Michele M Moore, Senior Vice President Communications & Marketing
Community-based movement devoted to empowering African Americans to enter the economic & social mainstream

Nelson A Rockefeller Inst of Govt, Federalism Research Grp
411 State St, Albany, NY 12203-1003
518-443-5522 Fax: 518-443-5788
e-mail: gaist@rockinst.org
Web site: www.rockinst.org
Thomas L Gais, Co-Director
State management systems for social service programs

New York Association of Homes & Services for the Aging
150 State St, Ste 301, Albany, NY 12207-1698
518-449-2707 Fax: 518-455-8908
e-mail: cyoung@nyahsa.org
Web site: www.nyahsa.org
Carl Young, President
Long term care

New York Community Trust (The)
909 Third Avenue, 22nd Fl, New York, NY 10022
212-686-0010 Fax: 212-532-8528
e-mail: info@nycommunitytrust.org
Web site: www.nycommunitytrust.org
Lorie A Slutsky, President/Director
Administrators of philanthropic funds

New York Public Welfare Association
130 Washington Ave, Albany, NY 12210
518-465-9305 Fax: 518-465-5633
e-mail: nypwa@nycap.rr.com
Web site: www.nypwa.com
Sheila Harrigan, Executive Director
Partnership of local social services districts dedicated to improve the quality & effectiveness of social welfare policy

New York Society for the Deaf
161 William St, 11th Fl, New York, NY 10038
646-278-8172 or TTY: 646-278-8171 Fax: 212-777-5740
Web site: www.nysd.org
Kathleen Cox, Executive Director
Ensure full & equal access to appropriate, comprehensive clinical, residential & support services for deaf & deaf-blind persons

New York State Association of Family Services Agencies Inc
95 Columbia Street, Albany, NY 12210
518-465-5340 Fax: 518-465-6023
Web site: www.nysafsa.org
Michael Barrett, Governmental Affairs Representative
Social & human services assistance & advocacy

Offices and agencies generally appear in alphabetical order, except when specific order is requested by listee.

SOCIAL SERVICES / Private Sector

New York State Catholic Conference
465 State St, Albany, NY 12203-1004
518-434-6195 Fax: 518-434-9796
e-mail: info@nyscatholic.org
Web site: www.nyscatholic.org
Richard E Barnes, Executive Director
Identify, formulate & implement public policy objectives of the NYS Bishops in health, education, welfare, human & civil rights

New York State Citizens' Coalition for Children Inc
410 East Upland Road, Ithaca, NY 14850-2551
607-272-0034 Fax: 607-272-0035
e-mail: office@nysccc.org
Web site: www.nysccc.org
Judith Ashton, Executive Director
Adoption & foster care advocacy

New York State Community Action Association
2 Charles Blvd, Guilderland, NY 12084
518-690-0491 Fax: 518-690-0498
e-mail: dan@nyscaaonline.org
Web site: www.nyscaaonline.org
Daniel Maskin, Chief Executive Officer
Dedicated to the growth & education of community action agencies in NYS to sustain their efforts in advocating & improving the lives of low-income New Yorkers

New York State Rehabilitation Association
155 Washington Ave, Suite 410, Albany, NY 12210
518-449-2976 Fax: 518-426-4329
e-mail: nysra@nyrehab.org
Web site: www.nyrehab.org
Jeff Wise, JD, Vice President
Political advocacy, education, communications, networking & referral services for people with disabilities

New York Urban League
204 W 136th St, New York, NY 10030
212-926-8000 Fax: 212-283-2736
Web site: www.nyul.org
Darwin M Davis, President & Chief Executive Officer
Social services, job training, education & advocacy

Nonprofit Coordinating Committee of New York
1350 Broadway, Rm 1801, New York, NY 10018-7802
212-502-4191 Fax: 212-502-4189
e-mail: mclark@npccny.org
Web site: www.npccny.org
Michael Clark, Executive Director/President
Advocacy & government activities monitoring for NYC nonprofits

North Shore Animal League America
25 Lewyt Street, Port Washington, NY 11050
516-883-7900 x257 Fax: 516-944-5732
e-mail: webmaster@nsalamerica.org
Web site: www.nsalamerica.org
Perry Fina, Director, Marketing
Rescue, care & adoption services for orphaned companion animals

Planned Parenthood of NYC, Inc
26 Bleecker St, New York, NY 10012
212-274-7292 Fax: 212-274-7276
e-mail: carla.goldstein@ppnyc.org
Web site: www.ppnyc.org
Carla Goldstein, Vice President, Public Affairs

Prevent Child Abuse New York
134 S Swan St, Albany, NY 12210
518-445-1273 or 800-CHILDREN Fax: 518-436-5889
e-mail: info@preventchildabuseny.org
Web site: www.preventchildabuseny.org
Christine Deyss, Executive Director
Child abuse prevention advocacy, education, technical assistance

ProLiteracy Worldwide
1320 Jamesville Ave, Syracuse, NY 13210-4224
315-422-9121 Fax: 315-422-6369
e-mail: info@proliteracy.org
Web site: www.proliteracy.org
Rochelle A Cassella, Director, Corporate Communications
Sponsors educational programs & services to empower adults & families through the acquisition of literacy skills & practices

Public/Private Ventures
The Chanin Building, 122 East 42nd St, 42nd Fl, New York, NY 10168
212-822-2400 Fax: 212-949-0439
e-mail: melliott@ppv.org
Web site: www.ppv.org
Mark Elliott, Executive Vice President
Action-based research, public policy & program development organization

Resource Center for Independent Living (RCIL)
401-409 Columbia St, PO Box 210, Utica, NY 13503-0210
315-797-4642 or TTY 315-797-5837 Fax: 315-797-4747
e-mail: burt.danovitz@rcil.com
Web site: www.rcil.com
Burt Danovitz, Executive Director
Services & advocacy for the disabled; public information & community education and awareness.

Roman Catholic Diocese of Albany, Catholic Charities
40 N Main Ave, Albany, NY 12203
518-453-6650 Fax: 518-453-6792
Web site: www.ccrcda.org
Sister Maureen Joyce, Chief Executive Officer
Social & human services assistance: housing, shelters, day care, counseling, transportation, health & emergency

Rural & Migrant Ministry Inc
PO Box 4757, Poughkeepsie, NY 12602
845-485-8627 Fax: 845-485-1963
e-mail: hope@ruralmigrantministry.org
Web site: www.ruralmigrantministry.org
Richard Witt, Executive Director
Working to end poverty & increase self-determination, education & economic resources for migrant farmworkers & the rural poor

Offices and agencies generally appear in alphabetical order, except when specific order is requested by listee.

SOCIAL SERVICES / Private Sector

Rural Opportunities Inc
400 East Ave, Rochester, NY 14607
585-546-7180 Fax: 585-340-3335
e-mail: smitchell@ruralinc.org
Web site: www.ruralinc.org
Stuart J Mitchell, President & Chief Executive Officer
Advance self-sufficiency of farm workers, low-income & other disenfranchised people & communities through advocacy & programs including training & employment, child development, health & safety, & home ownership

Salvation Army, Empire State Division
PO Box 148, Syracuse, NY 13206-0148
315-434-1300 x310 Fax: 315-434-1399
Web site: www.salvationarmy.org
Norman E Wood, Divisional Commander

Statewide Emergency Network for Social & Economic Security (SENSES)
275 State St, Albany, NY 12210
518-463-5576 Fax: 518-432-9073
e-mail: rdeutsch@sensesny.org
Web site: www.sensesny.org
Ron Deutsch, Executive Director
Poverty, welfare reform, tax policy, homelessness, community economic development

Syracuse University, Maxwell School of Citizenship & Public Affairs
200 Eggers Hall, Syracuse, NY 13244-1020
315-443-2552 Fax: 315-443-1081
e-mail: ctrpol@syr.edu
Web site: www.maxwell.syr.edu
Timothy Smeeding, Professor of Public Policy; Director
Education, healthcare, entrepreneurship policies, social welfare, income distribution & comparative social policies

United Jewish Appeal-Federation of Jewish Philanthropies of NY
155 Washington Ave, Albany, NY 12210
518-436-1091 Fax: 518-463-1266
e-mail: solowayr@ujafedny.org
Web site: www.ujafedny.org
Ronald Soloway, Managing Director, Government & External Relations

United Neighborhood Houses - Not For Profit
70 W 36th St, 5th Fl, New York, NY 10018
212-967-0322 Fax: 212-967-0792
e-mail: nwackstein@unhny.org
Web site: www.unhny.org
Nancy Wackstein, Executive Director
Federation of NYC settlement houses that provides issue advocacy & management assistance for member agencies' social, educational & cultural programs

United Way of Central New York
518 James St, PO Box 2129, Syracuse, NY 13220-2227
315-428-2216 Fax: 315-428-2227
e-mail: ccollie@unitedway-cny.org
Web site: www.unitedway-cny.org
Craig E Collie, Vice President, Volunteer Resource Development
Fundraising & support to human & social services organizations

United Way of New York City
2 Park Ave, New York, NY 10016
212-251-2500 Fax: 212-696-1220
e-mail: lmandell@uwnyc.org
Web site: www.unitedwaynyc.org
Lawrence Mandell, President & Chief Executive Officer
Works with partners from all sectors to create, support, & execute strategic initiatives that seek to achieve measurable improvement in the lives of the city's most valuable residents and communities

Upstate Homes for Children & Adults Inc
2705 State Hwy 28, Oneonta, NY 13820
607-286-7171 Fax: 607-286-7166
e-mail: kennedyp@upstatehome.org
Web site: www.upstatehome.org
Patricia E Kennedy, Executive Director
Education/mental hygiene

Welfare Research Inc
112 State St, Rm 1020, Albany, NY 12207
518-432-2563 Fax: 518-432-2564
e-mail: administration@welfareresearch.org
Web site: www.welfareresearch.org
Virginia Hayes Sibbison, Executive Director
Contract research in social service & related policy areas

World Hunger Year Inc
505 Eighth Ave, Suite 2100, New York, NY 10018-6582
212-629-8850 Fax: 212-465-9274
e-mail: why@worldhungeryear.org
Web site: www.worldhungeryear.org
Bill Ayres, Executive Director
Addresses root causes of hunger & poverty by promoting effective & innovative community-based solutions

YAI/National Institute for People with Disabilities
460 W 34th St, New York, NY 10001-2382
212-273-6110 or 866-2-YAI-LINK Fax: 212-947-7524
e-mail: jmlcares@yai.org
Web site: www.yai.org
Joel M Levy, Chief Executive Officer
Programs, services & advocacy for people with autism, mental retardation & other developmental disabilities of all ages, and their families; special education & early learning programs

Offices and agencies generally appear in alphabetical order, except when specific order is requested by listee.

TAXATION & REVENUE

New York State

GOVERNOR'S OFFICE

Governor's Office
Executive Chamber
State Capitol
Albany, NY 12224
518-474-8390 Fax: 518-474-1513
Web site: www.state.ny.us

Governor:
  Eliot Spitzer 518-474-8390
Secretary to the Governor:
  Richard Baum 518-474-4246
Counsel to the Governor:
  David Nocenti 518-474-8343
Director, Policy:
  Peter Pope 518-486-9671
Senior Advisor to the Governor:
  Lloyd Constantine 518-486-9671
Director, Communications:
  Darren Dopp 518-474-8418
Deputy Secretary, Appointments:
  Francine James 518-474-0491
Deputy Secretary, Intergovernmental Affairs:
  Martin Mack 518-408-2555

EXECUTIVE DEPARTMENTS AND RELATED AGENCIES

Alcoholic Beverage Control, Division of (State Liquor Authority)
80 S Swan St, Ste 900
Albany, NY 12210-8002
518-486-4767 Fax: 518-402-4015
Web site: www.abc.state.ny.us

317 Lenox Ave
New York, NY 10027
212-961-8385
Fax: 212-961-8299

Chair:
  Daniel B Boyle .... 212-961-8347 or 518-473-6559
  fax: 212-961-8283
Commissioner:
  Lawrence J Gedda 212-961-8347
Commissioner:
  Noreen Healey 212-961-8355
Counsel:
  Thomas J Donohue 518-402-4429

Administration
Senior Deputy Commissioner, Administration:
  J Mark Anderson 518-474-4139

Director, Financial Administration:
  Franklin A Hecht 518-474-4546
Director, Human Resources:
  Dan Cunningham 518-473-5995
Director, Communications:
  William Crowley 518-486-4767

Licensing & Enforcement

Albany (Zone II)
80 S Swan St, Ste 900, Albany, NY 12210-8002
Director, Licensing:
  Kerri O'Brien 518-474-3114
Associate Counsel:
  Leslie Trebby 518-474-6750
Assistant Director, ABC Compliance:
  Daniel Malay 518-473-0385/fax: 518-473-7527
Supervising Beverage Ctrl Investigator:
  Robert Benedetto 518-474-0385/fax: 518-473-7527

Buffalo (Zone III)
Iskalo Electric Tower, 535 Washington St, Ste 303, Buffalo, NY 14203
716-847-3035
Executive Officer:
  Brandon Noyes 716-847-3060
Senior Beverage Control Investigator:
  Gary Bartikofsky 716-847-3039

New York City (Zone I)
317 Lenox Avenue, New York, NY 10027
212-961-8385
Deputy Commissioner:
  Fred Gioffre 212-961-8301
Supervising Attorney:
  Stephen Kalinsky 212-961-8351

Budget, Division of the
State Capitol
Albany, NY 12224
518-473-3885
e-mail: bdgord@budget.state.ny.us
Web site: www.budget.state.ny.us

Director:
  Paul E Francis 518-474-2300
First Deputy Director:
  Laura L Anglin 518-474-6323
Deputy Director:
  Ron Rock 518-474-6300
Deputy Director:
  Kim Fine 518-474-6300
Counsel:
  Kathy Bennett 518-474-2300
Director, Communications:
  Jeffrey Gordon 518-473-3885
Press Officer:
  Scott Reif 518-473-3885

Offices and agencies generally appear in alphabetical order, except when specific order is requested by listee.

TAXATION & REVENUE / New York State

Law Department
120 Broadway
New York, NY 10271-0332
212-416-8000 Fax: 212-416-8796

State Capitol
Albany, NY 12224-0341
518-474-7330
Fax: 518-402-2472

Attorney General:
  Andrew M Cuomo 518-474-7330

Public Advocacy Division
Deputy Attorney General:
  Dietrich Snell. 212-416-8041/fax: 212-416-8068
Special Counsel:
  Mary Ellen Burns 212-416-6155

Charities Bureau
Bureau Chief:
  Gerald Rosenberg 212-416-8490/fax: 212-416-8393

Internet Bureau
Bureau Chief:
  Jane Azia 212-416-8433/fax: 212-416-8369

Investment Protection Bureau
Bureau Chief:
  David Brown 212-416-8198/fax: 212-416-6377

State Counsel Division
Deputy Attorney General:
  Richard Rifkin 518-473-7190
Assistant Deputy Attorney General:
  Patricia Martinelli 518-473-0648/fax: 518-486-9777
Assistant Deputy Attorney General:
  Susan L Watson 212-416-8579/fax: 212-416-6001

Civil Recoveries Bureau
Bureau Chief:
  Mary E House 518-474-7131/fax: 518-473-1635

Litigation Bureau
Bureau Chief, Albany:
  Bruce D Feldman 518-473-8328/fax: 518-473-1572
Bureau Chief, NYC:
  James B Henley 212-416-8523/fax: 212-416-6075

Lottery, Division of
One Broadway Center
PO Box 7500
Schenectady, NY 12301-7500
518-388-3300 Fax: 518-388-3423
Web site: www.nylottery.org

Director:
  Robert J McLaughlin 518-388-3400
Executive Deputy Director:
  Susan E Miller 518-388-3404
Acting General Counsel:
  Julie B Silverstein Barker 518-388-3408
Deputy Director, Finance & Administration:
  Gardner Gurney 518-388-3406
Director, Operations:
  Joe Seeley 518-388-3411

Director, Advertising:
  Fred Chick 518-388-3430
Director, Administration:
  Art DelSignore 518-388-3404
Director, Communications:
  Vacant 518-388-3415/fax: 518-388-3423
Director, Marketing:
  Randall Lex 518-388-3430/fax: 518-388-3403

Regional Offices

Adirondack-Capital District Region
One Broadway Center, Suite 700, Schenectady, NY 12305
Contact:
  Judy Drislane 518-388-3420

Central/Finger Lakes/Genesee Valley Regions
Rochester Office
First Federal Plaza Bldg, 28 E Main St, Rochester, NY 14614
Contact:
  George Popp 585-246-4200
Syracuse Office
Deys Centennial Bldg, 401 S Salina St, Syracuse, NY 13202
Contact:
  Robin Sywulski 315-448-4300

Hudson Valley Region
18 Westage Drive, Ste 6, Fishkill, NY 12524
Contact:
  Georgene Perlman 845-897-2412

Long Island Region
1000 Zeckendorf Blvd, Garden City, NY 11530
Contact:
  Jim Benoit 516-222-8260

New York City Region
175 Varick St, 5th Fl, New York, NY 10014
Contact:
  Thomas Breig 646-486-6100

Western Region
Ellicott Sq Bldg, 295 Main St, Ste 120, Buffalo, NY 14203
Contact:
  Doug Bautz 716-847-3469

Racing & Wagering Board
1 Broadway Center
Ste 600
Schenectady, NY 12305-2553
518-395-5400 Fax: 518-347-1250
e-mail: info@racing.state.ny.us
Web site: www.racing.state.ny.us

Chair:
  Daniel D Hogan 518-395-5400
Member:
  Michael J Hoblock, Jr 518-395-5400
Member:
  John B Simoni 518-395-5400
Executive Director:
  John G Cansdale 518-395-5400
Counsel:
  Robert A Feuerstein 212-417-2103
Secretary to the Board:
  Gail Pronti 518-395-5400
Public Information Officer:
  Dan Toomey 518-395-5400

Offices and agencies generally appear in alphabetical order, except when specific order is requested by listee.

TAXATION & REVENUE / New York State

Chief, Racing Operations:
  Joseph Lynch 518-395-5400
Director, Audits & Investigations:
  Tom Casaregola 518-395-5400
Director, Administration:
  Kevin Dempsey 518-395-5400
Manager, Licensing:
  Nicole Robilotto 518-395-5400
Director, Gaming Regulation:
  Bruce Samboy 518-395-5400
Director, Racing Officials:
  Brian Barry 518-395-5400

Real Property Services, Office of
16 Sheridan Ave
Albany, NY 12210-2714
518-486-5446 Fax: 518-474-9276
Web site: www.orps.state.ny.us

Executive Director:
  Donald C DeWitt 518-474-5711
Executive Deputy Director:
  Steve King 518-473-6914
Acting Counsel:
  James O'Keefe 518-474-6753
Director, Public Information:
  Geoffrey T Gloak 518-486-5446
  e-mail: geoffrey.gloak@orps.state.ny.us

Research, Information & Policy Development
Director:
  James Dunne 518-473-4532
  e-mail: jim.dunne@orps.state.ny.us

Regional Customer Service Delivery
Director:
  David Williams 518-473-8743
  e-mail: dave.williams@orps.state.ny.us

Albany (Northern Region) . . . . fax: 518-486-7752
16 Sheridan Ave, Albany, NY 12210-2714
Regional Director:
  Jeffrey Green 518-486-4403
  e-mail: internet.northern@orps.state.ny.us

Batavia (Western Region)
Genesee County Bldg 2, 3837 W Main Rd, Batavia, NY 14020
Regional Director:
  Joseph Muscarella 585-343-6329/fax: 585-343-9740
  e-mail: internet.western@orps.state.ny.us

Long Island Satellite Office . . . . fax: 631-952-3729
250 Veterans Memorial Hgwy, Rm 2B-44, Hauppauge, NY 11788
Manager:
  Louis Cubello 631-952-3650
  e-mail: internet.metro@orps.state.ny.us

Newburgh (Southern Region) . . . . fax: 845-567-2690
263 Route 17K, Ste 2001, Newburgh, NY 12550
Regional Director:
  John Wolham 845-567-2648
  e-mail: internet.southern@orps.state.ny.us

Saranac Lake Satellite Office . . . . fax: 518-891-2639
43 Broadway, Saranac Lake, NY 12983
Office Manager:
  Dan Lancor 518-891-1780
  e-mail: internet.saranac@orps.state.ny.us

Syracuse (Central Region) . . . . fax: 315-471-3634
401 South Salina St, Syracuse, NY 13202
Regional Director:
  Teresa Frank 315-471-2347
  e-mail: internet.central@orps.state.ny.us

State Board of Real Property Services
Chair:
  George E Herren 518-474-5711
Executive Secretary:
  Donald C DeWitt 518-474-5711
Asst to the Board:
  Darlene A Maloney 518-474-3793/fax: 518-474-9276

Tax Appeals, Division of
Riverfront Professional Tower
500 Federal St, 4th Fl
Troy, NY 12180
518-266-3000 Fax: 518-271-0886
e-mail: nysdota@nysdta.org
Web site: www.nysdta.org

Tax Appeals Tribunal
President & Commissioner:
  Charles H Nesbitt 518-266-3050
Commissioner:
  Carroll R Jenkins 518-266-3050
Commissioner:
  Robert J McDermott 518-266-3050
Counsel:
  Donna M Gardiner 518-266-3052
Secretary to the Tribunal:
  Jean A McDonnell 518-266-3036

Administrative Law Judges & Officers
Chief Administrative Law Judge:
  Andrew F Marchese 518-266-3000
Asst Chief Administrative Law Judge:
  Daniel J Ranalli 518-266-3000
Director, Administration:
  George J Cannon 518-266-3041

Taxation & Finance Department
State Campus
Bldg 9, Rm 227
Albany, NY 12227
518-457-4242 Fax: 518-457-2486
Web site: www.tax.state.ny.us

Acting Commissioner:
  Barbara G Billet 518-457-2244
Executive Deputy Commissioner:
  Barbara G Billet 518-457-7358
Deputy Commissioner & Counsel:
  Daniel Smirlock 518-457-3746/fax: 518-457-8247
Special Asst to Commissioner for Business:
  Holly Chamberlin 518-485-5080
Director, Conciliation & Mediation Services:
  Barry M Bresler 518-485-8063
Director, Executive Correspondence Control Unit:
  Elizabeth Amodeo 518-457-6118
Director, Legislative Affairs:
  Maryann Tucker 518-457-2398
Director, Public Information:
  Thomas Bergin 518-457-4242

Offices and agencies generally appear in alphabetical order, except when specific order is requested by listee.

TAXATION & REVENUE / New York State

Information Office
Chief Information Officer:
Brian Digman 518-457-4362

Office of Administration (OOA)
Deputy Commissioner:
Margaret Sherman 518-457-1000

Human Resources Management
Director:
Kiaran Johnson-Lew 518-457-2786

Operations Support Bureau
Director:
Lisa Negus 518-485-7891

Office of Budget & Management Analysis
Chief Financial Officer:
Patricia Mitchell 518-457-1000

Budget & Accounting Services
Director:
Eric Mostert 518-485-6731

Planning & Management Analysis Bureau
Director:
Mary Ellen Nagengast 518-457-8660

Tax Enforcement, Office of
Deputy Commissioner:
William Comisky 518-457-9692

Audit Division
Director, Tax Audits:
Nonie Manion 518-457-2750

Tax Compliance Division
Director:
Joseph F Gecewicz 518-457-1138

Tax Policy Analysis, Office of
Deputy Commissioner:
Robert D Plattner 518-457-4357

Technical Services Division
Director:
Marilyn M Kaltenborn 518-457-1153

Taxpayer Services & Revenue Division
Director:
Jamie Woodward 518-457-2261

Treasury Division
Deputy Commissioner & Treasurer:
Aida Brewer 518-474-4250/fax: 518-402-4118

E-MPIRE
Director:
Terry Atwater 518-457-7929

CORPORATIONS, AUTHORITIES AND COMMISSIONS

New York State Financial Control Board
123 William St
23rd Fl
New York, NY 10038-3804
212-417-5046 Fax: 212-417-5055
e-mail: nysfcb@fcb.state.ny.us
Web site: www.fcb.state.ny.us

Acting Executive Director:
Jeffrey Sommer 212-417-5066
Deputy Director, Expenditure Analysis:
Dennis DeLisle 212-417-5069
Acting Deputy Director, Economic & Revenue Analysis:
Martin Fischman 212-417-5068
Associate Director:
Mattie W Taylor 212-417-5053

New York State Project Finance Agency
641 Lexington Ave
New York, NY 10022
212-688-4000 Fax: 212-872-0678

Chair:
Judd Levy 212-688-4000
President & CEO:
Priscilla Almodovar 212-688-4000
Senior VP, COO & CFO:
Ralph J Madalena 212-688-4000
Senior VP & General Counsel:
Justin Driscoll 212-688-4000
Senior VP & Special Asst to Pres/CEO for Policy Dev & Programs:
James P Angley 212-688-4000
Senior VP, Debt Issuance:
Bernard Abramowitz 212-688-4000 x530
Vice President, Director of Development:
Jonathan Cortrell 212-688-4000 x688
Vice President, Policy & Planning:
Tracy A Oats 212-688-4000 x678

NEW YORK STATE LEGISLATURE

See Legislative Branch in Section 1 for additional Standing Committee and Subcommittee information.

Assembly Standing Committees

Racing & Wagering
Chair:
James Gary Pretlow (D) 518-455-5291
Ranking Minority Member:
Robert Barra (R) 518-455-4656

Real Property Taxation
Chair:
Sandra R Galef (D) 518-455-5348
Ranking Minority Member:
Nancy Calhoun (R) 518-455-5441

Ways & Means
Chair:
Herman D Farrell, Jr (D) 518-455-5491
Ranking Minority Member:
James P Hayes (R) 518-455-4618

Offices and agencies generally appear in alphabetical order, except when specific order is requested by listee.

TAXATION & REVENUE / U.S. Government

Senate Standing Committees

Finance
Chair:
 Owen H Johnson (R) 518-455-3411
Ranking Minority Member:
 William Stachowski (D) 518-455-2426

Racing, Gaming & Wagering
Chair:
 William J Larkin, Jr (R) 518-455-2770
Ranking Minority Member:
 John D Sabini (D) 518-455-2529

U.S. Government

EXECUTIVE DEPARTMENTS AND RELATED AGENCIES

US Department of Homeland Security (DHS)
Web site: www.dhs.gov

Bureau of Immigration & Customs Enforcement (ICE)
Web site: www.ice.gov

New York District Office
601 W 26th St, Ste 700, New York, NY 10001
Special Agent-in-Charge:
 Martin Ficke 646-230-3200
Albany Sub Office
 1086 Troy-Schenectady Rd, Latham, NY 12110
 Group Supervisor:
  LeRoy Tario 518-220-2100
 Resident Agent-in-Charge:
  Jack McQuade 518-220-2100

Customs & Border Protection (CBP)
202-354-1000
Web site: www.cbp.gov

Buffalo Field Office
4455 Genesee St, Buffalo, NY 14225
716-626-0400
Director:
 Michael D'Ambrosio 716-626-0400 x201/fax: 716-626-9281
Albany, Port of
 445 Broadway, Room 216, Albany, NY 12207
 518-431-0200
 Port Director:
  Drew Wescott 518-431-0200/fax: 518-431-0203
Buffalo, Port of
 Larkin at Exchange, 726 Exchange, Suite 400, Buffalo, NY 14210
 716-843-8300
 Area Port Director:
  Joseph Wilson 716-843-8300
Champlain, Port of .... fax: 518-298-8395
 198 W Service Rd, Champlain, NY 12919
 518-298-8327 Fax: 518-298-8395
 Area Port Director:
  Christopher Perry 518-298-8347/fax: 518-298-8314
Ogdensburg, Port of
 104 Bridge Approach Rd, Ogdensburg, NY 13669
 Port Director:
  William Mitchell 315-393-1390/fax: 315-393-7472

New York Field Office .... fax: 646-733-3245
1 Penn Plaza, 11th Fl, New York, NY 10119
646-733-3100 Fax: 646-733-3245
Director, Field Operations:
 Susan T Mitchell 646-733-3100

Field Public Affairs Officer:
 Janet Rapaport 212-514-8324/fax: 212-344-3755
Field Counsel - New York
 Associate Chief Counsel:
  Judith Altman 646-733-3200
Laboratory Division
 Director:
  Tom Governo 973-368-1901

US Justice Department
Web site: www.usdoj.gov

Bureau of Alcohol, Tobacco, Firearms & Explosives
Web site: www.atf.gov

New York Field Division .... fax: 718-650-4041
241 37th St, 3rd Floor, Brooklyn, NY 11232
718-650-4040 Fax: 718-650-4041
Spec Agent-in-Chg:
 William McMahon 718-650-4040/fax: 718-650-4071
Public Information Officer:
 Joseph G Green 718-650-4040

US Treasury Department
Web site: www.ustreas.gov

Internal Revenue Service
Web site: www.irs.gov

Appeals Unit - Office of Directors
290 Broadway, 13th Fl, New York, NY 10007
Director, Appeals, Area 1 (Large Business & Specialty):
 Richard Guevara 212-298-2270/fax: 212-298-2282
Director, Appeals, Area 1 (General):
 Raymond Wolff 212-298-2400/fax: 212-298-2648

Criminal Investigation Unit - New York Field Office
Spec Agent-in-Chg:
 Michael J Thomas 212-436-1633/fax: 212-436-1957
Public Information Officer:
 Joseph Foy 212-436-1032/fax: 212-436-1582

Large & Mid-Size Business Division (LMSB)
290 Broadway, 12th Fl, New York, NY 10007
Director, Financial Services:
 Paul Denard 212-298-2130/fax: 212-298-2124
Communications Manager:
 Louise Kaminskyj 212-298-2220
 e-mail: louise.kaminskyj@irs.gov
Office of Chief Counsel LMSB Area 1 .... fax: 917-421-3937
 33 Maiden Ln, 12th Fl, New York, NY 10038
 Area Counsel:
  Roland Barral 917-421-4667
 Assoc Area Counsel:
  Peter J Graziano 917-421-4632

Offices and agencies generally appear in alphabetical order, except when specific order is requested by listee.

TAXATION & REVENUE / U.S. Government

Management Information Technology Services - Northeast Area
290 Broadway, 12th Fl, New York, NY 10007
Director, Information Technology:
 Vacant 212-298-2050/fax: 212-298-2595

Office of Chief Counsel
33 Maiden Ln, 14th Fl, New York, NY 10038
Area Counsel for SBSE & W & I:
 Frances Regan.................. 917-421-4737/fax: 917-421-3944
Associate Area Counsel for SBSE & W & I:
 Janet F Appel 516-688-1707

Small Business & Self-Employed Division (SBSE)
 New York SBSE Compliance Services
  290 Broadway, 14th Fl, New York, NY 10007
  Program Manager, Compliance Centers Document Matching Programs:
   Shirley Greene 212-298-2001/fax: 212-298-2062
 SBSE-Compliance Area 2/New York
  290 Broadway, 7th Fl, New York, NY 10007
  Director, Compliance Area 2:
   Michael Donovan............ 212-436-1886/fax: 212-436-1046
 SBSE-Taxpayer Education & Communication (TEC)
  10 Metro Tech Center, 625 Fulton St, 6th Fl, Brooklyn, NY 11201
  Area Director:
   Ellen Murphy 718-488-2000/fax: 718-488-2077

Tax Exempt & Government Entities Div (TEGE)-Northeast Area
10 Metro Tech Center, 625 Fulton St, Brooklyn, NY 11201
Area Manager, Employee Plans:
 Robert Henn..................................... 718-488-2014
 TEGE Area Counsel's Office
  1600 Stewart Ave, Ste 601, Westbury, NY 11590
  Area Counsel:
   Laurence Ziegler........... 516-688-1701/fax: 516-688-1750

Taxpayer Advocate Service (TAS)
 Andover Campus Service Center
  310 Lowell St, Stop 120, Andover, MA 1812
  Taxpayer Advocate for Upstate NY:
   Vicki L Coss................ 973-474-5549/fax: 978-691-6961
 Brookhaven Campus Service Center
  1040 Waverly Ave, Stop 02, Holtsville, NY 11742
  Taxpayer Advocate for Downstate NY:
   Ed Safrey 631-654-6686/fax: 631-447-4879
 Brooklyn & Long Island Office
  10 Metro Tech Center, 625 Fulton St, Brooklyn, NY 11201
  Taxpayer Advocate:
   Anita Kitson 718-488-2080/fax: 718-488-3100
 Manhattan Office
  290 Broadway, 5th Fl, New York, NY 10007
  Taxpayer Advocate:
   Peter L Gorga, Jr............ 212-436-1011/fax: 212-436-1900
 Office of Director, Area 1 (New York State & New England)
  290 Broadway, 14th Fl, New York, NY 10007
  Area Director:
   Mary Ann Silvaggio......... 212-298-2015/fax: 212-298-2016
 Upstate New York Office
  Leo O'Brien Federal Bldg, Rm 354, 1 Clinton Sq, Albany, NY 12207
  Taxpayer Advocate:
   Georgeann Smith 518-427-5413/fax: 518-427-5494
 Western New York State Office
  201 Como Park Blvd, Buffalo, NY 14227-1416
  Taxpayer Advocate:
   William Wirth............... 716-686-4850/fax: 716-686-4851

Wage & Investmnt Div-Stakehldr Partnership Ed & Comm (SPEC)
 Albany Territory
  1 Clinton Ave, Rm 600, Albany, NY 12207
  Territory Manager:
   Peter Stevens 518-427-4109/fax: 518-427-5421

 Area 1 Director's Office
  135 High St, Hartford, CT 06103
  Area Director:
   Richard L Rodriguez 860-756-4666/fax: 860-756-4567
 Buffalo Territory
  201 Como Park Blvd, Cheektowaga, NY 14227
  Territory Manager:
   Thomas Kerr................. 716-686-4800/fax: 716-686-4705
 New York Territory
  290 Broadway, 7th Fl, New York, NY 10007
  Territory Mgr:
   Michael McCormick.......... 212-436-1031/fax: 212-436-1629

US Mint.. fax: 845-446-6258
Rte 218, PO Box 37, West Point, NY 10996
Fax: 845-446-6258
Web site: www.usmint.gov
Superintendent:
 Ellen McCullom.................................... 845-446-6201
Chief, Mint Police:
 John Bennett...................................... 845-446-6235

U.S. CONGRESS

See U.S. Congress Chapter for additional Standing Committee and Subcommittee information.

House of Representatives Standing Committees

Appropriations
Chair:
 David R Obey (D-WI) 202-225-3365
Ranking Minority Member:
 Jerry Lewis (R-CA) 202-225-5861
New York Delegate:
 Maurice D Hinchey (D) 202-225-6335
New York Delegate:
 Nita M Lowey (D) 202-225-6506
New York Delegate:
 Jose E Serrano (D) 202-225-4361
New York Delegate:
 John E Sweeney (R) 202-225-5614
New York Delegate:
 James T Walsh (R) 202-225-3701

Budget
Chair:
 John M Spratt, Jr (D-SC) 202-225-5501
Ranking Minority Member:
 Paul Ryan (R-WI)................................. 202-225-3031

Ways & Means
Chair:
 Charles B Rangel (D-NY) 202-225-4365
Ranking Minority Member:
 Charles B Rangel (D-NY) 202-225-4365
New York Delegate:
 Michael R McNulty (D) 202-225-5076
New York Delegate:
 Thomas M Reynolds (R) 202-225-5265

Joint Senate & House Standing Committees

Joint Committee on Taxation
Chair:
 Sen Charles B Rangel (D-NY) 202-225-4365

Offices and agencies generally appear in alphabetical order, except when specific order is requested by listee.

TAXATION & REVENUE / Private Sector

Vice Chair:
   Max Baucus (R-MT) 202-224-2651
New York Delegate:
   Rep Charles B Rangel (D) 202-225-4365

Senate Standing Committees

Appropriations
Chair:
   Robert C Byrd (D-WV) 202-224-3954
Ranking Minority Member:
   Thad Cochran (R-MS) 202-224-5054

Budget
Chair:
   Kent Conrad (D-ND) 202-224-2043
Ranking Minority Member:
   Judd Gregg (R-NH) 202-224-3324

Finance
Chair:
   Max Baucus (R-MT) 202-224-2651
Ranking Minority Member:
   Chuck Grassley (R-IA) 202-224-3744

Subcommittee
Taxation & IRS Oversight and Long-Term Growth
Chair:
   Kent Conrad (D-ND) 202-224-2043
Ranking Minority Member:
   Jon Kyl (R-AZ) 202-224-4521

Homeland Security & Governmental Affairs
Chair:
   Joseph I Liberman (D-CT) 202-224-4041
Ranking Minority Member:
   Susan Collins (R-ME) 202-224-2523

Private Sector

NYS Bar Assn, Pension Simplification Cmte
Alvin D Lurie PC
13 Country Club Drive, Larchmont, NY 10538
914-834-6725 Fax: 914-834-6725
e-mail: allurie@verizon.net
Alvin D Lurie,

Association of Towns of the State of New York
150 State St, Albany, NY 12207
518-465-7933 Fax: 518-465-0724
e-mail: jhaber@nytowns.org
Web site: www.nytowns.org
G Jeffrey Haber, Executive Director
Advocacy, education for local government

Business Council of New York State Inc
152 Washington Ave, Albany, NY 12210
518-465-7511 x215 Fax: 518-465-4389
e-mail: rich.schwarz@bcnys.org
Web site: www.bcnys.org
Richard Schwarz, Director, Government & Fiscal Affairs/Tax Counsel

Citizens Budget Commission
One Penn Plaza, Ste 640, New York, NY 10119
212-279-2605 Fax: 212-868-4745
e-mail: cmb2@ls2.nyu.edu
Web site: www.cbcny.org
Charles Brecher, Executive VP & Director, Research
Nonpartisan, nonprofit civic organization devoted to influencing constructive change in the finances and services of New York City and New York State government

Council of State Governments, Eastern Conference
100 Wall St, 20th Fl, New York, NY 10005
212-482-2320 Fax: 212-482-2344
e-mail: alan@csgeast.org
Web site: www.csgeast.org
Alan V Sokolow, Regional Director
Economic & fiscal programs

NYS Bar Assn, Tax Section
Sullivan & Cromwell LLP
125 Broad Street, New York, NY 10004
212-558-4000 Fax: 212-558-3588
Web site: www.sullcrom.com
David P Hariton, Chair

NYS Bar Assn, Trusts & Estates Law Section
Day Pitney LLP
7 Times Square, 41st & 42nd St, New York, NY 10036
212-297-5800 Fax: 212-916-2940
e-mail: gwwhitaker@dbh.com
Web site: www.daypitney.com
G Warren Whitaker,
Domestic and international trusts and estates.

Fiscal Policy Institute
1 Lear Jet Lane, Latham, NY 12110
518-786-3156
e-mail: mauro@fiscalpolicy.org
Web site: www.fiscalpolicy.org
Frank Mauro, Executive Director
Nonpartisan research & education; tax, budget, economic & related public policy issues

Community Bankers Assn of NY State, Accounting & Taxation Cmte
North Fork Bank
275 Broadhollow Road, Melville, NY 11747
631-844-1004
Web site: www.greenpoint.com
Aurelie Campbell, Co-Chair

Hawkins Delafield & Wood LLP
One Chase Manhattan Plaza, 43rd Floor, New York, NY 10005
212-820-9434 Fax: 212-820-9666
e-mail: jprogers@hawkins.com
Web site: www.hawkins.com
Joseph P Rogers, Jr, Counsel
Tax law; public finance & municipal contracts

Offices and agencies generally appear in alphabetical order, except when specific order is requested by listee.

TAXATION & REVENUE / Private Sector

Manhattan Institute, Center for Civic Innovation
52 Vanderbilt Ave, 2nd Fl, New York, NY 10017
212-599-7000 Fax: 212-599-3494
Web site: www.manhattan-institute.org
Lindsay Young, Executive Director, Communications
NY city & state tax, fiscal policy

Moody's Investors Service, Public Finance Group
99 Church St, New York, NY 10007
212-553-7780 Fax: 212-298-7113
e-mail: dennis.farrell@moodys.com
Web site: www.moodys.com
Dennis M Farrell, Group Managing Director
Municipal debt ratings & analysis

NYS Conference of Mayors & Municipal Officials
119 Washington Ave, Albany, NY 12210
518-463-1185 Fax: 518-463-1190
e-mail: info@nycom.org
Web site: www.nycom.org
Peter A Baynes, Executive Director
Legislative advocacy for NYS cities & villages

National Federation of Independent Business
1 Commerce Plaza, Ste 1119, Albany, NY 12260-1000
518-434-1262 Fax: 518-426-8799
e-mail: mike.elmendorf@nfib.org
Web site: www.nfib.org
Michael Elmendorf, State Director
Small business advocacy; supporting pro-small business candidates at the state & federal levels

Nelson A Rockefeller Institute of Government
411 State St, Albany, NY 12203-1003
518-443-5522 Fax: 518-443-5788
e-mail: nathanr@rockinst.org
Web site: www.rockinst.org
Richard P Nathan, Director
Management & finance of welfare, health & employment of state & local governments nationally & especially in NY

New York State Assessors' Association
PO Box 888, Middletown, NY 10940
845-344-0292 Fax: 845-343-8238
e-mail: nysaa@nyassessor.com
Web site: www.nyassessor.com
Thomas Frey, Executive Secretary
Real property tax issues

New York State Government Finance Officers Association Inc
7 Elk St, #2, Albany, NY 12207
518-465-1512 Fax: 518-434-4640
e-mail: info@nysgfoa.org
Web site: www.nysgfoa.org
John C Cochrane, President
Membership organization dedicated to the professional management of governmental resources

New York State Society of Certified Public Accountants
3 Park Avenue, 18th Floor, New York, NY 10016-5991
212-719-8418 Fax: 212-719-3364
e-mail: doleary@nysscpa.org
Web site: www.nysscpa.org
Dennis O'Leary, Director, Government Relations

New York State Society of Municipal Finance Officers
13 West Oneida Street, Oswego, NY 13126
315-342-8107 Fax: 315-342-8171
e-mail: dcoad@oswegony.org
Web site: www.nysmunicipalfinanceofficers.org
Deborah Coad, Secretary & Treasurer
Improve municipal financial & accounting operations & procedures in NYS

New York State Society of Enrolled Agents
Office of David J Silverman
866 UN Plaza, #415, New York, NY 10017
212-752-6983 Fax: 212-758-5478
e-mail: taxproblm@aol.com
Web site: www.nyssea.org
David J Silverman, Chair, Legislative/Government Relations Committee

Robert Schalkenbach Foundation
149 Madison Ave, Ste 601, New York, NY 10016
212-683-6424 Fax: 212-683-6454
e-mail: msullivan@schalkenbach.org
Web site: www.schalkenbach.org
Mark A Sullivan, Administrative Director
Land value taxation, real property & economic publications

SCAA - Schuyler Center for Analysis & Advocacy
150 State St, 4th Fl, Albany, NY 12207-1626
518-463-1896 x24 Fax: 518-463-3364
e-mail: kschimke@scaany.org
Web site: www.scaany.org
Karen Schimke, President & Chief Executive Officer
Advocacy, analysis & forums on economic security, education, child care, child support, revenue & taxation issues

Urbanomics
115 Fifth Ave, 3rd Fl, New York, NY 10003
212-353-7462 Fax: 212-353-7494
e-mail: r-armstrong@peapc.com
Web site: www.urbanomics.org
Regina B Armstrong, Principal
Economic development planning studies, market studies, tax policy analyses, program evaluations, economic & demographic forecasts

Wachtell, Lipton, Rosen & Katz
51 W 52nd St, New York, NY 10019
212-403-1241 Fax: 212-403-2241
e-mail: pccanellos@wlrk.com
Web site: www.wlrk.com
Peter C Canellos, Partner
Tax law

Offices and agencies generally appear in alphabetical order, except when specific order is requested by listee.

TOURISM, ARTS & SPORTS

New York State

GOVERNOR'S OFFICE

Governor's Office
Executive Chamber
State Capitol
Albany, NY 12224
518-474-8390 Fax: 518-474-1513
Web site: www.state.ny.us

Governor:
  Eliot Spitzer 518-474-8390
Secretary to the Governor:
  Richard Baum 518-474-4246
Counsel to the Governor:
  David Nocenti......................................518-474-8343
Senior Advisor to the Governor:
  Lloyd Constantine 518-486-9671
Director, Communications:
  Darren Dopp..518-474-8418
Deputy Secretary, Economic Development & Infrastructure:
  Timothy Gilchrist..................................518-408-2552
Deputy Secretary, Environment:
  Judith Enck...518-472-5442
Assistant Counsel to the Governor-Housing, Local Governments & Arts:
  Amanda Hiller 518-474-8494

EXECUTIVE DEPARTMENTS AND RELATED AGENCIES

Council on the Arts
175 Varick St
3rd Fl
New York, NY 10014-4604
212-627-4455 or TDD: 800-895-9838 Fax: 212-620-5911
Web site: www.nysca.org

Chair:
  Richard J Schwartz................................212-627-4455
Vice Chair:
  Debra R Black 212-627-4455
Acting Executive Director:
  Richard J Schwartz................................212-627-4440
  e-mail: rschwartz@nysca.org
Deputy Director:
  Al Berr 212-627-8444
  e-mail: aberr@nysca.org
Deputy Director:
  Jack Lindahl..212-627-3338
  e-mail: glindahl@nysca.org
Deputy Director:
  Debby Silverfine...................................212-627-7778
  e-mail: dsilverfine@nysca.org
Director, Special Projects/Assistant to Chair:
  Sasha Soreff 212-627-5656
  e-mail: ssoreff@nysca.org

Administrative Services
Director:
  Tracy Hamilton-Thompson 212-627-3131
  e-mail: thamilton@nysca.org

Fiscal Management
Contracts:
  Michael Cummings 212-627-4994
  e-mail: mcummings@nysca.org
Final Reports:
  Edward Leung 212-627-8783
  e-mail: eleung@nysca.org

Information Technology
Director:
  Lenn Ditman.......................................212-627-5545
  e-mail: lditman@nysca.org

Program Staff

Architecture, Planning & Design/Capital Projects
Director:
  Anne Van Ingen 212-741-7013
  e-mail: avaningen@nysca.org

Arts in Education
Director:
  Amy Duggins Pender............................212-741-5256
  e-mail: aduggins@nysca.org

Dance
Director:
  Beverly D'Anne...................................212-741-3232
  e-mail: bdanne@nysca.org

Electronic Media & Film
Director:
  Karen Helmerson 212-741-3003
  e-mail: khelmerson@nysca.org

Folk Arts
Director:
  Robert Baron 212-741-7755
  e-mail: rbaron@nysca.org

Individual Artists
Director:
  Don Palmer..212-741-6633
  e-mail: dpalmer@nysca.org

Literature
Director:
  Kathleen Masterson 212-741-2622
  e-mail: kmasterson@nysca.org

Museum
Associate:
  Fabiana Chiu-Rinaldi.............................212-741-7847
  e-mail: fchiu@nysca.org

Offices and agencies generally appear in alphabetical order, except when specific order is requested by listee.

TOURISM, ARTS & SPORTS / New York State

Music
Director:
Lisa Johnson.................................. 212-741-6562
e-mail: ljohnson@nysca.org

Presenting
Director:
Nancy Cohn.................................... 212-741-7014
e-mail: ncohn@nysca.org

Special Arts Services
Director:
Helen Cash Jackson........................... 212-741-7148
e-mail: hcash@nysca.org

State & Local Partnerships/Decentralization
Director:
Megan White.................................. 212-741-7143
e-mail: mwhite@nysca.org

Theatre
Director:
Robert Zukerman.............................. 212-741-7077
e-mail: rzukerman@nysca.org

Visual Artists
Director:
Elizabeth Merena............................. 212-741-5222
e-mail: emerena@nysca.org

Education Department
State Education Bldg
89 Washington Ave
Albany, NY 12234
518-474-5215 Fax: 518-486-5631
Web site: www.nysed.gov

Commissioner, University President:
Richard P Mills............................. 518-474-5844
e-mail: rmills@mail.nysed.gov
Assistant to the Commissioner:
Peggy Rivers................................ 518-474-5845
e-mail: privers@mail.nysed.gov
Counsel & Deputy Commissioner, Legal Affairs:
Kathy A Ahearn.............................. 518-474-6400
e-mail: kahearn@mail.nysed.gov
Chief of Staff & Deputy Commissioner, Innovation:
David Miller................................ 518-486-1713
e-mail: dmiller@mail.nysed.gov

Cultural Education Office
10A 33 Cultural Education Center, Madison Ave, Albany, NY 12230
Web site: www.oce.nysed.gov
Deputy Commissioner:
Jeffrey Cannell................. 518-474-5976/fax: 518-486-4850
e-mail: jcannell@mail.nysed.gov

State Museum Office
Assistant Commissioner & Director:
Clifford A Siegfried........................ 518-474-5812
e-mail: csiegfri@mail.nysed.gov
Exhibits/Public Programs Director:
Mark Schaming............................... 518-402-5952
State Geologist:
William Kelly............................... 518-474-5816
Director:
John Hart................................... 518-474-5816
Assistant Director:
Robert Daniels.............................. 518-474-5816
Assistant Director:
Penelope Drooker............................ 518-474-5816
Operations & Museum Administration Center:
Clifford Siegfried.......................... 518-474-5812
Chartering:
David Palmquist............................. 518-473-3131
Museum Education Director:
Jeanine Grinage............................. 518-486-2003
Registrar:
Vacant...................................... 518-474-4812

Empire State Development Corporation
633 Third Ave
New York, NY 10017
212-803-3100
Web site: www.empire.state.ny.us

30 South Pearl Street
Albany, NY 12245
518-292-5100

420 Main St, Ste 717
Buffalo, NY 14202
716-856-8111

Co-Chair Downstate:
Patrick J Foye.............................. 212-803-3700
Co-Chair Upstate:
Daniel C Gundersen............. 518-292-5100 or 716-856-8111
Director, Communications:
A J Carter.................................. 212-803-3740
Chief Financial Officer:
Frances A Walton............................ 212-803-3510

General Services, Office of
Corning Tower, 41st Fl
Empire State Plaza
Albany, NY 12242
518-474-3899 Fax: 518-474-1546
Web site: www.ogs.state.ny.us

633 Third Ave
New York, NY 10017
212-681-4580
Fax: 212-681-4558

Commissioner:
John C Egan................................. 518-474-5991
e-mail: john.egan@ogs.state.ny.us
First Deputy Commissioner:
Robert J Fleury............................. 518-473-6953
e-mail: robert.fleury@ogs.state.ny.us
Assistant Commissioner, Public Affairs:
Brad Maione.................... 518-474-5987/fax: 518-474-3187
e-mail: brad.maione@ogs.state.ny.us

Empire State's Convention & Cultural Events Office
Director:
Heather Flynn............................... 518-474-3195
Manager, Convention Center:
Dick Hallock................................ 518-474-0558
Director, Marketing:
Michael J Snyder............................ 518-474-0538

Offices and agencies generally appear in alphabetical order, except when specific order is requested by listee.

TOURISM, ARTS & SPORTS / New York State

Director, Curatorial & Tour Services:
  Dennis Anderson 518-473-7521
Curator, NYS Vietnam Memorial:
  Robert Allyn 518-473-5546/fax: 518-486-3948

Hudson River Valley Greenway
Capitol Building, Rm 254
Capitol Station
Albany, NY 12224
518-473-3835 Fax: 518-473-4518
e-mail: hrvg@hudsongreenway.state.ny.us
Web site: www.hudsongreenway.state.ny.us

Greenway Conservancy for the Hudson River Valley
Board Chair:
  Kevin J Plunkett 518-473-3835
Executive Director:
  Mary Mangione 518-473-3835

Hudson River Valley Greenway Communities Council
Board Chair:
  Barnabas McHenry 518-473-3835
Executive Director:
  Mary Mangione 518-473-3835

Parks, Recreation & Historic Preservation, NYS Office of
Empire State Plaza
Bldg 1
Albany, NY 12238
518-486-0456 Fax: 518-486-2924
Web site: www.nysparks.com

Commissioner:
  Carol Ash 518-474-0443
Executive Deputy Commissioner:
  Andy Beers 518-473-5385
Deputy Commissioner, Finance & Administration:
  Pete Finn 518-474-0440
Deputy Commissioner, Operations:
  Daniel Kane 518-474-0414
Deputy Commissioner, Open Space:
  Erik Kulleseid 518-474-0402
Counsel:
  Glen Bruening 518-474-0447
Director, Communication:
  Eileen Larrabee 518-486-1868
Acting Director, Natural Heritage Trust:
  Elaine Bartley 518-474-2997
Director, Natural Resources:
  Ralph Odell 845-889-4100
Director, Law Enforcement:
  James Warwick 518-474-4029

Concession Management
Director:
  Harold Hagemann 518-486-2932

Empire State Games
Director:
  Frederick W Smith 518-474-8889

Historic Preservation
Field Services
Peebles Island, Waterford, NY 12118
Director:
  Ruth Pierpont 518-237-8643

Historic Sites Bureau
Peebles Island, Waterford, NY 12118
Director:
  James P Gold 518-237-8643

Marine & Recreational Vehicles
Director:
  Brian Kempf 518-474-0445

Regional Offices-Downstate District
New York City Region
A C Powell State Ofc Bldg, 163 W 125th St, New York, NY 10027
212-866-2720

Taconic Region
PO Box 308, Staatsburg, NY 12580
845-889-4100

Regional Offices-Not Within Districts
Central Region . . . . fax: 315-492-3277
Clark Reservation, 6105 E Seneca Turnpike, Jamesville, NY 13078-9516
315-492-1756 Fax: 315-492-3277

Finger Lakes Region . . . . fax: 607-387-3390
2221 Taughannock Park Rd, Box 1055, Trumansburg, NY 14886
607-387-7041 Fax: 607-387-3390

Long Island Region . . . . fax: 631-667-2066
Belmont Lake St Park, Box 247, Babylon, NY 11702-0247
631-669-1000 Fax: 631-667-2066

Palisades Interstate Park Commission
Administration Headquarters, Bear Mountain, NY 10911
Executive Director:
  Jim Hall 845-786-2701

Saratoga/Capital District Region
19 Roosevelt Drive, Saratoga Springs, NY 12866
518-584-2000

Thousand Islands Region
Keewaydin State Park, Alexandria Bay, NY 13607
315-482-2593

Regional Offices-Western District
Allegany Region . . . . fax: 716-354-2255
Allegany State Park, Salamanca, NY 14779
716-354-6575 Fax: 716-354-2255

Genesee Region . . . . fax: 585-493-5272
One Letchworth State Park, Castile, NY 14427-1124
585-493-3600 Fax: 585-493-5272

Niagara Region & Western District Office . . . . fax: 716-278-1725
Niagara Frontier Park Region, Prospect P, PO Box 1132, Niagara Falls, NY 14303-0132
716-278-1770 Fax: 716-278-1725

Resource Management
Environmental Management
Director:
  Thomas Lyons 518-474-0409

Offices and agencies generally appear in alphabetical order, except when specific order is requested by listee.

TOURISM, ARTS & SPORTS / New York State

Planning & Development
Director:
Robert W Reinhardt 518-474-0415

Advisory Groups

State Board for Historic Preservation
Chairman:
Robert MacKay 631-692-4664

State Council of Parks, Recreation & Historic Preservation
Agency Contact:
Carol Ash 518-486-1868

Racing & Wagering Board
1 Broadway Center
Ste 600
Schenectady, NY 12305-2553
518-395-5400 Fax: 518-347-1250
e-mail: info@racing.state.ny.us
Web site: www.racing.state.ny.us

Chair:
Daniel D Hogan 518-395-5400
Member:
Michael J Hoblock, Jr. 518-395-5400
Member:
John B Simoni 518-395-5400
Executive Director:
John G Cansdale 518-395-5400
Counsel:
Robert A Feuerstein 212-417-2103
Secretary to the Board:
Gail Pronti 518-395-5400
Public Information Officer:
Dan Toomey 518-395-5400
Chief, Racing Operations:
Joseph Lynch 518-395-5400
Director, Audits & Investigations:
Tom Casaregola 518-395-5400
Director, Administration:
Kevin Dempsey 518-395-5400
Manager, Licensing:
Nicole Robilotto 518-395-5400
Director, Gaming Regulation:
Bruce Samboy 518-395-5400
Director, Racing Officials:
Brian Barry 518-395-5400

CORPORATIONS, AUTHORITIES AND COMMISSIONS

Adirondack Park Agency
1133 NYS Route 86
Ray Brook, NY 12977
518-891-4050 Fax: 518-891-3938
Web site: www.apa.state.ny.us

Chair:
Vacant 518-891-4050
Executive Director:
Vacant 518-891-4050
Counsel:
John S Banta 518-891-4050

Associate Counsel:
Barbara A Rottier 518-891-4050
Public Relations:
Keith McKeever 518-891-4050

Agriculture & NYS Horse Breeding Development Fund
90 State St, Ste 809
Albany, NY 12207
518-436-8713 Fax: 518-426-1490
e-mail: agfund@nysirestakes.com
Web site: www.nysirestakes.com

Executive Director:
Peter Goold 518-436-8713
Counsel:
Steven Losquadro 518-436-8713

Battery Park City Authority (Hugh L Carey)
One World Financial Center, 24th Fl
New York, NY 10281
212-417-2000 Fax: 212-417-2001
e-mail: info@bpcauthor.org
Web site: www.batteryparkcity.org

Chair:
James F Gill 212-417-2000
Vice Chairman:
Charles J Urstadt 212-417-2000
President & Chief Executive Officer:
James E Cavanaugh 212-417-4205/fax: 212-417-4153
Member:
David B Cornstein 212-417-2000
Member:
Andy K Shenoy 212-417-2000
Member:
Evelyn K Rollins 212-417-2000
Member:
Frank J Branchini 212-417-2000
Member:
Robert J Mueller 212-417-2000
Press Liaison:
Leticia M Remauro 212-417-2276/fax: 212-417-2279
e-mail: remaurol@bpcauthor.org

Capital District Regional Off-Track Betting Corporation
510 Smith St
Schenectady, NY 12305
518-370-5151 or 800-292-2387 Fax: 518-370-5460
Web site: www.capitalotb.com

Chair:
Marcel Webb 518-344-5225
President & Chief Executive Officer:
Michael J Connery 518-344-5225
Vice President/CFO:
John F Signor 518-344-5224
Executive Assistant to the President:
Tod Grenci 518-344-5408
Board Secretary:
Willis Vermilyea 518-482-5615

Offices and agencies generally appear in alphabetical order, except when specific order is requested by listee.

335

TOURISM, ARTS & SPORTS / New York State

Comptroller:
Nancy Priputen-Madrian 518-344-5233

Catskill Off-Track Betting Corporation
Park Place
Box 3000
Pomona, NY 10970
845-362-0400 Fax: 845-362-0419
e-mail: otb@interbets.com
Web site: www.interbets.com

President & Chief Executive Officer:
Donald J Groth 845-362-0400

Nassau Regional Off-Track Betting Corporation
220 Fulton Ave
Hempstead, NY 11550
516-572-2800 Fax: 516-572-2840
e-mail: webmaster@nassauotb.com
Web site: www.nassauotb.com

President:
Dino G Amoroso 516-572-2800
Executive Director of Operations:
Richard T Bennett, Jr. 516-572-2800 x155
Director, Public Affairs:
Joseph Galante 516-572-2800 x152
Comptroller:
Joah Sapphire 516-572-2800 x141

New York City Off-Track Betting Corporation
1501 Broadway
New York, NY 10036-5572
212-221-5200 Fax: 212-221-8025
Web site: www.nycotb.com

President:
Raymond V Casey 212-704-5101
Executive VP & COO:
John Van Lindt 212-704-5108
Chief of Staff:
Denise DePrima 212-704-5107
Executive Vice President & CFO:
Vacant 212-221-5200 x5214
Executive VP, General Counsel:
Ira H Block 212-221-5200 x5311
Executive Director, Legislative Affairs:
Daniel Wray 212-221-5200 x5230
Acting Inspector General:
Norma Papamichael-Walsh 212-704-5642
Senior VP, Marketing, Media & Communications:
Ron Ceisler 212-704-5152
Senior VP, New Business, Real Estate, Facilities & Community Affairs:
Robert E Unger 212-704-5642

New York Convention Center Operating Corporation
655 W 34th St
New York, NY 10001-1188
212-216-2000 Fax: 212-216-2588
e-mail: moreinfo@javitscenter.com
Web site: www.javitscenter.com

President & Chief Executive Officer:
Gerald T McQueen 212-216-2130
General Manager:
Anthony Bracco 212-216-2217
Chief Financial Officer:
Edward B MacDonald 212-216-2369
General Counsel:
Elizabeth Bradford 212-216-2125
Vice President, Sales & Marketing:
Doreen Guerin 212-216-2103

New York State Athletic Commission
123 William St
20th Fl
New York, NY 10038-3804
212-417-5700 Fax: 212-417-4987
e-mail: athletic@dos.state.ny.us
Web site: www.dos.state.ny.us/athletic.html

Chair:
Ron Scott Stevens 212-417-5700

New York State Commission on the Restoration of the Capitol
Corning Tower, 31st Fl
Empire State Plaza
Albany, NY 12242
518-473-0341 Fax: 518-486-5720

Executive Director:
Andrea J Lazarski 518-473-0341
e-mail: andrea.lazarski@ogs.state.ny.us

New York State Olympic Regional Development Authority
Olympic Center
2634 Main St
Lake Placid, NY 12946
518-523-1655 Fax: 518-523-9275
e-mail: info@orda.org
Web site: www.orda.org

Chair:
Pat Barrett 518-523-1655 x201
President & CEO:
Ted Blazer 518-523-1655 x201
e-mail: blazer@orda.org
Senior Vice President:
Jeffrey Byrne 518-523-1655 x203
e-mail: byrne@orda.org
Olympic Center Manager:
Denny Allen 518-523-1655 x222
e-mail: allen@orda.org
Marketing Director:
Fran Sayers 518-523-1655 x209
e-mail: sayers@orda.org

Offices and agencies generally appear in alphabetical order, except when specific order is requested by listee.

Director, Events:
    Jim Goff...518-523-1655 x212
    e-mail: jgoff@orda.org
Director, Finance:
    Kathy Bushy.....................................518-523-1655 x217
    e-mail: bushy@orda.org
Director, Communications:
    Sandy Caligiore..................................518-523-1655 x213
    e-mail: sandyc@orda.org

New York State Thoroughbred Breeding & Development Fund Corporation
Saratoga Spa State Park
19 Roosevelt Dr, Ste 250
Saratoga Springs, NY 12866
518-580-0100 Fax: 518-580-0500
e-mail: nybreds@nybreds.com
Web site: www.nybreds.com

Executive Director:
    Martin G Kinsella...............................518-580-0100

New York State Thruway Authority
200 Southern Blvd
Albany, NY 12209
518-436-2700 Fax: 518-436-2899
Web site: www.nysthruway.gov

Chair:
    John L Buono....................................518-436-3000
Executive Director:
    Michael R Fleischer.............................518-436-2900
General Counsel:
    Sharon O'Conor..................................518-436-2840
Deputy Counsel:
    Katherine McCartney.............................518-436-3188
Director, Government Relations:
    Pamela Davis....................518-436-2860/fax: 518-471-4340
Director, Public Information:
    Vacant..........................518-436-2983/fax: 518-426-3995

New York State Canal Corporation
    Web site: www.nyscanals.gov
Director:
    Carmella Mantello...............................518-436-3055

Northeastern Queens Nature & Historical Preserve Commission
Bldg 635, Bayside St, Box 5
Fort Totten, NY 11359-1012
718-229-8805 Fax: 718-229-6131
e-mail: sneq@aol.com
Web site: www.sneq.com

Chair:
    Bernard Haber...................................718-229-8805
Vice Chair:
    William Nieter..................................718-229-8805
Executive Director:
    Joan M Vogt.....................................718-229-8805

TOURISM, ARTS & SPORTS / New York State

Roosevelt Island Operating Corporation (RIOC)
591 Main St
Roosevelt Island, NY 10044
212-832-4540 Fax: 212-832-4582
e-mail: info@roosevelt-island.ny.us
Web site: www.rioc.com

President:
    Stephen H Shane.................................212-832-4540
Vice President, Operations:
    Vacant..212-832-4540
Chairperson, Board of Directors (ex officio):
    Deborah VanAmerogen.............................212-480-6705
General Counsel:
    Kenneth A Leitner..........................212-832-4540 x311
Chief Financial Officer:
    Carla Van de Walle..............................212-832-4540
Public Information Officer:
    Vacant..212-832-4540

Suffolk Regional Off-Track Betting Corporation
5 Davids Dr
Hauppauge, NY 11788-2004
631-853-1000 Fax: 631-853-1086
e-mail: customerservice@suffolkotb.com
Web site: www.suffolkotb.com

President/CEO:
    Jeffrey A Casale................................631-853-1000
Vice President:
    Marietta M Seaman...............................631-853-1000
Corporate Counsel/Executive Director, External Affairs:
    Neil H Tiger....................................631-853-1000
Comptroller:
    Celine M Gazes..................................631-853-1000

Western Regional Off-Track Betting Corp
8315 Park Road
Batavia, NY 14020-1272
585-343-1423 Fax: 585-344-6188
e-mail: info@westernotb.com
Web site: www.westernotb.com

Chair:
    Joseph Gallo....................................585-343-1423
President & Chief Executive Officer:
    Martin C Basinait...............................585-343-1423
Executive Vice President:
    Patrick T Murphy................................585-343-1423
Vice President, Racing & Gaming:
    Michael Kane....................................585-343-1423
General Counsel:
    Timothy A McCarthy..............................585-343-1423
Comptroller:
    Jacquelyne A Leach..............................585-343-1423
Director Marketing:
    Martin Biniasz..................................585-343-1423
Mutuels/Communications:
    James M Haas....................................585-343-1423

Offices and agencies generally appear in alphabetical order, except when specific order is requested by listee.

TOURISM, ARTS & SPORTS / New York State

CONVENTION & VISITORS BUREAUS

Convention Centers & Visitors Bureaus

Albany County Convention & Visitors Bureau
25 Quackenbush Sq, Albany, NY 12207
800-258-3582
Web site: www.albany.org
President & CEO:
  Michele Vennard................... 518-434-1217/fax: 518-434-0887
  e-mail: accvb@albany.org

Greater Binghamton New York Convention and Visitors Bureau
49 Court St 2nd Floor, PO Box 995, Binghamton, NY 13902
800-836-6740
Web site: www.binghamtoncvb.com
Senior Vice President Chamber Services:
  Louis Santoni................ 607-772-8860 x312/fax: 607-722-4513
  e-mail: lou@visitbinghamton.org

Buffalo Niagara Convention & Visitors Bureau
617 Main St, Ste 200, Buffalo, NY 14203-1496
800-283-3256
Web site: www.visitbuffaloniagara.com
President & CEO:
  Richard Geiger............... 716-852-0511 x275/fax: 716-852-0131
  e-mail: geiger@buffalocvb.org

Chautauqua County Visitors Bureau
Chautauqua County Visitors Bureau, PO Box 1441 Chautauqua, Route 394, Chautauqua, NY 14722
866-908-4569
Web site: www.tourchautauqua.com
Executive Director:
  R Andrew Nixon.................. 716-357-4569/fax: 716-357-2284
  e-mail: nixon@tourchautauqua.com

Greater Rochester Visitors Association
45 East Ave, Ste 400, Rochester, NY 14604-2294
800-677-7282
Web site: www.visitrochester.com
President & CEO:
  T Edward Hall..................... 585-279-8316/fax: 585-232-4822
  e-mail: edh@visitrochester.com

Ithaca/Tompkins County Convention & Visitors Bureau
904 E Shore Dr, Ithaca, NY 14850
800-28-ITHACA
Web site: www.visitithaca.com
Director:
  Fred Bonn........................ 607-272-1313/fax: 607-272-7617
  e-mail: fred@visitithaca.com

Lake Placid/Essex County Convention & Visitors Bureau
2610 Main St, Ste 2, Lake Placid, NY 12946
800-447-5224
Web site: www.lakeplacid.com
President & CEO:
  James McKenna.................... 518-523-2445/fax: 518-523-2605

Long Island Convention & Visitors Bureau & Sports Commission
330 Motor Pkwy, Ste 203, Hauppauge, NY 11788
877-FUN-ON-LI
Web site: www.funonli.com
President:
  R Moke McGowen 631-951-3900/fax: 631-951-3439
  e-mail: mmcgowen@discoverlongisland.com

NYC & Company/Convention & Visitors Bureau
810 Seventh Ave, New York, NY 10019
212-484-1200
Web site: www.nycvisit.com
CEO:
  George Fertitta..................... 212-484-1265/fax: 212-245-5943

Oneida County Convention & Visitors Bureau
PO Box 551, Utica, NY 13503-0551
800-426-3132
Web site: www.oneidacountycvb.com
President:
  Paul E Ziegler 315-724-7221/fax: 315-724-7335
  e-mail: paulzieg@dreamscape.com

Ontario County/Finger Lakes Visitor's Connection
25 Gorham St, Canandaigua, NY 14424
877-FUN-IN-NY
e-mail: info@visitfingerlakes.com
Web site: www.visitfingerlakes.com
President:
  Valerie Knoblauch.................. 585-394-3915/fax: 585-394-4067

Saratoga Convention & Tourism Bureau
60 Railroad Pl, Ste 100, Saratoga Springs, NY 12866-3048
Web site: www.discoversaratoga.org
President:
  Gavin Landry...................... 518-584-1531/fax: 518-584-2969
  e-mail: mail@discoversaratoga.org

Steuben County Conference & Visitors Bureau
1 West Market St, Ste 301, Corning, NY 14830
866-946-3386
Web site: www.corningfingerlakes.com
President:
  Peggy Coleman 607-936-6544/fax: 607-936-6575
  e-mail: pcoleman@corningfingerlakes.com

Sullivan County Visitors Association
100 North Street, PO Box 5012, Monticello, NY 12701
800-882-2287
Web site: www.scva.net
President & CEO:
  Roberta Byron Lockwood 845-794-3000 x5010/fax: 845-794-1058
  e-mail: sctoursim@scva.net

Syracuse Convention & Vistors Bureau
572 S Salina St, Syracuse, NY 13202
800-234-4797
Web site: www.visitsyracuse.org
President:
  David C. Holder.................... 315-470-1911/fax: 315-471-8545
  e-mail: Dholder@visitsyracuse.org

Thousand Islands Int'l Tourism Council
Box 400, 43373 Collins Landing, Alexandria Bay, NY 13607
800-847-5263
Web site: www.visit1000islands.com
Director:
  Gary DeYoung..................... 315-482-2520/fax: 315-482-5906
  e-mail: gary@visit1000islands.com

Westchester County Office of Tourism
222 Mamaroneck Ave, Ste 100, White Plains, NY 10605
800-833-9282
Web site: www.westchestertourism.com
Director:
  Margo Jones...................... 914-995-8500/fax: 914-995-8505
  e-mail: tourism@westchestergov.com

Offices and agencies generally appear in alphabetical order, except when specific order is requested by listee.

TOURISM, ARTS & SPORTS / U.S. Government

NEW YORK STATE LEGISLATURE

See Legislative Branch in Section 1 for additional Standing Committee and Subcommittee information.

Assembly Standing Committees

Racing & Wagering
Chair:
James Gary Pretlow (D) 518-455-5291
Ranking Minority Member:
Robert Barra (R) 518-455-4656

Tourism, Arts & Sports Development
Chair:
Joseph D Morelle (D) 518-455-5373
Ranking Minority Member:
Rob Walker (R) 518-455-4684

Senate Special Committees

Arts & Cultural Affairs, Special Committee on the
Chair:
Serphin R Maltese (R) 518-455-3281
Chief of Staff:
Victoria Vattimo 518-455-3281

Senate Standing Committees

Racing, Gaming & Wagering
Chair:
William J Larkin, Jr (R) 518-455-2770
Ranking Minority Member:
John D Sabini (D) 518-455-2529

Tourism, Recreation & Sports Development
Chair:
Mary Lou Rath (R) 518-455-3161
Ranking Minority Member:
Jose E Serrano (D) 518-455-2795

U.S. Government

EXECUTIVE DEPARTMENTS AND RELATED AGENCIES

National Archives & Records Administration

Franklin D Roosevelt Presidential Library & Museum
4079 Albany Post Rd, Hyde Park, NY 12538
845-486-7770
Web site: www.fdrlibrary.marist.edu
Director:
Cynthia M Koch 845-486-7770/fax: 845-486-1147
e-mail: roosevelt.library@nara.gov

Smithsonian Institution

Cooper-Hewitt National Design Museum
2 East 91st St, New York, NY 10128
Web site: www.cooperhewitt.org
Director:
Paul W Thompson 212-849-8370/fax: 212-849-8367

National Museum of the American Indian-George Gustav Heye Center
US Custom House, One Bowling Green, New York, NY 10004
Web site: www.nmai.si.edu
GGHC Director:
John Haworth 212-514-3700/fax: 212-514-3800

US Department of the Interior
202-208-3100
e-mail: webteam@ios.doi.gov
Web site: www.doi.gov

Fish & Wildlife Service-Northeast Region . . fax: 413-253-8308
300 Westgate Center Dr, Hadley, MA 01035-9589
413-253-8200 Fax: 413-253-8308
e-mail: northeast@fws.gov
Regional Director:
Marvin Moriarty 413-253-8200

National Park Service-Northeast Region
200 Chestnut St, US Custom House, Philadelphia, PA 19106
Web site: www.nps.gov
Acting Northeast Regional Director:
Mary A Bomar 215-597-7013/fax: 215-597-0815
Asst Regional Director, Communications & Tourism:
Edie Shean-Hammond 215-597-7989

Fire Island National Seashore . . . . fax: 631-289-4898
120 Laurel St, Patchogue, NY 11772
631-289-4810 Fax: 631-289-4898
Web site: www.nps.gov/fiis/
Superintendent:
Michael T Reynolds 631-289-4810/fax: 631-289-4898

Fort Stanwix National Monument . . . . fax: 315-334-5051
112 E Park St, Rome, NY 13440
315-338-7730 Fax: 315-334-5051
Web site: www.nps.gov/fost/
Superintendent:
James Perry 315-338-7730/fax: 315-334-5051

Gateway National Recreation Area
210 New York Ave, Staten Island, NY 10305
Web site: www.nps.gov/gate
General Superintendent:
Barry Sullivan 718-354-4665/fax: 718-354-4764
Jamaica Bay Unit
Superintendent:
Lisa Eckert 718-338-3338/fax: 718-338-3876
Sandy Hook Unit
Superintendent:
Richard Wells 732-872-5913/fax: 732-872-5915
Staten Island Unit
Superintendent:
Dave Avrin 718-354-4640/fax: 718-354-4639

Manhattan Sites
26 Wall St, New York, NY 10005

Offices and agencies generally appear in alphabetical order, except when specific order is requested by listee.

TOURISM, ARTS & SPORTS / Private Sector

212-825-6990
Web site: www.nps.gov/masi
Superintendent:
   Jim Pepper 212-825-6888/fax: 212-825-6874

Martin Van Buren National Historic Site . . . . fax: 518-758-6986
1013 Old Post Rd, Kinderhook, NY 12106
518-758-9689 Fax: 518-758-6986
Web site: www.nps.gov/mava
Superintendent:
   Daniel J Dattilio 518-758-9689/fax: 518-758-6986

Roosevelt-Vanderbilt National Historic Sites
4097 Albany Post Rd, Hyde Park, NY 12538
800-337-VISIT
Web site: www.nps.gov/hofr
Superintendent:
   Sarah Olson 845-229-9115/fax: 845-229-0739

Sagamore Hill National Historic Site . . . . fax: 516-922-4792
20 Sagamore Hill Road, Oyster Bay, NY 11771-1807
516-922-4788 Fax: 516-922-4792
Web site: www.nps.gov/sahi
Superintendent:
   Greg Marshall 516-922-4788/fax: 516-922-4792

Saratoga National Historical Park . . . . fax: 518-664-3349
648 Rt 32, Stillwater, NY 12170
518-664-9821 X224 Fax: 518-664-3349
Web site: www.nps.gov/sara
Superintendent:
   Frank Dean . . . . 518-664-9821 ext 224/fax: 518-664-9830

Statue of Liberty National Monument & Ellis Island
Liberty Island, New York, NY 10004
TTY: 212-363-3211 or 212-363-3200
Web site: www.nps.gov/stli/
Superintendent:
   Cynthia Garrett 212-363-3206/fax: 212-363-8347

Theodore Roosevelt Inaugural National Historic Site fax: 716-884-0330
641 Delaware Ave, Buffalo, NY 14202
716-884-0095 Fax: 716-884-0330
Web site: www.nps.gov/thri/
Superintendent:
   Molly Quackenbush 716-884-0095/fax: 716-884-0330

Women's Rights National Historical Park . . . . fax: 315-568-2141
136 Fall St, Seneca Falls, NY 13148
315-568-2991 Fax: 315-568-2141
Web site: www.nps.gov/wori
Superintendent:
   Tina Orcutt 315-568-2991/fax: 315-568-2141

U.S. CONGRESS

See U.S. Congress Chapter for additional Standing Committee and Subcommittee information.

House of Representatives Standing Committees

Resources
Chair:
   Richard W Pombo (R-CA) 202-225-2761
Ranking Minority Member:
   Nick J Rahall, II (D-WV) 202-225-3452

  Subcommittee
   Forests & Forest Health
    Chair:
      Greg Walden (R-OR) 202-225-6730
    Ranking Minority Member:
      Tom Udall (D-NM) 202-225-6190
   National Parks, Recreation & Public Lands
    Chair:
      Steve Pearce (R-NM) 202-225-2365
    Ranking Min Member:
      Donna M Christensen (D-VI) 202-225-1790

Senate Standing Committees

Energy & Natural Resources
Chair:
   Pete V Domenici (R-NM) 202-224-6621
Ranking Minority Member:
   Jeff Bingaman (D-NM) 202-224-5521
New York Delegate:
   Charles E Schumer (D) 202-224-6542

  Subcommittees
   National Parks
    Chair:
      Craig Thomas (R-WY) 202-224-6441
    Ranking Minority Member:
      Daniel K Akaka (D-HI) 202-224-6361
   Public Lands & Forests
    Chair:
      Larry E Craig (R-ID) 202-224-2752
    Ranking Minority Member:
      Ron Wyden (D-OR) 202-224-5244

Private Sector

AAA Northway
1626 Union St, Schenectady, NY 12309
518-374-4575 Fax: 518-374-3140
Web site: www.aaanorthway.com
Eric Stigberg, Marketing, Public & Government Affairs Manager
Capital region membership, travel & touring sales & services

AAA Western and Central NY
100 International Dr, Buffalo, NY 14221
716-626-3225 Fax: 716-631-5925
e-mail: wsmith@nyaaa.com
Web site: www.aaa.com
Wallace Smith, Vice President

Offices and agencies generally appear in alphabetical order, except when specific order is requested by listee.

TOURISM, ARTS & SPORTS / Private Sector

Adirondack Lakes Center for the Arts
Rte 28, PO Box 205, Blue Mountain Lake, NY 12812-0205
518-352-7715 Fax: 518-352-7333
e-mail: alca@frontiernet.net
Web site: www.adk-arts.org
Anisia Kelly, Executive Director
Multi/Arts Center

Adirondack Mountain Club Inc
301 Hamilton Street, Albany, NY 12210-1738
518-449-3870 Fax: 518-449-3875
e-mail: adk@nycapp.rr.com; marisatedesco@nycapp.rr.com
Web site: www.adk.org
Neil F Woodworth, Executive Director;, Marisa Tedesco, Conservation and Legislative Director; Ian Brown, Land Use Planner
Hiking, nonmotorized recreation, conservation & education

Adirondack/Pine Hill/NY Trailways
499 Hurley Ave, Hurley, NY 12443-5119
845-339-4230 Fax: 845-853-7035
e-mail: info@trailwaysny.com
Web site: www.trailwaysny.com
Eugene J Berardi, Jr, President
Tour & charter service

Alliance for the Arts
330 W 42nd St, Ste 1701, New York, NY 10036
212-947-6340 Fax: 212-947-6416
e-mail: info@allianceforarts.org
Web site: www.allianceforarts.org
Randall Bourscheidt, President
Advocacy, promotion, research, information, referrals & publications

Alliance of NYS Arts Organizations
PO Box 96, Mattituck, NY 11952-0096
631-298-1234 Fax: 631-298-1101
e-mail: jkweiner@thealliancenys.org
Web site: www.thealliancenys.org
Judith Kaufman Weiner, Executive Director
Technical assistance, professional development & advocacy services

Alliance of Resident Theatres/New York (ART/New York)
575 Eighth Ave, Ste 1720, New York, NY 10018
212-244-6667 Fax: 212-714-1918
Web site: www.offbroadwayonline.com
Virginia P Louloudes, Executive Director
Services & advocacy for New York City's not-for-profit theatre community

American Federation of Musicians, Local 802
322 West 48th St, 5th Fl, New York, NY 10036
212-245-4802 Fax: 212-245-6255
e-mail: jsmith@local802afm.org
Web site: www.local802afm.org
Julia Smith, Director, Public Relations

American Museum of Natural History
Central Park West at 79th St, New York, NY 10024-5192
212-769-5100 Fax: 212-769-5018
e-mail: info@amnh.org
Web site: www.amnh.org
Ellen V Futter, President
Education, exhibition & scientific research

Art & Science Collaborations Inc
130 East End Ave 1A, New York, NY 10028
505-988-2994
e-mail: asci@asci.org
Web site: www.asci.org
Cynthia Pannucci, Director
Raising public awareness of art & artists using science & technology to explore new forms of creative expression

ArtsConnection Inc (The)
520 8th Ave, #321, New York, NY 10018
212-302-7433 Fax: 212-302-1132
e-mail: artsconnection@artsconnection.org
Web site: www.artsconnection.org
Steven Tennen, Executive Director
Arts-in-education programming & training for children, teachers & artists

Association of Independent Video & Filmmakers (AIVF), (The)
304 Hudson St, 6th Fl, New York, NY 10013
212-807-1400 Fax: 212-463-8519
e-mail: info@aivf.org
Web site: www.aivf.org
Beni Matias, Executive Director
Membership service organization for independent producers & filmmakers

Automobile Club of New York
1415 Kellum Place, Garden City, NY 11530
516-873-2252 Fax: 516-873-2375
Web site: www.aaany.com
Dennis J Crossley, President

Brooklyn Botanic Garden
1000 Washington Ave, Brooklyn, NY 11225-1009
718-623-7200 Fax: 718-857-2430
Web site: www.bbg.org
Scot Medbury, President & CEO
Comprehensive study of plant biodiversity in metropolitan New York; home gardener's resource center

Brooklyn Museum of Art
200 Eastern Pkwy, Brooklyn, NY 11238
718-638-5000 Fax: 718-501-6136
Web site: www.brooklynmuseum.org
Schawannah Wright, Manager, Community Involvement

Buffalo Bills
One Bills Drive, Orchard Park, NY 14127
716-648-1800 x8701 Fax: 716-648-3202
Web site: www.buffalobills.com
Scott Berchtold, Vice President-Communications

Offices and agencies generally appear in alphabetical order, except when specific order is requested by listee.

TOURISM, ARTS & SPORTS / Private Sector

Buffalo Sabres
One Seymour H Knox III Plz, Buffalo, NY 14203
716-855-4100 x526 Fax: 716-855-4110
e-mail: michael.gilbert@sabres.com
Web site: www.sabres.com
Michael Gilbert, Director Public Relations

Buffalo Trotting Association Inc
5600 McKinley Parkway, PO Box 38, Hamburg, NY 14075
716-649-1280 Fax: 716-649-0033
e-mail: mangoj@buffaloraceway.com
Web site: www.buffaloraceway.com
James Mango, General Manager
Harness horse racing

CUNY New York City College of Technology, Hospitality Mgmt
300 Jay St, Room 220, Brooklyn, NY 11201-2983
718-260-5630 Fax: 718-260-5997
Web site: www.nyct.cuny.edu
Jerry Van Loon, Professor & Chair
Hospitality & food service management; tourism

CUNY New York City College of Technology, Hospitality Mgmt
300 Jay St, Room 621, Brooklyn, NY 11201-2983
718-260-5637 Fax: 718-260-5995
e-mail: jjordan@citytech.cuny.edu
Web site: www.cuny.edu
Julia Jordan, NYC Advisory Board Member & Professor
Spoons Across America; American Institute of Wine & Food (The); James Beard Foundation (The)

Campground Owners of New York
1 Grove Street, Suite 200, Pittsford, NY 14534
585-586-4360 Fax: 585-586-4360
e-mail: cony@frontiernet.net
Web site: www.nycampgrounds.com
Donald G Bennett Jr, Executive Administrator

Cendant Car Rental Group Inc
9 West 57th Street, New York, NY 10019
973-428-9700
e-mail: elliot.bloom@cendant.com
Web site: www.cendant.com
Elliot Bloom, Senior Vice President, Corporate Communications
Travel & rental car services

Coalition of Living Museums
1000 Washington Ave, Brooklyn, NY 11225
718-623-7225 or 718-623-7373 Fax: 718-857-2430
e-mail: loiscarswell@bbg.org
Web site: www.livingmuseums.org
Lois Carswell, Chair, Steering Committee
Advocacy organization for living museums (zoos, botanical gardens, aquaria, arboreta & nature centers) in NYS

Cold Spring Harbor Fish Hatchery & Aquarium
1660 Route 25A, Cold Spring Harbor, NY 11724
516-692-6768 Fax: 516-692-6769
e-mail: cshfha@optonline.net
Web site: www.cshfha.org
Norman Soule, Director
Largest living collection of NYS freshwater fish, amphibians & turtles

Columbia University, School of the Arts
305 Dodge Hall, 2960 Broadway, MC1808, New York, NY 10027
212-854-2134 Fax: 212-854-7733
e-mail: bwf3@columbia.edu
Web site: www.columbia.edu/cu/arts
Bruce W Ferguson, Dean

Culinary Institute of America
1946 Campus Dr, Hyde Park, NY 12538-1499
845-451-1203 Fax: 845-451-1052
e-mail: admissions@culinary.edu
Web site: www.ciachef.edu
Vance T Peterson, Vice President for Advancement
Four-year regionally accredited college offering Associate and Occupational Studies and Bachelor of Professional Studies in culinary and baking/pastry arts management. Campuses in Hyde Park, New York, and St Helena, California.

Darien Lake Theme Park Resort
9993 Allegheny Rd, PO Box 91, Darien Center, NY 14040
585-599-4641 Fax: 585-599-4053
Bradley Paul, Vice President & General Manager

Egg (The), Center for the Performing Arts
Empire State Plaza, PO Box 2065, Albany, NY 12220
518-473-1061 Fax: 518-473-1848
e-mail: info@theegg.org
Web site: www.theegg.org
Peter Lesser, Executive Director
Dance, theatre, family entertainment, music, special events

NYS Bar Assn, Entertainment, Arts & Sports Law Section
Elissa D Hecker, Esq
90 Quail Close, Irvington, NY 10533
914-478-0457
e-mail: eheckeresq@yahoo.com
Elissa D Hecker, Chair

Empire State Restaurant & Tavern Association Inc
40 Sheridan Ave, Albany, NY 12210
518-436-8121 Fax: 518-436-7287
e-mail: esrta@verizon.net
Web site: www.esrta.org
Scott Wexler, Executive Director

Entertainment Software Association
317 Madison Ave, 22nd Fl, New York, NY 10017
917-522-3250 Fax: 917-522-3258
Web site: www.theesa.com
Gail Markels, Senior Vice President & General Counsel

Offices and agencies generally appear in alphabetical order, except when specific order is requested by listee.

TOURISM, ARTS & SPORTS / Private Sector

Exhibition Alliance Inc (The)
Route 12B South, PO Box 345, Hamilton, NY 13346
315-824-2510 Fax: 315-824-1683
e-mail: donnao@exhibitionalliance.org
Web site: www.exhibitionalliance.org
Donna Ostraszewski Anderson, Executive Director
Exhibit-related services for museums in NYS & the surrounding region

Farmer's Museum (The)
PO Box 30, Cooperstown, NY 13326
607-547-1400 Fax: 607-547-1404
e-mail: m.bruce@nysha.org
Web site: www.farmersmuseum.org
D Stephen Elliott, President
Historical & cultural exhibition, preservation and education

Film/Video Arts
270 W 96th St, New York, NY 10025
212-941-8787
e-mail: mariopaoli@fva.com
Web site: www.fva.com
Chloe Kurabi, Programs Director, Fiscal Sponsorship and Filmmaker
Low cost training, postproduction suites, fiscal sponsorship, mentorship, internships

Finger Lakes Racing Association
PO Box 25250, Farmington, NY 14425
585-924-3232 Fax: 585-924-3239
Web site: www.fingerlakesracetrack.com
Christian Riegle, General Manager
Horse racing & video lottery gaming

Finger Lakes Tourism Alliance
309 Lake St, Penn Yan, NY 14527
315-536-7488 Fax: 315-536-1237
e-mail: info@fingerlakes.org
Web site: www.fingerlakes.org
Michael Rusinko, President
Regional tourism promotion

Gertrude Stein Repertory Theatre (The)
15 West 26th St, 2nd Fl, New York, NY 10010
212-725-0436 Fax: 212-725-7267
e-mail: info@gerstein.org
Web site: www.gertstein.org
Liz Dreyer, General Manager
Avant garde theater emphasizing international collaboration in experimental works incorporating new technologies

Great Escape Theme Park LLC (The)
PO Box 511, Lake George, NY 12845
518-792-3500 Fax: 518-792-3404
Web site: www.thegreatescape.com
John Collins, General Manager

Harvestworks
596 Broadway, Suite 602, New York, NY 10012
212-431-1130 Fax: 212-431-8473
e-mail: info@harvestworks.org
Web site: www.harvestworks.org
Carol Parkinson, Director
Nonprofit arts organization providing computer education & production studios for the digital media arts

Historic Hudson Valley
150 White Plains Rd, Tarrytown, NY 10591
914-631-8200 Fax: 914-631-0089
e-mail: mail@hudsonvalley.org
Web site: www.hudsonvalley.org
Waddell Stillman, President
Tourism promotion

Hotel Association of New York City Inc
320 Park Ave, 22nd Fl, New York, NY 10022-6838
212-754-6700 Fax: 212-688-2838
e-mail: jspinnato@hanyc.org
Web site: www.hanyc.org
Joseph E Spinnato, President

Hudson River Cruises
5 Rondout Landing, Kingston, NY 12401-3605
845-340-4700 or 800-843-7472 Fax: 845-340-4702
e-mail: hudsonrivercruises@hvc.rr.com
Web site: www.hudsonrivercruises.com
Sandra Henne, Owner
Sightseeing, music & dinner cruises and Private Charters

Hunter Mountain Ski Bowl
PO Box 295, Hunter, NY 12442
888-486-8376 or 518-263-4223 Fax: 518-263-3704
e-mail: info@huntermtn.com
Web site: www.huntermtn.com
Orville A Slutzky, General Manager
Skiing, snowshoeing, snowboarding & snowtubing; coaching & race camps; summer & fall festivals; Kaatskill Mountain Club/Hotel, Loftside Village Condominiums, and other Four Season Mountain Resort activities.

Jewish Museum (The)
1109 Fifth Ave, New York, NY 10128-0117
212-423-3271 Fax: 212-423-3233
e-mail: ascher@thejm.org
Web site: www.thejewishmuseum.org
Anne Scher, Director, Communications
Museum of art and Jewish culture

Lincoln Center for the Performing Arts Inc
70 Lincoln Center Plaza, New York, NY 10023-6583
212-875-5370 or 212-875-5319 Fax: 212-875-5534
e-mail: mwiertz@lincolncenter.org
Web site: www.lincolncenter.org
Michael Wiertz, Director, Visitor Services
Guided tours of Lincoln Center; Meet-the-Artist programs

Offices and agencies generally appear in alphabetical order, except when specific order is requested by listee.

TOURISM, ARTS & SPORTS / Private Sector

Lower Manhattan Cultural Council
125 Maiden Lane, 2nd Floor, New York, NY 10038
212-219-9401 Fax: 212-219-2058
e-mail: info@lmcc.net
Web site: www.lmcc.net
Mark Vevle, Director, Marketing & Communications
Supporting Manhattan arts organizations through funding assistance, support for creation & presentation of work & audience development

Madison Square Garden Corp
Two Penn Plaza, Madison Square Garden, New York, NY 10121
212-465-6000 Fax: 212-465-4423
Web site: www.thegarden.com
Barry Watkins, Senior Vice President, Communications
NY Knicks, NY Rangers, concerts, special events

Major League Baseball
245 Park Ave, New York, NY 10167
212-931-7800 Fax: 212-949-5654
Web site: www.mlb.com
Rich Levin, Senior Vice President, Public Relations

Metropolitan Museum of Art (The)
1000 Fifth Ave, New York, NY 10028
212-535-7710 Fax: 212-650-2102
Web site: www.metmuseum.org
Philippe de Montebello, Director;, Harold Holzer, Senior Vice President for External Affairs

Monticello Raceway
204 Rte 17-B, PO Box 5013, Monticello, NY 12701
845-794-4100 Fax: 845-791-1402
Web site: www.monticelloraceway.com
Clifford Ehrlich, President
Horse racing and video gaming machines.

Museum Association of New York
265 River St, Troy, NY 12180
518-273-3400 Fax: 518-273-3416
e-mail: info@manyonline.org
Web site: www.manyonline.org
Anne Ackerson, Director
Provides information, advocacy & training to strengthen the diverse museum community & enable museums to fulfill their missions

NY Film Academy
100 East 17th St, New York, NY 10003-2160
212-674-4300 Fax: 212-477-1414
e-mail: film@nyfa.com
Web site: www.nyfa.com
Jerry Sherlock, President & Founder
Film making

NY State Historical Association/Fenimore Art Museum
PO Box 800, Cooperstown, NY 13326-0800
607-547-1400 Fax: 607-547-1404
e-mail: m.bruce@nysha.org
Web site: www.nysha.org; www.farmersmuseum.org
D Stephen Elliott, President
Historical & cultural exhibition, preservation & education

NYC Arts Coalition
351 West 54th St, New York, NY 10019
212-246-3788 Fax: 212-246-3366
e-mail: info@nycityartscoalition.org
Web site: www.nycityartscoalition.org
Norma P Munn, Chair
Develops public policy analysis, provides reports on arts policy & funding issues & acts as an advocacy vehicle for a united voice for the nonprofit arts sector

NYS Alliance for Arts Education
PO Box 2217, Albany, NY 12220-0217
800-ARTS-N-ED or 518-473-0823 Fax: 518-486-7329
e-mail: info@nysaae.org
Web site: www.nysaae.org
Amy Williams, Executive Director
Advocacy, professional development, technical assistance & information for educators, organizations, artists, parents, policymakers

NYS Outdoor Guides Association
1936 Saranac Ave, Suite 2 PO Box 150, Lake Placid, NY 12946-1402
866-469-7642 or 518-359-8194 Fax: 518-359-8194
e-mail: info@nysoga.org
Web site: www.nysoga.org
Sonny Young, President
Provides information about member guide services & the profession of guiding through distribution of printed/electronic material and educational programs. Provides NYS licensed guides with support services, representation and sense of community

NYS Passenger Vessel Association
PO Box 98, Brightwaters, NY 11718
631-321-9005
e-mail: info@cruisenewyork.com
Web site: www.cruisenewyork.com
Mike Eagan, Treasurer
Promote cruises on NYS's waterways

NYS Theatre Institute
37 First St, Troy, NY 12180
518-274-3200 Fax: 518-274-3815
e-mail: nysti@capital.net
Web site: www.nysti.org
Patricia Di Benedetto Snyder, Producing Artistic Director
Professional theater productions for family and school audiences; training & education, internships, community/school outreach & cultural exchange programs

NYS Turfgrass Association
PO Box 612, Latham, NY 12110
518-783-1229 Fax: 518-783-1258
e-mail: nysta@nysta.org
Web site: www.nysta.org
Beth Seme, Executive Director
Grow & manage turf for golf courses, ball fields & landscape

Offices and agencies generally appear in alphabetical order, except when specific order is requested by listee.

TOURISM, ARTS & SPORTS / Private Sector

National Basketball Association
645 5th Ave, New York, NY 10022
212-407-8000 Fax: 212-826-0579
Web site: www.nba.com
Brian McIntyre, Senior Vice President, Communications

National Football League
280 Park Ave, New York, NY 10017
212-450-2000 Fax: 212-681-7599
e-mail: aiellog@nfl.com
Web site: www.nfl.com
Greg Aiello, Vice President, Public Relations

National Hockey League
1251 Ave of the Americas, 47th Fl, New York, NY 10020
212-789-2000 Fax: 212-789-2020
e-mail: fbrown@nhl.com
Web site: www.nhl.com
Frank Brown, Vice President, Media Relations

National Women's Hall of Fame
PO Box 335, 76 Fall Street, Seneca Falls, NY 13148
315-568-8060 Fax: 315-568-2976
Web site: www.greatwomen.org
Billie Luisi-Potts, Executive Director
The hall celebrates outstanding American women & their achievements

New School University, Department of Sociology
65 Fifth Ave, New York, NY 10003
212-229-5782 or 212-229-5737 Fax: 212-229-5595
e-mail: zolbergv@newschool.edu
Web site: www.newschool/edu
Vera Zolberg, Professor, Sociology & Liberal Studies
Sociology of the arts; censorship; collective memory; outsider art

New York Academy of Art Inc
111 Franklin St, New York, NY 10013-2911
212-966-0300 Fax: 212-966-3217
e-mail: info@nyaa.edu
Web site: www.nyaa.edu
Wayne A Linker, Executive Director

New York Aquarium
Surf Ave at West 8th St, Brooklyn, NY 11224
718-265-3428 Fax: 718-265-3400
e-mail: fhackett@wcs.org
Web site: www.nyaquarium.com
Fran Hackett, Communications
Conservation, education & research

New York Artists Equity Association Inc
498 Broome St, New York, NY 10013
212-941-0130 Fax: 212-941-0138
e-mail: reginas@tiac.net
Web site: www.anny.org
Regina Stewart, Executive Director
Web based advocacy for visual arts & cultural organizations; Call first to send fax

New York City Opera
20 Lincoln Center, New York, NY 10023
212-870-5600 Fax: 212-724-1120
Web site: www.nycopera.com
Susan Woelzl, Director, Press & Public Relations

New York Foundation for the Arts
155 Ave of the Americas, 14th Floor, New York, NY 10013-1507
212-366-6900 Fax: 212-366-1778
e-mail: nyfainfo@nyfa.org
Web site: www.nyfa.org
Theodore S Berger, Executive Director
Advocacy, leadership, financial & resource support & collaborative relationships with those committed to the arts

New York Giants
Giants Stadium, East Rutherford, NJ 07073
201-935-8111 Fax: 201-935-8493
Web site: www.giants.com
Pat Hanlon, Vice President, Communications

New York Hall of Science
4701 111th Street, Queens, NY 11368
718-699-0005 x323 Fax: 718-699-1341
e-mail: wbrez@nyscience.org
Web site: www.nyscience.org
Wendy J Brez, Manager, Public Relations
Hands-on science exhibits & education program

New York Islanders
1535 Old Country Rd, Plainview, NY 11803
516-501-6700 Fax: 516-501-6762
e-mail: customerservice@newyorkislanders.com
Web site: www.newyorkislanders.com
Chris Botta, Vice President, Communications

New York Jets
1000 Fulton Ave, Hempstead, NY 11550
516-560-8100 Fax: 516-560-8197
e-mail: rcolangelo@jets.nfl.com
Web site: www.newyorkjets.com
Bruce Speight, Public Relations

New York Marine Trades Association
194 Park Ave, Suite B, Amityville, NY 11701
631-691-7050 Fax: 631-691-2724
e-mail: csqueri@aol.com
Web site: www.nymta.com
Christopher Squeri, Executive Director
Promote & protect the marine & boating industry; own & operate two boat shows; monitor local, state & federal marine legislation

New York Mets
Shea Stadium, 123-01 Roosevelt Ave, Flushing, NY 11368
718-507-6387 Fax: 718-639-3619
Web site: www.mets.com
Fred Wilpon, Chairman & Chief Executive Officer

Offices and agencies generally appear in alphabetical order, except when specific order is requested by listee.

TOURISM, ARTS & SPORTS / Private Sector

New York Racing Association
PO Box 90, Jamaica, NY 11417
718-641-4700 Fax: 718-843-7673
e-mail: nyra@nyraing.com
Web site: www.nyra.com
Francis LaBelle, Jr, Director, Communications
Horse racing at Aqueduct, Belmont Park, and Saratoga.

New York State Hospitality & Tourism Association
80 Wolf Rd, Albany, NY 12205
800-642-5313 x13 or 518-465-2300 Fax: 518-465-4025
e-mail: dan@nyshta.org
Web site: www.nyshta.org
Daniel C Murphy, President
Hotels, motels, amusement parks & attractions

New York State Restaurant Association
409 New Karner Rd, Albany, NY 12205
518-452-4222 Fax: 518-452-4497
e-mail: ricks@nysra.org
Web site: www.nysra.org
Rick J Sampson, President & Chief Executive Officer

New York State School Music Association (NYSSMA)
718 The Plain Rd, Westbury, NY 11590-5931
888-697-7621 Fax: 516-997-1700
e-mail: executive@nyssma.org
Web site: www.nyssma.org
Steven Schopp, Executive Administrator
Advocacy for a quality school music education for every student

New York State Snowmobile Association
PO Box 612, Long Lake, NY 12847
518-624-3849 Fax: 518-624-2441
e-mail: jimjennings@nyssnowassoc.org
Web site: www.nyssnowassoc.org
Jim Jennings, Executive Director
Working to preserve & enhance snowmobiling & improve trails, facilities & services for participants

New York State Theatre Education Association
63 Hecla St, Buffalo, NY 14216
716-837-9434 Fax: 716-626-8207
e-mail: rogersouth@aol.com
Web site: www.nystea.org
Roger Paolini, President
Working to preserve & enhance drama & theater education & opportunities in NY schools & communities

New York State Travel & Vacation Association
PO Box 285, Akron, NY 14001
716-542-1586 or 888-698-2970 Fax: 716-542-4808
e-mail: info@nystva.org
Web site: www.nystva.org
Dawn L Borchert, Executive Director
The NYSTVA is the tourism industry's leader in communication, legislative awareness, professional development, and promotion.

New York University, Tisch School of the Arts
721 Broadway, New York, NY 10003-6807
212-998-1800 Fax: 212-995-4064
e-mail: mary.campbell@nyu.edu
Web site: www.nyu.edu/tisch
Mary Schmidt Campbell, Dean Associate Provost for the Arts, NYU

New York Wine & Grape Foundation
800 S Main St, Ste 200, Canandaigua, NY 14424
585-394-3620 Fax: 585-394-3649
e-mail: info@newyorkwines.org
Web site: www.newyorkwines.org
James Trezise, President
Promotion of wine & grape products of New York; research for wine & grape related products & issues

New York Yankees
800 Ruppert Place, Bronx, NY 10451
718-293-4300 Fax: 718-293-8431
Web site: www.yankees.com
Randy Levine, President

Resources for Artists with Disabilities Inc
77 7th Ave, Suite PHH, New York, NY 10011-6644
212-691-5490 Fax: 212-691-5490
Dr Lois Kaggen, President & Founder
Organizes & promotes exhibition opportunities for visual artists with physical disabilities

Saratoga Gaming & Raceway
PO Box 356, Saratoga Springs, NY 12866
518-584-2110 or 518-581-5748 Fax: 518-583-1269
e-mail: info@saratogaraceway.com
Web site: www.saratogaraceway.com
John R Matarazzo, Director of Racing Operations
Horse racing

Seaway Trail Inc
401 West Main Street, Ray & West Main Streets, PO Box 660, Sackets Harbor, NY 13685
315-646-1000 or 800-SEAWAY-T Fax: 315-646-1004
e-mail: info@seawaytrail.com
Web site: www.seawaytrail.com
Teresa Mitchell, President
Promotes coastal recreation, economic development, resource management & heritage, cultural, agricultural & culinary tourism along a 454 mile NYS highway system

Ski Areas of New York Inc
2144 Currie Rd, Tully, NY 13159
315-696-6550 Fax: 315-696-6567
e-mail: dirk@iskiny.com
Web site: www.iskiny.com
Dirk Gouwens, President
Promote skiing in NYS

Offices and agencies generally appear in alphabetical order, except when specific order is requested by listee.

TOURISM, ARTS & SPORTS / Private Sector

Solomon R Guggenheim Foundation
1071 5th Ave, New York, NY 10128
212-423-3500
e-mail: publicaffairs@guggenheim.org
Web site: www.guggenheim.org
Thomas Krens, Director

Special Olympics New York, Inc
504 Balltown Road, Schenectady, NY 12304-2290
518-388-0790 Fax: 518-388-0795
Web site: www.nyso.org
Neal J Johnson, President & Chief Executive Officer
Not-for-profit organization provides year-round sports training & competition in Olympic-style sports for athletes with mental retardation

Sports & Arts in Schools Foundation
58-12 Queens Blvd, Suite 1 - 59th Entrance, Woodside, NY 11377
718-786-7110 Fax: 718-786-7635
e-mail: info@sasfny.org
Web site: www.sasfny.org
James R O'Neill, Executive Director
After-school, summer camps & clinics, winter-break festival

Staten Island Zoo
614 Broadway, Staten Island, NY 10310
718-442-3101 Fax: 718-981-8711
e-mail: sizoodir@aol.com
Web site: www.statenislandzoo.org
John J Caltabiano, Director

Tribeca Film Institute
375 Greenwich St, New York, NY 10013
212-941-2400 Fax: 212-941-3892
Web site: www.tribecafilminstitute.org
Madeyln Wils, President & Chief Executive Officer

USA Track & Field, Adirondack Association Inc
233 Fourth St, Troy, NY 12180
518-273-5552 Fax: 518-273-0647
e-mail: info@usatfadir.org
Web site: www.usatfadir.org
George Regan, President
Leadership & opportunities for athletes pursuing excellence in running, race walking & track & field

Vernon Downs/Gaming-Racing-Entertainment
4229 Stuhlman Rd, PO Box 1040, Vernon Downs, NY 13476
315-829-2201 Fax: 315-829-3787
e-mail: vernonevents@vernondowns.com
Web site: www.vernondowns.com
Ursula Hardin, President
Horse racing, concerts, motorcross, motorcycle, craft fairs & other entertainment

Willow Mixed Media Inc
PO Box 194, Glenford, NY 12433
845-657-2914
e-mail: video@hvc.rr.com
Web site: www.willowmixedmedia.org
Tobe Carey, President
Not-for-profit specializing in documentary video & arts projects addressing social concerns

Yonkers Raceway
810 Central Park Ave, Yonkers, NY 10704
914-968-4200 Fax: 914-968-4479
Web site: www.yonkersraceway.com
Timothy Rooney, President
Horse racing and video gaming entertainment

Offices and agencies generally appear in alphabetical order, except when specific order is requested by listee.

TRANSPORTATION

New York State

GOVERNOR'S OFFICE

Governor's Office
Executive Chamber
State Capitol
Albany, NY 12224
518-474-8390 Fax: 518-474-1513
Web site: www.state.ny.us

Governor:
  Eliot Spitzer 518-474-8390
Secretary to the Governor:
  Richard Baum. 518-474-4246
Counsel to the Governor:
  David Nocenti. 518-474-8343
Senior Advisor to the Governor:
  Lloyd Constantine 518-486-9671
Director, Communications:
  Darren Dopp. 518-474-8418
Assistant Counsel to the Governor-Transportation & Infrastructure:
  Timothy B Lennon 518-474-1310
Special Advisor, Public Safety:
  James Sherry. 518-474-3522
Deputy Secretary, Intergovernmental Affairs:
  Martin Mack 518-408-2555
Assistant Secretary, Homeland Security:
  William Howard 518-408-2552

EXECUTIVE DEPARTMENTS AND RELATED AGENCIES

Motor Vehicles Department
Swan Street Building
6 Empire State Plaza
Room 411
Albany, NY 12228
518-474-0841 or 800-225-5368
Web site: www.nysdmv.com

Commissioner:
  David J Swarts. 518-474-0841/fax: 518-474-0712
Executive Deputy Commissioner:
  Wayne Benjamin 518-474-0846/fax: 518-474-0712
Associate Commissioner, Communications:
  Gail Tyner-Taylor 518-473-7000/fax: 518-473-1930
Director, Quality Development:
  Mike Graziade 518-486-7402

Administration, Office for
Deputy Commissioner:
  Gregory J Kline 518-474-6876
Director, Audit Services:
  Edward Wade 518-474-0881
CFO & Director, Fiscal Management:
  Kathy Gilchrist 518-474-0990

Director, Human Resources Management:
  Bob Hoffmeister 518-474-7602
Director, Information Technology:
  Adam Gigandet. 518-474-0605
Director, Labor Relations:
  Steve France 518-474-2902
Director, Program Analysis:
  Thea Rosenberg 518-474-0623

Governor's Traffic Safety Committee
Web site: www.nysgtsc.state.ny.us/index.htm
Chair:
  Kenneth Carpenter 518-474-5111

Legal Affairs, Office for
Deputy Commissioner, Legal Affairs:
  Jill A Dunn 518-474-1003
Legislative Counsel:
  Meg Murray 518-474-7726
Director, Legal:
  Neal W Schoen 518-486-3131

  Appeals Board
  Chairman:
    Deb Dugan 518-474-0645

Operations & Customer Service, Office for
Deputy Commissioner:
  Jack Hope 518-402-2379
Asst Commissioner & Clerks Liaison:
  Vacant 518-473-1489
Director, Field Operations:
  Robert McDonough 518-474-0953
Director, Field Operations:
  Joseph Crisafulli 518-473-7254
Director, Central Office Operations:
  Steve Berletic 518-486-6582
Director, Document Production & Mail Operations:
  Mike Filmer 518-486-9731

Safety, Consumer Protection & Clean Air, Office for
Deputy Commissioner:
  Terri Egan 518-402-4860
Director, Driver/Vehicle Safety/Clean Air:
  Jean Rosenthal 518-473-3347
Project Manager, Real ID Project Team:
  Kelly Smith-Lawless 518-474-8328
Director, Field Investigation:
  Owen McShane 518-474-8805
Director, Motor Carrier & Driver Safety Services:
  Kevin P O'Brien 518-474-0855
Director, Vehicle Safety & Clean Air:
  Steve Cooper 518-474-3785

Transportation Department
50 Wolf Road
6th Fl
Albany, NY 12232

Offices and agencies generally appear in alphabetical order, except when specific order is requested by listee.

TRANSPORTATION / New York State

518-457-5100 or 518-457-6195 Fax: 518-457-5583
Web site: www.nysdot.gov

Commissioner:
  Astrid C Glynn 518-457-4422
Deputy Commissioner:
  Stanley Gee 518-457-4422
Chief Counsel:
  Bruce Feldman 518-457-4422
Chief Operating Officer:
  Brian O Rowback 518-485-0887
  e-mail: browback@dot.state.ny.us
Acting Chief, Policy & Transportation Strategy:
  Karen Rae 518-457-6700
Chief Engineer:
  Robert Dennison 518-457-4430
Acting Chief Regional Director:
  Dave Ligeikis 585-272-3333
CFO:
  Michael Novakowski 518-457-2320

Administrative Services Division
Chief Administrative Officer:
  Michael J McCarthy 518-457-6300
Director, Contract Mgmt & Accounting Office:
  Richard D Albertin 518-457-2600
Director, Human Resources Office:
  Lou DeSol 518-457-6460
Director, External Affairs Office:
  Steven J Hewitt 518-457-2345
Director, Organizational Effectiveness:
  Michael J McCarthy 518-457-2787
Director, Audit & Risk Management Office:
  John S Samaniuk 518-457-4682
Director, Information Services Office:
  Donald Wells 518-457-2800
Director, Media Relations Office:
  Jennifer Post 518-457-6400/fax: 518-457-6506
  e-mail: jpost@dot.state.ny.us

Engineering Division
Chief Engineer:
  Michael Shamma 518-457-4430
Director, Design:
  Daniel D'Angelo 518-457-6452
Director, Structures:
  George A Christian 518-457-6827
Director, Environmental Analysis:
  Mary E Ivey 518-457-5672
Director, Real Estate:
  Mary Marocco 518-457-2430
Director, Technical Services Office:
  Robert L Sack 518-457-4445
Director, Construction Office:
  James Tynan 518-457-6472

Legal Affairs Division
Chief Counsel:
  Bruce Feldman 518-457-2412
Director, Legal Affairs Office:
  Thomas Perreault 518-457-2412
Director, Proceedings Office:
  Peter Loomis 518-457-1182
Director, Claims unit:
  Eric Celia 518-457-2411

Operations Division
Chief Operating Officer:
  Brian O Rowback 518-485-0887
Director, Safety & Security Services:
  Donald Baker 518-457-6512
Director, Fleet Administration & Support Office:
  Joseph L Darling 518-457-2875
Director, Emergency Management:
  Roberta Fox 518-485-1379
Director, Program Development & Mgmt Office:
  Donald Hannon 518-457-7664
Director, Operations Management Office:
  Gary McVoy 518-457-2779
Director, Employee Health & Safety:
  Daniel Mencucci 518-457-2420

Policy & Strategy Division
Acting Chief:
  Karen Rae 518-457-6700
Director, Southern Tier & Western Trans Strategy:
  Ronald Hayes 518-457-9307
CFO:
  Michael Novakowski 518-457-2320
Director, Downstate Transportation Strategy:
  Heather Sporn 212-267-4113
Director, Central & Northeastern Transportation Strategy:
  Clifford A Thomas 518-457-7475
Director, Transportation Policy & Performance Office:
  Robert Zerrillo 518-457-6700

Delivery Division
Director:
Mark Silo

Regional Offices
Region 1
328 State St, Schenectady, NY 12305
Acting Director:
  Dick Fredericks 518-388-0388/fax: 518-388-0347
Region 2
Utica State Ofc Bldg, 207 Genesee St, Utica, NY 13501
Director:
  Michael Shamma 315-793-2447/fax: 315-793-2182
Region 3
State Ofc Bldg, 333 E Washington St, Syracuse, NY 13202
Director:
  Carl F Ford 315-428-4351/fax: 315-428-4834
Region 4
1530 Jefferson Rd, Rochester, NY 14623
Director:
  Kevin O'Buckley 585-272-3310/fax: 585-427-8480
Region 5
Buffalo State Ofc Bldg, 125 Main St, Buffalo, NY 14203
Director:
  Alan E Taylor 716-847-3238/fax: 716-847-3961
Region 6
107 Broadway, Hornell, NY 14843
Director:
  Peter E White 607-324-8404/fax: 607-324-0790
Region 7
Dulles State Ofc Bldg, 317 Washington St, Watertown, NY 13601
Director:
  R Carey Babyak 315-785-2333/fax: 315-785-2507
Region 8
Eleanor Roosevelt State Ofc Bldg, 4 Burnett Blvd, Poughkeepsie, NY 12603
Director:
  Mike Cotton 845-431-5750/fax: 845-431-5703

Offices and agencies generally appear in alphabetical order, except when specific order is requested by listee.

TRANSPORTATION / New York State

Region 9
44 Hawley St, Binghamton, NY 13901
Director:
  Jack Williams 607-721-8116/fax: 607-721-8119

Region 10
State Ofc Bldg, 250 Veterans Memorial Hwy, Hauppauge, NY 11788
Director:
  Subi Chakraborti 631-952-6632/fax: 631-952-6311

Region 11
Hunters Point Plaza, 47-40 21st St, Long Island City, NY 11101
Director:
  Douglas Currey 718-482-4526/fax: 718-482-4525

CORPORATIONS, AUTHORITIES AND COMMISSIONS

Albany County Airport Authority
Administration Bldg, 2nd Fl
Albany International Airport
Albany, NY 12211-1507
518-242-2222 x1 Fax: 518-242-2641
e-mail: info@albanyairport.com
Web site: www.albanyairport.com

Chief Executive Officer:
  John A O'Donnell PE 518-242-2222 x1
Chief Fiscal Officer:
  J Dwight Hadley 518-242-2222 x1
Director, Public Affairs:
  Doug Myers 518-242-2222 x1
Counsel:
  Peter F Stuto 518-242-2222 x1
Airport Planner:
  Stephen A Iachetta 518-242-2222 x1
Purchasing Agent:
  Mary Ann Mysliwiec 518-242-2222 x2
Administrative Services Manager:
  Ginger Olthoff CM, A.C.E. Ops 518-242-2222 x1

Albany Port District Commission
Administration Bldg
Port of Albany
Albany, NY 12202
518-463-8763 Fax: 518-463-8767
e-mail: portofalbany@portofalbany.com
Web site: www.portofalbany.com

Chair:
  Robert F Cross 518-463-8763
General Manager:
  Frank W Keane 518-463-8763
Counsel:
  Thomas Owens 518-694-0910

Buffalo & Fort Erie Public Bridge Authority (Peace Bridge Authority)
One Peace Bridge Plaza
Buffalo, NY 14213-2494
716-884-6744 Fax: 716-884-2089
Web site: www.peacebridge.com

Chair (Canadian):
  John A Lopinski 716-884-6744/fax: 716-883-7246
Vice Chair (US):
  Paul J Koessler 716-884-6744/fax: 716-883-7246
General Manager:
  Ron Rienas 716-884-6744

Capital District Transportation Authority
110 Watervliet Ave
Albany, NY 12206
518-437-8300 Fax: 518-437-8318
Web site: www.cdta.org

Chair:
  David M Stackrow 518-437-8311
Vice Chair:
  Donald C MacElroy 518-437-8311
Executive Director:
  Ray Melleady 518-437-8300
General Counsel:
  David Winans 518-437-8300
Chief Financial Officer:
  Milt Pratt 518-437-8300
Deputy Executive Director, Business Development:
  Carm Basile 518-437-8300

Central New York Regional Transportation Authority
200 Cortland Ave
PO Box 820
Syracuse, NY 13205-0820
315-442-3300 Fax: 315-442-3337
Web site: www.centro.org

Chair, Board of Directors:
  Robert E Colucci 315-442-3300
Executive Director:
  Frank Kobliski 315-442-3360
  e-mail: fkobliski@centro.org
Senior VP, Finance & Administration:
  Steven M Share 315-442-3358
Senior VP, Corporation Operations:
  John Renock 315-442-3388

MTA Bridges & Tunnels
2 Broadway
22nd Floor
New York, NY 10004-2801
646-252-7000 Fax: 646-252-7408
Web site: www.mta.info/bandt

Chairman & CEO:
  Peter S Kalikow 212-878-7200
President:
  Susan Kupferman 212-360-3100
Vice President & Chief Engineer:
  Thomas Bach 212-360-3080
Vice President, Labor Relations:
  Sharon Gallo-Kotcher 212-360-3015
Executive Vice President, Operations:
  Martha Walther 212-360-3060
Vice President, Procurement & Materials:
  Roy Parks 646-252-7084

Offices and agencies generally appear in alphabetical order, except when specific order is requested by listee.

TRANSPORTATION / New York State

Vice President, Staff Services & Chief of Staff:
   Catherine T Sweeney 646-252-7421
Chief Financial Officer:
   David Moretti 646-252-7100
Chief Technology Officer:
   Tariq Habib 646-252-7230
General Counsel:
   Robert O'Brien 646-252-7617
Director, Public Affairs:
   Frank Pascual 646-252-7416
Executive Director, MTA:
   Katherine N Lapp 646-252-7000

MTA Bus Company
341 Madison Avenue
New York, NY 10017
212-878-7174 Fax: 2512-878-0205
Web site: www.mta.info/busco

Chairman & CEO:
   Peter S Kalikow 212-878-7200
President:
   Thomas J Savage 212-878-7174
Administrative Assistant:
   Marian Noel 212-878-7174

MTA Capital Construction
2 Broadway
8th Fl
New York, NY 10002
646-252-4200
Web site: www.mta.info/capconstr

Chairman & CEO:
   Peter S Kalikow 212-878-7200
President:
   Mysore L Nagaraja 646-252-4277
Chief Financial Officer:
   Anthony D'Amico 646-252-4200
Vice President & General Counsel:
   Veronique Hakim 646-252-4278
Vice President, Project Controls:
   Shawn Kildare 646-252-3723
Vice President, Program Executive & Chief Engineer:
   Joseph Trainor 646-252-3467
Program Executive, Fulton Street & Special Projects:
   Richard Miras 646-252-4556
Executive Assistant to the President:
   Vacant 646-252-4278
Deputy Vice President, Finance & Administration:
   Joseph Petrocelli 646-252-3813
Deputy Program Executive, Design Integrity:
   Mike Kyriacou 646-252-4500
Program Manager, Security Projects:
   Ron Pizak 646-252-4756
Program Manager, Security Projects:
   Joe Christen 646-252-3841
Program Manager, Manhattan East Side Access:
   Dilip Patel 212-967-0236
Program Manager, Fulton Street Transit Center:
   Uday Durg 646-252-4932
Program Manager, 7 West Extension Street:
   Philip McGrade 646-252-4107
Program Manager, 2nd Avenue Subway:
   Anil Parikh 212-510-2154

Chief Budget Officer:
   Susan Jurman 646-252-4260
Senior Director, Policy & Implementation:
   Patricia Hoag 646-252-4656

MTA Long Island Bus
700 Commercial Ave
Garden City, NY 11530
516-542-0100 Fax: 516-542-1428
Web site: www.mta.info/libus

Chairman & CEO:
   Peter S Kalikow 212-878-7200
President:
   Neil S Yellin 516-542-0100 x4525
Senior VP, Operations:
   William Norwich 516-542-0100 x4334
Vice President, Finance:
   Joseph Pokorny 516-542-0100 x4439
General Counsel & VP, Legal/Human Resources:
   Cheryl Hartell 516-542-0100 x4429

MTA Long Island Rail Road
Jamaica Station
Jamaica, NY 11435
718-558-7400 Fax: 718-558-8212
Web site: www.mta.info/lirr

Chairman & CEO:
   Peter S Kalikow 212-878-7200
Acting President:
   Raymond P Kenny 718-558-8252
Executive Vice President:
   Albert Cosenza 718-558-7993
   e-mail: accosen@lirr.org
Chief Information Officer:
   Frederick A Wedley 718-588-8166
   e-mail: fawedley@lirr.org
Vice President & Chief Fiscal Officer:
   Nicholas DiMola 718-558-7777
   e-mail: ndimola@lirr.org
Acting Vice President, General Counsel & Secretary:
   Frank Kronenberg 718-558-8264
Acting Vice President, Labor Relations:
   Steve Drayzen 718-558-7405
Acting Vice President, Market Development & Public Affairs:
   Susan McGowan 718-558-7301
Vice President, Service, Planning, Technology & Capital Program
   Management:
   John Coulter 718-558-7363
   e-mail: jwcoult@lirr.org
Vice President, Safety System:
   Jose R Fernandez 718-588-7711
   e-mail: jrferna@lirr.org
Chief Fire Marshal:
   William Rice 718-558-3094

MTA Metro-North Railroad
347 Madison Ave
New York, NY 10017
212-340-2677 Fax: 212-340-4995
Web site: www.mta.info/mnr

Offices and agencies generally appear in alphabetical order, except when specific order is requested by listee.

TRANSPORTATION / New York State

Chairman & CEO:
  Peter S Kalikow 212-878-7200
President:
  Peter A Cannito 212-340-2677
Vice President & General Counsel:
  Richard Bernard 212-340-4933
VP, Finanace & Informational Systems:
  Leonard DeSimone 212-340-2636
Director, Operating Capital Projects:
  George Walker 212-499-4300
Senior VP, Planning Procurement & Business Development:
  Howard Permut 212-340-2500
Chief of Staff & Director, Corporate Communications:
  Donna Evans 212-340-2766/fax: 212-340-3460
Chief Safety Officer:
  Mark Campbell 212-340-4913
Senior Director, Capital Programs:
  Ronald T Yutko 212-499-4403
Senior Director, Customer Service:
  Thomas Tendy 212-672-1251

MTA New York City Transit
370 Jay St
Brooklyn, NY 11201
718-330-3000 Fax: 718-596-2146
Web site: www.mta.info/nyct

Chairman & CEO:
  Peter S Kalikow 212-878-7200
President:
  Howard H Roberts Jr 646-252-5800
Executive Vice President:
  Barbara R Spencer 646-252-5888
Senior Vice President, Buses:
  Millard Seay 646-252-5872
Senior Vice President, Capital Program Management:
  Cosema Crawford 646-252-3034
Vice President, Corporate Communications:
  Paul Fleuranges 646-252-5873
Senior Vice President, Subways:
  Michael Lombardi 646-252-5860
Senior Vice President, System Safety:
  Cheryl Kennedy 646-252-5934
Vice President & General Counsel:
  Martin Schnabel 718-694-3900
Vice President, Labor Relations:
  Ralph Agritelley 646-252-5880
Chief Officer, Staten Island Railway:
  John McCabe 718-876-8239

MTA (Metropolitan Transportation Authority)
347 Madison Ave
New York, NY 10017
212-878-7000 Fax: 212-878-7030
Web site: www.mta.info

Chairman & CEO:
  Peter S Kalikow 212-878-7200
Executive Director/Chief Operating Officer:
  Elliot Sander 212-878-7274
Deputy Executive Director, Director of Security:
  William Morange 212-878-7155
Deputy Executive Director, Corporate & Community Affairs:
  Christopher P Boylan 212-878-7160
Deputy Executive Director, Policy/Special Advisor, Safety & Environmental Issues:
  Linda Kleinbaum 212-878-7206
Chief of Staff:
  Maureen E Boll 212-878-7420
Director, Labor Relations:
  Gary Dellaverson 212-878-7438
Director, Budgets & Financial Management:
  Gary Lanigan 212-878-7236
Director, Finance:
  Vacant 212-878-7278
Director, Human Resources:
  Margaret Connor 212-878-7017
Director, Government Affairs:
  Hilary Ring 212-878-7313/fax: 212-878-7050
MTA Chief of Police:
  Kevin J McConville 212-878-1084
Press Secretary:
  Jeremy Soffin 212-878-7145

MTA Office of the Inspector General
111 West 40th St
5th Fl
New York, NY 10018
212-878-0000 or 800-682-4448 Fax: 212-878-0003
Web site: www.mtaig.state.ny.us

Inspector General:
  Barry L Kluger 212-878-0007

New York Metropolitan Transportation Council
199 Water St, 22nd Fl
New York, NY 10038
212-383-7200 Fax: 212-383-2418
e-mail: nymtc-web@dot.state.ny.us
Web site: www.nymtc.org

Executive Director:
  Joel Ettinger 212-383-7236
Deputy Director, Adminstration Group:
  Alan Borenstein 212-383-7294
  e-mail: aborenstein@dot.state.ny.us
Assistant Director, Planning Group:
  Gerard J Bogacz 212-383-7260
  e-mail: gbogacz@dot.state.ny.us
Assistant Director, Technical Group:
  Kuo-Ann Chiao 212-383-7212
  e-mail: kchiao@dot.state.ny.us

New York State Bridge Authority
Mid-Hudson Bridge Plaza
PO Box 1010
Highland, NY 12528
845-691-7245 Fax: 845-691-3560
Web site: www.nysba.net

Chair:
  James P Sproat 845-691-7245
Vice Chair:
  Roderick O Dressel 845-691-7245
Executive Director:
  George C Sinnott 845-691-7245

Offices and agencies generally appear in alphabetical order, except when specific order is requested by listee.

TRANSPORTATION / New York State

Deputy Executive Director:
 James J Bresnan 845-691-7245
 e-mail: jbresnan@nysba.state.ny.us
General Counsel:
 Carl Whitbeck 518-828-4107
Public Information Officer, Planning & Public Relations:
 John R Bellucci 845-691-5953/fax: 845-691-3636
 e-mail: jbellucci@nysba.state.ny.us

New York State Thruway Authority
200 Southern Blvd
Albany, NY 12209
518-436-2700 Fax: 518-436-2899
Web site: www.nysthruway.gov

Chair:
 John L Buono 518-436-3000
Executive Director:
 Michael R Fleischer 518-436-2900
General Counsel:
 Sharon O'Conor 518-436-2840
Deputy Counsel:
 Katherine McCartney 518-436-3188
Director, Government Relations:
 Pamela Davis 518-436-2860/fax: 518-471-4340
Director, Public Information:
 Vacant 518-436-2983/fax: 518-426-3995
 e-mail: publicinfo@thruway.state.ny.us

New York State Canal Corporation
Web site: www.nyscanals.gov
Director:
 Carmella Mantella 518-436-3055

Niagara Falls Bridge Commission
PO Box 1031
Niagara Falls, NY 14302
716-285-6322 Fax: 716-282-3292
e-mail: general_inquiries@niagarafallsbridges.com
Web site: www.niagarafallsbridges.com

Chair:
 Janice A Thomson 716-285-6322
General Manager/Secretary/Treasurer:
 Thomas E Garlock 716-285-6322

Niagara Frontier Transportation Authority
181 Ellicott St
Buffalo, NY 14203
716-855-7300 Fax: 716-855-6655
e-mail: info@nfta.com
Web site: www.nfta.com

Chair:
 Gregory Stamm 716-855-7232
Executive Director:
 Lawrence M Meckler 716-855-7369
 e-mail: lawrence_meckler@nfta.com
Chief Financial Officer:
 Deborah Leous 716-855-7250
General Counsel:
 David M Gregory 716-855-7230
Director, Aviation:
 William Vanecek 716-630-6030

Director, Human Resources:
 Diane Ruszala 716-855-7373
Director, Surface Transportation:
 Walter D Zmuda 716-855-7252
Director, Engineering:
 Michael Bykowski 716-855-7412
Director, Public Affairs:
 C Douglas Hartmayer 716-855-7420

Ogdensburg Bridge & Port Authority
One Bridge Plaza
Ogdensburg, NY 13669
315-393-4080 Fax: 315-393-7068
e-mail: obpa@ogdensport.com
Web site: www.ogdensport.com

Chair:
 Fredrick J Carter 315-393-4080
Deputy Executive Director:
 Wade A Davis 315-393-4080
 e-mail: wadavis@ogdensport.com

Port Authority of New York & New Jersey
225 Park Ave South
18th Fl
New York, NY 10003
212-435-7000 Fax: 212-435-4032
Web site: www.panynj.gov

Chair, New Jersey:
 Anthony R Coscia 212-435-7000
Vice Chair, New York:
 Henry R Silverman 212-435-7000
Executive Director:
 Anthony E Shorris 212-435-7271
First Deputy Executive Director:
 James P Fox 212-435-6667
Deputy Executive Director:
 William H Goldstein 212-435-6668
Deputy Executive Director:
 Ernesto Butcher 212-435-7887
Director Gov't & Community Relations:
 Shawn K Laurenti 212-435-6903
General Counsel:
 Darrell Buchbinder 212-435-3515
Chief Financial Officer:
 A Paul Blanco 212-435-7738
Chief Administrative Officer:
 Louis J LaCapra 212-435-8140
Chief of Public & Government Affairs:
 Stephen Sigmund 212-435-8041
Chief Engineer:
 Francis J Lombardi 212-435-7449
Director, Public Affairs:
 John J McCarthy 212-435-6502
Office of Secretary:
 Karen E Eastman 212-435-6528

Port of Oswego Authority
1 East Second St
Oswego, NY 13126

Offices and agencies generally appear in alphabetical order, except when specific order is requested by listee.

TRANSPORTATION / New York State

315-343-4503 Fax: 315-343-5498
e-mail: shipping@portoswego.com
Web site: www.portoswego.com

Chair:
  Richard Tesoriero 315-343-8095
Acting Executive Director:
  James Cloonan 315-343-4503
Counsel:
  Timothy Fennell 315-343-6363

Rochester-Genesee Regional Transportation Authority

1372 E Main St
PO Box 90629
Rochester, NY 14609
585-654-0200 Fax: 585-654-0224
Web site: www.rgrta.com

Chair:
  John G Doyle, Jr. 585-654-0200
Chief Executive Officer:
  Mark R Aesch 585-654-0200
Chief Operating Officer:
  Stephen W Hendershott 585-654-0200
Chief Financial Officer:
  Robert W Frye 585-654-0200
Director, Transit Operations:
  Bruce G Philpott 585-654-0200

Thousand Islands Bridge Authority

PO Box 428, Collins Landing
43530 Interstate 81
Alexandria Bay, NY 13607
315-482-2501 or 315-658-2281 Fax: 315-482-5925
e-mail: info@tibridge.com
Web site: www.tibridge.com

Chair:
  Donald J Grant 315-482-2501
Executive Director:
  Robert G Horr, III 315-482-2501
  e-mail: roberthorr@tibridge.com
Legal Counsel:
  Anderson Wise 315-482-2501

Waterfront Commission of New York Harbor

39 Broadway
4th Fl
New York, NY 10006
212-742-9280 Fax: 212-480-0587
Web site: www.wcnyh.org

Commissioner, New York:
  Michael C Axelrod 212-742-9280
Commissioner, New Jersey:
  Michael J Madonna 212-742-9280

Executive Director:
  Thomas De Maria 212-905-9201

NEW YORK STATE LEGISLATURE

See Legislative Branch in Section 1 for additional Standing Committee and Subcommittee information.

Assembly Standing Committees

Corporations, Authorities & Commissions
Chair:
  Richard L Brodsky (D) 518-455-5753
Ranking Minority Member:
  Stephen Hawley (R) 518-455-5811

Economic Development, Job Creation, Commerce & Industry
Chair:
  Robin L Schimminger (D) 518-455-4767
Ranking Minority Member:
  Marc Butler (R) 518-455-5393

Transportation
Chair:
  David F Gantt (D) 518-455-5606
Ranking Minority Member:
  David G McDonough (R) 518-455-4633

Joint Legislative Commissions

Critical Transportation Choices, Legislative Commission on
Senate Chair:
  Thomas W Libous (R) 518-455-2091
Assembly Vice Chair:
  Vacant 518-455-0000
Program Manager:
  Heidi Kromphardt 518-455-4031

Senate Standing Committees

Commerce, Economic Development & Small Business
Chair:
  James S Alesi (R) 518-455-2015
Ranking Minority Member:
  Efrain Gonzalez, Jr (D) 518-455-3395

Corporations, Authorities & Commissions
Chair:
  John J Flanagan (R) 518-455-3341
Ranking Minority Member:
  Bill Perkins (D) 518-455-2441

Transportation
Chair:
  Thomas W Libous (R) 518-455-2677
Ranking Minority Member:
  John D Sabini (D) 518-455-2529

Offices and agencies generally appear in alphabetical order, except when specific order is requested by listee.

TRANSPORTATION / U.S. Government

U.S. Government

EXECUTIVE DEPARTMENTS AND RELATED AGENCIES

Federal Maritime Commission
Web site: www.fmc.gov

New York Area Office
Bldg 75, Rm 205B, JFK Intl Airport, Jamaica, NY 11430
Area Rep:
  Emanuel J Mingione 718-553-2228/fax: 718-553-2229

National Transportation Safety Board
Web site: www.ntsb.gov

Aviation Division, Northeast Regional Office
2001 Route 46, Ste 504, Parsippany, NJ 07054-1315
Regional Director:
  Robert Pearce. 973-334-6531/fax: 973-334-6759

Office of Administrative Law Judges
490 L'Enfant Plaza, ESW, Washington, DC 20594
Chief Judge:
  William E Fowler, Jr 202-314-6151/fax: 202-314-6158

US Department of Homeland Security (DHS)
Web site: www.dhs.gov

Transportation Security Administration (TSA)
201 Varick St, Rm 603, New York, NY 10014
Regional Spokesperson:
  Mark Hatfield 212-337-2260/fax: 212-337-2261
  e-mail: mark.hatfield@dhs.gov

US Transportation Department
Web site: www.dot.gov

Federal Aviation Administration-Eastern Region . . . . . . fax: 718-553-3220
One Aviation Plaza Room 520, Jamaica, NY 11434
718-553-3200 Fax: 718-553-3220
Web site: www.faa.gov
Regional Administrator:
  Arlene B Feldman. 718-553-3000
Regional Executive Manager:
  Manny Weiss 718-553-3001
Manager, Public Affairs:
  Arlene Murry 718-553-3010

  Accounting Division
  Manager:
    Fred Glassberg 718-553-4190

  Aerospace Medicine Division
  Regional Flight Surgeon:
    Harriet Lester 718-553-3300

  Air Traffic Division
  Acting Area Director:
    John G McCartney 718-553-4500

Airports Division
Manager:
  William Flanagan 718-553-3331

Aviation Information & Services Division
Manager:
  Alan Siperstein 718-553-3358

Engineering Services
Manager:
  Selin Haber 718-553-3400

Flight Standards Division
Manager:
  Lawrence Fields 718-553-3200

Human Resource Management Division
Manager:
  Gloria Quay 718-553-3130

Logistics Division
Manager:
  Vacant 718-553-3050

Military Liaison Officers to the Federal Aviation Admin (NYS)
12 New England Executive Park, Burlington, MA 1803
  Air Force Regional Representatives
  Representative:
    Vacant 781-238-7901/fax: 781-238-7903
  Transportation Specialist:
    Cheryl W Carpenter 781-238-7910
    e-mail: cheryl.w.carpenter@faa.gov
  Army Regional Representatives
  Liaison Officer:
    LTC Bill Walsh 781-238-7906
    e-mail: bill.walsh@faa.gov
  Liaison Officer:
    MSGT Jason Williams 781-238-7905
    e-mail: jason.williams@faa.gov
  Navy Regional Representatives
  Liaison Officer:
    CDR Rick Perez 781-238-7907
    e-mail: rick.perez@faa.gov
  Liaison Officer:
    ACCS Mark Moon 781-238-7908/fax: 781-238-7902
    e-mail: mark.moon@faa.gov

Runway Safety Manager
Manager:
  Bill DeGraaff 718-553-3326

Federal Highway Administration-New York Division . . fax: 518-431-4121
Leo W O'Brien Federal Bldg, Rm 719 Clinton Ave & N Pearl St, Albany, NY 12207
518-431-4125 Fax: 518-431-4121
Web site: www.fhwa.dot.gov
Division Administrator:
  Robert Arnold. 518-431-4127
  e-mail: robert.arnold@fwha.dot.gov
Asst Division Administrator:
  Amy D Jackson-Grove 518-431-4131
  e-mail: amy.jackson-grove@fwha.dot.gov
Senior Attorney:
  Kenneth Dymond. 518-431-4125 x224
  e-mail: ken.dymond@fwha.dot.gov

Offices and agencies generally appear in alphabetical order, except when specific order is requested by listee.

TRANSPORTATION / U.S. Government

Engineer Coordinator:
 Thomas G Herritt, Jr 518-431-4125 x233
 e-mail: thomas.g.herritt@fwha.dot.gov

Federal Motor Carrier Safety Admin-New York Division . . . . fax: 518-431-4140
Leo O'Brien Federal Bldg, Rm 742, Albany, NY 12207
518-431-4145 Fax: 518-431-4140
Web site: www.fmcsa.dot.gov
Division Administrator:
 Brian Temperine 518-431-4145 x311
Field Office Supervisor, Upstate:
 Pamela Noyes 518-431-4145 x316
State Program Specialist:
 Andrew Choquette 518-431-4145 x313
Manager, Intelligent Transportation Systems Commercial Vehicle Operati:
 Carolyn Temperine 518-431-4145 x270

Federal Railroad Administration-Field Offices
Web site: www.fra.dot.gov

Hazardous Material
111 W Huron St, Rm 909B, Buffalo, NY 14202
Inspector:
 Michael J Ziolkowski 716-551-3955

Highway-Rail Grade Crossing
PO Box 2144, Ballston Spa, NY 12020
Program Manager:
 Randall L Dickinson 518-899-5372/fax: 518-899-5372

Federal Transit Administration, Region II-New York
One Bowling Green, Rm 429, New York, NY 10004-1415
Web site: www.fta.dot.gov
Regional Admin:
 Letitia Thompson 212-668-2170/fax: 212-668-2136

Maritime Administration
Web site: www.marad.dot.gov

Great Lakes Region (includes part of New York State)
1701 E Woodfield Rd, Ste 203, Schaumburg, IL 60173-5127
Regional Director:
 Doris J Bautch 847-995-0122/fax: 847-995-0133
 e-mail: doris.bautch@marad.dot.gov

North Atlantic Region
One Bowling Green, Rm 418, New York, NY 10004-1415
Regional Director:
 Robert F McKeon 212-668-3330/fax: 212-668-3382
 e-mail: robert.mckeon@marad.dot.gov

US Merchant Marine Academy . . . . fax: 516-773-5774
300 Steamboat Rd, Kings Point, NY 11024-1699
516-773-5000 Fax: 516-773-5774
Web site: www.usmma.edu
Superintendent:
 VAdm Joseph D Stewart 516-773-5348/fax: 516-773-5347

National Highway Traffic Safety Administration, Reg II-NY
222 Mamaroneck Ave, Suite 204, White Plains, NY 10605
Web site: www.nhtsa.dot.gov
Reg Admin:
 Thomas M Louizou 914-682-6162/fax: 914-682-6239

Office of Inspector General, Region II-New York
201 Varick Street, Room 1161, New York, NY 10014
Web site: www.oig.dot.gov
Regional Audit Manager:
 Vacant 212-337-1280/fax: 212-620-3252

Saint Lawrence Seaway Development Corporation
180 Andrews St, PO Box 520, Massena, NY 13662-0520
Web site: www.seaway.dot.gov; www.greatlakes-seaway.com
Assoc Administrator:
 Salvatore Pisani 315-764-3209/fax: 315-764-3235
 e-mail: sal.pisani@sls.dot.gov

U.S. CONGRESS

See U.S. Congress Chapter for additional Standing Committee and Subcommittee information.

House of Representatives Standing Committees

Transportation & Infrastructure
Chair:
 James L Oberstar (D-MN) 202-225-4472
Ranking Minority Member:
 John L Mica (R-FL)
New York Delegate:
 Timothy H Bishop (D) 202-225-3826
New York Delegate:
 Sherwood L Boehlert (R) 202-225-3665
New York Delegate:
 Brian M Higgins (D) 202-225-3306
New York Delegate:
 Sue W Kelly (R) 202-225-5441
New York Delegate:
 John R (Randy) Kuhl (R) 202-225-3161
New York Delegate:
 Jerrold Nadler (D) 202-225-5635
New York Delegate:
 Anthony D Weiner (D) 202-225-6616

Senate Standing Committees

Commerce, Science & Transportation
Chair:
 Daniel K Inouye (D-HI)
Ranking Minority Member:
 Ted Stevens

Environment & Public Works
Chair:
 Barbara Boxer (CA) 202-224-8832
Ranking Minority Member:
 James M Inhofe (OK) 202-224-6176
New York Delegate:
 Hillary Rodham Clinton (D) 202-224-4451

 Subcommittee
 Transportation & Infrastructure
 Chair:
  Max Baucus (D-MT) 202-224-2651
 Ranking Minority Member:
  Johnny Isakson (R-GA) 202-224-3643

Offices and agencies generally appear in alphabetical order, except when specific order is requested by listee.

TRANSPORTATION / Private Sector

Private Sector

AAA Western and Central NY
100 International Dr, Buffalo, NY 14221
716-626-3225 Fax: 716-631-5925
e-mail: wsmith@nyaaa.com
Web site: www.aaa.com
Wallace Smith, Vice President

ALSTOM Transportation Inc
1 Transit Dr, Hornell, NY 14843
607-281-2487 Fax: 607-324-2641
e-mail: chuck.wochele@transport.alstom.com
Web site: www.transport.alstom.com
Chuck Wochele, Vice President Business Development
High-speed trains, rapid transit vehicles, commuter cars, AC propulsion & signaling, passenger locomotives

Ammann & Whitney
96 Morton St, New York, NY 10014
212-462-8500 Fax: 212-929-5356
e-mail: nivanoff@ammann-whitney.com
Web site: www.ammann-whitney.com
Nick Ivanoff, President & Chief Executive Officer
Planning, engineering & construction mgmt for airport, transit, gov't, recreation & commercial facilities; highways; bridges

Automobile Club of New York
1415 Kellum Place, Garden City, NY 11530
516-873-2259 Fax: 516-873-2355
Web site: www.aaany.com
John Corlett, Director Government Affairs

Automotive Technology & Energy Group of Western NY
2568 Walden Avenue, Suite 103, Cheektowaga, NY 14225
716-651-4645 Fax: 716-651-4662
Robert Gliss, Executive Director
Garage & service station owners

British Airways PLC
75-20 Astoria Blvd, Jackson Heights, NY 11370
347-418-4729 Fax: 347-418-4204
e-mail: john.lampl@ba.com
Web site: www.ba.com
John Lampl, Vice President, Communications-North America

CP Rail System
200 Clifton Corporate Parkway, PO Box 8002, Clifton Park, NY 12065
518-383-7200 Fax: 518-383-7222
Brent Szafron, Service Area Manager
Freight transport

DKI Engineering & Consulting USA, PC, Corporate World Headquarters
632 Plank Rd, Ste 208, Clifton Park, NY 12065
518-373-4999 Fax: 518-373-8989
e-mail: dki123@aol.com
Web site: www.dkitechnologies.com
D K Gupta, President & Chief Executive Officer
Design, engineering, planning, construction management & program management oversight for airports, bridges, highways, railroads, transit, tunnels, water & wastewater facilities

Empire State Passengers Association
PO Box 434, Syracuse, NY 13209
716-741-6384 Fax: 716-632-3044
e-mail: bbecker@esparail.org
Web site: www.esparail.org
Bruce Becker, President
Advocacy for improvement of rail passenger service

Ethan C Eldon Associates Inc
1350 Broadway, Ste 612, New York, NY 10018
212-967-5400 Fax: 212-967-2747
e-mail: eceaethan@aol.com
Ethan C Eldon, President
Environmental, EIS, traffic, hazardous & solid waste consulting

Gandhi Engineering Inc
111 John St, 3rd Fl, New York, NY 10038-3002
212-349-2900 Fax: 212-285-0205
e-mail: gandhi@gandhieng.com
Web site: www.gandhieng.com
Kirti Gandhi, President
Consulting architects & engineers; infrastructure projects & transportation facilities

General Contractors Association of NY
60 East 42nd St, Rm 3510, New York, NY 10165
212-687-3131 Fax: 212-808-5267
e-mail: felice@gca.gcany.net
Felice Farber, Director, Government Relations
Heavy construction, transportation

Jacobs Engineering
260 Madison Ave, 12th Floor, Suite 1200, New York, NY 10016
212-268-1500 Fax: 212-481-9484
Web site: www.jacobs.com
Vincent Mangieri, Vice President
Multi-modal surface transportation planning, design, engineering, construction & inspection services

Komanoff Energy Associates
636 Broadway, Rm 602, New York, NY 10012-2623
212-260-5237
e-mail: kea@igc.org
Charles Komanoff, Director
Energy, utilities & transportation consulting

Offices and agencies generally appear in alphabetical order, except when specific order is requested by listee.

TRANSPORTATION / Private Sector

Konheim & Ketcham Inc
175 Pacific St, Brooklyn, NY 11201
718-330-0550 Fax: 718-330-0582
e-mail: csk@konheimketcham.com
Web site: www.konheimketcham.com
Carolyn Konheim, President
Environmental impact analysis, traffic engineering, transportation planning & technical assistance to community groups

Kriss, Kriss, Brignola & Persing, LLP
350 Northern Blvd, Ste 306, Albany, NY 12204
518-449-2037 Fax: 518-449-7875
e-mail: office@krisslaw.com
Web site: www.krisslawoffice.com
Mark C Kriss, Partner
Advocates for highway & auto safety

Long Island Rail Road Commuter's Council
347 Madison Ave, 8th Fl, New York, NY 10017
212-878-7087 Fax: 212-878-7461
e-mail: mail@pcac.org
Web site: www.pcac.org
Gerard P Bringmann, Chairman
Represent interest of LIRR riders

Metro-North Railroad Commuter Council
347 Madison Ave, New York, NY 10017
212-878-7077 or 212-878-7087 Fax: 212-878-7461
e-mail: mail@pcac.org
Web site: www.pcac.org
William Henderson, Chair
Represent interests of MNR riders

NY Airport Service
15 Second Ave, Brooklyn, NY 11215
718-875-8200 Fax: 718-875-7056
Web site: www.nyairportservice.com
Mark Marmurstein, Vice President
Airport shuttle bus services

NY State Association of Town Superintendents of Highways Inc
119 Washington Avenue, Suite 300, Albany, NY 12210
518-694-9313 Fax: 518-694-9314
e-mail: info@nystownhwys.org
Web site: www.nystownhwys.org
Michael K Thompson, Executive Secretary & Treasurer

NYS Association of Service Stations & Repair Shops
6 Walker Way, Albany, NY 12205-4946
518-452-4367 Fax: 518-452-1955
e-mail: nysassn@together.net
Web site: www.nysassrs.com
Ralph Bombardiere, Executive Director
Protect the interests of independent service stations & repair shops & the motoring public

NYS County Hwy Super Assn / NY Aviation Mgt Assn / NY Public Transit Assn
119 Washington Ave, Ste 100, Albany, NY 12210
518-465-1694 Fax: 518-465-1942
e-mail: info@countyhwys.org; info@nyama.com; nypta@atdial.net
Web site: www.countyhwys.org; www.nyama.com; www.nytransit.org
Kathleen A Van De Loo, Communications Director
County highways & bridges in NYS; aviation industry in NYS; public transit industry in NYS

National Economic Research Associates
308 N Cayuga St, Ithaca, NY 14850
607-277-3007 Fax: 607-277-1581
e-mail: alfred.kahn@nera.com
Web site: www.nera.com
Alfred E Kahn, Professor Emeritus & Special Consultant
Utility & transportation regulation, deregulation & antitrust

New England Steamship Agents Inc
730 Downing St, Niskayuna, NY 12309
518-463-5749 Fax: 518-463-5751
e-mail: nesa0025@aol.com
Diane Delory, President
Domestic transportation, vessel agency/husbandry, customs brokerage & vessel brokerage

New York & Atlantic Railway (NYA)
68-01 Otto Rd, Glendale, NY 11385
718-928-2305 Fax: 718-497-3364
e-mail: mwesterfield@anacostia.com
Web site: www.anacostia.com
Mark H Westerfield, President
Freight transport

New York Public Interest Research Group Straphangers Campaign
9 Murray St, 3rd Fl, New York, NY 10007
212-349-6460 Fax: 212-349-1366
e-mail: grussian@nypirg.org
Web site: www.straphangers.org; www.nypirg.org
Gene Russianoff, Senior Staff Attorney
Mass transit & government reform

New York Roadway Improvement Coalition (NYRIC)
629 Old White Plains Road, Tarrytown, NY 10591
914-631-6070 Fax: 914-631-5172
e-mail: cicwhv@cicnys.org
Robert F Carlino, President
Heavy highway & bridge construction

New York Shipping Association Inc
100 Wood Ave South, Ste 304, Iselin, NJ 08830-2716
732-452-7800 Fax: 732-452-6312
e-mail: jcobb@nysanet.org
Web site: www.nysanet.org
James H Cobb, Jr, Director, Governmental Affairs
Maximizing the efficiency, cost competitiveness, safety & quality of marine cargo operations in the Port of New York & New Jersey

Offices and agencies generally appear in alphabetical order, except when specific order is requested by listee.

TRANSPORTATION / Private Sector

New York State Auto Dealers Association
37 Elk St, Albany, NY 12207
518-463-1148 x204 Fax: 518-432-1309
e-mail: bob@nysada.com
Web site: www.nysada.com
Robert Vancavage, President

New York State Motor Truck Association
828 Washington Ave, Albany, NY 12203-1622
518-458-9696 Fax: 518-458-2525
e-mail: nytrucks@aol.com
Web site: www.nytrucks.org
William G Joyce, Jr, President & Chief Executive Officer
Safety & regulatory compliance

New York State Transportation Engineering Alliance (NYSTEA)
99 Pine St, Ste 207, Albany, NY 12207
518-436-0786 Fax: 518-427-0452
e-mail: sdm@fcwc-law.com
Stephen D Morgan, Executive Director
Transportation & infrastructure

New York, Susquehanna & Western Railway
1 Railroad Ave, Cooperstown, NY 13326-1110
607-547-2555 Fax: 607-547-9834
e-mail: wrich@nysw.com
Web site: www.nysw.com
Walter G Rich, President & Chief Executive Officer
Subsidiaries operate freight & passenger railroad system

Parsons Brinckerhoff
One Penn Plaza, New York, NY 10119
212-465-5000 Fax: 212-465-5096
e-mail: bennett@pbworld.com
Web site: www.pbworld.com
Joel H Bennett, Senior Vice President
Engineering, planning, construction management & consulting for transit & transportation, power & telecom projects

Regional Plan Association
4 Irving Place, 7th Fl, New York, NY 10003
212-253-2727 Fax: 212-253-5666
e-mail: jeff@rpa.org
Web site: www.rpa.org
Jeffrey M Zupan, Senior Fellow, Transportation
Regional transportation planning & development issues

Seneca Flight Operations
2262 Airport Dr, Penn Yan, NY 14527
315-536-4471 Fax: 315-536-4558
e-mail: flight@senecafoods.com
Web site: www.senecafoods.com
Richard Leppert, General Manager
Executive air transportation

Simmons-Boardman Publishing Corp
345 Hudson St, 12th Fl, New York, NY 10014-4590
212-620-7200 Fax: 212-633-1863
e-mail: sbrailgroup@sbpub.com
Web site: www.railwayage.com or www.rtands.com or www.railjournal.com
Robert DeMarco, Publisher
Publisher of: Railway Age, International Railway Journal & Rapid Transit Review, Railway Track & Structures

Systra Consulting Inc
470 Seventh Ave, 10th Floor, New York, NY 10018
212-494-9111 Fax: 212-494-9112
Web site: www.systraconsulting.com
Peter Allibone, Executive Vice President
Engineering consultants specializing in urban rail & transit systems, passenger & freight railroads & high speed rail

Transport Workers Union of America, AFL-CIO
1700 Broadway, 2nd Fl, New York, NY 10019
212-259-4900 Fax: 212-265-5704
Web site: www.twu.com
James C Little, International President
Bus, train, railroad & airline workers' union

Transportation Alternatives
115 W 30th St, 12th Fl, New York, NY 10001-4010
212-629-8080 Fax: 212-629-8334
e-mail: info@transalt.org
Web site: www.transalt.org
John Kaehny, Executive Director
NYC commute alternatives, traffic calming, pedestrian safety issues

Tri-State Transportation Campaign
350 W 31st St, Room 802, New York, NY 10001-2726
212-268-7474 Fax: 212-268-7333
e-mail: tstc@tstc.org
Web site: www.tstc.org
Jon Orcutt, Executive Director
Public interest, transit advocacy, planning & environmental organizations working to reform transportation policies

United Transportation Union
35 Fuller Road, Suite 205, Albany, NY 12205
518-438-8403 Fax: 518-438-8404
e-mail: sjnasca@aol.com
Web site: www.utu.org
Samuel Nasca, Legislative Director
Federal government railroad, bus & airline employees; public employees

Urbitran Group
71 West 23rd St, 11th Fl, New York, NY 10010
212-366-6200 Fax: 212-366-6214
e-mail: mhorodnicaenu@urbitran.com
Web site: www.urbitran.com
Michael Horodnicaenu, President & Chief Executive Officer
Engineering, architecture & planning

Offices and agencies generally appear in alphabetical order, except when specific order is requested by listee.

VETERANS AND MILITARY

New York State

GOVERNOR'S OFFICE

Governor's Office
Executive Chamber
State Capitol
Albany, NY 12224
518-474-8390 Fax: 518-474-1513
Web site: www.state.ny.us

Governor:
  Eliot Spitzer 518-474-8390
Secretary to the Governor:
  Richard Baum. 518-474-4246
Counsel to the Governor:
  David Nocenti. 518-474-8343
Senior Advisor to the Governor:
  Lloyd Constantine 518-486-9671
Director, Communications:
  Darren Dopp. 518-474-8418
Deputy Secretary, Intergovernmental Affairs:
  Martin Mack 518-408-2555
Director, Legislative Affairs:
  James Clancy 518-486-9896

EXECUTIVE DEPARTMENTS AND RELATED AGENCIES

Health Department
Corning Tower
Empire State Plaza
Albany, NY 12237
518-474-7354
Web site: www.nyhealth.gov

Health Facilities Management
Director:
  Val S Gray 518-474-2772/fax: 518-474-0611

  New York State Veterans' Home at Batavia
  220 Richmond Ave, Batavia, NY 14020
  585-345-2000
  Administrator:
    Joanne I Hernick 585-345-2076/fax: 585-345-9030
  Medical Director:
    Bruce Small MD 585-345-2042
  Director, Nursing:
    Barbara Bates 585-345-2000 x2041

  New York State Veterans' Home at Montrose . . . . . . fax: 914-788-6025
  2090 Albany Post Rd, Montrose, NY 10548
  Administrator:
    Nancy Baa-Danso 914-788-6003/fax: 914-788-6100
  Medical Director:
    Wellington Liu MD 914-788-6025

  New York State Veterans' Home at Oxford
  4211 State Highway 220, Oxford, NY 13830-4305
  607-843-3100
  Administrator:
    Vathsala Venugopalan 607-843-3129/fax: 607-843-3199
  Medical Director:
    Philip Dzwonczyk 607-843-3140

  New York State Veterans' Home at St Albans
  178-50 Linden Blvd, Jamaica, NY 11434-1467
  718-990-0300
  Administrator:
    Neville Goldson 718-990-0329
  Medical Director:
    Thomas Bizarro MD 718-990-0328
  Director, Nursing:
    Elaine Boy-Brown 718-990-0316

Labor Department
Building 12, Room 500
State Campus
Albany, NY 12240
518-457-2741 Fax: 518-457-6908
e-mail: nysdol@labor.state.ny.us
Web site: www.labor.state.ny.us

Commissioner:
  M Patricia Smith. 518-457-2746
Executive Deputy Commissioner:
  Mario Musolino 518-457-4318
Deputy Commissioner, Veterans Affairs:
  Ronald Tocci 518-457-1343

Military & Naval Affairs, Division of
330 Old Niskayuna Rd
Latham, NY 12110-2224
518-786-4500 Fax: 518-786-4325
Web site: www.dmna.state.ny.us

Adjutant General:
  Maj Gen Joseph J Taluto 518-786-4502
Deputy Adjutant General:
  Maj Gen Robert A Knauff 518-786-4502
Inspector General, Federal:
  Col James D McDonough Jr 518-786-4679/fax: 518-786-4694
Legal Counsel:
  Robert G Conway, Jr 518-786-4541
Director, Budget & Finance:
  Robert A Martin 518-786-4513
Director, Governmental Affairs:
  Michael Ostrander 518-786-4580
Director, Public Affairs:
  Scott Sandman 518-786-4581/fax: 518-786-4649

Offices and agencies generally appear in alphabetical order, except when specific order is requested by listee.

VETERANS AND MILITARY / New York State

Veterans' Affairs, Division of
5 Empire State Plaza
Ste 2836
Albany, NY 12223-1551
518-474-6114 Fax: 518-473-0379
e-mail: info@veterans.state.ny.us
Web site: www.veterans.state.ny.us

Director:
  George P Basher.................................518-474-6114
Counsel:
  William J Brennan..............................518-474-6114

Bureau of Veterans Education

Albany Office
5 Empire State Plaza, Ste 2836, Albany, NY 12223-1551
Supervisor:
  Craig Farley.....................518-474-5322/fax: 518-474-5583

New York Office
116 W 32nd St, 14th Fl, New York, NY 10001
Chief:
  James Bombard.................................212-564-8414

Counseling & Claims Service
Web site: www.veterans.state.ny.us/ofcs.htm

Eastern Region
VA Regional Ofc, 245 W Houston St, Rm 206, New York, NY 10014
Deputy Director:
  Benjamin Weisbroth..............212-807-3162/fax: 212-807-4021
Senior Counselor:
  Steven Strandberg.......................845-831-2000 x5449
Senior Counselor:
  L Ray Colon...................................212-807-3162

New York State Claims Offices
Buffalo VA Regional Office
  307-06, 111 W Huron St, Buffalo, NY 14202-2638
  Senior Counselor:
    Gerald Grace............................716-857-3330
  Senior Counselor:
    John Rudy..............................716-857-3330
New York City VA Regional Office...............fax: 212-807-4021
  245 W Houston St, Rm 206, New York, NY 10014
  Senior Counselor:
    Christopher Podgus.....................212-807-3162
  Senior Counselor:
    Joanne C Reich.........................212-807-3162

Western Region
Mahoney Office Bldg, 65 Court St, Buffalo, NY 14202-3406
Deputy Director:
  Joseph Vogtli Jr.................716-847-3414/fax: 716-847-3410
Senior Counselor:
  Bernie Dotterweich............................716-847-3414
Senior Counselor:
  Harry Rudy...................................716-847-3414

Public Information, Field Support, Budget, Finance, Personnel, Blind Annuity
Executive Deputy Director:
  Vacant.........................518-474-6784/fax: 518-473-0379
Training Coordinator:
  Chris Stirling................................518-486-3720
Deputy Director:
  Michelle LaRock..............................518-474-6114

Veterans' Service Organizations

Albany Housing Coalition Inc................fax: 518-465-6499
278 Clinton Ave, Albany, NY 12210
Executive Director:
  Lynn Mack...................................518-465-5251
Director, Veterans Svcs:
  Kevin Norfleet...............................518-465-5251

COPIN HOUSE (Homeless Veterans)........fax: 716-283-5712
5622 Buffalo Ave, Niagara Falls, NY 14304
Executive Director:
  Sharon McGrath..............................716-283-5622

Continuum of Care for Homeless Veterans in New York City

30th Street Shelter
400-430 East 30th St, New York, NY 10016
Director:
  Yvonne Ballard..............................212-481-4730

Project TORCH, Veterans Health Care Center
40 Flatbush Ave Ext, 8th Fl, Brooklyn, NY 11201
Program Coordinator:
  Julie Irwin.....................718-439-4345/fax: 718-439-4356

Hicksville Counseling Center, Veterans' Resource Center.................................fax: 516-935-2717
385 West John St, Hicksville, NY 11801
Director, Substance Abuse Program & Veterans Resource Center:
  Geryl Pecora.................................516-935-6858

Saratoga Cnty Rural Preservation Co (Homeless Veterans)
36 Church Ave, Ballston Spa, NY 12020
Executive Director:
  Dottie Nixon....................518-885-0091/fax: 518-885-0998
e-mail: rpc36@aol.com

Suffolk County United Veterans Halfway House Project Inc
PO Box 598, Patchogue, NY 11772
Executive Director:
  John Lynch.....................631-924-8088/fax: 631-924-0160

Veterans House (The).......................fax: 518-465-6499
180 First St, Albany, NY 12210
House Manager:
  John Jacobie................................518-449-8430

Veterans Outreach Center Inc...............fax: 585-546-5234
459 South Ave, Rochester, NY 14620
Fax: 585-546-5234
Web site: www.eflagstore.com
President & Chief Executive Officer:
  Thomas Cray.................................585-546-1081
e-mail: voc.frontiernet.net

Veterans Services Center of the Southern Tier........fax: 607-771-9395
174 Clinton St, Binghamton, NY 13905
Executive Director:
  Patricia Gaven..............................607-771-8387

Veterans' Coalition of the Hudson Valley...fax: 845-471-6113
9 Vassar St, Poughkeepsie, NY 12601
845-471-6113 Fax: 845-471-6113

Offices and agencies generally appear in alphabetical order, except when specific order is requested by listee.

VETERANS AND MILITARY / U.S. Government

Administrator:
  Marilyn Wickman..................................845-471-6113
  e-mail: vetcoal@aol.com

CORPORATIONS, AUTHORITIES AND COMMISSIONS

Brooklyn Navy Yard Development Corporation
63 Flushing Ave, Unit #300
Bldg 292, 3rd Fl
Brooklyn, NY 11205-1054
718-907-5900 Fax: 718-643-9296
Web site: www.brooklynnavyyard.com

Chair:
  Alan H Fishman...................................718-907-5900
President & Chief Executive Officer:
  Andrew H Kimball.................................718-907-5900
Senior Vice President, External Affairs:
  Richard Drucker..................................718-907-5936
  e-mail: rdrucker@brooklynnavyyard.org

NEW YORK STATE LEGISLATURE

See Legislative Branch in Section 1 for additional Standing Committee and Subcommittee information.

Assembly Standing Committees

Veterans Affairs
Chair:
  Felix Ortiz (D)..................................518-455-3821
Ranking Minority Member:
  Greg Ball (R)....................................518-455-5783

Senate Standing Committees

Veterans, Homeland Security & Military Affairs
Chair:
  Vincent L Leibell, III (R).......................518-455-3111
Ranking Minority Member:
  Eric Adams (D)...................................518-455-2431

U.S. Government

EXECUTIVE DEPARTMENTS AND RELATED AGENCIES

US Defense Department
e-mail: www.defenselink.mil

AIR FORCE-National Media Outreach.....fax: 212-784-0149
805 Third Ave, 9th Fl, New York, NY 10022-7513
Director:
  Maj John J Thomas................................212-784-0147
  e-mail: john.thomas@afnews.af.mil
Deputy Director:
  Capt Jason Medina................................212-784-0143
  e-mail: jason.medina@afnews.af.mil

Air National Guard

Francis S Gabreski Airport, 106th Rescue Wing....fax: 631-723-7179
150 Old Riverhead Rd, Westhampton Beach, NY 11978
Commander:
  Col Michael F Canders............................631-723-7400
Public Affairs Officer:
  Major Emily Desrosier............................631-723-7402

Hancock Field, 174th Fighter Wing
6001 E Molloy Rd, Syracuse, NY 13211-7099
315-233-2100
Commander:
  Col Anthony Basile...............315-233-2599/fax: 315-233-2145

Army

Fort Drum....................................fax: 315-772-5165
Bldg P-10000, Rm 203, Fort Drum, NY 13602-5028
Fax: 315-772-5165
Web site: www.drum.army.mil
Commander:
  Maj Benjamin C Freakley..........................315-772-5565

Public Affairs Officer:
  Lt Col Paul Fitzpatrick..........................315-772-5461

Fort Hamilton................................fax: 718-630-4709
Bldg 113, 2nd Flr, Brooklyn, NY 11252-5000
Commander:
  Col Tracy E Nicholson............................718-630-4706

Fort Totten-77th Regional Support Command.....fax: 718-352-5830
Headquarters, Bldg 200, Flushing, NY 11359-1016
Fax: 718-352-5830
Web site: www.usarc.army.mil/77thrsc
Commander:
  Maj Gen William Terpeluk.........................718-352-5077
Public Affairs Officer:
  LTC Virginia Zoller..............................718-352-5072
Community Relations Officer:
  Chet Marcus......................................718-352-5226

Watervliet Arsenal
CO Bldg 10, Watervliet, NY 12189-4000
518-266-5111
Commander:
  Col Donald C Olson...............................518-266-4294
Public Affairs Officer:
  John E Swantek.................518-266-5418/fax: 518-266-5859

Marine Corps

1st Marine Corps District....................fax: 516-228-4201
605 Stewart Ave, Garden City, NY 11530
Commander:
  Col Rickey L Grabowski...........................516-228-5652
Public Affairs Officer:
  Captain Don Caetano..............................516-228-5640

Public Affairs Office........................fax: 212-784-0169
805 Third Ave, 9th Fl, New York, NY 10022-7513
Director:
  Maj David C Andersen.............................212-784-0160

Offices and agencies generally appear in alphabetical order, except when specific order is requested by listee.

VETERANS AND MILITARY / U.S. Government

Public Affairs Chief:
Gy Sgt John Jamison 212-784-0160

Navy

Saratoga Springs Naval Support Unit
19 JF King Dr, Saratoga Springs, NY 12866-9267
Officer-in-Charge & Public Affairs Officer:
LCDR Tonya N Cook 518-886-0200/fax: 518-886-0120

US Department of Veterans Affairs
Web site: www.va.gov

National Cemetery Administration
Web site: www.cem.va.gov

Bath National Cemetery
San Juan Ave, Bath, NY 14810
Director:
Walter Baroody 607-664-4853/fax: 607-664-4761

Calverton National Cemetery
210 Princeton Blvd, Calverton, NY 11933-1031
Director:
Michael G Picerno 631-727-5410 x31/fax: 631-369-4397

Cypress Hills National Cemetery
625 Jamaica Ave, Brooklyn, NY 11208
631-454-4949 or 631-454-4950
Director:
Michael G Picerno. 631-454-4949/fax: 631-694-5422

Gerald B.H. Solomon Saratoga National Cemetery
200 Duell Rd, Schuylerville, NY 12871-1721
Director:
Roseann Santore 518-581-9128/fax: 518-583-6975

Long Island National Cemetery
2040 Wellwood Ave, Farmingdale, NY 11735-1211
631-454-4949
Director:
Michael G Picerno. 631-454-4949/fax: 631-694-5422

Woodlawn National Cemetery
1825 Davis St, Elmira, NY 14901
Director:
Walter Baroody 607-664-4853/fax: 607-664-4761

VA Regional Office of Public Affairs, Field Operations Svc
245 W Houston St, Ste 315B, New York, NY 10014
Regional Director:
Lawrence M Devine 212-807-3429/fax: 212-807-4030
Public Affairs Specialist:
James A Blue 212-807-3429
Public Affairs Specialist:
Leo Marinacci. 212-807-3429

Veterans Benefits Administration

Buffalo Regional Office
Niagara Square Center, 130 South Elmwood Ave, Buffalo, NY 14202
800-827-1000
Regional Director:
Donna Ferrell 716-857-3020/fax: 716-551-3072
Assistant Director:
Thomas D Brownell. 800-827-1000
Veterans Service Center Manager:
James Rogers 800-827-1000
Regional Counsel:
Joseph Moreno. 800-827-1000

Vocational Rehabilitation & Employment Division:
Joseph Senulis 800-827-1000
Chief, Education Division:
Robert Quall. 800-827-1000

New York City Regional Office . . . . fax: 212-807-4024
245 West Houston St, New York, NY 10014
Director:
Patricia Amberg-Blyskal 212-807-3055
Veterans Benefits & Services Officer:
Joseph Collorafi 212-807-3420
Vocational Rehabilitation & Counseling Division:
Bernard Finger 212-807-3030

Veterans Health Admin Integrated Svc Network (VISN)

VA Healthcare Network Upstate New York (VISN2)
113 Holland Ave, Bldg 7, Albany, NY 12208
Web site: www.va.gov/visns/visn02
Acting Network Director:
Michael Finegan 518-626-7317 x67317
Network Communications Manager:
Kathleen Hider 585-463-2642/fax: 585-463-2649

Albany VA Medical Center
113 Holland Ave, Albany, NY 12208
Director:
Mary-Ellen Piche. 518-626-6731
e-mail: mary-ellen.piche@med.va.gov
Public Affairs Officer:
Peter Potter 518-626-5522

Batavia VA Medical Center . . . . fax: 585-344-3305
222 Richmond Ave, Batavia, NY 14020
716-343-7500 Fax: 585-344-3305
Acting Director:
Timothy W Liezert 716-862-8529
Public Affairs Liaison:
Kathleen Martin. 585-344-3330

Bath VA Medical Center
76 Veterans Ave, Bath, NY 14810
Acting Director:
Craig Howard 607-664-4722
Public Affairs Officer:
Carl Haneline. 607-664-4869

Buffalo VA Medical Center . . . . fax: 716-862-8759
3495 Bailey Ave, Buffalo, NY 14215
716-834-9200 Fax: 716-862-8759
Acting Director:
Timothy W Liezert 716-862-8529
Public Affairs Officer:
Evange Conley. 716-862-8751

Canandaigua VA Medical Center
400 Fort Hill Ave, Canandaigua, NY 14424
Director:
Craig Howard 585-393-7208/fax: 585-393-8328
Chief of Staff:
Robert Babcock 585-393-7211
e-mail: robert.babcock2@med.va.gov

Syracuse VA Medical Center & Clinics
800 Irving Ave, Syracuse, NY 13210
Director:
James Cody 315-425-4892
e-mail: james.cody@med.va.gov
Public Affairs Officer:
Gordon Sclar 315-425-2422

VA NY/NJ Veterans Healthcare Network (VISN3)
Bldg 16, 130 W Kingsbridge Rd, Bronx, NY 10468
Web site: www.va.gov/visns/visn03
Network Director:
James J Farsetta. 718-741-4143/fax: 718-741-4141

Offices and agencies generally appear in alphabetical order, except when specific order is requested by listee.

VETERANS AND MILITARY / U.S. Government

Deputy Network Director:
  Gerald Culliton..718-741-4134
Bronx VA Medical Center ....fax: 718-741-4269
  130 W Kingsbridge Rd, Bronx, NY 10468
  Director:
    MaryAnn Musumeci.....................718-584-9000 x6512
  Chief of Staff:
    Eric Langhoff..........................718-584-9000 x6522
Brooklyn Campus of the NY Harbor Healthcare System
  800 Poly Pl, Brooklyn, NY 11209
  718-836-6600
  Director:
    John J Donnellan, Jr..........718-630-3521/fax: 718-630-2840
  Associate Director:
    Veronica J Foy......................................718-630-3524
Castle Point Campus of the VA Hudson Vly Healthcare System..fax: 845-838-5180
  PO Box 100, 100 Rte 9D, Castle Point, NY 12511
  845-831-2000 Fax: 845-838-5180
  Executive Director:
    Michael A Sabo 845-737-4400 x2460
Montrose Campus of the VA Hudson Valley Healthcare System..fax: 914-788-4244
  2094 Albany Post Rd, Rte 9A, PO Box 100, Montrose, NY 10548
  Director:
    Michael A Sabo 914-737-4400 x2400
  Public Affairs:
    Nancy A Winter 914-737-4400 x2255
New York Campus of the NY Harbor Healthcare System ....fax: 212-951-3487
  423 East 23rd St, New York, NY 10010
  212-686-7500 Fax: 212-951-3487
  Executive Chief of Staff:
    Michael S Simberkoff 212-951-3417
  Associate Director:
    Martina A Parauda..........................212-951-3240
Northport VA Medical Center ....fax: 631-754-7933
  79 Middleville Rd, Northport, NY 11768
  Director:
    Robert Schuster 631-261-4400 x2747
  Chief of Staff:
    Edward Mack 631-261-4400 x2737

US Labor Department
Web site: www.dol.gov/vets/

New York State Field Offices
  Albany
    Harriman State Campus, Bldg 12, Rm 518, Albany, NY 12240-0099
    Director:
      Vacant.....................518-435-0831 or 518-457-7465
      fax: 518-435-0833
    Veteran's Program Assistant:
      Joan M Cramer 518-457-7465
    e-mail: cramer.joan@dol.gov
  New York City
    345 Hudson St, Rm 8209, PO Box 668, MS 8C, New York, NY 10014-0668
    Assistant Director:
      Alice F Jones 212-352-6184/fax: 212-352-6185
    e-mail: jones.alice@dol.gov

Assistant Director:
  Daniel A Friedman 212-352-6183
  e-mail: friedman.daniel@dol.gov
Veteran's Program Specialist:
  Timothy D Hays 212-352-6183
  e-mail: hays.timothy@dol.gov

US State Department
Web site: www.state.gov

US Mission to the United Nations
140 East 45th St, New York, NY 10022
US Representative to the United Nations:
  Acting Ambassador Ann Patterson 212-415-4404
Director, Communications, Spokesman:
  Richard Grenell 212-415-4058
Military Staff Committee:
  Col John B O'Dowd..................................212-415-4147

U.S. CONGRESS

See U.S. Congress Chapter for additional Standing Committee and Subcommittee information.

House of Representatives Standing Committees

Armed Services
Chair:
  Ike Skelton (D-MO)..................................202-225-2876
Ranking Minority Member:
  Duncan Hunter (R-CA) 202-225-5672
New York Delegate:
  John M McHugh (R) 202-225-4611
New York Delegate:
  Steve Israel (D)......................................202-225-3335

Veterans' Affairs
Chair:
  Bob Filner (D-CA) 202-225-8045
Ranking Minority Member:
  Steve Buyer (R-IN)..................................202-225-5037

Senate Standing Committees

Armed Services
Chair:
  Carl Levin (D-MI) 202-224-6221
Ranking Minority Member:
  John McCain (R-AZ) 202-224-2235
New York Delegate:
  Hillary Rodham Clinton (D)..........................202-224-4451

Veterans' Affairs
Chair:
  Daniel Akaka (D-HI) 202-224-6361
Ranking Minority Member:
  Larry Craig (R-ID) 202-224-2752

Offices and agencies generally appear in alphabetical order, except when specific order is requested by listee.

VETERANS AND MILITARY / Private Sector

Private Sector

369th Veterans Association Inc
PO Box 91, Lincolnton Station, New York, NY 10037
212-281-3308 Fax: 212-281-6308
e-mail: jamnat@earthlink.net
Web site: www.home.earthlink.net/~natlvets/
Nathaniel James, National President
Assistance & referrals for all veterans

Air Force Association (AFA)
1501 Lee Highway, Arlington, VA 22209-1198
703-247-5800 Fax: 703-247-5853
Web site: www.afa.org
Donald L Peterson, Executive Director
Support & advance the interest & recognition of the US Air Force

Air Force Sergeants Association (AFSA), Division 1
557 Sixth St, Dover, NH 3820
603-742-4844
e-mail: acaldwell557@comcast.net
Web site: www.afsahq.org
Alfred B Caldwell, President Division 1
Protect rights & benefits of enlisted personnel-active, retired, National Guard, reserve & their families

Air Force Women Officers Associated (AFWOA)
PO Box 780155, San Antonio, TX 78278
210-493-8125
e-mail: patriciamurphy@afwoa.com
Web site: www.afwoa.org
Col Patricia M Murphy, USAF Retired, President
Represent interests of active duty, retired & former women officers of the Air Force; preserve the history & promote recognition of the role of military women

Albany Housing Coalition Inc
278 Clinton Ave, Albany, NY 12210
518-465-5251 Fax: 518-465-6499
e-mail: admin@ahcvets.org
Web site: www.ahcvets.org
Bryon Koshgarian, Phd, Director, Veterans Services
Providing a continuum of affordable housing for veterans & their families; rental housing referrals

American Legion, Department of New York
112 State St, Suite 1300, Albany, NY 12207
518-463-2215 Fax: 518-427-8443
e-mail: info@nylegion.org
Web site: www.ny.legion.org
Richard M Pedro, New York State Adjutant
Advocate for veterans; entitlements for wartime veterans, their families & service to the community, children & youth of our nation

American Military Retirees Association Inc
5436 Peru St, Ste 1, Plattsburgh, NY 12901
800-424-2969 or 518-563-9479 Fax: 518-324-5204
e-mail: info@amra1973.org
Web site: www.amra1973.org
John E Campbell, Executive Director
Protecting the benefits of all military retirees & veterans

Army Aviation Association of America (AAAA)
755 Main St, Ste 4D, Monroe, CT 06468-2830
203-268-2450 Fax: 203-268-5870
William R Harris, Executive Director
Advance the cause & recognition of US Army aviation; benefit all personnel, current, retired, families & survivors

Army Aviation Association of America (AAAA), North Country Chapter
Bldg P10420, So Riva Ridge Dr, Fort Drum, NY 13602
315-772-8252 or 315-772-3177 Fax: 315-772-9093
Col Anthony Crutchfield, USA, Chapter President
Advance the cause & recognition of US Army aviation; benefit all Army aviation personnel, current, retired, families & survivors

Army Aviation Association of America (AAAA), Western NY Chapter
3 Glendale Dr, Clifton Park, NY 12065
518-786-4397 Fax: 518-786-4393
e-mail: nysaao@yahoo.com
COL Mike Bobeck, NYARNG, Chapter President
Advance the cause & recognition of US Army aviation; benefit all Army aviation personnel, current, retired, families & survivors

Association of Military Surgeons of the US (AMSUS), NY Chapter
105 Franklin Ave, Malverne, NY 11565-1926
516-542-0025 Fax: 516-593-3114
e-mail: amsusny@aol.com
Col John J Hassett, USAR, President NY Chapter
Improve federal healthcare service; support & represent military & other health care professionals

Association of the US Army (AUSA)
2425 Wilson Blvd, Arlington, VA 22201
703-841-4300 x639 or 800-336-4570 Fax: 703-525-9039
e-mail: wloper@ausa.org
Web site: www.ausa.org
William Loper, Director Government Affairs
Champion the cause & objectives of the US Army by public relations, communications & legislative action

Black Veterans for Social Justice Inc
665 Willoughby Street, Brooklyn, NY 11221
718-852-6004 Fax: 718-852-4805
e-mail: admin@bvsj.org; cfo@bvsj.org
Web site: www.bvsj.org
Job Mashariki, President & Chief Executive Officer
Assist all veterans in obtaining benefits, entitlements, employment & housing

Offices and agencies generally appear in alphabetical order, except when specific order is requested by listee.

VETERANS AND MILITARY / Private Sector

Blinded Veterans Association New York Inc
245 W Houston St, 2nd Fl, Rm 208, New York, NY 10014
212-807-3173 Fax: 212-807-4022
Web site: www.bva.org
Jack Shapiro, Director

Catholic War Veterans of the United States of America
c/o James C Finkel, Sr Adjutant, 346 Broadway, Ste 812, New York, NY 10013
212-962-0988 Fax: 212-894-0517
e-mail: nyscwv@aol.com
Web site: www.nycatholicwarvets.org
George Weihs, State Commander
Veterans & auxiliary of the Roman Catholic faith; assisting all veterans & their families

Commissioned Officers Assn of the US Public Health Svc Inc (COA)
8201 Corporate Dr, Ste 200, Landover, MD 20785
301-731-9080 Fax: 301-731-9084
e-mail: gfarrell@coausphs.org
Web site: www.coausphs.org
Jerry Farrell, Executive Director
Committed to improving the public health of the US; supports corps officers & advocates for their interests through leadership, education & communication

Disabled American Veterans, Department of New York
200 Atlantic Ave, Studio #1, Lynbrook, NY 11563-3597
516-887-7100 Fax: 516-887-7175
e-mail: davny@optonline.net
Web site: www.davny.org
Sidney Siller, Adjutant
Service, support & enhance healthcare & benefits for wartime disabled veterans

Fleet Reserve Association (FRA)
125 North West St, Alexandria, VA 22314
703-683-1400 Fax: 703-549-6610
e-mail: news-fra@fra.org
Web site: www.fra.org
Joseph L Barnes, National Executive Secretary & Chief Lobbyist
Serving the interests of active duty, retired & reserve enlisted members of the US Navy, Marine Corps & Coast Guard

Fleet Reserve Association (FRA), NE Region (NJ, NY, PA)
1118 West Jefferson Street, Philadelphia, PA 19122-3442
215-235-7796 Fax: 215-765-2671
e-mail: charleserainey@post.com
Web site: www.fra.org
Charles Rainey, Regional President
Serving the interests of active duty, retired & reserve enlisted members of the US Navy, Marine Corps & Coast Guard

Gold Star Wives of America Inc
763B Blackberry Lane, Yorktown, NY 10598
914-962-8083
Mary Dwyer, New York Contact
National nonprofit working to advance issues important to military service widows

Gold Star Wives of America Inc
PO Box 361986, Birmingham, AL 35236-1986
205-823-1778 or 888-751-6350 Fax: 205-823-2760
e-mail: info@goldstarwives.org
Web site: www.goldstarwives.org
Jim Ranieri, Office Manager
Support for widows of American Servicemen

Jewish War Veterans of the USA
1811 R St NW, Washington, DC 20009
202-265-6280 Fax: 202-234-5662
e-mail: jwv@jwv.org
Web site: www.jwv.org
Norman Rosenshein, National Commander
Honoring & supporting all Jewish war veterans, their benefits & rights; fight bigotry & discrimination; patriotic voice of American Jewry

Jewish War Veterans of the USA, State of NY
346 Broadway, Rm 817, New York, NY 10013
212-349-6640 Fax: 212-577-2575
e-mail: deptny.jwv@juno.com
Web site: www.jwv.org
Saul Rosenberg, Department Commander
Honoring & supporting Jewish war veterans

Korean War Veterans
54 Lyncrest Drive, Rochester, NY 14616-5238
e-mail: kwvfn@aol.com
Web site: www.kwva.org
Frank Nicalozzo, President
Ensuring that Korean war vets are remembered

Marine Corps League
PO Box 505, White Plains, NY 10602
914-941-2118 Fax: 914-864-7173
e-mail: llc1@mclwestchester.com
Web site: www.mclwestchester.org
Lu Caldara, Commandant
Marine Corps fraternal/veterans association

Marine Corps League (MCL)
PO Box 3070, Merrifield, VA 22116
703-207-9588 or 800-625-1775 Fax: 703-207-0047
e-mail: mcl@mcleague.org
Web site: www.mcleague.org
Michael Blum, Executive Director
Support & promote the interests, history & tradition of the Marine Corps & all Marines

Marine Corps League (MCL), Department of NY
46 Marine Corp Blvd, Staten Island, NY 10301
718-447-2306 Fax: 718-556-0590
Bob Powell, Commandant, Department of NY
Support & promote the interests, history & tradition of the Marine Corps & all Marines

Offices and agencies generally appear in alphabetical order, except when specific order is requested by listee.

VETERANS AND MILITARY / Private Sector

Military Chaplains Association of the USA (MCA)
PO Box 7056, Arlington, VA 22207
703-533-5890
e-mail: chaplains@mca-usa.org
Web site: www.mca-usa-org
David White, Executive Director
Promotes the recognition & interests of military, Civil Air Patrol & VA chaplains; develops & encourages candidates through national institutes, scholarships & outreach

Military Officers Association of America
201 N Washington St, Alexandria, VA 22314-2539
703-549-2311 or 800-234-6622 Fax: 703-838-8173
Web site: www.moaa.org
Col Steve Strobridge, USAF Retired, Director Government Relations
Preserve earned entitlements of members of the uniformed services, their families & survivors; support of strong national defense; scholarship & support to members' families

Military Officers Association of America (MOAA), NYS Council
258 Randwood Dr, Williamsville, NY 14221
716-689-6295 Fax: 716-847-6405
e-mail: patc258@aol.com
Col Patrick Cunningham, USA Retired, President, NYS Council of Chapters
Benefit members of uniformed services, active & retired, family & survivors; promote strong national defense

Military Order of the Purple Heart
Syracuse Veterans Administration Medical, 800 Irving Ave, Room A176, Syracuse, NY 13210-2796
315-425-4685 Fax: 315-472-2356
e-mail: lois.reinhardt-reyes@med.va.gov
Lois Reinhardt-Reyes, National Service Officer
Veterans' benefits & rehabilitation

Military Order of the Purple Heart (MOPH)
5413B Backlick Rd, Springfield, VA 22151
703-642-5360 Fax: 703-642-1841
e-mail: goberh@aol.com
Web site: www.purpleheart.org
Hershel Gober, National Legislative Director
Congressionally chartered organization representing the interests of America's combat-wounded veterans

Montford Point Marine Association
346 Broadway St, New York, NY 10013
212-267-3318 Fax: 212-566-4903
Web site: www.montfordpointmarines.com
James Maillard, Financial Secretary

National Amputation Foundation Inc
40 Church St, Malverne, NY 11565
516-887-3600 Fax: 516-887-3667
e-mail: amps76@aol.com
Web site: www.nationalamputation.org
Paul Bernacchio, President
Programs & services geared to help the amputee; donated medical equipment give-away program. Items must be picked up at the office-for anyone in need.

National Guard Association of the US (NGAUS)
One Massachusetts Ave NW, Washington, DC 20001
202-789-0031 Fax: 202-682-9358
e-mail: ngaus@ngaus.org
Web site: www.ngaus.org
Bill Goss, Director, Legislative Affairs
Promote the interests of the Army National Guard through legislative action;

National Military Family Association (NMFA)
2500 North Van Dorn St, Ste 102, Alexandria, VA 22302-1601
703-931-6632 or 800-260-0218 Fax: 703-931-4600
e-mail: families@nmfa.org
Web site: www.nmfa.org
Joyce Raezer, Director Government Relations
Service to the families of active duty, retirees, reserve & National Guard uniformed personnel

Naval Enlisted Reserve Association (NERA)
6703 Farragut Ave, Falls Church, VA 22042-2189
703-534-1329 or 800-776-9020
e-mail: members@nera.org
Web site: www.nera.org
Stephen R Sandy, Executive Director
Ensuring strong & well-trained Naval, Coast Guard & Marine Corps Reserves; improving reserve equipment, promotion, pay & retirement benefits through legislative action

Naval Reserve Association (NRA)
1619 King St, Alexandria, VA 22314-3647
703-548-5800 or 866-672-4968 Fax: 866-683-3647
e-mail: membership@navy-reserve.org
Web site: www.navy-reserve.org
Ike Puzon, USNR Retired, Director of Legislation
Premier education & professional organization for Naval Reserve officers & the association voice of the Naval Reserve

Navy League of the US (NLUS)
2300 Wilson Blvd, Arlington, VA 22201-3308
703-528-1775 or 800-356-5760 Fax: 703-528-2333
e-mail: jfleet@navyleague.org
Web site: www.navyleague.org
John Fleet, Director for Legislative Affairs
Citizens in support of the Sea Services

Navy League of the US (NLUS), New York Council
c/o US Coast Guard, Battery Park Bldg, 1 South St, Rm 314, New York, NY 10004
212-825-7333 Fax: 212-668-2138
e-mail: nlnyc1902@msn.com
Web site: www.nynavyleague.org
Dr Daniel Thys, President
Represent citizens in support of the Sea Services

New Era Veterans, Inc
1150 Commonwealth Ave, Bronx, NY 10472
718-904-7036 Fax: 718-904-7024
e-mail: neweravets@verizon.net
Web site: www.neweraveterans.org
John M Laguna, Chief Executive Officer
Housing and services for homeless veterans.

Offices and agencies generally appear in alphabetical order, except when specific order is requested by listee.

367

VETERANS AND MILITARY / Private Sector

New York State Air Force Association
PO Box 539, Merrick, NY 11566-0539
516-623-5714
e-mail: brave3@aaahawk.com
Web site: www.nysafa.org
Robert Braverman, Vice President Government Relations
Support & advance the interest & recognition of the US Air Force

North Country Vietnam Veterans Association, Post 1
PO Box 1161, 27 Town Line Rd, Plattsburgh, NY 12901
518-563-3426
e-mail: kenhynes@charter.net; secretary@ncvva.org
Web site: www.ncvva.org
Ken Hynes, Contact
Peer counseling & referral

Reserve Officers Association (ROA)
One Constitution Ave, NE, Washington, DC 20002
202-479-2200 or 800-809-9448 Fax: 202-547-1641
Web site: www.roa.org
Susan Lukas, Legislative Director
Advance the cause of reserve officers through legislative action; promote the interests & recognition of ROTC & military academy students

Reserve Officers Association (ROA), Department of NY
3 Wildwood Rd, Congers, NY 10920
845-638-5215 Fax: 845-638-5035
e-mail: robert.j.winzinger@us.army.mil
Brig Gen Robert J Winzinger, AUS Retired President
Advance the cause of reserve officers of the US Armed Forces; promote the interests & recognition of ROTC & military academy students

United Spinal Association
75-20 Astoria Blvd, Jackson Heights, NY 11370
718-803-3782 Fax: 718-803-0414
e-mail: info@unitedspinal.org
Web site: www.unitedspinal.org
Linda Gutmann, Advocacy
Managed & long-term care, disability assistance & benefits, advocacy & legislation

Veterans of Foreign Wars
1044 Broadway, Albany, NY 12204
518-463-7427 Fax: 518-426-8904
Web site: www.vfwny.com
Art Koch III, State Adjutant

Veterans of Foreign Wars (VFW)
200 Maryland Ave, NE, Washington, DC 20002
202-543-2239 Fax: 202-543-0961
e-mail: dcullinan@vfw.org
Web site: www.vfw.org
Dennis Cullinan, Director National Legislative Affairs
Legislative action, community service & volunteerism in support of the nation's veterans, their families & survivors

Veterans of Foreign Wars Auxiliary
1044 Broadway, Albany, NY 12204
518-462-2668 Fax: 518-427-1994
e-mail: nylavfw@hotmail.com
Marna Szewczyk, Treasurer
Rights & benefits of veterans

Veterans' Widows International Network Inc (VWIN), New York
3657 E South Laredo, Aurora, CO 80013
303-693-4745
e-mail: vwin95@aol.com
Web site: www.vetsurvivors.com
Outreach to American veterans' survivors; assist with obtaining benefits; provide local contacts & support

Vietnam Veterans of America, NYS Council
8 Queen Dian Lane, Queensbury, NY 12804
518-293-7801
e-mail: nedvva@adelphia.net
Ned Poope, President

Women Marines Association
59 Sawyer Ave, Dorchester, MA 02125-2040
617-265-1572
e-mail: sgtkwm@aol.com
Web site: www.womenmarines.org
Catherine Carpenter, Area 1 Director

Women's Army Corps Veterans Association - Empire Chapter
121-16 Ocean Promenade, Unit 3H, Rockaway Park, NY 11694
718-634-0353
e-mail: adelewac@aol.com
Adele Brenner, President, WAC Chapter #89

Offices and agencies generally appear in alphabetical order, except when specific order is requested by listee.

Section 3:
STATE & LOCAL GOVERNMENT PUBLIC INFORMATION

PUBLIC INFORMATION OFFICES

This chapter includes state public information contacts with telephone and fax numbers as well as e-mail and Web site addresses, if available. For additional information, please refer to the related policy area or the indexes.

New York State

GOVERNOR'S OFFICE

Governor's Office
Web site: www.ny.gov/governor

Director, Communications:
  Darren Dopp 518-474-8418
Press Secretary:
  Christine Anderson 518-474-8418
Press Secretary:
  Paul Larrabee 518-474-8418
Press Secretary:
  Mark Violette 518-474-8418
Director, Executive Chamber Operations:
  Peter Drago 518-474-4727
Director, Correspondence:
  Tricia Curley 518-474-3612

New York City Office
NYC Press Secretary:
  Christine Anderson 212-681-4640/fax: 212-681-4608

New York State Office of Federal Affairs
Director:
  Derek Douglas 202-434-7100

Lieutenant Governor's Office
Chief of Staff:
  Charles O'Bryne 518-474-4623/fax: 212-681-4533
Director, Communications & Intergovernmental Affairs:
  Richard Schwabacher 518-474-4623

EXECUTIVE & ADMINISTRATIVE DEPARTMENTS & AGENCIES

Aging, Office for the
Web site: www.aging.state.ny.us

Public Information Officer:
  Reza Mizbani 518-474-7181/fax: 518-473-6565

Agriculture & Markets Department
Web site: www.agmkt.state.ny.us

Public Information Officer:
  Jessica Chittenden 518-457-3136/fax: 518-457-3087
  e-mail: jessica.chittenden@agmkt.state.ny.us

Alcoholic Beverage Control, Division of (State Liquor Authority)
Web site: www.abc.state.ny.us

Director, Communications:
  William Crowley 518-486-4767/fax: 518-402-4015
  e-mail: pressoffice@abc.state.ny.us

Alcoholism & Substance Abuse Services, Office of
Web site: www.oasas.state.ny.us

Director, Communications:
  Jennifer Farrell 518-485-1768
  e-mail: jenniferfarrell@oasas.state.ny.us
Public Information Officer:
  Joseph Morrissey 518-485-1768
  e-mail: josephmorrissey@oasas.state.ny.us

Banking Department
Web site: www.banking.state.ny.us

Press Secretary, Communications & Media Relations:
  Vacant 212-709-1691
Director, Communications:
  James Fuchs 212-709-1690
  e-mail: james.fuchs@banking.state.ny.us

Budget, Division of the
Web site: www.budget.state.ny.us

Director, Communications:
  Jeffrey Gordon 518-473-3885/fax: 518-474-9041

CIO Office & Office for Technology
Web site: www.cio.state.ny.us

CIO Office
Web site: www.cio.state.ny.us
Chief Information Officer:
  Melodie Mayberry-Stewart, PhD 518-408-2140/fax: 518-402-2976
  e-mail: cio@cio.state.ny.us

Office for Technology
Web site: www.oft.state.ny.us
Acting Director:
  Melodie Mayberry-Stewart, PhD 518-473-9450/fax: 518-402-2976
  e-mail: oft@oft.state.ny.us

Offices and agencies generally appear in alphabetical order, except when specific order is requested by listee.

PUBLIC INFORMATION OFFICES / New York State

Children & Family Services, Office of
Web site: www.ocfs.state.ny.us

Council on Children & Families
Web site: www.ccf.state.ny.us
Assistant Commissioner, Public Affairs:
 Sandra A Brown 518-402-3130/fax: 518-486-7550

Civil Service Department
Web site: www.cs.state.ny.us

Director, Public Information:
 Erin Barlow 518-457-9375/fax: 518-457-6654
 e-mail: erin.barlow@cs.state.ny.us

Consumer Protection Board
Web site: www.nyconsumer.gov

Director, Marketing & Public Relations:
 Jon Sorensen 518-473-9472/fax: 518-474-2986

Correctional Services Department
Web site: www.docs.state.ny.us

Public Information Officer:
 Linda Foglia...................... 518-457-8182/fax: 518-457-7070
 e-mail: lmfoglia@docs.state.ny.us

Council on the Arts
Web site: www.nysca.org

Director, Information Technology:
 Lenn Ditman 212-627-5545/fax: 212-620-5911
 e-mail: lditman@nysca.org

Crime Victims Board
Web site: www.cvb.state.ny.us

General Counsel:
 John Watson 518-457-8066/fax: 518-457-8658

Criminal Justice Services, Division of
Web site: www.criminaljustice.state.ny.us

Public Information Officer:
 John Caher....................... 518-457-8828/fax: 518-485-7715

Developmental Disabilities Planning Council
Web site: www.ddpc.state.ny.us

Public Information Officer:
 Thomas F Lee 518-486-7505/fax: 518-402-3505
 e-mail: tlee@ddpc.state.ny.us

Education Department
Web site: www.nysed.gov

Director, Communications:
 Alan Ray 518-474-1201/fax: 518-473-2977
 e-mail: aray@mail.nysed.gov

Secretary to the Board of Regents:
 David Johnson 518-474-5889
 e-mail: djohnson@mail.nysed.gov

State Library
Web site: www.nysl.nysed.gov
Assistant Commissioner & State Librarian:
 Janet Welch 518-474-5930
 e-mail: jwelch@mail.nysed.gov
Public Information Officer:
 Valerie Chevrette................... 518-474-5961/fax: 518-486-2152

Elections, State Board of
Web site: www.elections.state.ny.us

Director, Public Information:
 Lee Daghlian 518-474-1953/fax: 518-473-8315
 e-mail: ldaghlian@elections.state.ny.us

Emergency Management Office, NYS (SEMO)
Web site: www.semo.state.ny.us

Asst Director, Community Affairs:
 Dennis J Michalski............................... 518-292-2310
Public Information Officer:
 Donald L Mauer 518-292-2312/fax: 518-457-4923
 e-mail: donald.maurer@semo.state.ny.us

Empire State Development Corporation
Web site: www.empire.state.ny.us

Director, Communications:
 A J Carter 212-803-3740

Employee Relations, Governor's Office of
Web site: www.goer.state.ny.us

Management/Confidential Affairs:
 Craig Dickinson.................... 518-473-3130/fax: 518-473-6795

Environmental Conservation Department
Web site: www.dec.ny.gov

Assistant Commissioner, Press Operations:
 Maureen Wren..................... 518-402-8000/fax: 518-402-9016
Director, Public Affairs & Education Division:
 Laurel Remus..................... 518-402-8049/fax: 518-402-8050

Freshwater Wetlands Appeals Board
Web site: www.dec.state.ny.us/website/fwab/

Counsel:
 Michele M Stefanucci 518-402-0566/fax: 518-402-0588

General Services, Office of
Web site: www.ogs.state.ny.us

Assistant Commissioner, Public Affairs:
 Brad Maione 518-474-5987/fax: 518-474-3187
 e-mail: brad.maione@ogs.state.ny.us

Offices and agencies generally appear in alphabetical order, except when specific order is requested by listee.

PUBLIC INFORMATION OFFICES / New York State

Health Department
Web site: www.nyhealth.gov

Director, Public Affairs:
Claudia Hutton.................................518-474-7354 x1

Housing & Community Renewal, NYS Division of
Web site: www.dhcr.state.ny.us

Director, Communications:
James Plastiras.....................518-473-2526/fax: 518-474-5752

Hudson River Valley Greenway
Web site: www.hudsongreenway.state.ny.us

Executive Director, Communities Council:
Mary Mangione...................518-473-3835/fax: 518-473-4518
Executive Director, Greenway Conservancy:
Mary Mangione...................518-473-3835/fax: 518-473-4518

Human Rights, State Division of
Web site: www.dhr.state.ny.us

Deputy Commissioner, External Relations:
Thomas D Shanahan...............718-741-3223/fax: 718-741-3214

Inspector General (NYS), Office of the
Web site: www.ig.state.ny.us

Director, Public Information:
Stephen Del Giacco................518-474-1010/fax: 518-486-3745
e-mail: steve.delgiacco@ig.state.ny.us

Insurance Department
Web site: www.ins.state.ny.us

Director, Communications:
David Neustadt.....................212-480-5262/fax: 212-480-6077
e-mail: public-affairs@ins.state.ny.us

Insurance Fund (NYS)
Web site: www.nysif.com

Public Information Officer:
Robert Lawson.....................518-437-3504/fax: 518-437-1849

Labor Department
Web site: www.labor.state.ny.us

Deputy Commissioner, Administration & CFO:
Vacant.........................518-457-3905/fax: 518-485-6297
Director, Communications:
Leo Rosales......................518-457-5519/fax: 518-485-1126

Law Department
Web site: www.oag.state.ny.us

Director, Public Information & Correspondence:
Peter A Drago....................518-474-7330/fax: 518-402-2472

Director, Communications:
Darren Dopp.......................212-416-8060/fax: 212-416-6005

APPEALS & OPINIONS DIVISION Law Library
Chief, Library Services:
Sarah Browne.....................518-474-3840/fax: 518-402-2271
Senior Librarian, New York City Office:
Franette Sheinwald................212-416-8012/fax: 212-416-6130

Lottery, Division of
Web site: www.nylottery.org

Director, Communications:
Vacant........................518-388-3415/fax: 518-388-3423
Chief Informaiton Officer:
Ray Sestak.......................................518-388-3441

Mental Health, Office of
Web site: www.omh.state.ny.us

Deputy Commissioner, Public Affairs & Planning:
Keith E Simons...................518-473-7612/fax: 518-473-4690
Acting Director, Public Affairs:
Jill Daniels......................518-474-6540/fax: 518-473-3456

Mental Retardation & Developmental Disabilities, Office of
Web site: www.omr.state.ny.us

Director, Public Affairs:
Deborah Sturm Rausch.............518-474-6601/fax: 518-474-1335

Military & Naval Affairs, Division of
Web site: www.dmna.state.ny.us

Director, Public Affairs:
Scott Sandman....................518-786-4581/fax: 518-786-4649
e-mail: scott.sandman1@us.army.mil

Motor Vehicles Department
Web site: www.nysdmv.com

Deputy Director, Communications:
Ken Brown........................518-473-7000/fax: 518-473-1930

NYS Commission on Quality of Care & Advocacy for Persons with Disabilities
Web site: www.cqcapd.state.ny.us; www.oapwd.org

Deputy Advocate, Counsel & Public Information Officer:
Gary Masline.....................................518-388-1270
e-mail: oapwdinfo@oapwd.org

NYS Foundation for Science, Technology & Innovation
Web site: www.nystar.state.ny.us

Director, Communications:
Jannette Rondo...................518-292-5700/fax: 518-292-5798

Offices and agencies generally appear in alphabetical order, except when specific order is requested by listee.

PUBLIC INFORMATION OFFICES / New York State

Parks, Recreation & Historic Preservation, NYS Office of
Web site: www.nysparks.state.ny.us

Director, Communication:
  Eileen Larrabee 518-486-1868/fax: 518-486-2924

Parole, Division of
Web site: www.parole.state.ny.us

Public Information Officer:
  Mark Johnson 518-486-4631/fax: 518-473-6037

Prevention of Domestic Violence, Office for the
Web site: www.opdv.state.ny.us

Public Information Officer:
  Suzanne Cecala 518-457-5744/fax: 518-457-5810
  e-mail: suzanne.cecala@opdv.state.ny.us

Probation & Correctional Alternatives, Division of
Web site: www.dpca.state.ny.us

Administrative Officer:
  Howard Bancroft 518-485-5145/fax: 518-485-5140

Public Employment Relations Board
Web site: www.perb.state.ny.us

Executive Director:
  James R Edgar 518-457-2676/fax: 518-457-2664

Public Service Commission
Web site: www.dps.state.ny.us

Director, Telecommunications:
  Robert H Mayer 518-474-1668/fax: 518-474-5616
Director, Public Affairs:
  James Denn 518-474-7080/fax: 518-473-2838
  e-mail: james_denn@dps.state.ny.us

Racing & Wagering Board
Web site: www.racing.state.ny.us

Public Information Officer:
  Dan Toomey 518-395-5400

Real Property Services, Office of
Web site: www.orps.state.ny.us

Director, Public Information:
  Geoffrey T Gloak 518-486-5446/fax: 518-474-9276
  e-mail: geoffrey.gloak@orps.state.ny.us

Regulatory Reform, Governor's Office of
Web site: www.gorr.state.ny.us

Public Information Officer:
  Tim Beadnell 518-486-3292/fax: 518-473-9342
  e-mail: tbeadnell@gorr.state.ny.us

Small Cities, Office for
Web site: www.nysmallcities.com

Director, Communications:
  Joseph Picchi 518-474-2057/fax: 518-474-5247

State Comptroller, Office of the
Web site: www.osc.state.ny.us

Director, Communications:
  Daniel Weiller 518-474-4015/fax: 518-473-8940
Press Secretary:
  Jeffrey Gordon 518-474-4015/fax: 518-473-8940
  e-mail: jgordon@osc.state.ny.us

State Department
Web site: www.dos.state.ny.us

Assistant Secretary of State, Communications:
  Laurence Sombke 518-474-4752/fax: 518-474-4597
  e-mail: info@dos.state.ny.us

State Police, Division of
Web site: www.troopers.state.ny.us

Director & Technical Lieutenant, Public Information:
  Glenn R Miner 518-457-2180/fax: 518-485-7818
  e-mail: piooffice@troopers.state.ny.us
Crime Prevention Coordinator:
  Sgt Kern Swoboda 518-457-2180/fax: 518-485-7818

Tax Appeals, Division of
Web site: www.nysdta.org

Secretary to the Tribunal:
  Jean A McDonnell 518-266-3036

Taxation & Finance Department
Web site: www.tax.state.ny.us

Director, Public Information:
  Thomas Bergin 518-457-4242/fax: 518-457-2486

Temporary & Disability Assistance, Office of
Web site: www.otda.state.ny.us

Director, Public Information:
  Michael Hayes 518-474-9516/fax: 518-486-6935

Transportation Department
Web site: www.nysdot.gov

Director, Public Affairs:
  Jennifer Post 518-457-6400/fax: 518-457-6506
  e-mail: jpost@dot.state.ny.us

Veterans' Affairs, Division of
Web site: www.veterans.state.ny.us

Executive Deputy Director, Public Information:
  Vacant 518-474-6784/fax: 518-473-0379

Offices and agencies generally appear in alphabetical order, except when specific order is requested by listee.

PUBLIC INFORMATION OFFICES / New York State

Welfare Inspector General, Office of NYS
Chief Investigator:
  Joseph R Bucci 212-417-2026/fax: 212-417-5849

Workers' Compensation Board
Web site: www.wcb.state.ny.us

Director, Public Information:
  Vacant 518-474-6670/fax: 518-473-1415

JUDICIAL SYSTEM AND RELATED AGENCIES

Unified Court System
Web site: www.nycourts.gov

Director, Public Affairs:
  Greg Murray 212-428-2116/fax: 212-428-2117
Director, Communications:
  David Bookstaver 212-428-2500/fax: 212-428-2507
Chief Law Librarian:
  Ellen Robinson 518-238-4373/fax: 518-238-2894

LEGISLATIVE BRANCH

Assembly
Press Secretary to the Speaker:
  Charles Carrier 518-455-3888/fax: 518-455-3858
Director, Minority Communications:
  Phil Olivia 518-455-3756/fax: 518-455-3750
Assembly Public Information Officer:
  Sharon Walsh 518-455-4218/fax: 518-455-5175
Director, Assembly Communication & Information Services:
  John Longo 518-455-5767/fax: 518-455-4963

Legislative Library
Legislative Librarian:
  Ellen Breslin 518-455-2468/fax: 518-426-6901
Legislative Librarian:
  James Giliberto 518-455-2468
Law Librarian:
  Kate Balassie 518-455-2468
Law Librarian:
  Stephen Gersztoff 518-455-2468

Senate
Director, Majority Communications:
  John E McArdle 518-455-2264/fax: 518-455-2260
Majority Press Secretary:
  Kris Thompson 518-455-3191/fax: 518-455-2448
Director, Minority Communications:
  Curtis Taylor 518-455-2415/fax: 518-426-6933
Minority Press Secretary:
  James Plastiras 518-455-2415/fax: 518-426-6955
Director, Student Programs Office:
  Krista Ketterer 518-455-2611/fax: 518-432-5470

CORPORATIONS, AUTHORITIES AND COMMISSIONS

Adirondack Park Agency
Web site: www.apa.state.ny.us

Public Relations:
  Keith McKeever 518-891-4050/fax: 518-891-3938

Agriculture & NYS Horse Breeding Development Fund
Web site: www.nysirestakes.com

Executive Director:
  Peter Goold 518-436-8713/fax: 518-426-1490

Albany County Airport Authority
Web site: www.albanyairport.com

Director, Public Affairs:
  Doug Myers 518-242-2222 x1/fax: 518-242-2641
  e-mail: info@albanyairport.com

Albany Port District Commission
Web site: www.portofalbany.com

General Manager:
  Frank W Keane 518-463-8763/fax: 518-463-8767
  e-mail: portofalbany@portofalbany.com

Atlantic States Marine Fisheries Commission
Web site: www.asmfc.org

Public Affairs & Resource Specialist:
  Tina Berger 202-289-6400/fax: 202-289-6051
  e-mail: tberger@asmfc.org

Battery Park City Authority (Hugh L Carey)
Web site: www.batteryparkcity.org

Press Liaison:
  Leticia Remauro 212-417-2276/fax: 212-417-2279
  e-mail: remaurol@pbcauthor.org

Brooklyn Navy Yard Development Corporation
Web site: www.brooklynnavyyard.org

Senior Vice President, External Affairs:
  Richard Drucker 718-907-5936/fax: 718-643-9296
  e-mail: rdrucker@brooklynnavyyard.org

Buffalo & Fort Erie Public Bridge Authority (Peace Bridge Authority)
Web site: www.peacebridge.com

General Manager:
  Ron Rienas 716-884-6744/fax: 716-884-2089

Capital Defender Office
Web site: www.nycdo.org

Offices and agencies generally appear in alphabetical order, except when specific order is requested by listee.

PUBLIC INFORMATION OFFICES / New York State

First Deputy Capital Defender, New York City Office:
  Susan Salomon 212-608-3352 x206/fax: 212-608-4558

Capital District Regional Off-Track Betting Corporation
Web site: www.capitalotb.com

Secretary:
  Willis Vermilyea 518-482-5615/fax: 518-370-5460

Capital District Regional Planning Commission
e-mail: cdrpc@cdrpc.org
Web site: www.cdrpc.org

Executive Director:
  Rocco Ferraro 518-453-0850/fax: 518-453-0856
  e-mail: cdrpc@cdrpc.org

Capital District Transportation Authority
Web site: www.cdta.org

Deputy Executive Director, Business Development:
  Carm Basile 518-437-8300/fax: 518-437-8318

Catskill Off-Track Betting Corporation
Web site: www.interbets.com

President & Chief Executive Officer:
  Donald J Groth 845-362-0400/fax: 845-362-0419
  e-mail: otb@interbets.com

Central New York Regional Market Authority
Executive Director:
  Benjamin Vitale 315-422-8647/fax: 315-442-6897
  e-mail: cnyrma@aol.com

Central New York Regional Transportation Authority
Web site: www.centro.org

Executive Director:
  Frank Kobliski 315-442-3360/fax: 315-422-3337
  e-mail: fkobliski@centro.org

Central Pine Barrens Joint Planning & Policy Commission
Web site: www.pb.state.ny.us

Executive Director:
  Ray Corwin 631-224-2604/fax: 631-224-7653

City University Construction Fund
Administrative Officer:
  Denise Phillips 212-541-0190/fax: 212-541-1014
  e-mail: denise.phillips@mail.cuny.edu

Delaware River Basin Commission
Web site: www.drbc.net

Communications Manager:
  Clarke Rupert 609-883-9500 x260/fax: 609-883-9522
  e-mail: clarke.rupert@drbc.state.nj.us

Development Authority of the North Country
Web site: www.danc.org

Executive Director:
  Robert S Juravich 315-785-2593/fax: 315-785-2591
  e-mail: juravich@danc.org

Empire State Development Corporation
Web site: www.empire.state.ny.us

Director, Communications:
  A J Carter 212-803-3740

Great Lakes Commission
Web site: www.glc.org

Program Manager, Communications & Internet Technology:
  Christine Manninen 734-971-9135/fax: 734-971-9150
  e-mail: manninen@glc.org

Hudson River-Black River Regulating District
Web site: www.hrbrrd.com

Executive Director:
  Glenn A LaFave 518-465-3491/fax: 518-432-2485
  e-mail: hrao@hrbrrd.com

Interest on Lawyer Account (IOLA) Fund of the State of NY
Web site: www.iola.org

Executive Director:
  Lorna Blake 646-865-1541/fax: 646-865-1545
  e-mail: lblake@iola.org

Interstate Environmental Commission
Web site: www.iec-nynjct.org

Executive Director & Chief Engineer:
  Howard Golub 212-582-0380/fax: 212-581-5719
  e-mail: iecmail@iec-nynjct.org

Interstate Oil & Gas Compact Commission
Web site: www.iogcc.state.ok.us

Executive Director:
  Christine Hansen 405-525-3556/fax: 405-525-3592
  e-mail: iogcc@iogcc.state.ok.us

Lake George Park Commission
Web site: www.lgpc.state.ny.us

Executive Director:
  Michael P White 518-668-9347/fax: 518-668-5001
  e-mail: info@lgpc.state.ny.us

Offices and agencies generally appear in alphabetical order, except when specific order is requested by listee.

PUBLIC INFORMATION OFFICES / New York State

Lawyers' Fund for Client Protection
Web site: www.nylawfund.org

Executive Director & Counsel:
Timothy O'Sullivan 518-434-1935/fax: 518-434-5641
e-mail: info@nylawfund.org

Legislative Bill Drafting Commission
Counsel:
Jamie-Lynne Elacqua 518-455-7538/fax: 518-455-7598
e-mail: elacqua@lbdc.state.ny.us

Long Island Power Authority
Web site: www.lipower.org

Vice President, Communications:
Bert Cunningham 516-719-9838/fax: 516-222-9137
e-mail: bcunningham@lipower.org

MTA (Metropolitan Transportation Authority)
Web site: www.mta.info

Deputy Executive Director, Corporate & Community Affairs:
Christopher Boylan 212-878-7160/fax: 212-878-7030
Press Secretary:
Jeremy Soffin 212-878-7145/fax: 212-878-7030

MTA Bridges & Tunnels
Web site: www.mta.info/bandt

Director, Public Affairs:
Frank Pascual 646-252-7416/fax: 646-252-7408

MTA Long Island Bus
Web site: www.mta.info/libus

General Counsel & VP, Legal/Human Resources:
Cheryl Hartell 516-542-0100 x4429/fax: 516-542-1428

MTA Bus Company
Web site: www.mta.info/busco

Media Relations:
Jeremy Soffin 212-878-7440/fax: 212-878-7030

MTA Capital Construction
Web site: www.mta.info/capconstr

Chief Financial Officer:
Anthony D'Amico 646-252-4200

MTA Long Island Rail Road
Web site: www.mta.info/lirr

Acting Vice President, Market Development & Public Affairs:
Susan McGowan 718-558-7301/fax: 718-558-8212

MTA Metro-North Railroad
Web site: www.mta.info/mnr

Chief of Staff & Director, Corporate Communications:
Donna Evans 212-340-2766/fax: 212-340-3460
Senior Director, Customer Service:
Thomas Tendy 212-672-1251

MTA New York City Transit
Web site: www.mta.info/nyct

Vice President, Corporate Communications:
Paul Fleuranges 646-252-5873/fax: 646-252-5845

MTA Office of the Inspector General
Web site: www.mtaig.state.ny.us

Inspector General:
Barry L Kluger 212-878-0007/fax: 212-878-0003

Municipal Assistance Corporation for the City of New York
Executive Director:
Nancy H Henze 212-840-8255/fax: 212-840-8570
e-mail: macnyc@earthlink.net

NYS Commission on Quality of Care & Advocacy for Persons with Disabilities
Web site: www.cqcapd.state.ny.us

Press Officer:
Gary W Masline 518-388-1270/fax: 518-388-1275

Nassau Regional Off-Track Betting Corporation
Web site: www.nassauotb.com

Director, Public Affairs:
Joseph Galante 516-572-2800 x152/fax: 516-572-2840

New England Interstate Water Pollution Control Commission
Web site: www.neiwpcc.org

Deputy Director:
Susan Sullivan 978-323-7929/fax: 978-323-7919
e-mail: mail@neiwpcc.org
Commissioner, New York State:
Denise M Sheehan 518-485-8940

New York City Housing Development Corporation
e-mail: info@nychdc.com
Web site: www.nychdc.org

Director, Communications:
Aaron Donovan 212-227-9496/fax: 212-227-8580
e-mail: info@nychdc.com

New York City Off-Track Betting Corporation
Web site: www.nycotb.com

Senior VP, Marketing, Media & Communications:
Ron Ceisler 212-704-5152/fax: 212-704-5141

Offices and agencies generally appear in alphabetical order, except when specific order is requested by listee.

PUBLIC INFORMATION OFFICES / New York State

New York City School Construction Authority
Web site: schools.nyc.gov/Offices/SCA

Senior Director, Business Development:
  Michael Garner....................................718-472-8048

New York Convention Center Operating Corporation
Web site: www.javitscenter.com

General Manager:
  Anthony Bracco....................212-216-2217/fax: 212-216-2588
  e-mail: moreinfo@javitscenter.com

New York Metropolitan Transportation Council
Web site: www.nymtc.org

Public Information Officer:
  Carol Wilkinson....................212-383-7241/fax: 212-383-2418

New York Power Authority
Web site: www.nypa.gov

Director, Media Relations:
  Michael Saltzman..................914-390-8181/fax: 914-390-8190

New York State Assn of Fire Districts
Web site: www.firedistnys.com

Counsel:
  William N Young....................800-349-2904 or 518-456-6767
  fax: 518-869-5142
  e-mail: byoung@wyfklaw.com

New York State Athletic Commission
Web site: www.dos.state.ny.us/athletic.html

Chair:
  Ron Scott Stevens...................212-417-5700/fax: 212-417-4987
  e-mail: athletic@dos.state.ny.us

New York State Board of Law Examiners
Web site: www.nybarexam.org

Executive Director:
  John J McAlary....................518-452-8700/fax: 518-452-5729

New York State Bridge Authority
Web site: www.nysba.state.ny.us

Public Information Officer, Public Relations & Planning:
  John R Bellucci....................845-691-5953/fax: 845-691-3636
  e-mail: jbellucci@nysba.state.ny.us

New York State Commission of Correction
Web site: www.scoc.state.ny.us

Director, Human Resource Management:
  Alyce Ashe......................518-457-6110/fax: 518-485-2467
  e-mail: infoscoc@scoc.state.ny.us

New York State Commission on Judicial Nomination

Senior Counsel:
  Stuart A Summit...................212-977-9700/fax: 212-262-5152
  e-mail: ssummit@phillipsnizer.com

New York State Commission on the Restoration of the Capitol
Executive Director:
  Andrea J Lazarski..................518-473-0341/fax: 518-486-5720
  e-mail: andrea.lazarski@ogs.state.ny.us

New York State Disaster Preparedness Commission
Web site: www.semo.state.ny.us/dpc/

Chairman:
  John R Gibb..518-292-2301

New York State Dormitory Authority
Web site: www.dasny.org

Director, Communications & Marketing:
  Paul Burgdorf....................518-257-3380/fax: 518-257-3387
  e-mail: pburgdor@dasny.org

New York State Energy Research & Development Authority
Web site: www.nyserda.org

Director, Communications (Acting):
  Colleen Q Ryan............518-862-1090 x3359/fax: 518-464-8249
  e-mail: cqr@nyserda.org

New York State Environmental Facilities Corp
Web site: www.nysefc.org

Director, Corporate Communications:
  Susan Mayer......................518-402-6957/fax: 518-486-9323

New York State Ethics Commission
Web site: www.dos.state.ny.us/ethc/ethics.html

Public Information Officer:
  Walter C Ayres...................518-474-4418/fax: 518-474-8322
  e-mail: wayres@dos.state.ny.us

New York State Financial Control Board
Web site: www.fcb.state.ny.us

Acting Executive Director:
  Jeffrey Sommer....................212-417-5066/fax: 212-417-5055

New York State Higher Education Services Corp (NYSHESC)
Web site: www.hesc.org

Senior Vice President, Communications:
  Ronald Kermani....................518-473-1264/fax: 518-474-2839
  e-mail: rkermani@hesc.org

Offices and agencies generally appear in alphabetical order, except when specific order is requested by listee.

PUBLIC INFORMATION OFFICES / New York State

New York State Housing Finance Agency (HFA)
Web site: www.nyhomes.org

Vice President, Policy & Planning:
  Tracy A Oats 212-688-4000 x678/fax: 212-872-0678

New York State Judicial Conduct Commission
Web site: www.scjc.state.ny.us

Administrator & Counsel:
  Robert H Tembeckjian 212-809-0566
  e-mail: scjc@scjc.state.ny.us

New York State Law Reporting Bureau
Web site: www.courts.state.ny.us/reporter

State Reporter:
  Gary D Spivey 518-474-8211
Deputy State Reporter:
  Charles A Ashe 518-474-8211/fax: 518-463-6869
  e-mail: Reporter@courts.state.ny.us

New York State Law Revision Commission
Web site: www.lawrevision.state.ny.us

Executive Director:
  Rose Mary Bailly 518-472-5858/fax: 518-445-2303

New York State Liquor Authority
Web site: www.abc.state.ny.us

Public Information Officer, NYC:
  Kimberly Morella 212-961-8331
Director, Communications:
  William Crowley 518-486-4767
  e-mail: pressoffice@abc.state.ny.us

New York State Mortgage Loan Enforcement & Administration Corporation
Web site: www.empire.state.ny.us

Senior Deputy & Director, Communications:
  Vacant 212-803-3700/fax: 212-803-3775

New York State Olympic Regional Development Authority
Web site: www.orda.org

Director, Communications:
  Sandy Caligiore 518-523-1655 x213/fax: 518-523-9275
  e-mail: sandyc@orda.org

New York State Teachers' Retirement System
Web site: www.nystrs.org

Manager, Public Information:
  John Cardillo 518-447-4743/fax: 518-447-2695

New York State Temporary Commission of Investigation
Web site: www.sic.state.ny.us

Deputy Commissioner & Chief Counsel:
  Anthony T Cartusciello 212-344-6670/fax: 212-344-6868

New York State Temporary Commission on Lobbying
Web site: www.nylobby.state.ny.us

Public Information Officer:
  David Grandeau 518-474-7126/fax: 518-473-6492
  e-mail: lobcom@nytscol.org

New York State Thoroughbred Breeding & Development Fund Corporation
Web site: www.nybreds.com

Executive Director:
  Martin G Kinsella 518-580-0100/fax: 518-580-0500

New York State Thruway Authority
Web site: www.nysthruway.gov

Director, Public Information:
  Vacant 518-436-2983/fax: 518-426-3995
  e-mail: publicinfo@thruway.state.ny.us

New York State Tug Hill Commission
Web site: www.tughill.org

Executive Director:
  John K Bartow, Jr 315-785-2380/fax: 315-785-2574
  e-mail: john@tughill.org

Niagara Falls Bridge Commission
Web site: www.niagarafallsbridges.com

General Manager/Secretary/Treasurer:
  Thomas E Garlock 716-285-6322/fax: 716-282-3292

Niagara Frontier Transportation Authority
Web site: www.nfta.com

Director, Public Affairs:
  C Douglas Hartmayer 716-855-7420/fax: 716-855-6655
  e-mail: info@nfta.com

Northeastern Forest Fire Protection Commission
Web site: www.nffpc.org

Executive Director:
  Thomas G Parent 207-968-3782/fax: 207-968-3782
  e-mail: necompact@fairpoint.net

Offices and agencies generally appear in alphabetical order, except when specific order is requested by listee.

PUBLIC INFORMATION OFFICES / New York State

Northeastern Queens Nature & Historical Preserve Commission
Web site: www.sneq.com

Executive Director:
Joan M Vogt 718-229-8805/fax: 718-229-6131
e-mail: sneq@aol.com

Ogdensburg Bridge & Port Authority
Web site: www.ogdensport.com

Executive Director:
Wade A Davis 315-393-4080/fax: 315-393-7068
e-mail: wadavis@ogdensport.com

Ohio River Valley Water Sanitation Commission
Web site: www.orsanco.org

Public Information Programs Manager:
Jeanne Ison 513-231-7719/fax: 513-231-7761
e-mail: jison@orsanco.org

Port Authority of New York & New Jersey
Web site: www.panynj.gov

Director, Public Affairs:
John J McCarthy 212-435-6502/fax: 212-435-6543

Port of Oswego Authority
Web site: www.portoswego.com

Acting Executive Director:
James Cloonan 315-343-4503/fax: 315-343-5498
e-mail: shipping@portoswego.com

Rochester-Genesee Regional Transportation Authority
Web site: www.rgrta.com

Chief Executive Officer:
Mark R Aesch 585-654-0200/fax: 585-654-0224

Roosevelt Island Operating Corporation (RIOC)
Web site: www.rioc.com

Public Information Officer:
Vacant 212-832-4540/fax: 212-832-4582
e-mail: info@roosevelt-island.ny.us

State University Construction Fund
Web site: www.sucf.suny.edu

Acting General Counsel:
William K Barczak 518-689-2514/fax: 518-689-2634

State of New York Mortgage Agency (SONYMA)
Web site: www.nyhomes.org

Vice President, Policy & Planning:
Tracy A Oats 212-688-4000 x678/fax: 212-872-0686

State of New York Municipal Bond Bank Agency (MBBA)
Web site: www.nymbba.org

Vice President, Policy & Planning:
Tracy A Oats 212-688-4000 x678/fax: 212-872-0686

Suffolk Regional Off-Track Betting Corporation
Web site: www.suffolkotb.com

Corporate Counsel/Executive Director, External Affairs:
Neil H Tiger 631-853-1000/fax: 631-853-1086
e-mail: customerservice@suffolkotb.com

Thousand Islands Bridge Authority
Web site: www.tibridge.com

Executive Director:
Robert G Horr, III 315-482-2501/fax: 315-482-5925
e-mail: roberthorr@tibridge.com

Uniform State Laws Commission
Chair:
Richard B Long 607-584-4193/fax: 607-723-1530
e-mail: rlong@cglawllp.com

United Nations Development Corporation
Web site: www.undc.org

Senior VP, Operations:
Robert M Preissner 212-888-1618/fax: 212-588-0758

Waterfront Commission of New York Harbor
Web site: www.wcnyh.org

Executive Director:
Thomas De Maria 212-905-9201/fax: 212-480-0587

Western Regional Off-Track Betting Corp
Web site: www.westernotb.com

General Counsel:
Timothy A McCarthy 585-343-1423/fax: 585-344-6188

Offices and agencies generally appear in alphabetical order, except when specific order is requested by listee.

U.S. CONGRESS

U.S. Senate: New York Delegation

Internet access, including e-mail addresses, is available at: www.senate.gov

Charles E Schumer (D) 202-224-6542/fax: 202-228-3027
313 Hart Senate Office Bldg, Washington, DC 20510
Committees: Banking, Housing and Urban Affairs; Finance; Judiciary; Rules and Administration

Hillary Rodham Clinton (D) . . . . . (202) 224-4451/fax: 202-228-0282
476 Russell Senate Office Bldg, Washington, DC 20510
Committees: Health, Education, Labor and Pensions; Environment and Public Works; Special Committee on Aging; Senate Armed Services

U.S. House of Representatives: New York Delegation

Internet access, including e-mail addresses, is available at: www.house.gov

Gary L Ackerman (D) 202-225-2601/fax: 202-225-1589
2243 Rayburn House Office Bldg, Washington, DC 20515
Congressional District: 5
Committees: Foreign Affairs; Financial Services

Timothy H Bishop (D) 202-225-3826/fax: 202-225-3143
225 Canon House Office Building, Washington, DC 20515-3201
Congressional District: 1
Committees: Education and the Workforce; Transportation and Infrastructure

Sherwood L Boehlert (R) 202-225-3665/fax: 202-225-1891
2246 Rayburn House Office Bldg, Washington, DC 20515-3223
Congressional District: 24
Committees: Science; Transportation and Infrastructure

Joseph Crowley (D) 202-225-3965/fax: 202-225-1909
312 Cannon House Office Bldg, Washington, DC 20515
Congressional District: 7
Committees: Financial Services; Foreign Affairs

Eliot L Engel (D) 202-225-2464/fax: 202-225-5513
2264 Rayburn House Office Bldg, Washington, DC 20515
Congressional District: 17
Committees: Energy and Commerce; Foreign Affairs

Vito J Fossella (R) 202-225-3371/fax: 202-226-1272
2453 Rayburn House Office Building, Washington, DC 20515
Congressional District: 13
Committees: Energy and Commerce

Brian Higgins (D) 202-225-3306/fax: 202-226-0347
431 Cannon House Office Bldg, Washington, DC 20515-3227
Congressional District: 27
Committees: Government Reform; Transportation & Infrastructure

Maurice D Hinchey (D) 202-225-6335/fax: 202-226-0774
2431 Rayburn House Office Bldg, Washington, DC 20515
Congressional District: 22
Committees: Appropriations; Natural Resources

Steve Israel (D) 202-225-3335/fax: 202-225-4669
432 Cannon House Office Bldg, Washington, DC 20515
Congressional District: 2
Committees: Apropriations

John Hall (D) 202-225-5441/fax: 202-225-3289
1217 Longworth House Office Building, Washington, DC 20515
Congressional District: 19
Committees: Veteran's Affairs, Transportation and Infrastructure, Energy Independence and Global Warming

Peter T King (R) 202-225-7896/fax: 202-226-2279
436 Cannon House Office Bldg, Washington, DC 20515
Congressional District: 3
Committees: Homeland Security; Financial Services

John R (Randy) Kuhl (R) 202-225-3161/fax: 202-226-6599
1505 Longworth House Office Bldg, Washington, DC 20515
Congressional District: 29
Committees: Agriculture; Education & Labor; Transportation & Infrastructure

Nita M Lowey (D) 202-225-6506/fax: 202-225-0546
2329 Rayburn House Office Bldg, Washington, DC 20515
Congressional District: 18
Committees: Appropriations; Homeland Security

Carolyn B Maloney (D) 202-225-7944/fax: 202-225-4709
2331 Rayburn House Office Bldg, Washington, DC 20515-3214
Congressional District: 14
Committees: Financial Services; Oversight and Government Reform

Carolyn McCarthy (D) 202-225-5516/fax: 202-225-5758
106 Cannon House Office Bldg, Washington, DC 20515-3207
Congressional District: 4
Committees: Education and Labor; Financial Services

Offices and agencies generally appear in alphabetical order, except when specific order is requested by listee.

U.S. CONGRESS / U.S. Senate Standing Committees

John M McHugh (R)................202-225-4611/fax: 202-226-0621
2366 Rayburn House Office Bldg, Washington, DC 20515-3223
Congressional District: 23
Committees: Armed Services; Government Reform

Michael R McNulty (D)...........202-225-5076/fax: 202-225-5077
2210 Rayburn House Office Bldg, Washington, DC 20515-3221
Congressional District: 21
Committees: Ways and Means

Gregory W Meeks (D)............202-225-3461/fax: 202-226-4169
2342 Rayburn House Office Building, Washington, DC 20515
Congressional District: 6
Committees: Financial Services; International Relations

Jerrold Nadler (D)................................202-225-5635
2334 Rayburn House Office Bldg, Washington, DC 20515
Congressional District: 8
Committees: Judiciary; Transportation

Yvette Clark (D).....................202-225-6231/fax: 202-226-0112
1209 Longworth House Office Building, Washington, DC 20515
Congressional District: 11
Committees: Education and Labor, Homeland Security, Small Business

Charles B Rangel (D)............202-225-4365/fax: 202-225-0816
2354 Rayburn House Office Bldg, Washington, DC 20515
Congressional District: 15
Committees: Ways and Means

Thomas M Reynolds (R).........202-225-5265/fax: 202-225-5910
332 Cannon House Office Bldg, Washington, DC 20515
Congressional District: 26
Committees: Ways and Means

Jose E Serrano (D)................202-225-4361/fax: 202-225-6001
2227 Rayburn House Office Bldg, Washington, DC 20515-3216
Congressional District: 16
Committees: Appropriations

Louise McIntosh Slaughter (D)...202-225-3615/fax: 202-225-7822
2469 Rayburn House Office Bldg, Washington, DC 20515
Congressional District: 28
Committees: Rules

Kirsten E Gillibrand (D)..........202-225-5614/fax: 202-225-1168
120 Cannon House Office Building, Washington, DC 20515
Congressional District: 20
Committees: Armed Services, Agriculture

Edolphus Towns (D).............202-225-5936/fax: 202-225-1018
2232 Rayburn House Office Bldg, Washington, DC 20515
Congressional District: 10
Committees: Energy and Commerce; Government Reform

Nydia M Velazquez (D)..........202-225-2361/fax: 202-226-0327
2466 Rayburn House Office Bldg, Washington, DC 20515-2104
Congressional District: 12
Committees: Small Business

James T Walsh (R)...............202-225-3701/fax: 202-225-4042
2372 Rayburn House Office Bldg, Washington, DC 20515
Congressional District: 25
Committees: Appropriations

Anthony D Weiner (D)...............................202-225-6616
1122 Longworth House Office Bldg, Washington, DC 20515
Congressional District: 9
Committees: Energy and Commerce; Judiciary

U.S. Senate Standing Committees

Agriculture, Nutrition & Forestry
Web site: www.agriculture.senate.gov

Chair:
  Tom Harkin (D-IA) 202-224-3254
Ranking Republican Member:
  Saxby Chambliss (R-GA)..........................202-224-3521

Subcommittees

Domestic and Foreign Marketing, Inspection and Plant & Animal Health
Chair:
  Max Baucus (D-MT) 202-224-2651
Ranking Minority Member:
  Lindsey Graham (R-SC) 202-224-5972

Energy, Science and Technology
Chair:
  Kent Conrad (D-ND).............................202-224-2043
Ranking Minority Member:
  John Thune (R-SD)..............................202-224-2321

Nutrition & Food Assistance, Sustainable & Organic Agriculture & Gen Legis
Chair:
  Patrick J Leahy (D-VT) 202-224-4242
Ranking Member:
  Norm Coleman (R-MN)...........................202-224-5641

Production, Income Protection and Price Support
Chair:
  Blanche L Lincol (D-AR) 202-224-4843
Ranking Minority Member:
  Pat Roberts (R-KS) 202-224-4774

Rural Revitalization, Conservation, Forestry and Credit
Chair:
  Debbie Stabenow (D-MI)..........................202-224-4822
Ranking Minority Member:
  Mike Crapo (R-ID)...............................202-224-6142

Appropriations
Web site: www.appropriations.senate.gov

Chair:
  Robert C Byrd (D-WV) 202-224-3954

Offices and agencies generally appear in alphabetical order, except when specific order is requested by listee.

U.S. CONGRESS / U.S. Senate Standing Committees

Ranking Minority Member:
Thad Cochran (R-MS) 202-224-5054

Subcommittees
Chair:
Herb Kohl (D-WI) 202-224-5653
Ranking Minority Member:
Robert Bennett (R-UT) 202-224-5444

Commerce, Justice, Science and Related Agencies
Chair:
Barbara Mikulski (D-MD) 202-224-4564
Ranking Minority Member:
Richard Shelby (R-AL) 202-224-5744

Defense
Chair:
Daniel Inouye (D-HI) 202-224-3934
Ranking Minority Member:
Ted Stevens (R-AK) 202-224-3004

Energy and Water Development
Chair:
Byron Dorgan (D-ND) 202-224-2551
Ranking Minority Member:
Pete V Domenici (R-NM) 202-224-6621

Financial Services and General Government
Chair:
Richard Durbin (D-IL) 202-224-2152
Ranking Minority Member:
Sam Brownback (R-KS) 202-224-6521

Homeland Security
Chair:
Robert C Byrd (D-WV) 202-224-3954
Ranking Minority Member:
Thad Cochran (R-MS) 202-224-5054

Interior, Environment and Related Agencies
Chair:
Dianne Feinstein (D-CA) 202-224-3841
Ranking Minority Member:
Larry Craig (R-ID) 202-224-2752

Labor, Health and Human Services, Education and Related Agencies
Chair:
Tom Harkin (D-IA) 202-224-3254
Ranking Minority Member:
Arlen Specter (R-PA) 202-224-4254

Legislative Branch
Chair:
Mary Landrieu (D-LA) 202-224-5824
Ranking Minority Member:
Wayne Allard (R-CO) 202-224-5941

Military, Construction, Veterans Affairs and Related Agencies
Chair:
Tim Johnson (D-SD) 202-224-5842
Ranking Minority Member:
Kay Bailey Hutchison (R-TX) 202-224-5922

State, Foreign Operations and Related Programs
Chair:
Patrick Leahy (D-VT) 202-224-4242
Ranking Minority Member:
Judd Gregg (D-VT) 202-224-3324

Transportation, Housing and Urban Development, and Related Agencies
Chair:
Patty Murray (D-WA) 202-224-2621

Ranking Minority Member:
Christopher Bond (R-MO) 202-224-5721

Armed Services
Web site: www.armed-services.senate.gov

Chair:
Carl Levin (D-MI) 202-224-6221
Ranking Minority Member:
John McCain (R-AZ) 202-224-2235
New York Delegate:
Hillary Rodham Clinton (D) 202-224-4451

Subcommittees

Airland
Chair:
Joseph I Liberman (D-CT) 202-224-4041
Ranking Minority Member:
John Cornyn (R-TX) 202-224-2934
New York Delegate:
Hillary Rodham Clinton (D-NY) 202-224-4451

Emerging Threats & Capabilities
Chair:
Jack Reed (D-RI) 202-224-4642
Ranking Minority Member:
Elizabeth Dole (R-NC) 202-224-6342

Personnel
Chair:
Ben Nelson (D-FL) 202-224-5274
Ranking Minority Member:
Lindsey O Graham (R-SC) 202-224-5972

Readiness & Management Support
Chair:
Daniel K Akaka (D-HI) 202-224-6361
Ranking Minority Member:
John Ensign (R-NV) 202-224-6244
New York Delegate:
Hillary Rodham Clinton (D-NY) 202-224-4451

SeaPower
Chair:
Edward M Kennedy (D-MA) 202-224-4543
Ranking Minority Member:
John Thune (R-SD) 202-224-2321

Strategic Forces
Chair:
Bill Nelson (D-FL) 202-224-5274
Ranking Minority Member:
Jeff Sessions (R-AL) 202-224-4124

Banking, Housing & Urban Affairs
Web site: www.banking.senate.gov

Chair:
Christopher J Dodd (D-CT) 202-224-2823
Ranking Minority Member:
Richard C Shelby (R-AL) 202-224-5744
New York Delegate:
Charles E Schumer (D) 202-224-6542

Subcommittees

Economic Policy
Chair:
Tom Carper (D-DE) 202-224-2441

Offices and agencies generally appear in alphabetical order, except when specific order is requested by listee.

U.S. CONGRESS / U.S. Senate Standing Committees

Ranking Minority Member:
  Jim Bunning (R-KY) 202-224-4343

Financial Institutions
Chair:
  Tim Johnson (D-SD) 202-224-5842
Ranking Minority Member:
  Chuck Hagel (R-NE) 202-224-4224

Housing, Transportation and Community Development
Chair:
  Charles E Schumer (D-NY) 202-224-6542
Ranking Minority Member:
  Mike Crapo (R-ID) 202-224-6142
New York Delegate:
  Charles E Schumer (D) 202-224-6542

Securities, Insurance and Investment
Chair:
  Jack Reed (D-RI) 202-224-4642
Ranking Minority Member:
  Wayne Allard (R-CO) 202-224-5941

Security, International Trade & Finance
202-224-6542
Chair:
  Evan Bayh (D-IN) 202-224-5623
Ranking Minority Member:
  Mel Martinez (R-FL) 202-224-3041

Budget
Web site: www.budget.senate.gov

Chair:
  Kent Conrad (D-ND) 202-224-2043
Ranking Minority Member:
  Judd Gregg (R-NH) 202-224-3324

Commerce, Science & Transportation
Web site: http://commerce.senate.gov

Chair:
  Daniel K Inouye (D-HI) 202-224-3934
Ranking Minority Member:
  Ted Stevens (R-AL) 202-224-3004

Subcommittees

Aviation Operations, Safety & Security
Chair:
  John D Rockefeller, IV (D-WV) 202-224-6472
Ranking Minority Member:
  Trent Lott (R-MS) 202-224-6253

Consumer Affairs, Insurance & Automotive Safety
Chair:
  Mark Pryor (D-AR) 202-224-2353
Ranking Minority Member:
  John E Sununu (R-NH) 202-224-2841

Interstate Commerce, Trade and Tourism
Chair:
  Byron L Dorgan (D-ND) 202-224-2551
Ranking Minority Member:
  Jim DeMint (R-SC) 202-224-6121

Oceans, Atmosphere, Fisheries and Coast Guard
Chair:
  Maria Cantwell (D-WA) 202-224-3441

Ranking Minority Member:
  Olympia J Snowe (R-ME) 202-224-5344

Science, Technology and Innovation
Chair:
  John F Kerry (D-MA) 202-224-2742
Ranking Minority Member:
  John Ensign (R-NV) 202-224-6244

Space, Aeronautics and Related Sciences
Chair:
  Bill Nelson (D-FL) 202-224-5721
Ranking Minority Member:
  Kay Bailey Hutchison (R-TX) 202-224-5922

Surface Transportation & Merchant Marine Infrastructure, Safety & Security
Chair:
  Frank R Lautneberg (D-NJ) 202-224-3224
Ranking Minority Member:
  Gordon H Smith (R-OR) 202-224-3753

Energy & Natural Resources
Web site: http://energy.senate.gov

Chair:
  Jeff Bingaman (D-NM) 202-224-4971
Ranking Minority Member:
  Pete V Domenici (R-NM) 202-224-4971

Subcommittees

Energy
Chair:
  Bryon L Dorgan (D-ND) 202-224-2551
Ranking Minority Member:
  Lisa Murkowski (R-AK) 202-224-6665

National Parks
Chair:
  Daniel K Akaka (D-HI) 202-224-6361
Ranking Minority Member:
  Craig Thomas (R-WY) 202-224-6441

Public Lands & Forests
Chair:
  Ron Wyden (D-OR) 202-224-5244
Ranking Minority Member:
  Richard Burr (R-NC) 202-224-3154

Water & Power
Chair:
  Tim Johnson (D-SD) 202-224-5842
Ranking Minority Member:
  Bob Corker (R-TN) 202-224-3344

Environment & Public Works
Web site: http://epw.senate.gov

Chair:
  Barbara Boxer (D-CA) 202-224-8832
Ranking Minority Member:
  James M Inhofe (R-OK) 202-224-6176
New York Delegate:
  Hillary Rodham Clinton (D) 202-224-4451

Offices and agencies generally appear in alphabetical order, except when specific order is requested by listee.

U.S. CONGRESS / U.S. Senate Standing Committees

Subcommittees

Clean Air and Nuclear Safety
Chair:
　Thomas R Carper (D-DE) 202-224-2441
Ranking Minority Member:
　George V Voinovich (R-OH) 202-224-3353

Private Sector & Consumer Solutions to Global Warming & Wildlife Protection
Chair:
　Joseph I Lieberman (D-CT) 202-224-4041
Ranking Minority Member:
　John Warner (R-VA) 202-224-2023
Chair:
　Barbara Boxer (D-CA) 202-224-8832
Ranking Minority Member:
　Lamar Alexander (R-TN) 202-224-4944

Superfund & Environmental Health
Chair:
　Hillary Rodham Clinton (D-NY) 202-224-4451
Ranking Minority Member:
　Larry E Craig (R-ID) 202-224-2752

Transportation & Infrastructure
Chair:
　Max Baucus (D-MT) 202-224-2651
Ranking Minority Member:
　Johnny Isakson (R-GA) 202-224-3643

Transportation Safety, Infrastructure Security and Water Quality
Chair:
　Frank R Lautenberg (D-NJ) 202-224-3224
Ranking Minority Member:
　David Vitter (R-LA) 202-224-4623

Finance
Web site: www.finance.senate.gov

Chair:
　Max Baucus (D-MT) 202-224-2651
Ranking Minority Member:
　Chuck Grassley (R-IA) 202-224-3744

Subcommittees

Energy, Natural Resources and Infrastructure
Chair:
　Jeff Bingaman (D-NM) 202-224-5521
Ranking Minority Member:
　Craig Thomas (R-WY) 202-224-6441

Health Care
Chair:
　John D Rockefeller, IV (D-WV) 202-224-6472
Ranking Minority Member:
　Orrin G Hatch (R-UT) 202-224-5251

International Trade and Global Competitiveness
Chair:
　Blanche L Lincoln (D-AR) 202-224-4843
Ranking Minority Member:
　Gordon Smith (R-OR) 202-224-3753

Social Security, Pensions and Family Policy
Chair:
　John F Kerry (D-MA) 202-224-2742
Ranking Minority Member:
　Jim Bunning (R-KY) 202-224-4343

Taxation and IRS Oversight and Long-Term Growth
Chair:
　Kent Conrad (D-ND) 202-224-2043
Ranking Minority Member:
　Jon Kyl (R-AZ) 202-224-4521

Foreign Relations
Web site: www.foreign.senate.gov

Chair:
　Joseph R Biden, Jr (D-DE) 202-224-5042
Ranking Minority Member:
　Richard G Lugar (R-IN) 202-228-0360

Subcommittees

African Affairs
Chair:
　Mel Martinez (R-FL) 202-224-3041
Ranking Minority Member:
　Russell D Feingold (D-WI) 202-224-5323

East Asian & Pacific Affairs
Chair:
　Lisa Murkowski (R-AK) 202-224-6665
Ranking Minority Member:
　John F Kerry (D-MA) 202-224-2742

European Affairs
Chair:
　George Allen (R-VA) 202-224-4024
Ranking Minority Member:
　Joseph R Biden, Jr (D-DE) 202-224-5042

International Economic Policy, Export & Trade Promotion
Chair:
　Charles E Hagel (R-NE) 202-224-4224
Ranking Minority Member:
　Paul S Sarbanes (D-MD) 202-224-4524

International Operations & Terrorism
Chair:
　John Sununu (R-NH) 202-224-2841
Ranking Minority Member:
　Bill Nelson (D-FL) 202-224-5274

Near Eastern & South Asian Affairs
Chair:
　Lincoln D Chafee (R-RI) 202-224-2921
Ranking Minority Member:
　Barbara Boxer (D-CA) 202-224-3553

Western Hemisphere, Peace Corps & Narcotics Affairs
Chair:
　Norm Coleman (R-MN) 202-224-5641
Ranking Minority Member:
　Christopher J Dodd (D-CT) 202-224-2823

Health, Education, Labor & Pensions
Web site: www.help.senate.gov

Chair:
　Edward M Kennedy (D-MA) 202-224-4543
Ranking Minority Member:
　Michael B Enzi (R-WY) 202-224-3424
New York Delegate:
　Hillary Rodham Clinton (D) 202-224-4451

Offices and agencies generally appear in alphabetical order, except when specific order is requested by listee.

U.S. CONGRESS / U.S. Senate Standing Committees

Subcommittees

Children and Families
Chair:
Christopher J Dodd (D-CT) 202-224-2823
Ranking Minority Member:
Lamar Alexander (R-TN) 202-224-4944

Employment & Workplace Safety
Chair:
Patty Murray (D-WA) 202-224-2621
Ranking Minority Member:
Johnny Isakson (R-GA) 202-224-3643

Retirement and Aging
Chair:
Barbara Mikulski (D-MD) 202-224-4654
Ranking Minority Member:
Richard Burr (R-NC) 202-224-3154
New York Delegate:
Hillary Rodham Clinton (D) 202-224-4451

Homeland Security & Governmental Affairs
Web site: www.hsgac.senate.gov

Chair:
Joseph I Lieberman (D-CT) 202-224-4041
Ranking Minority Member:
Susan Collins (R-ME) 202-224-2523

Subcommittees

Disaster Recovery
Chair:
Mary L Landrieu (D-LA) 202-224-5824
Ranking Minority Member:
Ted Stevens (R-AK) 202-224-3004

Federal Financial Mgt, Govt Info, Federal Services & International Society
Chair:
Thomas R Carper (D-DE) 202-224-2441
Ranking Minority Member:
Tom Coburn (R-OK) 202-224-5754

Oversight of Government Management, Federal Workforce & District of Columbia
Chair:
Daniel K Akaka (D-HI) 202-224-6361
Ranking Minority Member:
George V Voinovich (R-OH) 202-224-3353

Permanent Subcommittee on Investigations
Chair:
Carl Levin (D-MI) 202-224-6221
Ranking Minority Member:
Norm Coleman (R-MN) 202-224-5641

State, Local and Private Sector Preparedness and Integration
Chair:
Mark L Pryor (D-AR) 202-224-2353
Ranking Minority Member:
John E Sununu (R-NH) 202-224-2841

Judiciary
Web site: www.judiciary.senate.gov

Chair:
Patrick J Leahy (D-VT) 202-224-4242
Ranking Minority Member:
Arlen Specter (R-PA) 202-224-4254
New York Delegate:
Charles E Schumer (D) 202-224-6542

Subcommittees

Administrative Oversight & the Courts
Chair:
Charles E Schumer (D-NY) 202-224-6542
Ranking Minority Member:
Jeff Sessions (R-AL) 202-224-4124

Antitrust, Competition Policy & Consumer Rights
Chair:
Herb Kohl (D-WI) 202-224-5653
Ranking Minority Member:
Orrin G Hatch (R-UT) 202-224-5251

Constitution, The
Chair:
Russell D Feingold (D-WI) 202-224-5323
Ranking Minority Member:
Sam Brownbeck (R-KS) 202-224-6521

Crime & Drugs
Chair:
Joseph R Biden, Jr (D-DE) 202-224-5042
Ranking Minority Member:
Lindsey O Graham (R-SC) 202-224-5972

Human Rights and the Law
Chair:
Richard J Durbin (D-IL) 202-224-2152
Ranking Minority Member:
Tom Coburn (R-OK) 202-224-5754

Immigration, Refugees and Border Security
Chair:
Edward M Kennedy (D-MA) 202-224-4543
Ranking Minority Member:
John Cornyn (R-TX) 202-224-2934
New York Delegate:
Charles E Schumer (D) 202-224-6542

Terrorism, Technology & Homeland Security
Chair:
Dianne Feinstein (D-CA) 202-224-3841
Ranking Minority Member:
Jon Kyl (R-AZ) 202-224-4521

Rules & Administration
Web site: www.rules.senate.gov

Chair:
Dianne Feinstein (D-CA) 202-224-3841
Ranking Minority Member:
Bob Bennett (R-UT) 202-224-5444
New York Delegate:
Charles E Schumer (D) 202-224-6542

Small Business & Entrepreneurship
Web site: www.sbc.senate.gov

Chair:
John F Kerry (D-MA) 202-224-2742
Ranking Minority Member:
Olympia J Snowe (R-ME) 202-224-5344

Offices and agencies generally appear in alphabetical order, except when specific order is requested by listee.

U.S. CONGRESS / U.S. House of Representatives Standing Committees

Veterans' Affairs
Web site: www.veterans.senate.gov

Chair:
  Daniel Akaka (D-HI) 202-224-6361
Ranking Minority Member:
  Larry Craig (R-ID) 202-224-2752

OTHER, SELECT & SPECIAL COMMITTEES

Aging, Special Committee on
Web site: www.aging.senate.gov

Chair:
  Herb Kohl (D-WI) 202-224-5653
Ranking Minority Member:
  Gordon Smith (R-OR) 202-224-3753

Ethics, Select Committee on
Web site: www.ethics.senate.gov

Chair:
  Barbara Boxer (D-CA) 202-224-3553
Vice Chair:
  John Cornyn (R-TX) 202-224-2934

Indian Affairs, Committee on
Web site: http://indian.senate.gov

Chair:
  Bryon L Dorgan (D-ND) 202-224-2251
Vice Chair:
  Craig Thomas (R-WY) 202-224-6441

Intelligence, Select Committee on
Web site: www.intelligence.senate.gov

Chair:
  John D Rockefeller, IV (D-WV) 202-224-6472
Vice Chair:
  Christopher S Bond (R-MO) 202-224-5721

U.S. House of Representatives Standing Committees

Agriculture
Web site: http://agriculture.house.gov

Chair:
  Collin C Peterson (D-MN) 202-225-2165
Ranking Minority Member:
  Bob Goodlatte (R-VA) 202-225-5431

Subcommittees

Conservation, Credit, Energy and Research
Chair:
  Tim Holden (D-PA) 202-225-5546
Ranking Minority Member:
  Frank D Lucas (R-OK) 202-225-5565

Department Operations, Oversight, Nutrition & Forestry
Chair:
  Joe Baca (D-CA) 202-225-6161
Ranking Minority Member:
  Jo Bonner (R-AL) 202-225-4931

General Farm Commodities & Risk Management
Chair:
  Bob Etheridge (D-NC) 202-225-4531
Ranking Minority Member:
  Jerry Moran (R-KS) 202-225-2715

Horticulture and Organic Agriculture
Chair:
  Dennnis A Cardoza (D-CA) 202-225-6131
Ranking Minority Member:
  Randy Neugebauer (R-TX) 202-225-4005

Specialty Crops, Rural Development and Foreign Agriculture
Chair:
  Mike McIntyre (D-NC) 202-225-2731
Ranking Minority Member:
  Marilyn N Musgrave (R-CO) 202-225-4676

Appropriations
Web site: http://appropriations.house.gov

Chair:
  David R Obey (D-WI) 202-225-3365
Ranking Minority Member:
  Jerry Lewis (R-CA) 202-225-5861
New York Delegate:
  Maurice D Hinchey (D) 202-225-6335
New York Delegate:
  Nita M Lowey (D) 202-225-6506
New York Delegate:
  Jose E Serrano (D) 202-225-4361
New York Delegate:
  James T Walsh (R) 202-225-3701

Subcommittees

Agriculture, Rural Development, FDA & Related Agencies
Chair:
  Rosa DeLauro (D-CT) 202-225-3661
Ranking Minority Member:
  Jack Kingston (R-GA) 202-225-5831
New York Delegate:
  Maurice D Hinchey (D) 202-225-6335

Commerce, Justice, Science and Related Agencies
Chair:
  Alan B Mollohan (D-WV) 202-225-4172
Ranking Minority Member:
  Rodney P Frelinghuysen (R-NJ) 202-225-5034

Defense
Chair:
  John P Murtha (D-PA) 202-225-2847
Ranking Minority Member:
  C W Bill Young (R-FL) 202-225-5961

Offices and agencies generally appear in alphabetical order, except when specific order is requested by listee.

U.S. CONGRESS / U.S. House of Representatives Standing Committees

Energy and Water Development
Chair:
 Peter J Visclosky (D-IN) 202-225-2461
Ranking Minority Member:
 David L Hobson (R-OH)

Financial Services and General Government
Chair:
 Jose Serrano (D-NY) 202-225-7245
Ranking Minority Member:
 Ralph Regula (R-OH) 202-225-3876

Homeland Security
Chair:
 David E Price (D-NC) 202-225-1784
Ranking Minority Member:
 Harold Rogers (R-KY) 202-225-4601
New York Delegate:
 Jose E Serrano (D) 202-225-5614

Interior, Environment and Related Agencies
Chair:
 Norman D Dicks (D-WA) 202-225-5916
Ranking Minority Member:
 Todd Tiahrt (R-KS) 202-225-6216
New York Delegate:
 Maurice D Hinchey (D) 202-225-6335

Labor, Health & Human Services, Education and Related Agencies
Chair:
 David R Obey (D-WI) 202-225-3365
Ranking Minority Member:
 James T Walsh (R-NY) 202-225-3701
New York Delegate:
 Nita M Lowey (D) 202-225-6506
New York Delegate:
 James T Walsh (R) 202-225-3701

Military Construction, Veterans Affairs and Related Agencies
Chair:
 Chet Edwards (D-TX) 202-225-6105
Ranking Minority Member:
 Roger F Wicker (R-MS) 202-225-4306

State, Foreign Operations and Related Programs
Chair:
 Nita M Lowey (D-NY) 202-225-6506
Ranking Minority Member:
 Frank R Wolf (R-VA) 202-225-5136

Transportation, Housing and Urban Development, and Related Agencies
Chair:
 John W Olver (D-MA) 202-225-5335
Ranking Minority Member:
 Joe Knollenberg (R-MI) 202-225-5802
New York Delegate:
 John E Sweeney (R) 202-225-5614

Armed Services
Web site: www.armedservices.house.gov

Chair:
 Ike Skelton (D-MO) 202-225-2876
Ranking Minority Member:
 Duncan Hunter (R-CA) 202-225-5672
New York Delegate:
 John M McHugh (R) 202-225-4611

Subcommittees

Air and Land Forces
Chair:
 Neil Abercrombie (D-HI) 202-225-2726
Ranking Minority Member:
 Jim Saxton (R-NJ) 202-225-4765

Military Personnel
Chair:
 Vic Snyder (D-AR) 202-225-2506
Ranking Minority Member:
 John M McHugh (R-NY) 202-225-4611

Oversight and Investigations
Chair:
 Marty Meehan (D-MA) 202-225-3411
Ranking Minority Member:
 Todd Akin (R-MO) 202-225-2561

Readiness
Chair:
 Solomon P Ortiz (D-TX) 202-225-7742
Ranking Minority Member:
 Jo Ann Davis (R-VA) 202-225-4261
New York Delegate:
 John M McHugh (R) 202-225-4611

Seapower and Expeditionary Forces
Chair:
 Gene Taylor (D-MS) 202-225-5772
Ranking Minority Member:
 Roscoe G Bartlett (R-MD) 202-225-2721

Strategic Forces
Chair:
 Ellen O Tauscher (D-CA) 202-225-1880
Ranking Minority Member:
 Terry Everett (R-AL) 202-225-2901

Terrorism, Unconventional Threats and Capabilities
Chair:
 Adam Smith (D-WA) 202-225-8901
Ranking Minority Member:
 Mac Thornberry (R-TX) 202-225-3706

Budget
Web site: http://budget.house.gov

Chair:
 John M Spratt, Jr (D-SC) 202-225-5501
Ranking Minority Member:
 Paul Ryan (R-WI) 202-225-3031

Education & Labor
Web site: http://edworkforce.house.gov

Chair:
 George Miller (D-CA) 202-225-2095
Ranking Minority Member:
 Howard P (Buck) McKeon (R-CA) 202-225-1956
New York Delegate:
 Timothy H Bishop (D) 202-225-3826
New York Delegate:
 Carolyn McCarthy (D) 202-225-5516
New York Delegate:
 John R (Randy) Kuhl (R) 202-225-3161

Offices and agencies generally appear in alphabetical order, except when specific order is requested by listee.

U.S. CONGRESS / U.S. House of Representatives Standing Committees

Subcommittees

Early Childhood, Elementary and Secondary Education
Chair:
Dale E Kildee (D-MI) 202-225-3611
Ranking Minority Member:
Michael N Castle (R-DE) 202-225-4165

Healthy Families and Communities
Chair:
Carolyn McCarthy (D-NY) 202-225-5516
Ranking Minority Member:
Todd (Russell) Platts (R-PA) 202-225-5836

Higher Education, Lifelong Learning, and Competitiveness
Chair:
Ruben Hinojosa (D-TX) 202-225-2531
Ranking Minority Member:
Ric Keller (R-FL) 202-225-2176

Health, Employment, Labor and Pensions
Chair:
Robert Andrews (R-NJ) 202-225-6501
Ranking Minority Member:
John Kline (R-MN) 202-225-2271

Workforce Protections
Chair:
Lynn C Woolsey (D-CA) 202-225-5161
Ranking Minority Member:
Joe Wilson (R-SC) 202-225-2452
New York Delegate:
Timothy H Bishop (D) 202-225-3826

Energy & Commerce
Web site: http://energycommerce.house.gov

Chair:
John D Dingell (D-MI) 202-225-2927
Ranking Minority Member:
Joe Barton (R-TX) 202-225-2002
New York Delegate:
Eliot L Engel (D) 202-225-2464
New York Delegate:
Vito Fossella (R) 202-225-3371
New York Delegate:
Edolphus Towns (D) 202-225-5936

Subcommittees

Commerce, Trade & Consumer Protection
Chair:
Bobby L Rush (D-IL) 202-225-4372
Ranking Minority Member:
Cliff Stearns (R-FL) 202-225-5744
New York Delegate:
Edolphus Towns (D-NY) 202-225-5936

Energy & Air Quality
Chair:
Rick Boucher (D-VA) 202-225-3861
Ranking Minority Member:
J Dennis Hastert (R-IL) 202-225-2976
New York Delegate:
Eliot L Engel (D) 202-225-2464
New York Delegate:
Vito Fossella (R) 202-225-3371

Environment & Hazardous Materials
Chair:
Albert R Wynn (D-MD) 202-225-8699

Ranking Minority Member:
John Shimkus (R-IL) 202-225-5271
New York Delegate:
Vito Fossella (R) 202-225-3371

Health
Chair:
Frank J Pallone, Jr (D-NJ) 202-225-4671
Ranking Minority Member:
Nathan Deal (R-GA) 202-225-5211
New York Delegate:
Edolphus Towns (D) 202-225-5936

Oversight & Investigations
Chair:
Bart Stupak (D-MI) 202-225-2927
Ranking Minority Member:
Ed Whitfield (R-KY) 202-225-3115

Telecommunications & the Internet
Chair:
Edward J Markey (D-MA) 202-225-2836
Ranking Minority Member:
Fred Upton (R-MI) 202-225-3761
New York Delegate:
Edolphus Towns (D-NY) 202-225-5936
New York Delegate:
Vito Fossella (R) 202-225-3371
New York Delegate:
Eliot L Engel (D) 202-225-2464

Financial Services
Web site: http://financialservices.house.gov

Chair:
Barney Frank (D-MA) 202-225-5931
Ranking Minority Member:
Spencer Bachus (R-AL) 202-225-4921
New York Delegate:
Gary L Ackerman (D) 202-225-2601
New York Delegate:
Joseph Crowley (D) 202-225-3965
New York Delegate:
Peter T King (R) 202-225-7896
New York Delegate:
Carolyn B Maloney (D) 202-225-7944
New York Delegate:
Carolyn B Maloney (D) 202-225-7944
New York Delegate:
Carolyn McCarthy (D) 202-225-5516
New York Delegate:
Gregory W Meeks (D) 202-225-3461

Subcommittees

Capital Markets, Insurance & Government Sponsored Enterprises
Chair:
Paul E Kanjorski (D-PA) 202-225-6511
Ranking Minority Member:
Deborah E Pryce (R-OH) 202-225-2015
New York Delegate:
Gary L Ackerman (D) 202-225-2601
New York Delegate:
Joseph Crowley (D) 202-225-3965
New York Delegate:
Peter T King (R) 202-225-7896
New York Delegate:
Carolyn B Maloney (D) 202-225-4709

Offices and agencies generally appear in alphabetical order, except when specific order is requested by listee.

U.S. CONGRESS / U.S. House of Representatives Standing Committees

New York Delegate:
    Carolyn McCarthy (D).............................202-225-5516
New York Delegate:
    Gregory W Meeks (D)............................202-225-3461

Domestic & International Monetary Policy, Trade & Technology
Chair:
    Luis V Gutierrez (D-IL).............................202-225-8203
Ranking Minority Member:
    Carolyn B Maloney (D-NY).........................202-225-7944
New York Delegate:
    Joseph Crowley (D)..................................202-225-3965

Financial Institutions & Consumer Credit
Chair:
    Carolyn B Maloney (D-NY).........................202-225-2201
Ranking Minority Member:
    Paul Gillmor (R-OH).................................202-225-6405
New York Delegate:
    Gary L Ackerman (D)................................202-225-2601
New York Delegate:
    Joseph Crowley (D)..................................202-225-3965
New York Delegate:
    Vito Fossella (R).......................................202-225-3371
New York Delegate:
    Carolyn B Maloney (D)............................202-225-7944
New York Delegate:
    Carolyn McCarthy (D)..............................202-225-5516
New York Delegate:
    Gregory W Meeks (D)...............................202-225-3461
New York Delegate:
    Steve Israel (D)...202-225-3335

Housing & Community Opportunity
Chair:
    Maxine Waters (D-CA)..............................202-225-2201
Ranking Minority Member:
    Judy Biggert (R-IL)...................................202-225-3515
New York Delegate:
    Nydia M Velazquez (D).............................202-225-2361

Oversight & Investigations
Chair:
    Melvin L Watt (NC)..................................202-225-1510
Vice Chair:
    Ron Paul (R-TX).......................................202-225-2831
New York Delegate:
    Carolyn B Maloney (D)............................202-225-7944

Homeland Security
Web site: www.hsc.house.gov

Chair:
    Bennie G Thompson (D-MS)......................202-225-5876
Ranking Minority Member:
    Peter T King (R-NY).................................202-225-7896
New York Delegate:
    Nita M Lowey (D)....................................202-225-6506

Subcommittees

Border, Maritime and Global Counterterrorism
Chair:
    Loretta Sanchez (D-CA)............................202-225-2965
Ranking Minority Member:
    Mark Souder (R-IN).................................202-225-4436

Emergency Communications, Preparedness and Response
Chair:
    Henry Cuellar (D-TX)...............................202-225-1640

Ranking Minority Member:
    Charlie Dent (R-PA)..................................202-225-6411

Emerging Threats, Cybersecurity and Science and Technology
Chair:
    James R Langevin (D-RI)..........................202-225-2736
Ranking Minority Member:
    Michael McCaul (R-TX)............................202-225-2401

Intelligence, Information Sharing and Terrorism Risk Assessment
Chair:
    Jane Harman (D-CA).................................202-225-8220
Ranking Minority Member:
    Dave Reichert (R-WA)..............................202-225-7761

Management, Investigations and Oversight
Chair:
    Christopher P Carney (D-PA).....................202-225-3731
Ranking Minority Member:
    Mike Rogers (R-AL).................................202-225-3261

Transportation Security and Infrastructure Protection
Chair:
    Sheila Jackson Lee (D-TX).........................202-225-3816
Ranking Minority Member:
    Dan Lungren (R-CA)................................202-225-5716

House Administration
Web site: http://cha.house.gov

Chair:
    Robert A Brady (D-PA).............................202-225-4731
Ranking Minority Member:
    Vernon Ehlers (R-MI)................................202-225-3831
New York Delegate:
    Thomas M Reynolds (R)..........................202-225-5265

International Relations
Web site: www.internationalrelations.house.gov

Chair:
    Tom Lantos (D-CA)..................................202-225-3531
Ranking Minority Member:
    Ileana Ros Lehtinen (R-FL)........................202-225-3931
New York Delegate:
    Gary L Ackerman (D)................................202-225-2601
New York Delegate:
    Joseph Crowley (D)..................................202-225-3965
New York Delegate:
    Eliot L Engel (D).......................................202-225-2464
New York Delegate:
    Amory Houghton (R)...............................202-225-3161
New York Delegate:
    Peter T King (R).......................................202-225-7896
New York Delegate:
    Gregory W Meeks (D)...............................202-225-3461

Subcommittees

Africa & Global Health
Chair:
    Donald M Payne (D-NJ)...........................202-225-3436
Ranking Minority Member:
    Christopher J Smith (R-NJ).......................202-225-3765
New York Delegate:
    Gregory W Meeks (D)...............................202-225-3461

Offices and agencies generally appear in alphabetical order, except when specific order is requested by listee.

U.S. CONGRESS / U.S. House of Representatives Standing Committees

Asia, the Pacific, and the Global Environment
Chair:
Eni F H Faleomavaega (D-AS) 202-225-8577
Ranking Minority Member:
Donald A Manzullo (R-IL) 202-225-5676
New York Delegate:
Gary L Ackerman (D) 202-225-2601

Europe
Chair:
Robert Wexler (D-FL) 202-225-3001
Ranking Minority Member:
Elton Gallegly (R-CA) 202-225-5811
New York Delegate:
Eliot L Engel (D) 202-225-2464
New York Delegate:
Peter T King (R) 202-225-7896
New York Delegate:
Joseph Crowley (D) 202-225-3965

International Organizations, Human Rights and Oversight
Chair:
Bill Delahunt (D-MA) 202-225-3111
Ranking Minority Member:
Dana Rohrabacher (R-CA) 202-225-2415
New York Delegate:
Peter T King (R) 202-225-7896

Middle East and South Asia
Chair:
Gary Ackerman (D-NY) 202-225-2601
Ranking Minority Member:
Mike Pence (R-IN) 202-225-3021
New York Delegate:
Joseph Crowley (D) 202-225-3965

Terrorism, Nonproliferation and Trade
Chair:
Brad Sherman (D-CA) 202-225-5911
Ranking Minority Member:
Edward R Royce (R-CA) 202-225-4111

Western Hemisphere
Chair:
Eliot Engel (D-NY) 202-225-2464
Ranking Minority Member:
Dan Burton (R-IN) 202-225-2276
New York Delegate:
Gregory W Meeks (D) 202-225-3461

Judiciary
Web site: www.judiciary.house.gov

Chair:
John Conyers, Jr (D-MI) 202-225-5126
Ranking Minority Member:
Lamar S Smith (R-TX) 202-225-4236
New York Delegate:
Jerrold Nadler (D) 202-225-5635
New York Delegate:
Anthony D Weiner (D) 202-225-6616

Subcommittees

Commercial & Administrative Law
Chair:
Linda T Sanchez (D-CA) 202-225-6676
Ranking Minority Member:
Chris Cannon (R-UT) 202-225-7751

New York Delegate:
Jerrold Nadler (D) 202-225-5635

Constitution, Civil Rights and Civil Liberties
Chair:
Jerrold Nadler (D-NY) 202-225-5635
Ranking Minority Member:
Trent Franks (R-AZ)
Chair:
Howard L Berman (D-CA) 202-225-4695
Ranking Minority Member:
Howard Coble (R-NC) 202-225-3065

Crime, Terrorism and Homeland Security
Chair:
Robert C Scott (D-VA) 202-225-8351
Ranking Minority Member:
J Randy Forbes (R-VA) 202-225-6365

Immigration, Citizenship, Refugees, Border Security and International Law
Chair:
Zoe Lofgren (D-CA) 202-225-3072
Ranking Minority Member:
Steve King (R-IA) 202-225-4426

Natural Resources
Web site: http://resourcescommittee.house.gov

Chair:
Nick J Rahall, II (D-WV) 202-225-6065
Ranking Minority Member:
Don Young (R-AK) 202-225-5765

Subcommittees

Energy & Mineral Resources
Chair:
Jim Costa (D-CA) 202-225-9297
Ranking Minority Member:
Stevan Pearce (R-NM) 202-225-2365

Fisheries, Wildlife and Oceans
Chair:
Madeleine Z Bordallo (D-GU) 202-226-0200
Ranking Minority Member:
Henry E Brown, Jr (R-SC) 202-225-3176

Insular Affairs
Chair:
Donna M Christensen (D-VI) 202-225-0691
Ranking Republican Member:
Luis F Fortuno (R-PR)

National Parks, Forests and Public Lands
Chair:
Raul M Grijalva (R-AZ) 202-226-7736
Ranking Minority Member:
Rob Bishop (R-UT) 202-225-0453

Water & Power
Chair:
Grace F Napolitano (D-CA) 202-225-8331
Ranking Minority Member:
Cathy McMorris Rodgers (R-WA) 202-225-2006

Oversight and Government Reform
Web site: http://oversight.house.gov

Offices and agencies generally appear in alphabetical order, except when specific order is requested by listee.

U.S. CONGRESS / U.S. House of Representatives Standing Committees

Chair:
    Henry A Waxman (D-CA)..........................202-225-3976
Ranking Minority Member:
    Thomas M Davis, III (R-VA)......................202-225-1492
New York Delegate:
    Brian M Higgins (D)..................................202-225-3306
New York Delegate:
    Carolyn B Maloney (D)..............................202-225-7944
New York Delegate:
    John M McHugh (R)..................................202-225-4611
New York Delegate:
    Edolphus Towns (D)..................................202-225-5936

Subcommittees

Domestic Policy
Chair:
    Dennis J Kucinich (D-OH).........................202-225-5871
Ranking Minority Member:
    Darrell E Issa (R-CA)..................................202-225-3906

Federal Workforce, Postal Service and the District of Columbia
Chair:
    Danny K Davis (D-IL)................................202-225-5006
Ranking Minority Member:
    Kenny Marchant (R-TX)............................202-225-6605

Government Management, Organization and Procurement
Chair:
    Edolphus Towns (D-NY)............................202-225-5936
Ranking Minority Member:
    Brian Bilbray (R-CA)..................................202-225-0508

Information Policy, Census and National Archives
Chair:
    Wm Lacy Clay (D-MO)..............................202-225-2406
Ranking Minority Member:
    Michael Turner (R-OH)..............................202-225-6465

National Security and Foreign Affairs
Chair:
    John F Tierney (D-MA)..............................202-225-8020
Ranking Minority Member:
    Christopher Shays (R-CT)..........................202-225-5541
New York Delegate:
    Brian M Higgins (D)..................................202-225-3306
New York Delegate:
    Carolyn B Maloney (D)..............................202-225-7944
New York Delegate:
    John M McHugh (R)..................................202-225-4611

Rules
Web site: www.rules.house.gov

Chair:
    Louise M Slaughter (D-NY)........................202-225-9091
Ranking Minority Member:
    David Dreier (R-CA)..................................202-225-2305

Subcommittees

Legislative & Budget Process
Chair:
    Alcee L Hastings (D-FL)............................202-225-1313
Ranking Minority Member:
    Lincoln Diaz-Balart (R-FL)........................202-225-4211

Rules & Organization of the House
Chair:
    James F McGovern (D-MA)......................202-225-6101

Ranking Minority Member:
    Doc Hastings (R-WA)................................202-225-5816

Science & Technology
Web site: www.house.gov/science

Chair:
    Bart Gordon (D-TN)..................................202-225-4231
Ranking Minority Member:
    Ralph M Hall (R-TX)..................................202-225-6673

Subcommittees

Energy & Environment
Chair:
    Nick Lampson (D-TX)................................202-225-5951
Ranking Minority Member:
    Bob Inglis (R-SC)......................................202-225-6030

Investigations and Oversights
Chair:
    Brad Miller (D-NC)....................................202-225-3032
Ranking Minority Member:
    F James Sensenbrenner, Jr (R-WI)............202-225-5101

Research and Science Education
Chair:
    Brian Baird (D-WA)..................................202-225-3536
Ranking Minority Member:
    Vernon J Ehlers (R-MI)..............................202-225-3831

Space and Aeronautics
Chair:
    Mark Udall (D-CO)....................................202-225-2161
Ranking Minority Member:
    Ken Calvert (R-CA)..................................202-225-1986

Technology and Innovation
Chair:
    David Wu (D-OR)......................................202-225-0855
Ranking Minority Member:
    Phil Gingrey (R-GA)..................................202-225-2931

Small Business
Web site: www.house.gov/smbiz

Chair:
    Nydia Velazquez (D-NY)............................202-225-2361
Ranking Minority Member:
    Steve Chabot (R-OH)................................202-225-2216

Subcommittees

Contracting and Technology
Chair:
    Bruce Braley (D-IA)..................................202-225-2911
Ranking Minority Member:
    David Davis (R-TN)..................................202-225-6356

Finance and Tax
Chair:
    Melissa Bean (D-IL)..................................202-225-3711
Ranking Minority Member:
    Dean Heller (R-NV)..................................202-225-6155

Investigations and Oversight
Chair:
    Jason Altmire (D-PA)................................202-225-2565
Ranking Minority Member:
    Louie Gohmert (R-TX)..............................202-225-3035

Offices and agencies generally appear in alphabetical order, except when specific order is requested by listee.

U.S. CONGRESS / U.S. House of Representatives Standing Committees

Regulations, Health Care and Trade
Chair:
Charlie Gonzalez (D-TX)..........................202-225-3236
Ranking Minority Member:
Lynn Westmoreland (R-GA)......................202-225-5901

Standards of Official Conduct
Web site: www.house.gov/ethics

Chair:
Stephanie Tubbs Jones (D-OH).....................202-225-7032
Ranking Minority Member:
Doc Hastings (R-WA)................................202-225-5816

Transportation & Infrastructure
Web site: www.transportation.house.gov

Chair:
James L Oberstar (D-MN)..........................202-225-4472
Ranking Minority Member:
John L Mica (R-FL)..................................202-225-4035
New York Delegate:
Timothy H Bishop (D)...............................202-225-3826
New York Delegate:
Sherwood L Boehlert (R)............................202-225-3665
New York Delegate:
Brian M Higgins (D).................................202-225-3306
New York Delegate:
John R (Randy) Kuhl (R)............................202-225-3161
New York Delegate:
Jerrold Nadler (D)....................................202-225-5635
New York Delegate:
Anthony D Weiner (D)..............................202-225-6616

Subcommittees

Aviation
Chair:
Jerry F Costello (D-IL)..............................202-225-5661
Ranking Minority Member:
Thomas E Petri (R-WI).............................202-225-2476
New York Delegate:
John R (Randy) Kuhl (R)............................202-225-3161
New York Delegate:
Anthony D Weiner (D)..............................202-225-6616

Coast Guard & Maritime Transportation
Chair:
Elijah E Cummings (D-MD)........................202-225-4741
Ranking Minority Member:
Steve LaTourette (R-OH)...........................202-225-5731
New York Delegate:
Anthony D Weiner (D)..............................202-225-6616
New York Delegate:
Brian Higgins (D).....................................202-225-3306

Economic Development, Public Buildings & Emergency Management
Chair:
Eleanor Holmes Norton (D-DC)....................202-225-9961
Ranking Minority Member:
Sam Graves (R-MO)................................202-225-7041
New York Delegate:
John R (Randy) Kuhl Jr (R).........................202-225-3161

Highway and Transit
Chair:
Peter A DeFazio (D-OR)............................202-225-9989

Ranking Minority Member:
John J Duncan, Jr (R-TN)..........................202-225-5435
New York Delegate:
Timothy H Bishop (D)...............................202-225-3826
New York Delegate:
Jerrold Nadler (D)....................................202-225-5635
New York Delegate:
Sherwood Boehlert (R)..............................202-225-3665
New York Delegate:
Anthony D Weiner (D)..............................202-225-6616
New York Delegate:
Brian Higgins (D).....................................202-225-3306

Railroads, Pipelines and Hazardous Materials
Chair:
Corrine Brown (D-FL)..............................202-225-3274
Ranking Minority Member:
Bill Schuster (PA)....................................202-225-2431
New York Delegate:
Sherwood L Boehlert (R)............................202-225-3665
New York Delegate:
Jerrold Nadler (D)....................................202-225-5635

Water Resources & Environment
Chair:
Eddie Bernice Johnson (D-TX).....................202-225-0060
Ranking Minority Member:
Richard H Baker (R-LA)............................202-225-3901
New York Delegate:
Timothy H Bishop (D)...............................202-225-3826
New York Delegate:
Sherwood L Boehlert (R)............................202-225-3665
New York Delegate:
Brian M Higgins (D).................................202-225-3306

Veterans' Affairs
Web site: www.veterans.house.gov

Chair:
Bob Filner (D-CA)...................................202-225-8045
Ranking Minority Member:
Steve Buyer (D-IL)...................................202-225-5037

Subcommittees

Disability Assistance & Memorial Affairs
Chair:
John Hall (D-NY).....................................202-225-5441
Ranking Minority Member:
Doug Lamborn (R-CO).............................202-225-4422

Economic Opportunity
Chair:
Stephanie Herseth Sandlin (D-SD)................202-225-2801
Ranking Minority Member:
John Boozman (R-AR)..............................202-225-4301

Health
Chair:
Mike Michaud (D-ME)..............................202-225-6306
Ranking Minority Member:
Jeff Miller (R-FL).....................................202-225-4136

Oversight & Investigations
Chair:
Harry E Mitchell (D-AZ)............................202-225-2190
Ranking Minority Member:
Ginny Brown Waite (R-FL).........................202-225-1002

Offices and agencies generally appear in alphabetical order, except when specific order is requested by listee.

U.S. CONGRESS / Joint Senate and House Committees

Ways & Means
Web site: http://waysandmeans.house.gov

Chair:
　Charles B Rangel (D-NY) 202-225-4365
Ranking Minority Member:
　Charles B Rangel (D-NY) 202-225-4365
New York Delegate:
　Thomas M Reynolds (R) 202-225-5265
New York Delegate:
　Michael R McNulty (D) 202-225-5076

Subcommittees

Health
Chair:
　Fortney Pete Stark (D-CA) 202-225-5065
Ranking Minority Member:
　Dave Camp (R-MI) 202-225-3561

Income Security and Family Support
Chair:
　Jim McDermott (D-WA) 202-225-3106
Ranking Minority Member:
　Jerry Weller (R-IL) 202-225-3635

Oversight
Chair:
　John Lewis (D-GA) 202-225-3801
New York Delegate:
　Michael R McNulty (D) 202-225-5076
New York Delegate:
　Charles B Rangel (D) 202-225-4365

Select Revenue Measures
Chair:
　Richard E Neal (D-MA) 202-225-5601
Ranking Minority Member:
　Phil English (R-PA) 202-225-5406

Social Security
Chair:
　Michael R McNulty (D-NY) 202-225-5076
Ranking Minority Member:
　Sam Johnson (R-TX) 202-225-4201

Trade
Chair:
　Sander M Levin (MI) 202-225-4961

Ranking Minority Member:
　Wally Herger (R-CA) 202-225-3076
New York Delegate:
　Thomas M Reynolds (R) 202-225-5265

OTHER, SELECT & SPECIAL COMMITTEES

Intelligence, House Permanent Select Committee on
Web site: http://intelligence.house.gov

Chair:
　Silvestre Reyes (D-TX) 202-225-4831
Ranking Minority Member:
　Pete Hoekstra (R-MI) 202-225-4401
New York Delegate:
　John McHugh (R) 202-225-4611

Subcommittees

Intelligence Community Management
Chair:
　Anna G Eshoo (D-CA) 202-225-8104
Ranking Minority Member:
　Darrell Issa (R-CA) 202-225-3906

Oversight and Investigations
Chair:
　Robert E (Bud) Cramer, Jr (D-AL) 202-225-4801
Ranking Minority Member:
　Peter Hoekstra (R-MI) 202-225-4401

Technical and Tactical Intelligence
Chair:
　C A Dutch Ruppersberger (D-MD) 202-225-3061
Ranking Minority Member:
　Heather Wilson (R-NM) 202-225-6316

Terrorism/HUMIT, Analysis and Counterintelligence
Chair:
　Mike Thompson (D-CA) 202-225-3311
Ranking Minority Member:
　Mike Rogers (R-MI) 202-225-4872

Joint Senate and House Committees

Economic Committee, Joint
Web site: www.house.gov/jec

Chair:
　Sen Charles E Schumer (D-NY) 202-224-6542
Vice Chair:
　Rep Carolyn B Maloney (D-NY) 202-225-7944
Ranking Minority Member:
　Rep Jim Saxton (R-NJ) 202-225-4765
New York Delegate:
　Maurice D Hinchey (D) 202-225-6335
New York Delegate:
　Carolyn Maloney (D) 202-225-7944

Library, Joint Committee on the
Chair:
　Rep Vernon J Ehlers (R-MI) 202-224-3831
Vice Chair:
　Sen Ted Stevens (R-AK) 202-224-3004
New York Delegate:
　Charles Schumer (D) 202-224-6542

Printing, Joint Committee on
Web site: www.jcp.senate.gov

Chair:
　Sen Trent Lott (R-MS) 202-224-6253

Offices and agencies generally appear in alphabetical order, except when specific order is requested by listee.

U.S. CONGRESS / Joint Senate and House Committees

Vice Chair:
  Rep Vernon Ehlers 202-225-3831
New York Delegate:
  Rep Thomas Reynolds (R) 202-225-5265

Chair:
  Sen Charles B Rangel (D-NY) 202-225-4365
Vice Chair:
  Max Baucus (R-MT) 202-224-2651

Taxation, Joint Committee on
Web site: www.house.gov/jct

Offices and agencies generally appear in alphabetical order, except when specific order is requested by listee.

COUNTY GOVERNMENT

County Government

Albany County
112 State Street
Albany, NY 12207
518-447-7040 Fax: 518-447-5589
Web site: www.albanycounty.com

Chairman, County Legislature (D):
  Charles E Houghtaling, Jr. 518-447-7117
Majority Leader (D):
  Frank J Commisso . . . . 518-447-7117 or 518-438-5387
Minority Leader (R):
  Christine M Benedict 518-447-7164
  e-mail: cbenedic@nycap.rr.com
Clerk, Legislature:
  Paul T Devane 518-447-7168
County Executive:
  Michael G Breslin 518-447-7040/fax: 518-447-5589
  e-mail: countyexec@albanycounty.com
County Clerk:
  Thomas G Clingan. 518-487-5100/fax: 518-487-5099
  e-mail: countyclerk@albanycounty.com
County Attorney:
  Kristina A Burns 518-447-7110/fax: 518-447-5564
District Attorney:
  P David Soares 518-487-5460/fax: 518-487-5093
Sheriff:
  James L Campbell 518-487-5400/fax: 518-487-5037
Comptroller:
  Michael F Conners, II 518-447-7130/fax: 518-433-1554
  e-mail: mconners@albanycounty.com
General Services Commissioner:
  Edward Lynch 518-447-7210
Commissioner, Management & Budget:
  John W Rodat 518-447-5525/fax: 518-447-5589
  e-mail: budget@albanycounty.com

Allegany County
County Office Bldg, 7 Court St
Belmont, NY 14813
585-268-9222 Fax: 585-268-9446
Web site: www.alleganyco.com

Chairman, Board of Legislators (R):
  Curtis Crandall 585-268-9222
Majority Leader (R):
  Brent L Reynolds 585-268-9222
Minority Leader (D):
  Michael J McCormick 585-268-9222
Clerk, Board of Legislators:
  Brenda A Rigby Riehle 585-268-9222/fax: 585-268-9446
  e-mail: rigbyba@alleganyco.com
County Administrator:
  John E Margeson 585-268-9217
  e-mail: margesonje@alleganyco.com
County Clerk:
  Robert L Christman. 585-268-9270/fax: 585-268-9659
  e-mail: christr@alleganyco.com
District Attorney:
  Terrance M Parker 585-268-9225
  e-mail: parkertm@alleganyco.com
Public Defender:
  Barbara J Kelley. 585-268-9246
  e-mail: kelleyb@alleganyco.com
Sheriff:
  William Tompkins 585-268-9200
  e-mail: tompkiw@alleganyco.com
Treasurer:
  Terri L Ross 585-268-9289
  e-mail: rosstl@alleganyco.com
County Attorney:
  Daniel J Guiney 585-268-9410
  e-mail: guineydj@alleganyco.com
Director, Emergency Services:
  John C Tucker. 585-268-7658
  e-mail: tuckerj@alleganyco.com
Superintendent, Public Works:
  David Roeske 585-268-9230
  e-mail: roeskeds@alleganyco.com
Fire Coordinator:
  Paul W Gallmann 585-268-5290
  e-mail: gallmapw@alleganyco.com
County Historian:
  Craig R Braack 585-268-9293
  e-mail: historian@alleganyco.com

Bronx County (NYC Borough of the Bronx)
851 Grand Concourse
Bronx, NY 10451
718-590-3500 Fax: 718-590-3537
Web site: www.bronxcountyclerksoffice.com

Borough President:
  Adolfo Carrion, Jr 718-590-3557/fax: 718-590-3537
Deputy Borough President:
  Earl D Brown 718-590-3565
County Clerk:
  Hector L Diaz 718-590-3648/fax: 718-590-8122
  e-mail: hdiaz@courts.state.ny.us
District Attorney:
  Robert T Johnson 718-590-2000
Public Administrator:
  John Raniolo 718-293-7660
  e-mail: jraniolo@bronxpa.com

Broome County
County Office Bldg
44 Hawley St
PO Box 1766
Binghamton, NY 13902-1766
607-778-2131 Fax: 607-778-8869
Web site: www.gobroomecounty.com

Offices and agencies generally appear in alphabetical order, except when specific order is requested by listee.

COUNTY GOVERNMENT / County Government

Chairman, County Legislature (D):
  Mark R Whalen 607-778-2131
  e-mail: mwhalen2@co.broome.ny.us
Majority Leader (D):
  Daniel Reynolds 607-778-2131
  e-mail: dreynolds@co.broome.ny.us
Minority Leader (R):
  Daniel A Schofield 607-778-2131
  e-mail: daschofield@co.broome.ny.us
Clerk, Legislature:
  Eric S Denk 607-778-2131
  e-mail: legclerk@co.broome.ny.us
County Executive:
  Barbara J Fiala 607-778-2109/fax: 607-778-2044
  e-mail: bfiala@co.broome.ny.us
County Clerk:
  Richard R Blythe 607-778-2451/fax: 607-778-2243
  e-mail: clerkinfo@co.broome.ny.us
County Attorney:
  Joseph Sluzar 607-778-2117/fax: 607-778-6122
  e-mail: jsluzar@co.broome.ny.us
District Attorney:
  Gerald F Mollen 607-778-2423/fax: 607-778-8870
  e-mail: gmollen@co.broome.ny.us
Public Defender:
  Jay L Wilber 607-778-2403/fax: 607-778-2432
  e-mail: jwilber@co.broome.ny.us
Sheriff:
  David E Harder 607-778-1911/fax: 607-778-2100
  e-mail: bcsheriff@co.broome.ny.us
Director, Emergency Services:
  Brett B Chellis 607-778-2170/fax: 607-778-1150
  e-mail: bchellis@co.broome.ny.us
Comptroller:
  Alex McLaughlin 607-778-2178/fax: 607-778-2236
  e-mail: amclaughlin@co.broome.ny.us
Finance Commissioner:
  Jerome Z Knebel 607-778-2161/fax: 607-778-2176
  e-mail: jknebel@co.broome.ny.us
County Historian:
  Gerald R Smith 607-778-2076/fax: 607-778-6249
  e-mail: gsmith@co.broome.ny.us

Cattaraugus County
County Center
303 Court St
Little Valley, NY 14755
716-938-9111 Fax: 716-938-9698
Web site: www.cattco.org

Chair, County Legislature (R):
  Crystal Abers 716-938-9111 x2385
Vice Chairperson (R):
  Michael T O'Brien 716-938-9111
Majority Leader (R):
  Jon K Baker 716-938-9111 x2333
Minority Leader (D):
  Linda L Witte 716-938-9111 x2397
County Administrator & Clerk, Legislature:
  John R Searles 716-938-9111 x2577/fax: 716-938-9306
  e-mail: jrsearles@cattco.org
County Clerk:
  James Griffith 716-938-9111 x2293/fax: 716-938-6009
County Attorney:
  Dennis V Tobolski 716-938-9111 x2391/fax: 716-938-9438

District Attorney:
  Edward M Sharkey 716-938-9111 x2222/fax: 716-938-6555
  e-mail: emsharkey@cattco.org
Sheriff:
  Dennis B John 716-938-9191/fax: 716-938-6420
Director Emergency Svcs/Fire Coordinator:
  Edward G Koorse 716-938-9111 x2240/fax: 716-938-9170
Treasurer:
  Joseph Keller 716-373-8010/fax: 716-938-6897
Public Defender:
  Mark S Williams 716-373-0004/fax: 716-373-3462
  e-mail: pubdef@ccpd.cattco.org
County Historian:
  Carol Ruth 716-353-8200 x4721
  e-mail: cruth@cattco.org

Cayuga County
160 Genesee St
Auburn, NY 13021
315-253-1308 Fax: 315-253-1586
Web site: www.cayugacounty.us

Chairman, County Legislature (R):
  George Fearon 315-253-1273/fax: 315-253-1586
  e-mail: chairman@co.cayuga.ny.us
Majority Leader (R):
  Linda Murphy 315-253-1273
  e-mail: ccdistrict11@co.cayuga.ny.us
Minority Leader (D):
  Michele Sedor 315-253-1273
  e-mail: ccdistrict06@co.cayuga.ny.us
Clerk, Legislature:
  Lee Brew . . . . 315-253-1498 or 315-253-1308
  fax: 315-253-1586
  e-mail: lclerk@co.cayuga.ny.us
County Manager:
  Wayne D Allen 315-253-1273
  e-mail: wallen@cayugacounty.us
County Clerk:
  Susan M Dwyer 315-253-1271/fax: 315-253-1006
  e-mail: sdwyer@co.cayuga.ny.us
County Attorney:
  Fredrick Westphal 315-253-1274/fax: 315-253-1098
  e-mail: coatty@co.cayuga.ny.us
District Attorney:
  James B Vargason 315-253-1391/fax: 315-253-1521
  e-mail: cayugada@co.cayuga.ny.us
Director, Planning & Development:
  Steve Lynch 315-253-1276/fax: 315-253-1499
  e-mail: planning@co.cayuga.ny.us
Emergency Management Director:
  Brian Dahl 315-255-1161/fax: 315-253-1551
  e-mail: ccemo@co.cayuga.ny.us
Sheriff:
  David S Gould 315-253-1222/fax: 315-253-3022
  e-mail: sheriff@co.cayuga.ny.us
Treasurer:
  Jim H Orman 315-253-1211/fax: 315-253-1369
  e-mail: treasurer@co.cayuga.ny.us
County Historian:
  Sheila Tucker 315-253-1300
  e-mail: historian@co.cayuga.ny.us

Offices and agencies generally appear in alphabetical order, except when specific order is requested by listee.

397

COUNTY GOVERNMENT / County Government

Chautauqua County
3 N Erie St
Mayville, NY 14757-1007
716-753-4000 Fax: 716-753-4277
Web site: www.co.chautauqua.ny.us

Chairman, County Legislature (D):
   Keith D Ahlstrom 716-753-4215/fax: 716-753-4539
   e-mail: leg.keith@verizon.net
Majority Leader (D):
   Chuck Cornell. 716-753-4215
   e-mail: chuckcornell@hotmail.com
Minority Leader (R):
   Fred Croscut 716-753-4215
   e-mail: croscut@cecomet.net
Clerk, Legislature:
   Janet Jankowski George 716-753-4215
   e-mail: jankowsj@co.chautauqua.ny.us
County Executive:
   Gregory J Edwards 716-753-4211
   e-mail: edwardsg@co.chautauqua.ny.us
County Clerk:
   Sandra K Sopak 716-753-4331/fax: 716-753-4293
   e-mail: lorenzot@co.chautauqua.ny.us
County Attorney:
   Steve Abdella 716-753-4247
District Attorney:
   David Foley 716-753-4241
   e-mail: foleyd@co.chautauqua.ny.us
Public Defender:
   William Coughlin 716-753-4376
Director, Emergency Services:
   Julius Leone 716-753-4341
Sheriff:
   Joseph A Gerace . . . . 716-753-2131 or 716-753-4900
Comptroller:
   Dennis E Goggin 716-753-4433
   e-mail: goggind@co.chautauqua.ny.us
Finance Director:
   Darin Schulz 716-753-4223
   e-mail: ccfin@co.chautauqua.ny.us

Chemung County
John H Hazlett Bldg, 203 Lake St
PO Box 588
Elmira, NY 14902
607-737-2912 Fax: 607-737-0351
e-mail: info@chemungcounty.com
Web site: www.chemungcounty.com

Chairman, County Legislature (R):
   Cornelius J Milliken 607-737-2066/fax: 607-737-2851
   e-mail: cmilliken@co.chemung.ny.us
Majority Leader (R):
   Donna L Draxler. 607-737-2066
   e-mail: ddraxler@aol.com
Minority Leader (D):
   Theodore A Bennett 607-737-2066
   e-mail: ted.benn@verizon.net
Clerk, Legislature:
   Linda D Palmer. 607-737-2066
   e-mail: lpalmer@co.chemung.ny.us
County Executive:
   Thomas J Santulli 607-737-2912
   e-mail: tsantulli@co.chemung.ny.us

County Clerk:
   Catherine K Hughes 607-737-2920/fax: 607-737-2897
   e-mail: chughes@co.chemung.ny.us
County Attorney:
   Weeden Wetmore 607-737-2982
District Attorney:
   John R Trice 607-737-2944/fax: 607-737-2965
Public Defender:
   Nancy Braca-Cornish 607-737-2969
Fire & Emergency Services:
   Michael Smith 607-737-2096
   e-mail: msmith@co.chemung.ny.us
Sheriff:
   Christopher Moss. 607-737-2987/fax: 607-737-2931
   e-mail: cmoss@co.chemung.ny.us
Treasurer:
   Joseph E Sartori, III 607-737-2927/fax: 607-737-2846
   e-mail: jsartori@co.chemung.ny.us

Chenango County
County Office Bldg
5 Court St
Norwich, NY 13815
607-337-1700 Fax: 607-334-8768
Web site: www.co.chenango.ny.us

Chairman, Board of Supervisors (R):
   Richard B Decker 607-337-1401
Clerk, Board of Supervisors:
   R C Woodford 607-337-1430
County Clerk:
   Mary C Weidman 607-337-1450
   e-mail: countyclerk@co.chenango.ny.us
County Attorney:
   Richard W Breslin 607-337-1405/fax: 607-334-4534
District Attorney:
   Joseph A McBride 607-337-1745/fax: 607-337-1746
Public Defender:
   Alan E Gordon . . . . 607-843-8955 or 607-337-1870
Sheriff & Director Emergency Management:
   Thomas J Loughren 607-334-2000
Treasurer:
   William E Evans. 607-337-1414
Director, Public Works:
   Randy Gibbon. 607-337-1710
County Historian:
   Dale C Storms 607-337-1845

Clinton County
County Government Ctr
137 Margaret St, Ste 208
Plattsburgh, NY 12901
518-565-4600 Fax: 518-565-4616
Web site: www.co.clinton.ny.us

Chairman (R):
   James R Langley, Jr . . . . 518-565-4600 or 518-643-9052
   e-mail: langleyins@charter.net
Majority Leader (R):
   Samuel J Trombley 518-594-7109/fax: 518-594-7742
   e-mail: trombleyma@aol.com
Minority Leader (D):
   Keith M Defayette 518-565-4600
   e-mail: keith2125@charter.net

Offices and agencies generally appear in alphabetical order, except when specific order is requested by listee.

COUNTY GOVERNMENT / County Government

Clerk, Board of Legislators & County Administrator:
  Michael E Zurlo 518-565-4600
  e-mail: legislature@co.clinton.ny.us
County Clerk:
  John H Zurlo 518-565-4700/fax: 518-565-4718
County Attorney:
  Dennis D Curtin 518-561-4400/fax: 518-561-4848
District Attorney:
  Andrew J Wylie 518-565-4770/fax: 518-565-4777
  e-mail: da@co.clinton.ny.us
Director, Emergency Services:
  Eric Day 518-565-4791/fax: 518-566-1202
  e-mail: e911@co.clinton.ny.us
Sheriff:
  David N Favro 518-565-4300/fax: 518-565-4333
  e-mail: sheriff@co.clinton.ny.us
Treasurer:
  Joseph W Giroux 518-565-4730/fax: 518-565-4516
  e-mail: treasurer@co.clinton.ny.us
County Historian:
  Addie L Shields 518-565-4749/fax: 518-565-4616
  e-mail: historian@co.clinton.ny.us

Columbia County
401 State St
Hudson, NY 12534
518-828-1527 Fax: 518-822-0684
e-mail: dicosmo@govt.co.columbia.ny.us
Web site: www.columbiacountyny.com

Chairman, Board of Supervisors (R):
  James W Keegan 518-828-1527
  e-mail: dicosmo@govt.co.columbia.ny.us
Majority Leader (R):
  Elizabeth Young 518-828-1527
Minority Leader (D):
  Douglas McGivney 518-758-6385
Clerk, Board of Supervisors:
  Gail DiCosmo 518-828-1527
County Clerk:
  Holly C Tanner 518-828-3339/fax: 518-828-5299
  e-mail: htanner@govt.co.columbia.ny.us
County Attorney:
  Daniel J Tuczinski 518-828-3303/fax: 518-828-9535
District Attorney:
  Beth G Cozzolino 518-828-3414
Public Defender:
  Charles E Inman 518-828-3410/fax: 518-828-1279
Sheriff:
  David W Harrison Jr 518-828-0601/fax: 518-828-9088
Fire Coordinator:
  James Van Deusen 518-822-8610/fax: 518-828-1279
Director, Emergency Management:
  William Black 518-828-1212/fax: 518-828-1279
Treasurer:
  Kenneth H Wilber 518-828-0513/fax: 518-822-1110
County Historian:
  Mary Howell 518-828-3442/fax: 518-828-2969
  e-mail: mhowell@govt.co.columbia.ny.us

Cortland County
County Office Bldg
60 Central Ave
Cortland, NY 13045
607-753-5048 Fax: 607-756-3492
Web site: www.cortland-co.org

Chairperson, County Legislature (D):
  Marilyn E Brown 607-753-5048
  e-mail: mbrown@cortland-co.org
Majority Leader (D):
  Ronald J VanDee 607-753-1328
  e-mail: rvandee@cortland-co.org
Minority Leader (R):
  Danny G Ross 607-836-6433
  e-mail: dross@cortland-co.org
County Administrator:
  Scott A Schrader 607-753-5510
  e-mail: sschrader@cortland-co.org
Clerk, Legislature:
  Susan Morgan 607-753-5049/fax: 607-756-3492
  e-mail: sdmorgan@cortland-co.org
County Clerk:
  Elizabeth P Larkin 607-753-5021/fax: 607-753-5378
  e-mail: elarkin@cortland-co.org
County Attorney:
  Richard C VanDonsel 607-753-5095
  e-mail: rvandonsel@cortland-co.org
District Attorney:
  David S Hartnett 607-753-5008/fax: 607-756-3477
  e-mail: districtattorney@cortland-co.org
Public Defender:
  Keith D Dayton 607-753-5046/fax: 607-753-0781
  e-mail: kdayton@cortland-co.org
Sheriff:
  Lee A Price 607-758-5599
  e-mail: lprice@cortland-co.org
Fire/Emergency Management Coordinator:
  G Robert Duell 607-753-5064/fax: 607-756-8457
  e-mail: grduell@cortland-co.org
Treasurer:
  Donald F Ferris 607-753-5070/fax: 607-758-5512
  e-mail: dferris@cortland-co.org
County Historian:
  Jeremy Boylan 607-753-5360
  e-mail: jboylan@cortland-co.org

Delaware County
County Office Bldg
111 Main St
Delhi, NY 13753
607-746-2603 Fax: 607-746-7012
Web site: www.co.delaware.ny.us

Chairman, Board of Supervisors (R):
  James E Eisel, Sr . . . . 607-746-6691 or 607-652-3198
  e-mail: cob@co.delaware.ny.us
Vice Chairman, Board of Supervisors (R):
  Tina Mole . . . . 607-746-2603 or 607-832-4312
Clerk, Board of Supervisors:
  Christa M Schafer 607-746-2603
  e-mail: cob@co.delaware.ny.us
County Clerk:
  Sharon O'Dell 607-746-2123/fax: 607-746-6924
  e-mail: clerk@co.delaware.ny.us
County Attorney:
  Richard B Spinney 607-652-3443/fax: 607-652-3334
District Attorney:
  Richard D Northrup, Jr 607-746-3557/fax: 607-746-2297

Offices and agencies generally appear in alphabetical order, except when specific order is requested by listee.

COUNTY GOVERNMENT / County Government

Sheriff:
   Thomas E Mills 607-746-2336/fax: 607-746-2632
   e-mail: shrf@co.delaware.ny.us
County Treasurer:
   Beverly J Shields 607-746-2121/fax: 607-746-7433
   e-mail: treas@co.delaware.ny.us
Director, Emergency Services:
   Nelson Delameter 607-746-9600
Commissioner, Public Works:
   Wayne Reynolds 607-746-2128/fax: 607-746-7212
County Historian:
   Patrick H Grimes 845-676-3790
   e-mail: hist@co.delaware.ny.us

Dutchess County
County Office Bldg
22 Market St, 6th Fl
Poughkeepsie, NY 12601
845-486-2100 Fax: 845-486-2113
e-mail: countylegislature@co.dutchess.ny.us
Web site: www.dutchessny.gov

Chairman, County Legislature (R):
   Gary Cooper 518-943-0155/fax: 518-398-0053
   e-mail: gcooper@co.dutchess.ny.us
Majority Leader (R):
   Noreen H Reilly 845-229-0042
   e-mail: repcon35@aol.com
Minority Leader (D):
   Roger Higgins 845-297-8757/fax: 845-486-2113
   e-mail: rogerhig@optonline.net
County Executive:
   William R Steinhaus . . . . 845-486-2000 or 866-694-4600
   fax: 845-486-2021
   e-mail: countyexec@co.dutchess.ny.us
Clerk, Legislature:
   Patricia J Hohmann 845-486-2100
County Clerk:
   Bradford Kendall 845-486-2120/fax: 845-486-2138
   e-mail: bkendall@co.dutchess.ny.us
County Attorney:
   Ronald L Wozniak 845-486-2110/fax: 845-486-2002
   e-mail: countyattorney@co.dutchess.ny.us
District Attorney:
   William V Grady 845-486-2300/fax: 845-486-2324
Public Defender:
   David Goodman . . . . 845-486-2280 or 800-660-8818
   fax: 845-486-2266
   e-mail: publicdefender@co.dutchess.ny.us
Sheriff:
   Adrian H Anderson 845-486-3800/fax: 845-452-2987
   e-mail: sheriff@co.dutchess.ny.us
Comptroller:
   Diane Jablonski 845-486-2050/fax: 845-486-2055
   e-mail: comptroller@co.dutchess.ny.us
Finance Commissioner:
   Pamela Barrack 845-486-2025/fax: 845-486-2198
   e-mail: rptaxfinance@co.dutchess.ny.us
Emergency Response Coordinator:
   John Murphy 845-486-2080/fax: 845-486-3998
   e-mail: emergency911@co.dutchess.ny.us
County Historian:
   Stan Mersand 845-486-3669/fax: 845-486-3679
   e-mail: dchistory@co.dutchess.ny.us

Erie County
County Office Bldg
95 Franklin St
Buffalo, NY 14202
716-858-7500 Fax: 716-858-8895
Web site: www.erie.gov

Chair, County Legislature (D):
   Lynn M Marinelli 716-832-0493/fax: 716-832-0494
   e-mail: marinelli@erie.gov
Majority Leader, County Legislature (D):
   Maria R Whyte 716-874-3257/fax: 716-874-4779
   e-mail: whytem@erie.gov
Minority Leader, County Legislature (R):
   Barry Weinstein 716-633-0617/fax: 716-633-0618
   e-mail: drbarry15@erie.gov
Clerk, Legislature:
   Robert M Graber 716-858-7045/fax: 716-858-8895
County Executive:
   Joel A Giambra 716-858-8500/fax: 716-858-8411
   e-mail: cereception@erie.gov
County Clerk:
   Kathy Hochul 716-858-8865/fax: 716-858-6550
   e-mail: eriecountyclerk@erie.gov
County Attorney:
   Laurence Rubin 716-858-2200
District Attorney:
   Frank J Clark 716-858-2424/fax: 716-858-7425
Sheriff:
   Timothy B Howard 716-858-7608/fax: 716-662-5554
Civil Defense/Disaster Preparedness Deputy Commissioner:
   Dean Messing 716-858-8477/fax: 716-858-7937
   e-mail: messingd@erie.gov
Comptroller:
   Mark C Poloncarz 716-858-8400/fax: 716-858-8507

Essex County
County Government Ctr
7551 Court St
PO Box 217
Elizabethtown, NY 12932
518-873-3350 Fax: 518-873-3356
Web site: www.co.essex.ny.us

Chairman, Board of Supervisors (R):
   Noel H Merrihew III . . . . 518-873-3350 or 518-873-6555
   e-mail: chair@co.essex.ny.us
Vice Chairman, Board of Supervisors (R):
   Catherine L Moses . . . . 518-873-3350 or 518-532-7737
   e-mail: cmoses@schroon.net
Clerk, Board of Supervisors:
   Deborah L Palmer 518-873-3353/fax: 518-873-3356
   e-mail: dpalmer@co.essex.ny.us
County Manager:
   Clifford Donaldson Jr 518-873-3333/fax: 518-873-3339
   e-mail: cdonaldson@co.essex.ny.us
County Clerk:
   Joseph A Provoncha 518-873-3601/fax: 518-873-3584
   e-mail: jprovon@co.essex.ny.us
County Attorney:
   Daniel Manning III 518-873-3380/fax: 518-873-3894
   e-mail: dmanning@co.essex.ny.us
District Attorney:
   Julie Garcia 518-873-3335/fax: 518-873-3788
   e-mail: jgarcia@co.essex.ny.us

Offices and agencies generally appear in alphabetical order, except when specific order is requested by listee.

COUNTY GOVERNMENT / County Government

Public Defender:
   Livingston Hatch...................518-873-3880/fax: 518-873-3888
Sheriff:
   Henry H Hommes...................518-873-3348/fax: 518-873-3340
   e-mail: hhommes@co.essex.ny.us
Director, Emergency Services:
   Raymond Thatcher...................518-873-3660/fax: 518-873-3663
   e-mail: emerserv@co.essex.ny.us
Treasurer:
   Michael G Diskin...................518-873-3317/fax: 518-873-3318
   e-mail: mdiskin@co.essex.ny.us

Franklin County
Courthouse
355 W Main St
Malone, NY 12953
518-481-1641 or 800-397-8686 Fax: 518-483-0141
Web site: www.franklincony.org

Chairman, County Legislature (D):
   Guy Smith..518-481-1641
Vice Chairman, County Legislature (D):
   Raymond Susice..................................518-481-1641
Majority Leader, County Legislature (D):
   Earl J Lavoie...................................518-481-1641
Minority Leader, County Legislature (R):
   Paul A Maroun...................................518-481-1641
   e-mail: wawbeek@aol.com
Clerk, Legislature:
   Gloria Valone..................518-481-1640/fax: 518-481-1639
County Manager:
   James N Feeley................518-481-1693/fax: 518-483-0141
   e-mail: jfeeley@co.franklin.ny.us
County Clerk:
   Wanda D Murtagh................518-481-1684/fax: 518-483-9143
   e-mail: wmurtagh@co.franklin.ny.us
County Attorney:
   Jonathan J Miller..............518-483-8400/fax: 518-483-2054
District Attorney:
   Derek P Champagne..............518-481-1544/fax: 518-481-1545
   e-mail: da@co.franklin.ny.us
Public Defender:
   Mark McCormick.................518-481-1624/fax: 518-483-4690
Sheriff:
   Jack Pelkey....................518-483-3304/fax: 518-483-3205
   e-mail: jpelkey@co.franklin.ny.us
Director, Emergency Preparedness/Fire Coordinator:
   Malcolm Jones....................................518-483-2580
   e-mail: mjones@co.franklin.ny.us
Treasurer:
   Byron A Varin..................518-481-1513 or 518-481-1511
   e-mail: bvarin@co.franklin.ny.us

Fulton County
County Office Bldg
223 W Main St
Johnstown, NY 12095
518-736-5540 Fax: 518-762-0224
e-mail: fultbos@co.fulton.ny.us
Web site: www.fulcony.com

Chairman, Board of Supervisors (R):
   Stephen L Barker...............518-736-5540 or 518-736-5544
Administrative Officer/Clerk of Board:
   Jon R Stead....................518-736-5540/fax: 518-736-5544

County Clerk:
   William E Eschler..............518-736-5555/fax: 518-762-3839
County Attorney:
   Arthur Spring..................518-736-5803/fax: 518-762-4504
District Attorney:
   Louise Kauffman-Sira...........518-736-5511/fax: 518-762-2042
Public Defender:
   J Gerard McAuliffe, Jr.........518-736-5820/fax: 518-762-0122
Sheriff:
   Thomas Lorey...................518-736-2100/fax: 518-736-2126
Treasurer:
   Bruce Ellsworth................518-736-5580/fax: 518-736-1794
Fire Coordinator & Director, Civil Defense:
   Allan Polmateer................518-736-5858 or 518-736-5850
   fax: 518-762-4938
County Historian:
   Peter Betz.......................................518-736-5667

Genesee County
Old Courthouse, 7 Main Street
Batavia, NY 14020
585-344-2550 x2202 Fax: 585-344-8582
e-mail: legis@co.genesee.ny.us
Web site: www.co.genesee.ny.us

Chairman, County Legislature (R):
   Mary Pat Hancock.................................585-343-1011
Vice Chairman, County Legislature (R):
   Hollis D Upson...................................585-343-6211
County Manager:
   Jay Gsell.....................585-344-2550 x2204/fax: 585-344-8582
   e-mail: comanager@co.genesee.ny.us
Clerk, Legislature:
   Carolyn Pratt..............................585-344-2550 x2202
County Clerk:
   Don Read......................585-344-2550 x2242/fax: 585-344-8521
   e-mail: coclerk@co.genesee.ny.us
County Attorney:
   John L Rizzo..............................585-344-2550 x2205
District Attorney:
   Lawrence Friedman.............585-344-2550 x2250/fax: 585-344-8544
Public Defender:
   Gary Horton...................585-344-2550 x2280/fax: 716-344-8553
   e-mail: publicdefender@co.genesee.ny.us
Sheriff:
   Gary Maha......................585-345-3000/fax: 585-343-9129
   e-mail: sheriff@co.genesee.ny.us
Treasurer:
   Scott German..............................585-344-2550 x2210
   e-mail: treas@co.genesee.ny.us
County Historian:
   Susan L Conklin...........................585-344-2550 x2613
   e-mail: history@co.genesee.ny.us

Greene County
411 Main St, 4th Fl
PO Box 467
Catskill, NY 12414
518-719-3270 Fax: 518-719-3793
e-mail: government@discovergreene.com
Web site: www.greenegovernment.com

Chairman, County Legislature (R):
   Wayne Speenburgh.................................518-719-3270
   e-mail: wspeenburgh@discovergreene.com

Offices and agencies generally appear in alphabetical order, except when specific order is requested by listee.

COUNTY GOVERNMENT / County Government

Majority Leader (R):
   Keith Valentine...................................518-719-3270
   e-mail: kvalentine@discovergreene.com
Minority Leader (D):
   Larry Gardner.......................518-719-3270 or 518-263-3747
Acting Clerk, Legislature:
   Tammy Sciavallo..................................518-719-3270
   e-mail: legislature@discovergreene.com
County Administrator:
   Douglas J Brewer..................................518-719-3270
   e-mail: countyadministrator@discovergreene.com
County Clerk:
   Mary Ann Kordich..................518-719-3255/fax: 518-719-3284
   e-mail: countyclerk@discovergreene.com
County Attorney:
   Carol Stevens.....................518-719-3540/fax: 518-719-3790
   e-mail: cstevens@discovergreene.com
District Attorney:
   Terry J Wilhelm...................518-719-3590/fax: 518-719-3792
   e-mail: da@discovergreene.com
Public Defender:
   Dominic Cornelius.................518-719-3220/fax: 518-719-3785
   e-mail: publicdefender@discovergreene.com
Sheriff:
   Richard H Hussey.................518-943-3300/fax: 518-943-6832
   e-mail: sheriff@discovergreene.com
Director, Emergency Services:
   John P Farrell Jr..................518-622-3643/fax: 518-622-0572
   e-mail: emergency@discovergreene.com
Treasurer:
   Willis Vermilyea..................................518-719-3530
   e-mail: wvermilyea@discovergreene.com
County Historian:
   Raymond Beecher................................518-731-6822

Hamilton County

County Courthouse, Rte 8
PO Box 205
Lake Pleasant, NY 12108
518-548-6651 Fax: 518-548-7608
e-mail: hamcosup@klink.net

Chairman, Board of Supervisors (R):
   William G Farber.....................518-548-6651 or 518-548-6385
Vice Chairman, Board of Supervisors (R):
   J R Risley............................518-548-6651 or 315-357-2204
   e-mail: inletsupervisor@eagle-wireless.com
Clerk, Board of Supervisors:
   Laura A Abrams...................................518-548-6651
County Clerk:
   Jane Zarecki......................................518-548-7111
County Attorney:
   Charles Getty Jr...................................315-336-3900
District Attorney:
   James T Curry....................................518-648-5113
Sheriff:
   Douglas A Parker.................................518-548-3113
Treasurer:
   Beth A Hunt......................................518-548-7911

Herkimer County

109 Mary St, Ste 1310
Herkimer, NY 13350
315-867-1112 Fax: 315-867-1109
e-mail: herkimercounty@herkimercounty.org
Web site: www.herkimercounty.org

Chairman, County Legislature (R):
   Leonard R Hendrix................................315-867-1108
   e-mail: diggerhend@aol.com
Majority Leader (R):
   Patrick E Russell..................................315-867-1108
   e-mail: perussell@frontiernet.net
Minority Leader (D):
   Claudine F Grande................................315-867-1108
Clerk, Legislature:
   Carole L LaLonde.................................315-867-1108
County Administrator:
   James W Wallace, Jr..............................315-867-1112
County Clerk:
   Sylvia M Rowan...................315-867-1129/fax: 315-866-4396
County Attorney:
   Robert J Malone..................................315-867-1123
District Attorney:
   John Crandall.....................315-867-1155/fax: 315-867-1348
Sheriff:
   Christopher Farber................315-867-1167/fax: 315-867-1354
Director, Emergency Management:
   Robert Vanderwalker..............315-867-1212/fax: 315-867-5873
Treasurer:
   Jennifer J Haggerty................315-867-1145/fax: 315-867-1315
Administrator Public Defender Program:
   Keith Bowers.....................................315-866-0006
County Historian:
   James M Greiner.................................315-866-1398

Jefferson County

County Office Bldg
175 Arsenal St
Watertown, NY 13601
315-785-3075 Fax: 315-785-5070
Web site: www.co.jefferson.ny.us

Chairman, Board of Legislators (R):
   Kent D Burto.......................315-785-3075 or 315-493-6550
Vice Chairman, Board of Legislators (R):
   Carolyn D Fitzpatrick................315-785-3075 or 315-782-3636
County Administrator/Budget Officer & Clerk, Board:
   Robert F Hagemann, III...........................315-785-3075
   e-mail: roberth@co.jefferson.ny.us
Deputy County Administrator:
   Michael E Kaskan.................................315-785-3075
County Clerk:
   Jo Ann M Wilder..................315-785-3081/fax: 315-785-5145
County Attorney:
   David J Paulsen...................315-785-3088/fax: 315-785-5178
District Attorney:
   Cindy Intschert...................315-785-3053/fax: 315-785-3371
Public Defender:
   Julie Hutchins.....................315-785-3152/fax: 315-785-5060
   e-mail: joannem@co.jefferson.ny.us
Sheriff:
   John P Burns.....................315-786-2700/fax: 315-786-2775
Director, Fire & Emergency Management:
   Greg Brunelle....................................315-786-2654
Treasurer:
   Nancy Brown....................................315-785-3055

Offices and agencies generally appear in alphabetical order, except when specific order is requested by listee.

COUNTY GOVERNMENT / County Government

Kings County (NYC Borough of Brooklyn)
209 Joralemon St
Brooklyn, NY 11201
718-802-3883 Fax: 718-802-3805
Web site: www.brooklyn-usa.org

Borough President (D):
  Marty Markowitz.................................718-802-3700
  e-mail: askmarty@brooklynbp.nyc.gov
Deputy Borough President:
  Yvonne J Graham.................................718-802-3842
  e-mail: ygraham@brooklynbp.nyc.gov
County Clerk:
  Nancy T Sunshine.................................347-404-9760
District Attorney:
  Charles J Hynes...................................718-250-2000
Director, Public Information:
  Jerry Schmetterer.................................718-250-2000
  e-mail: schmetj@brooklynda.org

Lewis County
Courthouse
7660 N State St
Lowville, NY 13367
315-376-5666 Fax: 315-376-5445
e-mail: computer@lewiscountyny.org
Web site: www.lewiscountyny.org

Chairman, Legislative Board (D):
  Jack T Bush..315-348-8033
  e-mail: j.bush@lewiscountyny.org
Clerk, Board of Legislature:
  Teresa L Clark....................................315-376-5356
County Clerk:
  Douglas Hanno..................315-376-5333/fax: 315-376-3768
  e-mail: clerk@lewiscountyny.org
County Attorney:
  Richard Graham................315-376-5282/fax: 315-376-3857
  e-mail: rgraham@lewiscountyny.org
District Attorney:
  Michael F Young................315-376-5390/fax: 315-376-5873
  e-mail: myoung@lewiscountyny.org
Public Defender:
  Danial King......................315-376-6565/fax: 315-376-8418
Sheriff:
  L Michael Tabolt................315-376-3511/fax: 315-376-5232
  e-mail: LCSD@lewiscountyny.org
Treasurer:
  Vickie Roy........................315-376-5325/fax: 315-376-3768
  e-mail: treasurer@lewiscountyny.org
County Manager:
  Joe Baruth.......................315-376-5354/fax: 315-376-5445
  e-mail: county.manager@lewiscountyny.org
Fire & Emergency Management:
  James Martin....................315-376-5305/fax: 315-376-5293
  e-mail: jmartin@lewiscountyny.org
County Historian:
  Lisa Becker..315-376-2825

Livingston County
Government Center
6 Court St
Geneseo, NY 14454
585-243-7000 Fax: 585-243-7045
e-mail: info@co.livingston.ny.us
Web site: www.co.livingston.state.ny.us

Chairman, Board of Supervisors (R):
  James C Merrick..................................585-243-7030
Vice Chairman, Board of Supervisors (R):
  Gary D Moore.....................................585-243-7030
Clerk, Board of Supervisors:
  Virginia O Amico..................................585-243-7030
  e-mail: vamico@co.livingston.ny.us
County Administrator:
  Dominic F Mazza................585-243-7040/fax: 585-243-7045
  e-mail: dmazza@co.livingston.ny.us
County Clerk:
  James A Culbertson...............585-243-7010 or 585-243-7000
  fax: 585-243-7928
  e-mail: jculbertson@co.livingston.ny.us
County Attorney:
  David J Morris...................585-243-7033 or 585-468-2770
  e-mail: dmorris@co.livingston.ny.us
District Attorney:
  Thomas E Moran................585-243-7020/fax: 585-243-7199
  e-mail: da@co.livingston.ny.us
Public Defender:
  Marcea A Clark..................585-243-7028/fax: 585-243-7193
  e-mail: lcpd@co.livingston.ny.us
Emergency Management Services:
  Kevin Niedermaier.................................585-243-7160
  e-mail: kniedermaier@co.livingston.ny.us
Sheriff:
  John M York......................585-243-7120/fax: 585-243-7104
  e-mail: sheriffyork@co.livingston.ny.us
Treasurer:
  Carolyn D Taylor................585-243-7050/fax: 585-243-7597
  e-mail: ctaylor@co.livingston.ny.us
Historian:
  Amie Alden......................585-243-7955/fax: 585-243-7956
  e-mail: historian@co.livingston.ny.us

Madison County
County Office Bldg
138 N Court St
PO Box 635
Wampsville, NY 13163
315-366-2201 Fax: 315-366-2502
e-mail: supervisors@co.madison.ny.us
Web site: www.madisoncounty.org

Chairman, Board of Supervisors (R):
  Rocco J DiVeronica................315-366-2201 or 315-697-9291
  e-mail: rocco.diveronica@co.madison.ny.us
Clerk, Board of Supervisors:
  Cindy Urtz..315-366-2201
County Clerk:
  Kenneth J Kunkel Jr...............................315-366-2261
County Attorney:
  S John Campanie................315-366-2203/fax: 315-366-2502
District Attorney:
  Donald F Cerio, Jr...............315-366-2236/fax: 315-366-2503
Public Defender Director:
  Paul H Hadley..................315-366-2585/fax: 315-366-2583
Fire Coordinator/Emergency Preparedness:
  Joe DiFrancisco.................315-366-2258/fax: 315-366-2452

Offices and agencies generally appear in alphabetical order, except when specific order is requested by listee.

COUNTY GOVERNMENT / County Government

Sheriff:
  Ronald Cary........................315-366-2318/fax: 315-366-2286
Treasurer:
  Harold C Landers..................315-366-2371/fax: 315-366-2705
Public Information Officer:
  Sharon A Driscoll.................................315-366-2788
County Historian:
  Sarah Davies......................315-366-2453/fax: 315-366-2742
  e-mail: sarah.davies@co.madison.ny.us

Monroe County
County Office Bldg
39 W Main St
Rochester, NY 14614
585-753-1950 Fax: 585-753-1932
Web site: www.monroecounty.gov

President, County Legislature (R):
  Wayne E Zyra.....................................585-753-1950
  e-mail: mclegislature@monroecounty.gov
Majority Leader (R):
  Andrew Moore..................585-753-1922/fax: 585-753-1960
  e-mail: AMoore@monroecounty.gov
Minority Leader (D):
  Jennifer Skoog-Harvey..........585-753-1940/fax: 585-753-1946
Clerk, Legislature:
  David M Barry....................................585-753-1950
County Executive:
  Maggie Brooks.................585-753-1000/fax: 585-753-1014
  e-mail: countyexecutive@monroecounty.gov
County Clerk:
  Cheryl Dinolfo................585-753-1600/fax: 585-753-1624
  e-mail: mcclerk@monroecounty.gov
County Attorney:
  Daniel M DeLaus, Jr..............................585-753-1380
  e-mail: mclawdept@monroecounty.gov
District Attorney:
  Michael C Green...............585-753-4500/fax: 585-753-4576
  e-mail: districtattorney@monroecounty.gov
Sheriff:
  Patrick M O'Flynn.............585-753-4178/fax: 585-753-4524
  e-mail: sherriff@monroecountysheriff.info
Public Defender:
  Edward J Nowak................585-753-4210/fax: 585-753-4234
  e-mail: mcpublicdefender@monroecounty.gov
Chief Financial Officer:
  Stephen W Gleason.............585-753-1157/fax: 585-753-1133
  e-mail: mcfinance@monroecounty.gov
Director, Communications:
  John R Durso Jr...............585-753-1080/fax: 585-753-1068
  e-mail: communications@monroecounty.gov
County Historian:
  Carolyn Vacca.................585-428-8352/fax: 585-428-8353

Montgomery County
County Annex Bldg 20 Park St
PO Box 1500
Fonda, NY 12068-1500
518-853-4304 Fax: 518-853-8220
Web site: www.co.montgomery.ny.us

Chairman, Board of Supervisors:
  Thomas P DiMezza.................................518-853-4304
Clerk, Board of Supervisors:
  Kimberly Sanborn.................................518-853-4304

County Clerk:
  Helen A Bartone...............518-853-8111/fax: 518-853-8171
County Attorney:
  Douglas E Landon..............518-843-3717 or 518-843-1300
  fax: 518-842-5331
District Attorney:
  James E Conboy................518-853-8250/fax: 518-853-8212
Public Defender:
  William Martuscello...........518-853-8305/fax: 518-853-8308
Sheriff:
  Michael J Amato...............518-853-5500 or 518-853-4312
  fax: 518-853-4096
Director, Emergency Management/Fire Coordinator:
  Gary Nestle...................518-853-4011/fax: 518-853-4714
Treasurer:
  Shawn J Bowerman..............518-853-8175/fax: 518-853-8344
County Historian:
  Kelly Y Farquhar..............518-853-8187/fax: 518-853-8392
  e-mail: kfarquhar@co.montgomery.ny.us

Nassau County
One West St
Mineola, NY 11501
516-571-3000 or 516-571-6200 Fax: 516-739-2636
Web site: www.nassaucountyny.gov

Presiding Officer of the Legislature (D):
  Judith A Jacobs...............516-571-6216/fax: 516-571-6636
Deputy Presiding Officer of the Legislature (D):
  Roger Corbin..................516-571-6202/fax: 516-571-6761
Minority Leader (R):
  Peter J Schmitt..................................516-571-6212
Clerk, Legislature:
  William P Geier..................................516-571-4252
County Executive:
  Thomas R Suozzi..................................516-571-3131
County Clerk:
  Maureen O'Connell................................516-571-2664
County Attorney:
  Lorna Goodman....................................516-571-3056
District Attorney:
  Kathleen M Rice...............516-571-3800/fax: 516-571-5065
  e-mail: nassauda@nassauda.org
Emergency Management Commissioner:
  James J Callahan II...........516-573-0636/fax: 516-573-0696
Police Commissioner:
  James H Lawrence.................................516-573-7000
Comptroller:
  Howard S Weitzman.............516-571-2386 or 516-571-2679
  e-mail: nccomptroller@nassaucountyny.gov
Treasurer:
  Steven D Conkling.............516-571-2090/fax: 516-571-1528
  e-mail: nctreasurer@nassaucountyny.gov

New York County (NYC Borough of Manhattan)
Municipal Bldg
One Centre St, 19th Fl S
New York, NY 10007
212-669-8300 Fax: 212-669-4900
Web site: www.mbpo.org

Borough President:
  Scott M Stringer.................................212-669-8155
  e-mail: bp@manhattanbp.org

Offices and agencies generally appear in alphabetical order, except when specific order is requested by listee.

404

COUNTY GOVERNMENT / County Government

County Clerk:
  Norman Goodman 646-386-5956
Chief Deputy County Clerk:
  James A Rossetti.................................. 646-386-5956
District Attorney:
  Robert M Morgenthau 212-335-9000
Public Advocate:
  Betsy Gotbaum 212-669-7200/fax: 212-669-4091

Niagara County
County Courthouse
175 Hawley Street
Lockport, NY 14094-2740
716-439-7000 Fax: 716-439-7124
Web site: www.niagaracounty.com

Chairman, County Legislature (R):
  Clyde L Burmaster 716-791-3111
    e-mail: clyde.burmaster@niagaracounty.com
Majority Leader (R):
  Richard Updegrove 716-434-2140
    e-mail: richard.updegrove@niagaracounty.com
Minority Leader (D):
  Dennis F Virtuoso.................................. 716-284-1582
    e-mail: dennis.virtuoso@niagaracounty.com
Clerk, Legislature:
  James Sobczyk................... 716-439-7177/fax: 716-439-7124
County Manager:
  Gregory Lewis.................... 716-439-7006/fax: 716-439-7212
    e-mail: greg.lewis@niagaracounty.com
County Clerk:
  Wayne F Jagow 716-439-7022/fax: 716-439-7035
    e-mail: niagaracountyclerk@niagaracounty.com
County Attorney:
  Claude A Joerg 716-439-7105/fax: 716-439-7114
    e-mail: claude.joerg@niagaracounty.com
District Attorney:
  Matthew J Murphy, III 716-439-7085/fax: 716-439-7102
Public Defender:
  Michael J Violante 716-439-7071
Sheriff:
  Thomas A Beilein 716-438-3370/fax: 716-438-3357
Emergency Services, Assistant Director:
  James C Volkosh................. 716-438-3171/fax: 716-438-3173
Treasurer:
  David S Broderick 716-439-7018/fax: 716-439-7021
Historian:
  Catherine L Emerson 716-439-7324

Oneida County
County Office Bldg
800 Park Ave
Utica, NY 13501
315-798-5900 Fax: 315-798-5924
e-mail: bol@co.oneida.ny.us or bol@ocgov.net
Web site: www.co.oneida.ny.us or www.ocgov.net

Chairman, County Legislature (R):
  Gerald J Fiorini.................................... 315-798-5900
Majority Leader (R):
  James M D'Onofrio 315-798-5535
Minority Leader (D):
  Harry A Hertline................................... 315-798-5049
Clerk, Legislature:
  Susan L Crabtree 315-798-5404

County Executive:
  Anthony J Picente Jr 315-798-5800/fax: 315-798-2390
    e-mail: ce@ocgov.net
County Clerk:
  Sandra J DePerno 315-798-5794
    e-mail: countyclerk@ocgov.net
County Attorney:
  Linda M H Dillon 315-798-5910/fax: 315-798-5603
    e-mail: coatty@ocgov.net
District Attorney:
  Scott D McNamara 315-798-5766/fax: 315-798-5582
    e-mail: distatty@ocgov.net
Public Defender-Criminal Division:
  Frank J Nebush Jr 315-798-5870/fax: 315-798-0364
    e-mail: pubdef@ocgov.net
Public Defender-Civil Division:
  Frank J Furno.................... 315-266-6100/fax: 315-266-6105
    e-mail: pdcivil@ocgov.net
Sheriff:
  Daniel G Middaugh .... 315-738-7804 or 315-765-2222
    fax: 315-765-2205
Emergency Services Director:
  Frederic A Van Namee 315-765-2526/fax: 315-765-2529
    e-mail: 911@ocgov.net
Comptroller:
  Joseph J Timpano 315-798-5780/fax: 315-798-6415
    e-mail: comptroller@ocgov.net
Finance Commissioner:
  Anthony R Carvelli................................. 315-798-5750
    e-mail: finance@ocgov.net

Onondaga County
401 Montgomery Street
Room 407
Syracuse, NY 13202
315-435-2070 Fax: 315-435-8434
Web site: www.ongov.net

Chairman, County Legislature (R):
  Dale A Sweetland.................................. 315-435-2070
    e-mail: dalesweetland@ongov.net
Majority Leader (R):
  Bernard Kraft .... 315-435-2070 or 315-652-9768
    e-mail: berniekraft@msn.com
Minority Leader (D):
  Edward F Ryan.................... 315-435-2070 or 315-471-1315
County Executive:
  Nicholas J Pirro 315-435-3516/fax: 315-435-8582
Clerk, Legislature:
  Deborah L Maturo 315-435-2070
    e-mail: debbiematuro@ongov.net
County Clerk:
  M Ann Ciarpelli 315-435-2229
County Attorney:
  Anthony P Rivizzigno 315-435-2170
District Attorney:
  William J Fitzpatrick 315-435-2470
    e-mail: daweb@ongov.net
Emergency Management Director:
  Peter P Alberti 315-435-2525/fax: 315-435-3309
Sheriff:
  Kevin E Walsh 315-435-3044
Comptroller:
  Donald F Colon 315-435-2130/fax: 315-435-2250
Chief Fiscal Officer:
  Joe C Mareane 315-435-2426/fax: 315-435-2421

Offices and agencies generally appear in alphabetical order, except when specific order is requested by listee.

COUNTY GOVERNMENT / County Government

Ontario County
Ontario Co Municipal Bldg
20 Ontario St
1st Fl Mezzanine
Canandaigua, NY 14424
585-396-4447 Fax: 585-396-8818
e-mail: bos@co.ontario.ny.us
Web site: www.co.ontario.ny.us

Chairman, Board of Supervisors (R):
 Theodore Fafinski 585-396-4447/fax: 585-396-8818
Vice Chairman, Board of Supervisors (R):
 Wayne F Houseman 585-396-4447
Clerk, Board of Supervisors:
 Karen R DeMay 585-396-4447
 e-mail: karen.demay@co.ontario.ny.us
County Administrator:
 Geoffrey C Astles 585-396-4400
 e-mail: county.administrator@co.ontario.ny.us
County Clerk:
 Jack H Cooley 585-396-4200
County Attorney:
 John W Park 585-396-4411/fax: 585-396-4481
District Attorney:
 R Michael Tantillo 585-396-4010/fax: 585-396-4860
 e-mail: michael.tantillo@co.ontario.ny.us
Treasurer:
 Gary G Baxter 585-396-4422
Emergency Management Director:
 Jeff Harloff 585-396-4310
Sheriff:
 Philip C Povero 585-394-4560
 e-mail: sheriff@co.ontario.ny.us
Public Works:
 William C Wright 585-396-4000
Historian:
 Dr Preston Pierce 585-396-4034
 e-mail: pep646@frontiernet.net

Orange County
County Government Center
255 Main St
Goshen, NY 10924
845-291-3000 Fax: 845-291-4809
e-mail: legislature@co.orange.ny.us
Web site: www.co.orange.ny.us

Chairman, County Legislature (R):
 M William Lahey 845-291-4800
Majority Leader (R):
 Michael R Pillmeier 845-291-4800
Minority Leader (D):
 Wayne A Decker 845-291-4800
Clerk, Legislature:
 Laurie M Whightsil 845-291-4800
County Executive:
 Edward A Diana 845-291-2700/fax: 845-291-2724
 e-mail: ceoffice@co.orange.ny.us
County Clerk:
 Donna L Benson 845-291-2690/fax: 845-291-2691
County Attorney:
 David Darwin 845-291-3150
District Attorney:
 Francis D Phillips, II 845-291-2050
Emergency Services Commissioner:
 Walter C Koury 845-291-3001/fax: 845-294-8927
Sheriff:
 Carl E DuBois 845-291-4033/fax: 845-294-1590
Finance Commissioner:
 Joel Kleiman 845-291-2485/fax: 845-291-2516
Historian:
 Theodore W Sly 845-291-2388/fax: 845-291-2027

Orleans County
Courthouse Sq
3 South Main St
Albion, NY 14411-1495
585-589-7053 Fax: 585-589-1618
Web site: www.orleansny.com

Chairman, County Legislature (R):
 George R Bower . . . . 585-589-7053 or 585-638-6051
Vice Chairman (R):
 Kenneth E Rush . . . . 585-589-7053 or 585-682-5546
Majority Leader (R):
 David B Callard . . . . 585-589-7053 or 585-789-1507
Minority Leader (D):
 Donald J Allport . . . . 585-589-7053 or 585-589-5496
Clerk, Legislature:
 Nadine P Hanlon 585-589-7053
 e-mail: hanlonn@orleansny.com
Chief Administrative Officer:
 Charles H Nesbitt Jr 585-589-7053
 e-mail: cnesbitt@orleansny.com
County Clerk:
 Karen Lake-Maynard 585-589-3214/fax: 585-589-2824
County Attorney:
 David C Schubel 585-798-2250/fax: 585-798-0776
 e-mail: occoa@orleansny.com
District Attorney:
 Joseph V Cardone 585-590-4127/fax: 585-590-4129
 e-mail: da@orleansny.com
Public Defender:
 Sanford A Church 585-589-7335/fax: 585-589-2592
Emergency Management Director:
 Paul Wagner 585-589-4414/fax: 585-589-7671
 e-mail: pwagner@orleansny.com
Sheriff:
 Scott D Hess 585-590-4142/fax: 585-590-4178
 e-mail: ocsher@orleansny.com
Treasurer/Deputy Budget Officer:
 Susan M Heard 585-589-5353/fax: 585-589-9220
 e-mail: sheard@orleansny.com
County Historian:
 C W Lattin 585-589-4174

Oswego County
46 E Bridge St
Oswego, NY 13126
315-349-8230 Fax: 315-349-8237
Web site: www.co.oswego.ny.us

Chairman, County Legislature (R):
 Russ W Johnson . . . . 315-349-8230 or 315-598-4295
 e-mail: rjohnson@oswegocounty.com
Majority Leader (R):
 Barry Leemann . . . . 315-349-8230 or 315-964-2850
 e-mail: dist4legislator@aol.com

Offices and agencies generally appear in alphabetical order, except when specific order is requested by listee.

COUNTY GOVERNMENT / County Government

Minority Leader (D):
  Mike Kunzwiler . . . . 315-349-8230 or 315-343-8385
  e-mail: mikekunzwiler@twcny.rr.com
Clerk, Legislature:
  Theodore I Jerrett 315-349-8230
  e-mail: tjerrett@oswegocounty.com
County Administrator:
  Stephen P Lyman. 315-349-8235/fax: 315-349-8237
  e-mail: slyman@oswegocounty.com
County Clerk:
  George J Williams 315-349-8385/fax: 315-349-8383
  e-mail: williamsg@oswegocounty.com
County Attorney:
  Richard C Mitchell 315-349-8296
  e-mail: rich@oswegocounty.com
Assigned Counsel Administrator:
  Stephen C Greene Jr 315-349-8575/fax: 315-349-8298
  e-mail: sgreene@oswegocounty.com
District Attorney/Coroner:
  Donald H Dodd 315-349-3200/fax: 315-349-3212
  e-mail: doddd@oswegocounty.com
Treasurer:
  John Kruk 315-349-8393/fax: 315-349-8255
  e-mail: marthas@oswegocounty.com
Director, Emergency Management:
  Patricia Egan 315-591-9150/fax: 315-591-9176
  e-mail: eganp@oswegocounty.com
Fire Coordinator:
  John Hinds 315-591-9142/fax: 315-591-9146
Sheriff:
  Reuel A Todd . . . . 315-349-3302 or 800-582-7583
  fax: 315-349-3303
  e-mail: sheriff@oswegocounty.com

Otsego County
County Office Bldg
197 Main St
Cooperstown, NY 13326-1129
607-547-4202 Fax: 607-547-4260
e-mail: childl@otsegocounty.com
Web site: www.otsegocounty.com

Chairman, Board of Representatives (R):
  Donald Lindberg. . . . . 607-547-4202 or 607-397-9467
  e-mail: lindbergd@otsegocounty.com
Vice Chairman, Board of Representatives (R):
  Ronald Feldstein. . . . . 607-547-4202 or 607-431-2540
  e-mail: feldsteinr@otsegocounty.com
Clerk, Board of Representatives:
  Laura A Child 607-547-4202
  e-mail: childl@otsegocounty.com
County Clerk:
  Kathleen Sinnott Gardner 607-547-4276/fax: 607-547-7544
  e-mail: gardnerk@otsegocounty.com
County Attorney:
  Rodney Klafehn 607-547-4208/fax: 607-547-7572
  e-mail: klafehnr@otsegocounty.com
District Attorney:
  John M Muehl 607-547-4249/fax: 607-547-4373
  e-mail: distatty@otsegocounty.com
Public Defender:
  Richard A Rothermel. 607-432-7410/fax: 607-433-2168
Sheriff:
  Richard Devlin Jr. 607-547-4271/fax: 607-547-6413
Coordinator, Emergency Services:
  Lyle W Jones Jr 607-547-4226

Treasurer:
  Myrna Thayne 607-547-4235/fax: 607-547-7579
  e-mail: thaynem@otsegocounty.com
County Historian:
  Nancy S Milavec 607-397-9705

Putnam County
40 Gleneida Avenue
Carmel, NY 10512
845-225-8690 Fax: 845-225-0715
e-mail: putcoleg@putnamcountyny.com
Web site: www.putnamcountyny.com

Chairman, County Legislature (R):
  Dan Birmingham 845-225-8690
Deputy Chairman, County Legislature (R):
  Terry Intrary 845-225-8690
Clerk, Legislature:
  M Chris Marrone 845-225-8690
Legislative Counsel:
  Clement Van Ross 845-225-8690
County Executive:
  Robert J Bondi 845-225-3641 x200/fax: 845-225-0294
County Clerk:
  Dennis J Sant. 845-225-3641 x300
County Attorney:
  Carl F Lodes 845-225-3641 x251
District Attorney:
  Kevin Wright. 845-225-3641 x277
Emergency Services Bureau Commissioner:
  Robert McMahon. 845-808-4000/fax: 845-808-4010
  e-mail: administration@pcbes.org
Sheriff:
  Donald Blaine Smith 845-225-4300/fax: 845-225-4399
Finance Commissioner:
  William J Carlin, Jr . . . . 845-225-3641 x321 or 845-225-3848
  fax: 845-225-8290
County Historian:
  Allan J Warnecke 845-278-7209/fax: 845-278-4865
  e-mail: putpast@bestweb.net

Queens County (NYC Borough of Queens)
120-55 Queens Blvd
Kew Gardens, NY 11424
718-286-3000 Fax: 718-286-2876
e-mail: info@queensbp.org
Web site: www.queensbp.org

Borough President:
  Helen M Marshall. 718-286-3000
Deputy Borough President:
  Karen Koslowitz. 718-286-3000
Public Information Officer/Press Office:
  Daniel Andrews 718-286-2640
County Clerk:
  Gloria D'Amico . . . . 718-298-0600 or 718-298-0605
District Attorney:
  Richard A Brown 718-286-6000
Public Administrator:
  Lois M Rosenblatt . . . . 718-526-5037 or 718-520-3710
  fax: 718-526-5043
  e-mail: mail@queenscountypa.com
Counsel:
  Gerard J Sweeney 718-459-9000/fax: 718-459-3163

Offices and agencies generally appear in alphabetical order, except when specific order is requested by listee.

COUNTY GOVERNMENT / County Government

Rensselaer County
County Office Bldg
1600 Seventh Ave
Troy, NY 12180
518-270-2880 Fax: 518-270-2983
Web site: www.rensco.com or www.rensselaercounty.org

Chairperson, County Legislature (R):
  Neil J Kelleher 518-270-2880
  e-mail: nkelleher@rensco.com
Vice Chairman (R):
  Thomas M Walsh Sr 518-270-2880
  e-mail: twalsh@rensco.com
Vice Chairman-Finance (R):
  Richard Salisbury 518-270-2880
  e-mail: rsalisbury@rensco.com
Majority Leader (C):
  Robert Mirch 518-270-2880
  e-mail: rmirch@rensco.com
Minority Leader (D):
  Virginia O'Brien 518-270-2890
  e-mail: gobrien@rensco.com
Clerk, Legislature:
  Jenet N Allard 518-270-2880
  e-mail: jallard@rensco.com
County Executive:
  Kathleen M Jimino 518-270-2900/fax: 518-270-2961
County Clerk:
  Frank Merola 518-270-4080/fax: 518-271-7998
County Attorney:
  Robert A Smith 518-270-2950/fax: 518-270-2954
District Attorney:
  Patricia A DeAngelis 518-270-4040
Public Defender:
  Jerome K Frost 518-270-4030
Sheriff:
  Jack Mahar 518-270-5448
Chief Fiscal Officer:
  Michael J Slawson 518-270-2750/fax: 518-270-2728

Richmond County (NYC Borough of Staten Island)
Borough Hall
10 Richmond Terrace
Staten Island, NY 10301
718-876-2000 Fax: 718-876-2026
Web site: www.statenislandusa.com

Borough President:
  James P Molinaro 718-816-2000
County Clerk:
  Stephen J Fiala 718-390-5396
District Attorney:
  Daniel M Donovan Jr 718-876-6300
  e-mail: info@rcda.nyc.gov
Public Administrator:
  Gary D Gotlin 718-876-7228/fax: 718-876-8377

Rockland County
County Office Bldg
11 New Hempstead Rd
New City, NY 10956
845-638-5100 Fax: 845-638-5675
Web site: www.co.rockland.ny.us

Chairwoman, County Legislature (D):
  Harriet D Cornell 845-638-5100
Majority Leader (D):
  Michael M Grant 845-638-5100
Minority Leader (R):
  Gerold M Bierker 845-638-5100
Clerk, Legislature:
  Laurence O Toole 845-638-5100
  e-mail: legclerk@co.rockland.ny.us
County Executive:
  C Scott Vanderhoef 845-638-5122
  e-mail: vanderhs@co.rockland.ny.us
County Clerk:
  Paul Piperato 845-638-5070/fax: 845-638-5647
  e-mail: rocklandcountyclerk@co.rockland.ny.us
County Attorney:
  Patricia Zugibe 845-638-5180
District Attorney:
  Michael E Bongiorno 845-638-5001
Public Defender:
  James D Licata 845-638-5660
  e-mail: licataj@co.rockland.ny.us
Director, Fire & Emergency:
  Gordon Wren 845-364-8800/fax: 845-364-8961
  e-mail: wreng@co.rockland.ny.us
Sheriff:
  James F Kralik 845-638-5400/fax: 845-638-5035
Finance/Budget Commissioner:
  Robert E Bergman, Jr 845-638-5262
  e-mail: bergmanr@co.rockland.ny.us

Saratoga County
County Municipal Center
40 McMaster St
Ballston Spa, NY 12020
518-885-2240 Fax: 518-884-4771
e-mail: sarckbd1@govt.co.saratoga.ny.us
Web site: www.co.saratoga.ny.us

Chairman, Board of Supervisors (R):
  Phil Barrett 518-885-2240
  e-mail: pbarrett@cliftonpark.org
County Administrator:
  David A Wickerham 518-884-4742
Clerk, Board of Supervisors:
  Barbara J Plummer 518-885-2240
County Clerk:
  Kathleen A Marchione 518-885-2213/fax: 518-884-4726
  e-mail: marchiok@govt.co.saratoga.ny.us
County Attorney:
  Mark Rider 518-884-4770
  e-mail: saracaty@govt.co.saratoga.ny.us
District Attorney:
  James A Murphy, III 518-885-2263/fax: 518-884-8627
  e-mail: disatty@govt.co.saratoga.ny.us
Public Defender:
  John Ciulla 518-884-4795
  e-mail: sarpdinfo@govt.co.saratoga.ny.us
Sheriff:
  James Bowen 518-885-6761
Emergency Services:
  Paul Lent 518-885-2232
  e-mail: saremer@govt.co.saratoga.ny.us

Offices and agencies generally appear in alphabetical order, except when specific order is requested by listee.

COUNTY GOVERNMENT / County Government

County Treasurer:
  Sam Pitcheralle...................................518-884-4724
  e-mail: sartreas@govt.co.saratoga.ny.us

Schenectady County
County Legislature
620 State St
Schenectady, NY 12305
518-388-4280 Fax: 518-388-4591
Web site: www.schenectadycounty.com

Chairperson, County Legislature (D):
  Susan E Savage....................................518-388-4280
Majority Leader (D):
  Kent W Gray.......................................518-388-4280
Minority Leader (R):
  Robert T Farley...................................518-388-4280
Clerk, Legislature:
  Goeffrey Hall.....................................518-388-4282
County Manager:
  Kathleen Rooney...................518-388-4355/fax: 518-388-4590
County Clerk:
  John J Woodward...................518-388-4220/fax: 518-388-4224
  e-mail: john.woodward@schenectadycounty.com
County Attorney:
  Christopher H Gardner.............518-388-4700/fax: 518-388-4493
District Attorney:
  Robert M Carney...................518-388-4364/fax: 518-388-4569
  e-mail: districtattorney@schenectadycounty.com
Public Defender:
  Mark J Caruso.....................................518-386-2266
Sheriff:
  Harry C Buffardi..................518-388-4300/fax: 518-388-4593
Director, Emergency Management:
  Bill VanHoesen....................................518-370-3113
Finance Commissioner:
  George Davidson...................518-388-4262/fax: 518-388-4248

Schoharie County
284 Main St
PO Box 429
Schoharie, NY 12157
518-295-8421 Fax: 518-295-8482
e-mail: www.schohariecounty-ny.gov

Chairman, Board of Supervisors (R):
  Earl VanWormer, III...............................518-875-6109
Majority Leader (R):
  Martin Shrederis..................................518-295-7310
Minority Leader (D):
  Philip Skowfoe....................................518-827-4896
Clerk, Board of Supervisors:
  Karen Miller......................518-295-8421/fax: 518-295-8482
  e-mail: millerk@co.schoharie.ny.us
County Clerk:
  M Indica Jaycox...................518-295-8316 or 518-295-8317
  fax: 518-295-8338
  e-mail: indyjaycox@co.schoharie.ny.us
County Attorney:
  Michael West......................518-296-8844/fax: 518-296-8855
District Attorney:
  James L Sacket....................518-295-8257/fax: 518-295-8266
Sheriff:
  John S Bates, Jr..................518-295-7066/fax: 518-295-7094

Director, Emergency Management:
  Judith Warner.....................518-295-8323 or 518-295-8344
  fax: 518-295-8308
Treasurer:
  William E Cherry..................518-295-8386 or 518-295-8363
  fax: 518-295-8364
Administrator Legal Defense:
  Raynor B Duncombe.................518-295-7515/fax: 518-295-7519

Schuyler County
County Bldg
105 Ninth St, Unit 6
Watkins Glen, NY 14891
607-535-8100 Fax: 607-535-8109
e-mail: legislature@co.schuyler.ny.us
Web site: www.schuylercounty.us

Chairman, County Legislature (R):
  Thomas M Gifford..................................607-535-8100
  e-mail: t5141@aol.com
Clerk, Legislature:
  Stacey B Husted...................................607-535-8100
  e-mail: legislature@co.schuyler.ny.us
County Clerk:
  Linda M Compton...................................607-535-8133
County Administrator/Budget Officer:
  Timothy M O'Hearn.................607-535-8106/fax: 607-535-8108
  e-mail: TOhearn@co.schuyler.ny.us
County Attorney:
  James P Coleman...................................607-535-8121
District Attorney:
  Joseph G Fazzary..................................607-535-8383
Public Defender:
  Connie Fern Miller................607-535-0057/fax: 607-535-4218
Sheriff:
  William Yessman Jr................................607-535-8222
  e-mail: wyessman@co.schuyler.ny.us
Treasurer:
  Margaret Starbuck.................................607-535-8181
County Historian:
  Barbara Bell......................................607-535-4577

Seneca County
County Office Bldg
1 DiPronio Dr
Waterloo, NY 13165
315-539-1800 Fax: 315-539-0207
e-mail: supervisors@co.seneca.ny.us
Web site: www.co.seneca.ny.us

Chairman, Board of Supervisors (R):
  Edward L Barto....................315-549-7681/fax: 315-539-0207
  e-mail: seylea@aol.com
Majority Leader (R):
  James H Mooney....................................315-539-1700
Minority Leader (D):
  Peter W Same......................................315-539-1700
  e-mail: psame@seneca24.net
Clerk, Board of Supervisors:
  Margaret E Li.....................315-539-1700/fax: 315-539-0207
  e-mail: mli@co.seneca.ny.us
County Clerk:
  Christina L Lotz..................315-539-1771/fax: 315-539-3789
  e-mail: clerk@co.seneca.ny.us

Offices and agencies generally appear in alphabetical order, except when specific order is requested by listee.

COUNTY GOVERNMENT / County Government

County Manager:
  Sharon L Secor 315-539-1701/fax: 315-539-0207
  e-mail: ssecor@co.seneca.ny.us
County Attorney:
  Steven J Getman 315-539-1989
  e-mail: sgetman@co.seneca.ny.us
District Attorney:
  Richard E Swinehart 315-539-1300/fax: 315-539-0531
  e-mail: rswinehart@co.seneca.ny.us
Sheriff:
  Leo T Connolly . . . . 315-539-9241 or 315-869-3721
  e-mail: lconnolly@co.seneca.ny.us
Public Defender:
  Michael J Mirras 315-568-4975
Treasurer:
  Nicholas A Sciotti 315-539-1735/fax: 315-539-1731
  e-mail: nsciotti@co.seneca.ny.us
County Historian:
  Walter Gable 315-539-1700
  e-mail: wgable@co.seneca.ny.us

St Lawrence County
County Courthouse
48 Court St
Canton, NY 13617-1169
315-379-2276 Fax: 315-379-2333
Web site: www.co.st-lawrence.ny.us

Chair, Board of Legislators (D):
  J Patrick Turbett 315-267-2567
  e-mail: turbetjp@potsdam.edu
Vice Chair, Board of Legislators (D):
  Tedra L Cobb 315-267-2740
  e-mail: tedra@tedracobb.com
Acting County Administrator:
  Robert O McNeil 315-379-2276/fax: 315-379-2463
  e-mail: bmcneil@co.st-lawrence.ny.us
County Clerk:
  Patricia Ritchie 315-379-2237/fax: 315-379-2302
  e-mail: pritchie@co.st-lawrence.ny.us
Deputy Clerk of the Board:
  Chandra L Wirtz 315-379-2276
Deputy Clerk of the Board:
  Ruth Doyle 315-379-2276
County Attorney:
  Andrew W Silver 315-379-2269/fax: 315-379-2254
  e-mail: asilver@co.st-lawrence.ny.us
District Attorney:
  Nicole M Duve 315-379-2225/fax: 315-379-2301
Public Defender:
  Michael Bass 315-379-2393/fax: 315-379-0401
Emergency Services, Dept Head:
  Michael F Wassus 315-379-2240/fax: 315-379-0681
  e-mail: tlabrake@co.st-lawrence.ny.us
Sheriff:
  Gary Jarvis 315-379-2222/fax: 315-379-0335
Treasurer:
  Robert O McNeil 315-379-2234/fax: 315-379-5274
  e-mail: jnarrow@co.st-lawrence.ny.us

Steuben County
County Office Bldg
3 East Pulteney Square
Bath, NY 14810
607-776-9631 Fax: 607-776-6926
e-mail: scplanning@co.steuben.ny.us
Web site: www.steubencony.org

Chairman, County Legislature (R):
  Philip J Roche 607-776-9631
Vice Chair, County Legislature (R):
  Patrick Donnelly 607-776-9631
Majority Leader (R):
  Gary D Swackhamer 607-776-9631
Minority Leader (D):
  Richard A Argentieri 607-776-9631
Clerk, County Legislature:
  Christine Kane 607-776-9631 ext2247
  e-mail: chris@co.steuben.ny.us
County Administrator:
  Mark R Alger 607-776-9631 ext2245
County Clerk:
  Judith M Hunter 607-776-9631 ext3203
County Attorney:
  Frederick H Ahrens, Jr 607-776-9631 ext2355
District Attorney:
  John C Tunney 607-776-9631 ext2270
Public Defender:
  Byrum W Cooper Jr 607-776-9631 ext2413
Director, Emergency Services/Fire Coordinator:
  Michael A Sprague 607-664-2700
Sheriff:
  Richard C Tweddell . . . . 607-776-7009 or 800-724-7777
Treasurer:
  Carol S Whitehead 607-776-9631 ext2488
Historian:
  Twila O'Dell 607-664-2199
  e-mail: historian@co.steuben.ny.us

Suffolk County
Rogers Legislature Bldg
725 Veterans Memorial Hwy
Smithtown, NY 11787
631-853-4070 Fax: 631-853-4899
Web site: www.co.suffolk.ny.us

Presiding Officer, County Legislature (D):
  William J Lindsay 631-854-9611/fax: 631-854-9687
  e-mail: william.lindsay@suffolkcountyny.gov
Deputy Presiding Officer, County Legislature (D):
  Vivian Viloria-Fisher 631-854-1650/fax: 631-854-1653
  e-mail: vivian.viloria-fisher@suffolkcountyny.gov
Majority Leader (D):
  Jon Cooper 631-854-4500/fax: 631-854-4503
  e-mail: jon.cooper@co.suffolk.ny.us
Minority Leader (R):
  Daniel P Losquadro 631-854-1600/fax: 631-854-1603
  e-mail: daniel.losquadro@suffolkcountyny.gov
Clerk, County Legislature:
  Tim Laube 631-853-4074/fax: 631-853-4899
  e-mail: tim.laube@co.suffolk.ny.us
County Executive:
  Steve Levy 631-853-4000
  e-mail: county.executive@suffolkcountyny.gov
County Clerk:
  Judith A Pascale 631-852-2000/fax: 631-852-2004
County Attorney:
  Christine Malafi 631-853-4049/fax: 631-853-5169

Offices and agencies generally appear in alphabetical order, except when specific order is requested by listee.

COUNTY GOVERNMENT / County Government

District Attorney:
  Thomas J Spota. 631-853-4161
  e-mail: infoda@co.suffolk.ny.us
Director, Emergency Management:
  Belinda Pagdanganan 631-852-4900
Sheriff:
  Vincent F DeMarco 631-852-2200
Comptroller:
  Joseph Sawicki Jr 631-853-5040/fax: 631-853-5057
  e-mail: joseph.sawicki@suffolkcountyny.gov
Treasurer:
  Angie M Carpenter 631-852-1500/fax: 631-852-1507
  e-mail: treasurer@co.suffolk.ny.us

Sullivan County
County Gov't Center
100 North St
PO Box 5012
Monticello, NY 12701-5192
845-794-3000 Fax: 845-794-3459
e-mail: info@co.sullivan.ny.us
Web site: www.co.sullivan.ny.us

Chairman (D):
  Christopher A Cunningham 845-794-3000 x3300/fax: 845-794-0650
  e-mail: christopher.cunningham@co.sullivan.ny.us
Vice-Chairman (D):
  Jonathan Rouis. 845-794-3000 x3300
Majority Leader (D):
  Kathleen LaBuda. 845-794-3000 x3306
Minority Leader (R):
  Rodney Gaebel 845-794-3000 x3300
Clerk, County Legislature:
  AnnMarie Martin. 845-794-3000 x3300
  e-mail: annmarie.martin@co.sullivan.ny.us
County Manager:
  David P Fanslau 845-794-3000 x3322/fax: 845-794-0230
County Clerk:
  George L Cooke, II. 845-794-3000 x5012/fax: 845-794-0230
  e-mail: george.cooke@co.sullivan.ny.us
County Attorney:
  Samuel S Yasgur 845-794-3000 x3565/fax: 845-794-4924
District Attorney:
  Stephen F Lungen 845-794-3344/fax: 845-794-3646
Emergency Mgmt Director & Public Safety Commissioner:
  Richard A Martinkovic 845-794-3000 x3100
Sheriff:
  Michael A Schiff . . . . 845-794-7100 or 845-794-7102
  fax: 845-791-7979
Treasurer:
  Ira J Cohen. 845-794-3000 x5016
County Historian:
  John Conway 845-557-3434

Tioga County
County Office Bldg
56 Main St
Owego, NY 13827
607-687-8200 or 607-687-8240 Fax: 607-687-8232
Web site: www.tiogacountyny.com

Chair, County Legislature (R):
  Dale N Weston 607-687-8240

Clerk, County Legislature:
  Maureen L Dougherty 607-687-8240
County Clerk:
  Robert L Woodburn. 607-687-8660/fax: 607-687-4612
County Attorney:
  Mark Dixson 607-687-8253/fax: 607-223-7003
District Attorney:
  Gerald A Keene. 607-687-8650/fax: 607-687-1614
Public Defender:
  Robert L Miller. 607-565-2455
Emergency Management:
  Richard LeCount 607-687-2023
Sheriff:
  Gary Howard 607-687-1010/fax: 607-687-6755
Treasurer:
  James P McFadden 607-687-8670/fax: 607-223-7035
  e-mail: mcfaddenj@co.tioga.ny.us

Tompkins County
125 E Court St
Ithaca, NY 14850
607-274-5551 Fax: 607-274-5558
Web site: www.co.tompkins.ny.us

Chairman, County Legislature (D):
  Tim J Joseph. 607-274-5434
  e-mail: joseph@tompkins-co.org
Clerk, Board of Representatives:
  Catherine Covert. 607-274-5434
County Administrator:
  Stephen F Whicher 607-274-5551/fax: 607-274-5558
  e-mail: ctyadmin@tompkins-co.org
County Clerk:
  Aurora R Valenti 607-274-5431/fax: 607-274-5445
  e-mail: countyclerk@tompkins-co.org
County Attorney:
  Jonathan Wood. 607-274-5546
  e-mail: countyattorney@tompkins-co.org
District Attorney:
  Gwen Wilkinson 607-274-5461/fax: 607-274-5429
  e-mail: distatty@tompkins-co.org
Sheriff:
  Peter Meskill 607-257-1345/fax: 607-266-5436
  e-mail: pmeskill@tompkins-co.org
Finance Director:
  David Squires 607-274-5545
  e-mail: finance@tompkins-co.org
Finance Director:
  Carol Kammen 607-274-5434
  e-mail: historian@tompkins-co.org

Ulster County
County Office Bldg
244 Fair Street
Kingston, NY 12401
845-340-3900 Fax: 845-340-3651
e-mail: egov@co.ulster.ny.us
Web site: www.co.ulster.ny.us

Chairman, County Legislature (D):
  David Donaldson 845-340-3900
Majority Leader (D):
  Jeanette Provenzano 845-340-3900
Minority Leader (R):
  Glenn P Noonan 845-340-3900

Offices and agencies generally appear in alphabetical order, except when specific order is requested by listee.

COUNTY GOVERNMENT / County Government

Clerk of the County Legislature:
  Kathleen Carey Mihm 845-340-3900/fax: 845-340-3651
County Administrator:
  Michael P Hein 845-340-3800/fax: 845-340-3651
County Clerk:
  Nina Postupack 845-340-3288/fax: 845-340-3299
  e-mail: countyclerk@co.ulster.ny.us
County Attorney:
  Joshua Koplovitz 845-340-3685/fax: 845-340-3691
  e-mail: jkop@co.ulster.ny.us
District Attorney:
  Donald A Williams, Jr 845-340-3280/fax: 845-340-3185
Public Defender:
  Andrew Kossover 845-340-3232/fax: 845-340-3744
  e-mail: akos@co.ulster.ny.us
Director, Emergency Management:
  Arthur R Snyder 845-338-1440/fax: 845-331-1738
  e-mail: asny@co.ulster.ny.us
Sheriff:
  Paul Van Blarcum 845-338-3640/fax: 845-331-2810
  e-mail: sheriff@co.ulster.ny.us
Treasurer:
  Lewis C Kirschner 845-340-3460/fax: 845-340-3430
  e-mail: lkir@co.ulster.ny.us
Historian:
  Karlyn Knaust Elia 845-246-9893/fax: 845-246-4754
  e-mail: ulsterhistorian@aol.com

Warren County
Municipal Center, 1340 State Rte 9
Lake George, NY 12845
518-761-6535 Fax: 518-761-7652
e-mail: boardofsupervisors@co.warren.ny.us
Web site: www.co.warren.ny.us

Chairman, Board of Supervisors (R):
  William H Thomas 518-761-6535
Clerk, Board of Supervisors:
  Joan Sady 518-761-6563
Commissioner, Administrative & Fiscal Services:
  Hal Payne 518-761-6535
County Clerk:
  Pamela J Vogel 518-761-6427/fax: 518-761-6551
County Attorney:
  Paul Dusek 518-761-6463/fax: 518-761-6377
District Attorney:
  Kathleen B Hogan 518-761-6405/fax: 518-761-6254
Public Defender:
  John P M Wappett 518-761-6207/fax: 518-761-6208
Sheriff:
  Larry J Cleveland 518-743-2500/fax: 518-743-2589
Treasurer:
  Francis X O'Keefe 518-761-6379/fax: 518-761-6470
Historian:
  John Austin 518-761-6544

Washington County
383 Broadway
Fort Edward, NY 12828
518-746-2100 Fax: 518-746-2108
Web site: www.co.washington.ny.us

Chairman, Board of Supervisors (R):
  JoAnn C Trinkle 518-746-2210
Vice Chairman:
  Donald Wilbur 518-746-2210
Clerk, Board of Supervisors:
  Debra R Prehoda 518-746-2210
County Administrator:
  Kevin G Hayes 518-746-2100/fax: 518-746-2590
County Clerk/Historian:
  Deborah R Beahan 518-746-2170/fax: 518-746-2177
County Attorney:
  Roger A Wickes 518-746-2216
District Attorney:
  Kevin C Kortright 518-746-2525
Public Defender:
  Patrick Barber 518-747-2823
Sheriff:
  Roger W LeClaire 518-746-2475
Fire Coordinator:
  Raymond Rathburn 518-746-2255
Treasurer:
  Phyllis Cooper 518-746-2220

Wayne County
Wayne County Courthouse
26 Church St
Lyons, NY 14489
315-946-5400 Fax: 315-946-5407
Web site: www.co.wayne.ny.us

Chairman, Board of Supervisors (R):
  James Hoffman 315-946-5400
  e-mail: jhoffman@co.wayne.ny.us
Majority Leader (R):
  David Lyon 315-597-2324/fax: 315-597-5550
  e-mail: palmyrasupv@palmyrany.com
Minority Leader (D):
  Joseph DeSanto 315-331-7369/fax: 315-331-8854
  e-mail: superar@rochester.rr.com
Clerk, Board of Supervisors:
  Sandra Sloane 315-946-5403
Interim County Administrator/Fiscal Officer:
  Keith Kubasik 315-946-5400/fax: 315-946-5407
County Clerk:
  Michael Jankowski 315-946-7470/fax: 315-946-5978
  e-mail: mjankowski@co.wayne.ny.us
County Attorney:
  Daniel M Wyner 315-946-7442
  e-mail: dwyner@co.wayne.ny.us
District Attorney:
  Richard Healy 315-946-5905/fax: 315-946-5911
  e-mail: rhealy@co.wayne.ny.us
Public Defender:
  Ronald C Valentine 315-946-7472/fax: 315-946-7478
  e-mail: rvalentine@co.wayne.ny.us
Director, Emergency Management:
  Thelma Wildeman 315-946-5663/fax: 315-946-9721
Sheriff:
  Richard J Pisciotti 315-946-9711/fax: 315-946-5811
  e-mail: rjpisciotti@co.wayne.ny.us
Treasurer:
  Thomas A Warnick 315-946-7441/fax: 315-946-5949
  e-mail: warnicktreasurer@co.wayne.ny.us
County Historian:
  Peter Evans 315-946-5470/fax: 315-946-5460
  e-mail: historian@co.wayne.ny.us

Offices and agencies generally appear in alphabetical order, except when specific order is requested by listee.

COUNTY GOVERNMENT / County Government

Westchester County
800 Michaelian Bldg
148 Martine Ave
White Plains, NY 10601
914-995-2800 Fax: 914-995-3884
e-mail: pmol@westchestergov.com
Web site: www.westchestergov.com/bol

Chair, Board of Legislators (D):
  William J Ryan.....................914-995-2827
    e-mail: wjr1@westchestergov.com
Majority Leader (D):
  Martin Rogowsky..................914-995-2834
    e-mail: cyy9@westchestergov.com
Minority Leader (R):
  George Oros......................914-995-2828
    e-mail: goo6@westchestergov.com
Clerk, Board of Legislature & Chief of Staff:
  Tina Seckerson...................914-995-2823
    e-mail: tinas@westchesterlegislators.com
County Executive:
  Andrew J Spano...................914-995-2900
    e-mail: ceo@westchestergov.com
Deputy County Executive:
  Lawrence Schwartz...........914-995-2900/fax: 914-995-3372
County Clerk:
  Timothy C Idoni..............914-995-3081/fax: 914-995-4030
    e-mail: cclerk@westchestergov.com
County Attorney:
  Charlene M Indelicato............914-995-2690
    e-mail: cai2@westchestergov.com
District Attorney:
  Janet Difiore................914-995-3414/fax: 914-995-2116
Sheriff/Public Safety Commissioner:
  Thomas Belfiore..................914-864-7858
    e-mail: teb1@westchestergov.com
Finance Commissioner:
  Peter P Pucillo..................914-995-2756
    e-mail: ppp7@westchestergov.com
Public Works Commissioner:
  Ralph Butler.....................914-995-2546
    e-mail: rlb3@westchestergov.com
Emergency Management Office:
  Anthony W Sutton............914-813-1850 or 914-231-1688
    e-mail: aws1@westchestergov.com

Wyoming County
Gov't Center, 143 N Main St
Warsaw, NY 14569
585-786-8800 Fax: 585-786-8802
Web site: www.wyomingco.net

Chairman, Board of Supervisors (R):
  A Douglas Berwanger..........585-786-8800 or 585-492-4685
    e-mail: adberwanger@wyomingco.net
Vice Chairman, Board of Supervisors (R):
  Jerry Davis......................585-786-8800
Clerk, Board of Supervisors:
  Cheryl Ketchum...................585-786-8800
    e-mail: cketchum@wyomingco.net

County Clerk:
  Janet Coveny.................585-786-8810/fax: 585-786-3703
    e-mail: jcoveny@wyomingco.net
County Attorney:
  Eric T Dadd..................585-591-1724/fax: 585-591-1722
District Attorney:
  Gerald L Stout...............585-786-8822/fax: 585-786-8842
    e-mail: gstout@wyomingco.net
Public Defender:
  Norman P Effman..............585-591-1600/fax: 585-591-1602
    e-mail: attlegal@iinc.com
Acting Director, Fire & Emergency Management:
  William Streicher............585-786-8867/fax: 585-786-8961
Sheriff:
  Farris H Heimann.............585-786-8989/fax: 585-786-8961
    e-mail: fheimann@wyomingco.net
Treasurer:
  Cheryl Mayer.................585-786-8812/fax: 585-786-0466
    e-mail: cdmayer@wyomingco.net
County Historian:
  Doris Bannister..................585-786-8818

Yates County
417 Liberty St
Penn Yan, NY 14527
315-536-5150 Fax: 315-536-5166
Web site: www.yatescounty.org

Chairman, County Legislature (R):
  Robert N Multer..................315-536-5150
    e-mail: legislature@yatescounty.org
Vice Chairman, County Legislature (R):
  Patrick H Flynn..................315-536-5150
County Administrator:
  Sarah Purdy..................315-536-5100/fax: 315-536-5118
    e-mail: ycadministrator@yatescounty.org
Clerk, County Legislature:
  Connie C Hayes...............315-536-5150/fax: 315-536-5166
    e-mail: legislature@yatescounty.org
County Clerk:
  Julie D Betts................315-536-5120/fax: 315-536-5545
    e-mail: countyclerk@yatescounty.org
County Attorney:
  Bernetta A Bourcy............315-531-3233 or 315-536-0070
  fax: 315-536-5166
District Attorney:
  Susan H Lindenmuth...........315-536-5550/fax: 315-536-5556
Public Defender:
  Edward J Brockman............585-374-6439 or 315-536-0352
Sheriff:
  Ronald G Spike...............315-536-4438/fax: 315-536-5191
    e-mail: sheriff@yatescounty.org
Treasurer:
  Bonnie L Percy...............315-536-5192/fax: 315-536-5527
    e-mail: treasurer@yatescounty.org
Emergency Management Director:
  Glen Miller..................315-536-3000/fax: 315-536-5106
    e-mail: emergencymanagement@yatescounty.org
Historian:
  Frances Dumas................315-536-5147/fax: 315-531-3226
    e-mail: history@yatescounty.org

Offices and agencies generally appear in alphabetical order, except when specific order is requested by listee.

MUNICIPAL GOVERNMENT

Municipal Government

Albany, City of
City Hall
24 Eagle St, Rm 102
Albany, NY 12207
518-434-5100 Fax: 518-434-5013
e-mail: webmaster@ci.albany.ny.us
Web site: www.albanyny.org

Mayor:
　Gerald D Jennings 518-434-5100/fax: 518-434-5013
Deputy Mayor:
　Philip F Calderone 518-434-5077/fax: 518-434-5074
Executive Asst to the Mayor:
　Joseph J Rabito 518-434-5100
President, Common Council:
　Shawn Morris 518-426-0530/fax: 518-434-5081
　e-mail: hdesfosses@aol.com
City Clerk:
　John Marsolais 518-434-5090/fax: 518-434-5081
Corporation Counsel:
　John Reilly 518-434-5050/fax: 518-434-5070
City Comptroller:
　Thomas Nitido 518-434-5023/fax: 518-434-5098
City Treasurer:
　Betty Barnette 518-434-5036/fax: 518-434-5041
Commissioner, General Services:
　Willard Bruce . . . . 518-432-2489 or 518-427-7499
　fax: 518-427-7499
Commissioner, Assessment & Taxation:
　Keith McDonald 518-434-5155/fax: 518-434-5098
Police Chief:
　James E Tuffey 518-462-8013/fax: 518-447-7801
Fire Chief/Emergency Services:
　Robert Forezzi 518-447-7877/fax: 518-434-8675
Director, Community Development:
　Joseph Montana 518-434-5240
Director, Building & Codes:
　Nicholas DiLello 518-434-5165/fax: 518-434-6015

Amherst, Town of
5583 Main St
Williamsville, NY 14221
716-631-7000 Fax: 716-631-7146
e-mail: webmaster@amherst.ny.us
Web site: www.amherst.ny.us

Town Supervisor:
　Satish B Mohan 716-631-7032
　e-mail: smohan@amherst.ny.us
Town Clerk:
　Susan K Jaros 716-631-7045/fax: 716-631-7152
　e-mail: sjaros@amherst.ny.us
Town Attorney:
　E Thomas Jones 716-631-7030/fax: 716-631-7101
　e-mail: tjones@amherst.ny.us

Comptroller:
　Francis Belliotti 716-631-7005/fax: 716-631-7012
　e-mail: fbelliotti@amherst.ny.us
Director Emergency Services & Safety:
　James J Zymanek 716-631-7121/fax: 716-631-7076
　e-mail: jzymanek@amherst.ny.us
Police Chief:
　John J Moslow 716-689-1311/fax: 716-689-1310
　e-mail: jmoslow@apdny.org

Auburn, City of
Memorial City Hall
24 South Street
Auburn, NY 13021
315-255-4100 Fax: 315-255-4181
Web site: auburnny.virtualtownhall.net

Mayor:
　Timothy C Lattimore 315-255-4104/fax: 315-253-8345
　e-mail: mayor@ci.auburn.ny.us
City Manager:
　Mark Palesh 315-255-4146/fax: 315-255-4735
　e-mail: citymanager@ci.auburn.ny.us
City Clerk:
　Debra A McCormick 315-255-4100/fax: 315-255-4181
　e-mail: dmccormick@ci.auburn.ny.us
Acting Corporation Counsel:
　John Rossi 315-255-4176/fax: 315-255-4735
　e-mail: corpcounsel@ci.auburn.ny.us
Planning & Economic Development Program Manager:
　Jennifer Haines 315-255-4115/fax: 315-253-0282
　e-mail: jhaines@ci.auburn.ny.us
Comptroller:
　Lisa Green 315-255-4138/fax: 315-255-4727
　e-mail: lgreen@ci.auburn.ny.us
Treasurer:
　Marie Nellenback 315-255-4143/fax: 315-255-4727
　e-mail: mnellenback@ci.auburn.ny.us
Police Chief:
　Gary J Giannotta 315-253-3231/fax: 315-255-0022
　e-mail: chief@auburnpolice.com
Interim Fire Chief:
　Terri Winslow 315-253-4031/fax: 315-252-0318
　e-mail: twinslow@ci.auburn.ny.us

Babylon, Town of
200 E Sunrise Highway
Lindenhurst, NY 11757-2598
631-957-3000 Fax: 631-957-7440
e-mail: info@townofbabylon.com
Web site: www.townofbabylon.com

Town Supervisor:
　Steven Bellone 631-957-3072
Chief of Staff:
　Ronald Kluesner 631-957-3072

Offices and agencies generally appear in alphabetical order, except when specific order is requested by listee.

MUNICIPAL GOVERNMENT / Municipal Government

Town Clerk:
   Janice Tinsley-Colbert 631-957-3005
Town Attorney:
   Dennis Cohen 631-957-3029
Comptroller:
   Victoria Marotta 631-957-3179
Commissioner, Public Works:
   Phil Berdolt 631-957-3161
Director, Public Safety:
   Pat Farrell 631-422-7600/fax: 631-893-1031
Commissioner, General Services:
   Patricia Kaphan 631-957-3025

Bethlehem, Town of
445 Delaware Ave
Delmar, NY 12054-3098
518-439-4955 Fax: 518-439-1699
Web site: www.townofbethlehem.org

Town Supervisor:
   Theresa Egan 518-439-4955 x1164
   e-mail: tegan@townofbethlehem.org
Town Clerk:
   Kathleen A Newkirk 518-439-4955 x1183
   e-mail: knewkirk@townofbethlehem.org
Town Attorney:
   James Potter 518-436-4955 x1164/fax: 518-436-4751
   e-mail: jpotter@townofbethlehem.org
Comptroller:
   Judith E Kehoe 518-439-4955 x1123
   e-mail: jkehoe@townofbethlehem.org
Police Chief:
   Louis G Corsi 518-439-9973/fax: 518-439-6965
Emergency Management Director:
   John E Brennan 518-439-4955 x1166
   e-mail: jbrennan@townofbethlehem.org
Commissioner, Public Works:
   Oliver Holmes 518-439-4955 x1132
   e-mail: oholmes@townofbethlehem.org
Historian:
   Raymond C Houghton 518-478-9798
   e-mail: rhoughton@townofbethlehem.org

Binghamton, City of
City Hall
38 Hawley St
Binghamton, NY 13901
607-772-7005 Fax: 607-772-0508
Web site: www.cityofbinghamton.com

Mayor:
   Matthew T Ryan 607-772-7001
   e-mail: mayor@cityofbinghamton.com
Executive Assistant to the Mayor:
   Tarik Abdelazim 607-772-7001
   e-mail: tabdelazim@cityofbinghamton.com
City Clerk:
   Sheila Keatings 607-772-7005
   e-mail: clerk@cityofbinghamton.com
Corporation Counsel:
   Kenneth Frank 607-772-7013
City Treasurer:
   Delorme Taylor 607-772-7027
   e-mail: treasurer@cityofbinghamton.com

City Assessor:
   Mark Minoia 607-772-7002/fax: 607-772-7106
   e-mail: assessor@cityofbinghamton.com
Commissioner, Public Works:
   Luke Day 607-772-7021/fax: 607-772-7023
   e-mail: dpw@cityofbinghamton.com
Police Chief:
   Steven Tronovitch 607-772-7090/fax: 607-772-7169
   e-mail: police@cityofbinghamton.com
Administrator, Civil Service:
   Scott McNerney 607-772-7008
   e-mail: cs@cityofbinghamton.com
Director, Finance/Comptroller:
   John Cox 607-772-7011/fax: 607-772-7106
   e-mail: finance@cityofbinghamton.com
Director, Planning/Housing/Community Development:
   James Dessauer 607-772-7028/fax: 607-772-7063
   e-mail: planning@cityofbinghamton.com
Director, Economic Development:
   Merry Harris 607-772-7161/fax: 607-772-7244
   e-mail: ecodev@cityofbinghamton.com

Brighton, Town of
2300 Elmwood Ave
Rochester, NY 14618
585-784-5250 Fax: 585-784-5373
e-mail: brtown@rochester.rr.com
Web site: www.townofbrighton.org

Town Supervisor:
   Sandra L Frankel 585-784-5251
   e-mail: sfrankel@rochester.rr.com
Town Clerk:
   Susan Kramarsky . . . . 585-784-5247 or 585-784-5240
   e-mail: skramar@rochester.rr.com
Acting Director, Finance:
   Daniel Goebert 585-784-5210
   e-mail: dgoebert@rochester.rr.com
Police Chief:
   Thomas W Voelkl 585-784-5101
Fire Marshal:
   Jim Quinn . . . . 585-784-5220 or 585-381-3200
Town Attorney:
   William Moehle 585-784-5258/fax: 585-271-0847
Commissioner, Public Works:
   Tom Low 585-784-5225
   e-mail: tlow@rochester.rr.com
Director, Communications:
   Melissa Hantman 585-784-5253

Brookhaven, Town of
One Independence Hill
Farmingville, NY 11738
631-451-6655 Fax: 631-451-6677
Web site: www.brookhaven.org

Town Supervisor:
   Brian X Foley 631-451-6955
Town Clerk/Registrar:
   Pam Betheil 631-451-9101/fax: 631-451-9264
Town Attorney:
   Robert Quinlan 631-451-6500/fax: 631-698-4489
Commissioner of Finance:
   Kim Brandeau 631-451-6680/fax: 631-451-6692

Offices and agencies generally appear in alphabetical order, except when specific order is requested by listee.

415

MUNICIPAL GOVERNMENT / Municipal Government

Commissioner, Public Safety:
  Kevin M Cronin..................631-451-6291/fax: 631-451-6908
Receiver of Taxes:
  George A Davis..................631-451-9009/fax: 631-451-9008

Buffalo, City of
City Hall
65 Niagara Square
Buffalo, NY 14202
716-851-4200 Fax: 716-851-4360
Web site: www.ci.buffalo.ny.us

Mayor:
  Byron W Brown................................716-851-4841
Council President:
  David Franczyk...............................716-851-4138
  e-mail: dfranczyk@city-buffalo.com
City Clerk:
  Gerald Chwalinski............................716-851-5431
  e-mail: gchwalinski@city-buffalo.com
Corporation Counsel:
  Alisa Lukasiewicz............................716-851-4333
Comptroller:
  Andrew A SanFilippo.............716-851-5255/fax: 716-851-4031
  e-mail: asanfilippo@city-buffalo.com
Commissioner, Administration, Finance & Urban Affairs:
  Janet Penska.................................716-851-5922
Police Commissioner:
  H McCarthy Gipson............................716-851-4571
Fire Commissioner:
  Michael L Lombardo...........................716-851-5333
Director Emergency Preparedness:
  Roger Lander....................716-851-6510/fax: 716-851-4360
  e-mail: rlander@city-buffalo.com
Acting Commissioner, Public Works/Parks & Streets:
  Dan Kreuz...................716-851-5636 or 716-884-9660
Director, Communications:
  Peter K Cutler...............................716-851-4841

Camillus, Town of
4600 W Genesee Street
Syracuse, NY 13219
315-488-1335 Fax: 315-488-8768
Web site: www.townofcamillus.com

Town Supervisor:
  Mary Ann Coogan..............................315-488-1335
  e-mail: macoogan@townofcamillus.com
Town Clerk:
  Martha Dickson-McMahon..........315-488-1234/fax: 315-488-8983
  e-mail: mdickson@townofcamillus.com
Comptroller:
  Robert Kline....................315-488-2266/fax: 315-488-8983
  e-mail: rkline@townofcamillus.com
Town Attorney:
  Dirk Oudemool................................315-488-1234
Police Chief:
  Thomas Winn..................................315-487-0102
  e-mail: twinn@townofcamillus.com

Carmel, Town of
Town Hall
60 McAlpin Ave
Mahopac, NY 10541
845-628-1500 Fax: 845-628-7434
Web site: www.carmelny.org

Town Supervisor:
  Conny Munday...................845-628-1470/fax: 845-628-6836
Town Clerk:
  Ann Garris...................................845-628-1500
Town Counsel:
  Thomas Costello................845-328-5590/fax: 845-328-5591
Comptroller:
  Thomas Carey...................845-628-1500/fax: 845-628-7085
Police Chief:
  Michael R Johnson..............845-628-1300/fax: 845-628-2597
  e-mail: polcapt@bestweb.net

Cheektowaga, Town of
Town Hall
3301 Broadway
Cheektowaga, NY 14227
716-686-3465 Fax: 716-686-3515
Web site: www.tocny.org

Town Supervisor:
  James Jankowiak..............................716-686-3465
Town Clerk/Historian:
  Mary F Holtz.................................716-686-3434
  e-mail: mholtz@tocny.org
Town Attorney:
  Kevin Schenk...................716-686-3457/fax: 716-686-3997
Emergency Services Manager:
  Earl Loder...................................716-686-3465
Director, Administration & Finance:
  Brian Krause.................................716-686-3492
  e-mail: bkrause@tocny.org
Police Chief:
  Christine M Ziemba.............716-686-3557/fax: 716-686-3935
  e-mail: cziemba@tocny.org

Chili, Town of
3333 Chili Avenue
Rochester, NY 14624
585-889-3550 Fax: 585-889-8710
e-mail: info@townofchili.org
Web site: www.townofchili.org

Town Supervisor:
  Tracy L Logel................................585-889-6111
  e-mail: tlogel@townofchili.org
Clerk/Deputy Supervisor:
  Richard J Brongo.............................585-889-6125
  e-mail: rbrongo@townofchili.org
Director of Finance:
  Dianne O'Meara...............................585-889-6120
Town Attorney:
  Richard Stowe..................585-352-1831/fax: 585-352-1387
Commissioner, Public Works:
  Joseph Carr..................................585-889-2630
  e-mail: jcarr@townofchili.org
Town Historian:
  Anne Leach...................................585-889-6123
  e-mail: aleach@townofchili.org

Offices and agencies generally appear in alphabetical order, except when specific order is requested by listee.

MUNICIPAL GOVERNMENT / Municipal Government

Cicero, Town of
Town Hall
8236 S Main St
Cicero, NY 13039
315-699-1414 Fax: 315-699-0039
Web site: www.ciceronewyork.net

Town Supervisor:
   Chet Dudzinski..................................315-699-1414
   e-mail: supervisor@cynmail.com
Town Clerk:
   Tracy M Cosilmon..................315-699-8109/fax: 315-699-0039
   e-mail: clerk@cynmail.com
Comptroller:
   Christopher McCarthy...........................315-699-2759
Receiver of Taxes:
   Sharon Edick......................315-699-2756/fax: 315-699-9562
   e-mail: sharonedick@usadatanet.net
Police Chief:
   Joseph F Snell Jr..................315-699-3677/fax: 315-699-8128

Clarence, Town of
1 Town Place
Clarence, NY 14031
716-741-8930 Fax: 716-741-4715
Web site: www.clarence.ny.us

Town Supervisor:
   Kathleen E Hallock..............................716-741-8930
   e-mail: khallock@clarence.ny.us
Town Clerk:
   Nancy C Metzger...................716-741-8938/fax: 716-407-2190
   e-mail: nmetzger@clarence.ny.us
Town Attorney:
   Steven B Bengart....................716-741-8935/fax: 716-741-4715
   e-mail: sbengart@clarence.ny.us
Chief Security Officer:
   Joseph D Meacham.............................716-406-8928
   e-mail: jdmeacham@yahoo.com
Historian:
   Mark Woodward................................716-759-1118

Clarkstown, Town of
10 Maple Ave
New City, NY 10956
845-639-2050 Fax: 845-639-2008
Web site: www.town.clarkstown.ny.us

Town Supervisor:
   Alexander J Gromack............................845-639-2050
   e-mail: a_gromack@town.clarkstown.ny.us
Deputy Supervisor:
   Councilman John Maloney......................845-639-2049
   e-mail: towncouncil@town.clarkstown.ny.us
Town Clerk:
   David Carlucci.................................845-639-2010
   e-mail: d_carlucci@town.clarkstown.ny.us
Town Attorney:
   Amy Wagner Mele.............845-639-2060/fax: 845-639-2189
   e-mail: legal@town.clarkstown.ny.us
Comptroller:
   Edward Duer..................................845-639-2020
   e-mail: e_duer@town.clarkstown.ny.us

Police Chief:
   Peter T Noonan................................845-639-5800
   e-mail: cpd@town.clarkstown.ny.us

Clay, Town of
4401 State Route 31
Clay, NY 13041
315-652-3800 Fax: 315-622-7259
Web site: www.townofclay.org

Town Supervisor:
   James J Rowley...............................315-652-3800
   e-mail: supervisor@townofclay.org
Town Clerk:
   Vivian I Mason................................315-652-3800
   e-mail: townclerk@townofclay.org
Town Attorney:
   Robert M Germain.............................315-652-3800
   e-mail: legal@townofclay.org
Commissioner of Finance:
   John Shehadi.................................315-652-3800
Commissioner, Public Safety:
   Owen P Honors...............................315-652-3800
   e-mail: police@townofclay.org
Fire Marshall:
   Richard Mercer...............................315-652-4242

Clifton Park, Town of
1 Town Hall Plaza
Clifton Park, NY 12065
518-371-6651 Fax: 518-371-1136
Web site: www.cliftonpark.org

Town Supervisor:
   Philip Barrett..............................518-371-6651x240
   e-mail: pbarrett@cliftonpark.org
Deputy Town Supervisor:
   Roy A Speckhard............................518-371-6651
   e-mail: rspeckhard@cliftonpark.org
Town Administrator:
   Michael Shahen.........................518-371-6651 ext243
   e-mail: administrator@cliftonpark.org
Town Clerk:
   Patricia O'Donnell..................518-371-6681/fax: 518-383-5088
   e-mail: townclerk@cliftonpark.org
Town Attorney:
   Thomas McCarthy..................518-371-6651/fax: 518-371-1136
Comptroller:
   Mark Heggen.....................518-371-6651/fax: 518-371-1136
   e-mail: comptroller@cliftonpark.org
Historian:
   John Scherer................................518-371-2691
   e-mail: JLScherer@aol.com

Colonie, Town of
Memorial Town Hall
534 Loudon Rd
Newtonville, NY 12128
518-783-2700 Fax: 518-782-2360
e-mail: brizzellm@colonie.org
Web site: www.colonie.org

Offices and agencies generally appear in alphabetical order, except when specific order is requested by listee.

417

MUNICIPAL GOVERNMENT / Municipal Government

Town Supervisor:
   Mary Brizzell 518-783-2728
   e-mail: brizzellm@colonie.org
Town Clerk:
   Elizabeth A DelTorto 518-783-2734/fax: 518-786-6525
   e-mail: deltortoe@colonie.org
Town Attorney:
   Arnis Zilgme 518-783-2704/fax: 518-786-7324
   e-mail: attorney@colonie.org
Comptroller:
   Ronald Caponera 518-783-2708/fax: 518-783-2877
   e-mail: caponeraR@colonie.org
Emergency Management & Planning:
   Michael Rayball 518-782-2609
   e-mail: Rayballm@colonie.org
Police Chief:
   Steven H Heider 518-783-2800/fax: 518-786-7326
Public Works Commissioner:
   Robert S Mitchell 518-783-6292/fax: 518-785-3529
   e-mail: pworks@colonie.org
Town Historian:
   Kevin Franklin 518-782-2593
   e-mail: historian@colonie.org

Cortlandt, Town of
1 Heady St
Cortlandt Manor, NY 10567-1224
914-734-1002 Fax: 914-734-1025
e-mail: townhall@townofcortlandt.com
Web site: www.townofcortlandt.com

Town Supervisor:
   Linda D Puglisi 914-734-1002/fax: 914-734-1003
   e-mail: lindap@townofcortlandt.com
Town Clerk:
   Jo-Ann Dyckman 914-734-1020/fax: 914-734-1102
   e-mail: joannd@townofcortlandt.com
Town Attorney:
   Thomas F Wood 914-736-0930/fax: 914-736-9082
Comptroller:
   Glenn Cestaro 914-734-1071/fax: 914-734-1077
   e-mail: glennc@townofcortlandt.com
NY State Police Zone Commander:
   Michael Kopy 914-742-6340
DES/Coordinator of Homeland Security:
   Jeff Tkacs 914-734-2029/fax: 914-862-3376
   e-mail: jefft@townofcortlandt.com

DeWitt, Town of
5400 Butternut Drive
East Syracuse, NY 13057-8509
315-446-3428 Fax: 315-449-2065
Web site: www.townofdewitt.com

Town Supervisor:
   James G DiStefano 315-446-3428/fax: 315-449-2065
   e-mail: supervisor@townofdewitt.com
Town Clerk:
   Barbara K Klim 315-446-3826/fax: 315-446-3912
   e-mail: clerk@townofdewitt.com
Town Attorney:
   Gregory Scicchitano 315-428-8344/fax: 315-475-8230
Police Chief:
   Eugene J Conway 315-449-3640/fax: 315-449-3644
   e-mail: police@townofdewitt.com

Comptroller:
   John A Curulla 315-446-3392/fax: 315-449-2065
   e-mail: comptroller@townofdewitt.com
Town Historian:
   Frank Volcko 315-437-9820

East Fishkill, Town of
Town Hall
330 Route 376
Hopewell Junction, NY 12533
845-221-4303
Web site: www.eastfishkillny.org

Town Supervisor:
   John A Hickman Jr 845-221-4303
Town Clerk:
   Dorothy Mekeel 845-221-9191
Finance/Administration Manager:
   Christine Mitchell 845-226-2634
Police Chief:
   Brian C Nichols 845-221-2111
Fire Inspector:
   William Jackson 845-221-0378

East Hampton, Town of
159 Pantigo Rd
East Hampton, NY 11937
631-324-4140 Fax: 631-324-2789
e-mail: info@town.east-hampton.ny.us
Web site: www.town.east-hampton.ny.us

Town Supervisor:
   William McGintee 631-324-4141
Town Clerk:
   Fred Overton . . . . 631-324-4142 or 631-324-4143
   fax: 631-324-4128
   e-mail: Foverton@town.east-hampton.ny.us
Budget Officer:
   Ted Hults 631-324-4968
Town Attorney:
   Laura Molinari 631-324-8787/fax: 631-329-5371
Police Chief:
   Todd Sarris 631-537-7575
Emergency Services:
   Nat Raynor 631-324-1736
Chief Fire Marshall:
   David DiSunno 631-329-3473/fax: 631-329-9403

Eastchester, Town of
Town Hall
40 Mill Rd
Eastchester, NY 10709
914-771-3300 Fax: 914-771-3366
Web site: www.eastchester.org

Town Supervisor:
   Anthony S Colavita 914-771-3304/fax: 914-793-2168
   e-mail: supervisor@eastchester.org
Town Clerk:
   Linda Doherty 914-771-3351/fax: 914-771-3366
   e-mail: townclerk@eastchester.org

Offices and agencies generally appear in alphabetical order, except when specific order is requested by listee.

MUNICIPAL GOVERNMENT / Municipal Government

Town Attorney:
  John A Sarcone III.................914-771-3325/fax: 914-771-3367
  e-mail: legal@eastchester.org
Comptroller:
  Ann Marie Berg....................914-771-3330/fax: 914-771-9409
  e-mail: comptroller@eastchester.org
Police Chief:
  Chief Tim Bonci..914-961-3464
  e-mail: police@eastchester.org
Fire Chief:
  Michael P Grogan 914-793-6402/fax: 914-793-8012

Elmira, City of
City Hall
317 E Church St
Elmira, NY 14901
607-737-5644 Fax: 607-737-5824
Web site: www.cityofelmira.net

Mayor:
  John S Tonello...607-737-5644
City Manager:
  John J Burin..607-737-5644
City Clerk:
  Angela J Williams...................607-737-5673/fax: 607-737-5783
  e-mail: cityclerk@ci.elmira.ny.us
Corporation Counsel:
  J William O'Brien II....................................607-737-5674
Chamberlain:
  David Vandermark 607-737-5661/fax: 607-737-5783
Director, Public Services:
  Andrew P Avery...607-737-5679
Police Chief:
  W Scott Drake III ....607-735-8600 or 607-737-5630
Fire Chief:
  Gary E Blitz..607-737-5710

Fishkill, Town of
807 Route 52
Fishkill, NY 12524
845-831-7800 Fax: 845-831-6040
e-mail: tof@fishkill-ny.gov
Web site: www.fishkill-ny.gov

Town Supervisor:
  Joan A Pagones...................................845-831-7800 x3309
  e-mail: tof@fishkill-ny.gov
Town Clerk:
  Darlene Bellis 845-831-7800 x3329
  e-mail: dbellis@fishkill-ny.gov
Comptroller:
  Robert Wheeling 845-831-7800 x3339
  e-mail: rwheeling@fishkill-ny.gov
Police Chief:
  Donald Williams..845-831-1110

Freeport, Village of
46 North Ocean Ave
Freeport, NY 11520
516-377-2200 Fax: 516-377-2323
e-mail: freeportmail1@freeportny.gov
Web site: www.freeportny.com

Village Mayor:
  William F Glacken.......................................516-377-2252
  e-mail: wglacken@freeportny.gov
Village Clerk:
  Carolyn Thomas 516-377-2300/fax: 516-771-4127
  e-mail: cthomas@freeportny.gov
Village Attorney:
  Harrison J Edwards 516-377-2249/fax: 516-377-2366
Treasurer:
  Vilma I Lancaster.......................................516-377-2212
Superintendent, Public Works:
  Louis J DiGrazia..516-377-2289
  e-mail: dpw@vil.freeport.ny.us
Emergency Management Director:
  Richard E Holdener 516-377-2400
Police Chief:
  Michael Woodward 516-378-0700
Fire Chief:
  Allen Grosser 516-377-2190

Garden City, Village of
351 Stewart Ave
Garden City, NY 11530
516-465-4000 Fax: 516-742-5223
Web site: www.gardencityny.net

Mayor:
  Gerard P Lundquist......................................516-465-4051
Administrator & Treasurer:
  Robert L Schoelle, Jr 516-465-4051
Village Clerk:
  Brian Ridgway 516-465-4053
  e-mail: bridgway@gardencityny.net
Police Commissioner:
  Ernest J Cipullo 516-465-4100
Fire Chief:
  John P Casey..516-746-1301
Director, Public Works:
  Robert J Mangan....................516-465-4003 or 516-465-4031

Gates, Town of
1605 Buffalo Rd
Gates, NY 14624
585-247-6100 Fax: 585-247-0017
e-mail: admin@townofgates.org
Web site: www.townofgates.org

Town Supervisor:
  Ralph J Esposito..585-247-6100
Town Clerk:
  Richard A Warner.......................................585-247-6100
  e-mail: rwarner@townofgates.org
Town Attorney:
  John DiCaro 585-247-6100
Finance Director:
  Annie Sealy 585-247-6100
Police Chief:
  David R DiCaro 585-247-2262
Director, Building & Public Works:
  John Lathrop 585-247-6100 x241
Town Historian:
  Judy DeRooy 585-247-6100

Offices and agencies generally appear in alphabetical order, except when specific order is requested by listee.

MUNICIPAL GOVERNMENT / Municipal Government

Glen Cove, City of
9 Glen St
Glen Cove, NY 11542
516-676-2000 Fax: 516-676-0108
Web site: www.glencove-li.com

Mayor:
   Ralph V Suozzi..................................516-676-2004
City Clerk:
   Carolyn Willson...................516-676-3345/fax: 516-676-3357
   e-mail: cwillson@cityofglencove.ny.org
City Attorney:
   Vincent Taranto..................................516-676-2000
Controller:
   Sal Lombardi.....................................516-676-2000
Police Chief:
   Timothy Edwards.................................516-676-1000
Director, Public Works:
   Vacant...516-676-4278

Glenville, Town of
18 Glenridge Rd
Glenville, NY 12302
518-688-1200 Fax: 518-384-0140
Web site: www.townofglenville.org

Town Supervisor:
   Frank X Quinn....................................518-688-1201
   e-mail: fquinn@townofglenville.org
Town Clerk:
   Linda Neals..................................518-688-1200x402
   e-mail: lneals@townofglenville.org
Town Attorney:
   Eric J Dickson....................................518-382-0422
Town Planner:
   Kevin Corcoran..............................518-688-1200x407
   e-mail: kcorcoran@townofglenville.org
Comptroller:
   George W Phillips.................518-688-1206/fax: 518-384-0140
   e-mail: gphillips@townofglenville.org
Highway Superintendent & Commissioner, Public Works:
   Richard D LeClair..................518-382-1406/fax: 518-382-3015
   e-mail: highway@townofglenville.org
Historian:
   Joan Szablewski....................518-399-8555/fax: 518-384-0140
Police Chief:
   Michael Ranalli....................518-384-3444/fax: 518-384-0141
   e-mail: Jpaparella@townofglenville.org

Greece, Town of
1 Vince Tofany Blvd
Greece, NY 14612-5016
585-225-2000 Fax: 585-225-1915
Web site: www.townofgreece.org

Town Supervisor:
   John T Auberger..................................585-723-2311
Deputy Town Supervisor:
   Jeffery McCann...................................585-723-2311
Director, Constituent Services:
   Kathryn J Firkins.................................585-723-2361
Town Clerk:
   Patricia Anthony.................................585-723-2341
   e-mail: panthony@townofgreece.ny.gov

Town Attorney:
   Raymond DiRaddo.................................585-225-2000
Director, Finance:
   Rick Pellegrino..................................585-723-2335
Police Chief:
   Merritt Rahn....................................585-865-9200
Town Assessor:
   John Patton.....................................585-723-2308

Greenburgh, Town of
Town Hall, 177 Hillside Avenue
Greenburgh, NY 10607
914-993-1500 Fax: 914-993-1626
Web site: www.greenburghny.com

Town Supervisor:
   Paul J Feiner......................914-993-1540/fax: 914-993-1541
   e-mail: pfeiner@greenburghny.com
Town Clerk:
   Alfreda A Williams.................914-993-1500/fax: 914-993-1626
   e-mail: townclerk@greenburghny.com
Town Attorney:
   Timothy Lewis....................914-993-1546/fax: 914-993-1656
   e-mail: legal@greenburghny.com
Comptroller:
   James Heslop.....................914-993-1528/fax: 914-993-1647
   e-mail: jheslop@greenburghny.com
Comsnr, Public Works:
   Albert S Regula..................914-993-1573/fax: 914-993-1554
   e-mail: dpw@greenburghny.com
Chief of Police:
   John A Kapica....................914-682-5300/fax: 914-949-7116
   e-mail: gpdwebmail@greenburghny.com

Guilderland, Town of
Town Hall
5209 Western Turnpike
PO Box 339
Guilderland, NY 12084
518-356-1980 Fax: 518-356-3955
Web site: www.guilderland.org

Town Supervisor:
   Kenneth Runion.............518-356-1980 x1022/fax: 518-356-5514
   e-mail: runionk@townofguilderland.org
Town Clerk:
   Rosemary Centi...............................518-356-1980 x1024
   e-mail: centir@townofguilderland.org
Town Attorney:
   Richard Sherwood.................................518-356-1980
Comptroller:
   Jean Stearling...............................518-356-1980 x1054
   e-mail: stearlingj@townofguilderland.org
Police Chief:
   James Murley.....................518-356-1501/fax: 518-356-4668
Town Historian:
   Alice Begley.................................518-356-1980 x1050
   e-mail: abegley27@aol.com

Hamburg, Town of
S6100 South Park Ave
Hamburg, NY 14075

Offices and agencies generally appear in alphabetical order, except when specific order is requested by listee.

MUNICIPAL GOVERNMENT / Municipal Government

716-649-6111 Fax: 716-649-4087
Web site: www.townofhamburgny.com

Town Supervisor:
   Steven J Walters 716-649-6111 x2381
   e-mail: supervisor@townofhamburgny.com
Town Clerk:
   Catherine A Rybczynski 716-649-6111 x2360
   e-mail: townclerk@townofhamburgny.com
Town Attorney:
   Vincent J Sorrentino 716-649-6111 x2371/fax: 716-646-8559
   e-mail: legal@townofhamburgny.com
Director, Finance & Administration:
   James M Spute 716-649-6111 x2383/fax: 716-649-2522
Police Chief:
   Joseph Coggins 716-649-3800 x2501/fax: 716-646-6707
Senior Public Safety Dispatcher:
   Robert Mueller 716-649-6111 x2412
Town Historian:
   James Baker 716-646-5115

Harrison, Town/Village of
Alfred Sulla Municipal Bldg
1 Heineman Pl
Harrison, NY 10528
914-670-3000 Fax: 914-835-8067
Web site: www.townharrison.org

Supervisor/Mayor:
   Stephen Malfitano 914-670-3005
   e-mail: stephenmalfitano@harrison-ny.gov
Town Clerk:
   Joan B Walsh 914-670-3030/fax: 914-835-2009
   e-mail: clerk@harrison-ny.gov
Town Attorney:
   Frank Allegretti 914-670-3090 x3093/fax: 914-835-2738
   e-mail: law@harrison-ny.gov
Village Attorney:
   Fred Castiglia 914-670-3000 x3091/fax: 917835-2738
   e-mail: law@harrison-ny.gov
Comptroller/Treasurer:
   Maureen MacKenzie 914-670-3080/fax: 914-835-2759
   e-mail: comptroller@harrison-ny.gov
Police Chief:
   David R Hall 914-967-5110
Commissioner, Public Works:
   Robert G Wasp 914-670-3200/fax: 914-835-2387
   e-mail: dpw@harrison-ny.gov
Fire Marshal/Fire Prevention Dept:
   Steve Surace 914-670-3130
   e-mail: fire@harrison-ny.gov

Haverstraw, Town of
1 Rosman Rd
Garnerville, NY 10923
845-429-2200 Fax: 845-429-4701
Web site: www.townofhaverstraw.us

Town Supervisor:
   Howard T Phillips, Jr 845-429-2200
Town Clerk:
   Josephine E Carella . . . . 845-942-3727 or 845-942-3728
   fax: 845-429-4964
Town Attorney:
   William Stein 845-429-2200

Finance Director:
   Michael J Gamboli 845-429-2200
Police Chief:
   Charles B Miller 845-354-1500

Hempstead, Town of
Town Hall Plaza
1 Washington St
Hempstead, NY 11550
516-489-5000 Fax: 516-538-2908
Web site: www.townofhempstead.org; www.toh.li

Town Supervisor:
   Kate Murray 516-489-5000 x3260
Town Clerk:
   Mark A Bonilla 516-489-5000 x3046
   e-mail: markbon@hotmail.org
Town Attorney:
   Joseph J Ra 516-489-5000 x3209
Comptroller:
   John Mastromarino 516-489-5000
Director, Communications:
   Michael J Deery 516-812-3310/fax: 516-481-3183

Hempstead, Village of
Village Hall, 99 Nichols Court
PO Box 32
Hempstead, NY 11550
516-489-3400 Fax: 516-489-4285
Web site: www.villageofhempstead.org

Mayor:
   Wayne J Hall Sr 516-489-3400
Village Clerk:
   Tanya L Ford 516-478-6206
   e-mail: clerksoffice@villageofhempsteadny.gov
Village Attorney:
   Jillian Guthman 516-478-6275
Public Works Consulting Director:
   Harry Dickenson 516-478-6270
Chief of Police:
   James Russo 516-483-6200

Henrietta, Town of
475 Calkins Rd
PO Box 999
Henrietta, NY 14467
585-334-7700 Fax: 585-334-9667
Web site: www.townofhenrietta.org

Town Supervisor:
   James R Breese 585-359-7001
   e-mail: supervisor@townofhenrietta.org
Deputy Supervisor:
   Amber N Hutchinson 585-359-7036
Town Clerk & Receiver of Taxes:
   Patricia Shaffer 585-359-7700
   e-mail: pshaffer@townofhenrietta.org
Town Attorney:
   Daniel J Mastrella 585-232-8810
Commissioner, Public Works:
   Dean (Chuck) Marshall Jr 585-359-7005
   e-mail: cmarshall@townofhenrietta.org

Offices and agencies generally appear in alphabetical order, except when specific order is requested by listee.

421

MUNICIPAL GOVERNMENT / Municipal Government

Huntington, Town of
100 Main St
Huntington, NY 11743
631-351-3014 Fax: 631-424-7856
Web site: town.huntington.ny.us

Town Supervisor:
  Frank P Petrone 631-351-3030
  e-mail: fpetrone@town.huntington.ny.us
Town Clerk:
  Jo-Ann Raia 631-351-3206/fax: 631-351-3205
  e-mail: clerk@town.huntington.ny.us
Town Attorney:
  John J Leo 631-351-3042/fax: 631-351-3032
  e-mail: attorney@town.huntington.ny.us
Comptroller:
  Kathleen Cannon 631-351-3038/fax: 631-351-2898
  e-mail: audit@town.huntington.ny.us
Public Safety Director:
  Bruce Richard 631-351-3266
  e-mail: publicsafety@town.huntington.ny.us
Director, General Services:
  Thomas R Cavanaugh 631-351-3015/fax: 631-351-3337
  e-mail: genservices@town.huntington.ny.us
Historian:
  Robert C Hughes 631-351-3244/fax: 631-351-3245

Hyde Park, Town of
4383 Albany Post Rd
Hyde Park, NY 12538
845-229-5111 Fax: 845-229-7583
Web site: www.hydeparkny.us

Town Supervisor:
  Pompey Delafield 845-229-5111x7/fax: 845-229-0831
  e-mail: supervisor@hydeparkny.us
Town Clerk:
  Carole A Clearwater 845-229-2103/fax: 845-229-7583
  e-mail: tcc-1@hydeparkny.us
Town Attorney:
  George Rodenhausen 845-473-7766
Police Chief:
  James McKenna 845-229-9340/fax: 845-229-6953
Town Historian:
  Margaret Marquez 845-229-8438

Irondequoit, Town of
Town Hall
1280 Titus Ave
Rochester, NY 14617
585-467-8840 Fax: 585-467-7294
e-mail: feedback@irondequoit.org
Web site: www.irondequoit.org

Town Supervisor:
  Mary Ellen Heyman 585-336-6034
  e-mail: meheyman@irondequoit.org
Town Clerk/Receiver of Taxes:
  Barbara Genier 585-336-6045
  e-mail: bgenier@irondequoit.org
Town Attorney:
  Patrick Malgieri 585-987-2800
Comptroller:
  John Bovenzi 585-336-6010
  e-mail: jbovenzi@irondequoit.org
Police Chief:
  Richard Boyan 585-336-6000 x306/fax: 585-342-5699
  e-mail: rboyan@irondequoit.org
Fire Marshal:
  Greg Merrick 585-336-6097
  e-mail: gmerrick@irondequoit.org
Town Historian:
  Patricia Wayne 585-336-7269
  e-mail: pwayne@irondequoit.org

Islip, Town of
Town Hall
655 Main St
Islip, NY 11751
631-224-5500 or 631-224-5691 Fax: 631-581-8424
Web site: www.isliptown.org

Town Supervisor:
  Phil Nolan 631-224-5500
  e-mail: supervisorsoffice@townofislip-ny.gov
Town Clerk:
  Joan B Johnson 631-224-5490
  e-mail: J.B.Johnson@townofislip-ny.gov
Town Attorney:
  Pierce Cohalan 631-224-5550/fax: 631-224-5573
  e-mail: townattorney@townofislip-ny.gov
Comptroller:
  Douglas Celiberti 631-224-5575
Receiver of Taxes:
  Virginia E Allen 631-224-5580
Commissioner, Public Works:
  Donald Caputo 631-224-5610
  e-mail: commissioner-dpw@townofislip-ny.gov
Public Information:
  Catherine Green 631-224-5485/fax: 631-581-8424
Public Safety:
  Martin Raber 631-224-5300
Harbor Police Chief:
  Robert Sgroi 631-224-5656
  e-mail: harborpolice@townofislip-ny.gov

Ithaca, City of
City Hall
108 E Green St
Ithaca, NY 14850
607-274-6570 Fax: 607-272-7348
Web site: www.cityofithaca.org

Mayor:
  Carolyn K Peterson 607-274-6501/fax: 607-274-6526
  e-mail: mayor@cityofithaca.org
City Clerk:
  Julie Conley Holcomb 607-274-6570/fax: 607-272-7348
  e-mail: julieh@cityofithaca.org
City Chamberlain:
  Debra Parsons 607-274-6580/fax: 607-272-7348
  e-mail: debrap@cityofithaca.org
City Attorney:
  Daniel Hoffman 607-274-6504/fax: 607-274-6507
  e-mail: dawnt@cityofithaca.org

Offices and agencies generally appear in alphabetical order, except when specific order is requested by listee.

MUNICIPAL GOVERNMENT / Municipal Government

Controller:
   Steven P Thayer 607-274-6576
   e-mail: dredsicker@cityofithaca.org
Police Chief:
   Lauren E Signer 607-272-9973
   e-mail: laurens@cityofithaca.org

Jamestown, City of
Town Hall
215 North Tioga Street
Ithaca, NY 14850
607-273-1721
Web site: www.town.ithaca.ny.us

Town Supervisor:
   Cathy Valentino. 607-273-1721 x125
   e-mail: cvalentino@town.ithaca.ny.us
Town Clerk:
   Tee-Ann Hunter. 607-273-1721 x112
   e-mail: townclerk@town.ithaca.ny.us
Town Budget Officer:
   Al Carvill. 607-273-1721 x113
   e-mail: acarvill@town.ithaca.ny.us
Town Historian:
   Laura Johnson-Kelly
   e-mail: ljohnsonkelly@town.ithaca.ny.us

Jamestown, City of
Municipal Bldg
200 E Third St
Jamestown, NY 14701
716-483-7612 Fax: 716-483-7771
Web site: www.jamestownny.net

Mayor:
   Samuel Teresi 716-483-7600/fax: 716-483-7591
City Clerk:
   James Olson. 716-483-7612/fax: 716-483-7502
Corporation Counsel/Attorney:
   Marilyn Fiore-Nieves 716-483-7540/fax: 716-483-7591
Comptroller:
   Joseph A Bellitto 716-483-7738/fax: 716-483-7771
Director Financial Services:
   James N Olson. 716-483-7512/fax: 716-483-7502
Police Chief/Director Public Safety:
   Rex Rater. 716-483-7536/fax: 716-483-7722
Historian:
   B Dolores Thompson 716-484-8289

Kingston, City of
420 Broadway
Kingston, NY 12401
845-331-0080 Fax: 845-334-3904
Web site: www.ci.kingston.ny.us

Mayor:
   James M Sottile 845-334-3902/fax: 845-334-3904
   e-mail: mayor@ci.kingston.ny.us
Common Council Alderman-at-Large:
   James L Noble 845-331-4696
   e-mail: commoncouncil@ci.kingston.ny.us

City Clerk:
   Kathy Janeczek 845-334-3915/fax: 845-334-3918
   e-mail: cityclerk@ci.kingston.ny.us
Corporation Counsel:
   Daniel Heppner 845-334-3947/fax: 845-334-3959
   e-mail: corpcounsel@ci.kingston.ny.us
Comptroller:
   Penny M Radel 845-334-3935/fax: 845-334-3944
   e-mail: comptroller@ci.kingston.ny.us
Executive Director, Community Development:
   Daniel Mills. 845-334-3927/fax: 845-334-3932
   e-mail: dmills@ci.kingston.ny.us
Chief of Police/Commissioner:
   Gerald Keller . . . . 845-331-1671 or 845-331-2061
   e-mail: police@ci.kingston.ny.us
Fire Chief:
   Rick Salzmann 845-331-1326
   e-mail: fire@ci.kingston.ny.us

Lancaster, Town of
21 Central Ave
Lancaster, NY 14086
716-683-1610 Fax: 716-683-0512
e-mail: lookatus@lancasterny.com
Web site: www.erie.gov/lancaster/depts;
www.lancasterny.com

Town Supervisor:
   Robert H Giza. 716-683-1610
Town Clerk:
   Johanna M Coleman 716-683-9028/fax: 716-683-2094
   e-mail: jcoleman@lancaster.ny.com
Town Attorney:
   Richard J Sherwood. 716-684-3342/fax: 716-681-7475
   e-mail: townattorney@lancasterny.com
Director, Administration & Finance:
   David J Brown 716-683-1610
Police Chief:
   Gary Stoldt Jr. 716-683-2800/fax: 716-681-2352
Emergency Management/Nat'l Disaster Coordinator:
   Robert MacPeek 716-683-6363
Town Assessor:
   Christine A Fusco 716-683-1311/fax: 716-681-7054
Historian:
   Harley Scott 716-684-3281

LeRay, Town of
8650 LeRay Street
Evans Mill, NY 13637-3191
315-629-4052 Fax: 315-629-4393
Web site: www.townofleray.org

Town Supervisor:
   Ronald C Taylor 315-629-5532/fax: 315-629-4393
   e-mail: supervisor@townofleray.org
Town Clerk/Receiver/Registrar:
   Mary C Smith 315-629-4052/fax: 315-629-4393
   e-mail: lerayclerk@nnymail.com
Town Counsel:
   Hrabchak, Gebo & Langone. 315-788-5900/fax: 315-788-6085
   e-mail: gebolaw@nnyonline.net

Offices and agencies generally appear in alphabetical order, except when specific order is requested by listee.

MUNICIPAL GOVERNMENT / Municipal Government

Lindenhurst, Village of
430 S Wellwood Ave
Lindenhurst, NY 11757
631-957-7500 Fax: 631-957-4605
e-mail: info@villageoflindenhurst.com
Web site: www.villageoflindenhurst.com

Village Mayor:
  Thomas A Brennan..................................631-957-7500
Deputy Mayor:
  Kevin McCaffey.....................................631-957-7500
Clerk/Treasurer:
  Shawn Cullinane....................................631-957-7504
Deputy Clerk:
  Doug M Madlon.....................................631-957-7504
Village Attorney:
  Gerard Glass...................631-321-1400/fax: 631-321-1491
Fire Marshall:
  Richard Lyman......................................631-957-7530

Lockport, City of
Lockport Municipal Building
One Locks Plaza
Lockport, NY 14094
716-439-6665 Fax: 716-439-6668
Web site: www.elockport.com

Mayor:
  Michael W Tucker...................................716-439-6665
Common Council President:
  John Lombardi III..................................716-439-6628
City Clerk:
  Richard P Mullaney.................716-439-6676/fax: 716-439-6684
Corporation Counsel:
  John J Ottaviano...................................716-438-0488
Treasurer:
  Michael White.....................716-439-6744/fax: 716-439-6617
Police Chief:
  Neil B Merritt.....................................716-433-7700
Fire Department Chief:
  Thomas J Passuite..................................716-439-6724

Lockport, Town of
6560 Dysinger Rd
Lockport, NY 14094
716-439-9520 Fax: 716-439-0528
Web site: www.elockport.com/index_town.html

Town Supervisor:
  Marc Smith........................716-439-9520/fax: 716-439-0528
Town Clerk:
  Nancy Brooks......................716-439-9524/fax: 716-438-5221
Town Historian:
  Laurance Haseley...................................716-434-1547

Long Beach, City of
City Hall
1 West Chester St
Long Beach, NY 11561
516-431-1000 Fax: 516-431-1389
e-mail: info@longbeachny.org
Web site: www.longbeachny.org

City Manager:
  Edwin L Eaton.................................516-431-1000 x201
Council President:
  Leonard G Remo...............................516-431-1000 x264
City Clerk:
  David W Fraser...............................516-431-1000 x314
Corporation Counsel:
  Corey Klein................516-431-1800 x255/fax: 516-431-1016
Comptroller:
  Sandra Clarson...............................516-431-1000 x298
Police Commissioner:
  Thomas R Sofield Sr................516-431-1800/fax: 516-431-1459
  e-mail: lbpd@longbeachny.org

Lysander, Town of
Town Hall
8220 Loop Rd
Baldwinsville, NY 13027
315-638-4264 Fax: 315-635-1515
Web site: www.townoflysander.org

Town Supervisor:
  Barry Bullis......................315-638-4264/fax: 315-635-1515
  e-mail: supervisor@townoflysander.org
Town Clerk:
  Gale J Grice.....................315-638-0224/fax: 315-638-4965
  e-mail: townclerk@townoflysander.org
Comptroller:
  David J Rahrle...................315-635-1443/fax: 315-635-1515
  e-mail: comptroller@townoflysander.org
Town Historian:
  Bonnie Kisselstein.................................315-635-7669
  e-mail: localhistory@bville.lib.ny.us

Mamaroneck, Town of
Town Center
740 W Boston Post Rd
Mamaroneck, NY 10543
914-381-7805 Fax: 914-381-7809
e-mail: townclerk@townofmamaroneck.org
Web site: www.townofmamaroneck.org

Town Supervisor:
  Valerie Moore O'Keeffe.............................914-381-7805
  e-mail: townsupervisor@townofmamaroneck.org
Town Administrator/Emergency Manager:
  Stephen Altieri....................................914-381-7810
  e-mail: townadministrator@townofmamaroneck.org
Town Clerk:
  Patricia A DiCioccio..............914-381-7870/fax: 914-381-7813
  e-mail: townclerk@townofmamaroneck.org
Comptroller:
  Denis Brucciani....................................914-381-7850
  e-mail: towncomptroller@townofmamaroneck.org
Police Chief:
  Richard Rivera....................914-381-6100/fax: 914-381-7897
  e-mail: townpolice@townofmamaroneck.org
Emergency Management Coordinator:
  Michael Liverzani..................................914-381-7838
Town Counsel:
  William Maker Jr...................................914-381-7815
  e-mail: townattorney@townofmamaroneck.org

Offices and agencies generally appear in alphabetical order, except when specific order is requested by listee.

MUNICIPAL GOVERNMENT / Municipal Government

Manlius, Town of
301 Brooklea Dr
Fayetteville, NY 13066
315-637-3521 Fax: 315-637-0713
Web site: www.townofmanlius.org

Town Supervisor:
   Henry Chapman................315-637-3414/fax: 315-637-0713
   e-mail: supervisor@townofmanlius.org
Town Clerk:
   Terry Sloan......................315-637-3521/fax: 315-637-0713
   e-mail: tcsloan@townofmanlius.org
Town Attorney:
   Timothy A Frateschi..............315-637-1465/fax: 315-637-9807
Police Chief:
   Francis Marlowe..................315-682-2212/fax: 315-682-4527

Middletown, City of
City Hall
16 James St
Middletown, NY 10940
845-346-4100 Fax: 845-343-7439

Mayor:
   Marlinda Duncanson.............................845-346-4100
Common Council President:
   Robert Moson..................................845-346-4166
Common Council Clerk/Registrar:
   Charles Mitchell..................845-346-4166/fax: 845-344-5428
City Attorney:
   Thomas Farrell...................845-346-4140/fax: 845-346-4146
Treasurer:
   Vacant...........................845-346-4150/fax: 845-343-1101
Commissioner, Public Works:
   Jacob Tawil......................845-343-3169/fax: 845-343-4104
Chief of Police:
   Matthew Byrne....................845-343-3151/fax: 845-343-2660
Fire Chief:
   Ralph Parenti..................................845-343-4169

Monroe, Town of
11 Stage Road
Monroe, NY 10950
845-783-1900 Fax: 845-782-5590
Web site: www.monroeny.org

Town Supervisor:
   Sandy Leonard...............845-783-1900 x227/fax: 845-782-5597
   e-mail: ginny@monroeny.org
Town Clerk & Registrar:
   Mary Ellen Beams.........................845-783-1900 x221
   e-mail: maryellen@monroeny.org
Town Attorney:
   Kevin Dowd....................................845-778-5442
Chief of Police:
   Dominic Giudice Jr............................845-782-8644
Tax Collector:
   William Bollenbach............................845-782-4459
Historian:
   James Nelson..................................845-783-3406
   e-mail: nelsonja@fastmail.fm

Montgomery, Town of
110 Bracken Rd
Montgomery, NY 12549
845-457-2660 Fax: 845-457-2613
Web site: www.townofmontgomery.com

Town Supervisor:
   Susan L Cockburn..............................845-457-2660
   e-mail: tomsupervisor@frontiernet.net
Town Clerk:
   Amolia Miller.................................845-457-2660
   e-mail: tomtownclerk@frontiernet.net
Town Attorney:
   Charles T Bazydlo.............................845-361-3668
Receiver of Taxes:
   Jean Shafer...................................845-457-2630
   e-mail: tomtax@frontiernet.net
Police Chief:
   Leonard R Bauer...............................845-457-9211
   e-mail: TMPDChief@frontiernet.net
Town Historian:
   Suzanne Isaksen...................845-457-9211 or 845-457-9098
   e-mail: tomhistorian@frontiernet.net

Mount Pleasant, Town of
One Town Hall Plaza
Valhalla, NY 10595
914-742-2360 Fax: 914-769-3155
Web site: www.mtpleasant.americantowns.com

Town Supervisor:
   Robert F Meehan...............................914-742-2300
   e-mail: rmeehan@mtpleasantny.com
Town Clerk:
   Patricia June Scova..............914-742-2312/fax: 914-747-6172
   e-mail: pscova@mtpleasantny.com
Town Attorney:
   Gerald D Reilly..................914-742-2357/fax: 914-769-3155
Comptroller:
   Tina Peretti.....................914-742-2360 or 914-742-2359
   e-mail: tperetti@mtpleasantny.com
Police Chief:
   Louis Alagno.....................914-769-1941/fax: 914-769-7199
   e-mail: lalagno@mtpleasantny.com

Mount Vernon, City of
City Hall
1 Roosevelt Square
Mount Vernon, NY 10550
914-665-2300 Fax: 914-665-2496
Web site: www.ci.mount-vernon.ny.us

Mayor:
   Ernest D Davis...................914-665-2360 or 914-665-2361
   e-mail: mayor@cmvny.com
Council President:
   Steven Horton.................................914-665-2300
City Clerk/Registrar:
   Lisa A Copeland..................914-665-2348/fax: 914-668-6044
Corporation Counsel:
   Helen M Blackwood................914-665-2366/fax: 914-665-9142
Comptroller:
   Maureen Walker................................914-665-2312

Offices and agencies generally appear in alphabetical order, except when specific order is requested by listee.

MUNICIPAL GOVERNMENT / Municipal Government

Public Safety/Police Commissioner:
   David Chong...................................914-665-2500
Police Chief:
   Joseph P Pizzuti................................914-665-2500
Fire Chief:
   Nicholas Cicchetti..............................914-665-2626
Public Works Commissioner:
   James Finch.....................................914-665-2334
Civil Defense, Director:
   Peter W Sherrill.................................914-665-2390

New Hartford, Town of
Butler Hall
48 Genesee Street
New Hartford, NY 13413
315-733-7500
Web site: www.town.new-hartford.ny.us

Town Supervisor:
   Earle C Reed..........................315-733-7500 x2332
   e-mail: nhsupervisor@town.new-hartford.ny.us
Town Clerk:
   Gail Wolanin Young..........315-733-7500 x2322/fax: 315-797-9986
   e-mail: gyoung@town.new-hartford.ny.us
Receiver of Taxes:
   Hilarie Elefante...............315-733-7500 x2326/fax: 315-732-3979
   e-mail: hilarie@town.new-hartford.ny.us
Town Attorney:
   Gerald Green....................................315-735-6481
Police Chief:
   Raymond L Philo................315-724-7111/fax: 315-724-8618
   e-mail: rlp101@town.new-hartford.ny.us

New Rochelle, City of
City Hall
515 North Ave
New Rochelle, NY 10801
914-654-2000 Fax: 914-654-2174
Web site: www.newrochelleny.com

Mayor:
   Noam Bramson....................914-654-2150/fax: 914-654-2357
   e-mail: nbramson@ci.new-rochelle.ny.us
City Manager:
   Charles B Strome III...........................914-654-2145
   e-mail: cstrome@ci.new-rochelle.ny.us
City Clerk:
   Dorothy Allen...................................914-654-2159
Corporation Counsel:
   Bernis Shapiro..................................914-654-2125
   e-mail: bshapiro@ci.new-rochelle.ny.us
Finance/Administrative Services Commissioner:
   Howard Rattner.................................914-654-2063
   e-mail: hrattner@ci.new-rochelle.ny.us
Public Works Commissioner:
   Jeffrey C Coleman PE...........................914-654-2131
   e-mail: jcoleman@newrochelleny.com
Police Commissioner:
   Patrick J Carroll...............................914-654-2300
   e-mail: pcarroll@ci.new-rochelle.ny.us
Fire Commissioner:
   Raymond Kiernan.................................914-654-2211
   e-mail: rkiernan@ci.new-rochelle.ny.us

New Windsor, Town of
555 Union Avenue
New Windsor, NY 12553
845-565-8800 Fax: 845-563-4693
Web site: http://town.new-windsor.ny.us

Town Supervisor/Chief Fiscal Officer:
   George J Green..................................845-563-4610
   e-mail: ggreen@town.new-windsor.ny.us
Town Clerk:
   Deborah Green...................845-563-4611/fax: 845-563-4670
   e-mail: dgreen@town.new-windsor.ny.us
Town Attorney:
   Michael Blythe..................845-563-4630/fax: 845-563-4692
   e-mail: mblythe@town.new-windsor.ny.us
Comptroller:
   Lawrence Reis...................845-563-4626/fax: 845-563-4693
Police Chief:
   Michael C Biasotti..............845-565-7000 or 845-563-4654
   fax: 845-563-4694
   e-mail: mbiasotti@town.new-windsor.ny.us
Fire Inspector & Department Head:
   Michael Babcock.................845-563-4617/fax: 845-563-4695
   e-mail: dhamel@town.new-windsor.ny.us
Town Historian:
   Glenn Marshall..................................845-563-4609
   e-mail: historynw@aol.com

New York City
City Hall
New York, NY 10007
212-788-3000 Fax: 212-788-3247
Web site: www.nyc.gov

Mayor:
   Michael R Bloomberg...............212-788-3000/fax: 212-791-9628
First Deputy Mayor:
   Patricia E Harris..............................212-788-2990
Deputy Mayor, Economic Development & Rebuilding:
   Daniel L Doctoroff.............................212-788-3000
Deputy Mayor, Administration:
   Edward Skyler..................................212-788-3000
Deputy Mayor, Government Affairs:
   Kevin Sheekey..................................212-788-3063
Deputy Mayor, Legal Affairs:
   Carol A Robles-Roman...........................212-788-3000
Deputy Mayor, Operations:
   Marc V Shaw....................................212-788-3000
Deputy Mayor, Policy:
   Dennis M Walcott...............................212-788-3000
Director, Communications:
   James Anderson.................................212-788-3000
Special Advisor, Governance & Strategic Planning:
   Ester Fuchs....................................212-788-3000
Senior Advisor to Mayor:
   Shea Fink......................................212-788-3000
Chief of Staff:
   Peter J Madonia.................212-788-2728 or 212-788-3000
   fax: 212-788-2460
Press Secretary:
   Stu Loeser.....................................212-788-2958
City Clerk:
   Victor L Robles.................212-669-2400/fax: 212-669-3300

Aging, Dept for the, NYC...................fax: 212-442-1095
   2 Lafayette St, 7th Fl, New York, NY 10007

Offices and agencies generally appear in alphabetical order, except when specific order is requested by listee.

MUNICIPAL GOVERNMENT / Municipal Government

212-442-1322 Fax: 212-442-1095
Web site: www.nyc.gov/aging
Commissioner:
  Edwin Mendez-Santiago 212-442-1100
  e-mail: emendez@aging.nyc.gov
First Deputy Cmsr/General Counsel:
  Sally Renfro 212-442-1104
  e-mail: srenfro@aging.nyc.gov
Director, Management & Planning:
  Anne Fitzgibbon 212-442-0975
Executive Director, Aging in NY Fund:
  Ali Hodin-Baier 212-442-1375
Director, Public Affairs:
  Christopher Miller 212-442-1111/fax: 212-676-0685
  e-mail: cmiller@aging.nyc.gov

Art Commission, NYC . . . . fax: 212-788-3086
City Hall, 3rd Fl, New York, NY 10007
212-788-3071 Fax: 212-788-3086
Web site: www.nyc.gov/artcommission
Executive Director:
  Jackie Snyder 212-788-3071
  e-mail: jsnyder@cityhall.nyc.gov
President:
  Joyce Frank Menschel 212-788-3071
Project Manager:
  Sara Lev 212-788-3071
Project Coordinator:
  Meredith Topper 212-788-3071
Sculptor:
  Alice Aycock 212-788-3071
Painter:
  Byron Kim 212-788-3071
Mayor's Representative/VP:
  Nancy Rosen 212-788-3071
Architect:
  LeAnn Shelton 212-788-3071
Director, Tour Programs:
  Joan H Bright 212-788-3071

Buildings, Department of, NYC . . . . fax: 212-566-3784
280 Broadway, 7th Fl, New York, NY 10007-1801
212-566-5000 or TTY: 212-566-4769 Fax: 212-566-3784
Web site: www.nyc.gov/buildings
Commissioner:
  Patricia J Lancaster 212-566-3111/fax: 212-566-3784
First Deputy Cmsr, Operations:
  Robert LiMandri 212-566-3103/fax: 212-566-3785
Deputy Commissioner, Technology & Analysis:
  Marilyn King-Festa 212-566-4225/fax: 212-566-3865
Acting Dep Commissioner, Technical Affairs:
  Fatma Amer 212-566-3248/fax: 212-566-3796
General Counsel:
  Mona Sengal 212-566-3291/fax: 212-566-3843
Executive Director, Audits/Discipline:
  Leslie Torres 212-442-2000/fax: 212-442-2072
Assistant Cmsr, Safety & Emergency Operations:
  Robert Iulo 212-566-3364/fax: 212-566-3848

Campaign Finance Board, NYC . . . . fax: 212-306-7143
40 Rector St, 7th Fl, New York, NY 10006
212-306-7100 Fax: 212-306-7143
e-mail: info@nyccfb.info
Web site: www.nyccfb.info
Chair:
  Frederick A O Schwarz, Jr 212-306-7100
Executive Director:
  Amy M Loprest 212-306-7110

Director, Administrative Services:
  Man Wai Gin 212-306-7140
Press Secretary:
  Eric Friedman 212-306-7150

City Council, NYC . . . . fax: 212-788-7093
250 Broadway, 18th Fl, New York, NY 10007
212-788-7084 Fax: 212-788-7093
Web site: www.nyccouncil.info
Speaker:
  Christine C Quinn 212-788-7210
Majority Leader:
  Joel Rivera 212-788-7069
  e-mail: rivera@council.nyc.ny.us
Deputy Majority Leader:
  Leroy G Comrie 212-788-7084
  e-mail: comrie@council.nyc.ny.us
Minority Leader:
  James S Oddo 212-788-7159
  e-mail: oddo@council.nyc.ny.us
Majority Whip:
  Inez Dickens 212-788-7397

City Planning, Department of, NYC . . . . fax: 212-720-3219
22 Reade St, Rm 2W, New York, NY 10007-1216
212-720-3300 Fax: 212-720-3219
Web site: www.ci.nyc.ny.us/html/dcp
Chair, Planning Commission & Director, Dept of City Planning:
  Amanda M Burden 212-720-3200
Executive Director:
  Richard Barth 212-720-3500
Director, Operations:
  David J Zagor 212-720-3650
Director, Public Affairs:
  Rachaele Raynoff 212-720-3471
General Counsel:
  David Karnovsky 212-720-3400

Citywide Administrative Services, Department of, NYC . . . . fax: 212-669-8992
Municipal Bldg, One Centre St, 17th Fl S, New York, NY 10007
212-669-7000 Fax: 212-669-8992
Web site: www.nyc.gov/dcas
Commissioner:
  Martha K Hirst 212-669-7111
First Dep Commissioner/General Counsel:
  Lewis S Finkelman 212-669-4074/fax: 212-669-7898
Deputy Cmsr, Administration & Security:
  John Castellaneta 212-669-3098/fax: 212-669-3099
Communication Director:
  Mark Daly 212-669-7140/fax: 212-669-4664
  e-mail: mdaly@dcas.nyc.gov

Civil Service Commission, NYC . . . . fax: 212-669-2727
One Centre St, Rm 2300 N, New York, NY 10007
212-669-2609 Fax: 212-669-2727
e-mail: commission@nyc.csc.nyc.gov
Web site: www.nyc.gov/html/csc
Chair:
  Stanley K Schlein 212-669-2608
Acting Director & General Counsel:
  Norma I Lopez 212-669-3592
Office Manager:
  Evelyn Horowitz 212-669-2608

Collective Bargaining, Office of, NYC . . . . fax: 212-306-7167
40 Rector St, 7th Fl, New York, NY 10006

Offices and agencies generally appear in alphabetical order, except when specific order is requested by listee.

MUNICIPAL GOVERNMENT / Municipal Government

212-306-7160 Fax: 212-306-7167
e-mail: nyc-ocb@ocb.nyc.gov
Web site: www.ocb-nyc.org
Chair:
   Marlene A Gold 212-306-7170
Deputy Chair, Disputes Settlements:
   Susan Panepento 212-306-7190
General Counsel:
   Steven C DeCosta 212-306-7180
Director, Administration:
   Peter A Gilvarry 212-306-7177

Comptroller, NYC .... fax: 212-669-8878
Municipal Bldg, One Centre St, Rm 530, New York, NY 10007
212-669-3500 Fax: 212-669-8878
Web site: www.comptroller.nyc.gov
Comptroller:
   William C Thompson, Jr 212-669-3500
First Deputy Comptroller/Chief of Staff:
   Gayle Horwitz 212-669-2357
Deputy Comptroller/General Counsel:
   Phyllis Taylor 212-669-2048
Deputy Comptroller, External Affairs:
   Eduardo Castell 212-669-3858
Deputy Comptroller, Budget:
   Marcia Van Wagner 212-669-2038
Press Secretary:
   Jeff Simmons 212-669-3747

Conflicts of Interest Board, NYC .... fax: 212-442-1407
2 Lafayette St, Ste 1010, New York, NY 10007
212-442-1400 Fax: 212-442-1407
Web site: www.nyc.gov/ethics
Executive Director/Counsel:
   Mark Davies 212-442-1424
   e-mail: davies@coib.nyc.gov
Deputy Exec Director/General Counsel:
   Wayne G Hawley 212-442-1415
   e-mail: hawley@coib.nyc.gov
Director, Enforcement:
   Astrid B Gloade 212-442-1419
   e-mail: gloade@coib.nyc.gov
Director, Administration:
   Ute O'Malley 212-442-1427
   e-mail: omalley@coib.nyc.gov
Director, Information Technology:
   Christopher Lall 212-442-1605
Director, Training/Education Unit:
   Joel Rogers 212-442-1421

Consumer Affairs, Department of, NYC .... fax: 212-487-4221
42 Broadway, New York, NY 10004
212-487-4401 Fax: 212-487-4221
Web site: www.nyc.gov/html/dcas
Commissioner:
   Jonathan Mintz 212-487-4401
Deputy Director, Communications:
   Dina Improta 212-487-4283

Correction, Board of, NYC .... fax: 212-788-7860
51 Chambers St, Room 923, New York, NY 10007
212-788-7840 Fax: 212-788-7860
Chair:
   Hildy J Simmons 212-788-7840
   e-mail: nycboc@earthlink.net
Executive Director:
   Richard T Wolf 212-788-7845
Director, Field Operations:
   Carl G Niles 212-788-7867

Correction, Department of, NYC .... fax: 646-248-1219
60 Hudson St, 6th Fl, New York, NY 10013-4393
212-266-1500 Fax: 646-248-1219
Web site: www.nyc.gov/boldest
Commissioner:
   Martin F Horn 212-266-1212
Chief of Staff:
   Judith LaPook 212-266-1156
Senior Dep Commissioner:
   John J Antonelli 212-266-1271
Deputy Commissioner, Public Information:
   Thomas Antenen 212-266-1414/fax: 212-266-1597

Cultural Affairs, Department of, NYC
31 Chambers St, 2nd Fl, New York, NY 10007
212-513-9300
Web site: www.nyc.gov/html/dcla
Commissioner:
   Kate D Levin .... 212-643-2101 or 212-643-2102
Deputy Commissioner:
   Margaret Morgan 212-643-3924
Executive Secretary (Scheduling):
   Doris Littlejohn 212-643-2106

Design & Construction, Dept of, NYC ...... fax: 718-391-1608
30-30 Thomson Avenue, Long Island City, NY 11101
718-391-1000 Fax: 718-391-1608
Web site: www.nyc.gov/html/ddc
Commissioner:
   David J Burney 718-391-1000
Acting Chief of Staff:
   Ana Barrio 718-391-2300
Assistant Commissioner, Public Affairs:
   Matthew Monahan 718-391-1640/fax: 718-391-1892
Chief Contracting Officer:
   Donald Hooker 718-391-1501
General Counsel:
   David Varoli 718-391-1721

Disabilities, Mayor's Office, for People with fax: 212-341-9843
100 Gold Street, 2nd Floor, New York, NY 10038
212-788-2830 or TTY 212-788-2838 Fax: 212-341-9843
Web site: www.nyc.gov/html/mopd
Executive Director:
   Matthew P Sapolin 212-788-2830
Executive Assistant:
   Asma Quddus 212-788-2830

Economic Development Corp, NYC
110 William Street, New York, NY 10038
212-619-5000 or 888-692-0100
Web site: www.nycedc.com
President:
   Robert C Lieber 212-312-3500
CFO/CAO:
   John V Cirolia 212-312-3587
VP, Public Affairs:
   Michael Sherman 212-312-3804

Education, Dept of, NYC .... fax: 212-374-5588
52 Chambers St, New York, NY 10007
212-374-5110 Fax: 212-374-5588
Web site: www.nycenet.edu
Chancellor:
   Joel I Klein 212-374-5110
Deputy Chancellor, Finance/Admin:
   Kathleen Grimm 212-374-0209/fax: 212-374-5588

Offices and agencies generally appear in alphabetical order, except when specific order is requested by listee.

MUNICIPAL GOVERNMENT / Municipal Government

Deputy Chancellor, Operations:
   LaVerne Evans Srinivasan 212-374-5070
   e-mail: lsrinivasan@nycboe.net
Deputy Chancellor, Teaching/Learning:
   Carmen Farina 212-374-5115
Chief of Staff:
   Kristen Kane 212-374-6467
Senior Counselor Education Policy/Youth Development:
   Michele Cahill 212-374-0210
Senior Counselor, School Intervention & Development:
   Rose Albanese-DePinto 212-374-5090/fax: 212-374-5598
   e-mail: ralbane@nycboe.net
Director, Strategic Partnerships:
   Stephanie Dua 212-374-2874/fax: 212-374-5571
General Counsel & Legal Services Office:
   Michael Best 212-374-6888/fax: 212-374-5596
Executive Director, Intergovernmental Affairs:
   Terence D Tolbert 212-374-4946/fax: 518-374-5588
Communications & Media Relations:
   Jerry Russo 212-374-5141/fax: 212-374-5584
   e-mail: jrusso@nycboe.net

Educational Construction Fund, NYC . . . . fax: 718-391-6529
30-30 Thomson Ave, 4th Fl, Long Island City, NY 11101
718-472-8287 or 718-472-8285 Fax: 718-391-6529
Web site: www.nycenet.edu/offices/ecf
Chancellor:
   Joel I Klein 212-374-0200
Executive Director:
   Jamie A Smarr 212-374-5026
   e-mail: jsmarr@nycboe.net
General Counsel to Chancellor:
   Michael Best 212-374-0220/fax: 212-374-5588
   e-mail: mbest2@nycboe.net
Counsel:
   James P Cullen 212-278-1565/fax: 212-278-1733
   e-mail: jcullen@andersonkill.com
Director, Finance:
   Juanita Rosillo 718-472-8285
   e-mail: jrosillo@nycsca.org

Elections, Board of, NYC . . . . fax: 212-487-5349
32 Broadway, 7th Fl, New York, NY 10004-1609
212-487-5300 or TDD 212-487-5496 Fax: 212-487-5349
Web site: www.vote.nyc.ny.us
President, Commissioners:
   Terrence C O'Connor 212-487-5300
   e-mail: toconnor@boe.nyc.ny.us
Executive Director:
   John Ravitz 212-487-5412
   e-mail: webmail_ravitzj@boe.nyc.ny.us
Deputy Executive Director:
   George Gonzalez 212-487-5403
   e-mail: webmail_gonzalezg@boe.nyc.ny.us
Administrative Manager:
   Pamela Perkins 212-487-5406
   e-mail: webmail_perkinsp@boe.nyc.ny.us
Director, Public Affairs & Communications:
   Valerie Vazquez 212-487-5404
   e-mail: webmail_vazquezv@boe.nyc.ny.us

Environmental Protection, Department of, NYC . . . . fax: 718-595-3525
59-17 Junction Blvd, 13th Fl, Flushing, NY 11373-5108
718-595-6565 Fax: 718-595-3525
Web site: www.nyc.gov/dep
Commissioner:
   Emily Lloyd 718-595-6565
   e-mail: cward@dep.nyc.gov

First Dep Commissioner/Exec Dir Water Board:
   Vacant 718-595-6576
Chief of Staff:
   Kathryn Garcia 718-595-3480
General Counsel:
   Mark D Hoffer 718-595-6528
Director, Public & Intergovernmental Affairs:
   Charles G Sturcken 718-595-6568

Equal Employment Practices Commission, NYC . . . . fax: 212-788-8652
253 Broadway, Rm 301, New York, NY 10007
212-240-7902 Fax: 212-788-8652
Executive Director:
   Abraham May, Jr 212-788-8646
   e-mail: amay@eepc.nyc.gov
Deputy Director:
   Eric Matusewitch 212-788-8573
   e-mail: ematusewitch@eepc.nyc.gov
General Counsel:
   Lisa Badner 212-788-8644

Film, Theatre & Broadcasting, Mayor's Office of, NYC fax: 212-307-6237
1697 Broadway, Ste 602, New York, NY 10019
212-489-6710 Fax: 212-307-6237
e-mail: info@film.nyc.gov
Web site: www.nyc.gov/film
Commissioner:
   Katherine Oliver 212-489-6710
Deputy Commissioner:
   John Battista 212-489-6710
Director, Production:
   Dean McCann 212-489-6710

Finance, Department of, NYC . . . . fax: 212-669-2275
66 John St, 3rd Fl, New York, NY 10038
212-669-4855 Fax: 212-669-2275
e-mail: starkm@finance.nyc.gov
Web site: www.nyc.gov/finance
Commissioner:
   Martha E Stark 212-669-4855
First Deputy Commissioner:
   Rochelle Patricof 212-669-2525
Assistant Commissioner, Communications/Customer Service:
   Sam Miller 212-669-4763/fax: 212-669-2275
Budget Director:
   Pat Mattera-Russell 212-669-4472
Treasury Deputy Commissioner:
   Robert Lee 212-669-2746/fax: 212-669-4656

Fire Department, NYC . . . . fax: 718-999-2582
9 Metrotech Center, 8th Fl, Brooklyn, NY 11201
718-999-2000 Fax: 718-999-2582
Web site: www.nyc.gov/fdny
Commissioner:
   Nicholas Scoppetta 718-999-2004
First Deputy Commissioner:
   Frank Cruthers 718-999-2070/fax: 718-999-2582
Chief of NYC Fire Department:
   Peter E Hayden 718-999-2010
Deputy Commissioner, Administration:
   Douglas White 718-999-2007
Deputy Commissioner, Technology & Support Services:
   Milton Fischberger 718-999-2062
Deputy Commissioner, Intergovernmental Affairs:
   Daniel Shacknai 718-999-2013
Deputy Commissioner, Legal:
   Mylan Denerstein 718-999-2016

Offices and agencies generally appear in alphabetical order, except when specific order is requested by listee.

MUNICIPAL GOVERNMENT / Municipal Government

Deputy Commissioner, Public Information:
   Francis X Gribbon 718-999-2026
Chief of Operations:
   Salvatore J Cassano 718-999-2079

Health & Hospitals Corporation, NYC . . . . . . fax: 212-788-0040
   125 Worth St, Rm 514, New York, NY 10013
   212-788-3321 Fax: 212-788-0040
   Web site: www.nyc.gov/hhc
President:
   Alan D Aviles 212-788-3321
Senior VP, Corporate Planning/Community Health/Intergvt Relations:
   LaRay Brown 212-788-3449
Senior VP, Operations:
   Frank J Cirillo 212-788-3669
Senior VP, Medical & Professional Affairs:
   Van Dunn 212-788-3648
Senior VP, Finance/Capital:
   Marlene Zurack 212-788-3494
Acting General Counsel:
   Richard A Levy 212-788-3300
Corporate Communications & Marketing Director:
   Kate McGrath 212-788-3386
   e-mail: kate.mcgrath@nychhc.org

Health & Mental Hygiene, Dept of, NYC . . . . fax: 212-964-0472
   125 Worth St, New York, NY 10013
   212-788-5290 or 212-825-5400 Fax: 212-964-0472
   Web site: www.nyc.gov/html/doh
Commissioner/Chair:
   Thomas R Frieden 212-219-5261
Executive Deputy Commissioner, Mental Hygiene:
   Lloyd Sederer 212-219-5400
Chief of Staff:
   Christina Chang 212-788-5259
   e-mail: cchang@health.nyc.gov
Deputy Commissioner, Administrative Services:
   Scottie Owings-Leaks 212-788-5265
   e-mail: swings-leaks@health.nyc.gov
Deputy Commissioner, Disease Control:
   Isaac Weisfuse 212-788-4711
   e-mail: iweisfuse@health.nyc.gov
Deputy Commissioner, Health Care Access/Improvement:
   Vacant 212-788-2278/fax: 212-788-3241
   e-mail: jcapoziello@health.nyc.gov
Deputy Commissioner, Epidemiology:
   Lorna Thorpe 212-788-4788
Deputy Commissioner, Environmental Health:
   Vacant 212-788-4646
Deputy Commissioner, Health Promotion/Disease Prevention:
   Mary Travis Bassett 212-788-5323
Deputy Commissioner, Financial & Strategic Management:
   Andrew Rein 212-788-5347
General Counsel, Health:
   Wilfredo Lopez 212-788-5025
General Counsel, Mental Hygiene:
   William Martin 212-788-4285
Assoc Cmsr, Communications/Public Information Officer:
   Sandra Mullin 212-788-5290
   e-mail: smullin@health.nyc.gov

Homeless Services, Department of, NYC . . . . fax: 212-361-7950
   33 Beaver St, 17th Fl, New York, NY 10004
   212-361-8000 Fax: 212-361-7950
   Web site: www.nyc.gov/dhs
Acting Commissioner:
   Robert V Hess 212-361-8000
Chief of Staff:
   Angeles Pai 212-361-7973

Associate Commissioner, Communication/External Affairs:
   James Anderson 212-361-7971
Assistant Commissioner, Community Relations:
   Robert Mascali 212-361-7900
General Counsel:
   Clarke Bruno 212-361-7996
Deputy Commissioner, Prevention:
   Carine Barometre 212-361-7990
Deputy Commissioner, Adult Services:
   Mark Hurwitz 212-361-0617
Deputy Commissioner, Family Services:
   Roger Newman 212-361-0626
Deputy Commissioner, Facility Maint/Development:
   Robert Skallerup Jr 212-361-8394

Housing Authority, NYC . . . . fax: 212-306-8888
   250 Broadway, 12th Fl, New York, NY 10007
   212-306-3000 Fax: 212-306-8888
   Web site: www.nyc.gov/nycha
Chair:
   Tino Hernandez 212-306-3434
General Manager:
   Douglas Apple 212-306-3416
General Counsel:
   Ricardo Morales 212-776-5151
Chief of Staff:
   Y Stacey Cumberbatch 212-306-3423
Deputy General Mgr/Chief Information Officer:
   Avi Duvdevani 212-306-8833
Deputy General Mgr, Capital Projects & Development:
   Joseph Farro 212-306-8685
Deputy General Mgr, Finance:
   Felix Lam 212-306-3770
Deputy General Mgr, Operations:
   Robert Podmore 212-306-8874
Deputy General Mgr, Administration:
   Natalie Y Rivers 212-306-8786
Deputy General Mgr, Policy Planning/Management:
   Vacant 212-306-3302
Deputy General Mgr, Community Operations:
   Hugh Spence 212-306-7038
Public Information Officer:
   Howard Marder 212-306-3322

Housing Preservation & Development, Dept of, NYC . . fax: 212-863-6302
   100 Gold St, 5th Fl, New York, NY 10038
   212-863-6300 Fax: 212-863-6302
   Web site: www.nyc.gov/hpd
Commissioner:
   Shaun Donovan 212-863-6300
Firsy Deputy Commissioner:
   John Warren 212-863-8566
Deputy Commissioner/General Counsel:
   Matthew Shafit 212-863-8686
Deputy Commissioner, Intergovernmental Affairs:
   Joseph Rosenberg 212-863-5241
Deputy Commissioner, Housing Operations:
   Laurie LoPrimo 212-863-8570
Deputy Commissioner, Preservation Services:
   Luiz Aragon 212-863-7001
Deputy Commissioner, Administration:
   Bernard Schwarz 212-863-8610
Deputy Commissioner, Development:
   Rafael Cestero 212-863-6400
Deputy Commissioner, Community Partnerships:
   Kimberly D Hardy 212-863-5128/fax: 212-863-8907
Assistant Commissioner, Public Affairs:
   Carol Abrams 212-863-5176/fax: 212-863-8071

Offices and agencies generally appear in alphabetical order, except when specific order is requested by listee.

MUNICIPAL GOVERNMENT / Municipal Government

Chief of Staff:
Laurel Blatchford 212-863-7982

Human Resources Administration, Dept of, NYC . . . . . . fax: 212-331-6214
180 Water St, 17th Fl, New York, NY 10038
212-331-6000 Fax: 212-331-6214
Web site: www.nyc.gov/html/hra
Commissioner:
Robert Doar 212-331-6000
e-mail: egglestonv@hra.nyc.gov
First Deputy Commissioner:
Patricia M Smith 212-331-6230
Senior Exec Dep Commissioner, Operations & Administration:
Alexander Palumbo 212-331-6170
Exec Dep Commissioner, Medical Insur/Community Svcs Administration (Interim):
Mary Harper 212-273-0001
Executive Deputy Commissioner, Finance Office:
Frank Donno 212-331-3980
Executive Deputy Commissioner, Policy & Program Development:
Jane Corbett 212-331-5500
Executive Deputy Commissioner, Contracts & Procurement:
Sandra Glaves-Morgan 212-331-3434
Executive Deputy Commissioner, Family Independence Administration:
Seth Diamond 212-331-6180
Executive Deputy Commissioner, Program Reporting Analysis & Accountability:
Swati Desai 212-331-6075
Executive Deputy Commissioner, Office of Staff Resources:
Jean Matthews 212-331-3333
Executive Deputy Commissioner, Customized Assistance Services:
Frank R Lipton 212-495-2606
Executive Deputy Commissioner, Audit Services/Organizational Analysis:
Holly E Brown 212-331-6160
Deputy Commissioner, HIV AIDS Services Administration:
Elsie Del Campo 212-620-4644
Deputy Commissioner, General Support Services:
Paul J Harding 212-274-5200
Deputy Commissioner, Office of Constituency & Community Affairs:
Burton Blaustein . . . . 212-331-4640 or 212-331-4641
Deputy Commissioner, Domestic Violence & Emergency Intervention Office:
Cecile Noel 212-331-4500
Exec Deputy Commissioner, Investigation, Revenue & Enforcement Admin:
Peter Jenik 212-274-4740
Deputy Commissioner, Management Information Systems:
Richard Siemer 718-510-8614/fax: 718-510-0273
General Counsel, Office of Legal Affairs (Interim):
Maureen Walsh 212-331-6167
Inspector General:
Rebecca Holland 212-331-3002
Chief of Staff:
David Hansell 212-331-6225
Press Secretary, Public Information & Communication Office:
Vacant 212-331-6200

Human Rights Commission on, NYC . . . . . . fax: 212-306-7658
40 Rector St, 10th Fl, New York, NY 10006
212-306-7500 Fax: 212-306-7658
Web site: www.nyc.gov/cchr
Chair & Commissioner:
Patricia L Gatling 212-306-7560
Deputy Commissioner/General Counsel:
Cliff Mulqueen 212-306-7741
Deputy Commissioner, Law Enforcement:
Avery S Mehlman 212-306-7764
Deputy Commissioner, Public Affairs:
Lee Hudson 212-306-7773

Director, Public Information:
Betsy Herzog 212-306-7530
Managing Attorney:
Lanny R Alexander 212-306-7423

Information Technology & Telecommunications, Dept of, NYC . . . . fax: 212-788-8130
75 Park Place, 9th Fl, New York, NY 10007
212-788-6600 Fax: 212-788-8130
Web site: www.nyc.gov/doitt
Commissioner:
Paul J Cosgrave 212-788-6633
First Dep Commissioner:
Ron Bergmann 212-788-6624
Deputy Commissioner, Information Utility:
Peter Tighe 718-403-8100
Executive Director, NYC 3-1-1:
Dean Schloyer 212-504-4421
General Counsel:
Agostino Cangemi 212-788-6640
Deputy Commissioner, Finance/Admin:
Margery Brown 212-788-6616

Intergovernmental Affairs Ofc, NYC Mayor's . . . . fax: 212-788-9711
City Hall, 2nd Fl, New York, NY 10007
212-788-2162 Fax: 212-788-9711
Director:
Haeda B Mihaltses 212-788-2162

Investigation, Department of, NYC . . . . fax: 212-825-2823
80 Maiden Lane, 18th Fl, New York, NY 10038
212-825-5900 Fax: 212-825-2823
Web site: www.nyc.gov/html/doi
Commissioner:
Rose Gill Hearn 212-825-5913
e-mail: rghearn@doi.nyc.gov
First Dep Commissioner:
Elizabeth Glazer 212-825-5910
Deputy Commissioner, Investigations:
Daniel D Brownell 212-825-2147
General Counsel:
Marjorie Landa 212-825-2404
Public Information Officer:
Emily Gest 212-825-5931

Juvenile Justice, Department of, NYC . . . . . . fax: 212-431-4874
365 Broadway, 4th Fl, New York, NY 10013
212-925-7779 or TTY/TDD:212-334-6873 Fax: 212-431-4874
e-mail: nycdjj@djj.nyc.gov
Web site: www.nyc.gov/html/djj
Commissioner:
Neil Hernandez 212-925-7779 x254
First Deputy Commissioner:
Judith Pincus 212-925-7779 x210
Deputy Commissioner, Operations & Detention:
Thomas Tsotsoros 212-925-7779 x202
Deputy Commissioner, Administration & Policy:
Andrew A Gonzalez 212-925-7779 x294
General Counsel:
Herman Dawson 212-925-7779 x211/fax: 646-274-7160
Director, Public Affairs:
Scott Trent 212-925-7779 x205

Labor Relations, Office of, NYC . . . . fax: 212-306-7202
40 Rector St, 4th Fl, New York, NY 10006
212-306-7200 Fax: 212-306-7202
Web site: www.nyc.gov/html/olr

Offices and agencies generally appear in alphabetical order, except when specific order is requested by listee.

MUNICIPAL GOVERNMENT / Municipal Government

Commissioner:
   James F Hanley...................................212-306-7200
First Dep Commissioner:
   Pamela S Silverblatt 212-306-7220/fax: 212-306-7202
General Counsel:
   Deborah M Gaines..................212-306-7230/fax: 212-306-7223
Director, Employee Benefits Program:
   Dorothy A Wolfe 212-306-7200

Landmarks Preservation Commission, NYC fax: 212-669-7960
   One Centre Street, 9th Fl North, New York, NY 10007
   212-669-7700 Fax: 212-669-7960
   Web site: www.nyc.gov/landmarks
Chair:
   Robert B Tierney 212-669-7888
   e-mail: rtierney@lpc.nyc.gov
Executive Director:
   Ronda Wist..212-669-7922
Public Information Officer/311 Liaison:
   Doris Hernandez 212-669-7817/fax: 212-669-7818
   e-mail: dhernandez@lpc.nyc.gov
Director, Community Affairs:
   Diane Jackier 212-669-7923

Law, Department of, NYC....................fax: 212-788-0367
   100 Church St, New York, NY 10007-2601
   212-788-0303 Fax: 212-788-0367
   Web site: www.nyc.gov/html/law
Corporation Counsel:
   Michael A Cardozo................................212-788-0303
   e-mail: mcardozo@law.nyc.gov
Managing Attorney:
   G Foster Mills 212-788-0300/fax: 212-732-3097
   e-mail: gmills@law.nyc.gov
Chief of Operations:
   Kenneth J Majerus 212-788-0373
Director, Legal Recruitment:
   Stuart Smith 212-788-1687
Inspector General:
   Clive I Morrick....................212-825-2409 or 212-825-2177
   e-mail: cmorrick@doi.nyc.gov
Communications Director:
   Kathleen O'Brien Ahlers............212-788-0400/fax: 212-788-8716
   e-mail: kahlers@law.nyc.gov

Legislative Affairs Office, NYC Mayor's City..........fax: 212-788-2647
   253 Broadway, 14th Fl, New York, NY 10007
   212-788-3678 Fax: 212-788-2647
   e-mail: citylegislativeaffairs@cityhall.nyc.gov
   Web site: www.ci.nyc.ny.us
Director:
   Karen E Meara 212-788-3678

Legislative Affairs Office, NYC Mayor's State.........fax: 518-462-5870
   119 Washington Ave, 3rd Fl, Albany, NY 12210
   518-447-5200 Fax: 518-462-5870
Director:
   Anthony P Piscitelli 518-447-5200

Library, Brooklyn Public....................fax: 718-398-6798
   Grand Army Plaza, Brooklyn, NY 11238
   718-230-2100 Fax: 718-398-6798
   Web site: www.brooklynpubliclibrary.org
Executive Director:
   Ginnie Cooper 718-230-2403
   e-mail: g.cooper@brooklynpubliclibrary.org

Deputy Exec Director:
   Siobhan Reardon 718-230-2162
   e-mail: s.reardon@brooklynpubliclibrary.org
Deputy Director, Business Admin/CFO:
   John Vitali.......................................718-230-2100
   e-mail: j.vitali@brooklynpubliclibrary.org
President, BPL Foundation:
   Cindy Freidmutter 718-230-2158
   e-mail: c.freidmutter@brooklynpubliclibrary.org
Deputy Director, Public Service:
   Janet Kinney.....................................718-230-2442
   e-mail: j.kinney@brooklynpubliclibrary.org

Library, New York Public....................fax: 212-930-9299
   5th Ave & 42nd St, New York, NY 10018
   212-930-0800 or 212-340-0849 Fax: 212-930-9299
   Web site: www.nypl.org
President & CEO:
   Paul LeClerc.....................................212-930-0736
Senior VP, External Affairs:
   Catherine Carver Dunn............................212-930-0611
Senior VP/Chief Administrative Officer:
   David Offensend..................................212-930-0600
VP/COO:
   Robert Santos 212-930-9203
Vice President, Development:
   Heather Lubov 212-930-0692
   e-mail: hlubov@nypl.org
Vice President & General Counsel:
   Robert J Vanni 212-930-0744
Vice President, Budget & Planning:
   Jeffrey Roth 212-592-7501/fax: 212-592-7440
Director, Government & Community Affairs:
   Catherine Dente 212-930-0051
VP, Communications & Marketing:
   Anne Canty......................................212-704-8600

Library, Queens Borough Public............fax: 718-291-8936
   89-11 Merrick Blvd, Jamaica, NY 11432
   718-990-0700 or TTY 718-990-0809 Fax: 718-291-8936
   Web site: www.queenslibrary.org
Director:
   Thomas W Galante................................718-990-0796
   e-mail: thomas.w.galante@queenslibrary.org
Director, Government & Community Affairs:
   James Van Bramer.................718-990-8585/fax: 718-990-5147
Director, Marketing & Communications:
   Joanne King......................718-990-0704/fax: 718-291-2695
   e-mail: joanne.king@queenslibrary.org

Loft Board, NYC ....fax: 212-788-7501
   100 Gold St, 2nd Fl, New York, NY 10007
   212-788-7610 Fax: 212-788-7501
   Web site: www.nyc.gov/html/loft
Chairperson:
   Marc Rauch 212-788-7610
Executive Director:
   Dianne E Dixon 212-788-7619

Management & Budget, Office of, NYC.....fax: 212-788-6300
   75 Park Place, 8th Fl, New York, NY 10007
   212-788-5800 Fax: 212-788-6300
   Web site: www.nyc.gov/omb
Director:
   Mark Page.......................................212-788-5900
First Deputy Director:
   Stuart Klein.....................................212-788-5904
Deputy Director/General Counsel:
   Marjorie Henning.................................212-788-5880

Offices and agencies generally appear in alphabetical order, except when specific order is requested by listee.

MUNICIPAL GOVERNMENT / Municipal Government

Deputy Director:
　P V Anatharam....................................212-788-5894
Deputy Director:
　Michael Dardia....................................212-788-5891

Medical Examiner, Office of Chief, NYC ... fax: 212-447-2716
　520 First Ave, New York, NY 10016
　212-447-2030　Fax: 212-447-2716
　Web site: www.nyc.gov
Chief Medical Examiner:
　Charles S Hirsch..................................212-447-2034
First Deputy Commissioner:
　Barbara Sampson..................................212-447-2335
Deputy Commissioner, Administration/Finance:
　Janice English....................................212-447-5351
Director, Medicolegal Investigations:
　Barbara Butcher...................................212-447-2036
Director, Public Affairs:
　Ellen Borakove....................212-447-2401/fax: 212-447-2755
General Counsel:
　Jody Lipton......................................212-447-2046

Parks & Recreation, Department of, NYC .. fax: 212-360-1329
　The Arsenal, Central Park, 830 Fifth Ave, New York, NY 10021
　212-360-8111　Fax: 212-360-1329
　e-mail: commissioner@parks.nyc.gov
　Web site: www.nyc.gov/parks
Commissioner:
　Adrian Benepe....................212-360-1305/fax: 202-360-1345
First Deputy Commissioner, Operations:
　Liam Kavanagh....................................212-360-1307
Deputy Commissioner, Capital Projects:
　Amy Freitag......................................718-760-6602
Deputy Commissioner, Public Programs:
　Kevin Jeffrey....................................212-360-1381
Deputy Commissioner, Management/Budget:
　Robert L Garafola.................................212-360-1302
Director, Public Information:
　Warner Johnston..................212-360-1311/fax: 212-360-1333

Police Department, NYC......................fax: 646-610-5865
　One Police Plaza, New York, NY 10038
　646-610-5000　Fax: 646-610-5865
　Web site: www.nyc.gov/nypd
Police Commissioner:
　Raymond W Kelly..................................646-610-5410
First Dep Commissioner:
　George A Grasso..................................646-610-5420
Chief of Staff:
　Joseph P Wuensch.................................646-610-8534
Chief of Department:
　Joseph J Esposito................................646-610-6710
Deputy Chief Commissioner, Community Affairs:
　Joyce A Stephens.................................646-610-5323
Deputy Commissioner, Administration:
　Charles D DeRienzo...............................646-610-5577
Deputy Commissioner, Strategic Initiatives:
　Michael J Farrell................................646-610-8534
Deputy Commissioner, Counter Terrorism:
　Richard A Falkenrath.............................646-610-6169
Deputy Commissioner, Intelligence:
　David Cohen.....................................646-610-5403
Deputy Commissioner, Equal Employment Opportunity:
　Neldra M Zeigler.................................646-610-5330
Deputy Commissioner, Labor Relations:
　John P Beirne...................................646-610-5060
Deputy Commissioner, Trials:
　Martin G Karopkin................................646-610-5424

Deputy Commissioner, Training:
　Charles De Rienzo.................................646-610-4675
Deputy Commissioner, Legal Matters:
　S Andrew Schaffer.................................646-610-5336
Deputy Commissioner, Management & Budget:
　Edward J Allocco..................................646-610-6670
Deputy Commissioner, Operations:
　Phil T Pulaski....................................646-610-6100
Deputy Commissioner, Technological Development:
　V James Onalfo....................................646-610-6873
Deputy Commissioner, Public Information:
　Paul J Browne.....................................646-610-6700

Probation, Department of, NYC.............fax: 212-361-0686
　33 Beaver St, New York, NY 10004
　888-226-5395 or 212-232-0684　Fax: 212-361-0686
　Web site: www.nyc.gov/html/prob
Commissioner:
　Martin F Horn....................212-361-8977/fax: 212-361-8985
　e-mail: mhorn@probation.nyc.gov
First Deputy Commissioner:
　Richard Levy.....................................212-361-8970
　e-mail: rlevy@probation.nyc.gov
Director, Public Info/Records Access:
　Jack Ryan.......................................212-232-0684
　e-mail: jryan@probation.nyc.gov
Chief of Staff:
　Judith LaPook...................................212-361-8970
General Counsel:
　Florence Hutner.................................212-232-0700
Deputy Commissioner, Admin/Planning/Operations:
　Frank Marchiano.................................212-361-8965
Deputy Commissioner, Family Court Services:
　Patricia Brennan................................212-232-0486
Deputy Commissioner/Chief Information Officer:
　Kael S Goodman..................................212-266-1895

Public Advocate, Office of the...............fax: 212-669-4701
　Municipal Bldg, One Centre St, 15th Fl North, New York, NY 10007
　212-669-7200　Fax: 212-669-4701
　Web site: www.pubadvocate.nyc.gov
Public Advocate:
　Betsy Gotbaum...................................212-669-4102
　e-mail: bgotbaum@pubadvocate.nyc.gov
Counsel:
　Mary Mastropaolo................................212-669-7200
　e-mail: mmastropaolo@pubadvocate.nyc.gov
Chief of Staff:
　Anat Jacobson...................................212-669-4743
　e-mail: ajacobson@pubadvocate.nyc.gov
Director, Administration:
　Elba Feliciano..................................212-669-2179
　e-mail: elba@pubadvocate.nyc.gov
Ombudsman Services:
　Elizabeth Blaney................................212-669-7250
　e-mail: ombudsman@pubadvocate.nyc.gov
Executive Assistant:
　Jane Schatz.....................................212-669-4258
　e-mail: jschatz@pubadvocate.nyc.gov

Records & Information Services, Dept of, NYC........fax: 212-788-8614
　31 Chambers St, Rm 305, New York, NY 10007
　212-639-9675 or TTY: 212-788-8615　Fax: 212-788-8614
　Web site: www.nyc.gov/records
Commissioner:
　Brian G Andersson...............................212-788-8607
　e-mail: bgandersson@records.nyc.gov

Offices and agencies generally appear in alphabetical order, except when specific order is requested by listee.

MUNICIPAL GOVERNMENT / Municipal Government

Deputy Commissioner/Public Access Officer:
  Eileen M Flannelly................................. 212-788-8610
Director, Administration:
  Vickie Moore....................................... 212-788-8622
Director, Municipal Archives:
  Leonora Gidlund.................................... 212-788-8585
Director, Municipal Records Management Division:
  Pearl L Boatswain.................................. 212-788-8550
Director, City Hall Library:
  Paul C Perkus...................................... 212-788-8596

Rent Guidelines Board, NYC............... fax: 212-385-2554
  51 Chambers St, Ste 202, New York, NY 10007
  212-385-2934 Fax: 212-385-2554
  e-mail: ask@housingnyc.com
  Web site: www.housingnyc.com; www.nyc.gov/html/rgb
Chair:
  Marvin Markus..................................... 212-385-2934
Executive Director:
  Andrew McLaughlin........................... 212-385-2934 x12
Public Information Officer:
  Charmaine Frank................................... 212-385-2934
Senior Research Associate:
  Brian Hoberman.................................... 212-385-2934

Sanitation, Department of, NYC
  125 Worth St, New York, NY 10013
  e-mail: comroffc@dsny.nyc.gov
  Web site: www.nyc.gov/sanitation
Commissioner:
  John J Doherty.................................... 646-885-5020
First Deputy Commissioner, Operations:
  Michael A Bimonte................................. 646-885-4727
Deputy Commissioner, of Public Info & Community Affairs:
  Vito A Turso...................... 646-885-5020/fax: 212-791-3386

Small Business Services, Department of, NYC.......... fax: 212-618-8991
  110 William St, 7th Fl, New York, NY 10038
  212-513-6300 Fax: 212-618-8991
  Web site: www.nyc.gov/html/sbs
Commissioner:
  Robert W Walsh.................................... 212-513-6350
First Deputy Commissioner:
  Andrew Schwartz................................... 212-513-6428
Deputy Commissioner, Div of Neighborhood Development:
  Mark Newhouse..................................... 212-618-8802
Deputy Commissioner, Workforce Development:
  David Margalit.................................... 212-618-6710
General Counsel:
  David Farber...................................... 212-442-6432
Director, Business Relocation Assistance:
  Donald Giampetro.................................. 212-618-8778
Assistant Commissioner, External Affairs & Community Relations:
  Michael C Smith................................... 212-513-6368
Assistant Commissioner, Finance & Administration:
  Shaazad Ali....................................... 212-618-8735
Chief of Staff/Communications Director:
  Ethan Davidson.................................... 212-513-6374
Director, Business Outreach Team:
  Bernadette Nation................................. 212-618-8810

Sports Commission, NYC................... fax: 212-487-7090
  2 Washington Street, 15th Floor, New York, NY 10004
  877-692-7767 or 212-487-7120 Fax: 212-487-7090
  Web site: www.nyc.gov/sports
Commissioner:
  Kenneth J Podziba................................. 212-487-5676
  e-mail: kpodziba@cityhall.nyc.gov

Deputy Commissioner:
  Andrew Gould...................................... 212-487-5665

Standards & Appeals, Board of, NYC........ fax: 212-788-8769
  40 Rector Street, 9th Floor, New York, NY 10006
  212-788-8500 Fax: 212-788-8769
  e-mail: ppacific@dcas.nyc.gov
  Web site: www.nyc.gov/html/bsa
Chair/Commissioner:
  Meenakshi Srinivasan.............................. 212-788-8547
Executive Director:
  Jeff Mulligan..................................... 212-788-8805
Deputy Director:
  Roy E Starrin..................................... 212-788-8797
Counsel:
  Greg Belcamino.................................... 212-788-0296

Tax Commission, NYC...................... fax: 212-669-8636
  Municipal Building, 1 Centre St, Rm 936, New York, NY 10007
  212-669-4410 Fax: 212-669-8636
  Web site: www.nyc.gov/html/taxcomm
President:
  Glenn Newman...................................... 212-669-4401
Director, Operations:
  Myrna Hall..................... 212-669-4420/fax: 212-669-2003
Director, Information Technology:
  Iftikhar Ahmad.................................... 212-669-2954
Director, Appraisal & Hearings:
  Carlo Silvestri................................... 212-669-4412
General Counsel:
  Reed Schneider.................................... 212-669-4407

Taxi & Limousine Commission, NYC......... fax: 212-676-1100
  40 Rector St, New York, NY 10006
  212-639-9675 Fax: 212-676-1100
  Web site: www.nyc.gov/taxi
Commissioner/Chair/CEO:
  Matthew W Daus.................................... 212-676-1003
Chief of Staff:
  Ira Goldstein.................. 212-676-1017/fax: 212-676-2002
First Deputy Commissioner:
  Andrew Salkin................... 212-676-1147 or 212-676-1148
Deputy Commissioner, Legal Affairs:
  Charles Fraser.................................... 212-676-1117
Deputy Commissioner, Licensing:
  Barbara Schechter............... 718-391-5667 or 718-391-5666
Deputy Commissioner, Public Affairs:
  Allan J Fromberg................ 212-676-1013/fax: 212-676-1101
Deputy Commissioner of Financial Management & Administration:
  Louis Tazzi....................................... 212-676-1035

Transportation, Department of, NYC
  40 Worth St, New York, NY 10013
  212-639-9675
  Web site: www.nyc.gov/dot
Commissioner:
  Janette Sadik-Khan.............. 212-676-0868/fax: 212-442-7007
General Counsel:
  Phillip Damashek................ 212-442-7730/fax: 212-442-7733
First Deputy Commissioner:
  Judith Bergtraum................ 212-442-7042/fax: 212-442-5296
Deputy Commissioner, Procurement, Technology & Passenger Transport:
  Howard Altschuler................................. 212-442-3667
Deputy Commissioner, Sidewalks & Inspection Mgmt Division:
  Leon W Heyward.................................... 718-391-2701

Veterans' Affairs, Mayor's Office of, NYC.. fax: 212-442-4170
  100 Gold St, 2nd Fl, New York, NY 10038
  212-442-4171 Fax: 212-442-4170
  Web site: www.nyc.gov/veterans

Offices and agencies generally appear in alphabetical order, except when specific order is requested by listee.

MUNICIPAL GOVERNMENT / Municipal Government

Executive Director:
Clarice Joynes..............................212-442-4171
Deputy Director:
Jim Fuchs..................................212-442-4171

Voter Assistance Commission (VAC), NYC. fax: 212-788-2527
100 Gold Street, 2nd Floor, New York, NY 10038-1605
212-788-8384 Fax: 212-788-2527
e-mail: access via web site
Web site: www.nyc.gov/voter
Chairman:
Jeffrey F Kraus............................212-788-8384
Vice Chair:
Jane Kalmus...............................212-788-8384
Executive Director/Coordinator:
Onida Coward Mayers.......................212-788-8384
Office Manager:
Bibi N Yusuf..............................212-788-8384

Water Finance Authority, Municipal, NYC. fax: 212-788-9197
75 Park Place, 6th Fl, New York, NY 10007
212-788-5889 Fax: 212-788-9197
Web site: www.nyc.gov/nyw
Executive Director:
Alan L Anders.............................212-788-5889
Director, Investor Relations:
Raymond J Orlando.........................212-788-5875
e-mail: OrlandoR@omb.nyc.gov

Youth & Community Development, Department of, NYC...fax: 212-442-5998
156 William St, New York, NY 10038
212-442-5900 Fax: 212-442-5998
Web site: www.nyc.gov/dycd
Commissioner:
Jeanne B Mullgrav...............212-442-6006/fax: 212-442-6092
e-mail: jmullgrav@dycd.nyc.gov
General Counsel:
Everett Hughes............................212-442-5980
Chief of Staff:
Michael Ognibene..........................212-442-5989
Deputy Commissioner, Administration:
Regina Miller.............................212-442-8573
e-mail: rmiller@dycd.nyc.gov
Deputy Commissioner, Community Development:
Suzanne M Lynn............................212-442-6015

New York City Boroughs

Bronx (Bronx County).....................fax: 718-590-3537
Executive Division, 851 Grand Concourse, Bronx, NY 10451
718-590-3500 Fax: 718-590-3537
e-mail: webmail@bronxbp.nyc.gov
Web site: bronxboropres.nyc.gov
Borough President:
Adolfo Carrion Jr...............718-590-3557/fax: 718-590-3537
Deputy Borough President:
Earl D Brown..............................718-590-3565
Director, Communications:
Anne Fenton...............................718-590-3543
Counsel:
Lai-Sun Yee...............................718-590-8555
Press Secretary:
Ronnie Sykes..............................718-537-3386

Brooklyn (Kings County)...................fax: 718-802-3805
Borough Hall, 209 Joralemon St, Brooklyn, NY 11201
718-802-3883 Fax: 718-802-3805
Web site: www.brooklyn-usa.org
Borough President:
Marty Markowitz...........................718-802-3700
e-mail: askmarty@brooklynbp.nyc.gov
Deputy Borough President:
Yvonne J Graham...........................718-802-3842
Chief of Staff:
Gregory Atkins............................718-802-3862
General Counsel:
Fred Arriaga..............................718-802-3757
Director, Communications:
Eric Demby................................718-802-3835

Manhattan (New York County).............fax: 212-669-4900
Municipal Bldg, One Centre St, 19th Fl South, New York, NY 10007
212-669-8300 Fax: 212-669-4900
Web site: www.mbpo.org
Borough President:
Scott M Stringer..........................212-669-8155
e-mail: bp@manhattanbp.org
Deputy Borough President:
Rosemonde Pierre-Louis....................212-669-8137
e-mail: rpierre-louis@manhattanbp.org
Chief of Staff:
Alaina Colon..............................212-669-2527
e-mail: acolon@manhattanbp.org
General Counsel:
Jimmy Yan.................................212-669-8157
e-mail: jyan@manhattanbp.org
Director, Operations:
Leroy D Wilkes Jr.........................212-669-8300
e-mail: lwilkes@manhattanbp.org
Director, Policy & Research:
Megan Shane...............................212-669-8300
e-mail: mshane@manhattanbp.org
Director, Communications:
Eric Pugatch..............................212-669-8139
e-mail: epugatch@manhattanbp.org
Press Secretary:
Maibe Gonzalez Fuentes..........212-669-3882/fax: 212-669-3380
e-mail: mfuentes@manhattanbp.org

Queens (Queens County)...................fax: 718-286-2876
Executive Division, 120-55 Queens Blvd, Kew Gardens, NY 11424
718-286-3000 or TTY: 718-286-2656 Fax: 718-286-2876
e-mail: info@queensbp.org
Web site: www.queensbp.org
Borough President:
Helen M Marshall..........................718-286-3000
Deputy Borough President:
Karen Koslowitz...........................718-286-3000
Chief of Staff:
Alexandra Rosa............................718-286-3000
General Counsel:
Hugh Weinberg.............................718-286-3000
Director, Management & Budget:
Carol Ricci...............................718-286-2660
Director, Planning & Development:
Irving Poy................................718-286-2860
Immigration Affairs:
Susie Tanenbaum...........................718-286-2741
Public Information Officer/Press Office:
Daniel Andrews............................718-286-2640

Staten Island (Richmond County).........fax: 718-816-2026
Borough Hall, 10 Richmond Terrace, Staten Island, NY 10301
718-816-2000 Fax: 718-816-2026
Web site: www.statenislandusa.com
Borough President:
James P Molinaro..........................718-816-2200

Offices and agencies generally appear in alphabetical order, except when specific order is requested by listee.

MUNICIPAL GOVERNMENT / Municipal Government

Deputy Borough President:
  Edward Burke.........................718-816-2231
Chief of Staff:
  Meagan Devereaux.................718-816-2058
Legal Counsel:
  John Zaccone .... 718-816-2056 or 718-351-3900
Borough Commissioner, DOT:
  Thomas Curitore....................718-816-2387

Newburgh, City of
83 Broadway
Newburgh, NY 12550
845-569-7301 Fax: 845-569-7370
e-mail: info@mail.cityofnewburgh-ny.gov
Web site: www.newburgh-ny.com

Mayor:
  Nicholas J Valentine................845-569-7301
City Manager:
  Jean McGrane........................845-569-7301
Director, Planning & Development:
  Robert McKenna............845-569-9400/fax: 845-569-9700
City Clerk:
  Lorene Vitek...............845-569-7311/fax: 845-569-7314
  e-mail: lvitek@cityofnewburgh-ny.gov
Corporation Counsel:
  Geoffrey E Chanin............845-569-7335/fax: 845-569-7338
Comptroller:
  Dawn Gobeo.................845-569-7320/fax: 845-569-7490
  e-mail: dgobeo@cityofnewburgh-ny.gov
Chief of Police:
  Eric Paolilli................845-561-3131/fax: 845-565-5662
Fire Chief:
  James Merritt.......................845-562-1212
Historian:
  Mary McTamaney..................845-569-8090
  e-mail: newburghhistory@usa.com

Newburgh, Town of
1496 Rte 300
Newburgh, NY 12550
845-564-4552 Fax: 845-566-9486
Web site: www.townofnewburgh.org

Town Supervisor:
  Wayne C Booth......................845-564-4552
  e-mail: townsupervisor@hvc.rr.com
Town Clerk:
  Andrew J Zarutskie.........845-564-4554/fax: 945-564-8589
  e-mail: town-clerk@hvc.rr.com
Town Attorney:
  Mark Taylor................845-562-9100/fax: 845-565-1999
Accountant:
  Jacqueline Calarco.................845-564-5220
  e-mail: accountant@hvc.rr.com
Police Chief:
  Charles Kehoe.............845-565-1100/fax: 845-564-1870

Niagara Falls, City of
City Hall
745 Main St, PO Box 69
Niagara Falls, NY 14302-0069
716-286-4300 Fax: 716-286-4349
Web site: www.niagarafallsusa.org

Mayor:
  Vincenzo V Anello..................716-286-4310
City Administrator:
  William Bradberry..................716-286-4320
City Clerk:
  Carol Antonucci....................716-286-4396
  e-mail: cantonucci@falls.niagara.ny.us
Acting Corporate Counsel:
  Damon A Decastro.........716-286-4422/fax: 716-286-4424
Controller:
  Maria C Brown......................716-286-4340
Police Superintendent:
  John Chella........................716-286-4545
Public Works & Parks Manager:
  John Caso..........................716-286-4940

Niskayuna, Town of
One Niskayuna Circle
Niskayuna, NY 12309
518-386-4500 Fax: 518-386-4592
Web site: www.niskayuna.org

Town Supervisor:
  Luke Smith................518-386-4503/fax: 518-386-4592
Town Clerk:
  Helen Kopke...............518-386-4511/fax: 518-386-4592
  e-mail: hkopke@niskayuna.org
Comptroller:
  Paul Sebesta..............518-386-4508/fax: 518-386-4592
Town Attorney:
  Eric Dickson..............518-386-4505/fax: 518-386-4592
Police Chief:
  Lewis Moskowitz...........518-386-4585/fax: 518-386-4594

North Hempstead, Town of
220 Plandome Rd
PO Box 3000
Manhasset, NY 11030
516-627-0590 or 516-869-6311 Fax: 516-627-4204
e-mail: feedback@northhempstead.com
Web site: www.northhempstead.com

Town Supervisor:
  Jon Kaiman.........................516-869-7700
  e-mail: kaimanj@northhempstead.com
Town Clerk:
  Michelle Schimel...................516-869-7646
  e-mail: schimelm@northhempstead.com
Town Attorney:
  Richard S Finkel...................516-869-7600
  e-mail: finkelr@northhempstead.com
Director, Public Safety:
  Edward A Neidrich..................516-869-7628
  e-mail: neidriche@northhempstead.com
Commissioner, Public Works:
  Michael Martinaro..................516-739-6710
  e-mail: martinarom@northhempstead.com
Commissioner, Finance:
  Helene Raps-Beckerman..............516-869-7741
  e-mail: beckermh@northhempstead.com

Offices and agencies generally appear in alphabetical order, except when specific order is requested by listee.

MUNICIPAL GOVERNMENT / Municipal Government

Comptroller:
  Paul Pathe 516-869-7765
  e-mail: pathep@northhempstead.com
Commissioner, Community Services:
  Madge Kaplan 516-869-7715
  e-mail: commserve@northhempstead.com

North Tonawanda, City of
City Hall
216 Payne Ave
North Tonawanda, NY 14120
716-695-8000 Fax: 716-695-8557
Web site: www.northtonawanda.org

Mayor:
  Lawrence V Soos 716-695-8540/fax: 716-695-8541
  e-mail: larrysoos@northtonawanda.org
Common Council President:
  Brett M Sommer 716-692-4798
  e-mail: brettmsommer@adelhpia.net
City Clerk:
  Thomas M Jaccarino 716-695-8555
  e-mail: cityclerk@northtonawanda.org
City Attorney:
  Shawn P Nickerson 716-695-8590/fax: 716-695-8592
City Engineer:
  Dale W Marshall 716-695-8565/fax: 716-695-8568
  e-mail: dalemar@northtonawanda.org
Treasurer:
  Leslie J Stolzenfels 716-695-8575
Police Chief:
  Randy D Szukala 716-692-4111
Fire Chief:
  Gregory R Frank 716-693-2201
Historian:
  Daniel Bille 716-695-8000

Onondaga, Town of
5020 Ball Road
Syracuse, NY 13215
315-469-3888 Fax: 315-498-6129
Web site: www.townofonondagany.com

Town Supervisor:
  Thomas Andino 315-469-3888/fax: 315-498-6129
Town Clerk:
  Lisa Goodwin 315-469-1583/fax: 315-498-3461
  e-mail: lgoodwin@townofonondaga.com
Tax Receiver:
  Michele Kresser 315-469-0483/fax: 315-498-3461
Town Attorney:
  Kevin Gilligan 315-422-1152/fax: 315-422-1139
Town Historian:
  L Jane Tracy 315-214-2383

Orangetown, Town of
26 Orangeburg Rd
Orangeburg, NY 10962
845-359-5100 Fax: 845-359-2623
Web site: www.orangetown.com

Town Supervisor:
  Thom Kleiner 845-359-5100 x293/fax: 845-359-2623
  e-mail: supervisor@orangetown.com

Town Clerk:
  Charlotte E Madigan 845-359-5100/fax: 845-359-5126
  e-mail: cmadigan@orangetown.com
Town Attorney:
  Teresa M Kenny 845-359-5100 x215/fax: 845-359-2715
  e-mail: townattorney@orangetown.com
Director, Finance:
  Charles Richardson 845-359-5100 x205
  e-mail: findir@orangetown.com
Police Chief:
  Kevin A Nulty 845-359-3700/fax: 845-359-4563

Orchard Park, Town of
4295 S Buffalo Rd
Orchard Park, NY 14127
716-662-6400 Fax: 716-662-6479
e-mail: colarussoj@orchardparkny.org
Web site: www.orchardparkny.org

Town Supervisor:
  Mary Travers Murphy 716-662-6400
  e-mail: opsupervisor@orchardparkny.org
Town Clerk:
  Janis A Colarusso 716-662-6410
  e-mail: colarussoj@orchardpark.ny.org
Town Attorney:
  Leonard Berkowitz 716-662-9808/fax: 716-662-9546
Receiver of Taxes:
  Carol R Hutton 716-662-6406
  e-mail: optax@orchardparkny.org
Police Chief:
  Samuel McCune 716-662-6444
  e-mail: oppolice@orchardparkny.org

Ossining, Town of
16 Croton Ave
Ossining, NY 10562
914-762-6000 Fax: 914-762-7710
Web site: www.townofossining.com

Town Supervisor:
  John V Chervokas 914-762-6000
  e-mail: supervisor@townofossining.com
Town Clerk:
  MaryAnn Roberts 914-762-8428
  e-mail: townclerk@townofossining.com
Town Attorney:
  Thomas Beirne 914-762-6000
Receiver of Taxes:
  Gloria Fried 914-762-8790/fax: 914-762-0635
  e-mail: taxreceiver@townofossining.com
Police Chief:
  Kenneth Donato 914-762-6007/fax: 914-762-6900
  e-mail: topd@ossiningtownpolice.com

Ossining, Village of
16 Croton Ave
Ossining, NY 10562
914-941-3554
Web site: www.villageofossining.org

Mayor:
  William R Hanauer 914-941-3554

Offices and agencies generally appear in alphabetical order, except when specific order is requested by listee.

MUNICIPAL GOVERNMENT / Municipal Government

Village Manager:
   Linda Abels 914-941-3554
Village/Town Clerk:
   Mary Ann Roberts. 914-762-8428/fax: 914-762-7710
Treasurer:
   Rose Sickenius. 914-941-2581/fax: 914-941-3812
Corporation Counsel:
   Richard Leins. 914-941-3554/fax: 914-941-5940
Police Chief:
   Joseph Burton. 914-941-4099
Fire Chief:
   Mauro Santucci. 914-941-0215

Owego, Town of
2354 NYS Route 434
Apalachin, NY 13732
607-687-2194 Fax: 607-687-5191
Web site: www.townofowego.com

Town Supervisor:
   Carol Sweeney. 607-687-3535/fax: 607-687-5191
Town Clerk:
   Michael E Zimmer 607-687-2194
Town Attorney:
   Judy Quigley. 607-687-3575
Director, Utilities:
   Michael Trivisonno 607-625-2197
Town Historian:
   Emma Sedore 607-687-1961

Oyster Bay, Town of
Town Hall East
54 Audrey Ave
Oyster Bay, NY 11771
516-624-6498 Fax: 516-624-6387
Web site: www.oysterbaytown.com

Town Supervisor:
   John Venditto 516-624-6350
Town Clerk:
   Steven L Labriola. 516-624-6332
Attorney:
   Gregory J Giammalvo 516-624-6150
Comptroller:
   Thomas D Galasso 516-624-6440

Peekskill, City of
City Hall
840 Main Street
Peekskill, NY 10566
914-737-3400
Web site: www.ci.peekskill.ny.us

Mayor:
   John Testa. 914-737-3400
City Manager:
   Daniel W Fitzpatrick 914-737-3400
   e-mail: dfitzpatrick@cityofpeekskill.com
City Clerk:
   Pamela Beach 914-737-3400
Acting Corporation Counsel:
   William Florence 914-734-4180

Comptroller:
   Marcus A Serrano. 914-737-3400
Director, City Services:
   David Greener 914-737-3400
Police Chief:
   Eugene S Tumolo 914-737-8000

Penfield, Town of
3100 Atlantic Ave
Penfield, NY 14526
585-340-8600 Fax: 585-340-8667
Web site: www.penfield.org

Town Supervisor:
   George C Wiedemer. 585-340-8630
   e-mail: supervisor@penfield.org
Town Clerk:
   Cassie Williams 585-340-8629
   e-mail: clerk@penfield.org
Town Attorney:
   Richard Horwitz 585-264-0590
Town Comptroller:
   Robert P Beedon. 585-340-8620
   e-mail: finance@penfield.org
Fire Marshal:
   Pat Morris. 585-340-8643
   e-mail: firemarshal@penfield.org
Town Historian:
   Kathy Kanauer 585-340-8740
   e-mail: historian@penfield.org

Perinton, Town of
1350 Turk Hill Rd
Fairport, NY 14450
585-223-0770 or 585-223-5050 Fax: 585-223-3629
Web site: www.perinton.org

Town Supervisor:
   James E Smith 585-223-0770
   e-mail: jsmith@perinton.org
Town Clerk:
   Susan C Roberts 585-223-0770
   e-mail: sroberts@perinton.org
Town Attorney:
   Robert M Place 585-425-1060/fax: 585-223-3252
Public Works:
   Thomas C Beck 585-223-5115
   e-mail: tbeck@perinton.org
Director, Finance:
   Kevin Spacher 585-223-0770
   e-mail: kspacher@perinton.org
Historian:
   Jean Keplinger 585-223-0770
   e-mail: jkeplinger@perinton.org

Pittsford, Town of
11 S Main St
Pittsford, NY 14534
585-248-6200 Fax: 585-248-6247
Web site: www.townofpittsford.com

Town Supervisor:
   William A Carpenter 585-248-6220
   e-mail: bcarpenter@townofpittsford.org

Offices and agencies generally appear in alphabetical order, except when specific order is requested by listee.

MUNICIPAL GOVERNMENT / Municipal Government

Town Clerk:
   Patricia E Chuhta 585-248-6210/fax: 585-248-6215
   e-mail: pchuhta@townofpittsford.org
Town Attorney:
   Rich Williams 585-248-6216
   e-mail: rwilliams@townofpittsford.org
Director, Finance:
   Gregory J Duane 585-248-6225
   e-mail: gduane@townofpittsford.org
Commissioner, Public Works:
   Paul Schenkel 585-248-6250/fax: 585-248-6262
   e-mail: pschenkel@townofpittsford.org
Town Historian:
   Audrey M Johnson 585-248-6245
   e-mail: ajohnson@townofpittsford.org

Port Chester, Village of
10 Pearl Street
Port Chester, NY 10573
914-939-5202 Fax: 914-937-3169
e-mail: krang@villageofportchester-ny.com
Web site: www.portchesterny.com

Mayor:
   Gerald Logan 914-939-2200
Village Manager:
   William F Williams 914-939-2200
   e-mail: vilmgr@villageofportchester-ny.com
Village Clerk:
   Keith Rang 914-939-5202
Treasurer:
   Anthony S Siligato 914-939-5202
Corporation Counsel:
   Mario DeMarco 914-939-5201
Village Attorney:
   Anthony Cerreto 914-939-5201
Public Works General Foreman:
   Gary Racaniello 914-939-5207
Police Chief:
   Joseph Krzeminski 914-939-1000

Poughkeepsie, City of
Municipal Building
PO Box 300
Poughkeepsie, NY 12602
845-451-4200 Fax: 845-451-4201
e-mail: info@cityofpoughkeepsie.com
Web site: www.cityofpoughkeepsie.com

Mayor:
   Nancy Cozean 845-451-4076/fax: 845-451-4201
   e-mail: ncozean@cityofpoughkeepsie.com
City Administrator:
   James A Marquette 845-451-4072/fax: 845-451-4013
   e-mail: jmarquette@cityofpoughkeepsie.com
City Chamberlain/Clerk:
   Felicia M Santos 845-451-4200/fax: 845-451-4239
   e-mail: fsantos@cityofpoughkeepsie.com
Finance Commissioner:
   Jim Wijtowicz 845-451-4027/fax: 845-451-4028
City Attorney:
   Stephen Wing 845-451-4065/fax: 914-451-4070
Police Chief:
   Ronald Knapp 845-451-4132

Poughkeepsie, Town of
One Overocker Rd
Poughkeepsie, NY 12603
845-485-3600 Fax: 845-485-3701
Web site: www.townofpoughkeepsie.com

Town Supervisor:
   Patricia Myers 845-485-3607/fax: 845-485-3701
   e-mail: pmyers@townofpoughkeepsie.com
Town Clerk:
   Susan Miller 845-485-3620/fax: 845-485-8583
   e-mail: smiller@townofpoughkeepsie.ny.gov
Town Attorney:
   Thomas D Mahar, Jr 845-485-3633/fax: 845-486-7878
Comptroller:
   Charles Emberger 845-485-3610
Police Chief:
   Peter Wilkinson 845-485-3666/fax: 845-485-3756
   e-mail: townpolice@hotmail.com
Town Historian:
   Jean Murphy 845-485-3646

Queensbury, Town of
742 Bay Road
Queensbury, NY 12804
518-761-8200 Fax: 518-798-8359
Web site: www.queensbury.net

Town Supervisor:
   Dan Stec 518-761-8229
   e-mail: supervisor@queensbury.net
Town Clerk/Receiver of Taxes:
   Darleen Dougher 518-761-8234
   e-mail: townclerk@queensbury.net
Town Counsel, Legal Assistant:
   Pamela Hunsinger 518-761-8251/fax: 518-745-4408
   e-mail: towncounsel@queensbury.net
Town Fiscal Manager:
   Barbara Tierney 518-761-8240/fax: 518-745-4445
   e-mail: accounting@queensbury.net
Fire Marshal:
   Mike Palmer 518-761-8206/fax: 518-745-4437
   e-mail: firemarshal@queensbury.net
Historian:
   Marilyn VanDyke 518-761-8252
   e-mail: historian@queensbury.net

Ramapo, Town of
Town Hall, 237 Route 59
Suffern, NY 10901
845-357-5100 Fax: 845-357-3877
e-mail: supervisor@ramapo-ny.org
Web site: www.ramapo.org

Town Supervisor:
   Christopher P St Lawrence 845-357-5100
Town Clerk:
   Christian G Sampson 845-357-5100 x263/fax: 845-357-8513
   e-mail: townclerk@ramapo.org
Town Attorney:
   Michael L Klein 845-357-5100/fax: 845-357-2936
Director, Finance:
   Ilan Schoenberger 845-357-5100

Offices and agencies generally appear in alphabetical order, except when specific order is requested by listee.

MUNICIPAL GOVERNMENT / Municipal Government

Director, Public Works:
  Ted Dzurinko 845-357-0591
Police Chief:
  Peter Brower 845-357-2400

Riverhead, Town of
200 Howell Avenue
Long Island
Riverhead, NY 11901
631-727-3200
e-mail: info@riverheadli.com
Web site: www.riverheadli.com

Town Supervisor:
  Philip Cardinale 631-727-3200 x654
  e-mail: pjc@riverheadli.com
Town Clerk:
  Barbara Grattan 631-727-3200 x262/fax: 631-208-4034
  e-mail: grattan@riverheadli.com
Interim Financial Administrator:
  William Rothaar 631-727-3200 x270
  e-mail: rothaar@riverheadli.com
Town Attorney:
  Dawn Thomas 631-727-3200 x216
  e-mail: thomas@riverheadli.com
Town Attorney:
  David Hegermiller 631-727-4500
  e-mail: policechief@riverheadli.com

Rochester, City of
City Hall
30 Church St
Rochester, NY 14614
585-428-5990 Fax: 585-428-6059
e-mail: info@cityofrochester.gov
Web site: www.ci.rochester.ny.us

Mayor:
  Robert J Duffy 585-428-7045
Deputy Mayor:
  Patricia Malgieri 585-428-7163
  e-mail: malgierip@cityofrochester.gov
Council President:
  Lois Giess 585-428-7538
  e-mail: lois.giess@cityofrochester.gov
City Clerk:
  Daniel B Karin 585-428-7421
Corporation Counsel:
  Thomas Richards 585-428-6986
  e-mail: Richardt@cityofrochester.gov
City Treasurer:
  Charles A Benincasa 585-428-6705
Commissioner, Environmental Services:
  Paul Holahan 585-428-6855
  e-mail: Holahanp@cityofrochester.gov
Police Chief:
  David T Moore 585-428-7033
  e-mail: MooreD@cityofrochester.gov
Fire Chief:
  Floyd A Madison 585-428-7485
  e-mail: Madisonf@cityofrochester.gov
Director, Emergency Communications:
  John M Merklinger . . . . 585-528-2222 or 585-528-2200

Director, Finance:
  Vincent Carfagna 585-428-7151
  e-mail: vincent@cityofrochester.gov

Rockville Centre, Village of
1 College Place
Rockville Centre, NY 11571
516-678-9300 Fax: 516-678-9225
Web site: www.ci.rockville-centre.ny.us

Village Mayor:
  Eugene J Murray 516-678-9260
Deputy Clerk Treasurer:
  Carol Kramer 516-678-9263
Village Attorney:
  Martha Krisel 516-678-9206
Comptroller:
  Michael Schussheim 516-678-9226
Police Commissioner:
  John P McKeon 516-766-1500/fax: 516-678-9384
Superintendent, Public Works:
  Harry Weed 516-678-9293

Rome, City of
City Hall
Liberty Plaza
198 N Washington St
Rome, NY 13440
315-336-6000 Fax: 315-339-7788
Web site: www.romenewyork.com

Mayor:
  James F Brown 315-339-7676/fax: 315-339-7667
Common Council President:
  John J Mazzaferro 315-336-5275
City Clerk:
  Louise Glasso 315-339-7659
  e-mail: jreid@romecitygov.com
Corporation Counsel:
  Timothy A Benedict 315-339-7670/fax: 315-838-1166
Treasurer:
  John Nash 315-339-7678
Chief of Police:
  Gary DeMatteo 315-339-7705/fax: 315-339-7793
Public Safety Commissioner:
  James F Masucci 315-339-7697
Fire Chief:
  Roger Sabia 315-339-7784
Commissioner, Public Works:
  Frank Tallarino 315-336-6000

Rotterdam, Town of
Kirvin Gov't Center
1100 Sunrise Blvd
Rotterdam, NY 12306
518-355-7820 Fax: 518-355-7837
Web site: www.rotterdamny.org

Town Supervisor:
  Steven A Tommasone 518-355-7575
  e-mail: stommasone@rotterdamny.org

Offices and agencies generally appear in alphabetical order, except when specific order is requested by listee.

MUNICIPAL GOVERNMENT / Municipal Government

Town Clerk:
   Eunice O Esposito 518-355-7820
   e-mail: eesposito@rotterdamny.org
Town Attorney:
   Parisi, Coan & Saccocio 518-355-7575
Comptroller:
   Patrick Aragosa 518-355-0991
   e-mail: paragosa@rotterdamny.org
Police Chief:
   James Hamilton 518-355-7331
   e-mail: jhamilton@rotterdamny.org
Public Works Coordiantor:
   Michael Greisemer 518-355-9520
   e-mail: mgreisemer@rotterdamny.org

Rye, Town of
10 Pearl St
Port Chester, NY 10573
914-939-3075 Fax: 914-939-0786
e-mail: super@townofryeny.com
Web site: www.townofryeny.com

Town Supervisor:
   Robert A Morabito 914-939-3075
Town Clerk:
   Hope B Vespia 914-939-3570
Town Attorney:
   Monroe Y Mann 914-939-3075
Comptroller:
   Joseph M Granchelli 914-939-3075
Commissioner, Public Safety:
   Gene Branca 914-939-3098

Salina, Town of
201 School Rd
Liverpool, NY 13088
315-457-6661 Fax: 315-457-4317
Web site: www.salina.ny.us

Town Supervisor:
   Charles M Iavarone 315-457-6661/fax: 315-457-4476
Town Clerk:
   Jeannie Ventre 315-457-2710
   e-mail: jventre@salina.ny.us
Town Attorney:
   Coulter Ventre & McCarthy 315-475-8461
Comptroller:
   Daniel Nolan 315-451-4210

Saratoga Springs, City of
City Hall
474 Broadway
Saratoga Springs, NY 12866
518-587-3550 Fax: 518-587-1688
e-mail: email@saratoga-springs.org
Web site: www.saratoga-springs.org

Mayor:
   Valerie Keehn 518-587-3550 x520
   e-mail: valerie.keehn@saratoga-springs.org
City Clerk & Accounts Commissioner:
   John Franck 518-587-3550/fax: 518-587-6512
   e-mail: stephen.towne@saratogasprings.org

City Attorney:
   Michael Englert 518-587-3550 x516
Finance Commissioner:
   Matthew McCabe 518-587-3550/fax: 518-580-0781
   e-mail: matt.mccacbe@saratoga-springs.org
Public Safety Commissioner:
   Ron Kim 518-587-3550/fax: 518-587-1068
   e-mail: ron.kim@saratoga-springs.org
Public Works Commissioner:
   Thomas McTygue 518-587-3550/fax: 518-587-2417
   e-mail: thomas.mctygue@saratoga-springs.org
Chief of Police:
   Edward Moore 518-584-1800/fax: 518-584-1744

Saugerties, Town of
4 High Street
Saugerties, NY 12477
845-246-2800 Fax: 845-246-0355
Web site: www.saugerties.ny.us

Town Supervisor:
   Greg Helsmoortel 845-246-2800 x347
   e-mail: twood@saugerties.ny.us
Town Clerk:
   Lisa Stanley 845-246-2800 x343/fax: 845-246-0127
   e-mail: lstanley@saugerties.ny.us
Accounting Office:
   Deborah Martino 845-246-2800 x348
   e-mail: dmartino@saugerties.ny.us
Police Chief:
   Gregory M Hulbert 845-246-9800/fax: 845-246-0159
   e-mail: info@saugertiespd.com

Schenectady, City of
City Hall
105 Jay St
Schenectady, NY 12305
518-382-5000 Fax: 518-382-5272
Web site: www.cityofschenectady.com

Mayor:
   Brian U Stratton 518-382-5000
   e-mail: mayor@nycap.rr.com
City Council President:
   Mark W Blanchfield 518-382-5089
City Clerk:
   Carolyn Friello 518-382-5199 x5303
   e-mail: cityclk1@nycap.rr.com
Corporation Counsel:
   L John Van Norden 518-382-5073/fax: 518-382-5074
Finance Commissioner:
   Ismat Alam 518-382-5010
Chief of Police:
   Michael N Geraci Sr 518-382-5200
Historian:
   Don Rittner 518-788-1255

Smithtown, Town of
99 W Main St
PO Box 575
Smithtown, NY 11787
631-360-7600 Fax: 631-360-7668
Web site: www.smithtowninfo.com

Offices and agencies generally appear in alphabetical order, except when specific order is requested by listee.

MUNICIPAL GOVERNMENT / Municipal Government

Town Supervisor:
   Patrick R Vecchio..............................631-360-7600
Town Clerk:
   Vincent Puleo 631-360-7620/fax: 631-360-7692
   e-mail: vpuleo@tosgov.com
Town Attorney:
   Yvonne Lieffrig..............631-360-7570/fax: 631-360-7719
Comptroller:
   Anthony A Minerva.............631-360-7530/fax: 631-360-7625
Director, Public Safety:
   John Valentine................631-360-7553/fax: 631-360-7677

Southampton, Town of
116 Hampton Rd
Southampton, NY 11968
631-283-6000 Fax: 631-283-5606
Web site: http://town.southampton.ny.us

Town Supervisor:
   Patrick A Heaney..............631-283-6055/fax: 631-287-5708
Town Clerk:
   Sundy A Schermeyer 631-287-5740
Deputy Town Attorney:
   Kathleen Murray...............................631-287-3065
Comptroller:
   Charlene Kagel................................631-283-6094
   e-mail: ckagel@town.southampton.ny.us
Commissioner, Public Works/Highway Superintendent:
   William H Masterson Jr........................631-728-3600
Police Chief:
   James P Overton...............................631-728-5000
Town Historian:
   Ronald Michne.................................631-287-5740
   e-mail: agee@town.southampton.ny.us

Southold, Town of
53095 Route 25
PO Box 1179
Southold, NY 11971
631-765-1800 Fax: 631-765-6145
Web site: southoldtown.northfork.net

Town Supervisor & Emergency Coordinator:
   Scott A Russell..............631-765-1800 or 631-765-2600
   e-mail: STOEM@town.southold.ny.us
Town Clerk/Registrar:
   Elizabeth A Neville..........631-765-1800/fax: 631-765-6145
   e-mail: e.neville@town.southold.ny.us
Comptroller:
   John Cushman 631-765-4333
   e-mail: accounting@town.southold.ny.us
Town Attorney:
   Patricia Finnegan............631-765-1939/fax: 631-765-6639
   e-mail: patricia.finnegan@town.southold.ny.us
Police Chief:
   Carlisle Cochran..............................631-765-2600
   e-mail: chiefcochran@town.southold.ny.us
Historian:
   Antonia Booth.................................631-765-1981
   e-mail: antonia.booth@town.southold.ny.us

Spring Valley, Village of
200 North Main Street
Spring Valley, NY 10977
845-573-5867
Web site: www.villagespringvalley.org

Mayor:
   George O Darden...............................845-573-5867
Village Clerk:
   Mae N Naber 845-573-5806
Treasurer:
   Sandra Bullock................................845-573-5805
Village Attorney:
   Bruce Levine 845-573-5861
Public Works:
   John Ackerson................845-573-5800/fax: 845-573-5802
Police Chief:
   Anthony Furco ....845-573-5833 or 845-356-7400

Syracuse, City of
203 City Hall
233 East Washington St
Syracuse, NY 13202
315-448-8005 Fax: 315-448-8067
e-mail: cityhall@ci.syracuse.ny.us
Web site: www.syracuse.ny.us

Mayor:
   Matthew J Driscoll............................315-448-8005
   e-mail: mayor@ci.syracuse.ny.us
Common Council President:
   Bethaida Gonzalez............315-448-8466/fax: 315-448-8423
City Clerk:
   John P Copanas...............315-448-8216/fax: 315-448-8489
   e-mail: jcopanas@ci.syracuse.ny.us
Corporation Counsel:
   Rory A McMahon 315-448-8400/fax: 315-448-8381
   e-mail: law@ci.syracuse.ny.us
Commissioner, Assessment:
   John C Gamage................315-448-8280/fax: 315-448-8190
   e-mail: assessment@ci.syracuse.ny.us
Commissioner, Community Development:
   Fernando Ortiz Jr............315-448-8766/fax: 315-448-8618
   e-mail: cd@ci.syracuse.ny.us
Commissioner, Finance:
   Brian Roulin 315-448-8304/fax: 315-448-8424
Acting Commissioner, Public Works:
   Jeff Wright..................315-448-8515/fax: 315-448-8531
   e-mail: cityhall@ci.syracuse.ny.us
Director, Administration & Budget Management:
   Ken Mokryzcki................315-448-8005 or 315-448-8252
Director, Government & Community Affairs:
   Christine Fix.................................315-448-8005
Police Chief:
   Gary W Miguel 315-442-5250/fax: 315-442-5198
Fire Chief:
   John T Cowin 315-473-5525 x700

Tonawanda, Town of
2919 Delaware Ave
Kenmore, NY 14217
716-877-8800 Fax: 716-877-0578
Web site: www.tonawanda.ny.us

Town Supervisor:
   Ronald H Moline...............................716-877-8804

Offices and agencies generally appear in alphabetical order, except when specific order is requested by listee.

MUNICIPAL GOVERNMENT / Municipal Government

Town Clerk:
   Cal Champlin 716-877-8800
   e-mail: cchamplin@tonawanda.ny.us
Town Attorney:
   Daniel T Cavarello 716-875-9947
   e-mail: dcavarello@tonawanda.ny.us
Comptroller:
   Edward D Mongold 716-877-8810
   e-mail: emongold@tonawanda.ny.us
Police Chief:
   Anthony J Palombo 716-876-5300
Fire/Public Safety Dispatch Bureau Head:
   Dennis Carson 716-876-1212
Town Historian:
   John W Percy 716-873-5774
   e-mail: JohnWPercy@aol.com

Troy, City of
City Hall
One Monument Square
Troy, NY 12180
518-270-4401 Fax: 518-270-4609
Web site: www.troyny.gov

Mayor:
   Harry J Tutunjian 518-270-4401
   e-mail: mayorsoffice@troyny.gov
President, City Council:
   Henry Bauer . . . . 518-270-4493 or 518-273-1338
   fax: 518-270-4639
   e-mail: citycouncil@troyny.gov
City Clerk:
   Flora O'Malley 518-270-4541
   e-mail: teri.kippen@troyny.org
Corporation Counsel:
   Dave Mitchell 518-270-4606
Comptroller:
   Debbie Witkowski 518-270-4631
Chief of Police:
   Nicholas F Kaiser 518-270-4421
Fire Chief:
   Thomas O Garrett 518-270-4471

Union, Town of
3111 E Main St
Endwell, NY 13760
607-786-2900 Fax: 607-786-2998
Web site: www.townofunion.com

Town Supervisor:
   John M Bernardo 607-786-2995
   e-mail: supervisor@townofunion.com
Town Clerk:
   Gail L Springer 607-786-2915/fax: 607-786-2913
   e-mail: townclerk@townofunion.com
Town Attorney:
   Alan J Pope 607-786-2910
   e-mail: attorney@townofunion.com
Comptroller/Finance:
   Gary E Leighton 607-786-2930
Commissioner, Public Works:
   Peter Olevano 607-786-2950
   e-mail: cpw@townofunion.com
Historian:
   Suzanne Meredith 607-786-5786

Utica, City of
City Hall
One Kennedy Plz
Utica, NY 13502
315-797-5847 Fax: 315-734-9250
Web site: www.cityofutica.com

Mayor:
   Timothy J Julian 315-792-0100
   e-mail: mayor@cityofutica.com
Common Council President:
   Patrick J Donavan 315-792-0113
City Clerk:
   Joan M Brenon 315-792-0117/fax: 315-792-0220
   e-mail: clerk@cityofutica.com
Corporation Counsel:
   Linda Fatata 315-792-0171/fax: 315-792-0175
   e-mail: ulaw@cityofutica.com
Comptroller:
   Mike Cerminaro 315-792-0133
City Assessor:
   David H Williams 315-792-1025/fax: 315-792-9028
   e-mail: assessor@cityofutica.com
Commissioner, Parks:
   David Short 315-738-0172
   e-mail: dshort@cityofutica.com
Director, Community Development:
   Regina Clark 315-792-0181/fax: 315-797-6607
   e-mail: rclark@cityofutica.com
Commissioner, Public Works:
   William Schrader 315-738-1341/fax: 315-738-1346
   e-mail: bschrader@cityofutica.com
Deputy City Engineer:
   Mike Mahoney 315-792-0152/fax: 315-792-0236
   e-mail: engineering@cityofutica.com
Police Chief:
   Allen C Pylman . . . . 315-735-3301 or 315-223-3400
Fire Chief:
   Russell Brooks . . . . 315-731-2000 or 315-792-0264

Valley Stream, Village of
123 S Central Ave
Valley Stream, NY 11580
516-825-4200 Fax: 516-825-8316
Web site: www.valleystreamvillage.org;
www.valleystream-govoffice.com

Mayor:
   Edward W Cahill 516-825-4200
Village Clerk/Administrator:
   Vincent W Ang 516-825-4200
   e-mail: vsclerk@valleystream.govoffice.com
Village Attorney:
   Michael McKenna 516-825-4200
Treasurer:
   John Mastromarino 516-825-4200
Emergency Management Program Coordinator:
   Frank Roca 516-825-8245

Vestal, Town of
605 Vestal Parkway West
Vestal, NY 13850
607-748-1514 Fax: 607-786-3631
Web site: www.vestalny.com

Offices and agencies generally appear in alphabetical order, except when specific order is requested by listee.

MUNICIPAL GOVERNMENT / Municipal Government

Town Supervisor:
  Peter Andreasen 607-748-1514
  e-mail: pandreasen@vestalny.com
Town Clerk:
  Constance Lightner 607-748-1514
  e-mail: clightner@vestalny.com
Town Attorney:
  David Berger . . . . 607-748-1514 or 607-217-0782
  e-mail: dberger@vestalny.com
Comptroller:
  Laura McKane 607-748-1514
  e-mail: lmckane@vestalny.com
Police Chief:
  John Butler 607-754-2386
Fire Chief:
  Charles Paffie 607-748-1514
Historian:
  Margaret Hadsell 607-748-1514
  e-mail: mhadsell@vestalny.com

Wallkill, Town of
99 Tower Drive
Building A
Middletown, NY 10941
845-692-7800
Web site: www.townofwallkill.com

Town Supervisor:
  John Ward 845-692-7830
  e-mail: supervisor@townofwallkill.com
Town Clerk:
  Louisa Ingrassia 845-692-7826
  e-mail: townclerk@townofwallkill.com
Director, Public Works:
  John Lippert 845-361-1106
Chief of Police:
  Robert Hertman 845-692-6757/fax: 845-692-4166
  e-mail: chiefofpolice@townofwallkill.com

Wappinger, Town of
20 Middlebush Road
Wappinger Falls, NY 12590
845-297-5771 Fax: 845-298-1478
Web site: www.townofwappinger.us

Town Supervisor:
  Joseph Ruggiero 845-297-2744
Town Clerk:
  Chris Masterson 845-297-5771/fax: 845-298-1478
  e-mail: cmasterson@townofwappinger.us
Receiver of Taxes:
  Patricia Maupin 845-297-4342
Fire Inspector:
  Mark Liebermann 845-297-1373/fax: 845-297-0579
  e-mail: mliebermann@townofwappinger.us
Comptroller:
  Jean Gallucci 845-297-0060
Historian:
  Janice Hilderbrand 845-297-8773

Warwick, Town of
132 Kings Highway
Warwick, NY 10990
845-986-1124
e-mail: townhall@townofwarwick.org
Web site: www.townofwarwick.org

Town Supervisor:
  Michael Sweeton 845-986-1120 x240
Deputy Supervisor:
  James Gerstner 845-986-1120 x353
Town Clerk:
  Marjorie Quackenbush 845-986-1124 x246
Public Works Commissioner:
  Jeffrey Feagles 845-986-3358 x21
Police Chief:
  Thomas McGovern Jr 845-986-3423 x221

Watertown, City of
245 Washington St, Rm 302
Watertown, NY 13601
315-785-7730 Fax: 315-785-7796
Web site: www.citywatertown.org

Mayor:
  Jeffrey E Graham 315-785-7720
  e-mail: jgraham@watertown-ny.gov
City Manager:
  Mary M Corriveau 315-785-7730
City Clerk:
  Donna M Dutton 315-785-7780
  e-mail: ddutton@watertown-ny.com
City Attorney:
  Robert J Slye 315-786-0266/fax: 315-786-3488
Comptroller:
  James Mills 315-785-7754
  e-mail: jmills@watertown-ny.gov
Police Chief:
  Joseph J Goss 315-782-2233
Fire Chief:
  Dan Gaumont 315-785-7800
  e-mail: dgaumont@watertown-ny.gov

Webster, Town of
1000 Ridge Rd
Webster, NY 14580
585-872-1000 Fax: 585-872-1352
Web site: www.ci.webster.ny.us

Supervisor:
  Ronald Nesbitt 585-872-7068
  e-mail: supervisor@ci.webster.ny.us
Town Clerk:
  Barbara Ottenschot 585-872-7064
  e-mail: townclerk@ci.webster.ny.us
Town Attorney:
  Charles Genese 585-670-9583
Director, Finance:
  Kathy Tanea 585-872-7067
  e-mail: finance@ci.webster.ny.us
Public Works:
  Gary Kleist 585-872-7027
Police:
  Gerald Pickering 585-872-1216
  e-mail: chief@websterpolice.org
Historian:
  Lynn Barton 585-265-3308

Offices and agencies generally appear in alphabetical order, except when specific order is requested by listee.

West Seneca, Town of
1250 Union Rd
West Seneca, NY 14224
716-674-5600 Fax: 716-677-4330
Web site: www.westseneca.net

Town Supervisor:
  Paul T Clark 716-558-3202
  e-mail: pclark@twsny.org
Town Clerk:
  Patricia C DePasquale 716-558-3215
  e-mail: pdepasqu@twsny.org
Town Attorney:
  Timothy J Greenan 716-558-3240
Comptroller:
  Charles Koller 716-558-3205
Police Chief:
  Edward F Gehen 716-674-2280
  e-mail: denz@wspolice.com

White Plains, City of
City Hall
255 Main St
White Plains, NY 10601
914-422-1200 Fax: 914-422-1395
e-mail: webpo@white-plains.ny.us
Web site: www.cityofwhiteplains.com

Mayor:
  Joseph M Delfino 914-422-1411
  e-mail: jdelfino@ci.white-plains.ny.us
City Clerk:
  Anne McPherson 914-422-1227
Common Council President:
  Rita Z Malmud 914-946-0642
  e-mail: rmalmud@ci.white-plains.ny.us
Corporation Counsel:
  Edward Dunphy 914-422-1241/fax: 914-422-1231
Commissioner, Finance:
  Gina Cuneo-Harwood 914-422-1235
Commissioner, Public Works:
  Joseph Nicoletti Jr 914-422-1206
Commissioner, Public Safety:
  Frank G Straub 914-422-6400/fax: 914-422-6373
Chief of Police:
  James Bradley . . . . 914-422-6111 or 914-422-6230

Yonkers, City of
City Hall
40 S Broadway
Yonkers, NY 10701-3700
914-377-6000 Fax: 914-377-6048
Web site: www.cityofyonkers.com

Mayor:
  Philip A Amicone 914-377-6300
Chief of Staff:
  Lisa Mrijaj 914-377-6300
President, City Council:
  Chuck Lesnick 914-377-6060
City Clerk:
  Joan C Deierlen 914-377-6020
  e-mail: joan.deierlen@cityofyonkers.com
Corporation Counsel:
  Frank J Rubino 914-377-6240/fax: 914-964-0563
City Assessor:
  Mark Russell 914-377-6200
Commissioner, Affordable Housing:
  Vacant 914-377-6693
Commissioner, Finance & Mgmt Services:
  James LaPerche 914-377-6100
Commissioner, Parks, Recreation & Conservation:
  Mitch Tutoni 914-377-6425
Commissioner, Public Works:
  John Liszewski 914-377-6270
Commissioner, Planning & Development:
  Vacant 914-377-6650
Director, Public Affairs & Community Relations:
  Richard Halevy 914-377-6053
Assistant Director Economic Development:
  Helen Tvedt 914-377-6797/fax: 914-377-6003
Emergency Management Director:
  John Donaghy 914-377-7325/fax: 914-965-8430
Police Commissioner:
  Edmund Hartnett 914-377-7200
Fire Commissioner:
  Anthony Pagano 914-377-7500

Yorktown, Town of
363 Underhill Avenue
Yorktown Heights, NY 10598
914-962-5722 Fax: 914-962-1731
Web site: www.yorktownny.org

Town Supervisor:
  Linda Cooper 914-962-5722 x271/fax: 914-962-1004
Town Clerk:
  Alice Roker 914-962-5722 x209/fax: 914-962-6591
Comptroller:
  Joan Cavorti Goldberg 914-962-5722 x205/fax: 914-962-1004
Town Attorney:
  Kevin Sweeney 914-962-5722 x241/fax: 914-962-3473
Chief of Police:
  Daniel McMahon 914-962-4141/fax: 914-962-4458
  e-mail: info@yorktownpd.org

Offices and agencies generally appear in alphabetical order, except when specific order is requested by listee.

NEW YORK POLITICAL PARTIES

New York State Conservative Party

New York State Conservative Party
486 78th St
Ft Hamilton Station, NY 11209
718-921-2158 Fax: 718-921-5268
e-mail: info@cpnys.org
Web site: www.cpnys.org

Capital District Office
325 Parkview Dr
Schenectady, NY 12303
518-356-7882
Fax: 518-356-3773

Statewide Party Officials

State Chairman:
  Michael R Long 718-921-2158/fax: 718-921-5268
  486 78th St, Brooklyn, NY 11209
Executive Committee Member:
  Carol Birkholz 518-623-9151
  1 Pucker St, Warrensburg, NY 12885
State Exec Vice Chairman:
  James P Molinaro 718-442-3676
  85 Lyman Ave, Staten Island, NY 10305
State Vice Chairman:
  Pasquale J Curcio 631-789-2788
  10 Hampden Rd, Copiague, NY 11726
State Executive Director:
  Shaun Marie Levine 518-356-7882/fax: 518-356-3773
  325 Parkview Dr, Schenectady, NY 12303
Regional Vice Chairman:
  Daniel F Fitzgerald 315-853-8816
  118 Sanford Ave, Clinton, NY 13323
Secretary:
  Howard Lim, Jr. 914-939-7180
  83 Valley Terrance, Rye Brook, NY 10573
Treasurer:
  James M Gay 718-921-2158/fax: 718-921-5268
  486 78th St, Brooklyn, NY 11209
Law Chairman:
  Thomas A Bolan 212-682-8184
  521 5th Avenue, New York, NY 10175
National Affairs Chair:
  Allen Roth 516-776-2784
  43 Lehigh Court, Rockville Centre, NY 11570
Deputy Counsel:
  Michael V Ajello 718-258-9804
  1970 Flatbush Ave, Brooklyn, NY 11234

County Chairs

Albany
Richard Stack 518-463-8679
53 Nicholas Dr, Colonie, NY 12205

Allegany
Glen Hall 585-593-5259
472 Alma Hill Rd, Wellsville, NY 14895

Bronx
William Newmark 718-822-0504
3252 Philip Ave, Bronx, NY 10465

Broome
James M Thomas 607-648-5308
25 Woodland Rd, Binghamton, NY 13901

Cattaraugus
Warren G Schmidt 716-492-3812
1244 Eagle St, Arcade, NY 14009

Cayuga
Gregory S Rigby 315-253-0736
124 Owasco St, Auburn, NY 13021

Chautauqua
Jan R Potter 716-664-9550
22 W 18th St, Jamestown, NY 14701

Chemung
Louis F DeCiccio 607-796-5129
4905 Hillview Rd, Millport, NY 14864

Clinton
Robert Church 518-846-8944
22 Ladd Dr, Chazy, NY 12921

Columbia
Matthew G Torrey 518-392-9610
91 Nelson Avenue, Ghent, NY 12075

Cortland
Kurt Van Hamlin 607-756-6870
227 Port Watson St, Cortland, NY 13045

Delaware
John Bjorkander 845-676-4604
Wolf Hollow Rd, PO Box 180, Andes, NY 13731

Dutchess
Patricia K Killian 845-454-2697
20 Hillview Dr, Poughkeepsie, NY 12603

Erie
Ralph C Lorigo 716-824-7200
101 Slade Avenue, West Seneca, NY 14224

Essex
Tom Sullivan 518-946-8336
3 Orchard Lane, Jay, NY 12941

Fulton
Wayne Brooks 518-725-1270
95 E Fulton St, Gloversville, NY 12078-3217

Genesee
Arthur Munger 716-762-9323
2753 Pearl St Rd, Batavia, NY 14020

Greene
Nicholas J Passero 518-622-9407
Carylday Lane, PO Box 187, Round Top, NY 12473

Offices and agencies generally appear in alphabetical order, except when specific order is requested by listee.

NEW YORK POLITICAL PARTIES

Herkimer
Daniel Pollak 315-866-0936
RD#1, Box 71, Folts Road, Herkimer, NY 13350

Jefferson
Raymond C Carpenter 315-767-2204
933 Leray St, Watertown, NY 13601

Kings
Gerard Kassar 718-748-9010
7521 10th Ave, Brooklyn, NY 11228

Lewis
James H Koch 315-668-4131
RR #1, Box 88, Copaigue, NY 13626

Livingston
Doug Straight 585-226-2517
151 Genessee St, Avon, NY 14414

Madison
John Mulhall 315-655-4859
Evergreen Lane, Cazinovia, NY 13035

Monroe
Thomas D Cook 585-381-6850
7 State St, Pittsford, NY 14534

Montgomery
Robert Mead 518-842-4345
1 Northhampton Road, Amsterdam, NY 12010

Nassau
Roger Bogsted 516-796-3155
105 Bobolink Lane, Levittown, NY 11756

New York
Stuart Avrick 212-912-0022
375 S End Ave, Apt 9E, New York, NY 10280

Niagara
Karl Hoefer 716-434-3765
4299 Purdy Rd, Lockport, NY 14094

Oneida
Julie Miller 315-735-7367
466 Tryon Rd, Utica, NY 13502

Onondaga
Austin W Olmsted 315-696-8417
6519 Route 80, Apulia Station, NY 13020

Ontario
Tom Whipple 585-394-3308
4595 County Rd, Canandaigua, NY 14424

Orange
John P DeLessio 845-562-4963
7 Hill Street, Newburgh, NY 12550

Orleans
Karen L McAllister 585-638-2468
16111 Lynch Rd, Holley, NY 14470

Oswego
H Leonard Schick 315-593-0770
17 E Edgewater Dr, Fulton, NY 13069

Otsego
Stan Konopka 607-287-1045
45 Pioneer St, PO Box 566, Cooperstown, NY 13326

Putnam
James Maxwell 845-628-7716
117 Vista Terrace, Mahopac, NY 10541

Queens
Thomas M Long 718-474-3826
6 Beach 219th St, Rockaway Point, NY 11697

Richmond
Carmine F Ragucci 718-818-8888
32 Hylan Boulevard, Staten Island, NY 10304

Rockland
Mary G Loeffler 845-634-6715
15 Oak Rd, New City, NY 10956

Saratoga
Robert D Roe 518-581-1941
PO Box 1326, Saratoga Springs, NY 12866

Schenectady
Randy F Pascarella . . . .
610 Becker Crossing, Schenectady, NY 12306

Schoharie
William Hanson 518-827-5951
PO Box 151, Middleburgh, NY 12122

Schuyler
Linda D Moore 607-535-7591
2485 Irelandville Rd, Watkins Glen, NY 14891

Seneca
William R White 315-539-2534
19 Brookside Dr, Waterloo, NY 13165

St Lawrence
Henry Ford 315-262-2824
Stowe Bay Rd, Colton, NY 13625

Steuben
Donald E Gwinner 607-329-6765
5582 Sanford Rd, Savona, NY 14879

Suffolk
Edward M Walsh, Jr . . . .
211 Apex Lane, East Islip, NY 11730-3304

Sullivan
Robert W Hoose 845-794-2500
10 Myrtle Ave, Monticello, NY 12701

Tompkins
Thomas Straight 607-838-3426
45 McLean Rd, Cortland, NY 13045

Ulster
Debra L Hewitt 845-339-3074
PO Box 668, Adorn Lane, Port Ewen, NY 12466

Warren
Carol Birkholz 518-623-9151
1 Pucker St, Warrensburg, NY 12885

Washington
Louis Imhof 518-692-7251
217 Kenyon Rd, Greenwich, NY 12834

Wayne
James F Quinn, Jr 315-483-2240
8239 Lake St, Sodus Point, NY 14555

Westchester
Gail M Burns 914-965-7273/fax: 914-751-2356
510 Midland Avenue, Yonkers, NY 10704

Wyoming
Wayne O Chapple 585-495-6938
838 N Academy Street, Wyoming, NY 14591-9502

Offices and agencies generally appear in alphabetical order, except when specific order is requested by listee.

NEW YORK POLITICAL PARTIES

Yates
Vacant

New York State Democratic Party

New York State Democratic Committee

60 Madison Ave
New York, NY 10010
212-725-8825 Fax: 212-725-8867
e-mail: nydems@nydems.org
Web site: www.nydems.org

Statewide Party Officials

State Chair:
  June O'Neill.....................212-725-8825/fax: 212-725-8867
  60 Madison Ave, Ste 1201, New York, NY 10010
Executive Director:
  Edna Ishayik..................212-725-8825 x235/fax: 212-725-8867
  60 Madison Ave, Ste 1201, New York, NY 10010
Young Democrats:
  Evan Lederman...................212-725-8825/fax: 212-725-8867
  60 Madison Avenue, Ste 1201, New York, NY 10010
Executive Committee Chair:
  Denise King................518-392-1560 x2139/fax: 518-392-3978
  12 Mill Street, Chatham, NY 12037
First Vice Chair:
  Inez E Dickens....................212-749-2580/fax: 212-283-1151
  2153 Adam Clayton Powell Jr Blvd, New York, NY 10027
Vice Chair:
  Betty Barnette......................................518-438-5150
  3 Oxford Rd, Albany, NY 12203
Secretary:
  Peter Stein........................807-255-4843/fax: 807-255-9412
  315 Day Hall, Ithaca, NY 14850
Treasurer:
  David A Alpert....................914-946-8300/fax: 914-946-8090
  170 East Post Rd, White Plains, NY 10601
Sergeant-at-Arms:
  Michael Reich.....................718-631-0694/fax: 718-729-0871
  46-12 Queens Blvd, Ste 205, Sunnyside, NY 11104
Counsel & Law Chair:
  Gerard Harper.....................212-373-3263/fax: 212-379-2769
  1285 Ave of the Americas, New York, NY 10019
Policy Cmte Co-Chair:
  Mike Schell...315-782-0004
  316 Sherman St, Watertown, NY 13601
Policy Cmte Co-Chair:
  Harriet Cornell.....................................315-782-0004
  316 Sherman St, Watertown, NY 13601
Labor Task Force Representative:
  Suzy Ballantyne...................518-436-8516/fax: 518-463-6901
  100 S Swan St, Albany, NY 12210

County Chairs

Albany
  Frank Commisso David Bosworth.....518-438-8282/fax: 518-438-8375
  22 Colvin Avenue, Albany, NY 12206

Allegany
  Lisa Feinberg-Duckett................................585-593-3112
  429 N Main St, Wellsville, NY 14895

Bronx
  Jose Rivera.......................718-931-5200/fax: 718-792-3882
  135 Westchester Sq, Bronx, NY 10461

Broome
  Michael A Najarian................607-773-8369/fax: 607-772-0183
  39 Washington St, Binghamton, NY 13901

Cattaraugus
  Daniel W McCandless................................716-676-5716
  8003 Rogers Rd, Franklinville, NY 14737

Cayuga
  Laurie A Michelman.................................315-252-1774
  PO Box 547, Auburn, NY 13021

Chautauqua
  Keith Ahlstrom.....................................716-366-7030
  25 Cedar St, Dunkirk, NY 14048

Chemung
  Cynthia Emmer....................607-733-2844/fax: 607-734-6330
  858 Davis St, Elmira, NY 14901

Chenango
  Cathy Ulfik..607-843-7202
  PO Box 627, Oxford, NY 13830

Clinton
  Doug Brockway.....................................518-563-3603
  2 Sunnyside Rd, Plattsburgh, NY 12901

Columbia
  Ken Dow..518-828-6778
  PO Box 25, Mellenville, NY 12544

Cortland
  Bill Wood..607-756-6537
  26 Madison St, Cortland, NY 13045

Delaware
  William Buccheri...................................607-326-7935
  PO Box 254, Roxbury, NY 12474

Dutchess
  Joseph Ruggiero...................845-485-1934/fax: 845-485-3398
  2 LaGrange Ave, Ste 201, Poughkeepsie, NY 12603

Erie
  Leonard R Lenihan.................716-853-2511/fax: 716-853-2448
  Ellicott Square Bldg, Ste 115, Buffalo, NY 14203

Essex
  Rita Fitzgerald...................518-963-7479/fax: 518-963-7099
  PO Box 737, Elizabethtown, NY 12932

Franklin
  Joseph Pickreign..................518-891-1174/fax: 518-891-1174
  Rt 86 RFD 1, Box 322A, Saranac Lake, NY 12983

Fulton
  Albert Hays, Sr...................518-762-7598/fax: 518-762-7598
  2470 State Highway 29, Johnstown, NY 12095

Offices and agencies generally appear in alphabetical order, except when specific order is requested by listee.

NEW YORK POLITICAL PARTIES

Genesee
Raymond E Yacuzzo 716-768-8377/fax: 716-768-8377
4 East Ave, LeRoy, NY 14482

Greene
Tom Poelker . . . .
PO Box 220, Old Rd, Windham, NY 12496

Hamilton
Linda M Mitchell 518-648-5327
Tower Hill Rd, PO Box 163, Indian Lake, NY 12842

Herkimer
Toni Scalise 315-866-9663
PO Box 216, Mohawk, NY 13407

Jefferson
Sean Hennessey 315-775-0570
PO Box 603, Black River, NY 13612

Kings
Vito J Lopez 718-875-5870/fax: 718-596-4013
16 Court St, Rm 9, Brooklyn, NY 11241

Lewis
Ed Murphy 315-376-3051
5510 Jackson St, Lowville, NY 13367

Livingston
Phil Jones 585-243-5191
19 Elm St, Geneseo, NY 14454

Madison
Mary Anne Simberg 315-363-9722
433 Florence Ave, Oneida, NY 13421

Monroe
Joseph D Morelle 585-232-2410
1150 University Ave, Bldg 5, Rochester, NY 14607

Montgomery
Bethany Schumann 518-842-6084
286 Guy Park Avenue, Amsterdam, NY 12010

Nassau
Jay Jacobs 516-294-3366/fax: 516-873-0810
1 Old County Rd, Ste 430, Carle Place, NY 11514

New York
Herman D Farrell, Jr 212-725-8825/fax: 212-725-8867
60 Madison Ave, Ste 1201, New York, NY 10010

Niagara
Cindy Lenhart 716-692-0134
PO Box 26, Niagara Falls, NY 14304

Oneida
Bill Morris 315-732-4171/fax: 315-732-4190
PO Box 505, New Hartford, NY 13413

Onondaga
Diane M Dwire 315-422-0345/fax: 315-422-3503
248 East Water St, Syracuse, NY 13202

Ontario
Charles Evangelista 585-394-7500
60 North Main St, Geneva, NY 14456

Orange
Jonathan G Jacobson 845-567-6778/fax: 845-567-7721
843 Union Ave, 2nd Floor, New Windsor, NY 12553

Orleans
Sally Rytlewski 585-589-4534
432 E State St, Albion, NY 14411

Oswego
William W Scriber 315-342-8261
147 West 5th St, Oswego, NY 13126

Otsego
Henry J Nicols 607-547-4675/fax: 607-547-4616
2515 State Highway 28, Oneonta, NY 13820

Putnam
Ken Harper 845-628-0432
36 Astor Dr, Mahopac, NY 10541

Queens
Joseph Crowley 718-268-5100/fax: 718-268-7363
72-50 Austin St, Forest Hills, NY 11375

Rensselaer
Thomas W Wade 518-273-2797
PO Box 846, Troy, NY 12181

Richmond
John W Lavelle 718-983-5009/fax: 718-983-5541
274 Watchogue Rd, Staten Island, NY 10314

Rockland
Vincent Monte 845-634-1981/fax: 845-624-6228
PO Box 266, New City, NY 10956

Saratoga
Larry Bulman 518-792-9157/fax: 518-792-4876
13 Moreau Dr, South Glens Falls, NY 12803

Schenectady
Bob Brehm 518-785-9845
831 Maxwell Dr, Niskayuna, NY 12309

Schoharie
Cliff Hay 518-234-7165
RR3 Box 261, Cobleskill, NY 12043

Schuyler
Ruth Young 607-535-9566
1580 Sugar Hill Rd, Watkins Glen, NY 14891

Seneca
Theodore H Young 315-539-9614/fax: 315-539-9614
PO Box 555, Waterloo, NY 13165

St Lawrence
June O'Neill 315-386-3882
2262 County Rte 14, Canton, NY 13617

Steuben
Shawn Hogan 607-324-3150/fax: 607-324-3150
12 Mays Ave, Hornell, NY 14843

Suffolk
Richard H Schaffer 631-439-0400/fax: 631-439-0404
4250 Veterans Mem Hwy, Ste 155, Holbrook, NY 11741

Sullivan
Christopher Cunningham 845-794-3000/fax: 845-794-3459
100 North St, PO Box 5012, Monticello, NY 12701

Tioga
Gloria L Whitmore 607-687-1476
3058 Valley Rd, Owego, NY 13827

Tompkins
Irene W Stein 607-272-5309
371 Elmira Rd, PO Box 6798, Ithaca, NY 14851

Ulster
John R Parette 845-331-8275

Offices and agencies generally appear in alphabetical order, except when specific order is requested by listee.

NEW YORK POLITICAL PARTIES

Warren
Bill Montfort. 518-251-3138
1664 South Johnsburg Rd, Johnsburg, NY 12843

Washington
Sheila Comar 518-642-9566
29 Depot St, Middle Granville, NY 12849

Wayne
Gaye Chapman. 315-589-9649
5357 Contant Lane, North Rose, NY 14516

Westchester
Reginald A LaFayette 914-946-8300/fax: 914-946-8090
170 East Post Rd, Ste 210, White Plains, NY 10601

Wyoming
Anne R Weidman. 585-786-2782
PO Box 39, Wyoming, NY 14591

Yates
Carolyn Schaffer. 315-536-0007
2997 Merritt Hill Rd, Penn Yan, NY 14527

New York State Independence Party

New York State Independence Party
PO Box 871
Lindenhurst, NY 11757
Web site: www.ipny.org

Statewide Party Officials
Chairman:
Frank MacKay 631-821-5187
PO Box 871, Lindenhurst, NY 11757
Secretary:
Bill Bogardt
Treasurer:
Maclain Nichols
Vice Chair:
Rafael Colon. 585-594-8219
2 Loring Pl, Rochester, NY 14624
Vice Chair:
Thomas S Connolly
Vice Chair:
Paul Caputo
Vice Chair:
John Dotte
Vice Chair:
Anthony Orsini

County Chairs
Chautauqua
Maclain Nichols

Manhattan
Cathy L Stewart. 212-962-1699/fax: 212-803-1899
225 Broadway, Ste 2010, New York, NY 10007

Monroe
Rafael Colon
2 Loring Place, Rochester, NY 14624

Putnam
William G Sayegh

Richmond
Sarah Lyons 718-447-9689
36 Hamilton Ave, 3N, Staten Island, NY 10305

Suffolk
Frank MacKay 631-821-5187
PO Box 871, Lindenhurst, NY 11757

Offices and agencies generally appear in alphabetical order, except when specific order is requested by listee.

NEW YORK POLITICAL PARTIES

New York State Republican Party

New York State Republican Party
315 State St
Albany, NY 12210
518-462-2601 Fax: 518-449-7443
e-mail: info@nygop.org
Web site: www.nygop.org

Statewide Party Officials
Chairman:
Stephen Minarik 518-462-2601
315 State St, Albany, NY 12210
Executive Director:
Ryan Moses 518-462-2601/fax: 518-449-7443
315 State St, Albany, NY 12210
Secretary:
Elizabeth Brilliant 315-866-2056
402 Prospect St, Herkimer, NY 13350
Treasurer:
Michael Avella 518-462-2601
315 State St, Albany, NY 12210
Counsel:
Jeffrey T Buley 518-462-2601/fax: 518-449-7443
315 State St, Albany, NY 12210
National Committeeman:
Sandy Treadwell 516-334-5800/fax: 516-334-4406
164 Post Ave, Westbury, NY 11590
National Committeewoman:
Jennifer Saul Yaffa 516-334-5800/fax: 516-334-4406
164 Post Ave, Westbury, NY 11590

County Officials

Albany
Peter Kermani 518-626-0720/fax: 518-626-0300
915 Broadway, 1st Fl Box 9, Albany, NY 12207

Allegany
John W Hasper 585-365-2520
PO Box 425, Belfast, NY 14711

Bronx
Jay Savino 718-792-5800/fax: 718-863-2301
2113 Williamsbridge Rd, Bronx, NY 10461-1606

Broome
Anthony J Capozzi 607-723-8201/fax: 607-723-3036
59-61 Court St, 7th Floor, Ste 707, Binghamton, NY 13901

Cattaraugus
Jerry Burrell 716-676-2925/fax: 716-676-3541
4 S Main Street, 2361 Lyndon Rd, Franklinville, NY 14737

Cayuga
Cherl Heary 315-255-1103/fax: 315-364-5164
1171 Ledyard Rd, PO Box 420, King Ferry, NY 13081

Chautauqua
John H Walker, II 716-410-2827
PO Box 252, Fredonia, NY 14063

Chemung
John H Meier 607-732-1245/fax: 607-739-4583
9 Longmeadow Dr, Elmira, NY 14905

Chenango
Thomas L Morrone 607-334-3234/fax: 607-334-4625
213 Randall Ave, Norwich, NY 13815-1613

Clinton
William Favreau 518-562-0600/fax: 518-562-0657
206 West Bay Plaza, Plattsburgh, NY 12901

Columbia
Angelo Valentino 518-329-1636/fax: 518-329-1636
56 Chrysler Pond Rd, Copake, NY 12516

Cortland
Robert Howe 607-756-6188/fax: 607-758-9007
2188 East River Rd, Cortland, NY 13045

Delaware
Martin Donnelly 845-676-4647/fax: 845-676-4796
PO Box 525, Andes, NY 13731

Dutchess
Corinne Weber 845-464-7058/fax: 845-897-4792
158 Yantz Rd, Red Hook, NY 12571

Erie
James Domagalski 716-856-8700/fax: 716-856-8703
107 Delaware Ave, Ste 17, Buffalo, NY 14202

Essex
Ronald Jackson 518-963-7104
PO Box 123, Essex, NY 12936

Franklin
James Ellis 518-359-2580/fax: 518-359-2289
58 Broad St, Tupper Lake, NY 12986

Fulton
Dexter Risedorph 518-725-8882/fax: 518-725-8838
PO Box 488, Gloversville, NY 12078

Genesee
Richard Siebert 585-343-5925/fax: 585-344-8521
8585 Seven Springs Rd, Batavia, NY 14020

Greene
Brent Bogardus 518-369-6098
7 Molly White Drive, Coxsackie, NY 12051

Hamilton
William Farber 315-826-7744/fax: 315-826-3215
Mountain Home Rd, Hoffmeister, NY 13353

Herkimer
Marty Smith 315-866-2056/fax: 315-866-2056
15 S Park Place, Herkimer, NY 13350

Jefferson
Sandra Corey 315-788-4120/fax: 315-786-1387
161 Clinton St, Ste 204, Watertown, NY 13601

Kings
Hy Singer 718-582-9454/fax: 718-858-5144
26 Court St, Ste 2305, Brooklyn, NY 11242

Lewis
Sam Villanti 315-348-8984/fax: 315-348-8984
PO Box 332, Brantingham, NY 13312

Offices and agencies generally appear in alphabetical order, except when specific order is requested by listee.

NEW YORK POLITICAL PARTIES

Livingston
Lowell Conrad 716-243-2665/fax: 716-243-2711
123 Main St, PO Box 123, Geneseo, NY 14454-1113

Madison
Michael St Leger 315-655-4522/fax: 315-363-4195
5880 Fieldstone Dr, Cazenovia, NY 13035-9625

Monroe
Stephen Minarik, III 585-546-8040/fax: 585-546-8519
301 Exchange Blvd, Rochester, NY 14608

Montgomery
Lore Koppel 518-993-3233/fax: 518-993-4216
PO Box 390, Fort Plain, NY 13339

Nassau
Joseph Mondello 516-334-5800/fax: 516-333-4406
164 Post Ave, Westbury, NY 11590-3170

New York
Jennifer Saul Yaffa 212-517-8444/fax: 212-517-3142
122 East 83rd Street, New York, NY 10028

Niagara
Henry Wojtaszek 716-946-5576
150 Payne Ave, North Tonowanda, NY 14120

Oneida
Mark Scheidleman 315-724-5714/fax: 315-732-7427
PO Box 6, Clinton, NY 13323

Onondaga
John DeSpurito, III 315-471-2020/fax: 315-471-2033
375 West Onondaga St, Syracuse, NY 13202-3207

Ontario
Jay Dutcher 585-415-9803/fax: 585-394-8830
4946 Wyffels Rd, Canandaigua, NY 14424

Orange
William L DeProspo 845-294-6467/fax: 845-294-7928
75 Main St, Goshen, NY 10924

Orleans
Edward Morgan 585-638-5352/fax: 585-638-6214
3132 Hurlburton Rd, Holley, NY 14470

Oswego
George Williams 315-342-0840/fax: 315-342-2143
102 W Utica St, Downstairs, Oswego, NY 13126

Otsego
Charlotte Koniuto 607-286-7522/fax: 607-286-7522
3650 State Hwy 28, Milford, NY 13807

Putnam
Anthony Scannapieco 914-225-2002/fax: 914-225-2002
PO Box 203, Carmel, NY 10512-0203

Queens
Philip Ragusa 718-746-1741/fax: 718-746-6356
150-12 14th Ave, Whitestone, NY 11357

Rensselear
Jack Casey 518-272-2111/fax: 518-272-7522
PO Box 686, Troy, NY 12181

Richmond
John Scott Friscia 718-442-9000
58 471 Bemet Avenue, Staten Island, NY 10310

Rockland
Vincent Reda 845-634-7100/fax: 845-634-2423
172 S Main St, PO Box 201, New City, NY 10956

Saratoga
John Nolan 518-584-7900/fax: 518-581-0748
77 Van Dam St, Saratoga Springs, NY 12866

Schenectady
Thomas Buchanan 518-783-3843/fax: 518-783-8101
1343 Lilac St EE, Rotterdam, NY 12306

Schoharie
Lewis Wilson 518-234-2534/fax: 518-234-3422
826 E Main St, Cobleskill, NY 12043-0039

Schuyler
Philip Barnes 607-535-4600
203 Lakeview Avenue, Watkins Glen, NY 14891

Seneca
Angelo Bianchi 315-539-9301/fax: 315-539-9725
PO Box 504, Waterloo, NY 13165

St Lawrence
Janet Kelly 315-393-1197/fax: 315-393-3447
PO Box 147, Ogdensburg, NY 13669

Steuben
William O Hatch 607-698-2100/fax: 607-698-2355
6550 Hughes Rd, PO Box 98, Canisteo, NY 14823

Suffolk
Harry Withers 631-580-1482/fax: 631-580-1490
3340 Veterans Memorial Hwy, Bohemia, NY 11716

Sullivan
John LiGreci 845-856-4777/fax: 845-856-7118
PO Box 363, Glen Spey, NY 12737

Tioga
Don Leonard 607-589-4501/fax: 607-723-3246
PO Box 361, Spencer, NY 14883

Tompkins
Elizabeth Cree 607-257-4068/fax: 607-697-0059
9 Fairwinds Way, Ithaca, NY 14850

Ulster
Peter Savago 845-338-6245/fax: 845-255-4792
307 Wall St, PO Box 3413, Kingston, NY 12402

Warren
Michael Grasso 518-656-9093/fax: 518-783-8754
22 Rapaport Drive, Lake George, NY 12845

Washington
Michael Bittel 518-692-7612/fax: 518-692-9273
10544 State Rt 149, Fort Ann, NY 12827

Wayne
Daniel Olson 315-946-4937/fax: 315-946-4937
12 William St, PO Box 200, Lyons, NY 14489

Westchester
RoseMarie Panio 914-949-3020/fax: 914-949-2275
214 Mamaroneck Ave, White Plains, NY 10601

Wyoming
Gordon Brown 716-675-8620/fax: 716-675-1619
PO Box 191, Warsaw, NY 14569

Yates
Jack Clancy 315-536-6265/fax: 315-536-6265
PO Box 127, Penn Yan, NY 14527

Offices and agencies generally appear in alphabetical order, except when specific order is requested by listee.

LOBBYISTS

Each entry includes the name of the registered principal lobbyist, then lists names of additional lobbyists as well as all clients.

1199/SEIU & GNYHA Healthcare Education Project
330 W 42nd St, Rm 739
New York, NY 10036
212-603-1741 Fax: 212-603-1764
e-mail: debra@healtheducation.org
Web site: www.healtheducationproject.org

Clients:
1199/SEIU & GNYHA Healthcare Education Project

Lobbyists:
Debra Pucci

1199 SEIU United Healthcare Workers East (FKA 1199/SEIU New York's Health & Human Service Union)
330 W 42nd St, 7th Fl
New York, NY 10036
212-582-1890 Fax: 212-956-5140
Web site: www.1199seiuonline.org

Clients:
1199/SEIU New York's Health & Human Service Union

Lobbyists:
Dick Farfaglia
Patrick Gaspard
Dennis Rivera

92nd Street Y Young Men's and Young Women's Hebrew Association
1395 Lexington Ave
New York, NY 10128
212-415-5470

Clients:
92nd Street Y

Lobbyists:
Sol Adler

AAA Western and Central NY
100 International Dr
Amherst, NY 14221
716-626-3225 Fax: 716-631-5925
e-mail: wsmith@nyaaa.com

Clients:
AAA Western and Central NY

Lobbyists:
Wallace D Smith

AIA New York State, Inc
33 Elk Street
Ste 203
Albany, NY 12207
518-449-3334

Clients:
AIA New York State, Inc (FKA Rodriguez, Barbara J)

Lobbyists:
Edward C Farrell

AIDS Coalition (NY)
231 West 29th St, Ste 1002
New York, NY 10001
212-629-3075 Fax: 212-629-8403
e-mail: ckazanas@nyaidsc.org
Web site: www.nyaidscoalition.org

Clients:
AIDS Coalition (NY)

Lobbyists:
Kacie Winsor
Marie St Cyr

AMDeC Foundation
10 Rockefeller Plaza, Ste 1120
New York, NY 10020
212-218-5640 Fax: 212-218-5644
e-mail: info@amdec.org
Web site: www.amdec.org

Clients:
AMDeC Foundation

Lobbyists:
Maria K Mitchell
Robin C Gelburd

ANHD Inc
50 Broad St, Ste 1125
New York, NY 10004
212-747-1117

Clients:
ANHD Inc

Lobbyists:
Benjamin Dulchin
David Schuffler Jr

Offices and agencies generally appear in alphabetical order, except when specific order is requested by listee.

LOBBYISTS

Accenture LLP
800 Coonecticut Ave NW
Ste 600
Washington, DC 20006
202-553-1113

Clients:
Accenture LLP

Lobbyists:
Steve Hurst
Bill Killmartin
David Moskovitz
Rick Webb
Barry J Webster
Beth N Wright

Adams, Daniel J
47 Sweetbrier Dr
Ballston Lake, NY 12019
518-877-8225 Fax: 518-877-8225

Clients:
Brewers Association, Inc (NYS)
Coors Brewing Co
Illinois Tool Works Inc
Matt Brewing Co (The)

Adirondack Council Inc (The)
103 Hand Ave, PO Box D2
Elizabethtown, NY 12932
518-873-2240 or 518-432-6757 Fax: 518-873-6675
e-mail: info@adirondackcouncil.org
Web site: www.adirondackcouncil.org

Clients:
Adirondack Council Inc (The)

Lobbyists:
John Davis
Brian L Houseal
Scott Lorey

Adirondack Mountain Club Inc
301 Hamilton St
Albany, NY 12210-1738
518-449-3870 Fax: 518-449-3875
e-mail: nwoodwor@nycap.rr.com
Web site: www.adk.org

Clients:
Adirondack Mountain Club Inc
Trail Conference (NY/NJ)

Lobbyists:
Wes Lampman
Marisa Tedesco
Neil F Woodworth

Adolf, Jay
350 Broadway, Ste 900
New York, NY 10007
212-897-5848

Clients:
Big Apple Circus

Lobbyists:
Robert J Poulson, Jr

Advance Group Inc (The)
481 Eighth Ave, Ste 1202
New York, NY 10001
212-239-7323

Clients:
American Red Cross in Greater NY
Assn of Community Organizations for Reform Now (NY)
Community Health Care Assn of NYS
Hotel Trades Council (NYC)
Local 6 Hotel Restaurant & Club Employyes & Bartenders Union, AFL-CIO
Primary Care Development Corporation

Lobbyists:
Lauren Bierman
Laura Kavanagh
Peter Krokondelas
Scott Levenson
Rachel Mann
Nick Vagelatos

Advanced Micro Devices Inc
5204 E Ben White Blvd
MS 500
Austin, TX 78741-7306
512-602-4159

Clients:
Advanced Micro Devices Inc

Lobbyists:
Susan Snyder

Affinity Health Plan
2500 Halsey St
Bronx, NY 10461
718-794-7696 Fax: 718-794-7800

Clients:
Affinity Health Plan

Lobbyists:
Abenaa Abboa-Offei
Maura Bluestone

After-School Corporation (The)
925 Ninth Ave
New York, NY 10019
212-547-6950 Fax: 212-548-4657

Clients:
After-School Corporation (The)

Lobbyists:
John Albert

Offices and agencies generally appear in alphabetical order, except when specific order is requested by listee.

455

LOBBYISTS

Lucy Friedman
Rachel Sabella

Agostine Jr, Joseph A
Nghbhd Preserv Coalition of NYS
40 Colvin Ave
Albany, NY 12206
518-432-6757 Fax: 518-432-6758
e-mail: agostine@npcnys.org
Web site: www.npcnys.org

Clients:
Neighborhood Preservation Coalition of NYS Inc

Ahern, Barbara J
One Commerce Plaza, Ste 400
Albany, NY 12210
518-463-0723 Fax: 518-463-7809
e-mail: bjahern@albany.net

Clients:
Croplife America
First Data Corporation & Subsidiaries
Group Self Insurance Assn of NY Inc (GSIANY)
Hearing Healthcare Alliance of NY Inc (HHCANY)
Hearth, Patio & Barbeque Assn
Heineken USA, Inc
National Marine Manufacturers Assn
Personal Watercraft Industry Assn
Responsible Industry for a Sound Environment (RISE)

Albany Law School of Union University
80 New Scotland Ave
Albany, NY 12208
518-445-2380

Clients:
Albany Law School

Lobbyists:
Thomas Guernsey
Helen A Keane
Patricia Salkin

Allegretti, Daniel
111 Market St
Baltimore, MD 21202
410-468-3306

Clients:
Constellation Energy Group

Allegue, Raul R
St Paul Travelers Companies
1 Tower Sq-8MS
Hartford, CT 06183
860-277-4738 Fax: 860-277-4563

Clients:
Travelers Companies Inc (The)

Lobbyists:
John D Miletti

Alliance for Quality Education (FKA Easton, Regina N)
94 Central Ave
Albany, NY 12206
518-432-5315

Clients:
Alliance for Quality Education (FKA Easton, Regina N)

Lobbyists:
William Easton

Allinger, Stephen (FKA Nelson, Debra)
United Teachers (NYS)
800 Troy-Schenectady Rd
Latham, NY 12110-2455
518-213-6000

Clients:
Professional Staff Congress (The)
United Teachers (NYS)

Lobbyists:
Christopher Black
Floyd Cameron
John Costello
Joseph Garba
John Green
Richard Iannuzzi
Alan Lubin
Patrick Lyons
Maria Neira
Melinda Person
Charles Santelli
Paul Webster

Allocco, Carol
13 Sky Hollow Dr
Menands, NY 12204
518-432-8636 Fax: 518-432-8637
e-mail: callocco@corus.jnj.com

Clients:
Johnson & Johnson

Alteri, Richard
Cable Telecom Assn of NY
80 State St
Albany, NY 12207
518-463-6676 Fax: 518-463-0574
e-mail: rfa@nycap.rr.com

Clients:
Cable Telecommunications Assn of NY Inc

Altman, Frederick M
6 Walker Way
Albany, NY 12205-4946

Offices and agencies generally appear in alphabetical order, except when specific order is requested by listee.

LOBBYISTS

518-690-2828

Clients:
Associated Licensed Detectives of NYS, Inc

Altman, Robert S
Robert S Altman, Esq
27 Whitehall St
New York, NY 10004
212-232-8713

Clients:
Building Industry Assn of NY Inc
Queens & Bronx Building Assn

Altria Corporate Services
120 Park Ave
New York, NY 10017
917-663-3406 Fax: 917-663-5716

Clients:
Altria Corporate Services, Inc

Lobbyists:
Armando Mejia-Gallardo

Amalgamated Transit Union
5025 Wisconsin Ave NW
Washington, DC 20016
202-537-1645

Clients:
Amalgamated Transit Union

Lobbyists:
Luis Alzate
Joseph Carey
Daniel Cassella
Francis Falzone
Steven Green
Lawrence Hanley
Mark Henry
Angelo Tanzi

AmeriChoice of NY (United Healthcare Services Affiliate)
284 State St
Albany, NY 12210
518-432-0893 Fax: 518-432-0895
e-mail: vgrey@americhoice.com

Clients:
AmeriChoice of NY (United Healthcare Services Affiliate)

Lobbyists:
Mara Ginsberg

American Academy of Pediatrics District II (NYS)
420 Lakeville Rd, Rm 244
Lake Success, NY 11042
516-326-0310

Clients:
American Academy of Pediatrics District II (NYS)

Lobbyists:
George Dunkel

American College of Ob & Gyn, District II
152 Washington Ave
Albany, NY 12210-2203
518-436-3461 Fax: 518-426-4728
e-mail: info@ny.acog.org
Web site: www.acog.org/goto/nys

Clients:
American College of Ob & Gyn, District II/NY

Lobbyists:
Christa Chritakis
Serena Houle
Donna M Williams

American Continental Group
900 19th St NW
Ste 800
Washington, DC 20006
202-327-8100

Clients:
American Standard Companies Inc

Lobbyists:
Shawn Smeallie

American Diabetes Association
330 Congress St, 5th Fl
Boston, MA 02210
617-482-4580

Clients:
American Diabetes Association

Lobbyists:
Stephen Habbe
Jamie Depasquale

American Farmland Trust
112 Spring St
Ste 207
Saratoga Springs, NY 12866
518-581-0078

Clients:
Ameican Farmland Trust

Lobbyists:
Elizabeth Brock
Jeremiah Cosgrove
David Haight

Offices and agencies generally appear in alphabetical order, except when specific order is requested by listee.

LOBBYISTS

American Heart Assn/American Stroke Assn
440 New Karner Rd
Albany, NY 12205
518-869-4040 Fax: 518-869-8180
e-mail: paul.hartman@heart.org
Web site: www.americanheart.org;
www.strokeassociation.org

Clients:
American Heart Assn/American Stroke Assn

Lobbyists:
Tamiko Byrd
Amit Chitre
David Day
Ramona Englebrecht
Jeff Foley
Paul Hartman
Gabrielle Garland
Bryan Keane
Zainab Magdon-Ismail
Jeff Masline
June McKenley
Sheree Murphy
Michelle Nicholls
Joanna Rush
Christina Rutan
Kelvin Sapp
Suzanne Sawyer
Roseanne Stephan
Merrilee Sweet
Trina Tardone-Steinhart
Jim Versteeg
Duncan Ververs
Simon Vukelj

American Insurance Assn
95 Columbia St
Albany, NY 12210-2707
518-462-1695 Fax: 518-465-6023
e-mail: ghenning@aiadc.org
Web site: www.aiadc.org

Clients:
American Insurance Assn

Lobbyists:
Gary Henning
Michael Moran

American Lung Assn of the City of New York
116 John St, 30th Fl
New York, NY 10038
212-889-3370 Fax: 212-889-3375

Clients:
American Lung Assn of the City of New York

Lobbyists:
Irwin Berlin MD
Corrina Freedman
Peter Iwanowicz
Lauralee Munson
Robert Roth
Neil Schacter MD
Neil Schluger MD
Louise A Vetter

American Museum of Natural History
79th St & Central Park W
New York, NY 10024-5192
212-769-5333 Fax: 212-313-7990
Web site: www.amnh.org

Clients:
American Museum of Natural History

Lobbyists:
Lisa Guggenheim
Barbara Gunn
Daniel Slippen

Ames, Margery E
Interagency Cncl Mental Retard/Dev Disab
275 7th Ave, 19th Fl
New York, NY 10001
212-645-6360

Clients:
Interagency Council of Mental Retardation & Dev Disabilities

Lobbyists:
Margery E Ames
Charles Archer

Anderson, David
23 Hunters Run Blvd
Cohoes, NY 12407
518-785-4589 Fax: 518-785-0883
e-mail: david.anderson@astrazeneca.com

Clients:
Astrazeneca Pharmaceuticals

Andrew, Ralph
Eye & Ear Infirmary (NY)
310 East 14th St
New York, NY 10003
212-979-4578 Fax: 212-353-5779

Clients:
Eye & Ear Infirmary (NY)

Animal Welfare Advocacy
PO Box 737
Mamaroneck, NY 10543
914-381-6177

Clients:
Animal Welfare Advocacy

Lobbyists:
Brad Goldberg
Kelley Wind

Offices and agencies generally appear in alphabetical order, except when specific order is requested by listee.

LOBBYISTS

Ann Breeswine
153 N Broadway
Nyack, NY 10960
845-461-6883

Clients:
Dental Hygienists' Association of the State of NY, Inc

Anson, Joseph L
10 Applewood Dr
Rexford, NY 12148-1601
518-371-0393 Fax: 518-371-5070

Clients:
BayerCorp Pharmaceutical Div, Bayer Healthcare LLC

Apple Assn Inc (NY)
7645 Main St, PO Box 350
Fishers, NY 14453-0350
585-924-2171 Fax: 585-924-1629
e-mail: jimallen@nyapplecountry.com
Web site: www.nyapplecountry.com

Clients:
Apple Assn Inc (NY)

Lobbyists:
James Allen

Apple Inc (FKA Apple Computer Inc)
591 Redwood Hwy, Bldg 4000
Mill Valley, CA 94941-3039
415-389-6800

Clients:
Apple Inc

Lobbyists:
Scott Hughes

Arts Coalition (NYC)
351-A West 54 St
New York, NY 10019
212-246-3788

Clients:
Arts Coalition (NYC)

Lobbyists:
Norma Munn

Arzt, George Communications Inc
123 William St, 22nd Fl
New York, NY 10038
212-608-0333 Fax: 212-608-0458
e-mail: chief@arztcomm.com

Clients:
6-16 West 77th Street Corporation
62 Imlay Street Real Estate, LLC
Blood Center (NY)
Bovis Lend Lease
Broadway Concrete Corp
Circle Line Harbor Cruises, LLC
Crossroads Ventures, LLC
Defenders Justice Fund (NY)
Downtown Hospital (NY)
Extell Development Company
Institute of Technology (NY)
Jazz Museum in Harlem (The)
Legal Assistance Group (NY)
Lower East Side Tenement Museum
Madison Avenue Leasehold LLC
New School University
New Yorkers Against the Death Penalty
New Yorkers for Responsible Development
Prestige Properties & Development Co Inc
Rose Group (The)
St Barnabas Hospital
Scotto Brothers Site 16/17 Development LLC
Tempositions, Inc
United Way of NYC
Water/Pearl Associates, LLC

Lobbyists:
George Arzt
Jane Crotty
Brian Krapf
Bob Liff
Fred Winters

Asciutto, Georgia M
Conf Big 5 Sch Dist
1 Steuben Pl, 5th Fl Loft
Albany, NY 12207
518-465-4274 Fax: 518-465-0638
e-mail: big5schools@mindspring.com

Clients:
Conference of Big 5 School Districts

Lobbyists:
Jennifer Pyle

Assn for Community Living
632 Plank Rd, Ste 110
Clifton Park, NY 12065
518-688-1682

Clients:
Assn for Community Living

Lobbyists:
Antonia M Lasicki

Assn of Community & Residential Agencies (NYS)
99 Pine St, Ste C110
Albany, NY 12207
518-449-7551 Fax: 518-449-1509
Web site: www.nysacra.org

Clients:
Assn of Community & Residential Agencies (NYS)

Offices and agencies generally appear in alphabetical order, except when specific order is requested by listee.

459

LOBBYISTS

Lobbyists:
Forest Cotten
Ann Hardiman
James Kosakoski

Assn of Counties & Its Affiliated Organizations (NYS)
111 Pine St
Albany, NY 12207
518-465-1473 Fax: 518-465-0506
Web site: www.nysac.org

Clients:
Assn of Counties & Its Affiliated Organizations (NYS)

Lobbyists:
Stephen Acquario
Adriano Bongiorno
Kenneth Crannell
Mark Lavigne
Jeffrey Osinski
Peter Savage

Assn of PBAS, Inc (NYS)
111 Washington Ave
Albany, NY 11210-2207
518-465-1141 Fax: 518-465-3048

Clients:
Assn of PBAS, Inc (NYS)

Lobbyists:
Gus Danese
Gary Dela Raba
William Diebold
Nick Even
Jeff Frayler
Ray Gimmler
Patrick Hall
Chris Heimgartner
Brian Hoesl
James Hughes
Lou Matarazzo
Tim Morris
Michael O'Meara
Peter B Paterson
Frederick A Sales
Gordon Warnock
Thomas Willdigg

Assn of School Business Officials (NYS)
7 Elk St
Albany, NY 12207-1002
518-434-2281 Fax: 518-434-1303
e-mail: asbomail@nysasbo.org
Web site: www.nysasbo.org

Clients:
Assn of School Business Officials (NYS)

Lobbyists:
Gregory Beal
Margaret Boice
Deedrick Bertholf
Jennifer Bolton
Greg Carlson
Lynn Derway
Carl Fraser
Dick Lasselle
Greg Race
Terry Schruers
Michael Sheperd
Sheila Tufankjian
Steven Van Hoesen

Assn of Towns of the State of NY
150 State St
Albany, NY 12207
518-465-7933 Fax: 518-465-0724

Clients:
Assn of Towns of the State of NY

Lobbyists:
Thomas Bodden
Kevin A Crawford
Jeffrey G Haber
Mike Kenneally
Lori Mithen

Association on Independent Living
99 Washington Ave, Ste 806A
Albany, NY 12210
518-465-4650

Clients:
Association on Independent Living (NY)

Lobbyists:
Jill Poklemba
Melanie Shaw

Automobile Dealers Assn (NYS)
37 Elk St, PO Box 7347
Albany, NY 12224-0347
518-463-1148 Fax: 518-432-1309
Web site: www.nysada.com

Clients:
Automobile Dealers Assn (NYS)

Lobbyists:
Robert E Vancavage

Ayers, Deborah
Delphi Corp
200 Upper Mountain Rd, Bldg 6
Lockport, NY 14094
716-439-3245

Clients:
Delphi Corporation

Offices and agencies generally appear in alphabetical order, except when specific order is requested by listee.

LOBBYISTS

BP America Inc
PO Box 6596
Wiiliamsburg, VA 23188
757-645-4300

Clients:
BP America Inc

Lobbyists:
Bruce C Johnson

Baker & Hostetler, LLP
1050 Connecticut Ave NW
Ste 1100
Washington, DC 20036
202-861-1500

Clients:
National Paint & Coatings Assn

Lobbyists:
Tom McDonald
Bill Weber

Baldwin, Kristina
24 Marquis Dr
Slingerlands, NY 12159
518-446-1105

Clients:
Property Casualty Insurers Assn of America (PCIAA)

Banks, Steven
Legal Aid Society (The)
199 Water St
New York, NY 10038
212-577-3277 Fax: 212-809-1574
e-mail: sbanks@legal-aid.org

Clients:
Legal Aid Society (The)

Barba, James J
Albany Medical Ctr
43 New Scotland Ave
Albany, NY 12208-3478
518-262-3830

Clients:
Albany Medical Center

Lobbyists:
Richard Cook

Barnes, Richard E
NYS Catholic Conference
465 State St
Albany, NY 12203-1004
518-434-6195 Fax: 518-434-9796
Web site: www.nyscatholic.org

Clients:
Catholic Conference (NYS)

Lobbyists:
James Cultrara
S Earl Eichelberger
Kathleen M Gallagher
Ronald Guglielmo
Kyle McCauley
Dennis Poust

Barnett, Claire L
Healthy Schools Network, Inc
773 Madison Ave
Albany, NY 12208
518-462-0632 Fax: 518-462-0433
e-mail: info@healthyschools.org
Web site: www.healthyschools.org

Clients:
Healthy Schools Network Inc

Lobbyists:
Stephen Boese

Barrett Associates
95 Columbia St
Albany, NY 12210-2707
518-465-5340 Fax: 518-465-6023

Clients:
Acadia Insurance Company
America's Health Insurance Plans
Assn of Family Service Agencies (NYS)
Automobile Insurance Plan (NY)
Central Mutual Fire Insurance Co (NY)
Construction Contractors Assn of the Hudson Valley Inc
IAAC Inc
Independent Insurance Agents & Brokers of NY
Insurance Brokers' Association of the State of New York
Property Insurance Underwriting Assn (NY)

Lobbyists:
Michael V Barrett
Todd Gold
Gregory Sehr

Bauer, Peter
Residents Cmte Protect Adirondack
PO Box 27
North Creek, NY 12853
518-251-4257 Fax: 518-251-5068

Clients:
Residents Committee to Protect the Adirondacks

Behan Communications Inc
13 Locust St, PO Box 2077
Glens Falls, NY 12801
518-792-3856

Offices and agencies generally appear in alphabetical order, except when specific order is requested by listee.

LOBBYISTS

Clients:
Catholic Conference Policy Group, Inc

Lobbyists:
Mark Behan
John Brodt
Joan Gerhardt
Peter Lanahan

Bennett Firm, Inc (The)
PO Box 38004
Albany, NY 12207
518-439-0077

Clients:
Long Island Ophthalmological Society
Society of Orthopaedic Surgeons (NYS)

Lobbyists:
Heather Bennett

Bennett, Michael
33 South Clinton Ave
Hastings-on-Hudson, NY 10706-3602
914-478-0056

Clients:
Assn of Electrical Contractors, Inc (NYS)
Council of NECA Chapters (NYS)

Bergin, Robert J
Rochester Gas & Electric Corp
89 East Ave
Rochester, NY 14649-0001
585-771-2294 Fax: 585-724-8668
e-mail: robert_bergin@rge.com
Web site: www.rge.com

Clients:
Rochester Gas & Electric

Lobbyists:
James Laurito

Berry, Sally
Loretto Management Corp
700 E Brighton Ave
Syracuse, NY 13205
315-413-3145

Clients:
Loretto Management Corporation

Bigelsen, Jayne
Assn Bar of City NY
42 W 44th St
New York, NY 10036
212-382-6655

Clients:
NYC Bar Association

Lobbyists:
Jayne Bigelsen
Alan Rothstein

Biggerstaff Law Firm, LLP (The)
Main Sq, 318 Delaware Ave
Delmar, NY 12054
518-475-9500

Clients:
Association of Small City School Districts (NYS)

Lobbyists:
Laura Biggerstaff
Robert E Biggerstaff

Billig, Jacob
146 Rock Hill Dr
Rock Hill, NY 12738
845-794-3833

Clients:
Trading Cove NY, LLC

Clients:
Allen Health Care Services
Any-Time Home Care Inc
Bestcare, Inc
City of Yonkers
Comprehensive Home Care
Family Service Society of Yonkers
James F Capalino & Associates
Maxim of NY, LLC
Personal Touch Home Care of Westchester
Recco Home Care Services, Inc
Richmond UNI Home Care Inc
VIP Health Care Services
Wartburg Residential Community, Inc
Westchester Jewish Community Services

Lobbyists:
Marc Bloom

Blumenthal, Karen
Student Advocacy
3 West Main St, Ste 212
Elmsford, NY 10523-2414
914-347-7039

Clients:
Student Advocacy

Bogdan Lasky & Kopley, LLC
111 Washington Ave, Ste 750
Albany, NY 12210-2213
518-434-9000 Fax: 518-434-2510
e-mail: etricomi@blklobby.com
Web site: www.blklobby.com

Clients:
Academic Health Center Consortium
Alfred University
American Chemistry Council

Offices and agencies generally appear in alphabetical order, except when specific order is requested by listee.

LOBBYISTS

Anheuser-Busch Companies Inc
Assn of Nurse Anesthetists Inc (NYS)
AstraZeneca Pharmaceuticals, LP
Capital One Financial Corporation
Concentra Health Services Inc
Constellation Energy Group
Coventry
eBay
Entertainment Software Assn
Girl Scout Legislative Network (NYS)
HLR Service Corporation (Roche)
International Council of Shopping Centers
Jackson Hewitt Tax Service Inc
Medimmune Inc
McLane Company Inc
Merrill Lynch & Co Inc
Motion Picture Assn of America Inc
National Assn of Theatre Owners of NYS (NATO)
Netflix Inc
Northeastern Retail Lumber Assn
Plumbing & Mechanical Contractors Association of the Hudson Valley
Progressive Bag Alliance
Proctor & Gamble Company (The)
Realogy Corporation
SCAA Tissue North America
Sergeants Benevolent Assn
Sprint Nextel
St Paul Travelers
Thoroughbred Breeders Inc (NY)
Travelport LTD
University of Rochester
US Interactive Inc
Union Graduate University
Wine Institute
Wyndham Worldwide Corporation

Lobbyists:
Edward A Bogdan, III
Peter V Carr, Jr
Diane E Frazier
Mary K Kopley
James A Lasky
Denise Murphy McGraw
Erica Tricomi

Boilermakers Local Lodge #5
24 Van Siclen Ave
Floral Park, NY 11001
516-326-2500

Clients:
Boilermakers Local Lodge #5

Lobbyists:
Gerald Connolly

Bolton St Johns Inc
146 State St
Albany, NY 12207
518-462-4620 Fax: 518-426-1631
e-mail: mail@boltonstjohns.com
Web site: www.boltonstjohns.com

Clients:
1199 SEIU United Healthcare Workers East
AMDEC Foundation Inc
Adult Day Health Care Council (ADHCC)
Agencies for Children's Therapy Services
Anthony J Costello & Son Development LLC
Air Liquide Large Industries USLP
Continuing Care Leadership Coalition
Capital District Regional Off-Track Betting Corporation
Citigroup Washington Inc
City Ctr of Music & Drama Inc
Committee for Taxi Safety
Cultural Institution Group
County Nursing Facilities of New York
Express Scripts Inc
Fuel Cell Energy Inc
Gay & Lesbian Anti-Violence Project (NYC)
Globe Institute of Technology
Harm Reduction Coalition
Rochester Rhinos Stadium, LLC
Greater New York Hospital Assn
Health Insurance Plan of Greater NY (HIP)
Island Peer Review Organization Inc
Keyspan Energy
Kingsbrook Jewish Medical Ctr
Kaleida Health
Local 32-BJ
Local 338 RWDSU
Mentoring Partnership Coalition
Metropolitan Museum of Art
Moms Pharmacy
Medicare Rights Center
Monroe County Airport Authority
Village Care of New York
New School (The)
New England Stone LLC
OC Inc of NY
Phelps Dodge Refining Corporation
Pipe Trades Assn
Verizon NY
Recording Industry Assn of America Inc
Rosies for All Kids Foundation
Satellite Tracking of People LLC
Shawanga Lodge, LLC
Siemens Corporation
Workers' Compensation Pharmacy Alliance (WCPA)
Working Poor Legal Assistance Project
St. Elizabeth Medical Center
Suffolk County Assn of Municipal Employees PAC Inc
Sysco Food Services of Albany, LLC
Trustees of Columbia University in the City of NY (The)
Unity Health System
ValueOptions Inc
Verizon Wireless
Visy Paper (NY)
YMCA of New York State
Yum! Brands Inc

Lobbyists:
Norman M Adler
Jay Adolf
David Beier
Tom Connolly
Georgio DeRosa
Melissa DeRosa
Edward Draves
Emily Giske
Leshaun Lesley
Bill McCarthy
Melvin Miller

Offices and agencies generally appear in alphabetical order, except when specific order is requested by listee.

463

LOBBYISTS

John Wright

Boltz, John J Consulting
14 Linden Ct
Clifton Park, NY 12065
518-371-2790 Fax: 518-373-1536

Clients:
Altria Corporate Services, Inc
Business Council of Westchester (The)
First Data Corp & Its Subsidiaries
Hearth, Patio & Barbecue Association (HPBA)(Ahern, Barbara J)
Building & Realty Institute
Kraft Foods Global, Inc
Miller Brewing Company
National Assn of Marine Manufacturers (Ahern, Barbara J)
Personal Watercraft Industry Association

Lobbyists:
John J Boltz

Bombardiere, Ralph
NYSASSRS
6 Walker Way
Albany, NY 12205-4946
518-452-1979 Fax: 518-452-1955
e-mail: nysassn@together.net
Web site: www.nysassrs.com

Clients:
Assn of Service Stations & Repair Shops Inc (NYS)

Bonagura, David (FKA Hoops, Jeffrey)
Ernst & Young LLP
395 N Service Rd
Melville, NY 11747
631-752-6125

Clients:
Ernst & Young LLP

Lobbyists:
Robert Michael Duffey
Peter Lease
Mark Manoff
Michael R Press

Bond, Schoeneck & King, PLLC
111 Washington Ave
Albany, NY 12210
518-533-3036 Fax: 518-462-7441

Clients:
Besicorp-Empire Newsprint LLC
Brooklyn Navy Yard Cogeneration Partners LP
Collectors Assn Inc (NYS)
Dairylea Cooperative Inc
First Cardinal Corporation
H & R Block Eastern Enterprises
Indeck-Corinth Limited Partnership
Financial Service Centers of NY Inc
Ski Areas of NY Inc

Trivin Inc

Lobbyists:
Frank Breselor
Hermes Fernandez
Edwin Kelley
Virginia Robbins
Richard L Smith
Courtney Weller

Bookman, Robert S
Newsstand Operators
325 Broadway, Ste 501
New York, NY 10007
212-513-1988 Fax: 212-385-0564

Clients:
Newsstand Operators Assn (NYC)
Nightlife Association (NY)

Bopp, Linda (FKA Mesick, Edie)
235 Lark St
Albany, NY 12210
518-436-8757

Clients:
Nutrition Consortium of NYS Inc

Lobbyists:
Gail Cooney
Mark Denley
Casey Dinkin
Yvette James
Misha Marvel
Catherine Roberts

Botanical Garden (The) (NY)
200th St & Kazimiroff Blvd
Bronx, NY 10458
718-817-8962

Clients:
Botanical Garden (The)

Lobbyists:
Michael Alderstein
J V Cossaboom
Rosemary Ginty
Gregory Long
Janet Torres

Boykin-Towns, Karen
Pfizer, Inc
235 East 42nd St, 12th Fl
New York, NY 10017
212-573-7627 Fax: 212-808-8880
e-mail: karen.boykin-towns@phizer.com
Web site: www.pfizer.com

Clients:
Pfizer, Inc

Offices and agencies generally appear in alphabetical order, except when specific order is requested by listee.

LOBBYISTS

Brendel & Associates
407 Forst Ave
Rye, NY 10580
914-403-1700

Clients:
Keyspan Corporation

Lobbyists:
Joseph Brendel

Brescia, Richard
321 Loudon Rd
Loudonville, NY 12211
518-436-6733

Clients:
New York Propane Gas Assn

Clients:
American Red Cross in Greater NY

Lobbyists:
Mark Walter

Bronx Health Reach
16 East 16th St
New York, NY 10003
212-633-0800

Clients:
Bronx Health Reach

Lobbyists:
Neil Calman
Maxine Golub
Lorraine Gonzalez
Charmaine Ruddock

Brower, Michael R
SUNY College of Environ Science & Forest
1 Forestry Dr
Syracuse, NY 13210-2778
315-470-6681 Fax: 315-470-6977

Clients:
SUNY College of Environmental Science & Forestry

Brown McMahon & Weinraub, LLC
79 Columbia St
Albany, NY 12210
518-427-7350 Fax: 518-427-7792

Clients:
American Chemistry Council Inc
American Electronics Association/NY Council
Assn of Alcoholism & Substance Abuse Providers Inc (NY)
Astellas Pharma US Inc
Authentix Inc
Brooklyn Psychiatric Center
Cephalon Inc
Chinese-American Planning Council Inc
Church Avenue Merchants Block Assn
Clearing House Association LLC (The)
Committee for Safe Streets
Court Officers Benevolent Assn of Nassau Cnty Inc
Educational Broadcasting Corporation
Episcopal Health Services Inc
Eyemed Vision Care LLC
Entergy Nuclear Operations
Feld Entertainment Inc
Fortune Society (The)
Goldman Sachs & Company Inc
Government Payment Service Inc
Greater New York Hospital Association
Hospice & Palliative Care Assn of NYS
Hospitals Insurance Company Inc
Industrial Retention Network (NY)
Injured Workers Pharmacy
Instructional Systems Inc
Interfaith Medical Center
LB Furniture Industries LLC
Legal Services for NYC
Liberty Helicopters Inc
Long Island Gay & Lesbian Youth
Merscorp Inc
Mortgage Bankers Association
NADAP
Nat Sherman Inc
Oracle USA Inc
Premium Finance Association
Psychotherapy & Counseling Center (NY)
Sequoia Voting Systems Inc
Sprint Nextel
Pharmaceutical Research & Manufacturers Assn of America
Northrop Grumman Corporation
Real Estate Tax Review Bar Assn
Snapple Beverage Corp, Dr Pepper/Seven U Inc & Motts, LLP
Tier Technologies Inc
Trading Cove New York, LLC
United Water
Verizon
Women's Bar Assn of the State of NY

Lobbyists:
Patrick Brown
Jeffrey Buley
Sheila Healy
James McMahon
Sandra Rivera
Emily Saltzman
David Weinraub

Browne, Brian
St John's University-Manhattan Campus
101 Murray St
New York, NY 10007
212-284-7005
Web site: www.stjohns.edu

Clients:
St John's University

Bryan Cave, LLP
1290 Avenue of the Americas
New York, NY 10104
212-541-2386

Offices and agencies generally appear in alphabetical order, except when specific order is requested by listee.

LOBBYISTS

Clients:
3500 Park Avenue LLC
44th and 11th LLC
625 East Fordham LLC
American Self Storage Landing Road LLC
Fiam Building Associates
Flushing Commons LLC
Gerard Avenue LLC
Jamestown Chelsea Market Corporation
Metrovest Equities Inc

Lobbyists:
Robert Davis
Judith Gallent
Charla Beth Mobley
Margery Perlmutter
Ivan Schonfeld

Buffalo Niagara Assn of Realtors, Inc
100 Sylvan Pkwy
Amherst, NY 14228
716-636-9000

Clients:
Buffalo Niagara Assn of Realtors, Inc

Lobbyists:
Daniel Locche

Build PAC (NY)
One Commerce Plaza, Ste 704
Albany, NY 12210
518-465-2492 Fax: 518-465-0635
e-mail: info@nysba.com
Web site: www.nysba.com

Clients:
Builders Association (NYS)

Lobbyists:
Philip LaRocque

Burgos, Tonio & Associates
Trinity Center
115 Broadway, Ste 1504
New York, NY 10006
212-566-5600

Clients:
American Recycling Technologies Inc
American Red Cross in Greater New York
Change to Win
Clean Energy (DCI Group)
Cooper Tank & Welding Corp
Educational Housing Services
Greater New York Hospital Association
HF Management Services LLC
HIP Health Plan of NY
International Alliance of Theatrical & Stage Employees Local 4
Interstate Waste Technologies Inc
JCDecaux North America Inc
Keane Inc
Museum for African Arts
NJ Transit
Nielsen Media Research
Pfizer
Sims Hugo Neu
Theatre Workshop (NY)
T-Mobile USA Inc
Verizon

Lobbyists:
Tonio Burgos
Francisco Diaz

Burns, Miriam P
Selfhelp Community Svcs Inc
520 8th Ave
New York, NY 10018
212-971-7610 Fax: 212-967-1723

Clients:
Selfhelp Community Services, Inc

Business Council of NYS Inc
152 Washington Ave
Albany, NY 12210-2289
518-465-7511 Fax: 518-465-4389

Clients:
Business Council of NYS Inc (The)

Lobbyists:
Kenneth Adams
Margarita Mayo
Kenneth Pokalsky
Edward Reinfurt
Richard Schwarz
Elliott Shaw
Anne Van Buren
Robert Ward

CNA
CNA Plaza
43rd Fl
Chicago, IL 60685
312-822-1739 Fax: 312-822-1186

Clients:
CNA

Lobbyists:
Andrew Boron
Heather Davis

COFCCA Inc
254 west 31st St, 5th Fl
New York, NY 10001
212-929-2626

Clients:
COFCCA Inc

Lobbyists:
Mary Jane Dessables
Dianne Heggie
Edith Holzer

Offices and agencies generally appear in alphabetical order, except when specific order is requested by listee.

LOBBYISTS

William Pryylucki
James Purcell

CSC Holdings, Inc
1111 Stewart Ave
Bethpage, NY 11714
516-803-2387 Fax: 516-803-2667

Clients:
CSC Holdings, Inc

Lobbyists:
Theodore Baecher
Jeff Clark
Roger Connor
Claire Dorfman
Elizabeth Ferrier
Joan Gilroy
Elizabeth Losinski
Helena Williams
Michael Olsen
Lisa Rosenblum
Lee Schroeder
Emilie Spalding
Dodie Tschirch

CTIA - The Wireless Assn
CTIA The Wireless Assn
1400 16th St NW, Ste 600
Washington, DC 20036
202-785-0081

Clients:
CTIA - The Wireless Assn

Lobbyists:
William R Barnes
K Dane Snowden

Calvin, James S
Assn of Convenience Stores
130 Washington Ave, Ste 300
Albany, NY 12210
518-432-1400 Fax: 518-432-7400
e-mail: jim@nyacs.org
Web site: www.nyacs.org

Clients:
Assn of Convenience Stores (NY)

Campaign for Fiscal Equity, Inc
110 Williams St, Ste 2602
New York, NY 10038
212-867-8455
Web site: www.cfequity.org

Clients:
Campaign for Fiscal Equity, Inc

Lobbyists:
Helaine Doran
Geri Palast

Capalino, James F & Associates Inc
850 Third Ave, 19th Floor
New York, NY 10022-6222
212-822-2285
e-mail: james@capalino.com
Web site: www.capalino.com

Clients:
117 W 89th Street LLC (AS Realty Partners)
346 West 17th Street, LLC
361-363 West 50th Street Redevelopment Company L.P.
44th & 11th LLC
Actors' Equity Association
Adfleet Advertising USA Inc
Alchemy Properties, Inc
All Stars Project Inc (The)
Alliance for the Arts
Apthrop Associates, LLC
Axis Group Inc
CTK Properties
CBS Outdoor, Inc (FKA Viacom Outdoor, Inc)
Citizens for NYC
Computers for Youth
Coral Realty, LLC
Coro New York
Creative Time
Diebold Election Systems, Inc
Ecomedia Direct
Elaine Kaufman Cultural Center
Ferrara Bros. Buildings Material Corp
Gaia House, LLC
Gansevoort Market, Inc
Gene Kaufman Architect PC
Horizen Global
Housing & Services, Inc
Industry City Associates, LLC
Interim Housing
Inwood House
Jamestown Management
Lands End Associates L.P.
Lavin Properties
Leader House Associates, L.P.
Liberty Helicopter
Literacy Assistance Center
Magnum Management LLC
Manhattan Music Society
Merker Advisory Services
Metropolitan Events
Moynihan Station Developers, LLC
Museum of the Moving Image
Ninth K Realty LLC
Related Companies (The)
Rockrose Development Corp
Romanoff Equities, Inc
Safe Space
Saint Vincent Catholic Medical Centers
SH Ludlow Street, LLC
Solomon R Guggenheim Museum
Sunnyside Community Services Inc
Tavern on the Green
Theracare
Time Warner Cable
Two Trees Management Inc
Uniformed EMS Officers Union, FDNY, Local
Witkoff Group (The)
Worldwide Group Holdings Corp

Offices and agencies generally appear in alphabetical order, except when specific order is requested by listee.

LOBBYISTS

Lobbyists:
James Capalino
George Fontas
Travis Terry
Mark Thompson

Capital District Physicians' Health Plan Inc
500 Patroon Creek Blvd
Albany, NY 12206-1057
518-641-5211 Fax: 518-641-5205
Web site: www.cdphp.com

Clients:
Capital District Physicians' Health Plan Inc

Lobbyists:
William J Cromie
Robert R Hinckley

Capital Public Affairs
111 Washington Ave, Rm 104
Albany, NY 12210
518-465-8760 Fax: 518-427-6931

Clients:
Aetna Inc
Amgen
ING America Insurance Holdings
Medical Liability Mutual Insurance Co (MLMIC)
Pharmacists Society of the State of NY
Ticketmaster
Wyeth

Lobbyists:
Elizabeth M Lasky
Roy E Lasky

Capitol Consultants Inc (NY)
120 Washington Ave
Albany, NY 12210
518-449-3333 Fax: 518-427-6781
e-mail: judith@nycapcon.com

Clients:
American Lawyer Media
Astoria Energy
BP America Inc
Bus Distributors Assn Inc (NYS)
Independent Automobile Dealers Assn Inc (NY)
Parallel Park, LLC
Self Storage Assn Inc (NY)
Sunoco Inc
Unions for Jobs & the Environment
Monroe County Deputy Sheriff's Association Inc

Lobbyists:
M Joe Landry
Murray LeWinter
Christopher G McGrath

Capitol Group, LLC
120 Washington Ave
Albany, NY 12210
518-463-4841 Fax: 518-463-5301
e-mail: nick@capitolgroupllc.com; tim@capitolgroupllc.com
Web site: www.capitolgroupllc.com

Clients:
Acupuncture Society of NY Inc
American Safety Institute Inc
Association for the Help of Retarded Children NYC Chapter (NYS)
Bearingpoint
Column Technologies, Inc
Citrix Systems
Consumer Healthcare Products Assn
ECOR Solutions Inc
Empire State Marine Trades Assn
Grocery Manufacturers Assn (FKA Grocery Manufacturers of America)
Long Island Forum for Technology
National Association of Professional Employer Organizations
Rent-A-Center (Stateside Associates)
Rite Aid Corporation
Senior Associates
Snowmobile Assn (NYS)
Waste Management
Wendy's Internatioal

Lobbyists:
Nicholas Barrella
Timothy Sheridan

Capitol Hill Management Services Inc
90 State St, Ste 1009
Albany, NY 12207
518-463-8644 Fax: 518-463-8656
e-mail: chms@caphill.com
Web site: www.caphill.com

Clients:
Apollo Group Inc
Baden Street Settlement of Rochester Inc
Campus Auxiliary Services Inc
Coordinated Court Services
Coventry Health Care
Dewolff Partnership, Architects LLP (The)
Epilepsy Foundation of Northeastern NY Inc
Higher Education Opportunity Program - Professional Organization
Lamar Advertising Company
Malcolm Pirnie Inc
Outdoor Advertising Council of NY Inc
Public Adjusters Assn (NY)
Society of Opticians Inc (NYS)
Teamsters Local 317
Voth Inc

Lobbyists:
R Scott Gaddy
John A Graziano, Jr
Douglas Mercado
Ronald Ochrym

Capitol Strategies Group, LLC
30 S Pearl St
PO Box 445
Albany, NY 12207
518-432-3676

Offices and agencies generally appear in alphabetical order, except when specific order is requested by listee.

LOBBYISTS

Clients:
Alcatel-Lucent
Bryant & Stratton College
E-Bizdocs
Foundry Networks
Gartner Inc
IP Logic LLC
Keane Inc
Linium LLC
Map Info Corporation
MRV
Netsmart
Nfrastructure
Novell
Oracle USA, Inc
Poetic Holding Corp
Science Application International Corp (SAIC)
Serverware
Sun Microsystems Inc
Technology Enterprise Corporation (NYS)
Waste Management & Recycling Products

Lobbyists:
Robert Burdick
Christopher Cotrona
Louis Cotrona
Joseph Magno

Cappelli, Allen
148 Kissel Ave
Staten Island, NY 10310
917-355-2720

Clients:
Building Industry Assn of NYC, Inc
R Randy Lee
Senior Housing Resource Corp
Staten Island Chamber of Commerce

Carpenters Labor-Management Council, NYS
1284 Central Ave
Albany, NY 12205
518-459-7182 Fax: 518-459-7798
e-mail: kevinhicks@usa.com

Clients:
Carpenters Labor-Management Council, NYS

Lobbyists:
Kevin Hicks

Carpino, Peter
United Way of Greater Rochester
75 College Ave
Rochester, NY 14607
585-242-6400

Clients:
United Way of Greater Rochester

Lobbyists:
Enrique Brouwer
Nissa Youngren

Carr Public Affairs Inc
388 Broadway, 4th Floor
Albany, NY 12207-2941
518-434-8830 Fax: 518-434-0072
e-mail: john@carrpublicaffairs.com
Web site: www.carrpublicaffairs.com

Clients:
4201 Schools Assn
American Forest & Paper Assn (Multistate Associates Inc)
American Massage Therapy Assn (NY Chapter)
Assn of Supts of School Buildings & Grounds (NYS)
Caterpillar, Inc (Multistate Associates Inc)
Coalition of Special Act School Districts of NYS
Community Blood Services
Concepts of Independent Choices
Consumer Electronics Association (Multistate Associates Inc)
Dietetic Assn (NYS)
English Schools Assn (NY)
Federation of School Administrators (NYS)
Grow/Network/McGraw-Hill Companies (The)
Healthcare Distribution Management Assn (HDMA)
Heights Hill Mental Health Services Community Advisory Board (Dames Reid)
Home Care Council of New York City
Job Path (Dames Reid)
Literacy NY Inc
National Confectioners Assn
North American Insulation Manufacturers Assn
NY Mental Health Counselors Association
Toyota Motor Sales

Lobbyists:
James J Carr
John C Carr
Jean M Cox
Heather Evans
Vincent G Graber

Carr, Bernard
Assn for Affordable Housing
5925 Broadway
Bronx, NY 10463
718-432-2100 Fax: 718-432-2400
Web site: www.nysafah.org

Clients:
Assn for Affordable Housing (NYS)

Carson, Martin
105 Fiddlers Elbow Rd
Middle Falls, NY 12848
518-692-3162 Fax: 518-692-3164

Clients:
Lorillard Tobacco Co

Caruso, David A
Golub Corporation
501 Duanesburg Rd
Schenectady, NY 12306
518-379-1391 Fax: 518-379-3536

Offices and agencies generally appear in alphabetical order, except when specific order is requested by listee.

469

LOBBYISTS

Clients:
Golub Corporation (The)

Lobbyists:
Lewis Golub
Neil M Golub

Castelbuono, A J
10 Airline Dr, Ste 203
Albany, NY 12205-1025
518-456-1134 Fax: 518-456-1198
e-mail: ajcastel@agcnys.org
Web site: www.agcnys.org

Clients:
Associated Gen'l Contractors of America Inc (NYS)
Crisis Program (The)

Lobbyists:
Steven Stallmer

Chadwick, Cindy
NYSEG
18 Link Dr, PO Box 5224
Binghamton, NY 13902-5224
607-762-7310 Fax: 607-762-8751
e-mail: ctchadwick@nyseg.com
Web site: www.nyseg.com

Clients:
Electric & Gas Corp (NYS)
Rochester Gas & Electric Corp

Lobbyists:
Robert Bergin

Charter Schools Assn (NY)
One Commerce Plaza
99 Washington Ave, Ste 402
Albany, NY 12210
518-694-3110 Fax: 518-465-3383

Clients:
Charter Schools Assn (NY)

Lobbyists:
William A Phillips

Child Care Coordinating Council (NYS)
230 Washington Ave Ext
Albany, NY 12203
518-690-4217 Fax: 518-427-6603

Clients:
Child Care Coordinating Council (NYS)

Lobbyists:
Susan Antos
Jan Barbieri
Jane Brown
Rhonda Carloss-Smith
Karen Carpenter-Palumbo
Mon Cochran
Valerie Cooley
Dana Friedman
Sue Dale Hall
Lottie Harris
Carla Hibbard
Sue Kowaleski
Peggy Liuzzi
Howard Milbert
Sandra Murrin
Deborah Rojas
Carol Saginaw
Patricia Skinner
James Sonneborn
Lori Van Auken
Jeanne Wagner
Lynda Weismantel
Doris Woo

Child Care Inc
322 Eighth Ave
New York, NY 10001
212-929-7604 x3010 Fax: 212-929-5785
e-mail: info@childcareinc.org
Web site: www.childcareinc.org

Clients:
Child Care Inc

Lobbyists:
Betty Holcomb
Nancy Kolben
Rhonda Carloss-Smith

Children's Health Fund (The)
317 E 64th St
New York, NY 10021
212-535-9400

Clients:
Children's Health Fund (The)

Lobbyists:
Dennis Johnson
Violet Moss

Church Avenue Merchants Block Association
1720 Church Ave
Brooklyn, NY 11226
718-287-2600

Clients:
Church Avenue Merchants Block Association (CAMBA)

Lobbyists:
Valerie Barton-Richardson
Kevin Coffey
Dany Cunningham
Sharon Daly-Browne
Thomas Dambakly
Kathy Dros
Kaida Edwards
Michael Erhard
Kemar Hamilton
Claire Harding-Keefe

Offices and agencies generally appear in alphabetical order, except when specific order is requested by listee.

LOBBYISTS

Andrew Haupt
Christie Hodgkins
Robin Landes
Kathleen Masters
Janet Miller
Marjorie Momplaisir-Ellis
Reginald Murray
Joanne Oplustil
Jude Pierre
Eileen Reilly
Jessie Weisstein

Ciccone, Stephen J
1250 H St NW, Ste 800
Washington, DC 20005
202-857-3474 Fax: 202-857-3401
e-mail: stephen.ciccone@kodak.com
Web site: www.kodak.com

Clients:
Eastman Kodak Co

Lobbyists:
Richard Jarman
John Richardson

Citizens Budget Commission
One Penn Plaza
Suite 640
New York, NY 10119
212-279-2605

Clients:
Citizens Budget Commission

Lobbyists:
Charles Brecher
Diana Fortuna
Elizabeth Lynam

Citizens Campaign for the Environment
225A Main St
Farmingdale, NY 11735
516-390-7150 Fax: 516-390-7160
e-mail: ccefli@citizenscampaign.org
Web site: www.citizenscampaign.org

Clients:
Citizens Campaign for the Environment

Lobbyists:
William Cooke
Maureen Dolan
Adrienne Esposito
Dereth Glance
Kasey Jacobs
Emmett Pepper
Brian Smith

Citizens' Committee for Children of New York Inc
105 E 22nd St, 7th Fl
New York, NY 10010-5413
212-673-1800 Fax: 212-979-5063
Web site: www.cccnewyork.org

Clients:
Citizens' Committee for Children of New York Inc

Lobbyists:
Tina Huang
Jennifer March-Joly
Danielle Marchione
Gail Nayowith

City University of New York (CUNY)
111 Washington Ave, Ste 605
Albany, NY 12210
518-463-2177 Fax: 518-463-2170
Web site: www.cuny.edu

Clients:
City University of New York (CUNY)

Lobbyists:
Perminda Ahluwalia
Michelle Anderson
Scott Anderson
William Boone
Selma Botman
Stephen Brier
Emmanuel Conslues
Ben Corpus
Eduardo De Valle
Terry Rosen Deutsch
Allan Dobrin
Dolores M Fernandez
Ricardo R Fernandez
John Flateau
Eileen Goldmann
Matthew Goldstein
Carlos Hargraves
Sue Henderson
Jay Hershenson
Russell Hotzler
Bonnie Impagliazzo
Edison O Jackson
Richard Jones
Marcia Keizs
MaryKaye Kellogg
William P Kelly
Christoph M Kimmich
Oliver Klapper
John Kotowski
Andre Lake
Eric Lugo
Patrick S Madama
Ernesto Malave
Brenda Malone
Eduardo Marti
Matthew McGee
Lavita McMath
Gail Mellow
Meghan Moore Wilke

Offices and agencies generally appear in alphabetical order, except when specific order is requested by listee.

LOBBYISTS

Garrie Moore
James Muyskens
Dale Nussbaum
Gbubemi Okatieuro
Jose Orengo
Sandra Palleja
Angelo Pappagallo
Antonio Perez
Regina Peruggi
Frederick Price
Jennifer J Raab
Anne Garcia Reyes
Eneida Rivas
Augie Rivera
A William Rogers
Sanford A Roman, Jr
Fred Rooney
Chris Rosa
Sandra Ruiz
Angela Sales
Milton Santiago
Matthew Sapienza
Frederick Schaffer
Maureen Shields
Marlene Springer
Doris Torres
Jeremy Travis
Doreen Vinas
Carol White
Carolyn Williams
Gregory Williams
Karen Witherspoon
Roger Witherspoon

Civil Service Employees Assn, Inc
143 Washington Ave
Albany, NY 12210
518-257-1319 Fax: 518-465-2382

Clients:
Civil Service Employees Assn, Inc

Lobbyists:
George Boncoraglio
Danny Donohue
Kathy Garrison
Diane Hewitt
Nicholas Lamorte
Joseph McMullen
Barbara Reeves
Virginia Sheffey
Mary Sullivan
Florence Tripi

Clark, Frank A
Adirndk Landowner's Assn
One Park Pl, Ste 350
Syracuse, NY 13202
315-701-5990

Clients:
Adirondack Landowners Assn Inc

Clarke, Donald
Exxon Mobile
1400 Old Country Rd, Ste 203
Westbury, NY 11590
516-333-3177 Fax: 516-333-3428

Clients:
Exxon Mobile Corp

Clarkson University
8 Clarkson Ave
Potsdam, NY 13699-5537
315-268-6474 Fax: 315-268-6515

Clients:
Clarkson University

Lobbyists:
Anthony G Collins
Robert H Wood, Jr

Cleary, Kevin Government Relations, LLC
111 Washington Ave, Ste 700
Albany, NY 12210
518-463-2399 Fax: 518-463-2397

Clients:
AIDS Service Network, NYC
Assn of Independent Living Inc
Assn of Psychiatric Rehabilitation Svcs (NY)
CVS/Caremark Rx
Camphill Village USA Inc
Fountain House
Medical Equipment Providers Assn (NY)
Rochester City School District
United Healthcare Services Inc
University of Rochester

Lobbyists:
Kevin J Cleary

Coalition Against Domestic Violence (NYS)
350 New Scotland Ave
Albany, NY 12208
518-482-5465 Fax: 518-482-3807

Clients:
Coalition Against Domestic Violence (NYS)

Lobbyists:
Patti Jo Newell
Sherri Salvione
Jessica Vasquez

Coalition Against Hunger (NYC)
16 Beaver St, 3rd Fl
New York, NY 10004
212-825-0028

Clients:
Coalition Against Hunger (NYC)

Offices and agencies generally appear in alphabetical order, except when specific order is requested by listee.

Lobbyists:
Joel Berg

Coalition for Children's Mental Health Services (NYS)
PO Box 7124
Albany, NY 12224-0124
518-436-8715

Clients:
Coalition for Children's Mental Health Services (NYS)

Lobbyists:
Andrea Smyth

Coalition for Education Reform & Accountability
4 Chelsea Pl
Clifton Park, NY 12065
518-383-2598 Fax: 518-383-2841

Clients:
Coalition for Education Reform & Accountability

Lobbyists:
Brian D Backstrom
Maureen Blum
Thomas W Carroll

Coalition for the Homeless
146 Washington Ave
Albany, NY 12210
518-436-5612 Fax: 518-436-5615

Clients:
Coalition for the Homeless

Lobbyists:
Mary Brosnahan-Sullivan
Lindsey Davis
Patrick Markee
Ann Nortz
Diana Olaizola
Maryann White

Coalition of Voluntary Mental Health Agencies, Inc
90 Broad St, 8th Fl
New York, NY 10004
212-742-1600 Fax: 212-742-2080

Clients:
Coalition of Voluntary Mental Health Agencies, Inc

Lobbyists:
Patricia Gallo Goldstein
Michael Polenberg
Phillip Saperia

Cobb Jr, James H
Shipping Assn, Inc (NY)
100 Wood Ave, Ste 304
Iselin, NJ 08830-2716
732-452-7808

Clients:
Shipping Association, Inc (NY)

Cohen, Marsha A
Reinsurance Assn of America
1301 Pennsylvania Ave, NW, Ste 900
Washington, DC 20004-1701
202-683-3690 Fax: 202-638-0936
e-mail: cohen@reinsurance.org
Web site: www.reinsurance.org

Clients:
Reinsurance Assn of America

Committee for an Independent Public Defense Commission
One Commerce Plaza, Ste 1900
Albany, NY 12260
518-487-7738 Fax: 518-487-7777

Clients:
Committee for an Independent Public Defense Commission

Lobbyists:
Michael Whiteman

Community Advocacy & Advisory Services
247 Lark St, 1st Fl
Albany, NY 12210
518-449-2772 Fax: 518-449-2710
e-mail: kmk@communityadvocacy.com
Web site: www.communityadvocacy.com

Clients:
AIDS Day Services Assn Advocacy Committee
Prevent Child Abuse New York

Lobbyists:
Christine Deyss
Charles King
Michael Kink

Community Health Care Association of NYS
254 West 31st St, 9th Fl
New York, NY 10001
212-279-9686
e-mail: kbreslin@chcanys.org
Web site: www.chcanys.org

Clients:
Community Health Care Association of NYS

Lobbyists:
Katherine Breslin

Offices and agencies generally appear in alphabetical order, except when specific order is requested by listee.

LOBBYISTS

Beverly Grossman
Elizabeth Swain

Community Healthcare
79 Madison Ave, 6th Fl
New York, NY 10016
212-366-4500 Fax: 212-366-4616
Web site: www.chnnyc.org

Clients:
Community Healthcare Network

Lobbyists:
Catherine Abate
Elizabeth Howell
Phuong Tran

Community Preservation Corporation (The)
28 East 28th St, 9th Fl
New York, NY 10016-7943
212-869-5300 x511 Fax: 212-683-0694
e-mail: mlappin@communityp.com
Web site: www.communityp.com

Clients:
Community Preservation Corporation (The)

Lobbyists:
Barbara Baer
Kathleen Dunn
Richard A Kumro
Michael D Lappin
John M McCarthy
Brenda Ratliff

Community Voices Heard
170 East 116th St, Ste 1E
New York, NY 10029
212-860-6001 Fax: 212-996-9481

Clients:
Community Voices Heard

Lobbyists:
David Dodge
Anita Graham
Alexa Kasdan
Henry Serrano
Sondra Youdelman

Compensation Action Network (NY)
5784 Widewaters Pkwy, 1st Fl
Dewitt, NY 13214
800-962-7950

Clients:
Compensation Action Network (NY)

Lobbyists:
Lawrence Gilroy
Richard Poppa

Conference of Mayors & Municipal Officials (NYS)
119 Washington Ave
Albany, NY 12210
518-463-1185

Clients:
Conference of Mayors & Municipal Officials (NYS)

Lobbyists:
Peter Baynes
Wade Beltramo
Mary Carmel
Lynn Flansburg
John H Galligan
Donna M C Giliberto
Jennifer Mabee
Lynn Marco
Riele Morgiewicz
Jennifer Purcell
Barbara Van Epps
Deanna Walker

Connelly & McLaughlin
64 Fulton St
New York, NY 10038
212-437-7373

Clients:
50 West Street Development LLC
Alexico Management Group
BFC Construction Corp
Building Trades Employers Assn
Cadence Cycling & Multisport Centers
Chetrit Group (The)
Chip-Community Housing Improvement Program, Inc
Clarke's Group (The)
CMT-Creative Mobile Technology
Cohen Brothers Realty & Construction
Corporate Housing Providers Association
Douglaston Development LLC
Edward J Minskoff Equities, Inc
Entertainment Software Association
General Contractors Assn of NY, Inc (The)
Hunter College
Independence Plaza Associates LLC (FKA Stellar Management)
Metro Terminals Corporation
Metropolitan Taxicab Board of Trade
Millennium Partners
Oil Heating Assn (NY)
Philips International Holding Corp/40 Rector Owners LLC
RFR Holding Corp
SDS Investments LLC
Seventh Regiment Armory Conservancy
Starrett City Associates
Strategic 56 LP
Truffles LLC/Jackson Parker Co
Valeray Real Estate Company, Inc

Lobbyists:
Maureen Connelly
Kathy Cudahy
Martin McLaughlin
Michael Woloz

Offices and agencies generally appear in alphabetical order, except when specific order is requested by listee.

LOBBYISTS

Connelly Communications, Inc
64 Fulton St
New York, NY 10038
212-437-7373

Clients:
Doctors Council

Lobbyists:
Maureen Connelly
Michael Woloz

Constantinople & Vallone Consulting LLC (FKA Constantinople Consulting)
123 William St, 22nd Fl
New York, NY 10038
212-393-6500 Fax: 212-393-6501
e-mail: constantinople@worldnet.att.net

Clients:
151-45 Sixth Road Whitestone Partners LLC
380 Development LLC
43rd Ave Development LLC
Agusta & Ross
Bartlett Dairy Inc
Boymelgreen Developers LLC
Coach USA
Commerce Bank
Eagle One Roofing Contractors Inc
First City Developers Incorp
Jackson Development Group LTD
Junior Tennis League (NY)
K Hovnanian Companies NE Inc
LB Northeast Developers Vistamar Complex LTD
LLJ Realty Corp
Plaza 75 Realty Inc
Sapir Organization
Sports & Arts in Schools Foundation
St. Michael's Cemetery
TA Ahern Contractors/Ahern Painting
Tully Construction
Waste Management
Willets Point Industrial & Realty Corp

Lobbyists:
Anthony J Constantinople III
Anthony J Constantinople, Jr
Raymond Frier
Laura Imperiale
Paul Vallone
Peter F Vallone, Sr

Conway, Gerard L, Jr
Plug Power, Inc
968 Albany Shaker Rd
Latham, NY 12110
518-782-7700 Fax: 518-690-4446
e-mail: gerard.conway@plugpower.com
Web site: www.plugpower.com

Clients:
Plug Power Inc

Lobbyists:
Robert Berger
John Elter
Katrina Fritz Intwala
Roger Saillant

Coppola Ryan McHugh Riddell
119 Washington Avenue, 2nd Fl
Albany, NY 12210
518-434-7400 Fax: 518-434-0558
e-mail: crmlobby@aol.com
Web site: www.nylobbyist.com

Clients:
Aeralert US, LLC
Air Pegasus
America Online (AOL)
Assn of Convenience Stores (NY)
Assn of Mortgage Brokers (NY)
Assn of Surrogate's & Supreme Court Reporters
BJK Inc/dba Chem Rx
Building & Realty Institute of Westchester & Mid-Hudson Region
C&S Engineers Inc
Catskill Regional Off-Track Betting Corporation
Children's Institute
Exxon Mobil Corporation
Group for Equitable Tax Practices
Law School Admission Council
Mastercard International Inc
McDonald's Corporation
Metropolitan Transportation Authority
NRG Energy Inc
New York Chiropractic Political Action Fund
Norfolk Southern Corporation
Oppidan Investment Company (Ewald Consulting)
Pfizer Inc
Reckitt Benckiser Inc
Supreme Court Officers Assn (NYS)
Trustees of Columbia University in City of NY (The)
Verizon
Williams Companies (The)

Lobbyists:
Charles Coppola
Diana Georgia
Patrick J McHugh
Glenn T Riddell

Coppola, John J
ASAPNYS
1 Columbia St
Albany, NY 12207
518-426-3122 Fax: 518-426-1046
e-mail: jcoppola@asapnys.org
Web site: www.asapnys.org

Clients:
Assn of Alcoholism & Substance Abuse Providers Inc (NY)

Cordo, John
99 Pine St
Albany, NY 12207
518-436-0786

Offices and agencies generally appear in alphabetical order, except when specific order is requested by listee.

LOBBYISTS

Clients:
Cigar Assn of America Inc
Swisher International, Inc

Corning Place Consulting, LLC
121 State St
Albany, NY 12207-0693
518-432-9086

Clients:
Assn of Proprietary Colleges
Home Care Assn of NYS, Inc
NYSCOP Inc

Lobbyists:
Mark Amodeo
Basil Anastassiou

Couch White, LLP
540 Broadway
PO Box 22222
Albany, NY 12201
518-426-4600 Fax: 518-426-0376
e-mail: bbrenner@couchwhite.com
Web site: www.couchwhite.com

Clients:
Regional Interconnect, Inc (NY)

Lobbyists:
Leonard Singer

Council for Community Behavioral Healthcare
155 Washington Ave, 2nd Fl
Albany, NY 12210
518-445-2642 Fax: 518-445-2642

Clients:
Council for Community Behavioral Healthcare

Lobbyists:
Lauri Cole

Council of Senior Ctrs & Services of NYC, Inc
49 W 45th St, 7th Fl
New York, NY 10036
212-398-6565 Fax: 212-398-8395

Clients:
Council of Senior Ctrs & Services of NYC, Inc

Lobbyists:
Bobbie Sackman

Council of the City of New York (The)
111 Washington Ave, Ste 410
Albany, NY 12210-2208
518-462-5461 Fax: 518-462-1398
Web site: www.council.nyc.ny.us

Clients:
Council of the City of New York (The)

Lobbyists:
Rodney Capel
Natasha Kerry

Crane & Vacco, LLC
90 State St, Ste 1507
Albany, NY 12207
518-426-0606 Fax: 518-432-0086

Clients:
American Racing & Entertainment, LLC
ARE-East River Science Park LLC
Cable Telecommunications Assn of NY, Inc (The)
Council of School Supervisors & Administrators
Delaware North Companies, Inc
Duane Reade, Inc
Empire Racing Associates
Institutional Life Markets Association, Inc
Ivy Street Development Corp
Judge Rotenberg Center
Library Association (NY)
MetSchools, Inc
St Regis Mohawk Tribe (Empire Resorts Inc)
The New York Children's Vision Coalition
United NY Ambulance Network

Lobbyists:
Constance Crane
James B Crane
Andrea Debow
Christopher Duryea
Andrea Kosier
George Penn
Steven Sanders
Dennis Vacco

Credit Union League Inc & Affiliates (NYS)
19 British American Blvd
Latham, NY 12110
518-437-8122 Fax: 518-782-4212

Clients:
Members United Corporate FCU (Formerly Empire Corporate FCU)

Lobbyists:
Joseph Herbst
Amy Hines-Kramer
Michael Lanotte
William Mellin
Dirck VanDeusen

Crosier, Barbara V
United Cerebral Palsy Assn of NYS
90 State St, Ste 929
Albany, NY 12207
518-436-0178 Fax: 518-436-8619
e-mail: bcrosier@cerebralpalsynys.org
Web site: www.cerebralpalsynys.org

Clients:
United Cerebral Palsy Assns of NYS

Offices and agencies generally appear in alphabetical order, except when specific order is requested by listee.

LOBBYISTS

Lobbyists:
Michael Alvaro
Susan Constantino
Joanne Genovese

Crossett, Susan M
300 Erie Blvd W
Syracuse, NY 13202
315-428-5430 Fax: 315-428-3406
e-mail: susan.crossett@us.ngrid.com
Web site: www.niagaramohawk.com

Clients:
Niagara Mohawk Holdings & Power Co (dba National Grid)

Lobbyists:
William Flynn

Curran, Brian F
Public Employees Federation
100 State St
Albany, NY 12207-1806
518-432-4003 Fax: 518-432-7739
e-mail: bcurran@pef.org

Clients:
Public Employees Federation (NYS)

Lobbyists:
Kenneth Brynien
Ryan Delgado
John Murphy

D'Ambrosio, John A
Orange County Chamber of Commerce
11 Racquet Rd
Newburgh, NY 12550
845-567-6229

Clients:
Orange County Chamber of Commerce (The)

Lobbyists:
Debra Bogdanski

D'Onofrio, Paul
67 Chestnut St
Albany, NY 12210
518-432-7393

Clients:
Assn of Electrical Workers (NYS)
Council of Sheet Metal Workers Int'l Assn (NYS)
Monticello Raceway Management Inc

Dadey, Dick
Citizens Union of NYC
299 Broadway, Ste 700
New York, NY 10007
212-227-0342 Fax: 212-227-0345

Clients:
Citizens Union of the City of New York

Lobbyists:
Doug Israel

Dahill, Kevin
1383 Veterans Memorial Hwy, Ste 26
Hauppauge, NY 11788
631-435-3000 Fax: 631-435-2343
Web site: www.nshc.org

Clients:
Nassau-Suffolk Hospital Council Inc

Lobbyists:
Paul Rowland

Dames, Reid, LLC
1285 6th Ave, 35th Fl
New York, NY 10019
212-554-4244 Fax: 212-554-4245

Clients:
Alzheimer's Assn, NYC Chapter
Arthritis Foundation (NY Chapter)
Coalition of Behavioral Health Agencies, Inc (The) (FKA Coalition of Voluntary Mental Health Agen)
Diaspora Community Services
Empire State Pride Agenda
Heights Hill Mental Health Services Community Advisory Board Inc
Human Services Council of NYC
Institute for Community Living
Jewish Board of Family & Children's Services Inc
Job Path
Mental Health Assn of NYC (The)
National Assn of Social Workers (NYC Chapter)
Safe Horizon
Therapeutic Communities Assn of NY Inc
Women in Need Inc

Lobbyists:
Cynthia Dames
Lisa Reid

Dan Klores Communications Inc
386 Park Ave South, 10th Fl
New York, NY 10016
212-685-4300

Clients:
Cable Television & Telecommunications Assn of NY

Lobbyists:
William Cunningham
John Marino

Darwak, Stephanie
3 Independence Row
Stillwater, NY 12170
518-664-5880

Offices and agencies generally appear in alphabetical order, except when specific order is requested by listee.

LOBBYISTS

Clients:
Pfizer, Inc

Davidoff, Malito & Hutcher, LLP
150 State St, 4th Fl
Albany, NY 12207
518-465-8230 Fax: 518-465-8230

Clients:
Abbott Laboratories
Adelphi University
Altria Corporate Services Inc
American Society for Dermatological Surgery
American Tax Funding Servicing LLC
Association of Water & Sewer Excavators, Inc
Astor Terrace Condominium
Astroland, Inc
Augusta & Ross
Authentix Inc
Boundary Fence & Railing Systems, Inc
Camarda Realty Investments
Certified Lumber
Certilman Balin Adler & Hyman, LLP
Child Center of New York
City Bar Justice Center
Clear Channel Outdoor
Columbia Grammar & Preparatory School
Construction Materials Association (NY)
Council of School Supervisors & Administrators
Court Reporters Association
Crystal Window & Door Systems, LTD
Cyclone Coasters, Inc
Data Trace Information Services, LLC
Diamond Asphalt Corp.
Docking Pilots of NJ/NY
Election Systems & Software Inc
Epilepsy Foundation of Long Island
Fairmont Capital LLC
Family Support Systems Unlimited, Inc
Ferrara Bros. Building Materials Corp.
First American Property Information & Services Grp
Greater Jamaica Development Corporation
Greater NY Hospital Assn
Helen Keller Services for the Blind
Hillside Manor Rehabilitation & Extended Care Center, LLC
IDT Corporation
Incorporated Village of Freeport (The)
Incorporated Village of Westbury (The)
International Bottled Water Association
Life Insurance Settlement Association
Lowell School
Megrant Corporation
Mental Health Association of Nassau County
Nassau County Village Officials Assn
National Center for Disability Services
National Foundation for Teaching Entreprenership
Nestle Waters North America Holdings Inc
Palladia Inc (Formerly Project Return Foundation Inc)
Polytechnic University
Queens Borough Public Library
Queens Botanical Garden
Rainbow Chimes Inc, Child Care Ctr
RCN
S & J Sheet Metal Supply, Inc
Source Financing Corp
South Queens Boys & Girls Club, Inc
St John's Hospital/Yonkers General Hospital
St Vincent Catholic Medical Centers
Staffing Assn (NY)
Taxicab Service Assn
Thoroughbred Racing-New York (Vornado Realty Trust)
Ticket brokers (NY)
Touro College
Town of North Hempstead
United Charities Corporation
Vision Rehabilitation Assn (NYVRA) (NY)
Web Holdings
Westbury Union Free School District
Westchester County Health Care Corp
WSHU Public Radio (Long Island Friends of WSUF)
YAI/National Institute for People with Disabilities

Lobbyists:
Jeff Citron
Peter R Crouse
Sean Crowley
Sid Davidoff
Arthur Goldstein
John B Kiernan
Robert J Malito
Stephen A Malito
Ricardo Oquendo
Juan Reyes
Keith Sernick
Howard Weiss

Davis, Michael J
6790 Lainhart Rd
Altamont, NY 12009
518-356-1508
e-mail: mdavis10@rdg.boehringer-ingelheim.com

Clients:
Boehringer Ingelheim Pharmaceuticals, Inc

Demos:A Network for Ideas & Action
220 Fifth Ave, 5th Fl
New York, NY 10001
212-633-1405

Clients:
Demos:A Network for Ideas & Action

Lobbyists:
Steven Carbo
Miles Rapoport

Deutsch, Ronald
212 Great Oaks Blvd
Albany, NY 12203
518-452-2130

Clients:
New Yorkers for Fiscal Fairness

Offices and agencies generally appear in alphabetical order, except when specific order is requested by listee.

LOBBYISTS

Dewey Ballantine LLP
1301 Avenue of the Americas
New York, NY 10019-6022
212-259-8000

Clients:
New York Racing Assn Inc (The)
General Electric Co

Lobbyists:
Mary Caplan
Andrew Kentz
Kevin O'Connor
Eamon O'Kelly
Bradford Race

DiPalermo, Christian
NY'ers for Parks
355 Lexington Ave, 14th Fl
New York, NY 10017
212-838-9410 Fax: 212-371-6048

Clients:
New Yorkers for Parks

Lobbyists:
Micaela Birmingham
Sheelah Fienberg
Okenfe Lebarty

Diamond Asphalt Corp
91 Paidge Ave
Brooklyn, NY 11222
718-383-4198

Clients:
Diamond Asphalt Corp

Lobbyists:
John Labozza

Digiovanni, Joseph
Liberty Mutual Group
175 Berkeley St
Boston, MA 02117
617-357-9500 Fax: 617-574-5783
Web site: www.libertymutual.com

Clients:
Liberty Mutual Group

Diorio, L Todd
451 Little Britian Rd
Newburgh, NY 12550
845-565-2737

Clients:
Hudson Valley Building & Construction Trades Council
Laborers Int'l Union of North America AFL-CIO, Local 17

District Council 37, AFSCME
125 Barclay St
New York, NY 10007
212-815-1500 Fax: 212-815-1516
Web site: www.district37.net

Clients:
District Council 37, AFSCME

Lobbyists:
Leonard Allen
Susan Graham
Oliver Gray
Wanda Williams

Donnellan, James
Metropolitan Life Ins Co
27-01 Queens Plz N, Area 4D
Long Island City, NY 11101-4015
212-578-3968

Clients:
Metropolitan Life Insurance Co

Lobbyists:
Robert Henrikson
Ellie Jurado-Nieves
James L Lipscomb
Joseph Reali
Timothy Ring
Michael Zarcone

Donnelly, Edwin
AFL-CIO (NYS)
100 S Swan St
Albany, NY 12210
518-436-8516 Fax: 516-436-8470
e-mail: edonnelly@nysaflcio.org
Web site: www.nysaflcio.org

Clients:
AFL-CIO (NYS)

Lobbyists:
Denis Hughes
Arthur Wilcox

Donohue, Gavin J
Independent Power Prod of NY
19 Dove St, Ste 302
Albany, NY 12210
518-436-3749 Fax: 518-436-0369
e-mail: gavin@ippny.org
Web site: www.ippny.org

Clients:
Independent Power Producers of NY Inc

Lobbyists:
Radmila Miletich

Offices and agencies generally appear in alphabetical order, except when specific order is requested by listee.

LOBBYISTS

Doyle, Michael R
NYS Petroleum Council
150 State St
Albany, NY 12207-1675
518-465-3563 Fax: 518-465-4022
e-mail: doylem@api.org
Web site: www.api.org

Clients:
American Petroleum Institute

Lobbyists:
Cathy A Kenny

Dryfoos Group
444 Park Ave South, Ste 301
New York, NY 10016
646-742-3715 Fax: 718-786-7633
e-mail: bob@thedryfoosgroup.com

Clients:
ASPCA
Big Brothers Big Sisters of NYC
Brooklyn Children's Museum
Community Works
Ctr for Educational Innovation-Public Education Assn
Harmonie Ensemble/New York
Inside Broadway
Institute for Student Achievement
Junior Tennis League (NY)
Midori and Friends
Performance Space 122
Shareing & Careing Inc
Sports & Arts in School Foundation
Young Women's Leadership Foundation

Lobbyists:
Paul E Greenfield
Laura Jean Hawkins
Synge Maher
Carol Swift

Dudley Associates P.C.
146 State Street
Albany, NY 12207
518-463-2203 Fax: 518-449-4941
e-mail: dudleyassoc@worldnet.att.net

Clients:
Albany College of Pharmacy
American Standard Company
Florence Covell
Trial Lawyers' Assn (NYS)
UST Public Affairs Inc

Lobbyists:
David R Dudley
Kathleen M Haggerty

Duncan, Craig A
127 Eastern Union Tpk
Averill Park, NY 12018
518-674-5261

Clients:
Northeast Health & Affiliates

Dunne, Richard C
15 Trues Dr
West Islip, NY 11795
631-422-1320

Clients:
Northrop Grumman Corporation

E-3 Communications
43 Court St, Ste 910
Buffalo, NY 14202
716-854-8182 Fax: 716-852-6985
Web site: www.e3communications.com

Clients:
Apsire of WNY
Capitol Hill Management Services
Centerstone Development LLC
Independent Oil & Gas Assn of NY
NOCO Energy Corp
Niagara Tourism & Convention Corp
Power for Economic Prosperity Group

Lobbyists:
Margaret Duffy
Earl Wells

Economic Development Council Inc (NYS)
19 Dove St, Ste 101
Albany, NY 12210
518-426-4058 Fax: 518-426-4059
e-mail: mcmahon@nysedc.org
Web site: www.nysedc.org

Clients:
Economic Development Council Inc (NYS)

Lobbyists:
Brian T McMahon

Educational Conference Board (NYS)
NYS Assn of School Business Officials
7 Elk St
Albany, NY 12207-1002
518-434-2281 Fax: 518-434-1303

Clients:
Educational Conference Board (NYS)

Lobbyists:
Maria Dewald
Timothy Kremer
Alan Lubin
Edward McCormick
Steven Van Hoesen

Offices and agencies generally appear in alphabetical order, except when specific order is requested by listee.

LOBBYISTS

Elinski, Karen
TIAA/CREF
730 Third Ave
New York, NY 10017-3206
212-916-6476 Fax: 212-916-5952
e-mail: kelinski@tiaa-creff.org
Web site: www.tiaa-cref.org

Clients:
College Retirement Equities Fund Teachers Ins & Annuity Assn

Lobbyists:
Malcolm O Campbell

Empire State College, State University of NY
1 Union Ave
Saratoga Springs, NY 12866
518-587-2100 Fax: 518-587-2886
e-mail: marycaroline.powers@esc.edu
Web site: www.esc.edu

Clients:
Empire State College, State University of NY

Lobbyists:
Joseph B Moore
Mary Powers

Empire State Forest Products Association
828 Washington Ave
Albany, NY 12203
518-463-1297 Fax: 518-426-9502
Web site: www.esfpa.org

Clients:
Empire State Forest Products Association

Lobbyists:
Kevin King

Employer Alliance for Affordable Health Care
PO Box 1412
Albany, NY 12201-1412
518-462-2296 Fax: 518-462-2150
Web site: employeralliance.com

Clients:
Employer Alliance for Affordable Health Care

Lobbyists:
Jeffrey Leland

Energy Assn of NYS (The)
111 Washington Ave, Ste 601
Albany, NY 12210-2276
518-449-3440 Fax: 518-449-3446

Clients:
Energy Assn of NYS (The)

Lobbyists:
Patrick Curran
Sharon Foley

Entergy Nuclear Operations, Inc
440 Hamilton Ave
White Plains, NY 10601
914-272-3350

Clients:
Entergy Nuclear Operations, Inc

Lobbyists:
Debbie Fay
Joanne Fernandez
Michael Kansler
Michael Slobodien
Jim Steets
Kenneth Theobalds

Enterprise Rent-A-Car
1550 Route 23 North
Wayne, NJ 07470
973-709-2396 Fax: 973-709-2455

Clients:
Enterprise Rent-A-Car

Lobbyists:
Thomas Cantilli
John Carmichael
Judson Church
Tomi Gerber
Dean Thompson

Environmental Advocates of NY
353 Hamilton St
Albany, NY 12210
518-462-5526

Clients:
Environmental Advocates of NY

Lobbyists:
David Gahl
Erica Gulseth
Robert Moore
Katherine Nacleau
Erica Ringewald
Tim Sweeney

Equinox Inc
95 Central Ave
Albany, NY 12206
518-434-6135 Fax: 518-432-5607
e-mail: mseeley@equinoxinc.org
Web site: www.equinoxinc.org

Clients:
Equinox Inc

Lobbyists:
Wendy Ball

Offices and agencies generally appear in alphabetical order, except when specific order is requested by listee.

LOBBYISTS

Alicia Borns
Shalon Davis
Jaclyn Dechiro
Bernadette Felch
Danyelle Gipson
Mark Holeman
Maribel Jerominek
Kathy Magee
Claudia Mendonca
Kim Ploussard
Ramona Ramos
Christine Rodriguez
Carolyn Schimanski
Mary Seeley
Caitlin Sutton

Ewashko, John J
111 Washington Ave, Ste 700
Albany, NY 12210
518-434-8435 Fax: 518-434-8462

Clients:
Eli Lilly & Co

Lobbyists:
Steve Abington
Tamara Atkins
Victor Gladstone
Vince Matteo

Fahey, William C
3 Gannett Dr
Ste 400
White Plains, NY 10604
914-323-7000 Fax: 914-323-7001

Clients:
School Bus Contractors Assn (NY)

Faist Government Affairs Group, LLC
54 Willett St
Albany, NY 12210-1104
518-432-0599 Fax: 518-449-2294
e-mail: tfaist@aol.com

Clients:
American Int'l Grp, Inc
Combined Life Insurance Co of NY
Council of Insurance Brokers of Greater NY, Inc
Chemical Alliance (NYS)
Guardian Life Insurance Co of America
National Assn of Health Underwriters
Partnership for NYC, Inc

Lobbyists:
Thomas W Faist

Families Together in NYS Inc
737 Madison Ave
Albany, NY 12208
518-432-0333 Fax: 518-434-6478
Web site: www.ftnys.org

Clients:
Families Together in NYS Inc

Lobbyists:
Ruth Foster
Paige MacDonald

Farrell, Pamela
30 Rockefeller Plaza
New York, NY 10112
212-664-2823

Clients:
General Electric Co

Lobbyists:
Mark Colananni
Amy Eisenstadt
Tom Feist
Brian O'Leary
Scott Roberti
Kay Schmidt
Jerry Trant
Frank Yanover

Fashion Institute of Technology
Seventh Ave @ 27th St
New York, NY 10001-5992
212-217-7637 Fax: 212-217-7639
Web site: www.fitnyc.edu

Clients:
Fashion Institute of Technology

Lobbyists:
Joanne Arbuckle
Joyce F Brown
Herbert Cohen
Judith Ellis
Edwin A Goodman
Reginetta Haboucha
Alan Kane
Loretta Lawrence Keane
Harvey Spector
Lisa Wager

Fassler, Michael S
Beth Abraham Family Health Svcs
612 Allerton Ave
Bronx, NY 10467-7404
718-519-4001

Clients:
Beth Abraham Family of Health Services

Lobbyists:
Susan Aldrich

Featherstonhaugh Wiley Clyne & Cordo, LLP
99 Pine St
Albany, NY 12207
518-436-0786 Fax: 518-427-0452

Offices and agencies generally appear in alphabetical order, except when specific order is requested by listee.

LOBBYISTS

Clients:
1199 SEIU United Healthcare Workers East
1199/SEIU & GNYHA Healthcare Education Project
AAA New York State Inc
Academy of Trial Lawyers (NYS)
Ambulette Coalition Inc (NY)
American Alternative Fuels
Assn of Cemeteries (NYS)
Beer Wholesalers Association Inc (NYS) (Steven W Harris, LLC)
Bottlers Assn (NYS)
Building Congress (NY) (The)
Campaign for Fiscal Equity, Inc
Careplus, LLC
Charmer Industries, Inc
Cigar Assn of America Inc
Consortium for Worker Education (The)
Construction Ind Cncl of Westchester & Hudson Valley Inc
Cornerstone Real Estate Advisers LLC
Council for the Humanities (NY)
District Council of Carpenter's PAC (NYC) (Formerly Carpenters Civil Action Fund (NYC))
Dormitory Authority of the State of NY
Empire Merchants, LLC
Empire State Mortgage Bankers Assn
Entergy Nuclear Operations Inc
Feld Entertainment, Inc
Free Community Papers of NY
General Contractors Association of NY, Inc (The)
Goldman Sachs Group, Inc (The)
Gtech Corporation
Hotel Trades Council (NY)
Institute for Integrative Nutrition
Liberty Election Systems
Long Island Contractor's Assn
Medco Health Solutions Inc (Formerly Merck-Medco Managed Care, LLC)
Metropolitan Life Insurance Co
New Yorkers for Justice
Peerless Importers
Property Casualty Insurers Association of America (PCIAA)
Roadway Improvement Coalition (NY)
Saratoga Harness Racing Inc
Society of Physician Assistants (NYS)
Spectra Architecture, Engineering & Surveying PC
Stock Exchange Group (NY)
Thoroughbred Horsemen's Assn Inc (NY)
Tracfone Wireless Inc
Transportation Engineering Alliance (NYS)
Unite Here
Visiting Nurse Service of NY

Lobbyists:
Elizabeth K Clyne
John Cordo
Jennifer Cunningham
Denise DiPace
James D Featherstonhaugh
David F Fleming, Jr
Stephen Hanse
John L Hardy
Steven Harris
Stephen D Morgan
Elizabeth O'Flaherty
Bryan Poole

Federation of Protestant Welfare Agencies Inc
281 Park Ave South
New York, NY 10010
212-801-1311
e-mail: fgoldman@fpwa.org
Web site: www.fpwa.org

Clients:
Federation of Protestant Welfare Agencies Inc

Lobbyists:
Caitlyn Brazill
Kathleen Fitzgibbons
Fatima Goldman
Rachelle House
Terri Jackson
Esther Lok
Vani Sankarapandian
Jillynn Stevens

Feld Entertainment
8607 Westwood Center Dr
Vienna, VA 22182
703-749-5570

Clients:
Feld Entertainment, Inc

Lobbyists:
Thomas Albert
Cassie Folk

Ferris, William E
AARP
One Commerce Plaza, Ste 706
Albany, NY 12260
518-434-4194 Fax: 518-434-6949
e-mail: wferris@aarp.org
Web site: www.aarp.org/ny

Clients:
AARP

Lobbyists:
William E Ferris
David T McNally

Fisher Development Strategies
21 Choir Lane
Westbury, NY 11590
516-238-0186

Clients:
Nassau Community College
Nassau County Firefighters Museum & Education Ctr
Chamber Players International

Lobbyists:
Daniel M Fisher, Jr

Fitzgerald, Gary J
Iroquois Healthcare Alliance
17 Halfmoon Executive Park Dr
Clifton Park, NY 12065

Offices and agencies generally appear in alphabetical order, except when specific order is requested by listee.

LOBBYISTS

518-383-5060 Fax: 518-383-2616
e-mail: gfitzgerald@iroquois.org
Web site: www.iroquois.org

Clients:
Iroquois Healthcare Alliance

Fitzpatrick, Christine M
Adult Day Hlth Care Cncl
150 State St, Ste 301
Albany, NY 12207-1698
518-449-2707 x130 Fax: 518-449-8210
e-mail: cfitzpatrick@nyahsa.org
Web site: www.nyahsa.org

Clients:
Adult Day Health Care Council (ADHCC)

Food Industry Alliance of NYS Inc
130 Washington Ave
Albany, NY 12210
518-434-1900 Fax: 518-434-9962

Clients:
New Yorkers for Real Recycling Reform (Food Industry Alliance of NYS Inc)

Lobbyists:
Patricia Brodhagen
James T Rogers
Michael E Rosen

Frank, Robin
Healthcare Assn of NYS
One Empire Dr
Rensselaer, NY 12144
518-431-7600

Clients:
Healthcare Association of NYS

Lobbyists:
Renee Bernard
Karen Bonilla
Jennifer Carter
Ju-Ming Chang
Kathleen Ciccone
Joanne Cunningham
Julia Donnaruma
Rose Duhan
Jeffrey Gold
Stephen Harwell
Frederick Heigel
Nicholas Henley
Darcie Hurteau
Steven Kroll
Nancy Landor
Debora Lebarron
Cindy Levernois
Edward McGill
Stacey Montalto
Robert McLeod
Molly Poleto
Karen Roach
Lee Santos
Daniel Sisto
Christopher Smith
Raymond Sweeney
Mary Therriault
William Van Slyke
Shelby Wafer
Sue Ellen Wagner
Ruth Welch
Mary Jane Wurth

Fried Frank Harris Shriver & Jacobson, LLP
One New York Plaza
New York, NY 10004-1980
212-859-8102

Clients:
AGB 15th Street LLC
Dermot Company (The)
Durst Organization (The)
Forest City Ratner Companies
Georgetown Company
Joseph P Day Realty Corp
Park Tower Group
Pulte Homes of NY Inc
R/V Moynihan Station Developer LLC
R Squared LLC

Lobbyists:
Adrienne Bernard
Frank Chaney
Stephen Lefkowitz
Melanie Meyers
Paulina Williams

Friedell, Andrew
1434 Narragansett Blvd
Cranston, RI 02905
401-941-9720

Clients:
Medco Health Solutions, Inc

Friedman, John P
USAA
325 Columbia Tpk
Florham Park, NJ 07932
973-377-6662 Fax: 973-377-6607
e-mail: john.friedman@usaa.com

Clients:
United Services Automobile Assn (USAA)

Friedman, Michael B
12 Old Mamaroneck Rd
White Plains, NY 10605
914-686-2886 Fax: 914-948-4956
e-mail: mbfriedman@aol.com

Clients:
Mental Health Association of NYC, Inc

Offices and agencies generally appear in alphabetical order, except when specific order is requested by listee.

Mental Health Assn of Westchester Co, Inc

Funeral Directors Assn Inc (NYS)
426 New Karner Rd
Albany, NY 12205
518-452-8230 Fax: 518-452-8667
e-mail: info@nysfda.org
Web site: www.nysfda.org

Clients:
Funeral Directors Assn Inc (NYS)

Lobbyists:
Bonnie L McCullough
Randy L McCullough

Gallo, Richard J
123 State St
Albany, NY 12207-1622
518-465-3545 Fax: 518-465-3584
e-mail: rjgallo@msn.com

Clients:
Davita Inc
Psychiatric Assn Inc (NYS)

Gaughran, James F
191 New York Ave
Huntington, NY 11743
631-385-7004

Clients:
CSC Holdings Inc

Gay Men's Health Crisis Inc
119 W 24th St
New York, NY 10011-1995
212-367-1250 Fax: 212-367-1247
e-mail: ronaldj@gmhc.org
Web site: www.gmhc.org

Clients:
Gay Men's Health Crisis Inc

Lobbyists:
Gina Arias
Robert Bank
Daryl Cochrane
Marjorie Hill
Michelle O'Brien
Nancy Ordover
Janet Weinberg
Darryl Ng

Geiger, Bruce W & Associates
120 Washington Ave, Ste 100
Albany, NY 12210
518-432-1607 Fax: 518-463-5301

Clients:
Aviation Management Assn (NY)
City Highway Superintendents Assn (NYS)
Dollar Thrifty Automotive Group Inc
Long Island Gasoline Retailers Assn Inc
Nurse Practitioners Assn of NYS (The)
Pinelawn Cemetery
Refinance.com
Snowmobile Assn (NYS)

Lobbyists:
Bruce W Geiger

General Motors Corporation
MC 482-C27-D21
PO Box 300
Detroit, MI 48265-3000
313-665-2979

Clients:
General Motors Corporation

Lobbyists:
Bruce Edwards
Eric Henning
Pam Hughes
Jim Kiley

Genovese, Marta
1415 Kellum Place
Garden City, NY 11530-1690
516-873-2259 Fax: 516-873-2355
e-mail: mgenovese@aaany.com
Web site: www.aaanys.com

Clients:
AAA New York State Inc
Automobile Club of New York Inc

Lobbyists:
John A Corlett
Antoanela Vaccaro
Edward Welsh

Gergela III, Joseph
Long Island Farm Bureau
104 Edwards Ave, Ste 3
Calverton, NY 11933
631-727-3777

Clients:
Long Island Farm Bureau

Geto & deMilly Inc
130 East 40th St, 16th Fl
New York, NY 10016-1726

Offices and agencies generally appear in alphabetical order, except when specific order is requested by listee.

LOBBYISTS

212-686-4551 Fax: 212-213-6850
e-mail: pr@getodemilly.com
Web site: www.getodemilly.com

Clients:
122 Greenwich Owner LLC
AMDeC Foundation Inc
Brodsky Organization
Callen-Lorde Community Health Ctr
Ctr Against Domestic Violence
Common Ground Community Inc
East River Realty Company LLC
Eldridge Street Project
Forest City Ratner Companies
Jewish Home and Hospital for the Aged (The)
Plumbing Foundation of the City of NY
Refinery LLC (CPC Resorces Inc)
SJP Properties
SJP Residential Properties
Taconic Investment Partners LLC
Toll Brooklyn LP
W2001Z/15CPW Realty LLC
West 60th Street Associates LLC/West End Enterprises LLC

Lobbyists:
Joyce Baumgarten
Ethan Geto
Julie Hendricks
Peter Krokondelas
Phil Lentz
Michele deMilly

Gilberti Stinziano Heintz & Smith, PC
555 E Genesee St
Syracuse, NY 13202-2159
518-476-2001

Clients:
Catskill Off-Track Betting Corporation
Center for Jewish History (The)
Gomez Foundation for Mill House
General Society of Mechanics & Tradesmen of the City of NY (The)
Museum of Arts and Design
Solomon R Guggenheim Museum

Lobbyists:
Tarky Lombardi, Jr
Carol Philippi

Gilligan, Donald
610 Mountain St
Sharon, MA 02067
781-793-0250 Fax: 781-793-0600
e-mail: donaldg@ma.ultranet.com

Clients:
Nat'l Assn of Energy Service Companies

Glusko, John P
Central Hudson Gas & Elec
284 South Ave
Poughkeepsie, NY 12601
845-486-5218 Fax: 845-486-5544
e-mail: jglusko@cenhud.com
Web site: www.cenhud.com

Clients:
Central Hudson Gas & Electric Corp

Lobbyists:
Steven Lant
Denise VanBuren

Golden, Ben
NYSARC
393 Delaware Ave
Delmar, NY 12054-3094
518-439-8311

Clients:
Arc Inc (NYS)

Lobbyists:
John Kemmer
Tania Seaburg
John Von Ahn

Goldman, Gerald
10 East 40th St, Ste 1308
New York, NY 10016
212-268-1911 Fax: 201-487-3954

Clients:
Financial Service Centers of NY, Inc

Lobbyists:
Richard Smith

Goodwin, Jeffrey
Group Health Incorporated
441 9th Ave
New York, NY 10001-1681
212-615-0891 Fax: 212-563-8561
e-mail: jgoodwin@ghi.com

Clients:
Group Health Incorporated

Lobbyists:
Frank J Branchini
Ilene Margolin
William Mastro
Aran Ron

Greater NY Auto Dealers' Assn Inc
18-10 Whitestone Expwy
Whitestone, NY 11357-3067
718-746-5900 Fax: 718-746-5557
Web site: www.gnyada.com

Clients:
Greater NY Auto Dealers' Assn

Offices and agencies generally appear in alphabetical order, except when specific order is requested by listee.

LOBBYISTS

Lobbyists:
Stuart Rosenthal
Mark Schienberg

Green & Seifter Attorneys, PLLC
900 One Lincoln Ctr
110 W Fayette St
Syracuse, NY 13202
315-422-1391

Clients:
Cable Telecommunications Assn of NY Inc
Noble Environmental Power Inc
Regional Interconnect Inc (NY)

Lobbyists:
Maureen Helmer

Greenberg Traurig, LLP
54 State St, 6th Fl
Albany, NY 12207
518-689-1400 Fax: 518-689-3499
Web site: www.gtlaw.com

200 Park Avenue
New York, NY 10166
212-801-9200
Fax: 212-801-6400

Clients:
555 West 59th Street Holdings LLC
ACS State Healthcare (Multistate Associates Inc)
AES New York LLC
Advanced Micro Devices, Inc
Affinity Health Plan
Alliance for Child with Special Needs-School Age (NYS)
American Medical Alert Corporation
Anchor Contractors
Arker Companies (The)
Assoc General Contractors of America, Inc (NYS Chapter)
Assn for Marriage & Family Therapy, Inc (NYD)
Association of American Publishers
Assn of Health Information Outsourcing Services
Assn of Licensed Midwives (NYS)
Assn of School Psychologists (NY)
AT&T Inc & Its Affiliates
Auto Collision Technician's Assn, Inc (NYS)
Bank of New York
Bar Association (NYS)
Bearing Point Consulting
Bovis Lend Lease
CNA
Canadian Pacific Railway
Capital Region Council for Children with Special Needs
Children's Day Treatment Coalition
ChoicePoint
Cingular Wireless
Cisco Systems Inc
Coalition for Children with Special Needs (NYC)
ConocoPhillips
Council of Probation Administrators (NYS)
Credit Union League, Inc (NYS)
Crisis Program (The)
Doe Fund, Inc (The)
Drinking Driver Program Directors Assn (NYS)
Empire State Water Well Drillers' Assn, Inc
Enterprise Rent-A-Car
Ferry Point Partners LLC
Four Seasons Nursing & Rehabilitation Center
General Building Contractors of NYS, Inc
Geneva Worldwide Inc
GKC Industries
Harris & Harris LTD
Health Plan Assn (NY)
Honda North America, Inc
Housing Assn Inc (NY)(Mfg Housing Assn)
Hudson Alliance for Children with Special Needs
Hunts Point Cooperative Market, Inc
Hunts Point Produce Market
IMS Health Incorporated (Multistate Associates Inc)
Industries for the Disabled (NYS)
JCDecaux North America
Just Kids Diagnostic & Treatment Center
Just Kids Early Childhood Learning Ctr
Leewood Real Estate Group/NY, LLC & Affiliates
Liberty Mutual
Life Insurance Council of NY, Inc
Long Island Coalition for Children with Special Needs
Manhattan Youth Recreation & Resources
March of Dimes Birth Defects Foundation (NYS Chapters)
Microsoft Corporation
Mirant New York, Inc
Moving Media, LLC
National Academy of Elder Law Attorneys-NY Chapter
National Conference of Commissioners on Uniform State Laws
New York Philharmonic
North County Alliance for Children with Special Needs
Podiatric Medical Assn (NYS)
Primerica Financial Services
Quincunx
RLJ Development LLC
Rawlings Company LLC (The)
S&H Equities Inc
Sanofi Pasteur (Multistate Associates Inc)
Schnectady Museum and Planetarium
Servicemaster Co (The)
Sotheby's
Stop DWI Coordinators Assn (NYS)
STU Weissman Productions II Inc
Technology Enterprise Corp (NYS)
The Association of Settlement Companies (Multistate Associates Inc)
Thrivent Financial for Lutherans
Tomra
Union College
United Healthcare Services Inc
United Healthcare Services Inc (Ovations)
Verifone Transportation Systems Inc
Viasys Healthcare Inc
Wellcare Health Plans, Inc
Western Central Coalition for Children with Special Needs
Zurich

Lobbyists:
Tricia Asaro
Agostino Cangemi
Deidre Carson
Christopher Cernik
Margo Flug
Mark Glaser
Valerie Grey
Robert Harding
Harold Iselin

Offices and agencies generally appear in alphabetical order, except when specific order is requested by listee.

LOBBYISTS

Pamela Madeiros
John Mascialino
Michael Murphy
Joshua Oppenheimer
Doreen Saia
Elizabeth Sacco
Jay Segal
Edward Wallace

Griffin Plummer & Associates, LLC
61 Columbia St, Ste 403
Albany, NY 12210-2736
518-463-5949 Fax: 518-463-5991

Clients:
Clark Patterson Associates
Computer Aid Inc
Delaware Engineering
Funeral Directors Assn (NYS)
Genworth Financial
General Electric Co
Green County IDA
Hunter Mountain Ski Bowl
Land America Financial Group Inc
MH Corbin Enterprises
Railroads of NY, (RONY)

Lobbyists:
John Griffin
Daniel Plummer
Norman Schneider
Scott Wigger

Griffin, Mary A
Citigroup Mgmt Corp
95 Columbia St
Albany, NY 12210
518-432-1286 Fax: 518-465-6023

Clients:
Citigroup Management Corp

Hager, Susan
UWNYS
155 Washington Ave
Albany, NY 12210
518-463-2522 Fax: 518-463-2534
e-mail: hagers@uwnys.org
Web site: www.uwnys.org

Clients:
United Way of NYS

Hancock Public Affairs, LLC
201 W Genesse St
Fayetteville, NY 13066
315-447-6057

Clients:
Northeast Biofuels LP

Lobbyists:
Stewart Hancock III

Hannan, K T Public Affairs Inc
107 Washington Ave
Albany, NY 12210-2200
518-465-6550 Fax: 518-465-6557
e-mail: khannan401@aol.com
Web site: www.kthpa.com

Clients:
Assurant Solutions
Auxiliary Campus Enterprises and Services (FKA Alfred State College)
Conpor Conference of Private Organizations (NYS)
Consumer Finance Assn (NYS)
Credit Union League Inc (NYS)
Davita Inc
FASNY Federal Credit Union
Firemen's Assn of the State of NY
National Safety Council
Hannaford Bros Co
National Traffic Safety Administration
Owens-Illinois (Albers & Co)
Usinpac (Albers & Co)

Lobbyists:
Kirby T Hannan
Ross Hannan
Jan VanDeCarr

Harris, Steven W, LLC
99 Pine St, Ste 207
Albany, NY 12207
518-436-0786

Clients:
Beer Wholesalers Association Inc (NYS)
Reynolds America Inc

Harris, O Lewis
Queens Community House
108-25 62nd Dr
Forest Hills, NY 11375
718-592-5757 Fax: 718-592-2933

Clients:
Queens Community House Inc

Lobbyists:
Mary Abbate
Susan Matloff
Irma Rodriguez
Christine Roland
Hannah Weinstock
Kathryn-Celia Williams

Harter Secrest & Emery, LLP
1600 Bausch & Lomb Place
Rochester, NY 14604-2711
585-232-6500 Fax: 585-232-2152
e-mail: admin@hselaw.com
Web site: www.hartersecrest.com

Offices and agencies generally appear in alphabetical order, except when specific order is requested by listee.

LOBBYISTS

Clients:
Alliance for Fine Wine Wholesalers, Ltd (NY)
Association for Affordable Housing (NY)
ATU NY State Legislative Conference Board
Association of Safety Group Managers
Biotechnology Assn Inc (NY)
Buffalo & Pittsburgh Railroad Inc
Chiropractic Assn Inc (NYS)
Clinical Laboratory Assn Inc (NYS)
Cold Spring Harbor Laboratory
County of Orleans Industrial Development Agency
DaimlerChrysler Corp
Delta Air Lines Inc
Emerging Industries Alliance of NYS
Finger Lakes Health Systems Agency
Finger Lakes Horsemen's Benv & Protective Assn Inc
Genesee & Wyoming Railroad Inc
GlaxoSmithKline, PLC
Hall of Science (NY)
Medstat (Marsh and Associates PC)
Movers' & Warehousemen's Assn Inc (NYS)
OSI Pharmaceuticals Inc
Restaurant Assn (NYS)
Rochester & Southern Railroad Inc
SAS Institute Inc
Telecommunications Assn Inc (NYS)
Upstate Niagara Cooperative Inc (FKA Upstate Farms Cooperative Inc)
Rochester Tooling & Machine Assn Inc

Lobbyists:
John Jennings
Amy Kellogg
Ross Lanzafame
Donald S Mazzulo
Richard E Scanlan

Hartford Financial Svcs Group Inc
Hartford Plaza HO 1-11
690 Asylum Ave
Hartford, CT 06115
860-547-2944

Clients:
Hartford Financial Svcs Group Inc

Lobbyists:
Carol Clapp

Hastings, Jamie
4 Sylvan Way
Parsippany, NJ 07054
973-292-8919

Clients:
T-Mobile USA Inc

Hawayek, Jonathan F
728 Main St
East Aurora, NY 14052
716-652-2038

Clients:
Allergan, Inc

Health Insurance Plan of Greater NY
111 Washington Ave, Ste 411
Albany, NY 12210
518-462-5611

Clients:
Health Insurance Plan of Greater NY

Lobbyists:
Felix Delacruz
Kerry DeWitt
Diane DiGregorio
Michael Fullwood
Daniel McGowan
Ralph Pisano
Bob Ronda
Leslie Strassberg
Anthony Watson

Health Plan Assn Inc (NY)
90 State St, Ste 825
Albany, NY 12207-1717
518-462-2293 Fax: 518-462-2150
e-mail: info@nyhpa.org
Web site: www.nyhpa.org

Clients:
Health Plan Assn Inc (NY)

Lobbyists:
Arlene Halpert
Kim Kelly
Paul F Macielak
Lee R Marks
Leslie S Moran
Sheila Nelson

Healthcare Tort Reform Coalition (NY)
Combined Coordinating Council
14 Penn Plaza, Ste 720
New York, NY 10122
212-643-8100

Clients:
Healthcare Tort Reform Coalition (NY)

Lobbyists:
Terence Kelleher
Lisa Kramer
Christopher Smith

Heimgartner, Christian
118 Willowwood Dr
PO Box 296
Oakdale, NY 11769-0296
631-567-3783

Clients:
Lieutenants Benevolent Assn

Offices and agencies generally appear in alphabetical order, except when specific order is requested by listee.

LOBBYISTS

Heyman, Neil
Southern NY Association
39 Broadway, Ste 1710
New York, NY 10006
212-425-5050 Fax: 212-968-7710
e-mail: njheyman@snya.com
Web site: www.snya.org

Clients:
Southern NY Assn

Higgins Roberts Beyerl & Coan, PC
1430 Balltown Rd
Niskayuna, NY 12309
518-374-3399 Fax: 518-374-9416

Clients:
Society of Anesthesiologists, Inc (NYS)

Lobbyists:
Charles J Assini Jr

Hightower, A Dirk
Children's Institute
274 N Goodman St, Ste D103
Rochester, NY 14607-1154
585-295-1000 Fax: 585-295-1090

Clients:
Children's Institute, Inc

Hill & Gosdeck
One Commerce Plaza
99 Washington Ave, Ste 400
Albany, NY 12210
518-463-5449 Fax: 518-463-0947
e-mail: nylobbyists@aol.com

Clients:
AT&T Inc & Its Affiliates
Alliance of Automobile Manufacturers
Altria Corporate Services Inc
Consumer Data Industry Assoc
Genocide Intervention Network
Group Self-Insurance Assn of NY (GSIANY)
International Business Machines Corp
International Paper Co.
Kraft Foods Global, Inc
Lexmark International Inc
Livonia, Avon & Lakeville Railroad Corp
Miller Brewing Co
Monsanto Co
National Nutritional Foods Association East
Peachtree Settlement Funding
Program Risk Mgmt Inc
SGS Testcom
Shell Oil Company
Soap & Detergent Assoc
USA Training Company Inc
Veterinary Medical Society (NYS)

Lobbyists:
Thomas J Gosdeck
Heidi Hellenberg
Jeffrey L Hill
Frank Nemeth

Hiller, Elise L
80 State St
Albany, NY 12207
518-463-6676 Fax: 518-463-0574
e-mail: elh@nycap.rr.com
Web site: www.cabletvny.com

Clients:
Cable Telecommunications Assn of NY

Hines-Kramer, Amy
Credit Union League
19 British American Blvd
Latham, NY 12110
518-437-8122 Fax: 518-782-4212
Web site: www.nycreditunions.org

Clients:
Credit Union League Inc (NYS)

Lobbyists:
Cheryl Halter
Michael Lanotte
William Mellin

Hinman Straub, PC
121 State St
Albany, NY 12207-1693
518-436-0751 Fax: 518-436-4751
e-mail: reception@hspm.com
Web site: www.hspm.com

Clients:
1199 SEIU United Healthcare Workers East
Academic Dental Centers (NYS)
American Insurance Association
American Safety Council
Associated Medical Schools of NY
Association of Proprietary Colleges
Association of Service Stations & Repair Shops, Inc (NYS)
Assurant Solutions, Inc
Binghamton University
Boys & Girls Clubs of America (Boys & Girls Clubs Inc (NYS))
Builders Association (NYS)
Capital District Physicians' Health Plan
Charmer Industries Inc
Charter Schools Assn (NY)
Children's Aid Society (The)
Cigna Companies
City of Rochester
Colgate University
Community Preservation Corporation (The)
Consolidated Edison Co of NY Inc
Consumer Specialty Products Association
Dell Inc
Deputies Association (NYS)
EDS

Offices and agencies generally appear in alphabetical order, except when specific order is requested by listee.

LOBBYISTS

Education & Research Network Inc (NYS)
Empire State Assn of Assisted Living (FKA Empire State Association of Adult Homes & Assisted Living)
Episcopal Social Services
Estee Lauder Companies Inc (The) (FKA Estee Lauder, Inc)
Excellus Health Plan Inc
Federation of Mental Health Ctrs Inc (The)
Financial Aid Administrators Association, Inc (NYS)
Foundling Hospital (NY) (The)
Fresenius Medical Care-North America
Gerber Life Insurance Company
HSBC North America
Hillside Family of Agencies
Industries for the Blind of NYS, Inc
Institute for Special Education (NY)
Jewish Home of Rochester (The)
Medford Hamlet ALP, LLC
Medical & Health Research Assn of NYC Inc
Medical College (NY)
National Heritage Academies
New York Life Insurance Company
One Communications Corp
Opthalmological Society (NYS)
Organization of NYS Management Confidential Employees Inc
Parker Jewish Institute for Health Care & Rehab
Pearson Education Inc
Pet Industry Joint Advisory Council
Pharmaceutical Research & Manufacturers of America
Professional Firefighters Association Inc (NYS)
Racing Association Inc (NY) (The)
Rent Stabilization Assn of NYC Inc
Retirees for Tier 1
SLE Foundation (The)
School Administrators Association of NYS
Seneca Nation of Indians
Sightlines LLC
Stonehenge Capital Corporation
Stony Brook University
Superpower Inc
Support Services Alliance Inc
Supreme Court Justices' Assn of the City of NY (Association of Justices of the Supreme Court of NY)
Technical Assistance Centers' Assn for Transferring Success
TransCanada Pipelines Ltd
WNYC
Wellpoint Inc
Whitney Museum of American Art (The)

Lobbyists:
John Black
James Clyne
Bartley J Costello, III
William Y Crowell III
Terri Crowley
Sean M Doolan
Michael Fallon
John Federman
Bruce N Gyory
Robert McCarthy
Elizabeth Misa
Marthea O'Conner
Janet Penska
Kevin P Quinn
Janet Silver

Hirshorn, Donald P
860 Hereford Way
Niskayuna, NY 12309-4904
518-265-9284
e-mail: mail@rpea.org
Web site: www.rpea.org

Clients:
Retired Public Employees Association

Hodes Associates
284 State St
Albany, NY 12210
518-465-8303 Fax: 518-465-8320
e-mail: nhodes@hodesassoc.org

Clients:
Assisted Living Federation of America (ALFA)
Education & Work Consortium (The)
Forba LLC
Home Care Association of NYS
Instructional Systems Inc
Metropolitan College of NY
McKesson Corporation
Northeast Spa and Pool Association
Sunrise Senior Living
Visiting Nurse Regional Health Care System

Lobbyists:
Nancy L Hodes
Virginia Lynch-Landy
Michele O'Connor

Hodgson Russ, LLP
One M&T Plaza, Ste 2000
Buffalo, NY 14203-2391
646-218-7501
Web site: www.hodgsonruss.com

Clients:
Group Health Incorporated
Rural/Metro Medical Services
Society of Certified Public Accountants, NYS

Lobbyists:
Frederick J Jacobs
Adam Perry

Holloway, Jr, Floyd
State Farm Insurance Co
225 Wilmington W Chester Park
Ste 300
Chadds Ford, PA 19317-9039
610-361-4150 Fax: 610-361-4110
e-mail: floyd.holloway.clxm@statefarm.com

Clients:
State Farm Insurance Companies

Lobbyists:
Brian Carlson
Michele Mehler

Offices and agencies generally appear in alphabetical order, except when specific order is requested by listee.

LOBBYISTS

Tom Thompson
Allison A Woelk
Vance Yoshikawa

Home Care Assn of NYS Inc
194 Washington Ave, Ste 400
Albany, NY 12210
518-426-8764 Fax: 518-426-8788
e-mail: info@hcanys.org
Web site: www.hcanys.org

Clients:
Home Care Assn of NYS Inc

Lobbyists:
Patrick Conole
Mark Kissinger
Andrew Koski

Honda North America Inc
1001 G St NW, Ste 950
Washington, DC 20001
202-661-4400

Clients:
Honda North America Inc

Lobbyists:
Kent Dellinger
Toni Harrington
Ember A Rosenberg

Hood, William L
American Airlines
9525 W Bryn Mawr Ave, #800
Rosemont, IL 60018
847-233-4640
e-mail: bill.hood@aa.com
Web site: www.aa.com

Clients:
American Airlines

Lobbyists:
Justin Bernback

Housing Conservation Coordinators
777 Tenth Ave
New York, NY 10019
212-541-5996

Clients:
Housing Conservation Coordinators

Lobbyists:
Sarah Desmond
Harvey Epstein
John Raskin

Housing Works, Albany Advocacy Ctr
247 Lark St, 1st Fl
Albany, NY 12210
518-449-4207 Fax: 518-449-4219
e-mail: kink@housingworks.org; hayes@housingworks.org
Web site: www.housingworks.org

Clients:
Housing Works

Lobbyists:
Mark Hayes
Michael Kink
Terri Smith-Caronia

Hudacs, John
61 Paxwood Rd
Delmar, NY 12054
518-439-7570

Clients:
College of Staten Island (Research Foundation of CUNY)

Human Services Council of NYC
130 East 59th St
New York, NY 10022
212-836-1230

Clients:
Human Services Council of NYC

Hunger Action Network of NYS
275 State St
Albany, NY 12210
518-431-7371 Fax: 518-434-7390

Clients:
Hunger Action Network of NYS

Lobbyists:
Mark Dunlea
Bich Ha Pham

Hurley, John R
Guardian Life Ins Co
7 Hanover Sq H23E
New York, NY 10004-2616
212-598-8854 Fax: 212-919-2693

Clients:
Guardian Life Insurance Co of America (The)

Lobbyists:
Armand Depalo
Ulysses Lee

Immigration Coalition, Inc (NY)
137-139 W 25th St, 12th Fl
New York, NY 10001
212-627-2227

Clients:
Immigration Coalition, Inc (NY)

Offices and agencies generally appear in alphabetical order, except when specific order is requested by listee.

LOBBYISTS

Lobbyists:
Milan Bhaft
Jose Davila
Avitia Deycy
Norman Eng
Maysoun Freij
Adam Gurvitch
Chung-Wha Hong
Alan Kaplan
Angela Lee
Margaret McHugh
Avideh Moussavian
Minerva Moya
Ericka Stallings
Javier Valdes
Jackie Wong

Island Public Affairs
277 Indian Head Rd
Kings Park, NY 11754
631-724-0017

Clients:
Adelante of Suffolk County, Inc
Catholic Health Services of Longh Island
Hands Across Long Island Inc
Clubhouse of Suffolk
Literacy Suffolk, Inc
National Foundation for Human Potential Inc
Verizon

Lobbyists:
Steven Moll

Island Strategies, Inc
1425 Reckson Plaza
East Tower, 15th Fl
Uniondale, NY 11556-0190
516-663-6688

Clients:
Archstone Smith
Bowling Proprietor's Assn (NYS)
Cherokee Northeast LLC
Fair Assessment Committee LLC
Specialty Tobacco Council Inc
Three Village Central School District

Lobbyists:
Keith Fink
Arthur Kremer
Mark Lieberman

J Adams Consulting, LLC
One Battery Park Plaza
New York, NY 10004
212-493-7777

Clients:
Centre Partners Management LLC
CHH Realty
Cobble Hill Health Center
College PT Holdings LLC
Continental Airlines, Inc
Exchange Blvd.com
Guardian Engineering Services
Hunter College
International Academy of Detoxification Specialists (IADS)
International Code Council
M.A. Angeliades, Inc
MBA Long Island City
Par Group (The)
Partnership for NYC
Project Renewal
Property Markets Group
Sheet Metal Workers ltnl Association
SPL
Steel Equities
Stuart Portfolio Consultants LP
Triangle Equities

Lobbyists:
Catherine Giuliani
Jennifer Lump

JLW Consulting, LLC
19 Book Hill Rd
Essex, CT 06426
860-767-2814

Clients:
Newspaper Publishers Assn (NY)

Lobbyists:
Jerome Wilson

Jenkins, Joanne E
NY Life Ins
111 Washington Ave, 3rd Fl
Albany, NY 12210
518-463-6649 Fax: 518-436-0226

Clients:
Life Insurance Co (NY)

Lobbyists:
Martin Claire
Melvin Feinberg
Alan Igielski
Theodore Mathas
George Nichols
Carol Mayer
Michael Oleske
Lee Parkin
Janis Rubin
Fred Sievert
Joel Steinberg
Seymour Sternberg
Gil Valdes
Paul Whitman
Lori Whittaker
Gayle Yeomans
Richard Zuccaro

Johnson, Stephen Philip
Cornell University
110 Day Hall
Ithaca, NY 14853-2801

Offices and agencies generally appear in alphabetical order, except when specific order is requested by listee.

LOBBYISTS

607-255-4347
e-mail: spj2@cornell.edu
Web site: www.cornell.edu

Clients:
Cornell University

Lobbyists:
Charles J Kruzansky
Myrna Manners
Jacqueline K Powers
Stanley W Telega
Paula A Willsie

Kantor Davidoff Wolfe Mandelker & Kass, PC
51 East 42nd St
New York, NY 10017-5497
212-682-8383 Fax: 212-949-5206

Clients:
Junior Tennis League (NY)
Metropolitan Retail Assn, LLC (NY)
Sports & Arts in School Foundation

Lobbyists:
Lawrence A Mandelker
Robert Straniere

Kaplan, Randy L
LI Bd of Realtors
300 Sunrise Hwy
West Babylon, NY 11704
631-661-4800 Fax: 631-661-5202
e-mail: rkaplan@mlslirealtor.com

Clients:
Long Island Board of Realtors

Lobbyists:
Meredith Dulberg

Kasirer Consulting
321 Broadway, Ste 201
New York, NY 10007
212-285-1800 Fax: 212-285-1818
e-mail: skasirer@kasirerconsulting.com

Clients:
184 Kent Fee LLC
77 Commercial Holding, LLC
92nd Street Y
ATCO Properties & Management Inc
American Cancer Society, Eastern Division, Inc
Apollo Real Estate Advisors
Arcadis G & M (National Strategies, Inc)
Bedford Stuyvesant Family Health Ctr
Blood Center (NY)
CBS Corporation
Cemusa Inc
Citymeals-on-Wheels
Clipper Equity LLC
CPS 5 LLC
Easton Sports
Elad Properties, LLC
Element West 59th St
Empire Racing Associates
Episcopal Social Services
Extell Development Corporation
GDC Properties Inc
Hamilton, Rabinovitz & Alschuler Inc
Historical Society (NY)
JC Studios, LLC
Keyspan Corporation
Lower Manhattan Cultural Council
Museum of Arts & Design
NBC Universal
Noble Communications/CGBP
Nontraditional Employment for Women
Northside Center for Child Development
Northstar Development Corp
Port Parties, Ltd
Project Renewal
Rescare/Arbor (Multistate Associates)
Restoration Project (NY)
S&R Medallion Corporation
Safe Horizon Inc
Scan New York
Silverite Construction
SL Green Realty Corp
Swig Equities, LLC
Taxi Technology Corporation
T-Mobile
US Power Generating
Vocational Foundation Inc

Lobbyists:
Justin Ettinger
Julie Greenberg
Patrick Jenkins
Sara Kasirer

Katz, Arthur H
Wholesale Marketers & Distributors
211 E 43rd St
New York, NY 10017-4707
212-682-3576 Fax: 212-867-7844

Clients:
Assn of Wholesale Marketers & Distributors (NYS)

Keycorp & Subsidiaries
127 Public Square
Cleveland, OH 44114
216-689-5091

Clients:
Keycorp & Subsidiaries

Lobbyists:
Christopher Pugliese

King, Barbara
555 W 57th St, 5th Fl
New York, NY 10019
212-523-5367 Fax: 212-523-2617
e-mail: bking@chpnet.org
Web site: www.wehealnewyork.org

Offices and agencies generally appear in alphabetical order, except when specific order is requested by listee.

Clients:
Beth Israel Medical Ctr
Long Island College Hospital
St Luke's-Roosevelt Hospital Ctrs

Lobbyists:
Bradley Korn

Kirsch, Richard
Citizen Action of NY
94 Central Ave
Albany, NY 12206
518-465-4600 Fax: 518-465-2890
Web site: www.citizenactionny.org

Clients:
Citizen Action of NY

Lobbyists:
Mary Clark
Robert Cohen
Fabiola Friot
Shanna Goldman
Joyce E Gould
Rosemary Rivera
Karen Scharff
Jessica Wisneski

Knighton, Ethel V
15811 Glacier Ct
North Potomac, MD 20878
301-840-9161

Clients:
Medco Health Solutions, Inc

Kramer Levin Naftalis & Frankel, LLP
1177 Ave of Americas
New York, NY 10036
212-715-7835 or 212-715-9100 Fax: 212-715-7850
Web site: www.kramerlevin.com

Clients:
1765 First Avenue Associates LLC
AMV Unitel, LLC
Apollo Real Estate Advisors LP
Archdiocese of NY (The)
Bayrock Group LLC
City Investment Fund, LP (The)
Credit Suisse Securities (USA) LLC
Davis Development Holdings
Dia Art Foundation
East River Realty Company, LLC
Forest Hills Jewish Center
Gowanus Canal Joint Venture LLC
Hakimian Organization (The)
Intrepid Museum Foundation
Jujamcyn Theaters LLC
Lennar Corporation
Leonard Litwin
LHL Realty Co., LLC
Real Estate Industrials Inc
Solow Management Corp
Taconic Investment Partners LLC
Tahl Propp Equities
Terra Cotta LLC
Toll Brothers Inc
Toys R' Us
Trustees of Columbia University in the City of NY (The)
University (NY)
Vornado Realty Trust
West 129th Street Realty LLC
Worldwide Foods

Lobbyists:
Valerie Campbell
Jeremiah Candreva
Robert E Flahive
Albert Fredericks
Marcie Kesner
Robin Kramer
Elizabeth Larsen
Samuel H Lindenbaum
James P Powers
Sheila Pozon
Paul D Selver
Michael T Sillerman
Patrick Sullivan
Gary R Tarnoff
Elise Wagner

Kriss, Kriss, Brignola & Persing, LLP
350 Northern Blvd, Ste 306
Albany, NY 12204
518-449-2037 Fax: 518-449-7875

Clients:
Chickering Group (The)
Collateral Loan Brokers Assn of NY
Society of Professional Engineers Inc (NYS)

Lobbyists:
Mark C Kriss

Kruly, Kenneth
2001 Main St, LY 207B
Buffalo, NY 14208-1098
716-888-3755 Fax: 716-888-3102
e-mail: krulyk@canisius.edu
Web site: www.canisius.edu

Clients:
Canisius College

Lobbyists:
Vincent M Cooke SJ
Patrick J Greenwald
John J Hurley
Kenneth C Kruly
Jerome L Neuner PhD

Krupke, Bruce W
Dairy Foods
201 S Main St, # 302
North Syracuse, NY 13212-2166
315-452-6455
e-mail: info@nysdfi.org
Web site: www.nysdfi.org

Offices and agencies generally appear in alphabetical order, except when specific order is requested by listee.

LOBBYISTS

Clients:
Dairy Foods Inc (NYS)

La Fuente, A Tri State Worker & Community Fund Inc
101 Ave of the Americas, 17th Fl
New York, NY 10013
212-388-3208

Clients:
La Fuente, A Tri State Worker & Community Fund

Lobbyists:
Alessandra De Almeida
Surgida Lozada
Zahida Pirani
Luz Rodriguez
Amy Sugimori

Labor-Religion Coalition, Inc (NYS)
800 Troy-Schenectady Rd
Latham, NY 12110-2455
518-213-6000 Fax: 518-213-6414
e-mail: info@labor-religion.org
Web site: www.labor-religion.org

Clients:
Labor-Religion Coalition, Inc (NYS)

Lobbyists:
Mark Looney
Brian O'Shaughnessy

Lambert, Linda A
Am College of Physicians
100 State St, Ste 700
Albany, NY 12207-1817
518-427-0366 Fax: 518-427-1991

Clients:
American College of Physicians Svcs Inc (NY Chapter)

Lanahan, Kevin
4 Irving Place, Rm 1650-S
New York, NY 10003
518-434-1193
Web site: www.coned.com

Clients:
Consolidated Edison Co of NY, Inc & its subsidiaries

Lobbyists:
John Banks
Dan Brown
Larry Carbone
Eric Dessen
Martin Heslin
Robert Hoglund
Stephen Ianello
Nelson Perez
Kenneth Reinhart
Joseph Segarra
William Talbot
Joseph Tringali

Land Trust Alliance Northeast Program
PO Box 792
Saratoga Springs, NY 12866
518-587-0774 Fax: 518-587-6467
e-mail: newyork@lta.org
Web site: www.lta.org

Clients:
Land Trust Alliance Northeast Program

Lobbyists:
Katrina Howey
Henrietta Jordan
Lynn Schumann
Ethan Winter

Landau-Painter, Cathy
2001 M St NW
Washington, DC 20036
518-427-4610

Clients:
KPMG, LLP

Lobbyists:
Theresa Ahlstrom
Eric Applewhite
Geno Armstrong
Robert Arning
Cassandra Arnold
David Bradford
Michael Breen
Frank Calvaruso
Wayne Cafran
Edward Constantino
Rory Costello
Jamie Cote
Anthony Dalessio
Manolet Dayrit
David DiCristofaro
John Direnzo
John Druke
John Eusanio
Donald Evans
Virginia Evans
Steven Fishner
Richard Girgenti
David Gmelich
Richard Hannmann
Jeffrey Hecht
Paul Hencoski
Paul Hernandez
Lisa Hinkson
Mark Holtzman
Brian Johnson
Ronald Joma
Marcella Junco
Charles Kavanaugh
Darin Kempke
Brendan Kennedy
Joseph Kuehn
Emily Kunchala

Offices and agencies generally appear in alphabetical order, except when specific order is requested by listee.

Natalie Lam
Al Landau
Stephen Langowski
Eric Leach
James Littley
Bryan Mahoney
Kevin Manzo
Shelly Masi
Andrew Matuszak
Kevin Max
Jim McGrath Jr
Terrill Menzel
Ramin Mirsaidi
Andrew Mistur
Anthony Monaco
Jennifer Morris
Brian Murphy
David Pondillo
Gordon Postle
Tom Randall
Anthony Ricci
Brian Shea
Scott D Showalter
Darren Skolnick
Erin Smith
David Souchik
Sudipto Srivastava
Christopher Stanley
Lorna Stark
Maria Tiso
Nancy Valley
Rico Viscusi
Shawn Warren
Meghan Watson
Michael Wiater
Abid Zaim

Landry, M Joe
120 Washington Ave
Albany, NY 12210
518-449-3333

Clients:
Empire State Passengers Assn

Langdon, David
491 State St, 3A
Albany, NY 12203-1019
518-432-5440

Clients:
Brighter Choice Foundation
Racing Association (NY)

Lasky, Roy E
NYS Dental Assn
121 State St, 4th Fl
Albany, NY 12207-1622
518-465-0044 Fax: 518-427-0461
e-mail: rlasky@nysdental.org
Web site: www.nysdental.org

Clients:
Dental Assn (NYS)

Lawyers for the Public Interest (NY)
151 W 30th St, 11th Fl
New York, NY 10001-4007
212-244-4664 Fax: 212-244-4570

Clients:
Bronx Committee for Toxic Free Schools
Disabled in Action of Metropolitan NY
Lawyers for the Public Interest (NY)
Organization of Waterfront Neighborhoods (OWN)

Lobbyists:
Nisha Agarwal
Dennis Boyd
Veronica Eady
John Gresham
Chris Johnson
Gavin Kearney
Marianne Lado
Jin Hee Lee
Amanda Masters
Jaclyn Okin
Kevin Olson
Dave Palmer
Michael Silverman
Kim Sweet

LeBoeuf Lamb Greene & MacRae, LLP
99 Washington Ave, Ste 2020
Albany, NY 12210
518-626-9000 Fax: 518-626-9010

125 W 55th St
New York, NY 10019
212-424-8000

Clients:
AFLAC NY
Assn of Financial Guaranty Insurors
Asurion
Chesapeake Appalachia LLC
Excess Line Assn of NY
Green Point of NY Inc
International Underwriting Assn of London
Lloyds of London
Medical Liability Mutual Insurance Co
Mortgage Insurance Companies of America
State Farm Insurance Companies
Cooper Union for Advancement of Science & Art (NYC Office)

Lobbyists:
Gordon J Davis (NY Office)
Thomas Dawson
Jay B Martin
John Mulhern
Edmond Valente
Thomas West

League of Women Voters of New York State
62 Grand Street
Albany, NY 12207

Offices and agencies generally appear in alphabetical order, except when specific order is requested by listee.

LOBBYISTS

518-465-4162

Clients:
League of Women Voters of New York State

Lobbyists:
Aimee Allaud
Heather Baker-Sullivan
Lenore Banks
Barbara Bartoletti
Paula Blum
Ruth Bonn
Ann Brandon
Marian Bott
Hillary Brizell-Delise
Jane Chase
Jeanette Conners
Gail Davenport
Georgia DeGregorio
Joan Elliott
Gladys Gifford
Lois Haignere
Anne Huberman
Carol Hurford
Joan Johnson
Martha Kennedy
Ellen Kotlow
Marcia Merrins
Jacki Moriarty
Donna Packard-Maloney
Anne Riordan
Sally Robinson
Carol Saginaw
Charlotte Shapiro
Helga Schroeter
Evelyn Stock
Betsey Swan
Barbara Thomas
Dare Thompson
Lyle Toohey
Edna Vincente
Elsie Wager
Mildred Whalen
Roberta Wiernak

Legal Action Ctr of the City of NY Inc
225 Varick St, 4th Fl
New York, NY 10014
212-243-1313 Fax: 212-675-0286
e-mail: tgardner@lac.org
Web site: www.lac.org

Clients:
Legal Action Ctr of the City of NY Inc

Lobbyists:
Tracie M Gardner
Glenn Martin
Anita R Marton
Paul N Samuels

Legal Services of the Hudson Valley
4 Cromwell Pl
White Plains, NY 10601
914-949-1305

Clients:
Legal Services of the Hudson Valley

Lobbyists:
Tara Baksh
Jill Bradshaw-Soto
Lewis G Creekmore
Mary Grace Ferone
Barbara Finkelstein
William Flynn
Peter M Frank
Lesley Graves
Erin Guven
Kathleen Healey
Ursula Inghem
Kathleen Jones
Nancy Marrone
Aida Ramirez
Barbara Shealy
Robin Stiebel
Judy Studebaker
Eileen Swan
Mary Jo Wheatley
David Wright

Leon, Rachel
Common Cause (NY)
155 Ave of the Americas
New York, NY 10013
212-691-6421

Clients:
Common Cause (NY)

Lobbyists:
Megan Quattlebaum

Levine, Laurence J
BTOBA
1140 Bay St, Ste A & B
Staten Island, NY 10305
718-727-7613 Fax: 718-727-7619
e-mail: btoba@inetmail.att.net
Web site: www.btoba.org

Clients:
Bridge & Tunnel Officers Benevolent Assn

Levine, Paul
Jewish Board of Family & Children Svcs
120 W 57th St
New York, NY 10019
212-632-4614

Clients:
Jewish Board of Family & Children's Services Inc

Levy, Norman PC
575 Madison Ave
New York, NY 10022
212-605-0313 Fax: 212-333-8720

Offices and agencies generally appear in alphabetical order, except when specific order is requested by listee.

LOBBYISTS

Clients:
First American Title Insurance Company of NY
Lighthouse International
United Neighborhood Houses
Versa Med Inc

Lobbyists:
Norman Levy

Lewinter Associates, Murray
120 Washington Ave
Albany, NY 12210
518-449-3333 Fax: 518-427-6781

Clients:
Cingular Wireless
International Longshoresmen's Association AFL-CIO
National Promotions & Advertising

Lobbyists:
Murray Lewinter

Liantonio, John J
5 Wood Hollow Rd
Parsippany, NJ 07054
973-637-9388

Clients:
Cingular Wireless

Library Assn (NY)
252 Hudson Ave
Albany, NY 12210-1802
518-432-6952 Fax: 518-427-1697
e-mail: nyladirector@pobox.com
Web site: www.nyla.org

Clients:
Library Assn (NY)

Lobbyists:
Michael J Borges

Lieberman, Mark L
900 Merchants Concourse, Ste 214
Westbury, NY 11590
516-228-4226 Fax: 516-228-6569

Clients:
American Lawyer Media
Court Clerks Assn (NYS)
EAC Inc
Forestcitydaly Housing
Glenwood Management Corp
Nassau Regional Off-Track Betting Corporation
Lockwood, Kessler & Bartlett Inc
Sanitary District No 6
Town of Hempstead

Lincoln Ctr for the Performing Arts Inc
70 Lincoln Center Plaza
New York, NY 10023-6583
212-875-5000 Fax: 212-875-5122
e-mail: efinkelstein@lincolncenter.org
Web site: www.lincolncenter.org

Clients:
Lincoln Ctr for the Performing Arts Inc

Lobbyists:
Rosemarie Garipoli
Maureen McCormack
Melissa Thornton

Lipsky, Richard Associates Inc
15 Avalon Gardens
Nanuet, NY 10954
914-572-2865 Fax: 845-639-0687

Clients:
National Restaurant Association
Neighborhood Retail Alliance
Red Apple Group
United Food & Commercial Workers Union, Dist Council of Region 1
Tuck-it-Away

Lobbyists:
Richard Lipsky

LoCicero & Tan Inc
123 William St, 22nd Fl
New York, NY 10038
212-608-0888 Fax: 212-608-0458

Clients:
Bluestone Organization (The)
Covanta Energy Corp
Community Preservation Corporation (The)
Council of Senior Ctrs & Services of NYC Inc
Erie Basin Marine Associates (Kelly & Roth)
Fashion Institute of Technology
Flushing Commons
Forest City Ratner Companies
Gannett Fleming Engineers & Architects PC
Hospital for Special Surgery
Kingston Avenue Development LLC
Knickerbocker Plaza Associates
Millenium Partners
NYU School of Medicine
New York Botanical Garden (The)
Sequoia Community Initiatives (Consumer Info & Dispute Resolution)
SL Green Realty Corp
Snug Harbor Cultural Center
TDC Development & Construction Corp
TKGG LLC
Towers at Spring Creek
Village Care of NY Inc
Yonkers Contracting Co Inc
JBI International

Lobbyists:
John LoCicero
Eva Tan

Offices and agencies generally appear in alphabetical order, except when specific order is requested by listee.

LOBBYISTS

Logan, Ernest
Council of School Supervs/Administrators
16 Court St
Brooklyn, NY 11241-1254
718-852-3000

Clients:
Council of School Supervisors & Administrators

Lobbyists:
Brian Gibbons
Barbara Jaccoma
Jill Levy
Peter McNally

Long Island Association
300 Broad Hollow Rd
Melville, NY 11747-4840
631-493-3002 Fax: 631-499-2194

Clients:
Long Island Association

Lobbyists:
Matthew Crosson
Michael Deering
Laureen Hill

Long Term Care Community Coalition
242 West 30th St, Ste 306
New York, NY 10001
212-385-0355 Fax: 212-732-6945
e-mail: crnhcc@aol.com
Web site: www.nhccnys.org

Clients:
Long Term Care Community Coalition (FKA Nursing Home Community Coalition)

Lobbyists:
Richard Mollot

Losquadro, Steven E
649 Route 25A
Suite 4
Rocky Point, NY 11778
631-744-9070

Clients:
Caithness Energy, LLC

Louloudes, Virginia
575 Eighth Ave, Ste 1720
New York, NY 10018-3011
212-244-6667 Fax: 212-714-1918
e-mail: questions@art-newyork.org
Web site: www.offbroadwayonline.com

Clients:
Alliance of Resident Theatres/New York

Lowry, Robert
Council of School Superintendents
7 Elk St, 3rd Fl
Albany, NY 12207-1002
518-449-1063

Clients:
Council of School Superintendents (NYS)

Lobbyists:
Douglas Gerhardt
Thomas Rogers

Luria, Robert S
12 Spruce Run
East Greenbush, NY 12061-9611
518-477-2581 Fax: 800-561-5825
e-mail: robert.s.luria@gsk.com

Clients:
GlaxoSmithKline, PLC

Lustig, Esther Public Affairs
86-29 155th Ave, Ste 6L
Lindenwood
Queens, NY 11414
718-845-2855 Fax: 718-845-0282
e-mail: lustigpa@aol.com

Clients:
Federation Employment & Guidance Service Inc (FEGS)
Jamaica Chamber of Commerce
Lexington School for the Deaf/Ctr for the Deaf Inc
Mosholu Montefiore Community Ctr
Partnership with Children
Reece School (The)

Lobbyists:
Esther Lustig

Luthin Associates, Inc
15 Walling Place
Avon by the Sea, NJ 07717
732-774-0005

Clients:
Consumer Power Advocates

Lobbyists:
Catherine Luthin

Lynch, Bill Associates, LLC
41 Hamilton Terrace
New York, NY 10031
212-283-7515

Clients:
CSC Holdings Inc
Downtown Brooklyn Partnership (The)
Industrial Technology Assistance Corp
Thor 280 Richards Street LLC
Trustees of Columbia University in the City of NY (The)

Offices and agencies generally appear in alphabetical order, except when specific order is requested by listee.

Lobbyists:
Lee Chong
Shom Dhampande
Paul Elliott
Karen Holman
Norman McConney
Luther Smith
Kevin Wandally
Jacqui Williams

Lynch, Patricia Associates
111 Washington Ave, Ste 606
Albany, NY 12210
518-432-9220 Fax: 518-432-9186
e-mail: plynch@plynchassociates.com

Clients:
ABC Inc
Accenture
Adirondack Optics
Advantage Travel
After-School Corporation (The)
Albany Law School
Albany Port District Commission
Alliance for Downtown New York Inc
American Waterways Operators
Baldwin-Grand Canal & Baldwin-West-End Canal Improvement District
Bechtel Infrastructure Corp (Macquarie Securities)
Buffalo Niagara Partnership
Cendant Car Rental Group Inc
Catholic Healthcare System
Catholic Health System, Sisters of Charity Hospital
Claremont Prepatory School
Clough Harbor & Associates LLP
Coca-Cola Bottling Co of NY (The)
Concerned Home Care Providers
Continental Industrial Capital, LLC
Deepdale Inc
Delaware North Companies Gaming & Entertainment Inc
Destiny USA
EW Enterprises
Eastern Paramedics Inc
Economic Development Council (NYS)
Educational Broadcasting Corporation Thirteen/WNET
Electric & Gas Corporation (NYS)
Empire Green Biofuels Inc
Empire Condominium
Empire State Distributors & Wholesalers Assn Inc
Engel Burman Group
Fennimore Art Museum (The Clark Estates)
Forest City Ratner Companies
Foundation for Accounting Practitioners
General Contractor's Assn
General Motors Corp
Granite Halmar Construction Company
Hetrick-Martin Institute, Home of Harvey Milk HS (The)
Historical Assn NYS (Farmers Museum)
King Ferry Winery
Kings College
Kingsway Arms Nursing Center
Kinney & Associates Inc
LCOR Inc
Lehman Brothers
Library Association (NY)
Long Island Children's Museum
Long Island Power Authority
LP Ciminelli Inc
Lower East Side Tenement Museum
M & T Bank
M/A-Com Inc
Macquarie Securities (USA) Inc
Madison Square Garden LP
Magna Entertainment Corp
Automotive Recyclers Association (NY)
Maritime Assn
Medical Answering Services
Medical Staff of the Long Island College (Arent Fox)
Mohawk Ambulance Service
Monroe County Executive
National Baseball Hall of Fame
Motor Truck Assn (NYS)
Nurse Practitioners Assn of NYS (The)
Oneida Indian Nation
BBL Construction Services Inc
Park Avenue Health Care Management
Pharmaceutical Research & Mfrs of America (PHRMA)
Plumb Engineering PC
Police Investigators Assn (NY)
Precision Jet Management Inc
Premier Home Health Care Inc
Preservation League of NYS
Pyramid Managing Group Inc
Rochester Gas & Electric Corp
SCI of New York Inc
Bersin Properties, LLC
Seneca Niagara Falls Gaming Corp
Seneca Park Zoo Society
Sequoia Voting Systems Inc
St Peter's Hospital
Subcontractor's Trade Assn Inc
Syracuse City School District
Walt Disney Company (The)
Watervliet Development Company LLC
Westchester County
Westchester School for Special Children
Western Regional Off-Track Betting
Yonkers Raceway
Cablevision (CSC Holdings Inc)
Caramoor
CH2M Hill
Criterion Strategies Inc (FKA First Responder Inc)
Golden Technology Management, LLC
Hudson Valley Fois Gras (HVFG, LLC)
Kidspeace
Lifespan
Lilac Corporation
Mark IV IVHS Inc
NYSCON Collaborative Care LLC
Transcare NY Inc (Metrocare Ambulance)
Norvest Financial Services Inc
NVR Inc
Professional Insurance Agents of NYS Inc
Radiant Energy Corporation
Rochester-Genesee Regional Transportation Authority c/o Renaissan
Spring Valley Homes
Suffolk County Executive
Legal Aid Society (The)
Witkoff Group (The)
Tyco international (USA) Inc
Wal-Mart
Waste Management of NY, LLC

Lobbyists:
Christopher Bombardier

Offices and agencies generally appear in alphabetical order, except when specific order is requested by listee.

LOBBYISTS

Michelle Cummings
Christopher Del Giudice
Christopher Grimaldi
Sherman Jewett
Fredy Kaplan
Allison Lee
Patricia Lynch
Samir S NeJame
Clarence D Rappleyea
Paul Tokasz
Michael Wilton
Patrick Zlogar

M & R Strategic Services
80 Broad St, 16th Fl
New York, NY 10004
212-764-3878

Clients:
AIDS Service Center of NYC
Defenders Association (NYS)
Homeless Services United
Naral Pro-Choice NY
Pratt Center for Community Direct Marketing Association

Lobbyists:
Arthur Malkin
Michael O'Loughlin
Rebecca Wallach

MacKenzie, Duncan R
NYS Assn of Realtors
130 Washington Ave
Albany, NY 12210-2220
518-463-0300 Fax: 518-462-5474
e-mail: govt@nysar.com
Web site: www.nysar.com

Clients:
Assn of Realtors (NYS)

Lobbyists:
Michael J Kelly
Charles M Staro

Mackin, Robert E
Mackin & Company
139 Lancaster St
Albany, NY 12210-1903
518-449-4698 Fax: 518-432-5651
e-mail: bmackin@mackinco.com

Clients:
Assn of Financial Guaranty Insurors

Lobbyists:
Teresa Casey

Madison Square Garden LP
2 Penn Plaza
New York, NY 10121
212-465-6310

Clients:
Madison Square Garden LP

Lobbyists:
Joel Fisher
Andrew Lynn

Maher, Daniel F, Jr
Excess Line Assn of NY
55 Broadway, 1 Exchange Plz, 29th Fl
New York, NY 10006-3728
646-292-5500 Fax: 646-292-5500
e-mail: dmaher@elany.org
Web site: www.elany.org

Clients:
Excess Line Assn of NY

Maier, Ronald S
1170 Main Street
Buffalo, NY 14209
716-882-1025 Fax: 716-882-5577

Clients:
Elizabeth Pierce Olmsted MD Ctr for the Visually Impaired

Make the Road by Walking Inc
301 Grove St
Brooklyn, NY 11237
718-418-7690

Clients:
Make the Road by Walking

Lobbyists:
Oona Chatterjee
Sara Cullinane
Geoff Davenport
Josephina Davila
Andrew Friedman
Jesse Goldman
Raquel Gomez
Julian Gonzalez
Julissa Gonzalez
Theodoro Oshiro
Nieves Padilla
David Perez
Maria Elana Perez
Placida Rodriguez
Irene Tung
Angel Vera
Yorelis Vidal

Malkin & Ross
100 State St, Ste 400
Albany, NY 12207-1801
518-449-3359 Fax: 518-449-5788
e-mail: amalkin@malkinross.com
Web site: www.malkinross.com

Clients:
Advocates for Adult Day Services

Offices and agencies generally appear in alphabetical order, except when specific order is requested by listee.

LOBBYISTS

Alliance for Quality Education
Alliance for Clean Energy New York Inc
American Jewish Committee
Ascension Health
Aseptic Packaging Council
Assc of Perioperative Registered Nurses
Bedford Stuyvesant Family Health Center Inc
Business Outreach Ctr Network
Camp Directors (NYS)
Center for Constitutional Rights
Center for the Independence of the Disabled NY Inc
Coalition of NYS Alzheimer's Assn Chapters
Coalition for Quality Assisted Living (NY)
Coalition for the Homeless
Council of Senior Centers & Services of NYC
Defenders Assn (NYS)
Direct Marketing Assoc Inc (Dehart & Darr Assoc Inc)
Drug Policy Alliance (Center for Policy Reform)
Family Decisions Coalition (Open Society Policy Ctr)
Friends of Hudson River Park
Gay Men's Health Crisis
Lesbian Gay Bisexual & Transgender Community Ctr (The)
New Yorkers Against the Death Penalty
New Yorkers for Accessible Health Coverage
Nurses Assn (NYS)
Occupational Health Clinic Network (NYS)
Oneida Tribe of Indians of Wisconsin (Power Plant Entertainment)
Pharmaceutical Research & Manufacturers of America
Regional Community Service Pgms (NYS)
Regional Food Bank of Northeastern NY
Rehabilitation Association (NYS)
School Nutrition Assn (NY)
Schuyler Center for Analysis & Advocacy
Taxpayers Against Fraud
Trial Lawyers' Assn (NYS)
VIP Community Services

Lobbyists:
Scott J Bonacic
John Cochran
Gene DeSantis
Arthur N Malkin
Donald K Ross

Maloney, Richard
County Nursing Facilities of NY
111 Pine St
Albany, NY 12207
518-465-1473 Fax: 518-465-0506
e-mail: rmaloney@nysac.org

Clients:
County Nursing Facilities of NY, Inc

Manatt, Phelps & Phillips, LLP
30 S pearl Street
12th Fl
Albany, NY 12207
518-431-6700

Clients:
83-30 Austin Street LLC
Assn of Public Broadcasting Stations of NY
American Council of Life Insurers
Bayer Healthcare

Brain Trauma Foundation
Brooklyn Information & Culture
Callen-Lorde Coomunity Health Center
Coalition for Medically Fragile Children
Concepts of Independent Choices
Community Health Care Assoc of NYS
Corporation for Supportive Housing
Coalition of Voluntary Safety Net Hospitals (NYS)
Coalition of Prepaid Health Svcs Plans (NYS)
East Side Rezoning Alliance
El Paso Corporation
Federation of Protestant Welfare Agencies Inc
Glimmerglass Coalition
Group Health Incorporated
Health & Hospitals Corp (NYC)
Hewlett-Packard Company
Independent Care System (ICS)
Living Independently Inc
Memorial Sloan-Kettering Cancer Center
Montefiore Medical Ctr
NYS Council of Health-System Pharmacists
National Multiple Sclerosis Society, NY MS Coalition Action Netwo
Primary Care Development Corporation
Project Samaritan AIDS Services Inc
Ralph Lauren Center for Cancer Care & Prevention
Samaritan Village Inc
St Raymond Community Outreach
Structured Employment Economic Development Corp
Sephardic Bikur Holim
Structural Biology Center (NY)
Verizon Wireless
Visiting Nurse Service of NY

Lobbyists:
Marcia Alazraki
Deborah Bachrach
Robert Belfort
William Bernstein
Mira Burghardt
Patti Boozang
Andrea Cohen
Melinda Dutton
John Faso (Exec Only)
Anthony Fiori
Julie Hudman
Rebecca Hutton
Karen Lipson
James Lytle
Shelley Mayer
David Oakley
Helen Pfister
Steve Polan
Carol Rosenthal
Vanessa Wisniewski

Manhattan Chamber of Commerce Inc
1375 Broadway, 3rd Fl
New York, NY 10018
212-473-7875

Clients:
Manhattan Chamber of Commerce Inc

Lobbyists:
Michael Littenberg
Ronald Paltrowitz
Nancy Ploeger

Offices and agencies generally appear in alphabetical order, except when specific order is requested by listee.

LOBBYISTS

Don Winter

Maniscalco, John D
14 Penn Plz, Ste 1102
New York, NY 10122
212-695-1380 Fax: 212-594-6583
e-mail: nyoilheating@nyoha.org
Web site: www.nyoha.org

Clients:
Oil Heating Assoc

Mannella, Peter F
NY Assn for Pupil Transportation
266 Hudson Ave
Albany, NY 12210
518-463-4937

Clients:
Assn for Pupil Transportation (NY)

Mannis, David
140 E 45th St
New York, NY 10017-3144
646-658-7128

Clients:
Cigna Corporation

Manufacturers Assn of Central NY Inc
One Webster's Landing, 5th Fl
Syracuse, NY 13202-1044
315-474-4201

Clients:
Council of Industry of Southeastern NY
Manufacturers Assn of Central NY Inc

Lobbyists:
Karen DeJarnette
Kristen Heath
Jordan Nott
Randall Wolken

Marcus Attorneys
13 Greene Ave
Brooklyn, NY 11238
718-643-6555 Fax: 718-643-9111
e-mail: law@marcusattorneys.com
Web site: www.marcusattorneys.com

Clients:
Ballet Hispanico of NY Inc
Manhattan Theatre Club Inc
United Jewish Organizations of Williamsburg
Haim Marcovici

Lobbyists:
Daniel Benjamin
Kenya Jui
Philip Lavender

Jed S Marcus
Andrew Weltchek
Leslie Wright

Margiotta, Joseph M
425 Broad Hollow Rd, Ste 400
Melville, NY 11747
631-470-3574

Clients:
Institute of Technology (NY)
Physicians' Reciprocal Insurers

Maritato, Anna Maria
Pfizer Inc
284 State St, 2nd Fl
Albany, NY 12210
518-463-9133 Fax: 518-463-9136

Clients:
Pfizer Inc

Lobbyists:
Aimee Falchuk

Marsh & Associates, PC
677 Broadway
Albany, NY 12207
518-436-6000 Fax: 518-436-6009
e-mail: marshpc@attglobal.net

Clients:
Amerigroup New York LLC/Amerigroup Community Care (FKA Care Plus Health Plan)
Assn of Independent Schools (NYS)
ATM Industry Association
Atomic Learning Inc
Auxilia
Canadian National Railway
Cardtronics LP
Chief Executives Network for Manufacturing
Education & Work Consortium (The)
Eyemed Vision Care LLC
Greater NY Health Care Facilities Assoc
Greene International Golf Assn
LB Furniture Industries LLC
Medstat
Metropolitan College of NY
Morton Grove Pharmaceuticals
National Safety Commission Inc
SSP Companies
Tier Technologies
Town Clerks Assn Inc (NYS)
UST Public Affairs Inc
Westerm Union

Lobbyists:
C Thomas Barletta
Kerry D Marsh

Offices and agencies generally appear in alphabetical order, except when specific order is requested by listee.

LOBBYISTS

Martens, Joseph J
Open Space Institute
1350 Broadway, Rm 201
New York, NY 10018
212-629-3981 Fax: 212-344-2441
Web site: www.osiny.org

Clients:
Open Space Institute Inc

Lobbyists:
Christopher Elliman
Jennifer Grossman

Massiah, Lesley A
Fordham University
441 E Fordham Rd, Admin Bldg, Room 220
Bronx, NY 10458-9993
718-817-3023 Fax: 718-817-5722
e-mail: massiah@fordham.edu
Web site: www.fordham.edu

Clients:
Fordham University

Lobbyists:
Brian J Byrne
Ronald Davis
Rev Joseph M McShane
Michael A Molina
Joseph P Muriana

Master, Robert
CWA, District 1
80 Pine St, 37th Fl
New York, NY 10005
212-344-2515 Fax: 212-425-2947

Clients:
Communications Workers of America, District 1

Lobbyists:
Kenneth Peres
Peter Sikora

Matarazzo, Louis
36 Muirfield Rd
Rockville Centre, NY 11570
516-642-3900

Clients:
Captains Endowment Assn, NYC Police Department
Detectives Endowment Assn, Police Dept of NYC
Public Employee Conference (NYS)

McCulley & Associates Inc
150 State St, 4th Fl
Albany, NY 12207
518-432-3300 Fax: 518-432-4007

Clients:
American Academy of Orthotists and Prosthetists-New York Chapter
Assn of Home Inspectors Inc (NYS)
Fortuna Energy Inc
International Health, Raquet & Sportsclub Assn
New York Burglar Fire Alarm Association

Lobbyists:
James McCulley

McDevitt, William L
Metro Pkg Store Assn
6 Xavier Dr, Ste 315
Yonkers, NY 10704-1392
914-423-4500 Fax: 914-423-4508

Clients:
Metropolitan Package Store Assn Inc

McEvoy, Frank
99 Washington Ave, Ste 400
Albany, NY 12210
518-427-9071

Clients:
Fair Isaac Corporation
USA Training Company, Inc

McGuire, Michael J
Mason Tenders DC of Greater NY
266 W 37th St, 7th Fl
New York, NY 10018
212-452-9501 Fax: 212-452-9552

Clients:
Mason Tenders District Council Greater NY & Long Island PAC

Lobbyists:
Robert Asaro-Angelo
Kris Kohler

McInnis, Stephen C
District Council of Carpenters, PAC(NYC)
395 Hudson St, 9th Fl
New York, NY 10014
212-366-3388

Clients:
District Council of Carpenters, PAC (NYC)

Lobbyists:
Marina Vranich

McSpedon, William J
100 South Swan St
Albany, NY 12210-1939
518-463-7551 Fax: 518-463-7556

Clients:
Conf of the Int'l Union of Operating Engineers (NYS)

Offices and agencies generally appear in alphabetical order, except when specific order is requested by listee.

LOBBYISTS

Meara, Brian R, Public Relations Inc
321 Broadway
New York, NY 10007
518-465-8760

Clients:
ABC Inc
Altria Corporate Services Inc (ALCS)
American Lawyer Media Co
Assurant Solutions
Black Car Assistance Corporation
Black Car Operators' Injury Compensation Fund (NY)
Bus Association of NYS Inc
CBS Corporation
Delaware North Companies Gaming & Entertainment Inc
Court Officers Assn (NYS)
EAC Inc
Empire State Assn of Adult Homes & Assist Living Facilities
Finger Lakes Racing Association
Glenwood Management Corporation
Insurance Premium Finance Assn Inc
Long Island Power Authority
Nassau Regional Off-Track Betting Corporation
NBC Universal
Jets LLC (NY)
NYU School of Medicine
Parker Jewish Inst for Health Care & Rehab
Physicians' Reciprocal Insurers
Reliant Resources Inc
Retailers Alliance (The)
Solow Management Company
Simon Weisenthal Ctr Museum of Tolerance
Shinnecock Nation Gaming Authority
Silvercup Studios
Southern Tier Acquisition, LLC
Suffolk County Court Employees
Transit Alliance
Uniformed Fire Officers Assn (NYC)
Vanguard Car Rental USA Inc
Verizon
Wilmorite Holdings, LP
Yankees Partnership (NY)
Educational Housing Services (Regional Programs Inc)
Empire Resorts Inc
Guardian Life Insurance Company of America (The)
Lincoln Center for the Performing Arts Inc
New York Medical Staff Leadership Council
NYC & Company
NYC 2012

Lobbyists:
James Clyne
John Black
Bartley J Costello, III
Terri Crowley
Sean M Doolan
Michael Fallon
John Federman
Bruce Gyory
Brian R Meara
Robert McCarthy
Kevin P Quinn
Janet Silver

Meinking, Rebecca A
Associated Builders & Contractors, Inc
6369 Collamer Drive
East Syracuse, NY 13057
315-463-7539

Clients:
Associated Builders & Contractors, Inc

Lobbyists:
Andrea Harvey
Ruth Mulford
Scott Zylka

Melchionni, William, III
Nationwide Insurance
125 State St
Albany, NY 12207
518-455-8930 Fax: 518-426-5891
e-mail: melchib@nationwide.com

Clients:
Nationwide Insurance & Nationwide Financial Services
Mental Health Assn of Westchester Co Inc

Clients:
Mental Health Assn of Westchester

Lobbyists:
Michael Friedman
Carolyn S Hedlund PhD

Mental Health Association in NYS
194 Washington Ave, Ste 415
Albany, NY 12210
518-434-0439 Fax: 518-427-8676
e-mail: mhapres@mhanys.org
Web site: www.mhanys.org

Clients:
Mental Health Association of NYC Inc

Lobbyists:
Glenn Liebman
Micheal Seereiter

Mercury Public Affairs
137 5th Ave, 3rd Fl
New York, NY 10010-7147
212-681-1380 Fax: 212-681-1381
Web site: www.mercurypublicaffairs.com

Clients:
AT&T Corp
Accent Stripe Inc
American Red Cross in Greater NY
Ammann & Whitney
Armienti, Debellis & Whiten LLP
Armor Dynamics Inc
Bodega Assoc of the US Inc (The)
CMA Consulting
Distilled Spirits Council of the US
Federation of Taxi Drivers Inc (NYS)

Offices and agencies generally appear in alphabetical order, except when specific order is requested by listee.

LOBBYISTS

Fluent Energy
Information Management Group
Intergraph Corporation
Izzo Construction
Lechase Construction Services
Liberty Lines Express Inc
Jets, LLC (NY)
Mercy College
Empire Resorts Inc
Buffalo Niagara Partnership
Greater NY Health Care Facilities Assn
Western Regional Off-Track Betting Corporation
Natural Resources Defense Council
Niagara Falls Memorial Medical Arts Center
Otis Elevator Company
Pfizer Inc
Police Benevolent Assn of the NYS Troopers Inc
Plaza Construction Corporation
Sallie Mae Inc
School Bus Contractors Assn (NY)
Sheldrake Organization Inc
Shinnecock Nation Gaming Authority
Slavco Construction
Source Corp
Spain Agency Inc

Lobbyists:
Peter Barden
Jennifer Carlson
Andre Claridge
Thomas Doherty
Dina Dossantos
John Hishta
John Lonergan
Kieran Mahoney
Michael McKeon
Mike Relyea
Kevin Schuler
Greg Strimple
Matt Watson

Mesick, Edie
Nutrition Consortium of NYS
235 Lark St
Albany, NY 12210
518-436-8757 Fax: 518-427-7992

Clients:
Nutrition Consortium of NYS Inc

Lobbyists:
Lisa Allison
Christine Barberio
Gail Cooney
Mark Denley
Casey Dunkin
Lisa Frank
Yvette James
Misha Marvel
Colleen Pawling
Catherine Roberts

Meyer Suozzi English & Klein, PC
One Commerce Plaza, Ste 1102
Albany, NY 12260
518-465-5551 Fax: 518-465-2033

Clients:
1199/SEIU New York's Health & Human Services Union
Actors Fund of America (The)
Brooklyn Public Library
City Works Foundation, (The)
Committee for Occupational Safety & Health (NY)
Committee for Workers' Compensation Reform
Conservation Service Group
Council for Unity
Consortium for Workers Education
Forest City Ratner Companies
Fractured Atlas
Friends of NY Racing Inc
Local 802, American Federation of Musicians of Greater NY
Int'l Brotherhood of Teamsters, AFL-CIO (Local 237)
Laborers' Political Action Committee (NYS)
Garment Industry Development Corporation
Local 1180, CWA, AFL-CIO
Mount Sinai Medical Center
Retail Wholesale Department Store Union
MFY Legal Services
Screen Actors Guild (National & Hollywood Offices)
Suffolk County Correction Officers Assn
Susquehanna & Western Railway Corp (NY)
Production Alliance (NY)
Unite Here
Utility Workers Union, Local 1-2, AFL-CIO
SEIU Local 200 United
Workers' Compensation Alliance
Working Today
SEIU, Local 300
Traffipax Inc

Lobbyists:
Thomas Hartnett
Julie Ruttan
Lawrence Scherer
Jacqueline Williams
Richard D Winsten

Mid-Hudson Catskill Rural & Migrant Ministry Inc
360 Noxon Rd
PO Box 4757
Poughkeepsie, NY 12602
845-485-8627 Fax: 845-485-1963
e-mail: hope@ruralmigrantministry.org
Web site: www.ruralmigrantministry.org

Clients:
Mid-Hudson Catskill Rural & Migrant Ministry Inc

Lobbyists:
Luis Torres
Richard Witt, Jr

Midtown Consultants, Inc
321 W 44th Street (203-B)
New York, NY 10036
212-582-1347

Clients:
GVA Williams, Inc/60 Hudson Owner, LLC

Offices and agencies generally appear in alphabetical order, except when specific order is requested by listee.

LOBBYISTS

Lobbyists:
Bernie Cohen
James McManus

Miller, Monica
4691 Route 66
PO Box 118
Malden Bridge, NY 12115
518-766-0322

Clients:
Foundation for the Advancement of Innovative Medicine
Health Freedom NY

Mills, Josephine
Avon Products, Inc
1345 Ave of the Americas
New York, NY 10105-0196
212-282-5609 Fax: 212-282-6086
e-mail: josephine.mills@avon.com

Clients:
Avon Products Inc

Mirant New York Inc
140 Samsondale Ave
West Haverstraw, NY 10993
845-786-8111
e-mail: louis.friscoe@mirant.com

Clients:
Mirant New York Inc

Lobbyists:
Louis Friscoe
Philip Smith

Mirram Global, LLC
895 Broadway, 5th Fl
New York, NY 10003
212-505-6633/212-260 Fax: 212-505-0845/21
e-mail: mirramglobal@aol.com

Clients:
Healthplex Inc
New York First
Coalition for the Homeless
Center Care Inc
Morris Heights Health Ctr
New Visions for Public Schools
Vote Here, Inc

Lobbyists:
Luis A Miranda Jr
Roberto Ramirez Jr
Roberto Ramirez Sr
Kim Ramos
Jon Silvan
Catherine Torres

Mirram Group, LLC (The)
895 Broadway, 5th Fl
New York, NY 10003
212-505-6633 Fax: 212-505-0845
e-mail: mirramgroup@aol.com

Clients:
Atlantic Development Co
Cable Telecommunications Association of NY
Coalition for the Homeless
First (NY)
Food Industry Alliance of NYS
Healthcare Education Project
Healthplex Inc
Monroe College
Morris Heights Health Center
New Visions for Public Schools
Protecting America.org
Transport Workers Union, Local 100
TVG Network
UBS Securities
Urban Health Plan Inc
World Trade Center Properties

Lobbyists:
Luis A Miranda Jr
Roberto Ramirez Sr
Kim Ramos

Montalbano Initiatives Inc
64 Fulton St, Ste 603
New York, NY 10038
212-587-0587 Fax: 212-587-0667
Web site: www.nyclobbyist.com

Clients:
Covenant House NY
Legal Services for NYC Inc
Social Service Employees Union, Local 371
Teamsters Local 237
Trust for Public Land

Lobbyists:
Vincent Montalbano

Morello, Charles J
NYS PFFA
111 Washington Ave, Ste 207
Albany, NY 12210
518-436-8827 Fax: 518-436-8830
e-mail: nyspffapres@aol.com
Web site: www.nyspffa.org

Clients:
Professional Fire Fighters Assn Inc (NYS)

Lobbyists:
Michael McManus

Morgan Associates
12 North Main St
Homer, NY 13077
518-426-1298

Offices and agencies generally appear in alphabetical order, except when specific order is requested by listee.

LOBBYISTS

Clients:
Park Outdoor Advertising of NY Inc
Westchester County Correctional Superior Officers Assn

Lobbyists:
Matthew A Morgan

Morgante, Samuel
700 12th St NW, Ste 710
Washington, DC 20005
202-662-2577

Clients:
Genworth Financial

Lobbyists:
David Sloane

Morris & McVeigh LLP
19 Dove St
Albany, NY 12210
518-426-8111 Fax: 518-426-5111
e-mail: rjm@mormc.com

Clients:
Collegiate Church Corp
Greenwich House, Inc
New Amsterdam History Cneter (The)

Lobbyists:
Richard J Miller Jr

Morris, Mark
Hanys Insurance Co
217 Great Oaks Blvd
Albany, NY 12203-5964
518-862-0676

Clients:
Healthcare Professional Insurance Company, Inc

Morse, Alan
Jewish Guild for the Blind (The)
15 W 65th St
New York, NY 10023
212-769-6215 Fax: 212-595-4907
e-mail: armorse@jgb.org
Web site: www.jgb.org

Clients:
Jewish Guild for the Blind (The)

Lobbyists:
Annemarie O'Hearn

Motley, Duane R
PO Box 107
Spencerport, NY 14559-0107
585-225-2340 Fax: 585-225-2810
e-mail: family@nyfrf.org
Web site: www.nyfrf.org

Clients:
New Yorkers for Constitutional Freedoms

Mount Sinai Medical Center
One Gustave L Levy Pl
Box 1499
New York, NY 10029-6574
212-659-9011

Clients:
Mount Sinai Medical Center

Lobbyists:
Brad Beckstrom

Muhs, Robert E
Avis Budget Group Inc
6 Sylvan Way
Parsippany, NJ 07054
973-496-3532 Fax: 973-496-3444
e-mail: rmuhs@avis.com

Clients:
Avis Budget Group Inc & Its Subsidiaries (FKA Cendant Car Rental Group Inc & Subsidiaries)

Mullane, Robert A
MEUA
445 Electronics Pkwy, Ste 207
Liverpool, NY 13080-6001
315-453-7851 Fax: 315-473-7849
e-mail: info@meua.org
Web site: www.meua.org

Clients:
Municipal Electric Utilities Assn of NYS (MEUA)

Municipal Art Society
457 Madison Ave
New York, NY 10022
212-935-3960 Fax: 212-753-1816

Clients:
Municipal Art Society

Lobbyists:
Eve Baron
Kent Barwick
Micaela Birmingham
Carter Craft
Jasper Goldman
Vanessa Gruen
Katie Kendall
Lisa Kersavage
Frank Sanchis

Murphy, Daniel C
NY Hosp & Tourism Assn
80 Wolf Rd
Albany, NY 12205

Offices and agencies generally appear in alphabetical order, except when specific order is requested by listee.

LOBBYISTS

518-465-2300 Fax: 518-465-4025
e-mail: dan@nyshta.org
Web site: nyshta.org

Clients:
Hospitality & Tourism Assn (NYS)

Murphy, Robert J
Health Facilities Assn
33 Elk St, Ste 300
Albany, NY 12207-1010
518-462-4800 Fax: 518-426-4051
e-mail: rmurphy@nyshfa.org

Clients:
Health Facilities Assn (NYS)

Lobbyists:
Bryan Boeskin
Edwin Graham
Richard Herrick
Nancy Leveille
Karen Morris
Carl Pucci

Murray, Claire
1501 Twelfth Ave
Watervliet, NJ 12189-2402
518-273-1525

Clients:
Organization of Nurse Executives Inc (NY)

NAMI-NYS
260 Washington Ave
Albany, NY 12210
518-462-2000 Fax: 518-462-3811

Clients:
NAMI-NYS

Lobbyists:
J David Seay

NARAL Pro-Choice, New York
470 Park Ave S
7th Fl
New York, NY 10016
212-343-0114
e-mail: info@prochoiceny.org
Web site: www.prochoiceny.org

Clients:
NARAL Pro-Choice, New York

Lobbyists:
Emily Alexander
Mary Alice Carr
Pauline DeMairo
Angela Hooton
Kelli Conlin
Robert Jaffe

Debbie Johnson
Cristina Tenuta
Andrew Stern

NYC & Company, Inc
810 Seventh Ave, 3rd Fl
New York, NY 10019
212-484-1280

Clients:

Nasca, Samuel J
United Transp Union
35 Fuller Rd
Albany, NY 12205
518-438-8403 Fax: 518-438-8404
e-mail: sjnasca@aol.com

Clients:
United Transportation Union

National Alliance for the Mentally Ill of NYC, Inc
505 Eighth Ave, Ste 1103
New York, NY 10018
212-684-3365

Clients:
National Alliance for the Mentally Ill of NYC, Inc

Lobbyists:
Amanda Bohlig
Wendy Brennan
Alison Burke
Rebecca Pietsch

National Assn of Chain Drug Stores
328 Still River Rd
Still River, MA 01467
978-456-9235
Web site: www.nacds.org

Clients:
National Assn of Chain Drug Stores

Lobbyists:
Anne Fellows

National Assn of Social Workers (NYS Chapter)
188 Washington Ave
Albany, NY 12210
518-463-4741 Fax: 518-463-6446

Clients:
National Assn of Social Workers (NYS Chapter)

Lobbyists:
Reinaldo Cardona
Karin Moran

Offices and agencies generally appear in alphabetical order, except when specific order is requested by listee.

LOBBYISTS

New York State Nurses Association
Nurses Assn (NYS)
11 Cornell Rd
Latham, NY 12110-1499
518-782-9400

Clients:
Nurses Association (NYS)

Lobbyists:
Ron Abrahall
Lydia Bellardo
Ellen Brickman
Tina Gerardi
Michelle Hart
Carol Pittman
Alithia Rolon

New Yorkers Against the Death Penalty
40 N Main Ave
Albany, NY 12203
518-453-6797

Clients:
New Yorkers Against the Death Penalty

Lobbyists:
Colleen Eren
David Kaczynski
Jim Michalek
Janice Minott
Laura Porter
Carrie Schneider
Les Ulm
Marie Verzulli

Newman-Limata, Nancy
PricewaterhouseCoopers LLP
300 Madison Ave
New York, NY 10017
646-471-0514

Clients:
PricewaterhouseCoopers

Lobbyists:
Gerard Bielak
Michael Bokina
David Chin
Nick Cifra
Ann Filiault
Chris Guiliano
Richard Grant
Steven Gurtman
Matthew Lusnar
Kevin McCadden
Frank Paterno
Russ Sapineza
Mordecai Soloff
Tim Weld
Daniel Czajkowski
Brendan Dougher
James Dreyer
Albert Farina
Kelly Fingerhut
Michael Hayes
Alan Hines
David Holtzman
Steve Jacques
Karen Lee
Art Leibowitz
Charles Lewis
John Mattie
Lisa Preddice
Gary Ryan
Andrew Sawyer
Jeff Short
Bethany Smith
Duaine Smith
Ryder Smith
Steven Sumner
Staci Weissman

Newspaper Publishers Assn (NY)
291 Hudson Ave, Ste A
Albany, NY 12210
518-449-1667 Fax: 518-449-5053

Clients:
Newspaper Publishers Assn (NY)

Lobbyists:
Diane Kennedy

Nixon Peabody, LLP
Omni Plaza
30 S Pearl St, 9th Fl
Albany, NY 12207
518-427-2650 Fax: 518-427-2666

Clients:
Assn of Laser Hair Removal Specialists, Inc (NYS)
Bellevue Women's Medical Center, Inc

Lobbyists:
Peter Millock

Nolan & Heller, LLP
39 North Pearl St
3rd Fl
Albany, NY 12207
518-449-3300
e-mail: tburke@nolanandheller.com

Clients:
Empire State Subcontractors Assn

Lobbyists:
Francis Brennan
Terence Burke

Norat, Cecilia E
American Int'l Group, Inc
70 Pine St, 6th Fl
New York, NY 10270
212-770-5235

Offices and agencies generally appear in alphabetical order, except when specific order is requested by listee.

LOBBYISTS

Clients:
American International Group, Inc

Lobbyists:
Paul S Brown

Norris, Kelly K
Society of Professional Engineers, Inc
RPI Technology Park, 385 Jordan Rd
Troy, NY 12180-7620
518-283-7490
Web site: www.nysspe.org

Clients:
Society of Professional Engineers, Inc (NYS)

Northeast Health Inc
2212 Burdett Ave
Troy, NY 12180
518-271-5000 Fax: 518-271-5088
Web site: www.nehealth.com

Clients:
Northeast Health

Lobbyists:
Jo-Ann Costantino
Norman E Dascher Jr

Northern Metropolitan Hospital Assn
400 Stony Brook Court
Newburgh, NY 12550-5162
845-562-7520 Fax: 845-562-0187
e-mail: awein@normet.org

Clients:
Northern Metropolitan Hospital Assn

Lobbyists:
Neil Abitabilo
Angela Skretta-Huck

Nurse Practitioner Assn of NYS (The)
12 Corporate Dr
Clifton Park, NY 12065-8603
518-348-0719 Fax: 518-348-0720
e-mail: info@thenpa.org
Web site: www.thenpa.org

Clients:
Nurse Practitioner Assn of NYS (The)

Lobbyists:
Seth Gordon

O'Connell, Peter B
130 Washington Ave
Albany, NY 12210-2219
518-436-7202 Fax: 518-436-7203

Clients:
Automatic Vending Assn (NYS)
Empire State Towing & Recovery Assn
Capital District Physicians' Health Plan Inc
Campground Owners of NY Inc
Long Island Pest Control Assn

O'Connor, John
12 Sheridan Ave
Albany, NY 12207
518-449-5370 Fax: 518-449-5413

Clients:
Pharmaceutical Research & Manufacturers of America

O'Mara, John F
84 Oak Hill
Horseheads, NY 14845
585-349-7700

Clients:
Eber Bros Wine & Liquor Corp
National Grid USA
Salient Technologies Inc

Ohrenstein & Brown, LLP
1010 Franklin Ave, 2nd Fl
PO Box 9243
Garden City, NY 11530-9243
516-873-6334

Clients:
Jamaica Hospital Medical Center
Marsh USA Inc

Lobbyists:
Michael Brown
Manfred Ohrenstein

Organization of NYS Management/Confidential Employees Inc
3 Washington Square
Albany, NY 12205-5523
518-456-5241 Fax: 518-456-3838
e-mail: omce@aol.com
Web site: www.nysomce.org

Clients:
Org of NYS Mgmt/Confidential Employees, Inc

Lobbyists:
Joseph Sano
Barbara Zaron

Ostroff, Hiffa & Associates Inc
12 Sheridan Ave
Albany, NY 12207
518-436-6202 Fax: 518-436-1956
e-mail: ostroff_associates@msn.com
Web site: www.ostroff-hiffa.com

Offices and agencies generally appear in alphabetical order, except when specific order is requested by listee.

LOBBYISTS

Clients:
380 Development LLC
Adirondack Pine Hill NY Trailways
Amerada Hess Corporation
Assn of Town Superintendents of Highways Inc (NYS)
CATS VLT, LLC (Canadian American Transportation Systems)
Catholic Family Center
Cemetery Employer Assn of Greater NY
Cephalon Inc
Courtroom Television Network
Creative Coalition (The)
Crisis Program (The)
Dreyfus Corporation (The)
Duke Energy Corporation
Empire State Restaurant & Tavern Assn
Fahs Construction Group (Fahs-Rolston Paving Corp)
FlexCare
Central NY Railroad
Greater NY Health Care Facilities Assn
Cross Harbor Railroad (NY)
Hubbell Galvanizing
International Imaging Technology Council (I-ITC)
Liquid Asphalt Distributors Assoc Inc of NY
Monument Builders Assn (NYS)
Mount St Mary's Hospital & Health Center
Cumberland Packing Corporation
Public Library (NY), Astor, Lenox & Tilden Foundations
Electric & Gas Corporation (NYS)
Eponymous Associates LLC (FKA Steiner Studios)
Pratt Institute
Riverside South Planning Corp
Rochester Gas & Electric Corp
Suit-Kote Corp
UST Public Affairs Inc
United Health Services
Washington Cemetery
Western NY Energy LLC

Lobbyists:
James Cantwell
Frederick T Hiffa
Richard L Ostroff
Erin T Waterhouse
Scott Wexler

Pappas, Marcia
3 Equality Ct
Albany, NY 12205
518-452-7055

Clients:
National Organization for Women (NYS)

Lobbyists:
Lori Gardner
Barbara Kirkpatrick

Park Strategies, LLC
101 Park Ave, Ste 2506
New York, NY 10178
212-883-5608 Fax: 212-883-5643

Clients:
Aetna Inc
Concerned Home Care Providers
Cendant Car Rental Group Inc
Correction Officers & Police Benevolent Assn Inc
Covanta Energy Corp
Energy East Corporation
Health Care Subrogation Group
Canadian American Transportation Systems, LLC
Lilac Capital LLC
LS Power Associates LLC
Madison Square Garden LP
Manhattan Theatre Club
Magna Entertainment Corp
NYU Child Study Center
Sheriff Officers Assn
Subway Surface Supervisors Assn
Vector Group, Ltd

Lobbyists:
Alfonse M D'Amato
Armand D'Amato
Christopher P D'Amato
David Poleto
Greg Serio
John Zagame

Parkside Group, LLC
132 Nassau St, Ste 619
New York, NY 10038
212-571-7717 Fax: 212-571-7757
Web site: www.theparksidegroup.com

Clients:
345 E 62nd Street Associate
AAFE Managment Co
AFSCME Local 2021
American Museum of the Moving Image Inc
Assn for the Advancement of Blind & Retarded Inc
Assn for Neurologically Impaired Brain Injured Children Inc
Brooklyn Public Library
Business Outreach Center Network Inc
Central Labor Council (NYC)
Coastal Communications Services Inc
Committee for Hispanic Children & Families
Communication Workers of America Local 1180
Community Bank (NY)
Council Management Inc
Communication Workers of America, Local 1182
Danaher Controls Inc
Flushing Commons LLC
Flushing Council on Culture & the Arts Inc
Fresh Direct, LLC
Gloria Wise Boys & Girls Club Inc
Hospital Medical Center of Queens (NY)
Jamaica Ctr for Arts & Learning Inc
Church Avenue Merchants Block Association Inc
Metropolitan Life Insurance Co
Mulvihill ICS Inc
New York Cares Inc
Plaza College
Queens Centers for Progress Inc
Queens Chamber of Commerce
Queens Child Guidance Center Inc
Queens Economic Development Corp
Queens Centers for Progress Inc
Queens Theatre in the Park
Queensborough Comm College Auxiliary Enterprise Assn Inc
Rockaway Development & Revitalization Corp
Service Employees International Union, Local 300
South Queens Boys & Girls Club Inc

Offices and agencies generally appear in alphabetical order, except when specific order is requested by listee.

LOBBYISTS

Strive
Supershuttle NY Inc
Telebeam Telecommunications Corp
United Food & Commercial Workers Dist Cncl of NY & Northern NJ
Community Financial Services Association of America
Crystal Window & Door Systems, Ltd
Educational Assistance Corporation
Entergy Nuclear Operations Inc
Gaucho LLC
Gowanus Village 1 Inc
Jets (NY)
National Council to Prevent Delinquency Inc
Nextel Operations Inc
NYC & Company
Pratt Institute for Community & Environment Development
Queens College Foundation-Research of CUNY

Lobbyists:
William Driscoll
Harry Giannoulis
Barry Grodenchik
Tiffany Raspberry
Evan Stavisky

Pastel & Rosen, LLP
130 Washington Ave
Albany, NY 12210
518-462-4715 Fax: 518-462-4756

Clients:
Carco Group Inc
Chubb & Son (Division of Federal Insurance Co)
Coalition for Mold Reform (State Farm Insurance Cos)
Fireman's Fund Insurance Co
Insurance Brokers' Association of the State of New York
Professional Insurance Wholesalers Assoc of NYS Inc
Progressive Insurance Companies

Lobbyists:
Robert S Pastel
Michael E Rosen

Patterson & McLaughlin
64 Fulton St
New York, NY 10038
212-437-7373

Clients:
Verizon Corporate Services Corp
Manhattan Theatre Club

Lobbyists:
Cathy Cudahy
Martin McLaughlin
Michael Woloz

Pepe, Ross J
CIC of Westchester
629 Old White Plains Rd
Tarrytown, NY 10591-5100
914-631-6070 Fax: 914-631-5172

Clients:
Construction Industry Cncl of Westchester & Hudson Valley Inc

Perkins, Janice C
One Far Mill Crossing
PO Box 904
Shelton, CT 06484
203-225-8630

Clients:
Health Net of the Northeast

Perry, Robert
CLU-NY
125 Broad St, 19th Fl
New York, NY 10004
212-607-3300

Clients:
Civil Liberties Union (NY)

Lobbyists:
Elizabeth Benjamin
Linda Berns
Dolores Bilges
John Curr
Christopher Dunn
Arthur Eisenberg
Jeff Fogel
Lisa Fox
Barrie Gewanter
Beth Haroules
Palyn Hung
Tara Keenan-Thomas
Lee Che Leong
Donna Lieberman
Darinka Maldonado
Udi Ofer
Ari Rosemarin
Galen Sherwin
Christian Smith-Socaris
Corey Stoughton
Irum Taqi
Melanie Trimble
Barbara Williams Deleeuw

Peters, Jeffrey R
212 N Third St, Ste 101
Harrisburg, PA 17101
717-232-5634 Fax: 717-232-0691

Clients:
SUNOCO Inc

Petraitis, Brian J
122 South Swan St
Albany, NY 12210
518-472-1515 Fax: 518-472-1516
e-mail: bpetraitis@collegeboard.org
Web site: www.collegeboard.com

Clients:
College Board (The)

Lobbyists:
Brian J Petraitis

Offices and agencies generally appear in alphabetical order, except when specific order is requested by listee.

Tom Rudin

Phillips & Associates, PLLC
50 Beaver St
Albany, NY 12207-2830
518-432-6857 Fax: 518-445-9143

Clients:
Occupational Therapy Assn (NYS)

Lobbyists:
Lois R Phillips
Melissa Zamdri

Phillips Nizer, LLP
666 Fifth Ave
New York, NY 10103-0084
212-977-9700

Clients:
CSC Holdings, Inc

Lobbyists:
Kevin McGrath

Pinsky & Pinsky, PC
5790 Widewaters Pkwy
PO Box 250
Syracuse, NY 13214
315-446-2384 Fax: 315-446-3016

Clients:
Radiological Society Inc (NYS)

Lobbyists:
Philip C Pinsky

Pinsky & Skandalis
5790 Widewaters Pkwy
PO Box 250
Syracuse, NY 13214-0250
315-446-2384 Fax: 315-446-3016
e-mail: pinskyskan@aol.com

Clients:
7-Eleven Inc
Adirondack League Club
Assn for Community Living
City of Yonkers
Board of Commissioners of Pilots of the State of NY
Cable Telecommunications Assn of NY Inc
Calpine Corporation
City of White Plains (The)
Erie Boulevard Hydro Power LP
Graduate Mgmt Admission Council
Health Insurance Plan of Greater NY
HDS Retail North America
Industries for the Disabled Inc (NYS)
Jets (NY)
Land Title Assn (NYS)
North Shore-Long Island Jewish Health System Inc
Phoenix House Foundation Inc
Plug Power Inc

Randi Weingarten, MLC Chair & UFT President
Sagem Morpho
Westchester County Health Care Corporation
Society of Certified Public Accountants (NYS)
Xerox Corp

Lobbyists:
Philip C Pinsky

Poklemba, John J
358 Broadway, Ste 307
Saratoga Springs, NY 12866
518-581-9797 Fax: 518-581-9590

Clients:
American Transit Insurance Company
Assn of Chiefs of Police (NYS)
Deputy Sheriff's Assn (NYC)
Patrolmen's Benevolent Assn (NYC)

Lobbyists:
Steven Watts

Police Benevolent Assn of the NYS Troopers Inc
120 State St
Albany, NY 12207
518-462-7448 Fax: 518-462-0790
e-mail: nystpba@capital.net
Web site: www.nystpba.org

Clients:
Police Benevolent Assn of the NYS Troopers Inc

Lobbyists:
Daniel DeFedericis
Gordon Warnock

Powers & Company
90 State St, Ste 1422
Albany, NY 12207
518-431-0720 Fax: 518-431-0721
Web site: www.powerscompany.com

Clients:
BearingPoint
Boulevard ALP Associates
Broadcasters Assn (NYS)
Building Contractors Assn Inc
Colony Liquor & Wine Distributors, LLC
Computer Associates
Empire State Liquor Store Assn
Funding Source (The)
Glenwood Management Corporation
Hodgson Russ LLP
Law Enforcement Officers Union, Distr Cncl 82 (NYS)
Lincoln Center for the Performing Arts
Laborers PAC (NYS)
Motorola Inc
Oneida Tribe of Indians of Wisconsin (Power Plant Entertainment NY)
Pollard Banknote Limited
Pro Tech Monitoring Inc
PSCH Inc
Racing and Gaming Services Inc
Shaker Museum (The)

Offices and agencies generally appear in alphabetical order, except when specific order is requested by listee.

LOBBYISTS

Siena College
Stratford Business Corp
Susan O'Dell Taylor School for Children
Trustco Bank
Verizon
WelchAllyn Inc
Wilmorite Holdings
Yankees Partnership (NY)

Lobbyists:
Heather C Briccetti
John J Curry
Thomas J Murphy
Jason A Powers
Matthew D Powers
William D Powers
Paul W Zuber

Powers Global Strategies, LLC
152 West 57th St, 11th Fl
New York, NY 10019
212-582-0833 Fax: 212-582-0199

Clients:
3M Company
ACS State & Local Solutions Inc
ADT Security Services Inc
American Continental Properties Inc
BearingPoint Inc
Beth Israel Medical Center
C/S 12th Avenue LLC
HNTB, New York
Juniper Networks Inc
Long Island College Hospital (The)
P&O Ports North America Inc
St Luke's-Roosevelt Hospital Centers
Simpson & Brown Inc
Site-Blauvelt Engineers
Tishman Speyer Properties
United Parcel Service
Valeray Real Estate Co Inc
Veolia Water
World Trade Center Properties, LLC

Lobbyists:
Seth Kaye
Sylvia Ng
Peter Powers

Pozzi, Brian M
100 Motor Pkwy, Ste 140
Hauppauge, NY 11788
631-233-6050
Web site: www.allstate.com

Clients:
Allstate Insurance Co

Lobbyists:
Vincent Fusco
Bill Vainisi
Tom Wilson

Presbyterian Hospital (NY)
Herbert Irving Pavillion
161 Ft Washington Ave
14th Fl, Rm 1428
New York, NY 10032
212-305-4223 Fax: 212-342-5265

Clients:
Presbyterian Hospital (NY)

Lobbyists:
Julio Batista
Willa Brody
David Liss
Helen Morik
Herbert Pardes
William A Polf

Psychological Assn (NYS)
6 Executive Park
Albany, NY 12203
518-437-1040 Fax: 518-437-0177

Clients:
Psychological Assn (NYS)

Lobbyists:
Stephen Allinger
Joseph Garba

Public Library, Astor, Lenox & Tilden Foundations (NY)
5th Ave & 42nd St
New York, NY 10018-2788
212-930-0552 Fax: 212-869-3567

Clients:
Public Library, Astor, Lenox & Tilden Foundations (NY)

Lobbyists:
Catherine Dente
Catherine Dunn
Paul Leclerc

Public Strategies, LLC
247 Murray Ave
Larchmont, NY 10538
914-912-0526 Fax: 914-834-8397
e-mail: vmarrone@publicstrategiesllc.net
Web site: www.publicstrategiesllc.net

Clients:
AIDS Coalition (NY)
Beginning with Children Foundation
Big Brothers Big Sisters of NYC
Center for Charter School Excellence (NYC)
Clinical Education Initiative Council
Compassion & Choices of NY (Compassion in Dying)
Gay & Lesbian Anti-Violence Project (NYC)
Legal Services for Working Poor New Yorkers Coalition
Marijuana Policy Project
Medicare Rights Center

Offices and agencies generally appear in alphabetical order, except when specific order is requested by listee.

Lobbyists:
Vincent Marrone

Public Utility Law Project of New York Inc
194 Washington Ave
Ste 420
Albany, NY 12210
518-449-3375 Fax: 518-449-1769
e-mail: info@pulp.tc
Web site: www.pulp.tc

Clients:
Public Utility Law Project of New York Inc

Lobbyists:
Charles J Brennan
Gerald A Norlander
Ben Wiles

Public Welfare Assn (NY)
130 Washington Ave
Albany, NY 12210
518-465-9305 Fax: 518-465-5633
e-mail: nypwa@nycap.rr.com
Web site: www.nypwa.com

Clients:
Public Welfare Assn (NY)

Lobbyists:
Sheila Harrigan

Puckett, Robert R
Telecommunications Assn
100 State St, Ste 650
Albany, NY 12207
518-443-2700 Fax: 518-443-2810
e-mail: rpuckett@nysta.com
Web site: www.nysta.com

Clients:
Telecommunications Assn Inc (NYS)

Raustiala, Margaret
428 River Rd
Nissequogue, NY 11780
631-724-7767

Clients:
Alliance of Long Island Agencies

Real Estate Board of NY Inc
570 Lexington Ave
New York, NY 10022
212-532-3100 Fax: 212-481-0420
e-mail: jdoyle@rebny.com
Web site: www.rebny.com

Clients:
Real Estate Board of NY Inc

Lobbyists:
Marolyn Davenport
John Doyle
Sean Lindstone
Michael Slattery
Steven Spinola
Carol Van Guilder

Rehabilitation Assn Inc (NYS)
155 Washington Ave, Ste 410
Albany, NY 12210-2332
518-449-2976 Fax: 518-426-4329
e-mail: nysra@nyrehab.org
Web site: www.nyrehab.org

Clients:
Rehabilitation Assn Inc (NYS)

Lobbyists:
Patricia Dowse
Jeffrey Wise

Reiter/Begun Associates, LLC
299 Broadway
Ste 607
New York, NY 10007
212-513-0080

Clients:
NYU School of Medicine & NYU Hospitals

Lobbyists:
Martin Begun
Fran Reiter

Rensselaer Polytechnic Institute
110 Eighth St
#2021
Troy, NY 12180-3590
518-276-8682 Fax: 518-276-2732
Web site: www.rpi.edu

Clients:
Rensselaer Polytechnic Institute

Lobbyists:
Shirley Ann Jackson
John MacEnroe

Rent Stabilization Assn of NYC Inc
123 William St, 14th Fl
New York, NY 10038
212-214-9266 Fax: 212-732-0617

Clients:
Rent Stabilization Assn of NYC Inc

Lobbyists:
Jack Freund
Mitchell Posilkin
Frank P Ricci
Joseph Strasburg

Offices and agencies generally appear in alphabetical order, except when specific order is requested by listee.

LOBBYISTS

Repas, Peter G
33 Elk St
Albany, NY 12207
518-462-1590 Fax: 518-462-1390
e-mail: apbs@wxxi.org

Clients:
Assn of Public Broadcasting Stations of NY

Rice & Justice
111 Washington Ave, Ste 700
Albany, NY 12210
518-434-8435 Fax: 518-434-8462

Clients:
Air Transport Assn Inc
Business Council of NYS Inc (The)
Container Terminal Inc (NY)
Eli Lilly & Co
Industry Ad Hoc Committee on Pilotage

Lobbyists:
Lawrence P Justice
Bradley F Rice
John Carter Rice

Right to Life Committee Inc (NYS)
41 State St, Ste M-100
Albany, NY 12207
518-434-1293 Fax: 518-426-1200
e-mail: lhougens1@aol.com
Web site: www.nysrighttolife.org

Clients:
Right to Life Committee Inc (NYS)

Lobbyists:
Christina Fitch
Lori Kehoe

Riverkeeper, Inc
828 S Broadway
Tarrytown, NY 10591
914-478-4501
e-mail: info@riverkeeper.org
Web site: www.riverkeeper.org

Clients:
Riverkeeper, Inc

Lobbyists:
Leila Goldmark
Robert Goldstein
Robert Kennedy
Alex Matthiessen
Phillip Musegaas
Basil Seggos
Victor Tafur
Lisa Van Suntum

Rochester Regional Healthcare Advocates
3445 Winton Place, Ste 222
Rochester, NY 14623
585-273-8180 Fax: 585-273-8189

Clients:
Rochester Regional Healthcare Advocates

Lobbyists:
Diane Ashley
Robert Swinnerton
Karen Yacono

Roffe, Andrew S, PC
111 Washington Ave, Ste 409
Albany, NY 12210
518-432-7841 Fax: 518-432-4267
e-mail: aroffe@rc.com

Clients:
7-Eleven Inc
Adirondack League Club
Apple Computer Inc
Assn for Community Living
City of Yonkers
Board of Commissioners of Pilots of the State of NY
CSX Transportation Inc
Cable Telecommunications Assn of NY Inc
Calpine Corporation
Chiropractic Council (NY)
City of White Plains (The)
Erie Boulevard Hydropower LP
Graduate Management Admission Council
Health Insurance Plan of NY
Independent Living Services Inc
Industries for the Disabled Inc (NYS)
JP Morgan Chase & Co
Jets (NY)
Land Title Assn Inc (NYS)
Loretto Management Corp
Museum of Modern Art (The)
North Shore-Long Island Jewish Health System Inc
Phoenix House Foundation Inc
Plug Power Inc
Sagem Morpho Inc
Westchester County Health Care Corp
Westchester Industrial Development Agency
Randi Weingarten
Society of Certified Public Accountants (NYS)
Xerox Corp

Lobbyists:
Andrew S Roffe
Joelle Zullo

Roos, David E
AT&T
111 Washington Ave, Ste 706
Albany, NY 12210-2213
518-463-3107 Fax: 518-463-5943
e-mail: droos@att.com

Clients:
AT&T Inc & Its Affiliates

Offices and agencies generally appear in alphabetical order, except when specific order is requested by listee.

LOBBYISTS

Lobbyists:
Deborah Bierbaum
Mary Burgess
John Liantano

Ropes & Gray
1 International Place
Boston, MA 02110-2624
617-951-7000

Clients:
Pfizer, Inc

Lobbyists:
Stephen A Warnke

Rosario, Stephen M
Am Chemistry Cncl
99 Washington Ave, Ste 701
Albany, NY 12210
518-432-7835 Fax: 518-426-2276
e-mail: steve_rosario@americanchemistry.org
Web site: www.americanchemistry.org

Clients:
American Chemistry Council

Rosenthal, Harvey
NYAPRS
1 Columbia Pl, 2nd Fl
Albany, NY 12207
518-436-0008 Fax: 518-436-0044
e-mail: nyaprs@aol.com
Web site: www.nyaprs.org

Clients:
Assn of Psychiatric Rehabilitation Services (NY)

Lobbyists:
Kevin Cleary

Rougeux, Elizabeth
Syracuse University
2-212 Center for Science & Technology
Syracuse, NY 13244-4100
315-443-3919

Clients:
Syracuse University

Lobbyists:
Nancy Cantor
Diana Napolitano
Eleanor Ware

Rubenstein Associates Inc
1345 Ave of the Americas
New York, NY 10105-0109
212-843-8000 Fax: 212-843-9300

Clients:
CDRN, LLC
Columbia University
Cubic Corporation
Gloria Wise Boys & Girls Club
Investments US Real Estate Venture V, LP
Millenium Hilton Hotel (The)
Metropolitan TV Alliance
NY Waterway
New York Historical Society
Park Tower Group
Path Medical
RFR Holdings
Tishman Speyer/Citigroup Alternative
World Product Centre

Lobbyists:
Cheri Fein
Howard J Rubenstein
Steven Rubenstein
Patrick Smith
Robin Verges

Rubenstein Communications Inc
1345 Ave of the Americas
New York, NY 10105-0109
212-843-8000 Fax: 212-843-9200

Clients:
Collegiate Church Corp
Cooper Union for Advancement of Science & Art (The)
Duane Street Realty
Tussaud's Group (The)
Olnick Organization Inc (The)
Van Wagner Communications, LLC
Gracie Piont Community Council
Congregation Shearith Israel
SEF Industries Inc

Lobbyists:
Amanita Duga-Carroll
Cheri Fein
Suzanne Halpin
Gerald McKelvey
Howard J Rubenstein
Steven Rubenstein
Patrick Smith
Robin Verges

Rubino, Cynthia A
78 N Broadway
White Plains, NY 10603
914-422-4105

Clients:
Pace University

Lobbyists:
David A Caputo
Meghan Q French

Runes, Richard
3 Kirby Ln N
Rye, NY 10580

Offices and agencies generally appear in alphabetical order, except when specific order is requested by listee.

LOBBYISTS

914-967-4900 Fax: 212-592-4900
e-mail: rrunes@amlaw.com

Clients:
American Lawyer Media

Rural Law Ctr of NY Inc
56 Cornelia St
Plattsburgh, NY 12901
518-561-5460 Fax: 518-561-5468
e-mail: rlc@capital.net
Web site: www.ruruallawcenter.org

Clients:
Rural Law Ctr of NY Inc

Lobbyists:
Susan L Patnode

Rutherford, Clyde E
Dairylea Co-op
5001 Brittonfield Pkwy, PO Box 4844
Syracuse, NY 13221-4844
315-433-0100 Fax: 315-433-2345
e-mail: clyde.rutherford@dairylea.com
Web site: www.dairylea.com

Clients:
Dairylea Cooperative Inc

Lobbyists:
Ed Gallagher
Leon Graves
Gregory Wickham

Rutnik Law Firm (The)
80 State St, 9th Fl
Albany, NY 12207
518-436-9646 Fax: 518-436-9655

Clients:
DMJM & Harris Inc
Genentech Inc

Lobbyists:
Douglas P Rutnik

Ryan, Desmond M
150 Motor Pkwy, Ste LL60
Hauppauge, NY 11772
631-951-2410 Fax: 631-951-2412

Clients:
Alliance of Long Island Agencies
Bethpage Federal Credit Union
Stop & Shop Supermarket Co (The)

Ryan, Marc
8725 Henderson Rd
Tampa, FL 33634
813-290-6271

Clients:
Wellcare Health Plans, Inc

SUNY College at Brockport
350 New Campus Dr
Brockport, NY 14420
585-395-2451

Clients:
SUNY College at Brockport

Lobbyists:
John Halstead
Roxanne Johnston

SUNY Upstate Medical
750 East Adams St
Syracuse, NY 13210-1834
315-464-4832 Fax: 315-464-4519

Clients:
SUNY Upstate Medical University

Lobbyists:
Kenneth Barker
Steven C Brady
Daniel N Hurley
Steven Scheinman
David Smith
Ronald R Young

SUNY at Stony Brook
Administrative Bldg, Rm 310
Stony Brook, NY 11794-0701
631-632-9115

Clients:
State University of NY at Stony Brook

Lobbyists:
Bridget Baio
Peter Baigent
Ruth Brandwein
Helen Carrano
Marie Chandick
Lisa Clark
David Conover
Paul Edelson
Diane Fabel
James Fiore
Patricia Gilbert
Ray Goldsteen
Gail Habicht
Gary Halada
Vanessa Herman
Susan Katz
Theresa Leonard
Robert McGrath
Fred Preston
Janice Rohlf
Joseph Scaduto
Bruce Schroeffel
Fred Sganga
Yacov Shamash
Shirley Strum Kenny

Offices and agencies generally appear in alphabetical order, except when specific order is requested by listee.

520

LOBBYISTS

Bruce Teifer

SUNY, System Administration
State University Plaza
Albany, NY 12246-0001
518-443-5355 Fax: 518-443-5360

Clients:
State University of NY, System Administration

Lobbyists:
James J Campbell
Stacey B Hengsterman
Lynn Kopka
John Ryan
Michael C Trunzo

Sabol, Sharon
Land Title Association
Two Rector St, Ste 901
New York, NY 10006-1819
212-964-3701 Fax: 212-964-7185
e-mail: nyslta@aol.com
Web site: www.nyslta.org

Clients:
Land Title Assn Inc (NYS)

Safe Horizon Inc
2 Lafayette St
New York, NY 10007
212-577-7738 Fax: 212-577-3039
Web site: www.safehorizon.org

Clients:
Safe Horizon Inc

Lobbyists:
Tracie Abbott
Nancy Arnow
Gordon Campbell
Eloisa Gordon
Beatrice Hanson
Lynn Neugebauer
Daniel Stewart

Sampson, Rick J
Restaurant Association (NYS)
409 New Karner Rd
Albany, NY 12205
518-452-4222 Fax: 518-452-4497
e-mail: ricks@nysra.org
Web site: www.nysra.org

Clients:
Restaurant Assn (NYS)

Lobbyists:
Melissa Fleischut
E Charles Hunt
Fred Sampson

Scenic Hudson Inc
One Civic Center Plaza
Ste 200
Poughkeepsie, NY 12601-3157
845-473-4440 Fax: 845-473-2648
e-mail: wreiss@scenichudson.org
Web site: www.scenichudson.org

Clients:
Scenic Hudson Inc

Lobbyists:
Jeff Anzevino
Andrew Bicking
James Burgess
Sarah Charlop-Powers
Joshua Clague
Richard Cook-Schiafo
Raymond Curran
Robert Elliott
Margery Groten
Joseph Kiernan
Maryanne McGovern
Seth McKee
Warren Reiss
Steven Rosenberg
Rita Shaheen
Reed Sparling
Edward O Sullivan
Cari Watkins-Bates

Schillinger, Lawrence R
5 Palisades Dr, Ste 300
Albany, NY 12205-6433
518-459-0600

Clients:
Institute of Scrap Recycling Industries-Empire Chapter
Institute of Scrap Recycling Industries-NY Chapter

Schlein, Stanley
481 King Ave
Bronx, NY 10464
917-359-3186

Clients:
Bronx Museum
Daimler Chrysler Corporation
Easton Bell Sports
Exxon Mobil Corporation
Hall of Sciences (NY)
SAS Institute Inc
Women's Housing & Economic Development Corporation

Schnell, William A & Associates Inc
51 E Main Street, 2nd Fl
Smithtown, NY 11787
631-724-6569 Fax: 631-724-8427
e-mail: wmasainc@earthlink.net

Clients:
Amusement & Music Owners Assn of NY

Offices and agencies generally appear in alphabetical order, except when specific order is requested by listee.

LOBBYISTS

Federation of Organizations Inc
Long Island Gasoline Retailers Assn Inc
SDR Pharmaceuticals Inc
Securitas
Suffolk County Ambulance Chiefs Assoc
Suffolk County Deputy Sheriff's Police Benevolent Assn

Lobbyists:
William A Schnell

Schomberg, Dora
PO Box 9029
Albany, NY 12209
518-478-9760 Fax: 518-478-9764

Clients:
Humane Society of the United States (The)

School Administrators Association of NYS
8 Airport Park Blvd
Latham, NY 12110
518-782-0600 Fax: 518-782-9552

Clients:
School Administrators Association of NYS

Lobbyists:
Kevin Banes
Casey Kevin
Don Nickson

School Boards Assn (NYS)
24 Century Hill Dr
Latham, NY 12210
518-783-0200 Fax: 518-783-0211
e-mail: nyssba@nyssba.org
Web site: www.nyssba.org

Clients:
School Boards Assn (NYS)

Lobbyists:
Charles Dawson
Christine DeCatur
David Ernst
Timothy G Kremer
David Little
Julie Marlette
Carl Onken
Diane Ward
Jay Worona

Schuyler Center for Analysis & Advocacy (SCAA)
150 State St, 4th Fl
Albany, NY 12208-1626
518-463-1896 Fax: 518-463-3364
e-mail: info@scaany.org
Web site: www.scaany.org

Clients:
Schuyler Center for Analysis & Advocacy (SCAA)

Lobbyists:
Thomas Hillard
Jenn O'Connor
Davin Robinson
Karen Schimke
Bridget Walsh

Shanahan Group
4019 County Rte 21
Schodack Landing, NY 12156
518-732-3312 Fax: 518-732-2859
e-mail: tom@shanahangroup.com
Web site: www.shanahangroup.com

Clients:
Brookhaven Science Associates Inc
Guide Dog Foundation for the Blind Inc
Irrigation Assn of New York
Long Island Water Conference
Rural Water Assn (NY)
Suffolk County Water Authority

Lobbyists:
Thomas Shanahan

Shannon, Michael J
Lorillard Tobacco
714 Green Valley Rd
PO Box 10529
Greensboro, NC 27408
336-335-7711 Fax: 336-335-7752

Clients:
Lorillard Tobacco Co

Shaw, Linda R
1125 Crossroads Bldg
2 State St
Rochester, NY 14614
585-546-8430 Fax: 585-546-4324

Clients:
Atlas Park, LLC
Dermot Company (The)
Struever Fidelco Cappelli, Inc

Sheinkopf, Ltd
152 Madison Ave
Ste 1603
New York, NY 10016
212-725-2378 Fax: 212-772-2334

Clients:
Committee to Save St Brigid's

Lobbyists:
Scott Gastel
Henry A Sheinkopf

Offices and agencies generally appear in alphabetical order, except when specific order is requested by listee.

LOBBYISTS

Sierra Club, Atlantic Chapter
353 Hamilton St
Albany, NY 12210-1709
518-426-9144 Fax: 518-426-3052

Clients:
Sierra Club, Atlantic Chapter

Lobbyists:
Moisha Blechman
Theresa Cassaick
Harold Cohen
Linda DiStefano
Frank Eadie
Laurie Farber
Joseph Gardella
Margaret Hayes-Young
Rhea Jezer
Elizabeth Kasubski
John Klotz
Charles Lamb
Susan Lawrence
Martha Loew
Timothy Logan
Suzanne Mattei
James Mays
Hugh Mitchell
Robert Muldoon
Don Pachner
Frank Regan
Marion Rose
Shannon Stone
Walter Simpson
Karen Schultz
Julius Schultz
John Stouffer
Yvonne Trasker-Rothenberg
Anne Wilson
Carolyn Zolas

Smith, Joann
17 Elk St
Albany, NY 12207
518-436-8408

Clients:
Family Planning Advocates of NYS, Inc

Lobbyists:
Carol Blowers
Susan Pedo

Smith, Michael P
NY Bankers Association
99 Park Ave, 4th Fl
New York, NY 10016-1502
212-297-1699 Fax: 212-297-1658
e-mail: msmith@nyba.com
Web site: www.nyba.com

Clients:
Bankers Assn (NY)

Lobbyists:
William J Bosies, Jr
Karen L Jannetty
Roberta Kotkin
Stephen W Rice

Smith, Robert
First Pioneer Farm Credit ACA
2668 State Rte 7, Ste 21
Cobleskill, NY 12043-9707
518-296-8188

Clients:
First Pioneer Farm Credit ACA

Smyth, A Advocacy
130 Washington Ave, Ste A
Albany, NY 12210
518-426-8354 Fax: 518-426-8355
e-mail: asmyth@capital.net

Clients:
AIDS Service Network (NYC)
Medical Equipment Providers Assn (NY)
Coalition for Natural Health
United Neighborhood Houses of NY Inc
Assn of NYS Youth Bureaus

Lobbyists:
Andrea Smyth

Solowan, Richard
GEICO
One Geico Plaza
Washington, DC 20076
301-986-3948 Fax: 301-718-5207
e-mail: rsolowan@geico.com

Clients:
Government Employees Insurance Co (GEICO)

Soloway, Ronald
155 Washington Ave
Albany, NY 12210
518-436-1091 Fax: 518-463-1266
e-mail: solowayr@ujafedny.org
Web site: www.ujafedny.org

Clients:
United Jewish Appeal Federation - Jewish Philanthropies NY

Lobbyists:
Anita Altman
Chantall Askins
Elana Broitman
Joshua Cohen
Jennifer Doeren
John Ruskay

Offices and agencies generally appear in alphabetical order, except when specific order is requested by listee.

LOBBYISTS

St Mary's Healthcare System for Children, Inc
29-01 216 St
Bayside, NY 11360
718-281-8865

Clients:
St Mary's Healthcare System for Children, Inc

Lobbyists:
Burton Grebin
Mark Hoffacker
Edwin Simpser

Statewide Corporate Strategies Inc
1111 Park Ave
Ste 10B
New York, NY 10128
212-987-4616 Fax: 212-987-4616
e-mail: suzan.kremer@verison.net
Web site: www.statewidestrat.com

Clients:
Brentwood Union Free School District
Educational Housing Services
Globe Metallurgical Inc
Heartland Business Center
Pinelawn Cemetery

Lobbyists:
Arthur Kremer
Phil Fuchs
Jack O'Donnell

Stegemoeller, Rudy
PO Box 359
Poestenkill, NY 12140
518-283-0933

Clients:
Electric & Gas Corp (NYS)
Plug Power, Inc
Rochester Gas & Electric Corp

Stendardi, Deborah M
30 Lomb Memorial Dr
Rochester, NY 14623-5604
585-475-5040 Fax: 585-475-2240
e-mail: dmsgrl@rit.edu

Clients:
Rochester Institute of Technology

Strategic Services, Inc
170 E Post Rd, Ste 207B
White Plains, NY 10601
914-946-8400

Clients:
City of Mount Vernon
Westchester Jewish Community Services

Lobbyists:
Arnold Linhardt

Stryker, Patricia
International Brotherhood of Teamsters
216 W 14th St
New York, NY 10011
212-924-2000 Fax: 212-242-8772

Clients:
Teamsters Local 237

Stuto, Diane D
111 Washington Ave, Ste 300
Albany, NY 12210
518-436-8417 Fax: 518-436-0226
Web site: www.licony.org

Clients:
Life Insurance Council of NY Inc

Lobbyists:
Elizabeth J Byrne
John Kisson
Thomas E Workman

Suffolk Community Council (FKA Pannullo, Judith)
180 Oser Ave, Ste 850
Hauppauge, NY 11788
631-434-9277

Clients:
Suffolk Community Council Inc

Lobbyists:
Judith Pannullo

Sullivan, Edward C
606 W 116th St, Ste 43
New York, NY 10027
212-678-6962

Clients:
Hello World Language Center
St Francis College

Sullivan, Veronica
11 Wall St
New York, NY 10005
212-656-4254

Clients:
Stock Exchange (NY)

Tenants & Neighbors Coalition (NYS)
236 W 27th St, 4th Fl
New York, NY 10001

Offices and agencies generally appear in alphabetical order, except when specific order is requested by listee.

LOBBYISTS

212-608-4320 Fax: 212-619-7476
e-mail: nystnc@aol.com
Web site: www.tandu.org

Clients:
Tenants & Neighbors Coalition (NYS)

Lobbyists:
Alexander Boyer
Amy Chan
Patrick Coleman
Mary Kolar
Michael McKee
Jumaane Williams
Natasha Winegar

Thorpe, Vernon
Transport Workers Union of Greater NY
80 West End Ave
New York, NY 10023
212-873-6000 Fax: 212-579-3363

Clients:
Transport Workers Union, Local 100

Lobbyists:
Roger Toussaint
Ed Watt

Tourism Industry Coalition (TIC)
80 Wolf Rd
Albany, NY 12205
518-465-2300 Fax: 518-465-4025

Clients:
Tourism Industry Coalition

Lobbyists:
Daniel C Murphy

Trading Cove NY, LLC
914 Hartford Turnpike
Waterford, CT 06385
860-442-1202

Clients:
Trading Cove NY, LLC

Lobbyists:
Len Wolman

Tranter, G Thomas, Jr
Corning Incorporated
MP-BH-06
Corning, NY 14831
607-974-7818 Fax: 607-974-4050
e-mail: trantergt@corning.com
Web site: www.corning.com

Clients:
Corning Incorporated

Tribeca Film Institute
375 Greenwich St
New York, NY 10013
212-941-2400

Clients:
Tribeca Film Institute

Lobbyists:
Sydney Meeks

Trustees of Columbia University in the City of NY (The)
535 West 116th St
302 Low Library
New York, NY 10027
212-854-3394

Clients:
Trustees of Columbia University in the City of NY (The)

Lobbyists:
Lisa Anderson
Peter Awn
Lee Bollinger
Alan Brinkley
Ronald Feldman
Bruce Ferguson
Loftin Flowers
Ross Frommer
Zvi Galil
Lee Goldman
Maxine Griffith
Sandra Harris
David Hirsch
Robert Kasdin
Elizabeth Keefer
Ira Lamster
Victoria Mason-Ailey
Nicholas Moustakas
Mary Mundinger
Henry Pinkham
Austin Quigley
Allan Rosenfield
Jeffrey Sachs
Janet Schinderman
Ellen Smith
Jeanette Takamura
Vincent Tomaselli
Frank Wolf

Tully Abdo, Susan
260 S Main Ave
Albany, NY 12208-2432
518-451-3019 Fax: 518-451-3604

Clients:
Aetna Inc

Turner, Francine
CSEA-PAC
143 Washington Ave
Albany, NY 12210

Offices and agencies generally appear in alphabetical order, except when specific order is requested by listee.

LOBBYISTS

518-436-8622 Fax: 518-427-1677
e-mail: turner@cseainc.org

Clients:
Civil Service Employees Political Action Fund

Lobbyists:
Adam Acquario
John Belmont
Courtney Brunell
Matthew D'Amico
Jason Haenel
Michael Neidl
Ricky Noreault
Gretchen Penn
Robert Scholz
William Walsh
Kevin Younis

Tyson, Lisa
90 Pennsylvania Ave
Massapequa, NY 11758-4978
516-541-1006 Fax: 516-541-2113
e-mail: lisa@lipc.org
Web site: www.lipc.org

Clients:
Long Island Progressive Coalition

Ungar, Robert A Associates Inc
200 Garden City Plaza
Ste 201
Garden City, NY 11530
516-227-2400 Fax: 516-227-2406
e-mail: fireandems@aol.com

Clients:
Assn of Plumbing Heating Cooling Contractors Inc (NYS)
Building & Construction Trades Council (NYS)
Building & Construction Trades Council of Greater NY
Building Contractors' Assn, Inc
Building Trades Employers' Assn
Civil Svc Technical Guild, Local 375 DC-37, AFSCME AFL-CIO
Council of Administrators & Supervisors
Local 3, IBEW Communications Electricians
Local 246, SEIU
Nassau County PHCC
Plumbing Contractors Assn of Long Island Inc
Plumbing Foundation City of NY Inc
Purvis Systems Inc
Service Station Dealers of Greater NY, Inc
TBTA Maintenance Employees, Local 1931, DC-37, AFSCME
Uniformed EMT's & Paramedics, Local 2507-FDNY
Uniformed Fire Alarm Dispatchers Benevolent Assn-FDNY
Uniformed Firefighters Assn

Lobbyists:
Robert A Ungar

United Healthcare Services, Inc (FKA Oxford LLC)
Oxford Health Plans LLC
48 Monroe Tpk
Trumbull, CT 06611
203-459-7271

Clients:
United Healthcare Services, Inc

Lobbyists:
Mara Ginsberg
Carl Mattson
Timothy Meyer
Alan Muney
Mike Turpin

United Neighborhood Houses of NY
70 West 36th St, 5th Fl
New York, NY 10018-8007
212-967-0322 Fax: 212-967-0792

Clients:
United Neighborhood Houses of NY

Lobbyists:
Anthony Ng
Roopal Patel
Susan Stamler
Nancy Wackstein
Jessica Walker

United Spinal Assn (FKA Eastern Paralyed Veterans Assn)
75-20 Astoria Blvd
Jackson Heights, NY 11370-1177
718-803-3782 Fax: 718-803-1089

Clients:
United Spinal Assn

Lobbyists:
Daniel Anderson

United University Professions
PO Box 15143
Albany, NY 12212-5143
518-640-6600
e-mail: input@uupmail.org
Web site: www.uupinfo.org

Clients:
United University Professions

Lobbyists:
Stephen Allinger
Christopher Black
William Schneuerman

LOBBYISTS

University at Buffalo
520A Capen Hall
Buffalo, NY 14260-1629
716-645-7730 Fax: 716-645-5877
Web site: www.government.buffalo.edu

Clients:
University at Buffalo

Lobbyists:
Wayne Anderson
Dennis Black
Michael Bruneau
Beth Delgenio
David Dunn
Michael Dupre
Kathryn Frost
Kathryn Friedman
Robert Genco
William Greiner
Marsha Henderson
Bruce Holm
Jorge Jose
Mark Karwan
Carol Kobrin
Kemper Lewis
Warde Manuel
Bruce McComb
Ryan McPherson
Gregory Michaelidis
Scott Morris
Scott Nostaja
Norma Nowak
Nils Olsen
Carole Petro
Michael Pietkiewicz
John Simpson
Nancy Smyth
Harvey Stenger
Ernie Sternberg
Graham Stewart
Sean Sullivan
Megan Toohey
Maurizio Trevisan
Satish Tripathi
James Willis

Upstate Niagara Cooperative (FKA Upstate Farms Cooperative)
25 Anderson Rd
Buffalo, NY 14225
716-892-3156 Fax: 716-892-3157

Clients:
Upstate Farms Cooperative Inc

Lobbyists:
Timothy R Harner

Kimberly Pickard-Dudley
Thomas J Rodak
William Young

Vandervort Group, LLC (The)
19 Dove St, Ste 202
Albany, NY 12210-2222
518-463-3202 Fax: 518-463-7952
e-mail: thevgroup@aol.com

Clients:
Alliance for Environmental Concerns (NY)
Amylin Pharmaceuticals
Aztec Software
CNA Surety/Western Surety Co
Covanta Energy Corp Inc
Data Niche Associates
Global Spectrum LP
Health Management Systems Inc
Hewlett-Packard Co
Mildred Elley
Merck & Co Inc
Moneygram International
National Education Loan Network (NELNET)
New Amsterdam History Center
Northeastern Retail Lumber Assn
Reed Elsevier Inc
US Fireworks Safety Commission Inc

Lobbyists:
Jeffrey M Lane
John W Vandervort
Todd H Vandervort

Ventresca-Ecroyd, Gilda
3 Park Ave, 15th Fl
New York, NY 10016
212-404-4077 Fax: 212-404-4061
e-mail: gilda-ventresca-ecroyd@med.nyu.edu
Web site: www.med.nyu.edu

Clients:
NYU Hospitals Ctr

Lobbyists:
Karen Ann Acker

Verizon
140 West Street, Floor 30
New York, NY 10007
518-396-1086

Clients:
Verizon

Lobbyists:
Monica Azare
John Butter
Thomas Clark
Thomas Dunne
Susan Hayes
David Lamendola
Thomas McCarroll
Melvin Norris

Offices and agencies generally appear in alphabetical order, except when specific order is requested by listee.

LOBBYISTS

Barbara Patton
Richard Windram

Vidal Group, LLC (The)
150 State St, 4th Fl
Albany, NY 12207
518-434-5856

Clients:
ALM Medica Inc
American College of Occupational Environmental Medicine
Circulo De La Hispanidad
Earthwatch LTD
Hispanic Counseling Center Inc
Hispanic Federation
Hispanic Information Telecommunications Network
Latino Commission on AIDS
Glenwood Management Corporation
Oasis Children's Service LLC
Rain Inc
Partnership for NYC
Sepracor

Lobbyists:
Alfredo Vidal

Visiting Nurse Service of NY
107 East 70th St
New York, NY 10021
212-609-1541 Fax: 212-794-6357

Clients:
Visiting Nurse Service of NY

Lobbyists:
Erica Aguilar
Edo Banach
Charles Blum
Joan Chaya
Christina Coons
Karl Dehm
Judith Duhl
Felicia Dyer
Iliana Edison
Laura Ensler
Judy Farrell
Luz Flores
Arthur Gitshyn
Barbara Heinkind
Debra Holland
Joan Komolafe
Tara Medizabal
Carol Odnoha
James O'Neal
Linda Reid

Walsh, John B
368 Pleasantview Dr
Lancaster, NY 14086
716-684-8060 Fax: 716-684-4832
e-mail: jbwalsh@ene.com

Clients:
Buffalo & Erie Cnty Naval & Military Park

Ecology & Environment Inc

Lobbyists:
Daniel R Castle
Julie A Chang
Currier Dale
Jeffrey Hammond
Amy E Mahl

Wang, Phyllis A
NYSHCP
99 Troy Rd
Ste 200
East Greenbush, NY 12061
518-463-1118 Fax: 518-463-1606
e-mail: hcp@nyshcp.org
Web site: www.nyshcp.org

Clients:
Assn of Health Care Providers Inc (NYS)

Lobbyists:
Margaret Clark
Nancy Erdoes
Christine L Johnston
Glenn Lefebvre
Courtney Ronner
Travis Wattie

Weekley, Daniel A
Dominion Resources
Rope Ferry Rd
Waterford, CT 06385
860-444-5271 Fax: 860-437-5813
e-mail: daniel_a_weekley@dom.com
Web site: www.dominion.com

Clients:
Dominion Resources

Weingarten, Reid & McNally, LLC
One Commerce Plaza
Ste 1103
Albany, NY 12210
518-465-7330 Fax: 518-465-0273
e-mail: bobr@lobbywr.com
Web site: www.lobbywr.com

Clients:
Academy of Family Physicians (NYS)
American Cancer Society-Eastern Division
American College of Emergency Physicians (NY Chapter)
American Diabetes Association
American Heart Assn/American Stroke Assn
Assn of Health Care Providers Inc (NYS)
Cerebral Palsy Assns of NYS Inc
Chain Pharmacy Assn of NYS
Community General Hospital
Corporation for Supportive Housing
County of Westchester
Delphi Corp
Diageo, PLC

Offices and agencies generally appear in alphabetical order, except when specific order is requested by listee.

LOBBYISTS

Elmhurst Dairy Group
Fidelity National Financial Inc
Independent Petroleum Marketers of NY
Integris Inc (Bull Services)
Iroquois Healthcare Alliance
Life Insurance Co (NY)
NOCO Energy Co
Northeast Health
Presbyterian Hosp/Coal for School-Based Primary Care (NY)
Program Risk Management, Inc & PRM Claim Services Inc
Public Transit Assn (NY)
Schering Corporation
Securities Industry & Financial Markets Association (FKA Securities Industry Assn)
Society of Anesthesiologists Inc (NYS)
Speech, Language Hearing Assn Inc (NYS)
Wildlife Conservation Society Inc
Wildwood Programs Inc

Lobbyists:
Padraic Bambrick
Shauneen M McNally
Robert W Reid
Marcy Wamp
Steven B Weingarten

Whitehead, David
65 Oak St
Rensselaer, NY 12144-9742
518-283-0946 Fax: 518-283-0171

Clients:
Bristol-Myers Squibb Co

Whiteman Osterman & Hanna LLP
One Commerce Plaza, 19th Fl
Albany, NY 12260
518-487-7741 Fax: 518-487-7777
Web site: www.woh.com

Clients:
American Express Co
AIA New York State Inc
Assn of Homes & Services for the Aging (NY)
Bristol-Myers Squibb Co
Central Boiler Inc
COFCCA Inc
Council of New York Cooperatives
Creosote Council III
Distilled Spirits Council of the US
Educational Testing Service
Empire State Petroleum Assn Inc
Gillen Brewer School (The)
Hertz Corporation (The)
Institute for Student Achievement
Johnson & Johnson
Long Island Life Sciences Initiative
MCI
Metropolitan Museum of Art (The)
NYS Coalition of 853 Schools Inc
NYS Funeral Directors Assn Inc
Physical Therapy Assn (NY)
Presbyterian Hospital (NY)
Preserve Associates LLC
Public Employer Risk Management Assn

Questar III
Quest Diagnostics Inc
Reinsurance Assn of America
Roundabout Theatre Co
SC Johnson & Son Inc
Society for Respiratory Care Inc (NYS)
Advantage Capital Partners
Syracuse University
Teachers Insurance & Annuity Assn/College Retirement Equities Fun
Thomson West
Haverstraw-Stony Point Central School District
Managed Funds Association
MBIA Insurance Corporation
Natural Resources Defense Council Inc
Sanofi Pasteur Inc
St Elizabeth Medical Center
Scotts Company (The)

Lobbyists:
William Y Crowell III
Philip Gitlen
Aggie Leahy
Richard E Leckerling
Brian J Lucey
Kevin Quinn
Michael Whiteman

Wieboldt, Robert
Long Island Builders Institute
1757-8 Veterans Memorial Hwy
Islandia, NY 11749
631-232-2345 Fax: 631-232-2349
e-mail: evp@libi.org
Web site: libi.org

Clients:
Long Island Builders Institute

Wiener, Judith R
1102 Palmer Ave
Larchmont, NY 10538
914-833-0094 Fax: 914-833-0104

Clients:
Lower Hudson Education Coalition

Wildlife Conservation Society
2300 Southern Blvd
Bronx, NY 10460
718-220-5113
Web site: www.wcs.org

Clients:
Wildlife Conservation Society

Lobbyists:
John F Calvelli
Rosemary DeLuca
Sara S Marinello
Cynthia Reich

Offices and agencies generally appear in alphabetical order, except when specific order is requested by listee.

LOBBYISTS

Williams, Carla (FKA Alliance for Donation (NY))
99 Troy Rd, Ste 200
East Greenbush, NY 12061
518-533-7878

Clients:
Alliance for Donation (NY)

Williams Esq, Christopher A
Long Island University
700 Northern Blvd
Brookville, NY 11548-1327
516-299-3834

Clients:
Long Island University

Williams, Samuel G
Region 9 UAW
35 George Karl Blvd
Ste 100
Amherst, NY 14221
716-632-1540

Clients:
Region 9, UAW

Wilson Elser Moskowitz Edelman & Dicker
677 Broadway
Albany, NY 12207
518-449-8893 Fax: 518-449-8927
Web site: www.wemed.com

Clients:
1765 1st Associates LLC
250 E 57th Street, LLC
Albany Medical Ctr
Albert Lindley Lee Memorial Hospital
Alice Hyde Medical Center
American Insurance Assn
American International Group Inc (AIG)
Alliance of Resident Theatres (NY)
Assn of Professional Land Surveyors Inc (NYS)
Assn of Realtors Inc (NYS)
Athletic Trainers' Assn (NYS)
Assn of Independent Commercial Producers Inc
Asurion Corp & Subsidiaries (FKA Lock/Line LLC (DST Systems))
Ballet Theatre Foundation Inc/American Ballet Theatre
Bankers Assn (NY)
Barnes & Noble College Book Sellers (Dewey Square Group)
Brooklyn Adult Care Center
Brooklyn Hospital Center (The)
Canton-Potsdam Hospital
Carnegie Hall
Cathedral Church of St John the Devine (The)
Catholic Conference Policy Group Inc
College Board
Combined Coordinating Council Inc
Community Hospital Network of NY Eductl & Rsch Fund Inc
Community Service Society of NY
Consolidated Edison Co of NY Inc
Cortland Regional Medical Center (FKA Cortland Memorial Hospital)
Crouse Hospital
Center for Disability Services
CGI (FKA CGI Group)
Children's Institute
City of Syracuse Industrial Development Agency
Dell Inc
David B Kriser Dental Center of NY University
DeVry Incorporated
Deloitte & Touche, LLP
Education Management LLC
Elant, Inc
Elliott Management
Epilepsy Institute
Elizabethtown Community Hospital
Ernst & Young, LLP
Excelsior Racing Association (Powers & Company)
Family Planning Advocates
Forest City Ratner Companies
Glens Falls Hospital
Greater New York Automobile Dealers Assn
Groton Community Health Care Center
HANYS Services, Inc; D/B/A HANYS Solutions, Inc
Harbar Motors, Ltd
Healthcare Assn of NYS
Hebrew Home for the Aged at Riverdale (The)
Hedgewood Home for Adults
Henry Schein Inc
Hertz Corporation (The)
Hospitality & Tourism Assn (NYS)
Hospitals Insurance Company Inc
Hudson Valley Economic Development Corp
Hotel Assn of NYC Inc
IMG Models
Intrepid Museum Foundation
JXQ Holding Company, Inc
Jewish Guild for the Blind (The)
KPMG, LLP
Law School Admissions Council
League of American Theatres & Producers Inc
Lesbian Gay Bisexual & Transgender Community Center (The)
Jewish Museum (The)
John T Mather Memorial Hospital
Long Island Health Network
Long Island University
MCIC Vermont Inc
Marshals Assn (NYC)
Merchants Protective Co, Inc (NY)
Medtronic Inc (FKA Medtronic Sofamor Danek)
Taconic IPA Inc
Metropolitan Parking Assn
Morgan Stanley (Multistate Associates)
Nassau-Suffolk Hospital Association
New Brookhaven Town House for Adults
Norwegian Cruise Line
Niagara Mohawk Holdings, Inc., & NMPC DBA National Grid
New York University-College of Nursing
Nassau County Firefighter's Museum & Education Center
Northern Metropolitan Hospital Assn
Northern Westchester Hospital
North Country Healthcare Providers Eductl & Rsch Fund Inc (North Country Healthcare Providers, LLC)
Peconic Bay Medical Center
Phelps Memorial Hospital Center
Planned Parenthood of NYC Inc
Pricewaterhouse Coopers, LLP
Queens Adult Care Center
Queens-Long Island Medical Group, P.C.

Offices and agencies generally appear in alphabetical order, except when specific order is requested by listee.

LOBBYISTS

Real Estate Board of NY
Rochester Institute of Technology
Samaritan Medical Center
Sanctuary for Families
School Bus Contractor's Coalition, Inc. (NY)
Segway Inc. (Multistate Associates)
Society for Clinical Social Work Inc (NYS)
St Luke's Cornwall Hospital
St Margaret's Center
St Mary's Healthcare System for Children Inc
T-Mobile USA Inc
To Life
Tanglewood Manor
United Hospital Fund
University (NY)
University School of Medicine (NY) & Hospitals (NY)
Viahealth

Lobbyists:
Nicholas Antenucci
Alexander L Betke
Douglas Clark
Donna Clyne
Laurie T Cohen
Victoria M Contino
Diana Georgia
Jerry S Hoffman
Darrell E Jeffers
Lisa M Marrello
Mary Ann Mclean
Paula O'Brien
Anthony Piscitelli
Peter A Piscitelli
Jason M Poliner
Philip Rosenberg
Theresa Russo
Jill Sandhaas
Kenneth L Shapiro
Cynthia D Shenker
Lester Skulklapper
Mark Thomas
Larisa Wick

Wolf, Block, Schorr & Solis-Cohen, LLP
250 Park Ave
New York, NY 10177
212-297-2696
e-mail: sshorenstein@wolfblock.com
Web site: www.wolfblock.com

Clients:
American Council of Engineering Companies of NY
MGM Mirage

Lobbyists:
David Bronston
Kenneth Fisher
Paul Proulx
Stuart Shorenstein

Wolf, Stacy
PO Box 100
Cropseyville, NY 12052
518-279-4999

Clients:
American Society for the Prevention of Cruelty to Animals (ASPCA)

Lobbyists:
Laura Hawkins (Dryfoos Group)
Michelle Villagomez
Lisa Weisberg

Wood Rafalsky & Wood
62 William St, 2nd Fl
New York, NY 10005-1547
212-248-3001 Fax: 212-248-3008

Clients:
Clinical Laboratory Assoc, Inc (NYS)

Lobbyists:
Thomas R Rafalsky

Working Assets Funding Service Inc
101 Market St, Ste 700
San Francisco, CA 94105
415-369-2000 Fax: 415-371-1048

Clients:
Working Assets Funding Service Inc

Lobbyists:
Sarah Clusen Buecher

YMCAS of NYS Inc
33 Elk St, Ste 200
Albany, NY 12207
518-462-8241 Fax: 518-462-8491

Clients:
YMCAs of NYS Inc

Lobbyists:
Kyle Stewart

Yavornitzki, Mark L
NYSAIFA
38 Sheridan Ave
Albany, NY 12210-2714
518-462-5567 Fax: 518-462-5569
e-mail: nysaifa@aol.com
Web site: www.nysaifa.com

Clients:
Assn of Insurance & Financial Advisors (NYS)

Yoswein New York Inc
150 Broadway
Ste 1300
New York, NY 10038
212-233-5700 Fax: 212-233-5757
e-mail: info@yosweinnewyork.com
Web site: www.yosweinnewyork.com

Offices and agencies generally appear in alphabetical order, except when specific order is requested by listee.

LOBBYISTS

Clients:
40th Street Development LLC
Academy of Medicine (NY)
BA Cypress Bronx Holdings LLC
Bailey House Inc
Brooklyn Chamber of Commerce
Brooklyn Philharmonic
Brooklyn Technical High School Alumni Assn
Business Council of NYS, Inc (The)
Ceruzzi Holdings
College Community Services, Inc (DBA Brooklyn Center for the Performing Arts)
Flushing Commons, LLC
Gateway Center Properties Phase II, LLC
Groundwork, Inc
Keyspan Energy
Maimonides Medical Center
Metropolitan Funeral Directors Assn
Mt Sinai Hospital of Queens
New 42nd Street Inc (The)
Outward Bound Center (NYC)
Pfizer Inc
St Francis College
Standardbred Owners Assn of NY
Starwood Ceruzzi, LLC
SUNY Downstate Medical Center

Lobbyists:
Christopher Grimm
Tyquana Henderson
Monique Jarvis
Jamie Van Bramer
Joni A Yoswein

Young Jr, William N
2400 Western Ave
Guilderland, NY 12084-0309
518-456-6767

Clients:
Assn of Fire Districts of the State of NY, Inc

Zaleski, Terence M
437 Old Albany Post Rd
Garrison, NY 10524
845-788-5070 Fax: 845-788-5071
e-mail: tzaleski@sprynet.com

Clients:
Coalition of NYS Career Schools
Full Spectrum of New York, LLC
Green Chimneys Children's Services Inc
League for the Hard of Hearing
Putnam Associated Resource Ctrs
Institute for the Study of Infection Control Inc (The)

Lobbyists:
Kathy Zamechansky

Zogg, Jeffrey
General Bldg Contractors
6 Airline Dr
Albany, NY 12205
518-869-2207 Fax: 518-869-0846
e-mail: joeh@gbcnys.agc.org
Web site: www.gbcnys.agc.org

Clients:
General Building Contractors of NYS Inc

Lobbyists:
Joseph Hogan
Brenda Manning

Offices and agencies generally appear in alphabetical order, except when specific order is requested by listee.

POLITICAL ACTION COMMITTEES

1170 PEC
John P Pusloskie, Treasurer
1451 Lake Avenue, Rochester, NY 14615
585-647-1170
Web site: www.thecityofrochester.org

1199/SEIU New York State Political Action Fund
George Gresham, Treasurer
330 West 42nd Street, 7th Floor, New York, NY 10036
212-261-2342

21st Century Democrats
Michael Lux, Treasurer
1731 Connecticut Ave NW, 2nd Floor, Washington, DC 20009
202-626-5620 Fax: 202-347-0956
Web site: www.21stcenturydems.org

500 Club
Edward L Barlow, Treasurer
C/O Judy Winslow, 603 Steamboat Road, #7, Greenwich, CT 06830
203-661-9416

504 Democratic Club Campaign Committee
Marty Sesmer, Treasurer
332 E 29th St, Ste 5A, New York, NY 10002
212-684-6287

ABO Build PAC Inc
Nicholas LaPorte, Jr, Treasurer
Assoc Builders & Owners, 80 Maiden Lane, Ste 1503, New York, NY 10038
212-385-4949 Fax: 212-385-1442
e-mail: associatedbuilders@abgony.com
Web site: www.abogny.com

ACEC New York PAC
Hannah O'Grady, Treasurer
ACEC New York, 60 East 42nd Street, Suite 1742, New York, NY 10165
212-682-6336 Fax: 212-818-0286
e-mail: hannah@acecny.org

ACENY-PAC
Jay J Simson, Treasurer
2356 Nott Street East, Niskayuna, NY 12309
518-372-4936

AES NYS PAC
Amy V Conley, Treasurer
7725 Lake Rd, Barker, NY 14012
716-795-9501 Fax: 716-795-3153
e-mail: aconley@aes.com

AFGI PAC
Robert E Mackin, Treasurer
139 Lancaster St, Albany, NY 12210-1903
518-449-4698 Fax: 518-432-5651
e-mail: bmackin@mackinco.com
Web site: www.mackinco.com

ALPAC (ALCAS PAC)
Jack A Lorenz, Treasurer
418 Cherry St, Olean, NY 14760
716-373-1406
e-mail: jlorenz@alcas.com

ASAPPAC
David N Weinraub, Treasurer
C/O Brown & Weinraub, LLC, 12 Sheridan Avenue, Albany, NY 12207
518-427-7350 Fax: 518-427-7792

ATPAM COPE State Fund
Gordon G Forbes, Treasurer
1560 Broadway, Ste 700, New York, NY 10036
212-719-3666 Fax: 212-302-1585
e-mail: gforbe@atpam.com
Web site: www.atpam.com

ATU-NY Cope Fund
Oscar Owens, Treasurer
5025 Wisconsin Ave NW, Washington, DC 20016
202-537-1645 Fax: 202-244-7824

Abate RRF Inc
Brian J Trafford, Treasurer
216 Lincoln St, Riverhead, NY 11901
516-369-0729

Academy of Trial Lawyers PAC
John Bonina, Treasurer
C/O Bonina & Bonina PC, 16 Court Street, Suite 1800, Brooklyn, NY 11241
718-522-1786
Web site: www.medlaw1.com

Action Fund for Good Government
David JG Chambers, Treasurer
164 Fruitwood Terrace, Williamsville, NY 14221
716-626-4893

Aetna Inc PAC
Jonathan M Topodas, Treasurer
1331 F Street, NW, Suite 450, Washington, DC 20005
202-419-7042 Fax: 202-223-4424
e-mail: jonathan.topodas@aetna.com

Affordable Housing PAC, LTD
Frank J Anelante Jr, Treasurer

Offices and agencies generally appear in alphabetical order, except when specific order is requested by listee.

POLITICAL ACTION COMMITTEES

c/o Lumley & Woolf, 5925 Broadway, Bronx, NY 10463
718-884-7676 x201

Allied Bldg Metal Industries Inc State PAC
Arthur Rubinstein, Treasurer
211 East 43rd St, Ste 804, New York, NY 10017
212-697-5551 Fax: 212-818-0976

Ambassador Club
Verna J Hyer, Treasurer
830 W German Street, Herkimer, NY 13350
315-866-2841

American Express Company PAC (AXP PAC)
Robert B Thompson, III, Treasurer
801 Pennsylvania Ave, NW, Suite 650, Washington, DC 20004
202-434-0156

American Insurance Assn New York PAC
Leigh Ann Pusey, Treasurer
1130 Connecticut Ave NW, Ste 1000, Washington, DC 20036
202-828-7100 Fax: 202-293-1219
Web site: www.aiadc.org

American International Group, Inc Employee PAC
Robert A Gender, Treasurer
70 Pine Street, 19th Floor, New York, NY 10270
212-770-8212

American Motorcyclist Assn PAC
C Alexandar Ernst, Treasurer
PO Box 250, 1937 Delaware Tpke, Clarksville, NY 12041
518-768-8191 Fax: 775-361-1342
e-mail: a.ernst@ernst.cc

American Resort Dev/Assn Resort Owners' Coalition PAC
Sandra Y Depoy, Treasurer
1201 15th St NW, Ste 400, Washington, DC 20005
202-371-6700 Fax: 202-289-8544
Web site: www.arda.org

American Telephone & Telegraph Co PAC NY
Frederick K Wallach, Treasurer
32 Avenue of the Americas, Room 2700, New York, NY 10013
212-387-5611

ARAMARK PAC
Rick Martella, Treasurer
1101 Market Street, ARAMARK Tower, 31st Floor, Philadelphia, PA 19107

Arts PAC Non-Federal
Peggy Kaplan, Treasurer
c/o R Feldman Fine Arts, 31 Mercer St, New York, NY 10013
212-226-3232

Asbestos Workers Local 12 Political Action Committee
Matthew P Aracich, Treasurer

25-19 43rd Avenue, Long Island City, NY 11101-4208
718-784-3456

ASGM PAC
Christopher Durnan, Treasurer
1075 W Park Avenue, East Atlantic Beach, NY 11561
516-431-2501

Assn for a Better Long Island - PAC (ABLI)
John V Klein, Treasurer
1505 Kellum Pl, Mineola, NY 11501
516-741-6565 Fax: 516-741-6706

Assn of Independent Commercial Producers Inc PAC
David L Gould, Treasurer
555 So Flower St, Ste 4210, Los Angeles, CA 90071-2300
213-489-4792 Fax: 213-489-4818

Assn of New York City Concrete Producers Inc State PAC
Joseph C Greco Jr, Treasurer
87-13 Rockaway Blvd, Ozone Park, NY 11416
718-849-5200
Web site: www.grecoreadymix.com

Association of Commuter Rail Employees PAC NY
John Gaines, Treasurer
420 Lexington Avenue, Suite 215, New York, NY 10017
845-656-2469

Association of New York State Young Republicans Inc
Daniel Butler, Treasurer
PO Box 4811, New York, NY 10185
212-465-3377
e-mail: info@nyyrc.com
Web site: www.nyyrc.com

Astoria Financial Corp PAC
Daniel J Quirk, Treasurer
C/O Astoria Fed S&L, 1 Astoria Fed Plz, Lake Success, NY 11042
516-327-7823 Fax: 516-328-2035

Asurion Employees PAC
Michael Ain, Treasurer
648 Grassmere Park Dr, Suite 300, Nashville, TN 37211
615-837-3000 Fax: 615-837-3001

Aurora Endorsed Republican Club
Jerry Thompson, II, Treasurer
164 Quaker Road, East Aurora, NY 14052
716-652-0232

Automobile Dealers of New York PAC
Robert E Vancavage, Treasurer
PO Box 7347, Albany, NY 12224
518-463-1148 Fax: 518-432-1309
e-mail: bobv@nysada.com

BAC Local 2 PAC
John Buck, Treasurer

Offices and agencies generally appear in alphabetical order, except when specific order is requested by listee.

POLITICAL ACTION COMMITTEES

302 Centre Dr, Albany, NY 12203
518-456-5477 Fax: 518-456-7420
Web site: www.bac2.org

BBL PAC
Stephen J Obermayer, Treasurer
504 Victory Circle, Ballston Spa, NY 12020
518-884-8018

BCSA-PAC
Thomas F Vitale, Treasurer
2495 Main Street, OTC Suite 100, Buffalo, NY 14201
716-833-9145

BMW PAC
David N Weinraub, Treasurer
79 Columbia Street, Albany, NY 12210
518-427-7350

BRAB PAC, INC
Michael Laub, Treasurer
C/O Bronx Realty Advisory Board, 6 Xavier Drive, Suite 301, Yonkers, NY 10704
914-966-2000
e-mail: brabpac@aol.com

BXNY PAC
John A Emrick, II, Treasurer
1469 East Ave, #2C, Bronx, NY 10462
718-829-5142

BX Rochester PAC
Vic Salerno, Treasurer
180 Linden Oaks, Suite 100, Rochester, NY 14625
585-586-5460 Fax: 585-586-1580

Bank of America NY PAC
Gregory E Swanson, Treasurer
600 Peachtree St, NE, 3rd Fl, Atlanta, GA 30308
404-607-5267
Web site: www.bankofamerica.com

BAPA
Marie Kalka, Treasurer
26 Acre Place, Binghamton, NY 13904
607-760-0162

Bear Stearns Political Campaign Committee
Michael J Abatemarco, Treasurer
1 Metrotech Center N, 9th Fl, Brooklyn, NY 11201
212-272-8750 Fax: 347-643-2524
e-mail: mabatemarco@bear.com

Bell Atlantic Corporation PAC
Sandra L Borders, Treasurer
1717 Arch Street, 47S, Philadelphia, PA 19103
215-963-6387

Bellmore Republican Club Inc
Anne M Davis, Treasurer
308 St Marks Ave, Bellmore, NY 11710
516-826-5307

Bethpage Federal Credit Union PAC
Brian Clarke, Treasurer
899 South Oyster Bay Rd, Bethpage, NY 11714
516-349-6767 Fax: 516-349-6765
e-mail: bclarke@bethpagefcu.com

Better Health Care PAC
Jesse Ellman, Treasurer
18 Lexington Road, New City, NY 10956
914-634-6916

Black Car PAC
Douglas Kramer
C/O Fox Horan & Camerini, 825 3rd Ave, 11th Fl, New York, NY 10005
212-363-7020 Fax: 212-797-3369

Bricklayers & Allied Craftsmen Local Union 1 PAC
Santo Lanzafame, Treasurer
4 Court Square, Long Island City, NY 11101
718-392-0525 Fax: 718-392-1068

Bricklayers & Allied Craftworkers Local 5 NY PAC
Tony Piacente, Treasurer
126 Innis Ave, Poughkeepsie, NY 12601
845-452-3689 Fax: 845-452-4771

Bricklayers Allied Craftworkers Local 3 Buffalo PAC
Daniel Rose, Treasurer
, Pittsford, NY 14534
716-873-1141

Bristol-Myers Squibb Co Employee PAC
Daphne Quimi, Treasurer
345 Park Avenue, 42nd Floor, Room 67, New York, NY 10154
212-546-4324

Bronx Coalition for Good Government
Egidio Sementilli, Treasurer
1754 Hobart Avenue, Bronx, NY 10461
718-239-7700

Kings County Democratic Party
Derrick Davis, Treasurer
16 Court St, Ste 1115, Brooklyn, NY 11241
718-875-5870 Fax: 718-596-4013
e-mail: ddavis@brooklyndems.com
Web site: www.brooklyndems.com

Buffalo Niagara Builders' Assn Build PAC
Joseph W McIvor, Jr, Treasurer
91 Eastwood Pkwy, Depew, NY 14043
716-668-3100 Fax: 716-636-9658
e-mail: joe@bnba.org
Web site: www.bnba.org

Buffalo Professional Firefighters PAC
Scott T Skinner, Secretary Treasurer

Offices and agencies generally appear in alphabetical order, except when specific order is requested by listee.

535

POLITICAL ACTION COMMITTEES

255 Delaware Ave, Buffalo, NY 14202
716-856-4130 Fax: 716-854-1783
e-mail: buffalo.firefighters@verizon.net
Web site: www.buffalofirefighters.com

Buffalo Teachers Federation PAC
Donna Stempniak, Treasurer
271 Porter Avenue, Buffalo, NY 14201
716-881-5400 Fax: 716-881-6678
Web site: www.btfny.org

Build New York PAC
Joan E Flowers, Treasurer
219-10 South Conduit Avenue, Springfield Gardens, NY 11413
718-527-5229

Builders' PAC
Robert A Wieboldt, Treasurer
1757-8 Veterans Hwy, Islandia, NY 11749
631-232-2345 Fax: 631-232-2349
e-mail: evp@libi.org
Web site: www.libi.org

Building & Construction Trades Council PAC
Edward Malloy, Treasurer
71 W 23rd St, Ste 501-03, New York, NY 10010
212-647-0700 Fax: 212-647-0705

Building Contractors Assn Inc
James Sugrue, Treasurer
451 Park Ave S, 4th Fl, New York, NY 10016
212-683-8080 Fax: 212-683-0404
e-mail: nybca1@aol.com
Web site: www.ny-bca.com

Building Industry Association of New York City, Inc
Jessica Fortino, Treasurer
2535 Victory Blvd, Staten Island, NY 10314
718-720-3070 Fax: 718-720-3088
e-mail: jfortino@webuildnyc.com

Business First PAC
Todd L Shimkus, Treasurer
PO Box 158, Glens Falls, NY 12801
518-798-1761 Fax: 518-792-4147

Business-Industry PAC of Central NY Inc
John F Osta, Treasurer
5161 Wagon Trails End, Syracuse, NY 13215
315-487-6551 Fax: 315-487-0802
e-mail: jfosta@realtyusa.com

CAPE PAC
William Phillips, Treasurer
Hinman Straub, PC, 121 State Street, Albany, NY 12207
518-694-3110

CAS PAC
Anthony Laurino, President

1 Huntington Quadrangle, Ste 3N0SA, Melville, NY 11747
631-293-2820 Fax: 631-293-2716
e-mail: casmelvill@aol.com

CIGNA Corporation Political Action Committee
David M Porcello, Treasurer
900 Cottage Grove Road, S-258, Hartford, CT 06152
860-226-4602

CNY Labor PAC
John Hutchings, Treasurer
404 Oak Street, Lower Level, Syracuse, NY 13203
315-422-3363 Fax: 315-422-2260

CWA Finger Lakes PAC
Garry L Cranker, Treasurer
C/O CWA Local 1170, 1451 Lake Avenue, Rochester, NY 14615
585-649-1170

CWA SSF (NY)
Robert Master, Treasurer
80 Pine Street, 37th Floor, New York, NY 10005
212-344-2515 Fax: 212-425-2947

Cable PAC
Richard F Alteri, Treasurer
18 Olive Tree Lane, Albany, NY 12208
518-463-6676 Fax: 518-463-0574
e-mail: ralteri@nycap.rr.com

Cablevision Systems New York PAC
Sheila A Mahony, Treasurer
1111 Stewart Avenue, Bethpage, NY 11714
516-803-2387

Campaign for Renewable Energy
William Bastuk, Treasurer
125 Eastman Estates, Rochester, NY 14622
585-342-1375

Capital City Committee
Theresa Devine, Treasurer
PO Box 77443, Washington, DC 20013
202-265-0200

Captain's Endowment Assn PAC
Francis Porcelli, Treasurer
Captain's Endowmt, 233 B Way, Ste 850, New York, NY 10027
212-964-7500 Fax: 212-406-3105

Carpenters Local No. 19 PAC
Kevin T Smith, Treasurer
52 Stone Castle Rd, Ste 3, Rock Tavern, NY 12575
845-567-6985

Carpenters' Local 747 PAC
Richard Waite, Treasurer

Offices and agencies generally appear in alphabetical order, except when specific order is requested by listee.

POLITICAL ACTION COMMITTEES

21 Jetview Drive, Syracuse, NY 13212
585-455-5797 Fax: 315-455-8326
e-mail: carpenters@local.747.com

Carpenters' Local Union 85 PAC
John Mattle, Treasurer
244 Paul Rd, Rochester, NY 14624
716-328-6251 Fax: 585-436-4231
e-mail: smcdade@rochestercarpenters.org

Cayuga Community College Faculty Assn PAC
Teresa R Hoercher, Treasurer
197 Franklin St, Auburn, NY 13021
315-255-1743 Fax: 315-255-2050

Cendant Corporation NY PAC
John McClain, Treasurer
1 Campus Way, Parsippany, NJ 7054
973-496-5040 Fax: 973-496-5080

Central Brooklyn Medical Group, PC
Martin Valdes MD, Treasurer
242 E 72nd St Apt 18, New York, NY 10021
212-737-3636
Web site: www.brooklyndocs.com

Central NY PAC Region 9 UAW
Samuel G Williams, Treasurer
35 George Karl Blvd, Ste 100, Amherst, NY 14221
716-632-1540 Fax: 716-632-1797

Chain Pharmacy Assn PAC
Steven B Weingarten, Treasurer
1 Commerce Plaza, Ste 2005, Albany, NY 12210
518-465-7330 Fax: 518-465-0273
e-mail: stevew@lobbywr.com
Web site: www.lobbywr.com

Charter PAC
Tracy Nagler, Treasurer
575 Lexington Ave, 33rd Fl, New York, NY 10022
212-318-9109
Web site: www.bncf.org

Cheektowaga Democratic Finance Committee
Robert Brandon, Treasurer
39 Betty Lou Lane, Cheektowaga, NY 14825
716-683-0572

Cingular Wireless LLC EPAC
James Hoeberling, Treasurer
Comerica Bank, PAC Svcs, PO Box 75000, Detroit, MI 48275-2250
248-371-5562

Citigroup Inc PAC - Federal/State
Theresa A Russell, Treasurer

101 Pennsylvania Avenue NW, # 1000, Washington, DC, DC 20004
212-291-2838
e-mail: PAC@citi.com

Citizen Action of NY Political Contribution Acct
Richard Kirsch, Treasurer
94 Central Ave, Albany, NY 12206
518-465-4600 Fax: 518-465-2890
e-mail: mail@citizenaction.org
Web site: www.citizenactionny.org

Citizens for Integrity in Politics
Jeffrey T Buley, Treasurer
27 Elk Street, Albany, NY 12208
518-432-4563

Citizens for Fiscal Intergrity
Angela Irvin, Treasurer
6367 Treefoil Court, Lakeview, NY 14085

Citizens for Public Broadcasting
Peter G Repas, Treasurer
33 Elk St, Ste 200, Albany, NY 12207
518-462-1590

Citizens for Responsible Representation
Diane Hunt, Treasurer
PO Box 280202, Brooklyn, NY 11228-0202
212-816-3826

Citizens for Sports & Arts, Inc
Barbara Dillon, Treasurer
6601 Broadway, Bronx, NY 10471

Citizens Leadership Council
Leslie Lohrer, Treasurer
335 Upper Boiceville Road, Boiceville, NY 12412
845-657-8680

Civil Service Employees' PAF
Joseph McMullen, Treasurer
143 Washington Ave, Albany, NY 12210
518-436-8622 Fax: 518-427-1677
Web site: www.csealocal1000.net

Civil Service Technical Guild PAC
Thomas Conatantine, Treasurer
125 Barclay Street, New York, NY 10007
212-815-7604

Clean PAC Inc
Nora Nealis, Treasurer
252 W 29th St, New York, NY 10001
212-967-3002 Fax: 212-967-2240
e-mail: ncaiclean@aol.com

Clear Channel Communications Inc PAC
Stu Olds, Treasurer

Offices and agencies generally appear in alphabetical order, except when specific order is requested by listee.

537

POLITICAL ACTION COMMITTEES

c/o Katz Media, 125 W 55th St, New York, NY 10019
212-424-6780 Fax: 212-424-6769
Web site: www.katz-media.com

Committee for Action for a Responsible Electorate (CARE)
Robert J Murphy, Treasurer
c/o NYSHFA, 33 Elk St, Ste 300, Albany, NY 12207-1010
518-462-4800 Fax: 518-426-4051

Committee for a Better Niagara
Thomas J Kraus, Treasurer
6311 Inducon Corporate Drive, Suite 2, Sanborn, NY 14132
716-285-9141 Fax: 716-285-0941

Committee for Effective City Council
John G Curran, Treasurer
310 Executive Office Bldg, Rochester, NY 14614
585-454-6187

Committee for Effective Leadership
William J Hevert, Treasurer
63 Carraige Place, Edison, NJ 08820
732-744-1413

Committee for Medical Eye Care PAC
Hobart A Lerner, Treasurer
121 State St, Albany, NY 12207
716-271-7892

Committee for Workers' Compensation Reform
Ronald Balter, Treasurer
132 Nassau St, Ste 1200, New York, NY 10038
212-732-8333 Fax: 212-962-5523
Web site: www.nyworkerscompensationalliance.org

Coalition of Fathers & Families NY
James Hays, Treasurer
PO Box 782, Clifton Park, NY 12065
518-383-8202 Fax: 518-383-8202
Web site: www.fafny.org

Coca-Cola Enterprise Employee NonPartisan Committee for Good Government
Eugene M Rackley IV, Treasurer
2500 Windy Ridge Pkwy, Atlanta, GA 30339
770-989-3408

Columbus Circle Agency, Inc
Edmund J Bergassi, Treasurer
35 Portman Road, New Rochelle, NY 10801
914-637-8100

Committee for Economic Growth
Anita M Genovese, Treasurer
665 Main Street, Suite 200, Buffalo, NY 14203-1487
716-852-7100

Committee of Interns & Residents SEIU Loc 1957 Health Care Advocacy Fund (CARE)
Mark Levy, Treasurer

Cir, 520 Eighth Avenue, Suite 1200, New York, NY 10018
212-356-8100

Communication Workers of America, District 1 PAC
Robert Master, Treasurer
80 Pine St, 37th Fl, New York, NY 10005
212-344-2515 Fax: 212-425-2947
e-mail: rmaster@cwa-union.org

Community Mental Health PAC
Antonia M Lasicki, Treasurer
52 Dublin Dr, Niskayuna, NY 12309
518-783-9166 Fax: 518-426-0504
e-mail: toni@aclnys.org

Compac, NJ
Douglas J Pauls, Treasurer
1701 Route 70 East, Cherry Hill, NJ 08034
856-751-9000 Fax: 856-751-9260

Conservative Action Fund
Ross Brady, Treasurer
2064 84th Street, Brooklyn, NY 11214
718-265-3378

Consolidated Edison, Inc. Employees' Political Action Committee (CEIPAC)
Edward J Rasmussen, Treasurer
4 Irving Place, Room 506, New York, NY 10003
212-460-4202 Fax: 212-475-1809
e-mail: rasmussene@coned.com

Construction Contractors Assn PAC
Richard O'Beirne, Treasurer
330 Meadow Ave, Newburgh, NY 12250
845-562-4280 Fax: 845-562-1448

Construction Industry Council - NYS PAC
Ross J Pepe, Treasurer
629 Old White Plains Rd, Tarrytown, NY 10591
914-631-6070 Fax: 914-631-5172

Consumer Advocacy PAC
Neil Reiff, Treasurer
50 E St SE, Ste 300, Washington, DC 20003
703-455-1327 Fax: 202-479-1115

Contractors, Agents, & Brokers PAC
Frank E O'Brien Jr, Treasurer
2 Valley View Drive, Albany, NY 12208
518-482-0686

Convenience PAC
James S Calvin, Treasurer
130 Washington Ave, Ste 300, Albany, NY 12210
518-432-1400 Fax: 518-432-7400
e-mail: jim@nyacs.org
Web site: www.nyacs.org

Cope 25
James Plant, Treasurer

Offices and agencies generally appear in alphabetical order, except when specific order is requested by listee.

POLITICAL ACTION COMMITTEES

269 Barn Swallow Road, Maporville, NY 11949
516-874-6131

Corning Incorporated Employees PAC (COREPAC)
Timothy J Regan, Treasurer
325 7th Street, NW, Ste 600, Washington, DC 20004
202-661-4150 Fax: 202-661-4165

Correction Captains Assn PAC
Ronald W Whitfield, Treasurer
233 Broadway, Ste 1701, New York, NY 10279
212-227-4090 Fax: 212-962-4819

Correction Officers' Benevolent Assn PAC
Elias Husamudeen, Treasurer
335 Broadway, Rm 915, New York, NY 10013
212-274-8000 Fax: 212-274-8255
e-mail: cobanyc@aol.com
Web site: www.cobanyc.org

Couch White PAC
Robert M Loughney, Treasurer
540 Broadway, PO Box 22222, Albany, NY 12201-2222
518-426-4600 Fax: 518-426-0533
e-mail: rloughney@couchwhite.com

Council of School Supervisors & Admin, Local 1 AFSA AFL-CIO
Manfred Korman, Treasurer
16 Court St, 4th Floor, Brooklyn, NY 11241-1003
718-852-3000 Fax: 718-403-0278
e-mail: ernest@csa-nyc.org
Web site: www.csa-nyc.org

Council of Urban Professionals
Taurus Richardson, Treasurer
C/O ICV Capital Partners, 666 Third Ave, 25th Floor, New York, NY 10017
212-455-9641 Fax: 212-455-9603

Credit Unions' PAC (CUPAC)
Eugene Gizzi, Treasurer
811 Croton St, Rome, NY 13440
315-336-7578 Fax: 315-336-7578
e-mail: governmentalaffairs@nyscul.org
Web site: www.nyscul.org

D&M P.A.C., LLC
Arthur Goldstein, Treasurer
C/O Davidoff Malito & Hutcher LLP, 605 Third Avenue, 34th Floor, New York, NY 10158
212-557-7200
e-mail: agg@dmlegal.com

D.R.I.V.E.-Democratic, Republican, Independent Voter Education
John C Keegel, Treasurer

25 Louisiana Avenue, NW, Washington, DC 20001
202-624-6905

DC 37 PAC
Oliver Gray, Treasurer
125 Barclay Street, Room 525, New York, NY 10007
212-815-1504 Fax: 212-815-1516
e-mail: ogray@dc37.net

Daimler Chrysler Corporation Political Support Committee-New York
Timothy P Dykstra, Treasurer
1000 Chrysler Drive, CIMS 485-09-82, Auburn Hills, MI 48326-2766
248-512-6130

Delois Brassell Political Action Committee
Robert Brassell Jr, Treasurer
40 Lantern Street, Huntington, NY 11743
631-271-5028

Democracy for America-New York
Ben Eisenberg, Treasurer
PO Box 8313, Burlington, VT 05402
802-651-3200 Fax: 802-651-3299
Web site: www.democracyforamerica.com

Democratic Caucus Committee
Francis E Lus, Treasurer
71 Peerless Street, Brocton, NY 14706
716-792-9305

Democratic Governors' Assn - NY
Kenneth Jarin, Treasurer
1401 K Street NW, Suite 200, Washington, DC 20005
202-772-5600 Fax: 202-772-5602
Web site: www.democraticgovernors.org

Democratic Rural Conference of New York State
Cynthia Emmer, Treasurer
858 Davis St, Elmira, NY 14901
607-733-2844

Detectives' Endowment Association COPE
Michael J Palladino, President
26 Thomas St, New York, NY 10007
212-587-1000 Fax: 212-732-4863
e-mail: info@nycdetectives.org
Web site: www.nycdetectives.org

Dewey Ballantine LLP Political Action Committee-New York
Andrew W Kentz, Treasurer
975 F Street, NW, Washington, DC 20004
202-862-1086

District Council 9 PAC
William Ecfeld, Treasurer

Offices and agencies generally appear in alphabetical order, except when specific order is requested by listee.

POLITICAL ACTION COMMITTEES

45 West 14th St, New York, NY 10011
212-255-2950 Fax: 212-255-1151
e-mail: jackDC9@aol.com
Web site: www.DC9.net

Diverse New York PAC
Alfredo M Vidal, Treasurer
PO Box 7194, Albany, NY 12224-0194

DLA Piper Rudnick Gray Cary US LLP NYSPAC
John A Merrigan, Treasurer
C/O 1251 Avenue of the Americas, Main Reception on 29th Floor, New York, NY 10020
202-861-6455 Fax: 202-689-8560
Web site: www.dlapiper.com

Dominion PAC-NY
James W Hoeberling, Treasurer
Comerica Bank PAC Services, MC 2250, PO Box 75000, Detroit, MI 48275-2250
248-371-7268

Drug Policy Alliance Network (SSF)
James F McCauley, Treasurer
70 West 36th Street, 16th Floor, New York, NY 10018
646-335-2262

Duane Morris LLP Government Committee NY Find
Charles J O'Donnell, Treasurer
30 South 17th Street, Philadelphia, PA 19103
215-979-1000 Fax: 215-979-1020
Web site: www.duanemorris.com

Dutchess Democratic Women's Caucas
Mary H Williams, Treasurer
PO Box 5284, Poughkeepsie, NY 12602
845-229-8174

Dynegy NY PAC
Martin W Daley, Treasurer
c/o Martin W Daley, 992 River Road, Newburgh, NY 12550
845-563-4903 Fax: 845-563-4992
e-mail: martin.w.daley@dynegy.com

EISPAC
Robert C Rosenberg, Treasurer
419 Park Ave South, Room 807, New York, NY 10016
212-689-7744 Fax: 212-679-5576

ESMBA PAC MOR
Jonathan Pinaro, Treasurer
21 Gladstone Avenue, West Islip, NY 11725
631-661-6950

ESPAC
David Tarsa, Chairman

80 Wolf Road, Albany, NY 12205
518-449-0702 Fax: 518-449-0779
e-mail: info@espa.net
Web site: www.espa.net

ESSAA - PAC (Empire State Supervisors & Admin Assn)
Thomas Vasiloff, Treasurer
7333 Dartmoor Crossing, Fayetteville, NY 13066
315-637-6911

EYP PAC NY
Timothy N Burditt, Treasurer
C/O Einhorn Yaffee Prescott, PO Box 617, Albany, NY 12201
518-431-3464

East Greenbush Republican Club Inc
Robert D Lapham, Treasurer
23 Capital Place, Rensselaer, NY 12144
518-426-5610

East Rockaway Republican Club
Rosanne Tully, Treasurer
389 Beebe Court, North Babylon, NY 11703
631-586-7133

East Side Republican District Leaders Committee
Debra I Heitner, Treasurer
122 East 83rd Street, New York, NY 10028
212-517-8444 Fax: 212-517-3142

Eastman Kodak Co Employee PAC
M Celeste Amaral, Treasurer
343 State Street, Rochester, NY 14650-0240
585-724-9808
e-mail: m.celeste.amaral@kodak.com

Ecology & Environment NYS Committee for Responsible Government
Ronald L Frank, Treasurer
368 Pleasantview Drive, Lancaster, NY 14086
716-684-8060 Fax: 716-684-0844

Educational Leadership (EL) PAC
Kevin G Banes, Executive Director
8 Airport Park Blvd, Albany Airport Park, Latham, NY 12110
518-782-0600 Fax: 518-782-9552
e-mail: kbanes@saanys.org
Web site: www.saanys.org

Eleanor Roosevelt Legacy Committee Inc
Margo Alexander, Treasurer
138 East 92nd St, New York, NY 10128
212-348-9179
Web site: www.eleanorslegacy.org

Elevator Constructors Union Local No 1 Political Action Committee
Anthony J Carudo, Treasurer

Offices and agencies generally appear in alphabetical order, except when specific order is requested by listee.

POLITICAL ACTION COMMITTEES

47-24 27th Street, Long Island City, NY 11101
e-mail: acarudo@iueclocal1.com

Elevator Constructors Union Local 14 PAC
Donald M Winkle Jr, Treasurer
C/O IUEC Local 14, 3527 Harlem Road, Suite 9, Buffalo, NY 14225
716-833-5528

Eli Lilly & Company PAC
James Davlin, Treasurer
Lilly Corp Ctr, Indianapolis, IN 46285
317-873-4845

Elmont South Republican Club
Joseph A Kolb, Treasurer
601 Keswick Road, Elmont, NY 11003
516-859-4649

Emigrant Savings Bank PAC
Daniel C Hickey, Treasurer
14 Ferris Lane, Bedford, NY 10506
914-234-9469

Emily's List
Callie Fines, Treasurer
1120 Connecticut Ave NW, #1100, Washington, DC 20036
Fax: 202-326-1415
e-mail: cfines@emilyslist.org
Web site: www.emilyslist.org

Empire Dental PAC
Warren M Shaddock, DDS, Treasurer
59 Winding Creek Lane, Rochester, NY 14625-2175
716-586-3941

Empire Leadership Council
Albert Nocciolino, Treasurer
PO Box 2598, Albany, NY 12220
e-mail: empireleadershipcouncil@gmail.com

Empire Liquor Store Association
Jim Mackenzie, Treasurer
PO Box 197, Amherst, NY 41226-0197
716-691-3396

Empire State ABC PAC
Rebecca A Meinking, Treasurer
200 Cooper Lane, Dewitt, NY 13214
315-569-4579

Empire State Association of Adult Homes, Inc PAC
James Vitale, Treasurer
170 Murray Street, Auburn, NY 13021
315-253-2755 Fax: 315-252-9970

Empire State Leadership PAC
Patricia Krzesinski, Treasurer

11 Hunters Lane, Williamsville, NY 14221
716-632-4762

Empire State Pride Agenda PAC
Alan Van Capelle, Treasurer
16 West 22nd St, 2nd Fl, New York, NY 10010
212-627-0305 Fax: 212-627-4136
e-mail: prideagenda@prideagenda.org
Web site: www.prideagenda.org

Empire State Regional Council of Carpenters Political Action Fund-NYS
Michael L Conroy, Treasurer
270 Motor Parkway, Hauppauge, NY 11788
631-952-0808 Fax: 631-952-9833

Energy Action Fund
Dennis J Bender, Treasurer
PO Box 5224, Binghamton, NY 13902-5224
607-762-4924 Fax: 607-762-8045
e-mail: djbender@nyseg.com

Energy for NY PAC
Patrick J Curran, III, Treasurer
111 Washington Ave, Ste 601, Albany, NY 12210
518-449-3440 Fax: 518-449-3446

Engineers PEF-Local 832
Ferne Fantauzzo, Treasurer
PO Box 93310, Rochester, NY 14692
716-272-9890

Engineers Voluntary Political Action Fund
Theron H Hogle, Treasurer
127 East Glen Avenue, Syracuse, NY 13205
315-492-1752

Entergy Corporation Political Committee NY (ENPAC-NY)
Kay Arnold, Treasurer
425 W Capitol, Ste 40B, Little Rock, AR 72201
501-377-3553 Fax: 501-377-5822

Enterprise Rent-A-Car Company NY PAC
William Snyder, Treasurer
600 Corporate Park Drive, St Louis, MO 63105
314-512-5000 Fax: 314-512-4897
Web site: www.enterprise.com
Rent, sell, lease vehicles

Erdman Anthony & Assoc Employees' PAC
Angelo Magagnoli, Treasurer
2165 Brighton Henrietta Rd, Rochester, NY 14623
585-427-8888 Fax: 585-427-8914

Ernst & Young Committee for Good Government
David G Bonagura, Treasurer

Offices and agencies generally appear in alphabetical order, except when specific order is requested by listee.

POLITICAL ACTION COMMITTEES

Ernst & Young LLP, 395 N Service Rd, Ste 400, Melville, NY 11747
631-752-6125 Fax: 631-752-6118
e-mail: david.bonagura@ey.com
Web site: www.ey.com

Excelsior 2000
Leon Ilnitzki, Treasurer
PO Box 2566, Syracuse, NY 13220
315-452-7825

Executive Political Action Committee (EPAC)
Bruno J LaSpina ESQ, Treasurer
PO Box 13476, Hauppauge, NY 11788
631-261-9709

FED PAC
Andrew Pardo, Treasurer
792 Columbus Ave, New York, NY 10025
212-866-3493

FUTURENY
Scott J Goodman, Treasurer
595 New Loudon Road, Box 263, Latham, NY 12110

Faculty Association PAC
Paul Waite, Treasurer
3111 Saunders Settlement Rd, Sanborn, NY 14132
716-731-3271 Fax: 716-731-4053
e-mail: waite@niagaracc.suny.edu

Faculty Assn of Suffolk Community College VOTE-COPE
Joyce Gabriele, Treasurer
533 College Road, Rm H224J, Selden, NY 11784
631-451-4151 or 631-732-4552 Fax: 631-732-4584
e-mail: info@fascc.org
Web site: www.fascc.org

Fair PAC
John G Neidhart, Treasurer
3085 Southwestern Blvd, Orchard Park, NY 14127
716-674-5500 Fax: 716-674-5501

Family Physicians PAC
Vito F Grasso, Treasurer
260 Osborne Rd, Loudonville, NY 12211
518-489-8945 Fax: 518-489-8961
e-mail: ft@nyfafp.org
Web site: www.nyfafp.org

Farrell Fritz PC
Thomas J Killeen, Treasurer
1320 Reckson Plaza, Uniondale, NY 11556
516-227-0631
Web site: www.farrellfritz.com

Federal Express New York State Political Action Committee
Robert T Molinet, Treasurer
942 South Shady Grove Road, Memphis, TN 38120
901-818-7407 Fax: 901-818-7194

Federations of Police PAC Fund
Ralph Purdy, Treasurer
540 North State Road, Briarcliff Manor, NY 10510
914-941-4103 Fax: 914-941-4472
e-mail: mailroom@policefederation.com

Finger Lakes Chapter NECA PAC Fund
Marilyn M Oppedisano, Treasurer
PO Box 222, 112 Pickard Dr East, Syracuse, NY 13211
315-451-4278 Fax: 315-451-1327
Web site: www.flneca.org

Finger Lakes PAC
Wilson E Mitchell, Treasurer
2729 Miller Road, Waterloo, NY 13165
315-539-8456

Fire Island Pines Property Owners Assn PAC
Jon Gilbert, Treasurer
114 W 76th St, New York, NY 10023
212-580-2024

First District Dental Society Political Action Committee
Robert B Raiber, Treasurer
6 East 43rd Street, 11th Floor, New York, NY 10017
e-mail: drrobertr@aol.com

Fleet Bank of New York PAC
Christian M Abeel, Treasurer
1125 US Route 22 West, Bridgewater, NJ 08807
908-253-4757

Food Industry PAC-NYC
Patricia Brodhagen, Treasurer
C/O Food Industry Alliance of NYC, 411 Theodore Fremd Ave, Suite 206 S, Rye, NY 10580
914-925-3442

Ford Motor Company Civic Action Fund
James W Hoeberling, Treasurer
PO Box 75000, Detroit, MI 48275-2250
248-371-5562 Fax: 248-371-7272
e-mail: martha_k_denbaas@comerica.com

Franklin Square Republican Club
Joseph Ra, Executive Leader
PO Box 214, Franklin Square, NY 11010
516-328-3205

Fraternal Order of Police Empire State Lodge Inc
James Bartkowski, Chairman
911 Police Plaza, Hicksville, NY 11801
516-433-4455 Fax: 516-433-4473

Free PAC
Joseph J O'Hara, Treasurer

Offices and agencies generally appear in alphabetical order, except when specific order is requested by listee.

POLITICAL ACTION COMMITTEES

PO Box 1187, Albany, NY 12201-1187
518-445-3840

Freedom America
Douglas J Pauls, Treasurer
1701 Route 70 East, Cherry Hill, NJ 08034
856-751-9000
Web site: www.freedomamerica.org

Friend of Cultural Institutions
Richard J Miller Jr, Treasurer
19 Dove St, Albany, NY 12210
518-426-8111 Fax: 518-426-5111

Friends of Lazio
Gerard Glass, Treasurer
72 East Main St, Babylon, NY 11702
631-321-1400 or 631-321-1400 Fax: 631-321-1491

Friends of New York Racing PAC
Timothy G Smith, Treasurer
211 East 70th Street, Apt 12B, New York, NY 10021
212-737-9098

Friends of Schumer
Steven D Goldenkranz, Treasurer
509 Madison Avenue, Suite 1902, New York, NY 10022
718-338-8138

Friends of Upstate Labor
Kenneth L Warner, Treasurer
1163 East Ave, #6, Rochester, NY 14607
716-737-8420

Friends of the Volunteer Firefighter
Kirby Hannan, Treasurer
c/o KTHPA Inc, 107 Washington Ave, Albany, NY 12210
518-465-6550 Fax: 518-465-6557

Fund for Better Transportation PAC
Nathan Fenno, Treasurer
1 Railroad Avenue, Cooperstown, NY 13326
607-547-2555 Fax: 607-547-9834
Web site: www.cnyk.com

GEICO NY PAC
Michael H Campbell, Treasurer
1303 Roosevelt St, Annapolis, MD 21403
410-268-3050

Gay and Lesbian Victory Fund
Brian A Johnson, Treasurer
1705 DeSales St NW, 5th Floor, Washington, DC 20036
202-842-8679 Fax: 202-289-3863
Web site: www.victoryfund.org

General Building Contractors of NYS PAC
Jeffrey J Zogg, Executive Director

Six Airline Drive, Albany, NY 12205
518-869-2207 Fax: 518-869-0846
e-mail: jeffz@gbcnys.agc.org
Web site: www.gbcnys.agc.org

General Contractors Assn of NY PAC
Felice Farber, Director, External Affairs
60 E 42nd St, Rm 3510, New York, NY 10165
212-687-3131 Fax: 212-808-5267

General Motors Corporation Political Action Committee-NY (GM PAC-NY)
Thomas Jeffers, Treasurer
1660 L Street NW, Suite 400, Washington, DC 20036
202-775-5086

Generation Project
Jason West, Treasurer
PO Box 1229, New Paltz, NY 12561

Glacier Creek PAC
Stephen J Siano, Treasurer
6723 Towpath Road, Box 66, Syracuse, NY 13214-0066
315-446-9120

GLBT Friends of Good Government
Harry B Bronson, Treasurer
96 Mount Vernon Ave, Rochester, NY 14620
585-244-3034

Go PAC Dutchess
David T Warshaw, Treasurer
13 Bird Ln, Poughkeepsie, NY 12603-5001
845-462-3769

Golden Apple Business Action Committee, PAC
Marsha Gordon, Treasurer
108 Corporate Park Drive, Suite 101, White Plains, NY 10604
914-948-2110 Fax: 914-948-0122
e-mail: mgordon@westchesterny.org
Web site: www.westchesterny.org

Goldman Sachs NY PAC
Judah C Sommer, Treasurer
101 Constitution Ave NW, Suite 1000 East, Washington, DC 20001
202-637-3760 Fax: 202-637-3773
e-mail: judah.sommer@gs.com
Web site: www.gs.com

Good Government NY
Timothy P Gordon, Treasurer
15 Beldale Road, Slingerlands, NY 12159
518-438-9004

Grassy Sprain PAC
Stephen R Brown, Treasurer
51 Pondfield Road, Bronxville, NY 10708
914-961-6100

Great Neck Democratic Club
Helene R Beckerman, Treasurer

Offices and agencies generally appear in alphabetical order, except when specific order is requested by listee.

POLITICAL ACTION COMMITTEES

65 Forest Row, Great Neck, NY 11024
516-487-2298

Great South Bay Republican Club PAC
Salvatore A Sperduto, Treasurer
127 Crystal Beach Blvd, Moriches, NY 11955
631-874-5120

Greater New Hyde Park Republican Club
Rebekah Perillo, Treasurer
7 Terrace Circle, Apt 1H, Great Neck, NY 11021
516-570-6278

Greater NY Auto Dealers' Assn Inc
Mark Schienberg, Treasurer
18-10 Whitestone Expwy, Whitestone, NY 11357
718-746-5900 Fax: 718-746-5557

Green Island Democratic Association
Theodore Koniowka, Treasurer
72 James Street, Green Island, NY 12183
518-271-1470 Fax: 518-271-1470
e-mail: info@tgkandassc.com
Web site: www.tgkandassc.com

Green Worlds Coalition Fund
Barbara W Bonfiglio, Treasurer
1155 21st St NW, Ste 300, Washington, DC 20036
202-659-8201 Fax: 202-659-5249

Greenberg, Traurig Political Action Committee
Clifford A Schulman, Treasurer
1221 Brickell Avenue, Miami, FL 33126
305-579-0500 Fax: 305-579-0717
Web site: www.gtlaw.com

Group Health Inc State PAC
Jeffrey L Goodwin, Treasurer
Group Health Inc, 441 Ninth Ave, New York, NY 10001
212-615-0891 Fax: 212-563-8561
e-mail: jgoodwin@ghi.com

Guardian Life PAC
John R Hurley, Treasurer
c/o Guardian Life Insurance, 7 Hanover Square, PO Box 300975,
New York, NY 10004
212-598-8854
e-mail: jrhurley@glic.com

HBA of CNY Local Build PAC
Robert F Tomeny, Treasurer
3675 James Street, Syracuse, NY 13206
315-463-6261 Fax: 315-463-6263
e-mail: hba@hbaofcny.com
Web site: www.hbaofcny.com

HIC PAC
Eugene Daly, Treasurer

50 Main Street, 12th Floor, White Plains, NY 10606
212-891-0800

HLA PAC
Christopher F Grimaldi, Treasurer
111 Washington Ave, Suite 606, Albany, NY 12210
518-432-9220

HPA PAC
Leslie Moran, Treasurer
90 State Street, Suite 825, Albany, NY 12207-1719
518-462-2150

HSBC North America, Inc PAC (H-PAC)
Janet St Amand, Treasurer
1401 I St, NW, Ste 520, Washington, DC 20005
202-466-3561 Fax: 202-466-3583

Haitian-American Association for Political Action (HAAPA-PAC)
Melissa Severe, Treasurer
PO Box 300975, Brooklyn, NY 11230
718-576-1966 Fax: 718-360-5811

Hamburg Conservative Club
Judith A Krautsack, Treasurer
3738 Salisbury Avenue, Blasdell, NY 14219
716-824-4483

Harris Beach Political Committee
William H Kedley, Treasurer
99 Garnsey Road, Pittsford, NY 14534
585-419-8904

Hartford Advocates Fund (The)
Robert J Price, Treasurer
Hartford Plaza, Hartford, CT 06115
860-547-8495
e-mail: robert.price@thehartford.com

Health Access Affiliates Good Government Fund
David K Smith, Treasurer
8735 Henderson Road, Ren 2, Tampa, FL 33634
800-960-2530

Health Care Providers' PAC
James Dwyer, Treasurer
99 troy Rd, Ste 200, East Greenbush, NY 12061
518-463-1118 Fax: 518-463-1606
e-mail: hcp@nyshcp.org
Web site: www.nyshcp.org

Healthcare Assn of NYS PAC (HANYS PAC)
Steven Kroll, Treasurer
HANYS PAC, One Empire Drive, Rensselaer, NY 12144
518-431-7600 Fax: 518-431-7915
e-mail: skroll@hanys.org
Web site: www.hanys.org

Healthy Kids NY
Marjorie W Shoemaker, Treasurer

Offices and agencies generally appear in alphabetical order, except when specific order is requested by listee.

POLITICAL ACTION COMMITTEES

80 Broad Street, Suite 1600, New York, NY 10004
917-438-4603

Healthy New York
Kathleen M Dougan, Treasurer
C/O Healthy New York PAC, 360 W 31st Street, Suite 303, New York, NY 10001
212-871-0310

Hearing Healthcare Alliance of NY PAC
Barbara J Ahern, Treasurer
1 Commerce Plz, Ste 400, Albany, NY 12210-2823
518-463-0723

Hellenic American PAC - State
Hercules Argyriou, Treasurer
1217 83rd St, Brooklyn, NY 11228
718-759-1802
e-mail: jacny@aol.com

Hempstead PBA PAC
Francis McNamee, Treasurer
PO Box 41, Hempstead, NY 11551
516-483-6200
e-mail: hemppba@aol.com

Hewlett Republican Club
Arnold Palleschi, Treasurer
1236 Waverly Street, Hewlett, NY 11557
516-569-5176

High-Need Hospital PAC Inc
Barbara King, Treasurer
12 Stuyvesant Oval, Apt 9A, New York, NY 10009
212-674-6122

HillPAC-NY
Janice Enright, Treasurer
The Ickes & Enright Group, 1300 Connecticut Ave #600, Washington, DC 20036
202-887-6726 Fax: 202-223-0358

HIP Health Plan PAC
Arthur J Bryd, Treasurer
55 Water Street, New York, NY 10041
646-447-6263

Holland & Knight Committee for Responsible Gov't (The)
James H Power, Treasurer
Holland & Knight, LLP, 195 Broadway, New York, NY 10007-3189
212-513-3494 Fax: 212-385-9010
e-mail: jhpower@hklaw.com
Web site: www.hklaw.com

Hotel Assn of NYC Inc PAC
Xavier S Lividini, Treasurer
320 Park Ave S, 22nd Fl, New York, NY 10022-6838
212-754-6700 Fax: 212-754-0243
Web site: www.hanyc.org

Hotel Employees Restaurant Int'l Union Tip Edu Fund
John W Wilhelm, Treasurer
1219 - 28th St NW, Washington, DC 20007
202-393-4373 Fax: 202-333-0468
e-mail: hereunion@hereunion.org

Hudson Valley Build PAC
Rachel Neuhaus, Director of Government Affairs
1161 Little Britain Road, New Windsor, NY 12553
547-567-6600 Fax: 845-562-1166
e-mail: rachel@hubuilder.com

Hudson Valley Chapter, Nat'l Electrical Contractors Assn (NECA), PAC
Salvatore J DiFede, Treasurer
375 Route 32, Central Valley, NY 10917
845-928-3575 Fax: 845-928-3581
e-mail: hudneca@frontiernet.net
Web site: www.electricnewyork.org

Hudson Valley Citizens for Change
Cathleen Parise, Treasurer
9 Scott Lane, Lagrangeville, NY 12540
845-227-5049

Huntington Chamber Committee for Better Gov't
William R Bohn II, Treasurer
2 Sherwood Drive, Huntington, NY 11743
631-367-2255

Hunts Point Produce Market Redevelopment PAC
Jeffrey B Haas, Treasurer
Henry Haas, Inc, 464 New York City Terminal Market, Bronx, NY 10474
718-378-2550

I Love Good Government
Tarky Lombardi, III, Treasurer
528 Plum Street, Syracuse, NY 13204
315-466-0812

I.U.O.E. Local 15 PAC
Daniel J Schneider, Treasurer
265 West 14th Street, Ste 505, New York, NY 10011
212-929-5327 Fax: 212-206-0357

IAFF Firepac NY Non-Federal
Vincent J Bollon, Treasurer
C/O IAFF, 1750 New York Ave NW, Washington, DC 20006
202-737-8484
Web site: www.iaff.org

IATSE Local 600 NY PAC
Paul V Ferrazzi, Treasurer

Offices and agencies generally appear in alphabetical order, except when specific order is requested by listee.

POLITICAL ACTION COMMITTEES

7755 Sunset Blvd, Los Angeles, CA 90046
323-876-0160 Fax: 323-876-6383

IBEW Local Union #1249 PAC
Harry D Saville, Treasurer
6518 Fremont Rd, PO Box 277, East Syracuse, NY 13057
315-656-7253 Fax: 315-656-7579

IBEW Local Union #237 Community Action Program
Darren P Aderman, Treasurer
7821 Porter Rd, Niagara Falls, NY 14304
716-298-5762 Fax: 716-297-8471
e-mail: ibew237@yahoo.com

IBEW Local Union 363 PAC
John Maraia, Treasurer
67 Commerce Drive South, Harriman, NY 10926
845-783-3500 Fax: 845-634-4924

ING America Insurance Holdings Inc PAC (ING NY PAC)
Kevin P Brown, Treasurer
151 Farmington Ave-TS31, Hartford, CT 06156
860-723-2246

IUOE Local 106 Voluntary PAF
Daniel J McGraw, II, Treasurer
1284 Central Ave, Albany, NY 12205
518-453-6518 Fax: 518-453-6549
e-mail: mail@iuoelocal106.org
Web site: www.iuoelocal106.org

IUOE Local 14-14B Voluntary PAC
Edwin Christian, President/Business Manager
141-57 Northern Blvd, Flushing, NY 11354
718-939-0600 Fax: 718-939-3131

IUOE Local 17 PAC
Mark N Kirsch, Treasurer
5959 Versailles Rd, Lakeview, NY 14085
716-627-2648
Web site: www.iuoe17.org

IUOE Local 463 State & Local PAC & PEF
Brett Brochey, Treasurer
3365 Ridge Rd, Ransomville, NY 14131
716-434-3327 Fax: 716-434-2160
e-mail: iuoe463diane@adlphia.net
Web site: www.iuoe463.org

IUOE Local 825 Political Action & Education Cmte
Joseph Whittles, Treasurer
65 Springfield Ave, Springfield, NJ 07081
973-921-1900 Fax: 973-921-2918
e-mail: markl@iuoe825.org

Independence for Bethlehem
Timothy P Gordon, Treasurer
15 Beldale Road, Slingerlands, NY 12159

Independent Agents PAC
Kathleen A Weinheimer, Treasurer
5784 Widewaters Pkwy, 1st Fl, Dewitt, NY 13214
800-962-7950 Fax: 888-432-0510
e-mail: kweinheimer@iiaany.org
Web site: www.iiaany.org

Independent Health Assn Inc Political Alliance
Sidney N Weiss, Treasurer
2495 Kensington Ave, Buffalo, NY 14226
716-839-2024 Fax: 716-839-3962

Independent Oil and Gas Association of NY, Inc Political Action Committee
R Stephan Gollaher, Treasurer
828 Four Mile Road, Gollaher Oil Bldg, Allegany, NY 14706
716-372-5354

Independent Petroleum Mktrs of NY PAC
Robert W Reid, Treasurer
41 Hawthorne Ave, Albany, NY 12203-2113
518-465-7330 Fax: 518-465-0273
e-mail: bobr@lobbywr.com

Independent Power Producers of NY PAC
Roger Kelley, Treasurer
19 Dove Street, Suite 302, Albany, NY 12210
518-436-3749 Fax: 518-436-0369
e-mail: rogerkk@aol.com
Web site: www.ippny.org

Insurance Brokers' Assn of NY PAC
Donald Privett, Treasurer
25 Chamberlain St, PO Box 997, Glenmont, NY 12077
212-962-7771 Fax: 877-644-0422
e-mail: ibany@global2000.net

Int'l Longshoremen's Assn AFL-CIO COPE
Robert E Gleason, Treasurer
17 Battery Place, New York, NY 10004
212-425-1200 Fax: 212-425-2928

Intercounty Health Facilities Assn PAC
Theresa M Santmann, Vice Chairman/Secretary
66 Cedar Lane, Babylon, NY 11702
631-422-1330 Fax: 631-581-6018

Intermagnetics State PAC
Arthur P Kazanjian, Treasurer
C/O Hinman Straub PC, 121 State Street, Albany, NY 12207
518-346-1414

International Council of Shopping Centers PAC NY
Melina Spadone, Treasurer
1221 Avenue of the Americas, 41st Floor, New York, NY 10020
646-728-3800 Fax: 732-694-1755
e-mail: icsc@icsc.org

International Paper Political Action Committee
John C Runyan, Treasurer

Offices and agencies generally appear in alphabetical order, except when specific order is requested by listee.

POLITICAL ACTION COMMITTEES

1101 Pennsylvania Avenue NW, Suite 200, Washington, DC 20004
202-628-1223 Fax: 202-628-1368
Web site: www.internationalpaper.com

International Union of Painters and Allied Trades Legislative & Educational Committee
George Galis, Treasurer
1750 New York Avenue NW, Washington, DC 20006
202-637-0725
Web site: www.iupat.org

Inwood-North Lawrence Republican Committee
RoseMarie Evola, Treasurer
545 Allen Road, Woodmere, NY 11598
516-374-6527

Iron Workers' Local 12 PAF
Garry M Simmons, Treasurer
900 Lark Drive, Albany, NY 12207
518-436-1294 Fax: 518-436-6781
e-mail: iron12@msn.com

Iron Workers' Local 40 Voluntary COPE
Edward W Walsh, Treasurer
451 Park Ave S, New York, NY 10016
212-889-1320 Fax: 212-779-3267

Iron Workers' Local 60 PAC
Gary E Robb, Treasurer
500 West Genesee St, Syracuse, NY 13204
315-471-3413 Fax: 315-478-2630
e-mail: iwl60@verizon.net

Ironworkers Political Action League
Walter W Wise, Treasurer
1750 New York Avenue NW, Suite 400, Washington, DC 20006
202-383-4800 Fax: 202-638-4856
Web site: www.ironworkers.org

Issues Mobilization Fund - Greater Rochester
Peter Stoller, Treasurer
930 East Avenue, Rochester, NY 14607
585-292-5000 Fax: 585-292-5008

J P Morgan Chase & Co State & Federal PAC
Bridget Lawless, Treasurer
270 Park Ave, 29th Fl, New York, NY 10017
212-270-0774 Fax: 646-534-2102
e-mail: bridget.lawless@jpmchase.com

JBDS NYS PAC
Margaret J O'Brien, Treasurer
633 Third Avenue, 16th Floor, New York, NY 10017
212-850-0604

JOE-PAC NON-Federal
Scott G Kaufmann, Treasurer
84-54 Grand Avenue, Elmhurst, NY 11373

JY Trans PAC
Dennis M Wheeler, Treasurer

201 Edgewater St, Staten Island, NY 10305
718-448-3900 Fax: 718-447-1582

Johnson & Johnson Employees' Good Gov't Fund PAC
Richard W Lloyd, Treasurer
1 Johnson & Johnson Plz, New Brunswick, NJ 08933
732-524-3726 Fax: 732-524-3005
e-mail: jsosa@corus.jnj.com

Keeping Americas' Promise Inc
Matthew S Butler, Treasurer
607 14th Street NW, Suite 800, Washington, DC 20005
202-654-1759

Keycorp Advocates Fund-NY
Erskine E Cade, Treasurer
127 Public Sq, Cleveland, OH 44114
216-689-4486 Fax: 216-689-8710
e-mail: erskine_cade@keybank.com

Keyspan Energy State PAC (KEYSPAC)
Edward A T Carr, Treasurer
175 E Old Country Road, Hicksville, NY 11801
516-545-4405 Fax: 516-545-5065
e-mail: ecarr@keyspanenergy.com

Keyspan Services PAC
Joseph Witt, Treasurer
Keyspan Service PAC, Riverfront Plaza, PO Box 200003, Newark, NJ 07102
732-560-9700

Kings County C-PAC
Harvey S Rossel, Treasurer
790 Carroll St, Brooklyn, NY 11215-1404
718-638-4626 Fax: 718-638-5036

Kitchen PAC
Eric James, Treasurer
1771 T Street NW, #1, Washington, DC 20009
202-332-8011

KleinPAC
Dominick Calderon, Treasurer
744 Lydis Ave, Bronx, NY 10462
718-319-1400 Fax: 718-239-0716

Laborers' Intl Union of North America 435 Voluntary PAF
Raymond Kuntz Jr, Treasurer
20 Fourth Street, Rochester, NY 14609
716-454-5800
Web site: www.nysliuna.org

Laborers' Local #91 PAC
Enrico Liberale, Treasurer
6676 Cloverleaf Court, Niagara Falls, NY 14304
716-731-8447

Laborers' Local 103 PAF Cmte
Donald Calabrese, Treasurer

Offices and agencies generally appear in alphabetical order, except when specific order is requested by listee.

POLITICAL ACTION COMMITTEES

PO Box 571, Geneva, NY 14456
315-539-4220 Fax: 315-539-4150

Laborers' Local 17 PAC
Joseph Libonati, Treasurer
PO Box 202, Marlboro, NY 12542
914-236-4747 Fax: 845-565-3099
e-mail: tdiorio555@aol.com

Laborers' Local Union 190 PAC
Anthony M Fresina, Treasurer
668 Wemple Rd, PO Box 339, Glenmont, NY 12077
518-465-1254 Fax: 518-465-1257

Land Surveyors PAC
John A Robinson, Treasurer
146 Washington Avenue, Albany, NY 12210
518-432-4046 Fax: 518-432-4055
e-mail: j24601@aol.com

Latina Political Action Committee
Nicholas L Arture, Treasurer
68-43 136th Street, Apt B, Flushing, NY 11367
646-382-8982

Latino Democratic Committee of Orange County
Jesus M Rivera, Treasurer
23 Helene Road, Warwick, NY 10990
845-987-2105

Latino Political Action Committee
Saul A Maneiro, Treasurer
35 Conklin Ave, Rochester, NY 14609
585-482-1865
e-mail: latinopac@yahoogroups.com

Lawyers' PAC (LAWPAC)
Arthur M Luxenberg, Treasurer
180 Maiden Ln, New York, NY 10038
212-558-5613 Fax: 212-344-5465
Web site: www.weitzlux.com

League of Humane Voters of New York City
Maryanne Byington, Treasurer
368 East 8th Street, #6A, New York, NY 10009
212-677-5542

LeBoeuf Lamb Greene & MacRae PAC
Christopher Tsakiris, Treasurer
125 W 55th St, New York, NY 10019
212-424-8187 Fax: 212-424-8500

Lesnick Leadership PAC
David C Rosenzweig, Treasurer
9 Melissa Drive, Ardsley, NY 10502
914-693-9450

Levittown West Republican Golf
Reid N Berglind, Treasurer

43 Wedgewood Lane, Wantaghe, NY 11753
516-735-4022

Liberty Mutual Insurance Co PAC - NY
Laurance Yahia, Treasurer
175 Berkeley St, Boston, MA 02117
617-357-9500

Life Insurance Council of NY PAC (LICONY)
Diane D Stuto, Treasurer
111 Washington Ave, Suite 300, Albany, NY 12210
518-436-8417 Fax: 518-436-0226
e-mail: dstuto@licony.org
Web site: www.licony.org

Life of the Party
Philip Blitz, Treasurer
404 Oakland Ave, Staten Island, NY 10310
718-273-1935

Local #30 PAC
Leslie Fletcher, Treasurer
213 Ontario Pl, Liverpool, NY 13088
315-457-2304 Fax: 315-475-4042

Local #41 Int'l Brotherhood of Electrical Workers' PAC
Anthony S Coppola, Treasurer
S-3546 California Rd, Orchard Park, NY 14127
716-662-6111 Fax: 716-662-9644

Local 137 PEF
Salvatore Santamorena, Treasurer
50 Finnerty Place, Putnam Valley, NY 10579
845-762-1268 Fax: 845-762-0524

Local 138, 138A & 138B International Union of Operating Engineers
Kenneth Huber, Treasurer
C/O Local 138, 138A & 138B Intl Union, PO Box 206, 137 Gazza Blvd, Farmingdale, NY 11735-0206
631-694-2480
Web site: www.local138.com

Local 147 PAF
Richard Fitzsimmons, Treasurer
32 Clarewood Drive, Hastings, NY 10706
914-478-4803

Local 1500 Political Candidates Education Fund
Anthony Speelman, Treasurer
UFCW Local 1500, 221-10 Jamaica Avenue, Queens Village, NY 11428
718-479-8700 or 800-522-0456 ext 204 Fax: 718-217-7316
e-mail: aspeelman@UFCW1500.org

Local 1814 Intl Longshoremens Assn AFL-CIO PA & ED Fund
Anthony Graffino, Treasurer

Offices and agencies generally appear in alphabetical order, except when specific order is requested by listee.

POLITICAL ACTION COMMITTEES

70 20th Street, Brooklyn, NY 11232
718-499-9600

Local 23-25, Unite State & Local Campaign Committee
Kevin McCann, Treasurer
1 Chestnut Ct, Monroe Twp, NJ 8831
732-521-9251

Local 237 I.B.T. PAC
Gregory Floyd, Treasurer
216 West 14th Street, New York, NY 10011
212-924-2000

Local 30 IUOE PAC
John Ahern, Treasurer
115-06 Myrtle Ave, Richmond Hill, NY 11418
718-847-8484
Web site: www.iuoe30.org

Local 32BJ SEIU NY/NJ American Dream Fund
Peter Colavito, Treasurer
Local 32BJ SEIU, 101 Ave of Americas, New York, NY 10013
212-388-2175 Fax: 212-388-3692
e-mail: pcolavito@seiu32bj.org

Local 420 Political Action Committee
Peter Da Leon, Treasurer
125 Barclay Street, New York, NY 10007
212-815-1420

Local 6 Committee on Political Education
James Donovan, Treasurer
709 8th Avenue, New York, NY 10036
212-957-8000

Local 7 PAC Fund
W Joi Shaffer, Treasurer
98 Main Street, Binghamton, NY 13905
607-723-7543

Local 73 Plumbers and Steamfitters PAC Fund
David J Decaire, Treasurer
PO Box 911, Oswego, NY 13126
315-343-4037 Fax: 315-343-5810

Local 891 Cope Fund
Gregory Sutton, Treasurer
320 7th Avenue PMB #361, Brooklyn, NY 11215
212-414-2564

Local Union #373 UA Political Action Fund
Daniel A Lawless, Treasurer
PO Box 58, 76 Pleasant Hill Rd, Mountainville, NY 10953
845-534-1050 Fax: 845-534-1053

Lockport Fire Dept PAC
Kevin W Pratt, Treasurer
97 Adam Street, Lockport, NY 14094
716-434-6503

Log Cabin Republicans Hudson Valley PAC
Robert A Arko, Treasurer
Martine Station, PO Box 8263, White Plains, NY 10602
914-206-4059

Log Cabin Republicans NY PAC
Robert A Arko, Treasurer
Radio City Station, PO Box 2321, New York, NY 10101
212-202-6431

Long Island Assn Action Committe
Michael J Deering, Treasurer
300 Broadhollow Road, Suite 110W, Melville, NY 11747
631-493-3002 Fax: 631-499-2196
e-mail: mdeering@longislandassociation.org
Web site: www.longislandassociation.org

Long Island Chapter/American Institute of Architects LIC (AIA PAC)
Michael W Spinelli, Treasurer
AIA Long Island, 499 Sericato Trnpk, Suite 101, Mineola, NY 11051
516-294-0971 Fax: 516-294-0973

Long Island Contractors Assn PAC Inc
Marc Herbst, Treasurer
2805 Veterans Memorial Hwy, Suite 2, Ronkonkoma, NY 11779
631-467-4230 Fax: 631-467-4211
e-mail: mherbst@licanys.org
Web site: www.licanys.org

Long Island Federation of Labor AFL-CIO
Dominick Macchia, Treasurer
1111 Route 110, Ste 320, Farmingdale, NY 11735
631-396-1170 Fax: 631-396-1174
Web site: www.lilabor.org

Long Island Gasoline Retailers Assn PAC
Robert Santasiero, Treasurer
270 Spagnoli Road, Melville, NY 11747
631-755-5550
e-mail: steve@sdautorepire.com

Long Island Prosperity
Alan S Kappel, Treasurer
108 S Franklin Avenue, Suite 1, Valley Stream, NY 11580
516-333-5511

Lynbrook P.B.A. PAC
Harold Comastri, Treasurer
PO Box 509, Lynbrook, NY 11563
516-599-3300

MAC PAC
Barbara Zaron, Treasurer

Offices and agencies generally appear in alphabetical order, except when specific order is requested by listee.

POLITICAL ACTION COMMITTEES

C/O OMCE, 3 Washington Sq, Albany, NY 12205-5523
518-456-5241 Fax: 518-456-3838
e-mail: nysomce@gmail.com
Web site: www.nysomce.org

M. Dolores Denman Democratic Lawyers Club
Patrick Bannister, Treasurer
69 East Girard Blvd, Kenmore, NY 14217
716-874-2955

MLCA PAC
Kenneth Theobalds, Treasurer
909 Webster Ave, New Rochelle, NY 10804
914-654-0868

MLMICPAC
Stanley L Grossman, Treasurer
82 Susan Dr, Newburgh, NY 12550-1409
845-562-2067 Fax: 845-562-3870
e-mail: slgrossman@verizon.net

MPAC
Jennifer Carlson, Treasurer
111 Washington Ave, 3rd Floor, Albany, NY 12210
518-436-8808 Fax: 518-463-6731

Maloney Committee NYS PAC
Andrew R Tulloch, Treasurer
C/O Lowenstein Sandler PC, 1251 Avenue of the Americas, 18th Floor, New York, NY 10020
646-414-6792

Manhattan Connection PAC
Marcia Coleman, Treasurer
31 Bleecker Place, Albany, NY 12202
518-436-3689

Manufactured Housing PAC
Nancy P Geer, Treasurer
35 Commerce Ave, Albany, NY 12206-2081
518-435-9858 or 800-721-4663 Fax: 518-435-9839
e-mail: info@nymha.com
Web site: www.nymha.org

Manufacturers & Traders Trust Company PAC
Marlene B Giglia, Treasurer
21 Jonathon Place, Amherst, NY 14228

Marx PAC
David M Stackrow, Treasurer
314 Hoosick St, Troy, NY 12180
518-274-9081 Fax: 518-274-9085

Mason Tenders' District Council of Greater NY PAC
Mike Prohaska, Treasurer

c/o MTDCPAC, 520 8th Avenue, Suite 650, New York, NY 10018
212-452-9400
e-mail: mtdcpac@juno.com
Web site: www.masontenders.org

Medical Society of the State of New York PAC
Anthony A Clemendor, Treasurer
125 East 80th St, New York, NY 10021
212-628-1210 Fax: 212-861-1140
e-mail: aclemendor@aol.com

MetLife Ins Co Political Fund B
Clara Cortes, Treasurer
27-01 Queens Plaza North, 4th Floor, Long Island City, NY 11101
212-578-2640 Fax: 212-578-9890
e-mail: msheridan@metlife.com
Web site: www.metlife.com

Metalic Lathers Local 46 PAC
Robert A Ledwith, Treasurer
1322 Third Ave, New York, NY 10021
212-928-9141

Metlife Inc Employees' Political Participation Fund A
Timothy J Ring, Treasurer
27-01 Queens Plaza North, Area 4-D, Long Island City, NY 11101
212-578-2640 Fax: 212-578-9890
Web site: www.metlife.com

Metret PAC, Inc
Robert A Strainere, Treasurer
Kantor Davidoff, 51 E. 42nd St, New York, NY 10017
212-682-8383 Fax: 212-949-5206
e-mail: straiere@kantorlawonline.com

Metropolitan Garage Owners Assn PAC
Hugh M Heller, Treasurer
C/O Cozen O'Connor, 909 Third Ave, New York, NY 10022
201-407-4429

Metropolitan Package Store, Inc Assoc PAF
William L McDevitt, Treasurer
6 Xavier Drive, Yonkers, NY 10704-1392
914-423-4500

Meyer, Suozzi, English & Klein, PC - Political Acct
Patricia Cairo, Treasurer
1505 Kellum Pl, Mineola, NY 11501
516-741-6565 Fax: 516-741-6706

Mid Island Democratic PAC (MIDPAC)
Kristy Cusick, Treasurer
937 Victory Blvd, Apt 4G, Staten Island, NY 10301
718-442-3219

Mirant Corporation State Political Action Committee Inc-NY
Greg Weber, Treasurer

Offices and agencies generally appear in alphabetical order, except when specific order is requested by listee.

POLITICAL ACTION COMMITTEES

1155 Perimeter Center West, Atlanta, GA 30338-5416
678-579-6530

Mohawk Valley Chamber PAC
Margaret E Francis, Treasurer
Mohawk Valley Chamber of Commerce, Radisson Hotel, 200 Genesee Street, Utica, NY 13502
315-724-3151
Web site: www.mvchamber.org

Monroe County Independence Caucas
Donald R Porto, Treasurer
6 Golf Stream Drive, Penfield, NY 14526
585-381-2138

Monument Industry PAC
John S Wallenstein, Treasurer
220 Old Country Rd, Mineola, NY 11501
516-742-5600 Fax: 516-742-5040
e-mail: johnlawli@aol.com

Morris & McVeigh NYS PAC
Richard J Miller Jr, Treasurer
19 Dove Street, Albany, NY 12210
518-426-8111 Fax: 518-426-5111

Mountaintop Democratic Club
William Haltermann Jr, Treasurer
PO Box 494, 299 Nauvoo Road, Windham, NY 12496
518-734-5481

Movers & Warehousemen Political Action Committee
Mark Motler, Treasurer
757 Chenango Street, Binghamton, NY 13901
607-723-1023 Fax: 607-723-1024
e-mail: newyorkmovers@stny.rr.com
Web site: newyorkstatemovers.com

NARAL/NY Multicandidate PAC
Barbara Klar, Treasurer
427 Broadway, 3rd Flr, New York, NY 10013
212-343-0114 Fax: 212-343-0119
e-mail: info@prochoiceny.org
Web site: www.prochoiceny.org

NASW-NYS Political Action for Candidate Election (PACE)
Fred Newdom, Treasurer
NASW-NYS, 188 Washington Avenue, Albany, NY 12210
518-463-4741 Fax: 518-463-6446

NATPAC 2000
Warren E O'Hearn, Treasurer
15602 Northgate Drive, Montclair, VA 22026-1832

NBT PAC State Fund
Brian J Page, Treasurer
52 South Broad St, Norwich, NY 13815
607-337-6258 Fax: 607-337-6294
e-mail: bpage@nbtbci.com

NEA of New York PAC
Bernie Mulligan
217 Lark Street, Albany, NY 12210
518-462-6451 Fax: 716-835-2811
e-mail: BMulligan@neany.org

NIC-PAC
Steven A Lessmann, Treasurer
NIC Holding, 25 Melville Park Rd, POB 2937, Melville, NY 11747
631-753-4250

NLOA-PAC
Charles Castro, Treasurer
30-71 49th Street, Astoria, NY 11103
866-579-5809 Fax: 646-772-3728
Web site: www.nloaus.org

NRA Political Victory Fund
Mary R Adkins, Treasurer
11250 Waples Mill Rd, Ste 5027, Fairfax, VA 22030
703-267-1152

NRG New York PAC
Jennifer A Gregson, Treasurer
3500 River Road, Tonawanda, NY 14150
716-879-3890 Fax: 716-879-3950

NYPT PAC
Susan E Bennett, Treasurer
5 Palisades Dr, Suite 330, Albany, NY 12205
518-459-4499 Fax: 518-459-8953
Web site: www.nypta.org

NY Chiropractic PAC
Margaret H Savitzky, Treasurer
70-25 Yellowstone Blvd, Apt 1F, Forest Hills, NY 11375
718-261-3911

NY EDPAC
Elizabeth A Sullivan, Treasurer
PO Box 32224, Washington, DC 20007
202-251-4534
Web site: www.nyedpac.org

NYFF
Kalman Yeger, Treasurer
303 Park Avenue South, Suite 1091, New York, NY 10010

NY Film PAC
Katherine Riffey, Treasurer
1600 Eye Street NW, Washington, DC 20006
202-378-9141
e-mail: tom_igner@mpaa.org

NY Independent Bankers' PAC
William Y Crowell, Treasurer

Offices and agencies generally appear in alphabetical order, except when specific order is requested by listee.

POLITICAL ACTION COMMITTEES

NY Independent Bankers PAC, 125 State St, Albany, NY 12207-1622
518-436-4646 Fax: 518-436-4648

NY Podiatry PAC
Leonard Thaler, Treasurer
1255 Fifth Ave, New York, NY 10029
866-996-4400 Fax: 646-672-9344
e-mail: nyspma@nyspma.org
Web site: www.nyspma.org

NY Region 9A UAW PAC Committee
Robert Madore, Treasurer
111 South Rd, Farmington, CT 06032-2560
860-674-0143 Fax: 860-674-1164
e-mail: bmador@uaw.net

NYAHSA PAC
Carl S Young, Treasurer
150 State Street, Suite 301, Albany, NY 12207
518-449-2707 Fax: 518-455-8908
Web site: www.nyahsa.org

NYC Americans for Democratic Action NYC ADA PAC
Stephen R Parker, Treasurer
275 7th Avenue, 15th Fl, New York, NY 10001-0001
212-367-8883 Fax: 212-807-6245
e-mail: nycada@earthlink.net
Web site: www.nycada.com

NYC Columbus Circle PAC
George D Skinner, Treasurer
35 Portman Road, New Rochelle, NY 10801
914-576-9300

NYC District Council of Carpenters' PAC
Peter Thomassen, Treasurer
395 Hudson Street, 9th Fl, New York, NY 10014
212-366-7500 Fax: 212-675-3118
Web site: www.nycdistrictcouncil.com

NYMTA Boat PAC
Walter Werner, Treasurer
194 B Park Avenue, Suite B, Amityville, NY 11701
631-691-7050
e-mail: dwall@nymta.com
Web site: www.nyboatshows.com

NYNHP-PAC
Shauneen McNally, Treasurer
c/o Weingarten & Reid, 1 Commerce Plz, #1103, Albany, NY 12210
518-465-9273 Fax: 518-427-7792

NYPD Lieutenants Benevolent Association PAC
Peter Martin, Treasurer
30 Carman Avenue, East Rockaway, NY 11518
516-593-2275

NYPD Superior Officers Assn, Retired PAC
John J Coughlin, Treasurer
124 Wright Ave, Deer Park, NY 11729
631-667-1829

NYS AFL-CIO COPE
Suzy Ballantyne, Treasurer
100 South Swan St, Albany, NY 12210
518-436-8516 Fax: 518-462-1824
e-mail: sballantyne@nysaflcio.org
Web site: www.nysaflcio.org

NYS Architects PAC
Barbara J Rodriguez, Treasurer
407 3rd St, Troy, NY 12180
518-449-3334 Fax: 518-426-8176
e-mail: aianys@aianys.org
Web site: www.aianys.org

NYS Assn of Tobacco & Candy Distributors Inc
Arthur H Katz, Treasurer
211 E 43rd Street, Ste 1101, New York, NY 10017
212-682-3576 Fax: 212-867-7844
e-mail: arthurkatz@covad.net

NYS Association of Service Stations & Repair Shops
Jordan Weine, Treasurer
6 Walker Way, Albany, NY 12205-4946
518-452-4367

NYS Automatic Vending Association PAC
Robert Desormeau, Treasurer
4 Deep Woods Drive, Latham, NY 12110
518-785-4569

NYS Bowling Proprietors Assn PAC
Richard L O'Neil, Treasurer
201 Manchester Road, Vestal, NY 13850
607-798-1838 or 607-687-5631

NYS Broadcasters Association
Joseph A Reilly, Treasurer
1805 Western Avenue, Albany, NY 12203
518-456-8888

NYS Cemeteries PAC
Frank Giglio, Treasurer
PO Box 780004, 65-40 Grand Avenue, Maspeth, NY 11378
718-326-1280 Fax: 718-326-7506

NYS Chapter AGC PAC
A J Castelbuono, Treasurer
10 Airline Dr, Ste 203, Albany, NY 12205-1025
518-456-1134 Fax: 518-456-1198
e-mail: ajcastel@agcnys.org
Web site: www.agcnys.org

NYS Committee for the Advancement of Mental Health Therapy
James J Carr, Treasurer

Offices and agencies generally appear in alphabetical order, except when specific order is requested by listee.

POLITICAL ACTION COMMITTEES

388 Broadway, 4th Fl, Albany, NY 12207
518-434-8830 Fax: 518-434-0072

NYS Conference of the IUOE Pol Action Acct
William J McSpedon, Treasurer
100 South Swan St, Albany, NY 12210
518-463-7551 Fax: 518-463-7556
e-mail: nysconiuoe@aol.com

NYS Council of Physiotherapists PAC
Allen Bistrong, Treasurer
142 Joralemm Street, Brooklyn, NY 11201
Web site: www.nycouncilpt.org

NYS Food Industry PAC
James T Rogers, Treasurer
50 Edison Place, Niskayuna, NY 12309
518-372-1764 Fax: 518-434-9962
e-mail: jim@fiany.com
Web site: www.fiany.com

NYS Funeral Directors Association PAC
Randy L McCullough, Treasurer
426 New Karner Road, Albany, NY 12205
518-452-8230 Fax: 518-452-8667
e-mail: info@nysfda.org
Web site: www.nysfda.org

NYS Hospitality & Tourism Assn PAC
Daniel C Murphy, Treasurer
80 Wolf Rd, Albany, NY 12205
518-465-2300 Fax: 518-465-4025
Web site: www.nyshta.org

NYS Occupational Therapy PAC
Peggy A Lounsbury, Treasurer
19 Washington Avenue, 2nd Floor, Albany, NY 12210
518-583-8371

NYS Optometric Assn PAC
Jan S Dorman, Treasurer
119 Washington Ave, Albany, NY 12210
518-449-7300 Fax: 518-432-5902
e-mail: nysoa2020@aol.com
Web site: www.nysoa.org

NYS Pest Management Association PAC
Charles Frommer, Treasurer
22 Roosevelt Avenue, Box 405, Roslyn, NY 11576
516-676-0149

NYS Pipe Trades Political Action Committee
Larry S Bulman, Secretary/Treasurer
PO Box 1343, S Glens Falls, NY 12803
518-792-0321 Fax: 518-792-4876
e-mail: info@nyspipetrades.org
Web site: nyspipetrades.org

NYS Plumbing, Heating & Cooling Contractors PAC
Mark Whalen, Treasurer

17 S Lynn St, Warwick, NY 10990
800-933-9040 Fax: 845-986-4050

NYS Psychiatric PAC Inc
Seeth Vivek, Treasurer
100 Quentin Roosevelt Blvd, Suite 509, Garden City, NY 11530
516-542-0077 Fax: 516-542-0094

NYS Right to Life PAC
41 State Street, M-100, Albany, NY 12207
518-434-1293 Fax: 518-426-1200
e-mail: admin@nysrighttolife.org
Web site: www.nysrighttolife.org

NYS Snowmobile PAC
Martin D Bull, Treasurer
123 Fairway View Drive, Clayville, NY 13322
315-839-5652

NYS Society for Clinical Social Workers PAC
Marsha Wineburgh, Treasurer
263 West End Ave, #1F, New York, NY 10023
212-595-6518

NYS Speech-Language-Hearing Assn Inc - COMPAC
Salvatore Gruttadauria, Treasurer
2 Northway Lane, Latham, NY 12110-4809
518-786-0947 Fax: 518-786-9126
e-mail: dan@nysslha.org
Web site: www.nysslha.org

NYS Telecommunications PAC
Robert R Puckett, Treasurer
100 State Street, Suite 650, Albany, NY 12207
518-443-2700 Fax: 518-443-2810
e-mail: rmoneymaker@nysta.com

NYS Troopers PAC
Daniel M De Federicis, Treasurer
120 State Street, Albany, NY 12207
518-462-7448 Fax: 518-462-0790
e-mail: nystpba@nystpba.org
Web site: www.nystpba.org

NYS Veterinary PEC
Thomas J Gosdeck, Treasurer
99 Washington Ave, Ste 1950, Albany, NY 12210
518-463-5449 Fax: 518-463-0947
e-mail: tjgosdeck@aol.com

NYSAIFA-PAC
Mark L Yavornitzki, Treasurer
14 Bridle Place, East Greenbush, NY 12061
518-477-2278

NYSALM State PAC
Dana Sidney, Treasurer

Offices and agencies generally appear in alphabetical order, except when specific order is requested by listee.

POLITICAL ACTION COMMITTEES

41 Park Ter W, New York, NY 10034
212-569-3065

NYSCHP PAC
Debra B Feinberg, Treasurer
432 New Karner Road, Albany, NY 12205
518-456-8819 Fax: 518-456-9319

NYSCOPBA PAC
L Flanagan Jr, Treasurer
c/o Hinman Straub, PC, 121 State St, Albany, NY 12207
518-689-0196
e-mail: nyscopba@nyscopba.org

NYSE State PAC
Veronica Sullivan, Treasurer
11 Wall Street, New York, NY 10005
212-656-3000
Web site: www.nyse.com

NYSFRW Women Power PAC
Jill W Jackson, Treasurer
265 Kissel Avenue, Staten Island, NY 10310
718-981-1849

NYSIA NY PAC
Thomas Flaherty, Treasurer
55 Broad Street, 10th Floor, New York, NY 10004
212-475-4503 Fax: 212-979-2372
Web site: www.nysia.org

Nassau County Detectives Association Inc
Frank Allaire, Treasurer
777 Old Country Road, Suite 202, Plainview, NY 11803
516-681-8442 Fax: 516-681-8446

Nassau County Lesbian & Gay Democrats
Sandra J Rideout, Treasurer
PO Box 334, Long Beach, NY 11561
Web site: www.nassaugaydems.com

Nassau County PBA PAC
Wayne Hartman, Treasurer
89 E Jericho Tpke, Mineola, NY 11501
516-294-6230
Web site: www.nassaupba.org

Nat'l Assn of Social Workers - New York City Chapter
David Roth, Treasurer
1064 E 19th St, Brooklyn, NY 11230-4502
718-338-1395 Fax: 212-558-9991

Nat'l Federation of Independent Business/NY Save America's Free Enterprises
Daniel Richardson, Treasurer
2100 Latta Rd, Rochester, NY 14612
585-225-0910

National Good Government Fund
Thomas P Marinis, Jr, Treasurer

C/O Vinson and Elkins LLP, First City Tower, 1001 Fannin St, Suite 2500, Houston, TX 77002
713-758-2462 Fax: 713-615-5228

National Fuel Gas New York PAC
Brenda L Spillman, Treasurer
6363 Main Street, Williamsville, NY 14221-5887
716-857-7705 Fax: 716-857-7439

National Marine Manufacturers Association PAC (NAT PAC)
Monita W Fontaine, Treasurer
444 North Capitol Street NW, Washington, DC 20001
202-737-9750

National Organization for Women- NYS PAC
Marcia Pappas, President
1500 Central Avenue, Albany, NY 12205
518-452-3944 Fax: 518-452-3861
e-mail: newyorkstatenow@aol.com
Web site: www.nownys.org

Nationwide NY Political Participation Fund
Carol L Dove, Treasurer
One Nationwide Plaza 1-32-06, Columbus, OH 43215
614-249-6963

Neighborhood Preservation PAF
Sandra K Paul, Treasurer
360 E 72nd St, A710, New York, NY 10021
212-472-1459

New York Ambulette Coalition PAC
Anthony Tufaro, Treasurer
110-18 Corona Ave, Corona, NY 11368
917-683-7025

New York Anesthesiologists Political Action Committee
David S Bronheim MD, Treasurer
85th Fifth Avenue, 8th Floor, New York, NY 10003
212-867-7140

New York Association of Independent Lumber Dealers PAC (NAIL PAC)
John J Maiuri, Treasurer
PO Box 523, 62 Water Street, Catskill, NY 12414
518-943-3800 Fax: 518-943-6610

New York Association of Mortgage Brokers Political Action Committee
Patrick J McHugh, Treasurer
99 Pine Street, 4th Floor, Albany, NY 12207
518-434-7400

New York Association of Temporary Services State PAC
Edward A Lenz, Treasurer
277 S Washington, Suite 200, Alexandria, VA 22314
703-253-2020 Fax: 703-253-2053

New York Bankers Political Action Committee
Karen L Jannetty, Treasurer

Offices and agencies generally appear in alphabetical order, except when specific order is requested by listee.

POLITICAL ACTION COMMITTEES

99 Park Avenue, 4th Floor, New York, NY 10016
212-297-1635 Fax: 212-297-1622
e-mail: kjannetty@nyba.com

New York Build PAC
Philip A Laraque, Treasurer
One Commerce Plaza #704, Albany, NY 12210
518-465-2492 Fax: 518-465-0635

New York Building Congress PAF
Richard T Anderson, Treasurer
44 West 28th Street, 12th Floor, New York, NY 10001
212-481-9230

New York Check PAC
Henry F Shyne, Treasurer
10 East 40th Street, Suite 1308, New York, NY 10016
212-268-1911

New York Children's Advocates Making Progress
Robert Wortman, Treasurer
484 South Wood Road, Rockville Centre, NY 11570
516-867-3895

New York Chiropratic Political Action Fund
Peter H Morgan DC, Treasurer
PO Box 756, 951 E Boston Post Road, Mamaroneck, NY 10543
914-698-6626

New York Choice PAC
Shelby White, Treasurer
1202 Lexington Ave, Box 246, New York, NY 10028
212-517-3522

New York City Central Labor Council Political Action Committee
Ted Jacobson, Treasurer
31 West 15th Street, Floor 3, New York, NY 10011
212-604-9552 Fax: 212-604-9550
e-mail: nycaflcio@aol.com
Web site: www.ycclc.org

New York City Deputy Sheriff's Assn, PAC
James R Davis III, Treasurer
C/O Kim Wegener, 25 Osborne Road, Garden City, NY 11530
718-802-3544 Fax: 718-359-6950

New York City, Partnership for, PAC
Brad Hoylman, Treasurer
One Battery Park Plaza, New York, NY 10004
212-493-7484

New York Emergency Medicine PAC
Joan Tarantelli, Treasurer
1070 Sibley Tower, Rochester, NY 14604
585-546-7241 Fax: 585-546-5141
e-mail: nysacep@aol.com

New York Financial Services PAC
Kirby Hannan, Treasurer

107 Washington Avenue, Albany, NY 12210
518-465-6550
e-mail: khannan401@aol.com

New York Good Hearing Political Education Committee
Albert Shrive, Treasurer
C/O PHI, 1020 W Lackawanna Avenue, Scranton, PA 18504
717-343-1414

New York Hotel & Motel Trades Council Committee on Political Education
Michael Goodwin, Treasurer
707 Eighth Avenue, 4th Floor, New York, NY 10036
212-245-8100 Fax: 212-541-8267

New York Hygiene PAC
Lynda Lederer, Treasurer
42 Hilltop Acres, Yonkers, NY 10704
914-966-7205

New York Insurance Assn Inc Political Action Committee
Bernard N Bourdeau, Treasurer
21 Grandview Avenue, Cohoes, NY 12047
518-237-5789

New York League of Conservation Voters Action Fund
John Ernst, Treasurer
NYLCV, 30 Broad Street, 30th Floor, New York, NY 10004
212-361-6350 Fax: 212-361-6363
Web site: www.nylcv.org

New York Life-New York State PAC
Jonathon Poane, Treasurer
51 Madison Ave, Rm 117M, New York, NY 10010
212-576-7842 Fax: 212-576-4473

New York Medical Equipment Providers PAC
Carol Napierski, Treasurer
NYMEP, 27 Elk Street, Albany, NY 12207
518-436-9637
e-mail: nymep@nymep.org
Web site: www.nymep.org

New York Mercantiles Exchange Political Action Committee, Inc
Kenneth Shifrin, Treasurer
One North End Avenue, 14th Floor, New York, NY 10282
212-299-2525

New York Pan Hel Political Action Committee
Leslie Wyche, Treasurer
1270 Fifth Avenue, New York, NY 10029
212-749-9120

New York Pepsi Cola PAC
Mark J Johnson, Treasurer
50-35 56th Rd, Maspeth, NY 11378
718-392-1018

New York Professional Engineers
Randolph W Rakaczynski, Treasurer

Offices and agencies generally appear in alphabetical order, except when specific order is requested by listee.

POLITICAL ACTION COMMITTEES

250 Ridgewood Drive, Snyder, NY 14226
716-633-5887

New York Professional Nurses Union Political Action Fund
Jill Kaplan, Treasurer
1104 Lexington Avenue, 2D, New York, NY 10021

New York Propane PAC
Thomas Heslop, Treasurer
c/o Amos Post Inc, PO Box 351, Catskill, NY 12414
518-943-3500 Fax: 518-943-7090

New York Respiratory Care PAC
George W Gaebler, III, Treasurer
PO Box 145, 1946 Preble Road, Preble, NY 13141
607-749-4562

New York Retailers for Effective Government
James R Sherin, Treasurer
460 Orchard Street, Delmar, NY 12054
Web site: www.retailcouncilnys.com

New York School Bus Operators for Effective Gov't
John J Corrado, Treasurer
677 Broadway, 9th Fl, Albany, NY 12201
877-699-7222

New York State Association of PBAs
Patrick Hall, Treasurer
23 Reynolds Rd, Glen Cove, NY 11542
516-609-2732 Fax: 516-676-3956

New York State Beer Wholesalers Assn PAC
Dominick Bertoline, Treasurer
99 Pine Street, Suite 210, Albany, NY 12207
518-465-6115 Fax: 518-465-1907
e-mail: nybeer@att.net

New York State BPW/PAC (NYSBPW/PAC)
Lucretia D Hunt, Treasurer
903 Bleecker St, Utica, NY 13501
315-732-1032 Fax: 315-738-7218

New York State Car Wash PAC
Michael A Benmosche, Treasurer
26 Valdepenas Lane, Clifton Park, NY 12065
518-371-6542
e-mail: mikebenmosche@manginsurance.com

New York State Clinical Laboratory Assn PAC
Thomas R Rafalsky, Treasurer
62 William St, 2nd Fl, New York, NY 10005
212-664-7999 Fax: 212-248-3008
e-mail: info@nyscla.com
Web site: www.nyscla.com

New York State Dairy Foods PAC
Bruce W Krupke, Treasurer

201 S Main St, Ste 302, North Syracuse, NY 13212-3105
315-452-6455 Fax: 315-452-1643
e-mail: bkrupke@nysdfi.org
Web site: www.nysdfi.org

New York State Coalition of PHSPS PAC Inc
Paul Dickstein, Treasurer
500 E 77th Street, Apt 6JK, New York, NY 10162
212-570-9599

New York State Dietetic Association
Susan Branning, Treasurer
935 S Pines Drive, Endicott, NY 13760
607-786-9793

New York State Federation of School Administrators Political Action Committee
Audrey Fuentes, Treasurer
245-78 63 Avenue, Douglaston, NY 11362
718-225-2905

New York State Laborers' PAC
Charles Coleman, Treasurer
215 Old Nyack Tpke, Chestnut Ridge, NY 10977
518-449-1715
e-mail: info@nysliuna
Web site: www.nysliuna.org

New York State Nurses Assn PAC
Mary J Finnin, Treasurer
11 Cornell Road, Latham, NY 12110-1499
518-782-9400 Fax: 518-783-5207
Web site: www.nysna.org

New York State Political Action Committee, Region 9, UAW
Samuel G Williams, Treasurer
35 George Karl Boulevard, Suite 100, Amherst, NY 14221
716-632-1540

New York State Public Employees' Federation PAC
Joe Fox, Vice President & PAC Chair
PO Box 12414, Albany, NY 12212-2414
518-785-1900 Fax: 518-783-1117
e-mail: joefoxvp@aol.com
Web site: www.pef.org

New York State Radiologists PAC
Philip C Pinsky, Treasurer
c/o Pinsky & Pinsky, PC, 5790 Widewaters Pwky, PO Box 250, Syracuse, NY 13214-0250
315-446-2384 Fax: 315-446-3016
e-mail: pinskyskan@aol.com

New York State Restaurant Industry PAC
Rick J Sampson, Treasurer

Offices and agencies generally appear in alphabetical order, except when specific order is requested by listee.

POLITICAL ACTION COMMITTEES

409 New Karner Rd, Albany, NY 12205
518-452-4222 Fax: 518-452-4497
e-mail: ricks@nysra.org
Web site: www.nysra.org

New York State Scrap Recyclers PAC
Lawrence R Schillinger, Treasurer
5 Palis Drive, Suite 300, Albany, NY 12205
518-459-0600

New York State Sheriffs' Good Government Fund
Charles J Gallo, Treasurer
27 Elk St, Albany, NY 12207
518-434-9091 Fax: 518-434-9093
e-mail: cgallo@nysheriffs.org

New York State Society CPA PAC Inc
Louis Grumet, Treasurer
530 Fifth Ave, 5th Floor, New York, NY 10036
212-719-8301 Fax: 212-719-3364

New York State Society of Physician Assistants PAC
David I Jackson, Treasurer
52 Polo Road, Massapequa, NY 11758
516-797-0218

New York Thoroughbred Horsemen's Assn, Inc Political Action Committee
Michael P Shanley, Treasurer
PO Box 70, Jamaica, NY 11417
718-848-5045

New York Thoroughbred Racing Industry PAC
Barry K Schwartz, Treasurer
C/O Hinman Straub, PC, 121 State Street, Albany, NY 12207
718-641-4700

New York State Transit & Tour Operators' PAC
Melvin Konner, Treasurer
PO Box 12035, Albany, NY 12212
201-816-0088
e-mail: ajkremer@rmfpc.com

New York Truck PAC
William G Joyce, Treasurer
828 Washington Ave, Albany, NY 12203
518-458-9696 Fax: 518-458-2525
e-mail: bjoyce@nytrucks.org
Web site: www.nytrucks.org

New York's Tomorrow
Michael A Avella, Treasurer
36 Silver Creek Drive, Selkirk, NY 12158
518-859-5179 Fax: 413-832-2102

New Yorkers Against Gun Violence PAC
Barbara E Hohlt, Treasurer

40 East 10th Street - PHC, New York, NY 10003
212-995-2297 Fax: 212-679-2484

New Yorkers for Better Libraries PAC
John Hammond, Treasurer
PO Box 795, Canton, NY 13617
315-212-0182
e-mail: jhammond85@netscape.net

New Yorkers for Constitutional Freedom PAC
Gary Parrett, Treasurer
1909 Westside Dr, Rochester, NY 14559
585-594-1678

New Yorkers for Fairness
S A Anderson, Treasurer
163 Amsterdam Ave #143, New York, NY 10023
212-724-2284

Niagara Falls Firefighters PAC
Jason J Cafarella, Treasurer
2259 Forest Avenue, Niagara Falls, NY 14301
716-285-8132

Niagara Mohawk Holdings, Inc Corp Voluntary State PAC
Jeffrey Williams, Treasurer
Niagara Mohawk Power Corp, 535 Washington St, 6th Fl, Buffalo, NY 14203
716-857-4295 Fax: 716-845-9748
e-mail: jeffrey.williams@US.ngrid.com

Niagara's Future Coalition
John K Rosebrouc, Treasurer
2643 Pinelake Drive, Niagara Falls, NY 14304
716-694-7183

Ninth Decade Fund
Arthur A Zatz, Treasurer
1650 Arch St, 22nd Fl, Philadelphia, PA 19103-2097
215-977-2274 Fax: 215-405-3874
e-mail: azatz@wolfblock.com

Nisource Inc PAC-NY
Timothy J Tokish Jr, Treasurer
200 Civic Center Drive, Columbus, OH 43215
614-460-6413

North Castle Democratic Club
Barry D Malvin, Treasurer
4 Green Valley Road, Armonk, NY 10504
914-273-3063

North Hempstead Century Club
Salvatore Iannucci Jr, Treasurer
164 Post Avenue, Westbury, NY 11590
516-334-5800 Fax: 516-333-4406

North Windmere Republican Club
Merik R Aaron, Treasurer

Offices and agencies generally appear in alphabetical order, except when specific order is requested by listee.

POLITICAL ACTION COMMITTEES

205 Richards Lane, Hewlett Harbor, NY 11557
516-374-1910

Northeastern PAC
David Pardi, Treasurer
5911 Airport Road, Oriskany, NY 13424
315-797-9600 Fax: 315-797-2820

Northeastern Subcontractors Assn, PAC
Lori E Mayott, Treasurer
7 Washington Square, Albany, NY 12205
518-456-6663 Fax: 518-456-3975

Nucor Corporation, PAC NY
Ron Colella, Treasurer
Nucor Steel - Auburn Inc, PO Box 2008, Auburn, NY 13021
315-258-4201 Fax: 315-258-4392

Nurse Anesthesia - CRNA - PAC Fund
Kathleen M O'Donnell, Treasurer
PO Box 8867, Albany, NY 12208
518-262-4303 Fax: 518-861-8876

Nurse Practitioners of NYS PAC
Seth Gordon, Treasurer
12 Corporate Dr, Clifton Park, NY 12065-8603
518-348-0719 Fax: 518-348-0720

OILHEATPAC
John Maniscalco, Treasurer
14 Penn Plaza, Suite 1102, New York, NY 10122
212-695-1380 Fax: 212-594-6583
e-mail: info@nyoha.org
Web site: www.nyoha.org

OMMLLP PAC
Jose W Fernandez, Treasurer
7 Times Square, 27th Fl, New York, NY 10036
212-326-2000 Fax: 212-326-2061
e-mail: jmarlin@omm.com

ONPAC
Charles M Iavarone, Treasurer
127 Circle Road, North Syracuse, NY 13212-4032
315-451-5617

OPEIU Local 153 (VOTE) Voice of the Electorate
Richard Lanigan, Treasurer
265 W 14th St, New York, NY 10011
212-741-8282 Fax: 212-463-9479

ORISKA PAC
James M Kernan, Treasurer
1310 Utica Street, PO Box 750, Oriskany, NY 13424
315-736-8823

Oil Heat Institute PAC
Kevin M Rooney, Treasurer

200 Parkway Drive S, Ste 202, Hauppauge, NY 11788
516-360-0200 Fax: 516-360-0781
e-mail: info@ohili.org
Web site: www.ohili.org

Oilheat PAC, Inc
John Maniscalco, Treasurer
14 Penn Plaza, Suite 1102, New York, NY 10122
212-695-1380

One Eleven PAC
Edward A Bogdan, III, Treasurer
111 Washington Ave, Ste 750, Albany, NY 12210
518-434-9000 Fax: 518-434-2510
e-mail: ebogdan@blklobby.com

Onondaga 2004
Leon C Ilnitzki, Treasurer
PO Box 2566, Syracuse, NY 13220
315-698-8192

Opticians PAC
Michael P Buenau, Treasurer
c/o Buenau's Opticians Inc, 228 Delaware Ave, Delmar, NY 12054
518-439-7012 Fax: 518-439-8471
e-mail: elvisbue1@aol.com
Web site: www.buenausopticians.com

Orange County Democratic Women Inc Campaign
Risa Sugarman, Treasurer
250 King Road, Middletown, NY 10941
845-361-1220

Orange County Legislative Republican Caucas
Leigh J Benton, Treasurer
158 High Point Circle, Newburgh, NY 12550
845-569-8036

Organization of Staff Analysts PAC
Sheila Gorsky, Treasurer
220 East 23rd St, Ste 707, New York, NY 10010
212-686-1229 Fax: 212-686-1231
e-mail: osart@earthlink.net
Web site: www.osaunion.org

Ortho-PAC of New York
Edward A Toriello, Treasurer
PO Box 38004, Albany, NY 12207
518-439-0000 Fax: 518-439-1400
Web site: www.nyssos.org

Outdoor Advertising NY PAC
Matthew Duddy, Treasurer
48 Howard St, Albany, NY 12207
518-783-7784 Fax: 518-783-7805

Oxford Health Plans Inc-NY Committee for Quality Health Care
Robert Della Corte, Treasurer

Offices and agencies generally appear in alphabetical order, except when specific order is requested by listee.

POLITICAL ACTION COMMITTEES

Oxford Health Plans, 48 Monroe Tpke, Trumbull, CT 06611
203-459-7424 Fax: 203-452-4688
e-mail: rdellaco@oxhp.com

P.A.F.S.A. NY PAC
Belinda Lynton, Treasurer
99 Lucille Street, Hempstead, NY 11550
516-489-0322

PAC Police Assoc City of Yonkers
Keith Olson, Treasurer
104 South Broadway, Yonkers, NY 10701
914-377-7938

PAC Port Washington PBA
Dennis F Gaynor Jr, Treasurer
88-15 69 Avenue, Forest Hills, NY 11375
718-263-5597

PAC of Nassau Police Conference
Jack B Grape, Treasurer
82 Garfield Avenue, Sayville, NY 11782
631-589-0239

PAC of the Assoc Building Contractors of the Triple Cities, Inc
Bradley P Walters, Treasurer
535 Vestal Parkway, Suite 1, Vestal, NY 13850
716-938-9912

PAC of the Patrolmen's Benevolent Association of the City of NY, Inc
Joseph A Alejandro, Treasurer
C/O PBA of the City of New York, Inc, 40 Fulton Street, New York, NY 10038
212-233-5531

PCI State Political Account I
June Holmes, Treasurer
2600 River Road, Des Plaines, IL 60018
847-297-7800

PSC PAC
Dr John Hyland, Treasurer
PSC-CUNY, 25 West 43rd Street, New York, NY 10036
212-354-1252

Parents and Children PAC, Inc
Eli D Greenberg, Treasurer
C/O Wolf Haldenstein Adler Freeman & Ho, 270 Madison Avenue, New York, NY 10016
212-545-4790 Fax: 212-545-4792

Parola PAC for Good Government
Michael Hortofilis, Treasurer
3429 Park Avenue, Wantagh, NY 11793
516-679-2497

Peckham Industries Inc PAC
John R Peckham, Treasurer
20 Harlem Ave, White Plains, NY 10603
914-949-2000 Fax: 914-949-2075

Pendeleton Democrat Club
James A Sacco, Jr, Treasurer
6944 Creekview Drive, Lockport, NY 14094
716-625-8852
e-mail: jasacco@adelphia.net

Pepsi-Cola Bottlers' PAC
Peter G Wilcox, Treasurer
3195 Woodfield Court, Yorktown Heights, NY 10598
914-243-0358 Fax: 914-249-8203
e-mail: pwilcox@pepsi.com

Pfizer PAC - NY
Richard A Passov, Treasurer
235 East 42nd St, New York, NY 10017
212-573-7073 Fax: 212-338-1558

Pharmacy PAC of New York State
Selig Corman, Treasurer
53 Fleetwood Ave, Albany, NY 12208
518-438-9759 Fax: 518-464-0618
e-mail: seligc@pssny.org
Web site: www.pssny.org

Physicians Fund
Robert B Bergmann, Treasurer
1200 Stewart Ave, Garden City, NY 11530
516-541-7181 Fax: 516-832-2323

Plumbers & Pipefitters Local No 13 Pol Fund
Brandon Tumia, Treasurer
16 Hunt Hollow, Rochester, NY 14624
585-338-2360 Fax: 585-544-0600

Plumbers & Pipefitters Local Union 112 PAC
James G Rounds, Jr, Treasurer
PO Box 670, Binghamton, NY 13902
607-723-9593 Fax: 607-723-9467

Plumbers and Steamfitters Local 7 PAC
Edward Nadeau, Treasurer
308 Wolf Road, Latham, NY 12110
518-785-9808 Fax: 518-785-9855
e-mail: enadeau@ualocal7.org

Plumbers & Steamfitters Local 267 PAC
Gregory R Lancette, Treasurer
150 Midler Park Dr, Syracuse, NY 13206
315-437-7397 Fax: 315-437-2951

Plumbers & Steamfitters Local 21 PAC
Robert Philp, Treasurer
1024 McKinley St, Peekskill, NY 10566
914-737-7220 Fax: 914-737-7299

Plumbers Local Union No 1 N.Y.C. PAC
John J Murphy, Treasurer

Offices and agencies generally appear in alphabetical order, except when specific order is requested by listee.

POLITICAL ACTION COMMITTEES

158-29 George Meany Blvd, Howard Beach, NY 11414
718-738-7500 Fax: 718-835-0896

Plumbers Local Union 200 PAF
Arthur Gipson, Treasurer
137 Willis Ave, Mineola, NY 11501
516-747-4910 Fax: 516-747-6825

Plumbing Contractors PAC of the City of NY Inc
Stewart D O'Brien, Treasurer
44 West 28th Street, 12th Floor, New York, NY 10007
212-481-4580 Fax: 212-481-7185
e-mail: acpcny@aol.com
Web site: www.acpcny.org

Police Conference of New York Inc PAC
Edward W Guzdek, Treasurer
112 State St, Ste 1120, Albany, NY 12207
518-463-3283
e-mail: pcntinfo@pcny.org
Web site: www.pcny.org

Political Action Committee of Broome County Assoc PHCC
Rudolph W Gaspar, Treasurer
20 Meadow Street, Binghamton, NY 13905

Political Action Committee Buffalo PBA
William J Misztal, Treasurer
72 Woodgate Road, Tonawanda, NY 14150
716-832-3379

Political Action Committee of Council 82
Thomas J McGraw, Treasurer
63 Colvin Ave, Albany, NY 12206
518-489-8424 Fax: 518-435-1523
Web site: www.council82.org

Port Authority PBA, Inc State of New York PAC
Robert E Morris, Treasurer
611 Palisade Avenue, Englewood Cliff, NJ 07632
201-871-2100

Port Authority Sergeants Benevolent Assn PAC
Stephen Pruspero, Treasurer
220 Bridge Plaza S, Fort Lee, NJ 07024
201-592-6191 Fax: 201-592-5982

Praxair PAC NY
James B Rouse, Treasurer
PO Box 44, Tonawanda, NY 14150-7891
716-879-4009

Preserve Ramapo
Martina M Frawley, Treasurer
83 Wilder Road, Suffern, NY 10901
845-354-8901
Web site: preserverramapo.org

Probation Political Action Committee (PROPAC)
Rocco Turso, Treasurer

PO Box 35, Yaphank, NY 11980
631-654-2080

Professional Insurance Agents of New York Political Action Committee
Robert Franzese, Treasurer
34 Cloverfield Dr, Loudonville, NY 12211
518-437-1767

Professionals Political Action Committee-NY
James Hoeberling, Treasurer
Comerica Bank, PAC Services, PO Box 75000, MC 2250, Detroit, MI 48275-2250
248-371-7268

Prudential New York Political Action Committee
Maureen E Madolf, Treasurer
751 Broad Street, 14th Floor, Newark, NJ 07102-3777
973-802-6504 Fax: 973-802-6303

Psychologists for Legislative Action in NY
Lester Schad, Treasurer
6 Executive Park Dr, Albany, NY 12203
518-437-1040 Fax: 518-437-0177

Quest Diagnostics NY PAC
Robin M Sexton, Treasurer
2330 Putnam Ln, Crofton, MD 21114
301-858-1942

RC Build PAC of the Rockland County Builders Assn
Thomas D Benedetto, Treasurer
337 N Main St, Ste 14A, New City, NY 10956
845-634-3849 Fax: 845-634-3329
e-mail: rcba@rcba.org
Web site: www.rcba.org

RG & E Employees' NYS Pol Comm Inc
Richard J Marion, Treasurer
4430 St. Paul Blvd, Rochester, NY 14617
716-266-4042

R-PAC
Lauren M Cacioppo, Treasurer
PO Box 57, Middle Village, NY 11379
718-628-9522

RPA-PAC
Patrick W Brophy, Treasurer
504 E 84th St, #3W, New York, NY 10028
212-879-4059

RSA - PAC
Frank P Ricci, Treasurer
123 William St, New York, NY 10038
212-214-9266
e-mail: www.rcdsa.org

RSA PAC City Account
Frank P Ricci, Treasurer

Offices and agencies generally appear in alphabetical order, except when specific order is requested by listee.

POLITICAL ACTION COMMITTEES

123 William St, 14th Floor, New York, NY 10038
212-219-9266

RWDSU, Local 338 PAC
John R Durso, Treasurer
Local 338, 97-45 Queens Blvd, Rego Park, NY 11374
718-997-7400

Rangel for Congress - NY State
Basil A Paterson, Treasurer
990 Stewart Ave, Suite 300, Garden City, NY 11530
516-741-6565 Fax: 516-741-6706
e-mail: bpaterson@msek.com

Real Estate Board PAC
Steven Spinola, Treasurer
570 Lexington Ave, New York, NY 10022
212-532-3100 Fax: 212-481-0122
Web site: www.rebny.com

Real Independence Party Club-Amherst Branch
Patricia H Potts, Treasurer
142 Ponderosa Drive, Williamsville, NY 14221
716-688-1554

Realtors PAC
Max W McGurvitch, Treasurer
130 Washington Ave, Albany, NY 12210
518-463-0300 Fax: 518-462-5474
e-mail: govt@nysar.com
Web site: www.nysar.com

Rehabilitation Associates PAC
Walter W Stockton, Treasurer
PO Box 82, 2953 Quogue Riverhead Rd, Quogue, NY 11959
631-653-6765

Renew NY PAC
Arthur W Jaspan, Treasurer
300 Garden City Plaza, 5th Fl, Garden City, NY 11530
516-393-8210

Repair Shop & Gasoline Dealers' PAC Fund
William J Adams, Treasurer
501 Main St, East Rochester, NY 14445
585-381-9110

Republican 100,000 Club of Oneida County
June P Balduf, Treasurer
PO Box 47, Verona Beach, NY 13162

Republican Lawyers Club
Emilio L Colaiacovo, Treasurer
350 Main Street, Suite 1400, Buffalo, NY 14202
716-856-1344

Republican Main Stream Coalition of New York
Lawrence E MacDonald, Treasurer

155 Drake Dr, Rochester, NY 14617
585-338-7676

Republican Majority for Choice PAC
Susan B Walrich, Treasurer
57 West 57th Street, Suite 1101, New York, NY 10019
212-207-8266

Responsible Government Coalition
Nowell Denker, Treasurer
220-55 46th Ave, Bayside, NY 11361
718-281-3073

Responsive Government In Gates
Chris M Hollfelder, Treasurer
23 Noel Drive, Rochester, NY 14606
585-426-6534

Retirees Association of DC 37 Political Action Committee
Robert S Pfefferman, Treasurer
125 Barclay Street, Room 414, New York, NY 10007
212-815-1578

Riverhead PBA PAC Inc
Dana Griffiths, Treasurer
210 Howell Ave, Riverhead, NY 11901
631-727-4500 Fax: 631-727-8630

Rochester Area Right to Life Committee-PAC
Wilda Liana, Treasurer
675 Ling Rd, Ste 3, Rochester, NY 14612
716-621-4690 Fax: 716-621-6966

Rochester Build PAC
Bruce G Boncke, Treasurer
2024 West Henrietta Rd, Ste 5H, Rochester, NY 14623
585-377-7360 Fax: 585-272-8206

Rochester Higher Education and Research PAC
Stephen B Mullen, Treasurer
C/O Nixon Peabody LLP, 1300 Clinton Square, PO Box 31051, Rochester, NY 14604
585-263-1573

Rochester Regional Joint Board State PAC
Christopher T Ferriter, Treasurer
750 East Ave, Rochester, NY 14607
585-473-3280
Web site: www.uniterrjb.org

Rockland County Correction Officers Benevolent Association PAC
Katherine Bruso, Treasurer
PO Box 2046, New City, NY 10956
845-708-2349

Rockland County PBA Association PAC NY
Christopher Brigando, Treasurer

Offices and agencies generally appear in alphabetical order, except when specific order is requested by listee.

POLITICAL ACTION COMMITTEES

500 Bradley Hill Road, Blauvelt, NY 10913
845-727-3960 Fax: 845-727-4140
Web site: www.rcpba.org

Rockland County Sheriff's Deputy Assn, PAC
Thomas G Rapelye, Treasurer
55 New Hempstead Rd, New City, NY 10956
845-638-5400 Fax: 845-638-5035

Roofers' Pol Education & Legislative Fund of NY
Grace Felschow, Treasurer
2800 Clinton Street, West Seneca, NY 14224
716-828-0488 Fax: 716-828-0487

Rough Rider PAC
Michael Moriarty, Treasurer
C/O Windels Marx Lane & Mittendorf, 156 West 56th Street, New York, NY 10019
212-237-1132 Fax: 212-262-1215

Royal Indemnity Comapny Voluntary PAC (Royal & Sun Alliance PAC)
Jeffrey M Klein, Treasurer
9300 Arrowpoint Blvd, Charlotte, NC 28273
704-522-3141

SBA Political Action Committee
Robert W Johnson, Treasurer
C/O Sergeants Benevolent Assoc, 35 Worth Street, New York, NY 10013
212-226-2180 Fax: 212-431-4280

SEIU Local 704 PAC
Angelo Arena, President
945 North Broadway, Yonkers, NY 10701
914-377-6290 Fax: 914-377-6299
e-mail: seiulocal704@optonline.net

SEIU PEA State Fund
Anna Burger, Treasurer
1313 L Street, NW, Washington, DC 20005

SPEAKERPAC
Howard Lazar, Treasurer
C/O Sheldon Silver, 17th Floor, 180 Maiden Lane, New York, NY 10038
212-677-4451

SPOA For A Better University Neighborhood II
Robert Frank, Treasurer
1011 E Adams Street, Syracuse, NY 13210
315-476-7400

SSL Political Action Committee
James L Burns, Treasurer

180 Maiden Lane, 34th Floor, New York, NY 10038
212-806-5851 Fax: 212-806-6006
e-mail: jburns@stroock.com

SAFE-PAC (Schools Are For Everyone Political Action Committee)
Joseph T Amodeo, Treasurer
1 Tall Oaks Road, Marlboro, NY 12542
845-625-8680

Save American Jobs PAC
Matthew J Bova, Treasurer
PO Box 2005, 12600 Clarence Center Road, Akron, NY 14001
716-542-5200

Save The Lake (Political Action Committee)
W Wrobel, Treasurer
24 Clark Street, Saratoga Springs, NY 12866
518-584-6419

Schools Are For Everyone
Jeffrey S McGowan, Treasurer
340 Crescent Avenue, Highland, NY 12528
845-532-6255
Web site: www.lgcsc.org

Securities Industry Assn PAC, NY District
Bernard Beal, Treasurer
120 Broadway, 35th Fl, New York, NY 10271
212-608-1500 Fax: 212-968-0703
Web site: www.sifma.org

Semper FI NY State PAC Inc
Peter J Johnson Jr, Treasurer
115 East 9th Street, New York, NY 10003
e-mail: pjjjr@aol.com

Sen Dem
Arnold J Ludwig, Treasurer
26 Court St, Brooklyn, NY 11242
201-303-4582

Service Station & Repair Shop Operators, Upstate NY Inc
Stewart D Hill, Treasurer
3650 James St, Ste 101, Syracuse, NY 13206
315-455-1301

Shandaken Democrat Club
Chandra Lencina, Treasurer
Elm Street, Pine Hill, NY 12465
845-254-4838
e-mail: chandra@cloudspinners.com

Sheet Metal Workers Int'l Assn Local 137 PAL Fund
Richard Quaresima, Treasurer
21-42 44th Drive, Long Island City, NY 11101-4710
718-937-4514 Fax: 718-937-4113

Sheet Metal Workers LU 38 -PAC
Stephen M Quaranto, Treasurer

Offices and agencies generally appear in alphabetical order, except when specific order is requested by listee.

POLITICAL ACTION COMMITTEES

38 Starr Ridge Road, PO Box 119, Brewster, NY 10509
845-278-6868
Web site: www.sheetmetallocal38.org

Sheet Metal Workers' Intl Assoc Local 28 Political Action Committee
Michael Belluzzi, Treasurer
Sheet Metal Workers LU 28, 500 Greenwich Street, New York, NY 10013
212-941-7700 Fax: 212-226-0304
Web site: www.smwialu28.org

Sheet Metal Workers' Local 46 PAF
Michael J Morgan, Business Manager
40 Rutter St, Rochester, NY 14606
585-254-9151 Fax: 585-254-8584
e-mail: mjmorgan@frontiernet.net
Web site: www.smw46.com

Sheet Metal Workers' Local Union 83 Political Action Committee
David B Mellon, Treasurer
C/O Sheet Metal Workers LU 83, 718 Third Avenue, Albany, NY 12206
518-489-1377 Fax: 518-453-9284
e-mail: www.smwia83@aol.com

Soft Drink & Brewery Workers' PAC
Warren Marsh, Treasurer
11 Stillwell Ave, Yonkers, NY 10704
914-776-7834

Solidarity Task Force
Gary Steszewski, Treasurer
95 Cresthaven Dr, Buffalo, NY 14225
716-837-1150 Fax: 716-836-4599
e-mail: garski@adelphia.net

Somers Democratic Club
Harvey Kriedberg, Treasurer
27 Heritage Hills, Unit F, Somers, NY 10589
914-277-7621

Southern Onondaga Republican Club
Robert S De More, Treasurer
PO Box 145, Fabius, NY 13063
315-683-5655 Fax: 315-683-5479

Southern Tier HB & REM Build-PAC
Gary Brownell, Treasurer
80 Rockwell Road, Vestal, NY 13850
607-772-0889

Southern Tier Business PAC
James J Lewis, Treasurer
30 Wisconsin Drive, Binghamton, NY 13901
607-648-2523

Southern Tier Leadership PAC
Jane Northrup, Treasurer

812 West Henley St, Olean, NY 14760
716-372-7955

Southhampton Town Young Republicans
Gary Bronat, Treasurer
9 Douglas Ct, Hampton Bays, NY 11946
631-728-2558
e-mail: info@southamptontownyrs.com
Web site: www.southamptontownyrs.com

Southold Town PBA Tax PAC.COM
Kevin J Lynch, Treasurer
PO Box 141, Peconic, NY 11958
631-765-2600

Southtowns Republican Chairman's Association
Jerrold R Thompson, II, Treasurer
164 Quaker Road, East Aurora, NY 14052
716-652-0232

Sprint Nextel Corporation PAC
Lonnie Taylor, Treasurer
2001 Edmund Halley Dr, Reston, VA 20191
703-433-4966 Fax: 703-433-4142

Stars & Stripes PAC
Albert A Annunziata, Treasurer
80 Business Park Dr, Ste 309, Armonk, NY 10504
914-273-0730 Fax: 914-273-7051

State & Local Election Fund AFSCME Local 2054, DC 37
Kenneth Lieb, Treasurer
Local 2054, DC 37, 125 Barclay St, New York, NY 10007
212-815-1060

State & Local Election Fund Local 1070
Steven Schwartz, Treasurer
Local 1070, 125 Barclay St, New York, NY 10007
212-815-1070 Fax: 212-341-4941

State Street Associates PAC
Sean M Doolan, Treasurer
121 State St, Albany, NY 12207
518-436-0751 Fax: 518-436-4751

Staten Island Political Action Committee
Lorraine A Witzak, Treasurer
32 Cunard Place, Staten Island, NY 10304
718-442-8713

Statewide Association of Minority Businesses PAC
Yuri C Martinez, Treasurer
133-54 41st Avenue, 4th Floor, Flushing, NY 11355
212-717-6846

Steamfitters' Union Local 638 PAC
John J Torpey James E Elder

Offices and agencies generally appear in alphabetical order, except when specific order is requested by listee.

POLITICAL ACTION COMMITTEES

32-32 48th Ave, Long Island City, NY 11101
718-392-3420 Fax: 718-784-7285

Steve Israel for Congress Committee-State Account
Joel Schleifer, Treasurer
C/O Perlman Schleifer & Perrone, 368 Veterans Hwy, Commack, NY 11725
631-543-6660

STA Subcontractors Trade Assn Inc State PAC
Ronald S Berger, Executive Director
1430 Broadway, Suite 1600, New York, NY 10018
212-398-6220 Fax: 212-398-6224
e-mail: stanyc.berger@verizon.net
Web site: www.stanyc.com

Success PAC
Walter J Edwards, Treasurer
C/O Walter Edwards, New York, NY 10524
212-864-7410

Suffolk County Republican Women PAC
Angela Guarino, Treasurer
PO Box 81, Holbrook, NY 11741
631-585-0450 Fax: 631-585-4335
e-mail: tillangels@aol.com

Suffolk & Nassau Counties Plumbing & Heating Contractors Assoc PAC
Joseph L Kaufman, Treasurer
16 Lucinda Dr, Babylon, NY 11702
516-422-3945 Fax: 516-422-3945

Suffolk Co Detective Investigators PBA Inc PAC
Peter Tartaglia, Treasurer
868 Church Street, Bohemia, NY 11716
631-853-4150

Suffolk Co Police Dept Superior Officers Assoc Public Affairs Cmte
Lawrence Faraone, Treasurer
2518 Montauk Hwy, Brookhaven, NY 11719
631-654-0400 Fax: 631-447-0977

Suffolk County Assn of Municipal Employees' PAC Inc
Daniel Farrell, Treasurer
30 Orville Dr, Suite A, Bohemia, NY 11716
631-589-8400 Fax: 631-589-3860
e-mail: cherylfelice@scame.org
Web site: www.scame.org
Labor union representing support staff, both white and blue color, for Suffolk County government.

Suffolk County Chapter Nat'l Womens Political Caucus
Donna Lent, Treasurer
7 Lawrence Drive, Nesconset, NY 11767
631-265-0802
Web site: www.nwpc.org

Suffolk County Correction Officers' Assn PAC
Charles J Sclafani, Treasurer

400 West Main St, Suite 202, Riverhead, NY 11901
631-208-1301 Fax: 631-208-1333
e-mail: csclafani@sccoa.net
Web site: www.sccoa.net

Suffolk County Deputy Sheriffs Benevolent Assn Inc PAC
Bernard Cinquemani, Treasurer
2650 Rt 112, Medford, NY 11763
631-289-1768 Fax: 631-289-1813
e-mail: scdsba@optonline.net
Web site: www.scdsba.com

Suffolk County Police Benevolent Assn PAC
Patricia A O'Donnell, Treasurer
868 Church St, Bohemia, NY 11716
516-563-4200 Fax: 516-563-4204

Suffolk County Police Conference PAC
Kevin J Sarlo, Treasurer
20 Boxwood Street, E Hampton, NY 11937
631-329-9215

Superior Officers Assoc-Nassau County Police
Brian J Hoesl, Treasurer
777 Old Country Road, Suite 201, Plainview, NY 11803
516-681-8624

Superior Officers' Benevolent Assn of the TBTA PAC
Matthew Cirelli, Treasurer
225 Jericho Trnpk, Floral Park, NY 11001
516-358-7097 Fax: 516-358-1258

Surgeon PAC
John D Nicholson, Treasurer
100 State St, Ste 405, Albany, NY 12207
518-433-0397

Syracuse Tomorrow
Michael J Lorenz, Treasurer
5109 Waterford Wood Way, Fayetteville, NY 13066
315-637-3965 Fax: 315-471-8545

T-Mobile New York PAC
Brian Gorczynski, Treasurer
4 Sylvan Way, Parsippany, NJ 07054
973-292-8992

TAP PAC-APC
John Crossley, Treasurer
121 State St, 2nd Fl, Albany, NY 12207
315-733-2446

TEAPAC
Anthony Puglisi, Treasurer
160 E 38th St, Apt 4E, New York, NY 10016
212-986-7528

THOROPAC - Thoroughbred Breeders' PAC
Jane Decoteau, Treasurer

Offices and agencies generally appear in alphabetical order, except when specific order is requested by listee.

POLITICAL ACTION COMMITTEES

57 Phila St, #2, Saratoga Springs, NY 12866
518-587-0777 Fax: 518-587-1551
e-mail: thoroughbred@acmenet.net
Web site: www.nybreds.com

TOW PAC
John H Beauman, Treasurer
175 Oakhurst Street, Lockport, NY 14094
716-433-6481

Taxpayers for an Affordable New York PAC
Steven Spinola, Treasurer
114 Meadbrook Road, Garden City, NY 11530
516-746-2925

Teaching Hospital Education PAC
William A Polf, Treasurer
80 Central Park West, Apt 16E, New York, NY 10023
212-580-0452

Teamsters Local 317 PAC
Gary R Staring, Treasurer
566 Spencer St, Syracuse, NY 13204
315-471-4164 Fax: 315-471-4328
e-mail: cindy@twcny.rr.com

Teamsters Local 72 PAC
Terrance R Eldridge, Jr, Treasurer
Local 72 IBOFT, 265 West 14th St, New York, NY 10011
212-691-4228 Fax: 212-645-5026

Technologists for New York
Michael P Ridley, Treasurer
10 Henkes Lane, Latham, NY 12110
518-220-9118

Telecommunications Improvement Council
Keith J Roland, Treasurer
7 Southwoods Blvd, Suite 301, Albany, NY 12211
518-465-7581
e-mail: kroland@rfkplaw.com

Telecommunications Int'l Union
Sarah Willacy, Treasurer
71 Warwick Road, Bronxville, NY 10708
914-961-4929

Tempo 802
William R Dennison, Treasurer
183 Rockne Rd, Yonkers, NY 10701
914-968-9126 Fax: 212-489-6030
e-mail: eprice@local802.org

The Business Council PAC Inc
Kathleen Carlitz, Treasurer
152 Washington Avenue, Albany, NY 12210
518-465-7511 or 800-358-1202 Fax: 518-465-4389

The Coalition for Responsible Development
Joel Latman, Treasurer
C/O The Johnson Company, 630 Fifth Avenue, Suite 1510, New York, NY 10111

The Coca-Cola Bottling Company of New York, PAC
Christopher Grimaldi, Treasurer
111 Washington Avenue, Suite 606, Albany, NY 12210
518-432-9220

The Delaware Club
Thomas M Agostino, Treasurer
335 Commonwealth Avenue, Buffalo, NY 14216
716-877-5349

The Italian American Poltical Action Committee of New York
James C Lisa, Treasurer
48-08 111th Street, Corona, NY 11368
718-592-2196

The Political Action Committee of The Fulton County Regional Chamber of Commerce
George W Hart, Treasurer
2 North Main Street, Gloversville, NY 12078
518-725-0641
Web site: www.fultoncountyny.org

The Real Conservatives
Thomas G Vossler, Treasurer
154 Morris Avenue, Buffalo, NY 14214
716-836-4843

The Republican Club of Bronxville
Doug Banbury, Treasurer
PO Box 23, Bronxville, NY 10708
917-692-2924

The Shaw Licitra PAC
George P Esernio, Treasurer
1475 Franklin Avenue, Garden City, NY 11530
516-742-0610 Fax: 516-742-2670
Web site: www.shaw-licitra.com

The Wine PAC
Leonard M Fogelman, Treasurer
305 Madison Avenue, New York, NY 10165
212-370-1530

The Young Democratic Rural Conference
John D Byrne, Treasurer
207A Kenville Road, Buffalo, NY 14215
315-323-3848 Fax: 866-517-8577

Theatrical Protective Union Local No One Iatse NYS Stagehands PAC
James J Claffey, Jr, Treasurer
320 West 46th Street, New York, NY 10036
212-333-2500

Thoroughbred Horsemen of Western NY PAC
Jonathan Buckley, Treasurer

Offices and agencies generally appear in alphabetical order, except when specific order is requested by listee.

POLITICAL ACTION COMMITTEES

PO Box 25250, Farmington, NY 14425
716-924-3004 Fax: 716-924-1433
e-mail: flhbpa@frontiernet.net

Tile Layers Subordinate Union Local 7 of New York and New Jersey PAC
Charles Hill, Treasurer
45-34 Court Square, Long Island City, NY 11101
516-485-9289

Tourism Advocacy Coalition PAC
George Lence, Treasurer
810 Seventh Ave, 3rd Fl, New York, NY 10019
212-484-1265 Fax: 212-247-6193
e-mail: glence@nycvisit.com

Town of Annsville Democratic Club
David N Kobernuss, Treasurer
PO Box 440, Taberg, NY 13471

Town of Hamburg Endorsed Cadidates Fund
Vincent J Sorrentino, Treasurer
4535 Hidden Hollow Road, Hamburg, NY 14075
716-649-3589

Town of Hurley Republican Club Inc
Diane Lacasse, Treasurer
32 Circle Drive, Hurley, NY 12443
845-331-4720

Transit Supervisors Organization PAC
Vincent Modafferi, Treasurer
5768 Mosholu Ave, Bronx, NY 10471
718-601-5700 Fax: 718-601-6300
e-mail: sld139@aol.com

Transport Workers Union Local 100 Political Contributions Committee
Ed Watt, Treasurer
140B 126th Street, Rockaway, NY 11694
718-634-8747

U.S.W.A. Local 420A PAC
David G Rabideau, Treasurer
24 Woodlawn Avenue, Massena, NY 13662
315-764-0531

UA Plumbers & Pipefitters LU 773 Voluntary NYS PAC Fund
Larry Bulman, Business Manager
Local 773, PO Box 1343, South Glens Falls, NY 12803
518-792-9157 Fax: 518-792-4876
Web site: www.lu773.org

UA Plumbers & Steamfitters Local 22 PAC Inc
Michael W McNally, Treasurer
3509 Human Rd, Sanborn, NY 14132
716-731-4683

UFCW Active Ballot Club
Anthony M Perrone, Treasurer

1775 K Street NW, Washington, DC 20006-1598
202-223-3111
Web site: www.ufcw.org

UFT COPE Local
Melvyn Aaronson, Treasurer
52 Broadway, New York, NY 10004
212-598-9528 Fax: 212-475-2320
Web site: www.uft.org

UHAP PAC
Gary J Fitzgerald, Treasurer
17 Halfmoon Exec Park Dr, Clifton Park, NY 12065
518-383-5060 Fax: 518-383-2616
e-mail: gfitzgerald@iroquois.org
Web site: www.upstatehealthcare.org

UNITE HERE TIP State & Local Fund
Thomas Snyder, Treasurer
275 Seventh Avenue, 10th Floor, New York, NY 10001
212-265-7000

UNYAN PAC
Edna Moyer, Treasurer
941 Pauline Ave, Pine City, NY 14871
607-734-8056

USB Fund for Good Government Inc
Harold J Peterson, Treasurer
Union State Bank, 100 Dutch Hill Road, Orangeburg, NY 10962
845-398-5812 Fax: 845-365-4671

USWA, SEIU, AFL-CIO, CLC-PAC
Edward L Byrne, Treasurer
138-50 Queens Blvd, Briarwood, NY 11435

UWUA Local 1-2 Non Federal PAC
Robert Conetta, Treasurer
5 W 37th St, New York, NY 10018
212-575-4400 Fax: 212-575-3852

Ulster County Democratic Women
Susanne L Herl, Treasurer
UCDW, PO Box 4464, Kingston, NY 12402
845-331-8275

Uniformed Fire Officers Association 527 Account
John J McDonnell, Treasurer
225 Broadway, Suite 401, New York, NY 10007
212-293-9300

Uniformed Firefighters Assoc State FirePAC Political Action Committee
Robert Straub, Treasurer
204 East 23rd Street, New York, NY 10010
212-545-6975

Union for a Better New York
Peter Ward, Treasurer

Offices and agencies generally appear in alphabetical order, except when specific order is requested by listee.

POLITICAL ACTION COMMITTEES

707 Eighth Ave, New York, NY 10036
212-245-8100 Fax: 212-977-5714

United New York Democratic Club Inc
Flora Schuster, Treasurer
1620 Avenue I, Apt 307, Brooklyn, NY 11230
718-252-7185

United Parcel Service Inc PAC NY
Clifford L Hinds, Treasurer
55 Glenlake Pkwy NE, Atlanta, GA 30328
404-828-6872

United Restaurant, Hotel & Tavern Association of NY Statewide PAC
John M Egan, Treasurer
40 Sheridan Avenue, Albany, NY 12210
518-436-8121 or 877-436-8121 Fax: 518-436-7287
e-mail: esrta@capital.net
Web site: www.esrta.org

United Steelworkers of America
James D English, Treasurer
USWA-Five Gateway Center, Pittsburgh, PA 15222
412-562-2325 Fax: 412-562-2317
e-mail: jenglish@uswa.org

United Steelworkers District 4 PAC
William J Pienta, Treasurer
305 Cayuga Rd, Ste 175, Cheektowaga, NY 14225
716-565-1720 Fax: 716-565-1727
Web site: www.usa.org

United Transportation Union Political Action Committee (UTU PAC)
Daniel E Johnson III, Treasurer
14600 Detroit Avenue, Cleveland, OH 44107-4250
216-228-9400

United for Good Government
James E Dellarmi, Treasurer
21 Water Street, Eastchester, NY 10709
914-337-7451

Unity PAC
Ellen M Faigle, Treasurer
PO Box 5000, Syracuse, NY 13250-5000
315-448-7000 Fax: 315-448-7100
e-mail: efaigle@unity-life.com
Web site: www.unity-life.com

Urbane Leadership
Tiffany Raspberry, Treasurer
442 Gates Avenue, 3rd Floor, Brooklyn, NY 11216
347-439-9358
e-mail: tiffanyraspberry@aol.com

Valley Democratic Club PAC
George E Matthews, Treasurer

711 W Seneca Tpke, Syracuse, NY 13207

Van Buren Womens Republican Club
Virginia M Lathrop, Treasurer
7404 State Fair Road, Baldwinsville, NY 13027
315-638-8403

Verizon Communications Good Government Club New York PAC
Sandra L Borders, Treasurer
Verizon Communications, 1717 Arch Street 47S, Philadelphia, PA 19103
215-963-6387

Victory 2005 Committee
Simon Shamoun, Treasurer
255 91 Street, Brooklyn, NY 11209
917-439-0952

Voice of Teachers for Educational/Comm on Political Education
Alan Lubin, Treasurer
NYSUT, 800 Troy-Schenectady Road, Latham, NY 12110
518-213-6000
Web site: www.nysut.org

WNY Majority Leader PAC
Mehrl King, Treasurer
71 W Melcourt Dr, Cheektowaga, NY 14225
716-892-6098

WRCC 21st Century Fund
Thomas Belcastro, Treasurer
214 Mamaroneck Ave, White Plains, NY 10601
914-949-3020 Fax: 914-949-2275
Web site: www.westchestergop.com

WYETH Good Gov't Fund
Jack M O'Connor, Treasurer
Five Giralda Farms, Madison, NJ 07940
973-660-5000 Fax: 973-660-6030

Wachovia New York Employees Good Government Fund
Neal Doherty, Treasurer
301 South College Street, Charlotte, NC 28288-0630
704-374-3234

Wantagh GOP Victory Committee
Michael Hortofilis, Treasurer
3429 Park Avenue, Wantagh, NY 11793
516-679-2497

Wantagh Republican Committeesmens Council
Michael Hortofilis, Treasurer
3429 Park Avenue, Wantagh, NY 11793
516-679-2497

Weingarten, Reid & McNally, LLC
Robert Reid, Treasurer

Offices and agencies generally appear in alphabetical order, except when specific order is requested by listee.

POLITICAL ACTION COMMITTEES

1 Commerce Plaza, Suite 1103, Albany, NY 12210
518-465-7330 Fax: 518-465-0273
e-mail: bobr@lobbywr.com
Web site: www.lobbywr.com

Wellpoint, Inc WELLPAC
Marjorie Maginn, Treasurer
120 Monument Circle, Indianapolis, IN 46204
317-488-6351 Fax: 317-488-6007
e-mail: marjorie.maginn@wellpoint.com

Westchester Black Womens' Political Caucas
Mary E Cheek, Treasurer
1 Wellington Terrace, White Plains, NY 10607
914-997-9130

Westchester Coalition for Legal Abortion PAC
Deborah Tarlow, Treasurer
237 Mamaroneck Avenue, White Plains, NY 10605
914-946-5363 Fax: 914-946-1256
Web site: www.choicematters.org

Westchester County Conservative Party PAC
Joseph J Malara, Treasurer
185 Albemarle Rd, White Plains, NY 10605
914-428-4870

Westchester County Womens Republican Club
Fujiko Presseau, Treasurer
27 Park Ave, White Plains, NY 10603
914-428-4807

Westchester Right to Life PAC
Margaret Maroldy, Treasurer
45 Longue Vue Avenue, New Rochelle, NY 10804
914-632-9498

Westcons PAC
Nicholas Caputo, Treasurer
80 Ferris Place, Ossining, NY 10562
914-941-7983

Western NY PAC Region 9 UAW
Samuel G Williams, Treasurer
35 George Karl Blvd, Ste100, Amherst, NY 14221
716-632-1540

Western NY Regional Council PAC Fund
David F Haines, Jr, Treasurer
23 Market St, Binghamton, NY 13905
607-798-6940 Fax: 607-729-2087

Western NY Safari Club PAC
Ann Boller, Treasurer

440 Winspear Rd, Elma, NY 14059-9110
716-685-8099 Fax: 718-683-6260

Western New Yorkers for Economic Growth
Robert J Fischer, Treasurer
400 Andrews Street, Suite 600, Rochester, NY 14604
585-325-0900

Wilson Elser Moskowitz Edelman & Dicker PAC
Cynthia D Shenker, Treasurer
677 Broadway, Suitw 901, Albany, NY 12207
518-449-8893 Fax: 518-449-4292
e-mail: cynthia.shenker@wilsonelser.com

Women PAC
Regina M Calcaterra, Treasurer
200 West 72nd Street, Suite 56, New York, NY 10023
646-672-2846
Web site: www.womenpac.org

Women's Campaign Fund
Claire Gershon, Treasurer
734 15th Street NW, Suite 500, Washington, DC 20005
202-393-8164 Fax: 202-393-0649
e-mail: info@wcfonline.org
Web site: www.wcfonline.org

Women's TAP Fund
Alice Kryzan, Treasurer
7 Cloister Ct, Amherst, NY 14226
716-832-4617

Woodward Workforce
Robert W Gromer, Treasurer
75 Carraige Hill East, Amherst, NY 14221
716-688-6819

Workers' Compensation Alliance
Ronald Balter, Treasurer
132 Nassau Street, Suite 1200, New York, NY 10038
212-732-8333

Working Families Party WNY Chapter
James A Duncan, Jr, Treasurer
3000 Genesee Street, Suite 207, Cheektowaga, NY 14225
716-479-8148

Yonkers Council of School Administrators PAC
Charles D Whelan, Treasurer
28 Barry Road, Scarsdale, NY 10583
914-723-2748

Young Democrats of Monroe County
Dennis M O'Brien, Treasurer
140 Field Street, Rochester, NY 14620
585-217-7880

Offices and agencies generally appear in alphabetical order, except when specific order is requested by listee.

CHAMBERS OF COMMERCE and ECONOMIC AND INDUSTRIAL DEVELOPMENT ORGANIZATIONS

Provides a combined listing of public and private organizations involved in regional economic development.

Adirondack Economic Development Corporation
60 Main St, Ste 200, PO Box 747, Saranac Lake, NY 12983-0747
518-891-5523 or 888-243-2332 Fax: 518-891-9820
e-mail: info@aedconline.com
Web site: www.aedconline.com

Adirondack Regional Chambers of Commerce
Todd L Shimkus, President & CEO
5 Warren St, Glens Falls, NY 12801
518-798-1761 Fax: 518-792-4147
e-mail: tshimkus@adirondackchamber.org
Web site: www.adirondackchamber.org

Adirondacks Speculator Region Chamber of Commerce
Lisa Turner, Director
PO Box 184, Rts 30 & 8, Speculator, NY 12164
518-548-4521 Fax: 518-548-4905
e-mail: info@speculatorchamber.com
Web site: www.adrkmts.com

African American Chamber of Commerce of Westchester & Rockland Counties
Robin L Douglas, Founder & CEO & President
100 Stevens Ave, Ste 202, Mount Vernon, NY 10550
914-699-9050 Fax: 914-699-6279
e-mail: robinldouglas@cs.com
Web site: www.africanamericanchamberofcommercenys.org

Albany County Industrial Development Agency
Fowler J Riddick, Chairman
112 State St, Suite 1116, Albany, NY 12207-2021
518-447-4841 Fax: 518-447-5695
Web site: www.albanycounty.com/IDA

Albany Industrial Development Agency (City of)
Joe Rabito, Commissioner
21 Lodge St, Albany, NY 12207
518-434-2532 Fax: 518-434-9846
Web site: www.albanyny.org

Albany-Colonie Regional Chamber of Commerce
Lyn Taylor, President
107 Washington Ave, Albany, NY 12210
518-431-1400 Fax: 518-434-1339
e-mail: lyn@ac-chamber.org
Web site: www.ac-chamber.org

Alexandria Bay Chamber of Commerce
Georgene McKinley, Executive Director
7 Market St, PO Box 365, Alexandria Bay, NY 13607
315-482-9531 or 800-541-2110 Fax: 315-482-5434
e-mail: info@alexbay.org
Web site: www.alexbay.org

Allegany County Office of Development
John E Foels, Director of Development & IDA
Crossroads Commerce Conference Center, 6087 NYS Rte 19 North, Belmont, NY 14813
585-268-7472 or 800-893-9484 Fax: 585-268-7473
e-mail: development@alleganyco.com
Web site: www.alleganyco.com

Amherst Chamber of Commerce
Colleen C DiPirro, CEO & President
Centerpointe Corporate Park, 350 Essjay Road, Suite 200, Williamsville, NY 14221
716-632-6905 Fax: 716-632-0548
e-mail: cdipirro@amherst.org
Web site: www.amherst.org

Amherst Industrial Development Agency (Town of)
James Allen, Executive Director
4287 Main Street, Amherst, NY 14226
716-688-9000 Fax: 716-688-0205
e-mail: jallen@amherstida.com
Web site: www.amherstida.com

Amsterdam Industrial Development Agency
Frank Valiante, Executive Director
City Hall, 61 Church St, Amsterdam, NY 12010
518-842-5011 Fax: 518-843-2862
Web site: www.amsterdamedz.com

Arcade Area Chamber of Commerce
Hugh Ely, Executive Director

Offices and agencies generally appear in alphabetical order, except when specific order is requested by listee.

CHAMBERS OF COMMERCE/ECONOMIC DEVELOPMENT ORGANIZATIONS

278 Main St, Arcade, NY 14009
585-492-2114 Fax: 585-492-5103
Web site: www.arcadechamber.org

Babylon Industrial Development Agency
Robert Stricoff, CEO
47 West Main St, Ste 3, Babylon, NY 11702
631-587-3679 Fax: 631-587-3675
e-mail: info@babylonida.org
Web site: www.babylonida.org

Baldwin Chamber of Commerce
Doris Duffy, Co-President; Virginia Foley, Co-President
PO Box 813, Baldwin, NY 11510
516-223-8080
Web site: www.baldwin.org

Baldwinsville Chamber of Commerce (Greater Baldwinsville)
Charlie Farrell, President
50 Oswego St, Baldwinsville, NY 13027
315-638-0550 Fax: 315-720-1450
e-mail: bchamber@gisco.net
Web site: www.baldwinsvillechamber.com

Bath Area Chamber of Commerce (Greater Bath Area)
Bill Caudill, President
10 Pulteney Square W, Bath, NY 14810
607-776-7122 Fax: 607-776-7122
e-mail: bathchamber@insoblzd.net
Web site: www.bathnychamber.com

Bayshore Chamber of Commerce
Donna Periconi, President
77 East Main St, PO Box 5110, Bayshore, NY 11706
631-665-7003 Fax: 631-665-5204
Web site: www.bayshorecommerce.com

Bellmores Chamber of Commerce
Tom Valenti, President
PO Box 861, Bellmore, NY 11710
516-679-1875 Fax: 516-409-0544
e-mail: bellmorecc@aol.com
Web site: www.bellmorechamber.com

Bethlehem Chamber of Commerce
Marty DeLaney, President
318 Delaware Ave, Main Square, Delmar, NY 12054
518-439-0512 or 888-439-0512 Fax: 518-475-0910
e-mail: info@bethlehemchamber.com
Web site: www.bethlehemchamber.com

Bethlehem Industrial Development Agency (Town of)
George E Leveille, Executive Director & CEO
445 Delaware Ave, Delmar, NY 12054
518-439-4955 Fax: 518-439-5808
e-mail: info@bethlehemida.com
Web site: www.bethlehemida.com

Binghamton Chamber of Commerce (Greater Binghamton)
Catherine Glover, President & CEO

Metrocenter-2nd Floor, PO Box 995, Binghamton, NY 13902
607-772-8863 Fax: 607-722-4513
e-mail: president@binghamtonchamber.com
Web site: www.binghamtonchamber.com

Black Lake Chamber of Commerce
William Dashnshaw, President
PO Box 12, Hammond, NY 13646
315-578-2895
e-mail: blcc@blacklake.com
Web site: www.blacklakeny.com

Blooming Grove Chamber of Commerce
Carole McCann, President
PO Box 454, Washingtonville, NY 10992
845-496-5449 Fax: 845-497-7718
e-mail: cmac@frontiernet.net

Blue Mountain Lake Association
John Collins, President
PO Box 156, Blue Mountain Lake, NY 12812
518-352-7717 Fax: 518-352-7385
e-mail: jrc@frontiernet.net

Bolton Landing Chamber of Commerce
Dave Forshay, President
PO Box 368, Bolton Landing, NY 12814-0368
518-644-3831 Fax: 518-644-5951
e-mail: mail@boltonchamber.com
Web site: www.boltonchamber.com

Boonville Area Chamber of Commerce
Kathy Graver, Executive Secretary
122 Main St, PO Box 163, Boonville, NY 13309
315-942-5112 Fax: 315-942-6823
e-mail: info@boonvillechamber.org
Web site: www.boonvillechamber.org

Brewster Chamber of Commerce
Beth Murtha, Executive Director
16 Mount Ebo Road S, Ste 12A, Brewster, NY 10509
845-279-2477 Fax: 845-278-8349
e-mail: info@brewsterchamber.com
Web site: www.brewsterchamber.com

Brockport Chamber of Commerce (Greater Brockport)
Elaine Bader, President
PO Box 119, Brockport, NY 14420
585-637-8684 Fax: 585-637-7389

Bronxville Chamber of Commerce
Michele MacMillion, Executive Director
81 Pondfield Rd, Suite 7, Bronxville, NY 10708
914-337-6040 Fax: 914-337-6040
e-mail: cocbville@aol.com
Web site: www.bronxvillechamber.com

Brookhaven Industrial Development Agency
Raymond C Donnelley, CEO

Offices and agencies generally appear in alphabetical order, except when specific order is requested by listee.

CHAMBERS OF COMMERCE/ECONOMIC DEVELOPMENT ORGANIZATIONS

1 Independence Hill, Farmingville, NY 11738
631-451-6563 Fax: 631-451-6925
Web site: www.brookhaven.org

Brooklyn Chamber of Commerce
Mark Kessler, COO & Interim President
25 Elm Place, Suite 200, 2nd Floor, Brooklyn, NY 11201
718-875-1000 Fax: 718-237-4274
e-mail: info@brooklynchamber.com
Web site: www.ibrooklyn.com

Brooklyn Economic Development Corporation
Joan G Bartolomeo, President
175 Remsen St, Ste 350, Brooklyn, NY 11201
718-522-4600 Fax: 718-797-9286
e-mail: info@bedc.org
Web site: www.bedc.org

Broome County Industrial Development Agency
Richard D'Attilio, Executive Director
PO Box 1510, Binghamton, NY 13902-1510
607-584-9000 Fax: 607-584-9009
e-mail: info@bcida.com
Web site: www.bcida.com

Buffalo Economic Renaissance Corporation
Timothy E Wanamaker, President
Office of Strategic Planning, City of Buffalo, 920 City Hall, Buffalo, NY 14202-3309
716-851-5035 Fax: 716-842-6942
e-mail: start@berc.org
Web site: www.berc.org

Buffalo Niagara Partnership
Andrew J Rudnick, President & CEO
665 Main Street, Suite 200, Buffalo, NY 14203-1487
716-852-7100 Fax: 716-852-2761
e-mail: arudnick@thepartnership.org
Web site: www.thepartnership.org

Canandaigua Area Chamber of Commerce
Allison Grumes, President & CEO
113 S Main St, Canandaigua, NY 14424
585-394-4400 Fax: 585-394-4546
e-mail: bwalters@canadaigua.com
Web site: www.canandaigua.com

Canastota Chamber of Commerce
Rick Stevens, President
222 S Peterboro St, PO Box 206, Canastota, NY 13032
315-697-3677
Web site: www.canastota.org

Canton Chamber of Commerce
Sally Roberson, Executive Director
PO Box 369, 60 Main Street, Canton, NY 13617
315-386-8255 Fax: 315-386-8255
e-mail: cantoncc@northnet.org
Web site: www.cantonnychamber.org

Cape Vincent Chamber of Commerce
Shelley Higgins, Executive Director
PO Box 482, Cape Vincent, NY 13618
315-654-2481 Fax: 315-654-4141
e-mail: thecape@tds.net
Web site: www.capevincent.org

Carthage Area Chamber of Commerce
Tammy Trowbridge, Associate Executive Secretary
313 State St, 2nd Floor, Carthage, NY 13619
315-493-3590 Fax: 315-493-3590
e-mail: carthage@gisco.net
Web site: www.carthageny.com

Cattaraugus Empire Zone Corporation
John Sayegh, Chief Operating Officer
120 N Union St, Olean, NY 14760
716-373-9260 Fax: 716-372-7912
e-mail: econdev@oleanny.com
Web site: www.cattempirezone.org

Cayuga County Chamber of Commerce
Terri Bridenbecker, Executive Director
36 South Street, Auburn, NY 13021
315-252-7291 Fax: 315-255-3077
e-mail: contact@cayugacountychamber.com
Web site: www.cayugacountychamber.com

Cazenovia Area Chamber of Commerce (Greater Cazenovia Area)
Paul C Brooks, Chairman
59 Albany St, Cazenovia, NY 13035
315-655-9243 or 888-218-6305 Fax: 315-655-9244
e-mail: cazchamber@alltel.net
Web site: www.cazenoviachamber.com

Central Adirondack Association
Jon Bailey, President
PO Box 68, Old Forge, NY 13420
315-369-6983 Fax: 315-369-2676
e-mail: info@caany.com
Web site: www.caany.com

Chautauqua County Chamber of Commerce
Pamela S Lydic, President
101 W Fifth St, Jamestown, NY 14701
716-484-1101 Fax: 716-487-0785
e-mail: cccc@chautauquachamber.org
Web site: www.chautauquachamber.org

Chautauqua County Chamber of Commerce, Dunkirk Branch
Pamela S Lydic, President

Offices and agencies generally appear in alphabetical order, except when specific order is requested by listee.

CHAMBERS OF COMMERCE/ECONOMIC DEVELOPMENT ORGANIZATIONS

10785 Bennett Road, Dunkirk, NY 14048
716-366-6200 Fax: 761-366-4276
e-mail: cccc@chautauquachamber.org
Web site: www.chautauquachamber.org

Chautauqua County Industrial Development Agency
William Daly, Administrative Director
200 Harrison St, Jamestown, NY 14701
716-664-3262 Fax: 716-664-4515
e-mail: ccida@ccida.com
Web site: www.co.chautauqua.ny.us/ccida

Cheektowaga Chamber of Commerce
Debra S Liegl, President & CEO
AppleTree Business Park, 2875 Union Road, Ste 50, Cheektowaga, NY 14227
716-684-5838 Fax: 716-684-5571
e-mail: chamber@cheektowaga.org
Web site: www.cheektowaga.org

Chemung County Chamber of Commerce
Kevin D Keeley, President & CEO
400 E Church St, Elmira, NY 14901-2803
607-734-5137 Fax: 607-734-4490
e-mail: info@chemungchamber.org
Web site: www.chemungchamber.org

Chemung County Industrial Development Agency
George Miner, President
400 E Church Street, Elmira, NY 14902
607-733-6513 Fax: 607-734-2698
e-mail: gminer@steg.com
Web site: www.steg.com

Chenango County Chamber of Commerce
Sewain Conklin, Interim President & CEO
19 Eaton Ave, Norwich, NY 13815
607-334-1400 or 877-243-6264 Fax: 607-336-6963
e-mail: chamberinfo@chenangony.org
Web site: www.chenangony.org

Clarence Chamber of Commerce
David Hartzell, President
8975 Main St, Clarence, NY 14031
716-631-3888 Fax: 716-631-3946
e-mail: info@clarence.org
Web site: www.clarence.org

Clarence Industrial Development Agency (Town of)
Henry Bourg, Chairman
1 Town Place, Clarence, NY 14031
716-741-8930 Fax: 716-741-4715
Web site: www.clarence.ny.us

Clayton Chamber of Commerce
Karen Goetz, Executive Director

517 Riverside Dr, Clayton, NY 13624
315-686-3771 or 800-252-9806 Fax: 315-686-5564
e-mail: info@1000islands-clayton.com
Web site: www.1000islands-clayton.com

Clifton Springs Area Chamber of Commerce
Brian Morris, President
PO Box 86, Clifton Springs, NY 14432
315-462-8200 Fax: 315-548-6429
e-mail: info@cliftonspringschamber.com
Web site: www.cliftonspringschamber.com

Clinton Chamber of Commerce Inc
Ferris J Betrus, Executive Vice President
PO Box 142, Clinton, NY 13323
315-853-1735 Fax: 315-853-1735
e-mail: info@clintonnychamber.org
Web site: www.clintonnychamber.org

Clinton County, The Development Corporation
Adore Flynn Kurtz, President
61 Area Development Dr, Plattsburgh, NY 12901
518-563-3100 or 888-699-6757 Fax: 518-562-2232
e-mail: tdc@thedevelopcorp.com
Web site: www.nyworks.biz

Clyde Chamber of Commerce
Rudolph A DeLisio, President
PO Box 69, Clyde, NY 14433
315-923-7238 Fax: 315-923-9863
e-mail: info@clydeontheerie.com
Web site: www.clydeontheerie.com/COC

Clyde Industrial Development Corporation
Kenneth DiSanto, President
PO Box 92, Clyde, NY 14433
315-923-7238 Fax: 315-923-7855
e-mail: kdisanto@tds.net
Web site: www.clydeontheerie.com

Cohoes Industrial Development Agency (City of)
John T McDonald, Chairman
97 Mohawk Street, Cohoes, NY 12047
518-233-2118 Fax: 518-233-2168
e-mail: jscavo@ci.cohoes.ny.us
Web site: www.ci.cohoes.ny.us

Colonie Chamber of Commerce
Robert Jaquay, Chair
950 New Loudon Rd, Latham, NY 12110
518-785-6995 Fax: 518-785-7173
e-mail: info@coloniechamber.org
Web site: www.coloniechamber.org

Columbia County Chamber of Commerce
David B Colby, President

Offices and agencies generally appear in alphabetical order, except when specific order is requested by listee.

CHAMBERS OF COMMERCE/ECONOMIC DEVELOPMENT ORGANIZATIONS

507 Warren St, Hudson, NY 12534
518-828-4417 Fax: 518-822-9539
e-mail: mail@columbiachamber-ny.com
Web site: www.columbiachamber-ny.com

Columbia Hudson Partnership
James P Galvin, Executive Director
444 Warren St, Hudson, NY 12534-2415
518-828-4718 Fax: 518-828-0301
e-mail: partner@chpartnership.com
Web site: www.chpartnership.com

Coney Island Chamber of Commerce
Al O'Hagan, Chairman of the Board
1015 Surf Ave, Brooklyn, NY 11224
718-266-1234 Fax: 718-714-0379
Web site: www.2chambers.com/coney_island

Cooperstown Chamber of Commerce
Polly Renckens, Director
31 Chestnut St, Cooperstown, NY 13326
607-547-9983 Fax: 607-547-6006
e-mail: info1@cooperstownchamber.org
Web site: www.cooperstownchamber.org

Corinth Industrial Development Agency (Town of)
Richard B Lucia, Chairman
600 Palmer Ave, Corinth, NY 12822
518-654-9232 Fax: 518-654-7615
Web site: www.townofcorinthny.com

Corning Area Chamber of Commerce
Coleen Fabrizi, President
1 West Market Street, Suite 302, Corning, NY 14830
607-936-4686 or 866-463-6264 Fax: 607-936-4685
e-mail: fabrizi@corningny.com
Web site: www.corningny.com

Cortland County Chamber of Commerce
Garry VanGorder, Executive Director
37 Church St, Cortland, NY 13045
607-756-2814 Fax: 607-756-4698
e-mail: info@cortlandchamber.com
Web site: www.cortlandchamber.com

Cutchogue-New Suffolk Chamber of Commerce
Jim Trentalange, President
PO Box 610, Cutchogue, NY 11935
631-734-2335
Web site: www.cutchoguenewsuffolk.org

Dansville Chamber of Commerce
William Bacon, President
126 Main St, PO Box 105, Dansville, NY 14437
585-335-6920 or 800-949-0174 Fax: 585-335-5863
e-mail: dansvillechamber@hotmail.com
Web site: www.dansvilleny.net

Delaware County Chamber of Commerce
Mary Beth Silano, Executive Director

5 1/2 Main Street, Delhi, NY 13753
607-746-2281 or 800-642-4443 Fax: 607-746-3571
e-mail: info@delawarecounty.org
Web site: www.delawarecounty.org

Delaware County Planning Department
Nicole Franzese, Director of Planning
PO Box 367, Delhi, NY 13753
607-746-2944 Fax: 607-746-8479
e-mail: pln.director@co.delaware.ny.us
Web site: www.co.delaware.ny.us

Deposit Chamber of Commerce
Rick Golding, President
PO Box 222, Deposit, NY 13754
607-467-2556
Web site: www.tds.net/depositchamber

Development Authority of the North Country
Robert S Juravich, Executive Director
Dulles State Office Bldg, Ste 414, 317 Washington Street,
Watertown, NY 13601
315-785-2593 Fax: 315-785-2591
e-mail: juravich@danc.org
Web site: www.danc.org

Dover-Wingdale Chamber of Commerce
Melanie Ryder, President
PO Box 643, Dover Plains, NY 12522
845-877-9800

Downtown-Lower Manhattan Association
Eric Deutsch, President
120 Broadway, Rm 3340, New York, NY 10271
212-406-9100 or 212-566-6700 Fax: 212-406-9103
Web site: downtownny.com

Dutchess County Economic Development Corporation
Anne N Conroy, President & CEO
3 Neptune Rd, Poughkeepsie, NY 12601
845-463-5410 Fax: 845-463-5401
e-mail: dcedc@dcedc.com
Web site: http://thinkdutchess.com

East Aurora Chamber of Commerce (Greater East Aurora)
Gary D Grote, Executive Director
431 Main Street, East Aurora, NY 14052-1783
716-652-8444 or 800-441-2881 Fax: 716-652-8384
e-mail: eanycc@choiceonemail.com
Web site: www.eanycc.com

East Hampton Chamber of Commerce
Marina Van, Executive Director
79-A Main St, East Hampton, NY 11937
631-324-0362 Fax: 631-329-1642
e-mail: info@easthamptonchamber.com
Web site: www.easthamptonchamber.com

East Islip Chamber of Commerce
Tony Fanni, President

Offices and agencies generally appear in alphabetical order, except when specific order is requested by listee.

CHAMBERS OF COMMERCE/ECONOMIC DEVELOPMENT ORGANIZATIONS

PO Box 88, East Islip, NY 11730
631-859-5000
Web site: www.isliplife.com/eastislipchamber

East Meadow Chamber of Commerce
Brandon Bloom, President
PO Box 77, East Meadow, NY 11554
516-794-3727
Web site: www.emchamber.com

Eastchester-Tuckahoe Chamber of Commerce
Elaina Marie Peruso, President
PO Box 66, Eastchester, NY 10709
914-779-7344

Ellenville/Wawarsing Chamber of Commerce
William Tochterman, President
PO Box 227, 5 Berme Rd, Ellenville, NY 12428
845-647-4620
e-mail: chamberofcommerce2@hvc.rr.com
Web site: www.wawarsing.ny.net

Ellicottville Chamber of Commerce
Lindsey Coburn, Administrative Assistant
9 W Washington St, PO Box 456, Ellicottville, NY 14731
716-699-5046 or 800-349-9099 Fax: 716-699-5636
e-mail: info@ellicottvilleny.com
Web site: www.ellicottvilleny.com

Erie County Industrial Development Agency
Alfred Culliton, Chair, Management Committee
275 Oak St, Buffalo, NY 14203
716-856-6525 Fax: 716-856-6754
e-mail: info@ecidany.com
Web site: www.ecidany.com

Erie County Planning & Economic Development
Andrew M Eszak, Commissioner
95 Franklin St, 10th Floor, Buffalo, NY 14202
716-858-8390 Fax: 716-858-7248
e-mail: eszaka@erie.gov
Web site: www.erie.gov

Erwin Industrial Development Agency (Town of)
Jack Benjamin, President
Three Rivers Dev Corp Inc, 114 Pine St Suite 201, Corning, NY 14830
607-962-4693 Fax: 607-936-9132
e-mail: info@threeriversdevelopment.com
Web site: www.threeriversdevelopment.com

Essex County Industrial Development Agency
Carol Calabrese; Jody Olcott, Co-Executive Directors
7566 Court Street, Elizabethtown, NY 12932
518-873-9114 Fax: 518-873-2011
e-mail: info@essexcountyida.com
Web site: www.essexcountyida.com

Fair Haven Area Chamber of Commerce
Chris Drogi, President

PO Box 13, Fair Haven, NY 13064
315-947-6037
e-mail: info@fairhavenny.com
Web site: www.fairhavenny.com

Farmington Chamber of Commerce
Rose M Kleman, President
1000 County Rd, #8, Farmington, NY 14425
315-986-8182 Fax: 315-986-4377

Farmingville/Holtsville Chamber of Commerce
Wayne Carrington, President
PO Box 66, Holtsville, NY 11742
631-758-0544 Fax: 631-758-0544
e-mail: fhcoc@fhcoc.com
Web site: www.fhcoc.com

Fort Brewerton/Greater Oneida Lake Chamber
Robert Walczyk, President
PO Box 655, Brewerton, NY 13029
315-668-3408 Fax: 315-668-3408
e-mail: info@oneidalakechamber.com
Web site: www.oneidalakechamber.com

Fort Edward Chamber of Commerce
Pamela Brooks, President
PO Box 267, Fort Edward, NY 12828
518-747-3000 Fax: 518-747-0622
Web site: www.ftedward.com

Franklin County Industrial Development Agency
Brad W Jackson, Executive Director
10 Elm Street, Suite 2, Malone, NY 12953
518-483-9472 Fax: 518-483-2900

Franklin Square Chamber of Commerce
Frank Cutolo, President
PO Box 11, Franklin Square, NY 11010
516-775-0001
Web site: www.franklinsquarechamber.org

Fredonia Chamber of Commerce
Mary Beth Fagan, Executive Director
5 East Main St, Fredonia, NY 14063
716-679-1565
e-mail: fredcham@netsync.net
Web site: www.fredoniachamber.org

French-American Chamber of Commerce
Martin Biscoff, Director
122 E 42nd St, Suite 2015, New York, NY 10168
212-867-0123 Fax: 212-867-9050
e-mail: info@faccnyc.org
Web site: www.cclife.org/usa.new_york

Fulton County Economic Development Corporation
Jeffrey Bray, Executive Vice President

Offices and agencies generally appear in alphabetical order, except when specific order is requested by listee.

CHAMBERS OF COMMERCE/ECONOMIC DEVELOPMENT ORGANIZATIONS

55 East Main St, Ste 110, Johnstown, NY 12095
518-762-8700 Fax: 518-762-8702
e-mail: fcedc@sites4u.org
Web site: www.sites4u.org

Fulton County Industrial Development Agency
James Mraz, Executive Secretary
One East Montgomery St, Johnstown, NY 12095
518-736-5660 Fax: 518-762-4597

Fulton County Reg Chamber of Commerce & Ind
Wally Hart, President
2 N Main St, Gloversville, NY 12078
518-725-0641 Fax: 518-725-0643
e-mail: info@fultoncountyny.org
Web site: www.fultoncountyny.org

Garden City Chamber of Commerce
Althea Robinson, Executive Director
230 Seventh Street, Garden City, NY 11530
516-746-7724 Fax: 516-746-7725
e-mail: gcchamber@verizon.net
Web site: www.gardencitychamber.org

Genesee County Chamber of Commerce
Lynn Freeman, President
210 E Main St, Batavia, NY 14020
585-343-7440 or 800-622-2686 Fax: 585-343-7487
e-mail: chamber@geneseeny.com
Web site: www.geneseeny.com

Genesee County Economic Development Center
Steven G Hyde, CEO
One Mill Street, Batavia, NY 14020
585-343-4866 or 877-343-4866 Fax: 585-343-0848
e-mail: gcedc@gcedc.com
Web site: www.gcedc.com

Geneva Area Chamber of Commerce
Rob Gladden, President & CEO
35 Lakefront Dr, PO Box 587, Geneva, NY 14456
315-789-1776 or 877-543-6382 Fax: 315-789-3993
e-mail: rgladden@genevany.com
Web site: www.genevany.com

Geneva Industrial Development Agency (City of)
Valerie Bassett, Excutive Director
47 Castle St, PO Box 273, Geneva, NY 14456
315-789-6104 Fax: 315-789-8373
e-mail: vbassett@geneva.ny.us
Web site: www.geneva.ny.us

Glen Cove Chamber of Commerce
Gabor Karsai, President
70 Glen Street, 2nd Floor, Glen Cove, NY 11542
516-676-6666 Fax: 516-676-5490
e-mail: info@glencovechamber.org
Web site: www.glencovechamber.info

Gore Mountain Region Chamber of Commerce
Patricia Connor, President

228 Main Street, PO Box 84, North Creek, NY 12853
518-251-2612 Fax: 518-251-5317
e-mail: goremtn@frontiernet.net
Web site: www.goremtnregion.org

Goshen Chamber of Commerce
Sharon Barbera, President
44 Park Place, PO Box 506, Goshen, NY 10924
845-294-7741 Fax: 845-294-3998
e-mail: chamber@goshennychamber.com
Web site: www.goshennychamber.com

Gouverneur Chamber of Commerce
Donna Lawrence, Executive Director
214 East Main St, Gouverneur, NY 13642
315-287-0331 Fax: 315-287-3694
e-mail: info@governcurchamber.net
Web site: www.gouverneurchamber.net

Gowanda Area Chamber of Commerce
Dale M Koch, President
28 Jamestown St, PO Box 45, Gowanda, NY 14070
716-532-2834 Fax: 716-532-2834
e-mail: gowandausa@yahoo.com
Web site: www.gowandachamber.org

Grand Island Chamber of Commerce
Joanne Kud, President
2257 Grand Island Blvd, Grand Island, NY 14072
716-773-3651 Fax: 716-773-3316
e-mail: info@gichamber.org
Web site: www.gichamber.org

Granville Chamber of Commerce
Dan Brown, President
One Main St, PO Box 13, Granville, NY 12832
518-642-2815 Fax: 518-642-2772
e-mail: info@granvillechamber.com
Web site: www.granvillechamber.com

Great Neck Chamber of Commerce
Valerie A Link, President
Kiosk Information Center, 1 Middle Neck Road, Great Neck, NY 11021
516-487-2000 Fax: 516-829-5472
e-mail: info@greatneckchamber.org
Web site: www.greatneckchamber.org

Greece Chamber of Commerce
Jody Perry, President
2496 West Ridge Rd, Ste 201, Greece, NY 14626-3053
585-227-7272 Fax: 585-227-7275
e-mail: info@greecechamber.org
Web site: www.greecechamber.org

Green Island Industrial Development Agency (Village of)
Sean E Ward, Chairman

Offices and agencies generally appear in alphabetical order, except when specific order is requested by listee.

CHAMBERS OF COMMERCE/ECONOMIC DEVELOPMENT ORGANIZATIONS

20 Clinton St, Green Island, NY 12183
518-273-2201 Fax: 518-273-2235

Greene County Department of Planning & Economic Development
Warren Hart, AICP Director
411 Main Street, Catskill, NY 12414
518-719-3290 Fax: 518-719-3789
e-mail: business@discovergreene.com
Web site: www.discovergreene.com

Greene County Tourism Promotion
Daniela Marino, Director
Rte 23B at NYS Thruway, Exit 21, PO Box 527, Catskill, NY 12414
518-943-3223 or 800-355-CATS Fax: 518-943-2296
e-mail: tourism@discovergreene.com
Web site: www.greenetourism.com

Greenwich Chamber of Commerce (Greater Greenwich)
Kathy Nichols-Tomkins, Secretary
6 Academy St, Greenwich, NY 12834
518-692-7979 Fax: 518-692-7979
e-mail: info@greenwichchamber.org
Web site: www.greenwichchamber.org

Greenwich Village-Chelsea Chamber of Commerce
Bob Zuckerman, Executive Director
853 Broadway, Suite 800, New York, NY 10003
212-255-5811 Fax: 212-255-5058
e-mail: info@igreenwichvillage.com
Web site: www.gvccc.com

Greenwood Lake Chamber of Commerce
PO Box 36, Greenwood Lake, NY 10925
845-477-0112 Fax: 845-477-2577
e-mail: info@greenwoodlakeny.org
Web site: www.greenwoodlakeny.org

Guilderland Chamber of Commerce
Jane M Schramm, Executive Director
2021 Western Ave, Ste 105, Albany, NY 12203
518-456-6611 Fax: 518-456-6690
e-mail: info@guilderlandchamber.com
Web site: www.guilderlandchamber.com

Guilderland Industrial Development Agency (Town of)
James Shahda, Chairman
Town Hall, PO Box 339, Guilderland, NY 12084
518-356-1980 Fax: 518-356-5514
e-mail: togida@guilderland.org
Web site: www.guilderland.org

Hamburg Chamber of Commerce
Betty Newell, President & CEO
8 South Buffalo St, Hamburg, NY 14075
716-649-7917 or 877-322-6890 Fax: 716-649-6362
e-mail: mail2007@hamburg-chamber.org
Web site: www.hamburg-chamber.org

Hamburg Industrial Development Agency
Michael J Bartlett, Executive Director

S6100 South Park Avenue, Hamburg, NY 14075
716-648-6216 Fax: 716-648-0151
e-mail: hamburgida@townofhamburgny.com
Web site: www.townofhamburgny.com

Hampton Bays Chamber of Commerce
Stan Glinka, President
140 West Main St, Hampton Bays, NY 11946
631-728-2211
Web site: www.hamptonbayschamber.com

Hancock Area Chamber of Commerce
Lori Ray, President
Box 525, Hancock, NY 13783-0525
607-637-4756 or 800-668-7624 Fax: 607-637-4756
e-mail: hancockchamber@hancock.net
Web site: www.hancockareachamber.com

Harlem Chamber of Commerce (Greater Harlem)
Lloyd Williams, President
200 A West 136th St, New York, NY 10030
212-862-7200 Fax: 212-862-8745
e-mail: info@harlemdiscover.com
Web site: www.harlemdiscover.com/chamber

Hastings-on-Hudson Chamber of Commerce
Joseph R LoCascio, Jr, President
PO Box 405, Hastings-on-Hudson, NY 10706
914-478-0900 Fax: 914-478-1720
Web site: www.hastingsgov.org

Hempstead Industrial Development Agency (Town of)
Frederick Parola, Executive Director
350 Front St, Rm 240, Hempstead, NY 11550
516-489-5000 x4200 Fax: 516-489-3179
e-mail: idamail@hotmail.org
Web site: www.tohida.org

Herkimer County Chamber of Commerce
John Scarano, Executive Director
PO Box 129, 28 W Main St, Mohawk, NY 13407
315-866-7820 or 877-984-4636 Fax: 315-866-7833
e-mail: jscarano@herkimercountychamber.com
Web site: www.herkimercountychamber.com

Herkimer County Industrial Development Agency
Mark Feane, Executive Director
320 N Prospect Street, Herkimer, NY 13350
315-867-1373 Fax: 315-867-1515
e-mail: ida@herkimercounty.org
Web site: www.herkimercountyida.com

Hicksville Chamber of Commerce
James Pavone, President

Offices and agencies generally appear in alphabetical order, except when specific order is requested by listee.

CHAMBERS OF COMMERCE/ECONOMIC DEVELOPMENT ORGANIZATIONS

10 W Marie St, Hicksville, NY 11801
516-931-7170 Fax: 516-931-8546
e-mail: hicksvillechamber@earthlink.net
Web site: www.hicksvillechamber.com

Hornell Area Chamber of Commerce/Hornell Industrial Development Agency (City of)
James W Griffin, President & Executive Director
40 Main St, Hornell, NY 14843
607-324-0310 or 877-HORNELL Fax: 607-324-3776
e-mail: griff@hornellny.com
Web site: www.hornellny.com

Hudson Valley Gateway Chamber of Commerce
Ron Forehand, CEO
One S Division St, Peekskill, NY 10566
914-737-3600 Fax: 914-737-0541
e-mail: info@hvgatewaychamber.com
Web site: www.hvgatewaychamber.com

Hunter Chamber of Commerce (Town of)
Michael McCrary, President
PO Box 177, Hunter, NY 12442
518-263-4900 Fax: 518-589-0117
e-mail: hunterch@mhonline.net
Web site: www.hunterchamber.org

Huntington Township Chamber of Commerce
Ellen O' Brien, Executive Director
164 Main St, Huntington, NY 11743
631-423-6100 Fax: 631-851-3276
e-mail: ellen@chamberli.com
Web site: www.huntingtonchamber.com

Hyde Park Chamber of Commerce
Elizabeth Roger, President
PO Box 17, Hyde Park, NY 12538
845-229-8612 Fax: 845-229-8638
e-mail: info@hydeparkchamber.org
Web site: www.hydeparkchamber.org

Indian Lake Chamber of Commerce
Brenda Lamphear, President
PO Box 724, Indian Lake, NY 12842
518-648-5112 or 800-328-5253 Fax: 518-648-5489
e-mail: indianlakechamber@frontiernet.net
Web site: www.indian-lake.com

Inlet Information Office
Adele Burnett, Director of Information & Tourism
Route 28, PO Box 266, Inlet, NY 13360
315-357-5501 or 866-GOINLET Fax: 315-357-3570
e-mail: inletny@eagle-wireless.com
Web site: www.inletny.com

Islip Chamber of Commerce
Tom Cilmi, President
PO Box 112, Islip, NY 11751-0112
631-581-2720 Fax: 631-581-2720
e-mail: info@islipchamberofcommerce.com
Web site: www.islipchamberofcommerce.com

Islip Economic Development Division & Industrial Development Agency (Town of)
William G Mannix, Director
40 Nassau Ave, Islip, NY 11751
631-224-5512 Fax: 631-224-5532
e-mail: ecodev@isliptown.org
Web site: www.isliptown.org

Islip Industrial Development Agency (Town of)
Bill Nolan, Chairman
40 Nassau Ave, Islip, NY 11751
631-224-5512 Fax: 631-224-5532
e-mail: ecodev@isliptown.org
Web site: www.isliptown.org

Jamaica Chamber of Commerce
Robert M Richards, President
90-25 161st St, Ste 505, Jamaica, NY 11432
718-657-4800 Fax: 718-658-4642
Web site: www.jccnewyork.net

Jamaica Development Corporation (Greater Jamaica)
Carlisle Towery, President
90-04 161st Street, Jamaica, NY 11432
718-291-0282 Fax: 718-658-1405
Web site: www.gjdc.org

Japanese Chamber of Commerce
Susumu Kato, President
145 W 57th St, New York, NY 10019
212-246-8001 Fax: 212-246-8002
e-mail: info@jcciny.org
Web site: www.jcciny.org

Kenmore-Town of Tonawanda Chamber of Commerce
Tracey M Lukasik, Executive Director
3411 Delaware Ave, Kenmore, NY 14217
716-874-1202 Fax: 716-874-3151
e-mail: info@ken-ton.org
Web site: www.ken-ton.org

Kings Park Chamber of Commerce
Dee Grasso, Executive Director
PO Box 322, Kings Park, NY 11754
631-269-7678 Fax: 631-269-5575
e-mail: kingsparkchamber@kingsparkli.com
Web site: www.kingsparkli.com

Lackawanna Area Chamber of Commerce
Aimee Gomlack-Brace, President

Offices and agencies generally appear in alphabetical order, except when specific order is requested by listee.

CHAMBERS OF COMMERCE/ECONOMIC DEVELOPMENT ORGANIZATIONS

638 Ridge Rd, Lackawanna, NY 14218
716-823-8841 Fax: 716-823-8848
e-mail: info@lackawannachamber.com
Web site: www.lackawannachamber.com

Lake George Regional Chamber of Commerce
Scott Wood, President
PO Box 272, Lake George, NY 12845
518-668-5755 or 800-705-0059 Fax: 518-668-4286
e-mail: info@lakegeorgechamber.com
Web site: www.lakegeorgechamber.com

Lake Luzerne Chamber of Commerce
George Beagle, President
PO Box 222, Lake Luzerne, NY 12846-0222
518-696-3500
e-mail: llcc@telenet.net
Web site: www.lakeluzernechamber.org

Lake Placid Chamber of Commerce
James McKenna, CEO
2610 Main St, Suite #2, Lake Placid, NY 12946-1592
518-523-2445 Fax: 518-523-2605
e-mail: info@lakeplacid.com
Web site: www.lakeplacid.com

Lancaster Area Chamber of Commerce
Kathy Konst, President & CEO
41 Central Ave, PO Box 284, Lancaster, NY 14086
716-681-9755 Fax: 716-684-3385
e-mail: info@laccny.org
Web site: www.laccny.org

Lancaster Industrial Development Agency (Town of)
Robert H Giza, Chairman
21 Central Avenue, Lancaster, NY 14086
716-683-1610 Fax: 716-683-0512
e-mail: lookatus@lancasterny.com
Web site: www.lancasterny.com

Lewis County Chamber of Commerce
Bethany Yost, Interim Executive Director
7383-C Utica Blvd, Lowville, NY 13367
315-376-2213 Fax: 315-376-0326
e-mail: info@lewiscountychamber.org
Web site: www.lewiscountychamber.org

Lewis County Industrial Development Agency
Ned E Cole, Executive Director
7642 State St, PO Box 106, Lowville, NY 13367
315-376-3014 Fax: 315-376-7880
e-mail: info@lcida.org
Web site: www.lcida.org

Liverpool Chamber of Commerce (Greater Liverpool)
Lucretia M Hudzinski, Executive Director

314 Second St, Liverpool, NY 13088
315-457-3895 Fax: 315-234-3226
e-mail: chamber@liverpoolchamber.com
Web site: www.liverpoolchamber.com

Livingston County Chamber of Commerce
Cynthia Oswald, President
4635 Millennium Dr, Geneseo, NY 14454-1134
585-243-2222 Fax: 585-243-4824
e-mail: coswald@frontiernet.net
Web site: www.livchamber.com

Livingston County Economic Development Office & Industrial Development Agency
Patrick J Rountree, Director
6 Court St, Room 306, Geneseo, NY 14454-1043
585-243-7124 or 877-284-5343 Fax: 585-243-7126
e-mail: info@build-here.com
Web site: www.build-here.com

Lockport Industrial Development Agency (Town of)
Lewis L Staley, Administrative Director
6560 Dysinger Rd, Lockport, NY 14094
716-439-9535 Fax: 719-439-9715
e-mail: town-lkptida@elockport.com
Web site: www.elockport.com

Long Beach Chamber of Commerce
Michael J Kerr, President
350 National Blvd, Long Beach, NY 11561-3312
516-432-6000 Fax: 516-432-0273
Web site: www.longbeachnychamber.com

Long Island Association
Matthew Crosson, President
300 Broadhollow Road, Suite 110 W, Melville, NY 11747-4840
631-499-4400 Fax: 631-499-2194
e-mail: mcrosson@longislandassociation.org
Web site: www.longislandassociation.org

Long Island Council of Dedicated Merchants Chamber of Commerce
Maureen Schneider, President
PO Box 512, Miller Place, Long Island, NY 11764
631-821-1313 or 631-331-2833 Fax: 631-331-0027
e-mail: sch1999@aol.com
Web site: www.cdmlongisland.com

Long Island Development Corporation
Roslyn D Goldmacher, President & CEO
45 Seaman Ave, Bethpage, NY 11714-3701
516-433-5000 Fax: 516-433-5046
e-mail: biz-loans@lidc.org
Web site: www.lidc.org

Madison County Industrial Development Agency
John Reinhardt, Director

Offices and agencies generally appear in alphabetical order, except when specific order is requested by listee.

CHAMBERS OF COMMERCE/ECONOMIC DEVELOPMENT ORGANIZATIONS

11 Madison Blvd, Canastota, NY 13032
315-697-9817 Fax: 315-697-8169
e-mail: director@twcny.rr.com
Web site: www.madisoncountyny.com/mcida

Mahopac-Carmel Chamber of Commerce
Robert Daniels, President
953 South Lake Blvd, PO Box 160, Mahopac, NY 10541-0160
845-628-5553 Fax: 845-628-5962
e-mail: mcchamber@computer.net
Web site: www.mahopacchamber.com

Malone Chamber of Commerce
Madeleine Davis, President
497 East Main Street, Malone, NY 12953
518-483-3760 or 877-625-6631 Fax: 518-483-3172
e-mail: info@malonenychamber.com
Web site: www.malonenychamber.com

Mamaroneck Chamber of Commerce
Thomas DeRosa, President
430 Center Ave, Mamaroneck, NY 10543
914-698-4400
e-mail: chamber@mamaroneckchamberofcommerce.org
Web site: www.mamaroneckchamberofcommerce.org

Manhasset Chamber of Commerce
Diane Harragan, Co-President; Bernard Rolston, Co-President
62 Manhasset Ave, Manhasset, NY 11030
516-627-1098 Fax: 516-365-7644
Web site: www.manhasset.org

Manhattan Chamber of Commerce Inc
Nancy Ploeger, President
1375 Broadway, Third Floor, New York, NY 10018
212-479-7772 Fax: 212-473-8074
e-mail: info@manhattancc.org
Web site: www.manhattancc.org

Massapequa Chamber of Commerce
Joseph Basile, President
674 Broadway, Massapequa, NY 11758
516-541-1443 Fax: 516-541-8625
Web site: www.massapequachamber.com

Massena Chamber of Commerce
Tina Cocoran, President
50 Main St, Massena, NY 13662
315-769-3525 Fax: 315-769-5295
e-mail: chamber@massenaworks.com
Web site: www.massenany.com

Mastics/Shirley Chamber of Commerce
Pat Peluso, President
PO Box 4, Mastic, NY 11950
631-399-2228

Mattituck Chamber of Commerce
Martin Finnegan, President

PO Box 1056, Mattituck, NY 11952
631-298-5230
e-mail: info@mattituckchamber.org
Web site: www.mattituckchamber.org

Mayville/Chautauqua Chamber of Commerce
Deborah Marsala, Coordinator
PO Box 22, Mayville, NY 14757
716-753-3113 Fax: 716-753-3113
e-mail: mccc@madbbs.com
Web site: www.mayville-chautauquachamber.org

Mechanicville Area Chamber of Commerce
Barbara Corsale, President
312 N 3rd Ave, Mechanicville, NY 12118
518-664-7791 Fax: 518-664-0826
e-mail: mechanicvillechamber@verizon.net
Web site: www.mechanicville.org

Mechanicville/Stillwater Industrial Development Agency
Barbara Zecca Corsale, Chair
City Hall, 36 North Main Street, Mechanicville, NY 12118
518-664-7303 Fax: 518-664-5362
Web site: www.mechanicville-stillwater-ida.org

Merrick Chamber of Commerce
Marian Farker-Gutin, President
PO Box 53, Merrick, NY 11566
516-771-1171 Fax: 516-868-6692
Web site: www.merrickchamber.org

Mid-Hudson Pattern for Progress
Jonathan Drapkin, President
Desmond Campus, 6 Albany Post Rd, Newburgh, NY 12550
845-565-4900 Fax: 845-565-4918
Web site: www.pattern-for-progress.org

Miller Place/Mt Sinai/Sound Beach/Rocky Point Chamber of Commerce
Maureen Schneider, President
PO Box 512, Miller Place, NY 11764
631-821-1313
e-mail: sch1999@aol.com
Web site: www.cdmlongisland.com

Mineola Chamber of Commerce
Steven Ford, President
PO Box 62, Mineola, NY 11501
516-408-3554 Fax: 516-408-3554
Web site: www.mineolachamber.com

Mohawk Valley Chamber of Commerce
Radisson Hotel, Suite 1, 200 Genessee St, Utica, NY 13502
315-724-3151 Fax: 315-724-3177
e-mail: info@mvchamber.org
Web site: www.mvchamber.org

Mohawk Valley Economic Development District
Michael Reese, Executive Director

Offices and agencies generally appear in alphabetical order, except when specific order is requested by listee.

CHAMBERS OF COMMERCE/ECONOMIC DEVELOPMENT ORGANIZATIONS

26 W Main St, PO Box 69, Mohawk, NY 13407-0106
315-866-4671 Fax: 315-866-9862
e-mail: mvedd@twcny.rr.com
Web site: www.mvedd.org

Mohawk Valley Economic Development Growth Enterprises
Shawna Candella Papale, Senior VP Mktg & Economic Develop
153 Brooks Rd, Rome, NY 13441-4105
315-338-0393 or 800-765-4990 Fax: 315-338-5694
e-mail: info@mvedge.org
Web site: www.mvedge.org

Monroe County Industrial Development Agency (COMIDA)
Judy Seil, Acting Executive Director
CityPlace, 50 W Main St, Suite 8100, Rochester, NY 14614
585-753-2022 Fax: 585-753-2028
Web site: www.growmonroe.org

Montgomery County Chamber of Commerce/Montgomery County Partnership
Deborah Auspelmyer, President
PO Box 836, Fonda, NY 12068
518-853-1800 x11 or 800-743-7337 Fax: 518-853-1813
Web site: www.montgomerycountyny.com

Moravia Chamber of Commerce
Mark Wood, President
PO Box 647, Moravia, NY 13118
315-497-1341 Fax: 315-497-9319
Web site: www.cayuganet.org

Mount Kisco Chamber of Commerce
Janet Deane, Executive Director
3 N Moger Ave, Mount Kisco, NY 10549
914-666-7525 Fax: 914-666-7663
e-mail: mtkiscochamber@aol.com
Web site: www.mtkisco.com

Mount Vernon Chamber of Commerce
Constance (Gerrie) Post, President
22 West First Street, Suite 210, PO Box 351, Mount Vernon, NY 10550
914-667-7500 Fax: 914-699-0139
e-mail: mvny.coc@verizon.net
Web site: www.mvnycoc.org

Mount Vernon Industrial Development Agency (City of)
Constance (Gerrie) Post, Secretary
City Hall, Roosevelt Square, Mount Vernon, NY 10550
914-665-2300 Fax: 914-665-2496
e-mail: gerriepost@ci.mount-vernon.ny.us
Web site: www.cmvny.com

Nassau Council of Chambers
Richard M Bivone, President

308 East Meadow Ave, East Meadow, NY 11554
516-396-0200 Fax: 516-396-5097
e-mail: rmbivone@ncchambers,org
Web site: www.ncchambers.org

Nassau County Industrial Development Agency
Joseph Gioino, Executive Director
1100 Franklin Ave, Suite 300, Garden City, NY 11530
516-571-4160 Fax: 516-571-4161
e-mail: jgioino@nassauida.com
Web site: www.nassauida.com

New City Chamber of Commerce
Michael DiBella, President
PO Box 2021, New City, NY 10956
845-638-1395 Fax: 845-638-1395
e-mail: mdibe@optonline.net
Web site: www.newcitychamberofcommerce.org

New Paltz Regional Chamber of Commerce
Joyce M Minard, President
124 Main St, New Paltz, NY 12561-1525
845-255-0243 Fax: 845-255-5189
e-mail: info@newpaltzchamber.org
Web site: www.newpaltzchamber.org

New Rochelle, Chamber of Commerce, Inc
Frank Dursi, President
459 Main St, New Rochelle, NY 10801-6412
914-632-5700 or 914-632-7222 Fax: 914-632-0708
Web site: www.newrochellechamber.org

New York Chamber of Commerce (Greater New York)
Mark S Jaffe, President & CEO
172 Madison Ave, 7th fl, New York, NY 10016
212-686-7220 Fax: 212-686-7232
e-mail: info@chamber.com
Web site: www.chamber.com

New York City, Partnership for
Kathryn S Wylde, President & CEO
One Battery Park Plaza, 5th Floor, New York, NY 10004
212-493-7400 Fax: 212-344-3344
e-mail: info@pfnyc.org
Web site: www.pfnyc.org

New Yorktown Chamber of Commerce (The)
Michael Turton, Executive Director
Parkside Corner, PO Box 632, Suite 203, Yorktown Heights, NY 10598
914-245-4599 Fax: 914-734-7171
e-mail: staff@yorktownchamber.org
Web site: www.yorktownchamber.org

Newark Chamber of Commerce
Gregory Gray, President

Offices and agencies generally appear in alphabetical order, except when specific order is requested by listee.

CHAMBERS OF COMMERCE/ECONOMIC DEVELOPMENT ORGANIZATIONS

203 W Miller St, Newark, NY 14513
315-331-2705 Fax: 315-331-2705
e-mail: newarkcc@redsuspenders.com
Web site: www.newarknychamber.org

Niagara County Ind Dev Agency
Samuel M Ferraro, Executive Director
6311 Inducon Corporate Dr, Ste 1, Sanborn, NY 14132-9099
716-278-8750 Fax: 716-278-8757
e-mail: sam.ferraro@niagaracounty.com
Web site: www.ncida.org

Niagara USA Chamber of Commerce
Thomas Kraus, President
6311 Inducon Corporate Dr, Sanborn, NY 14132
716-285-9141 Fax: 716-285-0941
e-mail: rlnewman@niagarachamber.org
Web site: www.niagarachamber.org

North Fork Chamber of Commerce
Sal Saporito, President
PO Box 1415, Southold, NY 11971
631-765-3161 Fax: 631-765-3161
e-mail: info@northforkchamber.org
Web site: www.northforkchamber.org

North Greenbush IDA
Paul Tazbir, Chairman
2 Douglas Street, Wynantskill, NY 12198-7561
518-283-5313 Fax: 518-283-5345
e-mail: tazbir@townofng.com

North Warren Chamber of Commerce
Greg Beckler, President
PO Box 490, Chestertown, NY 12817
518-494-2722 or 888-404-2722 Fax: 518-494-2722
e-mail: chamber@netheaven.com
Web site: www.adirondacklakesandrivers.com

Nyack Chamber of Commerce
Lorie Reynolds, Executive Director
PO Box 677, Nyack, NY 10960
845-353-2221 Fax: 845-353-4204
e-mail: info@nyack-ny.com
Web site: www.nyack-ny.com

Oceanside Chamber of Commerce
Robert E Towers, President
PO Box 1, Oceanside, NY 11572
516-763-9177 Fax: 516-766-4575
Web site: www.oceansidechamber.org

Ogdensburg Chamber of Commerce (Greater Ogdensburg)
Laura Ashley, Executive Director
1020 Park Street, Ogdensburg, NY 13669
315-393-3620 Fax: 315-393-1380
e-mail: chamber@gisco.net
Web site: www.ogdensburgny.com

Olean Area Chamber of Commerce (Greater Olean)
John Sayegh, COO
120 N Union Street, Olean, NY 14760
716-372-4433 Fax: 716-372-7912
e-mail: info@oleanny.com
Web site: www.oleanny.com

Oneida Chamber of Commerce (Greater Oneida Area)
Brett Bogardus, Executive Director
136 Lenox Ave, Oneida, NY 13421
315-363-4300 Fax: 315-361-4558
e-mail: oneidach@dreamscape.com
Web site: www.oneidachamber.com

Oneida Industrial Development Agency (City of)
John Haskell, Chairman
Municipal Bldg, 109 N Main St, Oneida, NY 13421
315-363-4800 Fax: 315-363-9558

Onondaga County Industrial Development Agency
Donald Western, Executive Director
421 Montgomery St, 14th Fl, Civic Ctr Bldg, Syracuse, NY 13202
315-435-3770 or 877-797-8222 Fax: 315-435-3669
e-mail: info@syracusecentral.com
Web site: www.syracusecentral.com

Ontario Chamber of Commerce
Jay Vanwagner, President
PO Box 100, Ontario, NY 14519-0100
315-524-5886

Ontario County Industrial Development Agency & Economic Development
Michael J Manikowski, Executive Director
20 Ontario Street, Suite 106-B, Canandaigua, NY 14424
585-396-4460 Fax: 585-396-4594
e-mail: golfbag@co.ontario.ny.us
Web site: www.ontariocountydev.org

Orange County Chamber of Commerce Inc
Dr John A D'Ambrosio, President
11 Racquet Rd, Newburgh, NY 12550
845-567-6229 Fax: 845-567-6271
e-mail: drjohn@orangeny.com
Web site: www.orangeny.com

Orange County Partnership
Maureen Halahan, President & CEO
40 Matthews St, Suite 108, Goshen, NY 10924
845-294-2323 Fax: 845-294-8023
e-mail: maureen@ocpartnership.org
Web site: www.ocpartnership.org

Orchard Park Chamber of Commerce
Marilyn Heim, President
4211 N Buffalo St, Ste 14, Orchard Park, NY 14127-2401
716-662-3366 Fax: 716-662-5946
e-mail: opcc@orchardparkchamber.com
Web site: www.orchardparkchamber.com

Orleans County Chamber of Commerce
Tango Hill, Interim Executive Director

Offices and agencies generally appear in alphabetical order, except when specific order is requested by listee.

CHAMBERS OF COMMERCE/ECONOMIC DEVELOPMENT ORGANIZATIONS

121 N Main St, #110, Albion, NY 14411
585-589-7727 Fax: 585-589-7326
e-mail: dkelly@orleanschamber.com
Web site: www.orleanschamber.com

Orleans Economic Development Agency (OEDA)
James Whipple, CEO & CFO
111 West Ave, Albion, NY 14411
585-589-7060 Fax: 585-589-5258
e-mail: jwhipple@orleansdevelopment.org
Web site: www.orleansdevelopment.org

Oswego-Fulton Chamber of Commerce
Jennifer B Hill, Executive Director
44 East Bridge Street, Oswego, NY 13126
315-343-7681 Fax: 315-342-0831
e-mail: gofcc@oswegofultonchamber.com
Web site: www.oswegofultonchamber.com

Oswego County, Operation/Oswego County Industrial Development Agency
L Michael Treadwell, Executive Director
44 West Bridge St, Oswego, NY 13126
315-343-1545 Fax: 315-343-1546
e-mail: ooc@oswegocounty.org
Web site: www.oswegocounty.org

Otsego County Chamber (The)
Tom Armao, Chairman
12 Carbon St, Oneonta, NY 13820
607-432-4500 or 877-5-OTSEGO Fax: 607-432-4506
e-mail: tocc@otsegocountychamber.com
Web site: www.otsegocountychamber.com

Otsego County Economic Development Department & Industrial Development Agency
Lynn Bass, Economic Developer
242 Main St, Oneonta, NY 13820
607-432-8871 Fax: 607-432-5117
e-mail: info@otsegoeconomicdevelopment.com
Web site: www.otsegoeconomicdevelopment.com

Oyster Bay Chamber of Commerce
Alex Gallego, President
PO Box 21, Oyster Bay, NY 11771
516-922-6464 Fax: 516-624-8082
e-mail: alex.gallego@oysterbaychamber.org
Web site: www.oysterbaychamber.org

Painted Post Area Board of Trade
Thomas Magnusen, President
304 South Hamilton Street, Painted Post, NY 14870
607-962-5021 Fax: 607-937-4080
e-mail: info@paintedpostny.com
Web site: www.paintedpostny.com

Patchogue Chamber of Commerce (Greater Patchogue)
Gail Hoag, Executive Director

15 N Ocean Ave, Patchogue, NY 11772
631-475-0121 Fax: 631-475-1599
e-mail: info@patchoguechamber.com
Web site: www.patchoguechamber.com

Peekskill Industrial Development Agency (City of)
Brian Havranek, Executive Director
840 Main Street, Room 31, Peekskill, NY 10566-2016
914-734-4210 Fax: 914-737-2688
Web site: www.cityofpeekskill.com

Perry Area Chamber of Commerce
Lorraine Sturm, Secretary
PO Box 35, Perry, NY 14530
585-237-5040
e-mail: perrchamberny@yahoo.com
Web site: www.perrychamber.com

Plattsburgh-North Country Chamber of Commerce
Garry Douglas, CEO & President
7061 Route 9, PO Box 310, Plattsburgh, NY 12901
518-563-1000 Fax: 516-563-1028
e-mail: chamber@westelcom.com
Web site: www.northcountrychamber.com

Port Chester-Rye Brook Chamber of Commerce
Michael Borrelli, President
110 Willett Ave, Port Chester, NY 10573
914-939-1900 Fax: 914-939-2733
e-mail: info@portchesterryebrookchamber.com
Web site: www.portchesterryebrookchamber.com

Port Jefferson Chamber of Commerce
William Monahan, President
118 W Broadway, Port Jefferson, NY 11777
631-473-1414 Fax: 631-474-4540
e-mail: info@portjeffchamber.com
Web site: www.portjeffchamber.com

Port Morris Local Development Corporation
Peggy Mason, Zone Coordinator
555 Bergen Ave, Bronx, NY 10455
718-292-3113 Fax: 718-292-3115
e-mail: info@sobro.org
Web site: www.sobro.org

Port Washington Chamber of Commerce
Warren Schein, Co-President
329 Main St, PO Box 121, Port Washington, NY 11050
516-883-6566 Fax: 516-883-6591
e-mail: pwcoc@optonline.net
Web site: pwguide.com

Potsdam Chamber of Commerce
James Theodore, President

Offices and agencies generally appear in alphabetical order, except when specific order is requested by listee.

CHAMBERS OF COMMERCE/ECONOMIC DEVELOPMENT ORGANIZATIONS

PO Box 717, One Market St, Potsdam, NY 13676
315-274-9000 Fax: 315-274-9222
e-mail: potsdam@slic.com
Web site: www.potsdam.ny.us/chamber

Poughkeepsie Area Chamber of Commerce
Charles S North, President & CEO
One Civic Center Plaza, Suite 400, Poughkeepsie, NY 12601
845-454-1700 Fax: 845-454-1702
e-mail: office@pokchamb.org
Web site: www.pokchamb.org

Pulaski-Eastern Shore Chamber of Commerce
Nancy Farrell, President
3044 State Route 13, PO Box 34, Pulaski, NY 13142-0034
315-298-2213
e-mail: pulaski@dreamscape.com
Web site: www.pulaskinychamber.com

Putnam County Economic Development Corporation
Kevin Bailey, President
34 Gleneida Ave, Carmel, NY 10512
845-225-2300 Fax: 845-225-0311
e-mail: pedc@computer.net
Web site: www.putnamedc.org

Queens Chamber of Commerce (Borough of)
Raymond J Irrera, President
75-20 Astoria Blvd, Suite 140, Jackson Heights, NY 11370
718-898-8500 Fax: 718-898-8599
e-mail: info@queenschamber.org
Web site: www.queenschamber.org

Red Hook Area Chamber of Commerce
Jeff Ackerly, President
PO Box 254, Red Hook, NY 12571-0254
845-758-0824 Fax: 845-758-0824
e-mail: info@redhookchamber.org
Web site: www.redhookchamber.org

Rensselaer County Regional Chamber of Commerce
Linda Hillman, President
255 River St, Troy, NY 12180
518-274-7020 Fax: 518-272-7729
e-mail: info@renscochamber.com
Web site: www.renscochamber.com

Rhinebeck Chamber of Commerce
Susie Linn, Executive Director
PO Box 42, 23F E Market Street, Rhinebeck, NY 12572
845-876-4778 or 845-876-5904 Fax: 845-876-8624
e-mail: info@rhinebeckchamber.com
Web site: www.rhinebeckchamber.com

Richfield Area Chamber of Commerce
E Lawrence Budro, Executive Director
PO Box 909, Richfield Springs, NY 13439-0909
315-858-2553

Riverhead Chamber of Commerce
Thomas Lennon, President

542 E Main St, Suite 2, Riverhead, NY 11901
631-727-7600 Fax: 631-727-7946
e-mail: info@riverheadchamber.com
Web site: www.riverheadchamber.com

Rochester Business Alliance Inc
Sandra Parker, President & CEO
150 State St, Ste 400, Rochester, NY 14614-1308
585-244-1800 Fax: 585-263-3679
Web site: www.rochesterbusinessalliance.com

Rochester Downtown Development Corporation
Heidi N Zimmer-Meyer, President
183 E Main St, Suite 1300, Rochester, NY 14604
585-546-6920 Fax: 585-546-4784
e-mail: rddc@rddc.org
Web site: www.rochesterdowntown.com

Rochester Economic Development Corporation
Carl Carballata, President
30 Church Street, Room 005A, Rochester, NY 14614
585-428-6808 Fax: 585-428-6042
Web site: www.redco.net

Rockaway Development & Revitalization Corporation
Ivor A Quashie, Zone Coordinator
1920 Mott Ave, 2nd Fl, Far Rockaway, NY 11691
718-327-5300 Fax: 718-327-4990
e-mail: rdrc1@netzero.net
Web site: www.rdrc.org

Rockaways, Chamber of Commerce, Inc
253 Beach 116th St, Rockaway Park, NY 11694
718-634-1300 Fax: 718-634-9623
e-mail: rockawaychamberofcommerce@gmail.com
Web site: www.rockawaychamberofcommerce.com

Rockland Chamber of Commerce
Martin Bernstein, President
PO Box 2001, New City, NY 10956
845-634-5175 Fax: 845-634-6481
e-mail: martreal@aol.com

Rockland Economic Development Corporation
Holly Freedman, President & CEO
1 Blue Hill Plaza, PO Box 1575, Pearl River, NY 10965-1575
845-735-7040 Fax: 845-735-5736
e-mail: info@redc.org
Web site: www.redc.org

Rockville Centre Chamber of Commerce
Michael Shenker, President
PO Box 226, Rockville Centre, NY 11571
516-766-0666 Fax: 516-706-2236
e-mail: info@rockvillecentrechamber.com
Web site: www.rvcchamber.com

Rome Area Chamber of Commerce
William K Guglielmo, President

Offices and agencies generally appear in alphabetical order, except when specific order is requested by listee.

CHAMBERS OF COMMERCE/ECONOMIC DEVELOPMENT ORGANIZATIONS

139 West Dominick St, Rome, NY 13440-5809
315-337-1700 Fax: 315-337-1715
e-mail: info@romechamber.com
Web site: www.romechamber.com

Rome Industrial Development Corporation
Mark Kaucher, Executive Director
139 West Dominick St, Rome, NY 13440-5809
315-337-6360 Fax: 315-337-0918
e-mail: mkaucher@romeny.org
Web site: www.romeny.org

Ronkonkoma Chamber of Commerce
Arnold Quaranta, President
PO Box 2546, Ronkonkoma, NY 11779
631-471-0302
e-mail: info@ronkonkomachamber.com
Web site: www.ronkonkomachamber.com

Sackets Harbor Chamber of Commerce
Cheryl Payne, President
PO Box 17, 301 W Main Street, Sackets Harbor, NY 13685
315-646-2321 Fax: 315-646-2160
e-mail: shvisit@gisco.net
Web site: www.sacketsharborny.com

Sag Harbor Chamber of Commerce
Robert Evjen, President
PO Box 2810, Sag Harbor, NY 11963
631-725-0011 Fax: 631-725-6663
e-mail: sagchamber@peconic.net
Web site: www.sagharborchamber.com

Salamanca Area Chamber of Commerce
Sue Zaprowski, President
26 Main St, Salamanca, NY 14779
716-945-2034 Fax: 716-945-2034
e-mail: sal.cofc@verizon.net
Web site: www.salamancachamber.com

Salamanca Industrial Development Agency
Janet Schmick, Office Manager
225 Wildwood Ave, Salamanca, NY 14779-1547
716-945-3230 Fax: 716-945-8289
Web site: www.salmun.com

Saranac Lake Area Chamber of Commerce
Sylvie D Nelson, Executive Director
39 Main St, Saranac Lake, NY 12983
518-891-1990 or 800-347-1992 Fax: 518-891-7042
e-mail: snelson@saranaclake.com
Web site: www.saranaclake.com

Saratoga County Chamber of Commerce
Joseph W Dalton, Jr, President

28 Clinton St, Saratoga Springs, NY 12866
518-584-3255 Fax: 518-587-0318
e-mail: info@saratoga.org
Web site: www.saratoga.org

Saratoga County Industrial Development Agency
Raymond F Callanan, Chairman
50 W High St, Ballston Spa, NY 12020
518-884-4705 Fax: 518-885-2220
Web site: www.saratogacountyida.org

Saratoga Economic Development Corporation
Kenneth A Green, President
28 Clinton St, Saratoga Springs, NY 12866
518-587-0945 Fax: 518-587-5855
Web site: www.saratogaedc.com

Sayville Chamber of Commerce (Greater Sayville)
William Hoover, President
Bud Van Wyen Memorial BUilding, PO Box 235, Sayville, NY 11782-0235
631-567-5257 Fax: 631-218-0881
e-mail: info@sayvillechamber.com
Web site: www.greatersayvillechamber.com

Schenectady County Chamber of Commerce
Charles P Steiner, President
306 State St, Schenectady, NY 12305-2302
518-372-5656 or 800-962-8007 Fax: 518-370-3217
e-mail: info@schenectadychamber.org
Web site: www.schenectadychamber.org

Schenectady County Industrial Development Agency/Economic Development Corporation
Aurelia Lazzari, Interim President
301 Knott Street, Schenectady, NY 12305
518-393-7252 Fax: 518-393-8687
e-mail: alazzarisedc@aol.com

Schoharie County Chamber of Commerce
Jodie Rutt, Executive Director
113 Park Place, Schoharie, NY 12157
518-295-6550 or 800-41-VISIT Fax: 518-295-7453
e-mail: info@schohariechamber.com
Web site: www.schohariechamber.com

Schoharie County Industrial Development Agency
Ronald Filmer, Director
349 Mineral Springs Rd, Cobleskill, NY 12043
518-234-3751 Fax: 518-234-3951
e-mail: rfscrpc@midtel.net
Web site: www.schohariebiz.com

Schroon Lake Area Chamber of Commerce
John Huston, President

Offices and agencies generally appear in alphabetical order, except when specific order is requested by listee.

CHAMBERS OF COMMERCE/ECONOMIC DEVELOPMENT ORGANIZATIONS

1075 US Rte 9, PO Box 726, Schroon Lake, NY 12870-0726
518-532-7675 or 888-SCHROON
e-mail: info@schroonlake.org
Web site: www.schroonlakechamber.com

Schuyler County Chamber of Commerce
Cynthia Kimble, President
100 N Franklin St, St Rte 14, Watkins Glen, NY 14891
607-535-4300 or 800-607-4552 Fax: 607-535-6243
e-mail: chamber@schuylerny.com
Web site: www.schuylerny.com

Schuyler County Industrial Development Agency
Kevin Murphy, Chairperson
2 N Franklin St, Ste 330, Watkins Glen, NY 14891
607-535-4341 Fax: 607-535-7221
e-mail: info@scoped.biz
Web site: www.scoped.biz

Schuyler County Partnership for Economic Development
Kevin Murphy, Chairperson
2 N Franklin St, Ste 330, Watkins Glen, NY 14891
607-535-4341 Fax: 607-535-7221
e-mail: info@scoped.biz
Web site: www.scoped.biz

Seaford Chamber of Commerce
Carla Powell, President
PO Box 1634, Seaford, NY 11783
516-826-7642 Fax: 516-221-8683
e-mail: chamber@seaford.li
Web site: www.seaford.li

Seneca County Chamber of Commerce
Cedric Alfred Gassney, Executive Director
2020 Rtes 5 & 20 West, PO Box 70, Seneca Falls, NY 13148-0070
315-568-2906 or 800-732-1848 Fax: 315-568-1730
e-mail: windmill@flare.net
Web site: www.senecachamber.org

Seneca County Industrial Development Agency
Glenn R Cooke, Executive Director
One Di Pronio Dr, Waterloo, NY 13165
315-539-1722 Fax: 315-539-4340
e-mail: gcooke@co.seneca.ny.us
Web site: www.senecacountyida.org

Sidney Chamber of Commerce
Greg Hitchcock, President
24 River St, PO Box 2295, Sidney, NY 13838
607-561-2642 Fax: 607-561-2644
e-mail: chambersidneyny@mkl.com
Web site: www.sidneychamber.org

Skaneateles Chamber of Commerce
Susan Dove, Executive Director

PO Box 199, 22 Jordan St, Skaneateles, NY 13152
315-685-0552 Fax: 315-685-0552
e-mail: skaneateles-chamber@worldnet.att.net
Web site: www.skaneateles.com

Sleepy Hollow Chamber of Commerce
JoAnne Murray, President
54 Main Street, Tarrytown, NY 10591-3660
914-631-1705 Fax: 914-366-4291
e-mail: info@sleepyhollowchamber.com
Web site: www.sleepyhollowchamber.com

Smithtown Chamber of Commerce
Barbara Franco, Executive Director
79 E Main Street, Suite E, PO Box 1216, Smithtown, NY 11787
631-979-8069 Fax: 631-979-2206
e-mail: info@smithtownchamber.com
Web site: www.smithtownchamber.com

South Jefferson Chamber of Commerce
Crystal Cobb, President
10924 US Rte 11, S.J. Plaza, Ste 2, Adams, NY 13605-3126
315-232-4215 Fax: 315-232-3967

Southampton Chamber of Commerce
Bob Schepps, President
76 Main St, Southampton, NY 11968
631-283-0402 Fax: 631-283-8707
e-mail: info@southamptonchamber.com
Web site: www.southamptonchamber.com

Southeastern New York, Council of Industry of
Frank Falatyn, President
6 Albany Post Rd, Newburgh, NY 12550
845-565-1355 Fax: 845-565-4918
e-mail: hking@councilofindustry.org
Web site: www.councilofindustry.org

Southern Dutchess Chamber of Commerce (Greater Southern Dutchess)
Frank Capone, Chairman
Nussbickel Building, 2582 S Ave (Route 9D), Wappingers Falls, NY 12590
845-296-0001 Fax: 845-296-0006
e-mail: webmaster@gsdcc.org
Web site: www.gsdcc.org

Southern Saratoga County Chamber of Commerce
Peter L Aust, President & CEO
PO Box 399, Clifton Park, NY 12065
518-371-7748 Fax: 518-371-5025
e-mail: info@southernsaratoga.org
Web site: www.ssccc.org

Southern Tier Economic Growth Inc
George Miner, President

Offices and agencies generally appear in alphabetical order, except when specific order is requested by listee.

CHAMBERS OF COMMERCE/ECONOMIC DEVELOPMENT ORGANIZATIONS

400 Church St, Elmira, NY 14901
607-733-6513 Fax: 607-734-2698
e-mail: into@steg.com
Web site: www.steg.com

Southern Ulster County Chamber of Commerce
William Farrell, President
33 Main St, Highland, NY 12528
845-691-6070 Fax: 845-691-9194
e-mail: info@southernulsterchamber.org
Web site: www.southernulsterchamber.org

Springville Area Chamber of Commerce
Duane W Fischer, Executive Director
PO Box 310, Springville, NY 14141-0310
716-592-4746 Fax: 716-592-4746
e-mail: dirascc@aol.com
Web site: www.springvillechamber.com

St James Chamber of Commerce
Marc S Taczanowski, President
PO Box 286, St James, NY 11780
631-584-8510 Fax: 631-862-9839
e-mail: info@stjames.org
Web site: www.stjameschamber.org

St Lawrence County Chamber of Commerce
Karen St Hilaire, Executive Director
101 Main Street, Canton, NY 13617-1248
315-386-4000 or 877-228-7810 Fax: 315-379-0134
e-mail: slccoc@northnet.org
Web site: www.northcountryguide.com

St Lawrence County Industrial Development Agency
Brian Staples, Chairman
80 State Highway 310, Ste 6, Canton, NY 13617-1496
315-379-9806 Fax: 315-386-2573
e-mail: info@slcida.com
Web site: www.slcida.com

Staten Island Chamber of Commerce
Linda M Baran, President & CEO
130 Bay St, Staten Island, NY 10301
718-727-1900 Fax: 718-727-2295
e-mail: info@sichamber.com
Web site: www.sichamber.com

Staten Island Economic Development Corporation
Cesar J Claro, President & CEO
900 South Ave, Ste 402, Staten Island, NY 10314
718-477-1400 Fax: 718-477-0681
e-mail: info@siedc.net
Web site: www.siedc.net

Steuben County Industrial Development Agency
James P Sherron, Executive Director

7234 Rte 54, PO Box 393, Bath, NY 14810-0390
607-776-3316 Fax: 607-776-5039
e-mail: scida@steubencountyida.com
Web site: www.steubencountyida.com

Suffern Chamber of Commerce
Mel Berkowitz, President
PO Box 291, 71 Lafayette Avenue, Suffern, NY 10901
845-357-8424
e-mail: suffernchamberofcommerce@yahoo.com
Web site: www.suffernchamberofcommerce.org

Sullivan County Chamber of Commerce
Terri Hess, President & CEO
452 Broadway, Monticello, NY 12701
845-791-4200 Fax: 845-791-4220
e-mail: chamber@catskills.com
Web site: www.catskills.com

Sullivan County Industrial Development Agency
Jennifer C S Brylinski, Executive Director & COO
1 Cablevision Ctr, Ferndale, NY 12734
845-295-2603 Fax: 845-295-2604
e-mail: scida@hvc.rr.com
Web site: www.sullivanida.com

Syracuse & Central NY, Metropolitan Development Association of
Irwin L Davis, President & CEO
1900 State Tower Bldg, Syracuse, NY 13202
315-422-8284 Fax: 315-471-4503
e-mail: rsimpson@mda-cny.com
Web site: www.mda-cny.com

Syracuse Chamber of Commerce (Greater Syracuse)
Darlene Kerr, President
572 S Salina St, Syracuse, NY 13202-3320
315-470-1800 Fax: 315-471-8545
e-mail: info@syracusechamber.com
Web site: www.syracusechamber.com

Syracuse Economic Development
Patrice Bey, Zone Coordinator
233 East Washington St, Room 312, City Hall, Syracuse, NY 13202
315-448-8100 Fax: 315-448-8036
e-mail: info@edsyracuse.com
Web site: www.edsyracuse.com

Syracuse Industrial Development Agency
David Michel, Administrative Director
City Hall, 233 E Washington St, Syracuse, NY 13202
315-448-8100 Fax: 315-448-8036
Web site: www.syracuse.ny.us

Three Rivers Development Foundation Inc
Jack Benjamin, President

Offices and agencies generally appear in alphabetical order, except when specific order is requested by listee.

CHAMBERS OF COMMERCE/ECONOMIC DEVELOPMENT ORGANIZATIONS

114 Pine St, Suite 201, Corning, NY 14830
607-962-4693 Fax: 607-936-9132
e-mail: info@threeriversdevelopment.com
Web site: www.threeriversdevelopment.com

Ticonderoga Area Chamber of Commerce
Debra Malaney, Executive Director
94 Montcalm Street, Suite 1, Ticonderoga, NY 12883
518-585-6619 Fax: 518-585-9184
e-mail: chamberinfo@bluemoo.net
Web site: www.ticonderogany.com

Tioga County Chamber of Commerce
Martha Sauerbrey, President & CEO
80 North Avenue, Owego, NY 13827
607-687-2020 Fax: 607-687-9028
e-mail: business@tiogachamber.com
Web site: www.tiogachamber.com

Tioga County Industrial Development Agency
Aaron Gowan, Chairman
County Office Bldg, 56 Main Street, Owego, NY 13827
607-687-8259 Fax: 607-687-1435
e-mail: ida@developtioga.com
Web site: www.developtioga.com

Tompkins County Area Development
Michael Stamm, President
200 E Buffalo St, Ste 102A, Ithaca, NY 14850
607-273-0005 Fax: 607-273-8964
e-mail: info@tcad.org
Web site: www.tcad.org

Tompkins County Chamber of Commerce
Jean McPheeters, President
904 E Shore Drive, Ithaca, NY 14850
607-273-7080 Fax: 607-272-7617
e-mail: jean@tompkinschamber.org
Web site: www.tompkinschamber.org

Tonawanda (Town Of) Development Corporation
Robert L Dimmig, Executive Director
169 Sheridan Parkside Dr, Tonawanda, NY 14150
716-871-8072 Fax: 716-871-8073
e-mail: ttdc@tonawanda.ny.us
Web site: www.tonawanda.com

Tonawandas, Chamber of Commerce of the
David Burgio, President
15 Webster St, North Tonawanda, NY 14120
716-692-5120 Fax: 716-692-1867
e-mail: chamber@the-tonawandas.com
Web site: www.the-tonawandas.com

Tri-State Chamber of Commerce
Michael Loftus, President

PO Box 386, Lakeville, CT 06039-0386
860-435-0740 or 860-435-2000
e-mail: info@tristatechamber.com
Web site: www.tristatechamber.com

Tupper Lake Chamber of Commerce
Marti Mozdzier, Executive Director
121 Park Street, PO Box 987, Tupper Lake, NY 12986
518-359-3328 Fax: 518-359-9099
e-mail: visittupper@tupperlakeinfo.com
Web site: www.tupperlakeinfo.com

Ulster County Chamber of Commerce
Ward Todd, President
55 Albany Ave, Kingston, NY 12401
845-338-5100 Fax: 845-338-0968
e-mail: info@ulsterchamber.org
Web site: www.ulsterchamber.org

Ulster County Development Corporation/Ulster County Industrial Development Agency
Lance Matteson, President
5 Development Court, Kingston, NY 12401
845-338-8840 or 800-7-ULSTER Fax: 845-338-0409
e-mail: develop@ulsterny.com
Web site: www.ulsterny.com

Union Local Development Corporation (Town of)
Joseph M Moody, Director of Economic Development
3111 E Main St, Endwell, NY 13760
607-786-2900 Fax: 607-786-2998
e-mail: economicdevelopment@townofunion.com
Web site: www.townofunion.com

Utica Industrial Development Agency (City of)
Joseph H Hobika, Jr, Executive Director
One Kennedy Plz, Utica, NY 13501
315-792-0287 Fax: 315-792-9819
e-mail: jhobikajr@cityofutica.com
Web site: www.cityofutica.com

Valley Stream Chamber of Commerce
Boris Klerer, President
PO Box 1016, Valley Stream, NY 11580-1016
516-825-1741 Fax: 516-825-1741
Web site: www.vscc.org

Victor Chamber of Commerce
Mike Vuolo, President
37 East Main Street, Victor, NY 14564
585-742-1476 Fax: 585-924-0523
e-mail: victorchamber@aol.com
Web site: www.victorchamber.com

Waddington Chamber of Commerce
Alicia Murphy, President

Offices and agencies generally appear in alphabetical order, except when specific order is requested by listee.

CHAMBERS OF COMMERCE/ECONOMIC DEVELOPMENT ORGANIZATIONS

PO Box 291, Waddington, NY 13694
315-388-4079 or 315-388-5576
e-mail: waddingtonchamber@gmail.com
Web site: www.waddingtonny.us/chamber

Wantagh Chamber of Commerce
Joseph Farinella, President
PO Box 660, Wantagh, NY 11793
516-679-0100 or 516-781-6145
e-mail: wantaghchamber@wantaghmall.org
Web site: www.wantaghmall.org

Warren & Washington Industrial Development Agency
Nicholas Caimano, Chairman
5 Warren St, Suite 210, Glens Falls, NY 12801
518-792-1312 Fax: 518-792-4147
e-mail: mail@warren-washingtonida.com
Web site: www.warren-washingtonida.com

Warren County Economic Development Corporation
Leonard Fosbrook, President
234 Glen Street, Glens Falls, NY 12801
518-761-6007 Fax: 518-761-9053
e-mail: info@warrencounty.org
Web site: www.warrencounty.org

Warrensburg Chamber of Commerce
Lynn Smith, President
3847 Main St, Warrensburg, NY 12885
518-623-2161 Fax: 518-623-2184
e-mail: info@warrensburgchamber.com
Web site: www.warrensburgchamber.com

Warsaw Chamber of Commerce (Greater Warsaw)
Dolly Pierson, President
PO Box 221, Warsaw, NY 14569
585-786-3080 Fax: 585-786-3083
e-mail: info@warsawchamber.com
Web site: warsawchamber.com

Warwick Valley Chamber of Commerce
Linda Glohs, Executive Director
South St, Caboose, PO Box 202, Warwick, NY 10990
845-986-2720 Fax: 914-986-6982
e-mail: info@warwickcc.org
Web site: www.warwickcc.org

Washington County Local Development Corporation
Mark Galough, Executive Director
383 Broadway, Building A, Fort Edward, NY 12828
518-746-2292 Fax: 518-746-2293
e-mail: info@wcldc.org
Web site: www.wcldc.org

Watertown Empire Zone
R Michael N'dolo, Zone Coodinator

PO Box 3367, Saratoga Springs, NY 12866
315-782-1167 Fax: 518-899-9642
e-mail: michael@camoinassociates.com
Web site: www.watertownempirezone.com

Watertown-North Country Chamber of Commerce (Greater Watertown)
Karen Delmonico, President & CEO
1241 Coffeen St, Watertown, NY 13601
315-788-4400 Fax: 315-788-3369
e-mail: chamber@watertownny.com
Web site: www.watertownny.com

Wayne County Industrial Development Agency & Economic Development
Margaret Churchill, Executive Director
16 William St, Lyons, NY 14489
315-946-5917 or 888-219-2963 Fax: 315-946-5918
e-mail: wedcny@co.wayne.ny.us
Web site: www.wedcny.org

Webster Chamber of Commerce
Elizabeth Bernard, Administrator
26 E Main St, Webster, NY 14580-3280
585-265-3960 Fax: 585-265-3702
e-mail: info@websterchamber.com
Web site: www.websterchamber.com

Wellsville Area Chamber of Commerce
Steven Havey, Executive Director
114 N Main St, Wellsville, NY 14895
585-593-5080 Fax: 585-593-5088
e-mail: wlsvchamber@adelphia.net
Web site: www.wellsvilleareachamber.com

West Seneca Chamber of Commerce
Michelle Monaco, President
950A Union Rd, Suite 5, West Seneca, NY 14224
716-674-4900 Fax: 716-674-5846
e-mail: michellemonaco@shellfab.com
Web site: www.westseneca.org

West Side Chamber of Commerce
Andrew Albert, Executive Director
PO Box 1060, Planetarium Station, New York, NY 10024
212-541-8880 Fax: 212-541-8883
e-mail: mail@westsidechamber.org
Web site: www.westsidechamber.org

Westchester County Association Inc (The)
William M Mooney, Jr, President
707 Westchester Ave, Suite 213, White Plains, NY 10604
914-948-6444 Fax: 914-948-6913
e-mail: wmooney@westchester.org
Web site: www.westchester.org

Westchester County Chamber of Commerce
Dr Marsha Gordon, President & CEO

Offices and agencies generally appear in alphabetical order, except when specific order is requested by listee.

CHAMBERS OF COMMERCE/ECONOMIC DEVELOPMENT ORGANIZATIONS

108 Corporate Park Dr, Ste 101, White Plains, NY 10604
914-948-2110 Fax: 914-948-0122
e-mail: mpgordon@westchesterny.org
Web site: www.westchesterny.org

Westchester County Industrial Development Agency
Theresa G Waivada, Executive Director
Room 903, Michaelian Office Building, 148 Martine Avenue, White Plains, NY 10601
914-995-2916 Fax: 914-995-3044
e-mail: mgg8@westchestergov.com
Web site: http://economic.westchestergov.com

Westfield/Barcelona Chamber of Commerce
Maureen DelBalso, President
27 East Main St, Westfield, NY 14787-1319
716-326-4000
e-mail: mdelbalso@westfieldrepublican.com
Web site: www.chautauquachamber.org

Westhampton Chamber of Commerce (Greater Westhampton)
Robert Murray, President
PO Box 1228, Westhampton Beach, NY 11978
631-288-3337 Fax: 631-288-3322
e-mail: info@whbcc.org
Web site: www.whbcc.org

Whiteface Mountain Regional Visitor's Bureau
Diane Buckley, Office Manager
PO Box 277, Wilmington, NY 12997
518-946-2255 Fax: 518-946-2683
e-mail: info@whitefaceregion.com
Web site: www.whitefaceregion.com

Willistons Chamber of Commerce
Maura Clancy, President
PO Box 207, Williston Park, NY 11596
516-739-1943 Fax: 516-747-3742
e-mail: info@chamberofthewillistons.org
Web site: www.chamberofthewillistons.org

Woodstock Chamber of Commerce & Arts
Barry Samuels, President
PO Box 36, Woodstock, NY 12498
845-679-2205
e-mail: info@woodstockchamber.com
Web site: www.woodstockchamber.com

Wyoming County Chamber of Commerce
James M Pierce, Executive Director
6470 Route 20A, Suite 2, Perry, NY 14530-9798
585-237-0230 or 800-951-9774 Fax: 585-237-0231
e-mail: info@wycochamber.org
Web site: www.wycochamber.org

Yates County Chamber of Commerce
Michael Linehan, President & CEO
2375 Rte 14A, Penn Yan, NY 14527
800-868-YATES Fax: 315-536-3791
e-mail: info@yatesny.com
Web site: www.yatesny.com

Yates County Industrial Development Agency
One Keuka Business Park, Suite 104, Penn Yan, NY 14527
315-536-7328 Fax: 315-536-2389
e-mail: info@yatesida.com
Web site: www.yatesida.com

Yonkers Chamber of Commerce
Kevin T Cacace, President
20 S Broadway, Ste 1207, Yonkers, NY 10701
914-963-0332 Fax: 914-963-0455
e-mail: info@yonkerschamber.com
Web site: www.yonkerschamber.com

Yonkers Economic Development/Yonkers Industrial Development Agency (City of)
Edward A Sheeran, Executive Director
City Hall, 40 South Broadway, Rm 416, Yonkers, NY 10701
914-377-6797 Fax: 914-377-6003
e-mail: info@cityofyonkersida.com
Web site: www.cityofyonkersida.com

Offices and agencies generally appear in alphabetical order, except when specific order is requested by listee.

NEWS MEDIA

This chapter identifies key journalists and editorial management for daily and weekly newspapers in New York State, major news services with reporters assigned to cover State government, radio stations with a news format and television stations with news staff.

Newspapers

Newspapers included in this chapter employ reporters who cover state and regional news. The newspapers are listed alphabetically by primary city served.

ALBANY

Legislative Gazette *Weekly Circulation: 14,200*

Legislative Gazette
Empire State Plaza, Concourse Level, Room 106, PO Box 7329, Albany, NY 12224
518-473-9739 Fax: 518-486-7394
e-mail: editor@legislativegazette.com
Web site: www.legislativegazette.com
Executive Publisher/Project Director . . . . Professor Alan S Chartock
Editor . . . . James Gormley
General Manager & Advertising Director . . . . Glenn S Vadney
 e-mail: gvadney@legislativegazette.com

Business Review (The) *Weekly Circulation: 10,500*

The Business Review
40 British American Blvd, Latham, NY 12210
518-640-6800 Fax: 518-640-6801
e-mail: albany@bizjournals.com
Web site: www.albany.bizjournals.com
Chairman . . . . Ray Shaw
Publisher . . . . Carolyn M Jones
Editor . . . . Michael Hendricks
Managing Editor . . . . Neil Springer

Times Union *Weekday Circulation: 96,974*

Times Union
PO Box 15000, Albany, NY 12212
518-454-5420 Fax: 518-454-5628
Web site: www.timesunion.com
Publisher . . . . Mark E Aldam
 e-mail: maldam@timesunion.com
Vice President & Editor . . . . Rex Smith
 e-mail: rsmith@timesunion.com
Managing Editor . . . . Mary Fran Gleason
 e-mail: mgleason@timesunion.com
Editor, Opinion Pages . . . . Joann M Crupi
 e-mail: jcrupi@timesunion.com
Vice President, Associate Publisher & General Manager . . George R Hearst, III
 e-mail: ghearst@timesunion.com
Vice President, Advertising . . . . Kathleen Hallion
 e-mail: khallion@timesunion.com
Circulation Director . . . . John DeAugustine
 e-mail: jdeaugustine@timesunion.com

AMSTERDAM

Recorder (The) *Weekly Circulation: 8,000*

Recorder (The)
One Venner Rd, Amsterdam, NY 12010
518-843-1100 or 800-453-6397 Fax: 518-843-6580
e-mail: news@recordernews.com
Web site: www.recordernews.com
Publisher . . . . Kevin McClary
 e-mail: kevin@recordernews.com
Director, News Operations . . . . Geoff Dylong
 e-mail: geoff@recordernews.com
Advertising/Marketing Director . . . . Brian Krohn
 e-mail: briankrohn@recordernews.com
Executive Editor . . . . Robert Lindsay
 e-mail: news@recordernews.com
Circulation Director . . . . Lisa Guadagno
 e-mail: circulation@recordernews.com

AUBURN

Citizen (The) *Circulation: Daily 11,770; Sunday 13,600*

Auburn Publishers Inc
25 Dill St, Auburn, NY 13021
315-253-5311 Fax: 315-253-6031
e-mail: rick.emanuel@lee.net
Web site: www.auburnpub.com
Publisher . . . . Rick Emanuel
 e-mail: rick.emanuel@lee.net
Circulation Director . . . . Mark Kukiela
 e-mail: mark.kukiela@lee.net
Executive Editor . . . . Jeremy Boyer
 e-mail: jeremy.boyer@lee.net
Advertising Director . . . . Michael Rifanburg
 e-mail: michael.rifanburg@lee.net

Offices and agencies generally appear in alphabetical order, except when specific order is requested by listee.

NEWS MEDIA / Newspapers

BATAVIA

Daily News (The) *Weekday Circulation: 13,018*

Batavia Newspapers Corp
2 Apollo Drive, PO Box 870, Batavia, NY 14020
585-343-8000 Fax: 585-343-2623 or
e-mail: news@batavianews.com
Publisher . . . . Thomas Turnbill
Editorial Page Editor . . . . Sharon Larsen
Managing Editor . . . . Mark Graczyk
News Editor . . . . Dirk Hoffman

BINGHAMTON

Press & Sun Bulletin *Weekday Circulation: 37,915*

Gannet Co Inc
PO Box 1270, Binghamton, NY 13902-1270
607-798-1151 Fax: 607-798-1113
Web site: www.pressconnects.com
Executive Editor . . . . Calvin Stovall
  e-mail: cstovall@binghamt.gannett.com
Assistant Managing Editor - Nights . . . . Al Vieira
  e-mail: avieira@binghamt.gannett.com
Assistant Managing Editor - Online . . . . Stephen W Spero
  e-mail: sspero@binghamt.gannett.com
Editorial Page . . . . Mary Pat Hyland
  e-mail: mphyland@binghamt.gannett.com
Advertising Director . . . . Jodie Riesbeck
  e-mail: jriesbec@binghant.gannett.com

BRONXVILLE-EASTCHESTER

Review Press *Weekday Circulation: 4,393*

Journal News (The)/Gannett Co Inc
One Gannett Drive, White Plains, NY 10604
914-694-9300 Fax: 914-694-5018
e-mail: reviewpress@journalnews.com
Web site: www.thejournalnews.com
Editor/Vice President, News . . . . Henry Freeman
President/Publisher . . . . Tom Donovan
Vice President Circulation . . . . Anthony Simmons
Vice President Marketing . . . . John Green

BROOKLYN

Brooklyn Phoenix *Weekly Circulation: 13,000*

Brooklyn Eagle Publications
30 Henry St, Brooklyn, NY 11201
718-858-2300 Fax: 718-858-4483
e-mail: edit@brooklyneagle.net

Brooklyn Daily Eagle *Weekly Circulation: 12,500*

Brooklyn Eagle Publications
30 Henry St, Brooklyn, NY 11201
718-858-2300 Fax: 718-858-4483
e-mail: edit@brooklyneagle.net

Brooklyn Heights Press *Weekly Circulation: 12,500*

Brooklyn Eagle Publications
30 Henry St, Brooklyn, NY 11201
718-858-2300 Fax: 718-858-4483
e-mail: edit@brooklyneagle.net
Managing Editor . . . . Raanan Geberer
Legal Editor . . . . Vacant

Canarsie Courier *Weekly Circulation: 10,000*

Canarsie Courier
1142 East 92nd Street, Brooklyn, NY 11236
718-257-0600 Fax: 718-272-0870
e-mail: canarsiec@aol.com
Web site: www.canarsiecourier.com
Publisher . . . . Sandra Greco
Publisher . . . . Donna M Marra
Managing Editor . . . . Charles Rogers

Daily Challenge *Weekday Circulation: 81,000*

Daily Challenge
1195 Atlantic Ave, Brooklyn, NY 11216
718-636-9500 Fax: 718-857-9115
e-mail: challengegroup@yahoo.com
Web site: www.challenge-group.com
Publisher . . . . Thomas H Watkins, Jr
Managing Editor . . . . Gary Brown

BUFFALO

Buffalo Business First *Weekly Circulation: 10,000*

Buffalo Business First
465 Main Street, Buffalo, NY 14203-1793
716-541-1600 Fax: 716-854-3394
e-mail: buffalo@bizjournals.com
Web site: buffalo.bizjournals.com
Publisher . . . . Jack Connors
Editor . . . . Jeff Wright
Managing Editor . . . . Tim O'Shei

Offices and agencies generally appear in alphabetical order, except when specific order is requested by listee.

NEWS MEDIA / Newspapers

Buffalo News (The) *Weekday Circulation: 191,000*

Buffalo News (The)
One News Plaza 3rd Fl, PO Box 100, Buffalo, NY 14240
716-849-4444 Fax: 716-856-5150
Web site: www.buffalo.com
Editor . . . . Margaret M Sullivan
Albany Bureau Chief. . . . . Tom Precious
Managing Editor . . . . Edward L Cuddihy
Managing Editor. . . . . Stephen W Bell
News Editor. . . . . John Neville
Political Editor. . . . . Robert McCarthy

CANANDAIGUA

Daily Messenger (The) *Weekday Circulation: 11,900*

Messenger Post Newspapers
73 Buffalo St, Canandaigua, NY 14424
585-394-0770 Fax: 585-394-1675
e-mail: messengerpost@mpnewspapers.com
Web site: www.mpnewspaper.com
President/Publisher . . . . Carl Helbig
Executive Editor. . . . . Robert C Matson
    e-mail: rmatson@mpnewspaper.com
Managing Editor . . . . Kevin Frisch
    e-mail: kfrisch@mpnewspaper.com
Editorial Page Editor . . . . Mike Murphy

CATSKILL

Daily Mail (The) *Weekday Circulation: 3,524*

Hudson Valley Newspapers Inc
414 Main St, PO Box 484, Catskill, NY 12414
518-943-2100 Fax: 518-943-2063
e-mail: publisher@thedailymail.net
Web site: www.thedailymail.net
Publisher . . . . Roger F Coleman
    e-mail: rpignone@thedailymail.net
Editor. . . . . Ray Pignone
    e-mail: rpignone@thedailymail.net
Executive Editor. . . . . Theresa Hyland
    e-mail: thyland@thedailymail.net
Advertising Director . . . . Pamela Geskie

CORNING

Leader (The) *Weekday Circulation: 13,585*

Liberty Group Publishing
34 W Pulteney St, Corning, NY 14830
607-936-4651 Fax: 607-936-9939
Web site: www.the-leader.com
Publisher . . . . Dennis Bruen
    e-mail: dbruen@the-leader.com
Managing Editor . . . . Joe Dunning
    e-mail: jdunning@the-leader.com
Circulation Director . . . . Elmer Kuehner
    e-mail: ekuehner@infoblvd.net

Advertising/Marketing Director . . . . Michelle Passmore
    e-mail: mpassmore@the-leader.net

CORTLAND

Cortland Standard *Weekday Circulation: 10,500*

Cortland Standard Printing Co Inc
110 Main St, PO Box 5548, Cortland, NY 13045
607-756-5665 Fax: 607-756-5665
e-mail: news@cortlandstandard.net
Web site: www.cortland.org/news
Publisher . . . . Kevin R Howe
Managing/News Editor . . . . Kevin Conlon
Opinion Page Editor. . . . . Skip Chapman

DUNKIRK-FREDONIA

Observer *Weekday Circulation: 11,648*

Ogden Newspapers Inc
10 E 2nd St, PO Box 391, Dunkirk, NY 14048-0391
716-366-3000 Fax: 716-366-3005
e-mail: editorial@observertoday.com
Web site: http://observertoday.com
Publisher. . . . . John D'Agostino
    e-mail: jdagostino@observertoday.com
Advertising Director . . . . Meredith V Patton
    e-mail: mvpatton@observertoday.com
News Editor. . . . . Bill Hammond
    e-mail: bhammond@observertoday.com
City Editor. . . . . Doug Coy
    e-mail: dcoy@observertoday.com
Circulation Manager. . . . . Jeffrey Dolley
    e-mail: jdolley@observertoday.com

Star-Gazette *Weekday Circulation: 73,000*

Gannett Co Inc
PO Box 295, Elmira, NY 14902
607-734-5151 or 866-254-0173 Fax: 607-733-4408
Web site: www.stargazette.com
Managing Editor . . . . Lois Wilson
    e-mail: lowilson@stargazette.com
Advertising Director . . . . Jon Spaulding
    e-mail: jspauldi@elmira.gannett.com
Circulation Manager . . . . Rockwell Linda
    e-mail: lcrockwe@elmira.gannett.com

GENEVA

Finger Lakes Times *Circulation: Sunday: 19,102; Daily: 16,185*

Finger Lakes Printing Co
218 Genesee St, PO Box 393, Geneva, NY 14456
800-388-6652 Fax: 315-789-4077
e-mail: fltimes@fltimes.com
Web site: www.fltimes.com
Publisher . . . . Wayne Hemstreet
Managaing Editor . . . . Anne Schuhle

Offices and agencies generally appear in alphabetical order, except when specific order is requested by listee.

NEWS MEDIA / Newspapers

GLENS FALLS

Post-Star (The) *Weekday Circulation: 33,825*

Lee Corporation
Lawrence & Cooper Sts, Glens Falls, NY 12801
518-792-3131 or 800-724-2543 Fax: 518-761-1255
Web site: www.poststar.com
Publisher/Editor.................................Rona Rahlf
   e-mail: rahlf@poststar.com
Managing Editor...............................Ken Tingley
   e-mail: tingley@poststar.com
Operations Director.........................David E Guay
   e-mail: dguay@poststar.com
Advertising Director..........................Jim Murphy
   e-mail: jmurphy@poststar.com

GLOVERSVILLE-JOHNSTOWN

Leader-Herald (The) *Weekday Circulation: 11,500*

William B Collins Co
8 E Fulton St, PO Box 1280, Gloversville, NY 12078
518-725-8616 Fax: 518-725-7407
Web site: www.leaderherald.com
Publisher.....................................Patricia Beck
   e-mail: publisher@leaderherald.com
Managing Editor.................................Tim Fonda
   e-mail: editor@leaderherald.com
Advertising Director............................Doug Hill
   e-mail: adman@leaderherald.com
Circulation Director........................Toni Mosconi
   e-mail: circmanager@leaderherald.com

HERKIMER

Evening Telegram (The) *Weekday Circulation: 6,000*

Liberty Group New York Holdings Inc
111 Green St, Herkimer, NY 13350
315-866-2220 Fax: 315-866-5913
e-mail: news@herkimertelegram.com
Web site: www.herkimertelegram.com
Publisher...................................Beth A Brewer
   e-mail: beth@herkimertelegram.com
Managing Editor.........................Richard A Petrillo
   e-mail: news@herkimertelegram.com
Advertising Director..........................Pam Grande
   e-mail: pam@herkimertelegram.com

HORNELL

Evening Tribune (The) *Weekday Circulation: 7,562*

Liberty Group Publishing
85 Canisteo St, Hornell, NY 14843
607-324-1425 Fax: 607-324-2317
Web site: www.eveningtribune.com
Publisher....................................Kelly Luvison
   e-mail: kellyl@infoblvd.net

General Manager & Marketing Director...........John Frungillo
   e-mail: frungillo@infoblvd.net
Managing Editor..........................Andrew Thompson
   e-mail: a_thompson@infoblvd.com

HUDSON

The Independent *Weekly Circulation: 8,500*

The Independent
PO Box 360, Hillsdale, NY 12529
518-325-4400 Fax: 518-325-4497
e-mail: news@indenews.com
Web site: www.indenews.com
Publisher.....................................Grant Cover
   e-mail: gcover@indenews.com
Editor.......................................Parry Teasdale
   e-mail: pteasdale@indenews.com
Managing Editor..............................Marcia Stamell
   e-mail: mstamell@indenews.com

Register-Star *Weekday Circulation: 6,100*

Johnson Newspaper Corporation
364 Warren St, Hudson, NY 12534
518-828-1616 Fax: 518-828-3870
Web site: www.registerstar.com
Publisher..................................Roger F Coleman
   e-mail: publisher@registerstar.com
Editor.....................................Theresa Hyland
   e-mail: thyland@registerstar.com
Circulation Director.......................Joseph Hoffmann
   e-mail: jhoffman@registerstar.com
Managing Editor........................Erica Freudenberger
   e-mail: efreud@registerstar.com

ITHACA

Ithaca Journal (The) *Weekday Circulation: 10,371*

Gannett Co Inc
123-127 W State St, Ithaca, NY 14850
607-274-9231 Fax: 607-272-4248
Web site: www.theithacajournal.com
President/Publisher............................Jim Fogler
   e-mail: jfogler@ithacajournal.com
Managing Editor...............................Bruce Estes
   e-mail: bestes@ithaca.gannett.com
Advertising Director..........................Carol Becker
   e-mail: cbecker@ithacajournal.com
Circulation Director..........................Steve Miller
   e-mail: stemill@ithaca.gannett.com

Offices and agencies generally appear in alphabetical order, except when specific order is requested by listee.

NEWS MEDIA / Newspapers

JAMESTOWN

Post-Journal *Weekday Circulation: 20,000*

Post-Journal
15 W Second St, PO Box 190, Jamestown, NY 14702-0190
716-487-1111 or 866-756-9600 Fax: 716-664-3119
Web site: www.post-journal.com
Publisher .... Michael Bird
Editor .... Chris Herbst
    e-mail: cherbst@post-journal.com
Circulation Director .... Sean Spielvogel
    e-mail: sspielvogel@post-journal.com

KINGSTON

Daily Freeman *Weekday Circulation: 20,391*

Daily Freeman
79 Hurley Ave, Kingston, NY 12401
845-331-5000 Fax: 845-331-3557
e-mail: publisher@freemanonline.com
Web site: www.dailyfreeman.com
Publisher .... Ira Fusfeld
    e-mail: ifusfeld@journalregister.com
Managing Editor .... Sam Daleo
    e-mail: sdaleo@freemanonline.com
Advertising Director .... Greg Appel
    e-mail: gappel@freemanonline.com
Acting Circulation Director .... David Fogden
    e-mail: dfogden@freemanonline.com
Political Editor .... Hugh Reynolds
    e-mail: hreynolds@freemanonline.com

LITTLE FALLS

Evening Times (The) *Weekday Circulation: 5,042*

Liberty Group Publishing
347 S 2nd St, Little Falls, NY 13365
315-823-3680 Fax: 315-823-4086
e-mail: lfet@twcny.rr.com
Web site: www.littlefallstimes.com
Publisher .... Beth Brewer
Editor .... Larry Neely

LOCKPORT

Lockport Union-Sun & Journal *Weekday Circulation: 12,300*

Greater Niagara Newspapers
170 East Ave, Lockport, NY 14094
716-439-9222 Fax: 716-439-9239
Web site: www.lockportjournal.com
Publisher .... Steve Hall
Managing Editor .... Tim Marren
    e-mail: marrent@gnnewspaper.com
Circulation Manager .... Sue Wadosky

LONG ISLAND

Newsday *Weekday Circulation: 470,316*

Newsday Inc
235 Pinelawn Rd, Melville, NY 11747-4250
631-843-2000 Fax: 631-843-2953
Web site: www.newsday.com
Publisher/President/CEO .... Timothy P Knight
    e-mail: publisher@newsday.com
Editor/Executive Vice President .... John Mancini
    e-mail: editor@newsday.com
Senior Vice President, Advertising .... Ray McCutcheon
    e-mail: advertising@newsday.com
Managing Editor .... Richard Galant
Assistant Managing Editor - Long Island .... Debbie Henley
New York Editor .... Les Payne
Albany Bureau Chief .... Jordan Rau
    e-mail: jordon.rau@newsday.com

Queens Gazette *Weekly Circulation: 90,000*

Queens Gazette
42-16 34th Avenue, Long Island City, NY 11101
718-361-6161 Fax: 718-784-7552
e-mail: qgazette@aol.com
Web site: www.qgazette.com
Publisher/Editor .... Tony Barsamian
Editor .... Linda Wilson
Advertising Director .... Julie Wager

MALONE

Malone Telegram *Weekday Circulation: 6,000*

Johnson Newspaper Corp
469 E Main St, Ste 4, PO Box 69, Malone, NY 12953
518-483-4700 Fax: 518-483-8579
e-mail: news@mtelegram.com
Web site: www.mtelegram.com
Publisher .... Charles Kelly
Editor .... Connie Jenkins

MASSENA

Daily Courier-Observer *Weekday Circulation: 7,800*

Johnson Newspaper Corporation
One Harrowgate Commons, PO Box 300, Massena, NY 13662
315-769-2451 Fax: 315-764-0337
Web site: www.mpcourier.com
Publisher/Editor .... Charles Kelly
Assistant General Manager .... Sean McNamara
Managing Editor-Massena/Pottsdam .... Ryne R Martin
Deputy Managing Editor-Massena/Potsdam .... Matt Akins

Offices and agencies generally appear in alphabetical order, except when specific order is requested by listee.

NEWS MEDIA / Newspapers

MEDINA

Journal-Register *Weekday Circulation: 3,500*

Greater Niagara Newspapers
409-413 Main St, Medina, NY 14103
585-798-1400 Fax: 585-798-0290
e-mail: thejournalregister@mail.com
Web site: www.journal-register.com
Sports Editor .... Michael Wertman
Circulation Director .... Kim Pendergrass
City Editor .... Tim Marren

MIDDLETOWN

Times Herald-Record *Weekday Circulation: 80,000*

Orange County Publications
40 Mulberry St, PO Box 2046, Middletown, NY 10940
845-341-1100 or 800-295-2181 Fax: 845-343-2170
Web site: www.recordonline.com
Publisher .... Joe Vanderhook
   e-mail: mlevine@th-record.com
Managing Editor .... Meg McGuire
   e-mail: mmcguire@th-record.com
City Editor .... Adrianne Reilly
   e-mail: areilly@th-record.com

MOUNT KISCO-NORTH SALEM

Patent Trader *Weekly Circulation: 30,323*

Journal News (The)/Gannett Co Inc
185 Kisco Ave, Mount Kisco, NY 10549
914-666-6222 Fax: 914-666-6013
e-mail: patenttrader@thejournalnews.com
Web site: www.thejournalnews.com
President/Publisher .... Tom Donovan
   e-mail: tdonovan@lohud.com
Editor & Vice President, News .... Henry Freeman
   e-mail: hfreeman1@lohud.com
Vice President, Advertising .... Charlie Rowe
   e-mail: crowe@lohud.com

NEW YORK CITY

New York Law Journal *Weekday Circulation: 16,000*

American Lawyer Media Inc
345 Park Ave, South, 7th Fl, New York, NY 10010
212-779-9200 or 800-888-8300 Fax: 212-696-4287
e-mail: cservice@nylj.com
Web site: www.law.com
Editor-in-Chief .... Kris Fischer
Executive Editor .... Jeff Storey
Senior Writer .... Daniel Wise

Journal of Commerce *Weekly Circulation: 10,000*

Commonwealth Business Media
33 Washington St, Newark, NJ 07102-3107
973-848-7000 Fax: 973-837-7004
Web site: www.joc.com
Vice President/Editorial Director .... Peter M Tirschwell
   e-mail: ptirschwell@joc.com
Editor-in-Chief .... Joseph Bonney
   e-mail: jbonney@joc.com
Editorial Operations Chief .... Barbara Wyker
   e-mail: bwyker@joc.com
Managing Editor .... Chris Brooks
   e-mail: cbrooks@joc.com

Wall Street Journal (The) *Daily Circulation: 2,000,000*

Dow Jones & Company
200 Liberty St, New York, NY 10281
212-416-2000 Fax: 212-416-2255
Web site: www.wsj.com
Vice President/Managing Editor .... Paul Steiger
Editorial Page Editor .... Paul Gigot

People's Weekly World *Weekly Circulation: 27,000*

Long View Publishing Co
235 W 23rd St, New York, NY 10011
212-924-2523 Fax: 212-645-5436
e-mail: pww@pww.org
Web site: www.pww.org
Editor .... Teresa Albano
Managing Editor .... Mark Almberg

New York Post *Weekday Circulation: 686,207*

NYP Holdings Inc
1211 Ave of the Americas, 10th Fl, New York, NY 10036-8790
212-930-8000 Fax: 212-930-8540
Web site: www.nypost.com
Publisher .... Lachlan Murdoch
Editor-in-Chief .... Col Allan
Associate Editor .... Anne Aquilina
Managing Editor .... Colin Myler
Metropolitan Editor .... Jesse Angelo
Editorial Page Editor .... Robert McManus
Bureau Chief & State News Editor .... Frederic Dicker

New York Daily News *Weekday Circulation: 688,584*

New York Daily News
450 West 33rd St, 3rd Fl, New York, NY 10001
212-210-2100 Fax: 212-643-7831 or
Web site: www.nydailynews.com
Publisher .... Mortimer Zuckerman
Deputy Publisher & Editorial Director .... Martin Dunn
Executive Editor .... Michael Goodwin
Senior Managing Editor .... Robert Sapio
Managing Editor .... Bill Boyle

Offices and agencies generally appear in alphabetical order, except when specific order is requested by listee.

NEWS MEDIA / Newspapers

The Independent News *Weekly Circulation: 50,000*

The Independent News
74 Montauk Highway, Suite 19, East Hampton, NY 11937
631-324-2500 Fax: 631-324-2351
Web site: www.indyeastend.com
Co-Publisher .... Jerry J Della Femina
Co-Publisher .... James J Mackin
Editor-in-Chief .... Rick Murphy
Editor .... Carey Landon

New York Observer (The) *Weekday Circulation: 50,000*

The New York Observer
915 Broadway, 9th Floor, New York, NY 10010
212-755-2400 or 800-542-0420 Fax: 212-688-4889
Web site: www.nyobserver.com
Publisher .... Jared Kushner
Editor .... Peter W Kaplan
Managing Editor .... Tom McGeveran
Executive Editor .... Peter Stevenson
National Correspondent .... Joe Conason

New York Times (The) *Weekday Circulation: 1,121,057*

The New York Times
229 W 43rd St, New York, NY 10036
212-556-1234 Fax: 212-556-3690
Web site: www.nytimes.com
Chairman/Publisher .... Arthur Sulzberger, Jr
  e-mail: publisher@nytimes.com
Executive Editor .... Bill Keller
Managing Editor .... Jill Abramson
Managing Editor .... John Geddes

The Putnam County News and Recorder *Weekly Circulation: 4,000*

The Putnam County News and Recorder
86 Main Street, PO Box 185, Cold Spring, NY 10516
845-265-2468 Fax: 845-265-2144
Web site: www.pcnr.com
Publisher .... Brian O'Donnell
Advertising Manager .... Margaret O'Sullivan

Village Voice (The) *Weekly Circulation: 250,000*

Village Voice Media, Inc
36 Cooper Sq, New York, NY 10003
212-475-3300 Fax: 212-475-8944
Web site: www.villagevoice.com
Editor-in-Chief .... Donald H Forst
Managing Editor .... Doug Simmons
Executive Editor .... Laura Conaway

Wave *Weekly Circulation: 12,300*

Wave
88-08 Rockaway Beach Blvd, Rockaway Beach, NY 11693-0097
718-634-4000 Fax: 718-945-0913
e-mail: editor@rockawave.com
Web site: www.rockawave.com
Publisher .... Susan B Locke
Managing Editor .... Howard Schwach

NIAGARA FALLS

Niagara Gazette *Weekday Circulation: 20,268*

Greater Niagara Newspapers
310 Niagara St, PO Box 549, Niagara Falls, NY 14302-0549
716-282-2311 Fax: 716-286-3895
e-mail: newsroom@gnnewspaper.com
Web site: www.niagara-gazette.com
Publisher .... Wayne Lowman
Managing Editor .... David Arkin
Production Director .... Les Rogers

NORWICH

Evening Sun *Weekday Circulation: 5,200*

Snyder Communications Corp
29 Lackawanna Ave, PO Box 151, Norwich, NY 13815
607-334-3276 or 800-836-6780 Fax: 607-334-8273
e-mail: news@evesun.com
Web site: www.evesun.com
Publisher/President .... Richard Snyder
  e-mail: dsnyder@evesun.com
Managing Editor .... Jeffrey Genung
  e-mail: jgenung@evesun.com
Circulation Manager .... Brad Dick
  e-mail: subscribe@evesun.com

OGDENSBURG

Ogdensburg Journal *Weekday Circulation: 5,200*

St Lawrence County Newspapers
308 Isabella St PO Box 409, Ogdensburg, NY 13669
315-393-1000 Fax: 315-393-5108
Web site: www.ogd.com
Editor .... Charles W Kelly
Managing Editor .... James E Reagen

Offices and agencies generally appear in alphabetical order, except when specific order is requested by listee.

NEWS MEDIA / Newspapers

OLEAN

Weekday Circulation: 15,000

Bradford Publications Inc
639 Norton Dr, Olean, NY 14760
716-372-3121 Fax: 716-373-6397
e-mail: news@oleantimesherald.com
Web site: www.oleantimesherald.com
Publisher/General Manager.....................Bill Fitzpatrick
Managing Editor...............................Jim Eckstrom
News Editor.....................................Rick Jozwiak

ONEIDA

Oneida Daily Dispatch *Weekday Circulation: 6,818*

Journal Register Co
130 Broad St, Oneida, NY 13421
315-363-5100 Fax: 315-363-9832
Web site: www.oneidadispatch.com
Publisher..Phillip R Austin
Managing Editor...............................Kurt W Wanfried
Advertising Director............................Karen Alvord
Circulation Director............................Marc Alvord

ONEONTA

Daily Star (The) *Weekday Circulation: 21,000*

Ottaway Newspapers Inc
102 Chestnut St, PO Box 250, Oneonta, NY 13820
607-432-1000 or 800-721-1000 Fax: 607-432-5847
Web site: www.thedailystar.com
Publisher..Al Getler
    e-mail: spollak@thedailystar.com
Editor...Sam Pollak
    e-mail: spollak@thedailystar.com
Managing Editor...............................Cary Brunswick
    e-mail: cary@thedailystar.com

OSWEGO-FULTON

Palladium-Times (The) *Weekday Circulation: 8,500*

The Palladium Times
140 W First St, Oswego, NY 13126
315-343-3800 Fax: 315-343-0273
e-mail: editorial@palltimes.com
Web site: www.pall-times.com
Publisher..Paul Scott
    e-mail: pscott@palltimes.com
Editor..Gary Catt
    e-mail: gary.catt@palltimes.com
Advertising Manager...........................Michael Russo
    e-mail: mrusso@palltimes.com
Circulation......................................Toby Clawson
    e-mail: tclawson@palltimes.com

PLATTSBURGH

Press-Republican *Weekday Circulation: 20,210*

Ottaway Newspapers (The)
170 Margaret St, Plattsburgh, NY 12901
518-561-2300 Fax: 518-561-3362
e-mail: news@pressrepublican.com
Web site: www.pressrepublican.com
Publisher..Robert Parks
Editor-in-Chief..................................Bob Grady
    e-mail: bgrady@pressrepublican.com
News Editor.....................................Lois Clermont
    e-mail: lclermont@pressrepublican.com

POUGHKEEPSIE

Greenwood Lake and West Milford News *Weekly Circulation: 5,000*

Greenwood Lake and West Milford News
61 Windermere Ave, PO Box 1117, Greenwood Lake, NY 10925
845-477-2575 Fax: 845-477-2577
e-mail: glnews@greenwoodlakenews.com
Web site: www.greenwoodlakenews.com
Publisher..Anne Chaimowitz
Editor..Ron Nowak

Poughkeepsie Journal *Weekday Circulation: 40,202*

Gannett Co Inc
85 Civic Center Plz, Poughkeepsie, NY 12601
845-454-2000 Fax: 845-437-4921
e-mail: newsroom@poughkee.gannett.com
Web site: www.poughkeepsiejournal.com
Publisher/President............................Barry Rothfeld
Executive Editor................................Stuart Shinske
    e-mail: newsroom@poughkee.gannett.com
Advertising Director............................Jan Dewey
    e-mail: jdewey@poughkeep.gannett.com
Managing Editor...............................Richard L Kleban
    e-mail: rkleban@poughkee.gannett.com
Circulation Director............................Paul Felicissimo
    e-mail: pfelicis@poughkee.gannett.com

ROCHESTER

Daily Record (The) *Weekly Circulation: 4,500*

Dolan Media Co
PO Box 30006, Rochester, NY 14603-3006
585-232-6920 Fax: 585-232-2740
Web site: www.nydailyrecord.com
Vice President/Publisher.......................Peter L Mio
    e-mail: kevin.momot@nydailyrecord.com
Publications Director...........................Kevin Momot
    e-mail: kevin.momot@nydailyrecord.com
Advertising & Marketing Manager..............Kara Krause

Offices and agencies generally appear in alphabetical order, except when specific order is requested by listee.

NEWS MEDIA / Newspapers

Democrat and Chronicle *Weekday Circulation: 170,000*

Gannett Co Inc
55 Exchange Blvd, Rochester, NY 14614
585-258-2220 Fax: 585-258-2485
e-mail: feedback@democratandchronicle.com
Web site: www.democratandchronicle.com
Editor, VP, News . . . . Karen Magnuson
Assistant Managing Editor, Administration . . . . Matt Dudek
Editoral Page Editor . . . . Jim Lawrence

Suburban News & Hamlin Clarkson Herald *Weekly Circulation: 32,000*

Westside News Inc
1835 North Union Street, PO Box 106, Spencerport, NY 14559
585-352-3411 Fax: 585-352-4811
e-mail: westside@netacc.net
Web site: www.westsidenewsonline.com
Publisher . . . . Keith Ryan
Editor . . . . Evelyn Dow

ROME

Daily Sentinel *Weekday Circulation: 16,500*

Rome Sentinel Co
333 W Dominick St, PO Box 471, Rome, NY 13442-0471
315-337-4000 Fax: 315-337-4704
e-mail: sentinel@rny.com
Web site: www.rny.com
Publisher . . . . Stephen Waters
   e-mail: dswanson@rny.com
Managing Editor . . . . David C Swanson
   e-mail: dswanson@rny.com
Editorial Page Editor . . . . Tom Merz
   e-mail: bcharzuk@rny.com

SALAMANCA

Salamanca Press *Weekday Circulation: 2,200*

Bradford Publishing Co
36 River St, PO Box 111, Salamanca, NY 14779
716-945-1644 Fax: 716-945-4285
e-mail: salpress@eznet.net
Web site: www.salamancapress.com
Publisher/Editor . . . . Laura Howard

SARANAC LAKE

Adirondack Daily Enterprise *Weekday Circulation: 5,000*

Adirondack Publishing Co Inc
54 Broadway, PO Box 318, Saranac Lake, NY 12983
518-891-2600 Fax: 518-891-2756
e-mail: adenews@adirondackguide.com
Web site: www.adirondackguide.com
Publisher . . . . Catherine Moore
   e-mail: cmoore@adirondackenterprise.com
Managing Editor . . . . Peter Crowley
   e-mail: pcrowley@adirondackguide.com
Circulation Manager . . . . Ruby Vann
   e-mail: circulation@adriondackenterprise.com

SARATOGA SPRINGS

Saratogian (The) *Weekday Circulation: 10,000*

Journal Register Company
20 Lake Ave, Saratoga Springs, NY 12866
518-584-4242 Fax: 518-587-7750
e-mail: news@saratogian.com
Web site: www.saratogian.com
Publisher . . . . Frank J McGivern, Sr
   e-mail: blombardo@saratogian.com
Managing Editor . . . . Barbara A Lombardo
   e-mail: blombardo@saratogian.com
Advertising Director . . . . Lauren Rose
   e-mail: lrose@saratogian.com
Circulation Director . . . . Dan Ives
   e-mail: dives@saratogian.com

SCHENECTADY

Daily Gazette (The) *Weekday Circulation: 53,800*

Daily Gazette Co
2345 Maxon Rd Ext, PO Box 1090, Schenectady, NY 12301-1090
518-374-4141 Fax: 518-395-3089
e-mail: gazette@dailygazette.com
Web site: www.dailygazette.com
Editor/Publisher . . . . John E N Hume, III
   e-mail: woodman@dailygazette.com
Managing Editor . . . . Thomas L Woodman
   e-mail: woodman@dailygazette.com
City Editor . . . . George Walsh
   e-mail: walsh1@dailygazette.com

STATEN ISLAND

Staten Island Advance *Circulation: Monday, Tuesday, Wednesday, Friday: 59,000; Thursday: 67,000; Sunday: 77,000*

Advance Publications Inc
950 Fingerboard Rd, Staten Island, NY 10305
718-981-1234 Fax: 718-981-5679
e-mail: newsroom@siadvance.com
Web site: www.silive.com
Publisher . . . . Caroline Harrison
Editor . . . . Brian J Laline
Managing Editor . . . . William A Huus
City Editor . . . . Marge Hack
Editorial Page Editor . . . . Mark Hanley
Political Reporter . . . . Thomas Wrobleski
Legislative Correspondent . . . . Robert Hart

Offices and agencies generally appear in alphabetical order, except when specific order is requested by listee.

NEWS MEDIA / News Services/Magazines

SYRACUSE

Post-Standard (The) *Weekday Circulation: 115,000*

Syracuse Newspapers Inc
1 Clinton Sq, PO Box 4915, Syracuse, NY 13221
315-470-0011 Fax: 315-470-3081
e-mail: letters@syracuse.com
Web site: www.syracuse.com
Executive Director . . . . Michael J Connor
Senior Managing Editor . . . . Stan Linhorst
Managing Editor/Systems . . . . Bart Pollock
Editor/Publisher . . . . Stephen Rogers

TONAWANDA

Tonawanda News *Weekday Circulation: 9,000*

Greater Niagara Newspapers
435 River Rd, North Tonawanda, NY 14120-6809
716-693-1000 Fax: 716-693-0124
Web site: www.tonawanda-news.com
Managing Editor . . . . Carlene Peterson
    e-mail: petersonc@gnnewspaper.com
Circulation Manager . . . . Paul Flaeser
Advertising Manager . . . . Matt Green

TROY

Record (The) *Weekday Circulation: 16,872*

Journal Register Co
501 Broadway, Troy, NY 12180
518-270-1200 Fax: 518-270-1202
e-mail: newsroom@capitalcentral.com
Web site: www.troyrecord.com
Publisher . . . . Michael F O'Sullivan
    e-mail: mosullivan@journalregister.com
Editor . . . . Lisa Robert Lewis
    e-mail: llewis@capitalcentral.com
Advertising Director . . . . Joan Marro Harris
    e-mail: jharris@capitalcentral.com
Circulation Director . . . . Bryan Brown
    e-mail: bbrown@capitalcentral.com

UTICA

Observer-Dispatch *Weekday Circulation: 45,956*

Gannett Co Inc
221 Oriskany Plz, Utica, NY 13501
315-792-5000 Fax: 315-792-5033
e-mail: o-d@uticaod.com
Web site: www.uticaod.com
Editor . . . . Jon Broadbooks
    e-mail: jbroadbo1@utica.gannett.com
President/Publisher . . . . Donna Donovan
    e-mail: ddonovan@utica.gannett.com
Advertising Director . . . . Emilia Borelli
    e-mail: eborelli@utica.gannett.com
Circulation Director . . . . Richard Procida
    e-mail: rprocida@utica.gannett.com

WATERTOWN

Watertown Daily Times *Weekday Circulation: 27,020*

Johnson Newspaper Corp
260 Washington St, Watertown, NY 13601
315-782-1000 Fax: 315-661-2523
e-mail: news@wdt.net
Web site: www.watertowndailytimes.com
Editor . . . . John B Johnson, Jr
Executive Editor . . . . Bert Gault
Managing Editor . . . . Robert Gorman
Legislative Correspondent . . . . Chris Garifo
Washington Correspondent . . . . Marc Heller

WELLSVILLE

Wellsville Daily Reporter/Spectator *Weekday Circulation: 4,400*

Liberty Group Publishing
159 N Main St, Wellsville, NY 14895
585-593-5300 Fax: 585-593-5303
Web site: www.wellsvilledaily.com
Publisher . . . . Oak Duke
Managing Editor . . . . John Anderson
Reporter . . . . Kathryn Ross
Reporter Page Editor . . . . Heather Matta

News Services/Magazines

ABC News (New York Bureau)
7 W 66th St, New York, NY 10023
212-456-7777 Fax: 212-456-2795
Web site: www.abc.com
Bureau Chief . . . . Kristen Sebastian

American Metal Market
1250 Broadway, 26th Floor, New York, NY 10001
212-213-6202 Fax: 212-213-6617
Web site: www.amm.com
Publisher . . . . Martin Abbott
Editor . . . . Jo Isenberg-O'Loughlin
    e-mail: jisenberg@amm.com
Deputy Editor . . . . David Brooks
    e-mail: dbrooks@amm.com

Offices and agencies generally appear in alphabetical order, except when specific order is requested by listee.

NEWS MEDIA / News Services/Magazines

Associated Press (Albany/Upstate Bureau)
645 Albany-Shaker Road, PO Box 11010, Albany, NY 12211-1158
518-458-7821 Fax: 518-438-5891
e-mail: info@ap.org
Web site: www.ap.org
Acting Bureau Chief .... Hank Ackerman
News Editor .... Rik Stevens
Political Editor .... Marc Humbert
Capitol Correspondent .... Michael Gormley

Associated Press (New York/Metro Bureau)
450 West 33rd St, New York, NY 10001
212-621-1670 or 212-621-1676 Fax: 212-621-1679
e-mail: info@ap.org
Web site: www.ap.org
Bureau Chief .... Howard Goldberg
News Editor .... Josh Hoffner
City Hall Reporter .... Sarah Kugler

BNA (formerly Bureau of National Affairs)
PO Box 7169, Albany, NY 12224
518-399-8414 Fax: 518-399-8403
Web site: www.bna.com
NYS Correspondent .... Gerald Silverman

Business Review
40 British American Blvd, Latham, NY 12110
518-640-6800 Fax: 518-640-6801
e-mail: albany@bizjournals.com
Web site: albany.bizjournals.com
Editor .... Mike Hendricks
Managing Editor .... Neil Springer

CBS News (New York Bureau)
524 West 57th St, New York, NY 10019
212-975-4321 Fax: 212-975-9387
Web site: www.cbsnews.com
Assignment Editor .... Brian Lowder
Assignment Editor .... Andrew Friedman

Central New York Business Journal
231 Walton Street, Syracuse, NY 13202
315-472-3104 or 800-836-3539 Fax: 315-472-3644
e-mail: info@cnybj.com
Web site: www.cnybj.com
Publisher .... Norm Poltenson
    e-mail: npoltenson@cnybj.com

City Journal (Manhattan Institute for Policy Research)
52 Vanderbilt Ave, New York, NY 10017
212-599-7000 Fax: 212-599-0371
e-mail: cj@city-journal.org
Web site: www.city-journal.org
Senior Editor .... Steven Malanga
Editor .... Brian C Anderson
Managing Editor .... Benjamin A Plotinsky

Crain's New York Business
711 Third Ave, New York, NY 10017
212-210-0277 Fax: 212-210-0799
Web site: www.crainsny.com
Publisher .... Alair Townsend
Editor .... Greg David
Managing Editor .... Richard Barbieri
Deputy Managing Editor .... Erik Ipsen
Deputy Managing Editor .... Valerie Block
Sr Reporter, Politics, Gov't, Utilities, Environment .. Anne Michaud

Cuyler News Service
PO Box 7205, State Capitol, Albany, NY 12224
518-465-2647 Fax: 518-465-6849
e-mail: efmnews@aol.com
Bureau Chief .... Elizabeth G Flood-Morrow
Legislative Correspondent .... Muriel Gibbons
Legislative Correspondent .... Maria McBride-Bucciferro

Dow Jones Newswires (Dow Jones & Company)
Harborside Financial Ctr, 800 Plaza Two, Jersey City, NJ 07311
201-938-5400 Fax: 201-938-5600
e-mail: spotnews@priority.dowjones.com
Web site: www.djnewswires.com
VP, News Strategy .... Paul J Ingrassia
President, Dow Jones Newspaper Fund .... Richard J Levine
Publisher .... Stephen Acunto

Empire State Report (CINN Worldwide Inc)
PO Box 9001, Mount Vernon, NY 10552
914-966-3180 Fax: 914-966-3264
e-mail: empire@cinn.com
Web site: www.empirestatereport.com

Gannett News Service
150 State St, 2nd Fl, Albany, NY 12207
518-436-9781 Fax: 518-436-0130
e-mail: gannett@albany.net
Web site: www.gannett.com
Bureau Chief .... Jay Gallagher
    e-mail: jgannett@yahoo.com
Correspondent .... Yancey Roy
Correspondent .... Cara Matthews

Hudson Valley Business Journal
86 East Main Street, Wappingers Falls, NY 12590
845-298-6236 Fax: 845-298-6238
e-mail: hvbjmail@aol.com
Web site: www.hvbj.com
Publisher .... Albert Osten
Managing Editor .... Debbie Kwiatoski

ITAR-TASS News Agency
780 Third Ave, 19th Fl, New York, NY 10017
212-245-4250 Fax: 212-245-4258
e-mail: itar@aol.com
Web site: www.itar-tass.com
Bureau Chief .... Vladimir Kikilo

Offices and agencies generally appear in alphabetical order, except when specific order is requested by listee.

NEWS MEDIA / Radio

Inside Albany Productions Inc
Capitol Station, PO Box 7328, Albany, NY 12224
518-426-3771 Fax: 518-426-5396
e-mail: mail@insidealbany.com
Web site: www.insidealbany.com
Reporter/Producer/Co-Host. . . . . Lise Bang-Jensen
Founding Producer/Reporter . . . . David Hepp
Videographer . . . . Gary Glinski

Legislative Correspondents Association
PO Box 7340, State Capitol, 3rd Fl, Albany, NY 12224
518-455-2388
Web site: www.nys.nys.com
Press Room Supervisor . . . . Jean Gutbtodt

Long Island Business News
2150 Smithtown Avenue, Suite 7, Ronkonkoma, NY 11779
631-737-1700 Fax: 631-737-1890
e-mail: www.libn.com
Director Circulation & Information Services . . . . . . Jo Ann Buynoch

Mid-Hudson News Network
42 Marcy Lane, Middletown, NY 10941
845-537-1500 or 845-695-2923 Fax: 845-692-2921
e-mail: news@midhudsonnews.com/news@empirestatesnews.net
Web site: www.midhudsonnews.com; www.empirestatenews.net
Managing Director/Publisher . . . . Hank Gross

NBC News (New York Bureau)
30 Rockefeller Plaza, 300 West, New York, NY 10112
212-664-5900 Fax: 212-790-4711
Web site: www.nbc.com
Bureau Chief . . . . Roxanne Garcia
Desk Producer . . . . Frank Salamone

NY Capitolwire (Associated Press)
PO Box 7248, Albany, NY 12224
518-432-0710 Fax: 518-432-0275
e-mail: info@capitolwire.com
Web site: www.capitolwire.com

New York Magazine (New York Metro LLC)
444 Madison Ave, 4th Floor, New York, NY 10022-6999
212-508-0700 Fax: 212-583-7507
Web site: www.newyorkmetro.com
Editor-in-Chief. . . . . Adam Moss
Executive Editor . . . . John Homans
Managing Editor . . . . Ann Clarke
Contributing Editor, 'The City Politic' . . . . Greg Sargent
Deputy Editor . . . . Jon Gluck

Newsweek Magazine (MSNBC, Microsoft Corp)
251 W 57th St, New York, NY 10019
212-445-4000 Fax: 212-445-4695
e-mail: letters@newsweek.com
Web site: www.newsweek.msnbc.com
Chairman/Editor-in-Chief . . . . Richard M Smith
Editor. . . . . Mark Whitaker
Director Communications . . . . Ken Weine

Ottaway News Service (NYS only)
State Capitol, 3rd Fl, Albany, NY 12224
518-463-1157 Fax: 518-463-7486

Reuters (New York Bureau)
Three Times Square, New York, NY 10036
646-223-6280 Fax: 646-223-6289
Web site: www.reuters.com
Correspondent . . . . Ellen Wulfhorst
Bureau Chief, Northeastern United States. . . . . Mark Egan
Correspondent, Sports . . . . Larry Fine
Correspondent . . . . Claudia Parsons
    e-mail: claudia.parsons@reuters.com
Correspondent . . . . Daniel Trotta

Rochester Business Journal
45 East Avenue, Suite 500, Rochester, NY 14604
585-546-8303 Fax: 585-546-3398
e-mail: rbj@rbj.net
Web site: www.rbj.net
President/Publisher . . . . Susan R Holliday
    e-mail: sholliday@rbj.net
Vice President & Editor . . . . Paul Ericson
    e-mail: pericson@rbj.net
Managing Editor . . . . Mike Dickinson
    e-mail: mdickinson@rbj.net

Scripps Howard News Service
1090 Vermont Ave NW, Ste 1000, Washington, DC 20005
202-408-1484 Fax: 202-408-5950
Web site: www.shns.com
Editor/General Manager . . . . Peter Copeland
    e-mail: copelandp@shns.com
Managing Editor . . . . Karen Timmons
    e-mail: timmonsk@shns.com
Assistant Managing Editor . . . . David Nielsen
    e-mail: nielsend@shns.com
Department News Editor. . . . . Jeff Woods
    e-mail: woodsj@shns.com

Radio

Stations included in this chapter produce news and/or public affairs programming and are listed alphabetically by primary service area.

Offices and agencies generally appear in alphabetical order, except when specific order is requested by listee.

NEWS MEDIA / Radio

ALBANY

WAMC (90.3 FM)
318 Central Ave, PO Box 66600, Albany, NY 12206
518-465-5233 or 800-323-9262 Fax: 518-432-6974
e-mail: mail@wamc.org
Web site: www.wamc.org
President/CEO .... Alan Chartock
Assistant Executive Director .... Selma Kaplan
Assistant Executive Director .... David Galletly
News Director .... Katie Britton
Executive Producer, Host .... Alan Chartock
Producer, (Legislative Gazette) .... David Guistina

WPTR (1540 AM)
4243 Albany Street, Albany, NY 12205-4609
518-862-1540 Fax: 518-862-1545
e-mail: info@1540wdcd.com
Web site: www.1540wdcd.com
Program Director .... Peter Kaye
    e-mail: peterkaye@967wptr.com

BALDWINSVILLE

WSEN (92.1 FM)
8456 Smokey Hollow Road, PO Box 1050, Baldwinsville, NY 13027
315-635-3971 Fax: 315-635-3490
Web site: www.wsenfm.com
General Manager .... Judy Kelly
    e-mail: jkelly@wsenfm.com
Production/Traffic Manager .... Bryan Richards
    e-mail: brichards@wsenfm.com
Programming .... Jim Tate
    e-mail: jtate@wsenfm.com

BATH

WCII (88.5 FM), WCOT (90.9 FM)
7634 Campbell Creek Rd, PO Box 506, Bath, NY 14810-0506
607-776-4151 Fax: 607-776-6929
e-mail: mail@fln.org
Web site: www.fln.org
Executive Director/General Manager .... Rick Snavely
Morning Show Co-Host/Program Director .... John Owens
Founder/CFO .... Dick Snavely

BEACON

WSPK (104.7 FM)
715 Rte 52, Beacon, NY 12508
845-838-6000 Fax: 845-838-2109
Web site: www.k104online.com
General Manager .... Jason Finkelberg
    e-mail: jfinkelberg@pamal.com
Promotion Director .... Steve Vittoria
    e-mail: svittoria@pamal.com
Director Marketing .... Don Napolitani
    e-mail: don@pamal.com

BINGHAMTON

WMRV (105.7)
320 N Jensen Road, Vestal, NY 13850
607-584-5800 Fax: 607-584-5900
Web site: www.whrw.org
General Manager .... Joanne Alloi
News Director .... Dave Lozzi

WNBF (1290 AM), WHWK (98.1FM), WYOS (1360 AM), WAAL (99.1 FM), WWYL (104.1)
59 Court St, Binghamton, NY 13901
607-772-8400 Fax: 607-772-3438
Web site: www.wnbf.com; www.991thewhale.com; www.981thehawk.com
News Director .... Bernard Fionti
    e-mail: bernie@wnbf.com
Program Director (WAAL) .... Don Morgan
    e-mail: kathy@wnbf.com
Program Director (WNBF) .... Roger Neel
    e-mail: roger@wnbf.com
Program Director (WHWK) .... Don Brake
Program Director (WWYL) .... Matt Johnson

WSKG (89.3 FM), WSQX (91.5 FM)
PO Box 3000, Binghamton, NY 13902
607-729-0100 Fax: 607-729-7328
e-mail: mail@wskg.pbs.org
Web site: www.wskg.org
Radio Manager .... Ken Campbell
    e-mail: ken_campbell@wskg.pb.org
Music Director .... Bill Snyder

BRONX

WFUV (90.7 FM)
Fordham University, Bronx, NY 10458
718-817-4550 Fax: 718-365-9815
e-mail: thefolks@wfuv.org
Web site: www.wfuv.org
General Manager .... Dr Ralph Jennings
News & Public Affairs Director .... Julianne Welby
Program Director .... Chuck Singleton

BUFFALO

**WBFO (88.7 FM) WOLN (91.3 FM), WUBJ (88.7 FM)
NPR/PRI - SUNY at Buffalo**
205 Allen Hall, 3435 Main St, Buffalo, NY 14214-3003
716-829-6000 or 888-829-6000 Fax: 716-829-2277
e-mail: mail@wbfo.org
Web site: www.wbfo.org
News Director .... Mark Scott
News Producer .... Eileen Buckley
Associate Vice President/General Manager .... Dr Carole Smith Petro
Assistant General Manager/Program Director .... David Benders
    e-mail: dbenders@wbfo.org

Offices and agencies generally appear in alphabetical order, except when specific order is requested by listee.

NEWS MEDIA / Radio

WBLK (93.7 FM), WJYE (96.1 FM)
14 Lafayette Sq, Ste 1300, Buffalo, NY 14203
716-852-9393 or 800-828-2191 Fax: 716-852-9390
Web site: www.wjye.com; www.wblk.com
Production & Program Director . . . . Chris Reynolds
Production Director. . . . . Frank Dawkins
Program Director (WJYE). . . . . Joe Chille

WDCX (99.5 FM)
625 Delaware Avenue, Suite 308, Buffalo, NY 14202
716-883-3010 Fax: 716-883-3606
e-mail: info@wdcxfm.com
Web site: www.wdcxfm.com
General Manager. . . . . Nev Larson
Afternoon Host/Music Director . . . . Alan Scott
Executive Writer/Producer. . . . . Erin Zilbauer

WHTT (104.1 FM)
50 James E Casey, Buffalo, NY 14206
716-881-4555 Fax: 716-885-6104
e-mail: whtt@whtt.com
Web site: www.whtt.com
Promotions Director . . . . Stacy Berent
News Director. . . . . Gail Ann Hubert
Program Director. . . . . Joe Siragusa
General Manager. . . . . Chet Osadchey

WNED (94.5 FM)
PO Box 1263, Buffalo, NY 14240-1263
716-845-7000 Fax: 716-845-7036
e-mail: classical@wned.org
Web site: www.wned.org
Senior Vice President, Broadcasting. . . . . Dick Daly
Program Director, Classical 94.5. . . . . Peter Goldsmith
Program Director, WNED-AM . . . . Al Wallack
President/CEO . . . . Donald K Boswell

WYRK (106.5 FM), WBUF (92.9 FM)
14 Lafayette Sq., Suite 1200, Buffalo, NY 14203
716-852-9292 Fax: 716-852-9290
Program Director (WYRK) . . . . RW Smith
Program Director (WBUF) . . . . Joe Russo
Sales Manager (WYRK) . . . . Mark Plimpton
General Sales Manager (WBUF) . . . . Rose Vecchiarelli

CHAMPLAIN

WCHP (760 AM)
PO Box 888, Champlain, NY 12919
518-298-2800 Fax: 518-298-2604
e-mail: info@wchp.com
Web site: www.wchp.com
General Manager . . . . Teri Billiter
  e-mail: teri@wchp.com
Program Director . . . . Brandi Lloyd
  e-mail: brandi@wchp.com
Business Manager. . . . . Tonya Billiter
  e-mail: tonya@wchp.com

CORTLAND

WKRT (920 AM), WIII (99.9 or 100.3 FM)
277 Tompkins Street, Cortland, NY 13045
607-756-2828 Fax: 607-756-2953
Web site: www.wiii.com; www.wkrt.com
General Manager . . . . Todd Mallinson
  e-mail: todd.mallinson@citcomm.com
Operations Manager/Program Director/On-Air Talent Mark Vanness
  e-mail: mark.vanness@citcomm.com
Director of Sales. . . . . Margaret Tollner
  e-mail: margaret.tollner@citcomm.com

ELMIRA

WNKI (106.1 FM), WPGI (100.9 FM), WNGZ (104.9 FM), WWLZ (820 AM)
2205 College Avenue, Elmira, NY 14903
607-732-4400 Fax: 607-732-5038
Web site: www.wink106.com
General Manager/Sales Manager . . . . Kevin White
  e-mail: kevin.white@bybradio.com
Promotions Director/Special Events Coordinator . . . . Caryl Sutterby
  e-mail: csutterby@onlineimage.com
Program Director (WNGZ). . . . . Vinny Pagano
  e-mail: vinny@bybradio.com
Program Director (WNKI) . . . . Scott Free
  e-mail: scottfree@bybradio.com

HORNELL

WKPQ (105.3 FM), WHHO (1320 AM)
PO Box 726, Hornell, NY 14843
607-324-2000 or 800-258-1430 Fax: 607-324-2001
Web site: www.wkpq.com
News Director . . . . Jonathon Mark
General Manager. . . . . Tim Thomas

HORSEHEADS

WMTT (94.7 FM)
734 Chemung Street, Horseheads, NY 14845
607-772-1005 Fax: 607-772-2945
e-mail: themetrocks@aol.com
Web site: www.themetrocks.com
General Manager. . . . . George Harris
Program/News/Music Director . . . . Stephen Shimer

ITHACA

WHCU (870 AM), WTKO (1470 AM), WYXL (97.3 FM), WQNY (103.7 FM)
1751 Hanshaw Rd, Ithaca, NY 14850
607-257-6400 Fax: 607-257-6497
Web site: www.whcu870.com; www.lite97fm.com;
www.qcountryfm.com
General Manager. . . . . Susan Johnston
  e-mail: sjohnston@cyradiogroup.com

Offices and agencies generally appear in alphabetical order, except when specific order is requested by listee.

News Director................................Geoff Dunn
    e-mail: gdunn@cyradiogroup.com

JAMESTOWN

WKZA (106.9 FM)
106 West 3rd Street, Suite 106, Jamestown, NY 14701
716-487-1106 or 866-367-1069 Fax: 716-488-2169
Web site: www.1069kissfm.com
General Manager............................John Newman
Program Director..........................Steve Rockford

LATHAM

WFLY (92.3 FM), WAJZ (96.3 FM), WROW (590 AM), WYJB (95.5 FM), WZMR (104.9)
6 Johnson Road, Latham, NY 12110
518-786-6600 or 518-786-6715 (news) Fax: 518-786-6610
Web site: www.pamal.com
General Manager..............................Dan Austin
Program Director (WFLY)..................Terry O'Donnell
Program Director (WAJZ)......................Rob Torres
Program Director (WROW)..............Paul Vandenburgh
Program Director (WYJB).....................Ric Mitchell
Program Director (WZMR)................Kevin Callahan

WGY (810 AM), WPYX (106.5 FM), WRVE (99.5 FM)
Riverhill Center, 1203 Troy-Schenectady Road, Latham, NY 12110
518-452-4800 Fax: 518-452-4859
e-mail: news@wgy.com
Web site: www.wgy.com; www.pyx106.com; www.wrve.com
Vice President/General Manager............Kristen Delaney
Station Manager (WGY & WPYX)/Program Director (WPYX) John Cooper
Station Manager/Program Director (WRVE)......Randy McCarten
    e-mail: randymccarten@clearchannel.com
News Director (WGY)........................Chuck Custer

NEW ROCHELLE

WVOX (1460 AM), WRTN (93.5 FM)
1 Broadcast Forum, New Rochelle, NY 10801
914-636-1460 or 914-235-3279 editor Fax: 914-636-2900
e-mail: info@wvox.com
Web site: www.wvox.com
News Director............................Larry Goldstein
    e-mail: larry@wvox.com
Senior Vice President, Operations & Programming....Don Stevens
    e-mail: don@wvox.com
Public Affairs Director............Nancy Curry O'Shaughnessy
General Manager......................Cindy Hall Gallagher
    e-mail: cindy@wvox.com (traffic)

NEW YORK CITY

WABC (770 AM)
2 Penn Plaza, New York, NY 10121
212-613-3800 Fax: 212-613-3823
e-mail: postmaster@wabcradio.com
Web site: www.wabcradio.com
President/General Manager..................Steve Boreman
Program Director..............................Phil Boyce

WAXQ (104.3 FM)
1180 Avenue of the Americas, 6th Floor, New York, NY 10036
212-575-1043 Fax: 212-302-7814
Web site: www.q1043.com
General Manager.............................Jim Condron
    e-mail: ericlemieux@clearchannel.com
Promotions Director..........................Eric Lemieux
    e-mail: ericlemieux@clearchannel.com
Program Director...........................Bob Buchmann
Music Director..............................Eric Wellman
    e-mail: ericwellman@clearchannel.com

WBBR (1130 AM) Bloomberg News
731 Lexington Avenue, New York, NY 10022
212-318-2000 Fax: 212-940-1994
Web site: www.wbbr.com
General Manager..............................Al Mayers
News Director...............................John Meehan
Program Director...........................Michael Lysak

WCBS (880 AM)
524 W 57th St, 8th Fl, New York, NY 10019
212-975-2127 (news) or 212-975-4321 Fax: 212-975-1907
e-mail: wcbs880@wcbs880.com
Web site: www.wcbs880.com
General Manager...........................Steve Swenson
Program Director............................Crys Quinby
News Director................................Tim Scheld

WINS (1010 AM)
888 Seventh Ave, New York, NY 10106
212-315-7000 Fax: 212-489-7034
e-mail: info@1010winsmail.com
Web site: www.1010wins.com
News Director.............................Ben Mevorach
Vice President/Executive Editor..............Mark Mason
Editor.....................................Jim Maloney

WLTW (106.7 FM)
1133 Avenue of the Americas, 34th Fl, New York, NY 10036
212-603-4600 Fax: 212-603-4602
e-mail: contact@1067litefm.com
Web site: www.1067litefm.com
Interim General Manager....................Rob Williams
Program Coordinator.........................Morgan Prue

Offices and agencies generally appear in alphabetical order, except when specific order is requested by listee.

NEWS MEDIA / Radio

WOR (710 AM)
111 Broadway, 3rd Fl, New York, NY 10006
212-642-4467 Fax: 212-392-6517
e-mail: news@wor710.com
Web site: www.wor710.com
Executive Director . . . . Chris Thompson
Vice President/General Manager . . . . Bob Bruno
    e-mail: bbruno@wor710.com
News Director . . . . Joe Bartlett
    e-mail: joebartlett@wor710.com

OLEAN

WPIG (95.7 FM), WHDL (1450 AM)
3163 NYS Route 417, Olean, NY 14760-1853
716-372-0161 or 800-877-9749 Fax: 716-372-0164
Web site: www.wpig.com www.whdl.com
General Manager . . . . John Morton
    e-mail: john.morton@bybradio.com
News Director . . . . Gary Nease

PEEKSKILL

WHUD (100.7 FM)
PO Box 188, Peekskill, NY 10566
845-838-6000 Fax: 845-838-2109
Web site: www.whud.com
Program Director . . . . Steve Petrone
Sales/General Manager . . . . Jason Finkleberg

MIDDLETOWN

WALL (1340 AM), WRRV (92.7 FM)
PO Box 416, Poughkeepsie, NY 12602-0416
845-471-1500 Fax: 845-454-1204
e-mail: wrrv@wrrv.com
Web site: www.wrrv.com
Program Director (WRRV) . . . . Andrew Boris
    e-mail: boris@wrrv.com

POUGHKEEPSIE

WPDH (101.5 FM)
2 Pendell Rd, PO Box 416, Poughkeepsie, NY 12602
845-471-1500 Fax: 845-454-1204
e-mail: gm@wpdh.com
Web site: www.wpdh.com
General Manager . . . . Chuck Benfer
    e-mail: gm@wpdh.com
Promotions Director . . . . Anthony Verano
    e-mail: anthony.verano@cumulus.com
Program Director . . . . Gary Cee
    e-mail: garycee@wpdh.com
Sales Director . . . . Rob Vanderbeck
    e-mail: rob.vanderbeck@cumulus.com

ROCHESTER

WHAM (1180 AM)
207 Midtown Plaza, Rochester, NY 14604-2016
585-454-4884 Fax: 585-454-5081
e-mail: wham@eznet.com
Web site: www.wham1180.com
Station Manager . . . . Jeff Howlett
    e-mail: jeffhowlett@clearchannel.com
Promotions Director . . . . Brian Guck
    e-mail: brianguck@clearchannel.com
News Director . . . . Randy Gorbman
    e-mail: randygorbman@clearchannel.com

SCHENECTADY

WGNA (107.7 FM)
1241 Kings Road, Schenectady, NY 12303
518-881-1515 or 800-476-1077 Fax: 518-881-1516
e-mail: wgna@aol.com
Web site: www.wgna.com
Regional Vice President/General Manager . . . . Robert Ausfeld
    e-mail: robert.ausfeld@regentcomm.com
Program Manager . . . . Buzz Brindle
    e-mail: bbrindle@wgna.com
Station Manager . . . . John Hirsh
    e-mail: johnhirsch@regentcomm.com
Music Director . . . . Bill Earley
    e-mail: bearley@wgna.com

SYRACUSE

WNTQ (93.1 FM), WAQX (95.7 FM)
1064 James St, Syracuse, NY 13203
315-472-0200 Fax: 315-478-5625
Web site: www.93Q.com; www.95x.com
General Manager . . . . David Calabrese
Program Director (WNTQ) . . . . Tom Mitchell
Program Director (WAQX) . . . . Alexis Thang

WVOA (105.1 FM)
7095 Myers Road, East Syracuse, NY 13057-9748
315-656-2231 Fax: 315-656-2259
Public Service Coordinator . . . . Susan Anderson
Music Director . . . . Allen Elson

WYYY (94.5 FM)
Y94FM Bridgewater Place, 500 Plum St, Suite 100, Syracuse, NY 13204
315-472-9797 Fax: 315-478-6455
e-mail: y94fm@clearchannel.com
Program Director . . . . Kathy Rowe
Music Director . . . . John Smith

Offices and agencies generally appear in alphabetical order, except when specific order is requested by listee.

NEWS MEDIA / Television

UTICA

WOUR (96.9 FM)
239 Genesee Street, Suite 500, Utica, NY 13501-3412
315-797-0803 Fax: 315-797-7813
Web site: www.wour.com
General Manager/Sales Manager . . . . Brian Delany
    e-mail: brianelany@clearchannel.com
Program Director . . . . Tom Starr
    e-mail: tomstarr@clearchannel.com

WATERTOWN

WFRY (97.5 FM)
134 Mullin Street, Watertown, NY 13601
315-788-0790 Fax: 315-788-4379
Web site: www.froggy97.com
General Manager . . . . Don Wagner
Program/Music Director . . . . Stan Sobelski

Television

Stations included in this chapter produce news and/or public affairs programming and are listed alphabetically by primary service area.

ALBANY

WMHT (17) Public Broadcasting-NY Capitol Region
4 Global View Road, Troy, NY 12180
518-880-3400 or 800-477-9648 Fax: 518-880-3409
e-mail: email@wmht.org
Web site: www.wmht.org
President/General Manager . . . . Deborah Onslow

WNYT (13)
715 N Pearl St, PO Box 4035, Albany, NY 12204
518-436-4791 Fax: 518-434-0659
e-mail: comments@wnyt.com
Web site: www.wnyt.com
General Manager . . . . Steve Baboulis
News Director . . . . Paul Lewis
Director, Public Affairs & Special Promotions . . . . . . Maryann Ryan

WRGB (6)
1400 Balltown Rd, Schenectady, NY 12309
518-346-6666 or 800-666-3355 Fax: 518-346-6249
Web site: www.cbs6albany.com
General Manager . . . . Robert J Furlong
News Director . . . . Beau Duffy
Production Manager . . . . Bill Brandt
Chief Political Reporter . . . . Morgan Hook

WTEN (10)
341 Northern Blvd, Albany, NY 12204
518-436-4822 Fax: 518-426-4792
e-mail: news@wten.com
Web site: www.wten.com
President/General Manager . . . . Rene LaSpina
    e-mail: dana.dieterle@wten.com
News Director . . . . Dana Dieterle
    e-mail: dana.dieterle@wten.com

WXXA (23)
28 Corporate Circle, Albany, NY 12203
518-862-2323 Fax: 518-862-0995
Web site: www.fox23news.com
News Director . . . . Gene Ross

Program Director . . . . Paul Pelliccia

WYPX (55)
1 Charles Blvd, Guilderland, NY 12084
518-464-0143 or 800-646-7296 Fax: 518-464-0633
Web site: www.paxalbany.tv
Public Affairs Director . . . . Chris Iorio
    e-mail: chrisiorio@pax.net

BINGHAMTON

WBNG (12), WBXI (11)
560 Columbia Dr, Johnson City, NY 13790
607-729-8812 Fax: 607-797-6211
e-mail: wbng@wbngtv.com
Web site: www.wbng.com
General Manager . . . . Robert Krumenacker
    e-mail: catlin@wbngtv.com
News Director . . . . Greg Catlin
    e-mail: catlin@wbngtv.com

WICZ (40)
4600 Vestal Pkwy E, Vestal, NY 13850
607-770-4040 Fax: 607-798-7950
e-mail: fox40@wicz.com
Web site: www.wicz.com
General Manager . . . . John Leet
News Director . . . . Suh Neubauer
    e-mail: newsdirector@wicz.com
Program Director . . . . Vernon Rowlands

WIVT/WBGH (34)
203 Ingraham Hill Rd, Binghamton, NY 13903
607-771-3434 Fax: 607-723-6403
e-mail: newschannel34@newschannel34.com
Web site: www.newschannel34.com
News Director . . . . Jim Ehmke
Program Director . . . . Chris Wurth

Offices and agencies generally appear in alphabetical order, except when specific order is requested by listee.

NEWS MEDIA / Television

WSKG (46) Public Broadcasting
Box 3000, Binghamton, NY 13902
607-729-0100 Fax: 607-729-7328
e-mail: mail@wskg.pbs.org
Web site: www.wskg.com
President/Chief Executive Officer . . . . Brian Sickora
Producer/Moderator . . . . William Jaker

BUFFALO

WGRZ (2)
259 Delaware Ave, Buffalo, NY 14202
716-849-2222 or 716-849-2200 (news) Fax: 716-849-7602
Web site: www.wgrz.com
News Director . . . . Ellen Crooke
Assignment Editor . . . . Maria Sisti
Program Coordinator . . . . Paulette Harris

WIVB (4), WNLO (23)
2077 Elmwood Ave, Buffalo, NY 14207
716-874-4410 Fax: 716-874-8173
e-mail: wivbweb@wivb.com
Web site: www.wivb.com
Business Manager . . . . Nancy Kenney

WKBW (7)
7 Broadcast Plaza, Buffalo, NY 14202
716-845-6100 Fax: 716-856-8784
e-mail: news@wkbw.com
Web site: www.wkbw.com
News Director . . . . Glenn Horn
  e-mail: johndis@wkbw.com
Head of Programming & Promotion . . . . John Disciullo
  e-mail: johndis@wkbw.com

WNED (17) Western NY Public Broadcasting
PO Box 1263, Buffalo, NY 14240-1263
716-845-7000 Fax: 716-845-7036
e-mail: news@wned.org
Web site: www.wned.org
President/CEO . . . . Donald K Boswell
Program Director-WNED, AM . . . . Al Wallack
News Director . . . . Jim Ranney

WETM (18)
101 E Water St, Elmira, NY 14901
607-733-5518 Fax: 607-734-1176
e-mail: news@wetmtv.com
Web site: www.wetmtv.com
Vice President/General Manager . . . . Randy Reid
  e-mail: rreid@wetmtv.com
News Director . . . . Scott Nichols
  e-mail: snichols@wetmtv.com

HORSEHEADS

WENY (36)
474 Old Ithaca Rd, Horseheads, NY 14845
607-739-3636 Fax: 607-796-6171
e-mail: info@weny.com
Web site: www.weny.com
General Manager . . . . Peter Veto
News Director . . . . Scott Cook

KINGSTON

WRNN (62)
800 Westchester Avenue, Suite S-640, Rye Brook, NY 10573
914-417-2700 Fax: 914-696-0279
Web site: www.rnntv.com
General Manager . . . . Richard French
Sports Director . . . . Ben Sosenko

LONG ISLAND

WLIW (21) Public Broadcasting
Box 21, Channel 21 Dr, Plainview, NY 11803-0021
516-367-2100 Fax: 516-692-7629
e-mail: viewersvoice@wliw.org
Web site: www.wliw.org
President/General Manager . . . . Terrel L Cass
Producer/Local Production . . . . Theresa Statz-Smith

MELVILLE

WLNY (55)
Box 1355, 270 S Service Rd, Melville, NY 11747
631-622-9442 Fax: 631-420-4822
Web site: www.wlnytv.com
News Director . . . . Richard Rose

NEW YORK CITY

Bloomberg Television
731 Lexington Avenue, New York, NY 10022
212-318-2319 Fax: 212-940-1757
Web site: www.bloomberg.com/tv
News Director . . . . John Meehan

Fox News Channel
1211 Ave of the Americas, C-1, New York, NY 10036
212-301-3000 Fax: 212-301-8274
Web site: www.foxnews.com
Vice President/News Operations . . . . Sharri Berg

New York 1 News (1)
75 Ninth Avenue, New York, NY 10011
212-691-6397 Fax: 212-379-3575
e-mail: ny1news@ny1.com
Web site: www.ny1.com
Political Reporter, Anchor & Co-Host, ... Dominic Carter
Political Reporter, Anchor & Co-Host, ... Davidson Goldin
Politcal Reporter . . . . Sandra Endo

Offices and agencies generally appear in alphabetical order, except when specific order is requested by listee.

NEWS MEDIA / Television

WABC (7)
7 Lincoln Sq, New York, NY 10023
212-456-1000 or 212-456-3100 Fax: 212-456-2381
e-mail: eyewitness.news@abc.com
Web site: www.7online.com
Program Vice President . . . . Art Moore

WCBS (2)
524 W 57th St, New York, NY 10019
212-975-4321 Fax: 212-975-9387
Web site: www.cbsnewyork.com
Executive Editor . . . . Philip O'Brien
    e-mail: pobrien@cbs.com
Director, Communications . . . . Audry Pass

WNBC (4)
30 Rockefeller Plaza, New York, NY 10112
212-664-4444 or 212-664-2731 (news) Fax: 212-664-2994
Web site: www.nbc.com
Senior VP, News & Station Manager . . . . Dan Forman
Program Director . . . . Adele Rifken
Vice President/Director of Press & Public Affairs . . Anna Carbonell

WNYW (5)
205 E 67th St, New York, NY 10021
212-452-5555 Fax: 212-717-5849
Web site: www.fox5ny.com
Vice President/News Director . . . . Scott Matthews

WPIX (11)
220 East 42nd St, New York, NY 10017
212-949-1100 Fax: 212-210-2591
e-mail: wpix@tribune.com or wpix@aol.com
Web site: www.wb11.com
News Director . . . . Karen Scott

WWOR (UPN 9)
9 Broadcast Plaza, Secaucus, NJ 7096
201-330-2214 Fax: 201-330-3844
e-mail: newsdesk@wwortv.com
Web site: www.upn9.tv
News Director . . . . Scott Matthews
Assignment Editor . . . . Kevin Schwab
Assignment Editor . . . . Kim Lowe
Planning Editor . . . . Adam Cousins

PLATTSBURGH

WPTZ (5) NBC
5 Television Dr, Plattsburgh, NY 12901
518-561-5555 Fax: 518-561-5940
e-mail: newstips@thechamplainchannel.com
Web site: www.thechamplainchannel.com
News Director . . . . Kyle Grimes
Assignment Editor . . . . Matt Morin

ROCHESTER

WHEC (10)
191 East Ave, Rochester, NY 14604
585-546-5670 Fax: 585-546-5688
e-mail: news1@news10nbc.com
Web site: www.10nbc.com
News Director . . . . Mike Goldrick
Program Director . . . . Lynette Baker

WHAM (13)
Box 20555, 4225 W Henrietta Rd, Rochester, NY 14623
585-334-8700 Fax: 585-334-8719
e-mail: news@wokr13.tv
Web site: www.wokr13.tv
General Manager . . . . Chuck Samuels
TV Community Affairs Director . . . . Charlotte Clarke
News Director . . . . Steve Dawe
Business Manager/Human Resources . . . . Anne Johnson

WXXI (21) Public Broadcasting
280 State St, PO Box 30021, Rochester, NY 14614
585-325-7500 Fax: 585-258-0335
e-mail: wxxinews@wxxi.org
Web site: www.wxxi.org
President/Chief Executive Officer . . . . Norm Silverstein
    e-mail: norms@wxxi.org
Vice President, Television . . . . Elissa Orlando
Director, Television News . . . . Julie Philipp-Clayton

SYRACUSE

WCNY (24)
Box 2400, 506 Old Liverpool Rd, Syracuse, NY 13220-2400
315-453-2424 Fax: 315-451-8824
Web site: www.wcny.org
Producer . . . . George Kilpatrick
Host . . . . Dan Cummings

WIXT (9)
5904 Bridge St, East Syracuse, NY 13057
315-446-9999 Fax: 315-446-9283
e-mail: newschannel9@wixt.com
Web site: www.wixt.com
Program Director . . . . Vince Spicola

WSTM (3)
1030 James St, Syracuse, NY 13203
315-474-5000 Fax: 315-474-5122
e-mail: wstmnews@wstm.com
Web site: www.wstm.com
General Manager . . . . Chris Geiger
News Director . . . . Peggy Phillip
    e-mail: pphillip@wstm.com

WSYT (68)
1000 James St, Syracuse, NY 13203
315-472-6800 Fax: 315-471-8889
Web site: www.foxsyracuse.com
Group Manager . . . . Aaron Olander

Offices and agencies generally appear in alphabetical order, except when specific order is requested by listee.

NEWS MEDIA / Television

WTVH (5)
980 James St, Syracuse, NY 13203
315-425-5555 Fax: 315-425-0129
e-mail: onyourside@whtv.com
Web site: www.wtvh.com
News Director................................. Frank Kracher

UTICA

WKTV (2)
Box 2, Utica, NY 13503
315-733-0404 Fax: 315-793-3498
e-mail: newslink@wktv.com
Web site: www.wktv.com
Program Director .... Tom Coyne
News Director............................. Steve McMurray
Vice President/General Manager .... Vic Vetters

WATERTOWN

WWNY (7)
120 Arcade St, Watertown, NY 13601
315-788-3800 Fax: 315-782-7468
e-mail: wwny@wwnytv.net
Web site: www.wwnytv.com
General Manager............................. Cathy Pircsuk
News Director .... Scott Atkinson
Program Director .... Jim Corbin

WWTI (50)
Box 6250, 1222 Arsenal St, Watertown, NY 13601
315-785-8850 Fax: 315-785-0127
e-mail: davidmales@clearchannel.com
Web site: www.newswatch50.com
General Manager .... David J Males
   e-mail: johnmoore@clearchannel.com
News Director................................ John Moore
   e-mail: johnmoore@clearchannel.com

Offices and agencies generally appear in alphabetical order, except when specific order is requested by listee.

COLLEGES AND UNIVERSITIES

State University of New York

SUNY Board of Trustees
State University of New York
State University Plz
Albany, NY 12246
518-443-5157 or 800-342-3811 Fax: 518-443-5131
e-mail: asksuny@suny.edu
Web site: www.suny.edu

Chair:
   Thomas F Egan (2013).............................212-661-4431
Vice Chair:
   Randy A Daniels (2011)..........................212-417-5804
Member:
   Alyssa Amyotte (2007)...........................518-578-4244
Member:
   Aminy I Audi (2009) 315-682-5500
Member:
   Robert J Bellafiore (2010) 518-449-3000
Member:
   Christopher P Conners (2008) 518-786-6000
Member:
   Edward F Cox (2013)..............................212-336-2000
Member:
   Father John J Cremins (2007)..................718-268-6143
Member:
   Candace de Russy (2007).......................914-779-9607
Member:
   Gordon R Gross (2008) 716-854-4300
Member:
   Stephen J Hunt (2013) 914-232-5563
Member:
   Michael E Russell (2009)........................631-689-9434
Member:
   Teresa Santiago (2007)..........................914-761-4758
Member:
   Kay Stafford (2008) 518-314-7008
Member:
   Harvey F Wachsman (2011).....................516-624-2999
Member:
   Gerri Warren-Merrick (2012)....................212-484-6480

SUNY System Administration & Executive Council
State University Plz
Albany, NY 12246
518-443-5555
Web site: www.suny.edu

Chancellor:
   John R Ryan 518-443-5355/fax: 518-443-5360
Vice Chancellor & Chief of Staff:
   Vacant..............................518-443-5328/fax: 518-443-5369
Vice Chancellor/Secretary of the University/President Research Foundation:
   John J O'Connor 518-443-5157/fax: 518-443-5131
   e-mail: oconnojj@sysadm.suny.edu

Provost & Vice Chancellor, Academic Affairs:
   Risa I Palm 518-443-5152/fax: 518-443-5321
Vice Chancellor & CFO, Enrollment/University Life:
   Kimberly R Cline 518-443-5150/fax: 518-443-5470
Vice Chancellor, Community Colleges:
   Dennis Golladay 518-443-5134/fax: 518-443-5250
Vice Chancellor, Legal Affairs & University Counsel:
   Nicholas Rostow 518-443-5400/fax: 518-443-5409
Senior Assoc Vice Chancellor, University Relations:
   Michael C Trunzo 518-443-5148/fax: 518-443-5151
   e-mail: trunzom@sysadm.suny.edu
Public Relations Office:
   David Henahan..................................518-443-5311
   e-mail: pi@sysadmin.suny.edu

New York African American Institute
41 State St, Rm 702, Albany, NY 12246

Director:
   Anne Pope 518-443-5798/fax: 518-443-5803
   e-mail: popean@spo.rf.suny.edu

New York Network
Empire State Plaza, S Concourse, Ste 146, PO Box 2058, Albany, NY 12223
e-mail: contact@nyn.suny.edu
Web site: www.nyn.suny.edu

Executive Director:
   William F Snyder 518-443-5333/fax: 518-426-4198
Director of Administration & Broadcast Svcs:
   Roy T Saplin.......................................518-443-5333
Senior Producer:
   Chris Conto..518-443-5333
Supervising Television Engineer:
   Patrick Roche 518-443-5333

Rockefeller Institute of Government .... fax: 518-443-5788
411 State St, Albany, NY 12203-1003
518-443-5522 Fax: 518-443-5788
Web site: www.rockinst.org

Co-Director:
   Richard P Nathan 518-443-5522
   e-mail: nathanr@rockinst.org
Co-Director:
   Thomas L Gais 518-443-5522
   e-mail: gaist@rockinst.org
Executive Director, NYS Forum for Info Res Mgmt:
   Gregory Benson 518-443-5522
   e-mail: gbensonb@nysfirm.org
Director, Higher Education Program:
   Joseph Burke 518-443-5522
   e-mail: burkejo@rockinst.org

SUNY Metropolitan Recruitment Center ... fax: 212-818-9079
420 Lexington Ave, Ste 1640, New York, NY 10017
212-818-1204 Fax: 212-818-9079
e-mail: mrc@suny.edu
Web site: www.suny.edu/student/mrc.cfm

Director:
   Randy H Miller 212-818-1204/fax: 212-818-9079
   e-mail: millerra@sysadm.suny.edu

Offices and agencies generally appear in alphabetical order, except when specific order is requested by listee.

COLLEGES AND UNIVERSITIES / State University of New York

Support Staff:
  Ana Sanchez.....................................212-818-1204

Small Business Development Center
State University Plaza, Administration Office, 22 Corporate Woods Bldg,
  3rd Fl, Albany, NY 12246
800-732-7232 or 518-443-5398
Web site: www.nyssbdc.org
State Director:
  James L King..............518-443-5398 x166/fax: 518-443-5275
  e-mail: j.king@nyssbdc.org

State University Construction Fund
353 Broadway, Albany, NY 12246
518-689-2500
Web site: www.sucf.suny.edu
General Manager:
  Philip W Wood....................518-689-2501/fax: 518-689-2634
Acting General Counsel/Director, Legal Svcs:
  William K Barczak................518-689-2514/fax: 518-689-2634

UNIVERSITY CENTERS

Binghamton University, State University of New York
Vestal Parkway East
PO Box 6000
Binghamton, NY 13902
607-777-2000 Fax: 607-777-4000
e-mail: info@binghamton.edu
Web site: www.binghamton.edu

President:
  Lois B DeFleur....................607-777-2131/fax: 607-777-2533
  e-mail: ldefleur@binghamton.edu

College of Agriculture & Life Sciences at Cornell University
Roberts Hall
Ithaca, NY 14853-5901
607-255-2241 Fax: 607-255-3803
Web site: www.cals.cornell.edu

Dean:
  Susan A Henry....................................607-255-2241
  e-mail: sah42@cornell.edu

College of Human Ecology at Cornell University
142 Martha Van Rensselaer Hall
Ithaca, NY 14853
607-255-2216 Fax: 607-255-3794
Web site: www.human.cornell.edu

Dean:
  Lisa Staiano-Coico...............................607-255-2138
  e-mail: lfs9@cornell.edu

College of Veterinary Medicine at Cornell University
Cornell University
Ithaca, NY 14853
607-253-3000 Fax: 607-253-3701
Web site: www.vet.cornell.edu

Dean:
  Michael I Kotlikoff..............................607-253-3771

NYS College of Ceramics at Alfred University
2 Pine St
Alfred, NY 14802
607-871-2137 Fax: 607-871-2339
Web site: www.nyscc.alfred.edu

Provost:
  Suzanne Buckley..................................607-871-2137

SUNY Downstate Medical Center
450 Clarkson Ave
Brooklyn, NY 11203
718-270-1000 or 718-270-3160 Fax: 718-270-4732
Web site: www.downstate.edu

President:
  John C LaRosa....................................718-270-2611
  e-mail: jclarosa@downstate.edu

SUNY State College of Optometry
33 West 42nd St
New York, NY 10036-8003
212-938-4000 or 212-938-4001
Web site: www.sunyopt.edu

President:
  David O Heath....................................212-938-5650
  e-mail: dheath@sunyopt.edu

SUNY Upstate Medical University
750 E Adams St
Syracuse, NY 13210
315-464-5540 Fax: 315-464-4838
Web site: www.upstate.edu

President:
  David R Smith....................315-464-4513/fax: 315-464-5275

School of Industrial & Labor Relations at Cornell University (ILR School)
309 Ives Hall
Ithaca, NY 14853
607-254-4636 Fax: 607-255-5396
e-mail: info@ilr.cornell.edu
Web site: www.ilr.cornell.edu

Dean:
  Harry C Katz.....................................607-255-2185
  e-mail: hck2@cornell.edu

Offices and agencies generally appear in alphabetical order, except when specific order is requested by listee.

COLLEGES AND UNIVERSITIES / State University of New York

State University of New York at Albany
1400 Washington Ave
UAB 430
Albany, NY 12222
518-442-3300 or TDD: 518-442-3366
Web site: www.albany.edu

Provost & Executive VP:
Susan V Herbst 518-956-8010
e-mail: herbst@uamail.albany.edu

State University of New York College of Environmental Science & Forestry
One Forestry Dr
Syracuse, NY 13210
315-470-6500 or TDD: 315-470-6966 Fax: 315-470-6933
e-mail: esfinfo@esf.edu
Web site: www.esf.edu

President:
Cornelius B Murphy Jr 315-470-6681/fax: 315-470-6977
e-mail: cbmurphy@esf.edu

Stony Brook University, SUNY
310 Administration Bldg
Nicolls Rd
Stony Brook, NY 11794
631-632-6000
Web site: www.sunysb.edu

President:
Shirley Strum Kenny 631-632-6265/fax: 631-632-6621
e-mail: shirley.kenny@stonybrook.edu

University at Buffalo, State University of New York
Capen Hall
Buffalo, NY 14260
716-645-2000 Fax: 716-645-3728
Web site: www.buffalo.edu

President:
John B Simpson 716-645-2901
e-mail: simpson@buffalo.edu

UNIVERSITY COLLEGES

Buffalo State College
1300 Elmwood Ave
Buffalo, NY 14222-1095
716-878-4000 or TTD 716-878-3182 Fax: 716-878-3039
e-mail: webadmin@buffalostate.edu
Web site: www.buffalostate.edu

President:
Muriel A Howard 716-878-4101/fax: 716-878-6527
e-mail: howardma@buffalostate.edu

Purchase College, State University of New York
735 Anderson Hill Rd
Purchase, NY 10577
914-251-6000
Web site: www.purchase.edu

President:
Thomas J Schwarz 914-251-6010/fax: 914-251-6014
e-mail: thomas.schwarz@purchase.edu

State University at Brockport
350 New Campus Dr
Brockport, NY 14420
585-395-2211 Fax: 585-395-2401
Web site: www.brockport.edu

President:
John R Halstead 585-395-2361
e-mail: halstead@brockport.edu

State University at Old Westbury
223 Store Hill Rd
PO Box 210
Old Westbury, NY 11568-0210
516-876-3000
Web site: www.oldwestbury.edu

President:
Calvin O Butts, III 516-876-3160/fax: 516-876-3347
e-mail: buttsc@oldwestbury.edu

State University at Potsdam
44 Pierrepont Ave
Potsdam, NY 13676
315-267-2000 or 877-768-7326
Web site: www.potsdam.edu

President:
John Schwaller 315-267-2100
e-mail: schwaljf@potsdam.edu

State University College at Cortland
Graham Ave
PO Box 2000
Cortland, NY 13045
607-753-2011 Fax: 607-753-5688
Web site: www.cortland.edu

President:
Erik J Bitterbaum 607-753-2201/fax: 607-753-5993
e-mail: bitterbaume@cortland.edu

State University College at Geneseo
1 College Circle
Geneseo, NY 14454-1450
585-245-5211 Fax: 585-245-5005
Web site: www.geneseo.edu

Offices and agencies generally appear in alphabetical order, except when specific order is requested by listee.

COLLEGES AND UNIVERSITIES / State University of New York

President:
   Christopher C Dahl 585-245-5501/fax: 585-245-5555
   e-mail: cdahl@geneseo.edu

State University College at New Paltz
1 Hawk Drive
New Paltz, NY 12561
845-257-7869 or 845-257-2121 Fax: 845-257-3009
Web site: www.newpaltz.edu

President:
   Steven G Poskanzer. 845-257-3288/fax: 845-257-3389
   e-mail: poskanzer@newpaltz.edu

State University Empire State College
One Union Ave
Saratoga Springs, NY 12866
518-587-2100 Fax: 518-587-3033
Web site: www.esc.edu

President:
   Joseph B Moore 518-587-2100 x2265/fax: 518-587-2886
   e-mail: president@esc.edu

State University of New York, Fredonia
280 Central Ave
Fredonia, NY 14063-1136
716-673-3111 Fax: 716-673-3156
Web site: www.fredonia.edu

President:
   Dennis L Hefner. 716-673-3456
   e-mail: dennis.hefner@fredonia.edu

State University of New York at Oneonta
Ravine Pkwy
Oneonta, NY 13820
607-436-3500
Web site: www.oneonta.edu

President:
   Alan B Donovan 607-436-2500/fax: 607-436-3089
   e-mail: donovaab@oneonta.edu

State University of New York at Oswego
7060 Route 104
Oswego, NY 13126
315-312-2500 Fax: 315-312-2863
e-mail: proffice@oswego.edu
Web site: www.oswego.edu

President:
   Deborah F Stanley 315-312-2211
   e-mail: stanley@oswego.edu

State University of New York at Plattsburgh
101 Broad St
Plattsburgh, NY 12901
518-564-2000 Fax: 518-564-2094
Web site: www.plattsburgh.edu

President:
   John Ettling 518-564-2010/fax: 518-564-3932
   e-mail: president_office@plattsburgh.edu

COLLEGES OF TECHNOLOGY

Alfred State College of Technology
10 Upper College Dr
Alfred, NY 14802
607-587-4215 or 800-425-3733 Fax: 607-587-4299
e-mail: admissions@alfredstate.edu
Web site: www.alfredstate.edu

Interim President:
   John B Clark. 607-587-4210
   e-mail: clarkjb@alfredstate.edu

Farmingdale State College of Technology
2350 Broadhollow Rd
Farmingdale, NY 11735-1021
631-420-2000 Fax: 631-420-2633
e-mail: regoff@farmingdale.edu
Web site: www.farmingdale.edu

President:
   W Hubert Keen 631-420-2239/fax: 631-420-2753
   e-mail: hubert.keen@farmingdale.edu

Morrisville State College
Administration Bldg, South St
PO Box 901
Morrisville, NY 13408
315-684-6000 or 800-258-0111 Fax: 315-684-6116
Web site: www.morrisville.edu

President:
   Raymond W Cross. 315-684-6044/fax: 315-684-6109
   e-mail: crossrw@morrisville.edu

SUNY College of Agriculture & Technology at Cobleskill
State Route 7
Cobleskill, NY 12043
518-255-5700 or 800-295-8988 Fax: 518-255-6769
Web site: www.cobleskill.edu

Provost & Officer-in-Charge:
   Anne C Myers. 518-255-5111

State University College of Technology at Canton
34 Cornell Dr
Canton, NY 13617
315-386-7123 or 800-388-7123 Fax: 315-386-7929
Web site: www.canton.edu

President:
   Joseph L Kennedy 315-386-7204/fax: 800-386-7934
   e-mail: president@canton.edu

Offices and agencies generally appear in alphabetical order, except when specific order is requested by listee.

COLLEGES AND UNIVERSITIES / State University of New York

State University College of Technology at Delhi
2 Main St
Delhi, NY 13753
607-746-4550 or 800-963-3544 Fax: 607-746-4104
Web site: www.delhi.edu

President:
  Candace S Vancko.................607-746-4090/fax: 607-746-4346
  e-mail: vanckocs@delhi.org

State University Institute of Technology
Horatio St, Marcy Campus
PO Box 3050
Utica, NY 13504-3050
315-792-7500 Fax: 315-792-7837
Web site: web2.sunyit.edu

Interim President:
  Peter A Spina.....................315-792-7400/fax: 315-792-7407
  e-mail: spinap@sunyit.edu

State University of New York Maritime College
6 Pennyfield Ave
Throgs Neck, NY 10465
718-409-7200 or 800-642-1874 Fax: 718-409-7465
Web site: www.sunymaritime.edu

President:
  Vice Adm John W Craine Jr.........................718-409-7270

COMMUNITY COLLEGES

Adirondack Community College
640 Bay Rd
Queensbury, NY 12804
518-743-2200 Fax: 518-745-1433
e-mail: info@sunyacc.edu
Web site: www.sunyacc.edu

President:
  Marshall E Bishop.................518-743-2237/fax: 518-743-2262
  e-mail: bishopm@acc.sunyacc.edu

Broome Community College
PO Box 1017
904 Upper Front St
Binghamton, NY 13902
607-778-5000 Fax: 607-778-5310
Web site: www.sunybroome.edu

President:
  Laurence D Spraggs................................607-778-5100
  e-mail: president@sunybroome.edu

Cayuga Community College
197 Franklin St
Auburn, NY 13021
315-255-1743 Fax: 315-255-2117
Web site: www.cayuga-cc.edu

Interim President:
  Philip E Gover............................315-255-1743 x2208
  e-mail: goverp@cayuga-cc.edu

Clinton Community College
136 Clinton Point Dr
Plattsburgh, NY 12901
518-562-4200 Fax: 518-562-4159
Web site: www.clinton.edu

President:
  Maurice B Hickey..................518-562-4100/fax: 518-561-4890

Columbia-Greene Community College
4400 Route 23
PO Box 1000
Hudson, NY 12534-0327
518-828-4181 Fax: 518-828-8543
e-mail: info@sunycgcc.edu
Web site: www.sunycgcc.edu

President:
  James R Campion............518-828-4181x3325/fax: 518-822-2006
  e-mail: campion@sunycgcc.edu

Corning Community College
1 Academic Dr
Corning, NY 14830
607-962-9222 or 800-358-7171 Fax: 607-962-9456
Web site: www.corning-cc.edu

President:
  Floyd F Amann................607-962-9232 x232/fax: 607-962-9485
  e-mail: amann@corning-cc.edu

Dutchess Community College
53 Pendell Rd
Poughkeepsie, NY 12601-1595
845-431-8000 Fax: 845-431-8984
Web site: www.sunydutchess.edu

President:
  D David Conklin....................................845-431-8980
  e-mail: conklin@sunydutchess.edu

Erie Community College
121 Ellicott St
Buffalo, NY 14203-2698
716-842-2770 Fax: 716-851-1170
e-mail: info@ecc.edu
Web site: www.ecc.edu

Interim President:
  William Reuter....................716-851-1200/fax: 716-851-1029
  e-mail: reuter@ecc.edu

Fashion Institute of Technology
7th Ave at 27th St
New York, NY 10001-5992

Offices and agencies generally appear in alphabetical order, except when specific order is requested by listee.

COLLEGES AND UNIVERSITIES / State University of New York

212-217-7999
e-mail: fitinfo@fitnyc.edu
Web site: www.fitnyc.edu

President:
Joyce F Brown 212-217-7660/fax: 212-217-7639

Finger Lakes Community College
4355 Lakeshore Dr
Canandaigua, NY 14424
585-394-3500 or 585-394-3522 Fax: 585-394-5017
e-mail: admissions@flcc.edu
Web site: www.fingerlakes.edu

President:
Daniel T Hayes 585-394-3500 x7201
e-mail: hayesdt@flcc.edu

Fulton-Montgomery Community College
2805 State Hwy 67
Johnstown, NY 12095-3790
518-762-4651 Fax: 518-762-4334
e-mail: geninfo@fmcc.suny.edu
Web site: www.fmcc.suny.edu

President:
Dustin Swanger 518-762-5310 x8000

Genesee Community College
One College Rd
Batavia, NY 14020-9704
585-343-0055 Fax: 585-343-4541
Web site: www.genesee.edu

President:
Stuart Steiner 585-343-0055 x6201
e-mail: ssteiner@genesee.edu

Herkimer County Community College
100 Reservoir Rd
Herkimer, NY 13350-9987
315-866-0300 or 888-464-4222 Fax: 315-866-0062
Web site: www.herkimer.edu

President:
Ronald F Williams 315-866-0300 x8261/fax: 315-866-5539
e-mail: williams@herkimer.edu

Hudson Valley Community College
80 Vandenburgh Ave
Troy, NY 12180
518-629-4822 or 877-325-4822 Fax: 518-629-8070
e-mail: input@hvcc.edu
Web site: www.hvcc.edu

President:
Andrew Matonak 518-629-4530
e-mail: matonand@hvcc.edu

Jamestown Community College
525 Falconer St
PO Box 20
Jamestown, NY 14702-0020
716-665-5220 or 800-388-8557 Fax: 716-338-1466
Web site: www.sunyjcc.edu

President:
Gregory T DeCinque 716-665-5220 x2315
e-mail: gregdecinque@mail.sunyjcc.edu

Jefferson Community College
1220 Coffeen St
Watertown, NY 13601
315-786-2200 Fax: 315-786-0158
Web site: www.sunyjefferson.edu

President:
Carole A McCoy 315-786-2230
e-mail: cmccoy@sunyjefferson.edu

Mohawk Valley Community College
1101 Sherman Dr
Utica, NY 13501-5394
315-792-5400 Fax: 315-792-5666
Web site: www.mvcc.edu

President:
Michael I Schafer 315-792-5333/fax: 315-792-5678
e-mail: mschafer@mvcc.edu

Monroe Community College
1000 E Henrietta Rd
Rochester, NY 14623
585-292-2000 Fax: 585-292-3060
Web site: www.monroecc.edu

President:
R Thomas Flynn 585-292-2100/fax: 585-424-5249
e-mail: tflynn@monroecc.edu

Nassau Community College
1 Education Dr
Garden City, NY 11530-6793
516-572-7501 Fax: 516-572-8118
e-mail: info@ncc.edu
Web site: www.ncc.edu

President:
Sean A Fanelli 516-572-7205
e-mail: presidentsoffice@ncc.edu

Niagara County Community College
3111 Saunders Settlement Rd
Sanborn, NY 14132
716-614-6222 Fax: 716-614-6700
Web site: www.niagaracc.suny.edu

Offices and agencies generally appear in alphabetical order, except when specific order is requested by listee.

COLLEGES AND UNIVERSITIES / State University of New York

President:
 James P Klyczek 716-614-5901
 e-mail: klyczek@niagaracc.suny.edu

North Country Community College
23 Santanoni Ave
PO Box 89
Saranac Lake, NY 12983-0089
518-891-2915 or 888-879-6222 Fax: 518-891-6562
Web site: www.nccc.edu

President:
 Gail Rogers Rice 518-891-2915 x201/fax: 518-891-5029
 e-mail: president@nccc.edu

Onondaga Community College
4585 West Seneca Turnpike
Syracuse, NY 13215
315-498-2622 Fax: 315-469-4475
e-mail: occinfo@sunyocc.edu
Web site: www.sunyocc.edu

President:
 Debbie L Sydow 315-498-2211
 e-mail: sydowd@sunyocc.edu

Orange County Community College
115 South St
Middletown, NY 10940
845-344-6222 Fax: 845-343-1228
Web site: orange.cc.ny.us

President:
 William Richards 845-341-4971
 e-mail: president@sunyorange.edu

Rockland Community College
145 College Rd
Suffern, NY 10901
845-574-4000
Web site: www.sunyrockland.edu

President:
 Cliff L Wood 845-574-4214
 e-mail: cwood@sunyrockland.edu

Schenectady County Community College
78 Washington Ave
Schenectady, NY 12305
518-381-1200 Fax: 518-346-0379
Web site: www.sunysccc.edu

President:
 Gabriel J Basil 518-381-1304/fax: 518-346-8680
 e-mail: basilgj@gw.sunysccc.edu

Suffolk County Community College
533 College Rd
Selden, NY 11784
631-451-4000 Fax: 631-451-4090
Web site: www3.sunysuffolk.edu

President:
 Shirley Robinson Pippins 631-451-4736
 e-mail: pippins@sunysuffolk.edu

Sullivan County Community College
112 College Rd
PO Box 4002
Loch Sheldrake, NY 12759
845-434-5750 or 800-577-5243 Fax: 845-434-4806
e-mail: sccc@sullivan.suny.edu
Web site: www.sullivan.suny.edu

President:
 Mamie Howard Golladay 845-434-5750 x4261/fax: 845-434-9308
 e-mail: mgollada@sullivan.suny.edu

Tompkins Cortland Community College
170 North St
PO Box 139
Dryden, NY 13053
607-844-8211 or 888-567-8211 Fax: 607-844-9665
Web site: www.sunytccc.edu

President:
 Carl E Haynes 607-844-8211 x4368/fax: 607-844-8237

Ulster County Community College
Cottekill Rd
Stone Ridge, NY 12484
845-687-5000 or 800-724-0833 Fax: 845-687-5083
Web site: www.sunyulster.edu

President:
 Donald C Katt 845-687-5050/fax: 845-687-5292
 e-mail: kattd@sunyulster.edu

Westchester Community College
75 Grasslands Rd
Valhalla, NY 10595-1693
914-606-6600 Fax: 914-785-6565
e-mail: info@sunywcc.edu
Web site: www.sunywcc.edu

President:
 Joseph N Hankin 914-606-6707/fax: 914-785-6780
 e-mail: joseph.hankin@sunywcc.edu

EDUCATIONAL OPPORTUNITY CENTERS

Bronx Educational Opportunity Center
1666 Bathgate Ave
Bronx, NY 10457
718-530-7000 Fax: 718-583-0783
Web site: www.brx.eoc.suny.edu

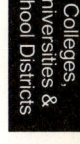

Offices and agencies generally appear in alphabetical order, except when specific order is requested by listee.

COLLEGES AND UNIVERSITIES / State University of New York

Executive Director:
 Wendell Joyner................................718-530-7045

Brooklyn Educational Opportunity Center
111 Livingston St
Brooklyn, NY 11201
718-246-2085 Fax: 718-246-2062
e-mail: henryd@bklyn.eoc.cuny.edu
Web site: www.bklyn.eoc.suny.edu

Executive Director/Dean:
 Lois Blades-Rosado...............................718-246-2057
 e-mail: rosadol@bklyn.eoc.cuny.edu

Buffalo Educational Opportunity Center
465 Washington St
Buffalo, NY 14203
716-849-6727 x500 Fax: 716-849-6755
Web site: www.eoc.buffalo.edu

Director:
 Sherryl D Weems.................................716-849-6727
 e-mail: weems@acsu.buffalo.edu

Capital District Educational Opportunity Center
145 Congress St
Troy, NY 12180
518-273-1900 Fax: 518-273-0244
Web site: www.alb.eoc.suny.edu

Executive Director/VP:
 Lucille A Marion.................................518-629-7768
 e-mail: marioluc@hvcc.edu

Educational Opportunity Center of Westchester
26 S Broadway
Yonkers, NY 10701
914-606-7600 Fax: 914-606-7640
Web site: www.ynk.sunyeoc.org

Director/Associate Dean:
 Renee Guy..914-606-7612
 e-mail: renee.guy@sunywcc.edu

Long Island Educational Opportunity Center
269 Fulton Ave
Hempstead, NY 11550
516-489-8705
Web site: www.li.sunyeoc.org

Dean/Executive Director:
 Veronica Henry...................................631-420-2507
 e-mail: henryv@farmingdale.edu

Manhattan Educational Opportunity Center
163 W 125th St
New York, NY 10027
212-961-4400 Fax: 212-961-4343
e-mail: info@meoc.suny.edu
Web site: www.meoc.suny.edu

Interim Director/Dean:
 Rodney Alexander................................212-961-1315
 e-mail: rodney.alexander@man.eoc.suny.edu

North Bronx Career Counseling & Outreach Center
3950 Laconia Ave
Bronx, NY 10466
718-547-1001 Fax: 718-547-1973
Web site: www.nbx.eoc.suny.edu

Director:
 Mitch Duren......................................718-547-1001

Queens Educational Opportunity Center
SUNY
158-29 Archer Ave
Jamaica, NY 11433
718-725-3300 Fax: 718-658-5604
Web site: www.qns.eoc.suny.edu

Director:
 Khayriyyah Ali...................................718-725-3403
 e-mail: ali_29@eoc.suny.edu

Rochester Educational Opportunity Center
305 Andrews St
Rochester, NY 14604
585-232-2730 Fax: 585-546-7824
Web site: www.rochestereoc.com

Dean/Executive Director:
 Melva L Brown................585-232-2730 x269/fax: 585-232-8154
 e-mail: mebrown@brockport.edu

SUNY College & Career Counseling Center
120 Emmons St
Schenectady, NY 12304
518-370-2654 Fax: 518-370-2661
e-mail: sunycccc@thebiz.net

Director:
 Lois M Tripp.....................................518-370-2654

Syracuse Educational Opportunity Center
100 New St
Syracuse, NY 13202
315-472-0130 Fax: 315-472-1241
Web site: www.syr.sunyeoc.org

Dean:
 Bill Harper.......................................315-472-0130
 e-mail: harperbg@morrisville.edu

Offices and agencies generally appear in alphabetical order, except when specific order is requested by listee.

COLLEGES AND UNIVERSITIES / The City University of New York

The City University of New York

CUNY Board of Trustees
535 E 80th St
New York, NY 10021
212-794-5450 Fax: 212-794-5678
Web site: www.cuny.edu

Chair:
   Benno C Schmidt Jr (2013) 212-794-5450
Member:
   Valerie Lancaster Beal (2009) 212-794-5450
Member:
   Philip Berry (2009)................................. 212-794-5450
Member:
   John S Bonnici (2008) 212-794-5450
Member:
   Wellington Z Chen (2010) 212-794-5450
Member:
   Rita DiMartino (2010) 212-794-5450
Member:
   Freida Foster-Tolbert (2012) 212-794-5450
Member:
   Joseph J Lhota (2011).............................. 212-794-5450
Member:
   Randy M Mastro (2006)............................ 212-794-5450
Member:
   Hugo M Morales MD (2007) 212-794-5450
Member:
   Kathleen M Pesile (2011)........................... 212-794-5450
Member:
   Carol A Robles-Roman (2008)..................... 212-794-5450
Member:
   Marc V Shaw (2007) 212-794-5450
Member:
   Sam A Sutton (2011) 212-794-5450
Member:
   Jeffrey Wiesenfeld (2013) 212-794-5450

CUNY Central Administration
535 E 80th St
New York, NY 10021
212-794-5555
Web site: www.cuny.edu

Chancellor:
   Matthew Goldstein 212-794-5311/fax: 212-794-5671
Executive Vice Chancellor/COO:
   Allan H Dobrin.................................... 212-794-5305
Executive Vice Chancellor/University Provost:
   Selma Botman 212-794-5414
Senior Vice Chancellor, University Relations/Board Secretary:
   Jay Hershenson................................... 212-794-5317
Senior Vice Chancellor, Legal Affairs & General Counsel:
   Frederick P Schaffer............................... 212-794-5506
Vice Chancellor, Budget & Finance:
   Ernesto Malave.................................... 212-794-5403
Vice Chancellor, Faculty & Staff Relations:
   Brenda Richardson Malone 212-794-5353
Vice Chancellor for Student Development:
   Garrie W Moore 212-794-5775
Interim Vice Chancellor, Facilities Planning, Construction & Mgmt:
   Eduardo del Valle................................. 212-794-5315

Special Counsel to the Chancellor:
   Dave Fields....................................... 212-794-5313
Vice Chancellor, Academic Administration & Planning:
   Michael J Zavelle 212-794-5326
Univeristy Dean, Research:
   Gillian Small...................................... 212-794-5417
University Dean, Faculty & Staff Relations:
   Gloriana Waters 212-794-5725
University Director, Admission Services:
   Richard P Alvarez................................. 212-794-5725
University Director, Communications & Marketing:
   Michael Arena 212-794-5685
Deputy COO:
   Ronald Spalter 212-794-5609

City University Construction Fund .... fax: 212-541-0401
555 W 57th St, 11th Fl, New York, NY 10019
212-541-0171 Fax: 212-541-0401

Interim Chairman:
   Philip Berry 212-541-0171
Executive Director:
   Iris Weinshall 212-541-5315
Counsel:
   Frederick Schaffer 212-794-5506
Special Assistant:
   Nancy Nichols 212-541-0171
   e-mail: nancy.nichols@mail.cuny.edu
Chief Administrative Officer:
   Denise Phillips 212-541-0190
   e-mail: denise.phillips@mail.cuny.edu

Bernard M Baruch College
One Bernard Baruch Way
New York, NY 10010
646-312-1000 Fax: 646-312-1362
Web site: www.baruch.cuny.edu

President:
   Kathleen M Waldron................ 646-312-3310/fax: 646-312-3311

Borough of Manhattan Community College
199 Chambers St
New York, NY 10007
212-220-8000 Fax: 212-220-1244
Web site: www.bmcc.cuny.edu

President:
   Antonio Perez 212-220-1230 x7079
   e-mail: aperez@bmcc.cuny.edu

Bronx Community College
West 181st St & University Ave
Bronx, NY 10453
718-289-5100
e-mail: webmaster@bcc.cuny.edu
Web site: www.bcc.cuny.edu

President:
   Carolyn G Williams................. 718-289-5151/fax: 718-289-6011

Offices and agencies generally appear in alphabetical order, except when specific order is requested by listee.

COLLEGES AND UNIVERSITIES / The City University of New York

Brooklyn College
2900 Bedford Ave
Brooklyn, NY 11210
718-951-5000
Web site: www.brooklyn.cuny.edu

President:
Christoph M Kimmich 718-951-5671/fax: 718-951-4872
e-mail: cmk@brooklyn.cuny.edu

City College of New York, The
Convent Ave & 138th St
New York, NY 10031
212-650-7000
Web site: www1.ccny.cuny.edu

President:
Gregory H Williams 212-650-7286/fax: 212-650-7680
e-mail: gwilliams@ccny.cuny.edu

College of Staten Island
2800 Victory Blvd
Staten Island, NY 10314
718-982-2000
Web site: www.csi.cuny.edu

President:
Marlene Springer 718-982-2400/fax: 718-982-2404
e-mail: springer@mail.csi.cuny.edu

Graduate Center
365 Fifth Ave
New York, NY 10016-4309
212-817-7000 or 877-428-6942
Web site: www.gc.cuny.edu

President:
William P Kelly 212-817-7100/fax: 212-817-1606
e-mail: pres@gc.cuny.edu

Graduate School of Journalism
230 W 41st Street
New York, NY 10036
646-758-7800
Web site: www.journalism.cuny.edu

Dean:
Steve Shepard 646-758-7816/fax: 646-758-7809
e-mail: steve.shepard@journalism.cuny.edu

Hostos Community College
500 Grand Concourse
Bronx, NY 10451
718-518-4444 or 718-518-4100
Web site: www.hostos.cuny.edu

President:
Dolores M Fernandez 718-518-4300
e-mail: dfernandez@hostos.cuny.edu

Hunter College
695 Park Ave
New York, NY 10021
212-772-4000
Web site: www.hunter.cuny.edu

President:
Jennifer J Raab 212-772-4242/fax: 212-772-4724
e-mail: jennifer.raab@hunter.cuny.edu

John Jay College of Criminal Justice
899 Tenth Ave
New York, NY 10019
212-237-8000 Fax: 212-237-8607
Web site: www.jjay.cuny.edu

President:
Jeremy Travis 212-237-8600
e-mail: jtravis@jjay.cuny.edu

Kingsborough Community College
2001 Oriental Blvd
Brooklyn, NY 11235-2398
718-265-5343
e-mail: info@kbcc.cuny.edu
Web site: www.kbcc.cuny.edu

President:
Regina S Peruggi 718-368-5109
e-mail: president@kingsborough.edu

LaGuardia Community College
31-10 Thomson Ave
Long Island City, NY 11101
718-482-7200
Web site: www.lagcc.cuny.edu

President:
Gail O Mellow 718-482-5050
e-mail: gmellow@lagcc.cuny.edu

Lehman College
250 Bedford Park Blvd West
Bronx, NY 10468
718-960-8000 or 877-534-6261
Web site: www.lehman.edu

President:
Ricardo R Fernandez 718-960-8111/fax: 718-584-1765
e-mail: president@lehman.cuny.edu

Medgar Evers College
1650 Bedford St
Brooklyn, NY 11225
718-270-4900
Web site: www.mec.cuny.edu

President:
Edison O Jackson 718-270-5000/fax: 718-270-5126

Offices and agencies generally appear in alphabetical order, except when specific order is requested by listee.

COLLEGES AND UNIVERSITIES / Independent Colleges & Universities

New York City College of Technology
300 Jay St
Brooklyn, NY 11201
718-260-5500
e-mail: connect@citytech.cuny.edu
Web site: www.citytech.cuny.edu

President:
   Russell K Hotzler 718-260-5400
   e-mail: rhotzler@citytech.cuny.edu

Queens College
65-30 Kissena Blvd
Flushing, NY 11367-1597
718-997-5000
Web site: www.qc.cuny.edu

President:
   James L Muyskens 718-997-5550/fax: 718-793-8044
   e-mail: james.muyskens@qc.cuny.edu

Queensborough Community College
222-05 56th Ave
Bayside, NY 11364-1497
718-631-6262
Web site: www.qcc.cuny.edu

President:
   Eduardo J Marti 718-631-6222/fax: 718-423-0363
   e-mail: emarti@qcc.cuny.edu

School of Law at Queens College
65-21 Main St
Flushing, NY 11367
718-340-4200 Fax: 718-340-4435
Web site: www.law.cuny.edu

Dean:
   Michelle J Anderson 718-340-4201
   e-mail: deansoffice@mail.law.cuny.edu

School of Professional Studies
365 Fifth Ave
New York, NY 10016
212-817-7255
Web site: sps.cuny.edu

Dean:
   John Mogulescu 212-817-7255

Sophie Davis School of Biomedical Education
160 Convent Ave
Room H-107
New York, NY 10031
212-650-5275 Fax: 212-650-6696
Web site: med.cuny.edu

Dean:
   Standford H Roman Jr 212-650-5275/fax: 212-650-6696
   e-mail: stanrom@ccny.cuny.edu

York College
94-20 Guy R Brewer Blvd
Jamaica, NY 11451
718-262-2000
Web site: york.cuny.edu

President:
   Marcia Keizs 718-262-2350/fax: 718-262-2352
   e-mail: president@york.cuny.edu

Independent Colleges & Universities

Adelphi University
1 South Ave
PO Box 701
Garden City, NY 11530
516-877-3050 or 800-233-5744 Fax: 516-877-3090
Web site: www.adelphi.edu

President:
   Robert A Scott 516-877-3838/fax: 516-877-3845

Albany College of Pharmacy
106 New Scotland Ave
Albany, NY 12208-3492
518-694-7200 or 888-203-8010 Fax: 518-694-7202
e-mail: info@acp.edu
Web site: www.acp.edu

President:
   James J Gozzo 518-694-7255
   e-mail: gozzoj@acp.edu

Albany Law School
80 New Scotland Ave
Albany, NY 12208-3494
518-445-2311 Fax: 518-445-2315
e-mail: info@albanylaw.edu
Web site: www.albanylaw.edu

President/Dean:
   Thomas F Guernsey 518-445-2380/fax: 518-472-5865

Albany Medical College
47 New Scotland Ave
Albany, NY 12208

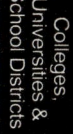

Offices and agencies generally appear in alphabetical order, except when specific order is requested by listee.

COLLEGES AND UNIVERSITIES / Independent Colleges & Universities

518-262-6008 Fax: 518-262-6515
Web site: www.amc.edu/Academic/AboutCollege/index.html

Dean:
Vincent P Verdile 518-262-6008
e-mail: verdilv@mail.amc.edu

Alfred University
1 Saxon Dr
Alfred, NY 14802-1205
800-541-9229 or 607-871-2111 Fax: 607-871-2198
Web site: www.alfred.edu

President:
Charles M Edmondson 607-871-2101
e-mail: edmondson@alfred.edu

American Academy McAllister Institute of Funeral Service
619 West 54th St, 6th Fl
New York, NY 10019
212-757-1190 Fax: 212-765-5923
e-mail: info@funeraleducation.org
Web site: www.funeraleducation.org

President/CEO:
Meg Dunn 212-757-1190

American Academy of Dramatic Arts
120 Madison Ave
New York, NY 10016-7004
212-686-9244 or 800-463-8990
Web site: www.aada.org

President:
Roger Croucher 212-686-9244

Bank Street College of Education/Graduate School
610 West 112th St
New York, NY 10025-1898
212-875-4400 Fax: 212-875-4678
e-mail: collegepubs@bankstreet.edu
Web site: www.bankstreet.edu

President:
Augusta Souza Kappner 212-875-4595/fax: 212-875-4594
e-mail: akappner@bankstreet.edu
Dean, Graduate School:
Jon Snyder 212-875-4400
e-mail: jsnyder@bankstreet.edu

Bard College
PO Box 5000
Annandale-on-Hudson, NY 12504-5000
845-758-6822 Fax: 845-758-5208
Web site: www.bard.edu

President:
Leon Botstein 845-758-7423
e-mail: president@bard.edu

Barnard College
3009 Broadway
New York, NY 10027
212-854-5262 Fax: 212-854-6220
Web site: www.barnard.edu

President:
Judith R Shapiro 212-854-2021
e-mail: jshapiro@barnard.edu

Boricua College
3755 Broadway
New York, NY 10032
212-694-1000 Fax: 212-694-1015
e-mail: acruz@boricuacollege.edu
Web site: www.boricuacollege.edu

President:
Victor G Alicea 212-694-1000
e-mail: valicea@boricuacollege.edu

Bramson ORT College
69-30 Austin St
Forest Hills, NY 11375-4239
718-261-5800 Fax: 718-575-5118
Web site: www.bramsonort.org

Director:
Ephraim Buhks 718-261-5800 x102
e-mail: ebuhks@bramsonort.edu

Brooklyn Law School
250 Joralemon St
Brooklyn, NY 11201-3798
718-625-2200 Fax: 718-780-0393
Web site: www.brooklaw.edu

Dean:
Joan G Wexler 718-780-7900
e-mail: joan.wexler@brooklaw.edu

Canisius College
2001 Main St
Buffalo, NY 14208-1098
716-883-7000 Fax: 716-888-2525
Web site: www.canisius.edu

President:
Rev Vincent M Cooke 716-888-2100/fax: 716-888-3220
e-mail: cookevm@canisius.edu

Cazenovia College
22 Sullivan St
Cazenovia, NY 13035

Offices and agencies generally appear in alphabetical order, except when specific order is requested by listee.

COLLEGES AND UNIVERSITIES / Independent Colleges & Universities

315-655-7000 or 800-654-3210 Fax: 315-655-4143
e-mail: admissions@cazenovia.edu
Web site: www.cazenovia.edu

President:
   Mark John Tierno.................................315-655-7116
   e-mail: mtierno@cazenovia.edu

Christ the King Seminary
711 Knox Rd
East Aurora, NY 14052-0607
716-652-8900 Fax: 716-652-8903
e-mail: cksacad@cks.edu
Web site: www.cks.edu

President/Rector:
   Rev Richard W Siepka...........................716-652-8900
   e-mail: rsiepka@cks.edu

Clarkson University
8 Clarkson Ave
Potsdam, NY 13699
315-268-6400 or 800-527-6577 Fax: 315-268-7993
Web site: www.clarkson.edu

President:
   Anthony G Collins..............................315-268-6444
   e-mail: tony.collins@clarkson.edu

Cochran School of Nursing
St John's Riverside Hospital
967 N Broadway, Andrus Pavilion
Yonkers, NY 10701
914-964-4296 Fax: 914-964-4266
e-mail: kvitola@riversidehealth.org
Web site: www.cochranschoolofnursing.org

Vice President & Dean:
   Kathleen Dirschel...............................914-964-4280
   e-mail: kdirschel@cochranschoolofnursing.org
Director, Administration:
   David T George.................................914-964-4296
   e-mail: dgeorge@riversidehealth.org

Colgate Rochester Crozer Divinity School
1100 S Goodman St
Rochester, NY 14620-2589
585-271-1320 Fax: 585-271-8013
Web site: www.crcds.edu

President:
   Eugene Bay................................585-271-1320 x340
   e-mail: gbay@crcds.edu

Colgate University
13 Oak Dr
Hamilton, NY 13346
315-228-1000 Fax: 315-228-7798
Web site: www.colgate.edu

President:
   Rebecca S Chopp................315-228-7444/fax: 315-228-6010
   e-mail: rchopp@mail.colgate.edu

College of Mount Saint Vincent
6301 Riverdale Ave
Riverdale, NY 10471-1093
800-665-2678 or 718-405-3267
Web site: www.mountsaintvincent.edu

President:
   Charles L Flynn Jr..............................718-405-3233

College of New Rochelle (The)
Brooklyn Campus
29 Castle Pl
New Rochelle, NY 10805-2339
914-654-5000 or 800-211-7077 Fax: 914-654-5833
e-mail: info@cnr.edu
Web site: www.cnr.edu

President:
   Stephen J Sweeny...............................914-654-5430
   e-mail: ssweeny@cnr.edu

College of Saint Rose (The)
432 Western Ave
Albany, NY 12203-1490
800-637-8556
Web site: www.strose.edu

President:
   R Mark Sullivan................................518-454-5120
   e-mail: sullivan@strose.edu

Columbia University
2960 Broadway
New York, NY 10027
212-854-9970 or 212-854-1754 Fax: 212-854-9973
Web site: www.columbia.edu

President:
   Lee C Bollinger................................212-854-9970
   e-mail: bollinger@columbia.edu

Concordia College
171 White Plains Rd
Bronxville, NY 10708
914-337-9300 Fax: 914-395-4500
Web site: www.concordia-ny.edu

President:
   Viji D George.............................914-337-9300 x2111
   e-mail: viji.george@concordia-ny.edu

Cooper Union for the Advancement of Science & Art
30 Cooper Sq
New York, NY 10003-7120

Colleges, Universities & School Districts

Offices and agencies generally appear in alphabetical order, except when specific order is requested by listee.

623

COLLEGES AND UNIVERSITIES / Independent Colleges & Universities

212-353-4100
Web site: www.cooper.edu

President:
George Campbell Jr 212-353-4100

Cornell University
300 Day Hall
Ithaca, NY 14853
607-254-4636 Fax: 607-255-5396
e-mail: info@cornell.edu
Web site: www.cornell.edu

President:
David J Skorton 607-255-5201/fax: 607-255-9924
e-mail: president@cornell.edu

Crouse Hospital School of Nursing
736 Irving Ave
Syracuse, NY 13210
315-470-7111 Fax: 315-470-7232
e-mail: crouseson@crouse.org
Web site: www.crouse.org/nursing

Director:
JoAnn Herne 315-470-7481

Culinary Institute of America
1946 Campus Dr
Hyde Park, NY 12538-1499
845-451-1401 or 800-285-4627 Fax: 845-451-1068
e-mail: alumni@culinary.edu
Web site: www.ciachef.edu

President:
Tim Ryan 845-451-1352

D'Youville College
320 Porter Ave
Buffalo, NY 14201
716-829-8000 or 800-777-3921 Fax: 716-881-7790
Web site: www.dyc.edu

President:
Sister Denise A Roche 716-829-7673
e-mail: roche@dyc.edu

Daemen College
4380 Main St
Amherst, NY 14226
716-839-3600 or 800-462-7652 Fax: 716-839-8516
Web site: www.daemen.edu

President:
Martin J Anisman 716-839-8210/fax: 716-839-8279
e-mail: manisman@daemen.edu

Davis College
400 Riverside Dr
Johnson City, NY 13790
607-729-1581 or 800-331-4137 Fax: 607-729-2962
e-mail: info@davisny.edu
Web site: www.davisny.edu

President:
George D Miller, III 607-729-1581 x316/fax: 607-729-1581

Dominican College
470 Western Highway
Orangeburg, NY 10962
845-359-7800 Fax: 845-359-2313
Web site: www.dc.edu

President:
Sister Mary Eileen O'Brien 845-359-7800/fax: 845-359-7988
e-mail: mary.eileen.obrien@dc.edu

Dorothea Hopfer School of Nursing at Mount Vernon Hospital
53 Valentine St
Mount Vernon, NY 10550
914-664-8000 x3220 Fax: 914-665-7047
e-mail: hopferadmissions@sshsw.org
Web site: www.ssmc.org

Dean of Nursing Education:
Joanna Scalabrini 914-664-8000 x3220
e-mail: hopfer@sshsw.org

Dowling College
Idle Hour Blvd
Oakdale, NY 11769
631-244-3030 or 800-369-5464 Fax: 631-589-6644
Web site: www.dowling.edu

President:
Albert E Donor 631-244-3200/fax: 631-589-7551
e-mail: donor@dowling.edu

Ellis Hospital School of Nursing
1101 Nott St
Schenectady, NY 12308
518-243-4471 Fax: 518-243-4470
Web site: www.ehson.org

Director:
Mary Lee Pollard 518-243-4471
e-mail: pollardm@ellishospital.org
CEO:
Robert Smanik 518-243-4471

Elmira College
One Park Pl
Elmira, NY 14901

Offices and agencies generally appear in alphabetical order, except when specific order is requested by listee.

COLLEGES AND UNIVERSITIES / Independent Colleges & Universities

607-735-1800 or 800-935-6472
e-mail: admissions@elmira.edu
Web site: www.elmira.edu

President:
 Thomas K Meier............................607-735-1790
 e-mail: tmeier@elmira.edu

Excelsior College
7 Columbia Cir
Albany, NY 12203-5159
518-464-8500 or 888-647-2388 Fax: 518-464-8777
e-mail: info@excelsior.edu
Web site: www.excelsior.edu

President:
 John F Ebersole 518-464-8500

Fordham University
Rose Hill
441 East Fordham Rd
Bronx, NY 10458
718-817-1000
Web site: www.fordham.edu

President:
 Joseph M McShane 718-817-3000/fax: 718-817-3005

General Theological Seminary of the Episcopal Church
175 Ninth Ave
Chelsea Sq
New York, NY 10011-4977
212-243-5150 Fax: 212-727-3907
Web site: www.gts.edu

President/Dean:
 Rev Ward B Ewing 212-243-5150/fax: 212-647-0294
 e-mail: ewing@gts.edu

Hamilton College
198 College Hill Rd
Clinton, NY 13323
315-859-4421 or 800-843-2655 Fax: 315-859-4457
Web site: www.hamilton.edu

President:
 Joan Hinde Stewart........................315-859-4105
 e-mail: jstewart@hamilton.edu

Hartwick College
One Hartwick Dr
Oneonta, NY 13820-4020
800-427-8942 or 607-431-4000 Fax: 607-431-4102
Web site: www.hartwick.edu

President:
 Richard P Miller, Jr 607-431-4990
 e-mail: president@hartwick.edu

Hebrew Union College - Jewish Institute of Religion
The Brookdale Center
One W 4th St
New York, NY 10012
212-674-5300 Fax: 212-388-1720
Web site: www.huc.edu

President:
 David Ellenson 800-424-1336 x2201/fax: 212-979-0853
 e-mail: presoff@huc.edu

Helene Fuld College of Nursing North General Hospital
1879 Madison Ave @ 120th St
New York, NY 10035
212-423-2700 Fax: 212-427-2453
Web site: www.helenefuld.edu

President:
 Margaret Wines 212-423-2750

Hilbert College
5200 South Park Ave
Hamburg, NY 14075
716-649-7900 Fax: 716-649-0702
Web site: www.hilbert.edu

President:
 Cynthia Zane 716-649-7900 x200
 e-mail: czane@hilbert.edu

Hobart & William Smith Colleges
629 S Main St
Geneva, NY 14456
315-781-3000 or 800-852-2256
Web site: www.hws.edu

President:
 Mark D Gearan............................315-781-3309
 e-mail: gearan@hws.edu

Hofstra University
100 Fulton Ave
Hempstead, NY 11550
800-463-7872 or 516-463-6600 Fax: 516-463-4867
Web site: www.hofstra.edu

President:
 Stuart Rabinowitz 516-463-6800/fax: 516-463-6096
 e-mail: president@hofstra.edu

Houghton College
1 Willard Ave
Houghton, NY 14744-0128
800-777-2556 Fax: 585-567-9572
Web site: www.houghton.edu

Offices and agencies generally appear in alphabetical order, except when specific order is requested by listee.

COLLEGES AND UNIVERSITIES / Independent Colleges & Universities

President:
   Shirley Mullen 585-567-9526
   e-mail: cindy.lastoria@houghton.edu

Institute of Design & Construction
141 Willoughby St
Brooklyn, NY 11201
718-855-3661 Fax: 718-852-5889
Web site: www.idc.edu

Executive Director:
   Vincent C Battista................................. 718-855-3661
   e-mail: vcbattista@idc.edu

Iona College
715 North Ave
New Rochelle, NY 10801
914-633-2000 or 800-231-4662 Fax: 914-633-2018
Web site: www.iona.edu

President:
   Br James A Liguori 914-633-2203
   e-mail: jliguori@iona.edu

Ithaca College
953 Danby Rd
Ithaca, NY 14850
607-274-3011 Fax: 607-274-1900
e-mail: thurston@ithaca.edu
Web site: www.ithaca.edu

President:
   Peggy R Williams 607-274-3111/fax: 607-274-1500
   e-mail: president@ithaca.edu

Jewish Theological Seminary
3080 Broadway
New York, NY 10027-4649
212-678-8000 Fax: 212-678-8947
Web site: www.jtsa.edu

Chancellor/President of Faculties:
   Ismar Schorsch.................................... 212-678-8071
   e-mail: isschorsch@jtsa.edu

Juilliard School (The)
60 Lincoln Center Plz
New York, NY 10023-6588
212-799-5000 Fax: 212-724-0263
Web site: www.juilliard.edu

President:
   Joseph W Polisi 212-799-5000
Dean:
   Stephen Clapp 212-799-5000 x204

Keuka College
141 Central Ave
Keuka Park, NY 14478
315-279-5000 or 800-335-3852 Fax: 315-279-5216
Web site: www.keuka.edu

President:
   Joseph Burke 315-279-5201/fax: 315-279-5335
   e-mail: president@mail.keuka.edu

King's College (The)
Empire State Bldg
350 Fifth Ave, Ste 1500
New York, NY 10118
888-969-7200 or 212-659-7200 Fax: 212-659-7210
e-mail: information@tkc.edu
Web site: www.tkc.edu

President:
   Jack Stanley Oakes Jr............................. 212-659-7200

Le Moyne College
1419 Salt Springs Rd
Syracuse, NY 13214-1301
315-445-4100 Fax: 315-445-4540
Web site: www.lemoyne.edu

President:
   Rev Charles J Beirne 315-445-4120/fax: 315-445-4691
   e-mail: beirnecj@lemoyne.edu

Long Island College Hospital School of Nursing
397 Hicks
Brooklyn, NY 11201
718-780-1953 Fax: 718-780-1936
Web site: www.wehealny.org

Dean:
   Janet MacKin 718-780-1998

Long Island University
University Center
700 Northern Blvd
Brookville, NY 11548-1326
516-299-2000 or 516-299-1926 Fax: 516-299-2072
Web site: www.liu.edu

President:
   David J Steinberg 516-299-2501/fax: 516-229-2590
   e-mail: president@liu.edu

Manhattan College
Manhattan College Pkwy
Riverdale, NY 10471
718-862-8000 or 800-622-9235
Web site: www.manhattan.edu

President:
   Brother Thomas J Scanlan........... 718-862-7301/fax: 718-862-8030
   e-mail: thomas.scanlan@manhattan.edu

Offices and agencies generally appear in alphabetical order, except when specific order is requested by listee.

COLLEGES AND UNIVERSITIES / Independent Colleges & Universities

Manhattan School of Music
120 Claremont Ave
New York, NY 10027
212-749-2802 Fax: 212-749-5471
Web site: www.msmnyc.edu

President:
Robert Sirota 212-749-2802 x4477
e-mail: officeofthepresident@msmnyc.edu

Manhattanville College
2900 Purchase St
Purchase, NY 10577
914-694-2200 Fax: 914-694-2386
Web site: www.manhattanville.edu

President:
Richard A Berman. 914-323-5230/fax: 914-694-6234
e-mail: president@mville.edu

Maria College of Albany
700 New Scotland Ave
Albany, NY 12208
518-438-3111 Fax: 518-453-1366
Web site: www.mariacollege.edu

President:
Sister Laureen A Fitzgerald. 518-438-3111 x213
e-mail: lfitz@mariacollege.edu

Marist College
3399 North Rd
Poughkeepsie, NY 12601
845-575-3000
e-mail: timmian.massie@marist.edu
Web site: www.marist.edu

President:
Dennis J Murray. 845-575-3600
e-mail: dennis.murray@marist.edu

Marymount Manhattan College
221 East 71st St
New York, NY 10021
800-627-9668 or 212-517-0400 Fax: 212-517-0567
Web site: www.mmm.edu

President:
Judson R Shaver. 212-517-0560
e-mail: jshaver@mmm.edu

Medaille College
18 Agassiz Cir
Buffalo, NY 14214
716-880-2000 or 800-292-1582
Web site: www.medaille.edu

Interim President:
Richard Davis. 716-880-2526

Memorial Hospital School of Nursing
600 Northern Blvd
Albany, NY 12204
518-471-3260 Fax: 518-447-3559
e-mail: dorseyp@nehealth.com
Web site: www.nehealth.com

Director:
Mary Harknett-Martin 518-471-3260
e-mail: martinm@nehealth.com

Mercy College
Main Campus
555 Broadway
Dobbs Ferry, NY 10522
800-637-2969 or 800-637-2969 Fax: 914-674-7382
e-mail: admissions@mercy.edu
Web site: www.mercy.edu

President:
Louise H Feroe 914-674-7307/fax: 914-674-5978
e-mail: LFeroe@mercy.edu

Metropolitan College of New York
75 Varick St
New York, NY 10013
212-343-1234 or 800-338-4465 Fax: 212-334-4890
Web site: www.metropolitan.edu

President:
Stephen R Greenwald 212-343-1234 x3301
e-mail: sgreenwald@metropolitan.edu

Mid-America Baptist Theological Seminary Northeast Branch
2810 Curry Rd
Schenectady, NY 12303
518-355-4000 or 800-209-3447 Fax: 518-355-8298
e-mail: paarrant@mabtsne.edu
Web site: www.mabts.edu

Director:
David H Shepherd 518-355-4000
e-mail: dshepherd@mabtsne.edu

Molloy College
1000 Hempstead Ave
PO Box 5002
Rockville Centre, NY 11571-5002
516-678-5000 or 888-466-5569
Web site: www.molloy.edu

President:
Drew Bogner 516-678-5000 x6200/fax: 516-678-5321
e-mail: presidentdrew@molloy.edu

Mount Saint Mary College
330 Powell Ave
Newburgh, NY 12550

Offices and agencies generally appear in alphabetical order, except when specific order is requested by listee.

COLLEGES AND UNIVERSITIES / Independent Colleges & Universities

845-561-0800 Fax: 845-562-6762
Web site: www.msmc.edu

President:
  Sister Ann Sakac.................................845-569-3201
  e-mail: sakac@msmc.edu

Mount Sinai School of Medicine of NYU
One Gustave L Levy Pl
New York, NY 10029-6574
212-241-6546
Web site: www.mssm.edu

President/CEO/Dean:
  Kenneth L Davis..................212-659-8888/fax: 212-803-6772
  e-mail: kenneth.davis@mssm.edu

Nazareth College of Rochester
4245 East Ave
Rochester, NY 14618-7390
585-389-2525 Fax: 585-586-2452
Web site: www.naz.edu

President:
  Daan Braveman....................585-389-2001/fax: 585-389-2015
  e-mail: dbravem7@naz.edu

New School University (The)
66 West 12th St
New York, NY 10011
212-229-5600 Fax: 212-229-5937
e-mail: kerreyb@newschool.edu
Web site: www.newschool.edu

President:
  Robert Kerrey.......................................212-229-5656
Dean:
  Linda Dunne...212-229-5613
  e-mail: dunnel@newschool.edu

New York Academy of Art Inc
111 Franklin St
New York, NY 10013
212-966-0300 Fax: 212-966-3217
e-mail: info@nyaa.edu
Web site: www.nyaa.edu

Executive Director:
  Wayne A Linker....................................212-966-0300
Dean:
  Erica Ehrenberg....................................212-966-0300

New York Chiropractic College
2360 Route 89
Seneca Falls, NY 13148
315-568-3000 or 800-234-6922 Fax: 315-568-3012
Web site: www.nycc.edu

President:
  Frank J Nicchi......................................315-568-3100
  e-mail: fnicchi@nycc.edu

New York College of Health Professions
6801 Jericho Tpke
Suite 300
Syosset, NY 11791
516-364-0808 or 800-922-7337 Fax: 516-364-0989
e-mail: info@nycollege.edu
Web site: www.nycollege.edu

President:
  Lisa E Pamintuan..................................516-364-0808
  e-mail: pamintuan@nycollege.edu

New York College of Podiatric Medicine
1800 Park Ave
New York, NY 10035-1940
212-410-8000 Fax: 212-722-4918
e-mail: admissions@nycpm.edu
Web site: www.nycpm.edu

President/CEO:
  Louis L Levine....................212-410-8024/fax: 212-876-7670
  e-mail: llevine@nycpm.edu

New York College of Traditional Chinese Medicine
13 E 37th St 2nd Fl
New York, NY 10016
212-685-0888
Web site: www.nyctcm.edu

President:
  Yemeng Chen......................................212-685-0888

New York Institute of Technology
Northern Blvd
PO Box 8000
Old Westbury, NY 11568-8000
516-686-1000 or 800-345-6948 Fax: 516-686-7613
Web site: www.nyit.edu

President/CEO:
  Edward Guiliano...................................516-686-7650
  e-mail: president@nyit.edu

New York Law School
57 Worth St
New York, NY 10013
212-431-2872 or 212-431-2100 Fax: 212-406-0103
e-mail: alevat@nyls.edu
Web site: www.nyls.edu

President/Dean:
  Richard A Matasar................212-431-2840/fax: 212-219-3752
  e-mail: ddean@nyls.edu

New York Medical College
Administration Bldg
40 Sunshine Cottage Rd
Valhalla, NY 10595

Offices and agencies generally appear in alphabetical order, except when specific order is requested by listee.

COLLEGES AND UNIVERSITIES / Independent Colleges & Universities

914-594-4000
Web site: www.nymc.edu

President/CEO:
Karl P Adler, M.D................................914-594-4600

New York School of Interior Design
170 East 70th St
New York, NY 10021
212-472-1500 or 800-336-9743 Fax: 212-472-3800
e-mail: admissions@nysid.edu
Web site: www.nysid.edu

President:
Inge Heckel..................212-472-1500 x401/fax: 212-472-1952

New York Theological Seminary
475 Riverside Dr, Ste 500
New York, NY 10115-0083
212-870-1211 Fax: 212-870-1236
e-mail: online@nyts.edu
Web site: www.nyts.edu

President:
Dale T Irvin..212-870-1211
e-mail: dirvin@nyts.edu

New York University
70 Washington Square South
New York, NY 10012
212-998-1212
Web site: www.nyu.edu

President:
John Sexton......................212-998-2345/fax: 212-995-4790
e-mail: john.sexton@nyu.edu

Niagara University
Lewiston Rd
Niagara University, NY 14109
716-285-1212 or 800-778-3450 Fax: 716-286-8710
Web site: www.niagara.edu

President:
Rev Joseph L Levesque.............716-286-8350/fax: 716-286-8350
e-mail: jll@niagara.edu

Northeastern Seminary
2265 Westside Dr
Rochester, NY 14624
585-594-6800 or 800-777-4792 Fax: 585-594-6801
e-mail: seminary@roberts.edu
Web site: www.nes.edu

President:
John A Martin......................................800-777-4792

Nyack College
1 South Blvd
Nyack, NY 10960-3698
845-358-1710 Fax: 845-358-1751
e-mail: president@nyack.edu
Web site: www.nyack.edu

President:
Michael Scales................................845-358-1710 x310

Pace University
1 Pace Plz
New York, NY 10038
212-346-1200 or 800-874-7223 Fax: 212-346-1933
Web site: www.pace.edu

President:
David A Caputo....................212-346-1097/fax: 212-346-1384
e-mail: president@pace.edu

Paul Smith's College
Routes 86 & 30
PO Box 265
Paul Smiths, NY 12970-0265
518-327-6227 or 800-421-2605 Fax: 518-327-6016
Web site: www.paulsmiths.edu

President/Acting Provost:
John W Mills.....................518-327-6223/fax: 518-327-6060
e-mail: millsj@paulsmiths.edu

Phillips Beth Israel School of Nursing
776 Ave of Americas
4th Fl
New York, NY 10001-6354
212-614-6110 Fax: 212-614-6109
Web site: www.futurenursebi.org

Dean:
Janet MacKin......................................212-614-6107
e-mail: jmackin@chpnet.org

Polytechnic University
Main Campus
6 MetroTech Ctr
Brooklyn, NY 11201-2999
718-260-3600 Fax: 718-260-3136
e-mail: inquiry@poly.edu
Web site: www.poly.edu

President:
Jerry MacArthur Hultin.............718-260-3500/fax: 718-260-3755
e-mail: hultin@poly.edu

Pratt Institute
200 Willoughby Ave
Brooklyn, NY 11205

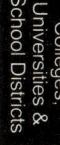
Colleges, Universities & School Districts

Offices and agencies generally appear in alphabetical order, except when specific order is requested by listee.

COLLEGES AND UNIVERSITIES / Independent Colleges & Universities

718-636-3600 Fax: 718-636-3785
e-mail: info@pratt.edu
Web site: www.pratt.edu

President:
    Thomas F Schutte.................................718-636-3647
    e-mail: tschutte@pratt.edu

Professional Business College
125 Canal St
New York, NY 10002
212-226-7300
Web site: www.pcbny.edu

President:
    Leon Y Lee..212-226-7300

Rensselaer Polytechnic Institute
110 8th St
Troy, NY 12180
518-276-6000
Web site: www.rpi.edu

President:
    Shirley Ann Jackson 518-276-6211/fax: 518-276-8702
    e-mail: president@rpi.edu

Roberts Wesleyan College
2301 Westside Dr
Rochester, NY 14624-1997
585-594-6000 or 800-777-4792 Fax: 585-594-6371
e-mail: admissions@roberts.edu
Web site: www.roberts.edu

President:
    John A Martin 585-594-6100/fax: 585-594-6780
    e-mail: presidentsoffice@roberts.edu

Rochester Institute of Technology
One Lomb Memorial Dr
Rochester, NY 14623-5603
585-475-2411 Fax: 585-475-5700
Web site: www.rit.edu

President:
    Albert J Simone 585-475-2394
    e-mail: ajspro@rit.edu

Rochester, University of
Wallis Hall
Administration
Rochester, NY 14627
585-275-2121 Fax: 585-275-0359
Web site: www.rochester.edu

President:
    Joel Seligman.....................585-275-8356/fax: 585-256-2473
    e-mail: seligman@rochester.edu

Rockefeller University
1230 York Ave
New York, NY 10021
212-327-8000 Fax: 212-327-7974
e-mail: pubinfo@rockefeller.edu
Web site: www.rockefeller.edu

President:
    Sir Paul Nurse.....................................212-327-8000
    e-mail: nurse@mail.rockefeller.edu

Sage Colleges (The)
45 Ferry St
Troy, NY 12180
518-244-2000 or 888-837-9724 Fax: 518-244-2470
Web site: www.sage.edu

President:
    Jeanne H Neff.....................................518-244-2214
    e-mail: pres@sage.edu

Salvation Army School for Officer Training
201 Lafayette Ave
Suffern, NY 10901
845-357-3501 Fax: 845-357-6644
Web site: www1.salvationarmy.org

Territorial Youth Candidates Secretary:
    Major Ivan Rock...................................845-620-7359
    e-mail: Ivan_Rock@use.salvationarmy.org

Samaritan Hospital School of Nursing
2215 Burdett Ave
Troy, NY 12180
518-271-3285 Fax: 518-271-3303
e-mail: dorseyp@nehealth.com
Web site: www.nehealth.com

Director:
    Mary Harknett-Martin 518-271-3285
    e-mail: martinm@nehealth.com

Sarah Lawrence College
1 Mead Way
Bronxville, NY 10708-5999
914-337-0700 Fax: 914-395-2515
e-mail: slcadmit@slc.edu
Web site: www.slc.edu

President:
    Michele Tolela Myers 914-395-2201/fax: 914-395-2668
    e-mail: mmyers@sarahlawrence.edu
Dean:
    Barbara Kaplan....................................914-395-2303
    e-mail: bkaplan@sarahlawrence.edu

Seminary of the Immaculate Conception
440 West Neck Rd
Huntington, NY 11743

Offices and agencies generally appear in alphabetical order, except when specific order is requested by listee.

COLLEGES AND UNIVERSITIES / Independent Colleges & Universities

631-423-0483 Fax: 631-423-2346
e-mail: info@icseminary.edu
Web site: www.icseminary.edu

Rector:
  Rev Msgr James McDonald 631-423-0483
    e-mail: jmcdonald@icseminary.edu

Siena College
515 Loudon Rd
Loudonville, NY 12211-1462
518-783-2300 Fax: 518-783-4293
Web site: www.siena.edu

President:
  Fr Kevin E Mackin 518-783-2302
    e-mail: mackin@siena.edu

Skidmore College
815 N Broadway
Saratoga Springs, NY 12866-1632
518-580-5000 Fax: 518-580-5699
e-mail: info@skidmore.edu
Web site: www.skidmore.edu

President:
  Philip A Glotzbach 518-580-5700/fax: 518-580-5699
    e-mail: pglotzba@skidmore.edu

St Bernard's School of Theology & Ministry
120 French Rd
Rochester, NY 14618
585-271-3657 Fax: 585-271-2045
Web site: www.stbernards.edu

President:
  Patricia A Schoelles 585-271-3657 x290
    e-mail: pschoelles@stbernards.edu

St Bonaventure University
3261 W State Rd
St Bonaventure, NY 14778-2284
716-375-2000 or 800-462-5050
Web site: www.sbu.edu

President:
  Sister Margaret Carney 716-375-2222
    e-mail: mcarney@sbu.edu

St Elizabeth College of Nursing
2215 Genesee St
Utica, NY 13501
315-798-8144 Fax: 315-798-8271
e-mail: conadmin@secon.edu
Web site: www.secon.edu

Dean:
  Marianne Monahan 315-798-8125
    e-mail: mmonahan@secon.edu

St Francis College
180 Remsen St
Brooklyn Heights, NY 11201
718-489-5200 or 718-522-2300 Fax: 718-237-8964
Web site: www.stfranciscollege.edu

President:
  Frank J Macchiarola 718-489-5354
    e-mail: fmacchia@stfranciscollege.edu

St John Fisher College
3690 East Ave
Rochester, NY 14618
585-385-8000 Fax: 585-385-8289
Web site: www.sjfc.edu

President:
  Donald E Bain 585-385-8010
    e-mail: bain@sjfc.edu

St John's University
Queens Campus
8000 Utopia Pkwy
Queens, NY 11439
718-990-2000 or 888-978-5646 Fax: 718-990-5723
e-mail: admhelp@stjohns.edu
Web site: www.new.stjohns.edu

President:
  Rev Donald J Harrington 718-990-6301
    e-mail: pres@stjohns.edu

St Joseph's College
Main Campus
245 Clinton Ave
Brooklyn, NY 11205-3688
718-636-6868 Fax: 718-636-7242
Web site: www.sjcny.edu

President:
  Elizabeth A Hill 718-636-6800/fax: 718-636-6102

St Joseph's Seminary Institute of Religious Studies
201 Seminary Ave
Yonkers, NY 10704-1896
914-968-6200 Fax: 914-376-2019
e-mail: sjs@archny.org
Web site: www.ny-archdiocese.org/seminary

Dean:
  Kevin P O'Reilly 914-968-6200

St Lawrence University
23 Romoda Dr
Canton, NY 13617
315-229-5011 or 800-285-1856 Fax: 315-229-7422
Web site: www.stlawu.edu

Offices and agencies generally appear in alphabetical order, except when specific order is requested by listee.

COLLEGES AND UNIVERSITIES / Independent Colleges & Universities

President:
   Daniel F Sullivan 315-229-5892
   e-mail: dsullivan@stlawu.edu

St Thomas Aquinas College
125 Route 340
Sparkill, NY 10976-1050
845-398-4000
Web site: www.stac.edu

President/CEO:
   Margaret M Fitzpatrick 845-398-4147/fax: 845-359-8136
   e-mail: mfitzpat@stac.edu

St Vladimir's Orthodox Theological Seminary
575 Scarsdale Rd
Crestwood, NY 10707-1699
914-961-8313 Fax: 914-961-4507
e-mail: info@svots.edu
Web site: www.svots.edu

Dean:
   John H Erickson 914-961-8313 X323
   e-mail: jhe@svots.edu

Sunbridge College
285 Hungry Hollow Rd
Chesnut Ridge, NY 10977
845-425-0055 Fax: 845-425-1413
e-mail: info@sunbridge.edu
Web site: www.sunbridge.edu

Administrator:
   John Greene 845-425-0055 x16
   e-mail: jgreene@sunbridge.edu

Syracuse University
Skytop Office Building
Syracuse, NY 13244-1100
315-443-1870 Fax: 315-443-3503
Web site: www.syr.edu

Chancellor & President:
   Nancy Cantor 315-443-2235
   e-mail: ncantor@syr.edu

Teachers College, Columbia University
525 W 120th St
New York, NY 10027
212-678-3000
Web site: www.tc.columbia.edu

President:
   Arthur E Levine 212-678-3131/fax: 212-678-3205
   e-mail: levine@exchange.tc.columbia.edu

Touro College
27-33 W 23rd St
New York, NY 10010
212-463-0400 Fax: 212-627-9144
Web site: www.touro.edu

President:
   Bernard Lander 718-820-4900
   e-mail: blander@touro.edu

Trocaire College
360 Choate Ave
Buffalo, NY 14220-2094
716-826-1200 Fax: 716-828-6109
e-mail: info@trocaire.edu
Web site: www.trocaire.edu

President:
   Paul B Hurley, Jr 716-826-1200
   e-mail: hurleyp@trocaire.edu

Unification Theological Seminary
30 Seminary Dr
Barrytown, NY 12507
845-752-3000 Fax: 845-752-3014
e-mail: registrar@uts.edu
Web site: www.uts.edu

President:
   Tyler O Hendricks 845-752-3000 x230
   e-mail: th@uts.edu

Union College
807 Union St
Schenectady, NY 12308-3107
518-388-6000 Fax: 518-388-6006
Web site: www.union.edu

President-Elect:
   Stephen C Ainlay 518-388-6101
   e-mail: ainlays@union.edu
Dean:
   Steve Leavitt 518-388-6116/fax: 518-388-6648
   e-mail: leavitts@union.edu

Union Theological Seminary
3041 Broadway at 121st St
New York, NY 10027
212-662-7100 Fax: 212-280-1416
e-mail: contactus@uts.columbia.edu
Web site: www.uts.columbia.edu

President:
   Joseph C Hough Jr 212-280-1403
   e-mail: jhough@uts.columbia.edu

Utica College
1600 Burrstone Rd
Utica, NY 13502-5159
315-792-3006 Fax: 315-792-3003
Web site: www.utica.edu

Offices and agencies generally appear in alphabetical order, except when specific order is requested by listee.

COLLEGES AND UNIVERSITIES / Proprietary Colleges

President:
Todd S Hutton 315-792-3222
e-mail: thutton@utica.edu

Vassar College
124 Raymond Ave
Poughkeepsie, NY 12604
845-437-7000 Fax: 845-437-7187
Web site: www.vassar.edu

President:
Catharine B Hill 845-437-7200

Vaughn College of Aeronautics & Technology
86-01 23rd Ave
Flushing, NY 11369
718-429-6600 or 866-682-8446 Fax: 718-779-2231
Web site: www.vaughn.edu

President:
John C Fitzpatrick. 718-429-6600 x104/fax: 718-429-4020
e-mail: john.fitzpatrick@vaughn.edu

Villa Maria College of Buffalo
240 Pine Ridge Rd
Buffalo, NY 14225
716-896-0700 Fax: 716-961-1871
e-mail: admissions@villa.edu
Web site: www.villa.edu

President:
Sr Marcella Marie Garus 716-961-1868
e-mail: smgarus@villa.edu

Wagner College
1 Campus Rd
Staten Island, NY 10301
718-390-3100 or 800-221-1010 Fax: 718-390-3105
Web site: www.wagner.edu

President:
Richard Guarasci 718-390-3131/fax: 718-390-3170
e-mail: guarasci@wagner.edu

Watson School of Biological Sciences at Cold Spring Harbor Laboratory
One Bungtown Rd
Cold Spring Harbor, NY 11724
516-367-6890 Fax: 516-367-6919
e-mail: gradschool@cshl.edu
Web site: gradschool.cshl.edu

President/CEO:
Bruce Stillman 516-367-6890

Webb Institute
298 Crescent Beach Rd
Glen Cove, NY 11542-1398
516-671-2213 or 866-708-9322 Fax: 516-674-9838
Web site: www.webb-institute.edu

President:
Admiral Robert Olsen 516-671-2213 x102
e-mail: rolsen@webb-institute.edu

Wells College
170 Main St
Aurora, NY 13026-0500
315-364-3266
Web site: www.wells.edu

President:
Lisa Marsh Ryerson. 315-364-3265/fax: 315-364-3335
e-mail: president@wells.edu

Yeshiva University
Wilf Campus
500 W 185th St
New York, NY 10033-3201
212-960-5400
e-mail: administration@yu.edu
Web site: www.yu.edu

President:
Richard M Joel 212-960-5300
e-mail: rjoel@yu.edu

Proprietary Colleges

ASA Institute of Business & Computer Technology
81 Willoughby St
Brooklyn, NY 11201
877-679-8772
Web site: www.asa-institute.com

President:
Alex Shchegol 877-679-8772

Art Institue of New York City (The)
75 Varick St, 16th Fl
New York, NY 10013
212-226-5500 or 800-654-2433 Fax: 212-966-0706
e-mail: ainycadm@aii.edu
Web site: www.artinstitutes.edu/newyork/

President:
Tim Howard 212-226-5500

Offices and agencies generally appear in alphabetical order, except when specific order is requested by listee.

COLLEGES AND UNIVERSITIES / Proprietary Colleges

Berkeley College, New York City Campus
3 East 43rd St
New York, NY 10017
212-986-4343 or 800-446-5400 Fax: 212-697-3371
e-mail: info@berkeleycollege.edu
Web site: www.berkeleycollege.edu

President:
  Mildred Garcia..................................212-986-4343 x4101
  e-mail: president@berkeleycollege.edu

Berkeley College, Westchester Campus
99 Church St
White Plains, NY 10601
914-694-1122 Fax: 914-328-9469
e-mail: info@berkeleycollege.edu
Web site: www.berkeleycollege.edu

SVP, Administration:
  Edward Imperiosi....................................914-694-1122

Briarcliffe College-Bethpage
1055 Stewart Ave
Bethpage, NY 11714
516-918-3600 Fax: 516-470-6020
e-mail: info@bcl.edu
Web site: www.bcbeth.com

Interim President:
  George Santiago Jr..................................516-918-3603

Briarcliffe College-Patchogue
225 West Main St
Patchogue, NY 11772
631-654-5300
Web site: www.bcpat.com

Interim President:
  George Santiago Jr..................................631-654-5300

Bryant & Stratton College-Albany Campus
1259 Central Ave
Albany, NY 12205
518-437-1802
Web site: www.bryantstratton.edu

Campus Director:
  Michael Gutierrez....................................518-437-1802
  e-mail: magutierrez@bryantstratton.edu

Bryant & Stratton College-Amherst Campus
Audubon Business Centre
40 Hazelwood Dr
Amherst, NY 14228
716-691-0012
Web site: www.bryantstratton.edu

Campus Director:
  Marvel Ross-Jones..................................716-691-0012

Bryant & Stratton College-Buffalo Campus
465 Main St, Ste 400
Buffalo, NY 14203
716-884-9120
Web site: www.bryantstratton.edu

Campus Director:
  Jeffrey Tredo..716-884-9120

Bryant & Stratton College-Greece Campus
150 Bellwood Dr
Rochester, NY 14606
585-720-0660
Web site: www.bryantstratton.edu

Campus Director:
  Marc Ambrosi......................................585-720-0660

Bryant & Stratton College-Henrietta Campus
1225 Jefferson Rd
Rochester, NY 14623
585-292-5627
Web site: www.bryantstratton.edu

Director of Rochester Colleges:
  Anne L Loria......................................585-292-5627

Bryant & Stratton College-Southtowns Campus
200 Red Tail
Orchard Park, NY 14127
716-677-9500
Web site: www.bryantstratton.edu

Campus Director:
  Paul Bahr..716-677-9500

Bryant & Stratton College-Syracuse Campus
953 James St
Syracuse, NY 13203-2502
315-472-6603
Web site: www.bryantstratton.edu

Campus Director:
  Michael Sattler....................................315-472-6603

Bryant & Stratton College-Syracuse North Campus
8687 Carling Rd
Liverpool, NY 13090
315-652-6500
Web site: www.bryantstratton.edu

Campus Director:
  Susan Cumoletti..................................315-652-6500

Business Informatics Center
134 S Central Ave
Valley Stream, NY 11580

Offices and agencies generally appear in alphabetical order, except when specific order is requested by listee.

COLLEGES AND UNIVERSITIES / Proprietary Colleges

516-561-0050 Fax: 516-561-0074
e-mail: info@thecollegeforbusiness.com
Web site: www.thecollegeforbusiness.com

President:
Joseph Brown 516-561-0050

Christie's Education Inc
20 Rockefeller Plaza
New York, NY 10020
212-636-2000 Fax: 212-636-2399
e-mail: info@christies.com
Web site: www.christies.com/education/ny_overview.asp

Head of Department:
Toby Usnik 212-636-2679
e-mail: tusnik@christies.com

College of Westchester (The)
325 Central Park Ave
PO Box 710
White Plains, NY 10606
914-831-0200 or 800-333-4924 Fax: 914-948-5441
Web site: www.cw.edu

President:
Karen J Smith 914-831-0200

DeVry Institute of Technology, Long Island City Campus
3020 Thomson Ave
Long Island City, NY 11101
718-269-4200 or 888-713-3879 Fax: 718-361-0004
Web site: www.ny.devry.edu

President:
Carol S Zajac PhD 718-269-4201

Elmira Business Institute
Langdon Plaza
303 N Main St
Elmira, NY 14901-2731
607-733-7177 or 800-843-1812 Fax: 607-733-7178
e-mail: info@ebi-college.com
Web site: www.ebi-college.com

President:
Brad C Phillips 607-733-7177 x202

Elmira Business Institute-Vestal
Vestal Executive Pk
4100 Vestal Rd
Vestal, NY 13850
607-729-8915 or 866-703-7550 Fax: 607-729-8916
e-mail: info@ebi-college.com
Web site: www.ebi-college.com

Campus Director:
Kathy Hamilton 607-729-8915 x202

Everest Institute
1630 Portland Ave
Rochester, NY 14621-3007
585-266-0430 or 888-741-4270 Fax: 585-266-8243
Web site: www.everest.edu

Five Towns College
305 N Service Rd
Dix Hills, NY 11746-5871
631-424-7000 Fax: 631-424-7008
e-mail: info@ftc.edu
Web site: www.ftc.edu

President:
Stanley G Cohen 631-424-7000

Globe Institute of Technology
291 Broadway
New York, NY 10007
212-349-4330 Fax: 212-227-5920
Web site: www.globe.edu

President:
Oleg Rabinovich 212-349-4330

ITT Technical Institute
13 Airline Dr
Albany, NY 12205
518-452-9300 or 800-489-1191 Fax: 518-452-9393
Web site: www.itt-tech.edu

Director:
Christopher Chang 518-452-9300
e-mail: cchang@itt-tech.edu

Interboro Institute
450 W 56th St
New York, NY 10019
212-399-0093
Web site: www.interboro.edu

CEO:
John J McGgrath 212-399-0093

Island Drafting & Technical Institute
128 Broadway, Route 110
Amityville, NY 11701-2704
631-691-8733 Fax: 631-691-8738
e-mail: info@idti.edu
Web site: www.idti.edu

President:
James G DiLiberto 631-691-8733
e-mail: dilibertoj@idti.edu

Jamestown Business College
7 Fairmount Ave
Jamestown, NY 14702

Offices and agencies generally appear in alphabetical order, except when specific order is requested by listee.

COLLEGES AND UNIVERSITIES / Proprietary Colleges

716-664-5100 Fax: 716-664-3144
Web site: www.jbcny.org

President:
   Tyler C Swanson 716-664-5100
   e-mail: tylerswanson@jbcny.org

Katharine Gibbs School-Melville
320 S Service Rd
Melville, NY 11747
631-370-3300 or 888-615-3444 Fax: 631-293-0429
Web site: www.gibbsmelville.com

President:
   Steven Kashlin 631-370-3300

Katharine Gibbs School-New York City
50 W 40th St
New York, NY 10018
212-867-9300 or 888-317-6444
Web site: www.gibbsny.edu

President:
   Wynn Blanton 212-867-9300

Laboratory Institute of Merchandising
216 E 45th St, 2nd Fl
New York, NY 10017
212-752-1530 or 800-677-1323 Fax: 212-750-3432
e-mail: info@limcollege.edu
Web site: www.limcollege.edu

President:
   Elizabeth S Marcuse 212-752-1530

Long Island Business Institute-Commack
6500 Jericho Tpke
Commack, NY 11725
631-499-7100 Fax: 631-499-7114
e-mail: info@libi.edu
Web site: www.libi.edu

President:
   Philip Stander 631-499-7100

Long Island Business Institute-Flushing
37-12 Prince St
Flushing, NY 11354
718-939-5100 Fax: 718-939-9235
Web site: www.libi.edu

President:
   Philip Stander 718-939-5100

Mandl School
254 W 54th St
New York, NY 10019
212-247-3434
Web site: www.mandlschool.com

Mildred Elley
800 New Loudon Rd, Ste 5120
Latham, NY 12110
518-786-0855 or 800-622-6327 Fax: 518-786-0898
e-mail: admissions@mildred-elley.edu
Web site: www.mildred-elley.edu

Director, External Program Development:
   Robert Giuffrida Jr 518-786-0855/fax: 518-785-7560
   e-mail: bob.giuffrida@mildred-elley.edu

Monroe College-Bronx
2501 Jerome Ave
Bronx, NY 10468
718-933-6700 or 800-556-6676 Fax: 718-295-5861
Web site: www.monroecollege.edu

President:
   Stephen J Jerome 718-933-6700 x8252

Monroe College-New Rochelle
434 Main St
New Rochelle, NY 10801
914-632-5400 Fax: 914-632-5457
Web site: www.monroecollege.edu

Executive VP:
   Marc M Jerome 914-632-5400 x6803

New York Career Institute
11 Park Place
4th Fl
New York, NY 10007
212-962-0002 Fax: 212-385-7574
e-mail: info@nyci.com
Web site: www.nyci.com

CEO:
   Ivan Londa 212-962-0002

Olean Business Institute
301 North Union St
Olean, NY 14760
716-372-7978 Fax: 716-372-2120
e-mail: admin@obi.edu
Web site: www.obi.edu

President:
   Jennifer L Madison 716-372-7978

Pacific College of Oriental Medicine
915 Broadway 2nd Floor
New York, NY 10010
212-982-3456 or 800-729-3468 Fax: 212-982-6514
Web site: www.pacificcollege.edu

President:
   Jack Miller 212-982-3456
   e-mail: jmiller@pacificcollege.edu

Offices and agencies generally appear in alphabetical order, except when specific order is requested by listee.

COLLEGES AND UNIVERSITIES / Proprietary Colleges

Plaza College
74-09 37th Ave
Jackson Heights, NY 11372
718-779-1430 Fax: 718-779-7423
e-mail: plazainfo@plazacollege.edu
Web site: www.plazacollege.edu

President:
Charles E Callahan 718-779-1430

School of Visual Arts
209 East 23rd St
New York, NY 10010
212-592-2000 or 888-220-5782 Fax: 212-725-3587
e-mail: admissions@sva.edu
Web site: www.schoolofvisualarts.edu

President:
David John Rhodes 212-592-2350

Simmons Institute of Funeral Service Inc
1828 South Ave at West Brighton Ave
Syracuse, NY 13207
315-475-5142 or 800-727-3536 Fax: 315-475-3817
e-mail: info@simmonsinstitute.com
Web site: www.simmonsinstitute.com

President/CEO:
Maurice C Wightman 315-475-5142

Swedish Institute
226 W 26th St
New York, NY 10001
212-924-5900 Fax: 212-924-7600
Web site: www.swedishinstitute.org

Dean, Administration and Operations:
Yick Pon Huey 212-924-5900

Taylor Business Institute
23 W 17th St, 7th Floor
New York, NY 10011
800-959-9999
e-mail: admission@tbiglobal.com
Web site: www.tbiglobal.com

President:
George Shu 800-959-9999

Technical Career Institutes Inc
320 W 31st St
New York, NY 10001
212-594-4000 or 800-878-8246
e-mail: admissions@tcicollege.edu
Web site: www.tcicollege.edu

President:
James Melville 212-594-4000

Tri-State College of Acupuncture
80th Ave, Ste 400
New York, NY 10011
212-242-2255 Fax: 212-242-2920
Web site: www.tsca.edu

President:
Mark D Seem 212-242-2255

Utica School of Commerce
201 Bleecker St
Utica, NY 13501
315-733-2300 or 800-321-4872 Fax: 315-733-9281
Web site: www.uscny.edu

President:
Philip M Williams 315-733-2309 x2214
e-mail: pwilliams@uscny.edu

Wood Tobe-Coburn
8 E 40th St
New York, NY 10016
212-686-9040 or 800-394-9663 Fax: 212-686-9171
Web site: www.woodtobecoburn.edu

President:
Sandi Gruninger 212-686-9040
e-mail: sgruninger@woodtobecoburn.edu

Offices and agencies generally appear in alphabetical order, except when specific order is requested by listee.

PUBLIC SCHOOL DISTRICTS
School District Administrators

ALBANY

Albany City SD
Eva Joseph, Superintendent
Academy Park, Albany, NY 12207-1099
518-475-6010 Fax: 518-475-7295
e-mail: ejoseph@albany.k12.ny.us
Web site: www.albanyschools.org

Berne-Knox-Westerlo CSD
Steven M Schrade, Superintendent
1738 Helderberg Trl, Berne, NY 12023-2926
518-872-1293 Fax: 518-872-0341
e-mail: sschrade@bkwcsd.k12.ny.us
Web site: www.bkwcsd.k12.ny.us

Bethlehem CSD
Leslie Loomis, Superintendent
90 Adams Pl, Delmar, NY 12054-3297
518-439-7098 Fax: 518-475-0352
e-mail: loomlco@bcsd.neric.org
Web site: bcsd.k12.ny.us

Cohoes City SD
Charles S Dedrick, Superintendent
21 Page Ave, Cohoes, NY 12047-3299
518-237-0100 Fax: 518-237-2912
e-mail: cdedrick@cohoes.org
Web site: www.cohoes.org

Green Island UFSD
John E McKinney, Superintendent
171 Hudson Ave, Green Island, NY 12183-1293
518-273-1422 Fax: 518-273-0818
e-mail: jmckinne@mum.neric.org
Web site: www.greenisland.org

Guilderland CSD
Gregory Aidala, Superintendent
6076 State Farm Rd, Guilderland, NY 12084-9533
518-456-6200 Fax: 518-456-1152
e-mail: aidalag@guilderlandschools.org
Web site: www.guilderlandschools.org

Maplewood-Colonie Common SD
Jerome D Steele, Superintendent
32 Cohoes Rd, Watervliet, NY 12189-1898
518-273-1512 Fax: 518-273-0269
e-mail: jsteele@choiceonemail.com
Web site: www.maplewoodschools.org

Menands UFSD
Andrea Kostik, Interim Superintendent
19 Wards Ln, Menands, NY 12204-2197
518-465-4561 Fax: 518-465-4572
e-mail: akostik@nycap.rr.com
Web site: www.menandsschool.nycap.rr.com

North Colonie CSD
Randy A Ehrenberg, Superintendent
91 Fiddler's Ln, Latham, NY 12110-5349
518-785-8591 Fax: 518-785-8502
e-mail: rehrenberg@ncolonie.org
Web site: www.northcolonie.org

Ravena-Coeymans-Selkirk CSD
Vicki Wright, Superintendent
26 Thatcher St, Selkirk, NY 12158-0097
518-756-5200 Fax: 518-767-2644
e-mail: vwright@rcscsd.org
Web site: www.rcscsd.org

South Colonie CSD
Michael Marcelle, Superintendent
102 Loralee Dr, Albany, NY 12205-2298
518-869-3576 Fax: 518-869-6577
e-mail: mjmcrs@aol.com
Web site: www.southcolonieschools.org

Voorheesville CSD
Linda Langevin, Superintendent
432 New Salem Rd, Voorheesville, NY 12186-0498
518-765-3313 Fax: 518-765-2751
e-mail: llang@vcsdk12.org
Web site: vcsd.neric.org

Watervliet City SD
Paul Padalino, Superintendent
1245 Hillside Dr, Watervliet, NY 12189
518-629-3201 Fax: 518-629-3265
e-mail: ppadalin@vliet.neric.org
Web site: vliet.neric.org

ALLEGANY

Alfred-Almond CSD
Richard A Nicol, Superintendent
6795 Rt 21, Almond, NY 14804-9716
607-276-2981 Fax: 607-276-6304
e-mail: rnicole@aacs.wnyric.org
Web site: www.aacs.org

Andover CSD
William C Berg, Superintendent

Offices and agencies generally appear in alphabetical order, except when specific order is requested by listee.

PUBLIC SCHOOL DISTRICTS / School District Administrators

31-35 Elm St, PO Box G, Andover, NY 14806-0508
607-478-8491 x222
e-mail: wberg@andovercsd.org
Web site: www.andovercsd.org

Belfast CSD
Judy May, Superintendent
1 King St, Belfast, NY 14711
585-365-9940
e-mail: jmay@belf.wnyric.org
Web site: www.belfast.wnyric.org

Bolivar-Richburg CSD
Joseph DeCerbo, Superintendent
100 School St, Bolivar, NY 14715
585-928-2561 Fax: 585-928-2411
e-mail: jdecerbo@brcs.wnyric.org
Web site: www.brcs.wnyric.org

Canaseraga CSD
Marie Blum, Superintendent
4-8 Main St, PO Box 230, Canaseraga, NY 14822-0230
607-545-6421 Fax: 607-545-6265
e-mail: mblum@canaseraga.wnyric.org

Cuba-Rushford CSD
Anne S Brungard, Superintendent
5476 Rt 305, Cuba, NY 14727-1014
585-968-2650 x4426
e-mail: abrungard@crcs.wnyric.org
Web site: www.crcs.wnyric.org

Fillmore CSD
David Hanks, Superintendent
104 Main St, Fillmore, NY 14735-0177
585-567-2251
e-mail: dhanks@fillmore.wnyric.org
Web site: www.fillmore.wnyric.org

Friendship CSD
Maureen Donahue, Superintendent
46 W Main St, Friendship, NY 14739-9702
716-973-3311 Fax: 716-973-2023
Web site: www.friendship.wnyric.org

Genesee Valley CSD
Michael Taylor, Superintendent
1 Jaguar Dr, Belmont, NY 14813-9788
585-268-7900
Web site: www.gvcs.wnyric.org

Scio CSD
Michael J McArdle, Superintendent
3968 Washington St, Scio, NY 14880-9507
716-593-5510 Fax: 716-593-3468
e-mail: mmcardle@scio.wnyric.org
Web site: scio.schooltools.us

Wellsville CSD
Byron Chandler, Superintendent
126 W State St, Wellsville, NY 14895
585-596-2170 Fax: 585-596-2177
Web site: www.wellsville.wnyric.org

Whitesville CSD
Douglas H Wyant Jr, Superintendent
692 Main St, Whitesville, NY 14897
607-356-3301 Fax: 607-356-3598
Web site: www.whitesville.wnyric.org

BROOME

Binghamton City SD
Peggy J Wozniak, Superintendent
164 Hawley St, Binghamton, NY 13901-2126
607-762-8100 x318
e-mail: wozniakp@binghamtonschools.org
Web site: www.binghamtonschools.org

Chenango Forks CSD
Robert Bundy, Superintendent
One Gordon Dr, Binghamton, NY 13901-5614
607-648-7543
e-mail: bundyr@cforks.org
Web site: www.cforks.org

Chenango Valley CSD
Carmen A Ciullo, Superintendent
1160 Chenango St, Binghamton, NY 13901-1653
607-779-4710 Fax: 607-779-8610
e-mail: cciullo@cvcsd.stier.org
Web site: www.cvcsd.stier.org

Deposit CSD
Bonnie Hauber, Superintendent
171 Second St, Deposit, NY 13754-1397
607-467-5380 Fax: 607-467-5535
e-mail: bhauber@deposit.stier.org
Web site: www.depositcsd.org

Harpursville CSD
Kathleen M Wood, Superintendent
54 Main St, Harpursville, NY 13787-0147
607-693-8101
Web site: www.hcs.stier.org

Johnson City CSD
Mary Kay Frys, Superintendent
666 Reynolds Rd, Johnson City, NY 13790-1398
607-763-1230 Fax: 607-763-8761
Web site: www.jcschools.org

Maine-Endwell CSD
Joseph F Stoner, Superintendent
712 Farm-to-Market Rd, Endwell, NY 13760-1199
607-754-1400 Fax: 607-754-1650
Web site: www.me.stier.org

Susquehanna Valley CSD
Gerardo Tagliaferri, Acting Superintendent

Offices and agencies generally appear in alphabetical order, except when specific order is requested by listee.

PUBLIC SCHOOL DISTRICTS / School District Administrators

1040 Conklin Rd, Conklin, NY 13748-0200
607-775-0170
Web site: www.svsabers.org

Union-Endicott CSD
James P Coon, Superintendent
1100 E Main St, Endicott, NY 13760-5271
607-757-2103 Fax: 607-757-2809
Web site: www.uetigers.stier.org

Vestal CSD
Mark Capobianco, Superintendent
201 Main St, Vestal, NY 13850-1599
607-757-2241
e-mail: markc@vcs.stier.org
Web site: www.vestal.stier.org

Whitney Point CSD
Carol A Eaton, Superintendent
10 Keibel Rd, Whitney Point, NY 13862-0249
607-692-8202 Fax: 607-692-4434
e-mail: caeaton@wpcsd.org
Web site: www.wpcsd.org

Windsor CSD
Jason A Andrews, Superintendent
1191 NY Route 79, Windsor, NY 13865-4134
607-655-8216 Fax: 607-655-3553
e-mail: jandrews@windsor-csd.org
Web site: www.windsor-csd.org

CATTARAUGUS

Allegany - Limestone CSD
Diane M Munro, Superintendent
3131 Five Mile Rd, Allegany, NY 14706-9627
716-375-6600 x2014
e-mail: dmunro@alli.wnyric.org
Web site: www.alli.wnyric.org

Cattaraugus-Little Valley CSD
Louis C McIntosh, Superintendent
207 Rock City St, Little Valley, NY 14755-1298
716-938-9155 x2210 Fax: 716-938-9367
Web site: qp.wnyric.org

Ellicottville CSD
Patricia Haynes, Superintendent
5873 Route 219, Ellicottville, NY 14731-9719
716-699-2368 Fax: 716-699-6017
e-mail: phaynes@eville.wnyric.org
Web site: www.ellicottvilecentral.com

Franklinville CSD
Dennis Johnson, Superintendent
31 N Main St, Franklinville, NY 14737-1096
716-676-8029 Fax: 716-676-3779
e-mail: djohnson@frkl.wnyric.org
Web site: www.tbafcs.org/franklinville/

Gowanda CSD
Charles J Rinaldi, Superintendent
10674 Prospect St, Gowanda, NY 14070
716-532-3325 Fax: 716-995-2156
e-mail: crinaldi@gowcsd.org
Web site: www.gowcsd.org

Hinsdale CSD
Judy McCarthy, Superintendent
3701 Main St, Hinsdale, NY 14743-0278
716-557-2227 x401
e-mail: jmccarthy@hinsdale.wnyric.org

Olean City SD
Mark J Ward, Superintendent
410 W Sullivan St, Olean, NY 14760-2596
716-375-8018
e-mail: mward@olean.wnyric.org
Web site: www.oleanschools.org

Pioneer CSD
Jeffrey Bowen, Superintendent
12125 County Line Rd, Yorkshire, NY 14173-0579
716-492-9304
e-mail: jbowen@pion.wnyric.org
Web site: www.pioneerschools.org

Portville CSD
Peter A Tigh, Superintendent
500 Elm Street, Portville, NY 14770-9791
716-933-6000 Fax: 716-933-7124
e-mail: ptigh@porterville.wnyric.org
Web site: staging.portervillecentral.wnyric.org

Randolph Academy UFSD
Lori DeCarlo, Superintendent
336 Main Street ER, Randolph, NY 14772-9696
716-358-6866 Fax: 716-358-9425
Web site: www.randoplhacademy.org

Randolph CSD
Sandra M Craft, Superintendent
18 Main St, Randolph, NY 14772-1188
716-358-7005 or 716-358-6161 Fax: 716-358-7072
e-mail: scraft@rand.wnyric.org
Web site: www.randolphcsd.org

Salamanca City SD
Rick T Moore, Superintendent
50 Iroquois Dr, Salamanca, NY 14779-1398
716-945-2403 Fax: 716-945-3964
e-mail: rmoore@salamancany.org
Web site: www.salamancany.org

West Valley CSD
Edward Ahrens, Superintendent

Offices and agencies generally appear in alphabetical order, except when specific order is requested by listee.

PUBLIC SCHOOL DISTRICTS / School District Administrators

5359 School St, West Valley, NY 14171-0290
716-942-3293 Fax: 716-942-3440
e-mail: eahrens@wvalley.wnyric.org
Web site: www.wvalley.wnyric.org

CAYUGA

Auburn Enlarged City SD
John B Plume, Superintendent
78 Thornton Ave, Auburn, NY 13021-4698
315-255-8835
e-mail: john_plume@auburn.cnyric.org

Cato-Meridian CSD
Deborah D Bobo, Superintendent
2851 NYS Rt 370, Cato, NY 13033-0100
315-626-3439 Fax: 315-626-2888
e-mail: dbobo@cm.cnyric.org

Moravia CSD
William P Tammaro, Superintendent
68 S Main St, Moravia, NY 13118-1189
315-497-2670 Fax: 315-497-2260

Port Byron CSD
Neil F O'Brien, Superintendent
30 Maple Ave, Port Byron, NY 13140-9647
315-776-5728 Fax: 315-776-4050
e-mail: nobrien@portbyron.cnyric.org

Southern Cayuga CSD
Mary Kay Worth, Superintendent
2384 Rt 34B, Aurora, NY 13026-9771
315-364-7211
e-mail: worthmk@southerncayuga.org

Union Springs CSD
Linda Rice, Superintendent
239 Cayuga St, Union Springs, NY 13160
315-889-4101
e-mail: lrice@unionspringscsd.org

Weedsport CSD
Shaun A O'Connor, Superintendent
2821 E Brutus St, Weedsport, NY 13166-9105
315-834-6637

CHAUTAUQUA

Bemus Point CSD
Albert D'Attilio, Superintendent
3980 Dutch Hollow Rd, Bemus Point, NY 14712
716-386-2375
Web site: www.mghs.org

Brocton CSD
Jack J Skahill Jr, Superintendent
138 W Main St, Brocton, NY 14716
716-792-2121 Fax: 716-792-7944
e-mail: jskahill@roc.wynric.org
Web site: www.brocton.wnyric.org

Cassadaga Valley CSD
John Brown, Superintendent
Route 60, PO Box 540, Sinclairville, NY 14782-0540
716-962-5155
e-mail: JBrown@cvcs.wnyric.org

Chautauqua Lake CSD
Benjamin B Spitzer, Superintendent
100 N Erie St, Mayville, NY 14757
716-753-5808 Fax: 716-753-5813
e-mail: bspitzer@clake.org
Web site: www.clake.org

Clymer CSD
Ralph Wilson, Superintendent
8672 E Main St, Clymer, NY 14724-0580
716-355-4444
e-mail: rwilson@clymer.wnyric.org
Web site: www.clymer.wnyric.org

Dunkirk City SD
Gary Cerne, Superintendent
620 Marauder Dr, Dunkirk, NY 14048-1396
716-366-9300
Web site: www.dunkirk.wnyric.org

Falconer CSD
Jane R Fosberg, Superintendent
2 East Ave N, Falconer, NY 14733
716-665-6624 x4101 Fax: 716-665-9265
e-mail: jfosberg@falcon.wynric.org
Web site: wwwfalconerschools.org

Forestville CSD
John O'Connor, Superintendent
12 Water St, Forestville, NY 14062-9674
716-965-2742
e-mail: jconnor@forestville.wnyric.org
Web site: www.forestville.com

Fredonia CSD
Paul Di Fonzo, Superintendent
425 E Main St, Fredonia, NY 14063
716-679-1581
Web site: www.fredonia.wnyric.org

Frewsburg CSD
Stephen Vanstrom, Superintendent
26 Institute St, Frewsburg, NY 14738
716-569-9241
Web site: www.frewsburg.wnyric.org

Jamestown City SD
Raymond J Fashano, Superintendent

Offices and agencies generally appear in alphabetical order, except when specific order is requested by listee.

PUBLIC SCHOOL DISTRICTS / School District Administrators

201 E Fourth St, Jamestown, NY 14701
716-483-4350
Web site: www.jamestownpublicschools.org

Panama CSD
Carol S Hay, Superintendent
41 North St, Panama, NY 14767-9775
716-782-2455 Fax: 716-782-4281
Web site: www.pancent.org

Pine Valley CSD (South Dayton)
Vincent J Vecchiarella, Superintendent
7755 Rt 83, South Dayton, NY 14138
716-988-3293 Fax: 716-988-3864
e-mail: pmorgante@pval.org
Web site: www.pval.org

Ripley CSD
John Hogan, Interim Superintendent
12 N State St, Ripley, NY 14775
716-736-6201
Web site: ripleycsd.wnyric.org

Sherman CSD
Thomas Schmidt, Superintendent
127 Park St, PO Box 950, Sherman, NY 14781-0950
716-761-6122 x1289 Fax: 716-761-6119
e-mail: Thomas_Schmidt@sherman.wnyric.org
Web site: www.sherman.wnyric.org

Silver Creek CSD
Gordon Salisbury, Superintendent
1 Dickinson St, PO Box 270, Silver Creek, NY 14136
716-934-2603 Fax: 716-934-2103
e-mail: gsalisbu@slcr.wnyric.org
Web site: www.silvercreek.wnyric.org

Southwestern CSD at Jamestown
Daniel A George, Superintendent
600 Hunt Rd, Jamestown, NY 14701
716-484-1136
Web site: swcs.wnyric.org

Westfield CSD
Laura Chabe, Superintendent
203 E Main St, Westfield, NY 14787
716-326-2151
Web site: www.wacs.wnyric.org

CHEMUNG

Elmira City SD
Raymond Bryant, Superintendent
951 Hoffman St, Elmira, NY 14905-1715
607-735-3010 Fax: 607-735-3002
e-mail: rbryant@elmiracityschools.org
Web site: www.elmiracityschools.org

Elmira Hts CSD
Mary Beth Fiore, Superintendent
100 Robinwood Ave, Elmira Heights, NY 14903-1598
607-734-7114 Fax: 607-734-7134
e-mail: mbfiore@gstboces.org
Web site: www.heightsschools.com

Horseheads CSD
Ralph Marino, Superintendent
One Raider Ln, Horseheads, NY 14845-2398
607-739-5601 x4200
e-mail: hcsdinfo@horseheadsdistrict.com
Web site: www.horseheadsdistrict.com

CHENANGO

Afton CSD
Elizabeth A Briggs, Superintendent
29 Academy St, PO Box 5, Afton, NY 13730-0005
607-639-8229
Web site: www.afton.stier.org

Bainbridge-Guilford CSD
Karl Brown, Superintendent
18 Juliand St, Bainbridge, NY 13733
607-967-6321 Fax: 607-967-4231
Web site: www.bgcsd.org

Greene CSD
Gary P Smith, Superintendent
40 S Canal St, Greene, NY 13778
607-656-4161
Web site: www.greenecsd.org

Norwich City SD
Gerard M O'Sullivan, Superintendent
19 Eaton Ave, Norwich, NY 13815
607-334-1600 Fax: 607-336-8652
Web site: www.norwichcityschooldistrict.com

Otselic Valley CSD
Lawrence Thomas, Superintendent
125 County Rd 13A, South Otselic, NY 13155-0161
315-653-7591 Fax: 315-653-7500
Web site: www.ovcs.org

Oxford Academy & CSD
Randall Squier, Superintendent
12 Fort Hill Park, PO Box 192, Oxford, NY 13830-0192
607-843-2025 x4041
Web site: www.oxac.org

Sherburne-Earlville CSD
Gayle H Hellert, Superintendent
15 School St, Sherburne, NY 13460-0725
607-674-7300 Fax: 607-674-7386
Web site: www.secsd.org

Unadilla Valley CSD
Rexford Hurlburt Jr, Superintendent

Offices and agencies generally appear in alphabetical order, except when specific order is requested by listee.

PUBLIC SCHOOL DISTRICTS / School District Administrators

4238 State Hwy 8, New Berlin, NY 13411
607-847-7500
Web site: www.uvstorm.org

CLINTON

Ausable Valley CSD
Paul D Savage II, Superintendent
1273 Rt 9N, Clintonville, NY 12924-4244
518-834-2845 Fax: 518-834-2843
e-mail: psavage@avcsk12.org
Web site: avcs.org

Beekmantown CSD
Mark A Sposato, Superintendent
37 Eagle Way, West Chazy, NY 12992-2577
518-563-8250 x5501 Fax: 518-563-8132
e-mail: sposato.mark@bcsdk12.org
Web site: www.bcsdk12.org

Chazy Central RSD
Kevin R Mulligan, Superintendent
609 Miner Farm Rd, Chazy, NY 12921-0327
518-846-7135 Fax: 518-846-8322
Web site: www.chazy.org

Northeastern Clinton CSD
Robert J Hebert, Superintendent
103 Route 276, Champlain, NY 12919
518-298-8242 Fax: 518-298-4293
Web site: www.nccscougars.org

Northern Adirondack CSD
William F Scott, Superintendent
Rt 11, Ellenburg Depot, NY 12935-0164
518-594-7060
Web site: www.nacs1.org

Peru CSD
A Paul Scott, Superintendent
17 School St, PO Box 68, Peru, NY 12972-0068
518-643-6000
Web site: www.perucsd.org

Plattsburgh City SD
James Short, Superintendent
49 Broad St, Plattsburgh, NY 12901-3396
518-957-6002 Fax: 518-561-6605
e-mail: jshort@plattscsd.org
Web site: www.plattscsd.org

Saranac CSD
Kenneth O Cringle, Superintendent
32 Emmons St, Dannemora, NY 12929
518-565-5600
e-mail: kcringle@saranac.org
Web site: www.saranac.org

COLUMBIA

Berkshire UFSD
James G Gaudette, Superintendent
13640 Rt 22, Canaan, NY 12029-0370
518-781-3511

Chatham CSD
Scott G Hunter, Superintendent
50 Woodbridge Ave, Chatham, NY 12037-1397
518-392-2400 Fax: 518-392-2413
e-mail: julianor@chatham.k12.ny.us
Web site: www.chathamcentralschools.com

Germantown CSD
Patrick Gabriel, Superintendent
123 Main St, Germantown, NY 12526
518-537-6280 Fax: 518-537-3284
Web site: germantowncsd.org

Hudson City SD
Fern Aefsky, Superintendent
215 Harry Howard Ave, Hudson, NY 12534-4011
518-828-4360 x2101
Web site: www.hudsoncityschooldistrict.com

Ichabod Crane CSD
James P Dexter, Superintendent
2910 Rt 9, Valatie, NY 12184-0137
518-758-7575 x3002
e-mail: icriders@ichabodcrane.org
Web site: www.berk.com~ichabod/

New Lebanon CSD
Karen McGraw, Superintendent
14665 Route 22, New Lebanon, NY 12125-2307
518-794-9016 Fax: 518-766-5574
e-mail: kmcgraw@newlebanoncsd.org
Web site: www.newlebanoncsd.org

Taconic Hills CSD
Mark Sposato, Superintendent
73 County Rt 11A, PO Box 482, Craryville, NY 12521
518-325-0313 Fax: 518-325-9051
e-mail: info@taconichills.k12.ny.us
Web site: www.taconichills.k12.ny.us

CORTLAND

Cincinnatus CSD
Steven V Hubbard, Superintendent

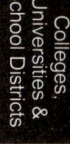
Colleges, Universities & School Districts

Offices and agencies generally appear in alphabetical order, except when specific order is requested by listee.

PUBLIC SCHOOL DISTRICTS / School District Administrators

2809 Cincinnatus Rd, Cincinnatus, NY 13040-9698
607-863-3200 Fax: 607-863-4109
e-mail: shubbard@cincynet.cnyric.org
Web site: www.cincynet.cbyric.org

Cortland Enlarged City SD
Laurence Spring, Superintendent
1 Valley View Dr, Cortland, NY 13045-3297
607-758-4100 Fax: 607-758-4128
e-mail: lspring@cortlandschools.org
Web site: www.cortlandschools.org

Homer CSD
Douglas Larison, Superintendent
Route 281, PO Box 500, Homer, NY 13077-0500
607-749-7241
e-mail: larison@homercentral.org
Web site: www.homercentral.org

Marathon CSD
Timothy Turecek, Superintendent
1 E Main St, PO Box 339, Marathon, NY 13803-0339
607-849-3251 Fax: 607-849-3305
e-mail: turecek@marathon.cnyric.org
Web site: www.marathonschools.org

McGraw CSD
Maria S Fragnoli-Ryan, Superintendent
W Academy St, PO Box 556, McGraw, NY 13101-0556
607-836-3636 Fax: 607-836-3635
e-mail: msfryan@mcgrawschools.org
Web site: www.mcgrawschools.org

DELAWARE

Andes CSD
John M Bernhardt, Superintendent
85 Delaware Ave, PO Box 248, Andes, NY 13731-0248
845-676-3167 Fax: 845-676-3181
e-mail: jbernhardt@catskill.net

Charlotte Valley CSD
Mark R Dupra, Superintendent
15611 St Hwy 23, Davenport, NY 13750-0202
607-278-5511 Fax: 607-278-5900
e-mail: dupra.mark@charlottevalley.org

Delhi CSD
Jack Mulholland, Superintendent
2 Sheldon Dr, Delhi, NY 13753-1276
607-746-1300 Fax: 607-746-6028
Web site: www.delhischools.org

Downsville CSD
Robert J Mackey, Superintendent
Maple St, Po Box J, Downsville, NY 13755
607-363-2101
Web site: www.dcseagles.org

Franklin CSD
Gordon Daniels, Superintendent

26 Institute St, Franklin, NY 13775-0888
607-829-3551 x302 Fax: 607-829-2101
Web site: www.franklincssd.org

Hancock CSD
Terrance Dougherty, Superintendent
67 Education Ln, Hancock, NY 13783
607-637-1301
Web site: hancock.stier.org

Margaretville CSD
John P Riedl, Superintendent
415 Main St, Margaretville, NY 12455-0319
845-586-2647 Fax: 845-586-2949
e-mail: jreidl@margaretvillecs.org

Roxbury CSD
Craig G Carr, Superintendent
53729 NYS Route 30, Roxbury, NY 12474-0207
607-326-4151 Fax: 607-326-4154
e-mail: ccarr@roxburycs.org

Sidney CSD
Sandra M Cooper, Superintendent
95 W Main St, Sidney, NY 13838-1699
607-563-2135 Fax: 607-563-4275
e-mail: smcooper@sidneycsd.org
Web site: www.sidneycsd.org

South Kortright CSD
Benjamin C Berliner, Superintendent
58200 State Hwy 10, South Kortright, NY 13842-0113
607-538-9111 Fax: 607-538-9205
e-mail: berliner@dmcom.net

Stamford CSD
Gregory J Sanik, Superintendent
1 River St, Stamford, NY 12167-1098
607-652-7301 Fax: 607-652-3446
e-mail: gjsanik@aol.com

Walton CSD
Jonathan W Buhner, Superintendent
47-49 Stockton Ave, Walton, NY 13856
607-865-4116 Fax: 607-865-8568
Web site: www.waltoncsd.stier.org

DUTCHESS

Arlington CSD
Frank Pepe Jr, Superintendent
696 Dutchess Tpke, Poughkeepsie, NY 12603
845-486-4460
Web site: www.arlingtonschools.org

Beacon City SD
Jean Parr, Superintendent

Offices and agencies generally appear in alphabetical order, except when specific order is requested by listee.

PUBLIC SCHOOL DISTRICTS / School District Administrators

10 Education Dr, Beacon, NY 12508
845-838-6900 x2010
e-mail: parr.j@beaconcityk12.org
Web site: www.beaconcityk12.org

Dover UFSD
Craig T Onofry, Superintendent
2368 Rt 22, Dover Plains, NY 12522
845-832-4500 Fax: 845-832-4511
Web site: www.doverschools.org

Hyde Park CSD
Carole Pickering, Superintendent
11 Boice Rd, Hyde Park, NY 12538-1632
845-229-4000 Fax: 845-229-4056
Web site: www.hydeparkschools.org

Millbrook CSD
Lloyd Jaeger, Superintendent
PO Box AA-3323 Franklin, Millbrook, NY 12545
845-677-4200 x101
e-mail: lloyd.jaeger@millbrookcsd.org
Web site: www.millbrookcsd.org

Pawling CSD
Joseph Sciortino, Superintendent
32 Holiday Hills Ln, Pawling, NY 12564
845-855-4600
Web site: www.pawlingschools.org

Pine Plains CSD
Linda Kaumeyer, Superintendent
2829 Church St, Pine Plains, NY 12567-5504
518-398-7181 Fax: 518-398-6592
Web site: www.pineplainsschools.org

Poughkeepsie City SD
Laval S Wilson, Superintendent
11 College Ave, Poughkeepsie, NY 12603-3313
845-451-4950 Fax: 845-451-4954
e-mail: lwilson@pcsd.k12.ny.us
Web site: www.poughkeepsieschools.org

Red Hook CSD
Paul Finch, Superintendent
7401 South Broadway, Red Hook, NY 12571-9446
845-758-2241 Fax: 845-758-4720
e-mail: pfinch@rhcsd.org
Web site: www.redhookcentralschools.org

Rhinebeck CSD
Joseph L Phelan, Superintendent
North Park Rd, Rhinebeck, NY 12572
845-871-5520 Fax: 845-876-4276
e-mail: jphelan@rcsd.dcboces.org
Web site: www.rhinebeckcsd.org

Spackenkill UFSD
Lois C Colletta, Superintendent
15 Croft Rd, Poughkeepsie, NY 12603-5028
845-463-7800 Fax: 845-463-7804
Web site: www.spekenkillschools.org

Wappingers CSD
Richard A Powell, Superintendent
167 Meyers Corners Rd, Wappingers Falls, NY 12590-3296
845-298-5000
Web site: www.wappingersschools.org

Webutuck CSD
Richard N Johns, Superintendent
194 Haight Rd, Amenia, NY 12501
845-373-4100
Web site: www.webutuckschools.org

ERIE

Akron CSD
George Batterson, Interim Superintendent
47 Bloomingdale Ave, Akron, NY 14001-1197
716-542-5010 Fax: 716-542-5018
e-mail: gbatterson@akronschools.org
Web site: www.akronschools.org

Alden CSD
Lynn Marie Fusco, Superintendent
13190 Park St, Alden, NY 14004
716-937-9116
Web site: aldenschools.org

Amherst CSD
Dennis Ford, Superintendent
55 Kings Hwy, Amherst, NY 14226
716-362-3051 Fax: 716-836-2537
Web site: www.amherstschools.org

Buffalo SD
James A Williams, Superintendent
713 City Hall, Buffalo, NY 14202-3375
716-816-3500 Fax: 716-816-3600
Web site: www.buffaloschools.org

Cheektowaga CSD
Delia G Bonenberger, Superintendent
3600 Union Rd, Cheektowaga, NY 14225-5170
716-686-3606 Fax: 716-681-5232
Web site: www.cheektowagaschools.org

Cheektowaga-Sloan UFSD
James P Mazgajewski, Superintendent
166 Halstead Ave, Sloan, NY 14212
716-891-6402
Web site: www.sloan.wnyric.org

Clarence CSD
Thomas G Coseo, Superintendent

Offices and agencies generally appear in alphabetical order, except when specific order is requested by listee.

PUBLIC SCHOOL DISTRICTS / School District Administrators

9625 Main St, Clarence, NY 14031-2083
716-407-9102
e-mail: tcoseo@clar.wnyric.org
Web site: www.clarenceschools.org

Cleveland Hill UFSD
Bruce Inglis, Superintendent
105 Mapleview Rd, Cheektowaga, NY 14225-1599
716-836-7200
Web site: www.clevehill.wnyric.org

Depew UFSD
Robert F Defilippo, Superintendent
591 Terrace Blvd, Depew, NY 14043-4535
716-686-2251
e-mail: RDeFilip@depew.wnyric.org
Web site: www.dpewschools.org

East Aurora UFSD
James Bodziak, Superintendent
430 Main St, East Aurora, NY 14052
716-687-2302
e-mail: james_bodziak@eaur.wnyric.org
Web site: www.eaur.wnyric.org

Eden CSD
Ronald Buggs, Superintendent
3150 Schoolview Rd, Eden, NY 14057
716-992-3629
Web site: www.edencentral.org

Evans-Brant CSD (Lake Shore)
Jeffrey Rabey, Superintendent
959 Beach Rd, Angola, NY 14006
716-549-2300 Fax: 716-549-6407
e-mail: jrabey@lakeshore.wnyric.org
Web site: www.lakeshore.wnyric.org

Frontier CSD
Ronald DeCarli, Superintendent
S 5120 Orchard Ave, Hamburg, NY 14075-5657
716-926-1711 Fax: 716-926-1776
Web site: www.frontier.wnyric.org

Grand Island CSD
Robert W Christmann, Superintendent
1100 Ransom Rd, Grand Island, NY 14072-1460
716-773-8801
e-mail: robertchristmann@k12.ginet.org
Web site: www.k12.ginet.org

Hamburg CSD
Gordon Kerr, Assistant Superintendent
5305 Abbott Rd, Hamburg, NY 14075
716-646-3220 Fax: 716-646-3209
Web site: www.hamburgschools.org

Holland CSD
Garry Stone, Superintendent

103 Canada St, Holland, NY 14080
716-537-8222
Web site: www.hlnd.wnyric.org

Hopevale UFSD at Hamburg
David S Frahm, Superintendent
3780 Howard Rd, Hamburg, NY 14075-2252
716-648-1930 Fax: 716-648-2361
e-mail: dfrahm@hopevale.com
Web site: www.hopevale.com

Iroquois CSD
Neil Rochelle, Superintendent
2111 Girdle Rd, Elma, NY 14059-0032
716-652-3000
e-mail: Neil_Rochelle@iroquois.wnyric.org
Web site: www.iroquois.wnyric.org

Kenmore-Tonawanda UFSD
Anne L Marotta, Interim Superintendent
1500 Colvin Blvd, Buffalo, NY 14223-1196
716-874-8400 Fax: 716-874-8621
Web site: www.kenton.k12.ny.us

Lackawanna City SD
Paul G Hashem, Superintendent
30 Johnson St, Lackawanna, NY 14218
716-827-6767 Fax: 716-827-6710
e-mail: phashem@lackawanna.wnyric.org
Web site: www.lackawannaschools.org

Lancaster CSD
Edward Myszka, Interim Superintendent
177 Central Ave, Lancaster, NY 14086-1897
716-686-3200
Web site: www.lancasterschools.org

Maryvale UFSD
Gary L Brader, Superintendent
1050 Maryvale Dr, Cheektowaga, NY 14225-2386
716-631-7407 Fax: 716-635-4699
e-mail: brader@maryvale.wnyric.org
Web site: www.maryvale.wnyric.org

North Collins CSD
Benjamin A Halsey, Superintendent
2045 School St, North Collins, NY 14111
716-337-0101
Web site: www.northcollins.com

Orchard Park CSD
Joan Thomas, Superintendent
3330 Baker Rd, Orchard Park, NY 14127
716-209-6280 Fax: 716-209-6353
Web site: www.opschools.org

Springville-Griffith Inst CSD
Brenda Peters, Superintendent

Offices and agencies generally appear in alphabetical order, except when specific order is requested by listee.

PUBLIC SCHOOL DISTRICTS / School District Administrators

307 Newman St, Springville, NY 14141
716-592-3230
Web site: www.spingvillegi.org

Sweet Home CSD
Geoffrey M Hicks, Superintendent
1901 Sweet Home Rd, Amherst, NY 14228
716-250-1402 Fax: 716-250-1361
e-mail: ghicks@shs.k12.ny.us
Web site: www.sweethomeschools.com

Tonawanda City SD
Barbara Peters, Superintendent
202 Broad St, Tonawanda, NY 14150-2098
716-694-7784
e-mail: bpeters@tona.wnyric.org
Web site: www.tona.wnyric.org

West Seneca CSD
James K Brotz, Superintendent
1397 Orchard Park Rd, West Seneca, NY 14224-4098
716-677-3101
Web site: www.wscschools.org

Williamsville CSD
Howard S Smith, Superintendent
105 Casey Rd, East Amherst, NY 14051-5000
716-626-8005 Fax: 716-626-8089
Web site: www.williamsvillek12.org

ESSEX

Crown Point CSD
Shari L Brannock, Superintendent
Main St, PO Box 35, Crown Point, NY 12928-0035
518-597-4200 Fax: 518-597-4121
e-mail: brannock@crownpointpanthers.com
Web site: www.crownpointpanthers.com

Elizabethtown-Lewis CSD
Gail J Else, Superintendent
7530 Court St, Elizabethtown, NY 12932-0158
518-873-6371
Web site: elcs.neric.org

Keene CSD
Cynthia Ford-Johnston, Superintendent
33 Market St, PO Box 67, Keene Valley, NY 12943-0067
518-576-4555 Fax: 518-576-4599
e-mail: cjohnsto@kcs.neric.org
Web site: www.kcs.neric.org

Lake Placid CSD
Ernest H Stretton, Superintendent
23 Cummings Rd, Lake Placid, NY 12946-1500
518-523-2475

Minerva CSD
Timothy Farrell, Superintendent
1466 County Rt 29, Olmstedville, NY 12857-0039
518-251-2000 Fax: 518-251-2395
e-mail: farrellt@minervasd.org
Web site: www.minervasd.org

Moriah CSD
William Larrow, Superintendent
39 Viking Ln, Port Henry, NY 12974
518-546-3301 Fax: 518-546-7895
Web site: www.moriahk12.org

Newcomb CSD
Clark Hults, Superintendent
5535 Rt 28 N, Newcomb, NY 12852-0418
518-582-3341 Fax: 518-582-2163
Web site: www.newcombcsd.org

Schroon Lake CSD
Michael Bonnewell, Superintendent
1125 US Rt 9, PO Box 338, Schroon Lake, NY 12870-0338
518-532-7164 Fax: 518-532-0284

Ticonderoga CSD
John C McDonald Jr, Superintendent
9 Amherst Ave, Ticonderoga, NY 12883-1444
518-585-6674

Westport CSD
Karen B Tromblee, Superintendent
25 Sisco St, Westport, NY 12993
518-962-8244 Fax: 518-962-4571
e-mail: wcs@westportcs.org
Web site: www.westportcs.org

Willsboro CSD
Stephen Broadwell, Superintendent
29 School Lane, Willsboro, NY 12996-0180
518-963-4456
Web site: www.willsborocsd.org

FRANKLIN

Brushton-Moira CSD
Robin Jones, Superintendent
758 County Rt 7, Brushton, NY 12916
518-529-8948 Fax: 518-529-6062
e-mail: district@bmcsd.org
Web site: www.bmcsd.org

Chateaugay CSD
Paul H Harrica, Superintendent
42 River St, PO Box 904, Chateaugay, NY 12920-0904
518-497-6611 Fax: 518-497-3170
Web site: chateau.neric.org

Malone CSD
Stephen Shafer, Superintendent

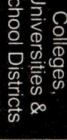

Offices and agencies generally appear in alphabetical order, except when specific order is requested by listee.

PUBLIC SCHOOL DISTRICTS / School District Administrators

42 Huskie Ln, PO Box 847, Malone, NY 12953-1118
518-483-7800 Fax: 518-483-3071
Web site: www.malone.k12.ny.us

Salmon River CSD
Glenn R Bellinger, Superintendent
637 County Rt 1, Fort Covington, NY 12937-9722
518-358-6610 Fax: 518-358-3492
Web site: www.srk12.org

Saranac Lake CSD
Scott A Amo, Superintendent
79 Canaras Ave, Saranac Lake, NY 12983-1500
518-891-5460

St Regis Falls CSD
Patricia A Dovi, Superintendent
92 N Main St, PO Box 309, St Regis Falls, NY 12980-0309
518-856-9421
Web site: www.fehb.org/stregis.htm

Tupper Lake CSD
Daniel Bower, Superintendent
294 Hosley Ave, Tupper Lake, NY 12986-1899
518-359-3371 Fax: 518-359-7862
e-mail: dbower@tupperlakecsd.net

FULTON

Broadalbin-Perth CSD
Sally Rojck, Superintendent
20 Pine St, Broadalbin, NY 12025-9997
518-954-2500 Fax: 51-954-2509
e-mail: rojck@bpcsd.org

Gloversville Enlarged SD
Daniel T Connor, Superintendent
243 Lincoln St, PO Box 593, Gloversville, NY 12078
518-775-5700 Fax: 518-725-8793

Greater Johnstown SD
John S Whelan, Superintendent
2 Wright Dr Ste 101, Johnstown, NY 12095
518-762-4611 Fax: 518-726-6379
Web site: www.johnstownschools.org

Mayfield CSD
Ralph Acquaro, Superintendent
27 School Street, Mayfield, NY 12117-0216
518-661-8207
e-mail: acquaro.ralph@mayfieldcsd.org
Web site: www.mayfieldk12.com

Northville CSD
Harry Brooks, Superintendent
131 S Third St, PO Box 608, Northville, NY 12134-0608
518-863-7000 x4121
e-mail: hbrooks@northvillecsd.k12.ny.us
Web site: northvillecsd.k12.ny.us

Oppenheim-Ephratah CSD
Dan M Russom, Superintendent
6486 State Hwy 29, St Johnsville, NY 13452-9309
518-568-2014 Fax: 518-568-2941
e-mail: dmrussom@oecs.k12.ny.us
Web site: www.oecs.k12.ny.us

Wheelerville UFSD
Robert A DeLilli, Superintendent
PO Box 756, Caroga Lake, NY 12032
518-835-2171 Fax: 518-835-3551
Web site: www.wufselementary.k12.ny.us

GENESEE

Alexander CSD
Richard Young, Superintendent
3314 Buffalo St, Alexander, NY 14005-9769
585-591-1551 Fax: 585-591-2257
e-mail: dyoung3@alexandercsd.org
Web site: www.alexandercsd.org

Batavia City SD
Richard G Stutzman Jr, Superintendent
39 Washington Ave, Batavia, NY 14020
585-343-2480 Fax: 585-344-8204
e-mail: rstutzman@bataviacsd.org
Web site: www.bataviacsd.org

Byron-Bergen CSD
Gregory C Geer, Superintendent
6917 W Bergen Rd, Bergen, NY 14416
585-494-1220 Fax: 585-494-2613
Web site: www.bbcs.k12.ny.us

Elba CSD
Joan Cole, Superintendent
57 S Main St, Elba, NY 14058
585-757-9967 x1034
e-mail: jcole@elbacsd.org
Web site: www.elbacsd.org

Le Roy CSD
Dave DeLoria, Interim Superintendent
2-6 Trigon Park, Le Roy, NY 14482
585-768-8133
e-mail: ddeloriad@leroycsd.org
Web site: www.leroycsd.org

Oakfield-Alabama CSD
Robert McIntosh, Superintendent

Offices and agencies generally appear in alphabetical order, except when specific order is requested by listee.

PUBLIC SCHOOL DISTRICTS / School District Administrators

7001 Lewiston Rd, Oakfield, NY 14125
585-948-5211 Fax: 585-948-9362
Web site: www.oacs.k12.ny.us

Pavilion CSD
Edward J Orman, Superintendent
7014 Big Tree Rd, Pavilion, NY 14525
585-584-3115
Web site: www.pavilioncsd.org

Pembroke CSD
Gary T Mix Sr, Superintendent
Rt 5 & 77, PO Box 308, Corfu, NY 14036
585-599-4525 Fax: 585-762-9993
Web site: www.pembroke.k12.ny.us

GREENE

Cairo-Durham CSD
Sally Sharkey, Superintendent
424 Main St, Cairo, NY 12413-0780
518-622-8534
e-mail: ssharkey@cairodurham.org
Web site: www.cairodurham,.org

Catskill CSD
Kathleen Farrell, Acting Superintendent
343 W Main St, Catskill, NY 12414-1699
518-943-4696 Fax: 518-943-7116
Web site: www.catskillcsd.org

Coxsackie-Athens CSD
Earle Gregory, Superintendent
24 Sunset Blvd, Coxsackie, NY 12051-1132
518-731-1710
Web site: www.coxsackie-athens.org

Greenville CSD
Cheryl Dudley, Superintendent
4976 Route 81, Greenville, NY 12083-0129
518-966-5070
Web site: www.greenville.k12.ny.us

Hunter-Tannersville CSD
Jim Piscitelli, Interim Superintendent
6094 Main St, Tannersville, NY 12485-1018
518-589-5400 Fax: 518-589-5403
e-mail: jpiscitelli@htcsd.org

Windham-Ashland-Jewett CSD
John Wiktorko, Superintendent
5411 State Route 23, Windham, NY 12496-0429
518-734-3403 Fax: 518-734-6050
e-mail: jwitkorko@wajcs.org

HAMILTON

Indian Lake CSD
Mark T Brand, Superintendent

28 W Main St, Indian Lake, NY 12842-9716
518-648-5024 Fax: 518-648-6346
e-mail: brandm@ilcsd.org
Web site: www.ilcsd.org

Inlet Common School
Donald Gooley, Superintendent
(Town of Webb UFSD), 220 Rt 28, Inlet, NY 13360-0207
315-369-3222 Fax: 315-369-6216
e-mail: dgooley@tows.moric.org

Lake Pleasant CSD
John E Brewer Jr, Superintendent
Elm Lake Rd, PO Box 140, Speculator, NY 12164-0140
518-548-7571 Fax: 518-548-3230
Web site: www.lpschools.com

Long Lake CSD
Kevin Crampton, Superintendent
20 School Lane, PO Box 217, Long Lake, NY 12847-0217
518-624-2221 Fax: 518-624-3896
Web site: www.longlakecsd.org

Piseco Common SD
Peter J Hallock, Superintendent
Rt 8, Piseco, NY 12139
518-548-7555 Fax: 518-548-5310
e-mail: bogriver13@yahoo.com
Web site: www.pisecoschool.com

Raquette Lake UFSD
Peter Hallock, Superintendent
PO Box 10, Raquette Lake, NY 13436-0010
315-354-4733

Wells CSD
Paul G Williamsen, Superintendent
Route 30, PO Box 300, Wells, NY 12190-0300
518-924-6000
Web site: www.wellscsd.com

HERKIMER

Dolgeville CSD
Theodore Kawryga, Superintendent
38 Slawson St, Dolgeville, NY 13329
315-429-3155 x128 Fax: 315-429-8473
e-mail: tkawryga@dolgeville.org
Web site: www.dolgeville.org

Frankfort-Schuyler CSD
Robert Reina, Superintendent
Palmer St, Frankfort, NY 13340
315-894-5083
e-mail: rreina@frankfort-schuyler.org
Web site: www.frankfort-schuyler.org

Herkimer CSD
Carol Zygo, Superintendent

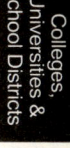

Offices and agencies generally appear in alphabetical order, except when specific order is requested by listee.

PUBLIC SCHOOL DISTRICTS / School District Administrators

801 W German St, Herkimer, NY 13350-2199
315-866-2230
Web site: www.herkimercsd.org

Ilion CSD
Robert J Service, Superintendent
1 Golden Bomber Dr, PO Box 480, Ilion, NY 13357-0480
315-894-9934 Fax: 315-894-2716
e-mail: rservice@ilioncsd.org
Web site: www.ilion-csd.org

Little Falls City SD
William A Gokey, Superintendent
15 Petrie St, Little Falls, NY 13365
315-823-1470
Web site: www.lfcsd.com

Mohawk CSD
Joyce M Caputo, Superintendent
28 Grove St, Mohawk, NY 13407-1782
315-867-2904
e-mail: jcaputo@mohawkcsd.org

Mount Markham CSD
Sandra Sampson, Superintendent
500 Fairground Rd, West Winfield, NY 13491-0500
315-867-2023
Web site: www.mmcsd.org

Poland CSD
John W Stewart, Superintendent
74 Cold Brook St, Poland, NY 13431
315-826-7900 Fax: 315-826-7516
Web site: www.polandcs.com

Town of Webb UFSD
Donald Gooley, Superintendent
Main St, PO Box 38, Old Forge, NY 13420-0038
315-369-3222 Fax: 315-369-6216
e-mail: dgooley@tows.moric.org
Web site: www.townschool.org

Van Hornesville-Owen D Young CSD
James Christmann, Superintendent
2316 State Rt 80, Van Hornesville, NY 13475-0125
315-858-0729 Fax: 315-858-2019
Web site: www.odyoung-csd.k12.ny.us

West Canada Valley CSD
Kenneth Slentz, Superintendent
5447 State Rt 28, Newport, NY 13416-0360
315-845-6800 Fax: 315-845-8652
e-mail: kslentz@westcanada.org
Web site: www.westcanada.org

JEFFERSON

Alexandria CSD
Robert Wagoner, Superintendent
34 Bolton Ave, Alexandria Bay, NY 13607-1699
315-482-9971
Web site: www.alexandriacentral.org

Belleville Henderson CSD
Robert R Ike, Superintendent
8372 County Rt 75, Belleville, NY 13611-0158
315-846-5826
e-mail: rike@bhpanthers.org
Web site: www.bhpanthers.org

Carthage CSD
Carl P Militello, Superintendent
25059 County Rt 197, Carthage, NY 13619-9527
315-493-5000
e-mail: cmilitello@carthagecsd.org
Web site: www.carthagecsd.org

General Brown CSD
Stephan J Vigliotti Sr, Superintendent
17643 Cemetery Rd, Dexter, NY 13634-9731
315-639-4711 Fax: 315-639-3444
e-mail: svigliotti@gblions.org
Web site: www.gblions.org

Indian River CSD
James Kettrick, Superintendent
32735-B County Rt 29, Philadelphia, NY 13673-0308
315-642-3441
Web site: www.ircsd.org

La Fargeville CSD
Susan Whitney, Superintendent
20414 Sunrise Ave, La Fargeville, NY 13656
315-658-2241 Fax: 315-658-4223
Web site: www.lafargevillecsd.org

Lyme CSD
Donnalee Dodson, Superintendent
11868 Academy St, PO Box 219, Chaumont, NY 13622-0219
315-649-2417 Fax: 315-649-2812
Web site: www.lymecsd.org

Sackets Harbor CSD
Suzanne C Tingley, Superintendent
215 S Broad St, PO Box 209, Sackets Harbor, NY 13685-0290
315-646-3575
Web site: www.sacketsharborschool.org

South Jefferson CSD
Jamie A Moesel, Superintendent
PO Box 10, Adams, NY 13605
315-583-6104
e-mail: jmoese@spartanpride.org
Web site: www.spartanpride.org

Thousand Islands CSD
John E Slattery, Superintendent

Offices and agencies generally appear in alphabetical order, except when specific order is requested by listee.

PUBLIC SCHOOL DISTRICTS / School District Administrators

8483 County Rt 9, PO Box 1000, Clayton, NY 13624-1000
315-686-5594 Fax: 315-686-5511
e-mail: jslattery@1000islandschools.org
Web site: www.1000islandschools.org

Watertown City SD
Terry N Fralick, Superintendent
376 Butterfield Ave, Watertown, NY 13601
315-785-3700 Fax: 315-785-6855
e-mail: tfralick@watertowncsd.org
Web site: www.watertowncsd.org

LEWIS

Beaver River CSD
Ray Borden, Interim Superintendent
9508 Artz Rd, Beaver Falls, NY 13305-0179
315-346-1211
Web site: www.brcsd.org

Copenhagen CSD
Lisa A Parsons, Superintendent
3020 Mechanic St, Copenhagen, NY 13626-0030
315-688-4411 Fax: 315-688-2001
e-mail: lparsons@ccsknights.org
Web site: www.ccsknights.org

Harrisville CSD
Rolf A Waters, Superintendent
14371 Pirate Lane, PO Box 200, Harrisville, NY 13648
315-543-2707
Web site: www.hcsk12.org

Lowville Academy & CSD
Kenneth J McAuliffe, Superintendent
7668 State St, Lowville, NY 13367
315-376-9000 Fax: 315-376-1933
Web site: www.lacs-ny.org

South Lewis CSD
Frank C House, Superintendent
PO Box 10, Turin, NY 13473-0010
315-348-2500
e-mail: fhouse@southlewis.org
Web site: www.southlewis.org

LIVINGSTON

Avon CSD
Bruce Amey, Superintendent
191 Clinton St, Avon, NY 14414
585-226-2455 x1318
e-mail: bamey@avoncsd.org
Web site: www.avoncsd.org

Caledonia-Mumford CSD
David V Dinolfo, Superintendent
99 North St, Caledonia, NY 14423
585-538-6811
e-mail: ddinolfo@cal-mum.org
Web site: www.cal-mum.org

Dansville CSD
Matthew McGarrity, Superintendent
284 Main St, Dansville, NY 14437-9787
585-335-4000 Fax: 585-335-4002
e-mail: mcgarritym@dansvillecsd.org
Web site: www.dansvillecsd.org

Geneseo CSD
Timothy Hayes, Superintendent
4050 Avon Rd, Geneseo, NY 14454
585-243-3450 Fax: 585-243-9481
e-mail: thayes@geneseo.k12.ny.us
Web site: www.geneseocsd.org

Keshequa CSD
Edward Stores, Acting Superintendent
13 Mill St, Nunda, NY 14517
585-468-2541 x1105 Fax: 585-468-3814
e-mail: estores@keshequa.org
Web site: www.keshequa.org

Livonia CSD
Scott Bischoping, Superintendent
2 Puppy Ln, PO Box E, Livonia, NY 14487
585-346-4001 Fax: 585-346-6145
e-mail: sbischoping@livoniacsd.org
Web site: www.livoniacsd.org

Mt Morris CSD
Renee Garrett, Superintendent
30 Bonadonna Ave, Mount Morris, NY 14510
585-658-2568 Fax: 585-658-4814
e-mail: rgarrett@mtmorriscsd.org
Web site: www.mtmorriscsd.org

York CSD
Thomas Manko, Superintendent
2578 Genesee St, PO Box 102, Retsof, NY 14539-0102
585-243-1730 x2223 Fax: 585-243-5269
e-mail: tjmanko@yorkcsd.org
Web site: www.yorkcsd.org

MADISON

Brookfield CSD
Sherri Scheibel, Superintendent
1910 Fairground Rd, Brookfield, NY 13314-0060
315-899-3323 x224
Web site: www.bcsbeavers.org

Canastota CSD
Frederick J Bragan, Superintendent

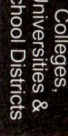

Offices and agencies generally appear in alphabetical order, except when specific order is requested by listee.

PUBLIC SCHOOL DISTRICTS / School District Administrators

120 Roberts St, Canastota, NY 13032-1198
315-697-2025
Web site: www.canastotacsd.org

Cazenovia CSD
Robert Dubik, Superintendent
31 Emory Ave, Cazenovia, NY 13035-1098
315-655-1317 Fax: 315-655-1375
e-mail: rdubik@caz.cnyric.org
Web site: www.caz.cnyric.org

Chittenango CSD
Thomas E Marzeski, Superintendent
1732 Fyler Rd, Chittenango, NY 13037-9520
315-687-2669 Fax: 315-687-2674
Web site: www.chittenangoschools.org

De Ruyter CSD
Bruce R Sharpe, Superintendent
711 Railroad St, Deruyter, NY 13052-0000
315-852-3410 Fax: 315-852-9600
e-mail: sandyw@deruyter.k12.ny.us
Web site: www.deruyter.k12.ny.us

Hamilton CSD
Diana Bowers, Superintendent
47 W Kendrick Ave, Hamilton, NY 13346-1299
315-824-3721
Web site: hcscolgate.edu

Madison CSD
Cynthia DeDominick, Superintendent
7303 State Route 20, Madison, NY 13402
315-893-1878
e-mail: cdedominick@madisoncentralny.org
Web site: www.madisoncentralny.org

Morrisville-Eaton CSD
Michael Drahos, Superintendent
PO Box 990, Morrisville, NY 13408-0990
315-684-9300 Fax: 315-684-9399
e-mail: mdrahos@m-ecs.org
Web site: www.m-ecs.org

Oneida City SD
Ronald R Spadafora Jr, Superintendent
565 Sayles St, Oneida, NY 13421-0327
315-363-2550
e-mail: rspadafora@oneida.high.moric.org
Web site: www.oneida.org

Stockbridge Valley CSD
Randy C Richards, Superintendent
6011 Williams Rd, Munnsville, NY 13409-0732
315-495-4400 Fax: 315-495-4492
e-mail: rrichards@stockbridgevalley.org
Web site: www.stockbridgevalley.org

MONROE

Brighton CSD
Christopher B Manaseri, Superintendent
2035 Monroe Ave, Rochester, NY 14618-2027
585-242-5080 Fax: 585-242-5212
e-mail: chris_manaseri@bcsd.org
Web site: www.bcsd.org

Brockport CSD
James C Fallon, Superintendent
40 Allen St, Brockport, NY 14420-2296
585-637-1810
e-mail: jfallon@bcs1.org
Web site: www.brockport.k12.ny.us

Churchville-Chili CSD
Phillip W Langton, Interim Superintendent
139 Fairbanks Rd, Churchville, NY 14428-9797
585-293-1800 Fax: 585-293-1013
Web site: www.cccsd.org

East Irondequoit CSD
Susan K Allen, Superintendent
600 Pardee Rd, Rochester, NY 14609
585-339-1210 Fax: 585-288-0713
Web site: www.eicsd.k12.ny.us

East Rochester UFSD
Howard S Maffucci, Superintendent
222 Woodbine Ave, East Rochester, NY 14445
585-248-6302 Fax: 585-586-3254
e-mail: carole_davis@er.monroe.edu
Web site: www.erschools.org

Fairport CSD
Jon Hunter, Superintendent
38 W Church St, Fairport, NY 14450-2130
585-421-2004 Fax: 585-421-3421
e-mail: jon_hunter@fairport.monroe.edu
Web site: www.fairport.org

Gates-Chili CSD
Richard A Stein, Superintendent
3 Spartan Way, Rochester, NY 14624
585-247-5050 x1217
Web site: www.gateschili.org

Greece CSD
Steven Achramoritch, Superintendent
PO Box 300, N Greece, NY 14515-0300
585-966-2301 Fax: 585-581-8203
Web site: www.greece.k12.ny.us

Hilton CSD
David Dimbleby, Superintendent

Offices and agencies generally appear in alphabetical order, except when specific order is requested by listee.

PUBLIC SCHOOL DISTRICTS / School District Administrators

225 West Ave, Hilton, NY 14468-1283
585-392-1000 Fax: 585-392-1038
Web site: www.hilton.k12.ny.us

Honeoye Falls-Lima CSD
Michelle Kavanaugh, Superintendent
20 Church St, Honeoye Falls, NY 14472-1294
585-624-7010
e-mail: michelle_kavanaugh@hflcsd.org
Web site: www.hflcsd.org

Penfield CSD
G Susan Gray, Superintendent
PO Box 900, Penfield, NY 14526-0900
585-249-5702 Fax: 585-248-8412
e-mail: susan_gray@penfield.monroe.edu
Web site: penfield.edu

Pittsford CSD
Mary Alice Price, Superintendent
42 W Jefferson Rd, Pittsford, NY 14534-1978
585-267-1000 Fax: 585-381-2105
e-mail: maryalice_price@pittsford.monroe.edu
Web site: www.pittsfordschools.com

Rochester City SD
Wiliam Cala, Interim Superintendent
131 W Broad St, Rochester, NY 14614
585-262-8378
Web site: www.rcsdk12.org

Rush-Henrietta CSD
Kenneth Graham, Superintendent
2034 Lehigh Station Rd, Henrietta, NY 14467-9692
585-359-5012 Fax: 585-359-5045
e-mail: kgraham@rhnet.org
Web site: www.rhnet.org

Spencerport CSD
Mary Ann Kermis, Superintendent
71 Lyell Ave, Spencerport, NY 14559-1899
585-349-5102 Fax: 585-349-5011
e-mail: mkermis@spencerportschools.org
Web site: www.spencerportschools.org

Webster CSD
Adele Borardz, Superintendent
119 South Ave, Webster, NY 14580-3594
585-265-3600 Fax: 585-265-6561
Web site: www.websterschools.org

West Irondequoit CSD
Jeffrey B Crane, Superintendent
321 List Ave, Rochester, NY 14617-3125
585-336-2983 Fax: 585-266-1556
e-mail: marykay_herman@westiron.monroe.edu
Web site: www.westirondequoit.org

Wheatland-Chili CSD
Thomas Gallagher, Superintendent
13 Beckwith Ave, Scottsville, NY 14546
585-889-4500 Fax: 585-889-6284
Web site: www.wheatland.k12.ny.us

MONTGOMERY

Canajoharie CSD
Richard Rose, Superintendent
136 Scholastic Way, Canajoharie, NY 13317
518-673-6302 Fax: 518-673-3177
e-mail: rrose@canajoharie.k12.ny.us
Web site: www.canajoharie.k12.ny.us

Fonda-Fultonville CSD
James Hoffman, Superintendent
112 Old Johnstown Rd, Fonda, NY 12068-1501
518-853-4415 Fax: 518-853-4461
e-mail: jhoffman@ffcsd.org

Fort Plain CSD
Douglas C Burton, Superintendent
25 High St, Fort Plain, NY 13339-1218
518-993-4000 Fax: 518-993-3393
e-mail: fpcsss@hotmail.com
Web site: www.fortplain.org

Greater Amsterdam SD
Ronald E Limoncelli, Superintendent
11 Liberty St, Amsterdam, NY 12010
518-843-5217 Fax: 518-842-0012
e-mail: rlimoncelli@gasd.org
Web site: gasd.neric.org

St Johnsville CSD
Christine Battisti, Superintendent
61 Monroe St, St Johnsville, NY 13452-1111
518-568-7023 Fax: 518-568-5407
Web site: www.sjcsd.org

NASSAU

Baldwin UFSD
Robert J Britto, Superintendent
960 Hastings St, Baldwin, NY 11510
516-377-9271 Fax: 516-377-9421
e-mail: brittor@baldwin.k12.ny.us
Web site: www.baldwin.k12.ny.us

Bellmore UFSD
Sheldon Dumain, Superintendent
580 Winthrop Ave, Bellmore, NY 11710-5099
516-679-2909 Fax: 516-679-3027
e-mail: sdumain@bellmoreschools.org
Web site: www.bellmore.k12.ny.us

Bellmore-Merrick Central HS District
Henry Kiernan, Superintendent

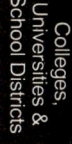

Offices and agencies generally appear in alphabetical order, except when specific order is requested by listee.

PUBLIC SCHOOL DISTRICTS / School District Administrators

1260 Meadowbrook Rd, North Merrick, NY 11566
516-992-1001
Web site: www.bellmore-merrick.k12.ny.us

Bethpage UFSD
Richard S Marsh, Superintendent
10 Cherry Ave, Bethpage, NY 11714
516-644-4001
e-mail: rmarsh@bethpage.ws
Web site: wwwbethpagecommunity.com/Schools

Carle Place UFSD
W Michael Mahoney, Superintendent
168 Cherry Ln, Carle Place, NY 11514
516-622-6575
Web site: www.cps.k12.ny.us

East Meadow UFSD
Robert R Dillon, Superintendent
718 The Plain Road, Westbury, NY 11590
516-478-5776
e-mail: rdillon@eastmeadow.k12.ny.us
Web site: www.eastmeadow.k12.ny.us

East Rockaway UFSD
Arnold Dodge, Superintendent
443 Ocean Ave, East Rockaway, NY 11518
516-887-8300
Web site: www.eastrockawayschools.org

East Williston UFSD
Carolyn S Harris, Superintendent
11 Bacon Rd, Old Westbury, NY 11568
516-333-3758 Fax: 516-333-1937
Web site: www.ewsdonline.org

Elmont UFSD
Al Harper, Superintendent
135 Elmont Rd, Elmont, NY 11003-1609
516-326-5500 Fax: 516-326-5574
Web site: www.elmontschools.org

Farmingdale UFSD
John Lorentz, Superintendent
50 Van Cott Ave, Farmingdale, NY 11735
516-752-6510
Web site: www.farmingdaleschools.org

Floral Park-Bellerose UFSD
Lynn Pombonyo, Superintendent
One Poppy Pl, Floral Park, NY 11001
516-327-9300 Fax: 516-327-9304
Web site: www.floralpark.k12.ny.us

Franklin Square UFSD
Thomas P Dolan, Superintendent
760 Washington St, Franklin Square, NY 11010
516-481-4100
e-mail: info@franklinsquare.k12.ny.us
Web site: franklinsquare.k12.ny.us

Freeport UFSD
Eric L Eversley, Superintendent
235 N Ocean Ave, Freeport, NY 11520
516-867-5205 Fax: 516-623-4759
Web site: www.freeportschools.org

Garden City UFSD
Robert Feirsen, Superintendent
56 Cathedral Ave, PO Box 216, Garden City, NY 11530-0216
516-478-1010
Web site: www.gardencity.k12.ny.us

Glen Cove City SD
Laurence W Aronstein, Superintendent
150 Dosoris Ln, Glen Cove, NY 11542
516-759-7217
e-mail: laronst@glencove.k12.ny.us
Web site: www.glencove.k12.ny.us

Great Neck UFSD
Ronald L Friedman, Superintendent
345 Lakeville Rd, Great Neck, NY 11020
516-773-1405 Fax: 516-773-6685
e-mail: rfriedman@greatneck.k12.ny.us
Web site: www.greatneck.k12.ny.us

Hempstead UFSD
Nathaniel Clay, Superintendent
185 Peninsula Blvd, Hempstead, NY 11550
516-292-7111 x1001
Web site: www.hempsteadschools.org

Herricks UFSD
John E Bierwirth, Superintendent
999 B Herricks Rd, New Hyde Park, NY 11040
516-248-3105
e-mail: jbierwirth@herricks.org
Web site: www.herricks.org

Hewlett-Woodmere UFSD
Lester M Omotani, Superintendent
1 Johnson Pl, Woodmere, NY 11598
516-374-8100 Fax: 516-374-8101
Web site: www.hewlett-woodmere.net

Hicksville UFSD
Maureen K Bright, Superintendent
200 Division Ave-Adm, Hicksville, NY 11801-4800
516-733-6600

Island Park UFSD
Edward Price, Superintendent

Offices and agencies generally appear in alphabetical order, except when specific order is requested by listee.

PUBLIC SCHOOL DISTRICTS / School District Administrators

150 Trafalgar Blvd, Island Park, NY 11558
516-431-8100 Fax: 516-431-7550
Web site: www.ips.k12.ny.us

Island Trees UFSD
James Parla, Superintendent
74 Farmedge Rd, Levittown, NY 11756
516-520-2100
e-mail: jparla@islandtrees.org
Web site: www.islandtrees.org

Jericho UFSD
Henry L Grishman, Superintendent
99 Cedar Swamp Rd, Jericho, NY 11753
516-203-3600 x3201
e-mail: hgrishman@jerichoschools.org
Web site: www.bestschools.org

Lawrence UFSD
John T Fitzsimons, Superintendent
195 Broadway, Lawrence, NY 11559
516-295-8000
Web site: www.lawrence.org

Levittown UFSD
Herman A Sirois, Superintendent
150 Abbey Ln, Levittown, NY 11756
516-520-8300 Fax: 516-520-8314
Web site: www.levittownschools.com

Locust Valley CSD
Richard Hirt, Superintendent
Horse Hollow Rd, Locust Valley, NY 11560
516-674-6310
e-mail: rhirt@lvcsd.k12.ny.us
Web site: www.lvcsd.k12.ny.us

Long Beach City SD
Robert Greenberg, Superintendent
235 Lido Blvd, Long Beach, NY 11561-5093
516-897-2104
Web site: www.lbeach.org

Lynbrook UFSD
Philip S Cicero, Superintendent
111 Atlantic Ave, Lynbrook, NY 11563
516-887-0253
Web site: www.lynbrook.k12.ny.us

Malverne UFSD
Mary Ellen Freeley, Superintendent
301 Wicks Ln, Malverne, NY 11565-2244
516-887-6405
Web site: www.malverne.k12.ny.us

Manhasset UFSD
Charles S Cardillo, Superintendent
200 Memorial Pl, Manhasset, NY 11030
516-627-7705 Fax: 516-627-8158
e-mail: ccardillo@manhasset.k12.ny.us
Web site: www.manhasset.k12.ny.us

Massapequa UFSD
Maureen Flaherty, Superintendent
4925 Merrick Rd, Massapequa, NY 11758
516-797-6160
e-mail: mflaherty@msd.k12.ny.us
Web site: www.msd.k12.ny.us

Merrick UFSD
Ranier W Melucci, Superintendent
21 Babylon Rd, Merrick, NY 11566
516-992-7240
Web site: www.merrick-k6.org

Mineola UFSD
Lorenzo Licopoli, Superintendent
121 Jackson Ave, Mineola, NY 11501
516-237-2001 Fax: 516-237-2008
Web site: www.mineola.k12.ny,us

New Hyde Park-Garden City Park UFSD
Regina Cohn, Superintendent
1950 Hillside Ave, New Hyde Park, NY 11040
516-352-6257 x221
e-mail: rcohn@nhp-gcp.org
Web site: www.nhp-gcp.org

North Bellmore UFSD
Dominic Mucci, Superintendent
2616 Martin Ave, Bellmore, NY 11710
516-992-3000 x4001
e-mail: dmucci@northbellmoreschools.org
Web site: www.northbellmoreschools.org

North Merrick UFSD
David S Feller, Superintendent
1057 Merrick Ave, Merrick, NY 11566
516-292-3694 Fax: 516-292-3097
Web site: www.north-merrick.k12.ny.us

North Shore CSD
Edward K Melnick, Superintendent
112 Franklin Ave, Sea Cliff, NY 11579
516-277-7800 or 516-277-7801
Web site: www.northshore.k12.ny.us

Oceanside UFSD
Herb R Brown, Superintendent
145 Merle Ave, Oceanside, NY 11572-2206
516-678-1215
e-mail: hbrown@oceanside.k12.ny.us
Web site: www.oceanside.k12.ny.us

Oyster Bay-East Norwich CSD
Phyllis Harrington, Superintendent

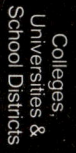

Colleges, Universities & School Districts

Offices and agencies generally appear in alphabetical order, except when specific order is requested by listee.

PUBLIC SCHOOL DISTRICTS / School District Administrators

1 McCouns Ln, Oyster Bay, NY 11771-3105
516-624-6505
e-mail: pharrington@obenschools.org
Web site: oben.schools.org

Plainedge UFSD
John A Richman, Superintendent
241 Wyngate Dr, PO Box 1669, North Massapequa, NY 11758
516-992-7455 Fax: 516-992-7445
Web site: www.plainedgeschools.org

Plainview-Old Bethpage CSD
Martin Brooks, Superintendent
106 Washington Ave, Plainview, NY 11803-3612
516-937-6301
Web site: www.pob.k12.ny.us

Port Washington UFSD
Geoffrey N Gordon, Superintendent
100 Campus Dr, Port Washington, NY 11050
516-767-5005 Fax: 516-767-5007
e-mail: gng@portnet.k12.ny.us
Web site: www.portnet.k12.ny.us

Rockville Centre UFSD
William H Johnson, Superintendent
128 Shepherd St, Rockville Centre, NY 11570-2298
516-255-8920
Web site: www.rvcschools.org

Roosevelt UFSD
Vacant, Superintendent
240 Denton Pl, Roosevelt, NY 11575-1539
516-867-8616 Fax: 516-379-0178
Web site: www.rooseveltufsd.com

Roslyn UFSD
Gerard W Dempsey Jr, Interim Superintendent
300 Harbor Hill Rd, Roslyn, NY 11576-1531
516-625-6303 Fax: 516-625-6336
e-mail: roslynsd@roslynschools.org
Web site: www.roslynschools.org

Seaford UFSD
Thomas J Markle, Superintendent
1600 Washington Ave, Seaford, NY 11783
516-592-4002
e-mail: Thomas_Markle@mail.seaford.k12.ny.us
Web site: www.seaford.k12.ny.us

Sewanhaka Central HS District
Warren A Meierdiercks, Superintendent
77 Landau Ave, Floral Park, NY 11001
516-488-9800 Fax: 516-488-9899
Web site: www.sewanhaka.k12.ny.us

Syosset CSD
Carole G Hankin, Superintendent
99 Pell Ln, PO Box 9029, Syosset, NY 11791
516-364-5605
Web site: www.syosett.k12.ny.us

Uniondale UFSD
William K Lloyd, Superintendent
933 Goodrich St, Uniondale, NY 11553-2499
516-560-8824 Fax: 516-564-8464
Web site: district.uniondaleschools.org

Valley Stream 13 UFSD
Elizabeth Lison, Superintendent
585 N Corona Ave, Valley Stream, NY 11580
516-568-6100 Fax: 516-825-2537
e-mail: elison@valleystream13.com
Web site: www.valleystream13.com

Valley Stream 24 UFSD
Edward M Fale, Superintendent
75 Horton Ave, Valley Stream, NY 11581-1420
516-256-0153
Web site: www.vsufsd.com

Valley Stream 30 UFSD
Lawrence R McGoldrick, Superintendent
175 N Central Ave, Valley Stream, NY 11580-3801
516-285-9881
Web site: www.valleystream30.com

Valley Stream Central HS District
Marc F Bernstein, Superintendent
One Kent Rd, Valley Stream, NY 11580-3398
516-872-5601 Fax: 516-872-5658
e-mail: bernstem@vschsd.org
Web site: www.vschsd.org

Wantagh UFSD
Carl Bonuso, Superintendent
3301 Beltagh Ave, Wantagh, NY 11793-3395
516-679-6300
e-mail: wantaghinfo@wantaghschools.org
Web site: www.wms.wantaghufsd.k12.ny.us

West Hempstead UFSD
Carol D Eisenberg, Superintendent
252 Chestnut St, West Hempstead, NY 11552-2455
516-390-3107 Fax: 516-489-1776
Web site: www.westhempstead.k12.ny.us

Westbury UFSD
Constance R Clark, Superintendent
2 Hitchcock Ln, Old Westbury, NY 11568-1624
516-876-5016 Fax: 516-876-5187
e-mail: cclark@westburyschools.org
Web site: www.westburyschools.org

NEW YORK CITY

NYC Chancellor's Office
Joel I Klein, Chancellor

Offices and agencies generally appear in alphabetical order, except when specific order is requested by listee.

PUBLIC SCHOOL DISTRICTS / School District Administrators

52 Chambers St, New York, NY 10007
212-374-0200 Fax: 212-374-5763

NYC Citywide Alternative HS District & Programs
Cami Anderson, Senior Superintendent
90-27 Sutphin Blvd, Jamaica, NY 11435
718-557-2681

NYC Citywide Special Ed District 75
Bonnie Brown, Superintendent
400 First Ave, New York, NY 10010
212-802-1503
Web site: schools.nycenet.edu/d75/

NYC Region 1
Yvonne Torres, Regional Superintendent
1 Fordham Plz, Rm 81, Bronx, NY 10458
718-741-7030

NYC Region 2
Laura Rodriguez, Regional Superintendent
1230 Zerega Ave, Bronx, NY 10462
718-828-2440

NYC Region 3
Judith J Chin, Regional Superintendent
30-48 Linden Pl, Flushing, NY 11354
718-281-7575

NYC Region 4
Charles A Amundsen, Regional Superintendent
28-11 Queens Plz N, Long Island City, NY 11101
718-391-8300
Web site: www.region4.nycenet.edu

NYC Region 5
Kathleen M Cashin, Regional Superintendent
82-01 Rockaway Blvd, Queens, NY 11416
718-270-5800 or 718-922-4960

NYC Region 6
Jean Claude Brizard, Regional Superintendent
5619 Flatlands Ave, Brooklyn, NY 11234
718-968-6100
Web site: www.region6nycdoe.net

NYC Region 7
Dorita Gibson, Regional Superintendent
715 Ocean Terr, Rm 1, Staten Island, NY 10301
718-556-8350 or 718-759-4900
Web site: www.region7online.com

NYC Region 8
Marcia V Lyles, Regional Superintendent
131 Livingston St, Brooklyn, NY 11201
718-935-3900

NYC Region 9
Peter Heaney Jr, Regional Superintendent
333 7th Ave & 28th St, Room 712, New York, NY 10001
212-356-7500

NYC Region 10
Gale Reeves, Regional Superintendent
4360 Broadway, Rm 52, New York, NY 10033
917-521-3700
Web site: www.r10nycdoe.org

NIAGARA

Barker CSD
Steven J La Rock, Superintendent
1628 Quaker Rd, Barker, NY 14012-0328
716-795-3832

Lewiston-Porter CSD
Don Rappold, Acting Superintendent
4061 Creek Rd, Youngstown, NY 14174-9799
716-754-8287
e-mail: rappoldd@lew-port.com
Web site: www.lew-port.com

Lockport City SD
Terry Carbone, Superintendent
130 Beattie Ave, Lockport, NY 14094-5099
716-478-4835 Fax: 716-478-4863
e-mail: tacarbone@lockport.wnyric.org
Web site: www.locport.k12.ny.us

Newfane CSD
Gary Pogorzelski, Superintendent
6273 Charlotteville Rd, Newfane, NY 14108
716-778-6850 Fax: 716-778-6852
Web site: www.newfane.wnyric.org

Niagara Falls City SD
Carmen A Granto, Superintendent
607 Walnut Ave, Niagara Falls, NY 14302-0399
716-286-4205 Fax: 716-286-4283
e-mail: cgranto@nfschools.net
Web site: www.nfschools.net

Niagara-Wheatfield CSD
Judith H Howard, Superintendent
2292 Saunders Settlement Rd, Sanborn, NY 14132
716-215-3003 Fax: 716-215-3039
e-mail: jhoward@nwcsd.wnyric.org
Web site: www.nwcsd.k12.ny.us

North Tonawanda City SD
Vincent Vecchiarella, Superintendent
175 Humphrey St, North Tonawanda, NY 14120-4097
716-807-3500
Web site: www.ntcityschools.wnyric.org

Royalton-Hartland CSD
Paul J Bona Jr, Superintendent

Offices and agencies generally appear in alphabetical order, except when specific order is requested by listee.

PUBLIC SCHOOL DISTRICTS / School District Administrators

54 State St, Middleport, NY 14105-1199
716-735-3031 Fax: 716-735-3660
e-mail: bonap@royhart.org
Web site: www.royhart.org

Starpoint CSD
C Douglas Whelan, Superintendent
4363 Mapleton Rd, Lockport, NY 14094
716-210-2352
e-mail: dwhelan@starpointcsd.org
Web site: www.starpointcsd.org

Wilson CSD
Michael Wendt, Superintendent
412 Lake St, Wilson, NY 14172
716-751-9341
Web site: www.wilson.wnyric.org

ONEIDA

Adirondack CSD
Frederick J Morgan, Superintendent
110 Ford St, Boonville, NY 13309-1200
315-942-9200 Fax: 315-942-5522
Web site: www.adirondackcsd.org

Camden CSD
Richard Keville, Superintendent
51 Third St, Camden, NY 13316-1114
315-245-4075
Web site: www.camdenschools.org

Clinton CSD
Jeffrey H Roudebush, Superintendent
75 Chenango Ave, Clinton, NY 13323
315-557-2253 Fax: 315-853-8727
e-mail: clinton@ccs.edu
Web site: www.ccs.edu

Holland Patent CSD
Kathleen M Davis, Superintendent
9601 Main St, Holland Patent, NY 13354-4610
315-865-7221
Web site: www.hpschools.org

NY Mills UFSD
David Langone, Superintendent
1 Marauder Blvd, New York Mills, NY 13417-1566
315-768-8127 Fax: 315-768-3521
Web site: www.newyorkmills.org

New Hartford CSD
Daniel Gilligan, Superintendent
33 Oxford Rd, New Hartford, NY 13413
315-624-1218
Web site: www.newhartfordschools.org

Oriskany CSD
Michael S Deuel, Superintendent
1313 Utica St, Oriskany, NY 13424-0539
315-768-2058 Fax: 315-768-2057
Web site: www.oriskanycsd.org

Remsen CSD
Ann P Turner, Superintendent
9733 Davis Dr, PO Box 406, Remsen, NY 13438
315-831-3797
Web site: www.remsencsd.org

Rome City SD
Thomas Gallagher, Superintendent
112 E Thomas St, Rome, NY 13440-5298
315-338-6500 Fax: 315-334-7409
e-mail: tgallagher@romecsd.org
Web site: www.romecsd.org

Sauquoit Valley CSD
Deborah S Flack, Superintendent
2601 Oneida St, Sauquoit, NY 13456-1000
315-839-6311
Web site: www.svcsd.org

Utica City SD
Marilyn A Skermont, Superintendent
1115 Mohawk St, Utica, NY 13501-3709
315-792-2222
Web site: www.uticaschools.org

Vernon-Verona-Sherrill CSD
Norman Reed, Superintendent
5275 State Rt 31, Verona, NY 13478-0128
315-829-2520
Web site: www.vvscentralschools.org

Waterville CSD
James Van Wormer, Superintendent
381 Madison St, Waterville, NY 13480-1100
315-841-3900
e-mail: districtoffice@watervilleschools.org
Web site: www.watervilleschools.org

Westmoreland CSD
Antoinette Kulak, Superintendent
5176 Rt 233, Westmoreland, NY 13490-0430
315-557-2601
e-mail: tkulak@westmorelandschool.org
Web site: www.westmorelandschool.org

Whitesboro CSD
Arnold L Kaye, Superintendent
67 Whitesboro St, PO Box 304, Yorkville, NY 13495-0304
315-266-3303 Fax: 315-768-9730
Web site: www.wboro.org

ONONDAGA

Baldwinsville CSD
Jeanne M Dangle, Superintendent

Offices and agencies generally appear in alphabetical order, except when specific order is requested by listee.

PUBLIC SCHOOL DISTRICTS / School District Administrators

29 E Oneida St, Baldwinsville, NY 13027-2480
315-638-6043 Fax: 315-638-6041
e-mail: jdangle@bville.org
Web site: www.bville.org

East Syracuse-Minoa CSD
Donna J DeSiato, Superintendent
407 Fremont Rd, East Syracuse, NY 13057-2631
315-656-7205 Fax: 315-656-3241
e-mail: ddesiato@esmschools.org
Web site: www.esmschools.org

Fabius-Pompey CSD
Martin L Swenson, Superintendent
1211 Mill St, PO Box 161, Fabius, NY 13063-8719
315-683-5301 Fax: 315-683-5827
e-mail: mswenson@fabius.cnyric.org
Web site: www.fabiuspompey.org

Fayetteville-Manlius CSD
Corliss Kaiser, Superintendent
8199 E Seneca Tpke, Manlius, NY 13104-2140
315-682-1200 Fax: 315-692-1227
e-mail: ckaiser@fmschools.org
Web site: www.fmschools.org

Jamesville-Dewitt CSD
Alice Kendrick, Superintendent
6845 Edinger Dr, PO Box 606, Dewitt, NY 13214-0606
315-445-8304 Fax: 315-445-8477
e-mail: ckendrick@jd.cnyric.org
Web site: www.jamesvilledewitt.org

Jordan-Elbridge CSD
Marilyn Dominick, Superintendent
130 E Main St, Elbridge, NY 13060
315-689-3978
e-mail: mdominick@jecsd.org
Web site: www.jecsd.org

LaFayette CSD
Mark P Mondanaro, Superintendent
5955 Rt 20 W, Lafayette, NY 13084-9701
315-677-9728 Fax: 315-677-3372
e-mail: mmondanaro@lafcs.cnyric.org
Web site: www.lafayetteschools.org

Liverpool CSD
Janice H Matousek, Superintendent
195 Blackberry Rd, Liverpool, NY 13090
315-622-7125 Fax: 315-622-7115
e-mail: jan@liverpool.k12.ny.us
Web site: www.liverpool.k12.ny.us

Lyncourt UFSD
Michael Sandore, Superintendent
2707-2709 Court St, Syracuse, NY 13208
315-455-7571 Fax: 315-455-7573
e-mail: msandore@lyncourt.cnyric.org
Web site: www.lyncourt.cnyric.org

Marcellus CSD
Carig J Tice, Superintendent
2 Reed Pkwy, Marcellus, NY 13108-1199
315-673-0201 Fax: 315-673-1727
e-mail: ctice@mcs.rway.com
Web site: mcs.rway.com

North Syracuse CSD
Jerome F Melvin, Superintendent
5355 W Taft Rd, North Syracuse, NY 13212-2796
315-218-2151
e-mail: jmelvin@nscsd.org
Web site: www.nscsd.org

Onondaga CSD
Donald Trombley, Interim Superintendent
4466 S Onondaga Rd, Nedrow, NY 13120-9715
315-492-1701 Fax: 315-492-4650
Web site: www.ocs.cnyric.org

Skaneateles CSD
Philip D D'Angelo, Superintendent
49 E Elizabeth St, Skaneateles, NY 13152
315-685-8361 Fax: 315-685-0347
Web site: www.skanschools.org

Solvay UFSD
J Francis Manning, Superintendent
103 3rd St, Solvay, NY 13209-1532
315-468-1111 Fax: 315-468-2755
e-mail: manningj@solvay.cnyric.org
Web site: www.solvayschools.org

Syracuse City SD
Daniel G Lowengard, Superintendent
725 Harrison St, Syracuse, NY 13210
315-435-4161 Fax: 315-435-4015
e-mail: dlowengard@scsd.org
Web site: www.syracusecityschools.com

Tully CSD
Kraig D Pritts, Superintendent
20 State St, PO Box 628, Tully, NY 13159-0628
315-696-6204
e-mail: kraig@pobox.com
Web site: www.tullyschools.org

West Genesee CSD
Rudolph Rubeis, Superintendent
300 Sanderson Dr, Camillus, NY 13031-1655
315-487-4562 Fax: 315-487-2999
e-mail: rrubeis@wgmail.cnyric.org
Web site: www.westgenesee.org

Westhill CSD
Stephen A Bocciolatt, Superintendent

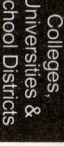

Offices and agencies generally appear in alphabetical order, except when specific order is requested by listee.

PUBLIC SCHOOL DISTRICTS / School District Administrators

400 Walberta Rd, Syracuse, NY 13219-2214
315-426-3218 Fax: 315-488-6411
e-mail: sbocciolatt@westhillschools.org
Web site: www.westhillschools.org

ONTARIO

Bloomfield CSD
Thomas Strining, Interim Superintendent
1 Oakmount Ave, East Bloomfield, NY 14443
585-657-6121 x4004
e-mail: tstrining@bloomfieldcsd.org
Web site: www.bloomfieldcsd.org

Canandaigua City SD
Ronald Raw Jr, Superintendent
143 N Pearl St, Canandaigua, NY 14424-1496
585-396-3700
e-mail: rawd@canandaiguaschools.org
Web site: www.canandaiguaschools.org

Geneva City SD
Robert Young, Superintendent
649 S Exchange St, Geneva, NY 14456-3492
315-781-0400 Fax: 315-781-4128
e-mail: ryoung@genevacsd.org
Web site: www.genevacsd.org

Honeoye CSD
William F Schofield, Superintendent
8523 Main St, Honeoye, NY 14471-0170
585-229-4125
Web site: www.honeoye.org

Manchester-Shortsville CSD
Robert E Leiby, Superintendent
1506 Rt 21, Shortsville, NY 14548-9502
585-289-3964 Fax: 585-289-6660
e-mail: rleiby@redjacket.org
Web site: www.redjacket.org

Marcus Whitman CSD
Oren Cook, Superintendent
4100 Baldwin Rd, Rushville, NY 14544-9799
585-554-4848
e-mail: ocook@mwcsd.org
Web site: www.mwcsd.org

Naples CSD
Brenda C Keith, Superintendent
136 N Main St, Naples, NY 14512-9201
585-374-7901
e-mail: bkeith@naples.k12.ny.us
Web site: www.naples.k12.ny.us

Phelps-Clifton Springs CSD
Michael J Ford, Superintendent

1490 Rt 488, Clifton Springs, NY 14432-9334
315-548-6420
Web site: www.midlakes.org

Victor CSD
Timothy J McElheran, Superintendent
953 High St, Victor, NY 14564-1167
585-924-3252 Fax: 585-742-7023
Web site: www.victorschools.org

ORANGE

Chester UFSD
Helen Ann Livingston, Superintendent
64 Hambletonian Ave, Chester, NY 10918
845-469-5052

Cornwall CSD
Timothy J Rehm, Superintendent
24 Idlewild Ave, Cornwall on Hudson, NY 12520
845-534-8000 Fax: 845-534-4231
e-mail: trehm@ccsd.ouboces.org
Web site: www.cornwallschools.com

Florida UFSD
Douglas Burnside, Superintendent
51 N Main St, PO Box 7, Florida, NY 10921-0757
845-651-3095
e-mail: dburnside@floridaufsd.org
Web site: www.floridaufsd.org

Goshen CSD
Roy Reese, Acting Superintendent
227 Main St, Goshen, NY 10924
845-294-2410 Fax: 845-294-1658
e-mail: rreese@gcsny.org
Web site: www.gcsny.org

Greenwood Lake UFSD
John Guarracino, Superintendent
80 Waterstone Rd, Greenwood Lake, NY 10925
845-477-7395 Fax: 845-477-7398
e-mail: JGuarracino@gwal.ouboces.org
Web site: gwl.ouboces.org

Highland Falls CSD
Philip B Arbolino, Superintendent
PO Box 287, Highland Falls, NY 10928
845-446-9575 Fax: 845-446-3321
Web site: www.hffmcsd.org

Kiryas Joel Village UFSD
Joel Petlin, Superintendent
51 Forest Rd, Ste 315, Monroe, NY 10950-0398
845-782-2300

Middletown City SD
Kenneth Eastwood, Superintendent

Offices and agencies generally appear in alphabetical order, except when specific order is requested by listee.

PUBLIC SCHOOL DISTRICTS / School District Administrators

223 Wisner Ave Ext, Middletown, NY 10940-3240
845-341-5300 Fax: 845-343-9938
e-mail: keastwood@ecsdm.org
Web site: middletowncityschools.org

Minisink Valley CSD
Dr Martha Murray, Superintendent
Rt 6, PO Box 217, Slate Hill, NY 10973-0217
845-355-5110
Web site: www.minisink.com

Monroe-Woodbury CSD
Joseph DiLorenzo, Superintendent
278 Rte 32, Education Ctr, Central Valley, NY 10917-1001
845-460-6200 Fax: 845-460-6080
e-mail: jdiloren@mw.k12.ny.us
Web site: www.mw.k12.ny.us

Newburgh Enlarged City SD
Annette M Saturnelli, Acting Superintendent
124 Grand St, Newburgh, NY 12550-4600
845-563-3400 Fax: 845-563-3501
e-mail: amsaturn@newburgh.k12.ny.us
Web site: www.newburgh.k12.ny.us

Pine Bush CSD
Rose Marie Stark, Superintendent
156 State Rt 302, PO Box 700, Pine Bush, NY 12566-0700
845-744-2031
Web site: www.pinebushschools.org

Port Jervis City SD
John P Xanthis, Superintendent
9 Thompson St, Port Jervis, NY 12771-3058
845-858-3175 Fax: 845-856-1885
e-mail: jxanthis@pj.ouboces.org
Web site: www.portjerviscsd.k12.ny.us

Tuxedo UFSD
Joseph P Zanetti, Superintendent
Route 17, Box 2002, Tuxedo Park, NY 10987
845-351-4799 x312 Fax: 845-351-5296
Web site: www.tuxedoschooldistrict.com

Valley CSD (Montgomery)
Richard M Hooley, Superintendent
944 State Rt 17k, Montgomery, NY 12549-2240
845-457-2400
Web site: www.vcsd.k12.ny.us

Warwick Valley CSD
Frank Greenhall, Superintendent
225 West St Ext, Warwick, NY 10990-0595
845-987-3010
e-mail: fgreenhall@wvcs.org
Web site: www.warwickvalleyschools.org

Washingtonville CSD
Roberta Green, Superintendent

52 W Main St, Washingtonville, NY 10992-1492
845-497-2200 Fax: 845-496-4031

ORLEANS

Albion CSD
Ada Grabowski, Superintendent
324 East Ave, Albion, NY 14411
585-589-2056
e-mail: agrabowski@albionk12.org
Web site: www.albionk12.org

Holley CSD
Robert C D'Angelo, Superintendent
3800 N Main St, Holley, NY 14470-9330
585-638-6316
Web site: www.holleycsd.org

Kendall CSD
Robert Thompson, Interim Superintendent
1932 Kendall Rd, Kendall, NY 14476-0777
585-659-2741
e-mail: kcsd@kendallschools.org
Web site: www.kendallschools.org

Lyndonville CSD
Barbara Deane-Williams, Superintendent
25 Housel Ave, Lyndonville, NY 14098-0540
585-765-2251 x3101
e-mail: bdeane-williams@lyndonville.wnyric.org
Web site: www.lyndonvillecsd.org

Medina CSD
Richard Galante, Superintendent
One Mustang Dr, Medina, NY 14103-1845
585-798-2700
e-mail: rgalante@medinacsd.org
Web site: www.medinacsd.org

OSWEGO

Altmar-Parish-Williamstown CSD
Deborah Haab, Superintendent
639 County Rt 22, Parish, NY 13131
315-625-5251
e-mail: dhaab@apw.cnyric.org

Central Square CSD
Carolyn Costello, Superintendent
642 S Main St, Central Square, NY 13036-3511
315-668-4220
e-mail: ccostello@cssd.org

Fulton City SD
William R Lynch, Superintendent

Offices and agencies generally appear in alphabetical order, except when specific order is requested by listee.

PUBLIC SCHOOL DISTRICTS / School District Administrators

167 S Fourth St, Fulton, NY 13069-1859
315-593-5510
e-mail: blynch@fulton.cnyric.org

Hannibal CSD
Michael J DiFabio, Superintendent
1051 Auburn St, PO Box 66, Hannibal, NY 13074
315-564-7900
e-mail: mdifabio@hannibal.cnyric.org

Mexico CSD
Nelson Bauersfeld, Superintendent
40 Academy St, Mexico, NY 13114-3432
315-963-8400 x5400
e-mail: nbauersf@mexico.cnyric.org

Oswego City SD
David Fischer, Superintendent
120 E 1st St, Oswego, NY 13126-2114
315-341-2001
e-mail: dfischer@oswego.org

Phoenix CSD
Rita Racette, Superintendent
116 Volney St, Phoenix, NY 13135-9778
315-695-1555
e-mail: rracette@phoenix.k12.ny.us

Pulaski CSD
Marshall Marshall, Superintendent
2 Hinman Rd, Pulaski, NY 13142-2201
315-298-5188
e-mail: mmarshal@pacs.cnyric.org

Sandy Creek CSD
Stewart R Amell, Superintendent
124 Salisbury St, Sandy Creek, NY 13145-0248
315-387-3445
e-mail: samell@sccs.cnyric.org

OTSEGO

Cherry Valley-Springfield CSD
Nicholas J Savin, Superintendent
597 County Hwy 54, Cherry Valley, NY 13320-0485
607-264-3265 Fax: 607-264-3458
e-mail: nsavin@cvscs.org

Cooperstown CSD
MaryJo A McPhail, Superintendent
39 Linden Ave, Cooperstown, NY 13326-1496
607-547-5364 Fax: 607-547-1000
e-mail: mjmcphail@cooperstowncs.org

Edmeston CSD
David Rowley, Superintendent
11 North St, Edmeston, NY 13335-0529
607-965-8931 Fax: 607-965-8942
e-mail: drowley@edmeston.net

Gilbertsville-Mount Upton CSD
Douglas A Exley, Superintendent
693 State Hwy 51, Gilbertsville, NY 13776
607-783-2207
e-mail: gmu@gmucsd.org
Web site: www.gmucsd.org

Laurens CSD
Romona N Wenck, Superintendent
55 Main St, Laurens, NY 13796-0301
607-432-2050 Fax: 607-432-4388
e-mail: rwenck@laurenscs.org

Milford CSD
Peter N Livshin, Superintendent
42 W Main St, Milford, NY 13807-0237
607-286-3341 Fax: 607-286-7879
e-mail: plishvin_99@yahoo.com

Morris CSD
Michael Virgil, Superintendent
65 Main St, Morris, NY 13808-0040
607-263-6100 Fax: 607-263-2483
e-mail: mvigil@morriscs.org

Oneonta City SD
Michael P Shea, Superintendent
189 Main St, Ste 302, Oneonta, NY 13820-1142
607-433-8232 Fax: 607-433-3641
e-mail: mshea@oneontacsd.org
Web site: www.oneontacsd.org

Richfield Springs CSD
Robert Barruco, Superintendent
93 Main St, PO Box 631, Richfield Springs, NY 13439-0631
315-858-0610
Web site: www.richfieldcsd.org

Schenevus CSD
Lynda Booknard, Superintendent
159 Main St, Schenevus, NY 12155-0008
607-638-5530 Fax: 607-638-5600
e-mail: lbooknard@schenevuscs.org

Unatego CSD
Rebecca R Furlong, Superintendent
2641 State Hwy 7, Otego, NY 13825
607-988-5000
e-mail: dfurlong@unatego.org
Web site: www.unatego.org

Worcester CSD
John Selover, Superintendent

Offices and agencies generally appear in alphabetical order, except when specific order is requested by listee.

PUBLIC SCHOOL DISTRICTS / School District Administrators

198 Main St, Worcester, NY 12197
607-397-8785 Fax: 607-397-9454
e-mail: seloverj@worcestercs.org

PUTNAM

Brewster CSD
Jane Sandbank, Superintendent
30 Farm-to-Market Rd, Brewster, NY 10509-9956
845-279-8000
e-mail: jsandbank@brewsterschools.org
Web site: www.brewsterschools.org

Carmel CSD
Marilyn C Terranova, Superintendent
81 South St, Patterson, NY 12563-0296
845-878-2094 Fax: 845-878-4337
e-mail: info@ccsd.k12.ny.us
Web site: www.ccsd.k12.ny.us

Garrison UFSD
Gloria J Colucci, Superintendent
1100 Rt 9 D, Garrison, NY 10524-0193
845-424-3689 Fax: 845-424-4733
e-mail: gcolucci@gufs.org
Web site: www.gufs.org

Haldane CSD
Mark Villanti, Superintendent
15 Craigside Dr, Cold Spring, NY 10516-1899
845-265-9254
Web site: www.haldaneschool.org

Mahopac CSD
Robert J Reidy Jr, Superintendent
179 East Lake Blvd, Mahopac, NY 10541-1666
845-628-3415 Fax: 845-628-5502
Web site: www.mahopac.k12.ny.us

Putnam Valley CSD
Gary Tutty, Superintendent
146 Peekskill Hollow Rd, Putnam Valley, NY 10579-3238
845-528-8143 Fax: 845-528-0274
e-mail: gtutty@pvcsd.org
Web site: www.putnamvalleyschools.org

RENSSELAER

Averill Park CSD
Josephine Moccia, Superintendent
8439 Miller Hill Rd, Averill Park, NY 12018-9798
518-674-7055 Fax: 518-674-3802
Web site: www.averillpark.k12.ny.us

Berlin CSD
Maria A Diamond, Superintendent
53 School St, PO Box 259, Berlin, NY 12022-0259
518-658-2690 Fax: 518-658-3822
e-mail: tdiamond@berlincentral.org
Web site: www.berlincentral.org

Brunswick CSD (Brittonkill)
Dave Burnham, Superintendent
3992 NY Rt 2, Troy, NY 12180-9034
518-279-4600 x602 Fax: 518-279-1918
e-mail: dburnham@brittonkill.k12.ny.us

East Greenbush CSD
Terrance Brewer, Superintendent
29 Englewood Ave, East Greenbush, NY 12061
518-477-2755 x131
e-mail: brewerte@egcsd.org
Web site: www.egcsd.org

Hoosic Valley CSD
James A Seeley, Superintendent
2 Pleasant Ave, Schaghticoke, NY 12154
518-753-4458 x1506
Web site: www.hoosickvalley.k12.ny.us

Hoosick Falls CSD
Roger E Thompson, Superintendent
21187 NY Rt 22, PO Box 192, Hoosick Falls, NY 12090-0192
518-686-7321 Fax: 518-686-9060

Lansingburgh CSD
Lee Bordick, Superintendent
576 Fifth Ave, Troy, NY 12182-3295
518-233-6850

North Greenbush Common SD (Williams)
Joseph Padalino, Superintendent
476 N Greenbush Rd, Rensselaer, NY 12144
518-283-6748

Rensselaer City SD
Gordon F Reynolds, Superintendent
555 Broadway, Rensselaer, NY 12144-2694
518-465-7509
e-mail: reynolds@rcsd.k12.ny.us
Web site: www.rcsd.k12.ny.us

Schodack CSD
Douglas B Hamlin, Superintendent
1216 Maple Hill Rd, Castleton, NY 12033-1699
518-732-2297 Fax: 518-732-7710
Web site: www.schodack.k12.ny.us

Troy City Enlarged SD
Lonnie Palmer, Interim Superintendent
2920 5th Ave, Troy, NY 12180
518-271-5210

Wynantskill UFSD
Christine Hamill, Superintendent

Offices and agencies generally appear in alphabetical order, except when specific order is requested by listee.

PUBLIC SCHOOL DISTRICTS / School District Administrators

East Ave, PO Box 345, Wynantskill, NY 12198-0345
518-283-4679 Fax: 518-283-3799
e-mail: chamill@wynantskillufsd.org
Web site: www.wynantskillufsd.org

ROCKLAND

Clarkstown CSD
Margaret Keller-Cogan, Superintendent
62 Old Middletown Rd, New City, NY 10956
845-639-6418 Fax: 845-639-6488
e-mail: mkeller@ccsd.edu
Web site: www.ccsd.edu

East Ramapo CSD (Spring Valley)
Mitchell J Schwartz, Superintendent
105 S Madison Ave, Spring Valley, NY 10977
845-577-6011
e-mail: mschwartz@ercsd.k12.ny.us
Web site: www.eram.k12.ny.us

Nanuet UFSD
Mark S McNeill, Superintendent
101 Church St, Nanuet, NY 10954-3000
845-627-9890
e-mail: mmcneil@nufsd.lhric.org
Web site: nanunet.lhric.org

North Rockland CSD
Brian Monahan, Superintendent
65 Chapel St, Garnerville, NY 10923
845-942-3000 Fax: 845-942-3047
e-mail: bmonahan@nrcsd.org
Web site: www.nrcsd.org

Nyack UFSD
Valencia F Douglas, Superintendent
13A Dickinson Ave, Nyack, NY 10960-2914
845-353-7000 Fax: 845-353-7019
Web site: www.nyackschools.org

Pearl River UFSD
Frank V Auriemma, Superintendent
275 E Central Ave, Pearl River, NY 10965-2799
845-620-3900 Fax: 845-620-3927
e-mail: auriemmaf@pearlriver.org
Web site: www.pearlriver.k12.ny.us

Ramapo CSD (Suffern)
Robert B MacNaughton, Superintendent
45 Mountain Ave, Hillburn, NY 10931-0935
845-357-7783 Fax: 845-357-5707
Web site: www.ramapocentral.org

South Orangetown CSD
Joseph Zambito, Superintendent

160 Van Wyck Rd, Blauvelt, NY 10913-1299
845-680-1050
e-mail: jzambito@socsd.org
Web site: www.socsd.org

SARATOGA

Ballston Spa CSD
Raymond Colucciello, Interim Superintendent
70 Malta Ave, Ballston Spa, NY 12020-1599
518-884-7195 Fax: 518-884-7101
e-mail: rcolucciello@bscsd.org
Web site: www.bscsd.org

Burnt Hills-Ballston Lake CSD
James Schultz, Superintendent
50 Cypress Dr, Glenville, NY 12302
518-399-9141 x5002
e-mail: jschultz@bhbl.org
Web site: www.bhbl.org

Corinth CSD
Daniel Starr, Superintendent
105 Oak St, Corinth, NY 12822-1295
518-654-2601 Fax: 518-654-6266
Web site: www.corinthcsd.org

Edinburg Common SD
Randy W Teetz, Superintendent
4 Johnson Rd, Edinburg, NY 12134-5390
518-863-8412

Galway CSD
Clifford Moses, Superintendent
5317 Sacandaga Rd, Galway, NY 12074-0130
518-882-1033 Fax: 518-882-5250
Web site: www.galwaycsd.org

Mechanicville City SD
Michael J McCarthy, Superintendent
25 Kniskern Ave, Mechanicville, NY 12118-1995
518-664-5727
Web site: www.mechanicville.org

Saratoga Springs City SD
John E MacFadden, Superintendent
3 Blue Streak Blvd, Saratoga Springs, NY 12866-5967
518-583-4709
Web site: www.saratogaschools.org

Schuylerville CSD
Leon J Reed, Superintendent
14 Spring St, Schuylerville, NY 12871-1098
518-695-3255 Fax: 518-695-6491
e-mail: administration@scuylerville.org
Web site: www.schuylervilleschools.org

Shenendehowa CSD
L Oliver Robinson, Superintendent

Offices and agencies generally appear in alphabetical order, except when specific order is requested by listee.

PUBLIC SCHOOL DISTRICTS / School District Administrators

5 Chelsea Pl, Clifton Park, NY 12065-3240
518-881-0610
e-mail: robioliv@shenet.org
Web site: www.shenet.org

South Glens Falls CSD
James P McCarthy, Superintendent
6 Bluebird Rd, South Glens Falls, NY 12803-5704
518-793-9617
Web site: www.sgfallssd.org

Stillwater CSD
Patrick DiCaprio, Interim Superintendent
334 N Hudson Ave, Stillwater, NY 12170-0490
518-373-6100
e-mail: pdicaprio@scsd.org
Web site: www.scsd.org

Waterford-Halfmoon UFSD
Carl J Klossner, Superintendent
125 Middletown Rd, Waterford, NY 12188-1590
518-237-0800
e-mail: cklossner@whufsd.org
Web site: www.whufsd.org

SCHENECTADY

Duanesburg CSD
Mark A Villanti, Superintendent
133 School Dr, Delanson, NY 12053-0129
518-895-2279 Fax: 518-895-2626
e-mail: mvillanti@mum.neric.org
Web site: dcs.neric.org

Mohonasen CSD
Kathleen A Spring, Superintendent
2072 Curry Rd, Schenectady, NY 12303-4400
518-356-8202 Fax: 518-356-8247
e-mail: kspring@mohonasen.org
Web site: www.mohonasen.org

Niskayuna CSD
Kevin S Baughman, Superintendent
1239 Van Antwerp Rd, Schenectady, NY 12309-5317
518-377-4666 x206 Fax: 518-377-4074
e-mail: baughman.k@nisk.k12.ny.us
Web site: www.niskayunaschools.org

Schalmont CSD
Valerie Kelsey, Superintendent
401 Duanesburg Rd, Schenectady, NY 12306-1981
518-355-9200 Fax: 518-355-9203
e-mail: vkelsey@sabrenet.net
Web site: www.schalmont.org

Schenectady City SD
Eric Ely, Superintendent
108 Education Dr, Schenectady, NY 12303-3442
518-370-8100 Fax: 518-370-8173
e-mail: elye@schenectady.k12.ny.us
Web site: www.schenectady.k12.ny.us

Scotia-Glenville CSD
Susan M Swartz, Superintendent
900 Preddice Pkwy, Scotia, NY 12302-1049
518-382-1215 Fax: 518-386-4336
e-mail: sshwartz@sgcsd.net
Web site: www.sgcsd.neric.org

SCHOHARIE

Cobleskill-Richmondville CSD
Samuel A Shevat, Superintendent
155 Washington Ave, Cobleskill, NY 12043-1099
518-234-4032 Fax: 518-234-7721
e-mail: shevats@crcs.k12.ny.us
Web site: www.crcs.k12.ny.us

Gilboa-Conesville CSD
M Matthew Murray, Superintendent
132 Wyckoff Rd, Gilboa, NY 12076-9703
607-588-7541 Fax: 607-588-6820
e-mail: mmatthew_murray@hotmail.com

Jefferson CSD
Carl J Mummenthey, Superintendent
1332 St Rt 10, Jefferson, NY 12093-0039
607-652-7821 Fax: 607-652-7806
e-mail: c.mummenthey@jeffersoncs.org

Middleburgh CSD
Douglas S Kelley, Superintendent
168 Main St, Middleburgh, NY 12122
518-827-5567 Fax: 518-827-6632
e-mail: d.kelley@yahoo.com

Schoharie CSD
Brian Sherman, Superintendent
136 Academy Drive, PO Box 430, Schoharie, NY 12157-0430
518-295-8132 Fax: 518-295-8178
e-mail: bsherman@schoharie.k12.ny.us
Web site: www.schoharieschools.org

Sharon Springs CSD
Patterson Green, Superintendent
514 State Rt 20, PO Box 218, Sharon Springs, NY 13459-0218
518-284-2266 Fax: 518-284-9033
e-mail: pgreen@sharonsprings.org
Web site: www.sharonsprings.org

SCHUYLER

Odessa-Montour CSD
James R Frame, Superintendent

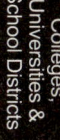

Offices and agencies generally appear in alphabetical order, except when specific order is requested by listee.

PUBLIC SCHOOL DISTRICTS / School District Administrators

300 College Ave, PO Box 430, Odessa, NY 14869-0430
607-594-3341 Fax: 607-594-3976
e-mail: jframe@gstboces.org
Web site: www.omschools.org

Watkins Glen CSD
Tom Phillips, Superintendent
303 12th St, Watkins Glen, NY 14891-1699
607-535-3219
e-mail: tphillips@watkinsglenschools.com
Web site: www.watkinsglenschools.com

SENECA

Romulus CSD
Michael Midey, Superintendent
5705 Rt 96, Romulus, NY 14541-9551
866-810-0345 x399
e-mail: mmidey@rcs.k12.ny.us
Web site: www.rcs.k12.ny.us

Seneca Falls CSD
Gerald Macaluso, Superintendent
98 Clinton St, Seneca Falls, NY 13148-1090
315-568-5500 Fax: 315-568-0535
e-mail: gmacaluso@sfcs.k12.ny.us
Web site: www.sfcs.k12.ny.us

South Seneca CSD
Janie L Nusser, Superintendent
7263 Main St, Ovid, NY 14521-9586
607-869-9636
e-mail: jnusser@southseneca.k12.ny.us
Web site: www.southseneca.com

Waterloo CSD
Terry MacNabb, Superintendent
109 Washington St, Waterloo, NY 13165
315-539-1500
Web site: www.waterloocsd.org

ST. LAWRENCE

Brasher Falls CSD
Stephen Putnam, Superintendent
1039 State Hwy 11C, Brasher Falls, NY 13613-0307
315-389-5131 Fax: 315-389-5245
e-mail: sputnam@bfcsd.org
Web site: www.bfcsd.org

Canton CSD
Wayne C Walbridge, Interim Superintendent
99 State St, Canton, NY 13617-1099
315-386-8561
Web site: www.ccsdk12.org

Clifton-Fine CSD
Paul J Alioto, Superintendent
11 Hall Ave, PO Box 75, Star Lake, NY 13690-0075
315-848-3335 x190
Web site: www.cfeagles.org

Colton-Pierrepont CSD
Martin Bregg, Superintendent
4921 State Hwy 56, Colton, NY 13625-0005
315-262-2100 Fax: 315-262-2644
e-mail: breggma@cpcs.k12.ny.us
Web site: www.cpcs.k12.ny.us

Edwards-Knox CSD
William Cartwright, Superintendent
2512 County Hwy 24, PO Box 630, Russell, NY 13684-0630
315-562-8326 Fax: 315-562-2477
e-mail: wcartwri@ekcsk12.org
Web site: www.ekcsk12.org

Gouverneur CSD
Christine J Larose, Superintendent
133 E Barney St, Gouverneur, NY 13642-1100
315-287-4870
e-mail: clarose@gcs.neric.org

Hammond CSD
Douglas McQueer, Superintendent
51 S Main St, PO Box 185, Hammond, NY 13646-0185
315-324-5931 x811
Web site: hammond.sllboces.org

Hermon-Dekalb CSD
Ann M Adams, Superintendent
709 E Dekalb Rd, Dekalb Junction, NY 13630-0213
315-347-3442 Fax: 315-347-3817
e-mail: aadams@mum.neric.org
Web site: www.hdcsk12.org

Heuvelton CSD
Vernice Church, Acting Superintendent
87 Washington St, Heuvelton, NY 13654-0375
315-344-2414 Fax: 315-344-2349
e-mail: stodd@heuvelton.k12.ny.us
Web site: www.heuvelton.k12.ny.us

Lisbon CSD
Ernest L Witkowski, Superintendent
6866 County Rt 10, Lisbon, NY 13658-0039
315-393-4951 x133 Fax: 315-393-7666
e-mail: witkowskie@lisbon.k12.ny.us
Web site: lisboncs.schoolwires.com

Madrid-Waddington CSD
Lynn Roy, Superintendent
2582 State Hwy 345, Madrid, NY 13660-0067
315-322-5746
e-mail: lroy@mwcsk12.org
Web site: www.mwcsk12.org

Massena CSD
Douglas W Huntley, Superintendent

Offices and agencies generally appear in alphabetical order, except when specific order is requested by listee.

PUBLIC SCHOOL DISTRICTS / School District Administrators

84 Nightengale Ave, Massena, NY 13662-1999
315-764-3700 x3005 Fax: 315-764-3701
e-mail: dhuntley@mcs.k12.ny.us
Web site: www.mcs.k12.ny.us

Morristown CSD
Beverly L Ouderkirk, Superintendent
408 Gouverneur St, Morristown, NY 13664-0217
315-375-8814

Norwood-Norfolk CSD
Elizabeth Kirnie, Superintendent
PO Box 194, 7852 State Hwy 56, Norwood, NY 13668-0194
315-353-9951
Web site: www.nncsk12.net

Ogdensburg City SD
Maurice H Barry, Superintendent
1100 State St, Ogdensburg, NY 13669-3398
315-393-0900 Fax: 315-393-2767
Web site: www.ogdensburg12.org/web

Parishville-Hopkinton CSD
Thomas R Burns, Superintendent
12 County Rt 47, Parishville, NY 13672-0187
315-265-4642 Fax: 315-268-1309
Web site: phcs.neric.org

Potsdam CSD
Patrick Brady, Superintendent
29 Leroy St, Potsdam, NY 13676-1787
315-265-2000 Fax: 315-265-2048
e-mail: pbrady@potsdam.k12.ny.us
Web site: www.potsdam.k12.ny.us

STEUBEN

Addison CSD
Betsey A Stiker, Superintendent
1 Colwell St, Addison, NY 14801-1398
607-359-2244 Fax: 607-359-2246
e-mail: bstiker@addison.wnyric.org

Arkport CSD
William S Locke, Superintendent
35 East Ave, Arkport, NY 14807-0070
607-295-7471 Fax: 607-295-7473
e-mail: willial_locke@stev.net

Avoca CSD
R Christopher Roser, Superintendent
17-29 Oliver St, Avoca, NY 14809-0517
607-566-2221 Fax: 607-566-8384
e-mail: croser@avoca.wnyric.org

Bath CSD
Marion Tunney, Superintendent

25 Ellas Ave, Bath, NY 14810-1107
607-776-3301 Fax: 607-776-5021
e-mail: mtunney@bathcsd.org

Bradford CSD
Charles Clemens, Interim Superintendent
2820 Rt 226, Bradford, NY 14815-9602
607-583-4616 Fax: 607-583-4013
e-mail: cclemens@bradfordcsd.org

Campbell-Savona CSD
Lynn Lyndes, Superintendent
8455 County Rt 125, Campbell, NY 14821-9518
607-527-4548 Fax: 607-527-8363
e-mail: llyndes@cscs.wnyric.org

Canisteo-Greenwood CSD
Lorraine A Patti, Superintendent
84 Greenwood St, Canisteo, NY 14823-1299
607-698-4225 Fax: 607-698-2833
e-mail: lpatti@cg.wnyric.org

Corning-Painted Post Area SD
Judith P Staples, Superintendent
165 Charles St, Painted Post, NY 14870-1199
607-936-3704 Fax: 607-654-2735
e-mail: jstaples@cppmail.com

Hammondsport CSD
Christopher R Brown, Superintendent
PO Box 368, Hammondsport, NY 14840-0368
607-569-5200 Fax: 607-569-5212
e-mail: cbrown@hport.wnyric.org

Hornell City SD
George Kiley, Superintendent
25 Pearl St, Hornell, NY 14843-1504
607-324-1302 Fax: 607-324-4060
e-mail: gkiley@hornell.wnyric.org

Jasper-Troupsburg CSD
Chad C Groff, Superintendent
3769 N Main St, Jasper, NY 14855
607-792-3675 Fax: 607-792-3749
e-mail: chadgroff@jt.wnyric.org

Prattsburgh CSD
Jeffrey A Black, Superintendent
1 Academy St, Prattsburgh, NY 14873-0249
607-522-3795 Fax: 607-522-6221
e-mail: jblack@pratts.wnyric.org

Wayland-Cohocton CSD
Michael J Wetherbee, Superintendent

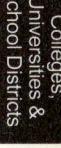

Offices and agencies generally appear in alphabetical order, except when specific order is requested by listee.

PUBLIC SCHOOL DISTRICTS / School District Administrators

2350 Rt 63, Wayland, NY 14572
585-728-2211
e-mail: mwetherbee@wccsk12.org
Web site: www.wccsk12.org

SUFFOLK

Amagansett UFSD
Judith S Wooster, Superintendent
320 Main St, PO Box 7062, Amagansett, NY 11930-7062
631-267-3572 Fax: 631-267-7504
Web site: www.amagansettschool.org

Amityville UFSD
Brian M DeSorbe, Superintendent
150 Park Ave, Amityville, NY 11701-3195
631-598-6507
Web site: www.amityvilleschools.org

Babylon UFSD
Ellen Best-Laimit, Superintendent
50 Railroad Ave, Babylon, NY 11702-2221
631-893-7925
Web site: www.babylon.k12.ny.us

Bay Shore UFSD
Evelyn B Holman, Superintendent
75 W Perkal St, Bayshore, NY 11706-6696
631-968-1100 Fax: 631-968-1129
Web site: www.bayshore.k12.ny.us

Bayport-Blue Point UFSD
Anthony Annunziato, Superintendent
189 Academy St, Bayport, NY 11705
631-472-7860 Fax: 631-472-7817
Web site: www.b-bp.k12.ny.us

Brentwood UFSD
Michael Cohen, Interim Superintendent
52 Third Ave, Brentwood, NY 11717-6198
631-434-2123 Fax: 631-434-6575
Web site: www.bufsd.org

Bridgehampton UFSD
Dianne B Youngblood, Superintendent
2685 Montauk Hwy, PO Box 3021, Bridgehampton, NY 11932-3021
631-537-0271 Fax: 631-537-1030
Web site: www.bridgehampton.k12.ny.us

Brookhaven-Comsewogue UFSD
Shelley Saffer, Superintendent
290 Norwood Ave, Port Jefferson, NY 11776-2999
631-474-8105 Fax: 631-474-8399

Central Islip UFSD
Fadhilika Atiba-Weza, Superintendent
50 Wheeler Road, Central Islip, NY 11722-9027
631-348-5112 Fax: 631-348-0366
Web site: www.cischools.us

Cold Spring Harbor CSD
Whitney K Vantine, Superintendent
75 Goose Hill Rd, Cold Spring Harbor, NY 11724-9813
631-692-8036 x122
Web site: www.csh.k12.ny.us

Commack UFSD
James A Feltman, Superintendent
Administration Ctr, Clay Pitts Rd, East Northport, NY 11731-3828
631-912-2010
e-mail: jfeltman@commack.k12.ny.us
Web site: www.commack.k12.ny.us

Connetquot CSD
Alan B Groveman, Superintendent
780 Ocean Ave, Bohemia, NY 11716
631-244-2215 Fax: 631-589-0683
Web site: www.connetquot.k12.ny.us

Copiague UFSD
William R Bolton, Superintendent
2650 Great Neck Rd, Copiague, NY 11726-1699
631-842-4015 x501
Web site: www.copiague.k12.ny.us

Center Moriches UFSD
Donald A James, Superintendent
529 Main St, Center Moriches, NY 11934-2206
631-878-0052 Fax: 631-878-4326
Web site: www.centermoriches.k12.ny.us

Deer Park UFSD
Elizabeth Marino, Superintendent
1881 Deer Park Ave, Deer Park, NY 11729-4326
631-274-4010
Web site: www.deerparkschools.org

East Hampton UFSD
Raymond D Gualtieri, Superintendent
4 Long Ln, East Hampton, NY 11937
631-329-4100 Fax: 631-329-0109
Web site: www.easthampton.k12.ny.us

East Islip UFSD
Dennis P Maloney, Superintendent
1 C B Gariepy Ave, Islip Terrace, NY 11752
631-581-1600 Fax: 631-581-1617
Web site: www.eischools.org

East Moriches UFSD
Charles Russo, Superintendent

Offices and agencies generally appear in alphabetical order, except when specific order is requested by listee.

PUBLIC SCHOOL DISTRICTS / School District Administrators

9 Adelaide Ave, East Moriches, NY 11940-1320
631-878-0162 Fax: 631-878-0186
e-mail: crusso@emo.ny.k12us.com
Web site: www.eastmoriches.k12.ny.us

East Quogue UFSD
Joseph F Donovan, Superintendent
6 Central Ave, East Quogue, NY 11942
631-653-5210 Fax: 631-653-8644
Web site: www.eastquogue.k12.ny.us

Eastport-South Manor CSD
James J Powers, Superintendent
149 Dayton Ave, Manorville, NY 11949
631-878-3782 Fax: 631-878-6308
e-mail: mannella@esmonline.org
Web site: www.esmonline.org

Elwood UFSD
William J Swart, Superintendent
100 Kenneth Ave, Greenlawn, NY 11740-2900
631-266-5402
e-mail: superintendent@elwood.k12.ny.us
Web site: www.elwood.k12.ny.us

Fire Island UFSD
Wendell Chu, Superintendent
Surf Rd, PO Box 428, Ocean Beach, NY 11770-0428
631-583-5626 Fax: 631-583-5167
e-mail: wchu@fi.k12.ny.us
Web site: www.fi.k12.ny.us

Fishers Island UFSD
Jeanne F Schultz, Superintendent
19 Greenwood Rd, Fishers Island, NY 06390
631-788-7444 Fax: 631-788-5562
Web site: www.fischool.com

Greenport UFSD
Charles Kozora, Superintendent
720 Front St, Greenport, NY 11944
631-477-1950 Fax: 631-477-2164
Web site: www.greenport.k12.ny.us

Half Hollow Hills CSD
Sheldon Karnilow, Superintendent
525 Half Hollow Rd, Dix Hills, NY 11746-5899
631-592-3008
e-mail: superintendent@hhh.k12.ny.us
Web site: www.halfhollowhills.k12.ny.us

Hampton Bays UFSD
Joanne S Loewenthal, Superintendent
86 E Argonne Rd, Hampton Bays, NY 11946
631-723-2100 Fax: 631-723-2109
Web site: www.hbschools.org

Harborfields CSD
Janet Ceparno Wilson, Superintendent
2 Oldfield Rd, Greenlawn, NY 11740
631-754-5320 x321
e-mail: wilsonj@harborfieldscsd.net
Web site: www.harborfieldscsd.net

Hauppauge UFSD
Patricia Sullivan-Kriss, Superintendent
600 Townline Rd, Hauppauge, NY 11788
631-761-8300 Fax: 631-265-3649
Web site: www.hauppauge.k12.ny.us

Huntington UFSD
John J Finello, Superintendent
50 Tower St, Huntington Station, NY 11746
631-673-2038
e-mail: jfinello@hufsd.edu
Web site: www.hufsd.edu

Islip UFSD
Alan Van Cott, Superintendent
215 Main St, Islip, NY 11751-3435
631-859-2200 Fax: 631-859-2224
Web site: www.islip.k12.ny.us

Kings Park CSD
Mary DeRose, Superintendent
101 Church St, Kings Park, NY 11754-1769
631-269-3210
e-mail: derose@mail.kpcsd.k12.ny.us
Web site: www.kpcsd.k12.ny.us

Lindenhurst UFSD
Neil Lederer, Superintendent
350 Daniel St, Lindenhurst, NY 11757-0621
631-226-6489 or 631-226-6490 Fax: 631-226-6865
e-mail: suptsecy@lindenhurstschools.org
Web site: www.lindenhurstschools.org

Little Flower UFSD
George Grigg, Superintendent
2450 N Wading River Rd, Wading River, NY 11792
631-929-4300 Fax: 631-929-0303
Web site: www.littleflowerufsd.org

Longwood CSD
Allan Gerstenlauer, Superintendent
35 Yaphank-Mid Isl Rd, Middle Island, NY 11953-2369
631-345-2172 Fax: 631-345-2166
Web site: www.longwood.k12.ny.us

Mattituck-Cutchogue UFSD
James McKenna, Superintendent
385 Depot Ln, PO Box 1438, Cutchogue, NY 11935
631-298-4242 Fax: 631-298-8520
Web site: www.mufsd.org

Middle Country CSD
Roberta Gerold, Superintendent

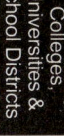
Colleges, Universities & School Districts

Offices and agencies generally appear in alphabetical order, except when specific order is requested by listee.

PUBLIC SCHOOL DISTRICTS / School District Administrators

Eight 43rd St, Centereach, NY 11720-2325
631-285-8005
Web site: www.middlecountry.k12.ny.us

Miller Place UFSD
Grace J Brindley, Superintendent
275 Route 25A, Miller Place, NY 11764-2036
631-474-2700 Fax: 631-331-8832
Web site: www.millerplace.k12.ny.us

Montauk UFSD
J Philip Perna, Superintendent
50 S Dorset Rd, Montauk, NY 11954
631-668-2474 Fax: 631-668-1107
Web site: www.montaukschool.org

Mt Sinai UFSD
Jonathan Van Eyk, Superintendent
150 N Country Rd, Mount Sinai, NY 11766-0397
631-870-2553 Fax: 631-473-0905
e-mail: mts@mtsinai.k12.ny.us
Web site: www.mtsinai.k12.ny.us

New Suffolk Common SD
Robert Feger, Superintendent
7605 New Suffolk Rd, PO Box 111, New Suffolk, NY 11956-0111
631-734-6940 Fax: 631-734-6940
e-mail: teach46@optonline.net

North Babylon UFSD
Joseph A Laria, Acting Superintendent
5 Jardine Pl, North Babylon, NY 11703-4203
631-321-3226
Web site: www.nbsd.org

Northport-East Northport UFSD
Marylou McDermott, Superintendent
158 Laurel Ave, Northport, NY 11768-3455
631-262-6604
e-mail: mmcdermott@northport.k12.ny.us
Web site: www.northport.k12.ny.us

Oysterponds UFSD
Stuart Rachlin, Superintendent
23405 Main Rd, PO Box 98, Orient, NY 11957
631-323-2410 Fax: 631-323-3713
Web site: www.oysterponds.k12.ny.us

Patchogue-Medford UFSD
Michael Mostow, Superintendent
241 S Ocean Ave, Patchogue, NY 11772-3787
631-687-6380
e-mail: mmostow@pmschools.org
Web site: www.pmschools.org

Port Jefferson UFSD
Robert Aloise, Superintendent
550 Scraggy Hill Rd, Port Jefferson, NY 11777-1969
631-476-4404
e-mail: raloise@portjeff.k12.ny.us
Web site: www.portjeff.k12.ny.us

Quogue UFSD
Richard J Benson, Superintendent
10 Edgewood Rd, PO Box 957, Quogue, NY 11959-0957
631-653-4285 Fax: 631-653-4864
e-mail: super@quogueschool.com
Web site: www.quogue.k12.ny.us

Remsenburg-Speonk UFSD
Katherine M Salomone, Superintendent
11 Mill Rd, PO Box 900, Remsenburg, NY 11960-0900
631-325-0203 Fax: 631-325-8439
Web site: www.rsufsd.org

Riverhead CSD
Joseph Singleton, Superintendent
700 Osborne Ave, Riverhead, NY 11901
631-369-6717 Fax: 631-369-6718
Web site: www.riverhead.net

Rocky Point UFSD
Carla D'Ambrosio, Superintendent
170 Rt 25A, Rocky Point, NY 11778-8401
631-744-1600
e-mail: cdambrosio@rockypoint.k12.ny.us
Web site: www.rockypointschools.org

Sachem CSD
Charles Murphy, Acting Superintendent
245 Union Ave, Holbrook, NY 11741
631-471-1300 Fax: 631-471-1341
e-mail: cmurphy@sachem.edu
Web site: www.sachem.edu

Sag Harbor UFSD
Kathryn Holden, Superintendent
200 Jermain Ave, Sag Harbor, NY 11963-3549
631-725-5300 Fax: 631-725-5307
Web site: www.sagharbor.k12.ny.us

Sagaponack Common SD
Lee Ellwood, Superintendent
Main St, PO Box 1500, Sagaponack, NY 11962-1500
631-537-0651 Fax: 631-537-2342

Sayville UFSD
Rosemary F Jones, Superintendent
99 Greeley Ave, Sayville, NY 11782
631-244-6510 Fax: 631-244-6504
Web site: www.sayville.k12.ny.us

Shelter Island UFSD
Sharon Clifford, Superintendent

Offices and agencies generally appear in alphabetical order, except when specific order is requested by listee.

PUBLIC SCHOOL DISTRICTS / School District Administrators

33 North Ferry Rd, PO Box 2015, Shelter Island, NY 11964-2015
631-749-0302 Fax: 631-749-1262
Web site: www.shelterisland.k12.ny.us

Shoreham-Wading River CSD
Harriet Copel, Superintendent
250B Rt 25A, Shoreham, NY 11786
631-821-8105 Fax: 631-929-3001
e-mail: mluhrs@swr.k12.ny.us
Web site: www.swrcsd.org

Smithtown CSD
Judith A Elias, Superintendent
26 New York Ave, Smithtown, NY 11787-3435
631-382-2005 Fax: 631-382-2010
Web site: www.smithtown.k12.ny.us

South Country CSD
Susan A Agruso, Superintendent
189 N Dunton Ave, East Patchogue, NY 11772
631-730-1510 Fax: 631-286-6394
e-mail: sagruso@southcountry.org
Web site: www.southcountry.org

South Huntington UFSD
Thomas C Shea, Superintendent
60 Weston St, Huntington Station, NY 11746-4098
631-425-5300 Fax: 631-425-5362
e-mail: tshea@shufsd.org
Web site: www.shuntington.k12.ny.us

Southampton UFSD
Linda J Bruno, Superintendent
70 Leland Ln, Southampton, NY 11968
631-591-4510 Fax: 631-287-2870
Web site: www.southhampton.k12.ny.us

Southold UFSD
Christopher Gallagher, Superintendent
420 Oaklawn Ave, PO Box 470, Southold, NY 11971-0470
631-765-5400 Fax: 631-765-5086
Web site: www.northfork.net/shs/

Springs UFSD
Thomas R Quinn, Superintendent
48 School St, East Hampton, NY 11937
631-324-0144 Fax: 631-324-0269
Web site: www.springs.k12.ny.us

Three Village CSD
Frank J Carasiti, Superintendent
200 Nicolls Rd, Stony Brook, NY 11790-3410
631-730-4010 Fax: 631-474-7784
e-mail: fcarasit@3villagecsd.k12.ny.us
Web site: www.3villagecsd.k12.ny.us

Tuckahoe Common SD
Linda J Rozzi, Superintendent
468 Magee St, Southampton, NY 11968-3216
631-283-3550 Fax: 631-283-3469
Web site: www.tuckahoe.k12.ny.us

Wainscott Common SD
Dominic Annacone, Superintendent
PO Box 79, Wainscott, NY 11975-0079
631-537-1080 Fax: 631-537-6977

West Babylon UFSD
Melvin S Noble, Superintendent
10 Farmingdale Rd, West Babylon, NY 11704-6289
631-321-3142 Fax: 631-661-5166
Web site: www.westbabylon.k12.ny.us

West Islip UFSD
Beth V Blau, Superintendent
100 Sherman Ave, West Islip, NY 11795-3237
631-893-3200 Fax: 631-893-3217
Web site: www.westislip.k12.ny.us

Westhampton Beach UFSD
Lynn Schwartz, Superintendent
340 Mill Rd, Westhampton Beach, NY 11978
631-288-3800 Fax: 631-288-8351
Web site: www.westhamptonbeach.k12.ny.us

William Floyd UFSD
Paul Casciano, Superintendent
240 Mastic Beach Rd, Mastic Beach, NY 11951
631-874-1201 Fax: 631-281-3047
Web site: www.wfsd.k12.ny.us

Wyandanch UFSD
Sherman Roberts, Superintendent
1445 MLK Jr Blvd, Wyandanch, NY 11798-3997
631-491-1013 Fax: 631-491-3032
Web site: www.wyandanch.k12.ny.us

SULLIVAN

Eldred CSD
Charlotte Gregory, Superintendent
600 Rt 55, Eldred, NY 12732-0249
845-557-6141 Fax: 845-537-3672
e-mail: cgregory@eldredschools.org
Web site: www.eldredschools.org

Fallsburg CSD
Ivan J Katz, Interim Superintendent
115 Brickman Rd, PO Box 124, Fallsburg, NY 12733-0124
845-434-5884 x1215
e-mail: ikatz@fallsburgcsd.net
Web site: www.fallsburg.net

Liberty CSD
Edward Rhine, Interim Superintendent

Offices and agencies generally appear in alphabetical order, except when specific order is requested by listee.

PUBLIC SCHOOL DISTRICTS / School District Administrators

115 Buckley St, Liberty, NY 12754-1600
845-292-6990 Fax: 845-292-1164
e-mail: rhineedw@libertyk12.org
Web site: www.libertyk12.org

Livingston Manor CSD
Debra Lynker, Superintendent
19 School St, Livingston Manor, NY 12758-0947
845-439-4400 Fax: 845-439-4717
e-mail: dlynker@lmcs.k12.ny.us
Web site: lmcs.k12.ny.us

Monticello CSD
Eileen P Casey, Superintendent
237 Forestburgh Rd, Monticello, NY 12701
845-794-7700 Fax: 845-794-7710
e-mail: pmichel@k12mcsd.net
Web site: www.monticelloschools.org

Roscoe CSD
Carmine C Giangreco, Superintendent
6 Academy St, Roscoe, NY 12776-0429
607-498-4126
e-mail: cagiang@roscoe.k12.ny.us
Web site: roscoe.k12.ny.us

Sullivan West CSD
Alan R Derry, Superintendent
33 Schoolhouse Rd, Jeffersonville, NY 12748
845-482-4610 x3000
Web site: www.swcsd.org

Tri-Valley CSD
Nancy S George, Superintendent
34 Moore Hill Rd, Grahamsville, NY 12740-5609
845-985-2296 x5101
Web site: tvcs.k12.ny.us

TIOGA

Candor CSD
Jeffrey J Kisloski, Superintendent
1 Academy St, PO Box 145, Candor, NY 13743-0145
607-659-5010
e-mail: jkisloski@candor.org
Web site: www.candor.org

Newark Valley CSD
Mary Ellen Grant, Superintendent
79 Whig St, Newark Valley, NY 13811-0547
607-642-3221
e-mail: mgrant@nvcs.stier.org
Web site: www.nvcs.stier.org

Owego-Apalachin CSD
Bill Russell, Superintendent

36 Talcott St, Owego, NY 13827-9965
607-687-6224
e-mail: russellw@oacsd.org
Web site: www.oacsd.org

Spencer-Van Etten CSD
Steven Schoonmaker, Superintendent
16 Dartts Crossroad, PO Box 307, Spencer, NY 14883
607-589-7100 Fax: 607-589-3010
e-mail: sschoonmaker@svecsd.org
Web site: www.svecsd.org

Tioga CSD
Patrick Dougherty, Superintendent
27 Fifth Ave, Tioga Center, NY 13845-0241
607-687-8001

Waverly CSD
Michael W McMahon, Superintendent
15 Frederick St, Waverly, NY 14892-1294
607-565-2841 Fax: 607-565-4997
e-mail: mmcmahon@gstboces.org
Web site: www.waverlyschools.com

TOMPKINS

Dryden CSD
Mark Crawford, Superintendent
2127 Drydn Rd, PO Box 88, Dryden, NY 13053
607-844-8694 x601
Web site: www.dryden.k12.ny.us

George Junior Republic UFSD
J Brad Herman, Superintendent
24 McDonald Rd, Freeville, NY 13068-9699
607-844-6200
Web site: www.georgejuniorrepublic.com

Groton CSD
Brenda Myers, Superintendent
400 Peru Rd, Groton, NY 13073-1297
607-898-5301 Fax: 607-898-4647
Web site: www.lightlink.com/grotonhs

Ithaca City SD
Judith C Pastel, Superintendent
400 Lake St, Ithaca, NY 14851-0549
607-274-6845
e-mail: jpastel@icsd.k12.ny.us
Web site: www.icsd.k12.ny.us

Lansing CSD
Mark S Lewis, Superintendent
264 Ridge Rd, Lansing, NY 14882-9021
607-533-3020 Fax: 607-533-3602
e-mail: mlewis@mail.lansingschools.org
Web site: wwwlansingschools.org

Newfield CSD
William Hurley, Superintendent

Offices and agencies generally appear in alphabetical order, except when specific order is requested by listee.

PUBLIC SCHOOL DISTRICTS / School District Administrators

247 Main St, Newfield, NY 14867-9313
607-564-9955
e-mail: whurley@newfieldschools.org
Web site: www.newschools.org

Trumansburg CSD
Cosimo Tangorra Jr, Superintendent
100 Whig St, Trumansburg, NY 14886-9179
607-387-7551 x421
e-mail: ctangorra@tburg.k12.ny.us
Web site: www.tburg.k12.ny.us

ULSTER

Ellenville CSD
Lisa A Wiles, Superintendent
28 Maple Ave, Ellenville, NY 12428
845-647-0100 Fax: 845-647-0105
Web site: www.ecs.k12.ny.us

Highland CSD
John McCarthy, Superintendent
320 Pancake Hollow Rd, Highland, NY 12528-2317
845-691-1012 Fax: 845-691-3904
e-mail: jmccarthy@highland-k12.org
Web site: www.highland-k12.org

Kingston City SD
Gerard M Gretzinger, Superintendent
61 Crown St, Kingston, NY 12401-3833
845-339-3000
Web site: www.kingstoncityschools.org

Marlboro CSD
Lou Ciota, Superintendent
50 Cross Rd, Marlboro, NY 12542-6009
845-236-5802
Web site: marlboroschools.schoolwires.com

New Paltz CSD
Maria Rice, Superintendent
196 Main St, New Paltz, NY 12561-1200
845-256-4020 Fax: 845-256-4025
Web site: www.newport.k12.ny.us/local/

Onteora CSD
Leslie Goldring Ford, Superintendent
PO Box 300, Boiceville, NY 12412-0300
845-657-6383 Fax: 845-657-9687
e-mail: lford@onteora.k12.ny.us
Web site: onteora.schoolwires.com

Rondout Valley CSD
Eileen L Camasso, Acting Superintendent
122 Kyserike Rd, PO Box 9, Accord, NY 12404-0009
845-687-2400 Fax: 845-687-9577
e-mail: ecamasso@rondout.k12.ny.us
Web site: www.rondout.k12.ny.us

Saugerties CSD
Richard R Rhau, Superintendent

Call Box A, Saugerties, NY 12477
845-247-6500 Fax: 845-246-8364
e-mail: rrhau@saugerties.k12.ny.us

Wallkill CSD
Anthony Argulewicz, Superintendent
19 Main St, Wallkill, NY 12589
845-895-7101
Web site: www.wallkillcsd.k12.ny.us

West Park UFSD
Joanne Petrelli, Assistant Superintendent
2112 Rt 9W, West Park, NY 12493-0010
845-384-6710

WARREN

Bolton CSD
Raymond Ciccarelli Jr, Superintendent
26 Horicon Ave, Bolton Landing, NY 12814-0120
518-644-2400
e-mail: info@boltoncsd.org
Web site: www.boltoncsd.org

Glens Falls City SD
Thomas F McGowan, Superintendent
15 Quade St, Glens Falls, NY 12801-2725
518-792-1212
e-mail: tmcgowan@gfsd.org
Web site: www.gfsd.org

Glens Falls Common SD
Ella W Collins, Superintendent
120 Lawrence St, Glens Falls, NY 12801-3758
518-792-3231 Fax: 518-792-2557
Web site: abewing.nycap.rr.com

Hadley-Luzerne CSD
Irwin H Sussman, Superintendent
273 Lake Ave, Lake Luzerne, NY 12846
518-696-2112 x134
Web site: www.hlcsd.org

Johnsburg CSD
Michael Markwica, Superintendent
165 Main St, North Creek, NY 12853-0380
518-251-2921
Web site: www.johnsburgcsd.org

Lake George CSD
Bruce Levin, Superintendent
381 Canada St, Lake George, NY 12845-1197
518-668-5456 Fax: 518-668-2285
e-mail: blevin@lkgeorge.org
Web site: www.lkgeorge.org

North Warren CSD
Joseph R Murphy, Superintendent

Offices and agencies generally appear in alphabetical order, except when specific order is requested by listee.

PUBLIC SCHOOL DISTRICTS / School District Administrators

6110 State Rt 8, Chestertown, NY 12817
518-494-3015
Web site: www.northwarren.k12.ny.us

Queensbury UFSD
Brian Howard, Superintendent
429 Aviation Rd, Queensbury, NY 12804-2914
518-824-5602 Fax: 518-793-4476
e-mail: bhoward@queensburyschool.org
Web site: www.queensburyschool.org

Warrensburg CSD
Timothy D Lawson, Superintendent
103 Schroon River Rd, Warrensburg, NY 12885-4803
518-623-2861
e-mail: lawsont@wcsd.org
Web site: www.wcsd.org

WASHINGTON

Argyle CSD
Ryan Sherman, Superintendent
5023 State Rt 40, Argyle, NY 12809-0067
518-638-8243 Fax: 518-638-6373
Web site: www.argylecsd.org

Cambridge CSD
Meoldy Troy, Superintendent
23 W Main St, Cambridge, NY 12816-1118
518-677-2653 x1014
Web site: www.cambridgecsd.org

Fort Ann CSD
Maureen VanBuren, Superintendent
One Catherine St, Fort Ann, NY 12827-5039
518-639-5594 Fax: 518-639-8911
e-mail: mvanburen@fortannschool.org
Web site: www.fortannschool.org

Fort Edward UFSD
Stanley W Maziejka, Superintendent
220 Broadway, Fort Edward, NY 12828-1598
518-747-4594 x100
e-mail: smaziejka@fortedward.org
Web site: www.fortedward.org

Granville CSD
Daniel A Teplesky, Superintendent
58 Quaker St, Granville, NY 12832-1596
518-642-1051 Fax: 518-642-2491
e-mail: dteplesky@granvillecsd.org
Web site: www.granvillecsd.org

Greenwich CSD
John McGuire, Superintendent
10 Gray Ave, Greenwich, NY 12834-1107
518-692-9542
e-mail: jmcguire@greenwichcsd.org
Web site: www.greenwichcsd.org

Hartford CSD
Thomas W Abraham, Administrator
4704 State Rt 149, Hartford, NY 12838-0079
518-632-5931
Web site: www.hartfordcsd.org

Hudson Falls CSD
Mark E Doody, Superintendent
1153 Burgoyne Ave, Hudson Falls, NY 12839-0710
518-747-2121
e-mail: mdoody@hfcsd.org
Web site: www.hfcsd.org

Putnam CSD
Matthew Boucher, Superintendent
, Putnam Station, NY 12861
518-547-8266 Fax: 518-547-8266
e-mail: mboucher@mum.neric.org
Web site: putnamcs.neric.org

Salem CSD
Richard Wheeler, Superintendent
41 E Broadway, Salem, NY 12865-0517
518-854-7855
Web site: www.salemcsdnyk-12.org

Whitehall CSD
James Watson, Superintendent
87 Buckley Rd, Whitehall, NY 12887-3633
518-499-1772
e-mail: jwatson@railroaders.net
Web site: www.railroaders.net

WAYNE

Clyde-Savannah CSD
Marilyn Barr, Superintendent
215 Glasgow St, Clyde, NY 14433-1222
315-902-3000
e-mail: mabarr@clydesavannah.org
Web site: www.clydesavannah.org

Gananda CSD
Patricia M Roach, Superintendent
PO Box 609, Macedon, NY 14502
315-986-3521
Web site: www.gananda.org

Lyons CSD
Richard Amundson, Superintendent

Offices and agencies generally appear in alphabetical order, except when specific order is requested by listee.

PUBLIC SCHOOL DISTRICTS / School District Administrators

10 Clyde Rd, Lyons, NY 14489-9371
315-946-2200
e-mail: ramundson@lyonscsd.org
Web site: www.lyonscsd.org

Marion CSD
J Richard Boyes, Superintendent
4034 Warner Rd, Marion, NY 14505-0999
315-926-2300
e-mail: rboyes@marioncs.org
Web site: www.marioncs.org

Newark CSD
Henry Hann, Acting Superintendent
100 E Miller St, Newark, NY 14513-1599
315-332-3217
e-mail: hhann@newark.k12.ny.us
Web site: www.newark.k12.ny.us

North Rose-Wolcott CSD
Lucinda Miner, Interim Superintendent
11669 Salter-Colvin Rd, Wolcott, NY 14590-9398
315-594-3141 Fax: 315-594-2352
e-mail: cminer@nrwcs.org
Web site: www.nrwcs.org

Palmyra-Macedon CSD
Harold Ferguson, Interim Superintendent
151 Hyde Pkwy, Palmyra, NY 14522-1297
315-597-3401
e-mail: hal.ferguson@plmaccsd.org
Web site: www.palmac.k12.ny.us

Red Creek CSD
David G Sholes, Superintendent
6815 Church St, PO Box 190, Red Creek, NY 13143-0190
315-754-2010 Fax: 315-754-8169
e-mail: dsholes@rccsd.org
Web site: www.redcreekcsd.k12.ny.us

Sodus CSD
Susan Kay Salvaggio, Superintendent
PO Box 220, Sodus, NY 14551-0220
315-483-5201 Fax: 315-483-4755
e-mail: ssalvaggio@soduscsd.org
Web site: www.sodus.k12.ny.us

Wayne CSD
Michael Havens, Superintendent
6076 Ontario Ctr Rd, Ontario Center, NY 14520-0155
315-524-1001
e-mail: mhavens@wayne.k12.ny.us
Web site: www.wayne.k12.ny.us

Williamson CSD
Maria Ehresman, Superintendent
PO Box 900, Williamson, NY 14589-0900
315-589-9661
e-mail: mehresman@williamsoncentral.org
Web site: www.williamsoncentral.org

WESTCHESTER

Abbott UFSD
Harold A Coles, Superintendent
100 N Broadway, Irvington, NY 10533-1254
914-591-7428
Web site: www.abbottufsd.org

Ardsley UFSD
Richard Maurer, Superintendent
500 Farm Rd, Ardsley, NY 10502-1410
914-693-6300
e-mail: maurerr@ardsleyschools.org
Web site: www.ardsleyschools.k12.ny.us

Bedford CSD
Debra Jackson, Superintendent
Route 172, Fox Lane Campus, Bedford, NY 10506
914-241-6000
Web site: www.bedford.k12.ny.us

Blind Brook-Rye UFSD
Ronald D Valenti, Superintendent
390 North Ridge St, Rye Brook, NY 10573-1105
914-937-3600 x3022
e-mail: rvalenti@blindbrook.org
Web site: www.blindbrook.org

Briarcliff Manor UFSD
Frances G Wills, Superintendent
45 Ingham Rd, Briarcliff Manor, NY 10510-2221
914-941-8880 x303
e-mail: fwills@briarcliffschools.org
Web site: www.briarcliffschools.org

Bronxville UFSD
David Quattrone, Superintendent
177 Pondfield Rd, Bronxville, NY 10708-4829
914-395-0500
e-mail: quattrod@bronxville.k12.ny.us
Web site: www.bronxville.lhric.org

Byram Hills CSD
John A Chambers, Superintendent
10 Tripp Ln, Armonk, NY 10504-2512
914-273-4198
e-mail: jchambers@byramhills.org
Web site: www.byramhills.org

Chappaqua CSD
David A Fleishman, Superintendent

Offices and agencies generally appear in alphabetical order, except when specific order is requested by listee.

PUBLIC SCHOOL DISTRICTS / School District Administrators

66 Roaring Brook Rd, Chappaqua, NY 10514-1703
914-238-7200 Fax: 914-238-7231
Web site: www.chappauqua.k12.ny.us/ccsd/

Croton-Harmon UFSD
Marjorie E Castro, Superintendent
10 Gerstein St, Croton-on-Hudson, NY 10520-2303
914-271-4793 Fax: 914-271-8685
e-mail: info@croton-harmonschools.org
Web site: www.croton-harmonschools.org

Dobbs Ferry UFSD
Debra Kaplan, Superintendent
505 Broadway, Dobbs Ferry, NY 10522-1118
914-693-1506 Fax: 914-693-1115
e-mail: kapland@dfsd.org
Web site: www.dfsd.org/home.aspx

Eastchester UFSD
Marilyn Terranova, Superintendent
580 White Plains Rd, Eastchester, NY 10709
914-793-6130
Web site: www2.lhric.org/eastchester

Edgemont UFSD
Nancy L Taddiken, Superintendent
300 White Oak Ln, Scarsdale, NY 10583-1725
914-472-7768 Fax: 914-472-6846
Web site: www.edgemont.org

Elmsford UFSD
Carol Franks-Randall, Superintendent
98 South Goodwin Ave, Elmsford, NY 10523-3711
914-592-8440
e-mail: cfrandal@elmsd.org
Web site: www.elmsd.org

Greenburgh 7 CSD
Josephine N Moffett, Superintendent
475 W Hartsdale Ave, Hartsdale, NY 10530-1398
914-761-6000 x3103
Web site: www.greenburgh.k12.ny.us

Greenburgh Eleven UFSD
Sandra G Mallah, Superintendent
Children's Vlg Campus-W, PO Box 501, Dobbs Ferry, NY 10522-0501
914-693-8500

Greenburgh-Graham UFSD
Frank DeLuca, Superintendent
One S Broadway, Hastings-on-Hudson, NY 10706-3809
914-478-4176

Greenburgh-North Castle UFSD
Robert Maher, Superintendent
71 S Broadway, Dobbs Ferry, NY 10522-2834
914-693-3030 x2244

Harrison CSD
Louis N Wool, Superintendent
50 Union Ave, Harrison, NY 10528-2032
914-630-3021
Web site: www.harrisoncsd.org

Hastings-On-Hudson UFSD
Robert I Shaps, Superintendent
27 Farragut Ave, Hastings-on-Hudson, NY 10706-2395
914-478-6200
Web site: www.hastings.k12.ny.us

Hawthorne-Cedar Knolls UFSD
Mark K Silverstein, Superintendent
226 Linda Ave, Hawthorne, NY 10532-2099
914-749-2900 Fax: 914-749-2904
Web site: district.hcks.org

Hendrick Hudson CSD
Daniel McCann, Superintendent
61 Trolley Rd, Montrose, NY 10548-1199
914-736-5200 Fax: 914-736-5242
e-mail: dmccann@henhudschools.org
Web site: www.henhudschools.org

Irvington UFSD
Kathleen Matusiak, Superintendent
40 N Broadway, Irvington, NY 10533-1328
914-591-8501
e-mail: kmatusiak@irvingtonschools.k12.ny.us
Web site: www.irvingtonschools.org

Katonah-Lewisboro UFSD
Robert V Lichtenfeld, Superintendent
PO Box 387, Katonah, NY 10536
914-763-7000 Fax: 914-763-7033
e-mail: blichtenfeld@klschools.org
Web site: www.klschools.org

Lakeland CSD
Kenneth Connolly, Superintendent
1086 Main St, Shrub Oak, NY 10588-1507
914-245-1700
Web site: www.lakelandschools.org

Mamaroneck UFSD
Paul Fried, Superintendent
1000 W Boston Post Rd, Mamaroneck, NY 10543-3399
914-220-3005
Web site: www.mamkschools.org

Mt Pleasant CSD
Alfred Lodovico, Superintendent
825 Westlake Drive, Thornwood, NY 10594
914-769-5500 Fax: 914-769-3733
e-mail: alodovico@mtplcsd.org
Web site: www.mtplcsd.org

Mt Pleasant-Blythedale UFSD
Ellen Bergman, Superintendent

Offices and agencies generally appear in alphabetical order, except when specific order is requested by listee.

PUBLIC SCHOOL DISTRICTS / School District Administrators

95 Bradhurst Ave, Valhalla, NY 10595-1697
914-347-1800 Fax: 914-592-5484
e-mail: ebergman@mpbschools.org
Web site: www.mpbschools.org

Mt Pleasant-Cottage UFSD
Norman Freimark, Superintendent
1075 Broadway, Pleasantville, NY 10570-0008
914-769-0456 Fax: 914-769-7331
e-mail: nfreimark@mail.mpcsny.org
Web site: www.mpcsny.org

Mt Vernon City SD
Brenda L Smith, Superintendent
165 N Columbus Ave, Mount Vernon, NY 10553-1199
914-665-5201
Web site: mtvernoncsd.org

New Rochelle City SD
Richard Organisciak, Superintendent
515 North Ave, New Rochelle, NY 10801-3416
914-576-4300 Fax: 914-632-4144
e-mail: rorganisciak@nred.org
Web site: www.nred.org

North Salem CSD
Sidney Freund, Interim Superintendent
230 June Rd, North Salem, NY 10560-1211
914-669-5414
Web site: www.northsalemschools.org

Ossining UFSD
Robert J Roelle, Superintendent
190 Croton Ave, Ossining, NY 10562
914-941-7700 Fax: 914-941-2794
e-mail: nreis@ossining.k12.ny.us
Web site: www.OssiningUFSD.org

Peekskill City SD
Judith Johnson, Superintendent
1031 Elm St, Peekskill, NY 10566-3499
914-737-3300 Fax: 914-737-3912
e-mail: jjohnson@peekskillcsd.org
Web site: www.peekskillcsd.org

Pelham UFSD
Charles T Wilson, Superintendent
18 Franklin Pl, Pelham, NY 10803
914-738-3434
e-mail: cwilson@pelhamschools.org
Web site: www.pelhamschools.org

Pleasantville UFSD
Donald Antonecchia, Superintendent
60 Romer Ave, Pleasantville, NY 10570-3157
914-741-1420 Fax: 914-741-1499
Web site: www2.lhric.org/Pleasantville/

Pocantico Hills CSD
Thomas C Elliott, Superintendent

599 Bedford Rd, Sleepy Hollow, NY 10591-1215
914-631-2440 Fax: 914-631-1619
e-mail: telliott@pocanticohills.org
Web site: www2.lhric.org/pocantico

Port Chester SD
Donald Carlisle, Superintendent
113 Bowman Ave, Port Chester, NY 10573-2851
914-934-7901 Fax: 914-934-0727
e-mail: dcarlisle@portchesterschools.org
Web site: www.portchesterschools.org

Rye City SD
Edward J Shine, Superintendent
324 Midland Ave, Rye, NY 10580-3899
914-967-6100 x6271
Web site: www.ryecityschools.lhric.org

Rye Neck UFSD
Peter J Mustich, Superintendent
310 Hornidge Rd, Mamaroneck, NY 10543-3898
914-777-5200
e-mail: pmustich@ryneck.k12.ny.us
Web site: www.ryeneck.k12.ny.us

Scarsdale UFSD
Michael V McGill, Superintendent
2 Brewster Rd, Scarsdale, NY 10583-3049
914-721-2400
e-mail: mmcgill@scarsdaleschools.k12.ny.us
Web site: www.scarsdaleschools.k12.ny.us

Somers CSD
Joanne Marien, Superintendent
334 Route 202, PO Box 620, Somers, NY 10589
914-277-2400
Web site: www.somers.k12.ny.us

Tarrytown UFSD
Howard W Smith, Superintendent
200 N Broadway, Sleepy Hollow, NY 10591-2696
914-332-6241 Fax: 914-332-4690
e-mail: hsmith@tufsd.org
Web site: www.tufsd.org

Tuckahoe UFSD
Michael Yazurlo, Superintendent
29 Elm St, Tuckahoe, NY 10707
914-337-6600 x251
Web site: www.tuckahoeschools.org

Valhalla UFSD
Diane Ramos-Kelly, Superintendent
316 Columbus Ave, Valhalla, NY 10595-1300
914-683-5040 Fax: 914-683-5075
e-mail: dramos-kelly@valhalla.k12.ny.us
Web site: valhalla.k12.ny.us

White Plains City SD
Timothy P Connors, Superintendent

Offices and agencies generally appear in alphabetical order, except when specific order is requested by listee.

PUBLIC SCHOOL DISTRICTS / BOCES District Superintendents

5 Homeside Ln, White Plains, NY 10605-4299
914-422-2019 Fax: 914-422-2024
e-mail: timconnors@wpcsd.k12.ny.us
Web site: www.wpcsd.k12.ny.us

Yonkers City SD
Bernard P Pierorazio, Superintendent
1 Larkin Center, Yonkers, NY 10701
914-376-8100
Web site: www.yonkerspublicschools.org

Yorktown CSD
Ralph Napolitano, Superintendent
2725 Crompond Rd, Yorktown Heights, NY 10598
914-243-8001
e-mail: rnapolitano@yorktown.org
Web site: www.yorktowncsd.org

WYOMING

Attica CSD
Bryce L Thompson, Superintendent
3338 E Main St, Attica, NY 14011
585-591-0400 x1000
Web site: www.atticacs.k12.ny.us

Letchworth CSD
Joseph W Backer, Superintendent
5550 School Rd, Gainesville, NY 14066
585-493-5450
Web site: www.letchworth.k12.ny.us

Perry CSD
Daniel White, Superintendent
33 Watkins Ave, Perry, NY 14530
585-237-0270 x1003 Fax: 585-237-6172
e-mail: dwhite@perry.k12.ny.us
Web site: www.perry.k12.ny.us

Warsaw CSD
Kevin McGowan, Superintendent
153 W Buffalo St, Warsaw, NY 14569
585-786-8000 Fax: 585-786-8008
Web site: www.warsaw.k12.ny.us

Wyoming CSD
Sandra B Duckworth, Superintendent
Route 19, PO Box 244, Wyoming, NY 14591-0244
585-495-6222 Fax: 585-495-6341
Web site: www.wyoming.k12.ny.us

YATES

Dundee CSD
Nancy R Zimar, Superintendent
55 Water St, Dundee, NY 14837-1099
607-243-5533 Fax: 607-243-7912
Web site: www.dundeecs.org

Penn Yan CSD
Ann E Orman, Superintendent
One School Dr, Penn Yan, NY 14527-1099
315-536-3371
e-mail: aorman@pennyan.k12.ny.us
Web site: www.pycsd.org

BOCES District Superintendents

Broome-Delaware-Tioga BOCES
Joseph R Busch
435 Glenwood Rd, Binghamton, NY 13905-1699
607-763-3309 Fax: 607-763-3691
e-mail: jbusch@btboces.org
Web site: www.btboces.org

Capital Region (Albany-Schoharie-Schenectady) BOCES
James Baldwin, Interim Superintendent
1031 Watervliet-Shaker Rd, Albany, NY 12205-2106
518-862-4900 Fax: 518-862-4903
Web site: www.capregboces.org

Cattaraugus-Allegany-Erie-Wyoming BOCES
Robert D Olczak
Olean Center, 1825 Windfall Rd, Olean, NY 14760-9303
716-376-8246 or 716-376-8200 Fax: 716-376-8452
e-mail: robert_olczak@caboces.org
Web site: www.caboces.org

Cayuga-Onondaga BOCES
Gary A Gilchrist
5980 South St Rd, Auburn, NY 13021-5699
315-253-0361 Fax: 315-252-6493
e-mail: ggilchrist@cayboces.org
Web site: www.cayboces.org

Champlain Valley Educational Svcs (Clinton-Essex-Warren-Washington)
Craig L King
1585 Military Tpk, PO Box 455, Plattsburgh, NY 12901-0455
518-561-0100 x210 Fax: 518-562-1471
Web site: www.cves.org

Delaware-Chenango-Madison-Otsego BOCES
Alan D Pole

Offices and agencies generally appear in alphabetical order, except when specific order is requested by listee.

PUBLIC SCHOOL DISTRICTS / BOCES District Superintendents

6678 County Rd #32, Norwich, NY 13815-3554
607-335-1233 Fax: 607-334-9848
e-mail: polea@dcmoboces.com
Web site: www.dcmoboces.com

Dutchess BOCES
John C Pennoyer
5 Boces Rd, Poughkeepsie, NY 12601-6599
845-486-4800 Fax: 845-486-4981
e-mail: john.pennoyer@dcboces.org
Web site: www.dcboces.org

Eastern Suffolk BOCES
Edward J Zero
James Hines Administration Ctr, 201 Sunrise Hwy, Patchogue, NY 11772-1868
631-687-3006 Fax: 631-289-2381
e-mail: ezero@esboces.org
Web site: www.esboces.org

Erie 1 BOCES
Donald A Ogilvie
355 Harlem Rd, West Seneca, NY 14224-1892
716-821-7000 Fax: 716-821-7242
Web site: www.erie1boces.org

Erie 2-Chautauqua-Cattaraugus BOCES
Robert S Guiffreda
8685 Erie Rd, Angola, NY 14006-9620
716-549-4454 or 800-228-1184 Fax: 716-549-5181
Web site: e2ccboces.wnyric.org

Franklin-Essex-Hamilton BOCES
David J DeSantis
3372 State Rte 11, PO Box 28, Malone, NY 12953-9608
518-483-6420 Fax: 518-483-2178
e-mail: cdurant@mail.fehb.org
Web site: www.fehb.org

Genesee-Livingston-Steuben-Wyoming BOCES
Michael A Glover
80 Munson St, LeRoy, NY 14482-8933
585-658-7903 Fax: 585-344-7903
Web site: www.gvboces.org

Greater Southern Tier BOCES
(Schuyler-Chemung-Tioga-Allegany-Steuben)
Anthony J Micha
9579 Vocational Dr, Painted Post, NY 14870
607-654-2283 or 607-962-3175 Fax: 607-962-1579
Web site: www.gstboces.org

Hamilton-Fulton-Montgomery BOCES
Geoffrey H Davis
25 West Main St, PO Box 665, Johnstown, NY 12095-0665
518-736-4300 Fax: 518-762-4724
e-mail: gdavis@admin.hfmboces.org
Web site: www.hfmboces.org

Herkimer-Fulton-Hamilton-Otsego BOCES
Sandra A Simpson

352 Gros Blvd, Herkimer, NY 13350-1499
315-867-2023 Fax: 315-867-2024
e-mail: ssimpson@herkimer-boces.org
Web site: www.herkimer-boces.org

Jefferson-Lewis-Hamilton-Herkimer-Oneida BOCES
Jack J Boak Jr
20104 State Rte 3, Watertown, NY 13601-5560
315-779-7000 or 800-356-4356 Fax: 315-779-7009
e-mail: jboak@mail.boces.com
Web site: www.boces.com

Madison-Oneida BOCES
Jacklin G Starks
4937 Spring Rd, PO Box 168, Verona, NY 13478-0168
315-361-5510 Fax: 315-361-5595
e-mail: districtsuperintendent@moboces.org
Web site: www.moboces.org

Monroe 1 BOCES
Frederick A Wille
41 O'Connor Rd, Fairport, NY 14450-1390
585-383-2200 Fax: 585-383-6404
e-mail: Fred-Wille@boces.monroe.edu
Web site: www.monroe.edu

Monroe 2-Orleans BOCES
Michael C O'Laughlin
3599 Big Ridge Rd, Spencerport, NY 14559-1799
585-352-2411 Fax: 585-352-2442
Web site: www.monroe2boces.org

Nassau BOCES
James D Mapes
71 Clinton Rd, PO Box 9195, Garden City, NY 11530-4757
516-396-2500 or 516-396-2200 Fax: 516-997-8742
e-mail: jmapes@mail.nasboces.org
Web site: www.nassauboces.org

Oneida-Herkimer-Madison BOCES
Howard D Mettelman
PO Box 70, 4747 Middle Settlement Rd, New Hartford, NY 13413-0070
315-793-8561 Fax: 315-793-8541
e-mail: hmettelman@oneida-boces.org
Web site: www.oneida-boces.org

Onondaga-Cortland-Madison BOCES
Jessica F Cohen
6820 Thompson Rd, PO Box 4754, Syracuse, NY 13221-4754
315-433-2602 Fax: 315-437-4816
e-mail: jcohen@ocmboces.org
Web site: ocmboces.org

Orange-Ulster BOCES
Robert J Hanna

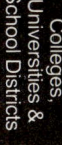
Colleges, Universities & School Districts

Offices and agencies generally appear in alphabetical order, except when specific order is requested by listee.

PUBLIC SCHOOL DISTRICTS / BOCES District Superintendents

53 Gibson Rd, Goshen, NY 10924-9777
845-291-0100 Fax: 845-291-0129
Web site: www.ouboces.org

Orleans-Niagara BOCES
Clark J Godshall
4232 Shelby Basin Rd, Medina, NY 14103-9515
800-836-7510 x 2201 Fax: 585-798-1317
Web site: www.onboces.org

Oswego BOCES
Joseph P Camerino
179 County Rte 64, Mexico, NY 13114-4498
315-963-4222 Fax: 315-963-7131
Web site: www.oswegoboces.org

**Otsego Northern Catskills BOCES
(Otsego-Delaware-Schoharie-Greene)**
Marie Wiles
159 W Main St, Frank W Cyr Center, Stamford, NY 12167-1027
607-652-7531 Fax: 607-652-1215
e-mail: info@oncboces.org
Web site: www.oncboces.org

Putnam-Northern Westchester BOCES
James T Langlois
200 Boces Dr, Yorktown Heights, NY 10598-4399
914-245-2700 or 914-248-2302 Fax: 914-248-2308
e-mail: jlanglois@pnwboces.org
Web site: www.pnwboces.org

Rensselaer-Columbia-Greene (Questar III) BOCES
James N Baldwin
10 Empire State Blvd, 2nd Fl, Castleton, NY 12033-2692
518-477-8771 Fax: 518-477-9833
e-mail: jbaldwin@questar.org
Web site: www.questar.org

Rockland BOCES
James M Ryan
65 Parrott Rd, West Nyack, NY 10994-0607
845-627-4700 Fax: 845-624-1764
e-mail: jryan@rocklandboces.org
Web site: www.rocklandboces.org

Southern Westchester BOCES
Ronald L Smalls
17 Berkeley Dr, Rye Brook, NY 10573-1422
914-937-3820 x535 Fax: 914-937-7850
e-mail: rsmalls@swboces.org
Web site: www.swboces.org

St Lawrence-Lewis BOCES
Linda R Gush
139 State Street Rd, PO Box 231, Canton, NY 13617
315-386-4504 Fax: 315-386-3395
e-mail: info@sllboces.org
Web site: www.sllboces.org

Sullivan BOCES
Martin D Handler
6 Wierk Ave, Liberty, NY 12754-2151
845-292-0082 Fax: 845-292-8694
e-mail: mhandler@scboces.org
Web site: www.scboces.org

Tompkins-Seneca-Tioga BOCES
Ellen O'Donnell
555 Warren Rd, Ithaca, NY 14850-1833
607-257-1551 x201 Fax: 607-257-2825
e-mail: eodonnell@mail.tstboces.org
Web site: www.tstboces.org

Ulster BOCES
Martin Ruglis
175 Rte 32 North, New Paltz, NY 12561-1034
845-255-1400 or 845-255-3040 Fax: 845-255-7942
e-mail: mruglis@mhric.org
Web site: www.ulsterboces.org

Washington-Saratoga-Warren-Hamilton-Essex BOCES
John L Stoothoff
1153 Burgoyne Ave, Ste 2, Fort Edward, NY 12828-1134
518-746-3310 or 518-581-3310 Fax: 518-746-3319
e-mail: jstoothoff@wswheboces.org
Web site: www.wswheboces.org

Wayne-Finger Lakes BOCES
Joseph J Marinelli
131 Drumlin Ct, Newark, NY 14513-1863
315-332-7284 Fax: 315-332-7425
Web site: www.wflboces.org

Western Suffolk BOCES
James D Mapes, Interim Superintendent
507 Deer Park Rd, PO Box 8007, Huntington Station, NY 11746-5207
631-549-4900 x201 Fax: 631-623-4996
e-mail: centraladmin@wsboces.org
Web site: www.wsboces.org

Offices and agencies generally appear in alphabetical order, except when specific order is requested by listee.

FINANCIAL PLAN OVERVIEW

CASH DISBURSEMENTS BY FUNCTION
ALL GOVERNMENTAL FUNDS
(thousands of dollars)

	2005-2006 Actuals	2006-2007 Actuals	2007-2008 Projected	2008-2009 Projected	2009-2010 Projected	2010-2011 Projected
ECONOMIC DEVELOPMENT AND GOVERNMENT OVERSIGHT						
Agriculture and Markets, Department of	85,677	94,967	122,415	132,022	106,183	106,587
Alcoholic Beverage Control	10,286	11,696	12,948	13,287	13,849	13,911
Banking Department	56,278	57,224	60,010	60,798	61,580	62,377
Consumer Protection Board	2,622	2,792	3,055	3,090	3,125	3,159
Economic Development, Department of	225,352	88,458	154,743	412,627	314,556	164,449
Empire State Development Corporation	45,829	169,786	778,720	538,900	335,840	252,981
Energy Research and Development Authority	26,151	28,865	28,623	27,950	27,950	27,950
Housing and Community Renewal, Division of	259,549	272,073	309,562	291,111	276,706	275,759
Insurance Department	124,142	145,590	262,421	262,594	263,718	264,860
Olympic Regional Development Authority	8,550	8,250	14,126	9,009	9,217	9,217
Public Service, Department of	50,453	50,931	56,884	58,427	59,765	61,705
Science, Technology and Academic Research, Office of	61,470	52,054	57,488	48,335	44,403	43,725
University Broadband	2,930	4,840	7,500	8,200	14,000	14,000
Functional Total	959,289	987,526	1,868,495	1,866,350	1,530,892	1,300,680
PARKS AND THE ENVIRONMENT						
Adirondack Park Agency	4,398	4,599	5,731	5,929	5,935	5,942
Environmental Conservation, Department of	816,091	818,004	896,910	875,694	894,001	902,647
Environmental Facilities Corporation	8,034	8,416	11,760	11,815	6,760	6,760
Parks, Recreation and Historic Preservation, Office of	248,425	284,161	272,031	269,640	250,908	242,053
Functional Total	1,076,948	1,115,180	1,186,432	1,163,078	1,157,604	1,157,402
TRANSPORTATION						
Motor Vehicles, Department of	238,186	257,839	288,051	298,568	302,683	337,234
Thruway Authority	1,671	1,775	1,734	1,778	1,822	1,868
Metropolitan Transportation Authority	38,078	0	93,700	188,550	258,700	278,922
Transportation, Department of	5,323,373	5,553,463	6,452,696	6,594,492	6,773,178	6,822,620
Functional Total	5,601,308	5,813,077	6,836,181	7,083,388	7,336,383	7,440,644
HEALTH AND SOCIAL WELFARE						
Advocate for Persons with Disabilities, Office of	18	0	0	0	0	0
Aging, Office for the	185,728	197,862	228,894	237,659	237,604	236,593
Blind, Office for the	0	0	0	0	0	0
Children and Family Services, Office of	3,196,604	2,711,049	2,997,831	3,180,910	3,311,746	3,445,400
Health, Department of	35,203,517	37,706,416	38,480,237	42,217,902	45,771,058	48,739,728
Medical Assistance	30,209,572	32,316,313	32,271,732	35,718,692	39,199,792	42,199,292
Medicaid Administration	575,158	745,398	840,600	859,800	880,200	901,900
All Other	4,418,787	4,644,705	5,367,905	5,639,410	5,691,066	5,638,536
Human Rights, Division of	14,942	16,226	15,166	15,677	15,677	15,677
Labor, Department of	573,213	513,840	583,624	576,803	577,041	574,350
Medicaid Inspector General, Office of	1,049	34,842	81,256	91,816	93,149	94,268
Prevention of Domestic Violence, Office of	1,985	2,315	2,556	2,584	2,584	2,577
Stem Cell Initiatives	0	0	25,000	125,000	50,000	0

681

FINANCIAL PLAN OVERVIEW

CASH DISBURSEMENTS BY FUNCTION
ALL GOVERNMENTAL FUNDS
(thousands of dollars)

	2005-2006 Actuals	2006-2007 Actuals	2007-2008 Projected	2008-2009 Projected	2009-2010 Projected	2010-2011 Projected
HEALTH AND SOCIAL WELFARE (Continued)						
Temporary and Disability Assistance, Office of	4,391,625	4,458,289	4,686,998	4,636,779	4,636,392	4,636,080
Welfare Assistance	2,979,052	3,110,913	3,284,923	3,228,074	3,222,743	3,218,456
Welfare Administration	368,537	380,495	377,933	377,933	377,933	377,933
All Other	1,044,036	966,881	1,024,142	1,030,772	1,035,716	1,039,691
Welfare Inspector General, Office of	1,004	1,074	1,295	1,321	1,347	1,374
Workers' Compensation Board	140,892	148,277	162,246	152,010	154,126	156,381
Functional Total	43,710,577	45,790,190	47,265,103	51,238,461	54,850,724	57,902,428
MENTAL HEALTH						
Mental Health, Office of	2,199,159	2,335,339	2,520,224	2,692,453	2,830,816	2,894,995
Mental Hygiene, Department of	9,370	8,442	7,800	7,800	7,800	7,800
Mental Retardation and Developmental Disabilities, Office of	2,930,056	3,168,254	3,369,167	3,560,454	3,676,258	3,788,938
Alcohol and Substance Abuse Services, Office of	484,034	521,906	595,007	655,669	704,897	687,400
Developmental Disabilities Planning Council	4,081	4,129	3,621	3,617	3,617	3,617
Quality of Care for the Mentally Disabled, Commission on	12,770	12,605	15,492	15,373	15,424	15,394
Functional Total	5,639,470	6,050,675	6,511,311	6,935,366	7,238,812	7,398,144
PUBLIC PROTECTION						
Capital Defenders Office	4,572	1,558	1,300	1,303	1,309	1,315
Correction, Commission of	2,515	2,621	2,629	2,674	2,674	2,674
Correctional Services, Department of	2,316,062	2,736,338	2,715,169	2,782,450	2,849,374	2,922,707
Crime Victims Board	55,565	60,073	62,709	62,248	62,269	62,294
Criminal Justice Services, Division of	193,492	267,326	254,005	265,162	245,525	235,356
Homeland Security	19,586	29,562	407,925	539,937	347,937	354,184
Investigation, Temporary State Commission of	3,586	3,551	3,929	4,152	4,219	4,242
Judicial Commissions	2,714	2,785	4,785	4,819	4,850	4,884
Military and Naval Affairs, Division of	209,562	401,610	396,929	291,930	146,845	166,777
Parole, Division of	193,231	194,729	205,978	220,361	233,189	250,269
Probation and Correctional Alternatives, Division of	72,254	72,752	74,649	74,702	74,726	73,484
Public Security, Office of	0	0	0	0	0	0
State Police, Division of	598,904	644,506	635,780	676,038	697,900	691,810
Functional Total	3,672,043	4,417,411	4,765,787	4,925,776	4,670,817	4,769,996
EDUCATION						
Arts, Council on the	42,825	49,244	55,766	54,665	54,845	54,826
City University of New York	619,871	1,064,544	1,186,315	1,245,860	1,301,014	1,332,761
Education, Department of	24,250,119	26,662,215	29,354,589	31,295,132	33,706,912	36,355,352
School Aid (includes EXCEL)	18,549,341	20,088,579	21,794,505	23,143,777	25,056,911	27,295,916
STAR Property Tax Relief	3,213,204	3,993,970	4,730,450	5,358,402	5,837,916	6,141,480
Handicapped	1,560,076	1,620,800	1,719,600	1,788,490	1,849,790	1,914,590
All Other	927,498	958,866	1,110,034	1,004,463	962,295	1,003,366
Higher Education Services Corporation	1,018,291	956,737	981,212	975,422	976,822	978,251
State University Construction Fund	10,013	13,157	12,493	12,628	12,756	12,884
State University of New York	4,964,540	5,447,926	5,901,289	5,996,243	6,164,116	6,130,560
Functional Total	30,905,659	34,193,823	37,491,664	39,579,950	42,216,465	44,864,634

FINANCIAL PLAN OVERVIEW

CASH DISBURSEMENTS BY FUNCTION
ALL GOVERNMENTAL FUNDS
(thousands of dollars)

	2005-2006 Actuals	2006-2007 Actuals	2007-2008 Projected	2008-2009 Projected	2009-2010 Projected	2010-2011 Projected
GENERAL GOVERNMENT						
Audit and Control, Department of	225,148	244,078	245,462	247,821	252,679	253,678
Budget, Division of the	37,423	54,817	94,137	109,900	112,400	115,800
Civil Service, Department of	26,391	24,363	23,653	23,857	24,037	24,270
Elections, State Board of	4,206	13,037	90,119	171,199	9,215	99,475
Employee Relations, Office of	3,579	3,852	4,000	4,025	4,062	4,103
Executive Chamber	13,937	14,517	20,320	20,930	21,560	22,200
General Services, Office of	260,359	255,060	234,558	236,355	222,064	233,375
Inspector General, Office of	5,336	5,933	6,908	6,980	7,059	7,127
Law, Department of	182,295	193,461	211,763	213,781	216,561	218,744
Lieutenant Governor, Office of the	348	360	1,378	1,420	1,460	1,500
Lottery, Division of	176,524	164,825	182,527	183,147	187,318	191,393
Racing and Wagering Board, State	13,093	16,899	19,489	19,497	19,967	20,148
Real Property Services, Office of	43,830	47,620	52,570	53,407	54,266	55,154
Regulatory Reform, Governor's Office of	3,661	3,509	3,781	3,825	3,871	3,895
State Labor Relations Board	3,508	3,376	4,077	4,118	4,156	4,198
State, Department of	158,651	148,140	193,507	176,781	155,666	141,851
Tax Appeals, Division of	2,958	3,228	3,233	3,228	3,263	3,298
Taxation and Finance, Department of	341,429	355,452	367,658	364,362	368,490	372,691
Technology, Office for	21,018	19,258	33,856	53,362	81,823	25,221
TSC Lobbying	1,572	2,338	2,314	2,324	2,351	2,370
Veterans Affairs, Division of	13,621	14,117	15,368	15,674	15,774	14,351
Functional Total	1,538,887	1,588,240	1,810,678	1,915,993	1,768,042	1,814,842
ALL OTHER CATEGORIES						
Legislature	210,051	213,118	220,258	223,168	225,841	225,887
Judiciary (excluding fringe benefits)	1,618,170	1,731,791	1,859,488	1,980,944	2,134,111	2,129,205
World Trade Center	38,003	37,020	135,450	82,950	55,500	34,150
Local Government Assistance	1,018,896	1,156,176	943,098	1,323,576	1,363,874	1,419,739
Long-Term Debt Service	3,701,385	4,450,737	4,133,998	4,798,128	5,250,500	5,877,446
General State Charges	4,735,317	5,222,834	5,385,856	5,824,962	6,230,090	6,544,433
Miscellaneous	(84,564)	(85,873)	261,566	251,825	234,109	440,996
Functional Total	11,237,258	12,725,803	12,939,714	14,485,553	15,494,025	16,671,856
TOTAL ALL GOVERNMENTAL FUNDS SPENDING	104,341,439	112,681,925	120,675,365	129,193,915	136,263,764	143,320,626

Note: This information is excerpted from the New York State 2007-08 Enacted Budget Financial Plan, published 4/19/2007. All Governmental Funds combines activity in the four governmental fund types: the General Fund; Special Revenue Funds; Capital Projects Funds; and Debt Service Funds.

683

BIOGRAPHIES
Executive Branch

ELIOT SPITZER (D)

New York Governor Eliot Spitzer was elected in November 2006, and took office on January 1, 2007. The Democratic former attorney general, who served two terms in that post, earned national accolades for his ground-breaking efforts to win victories that protect investors, consumers, the environment and low-wage workers. Among those was a 2002 settlement with ten of the nation's largest securities firms over charges of misleading investors, which led *Time Magazine* to name Spitzer "Crusader of the Year." He graduated from the Woodrow Wilson School at Princeton University and received his law degree from Harvard Law School. After law school, he clerked for U.S. District Judge Robert W. Sweet. He went on to serve as Assistant District Attorney in the Manhattan District Attorney's Office, where he rose to Chief of the Labor Racketeering Unit. In addition, he was an attorney in the New York City law firms of Paul, Weiss, Rifkind, Wharton & Garrison; Skadden, Arps, Slate, Meagher & Flom, and the firm of Constant Partners. The Bronx-born Spitzer has been married to his wife Silda Wall since 1987, and the couple has three daughters.

LORRAINE CORTES-VAZQUEZ (D)

New York Secretary of State Lorraine Cortes-Vazquez was appointed to office by Gov. Eliot Spitzer and took office in 2007. She graduated from Hunter College and holds a Master's degree from New York University's School of Public Administration. She served in the New York City Department of Aging from 1979 to 1992, becoming director of the Bureau of Program and Resource Development. She also served as executive director of ASPIRA, the oldest and largest non-profit youth leadership development and education organization in the city. From 1998 to 2004, she served as president of the Hispanic Federation, an umbrella organization of more than 60 health care and social service providers located in the northeast. Prior to becoming Secretary of State, she was vice president of Government and Public Affairs at Cablevision Systems Corporation.

DAVID A PATERSON (D)

Lieutenant Governor David A Paterson was elected to office on November 7, 2006, becoming the state's first African-American lieutenant governor. The former New York State Senator, first elected to that post to represent his district of Harlem in 1985, was elected Senate Minority leader in 2002, making him the first non-white legislative leader in New York's history. As Minority Leader, Paterson proposed legislation for a $1 billion voter-approved stem cell research initiative, worked toward a state-wide energy strategy, fought domestic violence, and served as a prime champion of minority- and women-owned businesses in New York. As lieutenant governor, he will continue to lead on these issues. Lt. Gov. Paterson, who is legally blind, graduated from Columbia University and Hofstra Law School. He advocates on behalf of the visually and physically impaired and serves as an adjunct professor at Columbia's School for International and Public Affairs. He and his wife, Michelle, have two children. The lieutenant governor's father, Basil Paterson, was New York State's first non-white Secretary of State.

THOMAS P DiNAPOLI (D)

New York State Comptroller Thomas P DiNapoli was sworn in as New York State's 54th Comptroller on February 7, 2007, taking over the state office responsible for many fiscal oversight functions. The lifelong resident of Nassau County formerly served in the New York State Assembly, to which he was first elected in 1986. For 15 years, he served on the Assembly's powerful Ways & Means Committee, where his duties focused on statewide fiscal issues including budgets, budget reform, and debt reform. He also chaired the Local Governments; the Governmental Operations; and the Environmental Conservation Committees. He helped draft and pass strengthened school district accountability laws and co-authored legislation creating the new Brownfield Cleanup Program. He holds a Bachelor's degree in history from Hofstra University and a Master's degree in human resources management from the New School University's Graduate School of Management and Urban Professions. He has been a manager in the telecommunications industry and an adjunct professor at Long Island University's CW Post College and Hofstra University. At age 18, he became New York State's youngest person to hold public office when he was elected a Trustee of the Mineola Board of Education, where he went on to serve for ten years, including two terms as president.

ANDREW M CUOMO (D)

Andrew M. Cuomo was elected New York State's 64th Attorney General on November 7, 2006. As the state's chief law enforcement official, Attorney General Cuomo represents the state and its residents in legal matters. He is the former U.S. Secretary of Housing and Urban Development during the Clinton Administration's second term, where he worked on behalf of reforms to make government efficient and competent while saving taxpayer dollars. Fighting racial discrimination was a key focus, with 2,000 anti-discrimination cases brought by the then-Secretary. Attorney General Cuomo graduated from Fordham University with a Bachelor of Arts degree, and received his law degree from Albany Law School. He first practiced law as an Assistant District Attorney in Manhattan, was a partner in a New York City law firm, and was of counsel at Fried, Frank, Harris, Shriver & Jacobson. He is the father of three children. His father is former three-term New York governor Mario Cuomo, for whom the current Attorney General served as campaign manager at the age of 24.

BIOGRAPHIES / New York State Assembly

New York State Assembly

PETER J ABBATE, JR (D)
49th - Part of Kings County

6419 11th Avenue, Brooklyn, NY 11219
718-232-9565/abbatep@assembly.state.ny.us

8500 18th Avenue, Brooklyn, NY 11214
718-236-1764

Peter Abbate was first elected to the New York State Assembly in 1986. He entered St. John's University in 1967 and graduated with a Bachelor of Arts degree in political science. From 1973 to 1974, he was Legislative Assistant to Assemblyman Stephen J Solarz and from 1974 to 1985 was District Representative for Mr Solarz while Mr Solarz was a US Congressman. Mr Abbate has been an active member of the Civitan Club of Brooklyn, the Boy Scouts of America, the Kiwanis Club of 18th Ave, the Statewide Homeowners & Tenants Assn, and the Guild for Exceptional Children. In the Assembly, he currently chairs the Committee on Governmental Employees, after earlier serving as chairman of the Committee on Real Property Taxation and the Committee on Cities. Mr Abbate is a lifelong resident of Bensonhurst.

MARC S ALESSI (D)
1st - Suffolk County

6144 Route 25A, Bldg A, Suite 5, Wading River, NY 11792
631-929-5540/alessim@assembly.state.ny.us

Marc Alessi was first elected to the New York State Assembly in a special election held September 13, 2005. He holds a Bachelor's degree from SUNY Albany, and a law degree from Touro Law School. He served as Downstate Director of Intergovernmental Affairs in the Office of the New York State Comptroller. He also interned at the Assembly, worked for an Albany law firm, and fought for working families with the Civil Service Employees Association. He lives in Manor Park.

THOMAS W ALFANO (R-I-C-WF)
21st - Part of Nassau County

Chase Building, 925 Hempstead Turnpike, Room 350, Franklin Sq, NY 11010
516-437-5577/alfanot@assembly.state.ny.us

Thomas W Alfano was first elected to the New York State Assembly in 1996. He received his undergraduate and JD degrees from Fordham University. He sits on two Assembly committees: Judiciary and Labor. Prior to his election, he worked as an attorney in several prominent New York City law firms including Skadden, Arps, Slate, Meagher & Flom. He is currently of counsel to the law firm of Entwistle & Cappucci, LLP, where he specializes in civil litigation. From 1988 to 1996, Mr Alfano served as staff counsel to NYS Senate Deputy Majority Leader Dean G Skelos, and from 1990 to 1996 he was also chairman of the Town of Hempstead Public Employees Relations Board. He has been active in the area of education, and his efforts have been recognized extensively by the groups, schools, and educational organizations throughout the 22nd Assembly district. He has been president of the North Valley Stream Kiwanis Club, and he is an advisory Board Member of United Cerebral Palsy Association of Nassau County, Inc., among other activities. He resides in North Valley Stream.

CARMEN E ARROYO (D)
84th - Part of Bronx County

384 E 149th St, Ste 608, Bronx, NY 10455
718-292-2901/arroyoc@assembly.state.ny.us

Carmen Arroyo was elected to the New York State Assembly in 1994, becoming the first and only Puerto Rican/Hispanic woman elected to the NY State Assembly. In the Assembly, she chairs the Subcommittee on Effective Treatment. She was born in Puerto Rico and arrived in the US in 1964. In 1966 she founded the South Bronx Action Group, in which she expanded the notion of tenant advocacy to include the interrelated services of employment, health, adult education, and welfare. In 1978 she became Executive Director of the South Bronx Community Corporation. At the same time, she continued her education, receiving her Associate of Arts degree from Eugenio Maria de Hostos Community College in 1978 and her BA from the College of New Rochelle in 1980. She served as member and president of Community School Board #7 for 20 years and was a member of the Lincoln Hospital Community Advisory Board for seventeen years. She is a member of the NYS Legislature's Black & Puerto Rican Caucus, the Women's Caucus, the NYS Assembly/Senate Puerto Rican/Hispanic Task Force, and the National Order of Women Legislators. She continues to reside in the South Bronx.

DARREL J AUBERTINE (D)
118th - Parts of Jefferson & St Lawrence Counties

200 Washington St, Ste 404B, Watertown, NY 13601
315-786-0284/aubertd@assembly.state.ny.us

70 Main St., Suite One, Canton, NY 13617
315-386-2037

Darrel J Aubertine was first elected to the New York State Assembly in November 2002. Prior to his election, he was a full-time dairy farmer for over thirty years at his family's Triple A Aubertine Farm, a sixth-generation heritage farm. He began public service in 1994 as a member of the Cape Vincent Town Board. In 1996 he became the Jefferson County Legislator for District 1, and he was elected chairman of the Jefferson County Board of Legislators in 1998 and 1999. As a lifelong resident of northern New York, his chief concern during his tenure in the State Assembly has been working on behalf of North Country families. This includes improving the region's economic climate. He currently chairs the Commission on State-Local Relations, co-chairs the New York Coalition of Great Lakes Legislators, and sits on numerous other committees. He resides in the town of Cape Vincent.

JEFFRION L AUBRY (D-L)
35th - Part of Queens County

98-09 Northern Blvd, Corona, NY 11368
718-457-3615/aubryj@assembly.state.ny.us

BIOGRAPHIES / New York State Assembly

Jeffrion Aubry was first elected to the New York State Assembly in a special election in 1992. He attended the College of Santa Fe, where he received his BA degree. Currently, he chairs the Committee on Correction and sits on numerous other committees, including the Task Force on Black, Puerto Rican, Hispanic & Asian Legislative Caucus. Formerly, he was employed by Elmcor Youth and Adult Activities, a not-for-profit multi-service corporation, for sixteen years, holding various positions including Executive Director. He also worked as a teacher in the New Mexico State Penitentiary for Eastern New Mexico University and as a consultant for Massand Associates, an engineering firm. He is former Director of Economic Development for the Borough President's Office of Queens, former Queens Representative to the Economic Development Corporation of the City of New York, and former Chairman of the Small Business Development Center's Advisory Board at York College. He is a member of organizations including the New York State Association of Black and Puerto Rican Legislators, Inc. and the New York State Assembly Puerto Rican/Hispanic Task Force.

JAMES G BACALLES (R-C)
136th - Steuben and Yates Counties

105 E. Steuben St., Bath, NY 14810
607-776-9691/bacallj@assembly.state.ny.us

James G Bacalles was elected to the New York State Assembly in 1995 in a special election. He attended Ithaca College. Currently, he is Assistant Minority Whip of the Assembly Minority Conference, and serves as Ranking Minority Member on the Committee on Health. Prior to his election, he served as major of the City of Corning since 1992. He began his political career in 1979 when he launched a ten-year stint as an elected member of the former Steuben County Board of Supervisors. He was appointed to the Medicaid and Welfare Reform Task Force of the New York State Association of Counties (NYSAC). He also served on the Steuben County committee studying alternate forms of government, leading to the transformation of the County Board of Supervisors into the Steuben County Legislature. He is involved in Boy Scout activities: he served as lodge adviser of the Order of the Arrow, the scouts' national honor society, and he is currently President of the Five Rivers Council. He has dedicated many hours to the Board of Directors of the Corning Hospital/Founders Pavilion, the Steuben County Youth Board, the Corning Area Youth Center, and the United Way. He is a lifelong resident of Corning.

GREGORY R BALL (R)
99th - Parts of Putnam, Dutchess, and Westchester Counties

Donald B Smith Government Center, Bldg.2, 110 Old Rte 6, Carmel, NY 10512
845-225-5038

Gregory R Ball was elected to the New York State Assembly in 2006. He graduated from the U.S. Air Force Academy with a Bachelor's degree, and is currently completing his thesis in International Affairs at Georgetown University in Washington, DC. Assemblyman Ball served as an Air Force protocol officer during his four years of active duty, which included work with four-star generals such as the Secretary of the Air Force and the Air Force Chief of Staff. Following his honorable discharge but prior to his election, he worked for an international redevelopment company that focuses on environmentally-friendly smart growth. His civic involvement includes founding the Courage Cup, an annual event that raises scholarship money for inner-city children. He resides in Carmel.

WILLIAM A BARCLAY (R-C-I)
124th - Parts of Onondaga & Oswego Counties

200 North Second St, Fulton, NY 13069
315-598-5185/barclaw@assembly.state.ny.us

William A Barclay was first elected to the New York State Assembly in 2002. A graduate of St. Lawrence University and Syracuse University College of Law, Assemblyman Barclay served as a clerk for Judge Roger Minor of the US Court of Appeals, Second Circuit, in Albany and New York City. He is currently a partner in the law firm of Hiscock and Barclay, specializing in business law, and he serves as a board member of Panthus Corporation and QMP Enterprises, Inc. He is on the boards of directors for the Friends of the Rosamond Gifford Zoo at Burnet Park, the Everson Museum of Art, and Northern Oswego County Health Services. He represents the eighth generation of his family living in Pulaski, Oswego County, where he resides.

ROBERT D BARRA (R-C-I)
14th - Nassau County

534 Merrick Rd, Lynbrook, NY 11563
516-561-8216/barrar@assembly.state.ny.us

Robert D Barra was first elected to the New York State Assembly in 2000. He earned his BA degree in Communications/Journalism from Hofstra University. He served as a councilman in the Town of Hempstead; while on the Town Board he also served as District Chief of Staff to State Senator Dean Skelos. He has been a Lynbrook Village Trustee and District Director for former Nassau Congressman David Levy. An active member of his community, Assemblyman Barra is a former member of the board of directors for the Nassau County Health Care Corporation, a former member of the St. Raymond School Board, and a charter member of the Lynbrook Kiwanis Club. He lives in North Lynbrook.

MICHAEL R BENEDETTO (D)
82nd - Part of Bronx County

177 Dreiser Loop, Rm 12, Bronx, NY 10475
718-320-2220

3369 E. Tremont Ave., Bronx, NY 10461
718-320-2220/benedem@assembly.state.ny.us

Michael R Benedetto was first elected to the New York State Assembly in 2004. He received his BA in History/Education from Iona College and in 1971 earned an MA in Social Studies/Education. He spent 35 years teaching career elementary and secondary school students. In 1974 he joined the New York City public school system as a teacher of mentally and physically challenged students; in 1977 he was assigned to PS 160, the Walt Disney School, and in 1988 became coordinator of the special education unit. He is currently on the staff of Mercy College as an adjunct instructor. While with the NYC schools, he ran the first "very special" Olympics for multiply handicapped children; he became an "in-service" instructor, teaching other teachers about special education, and he worked as a mentor teacher and taught in his schools' talented and gifted program. In his community, he established the Throggs Neck Community Players com-

BIOGRAPHIES / New York State Assembly

munity theater and served as member of Community Planning Board #10. He also started the Bronx Times Reporter, which became the largest community paper in the Bronx. He is a lifelong resident of Northeast Bronx.

MICHAEL A BENJAMIN (D)
79th - Part of Bronx County

540 E 169th St, Bronx, NY 10456
718-588-3119/benjamm@assembly.state.ny.us

Michael A Benjamin was first elected to the New York State Assembly in a special election in 2003. He earned a BA in Political Science from Syracuse University. Currently, he chairs the Subcommittee on Regulated Mortgage Lenders. Prior to his election to the Assembly, Assemblyman Benjamin was the first African American to head the Bronx Board of Elections. He continues to serve on the Election Law Committee in the Assembly, among other committee assignments, and chairs the Subcommittee on Regulated Mortgage lenders. His work has been honored by organizations such as the Bronx Branch of the NAACP, the New Covenant Board of Christian Education, and the Bronx Unity Democratic Club, and many other organizations.

JONATHAN L BING (D)
73rd - Part of New York City

360 E. 57th Street, Mezzanine Level, New York, NY 10022
212-605-0937 bingj@assembly.state.ny.us

Jonathan L Bing was first elected to the Assembly in 2002. He holds degrees from New York University School of Law and the University of Pennsylvania. Currently, he chairs the Mitchell-Lama Housing Subcommittee, and sits on numerous committees. Prior to his election, Mr Bing practiced law in Manhattan. He worked in the law firm of Torys LLP, and after September 11th organized over 250 attorneys as the New York Coordinator of the Federal Emergency Management Agency/American Bar Association's Disaster Legal Services Program. In 2006, his legislative accomplishments included passage of a bill he authored — now law — that expanded the statute of limitations for workers' compensation claims made by 9/11 rescue, recovery and clean-up workers, clearing the way for these people to get benefits they otherwise might have missed. He lives on Manhattan's East Side.

WILLIAM F BOYLAND, JR (D)
55th - Part of Kings County

467 Thomas S Boyland St, Brooklyn, NY 11212
718-498-8681

William F Boyland, Jr was first elected to the Assembly in a special election held in 2003. He chairs the Subcommittee on Outreach and Oversight of Senior Citizen Programs. Born in Brooklyn, he was initiated into public service by his father, William F. Boyland, Sr and his uncle, Thomas S. Boyland, both distinguished Assembly members. He attended Virginia State University, during which time worked for Virginia Governor Douglas Wilder and was also an intern in the offices of two US Congressmen, Major R Owens and Congressman Edolphus "Ed" Towns. As a member of Local 371, he was an eligibility specialist with the Department of Social Services. He has also worked on behalf of Wayside Baptist Church and the NAACP, among other organizations.

PHILIP BOYLE (R-C-I)
8th - Part of Suffolk

Legislative Office Building Room 718, Albany, NY 12240
518-455-4611/boylep@assembly.state.ny.us

Philip Boyle was first elected to the Assembly in 1994, where he served until his seat was redistricted in 2002. He returned to the legislative body following a special election in February 2006. He received his undergraduate degree from the University of North Carolina at Chapel Hill, a Master's degree in public administration from SUNY Albany, and his law degree from Albany Law School. During his first tenure in the Assembly, he served as Ranking Minority Member of the Committee on Environmental Conservation. Assemblyman Boyle, founding partner in the law firm of Stemberg & Boyle LLP, also has served as Assistant Town Attorney and Special Assistant District Attorney in Suffolk County. Among his civic service is duty as a volunteer firefighter and emergency medical technician (EMT) with the Great River Volunteer Fire Department. He lives in East Islip.

ADAM T BRADLEY (D)
89th - Part of Westchester County

4 New King St, Town of North Castle, White Plains, NY 10604
914-686-7335/bradlea@assembly.state.ny.us

Adam T Bradley was first elected to the New York State Assembly in 2002. He received both his BA and JD from Pace University, and he is an attorney in private practice specializing in family law. Currently, he chairs the Assembly's Subcommittee on Oversight of the Department of Environmental Conservation. Prior to his election to the Assembly, he was Assistant County Attorney in Westchester County. He has also handled many high-profile election law matters at trial and in appellate courts. He has been a member of the Advisory Board of the Coachman Family Center, which is a shelter for homeless families, and has been a member of the Board of Directors of the Law Guardian Association, which is devoted to representing children in legal proceedings. He lives in White Plains.

JAMES F BRENNAN (D)
44th - Part of Kings County

416 Seventh Avenue, Brooklyn, NY 11215
718-788-7221

1414 Cortelyou Road, Brooklyn, NY 11226
718-940-0641/brennaj@assembly.state.ny.us

James F Brennan was first elected to the New York State Assembly in 1984. He earned his law degree at Brooklyn Law School, and holds a B.A. from Yale University. Currently in the Assembly, he chairs the Committee on Cities, and sits on four other committees. Previously, Mr Brennan chaired the Assembly Committee on Mental Health, Mental Retardation and Developmental Disabilities. Among his accomplishments in that post was funding 5,000 housing units and allowing half-fares on the MTA system for those with mental illness. He was elected after working for his predecessor, Joseph Ferris.

RICHARD L BRODSKY (D)
92nd - Part of Westchester County

BIOGRAPHIES / New York State Assembly

5 West Main Street, Ste 205, Elmsford, NY 10523
914-345-0432/brodskr@assembly.state.ny.us

Richard Brodsky was first elected to the New York State Assembly in 1982. He is a graduate of Brandeis University and Harvard Law School. Prior to his election to the NYS Assembly, he served four terms on the Westchester County Board of Legislators. In the Assembly, he currently chairs the Committee on Corporations, Authorities and Commissions, which has oversight over major entities including public and private corporations and public authorities. Previously, he chaired the Assembly's Committee on Environmental Conservation from 1993 to 2002, as well as the Committee on Oversight, Analysis and Investigation. He has led efforts to investigate the Indian Point nuclear power plants. He has also been active on a national level, serving as co-chair of CLEAN (Coalition of Legislators for Environmental Action Now) and NCEL (National Coalition of Environmental Legislators). Mr Brodsky formerly served as Adjunct Professor at St. John's University School of Law and at Pace University Law School. Mr Brodsky was born in Brooklyn. His family later moved to Westchester County.

ALEC BROOK-KRASNY (D)
46th - Parts of Kings County

2823 West 12 Street, Suite 1F, Brooklyn, NY 11224
718-266-0267/BrookKrasnyA@assembly.state.ny.us

Alec Brook-Krasny was first elected to the New York State Assembly in 2006. He holds a Bachelor's degree in economics and engineering from Moscow Technological Institute, and graduated from the Institute for Not-for-Profit Management and Columbia University. Assemblyman Brook-Krasny immigrated to the United States from the former Soviet Union in 1989, and became a businessman operating a 14,000-square foot entertainment community center in Brooklyn known as "Fun-O-Rama." In 2001, he became founding Executive Director of The Council of Jewish Émigré Community Organizations, a coordinating body for 42 community-based Russian-speaking émigré organizations in New York.

DANIEL J BURLING (R-I-C)
147th - Parts of Allegany, Genesee, Livingston & Wyoming Counties

2371 N Main St, Warsaw, NY 14569
585-786-0180/http://assembly.state.ny.us/mem/?ad=147&sh=con

Daniel J Burling was first elected to the New York State Assembly in 1998. Currently, he serves as Vice-Chair of the Assembly Minority Conference and on four committees. A New York State registered pharmacist, Mr. Burling served in the United States Marine Corps from 1965 to 1969, which included a tour in Vietnam. He earned an honorable discharge as a Sergeant E-5m and then attended the Empire State Military Academy, graduating with a commission as a 2nd Lieutenant in the US Army Reserve, where he served until he was honorably discharged as Captain in 1994. Mr Burling also graduated from Herkimer County Community College and received his BS degree from the University of Buffalo School of Pharmacy. Mr Burling has been president and owner of Burling Drug since 1987. He has also served as an Intern/Staff Pharmacist at Genesee Memorial Hospital and as a consulting pharmacist for the Genesee County Nursing Home in Batavia. Prior to his election to the Assembly, Mr Burling served on the Genesee County Legislatue. He is a licensed private pilot and aircraft mechanic and served as airport manager for Nellis Airport in Fort Plain in 1972. He is also a licensed Charter Boat Captain and former owner/operator of Medicine Man Charters. Mr Burling is a member of the New York Pharmacists' Association, the National Association of Retail Druggists, and the Pharmacy Association of Western New York. Assemblyman Burling lives in the Town of Alexander.

MARC W BUTLER (R-I-C)
117th - Parts of Fulton, Herkimer & Otsego Counties

235 North Prospect Street, Herkimer, NY 13350
315-866-1632/butlerm@assembly.state.ny.us

33-41 East Main St, Johnstown, NY 12095
518-762-6486

Marc Butler was elected to the New York State Assembly in 1995. He holds a BA in English from SUNY Potsdam. Currently, Assemblyman Butler serves as ranking minority member of the Economic Development, Job Creation, Commerce, and Industry Committee. He also sits on the Assembly Minority Task Force on Hunting and Fishing and the Assembly Minority Task Force on Small Business. Prior to his election to the Assembly, his political career included service as a Newport Village Trustee and Deputy Mayor and two terms in the Herkimer County Legislature, where he was elected Majority Leader in 1993. Professionally, Mr Butler served as Corporate Communications Specialist to Utica National Insurance from 1986 until his election. In addition, he was a reporter from 1976 to 1986 for the Utica Observer-Dispatch, where he spent most of his time in the newspaper's Herkimer County Bureau reporting on local government and politics. A lifelong resident of the Mohawk Valley, he currently resides in the Village of Newport.

KEVIN A CAHILL (D)
101st - Dutchess & Ulster County

Gov Clinton Bldg, 1 Albany Ave, Ste G-4, Kingston, NY 12401
845-338-9610/ cahillk@assembly.state.ny.us

Kevin Cahill was first elected to the New York State Assembly in 1992, left in 1994, and was re-elected in 1998. A graduate of SUNY New Paltz and Albany Law School, he served from 1986 to 1992 in the Ulster County Legislature, where he was Minority Leader. Prior to his 1998 election, he directed a Medicare health plan under contract with the federal Health Care Financing Administration. Currently, he chairs the Committee on Ethics and Guidance. Among his previous Assembly posts, he served as Assembly spokesperson for Community Corrections, and was the longest tenured chair of the Legislative Task Force on People with Disabilities. Mr Cahill is a lifelong resident of Kingston, New York.

NANCY CALHOUN (R-C)
96th - Parts of Orange & Rockland Counties

1012 Little Britain Rd., Suite 900, New Windsor, NY 12553
845-567-3141/calhoun@assembly.state.ny.us

Nancy Calhoun was elected to the New York State Assembly in 1990. Born in Suffern, NY, she attended Empire State College, where she majored in Public and Business Administration. She is currently serving her second term as the Ranking Minority Member of the Committee on Standing Committees, and has previously served as Assistant Minority Whip and Secretary to the Minority Conference. Prior to her election to the Assembly, Ms Calhoun was

689

BIOGRAPHIES / New York State Assembly

Supervisor of the Town of Blooming Grove from 1986 to 1990, Councilwoman for the Town of Blooming Grove from 1982 to 1985, Blooming Grove Assessor's Clerk from 1978 to 1981, and Washington Central School District Tax Collector from 1976 to 1984. She has served as President of the Orange County Supervisors and Mayors Association, Orange Municipal Planning Federation Director, and other civic organizations. Currently she is executive committee member of the Women's Legislative Caucus, secretary to the American-Irish Legislators Society, and Assembly Minority Leader Tedisco's representative on the Hudson River Valley Greenway Council. She lives in Washingtonville.

KARIM CAMARA (D)
43 - Part of Kings

231 Empire Boulevard, Brooklyn, NY 11225
718-756-1776/camarak@assembly.state.ny.us

Karim Camara was first elected to the New York State Assembly in November, 2005. He received his Bachelor of Arts in English Literature and Chemistry from Xavier University of Louisiana and his Master's of Divinity from New York Theological Seminary. He also has studied at Alfred University, Fordham University and Wesley Theological Seminary. He sits on numerous Assembly committees. Prior to being elected to the Assembly, he was Director of Institutional Advancement for the Cush Campus Schools, a pre-K through 8th grade independent school in Crown Heights. He also has worked with the American Red Cross of Greater New York in their Emergency Family Center. He currently serves as Executive Pastor of the First Baptist Church of Crown Heights, where he previously served as Assistant Pastor. Assemblyman Camara also has served on the Community Advisory Board of the SUNY Downstate Medical Center and on the Faith Leader Advisory Committee of New Visions for Public Schools, among other organizations. He was born and raised in Crown Heights.

RONALD J CANESTRARI (D)
106th - Parts of Albany, Rensselaer & Saratoga Counties

Legislative Office Bldg, Rm 926, Albany NY 12248
518-455-4474/canestr@assembly.state.ny.us

Ron Canestrari was first elected to the New York State Assembly in 1988. He is a graduate of Fordham College and Fordham University School of Law. In January 2007, he was appointed Majority Leader by Assembly Speaker Sheldon Silver, a post that puts him in charge of the Assembly floor's day-to-day management during the legislative session. Previously, Assemblyman Canestrari chaired the Assembly's Higher Education Committee, where his achievements included backing the capital matching program that helps fund critical infrastructure for New York's independent colleges and universities, as well as an unprecedented five-year capital plan for maintenance and construction needs at SUNY and CUNY. The Majority Leader served in the US Army during the Vietnam era, and worked as an attorney with the federal government in Washington, DC. Prior to his election to the Assembly, he was Mayor of the City of Cohoes for thirteen years, where he served as President of the New York State Conference of Mayors.

ANN-MARGARET E CARROZZA (D)
26th - Part of Queens County

213-33 39th Avenue, Bayside, NY 11361
718-357-3588/carroza@assembly.state.ny.us

Ann Margaret E Carrozza was elected to the New York State Assembly in 1996. She received her JD from Hofstra University. She is an active member of legal organizations including the New York State Bar Association-Trusts and Estates and Elder Law sections, the Queens County Bar Association-Elderly and Disabled committee, the National Committee of Elder Law Attorneys. In the Assembly, she has sponsored numerous pieces of legislation focusing on health law issues, trusts and estates, and senior citizens' rights. Assemblywoman Carrozza is the host of a weekly cable television program in which she discusses budget & policy initiatives with guests. Currently, she chairs the Committee on Election Law.

JOAN K CHRISTENSEN (D)
119th - Part of Onondaga County

4317 E Genesee St, Rm 103, Syracuse, NY 13214
315-449-9536/christj@assembly.state.ny.us

Joan Christensen was first elected to the New York State Assembly in 1990. She is a graduate of Metropolitan Business College and attended Syracuse University. Prior to being elected to the Assembly, Assemblywoman Christensen served on City of Syracuse Board of Assessment Review and spent three terms on the Syracuse Common Council. In the Assembly, she chairs the Commission on Skills Development and Career Education, as well as numerous committees. The commission focuses on training and education issues as they impact economic and human development policy. Assemblywoman Christiensen chaired the Assembly's Task Force on Women's Issues from 1995 to 2000 and the Legislative Women's Caucus for two terms. She also chaired the Assembly's Administrative Regulation Review Commission (ARRC). Assemblywoman Christensen belongs to many organizations, including Women in Government and the National Order of Women's Legislators. She lives in Syracuse.

BARBARA M CLARK (D)
33rd - Part of Queens County

97-01 Springfield Blvd, Queens Village, NY 11429
718-479-2333/clarkb@assembly.state.ny.us

Barbara Clark was first elected to the New York State Assembly in 1986. She has chaired the Assembly Committees on Aging, State and Federal Relations and the New York State Legislative Caucus. Currently, she serves as Assistant Majority Whip. Nationally, she was vice-chair of the National Conference of State Legislators' (NCSL) Education, Labor and Job Training Committee, and is a member of the NCSL's policy group called the Education Partners. She also has been a Commissioner of the Education Commission of the States (ECS) since 1989. Assemblywoman Clark also sponsors the annual "Legislators Back to School" resolution, an initiative she coordinates that encourages legislators to go into their local schools and interact with students and faculty. She currently chairs the Education Committee of the Black, Puerto Rican and Hispanic Caucus, and is a member of the Majority Steering Committee. The health care administrator was born in Beckley, WV and lives in Cambria Heights.

MIKE COLE (R-I-C)
142 - Parts of Erie and Niagara

BIOGRAPHIES / New York State Assembly

5763 Seneca Street, Elma, NY 14059
716-675-7170/colem@assembly.state.ny.us

Mike Cole was elected to the New York State Assembly in a special election held on May 2, 2006. He earned a BS from the State University College at Brockport, and his JD from the State University at Buffalo Law School. Prior to his election to the Assembly, he served as an Alden Town Councilman starting in 1998, then served as Alden Town Supervisor where he worked to foster an improved economic climate. Chief among his accomplishments was working to bring Greatbatch Inc and its 400 new jobs to Alden. He also served as General Counsel and Senior Field Representative to former Congressman Jack Quinn, and has been a legislative assistant in the New York State Senate for the late Senator John B. Daley. He currently serves as Ranking Minority Member to the Alcoholism and Drug Abuse Committee, among his other committee assignments. He resides in Alden.

WILLIAM COLTON (D)
47th - Part of Kings County

155 Kings Highway, Brooklyn, NY 11223
718-236-1598/coltonw@assembly.state.ny.us

William Colton was elected to the New York State Assembly in November 1996. Currently, he chairs the Majority Conference. He received a BA degree from St John's University and an MS degree in Urban Education from Brooklyn College. He was a public school teacher for eleven years, serving as a UFT Chapter Chairperson for six years. While teaching, he attended St John's School of Law, and received his JD degree in 1978. Long active in community affairs, Assemblyman Colton was co-founder and organizer of the Bensonhurst Tenants Council and a member of the Bensonhurst Straphangers Committee for improving public transit. He fought for more money for public schools in Districts 20 and 21, as well as for numerous improvements such as traffic lights and pest control. He has been a member of the Board of Trustees of the Verrazano Lodge of the Order of the Sons of Italy and a member of the Board of Directors of the Cardinal Stritch Knights Corporation of the Cardinal Stritch Knights of Columbus Council.

JAMES D CONTE (R-C-I)
10th - Parts of Nassau & Suffolk Counties

1783 New York Ave, Huntington Station, NY 11746
631-271-8025/contej@assembly.state.ny.us

Jim Conte was first elected to the New York State Assembly in 1988 and currently serves as Assistant Minority Leader Pro Tempore. He holds a BA degree in Economics and Political Science from SUNY at Stony Brook, and worked for subsequently worked for Senator Martin Knorr and Assemblywoman Toni Rettaliata. He was later employed as an intergovernmental analyst for the office of the Suffolk County Executive Intergovernmental Relations Unit, acting as liaison between the State Legislature and executive departments. He has served on the Education Committee and is a member of the Higher Education Committee. Recipient of a kidney transplant, Assemblyman Conte was appointed by Governor Pataki to the New York State Transplant Council in 1997 and reappointed in 2001. His civic activities include membership in the Huntington Historical Society, Huntington Elks Club, and Constantino Brumidi Lodge Sons of Italy. He lives in Huntington Station.

VIVIAN E COOK (D)
32nd - Part of Queens County

142-15 Rockaway Blvd, Jamaica, NY 11436
718-322-3975

Vivian Cook was elected to the New York State Assembly in 1990. She was born in Rock Hill, South Carolina, and graduated from DeFrans Business Institute. Currently, she serves as Assistant Majority Leader in the Assembly, and previously served as Majority Whip. She has served as District Leader of Queens County since 1972. She is the founder and chair of the Board of Directors of the South Ozone Park Women's Association, and has been active in her community for many years. She supported community housing programs that provide residents with affordable homes. In 2000, Ms Cook was appointed Chair of the Task Force on Food, Farm and Nutrition Policy. She sits on a variety of standing committee including the Ways & Means Committee, and she serves as Treasurer of the Task Force on Black, Puerto Rican, Hispanic and Asian Legislative Caucus. She resides in Jamaica, Queens County.

CLIFFORD W CROUCH (R)
107th - Broome, Chenango, Delaware & Ulster Counties

1 Kattelville Rd, Ste 1, Binghamton, NY 13901
607-648-6080/crouchc@assembly.state.ny.us

Clifford Crouch was elected to the New York State Assembly in 1995. A 1965 graduate of Cornell University with an AAS degree in Dairy Science, he was owner and operator of a dairy farm from 1967 to 1989. He is Ranking Minority Member of the Agriculture Committee. Prior to serving in the Assembly, he served as Town Councilman for the Town of Bainbridge from 1982 to 1986 and Supervisor from 1986 until his election to the Assembly. He also served from 1993 until 1995 as Chairman of the Board of Supervisors in Chenango County. He has served on numerous committees throughout his career, such as the Chenango County Solid Waste Committee, the Human Resources Committee, the Planning and Safety Committee, and the Personnel Committee. He has been a member of the Bainbridge Local Development Corporation, the Board of Directors of the Broome Cooperative Fire Insurance Company, the American Agriculturist Foundation, the Bainbridge Lions Club, and the Bainbridge Methodist Church. He resides in the Town of Guilford.

MICHAEL J CUSICK (D)
63rd - Part of Richmond County

1911 Richmond Ave, Staten Island, NY 10314
718-370-1384/cusickm@assembly.state.ny.us

Michael Cusick was first elected to the New York State Assembly in 2002. He holds a B.A. from Villanova University, and launched into his public service career shortly after graduation when he served as Special Assistant to former President of the City Council Andrew J Stein. Later, he was chief of Staff to former Staten Island Assemblyman Eric N. Vitaliano. Finally, just before his election to the Assembly, he served as Director of Constituent Services for U.S. Senator Charles E Schumer, serving as Senator Schumer's liaison to various federal agencies and managing the daily operations of the senator's New York City Office. Currently, Assemblyman Cusick chairs the Subcommittee on Tuition Assistance Program. His civic interests include the Staten Island Board of Directors of the Catholic Youth Organization and the Boy Scouts of America. He is a lifelong resident of Staten Island.

BIOGRAPHIES / New York State Assembly

STEVEN H CYMBROWITZ (D)
45th - Kings County

1800 Sheepshead Bay Rd, Brooklyn, NY 11235
718-743-4078/cymbros@assembly.state.ny.us.

Steven Cymbrowitz was first elected to the New York State Assembly in November 2000. He holds a BA from CW Post College, a Master's degree in Social Work from Adelphi University, and a law degree from Brooklyn Law School. Currently, he chairs the Assembly's Subcommittee on Shoreline Protection of the Environmental Conservation Committee and is Secretary to the Assembly's Majority Conference. He has devoted his professional career to improving housing and protecting neighborhoods. Before his election to the Assembly, he served as Executive Director of the North Brooklyn Development Corporation, Director of Housing and Community Development for the Metropolitan New York Coordinating Council on Jewish Poverty, Assistant Commissioner of the Division of Homeless Housing Development for the New York City Department of Housing Preservation and Development (HPD), Assistant Commissioner of the Division of Housing Production and Finance for HPD, and Deputy Commissioner of Development at HPD. He also served as the New York City Housing Authority's Director of Intergovernmental Relations.

FRANCINE DELMONTE (D)
138th - Part of Niagara

1700 Pine Ave., Niagara Falls, NY 14301
716-282-6062/delmonf@assembly.state.ny.us

Francine DelMonte was first elected to the New York State Assembly in 2000. She graduated from Buffalo State College and completed course work for a Master of Arts degree from SUNY Albany. Currently, she is Secretary to the Majority Conference and chair of the Subcommittee on Export Trade. Prior to her election, she served for 20 years as Chief of Staff to retired Assemblyman Joseph T. Pillittere and staff aide to Majority Leader Paul A. Tokasz. Among her achievements, Assemblywoman DelMonte authored the 2001 legislation that created the Niagara Wine Trail in her district's growing wine industry. She has lived in Niagara County all of her life.

ROANN M DESTITO (D-WF)
116th - Part of Oneida County

101 West Liberty St, Rome, NY 13440
315-338-5779/destitr@assembly.state.ny.us

207 Genesee St, Rm 401, State Office Bldg, Utica, NY 13501
315-732-1055

RoAnn Destito was first elected to the New York State Assembly in 1992. She earned her BS degree in Industrial Relations at LeMoyne College. Currently, she chairs the Assembly's Committee on Governmental Operations. In the Assembly she has secured over $50 million to help redevelop the former Griffiss Air Force Base. She was part of the team that helped convince the Federal Base Realignment and Closure Commission (BRACC) to keep the Air Force Research Laboratory in Rome intact. She also is a member of the Griffiss Local Development Corporation's Executive Committee and Board of Directors. Active in her community, Assemblywoman Destito has served as many organizations, including as President of the Business and Professional Womens Club of Rome, a past board member and founder of the Mid-York Child Care Coordinating Council, and a board member of the Senior Citizens Council of Rome. Born in Utica, she now lives in Rome, New York.

LUIS M DIAZ (D)
86th - Bronx

2488 Grand Concourse, Room 310-11, Bronx, NY 10458
718-933-6909/diazl@assembly.state.ny.us

Luiz M Diaz was first elected to the Assembly in 2002. Born in Aguadilla, Puerto Rico and raised in the South Bronx, he holds a BA degree in Political Science from SUNY at Old Westbury. Among his committee assignments, Assemblyman Diaz sits on the Higher Education Committee and the Housing Committee. Prior to serving in the Assembly, he was the male district leader of the 76th Assembly District, as well as the Executive Director of N.E.T.S. Inc., a non-profit community-based organization that grew from a senior citizens service provider to one that serves both the young and elderly. He began his civic career when he joined the board of directors for the National Hispanic Voter Registration Drive, thereby helping 10,000 Hispanics register to vote. He also has been a board member of the League of United Latino American Citizens (LULAC), and served on the Bronx Council on the Arts and the Botanical Gardens Advisory Board.

RUBEN DIAZ, JR (D)
85th - Part of the Bronx

1163 Manor Avenue, Bronx, NY 10472
718-893-0202/diazr@assembly.state.ny.us

Ruben Diaz, Jr was first elected to the Assembly in 1996. He graduated from Lehman College, City University of New York, with a Bachelor's degree in political theory. Currently, he chairs the Assembly's Committee on State-Federal Relations, and numerous other committees. Among his many achievements has been his work to restore the Bronx River, which runs through his district. Assemblyman Diaz is a member of the Task Force on Black, Puerto Rican, Hispanic & Asian Legislative Caucus. He has lived in the Bronx all of his life.

JEFFREY DINOWITZ (D-L-WF)
81st - Part of Bronx County

3107 Kingsbridge Ave, Bronx, NY 10463
718-796-5345/dinowij@assembly.state.ny.us

Jeffrey Dinowitz was first elected to the New York State Assembly in 1994. He is a graduate of the Bronx High School of Science, City University, and Brooklyn Law School. Currently, he chairs the Assembly's Committee on Alcoholism and Drug Abuse, and serves on numerous other committees. Previously, he chaired the Legislative Commission on Government Administration, and currently chairs the Subcommittee on Protecting the Elderly Consumer. Prior to his election to the Assembly, he was an Administrative Law Judge for the State of New York for ten years. He has served in numerous community organizations, including Vice President of the Riverdale Community Council, member of Bronx Area Policy Board #7, and member of the Boards of Directors for the Bronx High school of Science Foundation and for the Bronx Council for Environmental Quality. His extensive community activity includes service on the Executive Committee of the Riverdale-Hudson Chapter of B'nai B'rith. In addition he has been a member of District Council 37 and

BIOGRAPHIES / New York State Assembly

the Public Employees Federation. He is a lifelong resident of the Bronx.

JANET L DUPREY (R - I - C)
114th - Parts of Clinton, Essex and Franklin Counties

176 U.S. Oval, Ste 1000, Plattsburg, NY 12903
518-562-1986

North Country Community College, 75 William St., Malone, NY 12953
518-483-9930/DupreyJ@assembly.state.ny.us

Janet L Duprey was first elected to the New York State Assembly in November 2006. Her long career in public service began when she was elected to the first of five terms on the Clinton County Legislature, including two years as the Legislature's chairperson. She went on to become County Treasurer, a post she held for 20 years after being elected in 1986. Assemblywoman Duprey has been a member of the New York State Office of Real Property Services Tax Enforcement Advisory Committee, the NYS Statewide Social Services Advisory Committee, and others. In her community, she has served on the boards of directors of the Champlain Valley physicians Hospital Medical Center, the Clinton-Northern Essex Chapter of the American Red Cross, among others. She resides in Peru.

PATRICIA A EDDINGTON (D-I-WF)
3rd - Part of Suffolk County

38 Oak Street, Suite 5, Patchogue, NY 11772
631-207-0073/eddingp@assembly.state.ny.us

Patricia Eddington was first elected to the New York State Assembly in 2000. She holds an AA degree in Women's Studies from Suffolk County Community College, a BA in Political Science from SUNY at Stony Brook, and an MA from the SUNY-Stony Brook School of Social Welfare. She is a NYS Certified Social Worker. Currently, she is vice chairman of the Majority Steering Committee. She is an Associate Professor of Philosophy and Women's Studies at Suffolk County Community College and spent 16 years as a social worker in the Islip School District. She served as a Patchogue-Medford school board member from 1980 to 1989 and for five years was a member of the Patchogue-Medford library board. She is past president of the National Organization for Women mid-Suffolk Chapter, as well as former Vice President of the National Women's Political Caucus, Suffolk County Chapter, and is President of the Legislative Women's Caucus.

STEVEN C ENGLEBRIGHT (D)
4th - Part of Suffolk County

149 Main Street, E Setauket, NY 11733
631-751-3094/engles@assembly.state.ny.us

Steve Englebright was elected to the New York State Assembly in 1992. He holds a BS degree from the University of Tennessee and an MS in Paleontology/Sedimentology from SUNY-Stony Brook. He was Founding Director of the Museum of Long Island Natural Sciences. First elected to public office in 1983, he served nine years in the Suffolk County Legislature, where his achievements included spearheading the county's open space program, which resulted in the doubling of the county's preserved open space. In the New York State Assembly, Assemblyman Englebright chairs the Committee on Aging and is focused on preparing the state for the coming demographic shift that will double New York's senior citizen population by 2015. Among his achievements is the 2004 Assisted Living Reform Act. He has also fought for a wide variety of other issues, including the Healthy Schools Initiative to protect kids from hazardous and toxic substances, and the Solar Choice Act, which allows for residential net-metering of solar photovoltaic cells. He lives in Setauket.

JOSEPH A ERRIGO (R-C)
130th - Parts of Livingston, Monroe & Ontario Counties

3045 East Henrietta Road, Henrietta, NY 14467
585-334-5210/errigoj@assembly.state.ny.us

Joseph Errigo was first elected to the New York State Assembly in November 2000. He graduated from Aquinas Institute in 1956 and joined the US Marine Corp Reserves, where he served until his honorable discharge in 1962. From 1965 until his retirement in 1995, he worked as an official Court Reporter for the State of New York in the Supreme, County, Family, and Surrogate Courts. This led to his first business venture (with two partners), Tiro Reporting Service, which existed until 1999; he still serves as a consultant for Midtown Reporting, Inc. Assemblyman Errigo's public service and political activities date back over four decades; in 1999, he was appointed Livingston County Commissioner to the Rochester Genesee Regional Transportation Authority. He also served on the Judicial Screening Committee of Livingston County. After joining the Assembly, he became Ranking Minority Member on the Children and Families Committee. He also continues to fight for the revitalization of Western New York's economy. Assemblyman Errigo lives in Conesus.

ADRIANO ESPAILLAT (D-WF)
72nd - Part of New York County

210 Sherman Ave, Ste A, New York, NY 10034
212-544-2278/espaila@assembly.state.ny.us

Adriano Espaillat was first elected to the Assembly in 1996, the first Dominican-American to be elected to a state house in the United States. He earned his BS degree in Political Science from Queens College and later completed postgraduate courses in Public Administration at the NYU Leadership for Urban Executives Institute. In 1980 he joined the New York City Criminal Justice Agency where he worked as the Manhattan Court Services Coordinator for eight years. In 1991 he was chosen as a member of then-Governor Mario Cuomo's Dominican Advisory Board, on which he served for two years. The following year, he was elected Democratic District Leader for the 72nd Assembly District Part-A, and he was reelected in 1995. From 1992 to 1994, he served as Director of the Washington Heights Victim Services Community Office and, in 1994, became Director of Project Right Start, a program aimed at combating substance abuse by education the parents of pre-school children. Since 1986, Assemblyman Espaillat has actively served on Community Planning Board 12 as a member of the Executive Board. Currently, he chairs the Assembly's Task Force on Black, Puerto Rican, Hispanic & Asian Legislative Caucus. In addition, he chairs the Oversight, Analysis and Investigation Committee, and sits on numerous others.

HERMAN D FARRELL, JR (D)
71st - Part of New York County

BIOGRAPHIES / New York State Assembly

2541-55 Adam Clayton Powell Jr Blvd, New York, NY 10039
212-234-1430/farrelh@assembly.state.ny.us

250 Broadway, 22nd Floor, New York, NY 10007
212-312-1441

Herman Farrell was first elected to the New York State Assembly in 1974. and has chaired the powerful Ways and Means Committee since 1994. Prior to his election, he served as Assistant Director of the Mayor's Office in Washington Heights. He has also been a Confidential Aide to a State Supreme Court Judge. Assemblyman Farrell is the former chair of the Assembly Banks Committee, and served on the Temporary Committee on Interstate Banking. From 1981 to 1982 he served as Chairman of the Subcommittee on Financial Institutions of the National Conference of State Legislators. He has been highly active in Democratic politics, serving in numerous capacities, and also has been honored by numerous organizations. Assemblyman Farrell also is a member of the Task Force on Black, Puerto Rican, Hispanic & Asian Legislative Caucus.

GINNY FIELDS (D-WF)
5th - Suffolk County

2 So Main St, Ste 2, Sayville, NY 11782
631-589-8685/fieldsg@assembly.state.ny.us

Assemblywoman Ginny Fields was elected in a special election on March 9, 2004. Currently, she chairs the Assembly's Subcommittee on Child Product Safety. A health care administrator for thirty-seven years, Assemblywoman Fields began elected public service in the Suffolk County Legislature in 1999, where she served two terms and sponsored a bill requiring Suffolk County to make available to the public comparison prices from local pharmacies for the top twenty-five drugs used by seniors. She is co-founder of the Oakdale Civic Association, and she has served on the Board of Directors of the Sayville Chamber of Commerce. She has been concerned with wetlands, habitat and open space and served as president of the Great South Bay Audubon Society. In 1999 she championed the acquisition by New York State of Benton Bay, a 127-acre parcel Assemblywoman Fields had worked ten years to help preserve. She is a lifelong resident of Suffolk County.

GARY D FINCH (R-C)
123rd - Parts of Cayuga, Broome, Chenango, Cortland & Tioga Counties

69 South Street, Auburn, NY 13021
315-255-3045/finchg@assembly.state.ny.us

Gary Finch was first elected to the New York State Assembly in 1999. He attended Cayuga Community College and received a degree from the Simmons School of Mortuary Science in Syracuse. He also earned a BS degree in Public Administration and Political Theory from SUNY Empire State College. Since 1970, Finch has been owner and chief operating officer of Brew-Finch Funeral Homes, Inc, which operates in northern, central, and southern New York State. He was first elected to public office in 1979 as a Village of Aurora Trustee, and in 1982 he was elected Mayor, a post he held for eight years. His extensive community service includes chairmanship of the Board of Trustees at Cayuga Community College. He also has served as Cayuga County United Way's president and campaign chair and as a member of its executive and finance committees. He is a past member of Leadership Cayuga's Curriculum Program; former chair of the membership committee for the Cayuga County Chamber of Commerce; and a charter member, past president, and big brother for Big Brothers and Big Sisters. He also is a member of the American Irish Legislators Society and the American Legislative Exchange Council. Born in Aurora, he lives in Springport.

MICHAEL J FITZPATRICK (R-C-I)
7th - Part of Suffolk County

50 Rte 111, Ste 202, Smithtown, NY 11787
631-724-2929/ fitzpam@assembly.state.ny.us

Michael J Fitzpatrick was first elected to the New York State Assembly in 2002. A graduate of St Michael's College in Colchester, Vermont with a BA in Business, he is an investment associate with UBS Financial Services Inc in its Port Jefferson office. Currently, he serves as Ranking Minority Member of the Assembly's Housing Committee. Prior to joining the Assembly, he served on the Smithtown Town Council for 15 years. He also is a member and past president of the Board of Trustees for the Cleary School for the Deaf in Nesconset, and he has also been the major gifts chairman for the Smithtown YMCA's capital campaign. He also was a member of the Suffolk County Charter Revision Commission. Assemblyman Fitzpatrick is active with the New York State American-Irish Legislators Society, and the Board of Directors of the Suffolk Sports Hall of Fame. Born in Jamaica, Queens, and raised in Hauppauge, Long Island, he now resides in St. James.

DENNIS H GABRYSZAK (D)
143rd - Part of Erie County

2560 Walden Ave., Ste 109, Cheektowaga, NY 14225
716-852-2791/GabryszakD@assembly.state.ny.us

Dennis H Gabryszak was first elected to the New York State Assembly in 2006. He studied business management at the University of Buffalo and business administration at Erie Community College. Prior to his election to the Assembly, he served as Cheektowaga Town Supervisor from 1993 to 2006, where his accomplishments included playing key roles constructing a library and gaining national recognition for the town's financial reporting from the Government Finance Officers Association, securing the highest municipal bond rating in Western New York, and spearheading construction of a town golf course. Assemblyman Gabryszak also served as a Councilman for the Cheektowaga Town Board and Trustee to the Village of Depew Board. For 12 years, he was Assistant Vice President for Citicorp Services, Inc., then became Deputy Erie County Clerk overseeing the Auto Bureau.

SANDRA R GALEF (D-I-WF)
90th - Parts of Putnam & Westchester Counties

2 Church Street, Ossining, NY 10562
914-941-1111/ galefs@assembly.state.ny.us

Sandy Galef was first elected to the Assembly in 1992. She graduated from Purdue University and earned a Master's degree in Education at the University of Virginia. Currently, she chairs the Assembly's Real Property Taxation Committee, and serves on the Assembly Majority Steering Committee as well as the Hudson Valley Greenway Communities Council. Before her election to the Assembly, she served on the Westchester County Legislature for 13 years, including eight as the Minority Leader. She also served as president of the New York State Association of Counties, and on the

BIOGRAPHIES / New York State Assembly

national level as chairperson of the Labor and Employee Benefits Steering Committee of the National Association of Counties. Her extensive community and civic also includes serving on the boards of the Westchester Medical Center Children's Hospital Foundation, the University of Virginia's Curry School of Education Foundation, and the State Task Force for Tobacco Free Women and Girls. Born in LaCross, Wisconsin, she has lived in Westchester County since 1944. She currently resides in Ossining.

DAVID F GANTT (D)
133rd - Part of Monroe County

74 University Ave, Rochester, NY 14605
585-454-3670

David Gantt was first elected to the New York State Assembly in 1983. He attended Roberts Wesleyan College and the Rochester Institute of Technology. Currently, he chairs the Assembly's Committee on Transportation. Assemblyman Gantt's professional experience has included service as Youth Counselor for the City of Rochester, as administrator for the Anthony L. Jordan Health Center, and as a member of Lithographers & Photoengravers International Union Local 230. Before joining the Assembly, he served nine years in the Monroe County Legislature. In the Assembly he previously has served as Co-Chair of the Legislative Task Force on Demographic Research and Reapportionment, thereby ushering the Assembly Majority through the 1990 Census and the subsequent reapportionment of legislative districts. He is a member of the Task Force on Black, Puerto Rican, Hispanic & Asian Legislative Caucus, and has lived in Rochester for many years.

MICHAEL N GIANARIS (D)
36th - Part of Queens County

21-77 31st Street, Suite 107, Astoria, NY 11105
718-545-3889/gianarm@assembly.state.ny.us

Michael Gianaris was first elected to the New York State Assembly in 2000. He received a Bachelor's Degree in Economics and Political Science from Fordham University and his JD degree from Harvard Law School. Currently, he chairs the Assembly's Subcommittee on Election Day Operations and Voter Disenfranchisement, a subcommittee of the Committee on Election Law, and the Commission on Administrative Regulations Review. He began his career in public service as an aide to Congressman Thomas Manton, and he later served as Governor Mario Cuomo's Queens County Regional Representative. Prior to his campaign and election to the Assembly, he served as Associate Counsel to the New York State Assembly, serving as Counsel to the committees on Consumer Affairs and Protection, Governmental Operations, Veterans Affairs, and Agriculture and Markets. He has served as a member of Queens Community Planning Board #1, as Legal Counsel to the United Community Civic Association, and as a board member of the Eastern Orthodox Lawyers Association. He is a lifelong resident of Astoria.

JOE GIGLIO (R-I-C)
149th - Cattaraugus County and parts of Allegany and Chautauqua Counties

700 West State Street, Olean, NY 14760
716-373-7103/GiglioJ@assembly.state.ny.us

Joe Giglio was first elected to the Assembly in 2005. He holds a Bachelor's degree from SUNY-Buffalo. Prior to his election, he served as a state deputy inspector general, investigating alleged criminal activity, fraud and abuse by individuals and company officials who deal with state agencies in a region stretching from Buffalo to Syracuse to the Pennsylvania border. He also has served as a special assistant to former state Attorney General Dennis Vacco. In addition, he has served in both the Erie and Cattaraugus county sheriffs' departments. He is also a small business owner, and has lived in Western New York all his life.

DEBORAH J GLICK (D)
66th - Part of New York County

853 Broadway, Suite 2120, New York, NY 10003
212-674-5153/glickd@assembly.state.ny.us

Deborah Glick was first elected to the Assembly in 1990, and is the first openly lesbian or gay member of the New York State Legislature. She graduated from Queens College of the City University of New York and earned her MBA from Fordham University. Prior to her election to the Assembly, she owned and managed a small printing business in TriBeCa, and then became Deputy Director of General Services at the City Department of Housing, Preservation and Development. Currently, she chairs the Assembly's Committee on Higher Education, and sits on several other important committees. Her legislative successes include her work on behalf of the Sexual Orientation Non-Discrimination Act (SONDA), which was signed into law in 2002, as well as the Women's Health and Wellness Act, which became law in 2003. Assemblywoman Glick has also served on Manhattan's Community Board #2, worked with the National Organization for Women, the Women's Political Caucus, and the National Abortion and Reproductive Rights Action League among others. A lifelong resident of New York, she lives in Greenwich Village.

DIANE M GORDON (D)
40th - Part of Kings County

669 Vermont Street, Brooklyn, NY 11207
718-257-5824/gordond@assembly.state.ny.us

Diane Gordon was first elected to the New York State Assembly in 2000. She graduated from New York City Technical College and is certified by the American Business Institute in Business Mathematics. Currently, she chairs the Assembly's Subcommittee on Transitional Services. Her civic involvement began in 1985, when she founded the Save our Homes Organization of East New York, which helped homeowners and businesses remain intact when rehabilitation was taking place. She has worked in daycare, taught fifth and sixth grades, and served as a senior-citizen caseworker and community liaison. She served on the Community School Board of District 19, was elected to the area policy board of Community Planning Board 5, and has been elected as New York State Committeewoman since 1996. She is currently a member of the New York State Black, Puerto Rican and Hispanic Legislative Caucus, the Puerto Rican/Hispanic Task Force, the Legislative Women's Caucus, and the Democratic Study Group. Born in Hemingway, South Carolina, she grew up in the East New York and Brownsville sections of Brooklyn.

TIMOTHY GORDON (I-D)
108th - Parts of Columbia, Rensselaer, Greene, Albany

BIOGRAPHIES / New York State Assembly

1654 Columbia Turnpike, Castleton-on-Hudson, NY 12033
518-479-0542/GordonT@assembly.state.ny.us

Tim Gordon was first elected to the New York State Assembly in November 2006, and is the Assembly's only Independence Party member. He is a graduate of SUNY Brockport, and the founder of an advertising and public relations firm for small business and non-profits called Albany Media Group. In the Assembly, he is committed to fighting on behalf of working families' interests ranging from tax relief to health care. Prior to his election, he served on the Bethlehem Town Council. He is active in his community in activities ranging from a Little League and Girls' Softball coach to being an active member in the North Bethlehem Volunteer Fire Department to membership in the Arise-Regionalism Committee. He resides in the Town of Bethlehem.

RICHARD N GOTTFRIED (D-WF)
75th - Part of New York County

242 W 27th Street, New York, NY 10001
212-807-7900/gottfrr@assembly.state.ny.us

Richard Gottfried was first elected to the New York State Assembly in 1970 when he was a 24-year-old Columbia Law School student. He graduated from law school the following year, having also earned a B.A. from Cornell. The full-time legislator focuses on health care policy, and chairs the Assembly's Health Committee. He was a major architect of New York's managed care reforms, the Prenatal Care Assistance Program for low income women, the Physician Profiling Law that gives patients access to information about a doctor's records, and Family Health Plus, which provides free health coverage for low-income adults. In addition, he is a member of the Assembly Democratic Steering Committee and sits on several other committees. He has previously served as Deputy Majority Leader, Assistant Majority Leader, and has chaired the committees on Codes and Children and Families. He is a Fellow of the New York Academy of Medicine, and a member of the American Public Health Association, the New York Civil Liberties Union, and the Association of the Bar of the City of New York, the Art Students League of New York, Stephen Wise Free Synagogue, and The China Institute. He lives in Manhattan.

AURELIA GREENE (D)
77th - Part of Bronx County

930 Grand Concourse, Ste E, Bronx, NY 10451
718-538-2000/greenea@assembly.state.ny.us

Aurelia Greene was elected to the New York State Assembly in 1982. She graduated from Livingston College at Rutgers University, where she majored in Community Development. In the Assembly, she is the Speaker Pro Tempore, the first African American to hold the leadership position. She also served as Deputy Majority Leader, and is the first woman to chair the Committee on Banks. In addition, she has chaired the Committee on Consumer Affairs & Protection and the Subcommittee on Adult Education. She serves as Chaplain to the Black, Puerto Rican, Hispanic & Asian Legislative Caucus. She is a former public agency administrator who also has taught at Antioch College, lectured at numerous universities in the metropolitan area, served as a major proposal writer, and is an experienced counselor. She is a native of the Bronx.

AILEEN M GUNTHER (D-WF)
98th - Sullivan County and Part of Orange County

19 South Street, Middletown, NY 10940
845-342-9304

20 Anawana Lake Road, Monticello, NY 12701
845-794-5807 GuntheA@assembly.state.ny.us

In November 2003, Aileen Gunther was elected to fill the vacancy created by the untimely death of her husband, Assemblyman Jake Gunther. She received her nursing degree from Orange County Community College, and studied liberal arts at the State University of New York at New Paltz. She is a registered nurse and the former Director of Performance Improvement and Risk Management for Catskill Regional Medical Center. Currently, she chairs the Assembly's Subcommittee on Women's Health, and sits on numerous other committees. Her healthcare knowledge has served her constituency: among the legislation she has introduced are measures to end mandatory overtime for nurses, require a circulating nurse in every emergency room, and force health insurance companies to provide coverage for prosthetics. Following the September 11, 2001 terrorist attacks, she was named a member of the Sullivan County Local Emergency Preparedness Council. Assemblywoman Gunther also has been a member of the AIDS Task Force and is a trained HIV Counselor. Among her many additional professional affiliations, she is the New York State Government Liaison for the Mid-Hudson Chapter of Infection Control Practitioners. She grew up in Orange County and raised her family with her late husband in Sullivan County.

STEPHEN HAWLEY (R-I-C)
139th - Niagara, Orleans, Genesee and Monroe Counties

121 N. Main Street, Albion, NY 14411
585-589-5780

Stephen Hawley was elected to the New York State Assembly during a special election held on Feb. 28, 2006. He holds a B.S. in Education from the University of Toledo, and served seven years in the Ohio Army National Guard and the U.S. Army Reserves, earning the rank of First Lieutenant. Prior to his election, the Batavia native served on the Genesee County Legislature. He also serves on the Genesee Community College Foundation Board of Directors, the county's Empire Zone Development Board and Planning Board, the Genesee Center for Independent Living, and the Genesee Valley BOCES Board of Education. He is a small businessman who formerly operated Hawley Farms, and now co-owns The Insurance Center with his wife, Crystal, and sells residential and commercial real estate in the Genesee Valley region. He has been active in community organizations such as the YMCA and Cornell Cooperative Extension Service, and lives in Batavia.

JAMES P HAYES (R-C-I)
148th - Parts of Erie & Niagara Counties

5555 Main St, Amherst, NY 14221
716-634-1895/hayesj@assembly.state.ny.us

Jim Hayes was first elected to the New York State Assembly in 1998. He holds a BA in political science from Canisius College. Currently, his committee memberships include a seat on the powerful Ways & Means Committee, which oversees tax revenues, as Ranking Minority Member. Prior to his election to the Assembly, he

BIOGRAPHIES / New York State Assembly

served as Campaign Finance Director and legislative assistant to former US Representative Bill Paxon, then went on to become development director for Catholic Charities of Buffalo. He served as trustee for the Village of Williamsville and as the village's deputy mayor, and then was twice elected to the Amherst Town Board. During his tenure, he was the Board's liaison to the highway department, the public library, the Amherst Museum, and citizen-based environmental and safety committees. Born and raised in Erie County, he lives in Amherst.

CARL E HEASTIE (D)
83rd - Part of Bronx County

1351 East Gun Hill Road, Bronx, NY 10469
718-654-6539/heastic@assembly.state.ny.us

Carl E Heastie was first elected to the New York State Assembly in 2000. He holds a BS degree in Applied Mathematics and Statistics from the State University of New York at Stony Brook, and he is presently enrolled in Baruch College's MBA program. He chairs the Assembly's Subcommittee on Emerging Workforce for the Assembly's Committee on Labor, as well as its Task Force on Demographic Research and Reapportionment, under the Committee on Governmental Operations. Prior to joining the Assembly, was employed as a budget analyst in the Office of the New York City Comptroller. He is a member of the Williamsbridge Branch of the NAACP, the National Council of Negro Women, and the Grace Baptist Church. He resides in the Bronx, where he was born.

ANDREW HEVESI (D)
28th - Parts of Queens County

98-08 Metropolitan Avenue, Forest Hills, NY 11375
718-263-5595

Andrew Hevesi was first elected to the New York State Assembly in a special election held in May 2005. Prior to his election to the Assembly, Assemblyman Hevesi served as Chief of Staff to former New York State Assemblyman Jeff Klein and Director of Community Affairs for New York City Public Advocate Betsy Gottbaum. In addition, he worked as a paralegal in the Queens County District Attorney's Office, Domestic Violence Bureau. The lifelong resident of Forest Hills, who played in youth athletics, now serves as Director of the Forest Hills Youth Athletic League Basketball Clinic.

DOV HIKIND (D)
48th - Part of Kings County

1310 48th Street, Brooklyn, NY 11219
718-853-9616/ hikindd@assembly.state.ny.us

Dov Hikind was first elected to the New York State Assembly in 1982. He graduated from Queens College, and earned a Master's degree in Urban Studies from Brooklyn College. In the Assembly, he serves as Deputy Majority Whip. A spokesman against discrimination, racism and anti-Semitism, Assemblyman Hikind formerly chaired the Subcommittee on Human Rights and published an in-depth study of the effects of the quota system and reverse discrimination on education, business, and the civil service. After the Crown Heights riots in 1991, he joined forces with other Jewish leaders and elected officials to address issues stemming from the violence. He is a strong proponent of Israel, has challenged the U.S. Coast Guard regarding its policies about wearing religious headgear during active service, and provided funds for closed-circuit cameras in nine subway stations on the N, D, and F lines following 9/11 and the ensuing terrorism concerns. He was born in New York.

EARLENE HOOPER (D-L)
18th - Part of Nassau County

50 Clinton St, Ste 214, Hempstead, NY 11550
516-489-6610

Earlene Hooper was elected to the New York State Assembly in 1988. She earned a BA in English from Norfolk State University, a Master's in Social Work from Adelphi University, and a Doctor of Humane Letters from Five Towns College in Dix Hills. Currently, Assemblywoman Hooper is the Deputy Majority Leader. A social worker, Assemblywoman Hooper has been an administrator in the NYS Department of Social Services' Division of Child and Family Services. As Legislative chair of the Nassau County Chapter of Jack and Jill of America, she established the DEALS project (Developing and Expanding Adult Life Skills). In the Assembly, she is a member of the Assembly Task Force on Women's Issues and the NYS Black and Puerto Rican Legislative Caucus, the Assembly Task Force on Women's Issues, and a member of the Permanent Commission on Justice for Children. She is an active member of the NAACP, the Central Nassau Chapter of the Negro Business and Professional Women's Association and Delta Sigma Theta Sorority. She resides in Hempstead.

WILLIAM B (SAM) HOYT, III (D)
144th - Part of Erie County

936 Delaware Avenue, Ste 005, Buffalo, NY 14209
716-885-9630/ hoyts@assembly.state.ny.us

Sam Hoyt was first elected to the New York State Assembly in 1992. He graduated from SUNY College at Buffalo with a BA degree in Political Science. Prior to his election, he served as Western New York regional director for the late U.S. Senator Daniel P Moynihan. In the Assembly, he chairs the Committee on Local Government, and sits on several other key committees. His primary priority in the Assembly is developing Western New York's economy, as a result of which he has introduced legislation promoting Smart Growth (which combats urban sprawl), as well as tax cuts and other bills. Assemblyman Hoyt also advocates on behalf of the environment, education, and against drug and alcohol abuse. He lives in Buffalo.

JANELE HYER-SPENCER (D)
60th - Parts of Richmond and Kings Counties

586 Midland Ave., Suite 1B, Staten Island, NY 10306
718-667-5891/HyerSpencerD@assembly.state.ny.us

Janele Hyer-Spencer was elected to the New York State Assembly in 2006. She graduated from the City of New York with a Master of Arts in Social Science/Public Policy, as also earned her law degree at CUNY. She has a private law practice specializing in family law and helping domestic violence victims. Previously, she served as legal director for My Sisters' Place, and was an attorney for the New York City Administration for Children's Services. She was appointed by the State of New York Commission on Quality of Care and Advocacy to its Surrogate Decision-Making Committee in 2005. She has been active in a variety of civic groups, including the Staten Island

BIOGRAPHIES / New York State Assembly

Welfare Action Network, and is a former board member of Community Health Action of Staten Island, where she resides.

RHODA S JACOBS (D)
42nd - Part of Kings County

2294 Nostrand Avenue, Brooklyn, NY 11210
718-434-0446/ jacobsr@assembly.state.ny.us

Rhoda Jacobs was first elected to the New York State Assembly in 1978. She received her Bachelor's and Master's degrees from Brooklyn College. She is currently Assistant Speaker in the Assembly. In the past, she has been chair of the Social Services Committee and Assistant Speaker Pro Tempore and Chair of the Majority Program Committee. She also formerly chaired the Assembly's Committee on Oversight, Analysis, and Investigation and the Task Force on Food, Farm, and Nutrition Policy. She served as Treasurer of the National Association of Jewish Legislators and remains a member, and also was an officer of the National Association of State Legislators. She also chaired the Budget Conference Committee on Health and Human Services in 1997. She was born and raised in Brooklyn.

ELLEN JAFFEE (D)
95th - Part of Rockland County

1 Blue Hill Plaza, Ste. 1116, PO Box 1549, Pearl River, NY 10965
845-624-4601/JeffeeE@assembly.state.ny.us

Ellen Jaffee was first elected to the New York State Assembly in November 2006. She holds a B.A. from Brooklyn College and an M.S. in Special Education from Fordham University. Prior to her election to the Assembly, she served as Rockland County Legislator from 1998 to 2006, where she chaired the Environmental Committee, served as vice-chair of the Budget and Finance Committee, co-chaired the Multi-Services Committee, and similarly led several other subcommittees. Assemblywoman Jaffee also served as a Suffern Village Trustee from 1995-1997. Her legislative accomplishments during the 2007 Assembly session included cosponsoring over 150 pieces of legislation, including a series of bills focused on reducing greenhouse gas emissions in the state. She resides in Suffern.

HAKEEM JEFFRIES (D)
57th - Part of Kings County

55 Hanson Place, Brooklyn, NY 11217
718-596-0100/JeffriesH@assembly.state.ny.us

Hakeem Jeffries was first elected to the New York State Assembly in 2006. He holds a Bachelor's degree in political science from SUNY, and a Master's degree in Public Policy from Georgetown University in Washington, DC. He earned his law degree from the New York University Law School, where he delivered the commencement speech for his graduating class. He then went on to clerk for U.S. District Judge Harold Baer, Jr. of the District Court for the Southern District of New York, worked as an associate in the litigation department of the New York City firm of Paul, Weiss, Rifkind, Wharton & Garrison, and served as an assistant general counsel in the litigation department of a major media company. His community involvement has included membership in the 77th Precinct Community Council, and he formerly was a civil rights/civil liberties instructor at the Crown Heights Youth Collective. He resides in Prospect Heights.

SUSAN V JOHN (D)
131st - Part of Monroe County

840 University Ave, Rochester, NY 14607
585-244-5255/ johns@assembly.state.ny.us

Susan John was first elected to the New York State Assembly in 1990. She earned her Bachelor's degree in Public Affairs from George Washington University and her JD from Syracuse University. She subsequently practiced law with a firm in Rochester. In the Assembly, she currently chairs the Labor Committee, where she authored The Empire State Wage Act of 2004. The bill was passed in bipartisan fashion, and raised the state's minimum wage to $7.15 per hour as of January 1, 2007. She also has worked with her colleagues to pass the Home Inspectors Licensing Act, which requires home inspectors be qualified to inspect houses during the home purchasing process. Assemblywoman John is also a member of the Office for the Prevention of Domestic Violence Advisory Council and the Visiting Committee for the State Archives. She is a strong supporter of the Women's Health and Wellness Act of 2002. Additionally, she serves on the Women's Network of the National Conference of State Legislatures, and other organizations. She resides in Rochester.

BRIAN P KAVANAGH (D)
74th - Part of New York

237 1st Avenue (14th Street), Room 407, New York, NY 10003
212-979-9696/KavanaughB@assembly.state.ny.us

Brian P Kavanaugh was first elected to the New York State Assembly in November 2006. He attended Princeton University on scholarship and earned his law degree from New York University. In the Assembly, he is a member of the Puerto Rican/Hispanic Task Force along with his standing committee memberships, and he is also a member of the American-Irish Legislators Society. Prior to his election to the Assembly, he served as Chief of Staff for New York City Councilmember Gale Brewer, where he drafted laws and negotiated enactment of the Domestic Worker Protection Act, among other accomplishments. He formerly served as an aide to New York City Mayors Ed Koch and David Dinkins. He also has been an attorney in the New York law firms of Kaye Scholer and Schulte Roth & Zabel. He is a lifelong resident of New York City.

THOMAS J KIRWAN (R-C)
100th - Parts of Dutchess, Orange and Ulster Counties

190 South Plank Road, Newburgh, NY 12550
845-562-0888/ kirwant@assembly.state.ny.us

Thomas Kirwan was first elected to the New York State Assembly in 1994. He received a BA degree in History & Political Science from Mount Saint Mary College in Newburgh, which is his hometown. He served with the New York State Police for twenty-eight years and retired as a lieutenant with the Bureau of Criminal Investigations. He spent his last four years in Manhattan with the New York Drug Enforcement Task Force investigating mid- to upper-level drug dealers in New York City. In the Assembly, he is the Ranking Minority Member of the Committee on Cities and a member of the committees on Education, and Alcoholism and Drug Abuse, among others. He is a member of the Board of Directors of Our Lady of Comfort, a women's shelter, and a member of the civic organization UNICO in Newburgh.

BIOGRAPHIES / New York State Assembly

BRIAN M KOLB (R-I-C)
129th - Cayuga, Cortland, Onondaga, Ontario & Seneca Counties

607 W Washington St, Ste 2, Geneva, NY 14456
315-781-2030/ kolbb@assembly.state.ny.us

Brian Kolb was elected to the Assembly in 2000. He holds a both a BS and MS from Roberts Wesleyan College in Rochester. In the Assembly, he serves as the Minority Leader Pro-Tempore, a signification leadership position also known as Floor Leader. Assemblyman Kolb also chairs the Minority Manufacturing Task Force. Prior to joining the Assembly, he was Supervisor for the Town of Richmond, Chairman of Leadership Rochester's Board of Directors, and a member of both the Ontario County Revolving Loan Fund Committee and the Ontario County Board of Supervisors. In the private sector, he is former President of Refraction Technologies and a co-founder of the North American Filter Corporation, and he is currently affiliated with Stone Bridge Business Partners of Rochester. Assemblyman Kolb also teaches as an Adjunct Professor of Adult and Graduate Education at Roberts Wesleyan College, and he was formerly a member of the Honeoye Central School Board and the Finger Lakes Community College Board of Trustees. Other community affiliations include membership of the Rochester District of Key Bank Board of Directors, the Canandaigua Rotary Club, the Honeoye Chapter of the Sons of the American Legion, the New York Guard and Ontario Charities Classic Board of Directors. He is a member of the Board of Directors of Thompson Health System Senior Living Services. He lives in Canandaigua.

DAVID R KOON (D-I)
135th - Part of Monroe County

268 Fairport Village Landing, Fairport, NY 14450
585-223-9130/ koond@assembly.state.ny.us

David Koon was elected to the New York State Assembly in 1996. Currently, he chairs the Assembly's Legislative Commission on Development of Rural Resources. A graduate of Fairmont State College in West Virginia, Assemblyman Koon began his career at Kelly Springfield Tire Company in Cumberland, Maryland. In 1982 he joined Bausch and Lomb as an Industrial Engineer in Oakland, Maryland, where his community service included participation as PTA president. In 1989 Bausch & Lomb transferred him to its Rochester office, and he and his family settled in the suburb of Fairport. In 1994, Assemblyman Koon was appointed to Rochester Mayor William Johnson's transition team on crime and violence, and he went on to become Co-Chair of the Task Force to Reduce Violence. He also helped to organize the Rochester Challenge Against Violence. In honor of their deceased daughter, David and his wife Suzanne created the Jennifer Patterson Koon Peacemaking Foundation through St John Fisher College, which awards scholarships for Peace Studies. He resides in Perinton.

IVAN C LAFAYETTE (D-WF)
34th - Queens County

33-46 92nd St, Ste 1W, Jackson Heights, NY 11372
718-457-0384/ lafayei@assembly.state.ny.us

Ivan Lafayette was elected to the New York State Assembly in 1976. He attended Brooklyn College and served in the US Army from 1952 to 1954. In the Assembly, he is Deputy Speaker, having previously served five years as Speaker Pro Tempore. In addition, he is the Dean of the Queens Delegation, the Assembly's former Majority Whip, and the former chair of the Committee on Standing Committees, Majority Steering Committee, and Consumer Affairs and Protection Committee. He has sponsored hundreds of bills that are now law, including the nationally acclaimed Truth in Testing Law for college applicants, the Uninsured Motorist Law, the Red Light Camera Law, and several laws on banking. His extensive community service includes being a founding member and Honorary President of the Jackson Heights/Elmhurst Kehillah and Trustee of the North Queens Homeowner and Civic Association. He also was responsible for the formation of the Air Services Committee for LaGuardia and Kennedy Airports under the Queens Office of the Economic Development Corporation. Assemblyman Lafayette resides in Jackson Heights.

RORY I LANCMAN (D)
25th - Part of Queens County

77-40 170th St., Fresh Meadows, NY 11366
718-820-0241/LancmanR@assembly.state.ny.us

Rory Lancman was first elected to the New York State Legislature in 2006. He graduated from CUNY's Queens College and Columbia Law School. Prior to his election to the Assembly, he served on Community Board 8 for more than 16 years where he chaired the Aging Committee and the Youth & Education Committee. He also chaired the Queens Hospital Community Center Advisory Board and led the community's successful fight to rebuild the hospital and prevent it from being privatized. Professionally, he has been an attorney in three law firms, including his own. His broad community service includes the vice presidency of the Flushing Heights Civic Association as well as volunteer coach for the Auburndale Soccer League. He also served in the New York Army National Guard Infantry, rising to the rank of First Lieutenant. He resides in Hillcrest.

GEORGE S LATIMER (D)
91st - Part of Westchester County

933 Mamaroneck Ave, Ste 102, Mamaroneck, NY 10534
914-777-3832/latimeg@assembly.state.ny.us

George Latimer was elected to the New York State Assembly in 2004. He holds a BA from Fordham University and a Master's in Public Administration from New York University's Wagner School. By profession, he is a marketing executive with over twenty years of experience working with major corporations that included Nestle, AT&T, ITT, IBM, and the former Shearson Lehman. His two decades of public service include a term on the Rye City Council (1988-1991) and seven terms as a Westchester County Legislator (1992-2004). From 1998 to 2001, he served as Chairman of the Westchester County Board of Legislators. He has received public recognition and awards from numerous Westchester and Hudson Valley organizations. He lives in Rye.

CHARLES D LAVINE (D)
13th - Part of Nassau County

70 Glen St., Suite 100, Glen Cove, NY 11542
516-676-0050/lavinec@assembly.state.ny.us

Charles D Lavine was elected to the New York State Assembly in 2004. He earned a BA in English Literature from the University of Wisconsin and a JD from New York Law School. His committee memberships include a seat on the Judiciary Committee, among oth-

BIOGRAPHIES / New York State Assembly

ers. Assemblyman Lavine retains his private legal practice in lower Manhattan, which he has operated since 1996, specializing in criminal defense work. From 1977 to 1995, he was a partner in a Forest Hills firm, Grossman, Lavine & Rinaldo. Early in his legal career, he was a staff attorney for the Legal Aid Society of New York. Active in his community, he has served as counsel for the Glen Cove Community Development Agency and the Industrial Development Agency, was appointed to the Glen Cove Planning Board, and also was selected to fill a vacancy on the Glen Cove City Council, a position to which he was subsequently elected. He also serves as an instructor at Cardozo Law School's Intensive Trial Advocacy Program. He resides in Glen Cove.

JOSEPH R LENTOL (D)
50th - Part of Kings County

619 Lorimer Street, Brooklyn, NY 11211
718-383-7474/ lentolj@assembly.state.ny.us

Joseph Lentol was first elected to the New York State Assembly in 1972. He holds a BA from the University of Dayton, and earned his JD from Baltimore University School of Law. Prior to being elected to the Assembly, he served as Kings County Assistant District Attorney. Assemblyman Lentol has chaired the Assembly's Committee on Codes since 1992, and also has chaired the Committee on Governmental Employees. In 2000 he was one of only two Assembly members chosen by the Assembly Speaker and Governor Pataki to participate in the Election Modernization Task Force, which investigated and analyzed operations and equipment used in recent elections. In 2001 he was elected by his colleagues to direct the Brooklyn Assembly Delegation, responsible for making decisions and advocating for funds and activities that benefit all areas of the borough. In the same year, he was appointed to the City's Community Action Board, and now serves as its chair. He has worked to preserve and enhance the waterfront in his North Brooklyn district, improve tenants' rights, deter crime, and revitalize commercial corridors. He is a lifelong resident of New York City.

BARBARA S LIFTON (D-WF)
125th - Cortland & Tompkins Counties

106 E Court St, Ithaca, NY 14850
607-277-8030/liftonb@assembly.state.ny.us

Barbara Lifton was first elected to the New York State Assembly in 2002. She received a BA degree from SUNY Geneseo with certification to teach Secondary English and an MA in English from the same institution. Currently, she chairs the Task Force on Women's Issues, along with her membership on several committees. She has been part of a 2007 effort to establish a proposed new commission to study aid to local governments. Prior to her election to the Assembly, she served as Chief of Staff to Assemblyman Marty Luster. She also was a public school teacher at Geneseo Central School and in Ithaca schools for many years. Her civic and professional activities include membership in the New York State United Teachers, the Ithaca Teachers Association, and the steering committee of the Tompkins County Nuclear Weapons Freeze Campaign. In addition, she co-founded the Coalition for Community Unity and worked with Justice for All, which fought Medicare and Social Security Cuts. She resides in Ithaca.

PETER D LOPEZ (R-C-I)
127th - Parts of Greene, Otsego, Delaware, Ulster, Columbia and Chenango Counties and all of Schoharie County

45 Five Mile Woods Rd., Ste 2, Catskill, NY 12414
518-943-1371

21 Liberty Street, Sidney, NY 13838
607-563-2929/lopezp@assembly.state.ny.us

Peter D. Lopez was first elected to the New York State Assembly in November 2006. He graduated from the State University College at Cobleskill and holds a Master's of Public Administration from the University at Albany. His extensive background in public service includes serving as Schoharie County Clerk. Prior to his election to the Assembly, he spent 21 years on the staff of the New York State Legislature, where his duties included service as Associate Director of the Senate Agriculture Committee, Assistant Director of the Legislative Commission on Rural Resources, and District Office Director for Assembly Minority Leader John J. Faso. He was also Executive Assistant to Senator John J. Bonacic. In his community, he has also been village trustee, town Councilman, and a member of the Schoharie County Board of Supervisors. His extensive volunteer service ranges from Red Cross water safety instructor to founding member of Habitat for Humanity of Schoharie County. He resides in the Village of Schoharie.

VITO J LOPEZ (D)
53rd - Part of Kings County

434 South Fifth St, Brooklyn, NY 11211
718-963-7029/ lopezv@assembly.state.ny.us

Vito Lopez was first elected to the New York State Assembly in 1984. He graduated from Long Island University with a BS in Business Administration and received his Master's degree in Social Work from Wurzweiler School of Social Work, Yeshiva University. Currently in the Assembly, he chairs the Housing Committee. He served as a part-time Adjunct Professor of Human Services at LaGuardia College and also as an Instructor at Molloy College, Empire State College, and Yeshiva University. Concerned about issues of aging, he founded the Ridgewood Bushwick Senior Center, City-Wide Advocates for Seniors, North Brooklyn Senior Citizens Coalition, and the Ridgewood Bushwick Senior Citizens Council. He has also established a community-based education program in Bushwick through Long Island University that gives district residents the chance to obtain an affordable college education. He helped establish Brooklyn Unidos, a leading advocacy group for Latinos within his district. Assemblyman Lopez was born and raised in Brooklyn.

DONNA LUPARDO (D)
126th - Part of Broome County

Binghamton State Office Building, 17th Fl, Binghamton, NY 13901
607-723-9047/lupardd@assembly.state.ny.us

Donna A Lupardo was elected to the New York State Assembly in 2004. She graduated from Wagner College and earned an MA n Philosophy at SUNY Binghamton. In the Assembly, she helped pass the Work Zone Safety Act and Yield-Right-Away legislation, which are designed to improve road safety. In addition, she introduced and passed the State Green Building Construction Act, which requires that new construction and substantial renovations undertaken by the state must comply with the United States Green Building Council

Leadership in Energy and Environmental Design Silver Rating Level. Prior to being elected to the Assembly, she was an adjunct lecturer at the university for ten years, as well as Director of Education for the Mental Health Association of the Southern Tier. She served on the Broome County Legislature from 1999 to 2000. She is the first woman to represent Broome County in the State Legislature, and resides in Endwell.

WILLIAM MAGEE (D)
111th - Madison County & parts of Oneida & Otsego Counties

214 Farrier Avenue, Oneida, NY 13421
315-361-4125, 607-432-1484/ mageew@assembly.state.ny.us

William Magee was elected to the New York State Assembly in 1990. He graduated from Cornell University with a degree in Agricultural Economics, and then became an auctioneer and small businessman in Madison County. Currently, he chairs the Assembly's Committee on Agriculture, a post he has held since 1999. Among his achievements, Assemblyman Magee sponsored and led the fight for approval of the Northeast Interstate Dairy Compact to provide a stable milk price for dairy farmers all over the state. In addition, he rallied support for the passage of the Farmland Viability Act, which provides assistance to farmers. Prior to his election to the Assembly, he was elected Supervisor for the Town of Nelson to the Madison County Board of Supervisors, where he served for nineteen years. From 1985 to 1990 he was also employed at the New York State Fair. He has served as a member of the SUNY Morrisville College Council and the Board of Directors of both the Community Memorial Hospital and the Crouse Community Center. He is a lifelong resident of Nelson.

WILLIAM B MAGNARELLI (D-WF)
120th - Part of Onondaga County

333 East Washington St, Rm 840,
Syracuse, NY 13202
315-428-9651/ magnarw@assembly.state.ny.us

William Magnarelli was first elected to the New York State Assembly in 1998. He received a BA from Syracuse University, and then received a JD degree from the Syracuse University Law School. Upon graduating, he entered the Army Reserves, retiring after six years with the rank of Captain. In the Assembly, he chairs the Legislative Commission on Science and Technology, and the Task Force on University-Industry Cooperation. In addition, he is vice chair of the Majority Conference, as well as a member of numerous standing committees. His concern for slower economic progress in Central New York than that found elsewhere in the state has led him to focus on generating jobs by securing funds for the major universities and high-tech companies in the region. In addition, in 2006, a bill he authored which would increase penalties for repeat drunk drivers who kill or injure others was passed into law. Prior to his election to the Assembly, Assemblyman Magnarelli was elected to the Syracuse Common Council and served as its Majority Leader. His community involvement includes serving on the board of the Arthritis Foundation and as president of Our Lady of Pompeii Church Parish Council. He is a lifelong resident of Syracuse.

ALAN MAISEL (D)
59th - Parts of Kings County

2424 Ralph Avenue, Brooklyn, NY 11234,
718-968-2770/maisela@assembly.state.ny.us

Alan Maisel was elected to the New York State Assembly in February 2006. He holds a BA in history from Long Island University, and an MA in Urban Studies from the same university. He also holds an Advanced Certificate of Administration and Supervision in Education from Brooklyn College. Assemblyman Maisel is a retired assistant school principal and teacher. He also served as Chief of Staff to his predecessor, Assemblyman Frank R Seddio, and as Administrative Assistant to Congressman Charles Schumer. He also served on the District 22 Community School Board and served two terms as its chairman. From 1979-1982, Assemblyman Maisel served as Assistant Director of the New York State Legislative Advisory Task Force on Reapportionment. His community service includes serving as Executive Vice President of the Brooklyn Staten Island Council of B'nai B'rith and Chairman of the New York City Anti-Defamation League - B'nai B'rith Coordinating Committee. He is a lifelong resident of Brooklyn.

MARGARET M MARKEY (D)
30th - Part of Queens County

55-19 69th St, Maspeth, NY 11378
718-651-3185/ markeym@assembly.state.ny.us

Margaret Markey was first elected to the New York State Assembly in 1998. She is a graduate of the Berkeley Business School of New York City. Currently, she chairs the Assembly's Committee on House Operations. She also has chaired the Subcommittee on Child Product Safety, and also is a member of the Legislative Women's College and president of the New York State American Irish Legislators Society. She began her civic involvement as a member of Community Board 2, and after new geographical lines were implemented she served on Community Board 5. In addition, she served as Assistant Director of Economic Development for former Queens Borough President Claire Shulman, then went on to become Director of Marketing & Tourism. Assemblywoman Markey is a member of the Maspeth Chapter of Kiwanis. She is a lifelong resident of Maspeth, where her family has lived for four generations.

NETTIE MAYERSOHN (D-L)
27th - Part of Queens County

159-06 71st Ave, Flushing, NY 11365
718-969-1508/mayersn@assembly.state.ny.us

Nettie Mayersohn was elected to the New York State Assembly in 1982. She received a BA degree from Queens College in 1978. Her committee memberships includes seats the Labor Committee and the Health Committee. Prior to her election to the Assembly, Ms Mayersohn was the Executive Director of the New York State Crime Victims Board; she was also Chairperson of the Pomonok Community Center and founded and helped organize the Pomonok Neighborhood Center, Inc. In the Assembly, she backed the Baby AIDS law, which requires that parents be notified when their newborns test positive for HIV, and she was prime sponsor of the HIV Partner Notification Law. She is a member of the Electchester Jewish Center and the Israel Center of Hillcrest Manor, and she is a member of the Board of Directors of the Harry Van Arsdale Jr Memorial Association. She has been a resident of the Electstchester Cooperative in Flushing, Queens, for more than forty-five years.

BIOGRAPHIES / New York State Assembly

ROY J McDONALD (R-I-C)
112th - Washington County and parts of Rensselaer & Saratoga Counties

383 Broadway, Rm 202, Fort Edward, NY 12828
518-747-7098 mcdonar@assembly.state.ny.us

Roy McDonald was elected to the New York State Assembly in 2002. He received his Bachelor's and Master's degrees from SUNY at Oneonta. He also served in the Vietnam War as an Artillery Forward Observer for the U.S. Army's First Cavalry Division. Currently, his committee memberships include the Ways & Means Committee, and the Racing & Wagering Committee. Prior to joining the Assembly, he served as the Town and County Supervisor of Wilton in Saratoga County. He is a member of numerous civic organizations including the Saratoga VFW, Saratoga/Wilton Elks, Vietnam Veterans of America, SUNY-Oneonta President's Advisory Committee, Saratoga Economic Development Corporation, and Saratoga County Chamber of Commerce. He is a native of the Lansingburgh section of Troy, New York.

DAVID G McDONOUGH (R-C-I)
19th - Part of Nassau County

3000 Hempstead Turnpike, Ste 110, Levittown, NY 11756
516-731-8830/McDonoD@assembly.state.ny.us

David G McDonough was elected to the New York State Assembly in 2002. He holds a BA in Economics from Columbia University, and he has served in the US Coast Guard and Air Force. His committee memberships include seats on the Banks Committee and as the Ranking Minority Member on the Consumer Affairs and Protection Committee. Assemblyman McDonough is past president of the Nassau County Council of Chambers of Commerce, a member of the Committee for the Merrick Downtown Revitalization Project, and four-term President for the Merrick Chamber of Commerce. In this role, his achievements included growing the membership ranks by 35 percent. In addition, he is a founding member and continuing board member of the Bellmore-Merrick Community Wellness Council and a member and past president of the Kiwanis Club of Merrick. He has served as Vice Chairman of the Assembly Minority Task force on Sex Crimes against Children and Women and a member of the Task Force on Successful Schools. He lives in Merrick.

JOHN J McENENY (D)
104th - Part of Albany County

Legislative Office Bldg, Rm 648, Albany, NY 12248
518-455-4178/ mcenenj@assembly.state.ny.us

John McEneny was first elected to the Assembly in 1992. He holds a BA in History from Siena College, and Certificates in Community Development and Public Administration from New Mexico State University School of Agriculture and the Kennedy School of Government at Harvard University. The former Albany County Historian has served as a member of the New York State Archives Partnership Trust, the Commission for the Restoration of the Capitol and the Albany Convention Center Authority. He chairs the Majority Steering Committee, and has authored numerous bills that have been signed into law including the Veterans' Bill of Rights. Prior to his election, served in the Peace Corps in Colombia, and he has been a social services caseworker, a counselor, and a director of the Albany County Neighborhood Youth Corps. From 1989 to 1991 he was Assistant Albany County Executive. In 1992 he was appointed Chief of Staff to State Assemblyman Richard J Connors, D-Albany, and was elected following Connor's decision not to seek re-election. He is active in many community organizations, and served as President of the New York State American-Irish Legislators Society. He resides in Albany.

TOM McKEVITT (R-C-I)
District 17

224 Seventh Street, Suite 200, Garden City, NY 11530;
516-739-5119/mckevit@assembly.state.ny.us

Tom McKevitt was elected to the New York State Assembly in a special election held Feb. 28, 2006. He holds a Bachelor's degree from Hofstra University and a JD from Hofstra Law School. In the Assembly, he serves as ranking minority member on the Committee on Mental Health, among other committee assignments. He served as Deputy Town Attorney in Hempstead for almost nine years. In addition, Assemblyman McKevitt has worked in the offices of state Senator Kemp Hannon and U.S. Senator Alfonse D'Amato. He is a member of the East Meadow Chamber of Commerce and the East Meadow Kiwanis Club. The Nassau County native resides in East Meadow.

JOEL M MILLER (R-I)
102nd - Part of Dutchess County

3 Neptune Road, Suite A19E, Poughkeepsie, NY 12601
845-463-1635/millerj@assembly.state.ny.us

Joel Miller was elected to the State Assembly in 1994. He earned a BS degree from the City College of New York and a DDS from Columbia University's School of Dental and Oral Surgery. His committee memberships include seats on the Education and Higher Education committees. He joined the military in 1963 and served on active duty in the US Air Force from 1967 to 1969, and remained in the Air Force reserve as a Captain until 1977. He is a Major in the New York State Guard. In 1969, Assemblyman Miller established a dental practice in the Town of Poughkeepsie. He has been a member of the Executive Committee of the Dutchess County Dental Society for many years, serving as Treasurer for five years and President for two years. Additionally, he served as President of the Mid-Hudson Dental Management and Marketing Corporation for five years and remains a member of its Executive Committee. He is a member and past president of the Harding Club, a philanthropic and social organization, as well as a member of the American Legion and several local chambers of commerce. He resides in the Town of Poughkeepsie.

JOAN L MILLMAN (D)
52nd - Part of Kings County

District Office: 341 Smith St, Brooklyn, NY 11231
718-246-4889/ millmaj@assembly.state.ny.us

Joan Millman was elected to the New York State Assembly in 1997. She holds a Bachelor's degree from Brooklyn College, a Master's degree in Library Science from Pratt Institute, and a Professional Diploma from Long Island University, Brooklyn Campus. Currently, Assemblywoman Millman chairs the Legislative Commission on Government Administration, and sits on several other Assembly committees. She has sponsored legislation to reform the Rockefeller Drug Laws, the Women's Health and Wellness Bill, and the Safe Weapon Storage Act. She was an early advocate for the creation of the Brooklyn Bridge Park and has worked to revitalize Brooklyn's entire waterfront. Assemblywoman Millman taught elementary school and served as school librarian at PS 10 in Brooklyn for many years, then became an educational consultant to New York City Council President Carol Bellamy and Senator Marty Connor. From 1995 to 1996, she was a member of the Citywide Advisory Committee on Middle School Initiatives. She is a Brooklyn native.

MARCUS MOLINARO (R-C-I)
103rd - Parts of Dutchess and Columbia Counties

7578 North Broadway, Suite 4, Red Hook NY 12571
845-758-9790

610 State Street, Hudson, NY 12534
518-822-8904/molinarom@assembly.state.ny.us

Marc Molinaro was first elected to the New York State Assembly in 2006. He graduated from Dutchess Community College and the PACE land Use law Center Community Leadership Alliance. Prior to being elected to the Assembly, Assemblyman Molinaro served as mayor of the Village of Tivoli for six terms, and served four terms of the Dutchess County Legislature. His achievements as mayor included computerizing village offices and repaving almost 75 percent of the community's roads. He was elected to the Tivoli Village Board of Trustees when he was only 18. His community service includes being an active member of the Tivoli Fire Department and Rescue Squad, as well as being a member of the Dutchess County Historical Greenway Conservation Council and other community organizations. He resides in Tivoli.

JOSEPH D MORELLE (D)
132nd - Part of Monroe County

1945 East Ridge Road, Rochester, NY 14622
585-467-0410/ morellj@assembly.state.ny.us

Joseph Morelle was elected to the Assembly in 1990. He received his Bachelor's degree from SUNY Geneseo. He is president and CEO of MMI Technologies, Inc, a software development company in Rochester. In the Assembly, he chairs the Committee on Tourism, Arts and Sports Development; previously he chaired the Subcommittee on Manufacturing. His focus on economic development has led to efforts such as creating the film production tax credit, which encourages motion picture companies to film in New York, as well as authoring a report detailing New York's decline as an economic power and offering prescriptions for change, entitled "Creating a State of Innovation: Unleashing the Power of New York's Entrepreneurial Economy." Prior to his election to the Assembly, he served in the Monroe County Legislature, including as its vice president and assistant majority leader. He lives in Irondequoit.

CATHERINE T NOLAN (D)
37th - Part of Queens County

45-25 47th Street, Woodside, NY 11377
718-784-3194/ nolanc@assembly.state.ny.us

61-08 Linden Street, Ridgewood, NY 11385
718-456-9492

Catherine Nolan was elected to the New York State Assembly in 1984. She graduated from New York University with a BA degree in Political Science. Currently, she chairs the Assembly's Committee on Education, and sits on several other committees including the powerful Ways & Means Committee. She is a member of the Assembly Majority Steering Committee. She also has chaired the Committee on Banks, focusing on enhancing consumer protections and maintaining a competitive balance among financial institutions. She also chaired the Committee on Labor and with her leadership the Assembly raised the minimum wage. Other assignments included representing the Assembly on the MTA Capital Program Review Board, and chairing the Assembly's Commission on State-Federal Relations. She lives in Ridgewood.

DANIEL J O'DONNELL (D)
69th - New York County

245 West 104th Street, New York, NY 10025;
212-866-3970/odonned@assembly.state.ny.us

Daniel J O'Donnell was first elected to the New York State Assembly in 2002. He holds a Bachelor of Arts degree in Public Affairs from George Washington University, and a JD from the City University of New York Law School. Currently in the Assembly, he chairs the Codes Committee's Subcommittee on Criminal Procedure, and sits on numerous other committees, including the powerful Judiciary Committee. He is a founding member of the New York City Chapter of Citizen Action and the Morningside Heights Historic District Committee. He formerly chaired the Community Board 9 Housing and Land Use Committee. Professionally, he was a staff attorney for the New York Legal Aid Society, then opened his own public interest law firm on Manhattan's Upper West Side, representing tenants and advocating on behalf of various civil rights cases. He resides in Morningside Heights.

THOMAS F O'MARA (R)
137th District - Chemung, Schuyler, part of Tioga

333 East Water Street, Suite 301, Elmira, NY 14901.
607-732-3500/omarat@assembly.state.ny.us

Thomas F O'Mara was first elected to the New York State Assembly in 2004. He holds a BA degree from the Catholic University of American and a JD from Syracuse University College of Law. The former Chemung County District Attorney also served as the Chemung County Attorney, Assistant District Attorney in both the New York County and Chemung County District Attorney's Office, and counsel to the Chemung County Industrial Development Agency. He is now a partner in the Elmira law firm of Davidson & O'Mara, P.C. He sits on numerous Assembly committees, including the powerful Judiciary Committee and the Banks Committee. Active in his community, he serves as Secretary to the board of St. Joseph's Hospital, trustee to the Horseheads Free Library, and a board member of the Wings of Eagles, formerly the National Warplane Museum. The Chemung County native lives in Horseheads.

ROBERT C OAKS (R-C)
128th - Wayne County and parts of Cayuga & Oswego Counties

10 Leach Rd, Lyons, NY 14489
315-946-5166; 800-767-6257/oaksr@assembly.state.ny.us

Robert Oaks was first elected to the New York State Assembly in 1992. He earned a Bachelor's degree in Political Science from Colgate University and a Master's degree in Recreation Administra-

BIOGRAPHIES / New York State Assembly

tion from the University of Montana. In the Assembly, he serves as Deputy Minority Leader and is Ranking Minority Member of the Committee on Ethics and Guidance. From 1983-1992, he served as Wayne County Clerk and during that time served as President of the New York State County Clerks Association. He is the owner and agent of the Robert C Oaks Insurance Agency, a third generation family-owned business. His extensive community involvement includes current service on the Board of Directors of the Finger Lakes Council Boy Scouts of America and the Wayne County Community Endowment Advisory Board. For nine years, he sat on the Wayne County United Way Board of Directors, and is the past President of the Wayne County Pre-Trial Services Board of Director. He's also a youth baseball and soccer coach, and lives in Macedon.

FELIX W ORTIZ (D)
51st - Part of Kings County

404 55th Street, Brooklyn, NY 11220
718-492-6334/ ortizf@assembly.state.ny.us

Felix Ortiz was elected to the New York State Assembly in 1994. He graduated from Boricua College in 1983 with a BS degree in Business Administration and received his Master's degree in Public Administration from New York University in 1986. Assemblyman Ortiz moved to the mainland U.S. from Puerto Rico in 1980, and joined the U.S. Army from 1986 to 1988 from which he was honorably discharged. Currently in the Assembly, he chairs the Committee on Veterans Affairs. Previously, he chaired the Subcommittee on Sweatshops, fighting to hold the industry accountable for labor violations and forcing employers to comply with labor laws and worker safety conditions. In 2000, he achieved passage of the nation's first law banning the use of handheld cell phones while driving a motor vehicle. His extensive service includes the presidency of the National Hispanic Caucus of State Legislators, Vice-President of COPA USA, Chair of the Labor and Workforce Committee of the National Conference of State Legislators (NCSL) and Executive Committee Board Member of the Council of State Governments (CSG). In addition, he serves as Parliamentarian for the Black, Puerto Rican, Hispanic & Asian Legislative Caucus. He resides in Brooklyn.

WILLIAM L PARMENT (D)
150th - Part of Chautauqua County

Hotel Jamestown Bldg, Rm 809, Jamestown, NY 14701
716-664-7773/parmentw@assembly.state.ny.us

William L Parment was first elected to the New York State Assembly in 1982. He graduated from Jamestown Community College, received an AAS degree from State University Agricultural and Technical College in Farmingdale, and a BS degree from SUNY New Paltz. Currently in the Assembly, he chairs the Committee on Standing Committees. His professional background includes working as a civil technician in the construction industry and as a facilities planner for the state university. For twelve years, he was employed by Chautauqua County, first as a planner, then as Deputy Director of Planning and Development. For six years, he was employed as Director of Public Works. Assemblyman Parment is a sixth-generation Chatauqua County native who lives in Jamestown.

AMY R PAULIN (D)
88th - Part of Westchester County

700 White Plains Road, Suite 252, Scarsdale, NY 10583
914-723-1115/paulina@assembly.state.ny.us

Amy Paulin was first elected to the New York State Assembly in 2000. She earned her B.A. from SUNY Albany, and a Master's degree in Criminal Justice from the same institution. Currently in the Assembly, she chairs the Libraries & Education Technology Committee. Prior to joining the Assembly, she served as Executive Director of My Sisters' Place, a comprehensive agency in White Plains working to end domestic violence, which has informed some of her efforts in the Assembly. For instance, Assemblywoman Paulin's legislation has increased the duration of orders of protection, or assured confidentiality of home addresses in civil proceedings. Prior to her election to the Assembly, she served for four years (1995-1999) as a Scarsdale village trustee, founder and former chair of the Westchester Women's Agenda and vice president of the League of Women Voters of New York State, where she was in charge of the League's issue advocacy. She lives in Scarsdale.

CRYSTAL D PEOPLES (D)
141st - Part of Erie County

792 E Delavan Ave, Buffalo, NY 14215
716-897-9714/peoplec@assembly.state.ny.us

Crystal Davis Peoples was first elected to the New York State Assembly in 2002. She received a Bachelor of Science in Elementary Education and Master's degree in Student Personnel Administration from Buffalo State College. In the Assembly, she chairs the Subcommittee on Oversight of Minority of Women-Owned Business Enterprises. Prior to her election, she was the 7th District Erie County Legislator from 1993 to 2002; she was Majority Leader and Chairperson of the Legislature's Finance Committee for five of the nine years she was in office. She sponsored public education campaigns that addressed social ills, housing and economic development; she also played an integral role in the inter-governmental economic development collaboration that brought a food market to an area where over 113,000 people had no immediate access to fresh meats, fruits, or vegetables. She serves as 2nd Vice Chairperson of the Black, Puerto Rican, Hispanic & Asian Legislative Caucus. She is a lifelong resident of Buffalo.

JOSE R PERALTA (D-WF)
39th - Part of Queens County

82-11 37th Ave, Jackson Heights, NY 11372
718-458-5367/ peraltj@assembly.state.ny.us

Jose Peralta was first elected to the New York State Assembly in 2002. He graduated from Queens College, where he was the first Latino Student Body President and also represented over 200,000 students within the CUNY system as a member of the University Student Senate. In the Assembly, he chairs the Subcommittee on Banking in Underserved Communities of the Committee on Banks. Before his election to the Assembly, he served as a community liaison for Assemblyman Brian McLaughlin. He was subsequently Director of the Commission on the Dignity for Immigrants at the New York City Labor Council, representing over 1.5 million union members. The Commission is a partnership between the labor unions and the Archdiocese of New York. He is a member of the Dominican American Society, the Gran Alliance of Queens, the Dominican American Hispanic Congress, Community Board 3, and the Inter-American Political and Civic Parliament. He resides in Queens.

BIOGRAPHIES / New York State Assembly

N NICKOLAS PERRY (D)
58th - Part of Kings County

903 Utica Avenue, Brooklyn, NY 11203
718-385-3336/ perryn@assembly.state.ny.us

N Nick Perry was elected to the New York State Assembly in 1992, and currently serves as the Majority Whip. Born in Jamaica, he moved to the United States in 1971. Drafted into the US Army in 1972, he was on active duty for two years and on inactive reserve until 1978 when he was honorably discharged. He earned a BA in political science and an MA in Public Policy and Administration from Brooklyn College. Prior to his election to the Assembly, he worked as a volunteer in several political campaigns, and in 1983 he was appointed a member of Community Board 17. He was unsuccessful in two bids for District Leader, but he served during this period as a member of the Executive Board of the 67th Police Precinct Community Council and as a director of the Flatbush East Community Development Corp. In 1988 he was elected Chairman of Community Board #17. In the Assembly, he has served as Vice-chair of the Assembly Majority Conference. He is a life member of Disabled American Veterans, and a former member of the Board of Directors of Nazareth Regional High School, and of the Caribbean Action Lobby. He is 1st Vice Chair of the Task Force on Black, Puerto Rican, Hispanic & Asian Legislative Caucus, among his other committee assignments. He resides in Brooklyn.

AUDREY I PHEFFER (D)
23rd - Part of Queens County

90-16 Rockaway Beach Blvd., Rockaway Beach, NY 11693
718-945-9550

108-14 Crossbay Blvd, Ozone Park, NY 11417
718-641-8755/Pheffea@assembly.state.ny.us

90-16 Rockaway Beach Blvd, Rockaway Beach, NY 11693
718-945-9550

Audrey Pheffer was first elected to the New York State Assembly in 1987. She graduated from Queens College of the City University of New York. In the Assembly, she chairs the Committee on Consumer Affairs and Protection, and is past chair of the Election Law Committee. Her community involvement spans four decades. In the early 1960s, she joined the Association for the Help of Retarded Children. She went on to work at the worked at the Rockaway Occupational Training Center where she advocated for special education and job placement for the mentally disabled. In 1977 she joined the New York City Commission on Human Rights-Neighborhood Stabilization Program and became Acting Director of the Far Rockaway Office. She has served as Special Assistant to New York City Council President Andrew Stein and Executive Assistant to State Senator Jeremy S Weinstein. She resides in Queens.

ADAM CLAYTON POWELL, IV (D)
68th - Part of New York County

87 East 116th Street, New York, NY 10029
212-828-3953/powella@assembly.state.ny.us

Adam Clayton Powell IV was first elected to the New York State Assembly in 2000. Born in Puerto Rico, he graduated from Howard University and earned a law degree from the Fordham University School of Law. In the Assembly, he chairs the Subcommittee on Insurer Investments and Market Practices in Underserved Areas. He is a member of the Task Force on Black, Puerto Rican, Hispanic & Asian Legislative Caucus. He is the author of the Senior Citizen Rent Increase Exemption, which exempts seniors from any rent increases if their income is under $24,000 per year and more than thirty percent of that goes to rent. From 1992 to 1997, he served on the New York City Council representing East Harlem and parts of the Upper West Side and South Bronx. He has served as Assistant District Attorney in the Bronx. He is bi-cultural and bi-lingual and uses his African American and Latino heritages to bring further parity to those communities. His civic involvement includes membership in the National Black Leadership Commission on AIDS and the Harlem Chapter of the American Red Cross. He resides in Manhattan.

JAMES GARY PRETLOW (D)
87th - Part of Westchester County

48 North Broadway, Yonkers, NY 10701
914-375-0456

6 Gramatan Ave, Mount Vernon, NY 10550
914-667-0127/ pretloj@assembly.state.ny.us

J Gary Pretlow was elected to the New York State Assembly in 1992. He earned a BA degree in Business Administration from Baruch College in 1972, and he is a licensed stockbroker and insurance agent. In the Assembly, he chairs the Committee on Racing and Wagering. Before entering politics, he was the Manager of Accounting for Bloomingdales Department Store, Assistant Controller of The Limited, and in 1985 started a partnership, Moncur-Pretlow & Company, a financial-planning and management-consulting firm. He served on the Mount Vernon City Council where he chaired the Finance and Planning Committee and Capital Projects Board. He is a member of the Association of Black & Puerto Rican Legislators and the New York State Senate and Assembly Hispanic Task Force. He resides in Mount Vernon.

JACK QUINN (R-C-I)
146th - Part of Erie County

3812 South Park Ave, Blasdell, NY 14219
716-826-1878/quinnj@assembly.state.ny.us

Jack Quinn was elected to the State Assembly in 2004. He earned a BA from Siena College and a JD from University at the Buffalo Law School. He is a former prosecutor in the Erie County District Attorney's office, where he served as Assistant District Attorney. He also served with the New York State Office of Science, Technology, and Academic Research. In the assembly, his committee assignments include service on the powerful Judiciary Committee. Active within his community, Assemblyman Quinn is a member of the St. Francis High School Alumni Association, the University at Buffalo Law School Alumni Association, and Ducks Unlimited. The lifelong resident of Erie County currently resides in Hamburg.

ANN G RABBITT (R-C-I)
97th - Parts of Orange and Rockland Counties

41 High St, Goshen, NY 10924
845-291-3631/rabbita@assembly.state.ny.us

Annie G Rabbitt was elected to the New York State Assembly in 2004. A third-generation woman business owner, Assemblywoman

BIOGRAPHIES / New York State Assembly

Rabbitt owns O'Hare's Pub in Greenwood Lake and is the past President of the Greenwood Lake Chamber of Commerce. In the Assembly, she serves as Ranking Minority Member of the Local Government Committee, and is a member of the American-Irish Legislators Society. Prior to her election, she served as a village trustee and deputy mayor of Greenwood Lake, and as a councilwoman and deputy supervisor for the town of Warwick where she was responsible for supervising maintenance of 103 square miles of infrastructure. She also organized a homeowners association for Greenwood Lake, became its president, and successfully lobbied to establish a bi-state commission to fund and regulate the cleanup of the lake. She's even organized the first-ever regatta held on the lake as a member of the East Arm Rowing Club. Assemblywoman Rabbitt resides in Greenwood Lake.

ANDREW P RAIA (R-I-C-WF)
9th - Part of Suffolk County

75 Woodbine Ave, Northport, NY 11768
631-261-4151/ raiaa@assembly.state.ny.us

Andrew P Raia was first elected to the New York State Assembly in 2002. He received a BA in Political Science from SUNY at New Paltz. His committee assignments include a seat on the Banks Committee, where he is Ranking Minority Member. Formerly, he was the ranking member on the Aging Committee. Assemblyman Raia spent 12 year as a staff member to legislative offices in the New York State Assembly and its Senate, as well as the Suffolk County Legislature. He serves on the Executive Boards of the Huntington Boys and Girls Club, the Huntington Freedom Day Care Center, the Huntington Station Enrichment Center, and Perspectives on Youth. He is also a member of both the Huntington and the East Northport Chambers of Commerce. He resides in East Northport.

PHILIP R RAMOS (D-WF)
6th - Part of Suffolk County

1010 Suffolk Ave, Brentwood, NY 11717
631-435-3214/ ramosp@assembly.state.ny.us

Phil Ramos was first elected to the New York State Assembly in 2002. In the Assembly, Assemblyman Ramos chairs the Subcommittee on Volunteer Emergency Services. He began his working career as a therapy aide and Emergency Medical Technician, and then joined the Suffolk County Police Department where he retired after twenty years. During his two decades in law enforcement, Assemblyman Ramos worked undercover in the Narcotics Unit for eight years, then went on to become a detective. He was elected president of the Suffolk County Police Hispanic Society in 1993. He also worked with the Long Island Guardians to create a mentoring program for Latino police officers to serve as role models for Latino and African American children. Ramos was born in the Bronx.

WILLIAM REILICH (R-C-I)
134th - Part of Monroe County

2737 W Ridge Rd, Rochester, NY 14626
585-225-4190/ reilicw@assembly.state.ny.us

Bill Reilich was first elected to the New York State Assembly in 2002. His committee memberships include seats on the Aging Committee, Banks Committee, and Small Business Committee. A businessman, he is the former owner of the Reilich Corporation, which he founded in 1975 as Upstate Alarm. Prior to joining the Assembly, he served in his community as a member of the Greece Zoning Board and the Monroe County Planning Board. In addition, he was a member of the Greece Chamber of Commerce and a Captain of the Marine Volunteer Fire Department. From 1997 to 2002, he was a Monroe County Legislator, serving as Chairman of the Ways and Means Committee and as Vice Chairman of the Intergovernmental Relations Committee. He lives with his family in Greece, New York.

ROBERT P REILLY (D-I-WF)
109th - Parts of Albany and Suffolk Counties

5 Halfmoon Executive Park Dr, Clifton Park, NY 12065
518-371-0568/reillyr@assembly.state.ny.us

Robert P Reilly was elected to the New York State Assembly in 2004. He received his BA from the University of Notre Dame and his MA from the College of Saint Rose; he completed all coursework for a PhD at Rensselaer Polytechnic Institute. His numerous committee assignments include seats on the Agriculture Committee and the Education Committee. He is chairman and CEO of Technofuture Enterprises Inc and 30-year owner of the Partridge Pub. He has taught in both public and private schools and also taught a stint in East Africa. He also served as director of the NYS Public Broadcasting Office for the State Education Department. A devoted runner, he was a cross country track coach at Siena College for seventeen years. Before election to the State Assembly, he was an Albany County Legislator, where he was the major force behind adoption of a new County Charter. He also initiated and chaired the OTB Committee, which eventually led to needed OTB reform. He has been president of the Shaker Heritage Society, and he has been a member of the National Erie Canal Commission, the Mohawk Valley Heritage Corridor Commission, Albany County Alternatives to Incarceration, and the Region 4 Fish and Wildlife Management Board. He resides in Latham.

JOSE RIVERA (D)
78th - Part of Bronx County

2488 Grand Concourse, Room 416, Bronx, NY 10458
718-933-2204/riveraj@assembly.state.ny.us

Jose Rivera was first elected to the New York State Assembly in 1982, where he served for five years. He then left office and was re-elected in 2000. Born in La Perla, Puerto Rico, Assemblyman Rivera was educated in the public schools of New York. In the Assembly, he chairs the Task Force on Food, Farm and Nutrition Policy, where he focuses on addressing issues such as food assistance for struggling working families and seniors, and sits on several other committees as well as the Task Force on Black, Puerto Rican, Hispanic & Asian Legislative Caucus. He has devoted his life to helping the people of the Bronx in their struggle for jobs, better housing and social justice. The longtime member of the Carpenters' Union founded the United Tremont Trades in 1975 and defended the Medallion Taxicab Industry and the "Bodegueros" of New York. During his first term in the Assembly, he was Treasurer, Vice Chair and Chairman of the Black and Puerto Rican Caucus. He was instrumental in helping to establish the Martin Luther King holiday in the state of New York. In 1987 he became a Council Member for the 15th District in the Bronx, where he was also President of the Black and Latino Caucus of the City Council and Chairman of the Council's Civil Service and Labor Committee and State and Federal Legislation Committee. His daughter is Assemblywoman Naomi Rivera.

BIOGRAPHIES / New York State Assembly

NAOMI RIVERA (D)
80th - Part of Bronx County

1126 Pelham Parkway South, Bronx, NY 10461
718-409-0109/RiveraN@assembly.state.ny.us

Naomi Rivera was elected to the New York State Assembly in 2004. Her committee memberships include seats on the Children & Families Committee and the Cities Committee. She also sits on the executive board of the Puerto Rican/Hispanic Task Force. Prior to her election to the Assembly, she worked for ten years as an accountant to large multinational corporations such as Sumitomo. As Director of Special Events for the Bronx Borough President's Office, she developed new events such as the Bronx Food and Art Festival and the Puerto Rican Film Festival. In addition, she produced the borough's annual ethnic pride celebrations. More recently, Assemblywoman Rivera served as the Deputy Chief Clerk of the Bronx Board of Elections. She is the co-chair of the Bronx Domestic Violence and creator of "DiVA" (Domestic Violence Awareness), a campaign designed to maximize community outreach through special events. She also served as Founder and Executive Director of the Children's Traveling Theater Project. She resides in the Pelham Parkway section of the Bronx.

PETER M RIVERA (D)
76th - Part of Bronx County

1973 Westchester Avenue, Bronx, NY 10462
718-931-2620/ riverap@assembly.state.ny.us

Peter Rivera was elected to the New York State Assembly in 1992. Born in Ponce, Puerto Rico, he migrated to New York City at an early age. He earned a BA in Business Administration from Pace College and a JD degree from St John's Law School. In the Assembly, he chairs the Mental Health Committee, as well as the Puerto Rican/Hispanic Task Force. In his role as chair of the mental health committee, he convened the Mental Hygiene Work Group to reorganize the state's mental health system. He formerly chaired the Cities Committee, as well as the Real Property Taxation Committee. Assemblyman Rivera's career in public service began in the late 1960s when he became a police officer in the South Bronx. He went on to become a detective, then became a federal agent with the DEA. Upon graduating from law school, he joined the Bronx District Attorney's Office, working as an Assistant District Attorney in the Homicide Bureau. Since 1978 he has practiced law privately. Assemblyman Rivera has served on the Mayor's Committee on City Marshals, the Gateway National Recreation Area Commission, the Spanish Progress Foundation, El Comite de la Providencia, the Governor's Committee on the Judiciary, and the Board of Directors of OTB.

ANNETTE M ROBINSON (D)
56th - Part of Kings County

1360 Fulton Street, Rm 417, Brooklyn, NY 11216
718-399-7630

Annette M Robinson was elected to the New York State Assembly in 2002. She received both her BS and Master's degrees from New Hampshire College. In the Assembly, she chairs the Subcommittee on Retention of Homeownership and Stabilization of Affordable Housing. She has long been involved in public service, having been elected to the first of three terms to the District 16 Community School Board in 1977, and then she was elected to the New York City Council in 1991. She is a District leader/State Committeewoman in the 56th A.D., has served as coordinator and liaison for former New York City Comptroller Harrison J. Goldin, and has been District Director for U.S. Congressman Major R. Owens. In the Assembly, she is also a member of the Black, Puerto Rican, Hispanic & Asian Legislative Caucus. She was born in Harlem and raised in Brooklyn.

LINDA B ROSENTHAL (D)
67th - Part of New York County

230 West 72nd Street, Suite 2F, New York, NY 10023
212-873-6368/RosentL@assembly.state.ny.us

Linda B Rosenthal was first elected to the New York State Assembly on Feb. 28, 2006. She holds a BA from the University of Rochester. Prior to her election to the Assembly, she served as Manhattan District Director and Director of Special Projects for U.S. Congressman Jerrold Nadler, focusing on issues that help to provide a livable community, promote tenant rights and affordable housing, and securing funding for major cultural institutions such as the Museum of Natural History and Jazz at Lincoln Center. She sits on numerous Assembly committees, including the committees on energy and housing.

JOSEPH S SALADINO (R)
12th - Part of Nassau County

200 Boundary Avenue, Massapequa, NY 11758
516-844-0635/saladij@assembly.state.ny.us

Assemblyman Joseph Saladino was elected in a special election held in March 2004. He studied at Tulane University and holds undergraduate and Master's degrees from New York Institute of Technology. Prior to his election to the Assembly, he had served as Director of Operations for the Town of Oyster Bay and Executive Assistant for the Town of Hempstead. Previously he had a career in broadcast journalism, working as a news anchor and broadcaster for some of Long Island's largest television and radio stations. He has been a member of the Massapequa Kiwanis Club for 16 years, where he has served as President. He is also a member of the Sons of Italy-Columbus Lodge, a former trustee of the Massapequa Historical Society, and co-founder of the Massapequa Anti-Graffiti Involvement Committee. In the Assembly, his committee assignments include service on the Environmental Conservation committee, reflecting one of his major interests. He is a lifelong resident of Massapequa.

TERESA R SAYWARD (R-I-C)
113th - Hamilton & Warren Counties, most of Essex County & part of Saratoga County

7559 Court St, Rm 203, PO Box 217, Elizabethtown, NY 12932
518-873-3803

21 Bay St, Ste 206, Glens Falls, NY 12801
518-792-4546/ saywart@assembly.state.ny.us

Teresa R Sayward was first elected to the New York State Assembly in 2002. In the Assembly, her committee memberships include seats on the Children and Families Committee and the Environmental Conservation Commission, where she is Ranking Minority Member. Prior to her election, she served as Town Supervisor in Willsboro for 11 years. In addition, she spent 11 years on the Board of Supervisors for Essex County, two as chair. Assemblywoman Sayward also

BIOGRAPHIES / New York State Assembly

served as chairwoman of the Inter-Governmental Affairs Committee at the New York State Association of Counties, the North County Advisory Council for the New York State Division for Women, and the Essex County Board of Supervisors' Legislative Committee. In the latter role she served as the lobbyist in Albany for Essex County. She also chaired Willsboro's Zoning Board of Appeals. Assemblywoman Sayward and her family owned and operated a large dairy farm in Willsboro for 20 years, and she also has held a New York state Realtor's License. Her extensive community involvement also includes serving as director on the Adirondack Association of Towns and Villages, director of the Plattsburgh North County Regional Chamber of Commerce, membership on the Board of Directors of the Smith House Health Care Center, and as a member on the Board of Directors for Cornell Cooperative Extension. She is a member of the Corporation of the Champlain Valley Physicians Hospital Medical Center and sits on the Board of Directors of the Willsboro Development Corporation. Ms Sayward was born in Willsboro and is a lifelong resident of the Adirondack North Country.

WILLIAM D SCARBOROUGH (D - WF)
29th - Part of Queens County

129-32 Merrick Blvd, Jamaica, NY 11434
718-723-5412 / scarbow@assembly.state.ny.us

William Scarborough was first elected to the New York State Assembly in 1994. He holds a BA degree in Psychology and Political Science from Queens College of the City University of New York. In the Assembly, he serves as chair of the Children & Families Committee, reflecting his focus on health care, education, and youth services. In the Assembly, Assemblyman Scarborough has focused his efforts in the areas of health care, education, and youth services. In addition, he serves as 2nd Vice Chair of the Black, Puerto Rican, Hispanic & Asian Legislative Caucus. Prior to his election to the Assembly, he was District Manager of Community Board 12, and during that time served as the Chairman of the Board's Human Services Cabinet. Assemblyman Scarborough also has been Chairman of Area Policy Board 12, and a member of Community School Board 28. In that post, he shared responsibility for over twenty-two elementary and middle schools with a budget of approximately $30 million. He was raised in Jamaica, Queens, and has since lived in St Albans and Rosedale.

MICHELLE SCHIMEL (D)
16th - Parts of Nassau

11 Middle Neck Rd., Suite 200, Great Neck, NY 1121
516-482-6966

Michelle Schimel was first elected to the New York State Assembly in a special election held March 27, 2007. She graduated from the University of Pennsylvania. Prior to her election to the Assembly, she served eight years as North Hempstead Town Clerk, where her numerous accomplishments included appointment by the state's Education Department to serve on the Local Government Records Advisory Council, which sets guidelines for municipalities regarding the security and accessibility of vital identity documents, as well as service on the New York State "Cyber-Security Panel" to review Internet policies for local governments throughout the state. She serves on the board of New Yorkers Against Gun Violence. She resides in Great Neck.

ROBIN L SCHIMMINGER (D-I-C)
140th - Parts of Erie & Niagara Counties

3514 Delaware Ave, Kenmore, NY 14217
716-873-2540/ schimmr@assembly.state.ny.us

Robin Schimminger was elected to the New York State Assembly in 1976. He earned a BA degree from Canisius College in Buffalo and also studied at Ireland's William Butler Yeats International School of Literature and the University College, Dublin. He received his JD degree from New York University Law School. In the Assembly, he chairs the Economic Development, Job Creation, Commerce and Industry Committee, a post he has held since 1997. His other committee assignments include the codes, health, and ways and means committees. Among his numerous legislative accomplishments is his Omnibus Procurement Act, which maximizes the opportunity for in-state firms to do business with New York State. He chairs the Western New York Delegation and is one of two Assembly representatives on the Council of State Governments. Prior to his election to the Assembly, he was twice elected to the Erie County Legislature, in 1973 and 1975. There, he chaired the Public Health Commission. He has served on the boards of numerous civic, community, educational, and cultural organizations. He is a co-founder of the Buffalo Dortmund Sister City Committee and is on the Board of Directors of Junior of Western New York. He resides in Kenmore.

MARK J F SCHROEDER (D)
145th - Part of Erie County

2019 Seneca Street, Buffalo, NY 14210
716-826-0152/schroem@assembly.state.ny.us

Mark Schroeder was elected to the New York State Assembly in 2004. He holds a Bachelor's Degree from Empire State College. In the Assembly, his committee memberships include seats on the Insurance Committee and the Veterans Affairs Committee. Prior to joining the Assembly, he served for three years on the Erie County Legislature, during which time he amassed a number of accomplishments. He started the South Buffalo Education Center, which offers free GED and computer classes. He also started The Greater South Buffalo Chamber of Commerce, and spearheaded the Seneca Street Redevelopment Project, a multi-million dollar project. He grew up and still lives in South Buffalo.

DIERDRE K SCOZZAFAVA (R)
122nd - Lewis County and parts of Jefferson, Oswego & St Lawrence Counties

93 East Main St, Gouverneur, NY 13642
315-287-2384/ scozzad@assembly.state.ny.us

Dierdre "Dede" Scozzafava was first elected to the New York State Assembly in 1998. She holds a BS degree from Boston University School of Management and a Master's in Business Administration from Clarkson Graduate School of Management. She is an investment adviser for RBC Dain Rausher Inc in Watertown, New York. Prior to her election to the Assembly, Ms Scozzafava served as a Village of Gouverneur Trustee for four years and as Mayor of the Village of Gouverneur from 1993 until her election to the Assembly. As Mayor, she carried the town budget from a deficit to a positive fund balance while also creating the Gouverneur Area Microenterprise Revolving Loan Fund to stimulate local job growth. In the Assembly, her committee assignments include membership of the powerful Ways & Means Committee, and the Codes Committee.

BIOGRAPHIES / New York State Assembly

She served on the Task Force on Education Standards and the Nursing Shortage Task Force. She is also an active member of the First United Methodist Church, a member of the Gouverneur BusinessWomen and an associate member of the Gouverneur Arts Club. Assemblywoman Scozzafava residents in Gouverneur.

ANTHONY S SEMINERIO (D-C)
38th - Part of Queens County

107-05 Jamaica Ave, Richmond Hill, NY 11418
718-847-0770

68-28 Myrtle Ave, Glendale, NY 11385
718-366-6725/ /seminea@assembly.state.ny.us

Anthony Seminerio was elected to the New York State Assembly in 1978. He holds a BS degree from the New York State Institute of Technology. In the Assembly, he chairs the Majority Program Committee in addition to his committee memberships. Prior to his election to the Assembly, he served as a corrections officer in the New York City Corrections System, and was elected to serve as a union executive board member for the Corrections Officers Benevolent Association. He handled grievance procedures, liaison duties, and collective bargaining negotiations for members of the Department of Correction with the City of New York. He was also a Founder and Treasurer of the New York State Peace Officers Association. He is involved in the Holy Name Society of Our Lady of Perpetual Help, the Boy Scouts, the Columbia Association of the Department of Corrections, and the New York State PTA. He resides in South Ozone Park.

SHELDON SILVER (D)
64th - Part of New York County

250 Broadway, Suite 2307, New York, NY 10007
212-312-1420/speaker@assembly.state.ny.us

Sheldon Silver was elected to the New York State Assembly in 1976. He holds a BA from Yeshiva University and his JD from Brooklyn Law School. In 1994, after climbing through the ranks of leadership, he assumed the Assembly's top leadership post, Speaker of the New York State Assembly. In this position, he works on behalf of the majority conference to reaffirm the Assembly's role as guardian of New York's middle class and working families. He chairs the powerful Rules Committee. He has made education the hallmark of his tenure. Through his comprehensive education initiative called LADDER, (Learning, Achieving, Developing By Directing Educational Resources), New York State has established the nation's first pre-kindergarten program for all four-year olds. The program has also targeted resources at reducing class size and making necessary school infrastructure repairs. Speaker Silver also staved off efforts to end rent control, and successfully fought for passage of the Clinic Access and Anti-Stalking Act, which ensures access to women's reproductive services and cracks down on violence against clinic workers. He achieved the enactment of a permanent cost-of-living adjustment for current and future retirees in all public retirement systems, and saw the enactment of the Bias Crime Law, which combats violence associated with hatred, bigotry and prejudice. Prior to his election to the Assembly, he was in private law practice and served as Law Secretary to Civil Court Judge Francis N Pecora. The Speaker's public service career has been marked by numerous awards and honors. He resides on Manhattan's Lower East Side.

MIKE SPANO (R - I - C)
93rd - Part of Westchester

35 East Grassy Sprain Rd, 4th Fl, Yonkers, NY 10710
914-779-8805/SpanoM@assembly.state.ny.us

Mike Spano was first elected to the New York State Assembly in 1992, where he saw his seat eliminated that same year due to the state's reapportionment plan. In 1994 he ran again, serving over a decade before deciding not to run for reelection to the Assembly. In 2006, he was once again elected to office. He attended Manhattan College. His professional service includes work at a governmental relations firm and service on the Board of Directors for the Leake and Watts Children's Services. His prior Assembly service has included being a lead advocate on behalf of the passage of New York's Megan's Law. He is a member of numerous community organizations. He resides in the Colonial Heights section of Yonkers.

ALBERT A STIRPE, JR (D)
121st - Part of Onondaga

5720 South Bay Rd., Cicero, NY 13039
315-452-1115/StirpeA@assembly.state.ny.us

Al Stirpe was first elected to the New York State Assembly in November 2006. He graduated from the University of Notre Dame with a degree in economics. Assemblyman Stirpe's career as an entrepreneur in the electronics field began when he was a financial analyst with General Electric in Syracuse, and subsequently, with four partners, spun off GE's Electronic Camera Operation to form CIT Technologies. He was the company's CFO until the owners sold the company in 1994. Stirpe then launched Qube Softward Inc., where, as president, he took the company from a start-up business to a multi-million dollar organization. His community involvement includes serving on the Board of Directors for Familycapped, a non-profit organization made up of parents of children with multiple disabilities that was formed to expand programs for handicapped children in Central New York. He resides in North Syracuse.

ROBERT K SWEENEY (D)
11th - Part of Suffolk County

270-B N Wellwood Ave, Lindenhurst, NY 11757-3708
631-957-2087/sweeney@assembly.state.ny.us

Robert Sweeney was elected to the New York State Assembly in 1988. A graduate of Adelphi University, he earned his Master's degree in Public Administration at CW Post. In the Assembly, he chairs the Committee on Environmental Conservation. Previously, he chaired the Local Governments Committee. Prior to his election to the Assembly, Assemblyman Sweeney served as Lindenhurst Village Clerk for fourteen years, during which time he received his designation as a Certified Municipal Clerk (CMC). He is also a former president of the New York State Association of City and Village Clerks. In the Assembly, he has been actively involved in health care, authoring legislation dealing with health insurance and care for diabetes. He sponsored boating safety legislation and worked to expand the law on drug-free school zones to include day care centers, Pre-K, and kindergarten. He has served on the Board of Directors of the Literacy Volunteers of America, Suffolk County; as a member of the advisory board of Children and Parents Together, Family Service League of Suffolk County; and on numerous other organizations. He is a lifelong resident of Babylon Town.

BIOGRAPHIES / New York State Assembly

JAMES N TEDISCO (R-I-C)
110th - Parts of Schenectady and Saratoga Counties

12 Jay Street, Schenectady, NY 12305
518-370-2812/ tediscj@assembly.state.ny.us

James Tedisco was elected to the New York State Assembly in 1982. He received a Master's degree in Special Education from the College of St Rose following his undergraduate studies in Psychology at Union College. In the Assembly, he serves as Minority Leader, a post to which he was unanimously elected in November 2005. Prior to his election to the Assembly, he worked in education as guidance counselor, varsity basketball coach and athletic director at Notre Dame-Bishop Gibbons High School in Schenectady, and as special education teacher, resource room instructor and varsity basketball coach at Bethlehem Central High School in Delmar. He also served as a Schenectady City Councilman from 1977 to 1982. Elected at the age of 27, he was, at the time, the youngest City Councilman in Schenectady's history. In the Assembly, he has worked on behalf of families and children, serving as Ranking Minority Member of the Children and Families Committee, chairing the Assembly Minority Task Force on Missing children, and, in 1996, authoring "Missing Children: A psychological approach to understanding the causes and consequences of stranger and non-stranger abduction of children." He is a member of the Sons of Italy Schenectady Lodge 321, the Ballston Spa NY Elks Lodge No 2619, the Schenectady Rotary Club, Schenectady Big Brothers/Big Sisters, and Friends of the Schenectady Museum. He lives in Schenectady.

FRED W THIELE, JR (R-I-WF)
2nd - Part of Suffolk County

2302 Main Street, Box 3062, Bridgehampton, NY 11932
631-537-2583/thielef@assembly.state.ny.us

Fred Thiele was elected to the New York State Assembly in 1995. He attended Cornell University and in 1976 received a BA degree in Political Science and History from Southampton College of Long Island University. In 1979 he received his law degree from Albany Law School. Prior to his election to the Assembly, he served as a counsel to former Assemblyman John L Behan, as Southampton Town Attorney, and as East Hampton town Planning Board attorney. He was elected to the Suffolk County Legislature in 1987. As a freshman legislator, he was appointed chairman of the County Legislature's Public Works and Transportation Committee. He went on to become Southampton Town Supervisor. He serves on the Assembly's Environmental Conservation, Education, and Ways and Means committees. Among his achievements has been his backing of the legislation he drafted that created the Peconic Bay Community Preservation Fund Act, responsible for generating more than $80 million for land preservation. He lives in Sag Harbor, New York.

MATTHEW TITONE (D)
61st - Part of Richmond County

853 Forest Avenue, Staten Island, NY 10310
718-442-9932

Mathew Titone was first elected to the New York State Assembly during a special election held March 27, 2007. He holds a law degree from St. John's University School. His law career includes working as senior trial associate and managing the labor law litigation department for the Wall Street firm of Morgan, Melhuish, Monahan, Arvidson, Abrutyn & Lisowski, and left the firm in 1998 to open his own practice. He has provided pro bono services for many years. He serves on the Board of Directors of Community Health Action of Staten Island - formerly known as the Staten Island AIDS Task Force - and has also served on the Board of Trustees for Legal Services of New York. He also sits on the Board of Trustees for the Snug Harbor Cultural Center, and currently chairs the Merger Committee overseeing the merger of the cultural center with the Staten Island Botanical Garden.

MICHELE R TITUS (D)
31st - Part of Queens County

19-31 Mott Avenue, Rm 301, Far Rockaway, NY 11691
718-327-1845/titusm@state.ny.us

Michele Titus was elected to the New York State Assembly in 2002. She received a Bachelor of Arts degree in Political Science from SUNY Binghamton, and a law degree from Albany Law School. Prior to her election, she served as Chief of Staff for NY State Senator Ada L Smith, and then served as the Executive Director of the New York State Black and Puerto Rican Legislative Caucus. She was an attorney for the New York City Board of Education, where she specialized in special education law. Other legal experience includes the Consumer Frauds Bureau of the NYS Attorney General's office and the Integrity Bureau at the Queens County District Attorney's office. In the Assembly, she chairs the Subcommittee on Foster Care and the Task Force on People with Disabilities, among other committee assignments including the powerful Judiciary Committee. She is a member of the New York State Black and Puerto Rican Legislative Caucus, the Women's Legislative Caucus, the New York State Puerto Rican/Hispanic Task Force, the Council of Black Elected Officials, and the New York State Trial Lawyers Association. She is a lifelong resident of Queens.

LOU TOBACCO (R)
62nd - Parts of Richmond

4345 Hylan Blvd, Staten Island, NY 10312
718-967-5194/tobaccol@assembly.state.ny.us

Lou Tobacco was first elected to the New York State Assembly in a special election held March 27, 2007. He holds a Bachelor of Arts degree from SUNY-Albany. He has served as an intern for Guy V Molinari when he was both Borough President and a Congressman. Assemblyman Tobacco has also served at Borough Hall as Assistant Director of Contract Oversight. He has been president of the Tottenville Civic Association and is active in the Staten Island Chamber of Commerce where he and his wife operate a small business. Formerly, he worked for Pfizer Inc as a senior professional healthcare representative. He resides in Tottenville.

PAUL D TONKO (D)
105th - Montgomery County & part of Schenectady County

Guy Park Manor, 366 West Main Street, Amsterdam, NY 12010
518-843-0227 tonkop@assembly.state.ny.us

Paul Tonko was first elected to the New York State Assembly in 1983. He attended Clarkson University and graduated with a BS degree in Mechanical and Industrial Engineering. He worked as an engineer for the New York State Dept. of Transportation, as well as on the staff of the Dept. of Public Service, prior to being elected to the Assembly. He was elected to the Montgomery County Board of Supervisors in 1975, and served as chair in 1981. In the Assembly, he has gained expertise on utility issues and is the author of comprehensive energy legislation that deregulates the electric industry in New York State. Since 1992 he has served as Chairman of the Assembly Committee on Energy. Active in civic affairs, Assemblyman Tonko is a member of the Knights of Columbus Council 209, the BPOE Lodge 101, Kiwanis Club of Amsterdam, the Montgomery County Chamber of Commerce, and Wildwood Programs. He also serves on the Board of Directors for Hispanic Outreach Services, the Horace J Inman Senior Citizens Center, the Montgomery Red Cross, and the Montgomery County Unit of the American Cancer Society. He is a lifelong resident of the city of Amsterdam.

DARRYL C TOWNS (D)
54th - Part of Kings County

840 Jamaica Avenue, Brooklyn, NY 11208
718-235-5627/townsd@assembly.state.ny.us

Darryl Towns was elected to the New York State Assembly in 1992. He is a 1990 graduate of North Carolina Agricultural & Technical State University with a degree in Economics, and served in the U.S. Air Force. In the Assembly, he chairs the NYS Black, Puerto Rican, Hispanic & Asian Legislative Caucus, as well as the Banks Committee. He spearheaded efforts to create the Bushwick Neighborhood Based Alliance, a coalition to improve local social and economic conditions. His ANCHOR Program bill, which was unanimously supported in both houses of the Legislature, is aimed at bolstering commercial revitalization in residential communities throughout New York City and supporting increased housing developments. Assemblyman Towns, soon of longtime U.S. Congressman Ed Towns, is a member of the National Black Caucus for State Legislators and the New York State Black, Puerto Rican & Hispanic Legislative Caucus. Prior to his election to the Assembly, he was Director of Community Affairs at Interfaith Hospital. Born and raised in his district, Assemblyman Towns resides in Brooklyn.

DAVID R TOWNSEND, JR (R-I-C-WF)
115th - Parts of Oneida & Oswego Counties

4767 State Rte 233, PO Box 597, Westmoreland, NY 13490
315-853-7260/townsed@assembly.state.ny.us

David Townsend was first elected to the New York State Assembly in November 1990. The Minority Whip, his committee assignments include seats on the Codes Committee and the Labor Committee. Prior to his election to the Assembly, he has a career in law enforcement. In 1966 he joined the Rome Police Department, and the following year, was appointed to the New York State Police. In January 1979 he was appointed to the Oneida County Sheriff's Department. Between January 1982 and April 1989, he worked as an undercover narcotics agent and was assigned to the Federal Drug Enforcement Administration Task Force in Syracuse in 1987. During this time he was elected president of the Oneida County Deputy Sheriffs Benevolent Association and president of the New York State Deputy's Association. . He resides in the Town of Kirkland.

ROBERT WALKER (R-C-I)
15th - Parts of Nassau County

111 Levittown Parkway, Hicksville, NY 11801
516-937-3571/walkerr2@assembly.state.ny.us

Rob Walker was first elected to the New York State Assembly on May 24, 2005. He holds a BA degree in education from Long Island University. His committee seats in the Assembly include the Aging Committee and the Energy Committee. Prior to his election, he served as deputy commissioner of parks for the town of Oyster Bay and spearheaded the town's Save Environmental Assets Fund Committee. Before that, he served three years as assistant to Oyster Bay Town Supervisor John Venditto, where he was director of traffic survey and constituent services. He also taught in the Syosset Central School District. In the community, Assemblyman Walker has volunteered with the Hicksville Football Association, the Hicksville Athletic Booster Club and the Hicksville Youth Council. A member of the Knights of Columbus, he resides in Hicksville.

HELENE E WEINSTEIN (D)
41st - Part of Kings County

3520 Nostrand Avenue, Brooklyn, NY 11229
718-648-4700/ weinsth@assembly.state.ny.us

Helene Weinstein was first elected to the New York State Assembly in 1980. She holds a Bachelor's degree in Economics from American University and a law degree from the New England School of Law. In the Assembly, she chairs the Judiciary Committee, the first woman in the state's history to be appointed to the post. The prestigious committee presides over virtually all legislation affecting the state's judicial system and civil practice in the courts. She is also a member of the Court Facilities Capital Review Board. Previously, she chaired the Committees on Governmental Employees and Election Law, and acted as the state's leading advocate for women and children as Chair of the Assembly Task Force on Women's Issues for seven years. She sponsored New York's landmark Family Protection and Domestic Violence Intervention Act, as well as the Child Support Standards Act, which established statewide guidelines to ensure that children receive fair and adequate support. She is a member of numerous organizations including the Leadership Council of NYC Chapter of the NYS Alzheimer's Association, the New York State Labor Commissioner's Task Force on Displaced Homemakers, the Brooklyn Women's Political Caucus, the Holocaust Survivors Association - The Next Generation, and the Jewish Women's Leadership Caucus. She resides in Brooklyn.

HARVEY WEISENBERG (D)
20th - Part of Nassau County

20 West Park Ave, Long Beach, NY 11561
516-431-0500/ weisenh@assembly.state.ny.us

Harvey Weisenberg was elected to the New York State Assembly in 1989. He graduated from New York University with a BS degree, and received an MS degree from Hofstra University. He also has a Professional Diploma in Administration from CW Post University. A former police officer in Long Beach, Assemblyman Weisenberg then entered the education field and worked for more than 20 years as a teacher and an administrator. He was elected to the Long Beach City Council in 1976, and served as president of that body in 1977 and 1980. In the Assembly, he has championed the needs of the disabled, and he is a staunch supporter of anti-drug programs. He chaired the Committee on Alcoholism and Drug Abuse until January of 2001, when Speaker Sheldon Silver appointed him to the post of Deputy Majority Whip. In 2003 he was appointed Assistant Speaker Pro Tempore, a position he still holds. He is active in the Lions Club, Kiwanis, the Long Beach Chamber of Commerce, the Nassau

BIOGRAPHIES / New York State Senate

County Juvenile Diabetes Foundation, Long Beach Hospital, Long Beach Breast Cancer Coalition, the American Legion, the Association for Help of Retarded Children, the Long Island Arthritis Foundation, the Alliance for the Mentally Ill, the March of Dimes, and the US Lifeguard Association. He lives in Long Beach.

MARK S WEPRIN (D)
24th - Part of Queens County

56-21 Marathon Parkway, Little Neck, NY 11362
718-428-7900/weprinm@assembly.state.ny.us

Mark Weprin was first elected to the New York State Assembly in March 1994 to fill the seat left vacant by the death of his father, Assembly Speaker Saul Weprin. He holds a BA from SUNY-Albany and his JD from Brooklyn Law School. Between college and law school, he was a public relations and marketing executive, then legislative representative in the office of former Mayor Edward Prior to his election, he was an associate with the law firm of Shea and Gould in their Labor and Employment Law Department. In the Assembly he chairs the Committee on Small Business, has chaired the Ethics and Guidance Committee, and co-chaired the Joint Senate/Assembly Legislative Ethics Committee. He is active on many issues within the community, including helping the autistic community by working with the United States Tennis Association to initiate a program of tennis instruction for autistic children. He resides in Queens.

KEITH L T WRIGHT (D)
70th - Part of New York County

163 W 125th St, Ste 911, Adam Clayton Powell Jr Bldg, New York, NY 10027
212-866-5809/wrightk@assembly.state.ny.us

Keith Wright was first elected to the Assembly in 1992. He graduated from Tufts University, where he received a Bachelor's degree, then earned a JD from Rutgers University. He chairs the Social Services Committee, formerly chaired the Election Law Committee and is a member of the Task Force on Black, Puerto Rican, Hispanic & Asian Legislative Caucus. He previously served as Assistant Majority Whip. Among other assignments, he has been on the S Task Force on Criminal Justice Reform, advocated for criminal justice reform; he introduced legislation to prevent "no knock" search warrants, which became part of the Community Relations Policing Package. As chair of the Harlem Community Development Corporation, he leveraged limited resources to create economic development in Harlem. Prior to his election to the Assembly, he held positions in the NYC Human Resources Administration (HRA), the Manhattan Borough President's Office and the New York City Transit Authority. Assemblyman Wright lives in Harlem.

ELLEN YOUNG (D)
22nd - Part of Queens County

29-07 Prince Street, Ste 5D, Flushing, NY 11354
718-939-0195/YoungE@assembly.state.ny.us

Ellen Young was first elected to the New York State Assembly in 2006. She is an immigrant from Taiwan who came to the U.S. with limited resources and has become a successful businesswoman. She co-founded the Chinese-American Women's Association and was the first female Asian Auxiliary Police Officer in Queens. She has served as a District leader to the 22nd Assembly District, District Administrator to Councilman John Liu, and board member to the Queens Borough President's Advisory Committee and other community and civic organizations. She is the first Asian-American woman elected to a state office.

KENNETH ZEBROWSKI (D)
94th - Rockland County

67 North Main Street, New City, NY 10956
845-634-9791/zebrowk@assembly.state.ny.us

Ken Zebrowski was first elected to the New York State Assembly on May 1, 2007 during a special election held to fill the seat of his late father, Assemblyman Kenneth P Zebrowski. He holds a B.A. in political science from SUNY Albany, and his J.D. from Seaton Hall University School of Law. In the Assembly, he holds a seat on the Judiciary Committee. Assemblyman Zebrowki served in the Rockland County Legislature in 2005, advocating on behalf of reduced property taxes and planning efforts aimed at limiting overdevelopment. He is a partner in the law firm of Zebrowski & Zebrowski, which he founded with his father, and is active in community groups including Rockland County Big Bothers-Big Sisters. He is a native of New City.

New York State Senate

ERIC L ADAMS (D)
20th - Part of King County

572 Flatbush Ave., Brooklyn, NY 11225
718-282-3585/eadams@senate.state.ny.us

Eric Adams was first elected to the New York State Senate in 2006. A graduate of New York City Technical College, John Jay College of Criminal Justice, Senator Adams received his Master's degree in Public Administration from Marist College. Prior to his election to the Senate, he served 22 years in the New York City Police Department. As a police captain, he created programs on issues ranging from conflict resolution to child abuse prevention, and worked with hundreds of community groups and civic organizations to assist with a wide range of issues. He co-founded 100 Blacks in Law Enforcement Who Care, which provides funding and grants to community-based organization. In addition, he formerly chaired the Grand Council for the Guardians, serves on the board of the Eastern District Counseling service which assists substance abusers. His expansive law enforcement background will now serve the Senate. Senator Adams is the Ranking Minority Member of the Crime Victims, Crime and Correction Committee, as well as the Veterans, Homeland Security & Military Affairs Committee. He resides in Prospect Heights.

JAMES S ALESI (R-I-C)
55th - Part of Monroe County and portions of the City of Rochester

220 Packett's Landing, Fairport, NY 14450
585-223-1800/ alesi@senate.state.ny.us

BIOGRAPHIES / New York State Senate

James S Alesi was first elected to the New York State Senate in 1996. A graduate of St John Fisher College in Rochester, Senator Alesi owns and operates Allstate Commercial Laundries, Inc, which operates in upstate New York. Prior to his election to the Senate, he served in the Monroe County Legislature from 1989 to 1992 then in the State Assembly from 1992 to 1996. In the Assembly, he was elected President of his class of freshman legislators. Currently, he chairs the Senate's Commerce, Economic Development and Small Business committee, as he has for the last eight years. Jobs creation and investing in education are only two issues on behalf of which he advocates in efforts to reform New York's business climate. Senator Alesi is active in numerous local community organizations, and has served on the Board of Directors of Big Brothers-Big Sisters, Mercy Flight, and Rochester Italian Charities. He is a lifelong resident of East Rochester.

JOHN J BONACIC (R-I-C)
42nd - Delaware, Sullivan and parts of Orange and Ulster Counties

279 Main Street, Suite 202, New Paltz, New York, NY 12561
845-255-9656/bonacic@senate.state.ny.us

111 Main Street, Delhi, NY 13753
(607) 746-6675

John Bonacic was first elected to the New York State Senate in 1998. He received his BA in Economics from Iona College, and his Doctorate of Law from Fordham University School of Law. Prior to his election to the Senate, he served seventeen years as an Orange County Legislator. In addition, he served as Assistant District Attorney for Orange County. In 1990 he was elected to the New York State Assembly, where he served until his election to the Senate. Currently, Senator Bonacic chairs the Senate's Housing, Construction and Community Development Committee, where he has sponsored legislation to all for the creation of thousands of new housing opportunities across the state. In addition, he sits on several other key committees. Senator Bonacic lives in the Town of Mount Hope in Orange County, New York.

NEIL D BRESLIN (D)
46th - Albany County

Room 414 State Capitol Bldg, Albany, NY 12247
518-455-2225/ breslin@senate.state.ny.us

Neil Breslin was first elected to the New York State Senate in 1996. The Albany native graduated from Fordham University in 1964 with a BS degree in Political Science. He received his JD from the University of Toledo in Toledo, Ohio. He has been an associate or partner in law firms, and currently is of counsel to the firm of Girvin and Ferlazzo. In the Senate, he currently serves as the Insurance Committee's Ranking Minority Member. In addition, he is a member of the National Conference of Insurance Legislators (NCOIL), where he serves on its Executive Committee and formerly chaired the State/Federal Relations Committee. His civic involvement includes serving for many years on the Board of Arbor House, a women's residence facility, including seven years as its president. In addition, he has been the attorney for St Anne's Institute in Albany. He also is active within the New York State Bar Association. He is a lifelong resident of Albany.

JOSEPH L BRUNO (R-I)
43rd - Rensselaer County and part of Saratoga County

368 Broadway, Saratoga Springs, NY 12866
518-583-1001/bruno@senate.state.ny.us

Senate Majority Leader Joseph L Bruno was first elected to the Senate in 1976. He holds a BA degree in Business Administration from Skidmore College and served in the Korean conflict as an infantry sergeant. In 1966 Majority Leader Bruno served on the campaign staff of Governor Nelson Rockefeller, and from 1969 to 1974 he served as Special Assistant to Speaker of the Assembly Perry B Duryea. Senator Bruno was elected Temporary President of the New York State Senate in January, 1995 and re-elected to that position in 1997, 1999, 2001, 2003, 2005, and 2007. In this capacity, he serves as Chairman of the Rules Committee and as an ex officio member of all of the Senate's standing committees and statutory commissions. Economic development has been a legislative priority, and Senator Bruno has helped lead efforts to cut state taxes. The result over his terms as Majority Leader have been more than $126 billion in cumulative tax savings and almost 800,000 new private sector jobs created. His legislative reforms also include the creation of joint legislative conference committees that have successfully resolved a range of issues. He resides in Brunswick.

MARTIN CONNOR (D-WF)
25th - Parts of Kings and New York Counties

250 Broadway, Suite 2011, New York, NY 10007
212-298-5565/ connor@senate.state.ny.us

Martin Connor was first elected to the Senate in 1978. He holds both a BA in Politics and a law degree from Catholic University of America in Washington, DC. Between 1970 and 1974, Senator Connor was associated with the large Wall Street law firm White & Case, where he practiced corporate and anti-trust litigation. In 1974 he joined the office of the General Counsel of Xerox Corporation, where he practiced antitrust law. In 1977 he left private practice upon his appointment as Assistant Counsel to the State Comptroller, a post he resigned upon his election to the Senate. Formerly the Senate Minority Leader for eight years, Senator Connor is the Ranking Minority Member of the Senate's standing Banks Committee. He resides in Brooklyn Heights.

JOHN A DeFRANCISCO (R-I-C-WF)
50th - Most of Onondaga County

800 State Office Bldg, 333 East Washington St, Syracuse, NY 13202
315-428-7632/jdefranc@senate.state.ny.us

John A DeFrancisco was elected to the New York State Senate in 1992. The lifetime Syracuse resident graduated with a BS degree from Syracuse University's College of Engineering and received his JD degree from Duke University in Durham, NC. Senator DeFrancisco worked in the law firm of Simpson, Thatcher and Bartlett in New York City before serving as a Judge Advocate in the United States Air Force from 1972 to 1975. He served as Assistant District Attorney in Onondaga County from 1975 until 1977, since which time he has practiced with the DeFrancisco Law Firm in Syracuse. Prior to his election to the Senate, he served eleven years on the Syracuse Common Council. Currently, he chairs the Senate's Standing Committee on Judiciary. In that position, he has advocated for reform in the way candidates for New York State Supreme Court Justice are nominated, as well as how town and village courts can be

BIOGRAPHIES / New York State Senate

improved. In addition, he is the Deputy Majority Leader for Intergovernmental Affairs. He resides in Syracuse.

RUBIN DIAZ, SR (D)
32nd - Part of Bronx County

1733 E. 172nd Street, Bronx, NY 10472
718-991-3161/ diaz@senate.state.ny.us

Rubin Diaz Sr was first elected to the New York State Senate in 2002. Prior to his election, he served the previous year on the New York City Council representing the 18th District in the Bronx. In the Senate, he currently serves as the Ranking Minority Member of the Committee on Aging. Born in Bayamon, Puerto Rico, he served in the US Army before moving to New York City in 1965. He received a BA degree from Herbert H Lehman College in 1976 and a Theological degree from The Damascus Bible Institute. In 1978, he became an ordained Minister of the Church of God. He founded and until recently has served as the Executive Director for the Christian Community Benevolent Association Inc, and he is also founder and pastor of the Christian Community Neighborhood Church. One of his children is Assemblyman Ruben Diaz, Jr.

MARTIN M DILAN (D-WF)
17th - Part of Kings County

786 Knickerbocker Ave, Brooklyn, NY 11207
718-573-1726/dilan@senate.state.ny.us

Martin M Dilan was first elected to the New York State Senate in November 2002. He is a graduate of Brooklyn College, where he participated in the Special Baccalaureate Degree Program. Currently, he chairs the Minority Conference, having been appointed Assistant Minority Leader of Conference Operations as a freshman. In addition, he is Ranking Minority member of the Elections Committee. Prior to his election to the Senate, he was a member of the New York City Council for ten years. He also served as a member of Community School Board #32 for fourteen years, seven as the Chair. He served as a Legislative Assistant for the US House of Representatives, as a Democratic District Leader, and as a Democratic State Committeeman.

THOMAS K DUANE (D-WF)
29th - Part of New York County

322 8th Avenue, Ste 1700, New York, NY 10001
212-633-8052/ duane@senate.state.ny.us

Thomas Duane was first elected to the New York State Senate in 1998. He was the Senate's first openly gay and HIV-positive member. He earned a Bachelor's degree from in Urban Studies and American Studies from Lehigh University. Prior to his election to the Senate, Senator Duane served seven years in the New York City Council. He currently serves as Assistant Minority Leader for Policy and Administration, as well as Ranking Minority Member of the Investigations and Government Operations Committee. During the 2006 legislature, he led the fight for passage of "Timothy's Law," which is comprehensive legislation that requires health insurance companies to provide mental health parity, thereby allowing those suffering from mental health illness to receive comprehensive coverage and treatment. In 2002, he advocated for passage of the Sexual Orientation Non-Discrimination Act (SONDA), which was signed into law. The lifetime New Yorker has lived in Chelsea since 1976, and served four terms as Male Democratic District Leader in the 64th Assembly District starting in 1982. In addition, he served seven years on his local community board.

HUGH T FARLEY (R-I-C)
44th - Schenectady, Montgomery and Fulton Counties, and part of Saratoga County

2430 Riverfront Center, Amsterdam, NY 12010
518-843-2188/farley@senate.state.ny.us

Senator Farley was elected to the New York State Senate in 1976 and was chosen Majority Whip in 1995. He holds a BS degree from the University of Albany, and also graduated from Mohawk Valley Community College. He received his JD degree from the American University Law School in Washington, DC. Senator Farley served in the US Army in Germany and has been a high school teacher. In 1965 he was appointed to the faculty of the State University at Albany's School of Business, where he became Full Professor, Law Area Coordinator, and in 2000 was named Professor Emeritus of Business Law. He is the author of continuing education texts in Business Law. First elected to public office in 1970, Senator Farley originally served as a Councilman and, later, Majority Leader in the Town of Niskayuna. He currently chairs the Senate Committee on Banks. In addition, he chairs the Senate Select Committee on Interstate Cooperation, as well as the Subcommittee on Libraries. The former Majority Whip, Senator Farley currently holds the Majority Conference leadership position of Chair of Senate Majority Program Development, in recognition of his expertise in legislative reform and modernization. He resides in Schenectady.

JOHN J FLANAGAN (R-I-C)
2nd - Part of Suffolk County

260 Middle Country Rd, Ste 203, Smithtown, NY 11787
631-361-2154/flanagan@senate.state.ny.us

John J Flanagan was first elected to the New York State Senate in 2002. Senator Flanagan received a BA in Economics from the College of William and Mary in Williamsburg, Virginia, and a law degree from Touro Law School in Huntington. He is Chairman of the Senate Corporations, Authorities and Commissions Committee. His Senate accomplishments including working with advocates to create legislation protecting stalking victims and their families, and efforts to expand public access to the New York State Sex Offenders Registry. Prior to his election to the Senate, Senator Flanagan - whose father, the late John Flanagan served in the New York State Assembly from 1972 to 1986 - himself served in the Assembly. There, he served as Ranking Minority Member of the Ways and Means Committee. He lives in East Northport, New York.

CHARLES J FUSCHILLO, JR (R-I-C)
8th - Part of Nassau and Suffolk Counties

30 South Ocean Avenue, Room 305, Freeport, NY 11520
516-546-4100/fuschill@senate.state.ny.us

Charles J Fuschillo, Jr, was first elected to the New York State Senate in 1998. Senator Fuschillo received his Bachelor's of Business Administration from Adelphi University. Currently, Senator Fuschillo chairs the Senate's Consumer Protection Committee. In that position, he has focused on sponsoring legislation to protect people's privacy. For instance, he is the author of the state's

Telemarketer "Do Not Call" Registry, as well as a law requiring business and government to notify consumers when security breaches compromise their personal information. Among other laws he has authored, Senator Fuschillo wrote the law to amend the New York State Clean Indoor Air Act to protect workers from secondhand smoke. Senator Fuschillo is active in his community, and serves on the board of directors and is a member of organizations including Kiwanis, the Community Wellness Council, Italian Americans in Government, and Order Sons of Italy in America.

MARTIN J GOLDEN (R-I-C)
22nd - Part of Kings County

7403 5th Avenue, Brooklyn, NY 11209
718-238-6044/golden@senate.state.ny.us

Martin J Golden was first elected to the New York Senate in November 2002. He attended John Jay College and St John's University, where he received an Associate's degree. In the Senate, he chairs the Aging Committee, where he has worked on issues such as assisted living, Senior Bill of Rights, and long-term care reform. Prior to his election, he served on the New York City Council representing the 43rd Council District. He is a former New York City police officer who retired after suffering a serious on-the-job injury. That professional background has helped him strengthen the Megan's law sex offender registry and expand the DNA databank to include all persons convicted of a felony and certain misdemeanors, back laws to increase penalties against gun-runners and people who injure or kill police officers, and to write the law mandating prison for the possession of a single loaded illegal firearm. He resides in Brooklyn.

EFRAIN GONZALEZ, JR (D)
33rd - Part of Bronx County

1780 Grand Concourse, 1st Floor, Bronx, NY 10457
718-299-7905/ gonzalez@senate.state.ny.us

Efrain Gonzalez was elected to the New York State Senate in 1989. At the age of 20, Senator Gonzalez was elected Union Representative for the Transport Worker's Union; he later served as Union Representative for Local 820 of the International Brotherhood of Teamsters. He is now Chairman of the New York State Senate Democratic Task Force on International Trade Development as well as the New York/Cuban Economic Development Task Force. In these roles, he has explored and engaged the untapped Caribbean and Latin American marketplaces. In addition, he sponsored key legislation that resulted in the creation of the Office of Minority Health to address people with AIDS or other health issues that predominantly impact low-income and minority residents. In addition, he sponsored the Security Guard Act, ensuring the accountability of personnel practices in the industry. Senator Gonzalez is founding member and of the National Hispanic Caucus of State Legislators (NHCSL), was born in Coamo, Puerto Rico and has lived in the Bronx since he was an infant.

JOSEPH A GRIFFO (R-C)
47th - Lewis and parts of Oneida and St. Lawrence Counties

207 Genesee St, State Office Building, Utica, NY 13501
315-793-9072/griffo@senate.state.ny.us

Joseph A. Griffo was elected to the New York State Senate in fall 2006. He holds a B.A. in Political Science from the State University of New York at Brockport. Currently in the Senate, he chairs the Elections Committee, and sits on numerous others. Prior to his election, Senator Griffo held key public service positions including Oneida County executive for over three years. In that position, his achievements included a key role in boosting the local economy by over 600 jobs by taking the principal role in efforts to protect U.S. Dept. of Defense-related jobs at the nearby Griffis Business and Technology Park. In his role as executive, he served on the Board of Directors of the New York State Association of Counties. Senator Griffo also served for 11 years as Mayor of Rome, NY, his hometown. Earlier, he also has served as an Oneida County legislator, director of community relations for the City of Rome, and as an administrative assistant to mayor. He resides in Rome.

KEMP HANNON (R-I-C)
6th - Part of Nassau County

224 Seventh St, 2nd Fl, Garden City, NY 11530
516-739-1700/hannon@senate.state.ny.us

Kemp Hannon was first elected to the New York State Senate in November 1989. He graduated from Boston College and holds a JD degree from Fordham Law School. In the Senate, he currently serves as Assistant Majority Whip, Chair of the Senate Committee on Health, and Chair of the Health Budget Subcommittee. His interest in health care has led him to various positions with the National Conference of State Legislators, including Chair of its Health Committee. He has been deeply involved with the New York State Health Care Reform Act, which improved all aspects of health care delivery and financing. During his Senate tenure, he has served as Chairman of the Committee for Housing and Community Development, among other key assignments. Prior to his Senate service, he was Minority Leader Pro Tempore in the Assembly. He lives in Garden City, New York.

RUTH HASSELL-THOMPSON (D-I-WF)
36th - Parts of Bronx and Westchester Counties

767 East Gunhill Road, Bronx, NY 10467
718-547-8854/hassellt@senate.state.ny.us

Ruth Hassell-Thompson was first elected to the New York State Senate in 2000. She is an alumna of Bronx Community College. Prior to her Senate service, Senator Hassell-Thompson was elected to the Mount Vernon City Council in 1993, where she served as both Council President and Acting Mayor. She currently serves as Ranking Minority Member of the Senate Judiciary Committee. Prior to her election, she was CEO of Whart Development Company, Inc, a real estate development company. She is also retired nurse and counselor at Mount Vernon Hospital for 35 years, specializing in pediatrics and helping women with substance abuse issues. She has served as President and CEO of The Gathering, a volunteer-staffed women's center in Mount Vernon that provides counseling and support services. Senator Hassell-Thompson was also a health educator for the Mount Vernon Neighborhood Health Center's health initiative working with persons affected by HIV/AIDS.

SHIRLEY L HUNTLEY (D)
10th - Part of Queens County

116-43 Sutphin Blvd, Jamaica, NY 11412
718-322-2537/shuntley@senate.state.ny.us

BIOGRAPHIES / New York State Senate

Shirley L. Huntley was first elected to the New York State Senate in 2006. The proud mother and grandmother has served many years as a community activist, including as a member of Community School Board 28, the president of Community School Board 27, the Community Education Council for District 28, and as that council's president. She and her husband operate a maintenance company called Huntley Enterprises, and the new senator intends to focus on health care, education and youth services. She currently serves as Ranking Minority Member of the Mental Health and Developmental Disabilities Committee, and as a member of the Education; Higher Education, and Transportation committees. She resides in Jamaica.

CRAIG M JOHNSON (D-W)
7th - Part of Nassau County

151 Herricks Rd., Ste 202, Garden City, NY 11040
516-746-5923/Johnson@senate.state.ny.us

Craig M Johnson was first elected to the New York State Senate in a special election in 2007. An attorney, he is Of Counsel to the law firm of Jaspan Schlesinger Hoffman LLP in Garden City. In the Senate, he is Ranking Member of the Environmental Conservation Committee, and is committed to ensuring that the state's air, land, and water remain clean for future generations. His priorities also include fighting for property tax relief for Nassau County's overtaxed homeowners. His other committee assignments include seats on the Senate Local Government, Ethics, and Environmental Conservation committees. Prior to being elected to the Senate, he served four terms in the Nassau County Legislature. There, as the youngest-ever chairman of the Finance Committee, he oversaw a $2.2 billion budget and was part of the team that brought Nassau's finances back from the brink of bankruptcy. Among his other achievements, he worked with local civic and environmental groups to pass a $50 million environmental bond initiative and authored a county law designed to protect Nassau County consumers by requiring all tax preparers to disclose all fees and charges for refund anticipation loans. Newsday's editorial board praised the law for its protection of Nassau County's working poor. He resides in Port Washington.

OWEN H JOHNSON (R-C)
4th - Part of Suffolk County

23-24 Argyle Square, Babylon, NY 11702
631-669-9200/ojohnson@senate.state.ny.us

Owen Johnson was first elected to the New York State Senate in 1972. Senator Johnson graduated from Hofstra University in 1956 with a BA degree in History-Political Science after being honorably discharged from service with the US Marine Corps. Since 2003, he has served as Chairman of the Senate Finance Committee. In this powerful position, Senator Johnson has taken the lead in reviewing the governor's budget proposals and developing the Senate Majority Conference's budget priorities. He also serves on the New York State Public Authorities Control Board and co-chairs the Legislative Audit Committee. He is also Chairman of the Senate Subcommittee on the Long Island Marine District, a Commissioner on the Atlantic States Marine Fisheries Commission, and Vice-Chair of the Legislative Commission on Government Administration. He is a National Director of the American Legislative Exchange Council, an organization for which he previously served as National Chairman. He is a member of Cross of Christ Lutheran Church in Babylon, and lives in West Babylon.

JEFFREY D KLEIN (D)
34th - Parts of Bronx and Westchester Counties

3713 East Tremont Avenue, Bronx, New York 10465
718-822-2049/jdklein@senate.state.ny.us

Jeff Klein was first elected to the New York State Senate in 2004. The lifelong Bronx resident received a BA from Queens College, an MPA from Columbia University's School of International and Public Affairs, and a JD from the City University of New York Law School. Currently, he serves as the Senate's Deputy Minority Leader. In addition, he is the Ranking Minority Member of the Senates Ethics Committee. Prior to his election to the Senate, Senator Klein spent ten years as a New York State Assemblyman, where he served as Chairman of the Subcommittee on Crime and the Elderly, the Committee on State-Federal Relations, and the Committee on Oversight, Analysis and Investigations. He has also served as Chief of Staff to Congress James Scheuer. Among his community and civil affiliations is membership on the New York regional board of the Anti-Defamation League. He is a partner in the law firm of Klein Calderoni & Santucci, LLP.

LIZ KRUEGER (D-WF)
26th - Part of New York County

211 East 43rd St, Ste 1300, New York, NY 10017
212-490-9535/lkrueger@senate.state.ny.us

Liz Krueger was elected to the New York State Senate in 2002. Senator Krueger graduated from Northwestern University in Chicago, Ill. with a Bachelor's degree in Social Policy and Human Development. She also holds a Master's degree from the University of Chicago's Harris Graduate School of Public Policy. She chairs the Minority Program Development and is the Ranking Minority Member on the Senate Committee on Housing, Construction and Community Development. She also serves as Chair of the Senate Minority Task Force on Legislative and Budgetary Reform. Her legislative initiatives look to supporting recycling and expanding the bottle bill, a bill that would repeal the Urstatdt Law and restore local control over New York City housing policy, and bills that would require a voter-verified paper trail for any new voting technology and eliminate the full-face ballot requirement. Prior to her election to the Senate, Senator Krueger was the Associate Director of the Community Food Resource Center (CFRC) for 15 years and the founding Director of the New York City Food Bank. She has served as Chair of the New York City Food Stamp Task Force and other community outreach organizations.

CARL KRUGER (D)
27th - Part of Kings County

2201 Avenue U, Brooklyn, NY 11229
718-743-8610 kruger@senate.state.ny.us

Senator Carl Kruger was first elected to the New York State Senate in 1994. Congressman Kruger holds a BS degree in Political Science. Prior to his election, Congressman Kruger served as an Assistant Director of Member Services for the New York State Assembly and for ten years was the Chairperson of Community Board #18. He currently chairs the Senate's Social Services, Children and Families Committee. Senator Kruger is a member of the SUNY Health Science Center Advisory Board, the Board of Trustees of the Flatlands Volunteer Ambulance Corporation, the Advisory Board of Visions and is Vice President of the Georgetowne Civic Association. Senator

BIOGRAPHIES / New York State Senate

Kruger is also a member of the Flatbush Park Jewish Center, the Knights of Pythias Excelsior Lodge, and a former board member of Temple Hillel. He resides in Brooklyn.

ANDREW J LANZA (R-I)
24th - Part of Richmond County

947 Legislative Office Building, Albany, NY 12247
518-455-3215/lanza@senate.state.ny.us

Senator Lanza was elected to the New York State Senate in November 2006. He holds a B.S. degree in accounting from St. John's University, and a J.D. from Fordham University School of Law. In the Senate, he chairs the Ethics Committee, and sits on several other committees. Prior to his election to the senate, he served as a New York City Council member, where his achievements included authoring and enacting comprehensive zoning laws to combat overdevelopment on Staten Island by preventing overly-dense and out-of-character construction. He also secured an agreement from New York City Michael Bloomberg to open a new police precinct on Staten Island. Senator Lanza is also a former assistant district attorney in the office of Manhattan District Attorney Robert Morgenthau. He resides in Great Kills.

WILLIAM J LARKIN, JR (R-C)
39th - Parts of Orange and Ulster Counties

1093 Little Britain Road, New Windsor, NY 12553
845-567-1270/larkin@senate.state.ny.us

Senator Larkin was first elected to the New York State Senate in 1990. Congressman Larkin graduated from LaSalle Institute in Troy and also attended the University of Maryland and the University of Denver. He currently chairs the Senate Committee on Racing, Gaming and Wagering, and is the Secretary of the Majority Conference. Until his appointment to this position in 2007, he had served since 1995 as Chairman of the Senate Majority Steering Committee. From 1993 to 1995, Senator Larkin chaired the Senate Committee on Local Governments, and authored a law to change the operations and procedures of local Industrial Development Agencies, or IDAS, thereby increasing their public accountability while allowing IDAS more flexibility to create jobs. Prior to his election to the Senate, Senator Larkin served in the New York State Assembly from 1979 to 1990. Additionally, he is recognized for his expertise relating to the insurance industry. For a year starting with his November 2001 election, he was president of the National Conference of Insurance Legislators. Senator Larkin is a veteran of 23 years of active military duty including combat assignments during World War II and the Korean War. He retired from the United States Army in 1967 with the rank of Lieutenant Colonel. Following his military service, Senator Larkin served as an Executive Assistant in the New York State Senate and as Supervisor of the Town of New Windsor in Orange County. Senator Larkin is a Troy native.

KENNETH P LaVALLE (R-I-C)
1st - Part of Suffolk County

325 Middle Country Road, Suite 4, Selden, NY 11784
631-696-6900/lavalle@senate.state.ny.us

Kenneth P LaValle was first elected to the New York State Senate in 1976. He holds an undergraduate degree from Adelphi College, a degree in Education from the State University College at New Paltz, and a JD from Touro College Jacob D Fuchsberg Law Center. Senator LaValle also has completed extensive graduate study in Government and International Relations at New York University. He currently serves as Chair of the Majority Conference, and chairs the Senate Committee on Higher Education. He has worked to establish a Burn Unit at University Hospital in Stony Brook. He also authored the Pine Barrens Preservation Act of 1993. He is a practicing attorney and resides in Port Jefferson.

VINCENT L LEIBELL, III (R-I-C)
40th - Putnam County, parts of Dutchess and Westchester Counties

1441 Route 22, Suite 205, Brewster, NY 10509
845-279-3773/leibell@senate.state.ny.us

Vincent L Leibell was first elected to the New York State Senate in 1994. He holds a Bachelor's degree in Economics, a Law degree from St John's University and a Master's degree in Public Administration from New York University. He currently serves as Chair of the Senate's Veterans, Homeland Security and Military Affairs Committee. Prior to his election, he served as an Associate Counsel to the New York State Senate, County Attorney of Putnam County, and as an Assistant District Attorney in Westchester County. From January 1983 until his election to the Senate, he served in the New York State Assembly and became Assistant Minority Leader Pro Tempore. The Navy veteran has commanded a U.S. Naval Reserve Unit in upstate New York. He lives in Patterson, New York.

THOMAS W LIBOUS (R-C)
52nd - Broome, Tioga and part of Chenango County

1607 State Ofc Bldg, 44 Hawley Street, Binghamton, NY 13901
607-773-8771/senator@senatorlibous.com

Senator Thomas W Libous was first elected to the New York State Senate in 1988. He graduated from Broome Community College and the State University of New York at Utica. He currently serves as Senior Assistant Majority Leader, Liason to the Executive Branch, as well as Chair of the Transportation Committee. In the past, he has chaired the Mental Health and Developmental Disabilities Committee, as well as the Alcoholism and Drug Abuse Committee. The Binghamton resident also worked to see the American Hockey League affiliate to the Ottawa Senators locate in his hometown. Prior to his election, he was employed by Chase-Lincoln First Bank and Johnson City Publishing.

ELIZABETH O'CONNOR LITTLE (R-I-C)
45th - Clinton, Essex, Franklin, Hamilton, Warren & Washington Counties

21 Bay Street, Glens Falls, NY 12801
518-743-0968/little@senate.state.ny.us

Elizabeth O'Connor Little was first elected to the New York State Senate in November 2002. She graduated from the College of Saint Rose with a degree in Elementary Education. Currently, she chairs the Senate's Local Government Committee, and thereby oversees committee work on legislation that affects local government entities, including counties, towns, villages, school districts, fire districts and special districts. Her legislative successes include adoption of a plan to encourage local governments to work cooperatively and share services in order to save tax money. Prior to her Senate election, she served in the New York State Assembly for seven years. She also

BIOGRAPHIES / New York State Senate

has served as At-Large-Supervisor to the Warren County Board of Supervisors for the Town of Queensbury. She is also now serving as a member of the Hudson-Fulton-Champlain Quadricentennial Commission planning and developing the 400th anniversary celebration of the historic discoveries of Henry Hudson and Samuel de Champlain, and also the 200th anniversary of Robert Fulton's landmark steamship voyage up the Hudson River.

SERPHIN R MALTESE (R-I-C)
15th - Part of Queens County

71-04 Myrtle Avenue, Glendale, NY 11385
718-497-1800/maltese@senate.state.ny.us

Serphin R Maltese was first elected to the New York State Senate in 1988. He holds a BA degree from Manhattan College. The Infantry veteran of the Korean War was awarded a War Service Scholarship and received his LLB and JD degrees from Fordham University Law School. Currently, he chairs the Senate's Cities Committee. Previously, he has chaired the Senate's Committee on Veterans and Committee on Consumer Protection. Senator Maltese. In addition, he is Vice Chair of the Majority Conference. During his many years in the Senate, he has authored 217 bills that have been signed into law. A recent achievement, in 2006, saw Senator Maltese secure a $55 million legislative grant for LaGuardia Community College, one of the largest legislative grants in CUNY history. He is currently a member of the American Legion's National Legislative Council. Prior to his election, Senator Maltese served as Queens Assistant District Attorney and Deputy Chief of the Homicide Bureau. He also has previously served as Counsel to US Senator Alfonse M D'Amato. As co-founder of the New York State Conservative Party in 1962, he went on to become State Chairman of the party from 1986 until his election to the Senate. The senator is affiliated with numerous civic and community organizations and has served in such positions as president of the New York Conference of Italian American State legislators. He resides in Middle Village, Queens.

CARL LOUIS MARCELLINO (R-I-C)
5th - Parts of Nassau and Suffolk Counties

250 Townsend Square, Oyster Bay, NY 11771
516-922-1811/marcelli@senate.state.ny.us

Carl Louis Marcellino was first elected to the New York State Senate in 1995. He received his BA and MS degrees from New York University, and received his Professional Diploma in Administration and Supervision from St John's University. Currently, he chairs the Senate's Environmental Conservation Committee. In the area of environmental legislation, his achievements including being the prime sponsor of the Brownfield/Superfund Reform Law, the Pesticide Notification law, and the first law in the county to phase out the groundwater contaminate MTBE from gasoline. He also focuses on health and safety issues, including efforts such as banning the use of handheld cell phones while driving in New York. Senator Marcellino is a former teacher and administrator and served as Oyster Bay Town Clerk prior to his election to the Senate. He is also the Oyster Bay Western Waterfront Committee, a founding member of the State Advisory Board of the National Environmental Policy Institute, and former President of the New York Conference of Italian American State Legislators. He is a longtime resident of Syosset.

GEORGE D MAZIARZ (R-I-C)
62nd - Orleans County and parts of Monroe and Niagara Counties

2578 Niagara Falls Blvd., Wheatfield, New York 14304
716-731-8740 maziarz@senate.state.ny.us

George D Maziarz was elected to the New York State Senate in 1995. He holds a BA degree in history from Niagara University. Prior to serving in the Senate, he was appointed City Clerk of North Tonawanda in 1978 and served in that capacity until elected Niagara County Clerk in 1989. He currently chairs the Senate's Labor Committee, and is also a member of the New York State Workforce Investment Board. Previously, he chaired the Committee on Tourism, Recreation and Sports Development, and the Senate Aging Committee. Senator Maziarz also has served as President of the Chamber of Commerce of the Tonawandas, has served on the board of directors of the United Way of the Tonawandas, and the corporate advisory board of DeGraff Memorial Hospital. Senator Maziarz also is a past officer and longtime member of Live Hose Co #4. He resides in Newfane, New York.

VELMANETTE MONTGOMERY (D-WF)
18th - Part of Kings County

30 3rd Ave, 11th Fl, Rm 615, Brooklyn, NY 11217
718-643-6140/montgome@senate.state.ny.us

Velmanette Montgomery was first elected to the New York State Senate in 1984. She received her Master's degree in Education from New York University and studied at the University of Accra in Ghana. She currently serves as the Ranking Minority Member on the Senate's Social Services, Children and Families Committee, and is Assistant Minority Leader for Policy and Administration. Before her election to the State Senate she was a Revson Fellow at Columbia University and received the Institute for Educational Leadership Fellowship. Prior to becoming a legislator, Senator Montgomery was a teacher, an adjunct professor, and a day care director. She co-founded the Day Care Forum of New York City. She also served as president of Community School Board 13. She resides in Brooklyn.

THOMAS P MORAHAN (R-I-C-WF)
38th - Rockland County and part of Orange County

158 Airport Executive Park, Nanuet, NY 10954
845-425-1818/morahan@senate.state.ny.us

Senator Thomas P Morahan was first elected to the New York State Senate in 1999. Senator Morahan attended Rockland Community College. He currently serves as Chair of the Senate Committee on Mental Health and Development Disabilities. In this position, he backed and ensured passage of the Geriatric Mental Health Act, which laid the groundwork for the state to provide high quality services to meet current and future senior mental health care needs. Senator Morahan previously served as Chairman of the Elections Committee. His previous public service experience includes serving as a member of the Clarkstown Zoning Board of Appeals, election to the Rockland County Legislature where he served from 1977 to 1980, and again from 1984 to 1999 where he was elected Chairman of the Legislature in 1996. He served in the New York State Assembly from 1980-1982.

MICHAEL F NOZZOLIO (R-I-C)
54th - Seneca and Wayne Counties and parts of Cayuga, Monroe, Ontario and Tompkins Counties

BIOGRAPHIES / New York State Senate

119 Fall Street, Seneca Falls, NY 13148
315-568-9816/nozzolio@senate.state.ny.us

Michael F Nozzolio was first elected to the New York State Senate in 1992. He received a BS degree in Labor Relations and an MS degree in Public Administration and Agricultural Economics from Cornell University. He also earned a JD degree from the Syracuse University College of Law. In the Senate, he has supported job development efforts that have created thousands of jobs in his district. Currently, he serves as Chairman of the Senate Crime Victims, Crime and Correction Committee. Prior to his Senate service, Congressman Nozzolio served in the New York Assembly for ten years. While in the Assembly, he served as Deputy Minority Leader. Senator Nozzolio serves on the Board of the Cornell Agricultural and Food Technology Park. He is a native of Seneca Falls.

GEORGE ONORATO (D)
12th - Part of Queens County

28-11 Astoria Boulevard, Long Island City, NY 11102
718-545-9706/onorato@senate.state.ny.us

George Onorato was elected to the New York State Senate in 1983. He served in the US Army, 118th Medical Battalion from 1950 to 1952 and received a Presidential Citation. Currently, Senator Onorato is Vice Chair of the Minority Conference, and is Ranking Minority Member on the Labor Committee. Throughout his many years in the Senate, Senator Onorato has advocated on behalf of New York's working families, consumers, senior citizens, veterans, and young people. He has served on the Senate Task Force on Legislative and Government Reform, and previously chaired the Insurance Committee. In his first year in the Senate, he was a prime co-sponsor of the Used Car lemon Law, thereby protecting consumers from defective automobiles when buying a car. He is past Treasurer and Past President of the Conference of Italian American Legislators. He served as Secretary/Treasurer of Bricklayer's Local #41 for 15 years, prior to his election to the New York State Senate. He was born in Astoria.

SUZI OPPENHEIMER (D-WF)
37th - Part of Westchester County

222 Grace Church Street, 3rd Floor, Port Chester, NY 10573
914-934-5250/ oppenhei@senate.state.ny.us

Suzi Oppenheimer was first elected to the New York State Senate in 1984. Senator Oppenheimer received her BA degree in Economics from Connecticut College for Women, and a Master's degree from Columbia University's Graduate School of Business. She served four terms as Mayor of the Village of Mamaroneck. She also served as President of the Westchester Municipal Officials Association, the Westchester Municipal Planning Federation, and the Mamaroneck League of Women Voters. She currently serves as Deputy Minority Whip; Ranking Minority Member on the Senate's standing Education Committee, and chairs the Senate Democratic Task Force on Women's Issues, and co-sponsored Kieran's law to protect children and families by providing for criminal background checks for nannies. Senator Oppenheimer's extensive community involvement includes service on several boards, including the Child Car Action Campaign and the Westchester Community Opportunity Program. She is a resident of Mamaroneck, New York.

FRANK PADAVAN (R-I-C)
11th - Part of Queens County

89-39 Gettysburg Street, Bellerose, NY 11426
718-343-0255/ padavan@senate.state.ny.us

Frank Padavan was first elected to the New York State Senate in 1972. He holds a Bachelor's degree in Electrical Engineering from Brooklyn Polytechnic University and Master's degree in Business Administration from New York University. Prior to his election to the Senate, Senator Padavan was employed by Westinghouse Electric Corporation for fourteen years. He also served as Deputy Commissioner of the New York City Department of Buildings. Senator Padavan currently serves as the Senate's Vice President Pro Tempore, and in 2006 became chairman of the newly-created Senate Majority Task Force on Port Security. In this capacity, he and his colleagues created legislature that became law which strengthens investigative powers of the Waterfront Commission and expands the commission's ability to revoke or deny the licenses of port employees with organized crime or terrorist ties. Senator Padavan also opposes casino gambling and the state lottery, and led recent opposition to expanding state-sanctioned gambling. During his many years in the Senate, he has chaired both the Cities Committee and the Mental Hygiene and Addiction Control Committee. He was a Colonel in the Army Corps of Engineers, and numerous other organizations. He is an ex-officio member of all Senate standing committees. Senator Padavan resides in Queens.

KEVIN S PARKER (D-WF)
21st - Part of Kings County

4515 Avenue D, Brooklyn NY 11203
718-629-6401/parker@senate.state.ny.us

Kevin S Parker was first elected to the New York State Senate in 2002. He received a Bachelor of Science degree in Public Service from Penn State University and a Master of Science degree from the New School for Social Research Graduate School of Management and Urban Policy. Senator Parker currently serves as the Ranking Minority Member of the Senate's Energy and Telecommunications Committee. Prior to his election, he served as Special Assistant to former New York State Comptroller H Carl McCall. As a New York City Urban Fellow, he served as a Special Assistant to Manhattan Borough President Ruth Messinger. Also, he was Legislative Aide to former New York City Council Member Una Clarke and Special Assistant to Assemblyman Nick Perry. He served as Project Manager with the New York State Urban Development Corporation. Currently, he teaches African-American Studies and Political Science at a variety of colleges. His community involvement includes service as the former second vice chairman of the board and chair of Community Board 17's Education Committee. He is a Brooklyn native, and resides in Flatbush.

BILL PERKINS (D)
30th - Part of New York County

163 West 125th Street, Harlem State office Bldg., Ste 932, New York, NY 10027
212-222-7315/perkins@senate.state.ny.us

Bill Perkins was first elected to the New York State Senate in November 2006. He holds a B.A. in political science from Brown University. His Senate committee memberships include Civil Service & Pensions; Codes; and Corporations, Authorities and Commissions

BIOGRAPHIES / New York State Senate

committees. Prior to his election to the Senate, he spent eight years on the New York City Council, serving as the Deputy Majority Leader. In this position, he was prime sponsor of the Childhood Lead Paint Poisoning Prevention Act of 2004. He has also advocated on behalf of public education, early cancer detection, and civil rights and civil liberties. He is a lifelong resident of Harlem.

MARY LOU RATH (R-I-C)
61st - Genesee and part of Erie Counties

5500 Main Street, Suite 260, Williamsville, NY 14221
716-633-0331/rath@senate.state.ny.us

Mary Lou Rath was first elected to the New York State Senate in 1993. She holds a BS degree from Buffalo State Teachers College. Prior to her election to the Senate, Senator Rath served as a Legislator in Erie County from 1979 to 1993, including four years as the Republican Leader of the Erie County Legislature. She currently chairs the Senate's Tourism, Recreation and Sports Development Committee. In addition, she serves as Deputy Majority Leader for State/Federal Relations, the first woman to serve in a leadership position in the Senate Majority. Her legislative goals include economic development, health care reform, drug and alcohol abuse prevention, and education. She serves on the Senate Task Force on Medicaid Reform, and established the Western New York "Fix Medicaid" Coalition. She resides in Williamsville, New York.

JOSEPH E ROBACH (R-I-C-WF)
56th - Part of Monroe County

2300 West Ridge Road, Rochester, NY 14626
585-225-3650/ robach@senate.state.ny.us

Joseph E Robach was first elected to the New York State Senate in November 2002. Senator Robach is a graduate of the State University of New York College at Brockport, where he received his Bachelor of Science and Master of Public Administration degrees. Currently, he chairs the Senate's Civil Service and Pensions committee. In his efforts to expand economic development in Rochester, he secured record increases in state aid for his district in 2006. Prior to his election, he served in the New York State Assembly from 1991-2002. His extensive community involvement includes membership on the boards of the Northwest YMCA, Norman Howard School and Flower City Down Syndrome Network. He lives in the Town of Greece.

JOHN D SABINI (D-WF)
13th - Part of Queens County

35-07 88th St, Jackson Heights, NY 11372
718-639-8469/ sabini@senate.state.ny.us

John D Sabini was first elected to the New York State Senate in 2002. Senator Sabini holds degrees from New York University's College of Business Administration, and attended its Graduate School of Public Administration. He currently serves as Ranking Minority Member of the Racing, Gaming and Wagering Committee, as well as the Transportation Committee. Prior to his election to the Senate, Senator Sabini served as a member of the New York City Council from 1992-2002. In addition, he served as District Administrator for Congressman James H Scheuer and Stephen J Solarz. He has been Director of the New York State Assembly Subcommittee on Senior Citizen Facilities. As a 16-year-old, he was elected to the Community Advisory Board at Elmhurst Hospital, and appointed to Community Board No. 3-Q at 19. Senator Sabini is a lifelong resident of Jackson Heights.

STEPHEN M SALAND (R-C-I)
41st - Columbia and part of Dutchess Counties

3 Neptune Road, Suite A19B, Poughkeepsie, NY 12601
845-463-0840/ saland@senate.state.ny.us

Stephen M Saland was first elected to the New York State Senate in 1990. He graduated from the University of Buffalo, and from Rutgers Law School. Currently in the Senate, Senator Saland chairs the Majority Steering Committee as well as the Education Committee. During his many years in the state Senate, he has authored more than 300 laws in the areas of criminal justice and victims' rights, domestic violence and child abuse, economic development, and environmental protection. He is the former chair of the Children and Families Committee, where he was responsible for reforming the state's domestic violence act by drafting the Family Protection and Domestic Violence Intervention Act. He served as president of the National Conference of State legislatures from 2001-2002. Prior to his election to the senate, he was a Town Councilman in the Town of Wappinger. In addition, he served in the New York State Assembly from 1980 to 1990. Senator Saland is of council to the Poughkeepsie law firm of Gellert & Klein, P.C., and resides in Poughkeepsie.

JOHN L SAMPSON (D-WF)
19th - Part of Kings County

9114 Flatlands Avenue, Brooklyn, NY 11236
718-649-7653/sampson@senate.state.ny.us

John L Sampson was first elected to the New York State Senate in 1996. He graduated from Brooklyn College with a BA degree in Political Science, and holds a law degree from Albany Law School. He currently serves as the Ranking Minority Member of the Senate Health Committee. In addition, he is the Secretary of the Minority Conference as well as a member of the Administrative Regulations Review Commission. Prior to his election, Senator Sampson worked as a staff attorney for the Legal Aid Society of New York. He has been an attorney at the law firm of Alter and Barbaro, Esqs, since 1993. He is a member of the Board of Trustees of Albany Law School.

DIANE J SAVINO (D-I-WF)
23rd District - Part of Kings and Richmond Counties

36 Richmond Terrace, 1st Floor, Staten Island, New York 10301
718-727-9406/savino@senate.state.ny.us

Diane J Savino was first elected to the New York State Senate in 2004. She graduated from St. John's University and the Cornell School of Industrial and Labor Relations. In the Senate, she currently serves as the Ranking Minority Member of the Civil Service and Pensions Committee. An advocate on behalf of working people, Senator Savino began her career as a caseworker for New York City's Child Welfare Administration, providing direct assistance to abused and neglected children in the Agency's Division of Foster Care and Adoption. In this position, she became involved in her local labor union, rising through the ranks to Vice President for Political Action & Legislative Affairs of the Social Service Employees Union, Local 371, DC 37 of AFSCME. In this capacity, she represented 16,000

BIOGRAPHIES / New York State Senate

public sector workers and their families at City Hall and the State Capital. She lives in the Fort Wadsworth section of Staten Island.

ERIC T SCHNEIDERMAN (D-WF)
31st - Parts of Bronx and New York Counties

80 Bennett Avenue, Ground Fl, New York, NY 10033
212-928-5578/schneide@senate.state.ny.us

Eric T Schneiderman was first elected to the New York State Senate in 1998. Senator Schneiderman graduated from Amherst College with degrees in English and Asian studies and received his JD from Harvard Law School. Currently in the senate, he serves as Ranking Minority Member of the Codes Committee. He advocates on behalf of tougher gun safety laws, and ensuring New York's children receive high-quality educations. To that end, he joined the Campaign for Fiscal Equity, a coalition of education advocates, in a successful lawsuit to obtain equitable funding for all of the state's public school students. He resides on the Upper West side of Manhattan.

JOSE M SERRANO (D-WF)
28th - Parts of Bronx and New York Counties

157 East 104th Street, Ground Floor, New York, New York, 10029
212-828-5829/ serrano@senate.state.ny.us

Senator Jose M Serrano was first elected to the New York State Senate in 2004. He graduated from Manhattan College with a BA in Government. Currently he serves as Ranking Minority Member of the Senate's Tourism, Recreation and Sports Development Committee. He is also Minority Policy Chair for the Senate Democratic Conference. In 2006, he was appointed to chair the Senate Minority Task Force on the Arts and Cultural Affairs, which is exploring a range of efforts including arts funding and economic development via the arts. Prior to his election to the Senate, he served on Community Board 4 and Chairman of the Board for the Institute of Family Health, a nonprofit community health services organization. In 2001 he was elected to the New York City Council for District 17, where he chaired the Council's Committee on Cultural Affairs, Libraries, and International Inter-group relations. He lives in the South Bronx.

JAMES L SEWARD (R-I-C)
51st - Cortland, Greene, Herkimer, Otsego, Schoharie, and parts of Chenengo and Tompkins Counties

41 South Main Street, Oneonta, NY 13820
607-432-5524/seward@senate.state.ny.us

James L Seward was first elected to the New York State Senate in 1986. He holds a BA degree from Hartwick College in political science, and he also studied at the Nelson Rockefeller Institute of Government at SUNY Albany. Currently, he chairs the Senate Committee on Insurance and serves as Majority Whip. He has chaired key Senate committees, including the Energy and Telecommunications Committee, as well as the Senate Majority Task Force on Volunteer Emergency Services. In that role, Senator Seward was instrumental in establishing a low-interest loan program for capital needs and equipment purchases of volunteer fire departments and emergency squads. He is a former Milford town justice, a director of the Wilber National Bank, a trustee of Glimmerglass Opera, and a board member for Pathfinder Village and the Catskill Symphony. He lives in Milford.

DEAN G SKELOS (R-I-C)
9th - Part of Nassau County

55 Front Street, Rockville Centre, NY 11570
516-766-8383/skelos@senate.state.ny.us

State Senator Dean Skelos was first elected to the New York State Senate in 1984. He received a BA in History from Washington College in Chestertown, Maryland and his JD degree from Fordham University School. Prior to being elected to the senate, he served two years in the New York State Assembly. He currently serves as Deputy Majority Leader for Legislative Operations, which allows him to play a key role in developing the Senate's legislative and governmental policy. Recently during his long legislative career, Senator Skelos in 2006 authored a sweeping law to fight fraud, waste and abuse in the state Medicaid program. He also helped to create the landmark new HELP program to make homeownership more affordable for Long Islanders. Also during his Senate tenure, Senator Skelos wrote New York State's Sex offender Registration Act, also known as "Megan's Law." Since 1998, he has served as the State Senate's representative on the Metropolitan Transportation Authority's Capital Program Review Board, and has chaired various committees and task forces. He is a member of the State Legislative Leaders Foundation, National Conference of State Legislators, and the National Conference of Insurance Legislators. He is of counsel to the firm of Ruskin Moscou Faltischeck PC and lives in Rockville Centre.

MALCOLM A SMITH (D-C-WF)
14th - Part of Queens County

205-19 Linden Blvd, St Albans NY 11412
718-528-4290/masmith@senate.state.ny.us

Malcolm A Smith was first elected to the New York State Senate in 2000. He received a BS in Business Administration with a concentration in economics from Fordham University, holds an MBA with a concentration in finance and operations from Adelphi University, and completed a certificate program on negotiations from Harvard Law School. In 2006, he became Senate Minority Leader, a position that makes him an ex officio member of all Senate standing committees, as well as the Ranking Minority Member of the Rules Committee. Prior to being elected to the senate, Senator Smith served as a senior aide to former Congressman Floyd H. Flake, chief aide to former City Councilman Archie Spigner, and a City Hall assistant to former Mayor Edward I. Koch. His focus is on community revitalization and affordable housing in addition to various other issues of interest to his constituents. In 2002, he collaborated with city and state officials to reach agreement on a $10 million cleanup of the Westside Corporation Toxic Site in Jamaica, Queens. Among his achievements, he is a founder of Peninsula Preparatory Academy, the first public charter school in the Rockaways, and serves on the Board of Trustees of the Merrick Academy-Queens public Charter School in Jamaica Queens. He resides in Queens.

WILLIAM T STACHOWSKI (D- C-WF)
58th - Part of Erie County

2030 Clinton Street, Buffalo, NY 14206
716-826-3344/stachows@senate.state.ny.us

William T Stachowski was first elected to the New York State Senate in 1981. He holds a BA degree in Political Science from College of the Holy Cross in Worcester, MA. He currently serves as the

BIOGRAPHIES / New York State Senate

Ranking Minority Member on the Finance Committee. He is also a member of the Legislative Commission on the Development of Rural Resources and the NYS Legislative Sportsmen's Caucus. Prior to his election, Senator Stachowski was a teacher/counselor at St Ann's Roman Catholic School in Buffalo. He was named to the Erie County Legislature (3rd District) in December 1974, where he served until November 1981. Senator Stachowski's community efforts include service on the Ilio DiPaolo Scholarship Committee, and the Western New York Delegation Hydro Re-Allocation Committee. He is a member of numerous organizations, including the Hunter's Hope Foundation, where he is a former director, and the Foundation's Community Advisory Board.

TOBY ANN STAVISKY (D-WF)
16th - Part of Queens County

144-36 Willets Point Blvd, Flushing, NY 11357
718-445-0004/stavisky@senate.state.ny.us

Toby Ann Stavisky was first elected to the Senate in 1999. She received her Bachelor's degree from Syracuse University and completed graduate school at Hunter and Queens Colleges. In the Senate, she was appointed Assistant Minority Whip in 2003, and she also currently serves as Ranking Minority Member of the Senate Committee on Higher Education. Prior to entering public life, Senator Stavisky worked in the actuarial department of a major insurance company and taught social studies in the New York City high schools, including Brooklyn Technical, Haaren, and Thomas Edison. She also served as District Manager in Northeast Queens for the 1980 Census. Senator Stavisky was a founder of the North Flushing Senior Center and served on its Board of Directors. She serves as a trustee of the Whitestone Hebrew Center where she and her husband, the late State Senator Leonard Price Stavisky, were honored as "Couple of the Year." She resides in Whitestone.

ANDREA STEWART-COUSINS (D)
35th - Part of Westchester County

35 East Grassy Sprain Rd., Ste 205, Yonkers, NY 10710
914-961-3355/scousins@senate.state.ny.us

Andrea Stewart-Cousins was first elected to the New York State Senate in 2006. She holds a B.S. from Pace University and received her teaching credentials in business education from Lehman College. Currently in the senate, she serves as Ranking Minority member of the Local Government Committee. Prior to her election to the Senate, she served on the Westchester County Board of legislators from 1996-2006. For six years, she chaired the Committee on Legislation, the Committee on Health, and the Committee on Families. She was also Majority Whip and Vice Chair of the legislature. The county's first human rights laws, smoke-free workplace laws, and tougher guns laws were among those passed during her chairmanship of the Legislation Committee. She sits on the boards of the Riverside Health Care System and Yonkers Community Action Program. She resides in Yonkers.

ANTOINE M THOMPSON (D-WF)
60th - Parts of Erie and Niagara Counties

213 Mahoney State Office Building, 65 Court St., Buffalo, NY 14202
716-854-8705/athompso@senate.state.ny.us

Antoine M Thompson was first elected to the New York State Senate in 2006. He holds a B.S. in history from SUNY Brockport, and studied at the University of Ghana, West Africa. Currently in the Senate, he is the Ranking Minority Member of the Cities Committee and Acting Ranking Minority Member of the Environmental Conservation Committee. In addition, he co-chairs the Democratic Senate Campaign Committee. Prior to his election, he served on the Buffalo Common Council, where he chaired the Committees on Education and Minority & Women-Owned Businesses. He also as served as Executive Director of the Office of Urban Initiatives, Inc., an economic development corporation, as well as legislative assistant for the Buffalo Common Council Central Staff. He is actively involved in numerous community organizations, and hosts a weekly radio broadcast called Western New York on the Move. He is a Buffalo native.

CAESAR TRUNZO (R-I-C)
3rd - Part of Suffolk County

NYS Office Bldg, Veterans Memorial Hwy, Hauppauge, NY 11788
631-360-3236/trunzo@senate.state.ny.us

Caesar Trunzo was first elected to the New York State Senate in 1972. He served in the US Army during World War II and graduated from Heffley & Browne Business College. Currently, he is Assistant Majority Leader of House Operations. He also sits on the Executive Committee of the Senate Task Force on Emergency Preparedness, and on the Senate Task Force on Voter Participation. He previously chaired the Senate Transportation Committee, and continues to make Long Island's transportation needs, such as congestion relief, a priority. He is also a former chairman of the Civil Service and Pensions Committee, the Government Operations Committee, and the Housing Committee. Senator Trunzo also served from 1978 to 1995 as Senate Chairman of the legislative Commission on Water Resource Needs of Long Island. Before his election to the Senate, Senator Trunzo was an Accounting Supervisor of Fairchild Stratos Corp, Bay Shore, New York, and Chief Accountant and Assistant Treasurer of Dayton T Brown, Inc, Bohemia, New York. He served as a member of the Islip Planning Board from 1959 until he became Councilman of the Town of Islip in 1965. He is a member of the Brentwood Lions Club, the Sons of Italy, the St Anne's Holy Name Society, and the St Anne's Council Knights of Columbus. He lives in Brentwood, New York.

DAVID J VALESKY (D-WF)
49th - Madison County and parts of Cayuga, Oneida and Onondaga Counties

805 State Office Building, 333 East Washington St, Syracuse, NY 13202
315-478-8745/valesky@senate.state.ny.us

Senator David J Valesky was elected to the New York State Senate in 2004. He received his Bachelor's degree from SUNY Potsdam and his Master's degree from the University of Connecticut. He currently serves as the Ranking Minority Member of the Senate's Committee on Agriculture. He is a member of the Senate Democratic Task Force on Legislative and Budgetary Reform. Prior to his election, Senator Valesky served as an aide to former State Assembly Majority Leader Michael Bragman. He then became Vice President of Communications at WCNY, the public television and radio station of Central New York, a post he occupied from 1995 to 2004. There,

BIOGRAPHIES / US Senate: New York Delegation

he hosted the midday talk show HOUR CNY. He lives in the Madison County city of Oneida.

DALE M VOLKER (R-I-C)
59th - Wyoming & parts of Erie, Livingston & Ontario Counties

4729 Transit Road, Suite 5, Depew NY 14043
716-656-8544/volker@senate.state.ny.us

Dale M Volker was first elected to the New York State Senate in 1975. He attended Niagara University and graduated from Canisius College. Subsequent to graduation, Senator Volker worked as a police officer in the Village of Depew while studying law at the University of Buffalo. After graduating, he continued to serve with the Depew Police Department for six years. Throughout his law enforcement career, he was a member of the Depew Police Benevolent Association and served a term as its President. Currently, he chairs the Senate's Codes Committee, a post he has held since 1987. During his Senate career, he has also chaired the Energy Committee and the Senate Subcommittee on Alcoholism. Prior to his Senate election, Senator Volker served three years in the Assembly. Active in his community and in his church, he has directed the United Fund Appeal in Depew and has served as Chairman of the Catholic Charities Appeal. He is a member of numerous civic organizations and sits on the Board of Regents-Canisius College. He lives in the village of Depew.

GEORGE H WINNER, JR (R-I-C)
53rd - includes Chemung, Schuyler, Steuben and Yates counties and part of Tompkins County

228 Lake Street, P.O. Box 588, Elmira, NY 14902
607-732-2765; winner@senate.state.ny.us

George H Winner, Jr was elected to the New York State Senate in 2004. He graduated from St Lawrence University and was admitted to practice law in New York after completing a legal clerkship. Currently, he chairs the Investigations and Government Operations Committee, and the Legislative Commission the Development of Rural Resources. Prior to his election to the Senate, Senator Winner spent twenty-six years in the New York State Assembly. There, he served as Minority Leader Pro Tempore, Deputy Minority Leader, and Ranking Minority Member of the Assembly Judiciary Committee. Before being elected to public office himself, Senator Winner was counsel and legislative assistant to then-Senate Deputy Majority Leader William T. Smith from 1971 to 1978. He is a partner in the law firm of Keyser, Maloney, Winner LLP in Elmira, where he resides.

JAMES W WRIGHT (R-I-C)
48th - Jefferson, Oswego and parts of St Lawrence Counties

State Office Bldg, 317 Washington St, 4th Floor, Watertown, NY 13601
315-785-2430/wright@senate.state.ny.us

James Wright was first elected to the New York State Senate in November 1992. He graduated from the State University of New York at Oswego in 1971 and attended the Maxwell School of Public Administration at Syracuse University. He was selected to participate in the Local Government Public Administration Internship at Harvard University's Kennedy School of Government Program for Senior Executives, and in the United States Army War College National Security Seminar. He has also served as an adjunct faculty member and a private consultant. In the Senate, he is currently Deputy Majority Leader for Policy and chairs the Senate Energy and Telecommunications Committee. In the latter position, he has taken a key role in dealing with issues such as New York's progression during the transition to deregulation, or increasing generating capacity. He chairs a bipartisan Senate task force to study and introduce new technology to the legislative process, and also is a member of the bipartisan Rural Resources Commission. He began his career as a caseworker in child protective services in Oswego County, and then became the first County Administrator of Oswego County, a post he held until his appointment as first County Administrator of Jefferson County. He resides in Watertown.

CATHARINE M YOUNG (R-I-C)
57th - Allegany, Cattaraugus & Chautauqua Counties and part of Livingston County

700 West State Street, Olean, NY 14760
716-372-4901/cyoung@senate.state.ny.us

Catharine Young was first elected to the Senate in 2005. She studied at SUNY Fredonia and earned a Bachelor's degree in mass communication from St. Bonaventure University. Currently, she chairs the Senate's Agriculture Committee and co-chairs the Administrative Regulations Review Commission. Prior to her election, she served in the New York State Assembly, where she was Minority Steering Committee Chair and Assistant Minority Leader Pro Tempore. Previously, she served on the Cattaraugus County Legislature, where she was Majority Whip. She serves as a Major in the Civil Air Patrol, is an advisory board member for the Alzheimer's Association Western New York Chapter, and has served on the board of the Olean Chamber of Commerce, the Cattaraugus County American Red Cross, and the Olean Rotary Club. She also has worked as a news reporter.

US Senate: New York Delegation

HILLARY RODHAM CLINTON (D)

476 Russell Senate Office Bldg, Washington, DC 20510
202-224-4451/fax: 202-228-0282

780 Third Avenue, Suite 2601, New York, NY 10017
212-688-6262/fax: 212-688-7444

Leo O'Brien Fed Ofc Bldg, 1 Clinton Sq, Rm 821, Albany, NY 12207
518-431-0120/fax: 518-431-0128

J M Hanley Fed Bldg, 100 South Clinton St, PO Box 7378, Syracuse, NY 13261-7378
315-448-0470/fax: 315-448-0476

BIOGRAPHIES / US House of Representatives: New York Delegation

Larkin at Exchange, 726 Exchange St, Suite 511, Buffalo, NY 14210
716-854-9725/fax 716-854-9731

Kenneth B. Keating Fed Ofc Bldg, 100 State St, Rm 3280, Rochester, NY 14614
585-263-6250/fax: 585-263-6247

PO Box 47, Nyack, NY 10960
845-613-0076/fax: 845-613-0110

PO Box 273, Lowville, NY 13367
315-376-6118/fax: 315-376-6118

PO Box 617, Hartsdale, NY 10530
914-725-9294/fax: 914-472-5073

155 Pinelawn Rd, Ste 250 N, Melville, NY 11747
631-249-2825/fax: 631-249-2847

Hillary Rodham Clinton was first elected to the United States Senate in November 2000. The wife of U.S. President Bill Clinton (1993-99), she is also the first former First Lady to be elected to public office. In 2007, she is widely considered to be a leading candidate for the Democratic presidential nomination. Senator Clinton graduated from Wellesley College and Yale Law School. In 1978 she was appointed to the board of the Legal Services Corporation by President Jimmy Carter. She joined the Rose Law Firm in 1976, became First Lady of Arkansas when her husband was elected governor in 1980, and served on the board of the Children's Defense Fund, among others. She became First Lady of the U.S. following her husband's 1992 ascension to the White House, where, among other duties, she chaired the Task Force on National Health Care Reform. As a U.S. Senator, she worked after 9/11 to secure $21.4 billion to assist cleanup and recovery, to provide health tracking for first responders and volunteers at Ground Zero, and to create redevelopment grants. She has visited U.S. troops in Afghanistan and Iraq, and worked on behalf of veterans. Working on behalf of the economy in New York and elsewhere, she led a bipartisan effort to bring next-generation broadband access to rural communities; co-sponsored the 21st Century Nanotechnology Research and Development Act; and won an extension of Unemployed Insurance for displaced workers. She has championed legislation to expand after-school programs, make high-quality childcare more accessible and affordable and provide respite care for the elderly. She is a co-sponsor of the bill expanding the Family and Medical leave Act to provide parents time off from work to take their children to the doctor. Her committee assignments include service on the Senate Arms Services Committee, making her the first New Yorker to take a seat on that key committee. In addition, she serves on the Health, Education, Labor and Pensions Committee; the Environment and Public Committee; and the Special Committee on Aging. An advocate for children and families for more than thirty years, she wrote the best-selling book, *It Takes A Village: And Other Lessons Children Teach Us*, contributing nearly $1 million of author proceeds to charities assisting children and families. She also is the author of *Living History*.

CHARLES E SCHUMER (D)

313 Hart Senate Office Bldg, Washington, DC 20510
202-224-6542/fax: 202-228-3027

757 Third Avenue, Suite 17-02, New York, NY 10017
212-486-4430; TDD: 212-486-7803/fax: 212-486-7693

Leo O'Brien Federal Building, Room 420, Albany, NY 12207
518-431-4070/fax: 518-431-4076

130 South Elmwood Avenue, #660, Buffalo, NY 14202
716-846-4111/fax: 716-846-4113

100 State Street, Room 3040, Rochester, NY 14614
585-263-5866/fax: 585-263-3173

100 S Clinton St, Rm 841, Syracuse, NY 13261-7318
315-423-5471/fax: 315-423-5185

15 Henry St., Rm M103, Binghamton, NY 13901
607-772-6792/fax: 607-772-8124

145 Pine Lawn Rd., #300, Melville, NY 11747
631-753-0978/fax: 631-753-0997

One Park Place, Suite 100, Peekskill, NY 10566
914-734-1532/fax: 914-734-1673

Charles E "Chuck" Schumer was first elected to the United States Senate in November 1998. He is a graduate of Harvard University and Harvard Law School. He was elected to the State Assembly in 1974 after graduating from law school, and the US House of Representatives in 1980. Early in his second Senate term, Senate Democratic Leader Harry Reid appointed Senator Schumer to the Democratic leadership team, and Schumer's committee assignments include a seat on the powerful Senate Finance Committee which oversees tax, trade, social security and health care legislation. Since his election to the Senate, Senator Schumer has made improving New York's economy his top priority. He has been successful in bringing affordable air service to Upstate New York, and he initiated a comprehensive effort to attract new businesses to that region. He also put together a group that developed a plan to boost New York City's office space shortage in order to accommodate 3000,000 new jobs over the next two decades. Improving access to quality education is another priority. He has worked to make college tuition tax deductible for most American families. Senator Schumer is also working to ensure that all Americans have quality health care and access to affordable prescription drugs under an initiative that increase the availability of generic drugs. He was a leader of the fight against privatization of Social Security, and has sought a bipartisan solution to ensure the long-term solvency of the program. He is working to retain Medicaid funding and the deductibility of state and local taxes on federal tax returns. In addition to the finance committee, Senator Schumer sits on the Judiciary Committee, and the Rules Committee, and on the Committee on Banking, Housing, and Urban Affairs. Born in Brooklyn, he is a lifelong resident of New York.

US House of Representatives: New York Delegation

GARY L ACKERMAN (D)
5 - Queens & Nassau Counties

BIOGRAPHIES / US House of Representatives: New York Delegation

2243 Rayburn House Office Bldg, Washington, DC 20515
202-225-2601/fax: 202-225-1589/www.house.gov/ackerman/contact.shtml

218-14 Northern Blvd, Bayside, NY 11361
718-423-2154/fax: 718-423-5053

Gary Ackerman was first elected to Congress in 1983. He graduated from Queens College and taught junior high school social studies and math in Queens. In 1970 he left his teaching position to start a weekly newspaper there. He was first elected to public office in 1978 as a member of the New York State Senate from a district that first included central Queens, then was reapportioned in 1992 to the north shore of Queens, Nassau and Suffolk Counties, then re-drawn again in 2002 to the current configuration. He chairs House Subcommittee on the Middle East and South Asia of the House Foreign Affairs Committee, which has jurisdiction over U.S. policy in these regions. He formerly chaired the Subcommittee on Asia and the Pacific, and remains on that panel. As chair, Congressman Ackerman made history in 1994 by traveling to North Korea to discuss with dictator Kim Il Sung the framework under which the country would stop building nuclear weapons. Congressman Ackerman is also well known for his efforts to feed the starving people of Ethiopia and the Sudan, for playing a leading role in the rescue of Ethiopian Jews and their emigration to Israel. He also convinced the German government to establish a $110 million fund to compensate 18,000 Holocaust survivors and to investigate whether 3,300 former Nazi soldiers collecting German pensions in the US are war criminals. In the wake of the September 11 attacks, he lobbied federal security officials to use ex-law enforcement officers as screeners at New York Airports. He persuaded the National Cancer Institute to fund and undertake the nation's first ever study of environmental factors causing breast cancer - a study that took place on Long Island, where the rate of breast cancer is among the highest in the nation. Congressman Ackerman was born in Brooklyn on western Long Island and resides in Jamaica Estates, Queens.

MICHAEL A ARCURI (D)
24th - Chenango, Cayuga, Cortland, Seneca and Herkimer Counties, and parts of Broom, Oneida, Ontario, Otsego, Tioga and Tompkins Counties.

327 Cannon House Office Bldg., Washington, DC 20515
202-225-3665/fax: 202-225-1892/arcuri.house.gov/contact.shtml

17 E. Genesee Street, Auburn, NY 13021
315-252-2777 or -2778/fax 315-252-2779

10 Broad Street, Utica, NY 13501
315-793-8146 or -8147/fax 315-798-4099

16 Church Street, Carriage House Right, Cortland, NY 13045
607-756-2470/fax 607-756-2472

Michael Acuri was first elected to the U.S. House of Representatives in 2006. He graduated from SUNY Albany and New York Law School in New York University. In his Utica-based law practice, he frequently advocated on behalf of children and families. In 1993, he was elected Oneida County District Attorney and was a strong advocate for crime prevention, as well as improving drug treatment programs and ending domestic violence and sexual assault. He sits on the Transportation and Infrastructure Committee as well as the House Rules Committee. He is a native of Utica.

TIMOTHY H BISHOP (D)
1 - Parts of Suffolk County

225 Cannon House Office Bldg, Washington, DC 20515
202-225-3826/fax: 202-225-3143/http://wwwc.house.gov/timbishop

3680 Route 112, Ste C, Coram, NY 11727
631-696-6500/fax: 631-696-4520

33 Flying Point Rd, Ste 104A, Southampton, NY 11968
631-259-8450

Timothy H Bishop was first elected to Congress in 2002. Congressman Bishop earned a Bachelor's degree in History from Holy Cross College in Worcester, MA, and a Masters degree in Public Administration from Long Island University. Prior to his election, he spent twenty-nice years at Southampton College, and held the post of Provost when he left the school to run for Congress. In Congress he serves on the Transportation and Infrastructure Committee and the Education and Labor Committee. In the former, he works to reduce congestion on Eastern Long Island. Congressman Bishop continues to fight on behalf of middle class families and seniors, improved education, homeland security, the environment, and veterans, as well as the concerns of his eastern Long Island district. He was born and raised in Southampton.

YVETTE D CLARKE (D)
11th - Part of Kings County

1029 Longworth House Office Building, Washington, DC 20515
202-225-6231/fax 202-226-0112/Clarke.house.gov

123 Linden Boulevard, Fourth Floor, Brooklyn, NY 11226
718-287-1142/fax 718-287-1223

Yvette D Clarke was first elected to Congress in 2006. She attended Oberlin College on a scholarship, and formerly served as the Bronx Empowerment Zone's first Director of Business Development. In that capacity, she administered the $51 million budget to revitalize the south Bronx. In 2001, she was elected to the New York City Council, where she served three terms. During her tenure there, she chaired the Contracts Committee and co-chaired the New York City Women's Caucus. In Congress, she sits on the Education & Labor Committee and its Healthy Families & Communities Subcommittee as well as its Healthy, Employment, Labor & Pension Subcommittee; the Homeland Security Committee and two of its subcommittees, and the Small Business Committee and two of its subcommittees. She is a Brooklyn native.

JOSEPH CROWLEY (D)
7 - Parts of the Bronx & Queens Counties

312 Cannon House Office Bldg, Washington, DC 20515
202-225-3965/write2joecrowley@mail.house.gov.

74-09 37th Avenue, Ste 306B, Jackson Heights, NY 11372
718-779-1400

3425 E. Tremont Avenue, Suite 1-3, Bronx, NY 10465
718-931-1400

Joseph Crowley was first elected to Congress in November 1998. A graduate of Queens College, he had previously served in the New York State Assembly from 1986 until his election to Congress. In 2003 he was selected to serve as Chief Deputy Whip, making him

725

BIOGRAPHIES / US House of Representatives: New York Delegation

the highest-ranking New York Member of the Democratic leadership. Congressman Crowley is using this post to promote sound policies to improve public education, make healthcare more affordable, and to protect Social Security. He serves on the powerful House Ways and Means Committee and the House Committee on Foreign Affairs. He has promoted stronger ties between the U.S. and India, taking an active role the Middle East Peace Process, and establishing greater EU-US ties. As a freshman member, Congressman Crowley passed his amendment to appropriate $25 million to the United Nation's Population Fund (UNFPA) to improve the health of over one million women and children in Third World nations. On the domestic front, he has authored the 9/11 Heroes Medal of Valor Act, passed unanimously in the House and Senate, which calls for a special Public Safety Office Medal of Valor, which was awarded to rescue workers who died while responding to the terrorist attacks. Congressman Crowley also has advocated for New York City's Homeland Security requirements, seeing his ideas issued in a May 2002 report become law through the creation of the High Threat Urban Area Account Program, now known as the Urban Area Security Initiative. Congressman Crowley lives in Woodside, New York.

ELIOT L ENGEL (D)
17 - Bronx, Rockland & Westchester Counties

2161 Rayburn House Office Bldg, Washington, DC 20515
202-225-2464/engle.house.gov

3655 Johnson Ave, Bronx, NY 10463
718-796-9700

261 West Nyack Rd, West Nyack, NY 10994
845-735-1000

6 Gramatan Ave, Ste 205, Mt Vernon, NY 10550
914-699-4100

Eliot Engel was first elected to the U.S. Congress in 1988. He graduated from Hunter-Lehman College with a BA in History. He holds a Master's degree in Guidance and Counseling from Herbert H Lehman College of the City University of New York and a law degree from New York Law School. Prior to his election to Congress, he was a teacher and guidance counselor in the New York City public school system and then served twelve years in the New York State Assembly (1977-1988). Congressman Engel sits on the Energy and Commerce Committee and the Foreign Affairs Committee, where he chairs the Subcommittee on the Western Hemisphere. He is also Vice-Chair of the Democratic Task Force on Homeland Security, and the founder and co-chair of the House Oil and National Security Caucus that is seeking clean energy-efficient alternatives to the United States' over-reliance on oil. He authored the Syria Accountability and Lebanese Sovereignty Restoration Act of 2003, which successfully sparked international pressure on Syria to withdraw from Lebanon. He also sponsored a key resolution recognizing Jerusalem as the undivided capital of Israel. Congressman Engel is a lifelong resident of the Bronx.

VITO J FOSSELLA (R)
13 - Richmond County & parts of Kings County

2453 Rayburn House Office Bldg, Washington, DC 20515
202-225-3371/fax: 202-226-1272/www.house.gov/fossella

8505 Fourth Ave, Brooklyn, NY 11209
718-630-5277/fax: 718-630-5388

4434 Amboy Road, 2nd Floor, Staten Island, NY 10312
718-356-8400/fax: 718-356-1928

Vito Fossella was first elected to Congress in 1997. He holds a BS degree from the University of Pennsylvania's Wharton School, and a JD degree from Fordham University's School of Law. His political career began in 1994, when he was elected to the New York City Council. In that capacity, he secured funding for construction of the first new schools built on Staten Island in over a decade, and authored the legislation that paved the way for the historic agreement to close Fresh Kills Landfill. In Congress, his priorities include, strengthening national security, protecting Social Security and Medicare, improving education, and securing federal aid to enhance New York's homeland security. He serves on the House Committee on Energy and Commerce. His legislative initiatives in Congress have included successfully saving the Fort Hamilton Military Base from closure; helping to secure $21 billion in federal funding to help rebuild and secure Lower Manhattan after 9/11; restoring $125 million in federal funding for monitoring and treatment of sick or injured first responders as a result of their Ground Zero service, and defeating a recommendation to close the Brooklyn Veterans Affairs Hospital while helping to secure funding for a new emergency room for local veterans. Congressman Fossella is a native of Staten Island.

KIRSTEN GILLIBRAND (D)
20 - Dutchess, Columbia, Greene, Delaware, Renssalaer, Washington, Saratoga, Warren, Essex, and Otsego Counties.

120 Cannon House Office Bldg, Washington, DC 20515
202-225-5614/fax 202-225-1168/gillibrand.house.gov

487 Broadway Street, Saratoga Springs, NY 12866
518-581-8247/fax 518-581-8430

446 Warren Street, Hudson, NY 12534
518-828-3109/fax 518-828-3985

333 Glen Street, Ste 302, Glens Falls, NY 12801
518-743-0964/fax 518-743-1391

Kirsten Gillibrand was first elected to the U.S. House of Representatives in 2006. She holds a Bachelor's degree from Dartmouth College and a law degree from UCLA. Prior to her election, during the Clinton Administration she served as Special Counsel to then-U.S. Secretary of Housing and Urban Development Andrew Cuomo. She then became partner in a law firm. In Congress, she serves on the House Armed Services Committee and the Agriculture Department. She resides in Hudson.

BRIAN M. HIGGINS (D)
27 - Chautauqua & Erie Counties

431 Cannon House Office Bldg, Washington, DC 20515
202-225-3306/fax: 202-226-0347/ http://higgins.house.gov

Larkin at Exchange, 726 Exchange St, Ste 601, Buffalo, NY 14210
716-852-3501/fax: 716-852-3929

Fenton Bldg, 2 E Second St, Ste 300, Jamestown, NY 14701
716-484-0729/fax: 716-484-1049

Brian Higgins was first elected to the United States Congress in 2004. He received his undergraduate and graduate education at Buffalo State College, studying political science and history, respectively. From 1987 to 1993 he served in the Buffalo Common

BIOGRAPHIES / US House of Representatives: New York Delegation

Council. In 1995 he was admitted to Harvard University's Kennedy School of Government on the inaugural Western New York Harvard Graduate Fellowship, and he received an MA in Public Policy and Administration in 1996. He lectured for a time at Buffalo State College, and in 1998 was elected to the New York State Assembly, where his priorities were economic development and job creation in western New York and the revitalization of Buffalo's waterfront. In the US Congress, he continues to make economic development and job creation throughout his district a priority, and secured more than $42 million for critical transportation projects. He serves on the Committee of Transportation and Infrastructure and on the Committee on Government Reform. He lives in South Buffalo.

MAURICE D HINCHEY (D)
22 - Ulster, Sullivan, Orange, Delaware, Broome, Tioga & Tompkins Counties

2431 Rayburn House Office Bldg, Washington, DC 20515
202-225-6335/fax
202-226-0774/http://www.house.gov/hinchey/contact/

100A Federal Building, Binghamton, NY 13901
607-773-2768

123 South Cayuga Street, Suite 201, Ithaca, NY 14850
607-273-1388

291 Wall St, Kingston, NY 12401
845-331-4466

18 Anawana Lake Road, Monticello, NY 12701
845-791-7116

Maurice Hinchey was first elected to Congress in 1992. He served in the US Navy after high school, serving in the Pacific on the destroyer U.S.S. Marshall, and then worked two years as a laborer before attending SUNY-New Paltz. There, he earned both his Bachelor's and Master's degrees. He later pursued advanced graduate studies in Public Administration and Economics at SUNY-Albany. In 1975 he began eighteen-year tenure in the New York State Assembly, where he chaired the Environmental Conservation Committee. Under his leadership, the committee conducted a successful investigation of Love Canal, one of the nation's first major toxic dumpsites, and developed the nation's first law to control acid rain. He also led an investigation into organized crime control of the waste-hauling industry that led to the conviction of more than twenty criminal figures. He was also responsible for the development of the statewide system of urban parks, now called heritage areas, and was the author of the act that created the Hudson River Greenway. In the US Congress, Congressman Hinchey sits on the House Appropriations Committee, which allocates federal budget funds. In addition, he sits on the House Natural Resources Committee, and is one of 20 members on the bicameral Joint Economic Committee. Early in his Congressional career, he successfully led the effort to preserve Sterling Forest, and introduced legislation to create the Hudson River Valley National Heritage Area, which was enacted. He advocated for the re-designation of New York's Route 17 as Interstate 86, legislation he and the late Senator Daniel Patrick Moynihan wrote and passed that could bring an additional $3.2 billion in additional economic activity to the Southern Tier and Catskills regions. At the time the legislation passed, Congressman Hinchey secured more than $17 million for highway upgrades. Congressman Hinchey was born on Manhattan's Lower West Side and was raised both there and in Saugerties. He now resides in Hurley, New York.

STEVE ISRAEL (D)
2 - Parts of Nassau & Suffolk Counties

432 Cannon House Office Bldg, Washington, DC 20515
202-225-3335/fax: 202-225-4669/ http://www.house.gov/israel

150 Motor Pkwy, Ste 108, Hauppauge, NY 11788
631-951-2210; 516-505-1448/fax: 631-951-3308

Steve Israel was first elected to Congress in November 2000. He holds a B.A. in Political Science from George Washington University and an AA in Liberal Arts from Nassau Community College. Prior to his election to national office, he served as a member of the Huntington Town Board from 1993 to 2000. He also worked as an assistant county executive, Congressional aide, and manager of a public relations and marketing firm. In the US Congress, he quickly rose to leadership positions and serves as Assistant Democratic Whip. He also sits on the powerful House Appropriations Committee; previously he served on the House Armed Services Committee and on the House Financial Services Committee. Among his other assignments, he chairs of the House Caucus Democratic Task Force on Defense and the Military, co-chairs the House Democratic Study Group on National Security, and co-chairs the Center Aisle Caucus (which he formed to foster respectful dialog), the Long Island Sound Caucus, and the House Cancer Caucus. Congressman Israel was an original sponsor of the Long Island Sound Stewardship Act, which authorizes $100 million over four years to protect the sound, and also sponsored and passed the "Save Our Women From Ovarian Cancer Act," which supports accelerated federal testing of new technologies to detect and diagnose ovarian cancer. Congressman Israel was raised on the South Shore of Long Island. He currently resides in Dix Hills.

JOHN J HALL (D)
19th - Dutchess, Putnam, Westchester, Rockland and Orange Counties

1217 Longworth House Office Bldg., Washington, DC 20515
202-225-5441/fax 202-225-3289/johnhall.house.gov

225 Main Street, Roome 3232G, Goshen, NY 10924
845-291-4100/845-291-4164

Putnam County Office Building, 40 Gleneida Avenue, 3rd Floor, New York, NY 10152
845-225-3641 ext 371/fax 845-228-1480

John J Hall was first elected to the U.S. House of Representatives in November 2006. He studied physics at Notre Dame University and studied at Loyola College before leaving school to pursue a full-time career as a professional musician. In Congress, he serves on the House Committees on Transportation and Infrastructure, Veterans' Affairs, and The Select Committee on Energy Independence and Global Warming. In addition, he chairs the Veterans' Subcommittee on Disability Assistance and Memorial Affairs. In spring 2007, he introduced legislation to freeze all fiscal year 2007 bonuses set to be paid to senior level Veterans Affairs Department officials until the VA has reduced its backlog of benefit cases to fewer than 100,000 claims. His positions include opposition to privatizing Social Security, withdrawing U.S. troops from Iraq in a swift and orderly fashion while renewing an emphasis on diplomacy, and intensifying efforts to produce more renewable energy. Prior to his election, he has had a long-term career in music, including as a songwriter, that included composing and directing music for Broadway, working as a session

BIOGRAPHIES / US House of Representatives: New York Delegation

artist with Janis Joplin among others, and founding the band Orleans in 1972 with three other musicians. His latest album was released in 2005.

PETER T KING (R)
3 - Nassau County

436 Cannon House Office Bldg, Washington, DC 20515
202-225-7896/fax: 202-226-2279

1003 Park Blvd, Massapequa Park, NY 11762
516-541-4225/fax: 516-541-6602

Peter King was first elected to Congress in 1992. He is a graduate of St Francis College and earned his J.D. University of Notre Dame Law School. He began his political career in November 1977 by winning election to the Hempstead Town Council. Subsequently, he was elected to three terms as Comptroller of Nassau County. In Congress, he is Ranking Member of the House Homeland Security Committee, and serves on the Financial Services Committee. He has been actively involved in efforts to secure Homeland Security funding based on threat analysis and is strongly opposed to amnesty for illegal immigrants. In 2005, the House passed legislation he co-authored called the Border Protection, Antiterrorism, and Illegal Immigration Control Act of 2005. Congressman King sits on the Board of Visitors for the U.S. Merchant Marine Academy among his varied civic and community activities. He is the author of three novels, a lifelong resident of New York and has lived in Nassau County for nearly forty years. He currently resides in Seaford.

JOHN R "RANDY" KUHL, JR (R)
29 - Allegany, Cattaraugus, Chemung, Schuyler, Steuben and Yates Counties; most of Ontario County, and parts of Monroe County.

1505 Longworth House Office Bldg, Washington, DC 20515
202-225-3161/fax: 202-226-6599/http://kuhl.house.gov

P.O. Box 153, 22 Buell Street, Bath, NY 14810
607-776-9142/fax:607-776-9159

220 Packett's Landing, Fairport, New York 14450
585-223-4760/fax: 585-223-2328

Westgate Plaza, 700 W State St, Olean, NY 14760
800-562-7431

Randy Kuhl was first elected to Congress in 2004. He received a BS in Civil Engineering from Union College in 1966 and a JD from Syracuse University College of Law in 1969. After serving in the New York State Assembly from 1980 to 1986, he was elected to the State Senate, where he was Assistant Majority Leader from 1995 to 2004. In Congress, he serves on the Transportation and Infrastructure Committee, where he is member of the Subcommittee on Economic Development, Public Buildings and Emergency Management, as well as the Subcommittee on Water Resources and the Environment. He also sits on the Agriculture Committee and the Committee on Education and Labor and subcommittees of each. In addition, he is Deputy Minority Whip in the 110th Congress. He is the former State Chairman of the American Legislative Exchange Council (ALEC) and was vice chairman of the National Conference of State Legislatures' (NCSL) Wine Industry Task Force. His professional career has included service as attorney for several municipalities, including Steuben County. He lives in Hammondsport.

NITA M LOWEY (D)
18 - Rockland & Westchester Counties

2329 Rayburn House Office Bldg, Washington, DC 20515
202-225-6506/fax: 202-225-0546/house.gov/lowey

222 Mamaroneck Ave, Ste 310, White Plains, NY 10605
914-428-1707/fax: 914-328-1505

Rockland: 845-639-3485

Yonkers: 914-779-9766

Nita Lowey was first elected to Congress in 1988. She received her Bachelor's degree from Mt Holyoke College. Prior to her election to Congress, she served as Assistant Secretary of State of New York from 1985 to 1988. In Congress she has taken a leadership role on a wide range of issues and chaired the Democratic Congressional Campaign Committee in 2001 and 2002, the first woman and the first New Yorker to do so. She sits on the powerful House Appropriations Committee and chairs the State and Federal Operations Subcommittee. Congresswoman Lowey also is a member of the House Homeland Security Committee. She advocates on behalf of transportation, nuclear and infrastructure security, and played a key leadership role in securing more than $20 billion for recovery after September 11 attacks. She also helped secure over $32 million in federal funding to develop local bioterrorism response plans and other assistance to local first responders. Under her leadership, federal funding for after-school programs has increased from $1 million in 1996 to $1 billion today. She staunchly defended the Public Broadcasting System (PBS), in the mid-1990s, even "inviting" Muppets Bert and Ernie to a Congressional hearing, and she has been equally strong in her defense of the National Endowment of the Arts (NEA). Her legislation requiring labeling of all food products with the eight most common food allergens was enacted in 2006. She is former Chair of the Congressional Women's Caucus and the House Pro-Choice Caucus. She was born in the Bronx and resides in Harrison.

CAROLYN B MALONEY (D)
14 - New York & Queens Counties

2331 Rayburn House Office Bldg, Washington, DC 20515
202-225-7944/fax: 202-225-4709/http://maloney.house.gov/

28-11 Astoria Blvd, Astoria, NY 11102-1933
718-932-1804/fax: 718-932-1805

1651 3rd Avenue, Suite 311, New York, NY 10128
212-860-0606/fax: 212-860-0704

Carolyn Maloney was first elected to Congress in 1992. A graduate of Greensboro College, she worked for several years as teacher and administrator for the New York City Board of Education. In 1977 she went to work for the New York State Legislature, serving in senior staff positions for both the Assembly and the Senate. In 1982 she won a seat on the New York City Council and served for ten years; her accomplishments included acting as principal author of the landmark New York City Campaign Finance Act. In the US Congress, she chairs the House Financial Service Committee's Financial Institutions Subcommittee, which has jurisdiction over the nation's banking system. She also is vice chair of the Joint Economics Committee, a bicameral Congressional panel that examines and addresses the nation's most pressing economic issues. She is also a senior member of the House Oversight and Government Reform Commit-

BIOGRAPHIES / US House of Representatives: New York Delegation

tee. Congresswoman Maloney has worked to ensure that New York's recovery from 9/11 is completed; in 2004 she obtained health monitoring and treatment for the workers at Ground Zero after 9/11. She became Chair of the House Democratic Caucus Task Force on Homeland Security in 2003. The former co-chair of the Women's Caucus spearheaded the effort to expedite use and processing of DNA rape kits. On the economic front, she has worked to including groundbreaking identity theft protections in legislation updating the nation's credit reporting system, and has advocated on behalf of New York's financial services community, playing a major role in legislation to modernize the deposit insurance system which passed the house. She lives in New York City.

CAROLYN McCARTHY (D)
4 - Nassau County

106 Cannon House Office Bldg, Washington, DC 20515
202-225-5516/fax 202-225-5758

200 Garden City Plaza, Ste 320, Garden City, NY 11530
516-739-3008/fax 516-739-2973

Carolyn McCarthy was elected to her first term in Congress in 1996. She is a licensed practical nurse with over thirty years of experience working in the health-care field. After her husband was killed and her son injured in the 1993 Long Island Railroad massacre, she turned her tragedy into a public campaign against gun violence. In addition to her activism against gun violence, she works on behalf of working families. In the US Congress, she chairs the Subcommittee on Healthy Families and Communities, is a senior member of the Committee on Education and Labor, and sits on the Committee on Financial Services. She is a lifelong resident of Mineola, New York.

JOHN M McHUGH (R)
23 - Clinton, Lewis, Jefferson, Franklin, Oswego, St Lawrence, Hamilton, & Madison Counties and parts of Essex, Fulton, and Oneida Counties.

2366 Rayburn House Office Bldg, Washington, DC 20515
202-225-4611/fax: 202-226-0621/ http://mchugh.house.gov

28 North School St, PO Box 800, Mayfield, NY 12117
518-661-6486/fax: 518-661-5704

104 Federal Building, Plattsburg, NY 12901
518-563-1406/fax: 518-561-9723

120 Washington St, Ste 200, Watertown, NY 13601
315-782-3150/fax: 315-782-1291

205 S Peterboro St, Canastota, NY 13032
315-697-2063/fax: 315-697-2064

John McHugh was first elected to Congress in 1992. He received a BA in Political Science from Utica College of Syracuse University in 1970, and earned a Master's degree in Public Administration from SUNY's Nelson A Rockefeller Graduate School of Public Affairs. He began his career in public service in 1971 in Watertown, where he served as confidential assistant to the city manager. Thereafter, he joined the staff of NYS Senator H Douglas Barclay, where he acted as chief of Research & Liaison with local government for nine years. He served in the New York State Senate from 1984 to 1992. In the US Congress, he has advocated for fiscal responsibility, lower taxes, stronger schools, and protection of Social Security and Medicare. He backs affordable and accessible health care for people residing in rural areas, and has fought to help farmers secure better prices, extend crop insurance protections to specialty crop farmers, and has rallied Congressional members from across the country to enact the Option 1-A pricing system, which provides higher payments to farmers for their milk. He is a senior member of the House Armed Services Committee and the House Oversight and Government Reform Committee. He also sits on the House Permanent Select Committee on Intelligence. Born in Watertown, Congressman McHugh lives in Pierrepont Manor in Jefferson County.

MICHAEL R McNULTY (D)
21 - Albany, Montgomery, Schenectady and Schoharie Counties and portions of Fulton, Renssalaer and Saratoga Counties

2210 Rayburn House Office Bldg, Washington, DC 20515
202-225-5076/fax: 202-225-5077/mike.mcnulty@mail.house.gov

O'Brien Fed Bldg, Room 827, Albany, NY 12207
518-465-0700/fax: 518-427-5107

2490 Riverfront Center, Amsterdam, NY 12010
518-843-3400/fax: 518-843-8874

376 Broadway, Suite 2, Schenectady, NY 12305
518-374-4547/fax: 518-374-7908

33 Second St, Troy, NY 12180-3975
518-271-0822/fax: 518-273-6150

Fulton Co Ofc Bldg, 223 W Main St, Rm 10, Johnstown, NY 12095
518-762-3568/fax: 518-736-2004

Michael McNulty was first elected to Congress in 1988. He is a graduate of the College of Holy Cross, where he earned a BA degree in Political Science. He is also a graduate of the Hill School of Insurance. He was first elected to public office in 1969, as Town Supervisor of Green Island. After eight years as Supervisor, he was elected Mayor of the Village of Green Island and served in that capacity until he won election to the New York State Assembly in 1982. In Congress, after having served as Freshman Majority Whip for the northern region of the country during the first session of the 101st Congress, he was named to the position of Majority Whip-At-Large and served in that capacity through the 103rd Congress. He now serves as At-Large-Whip. He has served on numerous committees: Armed Services, Small Business, International Relations, and Post Office and Civil Service. He serves on the powerful House Ways & Means Committee and chairs the Subcommittee on Social Security. He also sits on the Subcommittee on Income Security and Family Support. Congressman McNulty was born in Troy, and resides in Green Island.

GREGORY W MEEKS (D)
6 - Queens County

2324 Rayburn House Office Bldg, Washington, DC 20515
202-225-3461/fax: 202-226-4169/ http://www.house.gov/meeks

153-01 Jamaica Avenue 2nd Floor, Jamaica, NY 11432
718-327-9791/fax 718-327-4711

1931 Mott Ave, Rm 305, Far Rockaway, NY 11691
718-327-9791/fax: 718-327-4722

BIOGRAPHIES / US House of Representatives: New York Delegation

Gregory W Meeks was first elected to Congress in 1998. He received his BA degree in History with a minor in Political Science from Adelphi University and his JD from Howard University School of Law. He became an Assistant District Attorney in Queens and was promoted to the Office of the Special Narcotics Prosecutor for the City of New York. He later joined the State Investigations Commission responsible for investigations of public officials, state employees, and organized crime. He then became Supervising Judge for the New York State Worker's Compensation System. In 1992, he was elected to the NYS Assembly where he served five years. In Congress, Congressman Meeks serves on the House Financial Services Committee and the International Relations Committee, and advocates on behalf of economic opportunity and social justice for all people. He formerly chaired the Congressional Black Caucus' New Markets Initiatives, which focused on ensuring that the opinions of minority consumers, venture capitalists and entrepreneurs could be heard as Congress debated key financial and economic policy issues. He backed access to JFK Airport for the creation of Jet Blue Airlines, authored legislation to boost air service from New York City's two airports to communities in upstate New York, and assisted American Airlines as it began construction of a $1.4 billion terminal at JFK - which is located in Congressman Meeks's district. Born in East Harlem, he is a lifelong resident of New York and currently resides in Far Rockaway.

JERROLD L NADLER (D)
8 - New York & Kings Counties

2334 Rayburn House Office Bldg, Washington, DC 20515
202-225-5635/http://www.house.gov/nadler

445 Neptune Ave, Brooklyn, NY 11224
718-373-3198

201 Varick St, Ste 669, New York, NY 10014
212-367-7350

Jerrold Nadler was first elected to Congress in 1992. He graduated from Columbia University with a BA in government, and from Fordham Law School. In 1976, after a stint as a legislative assistant, he was elected to the New York State Assembly, where he served for sixteen years, during which time he was credited with authoring much of the state's body of law on domestic violence and child support enforcement and was one of the architects of the landmark "Child Support Standards Act." In Congress he is perhaps best known as a prominent member of the Judiciary Committee. He chairs the Constitution, Civil Rights, and Civil Liberties Subcommittee, which deals with such issues as religious freedom federal civil rights, abortion, and gay rights. He was one of the lead Democratic sponsors of the Religious Freedom Restoration Act and the Democratic sponsor of the Religious Land Use and Institutionalized Persons Act, signed into law by President Clinton and upheld by the U.S. Supreme Court. In addition, he serves on the Crime, Terrorism and Homeland Security Subcommittee. He is also a member of the House Committee on Transportation and Infrastructure and co-chairs the Congressional Transit Caucus, where he has fought for better subway service among other issues. After his district was attacked on 9/11, he dedicated his efforts to securing $20 billion for recovery work. Born in Brooklyn, he resides on Manhattan's West Side.

CHARLES B RANGEL (D)
15 - New York County

2354 Rayburn House Office Bldg, Washington, DC 20515
202-225-4365/fax: 202-225-0816/http://rangel.house.gov/contact.shtml

163 W 125th St, Suite 737, New York, NY 10027
212-663-3900/fax: 212-663-4277

Charles Rangel was first elected to Congress in 1970. He served in the US Army from 1948 to 1952 in Korea, and was awarded the Purple Heart and Bronze Star. He earned a BS degree from New York University School of Commerce in 1957 and a JD from St John's University School of Law. In 1961 he was appointed assistant US attorney in the Southern District of New York, and later served as General Counsel to the National Advisory Commission on Selective Service. In 1967, he was elected to the New York State Assembly. In the US Congress, he chairs the powerful House Ways and Means Committee. He is also Chairman of the Board of the Democratic Congressional Campaign Committee, and Dean of the New York State Congressional Delegation. He is the principal author of the $5 billion Federal Empowerment Zone demonstration project to revitalize urban neighborhoods, and author of the Low Income Housing Tax Credit that financed ninety percent of the nation's affordable housing built in the last decade. Congressman Rangel formerly chaired the Select Committee on Narcotics Abuse and Control and continues to fight against drug abuse and trafficking. He is a founding member and former chairman of the Congressional Black Caucus, was chairman of the NYS Council of Black Elected Democrats and was a member of the House Judiciary Committee during the hearings on the articles of impeachment against President Richard Nixon. He was born in Harlem and still lives there.

THOMAS M. REYNOLDS (R)
26 - Wyoming, Erie, Genesee, Monroe, Orleans, Niagara & Livingston Counties

332 Cannon House Office Bldg, Washington, DC 20515
202-225-5265/fax 202-225-5910/www.reynolds.house.gov

500 Essjay Rd, Suite 260, Williamsville, NY 14221
716-634-2324/7fax 16-631-7610

1577 West Ridge Rd, Greece, NY 14615
585-663-5570/fax 585-663-5711

Thomas Reynolds was first elected to Congress in 1998. Educated at Springville-Griffith Institute and Kent State University, he is a licensed real estate and insurance broker. After serving on the Concord Town board from 1974 to 1982, he joined the Erie County Legislature from 1982 to 1988. In 1988, soon after his arrival in the NYS Assembly, he became the Assembly Republican Leader in 1995. In Congress, he sits on the powerful Ways and Means Committee. A strong advocate for his home district, Congressman Reynolds has secured almost $500 million in federal funding for his district. Among his legislative initiatives signed into law was the Smith-Reynolds bill, which aids in the movement of people and goods over US borders with Canada. When his party was in the majority, he served in the Republican leadership as Chairman of the National Republican Congressional Committee. He lives in Clarence.

JOSE E SERRANO (D)
16 - Bronx County

2227 Rayburn House Office Bldg, Washington, DC 20515
202-225-4361/fax: 202-225-6001/Serrano.house.gov

BIOGRAPHIES / US House of Representatives: New York Delegation

788 Southern Blvd, Bronx, NY 10455
718-620-0084/fax: 718-620-0658

Jose E Serrano was first elected to Congress in 1990. Born in Mayaguez, Puerto Rico, he served in the 172nd Support Battalion of the US Army Medical Corps. He also attended Lehman College of CUNY. He was elected to the NYS Assembly in 1974 and served until 1990. In Congress, he serves on the House Appropriations Committee as a member of the Subcommittee on Financial Services and General Government. In addition, he is Senior Whip for the Majority Whip operation, and an active member of the Congressional Hispanic Caucus which he formerly chaired. As an appropriator, he has managed to secure millions of dollars in federal funding for his Bronx district; perhaps the most significant project has been the environmental restoration of the Bronx River. He is architect of the English-Plus Resolution, calling on government to encourage all Americans to learn and use multiple languages in addition to English. Since his earliest days in Congress, he has supported lifting the embargo against Cuba. He also proposed the bill, signed into law as part of a larger bill, which grants posthumous citizenship to non-citizens who died as a result of the 9/11 attack and who had already initiated the process to become US citizens. He resides in the Bronx.

LOUISE McINTOSH SLAUGHTER (D)
28 - Erie, Monroe, Niagara & Orleans Counties

2469 Rayburn House Office Bldg, Washington, DC 20515
202-225-3615/fax: 202-225-7822/www.louise.house.gov

3120 Federal Bldg, 100 State St, Rochester, NY 14614
585-232-4850/fax: 585-232-1954

465 Main St, Ste 105, Buffalo, NY 14203
716-853-5813/fax: 716-853-6347

1910 Pine Ave, Niagara Falls, NY 14301
716-282-1274/fax: 716-282-2479

Louise McIntosh Slaughter was first elected to Congress in 1986. She attended the University of Kentucky, where she received a BS degree in Microbiology and a Master of Science degree in Public Health. She served in the Monroe County Legislature from 1976 to 1979 and in the New York State Assembly from 1982 to 1986. In Congress, she chairs the powerful House Committee on Rules, the first woman to hold the post. She is also the Democratic chair of the Congressional Arts Caucus and the Bipartisan Congressional Pro-Choice Caucus. She was appointed to the new Select Committee on Homeland Security in 2003, at the time serving as Ranking Member. She advocates on behalf of fair coverage in the media, economic development, and health. A leading advocate for women's rights, she formerly co-chaired the Congressional Caucus for Women, and she co-authored the Violence Against Women Act in 1994. A member of the House Budget Committee in the early 1990s, she secured the first $500 million earmarked for breast cancer research at the National Institute of Health (NIH). Born in Harland County, Kentucky, she lives in Fairport, a suburb of Rochester.

EDOLPHUS TOWNS (D)
10 - Kings County

2232 Rayburn House Office Bldg, Washington, DC 20515
202-225-5936/fax: 202-225-1018/ http://www.house.gov/towns

1670 Fulton St, Brooklyn, NY 11213
718-774-5682

26 Court St, Ste 1510, Brooklyn, NY 11241
718-855-8018

1110 Pennsylvania Ave, Store 5, Brooklyn, NY 11207
718-272-1175

2294 Nostrand Ave, Brooklyn, NY 11210
718-434-7931

Edolphus Towns was first elected to Congress in November 1982. He is a veteran of the United States Army, an ordained Baptist Minister, holds his Bachelor's degree from North Carolina A&T University and a Master's degree in Social Work from Adelphi University. He has taught in the NYC public school system and is a former professor at Medgar Evers College in Brooklyn. He also has been an administrator at Beth Israel Hospital and Brooklyn District Deputy President - the first African American to hold that post. In the U.S. Congress, he is a member of the Energy and Commerce Committee, where he sits on the Commerce, Trade and Consumer Protection Subcommittee, the Health Subcommittee, and the Telecommunications and the Internet Subcommittee. His legislative successes include the Student Right to Know Act that mandates the reporting of student athletes' graduation rates, enhanced Medicare reimbursement rates for mid-level practitioners, creating new standards for the inclusion of children in clinical trials, and creating the Telecommunications Development Fund, which provides capital for small and minority telecommunications businesses. He is committed to protecting national parks and creating open space throughout Brooklyn, including the Brooklyn Bridge Park Project, of which he was an original incorporator. He was born in Chadbourn, North Carolina and lives Brooklyn.

NYDIA M VELAZQUEZ (D)
12 - New York, Queens & Kings Counties

2466 Rayburn House Office Bldg, Washington, DC 20515
202-225-2361/fax: 202-226-0327/ http://www.house.gov/velazquez

266 Broadway, Ste 201, Brooklyn, NY 11211
718-599-3658

173 Avenue B, New York, NY 10009
212-673-3997

16 Court Street, Suite 1006, Brooklyn, NY 11241
718-222-5819

Nydia Velazquez was first elected to Congress in 1992. Born in Yabucoa, Puerto Rico, she attended the University of Puerto Rico in Rio Piedras. In 1976 she earned her Master's degree from New York University. She went on to teach Puerto Rican Studies at CUNY's Hunter College before entering politics as a Special Assistant to Congressman Edolphus Towns in 1983. In 1984, she was appointed to serve on the New York City Council, the first Latina to do so. In 1986 she was the Director of the Department of Puerto Rican Community Affairs in the United States, where she initiated one of the most successful employment empowerment programs in the nation's history. As a Member of Congress, she has worked to promote economic development, to protect community health and the environment, and to secure access to affordable housing, quality education, and health care for all New York families. She chairs the House Small Business Committee, which oversees federal programs and

BIOGRAPHIES / US House of Representatives: New York Delegation

contracts worth an annual $200 billion. She also sits on the House Financial Services Committee and its Subcommittee on Housing and Community Opportunity. She resides in Brooklyn.

JAMES T WALSH (R)
25 - All of Onondaga and Wayne Counties, and parts of Cayuga & Monroe Counties

2372 Rayburn House Office Bldg, Washington, DC 20515
202-225-3701/fax: 202-225-4042/walsh.house.gov

PO Box 7306, Syracuse, NY 13261
315-423-5657/fax: 315-423-5669

1180 Canandaigua Road, Palmyra, New York 14522
315-597-6138/fax 315-597-6631

James Walsh was first elected to Congress in 1988. He earned his Bachelor's degree in history from St Bonaventure University, served in the Peace Corps in Nepal, and was director of the Telecommunications Institute SUNY's Institute of Technology at Utica-Rome. He also served as president of the Syracuse City Council. In Congress, he is a member of the Appropriations Committee and is Ranking Member of its Labor-health and Human Services-Education Subcommittee. In addition, he is a senior member of the Transportation-Housing and Urban Development Subcommittee. Congressman Walsh co-chairs the ad-hoc Committee on Ireland, is past chair of Friends of Ireland, and has been instrumental in the Irish Peace process. He also supports issues of interest to his district, such as clean water initiatives and projects to expand the region's reputation for renewable energy R&D. He lives in the town of Onondaga.

ANTHONY D WEINER (D)
9 - Kings & Queens Counties

1122 Longworth House Office Bldg, Washington, DC 20515
202-225-6616/weiner@mail.house.gov

1800 Sheepshead Bay Rd, Brooklyn, NY 11235
718-743-0441

80-02 Kew Gardens Rd, Ste 5000, Kew Gardens, NY 11415
718-520-9001

90-16 Rockaway Beach Blvd., Rockaway, NY 11693
718-318-9255

Anthony Weiner was first elected to Congress in 1998. He holds a B.A. from the University of New York, Plattsburg. Previously, he served as an aide to then-Representative Charles Schumer from 1985 to 1991. He was elected to the New York City Council in 1991 where he served until 1998. As a Congressman, he was the only New Yorker appointed by House leadership to the Homeland Security Task Force. He is a member of the Energy and Commerce Committee, and also sits on the Judiciary Committee. He's also brought millions in funding to New York to tackle such goals as restoring city parks and beaches, improve DNA collection to solve crimes against women, and more. In the latter role, he sits on the Aviation and Highways Subcommittees and is working to reduce airport air noise. He resides in Forest Hills Queens.

Name Index

Aaron, Merik R, 557
Aarons, Sharon A, 59
Aaronson, Melvyn, 566
Abate, Catherine, 222, 318, 474
Abatemarco, Cari, 22
Abatemarco, Michael J, 535
Abbate, Jr, Peter J, 36, 43, 44, 45, 47, 49, 297, 686
Abbate, Mary, 488
Abbati, Amy, 41
Abbitt, Viola, 134, 254
Abbitt, Viola I, 308
Abboa-Offei, Abenaa, 455
Abbott, Martin, 600
Abbott, Tracie, 521
Abdelazim, Tarik, 415
Abdella, Steve, 398
Abdus-Salaam, Sheila, 56
Abeel, Christian M, 542
Abels, Linda, 438
Abercrombie, Neil, 388
Abernethy, Samuel F, 109
Abers, Crystal, 397
Abington, Steve, 482
Abitabilo, Neil, 512
Abrahall, Ron, 511
Abraham, Thomas W, 674
Abram, Sam L, 5, 90
Abramowitz, Bernard, 91, 92, 124, 231, 291, 327
Abrams, Carol, 430
Abrams, David, 145
Abrams, Frank E, 237, 287, 295
Abrams, Laura A, 402
Abrams, William, 250
Abramson, Gilbert L, 67
Abramson, Jill, 597
Acampora, Patricia L, 14, 169
Achramoritch, Steven, 652
Acker, Karen Ann, 527
Acker, Ruth, 167
Ackerly, Jeff, 583
Ackerman, Gary, 391
Ackerman, Gary L, 93, 106, 232, 240, 249, 381, 389, 390, 391, 724
Ackerman, Hank, 601
Ackerson, Anne, 153, 344
Ackerson, John, 442
Ackey, Bruce, 79
Acosta, Rolando T, 56
Acquafredda, Nicholas, 290
Acquario, Adam, 526
Acquario, Stephen, 460
Acquario, Stephen J, 209, 294
Acquaro, Ralph, 648
Acunto, Stephen, 601
Adams, Andrew, 12, 269

Adams, Ann M, 666
Adams, Christopher, 219, 273
Adams, Eric, 21, 25, 26, 27, 32, 137, 239, 362
Adams, Eric L , 712
Adams, Eric R, 64
Adams, Jody, 61
Adams, Kenneth, 466
Adams, Michelle, 107, 233
Adams, Rachel Amy, 59
Adams, Thomas, 66
Adams, Toby, 85
Adams, William J, 561
Aderman, Darren P, 546
Adkins, Mary R, 551
Adler, Harold, 59
Adler, Lester B, 57
Adler, M.D., Karl P, 629
Adler, Norman M, 463
Adler, Sol, 454
Adolf, Jay, 463
Aefsky, Fern, 643
Aesch, Mark R, 127, 354, 380
Affronti, Francis A, 57
Agarwal, Nisha, 497
Agate, Augustus C, 58
Agins, Bruce D, 213
Agostine, Jr, Joseph A, 235
Agostino, John A, 9, 195, 289
Agostino, Thomas M, 565
Agostino, Tom, 248, 271
Agritelley, Ralph, 119, 352
Agruso, Susan A, 671
Aguilar, Erica, 528
Ahearn, Kathy A, 8, 144, 212, 279, 312, 333
Ahern, Barbara J, 545
Ahern, John, 549
Ahl, Caroline W, 6, 288, 296
Ahlers, Kathleen O'Brien, 432
Ahlstrom, Keith, 449
Ahlstrom, Keith D, 398
Ahlstrom, Theresa, 496
Ahluwalia, Perminda, 471
Ahmad, Iftikhar, 434
Ahrens, Edward, 640
Ahrens, Jr, Frederick H, 410
Aidala, Gregory, 638
Aiello, Greg, 345
Aiken, Doris, 142
Aikens, Patricia, 141, 265
Ain, Michael, 534
Ainlay, Stephen C, 632
Aison, Howard M, 71
Ajello, Michael V, 447
Akaka, Daniel, 364, 387
Akaka, Daniel K, 340, 383, 384, 386
Akin, Todd, 388

Akins, Matt, 595
Alagno, Louis, 425
Alam, Ismat, 441
Alamia, Salvatore A, 70
Alazraki, Marcia, 503
Albanese, Robert C, 93
Albanese-DePinto, Rose, 429
Albano, Teresa, 596
Albert, Andrew, 588
Albert, John, 455
Albert, John P, 151
Albert, Thomas, 483
Alberti, Peter P, 405
Albertin, Richard D, 349
Aldam, Mark E, 591
Alden, Amie, 403
Alderstein, Michael, 464
Aldous, Ken, 179, 215
Aldrich, Susan, 482
Alejandro, Joseph A, 559
Alesi, James S, 21, 26, 27, 28, 29, 30, 31, 103, 292, 303, 354, 712
Alessandro, Francis M, 59
Alessandro, Joseph, 57
Alessi, Marc A, 52
Alessi, Marc S, 36, 43, 44, 47, 49, 50, 52, 686
Alexander, Cedric, 8, 133, 253, 288
Alexander, Emily, 510
Alexander, George B, 14, 135
Alexander, Lamar, 385, 386
Alexander, Lanny R, 431
Alexander, Louis, 9, 177
Alexander, Margo, 540
Alexander, Rodney, 618
Alfano, John L, 74
Alfano, Robert R, 100, 148
Alfano, Thomas, 49
Alfano, Thomas W, 35, 36, 45, 48, 239, 248, 272, 297, 686
Algaze, Martin, 21
Alger, Mark R, 410
Alger, Robin L, 158
Ali, Khayriyyah, 618
Ali, Shaazad, 434
Alicea, Victor G, 622
Alioto, Paul J, 666
Aliotta, Thomas P, 56
Allaire, Frank, 554
Allan, Col, 596
Allard, Jenet N, 408
Allard, Wayne, 383, 384
Allaud, Aimee, 498
Allegretti, Frank, 421
Allen, Bruce, 60
Allen, Denny, 124, 336
Allen, Dorothy, 426

Name Index

Allen, George, 385
Allen, Gregory, 11, 213, 246, 268
Allen, James, 87, 459, 569
Allen, John, 281
Allen, Leonard, 479
Allen, Lora A, 160
Allen, Sandra, 178
Allen, Susan K, 652
Allen, Virginia E, 422
Allen, Wayne, 248, 271
Allen, Wayne D, 397
Allibone, Peter, 359
Allinger, Stephen, 516, 526
Allison, Lisa, 507
Allman, Richard N, 60
Allocco, Edward J, 433
Alloi, Joanne, 603
Allport, Donald J, 406
Allyn, Robert, 196, 334
Almberg, Mark, 596
Almodovar, Priscilla, 91, 92, 123, 127, 128, 230, 231, 291, 327
Aloi, Anthony F, 66
Aloise, Michael B, 58
Aloise, Robert, 670
Alonso, Esti, 48
Alpert, Allen G, 60
Alpert, Bruce D, 57
Alpert, David A, 449
Alpert, Paul L, 60
Altemus, Jim, 86
Alter, Eleanor Breitel, 117, 258
Alteri, Margaret M, 226
Alteri, Richard F, 173, 536
Alterman, Ava P, 60
Altieri, Stephen, 424
Altman, Anita, 523
Altman, Judith, 204, 328
Altmire, Jason, 274, 392
Altone, Edmund Russell, 214
Altschuler, Howard, 434
Alund, Chris, 270
Alvarado, Efrain L, 60
Alvarez, Richard P, 619
Alvaro, Michael, 221, 317, 477
Alverado, Ron, 184
Alvord, Karen, 598
Alvord, Marc, 598
Alworth, Tom, 188
Alzate, Luis, 457
Aman, Diane, 280
Amann, Floyd F, 615
Amarakoon, Vasantha, 100, 147
Amaral, M Celeste, 540
Amati, Patricia, 122, 137
Amato, Michael J, 404
Amberg-Blyskal, Patricia, 363
Ambrecht, Michael R, 58
Ambrosi, Marc, 634
Ambrosio, Michael A, 61
Ambuhl, Arthur, 224

Amell, Stewart R, 662
Amer, Fatma, 427
Ameroso, John, 84
Ames, Margery E, 284, 458
Ames, William F, 63
Amey, Bruce, 651
Amico, Virginia O, 403
Amicone, Philip A, 445
Amissah, Father Kofi, 310
Amler, Robert, 219
Amo, Scott A, 648
Amodeo, Damian J, 63
Amodeo, Elizabeth, 101, 326
Amodeo, Joseph T, 562
Amodeo, Mark, 476
Amodeo, Thomas P, 71
Amorosi, Greg, 36
Amoroso, Dino G, 120, 336
Amoroso, Rhonda K, 9, 178
Amstel, Heddy, 72
Amundsen, Charles A, 657
Amundson, Richard, 674
Amyotte, Alyssa, 611
Anastassiou, Basil, 476
Anatharam, P V, 433
Ancowitz, Richard, 49
Anders, Alan L, 435
Andersen, Maj David C, 362
Andersen, Ross, 80
Anderson, Adrian H, 400
Anderson, Brian C, 601
Anderson, Cami, 657
Anderson, Chris, 26, 30
Anderson, Christine, 3, 4, 157, 194, 371
Anderson, COS, Kristin, 41
Anderson, Daniel, 526
Anderson, Daniel S, 137
Anderson, Dennis, 196, 334
Anderson, Ellen, 213
Anderson, J Mark, 5, 98, 102, 124, 324
Anderson, James, 426, 430
Anderson, John, 600
Anderson, Kathleen, 161
Anderson, Lisa, 525
Anderson, Michelle, 471
Anderson, Michelle J, 621
Anderson, Richard T, 110, 235, 555
Anderson, S A, 557
Anderson, Scott, 471
Anderson, Susan, 606
Anderson, Wayne, 527
Andersson, Brian G, 433
Andino, Thomas, 437
Andreasen, Peter, 444
Andrews, Carl, 4, 157, 194, 287
Andrews, Daniel, 407, 435
Andrews, Jason A, 640
Andrews, Robert, 389
Andrews, Shelley, 22
Andrias, Richard T, 55
Andriola, Tom, 52

Andronaco, Mary Lee, 59
Andruili, Anthony, 160
Andrus, Matthew, 16, 101, 180, 199, 291
Anelante Jr, Frank J, 533
Anello, Vincenzo V, 436
Ang, Vincent W, 443
Angelo, Jeffrey, 215, 245
Angelo, Jesse, 596
Angiolillo, Daniel D, 55, 57
Angley, James P, 91, 92, 124, 127, 128, 231, 327
Anglin, Laura, 16, 198, 297
Anglin, Laura L, 6, 98, 194, 287, 324
Anisman, Martin J, 624
Annacone, Dominic, 671
Annetts, Paul, 130
Annucci, Anthony, 7, 129
Annunziata, Albert A, 304, 563
Annunziato, Anthony, 668
Ansty, Martha F, 185
Antalek, Sr, Frederick N, 93
Antenen, Thomas, 428
Antenucci, Nicholas, 531
Anthony, Barbara, 104, 109
Anthony, Patricia, 420
Antonecchia, Donald, 677
Antonelli, Debra, 71
Antonelli, John J, 428
Antonucci, Carol, 436
Antos, Susan, 470
Anzalone, Anna, 70
Anzevino, Jeff, 521
Apker, Craig, 138
Appel, Greg, 595
Appel, Janet F, 329
Appel, Larry, 197, 290
Apple, Douglas, 430
Applegate MD, Mary, 213
Applewhite, Eric, 496
Aquila, Evelyn, 157
Aquila, Evelyn J, 8
Aquilina, Anne, 596
Aracich, Matthew P, 534
Aragon, Luiz, 430
Aragosa, Patrick, 441
Arbolino, Philip B, 660
Arbuckle, Joanne, 482
Arcara, Richard J, 260
Arce, Mari, 4, 194
Archer, Charles, 458
Arcuri, Michae Al, 725
Arena, Angelo, 562
Arena, David, 304
Arena, Michael, 619
Argentieri, Richard A, 410
Argetsinger, J C, 68
Argulewicz, Anthony, 673
Argyriou, Hercules, 545
Arias, Gina, 485
Ark, John J, 57
Arkin, David, 597

734

Name Index

Arko, Robert A, 549
Armao, Tom, 582
Armstrong, Geno, 496
Armstrong, James, 83
Armstrong, Pamela J, 9, 178
Armstrong, Regina B, 331
Arning, Robert, 496
Arnold, Cassandra, 496
Arnold, Jacqueline J, 83
Arnold, Judith, 213
Arnold, Judith A, 10
Arnold, Kay, 541
Arnold, Robert, 355
Arnow, Nancy, 521
Aronowitz, Michelle, 134, 253
Aronson, Sam, 171
Aronson, Stephen D, 71
Aronstein, Laurence W, 654
Aronstein, Lois, 315
Arriaga, Fred, 435
Arroyo, Carmen E, 36, 43, 44, 45, 46, 686
Arture, Nicholas L, 548
Artus, Dale, 130
Arzt, George, 459
Asarch, Joel K, 70
Asaro, Tricia, 487
Asaro-Angelo, Robert, 505
Asciutto, Georgia, 152
Ash, Carol, 13, 179, 180, 334, 335
Ashe, Alyce, 122, 133, 137, 252, 288, 378
Ashe, Bernard F, 117, 258
Ashe, Charles A, 124, 201, 258, 379
Asheld, Barbara, 214
Asher, W Gerard, 70
Ashley, Diane, 518
Ashley, Laura, 581
Ashton, Judith, 322
Askins, Chantall, 523
Assini Jr, Charles J, 490
Assini, Jo Anne, 67
Astles, Geoffrey C, 406
Athens, Virginia, 67
Atherton, John J, 63
Atiba-Weza, Fadhilika, 668
Atkin, John, 116, 182
Atkins, Gregory, 435
Atkins, Tamara, 482
Atkinson, Scott, 610
Atlas, Jeffrey M, 60
Atwater, Terry, 102, 327
Auberger, John T, 420
Aubertine, Darrel, 203
Aubertine, Darrel J, 36, 44, 46, 47, 48, 52, 53, 292, 686
Aubry, Jeffrion L, 36, 46, 47, 51, 53, 137, 238, 686
Audi, Aminy I, 611
August, Stephen M, 52
Augustine, Pat, 113, 181
Aulisi, Richard T, 57
Auriemma, Frank V, 664

Ausfeld, Robert, 606
Auspelmyer, Deborah, 580
Aust, Peter L, 585
Austenberg, Nina, 85, 319
Austin, Dan, 605
Austin, James, 169
Austin, John, 123, 149, 412
Austin, Kelly J, 162
Austin, Leonard B, 57
Austin, Phillip R, 598
Avella, Michael, 20, 452
Avella, Michael A, 557
Avella, Mike, 30
Avery, Andrew P, 419
Aviles, Alan D, 430
Avner, Esq, Judith I, 221
Avner, Judith I, 283
Avrick, Stuart, 448
Avrin, Dave, 339
Awn, Peter, 525
Axelrod, Michael C, 128, 271, 354
Aycock, Alice, 427
Ayres, Bill, 323
Ayres, David J, 65
Ayres, Walter C, 123, 201, 378
Azare, Monica, 527
Azia, Jane, 99, 135, 169, 254, 325
Baa-Danso, Nancy, 214, 360
Babcock, Michael, 426
Babcock, Robert, 363
Baboulis, Steve, 607
Babu, S V, 100, 147
Babyak, R Carey, 349
Baca, Joe, 186, 219, 387
Bacalles, James, 45, 47, 48, 217
Bacalles, James G, 35, 36, 52, 687
Bach, Thomas, 117, 350
Bach, Victor, 234
Bacharach, Samuel B, 275
Bachrach, Deborah, 10, 213, 503
Bachus, Spencer, 93, 232, 249, 389
Backer, Joseph W, 678
Backes, William, 47
Backstrom, Brian D, 473
Bacon, William, 573
Bader, Elaine, 570
Badillo, Gilbert, 60
Badner, Lisa, 429
Baecher, Theodore, 467
Baer, Barbara, 474
Baer, Jack, 59
Baer, Kenneth J, 125, 163, 202
Baerman, Lawrence K, 259
Baggiano, Frank, 62
Bahr, Paul, 634
Bahren, Susan, 161
Baigent, Peter, 520
Bailey, Jack W, 162
Bailey, Jon, 571
Bailey, Jonathan, 45
Bailey, Kevin, 583

Bailey, Rosalie, 63
Bailie, Roger, 269
Bailly Jr, John P, 17, 313
Bailly, Rose Mary, 124, 258, 379
Baily-Schiffman, Loren, 59
Bain, Donald E, 631
Bain, Mark B, 188
Baio, Bridget, 520
Baird, Brian, 392
Baisley, Jr, Paul J, 57
Baker, Dale, 188
Baker, Debra D, 67
Baker, Donald, 349
Baker, Emily R, 205, 303
Baker, Francine, 73
Baker, III, Joseph R, 135, 216, 254
Baker, James, 421
Baker, Jon K, 397
Baker, Joseph, 3, 211, 237, 307
Baker, Lynette, 609
Baker, Paul, 86
Baker, Richard H, 186, 393
Baker-Sullivan, Heather, 498
Baksh, Tara, 498
Balassie, Kate, 375
Balbick, Robert J, 71
Balboni, Michael, 3, 129, 194
Baldauf, Gary A, 134, 216, 254
Balduf, June P, 561
Baldwin, Irene, 233
Baldwin, James, 678
Baldwin, James N, 680
Baldwin, Kristina, 29
Baldwin, Thomas W, 265, 294
Balkin, Ruth C, 55, 57
Ball, Greg, 36, 47, 49, 51, 52, 362
Ball, Gregory R, 687
Ball, Maureen, 72
Ball, Wendy, 481
Ballan, Jonathan A, 91, 119, 291
Ballantyne, Suzy, 449, 552
Ballard, Yvonne, 361
Balmas, Anna Mae, 163
Balter, Bruce M, 56
Balter, Ronald, 538, 568
Balzano, John S, 75
Bambrick, Padraic, 529
Banach, Edo, 528
Banbury, Doug, 565
Bancroft, Howard, 14, 136, 374
Bandhold, Stacy, 37
Banes, Kevin, 522
Banes, Kevin G, 540
Bang-Jensen, Lise, 602
Bank, Robert, 485
Banko, III, Stephen T, 232
Banks, John, 496
Banks, John H, 173
Banks, Lenore, 498
Bannister, Doris, 413
Bannister, Patrick, 550

Name Index

Banta, John S, 113, 180, 335
Baptiste, Mark S, 213
Barad, Rhonda, 243
Baran, Linda M, 586
Baran, Marie, 274
Baranowski, Marcia M, 160
Barasch, Esq, Amy, 14, 136, 312
Barash, Mark D, 185
Barber, Jerry, 16, 197, 198, 290, 297
Barber, Patrick, 412
Barbera, Sharon, 575
Barberio, Christine, 507
Barbieri, Jan, 470
Barbieri, Richard, 601
Barclay, Christopher, 11, 246, 268
Barclay, William, 248
Barclay, William A, 35, 36, 46, 47, 49, 53, 687
Barczak, William K, 128, 150, 380, 612
Barden, Peter, 507
Bardong, Charles, 245
Bargnesi, Mona, 248, 271
Barker, Jr, Lawrence L, 276, 321
Barker, Kenneth, 520
Barker, Stephen L, 401
Barkley, Warren D, 130
Barletta, C Thomas, 504
Barlow, Edward L, 533
Barlow, Erin, 6, 237, 287, 295, 372
Barnes, Allison, 63
Barnes, Joseph L, 366
Barnes, Philip, 453
Barnes, Richard E, 154, 322
Barnes, William R, 467
Barnette, Betty, 414, 449
Barnette, William, 212, 279, 308
Barney, Julie, 52
Barnhart, Gerald, 178
Barometre, Carine, 430
Baron, Eve, 509
Baron, Robert, 332
Barone, Inni, 146
Barone, John A, 58
Barone, Laurie, 47
Barone, Louis A, 57
Baroody, Walter, 363
Barr, Marilyn, 674
Barra, Robert, 44, 50, 327, 339
Barra, Robert D, 36, 50, 687
Barrack, Pamela, 400
Barral, Roland, 328
Barrella, Nicholas, 468
Barrett, Diane, 40
Barrett, Michael, 7, 133, 252, 288, 321
Barrett, Michael V, 461
Barrett, Pat, 124, 336
Barrett, Phil, 408
Barrett, Philip, 417
Barrett, RA, Bruce, 120, 149
Barrett, Steven Lloyd, 60
Barrett, William, 198

Barrio, Ana, 428
Barros, Betsy, 56
Barruco, Robert, 662
Barry, Brian, 15, 326, 335
Barry, David M, 57, 404
Barry, Maurice H, 667
Barsamian, Tony, 595
Barth, Richard, 427
Bartholomew, Edward, 26, 30
Bartikofsky, Gary, 98, 324
Bartkowski, James, 542
Bartle, Susan, 33, 54, 81, 103, 183
Bartlett, Henry, 222, 284
Bartlett, III, George R, 67
Bartlett, Joe, 606
Bartlett, Michael J, 576
Bartlett, Rickey, 130
Bartlett, Roscoe G, 388
Bartley, A Kirke, 60
Bartley, Elaine, 14, 180, 334
Barto, Edward L, 409
Bartoletti, Barbara, 498
Bartolomeo, Joan G, 571
Barton, Joe, 105, 171, 186, 219, 389
Barton, Lynn, 444
Barton, Patrick J, 70
Bartone, Helen A, 404
Barton-Richardson, Valerie, 470
Bartow, Jr, John K, 126, 183, 379
Baruth, Joe, 403
Barwick, Kent, 509
Basher, George P, 17, 361
Basil, Gabriel J, 617
Basile, Carm, 114, 350, 376
Basile, Col Anthony, 362
Basile, Joseph, 579
Basinait, Martin C, 128, 337
Basli, Andrea, 161
Bass, Christy Q, 68
Bass, Lynn, 582
Bass, Michael, 410
Bassett, Valerie, 575
Bastien, Sam, 281
Bastolla, Geraldine, 63
Bastuk, William, 536
Bately, Jr, Lionel, 205
Bates, Barbara, 214, 360
Bates, Jr, John S, 409
Batista, Julio, 516
Batt, John F, 65
Battaglia, Jack M, 59
Batterson, George, 645
Battista, John, 429
Battista, Vincent C, 626
Battiste, Phil, 132
Battisti, Christine, 653
Baucus, Max, 106, 249, 330, 356, 382, 385, 395
Bauer, Henry, 443
Bauer, Leonard R, 425
Bauersfeld, Nelson, 662

Baughman, Kevin S, 665
Baum, Hilary, 88
Baum, Richard, 3, 79, 90, 98, 129, 143, 157, 168, 177, 194, 211, 228, 237, 245, 252, 268, 278, 287, 295, 301, 307, 324, 332, 348, 360
Baumgarten, Ira, 296
Baumgarten, Joyce, 486
Baumol, William J, 111
Baur, Gene, 85
Bautch, Doris J, 356
Bautz, Doug, 325
Baxter, Andrew T, 138, 260
Baxter, Gary G, 406
Baxter, Kevin, 196
Bay, Eugene, 623
Bayh, Evan, 384
Bayne, Bernadette, 56
Baynes, Johnny Lee, 59
Baynes, Peter, 294, 474
Baynes, Peter A, 331
Bazydlo, Charles T, 425
Beach, Pamela, 438
Beadnell, Tim, 15, 99, 197, 374
Beagle, George, 578
Beahan, Deborah R, 412
Beal, Bernard, 562
Beal, Gregory, 460
Beal, Jr, Bruce A, 306
Beams, Mary Ellen, 425
Bean, Melissa, 392
Bean, Toni A, 70
Beaudoin, Raymond, 309
Beaulac, Lee, 88, 236
Beauman, John H, 565
Beaver, Sarah, 43, 49
Beck, Matt, 310
Beck, Patricia, 594
Beck, Susan, 208
Beck, Thomas C, 438
Becker, Bruce, 357
Becker, Carl F, 63
Becker, Carol, 594
Becker, Diane J, 161
Becker, Howard, 36, 43
Becker, Lisa, 403
Becker, Margaret, 6, 168, 195
Becker, Margaret A, 218, 314
Becker, Mindy, 282
Beckerman, Helene R, 543
Beckler, Greg, 581
Beckman, John, 154
Beckstrom, Brad, 224, 509
Bednar, Mary E, 61
Beebe, Matthew, 47
Beecher, Raymond, 402
Beedon, Robert P, 438
Beeler, Harold B, 59
Beeler, Patricia, 67
Beers, Andy, 13, 179, 334
Beganskas, Michael, 70

Name Index

Begley, Alice, 420
Begun, Martin, 517
Behan, Mark, 462
Behar Sr, Stephen M, 70
Behrle, Peter, 131
Beier, David, 463
Beilein, Thomas A, 405
Beinecke, Frances, 190
Beirne, John P, 433
Beirne, Rev Charles J, 626
Beirne, Thomas, 437
Belcamino, Greg, 434
Belcastro, Thomas, 567
Belen, Ariel, 56
Belfiore, Thomas, 413
Belfort, Marlene, 215
Belfort, Robert, 503
Bell, Barbara, 409
Bell, James, 19
Bell, Stephen W, 593
Bellafiore, Robert J, 611
Bellantoni, Orazio, 57
Bellantoni, Rory J, 69
Bellardo, Lydia, 511
Bellinger, Glenn R, 648
Bellini, Elma A, 65
Belliotti, Francis, 414
Bellis, Darlene, 419
Bellitto, Joseph A, 423
Bellone, Steven, 414
Belloni, Francis L, 225
Bellow, Bonnie, 186
Bellucci, John, 200
Bellucci, John R, 121, 353, 378
Belluzzi, Michael, 563
Belmont, John, 526
Belohlavek, Michael, 134, 253
Beltramo, Wade, 474
Beltz, Laura, 72
Ben-Amotz, Pico, 12, 216, 270, 312
Bender, Dennis F, 68
Bender, Dennis J, 541
Benders, David, 603
Bendit, Charles R, 143
Benedetto, Michael, 44, 45, 46, 48, 49
Benedetto, Michael R, 36, 687
Benedetto, Robert, 98, 324
Benedetto, Thomas D, 560
Benedict, Christine M, 396
Benedict, Timothy A, 440
Benedict, William L, 280
Benepe, Adrian, 433
Benfer, Chuck, 606
Bengart, Steven B, 417
Benincasa, Charles A, 440
Benitez, Jaime, 247, 271
Benitez, Peter J, 60
Benjamin, Daniel, 504
Benjamin, Elizabeth, 514
Benjamin, Gerald, 166, 210
Benjamin, Jack, 574, 586

Benjamin, Kennedy, 36
Benjamin, Michael, 44, 48
Benjamin, Michael A, 36, 45, 46, 47, 50, 688
Benjamin, Neil, 214
Benjamin, Wayne, 13, 348
Benjamin, Wayne L, 134, 253
Benmosche, Michael A, 556
Bennardo, Raymond, 22
Bennett Jr, Donald G, 342
Bennett, Bob, 386
Bennett, Heather, 462
Bennett, Joel H, 359
Bennett, John, 93, 329
Bennett, Jr, Richard T, 120, 336
Bennett, Kathy, 6, 99, 179, 194, 197, 254, 287, 324
Bennett, Lori, 137
Bennett, Richard, 5, 79
Bennett, Robert, 83, 383
Bennett, Robert J, 161
Bennett, Robert M, 143
Bennett, Susan E, 551
Bennett, Theodore A, 398
Bennison, JoAnn, 224
Benoit, Jim, 325
Benson Jr, Gregory M, 175
Benson, Deborah, 6, 311
Benson, Donna L, 406
Benson, Gregory, 611
Benson, John, 168, 195
Benson, Richard J, 670
Benson, Sarah, 146
Bentley, Robert, 144
Benton, Leigh J, 558
Berardi, Jr, Eugene J, 341
Berbary, James, 130
Berchtold, Scott, 341
Berdolt, Phil, 415
Berent, Stacy, 604
Berg, Ann Marie, 419
Berg, Deb, 296
Berg, James, 277, 305
Berg, Joel, 320, 473
Berg, Sharri, 608
Berg, Tomme, 57
Berg, William C, 638
Bergassi, Edmund J, 538
Berger, David, 444
Berger, Mary K, 21
Berger, Robert, 475
Berger, Ronald S, 564
Berger, Theodore S, 345
Berger, Tina, 113, 181, 375
Bergin, Robert, 470
Bergin, Shay, 43
Bergin, Thomas, 17, 101, 326, 374
Berglind, Reid N, 548
Bergman, Ellen, 676
Bergman, Jr, Robert E, 408
Bergmann, Robert B, 559

Bergmann, Ron, 431
Bergson, Howard M, 70
Bergtraum, Judith, 434
Berke, Philip A, 69
Berkman, Carol, 60
Berkowitz, Judy Roth, 152
Berkowitz, Leonard, 437
Berkowitz, Mel, 586
Berkowitz, Meryl J, 65
Berkowitz, Nancy, 235
Berler, Howard, 58
Berletic, Steve, 348
Berlin MD, Irwin, 458
Berlin, Gordon, 153, 276
Berliner, Benjamin C, 644
Berliner, Robert M, 67
Berlinski, Kenneth L, 42
Berman, Greg, 262
Berman, Howard L, 391
Berman, Richard A, 627
Berman, Stephen, 147
Bernacchio, Paul, 225, 367
Bernard Rolston, Diane Harragan, Co-President, 579
Bernard, Adrienne, 484
Bernard, Elizabeth, 588
Bernard, Renee, 484
Bernard, Richard, 119, 352
Bernardo, John M, 443
Bernback, Justin, 492
Bernet, Mary, 3
Bernhardt, John M, 644
Bernier, Lucy P, 74
Berns, Linda, 514
Berns, Michael T, 248, 271
Bern-Smith, Cathy, 29, 30
Bernstein, Lawrence H, 58
Bernstein, Marc F, 656
Bernstein, Martin, 583
Bernstein, Marvin, 256, 282
Bernstein, Stuart M, 259
Bernstein, William, 503
Berr, Al, 7, 332
Berrie, Jane, 229
Berry, Daniel, 16, 198, 297
Berry, Deborah, 66
Berry, Jeffrey G, 66
Berry, Philip, 115, 148, 619
Bertholf, Deedrick, 460
Bertoline, Dominick, 556
Berwanger, A Douglas, 413
Berwick, BG Bruce A, 184
Bessette, Ken, 251
Best, Billie, 88
Best, Jennifer, 43
Best, Michael, 429
Best, Miriam, 60
Best-Laimit, Ellen, 668
Betheil, Pam, 415
Betke, Alexander L, 531
Betrus, Ferris J, 572

Name Index

Betts, Julie D, 413
Betz, Peter, 401
Bey, Patrice, 586
Beyer, William D, 69
Bhaft, Milan, 493
Biamonte, William T, 160
Bianchi, Angelo, 453
Bianchi, Eileen, 70
Bianchi, Gina, 8, 133, 252, 288
Bianco, John, 184
Biasotti, Michael C, 426
Biberman, Nancy, 236
Bicking, Andrew, 521
Biden, Jr, Joseph R, 106, 385, 386
Bielak, Gerard, 511
Bienstock, Mark, 280
Bierbaum, Deborah, 519
Bierker, Gerold M, 408
Bierman, Joseph, 214
Bierman, Lauren, 455
Biersack, Robert, 164
Bierwirth, John E, 654
Bigelsen, Jayne, 262, 462
Biggerstaff, Laura, 462
Biggerstaff, Robert E, 462
Biggert, Judy, 233, 390
Bilbray, Brian, 392
Biletsky, Samantha, 197, 290
Bilges, Dolores, 514
Bilich, John, 134, 253
Bille, Daniel, 437
Billet, Barbara G, 17, 101, 326
Billings, John, 226
Billings, Lucy, 59
Billiter, Teri, 604
Billiter, Tonya, 604
Bimonte, Michael A, 434
Bing Newton, Juanita, 60
Bing, Jonathan L, 37, 44, 48, 49, 51, 52, 688
Bingaman, Jeff, 172, 187, 340, 384, 385
Biniasz, Martin, 128, 337
Bird, Michael, 595
Birkhead, Guthrie S, 10, 212, 213
Birkholz, Carol, 447, 448
Birmingham, Dan, 407
Birmingham, Micaela, 479, 509
Birnbaum, Arthur, 59
Birnbaum, Ronni D, 60
Bisceglia, Leo, 130
Bischoping, Scott, 651
Biscoff, Martin, 574
Bishop, John, 153
Bishop, Marshall E, 615
Bishop, Rob, 391
Bishop, Timothy, 186
Bishop, Timothy H, 151, 233, 240, 274, 356, 381, 388, 389, 393, 725
Bissram, Bette, 4
Bistrong, Allen, 553
BiTrolio, Robert, 260
Bittel, Michael, 453

Bitterbaum, Erik J, 613
Biviano, Corinne M, 123, 149
Bivona, Andrew P, 66
Bivona, John C, 58
Bivone, Richard M, 580
Bizarro MD, Thomas, 214, 360
Bizarro, Ralph, 200
Bjorkander, John, 447
Black, Christopher, 456, 526
Black, Debra R, 7, 332
Black, Dennis, 527
Black, Jeffrey A, 667
Black, John, 491, 506
Black, William, 399
Blackburn, Robert B, 105
Blackburne, Laura D, 58
Blackman, Albert, 247, 270
Blackwood, Helen M, 425
Blades-Rosado, Lois, 618
Blair, Jane, 146
Blake, Kathleen, 64
Blake, Lorna, 116, 258, 376
Blake, Thomas, 213
Blanchard, Timothy, 150
Blanchfield, Mark W, 441
Blanco, A Paul, 127, 353
Blanco-Bardia, France, 41
Bland, Toney, 93
Blaney, Elizabeth, 433
Blanton, Wynn, 636
Blatchford, Laurel, 431
Blau, Beth V, 671
Blau, Francine, 241
Blaustein, Burton, 431
Blausten, Frederica, 283
Blazer, Ted, 124, 336
Blechman, Moisha, 523
Bleiwas, Kenneth, 16, 199
Blitz, Gary E, 419
Blitz, Philip, 548
Bloch, Peter M, 134, 216, 254
Block, Arthur, 218, 314
Block, Ira H, 120, 336
Block, Valerie, 601
Bloom, Brandon, 574
Bloom, Elliot, 342
Bloom, Marc, 462
Bloomberg, Michael R, 426
Blot, Bob, 198, 290
Blower, Bruce G, 13, 119, 282
Blowers, Carol, 523
Blue, James A, 363
Bluestone, Maura, 455
Blum, Charles, 528
Blum, Marie, 639
Blum, Maureen, 473
Blum, Michael, 366
Blum, Paula, 498
Blumenfeld, Joel L, 60
Bluth, Arlene P, 59
Bluth, Randall G, 117, 200

Bly, Edward, 132
Blydenburgh, Donald R, 58
Blyer, Alvin P, 272
Blythe, Michael, 426
Blythe, Richard R, 397
Boak Jr, Jack J, 679
Boatswain, Pearl L, 434
Bobeck, COL Mike, 365
Bobins, Norman R, 234
Bobo, Deborah D, 641
Boccio, Frank J, 63
Bocciolatt, Stephen A, 659
Bochlert, Robert J, 282
Bochnak, Stephen, 50
Bockenstein, Mindy, 254
Bockstein, Mindy A, 7, 99, 168
Bodden, Thomas, 460
Bodrato, James Jay, 108
Bodziak, James, 646
Boehlert, Robert, 13
Boehlert, Robert J, 119
Boehlert, Sherwood, 186, 393
Boehlert, Sherwood L, 186, 233, 356, 381, 393
Boekmann, Monika, 220
Boese, Stephen, 461
Boeskin, Bryan, 510
Bogaard, Nancy, 79
Bogacz, Gerard J, 121, 352
Bogacz, Stephen J, 61
Bogardt, Bill, 451
Bogardus, Brent, 452
Bogardus, Brett, 581
Bogardus, Cynthia, 134, 253
Bogdan, III, Edward A, 463, 558
Bogdanski, Debra, 477
Boggess, Steven M, 19
Bogner, Drew, 627
Bogsted, Roger, 448
Bohlig, Amanda, 510
Bohman, Richard, 147
Bohn II, William R, 545
Bohren, Deborah, 222, 250
Boice, Margaret, 460
Boisi, Mark P, 304
Bokina, Michael, 511
Bolan, Thomas A, 447
Boland, David, 288, 295
Boland, Eileen, 40
Boll, Maureen E, 352
Bollenbach, William, 425
Boller, Ann, 568
Bollinger, Lee, 525
Bollinger, Lee C, 623
Bollon, Vincent J, 545
Bolton, Jennifer, 460
Bolton, William R, 668
Boltz, John J, 464
Bomar, Mary A, 185, 339
Bombard, James, 361
Bombardier, Christopher, 501

Name Index

Bombardiere, Ralph, 358
Bona Jr, Paul J, 657
Bonacic, John J, 21, 26, 28, 29, 30, 231, 292, 303, 713
Bonacic, Scott J, 503
Bonagura, David G, 541
Bonci, Chief Tim, 419
Boncke, Bruce G, 561
Boncoraglio, George, 472
Bond, Christopher, 383
Bond, Christopher S, 206, 387
Bond, Erin, 79
Bondi, Robert J, 407
Bonenberger, Delia G, 645
Bonfiglio, Barbara W, 544
Bongiorno, Adriano, 460
Bongiorno, Michael E, 408
Boniello, III, Ralph A, 57
Bonilla, Karen, 484
Bonilla, Mark A, 421
Bonina, John, 533
Bonn, Fred, 338
Bonn, Ruth, 498
Bonner, Jo, 186, 219, 387
Bonnewell, Michael, 647
Bonney, Joseph, 596
Bonnici, John S, 619
Bonuso, Carl, 656
Booknard, Lynda, 662
Bookstaver, David, 257, 375
Boone, William, 471
Boor, Kathryn, 86
Booth, Antonia, 442
Booth, David, 282
Booth, Wayne C, 436
Boozang, Patti, 503
Boozman, John, 393
Bopp, James, 281
Borakove, Ellen, 433
Borardz, Adele, 653
Borchert, Dawn L, 346
Bordallo, Madeleine Z, 391
Borden, Ray, 651
Borders, Sandra L, 535, 567
Bordick, Lee, 663
Borelli, Emilia, 600
Boreman, Steve, 605
Borenstein, Alan, 121, 352
Borges, Michael J, 154, 499
Boris, Andrew, 606
Borns, Alicia, 482
Boron, Andrew, 466
Borrelli, Kelley M, 162
Borrelli, Michael, 582
Borrello, Vito J, 318
Borsody, Robert P, 227
Bosanko, Michael, 287, 295
Bosies, Jr, William J, 523
Bosies, William J, 96
Bosse, Diane F, 121, 258
Bostic, Yolanda, 44

Boswell, Donald K, 604, 608
Bosworth, David A, 316
Bosy, Kim, 24
Botman, Selma, 471, 619
Botstein, Leon, 622
Bott, Marian, 498
Botta, Chris, 345
Bottar, Anthony S, 143
Boucher, Matthew, 674
Boucher, Rick, 171, 186, 389
Boufford, Jo Ivey, 226
Boughton, Jerry, 184
Bourcy, Bernetta A, 413
Bourdeau, Bernard N, 251, 555
Bourg, Henry, 572
Bourgeois, Theresa, 155
Bourscheidt, Randall, 341
Bova, Matthew J, 562
Bove, Jay, 28
Bovenzi, John, 422
Bowden, Gayle, 145
Bowen, C Scott, 246, 268
Bowen, James, 408
Bowen, Jeffrey, 640
Bowen, Mary Lu, 243
Bower, Daniel, 648
Bower, George R, 406
Bower, Laurie A, 66
Bowerman, Ella, 65
Bowerman, Shawn J, 404
Bowers, Diana, 652
Bowers, Keith, 402
Bowle, Johnathan, 233
Bowles, Johnathan, 275
Bowman, Janice L, 58
Bowman, Jr, Joseph E, 143
Boxer, Barbara, 164, 187, 206, 356, 384, 385, 387
Boxer, Michael, 11, 134, 197
Boyan, Richard, 422
Boy-Brown, Elaine, 214, 360
Boyce, Phil, 605
Boyd, Dennis, 497
Boyd, Mark, 24
Boyer, Alexander, 525
Boyer, Jeremy, 591
Boyes, J Richard, 675
Boylan, Christopher, 377
Boylan, Christopher P, 117, 352
Boylan, Jeremy, 399
Boyland, Jr, William F, 37, 43, 44, 46, 48, 50, 688
Boyle, Bill, 596
Boyle, Daniel B, 5, 98, 102, 124, 324
Boyle, Denis J, 60
Boyle, Philip, 37, 43, 45, 46, 50, 217, 238, 313, 688
Bozzolo, Ellis W, 69
Braack, Craig R, 396
Braca-Cornish, Nancy, 398
Bracco, Anthony, 121, 336, 378

Brace, Michael, 296
Brach, Ronald C, 33, 54, 81, 103, 183
Bracken, John P, 262
Brackman, Robert, 16, 197, 290
Bradberry, William, 436
Brader, Gary L, 646
Bradford, David, 496
Bradford, Dwight, 132
Bradford, Elizabeth, 336
Bradford, Elizaeth, 121
Bradley, Adam T, 37, 45, 47, 49, 52, 688
Bradley, Christian, 13
Bradley, James, 445
Bradley, John A K, 59
Bradley, Vincent, 57
Bradshaw-Soto, Jill, 498
Bradstreet, Peter C, 68
Brady, Patrick, 667
Brady, Robert A, 390
Brady, Ross, 538
Brady, Steven C, 520
Bragan, Frederick J, 651
Brake, Don, 603
Braley, Bruce, 274, 392
Bramson, Noam, 426
Branca, Gene, 441
Branchini, Frank J, 114, 335, 486
Branch-Muhammad, Gail, 310
Brand, Mark T, 649
Brandeau, Kim, 415
Brandon, Ann, 498
Brandon, Robert, 537
Brands, James V, 57
Brandt, Bill, 607
Brandt, Dorothy K Chin, 59
Brandt, Florence, 69
Brandt, Marc N, 285
Brandveen, Antonio I, 58
Brandwein, Ruth, 520
Brandwene, Merle, 310
Branning, Susan, 556
Brannock, Shari L, 647
Bransten, Eileen, 56
Braslow, Stephen L, 68
Brassard, Art, 161
Brassell Jr, Robert, 539
Brathwaite Nelson, Valerie, 58
Braun, Evelyn L, 58
Braun, Richard F, 56
Brauth, Sorelle, 169
Braveman, Daan, 628
Braverman, Robert, 368
Bray, Jeffrey, 574
Brazill, Caitlyn, 483
Brecher, Charles, 292, 330, 471
Bredenko, Patricia, 296
Bredhoff, Nancy, 191, 227
Breen, J Timothy, 69
Breen, Michael, 496
Breen, Peg, 235, 305
Breese, James R, 421

Name Index

Bregg, Martin, 666
Brehm, Bob, 450
Brehm, Robert, 157
Breig, Thomas, 325
Breiner, Charles, 309
Brencick, William J, 205
Brendel, Joseph, 465
Brennan, Charles J, 517
Brennan, Francis, 511
Brennan, James F, 37, 45, 46, 51, 103, 292, 688
Brennan, John E, 415
Brennan, Kevin, 219, 273
Brennan, Megan, 205
Brennan, Michael J, 56
Brennan, Patricia, 142, 433
Brennan, Theresa, 4, 287
Brennan, Thomas A, 424
Brennan, Thomas F, 6, 287, 295
Brennan, Wendy, 510
Brennan, William J, 17, 361
Brenner, Adele, 368
Brenon, Joan M, 443
Breselor, Frank, 464
Bresler, Barry M, 101, 326
Breslin, Dennis, 130
Breslin, Ellen, 19, 34, 375
Breslin, Katherine, 473
Breslin, Michael G, 396
Breslin, Neil D, 21, 25, 26, 29, 30, 248, 713
Breslin, Richard W, 398
Breslin, Thomas A, 61
Bresnan, James J, 121, 353
Bressman, Susan B, 227
Bretschneider, Stuart, 294, 300
Brettschneider, Eric B, 316
Brew, Lee, 397
Brewer Jr, John E, 649
Brewer, Aida, 102, 327
Brewer, Aida M, 17
Brewer, Beth, 595
Brewer, Beth A, 594
Brewer, Douglas J, 402
Brewer, Terrance, 663
Brewer, Vincent, 196
Brez, Wendy J, 345
Briand, Elizabeth H, 316
Briccetti, Heather, 26
Briccetti, Heather C, 516
Brickman, Ellen, 511
Bridenbecker, Terri, 571
Brier, Stephen, 471
Briffault, Richard, 165, 293
Brigando, Christopher, 561
Briganti-Hughes, Mary, 58
Briggs, Elizabeth A, 642
Briggs, Jane, 144
Briggs, Vernon, 275
Bright, Joan H, 427
Bright, Maureen K, 654
Brilliant, Elizabeth, 452

Brilliant, Harold, 136
Brilling, Jaclyn A, 15, 169
Brindle, Buzz, 606
Brindley, Grace J, 670
Bringmann, Gerard P, 358
Brinker, Laurence H, 107
Brinkley, Alan, 525
Brisky, Mike, 39
Britto, Robert J, 653
Britton, Katie, 603
Brizard, Jean Claude, 657
Brizell-Delise, Hillary, 498
Brizzell, Mary, 418
Broadbooks, Jon, 600
Broadwell, Stephen, 647
Brochey, Brett, 546
Brock, Elizabeth, 457
Brockett, Steven, 73
Brockman, Edward J, 413
Brockway, David M, 62
Brockway, Doug, 449
Broder, John P, 227
Broderick, David S, 405
Broderick, Kathleen M, 13, 281
Broderick, Peter L, 65
Brodhagen, Patricia, 484, 542
Brodie, Hal, 123, 170, 182
Brodsky, Richard L, 37, 44, 45, 52, 103, 202, 354, 688
Brodt, John, 462
Brody, Willa, 516
Broitman, Elana, 523
Bromirski, Timothy, 310
Bronat, Gary, 563
Bronfenbrenner, Kate, 275, 299
Brongo, Richard J, 416
Brongo, William, 65
Bronheim MD, David S, 554
Bronson, Harry, 49, 142
Bronson, Harry B, 543
Bronstein, Richard W, 305
Bronston, David, 531
Brook-Krasny, Alec, 37, 43, 45, 47, 49, 51
Brook-Krasny, Alec , 689
Brooks Hopkins, Karen, 143
Brooks, Albert, 198
Brooks, Chris, 596
Brooks, David, 600
Brooks, Harry, 648
Brooks, Kermitt, 11, 245
Brooks, Kermitt J, 12, 254
Brooks, Maggie, 404
Brooks, Martin, 656
Brooks, Nancy, 424
Brooks, Pamela, 574
Brooks, Paul C, 571
Brooks, Roberta, 79
Brooks, Russell, 443
Brooks, Stephen, 116, 258
Brooks, Tracey, 46
Brooks, Wayne, 447

Brophy, Patrick W, 560
Brosnahan-Sullivan, Mary, 473
Brotz, James K, 647
Brouwer, Enrique, 469
Brower, Peter, 440
Brown, Bonnie, 657
Brown, Bryan, 600
Brown, Byron W, 416
Brown, Cecil, 229
Brown, Christopher R, 667
Brown, Corrine, 393
Brown, Dan, 496, 575
Brown, David, 91, 99, 135, 254, 302, 325
Brown, David J, 423
Brown, Earl D, 396, 435
Brown, Frank, 345
Brown, Garry, 175
Brown, Gary, 255, 592
Brown, Gordon, 453
Brown, Herb R, 655
Brown, Holly E, 431
Brown, IV, David D, 122, 149, 201, 217
Brown, James F, 440
Brown, Jane, 470
Brown, Jeffrey S, 65
Brown, John, 641
Brown, Joseph, 635
Brown, Joyce F, 482, 616
Brown, Jr, Henry E, 391
Brown, Karl, 642
Brown, Ken, 373
Brown, Kevin P, 546
Brown, LaRay, 430
Brown, Larry G, 6, 143, 308
Brown, Linda C, 310
Brown, Margery, 431
Brown, Maria C, 436
Brown, Marilyn E, 399
Brown, Melva L, 618
Brown, Michael, 512
Brown, Mickey J, 81, 105, 184
Brown, Milton, 135
Brown, Nancy, 402
Brown, Patrick, 465
Brown, Paul S, 512
Brown, Peter, 129
Brown, Richard A, 407
Brown, Sandra A, 6, 143, 309, 372
Brown, Stephen R, 543
Brown, Thomas Paul, 61
Brown, W Ted, 282
Brown, William, 130
Brownback, Sam, 383
Brownbeck, Sam, 386
Brown-Clemons, Terryl, 4
Browne, Paul J, 433
Browne, Sarah, 134, 253, 373
Brownell, Daniel D, 431
Brownell, Gary, 563
Brownell, Thomas D, 363
Brown-Grant, Debora, 147, 279, 312

Name Index

Brucciani, Denis, 424
Bruce, Anthony M, 139, 261
Bruce, Raymond L, 59
Bruce, Thomas R, 263
Bruce, Willard, 414
Bruen, Dennis, 593
Bruening, Glen, 14, 179, 334
Bruhn, J Michael, 69
Bruneau, Michael, 527
Brunell, Courtney, 526
Brunell, John W, 158
Brunelle, Greg, 9, 195, 289, 402
Brunet, Pamela M, 221
Brunetti, John J, 57, 58
Brungard, Anne S, 639
Bruno, Bob, 606
Bruno, Clarke, 430
Bruno, Debra L, 158
Bruno, Joseph L, 19, 21, 31, 33, 54, 203, 217, 283, 713
Bruno, Linda J, 671
Brunswick, Cary, 598
Bruso, Katherine, 561
Bryan, Kathleen A, 262
Bryant, Diana, 188
Bryant, Michael, 138
Bryant, Raymond, 642
Bryce, Philip A, 126, 183
Bryd, Arthur J, 545
Brylinski, Jennifer C S, 586
Brynien, Kenneth, 477
Brynien, Kenneth D, 299
Bucaria, Stephen A, 58
Buccheri, William, 449
Buccheri, William J, 158
Bucci, Joseph R, 18, 200, 313, 375
Buchanan, Paul G, 63
Buchanan, Stuart, 178
Buchanan, Thomas, 453
Buchbinder, Darrell, 127, 353
Buchmann, Bob, 605
Buchter, Richard Lance, 58
Buck, John, 534
Bucki, Carl L, 259
Buckley, Diane, 589
Buckley, Eileen, 603
Buckley, John T, 55, 256
Buckley, Jonathan, 565
Buckley, Linda A, 41
Buckley, Peter C, 62
Buckley, Suzanne, 612
Buckley, Timothy J, 72
Buckman, Michael R, 136
Budd, Marlene, 68
Budro, E Lawrence, 583
Buenau, Michael P, 558
Buerkle, Thomas S, 96
Buettner, John F, 272
Buffardi, Harry C, 409
Bugbee, Larry A, 161
Buggs, Ronald, 646

Bugliosi, Edward, 185
Buhks, Ephraim, 622
Buhner, Jonathan W, 644
Buholtz, Eileen E, 249, 263
Buhrmaster, Neil E, 161
Buley, Cheryl A, 15
Buley, Jeffrey, 465
Buley, Jeffrey T, 452, 537
Bulgaro, Patrick J, 125, 163, 202
Bull, Martin D, 553
Bullard, Valerie, 70
Bullis, Barry, 424
Bullock, Sandra, 442
Bulman, Larry, 450, 566
Bulman, Larry S, 553
Bumbalo, Jackie, 146
Bundy, Robert, 639
Buniak, Kenneth R, 133, 252, 288
Bunn, Geraldine, 215
Bunning, Jim, 249, 384, 385
Bunyan, Bert A, 56
Buono, John L, 125, 337, 353
Buonpastore, Alan, 134, 216, 254
Burak, Janet L, 95
Burckard, Nicole, 29
Burden, Amanda M, 427
Burdi, Michael, 135
Burdick, Janice G, 158
Burdick, Richard, 20
Burdick, Rick, 21
Burdick, Robert, 469
Burditt, Timothy N, 540
Burgasser, R Thomas, 73
Burgdorf, Paul, 122, 149, 201, 217, 378
Burger, Anna, 562
Burgess, Dayle B, 42
Burgess, James, 521
Burgess, Mary, 519
Burgess, Michael, 4, 307
Burghardt, Mira, 503
Burgher Jr, John H, 18
Burgher, John, 247, 270
Burgio, David, 587
Burgos, Jose, 135
Burgos, Tonio, 466
Burin, John J, 419
Burke, Alison, 510
Burke, Edward, 436
Burke, Edward D, 58
Burke, Gerald, 228
Burke, III, William J, 70
Burke, James M, 60
Burke, Joseph, 212, 279, 308, 611, 626
Burke, Joseph C, 154
Burke, Robert E, 285
Burke, Terence, 511
Burke, Thomas J, 159
Burleson, Kevin, 158
Burling, Daniel J, 35, 37, 47, 51, 52, 53, 689
Burman, Janet, 248, 271
Burman, Steve, 94

Burmaster, Clyde L, 405
Burnett, Adele, 577
Burney, David J, 428
Burnham, Dave, 663
Burns, Brian D, 66
Burns, Christopher J, 57
Burns, Daniel, 198, 297
Burns, Elizabeth, 71
Burns, Gail M, 448
Burns, James A, 180, 199, 291
Burns, James L, 562
Burns, John P, 402
Burns, Karyn E, 109
Burns, Kristina A, 396
Burns, Mary Ellen, 91, 99, 134, 169, 179, 216, 229, 238, 254, 270, 301, 325
Burns, Robert, 136
Burns, Thomas R, 667
Burnside, Douglas, 660
Burr, Richard, 220, 384, 386
Burrell, Jerry, 452
Burridge, Craig, 226
Burris, Mary Ellen, 112
Burto, Kent D, 402
Burton, Dan, 391
Burton, Douglas C, 653
Burton, Joseph, 438
Burton, Nancy, 198, 297
Buscaglia, Russell P, 58
Busch, Joseph R, 678
Bush, Jack T, 403
Bush, Pamela, 115, 181
Bushy, Kathy, 125, 337
Busler, William L, 116, 181
Butcher, Barbara, 433
Butcher, Ernesto, 127, 353
Butler, Daniel, 534
Butler, Denis J, 59
Butler, John, 444
Butler, Marc, 103, 302, 354
Butler, Marc W, 37, 44, 46, 48, 49, 292, 689
Butler, Matthew S, 547
Butler, Ralph, 413
Butler, W R, 84
Butter, John, 527
Buttolph, Katherine, 185
Butts, III, Calvin O, 613
Buturla, John A, 62
Buyea, Cathy M, 100, 147
Buyer, Daniel P, 229
Buyer, Steve, 364, 393
Buynoch, Jo Ann, 602
Buzard, A Vincent, 264
Byington, Maryanne, 548
Bykowski, Michael, 126, 353
Bynum, Peter, 164
Byrd, Robert C, 83, 172, 330, 382, 383
Byrd, Tamiko, 458
Byrne, Brian J, 505
Byrne, Edward L, 566
Byrne, Elizabeth J, 524

741

Name Index

Byrne, Jeffrey, 124, 336
Byrne, John D, 565
Byrne, John N, 60
Byrne, Karen L, 158
Byrne, Matthew, 425
Byrne, Maureen A, 73
Byrne, Sean, 7, 133, 252, 288
Bystryn, Marcia, 166, 190
Cabrera, David, 10, 229
Cacace, Kevin T, 589
Cacace, Susan, 69
Cacioppo, Lauren M, 560
Cade, Erskine E, 547
Cade, Scott E, 17, 313
Cadle, Elizabeth, 239, 272
Caetano, Captain Don, 362
Cafarella, Jason J, 557
Cafaro, Angelo, 44, 45, 47
Cafasso, George, 61
Cafran, Wayne, 496
Caggana, Michele, 215
Caggiano-Siino, Kathleen, 5, 211, 278, 308
Caher, John, 8, 122, 133, 137, 252, 288, 372
Cahill, Edward W, 443
Cahill, John, 30
Cahill, Kevin A, 32, 37, 46, 47, 48, 53, 54, 202, 203, 689
Cahill, Michele, 429
Cahill, Thomas J, 255
Cahn, Herman, 56
Cail, Laura, 46, 48, 50
Caimano, Nicholas, 588
Cairo, Patricia, 550
Cala, Wiliam, 653
Calabrese, Alexander, 60
Calabrese, David, 606
Calabrese, Donald, 547
Calabrese, Joseph, 65
Calarco, Deborah, 158
Calarco, Jacqueline, 436
Calcaterra, Regina M, 568
Caldara, Lu, 366
Calderon, Dominick, 547
Calderone, Philip F, 414
Caldwell, Alfred B, 365
Caldwell, Elaine, 63
Caldwell, Freddie, 316
Caldwell, Lloyd, 184
Caldwell, Randall B, 66
Calhoun, Nancy, 35, 37, 49, 50, 53, 303, 327, 689
Caligiore, Sandy, 125, 337, 379
Call, Peter, 86
Callahan II, James J, 404
Callahan, Charles E, 637
Callahan, Heidi, 200
Callahan, Julie L, 71
Callahan, Kathleen, 185
Callahan, Kevin, 605
Callanan, Raymond F, 584
Callard, David B, 406

Callender, Robert, 123, 170, 182
Calman, Neil, 465
Calman, Neil S, 223
Caltabiano, John J, 347
Calvaruso, Edmund A, 65
Calvaruso, Frank, 496
Calvelli, John, 193
Calvelli, John F, 529
Calvert, Ken, 392
Calvin, James S, 538
Calvin, Jim, 110
Calvo, Joseph, 250
Camacho, Fernando M, 60
Camara, Karim, 37, 44, 45, 46, 48, 50, 690
Camasso, Eileen L, 673
Camerino, Joseph P, 680
Cameron, Floyd, 456
Cameron, Laura A, 321
Camilleri, Louis C, 106
Camoin, Linda, 48
Camp, Dave, 219, 394
Campana, Paul J, 139, 261
Campanie, S John, 403
Campano, Bob, 198, 290
Campbell Jr, George, 624
Campbell, Aurelie, 330
Campbell, Deborah J, 136
Campbell, Gordon, 521
Campbell, James J, 521
Campbell, James L, 396
Campbell, John E, 365
Campbell, Julie A, 63
Campbell, Kathleen, 246, 269
Campbell, Ken, 603
Campbell, Lew, 280
Campbell, Malcolm O, 481
Campbell, Mark, 119, 352
Campbell, Mary Schmidt, 346
Campbell, Michael H, 543
Campbell, Valerie, 495
Campbell, Victoria B, 74
Campbell, William, 9, 195, 289
Campbell, William J, 158
Campion, James R, 615
Canaday, Jeanette, 145
Candela, Alma, 213
Candella Papale, Shawna, 580
Canders, Col Michael F, 362
Candreva, Jeremiah, 495
Canellos, Peter C, 331
Canestrari, Ron, 34
Canestrari, Ronald J, 37, 51, 690
Canetto, Jay, 198
Cangemi, Agostino, 431, 487
Cannell, Jeffrey, 8, 144, 333
Cannito, Peter A, 119, 352
Cannon, Chris, 391
Cannon, George J, 17, 326
Cannon, Kathleen, 422
Cansdale, John G, 15, 325, 335
Cantilli, Thomas, 481

Cantor, Dan, 167
Cantor, Nancy, 519, 632
Cantore, Tony, 51
Cantwell, James, 513
Cantwell, Maria, 187, 384
Canty, Anne, 432
Capalino, James, 468
Capel, Rodney, 476
Capella, Joseph E, 60
Caplan, Mary, 479
Capobianco, Mark, 640
Capobianco, Paul, 197, 290
Capone, Don, 8, 133, 252, 288
Capone, Frank, 585
Caponera, Ronald, 418
Capozzi, Anthony J, 452
Caputo, David A, 519, 629
Caputo, Donald, 422
Caputo, Joyce M, 650
Caputo, Nicholas, 568
Caputo, Paul, 451
Caraley, Demetrios James, 206
Carasiti, Frank J, 671
Caravella, Donna, 65
Caravella, Patricia, 63
Carballata, Carl, 583
Carbo, Steven, 478
Carbone, Larry, 496
Carbone, Terry, 657
Carbonell, Anna, 609
Cardillo, Al, 217, 283
Cardillo, Charles S, 655
Cardillo, Dominic, 229
Cardillo, John, 125, 149, 297, 379
Cardillo, Robert, 232
Cardinale, Philip, 440
Cardinale, Philip J, 115, 181
Cardona, Anthony V, 56, 256
Cardona, David B, 61
Cardona, Reinaldo, 510
Cardona, Yessenia, 309
Cardone, Carolann, 160
Cardone, Joseph V, 406
Cardoza, Dennis A, 186
Cardoza, Dennnis A, 387
Cardozo, Michael A, 432
Carella, Josephine E, 421
Carey Mihm, Kathleen, 412
Carey, Joan B, 256
Carey, Joseph, 457
Carey, Sheila M, 8, 237, 279, 311
Carey, Thom, 228
Carey, Thomas, 416
Carey, Timothy S, 121, 170
Carey, Tobe, 347
Carfagna, Vincent, 440
Carlin, Jr, William J, 407
Carlino, Robert F, 358
Carlisle, Donald, 677
Carlitz, Kathleen, 565
Carloss-Smith, Rhonda, 470

Name Index

Carlsen, Scott C, 131
Carlson, Brian, 491
Carlson, G Anders, 179, 213
Carlson, Greg, 460
Carlson, Jennifer, 507, 550
Carlson, William, 273
Carlucci, David, 417
Carmack, Janet, 214
Carmel, Mary, 474
Carmichael, John, 481
Carmichael, LeRoy, 280
Carmody, Barbara A, 62
Carney, Christopher P, 206, 390
Carney, Patrick M, 71
Carney, Robert M, 409
Carney, Sister Margaret, 631
Carni, Edward D, 55, 57
Carpenter, Angie M, 411
Carpenter, Catherine, 368
Carpenter, Cheryl W, 355
Carpenter, John F, 246, 268
Carpenter, Kenneth, 348
Carpenter, Raymond C, 448
Carpenter, William A, 438
Carpenter-Palumbo, Karen, 470
Carpenter-Palumbo, Karen M, 5, 211, 278, 307
Carper, Thomas R, 385, 386
Carper, Tom, 383
Carpinello, Anthony J, 56
Carr, Allison, 163
Carr, Anne M, 196, 301
Carr, Craig G, 644
Carr, Edward A T, 547
Carr, Eleanor, 316
Carr, Erica, 116, 170, 182
Carr, Frederick, 169
Carr, Glynda, 23
Carr, James J, 469, 552
Carr, John C, 469
Carr, Joseph, 416
Carr, Jr, Peter V, 463
Carr, Mary Alice, 510
Carrano, Helen, 520
Carrier, Charles, 35, 375
Carrig, Bart M, 73
Carrillo, Victor, 116, 170, 182
Carrington, Wayne, 574
Carrion Jr, Adolfo, 435
Carrion, Esq, Gladys, 6, 143, 308
Carrion, Jr, Adolfo, 396
Carro, Gregory, 58
Carroll, Patrick J, 426
Carroll, Thomas J, 58
Carroll, Thomas W, 473
Carrozza, Ann Margaret, 46, 163
Carrozza, Ann Margaret E, 43, 49, 690
Carrozza, Ann-Margaret E, 37, 44, 47
Carruthers, Richard D, 60
Carson, Deidre, 487
Carson, Dennis, 443

Carswell, Lois, 342
Cartenuto, Michael, 32
Carter, A J, 9, 99, 116, 177, 230, 333, 372, 376
Carter, Brenda, 53, 150, 272
Carter, Dominic, 608
Carter, Fredrick J, 126, 353
Carter, Jennifer, 484
Carter, Jerald S, 65
Carter, John W, 60
Carter, Jr, John E, 256
Carter, Kevin M, 63
Carter, Michael, 218, 239, 315
Carter, William A, 70
Cartusciello, Anthony T, 125, 202, 297, 379
Cartwright, William, 666
Carucci, Peter, 214
Carudo, Anthony J, 540
Caruso, Mark J, 409
Caruso, Vito, 257
Caruso, Vito C, 57
Carvelli, Anthony R, 405
Carvill, Al, 423
Cary, Ronald, 404
Cary, Theresa, 145
Casale, Jeffrey A, 128, 337
Casamento, Mary Ann, 160
Casaregola, Tom, 15, 326, 335
Casciano, Paul, 671
Case, Laurie L, 63
Casella, Gary L, 255
Casey, Eileen P, 672
Casey, J Dennis, 135
Casey, Jack, 453
Casey, John P, 419
Casey, Kevin S, 155
Casey, Mary Beth, 162
Casey, Raymond V, 120, 336
Casey, Sean, 111
Casey, Teresa, 502
Casey, Thomas E, 196, 301
Casey, William M, 134, 254
Cash Jackson, Helen, 333
Cashin, Kathleen M, 657
Caso, John, 436
Cass, Stephen W, 62
Cass, Terrel L, 608
Cassaick, Theresa, 523
Cassano, Salvatore J, 430
Cassata, Joseph J, 75
Casscles, J Stephen, 31
Cassella, Daniel, 457
Cassella, LTC Kent, 150
Cassella, Rochelle A, 155, 322
Cassidy, Dawn E, 159
Cassidy, Linda, 14, 136, 313
Castelbuono, A J, 107, 552
Castell, Eduardo, 428
Castellaneta, John, 427
Castiglia, Fred, 421
Castiglione, Salvatore, 245

Castle, Daniel R, 528
Castle, Michael N, 151, 389
Castro, Charles, 551
Castro, Marjorie E, 676
Castro, Melchor E, 74
Cataldo, John, 60
Cataldo, Robert, 24
Catanise, Elaine M, 162
Catena, Felix J, 65
Cathcart, Kevin M, 242
Catlin, Greg, 607
Catone, Louis, 146
Catt, Gary, 598
Catterson, James M, 55
Caudill, Bill, 570
Cavallo, Ernest J, 60
Cavanaugh, James E, 113, 335
Cavanaugh, Thomas R, 422
Cavarello, Daniel T, 443
Cave, Cathy, 281
Cavorti Goldberg, Joan, 445
Cayne, James E, 94
Cecala, Suzanne, 14, 136, 313, 374
Cecile, James H, 75
Cee, Gary, 606
Ceisler, Ron, 120, 336, 377
Celia, Eric, 349
Celiberti, Douglas, 422
Celli, Jr, Andrew G, 125, 163, 202
Cellucci, Janice, 71
Cenci, Cathleen, 124, 258
Centi, Rosemary, 420
Centra, John V, 57
Ceparno Wilson, Janet, 669
Ceresia Jr, George B, 56, 57
Ceresia, George, 257
Cerio, Jr, Donald F, 403
Cerminaro, Mike, 443
Cerne, Gary, 641
Cernik, Christopher, 487
Cerone, James, 196
Cerrachio, Ronald M, 67
Cerrato, Robert C, 76
Cerreto, Anthony, 439
Cerro-Reehil, Patricia, 191
Cestaro, Glenn, 418
Cestero, Rafael, 430
Chabe, Laura, 642
Chabot, Steve, 106, 261, 274, 392
Chadwick, Cindy T, 175
Chafee, Lincoln D, 385
Chaikin, Bonnie P, 70
Chaimowitz, Anne, 598
Chaine, Marcel, 119, 282
Chakraborti, Subi, 350
Chamberlin, Holly, 101, 326
Chambers, Cheryl E, 56
Chambers, David JG, 533
Chambers, John A, 675
Chambliss, Saxby, 83, 187, 220, 382
Champagne, Derek P, 401

Name Index

Champlin, Cal, 443
Chan, Amy, 525
Chandick, Marie, 520
Chandler, Byron, 639
Chandler, Gloria, 67
Chandler, Marcia, 39
Chaney, Frank, 484
Chang, Christina, 430
Chang, Christopher, 635
Chang, Julie A, 528
Chang, Ju-Ming, 484
Chanin, Geoffrey E, 436
Chapey, Geraldine, 143
Chapman, Gaye, 451
Chapman, Henry, 425
Chapman, Langdon, 21, 29
Chapman, Skip, 593
Chapman-Minutello, Alice, 257
Chappelle, Robin, 41
Chapple, Wayne O, 448
Charlop-Powers, Sarah, 521
Charnetsky, Peter P, 61
Chartier, Jack, 16, 180, 198, 290, 297
Chartock, Alan, 603
Chartock, Professor Alan S, 591
Chase, Jane, 498
Chase, William, 137
Chatterjee, Oona, 502
Chauvin, Caroline, 27
Chavez, John, 273
Chaya, Joan, 528
Cheddie-Musall, Geeta, 158
Cheek, Mary E, 568
Chelales, Joseph, 211, 278, 308
Chella, John, 436
Chellis, Brett B, 397
Chen, Wellington Z, 619
Chen, Wesley, 95
Chen, Yemeng, 628
Chepiga, Stephen, 64
Chernoff, Mark, 199
Chernoff, Vida, 213
Cherry, John, 102, 116, 181
Cherry, William E, 409
Chervokas, John V, 437
Chevrette, Valerie, 144, 372
Chewning-Kulick, Brenda, 82, 232
Chiao, Kuo-Ann, 121, 352
Chiaro, Carla, 10, 196
Chick, Fred, 12, 325
Chief Executive Officer, , 226
Child, Laura A, 407
Chille, Joe, 604
Chin, David, 511
Chin, Judith J, 657
Chin, Oymin, 60
Chin, Rockwell J, 237
Chin, Shui-Kai, 100, 148
China, Susan, 288, 295
Chin-Chance, Shawn, 44
Chin-Kee-Fatt, Camille, 254

Chitre, Amit, 458
Chittenden, Jessica, 5, 79, 307, 371
Chiu-Rinaldi, Fabiana, 332
Chmura, Max, 13, 281
Cholakis, Catherine, 67
Chong, David, 426
Chong, Lee, 501
Chopp, Rebecca S, 623
Choquette, Andrew, 356
Christen, Joe, 118, 351
Christensen, Donna M, 340, 391
Christensen, Francis P, 16, 136
Christensen, Joan K, 37, 48, 49, 51, 53, 150, 272, 690
Christian, Catherine Ann, 265
Christian, Edwin, 546
Christian, George A, 349
Christman, Robert L, 396
Christmann, James, 650
Christmann, Robert W, 646
Christopher, Linda, 67
Chritakis, Christa, 457
Chu, Wendell, 669
Chuhta, Patricia E, 439
Chun, Danny K, 60
Church, Judson, 481
Church, Robert, 447
Church, Sanford A, 406
Church, Vernice, 666
Churchill, Margaret, 588
Chwalinski, Gerald, 416
Ciarpelli, M Ann, 405
Ciccarelli Jr, Raymond, 673
Cicchetti, Nicholas, 426
Ciccone, Kathleen, 484
Ciccone, LouAnn, 49
Ciccone, Stephen J, 108
Cicero, Philip S, 655
Cifra, Nick, 511
Cilmi, Tom, 577
Cimino, Joseph A, 225
Cinquemani, Bernard, 564
Ciota, Lou, 673
Ciparick, Carmen Beauchamp, 55
Cipollino, Michael, 68
Cipriano, Antoinette, 75
Ciprioni, Richard, 288, 295
Cipullo, Ernest J, 419
Cirelli, Matthew, 564
Cirigliano, Caesar, 58
Cirillo, Frank J, 430
Cirolia, John V, 428
Citron, Jeff, 478
Ciulla, John, 408
Ciullo, Carmen A, 639
Claffey, Jr, James J, 565
Clague, Joshua, 521
Claire, Judith S, 62
Claire, Martin, 493
Clancy, Jack, 453
Clancy, James, 4, 252, 360

Clancy, Margaret L, 58
Clancy, Maura, 589
Clancy-Botta, Jean, 132
Clapp, Carol, 489
Clapp, Stephen, 626
Claridge, Andre, 507
Clark, Barbara, 34
Clark, Barbara M, 37, 45, 46, 47, 49, 50, 690
Clark, Cheryl, 132
Clark, Christine, 75
Clark, Constance R, 656
Clark, Darcel D, 60
Clark, Douglas, 531
Clark, Frank J, 400
Clark, Jeff, 467
Clark, John B, 614
Clark, Lisa, 520
Clark, Marcea A, 403
Clark, Margaret, 528
Clark, Mary, 495
Clark, Michael, 322
Clark, Patricia K, 219, 273
Clark, Paul T, 445
Clark, Regina, 443
Clark, Richard E, 162
Clark, Steven B, 58, 61
Clark, Teresa L, 403
Clark, Thomas, 527
Clark, Yvette, 382
Clarke, Ann, 602
Clarke, Brian, 535
Clarke, Charlotte, 609
Clarke, Donald L, 173
Clarke, Yvette D, 725
Clarkson, John, 197, 290
Clarkson, Thomas, 192
Claro, Cesar J, 586
Clarson, Sandra, 424
Class, Amy, 22
Clawson, Toby, 598
Clay, Nathaniel, 654
Clay, Wm Lacy, 392
Cleare, Cordell, 24
Cleare, Michael, 107
Clearwater, Carole A, 422
Cleary, Jeff, 211, 278, 308
Cleary, Kevin, 519
Cleary, Kevin J, 472
Clemendor, Anthony A, 550
Clemens, Charles, 667
Clemente, Jeannine M, 125, 163, 202
Clements, Joanne, 162
Clements, Michael, 24
Clermont, Lois, 598
Cleveland, Kenneth, 224
Cleveland, Larry J, 412
Clifford, Sharon, 670
Cline, Kimberly R, 611
Clingan, Thomas G, 396

Name Index

Clinton, Hillary Rodham, 151, 187, 220, 274, 315, 356, 364, 381, 383, 384, 385, 386, 723
Cloonan, Edward T, 93, 249
Cloonan, James, 127, 354, 380
Clusen Buecher, Sarah, 531
Clute, Penelope D, 74
Clyne Jr, James W, 214
Clyne, Donna, 531
Clyne, Elizabeth K, 483
Clyne, James, 491, 506
Coad, Deborah, 294, 331
Cobb, Benjamin, 64, 294
Cobb, Crystal, 585
Cobb, Jr, James H, 358
Cobb, Tedra L, 410
Coble, Howard, 391
Coburn, Lindsey, 574
Coburn, Tom, 386
Coccoma, Michael V, 66
Cochran, Carlisle, 442
Cochran, John, 503
Cochran, Mon, 470
Cochran, Thad, 83, 172, 330, 383
Cochrane, Daryl, 485
Cochrane, John C, 331
Cockburn, Susan L, 425
Cocoran, Tina, 579
Cody, James, 363
Coffey, Kevin, 470
Coffey, Peter V, 263
Cofield, Milton L, 143
Coggins, Joseph, 421
Cohalan, Peter Fox, 58
Cohalan, Pierce, 422
Cohen MD, Michael D, 310
Cohen, Andrea, 503
Cohen, Bernie, 508
Cohen, David, 433
Cohen, David B, 60
Cohen, Dennis, 415
Cohen, Dennis S, 64
Cohen, H Rodgin, 96
Cohen, Harold, 523
Cohen, Herbert, 482
Cohen, Ira J, 411
Cohen, Jeffrey, 69
Cohen, Jessica F, 679
Cohen, Joshua, 523
Cohen, Laurie T, 531
Cohen, Linda J, 321
Cohen, Michael, 668
Cohen, Michael T, 304
Cohen, Rhoda J, 61
Cohen, Robert, 495
Cohen, Saul B, 143
Cohen, Stanley G, 635
Cohen, Steven, 188, 207
Cohen, Stuart M, 55
Cohn, Debra L W, 254
Cohn, Janet, 134, 253

Cohn, Janet S, 214
Cohn, Nancy, 333
Cohn, Regina, 655
Cohn, Thomas, 104
Coin, Ellen M, 60
Colabella, Nicholas, 57
Colaiacovo, Emilio L, 561
Colamaria, Nicholas, 211, 278, 308
Colananni, Mark, 482
Colangelo, John P, 73
Colarusso, Janis A, 437
Colarusso, Joseph, 282
Colavita, Anthony S, 418
Colavito, Maria, 12, 269, 312
Colavito, Peter, 549
Colby, David B, 572
Colby, Gerard, 276
Cole, Beverly, 93
Cole, Erin, 105
Cole, Joan, 648
Cole, Jr, Robert H, 71
Cole, Lauri, 476
Cole, Laurie, 285
Cole, Mike, 37, 44, 45, 48, 50, 52, 690
Cole, Ned E, 578
Cole, Steven, 112, 251
Colella, Ron, 558
Coleman PE, Jeffrey C, 426
Coleman, Charles, 556
Coleman, Elizabeth, 266
Coleman, James P, 409
Coleman, Johanna M, 423
Coleman, Marcia, 38, 52, 550
Coleman, Maureen, 9, 177
Coleman, Norm, 382, 385, 386
Coleman, Patrick, 525
Coleman, Peggy, 338
Coleman, Roger F, 593, 594
Coles, Harold A, 675
Colimon, Claude, 219, 315
Collazzi, John, 36
Colletta, Lois C, 645
Collie, Craig E, 323
Collier, Carol R, 115, 181
Colligan, John F, 157
Collini, Robert J, 58
Collins, Anthony G, 472, 623
Collins, Bill, 35
Collins, Brian, 247, 271
Collins, Cheryl, 64
Collins, Ella W, 673
Collins, Francis T, 58
Collins, John, 343, 570
Collins, John P, 58, 60, 257
Collins, Samuel J, 171
Collins, Scott, 82, 105, 171, 232, 303
Collins, Susan, 164, 206, 298, 330, 386
Collorafi, Joseph, 363
Colodner, Michael, 257
Colombo, Beth, 30
Colon, Alaina, 435

Colon, Donald F, 405
Colon, L Ray, 361
Colon, Linda, 218, 239, 315
Colon, Rafael, 451
Colon, Robert, 255
Colton, William, 33, 34, 37, 46, 47, 49, 53, 54, 183, 691
Colucci, Gloria J, 663
Colucci, Robert E, 115, 350
Colucciello, Raymond, 664
Colvin, Gordon C, 113, 181
Colvin, John O, 260
Comar, Sheila, 451
Comastri, Harold, 549
Comenzo, Susan, 296
Comiskey, William J, 254
Comisky, William, 17, 102, 327
Comisky, William J, 134, 216
Commisso, Frank J, 396
Como, Anthony, 160
Como, Joseph, 67
Compton, Linda M, 409
Comrie, Leroy G, 427
Conacchio, Barbara, 160
Conason, Joe, 597
Conatantine, Thomas, 537
Conaway, Laura, 597
Conboy, James E, 404
Condron, Jim, 605
Conerty, Thomas K, 117, 182
Conetta, Robert, 566
Coniglio, Donna, 235
Coniglio, Eleanor T, 74
Conklin, D David, 615
Conklin, John, 27
Conklin, Sewain, 572
Conklin, Susan L, 401
Conkling, Steven D, 404
Conley, Amy V, 533
Conley, Evange, 363
Conlin, Kelli, 510
Conlon, Kevin, 593
Connell, Joan, 269
Connell, John J, 65
Connell, Susan, 131
Connelly, Maureen, 474, 475
Conners, Christopher P, 611
Conners, II, Michael F, 396
Conners, Jeanette, 498
Connerton, Rita, 61
Connery, Michael J, 114, 335
Connolly, Gerald, 463
Connolly, Kenneth, 27, 32, 676
Connolly, Leo T, 410
Connolly, Thomas S, 451
Connolly, Tom, 463
Connolly, William, 130
Connor, Daniel T, 648
Connor, Margaret, 117, 352
Connor, Martin, 21, 25, 26, 29, 30, 31, 92, 713

Indexes & Demographic Maps

Name Index

Connor, Michael J, 600
Connor, Patricia, 575
Connor, Roger, 467
Connors, Gerard, 286
Connors, Jack, 592
Connors, Jr, John P, 263
Connors, Timothy P, 677
Connors-Wright, Lisa, 247, 269
Conole, Patrick, 492
Conover, David, 520
Conrad, Kent, 330, 382, 384, 385
Conrad, Lowell, 453
Conroe, Douglas E, 126, 183
Conroy, Anne N, 573
Conroy, John R, 10, 179, 214
Conroy, Kathleen, 39
Conroy, Martin J, 214
Conroy, Michael L, 541
Consentino, Richard, 32
Conslues, Emmanuel, 471
Constant, Donna, 132
Constantine, Christine, 256
Constantine, Lloyd, 3, 79, 90, 98, 143, 168, 177, 194, 211, 228, 237, 245, 252, 268, 278, 287, 295, 301, 307, 324, 332, 348, 360
Constantino, Edward, 496
Constantino, Susan, 152, 283, 477
Constantinople III, Anthony J, 475
Constantinople, Jr, Anthony J, 475
Conte, Anthony R, 185
Conte, James, 49
Conte, James D, 35, 37, 48, 691
Conte-Zimmer, Susan, 27
Conti, Richard, 39, 48
Conti, Steve, 310
Contino, Victoria M, 531
Conto, Chris, 611
Conway, Eugene J, 418
Conway, Gerard L, 224
Conway, James, 130, 145
Conway, John, 411
Conway, Jr, Gerard L, 175
Conway, Jr, Robert G, 13, 360
Conway, Thomas, 10, 214
Conway, Thomas G, 91, 99, 135, 229, 254
Conyers, Jr, John, 139, 261, 391
Coogan, Mary Ann, 416
Cook, Catherine, 130
Cook, Chris J, 19
Cook, Jen, 36
Cook, LCDR Tonya N, 363
Cook, Oren, 660
Cook, Richard, 461
Cook, Robert, 39
Cook, Scott, 608
Cook, Thomas D, 448
Cook, Vivian E, 34, 37, 45, 46, 48, 49, 51, 53, 691
Cooke SJ, Vincent M, 495
Cooke, Adrian, 145

Cooke, Glenn R, 585
Cooke, II, George L, 411
Cooke, Jacqueline, 273
Cooke, Rev Vincent M, 622
Cooke, William, 471
Cookfair, III, John R, 165
Cook-Schiafo, Richard, 521
Cooley, Jack H, 406
Cooley, Valerie, 470
Coon, James P, 640
Cooney, Gail, 464, 507
Coons, Christina, 528
Coons, Deborah, 129
Coons, Linda L, 159
Cooper Jr, Byrum W, 410
Cooper, Barbara J, 87
Cooper, Gary, 400
Cooper, Ginnie, 432
Cooper, John, 605
Cooper, Jon, 410
Cooper, Judy, 66
Cooper, Linda, 445
Cooper, Matthew F, 59
Cooper, Phyllis, 412
Cooper, Sam, 41
Cooper, Sandra M, 644
Cooper, Steve, 348
Cooper, Wendy E, 250
Cooperman, Arthur J, 58
Copanas, John P, 442
Copel, Harriet, 671
Copeland, Lisa A, 425
Copeland, Peter, 602
Copperman, Joel, 140
Coppola, Anthony S, 548
Coppola, Charles, 475
Copps, Anne Reynolds, 264, 320
Copps, Carl, 247, 270
Corbett, Cindy, 159
Corbett, Jane, 431
Corbin, Jim, 610
Corbin, Roger, 404
Corby, Joseph, 79
Corby, Laurel D, 37
Corcoran, Daniel, 168, 195
Corcoran, Eugene J, 139, 261
Corcoran, Kevin, 420
Corcoran, Michael, 130
Cordo, John, 483
Corellis, Cathy, 49
Corey, Sandra, 159, 452
Corey-Terry, Kandi, 26, 27
Corker, Bob, 384
Corker, Joyce, 37
Corlett, John, 357
Corlett, John A, 485
Corman, Selig, 559
Cornelius, Dominic, 402
Cornelius, Raymond E, 57, 65
Cornell, Chuck, 398
Cornell, Harriet, 449

Cornell, Harriet D, 408
Cornell, Marilyn J, 159
Corning, Peter E, 62
Cornstein, David B, 114, 335
Cornyn, John, 164, 206, 383, 386, 387
Corpus, Ben, 471
Corrado, John J, 556
Corriero, Michael A, 58
Corrigan, Michael T, 122, 149, 201, 217
Corriveau, Mary M, 444
Corsale, Barbara, 579
Corsi, Colleen, 153
Corsi, Louis G, 415
Cort, Rebecca, 8, 146, 279, 312
Cortes, Antonio, 199
Cortes, Clara, 550
Cortese, Maria T, 267
Cortese, Philip V, 65
Cortes-Vazquez, Lorraine, 685
Cortes-Vazquez, Lorraine A, 3, 16, 101, 180, 199, 291
Cortez, Diana, 219, 273
Cortrell, Jonathan, 91, 231, 327
Corwin, Ray, 115, 181, 376
Coscia, Anthony R, 127, 353
Cosentino, Frank T, 97
Cosenza, Albert, 118, 351
Coseo, Thomas G, 645
Cosgrave, Paul J, 431
Cosgrove, Jeremiah, 5, 79, 457
Cosilmon, Tracy M, 417
Coss, Vicki L, 329
Cossaboom, J V, 464
Costa, Jim, 109, 172, 391
Costantino, Jo-Ann, 512
Costello, Ann S, 95
Costello, Carolyn, 661
Costello, III, Bartley J, 491, 506
Costello, Jerry F, 393
Costello, John, 456
Costello, Laura P, 159
Costello, Ralph F, 58
Costello, Rory, 496
Costello, Susan A, 309
Costello, Thomas, 416
Costenbader, Katharine M, 185
Cote, Jamie, 496
Cotrona, Christopher, 469
Cotrona, Louis, 469
Cott, James, 138, 260
Cotten, Forest, 460
Cotton, Mike, 349
Coughlin, John J, 552
Coughlin, William, 398
Coulter, John, 118, 351
Couser, Cheryl, 48
Cousins, Adam, 609
Covello, Joseph, 55, 58
Coveny, Janet, 413
Cover, Grant, 594
Covert, Catherine, 411

Name Index

Covngold, Eric, 138, 260
Cowans, Mary Warr, 213
Coward, Kathryn, 26
Cowin, John T, 442
Cox, Edward F, 611
Cox, Jean M, 469
Cox, John, 415
Cox, Kathleen, 321
Cox, Maureen, 216, 270, 312
Coy, Doug, 593
Coyle, Ellen M, 228
Coyne, Tom, 610
Cozean, Nancy, 439
Cozzens, Robert B, 58
Cozzolino, Beth G, 399
Crabtree, Susan L, 405
Craft, Carter, 509
Craft, Sandra M, 640
Craig, Carla E, 259
Craig, Jane, 169
Craig, Larry, 364, 383, 387
Craig, Larry E, 340, 385
Craig, Lindsay Y, 109
Craig, T R, 138
Craine Jr, Vice Adm John W, 615
Cramer, Joan M, 364
Cramer, Jr, Robert E (Bud), 394
Crampton, Kevin, 649
Crandall, Charles E, 48, 50, 52
Crandall, Curtis, 396
Crandall, John, 402
Crane, Constance, 476
Crane, II, James B, 173, 207
Crane, James B, 476
Crane, Jeffrey B, 653
Crane, Stephen G, 55
Crane, Thomas R, 102, 116, 181
Cranker, Garry L, 536
Cranna, William F, 72
Crannell, Kenneth, 460
Crapo, Mike, 187, 382, 384
Crary, Marianne D, 37
Crawford, Cosema, 119, 352
Crawford, Kevin A, 460
Crawford, Mark, 672
Cray, Thomas, 361
Creahan, Emmett J, 256, 282
Crecca, Andrew A, 68
Cree, Elizabeth, 453
Cree, Elizabeth W, 162
Creedon, Richard, 251
Creekmore, Lewis G, 498
Cremins, Father John J, 611
Crescenzo, Bob, 276
Crespo, Marcos A, 22
Crew III, D Bruce, 56
Crimi, Charles F, 74
Crimmins, Keith F, 159
Cringle, Kenneth O, 643
Crisafulli, Joseph, 348
Cromie, William J, 468

Cronin, Kenneth J, 138
Cronin, Kevin M, 416
Crooke, Ellen, 608
Croscut, Fred, 398
Cross, Raymond W, 614
Cross, Robert F, 113, 350
Crossett, Susan, 175
Crossley, Dennis J, 341
Crossley, John, 564
Crosson, Matthew, 500, 578
Crotty, Jane, 459
Crotty, John, 120, 230
Crouch, Clifford, 35
Crouch, Clifford W, 38, 44, 46, 49, 51, 53, 80, 691
Croucher, Bruce, 86
Croucher, Roger, 622
Crounse, Marian, 150
Crouse, Peter R, 478
Crowell III, William Y, 491, 529
Crowell, III, William Y, 95
Crowell, William Y, 551
Crowley, Dennis, 131
Crowley, Joseph, 93, 106, 232, 240, 249, 381, 389, 390, 391, 450, 725
Crowley, Kevin J, 70
Crowley, Peter, 309, 599
Crowley, Sean, 478
Crowley, Terri, 491, 506
Crowley, William, 5, 98, 103, 124, 324, 371, 379
Crudele, Donna, 66
Crummey, Caron O'Brien, 29
Crupi, Joann M, 591
Crutchfield, Col Anthony, 365
Cruthers, Frank, 429
Cruz, Humberto, 212
Cruz, Raul, 59
Cubello, Louis, 289, 302, 326
Cudahy, Cathy, 514
Cudahy, Kathy, 474
Cuddihy, Edward L, 593
Cuellar, Henry, 206, 390
Cuevas, Michael, 51
Culbertson, James A, 403
Culkin, John, 132
Cullen, James P, 429
Cullen, Tracy, 25
Culley, Anna, 59
Cullinan, Dennis, 368
Cullinane, Sara, 502
Cullinane, Shawn, 424
Culliton, Alfred, 574
Culliton, Gerald, 364
Culliton, John T, 196, 301
Cully, Malcolm, 131
Cultrara, James, 461
Cumberbatch, Y Stacey, 430
Cummings, Dan, 609
Cummings, Elijah E, 393
Cummings, Michael, 332

Cummings, Michelle, 502
Cummings, Thomas, 92, 104
Cumoletti, Steven F, 16, 136
Cumoletti, Susan, 634
Cuneo-Harwood, Gina, 445
Cunningham, Bert, 117, 170, 377
Cunningham, Carmen, 307
Cunningham, Christopher, 450
Cunningham, Christopher A, 411
Cunningham, Col Patrick, 367
Cunningham, Dan, 98, 196, 324
Cunningham, Dany, 470
Cunningham, Deborah, 145
Cunningham, Glenn, 246, 269
Cunningham, Jennifer, 483
Cunningham, Joanne, 484
Cunningham, Katharine A, 65
Cunningham, Michael, 269
Cunningham, Raymond, 132
Cunningham, William, 477
Cuomo, Andrew M, 3, 12, 91, 99, 134, 169, 179, 197, 216, 229, 238, 247, 253, 270, 301, 325, 685
Curcio, Pasquale J, 447
Curitore, Thomas, 436
Curley, Marie, 43
Curley, Tricia, 371
Curr, John, 514
Curran, III, Patrick J, 541
Curran, John G, 538
Curran, John M, 57
Curran, Mary B, 68
Curran, Patrick, 481
Curran, Patrick J, 173
Curran, Raymond, 521
Curren, Kathryn F, 52
Curreri, Richard A, 14, 296
Currey, Douglas, 350
Currier, John V, 9, 296
Curry Jr, Robert E, 15
Curry, James T, 402
Curry, John J, 516
Curry, Patrick, 42
Curry, Sandra L, 15, 99, 197
Curry-Cobb, Sarah, 39
Curtin, Dennis D, 399
Curtis, Jeffrey J, 162
Curtis, Thomas, 94
Curulla, John A, 418
Cusack, Joan A, 7, 132, 311
Cushing, M Scott, 36
Cushman, John, 442
Cusick, Kristy, 550
Cusick, Michael J, 38, 47, 48, 50, 52, 691
Custer, Chuck, 605
Cutler, Peter K, 416
Cutolo, Frank, 574
Cutrona, Anthony J, 56
Cymbrowitz, Steven, 35, 45, 47, 48
Cymbrowitz, Steven H, 38, 49, 692
Cyrulnik, Miriam, 60

Name Index

Czajka, Paul, 62
Czajkowski, Daniel, 511
Czauski, Henry, 232
Czygier, Jr, John M, 68
D'Agati, John, 29
D'Agati, Rebecca, 36
D'Agati, Rebecca P, 53
D'Agostino, Carolyn, 198
D'Agostino, John, 593
D'Alauro, Veronica, 198, 297
D'Amato, Alfonse M, 513
D'Amato, Armand, 513
D'Amato, Christopher P, 513
D'Ambro, Evelyn, 308
D'Ambrosio, Carla, 670
D'Ambrosio, Dr John A, 581
D'Ambrosio, Michael, 328
D'Amico, Anthony, 118, 351, 377
D'Amico, Gloria, 407
D'Amico, Matthew, 526
D'Amico, Michael L, 63
D'Angelis, Anthony, 58
D'Angelo, Daniel, 302, 349
D'Angelo, Frank G, 264
D'Angelo, Philip D, 659
D'Angelo, Robert C, 661
D'Anne, Beverly, 332
D'Arcy, Wayne, 136
D'Attilio, Albert, 641
D'Attilio, Richard, 571
D'Emic, Matthew J, 58
D'Onofrio, James M, 405
Da Leon, Peter, 549
Dabiri, Gloria, 56
Dadd, Eric T, 413
Dadd, Mark H, 69
Dadey, Dick, 207, 293
Daghlian, Lee, 8, 157, 372
Dahl, Brian, 397
Dahl, Christopher C, 614
Dahl, Patricia, 222
Daimwood, Diana, 285
Daines, MD, Richard F, 10, 179, 212
Dale, Currier, 528
Daleo, Sam, 595
Dalessio, Anthony, 496
Daley, Martin W, 540
Daley, Mary, 145
Daley, Michael E, 57
Dalton, John K, 198
Dalton, Jr, Joseph W, 584
Daly, Dick, 604
Daly, Eugene, 544
Daly, Mark, 427
Daly, Terri, 168, 195
Daly, Thomas R, 76
Daly, William, 572
Daly-Browne, Sharon, 470
Damashek, Phillip, 434
Dambakly, Thomas, 470
Dame, Ginger, 199, 297

Dames, Cynthia, 477
Damiani, Lisa, 215
Damico, Robert, 229
Damrath, Joseph E, 72
Danese, Gus, 460
Dangle, Jeanne M, 658
Daniels, Brian, 6, 309
Daniels, Gordon, 644
Daniels, Jill, 12, 281, 373
Daniels, Randy A, 611
Daniels, Robert, 144, 333, 579
Danoff, Susan S, 61
Danovitz, Burt, 243, 322
Danzinger, Mitchell, 59, 60
Darcy, Martin, 280
Darden, George O, 442
Darden, James, 225
Darden, Lawrence, 73
Dardia, Michael, 433
Darling, Joseph L, 349
Darrell, Andrew, 189
Darwin, David, 406
Dascher Jr, Norman E, 512
Dashnshaw, William, 570
Dassin, Lev, 138, 260
Dattilio, Daniel J, 340
Daus, Matthew W, 434
Davenport, Gail, 498
Davenport, Geoff, 502
Davenport, Heyward B, 104, 239
Davenport, Marolyn, 517
David Bosworth, Frank Commisso, 449
David, Alphonso B, 11, 237
David, Greg, 601
Davidoff, Sid, 478
Davidowitz, Edward, 58
Davidson, Arlene, 188
Davidson, Ethan, 434
Davidson, George, 409
Davidson, Kathie E, 69
Davidson, Robert, 315
Davidson, Robert L, 219, 315
Davidson, William, 117, 170
Davie, Duncan, 24
Davies, James, 10
Davies, James M, 196
Davies, Mark, 428
Davies, Robert, 178
Davies, Sarah, 404
Davila, Jose, 493
Davila, Josephina, 502
Davis III, James R, 555
Davis, Anne M, 535
Davis, Danny K, 164, 298, 392
Davis, Darwin M, 322
Davis, David, 274, 392
Davis, Derrick, 535
Davis, Dr Kenneth, 82
Davis, Ernest D, 425
Davis, Geoffrey H, 679
Davis, George A, 416

Davis, Gordon J, 497
Davis, Heather, 466
Davis, III, Thomas M, 164, 298, 392
Davis, Irwin L, 586
Davis, Ivy, 164, 239
Davis, Jerry, 413
Davis, Jo Ann, 388
Davis, John, 455
Davis, Karen, 222
Davis, Kathleen M, 658
Davis, Kenneth A, 58
Davis, Kenneth L, 628
Davis, Lindsey, 473
Davis, Madeleine, 579
Davis, Pamela, 125, 337, 353
Davis, Perry, 111
Davis, Richard, 627
Davis, Robert, 73, 466
Davis, Robert E, 123, 182
Davis, Ronald, 505
Davis, Shalon, 482
Davis, Wade A, 126, 353, 380
Davis, William J, 56
Davitian, Harry, 173
Davlin, James, 541
Dawe, Steve, 609
Dawkins, Frank, 604
Dawson, Charles, 522
Dawson, Herman, 431
Dawson, James C, 143
Dawson, James P, 57
Dawson, Joseph J, 60
Dawson, Tandra L, 61
Dawson, Thomas, 497
Dax, Jocelyn, 52
Day, David, 458
Day, Eric, 399
Day, Julia, 238
Day, Luke, 415
Dayrit, Manolet, 496
Dayton, Keith D, 399
De Almeida, Alessandra, 496
De Federicis, Daniel M, 553
De Maria, Thomas, 128, 271, 354, 380
De More, Robert S, 563
De Rienzo, Charles, 433
de Russy, Candace, 611
de Torrente, Nicolas, 222
De Valle, Eduardo, 471
Deal, Nathan, 219, 389
Dean, Frank, 340
Dean, William J, 267
Deane, Janet, 580
Deane-Williams, Barbara, 661
DeAngelis, James, 188
DeAngelis, Patricia A, 408
DeAugustine, John, 591
DeBenedetto, Karen, 75
DeBenedictus, Frank, 159
Debow, Andrea, 476
Decaire, David J, 549

Name Index

DeCarli, Ronald, 646
DeCarlo, Donald T, 11, 246, 268
DeCarlo, Lori, 640
Decastro, Damon A, 436
DeCataldo, Robert T, 58
DeCatur, Christine, 522
DeCerbo, Joseph, 639
deChants, Joseph M, 257
Dechiro, Jaclyn, 482
DeCiccio, Louis F, 447
DeCinque, Gregory T, 616
Decker, Linda, 196
Decker, Richard B, 398
Decker, Wayne A, 406
DeCosta, Steven C, 428
Decoteau, Jane, 564
DeCotis, Henry A, 135, 229, 247, 255, 302
DeDominick, Cynthia, 652
Dedrick, Charles S, 638
Dedvukaj, Mick, 204, 240
Deering, Michael, 500
Deering, Michael J, 549
Deery, Michael J, 421
Defayette, Keith M, 398
DeFazio, Peter A, 393
DeFedericis, Daniel, 515
DeFelice, Paul, 260
Defilippo, Robert F, 646
DeFleur, Lois B, 612
DeFrancisco, John A, 20, 22, 26, 28, 29, 30, 31, 259, 713
DeFrancisco, John D, 28
DeGraaff, Bill, 355
DeGrace, John A, 160
DeGrasse, Leland G, 56
DeGregorio, Georgia, 498
Dehm, Karl, 528
Deierlen, Joan C, 445
DeIorio, Vincent A, 122, 170, 182
DeJarnette, Karen, 504
DeJesu, Thomas, 174
DeJoseph, Brian F, 57
Del Campo, Elsie, 431
Del Giacco, Stephen, 11, 134, 197, 373
Del Giudice, Christopher, 502
Del Guidice, Vincent M, 58
del Valle, Eduardo, 619
Dela Raba, Gary, 460
Delacruz, Felix, 489
Delafield, Pompey, 422
Delahunt, Bill, 391
Delameter, Nelson, 400
Delaney, Constance L, 69
Delaney, John, 145
Delaney, Kristen, 605
DeLaney, Marty, 570
Delaney, Nancy, 62
Delany, Brian, 607
DeLauro, Rosa, 83, 387
DeLaus, Jr, Daniel M, 404
DelBalso, Maureen, 589

DelDuca, Paul, 38
DeLessio, John P, 448
Delfino, Joseph M, 445
Delgado, Melba, 80
Delgado, Ryan, 477
Delgenio, Beth, 527
DeLilli, Robert A, 648
DeLisio, Rudolph A, 572
DeLisle, Dennis, 123, 201, 327
Della Corte, Robert, 558
Della Femina, Jerry J, 597
Dellarmi, James E, 567
Dellaverson, Gary, 117, 352
DelliBovi, Alfred A, 94
Dellinger, Kent, 492
Delmonico, Karen, 588
DelMonte, Francine, 35, 38, 44, 46, 47, 50, 52, 692
DeLorenzo, James, 146, 279, 312
DeLoria, Dave, 648
Delory, Diane, 358
DelPlato, Michael A, 71
DelSignore, Art, 12, 325
DelTorto, Elizabeth A, 418
DeLuca, Frank, 676
DeLuca, Rosemary, 529
DeMagistris, Tony, 196
DeMairo, Pauline, 510
DeMarco, Mario, 439
DeMarco, Robert, 359
DeMarco, Vincent F, 411
Demarest, Carolyn E, 56
Demarest, David R, 57
DeMaro, Joseph A, 58
DeMartino III, Michael James, 27
DeMartino, Michael James, 22
DeMass, Christina, 63
DeMatteo, Gary, 440
Demauro Busketta, Carol, 160
DeMay, Karen R, 406
Demby, Eric, 435
DeMers, Lawrence, 146, 212
deMilly, Michele, 486
DeMint, Jim, 384
Dempsey Jr, Gerard W, 656
Dempsey, Kevin, 15, 326, 335
Demrino, Yvonne, 82
Denard, Paul, 328
Denerstein, Mylan, 429
Deninger, William, 68
Denk, Eric S, 397
Denker, Nowell, 561
Denley, Mark, 464, 507
Denn, James, 15, 169, 374
Dennison, Robert, 349
Dennison, William R, 565
Dent, Charlie, 206, 390
Dente, Catherine, 432, 516
Denton, Lillian, 310
Depalo, Armand, 492
Depasquale, Jamie, 457

DePasquale, Patricia C, 445
DePerno, Sandra J, 405
DePhillips, Guy P, 61
Depoy, Sandra Y, 534
DePrima, Denise, 120, 336
DeProspo, William L, 453
Derbyshire, Vicky, 215
Deren, Joseph V, 73
DeRienzo, Charles D, 433
DeRienzo, Harold, 236
DeRiso, Frank C, 277
DeRooy, Judy, 419
DeRosa, Georgio, 463
DeRosa, Melissa, 463
DeRosa, Nicholas, 66
DeRosa, Thomas, 579
DeRose, Mary, 669
Derry, Alan R, 672
Derway, Lynn, 460
Desai, Swati, 431
DeSantis, David J, 679
DeSantis, Gene, 503
Desantis, Vincent, 72
DeSanto, Joseph, 412
Desch, Carol, 144
DeSiato, Donna J, 659
DeSimone, Leonard, 119, 352
Desmond, Sarah, 492
Desnoyers, Dale, 177
DeSol, Lou, 349
DeSole, Lauren, 257
DeSorbe, Brian M, 668
Desormeau, Robert, 552
DeSpurito, III, John, 453
Desrosier, Major Emily, 362
Dessables, Mary Jane, 466
Dessauer, James, 415
Dessen, Eric, 496
Destefano, Vito M, 70
Destito, RoAnn M, 38, 43, 44, 46, 48, 53, 202, 692
Deuel, Michael S, 658
Deutsch, Eric, 573
Deutsch, Ron, 323
Deutsch, Terry Rosen, 471
Devane, Paul T, 396
Devaney, James M, 152
Devereaux, Meagan, 436
Devine, Deb, 52, 228
Devine, Lawrence M, 363
Devine, Theresa, 536
Devlin Jr, Richard, 407
Devlin, Diane Y, 57
DeVore, Barbara, 212
Dewald, Maria, 480
DeWald, Maria L, 154
Dewey, Jan, 598
DeWitt, Donald C, 15, 289, 302, 326
DeWitt, Kerry, 489
DeWitt, Stephen M, 162
Dexter, James P, 643

Name Index

Deycy, Avitia, 493
Deyo, Gabriel, 213
DeYoung, Gary, 338
Deyss, Christine, 322, 473
Dhampande, Shom, 501
Di Bacco, Michelle, 25
Di Bella, Robert M, 69
Diamond, Arthur M, 58
Diamond, Charles, 61
Diamond, Maria A, 663
Diamond, Martin, 226
Diamond, Marylin G, 59
Diamond, Seth, 431
Diana, Edward A, 406
Diaz Jr, Ruben, 692
Diaz, Francisco, 466
Diaz, Hector L, 396
Diaz, Jr, Ruben, 38, 45, 46, 47, 52, 53
Diaz, Luis M, 38, 43, 44, 48, 49, 51, 692
Diaz, Sr, Ruben, 22, 25, 26, 29, 30, 31, 32, 217, 239, 283, 313
Diaz, Sr, Rubin, 714
Diaz-Balart, Lincoln, 392
DiBacco, Michelle, 31
DiBella, Michael, 580
DiBianco, Gustave J, 259
DiCaprio, Patrick, 665
DiCaro, David R, 419
DiCaro, John, 419
DiCioccio, Patricia A, 424
Dick, Brad, 597
Dickens, Inez, 427
Dickens, Inez E, 449
Dickenson, Harry, 421
Dicker, Frederic, 596
Dickerson, Ruth, 62
Dickerson, Thomas A, 55, 57
Dickinson, Christina, 27, 30
Dickinson, Craig, 9, 296, 372
Dickinson, Mike, 602
Dickinson, Randall L, 356
Dickinson, Toni, 24
Dicks, Norman D, 388
Dickson, Charles, 15
Dickson, Charles M, 169
Dickson, Eric, 436
Dickson, Eric J, 420
Dickson-McMahon, Martha, 416
Dickstein, Paul, 556
Dicob, Joanne, 200
DiCosmo, Gail, 399
DiCristofaro, David, 496
DiDomenico, Catherine M, 59
Diebold, William, 460
Dieterle, Dana, 607
Dietrich, David, 228
Dietrich, Martin A, 96
DiFabio, Michael J, 662
DiFede, Salvatore J, 545
Difiore, Janet, 413
DiFrancesco, Rob, 36

DiFrancisco, Joe, 403
Digman, Brian, 101, 327
Digman, John R, 133, 253
DiGrazia, Louis J, 419
DiGregorio, Diane, 489
Dilan, Martin M, 22, 26, 27, 29, 30, 32, 714
Dilan, Martin Malave, 20, 163
DiLello, Art, 25, 27, 29
DiLello, Nicholas, 414
DiLiberto, James G, 635
Dill, Jean, 72
Dillard, Helene, 82, 84
Dillon, Barbara, 537
Dillon, James H, 63
Dillon, Kevin M, 57
Dillon, Linda, 123, 149
Dillon, Linda M H, 405
Dillon, Mark, 57
Dillon, Mark C, 55
Dillon, Robert R, 654
DiLorenzo, Joseph, 661
DiMango, Patricia, 56
DiMartino, Margaret D, 70
DiMartino, Rita, 619
Dimaya, Leon, 238
Dimbleby, David, 652
DiMeglio, Albert K, 246, 268
DiMezza, Thomas P, 404
DiMillo, Thomas M, 73
Dimmig, Robert L, 587
DiMola, Nicholas, 118, 351
DiMura, Paul, 129
Dinallo, Eric R, 11, 215, 245
DiNapoli, Thomas, 180
DiNapoli, Thomas P, 3, 16, 197, 290, 297, 685
Ding, George, 146
Dingell, John D, 105, 186, 389
Dingell, Jr, John D, 171, 219
Dinin, John, 5, 90
Dinkin, Casey, 464
Dinolfo, Cheryl, 404
Dinolfo, David V, 651
Dinowitz, Jeffrey, 38, 44, 47, 48, 49, 137, 217, 282, 313, 692
Diomande, Ahmed, 28
DiPace, Denise, 483
DiPirro, Colleen C, 569
DiRaddo, Raymond, 420
Director
, Philippe de Montebello,, 344
Direnzo, John, 496
Dirolf, James, 196
DiRose, Marcia, 62
Dirschel, Kathleen, 623
DiSanto, Kenneth, 572
Disciullo, John, 608
DiSento, Carol, 305
Diskin, Michael G, 401
Disman, Beatrice M, 314
DiSpirito, Patricia Ann, 160

Dissek, Philip C, 274
DiStefano, Biagio J, 64
DiStefano, James G, 418
DiStefano, Linda, 523
DiSunno, David, 418
Ditman, Lenn, 7, 332, 372
DiTullio, Sheila, 63
DiVeronica, Rocco J, 403
DiVirgilio, Michael, 145
Dixon, Dianne E, 432
Dixon, Mija, 74
Dixson, Mark, 411
Dmytrenko, Orysia, 150
Doar, Robert, 431
Dobriko, Lynn, 309
Dobrin, Allan, 471
Dobrin, Allan H, 619
Dobrucki, Mary Beth, 79
Doctoroff, Daniel L, 426
Dodd, Christopher J, 93, 233, 383, 385, 386
Dodd, Donald H, 407
Dodge, Arnold, 654
Dodge, David, 474
Dodson, Donnalee, 650
Dodson, Thomas, 280
Doeren, Jennifer, 523
Doern, James E, 75
Doersam, Paul M, 314
Dogias, Nicholas, 247, 271
Doherty, John J, 434
Doherty, Linda, 418
Doherty, Marian C, 60
Doherty, Neal, 567
Doherty, Thomas, 507
Dolan, Maureen, 471
Dolan, Thomas J, 63
Dolan, Thomas P, 654
Dolci, Joel A, 110
Dole, Elizabeth, 383
Dolfman, Michael L, 273
Dollard, James P, 58
Dolley, Jeffrey, 593
Domagalski, James, 452
Domenici, Pete V, 172, 187, 340, 383, 384
Dominelli, Joseph S, 299
Dominick, Marilyn, 659
Domkowski, Jacqueline, 69
Donaghy, John, 445
Donahue, Maureen, 639
Donaldson Jr, Clifford, 400
Donaldson, David, 411
Donalty, Barry M, 66
Donato, Kenneth, 437
Donato, Stephanie, 309
Donavan, Patrick J, 443
Donegan, Michael F, 122, 137
Donelli, John, 130
Dong, Helen, 48
Donnaruma, Julia, 484
Donnaruma, Mary Ann, 53
Donnellan, James F, 250

Name Index

Donnellan, Jr, John J, 364
Donnellan, Susan, 11, 245
Donnelley, Raymond C, 570
Donnelly, Dennis, 257
Donnelly, Martin, 452
Donnelly, Patricia, 25
Donnelly, Patrick, 410
Donnino, William C, 58
Donno, Frank, 431
Donofrio, Gail A, 65
Donohue, Danny, 275, 299, 472
Donohue, David M, 247, 271
Donohue, Gavin J, 174
Donohue, Helena M, 8, 157
Donohue, Lawrence, 70
Donohue, Thomas J, 5, 98, 102, 124, 324
Donor, Albert E, 624
Donovan Jr, Daniel M, 408
Donovan, Aaron, 120, 230, 377
Donovan, Alan B, 614
Donovan, Donna, 600
Donovan, James, 549
Donovan, Joseph F, 669
Donovan, Michael, 329
Donovan, Shaun, 120, 230, 430
Donovan, Tom, 592, 596
Donovan, W Denis, 57
Doody, Mark E, 674
Dooha, Susan, 241, 316
Doolan, Sean M, 491, 506, 563
Dopp, Darren, 3, 12, 79, 90, 98, 99, 129, 143, 157, 168, 177, 194, 211, 228, 237, 245, 252, 254, 268, 278, 287, 295, 301, 307, 324, 332, 348, 360, 371, 373
Doran III, Arthur J, 76
Doran, Arthur J, 76
Doran, Craig, 66
Doran, Helaine, 467
Dorfman, Claire, 467
Dorgan, Bryon L, 384, 387
Dorgan, Byron, 172, 383
Dorgan, Byron L, 206, 240, 384
Dorman, Jan, 86, 224
Dorman, Jan S, 553
Dorsa, Joseph P, 58
Doss, Matthew, 102, 116, 181
Dossantos, Dina, 507
Dotte, John, 451
Dotterweich, Bernie, 361
Dougan, Kathleen M, 545
Dougher, Brendan, 511
Dougher, Darleen, 439
Dougherty, Maureen L, 411
Dougherty, Patrick, 672
Dougherty, Ruth, 86
Dougherty, Stephen J, 75
Dougherty, Terrance, 644
Douglas, Derek, 4, 194, 371
Douglas, Garry, 582
Douglas, Jewel A, 123
Douglas, Laura G, 58

Douglas, Robin L, 569
Douglas, Valencia F, 664
Douglass, Lewis L, 56
Dove, Carol L, 554
Dove, Cheryl, 72
Dove, Susan, 585
Dovi, Patricia A, 648
Dow, Debra, 68
Dow, Evelyn, 599
Dow, Ken, 449
Dow, Kenneth J, 158
Dowd, Kevin, 425
Dowd, Kevin M, 57
Dowery-Rodriquez, Brenda L, 73
Dowling, Deborah A, 56
Downes, Brien R, 53
Downey, Caroline, 11, 237
Downey, James, 73
Downs, Jennifer, 23
Dowse, Patricia, 517
Doyle, Cathryn M, 61
Doyle, III, Vincent E, 207
Doyle, James F X, 68
Doyle, John, 517
Doyle, Jr, John G, 127, 354
Doyle, Kathleen M, 146, 212
Doyle, Kevin, 114, 137, 257
Doyle, Michael R, 175
Doyle, Pat, 228
Doyle, Patti L, 159
Doyle, Robert W, 58
Doyle, Ruth, 410
Doyle, Vincent E, 57
Drag, Walter F, 71
Drager, Laura E, 60
Drago, Karen A, 67
Drago, Peter, 4, 179, 371
Drago, Peter A, 12, 91, 99, 134, 169, 216, 229, 238, 247, 254, 270, 373
Drago, Samuel J, 270
Drahos, Michael, 652
Draiss, Barbara, 196
Drake III, W Scott, 419
Drake, Daniel A, 255
Drake, Sally, 37
Drakes, Jennifer, 92, 104
Drapkin, Jonathan, 109, 234, 579
Draves, Edward, 463
Draxler, Donna L, 398
Drayzen, Steve, 118, 351
Dreier, David, 392
Drescher, Debbie, 122
Dresel, Carolyn, 95
Dress, James, 135
Dressel, Roderick O, 121, 352
Drexelius, J R, 26
Drexielius, John R, 25
Dreyer, James, 511
Dreyer, Liz, 343
Drillings, Robert M, 291
Drinane, Monica, 59

Driscoll, Justin, 91, 92, 124, 127, 128, 231, 327
Driscoll, M Colleen, 214
Driscoll, Matthew J, 442
Driscoll, Sharon A, 404
Driscoll, William, 514
Drislane, Judy, 325
Drogi, Chris, 574
Drooker, Penelope, 144, 333
Dros, Kathy, 470
Drucker, Richard, 114, 362, 375
Druke, John, 496
Drury, Timothy J, 63
Dua, Stephanie, 429
Duane, Gregory J, 439
Duane, Thomas K, 20, 22, 26, 28, 29, 30, 31, 714
Dube, Art, 219, 273
Dubensky, Joyce S, 243
Dubey, PhD, Dennis, 281
Dubik, Robert, 652
DuBois, Carl E, 406
Dubois, Robert, 6
DuBois, Robert, 287, 295
Duckworth, Sandra B, 678
Duddy, Matthew, 558
Dudek, Matt, 599
Dudley, Cheryl, 649
Dudley, David R, 480
Dudzinski, Chet, 417
Duell, G Robert, 399
Duer, Edward, 417
Duffey, Robert Michael, 464
Dufficy, Timothy J, 59
Duffy, Beau, 607
Duffy, Colleen, 69
Duffy, Margaret, 480
Duffy, Robert J, 440
Duga-Carroll, Amanita, 519
Dugan, Deb, 348
Dugan, Dot, 43
Dugan, Margaret, 280
Dugan, Suzanne, 123, 199, 201, 291
Duggan, W Dennis, 61
Duhan, Rose, 484
Duhl, Judith, 528
Duitz, Mindy, 153
Duke, Oak, 600
Dulberg, Meredith, 494
Dulchin, Benjamin, 454
Dumain, Sheldon, 653
Dumas, Cheryl A, 159
Dumas, Frances, 413
Dumka, Catherine A, 160
Dunbar, Gerald J, 59
Duncan, Jr, James A, 568
Duncan, Jr, John J, 393
Duncan, Liza, 144
Duncan, Thomasenia P, 164
Duncan-Poiter, Johanna, 145
Duncan-Poitier, Johanna, 8

Name Index

Duncanson, Marlinda, 425
Duncker, Karin A, 110
Duncombe, Raynor B, 409
Dunham, Carole S, 62
Dunkel, George, 457
Dunkin, Casey, 507
Dunlea, Mark, 492
Dunlop, Roberta L, 58
Dunn, Catherine, 516
Dunn, Catherine Carver, 432
Dunn, Christopher, 514
Dunn, David, 527
Dunn, Geoff, 605
Dunn, Jill A, 13, 348
Dunn, Kathleen, 474
Dunn, Martin, 596
Dunn, Meg, 622
Dunn, Van, 430
Dunne, James, 289, 302, 326
Dunne, James F, 15
Dunne, John P, 58
Dunne, Linda, 628
Dunne, Thomas, 527
Dunning, Joe, 593
Dunphy, Edward, 445
Dunwell, Frances, 178
Dupra, Mark R, 644
Dupre, Michael, 527
Duprey, Janet L, 38, 44, 46, 50, 51
Duprey, Janet L , 693
Durand, Catherine, 5, 79
Durbin, Richard, 383
Durbin, Richard J, 386
Duren, Mitch, 618
Durfee, Tracy, 13, 281
Durg, Uday, 118, 351
Durham, Kimberly, 191
Durnan, Christopher, 534
Dursi, Frank, 580
Durso Jr, John R, 404
Durso, John R, 561
Duryea, Christopher, 476
Dusablon, Robert, 208
Dusek, Paul, 412
Dustin, Daniel J, 146
Dutcher, Jay, 453
Dutton, Donna M, 444
Dutton, Melinda, 503
Duvdevani, Avi, 430
Duve, Nicole M, 410
Dvorsky, Thomas, 15, 169
Dwire, Diane M, 450
Dworkin, David M, 305
Dwyer, James, 544
Dwyer, Mary, 366
Dwyer, Michael L, 66
Dwyer, Susan M, 397
Dybas, Dolores C, 80
Dyckman, Jo-Ann, 418
Dyer, Denise, 311
Dyer, Felicia, 528

Dyer, Marilyn, 24
Dykstra, Timothy P, 539
Dylong, Geoff, 591
Dymond, Kenneth, 355
Dzurinko, Ted, 440
Dzus, Lydia, 311
Dzwonczyk MD, Philip, 214
Dzwonczyk, Philip, 360
Eadie, Frank, 523
Eady, Veronica, 497
Eagan, Mike, 344
Eannace, Ralph J, 75
Earl, Ruth, 178
Earle, Steven, 145
Earley, Bill, 606
Early, Rodney C, 260
Easley, David, 94, 108
Eastman, Karen E, 127, 353
Easton, Robert H, 11, 245
Easton, William, 456
Eastwood, Kenneth, 660
Eaton, Carol A, 640
Eaton, Edwin L, 424
Ebersole, John F, 625
Ebert, Loretta, 144
Ecfeld, William, 539
Eckert, Lisa, 339
Eckstrom, Jim, 598
Eddington, Patricia, 35
Eddington, Patricia A, 38, 46, 48, 49, 150, 693
Edelson, Paul, 520
Eder, Tim A, 102, 116, 181
Edert, James P, 219, 315
Edgar, James R, 14, 296, 374
Edick, Sharon, 417
Edison, Iliana, 528
Edlitz, Sandra B, 69
Edman, Peter A, 25
Edmead, Carol R, 56
Edmondson, Charles M, 622
Edwards, Bruce, 485
Edwards, Chet, 388
Edwards, Gregory J, 398
Edwards, Harrison J, 419
Edwards, Janet E, 41
Edwards, Kaida, 470
Edwards, Timothy, 420
Edwards, Walter J, 564
Edwards, William, 73
Effler, Steven, 192
Effman, Norman P, 413
Efman, Martin I, 70
Efner, Christine, 147
Egan Jr, John C, 57
Egan, David D, 57
Egan, John C, 10, 195, 301, 333
Egan, John M, 567
Egan, Jr, John, 70
Egan, Mark, 602
Egan, Patricia, 407

Egan, Terri, 13, 348
Egan, Theresa, 415
Egan, Thomas F, 611
Egeland, June, 34, 51
Eggert, Diane, 85
Eggler, William, 44
Eggleston, Alan P, 94
Egri, Marianne, 120, 149
Ehlers, Rep Vernon, 395
Ehlers, Rep Vernon J, 394
Ehlers, Vernon, 390
Ehlers, Vernon J, 392
Ehlinger, Elaine, 168, 195
Ehmke, Jim, 607
Ehrenberg, Erica, 628
Ehrenberg, Randy A, 638
Ehresman, Maria, 675
Ehrlich, Clifford, 344
Ehrlich, Mary-Jo, 39
Eichelberger, S Earl, 461
Eigendorff, Donald W, 205, 303
Eisel, Sr, James E, 399
Eisenberg, Arthur, 514
Eisenberg, Ben, 539
Eisenberg, Carol D, 656
Eisenhut, Ann, 23
Eisenstadt, Amy, 482
Eisgruber, Judith A, 233
Eisman, Julianne S, 65
Ekpe, Ekpe, 131
Elacqua, Jamie-Lynne, 117, 200, 377
Elder, Lance W, 140, 318
Eldon, Ethan C, 189, 357
Eldridge, Jr, Terrance R, 565
Elefante, Hilarie, 426
Elias, Judith A, 671
Elkins, Carolyn, 161
Elkins, Lee Hand, 61
Ellenson, David, 625
Ellerin, Betty W, 55
Elliman, Christopher, 505
Elliman, Christopher J, 191
Elliot, David, 58
Elliott, D Stephen, 343, 344
Elliott, Joan, 498
Elliott, John E, 74
Elliott, John J, 57, 66
Elliott, Mark, 277, 322
Elliott, Paul, 501
Elliott, Robert, 521
Elliott, Thomas C, 677
Ellis, James, 452
Ellis, Judith, 482
Ellis, Robert, 310
Ellis, Timothy, 27
Ellman, Jesse, 535
Ellsworth, Bruce, 401
Ellsworth, Lisa, 246, 269
Ellwood, Lee, 670
Elmendorf, Michael, 110, 276, 331
Else, Gail J, 647

Name Index

Elsner, Timmie E, 60
Elson, Allen, 606
Elter, John, 475
Ely, Eric, 665
Ely, Hugh, 569
Emanuel, Rahm, 165
Emanuel, Rick, 591
Emberger, Charles, 439
Emerson, Catherine L, 405
Emerson, Cathy, 68
Emerson, Elizabeth H, 58
Emery, Jean, 53, 239, 272, 313
Emery, John, 31
Emmer, Cynthia, 449, 539
Emrick, II, John A, 535
Enck, Judith, 3, 79, 177, 332
Endal, Charlene, 283
Endo, Sandra, 608
Endries, Laurie, 246, 268
Eng, Norman, 493
Eng, Randall T, 58
Engel, Eliot, 391
Engel, Eliot L, 105, 106, 171, 186, 219, 240, 381, 389, 390, 391, 726
Engel, Kevin, 30
Englebrecht, Ramona, 458
Englebright, Steven C, 38, 43, 46, 47, 48, 52, 217, 238, 313, 693
Engleman, James, 204
Englert, Michael, 441
English, Donna, 162
English, James D, 567
English, Janice, 433
English, Phil, 394
Engoron, Arthur F, 59
Ennis, Graham, 26, 32
Enright, Janice, 545
Ensign, John, 383, 384
Ensler, Laura, 528
Enzi, Michael B, 151, 220, 274, 315, 385
Epplemann, Christine, 47
Eppler, Klaus, 111, 266
Eppolito, Anthony P, 74
Epstein, Harvey, 492
Epstein, James E, 185
Ercole, Robert, 130
Erdman, Joseph, 30
Erdoes, Nancy, 528
Eren, Colleen, 511
Erhard, Michael, 470
Erickson, Anne, 263, 318
Erickson, John H, 632
Erickson, Mitchell D, 185, 204
Ericson, Paul, 602
Erlbaum, William M, 58
Ernst, C Alexandar, 534
Ernst, David, 522
Ernst, John, 212, 279, 308, 555
Errigo, Joseph A, 38, 44, 46, 52, 217, 313, 693
Eschler, William E, 401

Esernio, George P, 565
Eshoo, Anna G, 394
Espaillat, Adriano, 38, 44, 46, 47, 49, 50, 53, 202, 693
Esposito, Adrienne, 471
Esposito, Eunice O, 441
Esposito, Joseph J, 59, 433
Esposito, Ralph J, 419
Esposito, Vincent, 4, 168, 177
Estepa, Sandra, 219, 315
Estes, Bruce, 594
Estes, William, 4, 98
Estey, Cynthia A, 82
Eszak, Andrew M, 574
Etheridge, Bob, 186, 387
Etheridge, William H, 60
Ettinger, Joel, 121, 352
Ettinger, Justin, 494
Ettling, John, 614
Euken, James E, 61
Eusanio, John, 496
Evangelista, Charles, 450
Evans, Donald, 496
Evans, Donna, 119, 352, 377
Evans, Dwight, 22
Evans, Ellen J, 16, 198, 290, 297
Evans, Heather, 469
Evans, Jeff, 310
Evans, Mary Selden, 192
Evans, Peter, 412
Evans, Saralee, 59
Evans, Virginia, 496
Evans, William E, 398
Evans-Tranumn, Shelia, 145
Even, Nick, 460
Everett, Terry, 388
Everitt, Gayle, 285
Eversley, Eric L, 654
Evjen, Robert, 584
Evola, RoseMarie, 547
Ewashko, Dianne, 310
Ewing, Rev Ward B, 625
Executive Director
, Neil F Woodworth,, 187, 341
Exley, Douglas A, 662
Fabel, Diane, 520
Fabrizi, Coleen, 573
Fabrizio, Ralph A, 60
Factor, Mallory, 95
Fafinski, Theodore, 406
Fagan, Mary Beth, 574
Fahey, Eugene M, 57
Fahey, Joseph E, 66
Fahs, Marianne, 320
Faigle, Ellen M, 567
Fairgrieve, Scott, 70
Faist, Thomas W, 482
Falanga, Anthony, 58
Falatyn, Frank, 585
Falbo, Bruce, 229
Falchuk, Aimee, 504

Fale, Edward M, 656
Faleomavaega, Eni F H, 391
Falkenrath, Richard A, 433
Falkouski, Linda, 162
Fallon, James C, 652
Fallon, Michael, 491, 506
Falvey, W Patrick, 70
Falzone, Francis, 457
Fandrich, Mark H, 62
Fanelli, Sean A, 616
Fanni, Tony, 573
Fanning, Walter, 126, 183
Fanshawe, Helen, 198
Fanslau, David P, 411
Fantauzzo, Ferne, 541
Faraone, Lawrence, 564
Farber, Christopher, 402
Farber, David, 434
Farber, Felice, 109, 357, 543
Farber, Laurie, 523
Farber, Thomas A, 60
Farber, William, 452
Farber, William G, 402
Farbo-Lincoln, Martha J, 73
Farfaglia, Dan, 51
Farfaglia, Dick, 454
Fargione, Thomas, 9, 195, 289
Farina, Albert, 511
Farina, Carmen, 429
Farinella, Joseph, 588
Farker-Gutin, Marian, 579
Farley, Craig, 361
Farley, Hugh T, 19, 22, 25, 28, 29, 30, 31, 32, 92, 150, 203, 714
Farley, Robert, 32
Farley, Robert T, 409
Farnetti, Joseph, 68
Faron, Barbara, 284
Farquhar, Kelly Y, 404
Farrell Jr, John P, 402
Farrell, Charlie, 570
Farrell, Daniel, 564
Farrell, Dennis M, 293, 331
Farrell, Edward C, 106, 233, 454
Farrell, Jennifer, 5, 211, 278, 308, 371
Farrell, Jerry, 221, 366
Farrell, Jr, Herman D, 34, 38, 51, 52, 202, 292, 327, 450, 693
Farrell, Judy, 528
Farrell, Kathleen, 649
Farrell, Michael J, 433
Farrell, Nancy, 583
Farrell, Pat, 415
Farrell, Thomas, 425
Farrell, Timothy, 647
Farrell, William, 586
Farrell-Willoughby, Kathleen, 259
Farrington, Aurora, 147
Farro, Joseph, 430
Farsetta, James J, 363
Farthing, Lester A, 104

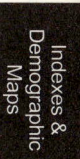

Indexes & Demographic Maps

753

Name Index

Fashano, Raymond J, 641
Faso, John, 503
Fatata, Linda, 443
Faughnan, Eugene D, 157
Faulkner, Mary, 147
Fauss, Rachael, 37
Favreau, William, 452
Favro, David N, 399
Fay, Debbie, 481
Fazzary, Joseph, 161
Fazzary, Joseph G, 409
Feagles, Jeffrey, 444
Feane, Mark, 576
Fearon, George, 397
Featherstonhaugh, James D, 483
Federman, John, 491, 506
Feeley, James N, 401
Feeney, Andrew X, 8, 195, 289
Feeney, Edward T, 72
Feerick, John D, 123, 199, 201, 291
Feger, Robert, 670
Fehrer, James, 246, 269
Feigel, Stewart, 59
Fein, Cheri, 519
Feinberg, Debra B, 554
Feinberg, Melvin, 493
Feinberg, Priscilla, 296
Feinberg-Duckett, Lisa, 449
Feiner, Paul J, 420
Feingold, Russell D, 385, 386
Feinman, Paul G, 59
Feinman, Thomas, 58
Feinstein, Dianne, 206, 383, 386
Feinzig, Margery, 139
Feinzig, Margery B, 260
Feirsen, Robert, 654
Feist, Tom, 482
Felch, Bernadette, 482
Felder, Esq, Raoul Lionel, 124, 258
Feldman, Anne G, 56
Feldman, Arlene B, 355
Feldman, Bruce, 17, 349
Feldman, Bruce D, 135, 216, 229, 255, 325
Feldman, Ira, 213
Feldman, Jeffrey, 103, 128, 202
Feldman, Ronald, 525
Feldstein, Ronald, 407
Feldstein, S Peter, 64
Feliciano, Elba, 433
Felicissimo, Paul, 598
Feller, David S, 655
Fellows, Anne, 510
Felschow, Grace, 562
Felter, Laurie, 211, 278, 308
Feltman, James A, 668
Felton, Chip, 12
Felton, Chip J, 280
Felton, Preston L, 16, 136
Fennell, Timothy, 127, 354
Fennell, Timothy J, 262
Fenno, Nathan, 543

Fenton, Anne, 435
Ferdinand, Joann, 60
Ferguson, Bruce, 525
Ferguson, Bruce W, 342
Ferguson, Dorothy H, 304
Ferguson, Harold, 675
Ferguson, Jodi L, 72
Ferguson, Marcus, 27
Fernandez, Dolores M, 471, 620
Fernandez, Hermes, 464
Fernandez, Joanne, 481
Fernandez, Jose R, 118, 351
Fernandez, Jose W, 558
Fernandez, Ricardo R, 471, 620
Feroe, Louise H, 627
Feroleto, Paula L, 57
Ferone, Mary Grace, 498
Ferradino, Stephen A, 57
Ferrara, Anthony J, 59
Ferrara, Donna, 18, 150, 247, 248, 270, 271
Ferrara, Richard J, 116
Ferrara, Robert J, 181
Ferrara, Todd, 39
Ferrarese, Thomas F, 160
Ferraro, Rocco, 114, 230, 376
Ferraro, Samuel M, 581
Ferrazzi, Paul V, 545
Ferrell, Donna, 363
Ferrier, Elizabeth, 467
Ferrini, Nancylynn, 44, 45, 46, 51
Ferris, Donald F, 399
Ferris, William E, 483
Ferriter, Christopher T, 561
Fertal Sr, George E, 8, 237, 279, 311
Fertitta, George, 338
Fettinger, Mark, 133, 253
Fetyko, Lynnore, 304
Feuerstein, Robert A, 15, 325, 335
Feurey, Claudia, 166, 209
Fiala, Barbara J, 397
Fiala, Stephen J, 408
Ficalora, Joseph R, 96
Ficke, Martin, 203, 328
Field, Bradley J, 116, 170, 178, 182
Fields, Dave, 619
Fields, Ginny, 38, 44, 45, 46, 50, 51, 52, 694
Fields, Lawrence, 355
Fields, Phillip, 53
Fienberg, Sheelah, 479
Figge MD, James, 213
Figueroa, Nicholas, 56
File, Linda, 71
Fileccia-Flagg, Tana, 310
Filiault, Ann, 511
Filiberto, Patricia M, 70
Filler, Allan, 33, 54
Filmer, Mike, 348
Filmer, Ronald, 584
Filner, Bob, 364, 393
Fina, Perry, 322

Finazzo, Barbara A, 185
Finch, Doug, 40
Finch, Gary D, 35, 38, 44, 46, 47, 137, 217, 282, 313, 694
Finch, James, 426
Finch, Paul, 645
Fine, Kim, 6, 16, 99, 194, 198, 287, 290, 324
Fine, Larry, 602
Finegan, Michael, 363
Finello, John J, 669
Fines, Callie, 541
Finger, Bernard, 363
Fingerhut, Kelly, 511
Fink, Keith, 493
Fink, Shea, 426
Finke, Barbara, 37
Finkel, Richard S, 436
Finkelberg, Jason, 603
Finkelman, Lewis S, 427
Finkelstein, Arthur J, 164
Finkelstein, Barbara, 498
Finkelstein, Barbara D, 264
Finkelstein, Marc, 60
Finkleberg, Jason, 606
Finn, Pete, 13, 179, 334
Finnegan, Candace K, 248, 271
Finnegan, Martin, 579
Finnegan, Patricia, 442
Finnegan, Paul, 121, 170
Finnin, Mary J, 556
Fionti, Bernard, 603
Fiore, James, 520
Fiore, Mary Beth, 642
Fiorella Jr, Anthony J, 60
Fiorella, Joseph A, 71
Fiore-Nieves, Marilyn, 423
Fiori, Anthony, 503
Fiorini, Gerald J, 405
Fiozzo, Gregory, 8, 163
Firetog, Neil Jon, 56, 60, 256
Firkins, Kathryn J, 420
Fisch, Joseph, 58
Fischberger, Milton, 429
Fischer, Brian, 7, 129
Fischer, David, 662
Fischer, Duane W, 586
Fischer, Kris, 596
Fischer, Robert J, 568
Fischman, Martin, 123, 201, 327
Fishberg, Gerard, 275, 293
Fisher, Arnold, 304
Fisher, Donald A, 305
Fisher, Fern, 256
Fisher, Fern A, 59
Fisher, Joel, 502
Fisher, Jr, Daniel M, 483
Fisher, Kenneth, 531
Fisher, Kenneth R, 57
Fisher, Nancy, 41
Fisher, Steven, 55

Name Index

Fisher, Thomas, 119, 282
Fisher, Vikki, 38
Fishkin, Ira, 205
Fishman, Alan H, 114, 362
Fishman, Richard D, 101, 199
Fishman, William, 80
Fishner, Steven, 496
Fiske, David, 171
Fitch, Christina, 518
Fitts, James, 80
Fitzgerald, Brendan, 51
Fitzgerald, Daniel F, 447
Fitzgerald, Daniel P, 60
Fitzgerald, Gary, 223
Fitzgerald, Gary J, 566
Fitzgerald, Meagan, 27
FitzGerald, Peter D, 263
Fitzgerald, Rita, 449
Fitzgerald, Rosalie, 65
Fitzgerald, Sean, 228
Fitzgerald, Sister Laureen A, 627
Fitzgibbon, Anne, 427
Fitzgibbon, Madeleine A, 70
Fitzgibbons, Kathleen, 483
Fitzmaurice, Maryellen, 61
Fitzpatrick, Bill, 598
Fitzpatrick, Carolyn D, 402
Fitzpatrick, Daniel W, 438
Fitzpatrick, Diane L, 58
Fitzpatrick, James E, 159
Fitzpatrick, John C, 633
Fitzpatrick, Lt Col Paul, 362
Fitzpatrick, Margaret M, 632
Fitzpatrick, Michael J, 38, 48, 49, 50, 51, 231, 292, 302, 694
Fitzpatrick, Thomas M, 60
Fitzpatrick, William J, 405
Fitzsimmons, Eileen, 168, 195
Fitzsimmons, Richard, 548
Fitzsimons, John T, 655
Fix, Christine, 442
Flack, Deborah S, 658
Flaeser, Paul, 600
Flagg, Harith, 140, 316
Flaherty, Maureen, 655
Flaherty, Thomas, 554
Flaherty, Timothy J, 58
Flahive, Robert E, 495
Flanagan Jr, L, 554
Flanagan, James P, 70
Flanagan, John J, 22, 25, 27, 29, 30, 32, 103, 203, 354, 714
Flanagan, Jr, Larry, 299
Flanagan, William, 355
Flanigan, Barbara J, 14, 136
Flannelly, Eileen M, 434
Flansburg, Lynn, 474
Flateau, John, 471
Fleckenstein, Dr Marilynn P, 155
Fleet, John, 367
Fleischauer, Sheila, 160

Fleischer, Michael R, 125, 337, 353
Fleischli, Steve, 192
Fleischut, Melissa, 521
Fleishman, David A, 675
Fleming, Jr, David F, 483
Fleming, Mary Pat, 139, 261
Fletcher, Leslie, 548
Fletcher, Robert B, 213
Fleuranges, Paul, 119, 352, 377
Fleury, Kathy M, 159
Fleury, Robert J, 10, 195, 301, 333
Flood-Morrow, Elizabeth G, 601
Florek, Lindsay, 48
Florence, William, 438
Flores, Luz, 528
Florian, Mary Ellen, 65
Florio, Anita R, 55
Flowers, Joan E, 536
Flowers, Loftin, 525
Floyd, Gregory, 549
Flug, Margo, 487
Flug, Phyllis Orlikoff, 58
Flynn Jr, Charles L, 623
Flynn, Heather, 196, 333
Flynn, John, 270
Flynn, Mary Ellen, 135
Flynn, Patrick H, 413
Flynn, R Thomas, 616
Flynn, Terrance P, 139, 261
Flynn, Thomas, 215
Flynn, William, 477, 498
Foels, John E, 569
Fogden, David, 595
Fogel, Jeff, 514
Fogelman, Leonard M, 565
Fogler, Jim, 594
Foglia, Linda, 7, 129, 372
Foley, Brian X, 115, 181, 415
Foley, David, 398
Foley, Jeff, 458
Foley, Sharon, 481
Folk, Cassie, 483
Foltan, Robert S, 116, 181
Folts, James, 144
Fonda, Tim, 594
Fontaine, Monita W, 554
Fontas, George, 468
Fonzo, Paul Di, 641
Forand, Douglas, 21
Forbes, Gordon G, 533
Forbes, J Randy, 139, 391
Forbes, Marjorie, 41
Ford, Carl F, 349
Ford, Dennis, 645
Ford, Henry, 448
Ford, Michael J, 660
Ford, Steven, 579
Ford, Tanya L, 421
Ford-Johnston, Cynthia, 647
Forehand, Ron, 577
Forezzi, Robert, 414

Forkas, Lisa, 45
Forman, Dan, 609
Forman, Peter M, 63
Formel, Ann F, 11, 246, 268
Foro, Daniel, 8, 133, 252, 288
Forrest, Linda A, 158
Forrest, Steven W, 72
Forrestel, II, E Peter, 94
Forshaw, Robin, 4, 129
Forshay, Dave, 570
Forshey, Christy, 234, 319
Forsline, Philip, 81
Forst, Donald H, 597
Forster, Art, 164
Fortino, Jessica, 536
Fortuna, Diana, 471
Fortuna, Jane B, 73
Fortuno, Luis F, 391
Fosberg, Jane R, 641
Fosbrook, Leonard, 588
Foskey, Carnell, 65
Fosler, Gail, 107
Fossella, Vito, 93, 105, 171, 186, 219, 232, 249, 389, 390
Fossella, Vito J, 381, 726
Foster, Jerry, 168, 195
Foster, Phyllis M, 133, 252, 288
Foster, Ruth, 482
Foster-Tolbert, Freida, 619
Fowler, Jr, William E, 355
Fox, James P, 127, 353
Fox, Jimmy S, 137
Fox, Joe, 556
Fox, Lisa, 514
Fox, Michael, 27
Fox, Roberta, 349
Fox, Thomas J, 50
Foxman, Abraham H, 240
Foy, James, 4, 307
Foy, Joseph, 328
Foy, Veronica J, 364
Foye, Patrick J, 9, 99, 116, 177, 230, 333
Fragnoli-Ryan, Maria S, 644
Frahm, David S, 646
Fralick, Terry N, 651
Frame, James R, 665
France, Steve, 348
Francis, Margaret E, 551
Francis, Paul E, 6, 98, 194, 287, 324
Francis, Will, 80
Franck, John, 441
Franco, Barbara, 585
Franco, Felipe, 310
Franco, Victor, 52
Franczyk, David, 416
Franczyk, Thomas P, 71
Frank Menschel, Joyce, 427
Frank, Barney, 93, 232, 248, 389
Frank, Charmaine, 434
Frank, Gregory R, 437
Frank, Kenneth, 415

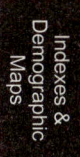
Indexes & Demographic Maps

Name Index

Frank, Lisa, 507
Frank, Paul M, 261
Frank, Peter M, 498
Frank, Robert, 562
Frank, Ronald L, 540
Frank, Teresa, 289, 302, 326
Frankel, Sandra L, 415
Franklin, Carol A, 158
Franklin, Kevin, 418
Franks, Martin, 172
Franks, Trent, 391
Franks-Randall, Carol, 676
Franzese, Nicole, 573
Franzese, Robert, 560
Franzman, Marjorie, 273
Fraser, Carl, 460
Fraser, Charles, 434
Fraser, David W, 424
Fraser, Lori, 245
Fraser, Stuart, 162
Frateschi, Timothy A, 425
Frawley, Martina M, 560
Frawley, Robert, 6, 311
Frayler, Jeff, 460
Frazee, Evelyn, 57
Frazer, Jr, Leroy, 141, 266, 299
Frazier, Diane E, 463
Frazier, Pauline, 215
Freakley, Maj Benjamin C, 362
Frederick, Bruce, 134, 253, 289
Fredericks, Albert, 495
Fredericks, Dick, 349
Fredericks, K L, 105
Fredsall, David, 90
Free, Scott, 604
Freed, Adam, 199
Freed, Kathryn E, 59
Freedman, Corrina, 458
Freedman, Helen E, 56
Freedman, Holly, 583
Freedman, Lynn P, 221, 241
Freedman, Spencer B, 11, 237
Freehill, Robert H, 66
Freeley, Mary Ellen, 655
Freeman, Edward, 212, 279, 308
Freeman, Henry, 592, 596
Freeman, Lynn, 575
Freeman, Nora L, 61
Freeman, Robert J, 199, 291
Freidmutter, Cindy, 432
Freij, Maysoun, 493
Freimark, Norman, 677
Freitag, Amy, 433
Frelinghuysen, Rodney P, 387
French, Daniel J, 158
French, Douglas E, 160
French, Mark, 310
French, Meghan Q, 519
French, Richard, 608
Fresina, Anthony M, 548
Freudenberger, Erica, 594

Freund, Jack, 517
Freund, Sidney, 677
Freundlich, David, 68
Frey, Joseph P, 8, 144
Frey, Thomas, 305, 331
Fricano, Amy J, 57
Friday, Shirley, 69
Fried, Bernard J, 60
Fried, Gloria, 437
Fried, Paul, 676
Friedberg, Alan W, 124, 258
Frieden, Thomas R, 430
Friedlander, Mark, 58
Friedman, Andrew, 502, 601
Friedman, Dana, 470
Friedman, Daniel A, 364
Friedman, David, 55
Friedman, Eby, 100, 148
Friedman, Eric, 427
Friedman, Kathryn, 527
Friedman, Lawrence, 401
Friedman, Lucy, 456
Friedman, Marcy S, 59
Friedman, Michael, 92, 127, 231, 506
Friedman, Rhea G, 61
Friedman, Ronald L, 654
Friedman, Sylvia, 44
Friello, Carolyn, 441
Frier, Raymond, 475
Fries, Sue A, 158
Friia, JoAnn, 75
Friot, Fabiola, 495
Frisch, Debra L, 199
Frisch, Kevin, 593
Friscia, John Scott, 453
Friscoe, Louis, 508
Friske, William, 283
Fritz Intwala, Katrina, 475
Froehlich, Richard, 120, 230
Fromberg, Allan J, 434
Frommer, Charles, 553
Frommer, Ross, 525
Frost, Jerome K, 408
Frost, Kathryn, 527
Fruci, William, 161
Frungillo, John, 594
Frye, Mary B, 287, 295
Frye, Robert W, 127, 354
Frys, Mary Kay, 639
Fuchs, Ester, 426
Fuchs, James, 5, 90, 371
Fuchs, Jim, 435
Fuchs, Phil, 524
Fuentes, Audrey, 556
Fugolo, Rev Joseph, 241
Fuleihan, Dean, 35, 52
Fuller, Michael, 41
Fuller, Paul, 229
Fullwood, Michael, 489
Fung, Margaret, 240, 262, 320
Furco, Anthony, 442

Furfure, Marianne, 68
Furlong, Rebecca R, 662
Furlong, Robert J, 607
Furnish, Mark, 22
Furno, Frank J, 405
Fuschillo, Jr, Charles J, 22, 26, 27, 29, 30, 32, 103, 203, 217, 714
Fusco, AnnMaria, 151
Fusco, Christine A, 423
Fusco, John A, 67
Fusco, Lynn Marie, 645
Fusco, Vincent, 516
Fusfeld, Ira, 595
Futter, Ellen V, 187, 341
Gabay, Donald D, 251
Gable, Walter, 410
Gabler, William J, 75
Gabriel, Patrick, 643
Gabriele, Joyce, 542
Gabrielsen, Peter, 81, 105
Gabryszak, Dennis, 44, 45, 50, 52
Gabryszak, Dennis H, 38
Gabryszak, Dennis H, 694
Gabryzsak, Dennis, 47
Gaddy, R Scott, 468
Gaebel, Rodney, 162, 411
Gaebler, III, George W, 556
Gaetano, Edward, 100, 148
Gaffney, Ed, 36
Gaffney, Mike, 34
Gage, Walter C, 72
Gahl, David, 481
Gaines, Deborah M, 432
Gaines, John, 534
Gais, Thomas L, 321, 611
Gaiss, Ralph F, 111
Galant, Richard, 595
Galante, Joseph, 120, 336, 377
Galante, Richard, 661
Galante, Thomas W, 432
Galarneau, Kenneth, 309
Galasso, John M, 65
Galasso, Thomas D, 438
Galef, Sandra R, 38, 46, 47, 48, 50, 303, 327, 694
Galil, Zvi, 525
Galis, George, 547
Gallagher, Christopher, 671
Gallagher, Cindy Hall, 605
Gallagher, Cynthia, 145
Gallagher, Ed, 520
Gallagher, James, 15, 169
Gallagher, Jay, 601
Gallagher, Joe, 216, 270
Gallagher, John, 300
Gallagher, Kathleen M, 461
Gallagher, Richard, 196, 301
Gallagher, Thomas, 653, 658
Gallati, Bob, 212, 279, 308
Gallegly, Elton, 391
Gallego, Alex, 582

Name Index

Gallent, Judith, 466
Galletly, David, 603
Galligan, John H, 474
Gallman, James, 157
Gallmann, Paul W, 396
Gallo Goldstein, Patricia, 473
Gallo, Charles J, 557
Gallo, Joseph, 128, 234, 337
Gallo-Kotcher, Sharon, 117, 350
Galloway, Harold, 57
Gallucci, Jean, 444
Galough, Mark, 588
Galu, Joe, 40
Galvin, James P, 573
Gamache, David J, 158
Gamage, John C, 442
Gamble, Diane, 42
Gamboli, Michael J, 421
Gandhi, Kirti, 357
Gangi, Robert, 140
Gannon, John C, 74
Gannon, Karen S, 159
Gantner, Mary Ann, 204, 240
Gantt, David F, 39, 46, 50, 51, 52, 53, 292, 354, 695
Garafola, Robert L, 433
Garba, Joseph, 456, 516
Garcia Reyes, Anne, 472
Garcia, Julie, 400
Garcia, Kathryn, 429
Garcia, Marisa, 76
Garcia, Michael, 138, 260
Garcia, Mildred, 634
Garcia, Roxanne, 602
Gardam, David, 211, 278, 308
Gardella, Joseph, 523
Gardella, Sheila, 125, 149, 297
Gardiner, Donna M, 16, 326
Gardner, Arnold B, 143
Gardner, Christopher H, 409
Gardner, Kathleen Sinnott, 407
Gardner, Kent, 207
Gardner, Larry, 402
Gardner, Lori, 513
Gardner, Ronald D, 84
Gardner, Tracie M, 498
Garfinkle, Gerald, 229
Garifo, Chris, 600
Garipoli, Rosemarie, 499
Garland, Gabrielle, 458
Garlock, Thomas E, 126, 353, 379
Garmon-Salaam, Christine, 310
Garner, Michael, 378
Garnett, William E, 60
Garoppolo, Tony, 259
Garretson, Sara, 101, 148
Garrett, Cynthia, 340
Garrett, Renee, 651
Garrett, Thomas O, 443
Garris, Ann, 416
Garrison, Kathy, 472

Garrity, John B, 74
Garson, Robin S, 59
Garth, David, 165
Gartner, Kenneth L, 70
Garus, Sr Marcella Marie, 633
Garvey, Margaret, 57
Gary, Michael A, 60
Gaspar, Rudolph W, 560
Gaspard, Patrick, 454
Gassney, Cedric Alfred, 585
Gastel, Scott, 522
Gatens, Michael, 281
Gatens, Michele, 13
Gatling, Patricia L, 431
Gaudet, Margaret, 11, 134, 197
Gaudette, James G, 643
Gault, Bert, 600
Gaumont, Dan, 444
Gauthier, Roger, 102, 116, 181
Gaven, Patricia, 361
Gavrin, Darrell L, 59
Gay, James M, 447
Gay, Janice W, 222
Gay, Timothy, 160
Gaynes, Elizabeth A, 141, 276
Gaynor Jr, Dennis F, 559
Gazes, Celine M, 128, 337
Gazzillo, Ralph T, 68
Gearan, Mark D, 625
Gebbie, Eric N, 221
Geberer, Raanan, 592
Gebhardt, James T, 123, 182
Gebo, Tanice A, 64
Gecewicz, Joseph F, 102, 327
Gedda, Lawrence J, 5, 98, 102, 124, 324
Geddes, John, 597
Geddis, Carol, 152
Gee, Stanley, 17, 349
Geer, Gregory C, 648
Geer, Nancy, 234
Geer, Nancy P, 550
Gehen, Edward F, 445
Geier, William P, 404
Geiger, Bruce W, 485
Geiger, Chris, 609
Geiger, Richard, 338
Geisinger, Ethel Z, 95, 293
Geithner, Timothy F, 92
Gelburd, Robin C, 454
Genchi, Joan M, 68
Genco, Robert, 527
Gender, Robert A, 534
Gendron, Dawn, 96
Generoso, James, 73
Genese, Charles, 444
Geneslaw, Robert, 236
Genier, Barbara, 422
Gennaovi, Mitchel, 245
Genovese, Anita M, 538
Genovese, Joanne, 477
Genung, Jeffrey, 597

George, Daniel A, 642
George, David T, 623
George, Nancy S, 672
George, Viji D, 623
Georgia, Diana, 475, 531
Gerace, Joseph A, 398
Geraci Sr, Michael N, 441
Geraci, Frank P, 65
Gerald, Lenora, 60
Gerard, Jerry, 196
Gerardi, Tina, 511
Gerber, Marlene S, 225
Gerber, Tomi, 481
Gerchak, Ralph, 273
Gergela, III, Joseph M, 86
Gerges, Abraham G, 56
Gerhardt, Douglas, 500
Gerhardt, Joan, 462
Gerling, Stephen D, 259
Germain, Robert M, 417
Germain, Robin, 74
German, Scott, 401
Gerold, Roberta, 669
Gershon, Claire, 568
Gerstein, Terri, 216, 270
Gerstenlauer, Allan, 669
Gerstman, Sharon Stern, 265
Gerstner, James, 444
Gersztoff, Stephen, 375
Geskie, Pamela, 593
Gesmer, Ellen Frances, 59
Gest, Emily, 431
Gesten MD, Foster, 213
Gesualdo, Hector, 151
Getler, Al, 598
Getman, Steven J, 410
Getnick, Michael E, 263
Geto, Ethan, 109, 208, 486
Gettman, Jr, William T, 6, 309
Getty Jr, Charles, 402
Gewanter, Barrie, 514
Giacobbe, Anthony, 58
Giacobbe, Joseph A, 260
Giacomo, William J, 57
Giambra, Joel A, 400
Giambrone, Linda M, 71
Giambruno, Michael, 132
Giammalvo, Gregory J, 438
Giammarino, Vincent, 229
Giampetro, Donald, 434
Gianaris, Michael N, 32, 39, 45, 47, 49, 52, 53, 695
Gianelli, Sharon MJ, 70
Giangreco, Carmine C, 672
Giannotta, Gary J, 414
Giannoulis, Harry, 514
Giardino, Richard C, 63
Gibb, John R, 8, 122, 195, 201, 289, 291, 378
Gibbon, Randy, 398
Gibbons, Brian, 500

757

Name Index

Gibbons, James D, 60
Gibbons, Muriel, 601
Gibson, Dorita, 657
Gibson, Kumiki, 11, 237
Gidlund, Leonora, 434
Giess, Lois, 440
Gifford, Gladys, 498
Gifford, Patricia G, 87
Gifford, Thomas M, 409
Gigandet, Adam, 13, 348
Gigante, Robert, 56
Giglia, Marlene B, 550
Gigliello, Teresa, 120, 230
Giglio, Frank, 552
Giglio, Joe, 39, 44, 46, 49, 52, 137, 238, 695
Gigliotti, Anthony J, 255
Gigot, Paul, 596
Gilbert, Hugh A, 57
Gilbert, Jon, 542
Gilbert, Michael, 342
Gilbert, Patricia, 520
Gilbride, John P, 137
Gilchrist, Gary A, 678
Gilchrist, Kathy, 348
Gilchrist, Timothy, 3, 90, 98, 332
Gilchrist, William, 257
Giliberto, Donna M C, 474
Giliberto, James, 19, 375
Gill, Bradley, 174
Gill, James F, 113, 335
Gillers, Stephen, 266
Gillibrand, Kirsten, 726
Gillibrand, Kirsten E, 382
Gilligan, Daniel, 658
Gilligan, Kevin, 437
Gillis, Carol, 87
Gillmor, Paul, 390
Gilpatric, James P, 72
Gilroy, Joan, 467
Gilroy, Lawrence, 474
Gilroy, Martin J, 196, 301
Gilvarry, Peter A, 428
Gimmler, Ray, 460
Gingrey, Phil, 392
Ginsberg, Mara, 457, 526
Ginsberg, William R, 189, 234
Ginty, Rosemary, 464
Gioffre, Fred, 98, 324
Gioffre, Fred J, 5, 102, 124
Gioino, Joseph, 580
Giordano, Christine, 42
Giordano, Ralph T, 105, 260
Giorgianni, Joseph J, 205, 303
Gipson, Arthur, 560
Gipson, Danyelle, 482
Gipson, H McCarthy, 416
Girgenti, Richard, 496
Giroux, Joseph W, 399
Gische, Judith J, 59
Giske, Emily, 463

Gitlen, Philip, 529
Gitshyn, Arthur, 528
Gittes, Marcia F, 185
Giudice Jr, Dominic, 425
Giuffra, Jr, Robert J, 123, 201
Giuffrida Jr, Robert, 636
Giuliani, Catherine, 493
Giuliano, Judi, 46
Givens, Debra L, 71
Givner, Jennifer, 4, 157, 194
Giza, Robert H, 423, 578
Gizzi, Eugene, 539
Glacken, William F, 419
Gladden, Rob, 575
Gladstone, Victor, 482
Glance, Dereth, 471
Glantz, Adam, 232
Glaser, Mark, 487
Glass, Gerard, 424, 543
Glassberg, Fred, 355
Glassnerg, Christine, 104
Glasso, Louise, 440
Glaves-Morgan, Sandra, 431
Glazer, Elizabeth, 431
Gleason, Mary Fran, 591
Gleason, Robert E, 546
Gleason, Stephen W, 404
Glenn, Kristin B, 65
Glennon, Robert, 255
Glick, Deborah J, 39, 45, 47, 48, 53, 150, 313, 695
Glinka, Stan, 576
Glinski, Gary, 602
Gliss, Robert, 357
Glisson, Carolyn, 309
Gloade, Astrid B, 428
Gloak, Geoffrey T, 15, 289, 302, 326, 374
Globerman, Ira R, 59
Gloeckner, Ingo, 147
Glohs, Linda, 588
Glotzbach, Philip A, 631
Glover, Catherine, 570
Glover, Michael A, 679
Glownia, Joseph R, 57
Gluchowski, Francis, 28
Gluchowski, Francis J, 20
Gluck, Jon, 602
Glusko, John P, 173
Glynn, Astrid C, 17, 302, 349
Gmelich, David, 496
Gobeo, Dawn, 436
Gober, Hershel, 367
Godambe, Megha, 27
Godshall, Clark J, 680
Goebert, Daniel, 415
Goetz, Karen, 572
Goff, Jim, 125, 337
Goggin, Dennis E, 398
Goggins, Charles P, 171
Gohmert, Louie, 274, 392
Gokey, William A, 650

Gold, James P, 180, 334
Gold, Jeffrey, 484
Gold, Lila P, 59
Gold, Marlene A, 428
Gold, Todd, 461
Goldberg, Arlene D, 60
Goldberg, Brad, 458
Goldberg, Edward Jay, 109
Goldberg, Howard, 601
Goldberg, Joel M, 60
Golden, Edward V, 53
Golden, Martin J, 22, 25, 26, 27, 29, 30, 32, 217, 239, 313, 715
Golden, Olivia, 3, 307
Goldenkranz, Steven D, 543
Goldfarb, Michael, 283
Goldfrank, Lewis, 221
Goldin, Davidson, 608
Golding, Rick, 573
Goldmacher, Roslyn D, 578
Goldman, Douglas, 47
Goldman, Douglas L, 47, 49
Goldman, Fatima, 318, 483
Goldman, Ilana, 167
Goldman, Jasper, 509
Goldman, Jesse, 502
Goldman, Lee, 525
Goldman, Shanna, 495
Goldmann, Eileen, 471
Goldmark, Leila, 518
Goldrick, Mike, 609
Goldring Ford, Leslie, 673
Goldsmith, Peter, 604
Goldson, Neville, 214, 360
Goldsteen, Ray, 520
Goldstein, Arthur, 478, 539
Goldstein, Carla, 322
Goldstein, Carol A, 9, 178
Goldstein, Ferne J, 59
Goldstein, Gloria, 55
Goldstein, Ira, 434
Goldstein, Larry, 605
Goldstein, Matthew, 471, 619
Goldstein, Robert, 518
Goldstein, William H, 127, 353
Golia, James J, 58
Golia, Joseph G, 58
Golladay, Dennis, 611
Golladay, Mamie Howard, 617
Gollaher, R Stephan, 546
Golub, Howard, 116, 182, 376
Golub, Lewis, 470
Golub, Maxine, 465
Golub, Neil M, 470
Gomez, Frank, 176
Gomez, Raquel, 502
Gomez-Velez, Natalie M, 143
Gomlack-Brace, Aimee, 577
Goncalves, Joseph, 251
Gonzalez Fuentes, Maibe, 435
Gonzalez Jr, Efrain, 27, 28, 29

Name Index

Gonzalez, Andrew A, 431
Gonzalez, Bethaida, 442
Gonzalez, Celia, 198
Gonzalez, Charlie, 393
Gonzalez, Dennis, 315
Gonzalez, Efrain, 26
Gonzalez, George, 160, 429
Gonzalez, Henry, 211, 278, 308
Gonzalez, Jr, Efrain, 22, 26, 28, 30, 103, 292, 303, 354, 715
Gonzalez, Julian, 502
Gonzalez, Julissa, 502
Gonzalez, Lizbeth, 59
Gonzalez, Lorraine, 465
Gonzalez, Luis A, 55
Gonzalez, Ralph, 286
Gonzalez, Yvonne, 58
Gooberman, Susan, 192
Good, Alicia, 120, 182
Goodbee, Arndreia M, 39
Goodlatte, Bob, 83, 186, 219, 387
Goodman, Budd G, 56
Goodman, David, 400
Goodman, Edwin A, 482
Goodman, Emily Jane, 56
Goodman, Kael S, 433
Goodman, Lorna, 404
Goodman, Norman, 56, 65, 405
Goodman, Roy M, 103, 128, 202
Goodman, Scott J, 542
Goodrich, Cinda Lou, 162
Goodsell, MaryBeth, 248, 271
Goodwin, Jeffrey, 223, 250
Goodwin, Jeffrey L, 544
Goodwin, Lisa, 437
Goodwin, Michael, 555, 596
Googas, Jr, John C, 23
Goold, Peter, 113, 335, 375
Gooley, Donald, 649, 650
Gorbman, Randy, 606
Gorczyea, Kathleen Barry, 64
Gorczynski, Brian, 564
Gordon, Alan E, 398
Gordon, Arthur, 169
Gordon, Bart, 172, 186, 392
Gordon, Diane, 44, 46
Gordon, Diane M, 39, 48, 51, 695
Gordon, Dr Marsha, 588
Gordon, Eloisa, 521
Gordon, Gail H, 122, 149, 201, 217
Gordon, Geoffrey N, 656
Gordon, Jeffrey, 6, 16, 99, 194, 198, 287, 290, 324, 371, 374
Gordon, Karen E, 317
Gordon, Marsha, 543
Gordon, Seth, 226, 512, 558
Gordon, Tim, 39, 44, 47, 50, 51
Gordon, Timothy N, 695
Gordon, Timothy P, 543, 546
Gorga, Jr, Peter L, 329
Gorman, Peter L, 300

Gorman, Robert, 600
Gormley, James, 591
Gormley, Michael, 601
Gormley-King, Margaret, 238
Gorski, Jerome C, 56
Gorsky, Sheila, 558
Gosdeck, Thomas J, 85, 490, 553
Goss, Bill, 367
Goss, Joseph J, 444
Gotbaum, Betsy, 405, 433
Gotlin, Gary D, 408
Gotlinsky, Alan, 248, 271
Gottfried, Richard N, 39, 48, 51, 217, 696
Gottlieb, Stephen S, 59
Gough, Darlene K, 63
Gould, Andrew, 434
Gould, Bruce, 176
Gould, David L, 534
Gould, David S, 397
Gould, Harry E, 120
Gould, Joyce, 42
Gould, Joyce E, 495
Gouldin, David M, 250, 264
Gouwens, Dirk, 346
Gover, Philip E, 615
Governo, Tom, 204, 328
Gowan, Aaron, 587
Gozzo, James J, 621
Graber, Robert M, 400
Graber, Vincent G, 469
Grabowski, Ada, 661
Grabowski, Col Rickey L, 362
Grabowski, Janice E, 161
Grace, Gerald, 361
Graczyk, Mark, 592
Gradess, Jonathan E, 141, 265
Gradwell, Lori, 29
Grady, Bob, 598
Grady, William V, 400
Graeson, Michael, 269
Graffeo, Paul, 19
Graffeo, Victoria A, 55
Graffino, Anthony, 548
Graham, Anita, 474
Graham, Bernard J, 59
Graham, Edwin, 510
Graham, Harold, 130
Graham, Jeffrey E, 444
Graham, Jr, Nero, 160
Graham, Kenneth, 653
Graham, Lindsey, 382
Graham, Lindsey O, 383, 386
Graham, Meg, 221
Graham, Richard, 403
Graham, Russell F, 205
Graham, Susan, 479
Graham, Yvonne J, 403, 435
Grainer, Joan M, 160
Gran Sinclair, Kristin, 30
Granchelli, Joseph M, 441
Grande, Claudine F, 402

Grande, Pam, 594
Grandeau, David, 379
Grandeau, David M, 125, 163, 202
Grannis, Alexander B, 102, 116, 123, 126, 181, 182, 183
Grannis, Alexander B (Pete), 9, 177
Grant, Donald J, 128, 354
Grant, Mary Ellen, 672
Grant, Michael M, 408
Grant, Rich, 209
Grant, Richard, 511
Granto, Carmen A, 657
Grape, Jack B, 559
Grassley, Chuck, 106, 249, 330, 385
Grasso, Dee, 577
Grasso, George A, 433
Grasso, Michael, 453
Grasso, Vito, 224
Grasso, Vito F, 542
Grattan, Barbara, 440
Graver, Kathy, 570
Graves, Leon, 520
Graves, Lesley, 498
Graves, Sam, 233, 393
Gray, Denise A, 102, 115, 230
Gray, G Susan, 653
Gray, Gregory, 580
Gray, Kent W, 409
Gray, Oliver, 479, 539
Gray, RA, James M, 122, 149, 201, 217
Gray, Val S, 10, 214, 360
Grays, Marguerite A, 58
Grayshaw, James R, 60
Graziade, Mike, 348
Graziano, Ellen, 157
Graziano, Jr, John A, 468
Graziano, Peter J, 328
Graziano, Sr, John A, 157
Greason, Michael, 247
Grebert, John, 141
Grebin, Burton, 524
Greco Jr, Joseph C, 534
Greco, Sandra, 592
Green, Alice P, 140, 262
Green, Catherine, 422
Green, Darcy L, 21
Green, David C, 161
Green, Deborah, 426
Green, Desmond A, 59
Green, George J, 426
Green, Gerald, 426
Green, Jeffrey, 289, 302, 326
Green, John, 456, 592
Green, Joseph G, 137, 328
Green, Kenneth A, 584
Green, Lisa, 414
Green, Matt, 600
Green, Michael C, 404
Green, Nelson L, 64
Green, Norman P, 158
Green, Patterson, 665

Name Index

Green, Richard, 197, 290
Green, Roberta, 661
Green, Samuel L, 56
Green, Stanley, 59
Green, Steven, 457
Greenan, Timothy J, 445
Greenberg, Elayne E, 263
Greenberg, Eli D, 559
Greenberg, Ethan, 60
Greenberg, Henry M, 208
Greenberg, Jamie, 310
Greenberg, Julie, 494
Greenberg, Robert, 655
Greenberg, Walter, 309
Greenberger, Sharon, 120, 149
Greene Jr, Stephen C, 407
Greene, Aurelia, 34, 39, 45, 46, 51, 53, 696
Greene, Courtney Canfield, 161
Greene, Donald R, 196
Greene, John, 632
Greene, Leonard M, 320
Greene, Norman L, 202, 258
Greene, Shirley, 329
Greene, Virginia, 79
Greener, David, 438
Greenfield, Paul E, 480
Greenhall, Frank, 661
Greenwald, Patrick J, 495
Greenwald, Stephen R, 627
Greenwood, Donald A, 57
Grega, Amy, 37
Gregg, Judd, 330, 383, 384
Gregory, Charlotte, 671
Gregory, David M, 126, 353
Gregory, Earle, 649
Gregson, Jennifer A, 551
Greiner, James M, 402
Greiner, William, 527
Greisemer, Michael, 441
Grella, Philip M, 58
Grenci, Tod, 114, 335
Grenell, Richard, 205, 364
Gresham, George, 533
Gresham, John, 497
Gresham, Julie, 198
Gretzinger, Gerard M, 673
Grey, Valerie, 487
Gribbon, Francis X, 430
Gribetz, Sidney, 61
Grice, Gale J, 424
Griffin, James P, 60
Griffin, James W, 577
Griffin, John, 488
Griffin, Kathleen, 247, 271
Griffin, Linda C, 67
Griffin, Thea, 321
Griffith, James, 397
Griffith, James R, 66
Griffith, Maxine, 525
Griffith, Michael F, 69
Griffith, Natatia, 208

Griffiths, Dana, 561
Griffo, Joseph A, 22, 26, 27, 28, 29, 31, 32, 163, 715
Grigg, George, 669
Grijalva, Raul M, 391
Grillo, Lorraine, 120, 149
Grimaldi, Christopher, 502, 565
Grimaldi, Christopher F, 544
Grimes, Kyle, 609
Grimes, Patrick H, 400
Grimm, Christopher, 532
Grimm, Kathleen, 428
Grinage, Jeanine, 144, 333
Grinnell, Richie, 218, 315
Grishman, Henry L, 655
Grisoli, William T, 184
Grobe, Sharon L, 38
Grodenchik, Barry, 514
Groenwegen, Nancy G, 6, 237, 287, 288, 295, 296
Groff, Chad C, 667
Grogan, Michael P, 419
Grogin, Neil, 211, 278, 308
Grogin, Neil C, 5
Gromack, Alexander J, 417
Gromer, Robert W, 568
Groski, Agatha Edel, 248, 271
Gross, Gordon R, 611
Gross, Hank, 602
Gross, Mark A, 73
Gross, Michael A, 60
Grosser, Allen, 419
Grossman, Beverly, 474
Grossman, Jennifer, 505
Grossman, Rachel, 120, 230
Grossman, Stanley L, 550
Grosso, Joseph A, 60
Grosvenor, Paul H, 61
Grote, Gary D, 573
Groten, Margery, 521
Groth, Donald J, 114, 336, 376
Groveman, Alan B, 668
Gruen, Vanessa, 509
Grumes, Allison, 571
Grumet, Louis, 110, 557
Grunfeld, Jeffrey S, 16, 198, 290, 297
Gruninger, Sandi, 637
Gruskin, Stuart, 9, 177
Gruttadauria, Salvatore, 553
Gsell, Jay, 401
Guadagno, Lisa, 591
Gualtieri, Raymond D, 668
Guarasci, Richard, 633
Guard, Josephine, 72
Guarinello, William R, 319
Guarino, Angela, 564
Guarracino, John, 660
Guastaferro, Lynette, 155
Guay, David E, 594
Gubbay, Josephe, 60
Guccione, Joseph R, 139, 261

Guck, Brian, 606
Guenther, Susan N, 159
Guerin, Doreen, 121, 336
Guernsey, Thomas, 456
Guernsey, Thomas F, 621
Guerra, III, Joseph M, 139, 261
Guevara, Richard, 328
Guggenheim, Lisa, 458
Guglielmo, Ronald, 461
Guglielmo, William K, 583
Guiffreda, Robert S, 679
Guiliano, Chris, 511
Guiliano, Edward, 628
Guiliano, Louise, 20
Guiney, Daniel J, 396
Guiney, John, 81, 105, 184
Guistina, David, 603
Gulezian, Dean, 81, 105, 184
Gulotty, Douglas C, 97
Gulseth, Erica, 481
Gump, Dan, 80
Gumson, Robert, 147
Gundersen, Daniel C, 9, 99, 116, 177, 230, 333
Gunn, Barbara, 458
Gunther, Aileen, 50
Gunther, Aileen M, 39, 44, 47, 48, 51, 52, 696
Gupta, D K, 357
Gurney, Gardner, 12, 325
Gurtman, Steven, 511
Gurvitch, Adam, 493
Gush, Linda R, 680
Gustavo-Rivera, Jose, 24
Gutbtodt, Jean, 602
Guthman, Jillian, 421
Gutierrez, Luis V, 390
Gutierrez, Michael, 634
Gutmann, Linda, 368
Gutterman, James M, 215, 245
Guven, Erin, 498
Guy, Renee, 618
Guzdek, Edward W, 142, 300, 560
Guzman, Raymond, 56
Guzman, Wilma, 59
Gwinner, Donald E, 448
Gyamfi, Alexander, 144
Gyory, Bruce, 506
Gyory, Bruce N, 491
Haab, Deborah, 661
Haas, James M, 128, 337
Haas, Jeffrey B, 545
Haaser, Brian L, 82
Habbe, Stephen, 457
Haber, Bernard, 126, 183, 337
Haber, G Jeffrey, 292, 330
Haber, Jeffrey G, 460
Haber, Selin, 355
Habib, Tariq, 118, 351
Habicht, Gail, 520
Haboucha, Reginetta, 482

Name Index

Hack, Marge, 599
Hackel, Arelene, 257
Hackeling, C Stephen, 70
Hackett, Fran, 345
Hadley, J Dwight, 113, 350
Hadley, Paul H, 403
Hadsell, Margaret, 444
Haendiges, Deborah A, 57
Haenel, Jason, 526
Hafner, Jr, Walter W, 66
Hagel, Charles E, 385
Hagel, Chuck, 384
Hagemann, Harold, 334
Hagemann, III, Robert F, 402
Hagenbeck, Lt Gen Franklin L, 150
Haggerty, Jennifer J, 402
Haggerty, John, 200
Haggerty, Kathleen M, 480
Haggerty, Leslie, 15
Haggerty, Robert, 79
Hagler, Shlomo S, 59
Hahn, Arlene H, 60
Haight, David, 83, 457
Haignere, Lois, 498
Haines, Jennifer, 414
Haines, Jr, David F, 568
Hakim, Veronique, 118, 351
Halada, Gary, 520
Halahan, Maureen, 581
Halayko, Kim, 45, 46
Halbritter, Jane A, 246, 268
Halbritter, Ray, 209
Hale, Barbara, 66
Hale, Gary, 204, 240
Hales, Thomas E, 97
Halevy, Richard, 445
Haley, Patricia A, 162
Halftown, Clint, 207
Hall Jr, John S, 69
Hall Sr, Wayne J, 421
Hall, Bob, 89
Hall, Carolyn, 67
Hall, Courtenay W, 67
Hall, David R, 421
Hall, Glen, 447
Hall, Goeffrey, 409
Hall, Jean, 222
Hall, Jerome, 310
Hall, Jim, 334
Hall, John, 381, 393
Hall, John J, 727
Hall, L Priscilla, 56
Hall, Myrna, 434
Hall, Patrick, 460, 556
Hall, PhD, Donna, 8, 133, 253, 288
Hall, Ralph M, 172, 186, 392
Hall, Steve, 595
Hall, Sue Dale, 470
Hall, T Edward, 338
Hallenbeck, Bruce, 196
Halligan, Caitlin J, 12, 134, 253

Hallion, Kathleen, 591
Hallman, Eric, 84
Hallock, Dick, 196, 333
Hallock, Gary, 10, 228
Hallock, Kathleen E, 417
Hallock, Peter, 649
Hallock, Peter J, 649
Halloran, Jean, 84, 108
Halpert, Arlene, 489
Halpin, Suzanne, 519
Halprin, Sheldon J, 60
Halsey, Benjamin A, 646
Halsey, Steven, 200
Halstead, John, 520
Halstead, John R, 613
Halter, Cheryl, 490
Haltermann Jr, William, 551
Hamann, Kristine, 11, 134, 197
Hamdani, Kausar, 92
Hamel, Thomas, 145
Hamer, Syliva, 268
Hamer, Sylvia, 3, 12, 99, 194, 197, 253, 254
Hamill, Bryanne A, 61
Hamill, Christine, 663
Hamilton, David, 146, 212
Hamilton, Edward J, 13, 100, 147
Hamilton, Henry, 9, 178
Hamilton, James, 441
Hamilton, Kathy, 635
Hamilton, Kemar, 470
Hamilton, Norma W, 88
Hamilton, Tracy M, 256
Hamilton-Thompson, Tracy, 332
Hamlin, Douglas B, 663
Hamlin, George W, 94
Hammond, Bill, 593
Hammond, Carol, 40
Hammond, Gail, 15, 101, 230, 290
Hammond, Jeffrey, 528
Hammond, John, 557
Hammond, Lawrence, 135
Hammond, Stephen, 177
Hanauer, William R, 437
Hance, Cathy, 81
Hancock III, Stewart, 488
Hancock, Mary Pat, 401
Hancox, David R, 198, 290
Hancox, Steve, 197, 290
Handal, Peter, 108
Handler, Martin D, 680
Haneline, Carl, 363
Hanin, Laurie, 223
Hankin, Carole G, 656
Hankin, Joseph N, 617
Hanks, David, 639
Hanley, James F, 432
Hanley, Lawrence, 457
Hanley, Mark, 599
Hanlon, Nadine P, 406
Hanlon, Pat, 345
Hann, Henry, 675

Hanna, Robert J, 679
Hanna, Sean, 178
Hannah, Craig D, 71
Hannan, Kirby, 543, 555
Hannan, Kirby T, 488
Hannan, Ross, 488
Hannigan, Anthony, 317
Hannmann, Richard, 496
Hanno, Douglas, 403
Hannon, Donald, 349
Hannon, Kemp, 20, 22, 26, 27, 28, 29, 30, 31, 217, 715
Hanophy, Robert J, 58
Hanor, Deborah J, 309
Hansbury, Brian, 75
Hanse, Stephen, 483
Hansell, David, 431
Hansell, David A, 17, 238, 313
Hansen, Christine, 116, 170, 182, 376
Hansen, Jr, Stanley S, 144
Hansen, Kristen, 165, 293
Hanson, Beatrice, 521
Hanson, William, 448
Hantman, Melissa, 415
Hanuszczak, Michael, 66
Haponik, Gayle, 7, 129
Harabin, Victor, 81
Harasek, Christine, 70
Harazin, Marcus, 4, 307
Harcrow, Richard, 141
Hard, Judith A, 58
Harder, David E, 397
Hardiman, Ann, 460
Hardiman, Ann M, 285
Hardin, Russell, 166
Hardin, Ursula, 347
Harding, Frances M, 5, 212, 279, 308
Harding, Paul J, 431
Harding, Robert, 487
Harding, Stella Chen, 6, 287, 295
Harding-Keefe, Claire, 470
Hardy, John L, 483
Hardy, Kimberly D, 430
Hargrave, Michael, 87
Hargraves, Carlos, 471
Hariton, David P, 330
Harkavy, Ira B, 56
Harkavy, Jonathan, 40, 48
Harkin, Tom, 83, 187, 220, 382, 383
Harknett-Martin, Mary, 627, 630
Harles, Charles W, 316
Harloff, Jeff, 406
Harman, Jane, 390
Harmon, Thomas, 119, 282
Harner, Timothy R, 527
Harney, James L, 16, 136
Haroules, Beth, 514
Harper, Al, 654
Harper, Bill, 618
Harper, Gerard, 449
Harper, Ken, 450

Name Index

Harper, Mary, 431
Harrica, Paul H, 647
Harrigan, Margaret, 288, 295
Harrigan, Sheila, 321, 517
Harrington, Phyllis, 655
Harrington, Rev Donald J, 631
Harrington, Toni, 492
Harrington, William M, 60
Harris Kluger, Judy, 256
Harris, Carolyn S, 654
Harris, David, 240
Harris, Evelyn M, 180, 199, 291
Harris, Frank, 41
Harris, George, 604
Harris, Gerald, 60
Harris, Joan Marro, 600
Harris, Lisa R, 7, 99, 168
Harris, Lorenda, 22
Harris, Lottie, 470
Harris, Maureen F, 14
Harris, Merry, 415
Harris, Patricia E, 426
Harris, Paulette, 608
Harris, Raymond H, 297
Harris, Sandra, 525
Harris, Steven, 483
Harris, William R, 365
Harrison Jr, David W, 399
Harrison, Caroline, 599
Harrison, Lorenzo, 273
Harrow, Richard, 134, 216, 254
Hart, Duane A, 58
Hart, George W, 565
Hart, John, 144, 333
Hart, Michelle, 511
Hart, Robert, 599
Hart, Wally, 575
Hart, Warren, 576
Hartell, Cheryl, 118, 351, 377
Hartman, Melanie, 71
Hartman, Paul, 458
Hartman, Wayne, 554
Hartmayer, C Douglas, 126, 353, 379
Hartnett, David S, 399
Hartnett, Edmund, 445
Hartnett, Thomas, 507
Hartzell, David, 572
Harvey, Andrea, 506
Harvey, Charlie R, 129
Harvey, James R, 66
Harwell, Stephen, 484
Hasanoeddin, Evelyn, 60
Haseley, Laurance, 424
Hashem, Paul G, 646
Haskell, John, 581
Haslett Rudiano, Diane, 160
Hasper, John W, 452
Hassell, Andrew, 60
Hassell-Thompson, Ruth, 22, 26, 27, 29, 30, 31, 259, 715
Hassett, Col John J, 221, 365

Hassett, Paul Michael, 107
Hastert, J Dennis, 171, 186, 389
Hastings, Alcee L, 392
Hastings, Doc, 164, 206, 392, 393
Hastings, Krystal, 162
Hatch, Gale M, 251, 294
Hatch, Livingston, 401
Hatch, Orrin G, 249, 385, 386
Hatch, William O, 453
Hatfield, Mark, 204, 355
Hattam, Victoria, 166
Hauber, Bonnie, 639
Haupt, Andrew, 471
Hauptman, Laurence, 210
Havens, Michael, 675
Haverly, Ferd, 283
Havey, Steven, 588
Havranek, Brian, 582
Hawkins, Dennis R, 263
Hawkins, Jacquelyn J, 198
Hawkins, Laura, 531
Hawkins, Laura Jean, 480
Hawley, Stephen, 39, 44, 45, 46, 48, 50, 52, 103, 202, 354, 696
Hawley, Wayne G, 428
Haworth, John, 339
Hay, Carol S, 642
Hay, Cliff, 450
Hay, Clifford C, 161
Hayden, James T, 62
Hayden, Michael, 135
Hayden, Peter E, 429
Hayes, Connie C, 413
Hayes, Daniel T, 616
Hayes, Darryl B, 29
Hayes, Gerald V, 63
Hayes, James P, 36, 39, 52, 202, 292, 327, 696
Hayes, Jim, 51
Hayes, John, 60
Hayes, Kathe, 281
Hayes, Kevin G, 412
Hayes, Larry, 310
Hayes, Mark, 492
Hayes, Michael, 17, 238, 313, 374, 511
Hayes, Roger S, 60
Hayes, Ronald, 349
Hayes, Susan, 527
Hayes, Timothy, 651
Hayes-Young, Margaret, 523
Hayner, David, 86
Haynes, Carl E, 617
Haynes, Patricia, 640
Hays, James, 207, 221, 263, 317, 538
Hays, Sr, Albert, 449
Hays, Timothy D, 364
Heady, Evelyn, 247, 269
Healey, Kathleen, 498
Healey, Noreen, 98, 102, 124, 324
Healy, Daniel, 168, 195
Healy, Richard, 412

Healy, Sheila, 465
Heaney Jr, Peter, 657
Heaney, Patrick A, 115, 181, 442
Heaney, William, 200
Heaphy, Alison, 207
Heard, Susan M, 406
Hearn, Rose Gill, 431
Hearst, III, George R, 591
Heary, Cherl, 158, 452
Heastie, Carl, 32, 53, 163
Heastie, Carl E, 39, 44, 45, 46, 49, 51, 697
Heath, David O, 612
Heath, Kristen, 504
Heath-Roland, Helena, 70
Hebert, Robert J, 643
Hecht, Franklin A, 98, 196, 324
Hecht, Jeffrey, 496
Heckel, Inge, 629
Hecker, Elissa D, 342
Hedges, Bryan R, 66
Hedlund PhD, Carolyn S, 506
Heerkens, Ronald, 215
Heffernan, Charles J, 60
Hefferon, Thomas, 102, 115, 230
Hefner, Dennis L, 614
Hegermiller, David, 440
Heggen, Mark, 417
Heggie, Dianne, 466
Heider, Steven H, 418
Heigel, Frederick, 484
Heilter, Sherry Klein, 56
Heim, Marilyn, 581
Heimann, Farris H, 413
Heimgartner, Chris, 460
Heimroth, Laurie, 29
Hein, Michael P, 412
Heinemann, Robert C, 259
Heinkind, Barbara, 528
Heitner, Carl, 246, 269
Heitner, Debra I, 540
Helbig, Carl, 593
Held, Gerald S, 56
Hellenberg, Heidi, 490
Heller, Dean, 392
Heller, Hugh M, 550
Heller, Marc, 600
Hellert, Gayle H, 642
Hellmer, Anthony, 125, 202, 297
Helmer, Maureen, 487
Helmerson, Karen, 332
Helrich, Todd G, 108
Helsmoortel, Greg, 441
Hemstead, George, 135
Hemstead, George W, 14
Hemstreet, Wayne, 593
Henahan, David, 611
Hencoski, Paul, 496
Hendershott, Stephen W, 127, 354
Henderson, Marsha, 527
Henderson, Meredith, 21
Henderson, Sue, 471

Name Index

Henderson, Tyquana, 532
Henderson, William, 358
Hendricks, James, 65
Hendricks, Julie, 486
Hendricks, Michael, 591
Hendricks, Mike, 601
Hendricks, Tyler O, 632
Hendrix, Anne W, 161
Hendrix, Leonard R, 402
Hengsterman, Stacey B, 521
Henley, Debbie, 595
Henley, James B, 135, 216, 229, 247, 255, 325
Henley, Nicholas, 484
Henn, Robert, 329
Henne, Sandra, 343
Hennessey, Sean, 450
Henning, Eric, 485
Henning, Gary, 458
Henning, Marjorie, 432
Henri, William F, 281
Henrikson, Robert, 479
Henry, Karl A, 248, 271
Henry, Mark, 457
Henry, Patricia E, 60
Henry, Patrick, 58
Henry, Susan A, 612
Henry, Sylvie, 320
Henry, Veronica, 618
Hensley, Paul M, 70
Henze, Nancy H, 91, 119, 291, 377
Hepner, Paula J, 61
Hepp, David, 602
Heppner, Daniel, 423
Herbert, Barbara, 169
Herbst, Chris, 595
Herbst, Joseph, 476
Herbst, Marc, 549
Herbst, Susan V, 613
Herdman, Elaine, 157
Herger, Wally, 394
Hering, LuAnn, 68
Heritage, Penny, 86
Herl, Susanne L, 566
Herlihy, Patricia S, 68
Herman, Frank, 135
Herman, J Brad, 672
Herman, Vanessa, 520
Hermann, Robert, 15, 99, 197
Hernandez, Doris, 432
Hernandez, Neil, 431
Hernandez, Paul, 496
Hernandez, Tino, 430
Hernandez, Wanda, 18, 200, 313
Herndon, Sandra, 145
Herne, JoAnn, 624
Hernick, Joanne I, 214, 360
Herren, George E, 15, 289, 302, 326
Herrick, Richard, 510
Herrick, Richard J, 226
Herrick, Stephen W, 61

Herritt, Jr, Thomas G, 356
Hershenson, Jay, 471, 619
Hertline, Harry A, 405
Hertman, Robert, 444
Herz, Robert, 25
Herzog, Betsy, 431
Herzog, Thomas, 132
Heslin, Martin, 496
Heslop, James, 420
Heslop, Thomas, 556
Hess, David, 191
Hess, John B, 172
Hess, Patricia, 213
Hess, Robert J, 20
Hess, Robert V, 430
Hess, Scott D, 406
Hess, Terri, 586
Heuer, Gary, 219, 315
Hevert, William J, 538
Hevesi, Andrew, 39, 44, 45, 46, 47, 49, 697
Hevesi, Andrew D, 45
Hewitt, Debra L, 448
Hewitt, Diane, 472
Hewitt, Steven J, 349
Heyman, Mary Ellen, 422
Heyman, Neil, 225
Heymann, George M, 60
Heyward, Leon W, 434
Heywood, Christine, 309
Hibbard, Carla, 470
Hickey, Christine, 224
Hickey, Daniel C, 541
Hickey, Maurice B, 615
Hickman Jr, John A, 418
Hicks, Christy, 165
Hicks, Geoffrey M, 647
Hicks, John, 133, 252, 288
Hicks, Kevin, 469
Hicks, Kevin R, 275
Hicks, Lisa U, 265
Hider, Kathleen, 363
Hiffa, Frederick T, 513
Higgins, Brian, 381, 393, 726
Higgins, Brian M, 164, 186, 187, 205, 233, 298, 356, 392, 393
Higgins, Christopher, 28, 31
Higgins, John J, 304
Higgins, MaryAnn, 218, 314
Higgins, Roger, 400
Higgins, Shelley, 571
Higgins, Thomas W, 75
Hikind, Dov, 34, 39, 697
Hilchey, Duncan, 84
Hilderbrand, Janice, 444
Hill Jr, William L, 10, 196, 301
Hill, Catharine B, 633
Hill, Charles, 566
Hill, Dennis, 80
Hill, Doug, 594
Hill, Elizabeth A, 631
Hill, Jeffrey L, 490

Hill, Jennifer B, 582
Hill, Laureen, 500
Hill, Marjorie, 485
Hill, Stewart D, 562
Hill, Tango, 581
Hill, Timothy E, 162
Hillard, Thomas, 522
Hiller, Amanda, 4, 157, 228, 301, 332
Hiller, Edward, 246, 268
Hillerman, Stephen R, 197, 290
Hillman, Linda, 583
Himelein, Larry M, 62
Himes, Jay L, 99, 134, 254
Hinchcliff, Diana, 144
Hinchey, Maurice D, 83, 106, 171, 329, 381, 387, 388, 394, 727
Hinckley, Robert R, 468
Hinds, Clifford L, 567
Hinds, John, 407
Hinds-Radix, Sylvia O, 56
Hines, Alan, 511
Hines, Mary, 9, 296
Hines-Kramer, Amy, 476
Hinkson, Lisa, 496
Hinojosa, Ruben, 389
Hinrichs, C Randall, 68
Hirsch, Charles S, 433
Hirsch, David, 525
Hirschfeld, Sidney, 256, 282
Hirsh, John, 606
Hirshman, Michele, 12, 91, 99, 134, 169, 179, 216, 229, 238, 247, 254, 270
Hirshorn, Donald, 300
Hirst, Martha K, 427
Hirt, Richard, 655
Hishta, John, 507
Hitchcock, Greg, 585
Hite, Patricia, 6, 237, 287, 295
Hite, Robert S, 14, 296
Ho, Wayne H, 317
Hoag, Bonnie, 188
Hoag, Gail, 582
Hoag, Patricia, 118, 351
Hobbs, Gary C, 72
Hoberman, Brian, 434
Hobika, Jr, Joseph H, 587
Hoblock, Jr, Michael J, 15, 325, 335
Hobson, David L, 171, 388
Hobson, Tracy, 316
Hochul, Kathy, 400
Hodes, Nancy L, 491
Hodgins, Pat, 145
Hodgkins, Christie, 471
Hodin-Baier, Ali, 427
Hoeberling, James, 537, 560
Hoeberling, James W, 540, 542
Hoefer, Karl, 448
Hoekstra, Pete, 394
Hoekstra, Peter, 206, 394
Hoercher, Teresa R, 537
Hoesl, Brian, 460

Name Index

Hoesl, Brian J, 564
Hoeven, John, 116, 170, 182
Hoffacker, Mark, 524
Hoffer, Mark D, 429
Hoffman, Daniel, 422
Hoffman, Dirk, 592
Hoffman, Douglas E, 60
Hoffman, James, 130, 412, 653
Hoffman, Jerry S, 531
Hoffman, Linda, 320
Hoffman, Martha R, 66
Hoffmann, Joseph, 594
Hoffmeister, Bob, 348
Hoffner, Josh, 601
Hogan, Daniel D, 15, 325, 335
Hogan, Elizabeth, 44, 48, 52
Hogan, John, 642
Hogan, Joseph, 532
Hogan, Kathleen B, 412
Hogan, Mike, 132
Hogan, PhD, Michael F, 12, 280
Hogan, Richard, 257
Hogan, Shawn, 450
Hogan, Tom, 145
Hogle, Dick, 211, 278, 308
Hogle, Theron H, 541
Hoglund, Robert, 496
Hohenstein, Anne, 180, 197, 290
Hohlt, Barbara E, 557
Hohmann, Judy, 144
Hohmann, Patricia J, 400
Holahan, Paul, 440
Holanchock, Howard, 280
Holbrook, Elizabeth, 66
Holcomb, Betty, 470
Holcomb, Julie Conley, 422
Holden, Kathryn, 670
Holden, Maria, 144
Holden, Ross J, 120, 149
Holden, Tim, 387
Holdener, Richard E, 419
Holder, David C., 338
Holdorf, Armin, 246, 268
Holeman, Mark, 482
Holland, Debra, 528
Holland, Michael, 171
Holland, Rebecca, 431
Hollander, Ellen, 152
Hollfelder, Chris M, 561
Holliday, Susan R, 602
Hollie, Ronald D, 58
Hollmen, Linda, 132
Hollyer, A Rene, 264
Holm, Bruce, 527
Holman, Evelyn B, 668
Holman, Karen, 501
Holman, Marcia, 285
Holmes Norton, Eleanor, 393
Holmes, Al, 280
Holmes, Grace, 220
Holmes, June, 559

Holmes, M Frances, 204, 239
Holmes, Oliver, 415
Holmes, Steve, 243, 286
Holst, Stephen L, 227
Holtz, Mary F, 416
Holtzman, David, 511
Holtzman, Mark, 496
Holzer, Edith, 466
Holzman, Lee L, 61
Homans, John, 602
Hommes, Henry H, 401
Hong, Chung-Wha, 243, 493
Honorof, Alan L, 58
Honors, Owen P, 417
Hood, Elizabeth, 144
Hood, Martha Walsh, 66
Hoogland, William, 215
Hook, Morgan, 607
Hooker, Donald, 428
Hooker, Patrick, 5, 79, 307
Hooley, Richard M, 661
Hooper, Earlene, 34, 39, 46, 49, 51
Hooper, Earlene , 697
Hoose, Robert W, 448
Hooton, Angela, 510
Hoover, William, 584
Hope, Jack, 13, 348
Hopkins, Kathryn D, 65
Hoppe, Lewis M, 32, 54, 163
Horan, Hon James F, 299
Horn, Glenn, 608
Horn, Martin F, 428, 433
Horodnicaenu, Michael, 359
Horohoe, William, 305
Horowitz, Evelyn, 427
Horowitz, Lawrence I, 57
Horowitz, Nilda Morales, 69
Horr, III, Robert G, 128, 354, 380
Hortofilis, Michael, 559, 567
Horton, Gary, 401
Horton, Steven, 425
Horwitz, Gayle, 428
Horwitz, Richard, 438
Hotzler, Russell, 471
Hotzler, Russell K, 621
Hough Jr, Joseph C, 632
Hough, Anthony, 310
Houghtaling, Jr, Charles E, 396
Houghton, Amory, 106, 240, 390
Houghton, Raymond C, 415
Houle, Serena, 457
House, Frank C, 651
House, Mary E, 135, 247, 255, 325
House, Rachelle, 483
Houseal, Brian L, 187, 455
Houseknecht, Michael, 91, 92, 231
Houseknecht, Michael R, 124, 127
Houseman, Wayne F, 406
Howard, Brian, 674
Howard, Craig, 363
Howard, Gary, 411

Howard, Jessica, 46
Howard, Jessica C, 52
Howard, Judith H, 657
Howard, Laura, 599
Howard, Matthew, 52
Howard, Muriel A, 613
Howard, Tim, 633
Howard, Timothy B, 400
Howard, William, 3, 348
Howe, Barbara, 63
Howe, Kevin R, 593
Howe, Robert, 452
Howe, Robert C, 158
Howe, Rod, 84, 234
Howell, Elizabeth, 474
Howell, Mary, 399
Howey, Katrina, 496
Howlett, Jeff, 606
Howley, Patricia, 101, 148
Hoye, Polly A, 63
Hoylman, Brad, 555
Hoyos, Inez, 60
Hoyt III, William (Sam), 50, 231, 292
Hoyt, III, William (Sam), 39, 45, 47, 52, 53
Hoyt, III, William B (Sam), 697
Hrabchak, Gebo & Langone, , 423
Hsiang, Willy, 82
Huang, Tina, 471
Hubbard, Steven V, 643
Huber, Kenneth, 548
Huberman, Anne, 498
Hubert, Gail Ann, 604
Hudder, John, 35
Hudman, Julie, 503
Hudson, James C, 68
Hudson, Lee, 431
Hudson, Michael E, 58
Hudzinski, Lucretia M, 578
Huether, Gregory J, 255
Huey, Yick Pon, 637
Huff, Carol E, 56
Huff, Charles, 80
Hughes, Catherine K, 398
Hughes, Denis, 479
Hughes, Everett, 435
Hughes, James, 460
Hughes, James F, 73
Hughes, Jr, Joseph R, 69
Hughes, Pam, 485
Hughes, Robert C, 422
Hughes, Scott, 459
Huguenin, Roger, 70
Hulbert, Gregory M, 441
Hull, Pam, 79
Hults, Clark, 647
Hults, Ted, 418
Humbert, Marc, 601
Hume, Chad, 169
Hume, III, John E N, 599
Hummel, Christian F, 67
Hummel, Edward, 104

Name Index

Humphreys, Brymer, 82
Humphreys, Glenn, 310
Hung, Palyn, 514
Hunsinger, Pamela, 439
Hunt, Beth A, 402
Hunt, Carl, 131
Hunt, Charles W, 274
Hunt, Diane, 537
Hunt, E Charles, 521
Hunt, John M, 61
Hunt, Lucretia D, 556
Hunt, Richard V, 64
Hunt, Stephen J, 611
Hunter, Alexander W, 58
Hunter, Duncan, 364, 388
Hunter, Jon, 652
Hunter, Judith M, 410
Hunter, Scott G, 643
Hunter, Tee-Ann, 423
Huntley, Douglas W, 666
Huntley, John, 79
Huntley, Shirley, 27, 29, 203
Huntley, Shirley L, 22, 31, 32, 715
Hurd, Gregory, 198
Hurd, Richard, 275
Hurford, Carol, 498
Hurkin-Torres, Allen Z, 56
Hurlburt Jr, Rexford, 642
Hurlbut, Robert H, 11, 246, 268
Hurlbutt, Robert G, 56
Hurley, Daniel N, 520
Hurley, John J, 495
Hurley, John R, 544
Hurley, Joseph P, 259
Hurley, Jr, Paul B, 632
Hurley, William, 672
Hurst, Steve, 455
Hurteau, Darcie, 484
Hurwitz, Mark, 430
Husamudeen, Elias, 539
Husar, Michael P, 62
Hussey, John F, 67
Hussey, Richard H, 402
Husted, Stacey B, 409
Huston, John, 584
Hutchings, John, 536
Hutchins, Julie, 402
Hutchinson, Amber N, 421
Hutchison, Kay Bailey, 172, 383, 384
Huth, Geoff, 144
Hutner, Florence, 433
Hutter, Adam, 185, 204
Huttner, Richard D, 58
Hutton, Carol R, 437
Hutton, Claudia, 10, 179, 215, 373
Hutton, Rebecca, 503
Hutton, Todd S, 633
Huus, William A, 599
Hwang, Jeffrey, 95
Hyde, Steven G, 575
Hyer, Verna J, 534

Hyer-Spencer, Janele, 39, 44, 45, 49, 697
Hyer-Spencer, Janelle, 52
Hyland, Dr John, 559
Hyland, Mary Pat, 592
Hyland, Theresa, 593, 594
Hynes, Charles J, 403
Hynes, Ken, 368
Iachetta, Stephen A, 113, 350
Iacovetta, Nicholas, 60
Ianello, Stephen, 496
Iannacci, Angela G, 58
Iannucci Jr, Salvatore, 557
Iannuzzi, Richard, 154, 300, 456
Iavarone, Charles M, 441, 558
Idoni, Timothy C, 413
Igielski, Alan, 493
Ignizio, Vincent, 313
Ike, Robert R, 650
Iliou, John, 70
Ilnitzki, Leon, 542
Ilnitzki, Leon C, 558
Imhof, Louis, 448
Impagliazzo, Bonnie, 471
Imperatrice, James, 56, 64
Imperiale, Laura, 475
Imperiosi, Edward, 634
Impicciatore, Joseph, 309
Improta, Dina, 428
Indelicato, Charlene M, 413
Infiesta, Julio, 314
Information, General, 19
Ingen, Anne Van, 332
Inghem, Ursula, 498
Inglis, Bob, 172, 186, 392
Inglis, Bruce, 646
Ingram, John G, 58
Ingrassia, Louisa, 444
Ingrassia, Paul J, 601
Inhofe, James M, 187, 356, 384
Inman, Charles E, 399
Inouye, Daniel, 383
Inouye, Daniel K, 106, 172, 187, 356, 384
Inserra, Theodore, 131
Intrary, Terry, 407
Intschert, Cindy, 402
Iorio, Chris, 607
Ipsen, Erik, 601
Ireland, Kim, 28
Irrera, Raymond J, 583
Irvin, Angela, 537
Irvin, Dale T, 629
Irvin, Thomas, 4
Irwin, Julie, 361
Isaksen, Suzanne, 425
Isakson, Johnny, 356, 385, 386
Iselin, Harold, 487
Isenberg, Andrew B, 57
Isenberg-O'Loughlin, Jo, 600
Ishayik, Edna, 166, 449
Ishmael, Cheryl, 122, 149, 201, 217
Ison, Jeanne, 126, 183, 380

Israel, Doug, 477
Israel, Laurie M, 134, 253
Israel, Steve, 93, 232, 249, 364, 381, 390, 727
Issa, Darrell, 394
Issa, Darrell E, 392
Issinger, Peter, 225
Itzo, Cynthia, 253
Iulo, Robert, 427
Ivanoff, Nick, 357
Iverson, Kathleen, 280
Ives, Dan, 599
Ivey, Mary E, 302, 349
Iwanowicz, Peter, 458
Izquierdo, Richard, 36
Jablonski, Diane, 400
Jaccarino, Thomas M, 437
Jaccoma, Barbara, 500
Jack, Howard A, 187
Jack, Kevin, 269
Jackier, Diane, 432
Jackman-Brown, Pam B, 60
Jackson, Brad W, 574
Jackson, David I, 557
Jackson, Debra, 675
Jackson, Edison O, 471, 620
Jackson, Edna, 26
Jackson, Jill W, 554
Jackson, Josephine, 157
Jackson, M Randolph, 56
Jackson, Melissa C, 60
Jackson, Patricia A, 204, 240
Jackson, Ronald, 452
Jackson, Sherree, 66
Jackson, Shirley Ann, 517, 630
Jackson, Terri, 483
Jackson, Wayne P, 34
Jackson, William, 418
Jackson-Grove, Amy D, 355
Jacob, Andrew, 126, 183
Jacob, Andrew T, 178
Jacob, Phyllis Gangel, 56
Jacobie, John, 361
Jacobosky, Anne, 314
Jacobs, Ann, 142
Jacobs, Frederick J, 491
Jacobs, Jay, 450
Jacobs, Judith A, 404
Jacobs, Kasey, 471
Jacobs, Rhoda S, 34, 39, 48, 49, 51, 698
Jacobsen, Susan, 133, 253
Jacobson, Anat, 433
Jacobson, Jonathan G, 450
Jacobson, Laura Lee, 56
Jacobson, Michael, 142, 267
Jacobson, Philip, 273
Jacobson, Ted, 555
Jacon, Robert M, 67
Jacques, Steve, 511
Jaeger, Kathleen, 223
Jaeger, Lloyd, 645

Name Index

Jaeger, Steven M, 65
Jaffarian, Robert, 145
Jaffe, Barbara, 59
Jaffe, Dana M, 70
Jaffe, Mark S, 580
Jaffe, Robert, 510
Jaffee, Ellen, 39, 45, 47, 50, 698
Jagow, Wayne F, 405
Jaker, William, 608
James E Elder, John J Torpey, 563
James, Daisy, 39
James, Debra A, 59
James, Donald A, 668
James, Eric, 547
James, Francine, 3, 12, 194, 252, 254, 287, 324
James, Kathrine A, 160
James, Nathaniel, 365
James, Yvette, 464, 507
Jamieson, Linda S, 57
Jamison, Gy Sgt John, 363
Janczak, Susan P, 67
Janeczek, Kathy, 423
Jankowiak, James, 416
Jankowski George, Janet, 398
Jankowski, Michael, 412
Jannetty, Karen L, 523, 554
Janowitz, Norman, 70
Jaquay, Robert, 572
Jaquith, Grant C, 138, 260
Jardine, Anne S, 134, 216, 254
Jarin, Kenneth, 539
Jarman, Richard, 471
Jaros, Susan K, 414
Jarvis, Gary, 410
Jarvis, Lucinda A, 161
Jarvis, Monique, 532
Jaspan, Arthur W, 561
Jaycox, M Indica, 409
Jayson, Larry, 233
Jecen, James R, 72
Jeffers, Darrell E, 531
Jeffers, Thomas, 543
Jefferson, Leah, 238
Jeffords, H Susan, 299
Jeffrey, Kevin, 433
Jeffries, Hakeem, 39, 44, 45, 46, 49, 698
Jenik, Peter, 431
Jenkins, Carroll R, 16, 326
Jenkins, Connie, 595
Jenkins, Harriet L, 158
Jenkins, Patrick, 494
Jennings, Dr Ralph, 603
Jennings, Gerald, 83, 204
Jennings, Gerald D, 414
Jennings, Jim, 346
Jennings, John, 489
Jennings, Molly, 203
Jerome, Edward, 219, 273
Jerome, Marc M, 636
Jerome, Stephen J, 636

Jerominek, Maribel, 482
Jerrett, Theodore I, 407
Jesep, Paul, 13, 100, 147
Jewett, Sherman, 502
Jezer, Rhea, 523
Jicha, Jean, 74
Jimenez, Dawn M, 60
Jiminez, Angela, 14, 135
Jimino, Kathleen M, 408
Joch, Nancy M, 69
Jody Olcott, Carol Calabrese, 574
Joel, Richard M, 633
Joerg, Claude A, 405
Johansen, Lawrence A, 125, 149, 297
John, Dennis B, 397
John, Sr, Maurice A, 210
John, Susan V, 39, 46, 47, 49, 50, 239, 248, 272, 297, 698
Johns, Richard N, 645
Johnson III, Daniel E, 567
Johnson Jr, Peter J, 562
Johnson, Allan C, 162
Johnson, Andrew, 310
Johnson, Anne, 609
Johnson, Audrey M, 439
Johnson, Bart R, 16, 136
Johnson, Brian, 496
Johnson, Brian A, 543
Johnson, Bruce A, 129
Johnson, Bruce C, 461
Johnson, Catherine, 10, 228
Johnson, Celeste M, 215
Johnson, Charlotte, 31
Johnson, Chris, 497
Johnson, Craig, 28, 183
Johnson, Craig M, 22, 30, 716
Johnson, Daniel, 146
Johnson, David, 143, 144, 372
Johnson, Debbie, 510
Johnson, Dennis, 470, 640
Johnson, Diana A, 56
Johnson, Eddie Bernice, 186, 393
Johnson, Gary, 9, 296
Johnson, Jeanine, 51
Johnson, Joan, 498
Johnson, Joan B, 422
Johnson, Jr, John B, 600
Johnson, Judith, 677
Johnson, Kathleen C, 61
Johnson, Kenneth, 81, 105
Johnson, Kevin, 251
Johnson, Lisa, 333
Johnson, Marc, 248, 271
Johnson, Mark, 14, 135, 374
Johnson, Mark J, 555
Johnson, Matt, 603
Johnson, Michael L, 52
Johnson, Michael R, 416
Johnson, Milton D, 138
Johnson, Neal J, 347

Johnson, Owen H, 19, 22, 26, 27, 28, 31, 32, 33, 54, 203, 292, 298, 328, 716
Johnson, Philip, 33, 54, 103, 203, 298
Johnson, Robert T, 396
Johnson, Robert W, 562
Johnson, Rosemary Ellis, 146, 279, 312
Johnson, Russ W, 406
Johnson, Sam, 315, 394
Johnson, Senator Owen H, 113, 181
Johnson, Stella, 74
Johnson, Stephen Philip, 152
Johnson, Susan, 142, 266
Johnson, Teresa D, 74
Johnson, Tim, 383, 384
Johnson, Troy, 160
Johnson, William H, 656
Johnson-Kelly, Laura, 423
Johnson-Lew, Kiaran, 101, 327
Johnston, Bonnie, 64
Johnston, Christine L, 528
Johnston, Christy, 224
Johnston, Roxanne, 520
Johnston, Stella, 75
Johnston, Susan, 604
Johnston, Warner, 433
Joma, Ronald, 496
Jonas, Rose I, 274
Jonas, Zelda, 58
Jones Jr, Lyle W, 407
Jones Ritter, Diana, 12, 281
Jones, Alice F, 364
Jones, Carolyn M, 591
Jones, E Thomas, 414
Jones, Jr, John J J, 58
Jones, Kathleen, 498
Jones, Loretta C, 189
Jones, Lynne M, 159
Jones, Malcolm, 401
Jones, Margo, 338
Jones, Michael, 80
Jones, Phil, 450
Jones, Richard, 471
Jones, Robin, 647
Jones, Rosemary F, 670
Jones, Stephanie Tubbs, 164, 206, 393
Jones, Theodore, 55
Jones, Theodore T, 56
Jones, Walter, 90
Jones, Wells B, 319
Jordan, Henrietta, 496
Jordan, Julia, 342
Jordan, Kevin J, 102, 115, 230
Jordan, Marilyn F, 57
Jordan, Mark, 39
Jordan, Patricia, 75
Jordan, Terry, 288, 295
Jose, Jorge, 527
Joseph, Arthur, 274, 298
Joseph, Burton S, 58
Joseph, Eva, 638
Joseph, Tim J, 411

Name Index

Joy, Debra, 132
Joyce, Edward, 247, 271
Joyce, John J, 40
Joyce, Jr, William G, 359
Joyce, Sister Maureen, 322
Joyce, William G, 557
Joyner, Wendell, 618
Joynes, Clarice, 435
Jozwiak, Rick, 598
Jui, Kenya, 504
Julian, Robert F, 57
Julian, Timothy J, 443
Junco, Marcella, 496
Jung, David F, 63
Jurado-Nieves, Ellie, 479
Juravich, Robert S, 102, 115, 230, 376, 573
Jurczynski, Al, 101, 199
Jurczynski, Albert P, 16
Jurman, Susan, 118, 351
Jurow, George L, 61
Justice, Lawrence P, 518
K. O, Cao, 316
Kacica, Marilyn A, 213
Kaczynski, David, 511
Kaehny, John, 359
Kafin, Robert, 85
Kafin, Robert J, 191
Kagel, Charlene, 442
Kaggen, Dr Lois, 346
Kahl, David B, 71
Kahn, Alfred E, 175, 358
Kahn, Barbara, 68
Kahn, Marcy L, 56
Kaiman, Jon, 436
Kaiser, Corliss, 659
Kaiser, Nicholas F, 443
Kaiser, Paul, 288, 295
Kalicin, Deborah, 85
Kalikow, Peter S, 117, 118, 119, 304, 350, 351, 352
Kalinsky, Stephen, 98, 324
Kalish, William, 60
Kalka, Marie, 535
Kallop, A George, 250
Kalmus, Jane, 435
Kaloyeros, Alain E, 100, 148
Kaltenborn, Marilyn M, 102, 327
Kaminskyj, Louise, 328
Kammen, Carol, 411
Kanauer, Kathy, 438
Kandel, Andrew, 95
Kane, Alan, 482
Kane, Anthony T, 56
Kane, Christine, 410
Kane, Daniel, 14, 179, 334
Kane, Kathleen G, 303
Kane, Kristen, 429
Kane, Michael, 128, 337
Kang, InBong, 52
Kanjorski, Paul E, 249, 389
Kanlian, Joan, 105

Kansler, Michael, 481
Kansler, Michael R, 173
Kantor, Paul, 293
Kaphan, Patricia, 415
Kapica, John A, 420
Kaplan, Alan, 493
Kaplan, Barbara, 630
Kaplan, Deborah A, 59
Kaplan, Debra, 676
Kaplan, Faith, 162
Kaplan, Fredy, 502
Kaplan, Jill, 556
Kaplan, Madge, 437
Kaplan, Peggy, 534
Kaplan, Peter W, 597
Kaplan, Richard, 211, 278, 308
Kaplan, Selma, 603
Kaplan, Tina, 296
Kaplewicz, Ron, 80
Kapnick, Barbara, 56
Kappel, Alan S, 549
Kappner, Augusta Souza, 622
Karalunas, Deborah H, 57
Karin, Daniel B, 440
Karnilow, Sheldon, 669
Karnovsky, David, 427
Karopkin, Martin G, 433
Karsai, Gabor, 575
Karwan, Mark, 527
Kasanof, Anton, 154
Kasdan, Alexa, 474
Kasdin, Robert, 525
Kase, John L, 65
Kashlin, Steven, 636
Kasirer, Sara, 494
Kaskan, Michael E, 402
Kassar, Gerard, 448
Kasubski, Elizabeth, 523
Kaszluga, Cathy, 155
Katcher, Marcie, 81, 105, 184
Kato, Susumu, 577
Katt, Donald C, 617
Kattleman, Ellen, 195
Kattleman, Ellen B, 6, 168
Katz, Anita S, 162
Katz, Anne, 60
Katz, Arthur H, 552
Katz, Bertram, 58
Katz, Harry C, 612
Katz, Ivan J, 671
Katz, Steven, 146
Katz, Susan, 520
Kaucher, Mark, 584
Kauffman-Sira, Louise, 401
Kaufman, Joseph L, 564
Kaufmann, Scott G, 547
Kaumeyer, Linda, 645
Kavanagh, Brian, 45
Kavanagh, Brian P, 39, 46, 47, 48, 698
Kavanagh, E Michael, 57
Kavanagh, Laura, 455

Kavanagh, Liam, 433
Kavanaugh, Brian P, 49
Kavanaugh, Charles, 496
Kavanaugh, Michelle, 653
Kavaney, Mary, 8, 133, 252, 255, 288
Kawryga, Theodore, 649
Kay, Jonathan, 273
Kaye, Arnold L, 658
Kaye, Judith S, 55, 256
Kaye, Peter, 603
Kaye, Seth, 516
Kayser, Kraig H, 88
Kazanjian, Arthur P, 546
Keane, Bryan, 458
Keane, Frank W, 113, 350, 375
Keane, Helen A, 456
Keane, Kevin J, 71
Keane, Loretta Lawrence, 482
Keane, William, 146
Kearley, Charles, 282
Kearney, Gavin, 497
Kearse, Diana M, 255
Keating, Robert G M, 257
Keatings, Sheila, 415
Kedley, William H, 544
Kedzierski, Linda, 229
Keefe, Thomas K, 70
Keefer, Elizabeth, 525
Keegan, James W, 399
Keegan, Mark, 119, 282
Keegel, John C, 539
Keehn, Valerie, 441
Keeley, Kevin D, 572
Keen, W Hubert, 614
Keenan, Richard A, 65
Keenan, Vicki R, 107
Keenan-Thomas, Tara, 514
Keene, Gerald A, 411
Kefi, Pamela, 242
Kehoe, Charles, 436
Kehoe, Dennis M, 69
Kehoe, Judith E, 415
Kehoe, Lori, 166, 518
Kehoe, Peter R, 141, 299
Keith, Brenda C, 660
Keizs, Marcia, 471, 621
Kelleher, Daniel, 146
Kelleher, Neil J, 408
Kelleher, Neil W, 8, 157
Kelleher, Terence, 489
Keller, Bill, 597
Keller, Gerald, 423
Keller, Joseph, 397
Keller, Ric, 389
Keller-Cogan, Margaret, 664
Kelley, Barbara J, 396
Kelley, Donna J, 161
Kelley, Douglas S, 665
Kelley, Edwin, 464
Kelley, Rebecca, 62
Kelley, Roger, 546

Name Index

Kellner, Douglas A, 8, 157
Kellogg, Amy, 489
Kellogg, MaryKaye, 471
Kelly, Anisia, 341
Kelly, Ann Marie, 161
Kelly, Carole, 200
Kelly, Charles, 595
Kelly, Charles W, 597
Kelly, Colleen, 73
Kelly, Janet, 453
Kelly, John, 68
Kelly, John W, 69
Kelly, Judy, 603
Kelly, Kim, 489
Kelly, Michael J, 502
Kelly, Michael T, 141, 265
Kelly, Michael W, 120
Kelly, Paul, 146
Kelly, Peter Joseph, 58
Kelly, Raymond W, 433
Kelly, Sue, 218, 314
Kelly, Sue W, 93, 106, 186, 187, 232, 233, 249, 274, 356
Kelly, William, 57, 144, 333
Kelly, William A, 67
Kelly, William P, 471, 620
Kelsey, Lorraine, 276
Kelsey, Valerie, 665
Kemmer, John, 486
Kemp, Whitney, 38
Kempf, Brian, 180, 334
Kempf, Jr, Stephen, 204, 219
Kempke, Darin, 496
Kendall, Bradford, 400
Kendall, Katie, 509
Kendrick, Alice, 659
Kennard, Rebecca, 144
Kenneally, Mike, 460
Kennedy Passantino, Holly, 88
Kennedy, Ambassador Patrick, 205
Kennedy, Brendan, 496
Kennedy, Cheryl, 119, 352
Kennedy, Daniel, 196
Kennedy, Diane, 175, 511
Kennedy, Edward M, 151, 206, 220, 274, 315, 383, 385, 386
Kennedy, John M, 158
Kennedy, Joseph L, 614
Kennedy, Martha, 498
Kennedy, Patricia E, 286, 323
Kennedy, Robert, 518
Kennerknecht, Michael, 40
Kenney, Joan M, 59
Kenney, Nancy, 608
Kenny, Cathy A, 480
Kenny, James E, 60
Kenny, Judith E, 199
Kenny, Raymond P, 118, 351
Kenny, Shirley Strum, 613
Kenny, Teresa M, 437
Kent, Fred I, 236

Kent, William J, 58
Kentoffio, Paul, 199, 297
Kentz, Andrew, 479
Kentz, Andrew W, 539
Kepich, Daniel J, 81
Keplinger, Jean, 438
Kerins, Martin J, 68
Kermani, Peter, 452
Kermani, Ronald, 123, 149, 378
Kermis, Mary Ann, 653
Kern, Cynthia S, 59
Kernan, James M, 558
Kerr, Darlene, 586
Kerr, Gordon, 646
Kerr, James T, 218, 314
Kerr, Michael J, 578
Kerr, Thomas, 329
Kerrey, Robert, 628
Kerrigan, Kevin, 59
Kerry, John F, 106, 249, 274, 384, 385, 386
Kerry, Natasha, 476
Kersavage, Lisa, 509
Kershaw, Lawrence R, 82
Kerwin, Kevin, 269
Kesner, Marcie, 495
Kesper, Raymond, 145
Kessel, Richard M, 117, 170
Kessler, Mark, 571
Ketchum, Cheryl, 413
Ketchum, Richard G, 96
Kett, Barbara, 160
Ketterer, Krista, 19, 375
Kettrick, James, 650
Ketzer, William, 44
Keville, Richard, 658
Kevin, Casey, 522
Keyser, Kathy, 37
Kidder, Stewart, 129
Kiedaisch, Debra, 66
Kiedrowski, Scott P, 160
Kienzle, Ken, 27
Kiernan, Henry, 653
Kiernan, John B, 478
Kiernan, Joseph, 521
Kiernan, Raymond, 426
Kiesel, Diane R, 60
Kiggins, Helen M, 160
Kikendall, Paul, 129
Kikilo, Vladimir, 601
Kildare, Shawn, 118, 351
Kildee, Dale E, 389
Kiley, George, 667
Kiley, Jim, 485
Kiley, Lawrence, 152
Kiley, Thomas M, 175
Killeen, Thomas J, 542
Killian, Patricia K, 447
Killmartin, Bill, 455
Kilpatrick, George, 609
Kim, Byron, 427
Kim, Nancy, 179, 213

Kim, Ron, 441
Kimball, Andrew H, 114, 362
Kimball, William, 79
Kimble, Cynthia, 585
Kimmich, Christoph M, 471, 620
Kincaid, Marianne, 65
King, Barbara, 545
King, Bernard T, 275
King, Carol, 86
King, Charles, 473
King, Craig L, 678
King, Danial, 403
King, Denise, 449
King, George, 198
King, George S, 198
King, Henry L, 108
King, Hon. James P, 125, 163, 202
King, James L, 612
King, Joanne, 432
King, Kathy J, 59
King, Kevin, 481
King, Kevin S, 189
King, Mehrl, 567
King, Peter T, 106, 206, 232, 240, 381, 389, 390, 391, 728
King, Randy, 210
King, Steve, 15, 289, 302, 326, 391
King, Veronica B, 159
King-Festa, Marilyn, 427
Kingston, Jack, 83, 387
Kink, Michael, 234, 319, 473, 492
Kinney, Alison, 266
Kinney, Cassie, 74
Kinney, Janet, 432
Kinsella, Martin G, 88, 125, 337, 379
Kirchgraber, Steven, 5, 90
Kirk, Patrick L, 64
Kirk, Timothy, 138
Kirkland, Galen, 197, 254
Kirkpatrick, Barbara, 513
Kirkpatrick, Robert, 131
Kirnie, Elizabeth, 667
Kirsch, Clifford P, 260
Kirsch, Mark N, 546
Kirsch, Richard, 165, 537
Kirschner, Lewis C, 412
Kirton, Lila, 4, 157, 194, 197, 254, 287
Kirton, Lila E, 243
Kirwan, Thomas J, 40, 44, 45, 46, 103, 292, 698
Kisloski, Jeffrey J, 672
Kisselstein, Bonnie, 424
Kissinger, Mark, 213, 492
Kissinger, Mark L, 223
Kisson, John, 524
Kitson, Anita, 329
Kitzes, Orin R, 58
Kiyonaga, Nancy B, 6, 287, 295
Klafehn, Rodney, 407
Klapper, Oliver, 471
Klar, Barbara, 551

768

Name Index

Kleban, Richard L, 598
Kleiman, Joel, 406
Klein, Barry, 37
Klein, Carol S, 66
Klein, Corey, 424
Klein, David, 69
Klein, George, 103, 128, 202
Klein, Jeffrey, 22, 28, 203
Klein, Jeffrey D, 20, 716
Klein, Jeffrey M, 562
Klein, Jerald R, 60
Klein, Joel I, 120, 149, 428, 429, 656
Klein, John V, 534
Klein, Lynne, 23
Klein, Michael A, 266
Klein, Michael L, 439
Klein, Monte, 14, 296
Klein, Stuart, 432
Klein, Sue, 213
Kleinbaum, Linda, 117, 352
Kleiner, Thom, 437
Kleinmann, Teri, 44, 46, 49, 51, 52
Kleist, Gary, 444
Kleman, Rose M, 574
Klerer, Boris, 587
Klim, Barbara K, 418
Kline, Donald R, 158
Kline, Gregory J, 13, 348
Kline, John, 389
Kline, Robert, 416
Kloch, Richard C, 59
Klonick, Thomas A, 124, 258
Klossner, Carl J, 665
Klotz, John, 523
Kluesner, Ronald, 414
Kluger, Barry L, 119, 352, 377
Klump, Jack, 311
Klyczek, James P, 617
Knab, Sheryl, 156
Knadler, John T, 31
Knapp, Frances A, 158
Knapp, Robert, 208
Knapp, Ronald, 439
Knapp-David, Terry, 132
Knauff, Maj Gen Robert A, 13, 360
Knaust Elia, Karlyn, 412
Knebel, Jerome Z, 397
Knight, Celeste, 21
Knight, Dave, 102, 116, 181
Knight, Michael J, 117, 258
Knight, Timothy P, 595
Knipel, Lawrence S, 56
Knobel, Gary F, 70
Knoblauch, Valerie, 338
Knoll, Patricia J, 66
Knollenberg, Joe, 388
Knopf, Stephen A, 59
Knowles, James, 146, 279, 312
Kobernuss, David N, 566
Kobliski, Frank, 115, 350, 376
Kobrin, Carol, 527

Koch III, Art, 368
Koch, Cynthia M, 150, 339
Koch, Dale M, 575
Koch, James H, 448
Kocsi, James A, 104
Koczak, Steven, 26, 30
Koeleveld, Celeste, 138, 260
Koenig, Thomas, 228
Koessler, Paul J, 114, 350
Kohen, Beverly, 104
Kohl, Herb, 83, 220, 315, 383, 386, 387
Kohl, Lynn M, 64
Kohler, Kris, 505
Kohm, Robert C, 58
Kohomban, PhD, Jeremy, 283, 317
Kohout, Joan S, 65
Kolar, Mary, 525
Kolb, Brian M, 35, 40, 49, 51, 53, 699
Kolb, Joseph A, 541
Kolben, Nancy, 470
Kolberg, Sarah, 39
Koller, Charles, 445
Komanoff, Charles, 174, 357
Komolafe, Joan, 528
Konev, Anton, 50
Konheim, Carolyn, 358
Koniowka, Theodore, 544
Koniuto, Charlotte, 161, 453
Konner, Melvin, 557
Konopka, Stan, 448
Konopko, Deborah, 218, 239, 315
Konst, Kathy, 578
Koon, David R, 33, 40, 44, 46, 50, 51, 54, 81, 103, 183, 217, 699
Koorse, Edward G, 397
Kopcza, Michael, 253
Kopec, Donna, 141
Kopka, Lynn, 521
Kopke, Helen, 436
Koplewicz, MD, Harold S, 280
Kopley, Mary K, 463
Koplovitz, Joshua, 412
Koppel, Jason, 23
Koppel, Lore, 453
Kopy, Michael, 418
Koral, Alan M, 277
Kordich, Mary Ann, 402
Koretz, Eileen, 60
Koris, Nancy, 221
Korman, Edward R, 259
Korman, Manfred, 539
Korn, Bradley, 495
Kornreich, Shirley W, 59
Korotkin, Bruce, 282
Korotkin, Paul, 132
Kortright, Kevin C, 412
Kosakoski, James, 460
Koser, Gail, 4, 307
Koshgarian, Phd, Bryon, 365
Kosier, Andrea, 476
Kosinski, Peter S, 8, 157

Koski, Andrew, 492
Kosky, Robert, 197, 290
Koslowitz, Karen, 407, 435
Kossover, Andrew, 412
Kostik, Andrea, 638
Kotkin, Roberta, 523
Kotlikoff, Michael I, 612
Kotlow, Ellen, 498
Kotlow, Richard, 112
Kotowski, John, 471
Kott, Alan, 212, 279, 308
Koury, John, 32, 53
Koury, Walter C, 406
Kowaleski, Sue, 470
Kozlowski, Mary, 228
Kozora, Charles, 669
Kracher, Frank, 610
Krafchin, Alan, 317
Kraft, Bernard, 405
Kralik, James F, 408
Kramarsky, Susan, 415
Kramer, Amy, 96
Kramer, Barry D, 67
Kramer, Bruce Marc, 60
Kramer, Carol, 440
Kramer, Douglas, 535
Kramer, Herbert, 56
Kramer, Lisa, 489
Kramer, Robin, 495
Krantz, Steve, 216, 254
Krantz, Steven, 4, 129, 134
Krapf, Brian, 459
Krasnopolski, Cathy, 37
Kraus, Jeffrey F, 435
Kraus, Thomas, 581
Kraus, Thomas J, 538
Kraus, William, 53, 203, 292
Krause, Brian, 416
Krause, Kara, 598
Krausman, Gabriel, 55
Krauss, Sarah L, 59
Krautsack, Judith A, 544
Krauza, Kathleen, 62
Krebbeks, Joyce A, 162
Kreitzer, Patricia, 62
Kremer, Arthur, 493, 524
Kremer, Timothy, 480
Kremer, Timothy G, 154, 522
Krens, Thomas, 347
Kreshik, Monica L, 177
Kresovich, Stephen, 100, 148
Kresser, Michele, 437
Kreuz, Dan, 416
Kriedberg, Harvey, 563
Krisel, Martha, 440
Kriss, Mark C, 358, 495
Krogmann, David B, 57
Krohn, Brian, 591
Krokondelas, Peter, 455, 486
Kroll, Steven, 223, 484, 544
Kromphardt, Heidi, 32, 53, 354

Name Index

Kron, Barry, 60
Kronenberg, Frank, 118, 351
Kronenberg, Marc B, 39
Krooks, Bernard A, 320
Krooks, Harold S, 264
Krough, Fred, 309
Krueger, Liz, 21, 22, 26, 27, 29, 31, 231, 292, 303
Kruger, Carl, 22, 25, 27, 28, 29, 31, 32, 103, 203, 217, 313, 716
Kruger, Liz, 716
Kruk, John, 407
Kruly, Kenneth C, 495
Krumenacker, Robert, 607
Krupke, Bruce W, 88, 556
Kruzansky, Charles J, 494
Kryzan, Alice, 568
Krzeminski, Joseph, 439
Krzesinski, Patricia, 541
Kubasik, Keith, 412
Kubecka, Jeff & Lindy, 87
Kucinich, Dennis J, 392
Kud, Joanne, 575
Kuehn, Joseph, 496
Kuehner, Elmer, 593
Kugler, Sarah, 601
Kuhl Jr, John R (Randy), 393
Kuhl, John R (Randy), 186, 233, 356, 381, 388, 393
Kuhl, John R "Randy", 728
Kuhl, Jr, John R (Randy), 151, 233, 240, 274
Kui, Christopher, 316
Kukiela, Mark, 591
Kulak, Antoinette, 658
Kulkin, Peter M, 73
Kulkus, Joseph, 287, 295
Kulleseid, Erik, 14, 179, 334
Kumro, Richard A, 474
Kunchala, Emily, 496
Kuniholm, Peter, 192
Kunkel Jr, Kenneth J, 403
Kunken, Gilbert, 218, 314
Kuntz Jr, Raymond, 547
Kunz, David, 208, 249
Kunzwiler, Mike, 407
Kupferman, Susan, 117, 350
Kurabi, Chloe, 343
Kurkul, Patricia A, 184
Kursky, Manuel, 5, 90
Kurtin, Peter, 138, 260
Kurtz, Adore Flynn, 572
Kurtz, Linda, 311
Kus, Christopher A, 213
Kushner, Jared, 597
Kusnierz, Todd, 25, 28
Kutter, Ann, 18, 247, 271
Kuzdale, John M, 71
Kwiatoski, Debbie, 601
Kyl, Jon, 206, 330, 385, 386
Kyriacou, Mike, 118, 351

La Rock, Steven J, 657
LaBarge, Martha A, 63
Labbe, Normand, 216, 270
LaBelle, Jr, Francis, 346
LaBelle, Kathleen M, 69
LaBelle, Thomas, 299
Labozza, John, 479
Labriola, Steven L, 438
Labuda, Frank J, 68
LaBuda, Kathleen, 411
LaCapra, Louis J, 127, 353
Lacasse, Diane, 566
LaCava, John R, 57
Laccetti, Michael J, 28
Lachanski, William, 211, 278, 308
Lack, James J, 59
Lackman, Abraham M, 152
Lackritz, Mark, 96
Laclair, Darwin, 130
Lacy, Susan E, 184
Lado, Marianne, 497
LaDue, Eddy L, 84
LaFave, Glenn A, 116, 181, 376
Lafayette, Ivan C, 34, 40, 44, 49, 51, 52, 53, 699
LaFayette, Reginald A, 163, 451
LaFrank, Jack, 146
LaGrou, Pamela, 39
Laguna, John M, 367
Lahey, M William, 406
Lahtinen, John A, 56
Lai, Lydia C, 60
Laird, Pete, 138
Lake, Andre, 471
Lake-Maynard, Karen, 406
Laline, Brian J, 599
Lall, Christopher, 428
Lally, Ute W, 58
LaLonde, Carole L, 402
Lalor, Daniel K, 64
Lam, Felix, 430
Lam, Natalie, 497
LaMancuso, John J, 72
Lamarca, William R, 58
Lamb, Charles, 523
Lamb, Rosemary, 13
Lamb, Thomas, 75
Lamberg, Carol, 236
Lambert, Linda, 220
Lamborn, Doug, 393
Lambright, W Henry, 192
Lamendola, David, 176, 527
Lamorte, Nicholas, 472
Lamot, William, 238
Lamphear, Brenda, 577
Lampl, John, 357
Lampman, Wes, 455
Lampson, Nick, 172, 186, 392
Lamster, Ira, 525
Lamy, Frederick C, 122, 137
Lanahan, Peter, 462

Lancaster Beal, Valerie, 619
Lancaster, Patricia J, 427
Lancaster, Vilma I, 419
Lancette, Gregory R, 559
Lancman, Rory I, 40, 44, 45, 48, 49, 699
Lancor, Dan, 289, 302, 326
Landa, Marjorie, 431
Landau, Al, 497
Lander, Bernard, 632
Lander, Brad, 236
Lander, Roger, 416
Landers, Harold C, 404
Landes, Robin, 471
Landin, Teri, 198, 297
Landman, Alan, 248, 271
Landon, Carey, 597
Landon, Douglas E, 404
Landor, Nancy, 484
Landrieu, Mary, 383
Landrieu, Mary L, 386
Landry, Gavin, 338
Landry, Kym, 199
Landry, M Joe, 468
Lane, Howard G, 59
Lane, Jeffrey M, 527
Lane, John P, 57
Lane, Peter, 74
Lane, Robin, 219, 315
Lang, Wilda, 45
Langan, Thomas R, 74
Langer-Smith, Eileen, 133, 252
Langevin, James R, 206, 390
Langevin, Linda, 638
Langhoff, Eric, 364
Langley, Jr, James R, 398
Langlois, James T, 680
Langone, David, 658
Langowski, Stephen, 497
Langton, Phillip W, 652
Lanigan, Gary, 117, 352
Lanigan, Richard, 558
Lanotte, Michael, 476, 490
Lanotte, Michael A, 96
Lansden, John S, 60
Lansley, Jason, 26
Lant, Steven, 486
Lantos, Tom, 106, 240, 390
Lanza, Andrew J, 23, 25, 26, 27, 28, 30, 32, 54, 203, 717
Lanzafame, Ross, 489
Lanzafame, Santo, 535
Lape, William, 130
Lapera, Richard, 65
LaPerche, James, 445
Lapham, Robert D, 540
Lapinski, Leonard, 146
Lapointe, George D, 113, 181
LaPointe, Laurence, 246, 268
LaPook, Judith, 428, 433
LaPorte, Evelyn J, 59
LaPorte, Jr, Nicholas, 533

Name Index

LaPosta, Dore, 185
Lapp, Katherine N, 118, 351
Lappin, Michael D, 234, 474
Larabee, Susan R, 61
LaRaia, Henry A, 64
Laranjo, Michelle, 26
Laraque, Philip A, 555
LaReau, Felicia D, 56
Laremont, Anita W, 9, 91, 99, 116, 124, 230, 231
Laria, Joseph A, 670
Larison, Douglas, 644
Lark, Dolores, 281
Larkin Jr, William J, 20, 31
Larkin, Elizabeth P, 399
Larkin, Jr, William J, 23, 26, 28, 29, 31, 32, 328, 339, 717
Larkin, William J, 25
LaRock, Michelle, 17, 361
LaRocque, Philip, 466
LaRocque, Philip A, 110
LaRosa, John C, 612
Larose, Christine J, 666
Larrabee, Eileen, 14, 179, 334, 374
Larrabee, Paul, 3, 371
Larrow, William, 647
Larsen, Christopher, 184
Larsen, Elizabeth, 495
Larsen, Richard, 185, 204
Larsen, Sharon, 592
Larson, Nev, 604
Lasak, Gregory L, 58
Lasicki, Antonia, 233, 283
Lasicki, Antonia M, 459, 538
Lasko, Kathy, 69
Lasky, Elizabeth M, 468
Lasky, James A, 463
Lasky, Roy E, 224, 468
LaSorsa, Maria, 91, 124, 231
LaSpina ESQ, Bruno J, 542
LaSpina, Rene, 607
Lasselle, Dick, 460
Latella, John B, 60
Latham, Joseph W, 68
Latham, Mike, 80
Lathrop, John, 419
Lathrop, Virginia M, 567
Latimer, George, 40
Latimer, George S, 47, 48, 49, 50, 52, 699
Latman, Joel, 565
LaTourette, Steve, 393
Lattanzio, Joe, 178
Latterman, Carol, 205
Lattimer, Robin, 36
Lattimore, Timothy C, 414
Lattin, C W, 406
Lau, Laurie L, 60
Laub, Michael, 535
Laube, Tim, 410
Lauer, Chaim, 152
Laughlin, Janice, 74

Laundree, Steven W, 159
Laurenti, Shawn K, 127, 353
Lauria, Joseph M, 60, 61, 257
Laurino, Anthony, 536
Laurito, James, 462
Lautenberg, Frank R, 385
Lautneberg, Frank R, 384
LaValle, Kenneth, 25
LaValle, Kenneth P, 19, 23, 25, 27, 28, 29, 30, 31, 150, 717
Lavelle, John W, 46, 50, 52, 450
Lavender, Philip, 504
Lavigne, Ann Marie, 69
Lavigne, Jan M, 62
Lavigne, Mark, 460
Lavine, Charles D, 40, 44, 45, 49, 50, 51, 699
Lavoie, Earl J, 401
Law, Kevin S, 117, 170
Law, Magaret, 20
Lawler, Michael, 5, 211, 278, 308
Lawless, Bridget, 547
Lawless, Daniel A, 549
Lawliss, Timothy J, 62
Lawlor, Brian, 10, 228
Lawney, Milton, 146, 212
Lawrence, C Bruce, 262
Lawrence, Donna, 575
Lawrence, James, 122, 137
Lawrence, James H, 404
Lawrence, Jim, 599
Lawrence, Mortimer, 21, 24
Lawrence, Peter, 139, 261
Lawrence, Peter A, 261
Lawrence, Richard S, 65
Lawrence, Susan, 523
Lawson, Robert, 11, 246, 268, 373
Lawson, Timothy D, 674
Lawton, Julie, 88
Layhee, Judith C, 158
Layton, J Mclane, 171
Layton, Jr, Daniel M, 274
Layton, Sandra, 136
Lazar, Howard, 562
Lazar, Robert W, 110
Lazarou, Robert, 196
Lazarou, Robert W, 301
Lazarski, Andrea J, 122, 201, 336, 378
Lazori, Barbara, 210
Lazzari, Aurelia, 584
Leach, Anne, 416
Leach, Eric, 497
Leach, Jacquelyne A, 128, 337
Leach, Leslie G, 58
Leahy, Aggie, 529
Leahy, Patrick, 383
Leahy, Patrick J, 139, 206, 261, 382, 386
Leak, Barbara A, 75
Lease, Kim, 45
Lease, Peter, 464
Leathersich, Nicolette, 147

Leavitt, Steve, 632
Lebarron, Debora, 484
LeBarron, Sandra L, 178
Lebarty, Okenfe, 479
LeBeau, Janet, 71
Lebedeff, Diane A, 59
Lebous, Ferris D, 57, 59
Lebovits, Gerald, 60
Lebowitz, Alan, 16, 198
Lebowitz, Don, 48
Lebowitz, Jeffrey, 60
Lebowitz, Richard, 57
Leckerling, Richard E, 529
LeClair, Richard D, 420
LeClaire, Lucien, 7, 129
LeClaire, Roger W, 412
LeClerc, Patricia A, 62
Leclerc, Paul, 516
LeClerc, Paul, 432
LeCount, Richard, 411
Leder, Darlene, 29
Lederer, Lynda, 555
Lederer, Neil, 669
Lederman, Evan, 449
Ledina, Burton, 68
Ledwith, Robert A, 550
Lee, Allison, 502
Lee, Angela, 493
Lee, Jin Hee, 497
Lee, Judith, 15, 169
Lee, Karen, 511
Lee, Leon Y, 630
Lee, Margaret, 218, 315
Lee, Robert, 429
Lee, Sheila Jackson, 206, 390
Lee, Thomas F, 8, 237, 279, 311, 372
Lee, Ulysses, 492
Leege, William, 138
Leemann, Barry, 406
Leet, John, 607
Lefebvre, Glenn, 528
Lefebvre, Lora K, 122, 149, 201, 217
Lefkowitz, Jerome, 14, 296
Lefkowitz, Joan B, 57
Lefkowitz, Stephen, 484
Legari, Gina, 159
Lehmann, Mary Anne, 71
Lehner, Edward H, 56
Lehner, Peter, 135, 179, 254
Lehtinen, Ileana Ros, 106, 240, 390
Leibell III, Vincent L, 28, 32
Leibell, III, Vincent L, 23, 25, 26, 28, 29, 362, 717
Leibowitz, Art, 511
Leiby, Robert E, 660
Leigh, Emma, 52
Leigh-Lewis, Benita, 51
Leighton, Gary E, 443
Leins, Richard, 438
Leinung, Mark, 4, 194
Leis III, H Patrick, 57

Name Index

Leis, III, H Patrick, 257
Leitner, Kenneth A, 127, 231, 337
Leland, Jeffrey, 481
Lemieux, Eric, 605
Lemke, John, 131
Lemson, Stephen, 93
Lenaghan, Matthew, 151
Lence, George, 566
Lencina, Chandra, 562
Lendler, Ernest, 164
Lenhard, Robert D, 164
Lenhart, Cindy, 450
Lenihan, Leonard R, 449
Lenior, John, 138, 260
Lennon, Thomas, 583
Lennon, Timothy B, 4, 348
Lent, Donna, 38, 564
Lent, Paul, 408
Lentivech, Douglas, 146
Lentol, Joseph R, 40, 45, 47, 51, 53, 137, 259, 700
Lentovich, Douglas, 212
Lentz, Phil, 486
Leny, Louis C, 82, 218
Lenz, Edward A, 554
Lenz, Michael A, 125, 163, 202
Leo, John J, 422
Leon, Rachel, 165, 207
Leonard, Don, 453
Leonard, Donald, 200
Leonard, Mark, 132
Leonard, Sandy, 425
Leonard, Theresa, 520
Leonard, Timothy J, 196, 301
Leone, Carmine, 184
Leone, Julius, 398
Leong, Lee Che, 514
Leous, Deborah, 126, 353
Lepore, J Robin, 185
Leppert, Richard, 359
Lerner, Aldred D, 202
Lerner, Alfred D, 125, 297
Lerner, Hobart A, 538
Lerner, Joel, 218, 315
Lerner, Robert G, 225
Lesley, Leshaun, 463
Lesnick, Chuck, 445
Lesser, Peter, 342
Lessmann, Steven A, 551
Lester, Harriet, 355
Letellier, Yonel, 41
Letson, Carl, 281
Leung, Edward, 332
Lev, Sara, 427
Leveille, George E, 570
Leveille, Nancy, 510
Leven, Nancy L, 159
Levenson, Scott, 455
Leventhal, John M, 56
Leverett, Ulysses B, 60
Levering, Carolyn, 225

Levernois, Cindy, 484
Levesque, Rev Joseph L, 629
Levin, A Thomas, 265
Levin, Bruce, 673
Levin, Carl, 364, 383, 386
Levin, Kate D, 428
Levin, Rich, 344
Levin, Sander M, 394
Levine, Alan, 58
Levine, Andrew T, 108
Levine, Arthur E, 632
Levine, Bruce, 442
LeVine, David M, 256, 282
Levine, Debra A, 32, 54, 163
Levine, James R, 123, 182
Levine, Joseph S, 56
Levine, Laurie, 41
Levine, Louis L, 628
Levine, Randy, 346
Levine, Richard J, 601
Levine, Shaun Marie, 165, 447
Levine, Theodore A, 264
Levitt, Judith A, 60
Levy, Jill, 500
Levy, Joel M, 286, 323
Levy, Judd, 91, 92, 123, 127, 230, 231, 291, 327
Levy, Mark, 538
Levy, Norman, 499
Levy, Richard, 433
Levy, Richard A, 430
Levy, Steve, 115, 181, 410
Lewinter, Murray, 499
LeWinter, Murray, 468
Lewis, Alan, 227
Lewis, Brett, 196
Lewis, Charles, 511
Lewis, Daniel, 58
Lewis, Evelyn R, 37
Lewis, Gregory, 405
Lewis, Hazel, 131
Lewis, James J, 563
Lewis, Jerry, 83, 171, 329, 387
Lewis, John, 394
Lewis, Jr, Spencer H, 239, 272
Lewis, Kemper, 527
Lewis, Mark S, 672
Lewis, Michael G, 174
Lewis, Paul, 256, 607
Lewis, Sarah, 4, 194
Lewis, Timothy, 420
Lewis, William R, 73
Lewis, Yvonne, 56
Lewis-Martin, Ingrid, 21
Lewyckyj, John D, 196
Lex, Randall, 325
Lhota, Joseph J, 619
Li, Margaret E, 409
Liana, Wilda, 561
Liantano, John, 519
Liberale, Enrico, 547

Liberman, Joseph I, 164, 206, 298, 330, 383, 386
Libonati, Joseph, 548
Libous, Fran, 18, 247, 248, 270, 271
Libous, Thomas W, 19, 23, 28, 29, 30, 31, 32, 53, 292, 354, 717
Licata, James D, 408
Lichtenfeld, Robert V, 676
Licopoli, Lorenzo, 655
Lieb, Judith S, 60
Lieb, Kenneth, 563
Lieber, Robert C, 428
Lieberman, Donna, 242, 514
Lieberman, Ellen, 140, 263
Lieberman, Joseph I, 385
Lieberman, Mark, 493
Lieberman, MD, Jeffrey A, 280
Liebermann, Mark, 444
Liebman, Glen, 284
Liebman, Glenn, 506
Lieffrig, Yvonne, 442
Liegl, Debra S, 572
Liezert, Timothy W, 363
Liff, Bob, 459
Lifson, Robert A, 55
Lifton, Barbara, 47, 53, 239, 272, 313
Lifton, Barbara A, 700
Lifton, Barbara S, 40, 44, 46, 47, 48, 50
Ligeikis, Dave, 349
Lightner, Constance, 444
LiGreci, John, 453
Liguori, Br James A, 626
Lilley, Earl L, 68
Lim, Arnold, 61
Lim, Jr, Howard, 447
Limage, Robert J, 198
LiMandri, Robert, 427
Limberger, Ron, 215
Limoncelli, Ronald E, 653
Lincol, Blanche L, 382
Lincoln, Blanche L, 385
Lind, Gary R, 281
Lind, Suzy A, 38
Linda, Rockwell, 593
Lindahl, Jack, 7, 332
Lindberg, Donald, 407
Lindberg, Thomas, 5, 79, 307
Lindenbaum, Samuel H, 495
Lindenmuth, Susan H, 413
Lindsay, Mark R, 133, 253, 288
Lindsay, Robert, 591
Lindsay, William J, 410
Lindstone, Sean, 517
Linehan, Michael, 589
Ling-Cohan, Doris, 56
Linhardt, Arnold, 524
Linhorst, Stan, 600
Link, Valerie A, 575
Linker, Wayne A, 345, 628
Linn, Susie, 583
Linton, Catherine, 64

Name Index

Lippert, John, 444
Lippman, Jonathan, 136, 256
Lippmann, Robert D, 59
Lipscomb, James L, 479
Lipsky, David, 275
Lipsky, David J, 184
Lipsky, Richard, 499
Lipson, Karen, 503
Lipton, Frank R, 431
Lipton, Jody, 433
Lirtzman, Harris, 16, 197, 290
Lisa, James C, 565
Liske, Anne, 140
Lison, Elizabeth, 656
Liss, David, 516
Liss, Stephen, 43, 47
Liszewski, John, 445
Littenberg, Michael, 503
Little, Bill, 177
Little, David, 522
Little, Elizabeth O'C, 717
Little, Elizabeth O'Connor, 23, 25, 27, 28, 30, 31, 232, 292
Little, James C, 277, 359
Little, Keith, 280
Littlejohn, Doris, 428
Littley, James, 497
Litwin, Leonard, 304
Liu MD, Wellington, 214, 360
Liu, Mike, 184
Liuzzi, Peggy, 470
Liverani, Lynette, 40
Liverzani, Michael, 424
Lividini, Xavier S, 545
Livingston, Helen Ann, 660
Livshin, Peter N, 662
Lloyd, Brandi, 604
Lloyd, Emily, 429
Lloyd, Richard W, 547
Lloyd, Tracy, 24
Lloyd, William K, 656
Lobdell, Robert, 196, 301
Lobis, Joan, 56
Lobosco, Anna, 8, 237, 279, 311
LoCascio, Jr, Joseph R, 576
Locche, Daniel, 466
LoCicero, John, 499
LoCicero, Robert, 212
Locke, Susan B, 597
Locke, William S, 667
Lockhart, Paula K, 133, 253
Lockwood, Roberta Byron, 338
Loder, Earl, 416
Lodes, Carl F, 407
Lodovico, Alfred, 676
Loeffler, Mary G, 448
Loehr, Gerald E, 69
Loeser, Stu, 426
Loew, Martha, 523
Loewenson, Jr, Carl H, 123, 201
Loewenthal, Joanne S, 669

Lofgren, Zoe, 206, 391
Lofrumento, Anthony, 146, 212, 279, 312
Loftus, Michael, 587
Logan, Ernest, 153
Logan, Gerald, 439
Logan, Timothy, 523
Logel, Tracy L, 416
Loglisci, David, 16, 198
Logus, Maria, 256
Lohrer, Leslie, 537
Loiodice, Charles L, 246, 268
Lok, Esther, 483
Lombardi III, John, 424
Lombardi, Francis J, 127, 353
Lombardi, III, Tarky, 545
Lombardi, Jr, Tarky, 486
Lombardi, Michael, 119, 352
Lombardi, Sal, 420
Lombardo, Barbara A, 599
Lombardo, Michael L, 416
Lometti, William V, 186
Londa, Ivan, 636
Lonergan, John, 507
Long, Gregory, 464
Long, Michael R, 447
Long, Richard B, 128, 202, 258, 380
Long, Sharon, 40
Long, Thomas M, 448
Longo, Angela Pedone, 160
Longo, John, 34, 375
Longo, Rosemarie, 38
Longo, Stephen M, 38
Longworth, Sandra, 307
Loomis, David, 7, 133, 311
Loomis, Leslie, 638
Loomis, Peter, 349
Looney, Mark, 496
Loper, William, 365
Lopez Torres, Margarita, 64
Lopez, Edgardo, 310
Lopez, Gene R, 60
Lopez, Norma I, 427
Lopez, Peter D, 40, 44, 45, 47, 51, 103, 202, 217, 700
Lopez, Robert, 146
Lopez, Stephen, 11, 237
Lopez, Vito J, 40, 46, 48, 51, 53, 231, 239, 272, 292, 302, 313, 450, 700
Lopez, Wilfredo, 430
Lopiccolo, Karen, 309
Lopinski, John A, 114, 350
Loprest, Amy M, 166, 427
LoPresti, Lynda, 68
LoPrimo, Laurie, 430
Lordahl, Gerard, 234
Lorentz, John, 654
Lorenz, Jack A, 533
Lorenz, Michael J, 564
Lorenzo, Albert, 59
Lorenzo, Faith, 255
Lorey, Scott, 455

Lorey, Thomas, 401
Loria, Anne L, 634
Lorigo, Ralph C, 447
Lorito, Thomas F, 57
Lorow, Catherine, 157
LoScalzo, John, 121, 291
Losinski, Elizabeth, 467
Losquadro, Daniel P, 410
Losquadro, Steven, 113, 335
Lott, Plummer E, 56
Lott, Sen Trent, 394
Lott, Trent, 172, 384
Lotto, Steven A, 70
Lotz, Christina L, 409
Loughlin, Daniel J, 58
Loughney, Robert M, 539
Loughren, Thomas J, 398
Louizou, Thomas M, 356
Louloudes, Virginia P, 341
Lounsbury, Lee, 143, 308
Lounsbury, Peggy A, 553
LoVallo, Sharon M, 71
Lovelett, Steven S, 200
Lovell, Jeffrey, 20, 28
Lovell, Kelly, 100, 148
Low, Tom, 415
Lowder, Brian, 601
Lowe, Kim, 609
Lowe, Richard B, 56
Lowengard, Daniel G, 659
Lowey, Nita M, 83, 171, 206, 329, 381, 387, 388, 390, 728
Lowman, Wayne, 597
Lowry, Marcia Robinson, 241, 317
Loyola, Guido A, 75
Lozada, Surgida, 496
Lozano, Julieta, 3, 134, 216, 253
Lozito, Gaetan B, 70
Lozzi, Dave, 603
Lubell, Lewis, 57
Lubin, Alan, 456, 480, 567
Lubov, Heather, 432
Lubow, Fran L, 61
Lucas, Frank D, 387
Lucey, Brian J, 529
Lucia, Janene, 86
Lucia, Richard B, 573
Luciano, Mark, 40
Luck, Candace, 200
Ludgate, Kathleen, 104
Ludington, Spencer J, 72
Ludwig, Arnold J, 562
Luft, Martha L, 68
Lugar, Richard G, 106, 385
Lugo, Eric, 471
Luisi-Potts, Billie, 345
Lukas, Susan, 368
Lukasiewicz, Alisa, 416
Lukasik, Tracey M, 577
Lukens, Daniel, 316
Luker, John, 80

Name Index

Lukiewski, Dave, 87
Luks, Allan, 316
Lump, Jennifer, 493
Lundberg, Marc G, 45
Lundberg, Mark G, 48, 51, 52
Lundquist, Gerard P, 419
Lungen, Stephen F, 411
Lungren, Dan, 206, 390
Lunn, Robert J, 57
Lupardo, Donna, 47, 48, 50, 52, 700
Lupardo, Donna A, 40
Lupi, Patricia, 75
Lupinetti, Patrick, 134, 216, 254
Lupkin, Stanley N, 141
Lurie, Alvin D, 330
Lurie, Edward S, 19, 20
Luryi, Serge, 100, 148
Lus, Francis E, 539
Lusnar, Matthew, 511
Lussier, Nancy, 178
Lustig, Esther, 500
Luther, Carole, 22, 30
Luther, Joan F, 161
Luthin, Catherine, 500
Lutz, David, 190
Lutzy, Doug, 169
Luvera, Joseph V, 196, 301
Luvison, Kelly, 594
Lux, Michael, 533
Luxenberg, Arthur M, 548
Lydic, Pamela S, 571
Lyles, Marcia V, 657
Lyman, James, 141
Lyman, Richard, 424
Lyman, Stephen P, 407
Lynam, Elizabeth, 471
Lynaugh, Barbara, 68
Lynch, Edward, 396
Lynch, Harold J, 61
Lynch, Jack, 307
Lynch, Jane G, 6, 309
Lynch, John, 361
Lynch, John P, 319
Lynch, Joseph, 15, 326, 335
Lynch, Kenneth, 178
Lynch, Kevin J, 563
Lynch, Margaret, 171
Lynch, Michael C, 57
Lynch, Patricia, 502
Lynch, Patrick, 142, 300
Lynch, Steve, 397
Lynch, Thomas J, 43
Lynch, William R, 661
Lynch-Landy, Virginia, 491
Lyndes, Lynn, 667
Lynker, Debra, 672
Lynn, Andrew, 502
Lynn, Suzanne M, 435
Lynton, Belinda, 559
Lyon, David, 412
Lyons, Patrick, 456
Lyons, Sarah, 451
Lyons, Thomas, 180, 334
Lyons, William, 79
Lysak, Michael, 605
Lytle, James, 503
Mabee, Jennifer, 474
Macaluso, Gerald, 666
MacArthur Hultin, Jerry, 629
MacAvoy, Harry, 36
MacAvoy, Harry J, 49
Maccarone, Robert, 14, 136
Macchia, Dominick, 549
Macchiarola, Frank J, 631
MacDonald, Edward B, 121, 336
MacDonald, Lawrence E, 561
MacDonald, Paige, 482
Mace, David, 159
MacElroy, Donald C, 114, 350
MacEnroe, John, 517
MacEnroe, Paul, 101, 148
MacFadden, John E, 664
Macielak, Paul F, 489
Mack, Edward, 364
Mack, John, 95
Mack, Lynn, 361
Mack, Martin, 3, 4, 157, 194, 252, 287, 295, 324, 348, 360
MacKay, Frank, 451
MacKay, Robert, 180, 335
MacKechnie, Roseann B, 259
Mackenzie, Jim, 541
Mackenzie, Leslie, 209
MacKenzie, Maureen, 421
Mackey, Robert J, 644
Mackin, Fr Kevin E, 631
Mackin, James J, 597
MacKin, Janet, 626, 629
Mackin, Robert E, 533
Mackle, Jon, 272
Macmillan, Gregor N, 214
MacMillan, Kelly, 37
MacMillion, Michele, 570
MacNabb, Terry, 666
MacNaughton, Robert B, 664
Macomber, Steve, 80
MacPeek, Robert, 423
MacPherson, Melanie, 198
Madalena, Ralph J, 91, 92, 124, 127, 128, 231, 291, 327
Madama, Patrick S, 471
Madden, Joan, 56
Madeiros, Pamela, 488
Madhaven, Jaya, 60
Madigan, Charlotte E, 437
Madison, Floyd A, 440
Madison, Jennifer L, 636
Madison, Linda M, 159
Madlon, Doug M, 424
Madolf, Maureen E, 560
Madonia, Peter J, 426
Madonna, Michael J, 128, 271, 354
Madore, Robert, 552
Madsen, Pamela, 220
Maffucci, Howard S, 652
Magagnoli, Angelo, 541
Magaliff, Gail, 318
Magdon-Ismail, Zainab, 458
Magee, Kathy, 482
Magee, William, 40, 44, 48, 50, 80, 701
Maginn, Marjorie, 568
Magnarelli, William B, 33, 40, 46, 48, 50, 52, 53, 54, 103, 150, 701
Magno, Joseph, 469
Magnusen, Thomas, 582
Magnuson, Karen, 599
Maguire, Raymond, 32
Maguire, Richard R, 71
Maha, Gary, 401
Mahany, David H, 133, 253
Mahar, Jack, 408
Mahar, Jr, Thomas D, 439
Mahar, Kevin W, 310
Mahar, Michael, 187
Maher, Daniel F, 250
Maher, Robert, 676
Maher, Synge, 480
Maher, William L, 74
Mahl, Amy E, 528
Mahon, Kate, 49
Mahon, Roy S, 58
Mahoney, Bryan, 497
Mahoney, Elizabeth, 215
Mahoney, Kieran, 507
Mahoney, Mike, 443
Mahoney, Tom, 198, 290
Mahoney, W Michael, 654
Mahony, Sheila A, 536
Maier, Christopher T, 75
Maier, Philip, 296
Maillard, James, 367
Main, Jr, Robert G, 63
Maione, Brad, 4, 10, 195, 301, 333, 372
Maione, Brad F, 254
Maisel, Alan, 40, 44, 46, 51, 52, 701
Maiuri, John J, 554
Majerus, Kenneth J, 432
Maker Jr, William, 424
Makinson, Carolyn, 244
Makowski, Joseph G, 57
Malafi, Christine, 410
Malaney, Debra, 587
Malanga, Steven, 601
Malara, Joseph J, 568
Malatras, Jim, 45
Malave, Ernesto, 471, 619
Malay, Daniel, 98, 324
Maldonado, Darinka, 514
Males, David J, 610
Maleve, Nelida, 59
Malfitano, Stephen, 421
Malgieri, Patricia, 440
Malgieri, Patrick, 422

Name Index

Malicki, Margaret, 153
Malinoski, Michael, 123, 182
Malito, Robert J, 478
Malito, Stephen A, 478
Malkin, Arthur, 502
Malkin, Arthur N, 503
Mallaber, Elaine, 161
Mallah, Sandra G, 676
Mallalieu, Julia, 45, 47, 50
Mallinson, Todd, 604
Mallison, Victor, 197, 290
Malloy, Alexander C, 232
Malloy, Edward, 536
Malloy, Edward J, 110, 276
Malmud, Rita Z, 445
Malone, Brenda, 471
Malone, Brenda Richardson, 619
Malone, Dr Beverly, 225
Malone, Robert J, 402
Maloney Jr, John C, 263
Maloney, Carolyn, 106, 394
Maloney, Carolyn B, 93, 164, 205, 232, 249, 298, 381, 389, 390, 392, 728
Maloney, Catherine R, 71
Maloney, Councilman John, 417
Maloney, Darlene A, 289, 302, 326
Maloney, Dennis P, 668
Maloney, Jim, 605
Maloney, Kathryn P, 184
Maloney, Rep Carolyn B, 106, 394
Maloney, Richard J, 222
Maloney, Sean, 3, 194
Maloney, Suzanne, 189
Maloney, Suzanne M, 87
Maltese, Joseph J, 59
Maltese, Serphin R, 20, 23, 26, 28, 29, 30, 31, 32, 103, 292, 339, 718
Malvin, Barry D, 557
Mammen, David, 208, 293
Manaseri, Christopher B, 652
Mance, James, 131
Mancini, John, 595
Mancuso, David C, 95
Mancuso, Tom, 304
Mandelker, Lawrence A, 494
Mandell, Lawrence, 323
Mandler, Jim, 222
Maneiro, Saul A, 548
Manella, Carmen, 215
Maney, Gerard E, 61
Maney, James, 285
Mangan, Robert J, 419
Mangano, Jr, Guy J, 59
Mangieri, Vincent, 357
Mangione, Jay, 110
Mangione, Kurt, 79
Mangione, Mary, 10, 11, 179, 334, 373
Mangler Jr, William, 104
Mango, James, 342
Mangold, Nancy M, 257
Manikowski, Michael J, 581

Manion, Nonie, 102, 327
Maniscalco, John, 174, 558
Manko, Thomas, 651
Mann, Monroe Y, 441
Mann, Rachel, 455
Mannella, Carmen, 215
Manners, Myrna, 494
Manninen, Christine, 102, 116, 181, 376
Manning III, Daniel, 400
Manning, Brenda, 532
Manning, J Francis, 659
Mannix, William G, 577
Manoff, Mark, 464
Mantella, Carmella, 353
Mantello, Carmella, 125, 337
Manuel, Warde, 527
Manz, David M, 71
Manzanet, Sallie, 58
Manzano, Venessa G, 241
Manzella, Vito, 211, 278, 308
Manzo, Kevin, 497
Manzullo, Donald A, 391
Mapes, James D, 679, 680
Marabon, Margo, 165
Maraia, John, 546
Marano, Anthony, 58
Marano, Anthony F, 57, 257
Marano, Linda, 20
Marber, Randy Sue, 70
Marcelle, Michael, 638
Marcellino, Carl L, 23, 26, 27, 28, 30, 31, 183, 718
Marchant, Kenny, 164, 298, 392
Marchant, Scott, 296
Marchese, Andrew F, 17, 326
Marchetti, Brian, 309
Marchiano, Frank, 433
Marchione, Danielle, 471
Marchione, Kathleen A, 408
Marchiony, Rob, 208
March-Joly, Jennifer, 471
Marco, Lynn, 474
Marcus, Chet, 362
Marcus, Jed S, 504
Marcus, Martin, 59
Marcus, Patricia, 265
Marcuse, Elizabeth S, 636
Marder, Howard, 430
Mareane, Joe C, 405
Margalit, David, 434
Margeson, John E, 396
Margolin, Ilene, 486
Margulis, Ira H, 59
Margulis, Reed, 190
Mariano, James C, 105
Marich, Cathy A, 161
Marien, Joanne, 677
Marik, Bethanne, 82
Marin, Alan C, 59
Marinacci, Leo, 363
Marinelli, Joseph J, 680

Marinelli, Lynn M, 400
Marinello, Sara S, 529
Marini, Michelle, 42
Marinis, Jr, Thomas P, 554
Marino, Daniela, 576
Marino, Elizabeth, 668
Marino, John, 477
Marino, Ralph, 642
Marino, Rebecca, 23
Marion, Dick, 176
Marion, Ira J, 286
Marion, Lucille A, 618
Marion, Richard J, 560
Mark, Jonathon, 604
Markee, Patrick, 473
Markels, Gail, 342
Markey, Edward J, 389
Markey, Margaret M, 40, 44, 45, 48, 49, 50, 52, 701
Markle, Thomas J, 656
Markowitz, Marty, 403, 435
Marks, John G, 65
Marks, Lawrence K, 256
Marks, Lee, 225
Marks, Lee R, 489
Marks, Patricia D, 65
Marks, Thomas, 198, 290
Markus, Marvin, 434
Markwica, Michael, 673
Marlette, Julie, 522
Marlow, George, 55
Marlowe, Francis, 425
Marmelstein, Joel L, 255
Marmurstein, Mark, 358
Marocco, Mary, 349
Maroldy, Margaret, 568
Maron, Edward A, 70
Maroney, Claudia, 173
Marotta, Anne L, 646
Marotta, Victoria, 415
Maroun, Paul A, 401
Marquette, James A, 439
Marquez, Margaret, 422
Marra, Donna M, 592
Marrano, Frederic J, 73
Marrello, Lisa M, 531
Marren, Tim, 595, 596
Marrero, Louis John, 56
Marrone, M Chris, 407
Marrone, Nancy, 498
Marrone, Vincent, 517
Marrus, Alan D, 60
Marsala, Deborah, 579
Marsh, Helen, 272
Marsh, Kerry D, 504
Marsh, Richard S, 654
Marsh, Warren, 563
Marshall Jr, Dean (Chuck), 421
Marshall, Charles, 44, 47
Marshall, Dale W, 437
Marshall, Frederick J, 57

Name Index

Marshall, Glenn, 426
Marshall, Greg, 340
Marshall, Harold J, 104
Marshall, Helen M, 407, 435
Marshall, Luis, 131
Marshall, Marshall, 662
Marsili, Denise, 68
Marsolais, John, 414
Martella, Rick, 534
Martello, Edward, 81
Marti, Eduardo, 471
Marti, Eduardo J, 621
Martin, Aaron, 32
Martin, Aaron M, 31
Martin, AnnMarie, 411
Martin, Christopher, 273
Martin, Clara L, 161
Martin, Daniel, 59
Martin, Glenn, 498
Martin, James, 403
Martin, Jay B, 497
Martin, Joanne, 52
Martin, John A, 629, 630
Martin, Kathleen, 363
Martin, La Tia W, 58
Martin, Larry D, 56
Martin, Peter, 552
Martin, Robert A, 13, 360
Martin, Robert J, 101, 148
Martin, Ryne R, 595
Martin, Virginia, 211, 278, 308
Martin, Will, 288, 295
Martin, William, 430
Martin, William C, 19
Martin, Willie J, 82, 203
Martinaro, Michael, 436
Martinelli, Esq, Patricia, 13, 281
Martinelli, Michael A, 76
Martinelli, Patricia, 99, 135, 229, 247, 255, 270, 302, 325
Martinez, Guillermo A, 42
Martinez, Mel, 384, 385
Martinez, Miriam, 246, 268
Martinez, Nancy W, 143, 310
Martinez, Yuri C, 563
Martinez-Perez, Myrna, 61
Martini, Deidre A, 261
Martinkovic, Richard A, 411
Martino, Deborah, 441
Martino, Ruben A, 61
Martland, Luke, 133, 253
Martoche, Mary Dee, 63
Martoche, Salvatore R, 56
Marton, Anita R, 498
Marton, Elana, 44, 50
Marton, Gary F, 60
Martuscello, Daniel, 129
Martuscello, William, 404
Martusewicz, Kim H, 64
Marvel, Misha, 464, 507
Marvin, Seth L, 60

Marzeski, Thomas E, 652
Mascali, Robert, 430
Mascialino, John, 488
Mashariki, Job, 365
Masi, Shelly, 497
Maskin, Daniel, 235, 322
Masline, Gary, 13, 238, 373
Masline, Gary W, 119, 282, 377
Masline, Jeff, 458
Mason, David M, 164
Mason, Mark, 605
Mason, Peggy, 582
Mason, Vivian I, 417
Mason-Ailey, Victoria, 525
Massaro, Dominic R, 59
Massell, Martin J, 70
Massetti, John, 246, 269
Massiah, Lesley A, 153
Master, Robert, 536, 538
Masters, Amanda, 497
Masters, Kathleen, 471
Masterson Jr, William H, 442
Masterson, Chris, 444
Masterson, Kathleen, 332
Mastic, Larry, 184
Mastrella, Daniel J, 421
Mastro, Randy M, 619
Mastro, William, 486
Mastro, William F, 55
Mastromarchi, James, 196
Mastromarino, John, 421, 443
Mastropaolo, Mary, 433
Mastropietro, Joseph, 205, 303
Masucci, James F, 440
Matarazzo, John R, 346
Matarazzo, Lou, 460
Matasar, Richard A, 628
Mathas, Theodore, 493
Mathews, Patrick H, 61
Mathison, Gary, 151
Matias, Beni, 341
Matloff, Susan, 488
Matonak, Andrew, 616
Matos, Milagros A, 59
Matott, Harold, 145
Matousek, Janice H, 659
Matson, Robert C, 593
Matta, Heather, 600
Mattei, Suzanne, 523
Matteo, Vince, 482
Mattera-Russell, Pat, 429
Matteson, Lance, 587
Matthews, Cara, 601
Matthews, George E, 567
Matthews, Jean, 431
Matthews, Scott, 609
Matthiessen, Alex, 192, 518
Mattie, John, 511
Mattina, Celeste J, 272
Mattina, Jacqueline C, 7, 132, 311
Mattle, John, 537

Mattson, Carl, 526
Maturo, Deborah L, 405
Matusewitch, Eric, 429
Matusiak, Kathleen, 676
Matuszak, Andrew, 497
Mauer, Donald L, 372
Maupin, Patricia, 444
Maurer, Donald L, 9, 195, 289
Maurer, Eric, 64
Maurer, Richard, 675
Mauro, Frank, 208, 330
Mauskopf, Roslynn R, 138, 260
Mawhinney, Bob, 184
Max, Kevin, 497
Maxwell, Daniel, 310
Maxwell, James, 448
Maxwell, Patricia A, 63
May, Douglas K, 169
May, Jr, Abraham, 429
May, Judy, 639
May, Lyn A, 160
May, MD, John, 87
Mayberry-Stewart, Melodie, 3
Mayberry-Stewart, PhD, Melodie, 6, 168, 195, 371
Mayer, Carol, 493
Mayer, Cheryl, 413
Mayer, Robert H, 15, 169, 374
Mayer, Shelley, 21, 503
Mayer, Susan, 123, 182, 378
Mayers, Al, 605
Mayers, Onida Coward, 435
Mayersohn, Lee A, 59
Mayersohn, Nettie, 40, 48, 49, 701
Mayeux, Richard, 223
Mayo, Margarita, 466
Mayott, Lori E, 558
Mays, James, 523
Mazgajewski, James P, 645
Maziarz, George, 30
Maziarz, George D, 23, 25, 27, 28, 30, 239, 248, 272, 298, 718
Maziejka, Stanley W, 674
Mazza, Dominic F, 403
Mazzaferro, John J, 440
Mazzarelli, Angela, 55
Mazzola, Larry, 184
Mazzulo, Donald S, 489
Mc Gann, Robert C, 60
McAlary, John J, 121, 258, 378
McAllister, James, 69
McAllister, Karen L, 448
McArdle, John E, 20, 375
McArdle, Michael J, 639
McAuliffe, Dennis, 81
McAuliffe, Jr, J Gerard, 401
McAuliffe, Kenneth J, 651
McBrearty, Judy M, 67
McBride, Joseph A, 398
McBride-Bucciferro, Maria, 601
McCabe, Dennis, 254

Name Index

McCabe, Edward G, 58
McCabe, John, 119, 352
McCabe, Matthew, 441
McCadden, Kevin, 511
McCaffey, Kevin, 424
McCain, John, 364, 383
McCandless, Daniel W, 449
McCandless, Frederick D, 123, 182
McCann, Barbara R, 162
McCann, Carole, 570
McCann, Daniel, 676
McCann, Dean, 429
McCann, Jeffery, 420
McCann, Karen, 35
McCann, Kevin, 549
McCann, William, 157
McCarroll, Thomas, 527
McCarten, Randy, 605
McCarthy, Bill, 463
McCarthy, Carolyn, 93, 151, 232, 240, 249, 274, 381, 388, 389, 390, 729
McCarthy, Christopher, 417
McCarthy, James P, 665
McCarthy, James W, 66
McCarthy, John, 673
McCarthy, John J, 127, 353, 380
McCarthy, John M, 474
McCarthy, Judy, 640
McCarthy, Justin, 27
McCarthy, Justin J, 23
McCarthy, Michael J, 17, 349, 664
McCarthy, Robert, 491, 506, 593
McCarthy, Thomas, 417
McCarthy, Timothy A, 128, 337, 380
McCarthy, William E, 55, 57
McCarthy, William F, 65
McCartney, Brian, 15, 101, 230, 289
McCartney, Brian P, 229
McCartney, John G, 355
McCartney, Katherine, 125, 337, 353
McCarty, Edward W, 58
McCarty, Kathleen, 34
McCaul, Michael, 206, 390
McCauley, James F, 540
McCauley, Kyle, 461
McClain, John, 537
McClanahan, Kevin C, 60
McClary, Kevin, 591
McClave, Michele, 220
McCloskey, Jon, 31
McClusky, James P, 126, 183
McClymonds, James, 177
McComb, Bruce, 527
McConney, Norman, 501
McConville, Kevin J, 117, 352
McCooe, William P, 56
McCord, Gerald, 135
McCord, Richard J, 72
McCormack, James P, 65
McCormack, Kathy B, 299
McCormack, Maureen, 499

McCormick, Debra A, 414
McCormick, Edward, 480
McCormick, James P, 86
McCormick, Mark, 401
McCormick, Mary, 173, 293
McCormick, Michael, 79, 329
McCormick, Michael J, 396
McCoy, Alyssa, 48
McCoy, Carole A, 616
McCrary, Michael, 577
McCue, Casey, 80
McCulley, James, 505
McCulloch, Carmen, 232
McCullom, Ellen, 93, 329
McCullough, Bonnie L, 485
McCullough, Jr, Frank S, 121, 170
McCullough, Randy L, 485, 553
McCune, Samuel, 437
McCurnin, Richmond, 229
McCutcheon, Burleigh, 117, 200
McCutcheon, Ray, 595
McDade III, Herbert H, 262
McDermott, Dennis K, 64
McDermott, Jim, 394
McDermott, Marylou, 670
McDermott, Robert J, 16, 326
McDevitt, William L, 550
McDonald Jr, John C, 647
McDonald, Anne B, 116, 181
McDonald, John T, 572
McDonald, Keith, 414
McDonald, Mary Pat, 30
McDonald, Rev Msgr James, 631
McDonald, Richard, 46
McDonald, Robert J, 58
McDonald, Roy, 35, 50
McDonald, Roy J, 40, 44, 52, 53, 702
McDonald, Tom, 461
McDonnell, Brian, 298
McDonnell, Jean A, 17, 326, 374
McDonnell, John J, 566
McDonnell, Patricia, 281
McDonough Jr, Col James D, 360
McDonough, David G, 40, 44, 45, 46, 48, 52, 292, 354, 702
McDonough, Edward G, 161
McDonough, Jr, Col James D, 13
McDonough, Robert, 348
McElheran, Timothy J, 660
McElligott, Denis, 255
McElroy, Edward J, 275
McEnany, John M, 138, 260
McEneny, John J, 35, 40, 44, 47, 51, 52, 53, 702
McFadden, James P, 411
McFarland, Lynne A, 164
McGarrity, Matthew, 651
McGarry, Bernard, 25, 28, 29
McGaw, Ronald J, 74
McGee, Matthew, 471
McGeveran, Tom, 597

McGgrath, John J, 635
McGill, Edward, 484
McGill, Michael V, 677
McGill, Patrick R, 62
McGinn, Irene, 281
McGintee, William, 418
McGinty, Anthony, 69
McGivern, Sr, Frank J, 599
McGivney, Douglas, 399
McGoldrick, Lawrence R, 656
McGovern Jr, Thomas, 444
McGovern, James F, 392
McGovern, Maryanne, 521
McGowan, Coreen, 88, 226
McGowan, Daniel, 489
McGowan, Jeffrey S, 562
McGowan, Kevin, 678
McGowan, Margaret P, 60
McGowan, Peter, 15, 169
McGowan, Susan, 118, 351, 377
McGowan, Thomas F, 673
McGowen, R Moke, 338
McGrade, Philip, 118, 351
McGrane, Jean, 436
McGrath Jr, Jim, 497
McGrath, Ann M, 52
McGrath, Christopher G, 468
McGrath, Dr John J, 108
McGrath, Kate, 430
McGrath, Kevin, 515
McGrath, Patrick J, 67
McGrath, Robert, 520
McGrath, Sharon, 361
McGraw, II, Daniel J, 546
McGraw, Karen, 643
McGraw, Kevin C, 35
McGraw, Thomas J, 560
McGrory, Rebecca, 43
McGuire Jr, William L, 60
McGuire, James M, 58
McGuire, John, 674
McGuire, Joseph D, 57
McGuire, Meg, 596
McGuirk, John, 57
McGurvitch, Max W, 561
McHenry, Barnabas, 11, 179, 334
McHugh, John, 206, 394
McHugh, John M, 205, 298, 364, 382, 388, 392, 729
McHugh, John R, 164
McHugh, Margaret, 493
McHugh, Patrick J, 475, 554
McIntosh, Louis C, 640
McIntosh, Robert, 648
McIntyre, Brian, 345
McIntyre, Mike, 186, 387
McIvor, Jr, Joseph W, 535
McKane, Laura, 444
McKay, Joseph K, 60
McKay, Sandy, 79
McKeage, Louis G, 110

Name Index

McKearin, Francis, 25, 27, 29, 31, 32
McKee, Michael, 525
McKee, Seth, 521
McKeever, Keith, 113, 180, 335, 375
McKelvey, Gerald, 519
McKenley, June, 458
McKenna, James, 338, 422, 578, 669
McKenna, Michael, 443
McKenna, Robert, 436
McKeon, Douglas E, 58
McKeon, Howard P (Buck), 151, 240, 274, 388
McKeon, Jack, 9, 178
McKeon, John P, 440
McKeon, Michael, 507
McKeon, Michael F, 71
McKeon, Robert F, 356
McKevitt, Tom, 41, 49, 50, 51, 239, 283, 702
McKillop, John P, 266, 300
McKinley, Georgene, 569
McKinney, Harold, 131
McKinney, John E, 638
McKinney, Langston C, 75
McKoy, Jeff, 131
McKoy, Richard A, 43
McLaughlin, Alex, 397
McLaughlin, Andrew, 434
McLaughlin, Bill, 143, 309
McLaughlin, Brian M, 52
McLaughlin, Edward J, 60
McLaughlin, John, 249
McLaughlin, Martin, 474, 514
McLaughlin, Robert J, 12, 325
Mclean, Mary Ann, 531
McLean, Mora, 151
McLear, Elaine M, 159
McLeod, James A, 71
McLeod, Maureen A, 61
McLeod, Robert, 484
McMahon, Brian, 110
McMahon, Brian T, 480
McMahon, Daniel, 445
McMahon, Edmund J, 108
McMahon, J Michael, 260
McMahon, James, 465
McMahon, John D, 175
McMahon, Judith N, 59
McMahon, Kathy A, 223, 319
McMahon, Michael W, 672
McMahon, Robert, 407
McMahon, Rory A, 442
McMahon, William, 137, 328
McManus, James, 508
McManus, Michael, 508
McManus, Robert, 596
McManus, Vicki, 71
McMath, Lavita, 471
McMillan, Susan D, 107
McMullen, Joseph, 472, 537
McMurdo, Lisa M, 214
McMurray, Steve, 610
McNally, David T, 483
McNally, Michael W, 566
McNally, Peter, 500
McNally, Shauneen, 552
McNally, Shauneen M, 529
McNamara, Jennifer, 200
McNamara, Scott D, 405
McNamara, Sean, 595
McNamara, Thomas J, 59
McNamee, Francis, 545
McNeil, Odette M, 116, 258
McNeil, Robert O, 410
McNeill, Mark S, 664
McNerney, Scott, 415
McNulty, Marion T, 58
McNulty, Michael R, 219, 315, 329, 382, 394, 729
McPhail, MaryJo A, 662
McPheeters, Jean, 587
McPherson, Anne, 445
McPherson, Ryan, 527
McQuade, Jack, 203, 328
McQuade, Sheila D, 73
McQueen, Gerald T, 121, 336
McQueer, Douglas, 666
McReynolds, John, 105, 260
McShane, Joseph M, 625
McShane, Lois M, 158
McShane, Owen, 348
McShane, Rev Joseph M, 505
McSpedon, William J, 553
McSweeney, Dennis, 273
McSweeney, Edward J, 7, 129
McSweeney, Mary M, 288, 295
McSweeney, Susan, 40
McTague, Barbara, 213
McTamaney, Mary, 436
McTigue, Thad, 198
McTygue, Thomas, 441
McVoy, Cullen, 229
McVoy, Gary, 349
Meacham, Joseph D, 417
Mead, Catherine, 253
Mead, Robert, 448
Mead, Trina, 10, 195
Meany, Dennis M, 109
Meara, Brian R, 506
Meara, Karen E, 432
Meckler, Lawrence M, 126, 353
Medbury, Scot, 187, 341
Meddaugh, Mark M, 68
Medina, Capt Jason, 362
Medizabal, Tara, 528
Meehan, John, 605, 608
Meehan, Marty, 388
Meehan, Robert F, 425
Meekins, Judy, 64
Meeks, Gregory W, 93, 106, 232, 240, 249, 382, 389, 390, 391, 729
Meeks, Sydney, 525
Mega, Christopher, 56
Mehler, Michele, 491
Mehlman, Avery S, 431
Mehltretter, Kathleen M, 139, 261
Meier, John H, 452
Meier, Thomas K, 625
Meierdiercks, Warren A, 656
Meinert, Barbara D, 144
Meinking, Rebecca, 107
Meinking, Rebecca A, 541
Meister, Cliff, 246, 269
Mejia-Gallardo, Armando, 457
Mekeel, Dorothy, 418
Meldrim, Thomas A, 71
Melendez, Edwin, 235
Melendez, Suzanne J, 60
Melita, Richard, 145
Melkonian, Michael, 28, 31
Melkonian, Michael H, 117, 200
Melleady, Ray, 114, 350
Mellin, William, 476, 490
Mellon, David B, 563
Mellow, Gail, 471
Mellow, Gail O, 620
Melnick, Edward K, 655
Melnitsky, Sheldon, 10, 229
Melucci, Ranier W, 655
Melville, James, 637
Melvin, Jerome F, 659
Mena, Carlos, 115, 148
Mencucci, Daniel, 349
Mendelson, Richard, 219, 273
Mendez, Manuel J, 59
Mendez-Santiago, Edwin, 427
Mendonca, Claudia, 482
Mengel, Darlene, 145
Mensch, Rebecca S, 71
Menzel, Terrill, 497
Mercado, Douglas, 468
Mercer, Richard, 417
Merchan, Juan, 255
Mercure, Thomas E, 56
Meredith, Suzanne, 443
Merena, Elizabeth, 333
Merkatz, Irwin R, 227
Merklinger, John M, 440
Merola, Frank, 408
Merola, Patricia, 296
Merrell, Bill C, 303
Merrell, Charles C, 64
Merrick, Greg, 422
Merrick, James C, 403
Merrigan, John A, 540
Merrihew III, Noel H, 400
Merrill, Jeffrey R, 75
Merrins, Marcia, 498
Merritt, James, 436
Merritt, Neil B, 424
Mersand, Stan, 400
Mershon, Mark J, 138
Merton, Vanessa, 141, 266

Name Index

Merz, Tom, 599
Meskill, Peter, 411
Messer, Sharon, 38
Messina, Joseph, 26
Messing, Dean, 400
Metcalf, James M, 74
Metcalf, Slade R, 174
Mettelman, Howard D, 679
Metzdorff, Howard, 257
Metzger, Mary Beth, 196
Metzger, Nancy C, 417
Metzko, Lori, 63
Metzler, Marie, 159
Mevorach, Ben, 605
Meyer, Alan J, 60
Meyer, Christopher, 191, 209
Meyer, Lisa Marie, 74
Meyer, Richard D, 63
Meyer, Timothy, 526
Meyers, Melanie, 484
Meyers, Michael, 243
Mica, John L, 186, 233, 356, 393
Micha, Anthony J, 679
Michaelidis, Gregory, 527
Michalek, Jim, 511
Michalek, John A, 57
Michalski, Dennis J, 9, 195, 289, 372
Michaud, Anne, 601
Michaud, Mike, 393
Michel, David, 586
Michelman, Laurie A, 449
Michne, Ronald, 442
Middaugh, Daniel G, 405
Midey Jr, Nicholas V, 59
Midey, Michael, 666
Mignano, Stephen J, 59
Miguel, Gary W, 442
Mihaltses, Haeda B, 431
Mikol, Gerald, 178
Mikulski, Barbara, 220, 383, 386
Milavec, Nancy S, 407
Milbert, Howard, 470
Miles, Evelyn, 80
Miles, George R, 236
Miletich, Radmila, 479
Miletti, John D, 456
Milin, Maria, 60
Militello, Carl P, 650
Miljoner, Irv, 273
Millan, Hector, 6, 237, 287, 295
Millane, Lynn, 123, 201
Millea, Matthew, 182
Millea, Matthew J, 123
Miller Jr, Richard J, 509, 543, 551
Miller, Amolia, 425
Miller, Brad, 392
Miller, Carolyn J, 61
Miller, Charles B, 421
Miller, Christopher, 427
Miller, Clifford, 97
Miller, Connie Fern, 409

Miller, David, 8, 82, 144, 171, 212, 232, 279, 312, 333
Miller, David J, 187
Miller, Deborah Long, 296
Miller, George, 151, 240, 274, 388
Miller, Glen, 413
Miller, Helen, 227
Miller, Howard, 55
Miller, Howard S, 70
Miller, III, George D, 624
Miller, Jack, 636
Miller, Janet, 471
Miller, Jeff, 393
Miller, Joel M, 41, 46, 48, 150, 163, 702
Miller, John R, 208
Miller, Jonathan J, 401
Miller, Jr, Richard P, 625
Miller, Julie, 448
Miller, Karen, 409
Miller, Marie, 213
Miller, Melvin, 463
Miller, Michael, 242
Miller, Michael S, 257
Miller, Paula, 67
Miller, Randy H, 611
Miller, Rebecca, 69
Miller, Regina, 435
Miller, Robert L, 411
Miller, Sam, 429
Miller, Stephen T, 74
Miller, Steve, 594
Miller, Susan, 439
Miller, Susan E, 12, 325
Miller, Virginia A, 7, 132, 311
Miller, William, 60
Millett, Eileen D, 116, 182
Millham, Joan M, 162
Milliken, Cornelius J, 398
Millman, Joan, 33, 54, 203, 298
Millman, Joan L, 41, 44, 46, 49, 51, 52, 702
Millock, Peter, 511
Mills, Beverly C, 159
Mills, Daniel, 423
Mills, Donna Marie, 56
Mills, Douglas C, 75
Mills, G Foster, 432
Mills, James, 444
Mills, John W, 629
Mills, Melissa, 67
Mills, Richard P, 8, 143, 144, 212, 279, 312, 333
Mills, Thomas E, 400
Milot, Michelle, 50
Milton, Karen, 259
Minard, Joyce M, 580
Minardo, Philip G, 56
Minarik, Hon Renee Forgensi, 265, 294
Minarik, III, Stephen, 453
Minarik, Renee Forgensi, 59
Minarik, Stephen, 452
Mincher, Rachael L, 300

Mincher, Rachel L, 142
Miner, George, 572, 585
Miner, Glenn R, 16, 136, 374
Miner, Lucinda, 675
Minerva, Anthony A, 442
Mingione, Emanuel J, 355
Minissale, Theodore T, 228
Minoia, Mark, 415
Minort, Donna, 69
Minott, Janice, 511
Mintz, Jonathan, 428
Mintz, Joseph D, 57
Mio, Peter L, 598
Mirabal, Jose, 218, 314
Mirabito, Jerome A, 72
Miraglia, Peter, 309
Miraglia, Richard, 280
Miranda Jr, Luis A, 508
Miranda, David P, 174
Miranda, Jr, Luis A, 176
Miras, Richard, 118, 351
Mirch, Robert, 408
Miringoff, Lee M, 165
Mirones, Matthew, 52
Mirras, Michael J, 410
Mirsaidi, Ramin, 497
Misa, Elizabeth, 491
Misiaszek, Michael J, 74
Mistur, Andrew, 497
Misztal, William J, 560
Mitchell, Charles, 425
Mitchell, Christine, 418
Mitchell, Dave, 443
Mitchell, Guy H, 255
Mitchell, Harry E, 393
Mitchell, Hugh, 523
Mitchell, III, Calvin, 92
Mitchell, Linda M, 450
Mitchell, Maria K, 454
Mitchell, Patricia, 17, 101, 327
Mitchell, Ric, 605
Mitchell, Richard C, 407
Mitchell, Robert S, 418
Mitchell, Stuart J, 323
Mitchell, Susan T, 204, 328
Mitchell, Teresa, 346
Mitchell, Thomas, 133, 253, 288, 311
Mitchell, Tom, 606
Mitchell, William, 204, 328
Mitchell, Wilson E, 542
Mitchell-Herzfeld, Sue, 310
Mithen, Lori, 460
Mitnick, Steve, 3, 168
Mittleman, Michael, 6, 168, 195
Mix Sr, Gary T, 649
Mizbani, Reza, 4, 307, 371
Mizel, Marianne O, 69
Mizerak, John, 282
Mobley, Charla Beth, 466
Moccia, Josephine, 663
Mock, Janice F, 63

Name Index

Modafferi, Vincent, 566
Modica, Deborah S, 60
Modica, Salvatore J, 60
Moehle, William, 415
Moerdler, Charles G, 120
Moesel, Jamie A, 650
Moffett, Josephine N, 676
Moffre, Dennis, 196
Mogulescu, John, 621
Mogulescu, William I, 60
Mohan, Satish B, 414
Mohr, Ralph M, 158
Mokhiber, Lawrence H, 146, 212
Mokryzcki, Ken, 442
Mole, Tina, 399
Molea, Richard, 57, 59
Molia, Denise F, 58
Molina, Michael A, 505
Molinari, Laura, 418
Molinaro, James P, 408, 435, 447
Molinaro, Marcus, 41, 45, 46, 48, 49, 50, 703
Moline, Ronald H, 442
Molineaux, Renea, 23
Molinet, Robert T, 542
Moll, Steven, 493
Mollen, Gerald F, 397
Mollenkopf, John Hull, 165
Mollohan, Alan B, 387
Mollot, Richard, 500
Molluso, Christopher, 25
Momot, Kevin, 598
Momplaisir-Ellis, Marjorie, 471
Monachino, Benedict J, 7, 132, 311
Monaco, Anthony, 497
Monaco, Eugene J, 286
Monaco, Michelle, 588
Monahan, Brian, 664
Monahan, Marianne, 631
Monahan, Matthew, 428
Monahan, William, 582
Monastra, Joseph, 59
Mondanaro, Mark P, 659
Mondello, Joseph, 453
Mondello, Joseph N, 166
Mondo, Suzanne M, 60
Mondrick, Lynne, 74
Mone, Lawrence J, 208
Mongold, Edward D, 443
Monroe, James E, 249
Monson, Charles, 211, 278, 308
Montalbano, Vincent, 508
Montalto, Stacey, 484
Montana, Joseph, 414
Monte, Vincent, 450
Monteiro, John, 309
Montes, Luis, 42
Montfort, Bill, 451
Montfort, William A, 162
Montgomery, Robyn L, 42

Montgomery, Velmanette, 21, 23, 27, 29, 31, 217, 314, 718
Montgomery-Costa, Veronica, 153, 299
Moody, Brian, 196
Moody, Joseph M, 587
Moody-Czub, Jacqueline, 5, 79
Moon, ACCS Mark, 355
Mooney, James H, 409
Mooney, Joan P, 162
Mooney, Jr, William M, 588
Moore Wilke, Meghan, 471
Moore, Andrew, 404
Moore, Art, 609
Moore, Catherine, 599
Moore, David T, 440
Moore, Edward, 441
Moore, Garrie, 472
Moore, Garrie W, 619
Moore, Gary D, 403
Moore, John, 610
Moore, John S, 60
Moore, Joseph B, 481, 614
Moore, Kathleen, 38
Moore, Linda D, 448
Moore, Michele M, 321
Moore, Rick T, 640
Moore, Robert, 481
Moore, Ruth, 5, 79
Moore, Tasha, 238
Moore, Vickie, 434
Morabito, Robert A, 441
Morahan, Thomas P, 23, 25, 26, 27, 28, 30, 32, 239, 283, 718
Morales MD, Hugo M, 619
Morales, Marisel, 232
Morales, Mirza Negron, 232
Morales, Ricardo, 430
Moran, James F, 13, 281
Moran, Jerry, 186, 387
Moran, Karin, 510
Moran, Leslie, 544
Moran, Leslie S, 489
Moran, Marc, 178
Moran, Michael, 458
Moran, Thomas E, 403
Morange, William, 117, 352
Mordue, Norman A, 259
Moreau, Karen, 25, 31
Moree, Margaret, 269, 312
Moree, Margaret M, 12
Morehouse, Max, 168, 195
Morella, Kimberly, 102, 124, 379
Morelle, Joseph D, 41, 46, 48, 51, 53, 339, 450, 703
Morello, Charles, 300
Moreno, Joseph, 363
Moretti, David, 118, 351
Morgan DC, Peter H, 555
Morgan Jr, Paul, 67
Morgan, Don, 603
Morgan, Edward, 453

Morgan, Frederick J, 658
Morgan, Karen H, 68
Morgan, Margaret, 428
Morgan, Matthew, 80
Morgan, Matthew A, 509
Morgan, Michael J, 563
Morgan, N Robin, 184
Morgan, Stephen D, 359, 483
Morgan, Susan, 399
Morgenthau, Robert M, 405
Morgiewicz, Riele, 474
Moriarity III, Jeremiah J, 59
Moriarity, Paul, 60
Moriarty, Jacki, 498
Moriarty, Marvin, 339
Moriarty, Marvin E, 185
Moriarty, Michael, 562
Morik, Helen, 516
Morin, Matt, 609
Morinello, Angelo J, 73
Morley MD, John N, 214
Moroney, Frank, 28
Morrick, Clive I, 432
Morris, Bill, 450
Morris, Brian, 572
Morris, David J, 403
Morris, Jennifer, 497
Morris, Karen, 510
Morris, Mitchell, 198
Morris, Pat, 438
Morris, Robert E, 560
Morris, Scott, 527
Morris, Shawn, 414
Morris, Tim, 460
Morrisey, Michael R, 66
Morrison, Gary L, 175
Morrison, Marvin D, 138
Morrissey, Deadra, 31
Morrissey, James, 130
Morrissey, Joseph, 5, 211, 278, 308, 371
Morrissey, Michael, 172
Morrone, Thomas L, 452
Morse, Geoff, 245
Morse, Joy V, 66
Morse, Jr, Richard D, 33, 54, 81, 183, 184, 217
Morse, Thomas R, 74
Morton, Cynthia, 130
Morton, John, 606
Moscicki, Ronald, 131
Mosconi, Toni, 594
Moser, Dan, 47, 49, 50
Moses, C Warren, 317
Moses, Catherine L, 400
Moses, Clifford, 664
Moses, Ryan, 452
Moses, Stanley, 233
Mosiello, Louis A, 7, 132, 311
Moskovitz, David, 455
Moskowitz, Karla, 56
Moskowitz, Lewis, 436

Name Index

Moskowitz, Steven, 153
Moslow, John J, 414
Moson, Robert, 425
Moss, Adam, 602
Moss, Christopher, 398
Moss, Dennis, 314
Moss, Mitchell, 235, 294
Moss, Ron, 218, 315
Moss, Violet, 470
Mostert, Eric, 101, 327
Mostow, Michael, 670
Motler, Mark, 551
Mottola Schacher, Nancy, 160
Mouillesseaux-Kunzman, Heidi, 84
Moulton, Peter H, 59
Mount, Chester, 257
Mountain III, William H, 74
Moussavian, Avideh, 493
Moustakas, Nicholas, 525
Mowl, Jr, Harold, 155
Moya, Minerva, 493
Moyer, Edna, 566
Moynihan, Eamon, 16, 101, 180, 199, 291
Moyse, Matthew W, 31
Mozdzier, Marti, 587
Mraz, James, 575
Mrijaj, Lisa, 445
Mucci, Dominic, 655
Muehl, John M, 407
Mueller, I Lynn, 108
Mueller, Robert, 421
Mueller, Robert J, 114, 335
Mugdan, Walter, 185
Mugglin, Carl J, 56
Mujica, Robert, 20, 28
Muldoon, Robert, 523
Mulford, Ruth, 506
Mulhall, John, 448
Mulhern, John, 497
Mulholland, Jack, 644
Mullally, Darlene, 51
Mullane, Robert, 174
Mullaney, Richard P, 424
Mullaney, Roxanne C, 82
Mullen, Joseph, 11, 246, 268
Mullen, Michael F, 59
Mullen, Shirley, 626
Mullen, Stephen B, 561
Muller, William J, 138, 260
Mullgrav, Jeanne B, 435
Mulligan, Bernie, 551
Mulligan, Jeff, 434
Mulligan, Kevin R, 643
Mullin, Sandra, 430
Mullings, Pauline, 60
Mulqueen, Cliff, 431
Mulroy, Martha E, 66
Multer, Robert N, 413
Mulvey, Robert C, 57
Mummenthey, Carl J, 665
Munday, Conny, 416

Mundinger, Mary, 525
Muney, Alan, 526
Mungari, Robert J, 80
Munger, Arthur, 447
Muniz-Hoyos, Inez, 60
Munn, Norma, 459
Munn, Norma P, 344
Munnelly, Ken, 49
Munoz, Frank, 146, 212, 279, 312
Munro, Diane M, 640
Munson, Lauralee, 458
Murad, David A, 66
Mural, Catherine, 25
Murdoch, Lachlan, 596
Murell, Matt, 6, 143, 310
Muriana, Joseph P, 505
Murkowski, Lisa, 384, 385
Murley, James, 420
Murphy Jr, Cornelius B, 613
Murphy McGraw, Denise, 463
Murphy, Alan, 56, 65
Murphy, Alicia, 587
Murphy, Barbara, 199, 291
Murphy, Brian, 497
Murphy, Charles, 670
Murphy, Col Patricia M, 365
Murphy, Daniel C, 346, 525, 553
Murphy, Diane, 64
Murphy, Ed, 450
Murphy, Ellen, 329
Murphy, Emy, 143, 309
Murphy, Glenn A, 70
Murphy, III, James A, 408
Murphy, III, Matthew J, 405
Murphy, J Emmett, 57
Murphy, James P, 57
Murphy, Jean, 439
Murphy, Jim, 594
Murphy, John, 400, 477
Murphy, John J, 559
Murphy, Joseph R, 673
Murphy, Karen, 58
Murphy, Kevin, 585
Murphy, Linda, 397
Murphy, Martin P, 61
Murphy, Michael, 488
Murphy, Mike, 593
Murphy, Patrick T, 128, 337
Murphy, Penny, 108
Murphy, Rich, 32, 53
Murphy, Rick, 597
Murphy, Robert C, 71
Murphy, Robert J, 538
Murphy, Sheree, 458
Murphy, Thomas J, 57, 516
Murray, Cheryl, 200
Murray, Dennis J, 627
Murray, Dr Martha, 661
Murray, Eugene J, 440
Murray, Greg, 375
Murray, Gregory, 257

Murray, JoAnne, 585
Murray, Kate, 421
Murray, Kathleen, 442
Murray, M Matthew, 665
Murray, Meg, 348
Murray, Patricia L, 157
Murray, Patty, 383, 386
Murray, Reginald, 471
Murray, Robert, 589
Murray, William, 198
Murrin, Sandra, 470
Murry, Arlene, 355
Murtagh, Wanda D, 401
Murtha, Beth, 570
Murtha, John P, 387
Muscarella, Joseph, 289, 302, 326
Musegaas, Phillip, 518
Musgrave, Marilyn N, 186, 387
Musolino, Mario, 12, 246, 269, 312, 360
Musser, Martha, 145
Mustich, Peter J, 677
Musumeci, MaryAnn, 364
Mutch, Susan, 9, 195, 289
Mutua, Makau, 243
Muyskens, James, 472
Muyskens, James L, 621
Myers, Anne C, 614
Myers, Brenda, 672
Myers, Doug, 113, 350, 375
Myers, Gail, 307
Myers, Michele Tolela, 630
Myers, Patricia, 439
Myers, Patricia A, 153
Myers, Robert, 280
Myersr, Gail, 307
Myler, Colin, 596
Mysliwiec, Mary Ann, 113, 350
Myszka, Edward, 646
N'dolo, R Michael, 588
Naber, Mae N, 442
Nabozny, Michael P, 158
Nacerino, Melissa, 163
Nacleau, Katherine, 481
Nadeau, Edward, 559
Nadel, S Michael, 59
Nadelson, Eileen N, 59
Nadler, Jerrold, 139, 186, 233, 261, 356, 382, 391, 393
Nadler, Jerrold L, 730
Naeris, Urmas, 120, 230
Nagaraja, Mysore L, 118, 351
Nagengast, Mary Ellen, 101, 327
Nagle, Richard, 180, 199, 291
Nagler, Tracy, 537
Nahman, Robert L, 67
Najarian, Michael A, 449
Nalamasu, Omkaram, 100, 148
Nanez, Irma, 184
Napierski, Carol, 555
Napoli, David, 131
Napoli, Katherine, 213

Name Index

Napolitani, Don, 603
Napolitano, Diana, 519
Napolitano, Grace F, 172, 391
Napolitano, Ralph, 678
Nardelli, Eugene, 55
Nardozzi, John, 147
Nasca, Samuel, 300, 359
Nash, John, 440
Nass, Melvin P, 89
Nastasi, Aldo, 57
Nathan, Larry, 224
Nathan, Richard P, 209, 331, 611
Nathan, Sandra, 296
Nation, Bernadette, 434
Natoli, David J, 28
Navone, Sperry J, 25
Nayowith, Gail, 471
Nayowith, Gail B, 241, 317
Nazarko, Michael, 214
Neal, Richard E, 394
Nealis, Nora, 537
Neals, Linda, 420
Nease, Gary, 606
Nebush Jr, Frank J, 405
Nedd, Michael D, 185
Neel, Roger, 603
Neely, Larry, 595
Neff, Jeanne H, 630
Negus, Lisa, 101, 327
Neidhart, John G, 542
Neidl, Michael, 526
Neidrich, Edward A, 436
Neiman, Richard H, 5, 90
Neira, Maria, 456
NeJame, Samir S, 502
Nellenback, Marie, 414
Nelligar, James, 281
Nelson, Ben, 383
Nelson, Bill, 172, 383, 384, 385
Nelson, James, 425
Nelson, Norman R, 96
Nelson, Robert F, 87
Nelson, Sheila, 489
Nelson, Stephen D, 11, 246, 268
Nelson, Sylvie D, 584
Nelson, William K, 67
Nemeth, Frank, 490
NeMoyer, Patrick H, 57
Nenno, Michael L, 62
Nephew, Kevin, 168, 195
Nesbitt Jr, Charles H, 406
Nesbitt, Charles H, 16, 326
Nesbitt, John B, 69
Nesbitt, Ronald, 444
Nesich, Jeffrey, 14, 135
Nestle, Gary, 404
Nestor, Christine, 63
Neubauer, Suh, 607
Neuburger, Jeffrey D, 262
Neugebauer, Lynn, 521
Neugebauer, Randy, 186, 387

Neuhaus, Rachel, 545
Neumaier, Gerhard J, 188
Neuner PhD, Jerome L, 495
Neustadt, David, 11, 215, 245, 373
Neville, Elizabeth A, 442
Neville, John, 593
Newcomb, Lisa, 222
Newdom, Fred, 551
Newell, Betty, 576
Newell, Donald, 285, 320
Newell, Patti Jo, 472
Newhouse, Mark, 434
Newkirk, Kathleen A, 415
Newman, Barbara F, 60
Newman, Glenn, 434
Newman, John, 605
Newman, Roger, 430
Newmark, William, 447
Newton, Juanita B, 59, 60
Newton, Juanita Bing, 256, 257
Ng, Anthony, 526
Ng, Darryl, 485
Ng, Sylvia, 516
Nicalozzo, Frank, 366
Nicchi, Frank J, 628
Nicholas, Wendy, 235
Nicholls, Michelle, 458
Nichols, Brian C, 418
Nichols, George, 493
Nichols, Jonathan D, 62
Nichols, Karen A, 67
Nichols, Maclain, 451
Nichols, Nancy, 619
Nichols, Scott, 608
Nichols, Tim, 42
Nichols, Timothy, 221
Nicholson, Col Tracy E, 362
Nicholson, John D, 564
Nicholson, Marsha, 234
Nicholson, Mary C, 36
Nichols-Tomkins, Kathy, 576
Nickerson, Shawn P, 437
Nicklas, Don, 309
Nickson, Amy, 50
Nickson, Don, 522
Nicol, Richard A, 638
Nicolai, Francis A, 57, 257
Nicolas, Sam, 197, 290
Nicolas, Samuel, 197, 290
Nicoletta, Gavin S, 169
Nicoletti Jr, Joseph, 445
Nicolino, Lynda, 117, 170
Nicols, Henry J, 161, 450
Niebel, Terry, 158
Niedermaier, Kevin, 403
Nielsen, David, 602
Nielsen, Peter, 188
Nielson Jr, Robert N, 23
Nieter, William, 126, 183, 337
Nieves, Ines, 6, 310
Nightingale, Thomas, 212, 279, 308

Niles, Carl G, 428
Nitido, Thomas, 414
Nixon, Dottie, 361
Nixon, R Andrew, 338
Noble, James L, 423
Noble, Melvin S, 671
Noble, Michael A, 96
Nocciolino, Albert, 541
Nocenti, David, 3, 4, 12, 79, 90, 98, 129, 143, 157, 168, 177, 194, 211, 228, 237, 245, 252, 254, 268, 278, 287, 295, 301, 307, 324, 332, 348, 360
Nocerino, Frank A, 121, 291, 292
Noel, Cecile, 431
Noel, Indira, 21, 46
Noel, Marian, 118, 351
Nojay, William R, 116, 258
Nolan, Bill, 577
Nolan, Catherine, 46, 150
Nolan, Catherine T, 41, 46, 51, 52, 53, 703
Nolan, Daniel, 441
Nolan, John, 453
Nolan, Phil, 422
Nolan, Thomas D, 57
Nolte, Betty, 41
Noonan, Glenn P, 411
Noonan, Peter T, 417
Noonan, Robert C, 64
Noonan, Rosemarie, 234, 293
Noreault, Ricky, 526
Norfleet, Kevin, 361
Norfleet, Sandra, 145
Noriega, Ruth, 310
Norlander, Gerald A, 175, 517
Norling, Peter, 138, 260
Norman, Juanita, 257
Normile, Michael, 17, 313
Norris, Kelly K, 111
Norris, Melvin, 527
Norris, Robert D, 84
North, Charles S, 583
Northrup, Jane, 563
Northrup, Jr, Richard D, 399
Northrup, Michael J, 160
Norton, Eleanor Holmes, 233
Norton, Lee, 63
Nortz, Ann, 473
Nortz, Ann M, 159
Norwich, William, 118, 351
Nostaja, Scott, 527
Notaro, Rosanne, 5, 90
Nott, Jordan, 504
Novacich, Steve, 147
Novack, Michael, 56
Novak, Greg, 165
Novakovic, Andrew, 85
Novakowski, Michael, 17, 349
Nowak, Christin, 44
Nowak, Edward J, 404
Nowak, Henry J, 71
Nowak, Kathy, 198, 297

Name Index

Nowak, Norma, 527
Nowak, Ron, 598
Nowogodzki, Susan, 48
Nowosilski, Audra, 52
Noyes, Brandon, 98, 324
Noyes, Pamela, 356
Nozzolio, Michael F, 20, 23, 27, 28, 30, 31, 32, 137, 239, 718
Nudelman, Jodi, 219, 315
Nulty, Kevin A, 437
Nunez, Bernie, 175
Nunez, Patricia M, 60
Nurse, Sir Paul, 630
Nussbaum, Dale, 472
Nussbaum, Steven, 69
Nusser, Janie L, 666
Nuttall, John, 7, 132
O' Brien, Ellen, 577
O'Beirne, Richard, 538
O'Brien II, J William, 419
O'Brien Jr, Frank E, 538
O'Brien, Dennis M, 568
O'Brien, Gary, 13, 119, 238, 282
O'Brien, James J, 225
O'Brien, Joseph E, 34
O'Brien, Kerri, 98, 324
O'Brien, Kevin P, 13, 348
O'Brien, Margaret J, 547
O'Brien, Mark, 266
O'Brien, Michael T, 397
O'Brien, Michelle, 485
O'Brien, Neil F, 641
O'Brien, Paul J, 107
O'Brien, Paula, 531
O'Brien, Philip, 609
O'Brien, Robert, 118, 351
O'Brien, Sean, 246, 268
O'Brien, Sean D, 214
O'Brien, Sister Mary Eileen, 624
O'Brien, Stewart D, 560
O'Brien, Timothy, 135
O'Brien, Virginia, 408
O'Brien, William J, 70
O'Brien, William S, 125, 149, 297
O'Brien-Jordan, Debora, 269
O'Bryne, Charles, 371
O'Buckley, Kevin, 349
O'Byrne, Charles J, 4, 194
O'Connell, Daniel, 104, 213
O'Connell, Estelle, 305
O'Connell, Geoffrey J, 58
O'Connell, Maureen, 404
O'Connell, Tom, 196, 301
O'Conner, Kelli, 200
O'Conner, Marthea, 491
O'Connor Little, Elizabeth, 29
O'Connor, Jack M, 567
O'Connor, Jenn, 522
O'Connor, John, 641
O'Connor, John J, 611
O'Connor, Karen, 67

O'Connor, Kevin, 196, 301, 479
O'Connor, Marilyn L, 65
O'Connor, Michele, 491
O'Connor, Shaun A, 641
O'Connor, Terrence C, 160, 429
O'Connor, Thomas, 5, 98
O'Connor, Thomas J, 102, 124
O'Conor, Sharon, 125, 337, 353
O'Dea, Katherin, 223
O'Dea, Katherine, 190
O'Dea, M Suzanne, 162
O'Dell, Mary, 158
O'Dell, Sharon, 399
O'Dell, Twila, 410
O'Donnell PE, John A, 113, 350
O'Donnell, Brian, 597
O'Donnell, Charles J, 540
O'Donnell, Daniel J, 41, 45, 47, 49, 50, 52, 703
O'Donnell, Denise E, 7, 133, 252, 288
O'Donnell, Ellen, 680
O'Donnell, Frances, 145
O'Donnell, Jack, 524
O'Donnell, Jeff, 45
O'Donnell, John F, 57
O'Donnell, Kathleen M, 558
O'Donnell, Kathy, 224
O'Donnell, Patricia, 417
O'Donnell, Patricia A, 564
O'Donnell, Terry, 605
O'Donoghue, Mary, 60
O'Donoghue, Peter, 58
O'Donovan, James, 305
O'Dowd, Col John B, 205, 364
O'Flaherty, Elizabeth, 483
O'Flynn, Patrick M, 404
O'Grady, Hannah, 533
O'Hagan, Al, 573
O'Hara, Daniel, 80
O'Hara, Joseph J, 542
O'Hare, Lauren, 53
O'Hearn, Annemarie, 509
O'Hearn, Timothy M, 409
O'Hearn, Warren E, 551
O'Keefe, Francis X, 412
O'Keefe, James, 15, 289, 302, 326
O'Keefe, Kathleen, 45, 47
O'Keefe, Timothy, 270
O'Keeffe, Valerie Moore, 424
O'Kelly, Eamon, 479
O'Laughlin, Michael C, 679
O'Leary, Brian, 482
O'Leary, Dennis, 331
O'Loughlin, Jr, William A, 246, 268
O'Loughlin, Michael, 502
O'Malley, Flora, 443
O'Malley, Ute, 428
O'Mara, John F, 122, 258
O'Mara, Marilyn, 158
O'Mara, Thomas, 47, 49, 170

O'Mara, Thomas F, 35, 41, 44, 47, 49, 52, 703
O'Meara, Dianne, 416
O'Meara, Michael, 460
O'Neal, James, 528
O'Neil, Richard L, 552
O'Neill, Barbara M, 36
O'Neill, James R, 155, 347
O'Neill, June, 449, 450
O'Neill, Kathleen, 28
O'Reilly, Eileen, 120, 230
O'Reilly, Kevin P, 631
O'Rourke, Andrew P, 57
O'Rourke, Deborah A, 159
O'Rourke, Jeanne, 162
O'Shaughnessy, Brian, 496
O'Shaughnessy, Nancy Curry, 605
O'Shea, Ann E, 59
O'Shea, John V, 113, 181
O'Shea, Judith F, 57, 257
O'Shei, Tim, 592
O'Sullivan, Gerard M, 642
O'Sullivan, Margaret, 597
O'Sullivan, Michael F, 600
O'Sullivan, Timothy, 117, 258, 377
Oakes Jr, Jack Stanley, 626
Oakley, David, 503
Oaks, Robert, 49, 202
Oaks, Robert C, 35, 41, 44, 47, 49, 51, 703
Oats, Tracy A, 91, 92, 124, 127, 128, 231, 291, 327, 379, 380
Obenauer, Cheryl Lidell, 69
Oberlander, Lynn, 266
Obermayer, Stephen J, 535
Oberstar, James L, 186, 233, 356, 393
Obertubbesing, Edward, 246, 268
Obey, David R, 83, 171, 329, 387, 388
Obie, Stephen J, 81, 104
Obus, Michael J, 60
Ochrym, Ronald, 468
Ochs, Mark S, 255
Oddo, James S, 427
Odell, Ralph, 180, 334
Odnoha, Carol, 528
Oechsle, G Russell, 57
Oechsner, Troy, 11, 245
Ofer, Udi, 514
Offensend, David, 432
Ogden, E Jeanette, 71
Ogilvie, Donald A, 679
Oglesby, Debra, 79
Ognibene, Michael, 435
Ohanesian, Susan, 142
Ohrenstein, Manfred, 512
Oing, Jeffrey K, 59
Okatieuro, Gbubemi, 472
Okin, Jaclyn, 497
Okoniewski, Patricia, 13, 119, 282
Olaizola, Diana, 473
Olander, Aaron, 609
Olazagasti, Robert, 9, 195, 289

783

Name Index

Olch, Norman A, 266
Olczak, Robert D, 678
Olds, Marjorie Z, 72
Olds, Stu, 537
Olek, Michael, 190
Oleske, Michael, 493
Olevano, Peter, 443
Oliva, Louis, 178
Oliva, Phil, 36
Oliver, Eugene, 60
Oliver, Katherine, 429
Oliver, Robert W, 58
Oliver, Russell, 269
Olivia, Phil, 375
Olmsted, Austin W, 448
Olsen, Admiral Robert, 633
Olsen, Bruce, 129
Olsen, Greg, 4, 307
Olsen, Michael, 467
Olsen, Nils, 527
Olshansky, Emily M, 61
Olson, Col Donald C, 362
Olson, Daniel, 453
Olson, James, 423
Olson, James N, 423
Olson, Keith, 559
Olson, Kevin, 497
Olson, Rich, 80
Olson, Richard, 80
Olson, Sandra, 18
Olson, Sarah, 340
Olson, Susan M, 248, 271
Olthoff CM, A.C.E. Ops, Ginger, 113, 350
Olver, John W, 388
Omotani, Lester M, 654
Onalfo, V James, 433
Onken, Carl, 522
Onofry, Craig T, 645
Onofry, Robert A, 74
Onorato, George, 20, 23, 26, 28, 29, 30, 31, 239, 248, 272, 298, 719
Onslow, Deborah, 607
Oplustil, Joanne, 471
Oppedisano, Marilyn M, 542
Oppenheimer, Joshua, 488
Oppenheimer, Suzi, 21, 23, 26, 27, 28, 29, 32, 150, 719
Oquendo, Ricardo, 478
Orcutt, Jon, 359
Orcutt, Tina, 340
Ordover, Nancy, 485
Orengo, Jose, 472
Orenstein, Michael L, 259
Organisciak, Richard, 677
Orlando, Elissa, 609
Orlando, Raymond J, 435
Orman, Ann E, 678
Orman, Edward J, 649
Orman, Jim H, 397
Oros, George, 413
Orsini, Anthony, 451

Orsini, Thomas, 145
Ortiz Jr, Fernando, 442
Ortiz, Claudia, 82, 218
Ortiz, Felix, 362
Ortiz, Felix W, 41, 44, 46, 49, 51, 52, 704
Ortiz, Jorge, 103, 128, 202
Ortiz, Solomon P, 388
Ortiz, Wilson, 238
Orton, Debi, 296
Osadchey, Chet, 604
Osborne, Keith H, 158
Oshiro, Theodoro, 502
Osinski, Jeffrey, 460
Ost, Chris, 310
Osta, John F, 536
Osten, Albert, 601
Osterhout, Tom, 196
Ostertag, Robert L, 266
Ostrander, Michael, 13, 360
Ostraszewski Anderson, Donna, 343
Ostroff, Richard L, 513
Oswald, Cynthia, 578
Otero, Maria, 112
Otis, Steven, 23
Ottaviano, John J, 424
Ottenschot, Barbara, 444
Ottman, Ronald, 196
Oudemool, Dirk, 416
Ouderkirk, Beverly L, 667
Ouimet, John, 309
Overton, Fred, 418
Overton, James P, 442
Owen, Joseph G, 57
Owens, Greg, 310
Owens, Javan, 163
Owens, John, 603
Owens, Kelli, 270
Owens, Major R, 151, 164, 205, 240, 274, 298
Owens, Oscar, 533
Owens, Thomas, 113, 350
Owens, Tom, 166
Owings-Leaks, Scottie, 430
Pace, Leonard A, 67
Pachner, Don, 523
Pacholczak, Walter A, 22
Packard-Maloney, Donna, 498
Packer, Mary Jeanne, 88, 191
Padalino, Joseph, 663
Padalino, Paul, 638
Padavan, Frank, 19, 23, 26, 28, 30, 31, 32, 719
Padden, Linda, 73
Paden, Deborah, 122
Padilla, Jose A, 59
Padilla, Nieves, 502
Padro, Eduardo, 56
Paffie, Charles, 444
Pagano, Anthony, 445
Pagano, Vinny, 604
Pagdanganan, Belinda, 411

Page, Brian J, 551
Page, JoAnne, 140
Page, Mark, 120, 432
Pagones, James D, 63
Pagones, Joan A, 419
Pagones, Timothy G, 71
Pahler, Deborah J, 161
Pai, Angeles, 430
Paige, Drue, 101, 230, 290
Palast, Geri, 467
Palazola, Jeannie L, 163
Palesh, Mark, 414
Palladino, Michael J, 539
Palladino, Peter A, 63
Palladino, Scott, 53
Palleja, Sandra, 472
Palleschi, Arnold, 545
Pallone, Jr, Frank J, 219, 389
Palm, Risa I, 611
Palmer, Dave, 497
Palmer, Deborah L, 400
Palmer, Don, 332
Palmer, Harold l, 191
Palmer, Linda D, 398
Palmer, Lonnie, 663
Palmer, Marcy, 28, 31
Palmer, Mary Lou, 41
Palmer, Mike, 439
Palmer, Robert, 196
Palmieri, Daniel, 65
Palmieri, Michael J, 218, 314
Palmquist, David, 144, 333
Palombo, Anthony J, 443
Palozzola, Joseph, 254
Paltrowitz, Ronald, 503
Palumbo, Alexander, 431
Palumbo, Carla M, 243
Palumbo, Daniel R, 74
Pamintuan, Lisa E, 628
Panebianco, George, 72
Panella, Joseph, 66
Panepento, Susan, 428
Panepinto, Barbara I, 59
Panepinto, Pat, 79
Panio, RoseMarie, 453
Pannucci, Cynthia, 341
Pannullo, Judith, 524
Panwar, Shivendra S, 100, 148
Paolangeli, Thomas M, 162
Paolilli, Eric, 436
Paolini, Roger, 346
Paolucci, John, 17, 238, 313
Papa, Mario J, 72
Papamichael-Walsh, Norma, 120, 336
Papandrea, Karen, 269
Paperin, Stewart, 243
Pappagallo, Angelo, 472
Pappas, Marcia, 166, 242, 554
Paprocki, Bernard J, 104
Paprocki, Ellen O, 248, 271
Paradiso, Anthony W, 70

Name Index

Parafinczuk, Raymond, 7, 132, 311
Parauda, Martina A, 364
Pardes, Herbert, 516
Pardes, Sondra K, 70
Pardi, David, 558
Pardo, Andrew, 542
Pardo, Tracy, 58, 61
Parent, Thomas G, 126, 183, 379
Parenti, Ralph, 425
Parete, John, 162
Parette, John R, 450
Parga, Anthony L, 58
Parikh, Anil, 118, 351
Paris, Anthony J, 57
Parise, Cathleen, 545
Parisi, Coan & Saccocio, , 441
Parisi, Frank, 281
Park, John W, 406
Park, Jr, George A, 248, 271
Parker, Dennis, 135, 229, 238, 254, 270, 302
Parker, Douglas A, 402
Parker, Elkin, 82
Parker, Johnatha, 165
Parker, Kevin S, 20, 23, 26, 28, 29, 32, 170, 719
Parker, Sandra, 583
Parker, Sheryl L, 60
Parker, Stephen R, 552
Parker, Terrance M, 396
Parkin, Lee, 493
Parkinson, Carol, 343
Parks, Robert, 598
Parks, Roy, 117, 350
Parla, James, 655
Parment, William L, 34, 41, 46, 47, 50, 52, 53, 704
Parmley, James J, 139, 261
Parola, Frederick, 576
Parr, Jean, 644
Parrett, Gary, 557
Parrington, Debbi, 288, 296
Parslow, William, 159
Parsons, Claudia, 602
Parsons, Debra, 422
Parsons, Lisa A, 651
Parsons, Patrick, 179, 215
Partnow, Mark I, 56
Pascale, Judith A, 410
Pascarella, Randy F, 448
Pascual, Frank, 118, 351, 377
Pasicznyk, John G, 122, 149, 201, 217
Pasquini, Julie, 134, 253
Pass, Audry, 609
Passenant, Jane, 65
Passero, Nicholas J, 447
Passmore, Michelle, 593
Passov, Richard A, 559
Passuite, Thomas J, 424
Pastel, Judith C, 672
Pastel, Robert S, 514

Pasti, Larry, 310
Pastoressa, Joseph C, 59
Patel, Dilip, 118, 351
Patel, Roopal, 526
Paterno, Frank, 511
Paterson, Basil A, 561
Paterson, David A, 3, 4, 194, 685
Paterson, Peter B, 460
Pathe, Paul, 437
Patience, Frank W, 19
Patnode, Susan L, 520
Patricof, Rochelle, 429
Patsos, James G, 89
Patterson, Acting Ambassador Ann, 205, 364
Patterson, Ambassador Ann, 205
Patterson, Gary, 85
Patterson, Michelle Weston, 56
Patti, Lorraine A, 667
Patti, Philip J, 59
Pattison, Mark P, 16, 197, 290
Patton, Barbara, 528
Patton, John, 420
Patton, Meredith V, 593
Patton, Roy, 184
Paul, Amy, 223, 319
Paul, Bradley, 342
Paul, Ron, 390
Paul, Sandra K, 554
Paulin, Amy, 45, 49
Paulin, Amy R, 41, 46, 48, 704
Pauls, Douglas J, 538, 543
Paulsen, David J, 402
Pavlou, George, 185
Pavone, James, 576
Pawelczak, Ronald W, 65
Pawling, Colleen, 507
Payant, Leo E, 131
Payne, Cheryl, 584
Payne, Donald M, 390
Payne, Hal, 412
Payne, Kibbie F, 59
Payne, Les, 595
Paynter, Steven W, 59
Peake, Catherine E, 40
Pearce, Robert, 355
Pearce, Stevan, 172, 391
Pearce, Steve, 340
Pearl, Jane, 61
Pearlman, Jeff, 4, 194
Pease, William H, 138, 260
Peaslee, Maurice, 198
Pecheone, Steven V, 75
Peck Kelleher, Deborah, 28
Peck, George R, 65
Peck, Judith L, 159
Peckham, Eugene E, 61
Peckham, John R, 559
Pecor, Peter, 270
Pecora, Geryl, 361
Pedo, Susan, 523

Pedro, Richard M, 365
Peet, JoAnn, 69
Pelella, William C, 71
Pelkey, Jack, 401
Pellegri, Michelle, 46, 49, 51
Pellegrini, Walter J, 9, 296
Pellegrino, Rick, 420
Pellegrino, Robin M, 226
Pelliccia, Paul, 607
Peluso, Pat, 579
Pelzer, James E, 55
Pence, Mike, 391
Pender, Amy Duggins, 332
Pendergrass, Kim, 596
Penn, George, 476
Penn, Gretchen, 526
Pennacchia, Robert, 214
Pennoyer, John C, 679
Penska, Janet, 416, 491
Peoples, Crystal D, 41, 44, 47, 48, 49, 51, 704
Pepe Jr, Frank, 644
Pepe, Ross J, 538
Pepper, Emmett, 471
Pepper, Jim, 340
Peradotto, Erin M, 57
Perales, Cesar, 243
Perales, Cesar A, 266
Peralta, Jose R, 41, 44, 45, 46, 47, 48, 49, 704
Peralta, Sherry Lynn, 318
Percy, Bonnie L, 413
Percy, John W, 443
Peres, Kenneth, 505
Peretti, Tina, 425
Perez, Ada, 130
Perez, Antonio, 472, 619
Perez, CDR Rick, 355
Perez, David, 502
Perez, Maria Elana, 502
Perez, Nelson, 496
Perez, Pedro J, 16, 136
Perez, Robert, 216, 270
Periconi, Donna, 570
Perillo, Rebekah, 544
Perkins, Bill, 24, 26, 27, 30, 32, 103, 203, 354, 719
Perkins, Pamela, 429
Perkins, Pamela Green, 160
Perkus, Paul C, 434
Perle, Ellen, 249
Perlman, Georgene, 325
Perlman, Kenneth, 131
Perlmutter, Barbara S, 250
Perlmutter, Margery, 466
Permut, Howard, 119, 352
Perna, J Philip, 670
Perreault, Thomas, 17, 349
Perrin, Richard, 293
Perrin, Uri, 3
Perrone, Anthony M, 566

Name Index

Perry, Adam, 491
Perry, Christopher, 204, 328
Perry, James, 339
Perry, Jody, 575
Perry, L Matthew, 110
Perry, N Nick, 34, 41, 44, 49, 52, 53
Perry, N Nickolas, 705
Perry, Nick N, 45
Person, Melinda, 456
Perticone, John, 157
Peruggi, Regina, 472
Peruggi, Regina S, 620
Perun, Vic, 145
Peruso, Elaina Marie, 574
Pesce, Michael L, 56
Pesile, Kathleen M, 619
Peters, Barbara, 647
Peters, Brenda, 646
Peters, David R, 309
Peters, Karen K, 56
Peters, Mark, 245
Peters, Thomas J, 173
Peterson, Carlene, 600
Peterson, Carolyn K, 422
Peterson, Collin C, 83, 186, 219, 387
Peterson, Donald L, 365
Peterson, Donna, 10, 213
Peterson, Harold J, 566
Peterson, Jr, Victor L, 304
Peterson, Keri, 41
Peterson, Vance T, 342
Petlin, Joel, 660
Petraitis, Brian J, 514
Petrella, Sandra, 74
Petrelli, Joanne, 673
Petri, Thomas E, 393
Petrillo, Richard A, 594
Petro, Carole, 527
Petrocelli, Joseph, 118, 351
Petrone, Frank P, 422
Petrone, Steve, 606
Petrosino, Larry, 184
Pettica, Jr, John A, 117, 182
Pettit, Patricia, 74
Pettit, Stacy L, 61
Pezdek, Eugene, 178
Pfau, Ann, 60
Pfau, Ann T, 256, 257
Pfefferman, Robert S, 561
Pfeifer, Maxwell S, 261
Pfendler, Lori, 64
Pferr, Laurie, 4, 307
Pfister, Helen, 503
Pfisterer, Kurt, 310
Pham, Bich Ha, 319, 492
Phaneuf, Joseph E, 191
Pheffer, Audrey I, 41, 44, 45, 47, 48, 52, 103, 202, 217, 705
Phelan, Jessica, 25
Phelan, Joseph L, 645
Phelan, Thomas P, 58

Philbrick, Steven, 135
Philip, George M, 125, 149, 297
Philipp-Clayton, Julie, 609
Philippi, Carol, 486
Phillip, Peggy, 609
Phillips, Brad C, 635
Phillips, Denise, 115, 148, 376, 619
Phillips, George W, 420
Phillips, II, Francis D, 406
Phillips, III, Harry, 143
Phillips, Jr, Howard T, 421
Phillips, Lois R, 515
Phillips, Maj R Brian, 184
Phillips, Sharon, 144
Phillips, Sr, Thomas J, 100, 148
Phillips, Susan, 250
Phillips, Tom, 666
Phillips, William, 536
Phillips, William A, 470
Philo, Raymond L, 426
Philp, Robert, 559
Philpott, Bruce G, 127, 354
Piacente, Tony, 535
Picchi, Joseph, 15, 101, 230, 290, 374
Piccirillo, Seth, 38
Picente Jr, Anthony J, 405
Picerno, Michael G, 363
Pichardo-Erskine, Katharine, 24
Piche, Mary-Ellen, 363
Pickard-Dudley, Kimberly, 527
Pickering, Carole, 645
Pickering, Gerald, 444
Pickering, Laurel, 225
Pickett, Adam, 126, 183
Pickett, Geraldine, 59
Pickholz, Ruth, 60
Pickreign, Joseph, 449
Piculell, Rob, 212, 279, 308
Piedimonte, Dennis J, 161
Pienta, William J, 567
Pierce, Dr Preston, 406
Pierce, Frances, 68
Pierce, Gene, 86
Pierce, James M, 589
Pierce, Lawrence, 121, 291
Pierce, Paige, 284
Pierce-Smith, Tracey, 21
Pieri, Brook, 485
Pierorazio, Bernard P, 678
Pierpont, Ruth, 180, 334
Pierre, Jude, 471
Pierre-Louis, Rosemonde, 435
Pierson, Dolly, 588
Piester, Ronald E, 199, 291
Pietanza, Kathleen, 161
Pietkiewicz, Michael, 527
Pietrafesa, Anthony, 309
Pietroluongo, Louis W, 11, 245
Pietruszka, Michael F, 63
Pietsch, Rebecca, 510
Pignone, Ray, 593

Pigott, Jr, Eugene F, 55
Pike, Kelly, 214
Pike, Susan, 314
Pillmeier, Michael R, 406
Pinaro, Jonathan, 540
Pinckney, Michael J, 60
Pincus, Judith, 431
Pine, Elizabeth W, 56
Pineda-Kirwan, Diccia T, 59
Pines, Emily, 58
Pines, Mary E, 158
Pines, Spero, 61
Pinkham, Henry, 525
Pinsky, Philip C, 515, 556
Pinson, Stephanie L, 109
Piper, Susan, 147
Piperato, Paul, 408
Pirani, Sylvia, 213
Pirani, Zahida, 496
Pircsuk, Cathy, 610
Pirro, Nicholas J, 405
Pisani, Salvatore, 356
Pisano, Ralph, 489
Pisciotti, Richard J, 412
Piscitelli, Anthony, 531
Piscitelli, Anthony P, 432
Piscitelli, Jim, 649
Piscitelli, Peter A, 531
Pitcheralle, Sam, 409
Pitkin, Jeffrey J, 123, 170, 182
Pitler, Robert M, 124, 258
Pittman, Carol, 511
Pitts, Arthur G, 58
Pizak, Ron, 118, 351
Pizzola, Lorrie, 10, 229
Pizzuti, Joseph P, 426
Place, Robert M, 438
Placke, Edward, 146, 279, 312
Plant, James, 538
Plante, Geoff, 174
Plastino, Thomas, 100, 148
Plastiras, James, 10, 21, 228, 373, 375
Plattner, Robert D, 17, 102, 327
Platts, Todd (Russell), 389
Pleasant, Kenneth, 138
Plescia, James, 131
Pleskach, Bart R, 64
Pleydle, Steven, 52
Plimpton, Mark, 604
Ploeger, Nancy, 503, 579
Ploetz, Ronald D, 75
Plotinsky, Benjamin A, 601
Plotzker, Michael, 146
Ploussard, Kim, 482
Plumadore, Jan, 256
Plume, John B, 641
Plummer, Barbara J, 408
Plummer, Daniel, 488
Plummer, Wilbert L, 137
Plunkett, Kevin J, 10, 179, 334
Poane, Jonathon, 555

Name Index

Podgus, Christopher, 361
Podmore, Robert, 430
Podziba, Kenneth J, 434
Poelker, Tom, 450
Pogoda, Susan, 99, 135, 216, 247, 255, 302
Pogorzelski, Gary, 657
Pohl, Jeffrey M, 122, 149, 201, 217
Pokalsky, Kenneth, 466
Pokalsky, Kenneth J, 187
Poklemba, Jill, 51, 460
Pokorny, Joseph, 118, 351
Polan, Steve, 503
Pole, Alan D, 678
Polenberg, Michael, 473
Poleto, David, 513
Poleto, Molly, 484
Polf, William A, 516, 565
Polimeni, Camille, 83, 204
Poliner, Jason M, 531
Polisi, Joseph W, 626
Poliski, Ellen, 215
Polito, William P, 57
Polizzi, Thomas V, 58
Polk, Ferris B, 260
Pollack, Robert, 310
Pollak, Daniel, 448
Pollak, Sam, 598
Pollard, Mary Lee, 624
Pollis, Adamantia, 242
Pollock, Bart, 600
Polmateer, Allan, 401
Poloncarz, Mark C, 400
Poltak, Ronald F, 120, 182
Poltenson, Norm, 601
Pombo, Richard W, 340
Pombonyo, Lynn, 654
Pondillo, David, 497
Poole, Bryan, 483
Poole, John F, 81
Poole, Thomas, 130
Poope, Ned, 368
Pope, Alan J, 443
Pope, Anne, 611
Pope, Peter, 3, 194, 324
Pope, Peter B, 12, 134, 216, 253
Popeo, Gerald J, 75
Popp, George, 325
Poppa, Richard, 474
Porcelli, Francis, 536
Porcello, David M, 536
Portelli, Terry, 310
Porter, Burt, 145
Porter, Elnora, 130
Porter, Kay-Ann, 257
Porter, Keith S, 190
Porter, Laura, 511
Porto, Donald R, 551
Posilkin, Mitchell, 517
Poskanzer, Steven G, 614
Posner, Michael, 242
Post, Constance (Gerrie), 580

Post, Jennifer, 17, 349, 374
Postel, John J, 124, 258
Postle, Gordon, 497
Postupack, Nina, 412
Potter, Barbara R, 68
Potter, James, 415
Potter, Jan R, 447
Potter, Marie, 6, 168, 195
Potter, Peter, 363
Potts, Patricia H, 561
Poulson, Jr, Robert J, 455
Poust, Dennis, 461
Povero, Philip C, 406
Powell, Bob, 366
Powell, Carla, 585
Powell, IV, Adam Clayton, 41, 46, 49, 51, 705
Powell, Richard A, 645
Powell, Tia, 214
Power, James H, 545
Powers, Jacqueline K, 494
Powers, James J, 669
Powers, James P, 495
Powers, Jason A, 516
Powers, Mark L, 67
Powers, Mary, 481
Powers, Matthew D, 516
Powers, Peter, 516
Powers, Phyllis, 147
Powers, William, 130
Powers, William D, 516
Powless, Jr, Irving, 209
Poy, Irving, 435
Pozon, Sheila, 495
Pozzi, Rocco, 136
Prager, Erica L, 70
Prather, J Christopher, 134, 254
Pratico, Jenifer J, 37
Pratt, Carolyn, 401
Pratt, Chip, 79
Pratt, Kevin W, 549
Pratt, Milt, 114, 350
Pratt, Susan, 40
Pratt, Terri, 7, 129
Pratts, Hasoni, 37
Preble, Judith, 141
Precious, Tom, 593
Preddice, Lisa, 511
Prehoda, Debra R, 412
Preissner, Robert M, 103, 128, 202, 380
Press, Eric P, 75
Press, Michael R, 464
Presseau, Fujiko, 568
Prestigiacomo, Dorothy, 62
Preston, Fred, 520
Preston, Jane, 22, 29
Preston, Kelley, 71
Preston, Larry D, 213
Pretlow, James Gary, 41, 45, 49, 50, 51, 53, 327, 339, 705
Price, Arnold N, 58

Price, David E, 388
Price, Edward, 654
Price, Frederick, 472
Price, Lee A, 399
Price, Mary Alice, 653
Price, Richard L, 58
Price, Robert J, 544
Priputen-Madrian, Nancy, 114, 336
Prisco, Michael L, 61
Pritchard, Christine, 3
Pritchett, Linda, 204, 240
Pritts, Kraig D, 659
Pritzker, Stanley L, 69
Privett, Donald, 546
Probst, Marian, 85
Prochera, Lee, 309
Procida, Richard, 600
Prohaska, Mike, 550
Proietti, Joseph, 310
Pronti, Gail, 15, 325, 335
Propper, Candyce, 23
Proulx, Paul, 531
Provenzano, Jeanette, 411
Provoncha, Joseph A, 400
Prudenti, A Gail, 55, 256
Prue, Morgan, 605
Prus, Eric I, 56
Pruspero, Stephen, 560
Pruzansky, Joshua M, 266
Pryce, Deborah, 249
Pryce, Deborah E, 389
Pryor, Mark, 384
Pryor, Mark L, 386
Pryor, Vikki, 251
Prystal, Tom, 158
Pryylucki, William, 467
Pucci, Carl, 510
Pucci, Debra, 454
Pucillo, Emilio, 218, 315
Pucillo, Peter P, 413
Puckett, Robert R, 175, 553
Puffer, Ray, 100, 148
Pugatch, Eric, 435
Pugliese, Christopher, 494
Pugliese, Melissa, 21, 26
Pugliese, Rosemary, 36
Puglisi, Anthony, 564
Puglisi, Linda D, 418
Pulaski, Phil T, 433
Puleo, Vincent, 442
Pulver, Jr, George J, 64
Punch, James P, 66
Purcell, Colleen, 26
Purcell, James, 467
Purcell, James F, 318
Purcell, Jennifer, 474
Purdy, Ralph, 542
Purdy, Sarah, 413
Pusey, Leigh Ann, 534
Pusloskie, John P, 533
Putnam, Stephen, 666

Name Index

Puzon, Ike, 367
Pyle, Jennifer, 459
Pyler, USPHS, Captain Bonita, 204, 219
Pylman, Allen C, 443
Quackenbush, Marjorie, 444
Quackenbush, Molly, 340
Quail, Brian, 161
Quall, Robert, 363
Quaranta, Arnold, 584
Quaranto, Stephen M, 562
Quaresima, Richard, 562
Quashie, Ivor A, 583
Quattlebaum, Megan, 498
Quattrone, David, 675
Quay, Gloria, 355
Quddus, Asma, 428
Quigley, Austin, 525
Quigley, Judy, 438
Quillen, Lori, 190
Quimi, Daphne, 535
Quinby, Crys, 605
Quinlan, George, 134, 216, 254
Quinlan, Joe, 198
Quinlan, Robert, 415
Quinn, Catherine, 74
Quinn, Christine C, 427
Quinn, Christopher G, 70
Quinn, Frank X, 420
Quinn, Jack, 41, 44, 48, 49, 259, 705
Quinn, Jeffrey, 248, 271
Quinn, Jim, 415
Quinn, Jr, James F, 448
Quinn, Kevin, 529
Quinn, Kevin P, 491, 506
Quinn, Michael F, 171
Quinn, Patrick, 102, 116, 181
Quinn, Peter M, 160
Quinn, Thomas R, 671
Quirk, Daniel A, 218, 314
Quirk, Daniel J, 534
Quirk, Donna, 308
Quirk, William J, 61
Quis, Nancy M, 161
Ra, Joseph, 542
Ra, Joseph J, 421
Raab, Jennifer J, 472, 620
Rabbitt, Ann G, 50, 705
Rabbitt, Annie, 41, 47, 49, 51, 52
Rabbitt, Annie G, 231, 292
Raber, Martin, 422
Rabey, Jeffrey, 646
Rabideau, David G, 566
Rabii, Robin R, 198, 297
Rabinovich, Oleg, 635
Rabinowitz, Stephen, 280
Rabinowitz, Stuart, 625
Rabito, Joe, 569
Rabito, Joseph J, 15, 101, 229, 289, 414
Rabsatt, Calvin, 131
Racaniello, Gary, 439
Race, Bradford, 479

Race, Greg, 460
Racette, Rita, 662
Rachlin, Stuart, 670
Rachmiel, William, 5, 90
Raciti, Robert M, 60
Rackley IV, Eugene M, 538
Raddant, Andrew L, 185
Radel, Penny M, 423
Radford, Les, 9, 195, 289
Rae, Karen, 349
Rae, Kathleen, 173
Raezer, Joyce, 367
Rafalsky, Thomas R, 531, 556
Rafalsky, Tom, 110
Rafferty, Thilde, 40
Raffo, Ellouise S, 161
Ragan, Sandra, 161
Ragazzo, Tim, 24
Ragazzo, Timothy, 26
Ragucci, Carmine F, 448
Ragusa, Philip, 453
Rahall, II, Nick J, 171, 186, 340, 391
Rahlf, Rona, 594
Rahn, Merritt, 420
Rahrle, David J, 424
Raia, Andrea P, 48
Raia, Andrew P, 42, 44, 46, 49, 92, 706
Raia, Jo-Ann, 422
Raiber, Robert B, 542
Rainey, Charles, 366
Rains, Michael T, 184
Rainville, Anne Marie, 168, 195
Rakaczynski, Randolph W, 555
Rake, Michael D V, 293
Rakower, Eileen A, 59
Ramich, Thomas E, 72
Ramirez Jr, Roberto, 508
Ramirez Sr, Roberto, 508
Ramirez, Aida, 498
Ramirez, Magdalena, 214
Ramondo, Patricia, 23
Ramos, Charles E, 56
Ramos, Kim, 508
Ramos, Philip R, 42, 44, 46, 49, 50, 706
Ramos, Ramona, 482
Ramos-Kelly, Diane, 677
Ramsey, B Harold, 73
Ranalli, Daniel J, 17, 326
Ranalli, Margie, 38
Ranalli, Michael, 420
Randall, Tom, 497
Rang, Keith, 439
Rangel, Charles B, 219, 315, 329, 382, 394, 730
Rangel, Rep Charles B, 330
Rangel, Sen Charles B, 329, 395
Ranieri, Jim, 366
Raniolo, John, 396
Ranney, Jim, 608
Rapacciulo, Charles, 215, 245
Rapaport, Janet, 204, 328

Rapelye, Thomas G, 562
Rapfogel, Judy R, 35, 42
Raphael, Ava S, 66
Rapoport, Miles, 478
Rappazzo, Sheila A, 169
Rappleyea, Clarence D, 502
Rappold, Don, 657
Raps-Beckerman, Helene, 436
Rashford, Eardell J, 60
Raske, Kenneth E, 223
Raskin, John, 492
Rasmussen, Edward J, 538
Rasmussen, Rebecca, 47
Raspberry, Tiffany, 514, 567
Ratanski, Robert, 60
Rater, Rex, 423
Rath, Mary Lou, 20, 24, 28, 29, 30, 31, 339, 720
Rathburn, Raymond, 412
Ratliff, Brenda, 474
Ratner, Judith, 6, 287, 295
Rattner, Howard, 426
Rau, Jordan, 595
Rauch, Marc, 432
Raufer, Susan, 204, 240
Ravin, Richard L, 109, 264
Ravitz, John, 160, 429
Raw Jr, Ronald, 660
Ray, Alan, 8, 144, 372
Ray, Carriann, 146
Ray, Herbert B, 61
Ray, Lori, 576
Rayball, Michael, 418
Raymond, Robert, 129
Raynoff, Rachaele, 427
Raynor, Bruce, 277
Raynor, Nat, 418
Rea, Michelle, 174
Read, Don, 401
Read, Susan Phillips, 55
Reagen, James E, 597
Reali, Joseph, 479
Reardon, Siobhan, 432
Rebell, Michael, 152
Rebisz, Donna L, 112
Rebolini, William B, 58
Record MS, RN, Victoria, 224
Recupero, Linda, 95
Reda, Vincent, 453
Redmond, Eileen, 196
Redmond, Suzanne, 38
Redstone, Sumner M, 176
Reed, Artis, 198
Reed, Earle C, 426
Reed, Frederick G, 66
Reed, Jack, 383, 384
Reed, Leon J, 664
Reed, Norman, 658
Reed, Robert W, 10, 179, 212
Reed, Ronald, 246, 268
Reed, Sharon, 73

Name Index

Reese, Michael, 579
Reese, Roy, 660
Reeves, Barbara, 472
Reeves, Gale, 657
Regan, Frances, 329
Regan, Frank, 523
Regan, George, 347
Regan, Timothy J, 539
Regula, Albert S, 420
Regula, Ralph, 388
Rehm, Timothy J, 660
Reich, Cynthia, 529
Reich, Joanne C, 361
Reich, Michael, 449
Reichbach, Gustin L, 56
Reicher, Andrew, 236
Reichert, Dave, 390
Reichert, Janet, 286
Reid, Brian, 190
Reid, John, 3, 143, 194
Reid, Linda, 528
Reid, Lisa, 477
Reid, Randy, 608
Reid, Robert, 567
Reid, Robert W, 529, 546
Reidbord, Kenneth, 105
Reidy Jr, Robert J, 663
Reif, Scott, 6, 99, 194, 287, 324
Reiff, Neil, 538
Reilich, William, 35, 42, 44, 46, 51, 103, 706
Reilich, William R, 52
Reilly, Adrianne, 596
Reilly, Edna Mae, 309
Reilly, Edward F, 139
Reilly, Edward T, 106
Reilly, Eileen, 471
Reilly, Gerald D, 425
Reilly, Geraldine, 46
Reilly, Geraldine A, 41
Reilly, Janet L, 20
Reilly, John, 414
Reilly, Joseph, 174
Reilly, Joseph A, 552
Reilly, Margaret C, 70
Reilly, Noreen H, 400
Reilly, Richard, 67
Reilly, Robert, 42
Reilly, Robert B, 706
Reilly, Robert P, 44, 46, 48, 50, 52
Reilly, Vincent J, 57
Reilly, William, 169
Rein, Andrew, 430
Reina, Robert, 649
Reinfurt, Edward, 466
Reinfurt, Susan B, 75
Reinhardt, Jessica, 44, 45, 52
Reinhardt, John, 578
Reinhardt, Robert W, 180, 335
Reinhardt-Reyes, Lois, 367
Reinhart, Kenneth, 496

Reis, Lawrence, 426
Reisman, Peter, 218, 314
Reiss, Dale Anne, 304
Reiss, Warren, 521
Reiter, Fran, 517
Reitz, James F, 67
Relihan Jr, Walter J, 57
Relyea, Michael J, 13, 100, 147
Relyea, Mike, 507
Relyea, Pamela, 309
Remauro, Leticia, 375
Remauro, Leticia M, 114, 335
Remo, Leonard G, 424
Remus, Laurel, 178, 372
Renckens, Polly, 573
Renfro, Sally, 427
Renner, Debra, 15, 169
Renock, John, 115, 350
Renwick, Dianne T, 58
Renzi, Alex R, 65
Renzi, Eugene R, 75
Repas, Peter, 172
Repas, Peter G, 537
Resnik, Kenneth H, 67
Ressos, Maria, 60
Restaino, Robert M, 73
Restani, Jane A, 259
Reuter, William, 615
Reville, Michael W, 175, 265
Reyes, Juan, 478
Reyes, Roberto, 145
Reyes, Ruben, 310
Reyes, Silvestre, 206, 394
Reynolds, Brent L, 396
Reynolds, Chris, 604
Reynolds, Daniel, 397
Reynolds, Gordon F, 663
Reynolds, Hugh, 595
Reynolds, Lorie, 581
Reynolds, Michael, 185
Reynolds, Michael T, 339
Reynolds, Rep Thomas, 395
Reynolds, Thomas A, 74
Reynolds, Thomas M, 219, 315, 329, 382, 390, 394, 730
Reynolds, Wayne, 400
Rhau, Richard R, 673
Rhine, Edward, 671
Rhodes, David John, 637
Ricci, Anthony, 497
Ricci, Carol, 435
Ricci, Frank P, 517, 560
Rice, Alicemarie E, 67
Rice, Bradley F, 518
Rice, Daniel, 79
Rice, Gail B, 73
Rice, Gail Rogers, 617
Rice, John Carter, 518
Rice, Kathleen M, 404
Rice, Linda, 641
Rice, Maria, 673

Rice, Natashua, 43
Rice, Stephen W, 523
Rice, William, 118, 351
Rich, Howard, 167
Rich, Sharon, 24
Rich, Walter G, 359
Richard, Bruce, 422
Richards, Arrah M, 162
Richards, Bryan, 603
Richards, Jerome J, 68
Richards, Randy C, 652
Richards, Robert M, 577
Richards, Thomas, 440
Richards, William, 617
Richardson, Charles, 437
Richardson, Clark V, 61
Richardson, Daniel, 554
Richardson, Edwina G, 61
Richardson, John, 471
Richardson, M Catherine, 241
Richardson, Taurus, 539
Richman, John A, 656
Richroath, Marybeth S, 61
Richter Geier, Cathy L, 162
Richter, Rosalyn H, 56
Ricigliano, Francis, 70
Rickert, Jody, 42
Ricketts, Rholda, 90
Riddell, Glenn T, 475
Riddick, Fowler J, 569
Rideout, Sandra J, 554
Rider, Mark, 408
Rider, Randall, 121
Rider, Randall J, 291
Rider, Renee, 309
Ridgeway, Mark, 147
Ridgway, Brian, 419
Ridley, Michael P, 565
Riedl, John P, 644
Riegelman, Elizabeth P, 154
Riegle, Christian, 343
Rienas, Ron, 114, 350, 375
Rienzi, Leonard P, 60
Riesbeck, Jodie, 592
Rifanburg, Michael, 591
Riffey, Katherine, 551
Rifken, Adele, 609
Rifkin, Richard, 3, 12, 99, 135, 216, 229, 247, 255, 270, 302, 325
Rigby Riehle, Brenda A, 396
Rigby, Gregory S, 447
Riley, Susan, 138, 260
Riley, Timothy J, 65
Rinaldi, Charles J, 640
Ring, Hilary, 117, 352
Ring, Timothy, 479
Ring, Timothy J, 550
Ringewald, Erica, 189, 481
Riordan, Anne, 498
Riordan, John, 304
Riordan, John B, 65

Name Index

Rios, Jaime Antonio, 58
Ripley, Maxine, 63
Risedorph, Dexter, 452
Risedorph, Dexter J, 159
Risi, Joseph J, 58
Risley, J R, 402
Ritchie, Patricia, 410
Ritholtz, Martin E, 58
Ritter, David S, 55
Ritter, Diana J, 16, 180, 198, 290, 297
Ritter, Harry, 309
Rittner, Don, 441
Ritzema, Ruth A, 232
Ritzko, Deborah, 101, 199
Rivas, Eneida, 472
Rivenburgh, Jeffrey, 96
Rivera, Augie, 472
Rivera, Dennis, 274, 454
Rivera, Francois A, 56
Rivera, Jesus M, 548
Rivera, Joel, 427
Rivera, Jose, 42, 44, 49, 51, 53, 80, 449, 706
Rivera, Jr, Reinaldo, 105, 260
Rivera, Manuel, 3, 143
Rivera, Naomi, 42, 45, 48, 51, 52, 707
Rivera, Peter M, 42, 44, 45, 49, 50, 51, 53, 239, 272, 283, 313, 707
Rivera, Reinaldo E, 55
Rivera, Richard, 424
Rivera, Rosemary, 495
Rivera, Sandra, 465
Rivers, Brenda, 309
Rivers, Natalie Y, 430
Rivers, Peggy, 8, 144, 212, 279, 312, 333
Rivet, Clayton, 49
Rivizzigno, Anthony P, 405
Rivkin, Richard, 194
Rivoli, John J, 65
Rizzo, John L, 401
Roach, Karen, 484
Roach, Patricia M, 674
Robach, Joseph, 27
Robach, Joseph E, 24, 26, 27, 29, 30, 31, 32, 203, 298, 720
Robb, Gary E, 547
Robbins, Tammy S, 65
Robbins, Virginia, 464
Roberson, Lucy, 79
Roberson, Sally, 571
Robert Lewis, Lisa, 600
Roberti, Scott, 482
Roberto Jr, Robert, 58
Roberts Jr, Howard H, 119, 352
Roberts, Alex, 133, 253
Roberts, Catherine, 464, 507
Roberts, Gayle P, 61
Roberts, Greg, 27, 29
Roberts, Mary Ann, 438
Roberts, MaryAnn, 437
Roberts, Pat, 382

Roberts, Sherman, 671
Roberts, Susan C, 438
Robichaud, Kathleen L, 74
Robillard, Deborah L, 71
Robillard, Robin, 75
Robilotto, Nicole, 15, 326, 335
Robinson Pippins, Shirley, 617
Robinson, Althea, 575
Robinson, Annette, 50
Robinson, Annette M, 42, 45, 49, 51, 707
Robinson, Christine, 136
Robinson, Davin, 286, 522
Robinson, Ellen, 257, 375
Robinson, John A, 548
Robinson, Kathleen, 226
Robinson, L Oliver, 664
Robinson, Nicholas, 191
Robinson, Robin M, 262, 316
Robinson, Sally, 498
Robles, Victor L, 426
Robles-Roman, Carol A, 426, 619
Roca, Frank, 443
Roche, Patrick, 611
Roche, Philip J, 410
Roche, Sister Denise A, 624
Rochelle, Neil, 646
Rock, Major Ivan, 630
Rock, Ron, 6, 98, 194, 287, 324
Rockefeller, IV, John D, 172, 206, 249, 384, 385, 387
Rockford, Steve, 605
Rodak, Thomas J, 527
Rodat, John W, 396
Rodenhausen, George, 422
Rodenhausen, Patricia M, 273
Rodgers, Cathy McMorris, 172, 391
Rodriguez Lopez, Lillian, 319
Rodriguez, Barbara J, 552
Rodriguez, Christine, 482
Rodriguez, Irma, 488
Rodriguez, Jose, 60
Rodriguez, Julia I, 59
Rodriguez, Laura, 657
Rodriguez, Luz, 496
Rodriguez, MarySol, 111
Rodriguez, Placida, 502
Rodriguez, Rafael W, 185
Rodriguez, Richard L, 329
Roe, Kathleen, 144
Roe, Robert D, 448
Roelle, Robert J, 677
Roeske, David, 396
Roest, Anne, 133, 252, 288
Roffe, Andrew S, 518
Roger, Elizabeth, 577
Rogers, A William, 472
Rogers, Cathleen E, 159
Rogers, Charles, 592
Rogers, Harold, 388
Rogers, James, 363
Rogers, James T, 484, 553

Rogers, Joel, 428
Rogers, Jr, Joseph P, 330
Rogers, Kathleen Martin, 68
Rogers, Les, 597
Rogers, Mark J, 74
Rogers, Mike, 206, 390, 394
Rogers, Stephen, 600
Rogers, Thomas, 500
Rogers, Thomas L, 154
Rogers, Wayne, 162
Rogowsky, Martin, 413
Rohde, Bridget, 138, 260
Rohlf, Janice, 520
Rohrabacher, Dana, 391
Rojas, Deborah, 470
Rojck, Sally, 648
Roker, Alice, 445
Roland Penta, John Hamilton, President, 174
Roland, Christine, 488
Roland, Keith J, 565
Roll, Kenneth, 70
Rollins, Evelyn K, 114, 335
Rolon, Alithia, 511
Romaine, Stephen S, 97
Roman Jr, Standford H, 621
Roman, David J, 66
Roman, Jr, Sanford A, 472
Roman, Nelson, 58
Roman, Sheri S, 58
Romano, Bernadette, 57
Romer, Lydia, 62
Ron, Aran, 486
Ronda, Bob, 489
Ronda, Linda, 296
Rondo, Jannette, 13, 100, 147, 373
Ronner, Courtney, 528
Roohan, J Thomas, 306
Rooney, Fred, 472
Rooney, James T, 67
Rooney, Kathleen, 409
Rooney, Kevin M, 175, 558
Rooney, Stephen J, 59
Rooney, Timothy, 347
Ropel, Stephen C, 80, 82
Rosa, Alexandra, 435
Rosa, Chris, 472
Rosa, Felix M, 14, 135
Rosa, Janice M, 57
Rosales, Leo, 12, 216, 246, 269, 312, 373
Rosario, Stephen, 106
Rosato, Peter P, 57
Rose, Daniel, 535
Rose, David, 4, 157, 245, 287
Rose, Edward J, 73
Rose, Lauren, 599
Rose, Marion, 523
Rose, Neal P, 75
Rose, Richard, 608, 653
Rose, Robert S, 56
Rosebrouc, John K, 557

Name Index

Rosemarin, Ari, 514
Rosen, Jay, 166
Rosen, Michael, 85, 109
Rosen, Michael E, 484, 514
Rosen, Nancy, 427
Rosen, Rae, 92
Rosenbaum, Marty, 45
Rosenbaum, Matthew A, 57
Rosenberg, Ember A, 492
Rosenberg, Gerald, 135, 254, 325
Rosenberg, Gerard H, 56
Rosenberg, Joseph, 430
Rosenberg, Philip, 531
Rosenberg, Phillip, 227, 267
Rosenberg, Robert C, 540
Rosenberg, Saul, 366
Rosenberg, Steven, 521
Rosenberg, Thea, 348
Rosenblatt, Lois M, 407
Rosenblatt, Michael, 229
Rosenblum, Lisa, 173, 467
Rosenfeld, Michel, 241
Rosenfield, Allan, 525
Rosengarten, Roger N, 58
Rosenshein, Norman, 366
Rosenthal, Carol, 503
Rosenthal, Cliff, 96
Rosenthal, Harvey, 285
Rosenthal, Jean, 348
Rosenthal, Kate, 75
Rosenthal, Linda, 707
Rosenthal, Linda B, 42, 44, 46, 47, 48, 49
Rosenthal, Stuart, 487
Rosenwald, Charles, 92, 127, 231
Rosenwasser, Stewart, 66
Rosenzweig, David C, 548
Roser, R Christopher, 667
Rosillo, Juanita, 429
Ross, Danny G, 399
Ross, Dixon J, 196
Ross, Donald K, 503
Ross, Gene, 607
Ross, James, 123, 149
Ross, Kathryn, 600
Ross, Kevin, 9, 195, 289
Ross, Laura Weigley, 257
Ross, Neil E, 60
Ross, Patricia A, 69
Ross, Robert A, 58
Ross, Sheila M, 161
Ross, Terri L, 396
Ross, Thomas H, 141, 299
Rossel, Harvey S, 547
Rossetti, James A, 405
Rossetti, Mario J, 59
Rossi, John, 414
Rossi, Robert J, 66
Rossiter, Judith A, 72
Ross-Jones, Marvel, 634
Rossomano, Victor, 68
Rostow, Charles Nicholas, 205

Rostow, Nicholas, 611
Roth, Allen, 447
Roth, David, 554
Roth, Jeffrey, 432
Roth, Kenneth, 242
Roth, Renee R, 65
Roth, Robert, 458
Rothaar, William, 440
Rothenberg, Karen B, 59
Rothenberg, Michael, 235, 243
Rothermel, Richard A, 407
Rothfeld, Barry, 598
Rothstein, Alan, 462
Rothstein, David, 185
Rotker, Seymour, 58
Rottier, Barbara A, 113, 180, 335
Roudebush, Jeffrey H, 658
Rougeux, Elizabeth A, 155
Rouis, Jonathan, 411
Roulin, Brian, 442
Rounds, Jr, James G, 559
Rountree, Patrick J, 578
Rouse, James B, 560
Rowan, Dawn, 309
Rowan, Sylvia M, 402
Rowback, Brian O, 17, 302, 349
Rowe, Charlie, 596
Rowe, Kathy, 606
Rowe, Laurie, 145
Rowe, Mona, 171
Rowe, Neil J, 256, 282
Rowland, Paul, 477
Rowlands, Vernon, 607
Rowley, David, 662
Rowley, James J, 417
Rowley, John C, 69
Rowse, Glenwood, 144
Roy, Lynn, 666
Roy, Richard D, 7, 129, 132
Roy, Vickie, 403
Roy, Yancey, 601
Royce, Edward R, 240, 391
Roys-Jones, Linda, 73
Rozzi, Linda J, 671
Rua, S Michael, 75
Rubeis, Rudolph, 659
Ruben, Maureen, 280
Rubenstein, Howard J, 519
Rubenstein, Steven, 519
Ruberto, Carmine, 270, 312
Rubin, Alice Fisher, 59
Rubin, Clinton T, 100, 148
Rubin, Janis, 493
Rubin, Laurence, 400
Rubin, Roberta, 16, 180, 198, 290, 297
Rubino, Frank J, 445
Rubinstein, Arthur, 534
Ruchelsman, Leon, 56
Ruddock, Charmaine, 465
Ruddy, Cort, 25
Ruderman, Hon Terry Jane, 263

Ruderman, Terry J, 59
Rudin, Tom, 515
Ruditzky, Howard A, 56
Rudnick, Andrew J, 571
Rudolph, Kenneth W, 57
Rudy, Harry, 361
Rudy, John, 361
Ruest, Penny M, 162
Ruff, Edwin, 18, 247, 270
Ruggiero, Joseph, 444, 449
Ruggiero, Steve, 205, 303
Ruglis, Martin, 680
Ruhlmann, Dandrea L, 65
Ruiz, Norma, 58
Ruiz, Pedro, 145
Ruiz, Sandra, 472
Rulon, Christopher, 245
Rulon, Diana, 90
Rumsey, Philip R, 57
Runion, Kenneth, 420
Runkel, Jay, 211, 278, 308
Runyan, John C, 546
Runyon, Dave, 195
Runyon, Dave A, 168
Runyon, David A, 6
Rupert, Clarke, 115, 181, 376
Rupert, Peter, 26, 30
Rupert, Peter L, 20
Ruppersberger, C A Dutch, 206, 394
Rush, Bobby L, 389
Rush, James, 216, 270
Rush, Joanna, 458
Rush, Kenneth E, 406
Rushdoony, Jonathan, 93
Rusinko, Michael, 343
Ruskay, John, 523
Ruskay, John S, 306
Ruskin, Lea, 70
Ruslander, Betsy R, 256
Russell, Bill, 672
Russell, Mark, 445
Russell, Michael E, 611
Russell, Patrick E, 402
Russell, Peter, 83
Russell, Robert T, 71
Russell, Scott A, 442
Russell, Theresa A, 537
Russi, Eugenio, 135
Russi, Teresa, 30
Russianoff, Gene, 358
Russo, Charles, 668
Russo, James, 421
Russo, Jerry, 429
Russo, Joe, 604
Russo, Michael, 598
Russo, Stephen, 72
Russo, Theresa, 531
Russom, Dan M, 648
Rustum, Youcef, 215
Ruszala, Diane, 126, 353
Rutan, Christina, 458

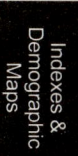

791

Name Index

Ruth, Carol, 397
Ruth, Lawrence, 185, 204
Rutherford, Clyde, 85
Rutigliano, Christine, 198, 290
Rutnik, Douglas P, 520
Rutt, Jodie, 584
Ruttan, Julie, 507
Rutter, Hillary, 220
Ruzow, Daniel A, 193, 294
Ryan, Barbara, 179, 215
Ryan, Beth, 8, 133, 253, 288
Ryan, Colleen Q, 123, 170, 182, 378
Ryan, Daniel J, 146, 312
Ryan, Dennis V, 159
Ryan, Edward F, 405
Ryan, Gary, 511
Ryan, Jack, 433
Ryan, James M, 680
Ryan, John, 521
Ryan, John R, 611
Ryan, Keith, 599
Ryan, Kevin K, 62
Ryan, Maryann, 607
Ryan, Matthew T, 415
Ryan, Melissa, 32, 54, 203
Ryan, Michael, 65
Ryan, Paul, 329, 388
Ryan, Tim, 624
Ryan, William J, 413
Ryan-Lynch, Blaine, 288, 295
Rybczynski, Catherine A, 421
Ryder, Melanie, 573
Rydl, Lubomira, 82
Ryerson, Lisa Marsh, 633
Rytlewski, Sally, 450
Rzepka, Patricia L, 39
Sabella, Rachel, 456
Sabesta, Rebecca, 199
Sabia, Roger, 440
Sabin, Deborah A, 14, 296
Sabini, John D, 20, 24, 27, 28, 31, 292, 328, 339, 354, 720
Sabo, Michael A, 364
Sabol, Sharon, 305
Sacco, Elizabeth, 488
Sacco, Jr, James A, 559
Sachs, Jeffrey, 525
Sack, Barry, 72
Sack, Robert L, 349
Sacket, James L, 409
Sackett, Robert A, 57, 58
Sackman, Bobbie, 476
Sacks Chapin, Deborah, 40
Saddlemire, Sandra, 162
Sadik-Khan, Janette, 434
Sady, Joan, 412
Safer-Espinoza, Laura, 59
Saffer, Shelley, 668
Safrey, Ed, 329
Saginaw, Carol, 321, 470, 498
Saia, Doreen, 488

Saidel, Judith R, 209
Saillant, Roger, 475
Sais, Michael, 39
Saitta, Wayne P, 56
Sakac, Sister Ann, 628
Saks, Alan J, 58
Saladino, Joseph S, 42, 45, 46, 47, 48, 297, 707
Salamone, Frank, 602
Saland, Stephen M, 20, 24, 26, 27, 28, 29, 30, 31, 150, 720
Saldana, Bertha A, 42
Salerno, George D, 58
Salerno, Vic, 535
Sales, Angela, 472
Sales, Frederick A, 460
Salinitro, Barbara, 61
Salis, Harry, 57
Salisbury, Gordon, 642
Salisbury, Richard, 408
Salkin, Andrew, 434
Salkin, Patricia, 206, 456
Salman, Barry, 58, 257
Salo, Terry, 133, 253
Salomon, Susan, 114, 137, 257, 376
Salomone, Katherine M, 670
Salotti, Mary Q, 160
Saltzman, Emily, 465
Saltzman, Michael, 121, 170, 378
Saltzman, Robert J, 209
Salvaggio, Susan Kay, 675
Salvione, Sherri, 472
Salzmann, Rick, 423
Sama, Jeffrey, 178
Samaniuk, John S, 349
Samboy, Bruce, 15, 326, 335
Same, Peter W, 409
Same, Ruth V, 162
Sammakia, Bahgat, 100, 148
Sammarco, Valentino T, 63
Sammons, Ann, 133, 252
Sampel, James Joseph, 160
Sampson, Barbara, 433
Sampson, Christian G, 439
Sampson, Fred, 521
Sampson, Frederick D R, 58
Sampson, John, 720
Sampson, John L, 20, 24, 26, 27, 29, 30, 31, 32, 217
Sampson, Rick J, 111, 346, 556
Sampson, Sandra, 650
Samuels, Barry, 589
Samuels, Chuck, 609
Samuels, Debrarose, 59
Samuels, Paul N, 141, 264, 498
Sanborn, Kimberly, 404
Sanchez, Ana, 612
Sanchez, Digna, 143, 308, 309
Sanchez, Linda T, 391
Sanchez, Loretta, 390
Sanchis, Frank, 509

Sandbank, Jane, 663
Sander, Elliot, 117, 352
Sanders, Lewis W, 159
Sanders, Lucia, 75
Sanders, Steven, 476
Sandhaas, Jill, 531
Sandlin, Stephanie Herseth, 393
Sandman, Scott, 13, 360, 373
Sandore, Michael, 659
Sandy, Stephen R, 367
SanFilippo, Andrew A, 416
Sanik, Gregory J, 644
Sankarapandian, Vani, 483
Sano, Joseph, 512
Sansom, Maston, 27
Sant, Dennis J, 407
Santamorena, Salvatore, 548
Santasiero, Robert, 549
Santelli, Charles, 456
Santiago Jr, George, 634
Santiago, Milton, 472
Santiago, Myrna, 16, 197, 290
Santiago, Nancy M, 23
Santiago, Teresa, 611
Santmann, Theresa M, 546
Santoni, Louis, 338
Santora, Frank R, 288, 295
Santore, Roseann, 363
Santorelli, Joseph A, 70
Santos, Felicia M, 439
Santos, Lee, 484
Santos, Robert, 432
Santucci, Fred T, 55
Santucci, Mauro, 438
Santulli, Thomas J, 398
Sanvidge, Brian P, 18, 200, 313
Sanzillo, Thomas, 16, 180, 198, 290, 297
Saperia, Phillip, 284, 473
Sapienza, Matthew, 472
Sapineza, Russ, 511
Sapio, Robert, 596
Sapio-Mayta, Janet, 6, 311
Saplin, Roy T, 611
Sapolin, Matthew P, 428
Saporito, Sal, 581
Sapp, Kelvin, 458
Sapphire, Joah, 120, 336
Saran, Melinda, 242
Sarbanes, Paul S, 385
Sarcone III, John A, 419
Sargent, Greg, 602
Sarlo, Kevin J, 564
Sarris, Todd, 418
Sartori, III, Joseph E, 398
Sassower, Elena Roth, 262
Satterfield, Patricia P, 58
Sattie, Maryrose, 160
Sattinger, Steve, 184
Sattler, Michael, 634
Saturnelli, Annette M, 661
Sauer, Doug, 318

Name Index

Sauerbrey, Martha, 587
Saul Yaffa, Jennifer, 452
Saunders, Wendy, 10, 179, 212, 213
Sauter, Thomas R, 102, 115, 230
Savage II, Paul D, 643
Savage, Peter, 460
Savage, Richard, 130
Savage, Susan E, 409
Savage, Thomas J, 118, 351
Savago, Peter, 453
Savanyu, Esq, Jean M, 124, 258
Savicki, Karen, 213
Saville, Dennis, 11, 134, 197
Saville, Harry D, 546
Savin, Nicholas J, 662
Savino, Diane J, 20, 24, 26, 28, 29, 30, 31, 32, 203, 298, 720
Savino, Jay, 452
Savitzky, Margaret H, 551
Savo, Theresa E, 8, 144, 145
Sawicki Jr, Joseph, 411
Sawyer, Andrew, 511
Sawyer, Donald, 280
Sawyer, Erin, 80
Sawyer, Suzanne, 458
Saxe, David B, 55
Saxton, Jim, 388
Saxton, Rep Jim, 106, 394
Sayegh, John, 571, 581
Sayegh, William G, 451
Sayers, Fran, 125, 336
Sayward, Teresa, 183
Sayward, Teresa R, 35, 42, 45, 46, 47, 52, 707
Scaduto, Joseph, 520
Scalabrini, Joanna, 624
Scalera, Lori, 146
Scalera, Patricia C, 192
Scales, Michael, 629
Scalione, Robert, 102, 115
Scalise, Toni, 450
Scalise, Toni M, 159
Scanlan, Brother Thomas J, 626
Scanlan, Richard E, 489
Scanlon, Sr, Kevin E, 265, 299
Scannapieco, Anthony, 453
Scannapieco, Jr, Anthony G, 161
Scarano Jr, Jerry J, 67
Scarano, John, 576
Scarborough, William, 44, 217, 313
Scarborough, William D, 42, 44, 46, 47, 708
Scarchilli, John M, 209
Scardino, Michael, 68
Scarlett, Juanita, 254
Scarpechi, Helen J, 163
Scarpino, Anthony A, 69
Scarpulla, Saliann, 59
Scarsella, Vincent L, 255
Schaaf, Eric, 186
Schachner, Larry S, 59
Schack, Arthur M, 56

Schacter MD, Neil, 458
Schad, Lester, 560
Schade, Michael, 188
Schaefer Hayes, Martha J, 281
Schaefer, Richard H, 119, 282
Schaefering, Lynn, 41
Schafer, Christa M, 399
Schafer, Michael I, 616
Schaff, Nancy, 87
Schaffer, Carolyn, 451
Schaffer, Frederick, 115, 148, 472, 619
Schaffer, Frederick P, 619
Schaffer, Richard H, 450
Schaffer, S Andrew, 433
Schaming, Mark, 144, 333
Schantz, Lawrence, 198, 297
Scharff, Karen, 495
Schassler, Steve, 178
Schatz, Jane, 433
Schechter, Barbara, 434
Schechter, Sara P, 61
Scheckowitz, Bruce E, 60
Scheibel, Sherri, 651
Scheidleman, Mark, 453
Schein, Warren, 582
Scheinman, Steven, 520
Scheld, Tim, 605
Schell, Catherine A, 62
Schell, Michael, 4, 287, 301
Schell, Mike, 449
Schenk, Kevin, 416
Schenkel, Paul, 439
Schensul, Joel, 309
Schepps, Bob, 585
Scher, Anne, 343
Scher, Preston S, 73
Scherer, John, 417
Scherer, Lawrence, 507
Scherer, Micki A, 56, 60, 256
Schermerhorn, Walter D, 82, 105, 232
Schermeyer, Sundy A, 442
Scheuer, Cynthia A, 174
Scheuerman, William E, 155, 300
Schiano, Anne, 145
Schick, Avi, 9, 99, 116, 177, 230, 254
Schick, H Leonard, 448
Schienberg, Mark, 487, 544
Schiff, Michael A, 411
Schiffer, Richard, 226
Schillinger, Lawrence R, 557
Schimanski, Carolyn, 482
Schimel, Michelle, 42, 47, 50, 52, 436, 708
Schimke, Karen, 155, 331, 522
Schimminger, Robin L, 42, 45, 46, 48, 53, 103, 292, 302, 354, 708
Schinderman, Janet, 525
Schleifer, Joel, 564
Schlein, Michael, 94
Schlein, Stanley K, 427
Schlesinger, Alice, 56
Schlesinger, Andrea Batista, 241

Schlesinger, Herbert J, 285
Schlick, James E, 163
Schlotter, Mary A, 40
Schloyer, Dean, 431
Schlueter, Thomas, 275
Schluger MD, Neil, 458
Schmetterer, Jerry, 403
Schmick, Janet, 584
Schmidt Jr, Benno C, 619
Schmidt, Kay, 482
Schmidt, Robert W, 55
Schmidt, Thomas, 642
Schmidt, Warren G, 447
Schmitt, Peter J, 404
Schnabel, Martin, 119, 352
Schneer, Errol, 221
Schneider, Carrie, 511
Schneider, Daniel J, 545
Schneider, Erasmus, 215
Schneider, Evan, 40
Schneider, Jean T, 60
Schneider, Maureen, 578, 579
Schneider, Norman, 488
Schneider, Reed, 434
Schneider, Wayne, 125, 149, 297
Schneiderman, Eric, 26, 29, 137, 259
Schneiderman, Eric T, 24, 26, 27, 30, 31, 721
Schneier, Martin, 56
Schnell, William A, 522
Schneuerman, William, 526
Schoelle, Jr, Robert L, 419
Schoelles, Patricia A, 631
Schoen, Neal W, 348
Schoenberger, Ilan, 439
Schoenfeld, Martin, 56
Schoetz, Kenneth, 254
Schoetz, Kenneth A, 9, 99, 116, 177, 230
Schofield, Daniel A, 397
Schofield, Thomas, 18, 248, 271
Schofield, William F, 660
Scholz, Robert, 526
Schonfeld, Ivan, 466
Schonfeld, Mark, 105
Schoolman, Maureen, 53, 103, 150
Schoonmaker, Steven, 672
Schoonover, Laura M, 159
Schopp, Steven, 154, 346
Schorsch, Ismar, 626
Schrade, Steven M, 638
Schrader, Scott A, 399
Schrader, William, 443
Schramm, Jane M, 576
Schreiber, Jane, 256
Schreiber, Michelle D, 60
Schroeder, Lee, 467
Schroeder, Mark J, 49, 50, 52
Schroeder, Mark J F, 42, 51, 708
Schroeffel, Bruce, 520
Schroeter, Helga, 498
Schruers, Terry, 460

Name Index

Schubel, David C, 406
Schuffler Jr, David, 454
Schuhle, Anne, 593
Schuler, Kevin, 507
Schulman, Clifford A, 544
Schulman, Martin J, 58
Schultz, Daniel, 151
Schultz, James, 664
Schultz, Jeanne F, 669
Schultz, Julius, 523
Schultz, Karen, 523
Schulz, Darin, 398
Schulz, William F, 240
Schumann, Bethany, 450
Schumann, Lynn, 190, 496
Schumer, Charles, 394
Schumer, Charles E, 93, 139, 206, 233, 261, 340, 381, 383, 384, 386, 724
Schumer, Sen Charles E, 106, 394
Schuppenhauer, John A, 71
Schussheim, Michael, 440
Schuster, Bill, 393
Schuster, Flora, 567
Schuster, Robert, 364
Schutte, Thomas F, 630
Schutz, Lisa, 71
Schwab, Kevin, 609
Schwabacher, Richard, 4, 194, 371
Schwach, Howard, 597
Schwaller, John, 613
Schwark, Linda M, 67
Schwartz, Andrew, 434
Schwartz, Barry K, 557
Schwartz, Ira, 145
Schwartz, John R, 74
Schwartz, Lawrence, 413
Schwartz, Lynn, 671
Schwartz, Mark, 273
Schwartz, Michael, 73
Schwartz, Mitchell J, 664
Schwartz, Richard J, 7, 332
Schwartz, Steven, 563
Schwarz, Bernard, 430
Schwarz, Jr, Frederick A O, 427
Schwarz, Richard, 330, 466
Schwarz, Thomas J, 613
Schweich, Thomas A, 205
Schweitzer, Melvin, 59
Schwenzfeier, Eric, 253
Schwerzmann, Peter A, 64
Sciara, Catherine, 213
Sciarrino Jr, Matthew, 60
Sciavallo, Tammy, 402
Scicchitano, Gregory, 418
Sciglibaglio, Eleanor, 160
Sciortino, Franklin J, 104
Sciortino, Joseph, 645
Sciotti, Nicholas A, 410
Sclafani, Charles J, 564
Sclar, Gordon, 363
Scofield, Robert, 232

Sconiers, Rose H, 57
Scoppetta, Nicholas, 429
Scorcia, John, 205, 303
Scott, A Paul, 643
Scott, Alan, 604
Scott, Bonita, 213
Scott, Brian Y, 214
Scott, Harley, 423
Scott, Karen, 609
Scott, Mark, 603
Scott, Michael, 169
Scott, Paul, 598
Scott, Robert A, 621
Scott, Robert C, 139, 391
Scott, William F, 643
Scova, Patricia June, 425
Scozzafava, Dede, 45, 51
Scozzafava, Deirdre K, 44
Scozzafava, Diedre K, 35
Scozzafava, Dierdre K, 42, 47, 53, 708
Screnci, Diane P, 171
Scriber, William W, 161, 450
Scuccimarra, Thomas H, 59
Scudder, Henry, 256
Scudder, Henry J, 56
Scully, Mona, 213
Scully, Peter A, 115, 178, 181
Seaburg, Tania, 486
Sealy, Annie, 419
Seaman, David E, 65
Seaman, Marietta M, 128, 337
Searles, John R, 397
Sears, Lawrence, 130
Seay, J David, 284, 510
Seay, Millard, 119, 352
Sebastian, Blair W, 235
Sebastian, Kristen, 600
Sebesta, Paul, 436
Seckerson, Tina, 413
Secor, Sharon L, 410
Sederer, Lloyd, 430
Sederer, MD, Lloyd I, 12, 280
Sedita, Frank A, 57
Sedor, Dennis, 158
Sedor, Michele, 397
Sedore, Emma, 438
Seehase, Jennifer, 4, 48, 307
Seeley, James A, 663
Seeley, Joe, 325
Seeley, Joseph E, 12
Seeley, Mary, 482
Seeley, Teresa B, 72
Seem, Mark D, 637
Seemann, Lisa, 49
Seereiter, Micheal, 506
Seewald, Robert G, 60
Segal, Elizabeth, 17, 238, 313
Segal, Jay, 488
Segal, Marvin E, 58
Segalla, David, 147
Segarra, Joseph, 496

Segermeister, David, 205, 303
Seggos, Basil, 518
Sehr, Gregory, 461, 527
Seibert, Harry W, 67
Seiden, Adam, 73
Seidenfeld, Stanley, 232
Seifried, E William, 102, 115, 230
Seil, Judy, 580
Seiter Jr, Norman W, 57
Sejan, John, 158
Seligman, Joel, 630
Selleck, Bruce, 188
Sellers, Corlis L, 273
Selover, John, 662
Selsky, Donald, 129
Selver, Paul D, 495
Selwood, Patricia, 163
Semansky, Joseph A, 273
Seme, Beth, 87, 344
Sementilli, Egidio, 535
Seminario, Anthony S, 51
Seminerio, Anthony S, 35, 42, 44, 45, 47, 50, 709
Sengal, Mona, 427
Sennett, John J, 169
Sennett, Peter, 296
Sennett, Suzanne, 143, 309
Sensenbrenner, Jr, F James, 392
Senulis, Joseph, 363
Serio, Greg, 513
Sernick, Keith, 478
Serrano, Henry, 474
Serrano, Jose, 388
Serrano, Jose E, 25, 27, 28, 29, 30, 31, 83, 171, 329, 339, 382, 387, 388, 730
Serrano, Jose M, 21, 24, 31
Serrano, Jose, M, 721
Serrano, Marcus A, 438
Serrano, Miriam, 235
Serrin, Bill, 276
Servatius, T Lee, 126, 183
Service, Constance L, 162
Service, Robert J, 650
Servis, Keith, 214
Sesmer, Marty, 533
Sessions, Jeff, 383, 386
Sestak, Ray, 373
Severe, Melissa, 544
Seward, James L, 20, 24, 25, 27, 28, 29, 31, 32, 248, 721
Sewell, Valerie, 270
Sexton, John, 629
Sexton, Michael, 215
Sexton, Robin M, 560
Sganga, Fred, 520
Sgroi, Robert, 422
Sgroi, Sandra L, 58
Sgueglia, Vincent, 68
Shacknai, Daniel, 429
Shaddock, DDS, Warren M, 541
Shafer, Jean, 425

Name Index

Shafer, Marilyn, 59
Shafer, Stephen, 647
Shaffer, David, 111
Shaffer, Patricia, 421
Shaffer, W Joi, 549
Shafit, Matthew, 430
Shahda, James, 576
Shaheen, Anthony F, 57
Shaheen, Caitlin, 45
Shaheen, Rita, 521
Shahen, Michael, 417
Shallman, John E, 314
Shamash, Yacov, 520
Shamma, Michael, 17, 302, 349
Shamon, Thomas J, 71
Shamoon, Alan, 94
Shamoun, Simon, 567
Shanahan, Thomas, 522
Shanahan, Thomas D, 11, 373
Shane, Megan, 435
Shane, Stephen H, 127, 231, 337
Shang, Debra J, 160
Shanley, Michael P, 557
Shapiro, Bernis, 426
Shapiro, Charlotte, 498
Shapiro, Daniel, 16, 101, 180, 199, 291
Shapiro, Daniel E, 101, 199
Shapiro, Jack, 366
Shapiro, James, 135
Shapiro, JoAnn, 41
Shapiro, Judith R, 622
Shapiro, Kenneth L, 531
Shapiro, Lois, 310
Shaps, Robert I, 676
Share, Steven M, 115, 350
Sharkey, Edward M, 397
Sharkey, Sally, 649
Sharp, Susan, 57
Sharp, Susan D, 11, 246, 268
Sharpe, Bruce R, 652
Shattuck, Barbara, 63
Shaver, Judson R, 627
Shaw, David, 177
Shaw, Elliott, 466
Shaw, John, 226
Shaw, Jr, Elliott A, 207
Shaw, Marc V, 426, 619
Shaw, Margaret L, 264
Shaw, Melanie, 460
Shaw, Ray, 591
Shays, Christopher, 392
Shchegol, Alex, 633
Shea, Brian, 497
Shea, Carol A, 75
Shea, James, 8, 133, 252, 288
Shea, Karen A, 157
Shea, Michael P, 662
Shea, Thomas C, 671
Shealy, Barbara, 498
Shean-Hammond, Edie, 339
Sheehan, Denise M, 120, 182, 377

Sheehan, Joseph W, 73
Sheehan, Kathy, 109
Sheehan, Neil A, 171
Sheehan-Nolan, Margaret, 269
Sheehy, Patricia, 311
Sheekey, Kevin, 426
Sheeran, Edward A, 589
Sheffer, Sharon, 67
Sheffey, Virginia, 472
Shehadi, John, 417
Sheifer, Charles, 196, 301
Sheinkopf, Henry A, 167, 522
Sheinwald, Franette, 134, 253, 373
Shelby, Richard, 383
Shelby, Richard C, 93, 233, 383
Sheltmire, Jack, 192
Shelton, Christopher, 275
Shelton, LeAnn, 427
Shelton, Marian R, 61
Shenker, Cynthia D, 531, 568
Shenker, Michael, 583
Shenoy, Andy K, 114, 335
Shenoy, Ram, 6, 168, 195
Shepard, Steve, 620
Shepard, Susan E, 123, 201
Sheperd, Michael, 460
Shepherd, David H, 627
Sher, Barry N, 166
Sher, Denise L, 70
Sheridan, John, 132
Sheridan, Timothy, 468
Sherin, James R, 111, 556
Sherlock, Jerry, 344
Sherman, Bill, 36
Sherman, Brad, 240, 391
Sherman, Brian, 665
Sherman, Howard E, 59
Sherman, M John, 69
Sherman, Margaret, 16, 17, 101, 327
Sherman, Michael, 428
Sherman, Ryan, 674
Sherrill, Peter W, 426
Sherron, James P, 586
Sherry, James, 3, 348
Sherwin, Galen, 514
Sherwin, Peter J W, 209
Sherwood, Richard, 420
Sherwood, Richard J, 423
Sherwood, William E, 57
Shevat, Samuel A, 665
Shields, Addie L, 399
Shields, Beverly J, 400
Shields, Maureen, 472
Shields, Robert, 228
Shifrin, Kenneth, 555
Shimer, Stephen, 604
Shimkus, John, 186, 389
Shimkus, Todd L, 536, 569
Shine, Edward J, 677
Shinske, Stuart, 598
Shirreffs, Donna, 205

Shoemaker, Marjorie W, 544
Sholes, David G, 675
Shorenstein, Stuart, 531
Shorris, Anthony E, 127, 353
Short, David, 443
Short, James, 643
Short, Jeff, 511
Shortliffe, Edward H, 100, 148
Showalter, Scott D, 497
Shrederis, Martin, 409
Shrive, Albert, 555
Shu, George, 637
Shubert, Patricia, 147
Shufro, Joel, 276
Shulman, Martin, 59
Shults, David A, 72
Shure, Kathleen, 213
Shyne, Henry F, 555
Siano, Stephen J, 543
Sibbison, Virginia Hayes, 323
Siciliano, Thomas G, 95
Sickenius, Rose, 438
Sickora, Brian, 608
Siconolfi, Patrick, 229
Siconolfi, Patrick J, 234
Sidney, Dana, 553
Siebert, Richard, 159, 452
Siegal, Bernice Daun, 59
Siegel, Lowell, 49
Siegel, Norman I, 59
Siegfried, Clifford, 144, 333
Siegfried, Clifford A, 144, 333
Siemer, Richard, 431
Siepka, Rev Richard W, 623
Sievert, Fred, 493
Sifontes, Jose, 104
Sigmund, Stephen, 127, 353
Signer, Lauren E, 423
Signor, John F, 114, 335
Sikora, Peter, 505
Sikowitz, Marcia, 60
Silano, Mary Beth, 573
Silber, Debra, 59
Silberman, Jacqueline W, 56
Silbermann, Jacqueline W, 256
Siligato, Anthony S, 439
Siller, Sidney, 366
Sillerman, Michael T, 495
Sillery, William, 8
Sillery, William J, 133, 252
Silo, Mark, 349
Silva, MD, Raul, 281
Silvaggio, Mary Ann, 329
Silvan, Jon, 508
Silver, Andrew W, 410
Silver, George, 73
Silver, George J, 59
Silver, Howard R, 58
Silver, Janet, 491, 506
Silver, Phyllis, 213
Silver, Sheldon, 34, 42, 51, 202, 709

Name Index

Silverblatt, Pamela S, 432
Silverfine, Debby, 7, 332
Silverman, Arlene, 60
Silverman, David J, 331
Silverman, Gerald, 601
Silverman, Harold, 58
Silverman, Henry R, 127, 353
Silverman, Joseph, 59
Silverman, Michael, 497
Silverstein Barker, Julie B, 12, 325
Silverstein, Larry A, 306
Silverstein, Mark K, 676
Silverstein, Norm, 609
Silvestri, Carlo, 434
Silvestri, Joan M, 161
Simberg, Mary Anne, 450
Simberkoff, Michael S, 364
Simmons, Anthony, 592
Simmons, Doug, 597
Simmons, Garry M, 547
Simmons, Hildy J, 428
Simmons, Jeff, 428
Simmons, Robert R, 206
Simms, Lenton D, 145
Simms, Philip, 72
Simone, Albert J, 630
Simoni, John B, 15, 325, 335
Simons, Hon Richard D, 208, 264
Simons, Keith E, 12, 281, 373
Simpser, Edwin, 524
Simpson, John, 527
Simpson, John B, 613
Simpson, Sandra A, 679
Simpson, ShawnDaya L, 59
Simpson, Walter, 523
Simpson, Wendy, 163
Simrany, Joe, 89
Simson, Jay J, 106, 533
Singer, Hy, 452
Singer, Leonard, 476
Singh, Anil C, 59
Singh, Mohan, 184
Singleton, Chuck, 603
Singleton, Joseph, 670
Sinisgalli, Erin, 224
Sinnott, George C, 121, 352
Siperstein, Alan, 355
Sippel, Leonard, 123, 149
Siragusa, Joe, 604
Sirkin, Stephen R, 69
Sirois, Herman A, 655
Sirota, Robert, 627
Sise, Joseph M, 57
Sise, Richard E, 58, 59, 256
Siskind, PhD, Alan B, 284
Sisti, Maria, 608
Sisto, Daniel, 484
Sitrin, Louis, 28
Siv, Ambassador Sichan, 205
Siwek, Donna M, 57
Skahill Jr, Jack J, 641

Skallerup Jr, Robert, 430
Skelos, Dean G, 19, 24, 26, 28, 29, 30, 31, 32, 54, 163, 721
Skelos, Gail M, 19
Skelos, Peter B, 55
Skelton, Ike, 364, 388
Skermont, Marilyn A, 658
Skinner, George D, 552
Skinner, Patricia, 470
Skinner, Scott T, 535
Sklar, Stanley L, 56
Skolnick, Darren, 497
Skoog-Harvey, Jennifer, 404
Skorton, David J, 624
Skowfoe, Philip, 409
Skretta-Huck, Angela, 512
Skulklapper, Lester, 531
Skyler, Edward, 426
Skype, Judith A, 36
Slade, Frank, 288, 295
Slater, Thomas, 14, 136
Slattery, John E, 650
Slattery, Michael, 517
Slaughter, Louise M, 392
Slaughter, Louise McIntosh, 382, 731
Slawson, Michael J, 408
Slentz, Kenneth, 650
Slingerland, David, 281
Slippen, Daniel, 458
Slivinski, Andrea, 65
Slizewski, Bea, 84
Sloan, Stephen R, 222, 250
Sloan, Terry, 425
Sloane, David, 509
Sloane, Sandra, 15, 169, 412
Sloat, Jr, Major Ellwood A, 136
Slobod, Elaine, 66
Slobodien, Michael, 481
Slocum, Peter, 220
Slutsky, Lorie A, 321
Slutzky, Orville A, 343
Sluzar, Joseph, 397
Sly, Theodore W, 406
Slye, Robert J, 444
Small MD, Bruce, 214, 360
Small, Andrea, 213
Small, Gillian, 619
Smalls, Ronald L, 680
Smanik, Robert, 624
Smarr, Jamie A, 429
Smeallie, Shawn, 457
Smeaton, Karen, 51
Smeeding, Timothy, 155, 210, 323
Smiley, Gregory O, 50
Smingler, David, 22
Smirensky, Nick, 198
Smirlock, Daniel, 17, 101, 134, 253, 326
Smith Petro, Dr Carole, 603
Smith, A T, 138
Smith, Adam, 388
Smith, Alan, 10, 229

Smith, Barbara, 69
Smith, Bethany, 511
Smith, Blair, 80
Smith, Brenda L, 677
Smith, Brian, 471
Smith, Christopher, 484, 489
Smith, Christopher J, 390
Smith, David, 520
Smith, David K, 544
Smith, David R, 612
Smith, Donald Blaine, 407
Smith, Donna M, 314
Smith, Duaine, 511
Smith, Ellen, 525
Smith, Erin, 497
Smith, Frederick W, 334
Smith, Gary P, 642
Smith, Georgeann, 329
Smith, Gerald L, 159
Smith, Gerald R, 397
Smith, Gordon, 220, 315, 385, 387
Smith, Gordon H, 384
Smith, Guy, 401
Smith, Howard S, 647
Smith, Howard W, 677
Smith, James E, 438
Smith, JoAnn M, 223, 241, 318
Smith, John, 606
Smith, Joseph, 131
Smith, Joseph V, 247, 271
Smith, Judy, 215
Smith, Julia, 341
Smith, Justin, 37
Smith, Karen, 59
Smith, Karen J, 635
Smith, Kevin T, 536
Smith, Lamar, 139
Smith, Lamar S, 261, 391
Smith, Lisa Margaret, 260
Smith, Lorrie, 37
Smith, Luke, 436
Smith, Luther, 501
Smith, Lynn, 588
Smith, M Patricia, 12, 135, 216, 246, 247, 255, 268, 269, 270, 312, 360
Smith, Malcolm A, 20, 24, 203, 721
Smith, Malcom A, 31
Smith, Marc, 424
Smith, Martin E, 61
Smith, Marty, 452
Smith, Marty L, 159
Smith, Mary C, 423
Smith, Mary H, 57
Smith, Michael, 398
Smith, Michael C, 434
Smith, Nancy A, 63
Smith, Nancy E, 56
Smith, Nancy L, 160
Smith, Onnolee, 296
Smith, Patricia M, 431
Smith, Patrick, 519

Name Index

Smith, Perry F, 213
Smith, Peter R, 123, 170, 182
Smith, Philip, 508
Smith, Rebecca, 79
Smith, Rex, 591
Smith, Richard, 486
Smith, Richard L, 464
Smith, Richard M, 602
Smith, Robert, 135
Smith, Robert A, 408
Smith, Robert S, 55
Smith, Ruth E, 59
Smith, RW, 604
Smith, Ryder, 511
Smith, Stuart, 432
Smith, Timothy G, 543
Smith, Valarie, 150
Smith, Wallace, 340, 357
Smith, Wallace D, 454
Smith-Caronia, Terri, 492
Smith-Lawless, Kelly, 13, 348
Smith-Socaris, Christian, 514
Smits, Stephen M, 281
Smolkin, Stanley A, 73
Smoller, Arlene, 3, 268, 295
Smyth, Andrea, 473, 523
Smyth, Nancy, 527
Snavely, Dick, 603
Snavely, Rick, 603
Snell Jr, Joseph F, 417
Snell, Dietrich, 12, 91, 99, 134, 169, 179, 216, 229, 238, 254, 270, 301, 325
Snowden, K Dane, 467
Snowe, Olympia J, 187, 274, 384, 386
Snowe, Oympia J, 106
Snyder, Arthur R, 412
Snyder, Bill, 603
Snyder, Connie, 133, 252
Snyder, Jackie, 427
Snyder, Jon, 622
Snyder, Leslea, 29
Snyder, Michael J, 196, 333
Snyder, Patricia Di Benedetto, 154, 344
Snyder, Phyllis, 242, 321
Snyder, Richard, 597
Snyder, Susan, 455
Snyder, Thomas, 566
Snyder, Vic, 388
Snyder, William, 541
Snyder, William F, 611
Soares, P David, 396
Sobczyk, James, 405
Sobelski, Stan, 607
Sobol, Thomas, 155
Soderberg, Carl-Axel P, 185
Soffin, Jeremy, 117, 352, 377
Sofield Sr, Thomas R, 424
Sohn, Jae, 90
Sokolow, Alan V, 207, 293, 330
Sola, David A, 151
Solarz, Ron, 286

Solecky, Richard, 200
Sollazzo, Robert A, 105
Soloff, Brenda S, 60
Soloff, Mordecai, 511
Solomkin, Bruce, 147
Solomon, Charles H, 60
Solomon, David L, 205
Solomon, Jane S, 59
Solomon, Jerry, 134, 216, 254
Solomon, Mark J, 264
Solomon, Martin M, 56
Soloway, Ronald, 323
Sombke, Laurence, 16, 101, 180, 199, 291, 374
Somers, Bob, 79
Sommer, Brett M, 437
Sommer, Jeffrey, 123, 201, 327, 378
Sommer, Judah C, 543
Son, Shin, 320
Sonberg, Michael R, 60
Sonneborn, James, 470
Sonnenblick, Arthur I, 306
Soos, Lawrence V, 437
Sopak, Sandra K, 398
Sopris, Kent, 44
Soreff, Sasha, 7, 332
Sorensen, Jon, 372
Sorrentino, Vincent J, 421, 566
Sosa-Lintner, Gloria, 61
Sosenko, Ben, 608
Sossei, Steve, 198, 290
Soto, Faviola, 59
Sottile, James M, 423
Souchik, David, 497
Souder, Mark, 390
Soule, Norman, 342
Soumas, Gregory C, 160
Southard-Kreiger, Rebecca, 38
Southard-Krieger, Rebecca, 51
Sovas, Gregory H, 192
Spacher, CPA, Kevin, 294
Spacher, Kevin, 438
Spadafora Jr, Ronald R, 652
Spadone, Melina, 546
Spain, Edward O, 56
Spalding, Emilie, 467
Spalter, Ronald, 619
Spano, Andrew J, 413
Spano, John J, 10, 196
Spano, Linda, 247, 271
Spano, Mike, 42, 44, 45, 46, 49, 50, 51, 202, 709
Spargo, Thomas J, 57
Sparling, Reed, 521
Spatz, Sara, 270
Spaulding, Jon, 593
Spears, Brenda S, 60
Speckhard, Roy A, 417
Specter, Arlen, 139, 206, 261, 383, 386
Specter, Marvin M, 265
Spector, Harvey, 482

Speelman, Anthony, 548
Speenburgh, Wayne, 401
Speicher, Brent, 82, 203
Speight, Bruce, 345
Spellman, G Ann, 70
Spence, Hugh, 430
Spencer, Barbara R, 119, 352
Spencer, Gary, 55
Spencer, Rick, 190
Sperduto, Salvatore A, 544
Spero, Stephen W, 592
Sperrazza, Sara S, 65
Speyer, Jerry I, 306
Spicola, Vince, 609
Spielvogel, Sean, 595
Spies, Christian F, 68
Spike, Ronald G, 413
Spilde, LCSWR, ACSW, Duane, 285
Spillman, Brenda L, 554
Spina, Peter A, 615
Spinelli, Michael W, 549
Spinnato, Joseph E, 343
Spinner, Jeffrey Arlen, 68
Spinney, Richard B, 399
Spinola, Joseph P, 58
Spinola, Steven, 305, 517, 561, 565
Spires, Mark H, 58
Spitler, William D, 105
Spitzer, Benjamin B, 641
Spitzer, Eliot, 3, 79, 90, 98, 115, 129, 143, 157, 168, 177, 181, 194, 211, 228, 237, 245, 252, 268, 278, 287, 295, 301, 307, 324, 332, 348, 360
Spitzer, Eliot , 685
Spivak, Barbara, 314
Spivey, Gary D, 124, 201, 258, 379
Spodek, Ellen M, 59
Spolzino, Robert A, 55
Spoor, James, 309
Sporn, Heather, 349
Sposato, Mark, 643
Sposato, Mark A, 643
Spota, Thomas J, 411
Spraggs, Laurence D, 615
Sprague, Michael A, 410
Spratt, Jr, John M, 329, 388
Spring, Arthur, 401
Spring, Kathleen A, 665
Spring, Laurence, 644
Springer, Gail L, 443
Springer, Marlene, 472, 620
Springer, Neil, 591, 601
Springle, Serena, 60
Sproat, Christine A, 57
Sproat, James, 196, 301
Sproat, James P, 121, 352
Spute, James M, 421
Squeri, Christopher, 345
Squier, Randall, 642
Squires, David, 411
Squires, William G, 82

Name Index

Srinivasan, LaVerne Evans, 429
Srinivasan, Meenakshi, 434
Srivastava, Sudipto, 497
St Amand, Janet, 544
St Andrews, Robin M, 161
St Cyr, Marie, 454
St George, Norman, 70
St Hilaire, Karen, 586
St John, Keith, 26, 27, 28, 30
St Lawrence, Christopher P, 439
St Leger, Michael, 453
Stabenow, Debbie, 187, 382
Stachowski, William, 28, 203, 292, 328
Stachowski, William T, 20, 24, 25, 29, 30, 31, 721
Stack, Derrick, 189
Stack, Elaine J, 58
Stack, Richard, 447
Stackhouse, John EH, 56
Stackrow, David M, 114, 350, 550
Stackrow, Karen, 269
Stadtmauer, David, 58
Staehr, Ed, 84
Stafford, George, 180, 199, 291
Stafford, Kay, 611
Stahr, Ed, 19
Staiano-Coico, Lisa, 612
Staley, Lewis L, 578
Stallings, Ericka, 493
Stallman, Michael D, 59
Stallmer, Steven, 470
Stamell, Marcia, 594
Stamler, Susan, 526
Stamm, Gregory, 126, 353
Stamm, Michael, 587
Stanco, James, 133, 252
Standard, Kenneth G, 265
Stander, Philip, 636
Stander, Thomas A, 57
Stanford, Eileen, 67
Stanley, Christopher, 497
Stanley, Deborah F, 614
Stanley, John, 60
Stanley, Lisa, 441
Stanton, Chris J, 260
Stanton, George, 163
Staples, Brian, 586
Staples, Douglas, 320
Staples, Judith P, 667
Starbuck, Margaret, 409
Staring, Gary R, 565
Stark, Fortney Pete, 219, 394
Stark, Lorna, 497
Stark, Martha E, 120, 429
Stark, Rose Marie, 661
Starkey, James G, 56
Starks, Jacklin G, 679
Staro, Charles M, 305, 502
Starr, Daniel, 664
Starr, Tom, 607
Starr, Tracy, 19

Starrin, Roy E, 434
Staton, Betty E, 61
Statz-Smith, Theresa, 608
Stavisky, Evan, 514
Stavisky, Toby A, 722
Stavisky, Toby Ann, 21, 24, 25, 26, 27, 29, 31, 32, 150
Stead, Jon R, 401
Stearling, Jean, 420
Stearns, Cliff, 389
Stec, Dan, 439
Stechel, Frank, 147
Steckman, Emma, 31
Steele, Dorothy, 146, 312
Steele, Jerome D, 638
Steele, Norman, 269
Steenstra, Chris, 108
Steets, Jim, 481
Stefano, Michael de, 138
Stefanucci, Michele M, 9, 178, 372
Steiger, Paul, 596
Steiger, Paul E, 176
Stein, Irene W, 450
Stein, Leslie E, 57
Stein, Peter, 449
Stein, Richard A, 652
Stein, William, 421
Steinbach, Maria C, 288, 295
Steinberg, Alan, 185
Steinberg, David J, 626
Steinberg, Joel, 493
Steiner, Charles P, 584
Steiner, Stuart, 616
Steinhardt, Marsha, 56
Steinhaus, William R, 400
Steinhause, Mitchell, 111
Stempel, Jr, Vincent F, 267
Stempniak, Donna, 536
Stenard, Karen, 80
Stenger, Harvey, 527
Stephan, Roseanne, 458
Stephen, Larry R, 60
Stephens, Joyce A, 433
Stephens, Theresa M, 66
Stergious, Lorraine, 59
Sterlin, Shrita, 41
Sterman, David, 123, 182
Stern, Amelia, 15, 99, 197
Stern, Andrew, 510
Stern, Robert, 53, 80
Stern, Sandra, 128, 202, 259
Sternberg, Ernie, 527
Sternberg, Kevin, 309
Sternberg, Seymour, 493
Steszewski, Gary, 563
Stevens, Carol, 402
Stevens, Deborah, 45
Stevens, Don, 605
Stevens, Jean, 8, 145
Stevens, Jillynn, 483
Stevens, Peter, 329

Stevens, Rick, 571
Stevens, Rik, 601
Stevens, Ron Scott, 121, 200, 336, 378
Stevens, Sen Ted, 394
Stevens, Ted, 106, 172, 187, 356, 383, 384, 386
Stevenson, Peter, 597
Stewart, Cathy L, 451
Stewart, Damon, 29
Stewart, Daniel, 521
Stewart, Daniel L, 122, 137
Stewart, Graham, 527
Stewart, Harry, 120, 182
Stewart, Joan Hinde, 625
Stewart, John W, 650
Stewart, Kyle, 531
Stewart, Regina, 345
Stewart, VAdm Joseph D, 151, 356
Stewart-Cousins, Andrea, 24, 26, 29, 30, 31, 232, 292, 722
Stich, Steve, 79
Stiebel, Robin, 498
Stigberg, Eric, 340
Stiglmeier, Gary F, 70
Stiker, Betsey A, 667
Stillman, Bruce, 633
Stillman, Charles A, 142
Stillman, Waddell, 343
Stirling, Chris, 361
Stirpe, Albert, 42, 44, 46, 48, 51, 52
Stirpe, Albert A, 709
Stix, Joseph D, 274, 298
Stock, Evelyn, 498
Stock, Richard, 196, 301
Stockbridge, F Joseph, 190
Stockton, Walter W, 561
Stokinger, Carol Ann, 61
Stoldt Jr, Gary, 423
Stoller, Peter, 547
Stolper, Giselle, 284
Stolz, Robert M, 60
Stolzenfels, Leslie J, 437
Stone, Deborah, 68
Stone, Edie, 85, 189
Stone, Garry, 646
Stone, Lewis Bart, 59
Stone, Regina A, 90
Stone, Shannon, 523
Stoner, Joseph F, 639
Stoothoff, John L, 680
Stores, Edward, 651
Storey, Jeff, 596
Storms, Dale C, 398
Stortecky, Frederick R, 72
Stouffer, John, 192, 523
Stoughton, Corey, 514
Stout, Gerald L, 413
Stovall, Calvin, 592
Stover, Princella, 311
Stowe, Richard, 416
Straight, Doug, 448

Name Index

Straight, Thomas, 448
Strainere, Robert A, 550
Strandberg, Steven, 361
Straniere, Philip S, 59
Straniere, Robert, 494
Strano, Anne Marie, 133, 252
Strano, AnneMarie, 134, 253, 289
Strasburg, Joseph, 236, 517
Strassberg, Leslie, 489
Stratton, Brian U, 441
Stratton, Martha, 138, 260
Straub, Frank G, 445
Straub, Robert, 566
Straus, Robert H, 60
Strauss, Janet, 72
Strauss, Sidney F, 58
Streicher, William, 413
Stretton, Ernest H, 647
Stricoff, Robert, 570
Strimple, Greg, 507
Stringer, Scott M, 404, 435
Strining, Thomas, 660
Strobel, Mary, 75
Strobridge, Col Steve, 367
Strohl, Richard, 280, 312
Strohl, Ronald, 147
Strome III, Charles B, 426
Strum Kenny, Shirley, 520
Stucchi, Victor, 123, 149
Studebaker, Judy, 498
Stuen, Cynthia, 224
Stupak, Bart, 389
Stupp, Hon. Herbert W, 320
Sturcken, Charles G, 429
Sturm Rausch, Deborah, 13, 281, 373
Sturm, Helen C, 61
Sturm, Lorraine, 582
Sturman, Lawrence S, 10, 179, 215
Stuto, Diane D, 548
Stuto, Peter F, 113, 350
Stutzman Jr, Richard G, 648
Suarez, Darren, 28
Suarez, Julie, 87
Suarez, Lucindo, 56
Suddaby, Glenn, 138, 260
Sudolnik, Joan C, 60
Sugarman, Risa, 558
Sugimori, Amy, 496
Sugrue, James, 536
Sugrue, Jr, William J, 220
Sullivan, Barry, 339
Sullivan, Charles, 177
Sullivan, Daniel F, 632
Sullivan, David, 256
Sullivan, David P, 65
Sullivan, Dennis, 299
Sullivan, Edward O, 521
Sullivan, Elizabeth A, 551
Sullivan, Frances, 122, 137
Sullivan, James P, 56
Sullivan, Joan, 198, 290
Sullivan, John, 255
Sullivan, Joseph P, 55
Sullivan, Margaret M, 593
Sullivan, Mark A, 306, 331
Sullivan, Mary, 472
Sullivan, Mary Brosnahan, 317
Sullivan, Mary Ellen, 69
Sullivan, Ned, 192
Sullivan, Patrick, 495
Sullivan, R Mark, 623
Sullivan, Sean, 527
Sullivan, Susan, 120, 182, 377
Sullivan, Tom, 447
Sullivan, Veronica, 554
Sullivan, W Howard, 62
Sullivan-Kriss, Patricia, 669
Sulzberger, Jr, Arthur, 597
Summit, Stuart A, 122, 258, 378
Sumner, Steven, 511
Sun Yee, Lai, 3, 129
Sundell, David, 294
Sunderland, Carolee C, 163
Sunkes, Lisa, 247, 271
Sunshine, Jeffrey S, 61
Sunshine, Nancy T, 403
Sununu, John, 385
Sununu, John E, 384, 386
Suozzi, Ralph V, 420
Suozzi, Thomas R, 404
Surace, Steve, 421
Surdey, Frank, 270
Suriano, Steve, 169
Surplus, Lisa, 232
Susice, Raymond, 401
Sussman, Irwin H, 673
Sutterby, Caryl, 604
Sutton, Anthony W, 413
Sutton, Caitlin, 482
Sutton, Charles C, 173
Sutton, Gregory, 549
Sutton, Ronald A, 65
Sutton, Sam A, 619
Svenson, Richard, 179, 213
Svizzero, Anna E, 163
Svizzero, Anne E, 8
Swackhamer, Gary D, 410
Swain, Elizabeth, 222, 474
Swan, Betsey, 498
Swan, Eileen, 498
Swan, Kim, 228
Swanger, Dustin, 616
Swanson, David C, 599
Swanson, Gregory E, 535
Swanson, Josephine, 222, 318
Swanson, Tyler C, 636
Swantek, John E, 362
Swanzey, Gregg, 189
Swart, William J, 669
Swarts, David J, 13, 348
Swartz, Greg, 88
Swartz, Susan M, 665
Sweeney, Carol, 438
Sweeney, Catherine T, 117, 351
Sweeney, Gerard J, 407
Sweeney, John E, 83, 171, 272, 329, 388
Sweeney, Kathleen D, 66
Sweeney, Kevin, 445
Sweeney, Patrick A, 68
Sweeney, Peter Paul, 59
Sweeney, Raymond, 484
Sweeney, Robert K, 43, 46, 47, 51, 52, 183, 709
Sweeney, Tim, 481
Sweeny, John W, 55
Sweeny, Stephen J, 623
Sweet, Kim, 497
Sweet, Merrilee, 458
Sweetland, Dale A, 405
Sweeton, Michael, 444
Sweitzer, Barbara A, 139, 261
Swenson, Martin L, 659
Swenson, Steve, 605
Swidorski, Theresa, 39
Swiers, George, 237, 287, 295
Swift, Carol, 480
Swift, William, 150
Swinehart, Richard E, 410
Swinnerton, Robert, 518
Swoboda, Sgt Kern, 136, 374
Sydow PhD, Debbie L, 152
Sydow, Debbie L, 617
Sykes, Ronnie, 435
Sykes, Russell, 17, 238, 313
Sywulski, Robin, 325
Szablewski, Joan, 420
Szady, Kimberly J, 8, 133, 252, 288
Szafron, Brent, 357
Szczesniak, Edward J, 160
Szczur, Margaret O, 63
Szesnat, Edward, 80
Szewczyk, Marna, 368
Szuberla, Charles, 145
Szuchman, David, 3
Szukala, Randy D, 437
Taber, Harry, 215
Tabolt, L Michael, 403
Taczanowski, Marc S, 586
Taddeo, Ann Marie, 57
Taddiken, Nancy L, 676
Tafur, Victor, 518
Tagliaferri, Gerardo, 639
Tait, Jeffrey A, 57
Takamura, Jeanette, 525
Talavera, Sheila, 14, 296
Talbot, William, 496
Tallarino, Frank, 440
Tallmer, Megan, 60
Tallon, Jr, James R, 143, 227
Taluto, Maj Gen Joseph J, 13, 360
Tamburlin, Mary Jo, 39
Tammaro, William P, 641
Tan, Eva, 499

Name Index

Tandy, Lewis, 81
Tanea, Kathy, 444
Tanenbaum, Melvyn, 58
Tanenbaum, Susie, 435
Tang, Angelica O, 273
Tangorra Jr, Cosimo, 673
Tanner, Holly C, 399
Tantillo, R Michael, 406
Tanzi, Angelo, 457
Tao, Elizabeth J Yalin, 60
Tapia, Fernando, 59
Taqi, Irum, 514
Tarantelli, Joan, 555
Tarantino, Richard P, 72
Taranto, Vincent, 420
Tardone-Steinhart, Trina, 458
Tario, LeRoy, 203, 328
Tarler, Howard A, 169
Tarlow, Deborah, 568
Tarnoff, Gary R, 495
Tarpinian, Anne S, 44, 47
Tarpley, Hugh D, 281
Tarsa, David, 540
Tartaglia, Peter, 564
Tate, Jim, 603
Tate, Sonia, 310
Tauriello, John, 12
Tauriello, John V, 280
Tauscher, Ellen O, 388
Tauzin, Dominique, 46
Tawil, Jacob, 425
Taylor, Alan E, 349
Taylor, Carolyn D, 403
Taylor, Curtis, 21, 375
Taylor, Delorme, 415
Taylor, Gene, 388
Taylor, Janice A, 58
Taylor, Jill, 179, 215
Taylor, Justin, 130
Taylor, Lonnie, 563
Taylor, Lyn, 569
Taylor, Mark, 436
Taylor, Mattie W, 123, 201, 327
Taylor, Michael, 639
Taylor, Phyllis, 428
Taylor, Ronald C, 423
Tazbir, Paul, 581
Tazzi, Louis, 434
Teall, Jon, 94
Teasdale, Parry, 594
Tedesco, Marisa, 455
Tedford, Jeff, 130
Tedisco, James N, 35, 43, 51, 202, 710
Teetz, Randy W, 664
Teifer, Bruce, 521
Tejada, Charles J, 59
Tekin, Jr, John V, 191
Telega, Stanley W, 494
Tembeckjian, Robert H, 124, 258, 379
Temperine, Brian, 356
Temperine, Carolyn, 356

Templeman, Leslie E, 145
Ten Eyck, Jeff, 80
Tendy, Thomas, 119, 352, 377
Tennen, Steven, 341
Tenney, Claudia, 43
Tenuta, Cristina, 510
Teplesky, Daniel A, 674
Tepper, Henry, 191
Tepper, Roy, 73
Teresi, Joseph C, 57
Teresi, Samuel, 423
Terpeluk, Maj Gen William, 362
Terranova, Marilyn, 676
Terranova, Marilyn C, 663
Terry, Billy, 184
Terry, III, Walter L, 74
Terry, Travis, 468
Terzer, Carl E, 94
Tesoriero, James, 213
Tesoriero, Richard, 127, 354
Testa, John, 438
Testo, Thomas A, 19
Thaler, Leonard, 226, 552
Thang, Alexis, 606
Tharp, Lorraine Power, 267
Thatcher, Raymond, 401
Thayer, Steven P, 423
Thayne, Myrna, 407
Theobald, Terri, 136
Theobalds, Kenneth, 481, 550
Theodore, James, 582
Therriault, Mary, 484
Therriault, Steve, 211, 278, 308
Thiele Jr, Fred W, 46, 47, 52, 150
Thiele, Jr, Fred W, 35, 43, 47, 53, 710
Thomas, Barbara, 498
Thomas, Carolyn, 419
Thomas, Charles J, 58
Thomas, Clifford A, 349
Thomas, Craig, 206, 240, 340, 384, 385, 387
Thomas, Dawn, 440
Thomas, Delores J, 59
Thomas, Denise, 82, 218
Thomas, Gail, 130
Thomas, Hanford, 168, 195
Thomas, James M, 447
Thomas, Joan, 646
Thomas, Kim, 309, 310
Thomas, Lawrence, 642
Thomas, Maj John J, 362
Thomas, Mark, 531
Thomas, Michael J, 328
Thomas, Sharon A, 71
Thomas, Tim, 604
Thomas, William H, 412
Thomassen, Peter, 552
Thompson, Alonzo W, 159
Thompson, Andrew, 594
Thompson, Antoine, 26, 29, 31, 32, 103, 292

Thompson, Antoine M, 24, 722
Thompson, B Dolores, 423
Thompson, Bennie G, 205, 390
Thompson, Bryce L, 678
Thompson, Chris, 606
Thompson, Dare, 498
Thompson, Dean, 481
Thompson, Frank J, 210
Thompson, II, Jerrold R, 563
Thompson, II, Jerry, 534
Thompson, III, Robert B, 534
Thompson, Jr, Kenneth, 58
Thompson, Jr, William C, 428
Thompson, Kris, 375
Thompson, Letitia, 356
Thompson, Mark, 468
Thompson, Michael K, 294, 358
Thompson, Mike, 394
Thompson, Paul W, 339
Thompson, Robert, 661
Thompson, Roger E, 663
Thompson, Sharlene J, 162
Thompson, Tom, 492
Thomson, Janice A, 126, 353
Thomson, Terri, 94
Thornberry, Mac, 388
Thornhill, Elizabeth M, 75
Thornton, Delores, 131
Thornton, Melissa, 499
Thornton, William, 45, 49, 52
Thorpe, Lorna, 430
Thrower, Ellen, 251
Thune, John, 382, 383
Thurlow, Winthrop, 255
Thurnau, Carl, 145
Thys, Dr Daniel, 367
Tiahrt, Todd, 388
Tice, Carig J, 659
Tichansky, Peter J, 107
Tierney, Barbara, 439
Tierney, John F, 392
Tierney, Robert B, 432
Tierno, Mark John, 623
Tiger, Neil H, 128, 337, 380
Tigh, Peter A, 640
Tighe, Peter, 431
Tilles, Roger B, 143
Tills, Ronald H, 59
Timber, Christine, 269
Timmons, Karen, 602
Timpano, Joseph J, 405
Tingley, Ken, 594
Tingley, Suzanne C, 650
Tingling, Milton A, 56
Tinsley-Colbert, Janice, 415
Tirschwell, Peter M, 596
Tisch, Merryl H, 143
Tiso, Maria, 497
Titone, Matthew, 43, 44, 47, 51, 52, 710
Tittler, Andrew, 185

Name Index

Titus, Michele R, 43, 45, 47, 49, 50, 51, 53, 710
Tkacs, Jeff, 418
Toal, Gloria S, 17, 313
Toas, Esq, Joshua B, 102, 124
Toas, Joshua B, 98
Tobacco, Lou, 710
Tobacco, Louis, 43, 45, 48, 51, 52
Tobias, Lou, 53
Tobin, Barbara, 136
Tobolski, Dennis V, 397
Tocci, Ronald, 269, 360
Tochterman, William, 574
Todd, Reuel A, 407
Todd, Ward, 587
Tokarski, Barbara L, 66
Tokasz, Paul, 502
Tokasz, Paul A, 51
Tokish Jr, Timothy J, 557
Tolbert, Bruce E, 57
Tolbert, Terence D, 429
Tolkoff, Andrew, 146
Tollner, Margaret, 604
Tolub, Walter, 59
Tom, Peter, 55
Tomaselli, Vincent, 525
Tomei, Albert, 56
Tomeny, Robert F, 544
Tomlinson, Guy P, 65
Tomlinson, James E, 260
Tommasone, Steven A, 440
Tompkins, William, 396
Tonello, John S, 419
Tonko, Paul D, 43, 44, 46, 47, 50, 52, 170, 710
Toohey, Lyle, 498
Toohey, Megan, 527
Toole, Elisabeth A, 72
Toole, Laurence O, 408
Toombs, Bernadette M, 162
Toomey, Dan, 15, 325, 335, 374
Toomey, Jr, John J, 70
Topodas, Jonathan M, 533
Topper, Meredith, 427
Toriello, Edward A, 558
Torino, Thomas M, 211, 278, 308
Tormey, III, James C, 257
Tormey, James C, 57
Torres, Analisa, 59
Torres, Anna, 160
Torres, Catherine, 508
Torres, Doris, 472
Torres, Edwin, 56
Torres, George, 24
Torres, Janet, 464
Torres, Leslie, 10, 229, 427
Torres, Luis, 507
Torres, Luis A, 248, 271
Torres, Maribel, 4
Torres, Rey, 237
Torres, Rey F, 237

Torres, Rob, 605
Torres, Robert E, 58
Torres, Yvonne, 657
Torrey, Matthew G, 447
Tortora, III, Ralph, 134, 216, 254
Toscano, Rose Marie, 8, 237, 279, 311
Tosi, Victor B, 160
Touchette, LTC Timothy B, 184
Touhey, Thomas, 59
Toussaint, Roger, 525
Toussaint, Wavny, 59
Towers, Robert E, 581
Towery, Carlisle, 577
Towns, Darryl C, 43, 44, 46, 48, 50, 92, 711
Towns, Edolphus, 106, 164, 171, 186, 205, 219, 298, 382, 389, 392, 731
Townsend Jr, David R, 35, 45, 46, 48, 49, 137, 259
Townsend, Alair, 601
Townsend, Barbara, 248, 271
Townsend, Jr, David R, 43, 49, 711
Townsend, Sharon, 257
Townsend, Sharon S, 57
Tracey, Patricia, 157
Trachtenberg, Robert I, 100, 148
Tracy, John, 147
Tracy, L Jane, 437
Tracy, Terrence X, 14, 135
Trafford, Brian J, 533
Trainor, Joseph, 118, 351
Traister, Pamela, 226
Tramontano, Ronald, 179, 213
Tran, Phuong, 474
Tranelli, CSJ, Sister Anne, 242
Tranelli, Sister Anne, 319
Trant, Jerry, 482
Trasker-Rothenberg, Yvonne, 523
Travers Murphy, Mary, 437
Travis Bassett, Mary, 430
Travis, Jeremy, 140, 472, 620
Travis, Jr, William E, 6, 309
Treadwell, L Michael, 582
Treadwell, Sandy, 452
Trebby, Leslie, 98, 324
Tredo, Jeffrey, 634
Treichel, Mark A, 93
Treisman, Mariya, 4, 157, 252
Trent, Scott, 431
Trentalange, Jim, 573
Trevisan, Maurizio, 527
Trezise, James, 88, 346
Triblet, Debra, 46
Trice, John R, 398
Tricomi, Erica, 463
Trimble, Melanie, 514
Trimble, Robert, 179, 215
Tringali, Joseph, 496
Trinkle, JoAnn C, 412
Tripathi, Satish, 527
Tripi, Florence, 472
Tripp, Lois M, 618

Trivisonno, Michael, 438
Troas, Joshua B, 5
Tromblee, Karen B, 647
Trombley, Donald, 659
Trombley, Samuel J, 398
Tronovitch, Steven, 415
Trotman, Michelle, 24
Trotta, Daniel, 602
Trotto, Hertha C, 70
Troutman, Shirley, 63
Trowbridge, Tammy, 571
Troy, Meoldy, 674
True, Sally T, 227
Truman, Joel S, 218, 239
Trump, Donald, 215
Trunzo, Caesar, 19, 25, 26, 27, 28, 30, 31, 32, 722
Trunzo, Michael C, 521, 611
Trzaskos, David J, 269
Tsakiris, Christopher, 548
Tsang, Marjorie, 198
Tschiember, Georgia A, 70
Tschirch, Dodie, 467
Tsotsoros, Thomas, 431
Tucker, F Michael, 107
Tucker, John C, 396
Tucker, Maryann, 101, 326
Tucker, Michael W, 424
Tucker, Sheila, 397
Tuczinski, Daniel J, 399
Tudor, Robert, 115, 181
Tudor, Tracey, 27, 28, 30
Tufankjian, Sheila, 460
Tufaro, Anthony, 554
Tuffey, James E, 414
Tuitt, Alison Y, 58
Tulis, Chelsey, 46, 48, 50
Tulloch, Andrew R, 550
Tully, Rosanne, 540
Tumia, Brandon, 559
Tumminia, Jr, Louis, 259
Tumolo, Eugene S, 438
Tung, Irene, 502
Tunney, John C, 410
Tunney, Marion, 667
Turbett, J Patrick, 410
Turbow, Daniel, 61
Turco, Thomas F, 162
Turecek, Timothy, 644
Turley, Michael, 178
Turnbill, Thomas, 592
Turner, Ann P, 658
Turner, Bonnie, 38
Turner, Lisa, 569
Turner, Marlene, 3, 194, 254
Turner, Matthew J, 75
Turner, Michael, 392
Turner, Pierre B, 60
Turney, Carol, 161
Turoski, John, 23
Turpin, Mike, 526

801

Name Index

Turso, Rocco, 560
Turso, Vito A, 434
Turton, Michael, 580
Tutoni, Mitch, 445
Tuttle, Carrie M, 102, 115, 230
Tutty, Gary, 663
Tutunjian, Harry J, 443
Tvedt, Helen, 445
Tweddell, Richard C, 410
Twomey, John, 276
Tyler, Bradley E, 139, 261
Tymeson, Michael, 133, 252
Tynan, James, 349
Tyner-Taylor, Gail, 13, 348
Tyrrell, Edward, 138, 260
Udall, Mark, 392
Udall, Tom, 340
Ulberg, John, 213
Ulfik, Cathy, 449
Ulianko, John A, 204
Ullman, Lisa, 4, 211, 278
Ulm, Les, 511
Uloops, Robert, 131
Umane, Frederic M, 160
Ungar, Robert A, 526
Unger, David, 131
Unger, Robert E, 120, 336
Updegrove, Richard, 405
Uplinger, Karen M, 75
Upson, Hollis D, 401
Upton, Fred, 389
Ursillo, William, 147
Urstadt, Charles J, 113, 335
Urtz, Cindy, 403
Uschakow, Peter, 281
Usher, Brad, 22
Usnik, Toby, 635
Uviller, Rena K, 59
Vacant, , 6, 7, 8, 9, 10, 12, 17, 18, 23, 29, 32, 33, 34, 36, 37, 38, 39, 42, 43, 46, 48, 49, 50, 53, 54, 64, 73, 79, 80, 81, 82, 83, 90, 91, 93, 95, 103, 105, 113, 117, 118, 119, 120, 125, 127, 129, 130, 131, 132, 133, 135, 144, 146, 147, 157, 160, 163, 169, 171, 177, 178, 179, 180, 183, 184, 185, 195, 196, 199, 202, 204, 205, 212, 213, 214, 217, 218, 228, 229, 231, 232, 245, 246, 247, 248, 252, 254, 257, 269, 270, 271, 279, 280, 282, 283, 288, 296, 301, 303, 307, 309, 310, 311, 312, 313, 314, 325, 329, 333, 335, 336, 337, 348, 351, 352, 353, 354, 355, 356, 361, 364, 371, 373, 374, 375, 379, 380, 420, 425, 429, 430, 431, 445, 592, 611, 656
Vacant, Bacqueline, 44
Vacca, Carolyn, 404
Vaccaro, Antoanela, 485
Vaccaro, Lori, 207
Vacco, Dennis, 476
Vadney, Glenn S, 591
Vagelatos, Nick, 455

Vagianelis, Nicholas J, 237, 287, 295
Vainisi, Bill, 516
Valdes MD, Martin, 537
Valdes, Gil, 493
Valdes, Javier, 493
Valente, Edmond, 497
Valenti, Aurora R, 411
Valenti, Linda, 14, 136
Valenti, Ronald D, 675
Valenti, Tom, 570
Valentine, John, 442
Valentine, Keith, 402
Valentine, Nicholas J, 436
Valentine, Ronald C, 412
Valentine, Todd D, 8, 157
Valentino, Angelo, 452
Valentino, Cathy, 423
Valentino, Joseph D, 57
Valeri, Peter, 171
Valesky, David J, 25, 26, 28, 29, 31, 32, 81, 722
Valiante, Frank, 569
Valle, Glenn P, 16, 136
Valley, Nancy, 497
Vallone, Paul, 475
Vallone, Sr, Peter F, 475
Valone, Gloria, 401
Van Auken, Lori, 470
Van Blarcum, Paul, 412
Van Bramer, James, 432
Van Bramer, Jamie, 532
Van Bramer, Jayne, 281
Van Buren, Anne, 172, 466
Van Buren, Diane, 129
Van Capelle, Alan, 541
Van Cott, Alan, 669
Van De Loo, Kathleen A, 107, 358
Van de Walle, Carla, 127, 231, 337
Van Deusen, James, 399
Van Epps, Barbara, 474
Van Erk, Nina, 154
Van Eyk, Jonathan, 670
Van Guilder, Carol, 517
Van Hamlin, Kurt, 447
Van Hoesen, Steve, 153
Van Hoesen, Steven, 460, 480
Van Leuven, David, 178
Van Lindt, John, 120, 336
Van Loon, Jerry, 342
Van Namee, Frederic A, 405
Van Norden, L John, 441
Van Ooyen, Marcel, 188
Van Ross, Clement, 407
Van Schaack, Rene, 189
Van Slyke, William, 484
Van Strydonck, Thomas M, 57
Van Suntum, Lisa, 518
Van Ullen, Stephen J, 71
Van Wagner, Marcia, 428
Van Wormer, James, 658
Van, Marina, 573

vanAlstyne, David, 133, 253, 288
VanAmburgh, Judy, 42
VanAmerogen, Deborah, 127, 228, 231, 337
VanAmerongen, Deborah, 10, 232
VanBrakle, Tina, 164
VanBuren, Denise, 486
VanBuren, Maureen, 674
Vancavage, Robert, 111, 359
Vancavage, Robert E, 460, 534
Vancko, Candace S, 615
VanDeCarr, Jan, 488
VanDee, Ronald J, 399
Vandenburgh, Paul, 605
Vanderbeck, Rob, 606
Vanderhoef, C Scott, 408
Vanderhook, Joe, 596
Vandermark, Brenda, 64
Vandermark, David, 419
Vandervort, John W, 527
Vandervort, Todd H, 527
Vanderwalker, Robert, 402
VanDeusen, Dirck, 476
VanDonsel, Richard C, 399
VanDyke, Marilyn, 439
Vanecek, William, 126, 353
VanGorder, Garry, 573
VanHoesen, Bill, 409
Vann, Mark, 131
Vann, Ruby, 599
Vanness, Mark, 604
Vanni, Robert J, 432
VanNortwick, Thomas H, 228
VanSickle, Darlene, 6, 168, 195
Vanstrom, Stephen, 641
VanStrydonck, Thomas M, 57, 257
Vantine, Whitney K, 668
VanVoorhis, Steven, 87
Vanvoorst, Mark, 284
Vanwagner, Jay, 581
VanWormer, III, Earl, 409
Vargason, James B, 397
Varin, Byron A, 401
Varoli, David, 428
Varricchio, Ronald, 63
Vasiloff, Thomas, 540
Vasisht, Gaurav, 4, 90
Vasko, Robert, 281
Vasquez, Jessica, 140, 317, 472
Vassell, William C, 140
Vattimo, Brian, 121, 170
Vattimo, Victoria, 23, 32, 339
Vaughan, Col Timothy G, 13
Vaughan, David B, 56
Vaughan, Peter B, 318
Vazquez, Valerie, 429
Vecchiarella, Vincent, 657
Vecchiarella, Vincent J, 642
Vecchiarelli, Rose, 604
Vecchio, Patrick R, 442
Velasquez, Nydia M, 93
Velazquez, Nydia, 106, 274, 392

Name Index

Velazquez, Nydia M, 232, 233, 249, 382, 390, 731
Velez, Laura, 143, 308
Venditto, John, 438
Vennard, Michele, 338
Ventre & McCarthy, Coulter, 441
Ventre, Jeannie, 441
Venugopalan, Vathsala, 214, 360
Vera, Angel, 502
Verano, Anthony, 606
Verdile, Vincent P, 622
Verges, Robin, 519
Vermilyea, Willis, 114, 335, 376, 402
Vernuccio, Jr, Frank, 248, 271
Versaci, Vincent W, 75
Versteeg, Jim, 458
Vertucci, Constance A, 64
Ververs, Duncan, 458
Verzulli, Marie, 511
Vescio, Marilyn A, 62
Vespia, Hope B, 441
Veto, Peter, 608
Vetter, Louise A, 458
Vetters, Vic, 610
Vevle, Mark, 344
Vezzetti, Ruth A, 161
Vicory, Jr, Alan H, 126, 183
Victor, Paul A, 58
Vidal, Alfredo, 528
Vidal, Alfredo M, 540
Vidal, Yorelis, 502
Vieira, Al, 592
Vietri, Joseph, 184
Vigdor, Justin L, 202, 259
Vigliotti Sr, Stephan J, 650
Vigus, Kenneth W, 125, 183
Villagomez, Michelle, 531
Villani, Miriam, 189
Villanti, Mark, 663
Villanti, Mark A, 665
Villanti, Sam, 452
Villegas, George R, 59
Viloria-Fisher, Vivian, 410
Vinas, Doreen, 472
Vincent, Curtis, 79
Vincente, Edna, 498
Viola, James, 145
Violante, Mark A, 73
Violante, Michael J, 405
Violette, Marc, 3, 254
Violette, Mark, 371
Virga, Kristie L, 158
Virgil, Michael, 662
Virginia Foley, Doris Duffy, Co-President, 570
Virtanen, John, 125, 149, 297
Virtuoso, Dennis F, 405
Visclosky, Peter J, 171, 388
Viscusi, Rico, 497
Visitacion-Lewis, Laura, 56
Vitale, Benjamin, 102, 114, 376

Vitale, James, 541
Vitale, Thomas F, 535
Vitali, John, 432
Vitaliano, Eric N, 59
Vitek, Lorene, 436
Vitello, Robert, 12, 269
Vitello, Robert J, 253
Vitter, David, 385
Vittoria, Steve, 603
Vivek, Seeth, 553
Vizian, Donna, 186
Vladeck, Judith, 277
Voelkl, Thomas W, 415
Vogel, Pamela J, 412
Vogt, Joan M, 126, 183, 337, 380
Vogt, Rosemary, 19
Vogtli Jr, Joseph, 361
Vogtli Jr, Joseph H, 17
Voinovich, George V, 385, 386
Vojta, George J, 94
Volcko, Frank, 418
Volker, Carol, 37
Volker, Dale M, 19, 25, 26, 27, 28, 30, 31, 137, 259, 723
Volkosh, James C, 405
Volpe, Edward J, 56, 64
Von Ahn, John, 486
Von Pless, George, 82, 232
Vona, John L, 161
Voninski, John R, 57
Vossler, Thomas G, 565
Vranich, Marina, 505
Vukelj, Simon, 458
Vuolo, Mike, 587
Wachsman, Harvey F, 611
Wachtler, Lauren J, 110, 265
Wackstein, Nancy, 323, 526
Wade, Diane, 161
Wade, Edward, 348
Wade, Thomas W, 450
Wadosky, Sue, 595
Wadsworth, Barrett, 50
Wafer, Shelby, 484
Waffner, Troy, 40
Wager, Elsie, 498
Wager, Julie, 595
Wager, Lisa, 482
Wagner Mele, Amy, 417
Wagner, Don, 607
Wagner, Elise, 495
Wagner, Jeanne, 470
Wagner, Paul, 406
Wagner, Sue Ellen, 484
Wagoner, Deborah, 280
Wagoner, Robert, 650
Wahl, JoAnn M, 56
Wai Gin, Man, 427
Waite, Ginny Brown, 393
Waite, Paul, 542
Waite, Richard, 536
Waithe, Deighton S, 60

Waithe, Wilma, 213
Waithe, Wilma E, 10
Waivada, Theresa G, 589
Waizer, PhD, Jonas, 284
Waks, Jay W, 276
Walbridge, Wayne C, 666
Walcott, Dennis M, 426
Walczyk, Robert, 574
Walden, Greg, 340
Waldman, Mark, 144
Waldon, Jr, Alton R, 59
Waldron, Jr, Alton R, 7, 132, 311
Waldron, Kathleen M, 619
Waldron, Sherryl, 66
Wales, Ross, 126, 183
Walker, Deanna, 474
Walker, Edgar G, 59
Walker, George, 119, 352
Walker, II, John H, 452
Walker, Jeff, 215
Walker, Jessica, 526
Walker, Maureen, 425
Walker, Rob, 35, 43, 44, 47, 51, 52, 339
Walker, Robert, 711
Walker, Sam D, 69
Wall, Daniel E, 6, 288, 296
Wall, Duane D, 97
Wallace, Campbell, 48, 49, 50
Wallace, Earl, 269
Wallace, Edward, 488
Wallace, Harry, 210
Wallace, Jr, James W, 402
Wallach, Frederick K, 534
Wallach, Rebecca, 502
Wallack, Al, 604, 608
Wallenstein, John S, 551
Wallin, Warren, 123, 149
Wallingford, David, 270
Walrich, Susan B, 561
Walsh Sr, Thomas M, 408
Walsh, Bridget, 522
Walsh, Christopher T, 12, 254
Walsh, Daniel, 205, 303
Walsh, Daniel B, 107
Walsh, David, 145
Walsh, Donald A, 33, 54, 81, 103, 183
Walsh, Edward W, 547
Walsh, George, 599
Walsh, James, 131
Walsh, James T, 83, 171, 329, 382, 387, 388, 732
Walsh, Joan B, 421
Walsh, John P, 60
Walsh, Jr, Edward M, 448
Walsh, Kevin E, 405
Walsh, LTC Bill, 355
Walsh, Margaret T, 61
Walsh, Maureen, 431
Walsh, Patricia M, 235
Walsh, Robert W, 434
Walsh, Sharon, 34, 375

Name Index

Walsh, Thomas C, 72
Walsh, Thomas P, 138, 260
Walsh, William, 526
Walsh, William D, 66
Walter, Mark, 465
Walter, Matthew, 20
Walters, Bradley P, 559
Walters, Steven J, 421
Walters, Tony, 257
Walther, Martha, 117, 350
Walton, Frances A, 9, 91, 99, 116, 124, 231, 333
Waltrous, Dolores L, 59
Wambua, Mathew, 120
Wamp, Marcy, 529
Wanamaker, Timothy E, 571
Wandally, Kevin, 501
Wanfried, Kurt W, 598
Wappett, John P M, 412
Ward, Christine, 144
Ward, Dennis, 158
Ward, Diane, 522
Ward, James E, 259
Ward, John, 444
Ward, John T, 62
Ward, Laura A, 60
Ward, Mark J, 640
Ward, Peter, 566
Ward, Robert, 466
Ward, Sean E, 575
Ward-Harper, Mikki, 309
Ware, Eleanor, 519
Warnecke, Allan J, 407
Warner, John, 385
Warner, Judith, 409
Warner, Kenneth L, 543
Warner, Richard A, 419
Warnick, Thomas A, 412
Warnke, Stephen A, 519
Warnock, Gordon, 460, 515
Warren, Glenn, 18, 247, 270
Warren, John, 430
Warren, Kenneth J, 115, 181
Warren, Paul R, 259
Warren, Shawn, 497
Warren, Vincent, 241
Warren, William P, 67
Warren-Merrick, Gerri, 611
Warrier, Sujata, 14, 313
Warshaw, David T, 543
Warshaw, Drew, 3
Warshawsky, Ira B, 58
Wart, Donald M, 161
Warwick, James, 14, 180, 334
Wasch, Ken, 112
Washburn, Richard, 228
Wasik, Joseph, 273
Wason, Jr, Jay, 251
Wasp, Robert G, 421
Wassus, Michael F, 410
Waterhouse, Erin T, 513

Waters, Gloriana, 619
Waters, Maxine, 233, 390
Waters, Rolf A, 651
Waters, Stephen, 599
Watford, Dolores, 154
Watkins, Barry, 344
Watkins, Edward A, 11, 237
Watkins, James C, 92
Watkins, Jr, Thomas H, 592
Watkins-Bates, Cari, 521
Watson, Anthony, 489
Watson, Duane, 147
Watson, James, 674
Watson, Jim, 25, 30
Watson, John, 7, 132, 311, 372
Watson, Margaret R, 227
Watson, Matt, 507
Watson, Meghan, 497
Watson, Susan, 16, 101, 180, 199, 291
Watson, Susan L, 99, 135, 229, 247, 255, 270, 302, 325
Watson, William J, 73
Watt, Ed, 525, 566
Watt, Melvin L, 390
Wattie, Travis, 528
Watts, Steven, 515
Waxman, Henry A, 164, 205, 298, 392
Wayne, Patricia, 422
Webb, George, 145
Webb, Jack H, 93
Webb, Marcel, 114, 335
Webb, Rick, 455
Webber, Troy K, 56
Weber, Bill, 461
Weber, Corinne, 452
Weber, Gary J, 68
Weber, Greg, 550
Weber, Michael, 21, 28
Webster, Barry J, 455
Webster, Paul, 456
Wedley, Frederick A, 118, 351
Weed, Harry, 440
Weems, Sherryl D, 618
Wegener, Thomas, 248, 271
Wehner, David P, 11, 246, 268
Weidman, Anne R, 451
Weidman, Mary C, 398
Weihs, George, 366
Weill, Charles B, 205, 303
Weiller, Daniel, 16, 198, 290, 374
Weinberg, David, 42
Weinberg, Hugh, 435
Weinberg, Janet, 485
Weinberg, Philip, 192
Weinberg, Richard M, 60
Weinberger, Harriet, 256
Weine, Jordan, 552
Weine, Ken, 602
Weiner, Alfred, 57
Weiner, Anthony, 186, 233

Weiner, Anthony D, 139, 261, 356, 382, 391, 393, 732
Weiner, Audrey, 223
Weiner, Judith Kaufman, 341
Weingarten, Randi, 155
Weingarten, Steven B, 529, 537
Weinheimer, Kathleen A, 546
Weinraub, David, 465
Weinraub, David N, 533, 535
Weinshall, Iris, 115, 148, 619
Weinstein, Barry, 400
Weinstein, David, 4, 268, 295, 307
Weinstein, Helene E, 43, 44, 45, 49, 51, 53, 259, 711
Weinstein, Jeremy, 257
Weinstein, Jeremy S, 58
Weinstein, Stewart H, 61
Weinstock, Dean, 280
Weinstock, Hannah, 488
Weirman, Jaye, 273
Weisberg, Lisa, 83, 140, 531
Weisbroth, Benjamin, 17, 361
Weisenberg, Harvey, 34, 43, 44, 46, 47, 50, 52, 711
Weisenberg, Maria, 38
Weisfuse, Isaac, 430
Weismantel, Lynda, 470
Weiss, Allan B, 58
Weiss, Andrew, 18
Weiss, Andrew J, 200, 313
Weiss, Howard, 478
Weiss, Luzer, 80
Weiss, Manny, 355
Weiss, Sidney N, 546
Weissman, George, 122
Weissman, Staci, 511
Weisstein, Jessie, 471
Weitz, Daniel M, 257
Weitzman, Howard S, 404
Wejko, Kelly J, 62
Welby, Julianne, 603
Welch, Janet, 144, 372
Welch, Robert, 215
Welch, Ruth, 484
Weld, Tim, 511
Welker, Pamela A, 163
Weller, Courtney, 464
Weller, Jerry, 394
Wellman, Eric, 605
Wells, Donald, 349
Wells, Earl, 480
Wells, Peter N, 66
Wells, Richard, 339
Wellspeak, John P, 34
Welsh, Edward, 485
Weltchek, Andrew, 504
Welter, John, 144
Wenck, Romona N, 662
Wendt, Michael, 658
Wendt, Peter M, 60
Weprin, Mark, 43, 44, 45, 49, 103

Name Index

Weprin, Mark S, 51, 712
Werner, Mary M, 58
Werner, Walter, 552
Wertman, Michael, 596
Weschler, David W, 264
Wescott, Drew, 204, 328
West, Jason, 543
West, Judi, 44
West, Lester J, 232
West, Michael, 409
West, Thomas, 497
Westerfield, Mark H, 358
Western, Donald, 581
Westmoreland, Lynn, 393
Weston, Dale N, 411
Westphal, Fredrick, 397
Westra, Alan, 88
Wetherbee, Michael J, 667
Wetmore, Weeden, 398
Wettenhall, Paul, 100, 148
Wetzel, William A, 59
Wexler, Joan G, 262, 622
Wexler, Robert, 391
Wexler, Scott, 108, 342, 513
Wexner, Ira H, 58
Whalen, Dennis, 3, 211, 237, 278, 307
Whalen, Gerald, 57
Whalen, Joseph A, 319
Whalen, Mark, 553
Whalen, Mark R, 397
Whalen, Mildred, 498
Wheatley, Jason, 26, 29, 31
Wheatley, Mary Jo, 498
Wheeler, Dennis M, 547
Wheeler, Janet, 281
Wheeler, Richard, 674
Wheeling, Robert, 419
Whelan, C Douglas, 658
Whelan, Charles D, 568
Whelan, John S, 648
Whelan, Rory P, 22
Whelan, Thomas F, 58
Whicher, Stephen F, 411
Whightsil, Laurie M, 406
Whipple, James, 582
Whipple, Tom, 448
Whitaker, G Warren, 263, 330
Whitaker, Mark, 602
Whitbeck, Carl, 121, 353
White, Carol, 472
White, Daniel, 678
White, David, 367
White, Douglas, 429
White, Kevin, 604
White, Maryann, 473
White, Megan, 333
White, Michael, 424
White, Michael P, 117, 182, 376
White, Peter E, 349
White, Phyllis W, 191
White, Renee A, 60

White, Sharon E, 159
White, Shelby, 555
White, William R, 448
Whitehead, Carol S, 410
Whitehead, James, 281
Whitehead, Merle, 305
Whiteman, Michael, 243, 473, 529
Whitfield, Ed, 389
Whitfield, Ronald W, 539
Whitman, Paul, 493
Whitmore, Gloria L, 450
Whitney, Susan, 650
Whittaker, Lori, 493
Whittles, Joseph, 546
Whyte, Maria R, 400
Wiater, Michael, 497
Wick, Edmund V, 45, 48, 50
Wick, Larisa, 531
Wicker, Roger F, 388
Wickerham, David A, 408
Wickes, Roger A, 412
Wickes, Vincent, 203
Wickham, Gregory, 520
Wickham, Melanie, 85
Wicklund, Diane, 270
Wickman, Marilyn, 362
Wieboldt, Robert A, 536
Wieda, Christopher, 199
Wiedemer, George C, 438
Wiederhorn, Jo, 152, 221
Wielk, Carol A, 227
Wiernak, Roberta, 498
Wiertz, Michael, 343
Wiesenfeld, Jeffrey, 619
Wiesmaier, Patricia, 74
Wigger, Scott, 488
Wiggins, Robert B, 64
Wightman, Maurice C, 637
Wigzell, Barbara, 228
Wijtowicz, Jim, 439
Wiktorek, David, 247, 271
Wiktorko, John, 649
Wilber, Jay L, 397
Wilber, Kenneth H, 399
Wilbur, Donald, 412
Wilcox, Arthur, 479
Wilcox, Peter G, 111, 559
Wildeman, Thelma, 412
Wilder, Jo Ann M, 402
Wiles, Ben, 517
Wiles, Lisa A, 673
Wiles, Marie, 680
Wiley, Linda, 62
Wiley, Maxwell T, 59
Wilhelm, John W, 545
Wilhelm, Terry J, 402
Wilkes Jr, Leroy D, 435
Wilkes, Monica, 196
Wilkins, Lottie E, 56
Wilkinson, Carol, 378
Wilkinson, Gwen, 411

Wilkinson, Peter, 439
Wilkinson, Steven, 39
Willacy, Sarah, 565
Willdigg, Thomas, 460
Wille, Frederick A, 679
Willey, Ann, 179, 215
Williams Deleeuw, Barbara, 514
Williams, Alfreda A, 420
Williams, Amy, 153, 344
Williams, Angela J, 419
Williams, Barbara S, 105, 260
Williams, Betty J, 59
Williams, Carolyn, 472
Williams, Carolyn G, 619
Williams, Cassie, 438
Williams, Cathy, 62
Williams, David, 289, 302, 326
Williams, David H, 443
Williams, Debbra, 273
Williams, Donald, 419
Williams, Donna M, 457
Williams, Donna Montalto, 220
Williams, Earl, 151
Williams, Frank B, 57
Williams, George, 453
Williams, George J, 407
Williams, Gregory, 472
Williams, Gregory H, 620
Williams, Helena, 467
Williams, Jack, 350
Williams, Jacqueline, 507
Williams, Jacqui, 501
Williams, James A, 645
Williams, Jeanne M, 163
Williams, Jeffrey, 557
Williams, Jerry W, 22
Williams, Joseph, 131
Williams, Jr, Donald A, 412
Williams, Judy, 9, 195, 289
Williams, Jumaane, 525
Williams, Katherine, 218, 239, 315
Williams, Kathryn-Celia, 488
Williams, Lloyd, 576
Williams, Lois Booker, 254
Williams, Mark S, 397
Williams, Mary H, 540
Williams, Melvin L, 132
Williams, Milton L, 55
Williams, MSGT Jason, 355
Williams, Patricia Anne, 60
Williams, Paulina, 484
Williams, Peggy R, 626
Williams, Philip M, 637
Williams, Rich, 439
Williams, Rob, 605
Williams, Robert F, 248, 271
Williams, Ronald F, 616
Williams, Samuel G, 537, 556, 568
Williams, Timothy P, 5, 212, 279, 308
Williams, Wanda, 298, 479
Williams, William F, 439

Name Index

Williamsen, Paul G, 649
Willis, James, 527
Wills, Frances G, 675
Wills, Randolph, 150
Wills, Ruben, 22
Willsie, Paula A, 494
Willson, Carolyn, 420
Wilmers, Robert G, 95
Wilpon, Fred, 345
Wils, Madeyln, 347
Wilson, Anne, 523
Wilson, Charles T, 677
Wilson, Daniel C, 74
Wilson, Donna, 97
Wilson, Heather, 206, 394
Wilson, Jerome, 493
Wilson, Joe, 389
Wilson, John, 179, 213
Wilson, John H, 59
Wilson, Joseph, 204, 328
Wilson, Laval S, 645
Wilson, Lewis, 453
Wilson, Lewis L, 161
Wilson, Linda, 595
Wilson, Lois, 593
Wilson, Loraine, 144
Wilson, Ralph, 641
Wilson, Stephen, 189
Wilson, Tom, 516
Wilton, Michael, 502
Wimpfheimer, Ruth, 43
Winans, David, 114, 350
Wind, Kelley, 458
Windram, Richard, 528
Wineburgh, Marsha, 553
Winegar, Natasha, 525
Wines, Margaret, 625
Wing, Stephen, 439
Wingender, Karen, 304
Winkle Jr, Donald M, 541
Winn, Thomas, 416
Winner Jr, George H, 25, 30, 33, 54, 81, 103, 183
Winner, George H, 28
Winner, George H, Jr, 723
Winner, Jr, George H, 27, 29, 30, 203
Winslow, F Dana, 58
Winslow, Terri, 414
Winsor, Kacie, 454
Winsten, Richard D, 507
Winter, Don, 504
Winter, Ethan, 496
Winter, Nancy A, 364
Winters, Fred, 459
Winzinger, Brig Gen Robert J, 368
Wirth, William, 329
Wirtz, Chandra L, 410
Wise, Anderson, 128, 354
Wise, Daniel, 596
Wise, Graham, 25
Wise, JD, Jeff, 285, 322

Wise, Jeffrey, 517
Wise, Kathleen J, 13, 100, 147
Wise, Walter W, 547
Wisneski, Jessica, 495
Wisniewski, Vanessa, 503
Wist, Ronda, 432
Withers, Harry, 453
Witherspoon, Karen, 472
Witherspoon, Roger, 472
Witkowski, Debbie, 443
Witkowski, Ernest L, 666
Witt, Joseph, 547
Witt, Jr, Richard, 507
Witt, Richard, 322
Witte, Linda L, 397
Wittenberg, Carol, 275
Wittner, Bonnie G, 60
Witzak, Lorraine A, 563
Wochele, Chuck, 357
Woda, Edward, 44
Woelk, Allison A, 492
Woelzl, Susan, 345
Wogick, Sandra A, 62
Wojnar, Eileen, 246, 269
Wojtaszek, Henry, 453
Wolanin Young, Gail, 426
Wolf, Frank, 525
Wolf, Frank R, 388
Wolf, Richard T, 428
Wolfe, Catherine O'Hagan, 55
Wolfe, Dorothy A, 432
Wolfersteig, Jean L, 280
Wolff, Raymond, 328
Wolfgang, Penny, 57
Wolham, John, 289, 302, 326
Wolken, Randall, 504
Wollman, Paul L, 71
Wollner, David V, 212
Wolman, Len, 525
Woloz, Michael, 474, 475, 514
Wong, Douglas S, 60
Wong, Jackie, 493
Woo, Doris, 470
Wood, Bill, 449
Wood, Cheryl, 18, 247, 270
Wood, Cliff L, 617
Wood, Jonathan, 411
Wood, Jr, Robert H, 472
Wood, Kathleen M, 639
Wood, Kimba M, 260
Wood, Laura, 45, 50, 51
Wood, Leslie, 224
Wood, Mark, 580
Wood, Meg, 42
Wood, Norman E, 323
Wood, Philip W, 128, 149, 612
Wood, Scott, 578
Wood, Thomas F, 418
Wood, William J, 158
Woodard, Jean, 3
Woodard, Jean M, 197, 253

Woodard, Michele M, 58
Woodburn, Robert L, 411
Woodford, R C, 398
Woodlock, David, 280
Woodman, Thomas L, 599
Woods, Jeff, 602
Woods, Lori Currier, 66
Woodward, Jamie, 102, 327
Woodward, John J, 409
Woodward, Marie M, 161
Woodward, Mark, 417
Woodward, Mary, 144
Woodward, Michael, 419
Woodworth, Neil F, 455
Wool, Louis N, 676
Woolsey, Lynn, 151
Woolsey, Lynn C, 389
Wooster, Judith S, 668
Work, Mary MacMaster, 69
Workman, Thomas E, 250, 524
Worona, Jay, 522
Worth, Mary Kay, 641
Wortman, Robert, 555
Woughter, Carol, 130, 131
Wozniak, Peggy J, 639
Wozniak, Ronald L, 400
Wray, Daniel, 120, 336
Wrege, Paul F, 82
Wren, Gordon, 408
Wren, Maureen, 9, 178, 372
Wright, Beth N, 455
Wright, Bob, 133, 252, 288
Wright, David, 498
Wright, David J, 235
Wright, G Stephen, 314
Wright, Geoffrey D, 60
Wright, Gwen, 14, 136, 312
Wright, James W, 20, 25, 26, 27, 28, 29, 30, 31, 32, 170, 723
Wright, Jeff, 442, 592
Wright, John, 464
Wright, Justin, 106, 172
Wright, Keith L, 45
Wright, Keith L T, 43, 46, 49, 51, 712
Wright, Kevin, 407
Wright, Leslie, 504
Wright, Lester, 7, 132
Wright, Pat, 247, 271
Wright, Schawannah, 341
Wright, Vicki, 638
Wright, William C, 406
Wrobel, Priscilla, 309
Wrobel, W, 562
Wrobleski, Thomas, 599
Wrona, Christine, 62
Wu, David, 392
Wuensch, Joseph P, 433
Wuerdeman, Teresa, 132
Wulfhorst, Ellen, 602
Wurth, Chris, 607
Wurth, Mary Jane, 484

Name Index

Wyant Jr, Douglas H, 639
Wyche, Leslie, 555
Wyden, Ron, 340, 384
Wyker, Barbara, 596
Wylde, Kathryn S, 580
Wylie, Andrew J, 399
Wyner, Daniel M, 412
Wynn, Albert R, 186, 389
Wynne, Brian, 60
Xanthis, John P, 661
Yacknin, Ellen, 74
Yacono, Karen, 518
Yacono, Tomlynn, 196
Yacuzzo, Raymond E, 450
Yaffa, Jennifer Saul, 453
Yahia, Laurance, 548
Yan, Jimmy, 435
Yanover, Frank, 482
Yaro, Robert D, 111, 236
Yasgur, Samuel S, 411
Yates, Carole, 144
Yates, James A, 56
Yavornitzki, Mark L, 251, 553
Yazurlo, Michael, 677
Yearwood, Alvin M, 60
Yee, Lai-Sun, 435
Yee, PE, Chester, 120, 149
Yee, Yue, 269, 312
Yeger, Kalman, 551
Yelich, Bruce, 130
Yellen, David N, 140
Yellin, Neil S, 118, 351
Yennella, Mary Ann, 160
Yeomans, Gayle, 493
Yeomans, Gayle A, 250
Yessman Jr, William, 409
Yeung, Miriam, 242, 284, 320
Yorio, Michael, 211, 278, 308
York, John M, 403
York, Louis B, 56
Yoshikawa, Vance, 492
Yost, Bethany, 578
Yoswein, Joni A, 532
Youdelman, Sondra, 474
Young, Bruce E, 117, 182
Young, C W Bill, 387
Young, Carl, 225, 321
Young, Carl S, 552
Young, Catharine M, 25, 28, 29, 31, 32, 53, 80, 723
Young, David, 53
Young, Don, 171, 186, 391
Young, Elizabeth, 399
Young, Elizabeth C, 68
Young, Ellen, 43, 44, 46, 49, 50, 712
Young, Kevin G, 75

Young, Lindsay, 293, 331
Young, Lindsay M, 208
Young, Michael F, 403
Young, Oliver C, 209
Young, Richard, 125, 149, 297, 648
Young, Robert, 660
Young, Ronald R, 520
Young, Ruth, 450
Young, Sonny, 344
Young, Theodore H, 450
Young, William, 527
Young, William N, 121, 291, 378
Youngblood, Dianne B, 668
Younger, Stephen P, 122, 258
Youngren, Nissa, 469
Younis, Kevin, 526
Younkins, Ron, 256
Youssouf, Emily, 120, 230
Yunis, Bebette, 200
Yusuf, Bibi N, 435
Yutko, Ronald T, 119, 352
Zaccone, John, 436
Zackoski, Colleen, 280
Zagame, John, 513
Zagor, David J, 427
Zaiger, Richard D, 272
Zaim, Abid, 497
Zajac PhD, Carol S, 635
Zalen, Stanley L, 8, 157
Zaleski, Terence M, 152, 317
Zambelli, Barbara G, 69
Zambito, Joseph, 664
Zamdri, Melissa, 515
Zamechansky, Kathy, 532
Zamm, Michael, 153
Zammit, Paul, 186
Zane, Cynthia, 625
Zanetti, Joseph P, 661
Zaprowski, Sue, 584
Zarcone, Michael, 479
Zarecki, Jane, 402
Zaremba, Agnes, 75
Zaron, Barbara, 300, 512, 549
Zarutskie, Andrew J, 436
Zatz, Arthur A, 557
Zavelle, Michael J, 619
Zayas, Joseph A, 60
Zdeb, Kathy, 179, 215
Zebrowski, Kenneth, 43, 712
Zecca Corsale, Barbara, 579
Zeh, Sr, Richard G, 259
Zeidman, Daniel, 309
Zeigler, Neldra M, 433
Zelazny, Donald, 178
Zelazny, Helen L, 161
Zeleke, Aster, 204, 240

Zeosky, Gerald M, 136
Zero, Edward J, 679
Zerrillo, Robert, 17, 349
Zeto, Keith, 198
Ziegler, Laurence, 329
Ziegler, Paul E, 338
Zielinksi, Kristin, 44
Zielinski, Kristin, 48, 50
Ziemba, Christine M, 416
Zigman, Alex J, 60
Zilbauer, Erin, 604
Zilgme, Arnis, 418
Zimar, Nancy R, 678
Zimmer, Michael E, 438
Zimmerman, Hope Schwartz, 65
Zimmerman, Joseph F, 166, 210
Zimmer-Meyer, Heidi N, 583
Zinck, Robert, 248, 271
Zinner, Joshua, 11, 237
Ziolkowski, Michael J, 356
Zittel, Barbara, 146, 212
Zlogar, Patrick, 502
Zmuda, Walter D, 126, 353
Zobel, John, 9, 195, 289
Zogby, John, 112, 167
Zogg, Jeffrey J, 109, 543
Zolas, Carolyn, 523
Zolberg, Aristide R, 242
Zolberg, Vera, 345
Zoller, LTC Virginia, 362
Zollo, Margaret, 145
Zuber, Michael P, 281
Zuber, Paul W, 516
Zuccaro, Richard, 493
Zuchlewski, Pearl, 263, 276
Zucker, Howard, 293
Zuckerman, Bob, 576
Zuckerman, Mortimer, 596
Zugibe, Patricia, 408
Zukerman, Robert, 333
Zukowski, Rosemary, 72
Zullo, Joelle, 518
Zupan, Jeffrey M, 359
Zurack, Marlene, 430
Zurlo, John H, 399
Zurlo, Michael E, 399
Zwack, Henry F, 211, 278, 308
Zweibel, Ronald A, 59
Zwickel, Howard, 10, 195
Zwiebel, David, 152
Zybert, Edmund, 214
Zygo, Carol, 649
Zylka, Scott, 506
Zymanek, James J, 414
Zyra, Tom, 215, 245
Zyra, Wayne E, 404

Organization Index

Includes the names of the top three levels in all New York State executive departments and agencies; public corporations; authorities; commissions; all organizations listed in the Private Sector sources segment of each policy chapter; lobbyist organizations; political action committees; chambers of commerce; newspapers; news services; radio and television stations; SUNY and CUNY locations; and private colleges.

10th Judicial District, 57
117 W 89th Street LLC (AS Realty Partners), 467
1170 PEC, 533
1199 SEIU United Healthcare Workers East, 274, 463, 483, 490
1199 SEIU United Healthcare Workers East (FKA 1199/SEIU New York's Health & Human Service Union), 454
1199/SEIU & GNYHA Healthcare Education Project, 454, 483
1199/SEIU New York State Political Action Fund, 533
1199/SEIU New York's Health & Human Service Union, 454
1199/SEIU New York's Health & Human Services Union, 507
11th Judicial District, 58
122 Greenwich Owner LLC, 486
12th Judicial District, 58
151-45 Sixth Road Whitestone Partners LLC, 475
1765 1st Associates LLC, 530
1765 First Avenue Associates LLC, 495
184 Kent Fee LLC, 494
1st Department, 55
1st Judicial District, 56
21st Century Democrats, 533
250 E 57th Street, LLC, 530
2nd Department, 55
2nd Judicial District, 56
345 E 62nd Street Associate, 513
346 West 17th Street, LLC, 467
3500 Park Avenue LLC, 466
361-363 West 50th Street Redevelopment Company L.P., 467
369th Veterans Association Inc, 365
380 Development LLC, 475, 513
3M Company, 516
3rd Department, 55
3rd Judicial District, 56
40th Street Development LLC, 532
4201 Schools Assn, 469
43rd Ave Development LLC, 475
44th & 11th LLC, 467
44th and 11th LLC, 466
4th Department, 56
4th Judicial District, 57
50 West Street Development LLC, 474
500 Club, 533

504 Democratic Club Campaign Committee, 533
555 West 59th Street Holdings LLC, 487
5th Judicial District, 57
6-16 West 77th Street Corporation, 459
62 Imlay Street Real Estate, LLC, 459
625 East Fordham LLC, 466
6th Judicial District, 57
77 Commercial Holding, LLC, 494
7-Eleven Inc, 515, 518
7th Judicial District, 57
83-30 Austin Street LLC, 503
8th Judicial District, 57
92nd Street Y, 454, 494
92nd Street Y Young Men's and Young Women's Hebrew Association, 454
9th Judicial District, 57
AAA New York State Inc, 483, 485
AAA Northway, 340
AAA Western and Central NY, 340, 357, 454
AAFE Managment Co, 513
AARP, 315, 483
Abate RRF Inc, 533
Abbott Laboratories, 478
Abbott UFSD, 675
ABC Inc, 501, 506
ABC News (New York Bureau), 600
Abilities Inc, National Center for Disability Services, 274, 316
ABO Build PAC Inc, 533
Academic Dental Centers (NYS), 490
Academic Health Center Consortium, 462
Academy of Family Physicians (NYS), 528
Academy of Medicine (NY), 532
Academy of Political Science, 206
Academy of Trial Lawyers (NYS), 483
Academy of Trial Lawyers PAC, 533
Acadia Insurance Company, 461
Accent Stripe Inc, 506
Accenture, 501
Accenture LLP, 455
ACEC New York PAC, 533
ACENY-PAC, 533
ACS State & Local Solutions Inc, 516
ACS State Healthcare (Multistate Associates Inc), 487
Action for a Better Community Inc, 316
Action Fund for Good Government, 533
Actors Fund of America (The), 507
Actors' Equity Association, 467

Acupuncture Society of NY Inc, 468
Adams, Daniel J, 455
Addison CSD, 667
Adelante of Suffolk County, Inc, 493
Adelphi NY Statewide Breast Cancer Hotline & Support Program, 220
Adelphi University, 478, 621
Adfleet Advertising USA Inc, 467
Adirondack Community College, 615
Adirondack Council Inc (The), 187, 455
Adirondack CSD, 658
Adirondack Daily Enterprise, 599
Adirondack Economic Development Corporation, 569
Adirondack Lakes Center for the Arts, 341
Adirondack Landowners Assn Inc, 472
Adirondack League Club, 515, 518
Adirondack Mountain Club Inc, 187, 341, 455
Adirondack Optics, 501
Adirondack Park Agency, 113, 180, 335, 375
Adirondack Pine Hill NY Trailways, 513
Adirondack Publishing Co Inc, 599
Adirondack Regional Chambers of Commerce, 569
Adirondack/Pine Hill/NY Trailways, 341
Adirondacks Speculator Region Chamber of Commerce, 569
Administrative Regulations Review, Legislative Commission on, 32, 53
Adolf, Jay, 455
ADT Security Services Inc, 516
Adult Day Health Care Council (ADHCC), 463, 484
Advance Group Inc (The), 455
Advance Publications Inc, 599
Advanced Micro Devices Inc, 455
Advanced Micro Devices, Inc, 487
Advantage Capital Partners, 529
Advantage Travel, 501
Advocates for Adult Day Services, 502
Advocates for Children of New York Inc, 151
AeA New York Council, 106, 172
Aeralert US, LLC, 475
AES New York LLC, 487
AES NYS PAC, 533
Aetna Inc, 468, 513, 525
Aetna Inc PAC, 533
Affinity Health Plan, 455, 487

Organization Index

Affordable Housing PAC, LTD, 533
AFGI PAC, 533
AFLAC NY, 497
AFL-CIO (NYS), 479
Africa-America Institute (The), 151
African American Chamber of Commerce of Westchester & Rockland Counties, 569
AFSCME District Council 37, 298
AFSCME Local 2021, 513
AFSCME, New York, 298
After-School Corporation (The), 151, 455, 501
Afton CSD, 642
AGB 15th Street LLC, 484
Agencies for Children's Therapy Services, 463
Agenda for Children Tomorrow, 316
Aging, 25, 43
   Committee Staff, 25, 43
   Key Assembly Staff Assignments, 43
   Key Senate Staff Assignments, 25
   Majority, 25, 43
   Membership, 25, 43
   Minority, 25, 44
Aging, Office for the, 4, 307, 371
   Advisory Groups, 307
   Aging Services Advisory Committee, 307
   Federal Relations, 307
   Finance & Administration Division, 307
   Governor's Advisory Committee, 307
   Local Program Operations, 307
   Targeting Services & Equal Opportunity Programs, 307
Aging, Special Committee on, 387
Agostine Jr, Joseph A, 456
Agricultural Affiliates, 83
Agriculture, 25, 44, 387
   Committee Staff, 25, 44
   Conservation, Credit, Energy and Research, 387
   Department Operations, Oversight, Nutrition & Forestry, 387
   General Farm Commodities & Risk Management, 387
   Horticulture and Organic Agriculture, 387
   Key Assembly Staff Assignments, 44
   Key Senate Staff Assignments, 25
   Majority, 25, 44
   Membership, 25, 44
   Minority, 25, 44
   Specialty Crops, Rural Development and Foreign Agriculture, 387
   Subcommittees, 387
Agriculture & Markets Department, 4, 79, 307, 371
   Agricultural Protection & Development Services, 79
   Agricultural Protection Unit, 79
   Animal Industry, 79

   Brooklyn, 80
   Buffalo, 80
   Counsel's Office, 79
   Field Operations, 80
   Fiscal Management, 79
   Food Laboratory, 79
   Food Safety & Inspection, 79
   Hauppauge, 80
   Human Resources, 80
   Information Systems, 80
   Internal Audit, 80
   Migrant Labor Programs, 79, 307
   Milk Control & Dairy Services, 80
   New York City Office, 80
   Plant Industry, 80
   Rochester, 80
   Soil & Water Conservation Committee, 80
   State Fair, 80
   Statistics, 80
   Syracuse, 80
   Weights & Measures, 80
Agriculture & NYS Horse Breeding Development Fund, 113, 335, 375
Agriculture, Nutrition & Forestry, 382
   Domestic and Foreign Marketing, Inspection and Plant & Animal Health, 382
   Energy, Science and Technology, 382
   Nutrition & Food Assistance, Sustainable & Organic Agriculture & Gen Legis, 382
   Production, Income Protection and Price Support, 382
   Rural Revitalization, Conservation, Forestry and Credit, 382
   Subcommittees, 382
Agudath Israel of America, 152
Agusta & Ross, 475
Ahern, Barbara J, 456
AIA New York State Inc, 529
AIA New York State, Inc, 454
AIA New York State, Inc (FKA Rodriguez, Barbara J), 454
AIDS Coalition (NY), 454, 516
AIDS Council of Northeastern New York, 220
AIDS Day Services Assn Advocacy Committee, 473
AIDS Service Center of NYC, 502
AIDS Service Network (NYC), 523
AIDS Service Network, NYC, 472
AIM Services Inc, 283
Air Force Association (AFA), 365
Air Force Sergeants Association (AFSA), Division 1, 365
Air Force Women Officers Associated (AFWOA), 365
Air Liquide Large Industries USLP, 463
Air Pegasus, 475
Air Transport Assn Inc, 518

Akron CSD, 645
Albany, 70
   Civil Court, 71
   Criminal Court, 71
   Traffic Court, 71
Albany City SD, 638
Albany College of Pharmacy, 480, 621
Albany County, 61, 396
   County Court, 61
   Family Court, 61
   Supreme & Surrogate's Courts, 61
Albany County Airport Authority, 113, 350, 375
Albany County Industrial Development Agency, 569
Albany County Rural Housing Alliance Inc, 233
Albany Housing Coalition Inc, 365
Albany Industrial Development Agency (City of), 569
Albany Law School, 456, 501, 621
Albany Law School of Union University, 456
Albany Law School, Government Law Center, 206
Albany Medical Center, 461
Albany Medical College, 621
Albany Medical Ctr, 530
Albany Port District Commission, 113, 350, 375, 501
Albany, City of, 414
Albany-Colonie Regional Chamber of Commerce, 569
Albert Lindley Lee Memorial Hospital, 530
Albion CSD, 661
Alcatel-Lucent, 469
Alchemy Properties, Inc, 467
Alcoholic Beverage Control, Division of (State Liquor Authority), 5, 98, 324, 371
   Administration, 98, 324
   Albany (Zone II), 98, 324
   Buffalo (Zone III), 98, 324
   Licensing & Enforcement, 98, 324
   New York City (Zone I), 98, 324
Alcoholism & Drug Abuse, 44
   Committee Staff, 44
   Key Assembly Staff Assignments, 44
   Majority, 44
   Membership, 44
   Minority, 44
Alcoholism & Substance Abuse Services, Office of, 5, 211, 278, 307, 371
   Bureau of ATCs, 212, 279, 308
   Bureau of Budget Management, 211, 278, 308
   Bureau of Capital Management, 211, 278, 308
   Bureau of Certification, 211, 278, 308
   Bureau of Counsel, 211, 278, 308
   Bureau of Enforcement, 211, 278, 308

Organization Index

Bureau of Evaluation & Practice Improvement, 212, 279, 308
Bureau of Financial & Emergency Management, 211, 278, 308
Bureau of Governmental & NYC Affairs, 211, 278, 308
Bureau of Health Care Financing & 3rd Party Reimbursement, 211, 278, 308
Bureau of Information Technology, 211, 278, 308
Bureau of Planning & Practice Improvement, 212, 279, 308
Bureau of Prevention, 212, 279, 308
Bureau of Quality Assurance, 211, 278, 308
Bureau of Statewide Field Operations, 212, 279, 308
Bureau of Systems Development & Public Education, 212, 279, 308
Bureau of Treatment, 212, 279, 308
Bureau of Workforce Development, 212, 279, 308
Financial, Capital & Information Tech Management Division, 211, 278, 308
Legal Affairs Division, 211, 278, 308
Management Resources & Quality Assurance Division, 211, 278, 308
Prevention & Treatment Services Division, 212, 279, 308
Systems/Program Performance & Analysis Division, 212, 279, 308
Alden CSD, 645
Alexander CSD, 648
Alexandria Bay Chamber of Commerce, 569
Alexandria CSD, 650
Alexico Management Group, 474
Alfred State College of Technology, 614
Alfred University, 462, 622
Alfred-Almond CSD, 638
Alice Hyde Medical Center, 530
All Stars Project Inc (The), 467
Allegany - Limestone CSD, 640
Allegany County, 61, 396
    Supreme, County, Family & Surrogate's Courts, 61
Allegany County Office of Development, 569
Allegretti, Daniel, 456
Allegue, Raul R, 456
Allen Health Care Services, 462
Allergan, Inc, 489
Alliance Bank, 93
Alliance for Child with Special Needs-School Age (NYS), 487
Alliance for Clean Energy New York Inc, 503
Alliance for Donation (NY), 530
Alliance for Downtown New York Inc, 501
Alliance for Environmental Concerns (NY), 527

Alliance for Fine Wine Wholesalers, Ltd (NY), 489
Alliance for Quality Education, 503
Alliance for Quality Education (FKA Easton, Regina N), 456
Alliance for the Arts, 341, 467
Alliance of Automobile Manufacturers, 490
Alliance of Long Island Agencies, 517, 520
Alliance of NYS Arts Organizations, 341
Alliance of Resident Theatres (NY), 530
Alliance of Resident Theatres/New York, 500
Alliance of Resident Theatres/New York (ART/New York), 341
Allied Bldg Metal Industries Inc State PAC, 534
Allinger, Stephen (FKA Nelson, Debra), 456
Allocco, Carol, 456
Allstate Insurance Co, 516
ALM Medica Inc, 528
ALPAC (ALCAS PAC), 533
ALSTOM Transportation Inc, 357
Alston & Bird LLP, 261
Alteri, Richard, 456
Altman, Frederick M, 456
Altman, Robert S, 457
Altmar-Parish-Williamstown CSD, 661
Altria Corporate Services, 106, 457
Altria Corporate Services Inc, 478, 490
Altria Corporate Services Inc (ALCS), 506
Altria Corporate Services, Inc, 457, 464
Alvin D Lurie PC, 330
Alzheimer's Assn, NYC Chapter, 477
Alzheimer's Association, Northeastern NY, 220
AMAC, Association for Metroarea Autistic Children, 283
Amagansett UFSD, 668
Amalgamated Transit Union, 457
Ambassador Club, 534
Ambulette Coalition Inc (NY), 483
AMDeC Foundation, 454
AMDeC Foundation Inc, 486
AMDEC Foundation Inc, 463
Amdursky Pelky Fennell & Wallen, 262
Ameican Farmland Trust, 457
Amerada Hess Corporation, 172, 513
America Online (AOL), 475
America's Health Insurance Plans, 461
American Academy McAllister Institute of Funeral Service, 622
American Academy of Dramatic Arts, 622
American Academy of Orthotists and Prosthetists-New York Chapter, 505
American Academy of Pediatrics District II (NYS), 457
American Airlines, 492
American Alternative Fuels, 483
American Cancer Society, Eastern Division, Inc, 494

American Cancer Society-Eastern Division, 220, 528
American Chemistry Council, 462, 519
American Chemistry Council Inc, 465
American Chemistry/American Plastics Council, 106
American College of Emergency Physicians (NY Chapter), 528
American College of Nurse-Midwives, NYC Chapter, 220
American College of Ob & Gyn, District II, 457
American College of Ob & Gyn, District II/NY, 457
American College of Obstetricians & Gynecologists/NYS, 220
American College of Occupational Environmental Medicine, 528
American College of Physicians Svcs Inc (NY Chapter), 496
American College of Physicians, New York Chapter, 220
American Continental Group, 457
American Continental Properties Inc, 516
American Council of Engineering Companies of NY, 531
American Council of Engineering Companies of NY (ACEC New York), 106
American Council of Life Insurers, 503
American Diabetes Association, 457, 528
American Electronics Association/NY Council, 465
American Express Co, 529
American Express Company, 93
American Express Company PAC (AXP PAC), 534
American Farmland Trust, 457
American Farmland Trust, Northeast Regional Office, 83
American Federation of Musicians, Local 802, 341
American Federation of Teachers, 275
American Fertility Association, 220
American Forest & Paper Assn (Multistate Associates Inc), 469
American Heart Assn/American Stroke Assn, 458, 528
American Heart Association Northeast Affiliate, 220
American Higher Education Development Corporation, 152
American Institute of Architects (AIA) New York State Inc, 106, 233
American Insurance Assn, 458, 530
American Insurance Assn New York PAC, 534
American Insurance Association, 490
American Int'l Grp, Inc, 482
American International Group Inc, 93, 249

811

Organization Index

American International Group Inc (AIG), 530
American International Group, Inc, 512
American International Group, Inc Employee PAC, 534
American Jewish Committee, 240, 503
American Lawyer Media, 468, 499, 520
American Lawyer Media Co, 506
American Lawyer Media Inc, 596
American Legion, Department of New York, 365
American Liver Foundation, Western NY Chapter, 221
American Lung Assn of the City of New York, 458
American Lung Association of NYS Inc, 221
American Management Association International, 106
American Massage Therapy Assn (NY Chapter), 469
American Medical Alert Corporation, 487
American Metal Market, 600
American Military Retirees Association Inc, 365
American Motorcyclist Assn PAC, 534
American Museum of Natural History, 187, 341, 458
American Museum of the Moving Image Inc, 513
American Petroleum Institute, 480
American Racing & Entertainment, LLC, 476
American Recycling Technologies Inc, 466
American Red Cross in Greater New York, 466
American Red Cross in Greater NY, 455, 465, 506
American Red Cross in NYS, 316
American Resort Dev/Assn Resort Owners' Coalition PAC, 534
American Safety Council, 490
American Safety Institute Inc, 468
American Self Storage Landing Road LLC, 466
American Society for Dermatological Surgery, 478
American Society for the Prevention of Cruelty to Animals (ASPCA), 83, 140, 531
American Standard Companies Inc, 457
American Standard Company, 480
American Tax Funding Servicing LLC, 478
American Telephone & Telegraph Co PAC NY, 534
American Transit Insurance Company, 515
American Waterways Operators, 501
AmeriChoice of NY (United Healthcare Services Affiliate), 457
Amerigroup New York LLC/Amerigroup Community Care (FKA Care Plus Health Plan), 504
Ames, Margery E, 458
Amgen, 468
Amherst Chamber of Commerce, 569
Amherst CSD, 645
Amherst Industrial Development Agency (Town of), 569
Amherst, Town of, 414
Amityville UFSD, 668
Ammann & Whitney, 357, 506
Amnesty International USA, 240
Amsterdam, 71
   Civil & Criminal Courts, 71
Amsterdam Industrial Development Agency, 569
Amusement & Music Owners Assn of NY, 521
AMV Unitel, LLC, 495
Amylin Pharmaceuticals, 527
Anchor Contractors, 487
Anderson, David, 458
Andes CSD, 644
Andover CSD, 638
Andrew, Ralph, 458
ANHD Inc, 454
Anheuser-Busch Companies Inc, 463
Animal Welfare Advocacy, 458
Ann Breeswine, 459
Anson, Joseph L, 459
Antalek & Moore Insurance Agency, 93
Anthony J Costello & Son Development LLC, 463
Anti-Defamation League, 240
Any-Time Home Care Inc, 462
Aon Services Corporation, 249
Apollo Group Inc, 468
Apollo Real Estate Advisors, 494
Apollo Real Estate Advisors LP, 495
Apple Assn Inc (NY), 459
Apple Banking for Savings, 94
Apple Computer Inc, 518
Apple Inc, 459
Apple Inc (FKA Apple Computer Inc), 459
Appraisal Education Network School & Merrell Institute, 303
Appropriations, 382, 387
   Agriculture, Rural Development, FDA & Related Agencies, 387
   Commerce, Justice, Science and Related Agencies, 383, 387
   Defense, 383, 387
   Energy and Water Development, 383, 388
   Financial Services and General Government, 383, 388
   Homeland Security, 383, 388
   Interior, Environment and Related Agencies, 383, 388
   Labor, Health & Human Services, Education and Related Agencies, 388
   Labor, Health and Human Services, Education and Related Agencies, 383
   Legislative Branch, 383
   Military Construction, Veterans Affairs and Related Agencies, 388
   Military, Construction, Veterans Affairs and Related Agencies, 383
   State, Foreign Operations and Related Programs, 383, 388
   Subcommittees, 383, 387
   Transportation, Housing and Urban Development, and Related Agencies, 383, 388
Apsire of WNY, 480
Apthrop Associates, LLC, 467
ARAMARK PAC, 534
Arc Inc (NYS), 486
Arcade Area Chamber of Commerce, 569
Arcadis G & M (National Strategies, Inc), 494
Archdiocese of NY (The), 495
Archstone Smith, 493
Ardsley UFSD, 675
ARE-East River Science Park LLC, 476
Argyle CSD, 674
Arker Companies (The), 487
Arkport CSD, 667
Arlington CSD, 644
Armed Services, 383, 388
   Air and Land Forces, 388
   Airland, 383
   Emerging Threats & Capabilities, 383
   Military Personnel, 388
   Oversight and Investigations, 388
   Personnel, 383
   Readiness, 388
   Readiness & Management Support, 383
   SeaPower, 383
   Seapower and Expeditionary Forces, 388
   Strategic Forces, 383, 388
   Subcommittees, 383, 388
   Terrorism, Unconventional Threats and Capabilities, 388
Armienti, Debellis & Whiten LLP, 506
Armor Dynamics Inc, 506
Army Aviation Association of America (AAAA), 365
Army Aviation Association of America (AAAA), North Country Chapter, 365
Army Aviation Association of America (AAAA), Western NY Chapter, 365
Art & Science Collaborations Inc, 341
Art Institue of New York City (The), 633
Arthritis Foundation (NY Chapter), 477
Arthur J Finkelstein & Associates Inc, 164
Arts & Cultural Affairs, Special Committee on the, 32
Arts Coalition (NYC), 459
Arts PAC Non-Federal, 534
ArtsConnection Inc (The), 341
Arzt, George Communications Inc, 459

Organization Index

ASA Institute of Business & Computer Technology, 633
ASAPPAC, 533
Asbestos Workers Local 12 Political Action Committee, 534
Ascension Health, 503
Asciutto, Georgia M, 459
Aseptic Packaging Council, 503
ASGM PAC, 534
Asian American Federation of New York, 316
Asian American Legal Defense and Education Fund, 240, 262
Asian Americans for Equality, 316
ASPCA, 480
ASPIRA of New York Inc, 151
Assc of Perioperative Registered Nurses, 503
Assembly, 375
Assembly Legislative Commissions, 292
    State-Local Relations, Legislative Commission on, 292
Assembly Standing Committees, 80, 92, 103, 137, 150, 163, 170, 183, 202, 217, 231, 238, 248, 259, 272, 282, 292, 297, 302, 313, 327, 339, 354, 362
    Aging, 217, 238, 313
    Agriculture, 80
    Alcoholism & Drug Abuse, 137, 217, 282, 313
    Banks, 92
    Children & Families, 217, 313
    Cities, 103, 292
    Codes, 137, 259
    Consumer Affairs & Protection, 103, 202, 217
    Corporations, Authorities & Commissions, 103, 202, 354
    Correction, 137, 238
    Economic Development, Job Creation, Commerce & Industry, 103, 292, 302, 354
    Education, 150
    Election Law, 163
    Energy, 170
    Environmental Conservation, 183
    Ethics & Guidance, 202
    Governmental Employees, 297
    Governmental Operations, 202
    Health, 217
    Higher Education, 150
    Housing, 231, 292, 302
    Insurance, 248
    Judiciary, 259
    Labor, 239, 248, 272, 297
    Libraries & Education Technology, 150
    Local Government, 231, 292
    Mental Health, 239, 283
    Oversight, Analysis & Investigation, 202
    Racing & Wagering, 327, 339
    Real Property Taxation, 303, 327
    Rules, 202
    Small Business, 103
    Social Services, 313
    Tourism, Arts & Sports Development, 339
    Transportation, 292, 354
    Veterans Affairs, 362
    Ways & Means, 202, 292, 327
Assembly Task Force, 80
    Food, Farm & Nutrition, Task Force on, 80
Assembly Task Forces, 103, 150, 239, 272, 313
    Puerto Rican/Hispanic Task Force, 239, 272, 313
    Skills Development & Career Education, Legislative Commission on, 150, 272
    University-Industry Cooperation, Legislative Task Force on, 150
    University-Industry Cooperation, Task Force on, 103
    Women's Issues, Task Force on, 239, 272, 313
Assembly Task Forces & Caucus, 203
    State-Local Relations, Legislative Commission on, 203
Assisted Living Federation of America (ALFA), 491
Assn for a Better Long Island - PAC (ABLI), 534
Assn for Affordable Housing (NYS), 469
Assn for Community Living, 459, 515, 518
Assn for Marriage & Family Therapy, Inc (NYD), 487
Assn for Neurologically Impaired Brain Injured Children Inc, 513
Assn for Pupil Transportation (NY), 504
Assn for the Advancement of Blind & Retarded Inc, 513
Assn of Alcoholism & Substance Abuse Providers Inc (NY), 465, 475
Assn of Cemeteries (NYS), 483
Assn of Chiefs of Police (NYS), 515
Assn of Community & Residential Agencies (NYS), 459
Assn of Community Organizations for Reform Now (NY), 455
Assn of Convenience Stores (NY), 467, 475
Assn of Counties & Its Affiliated Organizations (NYS), 460
Assn of Electrical Contractors, Inc (NYS), 462
Assn of Electrical Workers (NYS), 477
Assn of Family Service Agencies (NYS), 461
Assn of Financial Guaranty Insurors, 497, 502
Assn of Fire Districts of the State of NY, Inc, 532
Assn of Health Care Providers Inc (NYS), 528
Assn of Health Information Outsourcing Services, 487
Assn of Home Inspectors Inc (NYS), 505
Assn of Homes & Services for the Aging (NY), 529
Assn of Independent Commercial Producers Inc, 530
Assn of Independent Commercial Producers Inc PAC, 534
Assn of Independent Living Inc, 472
Assn of Independent Schools (NYS), 504
Assn of Insurance & Financial Advisors (NYS), 531
Assn of Laser Hair Removal Specialists, Inc (NYS), 511
Assn of Licensed Midwives (NYS), 487
Assn of Mortgage Brokers (NY), 475
Assn of New York City Concrete Producers Inc State PAC, 534
Assn of Nurse Anesthetists Inc (NYS), 463
Assn of NYS Youth Bureaus, 523
Assn of PBAS, Inc (NYS), 460
Assn of Plumbing Heating Cooling Contractors Inc (NYS), 526
Assn of Professional Land Surveyors Inc (NYS), 530
Assn of Proprietary Colleges, 476
Assn of Psychiatric Rehabilitation Services (NY), 519
Assn of Psychiatric Rehabilitation Svcs (NY), 472
Assn of Public Broadcasting Stations of NY, 503, 518
Assn of Realtors (NYS), 502
Assn of Realtors Inc (NYS), 530
Assn of School Business Officials (NYS), 460
Assn of School Psychologists (NY), 487
Assn of Service Stations & Repair Shops Inc (NYS), 464
Assn of Supts of School Buildings & Grounds (NYS), 469
Assn of Surrogate's & Supreme Court Reporters, 475
Assn of Town Superintendents of Highways Inc (NYS), 513
Assn of Towns of the State of NY, 460
Assn of Wholesale Marketers & Distributors (NYS), 494
Assoc General Contractors of America, Inc (NYS Chapter), 487
Associated Builders & Contractors, Construction Training Center of NYS, 275
Associated Builders & Contractors, Empire State Chapter, 107
Associated Builders & Contractors, Inc, 506
Associated Gen'l Contractors of America Inc (NYS), 470
Associated General Contractors of America, NYS Chapter, 107

Organization Index

Associated Licensed Detectives of New York State, 140
Associated Licensed Detectives of NYS, Inc, 457
Associated Medical Schools of New York, 152, 221
Associated Medical Schools of NY, 490
Associated New York State State Food Processors Inc, 83
Associated Press (Albany/Upstate Bureau), 601
Associated Press (New York/Metro Bureau), 601
Associated Risk Managers of New York Inc, 249
Association Development Group Inc, 107
Association for a Better New York, 107, 233
Association for Addiction Professionals of New York, 283
Association for Affordable Housing (NY), 489
Association for Community Living, 233, 283
Association for Eating Disorders - Capital Region, 283
Association for Neighborhood & Housing Development, 233
Association for the Help of Retarded Children NYC Chapter (NYS), 468
Association for the Help of Retarded Children/AHRC, 283
Association of American Publishers, 487
Association of Commuter Rail Employees PAC NY, 534
Association of Fire Districts of the State of NY Inc, 292
Association of Government Accountants, NY Capital Chapter, 207
Association of Graphic Communications, 107
Association of Independent Video & Filmmakers (AIVF), (The), 341
Association of Military Surgeons of the US (AMSUS), NY Chapter, 221, 365
Association of New York State Young Republicans Inc, 534
Association of Presidents of Public Community Colleges, 152
Association of Proprietary Colleges, 152, 490
Association of Public Broadcasting Stations of NY Inc, 172
Association of Safety Group Managers, 489
Association of Service Stations & Repair Shops, Inc (NYS), 490
Association of Small City School Districts (NYS), 462
Association of the Bar of the City of New York, 262
Association of the US Army (AUSA), 365
Association of Towns of the State of New York, 292, 330
Association of Water & Sewer Excavators, Inc, 478
Association on Independent Living, 460
Association on Independent Living (NY), 460
Assurant Solutions, 488, 506
Assurant Solutions, Inc, 490
Astellas Pharma US Inc, 465
Astor Terrace Condominium, 478
Astoria Energy, 468
Astoria Federal Savings & Loan, 94
Astoria Financial Corp PAC, 534
Astrazeneca Pharmaceuticals, 458
AstraZeneca Pharmaceuticals, LP, 463
Astroland, Inc, 478
Asurion, 497
Asurion Corp & Subsidiaries (FKA Lock/Line LLC (DST Systems)), 530
Asurion Employees PAC, 534
AT&T Corp, 506
AT&T Corporation, 172
AT&T Inc & Its Affiliates, 487, 490, 518
ATCO Properties & Management Inc, 494
Athletic Trainers' Assn (NYS), 530
Atlantic Development Co, 508
Atlantic States Marine Fisheries Commission, 113, 181, 375
Atlas Park, LLC, 522
ATM Industry Association, 504
Atomic Learning Inc, 504
ATPAM COPE State Fund, 533
Attica CSD, 678
Attorney Grievance Committee, 255
  1st Judicial Dept, Judicial Dist 1, 12, 255
  2nd Judicial Dept, Judicial Dist 2, 9, 10, 11, 255
  3rd Judicial Dept, Judicial Dist 3, 4, 6, 255
  4th Judicial Dept, Dist 5, 7, 8, 255
  Judicial Dist 10, 255
  Judicial Dist 2, 11, 255
  Judicial Dist 5, 255
  Judicial Dist 7, 255
  Judicial Dist 8, 255
  Judicial Dist 9, 255
ATU NY State Legislative Conference Board, 489
ATU-NY Cope Fund, 533
Auburn, 71
  Civil & Criminal Courts, 71
Auburn Enlarged City SD, 641
Auburn Publishers Inc, 591
Auburn, City of, 414
Audubon New York, 187
Audubon Society of NYS Inc (The) / Audubon International, 187
Augusta & Ross, 478
Aurora Endoresed Republican Club, 534
Ausable Valley CSD, 643
Authentix Inc, 465, 478
Auto Collision Technician's Assn, Inc (NYS), 487
Automatic Vending Assn (NYS), 512
Automobile Club of New York, 341, 357
Automobile Club of New York Inc, 485
Automobile Dealers Assn (NYS), 460
Automobile Dealers of New York PAC, 534
Automobile Insurance Plan (NY), 461
Automotive Recyclers Association (NY), 501
Automotive Technology & Energy Group of Western NY, 357
Auxilia, 504
Auxiliary Campus Enterprises and Services (FKA Alfred State College), 488
Averill Park CSD, 663
Aviation Management Assn (NY), 485
Avis Budget Group Inc & Its Subsidiaries (FKA Cendant Car Rental Group Inc & Subsidiaries), 509
Avoca CSD, 667
Avon CSD, 651
Avon Products Inc, 508
Axis Group Inc, 467
Ayers, Deborah, 460
Aztec Software, 527
BA Cypress Bronx Holdings LLC, 532
Babylon Industrial Development Agency, 570
Babylon UFSD, 668
Babylon, Town of, 414
BAC Local 2 PAC, 534
Baden Street Settlement of Rochester Inc, 468
Bailey House Inc, 532
Bainbridge-Guilford CSD, 642
Baker & Hostetler, LLP, 461
Baldwin Chamber of Commerce, 570
Baldwin UFSD, 653
Baldwin, Kristina, 461
Baldwin-Grand Canal & Baldwin-West-End Canal Improvement District, 501
Baldwinsville Chamber of Commerce (Greater Baldwinsville), 570
Baldwinsville CSD, 658
Ballet Hispanico of NY Inc, 504
Ballet Theatre Foundation Inc/American Ballet Theatre, 530
Ballston Spa CSD, 664
Bank of Akron, 94
Bank of America NY PAC, 535
Bank of New York, 487
Bank Street College of Education/Graduate School, 622
Bankers Assn (NY), 523, 530
Banking Department, 5, 90, 371
  Communication & Media Relations, 90
  Community and Regional Banks Division, 90
  Consumer Services Division, 90

Organization Index

Criminal Investigations Bureau, 90
Foreign and Wholesale Banks Division, 90
Human Resources, 90
Information Technology Division, 90
Licensed Financial Services Division, 90
London Office, 90
Mortgage Banking Division, 90
Regional Offices, 90
Research, Applications & Technical Assistance Division, 91
Upstate Office, 91
Banking, Housing & Urban Affairs, 383
Economic Policy, 383
Financial Institutions, 384
Housing, Transportation and Community Development, 384
Securities, Insurance and Investment, 384
Subcommittees, 383
Banks, 25, 44
Committee Staff, 25, 44
Key Assembly Staff Assignments, 44
Key Senate Staff Assignments, 25
Majority, 26, 44
Membership, 26, 44
Minority, 26, 44
Banks, Steven, 461
BAPA, 535
Bar Association (NYS), 487
Barba, James J, 461
Bard College, 622
Barker CSD, 657
Barnard College, 622
Barnes & Noble College Book Sellers (Dewey Square Group), 530
Barnes, Richard E, 461
Barnett, Claire L, 461
Barrett Associates, 461
Bartlett Dairy Inc, 475
Batavia, 71
Civil & Criminal Courts, 71
Batavia City SD, 648
Batavia Newspapers Corp, 592
Bath Area Chamber of Commerce (Greater Bath Area), 570
Bath CSD, 667
Battery Park City Authority (Hugh L Carey), 113, 335, 375
Bauer, Peter, 461
Bausch & Lomb Inc, 221
Bay Shore UFSD, 668
Bayer Healthcare, 503
BayerCorp Pharmaceutical Div, Bayer Healthcare LLC, 459
Bayport-Blue Point UFSD, 668
Bayrock Group LLC, 495
Bayshore Chamber of Commerce, 570
BBL Construction Services Inc, 501
BBL PAC, 535
BCSA-PAC, 535
Beacon, 71

Civil & Criminal Courts, 71
Beacon City SD, 644
Bear Stearns & Co Inc, 94
Bear Stearns Political Campaign Committee, 535
Bearing Point Consulting, 487
Bearingpoint, 468
BearingPoint, 515
BearingPoint Inc, 516
Beaver River CSD, 651
Bechtel Infrastructure Corp (Macquarie Securities), 501
Bedford CSD, 675
Bedford Stuyvesant Family Health Center Inc, 503
Bedford Stuyvesant Family Health Ctr, 494
Beekmantown CSD, 643
Beer Wholesalers Association Inc (NYS), 488
Beer Wholesalers Association Inc (NYS) (Steven W Harris, LLC), 483
Beginning with Children Foundation, 516
Behan Communications Inc, 461
Belfast CSD, 639
Bell Atlantic Corporation PAC, 535
Belleville Henderson CSD, 650
Bellevue Hospital Center, Department of Emergency Medicine Training Division, 221
Bellevue Women's Medical Center, Inc, 511
Bellmore Republican Club Inc, 535
Bellmore UFSD, 653
Bellmore-Merrick Central HS District, 653
Bellmores Chamber of Commerce, 570
Bemus Point CSD, 641
Bennett Firm, Inc (The), 462
Bennett, Michael, 462
Bergin, Robert J, 462
Berkeley College, New York City Campus, 634
Berkeley College, Westchester Campus, 634
Berkley Center for Entrepreneurial Studies NYU, Stern School of Business, 111
Berkshire Farm Center & Services for Youth, 140, 316
Berkshire UFSD, 643
Berlin CSD, 663
Bernard M Baruch College, 619
Berne-Knox-Westerlo CSD, 638
Berry, Sally, 462
Bersin Properties, LLC, 501
Besicorp-Empire Newsprint LLC, 464
Bestcare, Inc, 462
Beth Abraham Family of Health Services, 482
Beth Israel Medical Center, 516
Beth Israel Medical Ctr, 495
Bethlehem Chamber of Commerce, 570
Bethlehem CSD, 638

Bethlehem Industrial Development Agency (Town of), 570
Bethlehem, Town of, 415
Bethpage Federal Credit Union, 520
Bethpage Federal Credit Union PAC, 535
Bethpage UFSD, 654
Better Business Bureau of Metropolitan New York, 107
Better Health Care PAC, 535
BFC Construction Corp, 474
Big Apple Circus, 455
Big Brothers Big Sisters of NYC, 316, 480, 516
Bigelsen, Jayne, 462
Biggerstaff Law Firm, LLP (The), 462
Billig, Jacob, 462
Binghamton, 71
Civil & Criminal Courts, 71
Binghamton Chamber of Commerce (Greater Binghamton), 570
Binghamton City SD, 639
Binghamton University, 490
Binghamton University, State University of New York, 612
Binghamton, City of, 415
Biotechnology Assn Inc (NY), 489
Birds Eye Foods Inc, 84
BJK Inc/dba Chem Rx, 475
Black Car Assistance Corporation, 506
Black Car Operators' Injury Compensation Fund (NY), 506
Black Car PAC, 535
Black Lake Chamber of Commerce, 570
Black Veterans for Social Justice Inc, 365
Blind Brook-Rye UFSD, 675
Blinded Veterans Association New York Inc, 366
Blitman & King LLP, 275
Blood Center (NY), 459, 494
Bloomberg Television, 608
Bloomfield CSD, 660
Blooming Grove Chamber of Commerce, 570
Blue Mountain Lake Association, 570
Bluestone Organization (The), 499
Blumenthal, Karen, 462
BMW PAC, 535
BNA (formerly Bureau of National Affairs), 601
Board of Commissioners of Pilots of the State of NY, 515, 518
Board of Jewish Education of Greater New York, 152
Board of Regents, 143
Bodega Assoc of the US Inc (The), 506
Boehringer Ingelheim Pharmaceuticals, Inc, 478
Bogdan Lasky & Kopley, LLC, 462
Boilermakers Local Lodge #5, 463
Bolivar-Richburg CSD, 639
Bolton CSD, 673

815

Organization Index

Bolton Landing Chamber of Commerce, 570
Bolton St Johns Inc, 463
Boltz, John J Consulting, 464
Bombardiere, Ralph, 464
Bonagura, David (FKA Hoops, Jeffrey), 464
Bond Market Association (The), 94
Bond Schoeneck & King PLLC, 241
Bond, Schoeneck & King, PLLC, 464
Bookman, Robert S, 464
Boonville Area Chamber of Commerce, 570
Bopp, Linda (FKA Mesick, Edie), 464
Boricua College, 622
Borough of Manhattan Community College, 619
Botanical Garden (The), 464
Botanical Garden (The) (NY), 464
Bottlers Assn (NYS), 483
Boulevard ALP Associates, 515
Boundary Fence & Railing Systems, Inc, 478
Bovis Lend Lease, 459, 487
Bowling Proprietor's Assn (NYS), 493
Boykin-Towns, Karen, 464
Boylan Brown, 262
Boymelgreen Developers LLC, 475
Boys & Girls Clubs of America (Boys & Girls Clubs Inc (NYS)), 490
BP America Inc, 461, 468
BRAB PAC, INC, 535
Bracken & Margolin LLP, 262
Bradford CSD, 667
Bradford Publications Inc, 598
Bradford Publishing Co, 599
Brain Injury Association of NYS (BIANYS), 221, 283
Brain Trauma Foundation, 503
Bramson ORT College, 622
Branford Communications, 164
Brasher Falls CSD, 666
Brendel & Associates, 465
Brentwood UFSD, 668
Brentwood Union Free School District, 524
Brescia, Richard, 465
Brewers Association, Inc (NYS), 455
Brewster Chamber of Commerce, 570
Brewster CSD, 663
Briarcliff Manor UFSD, 675
Briarcliffe College-Bethpage, 634
Briarcliffe College-Patchogue, 634
Bricklayers & Allied Craftsmen Local Union 1 PAC, 535
Bricklayers & Allied Craftworkers Local 5 NY PAC, 535
Bricklayers Allied Craftworkers Local 3 Buffalo PAC, 535
Bridge & Tunnel Officers Benevolent Assn, 498
Bridgehampton UFSD, 668
Brighter Choice Foundation, 497

Brighton CSD, 652
Brighton, Town of, 415
Bristol-Myers Squibb Co, 221, 529
Bristol-Myers Squibb Co Employee PAC, 535
British Airways PLC, 357
Broadalbin-Perth CSD, 648
Broadcasters Assn (NYS), 515
Broadway Concrete Corp, 459
Brockport Chamber of Commerce (Greater Brockport), 570
Brockport CSD, 652
Brocton CSD, 641
Brodsky Organization, 486
Bronx Coalition for Good Government, 535
Bronx Committee for Toxic Free Schools, 497
Bronx Community College, 619
Bronx County, 61
 COUNTY & FAMILY COURTS: See New York City Courts, 61
 Supreme & Surrogate's Courts, 61
Bronx County (NYC Borough of the Bronx), 396
Bronx Educational Opportunity Center, 617
Bronx Health Reach, 465
Bronx Museum, 521
Bronx-Lebanon Hospital Center, 221
Bronxville Chamber of Commerce, 570
Bronxville UFSD, 675
Brookfield CSD, 651
Brookfield Properties Corporation, 303
Brookhaven Industrial Development Agency, 570
Brookhaven Science Associates Inc, 522
Brookhaven, Town of, 415
Brookhaven-Comsewogue UFSD, 668
Brooklyn Adult Care Center, 530
Brooklyn Botanic Garden, 187, 341
Brooklyn Chamber of Commerce, 532, 571
Brooklyn Children's Museum, 480
Brooklyn College, 620
Brooklyn Daily Eagle, 592
Brooklyn Eagle Publications, 592
Brooklyn Economic Development Corporation, 571
Brooklyn Educational Opportunity Center, 618
Brooklyn Heights Press, 592
Brooklyn Hospital Center (The), 530
Brooklyn Housing & Family Services Inc, 233
Brooklyn Information & Culture, 503
Brooklyn Law School, 262, 622
Brooklyn Museum of Art, 341
Brooklyn Navy Yard Cogeneration Partners LP, 464
Brooklyn Navy Yard Development Corporation, 114, 362, 375
Brooklyn Philharmonic, 532
Brooklyn Phoenix, 592

Brooklyn Psychiatric Center, 465
Brooklyn Public Library, 507, 513
Brooklyn Technical High School Alumni Assn, 532
Broome Community College, 615
Broome County, 61, 396
 County, Family & Surrogate's Courts, 61
 Supreme Court, 62
Broome County Industrial Development Agency, 571
Broome-Delaware-Tioga BOCES, 678
Brower, Michael R, 465
Brown & Kelly, LLP, 107
Brown Brothers Harriman & Co, Bank Asset Management Group, 94
Brown McMahon & Weinraub, LLC, 465
Browne, Brian, 465
Brunswick CSD (Brittonkill), 663
Brushton-Moira CSD, 647
Bryan Cave, LLP, 465
Bryant & Stratton College, 469
Bryant & Stratton College-Albany Campus, 634
Bryant & Stratton College-Amherst Campus, 634
Bryant & Stratton College-Buffalo Campus, 634
Bryant & Stratton College-Greece Campus, 634
Bryant & Stratton College-Henrietta Campus, 634
Bryant & Stratton College-Southtowns Campus, 634
Bryant & Stratton College-Syracuse Campus, 634
Bryant & Stratton College-Syracuse North Campus, 634
Budget, 384, 388
Budget, Division of the, 5, 98, 194, 287, 324, 371
Buffalo, 71
 Civil & Criminal Courts, 71
Buffalo & Erie Cnty Naval & Military Park, 528
Buffalo & Fort Erie Public Bridge Authority (Peace Bridge Authority), 114, 350, 375
Buffalo & Pittsburgh Railroad Inc, 489
Buffalo Bills, 341
Buffalo Business First, 592
Buffalo Economic Renaissance Corporation, 571
Buffalo Educational Opportunity Center, 618
Buffalo News (The), 593
Buffalo Niagara Assn of Realtors, Inc, 466
Buffalo Niagara Builders' Assn Build PAC, 535
Buffalo Niagara Partnership, 501, 507, 571
Buffalo Professional Firefighters PAC, 535
Buffalo Sabres, 342
Buffalo SD, 645

Organization Index

Buffalo State College, 613
Buffalo Teachers Federation PAC, 536
Buffalo Trotting Association Inc, 342
Buffalo, City of, 416
Build New York PAC, 536
Build PAC (NY), 466
Builders Association (NYS), 466, 490
Builders' PAC, 536
Building & Construction Trades Council (NYS), 526
Building & Construction Trades Council of Greater NY, 526
Building & Construction Trades Council PAC, 536
Building & Realty Institute, 304, 464
Building & Realty Institute of Westchester & Mid-Hudson Region, 475
Building Congress (NY) (The), 483
Building Contractors Assn Inc, 515, 536
Building Contractors Association, 107
Building Contractors' Assn, Inc, 526
Building Industry Assn of NY Inc, 457
Building Industry Assn of NYC, Inc, 469
Building Industry Association of New York City, Inc, 536
Building Industry Association of NYC Inc, 107
Building Trades Employers Assn, 474
Building Trades Employers' Assn, 526
Burgos, Tonio & Associates, 466
Burns, Miriam P, 466
Burnt Hills-Ballston Lake CSD, 664
Bus Association of NYS Inc, 506
Bus Distributors Assn Inc (NYS), 468
Business Council for International Understanding, 107
Business Council of New York State Inc, 107, 172, 187, 207, 330
Business Council of NYS Inc, 466
Business Council of NYS Inc (The), 466, 518
Business Council of NYS, Inc (The), 532
Business Council of Westchester (The), 464
Business First PAC, 536
Business Informatics Center, 634
Business Outreach Center Network Inc, 513
Business Outreach Ctr Network, 503
Business Review, 601
Business Review (The), 591
Business-Industry PAC of Central NY Inc, 536
BX Rochester PAC, 535
BXNY PAC, 535
Bynum, Thompson, Ryer, 164
Byram Hills CSD, 675
Byron-Bergen CSD, 648
C&S Engineers Inc, 475
C/S 12th Avenue LLC, 516
Cable PAC, 536
Cable Telecommunications Assn of NY, 490

Cable Telecommunications Assn of NY Inc, 456, 487, 515, 518
Cable Telecommunications Assn of NY, Inc (The), 476
Cable Telecommunications Association of New York Inc, 173
Cable Telecommunications Association of NY, 508
Cable Television & Telecommunications Assn of NY, 477
Cablevision (CSC Holdings Inc), 501
Cablevision Systems Corporation, 173
Cablevision Systems New York PAC, 536
Cadence Cycling & Multisport Centers, 474
Cairo-Durham CSD, 649
Caithness Energy, LLC, 500
Caledonia-Mumford CSD, 651
Callen-Lorde Community Health Ctr, 486
Callen-Lorde Coomunity Health Center, 503
Calpine Corporation, 515, 518
Calvin, James S, 467
Camarda Realty Investments, 478
Cambridge CSD, 674
Camden CSD, 658
Camillus, Town of, 416
Camp Directors (NYS), 503
Camp Venture Inc, 316
Campaign for Fiscal Equity, Inc, 152, 467, 483
Campaign for Renewable Energy, 536
Campbell-Savona CSD, 667
Campground Owners of New York, 342
Campground Owners of NY Inc, 512
Camphill Village USA Inc, 472
Campus Auxiliary Services Inc, 468
Canadian American Transportation Systems, LLC, 513
Canadian National Railway, 504
Canadian Pacific Railway, 487
Canajoharie CSD, 653
Canandaigua, 71
  Civil & Criminal Courts, 71
Canandaigua Area Chamber of Commerce, 571
Canandaigua City SD, 660
Canandaigua National Bank & Trust Co, 94
Canarsie Courier, 592
Canaseraga CSD, 639
Canastota Chamber of Commerce, 571
Canastota CSD, 651
Candor CSD, 672
Canisius College, 495, 622
Canisteo-Greenwood CSD, 667
Canton Chamber of Commerce, 571
Canton CSD, 666
Canton-Potsdam Hospital, 530
Capalino, James F & Associates Inc, 467
CAPE PAC, 536
Cape Vincent Chamber of Commerce, 571
Capital City Committee, 536

Capital Defender Office, 114, 136, 257, 375
Capital District Educational Opportunity Center, 618
Capital District Physicians' Health Plan, 490
Capital District Physicians' Health Plan Inc, 468, 512
Capital District Regional Off-Track Betting Corporation, 114, 335, 376, 463
Capital District Regional Planning Commission, 114, 230, 376
Capital District Transportation Authority, 114, 350, 376
Capital One Financial Corporation, 463
Capital Public Affairs, 468
Capital Region (Albany-Schoharie-Schenectady) BOCES, 678
Capital Region Council for Children with Special Needs, 487
Capitol Consultants Inc (NY), 468
Capitol Group, LLC, 468
Capitol Hill Management Services, 480
Capitol Hill Management Services Inc, 468
Capitol Strategies Group, LLC, 468
Cappelli, Allen, 469
Captain's Endowment Assn PAC, 536
Captains Endowment Assn, NYC Police Department, 505
Caramoor, 501
Carco Group Inc, 514
Cardozo School of Law, 241
Cardtronics LP, 504
Careplus, LLC, 483
Carle Place UFSD, 654
Carmel CSD, 663
Carmel, Town of, 416
Carnegie Hall, 530
Carpenters Labor-Management Council, NYS, 469
Carpenters Local No. 19 PAC, 536
Carpenters' Local 747 PAC, 536
Carpenters' Local Union 85 PAC, 537
Carpino, Peter, 469
Carr Public Affairs Inc, 469
Carr, Bernard, 469
Carson, Martin, 469
Carthage Area Chamber of Commerce, 571
Carthage CSD, 650
Caruso, David A, 469
CAS PAC, 536
CASA - Advocates for Children of NYS, 262, 316
Cassadaga Valley CSD, 641
Castelbuono, A J, 470
Caterpillar, Inc (Multistate Associates Inc), 469
Cathedral Church of St John the Devine (The), 530
Catholic Charities, 316
Catholic Conference (NYS), 461

Organization Index

Catholic Conference Policy Group Inc, 530
Catholic Conference Policy Group, Inc, 462
Catholic Family Center, 513
Catholic Health Services of Long Island, 493
Catholic Health System, 527
Catholic Health System, Sisters of Charity Hospital, 501
Catholic Healthcare System, 501
Catholic School Administrators Association of NYS, 152
Catholic War Veterans of the United States of America, 366
Cato-Meridian CSD, 641
CATS VLT, LLC (Canadian American Transportation Systems), 513
Catskill Center for Conservation & Development, 188
Catskill CSD, 649
Catskill Off-Track Betting Corporation, 114, 336, 376, 486
Catskill Regional Off-Track Betting Corporation, 475
Cattaraugus County, 62, 397
   Family Court, 62
   Supreme, County & Surrogate's Courts, 62
Cattaraugus Empire Zone Corporation, 571
Cattaraugus-Allegany-Erie-Wyoming BOCES, 678
Cattaraugus-Little Valley CSD, 640
Cayuga Community College, 615
Cayuga Community College Faculty Assn PAC, 537
Cayuga County, 62, 397
   Family Court, 62
Cayuga County Chamber of Commerce, 571
Cayuga Nation, 207
Cayuga-Onondaga BOCES, 678
Cazenovia Area Chamber of Commerce (Greater Cazenovia Area), 571
Cazenovia College, 622
Cazenovia CSD, 652
CBS Corporation, 172, 494, 506
CBS News (New York Bureau), 601
CBS Outdoor, Inc (FKA Viacom Outdoor, Inc), 467
CDRN, LLC, 519
Cemetery Employer Assn of Greater NY, 513
Cemusa Inc, 494
Cendant Car Rental Group Inc, 342, 501, 513
Cendant Corporation NY PAC, 537
Center Care Inc, 508
Center for Advanced Tech-Medical Biotechnology
   Center for Advanced Tech-Medical Biotechnology, 100

Center for Alternative Sentencing & Employment Services (CASES), 140
Center for an Urban Future, 233, 275
Center for Anti-Violence Education Inc, 316
Center for Charter School Excellence (NYC), 516
Center for Constitutional Rights, 241, 503
Center for Court Innovation, 262
Center for Disability Services, 317, 530
Center for Economic Growth Inc, 107
Center for Educational Innovation - Public Education Association, 152
Center for Environmental Information Inc, 188
Center for Family & Youth (The), 316
Center for Governmental Research Inc (CGR), 207
Center for Independence of the Disabled in NY (CIDNY), 241, 316
Center for Jewish History (The), 486
Center for Judicial Accountability Inc, 262
Center for Law & Justice, 140, 262
Center for Migration Studies of New York Inc, 241
Center for Technology in Government, University at Albany, SUNY, 207
Center for the Independence of the Disabled NY Inc, 503
Center for Urban Community Services, 317
Center Moriches UFSD, 668
Centerstone Development LLC, 480
Central Adirondack Association, 571
Central Boiler Inc, 529
Central Brooklyn Medical Group, PC, 537
Central Hudson Gas & Electric Corp, 486
Central Hudson Gas & Electric Corporation, 173
Central Islip UFSD, 668
Central Labor Council (NYC), 513
Central Mutual Fire Insurance Co (NY), 461
Central New York Business Journal, 601
Central New York Regional Market Authority, 102, 114, 376
Central New York Regional Transportation Authority, 115, 350, 376
Central NY PAC Region 9 UAW, 537
Central NY Railroad, 513
Central Pine Barrens Joint Planning & Policy Commission, 115, 181, 376
Central Square CSD, 661
Centre Partners Management LLC, 493
Century Foundation (The), 165
Cephalon Inc, 465, 513
Cerebral Palsy Assns of NYS Inc, 528
Cerebral Palsy Associations of New York State, 152, 221, 283, 317
Certified Lumber, 478
Certilman Balin Adler & Hyman, LLP, 478
Ceruzzi Holdings, 532
CGI (FKA CGI Group), 530

CH2M Hill, 501
Chadwick, Cindy, 470
Chain Pharmacy Assn of NYS, 528
Chain Pharmacy Assn PAC, 537
Chamber Players International, 483
Champlain Valley Educational Svcs (Clinton-Essex-Warren-Washington), 678
Change to Win, 466
Chappaqua CSD, 675
Charlotte Valley CSD, 644
Charmer Industries Inc, 490
Charmer Industries, Inc, 483
Charter PAC, 537
Charter Schools Assn (NY), 470, 490
Chateaugay CSD, 647
Chatham CSD, 643
Chautauqua County, 62, 398
   Family Court, 62
   Supreme & County Courts, 62
   Surrogate Court, 62
Chautauqua County Chamber of Commerce, 571
Chautauqua County Chamber of Commerce, Dunkirk Branch, 571
Chautauqua County Industrial Development Agency, 572
Chautauqua Lake CSD, 641
Chazy Central RSD, 643
Cheektowaga Chamber of Commerce, 572
Cheektowaga CSD, 645
Cheektowaga Democratic Finance Committee, 537
Cheektowaga, Town of, 416
Cheektowaga-Sloan UFSD, 645
Chemical Alliance (NYS), 482
Chemung County, 62, 398
   Family Court, 62
   Supreme & County Courts, 62
   Surrogate Court, 62
Chemung County Chamber of Commerce, 572
Chemung County Industrial Development Agency, 572
Chenango County, 62, 398
   Supreme, County, Family & Surrogate's Courts, 62
Chenango County Chamber of Commerce, 572
Chenango Forks CSD, 639
Chenango Valley CSD, 639
Cherokee Northeast LLC, 493
Cherry Valley-Springfield CSD, 662
Chesapeake Appalachia LLC, 497
Chester UFSD, 660
Chetrit Group (The), 474
CHH Realty, 493
Chickering Group (The), 495
Chief Executives Network for Manufacturing, 504
Child Care Coordinating Council (NYS), 470

Organization Index

Child Care Inc, 470
Child Center of New York, 478
Children & Families, 44
    Committee Staff, 44
    Key Assembly Staff Assignments, 44
    Majority, 45
    Membership, 45
    Minority, 45
Children & Family Services, Office of, 6, 143, 308, 372
    Administration Division, 309
    Adoption Services, 309
    Adult Protective Services, 309
    Albany Regional Office, 310
    Audit & Quality Control, 309
    Buffalo Regional Office, 310
    Bureau of Early Childhood Services (BECS), 309
    Bureau of Interagency Coordination & Case Resolution, 311
    Bureau of Management & Program Support, 310
    Bureau of Policy, Research & Planning, 311
    Central Services, 309
    Commission for the Blind & Visually Handicapped (CBVH), 309
    Connections, 309
    Contract Management, 309
    Council on Children & Families, 6, 372
    COUNCIL ON CHILDREN & FAMILIES, 311
    Development & Prevention Services Division, 309
    Executive Office, NYC, 308
    Facility Operations, 310
    Financial Management, 309
    Human Resources, 309
    Information Technology Division, 309
    Legal Affairs Division, 309
    Management & Support, 309
    Native American Services, 309, 310
    New York City Regional Office, 310
    Program Services, 310
    Program Support, 309
    Program Support & Community Partnerships, 310
    Public Information Division, 309
    Regional Offices, 310
    Regional Operations, 143, 309
    Regional Operations & Practice Improvement (ROPI), 309
    Rehabilitative Services Division, 310
    Rochester Regional Office, 311
    Special Investigations Unit, 310
    State Central Registry, 309
    Strategic Planning & Policy Development, Office of, 310
    Syracuse Regional Office, 311
    Yonkers Regional Office, 311
    Youth Development, 310, 311

Children's Aid Society (The), 317, 490
Children's Day Treatment Coalition, 487
Children's Health Fund (The), 470
Children's Institute, 475, 530
Children's Institute, Inc, 490
Children's Rights Inc, 241, 317
Children's Village (The), 283, 317
Chili, Town of, 416
Chinese-American Planning Council Inc, 465
Chip-Community Housing Improvement Program, Inc, 474
Chiropractic Assn Inc (NYS), 489
Chiropractic Council (NY), 518
Chittenango CSD, 652
ChoicePoint, 487
Christ the King Seminary, 623
Christie's Education Inc, 635
Christmas Tree Farmers Association of New York Inc, 84
Chubb & Son (Division of Federal Insurance Co), 514
Church Avenue Merchants Block Assn, 465
Church Avenue Merchants Block Association, 470
Church Avenue Merchants Block Association (CAMBA), 470
Church Avenue Merchants Block Association Inc, 513
Churchville-Chili CSD, 652
Ciccone, Stephen J, 471
Cicero, Town of, 417
CIDNY - Queens, 241, 316
Cigar Assn of America Inc, 476, 483
Cigna Companies, 490
Cigna Corporation, 504
CIGNA Corporation Political Action Committee, 536
Cincinnatus CSD, 643
Cingular Wireless, 487, 499
Cingular Wireless LLC EPAC, 537
CIO Office & Office for Technology, 6, 168, 195, 371
    Administration, 168, 195
    CIO Office, 6, 168, 195, 371
    Counsel, 168, 195
    Office for Technology, 6, 168, 195, 371
    Operations, 168, 195
    Statewide Initiatives, 168, 195
    Statewide Wireless Network, 168, 195
Circle Line Harbor Cruises, LLC, 459
Circulo De La Hispanidad, 528
Cisco Systems Inc, 487
Cities, 26, 45
    Committee Staff, 26, 45
    Key Assembly Staff Assignments, 45
    Key Senate Staff Assignments, 26
    Majority, 26, 45
    Membership, 26, 45
    Minority, 26, 45
Citigroup, 94

Citigroup Inc, 94
Citigroup Inc PAC - Federal/State, 537
Citigroup Management Corp, 488
Citigroup Washington Inc, 463
Citizen (The), 591
Citizen Action of New York, 165
Citizen Action of NY, 495
Citizen Action of NY Political Contribution Acct, 537
Citizens Budget Commission, 292, 330, 471
Citizens Campaign for the Environment, 471
Citizens for Fiscal Intergrity, 537
Citizens for Integrity in Politics, 537
Citizens for NYC, 467
Citizens for Public Broadcasting, 537
Citizens for Responsible Representation, 537
Citizens for Sports & Arts, Inc, 537
Citizens Housing & Planning Council of New York, 234
Citizens Leadership Council, 537
Citizens Union of the City of New York, 207, 293, 477
Citizens' Committee for Children of New York Inc, 241, 317, 471
Citizens' Environmental Coalition, 188
Citrix Systems, 468
City Bar Justice Center, 478
City College of New York, The, 620
City Ctr of Music & Drama Inc, 463
City Highway Superintendents Assn (NYS), 485
City Investment Fund, LP (The), 495
City Journal (Manhattan Institute for Policy Research), 601
City of Mount Vernon, 524
City of Rochester, 490
City of Syracuse Industrial Development Agency, 530
City of White Plains (The), 515, 518
City of Yonkers, 462, 515, 518
City University Construction Fund, 115, 148, 376
City University of New York (CUNY), 471
City Works Foundation, (The), 507
Citymeals-on-Wheels, 494
Civil Court, NYC, 59
    Bronx County, 59
    Housing Court Judges, 60
    Kings County, 59
    New York County, 59
    Queens County, 59
    Richmond County, 59
Civil Liberties Union (NY), 514
Civil Service & Pensions, 26
    Committee Staff, 26
    Key Senate Staff Assignments, 26
    Majority, 26
    Membership, 26
    Minority, 26

Organization Index

Civil Service Department, 6, 237, 287, 295, 372
  Administration, 287, 295
  Administrative Services Unit, 287, 295
  Civil Service Commission, 6, 288, 296
  Classification & Compensation Division, 237, 287, 295
  Commission Operations, 287, 295
  Diversity, Planning & Management Division, 237, 287, 295
  Employee Benefits Division, 287, 295
  Employee Health Services Division, 288, 295
  Information Resource Management, 288, 295
  Municipal Services Division, 288, 295
  Personnel, 288, 295
  Planning & Training Division, 295
  Planning Division, 288
  Staffing Services Division, 288, 295
  Testing Services Division, 288, 295
Civil Service Employees Assn of NY (CSEA), Local 1000, AFSCME, AFL-CIO, 299
Civil Service Employees Assn, Inc, 472
Civil Service Employees Political Action Fund, 526
Civil Service Employees Union (CSEA), Local 1000, AFSCME, AFL-CIO, 275
Civil Service Employees' PAF, 537
Civil Service Technical Guild PAC, 537
Civil Svc Technical Guild, Local 375 DC-37, AFSCME AFL-CIO, 526
Claremont Prepatory School, 501
Clarence Chamber of Commerce, 572
Clarence CSD, 645
Clarence Industrial Development Agency (Town of), 572
Clarence, Town of, 417
Clark Patterson Associates, 488
Clark, Frank A, 472
Clarke, Donald, 472
Clarke's Group (The), 474
Clarkson University, 472, 623
Clarkstown CSD, 664
Clarkstown, Town of, 417
Clay, Town of, 417
Clayton Chamber of Commerce, 572
Clean Energy (DCI Group), 466
Clean PAC Inc, 537
Clear Channel Communications Inc PAC, 537
Clear Channel Outdoor, 478
Clearing House Association LLC (The), 465
Cleary, Kevin Government Relations, LLC, 472
Cleveland Hill UFSD, 646
Clifton Park, Town of, 417
Clifton Springs Area Chamber of Commerce, 572
Clifton-Fine CSD, 666

Clinical Education Initiative Council, 516
Clinical Laboratory Assn Inc (NYS), 489
Clinical Laboratory Assoc, Inc (NYS), 531
Clinton Chamber of Commerce Inc, 572
Clinton Community College, 615
Clinton County, 62, 398
  Supreme, County, Family & Surrogate's Courts, 62
Clinton County, The Development Corporation, 572
Clinton CSD, 658
Clipper Equity LLC, 494
Clough Harbor & Associates LLP, 501
Clubhouse of Suffolk, 493
Clyde Chamber of Commerce, 572
Clyde Industrial Development Corporation, 572
Clyde-Savannah CSD, 674
Clymer CSD, 641
CMA Consulting, 506
CMT-Creative Mobile Technology, 474
CNA, 466, 487
CNA Surety/Western Surety Co, 527
CNY Labor PAC, 536
Coach USA, 475
Coalition Against Domestic Violence (NYS), 472
Coalition Against Domestic Violence, NYS, 140, 317
Coalition Against Hunger (NYC), 472
Coalition Against Sexual Assault (NYS), 140
Coalition for Asian American Children & Families, 317
Coalition for Children with Special Needs (NYC), 487
Coalition for Children's Mental Health Services (NYS), 473
Coalition for Education Reform & Accountability, 473
Coalition for Medically Fragile Children, 503
Coalition for Mold Reform (State Farm Insurance Cos), 514
Coalition for Natural Health, 523
Coalition for Quality Assisted Living (NY), 503
Coalition for the Homeless, 317, 473, 503, 508
Coalition of Animal Care Societies (The), 317
Coalition of Behavioral Health Agencies, Inc (The), 284
Coalition of Behavioral Health Agencies, Inc (The) (FKA Coalition of Voluntary Mental Health Agen), 477
Coalition of Fathers & Families NY, 221, 317, 538
Coalition of Fathers & Families NY, PAC, 207, 263
Coalition of Living Museums, 342

Coalition of New York State Career Schools (The), 152
Coalition of NYS Alzheimer's Assn Chapters, 503
Coalition of NYS Career Schools, 532
Coalition of Prepaid Health Svcs Plans (NYS), 503
Coalition of Special Act School Districts of NYS, 469
Coalition of Voluntary Mental Health Agencies, Inc, 473
Coalition of Voluntary Safety Net Hospitals (NYS), 503
Coastal Communications Services Inc, 513
Cobb Jr, James H, 473
Cobble Hill Health Center, 493
Cobleskill-Richmondville CSD, 665
Coca-Cola Bottling Co of NY (The), 501
Coca-Cola Enterprise Employee NonPartisan Committee for Good Government, 538
Cochran School of Nursing, 623
Codes, 26, 45
  Committee Staff, 26, 45
  Key Assembly Staff Assignments, 45
  Key Senate Staff Assignments, 26
  Majority, 26, 45
  Membership, 26, 45
  Minority, 26, 45
COFCCA Inc, 466, 529
Cohen Brothers Realty & Construction, 474
Cohen, Marsha A, 473
Cohoes, 71
  Civil, Criminal & Traffic Courts, 71
Cohoes City SD, 638
Cohoes Industrial Development Agency (City of), 572
Cold Spring Harbor CSD, 668
Cold Spring Harbor Fish Hatchery & Aquarium, 342
Cold Spring Harbor Laboratory, 489
Colgate Rochester Crozer Divinity School, 623
Colgate University, 490, 623
Colgate University, Department of Geology, 188
Collateral Loan Brokers Assn of NY, 495
Collectors Assn Inc (NYS), 464
College Board, 530
College Board (The), 514
College Community Services, Inc (DBA Brooklyn Center for the Performing Arts), 532
College of Agriculture & Life Sciences at Cornell University, 612
College of Human Ecology at Cornell University, 612
College of Mount Saint Vincent, 623
College of New Rochelle (The), 623
College of Saint Rose (The), 623
College of Staten Island, 620

Organization Index

College of Staten Island (Research Foundation of CUNY), 492
College of Veterinary Medicine at Cornell University, 612
College of Westchester (The), 635
College PT Holdings LLC, 493
College Retirement Equities Fund Teachers Ins & Annuity Assn, 481
Collegiate Church Corp, 509, 519
Colliers ABR Inc, 304
Colonie Chamber of Commerce, 572
Colonie, Town of, 417
Colony Liquor & Wine Distributors, LLC, 515
Colton-Pierrepont CSD, 666
Columbia County, 62, 399
   Supreme, County, Family & Surrogate's Courts, 62
Columbia County Chamber of Commerce, 572
Columbia Grammar & Preparatory School, 478
Columbia Hudson Partnership, 573
Columbia Law School, Legislative Drafting Research Fund, 165, 293
Columbia University, 519, 623
Columbia University, Exec Graduate Pgm in Public Policy & Administration, 207
Columbia University, Mailman School of Public Health, 221, 241
Columbia University, Mailman School of Public Health, Center for Public Health, 221
Columbia University, MPA in Environmental Science & Policy, 188
Columbia University, School of the Arts, 342
Columbia University, Science & Technology Ventures, 107
Columbia-Greene Community College, 615
Columbus Circle Agency, Inc, 538
Column Technologies, Inc, 468
Combined Coordinating Council Inc, 530
Combined Life Insurance Co of NY, 482
Commack UFSD, 668
Commerce Bank, 475
Commerce, Economic Development & Small Business, 26
   Committee Staff, 26
   Key Senate Staff Assignments, 26
   Majority, 26
   Membership, 26
   Minority, 26
Commerce, Science & Transportation, 384
   Aviation Operations, Safety & Security, 384
   Consumer Affairs, Insurance & Automotive Safety, 384
   Interstate Commerce, Trade and Tourism, 384

   Oceans, Atmosphere, Fisheries and Coast Guard, 384
   Science, Technology and Innovation, 384
   Space, Aeronautics and Related Sciences, 384
   Subcommittees, 384
   Surface Transportation & Merchant Marine Infrastructure, Safety & Security, 384
Commission on Economic Opportunity for the Greater Capital Region, 317
Commission on Independent Colleges & Universities, 152
Commissioned Officers Assn of the US Public Health Svc Inc (COA), 221, 366
Committee for a Better Niagara, 538
Committee for Action for a Responsible Electorate (CARE), 538
Committee for an Independent Public Defense Commission, 473
Committee for Economic Growth, 538
Committee for Effective City Council, 538
Committee for Effective Leadership, 538
Committee for Hispanic Children & Families, 513
Committee for Medical Eye Care PAC, 538
Committee for Occupational Safety & Health (NY), 507
Committee for Safe Streets, 465
Committee for Taxi Safety, 463
Committee for Workers' Compensation Reform, 507, 538
Committee of Interns & Residents SEIU Loc 1957 Health Care Advocacy Fund (CARE), 538
Committee of Methadone Program Administrators Inc of NYS (COMPA), 222, 284
Committee to Save St Brigid's, 522
Commodity Futures Trading Commission, 81, 104
   Eastern Region, 81, 104
Commodore Applied Technologies Inc, 188
Common Cause (NY), 498
Common Cause/NY, 165, 207
Common Ground Community Inc, 486
Commonwealth Business Media, 596
Commonwealth Fund, 222
Communication Workers of America Local 1180, 513
Communication Workers of America, District 1 PAC, 538
Communication Workers of America, Local 1182, 513
Communications Workers of America, District 1, 275, 505
Community & Rural Development Institute, 84
Community Advocacy & Advisory Services, 473
Community Bank (NY), 513

Community Bankers Assn of NY State, Accounting & Taxation Cmte, 95, 330
Community Bankers Assn of NY State, Bank Operations & Admin Cmte, 96
Community Bankers Assn of NY State, Banking Law & Regulations Cmte, 94
Community Bankers Assn of NY State, Government Relations Cmte, 96, 209
Community Bankers Assn of NY State, Mortgages & Real Estate Cmte, 96, 305
Community Blood Services, 469
Community Financial Services Association of America, 514
Community General Hospital, 528
Community Health Care Assn of NYS, 455
Community Health Care Assoc of NYS, 503
Community Health Care Association of NYS, 222, 473
Community Healthcare, 474
Community Healthcare Network, 222, 318, 474
Community Hospital Network of NY Eductl & Rsch Fund Inc, 530
Community Housing Improvement Program (CHIP), 234
Community Mental Health PAC, 538
Community Preservation Corporation (The), 234, 474, 490, 499
Community Service Society of New York, 234
Community Service Society of NY, 530
Community Voices Heard, 474
Community Works, 480
Compac, NJ, 538
Compassion & Choices of NY (Compassion in Dying), 516
Compensation Action Network (NY), 474
Comprehensive Home Care, 462
Computer Aid Inc, 488
Computer Associates, 515
Computers for Youth, 467
Concentra Health Services Inc, 463
Concepts of Independent Choices, 469, 503
Concerned Home Care Providers, 501, 513
Concordia College, 623
Coney Island Chamber of Commerce, 573
Conf of the Int'l Union of Operating Engineers (NYS), 505
Conference Board (The), 107
Conference of Big 5 School Districts, 152, 459
Conference of Mayors & Municipal Officials (NYS), 474
Congregation Shearith Israel, 519
Connelly & McLaughlin, 474
Connelly Communications, Inc, 475
Connetquot CSD, 668
Connors & Connors, PC, 263
Connors & Corcoran LLP, 249, 263
Connors & Vilardo, 207
ConocoPhillips, 487

Organization Index

Conpor Conference of Private Organizations (NYS), 488
Conservation Service Group, 507
Conservative Action Fund, 538
Conservative Party of NYS, 165
Consolidated Edison Co of NY Inc, 490, 530
Consolidated Edison Co of NY, Inc & its subsidiaries, 496
Consolidated Edison Energy, 173
Consolidated Edison, Inc. Employees' Political Action Committee (CEIPAC), 538
Consortium for Worker Education (The), 483
Consortium for Workers Education, 507
Constantinople & Vallone Consulting LLC (FKA Constantinople Consulting), 475
Constellation Energy Group, 456, 463
Constellation NewEnergy Inc, 173
Construction Contractors Assn of the Hudson Valley Inc, 461
Construction Contractors Assn PAC, 538
Construction Contractors Association of the Hudson Valley Inc, 108
Construction Ind Cncl of Westchester & Hudson Valley Inc, 483
Construction Industry Cncl of Westchester & Hudson Valley Inc, 514
Construction Industry Council - NYS PAC, 538
Construction Materials Association (NY), 478
Consumer Advocacy PAC, 538
Consumer Affairs & Protection, 45
  Committee Staff, 45
  Key Assembly Staff Assignments, 45
  Majority, 45
  Membership, 45
  Minority, 45
Consumer Data Industry Assoc, 490
Consumer Electronics Association (Multistate Associates Inc), 469
Consumer Finance Assn (NYS), 488
Consumer Healthcare Products Assn, 468
Consumer Power Advocates, 500
Consumer Product Safety Commission, 104
  Eastern Regional Center, 104
Consumer Protection, 27
  Committee Staff, 27
  Key Senate Staff Assignments, 27
  Majority, 27
  Membership, 27
  Minority, 27
Consumer Protection Board, 6, 99, 168, 372
Consumer Specialty Products Association, 490
Consumers Union, 84, 108
Container Terminal Inc (NY), 518
Continental Airlines, Inc, 493
Continental Industrial Capital, LLC, 501

Continuing Care Leadership Coalition, 463
Continuum Health Partners Inc, 222
Contractors, Agents, & Brokers PAC, 538
Convenience PAC, 538
Convention Centers & Visitors Bureaus, 338
  Albany County Convention & Visitors Bureau, 338
  Buffalo Niagara Convention & Visitors Bureau, 338
  Chautauqua County Visitors Bureau, 338
  Greater Binghamton New York Convention and Visitors Bureau, 338
  Greater Rochester Visitors Association, 338
  Ithaca/Tompkins County Convention & Visitors Bureau, 338
  Lake Placid/Essex County Convention & Visitors Bureau, 338
  Long Island Convention & Visitors Bureau & Sports Commission, 338
  NYC & Company/Convention & Visitors Bureau, 338
  Oneida County Convention & Visitors Bureau, 338
  Ontario County/Finger Lakes Visitor's Connection, 338
  Saratoga Convention & Tourism Bureau, 338
  Steuben County Conference & Visitors Bureau, 338
  Sullivan County Visitors Association, 338
  Syracuse Convention & Vistors Bureau, 338
  Thousand Islands Int'l Tourism Council, 338
  Westchester County Office of Tourism, 338
Conway, Gerard L, Jr, 475
Cookfair Media Inc, 165
Cooper Tank & Welding Corp, 466
Cooper Union for Advancement of Science & Art (NYC Office), 497
Cooper Union for Advancement of Science & Art (The), 519
Cooper Union for the Advancement of Science & Art, 623
Cooperstown Chamber of Commerce, 573
Cooperstown CSD, 662
Coordinated Court Services, 468
Coors Brewing Co, 455
Cope 25, 538
Copenhagen CSD, 651
Copiague UFSD, 668
Coppola Ryan McHugh Riddell, 475
Coppola, John J, 475
Coral Realty, LLC, 467
Cordo, John, 475
Corinth CSD, 664
Corinth Industrial Development Agency (Town of), 573

Cornell Cooperative Extension, 84
Cornell Cooperative Extension, College of Human Ecology, Nutrition, Health, 222, 318
Cornell Cooperative Extension, Community & Economic Vitality Program, 234
Cornell Cooperative Extension, Environment & Natural Resources Initiative, 188
Cornell Cooperative Extension, NY Sea Grant, 188
Cornell Cooperative Extension, Pesticide Management Education Program, 84
Cornell Cooperative Extension, Urban Agriculture & Markets Program, 84
Cornell Farmedic Training Program, 84
Cornell Law School, Legal Information Institute, 263
Cornell University, 152, 494, 624
Cornell University Center for the Environment, 188
Cornell University, College of Agriculture & Life Sciences, Animal Science, 84
Cornell University, Community, Food & Agriculture Program, 84
Cornell University, Department of Applied Economics & Management, 84
Cornell University, Development Sociology, 84
Cornell University, Economics Department, 94, 108
Cornell University, FarmNet Program, 84
Cornell University, Institute on Conflict Resolution, 275
Cornell University, Program on Dairy Markets & Policy, 85
Cornell University, Rural Schools Association of NYS, 152
Cornell University, Sch of Industr & Labor Relations Institute for Workplace Studies, 275
Cornell University, School of Industrial & Labor Relations, 153, 241, 275, 299
Cornerstone Real Estate Advisers LLC, 483
Corning, 71
  Civil & Criminal Courts, 71
Corning Area Chamber of Commerce, 573
Corning Community College, 615
Corning Incorporated, 525
Corning Incorporated Employees PAC (COREPAC), 539
Corning Place Consulting, LLC, 476
Corning-Painted Post Area SD, 667
Cornwall CSD, 660
Coro New York, 467
Corporate Housing Providers Association, 474
Corporation for National & Community Service, 314
  New York Program Office, 314

Organization Index

Corporation for Supportive Housing, 503, 528
Corporations, Authorities & Commissions, 27, 45
   Committee Staff, 27, 45
   Key Assembly Staff Assignments, 45
   Key Senate Staff Assignments, 27
   Majority, 27, 46
   Membership, 27, 46
   Minority, 27, 46
Correction, 46
   Committee Staff, 46
   Key Assembly Staff Assignments, 46
   Majority, 46
   Membership, 46
   Minority, 46
Correction Captains Assn PAC, 539
Correction Officers & Police Benevolent Assn Inc, 513
Correction Officers' Benevolent Assn PAC, 539
Correctional Association of New York, 140
Correctional Services Department, 7, 129, 372
   Adirondack Correctional Facility, 130
   Administrative Services, 129
   Agri-Business, 129
   Albion Correctional Facility, 130
   Altona Correctional Facility, 130
   Arthur Kill Correctional Facility, 130
   Attica Correctional Facility, 130
   Auburn Correctional Facility, 130
   Bare Hill Correctional Facility, 130
   Bayview Correctional Facility, 130
   Beacon Correctional Facility, 130
   Bedford Hills Correctional Facility, 130
   Budget & Finance Division, 129
   Buffalo Correctional Facility, 130
   Butler Correctional Facility, 130
   Camp Gabriels, 130
   Camp Georgetown, 130
   Camp Pharsalia, 130
   Cape Vincent Correctional Facility, 130
   Cayuga Correctional Facility, 130
   Chateaugay Correctional Facility, 130
   Classification & Movement/Transportation, 132
   Clinton Correctional Facility, 130
   Collins Correctional Facility, 130
   Correctional Facility Operations, 129
   Correctional Health Services, 132
   Correctional Industries Division, 129
   Coxsackie Correctional Facility, 130
   Dental Services, 132
   Diversity Management, 129
   Downstate Correctional Facility, 130
   Eastern NY Correctional Facility, 130
   Edgecombe Correctional Facility, 130
   Education, 132
   Elmira Correctional Facility, 130
   Facilities, 130
   Facilities Planning & Development, 132
   Fishkill Correctional Facility, 130
   Five Points Correctional Facility, 130
   Franklin Correctional Facility, 130
   Fulton Correctional Facility, 130
   Gouverneur Correctional Facility, 130
   Gowanda Correctional Facility, 130
   Great Meadow Correctional Facility, 130
   Green Haven Correctional Facility, 130
   Greene Correctional Facility, 131
   Groveland Correctional Facility, 131
   Guidance & Counseling, 132
   Hale Creek ASACTC, 131
   Health Services Division, 132
   Hudson Correctional Facility, 131
   Human Resources Management Division, 129
   Inmate Grievance, 129
   Internal Controls, 129
   Labor Relations Bureau, 129
   Lakeview Shock Incarceration Correctional Facility, 131
   Library Services, 132
   Lincoln Correctional Facility, 131
   Livingston Correctional Facility, 131
   Lyon Mountain Correctional Facility, 131
   Management Information Services, 132
   Marcy Correctional Facility, 131
   Mental Health, 132
   Mid-Orange Correctional Facility, 131
   Mid-State Correctional Facility, 131
   Ministerial & Family Services, 132
   Mohawk Correctional Facility, 131
   Monterey Shock Incarceration Correctional Facility, 131
   Moriah Shock Incarceration Correctional Facility, 131
   Mt McGregor Correctional Facility, 131
   Nursing & Ancillary Services, 132
   Ogdensburg Correctional Facility, 131
   Oneida Correctional Facility, 131
   Orleans Correctional Facility, 131
   Otisville Correctional Facility, 131
   Personnel Bureau, 129
   Population Management, 132
   Program Planning, Research & Evaluation, 132
   Program Services, 132
   Queensboro Correctional Facility, 131
   Riverview Correctional Facility, 131
   Rochester Correctional Facility, 131
   Security Staffing Unit, 132
   Shawangunk Correctional Facility, 131
   Sing Sing Correctional Facility, 131
   Southport Correctional Facility, 131
   Special Operations, 132
   Substance Abuse Treatment Services, 132
   Sullivan Correctional Facility, 131
   Summit Shock Incarceration Correctional Facility, 131
   Support Operations Division, 129
   Taconic Correctional Facility, 131
   Temporary Release, 132
   Training Academy, 129
   Ulster Correctional Facility, 131
   Upstate Correctional Facility, 131
   Volunteer Services, 132
   Wallkill Correctional Facility, 131
   Washington Correctional Facility, 131
   Watertown Correctional Facility, 131
   Wende Correctional Facility, 131
   Willard Drug Treatment Center, 132
   Woodbourne Correctional Facility, 132
   Workers' Compensation Investigation Unit, 129
   Wyoming Correctional Facility, 132
Cortland, 71
   Civil & Criminal Courts, 71
Cortland County, 63, 399
   Supreme, County, Family & Surrogate's Courts, 63
Cortland County Chamber of Commerce, 573
Cortland Enlarged City SD, 644
Cortland Regional Medical Center (FKA Cortland Memorial Hospital), 530
Cortland Standard, 593
Cortland Standard Printing Co Inc, 593
Cortlandt, Town of, 418
Couch White PAC, 539
Couch White, LLP, 476
Council for Community Behavioral Healthcare, 476
Council for the Humanities (NY), 483
Council for Unity, 507
Council Management Inc, 513
Council of Administrators & Supervisors, 526
Council of Community Services of NYS Inc, 318
Council of Family & Child Caring Agencies, 318
Council of Industry of Southeastern NY, 504
Council of Insurance Brokers of Greater NY, Inc, 482
Council of NECA Chapters (NYS), 462
Council of New York Cooperatives, 529
Council of Probation Administrators (NYS), 487
Council of School Superintendents (NYS), 500
Council of School Supervisors & Admin, Local 1 AFSA AFL-CIO, 539
Council of School Supervisors & Administrators, 153, 476, 478, 500
Council of Senior Centers & Services of NYC, 503
Council of Senior Ctrs & Services of NYC Inc, 499

Organization Index

Council of Senior Ctrs & Services of NYC, Inc, 476
Council of Sheet Metal Workers Int'l Assn (NYS), 477
Council of State Governments, Eastern Conference, 207, 293, 330
Council of the City of New York (The), 476
Council of Urban Professionals, 539
Council on the Arts, 7, 332, 372
   Administrative Services, 332
   Architecture, Planning & Design/Capital Projects, 332
   Arts in Education, 332
   Dance, 332
   Electronic Media & Film, 332
   Fiscal Management, 332
   Folk Arts, 332
   Individual Artists, 332
   Information Technology, 332
   Literature, 332
   Museum, 332
   Music, 333
   Presenting, 333
   Program Staff, 332
   Special Arts Services, 333
   State & Local Partnerships/Decentralization, 333
   Theatre, 333
   Visual Artists, 333
Council on the Environment of NYC (The), 188
Council on the Environment of NYC, Environmental Education, 153
Council on the Environment of NYC, Open Space Greening Program, 234
County Nursing Facilities of New York, 463
County Nursing Facilities of New York Inc, 222
County Nursing Facilities of NY, Inc, 503
County of Orleans Industrial Development Agency, 489
County of Westchester, 528
Court Clerks Assn (NYS), 499
Court of Appeals, 55
   Associate Judges, 55
Court of Claims, 58, 263
Court Officers Assn (NYS), 506
Court Officers Benevolent Assn of Nassau Cnty Inc, 465
Court Reporters Association, 478
Courtroom Television Network, 513
Covanta Energy Corp, 499, 513
Covanta Energy Corp Inc, 527
Covenant House NY, 508
Coventry, 463
Coventry Health Care, 468
Coxsackie-Athens CSD, 649
CP Rail System, 357
CPR, The International Institute for Conflict Prevention & Resolution, 262
CPS 5 LLC, 494

Crain's New York Business, 601
Crane & Vacco, LLC, 476
Crane, Parente & Cherubin, 173, 207
Creative Coalition (The), 513
Creative Time, 467
Credit Advocate Counseling Corporation, 94
Credit Suisse Securities (USA) LLC, 495
Credit Union League Inc & Affiliates (NYS), 476
Credit Union League Inc (NYS), 488, 490
Credit Union League, Inc (NYS), 487
Credit Unions' PAC (CUPAC), 539
Creosote Council III, 529
Crime Victims Board, 7, 132, 311, 372
Crime Victims, Crime & Correction, 27
   Committee Staff, 27
   Key Senate Staff Assignments, 27
   Majority, 27
   Membership, 27
   Minority, 27
Criminal Court, NYC, 60
   Bronx County, 60
   Kings County, 60
   New York County, 60
   Queens County, 60
   Richmond County, 60
Criminal Justice Services, Division of, 7, 133, 252, 288, 372
   Administration Office, 133, 252, 288
   Administrative Services, 133, 252, 288
   Advisory Groups, 133, 252
   Bureau of Justice Research & Innovation, 133, 253, 288
   Commission on Forensic Science, 133, 252
   Crime Reduction Strategies Unit, 133, 253, 288
   Funding & Program Assistance Office, 134, 253, 289
   Human Resources Management, 133, 252, 288
   Information Technology Development Group, 133, 252
   Information Technology Services Group, 133, 253
   Justice Systems Analysis Unit, 133, 253, 288
   Juvenile Justice Advisory Group, 133, 252
   Law Enforcement Accreditation Council, 133, 253, 288
   Legal Services, 133, 252, 288
   Missing & Exploited Children Clearinghouse, 133, 252, 288
   Municipal Police Training Council, 133, 253, 288
   NYS Motor Vehicle & Insurance Fraud Prevention Board, 133, 252
   Offender Management Analysis Unit, 134, 253, 289
   Office of Criminal Justice Operations, 133, 252, 288
   Office of Forensic Services, 133, 252, 288
   Office of Justice Information Services, 133, 252, 288
   Office of Justice Statistics & Performance, 133, 253
   Office of Operations, 133, 252
   Office of Public Safety, 133, 253, 288
   Office of Sex Offender Management, 133, 253
   Office of Strategic Planning, 133, 253, 288
   Operation IMPACT Coordinator, 134, 253
   Security Guard Advisory Council, 288
   State Committee for Coordination of Police Services for Elderly (TRIAD), 133, 253, 288
   State Finance & Budget, 133, 252, 288
   Statewide Law Enforcement Telecommunications Committee, 133, 253, 288
Crisis Program (The), 470, 487, 513
Criterion Strategies Inc (FKA First Responder Inc), 501
Critical Transportation Choices, Legislative Commission on, 32, 53
Croplife America, 456
Crosier, Barbara V, 476
Cross Harbor Railroad (NY), 513
Crossett, Susan M, 477
Crossroads Ventures, LLC, 459
Croton-Harmon UFSD, 676
Crouse Hospital, 530
Crouse Hospital School of Nursing, 624
Crown Point CSD, 647
Crystal Window & Door Systems, Ltd, 514
Crystal Window & Door Systems, LTD, 478
CSC Holdings Inc, 485, 500
CSC Holdings, Inc, 467, 515
CSX Transportation Inc, 518
CTIA - The Wireless Assn, 467
CTK Properties, 467
Ctr Against Domestic Violence, 486
Ctr for Educational Innovation-Public Education Assn, 480
Cuba-Rushford CSD, 639
Cubic Corporation, 519
Culinary Institute of America, 342, 624
Cullen & Dykman LLP, 275, 293
Cultural Institution Group, 463
Cumberland Packing Corporation, 513
CUNY Board of Trustees, 619
CUNY Central Administration, 619
   City University Construction Fund, 619
CUNY Graduate School, Center for Urban Research, 165
CUNY Hunter College, Urban Affairs & Planning Department, 233

Organization Index

CUNY John Jay College of Criminal Justice, 140
CUNY New York City College of Technology, Hospitality Mgmt, 342
Curran, Brian F, 477
Cutchogue-New Suffolk Chamber of Commerce, 573
Cuyler News Service, 601
CVS/Caremark Rx, 472
CWA Finger Lakes PAC, 536
CWA SSF (NY), 536
CWM Chemical Services LLC, 187
Cyclone Coasters, Inc, 478
D H Ferguson, Attorney, PLLC, 304
D&M P.A.C., LLC, 539
D.R.I.V.E.-Democratic, Republican, Independent Voter Education, 539
D'Ambrosio, John A, 477
D'Onofrio, Paul, 477
D'Youville College, 624
Dadey, Dick, 477
Daemen College, 624
Dahill, Kevin, 477
Daily Challenge, 592
Daily Courier-Observer, 595
Daily Freeman, 595
Daily Gazette (The), 599
Daily Gazette Co, 599
Daily Mail (The), 593
Daily Messenger (The), 593
Daily News (The), 592
Daily Record (The), 598
Daily Sentinel, 599
Daily Star (The), 598
Daimler Chrysler Corporation, 521
Daimler Chrysler Corporation Political Support Committee-New York, 539
DaimlerChrysler Corp, 489
Dairy Foods Inc (NYS), 496
Dairylea Cooperative Inc, 85, 464, 520
Dakota Software Corporation, 188
Dale Carnegie & Associates Inc, 108
Dames, Reid, LLC, 477
Dan Klores Communications Inc, 477
Danaher Controls Inc, 513
Dansville Chamber of Commerce, 573
Dansville CSD, 651
Darien Lake Theme Park Resort, 342
Darwak, Stephanie, 477
Data Niche Associates, 527
Data Trace Information Services, LLC, 478
David B Kriser Dental Center of NY University, 530
Davidoff, Malito & Hutcher, LLP, 478
Davis College, 624
Davis Development Holdings, 495
Davis Polk & Wardwell, 108
Davis, Michael J, 478
Davita Inc, 485, 488
Day Pitney LLP, 263, 330
DC 37 PAC, 539

De Ruyter CSD, 652
Debevoise & Plimpton LLP, 140, 263
Decision Strategies Group, 108
Deepdale Inc, 501
Deer Park UFSD, 668
Defenders Assn (NYS), 503
Defenders Association (NYS), 502
Defenders Justice Fund (NY), 459
DeGraff, Foy, Kunz & Devine, LLP, 208, 249
Delaware County, 63, 399
Supreme, County, Family & Surrogate's Courts, 63
Delaware County Chamber of Commerce, 573
Delaware County Planning Department, 573
Delaware Engineering, 488
Delaware North Companies Gaming & Entertainment Inc, 501, 506
Delaware North Companies, Inc, 476
Delaware River Basin Commission, 115, 181, 376
Delaware-Chenango-Madison-Otsego BOCES, 678
Delhi CSD, 644
Dell Inc, 490, 530
Delois Brassell Political Action Committee, 539
Deloitte & Touche, LLP, 530
Delphi Corp, 528
Delphi Corporation, 460
Delta Air Lines Inc, 489
Democracy for America-New York, 539
Democrat and Chronicle, 599
Democratic Caucus Committee, 539
Democratic Congressional Campaign Committee, 165
Democratic Governors' Assn - NY, 539
Democratic Rural Conference of New York State, 539
Demographic Research & Reapportionment, Legislative Task Force on, 32, 53
Demos: A Network for Ideas & Action, 478
Dental Assn (NYS), 497
Dental Hygienists' Association of the State of New York Inc, 222
Dental Hygienists' Association of the State of NY, Inc, 459
Depew UFSD, 646
Deposit Chamber of Commerce, 573
Deposit CSD, 639
Deputies Association (NYS), 490
Deputy Sheriff's Assn (NYC), 515
Dermot Company (The), 484, 522
Destiny USA, 501
Detectives Endowment Assn, Police Dept of NYC, 505
Detectives' Endowment Association COPE, 539
Deutsch, Ronald, 478
Deutsche Bank, 94

Development Authority of the North Country, 102, 115, 230, 376, 573
Development Counsellors International, 108
Developmental Disabilities Planning Council, 8, 237, 279, 311, 372
DeVry Incorporated, 530
DeVry Institute of Technology, Long Island City Campus, 635
Dewey Ballantine LLP, 479
Dewey Ballantine LLP Political Action Committee-New York, 539
DeWitt, Town of, 418
Dewolff Partnership, Architects LLP (The), 468
Dia Art Foundation, 495
Diageo, PLC, 528
Diamond Asphalt Corp, 479
Diamond Asphalt Corp., 478
Diaspora Community Services, 477
Diebold Election Systems, Inc, 467
Dietetic Assn (NYS), 469
Digiovanni, Joseph, 479
Dionondehowa Wildlife Sanctuary & School - Not For Profit, 188
Diorio, L Todd, 479
DiPalermo, Christian, 479
Direct Marketing Assoc Inc (Dehart & Darr Assoc Inc), 503
Disabled American Veterans, Department of New York, 366
Disabled in Action of Metropolitan NY, 497
Disabled, Select Committee on the, 32
Distilled Spirits Council of the US, 506, 529
District Council 37, AFSCME, 479
District Council 37, AFSCME, AFL-CIO, 299
District Council 9 PAC, 539
District Council of Carpenter's PAC (NYC) (Formerly Carpenters Civil Action Fund (NYC)), 483
District Council of Carpenters, PAC (NYC), 505
Diverse New York PAC, 540
DKI Engineering & Consulting USA, PC, Corporate World Headquarters, 357
DLA Piper Rudnick Gray Cary US LLP NYSPAC, 540
DMJM & Harris Inc, 520
Dobbs Ferry UFSD, 676
Docking Pilots of NJ/NY, 478
Doctors Council, 475
Doctors Without Borders USA, 222
Doe Fund, Inc (The), 487
Dolan Media Co, 598
Dolgeville CSD, 649
Dollar Thrifty Automotive Group Inc, 485
Dominican College, 624
Dominion PAC-NY, 540
Dominion Resources, 528
Donnellan, James, 479
Donnelly, Edwin, 479

Organization Index

Donohue, Gavin J, 479
Dormitory Authority of the State of NY, 483
Dorothea Hopfer School of Nursing at Mount Vernon Hospital, 624
Douglaston Development LLC, 474
Dover UFSD, 645
Dover-Wingdale Chamber of Commerce, 573
Dow Jones & Company, 596
Dow Jones Newswires (Dow Jones & Company), 601
Dowling College, 624
Downsville CSD, 644
Downtown Brooklyn Partnership (The), 500
Downtown Hospital (NY), 459
Downtown-Lower Manhattan Association, 573
Doyle, Michael R, 480
Dreyfus Corporation (The), 513
Drinking Driver Program Directors Assn (NYS), 487
Drug Policy Alliance (Center for Policy Reform), 503
Drug Policy Alliance Network (SSF), 540
Drum Major Institute for Public Policy - Not For Profit, 241
Dryden CSD, 672
Dryfoos Group, 480
Duane Morris LLP Government Committee NY Find, 540
Duane Reade, Inc, 476
Duane Street Realty, 519
Duanesburg CSD, 665
Dudley Associates P.C., 480
Duke Energy Corporation, 513
Duncan, Craig A, 480
Dundee CSD, 678
Dunkirk, 71
   Civil & Criminal Courts, 72
Dunkirk City SD, 641
Dunne, Richard C, 480
Dupee & Monroe, PC, 249
Durst Organization (The), 484
Dutchess BOCES, 679
Dutchess Community College, 615
Dutchess County, 63, 400
   Family Court, 63
   Supreme, County & Surrogate's Courts, 63
Dutchess County Economic Development Corporation, 573
Dutchess Democratic Women's Caucas, 540
Dynegy NY PAC, 540
E-3 Communications, 480
EAC Inc, 499, 506
Eagle One Roofing Contractors Inc, 475
Earthwatch LTD, 528
East Aurora Chamber of Commerce (Greater East Aurora), 573
East Aurora UFSD, 646

East Fishkill, Town of, 418
East Greenbush CSD, 663
East Greenbush Republican Club Inc, 540
East Hampton Chamber of Commerce, 573
East Hampton UFSD, 668
East Hampton, Town of, 418
East Irondequoit CSD, 652
East Islip Chamber of Commerce, 573
East Islip UFSD, 668
East Meadow Chamber of Commerce, 574
East Meadow UFSD, 654
East Moriches UFSD, 668
East Quogue UFSD, 669
East Ramapo CSD (Spring Valley), 664
East River Realty Company LLC, 486
East River Realty Company, LLC, 495
East Rochester UFSD, 652
East Rockaway Republican Club, 540
East Rockaway UFSD, 654
East Side Republican District Leaders Committee, 540
East Side Rezoning Alliance, 503
East Syracuse-Minoa CSD, 659
East Williston UFSD, 654
Eastchester UFSD, 676
Eastchester, Town of, 418
Eastchester-Tuckahoe Chamber of Commerce, 574
Eastern Contractors Association Inc, 108
Eastern Paramedics Inc, 501
Eastern Suffolk BOCES, 679
Eastman Kodak Co, 471
Eastman Kodak Co Employee PAC, 540
Eastman Kodak Company, 108
Easton Bell Sports, 521
Easton Sports, 494
Eastport-South Manor CSD, 669
eBay, 463
Eber Bros Wine & Liquor Corp, 512
E-Bizdocs, 469
Ecology & Environment Inc, 188, 528
Ecology & Environment NYS Committee for Responsible Government, 540
Ecomedia Direct, 467
Economic Committee, Joint, 394
Economic Development Council (NYS), 501
Economic Development Council Inc (NYS), 480
Economic Development, Job Creation, Commerce & Industry, 46
   Committee Staff, 46
   Key Assembly Staff Assignments, 46
   Majority, 46
   Membership, 46
   Minority, 46
ECOR Solutions Inc, 468
Eden CSD, 646
Edgemont UFSD, 676
Edinburg Common SD, 664
Edmeston CSD, 662

EDS, 490
Education, 27, 46
   Committee Staff, 27, 46
   Key Assembly Staff Assignments, 46
   Key Senate Staff Assignments, 27
   Majority, 27, 46
   Membership, 27, 46
   Minority, 27, 46
Education & Assistance Corp Inc, 318
Education & Assistance Corporation Inc, 140
Education & Labor, 388
   Early Childhood, Elementary and Secondary Education, 389
   Health, Employment, Labor and Pensions, 389
   Healthy Families and Communities, 389
   Higher Education, Lifelong Learning, and Competitiveness, 389
   Subcommittees, 389
   Workforce Protections, 389
Education & Research Network Inc (NYS), 491
Education & Work Consortium (The), 491, 504
Education Department, 8, 143, 212, 279, 311, 333, 372
   Administration, 145
   Adult Education & Workforce Development, 145
   Albany District Office, 147
   Architecture & Landscape Architecture, 146
   Bilingual Education, 145
   Bronx District Office, 147
   Brooklyn District Office, 147
   Buffalo District Office, 147
   Career & Technical Education, 145
   Central Regional Office, 146
   Child Nutrition Program Administration, 145
   Chiropractic, 146, 212
   College & University Evaluation, 144
   Cultural Education Office, 144, 333
   Curriculum & Instructional Support, 145
   Curriculum, Instruction & Instructional Technology, 145
   Deaf & Hard of Hearing Services, 312
   Dentistry & Optometry, 146, 212
   Early Education & Reading Initiatives, 145
   Eastern Regional Office, 147
   Educational Management Services, 145
   Educational Television & Public Broadcasting, 144
   Engineering & Land Surveying & Interior Design, 146
   Facilities & Management Services, 145
   Fiscal & Administrative Services, 146, 279, 312
   Fiscal Services, 145

Organization Index

Grants Management, 145
Hauppauge District Office, 147
Hempstead District Office, 147
Hudson Valley Regional Office, 147
Information & Reporting Services, 145
Information Technology Services, 145
Innovation, 144
Lifelong Services, 312
Long Island Regional Office, 147
Malone District Office, 147
Manhattan District Office, 147
Medicine, Diet-Nutrn, Athltc Trning, Medical Physics & Vet Med, 146, 212
Mid-Hudson District Office, 147
Native American Education, 145
New York City Regional Office, 147
Nonpublic School Services, 145
Nursing & Respiratory Therapy, 146, 212
NYC Intra/Interagency Group, 145
NYC School Improvement, 145
Office of Higher Education, 144
Office of K-16 Initiatives & Access Programs, 144
Office of Operations & Management Services, 144
Office of P-16 Education, 145
Office of Professional Responsibility, 146, 212, 279, 312
Office of Special Projects & Legislation, 146
Office of Teaching Initiatives, 144
Office of the Professions, 146, 212, 279, 312
Pharmacy & Midwifery, 146, 212
Planning & Policy Development, 145
Planning & Professional Development, 145
Professional Assistance Program, 146
Professional Discipline, 146
Professional Education Program Review, 146, 212, 279, 312
Professional Licensing Services, 146, 212, 279, 312
Program Develpmnt & Support Svcs/Special Ed Policy & Ptshps, 146, 279, 312
Proprietary School Supervision, 144
Psychology & Massage Therapy, 146, 212
Public Accountancy & Certified Shorthand Reporting, 146
Public School Choice, 145
Quality Assurance - Statewide Special Education, 146, 279, 312
Queens District Office, 147
Reference Services, 144
Research & Information Systems, 144
Research and Collections, 144
Rochester District Office, 147
School Improvement & Community Services (NYC), 145
School Improvements & Community Services (Regional), 145
School Operations & Management Services, 145
Social Work & Mental Health Practitioners, 146, 212
Southern Tier District Office, 147
Special Education Policy & Partnerships, 312
Special Education Quality Assurance Regional Offices, 146
Speech Language Pathology & Audiology, Acupuncture & Occupational Therapy, 146, 212
Standards, Assessment & Reporting, 145
State Archives, 144
State Assessment, 146
State Boards for the Professions, 146, 212
State Library, 144, 372
State Museum Office, 144, 333
State Review, 146
State School for the Blind at Batavia, 146, 279, 312
State School for the Deaf at Rome, 146
Student Support Services, 145
Summer Initiatives, 145
Syracuse District Office, 147
Teacher Certification, Teacher Policy & School Personnel Review, 144
Title I School & Community Services, 145
Utica District Office, 147
Vocational & Educational Services for Individuals With Disabilities Office (VESID), 146, 279, 312
Vocational Rehabilitation Operations, 147, 279, 312
Western Regional Office, 147
White Plains District Office, 147
Education Management LLC, 530
Educational Assistance Corporation, 514
Educational Broadcasting Corporation, 173, 465
Educational Broadcasting Corporation Thirteen/WNET, 501
Educational Conference Board (NYS), 480
Educational Housing Services, 466, 524
Educational Housing Services (Regional Programs Inc), 506
Educational Leadership (EL) PAC, 540
Educational Opportunity Center of Westchester, 618
Educational Testing Service, 529
Edward J Minskoff Equities, Inc, 474
Edwards-Knox CSD, 666
Egg (The), Center for the Performing Arts, 342
EISPAC, 540
El Paso Corporation, 503
Elad Properties, LLC, 494
Elaine Kaufman Cultural Center, 467
Elant, Inc, 530
Elayne E Greenberg, MS, Esq, 263
Elba CSD, 648
Eldred CSD, 671
Eldridge Street Project, 486
Eleanor Roosevelt Legacy Committee Inc, 540
Election Computer Services Inc, 165
Election Law, 46
   Committee Staff, 47
   Key Assembly Staff Assignments, 47
   Majority, 47
   Membership, 47
   Minority, 47
Election Systems & Software Inc, 478
Elections, 27
   Committee Staff, 27
   Key Senate Staff Assignments, 28
   Majority, 28
   Membership, 28
   Minority, 28
Elections, State Board of, 8, 157, 372
   Administrative Services, 157
   Albany, 157
   Allegany, 157
   Bronx, 160
   Broome, 157
   Campaign Finance, 157
   Cattaraugus, 158
   Cayuga, 158
   Chautauqua, 158
   Chemung, 158
   Chenango, 158
   Clinton, 158
   Columbia, 158
   Cortland, 158
   Counsel/Enforcement, 157
   County Boards of Elections, 157
   Delaware, 158
   Dutchess, 158
   Election Law Enforcement, 163
   Election Operations, 163
   Erie, 158
   Essex, 159
   Franklin, 159
   Fulton, 159
   General Information, 163
   Genesee, 159
   Greene, 159
   Hamilton, 159
   Herkimer, 159
   Information Technology Unit, 163
   Jefferson, 159
   Kings, 160
   Lewis, 159
   Livingston, 159
   Madison, 159
   Monroe, 159
   Montgomery, 160
   Nassau, 160
   New York, 160

Organization Index

New York City, 160
Niagara, 160
Oneida, 160
Onondaga, 160
Ontario, 160
Orange, 161
Orleans, 161
Oswego, 161
Otsego, 161
Putnam, 161
Queens, 160
Rensselaer, 161
Richmond, 160
Rockland, 161
Saint Lawrence, 161
Saratoga, 161
Schenectady, 161
Schoharie, 161
Schuyler, 161
Seneca, 161
Steuben, 162
Suffolk, 162
Sullivan, 162
Tioga, 162
Tompkins, 162
Ulster, 162
Warren, 162
Washington, 162
Wayne, 162
Westchester, 163
Wyoming, 163
Yates, 163
Electric & Gas Corp (NYS), 470, 524
Electric & Gas Corporation (NYS), 501, 513
Element West 59th St, 494
Elevator Constructors Union Local 14 PAC, 541
Elevator Constructors Union Local No 1 Political Action Committee, 540
Eli Lilly & Co, 482, 518
Eli Lilly & Company PAC, 541
Elinski, Karen, 481
Elissa D Hecker, Esq, 342
Elizabeth Pierce Olmsted MD Ctr for the Visually Impaired, 502
Elizabethtown Community Hospital, 530
Elizabethtown-Lewis CSD, 647
Ellenville CSD, 673
Ellenville/Wawarsing Chamber of Commerce, 574
Ellicottville Chamber of Commerce, 574
Ellicottville CSD, 640
Elliott Management, 530
Ellis Hospital School of Nursing, 624
Elmhurst Dairy Group, 529
Elmira, 72
  Civil & Criminal Courts, 72
Elmira Business Institute, 635
Elmira Business Institute-Vestal, 635
Elmira City SD, 642

Elmira College, 624
Elmira Hts CSD, 642
Elmira, City of, 419
Elmont South Republican Club, 541
Elmont UFSD, 654
Elmsford UFSD, 676
Elwood UFSD, 669
Emergency Management Office, NYS (SEMO), 8, 195, 289, 372
  Administration, 9, 195, 289
  Community Affairs, 9, 195, 289
  Preparedness, 9, 195, 289
  Support Services, 9, 195, 289
Emerging Industries Alliance of NYS, 489
Emigrant Savings Bank PAC, 541
Emily's List, 541
EMILY's List, 165
Empire Blue Cross & Blue Shield, 222, 250
Empire Center for New York State Policy, 108
Empire Condominium, 501
Empire Dental PAC, 541
Empire Green Biofuels Inc, 501
Empire Justice Center, 263, 318
Empire Leadership Council, 541
Empire Liquor Store Association, 541
Empire Merchants, LLC, 483
Empire Racing Associates, 476, 494
Empire Resorts Inc, 506, 507
Empire State ABC PAC, 541
Empire State Assn of Adult Homes & Assist Living Facilities, 506
Empire State Assn of Assisted Living (FKA Empire State Association of Adult Homes & Assisted Living), 491
Empire State Association of Adult Homes, Inc PAC, 541
Empire State Association of Assisted Living, 222
Empire State College, State University of NY, 481
Empire State Development Corporation, 9, 99, 115, 177, 230, 333, 372, 376
Empire State Distributors & Wholesalers Assn Inc, 501
Empire State Forest Products Association, 189, 481
Empire State Honey Producers Association, 85
Empire State Leadership PAC, 541
Empire State Liquor Store Assn, 515
Empire State Marine Trades Assn, 468
Empire State Mortgage Bankers Assn, 483
Empire State Passengers Assn, 497
Empire State Passengers Association, 357
Empire State Petroleum Assn Inc, 529
Empire State Petroleum Association Inc, 173
Empire State Potato Growers Inc, 85
Empire State Pride Agenda, 477
Empire State Pride Agenda PAC, 541

Empire State Regional Council of Carpenters, 275
Empire State Regional Council of Carpenters Political Action Fund-NYS, 541
Empire State Report (CINN Worldwide Inc), 601
Empire State Restaurant & Tavern Assn, 513
Empire State Restaurant & Tavern Association Inc, 108, 342
Empire State Society of Association Executives Inc, 108
Empire State Subcontractors Assn, 511
Empire State Towing & Recovery Assn, 512
Empire State Water Well Drillers' Assn, Inc, 487
Employee Relations, Governor's Office of, 9, 296, 372
  Family Benefits Committee, 296
  Labor/Management Committees, 296
  NYS/CSEA Discipline Unit, 296
  NYS/CSEA Partnership for Education & Training, 296
  NYS/SSU Joint Labor-Management Committee, 296
  NYS/UUP Labor-Management Committee, 296
  Statewide Employee Assistance Programs, 296
Employer Alliance for Affordable Health Care, 481
Energy, 47
  Committee Staff, 47
  Key Assembly Staff Assignments, 47
  Majority, 47
  Membership, 47
  Minority, 47
Energy & Commerce, 389
  Commerce, Trade & Consumer Protection, 389
  Energy & Air Quality, 389
  Environment & Hazardous Materials, 389
  Health, 389
  Oversight & Investigations, 389
  Subcommittees, 389
  Telecommunications & the Internet, 389
Energy & Natural Resources, 384
  Energy, 384
  National Parks, 384
  Public Lands & Forests, 384
  Subcommittees, 384
  Water & Power, 384
Energy & Telecommunications, 28
  Committee Staff, 28
  Key Senate Staff Assignments, 28
  Majority, 28
  Membership, 28
  Minority, 28

Organization Index

Energy Action Fund, 541
Energy Assn of NYS (The), 481
Energy Association of New York State, 173
Energy East Corporation, 513
Energy for NY PAC, 541
Engel Burman Group, 501
Engineers PEF-Local 832, 541
Engineers Voluntary Political Action Fund, 541
Englert Coffey & McHugh, 263
English Schools Assn (NY), 469
ENSR, 188
Entek Power Services, 173
Entergy Corporation Political Committee NY (ENPAC-NY), 541
Entergy Nuclear Northeast, 173
Entergy Nuclear Operations, 465
Entergy Nuclear Operations Inc, 483, 514
Entergy Nuclear Operations, Inc, 481
Enterprise Rent-A-Car, 481, 487
Enterprise Rent-A-Car Company NY PAC, 541
Entertainment Software Assn, 463
Entertainment Software Association, 342, 474
Environment & Public Works, 384
 Clean Air and Nuclear Safety, 385
 Private Sector & Consumer Solutions to Global Warming & Wildlife Protection, 385
 Subcommittees, 385
 Superfund & Environmental Health, 385
 Transportation & Infrastructure, 385
 Transportation Safety, Infrastructure Security and Water Quality, 385
Environmental Advocates of New York, 189
Environmental Advocates of NY, 481
Environmental Business Association of NYS Inc, 189
Environmental Conservation, 28, 47
 Committee Staff, 28, 47
 Key Assembly Staff Assignments, 47
 Key Senate Staff Assignments, 28
 Majority, 28, 47
 Membership, 28, 47
 Minority, 28, 47
Environmental Conservation Department, 9, 177, 372
 Air & Waste Management Office, 177
 Air Resources Division, 177
 Environmental Enforcement Division, 177
 Environmental Justice Division, 177
 Environmental Permits Division, 178
 Environmental Remediation Division, 177
 Fish, Wildlife & Marine Resources Division, 178
 Forest Protection & Fire Management Division, 178
 Freedom of Information Law, 178
 General Counsel's Office, 177
 Great Lakes Program, 178
 Hearings & Mediation Services Office, 177
 Hudson River Estuary Program, 178
 Information Services Division, 178
 Lands & Forests Division, 178
 Law Enforcement Division, 178
 Legal Affairs Division, 177
 Legislative Affairs Office, 177
 Management & Budget Services Division, 178
 Mineral Resources Division, 178
 Natural Resources & Water Quality Office, 177
 New York Natural Heritage Program, 178
 Office of Administration, 178
 Office of Employee Relations, 178
 Office of Media Affairs, 178
 Operations Division, 178
 Public Affairs & Education Division, 178
 Public Protection Office, 178
 Region 1, 178
 Region 2, 178
 Region 3, 178
 Region 4, 178
 Region 5, 178
 Region 6, 178
 Region 7, 178
 Region 8, 178
 Region 9, 178
 Regional Offices, 178
 Solid & Hazardous Materials Division, 177
 Special Programs, 178
 Water Division, 178
Environmental Defense, 189
EPIC-Every Person Influences Children Inc, 318
Epilepsy Coalition of New York State Inc, 222
Epilepsy Foundation of Long Island, 478
Epilepsy Foundation of Northeastern NY Inc, 468
Epilepsy Institute, 530
Episcopal Health Services Inc, 465
Episcopal Social Services, 491, 494
Eponymous Associates LLC (FKA Steiner Studios), 513
Equal Employment Opportunity Commission, 239, 272
 Buffalo Local, 239, 272
 New York District, 239, 272
Equinox Inc, 481
Equitable Life Assurance Society of the US, 250
Erdman Anthony & Assoc Employees' PAC, 541
Eric Mower & Associates, 108
Erie 1 BOCES, 679
Erie 2-Chautauqua-Cattaraugus BOCES, 679
Erie Basin Marine Associates (Kelly & Roth), 499
Erie Boulevard Hydro Power LP, 515
Erie Boulevard Hydropower LP, 518
Erie Community College, 615
Erie County, 63, 400
 County Court, 63
 Family Court, 63
 Supreme & Surrogate's Court, 63
Erie County Industrial Development Agency, 574
Erie County Planning & Economic Development, 574
Ernst & Young, 304
Ernst & Young Committee for Good Government, 541
Ernst & Young LLP, 464
Ernst & Young, LLP, 530
Erwin Industrial Development Agency (Town of), 574
ESMBA PAC MOR, 540
ESPAC, 540
ESSAA - PAC (Empire State Supervisors & Admin Assn), 540
Essex County, 63, 400
 Supreme, County, Family & Surrogate's Courts, 63
Essex County Industrial Development Agency, 574
Estee Lauder Companies Inc (The) (FKA Estee Lauder, Inc), 491
Ethan C Eldon Associates Inc, 189, 357
Ethics, 28
 Key Senate Staff Assignments, 28
 Majority, 28
 Membership, 28
 Minority, 28
Ethics & Guidance, 47
 Majority, 47
 Membership, 47
 Minority, 47
Ethics Committee, Legislative, 32, 54
Ethics, Select Committee on, 387
Evans-Brant CSD (Lake Shore), 646
EVCI Career Colleges Holding Corp, 108
Evening Sun, 597
Evening Telegram (The), 594
Evening Times (The), 595
Evening Tribune (The), 594
Everest Institute, 635
EW Enterprises, 501
Ewashko, John J, 482
Excellus Health Plan Inc, 222, 250, 491
Excelsior 2000, 542
Excelsior College, 625
Excelsior Racing Association (Powers & Company), 530
Excess Line Assn of NY, 497, 502

829

Organization Index

Excess Line Association of New York, 250
Exchange Blvd.com, 493
Executive Political Action Committee (EPAC), 542
Exhibition Alliance Inc (The), 343
Export Import Bank of the United States, 92, 104
  Northeast Regional Office, 92, 104
Express Scripts Inc, 463
Extell Development Company, 459
Extell Development Corporation, 494
Exxon Mobil Corporation, 173, 475, 521
Exxon Mobile Corp, 472
Eye & Ear Infirmary (NY), 458
Eye-Bank for Sight Restoration Inc (The), 222
Eyemed Vision Care LLC, 465, 504
EYP PAC NY, 540
Fabius-Pompey CSD, 659
Faculty Assn of Suffolk Community College VOTE-COPE, 542
Faculty Association PAC, 542
Fahey, William C, 482
Fahs Construction Group (Fahs-Rolston Paving Corp), 513
Fair Assessment Committee LLC, 493
Fair Haven Area Chamber of Commerce, 574
Fair Isaac Corporation, 505
Fair PAC, 542
Fairmont Capital LLC, 478
Fairport CSD, 652
Faist Government Affairs Group, LLC, 482
Falconer CSD, 641
Fallsburg CSD, 671
Families Together in NYS Inc, 284, 482
Family Court, NYC, 60
  Bronx County, 60
  Kings County, 60
  New York County, 60
  Queens County, 61
  Richmond County, 61
Family Decisions Coalition (Open Society Policy Ctr), 503
Family Physicians PAC, 542
Family Planning Advocates, 530
Family Planning Advocates of New York State, 223, 241, 318
Family Planning Advocates of NYS, Inc, 523
Family Service Society of Yonkers, 462
Family Support Systems Unlimited, Inc, 478
Farm Sanctuary, 85
Farmer's Museum (The), 343
Farmers' Market Federation of NY, 85
Farmingdale State College of Technology, 614
Farmingdale UFSD, 654
Farmington Chamber of Commerce, 574

Farmingville/Holtsville Chamber of Commerce, 574
Farrell Fritz PC, 542
Farrell Fritz, PC, 189
Farrell, Pamela, 482
Fashion Institute of Technology, 482, 499, 615
FASNY Federal Credit Union, 488
Fassler, Michael S, 482
Fayetteville-Manlius CSD, 659
Featherstonhaugh Wiley Clyne & Cordo, LLP, 482
FED PAC, 542
Federal Communications Commission, 170
  Office of Media Relations, 170
Federal Deposit Insurance Corporation, 92
  Division of Supervision & Consumer Protection, 92
Federal Election Commission, 164
Federal Express New York State Political Action Committee, 542
Federal Home Loan Bank of New York, 94, 234
Federal Labor Relations Authority, 272
  Boston Regional Office, 272
Federal Maritime Commission, 355
  New York Area Office, 355
Federal Mediation & Conciliation Service, 272
  Northeastern Region, 272
Federal Reserve System, 92
  Buffalo Branch, 92
  Federal Reserve Bank of New York, 92
Federal Trade Commission, 104, 109
  Northeast Regional Office, 104
Federation Employment & Guidance Service (FEGS) Inc, 284, 318
Federation Employment & Guidance Service Inc (FEGS), 500
Federation of Mental Health Ctrs Inc (The), 491
Federation of Organizations Inc, 284, 522
Federation of Protestant Welfare Agencies Inc, 318, 483, 503
Federation of School Administrators (NYS), 469
Federation of Taxi Drivers Inc (NYS), 506
Federations of Police PAC Fund, 542
Feld Entertainment, 483
Feld Entertainment Inc, 465
Feld Entertainment, Inc, 483
Fennimore Art Museum (The Clark Estates), 501
Ferrara Bros. Building Materials Corp., 478
Ferrara Bros. Buildings Material Corp, 467
Ferris, William E, 483
Ferry Point Partners LLC, 487
Fiam Building Associates, 466
Fidelity National Financial Inc, 529
Filipino American Human Services Inc, 241, 318

Fillmore CSD, 639
Film/Video Arts, 343
Finance, 28, 385
  Committee Staff, 28
  Energy, Natural Resources and Infrastructure, 385
  Health Care, 385
  International Trade and Global Competitiveness, 385
  Key Senate Staff Assignments, 28
  Majority, 28
  Membership, 28
  Minority, 28
  Social Security, Pensions and Family Policy, 385
  Subcommittees, 385
  Taxation and IRS Oversight and Long-Term Growth, 385
Financial Aid Administrators Association, Inc (NYS), 491
Financial Service Centers of NY Inc, 464
Financial Service Centers of NY, Inc, 486
Financial Services, 389
  Capital Markets, Insurance & Government Sponsored Enterprises, 389
  Domestic & International Monetary Policy, Trade & Technology, 390
  Financial Institutions & Consumer Credit, 390
  Housing & Community Opportunity, 390
  Oversight & Investigations, 390
  Subcommittees, 389
Financial Services Forum, 94
Finger Lakes Chapter NECA PAC Fund, 542
Finger Lakes Community College, 616
Finger Lakes Health Systems Agency, 489
Finger Lakes Horsemen's Benv & Protective Assn Inc, 489
Finger Lakes PAC, 542
Finger Lakes Printing Co, 593
Finger Lakes Racing Association, 343, 506
Finger Lakes Times, 593
Finger Lakes Tourism Alliance, 343
Fire Island Pines Property Owners Assn PAC, 542
Fire Island UFSD, 669
Fireman's Fund Insurance Co, 514
Firemen's Assn of the State of NY, 488
First (NY), 508
First American Property Information & Services Grp, 478
First American Title Insurance Company of NY, 499
First Cardinal Corporation, 464
First City Developers Incorp, 475
First Data Corp & Its Subsidiaries, 464
First Data Corporation & Subsidiaries, 456
First District Dental Society Political Action Committee, 542

Organization Index

First Pioneer Farm Credit ACA, 523
Fiscal Policy Institute, 208, 330
Fisher Brothers, 304
Fisher Development Strategies, 483
Fishers Island UFSD, 669
Fishkill, Town of, 419
FitzGerald Morris et al, 263
Fitzgerald, Gary J, 483
Fitzpatrick, Christine M, 484
Five Towns College, 635
Fleet Bank of New York PAC, 542
Fleet Reserve Association (FRA), 366
Fleet Reserve Association (FRA), NE Region (NJ, NY, PA), 366
FlexCare, 513
Floral Park-Bellerose UFSD, 654
Florence Covell, 480
Florida UFSD, 660
Fluent Energy, 507
Flushing Commons, 499
Flushing Commons LLC, 466, 513
Flushing Commons, LLC, 532
Flushing Council on Culture & the Arts Inc, 513
Fonda-Fultonville CSD, 653
Food Industry Alliance of New York State Inc, 85, 109
Food Industry Alliance of NYS, 508
Food Industry Alliance of NYS Inc, 484
Food Industry PAC-NYC, 542
Food, Farm & Nutrition, Task Force on, 53
Forba LLC, 491
Ford Motor Company Civic Action Fund, 542
Fordham University, 153, 505, 625
Fordham University, Department of Political Science, 208, 293
Fordham University, Graduate School of Social Service, 318
Foreign Relations, 385
 African Affairs, 385
 East Asian & Pacific Affairs, 385
 European Affairs, 385
 International Economic Policy, Export & Trade Promotion, 385
 International Operations & Terrorism, 385
 Near Eastern & South Asian Affairs, 385
 Subcommittees, 385
 Western Hemisphere, Peace Corps & Narcotics Affairs, 385
Forest City Ratner Companies, 484, 486, 499, 501, 507, 530
Forest Hills Jewish Center, 495
Forestcitydaly Housing, 499
Forestville CSD, 641
Fort Ann CSD, 674
Fort Brewerton/Greater Oneida Lake Chamber, 574
Fort Edward Chamber of Commerce, 574
Fort Edward UFSD, 674

Fort Plain CSD, 653
Fortuna Energy Inc, 505
Fortune Society (The), 140, 465
Foundation for Accounting Practitioners, 501
Foundation for the Advancement of Innovative Medicine, 508
Foundling Hospital (NY) (The), 491
Foundry Networks, 469
Fountain House, 472
Four Seasons Nursing & Rehabilitation Center, 487
Fox News Channel, 608
Fractured Atlas, 507
Frank, Robin, 484
Frankfort-Schuyler CSD, 649
Franklin County, 63, 401
 Supreme, County, Family & Surrogate's Courts, 63
Franklin County Industrial Development Agency, 574
Franklin CSD, 644
Franklin Square Chamber of Commerce, 574
Franklin Square Republican Club, 542
Franklin Square UFSD, 654
Franklin-Essex-Hamilton BOCES, 679
Franklinville CSD, 640
Fraternal Order of Police Empire State Lodge Inc, 542
Fredonia Chamber of Commerce, 574
Fredonia CSD, 641
Free Community Papers of NY, 483
Free PAC, 542
Freedom America, 543
Freeport UFSD, 654
Freeport, Village of, 419
French-American Chamber of Commerce, 574
Fresenius Medical Care-North America, 491
Fresh Direct, LLC, 513
Freshwater Wetlands Appeals Board, 9, 178, 372
Frewsburg CSD, 641
Fried Frank Harris Shriver & Jacobson, LLP, 484
Friedell, Andrew, 484
Friedman, John P, 484
Friedman, Michael B, 484
Friend of Cultural Institutions, 543
Friends & Relatives of Institutionalized Aged Inc (FRIA), 223, 319
Friends and Relatives of Institutionalized Aged Inc (FRIA), 485
Friends of Hudson River Park, 503
Friends of Lazio, 543
Friends of New York Racing PAC, 543
Friends of NY Racing Inc, 507
Friends of Schumer, 543
Friends of the Volunteer Firefighter, 543
Friends of Upstate Labor, 543

Friendship CSD, 639
Frontier CSD, 646
Frontier, A Citizens Communications Co, 173
Fuel Cell Energy Inc, 463
Full Spectrum of New York, LLC, 532
Fulton, 72
 Civil & Criminal Courts, 72
Fulton City SD, 661
Fulton County, 63, 401
 Family Court, 63
 Supreme, County & Surrogate's Courts, 63
Fulton County Economic Development Corporation, 574
Fulton County Industrial Development Agency, 575
Fulton County Reg Chamber of Commerce & Ind, 575
Fulton-Montgomery Community College, 616
Fund for Animals (The), 85
Fund for Better Transportation PAC, 543
Fund for Modern Courts (The), 263
Fund for the City of New York, 293
Fund for the City of New York, Center for Internet Innovation, 173
Funding Source (The), 515
Funeral Directors Assn (NYS), 488
Funeral Directors Assn Inc (NYS), 485
FUTURENY, 542
Gaia House, LLC, 467
Gallo, Richard J, 485
Galway CSD, 664
Gananda CSD, 674
Gandhi Engineering Inc, 357
Gannet Co Inc, 592
Gannett Co Inc, 593, 594, 598, 599, 600
Gannett Fleming Engineers & Architects PC, 499
Gannett News Service, 601
Gansevoort Market, Inc, 467
Garden City Chamber of Commerce, 575
Garden City UFSD, 654
Garden City, Village of, 419
Garden Gate Greenhouse, 85
Garment Industry Development Corporation, 507
Garrison UFSD, 663
Garth Group Inc (The), 165
Gartner Inc, 469
Gates, Town of, 419
Gates-Chili CSD, 652
Gateway Center Properties Phase II, LLC, 532
Gateway-Longview Inc, 527
Gaucho LLC, 514
Gaughran, James F, 485
Gay & Lesbian Anti-Violence Project (NYC), 463, 516
Gay and Lesbian Victory Fund, 543

831

Organization Index

Gay Men's Health Crisis, 503
Gay Men's Health Crisis Inc, 485
GDC Properties Inc, 494
GEICO NY PAC, 543
Geiger, Bruce W & Associates, 485
Gene Kaufman Architect PC, 467
Genentech Inc, 520
General Brown CSD, 650
General Building Contractors of NYS Inc, 532
General Building Contractors of NYS PAC, 543
General Building Contractors of NYS, Inc, 487
General Building Contractors of NYS/AGC, 109
General Contractor's Assn, 501
General Contractors Assn of NY PAC, 543
General Contractors Assn of NY, Inc (The), 474
General Contractors Association of NY, 109, 357
General Contractors Association of NY, Inc (The), 483
General Electric Co, 479, 482, 488
General Motors Corp, 501
General Motors Corporation, 485
General Motors Corporation Political Action Committee-NY (GM PAC-NY), 543
General Services, Office of, 10, 195, 301, 333, 372
   Administration, 195
   Design & Construction, 196
   Empire State's Convention & Cultural Events Office, 196, 333
   Information Resource Management, 196
   Information Technology & Procurement Services, 196
   Procurement Services Group, 196
   Real Estate Planning & Development Group, 196, 301
   Real Property Management Group, 196, 301
   Support Services, 196
General Society of Mechanics & Tradesmen of the City of NY (The), 486
General Theological Seminary of the Episcopal Church, 625
Generation Project, 543
Generic Pharmaceutical Association, 223
Genesee & Wyoming Railroad Inc, 489
Genesee Community College, 616
Genesee County, 64, 401
   Supreme, County, Family & Surrogate's Courts, 64
Genesee County Chamber of Commerce, 575
Genesee County Economic Development Center, 575
Genesee Transportation Council, 293

Genesee Valley CSD, 639
Genesee-Livingston-Steuben-Wyoming BOCES, 679
Geneseo CSD, 651
Geneva, 72
   Civil & Criminal Courts, 72
Geneva Area Chamber of Commerce, 575
Geneva City SD, 660
Geneva Industrial Development Agency (City of), 575
Geneva Worldwide Inc, 487
Genocide Intervention Network, 490
Genovese, Marta, 485
Genworth Financial, 488, 509
George Junior Republic UFSD, 672
Georgetown Company, 484
Gerard Avenue LLC, 466
Gerber Life Insurance Company, 491
Gergela III, Joseph, 485
Germantown CSD, 643
Gertrude H Sergievsky Center (The), 223
Gertrude Stein Repertory Theatre (The), 343
Getnick, Livingston, Atkinson, Gigliotti & Priore LLP, 263
Geto & deMilly Inc, 109, 208, 485
Getty Petroleum Marketing Inc, 174
Gilbert Tweed Associates Inc, 109
Gilberti Stinziano Heintz & Smith, PC, 486
Gilbertsville-Mount Upton CSD, 662
Gilboa-Conesville CSD, 665
Gillen Brewer School (The), 529
Gilligan, Donald, 486
Girl Scout Legislative Network (NYS), 463
GKC Industries, 487
Glacier Creek PAC, 543
GlaxoSmithKline, PLC, 489, 500
GLBT Friends of Good Government, 543
Glen Cove, 72
   Civil & Criminal Courts, 72
Glen Cove Chamber of Commerce, 575
Glen Cove City SD, 654
Glen Cove, City of, 420
Glens Falls, 72
   Civil & Criminal Courts, 72
Glens Falls City SD, 673
Glens Falls Common SD, 673
Glens Falls Hospital, 530
Glenville, Town of, 420
Glenwood Management Corp, 499
Glenwood Management Corporation, 304, 506, 515, 528
Glimmerglass Coalition, 503
Global Gardens Program, New York Botanical Garden (The), 85
Global Spectrum LP, 527
Globe Institute of Technology, 463, 635
Globe Metallurgical Inc, 524
Gloria Wise Boys & Girls Club, 519
Gloria Wise Boys & Girls Club Inc, 513
Gloversville, 72

   Civil & Criminal Courts, 72
Gloversville Enlarged SD, 648
Glusko, John P, 486
Go PAC Dutchess, 543
Gold Star Wives of America Inc, 366
Golden Apple Business Action Committee, PAC, 543
Golden Technology Management, LLC, 501
Golden, Ben, 486
Goldman Sachs & Co, 95
Goldman Sachs & Company Inc, 465
Goldman Sachs Group, Inc (The), 483
Goldman Sachs NY PAC, 543
Goldman, Gerald, 486
Golub Corporation (The), 470
Gomez Foundation for Mill House, 486
Good Government NY, 543
Goodman & Zuchlewski LLP, 263
Goodwin, Jeffrey, 486
Gore Mountain Region Chamber of Commerce, 575
Goshen Chamber of Commerce, 575
Goshen CSD, 660
Gouverneur Chamber of Commerce, 575
Gouverneur CSD, 666
Government Administration, Legislative Commission on, 33, 54
Government Employees Insurance Co (GEICO), 523
Government Payment Service Inc, 465
Governmental Employees, 47
   Committee Staff, 47
   Key Assembly Staff Assignments, 47
   Majority, 47
   Membership, 47
   Minority, 48
Governmental Operations, 48
   Committee Staff, 48
   Key Assembly Staff Assignments, 48
   Majority, 48
   Membership, 48
   Minority, 48
Governor's Office, 3, 79, 90, 98, 129, 143, 157, 168, 177, 194, 211, 228, 237, 245, 252, 268, 278, 287, 295, 301, 307, 324, 332, 348, 360, 371
   Appointments, 3
   Communications, 3
   Counsel, 4
   Intergovernmental Affairs, 4
   New York City Office, 4, 157, 194, 287, 371
   New York State Office of Federal Affairs, 371
   Office of the Secretary, 3
   Operations/Administration, 4
   Washington Office for the Governor, 4
   Washington Office of the Governor, 194
Gowanda Area Chamber of Commerce, 575
Gowanda CSD, 640
Gowanus Canal Joint Venture LLC, 495

Organization Index

Gowanus Village 1 Inc, 514
Gracie Piont Community Council, 519
Graduate Center, 620
Graduate Management Admission Council, 518
Graduate Mgmt Admission Council, 515
Graduate School of Journalism, 620
Grand Island Chamber of Commerce, 575
Grand Island CSD, 646
Granite Halmar Construction Company, 501
Granville Chamber of Commerce, 575
Granville CSD, 674
Grassy Sprain PAC, 543
Great Escape Theme Park LLC (The), 343
Great Lakes Commission, 102, 116, 181, 376
Great Lakes United, 189
Great Neck Chamber of Commerce, 575
Great Neck Democratic Club, 543
Great Neck UFSD, 654
Great South Bay Republican Club PAC, 544
Greater Amsterdam SD, 653
Greater Jamaica Development Corporation, 478
Greater Johnstown SD, 648
Greater New Hyde Park Republican Club, 544
Greater New York Automobile Dealers Assn, 530
Greater New York Hospital Assn, 463
Greater New York Hospital Association, 223, 465, 466
Greater Niagara Newspapers, 595, 596, 597, 600
Greater NY Auto Dealers' Assn, 486
Greater NY Auto Dealers' Assn Inc, 486, 544
Greater NY Health Care Facilities Assn, 507, 513
Greater NY Health Care Facilities Assoc, 504
Greater NY Hospital Assn, 478
Greater Rochester Association of Realtors Inc, 304
Greater Southern Tier BOCES (Schuyler-Chemung-Tioga-Allegany-Steuben), 679
Greater Syracuse Association of Realtors Inc, 304
Greece Chamber of Commerce, 575
Greece CSD, 652
Greece, Town of, 420
Green & Seifter Attorneys, PLLC, 487
Green Chimneys Children's Services Inc, 532
Green Chimneys School-Green Chimneys Children's Services Inc, 319
Green County IDA, 488
Green Island Democratic Association, 544
Green Island Industrial Development Agency (Village of), 575

Green Island UFSD, 638
Green Point of NY Inc, 497
Green Worlds Coalition Fund, 544
Greenberg Traurig, LLP, 208, 487
Greenberg, Traurig Political Action Committee, 544
Greenburgh 7 CSD, 676
Greenburgh Eleven UFSD, 676
Greenburgh, Town of, 420
Greenburgh-Graham UFSD, 676
Greenburgh-North Castle UFSD, 676
Greene County, 64, 401
  Supreme, County, Family & Surrogate's Courts, 64
Greene County Department of Planning & Economic Development, 576
Greene County Soil & Water Conservation District, 189
Greene County Tourism Promotion, 576
Greene CSD, 642
Greene International Golf Assn, 504
Greenmarket/Council on the Environment of NYC, 85
Greenport UFSD, 669
GreenThumb, 85, 189
Greenville CSD, 649
Greenwich Chamber of Commerce (Greater Greenwich), 576
Greenwich CSD, 674
Greenwich House, Inc, 509
Greenwich Village-Chelsea Chamber of Commerce, 576
Greenwood Lake and West Milford News, 598
Greenwood Lake Chamber of Commerce, 576
Greenwood Lake UFSD, 660
Griffin Plummer & Associates, LLC, 488
Griffin, Mary A, 488
Grocery Manufacturers Assn (FKA Grocery Manufacturers of America), 468
Groton Community Health Care Center, 530
Groton CSD, 672
Groundwork, Inc, 532
Group for Equitable Tax Practices, 475
Group Health Inc, 223, 250
Group Health Inc State PAC, 544
Group Health Incorporated, 486, 491, 503
Group Self Insurance Assn of NY Inc (GSIANY), 456
Group Self-Insurance Assn of NY (GSIANY), 490
Grow/Network/McGraw-Hill Companies (The), 469
Gtech Corporation, 483
Guardian Engineering Services, 493
Guardian Life Insurance Co of America, 482
Guardian Life Insurance Co of America (The), 492

Guardian Life Insurance Company of America (The), 506
Guardian Life PAC, 544
Guide Dog Foundation for the Blind Inc, 319, 522
Guilderland Chamber of Commerce, 576
Guilderland CSD, 638
Guilderland Industrial Development Agency (Town of), 576
Guilderland, Town of, 420
GVA Williams, 304
GVA Williams, Inc/60 Hudson Owner, LLC, 507
H & R Block Eastern Enterprises, 464
H J Kalikow & Co LLC, 304
Hadley-Luzerne CSD, 673
Hager, Susan, 488
Haim Marcovici, 504
Haitian-American Association for Political Action (HAAPA-PAC), 544
Hakimian Organization (The), 495
Haldane CSD, 663
Half Hollow Hills CSD, 669
Hall of Science (NY), 489
Hall of Sciences (NY), 521
Hamburg Chamber of Commerce, 576
Hamburg Conservative Club, 544
Hamburg CSD, 646
Hamburg Industrial Development Agency, 576
Hamburg, Town of, 420
Hamilton College, 625
Hamilton County, 64, 402
  Supreme, County, Family & Surrogate's Courts, 64
Hamilton CSD, 652
Hamilton, Rabinovitz & Alschuler Inc, 494
Hamilton-Fulton-Montgomery BOCES, 679
Hammond CSD, 666
Hammondsport CSD, 667
Hampton Bays Chamber of Commerce, 576
Hampton Bays UFSD, 669
Hancock Area Chamber of Commerce, 576
Hancock CSD, 644
Hancock Public Affairs, LLC, 488
Hands Across Long Island Inc, 493
Hannaford Bros Co, 488
Hannan, K T Public Affairs Inc, 488
Hannibal CSD, 662
HANYS Services, Inc
  D/B/A HANYS Solutions, Inc, 530
Harbar Motors, Ltd, 530
Harborfields CSD, 669
Harlem Chamber of Commerce (Greater Harlem), 576
Harm Reduction Coalition, 463
Harmonie Ensemble/New York, 480
Harpursville CSD, 639
Harris & Harris LTD, 487
Harris Beach LLP, 264
Harris Beach Political Committee, 544

833

Organization Index

Harris Interactive Inc, 165
Harris, O Lewis, 488
Harris, Steven W, LLC, 488
Harrison CSD, 676
Harrison, Town/Village of, 421
Harrisville CSD, 651
Harter Secrest & Emery, LLP, 488
Hartford Advocates Fund (The), 544
Hartford CSD, 674
Hartford Financial Svcs Group Inc, 489
Hartman & Winnicki, PC, 109, 264
Hartwick College, 625
Harvestworks, 343
Hastings, Jamie, 489
Hastings-on-Hudson Chamber of Commerce, 576
Hastings-On-Hudson UFSD, 676
Hauppauge UFSD, 669
Haverstraw, Town of, 421
Haverstraw-Stony Point Central School District, 529
Hawayek, Jonathan F, 489
Hawk Creek Wildlife Center Inc, 189
Hawkins Delafield & Wood LLP, 293, 330
Hawthorne-Cedar Knolls UFSD, 676
HBA of CNY Local Build PAC, 544
HDS Retail North America, 515
Health, 29, 48
   Committee Staff, 29, 48
   Key Assembly Staff Assignments, 48
   Key Senate Staff Assignments, 29
   Majority, 29, 48
   Membership, 29, 48
   Minority, 29, 48
Health & Hospitals Corp (NYC), 503
Health Access Affiliates Good Government Fund, 544
Health Care Financing, Council on, 33, 54
Health Care Providers' PAC, 544
Health Care Subrogation Group, 513
Health Department, 10, 179, 212, 360, 373
   Acute & Primary Care Services Division, 214
   Administrative Operations - Tower/Administrative Operations, 214
   AIDS Institute, 212
   Bureau of Production Systems Management, 214
   Capital District Regional Office, 215
   Center for Community Health, 213
   Center for Environmental Health, 179, 213
   Central New York Regional Office, 215
   Chronic Disease Prevention & Adult Health, 213
   Continuing Care Offices, 214
   Division of Environmental Health Investigation, 179, 213
   Environmental Disease Prevention, 179, 215
   Environmental Health Assessment Division, 179, 213
   Environmental Protection, 179, 213
   Epidemiology Division, 213
   Executive & Advisory Council Operations, 213
   Executive Offices, 213
   Family Health Division, 213
   Genetic Disorders, 215
   Health Care Quality & Safety Office, 214
   Health Care Standards & Surveillance Division, 214
   Health Facilities Management, 214, 360
   Health Facility Planning Division, 214
   Health Research Inc, 214
   Health Systems Management Office, 214
   HEALTHCOM Services, 214
   Helen Hayes Hospital, 214
   Herbert W Dickerman Library, 215
   HIV Health Care & Community Services, 213
   HIV Prevention, 213
   Home & Community Based Care Division, 214
   Human Resources & Operations, 214
   Human Resources Management Group, 214
   Infectious Disease, 215
   Information Systems & Health Statistics Group, 214
   Information Technology & Project Management, 213
   Laboratory Operations, 215
   Legal Affairs, 214
   Local Health Services, 213
   Metropolitan Area/Regional Office, 215
   Minority Health, 213
   Molecular Medicine, 215
   New York State Veterans' Home at Batavia, 214, 360
   New York State Veterans' Home at Montrose, 214, 360
   New York State Veterans' Home at Oxford, 214, 360
   New York State Veterans' Home at St Albans, 214, 360
   Nutrition Division, 213
   Office of Governmental Affairs, 213
   Office of Health Insurance Programs, 213
   Office of Long Term Care, 213
   Operations Management Group, 214
   Professional Medical Conduct, 214
   Public Affairs, 179, 215
   Quality & Surveillance for Nursing Homes & ICF/MRs, 214
   Regional/Area Offices, 215
   Roswell Park Cancer Institute Corporation, 215
   School of Public Health, SUNY at Albany, 213
   Task Force On Life & The Law, 213
   Wadsworth Center, 179, 215
   Western Regional Office, 215
Health Facilities Assn (NYS), 510
Health Freedom NY, 508
Health Insurance Plan of Greater NY, 489, 515
Health Insurance Plan of Greater NY (HIP), 463
Health Insurance Plan of NY, 518
Health Management Systems Inc, 527
Health Net of the Northeast, 514
Health Plan Assn (NY), 487
Health Plan Assn Inc (NY), 489
Health, Education, Labor & Pensions, 385
   Children and Families, 386
   Employment & Workplace Safety, 386
   Retirement and Aging, 386
   Subcommittees, 386
Healthcare Assn of NYS, 530
Healthcare Assn of NYS PAC (HANYS PAC), 544
Healthcare Association of New York State, 223
Healthcare Association of NYS, 484
Healthcare Distribution Management Assn (HDMA), 469
Healthcare Education Project, 508
Healthcare Professional Insurance Company, Inc, 509
Healthcare Tort Reform Coalition (NY), 489
Healthplex Inc, 508
Healthy Kids NY, 544
Healthy New York, 545
Healthy Schools Network Inc, 461
Hearing Healthcare Alliance of NY Inc (HHCANY), 456
Hearing Healthcare Alliance of NY PAC, 545
Hearth, Patio & Barbecue Association (HPBA)(Ahern, Barbara J), 464
Hearth, Patio & Barbeque Assn, 456
Heartland Business Center, 524
HeartShare Human Services of New York, Roman Catholic Diocese of Brooklyn, 319
Hebrew Home for the Aged at Riverdale (The), 530
Hebrew Union College - Jewish Institute of Religion, 625
Hedgewood Home for Adults, 530
Heights Hill Mental Health Services Community Advisory Board (Dames Reid), 469
Heights Hill Mental Health Services Community Advisory Board Inc, 477
Heimgartner, Christian, 489
Heineken USA, Inc, 456
Helen Keller Services for the Blind, 319, 478

Organization Index

Helene Fuld College of Nursing North General Hospital, 625
Hellenic American PAC - State, 545
Hello World Language Center, 524
Hempstead Industrial Development Agency (Town of), 576
Hempstead PBA PAC, 545
Hempstead UFSD, 654
Hempstead, Town of, 421
Hempstead, Village of, 421
Hendrick Hudson CSD, 676
Henrietta, Town of, 421
Henry Schein Inc, 530
Herkimer County, 64, 402
  Family Court, 64
  Supreme, County & Surrogate's Courts, 64
Herkimer County Chamber of Commerce, 576
Herkimer County Community College, 616
Herkimer County Industrial Development Agency, 576
Herkimer CSD, 649
Herkimer-Fulton-Hamilton-Otsego BOCES, 679
Hermon-Dekalb CSD, 666
Herricks UFSD, 654
Hertz Corporation (The), 529, 530
Heslin Rothenberg Farley & Mesiti PC, 174
Hetrick-Martin Institute, Home of Harvey Milk HS (The), 501
Heuvelton CSD, 666
Hewlett Republican Club, 545
Hewlett-Packard Co, 527
Hewlett-Packard Company, 503
Hewlett-Woodmere UFSD, 654
Heyman, Neil, 490
HF Management Services LLC, 466
HIC PAC, 544
Hicksville Chamber of Commerce, 576
Hicksville UFSD, 654
Higgins Roberts Beyerl & Coan, PC, 490
Higher Education, 29, 48
  Committee Staff, 29, 48
  Key Assembly Staff Assignments, 48
  Key Senate Staff Assignments, 29
  Majority, 29, 48
  Membership, 29, 48
  Minority, 29, 48
Higher Education Opportunity Program - Professional Organization, 468
Highland CSD, 673
Highland Falls CSD, 660
High-Need Hospital PAC Inc, 545
Hightower, A Dirk, 490
Hilbert College, 625
Hill & Gosdeck, 85, 490
Hiller, Elise L, 490
HillPAC-NY, 545
Hillside Family of Agencies, 491

Hillside Manor Rehabilitation & Extended Care Center, LLC, 478
Hilton CSD, 652
Hines-Kramer, Amy, 490
Hinman Straub, PC, 490
Hinsdale CSD, 640
HIP Health Plan of NY, 466
HIP Health Plan PAC, 545
Hirshorn, Donald P, 491
Hispanic Counseling Center Inc, 528
Hispanic Federation, 319, 528
Hispanic Information Telecommunications Network, 528
Hispanic Outreach Services, 242, 319
Historic Hudson Valley, 343
Historical Assn NYS (Farmers Museum), 501
Historical Society (NY), 494
HLA PAC, 544
HLR Service Corporation (Roche), 463
HNTB, New York, 516
Hobart & William Smith Colleges, 625
Hodes Associates, 491
Hodgson Russ LLP, 515
Hodgson Russ, LLP, 491
Hofstra University, 625
Hofstra University, School of Law, 140, 189, 234
Hogan & Hartson LLP, 174
Holland & Knight Committee for Responsible Gov't (The), 545
Holland CSD, 646
Holland Patent CSD, 658
Holley CSD, 661
Holloway, Jr, Floyd, 491
Hollyer Brady et al, 264
Home Care Assn of NYS Inc, 492
Home Care Assn of NYS, Inc, 476
Home Care Association of New York State Inc, 223
Home Care Association of NYS, 491
Home Care Council of New York City, 469
Homeland Security, 390
  Border, Maritime and Global Counterterrorism, 390
  Emergency Communications, Preparedness and Response, 390
  Emerging Threats, Cybersecurity and Science and Technology, 390
  Intelligence, Information Sharing and Terrorism Risk Assessment, 390
  Management, Investigations and Oversight, 390
  Subcommittees, 390
  Transportation Security and Infrastructure Protection, 390
Homeland Security & Governmental Affairs, 386
  Disaster Recovery, 386

  Federal Financial Mgt, Govt Info, Federal Services & International Society, 386
  Oversight of Government Management, Federal Workforce & District of Columbia, 386
  Permanent Subcommittee on Investigations, 386
  State, Local and Private Sector Preparedness and Integration, 386
  Subcommittees, 386
Homeless Services United, 502
Homer CSD, 644
Homes for the Homeless/Institute for Children & Parties, 234
Homes for the Homeless/Institute for Children & Poverty, 319
Honda North America Inc, 492
Honda North America, Inc, 487
Honeoye CSD, 660
Honeoye Falls-Lima CSD, 653
Hood, William L, 492
Hoosic Valley CSD, 663
Hoosick Falls CSD, 663
Hopevale UFSD at Hamburg, 646
Horizen Global, 467
Hornell, 72
  Civil & Criminal Courts, 72
Hornell Area Chamber of Commerce/Hornell Industrial Development Agency (City of), 577
Hornell City SD, 667
Horseheads CSD, 642
Hospice & Palliative Care Assn of NYS, 465
Hospice & Palliative Care Association of NYS Inc, 223, 319
Hospital for Special Surgery, 499
Hospital Medical Center of Queens (NY), 513
Hospitality & Tourism Assn (NYS), 510, 530
Hospitals Insurance Company Inc, 465, 530
Hostos Community College, 620
Hotel Assn of NYC Inc, 530
Hotel Assn of NYC Inc PAC, 545
Hotel Association of New York City Inc, 343
Hotel Employees Restaurant Int'l Union Tip Edu Fund, 545
Hotel Trades Council (NY), 483
Hotel Trades Council (NYC), 455
Houghton College, 625
House Administration, 390
House of Representatives Standing Committees, 83, 93, 105, 139, 151, 164, 171, 186, 205, 219, 232, 240, 248, 261, 274, 298, 315, 329, 340, 356, 364
  Agriculture, 83, 186, 219
  Agriculture, Rural Development, FDA & Related Agencies, 83

835

Organization Index

Appropriations, 83, 171, 329
Armed Services, 364
Budget, 329
Capital Markets, Insurance & Government Sponsored Enterprises, 249
Contracting and Technology, 274
Crime, Terrorism & Homeland Security, 139
Department Operations, Oversight, Nutrition & Forestry, 186, 219
Economic Development, Public Buildings & Emergency Management, 233
Education & Labor, 151, 240, 274
Education Reform, 151
Emergency Communications, Preparedness and Response, 206
Emerging Threats, Cybersecurity and Science & Technology, 206
Energy & Air Quality, 171, 186
Energy & Commerce, 105, 171, 186, 219
Energy & Environment, 172, 186
Energy & Mineral Resources, 172
Energy & Water Development, 171
Environment & Hazardous Materials, 186
Federal Workforce, Postal Service and the District of Columbia, 164, 298
Financial Services, 93, 232, 248
Foreign Affairs, 106, 240
Forests & Forest Health, 340
General Farm Commodities & Risk Management, 186
Government Reform, 164, 205
Health, 219
Homeland Security, 205
Horticulture and Organic Agriculture, 186
Housing & Community Opportunity, 233
Intelligence Information Sharing & Terrorism Risk Assessment, 206
Intelligence, Permanent Select Committee on, 206
Investigations and Oversight, 274
Judiciary, 139, 261
Management, Investigations and Oversight, 206
National Parks, Recreation & Public Lands, 340
Natural Resources, 171, 186
Resources, 340
Science & Technology, 172, 186
Small Business, 106, 274
Social Security, 315
Specialty Crops, Rural Development and Foreign Agriculture, 186
Standards of Official Conduct, 164, 206
Subcommittee, 83, 139, 151, 164, 171, 172, 186, 206, 219, 233, 240, 249, 261, 298, 315, 340
Subcommittees, 172, 186, 206, 274

Technical & Tactical Intelligence, 206
Terrorism, Nonproliferation and Trade, 240
The Constitution, 261
Transportation & Infrastructure, 186, 233, 356
Transportation Security and Infrastructure Protection, 206
Veterans' Affairs, 364
Water & Power, 172
Water Resources & Environment, 186
Ways & Means, 219, 315, 329
Housing, 48
   Committee Staff, 48
   Key Assembly Staff Assignments, 48
   Majority, 48
   Membership, 48
   Minority, 49
Housing & Community Renewal, Division of, 10, 228
   Administration, 228
   Albany Unit, 229
   Architecture & Engineering Bureau, 229
   Buffalo, 228
   Capital District, 228
   Community Development, 228
   Community Service Bureau/Technical Assistance Unit, 228
   Energy Services Bureau/Weatherization, 228
   Environmental Analysis Unit, 228
   Fair Housing & Equal Opportunity, 229
   General Law, 229
   Housing Audits & Accounts Bureau, 229
   Housing Information Systems, 228
   Housing Management Bureau, 229
   Housing Operations, 229
   Housing Trust Fund Program, 228
   Internal Audit, 228
   Legal Affairs, 229
   Luxury Decontrol/Overcharge, 229
   Mobile Home Unit, 229
   New York City, 228
   Office of Financial Administration, 228
   Office of Training & Professional Development, 228
   Owner Multiple Applications, 229
   Personnel, 228
   Policy & Intergovernmental Relations, 229
   Regional Offices, 228
   Rent Administration, 229
   Rent Control/ETPA, 229
   Rent Information & Mediation, 229
   Services Compliance Owner Restoration Enforcement/SCORE, 229
   Subsidy Services, 229
   Support Services/Processing Services Unit, 228
   Syracuse, 228

Housing & Community Renewal, NYS Division of, 373
Housing & Services, Inc, 467
Housing Action Council Inc - Not For Profit, 234, 293
Housing Assn Inc (NY)(Mfg Housing Assn), 487
Housing Conservation Coordinators, 492
Housing Works, 492
Housing Works Inc, 234, 319
Housing Works, Albany Advocacy Ctr, 492
Housing, Construction & Community Development, 29
   Committee Staff, 29
   Key Senate Staff Assignments, 29
   Majority, 29
   Membership, 29
   Minority, 29
HPA PAC, 544
HSBC Bank USA, 95
HSBC North America, 491
HSBC North America, Inc PAC (H-PAC), 544
HSBC USA Inc, 95
Hubbell Galvanizing, 513
Hudacs, John, 492
Hudson, 72
   Civil & Criminal Courts, 72
Hudson Alliance for Children with Special Needs, 487
Hudson City SD, 643
Hudson Falls CSD, 674
Hudson River Cruises, 343
Hudson River Environmental Society, 189
Hudson River Sloop Clearwater Inc, 189
Hudson River Valley Greenway, 10, 179, 334, 373
   Greenway Conservancy for the Hudson River Valley, 10, 179, 334
   Hudson River Valley Greenway Communities Council, 11, 179, 334
Hudson River-Black River Regulating District, 116, 181, 376
Hudson Valley Build PAC, 545
Hudson Valley Building & Construction Trades Council, 479
Hudson Valley Business Journal, 601
Hudson Valley Chapter, Nat'l Electrical Contractors Assn (NECA), PAC, 545
Hudson Valley Citizens for Change, 545
Hudson Valley Community College, 616
Hudson Valley Economic Development Corp, 530
Hudson Valley Fois Gras (HVFG, LLC), 501
Hudson Valley Gateway Chamber of Commerce, 577
Hudson Valley Grass Roots Energy & Environmental Network, 190
Hudson Valley Newspapers Inc, 593
Human Rights First, 242

Organization Index

Human Rights Watch, 242
Human Rights, State Division of, 11, 237, 373
  Albany, 237
  Binghamton, 237
  Brooklyn, 238
  Buffalo, 238
  Manhattan (Lower), 238
  Manhattan (Upper), 238
  Nassau County, 238
  Peekskill, 238
  Regional Offices, 237
  Rochester, 238
  Suffolk County, 238
  Syracuse, 238
Human Services Council of NYC, 477, 492
Humane Society of the United States (The), 522
Humane Society of the United States, Mid Atlantic Regional Office, 85, 319
Hunger Action Network of NYS, 492
Hunger Action Network of NYS (HANNYS), 319
Hunter Chamber of Commerce (Town of), 577
Hunter College, 474, 493, 620
Hunter College, Brookdale Center for Healthy Aging and Longevity, 320
Hunter Mountain Ski Bowl, 343, 488
Hunter-Tannersville CSD, 649
Huntington Chamber Committee for Better Gov't, 545
Huntington Township Chamber of Commerce, 577
Huntington UFSD, 669
Huntington, Town of, 422
Hunts Point Cooperative Market, Inc, 487
Hunts Point Produce Market, 487
Hunts Point Produce Market Redevelopment PAC, 545
Hurley, John R, 492
Hyde Park Chamber of Commerce, 577
Hyde Park CSD, 645
Hyde Park, Town of, 422
I Love Good Government, 545
I.U.O.E. Local 15 PAC, 545
IAAC Inc, 461
IAFF Firepac NY Non-Federal, 545
IATSE Local 600 NY PAC, 545
IBEW Local Union #1249 PAC, 546
IBEW Local Union #237 Community Action Program, 546
IBEW Local Union 363 PAC, 546
IBM Corporation, 109
Ichabod Crane CSD, 643
IDT Corporation, 478
Ilion CSD, 650
Illinois Tool Works Inc, 455
IMG Models, 530
Immigration Coalition, Inc (NY), 492

IMS Health Incorporated (Multistate Associates Inc), 487
Incorporated Village of Freeport (The), 478
Incorporated Village of Westbury (The), 478
Indeck-Corinth Limited Partnership, 464
Independence for Bethlehem, 546
Independence Plaza Associates LLC (FKA Stellar Management), 474
Independent Agents PAC, 546
Independent Automobile Dealers Assn Inc (NY), 468
Independent Bankers Association of NYS, 95
Independent Care System (ICS), 503
Independent Health Assn Inc Political Alliance, 546
Independent Insurance Agents & Brokers of NY, 461
Independent Living Services Inc, 518
Independent Oil & Gas Assn of NY, 480
Independent Oil & Gas Association of New York, 174
Independent Oil and Gas Association of NY, Inc Political Action Committee, 546
Independent Petroleum Marketers of NY, 529
Independent Petroleum Mktrs of NY PAC, 546
Independent Power Producers of NY Inc, 174, 479
Independent Power Producers of NY PAC, 546
Indian Affairs, Committee on, 387
Indian Lake Chamber of Commerce, 577
Indian Lake CSD, 649
Indian River CSD, 650
Industrial Retention Network (NY), 465
Industrial Technology Assistance Corp, 500
Industries for the Blind of NYS, Inc, 491
Industries for the Disabled (NYS), 487
Industries for the Disabled Inc (NYS), 515, 518
Industry Ad Hoc Committee on Pilotage, 518
Industry City Associates, LLC, 467
INFORM Inc, 190, 223
Information Management Group, 507
ING America Insurance Holdings, 468
ING America Insurance Holdings Inc PAC (ING NY PAC), 546
Injured Workers Pharmacy, 465
Inlet Common School, 649
Inlet Information Office, 577
Inside Albany Productions Inc, 602
Inside Broadway, 480
Inspector General (NYS), Office of the, 11, 134, 196, 373
Institute for Community Living, 477
Institute for Family Health (The), 223
Institute for Integrative Nutrition, 483

Institute for Socio-Economic Studies, 320
Institute for Special Education (NY), 491
Institute for Student Achievement, 480, 529
Institute for the Study of Infection Control Inc (The), 532
Institute of Design & Construction, 626
Institute of Ecosystem Studies, 190
Institute of Public Administration/NYU Wagner, 208, 293
Institute of Scrap Recycling Industries-Empire Chapter, 521
Institute of Scrap Recycling Industries-NY Chapter, 521
Institute of Technology (NY), 459, 504
Institutional Life Markets Association, Inc, 476
Instructional Systems Inc, 465, 491
Insurance, 29, 49
  Committee Staff, 29
  Key Assembly Staff Assignments, 49
  Key Senate Staff Assignments, 29
  Majority, 29, 49
  Membership, 29, 49
  Minority, 29, 49
Insurance Brokers' Assn of NY PAC, 546
Insurance Brokers' Association of the State of New York, 250, 461, 514
Insurance Department, 11, 215, 245, 373
  Administration & Operations, 245
  Consumer Services Bureau, 245
  Health Bureau, 215, 245
  Information Systems & Technology Bureau, 245
  Insurance Frauds Bureau, 245
  Licensing Services Unit, 245
  Life Bureau, 215, 245
  Liquidation Bureau, 245
  Property Bureau, 245
  Public Affairs & Research Bureau, 215, 245
  Taxes & Accounts Unit, 245
Insurance Fund (NYS), 11, 245, 268, 373
  Administration, 246, 268
  Albany, 246, 268
  Buffalo, 246, 268
  Claims & Medical Operations, 246, 268
  Confidential Investigations, 246, 268
  Endicott, 246, 269
  Field Services, 246, 268
  Information Technology Service, 246, 268
  Insurance Fund Board of Commissioners, 11, 246, 268
  Investments, 246, 268
  Nassau County, Long Island, 246, 269
  NYSIF District Offices, 246, 268
  Premium Audit, 246, 269
  Rochester, 246, 269
  Suffolk County, Long Island, 246, 269
  Syracuse, 246, 269
  Underwriting, 246, 269

Organization Index

White Plains, 246, 269
Insurance Premium Finance Assn Inc, 506
Int'l Brotherhood of Teamsters, AFL-CIO (Local 237), 507
Int'l Longshoremen's Assn AFL-CIO COPE, 546
Integris Inc (Bull Services), 529
Intelligence, House Permanent Select Committee on, 394
   Intelligence Community Management, 394
   Oversight and Investigations, 394
   Subcommittees, 394
   Technical and Tactical Intelligence, 394
   Terrorism/HUMIT, Analysis and Counterintelligence, 394
Intelligence, Select Committee on, 387
Interagency Council of Mental Retardation & Dev Disabilities, 458
InterAgency Council of Mental Retardatn & Developmental Disabilities, 284
Interboro Institute, 635
Intercounty Health Facilities Assn PAC, 546
Interest on Lawyer Account (IOLA) Fund of the State of NY, 116, 258, 376
Interfaith Medical Center, 465
Intergraph Corporation, 507
Interim Housing, 467
Intermagnetics General Corporation, 109
Intermagnetics State PAC, 546
International Academy of Detoxification Specialists (IADS), 493
International Alliance of Theatrical & Stage Employees Local 4, 466
International Bottled Water Association, 478
International Business Machines Corp, 490
International Code Council, 493
International Council of Shopping Centers, 463
International Council of Shopping Centers PAC NY, 546
International Flavors & Fragrances Inc, 109
International Health, Raquet & Sportsclub Assn, 505
International Imaging Technology Council (I-ITC), 513
International Institute of Buffalo, NY, Inc, 242
International Longshoresmen's Association AFL-CIO, 499
International Paper Co., 490
International Paper Political Action Committee, 546
International Relations, 390
   Africa & Global Health, 390
   Asia, the Pacific, and the Global Environment, 391
   Europe, 391

   International Organizations, Human Rights and Oversight, 391
   Middle East and South Asia, 391
   Subcommittees, 390
   Terrorism, Nonproliferation and Trade, 391
   Western Hemisphere, 391
International Underwriting Assn of London, 497
International Union of Painters and Allied Trades Legislative & Educational Committee, 547
Interstate Cooperation, Select Committee on, 32
Interstate Environmental Commission, 116, 181, 376
Interstate Oil & Gas Compact Commission, 116, 169, 182, 376
Interstate Waste Technologies Inc, 466
Intrepid Museum Foundation, 495, 530
Investigations & Government Operations, 30
   Committee Staff, 30
   Key Senate Staff Assignments, 30
   Majority, 30
   Membership, 30
   Minority, 30
Investments US Real Estate Venture V, LP, 519
Inwood House, 467
Inwood-North Lawrence Republican Committee, 547
Iona College, 626
IP Logic LLC, 469
Iron Workers' Local 12 PAF, 547
Iron Workers' Local 40 Voluntary COPE, 547
Iron Workers' Local 60 PAC, 547
Irondequoit, Town of, 422
Ironworkers Political Action League, 547
Iroquois CSD, 646
Iroquois Healthcare Alliance, 223, 484, 529
Irrigation Assn of New York, 522
Irvington UFSD, 676
IRX Therapeutics Inc, 95
Island Drafting & Technical Institute, 635
Island Park UFSD, 654
Island Peer Review Organization Inc, 463
Island Public Affairs, 493
Island Strategies, Inc, 493
Island Trees UFSD, 655
Islip Chamber of Commerce, 577
Islip Economic Development Division & Industrial Development Agency (Town of), 577
Islip Industrial Development Agency (Town of), 577
Islip UFSD, 669
Islip, Town of, 422
Issues Mobilization Fund - Greater Rochester, 547

ITAR-TASS News Agency, 601
Ithaca, 72
   Civil & Criminal Courts, 72
Ithaca City SD, 672
Ithaca College, 626
Ithaca Journal (The), 594
Ithaca, City of, 422
ITT Technical Institute, 635
IUOE Local 106 Voluntary PAF, 546
IUOE Local 14-14B Voluntary PAC, 546
IUOE Local 17 PAC, 546
IUOE Local 463 State & Local PAC & PEF, 546
IUOE Local 825 Political Action & Education Cmte, 546
Ivy Street Development Corp, 476
Izzo Construction, 507
J Adams Consulting, LLC, 493
J J Higgins Properties Inc, 304
J P Morgan Chase & Co State & Federal PAC, 547
Jackson Development Group LTD, 475
Jackson Hewitt Tax Service Inc, 463
Jacobs Engineering, 357
Jamaica Chamber of Commerce, 500, 577
Jamaica Ctr for Arts & Learning Inc, 513
Jamaica Development Corporation (Greater Jamaica), 577
Jamaica Hospital Medical Center, 512
James F Capalino & Associates, 462
Jamestown, 72
   Civil & Criminal Courts, 72
Jamestown Business College, 635
Jamestown Chelsea Market Corporation, 466
Jamestown City SD, 641
Jamestown Community College, 616
Jamestown Management, 467
Jamestown, City of, 423
Jamesville-Dewitt CSD, 659
JAMS, 264, 275
Japanese American Social Services Inc, 320
Japanese Chamber of Commerce, 577
Jasper-Troupsburg CSD, 667
Jazz Museum in Harlem (The), 459
JBDS NYS PAC, 547
JBI International, 499
JC Studios, LLC, 494
JCDecaux North America, 487
JCDecaux North America Inc, 466
Jefferson Community College, 616
Jefferson County, 64, 402
   County, Family & Surrogate's Courts, 64
   Supreme Court, 64
Jefferson CSD, 665
Jefferson-Lewis-Hamilton-Herkimer-Oneida BOCES, 679
Jenkins, Joanne E, 493
Jericho UFSD, 655
Jets (NY), 514, 515, 518
Jets LLC (NY), 506

Organization Index

Jets, LLC (NY), 507
Jewish Board of Family & Children's Services, 284
Jewish Board of Family & Children's Services Inc, 477, 498
Jewish Community Relations Council of NY Inc, 242
Jewish Guild for the Blind (The), 509, 530
Jewish Home & Hospital (The), 223
Jewish Home and Hospital for the Aged (The), 486
Jewish Home of Rochester (The), 491
Jewish Museum (The), 343, 530
Jewish Theological Seminary, 626
Jewish War Veterans of the USA, 366
Jewish War Veterans of the USA, State of NY, 366
JLW Consulting, LLC, 493
Job Path, 477
Job Path (Dames Reid), 469
JOE-PAC NON-Federal, 547
John Jay College of Criminal Justice, 620
John T Mather Memorial Hospital, 530
Johnsburg CSD, 673
Johnson & Johnson, 456, 529
Johnson & Johnson Employees' Good Gov't Fund PAC, 547
Johnson City CSD, 639
Johnson Newspaper Corp, 595, 600
Johnson Newspaper Corporation, 594, 595
Johnson, Stephen Philip, 493
Johnstown, 72
   Civil & Criminal Courts, 72
Joint Legislative Commissions, 354
   Critical Transportation Choices, Legislative Commission on, 354
Joint Senate & House Standing Committees, 106, 329
   Economic Committee, Joint, 106
   Joint Committee on Taxation, 329
Jordan-Elbridge CSD, 659
Joseph P Day Realty Corp, 484
Journal News (The)/Gannett Co Inc, 592, 596
Journal of Commerce, 596
Journal Register Co, 598, 600
Journal Register Company, 599
Journal-Register, 596
JP Morgan Chase & Co, 518
Judge Rotenberg Center, 476
Judiciary, 30, 49, 386, 391
   Administrative Oversight & the Courts, 386
   Antitrust, Competition Policy & Consumer Rights, 386
   Commercial & Administrative Law, 391
   Committee Staff, 30, 49
   Constitution, Civil Rights and Civil Liberties, 391
   Constitution, The, 386
   Crime & Drugs, 386
   Crime, Terrorism and Homeland Security, 391
   Human Rights and the Law, 386
   Immigration, Citizenship, Refugees, Border Security and International Law, 391
   Immigration, Refugees and Border Security, 386
   Key Assembly Staff Assignments, 49
   Key Senate Staff Assignments, 30
   Majority, 30, 49
   Membership, 30, 49
   Minority, 30, 49
   Subcommittees, 386, 391
   Terrorism, Technology & Homeland Security, 386
Juilliard School (The), 626
Jujamcyn Theaters LLC, 495
Junior Tennis League (NY), 475, 480, 494
Juniper Networks Inc, 516
Just Kids Diagnostic & Treatment Center, 487
Just Kids Early Childhood Learning Ctr, 487
JXQ Holding Company, Inc, 530
JY Trans PAC, 547
K Hovnanian Companies NE Inc, 475
Kaleida Health, 463
Kantor Davidoff Wolfe Mandelker & Kass, PC, 494
Kaplan, Randy L, 494
Kasirer Consulting, 494
Katharine Gibbs School-Melville, 636
Katharine Gibbs School-New York City, 636
Katonah-Lewisboro UFSD, 676
Katz, Arthur H, 494
Kaye Scholer LLP, 276
Keane Inc, 466, 469
Keene CSD, 647
Keeping Americas' Promise Inc, 547
Kendall CSD, 661
Kenmore-Tonawanda UFSD, 646
Kenmore-Town of Tonawanda Chamber of Commerce, 577
Keshequa CSD, 651
Keuka College, 626
Keycorp & Subsidiaries, 494
Keycorp Advocates Fund-NY, 547
Keyspan Corporation, 465, 494
KeySpan Corporation, 174
Keyspan Energy, 463, 532
Keyspan Energy State PAC (KEYSPAC), 547
Keyspan Services PAC, 547
Kidspeace, 501
King Ferry Winery, 501
King, Barbara, 494
King's College (The), 626
Kings College, 501
Kings County, 64
COUNTY & FAMILY COURTS: See New York City Courts, 64
Supreme Court, 64
Surrogate's Court, 64
Kings County (NYC Borough of Brooklyn), 403
Kings County C-PAC, 547
Kings County Democratic Party, 535
Kings Park Chamber of Commerce, 577
Kings Park CSD, 669
Kingsborough Community College, 620
Kingsbrook Jewish Medical Ctr, 463
Kingston, 72
   Civil & Criminal Courts, 72
Kingston Avenue Development LLC, 499
Kingston City SD, 673
Kingston, City of, 423
Kingsway Arms Nursing Center, 501
Kinney & Associates Inc, 501
Kirsch, Richard, 495
Kiryas Joel Village UFSD, 660
Kissling Interests, LLC, 527
Kitchen PAC, 547
KleinPAC, 547
Knickerbocker Plaza Associates, 499
Knighton, Ethel V, 495
Komanoff Energy Associates, 174, 357
Konheim & Ketcham Inc, 358
Korean Community Services of Metropolitan NY, 320
Korean War Veterans, 366
KPMG LLP, 208, 293
KPMG, LLP, 496, 530
Kraft Foods Global, Inc, 464, 490
Kramer Levin Naftalis & Frankel, LLP, 495
Kraus & Zuchlewski LLP, 276
Kriss, Kriss, Brignola & Persing, LLP, 358, 495
Kruly, Kenneth, 495
Krupke, Bruce W, 495
Kudlow & Company LLC, 95
La Fargeville CSD, 650
La Fuente, A Tri State Worker & Community Fund, 496
La Fuente, A Tri State Worker & Community Fund Inc, 496
Labor, 30, 49
   Committee Staff, 30, 49
   Key Assembly Staff Assignments, 49
   Key Senate Staff Assignments, 30
   Majority, 30, 49
   Membership, 30, 49
   Minority, 30, 49
Labor Department, 11, 216, 246, 269, 312, 360, 373
   Administration & Public Affairs, 269
   Asbestos Control Bureau, 216, 270
   Central/Mohawk Valley, 270
   Counsel's Office, 269
   Employability Development/Apprentice Training, 269

Organization Index

Employer Services, 270
Employment & Unemployment Insurance Advisory Council, 246, 269
Employment Relations Board, 247, 269
Employment Services Division, 269
Federal Programs, 269, 312
Finger Lakes Region, 270
Greater Capital District, 270
Hudson Valley, 270
Industrial Board of Appeals, 247, 269
Industry Inspection Unit, 216, 270
Inspector General's Office, 269
Labor Planning & Technology, 269
Labor Standards Division, 270, 312
Long Island Region, 270
New York City, 270
On-site Consultation Unit, 270
On-Site Consultation Unit, 216
Public Employees Safety & Health (PESH) Unit, 216, 270
Public Work Bureau, 270
Regional Offices, 270
Research & Statistics Division, 269
Safety & Health Division, 216, 270, 312
Southern Tier, 270
Unemployment Insurance Appeal Board, 247, 269
Unemployment Insurance Division, 247, 269, 312
Veterans Services, 269
Western Region, 270
Worker Protection, 216, 270
Workforce Development & Training Division, 269, 312
Workforce Protection, Standards & Licensing, 312
Laboratory Institute of Merchandising, 636
Laborers Int'l Union of North America AFL-CIO, Local 17, 479
Laborers PAC (NYS), 515
Laborers' Intl Union of North America 435 Voluntary PAF, 547
Laborers' Local #91 PAC, 547
Laborers' Local 103 PAF Cmte, 547
Laborers' Local 17 PAC, 548
Laborers' Local Union 190 PAC, 548
Laborers' Political Action Committee (NYS), 507
Labor-Religion Coalition, Inc (NYS), 496
Lackawanna, 73
  Civil & Criminal Courts, 73
Lackawanna Area Chamber of Commerce, 577
Lackawanna City SD, 646
LaFayette CSD, 659
LaGuardia Community College, 620
Lake George CSD, 673
Lake George Park Commission, 117, 182, 376
Lake George Regional Chamber of Commerce, 578

Lake Luzerne Chamber of Commerce, 578
Lake Placid Chamber of Commerce, 578
Lake Placid CSD, 647
Lake Pleasant CSD, 649
Lake Shore Savings, 95
Lakeland CSD, 676
Lamar Advertising Company, 468
Lambda Legal Defense & Education Fund Inc, 242
Lambert, Linda A, 496
Lanahan, Kevin, 496
Lancaster Area Chamber of Commerce, 578
Lancaster CSD, 646
Lancaster Industrial Development Agency (Town of), 578
Lancaster, Town of, 423
Lancer Insurance Co/Lancer Compliance Services, 276
Land America Financial Group Inc, 488
Land Surveyors PAC, 548
Land Title Assn (NYS), 515
Land Title Assn Inc (NYS), 518, 521
Land Trust Alliance Northeast Program, 190, 496
Landauer Realty Group Inc, 304
Landau-Painter, Cathy, 496
Landry, M Joe, 497
Lands End Associates L.P., 467
Langdon, David, 497
Lansing CSD, 672
Lansingburgh CSD, 663
Lasky, Roy E, 497
Latina Political Action Committee, 548
Latino Commission on AIDS, 528
Latino Democratic Committee of Orange County, 548
Latino Political Action Committee, 548
Laurens CSD, 662
Lavin Properties, 467
Law Department, 12, 91, 99, 134, 169, 179, 197, 216, 229, 238, 247, 253, 270, 301, 325, 373
  Administration, 197, 253
  Administrative Services, 253
  Antitrust Bureau, 99, 134, 254
  Appeals & Opinions Division, 134, 253
  APPEALS & OPINIONS DIVISION Law Library, 373
  Binghamton, 254
  Brooklyn, 254
  Budget & Fiscal Management, 253
  Buffalo, 254
  Charities Bureau, 135, 254, 325
  Civil Recoveries Bureau, 135, 247, 255, 325
  Civil Rights Bureau, 135, 229, 238, 254, 270, 302
  Claims Bureau, 99, 135, 216, 247, 255, 302
  Consumer Fraud & Protection Bureau, 91, 99, 229, 254

  Consumer Frauds & Protection Bureau, 135
  Criminal Division, 134, 216, 253
  Criminal Prosecutions Bureau, 134, 253
  Environmental Protection Bureau, 135, 179, 254
  Harlem, 255
  Healthcare Bureau, 135, 216, 254
  Human Resources, 253
  Intergovernmental Relations, 197, 254
  Internet Bureau, 99, 135, 169, 254, 325
  Investigations Bureau, 134, 254
  Investment Protection Bureau, 91, 99, 135, 254, 302, 325
  Labor Bureau, 135, 247, 255, 270
  Law Library, 134, 253
  Legal Technology & Systems Management, 253
  Litigation Bureau, 135, 216, 229, 247, 255, 325
  Medicaid Fraud Control Unit, 134, 216, 254
  Nassau, 255
  Office of the Attorney General, 254
  Organized Crime Task Force, 134, 254
  Plattsburgh, 255
  Poughkeepsie, 255
  Press Office, 254
  Public Advocacy Division, 91, 99, 134, 169, 179, 216, 229, 238, 254, 270, 301, 325
  Real Property Bureau, 135, 229, 247, 255, 302
  Regional Offices Division, 254
  Rochester, 255
  State Counsel Division, 99, 135, 216, 229, 247, 255, 270, 302, 325
  Suffolk, 255
  Syracuse, 255
  Telecommunications & Energy Bureau, 135, 169, 254
  Training & Staff Development, 253
  Utica, 255
  Watertown, 255
  Westchester, 255
Law Enforcement Officers Union, Distr Cncl 82 (NYS), 515
Law Guardian Program, 255
  1st Judicial Dept, 255
  2nd Judicial Dept, 256
  3rd Judicial Dept, 256
  4th Judicial Dept, 256
Law Office of Anne Reynolds Copps, 264, 320
Law Offices of Frank G. D'Angelo & Associates, 264
Law Offices of Stanley N Lupkin, 141
Law Offices of Wesley Chen, 95
Law School Admission Council, 475
Law School Admissions Council, 530
Lawrence UFSD, 655

Organization Index

Lawyers for the Public Interest (NY), 497
Lawyers' Fund for Client Protection, 117, 258, 377
Lawyers' PAC (LAWPAC), 548
LB Furniture Industries LLC, 465, 504
LB Northeast Developers Vistamar Complex LTD, 475
LCOR Inc, 501
Le Moyne College, 626
Le Roy CSD, 648
Leader (The), 593
Leader House Associates, L.P., 467
Leader-Herald (The), 594
League for the Hard of Hearing, 223, 532
League of American Theatres & Producers Inc, 530
League of Humane Voters of New York City, 548
League of Women Voters of New York State, 165, 208, 293, 497, 498
Learning Leaders, 153
LeBoeuf Lamb Greene & MacRae PAC, 548
LeBoeuf Lamb Greene & MacRae, LLP, 497
Lechase Construction Services, 507
Lee Corporation, 594
Leewood Real Estate Group/NY, LLC & Affiliates, 487
Legal Action Center Inc, 264
Legal Action Center of the City of NY Inc, 141
Legal Action Ctr of the City of NY Inc, 498
Legal Aid Society, 141, 264
Legal Aid Society (The), 461, 501
Legal Aid Society, Community Law Offices, 264
Legal Assistance Group (NY), 459
Legal Services for NYC, 465
Legal Services for NYC Inc, 508
Legal Services for Working Poor New Yorkers Coalition, 516
Legal Services of the Hudson Valley, 264, 498
Legislative Bill Drafting Commission, 117, 200, 377
Legislative Retrieval System, 117, 200
Legislative Correspondents Association, 602
Legislative Gazette, 591
Legislative Library, 375
Lehman Brothers, 501
Lehman College, 620
Lennar Corporation, 495
Leon, Rachel, 498
Leonard Litwin, 495
LeRay, Town of, 423
Lesbian Gay Bisexual & Transgender Community Center (The), 530
Lesbian Gay Bisexual & Transgender Community Ctr (The), 503

Lesbian, Gay, Bisexual & Transgender Community Ctr - Not For Profit, 242, 284, 320
Lesnick Leadership PAC, 548
Letchworth CSD, 678
Levene, Gouldin & Thompson LLP, 250, 264
Levine, Laurence J, 498
Levine, Paul, 498
Levittown UFSD, 655
Levittown West Republican Golf, 548
Levy, Norman PC, 498
Lewinter Associates, Murray, 499
Lewis County, 64, 403
Supreme, County, Family & Surrogate's Courts, 64
Lewis County Chamber of Commerce, 578
Lewis County Industrial Development Agency, 578
Lewiston-Porter CSD, 657
Lexington School for the Deaf/Ctr for the Deaf Inc, 500
Lexmark International Inc, 490
LHL Realty Co., LLC, 495
Liantonio, John J, 499
Liberty CSD, 671
Liberty Election Systems, 483
Liberty Group New York Holdings Inc, 594
Liberty Group Publishing, 593, 594, 595, 600
Liberty Helicopter, 467
Liberty Helicopters Inc, 465
Liberty Lines Express Inc, 507
Liberty Mutual, 487
Liberty Mutual Group, 479
Liberty Mutual Insurance Co PAC - NY, 548
Libraries & Education Technology, 49
Committee Staff, 49
Key Assembly Staff Assignments, 49
Majority, 50
Membership, 50
Minority, 50
Library Assn (NY), 499
Library Association (NY), 476, 501
Library, Joint Committee on the, 394
Lieberman, Mark L, 499
Lieutenant Governor's Office, 4, 194, 371
Lieutenants Benevolent Assn, 489
Life Insurance Co (NY), 493, 529
Life Insurance Council of New York, Inc, 250
Life Insurance Council of NY Inc, 524
Life Insurance Council of NY PAC (LICONY), 548
Life Insurance Council of NY, Inc, 487
Life Insurance Settlement Association, 478
Life of the Party, 548
Lifespan, 501
Lifespire, 284
Lighthouse International, 224, 499

Lilac Capital LLC, 513
Lilac Corporation, 501
Lincoln Center for the Performing Arts, 515
Lincoln Center for the Performing Arts Inc, 343, 506
Lincoln Ctr for the Performing Arts Inc, 499
Lindenhurst UFSD, 669
Lindenhurst, Village of, 424
Linium LLC, 469
Lipsky, Richard Associates Inc, 499
Liquid Asphalt Distributors Assoc Inc of NY, 513
Lisbon CSD, 666
Literacy Assistance Center, 467
Literacy NY Inc, 469
Literacy Suffolk, Inc, 493
Little Falls, 73
Civil & Criminal Courts, 73
Little Falls City SD, 650
Little Flower Children & Family Services, 320
Little Flower UFSD, 669
Littman Krooks LLP, 264, 320
Liverpool Chamber of Commerce (Greater Liverpool), 578
Liverpool CSD, 659
Living Independently Inc, 503
Livingston County, 64, 403
Supreme, County, Family & Surrogate's Courts, 64
Livingston County Chamber of Commerce, 578
Livingston County Economic Development Office & Industrial Development Agency, 578
Livingston Manor CSD, 672
Livonia CSD, 651
Livonia, Avon & Lakeville Railroad Corp, 490
LLJ Realty Corp, 475
Lloyds of London, 497
Local #30 PAC, 548
Local #41 Int'l Brotherhood of Electrical Workers' PAC, 548
Local 1180, CWA, AFL-CIO, 507
Local 137 PEF, 548
Local 138, 138A & 138B International Union of Operating Engineers, 548
Local 147 PAF, 548
Local 1500 Political Candidates Education Fund, 548
Local 1814 Intl Longshoremens Assn AFL-CIO PA & ED Fund, 548
Local 23-25, Unite State & Local Campaign Committee, 549
Local 237 I.B.T. PAC, 549
Local 246, SEIU, 526
Local 3, IBEW Communications Electricians, 526
Local 30 IUOE PAC, 549
Local 32-BJ, 463

841

Organization Index

Local 32BJ SEIU NY/NJ American Dream Fund, 549
Local 338 RWDSU, 463
Local 420 Political Action Committee, 549
Local 6 Committee on Political Education, 549
Local 6 Hotel Restaurant & Club Employyes & Bartenders Union, AFL-CIO, 455
Local 7 PAC Fund, 549
Local 73 Plumbers and Steamfitters PAC Fund, 549
Local 802, American Federation of Musicians of Greater NY, 507
Local 891 Cope Fund, 549
Local Government, 30, 50
  Committee Staff, 30, 50
  Key Assembly Staff Assignments, 50
  Key Senate Staff Assignments, 30
  Majority, 30, 50
  Membership, 30, 50
  Minority, 30, 50
Local Initiative Support Corporation, 234
Local Union #373 UA Political Action Fund, 549
LoCicero & Tan Inc, 499
Lockport, 73
  Civil & Criminal Courts, 73
Lockport City SD, 657
Lockport Fire Dept PAC, 549
Lockport Industrial Development Agency (Town of), 578
Lockport Union-Sun & Journal, 595
Lockport, City of, 424
Lockport, Town of, 424
Lockwood, Kessler & Bartlett Inc, 499
Locust Valley CSD, 655
Log Cabin Republicans Hudson Valley PAC, 549
Log Cabin Republicans NY PAC, 549
Logan, Ernest, 500
Long Beach, 73
  Civil & Criminal Courts, 73
Long Beach Chamber of Commerce, 578
Long Beach City SD, 655
Long Beach, City of, 424
Long Island Assn Action Committe, 549
Long Island Association, 500, 578
Long Island Board of Realtors, 494
Long Island Builders Institute, 529
Long Island Business Institute-Commack, 636
Long Island Business Institute-Flushing, 636
Long Island Business News, 602
Long Island Chapter/American Institute of Architects LIC (AIA PAC), 549
Long Island Children's Museum, 501
Long Island Coalition for Children with Special Needs, 487
Long Island College Hospital, 495

Long Island College Hospital (The), 516
Long Island College Hospital School of Nursing, 626
Long Island Contractor's Assn, 483
Long Island Contractors Assn PAC Inc, 549
Long Island Council of Dedicated Merchants Chamber of Commerce, 578
Long Island Development Corporation, 578
Long Island Educational Opportunity Center, 618
Long Island Farm Bureau, 86, 485
Long Island Federation of Labor AFL-CIO, 549
Long Island Forum for Technology, 468
Long Island Gasoline Retailers Assn Inc, 485, 522
Long Island Gasoline Retailers Assn PAC, 549
Long Island Gay & Lesbian Youth, 465
Long Island Health Network, 530
Long Island Life Sciences Initiative, 529
Long Island Nursery & Landscape Association Inc, 86
Long Island Ophthalmological Society, 462
Long Island Pest Control Assn, 512
Long Island Power Authority, 117, 170, 377, 501, 506
Long Island Progressive Coalition, 526
Long Island Prosperity, 549
Long Island Rail Road Commuter's Council, 358
Long Island University, 530, 626
Long Island Water Conference, 522
Long Lake CSD, 649
Long Term Care Community Coalition, 500
Long Term Care Community Coalition (FKA Nursing Home Community Coalition), 500
Long View Publishing Co, 596
Longwood CSD, 669
Loretto Management Corp, 518
Loretto Management Corporation, 462
Lorillard Tobacco Co, 469, 522
Losquadro, Steven E, 500
Lottery, Division of, 12, 325, 373
  Adirondack-Capital District Region, 325
  Central/Finger Lakes/Genesee Valley Regions, 325
  Hudson Valley Region, 325
  Long Island Region, 325
  New York City Region, 325
  Regional Offices, 325
  Rochester Office, 325
  Syracuse Office, 325
  Western Region, 325
Louloudes, Virginia, 500
Lowell School, 478
Lower East Side Tenement Museum, 459, 501
Lower Hudson Education Coalition, 529

Lower Manhattan Cultural Council, 344, 494
Lowry, Robert, 500
Lowville Academy & CSD, 651
LP Ciminelli Inc, 501
LS Power Associates LLC, 513
Luria, Robert S, 500
Lustig, Esther Public Affairs, 500
Luthin Associates, Inc, 500
Lyme CSD, 650
Lynbrook P.B.A. PAC, 549
Lynbrook UFSD, 655
Lynch, Bill Associates, LLC, 500
Lynch, Patricia Associates, 501
Lyncourt UFSD, 659
Lyndonville CSD, 661
Lyons CSD, 674
Lysander, Town of, 424
M & R Strategic Services, 502
M & T Bank, 501
M&T Bank Corporation, 95
M. Dolores Denman Democratic Lawyers Club, 550
M.A. Angeliades, Inc, 493
M/A-Com Inc, 501
MAC PAC, 549
MacKenzie, Duncan R, 502
Mackin, Robert E, 502
Macquarie Securities (USA) Inc, 501
Macy's East Inc, 109
Madison Avenue Leasehold LLC, 459
Madison County, 64, 403
  Supreme, County, Family & Surrogate's Courts, 64
Madison County Industrial Development Agency, 578
Madison CSD, 652
Madison Square Garden Corp, 344
Madison Square Garden LP, 501, 502, 513
Madison-Oneida BOCES, 679
Madrid-Waddington CSD, 666
Magna Entertainment Corp, 501, 513
Magnum Management LLC, 467
Maher, Daniel F, Jr, 502
Mahopac CSD, 663
Mahopac-Carmel Chamber of Commerce, 579
Maier, Ronald S, 502
Maimonides Medical Center, 532
Maine-Endwell CSD, 639
Major League Baseball, 344
Make the Road by Walking, 502
Make the Road by Walking Inc, 502
Malcolm Pirnie Inc, 468
Malkin & Ross, 502
Mallory Factor Inc, 95
Malone Chamber of Commerce, 579
Malone CSD, 647
Malone Telegram, 595
Maloney Committee NYS PAC, 550
Maloney, Richard, 503

842

Organization Index

Malverne UFSD, 655
Mamaroneck Chamber of Commerce, 579
Mamaroneck UFSD, 676
Mamaroneck, Town of, 424
Managed Funds Association, 529
Manatt, Phelps & Phillips, LLP, 503
Manchester-Shortsville CSD, 660
Mancuso Business Development Group, 304
Mandl School, 636
Manhasset Chamber of Commerce, 579
Manhasset UFSD, 655
Manhattan Chamber of Commerce Inc, 503, 579
Manhattan College, 626
Manhattan Connection PAC, 550
Manhattan Educational Opportunity Center, 618
Manhattan Institute (The), 208
Manhattan Institute for Policy Research, 109, 208
Manhattan Institute, Center for Civic Innovation, 293, 331
Manhattan Music Society, 467
Manhattan School of Music, 627
Manhattan Theatre Club, 513, 514
Manhattan Theatre Club Inc, 504
Manhattan Youth Recreation & Resources, 487
Manhattan-Bronx Minority Business Enterprise Center, 276
Manhattanville College, 627
Maniscalco, John D, 504
Manlius, Town of, 425
Mannella, Peter F, 504
Mannis, David, 504
Manufactured Housing PAC, 550
Manufacturers & Traders Trust Company PAC, 550
Manufacturers Assn of Central NY Inc, 504
Manufacturers Association of Central New York, 109
Map Info Corporation, 469
Maplewood-Colonie Common SD, 638
Marathon CSD, 644
Marcellus CSD, 659
March of Dimes Birth Defects Foundation, 320
March of Dimes Birth Defects Foundation (NYS Chapters), 487
Marcus Attorneys, 504
Marcus Whitman CSD, 660
Margaretville CSD, 644
Margiotta, Joseph M, 504
Maria College of Albany, 627
Marijuana Policy Project, 516
Marine Corps League, 366
Marine Corps League (MCL), 366
Marine Corps League (MCL), Department of NY, 366
Marion CSD, 675

Marion S Whelan School of Practical Nursing, 224
Marist College, 627
Marist Institute for Public Opinion, 165
Maritato, Anna Maria, 504
Maritime Assn, 501
Mark IV IVHS Inc, 501
Marlboro CSD, 673
Marsh & Associates, PC, 504
Marsh & McLennan Companies, 250
Marsh USA Inc, 512
Marshals Assn (NYC), 530
Martens, Joseph J, 505
Marx PAC, 550
Marymount Manhattan College, 627
Maryvale UFSD, 646
Mason Tenders District Council Greater NY & Long Island PAC, 505
Mason Tenders' District Council of Greater NY PAC, 550
Massapequa Chamber of Commerce, 579
Massapequa UFSD, 655
Massena Chamber of Commerce, 579
Massena CSD, 666
Massiah, Lesley A, 505
Master, Robert, 505
Mastercard International Inc, 475
Mastics/Shirley Chamber of Commerce, 579
Matarazzo, Louis, 505
Matt Brewing Co (The), 455
Mattituck Chamber of Commerce, 579
Mattituck-Cutchogue UFSD, 669
Maxim of NY, LLC, 462
Mayfield CSD, 648
Mayville/Chautauqua Chamber of Commerce, 579
MBA Long Island City, 493
MBIA Insurance Corporation, 95, 293, 529
McCormick Farms Inc, 86
McCulley & Associates Inc, 505
McDevitt, William L, 505
McDonald's Corporation, 475
McEvoy, Frank, 505
McGraw CSD, 644
McGuire, Michael J, 505
MCI, 529
MCIC Vermont Inc, 530
McInnis, Stephen C, 505
McKesson Corporation, 491
McLane Company Inc, 463
McMahon & Grow, 208, 264
McSpedon, William J, 505
MDRC, 153, 276
Meara, Brian R, Public Relations Inc, 506
Mechanical Technology Incorporated, 174
Mechanicville, 73
  Civil & Criminal Courts, 73
Mechanicville Area Chamber of Commerce, 579
Mechanicville City SD, 664

Mechanicville/Stillwater Industrial Development Agency, 579
Medaille College, 627
Medco Health Solutions Inc (Formerly Merck-Medco Managed Care, LLC), 483
Medco Health Solutions, Inc, 484, 495
Medford Hamlet ALP, LLC, 491
Medgar Evers College, 620
Medical & Health Research Assn of NYC Inc, 491
Medical Answering Services, 501
Medical College (NY), 491
Medical Equipment Providers Assn (NY), 472, 523
Medical Liability Mutual Insurance Co, 497
Medical Liability Mutual Insurance Co (MLMIC), 468
Medical Society of the State of New York PAC, 550
Medical Society of the State of New York, Div of Socio-Medical Economics, 250
Medical Society of the State of NY, Governmental Affairs Division, 224
Medical Staff of the Long Island College (Arent Fox), 501
Medicare Rights Center, 463, 516
Medimmune Inc, 463
Medina CSD, 661
Medstat, 504
Medstat (Marsh and Associates PC), 489
Medtronic Inc (FKA Medtronic Sofamor Danek), 530
Megrant Corporation, 478
Meinking, Rebecca A, 506
Melchionni, William, III, 506
Members United Corporate FCU (Formerly Empire Corporate FCU), 476
Memorial Hospital School of Nursing, 627
Memorial Sloan-Kettering Cancer Center, 224, 503
Menaker & Herrmann LLP, 109
Menands UFSD, 638
Mental Health, 50
  Committee Staff, 50
  Key Assembly Staff Assignments, 50
  Majority, 50
  Membership, 50
  Minority, 50
Mental Health & Developmental Disabilities, 30
  Committee Staff, 30
  Key Senate Staff Assignments, 30
  Majority, 30
  Membership, 30
  Minority, 31
Mental Health Assn of NYC (The), 477
Mental Health Assn of Westchester, 506
Mental Health Assn of Westchester Co Inc, 506
Mental Health Assn of Westchester Co, Inc, 485

843

Organization Index

Mental Health Association in NYS, 506
Mental Health Association of Nassau County, 478
Mental Health Association of NYC Inc, 284, 506
Mental Health Association of NYC, Inc, 484
Mental Health Association of NYS Inc, 284
Mental Health, Office of, 12, 280, 373
   Bronx Children's Psychiatric Center, 280
   Bronx Psychiatric Center, 280
   Brooklyn Children's Center, 280
   Buffalo Psychiatric Center, 280
   Capital District Psychiatric Center, 280
   Center for Human Resource Management, 280
   Center for Information Technology & Evaluation Research, 280
   Central New York Psychiatric Center, 280
   Creedmoor Psychiatric Center, 280
   Division of Adult Services, 280
   Division of Children and Family Services, 280
   Division of Forensic Services, 280
   Elmira Psychiatric Center, 280
   Facilities, 280
   Greater Binghamton Health Center, 280
   Hudson River Psychiatric Center, 280
   Hutchings Psychiatric Center, 280
   Kingsboro Psychiatric Center, 280
   Kirby Forensic Psychiatric Center, 280
   Manhattan Psychiatric Center, 280
   Mid-Hudson Forensic Psychiatric Center, 280
   Mohawk Valley Psychiatric Center, 280
   Nathan S Kline Institute for Psychiatric Research, 280
   New York Psychiatric Institute, 280
   Office of Consumer Affairs, 281
   Office of Financial Management, 281
   Office of Public Affairs and Planning, 281
   Office of Quality Management, 281
   Pilgrim Psychiatric Center, 280
   Queens Children's Psychiatric Center, 280
   Rochester Psychiatric Center, 281
   Rockland Children's Psychiatric Center, 281
   Rockland Psychiatric Center, 281
   Sagamore Children's Psychiatric Center, 281
   South Beach Psychiatric Center, 281
   St Lawrence Psychiatric Center, 281
   Western New York Children's Psychiatric Center, 281
Mental Hygiene Legal Service, 256, 282
   1st Judicial Dept, 256, 282
   2nd Judicial Dept, 256, 282
   3rd Judicial Dept, 256, 282
   4th Judicial Dept, 256, 282
Mental Retardation & Developmental Disabilities, Office of, 12, 281, 373
   Bernard Fineson Developmental Disabilities Services Office, 281
   Brooklyn Developmental Disabilities Services Office, 281
   Capital District Developmental Disabilities Services Office, 281
   Central New York Developmental Disabilities Services Office, 281
   Developmental Disabilities Services Offices, 281
   Finger Lakes Developmental Disabilities Services Office, 281
   Hudson Valley Developmental Disabilities Services Office, 281
   Information Support Services, 281
   Institute for Basic Research in Developmental Disabilities, 282
   Long Island Developmental Disabilities Services Office, 281
   Metro New York Developmental Disabilities Services Office, 281
   New York City Regional Office, 281
   Staten Island Developmental Disabilities Services Office, 282
   Sunmount Developmental Disabilities Services Office, 282
   Taconic Developmental Disabilities Services Office, 282
   Valley Ridge Developmental Disabilities Services Office, 282
   Western New York Developmental Disabilities Services Office, 282
Mentoring Partnership Coalition, 463
Merchants Protective Co, Inc (NY), 530
Merck & Co Inc, 527
Mercury Public Affairs, 506
Mercy College, 507, 627
Merker Advisory Services, 467
Merrick Chamber of Commerce, 579
Merrick UFSD, 655
Merrill Lynch & Co Inc, 95, 463
Merscorp Inc, 465
Mesick, Edie, 507
Messenger Post Newspapers, 593
Messinger Woods Wildlife Care & Education Center Inc, 190
Metalic Lathers Local 46 PAC, 550
MetLife, 250
Metlife Inc Employees' Political Participation Fund A, 550
MetLife Ins Co Political Fund B, 550
Metret PAC, Inc, 550
Metro Terminals Corporation, 474
Metro/Colvin Realty Inc, 304
Metro/Horohoe-Leimbach, 305
Metro-North Railroad Commuter Council, 358
Metropolitan College of New York, 627

Metropolitan College of NY, 491, 504
Metropolitan Events, 467
Metropolitan Funeral Directors Assn, 532
Metropolitan Garage Owners Assn PAC, 550
Metropolitan Life Insurance Co, 479, 483, 513
Metropolitan Museum of Art, 463
Metropolitan Museum of Art (The), 344, 529
Metropolitan Package Store Assn Inc, 505
Metropolitan Package Store, Inc Assoc PAF, 550
Metropolitan Parking Assn, 530
Metropolitan Retail Assn, LLC (NY), 494
Metropolitan Taxicab Board of Trade, 474
Metropolitan Transportation Authority, 475
Metropolitan TV Alliance, 519
Metrovest Equities Inc, 466
MetSchools, Inc, 476
Mexico CSD, 662
Meyer Suozzi English & Klein, PC, 265, 507
Meyer, Suozzi, English & Klein, PC - Political Acct, 550
MFY Legal Services, 507
MGM Mirage, 531
MH Corbin Enterprises, 488
Michael T Kelly, Esq, 141, 265
Microsoft Corporation, 487
Mid Island Democratic PAC (MIDPAC), 550
Mid-America Baptist Theological Seminary Northeast Branch, 627
Middle Country CSD, 669
Middleburgh CSD, 665
Middletown, 73
   Civil & Criminal Courts, 73
Middletown City SD, 660
Middletown, City of, 425
Mid-Hudson Catskill Rural & Migrant Ministry Inc, 507
Mid-Hudson News Network, 602
Mid-Hudson Pattern for Progress, 109, 234, 579
Midori and Friends, 480
Midtown Consultants, Inc, 507
Mildred Elley, 527, 636
Milford CSD, 662
Military & Naval Affairs, Division of, 13, 360, 373
Military Chaplains Association of the USA (MCA), 367
Military Officers Association of America, 367
Military Officers Association of America (MOAA), NYS Council, 367
Military Order of the Purple Heart, 367
Military Order of the Purple Heart (MOPH), 367
Millbrook CSD, 645

Organization Index

Millenium Hilton Hotel (The), 519
Millenium Partners, 499
Millennium Partners, 474
Miller Brewing Co, 490
Miller Brewing Company, 464
Miller Place UFSD, 670
Miller Place/Mt Sinai/Sound Beach/Rocky Point Chamber of Commerce, 579
Miller, Monica, 508
Mills, Josephine, 508
Mineola Chamber of Commerce, 579
Mineola UFSD, 655
Minerva CSD, 647
Minisink Valley CSD, 661
Mirant Corporation State Political Action Committee Inc-NY, 550
Mirant New York Inc, 508
Mirant New York, Inc, 487
Mirram Global, LLC, 508
Mirram Group, LLC (The), 508
MJ Peterson Corporation, 304
MLCA PAC, 550
MLMICPAC, 550
Modutank Inc, 190
Mohawk Ambulance Service, 501
Mohawk CSD, 650
Mohawk Valley Chamber of Commerce, 579
Mohawk Valley Chamber PAC, 551
Mohawk Valley Community College, 616
Mohawk Valley Economic Development District, 579
Mohawk Valley Economic Development Growth Enterprises, 580
Mohonasen CSD, 665
Molloy College, 627
Moms Pharmacy, 463
Moneygram International, 527
Monroe 1 BOCES, 679
Monroe 2-Orleans BOCES, 679
Monroe College, 508
Monroe College-Bronx, 636
Monroe College-New Rochelle, 636
Monroe Community College, 616
Monroe County, 65, 404
   Supreme, County, Family & Surrogate's Courts, 65
Monroe County Airport Authority, 463
Monroe County Deputy Sheriff's Association Inc, 468
Monroe County Executive, 501
Monroe County Independence Caucas, 551
Monroe County Industrial Development Agency (COMIDA), 580
Monroe, Town of, 425
Monroe-Woodbury CSD, 661
Monsanto Co, 490
Montalbano Initiatives Inc, 508
Montauk UFSD, 670
Montclare & Wachtler, 110, 265
Montefiore Medical Ctr, 503

Montford Point Marine Association, 367
Montgomery County, 65, 404
   Supreme, County, Family & Surrogate's Courts, 65
Montgomery County Chamber of Commerce/Montgomery County Partnership, 580
Montgomery, Town of, 425
Monticello CSD, 672
Monticello Raceway, 344
Monticello Raceway Management Inc, 477
Monument Builders Assn (NYS), 513
Monument Industry PAC, 551
Moody's Investors Service, Public Finance Group, 293, 331
Moravia Chamber of Commerce, 580
Moravia CSD, 641
Morello, Charles J, 508
Morgan Associates, 508
Morgan Stanley, 95
Morgan Stanley (Multistate Associates), 530
Morgante, Samuel, 509
Moriah CSD, 647
Morris & McVeigh LLP, 509
Morris & McVeigh NYS PAC, 551
Morris CSD, 662
Morris Heights Health Center, 508
Morris Heights Health Ctr, 508
Morris, Mark, 509
Morristown CSD, 667
Morrisville State College, 614
Morrisville-Eaton CSD, 652
Morse, Alan, 509
Mortgage Bankers Association, 465
Mortgage Insurance Companies of America, 497
Morton Grove Pharmaceuticals, 504
Mosholu Montefiore Community Ctr, 500
Mothers Against Drunk Driving (MADD) of NYS, 141
Motion Picture Assn of America Inc, 463
Motley, Duane R, 509
Motor Truck Assn (NYS), 501
Motor Vehicles Department, 13, 348, 373
   Administration, Office for, 348
   Appeals Board, 348
   Governor's Traffic Safety Committee, 348
   Legal Affairs, Office for, 348
   Operations & Customer Service, Office for, 348
   Safety, Consumer Protection & Clean Air, Office for, 348
Motorola Inc, 515
Mount Kisco Chamber of Commerce, 580
Mount Markham CSD, 650
Mount Pleasant, Town of, 425
Mount Saint Mary College, 627
Mount Sinai Medical Center, 224, 507, 509
Mount Sinai School of Medicine of NYU, 628

Mount St Mary's Hospital & Health Center, 513
Mount Vernon, 73
   Civil & Criminal Courts, 73
Mount Vernon Chamber of Commerce, 580
Mount Vernon Industrial Development Agency (City of), 580
Mount Vernon, City of, 425
Mountaintop Democratic Club, 551
Movers & Warehousemen Political Action Committee, 551
Movers' & Warehousemen's Assn Inc (NYS), 489
Moving Media, LLC, 487
Moynihan Station Developers, LLC, 467
MPAC, 550
MRV, 469
Mt Morris CSD, 651
Mt Pleasant CSD, 676
Mt Pleasant-Blythedale UFSD, 676
Mt Pleasant-Cottage UFSD, 677
Mt Sinai Hospital of Queens, 532
Mt Sinai UFSD, 670
Mt Vernon City SD, 677
MTA (Metropolitan Transportation Authority), 117, 352, 377
MTA Bridges & Tunnels, 117, 350, 377
MTA Bus Company, 118, 351, 377
MTA Capital Construction, 118, 351, 377
MTA Long Island Bus, 118, 351, 377
MTA Long Island Rail Road, 118, 351, 377
MTA Metro-North Railroad, 118, 351, 377
MTA New York City Transit, 119, 352, 377
MTA Office of the Inspector General, 119, 352, 377
Muhs, Robert E, 509
Mulholland & Knapp, LLP, 208
Mullane, Robert A, 509
Mulvihill ICS Inc, 513
Municipal Art Society, 509
Municipal Assistance Corporation for the City of New York, 91, 119, 291, 377
Municipal Credit Union, 95
Municipal Electric Utilities Assn of NYS (MEUA), 509
Municipal Electric Utilities Association, 174
Murphy, Daniel C, 509
Murphy, Robert J, 510
Murray, Claire, 510
Museum Association of New York, 153, 344
Museum for African Arts, 466
Museum of Arts & Design, 494
Museum of Arts and Design, 486
Museum of Modern Art (The), 518
Museum of the Moving Image, 467
My-T Acres Inc, 86
NADAP, 465
NAIFA - New York State, 251
NAMI-NYS, 284, 510

Organization Index

Nanuet UFSD, 664
Naples CSD, 660
Naral Pro-Choice NY, 502
NARAL Pro-Choice, New York, 510
NARAL/NY Multicandidate PAC, 551
Nasca, Samuel J, 510
Nassau BOCES, 679
Nassau Community College, 483, 616
Nassau Council of Chambers, 580
Nassau County, 65, 70, 404
   1st, 2nd & 4th District Courts, 70
   3rd District Court, 70
   County & Surrogate's Courts, 65
   Family Court, 65
   Supreme Court, 65
Nassau County Detectives Association Inc, 554
Nassau County Firefighter's Museum & Education Center, 530
Nassau County Firefighters Museum & Education Ctr, 483
Nassau County Industrial Development Agency, 580
Nassau County Lesbian & Gay Democrats, 554
Nassau County PBA PAC, 554
Nassau County PHCC, 526
Nassau County Village Officials Assn, 478
Nassau Regional Off-Track Betting Corporation, 119, 336, 377, 499, 506
Nassau-Suffolk Hospital Association, 530
Nassau-Suffolk Hospital Council Inc, 477
NASW-NYS Political Action for Candidate Election (PACE), 551
Nat Sherman Inc, 465
Nat'l Assn of Energy Service Companies, 486
Nat'l Assn of Social Workers - New York City Chapter, 554
Nat'l Federation of Independent Business/NY Save America's Free Enterprises, 554
National Academy of Elder Law Attorneys-NY Chapter, 487
National Academy of Forensic Engineers, 265
National Alliance for the Mentally Ill of NYC, Inc, 510
National Amputation Foundation Inc, 225, 367
National Archives & Records Administration, 150, 339
   Franklin D Roosevelt Presidential Library & Museum, 150, 339
National Assn of Chain Drug Stores, 510
National Assn of Health Underwriters, 482
National Assn of Marine Manufacturers (Ahern, Barbara J), 464
National Assn of Social Workers (NYC Chapter), 477

National Assn of Social Workers (NYS Chapter), 510
National Assn of Theatre Owners of NYS (NATO), 463
National Association of Black Accountants, NY Chapter, 110
National Association of Professional Employer Organizations, 468
National Association of Social Workers, NYS Chapter, 321
National Baseball Hall of Fame, 501
National Basketball Association, 345
National Center for Disability Services, 478
National Coffee Association, 87
National Confectioners Assn, 469
National Conference of Commissioners on Uniform State Laws, 487
National Council of Jewish Women, 242, 321
National Council to Prevent Delinquency Inc, 514
National Credit Union Administration, 93
   Albany Region, 93
National Economic Research Associates, 175, 358
National Education Loan Network (NELNET), 527
National Federation of Community Development Credit Unions, 96
National Federation of Independent Business, 110, 276, 331
National Football League, 345
National Foundation for Human Potential Inc, 493
National Foundation for Teaching Entreprenership, 478
National Fuel Gas, 175
National Fuel Gas Distribution, 175, 265
National Fuel Gas New York PAC, 554
National Good Government Fund, 554
National Grape Cooperative-Welch Foods Inc, 87
National Grid USA, 512
National Guard Association of the US (NGAUS), 367
National Heritage Academies, 491
National Hockey League, 345
National Labor Relations Board, 272
   Albany Resident Office, 272
   Region 2 - New York City Metro Area, 272
   Region 29 - Brooklyn Area, 272
   Region 3 - New York Except Metro Area, 272
National League for Nursing (NLN), 225
National Marfan Foundation, 225
National Marine Manufacturers Assn, 456
National Marine Manufacturers Association PAC (NAT PAC), 554
National Military Family Association (NMFA), 367

National Multiple Sclerosis Society, NY MS Coalition Action Netwo, 503
National Nutritional Foods Association East, 490
National Organization for Women (NYS), 513
National Organization for Women- NYS PAC, 554
National Organization for Women, NYS, 166, 242
National Paint & Coatings Assn, 461
National Potato Board, 86
National Promotions & Advertising, 499
National Restaurant Association, 499
National Safety Commission Inc, 504
National Safety Council, 488
National Traffic Safety Administration, 488
National Transportation Safety Board, 355
   Aviation Division, Northeast Regional Office, 355
   Office of Administrative Law Judges, 355
National Trust for Historic Preservation, 235
National Urban League Inc (The), 321
National Wildlife Federation, 190
National Women's Hall of Fame, 345
National Writers Union, 276
Nationwide Insurance & Nationwide Financial Services, 506
Nationwide NY Political Participation Fund, 554
NATPAC 2000, 551
Natural Resources, 391
   Energy & Mineral Resources, 391
   Fisheries, Wildlife and Oceans, 391
   Insular Affairs, 391
   National Parks, Forests and Public Lands, 391
   Subcommittees, 391
   Water & Power, 391
Natural Resources Defense Council, 190, 507
Natural Resources Defense Council Inc, 529
Nature Conservancy (The), 191
Naval Enlisted Reserve Association (NERA), 367
Naval Reserve Association (NRA), 367
Navy League of the US (NLUS), 367
Navy League of the US (NLUS), New York Council, 367
Nazareth College of Rochester, 628
NBC News (New York Bureau), 602
NBC Universal, 494, 506
NBT Bancorp Inc., 96
NBT PAC State Fund, 551
NEA of New York PAC, 551
Neighborhood Preservation Coalition of NYS Inc, 235, 456
Neighborhood Preservation PAF, 554
Neighborhood Retail Alliance, 499

846

Organization Index

Nelson A Rockefeller Inst of Government, NY Forum for Info, 175
Nelson A Rockefeller Inst of Govt, Federalism Research Grp, 321
Nelson A Rockefeller Inst of Govt, Higher Education Program, 154
Nelson A Rockefeller Inst of Govt, Urban & Metro Studies, 235
Nelson A Rockefeller Institute of Government, 209, 331
Nestle Waters North America Holdings Inc, 478
Netflix Inc, 463
Netsmart, 469
New 42nd Street Inc (The), 532
New Amsterdam History Center, 527
New Amsterdam History Cneter (The), 509
New Brookhaven Town House for Adults, 530
New City Chamber of Commerce, 580
New England Interstate Water Pollution Control Commission, 120, 182, 377
New England Steamship Agents Inc, 358
New England Stone LLC, 463
New Era Veterans, Inc, 367
New Hartford CSD, 658
New Hartford, Town of, 426
New Hyde Park-Garden City Park UFSD, 655
New Lebanon CSD, 643
New Paltz CSD, 673
New Paltz Regional Chamber of Commerce, 580
New Rochelle, 73
  Civil & Criminal Courts, 73
New Rochelle City SD, 677
New Rochelle, Chamber of Commerce, Inc, 580
New Rochelle, City of, 426
New School (The), 463
New School University, 459
New School University (The), 628
New School University, Department of Political Science, 166, 242
New School University, Department of Sociology, 345
New School University, Intl Center for Migration, Ethnicity & Citizenship, 242
New School University, Milano Graduate School of Mgmt & Urban Policy, 225, 235
New Suffolk Common SD, 670
New Visions for Public Schools, 508
New Windsor, Town of, 426
New York & Atlantic Railway (NYA), 358
New York 1 News (1), 608
New York Academy of Art Inc, 345, 628
New York Agriculture in the Classroom, 87
New York AIDS Coalition, 225
New York Ambulette Coalition PAC, 554

New York Anesthesiologists Political Action Committee, 554
New York Apple Association Inc, 87
New York Aquarium, 345
New York Artists Equity Association Inc, 345
New York Association for New Americans, Inc (NYANA), 320
New York Association of Convenience Stores, 110
New York Association of Homes & Services for the Aging, 225, 321
New York Association of Independent Lumber Dealers PAC (NAIL PAC), 554
New York Association of Mortgage Brokers Political Action Committee, 554
New York Association of Psychiatric Rehabilitation Services (NYAPRS), 285
New York Association of Temporary Services State PAC, 554
New York Bankers Association, 96
New York Bankers Political Action Committee, 554
New York Beef Industry Council Inc, 87
New York Biotechnology Association (The), 110
New York Botanical Garden (The), 499
New York Build PAC, 555
New York Building Congress, 110, 235
New York Building Congress PAF, 555
New York Burglar Fire Alarm Association, 505
New York Business Development Corporation, 110
New York Business Group on Health Inc, 225
New York Career Institute, 636
New York Cares Inc, 513
New York Center for Agricultural Medicine & Health, Bassett Healthcare, 87
New York Chamber of Commerce (Greater New York), 580
New York Check PAC, 555
New York Children's Advocates Making Progress, 555
New York Chiropractic College, 628
New York Chiropractic Political Action Fund, 475
New York Chiropratic Political Action Fund, 555
New York Choice PAC, 555
New York City, 426
  Aging, Dept for the, NYC, 426
  Art Commission, NYC, 427
  Buildings, Department of, NYC, 427
  Campaign Finance Board, NYC, 427
  City Council, NYC, 427
  City Planning, Department of, NYC, 427
  Citywide Administrative Services, Department of, NYC, 427
  Civil Service Commission, NYC, 427

  Collective Bargaining, Office of, NYC, 427
  Comptroller, NYC, 428
  Conflicts of Interest Board, NYC, 428
  Consumer Affairs, Department of, NYC, 428
  Correction, Board of, NYC, 428
  Correction, Department of, NYC, 428
  Cultural Affairs, Department of, NYC, 428
  Design & Construction, Dept of, NYC, 428
  Disabilities, Mayor's Office, for People with, 428
  Economic Development Corp, NYC, 428
  Education, Dept of, NYC, 428
  Educational Construction Fund, NYC, 429
  Elections, Board of, NYC, 429
  Environmental Protection, Department of, NYC, 429
  Equal Employment Practices Commission, NYC, 429
  Film, Theatre & Broadcasting, Mayor's Office of, NYC, 429
  Finance, Department of, NYC, 429
  Fire Department, NYC, 429
  Health & Hospitals Corporation, NYC, 430
  Health & Mental Hygiene, Dept of, NYC, 430
  Homeless Services, Department of, NYC, 430
  Housing Authority, NYC, 430
  Housing Preservation & Development, Dept of, NYC, 430
  Human Resources Administration, Dept of, NYC, 431
  Human Rights Commission on, NYC, 431
  Information Technology & Telecommunications, Dept of, NYC, 431
  Intergovernmental Affairs Ofc, NYC Mayor's, 431
  Investigation, Department of, NYC, 431
  Juvenile Justice, Department of, NYC, 431
  Labor Relations, Office of, NYC, 431
  Landmarks Preservation Commission, NYC, 432
  Law, Department of, NYC, 432
  Legislative Affairs Office, NYC Mayor's City, 432
  Legislative Affairs Office, NYC Mayor's State, 432
  Library, Brooklyn Public, 432
  Library, New York Public, 432
  Library, Queens Borough Public, 432
  Loft Board, NYC, 432
  Management & Budget, Office of, NYC, 432

Organization Index

Medical Examiner, Office of Chief, NYC, 433
Parks & Recreation, Department of, NYC, 433
Police Department, NYC, 433
Probation, Department of, NYC, 433
Public Advocate, Office of the, 433
Records & Information Services, Dept of, NYC, 433
Rent Guidelines Board, NYC, 434
Sanitation, Department of, NYC, 434
Small Business Services, Department of, NYC, 434
Sports Commission, NYC, 434
Standards & Appeals, Board of, NYC, 434
Tax Commission, NYC, 434
Taxi & Limousine Commission, NYC, 434
Transportation, Department of, NYC, 434
Veterans' Affairs, Mayor's Office of, NYC, 434
Voter Assistance Commission (VAC), NYC, 435
Water Finance Authority, Municipal, NYC, 435
Youth & Community Development, Department of, NYC, 435
New York City Boroughs, 435
　Bronx (Bronx County), 435
　Brooklyn (Kings County), 435
　Manhattan (New York County), 435
　Queens (Queens County), 435
　Staten Island (Richmond County), 435
New York City Central Labor Council Political Action Committee, 555
New York City College of Technology, 621
New York City Deputy Sheriff's Assn, PAC, 555
New York City Housing Development Corporation, 120, 230, 377
New York City Residential Mortgage Insurance Corporation, 120, 230
New York City Off-Track Betting Corporation, 120, 336, 377
New York City Opera, 345
New York City School Construction Authority, 120, 149, 378
New York City, Partnership for, 580
New York City, Partnership for, PAC, 555
New York Civil Liberties Union, 242
New York Civil Rights Coalition, 243
New York College of Health Professions, 628
New York College of Podiatric Medicine, 628
New York College of Traditional Chinese Medicine, 628
New York Committee for Occupational Safety & Health, 276
New York Community Bank, 96, 235, 305

New York Community College Trustees (NYCCT), 154
New York Community Trust (The), 321
New York Convention Center Operating Corporation, 120, 336, 378
New York Counties Registered Nurses Association, 225
New York County, 65
　COUNTY & FAMILY COURTS: See New York City Courts, 65
　SUPREME COURT, Civil Term, 65
　SUPREME COURT, Criminal Term, 65
　Surrogate's Court, 65
New York County (NYC Borough of Manhattan), 404
New York Daily News, 596
New York Emergency Medicine PAC, 555
New York Farm Bureau, 87
New York Field Corn Growers Association, 87
New York Financial Services PAC, 555
New York First, 508
New York Forest Owners Association Inc, 191
New York Foundation for the Arts, 345
New York Giants, 345
New York Good Hearing Political Education Committee, 555
New York Hall of Science, 345
New York Health Care Alliance, 225
New York Health Plan Association, 225
New York Historical Society, 519
New York Holstein Association, 87
New York Hotel & Motel Trades Council Committee on Political Education, 555
New York Hygiene PAC, 555
New York Immigration Coalition (The), 243
New York Independent System Operator - Not For Profit, 175
New York Institute of Technology, 628
New York Insurance Assn Inc Political Action Committee, 555
New York Insurance Association Inc, 251
New York Islanders, 345
New York Jets, 345
New York Landmarks Conservancy, 235, 305
New York Law Journal, 596
New York Law School, 628
New York Lawyers for the Public Interest, 235, 243
New York League of Conservation Voters Action Fund, 555
New York Library Association (The), 154
New York Life Insurance Company, 491
New York Life-New York State PAC, 555
New York Long-Term Care Brokers Ltd, 251
New York Magazine (New York Metro LLC), 602

New York Marine Trades Association, 345
New York Medical College, 225, 628
New York Medical College, Department of Community & Preventive Medicine, 225
New York Medical College, Department of Medicine, 225
New York Medical College, School of Public Health, 225
New York Medical Equipment Providers PAC, 555
New York Medical Staff Leadership Council, 506
New York Mercantile Exchange Inc, 111
New York Mercantiles Exchange Political Action Committee, Inc, 555
New York Metropolitan Transportation Council, 121, 352, 378
New York Mets, 345
New York Municipal Insurance Reciprocal (NYMIR), 251, 294
New York Newspaper Publishers Association, 175
New York Observer (The), 597
New York Pan Hel Political Action Committee, 555
New York Pepsi Cola PAC, 555
New York Philharmonic, 487
New York Pork Producers Coop, 87
New York Post, 596
New York Power Authority, 121, 170, 378
New York Presbyterian Hospital, 226
New York Presbyterian Hospital, Department of Psychiatry, 285
New York Press Photographers Association, 175
New York Professional Engineers, 555
New York Professional Nurses Union Political Action Fund, 556
New York Propane Gas Assn, 465
New York Propane PAC, 556
New York Public Interest Research Group, 191, 209
New York Public Interest Research Group Straphangers Campaign, 358
New York Public Welfare Association, 321
New York Racing Assn Inc (The), 479
New York Racing Association, 346
New York Republican State Committee, 166
New York Respiratory Care PAC, 556
New York Retailers for Effective Government, 556
New York Roadway Improvement Coalition (NYRIC), 358
New York School Bus Operators for Effective Gov't, 556
New York School of Interior Design, 629
New York Schools Insurance Reciprocal (NYSIR), 251

848

Organization Index

New York Seed Improvement Project, Cornell University, Plant Breeding Department, 88
New York Shipping Association Inc, 358
New York Society for the Deaf, 321
New York State Air Force Association, 368
New York State Assessors' Association, 305, 331
New York State Assn of Fire Districts, 121, 291, 378
New York State Association of Agricultural Fairs Inc, 88
New York State Association of Ambulatory Surgery Centers, 226
New York State Association of Family Services Agencies Inc, 321
New York State Association of Independent Schools, 154
New York State Association of PBAs, 556
New York State Athletic Commission, 121, 200, 336, 378
New York State Auto Dealers Association, 111, 359
New York State Beer Wholesalers Assn PAC, 556
New York State Board of Law Examiners, 121, 258, 378
New York State BPW/PAC (NYSBPW/PAC), 556
New York State Bridge Authority, 121, 352, 378
New York State Car Wash PAC, 556
New York State Catholic Conference, 154, 322
New York State Citizens' Coalition for Children Inc, 322
New York State Clinical Laboratory Assn PAC, 556
New York State Coalition of PHSPS PAC Inc, 556
New York State Commission of Correction, 122, 137, 378
New York State Commission on Judicial Nomination, 122, 258, 378
New York State Commission on the Restoration of the Capitol, 122, 201, 336, 378
New York State Community Action Association, 235, 322
New York State Congress of Parents & Teachers Inc, 154
New York State Conservation Council, 191
New York State Conservative Party, 447
   Albany, 447
   Allegany, 447
   Bronx, 447
   Broome, 447
   Cattaraugus, 447
   Cayuga, 447
   Chautauqua, 447
   Chemung, 447
   Clinton, 447
   Columbia, 447
   Cortland, 447
   County Chairs, 447
   Delaware, 447
   Dutchess, 447
   Erie, 447
   Essex, 447
   Fulton, 447
   Genesee, 447
   Greene, 447
   Herkimer, 448
   Jefferson, 448
   Kings, 448
   Lewis, 448
   Livingston, 448
   Madison, 448
   Monroe, 448
   Montgomery, 448
   Nassau, 448
   New York, 448
   Niagara, 448
   Oneida, 448
   Onondaga, 448
   Ontario, 448
   Orange, 448
   Orleans, 448
   Oswego, 448
   Otsego, 448
   Putnam, 448
   Queens, 448
   Richmond, 448
   Rockland, 448
   Saratoga, 448
   Schenectady, 448
   Schoharie, 448
   Schuyler, 448
   Seneca, 448
   St Lawrence, 448
   Statewide Party Officials, 447
   Steuben, 448
   Suffolk, 448
   Sullivan, 448
   Tompkins, 448
   Ulster, 448
   Warren, 448
   Washington, 448
   Wayne, 448
   Westchester, 448
   Wyoming, 448
   Yates, 449
New York State Council of Churches, 243
New York State Council of School Superintendents, 154
New York State Court of Claims, 265, 294
New York State Credit Union League Inc, 96
New York State Dairy Foods Inc, 88
New York State Dairy Foods PAC, 556
New York State Democratic Committee, 166, 449
   Albany, 449
   Allegany, 449
   Bronx, 449
   Broome, 449
   Cattaraugus, 449
   Cayuga, 449
   Chautauqua, 449
   Chemung, 449
   Chenango, 449
   Clinton, 449
   Columbia, 449
   Cortland, 449
   County Chairs, 449
   Delaware, 449
   Dutchess, 449
   Erie, 449
   Essex, 449
   Franklin, 449
   Fulton, 449
   Genesee, 450
   Greene, 450
   Hamilton, 450
   Herkimer, 450
   Jefferson, 450
   Kings, 450
   Lewis, 450
   Livingston, 450
   Madison, 450
   Monroe, 450
   Montgomery, 450
   Nassau, 450
   New York, 450
   Niagara, 450
   Oneida, 450
   Onondaga, 450
   Ontario, 450
   Orange, 450
   Orleans, 450
   Oswego, 450
   Otsego, 450
   Putnam, 450
   Queens, 450
   Rensselaer, 450
   Richmond, 450
   Rockland, 450
   Saratoga, 450
   Schenectady, 450
   Schoharie, 450
   Schuyler, 450
   Seneca, 450
   St Lawrence, 450
   Statewide Party Officials, 449
   Steuben, 450
   Suffolk, 450
   Sullivan, 450
   Tioga, 450
   Tompkins, 450
   Ulster, 450
   Warren, 451
   Washington, 451
   Wayne, 451

Organization Index

Westchester, 451
Wyoming, 451
Yates, 451
New York State Dietetic Association, 556
New York State Directory, 209
New York State Disaster Preparedness Commission, 122, 201, 291, 378
New York State Dormitory Authority, 122, 149, 201, 216, 378
New York State Electric & Gas Corporation (NYSEG), 175
New York State Energy Research & Development Authority, 122, 170, 182, 378
New York State Environmental Facilities Corp, 123, 182, 378
New York State Ethics Commission, 123, 201, 378
New York State Federation of School Administrators Political Action Committee, 556
New York State Financial Control Board, 123, 201, 327, 378
New York State Flower Industries Inc, 85
New York State Government Finance Officers Association Inc, 294, 331
New York State Health Facilities Association Inc, 226
New York State Higher Education Services Corp (NYSHESC), 123, 149, 378
New York State Hospitality & Tourism Association, 346
New York State Housing Finance Agency (HFA), 91, 123, 230, 379
　Affordable Housing Corporation, 91, 124, 231
New York State Independence Party, 451
　Chautauqua, 451
　County Chairs, 451
　Manhattan, 451
　Monroe, 451
　Putnam, 451
　Richmond, 451
　Statewide Party Officials, 451
　Suffolk, 451
New York State Judicial Conduct Commission, 124, 258, 379
New York State Laborers' PAC, 556
New York State Law Enforcement Council, 141, 266, 299
New York State Law Reporting Bureau, 124, 201, 258, 379
New York State Law Revision Commission, 124, 258, 379
New York State Liquor Authority, 102, 124, 379
New York State Maple Producers Association Inc, 88
New York State Mortgage Loan Enforcement & Administration Corporation, 91, 124, 231, 379

New York State Motor Truck Association, 359
New York State Nurses Assn PAC, 556
New York State Nurses Association, 226, 276, 511
New York State Olympic Regional Development Authority, 124, 336, 379
New York State Ophthalmological Society, 226
New York State Osteopathic Medical Society, 226
New York State Petroleum Council, 175
New York State Podiatric Medical Association, 226
New York State Political Action Committee, Region 9, UAW, 556
New York State Project Finance Agency, 91, 231, 327
New York State Public Employees Federation (PEF), 299
New York State Public Employees' Federation PAC, 556
New York State Radiological Society Inc, 226
New York State Radiologists PAC, 556
New York State Rehabilitation Association, 285, 322
New York State Republican Party, 452
　Albany, 452
　Allegany, 452
　Bronx, 452
　Broome, 452
　Cattaraugus, 452
　Cayuga, 452
　Chautauqua, 452
　Chemung, 452
　Chenango, 452
　Clinton, 452
　Columbia, 452
　Cortland, 452
　County Officials, 452
　Delaware, 452
　Dutchess, 452
　Erie, 452
　Essex, 452
　Franklin, 452
　Fulton, 452
　Genesee, 452
　Greene, 452
　Hamilton, 452
　Herkimer, 452
　Jefferson, 452
　Kings, 452
　Lewis, 452
　Livingston, 453
　Madison, 453
　Monroe, 453
　Montgomery, 453
　Nassau, 453
　New York, 453
　Niagara, 453

　Oneida, 453
　Onondaga, 453
　Ontario, 453
　Orange, 453
　Orleans, 453
　Oswego, 453
　Otsego, 453
　Putnam, 453
　Queens, 453
　Rensselear, 453
　Richmond, 453
　Rockland, 453
　Saratoga, 453
　Schenectady, 453
　Schoharie, 453
　Schuyler, 453
　Seneca, 453
　St Lawrence, 453
　Statewide Party Officials, 452
　Steuben, 453
　Suffolk, 453
　Sullivan, 453
　Tioga, 453
　Tompkins, 453
　Ulster, 453
　Warren, 453
　Washington, 453
　Wayne, 453
　Westchester, 453
　Wyoming, 453
　Yates, 453
New York State Restaurant Association, 111, 346
New York State Restaurant Industry PAC, 556
New York State Rural Advocates, 235
New York State Rural Development Council, 235
New York State Rural Housing Coalition Inc, 235
New York State School Boards Association, 154
New York State School Music Association (NYSSMA), 154, 346
New York State Scrap Recyclers PAC, 557
New York State Sheriffs' Good Government Fund, 557
New York State Snowmobile Association, 346
New York State Society CPA PAC Inc, 557
New York State Society of Certified Public Accountants, 331
New York State Society of Enrolled Agents, 331
New York State Society of Municipal Finance Officers, 294, 331
New York State Society of Physician Assistants PAC, 557
New York State Supreme Court Officers Association, 266, 300

850

Organization Index

New York State Teachers' Retirement System, 125, 149, 297, 379
New York State Telecommunications Association Inc, 175
New York State Temporary Commission of Investigation, 125, 202, 297, 379
New York State Temporary Commission on Lobbying, 125, 163, 202, 379
New York State Theatre Education Association, 346
New York State Thoroughbred Breeding & Development Fund Corporation, 125, 337, 379
New York State Thruway Authority, 125, 337, 353, 379
  New York State Canal Corporation, 125, 337, 353
New York State Transit & Tour Operators' PAC, 557
New York State Transportation Engineering Alliance (NYSTEA), 359
New York State Travel & Vacation Association, 346
New York State Trial Lawyers, 266
New York State Tug Hill Commission, 125, 182, 379
New York State United Teachers/AFT, AFL-CIO, 300
New York State United Teachers/AFT, NEA, AFL-CIO, 154
New York State Veterinary Medical Society, 88
New York State Woodsmen's Field Days Inc, 191
New York Stock Exchange, 96
New York Theological Seminary, 629
New York Thoroughbred Breeders Inc, 88
New York Thoroughbred Horsemen's Assn, Inc Political Action Committee, 557
New York Thoroughbred Racing Industry PAC, 557
New York Times (The), 597
New York Truck PAC, 557
New York University, 154, 629
New York University School of Law, 266
New York University, Departmentt of Politics, 166
New York University, Graduate School of Journalism, 166, 276
New York University, Graduate School of Public Service, 226
New York University, Law School, 266
New York University, Robert F Wagner Graduate School of Public Service, 226
New York University, Tisch School of the Arts, 346
New York University, Wagner Graduate School, 235, 294
New York University-College of Nursing, 530
New York Urban League, 322

New York Water Environment Association Inc (NYWEA), 191
New York Wine & Grape Foundation, 88, 346
New York Wired, 166
New York Yankees, 346
New York, Susquehanna & Western Railway, 359
New York's Tomorrow, 557
New Yorker, 266
New Yorkers Against Gun Violence PAC, 557
New Yorkers Against the Death Penalty, 459, 503, 511
New Yorkers for Accessible Health Coverage, 503
New Yorkers for Better Libraries PAC, 557
New Yorkers for Constitutional Freedom PAC, 557
New Yorkers for Constitutional Freedoms, 509
New Yorkers for Fairness, 557
New Yorkers for Fiscal Fairness, 478
New Yorkers for Justice, 483
New Yorkers for Parks, 479
New Yorkers for Real Recycling Reform (Food Industry Alliance of NYS Inc), 484
New Yorkers for Responsible Development, 459
New Yorktown Chamber of Commerce (The), 580
Newark Chamber of Commerce, 580
Newark CSD, 675
Newark Valley CSD, 672
Newburgh, 73
  Civil & Criminal Courts, 73
Newburgh Enlarged City SD, 661
Newburgh, City of, 436
Newburgh, Town of, 436
Newcomb CSD, 647
Newfane CSD, 657
Newfield CSD, 672
Newman-Limata, Nancy, 511
Newsday, 595
Newsday Inc, 595
Newspaper Publishers Assn (NY), 493, 511
Newsstand Operators Assn (NYC), 464
Newsweek Magazine (MSNBC, Microsoft Corp), 602
Next Wave Inc, 226
Nextel Operations Inc, 514
Nfrastructure, 469
Niagara County, 65, 405
  County, Family & Surrogate's Courts, 65
  Supreme & Family Courts, 65
Niagara County Community College, 616
Niagara County Ind Dev Agency, 581
Niagara Falls, 73
  Civil & Criminal Courts, 73
Niagara Falls Bridge Commission, 126, 353, 379

Niagara Falls City SD, 657
Niagara Falls Firefighters PAC, 557
Niagara Falls Memorial Medical Arts Center, 507
Niagara Falls, City of, 436
Niagara Frontier Transportation Authority, 126, 353, 379
Niagara Gazette, 597
Niagara Mohawk - A National Grid Company, 175
Niagara Mohawk Holdings & Power Co (dba National Grid), 477
Niagara Mohawk Holdings, Inc Corp Voluntary State PAC, 557
Niagara Mohawk Holdings, Inc., & NMPC DBA National Grid, 530
Niagara Tourism & Convention Corp, 480
Niagara University, 155, 629
Niagara USA Chamber of Commerce, 581
Niagara's Future Coalition, 557
Niagara-Wheatfield CSD, 657
NIC-PAC, 551
Nielsen Media Research, 466
Nightlife Association (NY), 464
Ninth Decade Fund, 557
Ninth K Realty LLC, 467
Niskayuna CSD, 665
Niskayuna, Town of, 436
Nisource Inc PAC-NY, 557
Nixon Peabody, LLP, 511
NJ Transit, 466
NLOA-PAC, 551
Noble Communications/CGBP, 494
Noble Environmental Power Inc, 487
NOCO Energy Co, 529
NOCO Energy Corp, 480
NOFA-NY Certified Organic LLC, 86
Nolan & Heller, LLP, 511
Nonprofit Coordinating Committee of New York, 322
Nontraditional Employment for Women, 494
Norat, Cecilia E, 511
Norddeutsche Landesbank Girozentrale, 96
Norfolk Southern Corporation, 475
Norman A Olch, Esq, 266
Norris, Kelly K, 512
North American Insulation Manufacturers Assn, 469
North Babylon UFSD, 670
North Bellmore UFSD, 655
North Bronx Career Counseling & Outreach Center, 618
North Castle Democratic Club, 557
North Collins CSD, 646
North Colonie CSD, 638
North Country Community College, 617
North Country Healthcare Providers Eductl & Rsch Fund Inc (North Country Healthcare Providers, LLC), 530
North Country Savings Bank, 96

Organization Index

North Country Vietnam Veterans Association, Post 1, 368
North County Alliance for Children with Special Needs, 487
North Fork Bank, 95, 330
North Fork Chamber of Commerce, 581
North Greenbush Common SD (Williams), 663
North Greenbush IDA, 581
North Hempstead Century Club, 557
North Hempstead, Town of, 436
North Merrick UFSD, 655
North Rockland CSD, 664
North Rose-Wolcott CSD, 675
North Salem CSD, 677
North Shore Animal League America, 322
North Shore CSD, 655
North Shore-Long Island Jewish Health System, 88, 226
North Shore-Long Island Jewish Health System Inc, 515, 518
North Syracuse CSD, 659
North Tonawanda, 73
  Civil & Criminal Courts, 73
North Tonawanda City SD, 657
North Tonawanda, City of, 437
North Warren Chamber of Commerce, 581
North Warren CSD, 673
North Windmere Republican Club, 557
Northeast Biofuels LP, 488
Northeast Equipment Dealers Association Inc, 111
Northeast Gas Association, 175
Northeast Health, 512, 529
Northeast Health & Affiliates, 480
Northeast Health Inc, 512
Northeast Organic Farming Association of New York, 88
Northeast Spa and Pool Association, 491
Northeastern Clinton CSD, 643
Northeastern Forest Fire Protection Commission, 126, 183, 379
Northeastern Loggers' Association, 191
Northeastern PAC, 558
Northeastern Queens Nature & Historical Preserve Commission, 126, 183, 337, 380
Northeastern Retail Lumber Assn, 463, 527
Northeastern Seminary, 629
Northeastern Subcontractors Assn, PAC, 558
Northern Adirondack CSD, 643
Northern Metropolitan Hospital Assn, 512, 530
Northern Westchester Hospital, 530
Northport-East Northport UFSD, 670
Northrop Grumman Corporation, 465, 480
Northside Center for Child Development, 494
Northstar Development Corp, 494
Northville CSD, 648
Norvest Financial Services Inc, 501

Norwegian Cruise Line, 530
Norwich, 73
  Civil & Criminal Courts, 73
Norwich City SD, 642
Norwood-Norfolk CSD, 667
Nostradamus Advertising, 166
Novell, 469
NRA Political Victory Fund, 551
NRG Energy Inc, 475
NRG New York PAC, 551
Nuclear Regulatory Commission, 171
  REGION I (includes New York State), 171
Nucor Corporation, PAC NY, 558
Nurse Anesthesia - CRNA - PAC Fund, 558
Nurse Practitioner Assn of NYS (The), 512
Nurse Practitioners Assn NYS (The), 226
Nurse Practitioners Assn of NYS (The), 485, 501
Nurse Practitioners of NYS PAC, 558
Nurses Assn (NYS), 503
Nurses Association (NYS), 511
Nutrition Consortium of NYS Inc, 464, 507
NVR Inc, 501
NY Airport Service, 358
NY Association of Local Government Records Officers, 294
NY Association of Training & Employment Professionals (NYATEP), 276
NY Capitolwire (Associated Press), 602
NY Chiropractic PAC, 551
NY Coalition of 100 Black Women - Not For Profit, 208
NY Commercial Association of Realtors, 305
NY Council on Problem Gambling, 285
NY Counseling Association Inc, 285, 320
NY County Lawyers' Association, 265
NY EDPAC, 551
NY Farms!, 86
NY Film Academy, 344
NY Film PAC, 551
NY Foundation for Senior Citizens Inc, 320
NY Health Information Management Association Inc, 224
NY Housing Association Inc, 234
NY Independent Bankers' PAC, 551
NY League of Conservation Voters/NY Conservation Education Fund, 166, 190
NY Life Insurance Co, 250
NY Mental Health Counselors Association, 469
NY Mills UFSD, 658
NY Oil Heating Association, 174
NY Physical Therapy Association, 224
NY Podiatry PAC, 552
NY Press Association, 174
NY Propane Gas Association, 174
NY Property Insurance Underwriting Association, 250
NY Region 9A UAW PAC Committee, 552

NY Society of Association Executives Inc (NYSAE), 110
NY State Association of Town Superintendents of Highways Inc, 294, 358
NY State Historical Association/Fenimore Art Museum, 344
NY State Society of Physician Assistants, 224
NY StateWatch Inc, 208
NY Waterway, 519
Nyack Chamber of Commerce, 581
Nyack College, 629
Nyack UFSD, 664
NYAHSA PAC, 552
NYC & Company, 506, 514
NYC & Company, Inc, 510
NYC 2012, 506
NYC Americans for Democratic Action NYC ADA PAC, 552
NYC Arts Coalition, 344
NYC Bar Association, 462
NYC Board of Education Employees, Local 372/AFSCME, AFL-CIO, 153, 299
NYC Campaign Finance Board, 166
NYC Chancellor's Office, 656
NYC Citywide Alternative HS District & Programs, 657
NYC Citywide Special Ed District 75, 657
NYC Coalition Against Hunger, 320
NYC Columbus Circle PAC, 552
NYC District Council of Carpenters' PAC, 552
NYC Neighborhood Open Space Coalition, 190
NYC Region 1, 657
NYC Region 10, 657
NYC Region 2, 657
NYC Region 3, 657
NYC Region 4, 657
NYC Region 5, 657
NYC Region 6, 657
NYC Region 7, 657
NYC Region 8, 657
NYC Region 9, 657
NYFF, 551
NYMAGIC Inc, 250
NYMTA Boat PAC, 552
NYNHP-PAC, 552
NYP Holdings Inc, 596
NYPD Lieutenants Benevolent Association PAC, 552
NYPD Superior Officers Assn, Retired PAC, 552
NYPT PAC, 551
NYS Academy of Family Physicians, 224
NYS AFL-CIO COPE, 552
NYS Agricultural Society, 86
NYS Alliance for Arts Education, 153, 344
NYS Arborists, 86
NYS Architects PAC, 552

Organization Index

NYS Assn of Tobacco & Candy Distributors Inc, 552
NYS Association For Food Protection, 86
NYS Association for Health, Physical Education, Recreation & Dance, 153
NYS Association for the Education of Young Children, 153
NYS Association of Area Agencies on Aging, 321
NYS Association of Chiefs of Police Inc, 141, 299
NYS Association of Community & Residential Agencies, 285
NYS Association of Counties, 209, 294
NYS Association of County Health Officials, 224
NYS Association of Criminal Defense Lawyers, 265
NYS Association of Electrical Contractors, 110
NYS Association of Fire Chiefs, 299
NYS Association of Health Care Providers, 224
NYS Association of Library Boards, 153
NYS Association of Nurse Anesthetists (NYSANA), 224
NYS Association of Realtors, 305
NYS Association of School Business Officials, 153
NYS Association of Service Stations & Repair Shops, 358, 552
NYS Association of Solid Waste Management, 190
NYS Association of Veterinary Technicians Inc, 86
NYS Automatic Vending Association PAC, 552
NYS Bar Assn, Alternative Dispute Resolution Cmte, 263
NYS Bar Assn, Antitrust Law Section, 109
NYS Bar Assn, Attorneys in Public Service Cmte, 299
NYS Bar Assn, Business Law Section, 109
NYS Bar Assn, Children & the Law Committee, 264, 320
NYS Bar Assn, Civil Practice Law & Rules Committee, 265
NYS Bar Assn, Civil Rights/Spec Cmte on Collateral Consequence of Criminal Proceedings, 209
NYS Bar Assn, Cmte on Diversity & Leadership Development, 265
NYS Bar Assn, Cmte on the Jury System, 263
NYS Bar Assn, Commercial & Federal Litigation Section, 110, 265
NYS Bar Assn, Court Operations Cmte, 263
NYS Bar Assn, Court Structure & Judicial Selection Cmte, 208, 264
NYS Bar Assn, Courts of Appellate Jurisdiction Cmte, 266

NYS Bar Assn, Criminal Justice Section, 141, 265
NYS Bar Assn, Cyberspace Law Cmte, 262
NYS Bar Assn, Diversity & Leadership Development Cmte, 267
NYS Bar Assn, Elder Law Section, 264
NYS Bar Assn, Electronic Communications Task Force, 174
NYS Bar Assn, Entertainment, Arts & Sports Law Section, 342
NYS Bar Assn, Environmental Law Section, 189
NYS Bar Assn, Family Law Section, 267
NYS Bar Assn, Federal Constitution & Legislation Cmte, 208, 263
NYS Bar Assn, Fiduciary Appointments Cmte, 266
NYS Bar Assn, Food, Drug & Cosmetic Law Section, 88, 226
NYS Bar Assn, Gender Equity Task Force Cmte, 241, 243
NYS Bar Assn, General Practice Section, 264
NYS Bar Assn, Health Law Section, 227, 267
NYS Bar Assn, Intellectual Property Law Section, 109, 264
NYS Bar Assn, International Law & Practice Section, 261
NYS Bar Assn, Issues Affecting People with Disabilities Cmte, 242
NYS Bar Assn, Issues Affecting Same Sex Couples, 243
NYS Bar Assn, Judicial Campaign Conduct Cmte, 266
NYS Bar Assn, Judicial Campaign Monitoring Cmte, 266
NYS Bar Assn, Judicial Independence Cmte, 261
NYS Bar Assn, Judicial Section, 263
NYS Bar Assn, Labor & Employment Law Section, 263, 276
NYS Bar Assn, Law Youth & Citizenship Committee, 209
NYS Bar Assn, Lawyer Referral Service Cmte, 262
NYS Bar Assn, Legal Aid Cmte/Funding for Civil Legal Svcs Cmte, 264
NYS Bar Assn, Legislative Policy Cmte, 208
NYS Bar Assn, Mass Disaster Response Committee, 209
NYS Bar Assn, Media Law Committee, 174, 266
NYS Bar Assn, Minorities in the Profession Cmte, 243
NYS Bar Assn, Multi-jurisdictional Practice Cmte, 111, 266
NYS Bar Assn, Municipal Law Section, 265, 294

NYS Bar Assn, Pension Simplification Cmte, 330
NYS Bar Assn, President's Cmte on Access to Justice, 262
NYS Bar Assn, Procedures for Judicial Discipline Cmte, 264
NYS Bar Assn, Public Relations Cmte, 107
NYS Bar Assn, Public Trust & Confidence in the Legal System, 140, 263
NYS Bar Assn, Public Utility Law Committee, 175, 265
NYS Bar Assn, Real Property Law Section, 304
NYS Bar Assn, Resolutions Committee, 265
NYS Bar Assn, Review Attorney Fee Regulation Cmte, 264
NYS Bar Assn, Review Judicial Nominations Cmte, 263
NYS Bar Assn, Review the Code of Judicial Conduct Cmte, 262
NYS Bar Assn, Task Force to Review Terrorism Legislation Cmte, 207
NYS Bar Assn, Tax Section, 330
NYS Bar Assn, Tort System Cmte, 262, 264
NYS Bar Assn, Torts, Insurance & Compensation Law Section, 249, 263
NYS Bar Assn, Trial Lawyers Section, 263
NYS Bar Assn, Trusts & Estates Law Section, 263, 330
NYS Bar Assn, Unlawful Practice of Law Cmte, 264
NYS Bar Association, 88
NYS Berry Growers Association, 86
NYS Bowling Proprietors Assn PAC, 552
NYS Broadcasters Association, 174, 552
NYS Builders Association Inc, 110
NYS Building & Construction Trades Council, 110, 276
NYS Cemeteries PAC, 552
NYS Chapter AGC PAC, 552
NYS Cheese Manufacturers Association, Department of Food Science, 86
NYS Child Care Coordinating Council, 321
NYS Clinical Laboratory Association Inc, 110
NYS Coalition of 853 Schools Inc, 529
NYS College of Ceramics at Alfred University, 612
NYS Commission on Quality of Care & Advocacy for Persons with Disabilities, 13, 119, 238, 282, 373, 377
Administrative Services Bureau, 119, 282
Advisory Council, 119, 282
Advocacy Services Bureau, 119, 282
Counsel, Policy Analysis, Fiscal Investigations, 119
Counsel/Policy Analysis/Fiscal Investigations, 282
Medical Review Board, 119, 282
Quality Assurance, 119, 282

Organization Index

Surrogate Decision-Making Committees Program, 119, 282
NYS Committee for the Advancement of Mental Health Therapy, 552
NYS Conference of Local Mental Hygiene Directors, 285
NYS Conference of Mayors & Municipal Officials, 294, 331
NYS Conference of the IUOE Pol Action Acct, 553
NYS Corps Collaboration, 321
NYS Correctional Officers & Police Benevolent Association Inc, 141, 299
NYS Council for Community Behavioral Healthcare, 285
NYS Council of Health-System Pharmacists, 503
NYS Council of Physiotherapists PAC, 553
NYS Council of Probation Administrators, 141, 265
NYS County Hwy Super Assn / NY Aviation Mgt Assn / NY Public Transit Assn, 358
NYS Court Clerks Association, 265, 299
NYS Credit Union League, 96
NYS Defenders Association, 141, 265
NYS Dental Association, 224
NYS Deputies Association Inc, 141, 299
NYS Dispute Resolution Association, 265
NYS Economic Development Council, 110
NYS Education Department, 242
NYS Federation of Physicians & Dentists, 224
NYS Food Industry PAC, 553
NYS Foundation for Science, Technology & Innovation, 13, 100, 147, 373
   Alliance for Manufacturing & Technology, 148
   Center for Advanced Ceramic Technology at Alfred University, 100, 147
   Center for Advanced Materials Processing at Clarkson Univ, 100, 147
   Center for Advanced Tech in Biomedical & Bioengineering, 100, 147
   Center for Advanced Tech in Electronic Imaging Systems, 100
   Center for Advanced Tech-Medical Biotechnology, 148
   Center for Advanced Technology in Electronic Imaging Systems, 148
   Center for Advanced Technology in Info Mgmt, 100
   Center for Advanced Technology in Information Management, 148
   Center for Advanced Technology in Life Science Enterprise, 100, 148
   Center for Advanced Technology in Photonic Applications, 100, 148
   Center for Automation Tech at Rensselaer Polytechnic Inst, 148
   Center for Automation Technologies at Rensselaer, 100
   Center for Computer Applications & Software Engineering, 148
   Center for Economic Growth, 148
   Center in Nanomaterials and Nanoelectronics, 148
   Centers for Advanced Technology, 100, 147
   Central New York Technology Development Organization, 148
   Council for Interntl Trade, Tech, Education & Communication, 148
   Ctr for Advanced Tech in Telecommunications at Polytech Univ, 100, 148
   Future Energy Systems CAT at Rensselaer Polytechnic Inst, 148
   High Technology of Rochester, 148
   Hudson Valley Technology Development Center, 148
   Industrial & Technology Assistance Corp, 148
   INSYTE Consulting (Western NY Technology Development Ctr), 148
   Integrated Electronics Engineering Center, 148
   Long Island Forum for Technology, 148
   Mohawk Valley Applied Technology Corp, 148
   Regional Technology Development Centers, 148
   Sensor CAT-Diagnostic Tools & Sensor Systems, 100, 147
NYS Funeral Directors Assn Inc, 529
NYS Funeral Directors Association PAC, 553
NYS Grange, 86
NYS Grievance Committee, 209
NYS Head Start Association, 153
NYS Health Department, 299
NYS Horticultural Society, 86
NYS Hospitality & Tourism Assn PAC, 553
NYS Industries for the Disabled (NYSID) Inc, 276, 321
NYS Land Title Association, 305
NYS Law Enforcement Officers Union, Council 82, AFSCME, AFL-CIO, 141, 299
NYS Magistrates Association, 265, 294
NYS Nursery/Landscape Association, 87
NYS Occupational Therapy PAC, 553
NYS Optometric Assn PAC, 553
NYS Optometric Association Inc, 224
NYS Outdoor Guides Association, 344
NYS Parole Officers Association, 299
NYS Passenger Vessel Association, 344
NYS Pest Management Association PAC, 553
NYS Pipe Trades Political Action Committee, 553
NYS Plumbing, Heating & Cooling Contractors PAC, 553
NYS Psychiatric PAC Inc, 553
NYS Psychological Association, 285
NYS Public Health Association, 224
NYS Public High School Athletic Association, 154
NYS Reading Association, 154
NYS Right to Life Committee, 166
NYS Right to Life PAC, 553
NYS Sheriffs' Association, 141, 299
NYS Snowmobile PAC, 553
NYS Society for Clinical Social Workers PAC, 553
NYS Society of Certified Public Accountants, 110
NYS Society of Real Estate Appraisers, 305
NYS Speech-Language-Hearing Assn Inc - COMPAC, 553
NYS Supreme Court, 209, 265
NYS Technology Enterprise Corporation (NYSTEC), 174
NYS Telecommunications PAC, 553
NYS Tenants & Neighbors Coalition, 235
NYS Theatre Institute, 154, 344
NYS Trade Adjustment Assistance Center, 110
NYS Troopers PAC, 553
NYS Turfgrass Association, 87, 344
NYS Vegetable Growers Association Inc, 87
NYS Veterinary PEC, 553
NYS Water Resources Institute of Cornell University, 190
NYS Weights & Measures Association, 87
NYSAIFA-PAC, 553
NYSALM State PAC, 553
NYSARC Inc, 285
NYSCHP PAC, 554
NYSCON Collaborative Care LLC, 501
NYSCOP Inc, 476
NYSCOPBA PAC, 554
NYSE State PAC, 554
NYSFRW Women Power PAC, 554
NYSIA NY PAC, 554
NYU Child Study Center, 513
NYU Hospitals Ctr, 527
NYU School of Medicine, 499, 506
NYU School of Medicine & NYU Hospitals, 517
O'Connell, Peter B, 512
O'Connor, John, 512
O'Mara, John F, 512
Oakfield-Alabama CSD, 648
Oasis Children's Service LLC, 528
Observer, 593
Observer-Dispatch, 600
OC Inc of NY, 463
Occupational Health Clinic Network (NYS), 503
Occupational Therapy Assn (NYS), 515

Organization Index

Oceanside Chamber of Commerce, 581
Oceanside UFSD, 655
Odessa-Montour CSD, 665
Office of David J Silverman, 331
Office of the Attorney General, 243
Ogden Newspapers Inc, 593
Ogdensburg, 73
   Civil & Criminal Courts, 73
Ogdensburg Bridge & Port Authority, 126, 353, 380
Ogdensburg Chamber of Commerce (Greater Ogdensburg), 581
Ogdensburg City SD, 667
Ogdensburg Journal, 597
Ohio River Valley Water Sanitation Commission, 126, 183, 380
Ohrenstein & Brown, LLP, 512
Oil Heat Institute of Long Island, 175
Oil Heat Institute PAC, 558
Oil Heating Assn (NY), 474
Oil Heating Assoc, 504
Oilheat PAC, Inc, 558
OILHEATPAC, 558
Olean, 74
   Civil & Criminal Courts, 74
Olean Area Chamber of Commerce (Greater Olean), 581
Olean Business Institute, 636
Olean City SD, 640
Olnick Organization Inc (The), 519
OMMLLP PAC, 558
One Communications Corp, 491
One Eleven PAC, 558
Oneida, 74
   Civil & Criminal Courts, 74
Oneida Chamber of Commerce (Greater Oneida Area), 581
Oneida City SD, 652
Oneida County, 66, 405
   Supreme & County Courts, 66
   Surrogate's Court, 66
Oneida Daily Dispatch, 598
Oneida Indian Nation, 209, 501
Oneida Industrial Development Agency (City of), 581
Oneida Tribe of Indians of Wisconsin (Power Plant Entertainment NY), 515
Oneida Tribe of Indians of Wisconsin (Power Plant Entertainment), 503
Oneida-Herkimer-Madison BOCES, 679
Oneonta, 74
   Civil & Criminal Courts, 74
Oneonta City SD, 662
Onondaga 2004, 558
Onondaga Community College, 617
Onondaga County, 66, 405
   County Court, 66
   Supreme, Family & Surrogate's Courts, 66
Onondaga County Industrial Development Agency, 581

Onondaga CSD, 659
Onondaga Nation, 209
Onondaga, Town of, 437
Onondaga-Cortland-Madison BOCES, 679
ONPAC, 558
Ontario Chamber of Commerce, 581
Ontario County, 66, 406
   Supreme, County, Family & Surrogate's Courts, 66
Ontario County Industrial Development Agency & Economic Development, 581
Onteora CSD, 673
OPEIU Local 153 (VOTE) Voice of the Electorate, 558
Open Society Institute, 243
Open Space Institute, 191
Open Space Institute Inc, 505
Oppenheim-Ephratah CSD, 648
Oppidan Investment Company (Ewald Consulting), 475
Opthalmological Society (NYS), 491
Opticians PAC, 558
Oracle USA Inc, 465
Oracle USA, Inc, 469
Orange & Rockland Utilities Inc, 175
Orange County, 66, 406
   Supreme, County & Family Courts, 66
   Surrogate's Court, 66
Orange County Chamber of Commerce (The), 477
Orange County Chamber of Commerce Inc, 581
Orange County Community College, 617
Orange County Democratic Women Inc Campaign, 558
Orange County Legislative Republican Caucas, 558
Orange County Partnership, 581
Orange County Publications, 596
Orangetown, Town of, 437
Orange-Ulster BOCES, 679
Orchard Park Chamber of Commerce, 581
Orchard Park CSD, 646
Orchard Park, Town of, 437
Org of NYS Mgmt/Confidential Employees, Inc, 512
Organization of Nurse Executives Inc (NY), 510
Organization of NYS Management Confidential Employees, 300
Organization of NYS Management Confidential Employees Inc, 491
Organization of NYS Management/Confidential Employees Inc, 512
Organization of Staff Analysts PAC, 558
Organization of Waterfront Neighborhoods (OWN), 497
ORISKA PAC, 558
Oriskany CSD, 658
Orleans County, 66, 406

   Supreme, County, Family & Surrogate's Courts, 66
Orleans County Chamber of Commerce, 581
Orleans Economic Development Agency (OEDA), 582
Orleans-Niagara BOCES, 680
Ortho-PAC of New York, 558
Osborne Association, 141, 276
OSI Pharmaceuticals Inc, 489
Ossining UFSD, 677
Ossining, Town of, 437
Ossining, Village of, 437
Ostertag O'Leary & Barrett, 266
Ostroff, Hiffa & Associates Inc, 512
Oswego, 74
   Civil & Criminal Courts, 74
Oswego BOCES, 680
Oswego City SD, 662
Oswego County, 66, 406
   Family Court, 66
   Supreme, County & Surrogate's Courts, 66
Oswego County, Operation/Oswego County Industrial Development Agency, 582
Oswego-Fulton Chamber of Commerce, 582
Otis Elevator Company, 507
Otsego County, 66, 407
   Supreme, County, Family & Surrogate's Courts, 66
Otsego County Chamber (The), 582
Otsego County Economic Development Department & Industrial Development Agency, 582
Otsego Northern Catskills BOCES (Otsego-Delaware-Schoharie-Greene), 680
Otselic Valley CSD, 642
Ottaway News Service (NYS only), 602
Ottaway Newspapers (The), 598
Ottaway Newspapers Inc, 598
Outdoor Advertising Council of NY Inc, 468
Outdoor Advertising NY PAC, 558
Outward Bound Center (NYC), 532
Oversight and Government Reform, 391
   Domestic Policy, 392
   Federal Workforce, Postal Service and the District of Columbia, 392
   Government Management, Organization and Procurement, 392
   Information Policy, Census and National Archives, 392
   National Security and Foreign Affairs, 392
   Subcommittees, 392
Oversight, Analysis & Investigation, 50
   Committee Staff, 50
   Majority, 50
   Membership, 50
Owego, Town of, 438

Organization Index

Owego-Apalachin CSD, 672
Owens-Illinois (Albers & Co), 488
Oxford Academy & CSD, 642
Oxford Health Plans Inc-NY Committee for Quality Health Care, 558
Oyster Bay Chamber of Commerce, 582
Oyster Bay, Town of, 438
Oyster Bay-East Norwich CSD, 655
Oysterponds UFSD, 670
P&O Ports North America Inc, 516
P.A.F.S.A. NY PAC, 559
PAC of Nassau Police Conference, 559
PAC of the Assoc Building Contractors of the Triple Cities, Inc, 559
PAC of the Patrolmen's Benevolent Association of the City of NY, Inc, 559
PAC Police Assoc City of Yonkers, 559
PAC Port Washington PBA, 559
Pace University, 519, 629
Pace University, School of Law Center for Environmental Legal Studies, 191
Pace University, School of Law, John Jay Legal Services Inc, 141, 266
Pacific College of Oriental Medicine, 636
Painted Post Area Board of Trade, 582
Palladia Inc, 142
Palladia Inc (Formerly Project Return Foundation Inc), 478
Palladium-Times (The), 598
Palmyra-Macedon CSD, 675
Panama CSD, 642
Pappas, Marcia, 513
Par Group (The), 493
Parallel Park, LLC, 468
Parents and Children PAC, Inc, 559
Parishville-Hopkinton CSD, 667
Park Avenue Health Care Management, 501
Park Outdoor Advertising of NY Inc, 509
Park Resident Homeowners' Association Inc, 236
Park Strategies, LLC, 513
Park Tower Group, 484, 519
Parker Jewish Inst for Health Care & Rehab, 506
Parker Jewish Institute for Health Care & Rehab, 491
Parks, Recreation & Historic Preservation, NYS Office of, 13, 179, 334, 374
  Advisory Groups, 180, 335
  Allegany Region, 334
  Central Region, 334
  Concession Management, 334
  Empire State Games, 334
  Environmental Management, 180, 334
  Field Services, 180, 334
  Finger Lakes Region, 334
  Genesee Region, 334
  Historic Preservation, 180, 334
  Historic Sites Bureau, 180, 334
  Long Island Region, 334

  Marine & Recreational Vehicles, 180, 334
  New York City Region, 334
  Niagara Region & Western District Office, 334
  Palisades Interstate Park Commission, 334
  Planning & Development, 180, 335
  Regional Offices-Downstate District, 334
  Regional Offices-Not Within Districts, 334
  Regional Offices-Western District, 334
  Resource Management, 180, 334
  Saratoga/Capital District Region, 334
  State Board for Historic Preservation, 180, 335
  State Council of Parks, Recreation & Historic Preservation, 180, 335
  Taconic Region, 334
  Thousand Islands Region, 334
Parkside Group, LLC, 513
Parodneck Foundation (The), 236
Parola PAC for Good Government, 559
Parole, Division of, 14, 135, 374
  Administrative Services, 135
  Board of Parole, 135
  Clemency Unit, 135
  Executive Office, 135
  Information Services, 135
  Office of Counsel, 135
  Parole Operations Unit, 135
  Policy Analysis, 136
  Victim Impact Unit, 136
Parsons Brinckerhoff, 359
Partnership for New York City, 111
Partnership for NYC, 493, 528
Partnership for NYC, Inc, 482
Partnership with Children, 500
Pastel & Rosen, LLP, 514
Patchogue Chamber of Commerce (Greater Patchogue), 582
Patchogue-Medford UFSD, 670
Patent Trader, 596
Path Medical, 519
Patrolmen's Benevolent Assn (NYC), 515
Patrolmen's Benevolent Association, 142, 300
Patterson & McLaughlin, 514
Paul Smith's College, 629
Pavilion CSD, 649
Pawling CSD, 645
PCI State Political Account I, 559
Peace Corps, 203
  New York Regional Office, 203
Peachtree Settlement Funding, 490
Pearl River UFSD, 664
Pearls' Prison Families of NY, 142
Pearson Education Inc, 491
Peckham Industries Inc PAC, 559
Peconic Bay Medical Center, 530
Peekskill, 74

  Civil & Criminal Courts, 74
Peekskill City SD, 677
Peekskill Industrial Development Agency (City of), 582
Peekskill, City of, 438
Peerless Importers, 483
Pelham UFSD, 677
Pembroke CSD, 649
Pendleton Democrat Club, 559
Penfield CSD, 653
Penfield, Town of, 438
Penn Yan CSD, 678
People with Disabilities Task Force, 53
People's Weekly World, 596
Pepe, Ross J, 514
Pepsi Co, 111
Pepsi-Cola Bottlers' PAC, 559
Performance Space 122, 480
Perinton, Town of, 438
Perkins, Janice C, 514
Perry Area Chamber of Commerce, 582
Perry CSD, 678
Perry Davis Associates, 111
Perry, Robert, 514
Personal Touch Home Care of Westchester, 462
Personal Watercraft Industry Assn, 456
Personal Watercraft Industry Association, 464
Peru CSD, 643
Pet Industry Joint Advisory Council, 491
Peters, Jeffrey R, 514
Petraitis, Brian J, 514
Pfizer, 466
Pfizer Inc, 475, 504, 507, 532
Pfizer PAC - NY, 559
Pfizer, Inc, 464, 478, 519
Pharmaceutical Research & Manufacturers Assn of America, 465
Pharmaceutical Research & Manufacturers of America, 491, 503, 512
Pharmaceutical Research & Mfrs of America (PHRMA), 501
Pharmacists Society of the State of New York, 226
Pharmacists Society of the State of NY, 468
Pharmacy PAC of New York State, 559
Phelps Dodge Refining Corporation, 463
Phelps Memorial Hospital Center, 530
Phelps-Clifton Springs CSD, 660
Philips International Holding Corp/40 Rector Owners LLC, 474
Phillips & Associates, PLLC, 515
Phillips Beth Israel School of Nursing, 629
Phillips Nizer, LLP, 515
Phoenix CSD, 662
Phoenix House Foundation Inc, 515, 518
Physical Therapy Assn (NY), 529
Physicians Fund, 559
Physicians' Reciprocal Insurers, 504, 506
Pine Bush CSD, 661

Organization Index

Pine Plains CSD, 645
Pine Valley CSD (South Dayton), 642
Pinelawn Cemetery, 485, 524
Pinsky & Pinsky, PC, 515
Pinsky & Skandalis, 515
Pioneer CSD, 640
Pioneer Savings Bank, 96, 209
Pipe Trades Assn, 463
Piseco Common SD, 649
Pittsford CSD, 653
Pittsford, Town of, 438
Plainedge UFSD, 656
Plainview-Old Bethpage CSD, 656
Planned Parenthood of NYC Inc, 530
Planned Parenthood of NYC, Inc, 322
Plattsburgh, 74
  Civil & Criminal Courts, 74
Plattsburgh City SD, 643
Plattsburgh-North Country Chamber of Commerce, 582
Plaza 75 Realty Inc, 475
Plaza College, 513, 637
Plaza Construction Corporation, 507
Pleasantville UFSD, 677
Plug Power Inc, 175, 475, 515, 518
Plug Power, Inc, 524
Plumb Engineering PC, 501
Plumbers & Pipefitters Local No 13 Pol Fund, 559
Plumbers & Pipefitters Local Union 112 PAC, 559
Plumbers & Steamfitters Local 21 PAC, 559
Plumbers & Steamfitters Local 267 PAC, 559
Plumbers and Steamfitters Local 7 PAC, 559
Plumbers Local Union 200 PAF, 560
Plumbers Local Union No 1 N.Y.C. PAC, 559
Plumbing & Mechanical Contractors Association of the Hudson Valley, 463
Plumbing Contractors Assn of Long Island Inc, 526
Plumbing Contractors PAC of the City of NY Inc, 560
Plumbing Foundation City of NY Inc, 526
Plumbing Foundation of the City of NY, 486
Pocantico Hills CSD, 677
Podiatric Medical Assn (NYS), 487
Poetic Holding Corp, 469
Poklemba, John J, 515
Poland CSD, 650
Police Benevolent Assn of the NYS Troopers Inc, 507, 515
Police Conference of New York Inc PAC, 560
Police Conference of NY Inc (PCNY), 142, 300
Police Investigators Assn (NY), 501

Political Action Committee Buffalo PBA, 560
Political Action Committee of Broome County Assoc PHCC, 560
Political Action Committee of Council 82, 560
Pollard Banknote Limited, 515
Polytechnic University, 478, 629
Pomeroy Appraisal Associates Inc, 305
Port Authority of New York & New Jersey, 127, 353, 380
Port Authority PBA, Inc State of New York PAC, 560
Port Authority Sergeants Benevolent Assn PAC, 560
Port Byron CSD, 641
Port Chester SD, 677
Port Chester, Village of, 439
Port Chester-Rye Brook Chamber of Commerce, 582
Port Jefferson Chamber of Commerce, 582
Port Jefferson UFSD, 670
Port Jervis, 74
  Civil & Criminal Courts, 74
Port Jervis City SD, 661
Port Morris Local Development Corporation, 582
Port of Oswego Authority, 127, 353, 380
Port Parties, Ltd, 494
Port Washington Chamber of Commerce, 582
Port Washington UFSD, 656
Portville CSD, 640
Postgrad Center for Mental Health, Child, Adolescent & Family-Couples, 285
Postgraduate Center for Mental Health, 285
Post-Journal, 595
Post-Standard (The), 600
Post-Star (The), 594
Potsdam Chamber of Commerce, 582
Potsdam CSD, 667
Poughkeepsie, 74
  Civil & Criminal Courts, 74
Poughkeepsie Area Chamber of Commerce, 583
Poughkeepsie City SD, 645
Poughkeepsie Journal, 598
Poughkeepsie, City of, 439
Poughkeepsie, Town of, 439
Power for Economic Prosperity Group, 480
Powers & Company, 515
Powers Global Strategies, LLC, 516
Pozzi, Brian M, 516
Pratt Center for Community Development, 236
Pratt Center for Community Direct Marketing Association, 502
Pratt Institute, 513, 629
Pratt Institute for Community & Environment Development, 514
Prattsburgh CSD, 667

Praxair PAC NY, 560
Precision Jet Management Inc, 501
Premier Home Health Care Inc, 501
Premium Finance Association, 465
Presbyterian Hosp/Coal for School-Based Primary Care (NY), 529
Presbyterian Hospital (NY), 516, 529
Preservation League of NYS, 501
Preserve Associates LLC, 529
Preserve Ramapo, 560
Press & Sun Bulletin, 592
Press-Republican, 598
Prestige Properties & Development Co Inc, 459
Prevent Child Abuse New York, 322, 473
Prevention of Domestic Violence, Office for the, 14, 136, 312, 374
Pricewaterhouse Coopers, LLP, 530
PricewaterhouseCoopers, 511
PricewaterhouseCoopers LLP, 209
Primary Care Development Corporation, 455, 503
Primerica Financial Services, 487
Printing, Joint Committee on, 394
Prisoners' Legal Services of New York, 142, 266
Pro Bono Net, 266
Pro Tech Monitoring Inc, 515
Probation & Correctional Alternatives, Division of, 14, 136, 374
  Interstate/Intrastate Transfers Unit, 136
  New York State Probation Commission, 136
Probation Political Action Committee (PROPAC), 560
Procter & Gamble Pharmaceuticals, 226
Proctor & Gamble Company (The), 463
Production Alliance (NY), 507
Professional Business College, 630
Professional Fire Fighters Assn Inc (NYS), 508
Professional Fire Fighters Association Inc (NYS), 300
Professional Firefighters Association Inc (NYS), 491
Professional Insurance Agents of New York Political Action Committee, 560
Professional Insurance Agents of New York State, 251
Professional Insurance Agents of NYS Inc, 501
Professional Insurance Wholesalers Assoc of NYS Inc, 514
Professional Staff Congress (The), 456
Professional Standards Review Council of America Inc (PSRC), 227
Professionals Political Action Committee-NY, 560
Program Risk Management, Inc & PRM Claim Services Inc, 529
Program Risk Mgmt Inc, 490

Organization Index

Progressive Bag Alliance, 463
Progressive Insurance Companies, 514
Project for Public Spaces, 236
Project Renewal, 493, 494
Project Samaritan AIDS Services Inc, 503
ProLiteracy Worldwide, 155, 322
Property Casualty Insurers Assn of America (PCIAA), 461
Property Casualty Insurers Association of America (PCIAA), 483
Property Insurance Underwriting Assn (NY), 461
Property Markets Group, 493
Proskauer Rose LLP, 111, 191, 209, 266
Protecting America.org, 508
Prudential New York Political Action Committee, 560
Pruzansky & Besunder LLP, 266
PSC PAC, 559
PSCH Inc, 515
Psychiatric Assn Inc (NYS), 485
Psychological Assn (NYS), 516
Psychologists for Legislative Action in NY, 560
Psychotherapy & Counseling Center (NY), 465
Public Adjusters Assn (NY), 468
Public Agenda, 166, 209
Public Employee Conference (NYS), 505
Public Employees Federation (NYS), 477
Public Employer Risk Management Assn, 529
Public Employment Relations Board, 14, 296, 374
- *Administration Section, 296*
- *Buffalo, 296*
- *Conciliation Section, 296*
- *District Offices, 296*
- *Employment Practices & Representation Section, 296*
- *Legal Section, 296*
- *New York City, 296*

Public Library (NY), Astor, Lenox & Tilden Foundations, 513
Public Library, Astor, Lenox & Tilden Foundations (NY), 516
Public Markets Partners / Baum Forum, 88
Public Policy Institute of NYS Inc, 111
Public Service Commission, 14, 169, 374
- *Accounting, Finance & Economics Office, 169*
- *Consumer Services Office, 169*
- *Electricity & Environment Office, 169*
- *Gas & Water Office, 169*
- *Hearings & Alternative Dispute Resolution Office, 169*
- *Office of Administration, 169*
- *Office of Telecommunications, 169*
- *Utility Security Office, 169*

Public Strategies, LLC, 516
Public Transit Assn (NY), 529
Public Utility Law Project of New York Inc, 175, 517
Public Welfare Assn (NY), 517
Public/Private Ventures, 277, 322
Puckett, Robert R, 517
Puerto Rican Legal Defense & Education Fund Inc (PRLDEF), 243, 266
Puerto Rican/Hispanic Task Force, 53
Pulaski CSD, 662
Pulaski-Eastern Shore Chamber of Commerce, 583
Pulte Homes of NY Inc, 484
Purchase College, State University of New York, 613
Purvis Systems Inc, 526
Putnam Associated Resource Ctrs, 532
Putnam County, 67, 407
- *Supreme, County, Family & Surrogate's Courts, 67*

Putnam County Economic Development Corporation, 583
Putnam CSD, 674
Putnam Valley CSD, 663
Putnam-Northern Westchester BOCES, 680
Pyramid Managing Group Inc, 501
Queens & Bronx Building Assn, 457
Queens Adult Care Center, 530
Queens Borough Public Library, 478
Queens Botanical Garden, 478
Queens Centers for Progress Inc, 513
Queens Chamber of Commerce, 513
Queens Chamber of Commerce (Borough of), 583
Queens Child Guidance Center Inc, 513
Queens College, 621
Queens College Foundation-Research of CUNY, 514
Queens Community House Inc, 488
Queens County, 67
- *COUNTY & FAMILY COURTS: See New York City Courts, 67*
- *Supreme & Surrogate's Courts, 67*

Queens County (NYC Borough of Queens), 407
Queens Economic Development Corp, 513
Queens Educational Opportunity Center, 618
Queens Gazette, 595
Queens Theatre in the Park, 513
Queensborough Comm College Auxiliary Enterprise Assn Inc, 513
Queensborough Community College, 621
Queensbury UFSD, 674
Queensbury, Town of, 439
Queens-Long Island Medical Group, P.C., 530
Quest Diagnostics Inc, 529
Quest Diagnostics NY PAC, 560
Questar III, 529
Quincunx, 487
Quogue UFSD, 670

R Randy Lee, 469
R Squared LLC, 484
R W Bronstein Corporation, 305
R/V Moynihan Station Developer LLC, 484
Racing & Wagering, 50
- *Committee Staff, 50*
- *Key Assembly Staff Assignments, 50*
- *Majority, 50*
- *Membership, 50*
- *Minority, 50*

Racing & Wagering Board, 15, 325, 335, 374
Racing and Gaming Services Inc, 515
Racing Association (NY), 497
Racing Association Inc (NY) (The), 491
Racing, Gaming & Wagering, 31
- *Committee Staff, 31*
- *Key Senate Staff Assignments, 31*
- *Majority, 31*
- *Membership, 31*
- *Minority, 31*

Radiac Environmental Services, 191
Radiant Energy Corporation, 501
Radiological Society Inc (NYS), 515
Radon Testing Corp of America Inc, 191, 227
Railroads of NY, (RONY), 488
Rain Inc, 528
Rainbow Chimes Inc, Child Care Ctr, 478
Ralph Lauren Center for Cancer Care & Prevention, 503
Ramapo CSD (Suffern), 664
Ramapo, Town of, 439
Randi Weingarten, 518
Randi Weingarten, MLC Chair & UFT President, 515
Randolph Academy UFSD, 640
Randolph CSD, 640
Rangel for Congress - NY State, 561
Raquette Lake UFSD, 649
Raustiala, Margaret, 517
Ravena-Coeymans-Selkirk CSD, 638
Rawlings Company LLC (The), 487
RC Build PAC of the Rockland County Builders Assn, 560
RCN, 478
Real Estate Board of New York Inc, 305
Real Estate Board of NY, 531
Real Estate Board of NY Inc, 517
Real Estate Board PAC, 561
Real Estate Industrials Inc, 495
Real Estate Tax Review Bar Assn, 465
Real Independence Party Club-Amherst Branch, 561
Real Property Services, Office of, 15, 289, 302, 326, 374
- *Albany (Northern Region), 289, 302, 326*
- *Batavia (Western Region), 289, 302, 326*
- *Long Island Satellite Office, 289, 302, 326*

Organization Index

Newburgh (Southern Region), 289, 302, 326
Regional Customer Service Delivery, 289, 302, 326
Research, Information & Policy Development, 289, 302, 326
Saranac Lake Satellite Office, 289, 302, 326
State Board of Real Property Services, 289, 302, 326
Syracuse (Central Region), 289, 302, 326
Real Property Taxation, 50
   Committee Staff, 51
   Key Assembly Staff Assignments, 51
   Majority, 51
   Membership, 51
   Minority, 51
Realogy Corporation, 463
Realtors PAC, 561
Realty Advisory Board on Labor Relations, 277, 305
Realty USA, 305
Recco Home Care Services, Inc, 462
Reckitt Benckiser Inc, 475
Record (The), 600
Recorder (The), 591
Recording Industry Assn of America Inc, 463
Red Apple Group, 499
Red Barn Properties, 305
Red Creek CSD, 675
Red Hook Area Chamber of Commerce, 583
Red Hook CSD, 645
Reece School (The), 500
Reed Elsevier Inc, 527
Refinance.com, 485
Refinery LLC (CPC Resorces Inc), 486
Regeneron Pharmaceuticals Inc, 227
Region 9, UAW, 530
Regional Community Service Pgms (NYS), 503
Regional Farm & Food Project, 88
Regional Food Bank of Northeastern NY, 503
Regional Interconnect Inc (NY), 487
Regional Interconnect, Inc (NY), 476
Regional Plan Association, 111, 236, 359
Register-Star, 594
Regulatory Reform, Governor's Office of, 15, 99, 197, 374
Rehabilitation Assn Inc (NYS), 517
Rehabilitation Associates PAC, 561
Rehabilitation Association (NYS), 503
Reinsurance Assn of America, 473, 529
Reiter/Begun Associates, LLC, 517
Related Companies (The), 467
Related Companies LP, 306
Reliant Resources Inc, 506
Remove Intoxicated Drivers (RID-USA Inc), 142

Remsen CSD, 658
Remsenburg-Speonk UFSD, 670
Renew NY PAC, 561
Rensselaer, 74
   Civil & Criminal Courts, 74
Rensselaer City SD, 663
Rensselaer County, 67, 408
   Family Court, 67
   Supreme, County & Surrogate's Courts, 67
Rensselaer County Regional Chamber of Commerce, 583
Rensselaer Polytechnic Inst, Ecological Economics, Values & Policy Program, 191
Rensselaer Polytechnic Institute, 155, 517, 630
Rensselaer-Columbia-Greene (Questar III) BOCES, 680
Rent Stabilization Assn of NYC Inc, 236, 491, 517
Rent-A-Center (Stateside Associates), 468
Repair Shop & Gasoline Dealers' PAC Fund, 561
Repas, Peter G, 518
Republican 100,000 Club of Oneida County, 561
Republican Lawyers Club, 561
Republican Main Stream Coalition of New York, 561
Republican Majority for Choice PAC, 561
Rescare/Arbor (Multistate Associates), 494
Research Foundation for Mental Hygiene Inc, 285
Research Foundation of SUNY, 155
Reserve Officers Association (ROA), 368
Reserve Officers Association (ROA), Department of NY, 368
Residents Committee to Protect the Adirondacks, 461
Resource Center for Independent Living (RCIL), 243, 322
Resources for Artists with Disabilities Inc, 346
Responsible Government Coalition, 561
Responsible Industry for a Sound Environment (RISE), 456
Responsive Government In Gates, 561
Restaurant Assn (NYS), 489, 521
Restoration Project (NY), 494
Retail Council of New York State, 111
Retail Wholesale Department Store Union, 507
Retailers Alliance (The), 506
Retired Public Employees Association, 300, 491
Retirees Association of DC 37 Political Action Committee, 561
Retirees for Tier 1, 491
Reuters (New York Bureau), 602
Review Press, 592

Reynolds America Inc, 488
RFR Holding Corp, 474
RFR Holdings, 519
RG & E Employees' NYS Pol Comm Inc, 560
Rhinebeck Chamber of Commerce, 583
Rhinebeck CSD, 645
Rice & Justice, 518
Richfield Area Chamber of Commerce, 583
Richfield Springs CSD, 662
Richmond County, 67
   COUNTY & FAMILY COURTS: See New York City Courts, 67
   Supreme & Surrogate's Courts, 67
Richmond County (NYC Borough of Staten Island), 408
Richmond UNI Home Care Inc, 462
Right to Life Committee Inc (NYS), 518
Ripley CSD, 642
Rite Aid Corporation, 468
Riverhead Chamber of Commerce, 583
Riverhead CSD, 670
Riverhead Foundation for Marine Research & Preservation (The), 191
Riverhead PBA PAC Inc, 561
Riverhead, Town of, 440
Riverkeeper Inc, 192
Riverkeeper, Inc, 518
Riverside South Planning Corp, 513
RLJ Development LLC, 487
Roadway Improvement Coalition (NY), 483
Robert P Borsody, PC, 227
Robert Schalkenbach Foundation, 306, 331
Roberts Wesleyan College, 630
Rochester, 74
   Civil Court, 74
   Criminal Court, 74
Rochester & Southern Railroad Inc, 489
Rochester Area Right to Life Committee-PAC, 561
Rochester Build PAC, 561
Rochester Business Alliance Inc, 583
Rochester Business Journal, 602
Rochester City School District, 472
Rochester City SD, 653
Rochester Downtown Development Corporation, 583
Rochester Economic Development Corporation, 583
Rochester Educational Opportunity Center, 618
Rochester Gas & Electric, 462
Rochester Gas & Electric Corp, 470, 501, 513, 524
Rochester Gas & Electric Corporation, 176
Rochester Higher Education and Research PAC, 561
Rochester Institute of Technology, 524, 531, 630
Rochester Interfaith Jail Ministry Inc, 142

Organization Index

Rochester Regional Healthcare Advocates, 518
Rochester Regional Joint Board State PAC, 561
Rochester Rhinos Stadium, LLC, 463
Rochester School for the Deaf, 155
Rochester Tooling & Machine Assn Inc, 489
Rochester, City of, 440
Rochester, University of, 630
Rochester-Genesee Regional Transportation Authority, 127, 354, 380
Rochester-Genesee Regional Transportation Authority c/o Renaissan, 501
Rockaway Development & Revitalization Corp, 513
Rockaway Development & Revitalization Corporation, 583
Rockaways, Chamber of Commerce, Inc, 583
Rockefeller University, 630
Rockland BOCES, 680
Rockland Chamber of Commerce, 583
Rockland Community College, 617
Rockland County, 67, 408
   Supreme, County, Family & Surrogate's Courts, 67
Rockland County Correction Officers Benevolent Association PAC, 561
Rockland County PBA Association PAC NY, 561
Rockland County Sheriff's Deputy Assn, PAC, 562
Rockland Economic Development Corporation, 583
Rockrose Development Corp, 467
Rockville Centre Chamber of Commerce, 583
Rockville Centre UFSD, 656
Rockville Centre, Village of, 440
Rocky Point UFSD, 670
Roffe, Andrew S, PC, 518
Roman Catholic Diocese of Albany, Catholic Charities, 322
Romanoff Equities, Inc, 467
Rome, 74
   Civil & Criminal Courts, 74
Rome Area Chamber of Commerce, 583
Rome City SD, 658
Rome Industrial Development Corporation, 584
Rome Sentinel Co, 599
Rome, City of, 440
Romulus CSD, 666
Rondout Valley CSD, 673
Ronkonkoma Chamber of Commerce, 584
Roofers' Pol Education & Legislative Fund of NY, 562
Roohan Realty, 306
Roos, David E, 518

Roosevelt Island Operating Corporation (RIOC), 127, 231, 337, 380
Roosevelt UFSD, 656
Ropes & Gray, 519
Rosario, Stephen M, 519
Roscoe CSD, 672
Rose Group (The), 459
Rosenthal, Harvey, 519
Rosies for All Kids Foundation, 463
Roslyn UFSD, 656
Rotterdam, Town of, 440
Rougeux, Elizabeth, 519
Rough Rider PAC, 562
Roundabout Theatre Co, 529
Roxbury CSD, 644
Royal Indemnity Comapny Voluntary PAC (Royal & Sun Alliance PAC), 562
Royalton-Hartland CSD, 657
R-PAC, 560
RPA-PAC, 560
RSA - PAC, 560
RSA PAC City Account, 560
Rubenstein Associates Inc, 519
Rubenstein Communications Inc, 519
Rubino, Cynthia A, 519
Rules, 31, 51, 392
   Committee Staff, 51
   Legislative & Budget Process, 392
   Majority, 31, 51
   Membership, 31, 51
   Minority, 31, 51
   Rules & Organization of the House, 392
   Subcommittees, 392
Rules & Administration, 386
Runes, Richard, 519
Rural & Migrant Ministry Inc, 322
Rural Housing Action Corporation, 236
Rural Law Ctr of NY Inc, 520
Rural Opportunities Inc, 88, 323
Rural Resources, Legislative Commission on, 33, 54
Rural Water Assn (NY), 522
Rural Water Association, 192
Rural/Metro Medical Services, 491
Rush-Henrietta CSD, 653
Rutherford, Clyde E, 520
Rutnik Law Firm (The), 520
RWDSU, Local 338 PAC, 561
Ryan, Desmond M, 520
Ryan, Marc, 520
Rye, 74
   Civil & Criminal Courts, 75
Rye City SD, 677
Rye Neck UFSD, 677
Rye, Town of, 441
S & J Sheet Metal Supply, Inc, 478
S&H Equities Inc, 487
S&R Medallion Corporation, 494
Sabol, Sharon, 521
Sachem CSD, 670
Sackets Harbor Chamber of Commerce, 584

Sackets Harbor CSD, 650
Safe Horizon, 477
Safe Horizon Inc, 494, 521
Safe Space, 467
SAFE-PAC (Schools Are For Everyone Political Action Committee), 562
Sag Harbor Chamber of Commerce, 584
Sag Harbor UFSD, 670
Sagaponack Common SD, 670
Sage Colleges (The), 630
Sagem Morpho, 515
Sagem Morpho Inc, 518
Saint Vincent Catholic Medical Centers, 467
Salamanca, 75
   Civil & Criminal Courts, 75
Salamanca Area Chamber of Commerce, 584
Salamanca City SD, 640
Salamanca Industrial Development Agency, 584
Salamanca Press, 599
Salem CSD, 674
Salient Technologies Inc, 512
Salina, Town of, 441
Sallie Mae Inc, 507
Salmon River CSD, 648
Salvation Army School for Officer Training, 630
Salvation Army, Empire State Division, 323
Samaritan Hospital School of Nursing, 630
Samaritan Medical Center, 531
Samaritan Village Inc, 286, 503
Sampson, Rick J, 521
Sanctuary for Families, 531
Sandy Creek CSD, 662
Sanitary District No 6, 499
Sanofi Pasteur (Multistate Associates Inc), 487
Sanofi Pasteur Inc, 529
Sapir Organization, 475
Sarah Lawrence College, 630
Saranac CSD, 643
Saranac Lake Area Chamber of Commerce, 584
Saranac Lake CSD, 648
Saratoga County, 67, 408
   Family Court, 67
   Supreme, County & Surrogate's Courts, 67
Saratoga County Chamber of Commerce, 584
Saratoga County Industrial Development Agency, 584
Saratoga Economic Development Corporation, 584
Saratoga Gaming & Raceway, 346
Saratoga Harness Racing Inc, 483
Saratoga Springs, 75
   Civil & Criminal Courts, 75
Saratoga Springs City SD, 664

Organization Index

Saratoga Springs, City of, 441
Saratogian (The), 599
SAS Institute Inc, 489, 521
Satellite Tracking of People LLC, 463
Saugerties CSD, 673
Saugerties, Town of, 441
Sauquoit Valley CSD, 658
Save American Jobs PAC, 562
Save The Lake (Political Action Committee), 562
Sawchuk Brown Associates, 111
Sayville Chamber of Commerce (Greater Sayville), 584
Sayville UFSD, 670
SBA Political Action Committee, 562
SBLI USA Mutual Life Insurance Company Inc, 251
SC Johnson & Son Inc, 529
SCAA - Schuyler Center for Analysis & Advocacy, 155, 331
SCAA Tissue North America, 463
Scan New York, 494
Scarsdale UFSD, 677
Scenic Hudson, 192
Scenic Hudson Inc, 521
Schalmont CSD, 665
Schenectady, 75
    Civil Court, 75
    Criminal Court, 75
Schenectady City SD, 665
Schenectady County, 67, 409
    Family Court, 67
    Supreme, County & Surrogate's Courts, 67
Schenectady County Chamber of Commerce, 584
Schenectady County Community College, 617
Schenectady County Industrial Development Agency/Economic Development Corporation, 584
Schenectady, City of, 441
Schenevus CSD, 662
Schering Corporation, 529
Schillinger, Lawrence R, 521
Schlather, Geldenhuys, Stumbar & Salk, 264
Schlein, Stanley, 521
Schnectady Museum and Planetarium, 487
Schnell, William A & Associates Inc, 521
Schodack CSD, 663
Schoharie County, 67, 409
    Supreme, County, Family & Surrogate's Courts, 68
Schoharie County Chamber of Commerce, 584
Schoharie County Industrial Development Agency, 584
Schoharie CSD, 665
Schomberg, Dora, 522

School Administrators Association of NYS, 155, 491, 522
School Boards Assn (NYS), 522
School Bus Contractor's Coalition, Inc. (NY), 531
School Bus Contractors Assn (NY), 482, 507
School Nutrition Assn (NY), 503
School of Industrial & Labor Relations at Cornell University (ILR School), 612
School of Law at Queens College, 621
School of Professional Studies, 621
School of Visual Arts, 637
Schools Are For Everyone, 562
Schroon Lake Area Chamber of Commerce, 584
Schroon Lake CSD, 647
Schuyler Center for Analysis & Advocacy, 503
Schuyler Center for Analysis & Advocacy (SCAA), 286, 522
Schuyler County, 68, 409
    Supreme, County, Family & Surrogate's Courts, 68
Schuyler County Chamber of Commerce, 585
Schuyler County Industrial Development Agency, 585
Schuyler County Partnership for Economic Development, 585
Schuylerville CSD, 664
SCI of New York Inc, 501
Science & Technology, 392
    Energy & Environment, 392
    Investigations and Oversights, 392
    Research and Science Education, 392
    Space and Aeronautics, 392
    Subcommittees, 392
    Technology and Innovation, 392
Science & Technology, Legislative Commission on, 33, 54
Science Application International Corp (SAIC), 469
Scio CSD, 639
Scotia-Glenville CSD, 665
Scotto Brothers Site 16/17 Development LLC, 459
Scotts Company (The), 529
Screen Actors Guild (National & Hollywood Offices), 507
Scripps Howard News Service, 602
SCS Engineers PC, 192
SDR Pharmaceuticals Inc, 522
SDS Investments LLC, 474
Seaford Chamber of Commerce, 585
Seaford UFSD, 656
Seaway Trail Inc, 346
Securitas, 522
Securities Industry & Financial Markets Association (FKA Securities Industry Assn), 529

Securities Industry & Financial Markets Association (SIFMA), 262
Securities Industry Assn PAC, NY District, 562
Securities Industry Association (SIA), 96
SEF Industries Inc, 519
Segway Inc. (Multistate Associates), 531
SEIU Local 200 United, 507
SEIU Local 704 PAC, 562
SEIU PEA State Fund, 562
SEIU, Local 300, 507
Self Advocacy Association of NYS, 243, 286
Self Storage Assn Inc (NY), 468
Selfhelp Community Services, Inc, 466
Seminary of the Immaculate Conception, 630
Semper FI NY State PAC Inc, 562
Sen Dem, 562
Senate, 375
Senate Select Committees, 203
    Interstate Cooperation, Select Committee on, 203
Senate Special Committees, 339
    Arts & Cultural Affairs, Special Committee on the, 339
Senate Standing Committees, 80, 83, 92, 93, 103, 106, 137, 139, 150, 151, 163, 164, 170, 172, 183, 187, 203, 206, 217, 220, 231, 233, 239, 240, 248, 249, 259, 261, 272, 274, 283, 292, 298, 303, 313, 315, 328, 330, 339, 340, 354, 356, 362, 364
    Aging, 217, 239, 313
    Aging, Special Committee on, 220, 315
    Agriculture, 80
    Agriculture, Nutrition & Forestry, 83, 187, 220
    Agriculture, Rural Development, FDA & Related Agencies, 83
    Appropriations, 83, 172, 330
    Armed Services, 364
    Aviation Operations, Safety & Security, 172
    Banking, Housing & Urban Affairs, 93, 233
    Banks, 92
    Budget, 330
    Cities, 103, 292
    Civil Service & Pensions, 203, 298
    Codes, 137, 259
    Commerce, Economic Development & Small Business, 103, 292, 303, 354
    Commerce, Science & Transportation, 106, 172, 187, 356
    Consumer Protection, 103, 203, 217
    Corporations, Authorities & Commissions, 103, 203, 354
    Crime Victims, Crime & Correction, 137, 239
    Education, 150
    Elections, 163

861

Organization Index

Energy & Natural Resources, 172, 187, 340
Energy & Telecommunications, 170
Energy & Water Development, 172
Environment & Public Works, 187, 356
Environmental Conservation, 183
Ethics, 203
Ethics, Select Committee on, 164, 206
Finance, 106, 203, 249, 292, 328, 330
Foreign Relations, 106
Health, 217
Health, Education, Labor & Pensions, 151, 220, 274, 315
Healthcare, 249
Higher Education, 150
Homeland Security & Governmental Affairs, 164, 206, 298, 330
Housing Construction & Community Development, 303
Housing, Construction & Community Development, 231, 292
Immigration, Refugees and Border Security, 206
Indian Affairs, Committee on, 206, 240
Insurance, 248
Intelligence, Select Committee on, 206
Investigations & Government Operations, 203
Judiciary, 139, 206, 259, 261
Labor, 239, 248, 272, 298
Libraries, 150
Local Government, 232, 292
Mental Health & Developmental Disabilities, 239, 283
National Parks, 340
Oceans, Atmosphere, Fisheries and Coast Guard, 187
Public Lands & Forests, 340
Racing, Gaming & Wagering, 328, 339
Retirement & Aging, 220
Rules, 203
Rural Revitalization, Conservation, Forestry and Credit, 187
Small Business & Entrepreneurship, 106, 274
Social Security, Pensions and Family Policy, 249
Social Services, Children & Families, 217, 313
Space, Aeronautics and Related Sciences, 172
Subcommittee, 83, 150, 172, 187, 330, 356
Subcommittees, 206, 220, 249, 340
Taxation & IRS Oversight and Long-Term Growth, 330
Terrorism, Technology & Homeland Security, 206
Tourism, Recreation & Sports Development, 339
Transportation, 292, 354

Transportation & Infrastructure, 356
Veterans, Homeland Security & Military Affairs, 362
Veterans' Affairs, 364
Senate/Assembly Legislative Commissions, 81, 103, 163, 183, 203, 217, 283, 298
Demographic Research & Reapportionment, Legislative Task Force on, 163
Ethics Committee, Legislative, 203
Government Administration, Legislative Commission on, 203, 298
Health Care Financing, Council on, 217, 283
Rural Resources, Legislative Commission on, 81, 103, 183
Science & Technology, Legislative Commission on, 103
Solid Waste Management, Legislative Commission on, 183
Toxic Substances & Hazardous Wastes, Legislative Commission on, 81, 183, 217
Water Resource Needs of NYS & Long Island, Legislative Commission on, 81, 183
Seneca County, 68, 409
Supreme, County, Family & Surrogate's Courts, 68
Seneca County Chamber of Commerce, 585
Seneca County Industrial Development Agency, 585
Seneca Falls CSD, 666
Seneca Flight Operations, 359
Seneca Foods Corporation, 88
Seneca Nation of Indians, 210, 491
Seneca Niagara Falls Gaming Corp, 501
Seneca Park Zoo Society, 501
Senior Associates, 468
Senior Housing Resource Corp, 469
Sephardic Bikur Holim, 503
Sepracor, 528
Sequoia Community Initiatives (Consumer Info & Dispute Resolution), 499
Sequoia Voting Systems Inc, 465, 501
Sergeants Benevolent Assn, 463
Serverware, 469
Service Employees International Union, Local 300, 513
Service Station & Repair Shop Operators, Upstate NY Inc, 562
Service Station Dealers of Greater NY, Inc, 526
Servicemaster Co (The), 487
Settlement Housing Fund Inc, 236
Seventh Regiment Armory Conservancy, 474
Sewanhaka Central HS District, 656
SGS Testcom, 490
SH Ludlow Street, LLC, 467
Shaker Museum (The), 515

Shanahan Group, 522
Shandaken Democrat Club, 562
Shannon, Michael J, 522
Shareing & Careing Inc, 480
Sharon Springs CSD, 665
Shaw, Linda R, 522
Shawanga Lodge, LLC, 463
Sheet Metal Workers Int'l Assn Local 137 PAL Fund, 562
Sheet Metal Workers Itnl Association, 493
Sheet Metal Workers LU 38 -PAC, 562
Sheet Metal Workers' Intl Assoc Local 28 Political Action Committee, 563
Sheet Metal Workers' Local 46 PAF, 563
Sheet Metal Workers' Local Union 83 Political Action Committee, 563
Sheinkopf Communications, 167
Sheinkopf, Ltd, 522
Sheldrake Organization Inc, 507
Shell Oil Company, 490
Shelter Island UFSD, 670
Shenendehowa CSD, 664
Sherburne-Earlville CSD, 642
Sheriff Officers Assn, 513
Sherman CSD, 642
Sherrill, 75
Civil & Criminal Courts, 75
Shinnecock Indian Nation, 210
Shinnecock Nation Gaming Authority, 506, 507
Shipping Association, Inc (NY), 473
Shoreham-Wading River CSD, 671
Sidney Chamber of Commerce, 585
Sidney CSD, 644
Siemens Corporation, 463
Siena College, 516, 631
Sierra Club, Atlantic Chapter, 192, 523
SIFMA, 94
Sightlines LLC, 491
Silver Creek CSD, 642
Silvercup Studios, 506
Silverite Construction, 494
Silverstein Properties Inc, 306
Simmons Institute of Funeral Service Inc, 637
Simmons-Boardman Publishing Corp, 359
Simon Weisenthal Ctr Museum of Tolerance, 506
Simon Wiesenthal Center, NY Tolerance Center, 243
Simpson & Brown Inc, 516
Sims Hugo Neu, 466
Site-Blauvelt Engineers, 516
Sithe Energies Inc, 176
SJP Properties, 486
SJP Residential Properties, 486
Skaneateles Chamber of Commerce, 585
Skaneateles CSD, 659
Ski Areas of New York Inc, 346
Ski Areas of NY Inc, 464
Skidmore College, 631

Organization Index

Skills Development & Career Education, Legislative Commission on, 53
SL Green Realty Corp, 494, 499
Slavco Construction, 507
SLE Foundation (The), 491
Sleepy Hollow Chamber of Commerce, 585
Small Business, 51, 392
   Committee Staff, 51
   Contracting and Technology, 392
   Finance and Tax, 392
   Investigations and Oversight, 392
   Key Assembly Staff Assignments, 51
   Majority, 51
   Membership, 51
   Minority, 51
   Regulations, Health Care and Trade, 393
   Subcommittees, 392
Small Business & Entrepreneurship, 386
Small Business Administration, 104
   Buffalo, 104
   District Offices, 104
   New Jersey, 104
   New York Business Information Center, 104
   New York City, 104
   Region II New York, 104
   Syracuse, 104
Small Cities, Office for, 15, 101, 229, 289, 374
Smith, Joann, 523
Smith, Michael P, 523
Smith, Robert, 523
Smithsonian Institution, 339
   Cooper-Hewitt National Design Museum, 339
   National Museum of the American Indian-George Gustav Heye Center, 339
Smithtown Chamber of Commerce, 585
Smithtown CSD, 671
Smithtown, Town of, 441
Smyth, A Advocacy, 523
Snapple Beverage Corp, Dr Pepper/Seven U Inc & Motts, LLP, 465
Snowmobile Assn (NYS), 468, 485
Snug Harbor Cultural Center, 499
Snyder Communications Corp, 597
Soap & Detergent Assoc, 490
Social Security Administration, 314
   Office of Hearings & Appeals, 314
   Office of Quality Assurance, 314
   Office of the General Counsel, 314
   Program Operations Center, 314
   Public Affairs, 314
   Region 2-New York, 314
Social Service Employees Union, Local 371, 508
Social Services, 51
   Committee Staff, 51
   Key Assembly Staff Assignments, 51
   Majority, 51
   Membership, 51
   Minority, 51
Social Services, Children & Families, 31
   Committee Staff, 31
   Key Senate Staff Assignments, 31
   Majority, 31
   Membership, 31
   Minority, 31
Society for Clinical Social Work Inc (NYS), 531
Society for Respiratory Care Inc (NYS), 529
Society of Anesthesiologists Inc (NYS), 529
Society of Anesthesiologists, Inc (NYS), 490
Society of Certified Public Accountants (NYS), 515, 518
Society of Certified Public Accountants, NYS, 491
Society of Opticians Inc (NYS), 468
Society of Orthopaedic Surgeons (NYS), 462
Society of Physician Assistants (NYS), 483
Society of Professional Engineers Inc (NYS), 111, 495
Society of Professional Engineers, Inc (NYS), 512
Sodus CSD, 675
Soft Drink & Brewery Workers' PAC, 563
Software & Information Industry Association, 112
Solid Waste Management, Legislative Commission on, 33, 54
Solidarity Task Force, 563
Solomon R Guggenheim Foundation, 347
Solomon R Guggenheim Museum, 467, 486
Solow Management Company, 506
Solow Management Corp, 495
Solowan, Richard, 523
Soloway, Ronald, 523
Solvay UFSD, 659
Somers CSD, 677
Somers Democratic Club, 563
Sonnenblick-Goldman Company, 306
Sophie Davis School of Biomedical Education, 621
Sotheby's, 487
Source Corp, 507
Source Financing Corp, 478
South Colonie CSD, 638
South Country CSD, 671
South Glens Falls CSD, 665
South Huntington UFSD, 671
South Jefferson Chamber of Commerce, 585
South Jefferson CSD, 650
South Kortright CSD, 644
South Lewis CSD, 651
South Orangetown CSD, 664
South Queens Boys & Girls Club Inc, 513
South Queens Boys & Girls Club, Inc, 478
South Seneca CSD, 666
Southampton Chamber of Commerce, 585
Southampton UFSD, 671
Southampton, Town of, 442
Southeastern New York, Council of Industry of, 585
Southern Cayuga CSD, 641
Southern Dutchess Chamber of Commerce (Greater Southern Dutchess), 585
Southern NY Assn, 490
Southern Onondaga Republican Club, 563
Southern Saratoga County Chamber of Commerce, 585
Southern Tier Acquisition, LLC, 506
Southern Tier Business PAC, 563
Southern Tier Economic Growth Inc, 585
Southern Tier HB & REM Build-PAC, 563
Southern Tier Leadership PAC, 563
Southern Ulster County Chamber of Commerce, 586
Southern Westchester BOCES, 680
Southhampton Town Young Republicans, 563
Southold Town PBA Tax PAC.COM, 563
Southold UFSD, 671
Southold, Town of, 442
Southtowns Republican Chairman's Association, 563
Southwestern CSD at Jamestown, 642
Spackenkill UFSD, 645
Spain Agency Inc, 507
Spanish Broadcasting System Network Inc, 176
SPEAKERPAC, 562
Special Committee on Animals & the Law, 88
Special Olympics New York, Inc, 347
Specialty Tobacco Council Inc, 493
Spectra Architecture, Engineering & Surveying PC, 483
Spectra Environmental Group Inc, 192
Speech, Language Hearing Assn Inc (NYS), 529
Spencerport CSD, 653
Spencer-Van Etten CSD, 672
SPL, 493
SPOA For A Better University Neighborhood II, 562
Sports & Arts in School Foundation, 480, 494
Sports & Arts in Schools Foundation, 155, 347, 475
Spring Valley Homes, 501
Spring Valley, Village of, 442
Springbrook, 286
Springs UFSD, 671
Springville Area Chamber of Commerce, 586
Springville-Griffith Inst CSD, 646
Sprint Nextel, 463, 465
Sprint Nextel Corporation PAC, 563

863

Organization Index

SSL Political Action Committee, 562
SSP Companies, 504
St Barnabas Hospital, 459
St Bernard's School of Theology & Ministry, 631
St Bonaventure University, 631
St Elizabeth College of Nursing, 631
St Elizabeth Medical Center, 529
St Francis College, 524, 532, 631
St James Chamber of Commerce, 586
St John Fisher College, 631
St John's Hospital/Yonkers General Hospital, 478
St John's University, 465, 631
St John's University, School of Law, 192
St John's University-Peter J Tobin College of Business, School of Risk Mgmt, 251
St Johnsville CSD, 653
St Joseph's College, 631
St Joseph's Rehabilitation Center Inc, 286
St Joseph's Seminary Institute of Religious Studies, 631
St Lawrence County, 68, 410
   Supreme, County, Family & Surrogate's Courts, 68
St Lawrence County Chamber of Commerce, 586
St Lawrence County Industrial Development Agency, 586
St Lawrence County Newspapers, 597
St Lawrence University, 631
St Lawrence-Lewis BOCES, 680
St Luke's Cornwall Hospital, 531
St Luke's-Roosevelt Hospital Centers, 516
St Luke's-Roosevelt Hospital Ctrs, 495
St Margaret's Center, 531
St Mary's Healthcare System for Children Inc, 531
St Mary's Healthcare System for Children, Inc, 524
St Paul Travelers, 463
St Peter's Hospital, 501
St Raymond Community Outreach, 503
St Regis Falls CSD, 648
St Regis Mohawk Tribe, 210
St Regis Mohawk Tribe (Empire Resorts Inc), 476
St Thomas Aquinas College, 632
St Vincent Catholic Medical Centers, 478
St Vladimir's Orthodox Theological Seminary, 632
St. Elizabeth Medical Center, 463
St. Michael's Cemetery, 475
STA Subcontractors Trade Assn Inc State PAC, 564
Staffing Assn (NY), 478
Stamford CSD, 644
Standardbred Owners Assn of NY, 532
Standards of Official Conduct, 393
Star-Gazette, 593
Starpoint CSD, 658

Starrett City Associates, 474
Stars & Stripes PAC, 563
Starwood Ceruzzi, LLC, 532
State & Local Election Fund AFSCME Local 2054, DC 37, 563
State & Local Election Fund Local 1070, 563
State Comptroller, Office of the, 16, 180, 197, 290, 296, 374
   Accounting Bureau, 198, 297
   Actuarial Bureau, 198, 297
   Administration, 197, 290
   Administration Services & Quality Performance, 198
   Advisory Counsel Affairs, 198
   Agency Analysis Bureau, 199
   Benefit Calculations & Disbursements, 198, 297
   Benefit Information Services, 198
   Bureau of Economic Development & Policy Analysis, 199
   Bureau of Tax & Economic Analysis, 199
   Disability Processing/Hearing Administration, 198, 297
   Division of Intergovernmental Affairs & Community Relations, 197, 290
   Division of Investigations, 197, 290
   Division of Local Govt Services & Economic Development, 197, 290
   Division of State Services, 197, 290, 297
   Executive Office, 180, 198, 290, 297
   Financial Administration, 197, 290
   Human Resources & Affirmative Action Office, 198
   Information Technology Services, 197, 290
   Infrastructure & Citywide Expenditure Analysis, 199
   Legal Services, 198
   Management Services, 197, 290
   Matrimonial & Hearing Review, 198
   Member & Employee Services, 199, 297
   Office of Budget & Policy Analysis, 198, 290
   Oil Spill Fund Office, 180, 197, 290
   Payroll & Revenue Services Div, 198
   Payroll & Revenue Services Division, 297
   Pension Investment & Public Finance, 198
   Press Office, 198, 290
   Retirement Communications, 199, 297
   Retirement Services, 198, 297
   State Audit Group, 198, 290
   State Deputy Comptroller for New York City, 199
   State Financial Services Group, 198, 290
State Department, 16, 101, 180, 199, 290, 374
   Administrative Rules Division, 101, 199
   Administrative Support Services, 199

   Affirmative Action, 199
   Albany, 200
   Binghamton, 200
   Buffalo, 200
   Business & Licensing Services Division, 101, 199
   Cemeteries Division, 101, 199
   Coastal Resources & Waterfront Revitalization Division, 180, 199, 291
   Code Enforcement & Administration Division, 199, 291
   Community Services Division, 180, 199, 291
   Corporations, State Records & UCC Division, 101, 199
   Ethics Commission, 199, 291
   Fire Prevention & Control Office, 180, 199, 291
   Fiscal Management, 199
   Hicksville, 200
   Human Resources Management, 199
   Internal Audit, 200
   Local Government & Community Services, 180, 199, 291
   Local Government Services Division, 199, 291
   New York State Academy of Fire Science, 180, 199, 291
   Olean, 200
   Open Government Committee, 199, 291
   Operations, 199
   Peekskill, 200
   Plattsburgh, 200
   Poughkeepsie, 200
   Regional Affairs Division, 200
   Regional Offices, 200
   Rochester, 200
   State Athletic Commission, 200
   Suffolk, 200
   Syracuse, 200
   Systems Management Bureau, 200
   Utica, 200
   Watertown, 200
State Employees Federal Credit Union, 300
State Farm Insurance Companies, 491, 497
State of New York Mortgage Agency (SONYMA), 91, 127, 231, 380
State of New York Municipal Bond Bank Agency (MBBA), 92, 127, 291, 380
State Police, Division of, 16, 136, 374
   Administration, 136
   Employee Relations, 136
   Field Command, 136
   Forensic Investigation Center, 136
   Human Resources, 136
   Internal Affairs, 136
   Public Information, 136
   State Police Academy, 136
State Street Associates PAC, 563
State University at Brockport, 613
State University at Old Westbury, 613

Organization Index

State University at Potsdam, 613
State University College at Cortland, 613
State University College at Geneseo, 613
State University College at New Paltz, 614
State University College of Technology at Canton, 614
State University College of Technology at Delhi, 615
State University Construction Fund, 128, 149, 380
State University Empire State College, 614
State University Institute of Technology, 615
State University of New York at Albany, 613
State University of New York at Oneonta, 614
State University of New York at Oswego, 614
State University of New York at Plattsburgh, 614
State University of New York College of Environmental Science & Forestry, 613
State University of New York Maritime College, 615
State University of New York, Fredonia, 614
State University of NY at Stony Brook, 520
State University of NY, System Administration, 521
State-Local Relations, Legislative Commission on, 53
Staten Island Advance, 599
Staten Island Chamber of Commerce, 469, 586
Staten Island Economic Development Corporation, 586
Staten Island Political Action Committee, 563
Staten Island Zoo, 347
Statewide Association of Minority Businesses PAC, 563
Statewide Black & Puerto Rican/Latino Substance Abuse Task Force, 286
Statewide Corporate Strategies Inc, 524
Statewide Emergency Network for Social & Economic Security (SENSES), 323
Steamfitters' Union Local 638 PAC, 563
Steel Equities, 493
Stegemoeller, Rudy, 524
Stendardi, Deborah M, 524
Steuben County, 68, 410
　Supreme, County, Family & Surrogate's Courts, 68
Steuben County Industrial Development Agency, 586
Steve Israel for Congress Committee-State Account, 564
Stillman, Friedman & Shechtman PC, 142
Stillwater CSD, 665
Stock Exchange (NY), 524

Stock Exchange Group (NY), 483
Stockbridge Valley CSD, 652
Stonehenge Capital Corporation, 491
Stony Brook University, 491
Stony Brook University, SUNY, 613
Stop & Shop Supermarket Co (The), 520
Stop DWI Coordinators Assn (NYS), 487
Strategic 56 LP, 474
Strategic Services, Inc, 524
Stratford Business Corp, 516
Strive, 514
Stroock & Stroock & Lavan LLP, 251
Structural Biology Center (NY), 503
Structured Employment Economic Development Corp, 503
Struever Fidelco Cappelli, Inc, 522
Stryker, Patricia, 524
STU Weissman Productions II Inc, 487
Stuart Portfolio Consultants LP, 493
Student Advocacy, 462
Stuto, Diane D, 524
Subcontractor's Trade Assn Inc, 501
Suburban News & Hamlin Clarkson Herald, 599
Subway Surface Supervisors Assn, 513
Success PAC, 564
Suffern Chamber of Commerce, 586
Suffolk & Nassau Counties Plumbing & Heating Contractors Assoc PAC, 564
Suffolk Co Detective Investigators PBA Inc PAC, 564
Suffolk Co Police Dept Superior Officers Assoc Public Affairs Cmte, 564
Suffolk Community Council (FKA Pannullo, Judith), 524
Suffolk Community Council Inc, 524
Suffolk County, 68, 70, 410
　1ST DISTRICT COURT, Civil Term, 70
　1ST DISTRICT COURT, Criminal Term, 70
　2nd District Court, 70
　3rd District Court, 70
　4th District Court, 70
　5th District Court, 70
　6th District Court, 70
　County Court, 68
　Family Court, 68
　Supreme Court, 68
　Surrogate's Court, 68
Suffolk County Ambulance Chiefs Assoc, 522
Suffolk County Assn of Municipal Employees PAC Inc, 463
Suffolk County Assn of Municipal Employees' PAC Inc, 564
Suffolk County Chapter Nat'l Womens Political Caucus, 564
Suffolk County Community College, 617
Suffolk County Correction Officers Assn, 507

Suffolk County Correction Officers' Assn PAC, 564
Suffolk County Court Employees, 506
Suffolk County Deputy Sheriff's Police Benevolent Assn, 522
Suffolk County Deputy Sheriffs Benevolent Assn Inc PAC, 564
Suffolk County Executive, 501
Suffolk County Police Benevolent Assn PAC, 564
Suffolk County Police Conference PAC, 564
Suffolk County Republican Women PAC, 564
Suffolk County Water Authority, 522
Suffolk Regional Off-Track Betting Corporation, 128, 337, 380
Suit-Kote Corp, 513
Sullivan & Cromwell, 96
Sullivan & Cromwell LLP, 330
Sullivan BOCES, 680
Sullivan County, 68, 411
　Family & Surrogate's Courts, 68
　Supreme & County Courts, 68
Sullivan County Chamber of Commerce, 586
Sullivan County Community College, 617
Sullivan County Industrial Development Agency, 586
Sullivan West CSD, 672
Sullivan, Edward C, 524
Sullivan, Veronica, 524
Sun Microsystems Inc, 469
Sunbridge College, 632
Sunnyside Community Services Inc, 467
Sunoco Inc, 468
SUNOCO Inc, 514
Sunrise Senior Living, 491
Sunwize Technologies Inc, 176
SUNY at Albany, Center for Women in Government & Civil Society, 209
SUNY at Albany, Nelson A Rockefeller College, 166
SUNY at Albany, Nelson A Rockefeller College of Public Affairs & Policy, 210
SUNY at Albany, Professional Development Program, NE States Addiction, 286
SUNY at Albany, Rockefeller College, 210
SUNY at Albany, School of Public Health, Center for Public Health Preparedness, 227
SUNY at Cortland, Center for Environmental & Outdoor Education, 192
SUNY at New Paltz, College of Liberal Arts & Sciences, 166, 210
SUNY at New Paltz, Department of History, 210
SUNY at Stony Brook, 520
SUNY at Stony Brook, NY State Drinking Driver Program, 142

Organization Index

SUNY Board of Trustees, 611
SUNY Buffalo Human Rights Center, 243
SUNY College & Career Counseling Center, 618
SUNY College at Brockport, 520
SUNY College of Agriculture & Technology at Cobleskill, 614
SUNY College of Environmental Science & Forestry, 465
SUNY Downstate Medical Center, 532, 612
SUNY State College of Optometry, 612
SUNY System Administration & Executive Council, 611
   New York African American Institute, 611
   New York Network, 611
   Rockefeller Institute of Government, 611
   Small Business Development Center, 612
   State University Construction Fund, 612
   SUNY Metropolitan Recruitment Center, 611
SUNY Upstate Medical, 520
SUNY Upstate Medical University, 520, 612
SUNY, System Administration, 521
Superior Officers Assoc-Nassau County Police, 564
Superior Officers' Benevolent Assn of the TBTA PAC, 564
Superpower Inc, 491
Supershuttle NY Inc, 514
Support Services Alliance Inc, 112, 251, 491
Supreme Court, 266
Supreme Court Justices' Assn of the City of NY (Association of Justices of the Supreme Court of NY), 491
Supreme Court Officers Assn (NYS), 475
Surgeon PAC, 564
Susan O'Dell Taylor School for Children, 516
Susquehanna & Western Railway Corp (NY), 507
Susquehanna Valley CSD, 639
Swedish Institute, 637
Sweet Home CSD, 647
Swig Equities, LLC, 494
Swisher International, Inc, 476
Syosset CSD, 656
Syracuse, 75
   Civil & Criminal Courts, 75
Syracuse & Central NY, Metropolitan Development Association of, 586
Syracuse Chamber of Commerce (Greater Syracuse), 586
Syracuse City School District, 501
Syracuse City SD, 659
Syracuse Economic Development, 586
Syracuse Educational Opportunity Center, 618
Syracuse Industrial Development Agency, 586

Syracuse Newspapers Inc, 600
Syracuse Tomorrow, 564
Syracuse University, 519, 529, 632
Syracuse University Press, 192
Syracuse University, Maxwell School of Citizenship & Public Affairs, 155, 192, 210, 294, 300, 323
Syracuse University, Office of Government & Community Relations, 155
Syracuse, City of, 442
Sysco Food Services of Albany, LLC, 463
Systra Consulting Inc, 359
TA Ahern Contractors/Ahern Painting, 475
Taconic Hills CSD, 643
Taconic Investment Partners LLC, 486, 495
Taconic IPA Inc, 530
Tahl Propp Equities, 495
Tanenbaum Center for Interreligious Understanding, 243
Tanglewood Manor, 531
TAP PAC-APC, 564
Tarrytown UFSD, 677
Tavern on the Green, 467
Tax Appeals, Division of, 16, 326, 374
   Administrative Law Judges & Officers, 17, 326
   Tax Appeals Tribunal, 16, 326
Taxation & Finance Department, 17, 101, 326, 374
   Audit Division, 102, 327
   Budget & Accounting Services, 101, 327
   E-MPIRE, 102, 327
   Human Resources Management, 101, 327
   Information Office, 101, 327
   Office of Administration (OOA), 101, 327
   Office of Budget & Management Analysis, 101, 327
   Operations Support Bureau, 101, 327
   Planning & Management Analysis Bureau, 101, 327
   Tax Compliance Division, 102, 327
   Tax Enforcement, Office of, 102, 327
   Tax Policy Analysis, Office of, 102, 327
   Taxpayer Services & Revenue Division, 102, 327
   Technical Services Division, 102, 327
   Treasury Division, 102, 327
Taxation, Joint Committee on, 395
Taxi Technology Corporation, 494
Taxicab Service Assn, 478
Taxpayers Against Fraud, 503
Taxpayers for an Affordable New York PAC, 565
Taylor Business Institute, 637
TBTA Maintenance Employees, Local 1931, DC-37, AFSCME, 526
TD Banknorth, 96
TDC Development & Construction Corp, 499
Tea Association of the USA Inc, 89

Teachers College, Columbia University, 155, 632
Teachers Insurance & Annuity Assn/College Retirement Equities Fun, 529
Teaching Hospital Education PAC, 565
Teaching Matters Inc, 155
Teamsters Local 237, 508, 524
Teamsters Local 317, 468
Teamsters Local 317 PAC, 565
Teamsters Local 72 PAC, 565
TEAPAC, 564
Technical Assistance Centers' Assn for Transferring Success, 491
Technical Career Institutes Inc, 637
Technologists for New York, 565
Technology Enterprise Corp (NYS), 487
Technology Enterprise Corporation (NYS), 469
Telebeam Telecommunications Corp, 514
Telecommunications Assn Inc (NYS), 489, 517
Telecommunications Improvement Council, 565
Telecommunications Int'l Union, 565
Tempo 802, 565
Temporary & Disability Assistance, Office of, 17, 238, 313, 374
   Budget, Finance & Data Management, 313
   Child Support Enforcement Division, 313
   Disability Determinations Division, 313
   Employment & Transitional Supports, 238, 313
   Information Technology Services, 313
   Legal Affairs Division, 313
   Program Support & Quality Improvement, 238, 313
   Public Information, 313
Tempositions, Inc, 459
Tenants & Neighbors Coalition (NYS), 524, 525
Terra Cotta LLC, 495
The Association of Settlement Companies (Multistate Associates Inc), 487
The Bachmann-Strauss Dystonia & Parkinson Foundation, 227
The Business Council PAC Inc, 565
The Business Review, 591
The Clearing House Association, LLC, 96
The Coalition for Responsible Development, 565
The Coca-Cola Bottling Company of New York, PAC, 565
The Delaware Club, 565
The Independent, 594
The Independent News, 597
The Italian American Poltical Action Committee of New York, 565
The Legal Aid Society, 243

Organization Index

The New York Children's Vision Coalition, 476
The New York Observer, 597
The New York Times, 597
The Palladium Times, 598
The Political Action Committee of The Fulton County Regional Chamber of Commerce, 565
The Putnam County News and Recorder, 597
The Real Conservatives, 565
The Republican Club of Bronxville, 565
The Shaw Licitra PAC, 565
The Wine PAC, 565
The Young Democratic Rural Conference, 565
Theatre Workshop (NY), 466
Theatrical Protective Union Local No One Iatse NYS Stagehands PAC, 565
Thelen Reid Brown Raysman & Steiner, 262
Theracare, 467
Therapeutic Communities Assn of NY Inc, 477
Thomson West, 529
Thor 280 Richards Street LLC, 500
THOROPAC - Thoroughbred Breeders' PAC, 564
Thoroughbred Breeders Inc (NY), 463
Thoroughbred Horsemen of Western NY PAC, 565
Thoroughbred Horsemen's Assn Inc (NY), 483
Thoroughbred Racing-New York (Vornado Realty Trust), 478
Thorpe, Vernon, 525
Thousand Islands Bridge Authority, 128, 354, 380
Thousand Islands CSD, 650
Three Rivers Development Foundation Inc, 586
Three Village Central School District, 493
Three Village CSD, 671
Thrivent Financial for Lutherans, 487
Ticket brokers (NY), 478
Ticketmaster, 468
Ticonderoga Area Chamber of Commerce, 587
Ticonderoga CSD, 647
Tier Technologies, 504
Tier Technologies Inc, 465
Tile Layers Subordinate Union Local 7 of New York and New Jersey PAC, 566
Time Warner Cable, 467
Times Herald-Record, 596
Times Union, 591
Tioga County, 68, 411
   Family & Surrogate's Courts, 68
   Supreme & County Courts, 69
Tioga County Chamber of Commerce, 587

Tioga County Industrial Development Agency, 587
Tioga CSD, 672
Tishman Speyer Properties, 306, 516
Tishman Speyer/Citigroup Alternative, 519
TKGG LLC, 499
T-Mobile, 494
T-Mobile New York PAC, 564
T-Mobile USA Inc, 466, 489, 531
To Life, 531
Toll Brooklyn LP, 486
Toll Brothers Inc, 495
Tompkins Cortland Community College, 617
Tompkins County, 69, 411
   Supreme, County, Family & Surrogate's Courts, 69
Tompkins County Area Development, 587
Tompkins County Chamber of Commerce, 587
Tompkins Trustco Inc, 97
Tompkins-Seneca-Tioga BOCES, 680
Tomra, 487
Tonawanda, 75
   Civil & Criminal Courts, 75
Tonawanda (Town Of) Development Corporation, 587
Tonawanda City SD, 647
Tonawanda News, 600
Tonawanda, Town of, 442
Tonawandas, Chamber of Commerce of the, 587
Tourism Advocacy Coalition PAC, 566
Tourism Industry Coalition, 525
Tourism Industry Coalition (TIC), 525
Tourism, Arts & Sports Development, 51
   Committee Staff, 51
   Key Assembly Staff Assignments, 51
   Majority, 52
   Membership, 52
   Minority, 52
Tourism, Recreation & Sports Development, 31
   Committee Staff, 31
   Key Senate Staff Assignments, 31
   Majority, 31
   Membership, 31
   Minority, 31
Touro College, 478, 632
TOW PAC, 565
Towers at Spring Creek, 499
Town Clerks Assn Inc (NYS), 504
Town of Annsville Democratic Club, 566
Town of Hamburg Endorsed Cadidates Fund, 566
Town of Hempstead, 499
Town of Hurley Republican Club Inc, 566
Town of North Hempstead, 478
Town of Webb UFSD, 650
Toxic Substances & Hazardous Waste, Legislative Commission on, 33

Toxic Substances & Hazardous Wastes, Legislative Commission on, 54
Toyota Motor Sales, 469
Toys R' Us, 495
Tracfone Wireless Inc, 483
Trading Cove New York, LLC, 465
Trading Cove NY, LLC, 462, 525
Traffipax Inc, 507
Trail Conference (NY/NJ), 455
TransCanada Pipelines Ltd, 491
Transcare NY Inc (Metrocare Ambulance), 501
Transit Alliance, 506
Transit Supervisors Organization PAC, 566
Transport Workers Union Local 100 Political Contributions Committee, 566
Transport Workers Union of America, AFL-CIO, 277, 359
Transport Workers Union, Local 100, 508, 525
Transportation, 31, 52
   Committee Staff, 31, 52
   Key Assembly Staff Assignments, 52
   Key Senate Staff Assignments, 31
   Majority, 32, 52
   Membership, 32, 52
   Minority, 32, 52
Transportation & Infrastructure, 393
   Aviation, 393
   Coast Guard & Maritime Transportation, 393
   Economic Development, Public Buildings & Emergency Management, 393
   Highway and Transit, 393
   Railroads, Pipelines and Hazardous Materials, 393
   Subcommittees, 393
   Water Resources & Environment, 393
Transportation Alternatives, 359
Transportation Department, 17, 302, 348, 374
   Administrative Services Division, 349
   Delivery Division, 349
   Engineering Division, 302, 349
   Legal Affairs Division, 349
   Operations Division, 349
   Policy & Strategy Division, 349
   Region 1, 349
   Region 10, 350
   Region 11, 350
   Region 2, 349
   Region 3, 349
   Region 4, 349
   Region 5, 349
   Region 6, 349
   Region 7, 349
   Region 8, 349
   Region 9, 350
   Regional Offices, 349
Transportation Engineering Alliance (NYS), 483

Organization Index

Tranter, G Thomas, Jr, 525
Travelers Companies Inc (The), 456
Travelport LTD, 463
Trees New York, 192
Trial Lawyers' Assn (NYS), 480, 503
Triangle Equities, 493
Tribeca Film Institute, 347, 525
Tri-State Chamber of Commerce, 587
Tri-State College of Acupuncture, 637
Tri-State Transportation Campaign, 359
Tri-Valley CSD, 672
Trivin Inc, 464
Trocaire College, 632
Trooper Foundation-State of New York Inc, 142, 300
Troy, 75
   Civil & Criminal Court, 75
Troy City Enlarged SD, 663
Troy, City of, 443
True & Walsh, LLP, 227
Truffles LLC/Jackson Parker Co, 474
Trumansburg CSD, 673
Trust for Public Land, 508
Trustco Bank, 516
Trustees of Columbia University in City of NY (The), 475
Trustees of Columbia University in the City of NY (The), 463, 495, 500, 525
Tuckahoe Common SD, 671
Tuckahoe UFSD, 677
Tuck-it-Away, 499
Tully Abdo, Susan, 525
Tully Construction, 475
Tully CSD, 659
Tupper Lake Chamber of Commerce, 587
Tupper Lake CSD, 648
Turner, Francine, 525
Turner/Geneslaw Inc, 236
Tussaud's Group (The), 519
Tuxedo UFSD, 661
TVG Network, 508
Two Trees Management Inc, 467
Tyco international (USA) Inc, 501
Tyson, Lisa, 526
U.S.W.A. Local 420A PAC, 566
UA Plumbers & Pipefitters LU 773 Voluntary NYS PAC Fund, 566
UA Plumbers & Steamfitters Local 22 PAC Inc, 566
UBS Securities, 508
UFCW Active Ballot Club, 566
UFT COPE Local, 566
UHAP PAC, 566
UHY Advisors, 112
Ulster BOCES, 680
Ulster County, 69, 411
   Family Court, 69
   Supreme & County Courts, 69
   Surrogate's Court, 69
Ulster County Chamber of Commerce, 587
Ulster County Community College, 617

Ulster County Democratic Women, 566
Ulster County Development Corporation/Ulster County Industrial Development Agency, 587
Ulster Savings Bank, 97
Unadilla Valley CSD, 642
Unatego CSD, 662
Ungar, Robert A Associates Inc, 526
Unification Theological Seminary, 632
Unified Court System, 256, 375
   10th Judicial District (Judicial Department 2), 257
   11th Judicial District (Judicial Department 2), 257
   12th Judicial District (Judicial Department 1), 257
   1st Judicial Department, 256
   1st Judicial District (Judicial Department 1), 256
   2nd Judicial Department, 256
   2nd Judicial District (Judicial Department 2), 256
   3rd Judicial Department, 256
   3rd Judicial District (Judicial Department 3), 257
   4th Judicial Department, 256
   4th Judicial District (Judicial Department 3), 257
   5th Judicial District (Judicial Department 4), 257
   6th Judicial District (Judicial Department 3), 257
   7th Judicial District (Judicial Department 4), 257
   8th Judicial District (Judicial Department 4), 257
   9th Judicial District (Judicial Department 2), 257
   Administrative Board of the Courts, 256
   Administrative Judge to the Court of Claims (NYS), 256
   Administrative Judges to the Courts in New York City, 256
   Administrative Judges to the Courts outside New York City, 257
   Administrative Services Office, 257
   Appellate Division, 256
   Civil Court, 256
   Counsel's Office, 257
   Court Administration, 256
   Court of Appeals, 256
   Court Operations, 257
   Criminal Court, 257
   Family Court, 257
   Financial Management & Audit Services, 257
   Human Resources & Employee Relations, 257
   Management Support, 257
   Public Affairs Office, 257

Uniform State Laws Commission, 128, 202, 258, 380
Uniformed EMS Officers Union, FDNY, Local, 467
Uniformed EMT's & Paramedics, Local 2507-FDNY, 526
Uniformed Fire Alarm Dispatchers Benevolent Assn-FDNY, 526
Uniformed Fire Officers Assn (NYC), 506
Uniformed Fire Officers Association, 300
Uniformed Fire Officers Association 527 Account, 566
Uniformed Firefighters Assn, 526
Uniformed Firefighters Assoc State FirePAC Political Action Committee, 566
Union College, 487, 632
Union for a Better New York, 566
Union Graduate University, 463
Union Local Development Corporation (Town of), 587
Union Springs CSD, 641
Union State Bank, 97
Union Theological Seminary, 632
Union, Town of, 443
Uniondale UFSD, 656
Union-Endicott CSD, 640
Unions for Jobs & the Environment, 468
Unite Here, 483, 507
UNITE HERE, 277
UNITE HERE TIP State & Local Fund, 566
United Cerebral Palsy Assns of NYS, 476
United Charities Corporation, 478
United Dairy Cooperative Services Inc, 89
United Federation of Teachers, 155
United Food & Commercial Workers Dist Cncl of NY & Northern NJ, 514
United Food & Commercial Workers Local 1, 277
United Food & Commercial Workers Union, Dist Council of Region 1, 499
United for Good Government, 567
United Health Services, 513
United Healthcare Services Inc, 472, 487
United Healthcare Services Inc (Ovations), 487
United Healthcare Services, Inc, 526
United Healthcare Services, Inc (FKA Oxford LLC), 526
United Hospital Fund, 531
United Hospital Fund of New York, 227
United Jewish Appeal Federation - Jewish Philanthropies NY, 523
United Jewish Appeal-Federation of Jewish Philanthropies, 306
United Jewish Appeal-Federation of Jewish Philanthropies of NY, 323
United Jewish Organizations of Williamsburg, 504
United Nations Development Corporation, 103, 128, 202, 380
United Neighborhood Houses, 499

Organization Index

United Neighborhood Houses - Not For Profit, 323
United Neighborhood Houses of NY, 526
United Neighborhood Houses of NY Inc, 523
United New York Ambulance Network (UNYAN), 227
United New York Democratic Club Inc, 567
United NY Ambulance Network, 476
United Parcel Service, 516
United Parcel Service Inc PAC NY, 567
United Restaurant, Hotel & Tavern Association of NY Statewide PAC, 567
United Services Automobile Assn (USAA), 484
United Spinal Assn, 526
United Spinal Assn (FKA Eastern Paralyed Veterans Assn), 526
United Spinal Association, 368
United Steelworkers District 4 PAC, 567
United Steelworkers of America, 567
United Teachers (NYS), 456
United Transportation Union, 300, 359, 510
United Transportation Union Political Action Committee (UTU PAC), 567
United University Professions, 155, 300, 526
United Water, 465
United Way of Central New York, 323
United Way of Greater Rochester, 469
United Way of New York City, 323
United Way of NYC, 459
United Way of NYS, 488
Unity Health System, 463
Unity Mutual Life Insurance Co, 251
Unity PAC, 567
University (NY), 495, 531
University at Buffalo, 527
University at Buffalo, Research Institute on Addictions, 286
University at Buffalo, State University of New York, 613
University of Rochester, 463, 472
University of Rochester School of Medicine, 192
University School of Medicine (NY) & Hospitals (NY), 531
University-Industry Cooperation, Task Force on, 53
Unkechauq Nation, 210
UNYAN PAC, 566
Upstate Farms Cooperative Inc, 527
Upstate Freshwater Institute, 192
Upstate Homes for Children & Adults Inc, 323
Upstate Niagara Cooperative (FKA Upstate Farms Cooperative), 527
Upstate Niagara Cooperative Inc, 89
Upstate Niagara Cooperative Inc (FKA Upstate Farms Cooperative Inc), 489
Urban Health Plan Inc, 508

Urban Homesteading Assistance Board, 236
Urbane Leadership, 567
Urbanomics, 294, 331
Urbitran Group, 359
US Commerce Department, 81, 104, 184, 239
   Boston Region (includes upstate New York), 104
   Buffalo US Export Assistance Center, 105
   Census Bureau, 104
   Economic Development Administration, 104
   Harlem US Export Assistance Center, 105
   Long Island US Export Assistance Center, 105
   Minority Business Development Agency, 104, 239
   National Marine Fisheries Svc, Northeast Region Headquarters, 184
   National Oceanic & Atmospheric Administration, 81, 105, 184
   National Weather Service, Eastern Region, 81, 105, 184
   New York Region, 104, 239
   New York US Export Assistance Center, 105
   Philadelphia Region (includes New York), 104
   Rochester US Export Assistance Center, 105
   Upstate New York Office, 104
   US Commercial Service - International Trade Administration, 105
   Westchester US Export Assistance Center, 105
US Commission on Civil Rights, 164, 239
   EASTERN REGION (includes New York State), 164, 239
US Defense Department, 150, 184, 362
   1st Marine Corps District, 362
   AIR FORCE-National Media Outreach, 362
   Air National Guard, 362
   Army, 362
   Army Corps of Engineers, 184
   Buffalo District Office, 184
   Fort Drum, 362
   Fort Hamilton, 362
   Fort Totten-77th Regional Support Command, 362
   Francis S Gabreski Airport, 106th Rescue Wing, 362
   Great Lakes & Ohio River Division (Western NYS), 184
   Hancock Field, 174th Fighter Wing, 362
   Marine Corps, 362
   Navy, 363
   North Atlantic Division, 184
   Program Directorate, 184
   Public Affairs Office, 362

   Regional Business Directorate, 184
   Saratoga Springs Naval Support Unit, 363
   US Military Academy, 150
   Watervliet Arsenal, 362
US Department of Agriculture, 81, 105, 171, 184, 217, 232, 303
   Agricultural Marketing Service, 81
   Agricultural Research Service, 81
   Albany Field Office, 82, 217
   Animal Plant Health Inspection Service, 81
   Avoca Work Unit, 81
   Batavia Work Station, 81
   Big Flats Work Station, 81
   Canandaigua Work Station, 82
   Cornell Cooperative Extension Service, 82
   Dairy Programs, 81
   Farm Service Agency, New York State Office, 82
   Field Operations - Albany District Office, 82
   Field Operations-Albany District Office, 218
   Finger Lakes National Forest, 184
   Food & Nutrition Service, 82, 217
   Food Safety & Inspection Service, 82, 218
   Forest Service-Northeastern Area State & Private Forestry, 184
   Forest Service-Northern Research Station, 184
   Forest Service-Region 9, 184
   Fresh Products Branch - Bronx Field Office, 81
   Fruit & Vegetable Division, 81
   Gastonia Region-New York Office, 81
   Green Mountain & Finger Lakes, 184
   Ithaca NY Research Units, 81
   JFK International Airport Inspection Station, 82
   Market News Branch-New York State, 81
   National Agricultural Statistics Service-NYS Office, 82
   Natural Resources Conservation Service, 184
   New York Area Office, 82
   New York City Field Office, 82, 218
   New York State Office, 82, 105, 171, 232, 303
   North Atlantic Area, 81
   Northeast Marketing Area, 81
   NY Animal Import Center, 82
   Office of the Inspector General, Northeast Region, 82
   Oneida Work Station, 82
   Plant Genetic Resources Unit, 81
   Plant Protection Quarantine (PPQ) Programs-Eastern Region, 81
   Rochester Field Office, 82, 218

Organization Index

Rural Development, 82, 105, 171, 232, 303
USDA/GIPSA, Packers & Stockyards Pgms-Atlantic Region, 82
USDA-AMS Poultry Grading Branch, 81
Veterinary Services, 82
Westhampton Beach Work Station, 82
US Department of Energy, 171
Brookhaven Group, 171
Brookhaven National Laboratory, 171
Community Involvement/Public Affairs, 171
Federal Energy Regulatory Commission, 171
Knolls Atomic Power Laboratory- KAPL Inc, 171
Laboratories, 171
New York Regional Office, 171
Office of External Affairs, 171
Office of the Director, 171
US Department of Health & Human Services, 218, 239, 314
Administration for Children & Families, 218, 314
Administration on Aging, 218, 314
Agency for Toxic Substances & Disease Registry-EPA Region 2, 218, 314
Centers for Disease Control & Prevention, 218, 314
Centers for Medicare & Medicaid Services, 218, 314
Food & Drug Administration, 218, 314
Health Resources & Svcs Admin Office of Performance Review, 218, 315
Indian Health Services-Area Office, 218, 315
Medicaid and Children's Health (DMCH), 218, 314
Medicare Financial Management (DMFM), 218, 314
Medicare Operations Division (DMO), 218, 314
New York District Office, 218, 314
New York Quarantine Station, 218, 314
Northeast Region, 218, 314
Northeast Regional Laboratory, 218, 314
Office for Civil Rights, 218, 239, 315
Office of General Counsel, 218, 315
Office of Inspector General, 219, 315
Office of Public Health & Science, 219, 315
Office of Secretary's Regional Representative-Region 2-NY, 218, 239, 315
US Department of Homeland Security (DHS), 82, 185, 203, 219, 239, 328, 355
Administration, 185, 204
Agricultural Inspections (AI), 82
Agriculture Inspections (AI), 203
Albany Sub Office, 203, 204, 240, 328
Albany, Port of, 204, 328
Brooklyn, Port of, 82, 203
Buffalo District Office, 204, 239
Buffalo Field Office, 204, 328
Buffalo, Port of, 82, 203, 204, 328
Bureau of Immigration & Customs Enforcement (ICE), 203, 328
Champlain, Port of, 82, 203, 204, 328
CIS Asylum Offices, 204, 240
Customs & Border Protection (CBP), 82, 203, 328
Environmental Measurements Laboratory, 185, 204
Federal Emergency Management Agency (FEMA), 204, 219
Federal Protective Service (The), 204
Field Counsel - New York, 204, 328
Garden City Satellite Office, 204, 240
JFK International Airport Area Office, 83, 204
Laboratory Division, 204, 328
National Disaster Medical System, 204, 219
New York Asylum Office, 204, 240
New York City District Office, 204, 240
New York District Office, 203, 328
New York Field Office, 204, 328
New York Regional Office, 204, 219
Newark Asylum Offc-Including NYS not served by New York City, 204, 240
Ogdensburg, Port of, 204, 328
Plum Island Animal Disease Center, 83, 204
Systems Division, 185, 204
Testbeds Division, 185, 204
Transportation Security Administration (TSA), 204, 355
US Citizenship & Immigration Services (USCIS), 204, 239
US Department of the Interior, 185, 339
Bureau of Land Management, 185
Coram Sub-District Office, 185
Eastern States Office (includes New York State), 185
Fire Island National Seashore, 185, 339
Fish & Wildlife Service, 185
Fish & Wildlife Service-Northeast Region, 339
Fort Stanwix National Monument, 339
Gateway National Recreation Area, 339
Geological Survey, 185
Ithaca Sub-District Office, 185
Jamaica Bay Unit, 339
Manhattan Sites, 339
Martin Van Buren National Historic Site, 340
National Park Service-Northeast Region, 185, 339
Northeast Region (includes New York State), 185
Office of the Secretary, Environmental Policy & Compliance, 185
Office of the Solicitor, 185
Roosevelt-Vanderbilt National Historic Sites, 340
Sagamore Hill National Historic Site, 340
Sandy Hook Unit, 339
Saratoga National Historical Park, 340
Staten Island Unit, 339
Statue of Liberty National Monument & Ellis Island, 340
Theodore Roosevelt Inaugural National Historic Site, 340
Water Resources Division - New York State District Office, 185
Women's Rights National Historical Park, 340
US Department of Veterans Affairs, 363
Albany VA Medical Center, 363
Batavia VA Medical Center, 363
Bath National Cemetery, 363
Bath VA Medical Center, 363
Bronx VA Medical Center, 364
Brooklyn Campus of the NY Harbor Healthcare System, 364
Buffalo Regional Office, 363
Buffalo VA Medical Center, 363
Calverton National Cemetery, 363
Canandaigua VA Medical Center, 363
Castle Point Campus of the VA Hudson Vly Healthcare System, 364
Cypress Hills National Cemetery, 363
Gerald B.H. Solomon Saratoga National Cemetery, 363
Long Island National Cemetery, 363
Montrose Campus of the VA Hudson Valley Healthcare System, 364
National Cemetery Administration, 363
New York Campus of the NY Harbor Healthcare System, 364
New York City Regional Office, 363
Northport VA Medical Center, 364
Syracuse VA Medical Center & Clinics, 363
VA Healthcare Network Upstate New York (VISN2), 363
VA NY/NJ Veterans Healthcare Network (VISN3), 363
VA Regional Office of Public Affairs, Field Operations Svc, 363
Veterans Benefits Administration, 363
Veterans Health Admin Integrated Svc Network (VISN), 363
Woodlawn National Cemetery, 363
US Education Department, 150
Civil Rights, 150
Federal Student Aid, 150
Financial Partner Services, 151
Office of Inspector General, 151
Region 2 - NY, NJ, PR, Vi, 150
Regional Grants Representative, 151
US Environmental Protection Agency, 185

Organization Index

Caribbean Environmental Protection Division (CEPD), 185
Division of Enforcement & Compliance Assistance (DECA), 185
Division of Environmental Planning & Protection (DEPP), 185
Division of Environmental Science & Assessment (DESA), 185
Emergency & Remedial Response Division (ERRD), 185
Inspector General, Office of (OIG), 186
OCEFT/Criminal Investigations Division, 186
Policy & Management, Office of, 186
Public Affairs Division (PAD), 186
Region 2 - New York, 185
Regional Counsel, Office of (ORC), 186
US Federal Courts, 259
   Eastern District, 259
   Northern District, 259
   Southern District, 259, 260
   US Bankruptcy Court - New York, 259
   US Court of Appeals for the Second Circuit, 259
   US Court of International Trade, 259
   US DISTRICT COURT - NEW YORK (part of the Second Circuit), 259
   US Tax Court, 260
   Western District, 259, 260
US Fireworks Safety Commission Inc, 527
US General Services Administration, 204, 303
   Administration, 205, 303
   Federal Supply Service, 205, 303
   Federal Technology Service, 205, 303
   Inspector General's Office, 205, 303
   Public Buildings Service, 205, 303
   Region 2-New York, 205, 303
US Government Printing Office, 205
   Printing Procurement Office, 205
   Region 2-I (New York), 205
US Housing & Urban Development Department, 232
   Administration (Admin Service Center 1), 232
   Albany Area Office & Financial Operations Center, 232
   Buffalo Area Office, 232
   Community Planning & Development, 232
   Fair Housing & Equal Opportunity Office, 232
   Field Offices, 232
   General Counsel, 232
   Housing, 232
   Inspector General, 232
   New York State Office, 232
   Public Housing, 232
US Interactive Inc, 463
US Justice Department, 105, 137, 260, 328
   Albany, 137, 138, 139, 260, 261

Antitrust Division-New York Field Office, 105
Antitrust Division-New York Field Office, 260
Audit Division, 260
Binghamton, 138, 260
Brooklyn, 139, 261
Brooklyn Metropolitan Detention Center, 138
Buffalo, 137, 138, 139, 261
Bureau of Alcohol, Tobacco, Firearms & Explosives, 137, 328
Central Islip, 139
Civil Division - Commercial Litigation Branch, 260
Civil Division-Commercial Litigation Branch, 105
Community Relations Service - Northeast & Caribbean Region, 260
Community Relations Service-Northeast & Carribean Region, 105
Drug Enforcement Administration - New York Task Force, 137
Eastern District, 138, 139, 260, 261
Federal Bureau of Investigation - New York Field Offices, 137
Federal Bureau of Prisons, 138
Federal Correctional Institution at Otisville, 138
Investigations Division, 260
JFK/LGA, 138
Melville, 138
Metropolitan Correctional Center, 138
New York City, 137, 138, 260
New York Field Division, 137, 328
Northern District, 138, 139, 260, 261
OFFICE OF INSPECTOR GENERAL (including New York State), 260
Ray Brook Federal Correctional Institution, 138
Rochester, 138, 139, 261
Secret Service - New York Field Offices, 138
Southern District, 138, 139, 260, 261
Syracuse, 138, 139, 260, 261
US Attorney's Office - New York, 138, 260
US Marshals' Service - New York, 139, 261
US Parole Commission, 139
US Trustee - Bankruptcy, Region 2, 261
Western District, 139, 261
White Plains, 138, 260
US Labor Department, 219, 272, 364
   Albany, 364
   Albany Area Office, 219, 273
   Albany District Office, 273
   Buffalo Area Office, 219, 273
   Buffalo District Office, 273
   Bureau of Labor Statistics (BLS), 272

Employee Benefits Security Administration (EBSA), 273
Employment & Training Administration (ETA), 273
Employment Standards Administration, 273
Federal Contract Compliance Programs Office (OFCCP), 273
Inspector General, 273
Inspector General's Office for Audit (OIG-A), 273
Inspector General's Office for Investigations (OIG-I), 273
Jobs Corps (JC), 273
Labor-Management Standards Office (OLMS), 273
Long Island District Office, 273
Manhattan Area Office, 219, 273
New York City, 364
New York City District Office, 273
New York District Office, 273
New York State Field Offices, 364
Occupational Safety & Health Administration (OSHA), 273
Occupational Safety & Health Adminstration (OSHA), 219
Office of Asst Secretary for Administration & Mgmt (OASAM), 273
Office of Public Affairs (OPA) (serving New York State), 273
Office of the Solicitor, 273
Queens Area Office, 219, 273
Region 2 - New York Office of Secretary's Representative, 273
Region 2 New York - Women's Bureau (WB), 273
Syracuse Area Office, 219, 273
Tarrytown Area Office, 219, 273
Wage-Hour Division (WHD)-Northeast Regional Office, 273
Workers' Compensation Programs (OWCP), 273
US Merit Systems Protection Board, 273, 298
   New York Field Office, 273, 298
US Office of Personnel Management, 274, 298
   PHILADELPHIA SERVICE CENTER (serving New York), 274, 298
US Postal Service, 205
   New York Metro Area, 205
   NORTHEAST AREA (Includes part of New York State), 205
US Power Generating, 494
US Railroad Retirement Board, 274
   Albany, 274
   Buffalo, 274
   New York, 274
   New York District Offices, 274
   Westbury, 274

Organization Index

US Securities & Exchange Commission, 105
  Broker-Dealer Inspection Program, 105
  Enforcement Division, 105
  Investment Management, 105
  Northeast Region, 105
US State Department, 205, 364
  Bureau of Educational & Cultural Affairs-NY Pgm Branch, 205
  US Mission to the United Nations, 205, 364
US Term Limits Foundation, 167
US Transportation Department, 151, 355
  Accounting Division, 355
  Aerospace Medicine Division, 355
  Air Force Regional Representatives, 355
  Air Traffic Division, 355
  Airports Division, 355
  Army Regional Representatives, 355
  Aviation Information & Services Division, 355
  Engineering Services, 355
  Federal Aviation Administration-Eastern Region, 355
  Federal Highway Administration-New York Division, 355
  Federal Motor Carrier Safety Admin-New York Division, 356
  Federal Railroad Administration-Field Offices, 356
  Federal Transit Administration, Region II-New York, 356
  Flight Standards Division, 355
  Great Lakes Region (includes part of New York State), 356
  Hazardous Material, 356
  Highway-Rail Grade Crossing, 356
  Human Resource Management Division, 355
  Logistics Division, 355
  Maritime Administration, 356
  Military Liaison Officers to the Federal Aviation Admin (NYS), 355
  National Highway Traffic Safety Administration, Reg II-NY, 356
  Navy Regional Representatives, 355
  North Atlantic Region, 356
  Office of Inspector General, Region II-New York, 356
  Runway Safety Manager, 355
  Saint Lawrence Seaway Development Corporation, 356
  US Merchant Marine Academy, 151, 356
US Treasury Department, 93, 328
  Albany Territory, 329
  Andover Campus Service Center, 329
  Appeals Unit - Office of Directors, 328
  Area 1 Director's Office, 329
  Brookhaven Campus Service Center, 329
  Brooklyn & Long Island Office, 329
  Buffalo Territory, 329
  Comptroller of the Currency, 93
  Criminal Investigation Unit - New York Field Office, 328
  Internal Revenue Service, 328
  Large & Mid-Size Business Division (LMSB), 328
  Management Information Technology Services - Northeast Area, 329
  Manhattan Office, 329
  New York SBSE Compliance Services, 329
  New York Territory, 329
  Northeast Region (serving NY), 93
  Northeastern District, 93
  Office of Chief Counsel, 329
  Office of Chief Counsel LMSB Area 1, 328
  Office of Director, Area 1 (New York State & New England), 329
  Office of Thrift Supervision, 93
  SBSE-Compliance Area 2/New York, 329
  SBSE-Taxpayer Education & Communication (TEC), 329
  Small Business & Self-Employed Division (SBSE), 329
  Tax Exempt & Government Entities Div (TEGE)-Northeast Area, 329
  Taxpayer Advocate Service (TAS), 329
  TEGE Area Counsel's Office, 329
  Upstate New York Office, 329
  US Mint, 93, 329
  Wage & Investmnt Div-Stakehldr Partnership Ed & Comm (SPEC), 329
  Western New York State Office, 329
USA Track & Field, Adirondack Association Inc, 347
USA Training Company Inc, 490
USA Training Company, Inc, 505
USB Fund for Good Government Inc, 566
Usinpac (Albers & Co), 488
UST Public Affairs Inc, 480, 504, 513
USWA, SEIU, AFL-CIO, CLC-PAC, 566
Utica, 75
  Civil & Criminal Courts, 75
Utica City SD, 658
Utica College, 632
Utica Industrial Development Agency (City of), 587
Utica Mutual Insurance Co, 251
Utica School of Commerce, 637
Utica, City of, 443
Utility Workers Union, Local 1-2, AFL-CIO, 507
UWUA Local 1-2 Non Federal PAC, 566
Valeray Real Estate Co Inc, 516
Valeray Real Estate Company, Inc, 474
Valhalla UFSD, 677
Valley CSD (Montgomery), 661
Valley Democratic Club PAC, 567
Valley National Bank, 97
Valley Stream 13 UFSD, 656
Valley Stream 24 UFSD, 656
Valley Stream 30 UFSD, 656
Valley Stream Central HS District, 656
Valley Stream Chamber of Commerce, 587
Valley Stream, Village of, 443
ValueOptions Inc, 463
Van Buren Womens Republican Club, 567
Van Hornesville-Owen D Young CSD, 650
Van Wagner Communications, LLC, 519
Vandervort Group, LLC (The), 527
Vanguard Car Rental USA Inc, 506
Vassar College, 633
Vaughn College of Aeronautics & Technology, 633
Vector Group, Ltd, 513
Vedder Price Kaufman & Kammholz PC, 277
Ventresca-Ecroyd, Gilda, 527
Venture Vineyards Inc, 89
Veolia Water, 516
Vera Institute of Justice, 142, 267
Verifone Transportation Systems Inc, 487
Verizon, 465, 466, 475, 493, 506, 516, 527
Verizon Communications, 176
Verizon Communications Good Government Club New York PAC, 567
Verizon Corporate Services Corp, 514
Verizon NY, 463
Verizon Wireless, 463, 503
Vernon Downs/Gaming-Racing-Entertainment, 347
Vernon-Verona-Sherrill CSD, 658
Versa Med Inc, 499
Vestal CSD, 640
Vestal, Town of, 443
Veterans of Foreign Wars, 368
Veterans of Foreign Wars (VFW), 368
Veterans of Foreign Wars Auxiliary, 368
Veterans, Homeland Security & Military Affairs, 32
  Committee Staff, 32
  Key Senate Staff Assignments, 32
  Majority, 32
  Membership, 32
  Minority, 32
Veterans' Affairs, 52, 387, 393
  Committee Staff, 52
  Disability Assistance & Memorial Affairs, 393
  Economic Opportunity, 393
  Health, 393
  Key Assembly Staff Assignments, 52
  Majority, 52
  Membership, 52
  Minority, 52
  Oversight & Investigations, 393
  Subcommittees, 393
Veterans' Affairs, Division of, 17, 361, 374
  Albany Office, 361
  Buffalo VA Regional Office, 361

Organization Index

Bureau of Veterans Education, 361
Counseling & Claims Service, 361
Eastern Region, 361
New York City VA Regional Office, 361
New York Office, 361
New York State Claims Offices, 361
Public Information, Field Support, Budget, Finance, Personnel, Blind Annuity, 361
Western Region, 361
Veterans' Service Organizations, 361
  30th Street Shelter, 361
  Albany Housing Coalition Inc, 361
  Continuum of Care for Homeless Veterans in New York City, 361
  COPIN HOUSE (Homeless Veterans), 361
  Hicksville Counseling Center, Veterans' Resource Center, 361
  Project TORCH, Veterans Health Care Center, 361
  Saratoga Cnty Rural Preservation Co (Homeless Veterans), 361
  Suffolk County United Veterans Halfway House Project Inc, 361
  Veterans House (The), 361
  Veterans Outreach Center Inc, 361
  Veterans Services Center of the Southern Tier, 361
  Veterans' Coalition of the Hudson Valley, 361
Veterans' Widows International Network Inc (VWIN), New York, 368
Veterinary Medical Society (NYS), 490
Viacom Inc, 176
Viahealth, 531
Viasys Healthcare Inc, 487
Victor Chamber of Commerce, 587
Victor CSD, 660
Victory 2005 Committee, 567
Vidal Group, LLC (The), 528
Vietnam Veterans of America, NYS Council, 368
Villa Maria College of Buffalo, 633
Village Care of New York, 463
Village Care of NY Inc, 499
Village Voice (The), 597
Village Voice Media, Inc, 597
Vincent F Stempel, Jr Esq, 267
VIP Community Services, 503
VIP Health Care Services, 462
Vision Rehabilitation Assn (NYVRA) (NY), 478
Visiting Nurse Regional Health Care System, 491
Visiting Nurse Service of NY, 483, 503, 528
Visy Paper (NY), 463
Vladeck, Waldman, Elias & Engelhard PC, 277
Vocational Foundation Inc, 494

Voice of Teachers for Educational/Comm on Political Education, 567
Volunteers of Legal Service, Inc, 267
Voorheesville CSD, 638
Vornado Realty Trust, 495
Vote Here, Inc, 508
Voth Inc, 468
W2001Z/15CPW Realty LLC, 486
WABC (7), 609
WABC (770 AM), 605
Wachovia New York Employees Good Government Fund, 567
Wachtell, Lipton, Rosen & Katz, 331
Waddington Chamber of Commerce, 587
Wagner College, 633
Wainscott Common SD, 671
WALL (1340 AM), WRRV (92.7 FM), 606
Wall Street Journal (The), 176, 596
Wallkill CSD, 673
Wallkill, Town of, 444
Wal-Mart, 501
Walsh, John B, 528
Walt Disney Company (The), 501
Walton CSD, 644
WAMC (90.3 FM), 603
Wang, Phyllis A, 528
Wantagh Chamber of Commerce, 588
Wantagh GOP Victory Committee, 567
Wantagh Republican Committeesmens Council, 567
Wantagh UFSD, 656
Wappinger, Town of, 444
Wappingers CSD, 645
Warren & Washington Industrial Development Agency, 588
Warren County, 69, 412
  Supreme, County, Family & Surrogate's Courts, 69
Warren County Economic Development Corporation, 588
Warrensburg Chamber of Commerce, 588
Warrensburg CSD, 674
Warsaw Chamber of Commerce (Greater Warsaw), 588
Warsaw CSD, 678
Wartburg Residential Community, Inc, 462
Warwick Valley Chamber of Commerce, 588
Warwick Valley CSD, 661
Warwick, Town of, 444
Washington Cemetery, 513
Washington County, 69, 412
  Supreme, County, Family & Surrogate's Courts, 69
Washington County Local Development Corporation, 588
Washington Mutual, 97
Washington-Saratoga-Warren-Hamilton-Essex BOCES, 680
Washingtonville CSD, 661
Waste Management, 468, 475

Waste Management & Recycling Products, 469
Waste Management of NY, LLC, 501
Water Resource Needs of NYS & Long Island, Legislative Commission on, 54
Water Resources Needs of New York State & Long Island, Legislative Commission, 33
Water/Pearl Associates, LLC, 459
Waterford-Halfmoon UFSD, 665
Waterfront Commission of New York Harbor, 128, 271, 354, 380
Waterkeeper Alliance, 192
Waterloo CSD, 666
Watertown, 75
  Civil & Criminal Courts, 75
Watertown City SD, 651
Watertown Daily Times, 600
Watertown Empire Zone, 588
Watertown, City of, 444
Watertown-North Country Chamber of Commerce (Greater Watertown), 588
Waterville CSD, 658
Watervliet, 75
  Civil & Criminal Courts, 75
Watervliet City SD, 638
Watervliet Development Company LLC, 501
Watkins Glen CSD, 666
Watson School of Biological Sciences at Cold Spring Harbor Laboratory, 633
Wave, 597
Waverly CSD, 672
WAXQ (104.3 FM), 605
Wayland-Cohocton CSD, 667
Wayne County, 69, 412
  Supreme, County, Family & Surrogate's Courts, 69
Wayne County Industrial Development Agency & Economic Development, 588
Wayne CSD, 675
Wayne-Finger Lakes BOCES, 680
Ways & Means, 52, 394
  Committee Staff, 52
  Health, 394
  Income Security and Family Support, 394
  Key Assembly Staff Assignments, 52
  Majority, 53
  Membership, 53
  Minority, 53
  Oversight, 394
  Select Revenue Measures, 394
  Social Security, 394
  Subcommittees, 394
  Trade, 394
WBBR (1130 AM) Bloomberg News, 605
WBFO (88.7 FM) WOLN (91.3 FM), WUBJ (88.7 FM) NPR/PRI - SUNY at Buffalo, 603
WBLK (93.7 FM), WJYE (96.1 FM), 604
WBNG (12), WBXI (11), 607

873

Organization Index

WCBS (2), 609
WCBS (880 AM), 605
WCHP (760 AM), 604
WCII (88.5 FM), WCOT (90.9 FM), 603
WCNY (24), 609
WDCX (99.5 FM), 604
We Move, 227
Web Holdings, 478
Webb Institute, 633
Webster Chamber of Commerce, 588
Webster CSD, 653
Webster, Town of, 444
Webutuck CSD, 645
Weedsport CSD, 641
Weekley, Daniel A, 528
Wegmans Food Markets Inc, 112
Weingarten, Reid & McNally, LLC, 528, 567
WelchAllyn Inc, 516
Welfare Inspector General, Office of NYS, 17, 200, 313, 375
Welfare Research Inc, 323
Wellcare Health Plans, Inc, 487, 520
Wellpoint Inc, 491
Wellpoint, Inc WELLPAC, 568
Wells College, 633
Wells CSD, 649
Wellsville Area Chamber of Commerce, 588
Wellsville CSD, 639
Wellsville Daily Reporter/Spectator, 600
Wendy's Internatioal, 468
WENY (36), 608
West 129th Street Realty LLC, 495
West 60th Street Associates LLC/West End Enterprises LLC, 486
West Babylon UFSD, 671
West Canada Valley CSD, 650
West Genesee CSD, 659
West Hempstead UFSD, 656
West Irondequoit CSD, 653
West Islip UFSD, 671
West Park UFSD, 673
West Seneca Chamber of Commerce, 588
West Seneca CSD, 647
West Seneca, Town of, 445
West Side Chamber of Commerce, 588
West Valley CSD, 640
Westbury UFSD, 656
Westbury Union Free School District, 478
Westchester Black Womens' Political Caucas, 568
Westchester Coalition for Legal Abortion PAC, 568
Westchester Community College, 617
Westchester County, 69, 413, 501
 Supreme, County & Family Courts, 69
 Surrogate's Court, 69
Westchester County Association Inc (The), 588

Westchester County Chamber of Commerce, 588
Westchester County Conservative Party PAC, 568
Westchester County Correctional Superior Officers Assn, 509
Westchester County Health Care Corp, 478, 518
Westchester County Health Care Corporation, 515
Westchester County Industrial Development Agency, 589
Westchester County Womens Republican Club, 568
Westchester Industrial Development Agency, 518
Westchester Jewish Community Services, 462, 524
Westchester Right to Life PAC, 568
Westchester School for Special Children, 501
Westcons PAC, 568
Westerm Union, 504
Western Central Coalition for Children with Special Needs, 487
Western New York Library Resources Council, 156
Western New Yorkers for Economic Growth, 568
Western NY Energy LLC, 513
Western NY PAC Region 9 UAW, 568
Western NY Regional Council PAC Fund, 568
Western NY Safari Club PAC, 568
Western Regional Off-Track Betting, 501
Western Regional Off-Track Betting Corp, 128, 337, 380
Western Regional Off-Track Betting Corporation, 507
Western Suffolk BOCES, 680
Westfield CSD, 642
Westfield/Barcelona Chamber of Commerce, 589
Westhampton Beach UFSD, 671
Westhampton Chamber of Commerce (Greater Westhampton), 589
Westhill CSD, 659
Westmoreland CSD, 658
Westport CSD, 647
Westside News Inc, 599
WETM (18), 608
WFLY (92.3 FM), WAJZ (96.3 FM), WROW (590 AM), WYJB (95.5 FM), WZMR (104.9), 605
WFRY (97.5 FM), 607
WFUV (90.7 FM), 603
WGNA (107.7 FM), 606
WGRZ (2), 608
WGY (810 AM), WPYX (106.5 FM), WRVE (99.5 FM), 605
WHAM (1180 AM), 606

WHAM (13), 609
WHCU (870 AM), WTKO (1470 AM), WYXL (97.3 FM), WQNY (103.7 FM), 604
Wheatland-Chili CSD, 653
WHEC (10), 609
Wheelerville UFSD, 648
White & Case LLP, 97
White Plains, 75
 Civil & Criminal Courts, 75
White Plains City SD, 677
White Plains, City of, 445
Whiteface Mountain Regional Visitor's Bureau, 589
Whitehall CSD, 674
Whitehead, David, 529
Whiteman Osterman & Hanna LLP, 193, 243, 267, 294, 529
Whitesboro CSD, 658
Whitesville CSD, 639
Whitney Museum of American Art (The), 491
Whitney Point CSD, 640
WHTT (104.1 FM), 604
WHUD (100.7 FM), 606
WICZ (40), 607
Wieboldt, Robert, 529
Wiener, Judith R, 529
Wilber National Bank, 97
Wildlife Conservation Society, 193, 529
Wildlife Conservation Society Inc, 529
Wildwood Programs Inc, 529
Willets Point Industrial & Realty Corp, 475
William B Collins Co, 594
William Floyd UFSD, 671
Williams Companies (The), 475
Williams Esq, Christopher A, 530
Williams, Carla (FKA Alliance for Donation (NY)), 530
Williams, Samuel G, 530
Williamson CSD, 675
Williamsville CSD, 647
Willistons Chamber of Commerce, 589
Willow Mixed Media Inc, 347
Willsboro CSD, 647
Wilmorite Holdings, 516
Wilmorite Holdings, LP, 506
Wilson CSD, 658
Wilson Elser Moskowitz Edelman & Dicker, 227, 267, 530
Wilson Elser Moskowitz Edelman & Dicker PAC, 568
Windham-Ashland-Jewett CSD, 649
Windsor CSD, 640
Wine Institute, 463
WINS (1010 AM), 605
Winthrop University Hospital, 227
Witkoff Group (The), 467, 501
WIVB (4), WNLO (23), 608
WIVT/WBGH (34), 607
WIXT (9), 609

Organization Index

WKBW (7), 608
WKPQ (105.3 FM), WHHO (1320 AM), 604
WKRT (920 AM), WIII (99.9 or 100.3 FM), 604
WKTV (2), 610
WKZA (106.9 FM), 605
WLIW (21) Public Broadcasting, 608
WLNY (55), 608
WLTW (106.7 FM), 605
WMHT (17) Public Broadcasting-NY Capitol Region, 607
WMRV (105.7), 603
WMTT (94.7 FM), 604
WNBC (4), 609
WNBF (1290 AM), WHWK (98.1FM), WYOS (1360 AM), WAAL (99.1 FM), WWYL (104.1), 603
WNED (17) Western NY Public Broadcasting, 608
WNED (94.5 FM), 604
WNKI (106.1 FM), WPGI (100.9 FM), WNGZ (104.9 FM), WWLZ (820 AM), 604
WNTQ (93.1 FM), WAQX (95.7 FM), 606
WNY Majority Leader PAC, 567
WNYC, 491
WNYT (13), 607
WNYW (5), 609
Wolf, Block, Schorr & Solis-Cohen, LLP, 531
Wolf, Stacy, 531
Women in Need Inc, 477
Women Marines Association, 368
Women PAC, 568
Women's Army Corps Veterans Association - Empire Chapter, 368
Women's Bar Assn of the State of NY, 465
Women's Bar Association of the State of New York, 267
Women's Business Training Center of New York State, 112
Women's Campaign Fund, 167, 568
Women's City Club of New York, 167
Women's Commission for Refugee Women & Children, 244
Women's Housing & Economic Development Corporation, 521
Women's Housing & Economic Development Corporation (WHEDCO), 236
Women's Issues, Task Force on, 53
Women's Prison Association & Home Inc, 142
Women's TAP Fund, 568
Women's Venture Fund Inc, 112
Wood Rafalsky & Wood, 531
Wood Tobe-Coburn, 637
Woodstock Chamber of Commerce & Arts, 589
Woodward Workforce, 568

WOR (710 AM), 606
Worcester CSD, 662
Workers' Compensation Alliance, 507, 568
Workers' Compensation Board, 18, 247, 270, 375
   Administration, 247, 271
   Albany, 247, 271
   Binghamton, 247, 271
   Brooklyn, 247, 271
   Buffalo, 248, 271
   District Offices, 247, 271
   Hauppauge, 248, 271
   Hempstead, 248, 271
   Manhattan, 248, 271
   Operations, 247, 271
   Peekskill, 248, 271
   Queens, 248, 271
   Rochester, 248, 271
   Syracuse, 248, 271
   Systems Modernization, 248, 271
   Workers' Compensation Board of Commissioners, 248, 271
Workers' Compensation Pharmacy Alliance (WCPA), 463
Working Assets Funding Service Inc, 531
Working Families Party, 167
Working Families Party WNY Chapter, 568
Working Poor Legal Assistance Project, 463
Working Today, 507
World Hunger Year Inc, 323
World Product Centre, 519
World Trade Center Properties, 508
World Trade Center Properties, LLC, 516
Worldwide Foods, 495
Worldwide Group Holdings Corp, 467
WOUR (96.9 FM), 607
WPDH (101.5 FM), 606
WPIG (95.7 FM), WHDL (1450 AM), 606
WPIX (11), 609
WPTR (1540 AM), 603
WPTZ (5) NBC, 609
WRCC 21st Century Fund, 567
WRGB (6), 607
WRNN (62), 608
WSEN (92.1 FM), 603
WSHU Public Radio (Long Island Friends of WSUF), 478
WSKG (46) Public Broadcasting, 608
WSKG (89.3 FM), WSQX (91.5 FM), 603
WSPK (104.7 FM), 603
WSTM (3), 609
WSYT (68), 609
WTEN (10), 607
WTVH (5), 610
WVOA (105.1 FM), 606
WVOX (1460 AM), WRTN (93.5 FM), 605
WWNY (7), 610
WWOR (UPN 9), 609
WWTI (50), 610
WXXA (23), 607
WXXI (21) Public Broadcasting, 609

Wyandanch UFSD, 671
Wyeth, 468
WYETH Good Gov't Fund, 567
Wynantskill UFSD, 663
Wyndham Worldwide Corporation, 463
Wyoming County, 69, 413
   Supreme, County, Family & Surrogate's Courts, 69
Wyoming County Chamber of Commerce, 589
Wyoming CSD, 678
WYPX (55), 607
WYRK (106.5 FM), WBUF (92.9 FM), 604
WYYY (94.5 FM), 606
Xerox Corp, 515, 518
YAI/National Institute for People with Disabilities, 286, 323, 478
Yankees Partnership (NY), 506, 516
Yates County, 70, 413
   Supreme, County, Family & Surrogate's Courts, 70
Yates County Chamber of Commerce, 589
Yates County Industrial Development Agency, 589
Yavornitzki, Mark L, 531
Yeshiva University, 633
Yeshiva University, A Einstein Clg of Med, Div of Subs Abuse, 286
Yeshiva University, A Einstein Clg of Med, OB/GYN & Wmn's Health, 227
YMCA of New York State, 463
YMCAs of NYS Inc, 531
YMCAS of NYS Inc, 531
Yonkers, 76
   Civil & Criminal Courts, 76
Yonkers Chamber of Commerce, 589
Yonkers City SD, 678
Yonkers Contracting Co Inc, 499
Yonkers Council of School Administrators PAC, 568
Yonkers Economic Development/Yonkers Industrial Development Agency (City of), 589
Yonkers Raceway, 347, 501
Yonkers, City of, 445
York College, 621
York CSD, 651
Yorktown CSD, 678
Yorktown, Town of, 445
Yoswein New York Inc, 531
Young Democrats of Monroe County, 568
Young Jr, William N, 532
Young Women's Leadership Foundation, 480
Yum! Brands Inc, 463
Zaleski, Terence M, 532
Zogby International, 112, 167
Zogg, Jeffrey, 532
Zurich, 487

Geographic Index

Includes the names of the top three levels in all New York State executive departments and agencies; public corporations; authorities; commissions; all organizations listed in the Private Sector sources segment of each policy chapter; lobbyist organizations; political action committees; chambers of commerce; newspapers; news services; radio and television stations; SUNY and CUNY locations; and private colleges.

Alabama

Birmingham
Gold Star Wives of America Inc, 366

Arkansas

Little Rock
Entergy Corporation Political Committee NY (ENPAC-NY), 541

California

Los Angeles
Assn of Independent Commercial Producers Inc PAC, 534
IATSE Local 600 NY PAC, 545

Mill Valley
Apple Inc (FKA Apple Computer Inc), 459

San Francisco
Working Assets Funding Service Inc, 531

Colorado

Aurora
Veterans' Widows International Network Inc (VWIN), New York, 368

Connecticut

Essex
JLW Consulting, LLC, 493

Fairfield
Kudlow & Company LLC, 95

Farmington
NY Region 9A UAW PAC Committee, 552

Greenwich
500 Club, 533

Hartford
Allegue, Raul R, 456
CIGNA Corporation Political Action Committee, 536
Hartford Advocates Fund (The), 544
Hartford Financial Svcs Group Inc, 489
ING America Insurance Holdings Inc PAC (ING NY PAC), 546
US Treasury Department
Area 1 Director's Office, 329

Lakeville
Tri-State Chamber of Commerce, 587

Monroe
Army Aviation Association of America (AAAA), 365

Shelton
Perkins, Janice C, 514

Trumbull
Oxford Health Plans Inc-NY Committee for Quality Health Care, 558
United Healthcare Services, Inc (FKA Oxford LLC), 526

Waterford
Trading Cove NY, LLC, 525
Weekley, Daniel A, 528

Windsor
US Postal Service
NORTHEAST AREA (Includes part of New York State), 205

District of Columbia

Washington
21st Century Democrats, 533
Accenture LLP, 455
Aetna Inc PAC, 533
Amalgamated Transit Union, 457
American Continental Group, 457
American Express Company PAC (AXP PAC), 534
American Federation of Teachers, 275
American Insurance Assn New York PAC, 534
American Resort Dev/Assn Resort Owners' Coalition PAC, 534
Atlantic States Marine Fisheries Commission, 113, 181
ATU-NY Cope Fund, 533
Baker & Hostetler, LLP, 461
Capital City Committee, 536
Ciccone, Stephen J, 471
Cohen, Marsha A, 473
Consumer Advocacy PAC, 538
Corning Incorporated Employees PAC (COREPAC), 539
CTIA - The Wireless Assn, 467
D.R.I.V.E.-Democratic, Republican, Independent Voter Education, 539
Democratic Congressional Campaign Committee, 165
Democratic Governors' Assn - NY, 539
Dewey Ballantine LLP Political Action Committee-New York, 539
Eastman Kodak Company, 108
Emily's List, 541
EMILY's List, 165
Federal Communications Commission
Office of Media Relations, 170
Federal Election Commission, 164
Gay and Lesbian Victory Fund, 543
General Motors Corporation Political Action Committee-N, 543
Goldman Sachs & Co, 95
Goldman Sachs NY PAC, 543
Governor's Office
Washington Office for the Governor, 4
Washington Office of the Governor, 194
Green Worlds Coalition Fund, 544
HillPAC-NY, 545
Honda North America Inc, 492
Hotel Employees Restaurant Int'l Union Tip Edu Fund, 545
HSBC North America, Inc PAC (H-PAC), 544
IAFF Firepac NY Non-Federal, 545
International Paper Political Action Committee, 546
International Union o, 547
Ironworkers Political Action League, 547
Jewish War Veterans of the USA, 366
Keeping Americas' Promise Inc, 547
Kitchen PAC, 547
Landau-Painter, Cathy, 496
Morgante, Samuel, 509
National Guard Association of the US (NGAUS), 367
National Marine Manufacturers Association PAC (NAT PAC), 554
National Transportation Safety Board

Listings appear in alphabetical order by state, then city.

Geographic Index

Office of Administrative Law Judges, 355
National Wildlife Federation, 190
NY EDPAC, 551
NY Film PAC, 551
Reserve Officers Association (ROA), 368
Scripps Howard News Service, 602
SEIU PEA State Fund, 562
Software & Information Industry Association, 112
Solowan, Richard, 523
UFCW Active Ballot Club, 566
US Commission on Civil Rights
 EASTERN REGION (includes New York State), 164, 239
US Department of Energy
 Office of External Affairs, 171
Veterans of Foreign Wars (VFW), 368
Women's Campaign Fund, 167, 568

Washington, DC
Citigroup Inc PAC - Federal/State, 537

Florida

Miami
Greenberg, Traurig Political Action Committee, 544

Tampa
Health Access Affiliates Good Government Fund, 544
Ryan, Marc, 520

Georgia

Atlanta
Bank of America NY PAC, 535
Coca-Cola Enterprise Employee NonPartisan Committee for Good Gove, 538
Mirant Corporation State Political Action Committee Inc-NY, 550
United Parcel Service Inc PAC NY, 567
US Department of Agriculture
 USDA/GIPSA, Packers & Stockyards Pgms-Atlantic Region, 82

Illinois

Chicago
CNA, 466

Des Plaines
PCI State Political Account I, 559

Glenview
US Term Limits Foundation, 167

Rosemont
Hood, William L, 492

Schaumburg
US Transportation Department
 Great Lakes Region (includes part of New York State), 356

Indiana

Indianapolis
Eli Lilly & Company PAC, 541
Wellpoint, Inc WELLPAC, 568

Maine

China Village
Northeastern Forest Fire Protection Commission, 126, 183

Maryland

Annapolis
GEICO NY PAC, 543

Baltimore
Allegretti, Daniel, 456

Chevy Chase
US Justice Department
 US Parole Commission, 139

Crofton
Quest Diagnostics NY PAC, 560

Landover
Commissioned Officers Assn of the US Public Health Svc Inc (COA), 221, 366

North Potomac
Knighton, Ethel V, 495

Massachusetts

Andover
US Treasury Department
 Andover Campus Service Center, 329

Boston
American Diabetes Association, 457
Digiovanni, Joseph, 479
Federal Labor Relations Authority
 Boston Regional Office, 272
Liberty Mutual Insurance Co PAC - NY, 548
National Trust for Historic Preservation, 235
Ropes & Gray, 519

US Commerce Department
 Boston Region (includes upstate New York), 104
US Department of the Interior
 Northeast Region (includes New York State), 185
US Labor Department
 Employment & Training Administration (ETA), 273
 Office of Public Affairs (OPA) (serving New York State), 273

Burlington
US Transportation Department
 Military Liaison Officers to the Federal Aviation Admin (NYS), 355

Concord
National Grape Cooperative-Welch Foods Inc, 87

Dorchester
Women Marines Association, 368

Gloucester
US Commerce Department
 National Marine Fisheries Svc, Northeast Region Headquarters, 184

Hadley
US Department of the Interior
 Fish & Wildlife Service-Northeast Region, 339
 Northeast Region (includes New York State), 185

Lowell
New England Interstate Water Pollution Control Commission, 120, 182

Needham
Northeast Gas Association, 175

Newton
US Department of the Interior
 Northeast Region (includes New York State), 185

Sharon
Gilligan, Donald, 486

Still River
National Assn of Chain Drug Stores, 510

Michigan

Ann Arbor
Great Lakes Commission, 102, 116, 181

Auburn Hills
Daimler Chrysler Corporation Political Support Committee-New York, 539

Listings appear in alphabetical order by state, then city.

Geographic Index

Detroit
Cingular Wireless LLC EPAC, 537
Dominion PAC-NY, 540
Ford Motor Company Civic Action Fund, 542
General Motors Corporation, 485
Professionals Political Action Committee-NY, 560

Missouri

St Louis
Enterprise Rent-A-Car Company NY PAC, 541

New Hampshire

Dover
Air Force Sergeants Association (AFSA), Division 1, 365

New Jersey

Avon by the Sea
Luthin Associates, Inc, 500

Bedminster
AT&T Corporation, 172

Bridgewater
Fleet Bank of New York PAC, 542

Cherry Hill
Compac, NJ, 538
Freedom America, 543

Clifton
Valley National Bank, 97

East Rutherford
New York Giants, 345

Edison
Committee for Effective Leadership, 538
US Environmental Protection Agency
  Division of Environmental Science & Assessment (DESA), 185

Englewood Cliff
Port Authority PBA, Inc State of New York PAC, 560

Flanders
Humane Society of the United States, Mid Atlantic Regional Office, 85, 319

Florham Park
Friedman, John P, 484

Fort Lee
Port Authority Sergeants Benevolent Assn PAC, 560

Iselin
Cobb Jr, James H, 473
Federal Mediation & Conciliation Service
  Northeastern Region, 272
New York Shipping Association Inc, 358

Jersey City
Dow Jones Newswires (Dow Jones & Company), 601
US Treasury Department
  Northeast Region (serving NY), 93

Lyndhurst
US Department of Homeland Security (DHS)
  Newark Asylum Offc-Including NYS not served by New York City, 204, 240

Madison
WYETH Good Gov't Fund, 567

Monroe Twp
Local 23-25, Unite State & Local Campaign Committee, 549

New Brunswick
Johnson & Johnson Employees' Good Gov't Fund PAC, 547

Newark
Commonwealth Business Media, 596
Journal of Commerce, 596
Keyspan Services PAC, 547
Prudential New York Political Action Committee, 560
Small Business Administration
  New Jersey, 104

Paramus
Hartman & Winnicki, PC, 109, 264
NYS Bar Assn, Intellectual Property Law Section, 109, 264

Parsippany
Cendant Corporation NY PAC, 537
Hastings, Jamie, 489
Liantonio, John J, 499
Muhs, Robert E, 509
National Transportation Safety Board
  Aviation Division, Northeast Regional Office, 355
T-Mobile New York PAC, 564

Secaucus
WWOR (UPN 9), 609

Springfield
IUOE Local 825 Political Action & Education Cmte, 546

Watervliet
Murray, Claire, 510

Wayne
Enterprise Rent-A-Car, 481

West Trenton
Delaware River Basin Commission, 115, 181

New York

Accord
Rondout Valley CSD, 673

Adams
South Jefferson Chamber of Commerce, 585
South Jefferson CSD, 650

Addison
Addison CSD, 667

Afton
Afton CSD, 642

Akron
Akron CSD, 645
Bank of Akron, 94
New York State Travel & Vacation Association, 346
Save American Jobs PAC, 562

Albany
3rd Department, 55
Adirondack Mountain Club Inc, 187, 341, 455
AeA New York Council, 106, 172
AFGI PAC, 533
AFSCME District Council 37, 298
AFSCME, New York, 298
Aging, Office for the, 4, 307
Agostine Jr, Joseph A, 456
Agriculture & Markets Department, 4, 79, 307
  Soil & Water Conservation Committee, 80
Agriculture & NYS Horse Breeding Development Fund, 113, 335
Ahern, Barbara J, 456
AIA New York State, Inc, 454
AIDS Council of Northeastern New York, 220
Albany
  Civil Court, 71
  Criminal Court, 71
  Traffic Court, 71
Albany City SD, 638
Albany College of Pharmacy, 621
Albany County, 396
  County Court, 61
  Family Court, 61

Listings appear in alphabetical order by state, then city.

Geographic Index

Supreme & Surrogate's Courts, 61
Albany County Airport Authority, 113, 350
Albany County Industrial Development Agency, 569
Albany Housing Coalition Inc, 365
Albany Industrial Development Agency (City of), 569
Albany Law School, 621
Albany Law School of Union University, 456
Albany Law School, Government Law Center, 206
Albany Medical College, 621
Albany Port District Commission, 113, 350
Albany, City of, 414
Albany-Colonie Regional Chamber of Commerce, 569
Alcoholic Beverage Control, Division of (State Liquor Authority), 5, 98, 324
Albany (Zone II), 98, 324
Alcoholism & Substance Abuse Services, Office of, 5, 211, 278, 307
Alliance for Quality Education (FKA Easton, Regina N), 456
Alteri, Richard, 456
Altman, Frederick M, 456
Alzheimer's Association, Northeastern NY, 220
American Cancer Society-Eastern Division, 220
American Chemistry/American Plastics Council, 106
American College of Ob & Gyn, District II, 457
American College of Obstetricians & Gynecologists/NYS, 220
American College of Physicians, New York Chapter, 220
American Council of Engineering Companies of NY (ACEC New York), 106
American Heart Assn/American Stroke Assn, 458
American Institute of Architects (AIA) New York State Inc, 106, 233
American Insurance Assn, 458
American Legion, Department of New York, 365
American Lung Association of NYS Inc, 221
American Red Cross in NYS, 316
AmeriChoice of NY (United Healthcare Services Affiliate), 457
ASAPPAC, 533
Asciutto, Georgia M, 459
Assn of Community & Residential Agencies (NYS), 459
Assn of Counties & Its Affiliated Organizations (NYS), 460
Assn of PBAS, Inc (NYS), 460

Assn of School Business Officials (NYS), 460
Assn of Towns of the State of NY, 460
Associated General Contractors of America, NYS Chapter, 107
Associated Press (Albany/Upstate Bureau), 601
Associated Risk Managers of New York Inc, 249
Association Development Group Inc, 107
Association for Addiction Professionals of New York, 283
Association of Government Accountants, NY Capital Chapter, 207
Association of Proprietary Colleges, 152
Association of Public Broadcasting Stations of NY Inc, 172
Association of Towns of the State of New York, 292, 330
Association on Independent Living, 460
Attorney Grievance Committee
   3rd Judicial Dept, Judicial Dist 3, 4, 6, 255
Audubon New York, 187
Automobile Dealers Assn (NYS), 460
Automobile Dealers of New York PAC, 534
BAC Local 2 PAC, 534
Banking Department, 5, 90
Barba, James J, 461
Barnes, Richard E, 461
Barnett, Claire L, 461
Barrett Associates, 461
Bennett Firm, Inc (The), 462
BMW PAC, 535
BNA (formerly Bureau of National Affairs), 601
Board of Regents, 143
Bogdan Lasky & Kopley, LLC, 462
Bolton St Johns Inc, 463
Bombardiere, Ralph, 464
Bond, Schoeneck & King, PLLC, 464
Bopp, Linda (FKA Mesick, Edie), 464
Brain Injury Association of NYS (BIANYS), 221, 283
Brown McMahon & Weinraub, LLC, 465
Bryant & Stratton College-Albany Campus, 634
Budget, Division of the, 5, 98, 194, 287, 324
Build PAC (NY), 466
Business Council of New York State Inc, 107, 172, 187, 207, 330
Business Council of NYS Inc, 466
Cable PAC, 536
Cable Telecommunications Association of New York Inc, 173
Calvin, James S, 467
CAPE PAC, 536
Capital District Physicians' Health Plan Inc, 468

Capital District Regional Planning Commission, 114, 230
Capital District Transportation Authority, 114, 350
Capital Public Affairs, 468
Capital Region (Albany-Schoharie-Schenectady) BOCES, 678
Capitol Consultants Inc (NY), 468
Capitol Group, LLC, 468
Capitol Hill Management Services Inc, 468
Capitol Strategies Group, LLC, 468
Carpenters Labor-Management Council, NYS, 469
Carr Public Affairs Inc, 469
CASA - Advocates for Children of NYS, 262, 316
Castelbuono, A J, 470
Center for Disability Services, 317
Center for Economic Growth Inc, 107
Center for Family & Youth (The), 316
Center for Law & Justice, 140, 262
Center for Technology in Government, University at Albany, SUNY, 207
Cerebral Palsy Associations of New York State, 221, 317
Chain Pharmacy Assn PAC, 537
Charter Schools Assn (NY), 470
Child Care Coordinating Council (NYS), 470
Children & Family Services, Office of
   Albany Regional Office, 310
   Information Technology Division, 309
CIO Office & Office for Technology, 6, 168, 195
Citizen Action of New York, 165
Citizen Action of NY Political Contribution Acct, 537
Citizens for Integrity in Politics, 537
Citizens for Public Broadcasting, 537
Citizens' Environmental Coalition, 188
City University of New York (CUNY), 471
Civil Service Department, 6, 237, 287, 295
Civil Service Employees Assn of NY (CSEA), Local 1000, AFSCME, AFL-, 299
Civil Service Employees Assn, Inc, 472
Civil Service Employees Union (CSEA), Local 1000, AFSCME, AFL-CIO, 275
Civil Service Employees' PAF, 537
Cleary, Kevin Government Relations, LLC, 472
Coalition Against Domestic Violence (NYS), 472
Coalition Against Domestic Violence, NYS, 140, 317
Coalition Against Sexual Assault (NYS), 140
Coalition for Children's Mental Health Services (NYS), 473
Coalition for the Homeless, 473

Listings appear in alphabetical order by state, then city.

Geographic Index

College of Saint Rose (The), 623
Commission on Independent Colleges & Universities, 152
Committee for Action for a Responsible Electorate (CARE), 538
Committee for an Independent Public Defense Commission, 473
Committee for Medical Eye Care PAC, 538
Committee of Methadone Program Administrators Inc of NYS (COMPA), 222, 284
Community Advocacy & Advisory Services, 473
Conference of Big 5 School Districts, 152
Conference of Mayors & Municipal Officials (NYS), 474
Consumer Protection Board, 6, 99, 168
Contractors, Agents, & Brokers PAC, 538
Convenience PAC, 538
Convention Centers & Visitors Bureaus
  Albany County Convention & Visitors Bureau, 338
Coppola Ryan McHugh Riddell, 475
Coppola, John J, 475
Cordo, John, 475
Corning Place Consulting, LLC, 476
Corporation for National & Community Service
  New York Program Office, 314
Correctional Services Department, 7, 129
  Correctional Industries Division, 129
  Facilities Planning & Development, 132
  Security Staffing Unit, 132
  Training Academy, 129
Couch White PAC, 539
Couch White, LLP, 476
Council for Community Behavioral Healthcare, 476
Council of Community Services of NYS Inc, 318
Council of the City of New York (The), 476
County Nursing Facilities of New York Inc, 222
Court of Appeals, 55
Court of Claims, 58
Crane & Vacco, LLC, 476
Crane, Parente & Cherubin, 173, 207
Crime Victims Board, 7, 132, 311
Criminal Justice Services, Division of, 7, 133, 252, 288
Crosier, Barbara V, 476
Curran, Brian F, 477
Cuyler News Service, 601
D'Onofrio, Paul, 477
Davidoff, Malito & Hutcher, LLP, 478
Decision Strategies Group, 108
DeGraff, Foy, Kunz & Devine, LLP, 208, 249
Deutsch, Ronald, 478
Developmental Disabilities Planning Council, 8, 237, 279, 311

Diverse New York PAC, 540
Donnelly, Edwin, 479
Donohue, Gavin J, 479
Doyle, Michael R, 480
Dudley Associates P.C., 480
Eastern Contractors Association Inc, 108
Economic Development Council Inc (NYS), 480
Education Department, 8, 143, 212, 279, 311, 333
  Albany District Office, 147
  Cultural Education Office, 144, 333
  Early Education & Reading Initiatives, 145
  Eastern Regional Office, 147
  Office of Higher Education, 144
  Office of P-16 Education, 145
  Office of the Professions, 146, 212, 279, 312
  State Library, 144
  Vocational & Educational Services for Individuals With Disabilities Office (VESID), 146, 279, 312
Educational Conference Board (NYS), 480
Egg (The), Center for the Performing Arts, 342
Elections, State Board of, 8, 157
  Albany, 157
Emergency Management Office, NYS (SEMO), 8, 195, 289
Empire Center for New York State Policy, 108
Empire Justice Center, 263, 318
Empire Leadership Council, 541
Empire State Development Corporation, 9, 99, 115, 177, 230, 333
Empire State Forest Products Association, 189, 481
Empire State Petroleum Association Inc, 173
Empire State Regional Council of Carpenters, 275
Empire State Restaurant & Tavern Association Inc, 108, 342
Empire State Society of Association Executives Inc, 108
Employee Relations, Governor's Office of, 9, 296
  Family Benefits Committee, 296
  NYS/CSEA Discipline Unit, 296
  NYS/CSEA Partnership for Education & Training, 296
  NYS/SSU Joint Labor-Management Committee, 296
  NYS/UUP Labor-Management Committee, 296
  Statewide Employee Assistance Programs, 296
Employer Alliance for Affordable Health Care, 481
Energy Assn of NYS (The), 481

Energy Association of New York State, 173
Energy for NY PAC, 541
Environmental Advocates of New York, 189
Environmental Advocates of NY, 481
Environmental Business Association of NYS Inc, 189
Environmental Conservation Department, 9, 177
  New York Natural Heritage Program, 178
Epilepsy Coalition of New York State Inc, 222
Equinox Inc, 481
ESPAC, 540
Ewashko, John J, 482
Excelsior College, 625
EYP PAC NY, 540
Faist Government Affairs Group, LLC, 482
Families Together in NYS Inc, 284, 482
Family Planning Advocates of New York State, 223, 241, 318
Featherstonhaugh Wiley Clyne & Cordo, LLP, 482
Ferris, William E, 483
Fitzpatrick, Christine M, 484
Food Industry Alliance of New York State Inc, 85, 109
Food Industry Alliance of NYS Inc, 484
Free PAC, 542
Freshwater Wetlands Appeals Board, 9, 178
Friend of Cultural Institutions, 543
Friends of the Volunteer Firefighter, 543
Funeral Directors Assn Inc (NYS), 485
Gallo, Richard J, 485
Gannett News Service, 601
Geiger, Bruce W & Associates, 485
General Building Contractors of NYS PAC, 543
General Building Contractors of NYS/AGC, 109
General Services, Office of, 10, 195, 301, 333
Governor's Office, 3, 79, 90, 98, 129, 143, 157, 168, 177, 194, 211, 228, 237, 245, 252, 268, 278, 287, 295, 301, 307, 324, 332, 348, 360
Greenberg Traurig, LLP, 487
Griffin Plummer & Associates, LLC, 488
Griffin, Mary A, 488
Guilderland Chamber of Commerce, 576
Hager, Susan, 488
Hannan, K T Public Affairs Inc, 488
Harris, Steven W, LLC, 488
Health Department, 10, 179, 212, 360
Health Insurance Plan of Greater NY, 489
Health Plan Assn Inc (NY), 489
Hearing Healthcare Alliance of NY PAC, 545
Heslin Rothenberg Farley & Mesiti PC, 174
Hill & Gosdeck, 85, 490

Listings appear in alphabetical order by state, then city.

Geographic Index

Hiller, Elise L, 490
Hinman Straub, PC, 490
Hispanic Outreach Services, 242, 319
HLA PAC, 544
Hodes Associates, 491
Home Care Assn of NYS Inc, 492
Home Care Association of New York State Inc, 223
Hospice & Palliative Care Association of NYS Inc, 223, 319
Housing & Community Renewal, Division of, 10, 228
 Capital District, 228
Housing Works, Albany Advocacy Ctr, 492
HPA PAC, 544
Hudson River Valley Greenway, 10, 179, 334
Hudson River-Black River Regulating District, 116, 181
Human Rights, State Division of
 Albany, 237
Hunger Action Network of NYS, 492
Hunger Action Network of NYS (HANNYS), 319
IBM Corporation, 109
Independent Bankers Association of NYS, 95
Independent Petroleum Mktrs of NY PAC, 546
Independent Power Producers of NY Inc, 174
Independent Power Producers of NY PAC, 546
Inside Albany Productions Inc, 602
Inspector General (NYS), Office of the, 11, 134, 196
Insurance Department, 11, 215, 245
Insurance Fund (NYS), 11, 245, 268
 Albany, 246, 268
Intermagnetics State PAC, 546
Iron Workers' Local 12 PAF, 547
ITT Technical Institute, 635
IUOE Local 106 Voluntary PAF, 546
Jenkins, Joanne E, 493
Kirsch, Richard, 495
KPMG LLP, 208
Kriss, Kriss, Brignola & Persing, LLP, 358, 495
Labor Department, 11, 216, 246, 269, 312, 360
 Greater Capital District, 270
Lambert, Linda A, 496
Land Surveyors PAC, 548
Landry, M Joe, 497
Langdon, David, 497
Lasky, Roy E, 497
Law Department, 12, 91, 99, 134, 169, 179, 197, 216, 229, 238, 247, 253, 270, 301, 325
 Administration, 197, 253
Law Guardian Program
 3rd Judicial Dept, 256
Law Office of Anne Reynolds Copps, 264, 320
Lawyers' Fund for Client Protection, 117, 258
League of Women Voters of New York State, 165, 208, 293, 497
LeBoeuf Lamb Greene & MacRae, LLP, 497
Legislative Bill Drafting Commission, 117, 200
 Legislative Retrieval System, 117, 200
Legislative Correspondents Association, 602
Legislative Gazette, 591
Lewinter Associates, Murray, 499
Library Assn (NY), 499
Lieutenant Governor's Office, 4, 194
Life Insurance Council of NY PAC (LICONY), 548
Lowry, Robert, 500
Lynch, Patricia Associates, 501
MAC PAC, 549
MacKenzie, Duncan R, 502
Mackin, Robert E, 502
Malkin & Ross, 502
Maloney, Richard, 503
Manatt, Phelps & Phillips, LLP, 503
Manhattan Connection PAC, 550
Mannella, Peter F, 504
Manufactured Housing PAC, 550
Maria College of Albany, 627
Maritato, Anna Maria, 504
Marsh & Associates, PC, 504
McCulley & Associates Inc, 505
McEvoy, Frank, 505
McSpedon, William J, 505
Mechanical Technology Incorporated, 174
Medical Society of the State of NY, Governmental Affairs Division, 224
Melchionni, William, III, 506
Memorial Hospital School of Nursing, 627
Mental Health Association in NYS, 506
Mental Health Association of NYS Inc, 284
Mental Health, Office of, 12, 280
 Capital District Psychiatric Center, 280
Mental Hygiene Legal Service
 3rd Judicial Dept, 256, 282
Mental Retardation & Developmental Disabilities, Office of, 12, 281
Mesick, Edie, 507
Meyer Suozzi English & Klein, PC, 507
Morello, Charles J, 508
Morris & McVeigh LLP, 509
Morris & McVeigh NYS PAC, 551
Morris, Mark, 509
Motor Vehicles Department, 13, 348
MPAC, 550
Murphy, Daniel C, 509
Murphy, Robert J, 510
NAIFA - New York State, 251
NAMI-NYS, 284, 510
Nasca, Samuel J, 510
NASW-NYS Political Action for Candidate Election (PACE), 551
National Assn of Social Workers (NYS Chapter), 510
National Association of Social Workers, NYS Chapter, 321
National Credit Union Administration
 Albany Region, 93
National Federation of Independent Business, 110, 276, 331
National Labor Relations Board
 Albany Resident Office, 272
National Organization for Women- NYS PAC, 554
National Organization for Women, NYS, 166, 242
Nature Conservancy (The), 191
NEA of New York PAC, 551
Neighborhood Preservation Coalition of NYS Inc, 235
Nelson A Rockefeller Inst of Government, NY Forum for Info, 175
Nelson A Rockefeller Inst of Govt, Federalism Research Grp, 321
Nelson A Rockefeller Inst of Govt, Higher Education Program, 154
Nelson A Rockefeller Inst of Govt, Urban & Metro Studies, 235
Nelson A Rockefeller Institute of Government, 209, 331
New York Association of Convenience Stores, 110
New York Association of Homes & Services for the Aging, 225, 321
New York Association of Mortgage Brokers Political Action Committee, 554
New York Association of Psychiatric Rehabilitation Services (NYAPRS), 285
New York Build PAC, 555
New York Business Development Corporation, 110
New York City
 Legislative Affairs Office, NYC Mayor's State, 432
New York Community College Trustees (NYCCT), 154
New York Farm Bureau, 87
New York Financial Services PAC, 555
New York Health Plan Association, 225
New York Insurance Association Inc, 251
New York Library Association (The), 154
New York Medical Equipment Providers PAC, 555
New York Municipal Insurance Reciprocal (NYMIR), 251, 294
New York Newspaper Publishers Association, 175
New York Power Authority, 121, 170
New York Public Welfare Association, 321

Listings appear in alphabetical order by state, then city.

Geographic Index

New York Republican State Committee, 166
New York School Bus Operators for Effective Gov't, 556
New York State Association of Family Services Agencies Inc, 321
New York State Auto Dealers Association, 111, 359
New York State Beer Wholesalers Assn PAC, 556
New York State Board of Law Examiners, 121, 258
New York State Catholic Conference, 154, 322
New York State Commission of Correction, 122, 137
New York State Commission on the Restoration of the Capitol, 122, 201, 336
New York State Congress of Parents & Teachers Inc, 154
New York State Council of Churches, 243
New York State Council of School Superintendents, 154
New York State Disaster Preparedness Commission, 122, 201, 291
New York State Dormitory Authority, 122, 149, 201, 216
New York State Energy Research & Development Authority, 122, 170, 182
New York State Environmental Facilities Corp, 123, 182
New York State Ethics Commission, 123, 201
New York State Government Finance Officers Association Inc, 294, 331
New York State Health Facilities Association Inc, 226
New York State Higher Education Services Corp (NYSHESC), 123, 149
New York State Hospitality & Tourism Association, 346
New York State Law Reporting Bureau, 124, 201, 258
New York State Law Revision Commission, 124, 258
New York State Liquor Authority, 102, 124
New York State Motor Truck Association, 359
New York State Ophthalmological Society, 226
New York State Petroleum Council, 175
New York State Public Employees Federation (PEF), 299
New York State Public Employees' Federation PAC, 556
New York State Rehabilitation Association, 285, 322
New York State Republican Party, 452
New York State Restaurant Association, 111, 346
New York State Restaurant Industry PAC, 556
New York State Rural Development Council, 235
New York State Rural Housing Coalition Inc, 235
New York State Scrap Recyclers PAC, 557
New York State Sheriffs' Good Government Fund, 557
New York State Teachers' Retirement System, 125, 149, 297
New York State Telecommunications Association Inc, 175
New York State Temporary Commission on Lobbying, 125, 163, 202
New York State Thruway Authority, 125, 337, 353
New York State Transit & Tour Operators' PAC, 557
New York State Transportation Engineering Alliance (NYSTEA), 359
New York State Veterinary Medical Society, 88
New York Thoroughbred Racing Industry PAC, 557
New York Truck PAC, 557
New York Wired, 166
New Yorkers Against the Death Penalty, 511
Newspaper Publishers Assn (NY), 511
Next Wave Inc, 226
Nixon Peabody, LLP, 511
Nolan & Heller, LLP, 511
Northeastern Subcontractors Assn, PAC, 558
Nurse Anesthesia - CRNA - PAC Fund, 558
NY Association of Training & Employment Professionals (NYATEP), 276
NY Capitolwire (Associated Press), 602
NY Commercial Association of Realtors, 305
NY Council on Problem Gambling, 285
NY Counseling Association Inc, 285, 320
NY Health Information Management Association Inc, 224
NY Housing Association Inc, 234
NY Independent Bankers' PAC, 551
NY Physical Therapy Association, 224
NY Press Association, 174
NY State Association of Town Superintendents of Highways Inc, 294, 358
NY State Society of Physician Assistants, 224
NY StateWatch Inc, 208
NYAHSA PAC, 552
NYNHP-PAC, 552
NYPT PAC, 551
NYS AFL-CIO COPE, 552
NYS Alliance for Arts Education, 153, 344
NYS Association for the Education of Young Children, 153
NYS Association of Area Agencies on Aging, 321
NYS Association of Community & Residential Agencies, 285
NYS Association of Counties, 209, 294
NYS Association of County Health Officials, 224
NYS Association of Library Boards, 153
NYS Association of Nurse Anesthetists (NYSANA), 224
NYS Association of Realtors, 305
NYS Association of School Business Officials, 153
NYS Association of Service Stations & Repair Shops, 358, 552
NYS Association of Solid Waste Management, 190
NYS Association of Veterinary Technicians Inc, 86
NYS Bar Assn, Children & the Law Committee, 264, 320
NYS Bar Assn, Cmte on Diversity & Leadership Development, 265
NYS Bar Assn, Diversity & Leadership Development Cmte, 267
NYS Bar Assn, Electronic Communications Task Force, 174
NYS Bar Assn, Health Law Section, 227, 267
NYS Bar Assn, Issues Affecting People with Disabilities Cmte, 242
NYS Bar Assn, Issues Affecting Same Sex Couples, 243
NYS Bar Association, 88
NYS Broadcasters Association, 174, 552
NYS Builders Association Inc, 110
NYS Chapter AGC PAC, 552
NYS Child Care Coordinating Council, 321
NYS Commission on Quality of Care & Advocacy for Persons wit, 13, 119, 238, 282
NYS Committee for the Advancement of Mental Health Therapy, 552
NYS Conference of Local Mental Hygiene Directors, 285
NYS Conference of Mayors & Municipal Officials, 294, 331
NYS Conference of the IUOE Pol Action Acct, 553
NYS Correctional Officers & Police Benevolent Association Inc, 141, 299
NYS Council for Community Behavioral Healthcare, 285
NYS Council of Probation Administrators, 141, 265
NYS County Hwy Super Assn / NY Aviation Mgt Assn / NY Public, 358
NYS Defenders Association, 141, 265
NYS Dental Association, 224

Listings appear in alphabetical order by state, then city.

883

Geographic Index

NYS Economic Development Council, 110
NYS Education Department, 242
NYS Foundation for Science, Technology & Innovation, 13, 100, 147
   Center for Economic Growth, 148
   Center in Nanomaterials and Nanoelectronics, 148
NYS Funeral Directors Association PAC, 553
NYS Head Start Association, 153
NYS Hospitality & Tourism Assn PAC, 553
NYS Industries for the Disabled (NYSID) Inc, 276, 321
NYS Law Enforcement Officers Union, Council 82, AFSCME, AFL-CIO, 141, 299
NYS Occupational Therapy PAC, 553
NYS Optometric Assn PAC, 553
NYS Optometric Association Inc, 224
NYS Parole Officers Association, 299
NYS Psychological Association, 285
NYS Public Health Association, 224
NYS Reading Association, 154
NYS Right to Life Committee, 166
NYS Right to Life PAC, 553
NYS Sheriffs' Association, 141, 299
NYS Society of Real Estate Appraisers, 305
NYS Technology Enterprise Corporation (NYSTEC), 174
NYS Telecommunications PAC, 553
NYS Troopers PAC, 553
NYS Veterinary PEC, 553
NYSCHP PAC, 554
NYSCOPBA PAC, 554
O'Connell, Peter B, 512
O'Connor, John, 512
One Eleven PAC, 558
Organization of NYS Management Confidential Employees, 300
Organization of NYS Management/Confidential Employees Inc, 512
Ortho-PAC of New York, 558
Ostroff, Hiffa & Associates Inc, 512
Ottaway News Service (NYS only), 602
Outdoor Advertising NY PAC, 558
Pappas, Marcia, 513
Parks, Recreation & Historic Preservation, NYS Office of, 13, 179, 334
Parole, Division of, 14, 135
   Clemency Unit, 135
Pastel & Rosen, LLP, 514
Petraitis, Brian J, 514
Pharmacists Society of the State of New York, 226
Pharmacy PAC of New York State, 559
Phillips & Associates, PLLC, 515
Police Benevolent Assn of the NYS Troopers Inc, 515
Police Conference of New York Inc PAC, 560

Police Conference of NY Inc (PCNY), 142, 300
Political Action Committee of Council 82, 560
Powers & Company, 515
Prevent Child Abuse New York, 322
Prevention of Domestic Violence, Office for the, 14, 136, 312
PricewaterhouseCoopers LLP, 209
Probation & Correctional Alternatives, Division of, 14, 136
Professional Fire Fighters Association Inc (NYS), 300
Psychological Assn (NYS), 516
Psychologists for Legislative Action in NY, 560
Public Employment Relations Board, 14, 296
Public Policy Institute of NYS Inc, 111
Public Service Commission, 14, 169
Public Utility Law Project of New York Inc, 175, 517
Public Welfare Assn (NY), 517
Puckett, Robert R, 517
Real Property Services, Office of, 15, 289, 302, 326
   Albany (Northern Region), 289, 302, 326
Realtors PAC, 561
Regional Farm & Food Project, 88
Regulatory Reform, Governor's Office of, 15, 99, 197
Rehabilitation Assn Inc (NYS), 517
Repas, Peter G, 518
Research Foundation of SUNY, 155
Retail Council of New York State, 111
Retired Public Employees Association, 300
Rice & Justice, 518
Right to Life Committee Inc (NYS), 518
Roffe, Andrew S, PC, 518
Roman Catholic Diocese of Albany, Catholic Charities, 322
Roos, David E, 518
Rosario, Stephen M, 519
Rosenthal, Harvey, 519
Rutnik Law Firm (The), 520
Sampson, Rick J, 521
Sawchuk Brown Associates, 111
SCAA - Schuyler Center for Analysis & Advocacy, 155, 331
Schillinger, Lawrence R, 521
Schomberg, Dora, 522
Schuyler Center for Analysis & Advocacy (SCAA), 286, 522
Sheet Metal Workers' Local Union 83 Political Action Committee, 563
Sierra Club, Atlantic Chapter, 192, 523
Small Business Administration
   New York Business Information Center, 104
Small Cities, Office for, 15, 101, 229, 289
Smith, Joann, 523

Smyth, A Advocacy, 523
Soloway, Ronald, 523
South Colonie CSD, 638
Special Committee on Animals & the Law, 88
State Comptroller, Office of the, 16, 180, 197, 290, 296
State Department, 16, 101, 180, 199, 290
   Albany, 200
   Ethics Commission, 199, 291
State Employees Federal Credit Union, 300
State Police, Division of, 16, 136
State Street Associates PAC, 563
State University Construction Fund, 128, 149
State University of New York at Albany, 613
Statewide Emergency Network for Social & Economic Security (SENSES), 323
Stuto, Diane D, 524
SUNY at Albany, Center for Women in Government & Civil Society, 209
SUNY at Albany, Nelson A Rockefeller College, 166
SUNY at Albany, Nelson A Rockefeller College of Public Affairs &, 210
SUNY at Albany, Professional Development Program, NE States Addiction, 286
SUNY at Albany, Rockefeller College, 210
SUNY Board of Trustees, 611
SUNY System Administration & Executive Council, 611
   New York African American Institute, 611
   New York Network, 611
   Rockefeller Institute of Government, 611
   Small Business Development Center, 612
   State University Construction Fund, 612
SUNY, System Administration, 521
Surgeon PAC, 564
TAP PAC-APC, 564
Taxation & Finance Department, 17, 101, 326
Telecommunications Improvement Council, 565
Temporary & Disability Assistance, Office of, 17, 238, 313
The Business Council PAC Inc, 565
The Coca-Cola Bottling Company of New York, PAC, 565
Times Union, 591
Tourism Industry Coalition (TIC), 525
Transportation Department, 17, 302, 348
Tully Abdo, Susan, 525
Turner, Francine, 525
UHY Advisors, 112
Unified Court System, 256
   3rd Judicial Department, 256
   Administrative Judge to the Court of Claims (NYS), 256

Listings appear in alphabetical order by state, then city.

Geographic Index

Financial Management & Audit Services, 257
United Jewish Appeal-Federation of Jewish Philanthropies of NY, 323
United New York Ambulance Network (UNYAN), 227
United Restaurant, Hotel & Tavern Association of NY Statewide PAC, 567
United Transportation Union, 300, 359
United University Professions, 155, 300, 526
US Department of Agriculture
  Albany Field Office, 82, 217
  Field Operations - Albany District Office, 82
  Field Operations-Albany District Office, 218
  Gastonia Region—New York Office, 81
  National Agricultural Statistics Service-NYS Office, 82
  New York Area Office, 82
  New York State Office, 82
  Northeast Marketing Area, 81
US Department of Homeland Security (DHS)
  Albany, Port of, 204, 328
US Department of Veterans Affairs
  Albany VA Medical Center, 363
  VA Healthcare Network Upstate New York (VISN2), 363
US Housing & Urban Development Department
  Albany Area Office & Financial Operations Center, 232
US Justice Department
  Albany, 137, 138, 139, 260, 261
US Labor Department
  Albany, 364
  Albany Area Office, 219, 273
  Albany District Office, 273
US Railroad Retirement Board
  Albany, 274
US Transportation Department
  Federal Highway Administration-New York Division, 355
  Federal Motor Carrier Safety Admin-New York Division, 356
US Treasury Department
  Albany Territory, 329
  Upstate New York Office, 329
Vandervort Group, LLC (The), 527
Veterans of Foreign Wars, 368
Veterans of Foreign Wars Auxiliary, 368
Veterans' Affairs, Division of, 17, 361
  Albany Office, 361
Veterans' Service Organizations
  Albany Housing Coalition Inc, 361
  Veterans House (The), 361
Vidal Group, LLC (The), 528
WAMC (90.3 FM), 603

Weingarten, Reid & McNally, LLC, 528, 567
Welfare Inspector General, Office of NYS, 18, 200, 313
Welfare Research Inc, 323
Whiteman Osterman & Hanna LLP, 193, 243, 267, 294, 529
Wilson Elser Moskowitz Edelman & Dicker, 227, 267, 530
Wilson Elser Moskowitz Edelman & Dicker PAC, 568
WNYT (13), 607
Workers' Compensation Board, 18, 247, 270
  Albany, 247, 271
WPTR (1540 AM), 603
WTEN (10), 607
WXXA (23), 607
Yavornitzki, Mark L, 531
YMCAS of NYS Inc, 531
Zogg, Jeffrey, 532

Albertson
Abilities Inc, National Center for Disability Services, 274, 316

Albion
Albion CSD, 661
Correctional Services Department
  Albion Correctional Facility, 130
  Orleans Correctional Facility, 131
Elections, State Board of
  Orleans, 161
Orleans County, 406
  Supreme, County, Family & Surrogate's Courts, 66
Orleans County Chamber of Commerce, 581
Orleans Economic Development Agency (OEDA), 582

Alden
Alden CSD, 645
Correctional Services Department
  Buffalo Correctional Facility, 130
  Wende Correctional Facility, 131

Alexander
Alexander CSD, 648

Alexandria Bay
Alexandria Bay Chamber of Commerce, 569
Alexandria CSD, 650
Convention Centers & Visitors Bureaus
  Thousand Islands Int'l Tourism Council, 338
Parks, Recreation & Historic Preservation, NYS Office of
  Thousand Islands Region, 334
Thousand Islands Bridge Authority, 128, 354

Alfred
Alfred State College of Technology, 614
Alfred University, 622
NYS College of Ceramics at Alfred University, 612
NYS Foundation for Science, Technology & Innovation
  Center for Advanced Ceramic Technology at Alfred University, 100, 147

Allegany
Allegany - Limestone CSD, 640
Independent Oil and Gas Association of NY, Inc Political Ac, 546

Almond
Alfred-Almond CSD, 638

Altamont
Davis, Michael J, 478
Hudson River Environmental Society, 189

Altona
Correctional Services Department
  Altona Correctional Facility, 130

Amagansett
Amagansett UFSD, 668

Amenia
Webutuck CSD, 645

Amherst
AAA Western and Central NY, 454
Amherst CSD, 645
Amherst Industrial Development Agency (Town of), 569
Bryant & Stratton College-Amherst Campus, 634
Buffalo Niagara Assn of Realtors, Inc, 466
Central NY PAC Region 9 UAW, 537
Daemen College, 624
Empire Liquor Store Association, 541
Manufacturers & Traders Trust Company PAC, 550
MJ Peterson Corporation, 304
New York State Political Action Committee, Region 9, UAW, 556
Sweet Home CSD, 647
Western NY PAC Region 9 UAW, 568
Williams, Samuel G, 530
Women's TAP Fund, 568
Woodward Workforce, 568

Amityville
Amityville UFSD, 668
Island Drafting & Technical Institute, 635
New York Marine Trades Association, 345
NYMTA Boat PAC, 552

Amsterdam
Amsterdam
  Civil & Criminal Courts, 71

Listings appear in alphabetical order by state, then city.

Geographic Index

Amsterdam Industrial Development Agency, 569
Criminal Justice Services, Division of
Juvenile Justice Advisory Group, 252
Greater Amsterdam SD, 653
Recorder (The), 591

Andes
Andes CSD, 644

Andover
Andover CSD, 638

Angola
Erie 2-Chautauqua-Cattaraugus BOCES, 679
Evans-Brant CSD (Lake Shore), 646

Annandale-on-Hudson
Bard College, 622

Apalachin
Owego, Town of, 438

Arcade
Arcade Area Chamber of Commerce, 569

Ardsley
Ardsley UFSD, 675
Lesnick Leadership PAC, 548

Argyle
Argyle CSD, 674

Arkport
Arkport CSD, 667

Arkville
Catskill Center for Conservation & Development, 188

Armonk
Building & Realty Institute, 304
Byram Hills CSD, 675
MBIA Insurance Corporation, 95, 293
North Castle Democratic Club, 557
Stars & Stripes PAC, 563

Astoria
NLOA-PAC, 551

Attica
Attica CSD, 678
Correctional Services Department
Attica Correctional Facility, 130
Wyoming Correctional Facility, 132

Auburn
Auburn
Civil & Criminal Courts, 71
Auburn Enlarged City SD, 641
Auburn Publishers Inc, 591
Auburn, City of, 414
Cayuga Community College, 615
Cayuga Community College Faculty Assn PAC, 537

Cayuga County, 397
Family Court, 62
Cayuga County Chamber of Commerce, 571
Cayuga-Onondaga BOCES, 678
Citizen (The), 591
Correctional Services Department
Auburn Correctional Facility, 130
Elections, State Board of
Cayuga, 158
Empire State Association of Adult Homes, Inc PAC, 541
Nucor Corporation, PAC NY, 558

Aurora
Southern Cayuga CSD, 641
Wells College, 633

Averill Park
Averill Park CSD, 663
Duncan, Craig A, 480

Avoca
Avoca CSD, 667
US Department of Agriculture
Avoca Work Unit, 81

Avon
Avon CSD, 651
Environmental Conservation Department
Region 8, 178

Babylon
Babylon Industrial Development Agency, 570
Babylon UFSD, 668
Friends of Lazio, 543
Intercounty Health Facilities Assn PAC, 546
Parks, Recreation & Historic Preservation, NYS Office of
Long Island Region, 334
Suffolk & Nassau Counties Plumbing & Heating Contractors Assoc PAC, 564

Bainbridge
Bainbridge-Guilford CSD, 642

Baldwin
Baldwin Chamber of Commerce, 570
Baldwin UFSD, 653

Baldwinsville
Baldwinsville Chamber of Commerce (Greater Baldwinsville), 570
Baldwinsville CSD, 658
Lysander, Town of, 424
Van Buren Womens Republican Club, 567
WSEN (92.1 FM), 603

Ballston Lake
Adams, Daniel J, 455

Ballston Spa
Ballston Spa CSD, 664
BBL PAC, 535
Elections, State Board of
Saratoga, 161
NYS Agricultural Society, 86
Saratoga County, 408
Family Court, 67
Supreme, County & Surrogate's Courts, 67
Saratoga County Industrial Development Agency, 584
US Transportation Department
Highway-Rail Grade Crossing, 356
Veterans' Service Organizations
Saratoga Cnty Rural Preservation Co (Homeless Veterans), 361

Barker
AES NYS PAC, 533
Barker CSD, 657

Barrytown
Unification Theological Seminary, 632

Batavia
Batavia
Civil & Criminal Courts, 71
Batavia City SD, 648
Batavia Newspapers Corp, 592
Daily News (The), 592
Education Department
State School for the Blind at Batavia, 146, 279, 312
Western Regional Office, 147
Elections, State Board of
Genesee, 159
Genesee Community College, 616
Genesee County, 401
Supreme, County, Family & Surrogate's Courts, 64
Genesee County Chamber of Commerce, 575
Genesee County Economic Development Center, 575
Health Department
New York State Veterans' Home at Batavia, 214, 360
Mancuso Business Development Group, 304
My-T Acres Inc, 86
Real Property Services, Office of
Batavia (Western Region), 289, 302, 326
US Department of Agriculture
Batavia Work Station, 81
US Department of Veterans Affairs
Batavia VA Medical Center, 363
Western Regional Off-Track Betting Corp, 128, 337

Listings appear in alphabetical order by state, then city.

Geographic Index

Bath
Bath Area Chamber of Commerce (Greater Bath Area), 570
Bath CSD, 667
Elections, State Board of
  Steuben, 162
Steuben County, 410
  Supreme, County, Family & Surrogate's Courts, 68
Steuben County Industrial Development Agency, 586
US Department of Veterans Affairs
  Bath National Cemetery, 363
  Bath VA Medical Center, 363
WCII (88.5 FM), WCOT (90.9 FM), 603

Bayport
Bayport-Blue Point UFSD, 668

Bayshore, 101
Bay Shore UFSD, 668
Bayshore Chamber of Commerce, 570
NYS Foundation for Science, Technology & Innovation
  Long Island Forum for Technology, 148

Bayside
Queensborough Community College, 621
Responsible Government Coalition, 561
St Mary's Healthcare System for Children, Inc, 524

Beacon
Antalek & Moore Insurance Agency, 93
Beacon
  Civil & Criminal Courts, 71
Beacon City SD, 644
Correctional Services Department
  Beacon Correctional Facility, 130
  Fishkill Correctional Facility, 130
WSPK (104.7 FM), 603

Bear Mountain
Parks, Recreation & Historic Preservation, NYS Office of
  Palisades Interstate Park Commission, 334

Beaver Dams
Correctional Services Department
  Monterey Shock Incarceration Correctional Facility, 131

Beaver Falls
Beaver River CSD, 651

Bedford
Bedford CSD, 675
Emigrant Savings Bank PAC, 541

Bedford Hills
Correctional Services Department
  Bedford Hills Correctional Facility, 130
  Taconic Correctional Facility, 131

Belfast
Belfast CSD, 639

Bellerose
Mental Health, Office of
  Queens Children's Psychiatric Center, 280

Belleville
Belleville Henderson CSD, 650

Bellmore
Bellmore Republican Club Inc, 535
Bellmore UFSD, 653
Bellmores Chamber of Commerce, 570
North Bellmore UFSD, 655

Belmont
Allegany County, 396
  Supreme, County, Family & Surrogate's Courts, 61
Allegany County Office of Development, 569
Elections, State Board of
  Allegany, 157
Genesee Valley CSD, 639

Bemus Point
Bemus Point CSD, 641

Bergen
Byron-Bergen CSD, 648

Berlin
Berlin CSD, 663

Berne
Berne-Knox-Westerlo CSD, 638

Bethpage
Bethpage Federal Credit Union PAC, 535
Bethpage UFSD, 654
Briarcliffe College-Bethpage, 634
Cablevision Systems Corporation, 173
Cablevision Systems New York PAC, 536
CSC Holdings, Inc, 467
Long Island Development Corporation, 578

Binghamton, 100
BAPA, 535
Binghamton
  Civil & Criminal Courts, 71
Binghamton Chamber of Commerce (Greater Binghamton), 570
Binghamton City SD, 639
Binghamton University, State University of New York, 612
Binghamton, City of, 415
Broome Community College, 615
Broome County, 396
  County, Family & Surrogate's Courts, 61
  Supreme Court, 62
Broome County Industrial Development Agency, 571
Broome-Delaware-Tioga BOCES, 678
Chadwick, Cindy, 470
Chenango Forks CSD, 639
Chenango Valley CSD, 639
Convention Centers & Visitors Bureaus
  Greater Binghamton New York Convention and Visitors Bureau, 338
Education Department
  Southern Tier District Office, 147
Elections, State Board of
  Broome, 157
Energy Action Fund, 541
Gannet Co Inc, 592
Human Rights, State Division of
  Binghamton, 237
Law Department
  Binghamton, 254
Levene, Gouldin & Thompson LLP, 250, 264
Local 7 PAC Fund, 549
Mental Health, Office of
  Greater Binghamton Health Center, 280
Movers & Warehousemen Political Action Committee, 551
New York State Electric & Gas Corporation (NYSEG), 175
NOFA-NY Certified Organic LLC, 86
NYS Bar Assn, Tort System Cmte, 264
NYS Foundation for Science, Technology & Innovation
  Alliance for Manufacturing & Technology, 148
  Integrated Electronics Engineering Center, 148
NYS Trade Adjustment Assistance Center, 110
Plumbers & Pipefitters Local Union 112 PAC, 559
Political Action Committee of Broome County Assoc PHCC, 560
Press & Sun Bulletin, 592
Southern Tier Business PAC, 563
State Department
  Binghamton, 200
Transportation Department
  Region 9, 350
Uniform State Laws Commission, 128, 202, 258
US Justice Department
  Binghamton, 138, 260
Veterans' Service Organizations
  Veterans Services Center of the Southern Tier, 361
Western NY Regional Council PAC Fund, 568
WIVT/WBGH (34), 607
WNBF (1290 AM), WHWK (98.1FM), WYOS (1360 AM), WAAL (, 603
Workers' Compensation Board
  Binghamton, 247, 271
WSKG (46) Public Broadcasting, 608

Listings appear in alphabetical order by state, then city.

Geographic Index

WSKG (89.3 FM), WSQX (91.5 FM), 603

Blasdell
Hamburg Conservative Club, 544

Blauvelt
Rockland County PBA Association PAC NY, 561
South Orangetown CSD, 664

Bliss
McCormick Farms Inc, 86
National Potato Board, 86

Bloomfield
NYS Berry Growers Association, 86

Blue Mountain Lake
Adirondack Lakes Center for the Arts, 341
Blue Mountain Lake Association, 570
New York State Rural Advocates, 235

Bohemia
Appraisal Education Network School & Merrell Institute, 303
Connetquot CSD, 668
Suffolk Co Detective Investigators PBA Inc PAC, 564
Suffolk County Assn of Municipal Employees' PAC Inc, 564
Suffolk County Police Benevolent Assn PAC, 564
US Commerce Department
  National Weather Service, Eastern Region, 81, 105, 184

Boiceville
Citizens Leadership Council, 537
Onteora CSD, 673

Bolivar
Bolivar-Richburg CSD, 639

Bolton Landing
Bolton CSD, 673
Bolton Landing Chamber of Commerce, 570

Boonville
Adirondack CSD, 658
Boonville Area Chamber of Commerce, 570
New York State Woodsmen's Field Days Inc, 191

Boston
US Labor Department
  Jobs Corps (JC), 273

Bowmansville
US Labor Department
  Buffalo Area Office, 273

Bradford
Bradford CSD, 667

Brasher Falls
Brasher Falls CSD, 666

Brentwood
Brentwood UFSD, 668

Brewerton
Fort Brewerton/Greater Oneida Lake Chamber, 574

Brewster
Brewster Chamber of Commerce, 570
Brewster CSD, 663
Elections, State Board of
  Putnam, 161
Green Chimneys School-Green Chimneys Children's Services Inc, 319
Sheet Metal Workers LU 38 -PAC, 562

Briarcliff Manor
Briarcliff Manor UFSD, 675
Federations of Police PAC Fund, 542

Briarwood
Samaritan Village Inc, 286
USWA, SEIU, AFL-CIO, CLC-PAC, 566

Bridgehampton
Bridgehampton UFSD, 668

Brightwaters
NYS Passenger Vessel Association, 344

Broadalbin
Broadalbin-Perth CSD, 648

Brockport
Brockport Chamber of Commerce (Greater Brockport), 570
Brockport CSD, 652
State University at Brockport, 613
SUNY College at Brockport, 520

Brocton
Brocton CSD, 641
Correctional Services Department
  Lakeview Shock Incarceration Correctional Facility, 131
Democratic Caucas Committee, 539

Bronx
Affinity Health Plan, 455
Affordable Housing PAC, LTD, 533
Botanical Garden (The) (NY), 464
Bronx Coalition for Good Government, 535
Bronx Community College, 619
Bronx County
  Supreme & Surrogate's Courts, 61
Bronx County (NYC Borough of the Bronx), 396
Bronx Educational Opportunity Center, 617
Bronx-Lebanon Hospital Center, 221
BXNY PAC, 535
Carr, Bernard, 469
Citizens for Sports & Arts, Inc, 537
Civil Court, NYC
  Bronx County, 59
Correctional Services Department
  Fulton Correctional Facility, 130
Criminal Court, NYC
  Bronx County, 60
Education Department
  Bronx District Office, 147
Elections, State Board of
  Bronx, 160
Family Court, NYC
  Bronx County, 60
Fassler, Michael S, 482
Fordham University, 153, 625
Fordham University, Department of Political Science, 293
Global Gardens Program, New York Botanical Garden (The), 85
Hostos Community College, 620
Human Rights, State Division of, 11, 237
Hunts Point Produce Market Redevelopment PAC, 545
KleinPAC, 547
Lehman College, 620
Massiah, Lesley A, 505
Mental Health, Office of
  Bronx Children's Psychiatric Center, 280
  Bronx Psychiatric Center, 280
Monroe College-Bronx, 636
New Era Veterans, Inc, 367
New York City Boroughs
  Bronx (Bronx County), 435
New York Yankees, 346
North Bronx Career Counseling & Outreach Center, 618
NYC Region 1, 657
NYC Region 2, 657
NYS Bar Assn, Judicial Independence Cmte, 261
Osborne Association, 141, 276
Port Morris Local Development Corporation, 582
Public Markets Partners / Baum Forum, 88
Schlein, Stanley, 521
Transit Supervisors Organization PAC, 566
Unified Court System
  12th Judicial District (Judicial Department 1), 257
US Department of Agriculture
  Fresh Products Branch - Bronx Field Office, 81
  Market News Branch—New York State, 81
US Department of Veterans Affairs
  Bronx VA Medical Center, 364
  VA NY/NJ Veterans Healthcare Network (VISN3), 363
WFUV (90.7 FM), 603
Wildlife Conservation Society, 193, 529

Listings appear in alphabetical order by state, then city.

Geographic Index

Women's Housing & Economic Development Corporation (WHEDCO), 236
Yeshiva University, A Einstein Clg of Med, Div of Subs Abuse, 286
Yeshiva University, A Einstein Clg of Med, OB/GYN & Wmn's Health, 227

Bronxville
Bronxville Chamber of Commerce, 570
Bronxville UFSD, 675
Concordia College, 623
Grassy Sprain PAC, 543
Sarah Lawrence College, 630
Telecommunications Int'l Union, 565
The Republican Club of Bronxville, 565

Brookfield
Brookfield CSD, 651

Brookhaven
Suffolk Co Police Dept Superior Officers Assoc Public Affairs Cmte, 564

Brooklyn
2nd Department, 55
Academy of Trial Lawyers PAC, 533
Agriculture & Markets Department
  Brooklyn, 80
  New York City Office, 80
American College of Nurse-Midwives, NYC Chapter, 220
ASA Institute of Business & Computer Technology, 633
Attorney Grievance Committee
  Judicial Dist 2, 11, 255
Bear Stearns Political Campaign Committee, 535
Black Veterans for Social Justice Inc, 365
Brooklyn Botanic Garden, 187, 341
Brooklyn Chamber of Commerce, 571
Brooklyn College, 620
Brooklyn Daily Eagle, 592
Brooklyn Eagle Publications, 592
Brooklyn Economic Development Corporation, 571
Brooklyn Educational Opportunity Center, 618
Brooklyn Heights Press, 592
Brooklyn Housing & Family Services Inc, 233
Brooklyn Law School, 262, 622
Brooklyn Museum of Art, 341
Brooklyn Navy Yard Development Corporation, 114, 362
Brooklyn Phoenix, 592
Canarsie Courier, 592
Center for Anti-Violence Education Inc, 316
Church Avenue Merchants Block Association, 470

Citizens for Responsible Representation, 537
Civil Court, NYC
  Kings County, 59
Coalition of Living Museums, 342
Coney Island Chamber of Commerce, 573
Conservative Action Fund, 538
Council of School Supervisors & Admin, Local 1 AFSA AFL-CIO, 539
Council of School Supervisors & Administrators, 153
Crime Victims Board, 7, 132, 311
Criminal Court, NYC
  Kings County, 60
CUNY New York City College of Technology, Hospitality Mgmt, 342
Daily Challenge, 592
Diamond Asphalt Corp, 479
Education Department
  Brooklyn District Office, 147
  New York City Regional Office, 147
  School Improvement & Community Services (NYC), 145
Elections, State Board of
  Kings, 160
Family Court, NYC
  Kings County, 60
Haitian-American Association for Political Action (HAAPA-PAC), 544
HeartShare Human Services of New York, Roman Catholic Dioce, 319
Helen Keller Services for the Blind, 319
Hellenic American PAC - State, 545
Housing Works Inc, 234, 319
Human Rights, State Division of
  Brooklyn, 238
Institute of Design & Construction, 626
Kings County
  Supreme Court, 64
  Surrogate's Court, 64
Kings County (NYC Borough of Brooklyn), 403
Kings County C-PAC, 547
Kings County Democratic Party, 535
Kingsborough Community College, 620
Konheim & Ketcham Inc, 358
Law Department
  Brooklyn, 254
Law Guardian Program
  2nd Judicial Dept, 256
Little Flower Children & Family Services, 320
Local 1814 Intl Longshoremens Assn AFL-CIO PA & ED Fund, 548
Local 891 Cope Fund, 549
Logan, Ernest, 500
Long Island College Hospital School of Nursing, 626
Make the Road by Walking Inc, 502
Marcus Attorneys, 504
Medgar Evers College, 620

Mental Health, Office of
  Brooklyn Children's Center, 280
  Kingsboro Psychiatric Center, 280
Mental Retardation & Developmental Disabilities, Office of
  Brooklyn Developmental Disabilities Services Office, 281
MTA New York City Transit, 119, 352
Nat'l Assn of Social Workers - New York City Chapter, 554
National Labor Relations Board
  Region 29 - Brooklyn Area, 272
New York Aquarium, 345
New York City
  Fire Department, NYC, 429
  Library, Brooklyn Public, 432
New York City Boroughs
  Brooklyn (Kings County), 435
New York City College of Technology, 621
NY Airport Service, 358
NYC Region 6, 657
NYC Region 8, 657
NYS Bar Assn, Mass Disaster Response Committee, 209
NYS Council of Physiotherapists PAC, 553
NYS Foundation for Science, Technology & Innovation
  Ctr for Advanced Tech in Telecommunications at Polytech Univ, 100, 148
NYS Grievance Committee, 209
Polytechnic University, 629
Pratt Center for Community Development, 236
Pratt Institute, 629
Public Employment Relations Board
  New York City, 296
Radiac Environmental Services, 191
Sen Dem, 562
St Joseph's College, 631
Statewide Black & Puerto Rican/Latino Substance Abuse Task Force, 286
SUNY Downstate Medical Center, 612
Unified Court System
  2nd Judicial Department, 256
  2nd Judicial District (Judicial Department 2), 256
United New York Democratic Club Inc, 567
Urbane Leadership, 567
US Defense Department
  Fort Hamilton, 362
  North Atlantic Division, 184
US Department of Homeland Security (DHS)
  Brooklyn, Port of, 82, 203
US Department of Veterans Affairs
  Brooklyn Campus of the NY Harbor Healthcare System, 364
  Cypress Hills National Cemetery, 363
US Federal Courts
  Eastern District, 259

Listings appear in alphabetical order by state, then city.

889

Geographic Index

US DISTRICT COURT - NEW YORK
(part of the Second Circuit), 259
US Justice Department
Brooklyn, 139, 261
Brooklyn Metropolitan Detention Center, 138
Eastern District, 138, 260
New York City, 138
New York Field Division, 137, 328
US Treasury Department
Brooklyn & Long Island Office, 329
SBSE-Taxpayer Education & Communication (TEC), 329
Tax Exempt & Government Entities Div (TEGE)-Northeast Area, 329
Veterans' Service Organizations
Project TORCH, Veterans Health Care Center, 361
Victory 2005 Committee, 567
Workers' Compensation Board
Brooklyn, 247, 271
Working Families Party, 167

Brooklyn Heights
St Francis College, 631

Brookville
Long Island University, 626
Williams Esq, Christopher A, 530

Browmansville
US Labor Department
Buffalo Area Office, 219

Brushton
Brushton-Moira CSD, 647

Buffalo
AAA Western and Central NY, 340, 357
Agriculture & Markets Department
Buffalo, 80
Alcoholic Beverage Control, Division of (State Liquor Authority)
Buffalo (Zone III), 98, 324
Attorney Grievance Committee
Judicial Dist 8, 255
BCSA-PAC, 535
Brown & Kelly, LLP, 107
Bryant & Stratton College-Buffalo Campus, 634
Buffalo
Civil & Criminal Courts, 71
Buffalo & Fort Erie Public Bridge Authority (Peace Bridge Authority), 114, 350
Buffalo Business First, 592
Buffalo Economic Renaissance Corporation, 571
Buffalo Educational Opportunity Center, 618
Buffalo News (The), 593
Buffalo Niagara Partnership, 571
Buffalo Professional Firefighters PAC, 535
Buffalo Sabres, 342
Buffalo SD, 645
Buffalo State College, 613
Buffalo Teachers Federation PAC, 536
Buffalo, City of, 416
Canisius College, 622
Children & Family Services, Office of
Buffalo Regional Office, 310
Committee for Economic Growth, 538
Connors & Vilardo, 207
Convention Centers & Visitors Bureaus
Buffalo Niagara Convention & Visitors Bureau, 338
Crime Victims Board, 7, 132, 311
D'Youville College, 624
E-3 Communications, 480
Education Department
Buffalo District Office, 147
Elections, State Board of
Erie, 158
Elevator Constructors Union Local 14 PAC, 541
Empire State Development Corporation, 9, 99, 116, 177, 230, 333
Environmental Conservation Department
Great Lakes Program, 178
Region 9, 178
EPIC-Every Person Influences Children Inc, 318
Equal Employment Opportunity Commission
Buffalo Local, 239, 272
Erie Community College, 615
Erie County, 400
County Court, 63
Family Court, 63
Supreme & Surrogate's Court, 63
Erie County Industrial Development Agency, 574
Erie County Planning & Economic Development, 574
Federal Reserve System
Buffalo Branch, 92
Great Lakes United, 189
Health Department
Roswell Park Cancer Institute Corporation, 215
Western Regional Office, 215
Hodgson Russ, LLP, 491
Housing & Community Renewal, Division of
Buffalo, 228
Human Rights, State Division of
Buffalo, 238
Independent Health Assn Inc Political Alliance, 546
Insurance Fund (NYS)
Buffalo, 246, 268
International Institute of Buffalo, NY, Inc, 242
Kenmore-Tonawanda UFSD, 646
Kruly, Kenneth, 495
Labor Department
Western Region, 270
Law Department
Buffalo, 254
Lottery, Division of
Western Region, 325
M&T Bank Corporation, 95
Maier, Ronald S, 502
Medaille College, 627
Mental Health, Office of
Buffalo Psychiatric Center, 280
Michael T Kelly, Esq, 141, 265
National Fuel Gas Distribution, 175, 265
National Labor Relations Board
Region 3 - New York Except Metro Area, 272
New York State Dormitory Authority, 122, 149, 201, 216
New York State Theatre Education Association, 346
Niagara Frontier Transportation Authority, 126, 353
Niagara Mohawk Holdings, Inc Corp
Voluntary State PAC, 557
NY Association of Local Government Records Officers, 294
NYS Bar Assn, Civil Practice Law & Rules Committee, 265
NYS Bar Assn, Criminal Justice Section, 141, 265
NYS Bar Assn, Law Youth & Citizenship Committee, 209
NYS Bar Assn, Public Relations Cmte, 107
NYS Bar Assn, Public Utility Law Committee, 175, 265
NYS Bar Assn, Task Force to Review Terrorism Legislation Cmte, 207
NYS Foundation for Science, Technology & Innovation
Center for Advanced Tech in Biomedical & Bioengineering, 100, 147
INSYTE Consulting (Western NY Technology Development Ctr), 148
NYS Supreme Court, 209, 265
Public Employment Relations Board
Buffalo, 296
Public Service Commission, 14, 169
R W Bronstein Corporation, 305
Republican Lawyers Club, 561
Small Business Administration
Buffalo, 104
Solidarity Task Force, 563
State Department
Buffalo, 200
SUNY Buffalo Human Rights Center, 243
The Delaware Club, 565
The Real Conservatives, 565
The Young Democratic Rural Conference, 565
Transportation Department
Region 5, 349

Listings appear in alphabetical order by state, then city.

Geographic Index

Trocaire College, 632
Unified Court System
   8th Judicial District (Judicial Department 4), 257
University at Buffalo, 527
University at Buffalo, Research Institute on Addictions, 286
University at Buffalo, State University of New York, 613
Upstate Niagara Cooperative (FKA Upstate Farms Cooperative), 527
Upstate Niagara Cooperative Inc, 89
US Commerce Department
   Buffalo US Export Assistance Center, 105
US Defense Department
   Buffalo District Office, 184
US Department of Homeland Security (DHS)
   Buffalo District Office, 204, 239
   Buffalo Field Office, 204, 328
   Buffalo, Port of, 82, 203, 204, 328
US Department of the Interior
   Theodore Roosevelt Inaugural National Historic Site, 340
US Department of Veterans Affairs
   Buffalo Regional Office, 363
   Buffalo VA Medical Center, 363
US Federal Courts
   Western District, 260
US Housing & Urban Development Department
   Buffalo Area Office, 232
US Justice Department
   Buffalo, 137, 138, 139, 261
US Labor Department
   Buffalo District Office, 273
US Railroad Retirement Board
   Buffalo, 274
US Transportation Department
   Hazardous Material, 356
US Treasury Department
   Western New York State Office, 329
Veterans' Affairs, Division of
   Buffalo VA Regional Office, 361
   Western Region, 361
Villa Maria College of Buffalo, 633
WBFO (88.7 FM) WOLN (91.3 FM), WUBJ (88.7 FM) NPR/PRI - SUNY at, 603
WBLK (93.7 FM), WJYE (96.1 FM), 604
WDCX (99.5 FM), 604
Western New York Library Resources Council, 156
WGRZ (2), 608
WHTT (104.1 FM), 604
WIVB (4), WNLO (23), 608
WKBW (7), 608
WNED (17) Western NY Public Broadcasting, 608
WNED (94.5 FM), 604
Workers' Compensation Board
   Buffalo, 248, 271
WYRK (106.5 FM), WBUF (92.9 FM), 604

Cairo
Cairo-Durham CSD, 649
Greene County Soil & Water Conservation District, 189

Caledonia
Caledonia-Mumford CSD, 651

Calverton
Gergela III, Joseph, 485
Long Island Farm Bureau, 86
US Department of Veterans Affairs
   Calverton National Cemetery, 363

Cambridge
Cambridge CSD, 674

Camden
Camden CSD, 658

Camillus
West Genesee CSD, 659

Campbell
Campbell-Savona CSD, 667

Canaan
Berkshire Farm Center & Services for Youth, 140, 316
Berkshire UFSD, 643

Canadaigua
New York Wine & Grape Foundation, 88

Canajoharie
Canajoharie CSD, 653

Canandaigua
Canandaigua
   Civil & Criminal Courts, 71
Canandaigua Area Chamber of Commerce, 571
Canandaigua City SD, 660
Canandaigua National Bank & Trust Co, 94
Convention Centers & Visitors Bureaus
   Ontario County/Finger Lakes Visitor's Connection, 338
Daily Messenger (The), 593
Elections, State Board of
   Ontario, 160
Finger Lakes Community College, 616
Messenger Post Newspapers, 593
New York Wine & Grape Foundation, 346
Ontario County, 406
   Supreme, County, Family & Surrogate's Courts, 66
Ontario County Industrial Development Agency & Economic Development, 581
US Department of Agriculture
   Canandaigua Work Station, 82
US Department of Veterans Affairs
   Canandaigua VA Medical Center, 363

Canaseraga
Canaseraga CSD, 639

Canastota
Canastota Chamber of Commerce, 571
Canastota CSD, 651
Madison County Industrial Development Agency, 578

Candor
Candor CSD, 672
NY Farms!, 86

Canisteo
Canisteo-Greenwood CSD, 667

Canton
Canton Chamber of Commerce, 571
Canton CSD, 666
Community Bankers Assn of NY State, Bank Operations & Admin Cmte, 96
Elections, State Board of
   Saint Lawrence, 161
New Yorkers for Better Libraries PAC, 557
North Country Savings Bank, 96
St Lawrence County, 410
   Supreme, County, Family & Surrogate's Courts, 68
St Lawrence County Chamber of Commerce, 586
St Lawrence County Industrial Development Agency, 586
St Lawrence University, 631
St Lawrence-Lewis BOCES, 680
State University College of Technology at Canton, 614

Cape Vincent
Cape Vincent Chamber of Commerce, 571
Correctional Services Department
   Cape Vincent Correctional Facility, 130

Carle Place
Carle Place UFSD, 654

Carmel
Putnam County, 407
   Supreme, County, Family & Surrogate's Courts, 67
Putnam County Economic Development Corporation, 583

Caroga Lake
Wheelerville UFSD, 648

Carthage
Carthage Area Chamber of Commerce, 571
Carthage CSD, 650

Castile
Parks, Recreation & Historic Preservation, NYS Office of
   Genesee Region, 334

Listings appear in alphabetical order by state, then city.

Geographic Index

Castle Point
US Department of Veterans Affairs
  Castle Point Campus of the VA Hudson Vly Healthcare System, 364

Castleton
Rensselaer-Columbia-Greene (Questar III) BOCES, 680
Schodack CSD, 663

Cato
Cato-Meridian CSD, 641

Catskill
Catskill CSD, 649
Daily Mail (The), 593
Elections, State Board of
  Greene, 159
Greene County, 401
  Supreme, County, Family & Surrogate's Courts, 64
Greene County Department of Planning & Economic Development, 576
Greene County Tourism Promotion, 576
Hudson Valley Newspapers Inc, 593
New York Association of Independent Lumber Dealers PAC (NAIL PAC), 554
New York Propane PAC, 556

Cazenovia
Cazenovia Area Chamber of Commerce (Greater Cazenovia Area), 571
Cazenovia College, 622
Cazenovia CSD, 652

Center Moriches
Center Moriches UFSD, 668

Centereach
Middle Country CSD, 669

Central Islip
Central Islip UFSD, 668
Suffolk County
  1ST DISTRICT COURT, Criminal Term, 70
  Family Court, 68
US Justice Department
  Central Islip, 139
  Eastern District, 261

Central Square
Central Square CSD, 661

Central Valley
Hudson Valley Chapter, Nat'l Electrical Contractors Assn (NECA), 545
Monroe-Woodbury CSD, 661

Champlain
Northeastern Clinton CSD, 643
US Department of Homeland Security (DHS)
  Champlain, Port of, 82, 203, 204, 328

WCHP (760 AM), 604

Chappaqua
Chappaqua CSD, 675

Chateaugay
Chateaugay CSD, 647
Correctional Services Department
  Chateaugay Correctional Facility, 130

Chatham
Chatham CSD, 643

Chaumont
Lyme CSD, 650

Chautauqua
Convention Centers & Visitors Bureaus
  Chautauqua County Visitors Bureau, 338

Chazy
Chazy Central RSD, 643

Cheektowaga
Automotive Technology & Energy Group of Western NY, 357
Cheektowaga Chamber of Commerce, 572
Cheektowaga CSD, 645
Cheektowaga Democratic Finance Committee, 537
Cheektowaga, Town of, 416
Cleveland Hill UFSD, 646
Maryvale UFSD, 646
United Steelworkers District 4 PAC, 567
US Treasury Department
  Buffalo Territory, 329
WNY Majority Leader PAC, 567
Working Families Party WNY Chapter, 568

Cherry Valley
Cherry Valley-Springfield CSD, 662

Chesnut Ridge
Sunbridge College, 632

Chester
Chester UFSD, 660

Chestertown
North Warren Chamber of Commerce, 581
North Warren CSD, 673

Chestnut Ridge
New York State Laborers' PAC, 556

Chittenango
Chittenango CSD, 652

Churchville
Churchville-Chili CSD, 652

Cicero
Cicero, Town of, 417

Cincinnatus
Cincinnatus CSD, 643

Clarence
Clarence Chamber of Commerce, 572
Clarence CSD, 645
Clarence Industrial Development Agency (Town of), 572
Clarence, Town of, 417

Clarksville
American Motorcyclist Assn PAC, 534

Claverack
Rural Water Association, 192

Clay
Clay, Town of, 417

Clayton
Clayton Chamber of Commerce, 572
Thousand Islands CSD, 650

Clayville
NYS Snowmobile PAC, 553

Clifton Park
Army Aviation Association of America (AAAA), Western NY Chapter, 365
Assn for Community Living, 459
Association for Community Living, 233, 283
Boltz, John J Consulting, 464
Clifton Park, Town of, 417
Coalition for Education Reform & Accountability, 473
Coalition of Fathers & Families NY, 221, 317, 538
Coalition of Fathers & Families NY, PAC, 207, 263
CP Rail System, 357
DKI Engineering & Consulting USA, PC, Corporate World Headquarters, 357
Empire State Association of Assisted Living, 222
Fitzgerald, Gary J, 483
Iroquois Healthcare Alliance, 223
New York Long-Term Care Brokers Ltd, 251
New York State Car Wash PAC, 556
Nurse Practitioner Assn of NYS (The), 512
Nurse Practitioners Assn NYS (The), 226
Nurse Practitioners of NYS PAC, 558
NY Propane Gas Association, 174
Shenendehowa CSD, 664
Southern Saratoga County Chamber of Commerce, 585
UHAP PAC, 566

Clifton Springs
Clifton Springs Area Chamber of Commerce, 572
Phelps-Clifton Springs CSD, 660

Clinton
Clinton Chamber of Commerce Inc, 572
Clinton CSD, 658

Listings appear in alphabetical order by state, then city.

Geographic Index

Hamilton College, 625

Clintonville
Ausable Valley CSD, 643

Clyde
Clyde Chamber of Commerce, 572
Clyde Industrial Development Corporation, 572
Clyde-Savannah CSD, 674

Clymer
Clymer CSD, 641

Cobleskill
Cobleskill-Richmondville CSD, 665
Northeast Organic Farming Association of New York, 88
Schoharie County Industrial Development Agency, 584
Smith, Robert, 523
SUNY College of Agriculture & Technology at Cobleskill, 614

Cohoes
Anderson, David, 458
Cohoes
  Civil, Criminal & Traffic Courts, 71
Cohoes City SD, 638
Cohoes Industrial Development Agency (City of), 572
New York Insurance Assn Inc Political Action Committee, 555

Cold Spring
Haldane CSD, 663
The Putnam County News and Recorder, 597

Cold Spring Harbor
Cold Spring Harbor CSD, 668
Cold Spring Harbor Fish Hatchery & Aquarium, 342
Watson School of Biological Sciences at Cold Spring Harbor, 633

Collins
Correctional Services Department
  Collins Correctional Facility, 130

Colton
Colton-Pierrepont CSD, 666

Commack
Long Island Business Institute-Commack, 636
Mental Retardation & Developmental Disabilities, Office of
  Long Island Developmental Disabilities Services Office, 281
Steve Israel for Congress Committee-State Account, 564

Comstock
Correctional Services Department
  Great Meadow Correctional Facility, 130
  Washington Correctional Facility, 131

Congers
Reserve Officers Association (ROA), Department of NY, 368

Conklin
Susquehanna Valley CSD, 639

Cooperstown
Cooperstown Chamber of Commerce, 573
Cooperstown CSD, 662
Elections, State Board of
  Otsego, 161
Farmer's Museum (The), 343
Fund for Better Transportation PAC, 543
New York Center for Agricultural Medicine & Health, Bassett He, 87
New York, Susquehanna & Western Railway, 359
NY State Historical Association/Fenimore Art Museum, 344
Otsego County, 407
  Supreme, County, Family & Surrogate's Courts, 66

Copenhagen
Copenhagen CSD, 651

Copiague
Copiague UFSD, 668

Coram
US Department of the Interior
  Coram Sub-District Office, 185

Corfu
Pembroke CSD, 649

Corinth
Corinth CSD, 664
Corinth Industrial Development Agency (Town of), 573

Corning
Convention Centers & Visitors Bureaus
  Steuben County Conference & Visitors Bureau, 338
Corning
  Civil & Criminal Courts, 71
Corning Area Chamber of Commerce, 573
Corning Community College, 615
Erwin Industrial Development Agency (Town of), 574
Leader (The), 593
Liberty Group Publishing, 593
Three Rivers Development Foundation Inc, 586
Tranter, G Thomas, Jr, 525
US Department of Agriculture
  Big Flats Work Station, 81

Cornwall on Hudson
Cornwall CSD, 660

Corona
Education Department
  Queens District Office, 147
New York Ambulette Coalition PAC, 554
The Italian American Poltical Action Committee of New York, 565

Cortland
Cortland
  Civil & Criminal Courts, 71
Cortland County, 399
  Supreme, County, Family & Surrogate's Courts, 63
Cortland County Chamber of Commerce, 573
Cortland Enlarged City SD, 644
Cortland Standard, 593
Cortland Standard Printing Co Inc, 593
Elections, State Board of
  Cortland, 158
NYS Grange, 86
State University College at Cortland, 613
SUNY at Cortland, Center for Environmental & Outdoor Education, 192
WKRT (920 AM), WIII (99.9 or 100.3 FM), 604

Cortlandt Manor
Cortlandt, Town of, 418

Coxsackie
Correctional Services Department
  Greene Correctional Facility, 131
Coxsackie-Athens CSD, 649

Craryville
Taconic Hills CSD, 643

Crestwood
St Vladimir's Orthodox Theological Seminary, 632

Cropseyville
Wolf, Stacy, 531

Croton-on-Hudson
Croton-Harmon UFSD, 676

Crown Point
Crown Point CSD, 647

Cuba
Cuba-Rushford CSD, 639

Cutchogue
Cutchogue-New Suffolk Chamber of Commerce, 573
Mattituck-Cutchogue UFSD, 669

Dannemora
Correctional Services Department
  Clinton Correctional Facility, 130

Listings appear in alphabetical order by state, then city.

Geographic Index

Saranac CSD, 643

Dansville
Dansville Chamber of Commerce, 573
Dansville CSD, 651

Darien Center
Darien Lake Theme Park Resort, 342

Davenport
Charlotte Valley CSD, 644

Deer Park
Deer Park UFSD, 668
NYPD Superior Officers Assn, Retired PAC, 552
Suffolk County
　2nd District Court, 70

Dekalb Junction
Hermon-Dekalb CSD, 666

Delanson
Duanesburg CSD, 665

Delhi
Delaware County, 399
　Supreme, County, Family & Surrogate's Courts, 63
Delaware County Chamber of Commerce, 573
Delaware County Planning Department, 573
Delhi CSD, 644
Elections, State Board of
　Delaware, 158
State University College of Technology at Delhi, 615

Delmar
Bethlehem Chamber of Commerce, 570
Bethlehem CSD, 638
Bethlehem Industrial Development Agency (Town of), 570
Bethlehem, Town of, 415
Biggerstaff Law Firm, LLP (The), 462
Golden, Ben, 486
Hudacs, John, 492
New York Retailers for Effective Government, 556
NYS Magistrates Association, 265, 294
NYSARC Inc, 285
Opticians PAC, 558

Depew
Buffalo Niagara Builders' Assn Build PAC, 535
Depew UFSD, 646

Deposit
Deposit Chamber of Commerce, 573
Deposit CSD, 639

Deruyter
De Ruyter CSD, 652

Dewitt
Compensation Action Network (NY), 474
Empire State ABC PAC, 541
Independent Agents PAC, 546
Jamesville-Dewitt CSD, 659

Dexter
General Brown CSD, 650

Dix Hills
Five Towns College, 635
Half Hollow Hills CSD, 669
Mental Health, Office of
　Sagamore Children's Psychiatric Center, 281

Dobbs Ferry
Children's Village (The), 283, 317
Dobbs Ferry UFSD, 676
Greenburgh Eleven UFSD, 676
Greenburgh-North Castle UFSD, 676
Mercy College, 627

Dolgeville
Dolgeville CSD, 649

Douglaston
New York State Federation of School Administrator, 556

Dover Plains
Dover UFSD, 645
Dover-Wingdale Chamber of Commerce, 573

Downsville
Downsville CSD, 644

Dryden
Dryden CSD, 672
Tompkins Cortland Community College, 617

Dundee
Dundee CSD, 678

Dunkirk
Chautauqua County Chamber of Commerce, Dunkirk Branch, 571
Dunkirk
　Civil & Criminal Courts, 72
Dunkirk City SD, 641
Lake Shore Savings, 95
Observer, 593
Ogden Newspapers Inc, 593

E Hampton
Suffolk County Police Conference PAC, 564

East Amherst
Williamsville CSD, 647

East Atlantic Beach
ASGM PAC, 534

East Aurora
Aurora Endoresed Republican Club, 534
Christ the King Seminary, 623
East Aurora Chamber of Commerce (Greater East Aurora), 573
East Aurora UFSD, 646
Hawayek, Jonathan F, 489
Hawk Creek Wildlife Center Inc, 189
Southtowns Republican Chairman's Association, 563

East Bloomfield
Bloomfield CSD, 660

East Greenbush
East Greenbush CSD, 663
Health Care Providers' PAC, 544
Luria, Robert S, 500
NYS Association of Health Care Providers, 224
NYSAIFA-PAC, 553
Wang, Phyllis A, 528
Williams, Carla (FKA Alliance for Donation (NY)), 530

East Hampton
East Hampton Chamber of Commerce, 573
East Hampton UFSD, 668
East Hampton, Town of, 418
Springs UFSD, 671
The Independent News, 597

East Islip
East Islip Chamber of Commerce, 573

East Meadow
East Meadow Chamber of Commerce, 574
Getty Petroleum Marketing Inc, 174
Nassau Council of Chambers, 580

East Moriches
East Moriches UFSD, 668

East Northport
Commack UFSD, 668

East Patchogue
South Country CSD, 671

East Quogue
East Quogue UFSD, 669

East Rochester
East Rochester UFSD, 652
Repair Shop & Gasoline Dealers' PAC Fund, 561

East Rockaway
East Rockaway UFSD, 654
NYPD Lieutenants Benevolent Association PAC, 552

East Schodack
NYS Association of Fire Chiefs, 299

Listings appear in alphabetical order by state, then city.

Geographic Index

East Setauket
Entek Power Services, 173

East Syracuse
American Heart Association Northeast Affiliate, 220
Associated Builders & Contractors, Construction Training Cen, 275
Associated Builders & Contractors, Empire State Chapter, 107
DeWitt, Town of, 418
East Syracuse-Minoa CSD, 659
IBEW Local Union #1249 PAC, 546
Meinking, Rebecca A, 506
WIXT (9), 609
WVOA (105.1 FM), 606

Eastchester
Eastchester UFSD, 676
Eastchester, Town of, 418
Eastchester-Tuckahoe Chamber of Commerce, 574
United for Good Government, 567

Eden
Eden CSD, 646

Edinburg
Edinburg Common SD, 664

Edmeston
Edmeston CSD, 662

Elba
Elba CSD, 648

Elbridge
Jordan-Elbridge CSD, 659

Eldred
Eldred CSD, 671

Elizabethtown
Adirondack Council Inc (The), 187, 455
Elections, State Board of
  Essex, 159
Elizabethtown-Lewis CSD, 647
Essex County, 400
  Supreme, County, Family & Surrogate's Courts, 63
Essex County Industrial Development Agency, 574

Ellenburg Depot
Northern Adirondack CSD, 643

Ellenville
Ellenville CSD, 673
Ellenville/Wawarsing Chamber of Commerce, 574

Ellicottville
Ellicottville Chamber of Commerce, 574
Ellicottville CSD, 640

Elma
Iroquois CSD, 646
Western NY Safari Club PAC, 568

Elmhurst
JOE-PAC NON-Federal, 547

Elmira
Chemung County, 398
  Family Court, 62
  Supreme & County Courts, 62
  Surrogate Court, 62
Chemung County Chamber of Commerce, 572
Chemung County Industrial Development Agency, 572
Correctional Services Department
  Elmira Correctional Facility, 130
Democratic Rural Conference of New York State, 539
Elections, State Board of
  Chemung, 158
Elmira
  Civil & Criminal Courts, 72
Elmira Business Institute, 635
Elmira City SD, 642
Elmira College, 624
Elmira, City of, 419
Gannett Co Inc, 593
Mental Health, Office of
  Elmira Psychiatric Center, 280
Southern Tier Economic Growth Inc, 585
Star-Gazette, 593
Unified Court System
  6th Judicial District (Judicial Department 3), 257
US Department of Veterans Affairs
  Woodlawn National Cemetery, 363
WETM (18), 608
WNKI (106.1 FM), WPGI (100.9 FM), WNGZ (104.9 FM), WWLZ (820 AM), 604

Elmira Heights
Elmira Hts CSD, 642

Elmont
Elmont South Republican Club, 541
Elmont UFSD, 654

Elmsford
Blumenthal, Karen, 462
Elmsford UFSD, 676
Mental Health Assn of Westchester Co Inc, 506
Radon Testing Corp of America Inc, 191, 227

Endicott
Insurance Fund (NYS)
  Endicott, 246, 269
Labor Department
  Southern Tier, 270
New York State Dietetic Association, 556
Union-Endicott CSD, 640

Endwell
Maine-Endwell CSD, 639
Union Local Development Corporation (Town of), 587
Union, Town of, 443

Evans Mill
LeRay, Town of, 423

Fabius
Fabius-Pompey CSD, 659
Southern Onondaga Republican Club, 563

Fair Haven
Fair Haven Area Chamber of Commerce, 574

Fairport
Fairport CSD, 652
Monroe 1 BOCES, 679
Perinton, Town of, 438

Falconer
Falconer CSD, 641

Fallsburg
Correctional Services Department
  Sullivan Correctional Facility, 131
Fallsburg CSD, 671

Far Rockaway
Rockaway Development & Revitalization Corporation, 583

Farmingdale
Citizens Campaign for the Environment, 471
Farmingdale State College of Technology, 614
Farmingdale UFSD, 654
Local 138, 138A & 138B International Union of Operating Engineers, 548
Long Island Federation of Labor AFL-CIO, 549
Long Island Nursery & Landscape Association Inc, 86
US Department of Veterans Affairs
  Long Island National Cemetery, 363

Farmington
Farmington Chamber of Commerce, 574
Finger Lakes Racing Association, 343
Thoroughbred Horsemen of Western NY PAC, 565

Farmingville
Brookhaven Industrial Development Agency, 570
Brookhaven, Town of, 415

Listings appear in alphabetical order by state, then city.

Geographic Index

Fayetteville
ESSAA - PAC (Empire State Supervisors & Admin Assn), 540
Hancock Public Affairs, LLC, 488
Manlius, Town of, 425
Syracuse Tomorrow, 564

Ferndale
Sullivan County Industrial Development Agency, 586

Fillmore
Fillmore CSD, 639

Fishers
Apple Assn Inc (NY), 459
New York Apple Association Inc, 87

Fishers Island
Fishers Island UFSD, 669

Fishkill, 100
Correctional Services Department
Downstate Correctional Facility, 130
Fishkill, Town of, 419
Lottery, Division of
Hudson Valley Region, 325
NYS Foundation for Science, Technology & Innovation
Hudson Valley Technology Development Center, 148

Floral Park
Boilermakers Local Lodge #5, 463
Floral Park-Bellerose UFSD, 654
Sewanhaka Central HS District, 656
Superior Officers' Benevolent Assn of the TBTA PAC, 564

Florida
Florida UFSD, 660

Flushing
CIDNY - Queens, 241, 316
IUOE Local 14-14B Voluntary PAC, 546
Latina Political Action Committee, 548
Long Island Business Institute-Flushing, 636
New York City
Environmental Protection, Department of, NYC, 429
New York Mets, 345
NYC Region 3, 657
Queens College, 621
School of Law at Queens College, 621
Statewide Association of Minority Businesses PAC, 563
US Defense Department
Fort Totten-77th Regional Support Command, 362
US Postal Service
New York Metro Area, 205
Vaughn College of Aeronautics & Technology, 633

Fonda
Elections, State Board of
Montgomery, 160
Fonda-Fultonville CSD, 653
Montgomery County, 404
Supreme, County, Family & Surrogate's Courts, 65
Montgomery County Chamber of Commerce/Montgomery County Partnership, 580

Forest Hills
Bramson ORT College, 622
Harris, O Lewis, 488
NY Chiropractic PAC, 551
PAC Port Washington PBA, 559

Forestville
Forestville CSD, 641

Fort Ann
Fort Ann CSD, 674

Fort Covington
Salmon River CSD, 648

Fort Drum
Army Aviation Association of America (AAAA), North Country Chapter, 365
US Defense Department
Fort Drum, 362

Fort Edward
Elections, State Board of
Washington, 162
Fort Edward Chamber of Commerce, 574
Fort Edward UFSD, 674
Washington County, 412
Supreme, County, Family & Surrogate's Courts, 69
Washington County Local Development Corporation, 588
Washington-Saratoga-Warren-Hamilton-Essex BOCES, 680

Fort Plain
Fort Plain CSD, 653

Fort Totten
Northeastern Queens Nature & Historical Preserve Commission, 126, 183, 337

Frankfort
Frankfort-Schuyler CSD, 649

Franklin
Franklin CSD, 644

Franklin Square
Franklin Square Chamber of Commerce, 574
Franklin Square Republican Club, 542
Franklin Square UFSD, 654

Franklinville
Franklinville CSD, 640

Fredonia
Fredonia Chamber of Commerce, 574
Fredonia CSD, 641
State University of New York, Fredonia, 614

Freeport
Freeport UFSD, 654
Freeport, Village of, 419

Freeville
George Junior Republic UFSD, 672

Frewsburg
Frewsburg CSD, 641

Friendship
Friendship CSD, 639

Ft Hamilton Station
New York State Conservative Party, 447

Fulton
Fulton
Civil & Criminal Courts, 72
Fulton City SD, 661

Gabriels
Correctional Services Department
Camp Gabriels, 130

Gainesville
Letchworth CSD, 678

Galway
Galway CSD, 664

Garden City
Adelphi NY Statewide Breast Cancer Hotline & Support Program, 220
Adelphi University, 621
Automobile Club of New York, 341, 357
Cullen & Dykman LLP, 275, 293
Garden City Chamber of Commerce, 575
Garden City UFSD, 654
Garden City, Village of, 419
Genovese, Marta, 485
Law Offices of Frank G. D'Angelo & Associates, 264
Lottery, Division of
Long Island Region, 325
Meyer Suozzi English & Klein, PC, 265
MTA Long Island Bus, 118, 351
Nassau BOCES, 679
Nassau Community College, 616
Nassau County Industrial Development Agency, 580
New York City Deputy Sheriff's Assn, PAC, 555
NYS Bar Assn, Family Law Section, 267
NYS Bar Assn, General Practice Section, 264

Listings appear in alphabetical order by state, then city.

Geographic Index

NYS Bar Assn, Resolutions Committee, 265
NYS Psychiatric PAC Inc, 553
Ohrenstein & Brown, LLP, 512
Physicians Fund, 559
Rangel for Congress - NY State, 561
Renew NY PAC, 561
Taxpayers for an Affordable New York PAC, 565
The Shaw Licitra PAC, 565
Ungar, Robert A Associates Inc, 526
US Defense Department
1st Marine Corps District, 362
US Department of Homeland Security (DHS)
Garden City Satellite Office, 204, 240
Vincent F Stempel, Jr Esq, 267

Garnerville
Haverstraw, Town of, 421
North Rockland CSD, 664

Garrison
Bynum, Thompson, Ryer, 164
Coalition of Animal Care Societies (The), 317
Coalition of New York State Career Schools (The), 152
Garrison UFSD, 663
Zaleski, Terence M, 532

Gates
Gates, Town of, 419

Geneseo
Elections, State Board of
Livingston, 159
Geneseo CSD, 651
Livingston County, 403
Supreme, County, Family & Surrogate's Courts, 64
Livingston County Chamber of Commerce, 578
Livingston County Economic Development Office & Indu, 578
State University College at Geneseo, 613

Geneva
Finger Lakes Printing Co, 593
Finger Lakes Times, 593
Geneva
Civil & Criminal Courts, 72
Geneva Area Chamber of Commerce, 575
Geneva City SD, 660
Geneva Industrial Development Agency (City of), 575
Hobart & William Smith Colleges, 625
Laborers' Local 103 PAF Cmte, 547
Marion S Whelan School of Practical Nursing, 224
NYS Horticultural Society, 86
US Department of Agriculture
Plant Genetic Resources Unit, 81

Georgetown
Correctional Services Department
Camp Georgetown, 130

Germantown
Germantown CSD, 643

Gilbertsville
Gilbertsville-Mount Upton CSD, 662

Gilboa
Gilboa-Conesville CSD, 665

Glen Cove
Glen Cove
Civil & Criminal Courts, 72
Glen Cove Chamber of Commerce, 575
Glen Cove City SD, 654
Glen Cove, City of, 420
New York State Association of PBAs, 556
Webb Institute, 633

Glendale
New York & Atlantic Railway (NYA), 358

Glenford
Willow Mixed Media Inc, 347

Glenmont
Insurance Brokers' Assn of NY PAC, 546
Laborers' Local Union 190 PAC, 548
Professional Insurance Agents of New York State, 251

Glens Falls
Adirondack Regional Chambers of Commerce, 569
Behan Communications Inc, 461
Business First PAC, 536
FitzGerald Morris et al, 263
Glens Falls
Civil & Criminal Courts, 72
Glens Falls City SD, 673
Glens Falls Common SD, 673
Lee Corporation, 594
NYS Bar Assn, Cmte on the Jury System, 263
Post-Star (The), 594
TD Banknorth, 96
Warren & Washington Industrial Development Agency, 588
Warren County Economic Development Corporation, 588

Glenville
Burnt Hills-Ballston Lake CSD, 664
Glenville, Town of, 420

Gloversville
Fulton County Reg Chamber of Commerce & Ind, 575
Gloversville
Civil & Criminal Courts, 72
Gloversville Enlarged SD, 648
Leader-Herald (The), 594
The Political Action Committee of The Ful, 565
William B Collins Co, 594

Goshen
Dupee & Monroe, PC, 249
Elections, State Board of
Orange, 161
Goshen Chamber of Commerce, 575
Goshen CSD, 660
Orange County, 406
Supreme, County & Family Courts, 66
Surrogate's Court, 66
Orange County Partnership, 581
Orange-Ulster BOCES, 679

Gouverneur
Correctional Services Department
Gouverneur Correctional Facility, 130
Gouverneur Chamber of Commerce, 575
Gouverneur CSD, 666

Gowanda
Correctional Services Department
Gowanda Correctional Facility, 130
Gowanda Area Chamber of Commerce, 575
Gowanda CSD, 640

Grahamsville
Tri-Valley CSD, 672

Grand Island
Grand Island Chamber of Commerce, 575
Grand Island CSD, 646

Granville
Granville Chamber of Commerce, 575
Granville CSD, 674

Great Neck
Elayne E Greenberg, MS, Esq, 263
Great Neck Chamber of Commerce, 575
Great Neck Democratic Club, 543
Great Neck UFSD, 654
Greater New Hyde Park Republican Club, 544
Law Offices of Stanley N Lupkin, 141
Nassau County
3rd District Court, 70
North Shore-Long Island Jewish Health System, 88, 226
NYS Bar Assn, Alternative Dispute Resolution Cmte, 263
NYS Bar Assn, Food, Drug & Cosmetic Law Section, 88, 226

Great River
Central Pine Barrens Joint Planning & Policy Commission, 115, 181

Greece
Greece Chamber of Commerce, 575
Greece, Town of, 420

Listings appear in alphabetical order by state, then city.

Geographic Index

Green Island
Green Island Democratic Association, 544
Green Island Industrial Development Agency (Village of), 575
Green Island UFSD, 638

Greenburgh
Greenburgh, Town of, 420

Greene
Greene CSD, 642

Greenlawn
Elwood UFSD, 669
Harborfields CSD, 669

Greenport
Greenport UFSD, 669
US Department of Homeland Security (DHS)
Plum Island Animal Disease Center, 83, 204

Greenville
Greenville CSD, 649

Greenwich
Greenwich Chamber of Commerce (Greater Greenwich), 576
Greenwich CSD, 674

Greenwood Lake
Greenwood Lake and West Milford News, 598
Greenwood Lake Chamber of Commerce, 576
Greenwood Lake UFSD, 660

Groton
Groton CSD, 672

Guilderland
Guilderland CSD, 638
Guilderland Industrial Development Agency (Town of), 576
Guilderland, Town of, 420
New York State Community Action Association, 235, 322
WYPX (55), 607
Young Jr, William N, 532

Hamburg
Buffalo Trotting Association Inc, 342
Frontier CSD, 646
Hamburg Chamber of Commerce, 576
Hamburg CSD, 646
Hamburg Industrial Development Agency, 576
Hamburg, Town of, 420
Hilbert College, 625
Hopevale UFSD at Hamburg, 646
Town of Hamburg Endorsed Cadidates Fund, 566

Hamilton
Colgate University, 623
Colgate University, Department of Geology, 188
Exhibition Alliance Inc (The), 343
Hamilton CSD, 652

Hammond
Black Lake Chamber of Commerce, 570
Hammond CSD, 666

Hammondsport
Hammondsport CSD, 667

Hampton Bays
Hampton Bays Chamber of Commerce, 576
Hampton Bays UFSD, 669
Southhampton Town Young Republicans, 563

Hancock
Hancock Area Chamber of Commerce, 576
Hancock CSD, 644

Hannibal
Hannibal CSD, 662

Harpursville
Harpursville CSD, 639

Harriman
IBEW Local Union 363 PAC, 546

Harrison
Harrison CSD, 676
Harrison, Town/Village of, 421

Harrisville
Harrisville CSD, 651
NYS Weights & Measures Association, 87

Hartford
Hartford CSD, 674

Hartsdale
Greenburgh 7 CSD, 676

Hastings
Local 147 PAF, 548

Hastings-on-Hudson
Bennett, Michael, 462
Greenburgh-Graham UFSD, 676
Hastings-on-Hudson Chamber of Commerce, 576
Hastings-On-Hudson UFSD, 676

Hauppauge
Agriculture & Markets Department
Hauppauge, 80
Attorney Grievance Committee
Judicial Dist 10, 255
Convention Centers & Visitors Bureaus
Long Island Convention & Visitors Bureau & Sports Commission, 338
Dahill, Kevin, 477
Dale Carnegie & Associates Inc, 108
Education Department
Hauppauge District Office, 147
Empire State Regional Council of Carpenters Political Action Fund-, 541
Executive Political Action Committee (EPAC), 542
Hauppauge UFSD, 669
Human Rights, State Division of
Suffolk County, 238
KeySpan Corporation, 174
Law Department
Suffolk, 255
Oil Heat Institute of Long Island, 175
Oil Heat Institute PAC, 558
Pozzi, Brian M, 516
Real Property Services, Office of
Long Island Satellite Office, 289, 302, 326
Ryan, Desmond M, 520
State Department
Suffolk, 200
Suffolk Community Council (FKA Pannullo, Judith), 524
Suffolk County
4th District Court, 70
Suffolk Regional Off-Track Betting Corporation, 128, 337
Transportation Department
Region 10, 350
Workers' Compensation Board
Hauppauge, 248, 271

Hawthorne
Hawthorne-Cedar Knolls UFSD, 676
National Academy of Forensic Engineers, 265

Hector
US Department of Agriculture
Finger Lakes National Forest, 184

Hempstead
Education & Assistance Corp Inc, 318
Education & Assistance Corporation Inc, 140
Education Department
Hempstead District Office, 147
Hempstead Industrial Development Agency (Town of), 576
Hempstead PBA PAC, 545
Hempstead UFSD, 654
Hempstead, Town of, 421
Hempstead, Village of, 421
Hofstra University, 625
Hofstra University, School of Law, 140, 189, 234
Human Rights, State Division of
Nassau County, 238
Long Island Educational Opportunity Center, 618
Nassau County

Listings appear in alphabetical order by state, then city.

Geographic Index

1st, 2nd & 4th District Courts, 70
Nassau Regional Off-Track Betting Corporation, 119, 336
New York Jets, 345
P.A.F.S.A. NY PAC, 559
Workers' Compensation Board
Hempstead, 248, 271

Henrietta
Henrietta, Town of, 421
Rush-Henrietta CSD, 653

Herkimer
Ambassador Club, 534
Elections, State Board of
Herkimer, 159
Evening Telegram (The), 594
Herkimer County, 402
Family Court, 64
Supreme, County & Surrogate's Courts, 64
Herkimer County Community College, 616
Herkimer County Industrial Development Agency, 576
Herkimer CSD, 649
Herkimer-Fulton-Hamilton-Otsego BOCES, 679
Liberty Group New York Holdings Inc, 594

Heuvelton
Heuvelton CSD, 666

Hewlett
Hewlett Republican Club, 545

Hewlett Harbor
North Windmere Republican Club, 557

Hicksville
Fraternal Order of Police Empire State Lodge Inc, 542
Hicksville Chamber of Commerce, 576
Hicksville UFSD, 654
Keyspan Energy State PAC (KEYSPAC), 547
Labor Department
Long Island Region, 270
State Department
Hicksville, 200
Veterans' Service Organizations
Hicksville Counseling Center, Veterans' Resource Center, 361

Highland
Highland CSD, 673
New York State Bridge Authority, 121, 352
Schools Are For Everyone, 562
Southern Ulster County Chamber of Commerce, 586

Highland Falls
Highland Falls CSD, 660

Hillburn
Ramapo CSD (Suffern), 664

Hillsdale
The Independent, 594

Hilton
Hilton CSD, 652

Hinsdale
Hinsdale CSD, 640

Hogansburg
St Regis Mohawk Tribe, 210

Holbrook
Sachem CSD, 670
Suffolk County Republican Women PAC, 564

Holland
Holland CSD, 646

Holland Patent
Holland Patent CSD, 658

Holley
Holley CSD, 661

Holtsville
Farmingville/Holtsville Chamber of Commerce, 574
US Treasury Department
Brookhaven Campus Service Center, 329

Homer
Homer CSD, 644
Morgan Associates, 508

Honeoye
Honeoye CSD, 660

Honeoye Falls
Honeoye Falls-Lima CSD, 653

Hoosick Falls
Hoosick Falls CSD, 663

Hopewell Junction
East Fishkill, Town of, 418

Hornell
ALSTOM Transportation Inc, 357
Evening Tribune (The), 594
Hornell
Civil & Criminal Courts, 72
Hornell Area Chamber of Commerce/Hornell Indus, 577
Hornell City SD, 667
Liberty Group Publishing, 594
Transportation Department
Region 6, 349
WKPQ (105.3 FM), WHHO (1320 AM), 604

Horseheads
Horseheads CSD, 642
O'Mara, John F, 512
WENY (36), 608
WMTT (94.7 FM), 604

Houghton
Houghton College, 625

Howard Beach
Plumbers Local Union No 1 N.Y.C. PAC, 559

Hudson
Columbia County, 399
Supreme, County, Family & Surrogate's Courts, 62
Columbia County Chamber of Commerce, 572
Columbia Hudson Partnership, 573
Columbia-Greene Community College, 615
Correctional Services Department
Hudson Correctional Facility, 131
Elections, State Board of
Columbia, 158
Hudson
Civil & Criminal Courts, 72
Hudson City SD, 643
Johnson Newspaper Corporation, 594
Register-Star, 594

Hudson Falls
Hudson Falls CSD, 674

Hunter
Hunter Chamber of Commerce (Town of), 577
Hunter Mountain Ski Bowl, 343

Huntington
Delois Brassell Political Action Committee, 539
Gaughran, James F, 485
Huntington Chamber Committee for Better Gov't, 545
Huntington Township Chamber of Commerce, 577
Huntington, Town of, 422
Seminary of the Immaculate Conception, 630

Huntington Station
Huntington UFSD, 669
South Huntington UFSD, 671
Suffolk County
3rd District Court, 70
Western Suffolk BOCES, 680

Hurley
Adirondack/Pine Hill/NY Trailways, 341
Town of Hurley Republican Club Inc, 566

Hyde Park
Culinary Institute of America, 342, 624

Geographic Index

Hyde Park Chamber of Commerce, 577
Hyde Park CSD, 645
Hyde Park, Town of, 422
National Archives & Records Administration
Franklin D Roosevelt Presidential Library & Museum, 150, 339
US Department of the Interior
Roosevelt-Vanderbilt National Historic Sites, 340

Ilion
Ilion CSD, 650
New York State Conservation Council, 191

Indian Lake
Hamilton County
Supreme, County, Family & Surrogate's Courts, 64
Indian Lake Chamber of Commerce, 577
Indian Lake CSD, 649

Inlet
Inlet Common School, 649
Inlet Information Office, 577

Irvington
Abbott UFSD, 675
Arthur J Finkelstein & Associates Inc, 164
Elissa D Hecker, Esq, 342
Irvington UFSD, 676
NYS Bar Assn, Entertainment, Arts & Sports Law Section, 342
Waterkeeper Alliance, 192

Island Park
Island Park UFSD, 654

Islandia
Bracken & Margolin LLP, 262
Builders' PAC, 536
NYS Bar Assn, Fiduciary Appointments Cmte, 266
NYS Bar Assn, Tort System Cmte, 262
Pruzansky & Besunder LLP, 266
Wieboldt, Robert, 529

Islip
Islip Chamber of Commerce, 577
Islip Economic Development Division & Industrial Devel, 577
Islip Industrial Development Agency (Town of), 577
Islip UFSD, 669
Islip, Town of, 422

Islip Terrace
East Islip UFSD, 668

Ithaca
College of Agriculture & Life Sciences at Cornell University, 612
College of Human Ecology at Cornell University, 612
College of Veterinary Medicine at Cornell University, 612
Community & Rural Development Institute, 84
Convention Centers & Visitors Bureaus
Ithaca/Tompkins County Convention & Visitors Bureau, 338
Cornell Cooperative Extension, 84
Cornell Cooperative Extension, College of Human Ecology, Nu, 222, 318
Cornell Cooperative Extension, Community & Economic Vitality Program, 234
Cornell Cooperative Extension, Environment & Natural Resource, 188
Cornell Cooperative Extension, NY Sea Grant, 188
Cornell Cooperative Extension, Pesticide Management Education Program, 84
Cornell Farmedic Training Program, 84
Cornell Law School, Legal Information Institute, 263
Cornell University, 152, 624
Cornell University Center for the Environment, 188
Cornell University, College of Agriculture & Life Sciences,, 84
Cornell University, Community, Food & Agriculture Program, 84
Cornell University, Department of Applied Economics & Management, 84
Cornell University, Development Sociology, 84
Cornell University, Economics Department, 94, 108
Cornell University, FarmNet Program, 84
Cornell University, Institute on Conflict Resolution, 275
Cornell University, Program on Dairy Markets & Policy, 85
Cornell University, Rural Schools Association of NYS, 152
Cornell University, School of Industrial & Labor Relations, 153, 241, 275, 299
Elections, State Board of
Tompkins, 162
Gannett Co Inc, 594
Ithaca
Civil & Criminal Courts, 72
Ithaca City SD, 672
Ithaca College, 626
Ithaca Journal (The), 594
Ithaca, City of, 422
Jamestown, City of, 423
Johnson, Stephen Philip, 493
National Economic Research Associates, 175, 358
New York Agriculture in the Classroom, 87
New York Holstein Association, 87
New York Seed Improvement Project, Cornell Univ, 88
New York State Citizens' Coalition for Children Inc, 322
NYS Association For Food Protection, 86
NYS Bar Assn, Unlawful Practice of Law Cmte, 264
NYS Cheese Manufacturers Association, Department of Food Science, 86
NYS Foundation for Science, Technology & Innovation
Center for Advanced Technology in Life Science Enterprise, 100, 148
NYS Water Resources Institute of Cornell University, 190
Prisoners' Legal Services of New York, 142, 266
Schlather, Geldenhuys, Stumbar & Salk, 264
School of Industrial & Labor Relations at Cornell University (, 612
Tompkins County, 411
Supreme, County, Family & Surrogate's Courts, 69
Tompkins County Area Development, 587
Tompkins County Chamber of Commerce, 587
Tompkins Trustco Inc, 97
Tompkins-Seneca-Tioga BOCES, 680
True & Walsh, LLP, 227
US Department of Agriculture
Cornell Cooperative Extension Service, 82
US Department of the Interior
Ithaca Sub-District Office, 185
WHCU (870 AM), WTKO (1470 AM), WYXL (97.3 FM), WQNY (103.7 FM), 604

Jackson Heights
British Airways PLC, 357
Plaza College, 637
Queens Chamber of Commerce (Borough of), 583
United Spinal Assn (FKA Eastern Paralyed Veterans Assn), 526
United Spinal Association, 368

Jamaica
Civil Court, NYC
Queens County, 59
Family Court, NYC
Queens County, 61
Federal Maritime Commission
New York Area Office, 355
Filipino American Human Services Inc, 241, 318
Health Department
New York State Veterans' Home at St Albans, 214, 360
Housing & Community Renewal, Division of
Rent Administration, 229
Jamaica Chamber of Commerce, 577

Listings appear in alphabetical order by state, then city.

Geographic Index

Jamaica Development Corporation (Greater Jamaica), 577
MTA Long Island Rail Road, 118, 351
New York City
   Library, Queens Borough Public, 432
New York Racing Association, 346
New York Thoroughbred Horsemen's Assn, Inc Political Action Committe, 557
NYC Citywide Alternative HS District & Programs, 657
Queens County
   Supreme & Surrogate's Courts, 67
Queens Educational Opportunity Center, 618
St John's University, School of Law, 192
Unified Court System
   11th Judicial District (Judicial Department 2), 257
US Department of Agriculture
   JFK International Airport Inspection Station, 82
US Department of Health & Human Services
   New York Quarantine Station, 218, 314
   Northeast Region, 218, 314
US Department of Homeland Security (DHS)
   JFK International Airport Area Office, 83, 204
US Justice Department
   Investigations Division, 260
US Transportation Department
   Federal Aviation Administration-Eastern Region, 355
Workers' Compensation Board
   Queens, 248, 271
York College, 621

Jamestown
Chautauqua County Chamber of Commerce, 571
Chautauqua County Industrial Development Agency, 572
Jamestown
   Civil & Criminal Courts, 72
Jamestown Business College, 635
Jamestown City SD, 641
Jamestown Community College, 616
Jamestown, City of, 423
Post-Journal, 595
Southwestern CSD at Jamestown, 642
WKZA (106.9 FM), 605

Jamesville
Parks, Recreation & Historic Preservation, NYS Office of
   Central Region, 334

Jasper
Jasper-Troupsburg CSD, 667

Jefferson
Jefferson CSD, 665

Jeffersonville
Sullivan West CSD, 672

Jericho
Jericho UFSD, 655
New York Community Bank, 235

Johnson City
Davis College, 624
Johnson City CSD, 639
WBNG (12), WBXI (11), 607

Johnstown
Correctional Services Department
   Hale Creek ASACTC, 131
Elections, State Board of
   Fulton, 159
Fulton County, 401
   Family Court, 63
   Supreme, County & Surrogate's Courts, 63
Fulton County Economic Development Corporation, 574
Fulton County Industrial Development Agency, 575
Fulton-Montgomery Community College, 616
Greater Johnstown SD, 648
Hamilton-Fulton-Montgomery BOCES, 679
Johnstown
   Civil & Criminal Courts, 72

Katonah
Katonah-Lewisboro UFSD, 676

Keene Valley
Keene CSD, 647

Kendall
Kendall CSD, 661

Kenmore
Kenmore-Town of Tonawanda Chamber of Commerce, 577
M. Dolores Denman Democratic Lawyers Club, 550
Metro/Colvin Realty Inc, 304
Metro/Horohoe-Leimbach, 305
Tonawanda, Town of, 442

Keuka Park
Keuka College, 626

Kew Gardens
Criminal Court, NYC
   Queens County, 60
Elections, State Board of
   Queens, 160
New York City Boroughs
   Queens (Queens County), 435
Queens County (NYC Borough of Queens), 407

Kinderhook
US Department of the Interior
   Martin Van Buren National Historic Site, 340

Kings Park
Island Public Affairs, 493
Kings Park Chamber of Commerce, 577
Kings Park CSD, 669

Kings Point
US Transportation Department
   US Merchant Marine Academy, 151, 356

Kingston
Daily Freeman, 595
Elections, State Board of
   Ulster, 162
Hudson River Cruises, 343
Kingston
   Civil & Criminal Courts, 72
Kingston City SD, 673
Kingston, City of, 423
Sunwize Technologies Inc, 176
Ulster County, 411
   Family Court, 69
   Supreme & County Courts, 69
   Surrogate's Court, 69
Ulster County Chamber of Commerce, 587
Ulster County Democratic Women, 566
Ulster County Development Corporation/Ulste, 587
Ulster Savings Bank, 97

Kirkville
NYS Vegetable Growers Association Inc, 87

La Fargeville
La Fargeville CSD, 650

Lackawanna
Lackawanna
   Civil & Criminal Courts, 73
Lackawanna Area Chamber of Commerce, 577
Lackawanna City SD, 646

Lafayette
LaFayette CSD, 659

Lagrangeville
Hudson Valley Citizens for Change, 545

Lake George
Elections, State Board of
   Warren, 162
Great Escape Theme Park LLC (The), 343
Lake George CSD, 673
Lake George Park Commission, 117, 182

Geographic Index

Lake George Regional Chamber of Commerce, 578
Warren County, 412
Supreme, County, Family & Surrogate's Courts, 69

Lake Luzerne
Hadley-Luzerne CSD, 673
Lake Luzerne Chamber of Commerce, 578

Lake Placid
Convention Centers & Visitors Bureaus
Lake Placid/Essex County Convention & Visitors Bureau, 338
Lake Placid Chamber of Commerce, 578
Lake Placid CSD, 647
New York State Olympic Regional Development Authority, 124, 336
NYS Outdoor Guides Association, 344

Lake Pleasant
Elections, State Board of
Hamilton, 159
Hamilton County, 402

Lake Success
American Academy of Pediatrics District II (NYS), 457
Astoria Federal Savings & Loan, 94
Astoria Financial Corp PAC, 534
Community Bankers Assn of NY State, Banking Law & Regulations Cmte, 94
Medical Society of the State of New York, Div of Socio-Me, 250

Lake View
Independent Oil & Gas Association of New York, 174

Lakeview
Citizens for Fiscal Intergrity, 537
IUOE Local 17 PAC, 546

Lancaster
Ecology & Environment Inc, 188
Ecology & Environment NYS Committee for Responsible Government, 540
Lancaster Area Chamber of Commerce, 578
Lancaster CSD, 646
Lancaster Industrial Development Agency (Town of), 578
Lancaster, Town of, 423
Walsh, John B, 528

Lansing
Lansing CSD, 672

Larchmont
Alvin D Lurie PC, 330
NYS Bar Assn, Pension Simplification Cmte, 330
Public Strategies, LLC, 516
Wiener, Judith R, 529

Latham
Allinger, Stephen (FKA Nelson, Debra), 456
Business Review, 601
Business Review (The), 591
Colonie Chamber of Commerce, 572
Conway, Gerard L, Jr, 475
Credit Union League Inc & Affiliates (NYS), 476
Educational Leadership (EL) PAC, 540
Fiscal Policy Institute, 208, 330
FUTURENY, 542
Hines-Kramer, Amy, 490
Intermagnetics General Corporation, 109
Labor-Religion Coalition, Inc (NYS), 496
Mildred Elley, 636
Military & Naval Affairs, Division of, 13, 360
Mothers Against Drunk Driving (MADD) of NYS, 141
New York State Credit Union League Inc, 96
New York State Nurses Assn PAC, 556
New York State Nurses Association, 226, 276, 511
New York State School Boards Association, 154
New York State United Teachers/AFT, AFL-CIO, 300
New York State United Teachers/AFT, NEA, AFL-CIO, 154
North Colonie CSD, 638
NYS Association of Electrical Contractors, 110
NYS Automatic Vending Association PAC, 552
NYS Corps Collaboration, 321
NYS Credit Union League, 96
NYS Public High School Athletic Association, 154
NYS Speech-Language-Hearing Assn Inc - COMPAC, 553
NYS Turfgrass Association, 87, 344
Plug Power Inc, 175
Plumbers and Steamfitters Local 7 PAC, 559
School Administrators Association of NYS, 155, 522
School Boards Assn (NYS), 522
Spectra Environmental Group Inc, 192
Technologists for New York, 565
The Business Review, 591
Trooper Foundation-State of New York Inc, 142, 300
US Department of Homeland Security (DHS)
Albany Sub Office, 203, 204, 240, 328
Voice of Teachers for Educational/Comm on Political Education, 567
WFLY (92.3 FM), WAJZ (96.3 FM), WROW (590 AM), WYJB (95.5, 605
WGY (810 AM), WPYX (106.5 FM), WRVE (99.5 FM), 605

Laurens
Laurens CSD, 662

Lawrence
Lawrence UFSD, 655

Le Roy
Le Roy CSD, 648

LeRoy
Genesee-Livingston-Steuben-Wyoming BOCES, 679

Levittown
Island Trees UFSD, 655
Levittown UFSD, 655

Liberty
Liberty CSD, 671
Sullivan BOCES, 680

Lima
New York Forest Owners Association Inc, 191

Lindenhurst
Babylon, Town of, 414
Education Department
Long Island Regional Office, 147
Lindenhurst UFSD, 669
Lindenhurst, Village of, 424
New York State Independence Party, 451

Lisbon
Empire State Honey Producers Association, 85
Lisbon CSD, 666

Little Falls
Evening Times (The), 595
Liberty Group Publishing, 595
Little Falls
Civil & Criminal Courts, 73
Little Falls City SD, 650
NYS Association for Health, Physical Education, Recreation & Dance, 153

Little Neck
US Labor Department
Queens Area Office, 219, 273

Little Valley
Cattaraugus County, 397
Supreme, County & Surrogate's Courts, 62
Cattaraugus-Little Valley CSD, 640
Elections, State Board of
Cattaraugus, 158

Liverpool
Bryant & Stratton College-Syracuse North Campus, 634

Listings appear in alphabetical order by state, then city.

Geographic Index

Greater Syracuse Association of Realtors Inc, 304
Insurance Fund (NYS)
Syracuse, 246, 269
Liverpool Chamber of Commerce (Greater Liverpool), 578
Liverpool CSD, 659
Local #30 PAC, 548
Mullane, Robert A, 509
Municipal Electric Utilities Association, 174
Northeast Equipment Dealers Association Inc, 111
Salina, Town of, 441

Livingston Manor
Livingston Manor CSD, 672

Livonia
Livonia CSD, 651

Loch Sheldrake
Sullivan County Community College, 617

Lockport
Ayers, Deborah, 460
Elections, State Board of
Niagara, 160
Greater Niagara Newspapers, 595
Lockport
Civil & Criminal Courts, 73
Lockport City SD, 657
Lockport Fire Dept PAC, 549
Lockport Industrial Development Agency (Town of), 578
Lockport Union-Sun & Journal, 595
Lockport, City of, 424
Lockport, Town of, 424
Niagara County, 405
County, Family & Surrogate's Courts, 65
Pendeleton Democrat Club, 559
Starpoint CSD, 658
TOW PAC, 565

Locust Valley
Locust Valley CSD, 655

Lodi
Venture Vineyards Inc, 89

Long Beach
Lancer Insurance Co/Lancer Compliance Services, 276
Long Beach
Civil & Criminal Courts, 73
Long Beach Chamber of Commerce, 578
Long Beach City SD, 655
Long Beach, City of, 424
Nassau County Lesbian & Gay Democrats, 554

Long Island
Long Island Council of Dedicated Merchants Chamber of Commerce, 578

Long Island City
Asbestos Workers Local 12 Political Action Committee, 534
Bricklayers & Allied Craftsmen Local Union 1 PAC, 535
Correctional Services Department
Queensboro Correctional Facility, 131
DeVry Institute of Technology, Long Island City Campus, 635
Donnellan, James, 479
Elevator Constructors Union Local No 1 Political Action Committee, 540
Environmental Conservation Department
Region 2, 178
LaGuardia Community College, 620
MetLife, 250
Metlife Inc Employees' Political Participation Fund A, 550
MetLife Ins Co Political Fund B, 550
Modutank Inc, 190
New York City
Design & Construction, Dept of, NYC, 428
Educational Construction Fund, NYC, 429
New York City School Construction Authority, 120, 149
NYC Region 4, 657
Queens Gazette, 595
Sheet Metal Workers Int'l Assn Local 137 PAL Fund, 562
Steamfitters' Union Local 638 PAC, 563
Tile Layers Subordinate Union Local 7 of New York and New Jer, 566
Transportation Department
Region 11, 350

Long Lake
Long Lake CSD, 649
New York State Snowmobile Association, 346

Loudonville
Brescia, Richard, 465
Family Physicians PAC, 542
NYS Academy of Family Physicians, 224
Professional Insurance Agents of New York Political Action Committ, 560
Siena College, 631

Lowville
Elections, State Board of
Lewis, 159
Lewis County, 403
Supreme, County, Family & Surrogate's Courts, 64
Lewis County Chamber of Commerce, 578
Lewis County Industrial Development Agency, 578
Lowville Academy & CSD, 651

Lynbrook
Disabled American Veterans, Department of New York, 366
Lynbrook P.B.A. PAC, 549
Lynbrook UFSD, 655

Lyndonville
Lyndonville CSD, 661

Lyon Mountain
Correctional Services Department
Lyon Mountain Correctional Facility, 131

Lyons
Elections, State Board of
Wayne, 162
Lyons CSD, 674
Wayne County, 412
Supreme, County, Family & Surrogate's Courts, 69
Wayne County Industrial Development Agency & Economic Development, 588

Macedon
Gananda CSD, 674

Madison
Madison CSD, 652

Madrid
Madrid-Waddington CSD, 666

Mahopac
Carmel, Town of, 416
Mahopac CSD, 663
Mahopac-Carmel Chamber of Commerce, 579

Malden Bridge
Miller, Monica, 508

Malone
Correctional Services Department
Bare Hill Correctional Facility, 130
Franklin Correctional Facility, 130
Upstate Correctional Facility, 131
Education Department
Malone District Office, 147
Elections, State Board of
Franklin, 159
Franklin County, 401
Supreme, County, Family & Surrogate's Courts, 63
Franklin County Industrial Development Agency, 574
Franklin-Essex-Hamilton BOCES, 679
Johnson Newspaper Corp, 595
Malone Chamber of Commerce, 579
Malone CSD, 647
Malone Telegram, 595

Listings appear in alphabetical order by state, then city.

Geographic Index

Malverne
Association of Military Surgeons of the US (AMSUS), NY Chapter, 221, 365
Malverne UFSD, 655
National Amputation Foundation Inc, 225, 367

Mamaroneck
Animal Welfare Advocacy, 458
Mamaroneck Chamber of Commerce, 579
Mamaroneck UFSD, 676
Mamaroneck, Town of, 424
New York Chiropractic Political Action Fund, 555
Rye Neck UFSD, 677

Manhasset
Manhasset Chamber of Commerce, 579
Manhasset UFSD, 655
North Hempstead, Town of, 436

Manlius
Fayetteville-Manlius CSD, 659

Manorville
Eastport-South Manor CSD, 669

Maporville
Cope 25, 538

Marathon
Marathon CSD, 644

Marcellus
Marcellus CSD, 659

Marcy
Correctional Services Department
  Marcy Correctional Facility, 131
  Mid-State Correctional Facility, 131
Mental Health, Office of
  Central New York Psychiatric Center, 280

Margaretville
Margaretville CSD, 644

Marion
Marion CSD, 675
Seneca Foods Corporation, 88

Marlboro
Laborers' Local 17 PAC, 548
Marlboro CSD, 673
SAFE-PAC (Schools Are For Everyone Political Action Committee), 562

Maspeth
New York Pepsi Cola PAC, 555
NYS Cemeteries PAC, 552

Massapequa
Dental Hygienists' Association of the State of New York Inc, 222
Massapequa Chamber of Commerce, 579

Massapequa UFSD, 655
New York State Assn of Fire Districts, 121, 291
New York State Society of Physician Assistants PAC, 557
Tyson, Lisa, 526

Massena
Daily Courier-Observer, 595
Johnson Newspaper Corporation, 595
Massena Chamber of Commerce, 579
Massena CSD, 666
U.S.W.A. Local 420A PAC, 566
US Transportation Department
  Saint Lawrence Seaway Development Corporation, 356

Mastic
Mastics/Shirley Chamber of Commerce, 579
Unkechauq Nation, 210

Mastic Beach
William Floyd UFSD, 671

Mattituck
Alliance of NYS Arts Organizations, 341
Mattituck Chamber of Commerce, 579

Mayfield
Mayfield CSD, 648

Mayville
Chautauqua County, 398
  Family Court, 62
  Supreme & County Courts, 62
  Surrogate Court, 62
Chautauqua Lake CSD, 641
Elections, State Board of
  Chautauqua, 158
Mayville/Chautauqua Chamber of Commerce, 579

McGraw
McGraw CSD, 644

Mechanicville
Mechanicville
  Civil & Criminal Courts, 73
Mechanicville Area Chamber of Commerce, 579
Mechanicville City SD, 664
Mechanicville/Stillwater Industrial Development Agency, 579

Medford
Suffolk County Deputy Sheriffs Benevolent Assn Inc PAC, 564

Medina
Greater Niagara Newspapers, 596
Journal-Register, 596
Medina CSD, 661
Orleans-Niagara BOCES, 680

Melville
Bonagura, David (FKA Hoops, Jeffrey), 464
CAS PAC, 536
Community Bankers Assn of NY State, Accounting & Taxation Cmte, 95, 330
Ernst & Young Committee for Good Government, 541
Insurance Fund (NYS)
  Nassau County, Long Island, 246, 269
  Suffolk County, Long Island, 246, 269
Katharine Gibbs School-Melville, 636
Long Island Assn Action Committee, 549
Long Island Association, 500, 578
Long Island Gasoline Retailers Assn PAC, 549
Margiotta, Joseph M, 504
Newsday, 595
Newsday Inc, 595
NIC-PAC, 551
North Fork Bank, 95, 330
US Justice Department
  Melville, 138
WLNY (55), 608

Menands
Allocco, Carol, 456
Correctional Services Department
  Support Operations Division, 129
Menands UFSD, 638
Research Foundation for Mental Hygiene Inc, 285

Merrick
Merrick Chamber of Commerce, 579
Merrick UFSD, 655
New York State Air Force Association, 368
North Merrick UFSD, 655

Mexico
Mexico CSD, 662
Oswego BOCES, 680

Middle Falls
Carson, Martin, 469

Middle Island
Longwood CSD, 669

Middle Village
R-PAC, 560

Middleburgh
Middleburgh CSD, 665

Middleport
Royalton-Hartland CSD, 657

Middletown
Frontier, A Citizens Communications Co, 173
Middletown
  Civil & Criminal Courts, 73
Middletown City SD, 660

Listings appear in alphabetical order by state, then city.

Geographic Index

Middletown, City of, 425
Mid-Hudson News Network, 602
New York State Assessors' Association, 305, 331
Orange County Community College, 617
Orange County Democratic Women Inc Campaign, 558
Orange County Publications, 596
Times Herald-Record, 596
Wallkill, Town of, 444

Milford
Milford CSD, 662

Millbrook
Institute of Ecosystem Studies, 190
Millbrook CSD, 645

Miller Place
Miller Place UFSD, 670
Miller Place/Mt Sinai/Sound Beach/Rocky Point Chamber of Commerce, 579

Millerton
New York State Directory, 209

Mineola
Assn for a Better Long Island - PAC (ABLI), 534
Elections, State Board of
   Nassau, 160
Law Department
   Nassau, 255
Long Island Chapter/American Institute of Architects LIC (AIA PAC), 549
Mental Hygiene Legal Service
   2nd Judicial Dept, 256, 282
Meyer, Suozzi, English & Klein, PC - Political Acct, 550
Mineola Chamber of Commerce, 579
Mineola UFSD, 655
Monument Industry PAC, 551
Nassau County, 404
   County & Surrogate's Courts, 65
   Supreme Court, 65
Nassau County PBA PAC, 554
Plumbers Local Union 200 PAF, 560
Winthrop University Hospital, 227

Mineville
Correctional Services Department
   Moriah Shock Incarceration Correctional Facility, 131

Model City
CWM Chemical Services LLC, 187

Mohawk
Herkimer County Chamber of Commerce, 576
Mohawk CSD, 650
Mohawk Valley Economic Development District, 579

Monroe
Kiryas Joel Village UFSD, 660
Monroe, Town of, 425

Montauk
Montauk UFSD, 670

Montgomery
Montgomery, Town of, 425
Valley CSD (Montgomery), 661

Monticello
Convention Centers & Visitors Bureaus
   Sullivan County Visitors Association, 338
Elections, State Board of
   Sullivan, 162
Monticello CSD, 672
Monticello Raceway, 344
Sullivan County, 411
   Family & Surrogate's Courts, 68
   Supreme & County Courts, 68
Sullivan County Chamber of Commerce, 586

Montour Falls
State Department
   New York State Academy of Fire Science, 180, 199, 291

Montrose
Health Department
   New York State Veterans' Home at Montrose, 214, 360
Hendrick Hudson CSD, 676
US Department of Veterans Affairs
   Montrose Campus of the VA Hudson Valley Healthcare System, 364

Moravia
Correctional Services Department
   Cayuga Correctional Facility, 130
Moravia Chamber of Commerce, 580
Moravia CSD, 641

Moriches
Great South Bay Republican Club PAC, 544

Morris
Morris CSD, 662

Morristown
Morristown CSD, 667

Morrisville
Morrisville State College, 614
Morrisville-Eaton CSD, 652

Mount Kisco
Journal News (The)/Gannett Co Inc, 596
Mount Kisco Chamber of Commerce, 580
Patent Trader, 596

Mount Morris
Mt Morris CSD, 651

Mount Sinai
Mt Sinai UFSD, 670

Mount Vernon
African American Chamber of Commerce of Westchester & Rockl, 569
Dorothea Hopfer School of Nursing at Mount Vernon Hospital, 624
Empire State Report (CINN Worldwide Inc), 601
Mount Vernon
   Civil & Criminal Courts, 73
Mount Vernon Chamber of Commerce, 580
Mount Vernon Industrial Development Agency (City of), 580
Mount Vernon, City of, 425
Mt Vernon City SD, 677

Mountainville
Local Union #373 UA Political Action Fund, 549

Munnsville
Stockbridge Valley CSD, 652

N Greece
Greece CSD, 652

Nanuet
Camp Venture Inc, 316
Lipsky, Richard Associates Inc, 499
Nanuet UFSD, 664

Napanoch
Correctional Services Department
   Agri-Business, 129
   Eastern NY Correctional Facility, 130
   Ulster Correctional Facility, 131

Naples
Naples CSD, 660

Nedrow
Onondaga CSD, 659
Onondaga Nation, 209

Nesconset
Suffolk County Chapter Nat'l Womens Political Caucus, 564

New Berlin
Unadilla Valley CSD, 642

New City
Better Health Care PAC, 535
Clarkstown CSD, 664
Clarkstown, Town of, 417
Elections, State Board of
   Rockland, 161
New City Chamber of Commerce, 580
RC Build PAC of the Rockland County Builders Assn, 560
Rockland Chamber of Commerce, 583
Rockland County, 408

Listings appear in alphabetical order by state, then city.

905

Geographic Index

Supreme, County, Family & Surrogate's Courts, 67
Rockland County Correction Officers Benevolent Association PAC, 561
Rockland County Sheriff's Deputy Assn, PAC, 562

New Hampton
Mental Health, Office of
Mid-Hudson Forensic Psychiatric Center, 280

New Hartford
New Hartford CSD, 658
New Hartford, Town of, 426
Oneida-Herkimer-Madison BOCES, 679

New Hyde Park
Glenwood Management Corporation, 304
Herricks UFSD, 654
New Hyde Park-Garden City Park UFSD, 655

New Lebanon
New Lebanon CSD, 643

New Paltz
Environmental Conservation Department
Hudson River Estuary Program, 178
Region 3, 178
Generation Project, 543
New Paltz CSD, 673
New Paltz Regional Chamber of Commerce, 580
State University College at New Paltz, 614
SUNY at New Paltz, College of Liberal Arts & Sciences, 166, 210
SUNY at New Paltz, Department of History, 210
Ulster BOCES, 680

New Rochelle
College of New Rochelle (The), 623
Columbus Circle Agency, Inc, 538
Iona College, 626
MLCA PAC, 550
Monroe College-New Rochelle, 636
New Rochelle
Civil & Criminal Courts, 73
New Rochelle City SD, 677
New Rochelle, Chamber of Commerce, Inc, 580
New Rochelle, City of, 426
NYC Columbus Circle PAC, 552
Westchester Right to Life PAC, 568
WVOX (1460 AM), WRTN (93.5 FM), 605

New Suffolk
New Suffolk Common SD, 670

New Windsor
Hudson Valley Build PAC, 545
New Windsor, Town of, 426

New York
1199 SEIU Unit, 454
1199 SEIU United Healthcare Workers East, 274
1199/SEIU & GNYHA Healthcare Education Project, 454
1199/SEIU New York State Political Action Fund, 533
1st Department, 55
369th Veterans Association Inc, 365
504 Democratic Club Campaign Committee, 533
92nd Street Y Young Men's and Young Women's Hebrew Association, 454
AARP, 315
ABC News (New York Bureau), 600
ABO Build PAC Inc, 533
Academy of Political Science, 206
ACEC New York PAC, 533
Adolf, Jay, 455
Advance Group Inc (The), 455
Advocates for Children of New York Inc, 151
Africa-America Institute (The), 151
After-School Corporation (The), 151, 455
Agenda for Children Tomorrow, 316
Agudath Israel of America, 152
AIDS Coalition (NY), 454
Alcoholic Beverage Control, Division of (State Liquor Authority), 5, 98, 324
New York City (Zone I), 98, 324
Alcoholism & Substance Abuse Services, Office of, 5, 211, 278, 307
Alliance for the Arts, 341
Alliance of Resident Theatres/New York (ART/New York), 341
Allied Bldg Metal Industries Inc State PAC, 534
Alston & Bird LLP, 261
Altman, Robert S, 457
Altria Corporate Services, 106, 457
AMAC, Association for Metroarea Autistic Children, 283
AMDeC Foundation, 454
Amerada Hess Corporation, 172
American Academy McAllister Institute of Funeral Service, 622
American Academy of Dramatic Arts, 622
American Express Company, 93
American Federation of Musicians, Local 802, 341
American Fertility Association, 220
American Higher Education Development Corporation, 152
American International Group Inc, 93, 249
American International Group, Inc Employee PAC, 534
American Jewish Committee, 240
American Lawyer Media Inc, 596
American Lung Assn of the City of New York, 458

American Management Association International, 106
American Metal Market, 600
American Museum of Natural History, 187, 341, 458
American Society for the Prevention of Cruelty to Animals (ASPCA), 83, 140
American Telephone & Telegraph Co PAC NY, 534
Ames, Margery E, 458
Ammann & Whitney, 357
Amnesty International USA, 240
Andrew, Ralph, 458
ANHD Inc, 454
Anti-Defamation League, 240
Aon Services Corporation, 249
Apple Banking for Savings, 94
Art & Science Collaborations Inc, 341
Art Institue of New York City (The), 633
Arts Coalition (NYC), 459
Arts PAC Non-Federal, 534
ArtsConnection Inc (The), 341
Arzt, George Communications Inc, 459
Asian American Federation of New York, 316
Asian American Legal Defense and Education Fund, 240, 262
Asian Americans for Equality, 316
ASPIRA of New York Inc, 151
Associated Licensed Detectives of New York State, 140
Associated Medical Schools of New York, 152, 221
Associated Press (New York/Metro Bureau), 601
Association for a Better New York, 107, 233
Association for Neighborhood & Housing Development, 233
Association for the Help of Retarded Children/AHRC, 283
Association of Commuter Rail Employees PAC NY, 534
Association of Graphic Communications, 107
Association of Independent Video & Filmmakers (AIVF), (The), 341
Association of New York State Young Republicans Inc, 534
Association of the Bar of the City of New York, 262
ATPAM COPE State Fund, 533
Attorney Grievance Committee
1st Judicial Dept, Judicial Dist 1, 12, 255
Bank Street College of Education/Graduate School, 622
Banking Department, 5, 90
Banks, Steven, 461
Barnard College, 622
Battery Park City Authority (Hugh L Carey), 113, 335

Listings appear in alphabetical order by state, then city.

Geographic Index

Bear Stearns & Co Inc, 94
Bellevue Hospital Center, Department of Emergency Med, 221
Berkeley College, New York City Campus, 634
Berkley Center for Entrepreneurial Studies NYU, Stern School, 111
Bernard M Baruch College, 619
Better Business Bureau of Metropolitan New York, 107
Big Brothers Big Sisters of NYC, 316
Bigelsen, Jayne, 462
Black Car PAC, 535
Blinded Veterans Association New York Inc, 366
Bloomberg Television, 608
Board of Jewish Education of Greater New York, 152
Bond Market Association (The), 94
Bookman, Robert S, 464
Boricua College, 622
Borough of Manhattan Community College, 619
Boykin-Towns, Karen, 464
Branford Communications, 164
Bristol-Myers Squibb Co Employee PAC, 535
Bronx Health Reach, 465
Brookfield Properties Corporation, 303
Brown Brothers Harriman & Co, Bank Asset Management Group, 94
Browne, Brian, 465
Bryan Cave, LLP, 465
Building & Construction Trades Council PAC, 536
Building Contractors Assn Inc, 536
Building Contractors Association, 107
Burgos, Tonio & Associates, 466
Burns, Miriam P, 466
Business Council for International Understanding, 107
Campaign for Fiscal Equity, Inc, 152, 467
Capalino, James F & Associates Inc, 467
Capital Defender Office, 114, 136, 257
Captain's Endowment Assn PAC, 536
Cardozo School of Law, 241
Catholic War Veterans of the United States of America, 366
CBS Corporation, 172
CBS News (New York Bureau), 601
Cendant Car Rental Group Inc, 342
Center for Alternative Sentencing & Employment Services (CASES), 140
Center for an Urban Future, 233, 275
Center for Constitutional Rights, 241
Center for Court Innovation, 262
Center for Educational Innovation - Public Education Association, 152
Center for Independence of the Disabled in NY (CIDNY), 241, 316

Center for Migration Studies of New York Inc, 241
Center for Urban Community Services, 317
Central Brooklyn Medical Group, PC, 537
Century Foundation (The), 165
Cerebral Palsy Associations of New York State, 152, 283
Charter PAC, 537
Child Care Inc, 470
Children & Family Services, Office of
Executive Office, NYC, 308
New York City Regional Office, 310
Children's Aid Society (The), 317
Children's Health Fund (The), 470
Children's Rights Inc, 241, 317
Christie's Education Inc, 635
Citigroup, 94
Citigroup Inc, 94
Citizens Budget Commission, 292, 330, 471
Citizens Housing & Planning Council of New York, 234
Citizens Union of the City of New York, 207, 293
Citizens' Committee for Children of New York Inc, 241, 317, 471
City College of New York, The, 620
City Journal (Manhattan Institute for Policy Research), 601
City University Construction Fund, 115, 148
Civil Court, NYC
New York County, 59
Civil Service Technical Guild PAC, 537
Clean PAC Inc, 537
Clear Channel Communications Inc PAC, 537
Coalition Against Hunger (NYC), 472
Coalition for Asian American Children & Families, 317
Coalition for the Homeless, 317
Coalition of Behavioral Health Agencies, Inc (The), 284
Coalition of Voluntary Mental Health Agencies, Inc, 473
COFCCA Inc, 466
Colliers ABR Inc, 304
Columbia Law School, Legislative Drafting Research Fund, 165, 293
Columbia University, 623
Columbia University, Exec Graduate Pgm in Public Policy & Adm, 207
Columbia University, Mailman School of Public Hea, 221
Columbia University, Mailman School of Public Health, 221, 241
Columbia University, MPA in Environmental Science & Policy, 188
Columbia University, School of the Arts, 342
Columbia University, Science & Technology Ventures, 107

Committee for Workers' Compensation Reform, 538
Committee of Interns & Residents SEIU Loc 1957, 538
Commodity Futures Trading Commission
Eastern Region, 81, 104
Commodore Applied Technologies Inc, 188
Common Cause/NY, 165, 207
Commonwealth Fund, 222
Communication Workers of America, District 1 PAC, 538
Communications Workers of America, District 1, 275
Community Health Care Association of NYS, 222, 473
Community Healthcare, 474
Community Healthcare Network, 222, 318
Community Housing Improvement Program (CHIP), 234
Community Preservation Corporation (The), 234, 474
Community Service Society of New York, 234
Community Voices Heard, 474
Conference Board (The), 107
Connelly & McLaughlin, 474
Connelly Communications, Inc, 475
Consolidated Edison Energy, 173
Consolidated Edison, Inc. Employees' Political Action Committ, 538
Constantinople & Vallone Consulting LLC (FKA Constantinople Cons, 475
Constellation NewEnergy Inc, 173
Consumer Product Safety Commission
Eastern Regional Center, 104
Consumer Protection Board, 7, 99, 168
Continuum Health Partners Inc, 222
Convention Centers & Visitors Bureaus
NYC & Company/Convention & Visitors Bureau, 338
Cooper Union for the Advancement of Science & Art, 623
Cornell Cooperative Extension, Urban Agriculture & Markets Program, 84
Cornell University, Sch of Industr &, 275
Correction Captains Assn PAC, 539
Correction Officers' Benevolent Assn PAC, 539
Correctional Association of New York, 140
Correctional Services Department
Bayview Correctional Facility, 130
Edgecombe Correctional Facility, 130
Lincoln Correctional Facility, 131
Council of Family & Child Caring Agencies, 318
Council of Senior Ctrs & Services of NYC, Inc, 476
Council of State Governments, Eastern Conference, 207, 293, 330
Council of Urban Professionals, 539
Council on the Arts, 7, 332

Listings appear in alphabetical order by state, then city.

907

Geographic Index

Council on the Environment of NYC (The), 188
Council on the Environment of NYC, Environmental Education, 153
Council on the Environment of NYC, Open Space Greening Program, 234
CPR, The International Institute for Conflict Prevention & Resoluti, 262
Crain's New York Business, 601
Credit Advocate Counseling Corporation, 94
Criminal Court, NYC
  New York County, 60
CUNY Board of Trustees, 619
CUNY Central Administration, 619
  City University Construction Fund, 619
CUNY Graduate School, Center for Urban Research, 165
CUNY Hunter College, Urban Affairs & Planning Department, 233
CUNY John Jay College of Criminal Justice, 140
CWA SSF (NY), 536
D&M P.A.C., LLC, 539
Dadey, Dick, 477
Dames, Reid, LLC, 477
Dan Klores Communications Inc, 477
Davis Polk & Wardwell, 108
Day Pitney LLP, 263, 330
DC 37 PAC, 539
Debevoise & Plimpton LLP, 140, 263
Demos: A Network for Ideas & Action, 478
Detectives' Endowment Association COPE, 539
Deutsche Bank, 94
Development Counsellors International, 108
Dewey Ballantine LLP, 479
DiPalermo, Christian, 479
District Council 37, AFSCME, 479
District Council 37, AFSCME, AFL-CIO, 299
District Council 9 PAC, 539
DLA Piper Rudnick Gray Cary US LLP NYSPAC, 540
Doctors Without Borders USA, 222
Dow Jones & Company, 596
Downtown-Lower Manhattan Association, 573
Drug Policy Alliance Network (SSF), 540
Drum Major Institute for Public Policy - Not For Profit, 241
Dryfoos Group, 480
East Side Republican District Leaders Committee, 540
Education Department
  Manhattan District Office, 147
  Professional Discipline, 146
Educational Broadcasting Corporation, 173
EISPAC, 540
Eleanor Roosevelt Legacy Committee Inc, 540

Elections, State Board of
  New York, 160
  New York City, 160
Elinski, Karen, 481
Empire Blue Cross & Blue Shield, 222, 250
Empire State Development Corporation, 9, 99, 115, 177, 230, 333
Empire State Pride Agenda PAC, 541
Entertainment Software Association, 342
Environmental Defense, 189
Equal Employment Opportunity Commission
  New York District, 239, 272
Equitable Life Assurance Society of the US, 250
Ernst & Young, 304
Ethan C Eldon Associates Inc, 189, 357
Excess Line Association of New York, 250
Export Import Bank of the United States
  Northeast Regional Office, 92, 104
Eye-Bank for Sight Restoration Inc (The), 222
Family Court, NYC
  New York County, 60
Farrell, Pamela, 482
Fashion Institute of Technology, 482, 615
FED PAC, 542
Federal Deposit Insurance Corporation
  Division of Supervision & Consumer Protection, 92
Federal Home Loan Bank of New York, 94, 234
Federal Reserve System
  Federal Reserve Bank of New York, 92
Federal Trade Commission, 109
  Northeast Regional Office, 104
Federation Employment & Guidance Service (FEGS) Inc, 284, 318
Federation of Protestant Welfare Agencies Inc, 318, 483
Film/Video Arts, 343
Financial Services Forum, 94
Fire Island Pines Property Owners Assn PAC, 542
First District Dental Society Political Action Committee, 542
Fisher Brothers, 304
Fordham University, Department of Political Science, 208
Fordham University, Graduate School of Social Service, 318
Fortune Society (The), 140
Fox News Channel, 608
French-American Chamber of Commerce, 574
Fried Frank Harris Shriver & Jacobson, LLP, 484
Friends & Relatives of Institutionalized Aged Inc (FRIA), 223, 319
Friends of New York Racing PAC, 543
Friends of Schumer, 543

Fund for Animals (The), 85
Fund for Modern Courts (The), 263
Fund for the City of New York, 293
Fund for the City of New York, Center for Internet Innovation, 173
Gandhi Engineering Inc, 357
Garth Group Inc (The), 165
Gay Men's Health Crisis Inc, 485
General Contractors Assn of NY PAC, 543
General Contractors Association of NY, 109, 357
General Services, Office of, 10, 195, 301, 333
General Theological Seminary of the Episcopal Church, 625
Gertrude H Sergievsky Center (The), 223
Gertrude Stein Repertory Theatre (The), 343
Geto & deMilly Inc, 109, 208, 485
Gilbert Tweed Associates Inc, 109
Globe Institute of Technology, 635
Goldman, Gerald, 486
Goodman & Zuchlewski LLP, 263
Goodwin, Jeffrey, 486
Governor's Office
  New York City Office, 4, 157, 194, 287
Graduate Center, 620
Graduate School of Journalism, 620
Greater New York Hospital Association, 223
Greenberg Traurig, LLP, 208, 487
Greenmarket/Council on the Environment of NYC, 85
GreenThumb, 85, 189
Greenwich Village-Chelsea Chamber of Commerce, 576
Group Health Inc, 223, 250
Group Health Inc State PAC, 544
Guardian Life PAC, 544
GVA Williams, 304
H J Kalikow & Co LLC, 304
Harlem Chamber of Commerce (Greater Harlem), 576
Harvestworks, 343
Hawkins Delafield & Wood LLP, 293, 330
Health Department
  Metropolitan Area/Regional Office, 215
  Task Force On Life & The Law, 213
Healthcare Tort Reform Coalition (NY), 489
Healthy Kids NY, 544
Healthy New York, 545
Hebrew Union College - Jewish Institute of Religion, 625
Helene Fuld College of Nursing North General Hospital, 625
Heyman, Neil, 490
High-Need Hospital PAC Inc, 545
HIP Health Plan PAC, 545
Hispanic Federation, 319
Hogan & Hartson LLP, 174

Listings appear in alphabetical order by state, then city.

Geographic Index

Holland & Knight Committee for Responsible Gov't (The), 545
Hollyer Brady et al, 264
Homes for the Homeless/Institute for Children & Parties, 234
Homes for the Homeless/Institute for Children & Poverty, 319
Hotel Assn of NYC Inc PAC, 545
Hotel Association of New York City Inc, 343
Housing & Community Renewal, Division of, 10, 228
  New York City, 228
Housing Conservation Coordinators, 492
HSBC Bank USA, 95
HSBC USA Inc, 95
Human Rights First, 242
Human Rights Watch, 242
Human Rights, State Division of
  Manhattan (Lower), 238
  Manhattan (Upper), 238
Human Services Council of NYC, 492
Hunter College, 620
Hunter College, Brookdale Center for Healthy Aging and Longevity, 320
Hurley, John R, 492
I.U.O.E. Local 15 PAC, 545
Immigration Coalition, Inc (NY), 492
INFORM Inc, 190, 223
Inspector General (NYS), Office of the, 11, 134, 197
Institute for Family Health (The), 223
Institute of Public Administration/NYU Wagner, 208, 293
Insurance Brokers' Association of the State of New York, 250
Insurance Department, 11, 215, 245
  Liquidation Bureau, 245
Insurance Fund (NYS), 11, 246, 268
Int'l Longshoremen's Assn AFL-CIO COPE, 546
InterAgency Council of Mental Retardatn & Developmental Disabilities, 284
Interboro Institute, 635
Interest on Lawyer Account (IOLA) Fund of the State of NY, 116, 258
International Council of Shopping Centers PAC NY, 546
International Flavors & Fragrances Inc, 109
Interstate Environmental Commission, 116, 181
Iron Workers' Local 40 Voluntary COPE, 547
IRX Therapeutics Inc, 95
ITAR-TASS News Agency, 601
J Adams Consulting, LLC, 493
J P Morgan Chase & Co State & Federal PAC, 547
Jacobs Engineering, 357
JAMS, 264, 275
Japanese American Social Services Inc, 320

Japanese Chamber of Commerce, 577
JBDS NYS PAC, 547
Jewish Board of Family & Children's Services, 284
Jewish Community Relations Council of NY Inc, 242
Jewish Home & Hospital (The), 223
Jewish Museum (The), 343
Jewish Theological Seminary, 626
Jewish War Veterans of the USA, State of NY, 366
John Jay College of Criminal Justice, 620
Juilliard School (The), 626
Kantor Davidoff Wolfe Mandelker & Kass, PC, 494
Kasirer Consulting, 494
Katharine Gibbs School-New York City, 636
Katz, Arthur H, 494
Kaye Scholer LLP, 276
King, Barbara, 494
King's College (The), 626
Komanoff Energy Associates, 174, 357
Korean Community Services of Metropolitan NY, 320
KPMG LLP, 293
Kramer Levin Naftalis & Frankel, LLP, 495
Kraus & Zuchlewski LLP, 276
La Fuente, A Tri State Worker & Community Fund Inc, 496
Labor Department
  New York City, 270
Laboratory Institute of Merchandising, 636
Lambda Legal Defense & Education Fund Inc, 242
Lanahan, Kevin, 496
Landauer Realty Group Inc, 304
Law Department, 12, 91, 99, 134, 169, 179, 197, 216, 229, 238, 247, 253, 270, 301, 325
  Harlem, 255
  Medicaid Fraud Control Unit, 134, 216, 254
Law Guardian Program
  1st Judicial Dept, 255
Law Offices of Wesley Chen, 95
Lawyers for the Public Interest (NY), 497
Lawyers' PAC (LAWPAC), 548
League for the Hard of Hearing, 223
League of Humane Voters of New York City, 548
Learning Leaders, 153
LeBoeuf Lamb Greene & MacRae PAC, 548
LeBoeuf Lamb Greene & MacRae, LLP, 497
Legal Action Center Inc, 264
Legal Action Center of the City of NY Inc, 141
Legal Action Ctr of the City of NY Inc, 498
Legal Aid Society, 141, 264

Legal Aid Society, Community Law Offices, 264
Leon, Rachel, 498
Lesbian, Gay, Bisexual & Transgender Community Ctr - Not For Profit, 242, 284, 320
Levine, Paul, 498
Levy, Norman PC, 498
Lieutenant Governor's Office, 4, 194
Life Insurance Council of New York, Inc, 250
Lifespire, 284
Lighthouse International, 224
Lincoln Center for the Performing Arts Inc, 343
Lincoln Ctr for the Performing Arts Inc, 499
Littman Krooks LLP, 320
Local 237 I.B.T. PAC, 549
Local 32BJ SEIU NY/NJ American Dream Fund, 549
Local 420 Political Action Committee, 549
Local 6 Committee on Political Education, 549
Local Initiative Support Corporation, 234
LoCicero & Tan Inc, 499
Log Cabin Republicans NY PAC, 549
Long Island Rail Road Commuter's Council, 358
Long Term Care Community Coalition, 500
Long View Publishing Co, 596
Lottery, Division of
  New York City Region, 325
Louloudes, Virginia, 500
Lower Manhattan Cultural Council, 344
Lynch, Bill Associates, LLC, 500
M & R Strategic Services, 502
Macy's East Inc, 109
Madison Square Garden Corp, 344
Madison Square Garden LP, 502
Maher, Daniel F, Jr, 502
Major League Baseball, 344
Mallory Factor Inc, 95
Maloney Committee NYS PAC, 550
Mandl School, 636
Manhattan Chamber of Commerce Inc, 503, 579
Manhattan Educational Opportunity Center, 618
Manhattan Institute (The), 208
Manhattan Institute for Policy Research, 109, 208
Manhattan Institute, Center for Civic Innovation, 293, 331
Manhattan School of Music, 627
Manhattan-Bronx Minority Business Enterprise Center, 276
Maniscalco, John D, 504
Mannis, David, 504
Marsh & McLennan Companies, 250
Martens, Joseph J, 505
Marymount Manhattan College, 627

Listings appear in alphabetical order by state, then city.

Geographic Index

Mason Tenders' District Council of Greater NY PAC, 550
Master, Robert, 505
McGuire, Michael J, 505
McInnis, Stephen C, 505
MDRC, 153, 276
Meara, Brian R, Public Relations Inc, 506
Medical Society of the State of New York PAC, 550
Memorial Sloan-Kettering Cancer Center, 224
Menaker & Herrmann LLP, 109
Mental Health Association of NYC Inc, 284
Mental Health, Office of
　New York Psychiatric Institute, 280
Mental Hygiene Legal Service
　1st Judicial Dept, 256, 282
Mental Retardation & Developmental Disabilities, Office of
　Metro New York Developmental Disabilities Services Office, 281
　New York City Regional Office, 281
Mercury Public Affairs, 506
Merrill Lynch & Co Inc, 95
Metalic Lathers Local 46 PAC, 550
Metret PAC, Inc, 550
Metro-North Railroad Commuter Council, 358
Metropolitan College of New York, 627
Metropolitan Garage Owners Assn PAC, 550
Metropolitan Museum of Art (The), 344
Midtown Consultants, Inc, 507
Mills, Josephine, 508
Mirram Global, LLC, 508
Mirram Group, LLC (The), 508
Montalbano Initiatives Inc, 508
Montclare & Wachtler, 110, 265
Montford Point Marine Association, 367
Moody's Investors Service, Public Finance Group, 293, 331
Morgan Stanley, 95
Morse, Alan, 509
Mount Sinai Medical Center, 224, 509
Mount Sinai School of Medicine of NYU, 628
MTA (Metropolitan Transportation Authority), 117, 352
MTA Bridges & Tunnels, 117, 350
MTA Bus Company, 118, 351
MTA Capital Construction, 118, 351
MTA Metro-North Railroad, 118, 351
MTA Office of the Inspector General, 119, 352
Mulholland & Knapp, LLP, 208
Municipal Art Society, 509
Municipal Assistance Corporation for the City of New York, 91, 119, 291
Municipal Credit Union, 95
NARAL Pro-Choice, New York, 510
NARAL/NY Multicandidate PAC, 551

National Alliance for the Mentally Ill of NYC, Inc, 510
National Association of Black Accountants, NY Chapter, 110
National Basketball Association, 345
National Coffee Association, 87
National Council of Jewish Women, 242, 321
National Federation of Community Development Credit Unions, 96
National Football League, 345
National Hockey League, 345
National Labor Relations Board
　Region 2 - New York City Metro Area, 272
National League for Nursing (NLN), 225
National Urban League Inc (The), 321
National Writers Union, 276
Natural Resources Defense Council, 190
Navy League of the US (NLUS), New York Council, 367
NBC News (New York Bureau), 602
Neighborhood Preservation PAF, 554
New School University (The), 628
New School University, Department of Political Science, 166, 242
New School University, Department of Sociology, 345
New School University, Intl Center for Migration, Ethnicity, 242
New School University, Milano Graduate School of Mgmt & Urban Policy, 225, 235
New York 1 News (1), 608
New York Academy of Art Inc, 345, 628
New York AIDS Coalition, 225
New York Anesthesiologists Political Action Committee, 554
New York Artists Equity Association Inc, 345
New York Association for New Americans, Inc (NYANA), 320
New York Bankers Association, 96
New York Bankers Political Action Committee, 554
New York Building Congress, 110, 235
New York Building Congress PAF, 555
New York Business Group on Health Inc, 225
New York Career Institute, 636
New York Chamber of Commerce (Greater New York), 580
New York Check PAC, 555
New York Choice PAC, 555
New York City, 426
　Aging, Dept for the, NYC, 426
　Art Commission, NYC, 427
　Buildings, Department of, NYC, 427
　Campaign Finance Board, NYC, 427
　City Council, NYC, 427
　City Planning, Department of, NYC, 427

　Citywide Administrative Services, Department of, NYC, 427
　Civil Service Commission, NYC, 427
　Collective Bargaining, Office of, NYC, 427
　Comptroller, NYC, 428
　Conflicts of Interest Board, NYC, 428
　Consumer Affairs, Department of, NYC, 428
　Correction, Board of, NYC, 428
　Correction, Department of, NYC, 428
　Cultural Affairs, Department of, NYC, 428
　Disabilities, Mayor's Office, for People with, 428
　Economic Development Corp, NYC, 428
　Education, Dept of, NYC, 428
　Elections, Board of, NYC, 429
　Equal Employment Practices Commission, NYC, 429
　Film, Theatre & Broadcasting, Mayor's Office of, NYC, 429
　Finance, Department of, NYC, 429
　Health & Hospitals Corporation, NYC, 430
　Health & Mental Hygiene, Dept of, NYC, 430
　Homeless Services, Department of, NYC, 430
　Housing Authority, NYC, 430
　Housing Preservation & Development, Dept of, NYC, 430
　Human Resources Administration, Dept of, NYC, 431
　Human Rights Commission on, NYC, 431
　Information Technology & Telecommunications, Dept of, NYC, 431
　Intergovernmental Affairs Ofc, NYC Mayor's, 431
　Investigation, Department of, NYC, 431
　Juvenile Justice, Department of, NYC, 431
　Labor Relations, Office of, NYC, 431
　Landmarks Preservation Commission, NYC, 432
　Law, Department of, NYC, 432
　Legislative Affairs Office, NYC Mayor's City, 432
　Library, New York Public, 432
　Loft Board, NYC, 432
　Management & Budget, Office of, NYC, 432
　Medical Examiner, Office of Chief, NYC, 433
　Parks & Recreation, Department of, NYC, 433
　Police Department, NYC, 433
　Probation, Department of, NYC, 433
　Public Advocate, Office of the, 433

Listings appear in alphabetical order by state, then city.

Geographic Index

Records & Information Services, Dept of, NYC, 433
Rent Guidelines Board, NYC, 434
Sanitation, Department of, NYC, 434
Small Business Services, Department of, NYC, 434
Sports Commission, NYC, 434
Standards & Appeals, Board of, NYC, 434
Tax Commission, NYC, 434
Taxi & Limousine Commission, NYC, 434
Transportation, Department of, NYC, 434
Veterans' Affairs, Mayor's Office of, NYC, 434
Voter Assistance Commission (VAC), NYC, 435
Water Finance Authority, Municipal, NYC, 435
Youth & Community Development, Department of, NYC, 435
New York City Boroughs
   Manhattan (New York County), 435
New York City Central Labor Council Political Action Committee, 555
New York City Housing Development Corporation, 120, 230
New York City Off-Track Betting Corporation, 120, 336
New York City Opera, 345
New York City, Partnership for, 580
New York City, Partnership for, PAC, 555
New York Civil Liberties Union, 242
New York Civil Rights Coalition, 243
New York College of Podiatric Medicine, 628
New York College of Traditional Chinese Medicine, 628
New York Committee for Occupational Safety & Health, 276
New York Community Trust (The), 321
New York Convention Center Operating Corporation, 120, 336
New York Counties Registered Nurses Association, 225
New York County
   SUPREME COURT, Civil Term, 65
   SUPREME COURT, Criminal Term, 65
   Surrogate's Court, 65
New York County (NYC Borough of Manhattan), 404
New York Daily News, 596
New York Foundation for the Arts, 345
New York Health Care Alliance, 225
New York Hotel & Motel Trades Council Committee on Political Educ, 555
New York Immigration Coalition (The), 243
New York Landmarks Conservancy, 235, 305
New York Law Journal, 596
New York Law School, 628

New York Lawyers for the Public Interest, 235, 243
New York League of Conservation Voters Action Fund, 555
New York Life-New York State PAC, 555
New York Magazine (New York Metro LLC), 602
New York Mercantile Exchange Inc, 111
New York Mercantiles Exchange Political Action Committee, Inc, 555
New York Metropolitan Transportation Council, 121, 352
New York Observer (The), 597
New York Pan Hel Political Action Committee, 555
New York Post, 596
New York Presbyterian Hospital, 226
New York Presbyterian Hospital, Department of Psychiatry, 285
New York Press Photographers Association, 175
New York Professional Nurses Union Political Action Fund, 556
New York Public Interest Research Group, 191, 209
New York Public Interest Research Group Straphangers Campaign, 358
New York School of Interior Design, 629
New York Society for the Deaf, 321
New York State Athletic Commission, 121, 200, 336
New York State Clinical Laboratory Assn PAC, 556
New York State Coalition of PHSPS PAC Inc, 556
New York State Commission on Judicial Nomination, 122, 258
New York State Democratic Committee, 166, 449
New York State Dormitory Authority, 122, 149, 201, 216
New York State Financial Control Board, 123, 201, 327
New York State Housing Finance Agency (HFA), 91, 123, 230
New York State Judicial Conduct Commission, 124, 258
New York State Law Enforcement Council, 141, 266, 299
New York State Mortgage Loan Enforcement & Administration Corporatio, 91, 124, 231
New York State Osteopathic Medical Society, 226
New York State Podiatric Medical Association, 226
New York State Project Finance Agency, 91, 231, 327
New York State Radiological Society Inc, 226
New York State Society CPA PAC Inc, 557

New York State Society of Certified Public Accountants, 331
New York State Society of Enrolled Agents, 331
New York State Supreme Court Officers Association, 266, 300
New York State Temporary Commission of Investigation, 125, 202, 297
New York State Trial Lawyers, 266
New York Stock Exchange, 96
New York Theological Seminary, 629
New York Times (The), 597
New York University, 154, 629
New York University School of Law, 266
New York University, Departmentt of Politics, 166
New York University, Graduate School of Journalism, 166, 276
New York University, Graduate School of Public Service, 226
New York University, Law School, 266
New York University, Robert F Wagner Graduate School of Public Se, 226
New York University, Tisch School of the Arts, 346
New York University, Wagner Graduate School, 235, 294
New York Urban League, 322
New Yorker, 266
New Yorkers Against Gun Violence PAC, 557
New Yorkers for Fairness, 557
Newman-Limata, Nancy, 511
Newsweek Magazine (MSNBC, Microsoft Corp), 602
Nonprofit Coordinating Committee of New York, 322
Norat, Cecilia E, 511
Norddeutsche Landesbank Girozentrale, 96
Norman A Olch, Esq, 266
Nostradamus Advertising, 166
NY Coalition of 100 Black Women - Not For Profit, 208
NY County Lawyers' Association, 265
NY Film Academy, 344
NY Foundation for Senior Citizens Inc, 320
NY League of Conservation Voters/NY Conservation Education Fund, 166, 190
NY Life Insurance Co, 250
NY Oil Heating Association, 174
NY Podiatry PAC, 552
NY Property Insurance Underwriting Association, 250
NY Society of Association Executives Inc (NYSAE), 110
NYC & Company, Inc, 510
NYC Americans for Democratic Action NYC ADA PAC, 552
NYC Arts Coalition, 344
NYC Board of Education Employees, Local 372/AFSCME, AFL-CIO, 153, 299

Listings appear in alphabetical order by state, then city.

911

Geographic Index

NYC Campaign Finance Board, 166
NYC Chancellor's Office, 656
NYC Citywide Special Ed District 75, 657
NYC Coalition Against Hunger, 320
NYC District Council of Carpenters' PAC, 552
NYC Neighborhood Open Space Coalition, 190
NYC Region 10, 657
NYC Region 9, 657
NYFF, 551
NYMAGIC Inc, 250
NYP Holdings Inc, 596
NYS Assn of Tobacco & Candy Distributors Inc, 552
NYS Association of Criminal Defense Lawyers, 265
NYS Bar Assn, Antitrust Law Section, 109
NYS Bar Assn, Business Law Section, 109
NYS Bar Assn, Civil Rights/Spec C, 209
NYS Bar Assn, Commercial & Federal Litigation Section, 110, 265
NYS Bar Assn, Courts of Appellate Jurisdiction Cmte, 266
NYS Bar Assn, Cyberspace Law Cmte, 262
NYS Bar Assn, Federal Constitution & Legislation Cmte, 208, 263
NYS Bar Assn, International Law & Practice Section, 261
NYS Bar Assn, Labor & Employment Law Section, 263, 276
NYS Bar Assn, Legislative Policy Cmte, 208
NYS Bar Assn, Media Law Committee, 174, 266
NYS Bar Assn, Minorities in the Profession Cmte, 243
NYS Bar Assn, Multi-jurisdictional Practice Cmte, 111, 266
NYS Bar Assn, Procedures for Judicial Discipline Cmte, 264
NYS Bar Assn, Public Trust & Confidence in the Legal System, 140, 263
NYS Bar Assn, Review the Code of Judicial Conduct Cmte, 262
NYS Bar Assn, Tax Section, 330
NYS Bar Assn, Trusts & Estates Law Section, 263, 330
NYS Building & Construction Trades Council, 110, 276
NYS Clinical Laboratory Association Inc, 110
NYS Court Clerks Association, 265, 299
NYS Federation of Physicians & Dentists, 224
NYS Foundation for Science, Technology & Innovation
   Center for Advanced Technology in Info Mgmt, 100
   Center for Advanced Technology in Information Management, 148

Center for Advanced Technology in Photonic Applications, 100, 148
Industrial & Technology Assistance Corp, 148
NYS Land Title Association, 305
NYS Society for Clinical Social Workers PAC, 553
NYS Society of Certified Public Accountants, 110
NYS Tenants & Neighbors Coalition, 235
NYSALM State PAC, 553
NYSE State PAC, 554
NYSIA NY PAC, 554
Office of David J Silverman, 331
Office of the Attorney General, 243
Oilheat PAC, Inc, 558
OILHEATPAC, 558
OMMLLP PAC, 558
OPEIU Local 153 (VOTE) Voice of the Electorate, 558
Open Society Institute, 243
Open Space Institute, 191
Organization of Staff Analysts PAC, 558
PAC of the Patrolmen's Benevolent Association of the City of NY, Inc, 559
Pace University, 629
Pacific College of Oriental Medicine, 636
Palladia Inc, 142
Parents and Children PAC, Inc, 559
Park Strategies, LLC, 513
Parks, Recreation & Historic Preservation, NYS Office of
   New York City Region, 334
Parkside Group, LLC, 513
Parodneck Foundation (The), 236
Parole, Division of, 135
Parsons Brinckerhoff, 359
Partnership for New York City, 111
Patrolmen's Benevolent Association, 142, 300
Patterson & McLaughlin, 514
Peace Corps
   New York Regional Office, 203
People's Weekly World, 596
Perry Davis Associates, 111
Perry, Robert, 514
Pfizer PAC - NY, 559
Phillips Beth Israel School of Nursing, 629
Phillips Nizer, LLP, 515
Planned Parenthood of NYC, Inc, 322
Plumbing Contractors PAC of the City of NY Inc, 560
Port Authority of New York & New Jersey, 127, 353
Postgrad Center for Mental Health, Child, Adolescent & Family-Coupl, 285
Postgraduate Center for Mental Health, 285
Powers Global Strategies, LLC, 516
Presbyterian Hospital (NY), 516
Prevention of Domestic Violence, Office for the, 14, 136

Pro Bono Net, 266
Professional Business College, 630
Professional Standards Review Council of America Inc (PSRC), 227
Project for Public Spaces, 236
Proskauer Rose LLP, 111, 191, 209, 266
PSC PAC, 559
Public Agenda, 166, 209
Public Library, Astor, Lenox & Tilden Foundations (NY), 516
Public Service Commission, 14, 169
Public/Private Ventures, 277, 322
Puerto Rican Legal Defense & Education Fund Inc (PRLDEF), 243, 266
Real Estate Board of New York Inc, 305
Real Estate Board of NY Inc, 517
Real Estate Board PAC, 561
Realty Advisory Board on Labor Relations, 277, 305
Regional Plan Association, 111, 236, 359
Reiter/Begun Associates, LLC, 517
Related Companies LP, 306
Rent Stabilization Assn of NYC Inc, 236, 517
Republican Majority for Choice PAC, 561
Resources for Artists with Disabilities Inc, 346
Retirees Association of DC 37 Political Action Committee, 561
Reuters (New York Bureau), 602
Robert P Borsody, PC, 227
Robert Schalkenbach Foundation, 306, 331
Rockefeller University, 630
Rough Rider PAC, 562
RPA-PAC, 560
RSA - PAC, 560
RSA PAC City Account, 560
Rubenstein Associates Inc, 519
Rubenstein Communications Inc, 519
Sabol, Sharon, 521
Safe Horizon Inc, 521
SBA Political Action Committee, 562
SBLI USA Mutual Life Insurance Company Inc, 251
School of Professional Studies, 621
School of Visual Arts, 637
Securities Industry & Financial Markets Association (SIFMA), 262
Securities Industry Assn PAC, NY District, 562
Securities Industry Association (SIA), 96
Semper FI NY State PAC Inc, 562
Settlement Housing Fund Inc, 236
Sheet Metal Workers' Intl Assoc Local 28 Political Action Committee, 563
Sheinkopf Communications, 167
Sheinkopf, Ltd, 522
SIFMA, 94
Silverstein Properties Inc, 306
Simmons-Boardman Publishing Corp, 359

Listings appear in alphabetical order by state, then city.

Geographic Index

Simon Wiesenthal Center, NY Tolerance Center, 243
Sithe Energies Inc, 176
Small Business Administration
   New York City, 104
   Region II New York, 104
Smith, Michael P, 523
Smithsonian Institution
   Cooper-Hewitt National Design Museum, 339
   National Museum of the American Indian-George Gustav Heye Center, 339
Social Security Administration
   Region 2—New York, 314
Solomon R Guggenheim Foundation, 347
Sonnenblick-Goldman Company, 306
Sophie Davis School of Biomedical Education, 621
Spanish Broadcasting System Network Inc, 176
SPEAKERPAC, 562
SSL Political Action Committee, 562
St John's University-Peter J Tobin College of Business,, 251
STA Subcontractors Trade Assn Inc State PAC, 564
State & Local Election Fund AFSCME Local 2054, DC 37, 563
State & Local Election Fund Local 1070, 563
State Comptroller, Office of the, 16, 180, 197, 290, 297
   State Deputy Comptroller for New York City, 199
State Department, 16, 101, 180, 199, 290
   State Athletic Commission, 200
State of New York Mortgage Agency (SONYMA), 91, 127, 231
State of New York Municipal Bond Bank Agency (MBBA), 92, 127, 291
Statewide Corporate Strategies Inc, 524
Stillman, Friedman & Shechtman PC, 142
Stroock & Stroock & Lavan LLP, 251
Stryker, Patricia, 524
Success PAC, 564
Sullivan & Cromwell, 96
Sullivan & Cromwell LLP, 330
Sullivan, Edward C, 524
Sullivan, Veronica, 524
SUNY State College of Optometry, 612
SUNY System Administration & Executive Council
   SUNY Metropolitan Recruitment Center, 611
Swedish Institute, 637
Systra Consulting Inc, 359
Tanenbaum Center for Interreligious Understanding, 243
Taylor Business Institute, 637
Tea Association of the USA Inc, 89

Teachers College, Columbia University, 155, 632
Teaching Hospital Education PAC, 565
Teaching Matters Inc, 155
Teamsters Local 72 PAC, 565
TEAPAC, 564
Technical Career Institutes Inc, 637
Tenants & Neighbors Coalition (NYS), 524
The Bachmann-Strauss Dystonia & Parkinson Foundation, 227
The Clearing House Association, LLC, 96
The Coalition for Responsible Development, 565
The New York Observer, 597
The New York Times, 597
The Wine PAC, 565
Theatrical Protective Union Local No One Iatse NYS Stagehands PAC, 565
Thelen Reid Brown Raysman & Steiner, 262
Thorpe, Vernon, 525
Tishman Speyer Properties, 306
Tourism Advocacy Coalition PAC, 566
Touro College, 632
Transport Workers Union of America, AFL-CIO, 277, 359
Transportation Alternatives, 359
Trees New York, 192
Tribeca Film Institute, 347, 525
Tri-State College of Acupuncture, 637
Tri-State Transportation Campaign, 359
Trustees of Columbia University in the City of NY (The), 525
UFT COPE Local, 566
Unified Court System, 256
   1st Judicial Department, 256
   Civil Court, 256
   Court of Appeals, 256
   Criminal Court, 257
   Family Court, 257
Uniformed Fire Officers Association, 300
Uniformed Fire Officers Association 527 Account, 566
Uniformed Firefighters Assoc State FirePAC Political Action Committ, 566
Union for a Better New York, 566
Union Theological Seminary, 632
UNITE HERE, 277
UNITE HERE TIP State & Local Fund, 566
United Federation of Teachers, 155
United Hospital Fund of New York, 227
United Jewish Appeal-Federation of Jewish Philanthropies, 306
United Nations Development Corporation, 103, 128, 202
United Neighborhood Houses - Not For Profit, 323
United Neighborhood Houses of NY, 526
United Way of New York City, 323
Urban Homesteading Assistance Board, 236
Urbanomics, 294, 331

Urbitran Group, 359
US Commerce Department
   Harlem US Export Assistance Center, 105
   Long Island US Export Assistance Center, 105
   New York Region, 104, 239
   New York US Export Assistance Center, 105
US Defense Department
   AIR FORCE-National Media Outreach, 362
   Public Affairs Office, 362
US Department of Agriculture
   New York City Field Office, 82, 218
   Office of the Inspector General, Northeast Region, 82
US Department of Energy
   New York Regional Office, 171
US Department of Health & Human Services
   Administration for Children & Families, 218, 314
   Administration on Aging, 218, 314
   Agency for Toxic Substances & Disease Registry-EPA Region 2, 218, 314
   Centers for Medicare & Medicaid Services, 218, 314
   Health Resources & Svcs Admin Office of Performance Review, 218, 315
   Office for Civil Rights, 218, 239, 315
   Office of General Counsel, 218, 315
   Office of Public Health & Science, 219, 315
   Office of Secretary's Regional Representative-Region 2-NY, 218, 239, 315
US Department of Homeland Security (DHS)
   Environmental Measurements Laboratory, 185, 204
   Federal Protective Service (The), 204
   National Disaster Medical System, 204, 219
   New York City District Office, 204, 240
   New York District Office, 203, 328
   New York Field Office, 204, 328
   New York Regional Office, 204, 219
   Transportation Security Administration (TSA), 204, 355
US Department of the Interior
   Manhattan Sites, 339
   Statue of Liberty National Monument & Ellis Island, 340
US Department of Veterans Affairs
   New York Campus of the NY Harbor Healthcare System, 364
   New York City Regional Office, 363
   VA Regional Office of Public Affairs, Field Operations Svc, 363
US Education Department

Listings appear in alphabetical order by state, then city.

Geographic Index

Region 2 - NY, NJ, PR, Vi, 150
US Environmental Protection Agency
  Region 2 - New York, 185
US Federal Courts
  Southern District, 259, 260
  US Court of Appeals for the Second Circuit, 259
  US Court of International Trade, 259
US General Services Administration
  Region 2—New York, 205, 303
US Government Printing Office
  Printing Procurement Office, 205
US Housing & Urban Development Department
  New York State Office, 232
US Justice Department
  Antitrust Division-New York Field Office, 105
  Antitrust Division—New York Field Office, 260
  Civil Division - Commercial Litigation Branch, 260
  Civil Division-Commercial Litigation Branch, 105
  Community Relations Service - Northeast & Caribbean Region, 260
  Community Relations Service-Northeast & Caribbean Region, 105
  Drug Enforcement Administration - New York Task Force, 137
  Metropolitan Correctional Center, 138
  New York City, 137, 260
  Southern District, 138, 139, 261
  US Trustee - Bankruptcy, Region 2, 261
US Labor Department
  Bureau of Labor Statistics (BLS), 272
  Employee Benefits Security Administration (EBSA), 273
  Federal Contract Compliance Programs Office (OFCCP), 273
  Inspector General's Office for Audit (OIG-A), 273
  Inspector General's Office for Investigations (OIG-I), 273
  Manhattan Area Office, 219, 273
  New York City, 364
  New York City District Office, 273
  New York District Office, 273
  Occupational Safety & Health Administration (OSHA), 273
  Occupational Safety & Health Adminstration (OSHA), 219
  Office of Asst Secretary for Administration & Mgmt (OASAM), 273
  Office of the Solicitor, 273
  Region 2 - New York Office of Secretary's Representative, 273
  Region 2 New York - Women's Bureau (WB), 273
  Workers' Compensation Programs (OWCP), 273
US Merit Systems Protection Board
  New York Field Office, 273, 298
US Railroad Retirement Board
  New York, 274
US Securities & Exchange Commission
  Northeast Region, 105
US State Department
  Bureau of Educational & Cultural Affairs-NY Pgm Branch, 205
  US Mission to the United Nations, 205, 364
US Transportation Department
  Federal Transit Administration, Region II-New York, 356
  North Atlantic Region, 356
  Office of Inspector General, Region II-New York, 356
US Treasury Department
  Appeals Unit - Office of Directors, 328
  Large & Mid-Size Business Division (LMSB), 328
  Management Information Technology Services - Northeast Area, 329
  Manhattan Office, 329
  New York SBSE Compliance Services, 329
  New York Territory, 329
  Northeastern District, 93
  Office of Chief Counsel, 329
  Office of Chief Counsel LMSB Area 1, 328
  Office of Director, Area 1 (New York State & New England), 329
  SBSE-Compliance Area 2/New York, 329
UWUA Local 1-2 Non Federal PAC, 566
Vedder Price Kaufman & Kammholz PC, 277
Ventresca-Ecroyd, Gilda, 527
Vera Institute of Justice, 142, 267
Verizon, 527
Verizon Communications, 176
Veterans' Affairs, Division of
  Eastern Region, 361
  New York City VA Regional Office, 361
  New York Office, 361
Veterans' Service Organizations
  30th Street Shelter, 361
Viacom Inc, 176
Village Voice (The), 597
Village Voice Media, Inc, 597
Visiting Nurse Service of NY, 528
Vladeck, Waldman, Elias & Engelhard PC, 277
Volunteers of Legal Service, Inc, 267
WABC (7), 609
WABC (770 AM), 605
Wachtell, Lipton, Rosen & Katz, 331
Wall Street Journal (The), 176, 596
Washington Mutual, 97
Waterfront Commission of New York Harbor, 128, 271, 354

WAXQ (104.3 FM), 605
WBBR (1130 AM) Bloomberg News, 605
WCBS (2), 609
WCBS (880 AM), 605
We Move, 227
Welfare Inspector General, Office of NYS, 17, 200, 313
West Side Chamber of Commerce, 588
White & Case LLP, 97
WINS (1010 AM), 605
WLTW (106.7 FM), 605
WNBC (4), 609
WNYW (5), 609
Wolf, Block, Schorr & Solis-Cohen, LLP, 531
Women PAC, 568
Women's Bar Association of the State of New York, 267
Women's City Club of New York, 167
Women's Commission for Refugee Women & Children, 244
Women's Prison Association & Home Inc, 142
Women's Venture Fund Inc, 112
Wood Rafalsky & Wood, 531
Wood Tobe-Coburn, 637
WOR (710 AM), 606
Workers' Compensation Alliance, 568
Workers' Compensation Board
  Manhattan, 248, 271
World Hunger Year Inc, 323
WPIX (11), 609
YAI/National Institute for People with Disabilities, 286, 323
Yeshiva University, 633
Yoswein New York Inc, 531

New York Mills
NY Mills UFSD, 658

Newark
New York Field Corn Growers Association, 87
Newark Chamber of Commerce, 580
Newark CSD, 675
Wayne-Finger Lakes BOCES, 680

Newark Valley
Newark Valley CSD, 672

Newburgh
Construction Contractors Assn PAC, 538
Construction Contractors Association of the Hudson Valley Inc, 108
D'Ambrosio, John A, 477
Diorio, L Todd, 479
Dynegy NY PAC, 540
Mid-Hudson Pattern for Progress, 109, 234, 579
MLMICPAC, 550
Mount Saint Mary College, 627
Newburgh

Listings appear in alphabetical order by state, then city.

Geographic Index

Civil & Criminal Courts, 73
Newburgh Enlarged City SD, 661
Newburgh, City of, 436
Newburgh, Town of, 436
Northern Metropolitan Hospital Assn, 512
Orange County Chamber of Commerce Inc, 581
Orange County Legislative Republican Caucas, 558
Real Property Services, Office of
Newburgh (Southern Region), 289, 302, 326
Southeastern New York, Council of Industry of, 585

Newcomb
Newcomb CSD, 647

Newfane
Newfane CSD, 657

Newfield
Newfield CSD, 672

Newport
West Canada Valley CSD, 650

Newtonville
Colonie, Town of, 417

Niagara Falls
Greater Niagara Newspapers, 597
IBEW Local Union #237 Community Action Program, 546
Laborers' Local #91 PAC, 547
Niagara County
Supreme & Family Courts, 65
Niagara Falls
Civil & Criminal Courts, 73
Niagara Falls Bridge Commission, 126, 353
Niagara Falls City SD, 657
Niagara Falls Firefighters PAC, 557
Niagara Falls, City of, 436
Niagara Gazette, 597
Niagara's Future Coalition, 557
Parks, Recreation & Historic Preservation, NYS Office of
Niagara Region & Western District Office, 334
Veterans' Service Organizations
COPIN HOUSE (Homeless Veterans), 361

Niagara University
Niagara University, 155, 629

Niskayuna
ACENY-PAC, 533
Community Mental Health PAC, 538
Higgins Roberts Beyerl & Coan, PC, 490
Hirshorn, Donald P, 491
New England Steamship Agents Inc, 358
Niskayuna, Town of, 436
NYS Food Industry PAC, 553

Nissequogue
Raustiala, Margaret, 517

North Babylon
East Rockaway Republican Club, 540
North Babylon UFSD, 670

North Collins
North Collins CSD, 646

North Creek
Bauer, Peter, 461
Gore Mountain Region Chamber of Commerce, 575
Johnsburg CSD, 673

North Massapequa
Association of Fire Districts of the State of NY Inc, 292
Plainedge UFSD, 656

North Merrick
Bellmore-Merrick Central HS District, 653

North Salem
North Salem CSD, 677

North Syracuse
Krupke, Bruce W, 495
New York State Dairy Foods Inc, 88
New York State Dairy Foods PAC, 556
North Syracuse CSD, 659
ONPAC, 558
US Labor Department
Syracuse Area Office, 219, 273

North Tonawanda
Greater Niagara Newspapers, 600
North Tonawanda
Civil & Criminal Courts, 73
North Tonawanda City SD, 657
North Tonawanda, City of, 437
Tonawanda News, 600
Tonawandas, Chamber of Commerce of the, 587

Northport
Northport-East Northport UFSD, 670
US Department of Veterans Affairs
Northport VA Medical Center, 364

Northville
Northville CSD, 648

Norwich
Chenango County, 398
Supreme, County, Family & Surrogate's Courts, 62
Chenango County Chamber of Commerce, 572
Delaware-Chenango-Madison-Otsego BOCES, 678
Elections, State Board of
Chenango, 158
Evening Sun, 597

Mental Retardation & Developmental Disabilities, Office of
Valley Ridge Developmental Disabilities Services Office, 282
NBT Bancorp Inc., 96
NBT PAC State Fund, 551
Norwich
Civil & Criminal Courts, 73
Norwich City SD, 642
Procter & Gamble Pharmaceuticals, 226
Snyder Communications Corp, 597

Norwood
Norwood-Norfolk CSD, 667

Nunda
Keshequa CSD, 651

Nyack
Ann Breeswine, 459
Nyack Chamber of Commerce, 581
Nyack College, 629
Nyack UFSD, 664

Oakdale
Dowling College, 624
Heimgartner, Christian, 489

Oakfield
Oakfield-Alabama CSD, 648

Ocean Beach
Fire Island UFSD, 669

Oceanside
Oceanside Chamber of Commerce, 581
Oceanside UFSD, 655

Odessa
Odessa-Montour CSD, 665

Ogdensburg
Correctional Services Department
Ogdensburg Correctional Facility, 131
Riverview Correctional Facility, 131
Mental Health, Office of
St Lawrence Psychiatric Center, 281
Ogdensburg
Civil & Criminal Courts, 73
Ogdensburg Bridge & Port Authority, 126, 353
Ogdensburg Chamber of Commerce (Greater Ogdensburg), 581
Ogdensburg City SD, 667
Ogdensburg Journal, 597
St Lawrence County Newspapers, 597
US Department of Homeland Security (DHS)
Ogdensburg, Port of, 204, 328

Old Forge
Central Adirondack Association, 571
Northeastern Loggers' Association, 191
Town of Webb UFSD, 650

Listings appear in alphabetical order by state, then city.

915

Geographic Index

Old Westbury
East Williston UFSD, 654
New York Institute of Technology, 628
State University at Old Westbury, 613
Westbury UFSD, 656

Olean, 598
ALPAC (ALCAS PAC), 533
Bradford Publications Inc, 598
Cattaraugus County
 Family Court, 62
Cattaraugus Empire Zone Corporation, 571
Cattaraugus-Allegany-Erie-Wyoming BOCES, 678
Olean
 Civil & Criminal Courts, 74
Olean Area Chamber of Commerce (Greater Olean), 581
Olean Business Institute, 636
Olean City SD, 640
Southern Tier Leadership PAC, 563
State Department
 Olean, 200
WPIG (95.7 FM), WHDL (1450 AM), 606

Olmstedville
Minerva CSD, 647

Oneida
Journal Register Co, 598
Oneida
 Civil & Criminal Courts, 74
Oneida Chamber of Commerce (Greater Oneida Area), 581
Oneida City SD, 652
Oneida Daily Dispatch, 598
Oneida Industrial Development Agency (City of), 581
US Department of Agriculture
 Oneida Work Station, 82

Oneonta
Daily Star (The), 598
Hartwick College, 625
Oneonta
 Civil & Criminal Courts, 74
Oneonta City SD, 662
Otsego County Chamber (The), 582
Otsego County Economic Development Department & Indu, 582
Ottaway Newspapers Inc, 598
Springbrook, 286
State University of New York at Oneonta, 614
Upstate Homes for Children & Adults Inc, 323
Wilber National Bank, 97

Ontario
Ontario Chamber of Commerce, 581
Park Resident Homeowners' Association Inc, 236

Ontario Center
Wayne CSD, 675

Orangeburg
Dominican College, 624
Mental Health, Office of
 Nathan S Kline Institute for Psychiatric Research, 280
 Rockland Children's Psychiatric Center, 281
 Rockland Psychiatric Center, 281
Orangetown, Town of, 437
Union State Bank, 97
USB Fund for Good Government Inc, 566

Orchard Park
Bryant & Stratton College-Southtowns Campus, 634
Buffalo Bills, 341
Fair PAC, 542
Local #41 Int'l Brotherhood of Electrical Workers' PAC, 548
Messinger Woods Wildlife Care & Education Center Inc, 190
Orchard Park Chamber of Commerce, 581
Orchard Park CSD, 646
Orchard Park, Town of, 437
Realty USA, 305

Orient
Oysterponds UFSD, 670

Oriskany
Northeastern PAC, 558
ORISKA PAC, 558
Oriskany CSD, 658
United Food & Commercial Workers Local 1, 277

Ossining
Correctional Services Department
 Sing Sing Correctional Facility, 131
Ossining UFSD, 677
Ossining, Town of, 437
Ossining, Village of, 437
Westcons PAC, 568

Oswego
Amdursky Pelky Fennell & Wallen, 262
Elections, State Board of
 Oswego, 161
Local 73 Plumbers and Steamfitters PAC Fund, 549
New York State Society of Municipal Finance Officers, 294, 331
NYS Bar Assn, Lawyer Referral Service Cmte, 262
Oswego
 Civil & Criminal Courts, 74
Oswego City SD, 662
Oswego County, 406
 Family Court, 66
 Supreme, County & Surrogate's Courts, 66
Oswego County, Operation/Oswego County Industrial Development Agency, 582
Oswego-Fulton Chamber of Commerce, 582
Palladium-Times (The), 598
Port of Oswego Authority, 127, 353
State University of New York at Oswego, 614
The Palladium Times, 598

Otego
Unatego CSD, 662

Otisville
Correctional Services Department
 Otisville Correctional Facility, 131
US Justice Department
 Federal Correctional Institution at Otisville, 138

Ovid
South Seneca CSD, 666

Owego
Elections, State Board of
 Tioga, 162
Owego-Apalachin CSD, 672
Tioga County, 411
 Family & Surrogate's Courts, 68
 Supreme & County Courts, 69
Tioga County Chamber of Commerce, 587
Tioga County Industrial Development Agency, 587

Oxford
Health Department
 New York State Veterans' Home at Oxford, 214, 360
Oxford Academy & CSD, 642

Oyster Bay
Oyster Bay Chamber of Commerce, 582
Oyster Bay, Town of, 438
Oyster Bay-East Norwich CSD, 655
US Department of the Interior
 Sagamore Hill National Historic Site, 340

Ozone Park
Assn of New York City Concrete Producers Inc State PAC, 534

Painted Post
Corning-Painted Post Area SD, 667
Greater Southern Tier BOCES (Schuyler-Chemung-Tioga-Allegany-St, 679
Painted Post Area Board of Trade, 582

Palmyra
Palmyra-Macedon CSD, 675

Listings appear in alphabetical order by state, then city.

Geographic Index

Panama
Panama CSD, 642

Parish
Altmar-Parish-Williamstown CSD, 661

Parishville
Parishville-Hopkinton CSD, 667

Patchogue
Briarcliffe College-Patchogue, 634
Eastern Suffolk BOCES, 679
Patchogue Chamber of Commerce (Greater Patchogue), 582
Patchogue-Medford UFSD, 670
Suffolk County
  6th District Court, 70
US Department of the Interior
  Fire Island National Seashore, 185, 339
Veterans' Service Organizations
  Suffolk County United Veterans Halfway House Project Inc, 361

Patterson
Carmel CSD, 663

Paul Smiths
Paul Smith's College, 629

Pavilion
Pavilion CSD, 649

Pawling
NYS Arborists, 86
Pawling CSD, 645

Pearl River
Orange & Rockland Utilities Inc, 175
Pearl River UFSD, 664
Rockland Economic Development Corporation, 583

Peconic
Southold Town PBA Tax PAC.COM, 563

Peekskill
Hudson Valley Gateway Chamber of Commerce, 577
Human Rights, State Division of
  Peekskill, 238
Peekskill
  Civil & Criminal Courts, 74
Peekskill City SD, 677
Peekskill Industrial Development Agency (City of), 582
Peekskill, City of, 438
Plumbers & Steamfitters Local 21 PAC, 559
State Department
  Peekskill, 200
WHUD (100.7 FM), 606
Workers' Compensation Board
  Peekskill, 248, 271

Pelham
Pelham UFSD, 677

Penfield
Monroe County Independence Caucas, 551
Penfield CSD, 653
Penfield, Town of, 438

Penn Yan
Elections, State Board of
  Yates, 163
Finger Lakes Tourism Alliance, 343
Penn Yan CSD, 678
Seneca Flight Operations, 359
Yates County, 413
  Supreme, County, Family & Surrogate's Courts, 70
Yates County Chamber of Commerce, 589
Yates County Industrial Development Agency, 589

Perry
Perry Area Chamber of Commerce, 582
Perry CSD, 678
Wyoming County Chamber of Commerce, 589

Perrysburg
Garden Gate Greenhouse, 85
New York State Flower Industries Inc, 85

Peru
Peru CSD, 643

Philadelphia
Indian River CSD, 650

Phoenix
Phoenix CSD, 662

Pine Bush
Pine Bush CSD, 661

Pine City
Correctional Services Department
  Southport Correctional Facility, 131
UNYAN PAC, 566

Pine Hill
Shandaken Democrat Club, 562

Pine Plains
Election Computer Services Inc, 165
Pine Plains CSD, 645

Piseco
Piseco Common SD, 649

Pittsford
Bricklayers Allied Craftworkers Local 3 Buffalo PAC, 535
Campground Owners of New York, 342
D H Ferguson, Attorney, PLLC, 304
Harris Beach LLP, 264
Harris Beach Political Committee, 544
J J Higgins Properties Inc, 304
NYS Bar Assn, Real Property Law Section, 304
NYS Bar Assn, Review Attorney Fee Regulation Cmte, 264
Pittsford CSD, 653
Pittsford, Town of, 438
Red Barn Properties, 305

Plainview
Nassau County Detectives Association Inc, 554
New York Islanders, 345
Plainview-Old Bethpage CSD, 656
Superior Officers Assoc-Nassau County Police, 564
WLIW (21) Public Broadcasting, 608

Plattsburgh
American Military Retirees Association Inc, 365
Champlain Valley Educational Svcs (Clinton-Essex-Warren-Washington), 678
Clinton Community College, 615
Clinton County, 398
  Supreme, County, Family & Surrogate's Courts, 62
Clinton County, The Development Corporation, 572
Elections, State Board of
  Clinton, 158
Law Department
  Plattsburgh, 255
North Country Vietnam Veterans Association, Post 1, 368
Ottaway Newspapers (The), 598
Plattsburgh
  Civil & Criminal Courts, 74
Plattsburgh City SD, 643
Plattsburgh-North Country Chamber of Commerce, 582
Press-Republican, 598
Rural Law Ctr of NY Inc, 520
State Department
  Plattsburgh, 200
State University of New York at Plattsburgh, 614
WPTZ (5) NBC, 609

Pleasantville
Mt Pleasant-Cottage UFSD, 677
Pleasantville UFSD, 677

Poestenkill
Stegemoeller, Rudy, 524

Poland
Poland CSD, 650

Pomona
Catskill Off-Track Betting Corporation, 114, 336

Port Byron
Port Byron CSD, 641

Listings appear in alphabetical order by state, then city.

917

Geographic Index

Port Chester
Port Chester SD, 677
Port Chester, Village of, 439
Port Chester-Rye Brook Chamber of Commerce, 582
Rye, Town of, 441

Port Henry
Moriah CSD, 647

Port Jefferson
Brookhaven-Comsewogue UFSD, 668
Port Jefferson Chamber of Commerce, 582
Port Jefferson UFSD, 670

Port Jervis
Port Jervis
 Civil & Criminal Courts, 74
Port Jervis City SD, 661

Port Washington
National Marfan Foundation, 225
North Shore Animal League America, 322
Port Washington Chamber of Commerce, 582
Port Washington UFSD, 656

Portville
Portville CSD, 640

Potsdam, 100
Clarkson University, 472, 623
NYS Foundation for Science, Technology & Innovation
 Center for Advanced Materials Processing at Clarkson Univ, 100, 147
 Council for Interntl Trade, Tech, Education & Communication, 148
Potsdam Chamber of Commerce, 582
Potsdam CSD, 667
State University at Potsdam, 613

Poughkeepsie
Arlington CSD, 644
Bricklayers & Allied Craftworkers Local 5 NY PAC, 535
Central Hudson Gas & Electric Corporation, 173
Dutchess BOCES, 679
Dutchess Community College, 615
Dutchess County, 400
 Family Court, 63
 Supreme, County & Surrogate's Courts, 63
Dutchess County Economic Development Corporation, 573
Dutchess Democratic Women's Caucus, 540
Education Department
 Mid-Hudson District Office, 147
Elections, State Board of
 Dutchess, 158
Gannett Co Inc, 598
Glusko, John P, 486

Go PAC Dutchess, 543
Hudson River Sloop Clearwater Inc, 189
Law Department
 Poughkeepsie, 255
Marist College, 627
Marist Institute for Public Opinion, 165
Mental Health, Office of
 Hudson River Psychiatric Center, 280
Mid-Hudson Catskill Rural & Migrant Ministry Inc, 507
NYS Bar Assn, Judicial Campaign Monitoring Cmte, 266
Ostertag O'Leary & Barrett, 266
Poughkeepsie
 Civil & Criminal Courts, 74
Poughkeepsie Area Chamber of Commerce, 583
Poughkeepsie City SD, 645
Poughkeepsie Journal, 598
Poughkeepsie, City of, 439
Poughkeepsie, Town of, 439
Rural & Migrant Ministry Inc, 322
Scenic Hudson, 192
Scenic Hudson Inc, 521
Spackenkill UFSD, 645
State Department
 Poughkeepsie, 200
Transportation Department
 Region 8, 349
Vassar College, 633
Veterans' Service Organizations
 Veterans' Coalition of the Hudson Valley, 361
WALL (1340 AM), WRRV (92.7 FM), 606
WPDH (101.5 FM), 606

Prattsburgh
Prattsburgh CSD, 667

Preble
New York Respiratory Care PAC, 556

Pulaski
Pulaski CSD, 662
Pulaski-Eastern Shore Chamber of Commerce, 583

Purchase
Manhattanville College, 627
Pepsi Co, 111
Purchase College, State University of New York, 613

Putnam Station
Putnam CSD, 674

Putnam Valley
Local 137 PEF, 548
Putnam Valley CSD, 663

Queens
Lustig, Esther Public Affairs, 500
New York Hall of Science, 345

NYC Region 5, 657
St John's University, 631
US Department of Health & Human Services
 Northeast Regional Laboratory, 218, 314

Queens Village
Local 1500 Political Candidates Education Fund, 548
Mental Health, Office of
 Creedmoor Psychiatric Center, 280

Queens Vlg
Mental Retardation & Developmental Disabilities, Office of
 Bernard Fineson Developmental Disabilities Services Office, 281

Queensbury
Adirondack Community College, 615
Queensbury UFSD, 674
Queensbury, Town of, 439
Vietnam Veterans of America, NYS Council, 368

Quogue
Quogue UFSD, 670
Rehabilitation Associates PAC, 561

Randolph
Randolph Academy UFSD, 640
Randolph CSD, 640

Ransomville
IUOE Local 463 State & Local PAC & PEF, 546

Raquette Lake
Raquette Lake UFSD, 649

Ray Brook
Adirondack Park Agency, 113, 180, 335
Correctional Services Department
 Adirondack Correctional Facility, 130
Environmental Conservation Department
 Region 5, 178
US Justice Department
 Ray Brook Federal Correctional Institution, 138

Red Creek
Christmas Tree Farmers Association of New York Inc, 84
Correctional Services Department
 Butler Correctional Facility, 130
Red Creek CSD, 675

Red Hook
Hudson Valley Grass Roots Energy & Environmental Network, 190
Red Hook Area Chamber of Commerce, 583
Red Hook CSD, 645

Listings appear in alphabetical order by state, then city.

Geographic Index

Rego Park
RWDSU, Local 338 PAC, 561

Remsen
Remsen CSD, 658

Remsenburg
Remsenburg-Speonk UFSD, 670

Rensselaer
Children & Family Services, Office of, 6, 143, 308
   Council on Children & Families, 6
   COUNCIL ON CHILDREN & FAMILIES, 311
   Youth Development, 310
East Greenbush Republican Club Inc, 540
Frank, Robin, 484
Health Department
   Health Research Inc, 214
   School of Public Health, SUNY at Albany, 213
Healthcare Assn of NYS PAC (HANYS PAC), 544
Healthcare Association of New York State, 223
New York Independent System Operator - Not For Profit, 175
North Greenbush Common SD (Williams), 663
Rensselaer
   Civil & Criminal Courts, 74
Rensselaer City SD, 663
SUNY at Albany, School of Public Health, Center, 227
Whitehead, David, 529

Retsof
York CSD, 651

Rexford
Anson, Joseph L, 459

Rhinebeck
Rhinebeck Chamber of Commerce, 583
Rhinebeck CSD, 645

Richfield Springs
Richfield Area Chamber of Commerce, 583
Richfield Springs CSD, 662

Richmond Hill
Local 30 IUOE PAC, 549

Ripley
Ripley CSD, 642

Riverdale
College of Mount Saint Vincent, 623
Manhattan College, 626

Riverhead
Abate RRF Inc, 533
Riverhead Chamber of Commerce, 583
Riverhead CSD, 670

Riverhead Foundation for Marine Research & Preservation (The), 191
Riverhead PBA PAC Inc, 561
Riverhead, Town of, 440
Suffolk County
   County Court, 68
   Supreme Court, 68
   Surrogate's Court, 68
Suffolk County Correction Officers' Assn PAC, 564

Rochester
1170 PEC, 533
4th Department, 56
Action for a Better Community Inc, 316
Agriculture & Markets Department
   Rochester, 80
American Liver Foundation, Western NY Chapter, 221
Attorney Grievance Committee
   Judicial Dist 7, 255
Bausch & Lomb Inc, 221
Bergin, Robert J, 462
Birds Eye Foods Inc, 84
Boylan Brown, 262
Brighton CSD, 652
Brighton, Town of, 415
Bryant & Stratton College-Greece Campus, 634
Bryant & Stratton College-Henrietta Campus, 634
BX Rochester PAC, 535
Campaign for Renewable Energy, 536
Carpenters' Local Union 85 PAC, 537
Carpino, Peter, 469
Center for Environmental Information Inc, 188
Center for Governmental Research Inc (CGR), 207
Children & Family Services, Office of
   Rochester Regional Office, 311
Chili, Town of, 416
Colgate Rochester Crozer Divinity School, 623
Committee for Effective City Council, 538
Connors & Corcoran LLP, 249, 263
Convention Centers & Visitors Bureaus
   Greater Rochester Visitors Association, 338
Correctional Services Department
   Rochester Correctional Facility, 131
CWA Finger Lakes PAC, 536
Daily Record (The), 598
Dakota Software Corporation, 188
Democrat and Chronicle, 599
Dolan Media Co, 598
East Irondequoit CSD, 652
Eastman Kodak Co Employee PAC, 540
Education Department
   Rochester District Office, 147
Elections, State Board of
   Monroe, 159

Empire Dental PAC, 541
Engineers PEF-Local 832, 541
ENSR, 188
Erdman Anthony & Assoc Employees' PAC, 541
Everest Institute, 635
Excellus Health Plan Inc, 222, 250
Friends of Upstate Labor, 543
Gannett Co Inc, 599
Gates-Chili CSD, 652
Genesee Transportation Council, 293
GLBT Friends of Good Government, 543
Greater Rochester Association of Realtors Inc, 304
Harris Interactive Inc, 165
Harter Secrest & Emery, LLP, 488
Hightower, A Dirk, 490
Human Rights, State Division of
   Rochester, 238
Insurance Fund (NYS)
   Rochester, 246, 269
Irondequoit, Town of, 422
Issues Mobilization Fund - Greater Rochester, 547
Korean War Veterans, 366
Labor Department
   Finger Lakes Region, 270
Laborers' Intl Union of North America 435 Voluntary PAF, 547
Latino Political Action Committee, 548
Law Department
   Rochester, 255
Law Guardian Program
   4th Judicial Dept, 256
Lottery, Division of
   Rochester Office, 325
Mental Health, Office of
   Rochester Psychiatric Center, 281
Mental Hygiene Legal Service
   4th Judicial Dept, 256, 282
Mental Retardation & Developmental Disabilities, Office of
   Finger Lakes Developmental Disabilities Services Office, 281
Monroe Community College, 616
Monroe County, 404
   Supreme, County, Family & Surrogate's Courts, 65
Monroe County Industrial Development Agency (COMIDA), 580
Nat'l Federation of Independent Business/NY Save Ameri, 554
Nazareth College of Rochester, 628
New York Emergency Medicine PAC, 555
New York State Court of Claims, 265, 294
New Yorkers for Constitutional Freedom PAC, 557
Northeastern Seminary, 629
NYS Bar Assn, Gender Equity Task Force Cmte, 243

Listings appear in alphabetical order by state, then city.

Geographic Index

NYS Bar Assn, Municipal Law Section, 265, 294
NYS Bar Assn, President's Cmte on Access to Justice, 262
NYS Bar Assn, Torts, Insurance & Compensation Law Section, 249, 263
NYS Deputies Association Inc, 141, 299
NYS Foundation for Science, Technology & Innovation
   Center for Advanced Tech in Electronic Imaging Systems, 100
   Center for Advanced Technology in Electronic Imaging Systems, 148
   High Technology of Rochester, 148
Pearls' Prison Families of NY, 142
Plumbers & Pipefitters Local No 13 Pol Fund, 559
Republican Main Stream Coalition of New York, 561
Responsive Government In Gates, 561
RG & E Employees' NYS Pol Comm Inc, 560
Roberts Wesleyan College, 630
Rochester
   Civil Court, 74
   Criminal Court, 74
Rochester Area Right to Life Committee-PAC, 561
Rochester Build PAC, 561
Rochester Business Alliance Inc, 583
Rochester Business Journal, 602
Rochester City SD, 653
Rochester Downtown Development Corporation, 583
Rochester Economic Development Corporation, 583
Rochester Educational Opportunity Center, 618
Rochester Gas & Electric Corporation, 176
Rochester Higher Education and Research PAC, 561
Rochester Institute of Technology, 630
Rochester Interfaith Jail Ministry Inc, 142
Rochester Regional Healthcare Advocates, 518
Rochester Regional Joint Board State PAC, 561
Rochester School for the Deaf, 155
Rochester, City of, 440
Rochester, University of, 630
Rochester-Genesee Regional Transportation Authority, 127, 354
Rural Housing Action Corporation, 236
Rural Opportunities Inc, 88, 323
Shaw, Linda R, 522
Sheet Metal Workers' Local 46 PAF, 563
St Bernard's School of Theology & Ministry, 631
St John Fisher College, 631
State Department
   Rochester, 200
Stendardi, Deborah M, 524
The Legal Aid Society, 243
Transportation Department
   Region 4, 349
Unified Court System
   4th Judicial Department, 256
   7th Judicial District (Judicial Department 4), 257
University of Rochester School of Medicine, 192
US Commerce Department
   Rochester US Export Assistance Center, 105
US Department of Agriculture
   Rochester Field Office, 82, 218
US Justice Department
   Rochester, 138, 139, 261
Veterans' Service Organizations
   Veterans Outreach Center Inc, 361
Wegmans Food Markets Inc, 112
West Irondequoit CSD, 653
Western New Yorkers for Economic Growth, 568
WHAM (1180 AM), 606
WHAM (13), 609
WHEC (10), 609
Workers' Compensation Board
   Rochester, 248, 271
WXXI (21) Public Broadcasting, 609
Young Democrats of Monroe County, 568

Rock Hill
Billig, Jacob, 462

Rock Tavern
Carpenters Local No. 19 PAC, 536
US Department of Agriculture
   NY Animal Import Center, 82

Rockaway
Transport Workers Union Local 100 Political Contributions Committee, 566

Rockaway Beach
Wave, 597

Rockaway Park
Rockaways, Chamber of Commerce, Inc, 583
Women's Army Corps Veterans Association - Empire Chapter, 368

Rockville Centre
Matarazzo, Louis, 505
Molloy College, 627
New York Children's Advocates Making Progress, 555
Rockville Centre Chamber of Commerce, 583
Rockville Centre UFSD, 656
Rockville Centre, Village of, 440

Rocky Point
Losquadro, Steven E, 500
Rocky Point UFSD, 670

Rome
Correctional Services Department
   Mohawk Correctional Facility, 131
   Oneida Correctional Facility, 131
Credit Unions' PAC (CUPAC), 539
Daily Sentinel, 599
Education Department
   State School for the Deaf at Rome, 146
McMahon & Grow, 208, 264
Mental Retardation & Developmental Disabilities, Office of
   Central New York Developmental Disabilities Services Office, 281
Mohawk Valley Economic Development Growth Enterprises, 580
NYS Bar Assn, Court Structure & Judicial Selection Cmte, 208, 264
Rome
   Civil & Criminal Courts, 74
Rome Area Chamber of Commerce, 583
Rome City SD, 658
Rome Industrial Development Corporation, 584
Rome Sentinel Co, 599
Rome, City of, 440
US Department of the Interior
   Fort Stanwix National Monument, 339

Romulus
Correctional Services Department
   Five Points Correctional Facility, 130
Romulus CSD, 666

Ronkonkoma
Long Island Business News, 602
Long Island Contractors Assn PAC Inc, 549
Ronkonkoma Chamber of Commerce, 584
Suffolk County
   1ST DISTRICT COURT, Civil Term, 70
   5th District Court, 70

Roosevelt
Roosevelt UFSD, 656

Roosevelt Island
Roosevelt Island Operating Corporation (RIOC), 127, 231, 337

Roscoe
Roscoe CSD, 672

Rosedale
US Department of Homeland Security (DHS)
   New York Asylum Office, 204, 240

Roslyn
NYS Pest Management Association PAC, 553
Roslyn UFSD, 656

Listings appear in alphabetical order by state, then city.

Geographic Index

Rotterdam
Rotterdam, Town of, 440

Roxbury
Roxbury CSD, 644

Rushville
Marcus Whitman CSD, 660

Russell
Edwards-Knox CSD, 666

Rye
Brendel & Associates, 465
Food Industry PAC-NYC, 542
Runes, Richard, 519
Rye
 Civil & Criminal Courts, 75
Rye City SD, 677

Rye Brook
Blind Brook-Rye UFSD, 675
Southern Westchester BOCES, 680
WRNN (62), 608

S Glens Falls
NYS Pipe Trades Political Action Committee, 553

Sackets Harbor
Sackets Harbor Chamber of Commerce, 584
Sackets Harbor CSD, 650
Seaway Trail Inc, 346

Sag Harbor
Sag Harbor Chamber of Commerce, 584
Sag Harbor UFSD, 670

Sagaponack
Sagaponack Common SD, 670

Salamanca
Bradford Publishing Co, 599
Parks, Recreation & Historic Preservation, NYS Office of
 Allegany Region, 334
Salamanca
 Civil & Criminal Courts, 75
Salamanca Area Chamber of Commerce, 584
Salamanca City SD, 640
Salamanca Industrial Development Agency, 584
Salamanca Press, 599
Seneca Nation of Indians, 210

Salem
Salem CSD, 674

Sanborn
Committee for a Better Niagara, 538
Faculty Association PAC, 542
Niagara County Community College, 616
Niagara County Ind Dev Agency, 581
Niagara USA Chamber of Commerce, 581

Niagara-Wheatfield CSD, 657
UA Plumbers & Steamfitters Local 22 PAC Inc, 566

Sandy Creek
Sandy Creek CSD, 662

Saranac Lake
Adirondack Daily Enterprise, 599
Adirondack Economic Development Corporation, 569
Adirondack Publishing Co Inc, 599
North Country Community College, 617
Real Property Services, Office of
 Saranac Lake Satellite Office, 289, 302, 326
Saranac Lake Area Chamber of Commerce, 584
Saranac Lake CSD, 648
St Joseph's Rehabilitation Center Inc, 286

Saratoga Springs
AIM Services Inc, 283
American Farmland Trust, 457
American Farmland Trust, Northeast Regional Office, 83
Association for Eating Disorders - Capital Region, 283
Convention Centers & Visitors Bureaus
 Saratoga Convention & Tourism Bureau, 338
Empire State College, State University of NY, 481
Journal Register Company, 599
Land Trust Alliance Northeast Program, 190, 496
New York State Thoroughbred Breeding & Development Fund Corporat, 125, 337
New York Thoroughbred Breeders Inc, 88
Parks, Recreation & Historic Preservation, NYS Office of
 Saratoga/Capital District Region, 334
Poklemba, John J, 515
Roohan Realty, 306
Saratoga County Chamber of Commerce, 584
Saratoga Economic Development Corporation, 584
Saratoga Gaming & Raceway, 346
Saratoga Springs
 Civil & Criminal Courts, 75
Saratoga Springs City SD, 664
Saratoga Springs, City of, 441
Saratogian (The), 599
Save The Lake (Political Action Committee), 562
Skidmore College, 631
State University Empire State College, 614
THOROPAC - Thoroughbred Breeders' PAC, 564
US Defense Department

 Saratoga Springs Naval Support Unit, 363
Watertown Empire Zone, 588

Saugerties
Saugerties CSD, 673
Saugerties, Town of, 441

Sauquoit
Sauquoit Valley CSD, 658

Sayville
PAC of Nassau Police Conference, 559
Sayville Chamber of Commerce (Greater Sayville), 584
Sayville UFSD, 670

Scarsdale
Edgemont UFSD, 676
Scarsdale UFSD, 677
Yonkers Council of School Administrators PAC, 568

Schaghticoke
Hoosic Valley CSD, 663
New York State Association of Agricultural Fairs Inc, 88

Schenectady
AAA Northway, 340
Capital District Regional Off-Track Betting Corporation, 114, 335
Caruso, David A, 469
Conservative Party of NYS, 165
Daily Gazette (The), 599
Daily Gazette Co, 599
Elections, State Board of
 Schenectady, 161
Ellis Hospital School of Nursing, 624
Englert Coffey & McHugh, 263
Environmental Conservation Department
 Region 4, 178
Lottery, Division of, 12, 325
 Adirondack-Capital District Region, 325
Mental Retardation & Developmental Disabilities, Office of
 Capital District Developmental Disabilities Services Office, 281
 Information Support Services, 281
Mid-America Baptist Theological Seminary Northeast Branch, 627
Mohonasen CSD, 665
New York State Association of Independent Schools, 154
New York State Conservative Party, 447
Niskayuna CSD, 665
NYS Association of Chiefs of Police Inc, 141, 299
NYS Bar Assn, Review Judicial Nominations Cmte, 263
Racing & Wagering Board, 15, 325, 335
Remove Intoxicated Drivers (RID-USA Inc), 142

Listings appear in alphabetical order by state, then city.

Geographic Index

Schalmont CSD, 665
Schenectady
   Civil Court, 75
   Criminal Court, 75
Schenectady City SD, 665
Schenectady County, 409
   Family Court, 67
   Supreme, County & Surrogate's Courts, 67
Schenectady County Chamber of Commerce, 584
Schenectady County Community College, 617
Schenectady County Industrial Developmen, 584
Schenectady, City of, 441
Self Advocacy Association of NYS, 243, 286
Special Olympics New York, Inc, 347
SUNY College & Career Counseling Center, 618
Transportation Department
   Region 1, 349
Unified Court System
   4th Judicial District (Judicial Department 3), 257
Union College, 632
US Department of Energy
   Knolls Atomic Power Laboratory- KAPL Inc, 171
WGNA (107.7 FM), 606
WRGB (6), 607

Schenevus
Schenevus CSD, 662

Schodack Landing
Shanahan Group, 522

Schoharie
Elections, State Board of
   Schoharie, 161
Schoharie County, 409
   Supreme, County, Family & Surrogate's Courts, 68
Schoharie County Chamber of Commerce, 584
Schoharie CSD, 665
Support Services Alliance Inc, 112, 251

Schroon Lake
Schroon Lake Area Chamber of Commerce, 584
Schroon Lake CSD, 647

Schuylerville
Schuylerville CSD, 664
US Department of Veterans Affairs
   Gerald B.H. Solomon Saratoga National Cemetery, 363

Scio
Scio CSD, 639

Scotia
Scotia-Glenville CSD, 665

Scottsville
Wheatland-Chili CSD, 653

Sea Cliff
North Shore CSD, 655

Seaford
Seaford Chamber of Commerce, 585
Seaford UFSD, 656

Selden
Faculty Assn of Suffolk Community College VOTE-COPE, 542
Suffolk County Community College, 617

Selkirk
Audubon Society of NYS Inc (The) / Audubon International, 187
New York's Tomorrow, 557
Ravena-Coeymans-Selkirk CSD, 638

Seneca Falls
National Women's Hall of Fame, 345
New York Chiropractic College, 628
New York Pork Producers Coop, 87
Seneca County Chamber of Commerce, 585
Seneca Falls CSD, 666
United Dairy Cooperative Services Inc, 89
US Department of the Interior
   Women's Rights National Historical Park, 340

Sharon Springs
Sharon Springs CSD, 665

Shelter Island
Shelter Island UFSD, 670

Sherburne
Sherburne-Earlville CSD, 642

Sherman
Sherman CSD, 642

Sherrill
Sherrill
   Civil & Criminal Courts, 75

Shoreham
Shoreham-Wading River CSD, 671

Shortsville
Manchester-Shortsville CSD, 660

Shrub Oak
Lakeland CSD, 676

Shushan
Dionondehowa Wildlife Sanctuary & School - Not For Profit, 188

Sidney
Sidney Chamber of Commerce, 585

Sidney CSD, 644

Silver Creek
Silver Creek CSD, 642

Sinclairville
Cassadaga Valley CSD, 641

Skaneateles
Skaneateles Chamber of Commerce, 585
Skaneateles CSD, 659

Slate Hill
Minisink Valley CSD, 661

Sleepy Hollow
Pocantico Hills CSD, 677
Tarrytown UFSD, 677

Slingerlands
Baldwin, Kristina, 461
Good Government NY, 543
Independence for Bethlehem, 546

Sloan
Cheektowaga-Sloan UFSD, 645

Smithtown
Guide Dog Foundation for the Blind Inc, 319
Schnell, William A & Associates Inc, 521
Smithtown Chamber of Commerce, 585
Smithtown CSD, 671
Smithtown, Town of, 441
Suffolk County, 410

Snyder
New York Professional Engineers, 555

Sodus
Sodus CSD, 675

Solvay
Solvay UFSD, 659

Somers
Somers CSD, 677
Somers Democratic Club, 563

Sonyea
Correctional Services Department
   Groveland Correctional Facility, 131
   Livingston Correctional Facility, 131

South Dayton
Pine Valley CSD (South Dayton), 642

South Glens Falls
South Glens Falls CSD, 665
UA Plumbers & Pipefitters LU 773
   Voluntary NYS PAC Fund, 566

South Kortright
South Kortright CSD, 644

South Otselic
Otselic Valley CSD, 642

Listings appear in alphabetical order by state, then city.

Geographic Index

South Plymouth
Correctional Services Department
Camp Pharsalia, 130

Southampton
Shinnecock Indian Nation, 210
Southampton Chamber of Commerce, 585
Southampton UFSD, 671
Southampton, Town of, 442
Tuckahoe Common SD, 671

Southold
North Fork Chamber of Commerce, 581
Southold UFSD, 671
Southold, Town of, 442

Sparkill
St Thomas Aquinas College, 632

Speculator
Adirondacks Speculator Region Chamber of Commerce, 569
Lake Pleasant CSD, 649

Spencer
Spencer-Van Etten CSD, 672

Spencerport
Associated New York State State Food Processors Inc, 83
Monroe 2-Orleans BOCES, 679
Motley, Duane R, 509
Spencerport CSD, 653
Suburban News & Hamlin Clarkson Herald, 599
Westside News Inc, 599

Spring Valley
East Ramapo CSD (Spring Valley), 664
Spring Valley, Village of, 442

Springfield Gardens
Build New York PAC, 536
US Justice Department
JFK/LGA, 138

Springville
Springville Area Chamber of Commerce, 586
Springville-Griffith Inst CSD, 646

St Bonaventure
St Bonaventure University, 631

St James
St James Chamber of Commerce, 586

St Johnsville
Oppenheim-Ephratah CSD, 648
St Johnsville CSD, 653

St Regis Falls
St Regis Falls CSD, 648

Staatsburg
Parks, Recreation & Historic Preservation, NYS Office of
Taconic Region, 334

Stamford
Otsego Northern Catskills BOCES (Otsego-Delaware-Schoharie-Greene), 680
Stamford CSD, 644

Stanley
Empire State Potato Growers Inc, 85

Star Lake
Clifton-Fine CSD, 666

Staten Island
Advance Publications Inc, 599
Building Industry Association of New York City, Inc, 536
Building Industry Association of NYC Inc, 107
Cappelli, Allen, 469
Civil Court, NYC
Richmond County, 59
College of Staten Island, 620
Connors & Connors, PC, 263
Correctional Services Department
Arthur Kill Correctional Facility, 130
Criminal Court, NYC
Richmond County, 60
Elections, State Board of
Richmond, 160
Family Court, NYC
Richmond County, 61
JY Trans PAC, 547
Levine, Laurence J, 498
Life of the Party, 548
Marine Corps League (MCL), Department of NY, 366
Mental Health, Office of
South Beach Psychiatric Center, 281
Mental Retardation & Developmental Disabilities, Office of
Institute for Basic Research in Developmental Disabilities, 282
Staten Island Developmental Disabilities Services Office, 282
Mid Island Democratic PAC (MIDPAC), 550
New York City Boroughs
Staten Island (Richmond County), 435
NYC Region 7, 657
NYS Bar Assn, Trial Lawyers Section, 263
NYSFRW Women Power PAC, 554
Richmond County
Supreme & Surrogate's Courts, 67
Richmond County (NYC Borough of Staten Island), 408
Staten Island Advance, 599
Staten Island Chamber of Commerce, 586

Staten Island Economic Development Corporation, 586
Staten Island Political Action Committee, 563
Staten Island Zoo, 347
US Department of the Interior
Gateway National Recreation Area, 339
Wagner College, 633

Stillwater
Darwak, Stephanie, 477
Stillwater CSD, 665
US Department of the Interior
Saratoga National Historical Park, 340

Stone Ridge
Ulster County Community College, 617

Stony Brook
Center for Advanced Tech-Medical Biotechnology
Center for Advanced Tech-Medical Biotechnology, 100
Environmental Conservation Department
Region 1, 178
New York Biotechnology Association (The), 110
NYS Foundation for Science, Technology & Innovation
Center for Advanced Tech-Medical Biotechnology, 148
Sensor CAT-Diagnostic Tools & Sensor Systems, 100, 147
Stony Brook University, SUNY, 613
SUNY at Stony Brook, 520
SUNY at Stony Brook, NY State Drinking Driver Program, 142
Three Village CSD, 671

Stormville
Correctional Services Department
Green Haven Correctional Facility, 130

Suffern
Preserve Ramapo, 560
Ramapo, Town of, 439
Rockland Community College, 617
Salvation Army School for Officer Training, 630
Suffern Chamber of Commerce, 586
Turner/Geneslaw Inc, 236

Summit
Correctional Services Department
Summit Shock Incarceration Correctional Facility, 131

Syosset
New York College of Health Professions, 628
Syosset CSD, 656

Syracuse
Agriculture & Markets Department

Listings appear in alphabetical order by state, then city.

Geographic Index

State Fair, 80
  Syracuse, 80
Alliance Bank, 93
Association of Presidents of Public Community Colleges, 152
Attorney Grievance Committee
  Judicial Dist 5, 255
Banking Department
  Upstate Office, 91
Berry, Sally, 462
Blitman & King LLP, 275
Bond Schoeneck & King PLLC, 241
Bristol-Myers Squibb Co, 221
Brower, Michael R, 465
Bryant & Stratton College-Syracuse Campus, 634
Business-Industry PAC of Central NY Inc, 536
Camillus, Town of, 416
Carpenters' Local 747 PAC, 536
Catholic Charities, 316
Central New York Business Journal, 601
Central New York Regional Market Authority, 102, 114
Central New York Regional Transportation Authority, 115, 350
Children & Family Services, Office of
  Syracuse Regional Office, 311
Clark, Frank A, 472
CNY Labor PAC, 536
Convention Centers & Visitors Bureaus
  Syracuse Convention & Vistors Bureau, 338
Cookfair Media Inc, 165
Crossett, Susan M, 477
Crouse Hospital School of Nursing, 624
Dairylea Cooperative Inc, 85
Education Department
  Central Regional Office, 146
  Syracuse District Office, 147
Elections, State Board of
  Onondaga, 160
Empire State Passengers Association, 357
Engineers Voluntary Political Action Fund, 541
Environmental Conservation Department
  Region 7, 178
Eric Mower & Associates, 108
Excelsior 2000, 542
Farmers' Market Federation of NY, 85
Finger Lakes Chapter NECA PAC Fund, 542
Gilberti Stinziano Heintz & Smith, PC, 486
Glacier Creek PAC, 543
Green & Seifter Attorneys, PLLC, 487
HBA of CNY Local Build PAC, 544
Health Department
  Central New York Regional Office, 215
Housing & Community Renewal, Division of
  Syracuse, 228

Human Rights, State Division of
  Syracuse, 238
I Love Good Government, 545
Iron Workers' Local 60 PAC, 547
Law Department
  Syracuse, 255
Le Moyne College, 626
Lottery, Division of
  Syracuse Office, 325
Lyncourt UFSD, 659
Manufacturers Assn of Central NY Inc, 504
Manufacturers Association of Central New York, 109
Mental Health, Office of
  Hutchings Psychiatric Center, 280
Military Order of the Purple Heart, 367
New York State Association of Ambulatory Surgery Centers, 226
New York State Radiologists PAC, 556
New York Water Environment Association Inc (NYWEA), 191
Niagara Mohawk - A National Grid Company, 175
NYS Bar Assn, Gender Equity Task Force Cmte, 241
NYS Bar Assn, Judicial Campaign Conduct Cmte, 266
NYS Foundation for Science, Technology & Innovation
  Center for Computer Applications & Software Engineering, 148
  Central New York Technology Development Organization, 148
Onondaga 2004, 558
Onondaga Community College, 617
Onondaga County, 405
  County Court, 66
  Supreme, Family & Surrogate's Courts, 66
Onondaga County Industrial Development Agency, 581
Onondaga, Town of, 437
Onondaga-Cortland-Madison BOCES, 679
Pinsky & Pinsky, PC, 515
Pinsky & Skandalis, 515
Plumbers & Steamfitters Local 267 PAC, 559
Pomeroy Appraisal Associates Inc, 305
Post-Standard (The), 600
ProLiteracy Worldwide, 155, 322
Real Property Services, Office of
  Syracuse (Central Region), 289, 302, 326
Rougeux, Elizabeth, 519
Rutherford, Clyde E, 520
Salvation Army, Empire State Division, 323
Service Station & Repair Shop Operators, Upstate NY Inc, 562
Simmons Institute of Funeral Service Inc, 637
Small Business Administration
  Syracuse, 104

SPOA For A Better University Neighborhood II, 562
State Department
  Syracuse, 200
State University of New York College of Environmental Science, 613
SUNY Upstate Medical, 520
SUNY Upstate Medical University, 612
Supreme Court, 266
Syracuse
  Civil & Criminal Courts, 75
Syracuse & Central NY, Metropolitan Development Association of, 586
Syracuse Chamber of Commerce (Greater Syracuse), 586
Syracuse City SD, 659
Syracuse Economic Development, 586
Syracuse Educational Opportunity Center, 618
Syracuse Industrial Development Agency, 586
Syracuse Newspapers Inc, 600
Syracuse University, 632
Syracuse University Press, 192
Syracuse University, Maxwell School of Citizenship & Public Affairs, 155, 192, 210, 294, 300, 323
Syracuse University, Office of Government & Community Relations, 155
Syracuse, City of, 442
Teamsters Local 317 PAC, 565
Transportation Department
  Region 3, 349
Unified Court System
  5th Judicial District (Judicial Department 4), 257
United Way of Central New York, 323
Unity Mutual Life Insurance Co, 251
Unity PAC, 567
Upstate Freshwater Institute, 192
US Commerce Department
  Upstate New York Office, 104
US Defense Department
  Hancock Field, 174th Fighter Wing, 362
US Department of Agriculture
  Farm Service Agency, New York State Office, 82
  Natural Resources Conservation Service, 184
  New York State Office, 82, 105, 171, 232, 303
US Department of Veterans Affairs
  Syracuse VA Medical Center & Clinics, 363
US Federal Courts
  Northern District, 259
US Justice Department
  Syracuse, 138, 139, 260, 261
Valley Democratic Club PAC, 567
WCNY (24), 609
Westhill CSD, 659

Listings appear in alphabetical order by state, then city.

Geographic Index

WNTQ (93.1 FM), WAQX (95.7 FM), 606
Workers' Compensation Board
  Syracuse, 248, 271
WSTM (3), 609
WSYT (68), 609
WTVH (5), 610
WYYY (94.5 FM), 606

Taberg
Town of Annsville Democratic Club, 566

Tannersville
Hunter-Tannersville CSD, 649

Tarrytown
Construction Industry Council - NYS PAC, 538
Historic Hudson Valley, 343
Housing Action Council Inc - Not For Profit, 234, 293
New York Roadway Improvement Coalition (NYRIC), 358
Pepe, Ross J, 514
Regeneron Pharmaceuticals Inc, 227
Riverkeeper Inc, 192
Riverkeeper, Inc, 518
Sleepy Hollow Chamber of Commerce, 585
US Labor Department
  Tarrytown Area Office, 219, 273

Thiells
Mental Retardation & Developmental Disabilities, Office of
  Hudson Valley Developmental Disabilities Services Office, 281

Thornwood
Mt Pleasant CSD, 676

Throgs Neck
State University of New York Maritime College, 615

Ticonderoga
Ticonderoga Area Chamber of Commerce, 587
Ticonderoga CSD, 647

Tioga Center
Tioga CSD, 672

Tonawanda
NRG New York PAC, 551
Political Action Committee Buffalo PBA, 560
Praxair PAC NY, 560
Tonawanda
  Civil & Criminal Courts, 75
Tonawanda (Town Of) Development Corporation, 587
Tonawanda City SD, 647

Troy
Brunswick CSD (Brittonkill), 663

Capital District Educational Opportunity Center, 618
Catholic School Administrators Association of NYS, 152
Commission on Economic Opportunity for the Greater Capital Region, 317
Community Bankers Assn of NY State, Government Relations Cmte, 96, 209
Elections, State Board of
  Rensselaer, 161
Health Department
  Capital District Regional Office, 215
  Center for Environmental Health, 179, 213
Hudson Valley Community College, 616
Journal Register Co, 600
Lansingburgh CSD, 663
Marx PAC, 550
Museum Association of New York, 153, 344
Norris, Kelly K, 512
Northeast Health Inc, 512
NYS Architects PAC, 552
NYS Bar Assn, Attorneys in Public Service Cmte, 299
NYS Dispute Resolution Association, 265
NYS Foundation for Science, Technology & Innovation
  Center for Automation Tech at Rensselaer Polytechnic Inst, 148
  Center for Automation Technologies at Rensselaer, 100
  Future Energy Systems CAT at Rensselaer Polytechnic Inst, 148
NYS Health Department, 299
NYS Theatre Institute, 154, 344
Pioneer Savings Bank, 96, 209
Record (The), 600
Rensselaer County, 408
  Family Court, 67
  Supreme, County & Surrogate's Courts, 67
Rensselaer County Regional Chamber of Commerce, 583
Rensselaer Polytechnic Inst, Ecological Economics, Values & P, 191
Rensselaer Polytechnic Institute, 155, 517, 630
Sage Colleges (The), 630
Samaritan Hospital School of Nursing, 630
Society of Professional Engineers Inc (NYS), 111
Tax Appeals, Division of, 16, 326
Troy
  Civil & Criminal Court, 75
Troy City Enlarged SD, 663
Troy, City of, 443
Unified Court System
  3rd Judicial District (Judicial Department 3), 257
US Department of the Interior

  Water Resources Division - New York State District Office, 185
USA Track & Field, Adirondack Association Inc, 347
WMHT (17) Public Broadcasting-NY Capitol Region, 607

Trumansburg
Parks, Recreation & Historic Preservation, NYS Office of
  Finger Lakes Region, 334
Trumansburg CSD, 673

Tuckahoe
Tuckahoe UFSD, 677

Tully
Ski Areas of New York Inc, 346
Tully CSD, 659

Tupper Lake
Mental Retardation & Developmental Disabilities, Office of
  Sunmount Developmental Disabilities Services Office, 282
Tupper Lake Chamber of Commerce, 587
Tupper Lake CSD, 648

Turin
South Lewis CSD, 651

Tuxedo Park
Tuxedo UFSD, 661

Union Springs
Union Springs CSD, 641

Uniondale
Farrell Fritz PC, 542
Farrell Fritz, PC, 189
Island Strategies, Inc, 493
Long Island Power Authority, 117, 170
New York Schools Insurance Reciprocal (NYSIR), 251
NYS Bar Assn, Environmental Law Section, 189
Uniondale UFSD, 656

Upton
US Department of Energy
  Brookhaven Group, 171
  Community Involvement/Public Affairs, 171
  Office of the Director, 171

Utica
Convention Centers & Visitors Bureaus
  Oneida County Convention & Visitors Bureau, 338
Education Department
  Utica District Office, 147
Elections, State Board of
  Oneida, 160
Gannett Co Inc, 600

Listings appear in alphabetical order by state, then city.

Geographic Index

Getnick, Livingston, Atkinson, Gigliotti & Priore LLP, 263
Labor Department
Central/Mohawk Valley, 270
Law Department
Utica, 255
Mental Health, Office of
Mohawk Valley Psychiatric Center, 280
Mohawk Valley Chamber of Commerce, 579
Mohawk Valley Chamber PAC, 551
Mohawk Valley Community College, 616
New York State BPW/PAC (NYSBPW/PAC), 556
NYS Bar Assn, Court Operations Cmte, 263
NYS Foundation for Science, Technology & Innovation
Mohawk Valley Applied Technology Corp, 148
Observer-Dispatch, 600
Oneida County, 405
Supreme & County Courts, 66
Surrogate's Court, 66
Resource Center for Independent Living (RCIL), 243, 322
St Elizabeth College of Nursing, 631
State Department
Utica, 200
State University Institute of Technology, 615
Transportation Department
Region 2, 349
Utica
Civil & Criminal Courts, 75
Utica City SD, 658
Utica College, 632
Utica Industrial Development Agency (City of), 587
Utica Mutual Insurance Co, 251
Utica School of Commerce, 637
Utica, City of, 443
WKTV (2), 610
Women's Business Training Center of New York State, 112
WOUR (96.9 FM), 607
Zogby International, 112, 167

Valatie
Ichabod Crane CSD, 643

Valhalla
Mount Pleasant, Town of, 425
Mt Pleasant-Blythedale UFSD, 676
New York Medical College, 225, 628
New York Medical College, Department of Community & Preventive, 225
New York Medical College, Department of Medicine, 225
New York Medical College, School of Public Health, 225
Valhalla UFSD, 677
Westchester Community College, 617

Valley Cottage
SCS Engineers PC, 192

Valley Stream
Business Informatics Center, 634
Long Island Prosperity, 549
Valley Stream 13 UFSD, 656
Valley Stream 24 UFSD, 656
Valley Stream 30 UFSD, 656
Valley Stream Central HS District, 656
Valley Stream Chamber of Commerce, 587
Valley Stream, Village of, 443

Van Hornesville
Van Hornesville-Owen D Young CSD, 650

Vernon
Oneida Indian Nation, 209

Vernon Downs
Vernon Downs/Gaming-Racing-Entertainment, 347

Verona
Madison-Oneida BOCES, 679
Vernon-Verona-Sherrill CSD, 658

Verona Beach
Republican 100,000 Club of Oneida County, 561

Versailles
Cayuga Nation, 207

Vestal
Elmira Business Institute-Vestal, 635
NYS Bowling Proprietors Assn PAC, 552
PAC of the Assoc Building Contractors of the Triple Cities, Inc, 559
Southern Tier HB & REM Build-PAC, 563
Vestal CSD, 640
Vestal, Town of, 443
WICZ (40), 607
WMRV (105.7), 603

Victor
Victor Chamber of Commerce, 587
Victor CSD, 660

Voorheesville
Albany County Rural Housing Alliance Inc, 233
NYS Nursery/Landscape Association, 87
Voorheesville CSD, 638

Waddington
Waddington Chamber of Commerce, 587

Wading River
Little Flower UFSD, 669

Wainscott
Wainscott Common SD, 671

Wallkill
Correctional Services Department
Shawangunk Correctional Facility, 131
Wallkill Correctional Facility, 131
Wallkill CSD, 673

Walton
Walton CSD, 644

Wampsville
Elections, State Board of
Madison, 159
Madison County, 403
Supreme, County, Family & Surrogate's Courts, 64

Wantagh
Parola PAC for Good Government, 559
Wantagh Chamber of Commerce, 588
Wantagh GOP Victory Committee, 567
Wantagh Republican Committeesmens Council, 567
Wantagh UFSD, 656

Wantaghe
Levittown West Republican Golf, 548

Wappinger Falls
Wappinger, Town of, 444

Wappingers Falls
Hudson Valley Business Journal, 601
Southern Dutchess Chamber of Commerce (Greater Southern Dutchess), 585
Wappingers CSD, 645

Wards Island
Mental Health, Office of
Kirby Forensic Psychiatric Center, 280
Manhattan Psychiatric Center, 280

Warrensburg
Warrensburg Chamber of Commerce, 588
Warrensburg CSD, 674

Warsaw
Elections, State Board of
Wyoming, 163
Warsaw Chamber of Commerce (Greater Warsaw), 588
Warsaw CSD, 678
Wyoming County, 413
Supreme, County, Family & Surrogate's Courts, 69

Warwick
Correctional Services Department
Mid-Orange Correctional Facility, 131
Latino Democratic Committee of Orange County, 548
NYS Plumbing, Heating & Cooling Contractors PAC, 553
Warwick Valley Chamber of Commerce, 588

Geographic Index

Warwick Valley CSD, 661
Warwick, Town of, 444

Washingtonville
Blooming Grove Chamber of Commerce, 570
Washingtonville CSD, 661

Wassaic
Mental Retardation & Developmental Disabilities, Office of
  Taconic Developmental Disabilities Services Office, 282

Waterford
Parks, Recreation & Historic Preservation, NYS Office of
  Field Services, 180, 334
  Historic Sites Bureau, 180, 334
Waterford-Halfmoon UFSD, 665

Waterloo
Elections, State Board of
  Seneca, 161
Finger Lakes PAC, 542
Seneca County, 409
  Supreme, County, Family & Surrogate's Courts, 68
Seneca County Industrial Development Agency, 585
Waterloo CSD, 666

Watertown
Correctional Services Department
  Watertown Correctional Facility, 131
Development Authority of the North Country, 102, 115, 230, 573
Elections, State Board of
  Jefferson, 159
Environmental Conservation Department
  Region 6, 178
Jefferson Community College, 616
Jefferson County, 402
  County, Family & Surrogate's Courts, 64
  Supreme Court, 64
Jefferson-Lewis-Hamilton-Herkimer-Oneida BOCES, 679
Johnson Newspaper Corp, 600
Law Department
  Watertown, 255
New York State Tug Hill Commission, 125, 182
State Department
  Watertown, 200
Transportation Department
  Region 7, 349
Watertown
  Civil & Criminal Courts, 75
Watertown City SD, 651
Watertown Daily Times, 600
Watertown, City of, 444
Watertown-North Country Chamber of Commerce (Greater Watertown), 588

WFRY (97.5 FM), 607
WWNY (7), 610
WWTI (50), 610

Waterville
Waterville CSD, 658

Watervliet
Maplewood-Colonie Common SD, 638
US Defense Department
  Watervliet Arsenal, 362
Watervliet
  Civil & Criminal Courts, 75
Watervliet City SD, 638

Watkins Glen
Elections, State Board of
  Schuyler, 161
Farm Sanctuary, 85
Schuyler County, 409
  Supreme, County, Family & Surrogate's Courts, 68
Schuyler County Chamber of Commerce, 585
Schuyler County Industrial Development Agency, 585
Schuyler County Partnership for Economic Development, 585
Watkins Glen CSD, 666

Watkins Glens
New York State Maple Producers Association Inc, 88

Waverly
Waverly CSD, 672

Wayland
Wayland-Cohocton CSD, 667

Webster
Webster Chamber of Commerce, 588
Webster CSD, 653
Webster, Town of, 444

Weedsport
Weedsport CSD, 641

Wells
Wells CSD, 649

Wellsville
Liberty Group Publishing, 600
Wellsville Area Chamber of Commerce, 588
Wellsville CSD, 639
Wellsville Daily Reporter/Spectator, 600

West Babylon
Federation of Organizations Inc, 284
Kaplan, Randy L, 494
West Babylon UFSD, 671

West Brentwood
Mental Health, Office of
  Pilgrim Psychiatric Center, 280

West Chazy
Beekmantown CSD, 643

West Coxsackie
Correctional Services Department
  Coxsackie Correctional Facility, 130

West Haverstraw
Health Department
  Helen Hayes Hospital, 214
Mirant New York Inc, 508

West Hempstead
West Hempstead UFSD, 656

West Islip
Dunne, Richard C, 480
ESMBA PAC MOR, 540
West Islip UFSD, 671

West Nyack
Rockland BOCES, 680

West Park
West Park UFSD, 673

West Point
US Treasury Department
  US Mint, 93, 329

West Seneca
Erie 1 BOCES, 679
Mental Health, Office of
  Western New York Children's Psychiatric Center, 281
Mental Retardation & Developmental Disabilities, Office of
  Western New York Developmental Disabilities Services Office, 282
Roofers' Pol Education & Legislative Fund of NY, 562
West Seneca Chamber of Commerce, 588
West Seneca CSD, 647
West Seneca, Town of, 445

West Valley
West Valley CSD, 640

West Winfield
Mount Markham CSD, 650

Westbury
Clarke, Donald, 472
Community Bankers Assn of NY State, Mortgages & Real Estate Cmte, 96, 305
East Meadow UFSD, 654
Exxon Mobil Corporation, 173
Fisher Development Strategies, 483
Lieberman, Mark L, 499
Nassau County
  Family Court, 65
New York Community Bank, 96, 305

Listings appear in alphabetical order by state, then city.

927

Geographic Index

New York State School Music Association (NYSSMA), 154, 346
North Hempstead Century Club, 557
US Labor Department
Long Island District Office, 273
US Railroad Retirement Board
Westbury, 274
US Treasury Department
TEGE Area Counsel's Office, 329

Westfield
Westfield CSD, 642
Westfield/Barcelona Chamber of Commerce, 589

Westhampton Beach
US Defense Department
Francis S Gabreski Airport, 106th Rescue Wing, 362
US Department of Agriculture
Westhampton Beach Work Station, 82
Westhampton Beach UFSD, 671
Westhampton Chamber of Commerce (Greater Westhampton), 589

Westmoreland
New York Beef Industry Council Inc, 87
Westmoreland CSD, 658

Westport
Westport CSD, 647

White Plains
Attorney Grievance Committee
Judicial Dist 9, 255
Berkeley College, Westchester Campus, 634
Center for Judicial Accountability Inc, 262
College of Westchester (The), 635
Convention Centers & Visitors Bureaus
Westchester County Office of Tourism, 338
Court of Claims, 263
Education Department
White Plains District Office, 147
Elections, State Board of
Westchester, 163
Entergy Nuclear Northeast, 173
Entergy Nuclear Operations, Inc, 481
Fahey, William C, 482
Friedman, Michael B, 484
Golden Apple Business Action Committee, PAC, 543
HIC PAC, 544
Institute for Socio-Economic Studies, 320
Insurance Fund (NYS)
White Plains, 246, 269
Journal News (The)/Gannett Co Inc, 592
Labor Department
Hudson Valley, 270
Law Department
Westchester, 255
Legal Services of the Hudson Valley, 264, 498
Littman Krooks LLP, 264
Log Cabin Republicans Hudson Valley PAC, 549
March of Dimes Birth Defects Foundation, 320
Marine Corps League, 366
New York Power Authority, 121, 170
NYS Bar Assn, Elder Law Section, 264
NYS Bar Assn, Judicial Section, 263
NYS Bar Assn, Legal Aid Cmte/Funding for Civil Legal Svcs Cmte, 264
Pace University, School of Law Center for Environmental Legal S, 191
Pace University, School of Law, John Jay Legal Services Inc, 141, 266
Peckham Industries Inc PAC, 559
Review Press, 592
Rubino, Cynthia A, 519
Strategic Services, Inc, 524
Unified Court System
9th Judicial District (Judicial Department 2), 257
US Commerce Department
Westchester US Export Assistance Center, 105
US Justice Department
White Plains, 138, 260
US Transportation Department
National Highway Traffic Safety Administration, Reg II-NY, 356
Westchester Black Womens' Political Caucas, 568
Westchester Coalition for Legal Abortion PAC, 568
Westchester County, 413
Supreme, County & Family Courts, 69
Surrogate's Court, 69
Westchester County Association Inc (The), 588
Westchester County Chamber of Commerce, 588
Westchester County Conservative Party PAC, 568
Westchester County Industrial Development Agency, 589
Westchester County Womens Republican Club, 568
White Plains
Civil & Criminal Courts, 75
White Plains City SD, 677
White Plains, City of, 445
WRCC 21st Century Fund, 567

Whitehall
Whitehall CSD, 674

Whitestone
Greater NY Auto Dealers' Assn Inc, 486, 544

Whitesville
Whitesville CSD, 639

Whitney Point
Whitney Point CSD, 640

Willard
Correctional Services Department
Willard Drug Treatment Center, 132

Williamson
Williamson CSD, 675

Williamsville
Action Fund for Good Government, 533
Amherst Chamber of Commerce, 569
Amherst, Town of, 414
Empire State Leadership PAC, 541
Military Officers Association of America (MOAA), NYS Council, 367
National Fuel Gas New York PAC, 554
Real Independence Party Club-Amherst Branch, 561

Williston Park
Willistons Chamber of Commerce, 589

Willsboro
Willsboro CSD, 647

Wilmington
Whiteface Mountain Regional Visitor's Bureau, 589

Wilson
Agricultural Affiliates, 83
Wilson CSD, 658

Wilton
Correctional Services Department
Mt McGregor Correctional Facility, 131

Windham
Mountaintop Democratic Club, 551
Windham-Ashland-Jewett CSD, 649

Windsor
Windsor CSD, 640

Wolcott
North Rose-Wolcott CSD, 675

Woodbourne
Correctional Services Department
Woodbourne Correctional Facility, 132

Woodmere
Hewlett-Woodmere UFSD, 654
Inwood-North Lawrence Republican Committee, 547

Woodside
Sports & Arts in Schools Foundation, 155, 347

Geographic Index

Woodstock
Woodstock Chamber of Commerce & Arts, 589

Worcester
Worcester CSD, 662

Wyandanch
Wyandanch UFSD, 671

Wynantskill
North Greenbush IDA, 581
Wynantskill UFSD, 663

Wyoming
Wyoming CSD, 678

Yaphank
Elections, State Board of
Suffolk, 162
Probation Political Action Committee (PROPAC), 560

Yonkers
BRAB PAC, INC, 535
Children & Family Services, Office of
Yonkers Regional Office, 311
Cochran School of Nursing, 623
Consumers Union, 84, 108
Educational Opportunity Center of Westchester, 618
EVCI Career Colleges Holding Corp, 108
McDevitt, William L, 505
Metropolitan Package Store, Inc Assoc PAF, 550
New York Hygiene PAC, 555
PAC Police Assoc City of Yonkers, 559
SEIU Local 704 PAC, 562
Soft Drink & Brewery Workers' PAC, 563
St Joseph's Seminary Institute of Religious Studies, 631
Tempo 802, 565
Yonkers
Civil & Criminal Courts, 76
Yonkers Chamber of Commerce, 589
Yonkers City SD, 678
Yonkers Economic Development/Yonkers Industrial Develo, 589
Yonkers Raceway, 347
Yonkers, City of, 445

Yorkshire
Pioneer CSD, 640

Yorktown
Gold Star Wives of America Inc, 366

Yorktown Heights
Education Department
Hudson Valley Regional Office, 147
New Yorktown Chamber of Commerce (The), 580
Pepsi-Cola Bottlers' PAC, 559
Putnam-Northern Westchester BOCES, 680

Yorktown CSD, 678
Yorktown, Town of, 445

Yorkville
Whitesboro CSD, 658

Youngstown
Lewiston-Porter CSD, 657

North Carolina

Charlotte
Royal Indemnity Comapny Voluntary PAC (Royal & Sun Alliance PAC), 562
Wachovia New York Employees Good Government Fund, 567

Greensboro
Shannon, Michael J, 522

Raleigh
US Department of Agriculture
Plant Protection Quarantine (PPQ) Programs-Eastern Region, 81

Ohio

Cincinnati
Ohio River Valley Water Sanitation Commission, 126, 183
US Defense Department
Great Lakes & Ohio River Division (Western NYS), 184

Cleveland
Keycorp & Subsidiaries, 494
Keycorp Advocates Fund-NY, 547
United Transportation Union Political Action Committee (UTU PAC), 567

Columbus
Nationwide NY Political Participation Fund, 554
Nisource Inc PAC-NY, 557

Oklahoma

Oklahoma City
Interstate Oil & Gas Compact Commission, 116, 169, 182

Pennsylvania

Chadds Ford
Holloway, Jr, Floyd, 491

Harrisburg
National Fuel Gas, 175

Peters, Jeffrey R, 514

King of Prussia
Nuclear Regulatory Commission
REGION I (includes New York State), 171

Newton Square
US Department of Agriculture
Forest Service-Northern Research Station, 184

Newtown Square
US Department of Agriculture
Forest Service-Northeastern Area State & Private Forestry, 184

Philadelphia
ARAMARK PAC, 534
Bell Atlantic Corporation PAC, 535
Duane Morris LLP Government Committee NY Find, 540
Fleet Reserve Association (FRA), NE Region (NJ, NY, PA), 366
Ninth Decade Fund, 557
US Commerce Department
Philadelphia Region (includes New York), 104
US Department of the Interior
National Park Service-Northeast Region, 185, 339
US Justice Department
Audit Division, 260
US Labor Department
Wage-Hour Division (WHD)-Northeast Regional Office, 273
US Office of Personnel Management
PHILADELPHIA SERVICE CENTER (serving New York), 274, 298
Verizon Communications Good Government Club New York PAC, 567

Pittsburgh
United Steelworkers of America, 567

Scranton
New York Good Hearing Political Education Committee, 555

Rhode Island

Cranston
Friedell, Andrew, 484

Tennessee

Memphis
Federal Express New York State Political Action Committee, 542

Listings appear in alphabetical order by state, then city.

Geographic Index

Nashville
Asurion Employees PAC, 534
US Department of Health & Human Services
Indian Health Services-Area Office, 218, 315

Texas

Austin
Advanced Micro Devices Inc, 455

Houston
National Good Government Fund, 554

San Antonio
Air Force Women Officers Associated (AFWOA), 365

United Kingdom

London
Banking Department
London Office, 90

Vermont

Burlington
Democracy for America-New York, 539

Rutland
US Department of Agriculture
Green Mountain & Finger Lakes, 184

Virginia

Alexandria
Fleet Reserve Association (FRA), 366
Military Officers Association of America, 367
National Military Family Association (NMFA), 367
Naval Reserve Association (NRA), 367
New York Association of Temporary Services State PAC, 554

Arlington
Air Force Association (AFA), 365
Association of the US Army (AUSA), 365
Generic Pharmaceutical Association, 223
Military Chaplains Association of the USA (MCA), 367
Navy League of the US (NLUS), 367

Fairfax
NRA Political Victory Fund, 551

Falls Church
Naval Enlisted Reserve Association (NERA), 367

Merrifield
Marine Corps League (MCL), 366

Montclair
NATPAC 2000, 551

Reston
Sprint Nextel Corporation PAC, 563

Springfield
Military Order of the Purple Heart (MOPH), 367
US Department of the Interior
Eastern States Office (includes New York State), 185

Vienna
Feld Entertainment, 483

Wiiliamsburg
BP America Inc, 461

Listings appear in alphabetical order by state, then city.

World Wide Web (URL) Index

1170 PEC	www.thecityofrochester.org
1199 SEIU United Healthcare Workers East	www.1199seiuonline.org
1199/SEIU & GNYHA Healthcare Education Project	www.healtheducationproject.org
21st Century Democrats	www.21stcenturydems.org
369th Veterans Association Inc	www.home.earthlink.net/~natlvets/
3rd Judicial Dept	www.courts.state.ny.us/ad3/lg
3rd Judicial Dept, Judicial Dist 3, 4, 6	www.courts.state.ny.us/ad3
4th Judicial Dept	www.courts.state.ny.us/ad4/
4th Judicial Dept, Dist 5, 7, 8	www.courts.state.ny.us/ad4
AAA Northway	www.aaanorthway.com
AAA Western and Central NY	www.aaa.com
AARP	www.aarp.org
Abbott UFSD	www.abbottufsd.org
ABC News (New York Bureau)	www.abc.com
Abilities Inc, National Center for Disability Services	www.abilitiesinc.org
ABO Build PAC Inc	www.abogny.com
Academy of Political Science	www.psqonline.org
Academy of Trial Lawyers PAC	www.medlaw1.com
Action for a Better Community Inc	www.abcinfo.org
Adelphi NY Statewide Breast Cancer Hotline & Support Program	www.adelphi.edu/nysbreastcancer
Adelphi University	www.adelphi.edu
Adirondack Community College	www.sunyacc.edu
Adirondack Council Inc (The)	www.adirondackcouncil.org
Adirondack CSD	www.adirondackcsd.org
Adirondack Daily Enterprise	www.adirondackguide.com
Adirondack Economic Development Corporation	www.aedconline.com
Adirondack Lakes Center for the Arts	www.adk-arts.org
Adirondack Mountain Club Inc	www.adk.org
Adirondack Park Agency	www.apa.state.ny.us
Adirondack Publishing Co Inc	www.adirondackguide.com
Adirondack Regional Chambers of Commerce	www.adirondackchamber.org
Adirondack/Pine Hill/NY Trailways	www.trailwaysny.com
Adirondacks Speculator Region Chamber of Commerce	www.adrkmts.com
Administration	www.senate.state.ny.us
Administration for Children & Families	www.acf.hhs.gov
Administration on Aging	www.aoa.gov
Advance Publications Inc	www.silive.com
Advocates for Children of New York Inc	www.advocatesforchildren.org; www.insideschools.org
AeA New York Council	www.aeanet.org
AFGI PAC	www.mackinco.com
Africa-America Institute (The)	www.aaionline.org
African American Chamber of Commerce of Westchester & Rockland Counties	www.africanamericanchamberofcommercenys.org
AFSCME, New York	www.afscme.org
After-School Corporation (The)	www.tascorp.org
Afton CSD	www.afton.stier.org
Agency for Toxic Substances & Disease Registry-EPA Region 2	www.atsdr.cdc.gov
Agenda for Children Tomorrow	www.actnyc.org
Aging, Dept for the, NYC	www.nyc.gov/aging
Aging, Office for the	www.aging.state.ny.us
Aging, Special Committee on	www.aging.senate.gov
Agostine Jr, Joseph A	www.npcnys.org
Agriculture	http://agriculture.house.gov

See Organization Index for page numbers.

World Wide Web (URL) Index

Agriculture & Markets Department	www.agmkt.state.ny.us
Agriculture & NYS Horse Breeding Development Fund	www.nysirestakes.com
Agriculture, Nutrition & Forestry	www.agriculture.senate.gov
AIDS Coalition (NY)	www.nyaidscoalition.org
AIDS Council of Northeastern New York	www.aidscouncil.org
AIM Services Inc	www.aimservicesinc.org
Air Force Association (AFA)	www.afa.org
Air Force Sergeants Association (AFSA), Division 1	www.afsahq.org
Air Force Women Officers Associated (AFWOA)	www.afwoa.org
Akron CSD	www.akronschools.org
Albany	www.albany.fbi.gov
Albany City SD	www.albanyschools.org
Albany College of Pharmacy	www.acp.edu
Albany County	www.albanycounty.com
Albany County Airport Authority	www.albanyairport.com
Albany County Convention & Visitors Bureau	www.albany.org
Albany County Industrial Development Agency	www.albanycounty.com/IDA
Albany County Rural Housing Alliance Inc	www.acrha.org
Albany Housing Coalition Inc	www.ahcvets.org
Albany Industrial Development Agency (City of)	www.albanyny.org
Albany Law School	www.albanylaw.edu
Albany Law School, Government Law Center	www.als.edu
Albany Medical College	www.amc.edu/Academic/AboutCollege/index.html
Albany Port District Commission	www.portofalbany.com
Albany, City of	www.albanyny.org
Albany-Colonie Regional Chamber of Commerce	www.ac-chamber.org
Albion CSD	www.albionk12.org
Alcoholic Beverage Control, Division of (State Liquor Authority)	www.abc.state.ny.us
Alcoholism & Substance Abuse Services, Office of	www.oasas.state.ny.us
Alden CSD	aldenschools.org
Alexander CSD	www.alexandercsd.org
Alexandria Bay Chamber of Commerce	www.alexbay.org
Alexandria CSD	www.alexandriacentral.org
Alfred State College of Technology	www.alfredstate.edu
Alfred University	www.alfred.edu
Alfred-Almond CSD	www.aacs.org
Allegany - Limestone CSD	www.alli.wnyric.org
Allegany County	www.alleganyco.com
Allegany County Office of Development	www.alleganyco.com
Alliance Bank	www.alliancebankna.com
Alliance for the Arts	www.allianceforarts.org
Alliance of NYS Arts Organizations	www.theallianceenys.org
Alliance of Resident Theatres/New York (ART/New York)	www.offbroadwayonline.com
ALSTOM Transportation Inc	www.transport.alstom.com
Altria Corporate Services	www.altria.com
Alzheimer's Association, Northeastern NY	www.alzneny.org
AMAC, Association for Metroarea Autistic Children	www.amac.org
Amagansett UFSD	www.amagansettschool.org
AMDeC Foundation	www.amdec.org
Amdursky Pelky Fennell & Wallen	www.apfwlaw.com
Amerada Hess Corporation	www.hess.com
American Academy McAllister Institute of Funeral Service	www.funeraleducation.org
American Academy of Dramatic Arts	www.aada.org
American Cancer Society-Eastern Division	www.cancer.org
American Chemistry/American Plastics Council	www.americanchemistry.com
American College of Nurse-Midwives, NYC Chapter	www.nysmidwives.org; www.nyc.org

See Organization Index for page numbers.

World Wide Web (URL) Index

American College of Ob & Gyn, District II	www.acog.org/goto/nys
American College of Obstetricians & Gynecologists/NYS	www.acogny.org
American College of Physicians, New York Chapter	www.acponline.org/chapters/ny
American Council of Engineering Companies of NY (ACEC New York)	www.acecny.org
American Express Company	www.americanexpress.com
American Farmland Trust, Northeast Regional Office	www.farmland.org
American Federation of Musicians, Local 802	www.local802afm.org
American Federation of Teachers	www.aft.org
American Fertility Association	www.theafa.org
American Heart Assn/American Stroke Assn	www.americanheart.org; www.strokeassociation.org
American Heart Association Northeast Affiliate	www.americanheart.org
American Institute of Architects (AIA) New York State Inc	www.aianys.org
American Insurance Assn	www.aiadc.org
American Insurance Assn New York PAC	www.aiadc.org
American International Group Inc	www.aig.com
American Jewish Committee	www.ajc.org
American Lawyer Media Inc	www.law.com
American Legion, Department of New York	www.ny.legion.org
American Liver Foundation, Western NY Chapter	www.liverfoundation.org
American Lung Association of NYS Inc	www.alanys.org
American Management Association International	www.amanet.org
American Metal Market	www.amm.com
American Military Retirees Association Inc	www.amra1973.org
American Museum of Natural History	www.amnh.org
American Resort Dev/Assn Resort Owners' Coalition PAC	www.arda.org
American Society for the Prevention of Cruelty to Animals (ASPCA)	www.aspca.org
Amherst Chamber of Commerce	www.amherst.org
Amherst CSD	www.amherstschools.org
Amherst Industrial Development Agency (Town of)	www.amherstida.com
Amherst, Town of	www.amherst.ny.us
Amityville UFSD	www.amityvilleschools.org
Ammann & Whitney	www.ammann-whitney.com
Amnesty International USA	www.amnestyusa.org
Amsterdam Industrial Development Agency	www.amsterdamedz.com
Andover CSD	www.andovercsd.org
Animal Plant Health Inspection Service	www.aphis.usda.gov
Antalek & Moore Insurance Agency	www.antalek-moore.com
Anti-Defamation League	www.adl.org
Aon Services Corporation	www.aon.com
Apple Assn Inc (NY)	www.nyapplecountry.com
Apple Banking for Savings	www.applebank.com
Appraisal Education Network School & Merrell Institute	www.merrellinstitute.com
Appropriations	www.appropriations.senate.gov
Arcade Area Chamber of Commerce	www.arcadechamber.org
Ardsley UFSD	www.ardsleyschools.k12.ny.us
Argyle CSD	www.argylecsd.org
Arlington CSD	www.arlingtonschools.org
Armed Services	www.armed-services.senate.gov
Army Corps of Engineers	www.usace.army.mil
Art & Science Collaborations Inc	www.asci.org
Art Commission, NYC	www.nyc.gov/artcommission
Art Instiue of New York City (The)	www.artinstitutes.edu/newyork/
ArtsConnection Inc (The)	www.artsconnection.org
ASA Institute of Business & Computer Technology	www.asa-institute.com
Asian American Federation of New York	www.aafny.org
Asian American Legal Defense and Education Fund	www.aaldef.org

See Organization Index for page numbers.

World Wide Web (URL) Index

Asian Americans for Equality	www.aafe.org
ASPIRA of New York Inc	www.nyaspira.org
Assn of Community & Residential Agencies (NYS)	www.nysacra.org
Assn of Counties & Its Affiliated Organizations (NYS)	www.nysac.org
Assn of New York City Concrete Producers Inc State PAC	www.grecoreadymix.com
Assn of School Business Officials (NYS)	www.nysasbo.org
Associated Builders & Contractors, Construction Training Center of NYS	www.abc.org/newyork
Associated Builders & Contractors, Empire State Chapter	www.abcnys.org
Associated General Contractors of America, NYS Chapter	www.agcnys.org
Associated Licensed Detectives of New York State	www.aldonys.org
Associated Medical Schools of New York	www.amsny.org
Associated New York State State Food Processors Inc	www.nyfoodprocessors.org
Associated Press (Albany/Upstate Bureau)	www.ap.org
Associated Press (New York/Metro Bureau)	www.ap.org
Associated Risk Managers of New York Inc	www.armnortheast.com
Association Development Group Inc	www.adgcommunications.com
Association for a Better New York	www.abny.org
Association for Addiction Professionals of New York	www.aapnycounselor.com
Association for Community Living	www.aclnys.org
Association for Eating Disorders - Capital Region	www.craed.org
Association for Neighborhood & Housing Development	www.anhd.org
Association for the Help of Retarded Children/AHRC	www.ahrcnyc.org
Association of Fire Districts of the State of NY Inc	www.firedistnys.com
Association of Government Accountants, NY Capital Chapter	www.aganycap.org
Association of Graphic Communications	www.agcomm.org
Association of Independent Video & Filmmakers (AIVF), (The)	www.aivf.org
Association of New York State Young Republicans Inc	www.nyyrc.com
Association of Proprietary Colleges	www.apc-colleges.org
Association of the Bar of the City of New York	www.nycbar.org
Association of the US Army (AUSA)	www.ausa.org
Association of Towns of the State of New York	www.nytowns.org
Astoria Federal Savings & Loan	www.astoriafederal.com
AT&T Corporation	www.att.com
Atlantic States Marine Fisheries Commission	www.asmfc.org
ATPAM COPE State Fund	www.atpam.com
Attica CSD	www.atticacs.k12.ny.us
Auburn Publishers Inc	www.auburnpub.com
Auburn, City of	auburnny.virtualtownhall.net
Audubon New York	ny.audubon.org
Audubon Society of NYS Inc (The) / Audubon International	www.auduboninternational.org
Ausable Valley CSD	avcs.org
Automobile Club of New York	www.aaany.com
Automobile Dealers Assn (NYS)	www.nysada.com
Averill Park CSD	www.averillpark.k12.ny.us
Avon CSD	www.avoncsd.org
Babylon Industrial Development Agency	www.babylonida.org
Babylon UFSD	www.babylon.k12.ny.us
Babylon, Town of	www.townofbabylon.com
BAC Local 2 PAC	www.bac2.org
Bainbridge-Guilford CSD	www.bgcsd.org
Baldwin Chamber of Commerce	www.baldwin.org
Baldwin UFSD	www.baldwin.k12.ny.us
Baldwinsville Chamber of Commerce (Greater Baldwinsville)	www.baldwinsvillechamber.com
Baldwinsville CSD	www.bville.org
Ballston Spa CSD	www.bscsd.org
Bank of Akron	www.bankofakron.com

See Organization Index for page numbers.

World Wide Web (URL) Index

Bank of America NY PAC	www.bankofamerica.com
Bank Street College of Education/Graduate School	www.bankstreet.edu
Banking Department	www.banking.state.ny.us
Banking, Housing & Urban Affairs	www.banking.senate.gov
Bard College	www.bard.edu
Barnard College	www.barnard.edu
Barnes, Richard E	www.nyscatholic.org
Barnett, Claire L	www.healthyschools.org
Batavia City SD	www.bataviacsd.org
Bath Area Chamber of Commerce (Greater Bath Area)	www.bathnychamber.com
Battery Park City Authority (Hugh L Carey)	www.batteryparkcity.org
Bausch & Lomb Inc	www.bausch.com
Bay Shore UFSD	www.bayshore.k12.ny.us
Bayport-Blue Point UFSD	www.b-bp.k12.ny.us
Bayshore Chamber of Commerce	www.bayshorecommerce.com
Beacon City SD	www.beaconcityk12.org
Bear Stearns & Co Inc	www.bearstearns.com
Beaver River CSD	www.brcsd.org
Bedford CSD	www.bedford.k12.ny.us
Beekmantown CSD	www.bcsdk12.org
Belfast CSD	www.belfast.wnyric.org
Belleville Henderson CSD	www.bhpanthers.org
Bellmore UFSD	www.bellmore.k12.ny.us
Bellmore-Merrick Central HS District	www.bellmore-merrick.k12.ny.us
Bellmores Chamber of Commerce	www.bellmorechamber.com
Bemus Point CSD	www.mghs.org
Bergin, Robert J	www.rge.com
Berkeley College, New York City Campus	www.berkeleycollege.edu
Berkeley College, Westchester Campus	www.berkeleycollege.edu
Berkley Center for Entrepreneurial Studies NYU, Stern School of Business	http://pages.stern.nyu.edu/~wbaumol
Berkshire Farm Center & Services for Youth	www.berkshirefarm.org
Berlin CSD	www.berlincentral.org
Bernard M Baruch College	www.baruch.cuny.edu
Berne-Knox-Westerlo CSD	www.bkwcsd.k12.ny.us
Bethlehem Chamber of Commerce	www.bethlehemchamber.com
Bethlehem CSD	bcsd.k12.ny.us
Bethlehem Industrial Development Agency (Town of)	www.bethlehemida.com
Bethlehem, Town of	www.townofbethlehem.org
Bethpage UFSD	wwwbethpagecommunity.com/Schools
Better Business Bureau of Metropolitan New York	www.newyork.bbb.org
Big Brothers Big Sisters of NYC	www.bigsnyc.org
Binghamton Chamber of Commerce (Greater Binghamton)	www.binghamtonchamber.com
Binghamton City SD	www.binghamtonschools.org
Binghamton University, State University of New York	www.binghamton.edu
Binghamton, City of	www.cityofbinghamton.com
Birds Eye Foods Inc	www.birdseyefoods.com
Black Lake Chamber of Commerce	www.blacklakeny.com
Black Veterans for Social Justice Inc	www.bvsj.org
Blind Brook-Rye UFSD	www.blindbrook.org
Blinded Veterans Association New York Inc	www.bva.org
Blitman & King LLP	www.bklawyers.com
Bloomberg Television	www.bloomberg.com/tv
Bloomfield CSD	www.bloomfieldcsd.org
BNA (formerly Bureau of National Affairs)	www.bna.com
Board of Jewish Education of Greater New York	www.bjeny.org
Board of Regents	www.regents.nysed.gov

See Organization Index for page numbers.

World Wide Web (URL) Index

Bogdan Lasky & Kopley, LLC	www.blklobby.com
Bolivar-Richburg CSD	www.brcs.wnyric.org
Bolton CSD	www.boltoncsd.org
Bolton Landing Chamber of Commerce	www.boltonchamber.com
Bolton St Johns Inc	www.boltonstjohns.com
Bombardiere, Ralph	www.nysassrs.com
Bond Market Association (The)	www.bondmarkets.com
Boonville Area Chamber of Commerce	www.boonvillechamber.org
Boricua College	www.boricuacollege.edu
Borough of Manhattan Community College	www.bmcc.cuny.edu
Boykin-Towns, Karen	www.pfizer.com
Boylan Brown	www.boylanbrown.com
Bracken & Margolin LLP	www.bracken-margolin.com
Bradford Publications Inc	www.oleantimesherald.com
Bradford Publishing Co	www.salamancapress.com
Brain Injury Association of NYS (BIANYS)	www.bianys.org
Bramson ORT College	www.bramsonort.org
Brasher Falls CSD	www.bfcsd.org
Brentwood UFSD	www.bufsd.org
Brewster Chamber of Commerce	www.brewsterchamber.com
Brewster CSD	www.brewsterschools.org
Briarcliff Manor UFSD	www.briarcliffschools.org
Briarcliffe College-Bethpage	www.bcbeth.com
Briarcliffe College-Patchogue	www.bcpat.com
Bridgehampton UFSD	www.bridgehampton.k12.ny.us
Brighton CSD	www.bcsd.org
Brighton, Town of	www.townofbrighton.org
Bristol-Myers Squibb Co	www.bms.com
British Airways PLC	www.ba.com
Brockport CSD	www.brockport.k12.ny.us
Brocton CSD	www.brocton.wnyric.org
Bronx (Bronx County)	bronxboropres.nyc.gov
Bronx Community College	www.bcc.cuny.edu
Bronx County (NYC Borough of the Bronx)	www.bronxcountyclerksoffice.com
Bronx Educational Opportunity Center	www.brx.eoc.suny.edu
Bronx-Lebanon Hospital Center	www.bronxcare.org
Bronxville Chamber of Commerce	www.bronxvillechamber.com
Bronxville UFSD	www.bronxville.lhric.org
Brookfield CSD	www.bcsbeavers.org
Brookfield Properties Corporation	www.brookfieldproperties.com
Brookhaven Industrial Development Agency	www.brookhaven.org
Brookhaven, Town of	www.brookhaven.org
Brooklyn (Kings County)	www.brooklyn-usa.org
Brooklyn Botanic Garden	www.bbg.org
Brooklyn Chamber of Commerce	www.ibrooklyn.com
Brooklyn College	www.brooklyn.cuny.edu
Brooklyn Economic Development Corporation	www.bedc.org
Brooklyn Educational Opportunity Center	www.bklyn.eoc.suny.edu
Brooklyn Housing & Family Services Inc	www.brooklynhousing.org
Brooklyn Law School	www.brooklaw.edu
Brooklyn Museum of Art	www.brooklynmuseum.org
Brooklyn Navy Yard Development Corporation	www.brooklynnavyyard.com
Broome Community College	www.sunybroome.edu
Broome County	www.gobroomecounty.com
Broome County Industrial Development Agency	www.bcida.com
Broome-Delaware-Tioga BOCES	www.btboces.org

See Organization Index for page numbers.

World Wide Web (URL) Index

Brown Brothers Harriman & Co, Bank Asset Management Group	www.bbh.com
Browne, Brian	www.stjohns.edu
Brushton-Moira CSD	www.bmcsd.org
Bryant & Stratton College-Albany Campus	www.bryantstratton.edu
Bryant & Stratton College-Amherst Campus	www.bryantstratton.edu
Bryant & Stratton College-Buffalo Campus	www.bryantstratton.edu
Bryant & Stratton College-Greece Campus	www.bryantstratton.edu
Bryant & Stratton College-Henrietta Campus	www.bryantstratton.edu
Bryant & Stratton College-Southtowns Campus	www.bryantstratton.edu
Bryant & Stratton College-Syracuse Campus	www.bryantstratton.edu
Bryant & Stratton College-Syracuse North Campus	www.bryantstratton.edu
Budget	www.budget.senate.gov
Budget, Division of the	www.budget.state.ny.us
Buffalo	www.buffalo.fbi.gov
Buffalo & Fort Erie Public Bridge Authority (Peace Bridge Authority)	www.peacebridge.com
Buffalo Bills	www.buffalobills.com
Buffalo Business First	buffalo.bizjournals.com
Buffalo Economic Renaissance Corporation	www.berc.org
Buffalo Educational Opportunity Center	www.eoc.buffalo.edu
Buffalo News (The)	www.buffalo.com
Buffalo Niagara Builders' Assn Build PAC	www.bnba.org
Buffalo Niagara Convention & Visitors Bureau	www.visitbuffaloniagara.com
Buffalo Niagara Partnership	www.thepartnership.org
Buffalo Professional Firefighters PAC	www.buffalofirefighters.com
Buffalo Sabres	www.sabres.com
Buffalo SD	www.buffaloschools.org
Buffalo State College	www.buffalostate.edu
Buffalo Teachers Federation PAC	www.btfny.org
Buffalo Trotting Association Inc	www.buffaloraceway.com
Buffalo, City of	www.ci.buffalo.ny.us
Build PAC (NY)	www.nysba.com
Builders' PAC	www.libi.org
Building & Realty Institute	www.buildersinstitute.org
Building Contractors Assn Inc	www.ny-bca.com
Building Contractors Association	www.ny-bca.com
Building Industry Association of NYC Inc	www.webuildnyc.com
Buildings, Department of, NYC	www.nyc.gov/buildings
Bureau of Alcohol, Tobacco, Firearms & Explosives	www.atf.gov
Bureau of Educational & Cultural Affairs-NY Pgm Branch	exchanges.state.gov
Bureau of Immigration & Customs Enforcement (ICE)	www.ice.gov
Bureau of Labor Statistics (BLS)	www.bls.gov
Bureau of Land Management	www.blm.gov
Burnt Hills-Ballston Lake CSD	www.bhbl.org
Business Council for International Understanding	www.bciu.org
Business Council of New York State Inc	www.bcnys.org
Business Council of Westchester	www.westchesterny.org
Business Informatics Center	www.thecollegeforbusiness.com
Business Review	albany.bizjournals.com
Business Review (The)	www.albany.bizjournals.com
Bynum, Thompson, Ryer	www.btrsc.com
Byram Hills CSD	www.byramhills.org
Byron-Bergen CSD	www.bbcs.k12.ny.us
Cable Telecommunications Association of New York Inc	www.cabletvny.com
Cablevision Systems Corporation	www.cablevision.com
Cairo-Durham CSD	www.cairodurham,.org
Caledonia-Mumford CSD	www.cal-mum.org

See Organization Index for page numbers.

World Wide Web (URL) Index

Calvin, James S. . . . . www.nyacs.org
Cambridge CSD . . . . www.cambridgecsd.org
Camden CSD . . . . www.camdenschools.org
Camillus, Town of . . . . www.townofcamillus.com
Camp Venture Inc . . . . www.campventure.org
Campaign Finance Board, NYC . . . . www.nyccfb.info
Campaign for Fiscal Equity, Inc . . . . www.cfequity.org
Campground Owners of New York . . . . www.nycampgrounds.com
Canajoharie CSD www.canajoharie.k12.ny.us
Canandaigua Area Chamber of Commerce . . . . www.canandaigua.com
Canandaigua City SD . . . . www.canandaiguaschools.org
Canandaigua National Bank & Trust Co . . . . www.cnbank.com
Canarsie Courier . . . . www.canarsiecourier.com
Canastota Chamber of Commerce . . . . www.canastota.org
Canastota CSD . . . . www.canastotacsd.org
Candor CSD . . . . www.candor.org
Canisius College . . . . www.canisius.edu
Canton Chamber of Commerce . . . . www.cantonnychamber.org
Canton CSD www.ccsdk12.org
Capalino, James F & Associates Inc . . . . www.capalino.com
Cape Vincent Chamber of Commerce . . . . www.capevincent.org
Capital Defender Office . . . . www.nycdo.org
Capital District Educational Opportunity Center . . . . www.alb.eoc.suny.edu
Capital District Physicians' Health Plan Inc . . . . www.cdphp.com
Capital District Regional Off-Track Betting Corporation . . . . www.capitalotb.com
Capital District Regional Planning Commission . . . . www.cdrpc.org
Capital District Transportation Authority . . . . www.cdta.org
Capital Region (Albany-Schoharie-Schenectady) BOCES . . . . www.capregboces.org
Capitol Group, LLC . . . . www.capitolgroupllc.com
Capitol Hill Management Services Inc . . . . www.caphill.com
Cardozo School of Law . . . . www.cardozo.yu.edu
Carle Place UFSD www.cps.k12.ny.us
Carmel CSD www.ccsd.k12.ny.us
Carmel, Town of . . . . www.carmelny.org
Carr Public Affairs Inc . . . . www.carrpublicaffairs.com
Carr, Bernard . . . . www.nysafah.org
Carthage Area Chamber of Commerce . . . . www.carthageny.com
Carthage CSD . . . . www.carthagecsd.org
CASA - Advocates for Children of NYS . . . . www.casanys.org
Castelbuono, A J . . . . www.agcnys.org
Catholic Charities . . . . www.ccoc.us
Catholic School Administrators Association of NYS . . . . www.csaanys.org
Catholic War Veterans of the United States of America . . . . www.nycatholicwarvets.org
Catskill Center for Conservation & Development . . . . www.catskillcenter.org
Catskill CSD . . . . www.catskillcsd.org
Catskill Off-Track Betting Corporation . . . . www.interbets.com
Cattaraugus . . . . www.cattco.org
Cattaraugus County . . . . www.cattco.org
Cattaraugus Empire Zone Corporation . . . . www.cattempirezone.org
Cattaraugus-Allegany-Erie-Wyoming BOCES . . . . www.caboces.org
Cattaraugus-Little Valley CSD . . . . qp.wnyric.org
Cayuga . . . . www.co.cayuga.ny.us/election
Cayuga Community College . . . . www.cayuga-cc.edu
Cayuga County . . . . www.cayugacounty.us
Cayuga County Chamber of Commerce . . . . www.cayugacountychamber.com
Cayuga Nation . . . . www.sixnations.org

See Organization Index for page numbers.

World Wide Web (URL) Index

Cayuga-Onondaga BOCES	www.cayboces.org
Cazenovia Area Chamber of Commerce (Greater Cazenovia Area)	www.cazenoviachamber.com
Cazenovia College	www.cazenovia.edu
Cazenovia CSD	www.caz.cnyric.org
CBS Corporation	www.cbs.com
CBS News (New York Bureau)	www.cbsnews.com
Cendant Car Rental Group Inc	www.cendant.com
Census Bureau	www.census.gov
Center for Alternative Sentencing & Employment Services (CASES)	www.cases.org
Center for an Urban Future	www.nycfuture.org
Center for Anti-Violence Education Inc	www.cae-bklyn.org
Center for Constitutional Rights	www.ccr-ny.org
Center for Court Innovation	www.courtinnovation.org
Center for Disability Services	www.cfdsny.org
Center for Economic Growth Inc	www.ceg.org
Center for Educational Innovation - Public Education Association	www.cei-pea.org
Center for Environmental Information Inc	www.ceinfo.org
Center for Governmental Research Inc (CGR)	www.cgr.org
Center for Independence of the Disabled in NY (CIDNY)	www.cidny.org
Center for Judicial Accountability Inc	www.judgewatch.org
Center for Law & Justice	www.timesunion.com/communities/cflj
Center for Migration Studies of New York Inc	www.cmsny.org
Center for Technology in Government, University at Albany, SUNY	www.ctg.albany.edu
Center for Urban Community Services	www.cucs.org
Center Moriches UFSD	www.centermoriches.k12.ny.us
Centers for Disease Control & Prevention	www.cdc.gov
Centers for Medicare & Medicaid Services	www.cms.hhs.gov
Central Adirondack Association	www.caany.com
Central Brooklyn Medical Group, PC	www.brooklyndocs.com
Central Hudson Gas & Electric Corporation	www.cenhud.com
Central Islip UFSD	www.cischools.us
Central New York Business Journal	www.cnybj.com
Central New York Regional Transportation Authority	www.centro.org
Central Pine Barrens Joint Planning & Policy Commission	www.pb.state.ny.us
Century Foundation (The)	www.tcf.org
Cerebral Palsy Associations of New York State	www.cpofnys.org
Chadwick, Cindy	www.nyseg.com
Chain Pharmacy Assn PAC	www.lobbywr.com
Champlain Valley Educational Svcs (Clinton-Essex-Warren-Washington)	www.cves.org
Chappaqua CSD	www.chappauqua.k12.ny.us/ccsd/
Charter PAC	www.bncf.org
Chateaugay CSD	chateau.neric.org
Chatham CSD	www.chathamcentralschools.com
Chautauqua	www.votechautauqua.com
Chautauqua County	www.co.chautauqua.ny.us
Chautauqua County Chamber of Commerce	www.chautauquachamber.org
Chautauqua County Chamber of Commerce, Dunkirk Branch	www.chautauquachamber.org
Chautauqua County Industrial Development Agency	www.co.chautauqua.ny.us/ccida
Chautauqua County Visitors Bureau	www.tourchautauqua.com
Chautauqua Lake CSD	www.clake.org
Chazy Central RSD	www.chazy.org
Cheektowaga Chamber of Commerce	www.cheektowaga.org
Cheektowaga CSD	www.cheektowagaschools.org
Cheektowaga, Town of	www.tocny.org
Cheektowaga-Sloan UFSD	www.sloan.wnyric.org
Chemung	www.chemungcounty.com

See Organization Index for page numbers.

World Wide Web (URL) Index

Chemung County	www.chemungcounty.com
Chemung County Chamber of Commerce	www.chemungchamber.org
Chemung County Industrial Development Agency	www.steg.com
Chenango	www.co.chenango.ny.us
Chenango County	www.co.chenango.ny.us
Chenango County Chamber of Commerce	www.chenangony.org
Chenango Forks CSD	www.cforks.org
Chenango Valley CSD	www.cvcsd.stier.org
Child Care Inc	www.childcareinc.org
Children & Family Services, Office of	www.ocfs.state.ny.us
Children's Aid Society (The)	www.childrensaidsociety.org
Children's Rights Inc	www.childrensrights.org
Children's Village (The)	www.childrensvillage.org
Chili, Town of	www.townofchili.org
Chittenango CSD	www.chittenangoschools.org
Christ the King Seminary	www.cks.edu
Christie's Education Inc	www.christies.com/education/ny_overview.asp
Christmas Tree Farmers Association of New York Inc	www.christmastreesny.org
Churchville-Chili CSD	www.cccsd.org
Ciccone, Stephen J	www.kodak.com
Cicero, Town of	www.ciceronewyork.net
CIDNY - Queens	www.cidny.org
Cincinnatus CSD	www.cincynet.cbyric.org
CIO Office	www.cio.state.ny.us
CIO Office & Office for Technology	www.cio.state.ny.us
Citigroup	www.citigroup.com
Citigroup Inc	www.citigroup.com
Citizen (The)	www.auburnpub.com
Citizen Action of New York	www.citizenactionny.org
Citizen Action of NY Political Contribution Acct	www.citizenactionny.org
Citizens Budget Commission	www.cbcny.org
Citizens Campaign for the Environment	www.citizenscampaign.org
Citizens Housing & Planning Council of New York	www.chpcny.org
Citizens Union of the City of New York	www.citizensunion.org
Citizens' Committee for Children of New York Inc	www.cccnewyork.org
Citizens' Environmental Coalition	www.cectoxic.org ; www.kodakstoxicolors.org
City College of New York, The	www1.ccny.cuny.edu
City Council, NYC	www.nyccouncil.info
City Journal (Manhattan Institute for Policy Research)	www.city-journal.org
City Planning, Department of, NYC	www.ci.nyc.ny.us/html/dcp
City University of New York (CUNY)	www.cuny.edu
Citywide Administrative Services, Department of, NYC	www.nyc.gov/dcas
Civil Service Commission, NYC	www.nyc.gov/html/csc
Civil Service Department	www.cs.state.ny.us
Civil Service Employees Assn of NY (CSEA), Local 1000, AFSCME, AFL-CIO	www.csealocal1000.org
Civil Service Employees Union (CSEA), Local 1000, AFSCME, AFL-CIO	www.csealocal1000.org
Civil Service Employees' PAF	www.csealocal1000.net
Clarence Chamber of Commerce	www.clarence.org
Clarence CSD	www.clarenceschools.org
Clarence Industrial Development Agency (Town of)	www.clarence.ny.us
Clarence, Town of	www.clarence.ny.us
Clarkson University	www.clarkson.edu
Clarkstown CSD	www.ccsd.edu
Clarkstown, Town of	www.town.clarkstown.ny.us
Clay, Town of	www.townofclay.org
Clayton Chamber of Commerce	www.1000islands-clayton.com

See Organization Index for page numbers.

World Wide Web (URL) Index

Clear Channel Communications Inc PAC	www.katz-media.com
Cleveland Hill UFSD	www.clevehill.wnyric.org
Clifton Park, Town of	www.cliftonpark.org
Clifton Springs Area Chamber of Commerce	www.cliftonspringschamber.com
Clifton-Fine CSD	www.cfeagles.org
Clinton	www.clintoncountygov.com
Clinton Chamber of Commerce Inc	www.clintonnychamber.org
Clinton Community College	www.clinton.edu
Clinton County	www.co.clinton.ny.us
Clinton County, The Development Corporation	www.nyworks.biz
Clinton CSD	www.ccs.edu
Clyde Chamber of Commerce	www.clydeontheerie.com/COC
Clyde Industrial Development Corporation	www.clydeontheerie.com
Clyde-Savannah CSD	www.clydesavannah.org
Clymer CSD	www.clymer.wnyric.org
Coalition Against Domestic Violence, NYS	www.nyscadv.org
Coalition Against Sexual Assault (NYS)	www.nyscasa.org
Coalition for Asian American Children & Families	www.cacf.org
Coalition for the Homeless	www.coalitionforthehomeless.org
Coalition of Behavioral Health Agencies, Inc (The)	www.coalitionny.org
Coalition of Fathers & Families NY	www.fafny.org/fafnypac.htm
Coalition of Fathers & Families NY, PAC	www.fafny.org/fafnypac.htm
Coalition of Living Museums	www.livingmuseums.org
Coalition of New York State Career Schools (The)	www.coalitionofnewyorkstatecareerschools.com
Cobleskill-Richmondville CSD	www.crcs.k12.ny.us
Cochran School of Nursing	www.cochranschoolofnursing.org
Cohen, Marsha A	www.reinsurance.org
Cohoes City SD	www.cohoes.org
Cohoes Industrial Development Agency (City of)	www.ci.cohoes.ny.us
Cold Spring Harbor CSD	www.csh.k12.ny.us
Cold Spring Harbor Fish Hatchery & Aquarium	www.cshfha.org
Colgate Rochester Crozer Divinity School	www.crcds.edu
Colgate University	www.colgate.edu
Colgate University, Department of Geology	departments.colgate.edu/geology
Collective Bargaining, Office of, NYC	www.ocb-nyc.org
College of Agriculture & Life Sciences at Cornell University	www.cals.cornell.edu
College of Human Ecology at Cornell University	www.human.cornell.edu
College of Mount Saint Vincent	www.mountsaintvincent.edu
College of New Rochelle (The)	www.cnr.edu
College of Saint Rose (The)	www.strose.edu
College of Staten Island	www.csi.cuny.edu
College of Veterinary Medicine at Cornell University	www.vet.cornell.edu
College of Westchester (The)	www.cw.edu
Colliers ABR Inc	www.colliersabr.com
Colonie Chamber of Commerce	www.coloniechamber.org
Colonie, Town of	www.colonie.org
Colton-Pierrepont CSD	www.cpcs.k12.ny.us
Columbia County	www.columbiacountyny.com
Columbia County Chamber of Commerce	www.columbiachamber-ny.com
Columbia Hudson Partnership	www.chpartnership.com
Columbia Law School, Legislative Drafting Research Fund	www.law.columbia.edu
Columbia University	www.columbia.edu
Columbia University, Exec Graduate Pgm in Public Policy & Administration	www.columbia.edu/~sc32
Columbia University, Mailman School of Public Health	cpmcnet.columbia.edu/dept/sph/popfam
Columbia University, Mailman School of Public Health, Center for Public Health	www.cpmcnet.columbia.edu/dept/sph
Columbia University, MPA in Environmental Science & Policy	www.columbia.edu/~sc32

See Organization Index for page numbers.

World Wide Web (URL) Index

Columbia University, School of the Arts .... www.columbia.edu/cu/arts
Columbia University, Science & Technology Ventures .... www.stv.columbia.edu
Columbia-Greene Community College .... www.sunycgcc.edu
Commack UFSD www.commack.k12.ny.us
Commerce, Science & Transportation .... http://commerce.senate.gov
Commission on Economic Opportunity for the Greater Capital Region .... www.ceo-cap.org
Commission on Independent Colleges & Universities .... www.cicu.org
Commissioned Officers Assn of the US Public Health Svc Inc (COA) .... www.coausphs.org
Committee for Workers' Compensation Reform .... www.nyworkerscompensationalliance.org
Committee of Methadone Program Administrators Inc of NYS (COMPA) .... www.compa-ny.org
Commodity Futures Trading Commission .... www.cftc.gov
Commodore Applied Technologies Inc .... www.commodore.com
Common Cause/NY .... www.commoncause.org/ny
Commonwealth Business Media .... www.joc.com
Commonwealth Fund .... www.cmwf.org
Communications Workers of America, District 1 .... www.cwa-union.org
Community & Rural Development Institute .... www.cardi.cornell.edu
Community Advocacy & Advisory Services .... www.communityadvocacy.com
Community Bankers Assn of NY State, Accounting & Taxation Cmte .... www.northforkbank.com
Community Bankers Assn of NY State, Bank Operations & Admin Cmte ..... www.northcountrysavings.com
Community Bankers Assn of NY State, Banking Law & Regulations Cmte ... www.astoriafederal.com
Community Bankers Assn of NY State, Government Relations Cmte .... www.pioneersb.com
Community Bankers Assn of NY State, Mortgages & Real Estate Cmte ..... www.mynycb.com
Community Health Care Association of NYS .... www.chcanys.org
Community Healthcare .... www.chnnyc.org
Community Healthcare Network .... www.chnnyc.org
Community Housing Improvement Program (CHIP) .... www.chipnyc.org
Community Preservation Corporation (The) .... www.communityp.com
Community Service Society of New York .... www.cssny.org
Comptroller of the Currency .... www.occ.treas.gov
Comptroller, NYC .... www.comptroller.nyc.gov
Concordia College .... www.concordia-ny.edu
Coney Island Chamber of Commerce .... www.2chambers.com/coney_island
Conference Board (The) .... www.conference-board.org
Conflicts of Interest Board, NYC .... www.nyc.gov/ethics
Connetquot CSD www.connetquot.k12.ny.us
Connors & Connors, PC .... www.connorslaw.com
Connors & Corcoran LLP .... www.connorscorcoran.com
Connors & Vilardo .... www.connors-vilardo.com
Conservative Party of NYS .... www.cpnys.org
Consolidated Edison Energy .... www.coned.com
Constellation NewEnergy Inc .... www.newenergy.com
Construction Contractors Association of the Hudson Valley Inc .... www.constructioncontractorsassociation.com
Consumer Affairs, Department of, NYC .... www.nyc.gov/html/dcas
Consumer Product Safety Commission .... www.cpsc.gov
Consumer Protection Board .... www.nyconsumer.gov
Consumers Union .... www.consumerreports.org;
                                                           www.consumersunion.org
Continuum Health Partners Inc .... wehealnewyork.org
Convenience PAC .... www.nyacs.org
Conway, Gerard L, Jr .... www.plugpower.com
Cooper Union for the Advancement of Science & Art .... www.cooper.edu
Cooper-Hewitt National Design Museum .... www.cooperhewitt.org
Cooperstown Chamber of Commerce .... www.cooperstownchamber.org
Copenhagen CSD .... www.ccsknights.org
Copiague UFSD www.copiague.k12.ny.us

See Organization Index for page numbers.

World Wide Web (URL) Index

Coppola Ryan McHugh Riddell	www.nylobbyist.com
Coppola, John J.	www.asapnys.org
Corinth CSD	www.corinthcsd.org
Corinth Industrial Development Agency (Town of)	www.townofcorinthny.com
Cornell Cooperative Extension	www.cce.cornell.edu
Cornell Cooperative Extension, College of Human Ecology, Nutrition, Health	www.cce.cornell.edu
Cornell Cooperative Extension, Community & Economic Vitality Program	www.cce.cornell.edu
Cornell Cooperative Extension, Environment & Natural Resources Initiative	www.dnr.cornell.edu/extension
Cornell Cooperative Extension, NY Sea Grant	www.nyseagrant.org
Cornell Cooperative Extension, Pesticide Management Education Program	pmep.cce.cornell.edu
Cornell Cooperative Extension, Urban Agriculture & Markets Program	www.cce.cornell.edu
Cornell Farmedic Training Program	www.farmedic.com
Cornell Law School, Legal Information Institute	www.law.cornell.edu
Cornell University	www.govrelations.cornell.edu
Cornell University Center for the Environment	environment.cornell.edu
Cornell University, College of Agriculture & Life Sciences, Animal Science	www.ansci.cornell.edu
Cornell University, Community, Food & Agriculture Program	www.cfap.org
Cornell University, Department of Applied Economics & Management	www.aem.cornell.edu/profiles/ladue.htm
Cornell University, Development Sociology	www.cfap.org
Cornell University, Economics Department	www.arts.cornell.edu/econ
Cornell University, FarmNet Program	www.nyfarmnet.org
Cornell University, Institute on Conflict Resolution	www.ilr.cornell.edu
Cornell University, Program on Dairy Markets & Policy	www.cpdmp.cornell.edu
Cornell University, Rural Schools Association of NYS	www.education.cornell.edu/rsp
Cornell University, Sch of Industr & Labor Relations Institute for Workplace Studies	www.ilr.cornell.edu/iws
Cornell University, School of Industrial & Labor Relations	www.ilr.cornell.edu
Corning Area Chamber of Commerce	www.corningny.com
Corning Community College	www.corning-cc.edu
Cornwall CSD	www.cornwallschools.com
Corporation for National & Community Service	www.cns.gov
Correction Officers' Benevolent Assn PAC	www.cobanyc.org
Correction, Department of, NYC	www.nyc.gov/boldest
Correctional Association of New York	www.correctionalassociation.org
Correctional Industries Division	www.corcraft.org
Correctional Services Department	www.docs.state.ny.us
Cortland County	www.cortland-co.org
Cortland County Chamber of Commerce	www.cortlandchamber.com
Cortland Enlarged City SD	www.cortlandschools.org
Cortland Standard	www.cortland.org/news
Cortland Standard Printing Co Inc	www.cortland.org/news
Cortlandt, Town of	www.townofcortlandt.com
Couch White, LLP	www.couchwhite.com
Council of Community Services of NYS Inc	www.ccsnys.org
Council of Family & Child Caring Agencies	www.cofcca.org
Council of School Supervisors & Admin, Local 1 AFSA AFL-CIO	www.csa-nyc.org
Council of School Supervisors & Administrators	www.csa-nyc.org
Council of State Governments, Eastern Conference	www.csgeast.org
Council of the City of New York (The)	www.council.nyc.ny.us
Council on Children & Families	www.ccf.state.ny.us
Council on the Arts	www.nysca.org
Council on the Environment of NYC (The)	www.cenyc.org
Council on the Environment of NYC, Environmental Education	www.cenyc.org
Council on the Environment of NYC, Open Space Greening Program	www.cenyc.org
Counseling & Claims Service	www.veterans.state.ny.us/ofcs.htm
County Nursing Facilities of New York Inc	www.nysac.org
Coxsackie-Athens CSD	www.coxsackie-athens.org

See Organization Index for page numbers.

World Wide Web (URL) Index

CPR, The International Institute for Conflict Prevention & Resolution . . . . www.cpradr.org
Crain's New York Business . . . . www.crainsny.com
Credit Advocate Counseling Corporation . . . . www.creditadvocates.com
Credit Unions' PAC (CUPAC) . . . . www.nyscul.org
Crime Victims Board . . . . www.cvb.state.ny.us
Criminal Justice Services, Division of . . . . www.criminaljustice.state.ny.us
Crosier, Barbara V . . . . www.cerebralpalsynys.org
Crossett, Susan M . . . . www.niagaramohawk.com
Croton-Harmon UFSD . . . . www.croton-harmonschools.org
Crouse Hospital School of Nursing . . . . www.crouse.org/nursing
Crown Point CSD . . . . www.crownpointpanthers.com
Cuba-Rushford CSD . . . . www.crcs.wnyric.org
Culinary Institute of America . . . . www.ciachef.edu
Cullen & Dykman LLP . . . . www.cullenanddykman.com
Cultural Affairs, Department of, NYC . . . . www.nyc.gov/html/dcla
Cultural Education Office . . . . www.oce.nysed.gov
CUNY Board of Trustees . . . . www.cuny.edu
CUNY Central Administration . . . . www.cuny.edu
CUNY Graduate School, Center for Urban Research . . . . www.gc.cuny.edu
CUNY Hunter College, Urban Affairs & Planning Department . . . . www.hunter.cuny.edu
CUNY John Jay College of Criminal Justice . . . . www.jjay.cuny.edu
CUNY New York City College of Technology, Hospitality Mgmt . . . . www.nyct.cuny.edu
Customs & Border Protection (CBP) . . . . www.cbp.gov
Cutchogue-New Suffolk Chamber of Commerce . . . . www.cutchoguenewsuffolk.org
CWM Chemical Services LLC . . . . www.cwmlandfill.com
D'Youville College . . . . www.dyc.edu
Daemen College . . . . www.daemen.edu
Dahill, Kevin . . . . www.nshc.org
Daily Challenge . . . . www.challenge-group.com
Daily Courier-Observer . . . . www.mpcourier.com
Daily Freeman . . . . www.dailyfreeman.com
Daily Gazette (The) . . . . www.dailygazette.com
Daily Gazette Co . . . . www.dailygazette.com
Daily Mail (The) . . . . www.thedailymail.net
Daily Messenger (The) . . . . www.mpnewspaper.com
Daily Record (The) . . . . www.nydailyrecord.com
Daily Sentinel . . . . www.rny.com
Daily Star (The) . . . . www.thedailystar.com
Dairy Programs . . . . www.ams.usda.gov
Dairylea Cooperative Inc . . . . www.dairylea.com
Dakota Software Corporation . . . . www.dakotasoft.com
Dale Carnegie & Associates Inc . . . . www.dale-carnegie.com
Dansville Chamber of Commerce . . . . www.dansvilleny.net
Dansville CSD . . . . www.dansvillecsd.org
Davis College . . . . www.davisny.edu
Davis Polk & Wardwell . . . . www.dpw.com
Day Pitney LLP . . . . www.daypitney.com
De Ruyter CSD www.deruyter.k12.ny.us
Debevoise & Plimpton LLP . . . . www.debevoise.com
Decision Strategies Group . . . . www.decisionstrategiesgroup.com
Deer Park UFSD . . . . www.deerparkschools.org
DeGraff, Foy, Kunz & Devine, LLP . . . . www.degraff-foy.com
Delaware . . . . www.co.delaware.ny.us
Delaware County . . . . www.co.delaware.ny.us
Delaware County Chamber of Commerce . . . . www.delawarecounty.org
Delaware County Planning Department . . . . www.co.delaware.ny.us

See Organization Index for page numbers.

World Wide Web (URL) Index

Delaware River Basin Commission	www.drbc.net
Delaware-Chenango-Madison-Otsego BOCES	www.dcmoboces.com
Delhi CSD	www.delhischools.org
Democracy for America-New York	www.democracyforamerica.com
Democrat and Chronicle	www.democratandchronicle.com
Democratic Congressional Campaign Committee	www.dccc.org
Democratic Governors' Assn - NY	www.democraticgovernors.org
Dental Hygienists' Association of the State of New York Inc	www.dhasny.org
Depew UFSD	www.dpewschools.org
Deposit Chamber of Commerce	www.tds.net/depositchamber
Deposit CSD	www.depositcsd.org
Design & Construction, Dept of, NYC	www.nyc.gov/html/ddc
Detectives' Endowment Association COPE	www.nycdetectives.org
Deutsche Bank	www.db.com
Development Authority of the North Country	www.danc.org
Development Counsellors International	www.aboutdci.com
Developmental Disabilities Planning Council	www.ddpc.state.ny.us
DeVry Institute of Technology, Long Island City Campus	www.ny.devry.edu
DeWitt, Town of	www.townofdewitt.com
Digiovanni, Joseph	www.libertymutual.com
Dionondehowa Wildlife Sanctuary & School - Not For Profit	www.dionondehowa.org
Disabilities, Mayor's Office, for People with	www.nyc.gov/html/mopd
Disabled American Veterans, Department of New York	www.davny.org
District Council 37, AFSCME	www.district37.net
District Council 37, AFSCME, AFL-CIO	www.dc37.net
District Council 9 PAC	www.DC9.net
DKI Engineering & Consulting USA, PC, Corporate World Headquarters	www.dkitechnologies.com
DLA Piper Rudnick Gray Cary US LLP NYSPAC	www.dlapiper.com
Dobbs Ferry UFSD	www.dfsd.org/home.aspx
Doctors Without Borders USA	www.doctorswithoutborders.org
Dolan Media Co	www.nydailyrecord.com
Dolgeville CSD	www.dolgeville.org
Dominican College	www.dc.edu
Donnelly, Edwin	www.nysaflcio.org
Donohue, Gavin J	www.ippny.org
Dorothea Hopfer School of Nursing at Mount Vernon Hospital	www.ssmc.org
Dover UFSD	www.doverschools.org
Dow Jones & Company	www.wsj.com
Dow Jones Newswires (Dow Jones & Company)	www.djnewswires.com
Dowling College	www.dowling.edu
Downsville CSD	www.dcseagles.org
Downtown-Lower Manhattan Association	downtownny.com
Doyle, Michael R	www.api.org
Drug Enforcement Administration - New York Task Force	www.usdoj.gov/dea/deahome.html
Drum Major Institute for Public Policy - Not For Profit	www.drummajorinstitute.org
Dryden CSD	www.dryden.k12.ny.us
Duane Morris LLP Government Committee NY Find	www.duanemorris.com
Duanesburg CSD	dcs.neric.org
Dundee CSD	www.dundeecs.org
Dunkirk City SD	www.dunkirk.wnyric.org
Dupee & Monroe, PC	www.dupeelaw.com
Dutchess	www.dutchesselections.com
Dutchess BOCES	www.dcboces.org
Dutchess Community College	www.sunydutchess.edu
Dutchess County	www.dutchessny.gov
Dutchess County Economic Development Corporation	http://thinkdutchess.com

See Organization Index for page numbers.

World Wide Web (URL) Index

E-3 Communications	www.e3communications.com
East Aurora Chamber of Commerce (Greater East Aurora)	www.eanycc.com
East Aurora UFSD	www.eaur.wnyric.org
East Fishkill, Town of	www.eastfishkillny.org
East Greenbush CSD	www.egcsd.org
East Hampton Chamber of Commerce	www.easthamptonchamber.com
East Hampton UFSD	www.easthampton.k12.ny.us
East Hampton, Town of	www.town.east-hampton.ny.us
East Irondequoit CSD	www.eicsd.k12.ny.us
East Islip Chamber of Commerce	www.isliplife.com/eastislipchamber
East Islip UFSD	www.eischools.org
East Meadow Chamber of Commerce	www.emchamber.com
East Meadow UFSD	www.eastmeadow.k12.ny.us
East Moriches UFSD	www.eastmoriches.k12.ny.us
East Quogue UFSD	www.eastquogue.k12.ny.us
East Ramapo CSD (Spring Valley)	www.eram.k12.ny.us
East Rochester UFSD	www.erschools.org
East Rockaway UFSD	www.eastrockawayschools.org
East Syracuse-Minoa CSD	www.esmschools.org
East Williston UFSD	www.ewsdonline.org
Eastchester UFSD	www2.lhric.org/eastchester
Eastchester, Town of	www.eastchester.org
Eastern Contractors Association Inc	www.ecainc.org
Eastern District	www.nyeb.uscourts.gov
Eastern Suffolk BOCES	www.esboces.org
Eastman Kodak Company	www.kodak.com
Eastport-South Manor CSD	www.esmonline.org
Ecology & Environment Inc	www.ene.com
Economic Committee, Joint	www.house.gov/jec
Economic Development Administration	www.doc.gov/eda/
Economic Development Corp, NYC	www.nycedc.com
Economic Development Council Inc (NYS)	www.nysedc.org
Eden CSD	www.edencentral.org
Edgemont UFSD	www.edgemont.org
Education & Assistance Corp Inc	www.eacinc.org
Education & Assistance Corporation Inc	www.eacinc.org
Education & Labor	http://edworkforce.house.gov
Education Department	www.nysed.gov
Education, Dept of, NYC	www.nycenet.edu
Educational Broadcasting Corporation	www.thirteen.org
Educational Construction Fund, NYC	www.nycenet.edu/offices/ecf
Educational Leadership (EL) PAC	www.saanys.org
Educational Opportunity Center of Westchester	www.ynk.sunyeoc.org
Edwards-Knox CSD	www.ekcsk12.org
Egg (The), Center for the Performing Arts	www.theegg.org
Elba CSD	www.elbacsd.org
Eldred CSD	www.eldredschools.org
Eleanor Roosevelt Legacy Committee Inc	www.eleanorslegacy.org
Elections, Board of, NYC	www.vote.nyc.ny.us
Elections, State Board of	www.elections.state.ny.us
Elinski, Karen	www.tiaa-cref.org
Elizabethtown-Lewis CSD	elcs.neric.org
Ellenville CSD	www.ecs.k12.ny.us
Ellenville/Wawarsing Chamber of Commerce	www.wawarsing.ny.net
Ellicottville Chamber of Commerce	www.ellicottvilleny.com
Ellicottville CSD	www.ellicottvilecentral.com

See Organization Index for page numbers.

World Wide Web (URL) Index

Ellis Hospital School of Nursing	www.ehson.org
Elmira Business Institute	www.ebi-college.com
Elmira Business Institute-Vestal	www.ebi-college.com
Elmira City SD	www.elmiracityschools.org
Elmira College	www.elmira.edu
Elmira Hts CSD	www.heightsschools.com
Elmira, City of	www.cityofelmira.net
Elmont UFSD	www.elmontschools.org
Elmsford UFSD	www.elmsd.org
Elwood UFSD	www.elwood.k12.ny.us
Emergency Management Office, NYS (SEMO)	www.semo.state.ny.us
EMILY's List	www.emilyslist.org
Empire Blue Cross & Blue Shield	www.empireblue.com
Empire Center for New York State Policy	www.empirecenter.org
Empire Justice Center	www.empirejustice.org
Empire State Association of Assisted Living	www.esaal.org
Empire State College, State University of NY	www.esc.edu
Empire State Development Corporation	www.empire.state.ny.us
Empire State Forest Products Association	www.esfpa.org
Empire State Honey Producers Association	www.eshpa.org
Empire State Passengers Association	www.esparail.org
Empire State Petroleum Association Inc	www.espa.net
Empire State Potato Growers Inc	www.empirepotatogrowers.com
Empire State Pride Agenda PAC	www.prideagenda.org
Empire State Report (CINN Worldwide Inc)	www.empirestatereport.com
Empire State Restaurant & Tavern Association Inc	www.esrta.org
Empire State Society of Association Executives Inc	www.essae.org
Employee Relations, Governor's Office of	www.goer.state.ny.us
Employer Alliance for Affordable Health Care	employeralliance.com
Energy & Commerce	http://energycommerce.house.gov
Energy & Natural Resources	http://energy.senate.gov
Englert Coffey & McHugh	www.englertcoffeymchugh.com
ENSR	www.ensr.aecom.com
Entek Power Services	www.entekpower.com
Entergy Nuclear Northeast	www.entergy.com
Enterprise Rent-A-Car Company NY PAC	www.enterprise.com
Entertainment Software Association	www.theesa.com
Environment & Public Works	http://epw.senate.gov
Environmental Advocates of New York	www.eany.org
Environmental Business Association of NYS Inc	www.eba-nys.org
Environmental Conservation Department	www.dec.ny.gov
Environmental Defense	www.environmentaldefense.org
Environmental Measurements Laboratory	www.eml.st.dhs.gov
Environmental Protection, Department of, NYC	www.nyc.gov/dep
EPIC-Every Person Influences Children Inc	www.epicforchildren.org
Epilepsy Coalition of New York State Inc	www.epilepsyny.org
Equal Employment Opportunity Commission	www.eeoc.gov
Equinox Inc	www.equinoxinc.org
Equitable Life Assurance Society of the US	www.axa-financial.com
Eric Mower & Associates	www.mower.com
Erie 1 BOCES	www.erie1boces.org
Erie 2-Chautauqua-Cattaraugus BOCES	e2ccboces.wnyric.org
Erie Community College	www.ecc.edu
Erie County	www.erie.gov
Erie County Industrial Development Agency	www.ecidany.com
Erie County Planning & Economic Development	www.erie.gov

See Organization Index for page numbers.

World Wide Web (URL) Index

Ernst & Young . . . . www.ey.com
Ernst & Young Committee for Good Government . . . . www.ey.com
Erwin Industrial Development Agency (Town of) . . . . www.threeriversdevelopment.com
ESPAC . . . . www.espa.net
Essex . . . . www.co.essex.ny.us/elect.asp
Essex County . . . . www.co.essex.ny.us
Essex County Industrial Development Agency . . . . www.essexcountyida.com
Ethan C Eldon Associates Inc . . . . www.ethanceldon.com
Ethics, Select Committee on . . . . www.ethics.senate.gov
Evans-Brant CSD (Lake Shore) . . . . www.lakeshore.wnyric.org
EVCI Career Colleges Holding Corp . . . . www.evcinc.com
Evening Sun . . . . www.evesun.com
Evening Telegram (The) . . . . www.herkimertelegram.com
Evening Times (The) . . . . www.littlefallstimes.com
Evening Tribune (The) . . . . www.eveningtribune.com
Everest Institute . . . . www.everest.edu
Excellus Health Plan Inc . . . . www.excellus.com
Excelsior College . . . . www.excelsior.edu
Excess Line Association of New York . . . . www.elany.org
Exhibition Alliance Inc (The) . . . . www.exhibitionalliance.org
Export Import Bank of the United States . . . . www.exim.gov
Exxon Mobil Corporation . . . . www.exxonmobil.com
Eye-Bank for Sight Restoration Inc (The) . . . . www.eyedonation.org
Fabius-Pompey CSD . . . . www.fabiuspompey.org
Faculty Assn of Suffolk Community College VOTE-COPE . . . . www.fascc.org
Fair Haven Area Chamber of Commerce . . . . www.fairhavenny.com
Fairport CSD . . . . www.fairport.org
Falconer CSD . . . . wwwfalconerschools.org
Fallsburg CSD . . . . www.fallsburg.net
Families Together in NYS Inc . . . . www.ftnys.org
Family Physicians PAC . . . . www.nyfafp.org
Family Planning Advocates of New York State . . . . www.fpaofnys.org
Farm Sanctuary . . . . www.farmsanctuary.org
Farmer's Museum (The) . . . . www.farmersmuseum.org
Farmers' Market Federation of NY . . . . www.nyfarmersmarket.com
Farmingdale State College of Technology . . . . www.farmingdale.edu
Farmingdale UFSD . . . . www.farmingdaleschools.org
Farmingville/Holtsville Chamber of Commerce . . . . www.fhcoc.com
Farrell Fritz PC . . . . www.farrellfritz.com
Farrell Fritz, PC . . . . www.farrellfritz.com
Fashion Institute of Technology . . . . www.fitnyc.edu
Fayetteville-Manlius CSD . . . . www.fmschools.org
Federal Aviation Administration-Eastern Region . . . . www.faa.gov
Federal Bureau of Investigation - New York Field Offices . . . . www.fbi.gov
Federal Bureau of Prisons . . . . www.bop.gov
Federal Communications Commission . . . . www.fcc.gov
Federal Deposit Insurance Corporation . . . . www.fdic.gov
Federal Election Commission . . . . www.fec.gov
Federal Emergency Management Agency (FEMA) . . . . www.fema.gov
Federal Highway Administration-New York Division . . . . www.fhwa.dot.gov
Federal Home Loan Bank of New York . . . . www.fhlbny.com
Federal Labor Relations Authority . . . . www.flra.gov
Federal Maritime Commission . . . . www.fmc.gov
Federal Mediation & Conciliation Service . . . . www.fmcs.gov
Federal Motor Carrier Safety Admin-New York Division . . . . www.fmcsa.dot.gov
Federal Railroad Administration-Field Offices . . . . www.fra.dot.gov

See Organization Index for page numbers.

World Wide Web (URL) Index

Federal Reserve Bank of New York	www.newyorkfed.org
Federal Trade Commission	www.ftc.gov
Federal Transit Administration, Region II-New York	www.fta.dot.gov
Federation Employment & Guidance Service (FEGS) Inc	www.fegs.org
Federation of Organizations Inc	www.fedoforg.org
Federation of Protestant Welfare Agencies Inc	www.fpwa.org
Ferris, William E.	www.aarp.org/ny
Filipino American Human Services Inc	www.fahsi.org
Fillmore CSD	www.fillmore.wnyric.org
Film, Theatre & Broadcasting, Mayor's Office of, NYC	www.nyc.gov/film
Film/Video Arts	www.fva.com
Finance	www.finance.senate.gov
Finance, Department of, NYC	www.nyc.gov/finance
Financial Services	http://financialservices.house.gov
Financial Services Forum	www.estandardsforum.com
Finger Lakes Chapter NECA PAC Fund	www.flneca.org
Finger Lakes Community College	www.fingerlakes.edu
Finger Lakes Printing Co	www.fltimes.com
Finger Lakes Racing Association	www.fingerlakesracetrack.com
Finger Lakes Times	www.fltimes.com
Finger Lakes Tourism Alliance	www.fingerlakes.org
Fire Department, NYC	www.nyc.gov/fdny
Fire Island National Seashore	www.nps.gov/fiis/
Fire Island UFSD	www.fi.k12.ny.us
Fiscal Policy Institute	www.fiscalpolicy.org
Fish & Wildlife Service	www.fws.gov
Fishers Island UFSD	www.fischool.com
Fishkill, Town of	www.fishkill-ny.gov
Fitzgerald, Gary J	www.iroquois.org
Fitzpatrick, Christine M	www.nyahsa.org
Five Towns College	www.ftc.edu
Fleet Reserve Association (FRA)	www.fra.org
Fleet Reserve Association (FRA), NE Region (NJ, NY, PA)	www.fra.org
Floral Park-Bellerose UFSD	www.floralpark.k12.ny.us
Florida UFSD	www.floridaufsd.org
Food & Drug Administration	www.fda.gov
Food Industry Alliance of New York State Inc	www.fiany.com
Food Safety & Inspection Service	www.fsis.usda.gov
Fordham University	www.fordham.edu
Fordham University, Department of Political Science	www.fordham.edu
Fordham University, Graduate School of Social Service	www.fordham.edu
Foreign Relations	www.foreign.senate.gov
Forest Service-Region 9	www.fs.fed.us
Forestville CSD	www.forestville.com
Fort Ann CSD	www.fortannschool.org
Fort Brewerton/Greater Oneida Lake Chamber	www.oneidalakechamber.com
Fort Drum	www.drum.army.mil
Fort Edward Chamber of Commerce	www.ftedward.com
Fort Edward UFSD	www.fortedward.org
Fort Plain CSD	www.fortplain.org
Fort Stanwix National Monument	www.nps.gov/fost/
Fort Totten-77th Regional Support Command	www.usarc.army.mil/77thrsc
Fortune Society (The)	www.fortunesociety.org
Fox News Channel	www.foxnews.com
Frankfort-Schuyler CSD	www.frankfort-schuyler.org
Franklin	franklincony.org

See Organization Index for page numbers.

World Wide Web (URL) Index

Franklin County	www.franklincony.org
Franklin CSD	www.franklincssd.org
Franklin D Roosevelt Presidential Library & Museum	www.fdrlibrary.marist.edu
Franklin Square Chamber of Commerce	www.franklinsquarechamber.org
Franklin Square UFSD	franklinsquare.k12.ny.us
Franklin-Essex-Hamilton BOCES	www.fehb.org
Franklinville CSD	www.tbafcs.org/franklinville/
Fredonia Chamber of Commerce	www.fredoniachamber.org
Fredonia CSD	www.fredonia.wnyric.org
Freedom America	www.freedomamerica.org
Freeport UFSD	www.freeportschools.org
Freeport, Village of	www.freeportny.com
French-American Chamber of Commerce	www.cclife.org/usa.new_york
Freshwater Wetlands Appeals Board	www.dec.state.ny.us/website/fwab/
Frewsburg CSD	www.frewsburg.wnyric.org
Friends & Relatives of Institutionalized Aged Inc (FRIA)	www.fria.org
Friendship CSD	www.friendship.wnyric.org
Frontier CSD	www.frontier.wnyric.org
Frontier, A Citizens Communications Co	www.frontieronline.com
Fulton County	www.fulcony.com
Fulton County Economic Development Corporation	www.sites4u.org
Fulton County Reg Chamber of Commerce & Ind	www.fultoncountyny.org
Fulton-Montgomery Community College	www.fmcc.suny.edu
Fund for Animals (The)	www.fund.org
Fund for Better Transportation PAC	www.cnyk.com
Fund for Modern Courts (The)	www.moderncourts.org
Fund for the City of New York	www.fcny.org
Fund for the City of New York, Center for Internet Innovation	www.fcny.org
Funeral Directors Assn Inc (NYS)	www.nysfda.org
Galway CSD	www.galwaycsd.org
Gananda CSD	www.gananda.org
Gandhi Engineering Inc	www.gandhieng.com
Gannet Co Inc	www.pressconnects.com
Gannett Co Inc	www.stargazette.com
Gannett News Service	www.gannett.com
Garden City Chamber of Commerce	www.gardencitychamber.org
Garden City UFSD	www.gardencity.k12.ny.us
Garden City, Village of	www.gardencityny.net
Garrison UFSD	www.gufs.org
Gates, Town of	www.townofgates.org
Gates-Chili CSD	www.gateschili.org
Gateway National Recreation Area	www.nps.gov/gate
Gay and Lesbian Victory Fund	www.victoryfund.org
Gay Men's Health Crisis Inc	www.gmhc.org
General Brown CSD	www.gblions.org
General Building Contractors of NYS PAC	www.gbcnys.agc.org
General Building Contractors of NYS/AGC	www.gbcnys.agc.org
General Services, Office of	www.ogs.state.ny.us
General Theological Seminary of the Episcopal Church	www.gts.edu
Generic Pharmaceutical Association	www.gphaonline.org
Genesee	www.co.genesee.ny.us
Genesee Community College	www.genesee.edu
Genesee County	www.co.genesee.ny.us
Genesee County Chamber of Commerce	www.geneseeny.com
Genesee County Economic Development Center	www.gcedc.com
Genesee Transportation Council	www.gtcmpo.org

See Organization Index for page numbers.

World Wide Web (URL) Index

Genesee Valley CSD	www.gvcs.wnyric.org
Genesee-Livingston-Steuben-Wyoming BOCES	www.gvboces.org
Geneseo CSD	www.geneseocsd.org
Geneva Area Chamber of Commerce	www.genevany.com
Geneva City SD	www.genevacsd.org
Geneva Industrial Development Agency (City of)	www.geneva.ny.us
Genovese, Marta	www.aaanys.com
Geological Survey	ny.usgs.gov
George Junior Republic UFSD	www.georgejuniorrepublic.com
Germantown CSD	germantowncsd.org
Gertrude Stein Repertory Theatre (The)	www.gertstein.org
Geto & deMilly Inc	www.getodemilly.com
Getty Petroleum Marketing Inc	www.getty.com
Gilbert Tweed Associates Inc	www.gilberttweed.com
Gilbertsville-Mount Upton CSD	www.gmucsd.org
Glen Cove Chamber of Commerce	www.glencovechamber.info
Glen Cove City SD	www.glencove.k12.ny.us
Glen Cove, City of	www.glencove-li.com
Glens Falls City SD	www.gfsd.org
Glens Falls Common SD	abewing.nycap.rr.com
Glenville, Town of	www.townofglenville.org
Glenwood Management Corporation	www.glenwoodmanagement.com
Global Gardens Program, New York Botanical Garden (The)	www.nybg.org
Globe Institute of Technology	www.globe.edu
Glusko, John P	www.cenhud.com
Gold Star Wives of America Inc	www.goldstarwives.org
Golden Apple Business Action Committee, PAC	www.westchesterny.org
Goldman Sachs & Co	www.gs.com
Goldman Sachs NY PAC	www.gs.com
Gore Mountain Region Chamber of Commerce	www.goremtnregion.org
Goshen Chamber of Commerce	www.goshennychamber.com
Goshen CSD	www.gcsny.org
Gouverneur Chamber of Commerce	www.gouverneurchamber.net
Governor's Office	www.ny.gov/governor
Governor's Traffic Safety Committee	www.nysgtsc.state.ny.us/index.htm
Gowanda Area Chamber of Commerce	www.gowandachamber.org
Gowanda CSD	www.gowcsd.org
Graduate Center	www.gc.cuny.edu
Graduate School of Journalism	www.journalism.cuny.edu
Grand Island Chamber of Commerce	www.gichamber.org
Grand Island CSD	www.k12.ginet.org
Granville Chamber of Commerce	www.granvillechamber.com
Granville CSD	www.granvillecsd.org
Great Escape Theme Park LLC (The)	www.thegreatescape.com
Great Lakes Commission	www.glc.org
Great Lakes United	www.glu.org
Great Neck Chamber of Commerce	www.greatneckchamber.org
Great Neck UFSD	www.greatneck.k12.ny.us
Greater Amsterdam SD	gasd.neric.org
Greater Binghamton New York Convention and Visitors Bureau	www.binghamtoncvb.com
Greater Johnstown SD	www.johnstownschools.org
Greater New York Hospital Association	www.gnyha.org
Greater Niagara Newspapers	www.lockportjournal.com
Greater NY Auto Dealers' Assn Inc	www.gnyada.com
Greater Rochester Association of Realtors Inc	www.homesteadnet.com
Greater Rochester Visitors Association	www.visitrochester.com

See Organization Index for page numbers.

World Wide Web (URL) Index

Greater Southern Tier BOCES (Schuyler-Chemung-Tioga-Allegany-Steuben)	www.gstboces.org
Greater Syracuse Association of Realtors Inc	www.cnyrealtor.com
Greece Chamber of Commerce	www.greecechamber.org
Greece CSD	www.greece.k12.ny.us
Greece, Town of	www.townofgreece.org
Green Chimneys School-Green Chimneys Children's Services Inc	www.greenchimneys.org
Green Island Democratic Association	www.tgkandassc.com
Green Island UFSD	www.greenisland.org
Greenberg Traurig, LLP	www.gtlaw.com
Greenberg, Traurig Political Action Committee	www.gtlaw.com
Greenburgh 7 CSD	www.greenburgh.k12.ny.us
Greenburgh, Town of	www.greenburghny.com
Greene County	www.greenegovernment.com
Greene County Department of Planning & Economic Development	www.discovergreene.com
Greene County Soil & Water Conservation District	www.gcswcd.com
Greene County Tourism Promotion	www.greenetourism.com
Greene CSD	www.greenecsd.org
Greenmarket/Council on the Environment of NYC	www.cenyc.org
Greenport UFSD	www.greenport.k12.ny.us
GreenThumb	www.greenthumbnyc.org
Greenville CSD	www.greenville.k12.ny.us
Greenwich Chamber of Commerce (Greater Greenwich)	www.greenwichchamber.org
Greenwich CSD	www.greenwichcsd.org
Greenwich Village-Chelsea Chamber of Commerce	www.gvccc.com
Greenwood Lake and West Milford News	www.greenwoodlakenews.com
Greenwood Lake Chamber of Commerce	www.greenwoodlakeny.org
Greenwood Lake UFSD	gwl.ouboces.org
Groton CSD	www.lightlink.com/grotonhs
Group Health Inc	www.ghi.com
Guide Dog Foundation for the Blind Inc	www.guidedog.org
Guilderland Chamber of Commerce	www.guilderlandchamber.com
Guilderland CSD	www.guilderlandschools.org
Guilderland Industrial Development Agency (Town of)	www.guilderland.org
Guilderland, Town of	www.guilderland.org
GVA Williams	www.gvawilliams.com
H J Kalikow & Co LLC	www.hjkalikow.com
Hadley-Luzerne CSD	www.hlcsd.org
Hager, Susan	www.uwnys.org
Haldane CSD	www.haldaneschool.org
Half Hollow Hills CSD	www.halfhollowhills.k12.ny.us
Hamburg Chamber of Commerce	www.hamburg-chamber.org
Hamburg CSD	www.hamburgschools.org
Hamburg Industrial Development Agency	www.townofhamburgny.com
Hamburg, Town of	www.townofhamburgny.com
Hamilton College	www.hamilton.edu
Hamilton CSD	hcscolgate.edu
Hamilton-Fulton-Montgomery BOCES	www.hfmboces.org
Hammond CSD	hammond.sllboces.org
Hampton Bays Chamber of Commerce	www.hamptonbayschamber.com
Hampton Bays UFSD	www.hbschools.org
Hancock Area Chamber of Commerce	www.hancockareachamber.com
Hancock CSD	hancock.stier.org
Hannan, K T Public Affairs Inc	www.kthpa.com
Harborfields CSD	www.harborfieldscsd.net
Harlem Chamber of Commerce (Greater Harlem)	www.harlemdiscover.com/chamber
Harpursville CSD	www.hcs.stier.org

See Organization Index for page numbers.

World Wide Web (URL) Index

Harris Beach LLP	www.nysba.org
Harris Interactive Inc	www.harrisinteractive.com
Harrison CSD	www.harrisoncsd.org
Harrison, Town/Village of	www.townharrison.org
Harrisville CSD	www.hcsk12.org
Harter Secrest & Emery, LLP	www.hartersecrest.com
Hartford CSD	www.hartfordcsd.org
Hartman & Winnicki, PC	www.hartmanwinnicki.com
Hartwick College	www.hartwick.edu
Harvestworks	www.harvestworks.org
Hastings-on-Hudson Chamber of Commerce	www.hastingsgov.org
Hastings-On-Hudson UFSD	www.hastings.k12.ny.us
Hauppauge UFSD	www.hauppauge.k12.ny.us
Haverstraw, Town of	www.townofhaverstraw.us
Hawk Creek Wildlife Center Inc	www.hawkcreek.org
Hawkins Delafield & Wood LLP	www.hawkins.com
Hawthorne-Cedar Knolls UFSD	district.hcks.org
HBA of CNY Local Build PAC	www.hbaofcny.com
Health & Hospitals Corporation, NYC	www.nyc.gov/hhc
Health & Mental Hygiene, Dept of, NYC	www.nyc.gov/html/doh
Health Care Providers' PAC	www.nyshcp.org
Health Department	www.nyhealth.gov
Health Plan Assn Inc (NY)	www.nyhpa.org
Health Research Inc	www.hrinet.org
Health, Education, Labor & Pensions	www.help.senate.gov
Healthcare Assn of NYS PAC (HANYS PAC)	www.hanys.org
Healthcare Association of New York State	www.hanys.org
HeartShare Human Services of New York, Roman Catholic Diocese of Brooklyn	www.heartshare.org
Hebrew Union College - Jewish Institute of Religion	www.huc.edu
Helen Hayes Hospital	www.helenhayeshospital.org
Helen Keller Services for the Blind	www.helenkeller.org
Helene Fuld College of Nursing North General Hospital	www.helenefuld.edu
Hempstead Industrial Development Agency (Town of)	www.tohida.org
Hempstead UFSD	www.hempsteadschools.org
Hempstead, Town of	www.townofhempstead.org; www.toh.li
Hempstead, Village of	www.villageofhempstead.org
Hendrick Hudson CSD	www.henhudschools.org
Henrietta, Town of	www.townofhenrietta.org
Herkimer County	www.herkimercounty.org
Herkimer County Chamber of Commerce	www.herkimercountychamber.com
Herkimer County Community College	www.herkimer.edu
Herkimer County Industrial Development Agency	www.herkimercountyida.com
Herkimer CSD	www.herkimercsd.org
Herkimer-Fulton-Hamilton-Otsego BOCES	www.herkimer-boces.org
Hermon-Dekalb CSD	www.hdcsk12.org
Herricks UFSD	www.herricks.org
Heslin Rothenberg Farley & Mesiti PC	www.hrfmlaw.com
Heuvelton CSD	www.heuvelton.k12.ny.us
Hewlett-Woodmere UFSD	www.hewlett-woodmere.net
Heyman, Neil	www.snya.org
Hicksville Chamber of Commerce	www.hicksvillechamber.com
Highland CSD	www.highland-k12.org
Highland Falls CSD	www.hffmcsd.org
Hilbert College	www.hilbert.edu
Hiller, Elise L	www.cabletvny.com
Hilton CSD	www.hilton.k12.ny.us

See Organization Index for page numbers.

World Wide Web (URL) Index

Hines-Kramer, Amy .... www.nycreditunions.org
Hinman Straub, PC .... www.hspm.com
Hirshorn, Donald P .... www.rpea.org
Hispanic Federation .... www.hispanicfederation.org
Hispanic Outreach Services .... www.hispanicoutreachservices.org
Historic Hudson Valley .... www.hudsonvalley.org
Hobart & William Smith Colleges .... www.hws.edu
Hodgson Russ, LLP .... www.hodgsonruss.com
Hofstra University .... www.hofstra.edu
Hofstra University, School of Law .... www.hofstra.edu/law
Holland & Knight Committee for Responsible Gov't (The) .... www.hklaw.com
Holland CSD .... www.hlnd.wnyric.org
Holland Patent CSD .... www.hpschools.org
Holley CSD .... www.holleycsd.org
Home Care Assn of NYS Inc .... www.hcanys.org
Home Care Association of New York State Inc .... www.hcanys.org
Homeland Security .... www.hsc.house.gov
Homeland Security & Governmental Affairs .... www.hsgac.senate.gov
Homeless Services, Department of, NYC .... www.nyc.gov/dhs
Homer CSD .... www.homercentral.org
Homes for the Homeless/Institute for Children & Parties .... www.homesforthehomeless.com
Homes for the Homeless/Institute for Children & Poverty .... www.homesforthehomeless.com
Honeoye CSD .... www.honeoye.org
Honeoye Falls-Lima CSD .... www.hflcsd.org
Hood, William L .... www.aa.com
Hoosic Valley CSD www.hoosickvalley.k12.ny.us
Hopevale UFSD at Hamburg .... www.hopevale.com
Hornell Area Chamber of Commerce/Hornell Industrial Development Agency (City of) . www.hornellny.com
Horseheads CSD .... www.horseheadsdistrict.com
Hospice & Palliative Care Association of NYS Inc .... www.hpcanys.org
Hostos Community College .... www.hostos.cuny.edu
Hotel Assn of NYC Inc PAC .... www.hanyc.org
Hotel Association of New York City Inc .... www.hanyc.org
Houghton College .... www.houghton.edu
House Administration .... http://cha.house.gov
Housing & Community Renewal, Division of .... www.dhcr.state.ny.us
Housing & Community Renewal, NYS Division of .... www.dhcr.state.ny.us
Housing Authority, NYC .... www.nyc.gov/nycha
Housing Preservation & Development, Dept of, NYC .... www.nyc.gov/hpd
Housing Works Inc .... www.housingworks.org
Housing Works, Albany Advocacy Ctr .... www.housingworks.org
HSBC USA Inc .... www.us.hsbc.com
Hudson City SD .... www.hudsoncityschooldistrict.com
Hudson Falls CSD .... www.hfcsd.org
Hudson River Cruises .... www.hudsonrivercruises.com
Hudson River Environmental Society .... www.hres.org
Hudson River Sloop Clearwater Inc .... www.clearwater.org
Hudson River Valley Greenway .... www.hudsongreenway.state.ny.us
Hudson River-Black River Regulating District .... www.hrbrrd.com
Hudson Valley Business Journal .... www.hvbj.com
Hudson Valley Chapter, Nat'l Electrical Contractors Assn (NECA), PAC .... www.electricnewyork.org
Hudson Valley Community College .... www.hvcc.edu
Hudson Valley Gateway Chamber of Commerce .... www.hvgatewaychamber.com
Hudson Valley Grass Roots Energy & Environmental Network .... www.hvgreentimes.org
Hudson Valley Newspapers Inc .... www.thedailymail.net
Human Resources Administration, Dept of, NYC .... www.nyc.gov/html/hra

See Organization Index for page numbers.

World Wide Web (URL) Index

Human Rights Commission on, NYC	www.nyc.gov/cchr
Human Rights First	www.humanrightsfirst.org
Human Rights Watch	www.hrw.org
Human Rights, State Division of	www.dhr.state.ny.us
Humane Society of the United States, Mid Atlantic Regional Office	www.hsus.org
Hunger Action Network of NYS (HANNYS)	www.hungeractionnys.org
Hunter Chamber of Commerce (Town of)	www.hunterchamber.org
Hunter College	www.hunter.cuny.edu
Hunter College, Brookdale Center for Healthy Aging and Longevity	www.brookdale.org
Hunter Mountain Ski Bowl	www.huntermtn.com
Huntington Township Chamber of Commerce	www.huntingtonchamber.com
Huntington UFSD	www.hufsd.edu
Huntington, Town of	town.huntington.ny.us
Hyde Park Chamber of Commerce	www.hydeparkchamber.org
Hyde Park CSD	www.hydeparkschools.org
Hyde Park, Town of	www.hydeparkny.us
IAFF Firepac NY Non-Federal	www.iaff.org
IBM Corporation	www.ibm.com
Ichabod Crane CSD	www.berk.com~ichabod/
Ilion CSD	www.ilion-csd.org
Independent Agents PAC	www.iiaany.org
Independent Bankers Association of NYS	ibanys.net
Independent Oil & Gas Association of New York	www.iogany.org
Independent Power Producers of NY Inc	www.ippny.org
Independent Power Producers of NY PAC	www.ippny.org
Indian Affairs, Committee on	http://indian.senate.gov
Indian Lake Chamber of Commerce	www.indian-lake.com
Indian Lake CSD	www.ilcsd.org
Indian River CSD	www.ircsd.org
INFORM Inc	www.informinc.org
Information Technology & Telecommunications, Dept of, NYC	www.nyc.gov/doitt
Inlet Information Office	www.inletny.com
Inside Albany Productions Inc	www.insidealbany.com
Inspector General (NYS), Office of the	www.ig.state.ny.us
Institute for Family Health (The)	www.institute2000.org
Institute for Socio-Economic Studies	www.socioeconomic.org
Institute of Design & Construction	www.idc.edu
Institute of Ecosystem Studies	www.ecostudies.org
Institute of Public Administration/NYU Wagner	www.wagner.nyu.edu
Insurance Brokers' Association of the State of New York	www.ibany.org
Insurance Department	www.ins.state.ny.us
Insurance Fund (NYS)	www.nysif.com
Intelligence, House Permanent Select Committee on	http://intelligence.house.gov
Intelligence, Select Committee on	www.intelligence.senate.gov
InterAgency Council of Mental Retardatn & Developmental Disabilities	www.iacny.org
Interboro Institute	www.interboro.edu
Interest on Lawyer Account (IOLA) Fund of the State of NY	www.iola.org
Intermagnetics General Corporation	www.igc.com
Internal Revenue Service	www.irs.gov
International Flavors & Fragrances Inc	www.iff.com
International Institute of Buffalo, NY, Inc	www.iibuff.org
International Paper Political Action Committee	www.internationalpaper.com
International Relations	www.internationalrelations.house.gov
International Union of Painters and Allied Trades Legislative & Educational Committee	www.iupat.org
Interstate Environmental Commission	www.iec-nynjct.org
Interstate Oil & Gas Compact Commission	www.iogcc.state.ok.us

See Organization Index for page numbers.

World Wide Web (URL) Index

Investigation, Department of, NYC .... www.nyc.gov/html/doi
Iona College .... www.iona.edu
Irondequoit, Town of .... www.irondequoit.org
Ironworkers Political Action League .... www.ironworkers.org
Iroquois CSD .... www.iroquois.wnyric.org
Iroquois Healthcare Alliance .... www.iroquois.org
Irvington UFSD .... www.irvingtonschools.org
IRX Therapeutics Inc .... www.irxtherapeutics.com
Island Drafting & Technical Institute .... www.idti.edu
Island Park UFSD www.ips.k12.ny.us
Island Trees UFSD .... www.islandtrees.org
Islip Chamber of Commerce .... www.islipchamberofcommerce.com
Islip Economic Development Division & Industrial Development Agency (Town of) ..... www.isliptown.org
Islip Industrial Development Agency (Town of) .... www.isliptown.org
Islip UFSD www.islip.k12.ny.us
Islip, Town of .... www.isliptown.org
ITAR-TASS News Agency .... www.itar-tass.com
Ithaca City SD www.icsd.k12.ny.us
Ithaca College .... www.ithaca.edu
Ithaca Journal (The) .... www.theithacajournal.com
Ithaca, City of .... www.cityofithaca.org
Ithaca/Tompkins County Convention & Visitors Bureau .... www.visitithaca.com
ITT Technical Institute .... www.itt-tech.edu
IUOE Local 106 Voluntary PAF www.iuoelocal106.org
IUOE Local 17 PAC www.iuoe17.org
IUOE Local 463 State & Local PAC & PEF www.iuoe463.org
J J Higgins Properties Inc .... www.jjhigginsproperties.com
Jacobs Engineering .... www.jacobs.com
Jamaica Chamber of Commerce .... www.jccnewyork.net
Jamaica Development Corporation (Greater Jamaica) .... www.gjdc.org
Jamestown Business College .... www.jbcny.org
Jamestown City SD .... www.jamestownpublicschools.org
Jamestown Community College .... www.sunyjcc.edu
Jamestown, City of .... www.town.ithaca.ny.us
Jamesville-Dewitt CSD .... www.jamesvilledewitt.org
JAMS .... www.jamsadr.com
Japanese American Social Services Inc .... www.jassi.org
Japanese Chamber of Commerce .... www.jcciny.org
Jefferson .... www.co.jefferson.ny.us
Jefferson Community College .... www.sunyjefferson.edu
Jefferson County .... www.co.jefferson.ny.us
Jefferson-Lewis-Hamilton-Herkimer-Oneida BOCES .... www.boces.com
Jericho UFSD .... www.bestschools.org
Jewish Board of Family & Children's Services .... www.jbfcs.org
Jewish Community Relations Council of NY Inc .... www.jcrcny.org
Jewish Home & Hospital (The) .... www.jewishhome.org
Jewish Museum (The) .... www.thejewishmuseum.org
Jewish Theological Seminary .... www.jtsa.edu
Jewish War Veterans of the USA .... www.jwv.org
Jewish War Veterans of the USA, State of NY .... www.jwv.org
John Jay College of Criminal Justice .... www.jjay.cuny.edu
Johnsburg CSD .... www.johnsburgcsd.org
Johnson City CSD .... www.jcschools.org
Johnson Newspaper Corp .... www.mtelegram.com
Johnson Newspaper Corporation .... www.registerstar.com
Johnson, Stephen Philip .... www.cornell.edu

See Organization Index for page numbers.

World Wide Web (URL) Index

Jordan-Elbridge CSD	www.jecsd.org
Journal News (The)/Gannett Co Inc	www.thejournalnews.com
Journal of Commerce	www.joc.com
Journal Register Co.	www.oneidadispatch.com
Journal Register Company	www.saratogian.com
Journal-Register	www.journal-register.com
Judiciary	www.judiciary.senate.gov
Juilliard School (The)	www.juilliard.edu
Juvenile Justice, Department of, NYC	www.nyc.gov/html/djj
Katharine Gibbs School-Melville	www.gibbsmelville.com
Katharine Gibbs School-New York City	www.gibbsny.edu
Katonah-Lewisboro UFSD	www.klschools.org
Kaye Scholer LLP	www.kayescholer.com
Keene CSD	www.kcs.neric.org
Kendall CSD	www.kendallschools.org
Kenmore-Tonawanda UFSD	www.kenton.k12.ny.us
Kenmore-Town of Tonawanda Chamber of Commerce	www.ken-ton.org
Keshequa CSD	www.keshequa.org
Keuka College	www.keuka.edu
King's College (The)	www.tkc.edu
King, Barbara	www.wehealnewyork.org
Kings County (NYC Borough of Brooklyn)	www.brooklyn-usa.org
Kings County Democratic Party	www.brooklyndems.com
Kings Park Chamber of Commerce	www.kingsparkli.com
Kings Park CSD	www.kpcsd.k12.ny.us
Kingsborough Community College	www.kbcc.cuny.edu
Kingston City SD	www.kingstoncityschools.org
Kingston, City of	www.ci.kingston.ny.us
Kirsch, Richard	www.citizenactionny.org
Komanoff Energy Associates	www.carbontax.org
Konheim & Ketcham Inc	www.konheimketcham.com
Korean Community Services of Metropolitan NY	www.kcsny.org
Korean War Veterans	www.kwva.org
KPMG LLP	www.kpmg.com
Kramer Levin Naftalis & Frankel, LLP	www.kramerlevin.com
Kriss, Kriss, Brignola & Persing, LLP	www.krisslawoffice.com
Kruly, Kenneth	www.canisius.edu
Krupke, Bruce W	www.nysdfi.org
Kudlow & Company LLC	www.kudlow.com
La Fargeville CSD	www.lafargevillecsd.org
Labor Department	www.labor.state.ny.us
Labor Relations, Office of, NYC	www.nyc.gov/html/olr
Labor-Management Standards Office (OLMS)	www.olms.dol.gov
Labor-Religion Coalition, Inc (NYS)	www.labor-religion.org
Laboratory Institute of Merchandising	www.limcollege.edu
Laborers' Intl Union of North America 435 Voluntary PAF	www.nysliuna.org
Lackawanna Area Chamber of Commerce	www.lackawannachamber.com
Lackawanna City SD	www.lackawannaschools.org
LaFayette CSD	www.lafayetteschools.org
LaGuardia Community College	www.lagcc.cuny.edu
Lake George CSD	www.lkgeorge.org
Lake George Park Commission	www.lgpc.state.ny.us
Lake George Regional Chamber of Commerce	www.lakegeorgechamber.com
Lake Luzerne Chamber of Commerce	www.lakeluzernechamber.org
Lake Placid Chamber of Commerce	www.lakeplacid.com
Lake Placid/Essex County Convention & Visitors Bureau	www.lakeplacid.com

See Organization Index for page numbers.

World Wide Web (URL) Index

Lake Pleasant CSD . . . . www.lpschools.com
Lake Shore Savings . . . . www.lakeshoresavings.com
Lakeland CSD . . . . www.lakelandschools.org
Lambda Legal Defense & Education Fund Inc . . . . www.lambdalegal.org
Lanahan, Kevin . . . . www.coned.com
Lancaster Area Chamber of Commerce . . . . www.laccny.org
Lancaster CSD . . . . www.lancasterschools.org
Lancaster Industrial Development Agency (Town of) . . . . www.lancasterny.com
Lancaster, Town of . . . . www.erie.gov/lancaster/depts; www.lancasterny.com
Land Trust Alliance Northeast Program . . . . www.lta.org
Landauer Realty Group Inc . . . . www.landauer.com
Landmarks Preservation Commission, NYC . . . . www.nyc.gov/landmarks
Lansing CSD . . . . wwwlansingschools.org
Lasky, Roy E . . . . www.nysdental.org
Law Department . . . . www.oag.state.ny.us
Law Office of Anne Reynolds Copps . . . . arcopps.net
Law, Department of, NYC . . . . www.nyc.gov/html/law
Lawrence UFSD . . . . www.lawrence.org
Lawyers' Fund for Client Protection . . . . www.nylawfund.org
Lawyers' PAC (LAWPAC) . . . . www.weitzlux.com
Le Moyne College . . . . www.lemoyne.edu
Le Roy CSD . . . . www.leroycsd.org
Leader (The) . . . . www.the-leader.com
Leader-Herald (The) . . . . www.leaderherald.com
League for the Hard of Hearing . . . . www.lhh.org
League of Women Voters of New York State . . . . www.lwvny.org
Learning Leaders . . . . www.learningleaders.org
Lee Corporation . . . . www.poststar.com
Legal Action Center Inc . . . . www.lac.org
Legal Action Center of the City of NY Inc . . . . www.lac.org
Legal Action Ctr of the City of NY Inc . . . . www.lac.org
Legal Aid Society . . . . www.legal-aid.org
Legal Aid Society, Community Law Offices . . . . www.legal-aid.org
Legal Services of the Hudson Valley . . . . www.lshv.org
Legislative Affairs Office, NYC Mayor's City . . . . www.ci.nyc.ny.us
Legislative Correspondents Association . . . . www.nys.nys.com
Legislative Gazette . . . . www.legislativegazette.com
Lehman College . . . . www.lehman.edu
LeRay, Town of . . . . www.townofleray.org
Lesbian, Gay, Bisexual & Transgender Community Ctr - Not For Profit . . . . . www.gaycenter.org
Letchworth CSD www.letchworth.k12.ny.us
Levene, Gouldin & Thompson LLP . . . . www.binghamtonlaw.com
Levine, Laurence J . . . . www.btoba.org
Levittown UFSD . . . . www.levittownschools.com
Lewis County . . . . www.lewiscountyny.org
Lewis County Chamber of Commerce . . . . www.lewiscountychamber.org
Lewis County Industrial Development Agency . . . . www.lcida.org
Lewiston-Porter CSD . . . . www.lew-port.com
Liberty CSD www.libertyk12.org
Liberty Group New York Holdings Inc . . . . www.herkimertelegram.com
Liberty Group Publishing . . . . www.the-leader.com
Library Assn (NY) . . . . www.nyla.org
Library, Brooklyn Public . . . . www.brooklynpubliclibrary.org
Library, New York Public . . . . www.nypl.org
Library, Queens Borough Public . . . . www.queenslibrary.org
Life Insurance Council of New York, Inc . . . . www.licony.org

See Organization Index for page numbers.

World Wide Web (URL) Index

Life Insurance Council of NY PAC (LICONY)	www.licony.org
Lifespire	www.lifespire.org
Lighthouse International	www.lighthouse.org
Lincoln Center for the Performing Arts Inc	www.lincolncenter.org
Lincoln Ctr for the Performing Arts Inc	www.lincolncenter.org
Lindenhurst UFSD	www.lindenhurstschools.org
Lindenhurst, Village of	www.villageoflindenhurst.com
Lisbon CSD	lisboncs.schoolwires.com
Little Falls City SD	www.lfcsd.com
Little Flower Children & Family Services	www.littleflowerny.org
Little Flower UFSD	www.littleflowerufsd.org
Littman Krooks LLP	www.lkrlaw.com
Liverpool Chamber of Commerce (Greater Liverpool)	www.liverpoolchamber.com
Liverpool CSD	www.liverpool.k12.ny.us
Livingston County	www.co.livingston.state.ny.us
Livingston County Chamber of Commerce	www.livchamber.com
Livingston County Economic Development Office & Industrial Development Agency	www.build-here.com
Livingston Manor CSD	lmcs.k12.ny.us
Livonia CSD	www.livoniacsd.org
Local 138, 138A & 138B International Union of Operating Engineers	www.local138.com
Local 30 IUOE PAC	www.iuoe30.org
Local Initiative Support Corporation	www.liscnet.org
Lockport City SD	www.locport.k12.ny.us
Lockport Industrial Development Agency (Town of)	www.elockport.com
Lockport Union-Sun & Journal	www.lockportjournal.com
Lockport, City of	www.elockport.com
Lockport, Town of	www.elockport.com/index_town.html
Locust Valley CSD	www.lvcsd.k12.ny.us
Loft Board, NYC	www.nyc.gov/html/loft
Long Beach Chamber of Commerce	www.longbeachnychamber.com
Long Beach City SD	www.lbeach.org
Long Beach, City of	www.longbeachny.org
Long Island Assn Action Committe	www.longislandassociation.org
Long Island Association	www.longislandassociation.org
Long Island Business Institute-Commack	www.libi.edu
Long Island Business Institute-Flushing	www.libi.edu
Long Island College Hospital School of Nursing	www.wehealny.org
Long Island Contractors Assn PAC Inc	www.licanys.org
Long Island Convention & Visitors Bureau & Sports Commission	www.funonli.com
Long Island Council of Dedicated Merchants Chamber of Commerce	www.cdmlongisland.com
Long Island Development Corporation	www.lidc.org
Long Island Educational Opportunity Center	www.li.sunyeoc.org
Long Island Farm Bureau	www.lifb.com
Long Island Federation of Labor AFL-CIO	www.lilabor.org
Long Island Power Authority	www.lipower.org
Long Island Rail Road Commuter's Council	www.pcac.org
Long Island University	www.liu.edu
Long Lake CSD	www.longlakecsd.org
Long Term Care Community Coalition	www.nhccnys.org
Long View Publishing Co	www.pww.org
Longwood CSD	www.longwood.k12.ny.us
Lottery, Division of	www.nylottery.org
Louloudes, Virginia	www.offbroadwayonline.com
Lower Manhattan Cultural Council	www.lmcc.net
Lowville Academy & CSD	www.lacs-ny.org
Lyme CSD	www.lymecsd.org

See Organization Index for page numbers.

World Wide Web (URL) Index

Lynbrook UFSD www.lynbrook.k12.ny.us
Lyncourt UFSD. . . . . www.lyncourt.cnyric.org
Lyndonville CSD . . . . www.lyndonvillecsd.org
Lyons CSD . . . . www.lyonscsd.org
Lysander, Town of . . . . www.townoflysander.org
M&T Bank Corporation . . . . www.mandtbank.com
MAC PAC . . . . www.nysomce.org
MacKenzie, Duncan R . . . . www.nysar.com
Madison County . . . . www.madisoncounty.org
Madison County Industrial Development Agency . . . . www.madisoncountyny.com/mcida
Madison CSD . . . . www.madisoncentralny.org
Madison Square Garden Corp. . . . . www.thegarden.com
Madison-Oneida BOCES . . . . www.moboces.org
Madrid-Waddington CSD. www.mwcsk12.org
Maher, Daniel F, Jr . . . . www.elany.org
Mahopac CSD. www.mahopac.k12.ny.us
Mahopac-Carmel Chamber of Commerce . . . . www.mahopacchamber.com
Maine-Endwell CSD. . . . . www.me.stier.org
Major League Baseball . . . . www.mlb.com
Malkin & Ross . . . . www.malkinross.com
Malone Chamber of Commerce . . . . www.malonenychamber.com
Malone CSD www.malone.k12.ny.us
Malone Telegram . . . . www.mtelegram.com
Malverne UFSD www.malverne.k12.ny.us
Mamaroneck Chamber of Commerce. . . . . www.mamaroneckchamberofcommerce.org
Mamaroneck UFSD . . . . www.mamkschools.org
Mamaroneck, Town of . . . . www.townofmamaroneck.org
Management & Budget, Office of, NYC . . . . www.nyc.gov/omb
Manchester-Shortsville CSD . . . . www.redjacket.org
Mancuso Business Development Group. . . . . www.mancusogroup.com
Mandl School . . . . www.mandlschool.com
Manhasset Chamber of Commerce. . . . . www.manhasset.org
Manhasset UFSD www.manhasset.k12.ny.us
Manhattan (New York County) . . . . www.mbpo.org
Manhattan Chamber of Commerce Inc. . . . . www.manhattancc.org
Manhattan College . . . . www.manhattan.edu
Manhattan Educational Opportunity Center . . . . www.meoc.suny.edu
Manhattan Institute (The) . . . . www.manhattan-institute.org
Manhattan Institute for Policy Research. . . . . www.manhattan-institute.org
Manhattan Institute, Center for Civic Innovation. . . . . www.manhattan-institute.org
Manhattan School of Music . . . . www.msmnyc.edu
Manhattan Sites. . . . . www.nps.gov/masi
Manhattan-Bronx Minority Business Enterprise Center. www.manhattanmbec.com
Manhattanville College. . . . . www.manhattanville.edu
Maniscalco, John D. . . . . www.nyoha.org
Manlius, Town of . . . . www.townofmanlius.org
Manufactured Housing PAC. . . . . www.nymha.org
Manufacturers Association of Central New York . . . . www.macny.org
Maplewood-Colonie Common SD . . . . www.maplewoodschools.org
Marathon CSD . . . . www.marathonschools.org
Marcellus CSD . . . . mcs.rway.com
March of Dimes Birth Defects Foundation. . . . . www.marchofdimes.com
Marcus Attorneys . . . . www.marcusattorneys.com
Marcus Whitman CSD . . . . www.mwcsd.org
Maria College of Albany . . . . www.mariacollege.edu
Marine Corps League . . . . www.mclwestchester.org

See Organization Index for page numbers.

World Wide Web (URL) Index

Marine Corps League (MCL)	www.mcleague.org
Marion CSD	www.marioncs.org
Marion S Whelan School of Practical Nursing	www.flhealth.org - Services & Programs
Marist College	www.marist.edu
Marist Institute for Public Opinion	www.maristpoll.marist.edu
Maritime Administration	www.marad.dot.gov
Marlboro CSD	marlboroschools.schoolwires.com
Marsh & McLennan Companies	www.mmc.com
Martens, Joseph J	www.osiny.org
Martin Van Buren National Historic Site	www.nps.gov/mava
Marymount Manhattan College	www.mmm.edu
Maryvale UFSD	www.maryvale.wnyric.org
Mason Tenders' District Council of Greater NY PAC	www.masontenders.org
Massapequa Chamber of Commerce	www.massapequachamber.com
Massapequa UFSD	www.msd.k12.ny.us
Massena Chamber of Commerce	www.massenany.com
Massena CSD	www.mcs.k12.ny.us
Massiah, Lesley A	www.fordham.edu
Mattituck Chamber of Commerce	www.mattituckchamber.org
Mattituck-Cutchogue UFSD	www.mufsd.org
Mayfield CSD	www.mayfieldk12.com
Mayville/Chautauqua Chamber of Commerce	www.mayville-chautauquachamber.org
MBIA Insurance Corporation	www.mbia.com
McGraw CSD	www.mcgrawschools.org
McMahon & Grow	www.mgglaw.com
MDRC	www.mdrc.org
Mechanical Technology Incorporated	www.mechtech.com
Mechanicville Area Chamber of Commerce	www.mechanicville.org
Mechanicville City SD	www.mechanicville.org
Mechanicville/Stillwater Industrial Development Agency	www.mechanicville-stillwater-ida.org
Medaille College	www.medaille.edu
Medgar Evers College	www.mec.cuny.edu
Medical Examiner, Office of Chief, NYC	www.nyc.gov
Medical Society of the State of New York, Div of Socio-Medical Economics	www.mssny.org
Medical Society of the State of NY, Governmental Affairs Division	www.mssny.org
Medina CSD	www.medinacsd.org
Memorial Hospital School of Nursing	www.nehealth.com
Memorial Sloan-Kettering Cancer Center	www.mskcc.org
Menaker & Herrmann LLP	www.mhjur.com
Menands UFSD	www.menandsschool.nycap.rr.com
Mental Health Association in NYS	www.mhanys.org
Mental Health Association of NYC Inc	www.mhaofnyc.org
Mental Health Association of NYS Inc	www.mhanys.org
Mental Health, Office of	www.omh.state.ny.us
Mental Retardation & Developmental Disabilities, Office of	www.omr.state.ny.us
Mercury Public Affairs	www.mercurypublicaffairs.com
Mercy College	www.mercy.edu
Merrick Chamber of Commerce	www.merrickchamber.org
Merrick UFSD	www.merrick-k6.org
Merrill Lynch & Co Inc	www.ml.com
Messenger Post Newspapers	www.mpnewspaper.com
Messinger Woods Wildlife Care & Education Center Inc	www.messingerwoods.org
MetLife	www.metlife.com
Metlife Inc Employees' Political Participation Fund A	www.metlife.com
MetLife Ins Co Political Fund B	www.metlife.com
Metro-North Railroad Commuter Council	www.pcac.org

See Organization Index for page numbers.

World Wide Web (URL) Index

Metro/Horohoe-Leimbach	metrohorohoe.com
Metropolitan College of New York	www.metropolitan.edu
Metropolitan Museum of Art (The)	www.metmuseum.org
Mid-America Baptist Theological Seminary Northeast Branch	www.mabts.edu
Mid-Hudson Catskill Rural & Migrant Ministry Inc	www.ruralmigrantministry.org
Mid-Hudson News Network	www.midhudsonnews.com; www.empirestatenews.net
Mid-Hudson Pattern for Progress	www.pattern-for-progress.org
Middle Country CSD	www.middlecountry.k12.ny.us
Middletown City SD	middletowncityschools.org
Mildred Elley	www.mildred-elley.edu
Military & Naval Affairs, Division of	www.dmna.state.ny.us
Military Chaplains Association of the USA (MCA)	www.mca-usa-org
Military Officers Association of America	www.moaa.org
Military Order of the Purple Heart (MOPH)	www.purpleheart.org
Millbrook CSD	www.millbrookcsd.org
Miller Place UFSD	www.millerplace.k12.ny.us
Miller Place/Mt Sinai/Sound Beach/Rocky Point Chamber of Commerce	www.cdmlongisland.com
Mineola Chamber of Commerce	www.mineolachamber.com
Mineola UFSD	www.mineola.k12.ny,us
Minerva CSD	www.minervasd.org
Minisink Valley CSD	www.minisink.com
Minority Business Development Agency	www.mbda.gov
MJ Peterson Corporation	www.mjpeterson.com
Modutank Inc	www.modutank.com
Mohawk Valley Chamber of Commerce	www.mvchamber.org
Mohawk Valley Chamber PAC	www.mvchamber.org
Mohawk Valley Community College	www.mvcc.edu
Mohawk Valley Economic Development District	www.mvedd.org
Mohawk Valley Economic Development Growth Enterprises	www.mvedge.org
Mohonasen CSD	www.mohonasen.org
Molloy College	www.molloy.edu
Monroe	www.monroe.county.gov
Monroe 1 BOCES	www.monroe.edu
Monroe 2-Orleans BOCES	www.monroe2boces.org
Monroe College-Bronx	www.monroecollege.edu
Monroe College-New Rochelle	www.monroecollege.edu
Monroe Community College	www.monroecc.edu
Monroe County	www.monroecounty.gov
Monroe County Industrial Development Agency (COMIDA)	www.growmonroe.org
Monroe, Town of	www.monroeny.org
Monroe-Woodbury CSD	www.mw.k12.ny.us
Montalbano Initiatives Inc	www.nyclobbyist.com
Montauk UFSD	www.montaukschool.org
Montclare & Wachtler	www.montclarewachtler.com
Montford Point Marine Association	www.montfordpointmarines.com
Montgomery County	www.co.montgomery.ny.us
Montgomery County Chamber of Commerce/Montgomery County Partnership	www.montgomerycountyny.com
Montgomery, Town of	www.townofmontgomery.com
Monticello CSD	www.monticelloschools.org
Monticello Raceway	www.monticelloraceway.com
Moody's Investors Service, Public Finance Group	www.moodys.com
Moravia Chamber of Commerce	www.cayuganet.org
Morello, Charles J	www.nyspffa.org
Morgan Stanley	www.morganstanley.com
Moriah CSD	www.moriahk12.org

See Organization Index for page numbers.

World Wide Web (URL) Index

Morrisville State College	www.morrisville.edu
Morrisville-Eaton CSD	www.m-ecs.org
Morse, Alan	www.jgb.org
Mothers Against Drunk Driving (MADD) of NYS	www.madd.org
Motley, Duane R.	www.nyfrf.org
Motor Vehicles Department	www.nysdmv.com
Mount Kisco Chamber of Commerce	www.mtkisco.com
Mount Markham CSD	www.mmcsd.org
Mount Pleasant, Town of	www.mtpleasant.americantowns.com
Mount Saint Mary College	www.msmc.edu
Mount Sinai Medical Center	www.mountsinaihospital.org
Mount Sinai School of Medicine of NYU	www.mssm.edu
Mount Vernon Chamber of Commerce	www.mvnycoc.org
Mount Vernon Industrial Development Agency (City of)	www.cmvny.com
Mount Vernon, City of	www.ci.mount-vernon.ny.us
Movers & Warehousemen Political Action Committee	newyorkstatemovers.com
Mt Morris CSD	www.mtmorriscsd.org
Mt Pleasant CSD	www.mtplcsd.org
Mt Pleasant-Blythedale UFSD	www.mpbschools.org
Mt Pleasant-Cottage UFSD	www.mpcsny.org
Mt Sinai UFSD	www.mtsinai.k12.ny.us
Mt Vernon City SD	mtvernoncsd.org
MTA (Metropolitan Transportation Authority)	www.mta.info
MTA Bridges & Tunnels	www.mta.info/bandt
MTA Bus Company	www.mta.info/busco
MTA Capital Construction	www.mta.info/capconstr
MTA Long Island Bus	www.mta.info/libus
MTA Long Island Rail Road	www.mta.info/lirr
MTA Metro-North Railroad	www.mta.info/mnr
MTA New York City Transit	www.mta.info/nyct
MTA Office of the Inspector General	www.mtaig.state.ny.us
Mulholland & Knapp, LLP	www.mklex.com
Mullane, Robert A	www.meua.org
Municipal Credit Union	www.nymcu.org
Municipal Electric Utilities Association	www.meua.org
Murphy, Daniel C	nyshta.org
Museum Association of New York	www.manyonline.org
NAIFA - New York State	www.naifanys.org
NAMI-NYS	www.naminys.org
Nanuet UFSD	nanunet.lhric.org
Naples CSD	www.naples.k12.ny.us
NARAL Pro-Choice, New York	www.prochoiceny.org
NARAL/NY Multicandidate PAC	www.prochoiceny.org
Nassau BOCES	www.nassauboces.org
Nassau Community College	www.ncc.edu
Nassau Council of Chambers	www.ncchambers.org
Nassau County	www.nassaucountyny.gov
Nassau County Industrial Development Agency	www.nassauida.com
Nassau County Lesbian & Gay Democrats	www.nassaugaydems.com
Nassau County PBA PAC	www.nassaupba.org
Nassau Regional Off-Track Betting Corporation	www.nassauotb.com
National Academy of Forensic Engineers	www.nafe.org
National Amputation Foundation Inc	www.nationalamputation.org
National Assn of Chain Drug Stores	www.nacds.org
National Association of Black Accountants, NY Chapter	www.nabany.org
National Association of Social Workers, NYS Chapter	www.naswnys.org

See Organization Index for page numbers.

World Wide Web (URL) Index

National Basketball Association . . . . www.nba.com
National Cemetery Administration . . . . www.cem.va.gov
National Coffee Association . . . . www.ncausa.org
National Council of Jewish Women . . . . www.ncjw.org
National Economic Research Associates . . . . www.nera.com
National Federation of Community Development Credit Unions . . . . www.cdcu.coop
National Federation of Independent Business . . . . www.nfib.org
National Football League . . . . www.nfl.com
National Fuel Gas . . . . www.nationalfuel.com
National Fuel Gas Distribution . . . . www.natfuel.com
National Grape Cooperative-Welch Foods Inc . . . . www.welchs.com
National Guard Association of the US (NGAUS) . . . . www.ngaus.org
National Highway Traffic Safety Administration, Reg II-NY . . . . www.nhtsa.dot.gov
National Hockey League . . . . www.nhl.com
National Labor Relations Board . . . . www.nlrb.gov
National League for Nursing (NLN) . . . . www.nln.org
National Marfan Foundation . . . . www.marfan.org
National Marine Fisheries Svc, Northeast Region Headquarters . . . . www.nero.noaa.gov/nero/
National Military Family Association (NMFA) . . . . www.nmfa.org
National Museum of the American Indian-George Gustav Heye Center . . . . www.nmai.si.edu
National Organization for Women, NYS . . . . www.nownys.com
National Organization for Women- NYS PAC . . . . www.nownys.org
National Park Service-Northeast Region . . . . www.nps.gov
National Transportation Safety Board . . . . www.ntsb.gov
National Trust for Historic Preservation . . . . www.nthp.org
National Urban League Inc (The) . . . . www.nul.org
National Weather Service, Eastern Region . . . . www.nws.noaa.gov
National Wildlife Federation . . . . www.nwf.org
National Women's Hall of Fame . . . . www.greatwomen.org
National Writers Union . . . . www.nwu.org
Natural Resources . . . . http://resourcescommittee.house.gov
Natural Resources Conservation Service . . . . www.ny.nrcs.usda.gov
Natural Resources Defense Council . . . . www.nrdc.org
Nature Conservancy (The) . . . . www.nature.org
Naval Enlisted Reserve Association (NERA) . . . . www.nera.org
Naval Reserve Association (NRA) . . . . www.navy-reserve.org
Navy League of the US (NLUS) . . . . www.navyleague.org
Navy League of the US (NLUS), New York Council . . . . www.nynavyleague.org
Nazareth College of Rochester . . . . www.naz.edu
NBC News (New York Bureau) . . . . www.nbc.com
NBT Bancorp Inc . . . . www.nbtbank.com
Neighborhood Preservation Coalition of NYS Inc . . . . www.npcnys.org
Nelson A Rockefeller Inst of Government, NY Forum for Info . . . . www.nysfirm.org
Nelson A Rockefeller Inst of Govt, Federalism Research Grp . . . . www.rockinst.org
Nelson A Rockefeller Inst of Govt, Higher Education Program . . . . www.rockinst.org
Nelson A Rockefeller Inst of Govt, Urban & Metro Studies . . . . www.rockinst.org
Nelson A Rockefeller Institute of Government . . . . www.rockinst.org
New City Chamber of Commerce . . . . www.newcitychamberofcommerce.org
New England Interstate Water Pollution Control Commission . . . . www.neiwpcc.org
New Era Veterans, Inc . . . . www.neweraveterans.org
New Hartford CSD . . . . www.newhartfordschools.org
New Hartford, Town of . . . . www.town.new-hartford.ny.us
New Hyde Park-Garden City Park UFSD . . . . www.nhp-gcp.org
New Lebanon CSD . . . . www.newlebanoncsd.org
New Paltz CSD www.newport.k12.ny.us/local/
New Paltz Regional Chamber of Commerce . . . . www.newpaltzchamber.org

See Organization Index for page numbers.

World Wide Web (URL) Index

New Rochelle City SD	www.nred.org
New Rochelle, Chamber of Commerce, Inc	www.newrochellechamber.org
New Rochelle, City of	www.newrochelleny.com
New School University (The)	www.newschool.edu
New School University, Department of Political Science	www.newschool.edu
New School University, Department of Sociology	www.newschool/edu
New School University, Intl Center for Migration, Ethnicity & Citizenship	www.newschool.edu/icmec
New School University, Milano Graduate School of Mgmt & Urban Policy	www.newschool.edu
New Windsor, Town of	http://town.new-windsor.ny.us
New York & Atlantic Railway (NYA)	www.anacostia.com
New York 1 News (1)	www.ny1.com
New York Academy of Art Inc	www.nyaa.edu
New York Agriculture in the Classroom	www.cerp.cornell.edu/aitc
New York AIDS Coalition	www.nyaidscoalition.org
New York Apple Association Inc	www.nyapplecountry.com
New York Aquarium	www.nyaquarium.com
New York Artists Equity Association Inc	www.anny.org
New York Association for New Americans, Inc (NYANA)	www.nyana.org
New York Association of Convenience Stores	www.nyacs.org
New York Association of Homes & Services for the Aging	www.nyahsa.org
New York Association of Psychiatric Rehabilitation Services (NYAPRS)	www.nyaprs.org
New York Bankers Association	www.nyba.com
New York Beef Industry Council Inc	www.nybeef.org
New York Biotechnology Association (The)	www.nyba.org
New York Building Congress	www.buildingcongress.com
New York Business Development Corporation	www.nybdc.com
New York Business Group on Health Inc	www.nybgh.org
New York Career Institute	www.nyci.com
New York Center for Agricultural Medicine & Health, Bassett Healthcare	www.nycamh.com
New York Chamber of Commerce (Greater New York)	www.chamber.com
New York Chiropractic College	www.nycc.edu
New York City	www.vote.nyc.ny.us
New York City Central Labor Council Political Action Committee	www.ycclc.org
New York City College of Technology	www.citytech.cuny.edu
New York City Housing Development Corporation	www.nychdc.com
New York City Off-Track Betting Corporation	www.nycotb.com
New York City Opera	www.nycopera.com
New York City School Construction Authority	schools.nyc.gov/Offices/SCA
New York City, Partnership for	www.pfnyc.org
New York Civil Liberties Union	www.nyclu.org
New York Civil Rights Coalition	www.nycivilrights.org
New York College of Health Professions	www.nycollege.edu
New York College of Podiatric Medicine	www.nycpm.edu
New York College of Traditional Chinese Medicine	www.nyctcm.edu
New York Committee for Occupational Safety & Health	www.nycosh.org
New York Community Bank	www.mynycb.com
New York Community Trust (The)	www.nycommunitytrust.org
New York Convention Center Operating Corporation	www.javitscenter.com
New York Counties Registered Nurses Association	www.nysna.org/districts/13.htm
New York County (NYC Borough of Manhattan)	www.mbpo.org
New York Daily News	www.nydailynews.com
New York Farm Bureau	www.nyfb.org
New York Field Corn Growers Association	www.nycorn.org
New York Forest Owners Association Inc	www.nyfoa.org
New York Foundation for the Arts	www.nyfa.org
New York Giants	www.giants.com

See Organization Index for page numbers.

World Wide Web (URL) Index

New York Hall of Science	www.nyscience.org
New York Health Care Alliance	www.nyhca.com
New York Health Plan Association	www.nyhpa.org
New York Holstein Association	www.nyholsteins.com
New York Immigration Coalition (The)	www.thenyic.org
New York Independent System Operator - Not For Profit	www.nyiso.com
New York Institute of Technology	www.nyit.edu
New York Insurance Association Inc	www.nyia.org
New York Islanders	www.newyorkislanders.com
New York Jets	www.newyorkjets.com
New York Landmarks Conservancy	www.nylandmarks.org
New York Law Journal	www.law.com
New York Law School	www.nyls.edu
New York Lawyers for the Public Interest	www.nylpi.org
New York League of Conservation Voters Action Fund	www.nylcv.org
New York Library Association (The)	www.nyla.org
New York Long-Term Care Brokers Ltd	www.nyltcb.com
New York Magazine (New York Metro LLC)	www.newyorkmetro.com
New York Marine Trades Association	www.nymta.com
New York Medical College	www.nymc.edu
New York Medical College, Department of Community & Preventive Medicine	www.nymc.edu
New York Medical College, Department of Medicine	www.nymc.edu
New York Medical College, School of Public Health	www.nymc.edu
New York Medical Equipment Providers PAC	www.nymep.org
New York Mercantile Exchange Inc	www.nymex.com
New York Metropolitan Transportation Council	www.nymtc.org
New York Mets	www.mets.com
New York Municipal Insurance Reciprocal (NYMIR)	www.nymir.org
New York Network	www.nyn.suny.edu
New York Newspaper Publishers Association	www.nynpa.com
New York Observer (The)	www.nyobserver.com
New York Post	www.nypost.com
New York Power Authority	www.nypa.gov
New York Presbyterian Hospital	www.med.cornell.edu; www.nyp.org
New York Press Photographers Association	www.nyppa.org
New York Public Interest Research Group	www.nypirg.org
New York Public Interest Research Group Straphangers Campaign	www.straphangers.org; www.nypirg.org
New York Public Welfare Association	www.nypwa.com
New York Racing Association	www.nyra.com
New York Republican State Committee	www.nygop.org
New York Retailers for Effective Government	www.retailcouncilnys.com
New York School of Interior Design	www.nysid.edu
New York Schools Insurance Reciprocal (NYSIR)	www.nysir.org
New York Seed Improvement Project, Cornell University, Plant Breeding Department	SeedPotato.NewYork.cornell.edu
New York Shipping Association Inc	www.nysanet.org
New York Society for the Deaf	www.nysd.org
New York State Air Force Association	www.nysafa.org
New York State Assessors' Association	www.nyassessor.com
New York State Assn of Fire Districts	www.firedistnys.com
New York State Association of Agricultural Fairs Inc	www.nyfairs.org
New York State Association of Ambulatory Surgery Centers	nysaasc.org
New York State Association of Family Services Agencies Inc	www.nysafsa.org
New York State Association of Independent Schools	www.nysais.org
New York State Athletic Commission	www.dos.state.ny.us/athletic.html
New York State Auto Dealers Association	www.nysada.com
New York State Board of Law Examiners	www.nybarexam.org

See Organization Index for page numbers.

World Wide Web (URL) Index

New York State Bridge Authority	www.nysba.net
New York State Canal Corporation	www.nyscanals.gov
New York State Catholic Conference	www.nyscatholic.org
New York State Citizens' Coalition for Children Inc	www.nysccc.org
New York State Clinical Laboratory Assn PAC	www.nyscla.com
New York State Commission of Correction	www.scoc.state.ny.us
New York State Community Action Association	www.nyscaaonline.org
New York State Congress of Parents & Teachers Inc	www.nyspta.org
New York State Conservation Council	www.nyscc.com
New York State Conservative Party	www.cpnys.org
New York State Council of Churches	www.nyscoc.org
New York State Council of School Superintendents	www.nyscoss.org
New York State Court of Claims	www.nyscourtofclaims.courts.state.ny.us/
New York State Credit Union League Inc	www.nyscul.org
New York State Dairy Foods Inc	www.nysdfi.org
New York State Dairy Foods PAC	www.nysdfi.org
New York State Democratic Committee	www.nydems.org
New York State Directory	www.greyhouse.com
New York State Disaster Preparedness Commission	www.semo.state.ny.us/dpc/
New York State Dormitory Authority	www.dasny.org
New York State Electric & Gas Corporation (NYSEG)	www.nyseg.com
New York State Energy Research & Development Authority	www.nyserda.org
New York State Environmental Facilities Corp	www.nysefc.org
New York State Ethics Commission	www.dos.state.ny.us/ethc/ethics.html
New York State Financial Control Board	www.fcb.state.ny.us
New York State Government Finance Officers Association Inc	www.nysgfoa.org
New York State Health Facilities Association Inc	www.nyshfa.org
New York State Higher Education Services Corp (NYSHESC)	www.hesc.org
New York State Hospitality & Tourism Association	www.nyshta.org
New York State Housing Finance Agency (HFA)	www.nyhomes.org
New York State Independence Party	www.ipny.org
New York State Judicial Conduct Commission	www.scjc.state.ny.us
New York State Laborers' PAC	www.nysliuna.org
New York State Law Enforcement Council	www.nyslec.org
New York State Law Reporting Bureau	www.courts.state.ny.us/reporter
New York State Law Revision Commission	www.lawrevision.state.ny.us
New York State Liquor Authority	www.abc.state.ny.us
New York State Maple Producers Association Inc	www.nysmaple.com
New York State Mortgage Loan Enforcement & Administration Corporation	www.empire.state.ny.us
New York State Motor Truck Association	www.nytrucks.org
New York State Nurses Assn PAC	www.nysna.org
New York State Nurses Association	www.nysna.org
New York State Olympic Regional Development Authority	www.orda.org
New York State Ophthalmological Society	www.nysos.com
New York State Osteopathic Medical Society	www.nysoms.org
New York State Petroleum Council	www.api.org
New York State Podiatric Medical Association	www.nyspma.org
New York State Public Employees Federation (PEF)	www.nyspef.org
New York State Public Employees' Federation PAC	www.pef.org
New York State Rehabilitation Association	www.nyrehab.org
New York State Republican Party	www.nygop.org
New York State Restaurant Association	www.nysra.org
New York State Restaurant Industry PAC	www.nysra.org
New York State Rural Development Council	www.dos.state.ny.us
New York State Rural Housing Coalition Inc	www.ruralhousing.org
New York State School Boards Association	www.nyssba.org

See Organization Index for page numbers.

World Wide Web (URL) Index

New York State School Music Association (NYSSMA)	www.nyssma.org
New York State Snowmobile Association	www.nyssnowassoc.org
New York State Society of Certified Public Accountants	www.nysscpa.org
New York State Society of Enrolled Agents	www.nyssea.org
New York State Society of Municipal Finance Officers	www.nysmunicipalfinanceofficers.org
New York State Supreme Court Officers Association	www.nysscoa.org
New York State Teachers' Retirement System	www.nystrs.org
New York State Telecommunications Association Inc	www.nysta.com
New York State Temporary Commission of Investigation	www.sic.state.ny.us
New York State Temporary Commission on Lobbying	www.nylobby.state.ny.us
New York State Theatre Education Association	www.nystea.org
New York State Thoroughbred Breeding & Development Fund Corporation	www.nybreds.com
New York State Thruway Authority	www.nysthruway.gov
New York State Travel & Vacation Association	www.nystva.org
New York State Trial Lawyers	www.nystla.org
New York State Tug Hill Commission	www.tughill.org
New York State United Teachers/AFT, AFL-CIO	www.nysut.org
New York State United Teachers/AFT, NEA, AFL-CIO	www.nysut.org
New York State Veterinary Medical Society	www.nysvms.org
New York State Woodsmen's Field Days Inc	www.starinfo.com/woodsmen/
New York Stock Exchange	www.nyse.com
New York Theological Seminary	www.nyts.edu
New York Thoroughbred Breeders Inc	www.nybreds.com
New York Times (The)	www.nytimes.com
New York Truck PAC	www.nytrucks.org
New York University	www.nyu.edu
New York University School of Law	www.law.nyu.edu/institutes/judicial
New York University, Departmentt of Politics	www.nyu.edu/gsas/dept/politics
New York University, Graduate School of Journalism	www.journalism.nyu.edu
New York University, Graduate School of Public Service	www.nyu.edu/wagner
New York University, Robert F Wagner Graduate School of Public Service	www.nyu.edu/wagner
New York University, Tisch School of the Arts	www.nyu.edu/tisch
New York University, Wagner Graduate School	www.nyu.edu/wagner
New York Urban League	www.nyul.org
New York Water Environment Association Inc (NYWEA)	www.nywea.org
New York Wine & Grape Foundation	www.newyorkwines.org
New York Wired	www.newyorkwired.com
New York Yankees	www.yankees.com
New York, Susquehanna & Western Railway	www.nysw.com
New Yorker	www.newyorker.com
New Yorktown Chamber of Commerce (The)	www.yorktownchamber.org
Newark Chamber of Commerce	www.newarknychamber.org
Newark CSD	www.newark.k12.ny.us
Newark Valley CSD	www.nvcs.stier.org
Newburgh Enlarged City SD	www.newburgh.k12.ny.us
Newburgh, City of	www.newburgh-ny.com
Newburgh, Town of	www.townofnewburgh.org
Newcomb CSD	www.newcombcsd.org
Newfane CSD	www.newfane.wnyric.org
Newfield CSD	www.newschools.org
Newsday	www.newsday.com
Newsday Inc	www.newsday.com
Newsweek Magazine (MSNBC, Microsoft Corp)	www.newsweek.msnbc.com
Next Wave Inc	www.nextwave.info
Niagara	www.elections.niagara.ny.us
Niagara County	www.niagaracounty.com

See Organization Index for page numbers.

World Wide Web (URL) Index

Niagara County Community College	www.niagaracc.suny.edu
Niagara County Ind Dev Agency	www.ncida.org
Niagara Falls Bridge Commission	www.niagarafallsbridges.com
Niagara Falls City SD	www.nfschools.net
Niagara Falls, City of	www.niagarafallsusa.org
Niagara Frontier Transportation Authority	www.nfta.com
Niagara Gazette	www.niagara-gazette.com
Niagara University	www.niagara.edu
Niagara USA Chamber of Commerce	www.niagarachamber.org
Niagara-Wheatfield CSD	www.nwcsd.k12.ny.us
Niskayuna CSD	www.niskayunaschools.org
Niskayuna, Town of	www.niskayuna.org
NLOA-PAC	www.nloaus.org
NOFA-NY Certified Organic LLC	www.nofany.org
Nonprofit Coordinating Committee of New York	www.npccny.org
Norddeutsche Landesbank Girozentrale	www.nordlbnewyork.com
Norris, Kelly K	www.nysspe.org
North Babylon UFSD	www.nbsd.org
North Bellmore UFSD	www.northbellmoreschools.org
North Bronx Career Counseling & Outreach Center	www.nbx.eoc.suny.edu
North Collins CSD	www.northcollins.com
North Colonie CSD	www.northcolonie.org
North Country Community College	www.nccc.edu
North Country Savings Bank	www.northcountrysavings.com
North Country Vietnam Veterans Association, Post 1	www.ncvva.org
North Fork Bank	www.northforkbank.com
North Fork Chamber of Commerce	www.northforkchamber.org
North Hempstead, Town of	www.northhempstead.com
North Merrick UFSD	www.north-merrick.k12.ny.us
North Rockland CSD	www.nrcsd.org
North Rose-Wolcott CSD	www.nrwcs.org
North Salem CSD	www.northsalemschools.org
North Shore Animal League America	www.nsalamerica.org
North Shore CSD	www.northshore.k12.ny.us
North Syracuse CSD	www.nscsd.org
North Tonawanda City SD	www.ntcityschools.wnyric.org
North Tonawanda, City of	www.northtonawanda.org
North Warren Chamber of Commerce	www.adirondacklakesandrivers.com
North Warren CSD	www.northwarren.k12.ny.us
Northeast Equipment Dealers Association Inc	www.ne-equip.com
Northeast Gas Association	www.northeastgas.org
Northeast Health Inc	www.nehealth.com
Northeast Organic Farming Association of New York	www.nofany.org
Northeastern Clinton CSD	www.nccscougars.org
Northeastern Forest Fire Protection Commission	www.nffpc.org
Northeastern Loggers' Association	www.northernlogger.com
Northeastern Queens Nature & Historical Preserve Commission	www.sneq.com
Northeastern Seminary	www.nes.edu
Northern Adirondack CSD	www.nacs1.org
Northern District	www.nynb.uscourts.gov
Northport-East Northport UFSD	www.northport.k12.ny.us
Northville CSD	northvillecsd.k12.ny.us
Norwich City SD	www.norwichcityschooldistrict.com
Norwood-Norfolk CSD	www.nncsk12.net
Nostradamus Advertising	www.nostradamus.net
Nuclear Regulatory Commission	www.nrc.gov

See Organization Index for page numbers.

World Wide Web (URL) Index

Nurse Practitioner Assn of NYS (The)	www.thenpa.org
Nurse Practitioners Assn NYS (The)	www.thenpa.org
NY Airport Service	www.nyairportservice.com
NY Association of Local Government Records Officers	www.nyalgro.org
NY Association of Training & Employment Professionals (NYATEP)	www.nyatep.org
NY Capitolwire (Associated Press)	www.capitolwire.com
NY Commercial Association of Realtors	www.nyscarxchange.com
NY Council on Problem Gambling	www.nyproblemgambling.org
NY Counseling Association Inc	www.nycounseling.org
NY County Lawyers' Association	www.nycla.org
NY EDPAC	www.nyedpac.org
NY Farms!	www.nyfarms.info
NY Film Academy	www.nyfa.com
NY Foundation for Senior Citizens Inc	www.nyfsc.org
NY Health Information Management Association Inc	www.nyhima.org
NY Housing Association Inc	www.nyhousing.org
NY League of Conservation Voters/NY Conservation Education Fund	www.nylcv.org
NY Life Insurance Co	www.newyorklife.com
NY Mills UFSD	www.newyorkmills.org
NY Oil Heating Association	www.nyoha.org
NY Physical Therapy Association	www.nypta.org
NY Podiatry PAC	www.nyspma.org
NY Press Association	www.nynewspapers.com
NY Propane Gas Association	www.nypropane.com
NY Property Insurance Underwriting Association	www.nypiua.com
NY Society of Association Executives Inc (NYSAE)	www.nysaenet.org
NY State Association of Town Superintendents of Highways Inc	www.nystownhwys.org
NY State Historical Association/Fenimore Art Museum	www.nysha.org; www.farmersmuseum.org
NY State Society of Physician Assistants	www.nysspa.org
NY StateWatch Inc	www.statewatch.com
Nyack Chamber of Commerce	www.nyack-ny.com
Nyack College	www.nyack.edu
Nyack UFSD	www.nyackschools.org
NYAHSA PAC	www.nyahsa.org
NYC & Company/Convention & Visitors Bureau	www.nycvisit.com
NYC Americans for Democratic Action NYC ADA PAC	www.nycada.com
NYC Arts Coalition	www.nycityartscoalition.org
NYC Board of Education Employees, Local 372/AFSCME, AFL-CIO	www.local372.com
NYC Campaign Finance Board	www.nyccfb.info
NYC Citywide Special Ed District 75	schools.nycenet.edu/d75/
NYC Coalition Against Hunger	www.nyccah.org
NYC District Council of Carpenters' PAC	www.nycdistrictcouncil.com
NYC Neighborhood Open Space Coalition	www.treebranch.com; www.walkny.org
NYC Region 10	www.r10nycdoe.org
NYC Region 4	www.region4.nycenet.edu
NYC Region 6	www.region6nycdoe.net
NYC Region 7	www.region7online.com
NYMAGIC Inc	www.nymagic.com
NYMTA Boat PAC	www.nyboatshows.com
NYP Holdings Inc	www.nypost.com
NYPT PAC	www.nypta.org
NYS Academy of Family Physicians	www.nysafp.org
NYS AFL-CIO COPE	www.nysaflcio.org
NYS Agricultural Society	www.nysagsociety.org
NYS Alliance for Arts Education	www.nysaae.org
NYS Arborists	www.newyorkstatearborists.com

See Organization Index for page numbers.

World Wide Web (URL) Index

NYS Architects PAC	www.aianys.org
NYS Association For Food Protection	www.foodscience.cornell.edu/nysfsanit/index.html
NYS Association for Health, Physical Education, Recreation & Dance	www.nysahperd.org
NYS Association for the Education of Young Children	www.nysaeyc.org
NYS Association of Area Agencies on Aging	www.nysaaaa.org
NYS Association of Chiefs of Police Inc	www.nychiefs.org
NYS Association of Community & Residential Agencies	www.nysacra.org
NYS Association of Counties	www.nysac.org
NYS Association of County Health Officials	www.nysacho.org
NYS Association of Criminal Defense Lawyers	www.nysacdl.org
NYS Association of Electrical Contractors	www.nysaec.org
NYS Association of Fire Chiefs	www.nysfirechiefs.com
NYS Association of Health Care Providers	www.nyshcp.org
NYS Association of Library Boards	www.nysalb.org
NYS Association of Nurse Anesthetists (NYSANA)	www.nysana.com
NYS Association of Realtors	www.nysar.com
NYS Association of School Business Officials	www.nysasbo.org
NYS Association of Service Stations & Repair Shops	www.nysassrs.com
NYS Association of Solid Waste Management	www.newyorkwaste.org
NYS Association of Veterinary Technicians Inc	www.nysavt.org
NYS Bar Assn, Business Law Section	www.mhjur.com
NYS Bar Assn, Children & the Law Committee	arcopps.net
NYS Bar Assn, Civil Rights/Spec Cmte on Clltrl Consequence of Criminal Proceedings	www.proskauer.com
NYS Bar Assn, Commercial & Federal Litigation Section	www.montclarewachtler.com
NYS Bar Assn, Court Structure & Judicial Selection Cmte	www.mgglaw.com
NYS Bar Assn, Cyberspace Law Cmte	www.thelen.com
NYS Bar Assn, Diversity & Leadership Development Cmte	www.woh.com
NYS Bar Assn, Elder Law Section	www.lkrlaw.com
NYS Bar Assn, Electronic Communications Task Force	www.hrfmlaw.com
NYS Bar Assn, Environmental Law Section	www.farrellfritz.com
NYS Bar Assn, Federal Constitution & Legislation Cmte	www.mklex.com
NYS Bar Assn, Intellectual Property Law Section	www.hartmanwinnicki.com
NYS Bar Assn, Issues Affecting Same Sex Couples	www.woh.com
NYS Bar Assn, Lawyer Referral Service Cmte	www.apfwlaw.com
NYS Bar Assn, Legal Aid Cmte/Funding for Civil Legal Svcs Cmte	www.lshv.org
NYS Bar Assn, Legislative Policy Cmte	www.gtlaw.com
NYS Bar Assn, Media Law Committee	www.newyorker.com
NYS Bar Assn, Multi-jurisdictional Practice Cmte	www.proskauer.com
NYS Bar Assn, Municipal Law Section	www.nyscourtofclaims.courts.state.ny.us/
NYS Bar Assn, President's Cmte on Access to Justice	www.boylanbrown.com
NYS Bar Assn, Public Trust & Confidence in the Legal System	www.debevoise.com
NYS Bar Assn, Public Utility Law Committee	www.natfuel.com
NYS Bar Assn, Review Attorney Fee Regulation Cmte	www.nysba.org
NYS Bar Assn, Review Judicial Nominations Cmte	www.englertcoffeymchugh.com
NYS Bar Assn, Review the Code of Judicial Conduct Cmte	www.sifma.org
NYS Bar Assn, Task Force to Review Terrorism Legislation Cmte	www.connors-vilardo.com
NYS Bar Assn, Tax Section	www.sullcrom.com
NYS Bar Assn, Tort System Cmte	www.bracken-margolin.com
NYS Bar Assn, Torts, Insurance & Compensation Law Section	www.connorscorcoran.com
NYS Bar Assn, Trial Lawyers Section	www.connorslaw.com
NYS Bar Assn, Trusts & Estates Law Section	www.daypitney.com
NYS Bar Assn, Unlawful Practice of Law Cmte	www.ithacalaw.com
NYS Bar Association	www.nysba.org
NYS Berry Growers Association	www.nysbga.org
NYS Broadcasters Association	www.nysbroadcasters.org
NYS Builders Association Inc	www.nysba.com

See Organization Index for page numbers.

World Wide Web (URL) Index

NYS Chapter AGC PAC	www.agcnys.org
NYS Cheese Manufacturers Association, Department of Food Science	www.newyorkcheese.org
NYS Child Care Coordinating Council	www.nyscccc.org
NYS Clinical Laboratory Association Inc	www.nyscla.com
NYS College of Ceramics at Alfred University	www.nyscc.alfred.edu
NYS Commission on Quality of Care & Advocacy for Persons with Disabilities	www.cqcapd.state.ny.us
NYS Conference of Local Mental Hygiene Directors	www.clmhd.org
NYS Conference of Mayors & Municipal Officials	www.nycom.org
NYS Corps Collaboration	www.nyscc.net
NYS Correctional Officers & Police Benevolent Association Inc	www.nyscopba.org
NYS Council for Community Behavioral Healthcare	www.nccbh.org
NYS Council of Physiotherapists PAC	www.nycouncilpt.org
NYS Council of Probation Administrators	www.nyscopa.org
NYS County Hwy Super Assn / NY Aviation Mgt Assn / NY Public Transit Assn	www.countyhwys.org; www.nyama.com; www.nytransit.org
NYS Credit Union League	www.nyscul.org
NYS Defenders Association	www.nysda.org
NYS Dental Association	www.nysdental.org
NYS Deputies Association Inc	www.nysdeputy.org
NYS Dispute Resolution Association	www.nysdra.org
NYS Economic Development Council	www.nysedc.org
NYS Food Industry PAC	www.fiany.com
NYS Foundation for Science, Technology & Innovation	www.nystar.state.ny.us
NYS Funeral Directors Association PAC	www.nysfda.org
NYS Grange	www.nysgrange.com
NYS Head Start Association	www.nysheadstart.org
NYS Horticultural Society	www.nyshs.org
NYS Hospitality & Tourism Assn PAC	www.nyshta.org
NYS Industries for the Disabled (NYSID) Inc	www.nysid.org
NYS Land Title Association	www.nyslta.org
NYS Law Enforcement Officers Union, Council 82, AFSCME, AFL-CIO	www.council82.org
NYS Magistrates Association	www.nysmagassoc.homestead.com
NYS Nursery/Landscape Association	www.nylandscaper.com
NYS Optometric Assn PAC	www.nysoa.org
NYS Optometric Association Inc	www.nysoa.org
NYS Outdoor Guides Association	www.nysoga.org
NYS Passenger Vessel Association	www.cruisenewyork.com
NYS Pipe Trades Political Action Committee	nyspipetrades.org
NYS Psychological Association	www.nyspa.org
NYS Public Health Association	www.nyspha.org
NYS Public High School Athletic Association	www.nysphsaa.org
NYS Reading Association	www.nysreading.org
NYS Right to Life Committee	www.nysrighttolife.org
NYS Right to Life PAC	www.nysrighttolife.org
NYS Sheriffs' Association	www.nysheriffs.org
NYS Society of Certified Public Accountants	www.nysscpa.org
NYS Society of Real Estate Appraisers	www.nyrealestateappraisers.com
NYS Speech-Language-Hearing Assn Inc - COMPAC	www.nysslha.org
NYS Technology Enterprise Corporation (NYSTEC)	www.nystec.com
NYS Tenants & Neighbors Coalition	www.tandn.org
NYS Theatre Institute	www.nysti.org
NYS Trade Adjustment Assistance Center	www.nystaac.org
NYS Troopers PAC	www.nystpba.org
NYS Turfgrass Association	www.nysta.org
NYS Water Resources Institute of Cornell University	wri.eas.cornell.edu
NYS Weights & Measures Association	lewiscountyny.net/wt-measures

See Organization Index for page numbers.

World Wide Web (URL) Index

NYSARC Inc	www.nysarc.org
NYSE State PAC	www.nyse.com
NYSIA NY PAC	www.nysia.org
Oakfield-Alabama CSD	www.oacs.k12.ny.us
Observer	http://observertoday.com
Observer-Dispatch	www.uticaod.com
Occupational Safety & Health Administration (OSHA)	www.osha.gov
Occupational Safety & Health Adminstration (OSHA)	www.osha.gov
Oceanside Chamber of Commerce	www.oceansidechamber.org
Oceanside UFSD	www.oceanside.k12.ny.us
Odessa-Montour CSD	www.omschools.org
Office for Civil Rights	www.hhs.gov/ocr
Office for Technology	www.oft.state.ny.us
Office of David J Silverman	www.nyssea.org
Office of Higher Education	www.highered.nysed.gov
Office of Inspector General, Region II-New York	www.oig.dot.gov
Office of Operations & Management Services	www.oms.nysed.gov
Office of the Professions	www.op.nysed.gov
Office of Thrift Supervision	www.ots.treas.gov
Ogden Newspapers Inc	http://observertoday.com
Ogdensburg Bridge & Port Authority	www.ogdensport.com
Ogdensburg Chamber of Commerce (Greater Ogdensburg)	www.ogdensburgny.com
Ogdensburg City SD	www.ogdensburg12.org/web
Ogdensburg Journal	www.ogd.com
Ohio River Valley Water Sanitation Commission	www.orsanco.org
Oil Heat Institute of Long Island	www.ohili.org
Oil Heat Institute PAC	www.ohili.org
OILHEATPAC	www.nyoha.org
Olean Area Chamber of Commerce (Greater Olean)	www.oleanny.com
Olean Business Institute	www.obi.edu
Olean City SD	www.oleanschools.org
Oneida	www.oneidacounty.org
Oneida Chamber of Commerce (Greater Oneida Area)	www.oneidachamber.com
Oneida City SD	www.oneida.org
Oneida County	www.co.oneida.ny.us or www.ocgov.net
Oneida County Convention & Visitors Bureau	www.oneidacountycvb.com
Oneida Daily Dispatch	www.oneidadispatch.com
Oneida Indian Nation	www.oneida-nation.org
Oneida-Herkimer-Madison BOCES	www.oneida-boces.org
Oneonta City SD	www.oneontacsd.org
Onondaga	www.ongov.net
Onondaga Community College	www.sunyocc.edu
Onondaga County	www.ongov.net
Onondaga County Industrial Development Agency	www.syracusecentral.com
Onondaga CSD	www.ocs.cnyric.org
Onondaga Nation	www.onondaganation.org
Onondaga, Town of	www.townofonondagany.com
Onondaga-Cortland-Madison BOCES	ocmboces.org
Ontario	www.co.ontario.ny.us/elections
Ontario County	www.co.ontario.ny.us
Ontario County Industrial Development Agency & Economic Development	www.ontariocountydev.org
Ontario County/Finger Lakes Visitor's Connection	www.visitfingerlakes.com
Onteora CSD	onteora.schoolwires.com
Open Society Institute	www.soros.org
Open Space Institute	www.osiny.org
Oppenheim-Ephratah CSD	www.oecs.k12.ny.us

See Organization Index for page numbers.

World Wide Web (URL) Index

Opticians PAC	www.buenausopticians.com
Orange & Rockland Utilities Inc	www.oru.com
Orange County	www.co.orange.ny.us
Orange County Chamber of Commerce Inc	www.orangeny.com
Orange County Community College	orange.cc.ny.us
Orange County Partnership	www.ocpartnership.org
Orange County Publications	www.recordonline.com
Orange-Ulster BOCES	www.ouboces.org
Orangetown, Town of	www.orangetown.com
Orchard Park Chamber of Commerce	www.orchardparkchamber.com
Orchard Park CSD	www.opschools.org
Orchard Park, Town of	www.orchardparkny.org
Organization of NYS Management Confidential Employees	www.nysomce.org
Organization of NYS Management/Confidential Employees Inc	www.nysomce.org
Organization of Staff Analysts PAC	www.osaunion.org
Oriskany CSD	www.oriskanycsd.org
Orleans County	www.orleansny.com
Orleans County Chamber of Commerce	www.orleanschamber.com
Orleans Economic Development Agency (OEDA)	www.orleansdevelopment.org
Orleans-Niagara BOCES	www.onboces.org
Ortho-PAC of New York	www.nyssos.org
Osborne Association	www.osborneny.org
Ossining UFSD	www.OssiningUFSD.org
Ossining, Town of	www.townofossining.com
Ossining, Village of	www.villageofossining.org
Ostroff, Hiffa & Associates Inc	www.ostroff-hiffa.com
Oswego BOCES	www.oswegoboces.org
Oswego County	www.co.oswego.ny.us
Oswego County, Operation/Oswego County Industrial Development Agency	www.oswegocounty.org
Oswego-Fulton Chamber of Commerce	www.oswegofultonchamber.com
Otsego County	www.otsegocounty.com
Otsego County Chamber (The)	www.otsegocountychamber.com
Otsego County Economic Development Department & Industrial Development Agency	www.otsegoeconomicdevelopment.com
Otsego Northern Catskills BOCES (Otsego-Delaware-Schoharie-Greene)	www.oncboces.org
Otselic Valley CSD	www.ovcs.org
Ottaway Newspapers (The)	www.pressrepublican.com
Ottaway Newspapers Inc	www.thedailystar.com
Oversight and Government Reform	http://oversight.house.gov
Owego, Town of	www.townofowego.com
Owego-Apalachin CSD	www.oacsd.org
Oxford Academy & CSD	www.oxac.org
Oyster Bay Chamber of Commerce	www.oysterbaychamber.org
Oyster Bay, Town of	www.oysterbaytown.com
Oyster Bay-East Norwich CSD	oben.schools.org
Oysterponds UFSD	www.oysterponds.k12.ny.us
Pace University	www.pace.edu
Pace University, School of Law Center for Environmental Legal Studies	www.law.pace.edu
Pace University, School of Law, John Jay Legal Services Inc	www.law.pace.edu
Pacific College of Oriental Medicine	www.pacificcollege.edu
Painted Post Area Board of Trade	www.paintedpostny.com
Palladia Inc	www.palladiainc.org
Palladium-Times (The)	www.pall-times.com
Palmyra-Macedon CSD	www.palmac.k12.ny.us
Panama CSD	www.pancent.org
Parishville-Hopkinton CSD	phcs.neric.org
Park Resident Homeowners' Association Inc	www.prho.com

See Organization Index for page numbers.

World Wide Web (URL) Index

Parks & Recreation, Department of, NYC	www.nyc.gov/parks
Parks, Recreation & Historic Preservation, NYS Office of	www.nysparks.com
Parkside Group, LLC	www.theparksidegroup.com
Parole, Division of	www.parole.state.ny.us
Parsons Brinckerhoff	www.pbworld.com
Partnership for New York City	www.partnershipfornyc.org
Patchogue Chamber of Commerce (Greater Patchogue)	www.patchoguechamber.com
Patchogue-Medford UFSD	www.pmschools.org
Patent Trader	www.thejournalnews.com
Patrolmen's Benevolent Association	www.nycpba.org
Paul Smith's College	www.paulsmiths.edu
Pavilion CSD	www.pavilioncsd.org
Pawling CSD	www.pawlingschools.org
Peace Corps	www.peacecorps.gov
Pearl River UFSD	www.pearlriver.k12.ny.us
Peekskill City SD	www.peekskillcsd.org
Peekskill Industrial Development Agency (City of)	www.cityofpeekskill.com
Peekskill, City of	www.ci.peekskill.ny.us
Pelham UFSD	www.pelhamschools.org
Pembroke CSD	www.pembroke.k12.ny.us
Penfield CSD	penfield.edu
Penfield, Town of	www.penfield.org
Penn Yan CSD	www.pycsd.org
People's Weekly World	www.pww.org
Pepsi Co	www.pepsi.com
Perinton, Town of	www.perinton.org
Perry Area Chamber of Commerce	www.perrychamber.com
Perry CSD	www.perry.k12.ny.us
Perry Davis Associates	www.perrydavis.com
Peru CSD	www.perucsd.org
Petraitis, Brian J	www.collegeboard.com
Pharmacists Society of the State of New York	www.pssny.org
Pharmacy PAC of New York State	www.pssny.org
Phelps-Clifton Springs CSD	www.midlakes.org
Phillips Beth Israel School of Nursing	www.futurenursebi.org
Pine Bush CSD	www.pinebushschools.org
Pine Plains CSD	www.pineplainsschools.org
Pine Valley CSD (South Dayton)	www.pval.org
Pioneer CSD	www.pioneerschools.org
Pioneer Savings Bank	www.pioneersb.com
Piseco Common SD	www.pisecoschool.com
Pittsford CSD	www.pittsfordschools.com
Pittsford, Town of	www.townofpittsford.com
Plainedge UFSD	www.plainedgeschools.org
Plainview-Old Bethpage CSD	www.pob.k12.ny.us
Planned Parenthood of NYC, Inc	www.ppnyc.org
Plattsburgh City SD	www.plattscsd.org
Plattsburgh-North Country Chamber of Commerce	www.northcountrychamber.com
Plaza College	www.plazacollege.edu
Pleasantville UFSD	www2.lhric.org/Pleasantville/
Plug Power Inc	www.plugpower.com
Plumbing Contractors PAC of the City of NY Inc	www.acpcny.org
Pocantico Hills CSD	www2.lhric.org/pocantico
Poland CSD	www.polandcs.com
Police Benevolent Assn of the NYS Troopers Inc	www.nystpba.org
Police Conference of New York Inc PAC	www.pcny.org

See Organization Index for page numbers.

World Wide Web (URL) Index

Police Conference of NY Inc (PCNY)	www.pcny.org
Police Department, NYC	www.nyc.gov/nypd
Political Action Committee of Council 82	www.council82.org
Polytechnic University	www.poly.edu
Pomeroy Appraisal Associates Inc	pomeroyappraisal.com
Port Authority of New York & New Jersey	www.panynj.gov
Port Chester SD	www.portchesterschools.org
Port Chester, Village of	www.portchesterny.com
Port Chester-Rye Brook Chamber of Commerce	www.portchesterryebrookchamber.com
Port Jefferson Chamber of Commerce	www.portjeffchamber.com
Port Jefferson UFSD	www.portjeff.k12.ny.us
Port Jervis City SD	www.portjerviscsd.k12.ny.us
Port Morris Local Development Corporation	www.sobro.org
Port of Oswego Authority	www.portoswego.com
Port Washington Chamber of Commerce	pwguide.com
Port Washington UFSD	www.portnet.k12.ny.us
Portville CSD	staging.portervillecentral.wnyric.org
Post-Journal	www.post-journal.com
Post-Standard (The)	www.syracuse.com
Post-Star (The)	www.poststar.com
Postgraduate Center for Mental Health	www.pgcmh-institute.org
Potsdam Chamber of Commerce	www.potsdam.ny.us/chamber
Potsdam CSD	www.potsdam.k12.ny.us
Poughkeepsie Area Chamber of Commerce	www.pokchamb.org
Poughkeepsie City SD	www.poughkeepsieschools.org
Poughkeepsie Journal	www.poughkeepsiejournal.com
Poughkeepsie, City of	www.cityofpoughkeepsie.com
Poughkeepsie, Town of	www.townofpoughkeepsie.com
Powers & Company	www.powerscompany.com
Pozzi, Brian M	www.allstate.com
Pratt Center for Community Development	www.prattcenter.edu
Pratt Institute	www.pratt.edu
Preserve Ramapo	preserverramapo.org
Press & Sun Bulletin	www.pressconnects.com
Press-Republican	www.pressrepublican.com
Prevent Child Abuse New York	www.preventchildabuseny.org
Prevention of Domestic Violence, Office for the	www.opdv.state.ny.us
PricewaterhouseCoopers LLP	www.pwc.com
Printing, Joint Committee on	www.jcp.senate.gov
Pro Bono Net	www.probono.net; www.lawhelp.org
Probation & Correctional Alternatives, Division of	www.dpca.state.ny.us
Probation, Department of, NYC	www.nyc.gov/html/prob
Procter & Gamble Pharmaceuticals	www.pg.com
Professional Business College	www.pcbny.edu
Professional Fire Fighters Association Inc (NYS)	www.nyspffa.org
Professional Insurance Agents of New York State	www.piany.org
Professional Standards Review Council of America Inc (PSRC)	www.psrc-of-america.org
Project for Public Spaces	www.pps.org
ProLiteracy Worldwide	www.proliteracy.org
Proskauer Rose LLP	www.proskauer.com
Public Advocate, Office of the	www.pubadvocate.nyc.gov
Public Agenda	www.publicagenda.org
Public Employment Relations Board	www.perb.state.ny.us
Public Markets Partners / Baum Forum	www.baumforum.org
Public Policy Institute of NYS Inc	www.ppinys.org
Public Service Commission	www.dps.state.ny.us

See Organization Index for page numbers.

World Wide Web (URL) Index

Public Strategies, LLC	www.publicstrategiesllc.net
Public Utility Law Project of New York Inc	www.pulp.tc
Public Welfare Assn (NY)	www.nypwa.com
Public/Private Ventures	www.ppv.org
Puckett, Robert R	www.nysta.com
Puerto Rican Legal Defense & Education Fund Inc (PRLDEF)	www.prldef.org
Pulaski-Eastern Shore Chamber of Commerce	www.pulaskinychamber.com
Purchase College, State University of New York	www.purchase.edu
Putnam County	www.putnamcountyny.com
Putnam County Economic Development Corporation	www.putnamedc.org
Putnam CSD	putnamcs.neric.org
Putnam Valley CSD	www.putnamvalleyschools.org
Putnam-Northern Westchester BOCES	www.pnwboces.org
Queens (Queens County)	www.queensbp.org
Queens Chamber of Commerce (Borough of)	www.queenschamber.org
Queens College	www.qc.cuny.edu
Queens County (NYC Borough of Queens)	www.queensbp.org
Queens Educational Opportunity Center	www.qns.eoc.suny.edu
Queens Gazette	www.qgazette.com
Queensborough Community College	www.qcc.cuny.edu
Queensbury UFSD	www.queensburyschool.org
Queensbury, Town of	www.queensbury.net
Quogue UFSD	www.quogue.k12.ny.us
R W Bronstein Corporation	www.bronstein.net
Racing & Wagering Board	www.racing.state.ny.us
Radon Testing Corp of America Inc	www.rtca.com
Ramapo CSD (Suffern)	www.ramapocentral.org
Ramapo, Town of	www.ramapo.org
Randolph Academy UFSD	www.randoplhacademy.org
Randolph CSD	www.randolphcsd.org
Ravena-Coeymans-Selkirk CSD	www.rcscsd.org
RC Build PAC of the Rockland County Builders Assn	www.rcba.org
Real Estate Board of New York Inc	www.rebny.com
Real Estate Board of NY Inc	www.rebny.com
Real Estate Board PAC	www.rebny.com
Real Property Services, Office of	www.orps.state.ny.us
Realtors PAC	www.nysar.com
Realty Advisory Board on Labor Relations	www.rabolr.com
Realty USA	www.realtyusa.com
Record (The)	www.troyrecord.com
Recorder (The)	www.recordernews.com
Records & Information Services, Dept of, NYC	www.nyc.gov/records
Red Barn Properties	www.redbarnproperties.com
Red Creek CSD	www.redcreekcsd.k12.ny.us
Red Hook Area Chamber of Commerce	www.redhookchamber.org
Red Hook CSD	www.redhookcentralschools.org
Regeneron Pharmaceuticals Inc	www.regeneron.com
Regional Farm & Food Project	www.farmandfood.org
Regional Plan Association	www.rpa.org
Register-Star	www.registerstar.com
Regulatory Reform, Governor's Office of	www.gorr.state.ny.us
Rehabilitation Assn Inc (NYS)	www.nyrehab.org
Related Companies LP	www.related.com
Remove Intoxicated Drivers (RID-USA Inc)	www.rid-usa.org
Remsen CSD	www.remsencsd.org
Remsenburg-Speonk UFSD	www.rsufsd.org

See Organization Index for page numbers.

World Wide Web (URL) Index

Rensselaer City SD www.rcsd.k12.ny.us
Rensselaer County . . . . www.rensco.com or www.rensselaercounty.org
Rensselaer County Regional Chamber of Commerce . . . . www.renscochamber.com
Rensselaer Polytechnic Inst, Ecological Economics, Values & Policy Program . . . . www.rpi.edu/dept/sts/eevp
Rensselaer Polytechnic Institute . . . . www.rpi.edu
Rensselaer-Columbia-Greene (Questar III) BOCES . . . . www.questar.org
Rent Guidelines Board, NYC . . . . www.housingnyc.com; www.nyc.gov/html/rgb
Rent Stabilization Assn of NYC Inc . . . . www.rsanyc.org
Research Foundation of SUNY . . . . www.rfsuny.org
Reserve Officers Association (ROA) . . . . www.roa.org
Resource Center for Independent Living (RCIL) . . . . www.rcil.com
Retail Council of New York State . . . . www.retailcouncilnys.com
Retired Public Employees Association . . . . www.rppa.org
Reuters (New York Bureau) . . . . www.reuters.com
Review Press . . . . www.thejournalnews.com
Rhinebeck Chamber of Commerce . . . . www.rhinebeckchamber.com
Rhinebeck CSD . . . . www.rhinebeckcsd.org
Richfield Springs CSD . . . . www.richfieldcsd.org
Richmond County (NYC Borough of Staten Island) . . . . www.statenislandusa.com
Right to Life Committee Inc (NYS) . . . . www.nysrighttolife.org
Ripley CSD . . . . ripleycsd.wnyric.org
Riverhead Chamber of Commerce . . . . www.riverheadchamber.com
Riverhead CSD . . . . www.riverhead.net
Riverhead Foundation for Marine Research & Preservation (The) . . . . www.riverheadfoundation.org
Riverhead, Town of . . . . www.riverheadli.com
Riverkeeper Inc . . . . www.riverkeeper.org
Riverkeeper, Inc . . . . www.riverkeeper.org
Robert P Borsody, PC . . . . www.borsodyhealthlaw.com
Robert Schalkenbach Foundation . . . . www.schalkenbach.org
Roberts Wesleyan College . . . . www.roberts.edu
Rochester Business Alliance Inc . . . . www.rochesterbusinessalliance.com
Rochester Business Journal . . . . www.rbj.net
Rochester City SD www.rcsdk12.org
Rochester Downtown Development Corporation . . . . www.rochesterdowntown.com
Rochester Economic Development Corporation . . . . www.redco.net
Rochester Educational Opportunity Center . . . . www.rochestereoc.com
Rochester Gas & Electric Corporation . . . . www.rge.com
Rochester Institute of Technology . . . . www.rit.edu
Rochester Regional Joint Board State PAC . . . . www.uniterrjb.org
Rochester School for the Deaf . . . . www.rsdeaf.org
Rochester US Export Assistance Center . . . . www.export.gov
Rochester, City of . . . . www.ci.rochester.ny.us
Rochester, University of . . . . www.rochester.edu
Rochester-Genesee Regional Transportation Authority . . . . www.rgrta.com
Rockaway Development & Revitalization Corporation . . . . www.rdrc.org
Rockaways, Chamber of Commerce, Inc . . . . www.rockawaychamberofcommerce.com
Rockefeller Institute of Government . . . . www.rockinst.org
Rockefeller University . . . . www.rockefeller.edu
Rockland . . . . www.co.rockland.ny.us
Rockland BOCES . . . . www.rocklandboces.org
Rockland Community College . . . . www.sunyrockland.edu
Rockland County . . . . www.co.rockland.ny.us
Rockland County PBA Association PAC NY . . . . www.rcpba.org
Rockland Economic Development Corporation . . . . www.redc.org
Rockville Centre Chamber of Commerce . . . . www.rvcchamber.com
Rockville Centre UFSD . . . . www.rvcschools.org

See Organization Index for page numbers.

World Wide Web (URL) Index

Rockville Centre, Village of	www.ci.rockville-centre.ny.us
Rocky Point UFSD	www.rockypointschools.org
Roman Catholic Diocese of Albany, Catholic Charities	www.ccrcda.org
Rome Area Chamber of Commerce	www.romechamber.com
Rome City SD	www.romecsd.org
Rome Industrial Development Corporation	www.romeny.org
Rome Sentinel Co	www.rny.com
Rome, City of	www.romenewyork.com
Romulus CSD	www.rcs.k12.ny.us
Rondout Valley CSD	www.rondout.k12.ny.us
Ronkonkoma Chamber of Commerce	www.ronkonkomachamber.com
Roohan Realty	www.roohanrealty.com
Roosevelt Island Operating Corporation (RIOC)	www.rioc.com
Roosevelt UFSD	www.rooseveltufsd.com
Roosevelt-Vanderbilt National Historic Sites	www.nps.gov/hofr
Rosario, Stephen M	www.americanchemistry.org
Roscoe CSD	roscoe.k12.ny.us
Rosenthal, Harvey	www.nyaprs.org
Roslyn UFSD	www.roslynschools.org
Roswell Park Cancer Institute Corporation	www.roswellpark.org
Rotterdam, Town of	www.rotterdamny.org
Royalton-Hartland CSD	www.royhart.org
Rules	www.rules.house.gov
Rules & Administration	www.rules.senate.gov
Rural & Migrant Ministry Inc	www.ruralmigrantministry.org
Rural Development	www.rurdev.usda.gov/ny
Rural Housing Action Corporation	www.ruralinc.org
Rural Law Ctr of NY Inc	www.ruruallawcenter.org
Rural Opportunities Inc	www.ruralinc.org
Rush-Henrietta CSD	www.rhnet.org
Rutherford, Clyde E	www.dairylea.com
Rye City SD	www.ryecityschools.lhric.org
Rye Neck UFSD	www.ryeneck.k12.ny.us
Rye, Town of	www.townofryeny.com
Sabol, Sharon	www.nyslta.org
Sachem CSD	www.sachem.edu
Sackets Harbor Chamber of Commerce	www.sacketsharborny.com
Sackets Harbor CSD	www.sacketsharborschool.org
Safe Horizon Inc	www.safehorizon.org
Sag Harbor Chamber of Commerce	www.sagharborchamber.com
Sag Harbor UFSD	www.sagharbor.k12.ny.us
Sagamore Hill National Historic Site	www.nps.gov/sahi
Sage Colleges (The)	www.sage.edu
Saint Lawrence	www.co.st-lawrence.ny.us
Saint Lawrence Seaway Development Corporation	www.seaway.dot.gov; www.greatlakes-seaway.com
Salamanca Area Chamber of Commerce	www.salamancachamber.com
Salamanca City SD	www.salamancany.org
Salamanca Industrial Development Agency	www.salmun.com
Salamanca Press	www.salamancapress.com
Salem CSD	www.salemcsdnyk-12.org
Salina, Town of	www.salina.ny.us
Salmon River CSD	www.srk12.org
Salvation Army School for Officer Training	www1.salvationarmy.org
Salvation Army, Empire State Division	www.salvationarmy.org
Samaritan Hospital School of Nursing	www.nehealth.com
Samaritan Village Inc	www.samaritanvillage.org

See Organization Index for page numbers.

World Wide Web (URL) Index

Sampson, Rick J	www.nysra.org
Sanitation, Department of, NYC	www.nyc.gov/sanitation
Sarah Lawrence College	www.slc.edu
Saranac CSD	www.saranac.org
Saranac Lake Area Chamber of Commerce	www.saranaclake.com
Saratoga	www.co.saratoga.ny.us
Saratoga Convention & Tourism Bureau	www.discoversaratoga.org
Saratoga County	www.co.saratoga.ny.us
Saratoga County Chamber of Commerce	www.saratoga.org
Saratoga County Industrial Development Agency	www.saratogacountyida.org
Saratoga Economic Development Corporation	www.saratogaedc.com
Saratoga Gaming & Raceway	www.saratogaraceway.com
Saratoga National Historical Park	www.nps.gov/sara
Saratoga Springs City SD	www.saratogaschools.org
Saratoga Springs, City of	www.saratoga-springs.org
Saratogian (The)	www.saratogian.com
Saugerties, Town of	www.saugerties.ny.us
Sauquoit Valley CSD	www.svcsd.org
Sawchuk Brown Associates	www.sawchukbrown.com
Sayville Chamber of Commerce (Greater Sayville)	www.greatersayvillechamber.com
Sayville UFSD	www.sayville.k12.ny.us
SBLI USA Mutual Life Insurance Company Inc	www.sbliusa.com
SCAA - Schuyler Center for Analysis & Advocacy	www.scaany.org
Scarsdale UFSD	www.scarsdaleschools.k12.ny.us
Scenic Hudson	www.scenichudson.org
Scenic Hudson Inc	www.scenichudson.org
Schalmont CSD	www.schalmont.org
Schenectady	www.schenectadyelections.com
Schenectady City SD	www.schenectady.k12.ny.us
Schenectady County	www.schenectadycounty.com
Schenectady County Chamber of Commerce	www.schenectadychamber.org
Schenectady County Community College	www.sunysccc.edu
Schenectady, City of	www.cityofschenectady.com
Schlather, Geldenhuys, Stumbar & Salk	www.ithacalaw.com
Schodack CSD	www.schodack.k12.ny.us
Schoharie County Chamber of Commerce	www.schohariechamber.com
Schoharie County Industrial Development Agency	www.schohariebiz.com
Schoharie CSD	www.schoharieschools.org
School Administrators Association of NYS	www.saanys.org
School Boards Assn (NYS)	www.nyssba.org
School of Industrial & Labor Relations at Cornell University (ILR School)	www.ilr.cornell.edu
School of Law at Queens College	www.law.cuny.edu
School of Professional Studies	sps.cuny.edu
School of Visual Arts	www.schoolofvisualarts.edu
Schools Are For Everyone	www.lgcsc.org
Schroon Lake Area Chamber of Commerce	www.schroonlakechamber.com
Schuyler Center for Analysis & Advocacy (SCAA)	www.scaany.org
Schuyler County	www.schuylercounty.us
Schuyler County Chamber of Commerce	www.schuylerny.com
Schuyler County Industrial Development Agency	www.scoped.biz
Schuyler County Partnership for Economic Development	www.scoped.biz
Schuylerville CSD	www.schuylervilleschools.org
Science & Technology	www.house.gov/science
Scio CSD	scio.schooltools.us
Scotia-Glenville CSD	www.sgcsd.neric.org
Scripps Howard News Service	www.shns.com

See Organization Index for page numbers.

World Wide Web (URL) Index

SCS Engineers PC	www.scsengineers.com
Seaford Chamber of Commerce	www.seaford.li
Seaford UFSD	www.seaford.k12.ny.us
Seaway Trail Inc	www.seawaytrail.com
Securities Industry & Financial Markets Association (SIFMA)	www.sifma.org
Securities Industry Assn PAC, NY District	www.sifma.org
Securities Industry Association (SIA)	www.sia.com
Self Advocacy Association of NYS	www.sanys.org
Seminary of the Immaculate Conception	www.icseminary.edu
Seneca	www.co.seneca.ny.us/boe
Seneca County	www.co.seneca.ny.us
Seneca County Chamber of Commerce	www.senecachamber.org
Seneca County Industrial Development Agency	www.senecacountyida.org
Seneca Falls CSD	www.sfcs.k12.ny.us
Seneca Flight Operations	www.senecafoods.com
Seneca Foods Corporation	www.senecafoods.com
Seneca Nation of Indians	www.sni.org
Sensor CAT-Diagnostic Tools & Sensor Systems	www.sensorcat.sunysb.edu
Settlement Housing Fund Inc	www.settlementhousingfund.org
Sewanhaka Central HS District	www.sewanhaka.k12.ny.us
Shanahan Group	www.shanahangroup.com
Sharon Springs CSD	www.sharonsprings.org
Sheet Metal Workers LU 38 -PAC	www.sheetmetallocal38.org
Sheet Metal Workers' Intl Assoc Local 28 Political Action Committee	www.smwialu28.org
Sheet Metal Workers' Local 46 PAF	www.smw46.com
Sheinkopf Communications	www.sheikopf.com
Shelter Island UFSD	www.shelterisland.k12.ny.us
Shenendehowa CSD	www.shenet.org
Sherburne-Earlville CSD	www.secsd.org
Sherman CSD	www.sherman.wnyric.org
Shinnecock Indian Nation	www.shinnecocknation.com
Shoreham-Wading River CSD	www.swrcsd.org
Sidney Chamber of Commerce	www.sidneychamber.org
Sidney CSD	www.sidneycsd.org
Siena College	www.siena.edu
Sierra Club, Atlantic Chapter	www.sierraclub.org/chapters/ny/
SIFMA	www.bondmarkets.com
Silver Creek CSD	www.silvercreek.wnyric.org
Simmons Institute of Funeral Service Inc	www.simmonsinstitute.com
Simmons-Boardman Publishing Corp	www.railwayage.com or www.rtands.com or www.railjournal.com
Simon Wiesenthal Center, NY Tolerance Center	www.wiesenthal.com
Sithe Energies Inc	www.sithe.com
Skaneateles Chamber of Commerce	www.skaneateles.com
Skaneateles CSD	www.skanschools.org
Ski Areas of New York Inc	www.iskiny.com
Skidmore College	www.skidmore.edu
Sleepy Hollow Chamber of Commerce	www.sleepyhollowchamber.com
Small Business	www.house.gov/smbiz
Small Business & Entrepreneurship	www.sbc.senate.gov
Small Business Administration	www.sba.gov
Small Business Development Center	www.nyssbdc.org
Small Business Services, Department of, NYC	www.nyc.gov/html/sbs
Small Cities, Office for	www.nysmallcities.com
Smith, Michael P	www.nyba.com
Smithtown Chamber of Commerce	www.smithtownchamber.com

See Organization Index for page numbers.

World Wide Web (URL) Index

Smithtown CSD	www.smithtown.k12.ny.us
Smithtown, Town of	www.smithtowninfo.com
Snyder Communications Corp	www.evesun.com
Social Security Administration	www.socialsecurity.gov
Society of Professional Engineers Inc (NYS)	www.nysspe.org
Sodus CSD	www.sodus.k12.ny.us
Software & Information Industry Association	www.siia.net
Soil & Water Conservation Committee	www.nys-soilandwater.org
Solomon R Guggenheim Foundation	www.guggenheim.org
Soloway, Ronald	www.ujafedny.org
Solvay UFSD	www.solvayschools.org
Somers CSD	www.somers.k12.ny.us
Sonnenblick-Goldman Company	www.sonngold.com
Sophie Davis School of Biomedical Education	med.cuny.edu
South Colonie CSD	www.southcolonieschools.org
South Country CSD	www.southcountry.org
South Glens Falls CSD	www.sgfallssd.org
South Huntington UFSD	www.shuntington.k12.ny.us
South Jefferson CSD	www.spartanpride.org
South Lewis CSD	www.southlewis.org
South Orangetown CSD	www.socsd.org
South Seneca CSD	www.southseneca.com
Southampton Chamber of Commerce	www.southamptonchamber.com
Southampton UFSD	www.southhampton.k12.ny.us
Southampton, Town of	http://town.southampton.ny.us
Southeastern New York, Council of Industry of	www.councilofindustry.org
Southern District	www.nysb.uscourts.gov
Southern Dutchess Chamber of Commerce (Greater Southern Dutchess)	www.gsdcc.org
Southern Saratoga County Chamber of Commerce	www.ssccc.org
Southern Tier Economic Growth Inc	www.steg.com
Southern Ulster County Chamber of Commerce	www.southernulsterchamber.org
Southern Westchester BOCES	www.swboces.org
Southhampton Town Young Republicans	www.southamptontownyrs.com
Southold UFSD	www.northfork.net/shs/
Southold, Town of	southoldtown.northfork.net
Southwestern CSD at Jamestown	swcs.wnyric.org
Spackenkill UFSD	www.spekenkillschools.org
Spanish Broadcasting System Network Inc	www.lamusica.com
Special Committee on Animals & the Law	www.nysba.org
Special Olympics New York, Inc	www.nyso.org
Spectra Environmental Group Inc	www.spectraenv.com
Spencer-Van Etten CSD	www.svecsd.org
Spencerport CSD	www.spencerportschools.org
Sports & Arts in Schools Foundation	www.sasfny.org
Sports Commission, NYC	www.nyc.gov/sports
Spring Valley, Village of	www.villagespringvalley.org
Springbrook	www.springbrookny.org
Springs UFSD	www.springs.k12.ny.us
Springville Area Chamber of Commerce	www.springvillechamber.com
Springville-Griffith Inst CSD	www.spingvillegi.org
St Bernard's School of Theology & Ministry	www.stbernards.edu
St Bonaventure University	www.sbu.edu
St Elizabeth College of Nursing	www.secon.edu
St Francis College	www.stfranciscollege.edu
St James Chamber of Commerce	www.stjameschamber.org
St John Fisher College	www.sjfc.edu

See Organization Index for page numbers.

World Wide Web (URL) Index

St John's University	www.new.stjohns.edu
St John's University-Peter J Tobin College of Business, School of Risk Mgmt	www.stjohns.edu
St Johnsville CSD	www.sjcsd.org
St Joseph's College	www.sjcny.edu
St Joseph's Rehabilitation Center Inc	www.sjrcrehab.org
St Joseph's Seminary Institute of Religious Studies	www.ny-archdiocese.org/seminary
St Lawrence County	www.co.st-lawrence.ny.us
St Lawrence County Chamber of Commerce	www.northcountryguide.com
St Lawrence County Industrial Development Agency	www.slcida.com
St Lawrence County Newspapers	www.ogd.com
St Lawrence University	www.stlawu.edu
St Lawrence-Lewis BOCES	www.sllboces.org
St Regis Falls CSD	www.fehb.org/stregis.htm
St Regis Mohawk Tribe	www.stregismohawktribe.com
St Thomas Aquinas College	www.stac.edu
St Vladimir's Orthodox Theological Seminary	www.svots.edu
STA Subcontractors Trade Assn Inc State PAC	www.stanyc.com
Standards & Appeals, Board of, NYC	www.nyc.gov/html/bsa
Standards of Official Conduct	www.house.gov/ethics
Star-Gazette	www.stargazette.com
Starpoint CSD	www.starpointcsd.org
State Comptroller, Office of the	www.osc.state.ny.us
State Department	www.dos.state.ny.us
State Employees Federal Credit Union	www.sefcu.com
State Fair	www.nysfair.org/fair
State Library	www.nysl.nysed.gov
State of New York Mortgage Agency (SONYMA)	www.nyhomes.org
State of New York Municipal Bond Bank Agency (MBBA)	www.nymbba.org
State Police, Division of	www.troopers.state.ny.us
State University at Brockport	www.brockport.edu
State University at Old Westbury	www.oldwestbury.edu
State University at Potsdam	www.potsdam.edu
State University College at Cortland	www.cortland.edu
State University College at Geneseo	www.geneseo.edu
State University College at New Paltz	www.newpaltz.edu
State University College of Technology at Canton	www.canton.edu
State University College of Technology at Delhi	www.delhi.edu
State University Construction Fund	www.sucf.suny.edu
State University Empire State College	www.esc.edu
State University Institute of Technology	web2.sunyit.edu
State University of New York at Albany	www.albany.edu
State University of New York at Oneonta	www.oneonta.edu
State University of New York at Oswego	www.oswego.edu
State University of New York at Plattsburgh	www.plattsburgh.edu
State University of New York College of Environmental Science & Forestry	www.esf.edu
State University of New York Maritime College	www.sunymaritime.edu
State University of New York, Fredonia	www.fredonia.edu
Staten Island (Richmond County)	www.statenislandusa.com
Staten Island Advance	www.silive.com
Staten Island Chamber of Commerce	www.sichamber.com
Staten Island Economic Development Corporation	www.siedc.net
Staten Island Zoo	www.statenislandzoo.org
Statewide Black & Puerto Rican/Latino Substance Abuse Task Force	www.nytaskforce.org
Statewide Corporate Strategies Inc	www.statewidestrat.com
Statewide Emergency Network for Social & Economic Security (SENSES)	www.sensesny.org
Statistics	www.nass.usda.gov/ny

See Organization Index for page numbers.

World Wide Web (URL) Index

Statue of Liberty National Monument & Ellis Island . . . . www.nps.gov/stli/
Steuben . . . . www.steubencony.org
Steuben County . . . . www.steubencony.org
Steuben County Conference & Visitors Bureau . . . . www.corningfingerlakes.com
Steuben County Industrial Development Agency . . . . www.steubencountyida.com
Stillman, Friedman & Shechtman PC . . . . www.stillmanfriedman.com
Stillwater CSD . . . . www.scsd.org
Stockbridge Valley CSD . . . . www.stockbridgevalley.org
Stony Brook University, SUNY . . . . www.sunysb.edu
Stuto, Diane D. . . . . www.licony.org
Suburban News & Hamlin Clarkson Herald . . . . www.westsidenewsonline.com
Suffern Chamber of Commerce . . . . www.suffernchamberofcommerce.org
Suffolk County . . . . www.co.suffolk.ny.us
Suffolk County Assn of Municipal Employees' PAC Inc . . . . www.scame.org
Suffolk County Chapter Nat'l Womens Political Caucus . . . . www.nwpc.org
Suffolk County Community College www3.sunysuffolk.edu
Suffolk County Correction Officers' Assn PAC . . . . www.sccoa.net
Suffolk County Deputy Sheriffs Benevolent Assn Inc PAC . . . . www.scdsba.com
Suffolk Regional Off-Track Betting Corporation . . . . www.suffolkotb.com
Sullivan & Cromwell . . . . www.sullcrom.com
Sullivan & Cromwell LLP . . . . www.sullcrom.com
Sullivan BOCES . . . . www.scboces.org
Sullivan County . . . . www.co.sullivan.ny.us
Sullivan County Chamber of Commerce . . . . www.catskills.com
Sullivan County Community College . . . . www.sullivan.suny.edu
Sullivan County Industrial Development Agency . . . . www.sullivanida.com
Sullivan County Visitors Association . . . . www.scva.net
Sullivan West CSD . . . . www.swcsd.org
Sunbridge College . . . . www.sunbridge.edu
Sunwize Technologies Inc . . . . www.sunwize.com
SUNY at Albany, Center for Women in Government & Civil Society . . . . www.cwig.albany.edu
SUNY at Albany, Nelson A Rockefeller College . . . . www.albany.edu/rockefeller
SUNY at Albany, Nelson A Rockefeller College of Public Affairs & Policy . . . . www.albany.edu/rockefeller
SUNY at Albany, Professional Development Program, NE States Addiction . . . . www.pdp.albany.edu
SUNY at Albany, School of Public Health, Center for Public Health Preparedness . . . . . www.ualbanycphp.org
SUNY at Cortland, Center for Environmental & Outdoor Education . . . . www.cortland.edu
SUNY at New Paltz, College of Liberal Arts & Sciences . . . . www.newpaltz.edu
SUNY Board of Trustees . . . . www.suny.edu
SUNY Buffalo Human Rights Center . . . . wings.buffalo.edu/law/bhrlc
SUNY College of Agriculture & Technology at Cobleskill . . . . www.cobleskill.edu
SUNY Downstate Medical Center . . . . www.downstate.edu
SUNY Metropolitan Recruitment Center . . . . www.suny.edu/student/mrc.cfm
SUNY State College of Optometry . . . . www.sunyopt.edu
SUNY System Administration & Executive Council . . . . www.suny.edu
SUNY Upstate Medical University . . . . www.upstate.edu
Support Services Alliance Inc . . . . www.smallbizgrowth.com
Susquehanna Valley CSD . . . . www.svsabers.org
Swedish Institute . . . . www.swedishinstitute.org
Sweet Home CSD . . . . www.sweethomeschools.com
Syosset CSD www.syosett.k12.ny.us
Syracuse & Central NY, Metropolitan Development Association of . . . . www.mda-cny.com
Syracuse Chamber of Commerce (Greater Syracuse) . . . . www.syracusechamber.com
Syracuse City SD . . . . www.syracusecityschools.com
Syracuse Convention & Vistors Bureau . . . . www.visitsyracuse.org
Syracuse Economic Development . . . . www.edsyracuse.com
Syracuse Educational Opportunity Center . . . . www.syr.sunyeoc.org

See Organization Index for page numbers.

World Wide Web (URL) Index

Syracuse Industrial Development Agency	www.syracuse.ny.us
Syracuse Newspapers Inc	www.syracuse.com
Syracuse University	www.syr.edu
Syracuse University Press	www.syracuseuniversitypress.syr.edu
Syracuse University, Maxwell School of Citizenship & Public Affairs	www.maxwell.syr.edu
Syracuse University, Office of Government & Community Relations	govt-comm.syr.edu
Syracuse, City of	www.syracuse.ny.us
Systra Consulting Inc	www.systraconsulting.com
Taconic Hills CSD	www.taconichills.k12.ny.us
Tanenbaum Center for Interreligious Understanding	www.tanenbaum.org
Tarrytown UFSD	www.tufsd.org
Tax Appeals, Division of	www.nysdta.org
Tax Commission, NYC	www.nyc.gov/html/taxcomm
Taxation & Finance Department	www.tax.state.ny.us
Taxation, Joint Committee on	www.house.gov/jct
Taxi & Limousine Commission, NYC	www.nyc.gov/taxi
Taylor Business Institute	www.tbiglobal.com
TD Banknorth	www.TDBanknorth.com
Tea Association of the USA Inc	www.teausa.com
Teachers College, Columbia University	www.tc.columbia.edu
Teaching Matters Inc	www.teachingmatters.org
Technical Career Institutes Inc	www.tcicollege.edu
Temporary & Disability Assistance, Office of	www.otda.state.ny.us
Tenants & Neighbors Coalition (NYS)	www.tandu.org
The Bachmann-Strauss Dystonia & Parkinson Foundation	www.dystonia-parkinsons.org
The Business Review	www.albany.bizjournals.com
The Clearing House Association, LLC	www.theclearinghouse.org
The Independent	www.indenews.com
The Independent News	www.indyeastend.com
The New York Observer	www.nyobserver.com
The New York Times	www.nytimes.com
The Palladium Times	www.pall-times.com
The Political Action Committee of The Fulton County Regional Chamber of Commerce	www.fultoncountyny.org
The Putnam County News and Recorder	www.pcnr.com
The Shaw Licitra PAC	www.shaw-licitra.com
Thelen Reid Brown Raysman & Steiner	www.thelen.com
Theodore Roosevelt Inaugural National Historic Site	www.nps.gov/thri/
THOROPAC - Thoroughbred Breeders' PAC	www.nybreds.com
Thousand Islands Bridge Authority	www.tibridge.com
Thousand Islands CSD	www.1000islandschools.org
Thousand Islands Int'l Tourism Council	www.visit1000islands.com
Three Rivers Development Foundation Inc	www.threeriversdevelopment.com
Three Village CSD	www.3villagecsd.k12.ny.us
Ticonderoga Area Chamber of Commerce	www.ticonderogany.com
Times Herald-Record	www.recordonline.com
Times Union	www.timesunion.com
Tioga	www.tiogacountyny.com/boardofelections.asp
Tioga County	www.tiogacountyny.com
Tioga County Chamber of Commerce	www.tiogachamber.com
Tioga County Industrial Development Agency	www.developtioga.com
Tishman Speyer Properties	www.tishmanspeyer.com
Tompkins	www.tompkins-co.org/boe
Tompkins Cortland Community College	www.sunytccc.edu
Tompkins County	www.co.tompkins.ny.us
Tompkins County Area Development	www.tcad.org
Tompkins County Chamber of Commerce	www.tompkinschamber.org

See Organization Index for page numbers.

World Wide Web (URL) Index

Tompkins Trustco Inc . . . . www.tompkinstrustco.com
Tompkins-Seneca-Tioga BOCES . . . . www.tstboces.org
Tonawanda (Town Of) Development Corporation . . . . www.tonawanda.com
Tonawanda City SD . . . . www.tona.wnyric.org
Tonawanda News . . . . www.tonawanda-news.com
Tonawanda, Town of . . . . www.tonawanda.ny.us
Tonawandas, Chamber of Commerce of the . . . . www.the-tonawandas.com
Touro College . . . . www.touro.edu
Town of Webb UFSD . . . . www.townschool.org
Transport Workers Union of America, AFL-CIO . . . . www.twu.com
Transportation & Infrastructure . . . . www.transportation.house.gov
Transportation Alternatives . . . . www.transalt.org
Transportation Department . . . . www.nysdot.gov
Transportation, Department of, NYC . . . . www.nyc.gov/dot
Tranter, G Thomas, Jr . . . . www.corning.com
Trees New York . . . . www.treesny.com
Tri-State Chamber of Commerce . . . . www.tristatechamber.com
Tri-State College of Acupuncture . . . . www.tsca.edu
Tri-State Transportation Campaign . . . . www.tstc.org
Tri-Valley CSD tvcs.k12.ny.us
Tribeca Film Institute . . . . www.tribecafilminstitute.org
Trocaire College . . . . www.trocaire.edu
Trooper Foundation-State of New York Inc . . . . www.nystrooperfoundation.org
Troy, City of . . . . www.troyny.gov
True & Walsh, LLP . . . . www.truewalshlaw.com
Trumansburg CSD www.tburg.k12.ny.us
Tuckahoe Common SD www.tuckahoe.k12.ny.us
Tuckahoe UFSD . . . . www.tuckahoeschools.org
Tully CSD . . . . www.tullyschools.org
Tupper Lake Chamber of Commerce . . . . www.tupperlakeinfo.com
Turner/Geneslaw Inc . . . . www.tgiplanning.com
Tuxedo UFSD . . . . www.tuxedoschooldistrict.com
Tyson, Lisa . . . . www.lipc.org
UA Plumbers & Pipefitters LU 773 Voluntary NYS PAC Fund www.lu773.org
UFCW Active Ballot Club . . . . www.ufcw.org
UFT COPE Local . . . . www.uft.org
UHAP PAC . . . . www.upstatehealthcare.org
UHY Advisors . . . . www.uhyadvisors-us.com
Ulster BOCES . . . . www.ulsterboces.org
Ulster County . . . . www.co.ulster.ny.us
Ulster County Chamber of Commerce . . . . www.ulsterchamber.org
Ulster County Community College . . . . www.sunyulster.edu
Ulster County Development Corporation/Ulster County Industrial Development Agency . www.ulsterny.com
Ulster Savings Bank . . . . www.ulstersavings.com
Unadilla Valley CSD . . . . www.uvstorm.org
Unatego CSD . . . . www.unatego.org
Unification Theological Seminary . . . . www.uts.edu
Unified Court System . . . . www.nycourts.gov
Uniformed Fire Officers Association . . . . www.ufoa.org
Union College . . . . www.union.edu
Union Local Development Corporation (Town of) . . . . www.townofunion.com
Union State Bank . . . . www.unionstate.com
Union Theological Seminary . . . . www.uts.columbia.edu
Union, Town of . . . . www.townofunion.com
Union-Endicott CSD . . . . www.uetigers.stier.org
Uniondale UFSD . . . . district.uniondaleschools.org

See Organization Index for page numbers.

World Wide Web (URL) Index

UNITE HERE	www.uniteunion.org
United Federation of Teachers	www.uft.org
United Food & Commercial Workers Local 1	www.ufcwone.org
United Hospital Fund of New York	www.uhfnyc.org
United Jewish Appeal-Federation of Jewish Philanthropies	www.ujafedny.org
United Jewish Appeal-Federation of Jewish Philanthropies of NY	www.ujafedny.org
United Nations Development Corporation	www.undc.org
United Neighborhood Houses - Not For Profit	www.unhny.org
United New York Ambulance Network (UNYAN)	unyan.net
United Restaurant, Hotel & Tavern Association of NY Statewide PAC	www.esrta.org
United Spinal Association	www.unitedspinal.org
United Steelworkers District 4 PAC	www.usa.org
United Transportation Union	www.utu.org
United University Professions	www.uupinfo.org
United Way of Central New York	www.unitedway-cny.org
United Way of New York City	www.unitedwaynyc.org
Unity Mutual Life Insurance Co	www.unity-life.com
Unity PAC	www.unity-life.com
University at Buffalo	www.government.buffalo.edu
University at Buffalo, Research Institute on Addictions	www.ria.buffalo.edu
University at Buffalo, State University of New York	www.buffalo.edu
University of Rochester School of Medicine	www2.envmed.rochester.edu
Upstate Freshwater Institute	www.upstatefreshwater.org
Upstate Homes for Children & Adults Inc	www.upstatehome.org
Upstate Niagara Cooperative Inc	www.upstateniagara.com
Urban Homesteading Assistance Board	www.uhab.org
Urbanomics	www.urbanomics.org
Urbitran Group	www.urbitran.com
US Citizenship & Immigration Services (USCIS)	www.uscis.gov
US Commerce Department	www.doc.gov
US Commercial Service - International Trade Administration	www.export.gov
US Commission on Civil Rights	www.usccr.gov
US Court of Appeals for the Second Circuit	www.ca2.uscourts.gov
US Court of International Trade	www.cit.uscourts.gov
US Department of Agriculture	www.usda.gov
US Department of Energy	www.doe.gov
US Department of Health & Human Services	www.os.dhhs.gov; www.hhs.gov/region2/
US Department of Homeland Security (DHS)	www.dhs.gov
US Department of the Interior	www.doi.gov
US Department of Veterans Affairs	www.va.gov
US DISTRICT COURT - NEW YORK (part of the Second Circuit)	www.nyed.uscourts.gov
US Education Department	www.ed.gov
US Environmental Protection Agency	www.epa.gov
US General Services Administration	www.gsa.gov
US Government Printing Office	www.gpo.gov
US Housing & Urban Development Department	www.hud.gov
US Justice Department	www.usdoj.gov
US Labor Department	www.dol.gov
US Merchant Marine Academy	www.usmma.edu
US Merit Systems Protection Board	www.mspb.gov
US Military Academy	www.usma.edu
US Mint	www.usmint.gov
US Office of Personnel Management	www.usajobs.opm.gov
US Postal Service	www.usps.gov
US Railroad Retirement Board	www.rrb.gov
US Securities & Exchange Commission	www.sec.gov

See Organization Index for page numbers.

World Wide Web (URL) Index

US State Department	www.state.gov
US Term Limits Foundation	www.ustermlimits.org
US Transportation Department	www.dot.gov
US Treasury Department	www.ustreas.gov
USA Track & Field, Adirondack Association Inc	www.usatfadir.org
Utica City SD	www.uticaschools.org
Utica College	www.utica.edu
Utica Industrial Development Agency (City of)	www.cityofutica.com
Utica Mutual Insurance Co	www.uticanational.com
Utica School of Commerce	www.uscny.edu
Utica, City of	www.cityofutica.com
VA Healthcare Network Upstate New York (VISN2)	www.va.gov/visns/visn02
VA NY/NJ Veterans Healthcare Network (VISN3)	www.va.gov/visns/visn03
Valhalla UFSD	valhalla.k12.ny.us
Valley CSD (Montgomery)	www.vcsd.k12.ny.us
Valley National Bank	www.valleynationalbank.com
Valley Stream 13 UFSD	www.valleystream13.com
Valley Stream 24 UFSD	www.vsufsd.com
Valley Stream 30 UFSD	www.valleystream30.com
Valley Stream Central HS District	www.vschsd.org
Valley Stream Chamber of Commerce	www.vscc.org
Valley Stream, Village of	www.valleystreamvillage.org; www.valleystream-govoffice.com
Van Hornesville-Owen D Young CSD	www.odyoung-csd.k12.ny.us
Vassar College	www.vassar.edu
Vaughn College of Aeronautics & Technology	www.vaughn.edu
Vedder Price Kaufman & Kammholz PC	www.vedderprice.com
Ventresca-Ecroyd, Gilda	www.med.nyu.edu
Vera Institute of Justice	www.vera.org
Verizon Communications	www.verizon.com
Vernon Downs/Gaming-Racing-Entertainment	www.vernondowns.com
Vernon-Verona-Sherrill CSD	www.vvscentralschools.org
Vestal CSD	www.vestal.stier.org
Vestal, Town of	www.vestalny.com
Veterans of Foreign Wars	www.vfwny.com
Veterans of Foreign Wars (VFW)	www.vfw.org
Veterans Outreach Center Inc	www.eflagstore.com
Veterans' Affairs	www.veterans.senate.gov
Veterans' Affairs, Division of	www.veterans.state.ny.us
Veterans' Affairs, Mayor's Office of, NYC	www.nyc.gov/veterans
Veterans' Widows International Network Inc (VWIN), New York	www.vetsurvivors.com
Viacom Inc	www.viacom.com
Victor Chamber of Commerce	www.victorchamber.com
Victor CSD	www.victorschools.org
Villa Maria College of Buffalo	www.villa.edu
Village Voice (The)	www.villagevoice.com
Village Voice Media, Inc	www.villagevoice.com
Vocational & Educational Services for Individuals With **Disabilities Office (VESID)**	www.vesid.nysed.gov
Voice of Teachers for Educational/Comm on Political **Education**	www.nysut.org
Voorheesville CSD	vcsd.neric.org
Voter Assistance Commission (VAC), NYC	www.nyc.gov/voter
WABC (7)	www.7online.com
WABC (770 AM)	www.wabcradio.com
Wachtell, Lipton, Rosen & Katz	www.wlrk.com
Waddington Chamber of Commerce	www.waddingtonny.us/chamber
Wagner College	www.wagner.edu

See Organization Index for page numbers.

World Wide Web (URL) Index

WALL (1340 AM), WRRV (92.7 FM)	www.wrrv.com
Wall Street Journal (The)	www.wsj.com
Wallkill CSD	www.wallkillcsd.k12.ny.us
Wallkill, Town of	www.townofwallkill.com
Walton CSD	www.waltoncsd.stier.org
WAMC (90.3 FM)	www.wamc.org
Wang, Phyllis A	www.nyshcp.org
Wantagh Chamber of Commerce	www.wantaghmall.org
Wantagh UFSD	www.wms.wantaghufsd.k12.ny.us
Wappinger, Town of	www.townofwappinger.us
Wappingers CSD	www.wappingersschools.org
Warren & Washington Industrial Development Agency	www.warren-washingtonida.com
Warren County	www.co.warren.ny.us
Warren County Economic Development Corporation	www.warrencounty.org
Warrensburg Chamber of Commerce	www.warrensburgchamber.com
Warrensburg CSD	www.wcsd.org
Warsaw Chamber of Commerce (Greater Warsaw)	warsawchamber.com
Warsaw CSD	www.warsaw.k12.ny.us
Warwick Valley Chamber of Commerce	www.warwickcc.org
Warwick Valley CSD	www.warwickvalleyschools.org
Warwick, Town of	www.townofwarwick.org
Washington County	www.co.washington.ny.us
Washington County Local Development Corporation	www.wcldc.org
Washington Mutual	www.wamu.com
Washington-Saratoga-Warren-Hamilton-Essex BOCES	www.wswheboces.org
Water Finance Authority, Municipal, NYC	www.nyc.gov/nyw
Waterford-Halfmoon UFSD	www.whufsd.org
Waterfront Commission of New York Harbor	www.wcnyh.org
Waterkeeper Alliance	www.waterkeeper.org
Waterloo CSD	www.waterloocsd.org
Watertown City SD	www.watertowncsd.org
Watertown Daily Times	www.watertowndailytimes.com
Watertown Empire Zone	www.watertownempirezone.com
Watertown, City of	www.citywatertown.org
Watertown-North Country Chamber of Commerce (Greater Watertown)	www.watertownny.com
Waterville CSD	www.watervilleschools.org
Watervliet City SD	vliet.neric.org
Watkins Glen CSD	www.watkinsglenschools.com
Watson School of Biological Sciences at Cold Spring Harbor Laboratory	gradschool.cshl.edu
Wave	www.rockawave.com
Waverly CSD	www.waverlyschools.com
WAXQ (104.3 FM)	www.q1043.com
Wayland-Cohocton CSD	www.wccsk12.org
Wayne	www.co.wayne.ny.us
Wayne County	www.co.wayne.ny.us
Wayne County Industrial Development Agency & Economic Development	www.wedcny.org
Wayne CSD	www.wayne.k12.ny.us
Wayne-Finger Lakes BOCES	www.wflboces.org
Ways & Means	http://waysandmeans.house.gov
WBBR (1130 AM) Bloomberg News	www.wbbr.com
WBFO (88.7 FM) WOLN (91.3 FM), WUBJ (88.7 FM) NPR/PRI - SUNY at Buffalo	www.wbfo.org
WBLK (93.7 FM), WJYE (96.1 FM)	www.wjye.com; www.wblk.com
WBNG (12), WBXI (11)	www.wbng.com
WCBS (2)	www.cbsnewyork.com
WCBS (880 AM)	www.wcbs880.com
WCHP (760 AM)	www.wchp.com

See Organization Index for page numbers.

World Wide Web (URL) Index

WCII (88.5 FM), WCOT (90.9 FM)	www.fln.org
WCNY (24)	www.wcny.org
WDCX (99.5 FM)	www.wdcxfm.com
We Move	www.wemove.org
Webb Institute	www.webb-institute.edu
Webster Chamber of Commerce	www.websterchamber.com
Webster CSD	www.websterschools.org
Webster, Town of	www.ci.webster.ny.us
Webutuck CSD	www.webutuckschools.org
Weekley, Daniel A	www.dominion.com
Wegmans Food Markets Inc	www.wegmans.com
Weingarten, Reid & McNally, LLC	www.lobbywr.com
Welfare Research Inc	www.welfareresearch.org
Wells College	www.wells.edu
Wells CSD	www.wellscsd.com
Wellsville Area Chamber of Commerce	www.wellsvilleareachamber.com
Wellsville CSD	www.wellsville.wnyric.org
Wellsville Daily Reporter/Spectator	www.wellsvilledaily.com
WENY (36)	www.weny.com
West Babylon UFSD	www.westbabylon.k12.ny.us
West Canada Valley CSD	www.westcanada.org
West Genesee CSD	www.westgenesee.org
West Hempstead UFSD	www.westhempstead.k12.ny.us
West Irondequoit CSD	www.westirondequoit.org
West Islip UFSD	www.westislip.k12.ny.us
West Seneca Chamber of Commerce	www.westseneca.org
West Seneca CSD	www.wscschools.org
West Seneca, Town of	www.westseneca.net
West Side Chamber of Commerce	www.westsidechamber.org
West Valley CSD	www.wvalley.wnyric.org
Westbury UFSD	www.westburyschools.org
Westchester Coalition for Legal Abortion PAC	www.choicematters.org
Westchester Community College	www.sunywcc.edu
Westchester County	www.westchestergov.com/bol
Westchester County Association Inc (The)	www.westchester.org
Westchester County Chamber of Commerce	www.westchesterny.org
Westchester County Industrial Development Agency	http://economic.westchestergov.com
Westchester County Office of Tourism	www.westchestertourism.com
Western District	www.nywb.uscourts.gov
Western New York Library Resources Council	www.wnylrc.org; www.wnylibraries.org;www.askus247.org
Western Regional Off-Track Betting Corp	www.westernotb.com
Western Suffolk BOCES	www.wsboces.org
Westfield CSD	www.wacs.wnyric.org
Westfield/Barcelona Chamber of Commerce	www.chautauquachamber.org
Westhampton Beach UFSD	www.westhamptonbeach.k12.ny.us
Westhampton Chamber of Commerce (Greater Westhampton)	www.whbcc.org
Westhill CSD	www.westhillschools.org
Westmoreland CSD	www.westmorelandschool.org
Westport CSD	www.westportcs.org
Westside News Inc	www.westsidenewsonline.com
WETM (18)	www.wetmtv.com
WFLY (92.3 FM), WAJZ (96.3 FM), WROW (590 AM), WYJB (95.5 FM), WZMR (104.9)	www.pamal.com
WFRY (97.5 FM)	www.froggy97.com
WFUV (90.7 FM)	www.wfuv.org
WGNA (107.7 FM)	www.wgna.com

See Organization Index for page numbers.

World Wide Web (URL) Index

WGRZ (2)	www.wgrz.com
WGY (810 AM), WPYX (106.5 FM), WRVE (99.5 FM)	www.wgy.com; www.pyx106.com; www.wrve.com
WHAM (1180 AM)	www.wham1180.com
WHAM (13)	www.wokr13.tv
WHCU (870 AM), WTKO (1470 AM), WYXL (97.3 FM), WQNY (103.7 FM)	www.whcu870.com; www.lite97fm.com; www.qcountryfm.com
Wheatland-Chili CSD	www.wheatland.k12.ny.us
WHEC (10)	www.10nbc.com
Wheelerville UFSD	www.wufselementary.k12.ny.us
White & Case LLP	www.whitecase.com
White Plains City SD	www.wpcsd.k12.ny.us
White Plains, City of	www.cityofwhiteplains.com
Whiteface Mountain Regional Visitor's Bureau	www.whitefaceregion.com
Whitehall CSD	www.railroaders.net
Whiteman Osterman & Hanna LLP	www.woh.com
Whitesboro CSD	www.wboro.org
Whitesville CSD	www.whitesville.wnyric.org
Whitney Point CSD	www.wpcsd.org
WHTT (104.1 FM)	www.whtt.com
WHUD (100.7 FM)	www.whud.com
WICZ (40)	www.wicz.com
Wieboldt, Robert	libi.org
Wilber National Bank	www.wilberbank.com
Wildlife Conservation Society	www.wcs.org
William B Collins Co	www.leaderherald.com
William Floyd UFSD	www.wfsd.k12.ny.us
Williamson CSD	www.williamsoncentral.org
Williamsville CSD	www.williamsvillek12.org
Willistons Chamber of Commerce	www.chamberofthewillistons.org
Willow Mixed Media Inc	www.willowmixedmedia.org
Willsboro CSD	www.willsborocsd.org
Wilson CSD	www.wilson.wnyric.org
Wilson Elser Moskowitz Edelman & Dicker	www.wemed.com
Windsor CSD	www.windsor-csd.org
WINS (1010 AM)	www.1010wins.com
Winthrop University Hospital	www.winthrop.org
WIVB (4), WNLO (23)	www.wivb.com
WIVT/WBGH (34)	www.newschannel34.com
WIXT (9)	www.wixt.com
WKBW (7)	www.wkbw.com
WKPQ (105.3 FM), WHHO (1320 AM)	www.wkpq.com
WKRT (920 AM), WIII (99.9 or 100.3 FM)	www.wiii.com; www.wkrt.com
WKTV (2)	www.wktv.com
WKZA (106.9 FM)	www.1069kissfm.com
WLIW (21) Public Broadcasting	www.wliw.org
WLNY (55)	www.wlnytv.com
WLTW (106.7 FM)	www.1067litefm.com
WMHT (17) Public Broadcasting-NY Capitol Region	www.wmht.org
WMRV (105.7)	www.whrw.org
WMTT (94.7 FM)	www.themetrocks.com
WNBC (4)	www.nbc.com
WNBF (1290 AM), WHWK (98.1FM), WYOS (1360 AM), WAAL (99.1 FM), WWYL (104.1)	www.wnbf.com; www.991thewhale.com; www.981thehawk.com
WNED (17) Western NY Public Broadcasting	www.wned.org
WNED (94.5 FM)	www.wned.org
WNKI (106.1 FM), WPGI (100.9 FM), WNGZ (104.9 FM), WWLZ (820 AM)	www.wink106.com

See Organization Index for page numbers.

World Wide Web (URL) Index

WNTQ (93.1 FM), WAQX (95.7 FM)	www.93Q.com; www.95x.com
WNYT (13)	www.wnyt.com
WNYW (5)	www.fox5ny.com
Wolf, Block, Schorr & Solis-Cohen, LLP	www.wolfblock.com
Women Marines Association	www.womenmarines.org
Women PAC	www.womenpac.org
Women's Bar Association of the State of New York	www.wbasny.org
Women's Business Training Center of New York State	www.nywbc.org
Women's Campaign Fund	www.wcfonline.org
Women's City Club of New York	www.wccny.org
Women's Commission for Refugee Women & Children	www.womenscommission.org
Women's Housing & Economic Development Corporation (WHEDCO)	www.whedco.org
Women's Prison Association & Home Inc	www.wpaonline.org
Women's Rights National Historical Park	www.nps.gov/wori
Women's Venture Fund Inc	www.womensventurefund.org
Wood Tobe-Coburn	www.woodtobecoburn.edu
Woodstock Chamber of Commerce & Arts	www.woodstockchamber.com
WOR (710 AM)	www.wor710.com
Workers' Compensation Board	www.wcb.state.ny.us
Working Families Party	www.workingfamiliesparty.org
World Hunger Year Inc	www.worldhungeryear.org
WOUR (96.9 FM)	www.wour.com
WPDH (101.5 FM)	www.wpdh.com
WPIG (95.7 FM), WHDL (1450 AM)	www.wpig.com www.whdl.com
WPIX (11)	www.wb11.com
WPTR (1540 AM)	www.1540wdcd.com
WPTZ (5) NBC	www.thechamplainchannel.com
WRCC 21st Century Fund	www.westchestergop.com
WRGB (6)	www.cbs6albany.com
WRNN (62)	www.rnntv.com
WSEN (92.1 FM)	www.wsenfm.com
WSKG (46) Public Broadcasting	www.wskg.com
WSKG (89.3 FM), WSQX (91.5 FM)	www.wskg.org
WSPK (104.7 FM)	www.k104online.com
WSTM (3)	www.wstm.com
WSYT (68)	www.foxsyracuse.com
WTEN (10)	www.wten.com
WTVH (5)	www.wtvh.com
WVOX (1460 AM), WRTN (93.5 FM)	www.wvox.com
WWNY (7)	www.wwnytv.com
WWOR (UPN 9)	www.upn9.tv
WWTI (50)	www.newswatch50.com
WXXA (23)	www.fox23news.com
WXXI (21) Public Broadcasting	www.wxxi.org
Wyandanch UFSD	www.wyandanch.k12.ny.us
Wynantskill UFSD	www.wynantskillufsd.org
Wyoming	www.wyoming.co.net
Wyoming County	www.wyomingco.net
Wyoming County Chamber of Commerce	www.wycochamber.org
Wyoming CSD	www.wyoming.k12.ny.us
WYPX (55)	www.paxalbany.tv
YAI/National Institute for People with Disabilities	www.yai.org
Yates County	www.yatescounty.org
Yates County Chamber of Commerce	www.yatesny.com
Yates County Industrial Development Agency	www.yatesida.com
Yavornitzki, Mark L	www.nysaifa.com

See Organization Index for page numbers.

World Wide Web (URL) Index

Yeshiva University	www.yu.edu
Yeshiva University, A Einstein Clg of Med, Div of Subs Abuse	www.aecom.yu.edu
Yeshiva University, A Einstein Clg of Med, OB/GYN & Wmn's Health	www.yu.edu
Yonkers Chamber of Commerce	www.yonkerschamber.com
Yonkers City SD	www.yonkerspublicschools.org
Yonkers Economic Development/Yonkers Industrial Development Agency (City of)	www.cityofyonkersida.com
Yonkers Raceway	www.yonkersraceway.com
Yonkers, City of	www.cityofyonkers.com
York College	york.cuny.edu
York CSD	www.yorkcsd.org
Yorktown CSD	www.yorktowncsd.org
Yorktown, Town of	www.yorktownny.org
Yoswein New York Inc	www.yosweinnewyork.com
Youth & Community Development, Department of, NYC	www.nyc.gov/dycd
Zogby International	www.zogby.com
Zogg, Jeffrey	www.gbcnys.agc.org

See Organization Index for page numbers.

DEMOGRAPHIC MAPS

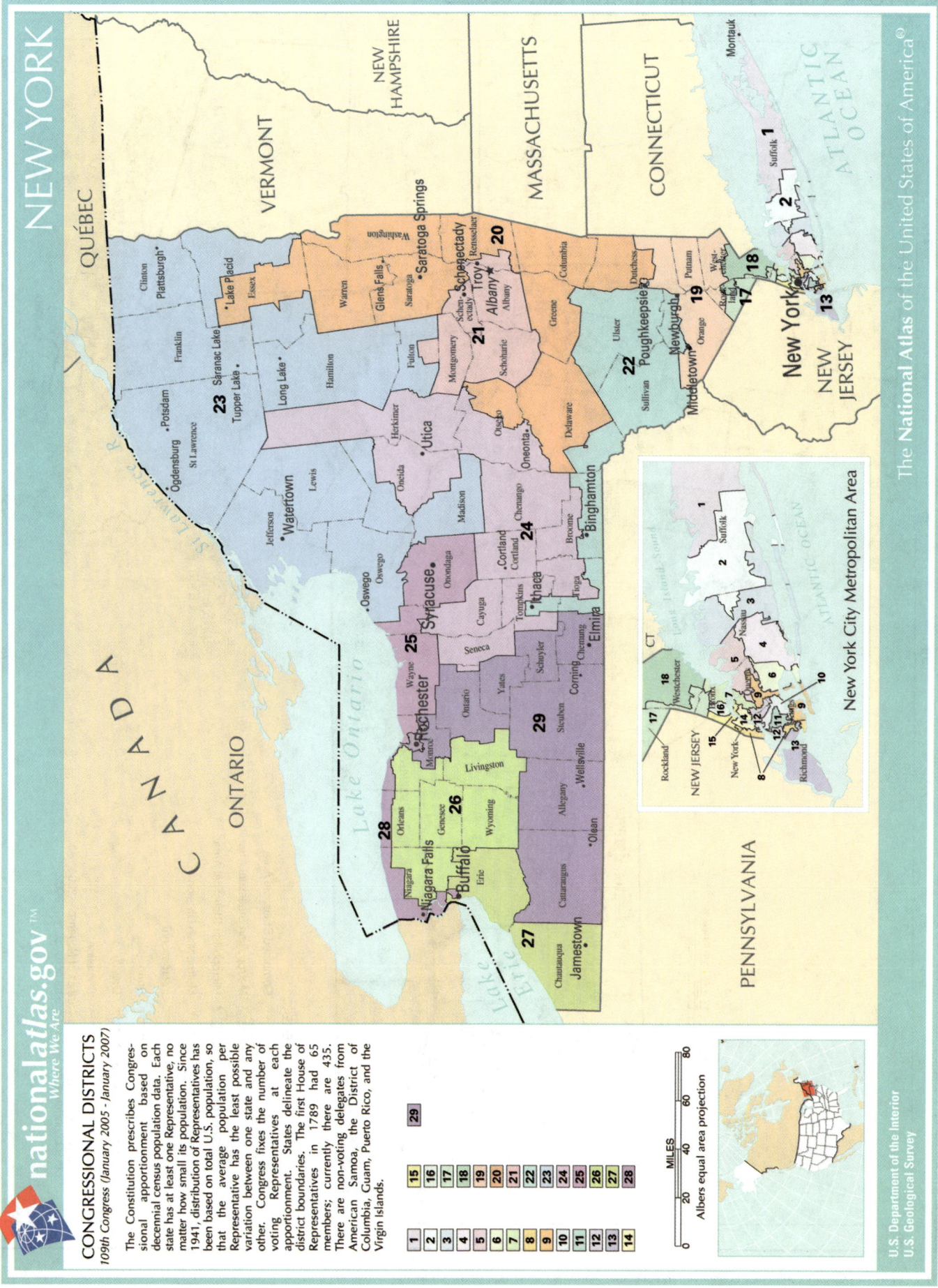

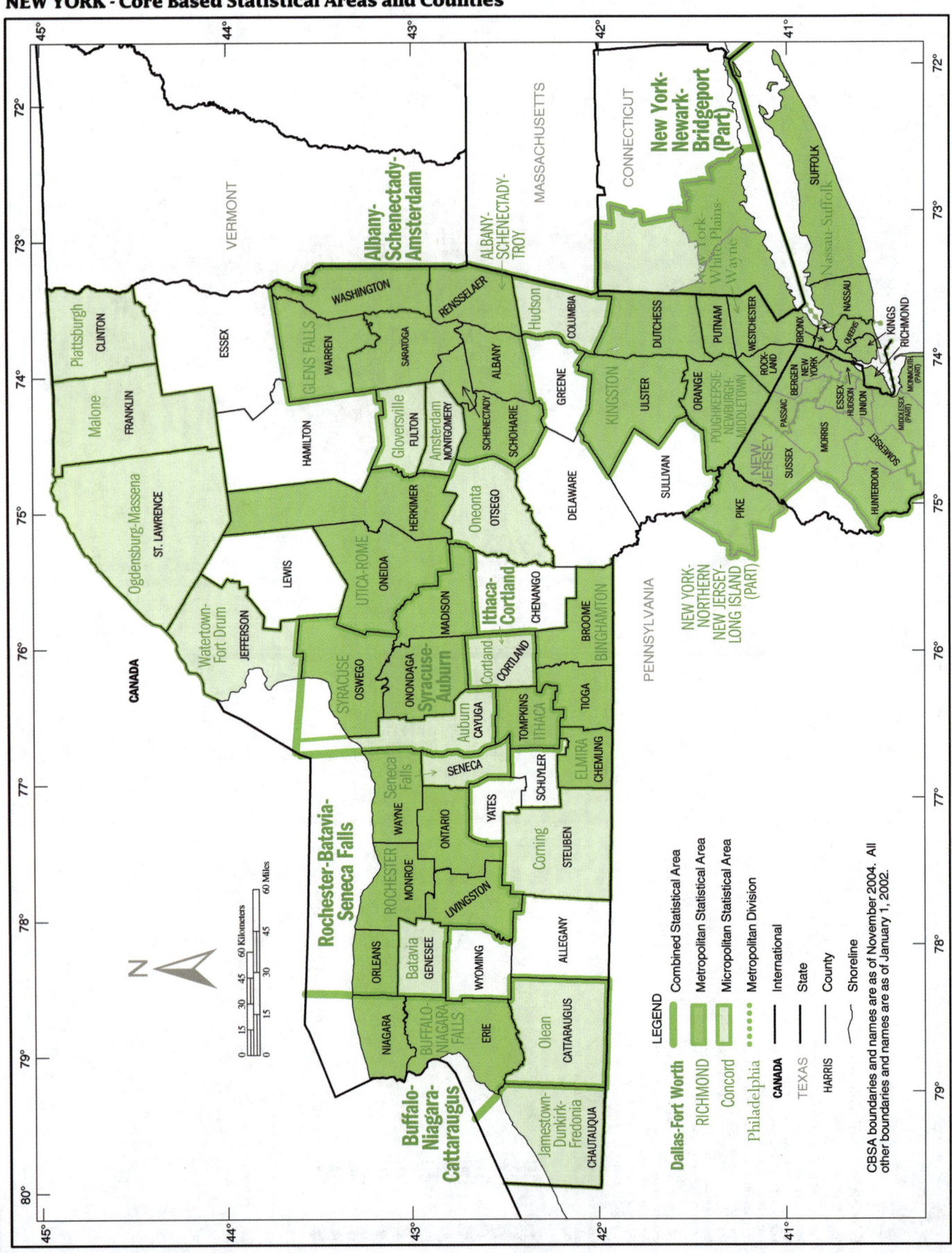

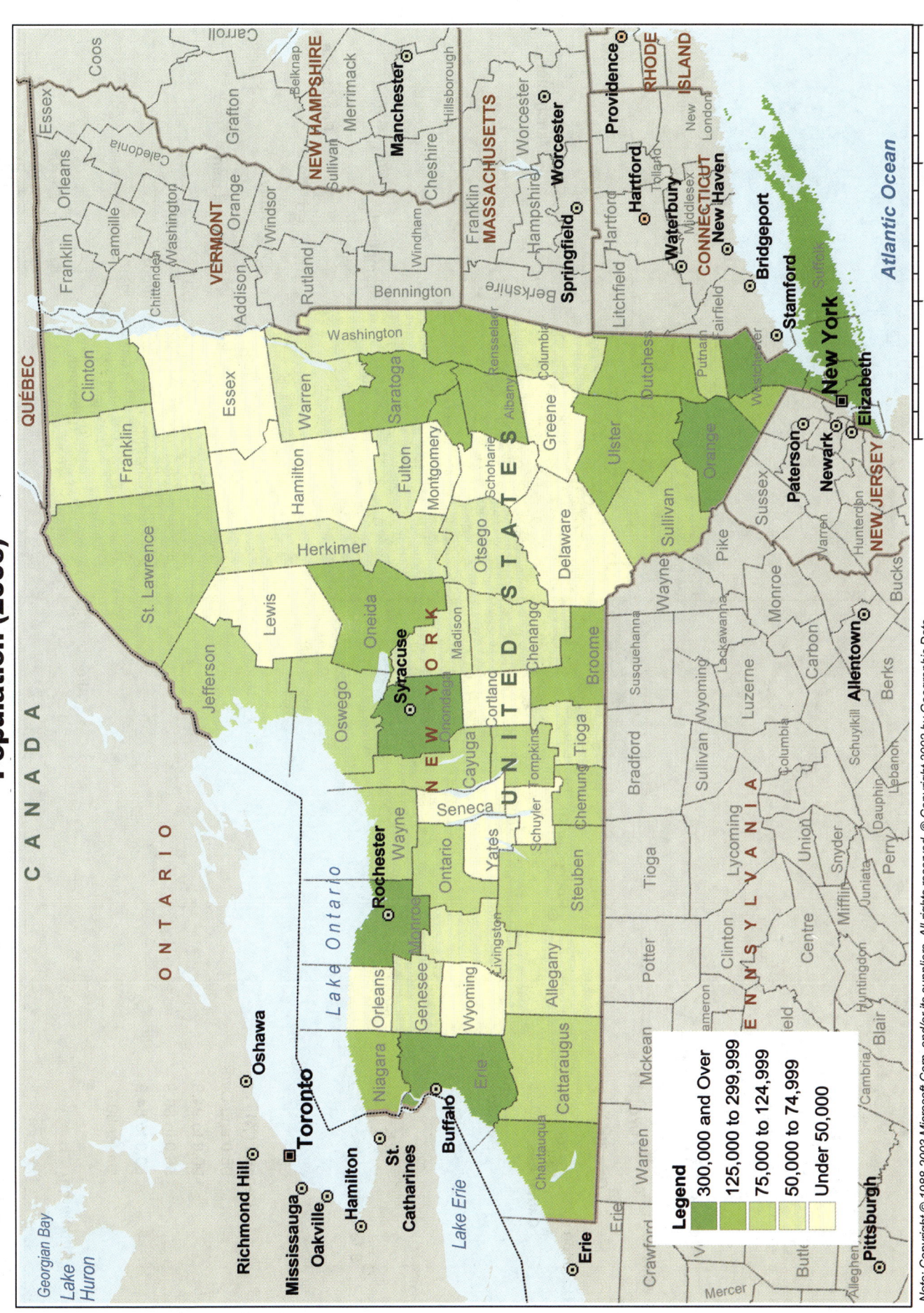

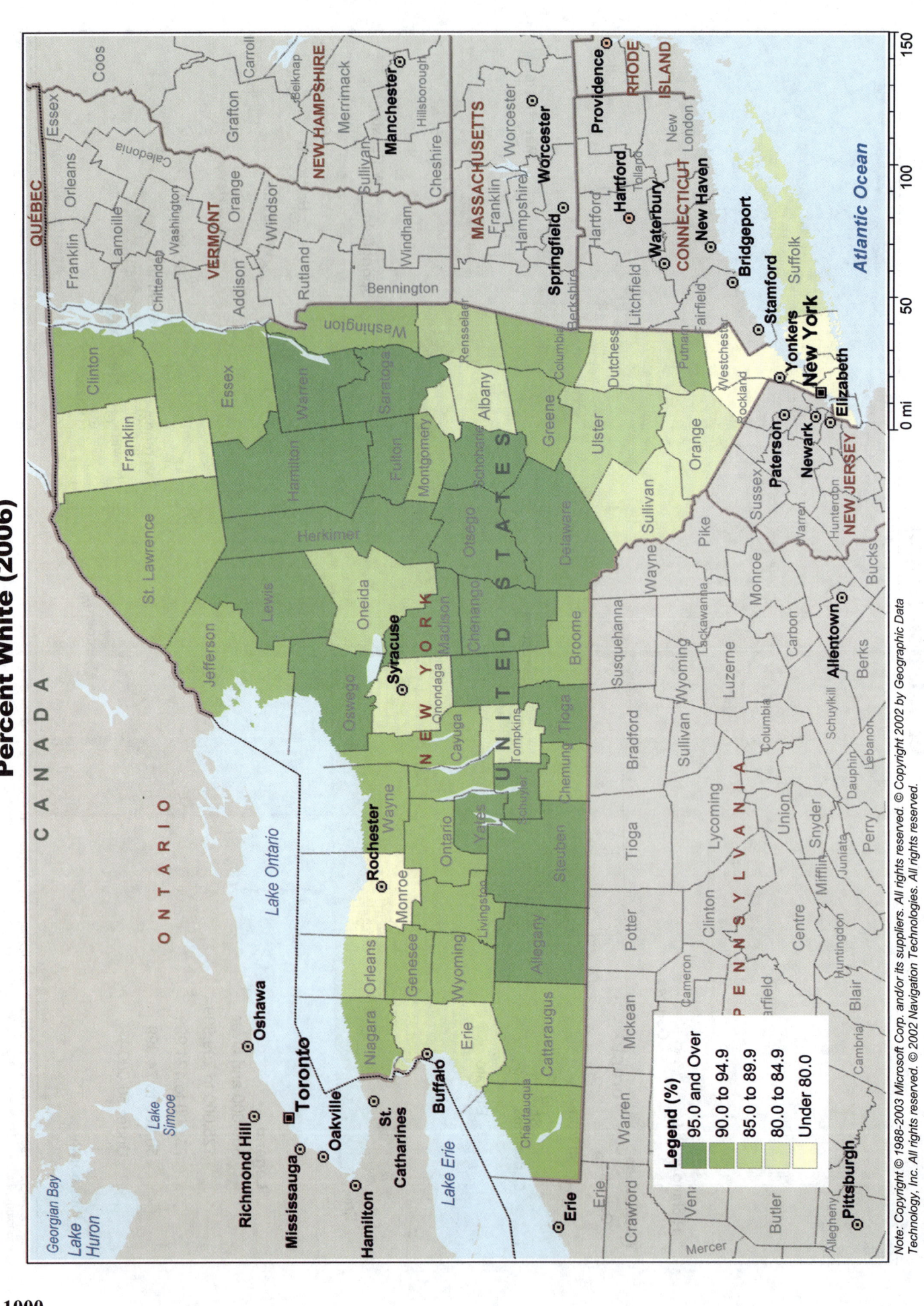

Percent Black (2006)

Legend (%)
- 8.0 and Over
- 6.0 to 7.9
- 4.0 to 5.9
- 2.0 to 3.9
- Under 2.0

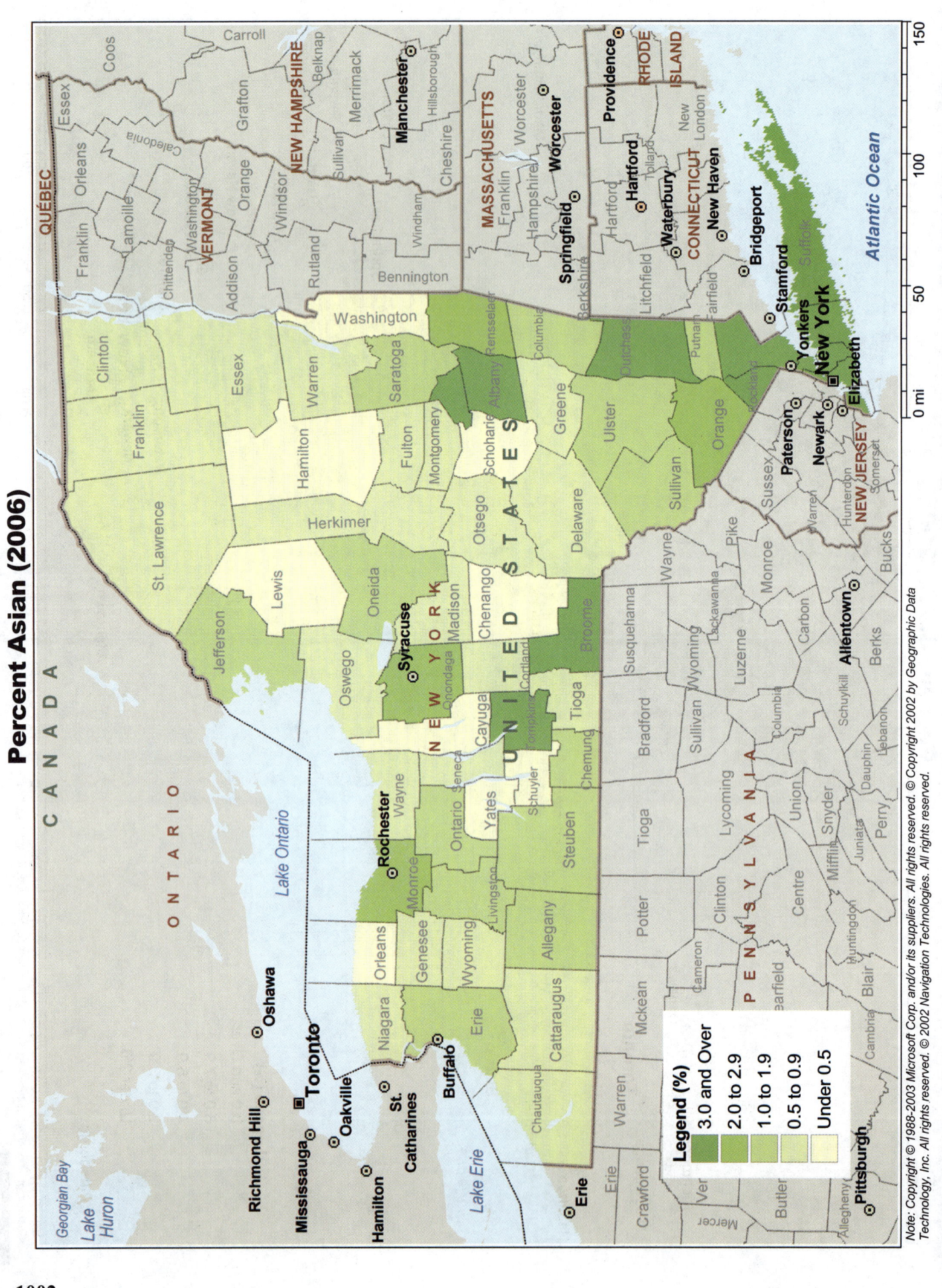

Percent Asian (2006)

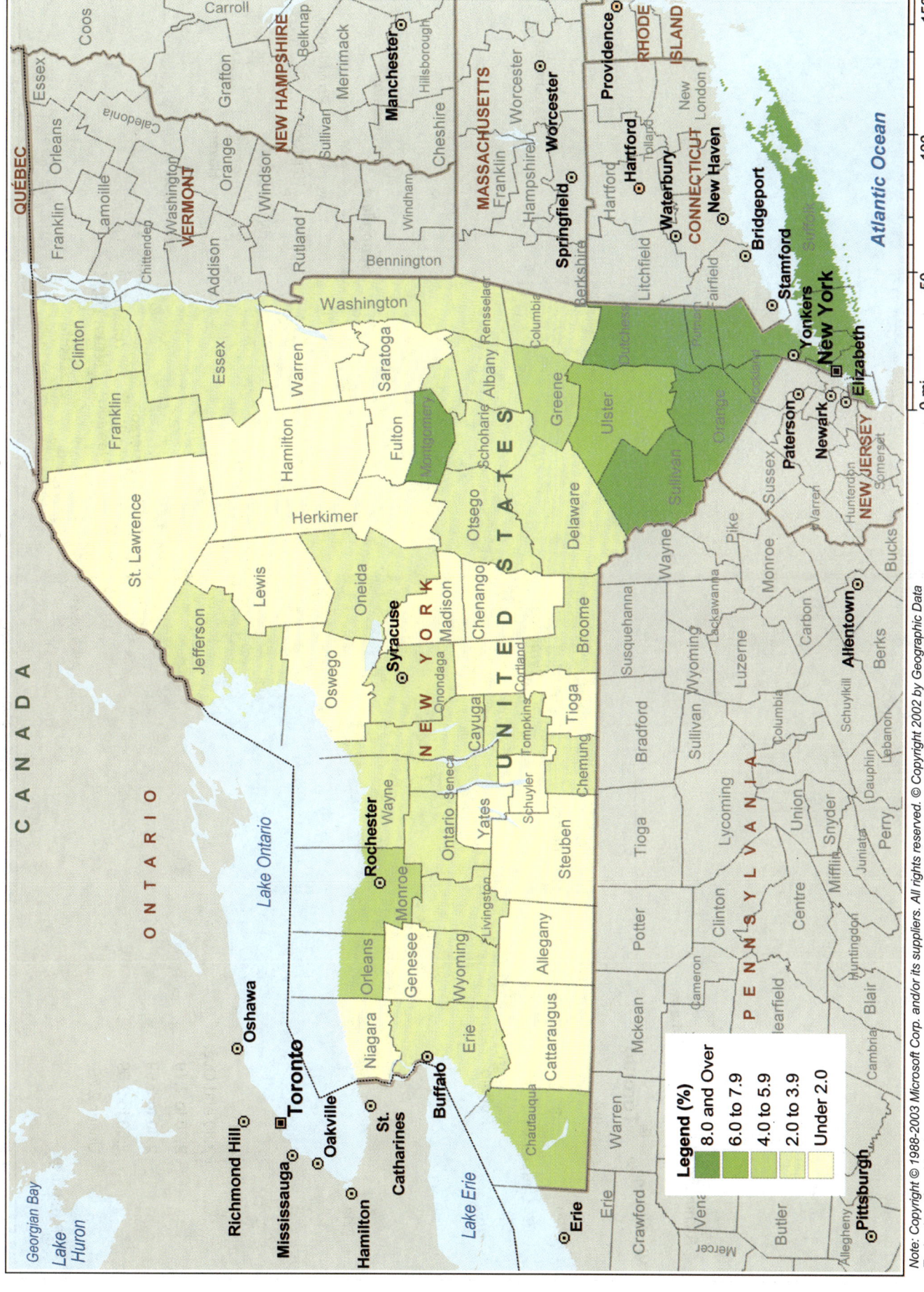

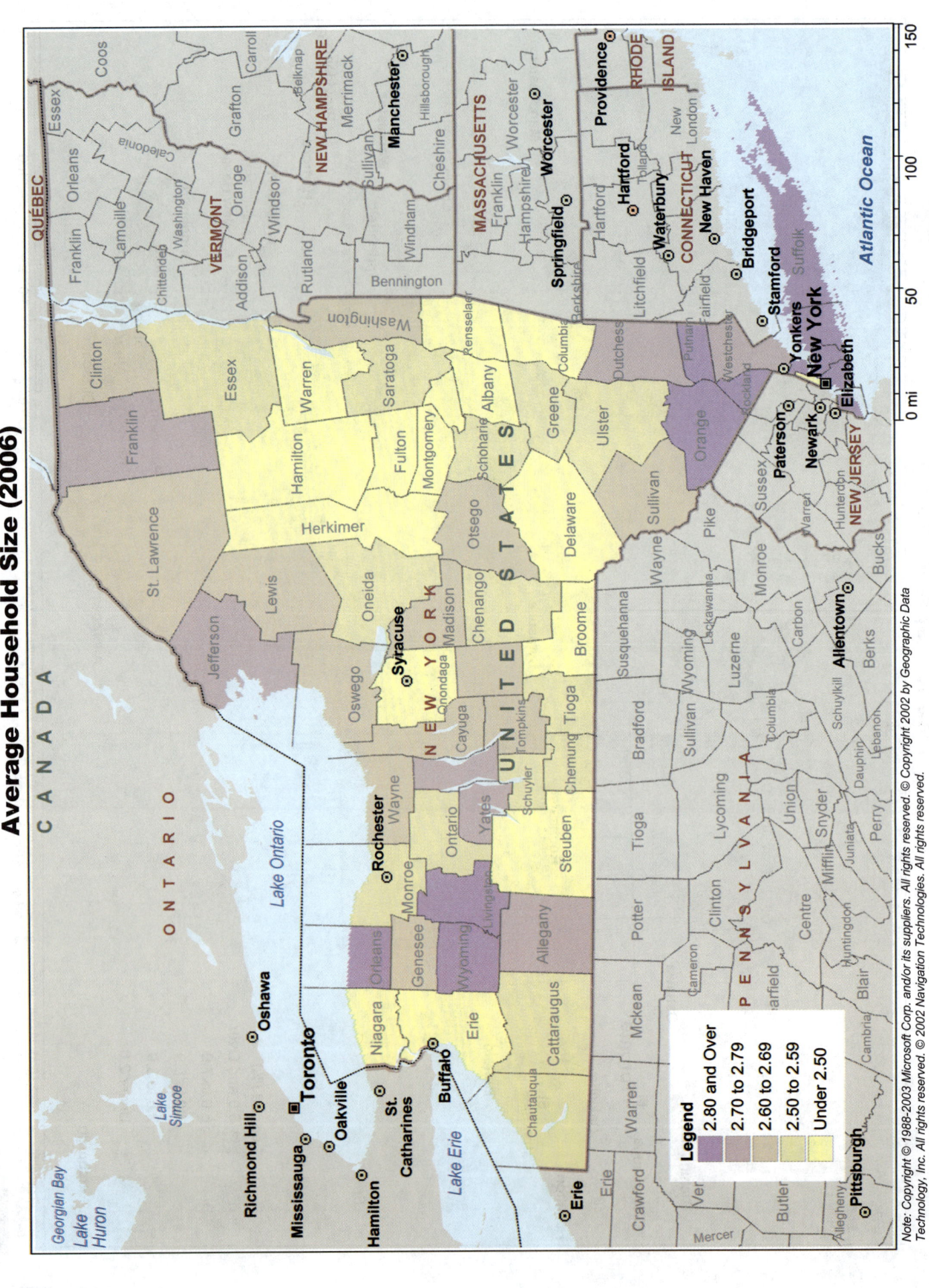

Median Age (2006)

Legend (years)
- 40.0 and Over
- 39.0 to 39.9
- 38.0 to 38.9
- 37.0 to 37.9
- Under 37.0

Note: Copyright © 1988-2003 Microsoft Corp. and/or its suppliers. All rights reserved. © Copyright 2002 by Geographic Data Technology, Inc. All rights reserved. © 2002 Navigation Technologies. All rights reserved.

Indexes & Demographic Maps

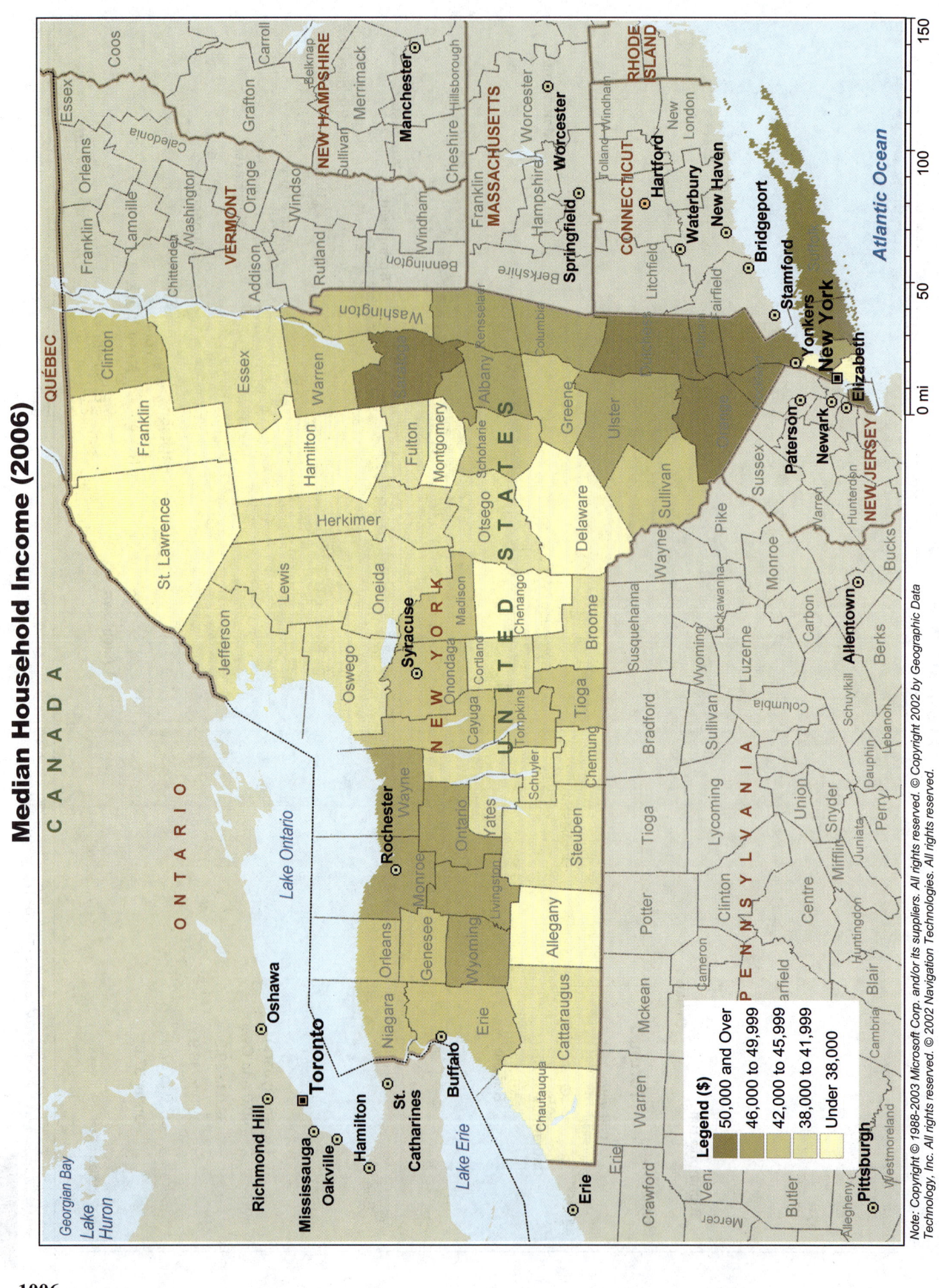

Percent of Population Living Below Poverty Level (2004)

Legend (%)
- 15.0 and Over
- 13.0 to 14.9
- 11.0 to 12.9
- 9.0 to 10.9
- Under 9.0

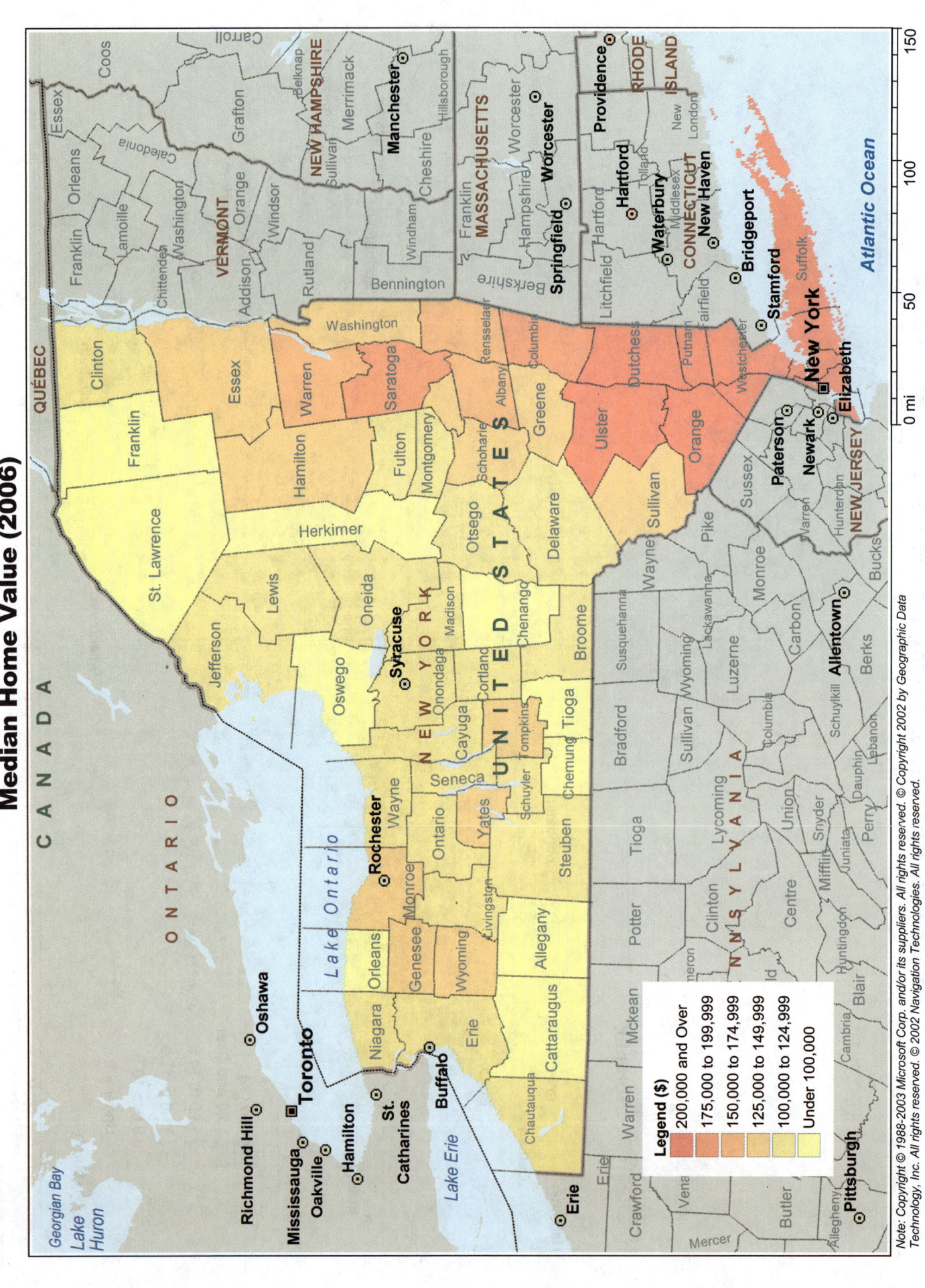

Percent of Population Who are Homeowners (2006)

Legend (%)
- 77.0 and Over
- 73.0 to 76.9
- 69.0 to 72.9
- 65.0 to 68.9
- Under 65.0

Note: Copyright © 1988-2003 Microsoft Corp. and/or its suppliers. All rights reserved. © Copyright 2002 by Geographic Data Technology, Inc. All rights reserved. © 2002 Navigation Technologies. All rights reserved.

Indexes & Demographic Maps

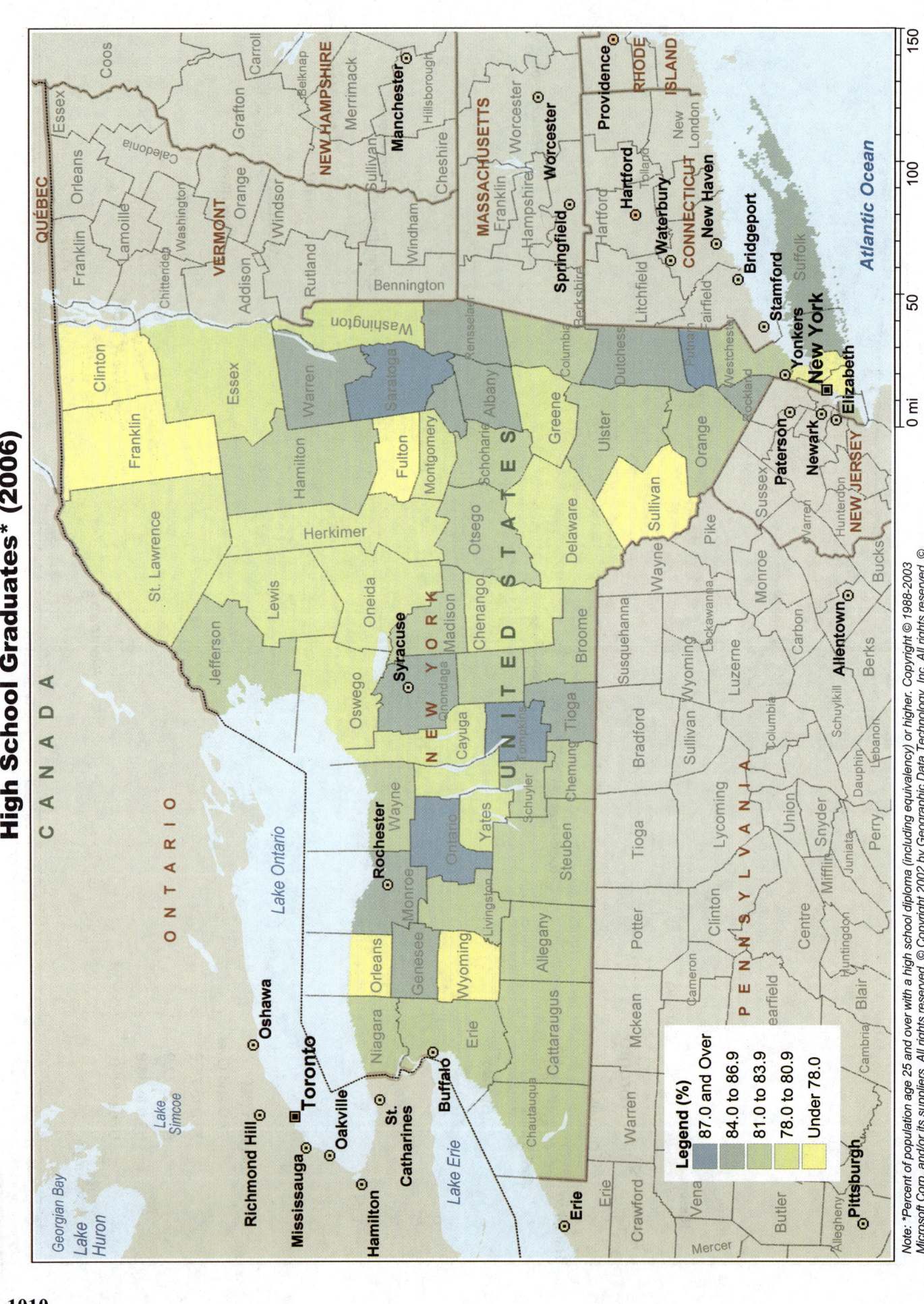

College Graduates* (2006)

Legend (%)
- 26.0 and Over
- 22.0 to 25.9
- 18.0 to 21.9
- 14.0 to 17.9
- Under 14.0

Note: *Percent of population age 25 and over with a Bachelor's Degree or higher. Copyright © 1988-2003 Microsoft Corp. and/or its suppliers. All rights reserved. © Copyright 2002 by Geographic Data Technology, Inc. All rights reserved. © 2002 Navigation Technologies. All rights reserved.

Indexes & Demographic Maps

1011

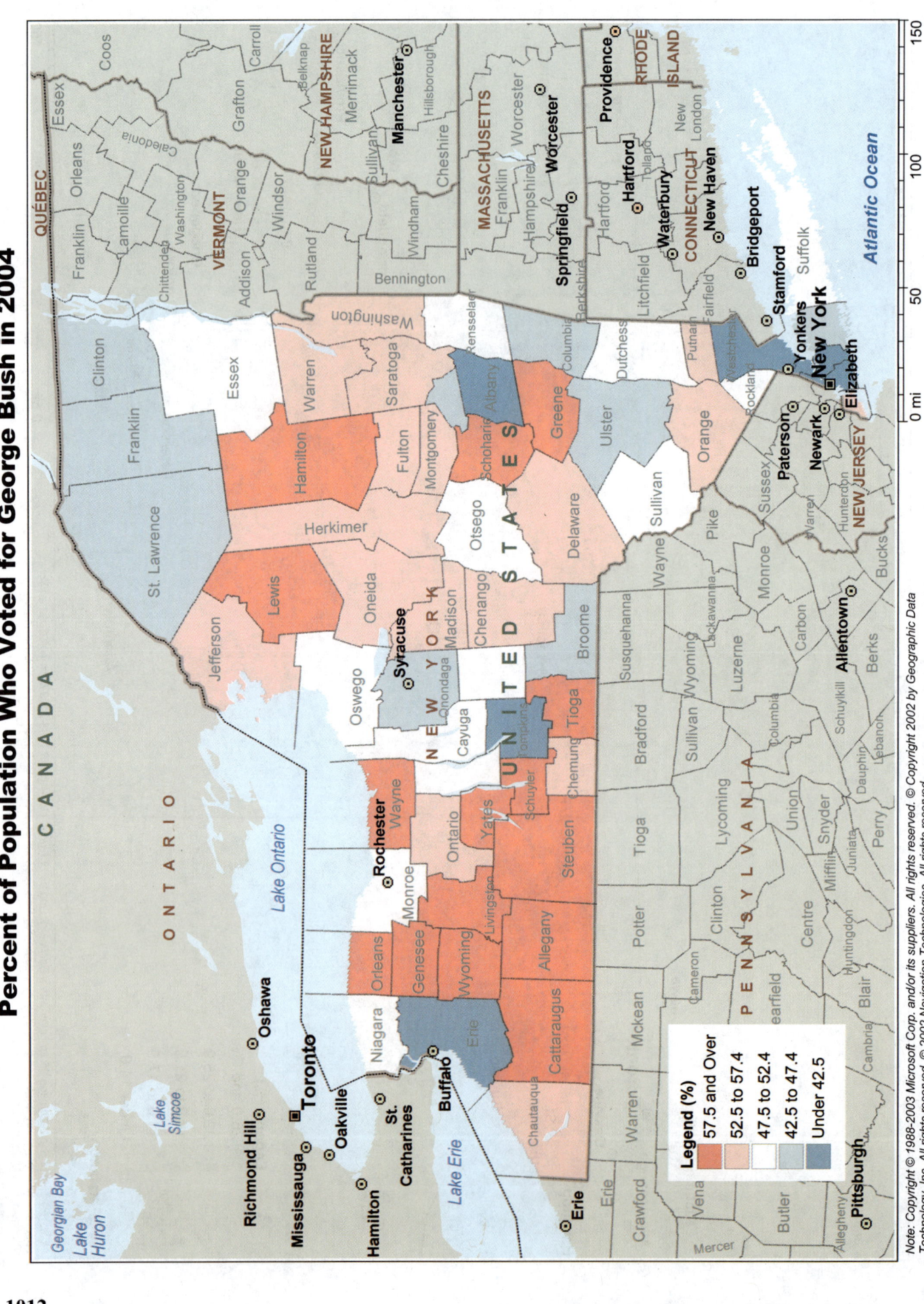

Grey House Publishing
Business Directories

Profiles of New York ♦ Profiles of Florida ♦ Profiles of Texas ♦ Profiles of Illinois ♦ Profiles of Michigan ♦ Profiles of Ohio ♦ Profiles of New Jersey ♦ Profiles of Massachusetts ♦ Profiles of Pennsylvania ♦ Profiles of Wisconsin ♦ Profiles of Connecticut ♦ Profiles of Indiana ♦ Profiles of North Carolina ♦ Profiles of Virginia ♦ Profiles of California

Packed with over 50 pieces of data that make up a complete, user-friendly profile of each state, these directories go even further by then pulling selected data and providing it in ranking list form for even easier comparisons between the 100 largest towns and cities! The careful layout gives the user an easy-to-read snapshot of every single place and county in the state, from the biggest metropolis to the smallest unincorporated hamlet. The richness of each place or county profile is astounding in its depth, from history to weather, all packed in an easy-to-navigate, compact format. No need for piles of multiple sources with this volume on your desk. Here is a look at just a few of the data sets you'll find in each profile: History, Geography, Climate, Population, Vital Statistics, Economy, Income, Taxes, Education, Housing, Health & Environment, Public Safety, Newspapers, Transportation, Presidential Election Results, Information Contacts and Chambers of Commerce. As an added bonus, there is a section on Selected Statistics, where data from the 100 largest towns and cities is arranged into easy-to-use charts. Each of 22 different data points has its own two-page spread with the cities listed in alpha order so researchers can easily compare and rank cities. Drawn from official census information, other government statistics and original research, you will have at your fingertips data that's available nowhere else in one single source.

Each Profiles of… title ranges from 400-800 pages, priced at $149.00 each

The Directory of Business Information Resources, 2007

With 100% verification, over 1,000 new listings and more than 12,000 updates, this 2007 edition of *The Directory of Business Information Resources* is the most up-to-date source for contacts in over 98 business areas – from advertising and agriculture to utilities and wholesalers. This carefully researched volume details: the Associations representing each industry; the Newsletters that keep members current; the Magazines and Journals - with their "Special Issues" - that are important to the trade, the Conventions that are "must attends," Databases, Directories and Industry Web Sites that provide access to must-have marketing resources. Includes contact names, phone & fax numbers, web sites and e-mail addresses. This one-volume resource is a gold mine of information and would be a welcome addition to any reference collection.

"This is a most useful and easy-to-use addition to any researcher's library." –The Information Professionals Institute

2,500 pages; Softcover ISBN 1-59237-146-9, $195.00 ♦ Online Database $495.00

Nations of the World, 2007/08 A Political, Economic and Business Handbook

This completely revised edition covers all the nations of the world in an easy-to-use, single volume. Each nation is profiled in a single chapter that includes Key Facts, Political & Economic Issues, a Country Profile and Business Information. In this fast-changing world, it is extremely important to make sure that the most up-to-date information is included in your reference collection. This edition is just the answer. Each of the 200+ country chapters have been carefully reviewed by a political expert to make sure that the text reflects the most current information on Politics, Travel Advisories, Economics and more. You'll find such vital information as a Country Map, Population Characteristics, Inflation, Agricultural Production, Foreign Debt, Political History, Foreign Policy, Regional Insecurity, Economics, Trade & Tourism, Historical Profile, Political Systems, Ethnicity, Languages, Media, Climate, Hotels, Chambers of Commerce, Banking, Travel Information and more. Five Regional Chapters follow the main text and include a Regional Map, an Introductory Article, Key Indicators and Currencies for the Region. As an added bonus, an all-inclusive CD-ROM is available as a companion to the printed text. Noted for its sophisticated, up-to-date and reliable compilation of political, economic and business information, this brand new edition will be an important acquisition to any public, academic or special library reference collection.

"A useful addition to both general reference collections and business collections." –RUSQ

1,700 pages; Print Version Only Softcover ISBN 1-59237-177-9, $155.00

To preview any of our Directories Risk-Free for 30 days, call (800) 562-2139 or fax to (518) 789-0556

The Directory of Venture Capital & Private Equity Firms, 2007

This edition has been extensively updated and broadly expanded to offer direct access to over 2,800 Domestic and International Venture Capital Firms, including address, phone & fax numbers, e-mail addresses and web sites for both primary and branch locations. Entries include details on the firm's Mission Statement, Industry Group Preferences, Geographic Preferences, Average and Minimum Investments and Investment Criteria. You'll also find details that are available nowhere else, including the Firm's Portfolio Companies and extensive information on each of the firm's Managing Partners, such as Education, Professional Background and Directorships held, along with the Partner's E-mail Address. *The Directory of Venture Capital & Private Equity Firms* offers five important indexes: Geographic Index, Executive Name Index, Portfolio Company Index, Industry Preference Index and College & University Index. With its comprehensive coverage and detailed, extensive information on each company, *The Directory of Venture Capital & Private Equity Firms* is an important addition to any finance collection.

"The sheer number of listings, the descriptive information provided and the outstanding indexing make this directory a better value than its principal competitor, Pratt's Guide to Venture Capital Sources. Recommended for business collections in large public, academic and business libraries." —Choice

1,300 pages; Softcover ISBN 1-59237-176-0, $565.00/$450.00 Library ☐ Online Database (includes a free copy of the directory) $889.00

The Directory of Mail Order Catalogs, 2007

Published since 1981, the *Directory of Mail Order Catalogs* is the premier source of information on the mail order catalog industry. It is the source that business professionals and librarians have come to rely on for the thousands of catalog companies in the US. New for 2007, The Directory of Mail Order Catalogs has been combined with its companion volume, *The Directory of Business to Business Catalogs* to offer all 13,000 catalog companies in one easy-to-use volume. Section I: Consumer Catalogs, covers over 9,000 consumer catalog companies in 44 different product chapters from Animals to Toys & Games. Section II: Business to Business Catalogs, details 5,000 business catalogs, everything from computers to laboratory supplies, building construction and much more. Listings contain detailed contact information including mailing address, phone & fax numbers, web sites, e-mail addresses and key contacts along with important business details such as product descriptions, employee size, years in business, sales volume, catalog size, number of catalogs mailed and more. Three indexes are included for easy access to information: Catalog & Company Name Index, Geographic Index and Product Index. *The Directory of Mail Order Catalogs*, now with its expanded business to business catalogs, is the largest and most comprehensive resource covering this billion-dollar industry. It is the standard in its field. This important resource is a useful tool for entrepreneurs searching for catalogs to pick up their product, vendors looking to expand their customer base in the catalog industry, market researchers, small businesses investigating new supply vendors, along with the library patron who is exploring the available catalogs in their areas of interest.

"This is a godsend for those looking for information." —Reference Book Review

1,700 pages; Softcover ISBN 1-59237-156-6 $350.00/$250.00 Library ☐ Online Database (includes a free copy of the directory) $495.00

Sports Market Place Directory, 2007

For over 20 years, this comprehensive, up-to-date directory has offered direct access to the Who, What, When & Where of the Sports Industry. With over 20,000 updates and enhancements, the *Sports Market Place Directory* is the most detailed, comprehensive and current sports business reference source available. In 1,800 information-packed pages, *Sports Market Place Directory* profiles contact information and key executives for: Single Sport Organizations, Professional Leagues, Multi-Sport Organizations, Disabled Sports, High School & Youth Sports, Military Sports, Olympic Organizations, Media, Sponsors, Sponsorship & Marketing Event Agencies, Event & Meeting Calendars, Professional Services, College Sports, Manufacturers & Retailers, Facilities and much more. *The Sports Market Place Directory* provides organization's contact information with detailed descriptions including: Key Contacts, physical, mailing, email and web addresses plus phone and fax numbers. Plus, nine important indexes make sure that you can find the information you're looking for quickly and easily: Entry Index, Single Sport Index, Media Index, Sponsor Index, Agency Index, Manufacturers Index, Brand Name Index, Facilities Index and Executive/Geographic Index. For over twenty years, *The Sports Market Place Directory* has assisted thousands of individuals in their pursuit of a career in the sports industry. Why not use "THE SOURCE" that top recruiters, headhunters and career placement centers use to find information on or about sports organizations and key hiring contacts.

1,800 pages; Softcover ISBN 1-59237-189-2, $225.00 ☐ Online Database $479.00

To preview any of our Directories Risk-Free for 30 days, call (800) 562-2139 or fax to (518) 789-0556

Food and Beverage Market Place, 2007

Food and Beverage Market Place is bigger and better than ever with thousands of new companies, thousands of updates to existing companies and two revised and enhanced product category indexes. This comprehensive directory profiles over 18,000 Food & Beverage Manufacturers, 12,000 Equipment & Supply Companies, 2,200 Transportation & Warehouse Companies, 2,000 Brokers & Wholesalers, 8,000 Importers & Exporters, 900 Industry Resources and hundreds of Mail Order Catalogs. Listings include detailed Contact Information, Sales Volumes, Key Contacts, Brand & Product Information, Packaging Details and much more. *Thomas Food and Beverage Market Place* is available as a three-volume printed set, a subscription-based Online Database via the Internet, on CD-ROM, as well as mailing lists and a licensable database.

> "An essential purchase for those in the food industry but will also be useful in public libraries where needed. Much of the information will be difficult and time consuming to locate without this handy three-volume ready-reference source." –ARBA

3,500 pages, 3 Volume Set; Softcover ISBN 1-59237-152-3, $595.00 ☐ Online Database $795.00 ☐ Online Database & 3 Volume Set Combo, $995.00

The Grey House Homeland Security Directory, 2007

This updated edition features the latest contact information for government and private organizations involved with Homeland Security along with the latest product information and provides detailed profiles of nearly 1,000 Federal & State Organizations & Agencies and over 3,000 Officials and Key Executives involved with Homeland Security. These listings are incredibly detailed and include Mailing Address, Phone & Fax Numbers, Email Addresses & Web Sites, a complete Description of the Agency and a complete list of the Officials and Key Executives associated with the Agency. Next, *The Grey House Homeland Security Directory* provides the go-to source for Homeland Security Products & Services. This section features over 2,000 Companies that provide Consulting, Products or Services. With this Buyer's Guide at their fingertips, users can locate suppliers of everything from Training Materials to Access Controls, from Perimeter Security to BioTerrorism Countermeasures and everything in between – complete with contact information and product descriptions. A handy Product Locator Index is provided to quickly and easily locate suppliers of a particular product. Lastly, an Information Resources Section provides immediate access to contact information for hundreds of Associations, Newsletters, Magazines, Trade Shows, Databases and Directories that focus on Homeland Security. This comprehensive, information-packed resource will be a welcome tool for any company or agency that is in need of Homeland Security information and will be a necessary acquisition for the reference collection of all public libraries and large school districts.

> "Compiles this information in one place and is discerning in content. A useful purchase for public and academic libraries." –Booklist

800 pages; Softcover ISBN 1-59237-151-5, $195.00 ☐ Online Database (includes a free copy of the directory) $385.00

The Grey House Transportation Security Directory & Handbook

This brand new title is the only reference of its kind that brings together current data on Transportation Security. With information on everything from Regulatory Authorities to Security Equipment, this top-flight database brings together the relevant information necessary for creating and maintaining a security plan for a wide range of transportation facilities. With this current, comprehensive directory at the ready you'll have immediate access to: Regulatory Authorities & Legislation; Information Resources; Sample Security Plans & Checklists; Contact Data for Major Airports, Seaports, Railroads, Trucking Companies and Oil Pipelines; Security Service Providers; Recommended Equipment & Product Information and more. Using the *Grey House Transportation Security Directory & Handbook*, managers will be able to quickly and easily assess their current security plans; develop contacts to create and maintain new security procedures; and source the products and services necessary to adequately maintain a secure environment. This valuable resource is a must for all Security Managers at Airports, Seaports, Railroads, Trucking Companies and Oil Pipelines.

800 pages; Softcover ISBN 1-59237-075-6, $195

To preview any of our Directories Risk-Free for 30 days, call (800) 562-2139 or fax to (518) 789-0556

The Grey House Safety & Security Directory, 2007

The Grey House Safety & Security Directory is the most comprehensive reference tool and buyer's guide for the safety and security industry. Arranged by safety topic, each chapter begins with OSHA regulations for the topic, followed by Training Articles written by top professionals in the field and Self-Inspection Checklists. Next, each topic contains Buyer's Guide sections that feature related products and services. Topics include Administration, Insurance, Loss Control & Consulting, Protective Equipment & Apparel, Noise & Vibration, Facilities Monitoring & Maintenance, Employee Health Maintenance & Ergonomics, Retail Food Services, Machine Guards Process Guidelines & Tool Handling, Ordinary Materials Handling, Hazardous Materials Handling, Workplace Preparation & Maintenance, Electrical Lighting & Safety, Fire & Rescue and Security. The Buyer's Guide sections are carefully indexed within each topic area to ensure that you can find the supplies needed to meet OSHA's regulations. Six important indexes make finding information and product manufacturers quick and easy: Geographical Index of Manufacturers and Distributors, Company Profile Index, Brand Name Index, Product Index, Index of Web Sites and Index of Advertisers. This comprehensive, up-to-date reference will provide every tool necessary to make sure a business is in compliance with OSHA regulations and locate the products and services needed to meet those regulations.

"Presents industrial safety information for engineers, plant managers, risk managers, and construction site supervisors..." –Choice

1,500 pages, 2 Volume Set; Softcover ISBN 1-59237-160-4, $225.00

The Grey House Biometric Information Directory

The Biometric Information Directory is the only comprehensive source for current biometric industry information. This 2006 edition is the first published by Grey House. With 100% updated information, this latest edition offers a complete, current look, in both print and online form, of biometric companies and products – one of the fastest growing industries in today's economy. Detailed profiles of manufacturers of the latest biometric technology, including Finger, Voice, Face, Hand, Signature, Iris, Vein and Palm Identification systems. Data on the companies include key executives, company size and a detailed, indexed description of their product line. Plus, the Directory also includes valuable business resources, and current editorial make this edition the easiest way for the business community and consumers alike to access the largest, most current compilation of biometric industry information available on the market today. The new edition boasts increased numbers of companies, contact names and company data, with over 700 manufacturers and service providers. Information in the directory includes: Editorial on Advancements in Biometrics; Profiles of 700+ companies listed with contact information; Organizations, Trade & Educational Associations, Publications, Conferences, Trade Shows and Expositions Worldwide; Web Site Index; Biometric & Vendors Services Index by Types of Biometrics; and a Glossary of Biometric Terms. This resource will be an important source for anyone who is considering the use of a biometric product, investing in the development of biometric technology, support existing marketing and sales efforts and will be an important acquisition for the business reference collection for large public and business libraries.

800 pages; Softcover ISBN 1-59237-121-3, $225

The Grey House Performing Arts Directory, 2007

The Grey House Performing Arts Directory is the most comprehensive resource covering the Performing Arts. This important directory provides current information on over 8,500 Dance Companies, Instrumental Music Programs, Opera Companies, Choral Groups, Theater Companies, Performing Arts Series and Performing Arts Facilities. Plus, this edition now contains a brand new section on Artist Management Groups. In addition to mailing address, phone & fax numbers, e-mail addresses and web sites, dozens of other fields of available information include mission statement, key contacts, facilities, seating capacity, season, attendance and more. This directory also provides an important Information Resources section that covers hundreds of Performing Arts Associations, Magazines, Newsletters, Trade Shows, Directories, Databases and Industry Web Sites. Five indexes provide immediate access to this wealth of information: Entry Name, Executive Name, Performance Facilities, Geographic and Information Resources. *The Grey House Performing Arts Directory* pulls together thousands of Performing Arts Organizations, Facilities and Information Resources into an easy-to-use source – this kind of comprehensiveness and extensive detail is not available in any resource on the market place today.

"Immensely useful and user-friendly ... recommended for public, academic and certain special library reference collections." –Booklist

1,500 pages; Softcover ISBN 1-59237-138-8, $185.00 ☐ Online Database $335.00

To preview any of our Directories Risk-Free for 30 days, call (800) 562-2139 or fax to (518) 789-0556

The Rauch Guide to the US Adhesives & Sealants, Cosmetics & Toiletries, Ink, Paint, Plastics, Pulp & Paper and Rubber Industries

The Rauch Guides are known worldwide for their comprehensive marketing information. Acquired by Grey House Publishing in 2005, new updated and revised editions will be published throughout 2005 and 2006. Each Guide provides market facts and figures in a highly organized format, ideal for today's busy personnel, serving as ready-references for top executives as well as the industry newcomer. *The Rauch Guides* save time and money by organizing widely scattered information and providing estimates for important business decisions, some of which are available nowhere else. Each Guide is organized into several information-packed chapters. After a brief introduction, the ECONOMICS section provides data on industry shipments; long-term growth and forecasts; prices; company performance; employment, expenditures, and productivity; transportation and geographical patterns; packaging; foreign trade; and government regulations. Next, TECHNOLOGY & RAW MATERIALS provide market, technical, and raw material information for chemicals, equipment and related materials, including market size and leading suppliers, prices, end uses, and trends. PRODUCTS & MARKETS provide information for each major industry product, including market size and historical trends, leading suppliers, five-year forecasts, industry structure, and major end uses. For easy access, each *Guide* contains a chapter on INDUSTRY ACTIVITIES, ORGANIZATIONS & SOURCES OF INFORMATION with detailed information on meetings, exhibits, and trade shows, sources of statistical information, trade associations, technical and professional societies, and trade and technical periodicals. Next, the COMPANY DIRECTORY profiles major industry companies, both public and private. Generally several hundred companies are analyzed. Information includes complete contact information, web address, estimated total and domestic sales, product description, and recent mergers and acquisitions. Each Guide also contains several APPENDICES that provide a cross-reference of suppliers, subsidiaries and divisions. The Rauch Guides will prove to be an invaluable source of market information, company data, trends and forecasts that anyone in these fast-paced industries.

The Rauch Guide to the U.S. Paint Industry Softcover ISBN 1-59237-127-2 $595 ☐ The Rauch Guide to the U.S. Plastics Industry Softcover ISBN 1-59237-128-0 $595 ☐ The Rauch Guide to the U.S. Adhesives and Sealants Industry Softcover ISBN 1-59237-129-9 $595 ☐ The Rauch Guide to the U.S. Ink Industry Softcover ISBN 1-59237-126-4 $595 ☐ The Rauch Guide to the U.S. Rubber Industry Softcover ISBN 1-59237-130-2 $595 ☐ The Rauch Guide to the U.S. Pulp and Paper Industry Softcover ISBN 1-59237-131-0 $595 ☐ The Rauch Guide to the U.S. Cosmetic and Toiletries Industry Softcover ISBN 1-59237-132-9 $895

Research Services Directory: Commercial & Corporate Research Centers

This Ninth Edition provides access to well over 8,000 independent Commercial Research Firms, Corporate Research Centers and Laboratories offering contract services for hands-on, basic or applied research. *Research Services Directory* covers the thousands of types of research companies, including Biotechnology & Pharmaceutical Developers, Consumer Product Research, Defense Contractors, Electronics & Software Engineers, Think Tanks, Forensic Investigators, Independent Commercial Laboratories, Information Brokers, Market & Survey Research Companies, Medical Diagnostic Facilities, Product Research & Development Firms and more. Each entry provides the company's name, mailing address, phone & fax numbers, key contacts, web site, e-mail address, as well as a company description and research and technical fields served. Four indexes provide immediate access to this wealth of information: Research Firms Index, Geographic Index, Personnel Name Index and Subject Index.

"An important source for organizations in need of information about laboratories, individuals and other facilities." –ARBA

1,400 pages; Softcover ISBN 1-59237-003-9, $395.00 ☐ Online Database (includes a free copy of the directory) $850.00

International Business and Trade Directories

Completely updated, the Third Edition of *International Business and Trade Directories* now contains more than 10,000 entries, over 2,000 more than the last edition, making this directory the most comprehensive resource of the worlds business and trade directories. Entries include content descriptions, price, publisher's name and address, web site and e-mail addresses, phone and fax numbers and editorial staff. Organized by industry group, and then by region, this resource puts over 10,000 industry-specific business and trade directories at the reader's fingertips. Three indexes are included for quick access to information: Geographic Index, Publisher Index and Title Index. Public, college and corporate libraries, as well as individuals and corporations seeking critical market information will want to add this directory to their marketing collection.

"Reasonably priced for a work of this type, this directory should appeal to larger academic, public and corporate libraries with an international focus." –Library Journal

1,800 pages; Softcover ISBN 1-930956-63-0, $225.00 ☐ Online Database (includes a free copy of the directory) $450.00

To preview any of our Directories Risk-Free for 30 days, call (800) 562-2139 or fax to (518) 789-0556

Grey House Publishing Canada
Canadian Information Resources

Canadian Almanac & Directory, 2007

The Canadian Almanac & Directory contains ten directories in one – giving you all the facts and figures you will ever need about Canada. No other single source provides users with the quality and depth of up-to-date information for all types of research. This national directory and guide gives you access to statistics, images and over 45,000 names and addresses for everything from Airlines to Zoos - updated every year. It's Ten Directories in One! Each section is a directory in itself, providing robust information on business and finance, communications, government, associations, arts and culture (museums, zoos, libraries, etc.), health, transportation, law, education, and more. Government information includes federal, provincial and territorial - and includes an easy-to-use quick index to find key information. A separate municipal government section includes every municipality in Canada, with full profiles of Canada's largest urban centers. A complete legal directory lists judges and judicial officials, court locations and law firms across the country. A wealth of general information, the Canadian Almanac & Directory also includes national statistics on population, employment, imports and exports, and more. National awards and honors are presented, along with forms of address, Commonwealth information and full color photos of Canadian symbols. Postal information, weights, measures, distances and other useful charts are also incorporated. Complete almanac information includes perpetual calendars, five-year holiday planners and astronomical information. Published continuously for 160 years, The Canadian Almanac & Directory is the best single reference source for business executives, managers and assistants; government and public affairs executives; lawyers; marketing, sales and advertising executives; researchers, editors and journalists.

Hardcover ISBN 978-1-89502-149-3; 1,600 pages; $315.00

Associations Canada, 2007

The Most Powerful Fact-Finder to Business, Trade, Professional and Consumer Organizations

Associations Canada covers Canadian organizations and international groups including industry, commercial and professional associations, registered charities, special interest and common interest organizations. This annually revised compendium provides detailed listings and abstracts for nearly 20,000 regional, national and international organizations. This popular volume provides the most comprehensive picture of Canada's non-profit sector. Detailed listings enable users to identify an organization's budget, founding date, scope of activity, licensing body, sources of funding, executive information, full address and complete contact information, just to name a few. Powerful indexes help researchers find information quickly and easily. The following indexes are included: subject, acronym, geographic, budget, executive name, conferences & conventions, mailing list, defunct and unreachable associations and registered charitable organizations. In addition to annual spending of over $1 billion on transportation and conventions alone, Canadian associations account for many millions more in pursuit of membership interests. Associations Canada provides complete access to this highly lucrative market. Associations Canada is a strong source of prospects for sales and marketing executives, tourism and convention officials, researchers, government officials - anyone who wants to locate non-profit interest groups and trade associations.

Hardcover ISBN 978-1-59237-219-5; 1,600 pages; $315.00

Financial Services Canada, 2007/08

Financial Services Canada is the only master file of current contacts and information that serves the needs of the entire financial services industry in Canada. With over 18,000 organizations and hard-to-find business information, Financial Services Canada is the most up-to-date source for names and contact numbers of industry professionals, senior executives, portfolio managers, financial advisors, agency bureaucrats and elected representatives. Financial Services Canada incorporates the latest changes in the industry to provide you with the most current details on each company, including: name, title, organization, telephone and fax numbers, e-mail and web addresses. Financial Services Canada also includes private company listings never before compiled, government agencies, association and consultant services - to ensure that you'll never miss a client or a contact. Current listings include: banks and branches, non-depository institutions, stock exchanges and brokers, investment management firms, insurance companies, major accounting and law firms, government agencies and financial associations. Powerful indexes assist researchers with locating the vital financial information they need. The following indexes are included: alphabetic, geographic, executive name, corporate web site/e-mail, government quick reference and subject. Financial Services Canada is a valuable resource for financial executives, bankers, financial planners, sales and marketing professionals, lawyers and chartered accountants, government officials, investment dealers, journalists, librarians and reference specialists.

900 pages; Hardcover ISBN 978-1-59237-221-8 $315.00

To preview any of our Directories Risk-Free for 30 days, call (800) 562-2139 or fax to (518) 789-0556

Directory of Libraries in Canada, 2007/08

The Directory of Libraries in Canada brings together almost 7,000 listings including libraries and their branches, information resource centers, archives and library associations and learning centers. The directory offers complete and comprehensive information on Canadian libraries, resource centers, business information centers, professional associations, regional library systems, archives, library schools and library technical programs. The Directory of Libraries in Canada includes important features of each library and service, including library information; personnel details, including contact names and e-mail addresses; collection information; services available to users; acquisitions budgets; and computers and automated systems. Useful information on each library's electronic access is also included, such as Internet browser, connectivity and public Internet/CD-ROM/subscription database access. The directory also provides powerful indexes for subject, location, personal name and Web site/e-mail to assist researchers with locating the crucial information they need. The Directory of Libraries in Canada is a vital reference tool for publishers, advocacy groups, students, research institutions, computer hardware suppliers, and other diverse groups that provide products and services to this unique market.

850 pages; Hardcover ISBN 978-1-59237-222-5; $315.00

Canadian Environmental Directory, 2007/08

The Canadian Environmental Directory is Canada's most complete and only national listing of environmental associations and organizations, government regulators and purchasing groups, product and service companies, special libraries, and more! The extensive Products and Services section provides detailed listings enabling users to identify the company name, address, phone, fax, e-mail, Web address, firm type, contact names (and titles), product and service information, affiliations, trade information, branch and affiliate data. The Government section gives you all the contact information you need at every government level – federal, provincial and municipal. We also include descriptions of current environmental initiatives, programs and agreements, names of environment-related acts administered by each ministry or department PLUS information and tips on who to contact and how to sell to governments in Canada. The Associations section provides complete contact information and a brief description of activities. Included are Canadian environmental organizations and international groups including industry, commercial and professional associations, registered charities, special interest and common interest organizations. All the Information you need about the Canadian environmental industry: directory of products and services, special libraries and resource, conferences, seminars and tradeshows, chronology of environmental events, law firms and major Canadian companies, The Canadian Environmental Directory is ideal for business, government, engineers and anyone conducting research on the environment.

Hardcover ISBN 978-1-59237-218-8; 900 pages; $315.00

To preview any of our Directories Risk-Free for 30 days, call (800) 562-2139 or fax to (518) 789-0556

Grey House Publishing
General Reference Titles

The Value of a Dollar 1600-1859, The Colonial Era to The Civil War

Following the format of the widely acclaimed, T*he Value of a Dollar, 1860-2004*, *The Value of a Dollar 1600-1859, The Colonial Era to The Civil War* records the actual prices of thousands of items that consumers purchased from the Colonial Era to the Civil War. Our editorial department had been flooded with requests from users of our Value of a Dollar for the same type of information, just from an earlier time period. This new volume is just the answer – with pricing data from 1600 to 1859. Arranged into five-year chapters, each 5-year chapter includes a Historical Snapshot, Consumer Expenditures, Investments, Selected Income, Income/Standard Jobs, Food Basket, Standard Prices and Miscellany. There is also a section on Trends. This informative section charts the change in price over time and provides added detail on the reasons prices changed within the time period, including industry developments, changes in consumer attitudes and important historical facts. This fascinating survey will serve a wide range of research needs and will be useful in all high school, public and academic library reference collections.

600 pages; Hardcover ISBN 1-59237-094-2, $135.00

The Value of a Dollar 1860-2004, Third Edition

A guide to practical economy, *The Value of a Dollar* records the actual prices of thousands of items that consumers purchased from the Civil War to the present, along with facts about investment options and income opportunities. This brand new Third Edition boasts a brand new addition to each five-year chapter, a section on Trends. This informative section charts the change in price over time and provides added detail on the reasons prices changed within the time period, including industry developments, changes in consumer attitudes and important historical facts. Plus, a brand new chapter for 2000-2004 has been added. Each 5-year chapter includes a Historical Snapshot, Consumer Expenditures, Investments, Selected Income, Income/Standard Jobs, Food Basket, Standard Prices and Miscellany. This interesting and useful publication will be widely used in any reference collection.

"Recommended for high school, college and public libraries." –ARBA

600 pages; Hardcover ISBN 1-59237-074-8, $135.00

Working Americans 1880-1999
Volume I: The Working Class, Volume II: The Middle Class, Volume III: The Upper Class

Each of the volumes in the *Working Americans 1880-1999* series focuses on a particular class of Americans, The Working Class, The Middle Class and The Upper Class over the last 120 years. Chapters in each volume focus on one decade and profile three to five families. Family Profiles include real data on Income & Job Descriptions, Selected Prices of the Times, Annual Income, Annual Budgets, Family Finances, Life at Work, Life at Home, Life in the Community, Working Conditions, Cost of Living, Amusements and much more. Each chapter also contains an Economic Profile with Average Wages of other Professions, a selection of Typical Pricing, Key Events & Inventions, News Profiles, Articles from Local Media and Illustrations. The *Working Americans* series captures the lifestyles of each of the classes from the last twelve decades, covers a vast array of occupations and ethnic backgrounds and travels the entire nation. These interesting and useful compilations of portraits of the American Working, Middle and Upper Classes during the last 120 years will be an important addition to any high school, public or academic library reference collection.

"These interesting, unique compilations of economic and social facts, figures and graphs will support multiple research needs. They will engage and enlighten patrons in high school, public and academic library collections." –Booklist

Volume I: The Working Class ◻ 558 pages; Hardcover ISBN 1-891482-81-5, $145.00 ◻ Volume II: The Middle Class ◻ 591 pages; Hardcover ISBN 1-891482-72-6; $145.00 ◻ Volume III: The Upper Class ◻ 567 pages; Hardcover ISBN 1-930956-38-X, $145.00

Working Americans 1880-1999 Volume IV: Their Children

This Fourth Volume in the highly successful *Working Americans 1880-1999* series focuses on American children, decade by decade from 1880 to 1999. This interesting and useful volume introduces the reader to three children in each decade, one from each of the Working, Middle and Upper classes. Like the first three volumes in the series, the individual profiles are created from interviews, diaries, statistical studies, biographies and news reports. Profiles cover a broad range of ethnic backgrounds, geographic area and lifestyles – everything from an orphan in Memphis in 1882, following the Yellow Fever epidemic of 1878 to an eleven-year-old nephew of a beer baron and owner of the New York Yankees in New York City in 1921. Chapters also contain important supplementary materials including News Features as well as information on everything from Schools to Parks, Infectious Diseases to Childhood Fears along with Entertainment, Family Life and much more to provide an informative overview of the lifestyles of children from each decade. This interesting account of what life was like for Children in the Working, Middle and Upper Classes will be a welcome addition to the reference collection of any high school, public or academic library.

600 pages; Hardcover ISBN 1-930956-35-5, $145.00

To preview any of our Directories Risk-Free for 30 days, call (800) 562-2139 or fax to (518) 789-0556

Working Americans 1880-2003 Volume V: Americans At War

Working Americans 1880-2003 Volume V: Americans At War is divided into 11 chapters, each covering a decade from 1880-2003 and examines the lives of Americans during the time of war, including declared conflicts, one-time military actions, protests, and preparations for war. Each decade includes several personal profiles, whether on the battlefield or on the homefront, that tell the stories of civilians, soldiers, and officers during the decade. The profiles examine: Life at Home; Life at Work; and Life in the Community. Each decade also includes an Economic Profile with statistical comparisons, a Historical Snapshot, News Profiles, local News Articles, and Illustrations that provide a solid historical background to the decade being examined. Profiles range widely not only geographically, but also emotionally, from that of a girl whose leg was torn off in a blast during WWI, to the boredom of being stationed in the Dakotas as the Indian Wars were drawing to a close. As in previous volumes of the *Working Americans* series, information is presented in narrative form, but hard facts and real-life situations back up each story. The basis of the profiles come from diaries, private print books, personal interviews, family histories, estate documents and magazine articles. For easy reference, *Working Americans 1880-2003 Volume V: Americans At War* includes an in-depth Subject Index. The *Working Americans* series has become an important reference for public libraries, academic libraries and high school libraries. This fifth volume will be a welcome addition to all of these types of reference collections.

600 pages; Hardcover ISBN 1-59237-024-1; $145.00
Five Volume Set (Volumes I-V), Hardcover ISBN 1-59237-034-9, $675.00

Working Americans 1880-2005 Volume VI: Women at Work

Unlike any other volume in the *Working Americans* series, this Sixth Volume, is the first to focus on a particular gender of Americans. *Volume VI: Women at Work*, traces what life was like for working women from the 1860's to the present time. Beginning with the life of a maid in 1890 and a store clerk in 1900 and ending with the life and times of the modern working women, this text captures the struggle, strengths and changing perception of the American woman at work. Each chapter focuses on one decade and profiles three to five women with real data on Income & Job Descriptions, Selected Prices of the Times, Annual Income, Annual Budgets, Family Finances, Life at Work, Life at Home, Life in the Community, Working Conditions, Cost of Living, Amusements and much more. For even broader access to the events, economics and attitude towards women throughout the past 130 years, each chapter is supplemented with News Profiles, Articles from Local Media, Illustrations, Economic Profiles, Typical Pricing, Key Events, Inventions and more. This important volume illustrates what life was like for working women over time and allows the reader to develop an understanding of the changing role of women at work. These interesting and useful compilations of portraits of women at work will be an important addition to any high school, public or academic library reference collection.

600 pages; Hardcover ISBN 1-59237-063-2; $145.00

Working Americans 1880-2005 Volume VII: Social Movements

The newest addition to the widely-successful *Working Americans* series, *Volume VII: Social Movements* explores how Americans sought and fought for change from the 1880s to the present time. Following the format of previous volumes in the Working Americans series, the text examines the lives of 34 individuals who have worked — often behind the scenes — to bring about change. Issues include topics as diverse as the Anti-smoking movement of 1901 to efforts by Native Americans to reassert their long lost rights. Along the way, the book will profile individuals brave enough to demand suffrage for Kansas women in 1912 or demand an end to lynching during a March on Washington in 1923. Each profile is enriched with real data on Income & Job Descriptions, Selected Prices of the Times, Annual Incomes & Budgets, Life at Work, Life at Home, Life in the Community, along with News Features, Key Events, and Illustrations. The depth of information contained in each profile allow the user to explore the private, financial and public lives of these subjects, deepening our understanding of how calls for change took place in our society. A must-purchase for the reference collections of high school libraries, public libraries and academic libraries.

600 pages; Hardcover ISBN 1-59237-101-9; $145.00
Seven Volume Set (Volumes I-VII), Hardcover ISBN 1-59237-133-7, $945.00

The Encyclopedia of Warrior Peoples & Fighting Groups

Many military groups throughout the world have excelled in their craft either by fortuitous circumstances, outstanding leadership, or intense training. This new second edition of The Encyclopedia of Warrior Peoples and Fighting Groups explores the origins and leadership of these outstanding combat forces, chronicles their conquests and accomplishments, examines the circumstances surrounding their decline or disbanding, and assesses their influence on the groups and methods of warfare that followed. This edition has been completely updated with information through 2005 and contains over 20 new entries. Readers will encounter ferocious tribes, charismatic leaders, and daring militias, from ancient times to the present, including Amazons, Buffalo Soldiers, Green Berets, Iron Brigade, Kamikazes, Peoples of the Sea, Polish Winged Hussars, Sacred Band of Thebes, Teutonic Knights, and Texas Rangers. With over 100 alphabetical entries, numerous cross-references and illustrations, a comprehensive bibliography, and index, the Encyclopedia of Warrior Peoples and Fighting Groups is a valuable resource for readers seeking insight into the bold history of distinguished fighting forces.

"This work is especially useful for high school students, undergraduates, and general readers with an interest in military history." –Library Journal

Pub. Date: May 2006; Hardcover ISBN 1-59237-116-7; $135.00

To preview any of our Directories Risk-Free for 30 days, call (800) 562-2139 or fax to (518) 789-0556

The Encyclopedia of Invasions & Conquests, From the Ancient Times to the Present

Throughout history, invasions and conquests have played a remarkable role in shaping our world and defining our boundaries, both physically and culturally. This second edition of the popular Encyclopedia of Invasions & Conquests, a comprehensive guide to over 150 invasions, conquests, battles and occupations from ancient times to the present, takes readers on a journey that includes the Roman conquest of Britain, the Portuguese colonization of Brazil, and the Iraqi invasion of Kuwait, to name a few. New articles will explore the late 20th and 21st centuries, with a specific focus on recent conflicts in Afghanistan, Kuwait, Iraq, Yugoslavia, Grenada and Chechnya. Categories of entries include countries, invasions and conquests, and individuals. In addition to covering the military aspects of invasions and conquests, entries cover some of the political, economic, and cultural aspects, for example, the effects of a conquest on the invade country's political and monetary system and in its language and religion. The entries on leaders – among them Sargon, Alexander the Great, William the Conqueror, and Adolf Hitler – deal with the people who sought to gain control, expand power, or exert religious or political influence over others through military means. Revised and updated for this second edition, entries are arranged alphabetically within historical periods. Each chapter provides a map to help readers locate key areas and geographical features, and bibliographical references appear at the end of each entry. Other useful features include cross-references, a cumulative bibliography and a comprehensive subject index. This authoritative, well-organized, lucidly written volume will prove invaluable for a variety of readers, including high school students, military historians, members of the armed forces, history buffs and hobbyists.

"Engaging writing, sensible organization, nice illustrations, interesting and obscure facts, and useful maps make this book a pleasure to read." –ARBA

Pub. Date: March 2006; Hardcover ISBN 1-59237-114-0; $135.00

Encyclopedia of Prisoners of War & Internment

This authoritative second edition provides a valuable overview of the history of prisoners of war and interned civilians, from earliest times to the present. Written by an international team of experts in the field of POW studies, this fascinating and thought-provoking volume includes entries on a wide range of subjects including the Crusades, Plains Indian Warfare, concentration camps, the two world wars, and famous POWs throughout history, as well as atrocities, escapes, and much more. Written in a clear and easily understandable style, this informative reference details over 350 entries, 30% larger than the first edition, that survey the history of prisoners of war and interned civilians from the earliest times to the present, with emphasis on the 19th and 20th centuries. Medical conditions, international law, exchanges of prisoners, organizations working on behalf of POWs, and trials associated with the treatment of captives are just some of the themes explored. Entries range from the Ardeatine Caves Massacre to Kurt Vonnegut. Entries are arranged alphabetically, plus illustrations and maps are provided for easy reference. The text also includes an introduction, bibliography, appendix of selected documents, and end-of-entry reading suggestions. This one-of-a-kind reference will be a helpful addition to the reference collections of all public libraries, high schools, and university libraries and will prove invaluable to historians and military enthusiasts.

"Thorough and detailed yet accessible to the lay reader. Of special interest to subject specialists and historians; recommended for public and academic libraries." - Library Journal

Pub. Date: March 2006; Hardcover ISBN 1-59237-120-5; $135.00

The Religious Right, A Reference Handbook

Timely and unbiased, this third edition updates and expands its examination of the religious right and its influence on our government, citizens, society, and politics. From the fight to outlaw the teaching of Darwin's theory of evolution to the struggle to outlaw abortion, the religious right is continually exerting an influence on public policy. This text explores the influence of religion on legislation and society, while examining the alignment of the religious right with the political right. A historical survey of the movement highlights the shift to "hands-on" approach to politics and the struggle to present a unified front. The coverage offers a critical historical survey of the religious right movement, focusing on its increased involvement in the political arena, attempts to forge coalitions, and notable successes and failures. The text offers complete coverage of biographies of the men and women who have advanced the cause and an up to date chronology illuminate the movement's goals, including their accomplishments and failures. This edition offers an extensive update to all sections along with several brand new entries. Two new sections complement this third edition, a chapter on legal issues and court decisions and a chapter on demographic statistics and electoral patterns. To aid in further research, The Religious Right, offers an entire section of annotated listings of print and non-print resources, as well as of organizations affiliated with the religious right, and those opposing it. Comprehensive in its scope, this work offers easy-to-read, pertinent information for those seeking to understand the religious right and its evolving role in American society. A must for libraries of all sizes, university religion departments, activists, high schools and for those interested in the evolving role of the religious right.

" Recommended for all public and academic libraries." - Library Journal

Pub. Date: November 2006; Hardcover ISBN 1-59237-113-2; $135.00

To preview any of our Directories Risk-Free for 30 days, call (800) 562-2139 or fax to (518) 789-0556

From Suffrage to the Senate, America's Political Women

From Suffrage to the Senate is a comprehensive and valuable compendium of biographies of leading women in U.S. politics, past and present, and an examination of the wide range of women's movements. Up to date through 2006, this dynamically illustrated reference work explores American women's path to political power and social equality from the struggle for the right to vote and the abolition of slavery to the first African American woman in the U.S. Senate and beyond. This new edition includes over 150 new entries and a brand new section on trends and demographics of women in politics. The in-depth coverage also traces the political heritage of the abolition, labor, suffrage, temperance, and reproductive rights movements. The alphabetically arranged entries include biographies of every woman from across the political spectrum who has served in the U.S. House and Senate, along with women in the Judiciary and the U.S. Cabinet and, new to this edition, biographies of activists and political consultants. Bibliographical references follow each entry. For easy reference, a handy chronology is provided detailing 150 years of women's history. This up-to-date reference will be a must-purchase for women's studies departments, high schools and public libraries and will be a handy resource for those researching the key players in women's politics, past and present.

"An engaging tool that would be useful in high school, public, and academic libraries looking for an overview of the political history of women in the US." —Booklist

Pub. Date: October 2006; Two Volume Set; Hardcover ISBN 1-59237-117-5; $195.00

An African Biographical Dictionary

This landmark second edition is the only biographical dictionary to bring together, in one volume, cultural, social and political leaders – both historical and contemporary – of the sub-Saharan region. Over 800 biographical sketches of prominent Africans, as well as foreigners who have affected the continent's history, are featured, 150 more than the previous edition. The wide spectrum of leaders includes religious figures, writers, politicians, scientists, entertainers, sports personalities and more. Access to these fascinating individuals is provided in a user-friendly format. The biographies are arranged alphabetically, cross-referenced and indexed. Entries include the country or countries in which the person was significant and the commonly accepted dates of birth and death. Each biographical sketch is chronologically written; entries for cultural personalities add an evaluation of their work. This information is followed by a selection of references often found in university and public libraries, including autobiographies and principal biographical works. Appendixes list each individual by country and by field of accomplishment – rulers, musicians, explorers, missionaries, businessmen, physicists – nearly thirty categories in all. Another convenient appendix lists heads of state since independence by country. Up-to-date and representative of African societies as a whole, An African Biographical Dictionary provides a wealth of vital information for students of African culture and is an indispensable reference guide for anyone interested in African affairs.

"An unquestionable convenience to have these concise, informative biographies gathered into one source, indexed, and analyzed by appendixes listing entrants by nation and occupational field." —Wilson Library Bulletin

Pub. Date: July 2006; Hardcover ISBN 1-59237-112-4; $125.00

American Environmental Leaders, From Colonial Times to the Present

A comprehensive and diverse award winning collection of biographies of the most important figures in American environmentalism. Few subjects arouse the passions the way the environment does. How will we feed an ever-increasing population and how can that food be made safe for consumption? Who decides how land is developed? How can environmental policies be made fair for everyone, including multiethnic groups, women, children, and the poor? American Environmental Leaders presents more than 350 biographies of men and women who have devoted their lives to studying, debating, and organizing these and other controversial issues over the last 200 years. In addition to the scientists who have analyzed how human actions affect nature, we are introduced to poets, landscape architects, presidents, painters, activists, even sanitation engineers, and others who have forever altered how we think about the environment. The easy to use A–Z format provides instant access to these fascinating individuals, and frequent cross references indicate others with whom individuals worked (and sometimes clashed). End of entry references provide users with a starting point for further research.

"Highly recommended for high school, academic, and public libraries needing environmental biographical information." —Library Journal/Starred Review

Two Volume Set; Hardcover ISBN 1-57607-385-8 $175.00

World Cultural Leaders of the Twentieth Century

An expansive two volume set that covers 450 worldwide cultural icons, World Cultural Leaders of the Twentieth Century includes each person's works, achievements, and professional careers in a thorough essay. Who was the originator of the term "documentary"? Which poet married the daughter of the famed novelist Thomas Mann in order to help her escape Nazi Germany? Which British writer served as an agent in Russia against the Bolsheviks before the 1917 revolution? These and many more questions are answered in this illuminating text. A handy two volume set that makes it easy to look up 450 worldwide cultural icons: novelists, poets, playwrights, painters, sculptors, architects, dancers, choreographers, actors, directors, filmmakers, singers, composers, and musicians. World Cultural Leaders of the Twentieth Century provides entries (many of them illustrated) covering the person's works, achievements, and professional career in a thorough essay and offers interesting facts and statistics. Entries are fully cross-referenced so that readers can learn how various individuals influenced others. A thorough general index completes the coverage.

"Fills a need for handy, concise information on a wide array of international cultural figures." -ARBA

Two Volume Set; Hardcover ISBN 1-57607-038-7 $175.00

To preview any of our Directories Risk-Free for 30 days, call (800) 562-2139 or fax to (518) 789-0556

Universal Reference Publications
Statistical & Demographic Reference Books

America's Top-Rated Cities, 2007
America's Top-Rated Cities provides current, comprehensive statistical information and other essential data in one easy-to-use source on the 100 "top" cities that have been cited as the best for business and living in the U.S. This handbook allows readers to see, at a glance, a concise social, business, economic, demographic and environmental profile of each city, including brief evaluative comments. In addition to detailed data on Cost of Living, Finances, Real Estate, Education, Major Employers, Media, Crime and Climate, city reports now include Housing Vacancies, Tax Audits, Bankruptcy, Presidential Election Results and more. This outstanding source of information will be widely used in any reference collection.

"The only source of its kind that brings together all of this information into one easy-to-use source. It will be beneficial to many business and public libraries." –ARBA

2,500 pages, 4 Volume Set; Softcover ISBN 1-59237-184-1, $195.00

America's Top-Rated Smaller Cities, 2006/07
A perfect companion to *America's Top-Rated Cities*, *America's Top-Rated Smaller Cities* provides current, comprehensive business and living profiles of smaller cities (population 25,000-99,999) that have been cited as the best for business and living in the United States. Sixty cities make up this 2004 edition of *America's Top-Rated Smaller Cities*, all are top-ranked by Population Growth, Median Income, Unemployment Rate and Crime Rate. City reports reflect the most current data available on a wide-range of statistics, including Employment & Earnings, Household Income, Unemployment Rate, Population Characteristics, Taxes, Cost of Living, Education, Health Care, Public Safety, Recreation, Media, Air & Water Quality and much more. Plus, each city report contains a Background of the City, and an Overview of the State Finances. *America's Top-Rated Smaller Cities* offers a reliable, one-stop source for statistical data that, before now, could only be found scattered in hundreds of sources. This volume is designed for a wide range of readers: individuals considering relocating a residence or business; professionals considering expanding their business or changing careers; general and market researchers; real estate consultants; human resource personnel; urban planners and investors.

"Provides current, comprehensive statistical information in one easy-to-use source... Recommended for public and academic libraries and specialized collections." –Library Journal

1,100 pages; Softcover ISBN 1-59237-135-3, $160.00

Profiles of America: Facts, Figures & Statistics for Every Populated Place in the United States
Profiles of America is the only source that pulls together, in one place, statistical, historical and descriptive information about every place in the United States in an easy-to-use format. This award winning reference set, now in its second edition, compiles statistics and data from over 20 different sources – the latest census information has been included along with more than nine brand new statistical topics. This Four-Volume Set details over 40,000 places, from the biggest metropolis to the smallest unincorporated hamlet, and provides statistical details and information on over 50 different topics including Geography, Climate, Population, Vital Statistics, Economy, Income, Taxes, Education, Housing, Health & Environment, Public Safety, Newspapers, Transportation, Presidential Election Results and Information Contacts or Chambers of Commerce. Profiles are arranged, for ease-of-use, by state and then by county. Each county begins with a County-Wide Overview and is followed by information for each Community in that particular county. The Community Profiles within the county are arranged alphabetically. *Profiles of America* is a virtual snapshot of America at your fingertips and a unique compilation of information that will be widely used in any reference collection.

A Library Journal Best Reference Book "An outstanding compilation." –Library Journal

10,000 pages; Four Volume Set; Softcover ISBN 1-891482-80-7, $595.00

The Comparative Guide to American Suburbs, 2007
The Comparative Guide to American Suburbs is a one-stop source for Statistics on the 2,000+ suburban communities surrounding the 50 largest metropolitan areas – their population characteristics, income levels, economy, school system and important data on how they compare to one another. Organized into 50 Metropolitan Area chapters, each chapter contains an overview of the Metropolitan Area, a detailed Map followed by a comprehensive Statistical Profile of each Suburban Community, including Contact Information, Physical Characteristics, Population Characteristics, Income, Economy, Unemployment Rate, Cost of Living, Education, Chambers of Commerce and more. Next, statistical data is sorted into Ranking Tables that rank the suburbs by twenty different criteria, including Population, Per Capita Income, Unemployment Rate, Crime Rate, Cost of Living and more. *The Comparative Guide to American Suburbs* is the best source for locating data on suburbs. Those looking to relocate, as well as those doing preliminary market research, will find this an invaluable timesaving resource.

"Public and academic libraries will find this compilation useful...The work draws together figures from many sources and will be especially helpful for job relocation decisions." – Booklist

1,700 pages; Softcover ISBN 1-59237-180-9, $130.00

To preview any of our Directories Risk-Free for 30 days, call (800) 562-2139 or fax to (518) 789-0556

The Asian Databook: Statistics for all US Counties & Cities with Over 10,000 Population

This is the first-ever resource that compiles statistics and rankings on the US Asian population. *The Asian Databook* presents over 20 statistical data points for each city and county, arranged alphabetically by state, then alphabetically by place name. Data reported for each place includes Population, Languages Spoken at Home, Foreign-Born, Educational Attainment, Income Figures, Poverty Status, Homeownership, Home Values & Rent, and more. Next, in the Rankings Section, the top 75 places are listed for each data element. These easy-to-access ranking tables allow the user to quickly determine trends and population characteristics. This kind of comparative data can not be found elsewhere, in print or on the web, in a format that's as easy-to-use or more concise. A useful resource for those searching for demographics data, career search and relocation information and also for market research. With data ranging from Ancestry to Education, *The Asian Databook* presents a useful compilation of information that will be a much-needed resource in the reference collection of any public or academic library along with the marketing collection of any company whose primary focus in on the Asian population.

,000 pages; Softcover ISBN 1-59237-044-6 $150.00

The Hispanic Databook: Statistics for all US Counties & Cities with Over 10,000 Population

Previously published by Toucan Valley Publications, this second edition has been completely updated with figures from the latest census and has been broadly expanded to include dozens of new data elements and a brand new Rankings section. The Hispanic population in the United States has increased over 42% in the last 10 years and accounts for 12.5% of the total US population. For ease-of-use, *The Hispanic Databook* presents over 20 statistical data points for each city and county, arranged alphabetically by state, then alphabetically by place name. Data reported for each place includes Population, Languages Spoken at Home, Foreign-Born, Educational Attainment, Income Figures, Poverty Status, Homeownership, Home Values & Rent, and more. Next, in the Rankings Section, the top 5 places are listed for each data element. These easy-to-access ranking tables allow the user to quickly determine trends and population characteristics. This kind of comparative data can not be found elsewhere, in print or on the web, in a format that's as easy-to-use or more concise. A useful resource for those searching for demographics data, career search and relocation information and also for market research. With data ranging from Ancestry to Education, *The Hispanic Databook* presents a useful compilation of information that will be a much-needed resource in the reference collection of any public or academic library along with the marketing collection of any company whose primary focus in on the Hispanic population.

"This accurate, clearly presented volume of selected Hispanic demographics is recommended for large public libraries and research collections."-Library Journal

,000 pages; Softcover ISBN 1-59237-008-X, $150.00

Ancestry in America: A Comparative Guide to Over 200 Ethnic Backgrounds

This brand new reference work pulls together thousands of comparative statistics on the Ethnic Backgrounds of all populated places in the United States with populations over 10,000. Never before has this kind of information been reported in a single volume. Section One, Statistics by Place, is made up of a list of over 200 ancestry and race categories arranged alphabetically by each of the 5,000 different places with populations over 10,000. The population number of the ancestry group in that city or town is provided along with the percent that group represents of the total population. This informative city-by-city section allows the user to quickly and easily explore the ethnic makeup of all major population bases in the United States. Section Two, Comparative Rankings, contains three tables for each ethnicity and race. In the first table, the top 150 populated places are ranked by population number for that particular ancestry group, regardless of population. In the second table, the top 150 populated places are ranked by the percent of the total population for that ancestry group. In the third table, those top 150 populated places with 10,000 population are ranked by population number for each ancestry group. These easy-to-navigate tables allow users to see ancestry population patterns and make city-by-city comparisons as well. Plus, as an added bonus with the purchase of *Ancestry in America*, a free companion CD-ROM is available that lists statistics and rankings for all of the 35,000 populated places in the United States. This brand new, information-packed resource will serve a wide-range or research requests for demographics, population characteristics, relocation information and much more. *Ancestry in America: A Comparative Guide to Over 200 Ethnic Backgrounds* will be an important acquisition to all reference collections.

"This compilation will serve a wide range of research requests for population characteristics ... it offers much more detail than other sources." –Booklist

1,500 pages; Softcover ISBN 1-59237-029-2, $225.00

To preview any of our Directories Risk-Free for 30 days, call (800) 562-2139 or fax to (518) 789-0556

The American Tally: Statistics & Comparative Rankings for U.S. Cities with Populations over 10,000

This important statistical handbook compiles, all in one place, comparative statistics on all U.S. cities and towns with a 10,000+ population. *The American Tally* provides statistical details on over 4,000 cities and towns and profiles how they compare with one another in Population Characteristics, Education, Language & Immigration, Income & Employment and Housing. Each section begins with an alphabetical listing of cities by state, allowing for quick access to both the statistics and relative rankings of any city. Next, the highest and lowest cities are listed in each statistic. These important, informative lists provide quick reference to which cities are at both extremes of the spectrum for each statistic. Unlike any other reference, *The American Tally* provides quick, easy access to comparative statistics – a must-have for any reference collection.

"A solid library reference." –Bookwatch

500 pages; Softcover ISBN 1-930956-29-0, $125.00

The Environmental Resource Handbook, 2007/08

The Environmental Resource Handbook is the most up-to-date and comprehensive source for Environmental Resources and Statistics. Section I: Resources provides detailed contact information for thousands of information sources, including Associations & Organizations, Awards & Honors, Conferences, Foundations & Grants, Environmental Health, Government Agencies, National Parks & Wildlife Refuges, Publications, Research Centers, Educational Programs, Green Product Catalogs, Consultants and much more. Section II: Statistics, provides statistics and rankings on hundreds of important topics, including Children's Environmental Index, Municipal Finances, Toxic Chemicals, Recycling, Climate, Air & Water Quality and more. This kind of up-to-date environmental data, all in one place, is not available anywhere else on the market place today. This vast compilation of resources and statistics is a must-have for all public and academic libraries as well as any organization with a primary focus on the environment.

"...the intrinsic value of the information make it worth consideration by libraries with environmental collections and environmentally concerned users." –Booklist

1,000 pages; Softcover ISBN 1-59237-195-7, $155.00 ☐ Online Database $300.00

Weather America, A Thirty-Year Summary of Statistical Weather Data and Rankings

This valuable resource provides extensive climatological data for over 4,000 National and Cooperative Weather Stations throughout the United States. *Weather America* begins with a new Major Storms section that details major storm events of the nation and a National Rankings section that details rankings for several data elements, such as Maximum Temperature and Precipitation. The main body of *Weather America* is organized into 50 state sections. Each section provides a Data Table on each Weather Station, organized alphabetically, that provides statistics on Maximum and Minimum Temperatures, Precipitation, Snowfall, Extreme Temperatures, Foggy Days, Humidity and more. State sections contain two brand new features in this edition – a City Index and a narrative Description of the climatic conditions of the state. Each section also includes a revised Map of the State that includes not only weather stations, but cities and towns.

"Best Reference Book of the Year." –Library Journal

2,013 pages; Softcover ISBN 1-891482-29-7, $175.00

Crime in America's Top-Rated Cities

This volume includes over 20 years of crime statistics in all major crime categories: violent crimes, property crimes and total crime. *Crime in America's Top-Rated Cities* is conveniently arranged by city and covers 76 top-rated cities. *Crime in America's Top-Rated Cities* offers details that compare the number of crimes and crime rates for the city, suburbs and metro area along with national crime trends for violent, property and total crimes. Also, this handbook contains important information and statistics on Anti-Crime Programs, Crime Risk, Hate Crimes, Illegal Drugs, Law Enforcement, Correctional Facilities, Death Penalty Laws and much more. A much-needed resource for people who are relocating, business professionals, general researchers, the press, law enforcement officials and students of criminal justice.

"Data is easy to access and will save hours of searching." –Global Enforcement Review

832 pages; Softcover ISBN 1-891482-84-X, $155.00

To preview any of our Directories Risk-Free for 30 days, call (800) 562-2139 or fax to (518) 789-0556

Sedgwick Press
Health Directories

The Complete Directory for People with Disabilities, 2007

A wealth of information, now in one comprehensive sourcebook. Completely updated, this edition contains more information than ever before, including thousands of new entries and enhancements to existing entries and thousands of additional web sites and e-mail addresses. This up-to-date directory is the most comprehensive resource available for people with disabilities, detailing Independent Living Centers, Rehabilitation Facilities, State & Federal Agencies, Associations, Support Groups, Periodicals & Books, Assistive Devices, Employment & Education Programs, Camps and Travel Groups. Each year, more libraries, schools, colleges, hospitals, rehabilitation centers and individuals add *The Complete Directory for People with Disabilities* to their collections, making sure that this information is readily available to the families, individuals and professionals who can benefit most from the amazing wealth of resources cataloged here.

"No other reference tool exists to meet the special needs of the disabled in one convenient resource for information." –Library Journal

1,200 pages; Softcover ISBN 1-59237-147-7, $165.00 ☐ Online Database $215.00 ☐ Online Database & Directory Combo $300.00

The Complete Directory for People with Chronic Illness, 2007/08

Thousands of hours of research have gone into this completely updated 2005/06 edition – several new chapters have been added along with thousands of new entries and enhancements to existing entries. Plus, each chronic illness chapter has been reviewed by an medical expert in the field. This widely-hailed directory is structured around the 90 most prevalent chronic illnesses – from Asthma to Cancer to Wilson's Disease – and provides a comprehensive overview of the support services and information resources available for people diagnosed with a chronic illness. Each chronic illness has its own chapter and contains a brief description in layman's language, followed by important resources for National & Local Organizations, State Agencies, Newsletters, Books & Periodicals, Libraries & Research Centers, Support Groups & Hotlines, Web Sites and much more. This directory is an important resource for health care professionals, the collections of hospital and health care libraries, as well as an invaluable tool for people with a chronic illness and their support network.

"A must purchase for all hospital and health care libraries and is strongly recommended for all public library reference departments." –ARBA

1,200 pages; Softcover ISBN 1-59237-183-3, $165.00 ☐ Online Database $215.00 ☐ Online Database & Directory Combo $300.00

The Complete Learning Disabilities Directory, 2007

The Complete Learning Disabilities Directory is the most comprehensive database of Programs, Services, Curriculum Materials, Professional Meetings & Resources, Camps, Newsletters and Support Groups for teachers, students and families concerned with learning disabilities. This information-packed directory includes information about Associations & Organizations, Schools, Colleges & Testing Materials, Government Agencies, Legal Resources and much more. For quick, easy access to information, this directory contains four indexes: Entry Name Index, Subject Index and Geographic Index. With every passing year, the field of learning disabilities attracts more attention and the network of caring, committed and knowledgeable professionals grows every day. This directory is an invaluable research tool for these parents, students and professionals.

"Due to its wealth and depth of coverage, parents, teachers and others… should find this an invaluable resource." -Booklist

900 pages; Softcover ISBN 1-59237-122-1, $145.00 ☐ Online Database $195.00 ☐ Online Database & Directory Combo $280.00

The Complete Mental Health Directory, 2006/07

This is the most comprehensive resource covering the field of behavioral health, with critical information for both the layman and the mental health professional. For the layman, this directory offers understandable descriptions of 25 Mental Health Disorders as well as detailed information on Associations, Media, Support Groups and Mental Health Facilities. For the professional, *The Complete Mental Health Directory* offers critical and comprehensive information on Managed Care Organizations, Information Systems, Government Agencies and Provider Organizations. This comprehensive volume of needed information will be widely used in any reference collection.

"… the strength of this directory is that it consolidates widely dispersed information into a single volume." –Booklist

800 pages; Softcover ISBN 1-59237-124-8, $165.00 ☐ Online Database $215.00 ☐ Online & Directory Combo $300.00

To preview any of our Directories Risk-Free for 30 days, call (800) 562-2139 or fax to (518) 789-0556

Older Americans Information Directory, 2006/07

Completely updated for 2006/07, this sixth edition has been completely revised and now contains 1,000 new listings, over 8,000 updates to existing listings and over 3,000 brand new e-mail addresses and web sites. You'll find important resources for Older Americans including National, Regional, State & Local Organizations, Government Agencies, Research Centers, Libraries & Information Centers, Legal Resources, Discount Travel Information, Continuing Education Programs, Disability Aids & Assistive Devices, Health, Print Media and Electronic Media. Three indexes: Entry Index, Subject Index and Geographic Index make it easy to find just the right source of information. This comprehensive guide to resources for Older Americans will be a welcome addition to any reference collection.

"Highly recommended for academic, public, health science and consumer libraries..." –Choi

1,200 pages; Softcover ISBN 1-59237-136-1, $165.00 ☐ Online Database $215.00 ☐ Online Database & Directory Combo $300.00

The Complete Directory for Pediatric Disorders, 2007

This important directory provides parents and caregivers with information about Pediatric Conditions, Disorders, Diseases and Disabilities, including Blood Disorders, Bone & Spinal Disorders, Brain Defects & Abnormalities, Chromosomal Disorders, Congenital Heart Defects, Movement Disorders, Neuromuscular Disorders and Pediatric Tumors & Cancers. This carefully written directory offers: understandable Descriptions of 15 major bodily systems; Descriptions of more than 200 Disorders and a Resources Section, detailing National Agencies & Associations, State Associations, Online Services, Libraries & Resource Centers, Research Centers, Support Groups & Hotlines, Camps, Books and Periodicals. This resource will provide immediate access to information crucial to families and caregivers when coping with children's illnesses.

"Recommended for public and consumer health libraries." –Library Journa

1,200 pages; Softcover ISBN 1-59237-150-7 $165.00 ☐ Online Database $215.00 ☐ Online Database & Directory Combo $300.00

The Directory of Drug & Alcohol Residential Rehabilitation Facilities

This brand new directory is the first-ever resource to bring together, all in one place, data on the thousands of drug and alcohol residential rehabilitation facilities in the United States. *The Directory of Drug & Alcohol Residential Rehabilitation Facilities* covers over 1,000 facilities, with detailed contact information for each one, including mailing address, phone and fax numbers, email addresses and web sites, mission statement, type of treatment programs, cost, average length of stay, numbers of residents and counselors, accreditation, insurance plans accepted, type of environment, religious affiliation, education components and much more. It also contains a helpful chapter on General Resources that provides contact information for Associations, Print & Electronic Media, Support Groups and Conferences. Multiple indexes allow the user to pinpoint the facilities that meet very specific criteria. This time-saving tool is what so many counselors, parents and medical professionals have been asking for. *The Directory of Drug & Alcohol Residential Rehabilitation Facilities* will be a helpful tool in locating the right source for treatment for a wide range of individuals. This comprehensive directory will be an important acquisition for all reference collections: public and academic libraries, case managers, social workers, state agencies and many more.

"This is an excellent, much needed directory that fills an important gap..." –Booklis

300 pages; Softcover ISBN 1-59237-031-4, $135.00

To preview any of our Directories Risk-Free for 30 days, call (800) 562-2139 or fax to (518) 789-0556

Sedgwick Press
Education Directories

The Comparative Guide to American Elementary & Secondary Schools, 2007

The only guide of its kind, this award winning compilation offers a snapshot profile of every public school district in the United States serving 1,500 or more students – more than 5,900 districts are covered. Organized alphabetically by district within state, each chapter begins with a Statistical Overview of the state. Each district listing includes contact information (name, address, phone number and web site) plus Grades Served, the Numbers of Students and Teachers and the Number of Regular, Special Education, Alternative and Vocational Schools in the district along with statistics on Student/Classroom Teacher Ratios, Drop Out Rates, Ethnicity, the Numbers of Librarians and Guidance Counselors and District Expenditures per student. As an added bonus, *The Comparative Guide to American Elementary and Secondary Schools* provides important ranking tables, both by state and nationally, for each data element. For easy navigation through this wealth of information, this handbook contains a useful City Index that lists all districts that operate schools within a city. These important comparative statistics are necessary for anyone considering relocation or doing comparative research on their own district and would be a perfect acquisition for any public library or school district library.

"This straightforward guide is an easy way to find general information. Valuable for academic and large public library collections." –ARBA

2,400 pages; Softcover ISBN 1-59237-223-6, $125.00

Educators Resource Directory, 2007/08

Educators Resource Directory is a comprehensive resource that provides the educational professional with thousands of resources and statistical data for professional development. This directory saves hours of research time by providing immediate access to Associations & Organizations, Conferences & Trade Shows, Educational Research Centers, Employment Opportunities & Teaching Abroad, School Library Services, Scholarships, Financial Resources, Professional Consultants, Computer Software & Testing Resources and much more. Plus, this comprehensive directory also includes a section on Statistics and Rankings with over 100 tables, including statistics on Average Teacher Salaries, SAT/ACT scores, Revenues & Expenditures and more. These important statistics will allow the user to see how their school rates among others, make relocation decisions and so much more. For quick access to information, this directory contains four indexes: Entry & Publisher Index, Geographic Index, a Subject & Grade Index and Web Sites Index. *Educators Resource Directory* will be a well-used addition to the reference collection of any school district, education department or public library.

"Recommended for all collections that serve elementary and secondary school professionals." –Choice

1,000 pages; Softcover ISBN 1-59237-179-5, $145.00 ☐ Online Database $195.00 ☐ Online Database & Directory Combo $280.00

To preview any of our Directories Risk-Free for 30 days, call (800) 562-2139 or fax to (518) 789-0556

Sedgwick Press
Hospital & Health Plan Directories

The Comparative Guide to American Hospitals, 2007

This is the first ever resource to compare all of the nation's hospitals by 17 measures of quality in the treatment of heart attack, heart failure and pneumonia. This data is based on the Hospital Compare study, produced by Medicare, and is available in print and in a unique and user-friendly format from Grey House Publishing, along with extra contact information from Grey House's *Directory of Hospital Personnel*. *The Comparative Guide to American Hospitals* provides a snapshot profile of each of the nations 6,000 hospitals. These informative profiles illustrate how the hospital rates in 17 important areas: Heart Attack Care (% who receive Aspirin at Arrival, Aspirin at Discharge, ACE Inhibitor for LVSD, Beta Blocker at Arrival, Beta Blocker at Discharge, Thrombolytic Agent Received, PTCA Received and Adult Smoking Cessation Advice); Heart Failure (% who receive LVF Assessment, ACE Inhibitor for LVSD, Discharge Instructions, Adult Smoking Cessation Advice); and Pneumonia (% who receive Initial Antibiotic Timing, Pneumococcal Vaccination, Oxygenation Assessment, Blood Culture Performed and Adult Smoking Cessation Advice). Each profile includes the raw percentage for that hospital, the state average, the US average and data on the top hospital. For easy access to contact information, each profile includes the hospitals address, phone and fax numbers, email and web addresses, type and accreditation along with 5 top key administrations. These profiles will allow the user to quickly identify the quality of the hospital and have the necessary information at their fingertips to make contact with that hospital. Most importantly, *The Comparative Guide to American Hospitals* provides an easy-to-use Ranking Table for each of the data elements to allow the user to quickly locate the hospitals with the best level of service. This brand new title will be a must for the reference collection at all public, medical and academic libraries.

2,500 pages; Softcover ISBN 1-59237-182-5; $225.00

The Directory of Hospital Personnel, 2007

The Directory of Hospital Personnel is the best resource you can have at your fingertips when researching or marketing a product or service to the hospital market. A "Who's Who" of the hospital universe, this directory puts you in touch with over 150,000 key decision-makers. With 100% verification of data you can rest assured that you will reach the right person with just one call. Every hospital in the U.S. is profiled, listed alphabetically by city within state. Plus, three easy-to-use, cross-referenced indexes put the facts at your fingertips faster and more easily than any other directory: Hospital Name Index, Bed Size Index and Personnel Index. *The Directory of Hospital Personnel* is the only complete source for key hospital decision-makers by name. Whether you want to define or restructure sales territories… locate hospitals with the purchasing power to accept your proposals… keep track of important contacts or colleagues… or find information on which insurance plans are accepted, *The Directory of Hospital Personnel* gives you the information you need – easily, efficiently, effectively and accurately.

"Recommended for college, university and medical libraries." -ARBA

2,500 pages; Softcover ISBN 1-59237-178-7 $325.00 ♦ Online Database $545.00 ♦ Online Database & Directory Combo, $650.00

The Directory of Health Care Group Purchasing Organizations, 2006

This comprehensive directory provides the important data you need to get in touch with over 800 Group Purchasing Organizations. By providing in-depth information on this growing market and its members, *The Directory of Health Care Group Purchasing Organizations* fills a major need for the most accurate and comprehensive information on over 800 GPOs – Mailing Address, Phone & Fax Numbers, E-mail Addresses, Key Contacts, Purchasing Agents, Group Descriptions, Membership Categorization, Standard Vendor Proposal Requirements, Membership Fees & Terms, Expanded Services, Total Member Beds & Outpatient Visits represented and more. Five Indexes provide a number of ways to locate the right GPO: Alphabetical Index, Expanded Services Index, Organization Type Index, Geographic Index and Member Institution Index. With its comprehensive and detailed information on each purchasing organization, *The Directory of Health Care Group Purchasing Organizations* is the go-to source for anyone looking to target this market.

"The information is clearly arranged and easy to access…recommended for those needing this very specialized information." -ARBA

1,000 pages; Softcover ISBN 1-59237-0091-8, $325.00 ♦ Online Database, $650.00 ♦ Online Database & Directory Combo, $750.00

To preview any of our Directories Risk-Free for 30 days, call (800) 562-2139 or fax to (518) 789-0556

The HMO/PPO Directory, 2007

The HMO/PPO Directory is a comprehensive source that provides detailed information about Health Maintenance Organizations and Preferred Provider Organizations nationwide. This comprehensive directory details more information about more managed health care organizations than ever before. Over 1,100 HMOs, PPOs, Medicare Advantage Plans and affiliated companies are listed, arranged alphabetically by state. Detailed listings include Key Contact Information, Prescription Drug Benefits, Enrollment, Geographical Areas Served, Affiliated Physicians & Hospitals, Federal Qualifications, Status, Year Founded, Managed Care Partners, Employer References, Fees & Payment Information and more. Plus, five years of historical information is included related to Revenues, Net Income, Medical Loss Ratios, Membership Enrollment and Number of Patient Complaints. Five easy-to-use, cross-referenced indexes will put this vast array of information at your fingertips immediately: HMO Index, PPO Index, Other Providers Index, Personnel Index and Enrollment Index. The HMO/PPO Directory provides the most comprehensive data on the most companies available on the market place today.

"Helpful to individuals requesting certain HMO/PPO issues such as co-payment costs, subscription costs and patient complaints. Individuals concerned (or those with questions) about their insurance may find this text to be of use to them." –ARBA

600 pages; Softcover ISBN 1-59237-158-2, $325.00 ♦ Online Database, $495.00 ♦ Online Database & Directory Combo, $600.00

Medical Device Register, 2007

The only one-stop resource of every medical supplier licensed to sell products in the US. This award-winning directory offers immediate access to over 13,000 companies - and more than 65,000 products – in two information-packed volumes. This comprehensive resource saves hours of time and trouble when searching for medical equipment and supplies and the manufacturers who provide them. Volume I: The Product Directory, provides essential information for purchasing or specifying medical supplies for every medical device, supply, and diagnostic available in the US. Listings provide FDA codes & Federal Procurement Eligibility, Contact information for every manufacturer of the product along with Prices and Product Specifications. Volume 2 - Supplier Profiles, offers the most complete and important data about Suppliers, Manufacturers and Distributors. Company Profiles detail the number of employees, ownership, method of distribution, sales volume, net income, key executives detailed contact information medical products the company supplies, plus the medical specialties they cover. Four indexes provide immediate access to this wealth of information: Keyword Index, Trade Name Index, Supplier Geographical Index and OEM (Original Equipment Manufacturer) Index. Medical Device Register, 2007 is the only one-stop source for locating suppliers and products; looking for new manufacturers or hard-to-find medical devices; comparing products and companies; know who's selling what and who to buy from cost effectively. This directory has become the standard in its field and will be a welcome addition to the reference collection of any medical library, large public library, university library along with the collections that serve the medical community.

"A wealth of information on medical devices, medical device companies… and key personnel in the industry is provide in this comprehensive reference work… A valuable reference work, one of the best hardcopy compilations available." -Doody Publishing

3,000 pages Two Volumes; Hardcover ISBN 1-59237-181-7; $325.00

The Directory of Independent Ambulatory Care Centers

This first edition of The Directory of Independent Ambulatory Care Centers provides access to detailed information that, before now, could only be found scattered in hundreds of different sources. This comprehensive and up-to-date directory pulls together a vast array of contact information for over 7,200 Ambulatory Surgery Centers, Ambulatory General and Urgent Care Clinics, and Diagnostic Imaging Centers that are not affiliated with a hospital or major medical center. Detailed listings include Mailing Address, Phone & Fax Numbers, E-mail and Web Site addresses, Contact Name and Phone Numbers of the Medical Director and other Key Executives and Purchasing Agents, Specialties & Services Offered, Year Founded, Numbers of Employees and Surgeons, Number of Operating Rooms, Number of Cases seen per year, Overnight Options, Contracted Services and much more. Listings are arranged by State, by Center Category and then alphabetically by Organization Name. Two indexes provide quick and easy access to this wealth of information: Entry Name Index and Specialty/Service Index. The Directory of Independent Ambulatory Care Centers is a must-have resource for anyone marketing a product or service to this important industry and will be an invaluable tool for those searching for a local care center that will meet their specific needs.

"Among the numerous hospital directories, no other provides information on independent ambulatory centers. A handy, well-organized resource that would be useful in medical center libraries and public libraries." –Choice

986 pages; Softcover ISBN 1-930956-90-8, $185.00 ♦ Online Database, $365.00 ♦ Online Database & Directory Combo, $450.00

To preview any of our Directories Risk-Free for 30 days, call (800) 562-2139 or fax to (518) 789-0556